ISBN 978-0-483-47442-0
PIBN 10782203

THE
CHRISTIAN-EVANGELIST

"IN FAITH, UNITY; IN OPINION AND METHODS, LIBERTY; IN ALL THINGS, CHARITY."

| Vol. XLIII. | July 5, 1906 | No. 27 |

1809 CENTENNIAL PROPAGANDA CHURCHES OF CHRIST 1909
: : : GEO. L. SNIVELY : : :

Looking Toward Pittsburg.

This Educational number of THE CHRISTIAN-EVANGELIST is sent forth with the prayers that it may help the brotherhood to a clearer vision of the duty of sending an educated ministry in the van of our great hosts soon to cross over the borders and into our second century. The captains of the Lord's army, the shepherds of his unifying flocks must be superior men intellectually as well as morally and spiritually. It is not only our duty to insist that young aspirants for these positions should thoroughly qualify themselves but to help them.

Here, as always, the severe angel of duty is accompanied by the good angel of privilege. How happy one would be to hand the struggling life saver a good oar to replace his broken one. What a gracious privilege it is to be a factor in proffering the Captain of our salvation a fully equipped young soldier, even superior to the old veteran whom age has mustered out of active service. In educating a candidate for the ministry you are doing for the church what they do elsewhere who give the reaper a sharper scythe, the miner a keener drill, the physician better herbs, the knight a stronger blade, the mariner a wider sail. No other feature of the great convention could be more inspirational than a corps of 5,000 young men brought from our colleges where they are preparing for the ministry of the word. It would create a world-wide sensation. Will not steps be taken to have this one of the great events of 1909?

As part of its contribution to our Centennial celebration, the Christian Publishing Company is maintaining its own living link evangelist. While it is desirable the churches should assist in his support, he is sent to poor but promising fields without financial conditions. We are pleased with this tribute to his efficiency: "I wish to congratulate you on maintaining an evangelist in the home field which is ripe unto harvest. Brother J. D. Lawrence is the right man in the right place. You were wise in the selection of this efficient soldier of the cross as your representative in the Lord. Brother Lawrence has encouraged and strengthened this congregation by his visits and series of sermons. We thank you very much for sending unto us such a blessing."—W. J. Waggoner (minister), Port Jefferson, Ohio.

It will be remembered that when at the San Francisco convention attention was called to the fact that there was not a single church of Christ in New Hampshire, Bro. J. H. Garrison, in the name of himself and friends, pledged an earnest effort for the establishment of a church patterned after the New Testament order of things in that commonwealth. Accordingly, Herbert Yeuell was engaged, a tabernacle rented, a sing-

ing evangelist employed and a meeting begun in Manchester last Lord's day. The prayers of God's people everywhere are asked for the success of this enterprise. The expenses of the meeting will be fully $1,000. So far but $511.10 have been pledged toward these expenses. We do not believe the brethren will permit this meeting to languish or prematurely close for lack of a few hundred dollars. Will not each reader of this paragraph send a gift at once to be placed on this altar? Dollar contributions will be thankfully accepted. Several $25.00 offerings have been forwarded us and others will be welcomed. Full reports will be given in this paper. If this emprise is successful we hope attempts will be made to establish a church in every county in the United States, where we are not now represented, before 1909.

Education and the Centennial.
BY W. R. WARREN,
Centennial Secretary.

Among the world's religions Christianity alone is equally adapted to every climate, every race and every century. Within the last hundred years a million and a quarter Christians have stood forth from their brethren to declare that essential Christianity is equally adapted to all nationalities, all temperaments, all classes and all conditions; that it must include all the truth and reject all error; that it is a divine system and that no human modification is allowable. Starting with no presupposition as to the character of this God-given religion, and every one claiming for himself and according to every other full liberty to search the Scripture and to teach and practice just what he finds to be taught and enjoined there we challenge the world to behold to-day a consensus of doctrine, a uniformity of practice and a consistency of organization unequalled in any creed-fenced or prelate-ruled body in the world. Others may account for this as they can, but we claim only and with all humility that this universal agreement is due to universal and glad submission to him who is the Way, the Truth, the Life. It is perfectly natural that the Truth should unify and harmonize those who hold it. Moreover no error and no partial truth can finally satisfy the human heart. It cries out for the whole truth as thirsty lips for water. Any apparent satisfaction with falsehood is thus to mistake as to its real character. Truth needs no other recommendation than the clear expression of itself.

In Christ Jesus the Word was made flesh and dwelt among us—all the fulness of the Godhead bodily. Only ignorance separates unbelievers from Christians and only ignorance divides believers into more or less hostile denominations.

Education, then, is the final evangelistic and missionary method and education is the only means by which Christian union may be realized. Then the Centennial of our Christian union movement should witness

unprecedented advancement in education. Preachers for this movement are demanded in ever increasing numbers, and their education should be as complete as possible. They must not only teach but train teachers. Theirs is not to merely impart knowledge but in the dread liberty of the Gospel to incite men to go themselves in quest of truth. It is not merely to kindle other torches but to start other torch kindlers. Jesus started a perpetual succession of teachers. There is much teaching in our Bible schools and churches, and a little in our homes, but in our schools and colleges there is nothing but teaching. Here at last is the test of the permanent strength and vital endurance of our plea. If it only wins the plaudits of the populace and the money of the rich it will pass, but having established a succession of teachers it is chained to the chariot of God's unfailing and unceasing progress.

Among the Disciples of Christ there have been built sorts of educational institutions: colleges with ministerial training, more or less closely joined in the program; Bible colleges independent of other schools; Bible colleges connected with secular institutions and female colleges. Worthy celebration of the centennial involves completing the creditable endowment of all these; but even more it requires the correction of that truly damnable heresy that material equipment is the first matter for the consideration in selecting a college for a young man or young woman. Look for the school that offers most of the things that money can not buy even in this trafficking age. To one who has come to love the liberty wherewith Christ has made us free and to plead for the union for which Christ prayed that means that he will make his choice within the closed circle of colleges that definitely stand for union in Christ and liberty under Christ. Money follows the man. Let us send all our children where the influence of our plea is dominant, enlist twice as many to take training in our Bible colleges for the coming year and witness how the material resources of all our schools are doubled before 1909.

Bissell Block, Pittsburg.

Our Centennial Co-laborers.

THE CHRISTIAN-EVANGELIST has the right and only view of this federation question. The —— has made too much out of it. Let us not grow radical, conservative, sectarian in ourselves. We need not give up any of our principles for which we are pleading to co-operate with the denominations. My support is with THE CHRISTIAN-EVANGELIST.—Hugh C. Gresham, minister.

I must tell you how I sympathize with you, because I know you are right. Keep up a stout heart and you will be vindicated some day. Bro. Isaac Errett was persecuted the same way by his brethren. I have taken THE CHRISTIAN-EVANGELIST a great many years and would not do without it. May your days be long in the land.
—Mrs. S. E. Turner, Pine Flats, Pa.

Current Events

Attorney-General Moody has sent to the Senate, by request, a list of the corporations

The War on Trusts.

against which proceedings have been instituted under the Sherman anti-trust act. They include the Standard Oil Company, against the officers of which criminal action has been begun, and the tobacco, drug, elevator, beef, paper and sugar trusts. In addition, several railroads are being prosecuted for granting rebates, and action is being taken against the St. Louis Terminal Association, which is a most egregious trust. This is a good record for the administration. It is reported that the Standard Oil Company has decided to abandon its policy of secrecy, publish its reports, increase its capital stock from $100,000,000 to $600,000,000, most of the new stock being divided in the form of stock dividend among the present holders, and list its stock upon the exchanges. And, speaking of trusts, the managers of five ice companies in Toledo, O., have been fined $5,000 each and sentenced to one year in the workhouse. As a result of a combination, the price of ice had gone up nearly 100 per cent, and as a result of the prosecution, the price has gone down again.

❧

Details about the massacre of Jews at Bialystok, Russia, have been coming in

The Jewish Massacre.

slowly. The Russian government is doing its best to prevent them coming in at all, but the most careful of censors can not do much more than delay the transmission of news. The total casualties are now put at 250, of which 100 were deaths—outright murders, many of them with torture. Besides the number killed and injured Jews, a considerable number of Christians were killed or wounded, partly by accident and partly in settlement of private grudges or in pursuit of spoil, for which the general chaos of the massacre afforded large opportunity. The real cause of this awful outbreak of savagery is not yet definitely known. It appears that some one threw a bomb at the Corpus Christi procession, but there is no evidence that it was done by a Jew or even that any one sincerely believed that it was done by a Jew. There are some indications that the massacre was deliberately planned, though no convincing proof that the plan was originated or known in St. Petersburg.

❧

Earthquake cures the suicide mania. It may not be a convenient or popular rem-

A Cure for Suicide.

edy, but it does the work. In San Francisco before the late quake there were, on an average, ten suicides every week. But in the two months since that event, only three persons in that city have found refuge in suicide from the insupportable ills of life. And yet there have been more troubles in San Francisco during these months than ever before. Why then? First, people have been busy. That prevents despair. Second, they have been interested. Every man in San Francisco,

however miserable, has been eager to see what would happen next. Third, when a whole city is engulfed in obvious and palpable calamity, the private sorrows of an individual look too small, even to himself, to justify suicide. Lastly, a misfortune that is big enough wakes the heroic in even little men and disinclines them to make a cowardly surrender to fate. There is a whole philosophy of life here, if one will stop to get it out.

❧

A picturesque suggestion, made by a member of the French Academy of Sci-

Christo-centric Geography.

ences, contemplates the establishment of the standard meridian for the measurement of longitude at Bethlehem instead of Greenwich. Greenwich means nothing except that the British royal observatory happens to be located there. There would be an obvious appropriateness in measuring distance from the place of Christ's birth as we measure years from the time of it.

❧

Japan is entering upon an aggressive program of subsidy and protection to get con-

Korean Trades.

trol of the trade with Korea and Manchuria. The plan includes free entry for Japanese goods at Walny, though other foreign goods must pay duty, free freight transportation for Japanese goods on that part of the Chinese Eastern railway in Manchuria which is under Japanese control, the payment by the government of half the marine freight on goods shipped from Japan, and the granting of government loans aggregating several million dollars to manufacturing and exporting companies. Such measures will obviously give Japanese merchants and manufacturers a vast advantage in the competition for trade in Korea and Manchuria. But whether the advantage will be worth what it costs, is another question. Here is where the "infant industries" begin to get their grip on Japan. The infants will flourish, beyond question, on this predigested food of subsidy and special favor. But it is just possible, in cases like this, that what is good for the infants may be bad for the family. A dozen great and prosperous Japanese exporting firms will not necessarily mean real prosperity for Japan. For solemn warning on the subject of infant industries Japan might well cast a studious eye on the present economic condition of this country.

❧

A carriage maker is quoted as saying that the coming in of the cheap automobile had

Autos and Horses.

given a great impetus to his business, especially in the manufacture of the finer grades of vehicles. Personally, we had not noticed the arrival of the cheap automobile. There are some that do not cost a great deal of money, but these are generally worth still less and are therefore not cheap. But accepting the premise, the argument is that, since the relatively poor can now afford automobiles, the rich are returning to thoroughbreds and fine carriages. Just like the fool rich. There always are those whose only interest in anything is the fact that they can afford it and other people can not. But these people who do things with real interest or vital motive just because other folks can't, are, after all, only a shade more despicable than

Christian Union: A Historical Study.

IV. THE PROTESTANT ERA: THE PERIOD OF REUNION.

13. External Motives to Union.

We have spoken of the inevitableness of the tendency toward unity in the church, by reason of the internal law of its life unfolding without, according to the divine order of progressive development. It remains to be said that this tendency of the internal law of life is mightily reinforced by external conditions in the world to which the church is called to minister. The needs of humanity make a powerful appeal to this inward law of life, which is the law of love. Love is always stimulated to make its greatest sacrifices and put forth its highest efforts to relieve from suffering, or protect from peril, the object of its affections. "God so loved the world that he gave his only begotten Son, that whosoever believeth in him might not perish, but have everlasting life." When will it be written that the Church "so loved the world" that it gave up its sectarian spirit, aims, ambitions, names, creeds, its half-hearted consecration, and whatever else hinders its unity and co-operation, that the world might not perish, but have everlasting life? Sometime that fact must be written if the world is ever to be redeemed by Christ. The infinite love of God, which found expression in Christ, must also find expression in his Church, which is to be the medium for conveying that love to a perishing world.

In the past, it must be confessed, the Church has been so much absorbed in defining and defending its theological position, so occupied with questions of organization and government, so exhausted by its efforts at denominational propaganda, that it has not caught a clear vision of the world's needs and of its own obligation to minister to these needs.

It is only recently that it seems to have become conscious of the stupendous tasks which Christ has laid upon it, and of its need of unity in order to the accomplishment of these tasks. What the Church of to-day needs, more than anything else, perhaps, to fill it with the spirit of consecration, unification, and co-operation, is to catch a clear and distinct vision of this world's needs as seen through the eyes of Jesus Christ. Such a vision would humble it, put it upon its knees in prayer, and cause it to cry to God for a fresh anointing of the Holy Spirit, to fit it to accomplish these great tasks. Let us look for a moment at some of these needs which appeal to the Church for united action.

Three men out of every five, of all the millions that dwell upon the globe, abide even yet in pagan darkness. So far as these three-fifths of the human race are concerned, God's love manifested in the sending of his Son, and Christ's death for the sins of men, in manifestation of that same love, were in vain. They have not yet heard the good news, and are "without God and without hope in the world." Christ has called out his Church from the world to carry to these hopeless millions the good news of salvation, and he prayed for its unity to the end that this sublime purpose might be accomplished. Oh, if we only had ears to hear the plaintive and inarticulate cry that comes from the heart of the heathen world—its deep moan of anguish because it knows not God nor the meaning and mystery of life! If we only had eyes to see the moral desolation that prevails, even yet in so-called Christian lands, and the gigantic evils which threaten our civilization and all that is dearest and most sacred in life! If we only had hearts to appreciate the religious indifference that lies like a blight upon so large a part of our population, and could realize that these great tasks remain unaccomplished, and these gigantic evils unremedied, because there has not been, and is not even yet, a united Church, how rapidly would our little differences and prejudices give way before these mighty motives for united action! The Church has lost its moral leadership in the great reforms of the age because of its divisions and internal strifes. That leadership can only be regained by closing up its divided ranks and undertaking seriously the overthrow of these great moral evils which oppose the progress of the kingdom of God. Every cry that comes from the desolate heart of orphanage; every moan of anguish that comes from neglected widowhood and poverty; every ruined life and wrecked home which may attribute its downfall to the open saloon and the gambling hell, is a challenge to the Church to vindicate its divine character and mission by rising to the needs of the hour. Every form of unbelief and of practical atheism which defies the law of God and tramples under its unhallowed feet the sacred rights of men, and all false "isms," philosophies and cults, that draw men away from the feet of Christ, are so many calls to the Church to rise to the height of its great opportunity and obligation. All this widespread corruption that has tarnished the fair fame of our nation and people, this mammon worship and public and private graft, is an awful impeachment of the fidelity of the Church in molding the lives and characters of men.

These are only a few of the external motives, in the great world without, which appeal with convincing power to the life within the Church to organize, mobilize and unify its forces to meet these needs. Once the Church comes to realize the magnitude of its responsibilities for the performance of these great tasks, how gladly would we all join hands with our brothers who differ with us in some things, but who agree with us in many more things, in order that we may work together, as far as possible, for the overthrow of Satan's kingdom and for bringing in the triumphant reign of the kingdom of God!

Just before a great naval conflict in which England was to measure the strength of her navy against that of another nation, Lord Nelson said to two of his high officers who were at enmity with each other, as he placed their hands together, "Be friends; yonder is your enemy!" Is not Jesus Christ to-day seeking to put the hands of his divided Church into his own wounded palm, and saying to all his followers, "Be ye friends; yonder are your enemies?" Lift us, lift all thy church, Oh Lord, to this Mount of Vision, that we may see the world and its needs as thou seest them, and send it forth, a united and consecrated force, to minister to human need, and subdue this whole earth to thy glorious and beneficent reign!

❋ ❋

Education, Patriotism, Religion.

In these three words are summed up the forces which have made this Republic what it is as a free, independent, liberty-loving, and united nation, occupying a prominent place in the vanguard of the world's highest civilization. Whatever of virtue, enlightenment, stability, reverence for God and respect for the rights of men, enter into and constitute the greatness of this nation owe their existence to the joint operation of these three mighty forces. It has been our custom for years, in our educational number, the first issue in July, to recognize the essential alliance of these powerful agencies in promoting the highest welfare of the nation and of the world.

We place education first because it is the first in order. Beginning at home, in infancy, it is developed through the agency of our public schools, colleges, and universities, or, if denied the latter, through such other educational influences as come from reading, travel, conversation, and experience. From the beginning of our government education has been recognized by our leading statesmen as essential to the perpetuity of our free institutions. Our whole public school system from the "little red school house" to the state university, is based on this theory. Other nations, ruled and guided by privileged classes, may exist in the absence of general education, but not so a republic in which all the people are the sovereigns, and in the government of which all have a part. Reason and experience both teach us that the higher institutions of learning are essential to the efficiency of the lower, seeing that only the highest educated minds are capable of managing wisely the rudimentary training of the young. Without a liberal supply of college and university-trained men in all the walks of life, making their influence felt in their various communities in behalf of the things that are most worth while, our country can never achieve the real greatness to which it should aspire.

One of the strongest passions in human life is love of country. Under its mighty influence men go to the battle field, and to death, chanting the songs of patriotism. No people on earth have furnished higher examples of lofty and heroic devotion to flag and country than the citizens of our own Republic. A nation whose citizens are animated by this principle needs no large standing army, for at the first call of their country, its citizens forsake their farms and factories, their schools and offices, and all the varied pursuits of peace, to defend its honor and rights against the invasion of any foreign, or domestic, foe. In the last analysis this love of country is love of one's fellowmen, and the country for their sakes. To this mighty, unselfish passion we are indebted for the existence of our own nation, whose independence we celebrate on the Fourth of July. As long as patriotism remains pure and unperverted, neither stifled by gross commercialism nor undermined by false political theories, the future of our country will be safe.

But back of education, and back of patriotism, as the underlying motive, and as a guiding principle, is religion—the love of God and of our fellowmen. The highest form of religion which the world knows is that revealed through Jesus Christ, and it is his religion that founded this nation and has given it whatever of true greatness it possesses. Christ alone, of all the world's teachers, has taught us the true relation of .man to God and of man to his fellowmen. It is easy to see how this recognition of our divine and human relationships lies at the basis of all true ideas of government and of religion. The Declaration of Independence and the American Republic lay, potentially, in the teaching of Jesus in relation to the great commandments—love God supremely and your neighbor as yourself. The greatest statesmen which this country has produced, from the "Father of His Country" to President Roosevelt, have recognized the vital relation of religion to the permanency and prosperity of our government. The present wide-extended exposure of corruption and dishonesty, in public office and in private monopolies, is but an illustration of the rising ethical standard among the people and of a quickened public conscience. This, of course, we owe to religion, and it is only in obedience to its stern demands for honesty and purity that these evils can be overcome and the life of the nation be preserved.

It is because our colleges combine, in a pre-eminent degree, these three mighty forces of civilization—education, patriotism, and religion—that we give this number of the paper to a presentation of their claims upon public patronage. They are among the greatest bulwarks of civil and religious liberty. They stand for the widest culture, for the highest altruistic ideals in love of country and fellowmen, and for the noblest form of religion—the Christianity of Christ and of the New Testament. They educate for service. They train their students with a view to their serving their fellowmen, whether in church or state, and teach them that in so doing they are serving God. They have received too little recognition at our hands. To them we are indebted for the men and the women who have done most to make known to the world, and to commend to the favorable consideration of thoughtful people, the principles of a Reformation which has for its aim the glory of God and the good of our fellowmen.

Education, patriotism, religion, these three; but the greatest of these is religion. But it is only as patriotism and religion are enlightened by education that they be-

Notes and Comments.

The last topic of the mid-week prayer-meeting—Jesus rebuking the narrowness of his disciples—contained two instructive incidents: His rebuke of John for forbidding one to cast out demons in his name "because he followed not us," and of John and James, who wished to "call down fire from heaven" on the Samaritans who refused to entertain Jesus and his disciples. The first incident teaches us that we are to rejoice in all the good that is being done in the name of Christ in all religious bodies and to regard them as co-workers with us, in so far as they are working the will of Christ. The second incident teaches us that we are not to return unkindness for unkindness shown to us. John and James, perhaps, felt that as they were out "on the firing-line," among the enemies of the Jews, they would be justified in resorting to extreme measures. "Back yonder in Jerusalem," they might have said, "it is all very well to be courteous; but out there among the Samaritans the thing to do is to call down fire!" But Jesus said in effect, "You misjudge the whole nature of my mission. The son of man came not to destroy men, but to save them. I would have you be kind and forgiving toward all men, but especially toward these Samaritans whose prejudices and ill-will are to be overcome." If we take the lesson in these two incidents to heart they will help to solve some of our current problems.

That old adage about "fighting the devil with fire" is one of Satan's own falsehoods. Nothing pleases his Satanic majesty better than to have his enemies attack him with the very element with which he is most familiar, and in which he is most at home. To use Satan's method and spirit in trying to overcome him is the very worst kind of tactics. "Overcome evil with good" is the divine method. Allowing that the devil is at the bottom of all bitterness and narrowness manifested toward us, how shall we most successfully overcome it? Not by calling down fire from heaven to destroy them, but by praying for them that despitefully use us, and by blessing them that curse us. "But that is contrary to human nature." Perhaps it is contrary to unregenerate human nature, but it is in exact harmony with the spirit of Christ, without which we are none of his. It would give a resistless power to our plea for Christian union by a return to the simplicity that is in Christ, if its advocates were able, by divine grace, to advocate it and overcome its enemies in this spirit. Why not try it? Why should not our pulpits and religious journals urge it as a duty to the cause we plead, and as an attainment worthy of those

who would be known as Christians, or Disciples of Christ?

There is a rebellion abroad against our doctored divinity, like our doctored meat products. One often wonders upon what principle some of our institutions of learning bestow their honorary degrees. Much as we admire Mr. Folk, we are bound to confess that there are a number of men not a dozen miles from the State University campus upon whom an honorary degree could be much more properly bestowed than upon the excellent young governor of this state. We have looked in vain for the names of Dr. J. B. Briney or Dr. J. H. O. Smith among the recipients of any marks of esteem from our own colleges at this degree giving season. Is this just another indication of the fallibility of the wise men of the colleges? And yet, sometimes some colleges do pick out the right man—even colleges of little repute.

That is where the trouble in England now is. John Clifford and Charles Aked, two of the most prominent of British preachers, have been strangely overlooked by American institutions of renown. No degree that Harvard has ever conferred has been more worthily earned than one that might be given to John Clifford. He has, by hard study, won the M. A., B. Sc. and LL. B., at the University of London, representing over ten years of steady university work and examinations. Yet, because Bates' College gave him a D. D., which, we may say from personal knowledge, Dr. Clifford himself never uses, some of his political opponents are trying to discredit Dr. Clifford by reason of this degree from a college hardly known in England. Dr. Clifford is easily the most prominent figure in the British religious world.

Mr. Aked, not a scholar, but a preacher whose abilities have forced him to the front rank, received a "D.D." from Temple College, Philadelphia. Instead of accepting the inevitable gracefully Mr. Aked, after acknowledging the degree and using it, had qualms of conscience, which worked on his whole system in such a way that he finally cast off the title. And yet Mr. Aked is far more worthy of the honor than many a man who receives it from an institution of standing. There is no reason why a reputable institution of learning may not give public recognition to men who have done something notable for the world, especially when they are college bred or of wide literary culture. But there needs to be more discrimination on the part of college authorities. It is just as true that no man of reputation would feel honored except an institution of the best repute was behind any honor bestowed.

Editor's Easy Chair.

The Easy Chair is convinced that there is an unconscious skepticism that is far more universal in its extent and subtle in its operations than any conscious infidelity that may exist. It may be doubted whether most of us accept, at their full value and meaning, many of the statements of Scripture which we constantly use. For instance, we quote as one of our favorite texts, "Seek ye first the kingdom of God," and straightway we seek first, either our personal interests or what we regard as our party or denominational interests, making the kingdom of God a subordinate consideration. If the religious world should "seek first the kingdom of God," then every religious body would regard itself as existing simply for the advancement of the kingdom of God, and its one question, concerning every action and movement, would be, "Will this tend to promote the interests of God's kingdom on earth?" But is that true? Do we indeed subordinate all party interests and party pride to the welfare of the kingdom? Perhaps the most fundamental mistake which religious people have made in the past has been the exaltation of denominational interests above those of the kingdom of God. Do we really believe, then, that the thing of first importance with every individual Christian and with every local church, and with every religious body is the kingdom of God and its righteousness? If we are to judge men's faith by their actions are we not compelled to the conclusion that there is a good deal of latent skepticism in the church as to the primacy of the kingdom of God? We submit this question as worthy of the serious consideration of all who accept the supremacy of Christ and profess to make his teaching the rule of their lives.

Let us take another inspired statement about which there is probably even more unconscious skepticism than about the former. In enumerating the things which abide, Paul mentions faith, hope and love, and says "the greatest of these is love." Do we believe that? Do we act like we believed it? Would not the passage conform more to our real practice if it read, "Now abideth faith, hope and accuracy in theological thinking, and the greatest of these is theological accuracy?" Let us suppose two men, one of whom is characterized by his love to God and men. The law of kindness is in his tongue and his hands are outstretched to relieve the wants of the needy, but he is known to be "unsound," as the phrase goes, in some of his theological opinions, though he holds to Christ with steadfast devotion. The other man is skilled in argument, and has a reputation for great "soundness in the faith," though his heart is as loveless as a stone. Which of the twain would have the better standing—the man that *loves* most or the man that

debates most? We make much of the phrase "sound in the faith," but how seldom we quote the other Scripture, "sound in love!" It is not our purpose, by any means, to discredit accuracy in theological thinking, but rather to magnify the supremacy of love. If we should give it its rightful place at the very head of the Christian virtues it would revolutionize our religious estimates, widen the circle of our Christian fellowship, and put us well forward on the road to Christian unity. If we believe in New Testament Christianity let us exalt love to its rightful and original place. Heresy of the heart is far worse, in the sight of God, than heresy of the head. Indeed, all real heresies emanate from the heart. "Out of the heart are the issues of life."

Why is love greatest? Evidently because it is the greatest force with which to do God's work in the world. It fulfils the law. Nothing else does. All the law and the prophets hang on love—Godward and manward. The law and the prophets had for their ultimate end the bringing about of right relations between God and man, and between man and man. Love is the only force that accomplishes this end. God wants his Church edified. Love edifies. He wants his Church united. Love unites. He wants the world evangelized. Love evangelizes. He wants us to bear each other's burdens. Love is a burden-bearer for others. He wants all wars throughout the earth to cease and men to live together in peace. Love is the great peacemaker. He wants the fatherless and the homeless cared for, the widows visited in their affliction, the sorrowing comforted, and the poor to have the Gospel preached to them. Love is evermore reaching out helpful hands to the poor and the needy, binding up broken hearts, wiping tears from the eyes of sorrow and pouring its wealth of affection upon friendless childhood and desolate old age, which would otherwise be unloved and uncared for. Love is the cohesive power in the family, in the church and in the society without which the social bonds would be disrupted and strife and confusion usurp the place of peace and order. He serveth best who loveth most. That church, or religious body, that is most dominated by love is most united within itself and with God, and has attained to the highest excellence in Christian life. Beloved, here is our standard. Let us emulate each other in loving, until this shall become our distinguishing mark, and men shall say of us, as they said of the disciples of old, "Behold, how they love one another!"

En route. Billowy plains of ripened wheat, ripening oats and growing corn, dotted with comfortable farm houses, green meadows, grazing herds, all passing in swift panoramic view as the train rushes on—that is Illinois to-day. It requires only the historic imagination to see what was once here—a vast inland sea—Lake Michigan continued—tenanted by such monsters of

the deep as inhabited these fresh water seas in prehistoric times. Then, after how many millenniums we know not, the dry land appeared and much later came man, savages first, and afterwards civilized man. He proved to be a farmer and tilled the soil, and his tribe multiplied and the wilderness was subdued, and cities were built, and school houses and churches were erected, and from its soil sprang into the national arena such men as Abraham Lincoln, Stephen A. Douglas and Ulysses S. Grant. What an evolution was that—from the low swampy marsh at the mouth of the sluggish stream that flowed into Lake Michigan at the southern end of it, to Chicago, and from the reptiles of primeval slime to Abraham Lincoln! An evolution we have called it, but not by "resident forces" altogether, but by the coming hither of a higher type of life and civilization, which, by utilizing natural resources, has developed what Illinois has been and is. Now here is the southern border of the present Lake Michigan, and shying away from Chicago to the east we pass up the eastern shore of the lake through many popular resorts and pause for a few hours at our first love of all the east side resorts—Macatawa Park.

In our brief stop-over at Macatawa we had the pleasure of greeting the Haleys, Hallacks, Rogers, Hollands, Combs, Clarks and Weeks; take down the shutters from "Edgewood-on-the-Lake," take in the wondrous sweep of vision from its upper veranda, including a storm-cloud approaching majestically over the watery plain, and hasten on to our train to continue our journey to the north. It seemed a great pity to break away from the association of such good people as we met there, and we indulge the hope that some of them, at least, may join the Pentwater colony of Disciples. T. P. Haley and George H. Combs were in *neglige* attire, so that their churches would hardly know them. Let them come up to Pentwater and we will theologize and ichthyologize by turns. There is a very close connection between these two sciences. One of the greatest revelations which the original disciples of Jesus ever had concerning his divinity, came to them while they were fishing. And is it not remarkable that when Jesus selected his apostles he chose so many fishermen? But hark! What sound is that which greets our ears? It is the roar of the surf on the beach at "Garrison Park," Pentwater. Here we are at last. "The Pioneer"—our humble cottage—seems as glad to see us as we to see it. The trees we love so much are nodding us a hearty welcome, and the waves are clapping their hands in joy! That is all there is to welcome us, as we are the first arrivals of the season, either at "Garrison Park" or our near neighbor, the "Oceana Beach" resort. The season here does not open, very widely at least, until after the glorious Fourth. We have not yet had time to open the cottage, as I am hastily penning these lines to get them away on the next mail train on this the last day of June. We notice a distinct change of temperature here and have already donned heavier clothing. We have just heard the whistle of "The Kansas," the steamer from Chicago, which is just making its first tri-weekly trip. Concerning all these things, more anon.

Our Colleges and Foreign Missions

By Archibald McLean
President of the Foreign Christian Missionary Society.

The first need of the mission field is the need of a sufficient number of thoroughly equipped men. No other need is comparable with this. Money is needful, and money is hard to get, but not so hard as men of the right kind. Money can be had if suitable men are ready for the service.

It is to the colleges that the society must look for men. What West Point does for the army, and what Annapolis does for the navy, our colleges must do for foreign missions. To be sure now and then a man may be sent who has not been to college. He may be a man of extraordinary ability. He may, by sheer force of intellect have acquired the education necessary, but men of that sort are very rare, and they would be none the worse, but all the better, for a collegiate education. In any case it is to the colleges that the societies must look for a steady supply of men. They can come from no other source.

In the early years of the present missionary era, mechanics and farmers were sent out in large numbers. No others were ready to go. Men trained in the colleges preferred to remain at home. It is not so now, men of ability and education are called for more and more, and they are responding, "Here am I, send me." The fields need such men. Most of the work done in the early period was done among savage and illiterate people. The missionaries now go to the people who have great schools and high educational ideals. These people must be addressed by men of culture and refinement if much good is to be done. The missionaries have to do with government officials and military officers, travelers and merchants. They should be men of broad and generous culture in order to favorably impress such people as they meet.

Pastors and evangelists and other helpers must be trained for the work. This can not be done by men of limited or no education. Wise master-builders are needed to lay foundations upon which others shall build. They are needed to train those who shall go out in the name of the Lord to preach the Gospel of his grace and glory to their own countrymen.

In most, if not all, of our schools, mission study classes are taught. In nearly every school there is a band of volunteers. The students meet once a week or once in two weeks to pray about the fields, to pray for the workers, and to prepare themselves in mind and heart for the service. In some of our schools missions are a part of the curriculum. This subject is taught as church history or exegesis is taught. Missions are having a larger place constantly in our colleges. This is one of the hopeful signs of the times.

Our Colleges and Home Missions

By Geo. B. Ranshaw
Field Secretary of the American Christian Missionary Society.

At the recent Texas convention addresses were made by the representatives of the various organized agencies through which we are endeavoring to do the Lord's work. Bro. Stephen J. Corey, with inimitable and convincing charm, showed how impossible it is for a congregation to live unless it have the spirit of missions, and unless, fired with enthusiasm for the Christ and the world, it send far and near its cheering, healing help. Immediately following him came Charles A. Finch, the successful pastor of the church at Topeka, presenting the cause of church extension. In an admirable address he proved how utterly impossible it would be to have a congregation to enthuse upon the subject of foreign missions without the help of the board of church extension, to gather into a nucleus under one roof the individuals that compose the effective congregation. Following this conviction so deeply driven home to the hearts of the most appreciative and responsive convention within our ranks, the representative of the American Christian Missionary Society boldly declared that unless the home missionary board sent out its faithful skirmishers, preaching the Gospel and gathering together the inarticulated elements, combining them skillfully into dynamic forces, there would be no need of church extension loans and no possibility of foreign missionary interest in a given locality. So that underneath all the work we are endeavoring to do, in a very essential way, is the work popularly spoken of as home missions. It seemed to be sound logic and the convention cheered the argument and endorsed the conclusion. But

T. E. Shirley, of Texas Christian University, presently arose to speak on Christian Education. Alluding to the addresses just mentioned, he said: "I agree with them all, and especially with the last one, which convincingly presented home missions as the foundation of all our co-operative work. But I would like to ask Brother Ranshaw where he is going to get the preacher who is to preach to those scattered people and bring them into effective union and relationship with the great brotherhood of workers, unless our colleges train up our young men for this work? Home missions is the foundation, but education is the bedrock." And this is the conclusion which experience in home missionary work forces upon every man.

Home missionary work is the vitally essential work before the church of Christ to-day, for, obviously upon it rests the development of the church, the future of the nation, and destiny of the world. A work so fundamentally important demands men of trained abilities. There was a time when the uneducated preacher could do effective evangelistic work and could give great aid in rapidly extending the borders of the kingdom. But that day has passed. Schools, colleges, newspapers, magazines, Chautauqua courses, libraries, interurban and transcontinental communication, have so broadened the culture, developed the capabilities, energized the minds and inspired the purposes of men, that the demand for an educated ministry comes with as much insistence from the firing line on the frontier as from the city centers. The untrained preacher, like the untrained mechanic, is relegated to secondary operations and reduced to the minimum wage. The most frequent complaints that reach our office are those which have their just lodgment against men who essay to fill positions for which they are ill qualified. Such men have, now and then, set back a hopeful missionary work a whole decade, and by their unwise conduct and illiterate speech have not infrequently repelled the very people whom they sought to reach.

The city becomes more and more the point of strategy in the conquest of the world. Trained men only can enter the cities, maintain the cause against the myriad antagonisms that here assail, compel attention from the world-distraught, set high the standard of the cross and by it conquer.

The difference between the skilled cabinet maker and the wheeler of sawdust in the pit is one of training. The one has skill and knowledge of tools, appreciation of proportion, initiative and inventive genius. He is not confined to a single round of employment of mind or body. He devises, builds, improves upon each piece of workmanship, and blesses thus his fellowmen while bettering himself. The wheeler in the pit toils in the rut of a single wheel day after day. His lack of training limits his usefulness. The difference is even greater between the trained and the untrained preacher. As we view the field of battle at every point we see the need of trained and seasoned men, we hear the call for leaders, well equipped and ready for the keenest problems of the day. The hope of the future in home missions is in our colleges.

Cincinnati, O.

Our Debt to Our Colleges

By J. G. Waggoner
Field Secretary of Eureka College.

"I am debtor both to the Greeks and barbarians. * * I am ready to preach."—Paul.

"Never was there such a demand for competent preachers of the Gospel."—D. R. Dungan.

"In the Christian colleges rests our hope of greater victories in evangelism. * * * Help the college if you would speed the world's evangelization."—W. J. Wright.

"The demand of the hour is educated men in the pulpit. * * One of the most potent methods of preaching the Gospel is by the support of the colleges where Christ is honored and his truth is taught."—Judge C. J. Scofield.

"First among the agencies for spreading the Gospel is the preacher, and first among the means of supplying the preachers is the Bible college."—W. F. Richardson.

"Our schools are our sources of pulpit supply. * * * Our schools and our faithful educators, to whom we owe immeasurable and unspeakable obligation, and whose work is the essential basis of all our enterprises and all our successes, receive scant attention."—F. D. Power.

"One thousand dollars brings $50 a year to the college which enables one student to graduate each year. If he preaches twenty years, he ought to add 1,000 members, put $10,000 into church property and $2,000 into missions. What better can $1,000 do?"—Gen. F. M. Drake.

Salvation being the *gift* of God does not release the receiver from *obligation*, but intensifies it. Therefore Paul's "*debt*" and ours—Paul's obligation expressed itself in passing the blessing on to others, so must ours. Our debt to our colleges arises from their contribution to preaching the Gospel.

If we appreciate the invaluable services rendered the church and the world by the great army of mighty men and leaders which our colleges have trained to preach the Gospel, if we appreciate the "unspeakable sacrifices" of our educators to produce such men, then we owe our colleges an everlasting debt of appreciation and gratitude.

If the college fills a difficult and a trying place, where selfish, or designing men may ruin the prospects and possibilities of young men by unfaithfulness, or pernicious doctrine, if our teachers and trustees need wisdom from on high, that they may train our young men to be mighty men of God, declaring his whole counsel, preaching his word faithfully, then we owe our colleges our most sincere and devout prayers to God to give grace and wisdom.

If the great truths and principles for which we stand are worthy to be occupied and promoted by our children; if our children are to be worthy and competent to be the leaders of the world's moral and spiritual life, then we owe them the opportunity of moral and spiritual training in colleges which give attention to these things. If we look to our colleges for leaders in divine things, ministers, leaders and missionaries for the world's life, then we owe the colleges the best material, our children, our patronage.

If the Christian college is at the basis of our progress, if every additional well trained minister adds strength and power to every department of our growth, if the foreign fields depend on our colleges for men and women, if every phase of home work is made stronger by the better educated, and better trained ministry, if all our children in whatever profession are made stronger in moral and spiritual life by being educated of our colleges, then we owe these institutions our financial support. If tuition pays only half the expenses of conducting colleges, as it does, and if every church and every Christian has better services and a better ministry because of our Christian colleges then we owe them our financial support. No Christian should be satisfied until, according to his ability, he has made a liberal donation in money, or annuity, or deed to property, or has put a bequest in his will to our colleges that have done so much for the kingdom of God in the past and on which so much depends for the future.

Eureka, Ill.

Education Day and How to Observe It

By W. P. Aylsworth
President of Cotner University.

Great advantage attaches to uniform and concerted action in any important task. Some of us who were brought up in the woods remember the eventful days when a whole neighborhood came together to do what a few could not possibly have done. The shout and rhythm of action, as willing hands raised huge beams to their places in the heavy framework had much to do with success.

Just such enthusiasm and unity of effort are needed in the observance of education day. To arouse interest and overcome inertia can not be accomplished by a few; it should be the work of a whole brotherhood. The lifting of our educational interests to the proper place in our organized work as a people is the duty of the hour. It is not too early to think it over and make some resolutions.

1. Resolve that without fail the cause shall be presented if possible on the day appointed. If not then as soon as possible afterward. It is not easy to make good such a resolve under some circumstances. Other things, even less important, crowd it out. The pastor will be advised to omit it "this time." Interest is lukewarm or courage fails and the opportunity to help our most needy cause goes over. Such is the case with a large number of our churches if returns are sure indications. Only through the ministry can the people be reached. What has been true of our missionary appeals is true of the cause of Christian education. Too often the people are more willing to help than we think. At any rate a duty is laid upon the ministry which can not be put aside without an almost criminal participation in defeat and failure of a great cause.

2. Present the facts in the case. Show how vital is the success of our schools to all other departments of Christian effort. Study the map, see how the communities of the brotherhood most populous and best organized have in their very heart school centers. Study history. See how all enduring reforms have sprung from centers of learning. The restoration movement is not an exception unless in its greater need of the strength and freedom of intelligence. Study our needs. The old guard of the ministry is passing away. Who shall fill their places in the harvest fields of humanity? Can we hope that the great secular and industrial schools will suffice to furnish trained and enthused workers? At least the initiative must be taken in the environment of Christian training or our brightest youth will be turned away from the spirit of sacrifice essential to success. Listen to the calls from empty pulpits and destitute mission fields. With such a preparation your observance of education day can not fail to arouse interest.

3. Present the bright side. We dwell upon discouragements too much. Difficulties and failures should be presented that our needs may be seen, but it is possible to dwell so much on the dark side that no courage remains to help. The fact remains that at tremendous odds our schools are doing a great work and are steadily gaining in influence and power. Let it be understood that to help on this work is to lend a hand to a winning cause. Consecrated money can find no safer or better investment. A better day is dawning for this much neglected part of our organized effort if all who can will lend a hand in a united effort to lift the burden.

4. Let the urgent need of this work be subject of prayer. May God help us each one to do his duty in presenting this paramount need as it has never been presented before.

Lincoln, Neb.

Our Colleges and Evangelism

By WM. J. WRIGHT
National Supt. of Evangelism

So far as the ministry is concerned, the college measurably takes the place of our Master in the training of the twelve. Its function is to take all possible things of God—in earth, in the universe, in man and in the book—and make them the property of the embryo preacher. Further, it is to show him the best methods of applying all truth and is to train and direct him in the application.

Evangelism is the process of making known to men God's purpose and plan for men, both for this world and life, and for the future and unseen. But this knowledge is not imparted simply that men may not be ignorant. The objective is to "turn" them from darkness to light and from the power of Satan to God;" to bring them to immediate, hearty and constant harmony and co-operation with God in making his purpose and plan operative and universal among men.

The college views all truth as being God's. It therefore rightly considers him who is in possession of the greatest measure of truth, with which his own life is consistent, best qualified to make God known to men, and best equipped to persuade them to commit their ways to him; to delight themselves also in the Lord in order that he may give them the desires of their hearts. The college stands for the best methods of acquiring and applying truth. Possibly this should be affirmed mainly of the truth which is commonly reckoned as not being vital to religion; for the possession and application of religious truth has not been as fully or scientifically treated in our colleges as its merits demand. Or, if religious truth has been satisfactorily

imparted to young preachers by our colleges, the best methods of applying this truth to other lives, and winning them to the service of the Lord, have been much neglected.

It is a common thing for preachers to be graduated from our colleges in almost absolute ignorance of the work of evangelism. Not only are many of them uninformed as to the thousand niceties which make the pastoral duties and public meetings smooth and attractive; but—and it is a thousand times more important—they are untaught and untrained in the fundamentals of evangelism. If a man be awkward, embarrassed, boorish in pastoral calling, pulpit ministration, performing the marriage ceremony or administering Christian baptism, he may be simply ludicrous or ridiculous; but if he does not know how to make his sermons evangelistic, flashing with conviction and throbbing with enticing and wooing notes, then he is out of place, pitiable; and he or his teachers, criminal. The college has failed to equip him for his most important task. If has not discovered and trained his latent powers for winning men to God. It has given truth but not spirit and method; it has made a scholar perhaps, but not an evangelist.

I once made a list of 57 words mispronounced by an evangelist in a single sermon, and even then the list was incomplete. An evangelist of national reputation, recently and repeatedly made three syllables of the word "microbes." Another says that "men have saw more than Moses seen when he clumb the mount and seen the Promised Land." Such talk is a rock of offence; yet the men who use it wield well the Spir-

it's sword and win vast throngs to God. On the other hand, here is a man whose knowledge is of wide range and deep; whose words are sweeter than honey, for pronunciation; grammar and rhetoric are all but faultless, but he does not make me see myself as I appear before God; he does not let me see Jesus. His sermons are "icily regular, splendidly null, dead perfection; no more." The former man offends my ear; the latter rives my heart. The former preaching is an offence to learning and culture; the latter is an insult to the high calling of the evangelist and an affront to God.

The best college, then, is the one which trains the brain and fires the heart; which fits a man not simply for acceptable public speech, in edifying saints, but which stamps indelibly upon his soul the vision of the lost, gives egress and direction to the fire once shut up within his bones, and which now breaks out and kindles like fires in countless other lives.

"Till every kindred, every tribe
   On this terrestrial ball,
To Him all majesty ascribe,
   And crown Him Lord of all."

Let this be the program in our colleges: *make our young preachers evangelistic.* Our national board of evangelism, in order to bring this to pass, extends herein to all our colleges a helping hand. The evangelistic institutes and schools of evangelism which we conduct will give your students new ideas of the ministry, and will influence their preaching for many years.

If you can use us we are "your servants for Jesus' sake," in all matters pertaining to "our colleges and evangelism."

Y. M. C. A. Bldg., Cincinnati, O.

The Elderburg Association

CHAPTER VII.

Brother Piano-Tuner Reviewed.

In the manner of Brother Lawyer, when he came to review Brother Piano-Tuner, there was, for once, none of the cocksureness of the great jurist laying down the law. He spoke, for the most part, musingly, hesitatingly, as if communing with his own soul rather than with his audience.

"Truthfulness," he said, "is a quality to make the man who possesses it respected in heaven and admired on earth. It is an essential part of a preacher's equipment, wanting which he must fail, though he speak with the tongues of men and of angels.

"Yet the people of Spinsterview, when they accused our brother of lying, were flagrantly unjust, whether they intended injustice or not. A charitable explanation of their conduct is that they were unable to distinguish between a falsehood and an erroneous prediction.

"We all utter prophecies at times, announcing them in such form that they seem like statements of fact; but if such of them as fail of fulfillment are to be accounted as lies, heaven help us all.

"'I shall die an old maid,' said a dear girl. She died at the age of 80, having buried two husbands, leaving behind her forty-three grandchildren and eleven great-grandchildren. A liar? No. She had uttered a prediction which lost its way amid a labyrinth of unforeseeable conditions, and so could not arrive at fulfillment.

"'I shall never take another to fill the place made vacant by the death of my beloved,' said the heartbroken widower. Twenty years later he buried his third wife. His hasty announcement of perpetual widowerhood had not been made with intent to deceive. Looking with tear-blurred eyes into a future heavily shadowed, much obscured by flying cloud-rack, he had mistaken a blooming orange tree for a weeping willow. Byron's lady, who, 'swearing she would ne'er consent, consented,' was not a perjurer but a poor prophet. A lie is an untruth uttered with intent to deceive.

"'When I said I would die a bachelor,' said Benedict, 'I did not think I should live till I were married.' That explanation secures Benedict from any condemnation for lying. When this witness declared he would die a bachelor, the declaration did

not emanate from a heart deceitful and desperately wicked; it was merely a forecast of the future which turned out to be wrong. If bad augury is a sin, then many an almanac maker that I know is damned. Shall we, in this enlightened age, take the poor, discredited augur to the summit of the Tarpeian rock and cast him down headlong? That were absurd, illogical, and wasteful.

"This case of Brother P-T brings us face to face with one of the deep mysteries of this life. Why is it that when a preacher marries he must presently leave the place where matrimony overtakes him? The human intellect has seldom had to grapple with a more perplexing problem than this. When the man in the parable said, 'I have married a wife, and therefore I can not come,' the Master did not pretend to discover any essential connection between the fact of marriage and the Therefore; and I think no one has since discovered it. So, in our day, when a preacher says, 'I have married a wife, and therefore I had to go,' we are confronted with the same problem. We can not discover the

(Continued on Page 848.)

As Seen From the Dome   By F. D. Power

Our party from the start has had excellent health. The ten cases of the bubonic plague reported in Alexandria even cause no uneasiness. Our venerable Doctor Divinitatis from Denver made the Samaritan trip on horseback for three days, and the last day was eleven hours in the saddle, and had to be helped into the hotel, but he is as bright as a lark in Maytime. Our patriarchal church dedicator went down to Jericho and broke his carriage down four times and had to walk four miles in the rain but no camel can make quicker or longer strides, and he is in better condition than the poor fellow who fell among thieves on the same journey. Our man from Oklahoma went in both the Dead Sea and the Jordan in one day, something few men can do, however long unwashed, but he seems to have felt no inconvenience from his contact with much water and consequent loss of real estate. Our men Hester and Medbury ran considerable risk in rescuing a young calf on the highway to Jericho, and restoring it to the arms of the shepherd, but they seem to have recovered from their act of heroism. One of our ladies tried to see the walls of Jerusalem from the back of a donkey and has settled the question as to the location of the Holy Sepulchre by the impression that Jerusalem has no walls. All of the little party of Disciples with a big D, belonging to the Restoration movement with a capital R, I am glad to say, are in good condition after a somewhat trying trip. We reached Egypt in good shape on Wednesday, March 21, landing in Alexandria, and cheered by the crews of our warships in the harbor.

Egypt is a most interesting land. "Egypt," said Herodotus, "contains more wonders than any other land, and is pre-eminent above all the countries of the world." We are on the Nile. Like the Amazon, the Congo and Mississippi, it is one of the longest of the world's rivers, only fifty miles less than the Father of Waters, being 4,062 miles in length. It supplies the daily needs of ten millions of people, and their horses and cattle, for without it the Libyan and Arabian deserts would blot out all Egypt. All Egypt, its very civilization, its social and political order have been determined by the Nile, and Egypt is old. It has its ancient, its middle and its new empire. Its beginning is placed with the reign of Menes 5004 B. C. Its ancient empire closed before Abraham was born, the period to which belong the Pyramids, B. C. 5,000 to 3,250. The middle empire with its shepherd kings covers the period to 2,000 B. C. Its new empire gave the world Thothmes III. and the great Seti I., and his greater Son Rameses II., the Sesostris of the Greeks; and in the Museum of Cairo we see the faces of these giants who flourished 3,000 years ago. In Egypt time is reckoned not by centuries, but millenniums. The Pyramids are twice as old as the ten commandments, and when they were built,

nearly 6,000 years ago, we are told Egypt had its written language, its grammar, its literature, its knowledge of mathematics and of the arts, its established hierarchy, and its social system. It worshipped the principle of life, hence the worship of the sacred bull, of the ibis, the crocodile, and the cat, and even the lotus. So Juvenal sang:

"O sacred nation whose gods grow in gardens!"

They believed in immortality and divided man into several elements that ultimately would be reunited and hence embalmed the body. Some one, skilled in figures, estimates the embalmed mummies in 4,700 years at 731,000,000. Egypt's architecture is massive. Temples and tombs are the notable examples. Cheops is a great tomb composed of 2,300,000 blocks of stone, each containing forty cubic feet. Cleopatra and Mark Antony, Joseph, Jacob and Abraham saw this Pyramid and the great Sphinx. Scores of volumes have been written to explain these monuments. These ancient people knew geometry and astronomy. They said: "The earth forms a part of the planetary system and is subject to the same law of motion," and in an inscription older than Abraham declared: "The earth navigates the celestial ocean in like manner with the sun and stars," and Ptah, they said: "moulded man, created the gods, made the sky, and formed the earth, *revolving in space.*" With the discovery of the Rosetta stone now in the British museum, scholars learned all the riches of Egyptian literature carved upon monuments and written upon papyrus, and these ancient writings confirm the teaching of our Bible. Explorers have discovered the ruins of the treasure cities of Pharaoh, Pithom and Raamses, which Exodus tells us Israel built. It is declared, "The Egyptians made the children of Israel to serve with rigour, and they made their lives bitter with hard bondage in mortar and in brick;" and while it was the custom of the Egyptians to lay brick in mud and not in mortar, it was found that the brick of Pithom was laid in *mortar and not in mud.* Straw was first furnished the Israelites to mix with their clay and then denied them and they had to collect "stubble" to mix with clay. These very bricks have come to light; the cellar walls of Pithom laid with brick mixed with chopped straw, and higher up, bricks made of clay mixed with "stubble," that part that still grow on the Nile; and then above them, bricks made of nothing but Nile mud! While Egypt is nominally subject to Turkey it is really self-governing. The Khedive, or King, is supposed to rule, but Great Britain administers the government as a trustee for the debts owing to her and to other nations. Lord Cromer is the real head. The international courts are composed of thirteen European powers and the United States. It has 400,000 square miles, and is a long oasis worn in the rocky desert by the ever-flowing Nile stream and varying from half a mile to fourteen miles in

width. Under the Ptolemies we are told there were 25,000,000 people, now there are 10,000,000. Only twelve per cent can read and write. The Nile valley has about 13,000 square miles; 5,700,000 acres are under cultivation, and they raise three crops a year by irrigation. It is as rich as an Illinois prairie. There are 5,219,113 date palms which are in themselves a great treasure. Egypt is the gift of the Nile. The very name "Neilos" from *nea ilus,* "new mud," tells the story of its fertilizing properties. In Homeric days the Nile was called *Aigyptos,* a name afterward transferred to the country. The present ruler is Abbas Hilmi II., who became Khedive in '92 at the age of 18. He is well qualified, popular and content with one wife though the Koran allows him four. He has six children.

Alexandria was our first sight of Egypt. Alexander the Great intended this city to be the capital of the world. Alexandria was the home of Ptolemy, of the great Library, of Philo, the great philosopher, of Cleopatra, of Hypatia, of Apollos and Barnabas, and of Mark who wrote the second gospel of the Septuagint translation

❀ ❀

WELL POSTED

A California Doctor With 40 Years Experience.

"In my 40 years' experience as a teacher and practitioner along hygienic lines," says a Los Angeles physician, "I have never found a food to compare with Grape-Nuts for the benefit of the general health of all classes of people. I have recommended Grape-Nuts for a number of years to patients with the greatest success and every year's experience makes me more enthusiastic regarding its use.

"I make it a rule to always recommend Grape-Nuts and Postum Food Coffee in place of coffee when giving my patients instructions as to diet for I know both Grape-Nuts and Postum can be digested by any one.

"As for myself, when engaged in much mental work my diet twice a day consists of Grape-Nuts and rich cream. I find it just the thing to build up gray matter and keep the brain in good working order.

"In addition to its wonderful effects as a brain and nerve food Grape-Nuts always keeps the digestive organs in perfect healthy tone. I carry it with me when I travel, otherwise I am almost certain to have trouble with my stomach." Name given by Postum Co., Battle Creek, Mich.

Strong endorsements like the above from physicians all over the country have stamped Grape-Nuts the most scientific food in the world.

"There's a reason."

Look in pkgs. for the famous little book, "The Road to Wellville."

of the Old Testament used by him of whom it was said, "Out of Egypt have I called my son." It is a modern city of 320,-000 people, 46,000 of whom are Europeans. It has its places of interest. One sees on entering the harbor of this great commercial port, on the left, the Phare or light-house, the direct descendant of the ancient Pharos which was nearly 600 feet high, illuminated at night with great fires to guide the ships, which was one of the seven wonders of the world; and one views on the right Pompey's Pillar, a shaft of red granite, 81 feet high, the twin of Cleopatra's Needle, which has no more connection with Caesar's rival than the shaft in Central Park has with the Egyptian sorceress. It is a singularly striking monument not unlike the Nelson Column in Trafalgar Square, London. The city is a hybrid. It has had a mushroom growth compared to the Old Alexandria, or the dead cities of the Nile Valley, Heliopolis, Memphis, Thebes, Karnak, Luxor, or Dendera. We think of Mark's Gospel, and Athanasius thundering against the Arians, and Cleopatra, "conqueror of the world's conquerors," and Kingsley's Hypatia. We think of it as the entrance to the Egypt of the Pharaoh's and of the Bible, of the Caliphates, and of the Arabian Nights. We think of it as the spot where we first view the great river whose delta, the seven mouths of the Nile, spread out like a seven-ribbed fan, pictures a green robe interwoven with silver threads—green fields of wheat and barley, of melons and cucumbers, of peas and grasses interspersed with palm groves and white minarets and intersected with canals and trenches with *dahabiehs* and *giassos* with their lateen sails apparently moving through the land. We think of Caliph Omar and the Great Library and his fallacious epigram: "If these writings agree with the Book of God they are useless, and need not be preserved; if they disagree, they are pernicious. In either case, let them be destroyed"; and the 300,000 parchments supplied fuel for the 4,000 baths of Alexandria. We think of the battle in which Octavius defeated the army of Antony near by, and gained for Rome a new empire; of the struggle near the same spot between 12,000 Britons and an equal number of French under Napoleon which gave the death blow to Napoleon's scheme of founding an eastern empire and converting the Mediterranean into a "French lake"; and of that greater conflict at Aboukir Bay, August 1, 1798, when Nelson met Brueys, and they illuminated the night by the incessant discharge of 2,000 cannon and the flames of burning French ships, and India was saved on the shores of Egypt. We think of the famous Rosetta stone, found near here, which furnished the key sought by archaeological students and Egyptologists for years to the hieroglyphic writings of this old land. We think finally of that "bridge of water" with which from Sesostris down men sought to span the Isthmus at last achieved by one heroic man, De Lesseps. Such thoughts come to us as we set foot on this shore.

The Elderburg Association.

(Continued from Page 846.)

relation between the wedding and the Therefore. There must be a lost premise in the formula by which the conclusion is reached; there must be an undiscoverable cog in the intellectual machinery that grinds out for us that particular grist of information; there must be a mysterious, invisible span in the bridge across the logical gulf between the fact of matrimony and the resultant hegira of the happy pair to fresh fields and pastures new.

"It is curious to observe how great intellects have fought shy of this problem. Darwin may have neglected it because it belongs to the domain of the metaphysical rather than to the physical. Huxley, Herbert Spencer, Jeremy Bentham, John Stuart Mill, Haeckel and Draper, maintain a silence on this theme that is almost cowardly, if not entirely criminal. Carlyle, Emerson and Immanuel Kant ignore it altogether. One might suppose that Swedenborg, who made a number of excusions into the Great Beyond, might have 'met-up' with something, over there, to elucidate this problem; if he did he failed to mention it. It is reasonable to believe, think you, that these great ones have not noticed a phenomenon so frequent and so singularly interesting? That were a poor compliment to their powers of discernment. Just between ourselves, they have been afraid to tackle it. Smart men do not like to be 'up the stump' (as the janitor might express it), any better than the rest of us. Therefore, they have thrown this puzzle into the intellectual scrap-heap, along with the problems of squaring the circle, perpetual motion, and the fourth dimension.

"I wish I could explain the thing myself. If I could I would, no matter what it might cost me.

"We are next to hear from Brother Paper-Hanger."

✸ ✸

Education at the Missouri Convention.

The educational session at the recent Missouri State Convention was not a prolonged one. President Carl Johann, in making the report of the Students' Aid Fund, said that the great percentage of the men who died in the war was through lack of knowledge and preparation on the part of leaders. The churches, he said, must not make the same mistake, but provide competent leaders for the work which they have to do. He dwelt on the insignificant amount of money which is provided for this purpose. All the money that has been spent for educational institutions will not meet the cost of a single battleship, and one battleship's maintenance a year would cost more than all our schools cost. The price of one torpedo would be more than is expended for a whole year in the maintenance of Christian University, of which he was the president.

Ralph Lozier, of Carrollton, made a brilliant and telling speech on behalf of education. He asked the ministers to rise, and some thirty or forty who had not departed for their homes did so. "Is this the

Our Budget

—Wanted: Attention to our colleges.

—Wanted: The brainiest and best young men for the ministry.

—Wanted: More skilled physicians for an abundance of sick churches.

—Wanted: Our religious papers to support Education Day. Name those that are giving special space to our educational interests? THE CHRISTIAN-EVANGELIST is easily first and "The Christian Century" second. "Silence is sinful when to speak is a duty."

—We present in this annual mid-summer Education Number a view of the work and the needs of the principal colleges and schools under the control of the Disciples of Christ in the United States. No cause among us is so neglected in comparison with its importance as our school interests. Read the testimony of McLean, Ranshaw, Wright, men at the head of our national societies.

—The Editor-in-Chief escaped from St. Louis just in time to avoid some of the extreme heat. For some time he will send "copy" from Garrison Park, Pentwater, Mich.

—May we again request our subscribers to address their communications that are not strictly personal "To the Editor," and not to J. H. Garrison or Paul Moore, or any individual. The various members of the staff are frequently absent from the office on special business and items that should receive immediate attention are delayed or perhaps lost, through being sent to an individual who may be a thousand miles from THE CHRISTIAN-EVANGELIST office.

—Looking over the matter we have on hand, we find a good deal of material on the subject of federation that might well claim place if the discussion were to continue, but in view of the fact that we have decided for the present to close the discussion we are sure these brethren will understand why their contributions are omitted.

—W. H. Gross begins the work at Oak Harbor, O.

—The San Marcos River camp meeting will be held July 6-22.

—The New York state convention has just been meeting at Elmira.

—The church at Stoutland, Mo., has lately put in a new lighting system.

—We regret very much to hear of the death of the wife of Milo W. Nethercutt, of Toulon, Ill.

—The church at Douglas, Ariz., has called Mart G. Smith, of Waco, Texas, and he has accepted.

—We hear that A. N. Lindsay, of New Franklin, will take charge at Clinton, Mo., September 1.

—W. C. Crerie has accepted a call to the church at Haverhill, Mass., and has entered upon the work.

—The corner-stone of a new building will be laid at Belle Center, O., July 8. H. E. Becker is the pastor.

—J. K. Hester has left Denver for Paonia, Colo., with the purpose of erecting a $3,000 church building.

—James N. Crutcher, of Chillicothe, Mo., preached the "Home-Coming" sermon for Hugh McClellan at Richmond, Ky.

—The corner-stone of the new addition to the church at Chanute, Kan., has been laid. G. W. Kitchen is the pastor.

—George E. Lyon, of Lyons, was elected president of the Kansas State Christian Endeavor Union at the recent convention.

—Old People's Day at the First Christian Church, Nelson, Neb., of which F. Elsworth Day is pastor, was a splendid success.

—The First Church, Pine Bluff, Ark., has given a call to C. C. Cline, which he has accepted.

—The Illinois Christian Missionary Society will hold its 56th annual convention at Paris, September 10-13.

—The convention of Missouri, District No. 2 will convene at Sweet Springs July 16-18. Address T. B. Elmore.

—T. W. Bellingham is proving popular for addresses on special occasions, he having been asked to deliver several of these recently.

—E. W. Finkle, who has been with the North Side Church of Lawrence, Kan., has been asked to remain another year at an increased salary.

—C. E. Smith, who has done a good work at Charleston, S. C., will make his headquarters at St. Stephens. Marcellus Ely has succeeded him.

—Austin, O., will be without a preacher September 1, unless in the meantime the church selects a successor to C. Burton Stevens, who has resigned.

—The latest report from Dean Van Kirk shows that the total amount received for the relief of our San Francisco churches up till June 25, was $4,152.16.

—The brethren at Sapulpa, I. T., expected to enter their new house of worship last Lord's day. Prospects have never been so bright for them as they are now.

—As a token of appreciation of his work the young people of our church at Knightstown, Ind., recently presented a handsome Morris chair to their pastor, E. S. Conner.

—M. M. Davis, of Dallas, Texas, has dedicated the church at Ponca City, Okla., and raised more than half the cost of the building. R. H. Love is the pastor at Ponca.

—Dr. Thomas B. McCartney, assistant professor in Greek at Kentucky University, will spend a month in Virginia as a lecturer and instructor in the State School for Teachers.

—E. T. McFarland celebrated his seventh anniversary as pastor of the Fourth Church, St. Louis, July 1. This is the longest pastorate of any of the present pastors in St. Louis, among our people.

—R. E. Hieronymus, president of Eureka College, will spend the summer in Europe with a small party of congenial spirits. They sailed on June 27, and will return the week before college opens.

—J. M. Monroe has dedicated the church at Mountain View, Okla. The former building was blown away by a cyclone last fall. All the indebtedness on the new structure was raised at the dedication.

—L. C. Swan has resigned at Fremont, Neb., to take effect by October 1. A good man will therefore be needed a little later for this church, which has done a good work in the past, and is a hopeful field.

—The church at Concord (Minier) Ill., has just had its annual rally. J. W. Street, pastor at Mackinaw, and Dr. J. M. Cody, of Tremont, were the chief speakers at the afternoon service. J. W. Pearson is the minister.

—Prof. E. L. Porter, of the department of science of Kentucky University, and Prof. Henry Lloyd, of the department of mathematics, will spend the summer at the University of Chicago, studying in the Graduate School.

—We regret to hear of the death of Lyda Gertrude Archer, daughter of Broth-

er and Sister George W. Brown, missionaries at Jubbulpore, India. She spent some time at Hiram and only returned to India about a year ago.

—F. W. Allen, the young pastor at Odessa, Mo., who recently passed through this city on his return bridal tour, announced that the church at Cairo, Ill., for which he preached in passing, is in need of a pastor and will be glad to secure the right man.

—W. P. Keeler writes us that churches might with advantage arrange for an entertainment in the form of an illustrated lecture on Gladstone, given by M. O. Naramore, with musical setting by his wife. The lecture has just been enjoyed by the church at Englewood, Chicago.

—We regret to learn that Harold Bell Wright has been ill with a slight attack of malaria. The total amount raised as a result of the "missionary week" held by the church at Lebanon, Mo., was $260, so that all the missionary and benevolent interests have been remembered. This church finds this way of raising money for missions the best it has tried.

❋ ❋

—Harold H. Griffis has just been ordained to the ministry by the church at
Middletown, Ind. He was the valedictor-
ian of this year's class at the Bible college,
Lexington. L. E. Murray predicts for him
fruitful ministry. He was to begin work
Kalispell, Mont., July 1.

—John L. Rose writes us from Atchison,
Kan., that they were just starting a big
meeting. Brother Scoville was to be on
and in a few days, and Brother Kendall
was already there. The tabernacle will
at two thousand.

—The Sunday-school at Watonga, Okla.,
is not observed children's day for many
years until this year. F. Douglas Wharton
now the pastor, and he makes it a point
take all missionary offerings. More than
the apportionment was raised, and the
school is rejoicing. D. J. Martz is the superintendent.

—W. E. M. Hackelman, during six
months in the field, has been in meetings
Cincinnati, Lexington, Washington,
Georgetown, Ky.; Worcester, Ohio; Philadelphia and New York city, wherein there
were 527 accessions. He is to be associated
with Herbert Yeuell at Union City, Tenn.,
where J. T. Castlebury is pastor, September 1.

—Among those spending the summer for
special work at Chicago University are
H. Winders, pastor at Columbia, Mo.;
H. Newton, pastor at Normal, Ill.;
Prof. A. D. Veatch and Prof. Walter Stairs,
Drake University; Richard Gentry, of
Sedalia, Mo., who has been studying at
Union Theological Seminary, and Professor
Amberson, of the Missouri State Normal
School, Kirksville, Mo.

—Charles Reign Scoville is to begin a
union revival at Monroe, Wis., August 1,
which will probably continue one month.
The Monroe Ministerial Association has
secured the use of the armory, the largest
auditorium in the city. It will be remembered that J. H. Berkey is pastor of the
union Church in Christ, and he desires the
prayers of the brotherhood in behalf of this
meeting.

—The latest report we have received
from N. M. Perry as to the condition of
G. Creason is that this brother, who has
been seriously ill for five months, was,
upon the advice of a Kansas City physician, removed from Lathrop to the home
of his mother in Kansas City. His condition is still critical. His family, who are
ill with him, and the congregation at
Lathrop, ask the continued prayers of the
brotherhood.

—The Island Church, Wheeling, W. Va.,
is in the most prosperous condition in its
history. It raised more money, had more
additions and larger audiences than in any
other year. C. Manley Rice, the minister,
has been granted a month's vacation. The
"Wheeling News" makes the following editorial comment: "Dr. Rice's sermons have
proved invaluable to 'The News.' The departments of any Sunday paper have won
such general approbation."

—"It seems so strange to me that so few
young men are preparing themselves for
the ministry. There is no profession in
which there is so much room at the top.
The demand for competent and consecrated
ministers is far greater than the supply
and is steadily increasing. I am satisfied
that, if we could graduate one hundred
ministers every year instead of eight or
ten, all of them would be engaged for permanent work before their last school year
had closed."—President Carl Johann.

—Bro. A. J. Bush, the financial agent of
the Juliet Fowler Home, Station A, Dallas,
Texas, writes us: "The problem before
us now is a house for the boys. Our lease
of the building now in use runs out January 1, 1907. We must have a place for

these twenty-five little boys before we have
to vacate the house in which they now live."
We hope the brethren of the southwest will
respond to this appeal. During the present
year the running expenses of the home have
been paid, and $5,600 on the land. There
are sixty happy, healthy children in the
home, but there is no room for other applicants.

—A note from Bro. W. C. MacDougall,
St. Thomas, Ont., informs us that he will
sail on the Pretorian, of the Allan line,
on July 11. He expects to remain in Scotland and England until the second week of
September, the month of August to be
spent at the "Summer Meeting" in Cambridge. The latter part of September will
be spent in Palestine, and he will sail from
Port Said for Bombay the first week of
October, and from Bombay to Calcutta.
Our esteemed brother will be followed by
the prayers and best wishes of his host of
friends in the United States and Canada
for a safe journey and for the prosperity of
his mission.

—A. K. Wright, of California, has received a call to the church recently established by George C. Ritchey at Meridian,
Idaho. As a result of the latter's meeting
thirty-three charter members organized
themselves and at the close of the meeting
the membership was sixty-three, with a
Bible school of forty-five, a Christian Endeavor of twenty-seven members and a lot
secured for a church site. Bro. L. K.
Dick, in sending us these particulars, says:
"We heartily thank God for our success, as
there were several of us who had carried
our church letters in our trunks for years,
and we were nearly starved out. We feel
now that we will be a wide-awake church."

—The last copy of "La Via de Paz" received says: "Just now things wear a little lonesome look around the mission.
Brother and Sister Moses are in Saltillo,
Brother Ireland, Miss Case and Miss Robertson in the States, and Monday Mrs. Cox,
Mrs. Inman's mother, left for Fort Worth,
Texas, to be at the bedside of Mrs. Knee-
land, Brother Inman's aunt, who is very
sick. * * * Brother Jimenez is rejoicing over
the birth of a daughter. This is the third
little one that has been added to our mission family in two months. Brother Enrique
Westrup and Brother Arellano, being the
proud fathers of the other two."

—After what seems to us many trials
and tribulations, a pastor has been called to
succeed Homer Wilson at the Central
Christian Church, San Antonio, Texas.
From time to time we have had reports
of this minister or that receiving a call,
but none of these reports seems to have
resulted in a minister taking up the work
definitely. We now understand that J. B.
Cleaver has begun his labors with the
church, and we trust the membership will
unite in supporting his hands. No good
can come from any division such as has
been manifested. We are glad to know
that the outlook is encouraging. Eight have
taken membership during the last two
Sundays, and Brother Furnish, who has
been quite sick for over six months, was
able to be present.

—Considering the obstacles to be overcome the work at Waukegan, Ill., where
E. N. Tucker has just closed his second
year, is a very successful one. During the
past twelve months forty were added to the
membership, which is now seventy-seven.
The Bible school has 175 enrolled and has
more than doubled in numbers. Endeavor
societies have also been organized. A basement for a commodious church building has
been erected at a cost of $5,000, and some
$3,000 additional have been raised for other
purposes. Brother Tucker has accepted
a unanimous call for a term of five years,
beginning August 1. T. B. Hutchison, an
elder of the church, writes that he has

brethren to meet with them; the entertainment will be free. This district is composed of the following counties: Cass, Bates, Lafayette, Johnson, Henry, Saline, Pettis, Benton, Cooper, Morgan, Camden, Moniteau, Miller, Cole, Osage, Maries and Gasconade.

Let all the churches take notice and let all come together and pray and plan for great things. A good program has been prepared.—T. A. Abbottt, corresponding secretary; J. H. Hardin, Bible school superintendent.

BATH OF BEAUTY
Is Cuticura Soap, assisted by Cuticura Ointment, Purest and Sweetest of Emollients.

Cuticura Soap combines delicate, medicinal, emollient, sanative, and antiseptic properties derived from Cuticura, the great Skin Cure, with the purest of cleansing ingredients and most refreshing of flower odors. For preserving, purifying, and beautifying the skin, scalp, hair, and hands, for irritations of the skin, for baby rashes, itchings, and chafings, for lameness and soreness, for sanative, antiseptic cleansing, and for all the purposes of the toilet, bath, and nursery, Cuticura Soap, assisted by Cuticura Ointment, is priceless.

Illinois—Sixth District

The sixth missionary district of the Illinois Christian Missionary Society met in annual convention with the Christian church at Farmer City, June 26, 27. The first afternoon and evening were given to the C. W. B. M. interests. Mrs. Sue Odor, of Decatur, presided; Miss Lura Thompson, of Carthage, and Mrs. Effie Cunningham, of Indianapolis, Ind., were the principal speakers. A good report was given of work done during the past year.

The second day was given entire to the missionary interests. The secretary was able to give a fine report of work done in the district during the past year. The year was closed with a balance to the credit of the district of about $180, a good nucleus for the work of the coming year. The principal addresses were made by the president, Harold E. Monser; F. W. Burnham, S. E. Fisher, Marion Stevenson and J. H. Gilliland. The old officers, C. L. H. Otto, president; J. H. Smart, vice president, and H. H. Peters, secretary, were succeeded by Finis Idleman, president; Charles Bloom, vice-president, and S. Elwood Fisher, secretary. The convention is to meet next year with the church at Sullivan.

Danville, Ill.   J. H. Smart.

Golden Wedding.

If they live until July 13, Brother and Sister J. C. Powell, of Norman, Okla., will celebrate their golden wedding. We regret that owing to the fact that Brother Powell has been on the sick list for the last ten weeks we are unable to present a photograph of this interesting couple, and the golden wedding will be a quiet occasion owing to the fact of the recent death of Brother Powell's sister; and that some of his children can not be present at the reunion. Brother Powell will be pleased to receive a letter from the pastor, or some old friend in each of the churches where he has worked, advising him of their present condition.

He was born in New Lisbon, Columbiana county, Ohio, July 9, 1831; a son of Joseph and Sarah (Paul) Powell. He united with the Christian church in Wooster, Ohio, in 1849, and married Josephine C. Stauber, daughter of Dr. C. F. and Catherine Stauber, in Columbus City, Iowa, July 13, 1856, by Elder M. N. Warren. Their mar-

ried life has been a busy, but happy one, and ten sons and four daughters have blessed their union. Three sons have died, and the eldest daughter, Sadie, is the wife of Bro. J. C. Hanna, of Arlington, Iowa. All save three are members of the Christian church.

Brother Powell was called to the ministry and ordained at Columbus City, Iowa, 1858. His first pastorate was at Honey Creek and Pleasant Hill. Then he served at Paris, Washington county; Lancaster and Bethel, Keokuk county, with visits to Lost Creek, and other points. In 1867 he spent some time at Hiram College, and on his return to Iowa built up the congregation at Big Springs, Jefferson county, and established new congregations in West Liberty and Nichols, Muscatine county, leaving each church with good meeting houses. He held successful meetings in Muscatine City, Springfield, and other places. After twenty-five years' service in Iowa, he moved to Barton county, Missouri, and established a church in the infidel town of Liberal, thence he moved to Sumner county, Kansas, and preached at Morris Center, his home, Corbin and South Haven. Thence he moved to Cowly county, and continued in the work, but rather spasmodically. Some thirteen years ago he moved to Cleveland county, Okla., established a congregation called Antioch, ten miles southwest of Oklahoma City, and three years ago built a good house of worship there. He now lives in Norman, helping on the cause of the Master in various ways, and preaching still for the congregation at Falls schoolhouse, one-half of his time. Brother Powell has always been a warm friend of missions and education. He has contributed every year since his first dollar was given to Dr. Barclay's Jerusalem mission in 1850. He and his beloved companion are now "Only waiting till the shadows are a little longer grown." They are associated with a fine congregation in Norman, working heartily with its pastor, R. E. McCorkle, and surrounded by pleasant and sympathetic neighbors. Many will be glad to know that these faithful workers in a good cause are so soon to realize all the hopes which must have been theirs during the past year, and we shall rejoice with them on the completion of fifty years of happy wedded life, and wish for them continued usefulness for years to come.

Rapid Method Bible Study

at our "Summer Normal Term," or by correspondence. Term opens June 11. Let us send you announcements. Write Pres. Chas. J. Burton, Christian College, Oskaloosa, Iowa.

Northeast Arkansas Convention.

The Northeast Arkansas Missionary District Convention of the Churches of Christ, will meet at Stuttgart, Ark., July 10-12. It is composed of the twenty-one counties of Clay, Randolph, Sharp, Lawrence, Greene, Mississippi, Craighead, Jackson, Independence, White, Woodruff, Poinsett, Crittenden, Cross, St. Francis, Lee, Phillips, Monroe, Prairie, Lonoke, Arkansas. James C. Creel, president; J. R. Crank, vice president; J. A. Houghton, treasurer; J. H. Brooks, corresponding secretary.

Tuesday evening, convention sermon, J. R. Crank; Wednesday morning, appointment of committees; report of district board, J. H. Brooks; report of treasurer; "How to Enlist the Churches in Missions," E. C. Browning; "Macedonian Calls," J. K. Pedrick; pledges for district work. C. W. B. M. session, Wednesday afternoon and evening. District convention sermon (continued) Thursday—Reports of committees; "The Go of the Commission," a discussion; "The Right Man in the Right Place," W. B. Mason; The Preaching for the Times," C. C. Cline; discussion.

Bethany Assembly—Season 1906.

July 19, opening day; July 20, soldiers' day; July 21, children's day; July 22, assembly day; July 23, temperance day; July 24, 25, state Sunday-school convention; July 26, 27, C. W. B. M. convention; July 28, law enforcement day; July 29, assembly day; July 30, 31, August 1, state ministerial association; August 2, 3, 4, school of evangelists; August 5, assembly day; August 6, Butler College day; August 7, school for pastors; Bethany jubilee and mortgage burning; August 8, school for pastors; August 9, 10, 11, Y. P. S. C. E. convention; August 12, assembly day; August 13, closing day. The Bethany jubilee and mortgage burning will be on Tuesday, August 7, at 2 p. m. It is intended to make it the greatest day in the history of "dear old Bethany."

Wabash, Ind.   L. L. Carpenter, President.

Music at Bethany.

The music at Bethany assembly will be under the direction of W. E. M. Hackleman. He has engaged the Netz sisters, Toledo, Ohio; Juanita Glee Club, Flora, Ind.; Miss Una Berry, Lafayette; Miss Bessie May, Warsaw; Miss Margaret Windsor, Muncie; Miss Gertrude Lennick, Union City; Miss Margaret Van Winkle, Indianapolis; Mrs. Nona Earhart, Indianapolis, and Messrs. J. R. Lynn, Indianapolis; H. K. Shields, Rochester; J. Walter Wilson, Rushville; Miss Yuba Wilhite, violin virtuso, Indianapolis; Mrs. Estelle Edmunds, reader, Chicago; Miss Tillie Purcell, Cincinnati, Ohio, pianist; Misses Myrtle Rader, Mabel Sweeney, Myrtle Castle, Lela Williams, Mary Shively, Edna Sweeney and Messrs. Byron Burditt, C. L. Truckess, J. L. Fink, Omar Day and Jacob Jones, all of Lafayette. It is especially desired that all who sing or play any small instrument who will be present at the assembly. If only for a day or so, will come prepared to join the assembly chorus choir, and that all such bring their repertoire of music and if possible report to the musical director before the opening day, July 19, stating what days they can be present.

College Work and Plans

Atlantic Christian College.

This college is located in the town of Wilson, N. C., It is owned by the Christian Church, and has been in operation four years. Its buildings are of brick, heated by steam, lighted by electricity, with water and sewerage, with dormitory on the second floor for ladies. It has a good health record, beautiful grounds and safe environments. It has a faculty of eleven teachers, preparatory, collegiate and post-graduate courses, and seven courses leading to the A. B. degree. It gives instruction in languages, sciences, mathematics, art, leather, music, elocution and physical culture, bookkeeping, shorthand and typewriting and preparation for the ministry. The buildings stand in the midst of a beautiful grassy plot of ground, and the property has been estimated at $50,000, and is increasing rapidly in value. During the four years of operation the patronage has ranged from 100 to 200. The college is growing in favor, and its future is bright and every way full of hope.   J. J. HARPER, President.

Bethany College.

Bethany's sixty-fifth commencement festivities were the best yet. Sunday, June 10, H. P. Atkins, of Richmond, Va., preached the baccalaureate. Tuesday, June 12, came the field day exercises, the annual meeting of trustees and the president's reception. Wednesday, class day and concert, and Thursday the great day of the week, when there was oratory "to burn," and twenty-nine sheepskins were distributed. Eighty young men matriculated during the year as students in the ministerial department. Of the graduates ten have chosen the ministry for their life work. There was a large attendance of the trustees and much good work accomplished. Only one change in the faculty occurs. Prof. Beatty retires from the chair of science, and Wren J. Grinstead takes his place. The board resolved to raise a second block of $100,000 on endorsement before the centennial at Pittsburg, in 1909. The new Carnegie library is being built and will be completed by January, 1907. It will be a beautiful structure, east of Phillips Hall, and will cost $40,000. The first floor will be a hall seating 1,000 for assembly and banqueting room; the second will be the library proper with stacks for 50,000 volumes and ample reading rooms; the third will have four lecture or society rooms. The structure will be built of broken brick with stone trimmings, and will add greatly to the group of buildings. Two hundred and sixty-four students were enrolled the past session, eighty-three of whom are ministerial and forty are already preaching. The college is self-sustaining, but has yet some debts to square up, and needs funds for equipment and necessary repairs on its buildings and for the better support of the faculty. A half million for Bethany would not more than supply its wants and make good the obligation of the brotherhood to this useful institution of learning. The alumni meeting, with W. R. Warren as president and Prof. Philip Johnson secretary, held a good session. It was resolved to get out a full attendance of old students next commencement and hold a great banquet in the new library, to solicit books for the library from the alumni and

Order a Free Bottle

to enlist all old Bethany's sons and daughters in raising this new block of $100,000. Mr. Carnegie's gift of $20,000 was conditioned on the raising of an equal sum on our endowment. This has been done, but $100,000 additional are needed to put Bethany well on the way to permanent prosperity. Among old students in attendance were B. T. Blanpied, George McCoard, H. P. Connelly, W. H. Fields, M. S. Decker, O. G. Hertzog, Carl Anderson, Alfred Place, V. G. Hostetter, C. C. Cowgill, Julia White, T. O. Whitaker, A. Linkletter, Mr. and Mrs. W. E. Pierce, R. H. and F. E. Wynne, Ray O. Miller, D. G. Miller, O. G. White, R. C. and Mrs. Mary Campbell Hagerman, Harvey Brown, W. B. Hendershott, Miss Myrtle Sprague, Miss Muriel Scott and Miss Catherine Miller, Commencement day brought a large attendance. The Bethany Band covered itself with glory. The speeches were well received and live roses showered upon the orators of the day. It was a typical day and a typical Bethany closing. Only three honorary degrees were conferred: on W. F. Cowden the doctor of laws, and on S. W. Brown and W. B. Taylor the master of arts. Every one speaks of the excellent service of W. B. Taylor as vice president of the college and pastor of the Bethany Church. By the way, one more thing must be done before 1909—a new Alexander Campbell memorial church, an up-to-date structure of stone, should take the place of the present dilapidated Bethany house of worship. The Vermont Avenue Church asks the privilege of making the first contribution toward it. Thirty-thousand dollars will be little enough to meet this great want.

President Cramblet has now served five years. The last has been the best. Five years ago the actual enrolment the previous year was less than 100. Every year since then has shown substantial increase. The session just closed shows 264 on the roll. The income for 1900-01 was $2,416 for tuition and room rent; the income for 1905-06 is little less than $12,000, or five times as great as five years ago. This does not take into account gifts and income from endowment, but only from tuition and rents. The college work done shows the same advance. A new course in civil and mining engineering will be inaugurated the coming session. Never were the prospects brighter for Bethany. Next year will see 300 students within its walls. Prof. Keith and Col. Nave were among the missing. Their work is done. Prof. Wynne and Prof. Pendleton, or "Miss Camnie," are still doing heroic service. Buffalo Creek and the Wellsburg road, the hills and the farms, the lovely scenery and the kindly people are still there.   F. D. POWER.

Berkeley Bible Seminary.

Berkeley Bible Seminary closed the year of 1905-6 in a very remarkable way. Our school year runs us really from August 20 to May 1, but when the great trembler of April 18 came we dismissed classes straightway, remitted examinations and faculty and students gave themselves to relief work. We were hurt in Berkeley in no way, and despite the loss of a few thousands in income, the seminary sustained no loss. We shall be running with full force August 21, when our next term opens.

During the last year Dean Van Kirk was compelled by press of seminary work to give up his classes in the university. Accordingly the seminary has experienced a marked development in growth. There were forty-two students enrolled. Of these fourteen are preparing for our own ministry, while the others came from the co-operating seminaries. Prof. A. M. Elston has added great strength to our teaching force. We look forward to the future with cheer and hope. Our faculty will be greatly enlarged. R. P. Shepherd, Ph.D., becomes lecturer on the English Bible, and W. P. Bentley, A. M., lecturer on missions. President McAneney continues in the field. This gives us a force of five well-known men which, with the equipment of the University of California and the co-operating seminaries, will furnish the facilities for a broad and thorough

students. We had the promise of a large entering class before the earthquake, but since then some have wavered, others have had their income cut off. There is no danger. Berkeley, as well as the greater part of California, was unhurt. There are numerous new fields opening here already. Let young men of devotion and courage come on. The Lord calls to distinguished service.

HIRAM VAN KIRK.

Bible College of Missouri.

This young institution is rapidly taking rank among the vigorous and aggressive in the brotherhood. A year ago it reported the erection and occupation of a most beautiful and commodious stone building. Lowry Hall has proved to be not only a home for the college and its work, but a financial success also, since it is a productive building. This year the college reports another great step in advance in its relation to the University of Missouri. Hereafter there will be an interchange of credits between the two institutions, ministerial students receiving credits for work done in the university and university students in the academic department receiving credit for work done in the more general of the Bible college courses. The Bible college management feels sure that this will greatly advance the work.

This interchange of credits is the beginning of an educational policy of which more will be heard in coming years. The inception of the plan in Columbia opens the way for other movements similar to our own, and extends the same privileges to the colleges of the Missouri College Union. For obvious reasons our growing state universities can not teach the Bible. Meanwhile young men and women continue to attend them in increasing numbers. Why should they not have the privilege of studying the Bible in affiliated institutions and receive credits for their work? The plan solves the double problem of Christianizing our universities and of building up strong Bible colleges and seminaries at reasonable cost.

Year by year the number of our ministerial and missionary students increases. Last year nineteen young men and women took studies with a view to distinctively Christian work. Between 200 and 300 other students received more or less help in Biblical ways. A number of the best known business men in the Christian Church in Missouri are fostering the work and are desirous of making it an institution of great power and beneficence. J. H. Garrison, the beloved Editor of THE CHRISTIAN-EVANGELIST, is a trustee of the institution and a liberal contributor to it. D. O. Smart, of Kansas City, president of the Board of Church Extension, is president also of the Bible College Board, and a large contributor. In the same capacity as members of the board and contributors J. T. Mitchell, of Centralia, may be named, and T. P. Haley, of Kansas City, with whom the plan originated, and C. H. Winders, pastor in Columbia, and I. A. Roberts, W. J. Stone and B. F. Lowry, all of Columbia.

By careful management, by earnest and constructive work, and by its growing usefulness, the Bible college seeks a warm place in the affections of the Missouri brotherhood, and of the brotherhood at large.   W. J. LHAMON, Dean.

Columbia, Mo.

Butler College's Fifty-first Year.

At this year's commencement exercises twenty-five graduates of the class, four recipients of the A. M. degree and one guest honored with the honorary degree of LL. D., represented in a measure the finished product of Butler's educational process. Five of these are our contribution to the ministry of the Christian church: Malo M. Amunson, H. H. Harmon, H. Maxwell Hall, G. W. Henry, post-graduate students, and Cloyd Goodnight, of the class of 1906, all men of exceptional ability and of the highest standing among their fellows. One graduate, Geo. B. Baird, is under appointment of the Foreign Christian Missionary Society for work in China, and expects to sail this fall. He will take with him the prayers of a host of Butler friends, and the memory of having done much for the stimulation of interest in our foreign work among the students of the college. It is a satisfaction to know that this interest will be maintained next year by the kindness of Mrs. Atwater, of the Christian Woman's Board of Missions, in leading the mission study class. The other graduates of 1906 show a good, healthy interest in the necessary and useful work of the world. A number will continue their studies at various institutions, Butler, the University of Chicago and Yale having been already decided upon by some. All of them, and the large number of friends and former students of Butler, will carry with them a long time the inspiration and help of the eloquent commencement address which E. L. Powell brought to us.

The year has been a most varied one. The attendance at all departments, preparatory, resident college work, teachers' college, art and music and the summer school, has been good, aggregating over 400. The teaching force was strengthened at the beginning of the year by the addition of Richard B. Moore, formerly of the University of Missouri, as professor of chemistry. We have been somewhat crippled, however, by the serious illness of Prof. Bruner, by the enforced absence of President Garrison, by the appointment of Prof. T. C. Howe as chairman of the endowment committee and by the work of Prof. W. D. Howe in finishing his edition of Hazlitt's works, which necessitated his going east the last half of the spring term. Instruction in all these cases, however, has been satisfactorily continued through the year by securing instructors from elsewhere and redividing the work affected.

The work of adding $250,000 to the endowment, to which President Garrison had devoted much of his energy, has gone on during the year. After President Garrison found it necessary to leave Indianapolis on account of his health, Prof. T. C. Howe was put at the head of the movement and has carried it on with increasing vigor and success for the last three months. In addition to the original conditional offer of Mr. Joseph I. Irwin of $100,000, Mrs. Andrew Carnegie has offered $25,000, property worth between $25,000 and

---

Texas Christian University
NORTH WACO, TEXAS

lectures free to students. Large library, four laboratories, twenty-four pianos, three grand pianos, a pipe organ and band instruments. Thoroughly equipped Business College in connection. Maintain own light, heat, laundry and sewerage plants. Pure Artesian Water for all purposes. Location high and healthful, overlooking the city. Fifteen acre campus and Athletic Field. Nine free scholarships. Ministers and ministers' children half tuition. Students below Junior rank in special care. Boarding will be good, rooms pleasant.

Address Box 171.

Thirty-fourth year, co-educational, thirty officers, professors and teachers from the leading institutions of America and Europe. Our work credited in the Universities of the East. Course of fifteen studies.

CLINTON LOCKHART, A. M., Ph. D., President.

$35,000 has been given the college on the annuity plan by Mr. Charles Whitsett, of Indianapolis (counted by actuaries as equal to a cash subscription of more than $12,000, and with rising real estate values sure to be a very valuable asset in the future), and more than $25,000 has been subscribed in smaller amounts by alumni and friends of the college. Of the remaining $80,000 necessary, at least $25,000 has been promised, though not yet subscribed, so that less than $60,000 remains to be canvassed for, a task which all are hopeful of accomplishing within the next year. Other gifts, not counting on the endowment fund, reported during the year are, $500 from William Jennings Bryan, the income of which is to be loaned without interest to students needing it, and a valuable lot adjacent to the library, now held in trust for the college.

One inexpressible regret and sense of loss comes at the close of the year. President W. E. Garrison, though he would probably have continued in his work and literally have given his life for the college, was compelled, for the sake of his health, by the direction of his physicians and the urgency of his personal friends, to go temporarily to another climate. It was hoped when he left in March that he might return within a few months; but though there has been improvement, his return within a couple of years has recently been pronounced out of the question. His resignation, therefore, has been tendered and finally accepted, after two years' work, a period which though short, has told decisively for the permanent welfare of Butler.   C. B. COLEMAN.

Christian University.

The year just closed has been one of strenuous work and intense application on the part of students and teachers alike. It seems to me that an earnest and faithful student does now nearly twice as much work in a given time as was done ten or twenty years ago. The course of studies in the collegiate department has again been lengthened by one year, so that we now offer four years of academic or preparatory work, followed by four full years of college work. The preparatory course has been so arranged that the graduates from it may be admitted without conditions, not only to our collegiate department, but also to the University of Missouri, Princeton College and many other universities of the highest rank.

Many have been under the impression that Christian University is a school for ministerial students only. That is a great mistake; two-thirds of our students have no thought of becoming ministers, but study such branches as are taught in all the better colleges. Last year forty of our students were preparing for the ministry, and all those who can preach acceptably found regular preaching points with neighboring congregations, earning thereby money enough to support themselves while attending school. Nearly 100 churches within seventy-five miles of Canton depend exclusively on our boys for their ministry. Indeed, we frequently have more calls for preachers than we can supply.

Christian University is now in better condition to do excellent work than ever before. Our large, new building is conceded to be the best owned anywhere by our brotherhood, the fourteen professors are all specialists in their respective branches and the 142 students last year are as fine and promising a

---

Butler College
Indianapolis (Irvington), Indiana

¶Elective courses in Literary, Scientific and Theological Departments.

¶University trained men in the Faculty.

¶Situation very advantageous in a city where concerts, lectures and conventions are very common.

¶Expenses moderate.

¶Address the President.

---

body of earnest Christian men and women as can be found anywhere.

We are striving to make Christian University the rallying point and center of Christian activity in Missouri and sincerely desire the advice, help and confidence of our great brotherhood in the state. The president will gladly answer any communications in reference to our educational work.

Canton, Mo.   CARL JOHANN, President Christian University.

An Instrument of Great Merit for the Cure of Diseased Eyes.

Any reader of this article who is afflicted with any impairment of his or her eyesight should not fail to address the New York and London Electric Association, Suite 203, 929 Walnut street, Kansas City, Mo., for detailed particulars and testimonials regarding the merits, reliability and efficiency of "Actina," the wonderful discovery which is now attracting the attention of the people, owing to the many cures of afflicted eyesight that it is performing. This method of treatment is used by patients in their own homes and without any trouble or expense beyond the small cost price of "Actina." No cutting or probing is involved in the use of this treatment, nor are any drugs or medicines required. It cures afflictions of the eyes, and cases of cures are reported where the patients had been pronounced by leading oculists as incurable. Your attention is called to this marvelous treatment for failing eyesight, cataracts, granulated lids, or sore eyes, etc., and the proprietors call particular attention to it in order that any of the readers of this paper who are troubled with eyesight difficulties may know where to procure immediate relief and a permanent cure without any use of knife or drugs, and at but little expense.

Christian College.

For fifty-five years Christian College has demonstrated the wisdom of its founders by the splendid results which show forth in the lives of its young women. The high standard of work done is more apparent with each passing session and the conduct of the young ladies beyond reproach. The past year there has been connected with Christian College a splendid faculty of thirty-two teachers and administrative officers, and the college has had a total enrollment of 218 students, 150 of whom were in the boarding department. Of these twelve supported themselves by domestic, clerical or monitor work, three were the recipients of full board, home and tuition scholarships four of half board, home and tuition scholarships, thirteen of full academic tuition scholarships and five of music scholarships.

Part of the year there has been one of our returned missionaries with her two children in the boarding department, and three young ladies preparing for foreign missionary work have been with us the entire year. These three will be joined by a fourth next year and all will go on with their studies, both in Christian College and the Bible college, looking to active missionary labor in some foreign field. Two of our missionaries who have been for years in a foreign land are sending their daughters back next September to be educated in Christian College.

Thirty of our young ladies have maintained a vigorous missionary society where missionary topics are studied and discussed and regular contributions made to the Christian Woman's Board of Missions, they having sent this year $36 to the national fund. A voluntary contribution of $25 was also sent by the young ladies of the school for the relief of the California sufferers.

The Christian College Daughters' League has carried on weekly meetings of praise and prayer and with a membership of over 100 has done much for the religious life of the school.

The building equipment of Christian College has long been in need of new class room facilities in harmony with the growth in numbers and advancement in work. This spring Mr. Andrew Carnegie promised $25,000 for a new academic hall at Christian College, provided $25,000 additional should be raised for endowment. Steps are being taken to fulfill this condition, and it is hoped that strong friends may rally to the call so that the building will soon be under way.

The health of the college family has been most excellent; harmony and right endeavor has prevailed, and work has been done which will, we trust, not only prepare our young women for greater future usefulness, but will honor the Master and further his cause.

MRS. W. T. MOORE, President.
Columbia, Mo.

Cotner University.

We have closed one of Cotner's best years. Situated as it is in the midst of perhaps the greatest educational center of the new west, it has been subjected to close competition. What at first seems to be a disadvantage turns out a benefit in some ways. To succeed means great energy and enthusiasm on the part of teachers and students alike. Nebraska also has a number of excellent private institutions. These, most of them, are banded together in a college union with the State University to sustain certain uniform standards as to length of courses and entrance requirements. Cotner, spite of difficulties which all have not encountered has held honorable rank among such schools and during the past year has received valuable recognition from strong centers of education, both east and west. It is the aim to hold and strengthen a high standing.

Contest in oratorical debates and athletic tournaments has been specially interesting. A move is on foot to erect a substantial gymnasium, costing when completed about $10,000. Quite an encouraging beginning has been made in raising money. It is hoped that it may at least be enclosed the year next year. Some progress has been made in the way of endowment, a few thousands in cash have been added, several thousand in wills and unfulfilled assurances of help in the near future have given encouragement, and it is hoped that a substantial increase may be secured during the coming year. Surely no investment of consecrated means could be safer or bring

greater returns than at Cotner. The Lincoln Medical College, affiliated as a department of the university from its organization, has done good work during the year. Dr. Wilmuth, one of our brethren, has recently been elected dean. A new building, very centrally located, has been purchased for lecture and hospital purposes. A prosperous year seems to be indicated by added enterprise and enthusiasm. The same prudence in business management has prevented the university from incurring debt. The prospect for the next year seems excellent, both as to attendance and other enlargements. The student body separated, charged with unbounded enthusiasm, and promise to return, bringing many others with them.

W. P. AYLSWORTH.

Drake University.

Drake University has just closed the twenty-fifth year of her history. In celebration of this, unusual preparation was made for commencement time. A large number of prominent men in and out of the church were present to rejoice with us during the week.

A review of the work of the University during the past year is most gratifying. The friends of the school have not failed to remember it in many and most helpful ways. The attendance has been large, and the spirit prevailing in the school has been exceedingly satisfactory. Every term has shown a small increase in the number enrolled, and in addition to that, we have had quite an increase in the total number of different students for the year. The whole number of different students registered was 1,634. Every term in the year has been larger than any previous like term in the history of the University, except the summer term.

The success of the student activities of the school was highly satisfactory. Mr. Clarence Eppard, after winning the home oratorical contest, won the State Prohibition Contest with a splendid oration. Mr. John Booth won the Home and the State Oratorical Contest, and followed these successes by winning the Inter-State Contest at Topeka, Kansas. Mr. Booth received the highest mark in thought and composition in the State Contest, and he received the highest in delivery in the Inter-State Contest. Mr. Booth will enter the ministry upon graduation, and it is certain that he will be a mighty force in that great work.

Many gifts for the University were received during the year. Gifts to the Bible Department running expense amounted to $2,018.31; to the Bible Building fund, $11,164.41; the Stadium fund, $7,665.57; the Bible endowment, $17.00; the Phoebe Lincoln scholarship, $1,000; 1903 scholarship, $575; Library endowment fund, $21,500. The total amount of gifts to the University for all purposes during the year amounted to $44,440.99. This makes the year one of the best from a financial standpoint, in the history of the University. The friends of the University were especially gratified that the institution was able to run within its income. The increase in tuitions and fees for the year amounted to over $5,000. It is the purpose during the present year to complete the Carnegie Library Endowment. $26,000 have been raised toward this endowment, but, as there are a number of annuities in this, it will be necessary to raise a larger amount in order to cover the requirements of Mr. Carnegie's gift. It is hoped that we may raise, altogether, $50,000 additional to put into this fund.

The College of Liberal Arts has had an unusually successful year, 464 different students having been enrolled in this department of the University. In the College of the Bible, 120 have been enrolled. The number of ministerial students

taking work in this department was thirty per cent greater than that of any previous year. The Colleges of Law, Medicine, Music, and Normal have all been unusually successful in their work.

In planning for the work of the ensuing year, the various departments have been strengthened in many ways. The most important matter receiving attention has been the courses of study. These, in many instances, have been lengthened and in others, the requirements for entrance to the schools have been increased. This is notably true in the Law and Medical Colleges.

A few new teachers have been called. Professor M. L. Hoblit, of Agricultural College, New Mexico, has been called to take the chair of Romance languages. He will teach French and Spanish. Professor Hoblit was connected with the University some years ago, and is well known here as a man unusually well qualified for these particular lines of work. Mrs. Emma Rosen-Kerr will teach voice in the Conservatory of Music. Mrs Kerr comes to us from Cincinnati, Ohio, and is most highly recommended. Miss Ida Mae Morrison will teach piano in the College of Music. One of the most eminent scholars in the brotherhood has been chosen to fill the chair of New Testament Greek vacated by Professor Walter Stairs, but as his acceptance is not at hand, we do not feel at liberty to announce his name. Suffice it to say that, should he not accept, another wholly competent to fill this position with great credit will be chosen.

The Bible College of the University is now adequately housed in Memorial-Hall, a beautiful building especially constructed for the use of this institution. It has just been completed at a cost of $30,000. It is our purpose to make the Bible College of Drake University strong in every way, and especially in the character of the work which shall be offered. Next year, an English Bible course, which is open to students who have not completed their preparatory school work; a diploma course, which is open to those who are taking work in the College of Liberal Arts; and a Bachelor of Divinity course, which is open to those who have completed a course in the College of Liberal Arts, will be offered, and the expectation is now that the patronage will be unusually large. Taken all together, the outlook for all the departments of the University is most promising.

Eugene Divinity School.

Eleven years ago President E. C. Sanderson, in an upper room in a residence, began teaching five young men who desired to prepare for the ministry of the Word. As an evangelistic missionary, he had seen the great need of the northwest for a ministry prepared in mind and heart to reach and win this wonderful, new and growing empire. During these years wise plans and management have increased every interest. Six classes have graduated. The school is located in Eugene, Lane county, Ore., 120 miles south of Portland, on the Southern Pacific Railroad, and at the head of the far-famed Willamette Valley. The school is adjacent to the State University, and our students have the same advantages on equal terms. The school has ample grounds and good buildings, free from debt and a growing endowment fund. Our watchword is $50,000 endowment by October, 1909. We have a most excellent Biblical library of 2,500 volumes. The students also have access to the university and city libraries.

The school has become the greatest missionary and evangelistic force in the northwest. To secure qualified preachers is the great problem in this vast field with multiplying churches. The school is solving this problem by sending out pastors, evangelists and many Sunday-school and church workers. The faculty is strong in pastoral, evangelistic and teaching experience. The confidence of the brethren is increasing the support. President Sanderson, by wise financial management, has closed each of the eleven free from debt on current expenses. Many parents, seeing the good work, are giving their sons to the ministry. A strong church joins the teachers and students in extending a cordial welcome to all.

I. M. MORRIS, Sec.

Eureka College.

One of the most pleasant sessions in the history of Eureka College has just closed. The character of the college is such that it attracts a superior class of young people from our best homes. Young people who wish their college days to count for as much as possible, yet under pleasant and happy conditions, come. They come to us from Canada, England, Japan, Australia, District of Columbia, Wisconsin and several other states besides our own. The character of work was of high order, as well as the deportment of the student body. The young ladies, who constitute about one-third of the number, conduct a very profitable Y. W. C. A., as also do the young gentlemen a Y. M. C. A. Our heating plant has proved very satisfactory, the senior class laid a fine granitoid walk from Burgess Hall to the chapel as a kind of farewell appreciation to alma mater, and other improvements are being made.

The faculty remains materially the same as last year. The Bible department has enlarged its course of study. Prof. Radford will devote most of his time to it, as will also Prof. Jones, and President Hieronymous will teach at least one class in the English Bible. College opened with an able lecture; Founders' day was duly observed, having several able addresses. The joint committee of the literary societies arranged a fine lecture course for the year. Marion Stevenson, state Sunday-school evangelist of Illinois, spent a month in Eureka, giving (1) a course of lectures on the Pentateuch, (2) on Sunday-school teaching and (3) a course to preachers on various Sunday-school problems. W. M. Forrest, late of Calcutta, India, gave two courses of lectures, one on the prophets, the other on the India people, life and habits. President J. W. McGarvey gave a course of popular Biblical lectures at the church and conducted a series of conferences at the college for a week. All these and other incidental lectures are most helpful, useful and enjoyable. Arrangements are already being made for such work for next year. The college, through two generous friends, has been able to install an elegant printing plant, which will be useful in publishing leaflets, bulletins, etc., as well as aidin' young men in getting their education.

The college conducted twenty-four educational conferences during the fall at as many places, which were well attended and helpful. Education day was observed by sixty-eight churches in the state, with an aggregate offering of $1,370.45. This shows a marked growth in spirit and sentiment in favor of education. Already a number of preachers have promised to observe the day in 1907. The financial condition of the college has steadily improved. The completion of the second Coleman proposition gave the college $3,000, besides the regular dues from about 2,000 members of the Educational Association. We want this association to have a membership of 3,000 as soon as possible, each paying $1 or more a year. Uncle William Britt gave us $2,000 endowment.

President R. E. Hieronymous accepted an unusually favorable opportunity to take a trip to Europe this summer, but will return before time for college to open in September. He made ample provision for his work and correspondence to be taken care of while he is away. He needs the rest and the trip will be of great educational value to him and to the college.   J. G. W.

Hamilton College.

The thirty-seventh annual session showed a total enrollment of 260 students from nineteen states and one foreign country. The demand for accommodations was so great that several teachers were placed in near-by rooms so that students need not be refused, and the 40 per cent increase during the past three years shows a steady and healthy growth. The teaching and administrative staff have numbered thirty-two, twenty-four of these being teachers. The following important changes on the faculty have been made for next year: Signor G. Aldo Randegger is the new dean of the school of music. Signor Randegger is a first-honor graduate at the Royal Conservatory, Italy, and has had a number of years of valuable teaching experience in this country, having taught in Atlanta, Ga., and New York City. He is a composer of merit and a brilliant pianist, and comes to the work at Hamilton with the highest endorsements. The school of music will have as the new director of the vocal department Mrs. Louise Cowan Bigelow, pupil of Mme. Ashforth,

New York; Norman McCloud and Henrietta Hascall, of Boston. Mrs. Bigelow is an experienced teacher and possesses a beautiful lyric soprano voice. The academic department will have two new instructors: Miss Jessie L. P. Brown, teacher of sacred and civil history, has an A. B. from Barnard College and an A. M. from Columbia University and a teacher's certificate from Teachers' College, New York. Miss Kate Galt Miller is the new head of the Latin department and is an A. B. of Vassar College, with a year of graduate study at Vassar.

The excellent scholastic standing of Hamilton has been thoroughly tested by higher institutions and our pupils have made, in every instance, excellent records. The health record has been phenomenal. Not a case of serious illness has occurred during the past year.

With the investment of $25,000 within the past three years the buildings have been enlarged and improved until they are in perfect condition. During the past year a magnificent portico of gray stone has replaced the old wooden structure, and this latest improvement gives great dignity to the main building. The portico, 40x17 feet, supported by massive Corinthian columns, cost $3,000 and is almost entirely the gift of the alumni. The morale of the student body has been of the highest order. We largely attribute this condition to the strong religious life of the school, numbering among its influences a large auxiliary to the C. W. B. M., a strong organization of the Y. W. C. A. and a mission study circle. These organizations have held weekly meetings, and some of the financial contributions for good causes have been as follows: Twenty-five dollars to the dormitory at Morehead, $35 to the Kentucky University Volunteer Association, $30 to the state budget of the Y. W. C. A., $20 to the national C. W. B. M. Besides this faithful work has been done in some local settlement interests.

The purchase of the residence property to the north of the Hamilton grounds (formerly the home of President Robert Graham) is the first step toward much-needed improvement. This valuable and beautiful corner lot should be made the site of a new building containing an entertainment hall, a gymnasium and additional class rooms. Somewhere the money is waiting to be used for this splendid purpose; somehow it must be enlisted for this purpose.

Lexington, Ky.   LUELLA WILCOX ST. CLAIR.

Hiram College.

June 22 was a beautiful day on Hiram Hill. A very large company, especially of old students, was present and the old "tabernacle" was never better filled. Six seniors gave orations which would do honor to any college class, and President Rowlinson gave diplomas certifying the bachelor's degree to twenty-four young men and women. It was a great disappointment that at the last moment President Burris A. Jenkins, who was to have been the commencement speaker, should have been kept away, but the large number of alumni present made afternoon meetings of unusual interest. On Wednesday five young men—Garry L. Cook, J. F. Baxter, S. L. Lyon, O. L. Hull and A. C. Young—were ordained to the ministry. They are most excellent young men. The ordination sermon, an unusually strong discourse, was preached by President E. V. Zollars. Indeed, the presence of President Zollars, as he moved genially and with warm welcomes amid scenes where he had achieved so much, was one of the brightest passages of the week. Hiram College owes him much and will follow him everywhere with grateful good will.

The meeting of the board of trustees was full and earnest and optimistic. It was the one expressed thought that Hiram should go steadily on in the line of her present work, and it was felt that means could be secured which would insure larger growth. The faculty will remain essentially as during the past year, except that Prof.

H. H. Lane, who has had charge of the work in biology, goes to fill a chair in Oklahoma University. He is a good man every way, and "a comer," and it is a privilege to say that much. C. T. Paul, returning from China, will take charge of the modern language department. Students are apt to love their college home, but it is not amiss to say that few are loved as Hiram is. There is reason for it. And that heart loyalty is the best possession a college ever has. May it never fail to Hiram!

How a Church may be a Seminary.

The Christian Temple Seminary at Baltimore, Md., offers a systematic and popular course of Bible study, covering three years, and divided as follows: The Freshman year is devoted to the Old Testament and there are four examinations, one after each period, the law, history, poetry and prophecy. The junior year is devoted to the New Testament and likewise has four examinations, biographical (the four Gospels), historical (the Acts), epistolary and apocalyptic. The senior year has its four periods, chart study of both Old and New Testament, ecclesiastical history, Christian evidence and Christian missions, with some supplementary work in the art galleries of Baltimore and Washington, making in all twelve written examinations for the entire course.

There is only one lecture a week given to each class. The Bible is the text-book. To know it only as a means to know him is the purpose of this study, which is conducted from the historical and devotional viewpoints, and persons of various denominational affiliations have been among the matriculates. On the completion of this three years' course diplomas are conferred on the graduates at the regular commencement exercises, and those holding diplomas may become members of the guild of the Round Table, which is a four years' reading course. The first year is the rereading of the Old Testament with helps from several other books; the second year is the New Testament, likewise with the reading of four or five other books; the third year is the reading of the missionary books of both Testaments, with four or five books on modern missions, and the fourth year is a study of Jesus Christ in history, poetry, art and personal living. On simply stating that one has read these books a second seal is added to his diploma.

This course of study is designed for busy people, and it is popular. A correspondence course is being arranged for and perhaps may be ready by September. Next to the saving of men the greatest business in the world is teaching the Bible. Last year there were forty matriculates and at the opening of the next season, in September, the indications already are that it will be greatly increased.   PETER AINSLIE, Dean.

Iowa Christian College.

Oskaloosa College was incorporated in 1856, and has graduated a large number, many of whom are filling important positions in life. As a new work opened up here, with a new management, new articles of incorporation were secured in July, 1902, under a new name, and the institution is now composed of the following departments: College of the Bible, Oskaloosa normal college, Oskaloosa business college, correspondence Bible college. Our work the past year has been in fine shape. Our third year closed at the commencement in June, with 130 enrollment in all departments of the resident work. We had fifteen graduates, five ministers, one teacher, four from the music department and the remainder from the business college.

While our normal and business work is growing rapidly the ministerial is by no means in the

JOSEPH REILLY
ATTORNEY-AT-LAW

background. We have a splendid ministerial course and fine opportunities here for those who wish to study for the ministry. Our motto is, "More work, better work, larger work." Consequently we are laying the foundation well for future building. Our building is in very good shape. It contains three stories and twenty rooms, all of which have been papered and painted the past two or three years. We have a beautiful campus at the west end of the new electric car line. It is our aim to give those who come here a good, thorough, practical education and to send them away prepared for their work and with better conceptions of duty and responsibility.

As to the correspondence school, that has been in fine shape all along. We have at present more than 1,000 enrollment in this department, representing every state of the Union and the following foreign countries: Canada, England, Scotland, Holland, Japan, India, Australia, Ceylon, Africa, Bermuda, Jamaica, Porto Rico and Hawaii. The practicability of this work is seen in the fact that it covers not only the Bible and sacred literature, but the languages, mathematics, sciences, history, literature, philosophy and commercial branches.
CHAS. J. BURTON, President.

Kentucky University.

Kentucky University has closed its most successful session since the seventies. At the mention of the board, June 13, it elected four young up-to-date men as curators, namely, W. K. Ellis, Hugh McLellan, J. A. Stucky and Charles R. Hudson. In the past five years the university has added to its assets something like $80,000, not counting the annexation of Hamilton College, which represents $65,000 or $70,000, nor the erection of the Carnegie public library on the lower end of the college lawn, a $60,000 building with an annual maintenance fund from the city of $6,000. It has just completed, also, the raising of the money required for the erection of a science building, donated by Mr. Carnegie, to cost $25,000. This gift was conditioned on raising $25,000 to add to the endowment. The condition has been fulfilled and the building will be erected as soon as plans can be arranged for.

The attendance in the university for the past year has been upward of 1,100 in all departments. The increase in mature and well-prepared students has been especially noticeable in the College of Liberal Arts and the College of the Bible. This is due, doubtless to the elevated standards of the university and to the increase in efficiency in the secondary schools of Kentucky. The attendance has embraced thirty-four states and territories and seven foreign countries. There were nineteen students from Australia—the largest Australian club that the university has yet possessed and these students are of very high type.

President Jenkins is to be in Lexington throughout the summer, directing the campaign for the coming session, and a large crop of canvassers have been sent out to all parts of the state and into some adjoining southern states. Large results are anticipated from this vigorous summer campaign.

The work of Secretary Walter White, which began January 1, has fulfilled the expectations of the authorities of the university in the highest degree. Brother White has made favorable impression wherever he has gone, and his work will doubtless be felt in the coming year in increased attendance and endowments.

The additions to the faculty during the past five years have proved satisfactory. There are now in the university five doctors of philosophy of large eastern institutions, vigorous, up-to-date young professors, who are ably supplementing the work done by the old-established professors whose reputation is already so well known in the brotherhood. The friends of the institution are confident of its future and especially hopeful for the approaching session.

The morale of the student body is higher than it has ever been. The students are a fine set of men, and there is little or no trouble in maintaining order among them. Their loyalty to the institution is marked, and every one of them goes out as an agent to bring others back. The attendance in the university next year will undoubtedly be the largest in the history of the institution of recent years. BURRIS A. JENKINS.

Louisville Christian Bible School.

This school was in its inception a creature of what is now the American Christian Missionary Society. Later it came under the care of the C. W. B. M. Its purpose was and is to assist young men of the colored race to be acceptable and efficient public servants of the church as Sunday-school teachers, Christian Endeavor workers, prayer-meeting leaders, elders, deacons and preachers. Friends who have visited the school in its daily work or witnessed its annual closing exercises have almost invariably expressed themselves as most agreeably surprised at the evidences of improvement and advancement which they have noted. C. C. Smith was present at the last closing exercises and publicly stated that the addresses of some of the students were as good as would be heard at college commencements of white people; but that he would not be believed if he should make that statement elsewhere. Mrs. Hagerman, vice president of Kentucky's C. W. B. M., spoke up, saying she would be believed in making it.

The claim is made by some of the older colored preachers who have known most of the work and results of the school that the Louisville Christian Bible school is the best gift of the white Christian Church to the colored people of the nation. Be this as it may, it is gratifying to those who are interested in the intellectual, moral and spiritual development of the negro to know that the Bible school has had and does have some part, however humble, in this great work. It is also gratifying to know that some of the colored people, those best acquainted with it, appreciate the help it affords them and are grateful for it. Up to the present time twelve of our home states and Jamaica and Australia besides have been represented in our classes.

The year just closed has been one of the most prosperous. There have been difficulties and discouragements confronting teachers and students, but the struggle against poverty, in which every student is involved, and the limitations imposed by it have, with the encouragement of teachers, tended to develop in the students that determination, industry, patience, perseverance and endurance which enter so largely into the composition of useful and heroic lives. A goodly portion of the enrollment of the year are students of more than average promise. Three colored churches out of four in the city were supplied with their regular preaching. A number of other pulpits, some of them regularly and others occasionally, were also filled by the students. Besides this they did Sunday-school, prayer-meeting, mission and open-air Sunday service in different parts of the city.

The prospects are hopeful for an increased attendance next year. Will not a number of friends call the attention of promising young negroes to the school? Speak a word of encouragement; ask them to send for a catalogue and investigate the opportunities open to them. A. J. THOMPSON.

Milligan College.

The past session of Milligan College was highly successful. The enrollment was larger than that of the previous year, the class of students was the best on the average we have had for years, the students were older, the class work was fine and the behavior of the student body was never better. All of our teachers are Christians, and none of them uses tobacco. They uphold a high standard of morality.

There are fine prospects of the next session. A large part of the old students will return to school, and a goodly number of new ones are expected. We are planning to enlarge the plant and the work in every way. We are now making brick for a new college building which we expect to erect next vacation. More than $11,000 has already been donated in cash and pledges for the purpose of erecting this building. The people are responding liberally to the calls of our financial agent, and everything is hopeful for the college. The old buildings are to be repaired and remodeled. New equipments, new heating apparatus, water and electric lights are to be put in as soon as the means are provided. We hope to make this small college here in this mountainous country where its good work is so much needed one of the best schools in every way in all this section. R. H. GARRETT, President.
Milligan, Tenn.

The College of the Bible.

The session of this institution which closed in June was the most prosperous in its history. The attendance ran up to 216, and the average attainments of the students in scholarship were higher than usual. Prof. Grubbs, on account of feeble health, had leave of absence, but the work of his professorship was successfully continued by his colleagues, who cheerfully bore the added burden for his sake. He is now in such a condition that, though still feeble, he proposes to resume his labors with the opening of the coming session. Like the lamented President Milligan during the last few years of his career, Prof. Grubbs has bravely borne the burden of his responsible work for several years, under the disadvantage of physical weakness, while the vigor of his mental powers has remained unimpaired.

The very efficient financial agent of the college, W. T. Donaldson, has continued his work of solicitation and has added a material sum to the college endowment; and although a large per cent of the subscriptions is not yet payable, the resources of the college are such as to justify the addition to the faculty of another professor in the person of W. C. Marrs, who has recently received, from Harvard University the degree of Ph.D. He was an honor graduate of Kentucky University in both the College of the Bible and the College of Liberal Arts, in 1898, and is in realization of a constant hope since that date that he is welcomed as a fellow laborer. We now have six professors. With this addition to the teaching force of the college, it is now prepared for an enlargement of its Biblical courses, while maintaining without diminution the thoroughness which has characterized it. It is confidently expected that, notwithstanding the multiplication of institutions which offer comparatively meager courses of Biblical study, its number of students will continue to steadily increase, and especially that the number of graduates from other colleges who seek its superior advantages will be multiplied.

Very many of the students now in attendance are preachers of some years' experience. Sixty-five of these filled regular preaching appointments last year and visited 113 churches. Quite a number of others could have done the same, but the number of churches within reach from Lexington that are without the labor of settled preachers is limited. The nineteen men who graduated last month are all preachers of much experience as they them for important positions, and to such they are already called.

The increasing number of young women who desire a good knowledge of the Bible in order to efficiency as Sunday-school teachers, and especially as missionaries to the heathen, has led to the opening of the College of the Bible to women on the same conditions as to men, and during the last session there were eight matriculates of this class, one of whom graduated.

The number of men studying for the ministry would be greatly increased if preachers and others would take pains to call the attention of all worthy young brethren to the opportunities for such study that are within their reach. We shall be grateful to any friend who will send us the

names of such persons, that we may communicate with them. For catalogues and other information address   J. W. McGarvey, President.
Lexington, Ky.

The Southern Christian Institute.

All through the south where there are white churches many negro churches have sprung up through the helpful influence of some of the best members of these churches. The provision our people have made for training ministers and teachers for these churches and communities was entirely inadequate to the demands, our entire expenditure since we began not amounting to more than what our religious neighbors expend annually. The negro churches have had to depend on men who have had no training for their work. As a result our churches have been disorganized, like sheep without a shepherd. But now there is a change. The churches are asking for ministers and teachers. There are fifty places to be filled where one can be filled. They are ready to co-operate if we can put a shepherd among them to show them what co-operation means. The negroes who have come from the various missionary schools are now leading their people and they are fast changing the ideal of the race. Fifteen or twenty years ago their ambition was to get something. Now the ambition is to do something and to show that they can. They humbly appreciate what we have done for them, and are asking us to help them to make themselves a useful factor in our society. What we do in the next twenty-five years will determine the condition of the Negro Church of Christ for 200 years to come, if not throughout the entire life of this American republic.

Let no one be discouraged because this question is an old one and has been harped on much. It is true the negro problem has been ever present from the foundation of the nation; but we are now in that stage of the battle when flank movements and assaults in force will decide the fate of the day and the issue of the war. Let

the reader stand with us on this beautiful hill and look out and see a stretch of country from Southern California to South Carolina beckoning for help, asking that preachers be sent to their churches and that prepared men and women be sent to school in their midst, and he will be in a frame of mind to understand more clearly what we mean when we tell of our work and what our purposes are.

Our attendance last year was 15 per cent better than any previous session. The morale also has been better. We have maintained strict discipline and those whose tendency was toward criminality were soon weeded out. We did all that could be done with the means at hand to perfect both our school work and our industries. As a result, much progress was manifested. Prof. T. M. Burgess has been enabled to devote his whole time to bringing our class room work, and the good results are very evident. Willis Prout, superintendent of industries, has brought out most excellent results in the one department of farming.

Our aim for the future must be twofold, yet with one result in view. We must go on and perfect the work at the school we have already undertaken, and we must organize the Negro Disciples for more effective work. The "Gospel Plea" must be made the medium through which much of this work will be done. The time is now ripe to do this provided we can be enabled to equip ourselves better so we can make it a better paper. The dawn of a new day has come. Our prayer is that when high noon comes we may be found ready to garner in the great harvest.

J. B. Lehman.

The School of the Evangelists.

We are slowly but surely recovering from the awful fire which, on December 1, 1904, swept away our splendid main building. On January 11, 1906, we were far enough along to reopen school, although we were by no means complete. We enrolled students from 25 states and countries —110 in all. We are now at work on the buildings. It is our purpose to have, by God's help, everything in readiness for the opening, September 19, 1906. We have built a power house, containing engine and boiler rooms, coal room, laundry, bakery, lavatory and shower bath, all

equipped with up-to-date necessities. We have built a large combined college building (three stories) and dormitory (four stories). These buildings are furnished with up-to-date furnishings, steam and electricity, steam cooking, etc. Some idea of the magnitude of the work may be seen in the fact that the buildings measure nearly 700,000 bricks.

In answer to prayer God has given us in labor, material and cash close to $30,000. We need about $3,000 more. We are getting it slowly but surely. We appeal to our friends to remember us in this last long, hard pull. We have planned a perfect equipment and accommodations for 160 young preachers. A young man can get help here. For example, if he can pay his tuition ($24) a year he can work out his room rent, board and plain washing by working a certain number of hours a week; or he can pay $85 and not work. We want to help the young men, and we are in a position to do it. We want clean young men—young men who do not use tobacco in any form. We want young men who have their minds made up to preach and to do nothing else, and we want them at the opening of next term. We want the address of every young man in the English-speaking world who desires to preach, whether he has money or not. The fact is, poverty, principle and purpose constitute the highest recommendation here.

The Lord and his people have graciously given us the equipment and the open door. Will not our brethren everywhere call the attention of the young men to the opportunity? Our new catalogue is free for the asking. It tells the whole story.   Ashley S. Johnson, President.

Kimberlin Heights, Tenn.

WILLIAM WOODS COLLEGE FOR YOUNG LADIES
FULTON, MISSOURI.

Just the place for your daughter. A college home of high moral character. An institution abreast of the times. A University and College training faculty. Handsome and commodious buildings with all modern conveniences. Large and beautiful campus. A new $20,000.00 Chapel in process of erection. Healthful location.

Articulates with the Missouri State University. Courses in literature, science, art, elocution, vocal and instrumental music, domestic science, art, book-keeping and shorthand and type-writing. Educates daughters of foreign missionaries. Endowment solicited. For catalogue or further information, address,   J. B. JONES, President.

The University of Virginia Bible Chair.

During the past session the Bible work at the University of Virginia has included one course of lectures by Dr. H. L. Willett, and two courses by me as regular lectures there. A variety of causes prevented my being present for systematic work throughout the year. Chief among them was the conviction that it was not worth while to maintain continuous work where the absence of academic credit made impossible regular study on the part of the students.

For the three years that I have had charge of the work I have endeavored to secure for it a place in the curriculum. It has been evident all along that in no other way could systematic Bible teaching of university grade be made possible. It is a satisfaction to all friends of the work that the university board has just put Bible teaching upon the same footing with other branches of learning by creating the John B. Cary chair of Biblical history and literature. They have apvided that candidates for the B. A. degree may elect one course in this department. The work is to be supported as heretofore by the C. W. B. M. Thus a new opportunity for Bible teaching, under circumstances worthy of its dignity and importance, has been afforded in this old and honorable state university.

Too much praise can not be given our brother, Dr. Charles W. Kent, professor of English literature, for his efforts to attain this end. From the very beginning of the Bible lectureship he has been its steadfast friend. Without his unfailing efforts it would not have been possible to secure this recognition. The friends of the Bible everywhere are his debtors. Much is also due to the efforts of President Alderman. Ever since he assumed the high office that he is so ably and successfully filling, he has interested himself in the Bible work. To his advocacy of the plan in the meetings of the board its adoption must be credited.

Necessarily this important step is in the nature of an experiment. If it succeeds it will become a permanent part of the university teaching. It has been demonstrated to the satisfaction of those who are acquainted with the facts that Bible teaching can not be sucessfully conducted at the University of Virginia without such recognition and credit as have now been granted. Under the present plan there is good reason to hope for an ever enlarging success. It seems fitting that the university which has led in so many important educational movements should also be a pioneer here. This advance step on the part of one of our oldest universities in the east, along with a somewhat similar move by one of the youngest institutions of the far west, shou.. open the way for a like move elsewhere. Friends of the Bible should see to it that it secures the same opportunity in other state institutions that it has at the University of California and the University of Virginia [and Missouri also.—EDITOR.] W. M. FORREST.

William Woods College.

With profound gratitude the managers of this institution recognize the achievements of the past and the improvements contemplated for the summer and fall are thrilling the donors and the patrons everywhere with supreme delight. The auditorium, which will be known as the "D. M. Dulany Auditorium," will rank among the best in the state and will have a capacity for seating at least 1,000 people, with two galleries, and its equipment throughout will be complete. The basement will for the present be used as a gymnasium. A grand piano and organ will in all probability be introduced this winter. This institution will be articulated with the university. Its curriculum meets every just demand. Preparations are being made to accommodate a larger enrollment than that of last year. New school rooms will be added and new apparatus will be introduced in the scientific department. The teaching force will be increased.

The most gratifying feature in the outlook for the institution is the continued friendship and generosity of Dr. W. S. Woods and wife. All told, from first to last, their gifts will amount to nearly $100,000. Other generous persons, like the Dulanys, Edwards and Adams, are co-operating with these good people. The brotherhood throughout the state should recognize the fact that this institution makes education possible to nearly every aspiring girl. Their generosity should kindle the deepest sympathy in the hearts of other benevolent persons who can duplicate what they have done by giving scholarships for the education of the daughters of foreign missionaries and for extending privileges to a larger number of dependent girls. It is expected that the patronage heretofore extended by those blessed with ample means will continue, since the co-education of the two classes has achieved the very best results. It is hoped that some day an endowment of $500,000 will be realized. An ample endowment, however, will in no wise cancel the obligations of preachers and churches to co-operate in this great work. The oft quoted expression of Alexander Campbell finds its fulfillment in the triumphs of this institution: "Attempt great things, expect great things and great things will follow." J. B. JONES.

Texas Christian University.

The sky of Christian education in the southwest is bright and hopeful. The past few years have been years of growth. Now some advance steps that have been hoped for for years will be undertaken, and the spirit of the work is permanency. We have had a period of building. Under the aggressive leadership of President Zollars improvements in buildings and equipments have gone on at a marvellous rate. During the past year no buildings have been added, but there has been much activity in raising funds for interior equipment, library, apparatus, etc. A few of our churches observed Educational day and quite a number of others made liberal pledges on the visits of President Zollars. There is much regret at losing this strong man from the work in Texas. His administration has contributed an invaluable element to T. C. U. at a period that was critical in her history. This year's work has sent out one of the strongest classes in the history of Texas Christian University, and leaves a student body coming on.

Toward the future our workers are looking with a large spirit of hopefulness and confidence, especially because of the definite lines of enlargement that are undertaken at this time. Some of these are the plans that have been in our prayers for years. The Bible college is greatly enlarged. The scarcity of funds has always limited this department below the requirements of the field. The demand for preachers in Texas and the imperative duty of training our own Texas boys for the ministry has caused the trustees to concentrate our improvements this year on the Bible college. There will be three men to give full time to it, besides some teaching that will be done by professors in other departments. With such men as Dr. Clinton Lockhart, Prof. Stairs and Ellsworth Faris to train the preacher boys, great and permanent work is looked for. This makes the department entirely new, as Prof. F. H. Marshall has gone to train the native workers in Norway, under the foreign society. Another help for the preacher boys is the establishment of a club boarding house for them. This will be ready by the opening in September and will help reduce the cost of living materially.

Another attestation of the strictly up-to-date character of the Texas educational work is the move of putting into the field this year an educational secretary. Only pioneer work along this line has been done by our people as yet, but the time is at hand for some fundamental effort to reach our people for education. The secretary was selected some time before the Indianapolis congress, thus anticipating the action of the educational society there in throwing the responsibility back upon the individual colleges.

The writer of this article was selected jointly by the T. C. U. trustees and the State Mission Board to represent the brotherhood of Texas and the southwest as educational secretary. He enters upon the work July 1. The direct effort at first will be to enlist the churches in the observance of Educational day, and to find and enlist a new crop of preachers. There may be a superabundance of preachers in some states, but there is not in Texas. This is because of the fact that so many of our churches that have been weak are getting able to support ministers. This great problem, vital and pressing, we feel will be solved by the present course and equipment. In additon to this, the secretary will have to enlist in the interest of our education large numbers of our people whose influence now is lost because of lack of touch with the work. In addition to this work Bro. T. E. Shirley, who has done such a magnificent work as financial agent, will be assisted by John L. Andrews. Brother Shirley has had to go to Hereford on account of the condition of his health. Announcement will be made before long of some large plans for securing much needed endowment in the next few years.

Dr. Clinton Lockhart has been in Texas only a few weeks, but he has made friends rapidly and his coming has inspired great confidence in the work. He was sought earnestly and secured as dean of the Bible college. This is where he is needed and where his chief work will be done. He has also been made acting president for the coming year. With such leaders and a strong, experienced faculty; with our two other schools incorporated with us, viz.: Carleton College and Panhandle Christian College; with other schools of our brethren closely allied, and with such fundamental problems as our task, we feel that great things are in store for this cause in the great southwest. We believe a period of solid and permanent growth is just ahead of us.

Hillsboro, Tex. COLBY D. HALL.

Washington Christian College.

The fourth year of educational work was the best session in every way the college has had. The college has won a large number of friends and patrons and the executive members of the board of trustees have manifested great faithfulness to the institution. The college is doing a much needed work, in that the majority of the students we get would certainly never be in a Christian college.

For the coming session there will be only two changes worth mention. The young ladies' home will be partly refurnished. There will be even more Bible and kindred studies than last session. A special additional fund is being raised for this work. The college, realizing there never was an age when able preachers were more needed, wishes thorough and strong courses for those preparing for the ministry. The emphasis of the institution is always put upon the quality of the work done. The faculty has proven so satisfactory and there will be no changes of importance. To it is added an associate professor of Latin and mathematics.

Miss Minna Schott is a very valuable addition to the music department.

Emerson W. Matthews, professor of Latin and Greek, who is one of the best language teachers in the country, is spending the summer in Germany doing special work in his favorite studies at Heidelberg University. He is a graduate of Harvard University

The prospects for the coming session are good. More than half of the young ladies' home is already contracted for.

Washington, D. C. DANIEL E. MOTLEY.

Ministerial Exchange.

R. R. Hamlin can be secured for meetings in the north after January 1, 1907. He may be addressed at Ft. Worth, Texas.

Charles E. McVey, singing evangelist, has open dates after July 15. He is now assisting in a meeting at Dalhart, Texas.

E. C. Tuckerman, singing evangelist, desires to correspond with churches or evangelists. Address him at Lincoln, Neb., General Delivery.

A preacher of experience and ability would like to correspond with churches, with view of locating at an early date. Salary, $1,000. Address T. R. W., General Delivery, Buffalo, N. Y.

Lawrence Wright has open dates for July and August. Address him at Bald Knob, Arkansas.

Harold E. Monser has canceled an engagement for August and can hold a meeting then if notified soon. He prefers a tent and can furnish one if desired.

G. W. Terrell, Stanberry, Mo., writes that a capable young married minister of experience would like to hold meetings in that and adjoining counties during July and August for free will offerings.

Evangelistic

We invite ministers and others to send reports of meetings, additions and other news of the churches. It is especially requested that additions be reported as "by confession and baptism" or "by letter."

Special to THE CHRISTIAN-EVANGELIST.

Long Beach, Cal., July 2.—Scoville closed meeting with twenty-three to-day; 256 altogether. He has captured the port. Smith and the Kendalls are great in song.—E. W. Thornton.

Arkansas.

Bald Knob, June 15.—I have just closed a good meeting at Paris and begin here to-night.—Lawrence Wright.

Bentonville, June 26.—Two additions last Lord's day.—J. W. Ellis.

Fordyce, June 30.—We are helping the pastor, E. M. Berry, in a protracted meeting. There is a new house of worship here. Brother Browning, the state evangelist, is with us. The church held a week of prayer to get ready for the meeting.—T. M. Myers.

Hope, June 28.—Four added recently—2 by baptism, 2 by statement. Midweek services are holding up well in attendance and inspiration.—Percy G. Cross.

California.

Ocean Park, 'une 25.—Two confessions yesterday; splendid Children's day offering.—George Ringo.

Ukiah, June 26.—A series of Sunday evening lectures has resulted in much good. Two baptisms last week. I will spend August and September in Kansas and Oklahoma.—Otha Wilkison.

Colorado.

Grand Junction, June 26.—Four additions yesterday; 65 since February, 11 of these being young people from the Indian school.—Frederic Grimes.

Idaho.

Meridian, June 24.—We have just closed a meeting with 27 additions—17 by confession.—L. K. Dick.

Illinois.

Effingham, June 25.—Seven additions since last report—5 by confession, 2 by statement.—Wilford Field.

Fisher, June 26.—One added by confession last night.—S. Elwood Fisher.

Concord, June 26.—Two additions yesterday.—J. W. Pearson.

Williamsville, June 25.—Two added by confession yesterday.—C. D. Kaskell.

Indiana.

Newcastle, June 27.—Seven additions recently—2 by confession; Sunday-school and Christian Endeavor Society growing.—L C. Howe.

Portland, June 1.—Our four weeks' meeting, conducted by L. O. Newcomer and Frank C. Huston, has just closed with 39 additions—32 by confession. Every department of the work was strengthened. There has been 1 added by statement since the meeting, making 73 additions in the past seven months. M. W. Harkins assisted us during the first week of the meeting.—C. H. Trout, Pastor.

Scottsburg, June 30.—We held a basket meeting with a special service for old people at Austin. There were 24 over 60 years of age present. On the following Tuesday I baptized two old men. The Sunday-schools at each of my preaching points, Austin, Scottsburg and Zoah, raised their apportionment for foreign missions. Scottsburg C. W. B. M. will also be on the honor roll this year.—C. O. Burton.

Indian Territory.

Sapulpa, June 28.—One by letter. The children met their apportionment.—A. M. Harral.

Kansas.

Chanute, June 22.—One confession recently.—G. W. Kitchen.

Plainville, June 26.—Five added recently.—N. Ferd Engle.

Harper, June 29.—We closed a meeting at Minneola with 24 added, the membership doubled, the Bible school organized, the house dedicated, all debts provided for and we left the strongest church in the place.—M. B. Ingle and H. A. Easton.

Logan.—Otha Wilkison, of Ukiah, Cal., and Charles E. McVay, singer, will begin a meeting

August 12. The opera house has been secured which seats 1,500 people.

Massachusetts.

Everett, June 25.—Twelve additions recently—7 by baptism. Our Bible school raised its apportionment, $45.—A. T. June.

Haverhill.—In a recent meeting conducted by Brother McKissick there were 12 additions, all by confession.—F. E. Giles.

Michigan.

Fremont, June 19.—One confession. The work is moving nicely; Sunday-school growing.—T. W. Bellingham.

Saginaw, June 25.—Six additions recently—4 by confession.—J. Murray Taylor.

Missouri.

Billings, June 20.—I began a meeting here a week ago; 6 additions. We hope to leave the brethren so sufficiently "revived" that they will employ a pastor for the ensuing year.—S. J. Vance, Carthage, Mo.

Dixon, June 24.—Last Sunday was a great day at Franks; largest crowd in years; preaching and roll call in the morning; basket dinner and Children's day exercises in the afternoon. Apportionment raised. All the work moves along well.

Twelve added since last report—11 by baptism.—Leon Couch.

Grant City, June 24.—Two added this week—1 by baptism, 1 by letter. Fine audiences and work opening up in excellent shape.—W. A. Shullenberger.

La Plata, June 26.—Three added by confession and baptism since last report.—Percy T. Carnes.

Richland.—My work is moving along nicely. We had 17 accessions at Crocker recently—15 by confession. Mrs. Julia Watkins, a former Junior worker at Fayetteville, Ark., is doing a marvelous work among the Juniors. The new Young People's Society is doing good work. There have been 10 additions at Richland in the past two months—2 by confession. We are preparing for a meeting this fall, with George H. Nicol, of Red Oak, Ia., as evangelist.—J. R. Blunt.

Flat River.—The Clerk family are in a meeting here. The new church building will be ready for use about the middle of J—uly. The possibilities of this place are limited only by a preacher's ability. A strong man is wanted at once to take charge of the work. Address Dr. Edward Griffin, Flat River, Mo.

Kansas City, June 26.—One added at Lewisburg yesterday from another religious body and two last Lord's day by confession and baptism. I begin a meeting there July 8.—Clyde Lee Fife.

Fredericktown.—After closing our meeting at Abilene, Texas, I visited my children at Fredericktown where I found R. O. Rogers in a meeting with 60 additions up to date. I sang in three services and at one of them had the great pleasure of taking the great confession from my two children and baptized them in the creek which runs through the town. Brother Rogers is doing some effective work. Among his converts was the lay reader of the Episcopalians and one member of the Catholic Church.—John S. Zeran.

Nebraska.

Trumbull.—The church is going ahead. Our Children's day apportionment was $30 and the offering over $50. George Poulson is the superintendent and E. J. Sias the minister.

New York.

Auburn, June 29.—Three additions by baptism since last report, making 73 during the past eight months. 53 of them through the regular services.—Arthur Braden.

New York City.—Up fill June 18 the Lenox Avenue Church had 17 additions since the Scoville meeting closed. It is now the third congregation in size in the state. A. Long has just been elected superintendent of the Bible school.

Ohio.

Marion, June 26.—One added by confession last Sunday.—O. D. Maple.

Ravenna, June 27.—Two confessions and 1 by letter.—M. E. Chatley, Pastor.

Pennsylvania.

Philadelphia, June 28.—There have been 46 additions to the Third Christian Church since January 1—all at the regular services. The church is in the best condition of its history. The Children's day offering was $182.—G. P. Rutledge.

South Carolina.

Bonneau, June 28.—My ministry at Charleston closed June 10, when there were 2 confessions, making 84 during the two years at that place. I am in my first meeting as state evangelist at this place. In ten days there have been 9 confessions—all young men but one. This is new work, as there is no congregation here of any kind. We continue.—Charles E. Smith.

Texas.

Amarillo, June 28.—Our four weeks' meeting,

conducted by R. R. Hamlin, has closed with 26 additions—Jewell Howard.

Dalhart, June 25.—Our meeting is starting well; 3 additions first day. John Auslien, the pastor, is doing the preaching.—Charles E. McVay, Singing Evangelist.

Fort Worth, June 25.—Seven additions at the Tabernacle Church yesterday.—A. E. Dubber.

Lockhart, June 26.—Two confessions last Sunday night.—J. F. Quisenberry.

Sulphur Springs, June 28.—Our meeting has been in progress two weeks. There is a splendid interest and 23 additions to date. J. W. Famuliner is the pastor. We go from here to Piano for a meeting. We expect to conduct meetings in Richmond, Ky., in September and St. Jos, Mo., in October.—H. A. Northcutt, Evangelist; J. S. Zeran and Wife, Singers.

Angleton, June 30.—We closed a meeting at Center, Texas, with 34 additions. We have organized a church here at Angleton with 32 members and will continue till Monday night. We begin the San Marcos River camp-meeting July 6.—R. V. Spicer and E. M. Douthit.

West Virginia.

Wheeling Island.—Eight additions recently—6 by baptism. There have been 57 additions this year—29 by confession, 13 by statement, 15 by letter. All bills and running expenses have been met with money still in the treasury.—C. Manly Rice.

TRANSIENT GOODNESS.—Hosea 6:4.

"My soul, it is the Lord
  Who calls thee by his grace;
Now loose thee from each cumbering load,
  And bend thee to the race.

"Thy crown of life hold fast,
  Thy heart with courage stay;
Nor let one trembling glance be cast
  Along the backward way."

One truly good hour in a penitent's to-day is a bright prophecy of a good, full month next year, and an eternity of goodness (or heaven) beyond the flood.

Transient goodness is evidence of power to be good, as it also is of lack of proper determination and stability of character. We are not drawn from the clear atmosphere of goodness out into the murkiness of evil—we go, and the responsibility rests on us. Let us strive to enlarge the area of the good stage in our pilgrimage till they become at last as a sky, cloudless from horizon to horizon.

A life shotted through with periods of transient goodness is vastly preferable to one that is a rayless story of wrong. There is reason to believe the doom of a wasted life will be mitigated by the record of every good thought and chivalrous deed the keen light of judgment day will reveal amidst the debris of the past. Let us encourage even those whom we have no hope of leading into the church to fulfill the promptings of every good impulse. If it does not add a new joy to their heaven, it will at least quench one fury in their hell.

It was good in Ananias and Sapphira to so enter into the spirit of giving as to promise the church the price of the field, but avarice retained half and they lost all and were borne to disgraceful graves. Achan, we take it, was a good man, but cupidity was his undoing. Saul was far happier living in obscurity but in divine favor than afterward in royal splendor but alienated from God. Though poor, unknown to fame, and not one of the great lights of the church, "Be thou faithful unto death, and thou shalt receive the crown of life."

Satan never sees us in our better estate, but it can be said of him, "He hath desired us that he might sift us as wheat." But he can not reach within the cordon of angels divine love hath placed about us to guard us and draw us out for destruction. The band will open to let us out but not to let him in. As an angel of light he now stands in the midst of illusions inviting us to bask with him in a wealth of false promises. Let us not be deceived by cunningly devised fables concerning the wages of sin, but rather give heed unto the words of the Savior: "Behold, I come quickly: hold that fast which thou hast that no man take thy crown."

have little reason to expect the sweets of virtue till all are eliminated. We must enter into the meaning of patient continuance in well doing. One more blow with the pick after one miner has yielded to discouragement has revealed storied wealth; one more round with the spade has opened fountains that have made deserts bloom. Continue in goodness, for in due time we, too, shall "reap if we faint not."

THE GOOD SAMARITAN.—Luke 10:25-37.

Memory verses, 33, 34.

GOLDEN TEXT.—Blessed are the merciful, for they shall obtain mercy.—Matt. 5:7.

Chapters 10 to 17, inclusive, in the Gospel of Luke, contain matter which is not paralleled by any of the other evangelists. It is represented that after Jesus had completed his ministry in Galilee and had turned his face toward Jerusalem to meet his death, he made first a direct journey to the vicinity of Jerusalem (perhaps to the city itself for the feast of dedication.—John 9 and 10): then a long and circuitous journey through Perea, the country east of the Jordan, and a return again to the neighborhood of Jerusalem; then a northern tour into Ephraim and a final return by way of Jericho to Jerusalem. The whole of this period is called the Perean ministry, and each of its three parts closed with a visit to Bethany. The first time he visited Mary and Martha; the second time he raised their brother Lazarus from the dead; the third time he was anointed by Mary.

It was after the final departure from Galilee, and after the sending out of seventy disciples to preach and heal, that Jesus spoke this parable of mercy. The good Samaritan has become, to all subsequent generations, the type of the merciful and unselfishly helpful man.

A lawyer came to Jesus to put him to a test. He asked a great question, how to secure eternal life, perhaps seeking to entangle the Master in some subtle argument about the law. But Jesus shunned subtleties, then as always. He was always profound, but never idly subtle. He led his inquirer at once to solid ground. Eternal life comes through love to God and one's neighbor. This was the highest word of the law, and, as a general principle, it was high enough. But it wanted application. It needed to be made concrete, definite and personal.

So Jesus spoke a parable to show how the obligation of man to man overleaps all bounds of creed and caste and is of universal validity. Even the despised Samaritan, by observing it, won the approval of God and compels the approbation of man. Our debt to our neighbors as fellow-townsmen, as fellow-Christians, as fellow-countrymen, as members of the same family, or club, or business organization, is something. But underlying all that is our debt to man *as man*. It is a man's manhood that is in the image of God—not his Americanism, or his membership in a political party or in a religious community, or in a social group. And it is to God's image in man that our

---

Christian Endeavor

By GEO. L. SNIVELY

FRIENDSHIP.—Prov. 17:17; 18:24; 27:9, 12, 19; Eccl, 4:9, 10

July 15, 1906.

DAILY READINGS.

M. Ruth and Naomi. .....Ruth 1:14-18.
T. David and Jonathan. .....1 Sam. 18:1-4.
W. David and Nahash. .....2 Sam. 10:1,2.
T. David and Hiram. .....1 Kings 5:1-12.
F. Paul and Epaphroditus. .....Phil. 2:25-30.
S. Paul and Timothy. .....1 Cor. 16:10-16.
S. Jesus and the Bethany Family. John 11:1-9.

"The only solid basis of true and lasting friendship is to be found in the mutual possession of right principles, virtuous character and a true life."

The immortalization of friendship in the sacred biographies of Ruth and Naomi, Esther and Mordecai, David and Jonathan, Paul and Timothy, Jesus and Lazarus, Martha and Mary are expressions of heaven's appreciation of the importance of this grace in effecting the brotherhood of man and right relations between man and the great "Friend" of all.

If it is evidence of friendship to help one into possession of a field, it is proof of a more exalted quality to help him to a heavenly inheritance. If it is an expression of friendship to cultivate in him a taste for music and art, how much nobler to help him up into an apprecia-

tion of God and his righteousness? In the commerce of friendship let us earnestly seek to secure and bestow "the best gifts."

You may make beneficiaries of many out of whom you can not make friends. There must be congeniality and much in common between men before they can be friends. Only fine metal can receive certain impressions, and only the higher natures can receive the seal of friendship. It is a high testimonial to one's worth to be the friend of a great and good man. To be a true friend is proof of a noble character. This is a touch stone helping us to know ourselves as we are.

"Never desert a friend under fire," was an admonition to the cadets by Gen. Grant that the world approves. Centuries before, he of whom the prophet philosopher had said, "There is a friend that sticketh closer than a brother," calmly remarked, "Lo, I am with you always, even unto the end of the world." If free from moral turpitude, he will commend us though all men should speak evil of us or forget us; and if we go down to our graves with our faces toward Zion he will raise us up into glory notwithstanding the hate of men or demons.

The quaint Hebrew parallelism has it:

"A friend loveth at all times,
And a brother is born for adversity."

It requires adversities to test friendships even as storms prove the stability

of ships. And when we have a friend who has weathered with us reverses of fortune or the aspersions of calumny and social ostracism we have one of life's greatest treasures. We have not counted all our "many blessings," if we leave our friendships out. This is one that gold can not buy nor other forms of power procure. It is the common heritage of us all. God give to us all friends who will rejoice with us when we are glad, and manfully stand by us and comfort us when we are sad.

It is well to get before us the real scope of friendship and then cultivate the help and joy it holds for the race. "Friendship is a deep, quiet, enduring affection founded upon mutual respect and esteem." Friendship is always mutual; there may be unreciprocated affection, unrequited love! but never unreciprocated or unrequited friendship; one may have friendly feelings toward an enemy, but while there is hostility or coldness on one side, there can be no friendship." "Affection may be purely natural; friendship is a growth." "Friendship is more intellectual and less emotional than love." "Friendship implies some degree of equality while love does not: we can speak of man's love toward God, but not his friendship for God."

❀ ❀

WHEN SLEEP FAILS

Take Horsford's Acid Phosphate

Half a teaspoon in half a glass of water just before retiring brings refreshing sleep.

The Home Departmei

Our Country.

With peace that comes of purity
    And strength to simple justice due,
So runs our royal dream of thee:
    God of our fathers! make it true.

O land of lands! to thee we give
    Our prayers, our hopes, our service free;
For thee thy sons shall nobly live,
    And at thy need shall die for thee!
                    —*John G. Whittier.*

Matt Crandal's Independence Day.

BY JESSIE CLAIRE GLASIER.

"I should like to know what a house full of girls can do to celebrate the Fourth?" said Rose, scornfully tipping her little chin up at the rest of the group. They were all in the kitchen, gathered around patient, steady-going Di, who had clucked after them like a motherly little hen ever since any of them could remember. Di's name was Diantha, really, after Grandmother Bristow, but in all her nineteen years she had scarcely ever heard it, for first it was too long for a baby, and then in two years there was wee Rose who could not get beyond the first syllable, and then Annette and Georgie and little Lide had kept up the nickname, so that the faithful eldest sister would have felt a little startled, as if she had suddenly had a telegram thrust into her hand, for instance, if any one had called her by the old-fashioned name that was hers by right.

This Fourth of July morning she held an open letter in her hand. Annette, on the run, had brought it in five minutes ago from the new rural delivery box at the farm yard gate. "It's a disappointment, of course," she said, knitting her pretty eyebrows, "but mother says they'll surely be back before night. Don't cry, Lide, they'll bring the rockets and pin wheels and things. I'm sure I don't wonder Aunt Maggie wanted them to stay a few hours longer. It's the first time in years that father has been there over night—think of it! His one sister, and only ten miles away! Of course they didn't want to come right off after breakfast. We'll see old Prince's white nose at the gate before sundown, so don't feel badly, Georgie."

"And here we were going to have such a splendiferous dinner," mourned Annette. "It'll be too late when they come, and they won't want anything, anyhow, after they've been to Aunt Maggie's. I know what she'll have—chicken pie, an' creamed potatoes an' store ice cream an' everything."

"Well, we'll have something good, too," soothed Di, "and we'll have it at noon, just as usual."

"And will you let us make a platform under the big chestnut tree and a-speak our pieces and all just like we planned?" piped patriotic Georgie, who stammered under excitement.

"Yes, we'll go this minute and put out the big flag. Now Rose, don't look thorny. We'll have a good time celebrating, if there isn't a man about the place. We've always had a rousing good Fourth, and we ought to feel happier than usual because father and mother are having a real holiday."

"Who do you think is going to fix that great heavy flag pole? It's all father can manage," said Rose, with a skeptical toss of her curly head.

"Me! Let me climb out on the roof! I can help hold it," cried Annette, whose daring feats were the despair of her elders and the admiration of the little sisters.

"Yes, you'd enjoy dancing on the ridgepole, I don't doubt," laughed Di, "but nobody's neck is going to be risked if it is Independence Day. I wish we'd known earlier, before Mrs. Bantry went home, and had her ask Hen to come over before they started for town."

"And I wish we could drive over," grumbled Rose. "There'll be lots going on. I wouldn't be afraid to drive the colt."

"Now, honey, do be reasonable," coaxed Di. "You know even father wouldn't take Jerry with fire-crackers and torpedoes snapping all around. He'd bolt in five minutes and string us all along the road. Besides, we couldn't just part of us go, and suppose father and mother got home earlier than we expected and nobody to welcome them?"

"There comes somebody," cried Georgie. "Goody! It's Hen! I'm going to make him stop!" She flew down the path, followed by 5-year-old Lide, yellow locks streaming, arms waving. "Say!" she called, "Come on in and help up put out the flag! Why, you're not Hen Bantry, after all!" She stopped and looked hard at the thin face and narrow shoulders of the young man, who had halted at sound of the eager little voice. "Hen is real straight and you're stoopy," she went on, with childish frankness, "and he's all tanned up and you're so white, but you do look a lot like him. Oh, dear! I did think you were Hen!"

A friendly smile came into the stranger's black eyes. "No, I'm Matt Crandal, and quite at your service." He took off his straw hat with a bow that won the hearts of the two little girls.

"Then, can you fix it? Father and mother are away and just us girls home and it's such a big flag, and we want to c-celebrate just the s-same," Georgie cried eagerly.

Bashful little Lide peeped out from behind her sister, "I'll give you some of my fire-cwackers if you will," she promised sweetly, raising her blue eyes for one instant and then dropping them to the toe of her dusty little shoe.

"Sure! This is the day we celebrate," said the young man with an odd little laugh. "I hadn't expected to be hanging out any flags, but show me what you want and I'll take a try at it."

Georgie led the way back to the house a little slowly. Maybe Di wouldn't like it because she asked a stranger—grown-up folks were so funny about things like that. But he looked so nice out of his eyes when he smiled. Lide had hold of his hand already. Georgie faced the group in the kitchen door steadily. "This is our friend, Lide's and mine, Mr. Matthew Crandal, and he's going to put out the flag," she announced, with dignity in every line of her 8-year-old figure.

Annette's round, freckled face dimpled. "Oh! He can help make our platform, can't he, Di?"

Before Di could answer the stranger spoke. "I have nothing at all to do this morning—I was looking for work but I haven't found it yet, and this isn't the day to expect it. I'll be glad to help you in any way that I can. I learned carpentry when —before—" he broke off and looked down at the trustful little hand that still clasped his own. The words came in a straightforward, cheery tone, but something in the black eyes hinted at discouragement and loneliness. Warm-hearted Di took a sudden resolve. This was no ordinary tramp; he was as neat and as pleasant-mannered as Professor Simmons at the Academy. He looked as though he might have been sick; some kind of bad luck had come, and he

needed hea:
stay and e;
here? And
get a job, i
"I'm glac
said cordial
the attic wi
up there. ;
Father alw:
It's heavy
plained as s
Georgia c
the open w
laughter, w
shrilly. "L
can l-look,
know how,"
deft turns
clicked into
proudly to
expressive :
fluttering c
"I'll neve:
to see my l
pines—I sa:
set. The b:
ner," and e
as a church.
but my lung
"It's awf
unteered Ge
out of wind
tiful view,
'way over :
Penfield. S
no, that wa;
And there's
that's the r
do wish our
hurry up a:
tion of the
voices o:
ly. "Was
go?" he as
tone.
"Oh, yes
show him h
the tree yo:
dinner."
The next
doors and c
moulded bi
the sawing
of voices o;
nut-tree. 7
who had dr
and could c
lowed to tu
holiday cak
gation hea:
"Will you p
he asked re
kerchief fro
coat and wi
Di gave
course it st
platform, a:
look! And
ton's picture
you'll have
dinner. "O;
we want yo:
When ha:
Matt Crand:
them all la:
in honor of
eye on his ;
mood, and t
pause with
self telling ;
petite was s
might last
the home-li:
been starvi:
It was a:

mounted the flower-decked platform and announced in her clear treble, "The exercises of this afternoon will now begin with a song, 'The S-star S-spangled B-banner.' All of you sing."

A pretty group they made—Di in a simple gown that matched her clear, innocent eys; Rose in pink muslin the very hue of her cheeks; Annette in last summer's pique sailor suit much let down, her brown braids tied with poppy-red ribbons, and the two little girls proudly disporting their best white frocks, while their new friend sat on the grass at their feet, his clear baritone leading the familiar chorus.

"Now, Babe, your turn next," whispered Rose, and without waiting to be heralded Lide took her place in front of the Father of His Country, and after a hurried bob of the head lifted her eyes to the big flag and began, in her sweet voice—

"I love this bonny flag!
    Its colors brightly glowing
Mean peace and freedom in our land
    As on the breeze they're blowing.
I hope its stars will eVer shine
    Above this little head of mine,
And when I'm bi~ you'll surely see
    I'll love and serve my own countree!"

"Rose! You wrote that!" cried Annette, as Lide finished with a sweeping courtesy and ran to hide her head in Rose's lap while the rest applauded vigorously.

"It came into my head this morning while we were making the platform," confessed the budding poet, turning a shade pinker. "Didn't Babe learn it quick? Now let's sing America."

"Sheridan's Ride," delivered by Annette with much spirit, came after the song. Then Georgia," trying her best to be deliberate and smooth of tongue, gave "Breathes there a man with soul so dead." Di, from her camp-chair, read a chapter from her birthday copy of "The Man Without a Country." "Hail Columbia" came next, and then Di turned to their guest. "Won't you help us celebrate? Sing or recite something?" she urged.

"Perhaps I could get through with 'Give me liberty or give me death'—I knew it by heart long ago at school."

"Splendid! But first, let's all drink to 'Our Country," Rose put in, appearing with an inviting pitcher of lemonade.

It is hardly to be imagined that Patrick Henry himself began his famous speech with more vigor than did Matt Crandal, inspired by the bright, friendly faces about him. As he went on he straightened himself unconsciously and threw back his dark head.

"Shall we gather strength by irresolution and inaction? Shall we acquire the means of effectual resistance by lying supinely on our backs and hugging the delusive phantom of hope until our enemies shall have bound us hand and foot? Sir, we are not weak if we make a proper use of those means which the God of nature hath placed in our power . . . . The battle is not to the strong alone, it is to the vigilant, the active, the brave."

More and more impassioned grew the dark eyes, the strong young voice, till, the immortal words ended, Matt stepped down with the air of a man who has thrown a weight off his shoulders. George and Lide fell upon him tumultuously.

"You're the b-best s-speaker I ever heard!" "Give us another!" "Don't you know some more?" chorused the girls. Rose drained the pitcher into his glass. "Here, drink this first!"

"Want to hear 'Sink or Swim, survive or perish?' I used to know a lot of Daniel Webster. My mother had her heart set on my being a lawyer." The glowing eyes sobered. "I learned them to please her. She was an angel of a woman. She died when I was fourteen."

"Oh! And did you give up being a law-

yer?" Annette asked, her gypsy face full of sympathy.

"Yes, it wasn't any use to think of it. My stepmother didn't give me any chance at school, and I made up my mind it was better to be a good mechanic than a poor lawyer," confessed the young carpenter as he sipped his lemonade. "It takes me back, though—these old speeches. I don't know when I've thought of them before."

Jumping to his feet he began the familiar defense of the Declaration. At the words, "We shall make this a glorious, an immortal day," Lide happened to look down the dusty road.

"There they come! Now we'll have our fireworks!" she cried, and made a dash for the gate. Matt laughed as he finished opportunely, "Our children will honor it. They will celebrate it with thanksgiving, with festivity, with bonfires and illuminations."

Hospitable Mrs. Deming did not heed the few words Di whispered in her ear to make her motherly face turn to the stranger with a smile of welcome, and as soon as the kind-eyed, grizzled farmer could free himself from his clamorous little daughters he drew the young man aside with a hearty clap on the shoulder. "You've done a good piece of work here. Some men never would 'a' taken time to plane those rough old boards. I'd like to help you find steady work, an' mebby I can. You better finish out the Fourth with us—there's a good bed in the back chamber—and to-morrow we'll look around."

The thin face changed again. "Thank you, sir. I ought to tell you first. I don't know as you'll want me under your roof when you know—I just came out of the reformatory there, yesterday."

George Deming gave a shrewd glance at the younger man. "Tell me about it," he said, briefly.

"It was assault. They made it intent to kill, but I never meant that. There was a girl—I hoped to marry—Oh, I've had my lesson! She wasn't worth it, but I don't want any worse hell than what she made me suffer! I'd have trusted her around the world, and when a dirty fellow at the shop made free with her name I couldn't help it, I pitched into him. I've an awful temper when it's going once. They thought first he was killed, but he got over it. I

had to stand my trial, and my stepmother, she always hated me, she told in court that I was a dangerous character." He laughed bitterly. "I've had reason enough to be angry with her, but I never yet laid hands on a woman. Well, one or two more fellows in the shop wanted to get me out before I let daylight in on some of their tricks, and they raked up everything they could. I pleaded not guilty, but by that time I'd found out about her. It was all true an' a lot more, and I didn't care much what became of me. I guess I looked like a pretty tough customer. Anyway, it was either the pen or the reformatory and the judge sent me down here because he was kind-hearted and seemed to want me to have the best chance I could."

George Deming was a good reader of human nature. His generous hand still lay on Matt Crandal's shoulder. "And you mean to make the most of your chance now you're your own man again?" he asked bluntly.

"Yes, sir, I do." There was an unmistakable note of determination in Matt's voice. "I didn't know which way to turn this morning—couldn't bear to go back to the old town, and didn't know how to make a beginning. Your girls there—well, I shan't forget what this day has been to me! I felt as though everybody'd be suspecting me now, and I'd most made up my mind to tramp it awhile if I didn't get an honest job about the next time I asked. I stopped at twenty places yesterday—sometimes they treated me decent and sometimes they didn't. One man looked me over and said he'd no use for anybody of my stripe. And then there was one old lady—I don't know when anything went against the grain like her taking me for a thief. She asked me in and gave me a glass of milk, kind as could be, but just as I got out of the gate she missed her gold-bowed glasses. I told her I never set eyes on them, but I could, see she didn't more than half believe me. Matt's face had hardened as he spoke.

"Le's see, now! White house, wa'n't it? Green blinds? A green house close by?" asked Farmer Deming with an odd chuckle.

"How on earth did you know?" Matt asked in turn.

"Well, you see, my sister, where ma and I've just been visiting, she's gettin' sort o' forgetful, an' she had the misfortune to lay her specs on the top shelf of the pantry, where she'd climbed up to get something, and didn't find 'em again till this morning. Then you just ought to heard her mourn over the innocent boy she'd mistrusted. Says she, 'He was a real honest, handy-looking young fellow, and I wish he'd come back and give me a chance to make up for being so quick to suspect him, when 'twas all my own fault,' she says. She's made up her mind they ought to have more help in the greenhouse, and says she, 'I'd like to try the boy if I had it to do over again! Think you'd like that?"

A great light shone in Matt's face. "It's what I loved most down there at Penfield! They let me work with the flowers some every day all the year, and it seemed as though they understood." His voice broke suddenly.

"Well, then, that's settled!" cried the farmer cheerily. "An' now you're free an' equal, so to speak, let's have the fireworks!"

❀ ❀

If we can not find God in house and mine, upon the roadside or the margin of the sea, in the bursting seed or opening flower, in the day duty and the night musing, I do not think we should discern him any more on the grass of Eden or beneath the moonlight of Gethsemane.—*James Martineau.*

July Wishes

These sultry days I wish I were
A water lily just astir
    Upon the ripples light that flow
    Along the quiet pool;
Or that I were a bird, to fly
Across the blue and breezy sky,
    Where merry winds forever blow
    So fresh and strong and cool.

And then, again, sometimes I wish
    I were a little silver fish
    At play among the corals tall,
    Down in the deep, cold sea.
But I am just a little lass
Curled up in grandpa's orchard grass;
And maybe that is, after all,
    The nicest place to be.
        —*Youth's Companion.*

❀ ❀

The Evolution of Independence Day.

BY JANE A. STEWART.

It is interesting to review the process of development which has marked our national celebration of Independence Day. When the nation's natal day was first observed, it was the spirit of independence which was recognized. The Independence Day of the revolutionary era was peculiarly and realistically patriotic. The celebration took on the nature of a serious and solemn ceremony, while it was pre-eminently a demonstration of rejoicing.

The first celebration of independence in the United States occurred just four days after the official adoption of the Declaration of Independence by the United States Congress in Philadelphia. It was in effect a welcome and jubilee, signalizing and endorsing the new era of liberty and self government for the burdened people of the American colonies. Rejoicing was its chief feature. The people gathered as on a holiday. All labor was suspended. The military and civil authorities were out in full force. The bells rang all day and almost all night, according to no less an authority than John Adams.

Col. John Nixon, of Westchester, Pa., an ardent patriot, who had served as head of a regiment at Long Island and at Valley Forge, a prominent banker, was appointed to read the Declaration of Independence on that historic occasion. He stood on a tall erection in Independence Square (the observatory which had been built by the American Philosophical Society for its famous study of the transit of Venus) as he read in a loud, clear voice the words of the most famous of state documents. The reading was followed by the shouts and cheers of the multitude, the roll of drums, and the roar of cannon.

A special committee of nine associators removed the King's arms from the state-house (now Independence Hall), conveying them to the top of a pile of casks erected upon the common (Independence Square) for the purpose of a bonfire. The scene around this great bonfire as the flames rose and consumed the hated emblem of kingly authority can readily be imagined. Patriotic feeling rose to a high pitch and was given vent in noisy demonstration by the less restrained part of the population.

Similar scenes, the records state, were enacted in New York and elsewhere throughout the country. And everywhere the Declaration of Independence was received with joyful acclamation and enthusiasm, as well as with the less demonstrative evidences of appreciation of its meaning and all that it involved.

This event (in which tradition tells us the Liberty Bell bore a conspicuous part) was preliminary to the permanent introduction of the Fourth of July holiday on our national calendar.

The first real anniversary of the Declaration of Independence was held on July 4, 1777. At that time the struggle for independence was well under way, and the battles of Brandywine and Germantown were imminent. Although the outlook was grave, courage and enthusiasm for the cause of independence ran high.

The first Fourth of July celebration had the background of a current revolution and was celebrated in the atmosphere of highest patriotic purpose. There were many of the more serious minded among the populace who, no doubt, took occasion to commemorate the anniversary as the day of deliverance, as did General Washington, to seek strength and protection by prayer and devotion in church and home.

Yet undoubtedly cheer and hope were imparted to all, also, by the public demonstrations. It is recorded that at Philadelphia the vessels in the harbor displayed all their bunting, manned their yards, formed in line of parade, and fired salutes. Congress adjourned and gave a dinner at the city tavern to civil and military authorities at which a band of Hessians captured by Washington at the battle of Trenton were the somewhat unwilling musicians.

After the banquet a military parade took place, whose chief companies were an artillery battalion, the Maryland light horse, and a North Carolina battalion. At night the bells were rung vociferously, houses were illuminated by candles set in the windows, and a display of fireworks was enjoyed. Lights, however, were ordered out at 11 o'clock, and extraordinary precautions were naturally taken to guard against fire and to prevent riots.

Ever since that initial celebration the holiday spirit has dominated Independence Day. In its evolution as a gala day it has been the occasion for the introduction of new and constantly changing recreation schemes, and unfortunately marked by abuses and excesses.

The bell ringing, the illuminations, the parade, and the fireworks still remain as perennial reminders of the early Independence Day; but other less felicitous features have been evolved.

Boat races, balloon ascensions, target shooting, the barbecue, baseball, and football are among the outdoor sports which have been received with most popular favor as features of a happy Fourth of July during succeeding years.

But noise, which was the natural concomitant of the Independence Day celebration at its very beginning, has unhappily shown no signs of remission. Instead of decreasing its volume has increased. And the rampant holiday spirit, not content with a single day of racket, has extended its ebullitions over a whole week.

As long ago as 1850, too, the problem of diminishing the danger from the increasing use of gunpowder and reducing the volume of racket and din was discussed by serious minded citizens.

As population has become more dense and cities have grown, the menace of gunpowder has been magnified. In a single recent year no less than 4,000 Independence Day injuries have been reported, about one-tenth of which caused death, in addition to several hundreds who sustained bodily mutilation by careless use of the dangerous devices introduced by inventive genius and enterprising dealers to swell the Fourth of July jollification.

This perversion of the real animus of a Fourth of July holiday is regarded as a serious indication that the people need to be reminded more strongly of the hardships and suffering that our noble and patriotic ancestors endured; and to realize more clearly the value of the inheritance that came to us from that band of sturdy statesmen who signed the Declaration of Independence and thus set an example of courage and character to the world for all ages.

This growing sentiment is having perennial manifestation in the many feasible as well as in impracticable and unpopular suggestions for "a saner Fourth of July." Chicago has set the pace for a more dignified and less dangerous observance. The funds raised it transpires were insufficient to carry out the plan, only $6,000 being subscribed when $50,000 was required. But the suggestion remains, and is open to application in modified form by local communities.

The plan, as outlined, included open celebrations in the parks, playgrounds, and vacant lots, with free selected fireworks for the children under the supervision of directors of the fetes with physicians and the fire department near at hand. A policeman, a fireman, a doctor, a teacher, and one member of the Illinois Naval Reserve in uniform (who would give the older children instruction in the use of firearms), made up the corps of attendants planned for each locality. The evening program listed a sham naval battle on Lake Michigan and a magnificent display of fireworks from several points in the city, so that as many as possible might be able to enjoy it.

A suggestion which has also won wide commendation is one which provides that in all communities (where the population is not so great as to make it impossible) all young men who have reached the age of 21 years during the year be invited to a great banquet, given seats of honor, and addressed by representative men upon the responsibilities which their coming of age imposes on them as citizens.

There is felicitous evidence that public sentiment is rising to a higher plane in its regard for the nation's natal day, in these valuable suggestions. The deadly toy pistol, the earsplitting cannon crackers, and dangerous cartridge cane have recently been legally tabooed in many enterprising communities. Other indications that a healthy reaction has set in against the incongruous features of the nineteenth century Fourth of July are happily not lacking. And in its natural evolution the celebration of Independence Day will take its appropriate place as an orderly and enthusiastic patriotic holiday.—*Epworth Herald.*

How to Break a Habit.

A minister offered a prize to the boy who would write the best composition in five minutes on, "How to overcome a habit." The prize went to a lad of nine years. The following is his essay:

"Well, sir, habit is hard to overcome. If you take off the first letter, it does not change 'a bit.' If you take off another, you still have a 'bit' left. If you take off still another, the whole of 'it' remains. If you take off another, it is wholly used up; all of which goes to show that if you want to get rid of habit you must throw it off altogether."

Not Up-to-Date.

Thomas Edison, Jr., is very fond of children. While on a visit to New York recently he was endeavoring to amuse the 6-year-old son of the host, when the youngster asked him to draw an engine for him.

Mr. Edison promptly set to work, and, thinking it would please the child to have an elaborate design, he added a couple of smokestacks and several imaginary parts.

When the plan was completed the boy took it and eyed it critically; then he turned to the inventor with disapproval in every feature.

"You don't know much about engines, do you?" he said with infantile frankness. "Engines may have been that way in your time, but they've changed a whole lot since then."

Picture of War Engine "General."

A beautiful colored picture, 18x25 inches, of the historic old engine "General" which was stolen at Big Shanty, Ga., by the Andrew's Raiders during the Civil War, and which is now on exhibition in the Union Depot, Chattanooga, Tenn., has been gotten out by the NASHVILLE, CHATTANOOGA & ST. LOUIS RY.— The "Battlefields Route" to the South. The picture is ready for framing and will be mailed for 25c. The "Story of the General" sent free. W. L. Danley, Gen'l Pass. Agent, Nashville, Tenn.

Jes' Plain Torpedoes.

The good old Fourth's a-comin'—the best day in
   the year,
And little chaps get anxious-like, when once it's
   drawin' near;
They talk of firecrackers and they dream about
   the noise,
The dear old Fourth was certainly jes' made fer
   little boys.
Bill's got a great big cannon, with fuse you have
   to light,
And lots of great big crackers that's filled with
   dynamite;
But I'm a little feller—ain't half as old as be,
And I guess that plain torpedoes will have to do
   fer me!

Pa says that giant crackers ain't fit fer little chaps,
He's sore on all toy pistols and hates these paper
   caps.
He don't intend his children shall ever celebrate
By blowin' off their fingers—he says they'll have
   to wait.
"You're nothin' but a baby," my father says,
   "as yet,
And your dady can't quite spare you; he needs
   you bad, you bet.
Bill's got some giant crackers? Well, that I know
   is true,
But I guess that plain torpedoes will have to do
   fer you."

It's hard to have big brothers and watch them at
   their play,
And jes' to be a little chap and sort o' in the way;
To have folks always tell you, you can't do thus
   and so.
Because you're·jes' a little chap—not old enough,
   you know.
But ma, she· sees I'm tearful, so she takes me in
   her lap
And says, "Why, what's the matter, you're cryin',
   little chap."
Then, as she bends to kiss me, I'm brave as I
   can be,
I·guess that plain torpedoes are good enough for
   me!
—*Louis E. Thayer in the Woman's Home Companion for July.*

* *

The Bronze Vase.

BY J. BRECKENRIDGE ELLIS.

PART III.

CHAPTER I.

Raymund Revore thrust his sister's letter
into his pocket and started toward the
Omer mansion with an agitated step. He
met the farmhand, Tom, coming from the
massive brick residence. Tom, catching
sight of the youth's face, exclaimed, "Don't
you worry about having to leave this farm,
Raymund. You won't have any trouble
finding a job, and you'll get more than Mr.
Omer ever gave you, too!"

"It isn't that," said Raymund, speaking
rapidly. "A letter has just come from
Rhoda. She has gone to work for a lady
in Kansas City, and she is in trouble,
somehow. She wants me to come to her
at once. I'm going on the first train."

"We'll walk to Crawley together," said
Fred, coming up. "I'm leaving for town."
Raymund hurriedly gathered together his
few possessions, and made them into a
bundle. He left the bundle in Tom's care
to be taken to Brother Bellfield's. Tom
and Baby would be driven to Crawley the
next day.

"I guess it's goodby," said Tom, as Raymund and Fred hesitated in the doorway.
Raymund carried the green umbrella under one arm, and a little package of what
he deemed necessities, swung from his
hand.

"I guess it is," said Fred in his high
key. "It's the lonesomest word in the language, I reckon." He stroked his whiskers
to conceal his emotion. "Tom, you and me
has lived and worked together four year,
ain't we?"

"Yep," said Tom, nervously scraping the
ground with one of his huge boots, and
stooping to look at the mark he had made.
"Well," said Fred, "be good to yourself,
Tom."

Just then Baby, now a boy of six·in his
first trousers, came from around the house.
"Come here, kid, and tell me goodby!"
cried Fred, setting his weather-beaten valise
in the path.

"Goodby," said ·Baby; "b'ing me something dood!"

"Was they ever such a kid!" cried Fred,
grinning. He bent his knees slightly outward, slowly lit his pipe and stared at the
child in speechless admiration. Baby finding himself the center of observation gave
a shout and turned a summersault.

"Well," said Tom, presently, "if Raymund
wants to ketch that there train, we'd better shake hands and part." Then they
shook hands all around, very mournfully
and Tom said to Raymund with deep feeling, "Be good to yourself!"

"Thank you," said Raymund, stooping to
give Baby a final hug. Then he and Fred
set forth upon their tramp to town. When
the high road was gained they looked back.
The sun was shining upon the mansion
where Raymund had gone day after day to
learn Latin and French. It was June and
the roses bloomed near the spot where he
and Jack Bellfield had parted from Nelsie
Loraine, the night of his thirteenth birthday. The Hands' House was in sight and,
in the doorway stood Tom waving his red
bandana, while Baby, with no troubles of
his own, and callous to the troubles of others, was strutting in his new trousers.

"Was they ever such a kid!" exclaimed Fred
with a sigh. It was a silent walk to Crawley. There was no time to lose and Raymund intrusted Fred with messages to be
delivered to the Bellfields. "I may bring
Rhoda back home to-morrow," he said;
"tell Brother Bellfield I may have to ask
him to take her in for a little while, until I
can find something to do. I know he will
be willing."

As they neared Crawley they heard the
whistle of an engine. "Train's comin,"
cried Fred· shrilly. They began to run.
Fortunately their road approached Crawley
from the side where the station stood. As
they panted up to the side platform the
engine bell was ringing. There· was no
time to buy a ticket. Raymund wrung
Fred's hand and jumped aboard. As he
found his seat the train started. Raymund
looked out and Fred shouted from the
platform, "Be good to yourself!" Then the
outskirts of Crawley whisked out of sight.

Raymund wished he had known of this
departure only the day before, when he had
been in Crawley. Then he could have told
all his friends goodby. But he had been in
such a hurry on that day he had only taken
time to draw the money on Mr. Omer's
hundred-dollar check. He had taken most
of. it in bank notes, and with one of his
five-dollar bills he paid his way to Kansas
City, receiving in change a little over two
dollars. With the caution of one unused
to the city, he had disposed of his money
in various parts of· his garments. There
was a ten-dollar bill in the bottom of each
of his shoes. Seventy dollars were sewed
in a little pocket of his undershirt. In·spite
of this caution he was on the lookout for
thieves and confidence ·men. He and
Rhoda were but six years old when their
widowed mother brought them from St.
Louis to Crawley. Since then Raymund
had never ridden on a train, and, of course;
had never been in a city. The ride through
strange fields, over high trestle work and
across the wide Missouri river, made his
brain hum with strange sensations. When
they rolled into Kansas City, the bewildering sights and clanging sounds dazed him.
He thought he must leave the car when
they drew among the many-storied buildings, but the train went on and on till it
seemed they would never ·stop in Kansas
City, but would go on to another place.
Even when a man came on board and requested, or rather demanded, to check their
baggage, it was no use for Raymund to
get up and start ·down the aisle, for the
train kept right on.

"Baggage? Baggage?" said the man, rattling his brass checks and hovering over
Raymund as if with half a mind to check
him.

"No," Raymund apologized, "I have no
baggage but this little ·bundle,"
"I'll check the little bundle," said the
man, drawing forward his cap to have a
better look at the boy.
"I don't think it is worth while," .said
Raymund.
"Not worth while? Of course it is worth
while! Now, where do you want to go?
Do you want a carriage?"
"I don't want anything ·checked," ·said
Raymund in a determined voice.
"Then why didn't you say so at first?"
scowled the man. "Let me by, will you?"
Raymund was not at all in the way, but he
made no·reply. ·At last the train *did* stop,
and the people began to pour out as ·if
they fancied there would be an attempt ·on
the part of the train crew to hold them as
prisoners. · Raymund did not like to
squeeze himself into the throng for fear of
being crowded upon some lady or child.
But after he had waited a good while and
everybody else was pushing himself or herself forward with no regard for those who·
might be inconvenienced by their frenzied
eagerness, Raymund left his seat and allowed himself to be borne along with the
rest. There was so much noise from the
outside, such deafening hiss of escaping
steam, and rush·of truck wheels and clash
of high voices that Raymund could hear
nothing distinctly. In front of him was a
very fat man who perspired freely and who
turned his bald head occasionally in his direction. Finally Raymund reached the
wooden flooring· that extended under the
great shed, and as he did·so the fat man
seized him·by the elbow and shouted in his
ear, "Come give me just one more jab with
that miserable umbrella of yours, sir, and
I'll break·it over your head!" Then Raymund realized that when the fat man's lips
had been moving it was not merely to gasp
for air but to remonstrate against the in-
fliction of physical injuries.

"I beg your pardon," said ·Raymund, re-
versing the umbrella.

"And it does no good when you·do," said·
the ·fat man, mopping his brow and still
glaring. "You have made my· leg·"black·
and blue, sir!"

Raymund crimsoned with shame and
hastened·away. He did ·not know which
way to go, but·it was his intention to escape the fat man. He followed the crowd

REGIMENTAL REUNIONS AND FORTY-
THIRD ANNIVERSARY BATTLE
CHICKAMAUGA,

CHATTANOOGA, SEPTEMBER 18-20, 1906.

On September 18, 1906, will occur the forty-
third anniversary of the Battle of Chickamauga.
It is proposed ·to celebrate this memorable event
with a reunion of the various regiments that participated in this memorable battle and the various
battles fought around Chattanooga. This reunion
will be held at Chickamauga National Park, September 18, 19 and 20, and the present indications
are that it will be the largest and most notable
gathering ever held in the South. On the above
dates, the remnants from the armies of twelve
states, comprising the following: Pennsylvania,
Ohio, Michigan, Indiana, Illinois, Wisconsin, Minnesota, Iowa, Nebraska, Missouri, Kansas and Kentucky, will assemble, many for the first and last
time since they marched from its blood-stained
fields, forty-three years ago.

Here is one of the great opportunities for the
education of the youth. Don't fail to take your
children and show them historic Chattanooga, with
all its historical connections. It is the opportunity of a lifetime. Go and see the old war generals
and other officers point out the places of interest
on the battlefield; let them show you and explain,
in person, the markers erected on the battlefield
showing the positions of the opposing armies at
the time of battle. It will not be long until none
will be left to do this noble work.

It will be many years, if ever again, that such
an opportunity will present itself. See that your
tickets read via the Louisville & Nashville R. R.,
the Battlefield Route. Call on your nearest railroad agent for rates and advertising matter pertaining to the reunion, or write nearest representative of the Louisville & Nashville R. R. ·
F. H. MILLIKEN, D. P. A., Louisville, Ky.
F. D. BUSH, D. P. A., Cincinnati, Ohio.
J. E. DAVENPORT, D. P. A., St. Louis, Mo.
H. C. BAILEY, N. W. P. A., Chicago, Ill. ·

which swept toward the iron gates. Presently he was walking along the flooring outside the Union Station, uncertain which of its many doors to enter. He presently tried one and found himself in a vast chamber which was thronged with people. Around the ticket windows was a solid mass, and at one side was another packed crowd, above the heads of which an official was shouting names. Whenever he called a name somebody in the crowd would respond. Raymund approached a man in uniform and asked how he could find the street. The officer stared at him crossly and said he didn't know, and walked away. It was nearing twilight and Raymund was uneasy lest he should fail to reach the house where Rhoda was staying, before dark. He was in a hurry to go out into the city, but the crowd prevented him from seeing that just across the room the door opened upon the street. He accosted another official with his inquiry and was again told, "I don't know." Just then the mass of excited travelers parted a little and he looked through a glass door and saw what he had been asking about.

On the street he inquired of a policeman the way to the house where Rhoda was working. The direction staggered him. He was told to go to a certain street, take a street car and be sure to get a transfer ticket to another car, and from it get a transfer ticket to another car, and so on till he came to Pennsylvania avenue, where he was to walk until he reached the house in question. If there was no misadventure he ought to reach his destination in an hour. Raymund had heard a vague mention of transfer tickets, but he did not know how or where to procure one. He believed from the tone of Rhoda's letter that no time was to be lost in reaching her, and he started upon his perplexing journey with dauntless resolution. He was so evidently from the country that those near him on the various street cars seemed, as they looked at him, to smell newmown hay, and hear the cows coming home to be milked. It was at least two hours before he stood in front of a respectable looking three-story brick, waiting for his ring to be answered. Already the street lights were lit, and the gathering darkness filled Raymund with uneasy foreboding. He heard some one raise a window above his head. He looked up and there was Rhoda! He had not seen her for three years. The tears came to his eyes. Her head disappeared like a flash. Almost immediately it seemed to him the door was flung open and Rhoda's arms went about his neck, and she was sobbing convulsively. "Oh, Raymund! Raymund!" she gasped. "Oh, Raymund! It is you! I knew you would come, I knew it! Come, quick!"

She shut the door behind her and they stood on the steps. She was barefooted. Her dress was in rags. Her head was uncovered. The miserable skirt came only a little way below her knees. Her face and hands and bare arms, as well as her feet, were soiled with streaks of soot. The light hair, once his mother's pride, was tangled and dingy. His heart stood still.

"Why, Rhoda!" he exclaimed. "What is the matter?"

"Quick! Quick!" panted Rhoda, dragging him away. "Let us get from this place as soon as possible. I will tell you all about it when we are safe."

She had grown up into a tall, slim girl of fifteen, but Raymund feared she had lost all her beauty. He could not be sure because she was so wretched of attire, so careless of her person and the street was so dark.

"Where will we go?" he asked in perplexity.

"I don't know," said Rhoda, still struggling to suppress her sobs.

(TO BE CONTINUED.)

Christian Publishing Company
2712 Pine St., St. Louis, Mo.

J. H. GARRISON, - - - - President
W. W. DOWLING, - - - Vice-President
GEO. L. SNIVELY, - - Sec. and Gen. Supt
R. P. CROW, - - - Treas. and Bus. Manager

Hundreds can find pleasant, useful and profitable employment through the summer representing the general interests of this company. Write us at once for particulars, mentioning this notice.

✦

Some of our W. W. Dowling series of Bible school papers and lesson helps show an increase in sales of thousands over those of the corresponding period last year. Samples sent on application. The price will be found as low as asked for greatly inferior kinds.

✦

Our own books are invaluable to all who would be schooled in the history and genius of this Restoration and should justly constitute the major part of a Disciple's library. We handle many attractive lines from other publishers, also. Catalogues sent on application. We aspire to be your bookseller and will grant our patrons favors that few houses can.

✦

Seven orders for the enlarged picture of Brother Garrison were filled Tuesday afternoon. One new subscription and a renewal accompanied by the $3.00 secures it. Though voiceless, this picture hung in study, library, church parlor or family living room will speak eloquently for gentleness and peace, for Bible study and loyalty, zeal for righteousness and all other of the virtues inculcated by primitive Christianity. Secure it while the present excellent edition lasts.

✦

The reduced price of Alexander Campbell's Debate with Purcell, Evidences of Christianity, Lectures on the Pentateuch, The Christian System and Christian Baptism is $1.00. During the summer we will sell either book and THE CHRISTIAN-EVANGELIST for $2. THE CHRISTIAN-EVANGELIST together with Campbell's Popular Lectures and Addresses, $3. Former price of book was $5. This great offer holds good through July and August. It is a fine edition of these great works.

✦

July weather has not wilted the flourishing growth of our subscription list. Though the great majority of our new subscribers are coming singly and in pairs, yet we are pleased to receive the following lists: Normal, Ill., 40 (R. H. Newton, minister); Moline, Kan., 5 (C. A. Beurgan, pastor); Danbury, Conn., 11 (E. J. Teagarden, minister); Camp Point, Ill., 23 (H. J. Reynolds, minister); Mt. Sterling, Ill., 14; Pittsfield, Ill., 30 (W. E. Spicer, pastor); Winchester, Ill., 27 (E.

O. Sharpe, minister); St. Thomas, Ontario, 3 (Colin Sinclair, minister); Mena, Ark., 6 (W. H. Williams, pastor).

✦

Our national conventions hold this year's sessions in Buffalo, from October 12th to 19th. THE CHRISTIAN-EVANGELIST Special goes over the Wabash. Our clients have choice of going from Detroit through Canada by rail, or across Lake Erie by ship. We naturally suppose most will take the water route. The rate will be one fare plus $1.00 for round trip east of the Mississippi and plus $2.00 west of the river. We have arranged for a fine equipment of new reclining chair cars and tourist sleepers. There will be a delightful company. You would better go over the Wabash. Write us when your mind is fully made up to join us.

THE
CHRISTIAN-
EVANGELIST

A WEEKLY RELIGIOUS NEWSPAPER.

Volume XLIII.   No. 28.

ST. LOUIS, JULY 12, 1906.

A Norwegian Church in the Old World.

The Christian-Evangelist.

J. H. GARRISON, Editor

PAUL MOORE, Assistant Editor

F. D. POWER,
B. B. TYLER, } Staff Correspondents.
W. DURBAN, }

Subscription Price, $1.50 a Year.

For foreign countries add $1.04 for postage.

Remittances should be made by money order, draft, or registered letter; not by local cheque, unless 10 cents is added to cover cost of collection

In Ordering Change of Post Office give both old and new address.

Matter for Publication should be addressed to THE CHRISTIAN-EVANGELIST. Subscriptions and remittances should be addressed to the Christian Publishing Company, 2712 Pine Street, St. Louis, Mo. Unused Manuscripts will be returned only if accompanied by stamps.

News Items, evangelistic and other rise, are solicited, and should be sent on a postal card, if possible.

Published by the Christian Publishing Company, 2712 Pine Street, St. Louis, Mo.

Entered at St. Louis P. O. as Second Class Matter

WHAT WE STAND FOR.

For the Christ of Galilee,
For the truth which makes men free,
For the bond of unity
Which makes God's children one.

For the love which shines in deeds,
For the life which this world needs,
For the church whose triumph speeds
The prayer: "Thy will be done."

For the right against the wrong,
For the weak against the strong,
For the poor who've waited long
For the brighter age to be.

For the faith against tradition,
For the truth 'gainst superstition,
For the hope whose glad fruition
Our waiting eyes shall see.

For the city God is rearing,
For the New Earth now appearing,
For the heaven above us clearing,
And the song of victory.

J. H. Garrison.

CONTENTS.

Centennial Propaganda 871
Current Events 872
Editorial—
Christian Union; A Historical Study.873
"One Baptism;" What is It?.....,...873
Current Religious Thought.........874
Notes and Comments...............874
Editor's Easy Chair 875
Original Contributions—
Our Plea Among Scandinavians; C. S.
Osterhus 876
Modern Religious Persecution. B. L.
Chase 879
Some of My Likings. William Durban 880
As Seen from the Dome. F. D. Power.881
What the Brethren are Saying and
Doing. B. B. Tyler...............882
Our Budget 883
Conventions 887
News from Many Fields.............889
Evangelistic 891
Sunday-school 892
Christian Endeavor 892
Midweek Prayer-meeting 893
Books by Disciples of Christ........894
People's Forum 896
Obituaries ,........................896
The Home Department 897

ON AND METHODS, LIBERTY, IN ALL THINGS, CHARITY."

July 12, 1906   No. 28

INIAL PROPAGANDA
HES OF CHRIST   1909

: : : GEO. L. SNIVELY : : :

1 in this country are many thousands
ering for those truths unmixed with
of which the Churches of Christ are
repositories in trust. Loyalty to this
involves our fellowship with Brothers
rhus, Stone and other great-hearts in
ng the souls of these Norsemen-Amer-
1 with the bread of life. It is true a
itude of calls come to us for help every
:, but many busy themselves more in
ing all these calls than in helping an-
any one of them. Will not some of
readers make actual personal sacrifices
·der to give our heroic brother the ad-
ages of a printing press in disseminat-
the Gospel among his countrymen?.
hope many will pray and earnestly
to the end that these people may
ne possessed of a religion that will
ort and satisfy their souls and make
great and holy in the Lord.
it not fitting, too, we should take some
for the redemption of the thousands
reeks who are crowding to our shores
iese latter years? Their fathers gave
ie plastic language in which will for-
be enshrined the Master's words of life.
have done nothing as yet to discharge
obligations to that virile race. Let us
pret to them meanings locked in their
vernacular that will prove their re-
ition from vice and coronation at the
hand of One infinitely greater than the
of their marvelous ancestors.
ly, also, rallied to the defense of
itianity at a time when to all human
irances it would otherwise have been
minated. From her shores are an-
y coming hordes who so need God and
ighteousness and the help we can best
nister to free them from superstition
vice. China, Japan, Africa and Lo,
oor red man from our own western
s, appeal to us through their actual
1 if they confess it not with the lips

confess the Son of God; increase in missionary offerings, that the church may be
built up in the dear homeland and the Gospel be spread in far-away regions by ancient rivers and over palmy plains; the
raising of church debts, lifting the burden
that is crushing many a congregation; the
endowment of colleges, that the young men
of the future may be more completely
equipped than were the best of their predecessors: O, what great things are on the
program of our brotherhood! Highly favored are we who live in these magnificent
times. Not divided by debateable questions, but knit together more firmly as we
realize with grateful pride how wide our
liberty is to differ, yet ever at one in loyalty
to the Son of God, as we bend the knee
and doff the helm to our Glorious Commander, while down all our long and eager
line there swells the acclaim, "Crown Him
Lord of All!"

Added to these and other achievements
that lie just before us, is not this a most
appropriate time for the building of mem-
oral churches? With the waning of 1909,
and when the great Pittsburg convention
shall pass away in echoes, why should not
memorial buildings thickly stud the land?
I am encouraged in my own work by the
prospect of a Centennial building for this
southern part of St. Louis. This field is
exceedingly difficult, more so than any I
have known elsewhere, all its conditions
make it so. Often have we felt that we
must surely let go our hold upon it, but
always has the vision of a strong, great
future for this congregation held us fast.
A church in the years that are coming
which shall be a trysting place for a host
of believers; a center of holy influence for
young and old; a church where "the people" shall find light and rest and strength.
This has been the vision, night and day.
And now this hope is almost changed into
sight. The city mission board has resolved

Current Events

The first session of the Fifty-ninth Congress closed Saturday night, June 30. It was

The Close of Congress. a record-breaking session for the amount of its appropriations, which were approximately $875,000,000, the number of bills introduced, which amounted to 27,600, and the volume of talk, which was no less than 40,000,000 words as recorded in the Congressional Record. The most important bills of the session, some of which had been before congress for the entire seven months of its duration, were passed at the last moment. The bill empowering the interstate commerce commission to review the rates of railroads and other common carriers, the pure food bill, the meat inspection bill, and the federal naturalization bill were all enacted into laws. The difference between the Senate and the House on the meat bill was removed by the former's accepting the provision that the government should bear the expense of the inspection and abandoning the demand for dated labels on canned products. The appropriation for carrying on the work on the Panama Canal carried with it the determination that the canal shall be of the lock type with an 80-foot level. The new state of Oklahoma was created and provision made for joint statehood for Arizona and New Mexico if both territories accept the offer. This will dispose of the last of the territories, except those which may be organized in our non-contiguous possessions. The consular service was re-organized; Niagara Falls were protected by limiting the amount of water which may be diverted for power; and an employer's liability law was enacted. After all that one feels compelled to say during the session about the dilatory tactics of congress, it must be admitted that this is a considerable body of important legislation. Most of it is in the direction of abolishing special privileges and compelling avaricious dividend.seekers to observe a decent regard for the rights of the public. Besides these acts that have been enumerated, congress passed about 300 others of a general or public nature, and nearly 4,000 private bills, mostly pension grants. The most important bills that failed to pass both houses were the Philippine tariff bill, the ship subsidy bill and the bills prohibiting compaign contributions by corporations and requiring publicity in campaign receipts and expenditures.

❦

The President will go to Panama for a three weeks' trip next October. This will be about as near as any President ever came to passing outside of the boundaries of the United States. It will be a great wonder if Mr. Roosevelt does not shatter that tradition before his term of office expires. With his new appropriation of $25,-000 for traveling expenses he could afford to take a summer trip to Europe.

The Topeka Public Library, according to newspaper reports, has barred out Upton Sinclair's "The Jun-

Pleasant Reading. gle" on the ground that it is a very unpleasant book. As newspaper dispatches about this sort of thing are not always either complete or accurate, we do not care to make special application of these remarks to the Topeka library board, but the incident serves as occasion for saying a thing that needs to be said often to the American reader. Pleasantness is not the criterion of excellence in literature. The contrary belief is doing more than anything else to degrade current literature and especially current fiction. A humorous book, which gladdens the heart, unburdens the mind and agitates the diaphragm to wholesome laughter, is always justifiable. But a merely pleasant book, which flows along from one triviality to another, neither offending the taste nor stimulating the mind, a bas with such. Literature must be a transcript of life—a very hackneyed statement, but still true. It must also be a transcript of life that is worth transcribing. That includes good life, bad life, high life, low life, but not the life which has nothing to recommend it except the fact that it is pleasant. If literature can be pleasant while it is also vital, so much the better. But as mere pleasantness can not make, so unpleasantness can not mar a book. "The Jungle" is not great literature, but it is alive. It touches things as they are and is quickened by the author's vision (right or wrong) of things as they should be. To ask, as a question of first importance, whether it is pleasant, is a sheer impertinence.

❦

A beer advertisement that is appearing in current papers quotes a certain Rev. Alexis W. Stein, an Episcopal rector, as saying that he is in favor of the use of beer. Perhaps the Rev. Mr. Stein is a belated convert to Bishop Potter's subway tavern scheme. Or again, perhaps he is only following the evil leadings of his own name.

❦

Some days before the Fourth it was estimated that not less than twelve million

Fireworks. dollars would be burned up in fireworks in celebrating our independence. And this did not include the inevitable losses from accidental fires which add to the glare of the Glorious Fourth, but are not exactly freewill offerings on the altar of Liberty. Twelve millions for fireworks! Enough to build and endow a first-rate university or a dozen good colleges. Enough to establish a number of free hospitals and dispensaries, or build a thousand moderate-priced churches, or support several "national theaters," which some people are so much interested in, or support all the foreign missionaries sent out from this Christian country, or do a great many other things. Is it a wise expenditure? Probably not. But certainly it is no more foolish than any sermon against it would be. If the buyers of fireworks were moved solely by patriotic motives, perhaps they would all put their money into one big fund and appoint com-

Christian Union: A Historical Study.

IV. THE PROTESTANT ERA; THE PERIOD OF REUNION.

14. How Shall the Union of Christians Come About?

If our premises have been true in the preceding articles, and the unity of Christians is rendered certain by the operation of the law of life within the Church, and by the mighty motives from without which appeal to the inner law of life, the question still obtrudes itself, how is it to come about? Indeed, there are those who lay so much stress upon the how of Christian union that they become skeptical about the *fact*, because they do not understand all the process. When certain Christians of Paul's day asked, "How are the dead raised and with what manner of body do they come?" the apostle replied, with a little sharpness, "Thou foolish one, that which thou thyself sowest is not quickened except it die: and that which thou sowest, thou sowest not the body that shall be, but the bare grain, it may chance of wheat, or of some other kind; but God giveth it a body even as it pleased him, and to each seed a body of its own."

There is an implication in this reply of the apostles that it is a very foolish thing for a Christian to doubt the possibility of God's carrying out his promises to us, because we can not see just how he will do it. or just what we shall be when he has done it. Would not the same great Christian philosopher, if he were on earth to-day, reply to the question which is so. often raised, "How will Christian union come about; and what will the united Church be like?" in very much the same way? We, of course, know more about the process of Christian union than that of the resurrection, because the latter is wholly God's work, while in the matter of Christian union we are to co-operate with God. The things revealed to us, however, relate to what manner of Christians we are to be, how we may cultivate the spirit of unity, and in what essential elements Christian unity consists. There remains much left for faith, as to what changes God is to lead his people through in order to their unification, and the exact nature of the form which that union shall take. If, however, there be the unity of the Spirit, God will give it a body as it pleaseth him.

There are some things, however, that are reasonably sure concerning the nature of that union that shall be. We call attention to a few of these characteristics.

1. The union must be vital, not mechanical. It must grow; it can not be manufactured. There can be no union among Christ's followers except as they are united with him and share in his life and enter into fellowship with his plans and purposes. We may promote its growth by deepening the spiritual life and by removing obstacles out of the way; but we may not force it, or seek to hasten it beyond the law of spiritual development.

2. It must be *Christian* union. That is to say, Christ must be the center of it and the circumference of it. He must be supreme, and no man must divide authority with him. A division in authority is certain to perpetuate existing divisions and may result in new ones. It is only by following a common master that we can have unity; and it is only by following Christ as that Master that we can have Christian unity. "Other foundation can no man lay than that is laid which is Jesus Christ."

3. The union which Christ prayed for and which is essential to the world's conversion, is not the union of denominations, having differing creeds, tests of fellowship, party names and party ambitions. Federation is not Christian union, though we believe it is an important step in that direction. We owe it to the Christ who prayed for the unity of his followers, that in so far as we have attained to unity in faith and purpose and doctrine, we seek to manifest it to the world in such co-operation as that unity makes possible; but we must not mistake the co-operation of distinct denominational bodies for Christian union, as Jesus prayed for it.

4. It is safe to say that Christian union is not to come about by any one religious body absorbing all other religious bodies. No doubt that hope is cherished by many in almost all the religious bodies of Christendom, but it is a hope destined never to be realized. Such a union would be both impracticable and undesirable. No religious body in Christendom is organized on a basis to adequately utilize and direct the religious forces of Christendom and administer wisely its vast interests. If history teaches anything, it teaches that this is not God's method of bringing about Christian union. No doubt he has a more excellent way which in time will commend itself to the approval of all his real followers. If we may judge from the history of the past what the divine plan of bringing about that unity of Christians is to be, it is their gradual approximation to a common divine standard, in which, as they come nearer to that standard, they necessarily come nearer to each other. That is the process which we see going on before our eyes and we have no right to suppose that any different plan is to be adopted. There will be a growing consciousness of the evils of division, which is only partially realized as yet; a growing sense of the need of unity, together with a clearer recognition among various religious bodies of the truths they already hold in common. With the growth in Christian knowledge and in spiritual discernment there will come new estimates of spiritual values, and a readjustment of doctrinal conceptions more in harmony with the mind of Christ, which will open the way for continuous progress toward unity. Denominational peculiarities will shrink to their proper dimensions, while the great fundamentals of Christian faith and character will rise to their true places, and this will bring the whole body of believers into closer fellowship and co-operation. This process is to be mightily stimulated by the free intermingling of Christians and their working together for common ends.

5. Christian union, when it comes, will not be *uniformity*. There will be room in it for differences of opinion, different methods of work and worship, different forms of organization and different degrees of emphasis. No other sort of union is possible among a free people, nor would it be desirable. Life everywhere takes on a variety of forms, and it must be so in the kingdom of God. Nature furnishes us infinite variety, and yet underlying it all is a wonderful unity. But we must get rid of the notion that this variety of opinions and freedom of action within the limitations of the spirit and teaching of Christ involves separate and distinct religious denominations. That idea belongs to the childhood period of the church. We are coming more and more to understand that if we have the common faith that unites us to Christ, that makes us obedient to him, we may hold differences of opinion, and work and worship in different ways, without interfering with our oneness in Christ or our fellowship with each other. How far denominational lines will be obliterated, and present forms of organization modified, in order to the realization of New Testament unity, is a question which would be answered differently by persons occupying different points of view; but one thing, we think, may be said with assurance, and that is that in so far as our existing denominationalism interferes with the freest and fullest fellowship between Christians, and with their hearty co-operation in advancing the kingdom of God by the diversion of resources or purely sectarian purposes, or by confusing the minds of those without by our differing names and creeds, it must give way to that unity of faith and purpose, of spirit and life, that subordinates everything else to the triumph of the kingdom of God on earth.

"One Baptism:" What Is It?

The Apostle Paul tells us in his list of unities in the Ephesian letter that there is "one baptism." What is it? One class of writers tells us it is Spirit baptism, and hence baptism in water is out of date. Another class tells us it is water baptism and, therefore, Spirit baptism is out of date. Both of them, in our judgment, are wrong. It is *Christian* baptism that is meant, and Christian baptism is neither Spirit-alone baptism, nor water-alone baptism, but a baptism in which both the water and the Spirit are united.

This agrees with the statement of Jesus in his famous conversation with Nicodemus: "Except one be born of water and the Spirit he can not enter into the kingdom of God." The baptism that admits into the kingdom of God is a birth in which, in its proper scriptural form, the body is buried in water and the Spirit comes into union with and under the control of the Holy Spirit. Nicodemus had probably heard of the baptism of John, and was willing to accept it if that would suffice to bring him into harmony with this new

Teacher, whom he recognized as one sent from God. Jesus tells him plainly that baptism in water does not suffice, but that the Holy Spirit has a necessary part in the important change, and that there must be a birth, both of the water and of the Spirit. This explains, too, why water is mentioned first in the passage. Jesus is following the historical order. John's baptism came first, and after that, as John prophesied, Jesus came with another baptism which John could not administer. Even the least of those who were subjects of Christ's baptism was greater than John the Baptist.

With this also agrees the statement of Paul in another place: "For in one Spirit were we all baptized into one body, whether Jews or Greeks, whether bond or free, and were all made to drink of one Spirit." (1. Cor. xii. 13). This was Paul's explanation of the unity of the "one body," namely: that all had been baptized with one Spirit, whether Jews or Greeks, bond or free, and were all made to drink of this one Spirit. It is self-evident that no mere baptism in water, without the corresponding action of the Spirit, would have accomplished the unification of these diverse elements that entered into the early church. In perfect harmony with this is Paul's reference to Christian baptism in his celebrated passage in the sixth of Romans, in which he argues that those who have been "buried with Christ in baptism" in the "likeness of his death" can not continue their old life of sin in order that grace may abound. It was the death to sin, accomplished through the action of the Spirit, that makes continuance in a life of sin impossible. The form of baptism is only incidental in this passage; the main point in its spiritual significance.

It is a great pity that the church in its controversy over the form of baptism has well nigh lost its deeper spiritual meaning, until one scarcely associates with it its real spiritual meaning—a deeper and truer consecration to God. The burial of the body in water means the submergence of the human spirit in the divine Spirit. It is time for us all to put away the controversial spirit in dealing with this vital subject and come to it on our knees, for a fresh study of it, that we may learn anew what the Apostle Paul taught the Romans, Corinthians and Ephesians, long ago, that our baptism commits us to a life of thorough consecration to God, of death to sin, and of union with Christ and with each other. This is the true relation of baptism to the union problem.

❦ ❦

ADMIRERS of Mark Twain believe he has never written anything more effective than the little verse he had cut in the modest block of marble which marks the resting-place of his wife in Woodlawn Cemetery, Elmira, N. Y.:

Warm summer sun,
Shine kindly here;
Warm southern wind,
Blow softly here.
Green sod above,
Lie light, lie light.
Good-night, dear heart,
Good-night, good-night.

Current Religious Thought.

At the request of many readers we re-open this department. Perhaps nothing else we could cull would inform us of a more practical, helpful idea being cherished by our religious contemporaries than the following from the "Chicago Record-Herald:"

A movement is on foot in New York City to secure a rule by the board of education providing for nonsectarian religious instruction in the public schools. An organization has been formed for the purpose of promoting a movement against what are called "Godless public schools." Prominent among the leaders are several Jewish rabbis, several Catholic priests and representatives of the Episcopalian, Presbyterian, Methodist and Congregational churches. It is proposed that the curriculum of the public schools be arranged so as to include at least one lesson a week on the great truths that are accepted by all denominations, and that a lesson in moral philosophy be given twice a week.

Bishop Greer, who is quite active in the movement, says: "There must be moral and religious training among the children of our public schools if we expect to continue to be a righteous nation. I am a strong believer in the public schools. I approve them as they are, and for what they stand for. They serve a great patriotic purpose in educating children of nearly every race in the world and making Americans of them. I know of one school where seventeen different nationalities are represented among the pupils. These schools are not entirely godless. They can not be where they have God-fearing teachers, and most of the teachers I know by their characters alone are exerting a wholesome moral, if not a religious, influence. That is good as far as it goes, but it does not go far enough. Moral training rests upon the knowledge and the reverence of a divinity, and every race believes in and every religion is based upon the recognition of a supreme being. And no harm can be done by teaching the children of the public schools their responsibility to their Creator."

Rabbi Mendes, who is a member of the committee, says that the Jews will gladly support the movement for "three new Rs" and want their children instructed in "Reverence, Righteousness and Responsibility," as well as in reading, 'riting and 'rithmetic. "This generation is irreverent," he says, "and irreverence leads to unrighteousness and immorality. We must not neglect to teach the masses of children that are thronging our public schools their obligations to their Creator and the object of their conscience."

Father McMillan, of the Paulist Catholic educational order, says that there will be no objection on the part of the members of his faith if character building is introduced into the public schools, and that the basis of all character is a recognition of a supreme power and reverence for religion. On account of religious differences we shall have to be very careful in preparing a text-book, but it will be easy. Everybody but atheists must readily admit the necessity of moral education, and religion is the basis of all morals."

The committee is now preparing a text-book which will be submitted to the criticism of clergymen of the different denominations, Protestant, Catholic, Jews and Greeks, and their indorsement will be obtained before the matter is brought into the Board of Education. It

has been thought best to settle the question as to what shall be taught before asking official permission to teach anything. If the proposed text-book commands the approval of every religious denomination the Board of Education naturally will feel less delicacy in treating the subject. One of the committee said that it would be based upon the Ten Commandments and the additional commandments proposed by the Savior.

❦ ❦

Notes and Comments.

Here is another report from the "firing line." It comes from the south, where the "firing" is supposed to be the fiercest. The attack is from the Methodists, and shows how our cause is sometimes assailed in the Sunny South. Through the courtesy of Bro. Claude E. Hill, our preacher at Mobile, Ala., we are permitted to publish this letter from the Methodist pastor at Whistler, Ala., a town of about 2,000 population, ten miles from Mobile. The letter is addressed to Rev. Claude E. Hill, Mobile, Ala., under date of June 26, and reads as follows:

Dear Sir and Brother—There are some of your 'flock' out here who desire a service from you. I told some of them that I would write and ask you in regard to the matter. If you can arrange to come the Methodist Church will be at your service. I know your time is well taken up with duties in town, but these out here would be glad to get a week night service from you. Write me what time to announce for you. Hoping that you are well and happy, I am yours fraternally,
A. B. BROWN, Pastor Methodist Church.

Brother Hill writes that he has never met this pastor, so far as he knows, but he evidently suspects no "trap," and is going out to preach in the Methodist Church, as invited. The fact is, Brother Hill writes, that all the religious bodies thereabouts "have been uniformly kind and courteous" and that he has no complaint whatever to make of the cause having been "slandered or misrepresented." This incident is refreshing. Of course, "it takes more than one swallow to make a summer," but there are many such swallows flitting through the air and building their nests under the eaves of our churches, and they prophesy that the winter of our sectarian strife is passing, and that the summer of Christian fraternity and co-operation is at hand.

❦

Referring to the above statement of Brother Hill concerning the kind and courteous treatment he is receiving from his religious neighbors, it reminds us of a story told us in boyhood, the moral of which we have never forgotten. A Quaker entertaining a man who was moving from one state to another, was told by the emigrant that he had very bad neighbors where he came from who were ill-natured and unaccommodating. Said the old Quaker, in reply: "Thou w t have bad neighbors in the new state where thou art going." A few days later he entertained another emigrant moving to a new state, who boasted of the good neighbors he had left behind, and expressed his sorrow in parting from them. "Well," said the Quaker host, "thou wilt find good neighbors where thou art going." The old Quaker had a simple philosophy which he acted upon, that kindness begets kindness, and that unkindness, likewise, begets unkindness. Is it not altogether probable that in this bit of Quaker wisdom, borrowed from Christ, we have the explanation of why it is that in some communities our churches are treated very courteously, and in others they claim to be misrepresented and persecuted? The suggestion is at least worth looking into.

Editor's Easy Chair.

The Easy Chair to-day rocks in its northern home beside the resounding Lake, whose tumultuous waves fill our ears with their ceaseless monotones. The wind is blowing a steady gale from the northwest and has filled the Lake with noisy billows which, like white maned steeds, chase each other shoreward in endless succession. The sky is clear, save a few white clouds which float high in the air like phantom ships in the upper deep. The sun shines through these vapor clouds and paints the surface of the Lake with nearly all the tints of the rainbow. And this is the scene that spreads itself out before us this afternoon, as we rest under the shade of the trees on the heights of "Garrison Park." Thank God for the trees! How gracefully they bend in the breeze that comes over the Lake, and how grateful are the shadows they cast for protection from the heat of the sun! How soothing is the rustle of their leaves, as if they were whispering to each other the secrets of their life and joy! For the time being the Easy Chair is converted into a hammock, and what is more restful than a hammock swung under the trees where one can gaze upward through their branches into the infinite blue? How easy it is, at such a time, when the imagination is kindled by the immensities which are stretched out above one, to believe in the infinities and the eternities! No creed of narrow negations measured up to the sublime realities which lie open to the gaze. At such a time, and under such circumstances, Nature, in her vastness, becomes a magnificent symphony in which roaring waves, sighing trees, and singing spheres, are but the different parts.

"Great and marvelous are Thy works, O Lord
   Almighty,
In wisdom hast Thou made them all."

"The Pioneer" has been almost the only inhabited cottage on the Lake shore since our arrival, though in a few days we expect our neighbors to the immediate north of us, of the Oceana Beach Company, to be in their cottages, and the club house, we believe, is being opened to-day and put in order for the entertainment of guests. As the name "Pioneer" suggests, we are the first to occupy a cottage in this park. Pioneer life has its attractions, but it has its drawbacks, also. The chief deprivation we feel here is the absence of a few familiar friends, whose faces we have been wont to see in these summer outings. No doubt, some of these will come later and, meanwhile, our companions must be the lakes and the trees and the birds and the squirrels. The birds, however, are not numerous, for they like human companionship, and there are not enough people here yet to attract them in large numbers. Speaking of pioneering reminds us that a good brother wrote us recently that he thought we were doing too much "pioneering" in the way of introducing new and disturbing ideas among the brethren. "Art thou he that disturbest Israel?" The prophet thus interrogated pleaded "not guilty," and laid the responsibility for the disturbance elsewhere. We certainly hope

that we have not been a disturber of Israel in any evil sense. God knows we have no motive for disturbing the brethren except for their good. Many years ago, we came to the conclusion that we could serve God and our fellowmen best by declaring his truth, as he gave us to see the truth. We have sought to do this with proper humility and respect for the judgment of others, and in the spirit of love. Of course, we may have erred both in our thinking and in our manner of expressing our thought, but in either case the error was unintentional and we certainly regret it. What we desire, above all things else, is to know the truth of God as it relates to human duty and destiny, and to speak that truth in love. If this course makes us enemies, that is one of the crosses we must bear for the sake of truth, and especially for his sake who was truth incarnate.

❦

The quietest Fourth of July we have known for many years, we experienced yesterday in "Garrison Park." As sole occupants of the resort, we felt it incumbent upon us that the day which celebrates our nation's birth should have some recognition at our hands. So we laid in a few firecrackers, skyrockets, Roman candles, and the stars and stripes, and after a quiet restful day, when the great red, round sun had sunk, like a ball of fire, in the west, and quenched its flame in the Lake, and night's candles were lighted in the blue dome above, we marched down to the beach, built a bonfire, planted our flag on the ramparts of a sand dune and sang patriotic airs. Then the junior member of our party, who in the evening had dressed herself as the Goddess of Liberty, sent up her skyrockets over the lake and felt that she had had a part in celebrating the Glorious Fourth. Over the live coals of the bonfire, we roasted a few marshmallows, and then the patriarch of the party was asked to relate some old war stories out of his experience as a soldier. All this accomplished, we covered our coals with the sand and retired to the cottage, feeling that we had appropriately expressed our approval of the Declaration of Independence and the birth of the American Republic. This recalls the Fourth of July of the olden times. There was a barbecue in the woods. The neighbors far and near came to celebrate the day and the dinner. There was a procession formed, and some old veteran of the Mexican war marched at the front playing a fife, and some younger man beat the drum, and so we marched to the barbecue. There was a platform erected in the woods and Old Glory was flung to the breeze. The village choir rendered a few patriotic airs and the school-master read the Declaration of Independence, following which some aspiring young orator turned loose the American eagle and let her scream and flap her wings to her heart's content! Then the parson pronounced the benediction and we all retired to the dinner and ate the American beef as only hungry patriots could eat it, before the days of packing-house scandals. This was the Fourth of July in ye olden times.

❦

Speaking of the Fourth, the American people never had greater reasons for celebrating the day than at the present time. The prosecutions of trusts and monopolies and grafters throughout the country, fur-

nish abundant reason for the belief that the American conscience is being stirred as never before. There is really reason to hope that public business and private corporations may be carried on in this "land of the free and the home of the brave" as honestly and decently as in the "effete monarchies" of the old world. We can not be too grateful for a Chief Executive that is leading forward in this work of redeeming the country from the bondage of public plunder and private graft. If the Stars and Stripes does not mean a government that can punish its evil doers, and enact and enforce wholesome laws, protecting the people from the ravages of greed, it ought to be lowered to half mast, at least, until we learn how to be honest and law-abiding, though rich and powerful. All honor to the President of the United States, to the governors of several of the states, to mayors and prosecuting attorneys, and other public officials, here and there over the country, who have undertaken this gigantic task of regenerating the business methods of the United States and of teaching corporations that they are creatures of law and must be subject to law or forfeit their chartered rights and privileges. Instead of rejoicing at this exposure of crime there are people appalled by it and discouraged, just as in religious matters some good people deprecate a discussion that brings to the surface a condition of things that requires immediate remedy. Whatever helps us politically or religiously to a knowledge of evils that need to be cured, we should count as a special favor of God.

❦

"After the storm the calm." This is the morning of a new day. The conflict between the wind and the Lake which raged all day yesterday, began to subside at sundown, when the wind showed a disposition to retire for the night. The Lake kept up its noise later but its troubles passed away with the night and this morning it smiles as placidly as an infant in its sleep. Far out toward the sky-line a steamer is passing north, carrying, no doubt, its cargo of passengers to the resorts farther north, while another headed in the opposite direction is going after others who are anxious to escape the heat of the cities. Nearer shore the little red boat of the fishermen, who have been out to their nets in the Lake opposite "Garrison Park," is making its way back with the result of the night's catch. A few days ago they showed us some ten and twelve pound trout they had caught with baited hooks on a trot-line just out in the lake in front of our cottage. This is a hint we shall act on. The reader may be prepared for fish stories! While rowing across Lake Pentwater last evening for the mail, we saw two men in a row boat just landing with four large pickerel and a basket full of smaller fish. Encouraged by this success, we put on an artificial minnow and trolled on our return trip and captured a sixteen inch pickerel, the odor of which now comes to us from the frying pan. We have had no trouble so far in supplying our table with fresh fish, although we have devoted little time to angling. With the perch and trout of Lake Michigan, the pickerel, croppie and small mouth black bass of Lake Pentwater, and the large mouthed bass of Bass Lake, four miles up, the lover of the fine art of angling will find here plenty to amuse him, and this is a prime requisite of an ideal summer resort.

Our Plea Among Scandinavians By C. S. Osterhus

During the past fifteen or twenty years thousands of our Scandinavian people of America have been converted to God. In hundreds of places this has meant a separation from the dead and formal churches, to which many of our people before belonged.. A family here, and two there, and probably ten or twenty families at the third and other places, have thus found themselves placed alone, as it were, in a cold and formal world, and in the immediate shadow of heartless and sometimes raging sectism. Besides these very discouraging influences surrounding them from the outside, they have had some bitter experiences from ravaging wolves from the inside. These thousands of families have found themselves in danger and peril from both without and within, between two fires.

How did these people get converted and get into this situation?

By the manifold and wonderful movings of the spirit of God among them, like as among so many other peoples in the last century. Many of our people are earnest believers before they immigrate into this country. Although the Lutheran Church is the state and predominating church of the three Scandinavian countries of Continental Europe, yet even within its walls there are thousands of believers to be found who are most devout and pious worshipers of the true God, worshiping him up to the measure of the light and knowledge they have had access to. Besides these, there are also thousands upon thousands of true disciples of Jesus of Nazareth, the true and only Christ, outside of the above-named church in these countries. In Norway, Sweden and Denmark there are a very large number of people who are truly converted to God, who worship him in spirit and also in truth, as far as they have knowledge of it.

Coming to this country, they are scattered in the various settlements of Scandinavian people, which are to be found mostly in the states of Iowa, Illinois, Wisconsin, Michigan, Minnesota, North and South Dakota, Nebraska and Kansas. Quite a few are along the states of the Atlantic coast; and in later years quite a few are to be found in the states of the Pacific coast, as also in Canada and Texas.

There are to-day at least about four millions of these good citizens in America. There are at least 7,000 organized churches or congregations among them, the greatest part of which are Lutherans. Some are Methodists, some Baptists, some Congregationalists, etc. There are at least 3,500 ministers working among them. They have many great synods, schools, colleges, seminaries and institutions of benevolence, etc.

But aside from all these things, there now exists among them a large company of believers, who would like to be Christians only, and who, for years, have searched to find the good old paths of the apostolic, primitive and real New Testament church. Some of them have read themselves out of denominationalism, and some have prayed themselves out of it; and many have been converted out of it, so to speak..

As aforesaid, many of our people were disciples of Christ before they came to this country. Some of them joined some

C. S. Osterhus.

denomination for a time (mostly Lutheran), others not; and whether they did or not, many of these have read and prayed themselves out of the questionable creeds of men. With the open Bible before them, many of them have set out to preach the Gospel, as best they could in their home district, and adjoining districts. Some have for years gone out to spend their entire time preaching in larger districts. This has been going on for many years, probably fifteen or twenty years, anyhow; in a larger degree especially during the last eight or ten years.

The result of it is that there is to-day (speaking especially for the Norwegians and Danes) at least 200 scattered groups of Disciples of Christ throughout the various states named above, who would like to be Christians only, and who stand independent of human creeds, etc. Some of them are only small groups of a few families, others larger ones from ten, fifteen and twenty families or more in each place. Some of them, especially the larger ones, are partially organized, and have nice church buildings, etc. Others are not organized at all. They simply come together and sing and pray and read the Scriptures, etc., as best they can, without any leader or local preacher. Some of them can testify well and give a Gospel exhortation. But few of them can preach or teach. Hence the large majority of these many

groups are almost literally "as sheep without a shepherd."

There are probably 100 or maybe 150 evangelistic preachers among these groups. Nearly all of them are so-called self-made evangelists, who have had no college or Bible school training. Yet some are very good preachers. But the greatest difficulty is that not all of them "speak the same thing," some causing considerable confusion. And nearly all of them teach erroneously as to the servants of the church which the Scriptures designate as "pastors and teachers." The result is there is no capable minister of Christ to care for the flock at each place; hence the flock is open to most any kind of influence from the straying preachers.

One great cause of this is the fact that there is no organic co-operation and systematic work done. Every evangelist teaches what he pleases, and goes where he pleases; some groups are visited often by sometimes two or three evangelists at a time, who happen to meet at one place, not knowing about each other. Other places are entirely neglected, not having preaching for six months. There is no Bible school yet among them where those going out to preach could learn to know the same truths, and work in harmony one with another. The great and good cause is therefore suffering greatly. The papers circulated among them teach the same errors as most of the evangelists on the subject named. What they despisingly call a paid ministry is strenuously opposed. They have seen the extreme on one side, so they go to the extreme on the other side.

This was the situation as I found it when, six years ago, I found myself standing isolated from everybody, as it seemed.

In order that the reader may see how the New Testament plea works its way even to the hearts of Lutheran ministers, I will give you

A Brief Sketch of My Life and Work.

I was born 34 years ago at this place, Ossian, Iowa, where I now live temporarily. My parents were both born in Norway. I understand the Dano-Norwegian language very well—a good deal better than I do English. My parents were Lutherans and I was faithfully taught the doctrines of that church from childhood. My father was an earnest preacher among the laity, so-called. I was trained at our splendid Norwegian seminary at Minneapolis, Minn. Yet I preached the Gospel for several years before I took the Bible course at the seminary. I began preaching publicly and regularly as assistant pastor of eight churches in Iowa, which my brother-in-law had charge of when I was 19 years of age, now fifteen years ago. Thus, I am not so very young in the Gospel work, although somewhat young in years. I was duly and regularly ordained to the Gospel ministry in 1897, and served churches in Iowa, Oregon and Washington as regular pastor in charge. I later traveled some as evangelist in Minnesota and North Dakota. God graciously blessed the ministry. Souls were saved and believers greatly strengthened and edified in Christ. (This latter, that of teaching and shepherding the believer, being, perhaps, my strongest side, the special gift of God.) I had two beautiful churches in Oregon. We had a nice home and were greatly loved by the people.

But now came severe trials of a new character to me. I had been severely tested in life before, even in a very young age, but not in this way. It was six years ago. By an incessant and deep study of the Bible, under increasing prayers and unbroken earnestness to know the truth and the truth only, God led me to see some of the errors of the doctrines of the Lutheran Church. My conscience, my Bible and my God bade me testify in word and deed against errors and sins. It was daring for me, a young man, a lonely preacher in one of the extreme western cities, to take a different view of these eternal matters than the whole powerful army of 70,000,000 of Lutherans in the world, with its thousands upon thousands of highly educated, well trained and skilled ministers, teachers and professors, colleges and seminaries. But almost unconsciously, in a way, I was brought face to face with a similar state of affairs, as our dear young Luther was when he said those never to be forgotten words:

"Here I stand; I can not do otherwise. God help me! Amen."

With my open Bible in hand, I could not revoke the truths it had revealed to me. The interpretations of men, councils and synods could not change my convictions.

Oh, those wonderful days and hours! It causes my tears to flow even now at this writing to think back upon those days of dreadful revolutions in my life six years ago. In my intense agony on the point of baptism, for instance, I could hardly help praying: "Oh, God, send some angel of heaven and once for all settle this question among men." But no angel came. But the Advocate with the Father and with men, the Spirit of Truth and the true Bible Commentator, the gentle, faithful Revealer of Truth as it is in Christ Jesus, the Holy Spirit, "took of Christ's (and God's word) and declared them unto me" (John 16:13,14). The New Testament plea was made plain to me, more than ever before.

So, after having passed through the agonies of our brother, young Martin Luther, and after many prayers, much searching and many tears, I took my stand, by the grace of God, with him who loved me so he died for me.

My wife and I were baptized by immersion. The act itself meant the nailing of at least one great thesis upon the

spacious door of the Lutheran Church. And this again meant the loss of home, friends and support for me and my family. But with Luther we sang:

"A mighty fortress is our God,
A bulwark never failing;
Our helper he amid the flood
Of mortal ills prevailing.
Let goods and kindred go,
This mortal life also;
The body they may kill;
God's truth abideth still,
His kingdom is forever."

Yes, we continued, by the grace of God and his courage, to sing even these words:

"And tho' this world with devils filled
Should threaten to undo us,
We will not fear, for God hath willed
His truth to triumph through us."

And dear old brother Paul Gerhardt helped us to word the next verse of our song:

"Commit thou all thy ways,
And all thy grief and care,
To him whom heaven obeys,
Whose love is everywhere.
For air, and clouds, and wind,
He findeth pathways meet;
Shall he not also find
The pathway for thy feet?"

I had just previously quietly resigned from my two churches in Oregon, as the heavy strain of work, and study and anxiety, now and before, had ruined my health. But I had not formally resigned from the church body in general. They let my name remain on the clergy list for about two years, when they quietly took it off. Hence the church really withdrew from me, when I lived up to the Bible faith. Financial support had, of course, been withdrawn long before. Nearly all the earnest Christians resigned from the local church in Oregon when

we did. They stood by us faithfully. They wept bitterly when we left. The home, or parsonage, belonged to the church, so we had to leave everything, of course. We have been a homeless family ever since, living most of these six years "on grace" in the crowded homes of others. You see, my health was broken, and my income gone immediately. We stood alone, had no church any more and lost many friends on account of our baptism. It has been some very, yes,

truly, very hard years. But I can not take space to relate any of that here. Suffice it to say God has wonderfully stood by us and borne us up.

"And none can stay his arm,
Nor bid his work be still,
When he will save from harm
His people Israel."

A wonderful and peculiar training it has been. Many a lesson of humility and patience has been taught us.

Although for a time thrown out of active pastoral work on account of this change in church matters and broken health, yet I was laboring day and night during all these hard years, searching for a way out. I carried on an extensive searching by correspondence in two languages, and by occasional journeys here and there attending special meetings and conventions, for weeks and sometimes months studying the various movements, as well as the religious situation and condition in America in general the last two years or more, especially among our own Scandinavian people.

This finally led me, by the wonderful leadings of God, to begin writing a series of articles for two of our large Norwegian weeklies of Chicago about two years ago. These papers are especially circulated among the 30,000 to 50,000 independently standing Disciples of Christ, referred to in the first part of this article. They were upon themes like "The True Church of God and His Christ," its "Officers," such as "Pastors and Teachers," and a great deal on "Unity of All Believers in Christ," etc., etc.

Hundreds of letters of appreciation soon came flooding in to me from all directions of the country. A great many were from preachers. All expressed a

A Scandinavian-American Church interested in the Christian Unity Movement.

deep longing for the true unity of all believers among us, having longed deeply for it in their hearts for years, but none of them had been given the courage or commission to speak the word and dare to be a spokesman for the sacred cause in general. The peculiar training I had had in God's school made it a matter of conscience for me to speak. God had enabled me, by his grace, to take a bold step six years ago against sectism and human creeddom. He seemed much pleased to enable me to take another one now. And again I had to obey the constraint of the love of God for the truth. So, in December, 1904, he encouraged me to call the first general unity convention or conference among our Norwegian and Danish Christians.

Although I was personally unacquainted with the majority of the readers of the papers I was permitted to have the loaned use of, yet they had listened intently to the sound of the trumpet which I had, like Gideon of old, blown. And they came together from more than five tribes of the religious dispersion among our people. At the earnest invitation of the Church of Christ at Chippewa Falls, Wis. (Julius Stone, pastor), the convention assembled there. And that never-to-be-forgotten conference was held there for seven whole days, in January, 1905, with almost all day and all night sessions every day of the seven.

I had most carefully prepared the program ahead and published it in the papers several weeks previous. The keynote of it was Christ's unity prayer in John 17:20-23. A wonderful spirit of God's love was prevalent throughout the whole conference. There were delegates present from all over this land and a noted evangelist from Denmark also. It set an indelible mark upon every one present.

Among other things done was that a committee of five was elected to arrange for another convention in June, 1905. Brother Stone, your humble writer and three others constituted the committee. Your humble writer was further elected to travel continually in the cause of unity among our scattered groups of Christians throughout our land and interest them all sincerely in the unity prayer of Jesus in John 17:20-23; hence to co-operate together in Christian work for lost mankind.

By the grace of God we carried it through with great success and much blessing.

I traveled continually up to the convention, and visited scores upon scores of real and genuine churches of Christ among our people throughout all these states. I traveled in three months over 6,000 miles in Iowa, Illinois, Wisconsin, Michigan, Minnesota, South Dakota, Nebraska and Kansas, and preached on an average more than once every day, besides the long distances traveled. Sometimes I held four long meetings inside of twenty-six hours, from Saturday night till Sunday night; and I seldom spoke less than one and a half hours to the hungry assembly in each meeting, besides the writing of hundreds of letters during these months (more than 1,000 for the year), and almost regular weekly articles for the two papers.

God was wonderfully with us in great power and blessing. Truly, he was.

The program for the second general unity convention, held at Hutchinson, Minn., last June, was carefully prepared by your humble brother, assisted by the other members of the committee, Brother Stone not the least. Delegates came again from all over these states, yes, even from the state of Washington; and greetings in the work have come to me by hundreds upon hundreds of letters from all over this land. For seven days the program was again carefully discussed with great educational value to our scattered Christians. Your humble brother was unanimously re-elected to travel continually in the cause of unity among our whole people.

After that immense work I had undertaken for months previous, and after acting as chairman of the conference for seven hot June days; my strength was pretty well worn down. For months I had not had more than about five or six hours good rest per night, besides the almost phenomenal amount of work done in traveling, meetings day and night, several times a day and all day, hundreds of letters to write in spare moments while riding on trains, etc., etc. I needed a few days rest. Arriving home June 8, I broke completely down with what had every appearance of tuberculosis of the lungs and my life doomed to death. I quickly wrote a request for prayer to our two papers, which yet stood by us. Thousands of prayers went up for me from those who had learned to love me everywhere in this work. Scores and scores wrote me letters of sympathy and love.

God heard the earnest prayers from our hearts. My lungs were soon perfectly well, and have been ever since. Glory be to God in the highest, ever and ever!

I am, therefore, among you, dear brethren, as a man redeemed from the grave almost literally. My life is truly a gift of God in a double sense to me.

But by this time the devil began to dislike this unity movement, seeing his craft of sectarianism was in danger of coming in disrepute at least. The Gospel of Christ had been preached with power, and divine force, and without fear. The spirit of the devil, called sectism, felt pinched and made a howl. The howl scared the papers we had the loaned use of. So now we have not for many months had any paper that will faithfully serve this sacred cause among our divided people.

I am praying day and night for God to supply us means to publish a real Church of Christ paper that will stand for all that Christ and his Gospel stands for. My own personal correspondence makes it a necessity. People write me from all over this land, asking me to explain to them this Scripture and that Scripture. People are hungry for light and teaching. But few are the capable teachers among them. For most of these thousands of Christians have, like myself, come out from the Lutheran Church; and they are most literally as sheep without a shepherd.

How it does pain me to read these hundreds of letters and hear these hundreds of Macedonian cries, "Come over and help us!" especially painful since I am utterly unable with my own pen or person to help them all as fully as I ought to.

One of the main causes for this has been the lack of money to carry on the work successfully and continually. Remember, that for more than six whole years I have received no salary or regular income from any source whatever. I labor hard with my hands for a support for the family, wife and six little children (with additional help and an aged mother, in all always ten, often twelve, at our table), laboring up to fifteen and eighteen hours daily. I labor all day for a support, even up to 9 p. m., then try to do all the spiritual work I can after 9 o'clock at night. I sit up and write till 12, 1, 2 and even 3 o'clock at night very often; in fact, most of the time till about midnight, writing, searching the Scriptures and praying.

This is when I am at home, which I have been compelled to be now for many months for lack of funds. You see, the scattered and mostly unorganized condition of these independent and divided groups make the financial arrangements as poor as their own religious situation. Besides, most of the unstable evangelists and papers working among them have for years taught error on finances in the kingdom of God. They are yet opposed to a steady and systematic way of giving. Hence a little collection here and there will not carry a steady and systematic and persistent work of this kind yet. My prayer has, therefore, for a long time been for several definite things relative to this work, two of which are these, namely:

1. That God would some way send me needed support so I could be free to spend my entire time as a special unity messenger among our people, with tongue and pen to assist in the formation of and the setting in proper and Biblical order real churches of God and his Christ among these hundreds of scattered groups of Christians, who are either wholly unorganized or at least only partially so.

2. That God would some way soon send me means for the publishing of a real Church of Christ paper in the Dano-Norwegian language for teaching of the full and pure Gospel of Christ and his kingdom, presenting the beautiful New Testament plea, without partiality or sectism. We have no such paper in all America in our language! We have a Scandinavian population of 4,000,000 in America alone to work among with such a paper.

We must have such a paper, and that soon if we shall be able to reap while the harvest is ripe, and before it is blown down by the devouring winds of error.

I humbly lay these desires before the throne of mercy and before the people

(Continued on Page 886.)

Modern Religious Persecution By B. L. Chase

I. Its Instruments.

It has become very popular in modern times to denounce persecution, and to say unkind things of persecutors. I fear it is because we misunderstand the persecutor. Sometime the history of persecution will be written from the standpoint of the persecutor instead of the persecuted; then the world will see it very differently. Up to the present time we have been made to see it in the light of the pains suffered by the guilty, rather than in the crimes committed by the guilty. Punishment for crime is one thing to the criminal, another thing to the judge. The readers of history have always viewed persecution from the side of the criminal. It is not just to the glorious company of persecutors who have saved the truth in the hour of its peril. It is we who owe the heritage of faith and truth which is ours to-day.

Let no one suppose the persecutor takes pleasure in his gruesome work any more than the hangman. It is a painful duty which he owes to his brethren, to his conscience and his God. It falls to him because to him belong the stronger conviction and the greater courage. Men are found congratulating themselves that they do not live in the age of the inquisition and the auto-da-fe; that heretics are no longer burned in civilized countries; and that there can be difference of religious opinion without banishment or confiscation of goods. Many of these men will be found to glory in their religious fancies and conceits, and to riot in their liberty. What a brood of fads and fancies in religion, of isms and ologies, have sprung up in the wake of modern religious liberty. A man can believe anything he pleases to-day, and no one can molest him. The result is that we have hundreds of denominations or sects teaching doctrines of every shade of color. It was not so in the days when persecutors could require every man to believe as every other man, on pain of death. We have gained liberty in modern times, but we have lost unity. We shall never have the glorious unity of the primitive church and of ancient times until there arises another order of faithful defenders of the faith.

Persecution is not what it used to be. Most of the objectionable features of mediaeval persecution have been removed to-day. Its instruments and methods have been refined under the refining influence of modern civilization, and all of its old-time horror has been eliminated. One who would be shocked at the sight of the thumbscrew, the branding iron, the iron boot, the flesh pinchers and many other instruments of torture used in ancient times upon the quivering flesh of men and maidens, could not possibly object to the instruments in use to-day. If modern persecutors keep within the law, no heretic's body is touched. He is made to feel no

physical pain, unless it be an indirect result of the refined process. No iron, or steel, not even wood, is sharpened and driven into the flesh. An ordinary pen and a little paper and ink is all the equipment a modern persecutor needs, as it is all the law allows. He uses only words. All that he attempts to do is to define and name the man's error, and warn the churches or the colleges.

That you may know how unobjectionable the modern instruments of torture are, I have copied the following list of choice and effective epithets used by a very distinguished persecutor among the Disciples: "Surrenderers" of the plea," "Revolutionary teachings," "Disturbers of the faith," "Destructive critics," "Subverters of our plea," "Sowers of discord," "Corruptionists," "Would-be clergymen," "Antagonists of the Bible," "Anti-Scriptural," "Subtle adversaries," "Traitors to our cause," "Betrayers of our Lord," "Enemies of the Simple Gospel," "Heretics," "Agnostics," "Infidels," "Followers of Bob Ingersoll," "Hypocrites," "Masquerading Infidels," "Retailers of agnosticism," "Defenders of infidelity and hypocrisy."

There are but few cases of heresy which require the application of some of the last of the foregoing terms; they are reserved for some of the more serious cases of departure from the faith. Not many men would have the courage to deal in this way with false teachers who are received into the bosoms of the churches and given places upon convention programs, or have the courage to continue the persecution when the persons so accused went about deceiving the people with smooth words, and in spite of the warnings of true and faithful brethren, were praised in many of the large city churches as Christian gentlemen. But few men would have the skill to unmask such false teachers and show the wolf beneath the sheep's clothing. Such persecutors show themselves to be true defenders of the faith by risking their all—their reputations for honesty and veracity, their publishing companies and the missionary work and unity of their church—in their determination to expose such heretics and prevent them from getting any chance to speak their errors to their brethren. They are to be congratulated that they possess one or two such true souls in the midst of the alarming apostasies of these last days, who are ready to lay down their lives and reputations for the plea.

There are few that can be made to believe that such men as receive the foregoing epithets exist outside of the penitentiary, much less hold membership in many churches where they are given office and respect. The few who do believe it are the salt of the earth and the true lights of the present darkened generation. So dull and insensible has the present generation become that they

seem no longer moved to righteous indignation against these men who are shown to be "infidels" and abettors of "agnostics." After being told that they are "Higher critics" churches will call them to deliver lectures, secretaries of missionary societies will retain them as friends and place their names on national convention programs. They seem to have forgotten what "infidel" means, and rather to court the title as a badge of honor than spurn it as a stigma of reproach.

One is almost ready to conclude that the treatment of heretics that is allowed to-day is altogether too mild; that the persecutor, as well as the public, has grown too sensitive to suffering. As soon as a heretic is exposed the people seem to rally around him to prevent his suffering from even a sense of loneliness. If one of his poisonous books is denounced as an "infidel publication," scholars continue to recommend it; and the people seem afraid that the sale of the book will suffer; so they buy and advise all their friends to buy copies of the book.

(Continued on Page 886.)

❀ ❀

DOCTOR'S SHIFT
Now Gets Along Without It.

A physician says: "Until last fall I used to eat meat for my breakfast and suffered with indigestion until the meat had passed from the stomach.

"Last fall I began the use of Grape-Nuts for breakfast and very soon found I could do without meat, for my body got all the nourishment necessary from the Grape-Nuts and since then I have not had any indigestion and am feeling better and have increased in weight.

"Since finding the benefit I derived from Grape-Nuts I have prescribed the food for all of my patients suffering from indigestion or over-feeding and also for those recovering from disease where I want a food easy to take and certain to digest and which will not overtax the stomach.

"I always find the results I look for when I prescribe Grape-Nuts. For ethical reasons please omit my name." Name given by mail by Postum Co., Battle Creek, Mich.

The reason for the wonderful amount of nutriment, and the easy digestion of Grape-Nuts is not hard to find.

In the first place, the starchy part of the wheat and barley goes through various processes of cooking, to perfectly change the starch into Dextrose or Post Sugar, in which state it is ready to be easily absorbed by the blood. The parts in the wheat and barley which Nature can make use of for rebuilding brain and nerve centres are retained in this remarkable food, and thus the human body is supplied with the powerful strength producers so easily noticed after one has eaten Grape-Nuts each day for a week or 10 days. "There's a reason."

Get the little book, "The Road to Wellville," in pkgs.

Some of My Likings

3. The Kind of Preaching I Like.

Though I once was young, and now am growing venerable, I find that in most respects I am just as youthful as I ever was. My conviction is that Christians who are total abstainers and philosophers as to rules of ordinary life do not grow old but have found the secret of perpetual juvenility. So I am beginning to appreciate all the meaning of dear old Cicero's treatise "De Senectute," which in my early days I read with delight because of its classic beauty, and now find that I shall be myself a subject of some of the choicest pleasures of the sunset of life.

My First Love and My Last in Theology.

I was cradled and trained in Puritanism. And I am not at all ashamed to say that I am a genuine Puritan to-day. I am many other things besides, for I am a broad churchman and a high churchman in certain applications of those terms; I am a free churchman or nonconformist and an ecclesiastical radical; I am an advanced Protestant and Disciple of Christ; I am a higher critic of the moderate or conservative type and a sympathizer with such men of research as Flinders Petrie and Professor Sayce; I am given to rejoicing in all the results of effort on the part of Christian socialists and present-day reformers who make religion an applied science. So let it not be thought that my persistent Puritanism has narrowed my outlook or cramped my sympathies. It was declared by a distinguished Frenchman, fifty years ago, Monod the elder, that poor France was dying for lack of Puritanism. Half a century earlier Napoleon uttered his famous dictum that France was dying for want of mothers. Had the great emperor understood his country and its need as well as did the great theologian he would have seen that a nation which had killed its Puritanism when it destroyed the Huguenots, must inevitably lose motherhood and much else. To slaughter the bulk of the Protestants and to expatriate the remnant of them was to ensure the decadence of the national life. A land which once has had the reformation and has rejected it must lie under a curse. Under such a curse France and Spain languish at this hour. I meet with only a few people who seem to realize, however, in all its force, the principle that the greatness, the glory, the happiness, and the prosperity of any people must depend positively on the theological type of the national faith.

How Theology Makes a Nation.

I have often wished that the point I am now emphasizing were more generally perceived by Christian people. If they understood it they might seek to impress it on politicians, statesmen, literary men and others who are for the most part utterly ignorant in this regard. Does history teach anything more clearly than this that national differentiations are shaped, happily or miserably, as the case may be, entirely by the trend of the national creed? Russia is what she is, and she fell under the withering vengeance of a pagan nation, simply through the superstitious doctrine of ikonolatry. The notion that saints could give all benedictions through the curious amulets known as ikons or picture-images of those saints, has ruined the vast nation. The type of doctrinal conviction ingrained in the very soul of the people has turned the whole course of Russian history. Let none of us imagine that it is of small consequence what a nation believes. This is the one vital consideration. Why is Scotland, a tiny country, influencing the thought and life of the whole world beyond all proportion to its size and its population? Because it with fiery enthusiasm adopted the reformation and flung off the yoke of the Pope. And why is there such indomitable grit in the Scottish character? Because of the sturdy factor incorporated in the national creed by Knox, called Calvinism. Knox had lived with Calvin for some time. Calvinism has its weak side, I well know, but so has each type of theology. We have to consider theology in its types all round. Why are the Welsh the most religious people on earth, for I feel well assured that there is nowhere so devout a community? Because of the Puritanic elements which form the backbone both of the Welsh Calvinistic Methodism in the north and of the faith of the great Welsh Baptist church which really possess the land in South Wales? Little Wales has been gallantly defying the worst efforts of Tory ecclesiasticism during the last three years until recently the Liberals came back to power. But this is because Wales is not merely Protestant, like Germany, like America, like Denmark, like England, like Scotland, but because Wales is even more Puritan in the theology of its preachers and of its churches than is any other country on earth. We have been in England witnessing the magnificent progress of a strenuous movement called the Passive Resistance Campaign. But I have noted that Puritanism was the mainspring of that movement. The free churches that care comparatively little, theologically speaking, for the Puritanism that made England great in the Cromwellian period, have taken languid interest in the struggle or have only been dragged into it by the force of example.

The Preaching That Converts.

Years ago I came to the conclusion that Puritanism is the secret of converting efficacy in preaching. There is no absolute, cast-iron Puritanism. Puritan theology has its variations. It is elastic so that it fits itself to the moulds of individual temperament, and adapts itself to the idiosyncracy of personality. The Puritan accent of Moody differed from that of Spurgeon. But Spurgeon was styled "the last of the English Puritans," and Moody certainly was in his theology an American replica of the great English preacher, as Dr. A. T.

As Seen From the Dome   By F. D. Power

Through a constant and ever-varying panorama of village and rural Egyptian life for 150 miles, on a comfortable railroad car, one journeys to Cairo from Alexandria, and soon gets a glimpse of the famous Pyramids and enters the White City of the East, with visions of Saladin and Harun-al-Rashid and Napoleon, of Oriental romance and poetry and history crowding his already overcrowded brain. On the east bank of the Nile, twelve miles from the apex of the Delta, stands this city of 600,000 people. It is built partly on the plain and partly on the slope of the Mokattem range. It is a city of walls and towers, gardens and squares, palaces and mosques, domes and minarets, with luxurious hotels and visitors from every clime; a city of pure air and perpetual sunshine, of Fellahs and Copts, of Turks and Jews, of Negroes and Bedouins. English and French and Germans and Americans. It was once a fortress called Babylon. Some say the Persians under Cambyses, who conquered Egypt in 525 A. D., founded it as "New Babylon"—but it existed before Cambyses and before Rameses II. It is pre-historic. Anir invaded Egypt 638 and on the site of Babylon pitched his tent and named his town Fostal. Then came the Khaliff Muizz 869, and named the place Masr-el-Kahira, and so we have Cairo, but the natives still say "Masr."

The city is called a precious diamond in the handle of the green fan of the Delta, and praised for the power of its princes, the beauty of its women, the charm of its climate, in all the Oriental imagery and extravagance of The Thousand and One Nights. "He who has not seen Cairo has not seen the world. Its earth is gold, its women are bewitching, and its Nile is a wonder." "As compared with a sight of Cairo what is the joy of setting eyes on your beloved!" We saw it from the citadel under the glowing Egyptian sun, and again on a fine evening, coming down the Nile from Memphis, as the sun went down behind the Pyramids, gleaming through the palm groves with cupolas and minarets glittering in airy robes of rose and violet; and again under the soft light of the stars; and it is beautiful.

What a mixture of people! My first stroll was along the Muski, without knowing where I was. Here was a continuous stream of riders, carriages, camels, donkeys, and foot passengers, with rustle and tramp and clatter and voices in a score of tongues and picturesque costumes of every race and tribe and people, tarboush and turban and hat, veiled women with their hideous nose pieces, Arab lancers, Soudanese infantry and Egyptian cavalry, vendors of all sorts of goods, great bazaars with thousands of dollars represented in oil of roses, perfumes and spices, glass and china, cloth and silks, jewelry and brasses, rugs and carpets, gold and silver and copper wares,

and noisy costermongers crying their stuff on every hand. Here is a scribe with his ink horn and reed pen; Bedouins from the desert with striped "Kufieh" and bare legs; Pashas in state, with runners going before him to prepare the way; a camel train laden with Oriental goods, passing in the midst of automobiles and bicycles; a turkey vendor driving his birds along the crowded thoroughfare with a palm branch; a little donkey wagon loaded with veiled women, and the driver feeding clover to his beast as he walks along; a milkman driving his goats, and milking them for you while you wait; sometimes the goat going up stairs to the second story and supplying the customer; a wedding procession preceded by dancing girls, or a funeral with black-shawled professional mourners, yelling their mercenary grief as they go—such are some sights one sees in Cairo.

Some of the mosques here are interesting. There is Sultan Hassan with the inscription, "Thi.- building is dedicated to Allah the Merciful, the Compassionate," with its quaint sublimity, its beautiful dome, 180 feet, its five windows and arches, its impressive religious atmosphere, and its minaret, 290 feet. There is El Azhar, the university founded in 975, perhaps the oldest of universities, with its 6,000 students and 225 teachers, from Algeria, Morocco, Nubia and elsewhere, all sitting and repeating in monotonous voices passages from the Koran, an exercise of memory with little original work or training in grammar, literature, philosophy or science. The great school is endowed, teachers get only their food, and many of the students are charity scholars. There is "the Alabaster Mosque, or Muhammad Ali, in the center of the citadel, built in imitation of St. Sophia, with beautiful columns and wall facings of alabaster, the most distinctive feature of Cairo. To see one mosque is to see all. They are built in uniform style. The plan is an oblong rectangle, in the center a vast court yard, in the middle of which is a fountain of ablutions. This court is enclosed by a colonnade which forms the Liwan, or place of prayer. The sanctuary is in the southeastern part of the Liwan looking toward Mecca. The most sacred part of the building, like the choir of a Catholic cathedral, is screened off from the rest, and contains the tomb of the founder. There is a richly sculptured and decorated niche of prayer, the "Kiblah," and on the right the "Mimbar," or preaching pulpit, of marquetry and richly carved. The reading desk of the Koran, "the Kursi," and chandeliers and lamps are often very rich and artistic. The floors are covered with the costliest rugs and we must wear slippers or remove our shoes, or slip off our rubbers; and they watch jealousy to prevent defilement. Doorways are richly decorated

and carved and doors studded with fretted and engraved bronze plates. Minarets have a great variety of design and at about two-thirds of the height is a balcony from which the Mueddin calls to prayer. Minarets and domes are capped with great copper crescents. Almost every mosque has its "Sebil," or fountain, where water is offered to the passer by, and there is generally a school where children study the Koran. The tombs are many of them most elaborate. For the plainer people through the head piece is a little hole, by which they say Israfel, the angel of the resurrection, enters and catches the occupant by the hair and brings him forth. So one sees the children of the lower classes with the head shaved, excepting a little tuft in the middle, an incipient pigtail or inverted tonsure, due to this superstition.

The Egyptian museum is one of the great institutions of the city. It is a monument to two men, Marietta and Maspero. Its contents are priceless. Here are statues and mummies of Pharaohs and kings and queens of thousands of years ago, sphinxes and gods and priests, domestic utensils, jewels, grains and fruits and mummied cats and alligators, gazelles and birds, s arabs and lotus flowers—an endless array of things gathered from old tombs buried under the sands. Here is a wooden statue of a village sheik, with round head, life-like face and in-set eyes of quartz, with rock crystal pupils; statues of scribes writing on papyrus; copper statues of kings, with in-set enamelled eyes; colossal figures of men who ruled thousands of years ago; limestone statues of Rahotep and his wife, Nofret, with pigments retaining their colors after five millenniums, and eyes of colored quartz, that stare at an American in a life-like way, as if resenting his intrusion. Madame Nofret has her arms folded, and "not a wave of trouble rolls across her peaceful breast." Here are the royal mummies, discovered in 1881 and 1898. An Arab, Ahmed, "the tomb robber," was digging among the Tombs of the Kings at Luxor, and struck a shaft. Seeing he had hit upon vast treasures which meant for him untold wealth, to conceal his discovery from his companions he shouted he had seen an evil spirit, and called to them to draw him to the surface. To give an additional color to the story he threw a dead donkey down the shaft, and so had a monopoly of the lucrative antiquities, which he disposed of to foreigners. Egyptologists learned of the find, explored, and lo, thirty-six coffins of kings and queens, Seti I, Ramses II, the great Merenptah, son and successor of Ramses II, the Pharaoh of the oppression, and many others; and we stand and look into their wrinkled faces. It is a great sight. Here also is the stele, or tablet, with inscriptions of Merenptah regarding his victories over Israel, with the words, "Israel is wasted and his seed is brought to nothing," and the stone with the decree of Canopus in three tongues, Egyptian, Greek and Demotic, which, had it not been for the famous Rosetta, would have furnished the key to the ancient Egyptian language. The decree was pronounced 238 B. C., and praises Ptolemy III. for his beneficent acts, and announces new festivals in honor of the king and queen. The jewels of the collection show the skill of Egyptian gold and silver smiths. One is simply amazed at the exquisite art of these ancient workmen. Then there is a vast wealth of papyrus writings, pottery, figures of animals, lamps and other treasures. There are many other things in Cairo of great interest to the visitor. The tombs of the sultans and khaliffs; the Island of Rhoda, which, according to tradition, knows the place where Moses was found among the bulrushes of the Nile; the old Nilometer, dating from 716 A. D., with its octagonal column in the center with Arabic measurements, which tells of the rise and fall of the glorious stream from 7 ells, or 12 feet, to 15 ells, or about 25 feet, an event celebrated with great popular rejoicing. The old Coptic hurch, where, according to tradition, Joseph and Mary and the boy Jesus rested when in Egypt, while given over hopelessly to dirt, is worth seeing. The Coptic church is the survival of the church founded by Mark 37 A. D., and next to the Mohammedan is the strongest in Egypt. It is believed the reference in 1 Pet. 5:13 is not the Babylon in Chaldea, but the Babylon in Egypt on the east side of the Nile. Peter here sends greetings to his old friend and amanuensis. The church became degenerate and there is little to show any connection with the apostles. Over a quarter of a million Copts, they say, have gone over to Islam. There are twenty-three of the churches of this faith in Cairo. Dean Stanley said "the Coptic race is the only living representative of the most venerable nation of antiquity." By apostasy and intermarriage with Moslems they are constantly decreasing. The Greek Church is strong in Egypt, about 50,000 Greek Christians being found among the traders and merchants. Roman Catholics have aggressive missions here, and there are Armenians represented, and the church missionary society. Who does not know of the work here of Miss Whately, daughter of the archbishop of Dublin? About 1860 she began her school work in Cairo for Mohammedan boys and girls, and its story for thirty years is one of the fascinating chapters of missionary history. The United Presbyterian Church, however, is doing the best work in this old country. We attended their Sunday-school, Christian Endeavor and church services. There were 223 at Sunday-school and the offering was $320. I caught one word, "Amen," and a baby cried in English. They have in Egypt 63 congregations, 75 native workers, a membership of 7,757, an attendance of 15,935, and contribute $28,256; average attendance at Sunday-schools 11,212. The work was begun in 1854.

What the Brethren Are Saying and Doing

By B. B. TYLER.

A most important meeting, and a meeting of unusual size and interest, was held in the Central Christian Church June 20. Representatives were present from seven congregations of Disciples in Denver and vicinity. The purpose of this meeting was to consider a plan of union for mutual help and aggressive work. The Kansas City plan, after a full and free discussion, was adopted unanimously and with enthusiasm. The seven congregations that will be represented in this "joint board" are the Central, the Highlands, the South Broadway, the Berkeley, the East Side, the Elyria and the Golden Christian churches. Each of these has a pastor and the pastors seem to be "settled." I make the statement in this form because no person knows what a day or an hour may bring forth. Four of the pastors own their homes. The Berkeley church owns its parsonage. The new pastor of the East Side congregation, J. B. Haston, will, I am informed, probably buy a home in Denver. The churches named own their houses of worship except Elyria and the East Side. The Golden church owned a house of worship which it sold and is now engaged in the work of building a better house and in a more eligible section of the town. The East Side is beginning to move in the direction of a home of its own. The present condition of our churches in this part of the world is good and the outlook is radiant.

The meeting mentioned above considered also the propriety and practicability of a simultaneous evangelistic campaign. The brethren resolved to conduct such a campaign to begin in the early part of January, 1907.

The brethren are saying and doing many interesting and good things in all sections of the country. One of the best of which I have heard is the fact that W. T. Moore has set about to work in earnest to write a comprehensive history of the Disciples of Christ. It is passing strange that no history of the Disciples has been written, and yet they are preparing to celebrate, in a fitting manner, the centennial of their beginning. Almost a hundred years old and no history in print. This is probably because they have been so busy making history that no time has been left for writing. There are sermons, leaflets, tracts, booklets, innumerable, telling who the Disciples are, when, where, under what circumstances, and for what purpose, they began. Again and again "Our Plea" has been set forth. Note has been made of their rapid numerical increase in the home land and of their work—educational, medical and evangelistic—in lands beyond the seas; but no comprehensive history has been written. This is a remarkable fact. The Cumberland Presbyterians had time, inclination and ability to write at least two histories of their church some years ago. W. T. Moore is the man to tell the story of the Disciples of Christ in a comprehensive way and free from prejudice and bias for or

against any school, or class, or person. His work will be, unless I am mistaken, judicially fair to all parties.

There is in "The Standard" (Baptist), of Chicago, under date of June 30, a notice of Dr. Moore's little book, entitled, "The Plea of the Disciples of Christ," recently from the press of the Christian Century Company, Chicago. The writer calls attention to the fact that Dr. Moore speaks of "The True Conception of the Bible," entertained by the Disciples, "The True Conception of God," "The True Conception of Christ," "The True Conception of the Holy Spirit," etc., and remarks that "Some of these true conceptions seem to us the common property of the Protestant world, and in no way peculiar to the Disciples; and others seem too indefinite and hazy to be called 'Conceptions' at all. But the failure of definition is not the fault of the author; it belongs to the protest of the Disciples against creeds. Dr. Moore brings not a little ability to the task of setting forth the plea of the Disciples and writes in a kindly spirit."

The remark about "The protest of the Disciples against creeds" has a strange sound coming from a Baptist. Dr. Thomas Armitage, in his "History of the Baptists," mentions among other things in the very beginning of his work, that Baptists have no creed as have Presbyterians, Methodists, Lutherans, Episcopalians, et cetera—that the only book of authority with Baptists is the Bible, especially the New Testament. His statement, as I remember it, as to the position of the Baptists on the creed question would satisfy the average Disciple. Now "the failure" of Dr. Moore in the matter "of definition" "belongs to the protest of the Disciples against creeds." How about the Baptists?

The same issue of "The Standard" notes the withdrawal of Professor Nathaniel Schmidt, of Cornell University, from the Baptist denomination. Professor Schmidt's pastor, Robert T. Jones, of the First Baptist church, Ithaca, New York, makes a statement of the case. He says that Professor Schmidt hesitated to leave the denomination because "he had never been requested, in any position he had held, or in uniting with any local church, to subscribe to a creed." "The Baptist brotherhood is not bound by a common creed," says Professor Schmidt, "nevertheless there is a general concensus of opinion as to the authority of the Bible, the person of Jesus, the way of salvation, and the manner of worship."

Is Professor Schmidt writing about Baptists or is he writing about the Disciples of Christ?

A tract has been issued by "The Pilgrim Press," Boston, entitled, "Congregational Faith and Practice," price 5 cents, which contains a hint for some scribe in "our brotherhood." The purpose of the booklet is to drill Congregationalists in the origin, history, distinctive principles and achievements of the denomination. Besides a clear statement of the fundamental principles, polity, belief and enterprises of the Congregationalists there are exercises and answers for thorough drill work. Would not something of this kind be good for "our people?"

Denver, Colo.

Our Budget

—Gateways to ruin do not close through summer time.

—Nevertheless, preachers should take vacations, but elders and other helpers should keep open house at the church.

—W. F. Richardson, of Kansas City, will make the principal address of the C. W. B. M. section of the Second District Convention at Sweet Springs, Mo., July 17.

—Bro. W. D. McCulley, formerly of Salisbury, Mo., has taken the important work at Cameron, Mo. This is a union of which great good may be safely predicted.

—Bro. E. W. Brickert has entered upon an active ministry with the Sullivan (Ind.) church. Brother Brickert is devoting years of exceeding usefulness to our churches.

—Bro. Claude Hill, of Mobile, Ala., in addition to taking care of that rapidly growing church and doing a work of which our whole brotherhood is proud, has recently organized a church at Citronelle.

—Bro. L. L. Carpenter and colleagues have prepared a very helpful Bethany assembly program for this year. The encampment continues from July 19 to August 13. Every attendant will be greatly benefited.

—Martin Gregory, of the Central, Walla Walla, Wash., writes: "I have given exceedingly careful examination to the Gloria in Excelsis, of which we bought 250 copies, and will say it is the finest hymnal I ever saw."

—Bro. A. H. Brown, of Greenwood, Ind., reports the church there greatly prospering under the ministry of Bro. George W. Winfrey. During June there were three additions to the membership by confession and baptism, and two otherwise.

—Bro. George W. Wise, of Leesville, La., spent ten days recently in Lodington, where he organized a church of forty members. He is a man well known in the northern part of the country and is a comparatively new man in the south.

—Marcellus Ely, recently at Soniat Avenue, New Orleans, has assumed charge of our church at Charleston. Bro. W. M. Taylor, who succeeds him in New Orleans, reports that work is in splendid condition and speaks highly of the retiring pastor.

—J. H. Coultard, formerly of Owasso, Mich., is now preaching for the congregation at Paw Paw, same state. Paw Paw will be in the van of the churches making contributions to what our centennial may justly expect of Michigan by 1909.

—J. L. McDonald, 1833 East Seventeenth street, Anderson, Ind., is available as a pastor. Brother McDonald is that man who has done good work in various states of the union and who is a pure and exemplary character. He ought to be set to work at once.

—Bro. H. A. Northcutt writes that J. W. Vance has recently located at Sulphur Springs, Tex., but will soon begin a meeting in Plano, Tex. He testifies to the great help Brother and Sister Zeran have been to him in a recent successful meeting at Sulphur Springs and elsewhere.

—The church at Deland, Fla., is without a preacher. No one but a well educated and capable man ought to go to that important place since it is the seat of a university and has a strong intellectual atmosphere. Men of the right type would do well to apply to W. H. Halsey.

—A young man of consecration and ability who can accept a salary of $650 or $700, where living is very cheap, is wanted for the ministry in Wiarton, Ontario, Canada. Address Bro. R. W. Stevenson, 568 Manning Avenue, Toronto.

—We call attention to the third report of the relief fund of the Christian churches at San Francisco, made by Hiram Van Kirk, financial secretary, in another column. One touch of misfortune makes all the world akin, but it makes brethren in the Lord particularly dear and helpful.

—O. L. Lyon, the tireless minister of the Newman (Ill.) church, reports six baptisms during the last two weeks and six other additions by letter. He testifies that Brother Brooks may still be used to great advantage even after Bro. Scoville has held a meeting for a church.

—Bros. J. J. Taylor and Arthur Haley are to hold another meeting, this time in a tent, in Montpelier, O., beginning July 29. These brethren held a meeting there last winter which resulted in the organization of a church in that place. The character of their work may well be understood by this return call within a year.

—T. F. Weaver writes that he has sold his interest in Grayson College and is no longer connected with that institution. He is now ready to serve any congregation that may need his help either in a pastoral or evangelistic capacity. We most cordially welcome Brother Weaver back into the ranks of our active ministry.

—Bro. M. B. Ingle, Harper, Kan., will hold a missionary protracted meeting in Wheatland, Wyo., during the summer. We have a few members in and about that town who are anxious to organize a church, secure a preacher and go to work. Brother Ingle has had much experience in this sort of pioneer work and will doubtless do it well.

—From "The Greeting," of Peoria, Ill., Harry Foster Burns, minister, we learn the church is agitating the question of a new building. Lacy Parks Schooling, the assistant pastor, will spend his vacation in study at the University of Chicago. Increased attention is being paid to the social life of the church and with very beneficial results.

—The church at Wilkesbarre, Pa., is two years old and has grown to a membership of two hundred under the ministry of E. E. Cowperthwaite. A more difficult field has probably never been entered by our people. It has required heroic work to bring things to their present condition. This baby church entertains the state convention July 31 to August 2.

—Bro. D. T. Stanley, our missionary in and about Birmingham, Ala., has made a splendid beginning in his work. He has organized a church at Woodlawn and is gathering people together in North Birmingham, where we have at least thirty members not yet organized into a church. We look for good permanent results in this important field.

—Bro. Finley Sapp was elected secretary of the South Dakota Christian Missionary Society during its recent convention in Carthage. Brother Sapp has had experience in this form of work in other states and brings to his new task both knowledge and capacity for the work. We will hope to hear good reports of the progress of the work in that important state.

—Bro. T. M. Johnson, of Quincy, Ill., a day or two ago went to his eternal reward. Brother Johnson was graduated from the Christian University, Canton, Mo., in 1874, and gave his life to the ministry from that time. He has been very successful as an evangelist and has done good work as a settled minister. Our sympathies go out to his wife and the children who mourn his departure.

—Bros. O. P. Spiegel and J. E. Sturgis, the latter singing evangelist, Butler, Ind., have recently closed a meeting in Jackson, Miss., where they organized a second church with fifty-two members. It is said that our people, during this meeting, had the best hearing in the history of our work in that city. A preacher has been called for the new congregation and the prospects are bright for a rapid and permanent growth.

—Bro. J. G. Wilson, Waldron, Mich., is familiar with many places in the state of Michigan in which we have no churches. His work among the Seventh Day Adventists took him to many towns in that state and revealed to him their religious conditions. He is desirous of going to Salt St. Marie to establish a church, however the support may come. We hope that he will not long be deterred and that ample support may be provided for him.

—Bro. C. A. Lowe, of St. Joseph, sends us a very interesting programme of the Seventh (Mo.) Missionary District, to be held at Camden Point, July 23-26. The names of many able men appear on the program. Excellent arrangements are made for the accommodation of visitors. The expense will not exceed 75 cents per day. Send name at once to Brother Lowe, 2316 South 15th St., and provision will be made for your entertainment.

—James A. Gordon, of Marshall, Mo., does not let his duties as cashier of the bank interfere seriously with his superintendency of the Bible school. During the year the school has paid $110 to our National Benevolent Association; $167 to foreign missions and $12.50 to state missions. The superintendent takes special pride in the fact that 85½ per cent of the average attendance of 194 read the Bible daily. This feature he commends to other schools.

—Bro. J. A. Banta, of Ten Sleep, Wyo., is probably the only settled minister among the disciples in that state. He knows of scores of places where we could organize churches if we could only find support for the preachers. The Home Society ought to have $5,000 to put into that field this year. Brother Banta begs for an evangelist to be sent to organize the churches and fully believes that they can be arranged into circuits which will be able to support the preachers.

—Elsewhere will be found an advertisement of Garrison Park on the east coast of Lake Michigan, but a day or night's ride from Chicago over the Pierre Marquette Railroad or by steamer daily to Muskagon by the Goodrich or Hackley line where connection is made with a small steamer or the railroad. This resort is winning golden opinions from all visitors because combining great beauty of scenery and perfect restfulness.

—Bro. C. V. Allison, of Mound City, Mo., reports the affairs of our church there to be most prosperous. Since the first of April three have been added to the membership, $60 given to home missions, a $75 Children's day offering and improvements made to the church and parsonage at a cost of $180. We safely expect such reports where a union has been effected between ministers like Brother Allison and such Disciples as he testifies constitute our Mound City church.

—Bernard P. Smith, who is in charge of our West End church in Atlanta, has voluntarily released the American Christian Missionary Society from any further aid for that work. The board had passed an appropriation for another year's work, but Brother Smith knowing the great pressure of appeals upon us and our inability to answer them, has come to our rescue by declaring the church self supporting, at least while he is minister. We commend this action to a hundred congregations among us.

—Bro. James P. Orr, one of the pioneers in the Church of Christ, being some 80 years of age, is removing from Lebanon, Ind, to the Pacific coast. He came to Cincinnati in the early fifties and was the publisher of Benjamin Franklin's paper for a number of years. He taught school and practiced medicine in Cincinnati and preached the Gospel far and wide without money and without price. In speaking of his acquaintance in Cincinnati he pathetically remarks, "Spring Grove Cemetery holds most of my friends and acquaintances."

—The Western Washington Christian Missionary Society at its recent convention elected the following board of officers: F. Waldon, president, Seattle; R. H. Ellett, C. H. Hilton, A. D. Skaggs, vice-presidents; R. E. Dunlap, corresponding secretary; A. L. Chapman, recording secretary; U. E. Harmon, treasurer; W. A. Moore, superintendent of Sunday-schools; E. E. Francis, superintendent of Christian Endeavor work. This is a strong organization and ought to mean much in the forwarding of the work in the western part of that state.

—Mrs. Mary Varney and her husband, of Baltimore, have recently presented the American Christian Missionary Society a corner lot, 75×115, in Port Huron, Mich. The society is under obligations to organize a Christian church in that city of 22,000 in-habitants within two years of the delivery of the deed. We ought to have had a church in this city long ago, for it is an important place and growing rapidly. It is hoped that one year hence a good church will be started in that city, it having been made possible by the beneficence of these two good persons.

—The editorial sanctum was brightened on the eve of the Fourth by a wedding party, in which Miss Elizabeth Wilhite and James Coe were the bright and particular stars. The young couple are members of the Jacksonville (Ill.) congregation, where our general superintendent formerly ministered, and came to the city that he might pronounce to them the magic ceremonial. Our confidence in their permanent happiness and usefulness is strengthened by their making THE CHRISTIAN-EVANGELIST one of the institutes of their new home.

—The Clifton church, in Louisville, Ky., Bro. T. S. Tinsley, pastor, has organized a mission at Crescent Hill. The Clifton church, on June 2, took up an offering of $134 for this new work. They have adopted as their "Centennial aim "Seven Hundred Members in the Local Church," "Found and Foster Another Congregation," "Keep United, Evangelistic and Missionary." They are urging all their members in the vicinity of the newly founded mission to cast in their influence there and make work a success. We commend this action to a hundred other churches.

—The state board of North Carolina is doing some splendid work in the way of extension. They are about to enter Wilmington, the largest city, and establish a church there. They have recently organized a church in Windsor and are building houses of worship at Freemont and Rocky Mount where congregations were recently established. Houses of worship are under way at the points where the churches were established last year. With the material development of North Carolina our people ought to enter the state and establish a church in every considerable community.

—J. A. L. Romig, of Manitoba, is in a meeting with C. C. Redgrave at Port Arthur, Ontario. Port Arthur will, ere long, be a city of 20,000 inhabitants, for it is a rapidly growing city. Within a few years it will be one of the great commercial centers of the British Northwest. Now is the time for us to lay the foundation of a great work. Brother Redgrave has need of assistance and could use with fine effect a small printing press if some one could furnish it. Who is the man who will supply leaves of healing for the nation by sending this good man the machine with which to print them?

—The Editor, writing from his new summer home at Pentwater, Michigan, advises that it will save him much writing if we will announce that persons preferring to come to Pentwater by steamer rather than railroad would better take the Goodrich or Hackley line of daily steamboats from Chicago to Muskegon which will connect with either the morning or evening trains for Pentwater. The "Kansas" has discontinued its trip directly to Pentwater until the channel is deepened, which may require some time. There are two or three desirable cottages in Pentwater for rent which yet be secured by prompt application.

—Roger H. Fife, evangelist, and Herbert H. Saunders, singer, recently closed an evangelistic meeting resulting in eighteen additions in Durand, Mich. This about doubles the membership of the church and insures its permanency. The pastor is J. A. Canby, a consecrated and able man. The prominent feature of this meeting was the street preaching. Many evenings during the continuance of the meeting the evangelist and a corps of workers repaired

For a Church in New Hampshire.

Already acknowledged $510 10
Hon. M. M Cochran............. 25 00
Wm. Carey 10 00

Total $545 10

—Brother Herbert T. Yeuell, one of our most successful evangelists, is now preaching the primitive Gospel to great audiences in Manchester, and trying to establish our first church in New Hampshire. On account of hall rents, advertising and other expenses being higher than anticipated, this meeting will cost probably much more than the original estimate of $1,000, if held long enough to give our plea a fair trial in that part of New England. Unless our people express greater financial interest we fear the meeting must come to a premature close. We ask our liberal-hearted brethren to make generous and immediate gifts for this purpose. They will be gladly acknowledged in this column.

❦ ❦

Sweet Spring (Mo.) Convention.

The convention of the district No. 2 convenes in Sweet Springs July 16-18. We are making preparation for the reception and the enjoyment of what promises to be a great convention. Sweet Springs has hospitality large enough and wide enough to include every Christian within the borders of the seventeen counties composing district No. 2. We desire that you come in large delegations, with overflowing enthusiasm, to enjoy the best of programs, as well as the most generous hospitality. The sessions are to be held in the Sweet Springs Park, one of "God's first temples."

If you are coming, write. Only those who announce their coming need expect to be met with a carriage and brass band. Finally, come! All come!!

               F. B. ELMORE.

❦ ❦

Eastern Ohio Ministerial Association.

In view of the fact that nearly fifty preachers, the most of whom are members of "The Ministerial Association of the Disciples of Christ in Eastern Ohio" have signed "A Call to Conference and Prayer in behalf of the special objects of the Century Movement," to be held in Hiram, Aug. 5-12, 1906, it has seemed best to hold the sessions of the Ministerial Association during the same week and at Hiram. The members of the association will take notice and are urged to be present. The place is an ideal one for a few days' rest and recreation. No formal program will be issued but questions of current importance will be considered, and such business transacted as may be necessary. In case of necessary absence members are asked to address the association by a letter to the corresponding secretary.

             F. M. GREEN, Cor. Sec.
221 Ash St., Akron, O.

❦ ❦

Annual Report of Liberty (Mo.) Church.

Although we have been worshiping in the court house for the past fourteen months pending the completion of our new church, we have had a good year. There have been forty-eight additions to the church. Our financial budget shows a total of $3,166. Our combined missionary offerings amount to $684. I have

preached 105 sermons here at home and 77 elsewhere. There have been seven deaths in the church during the last church year. The Liberty church is girding herself for greater things. Although we have been under the strain of erecting an expensive church, none of our missionary offerings have been neglected. Peace and harmony prevail and we begin our new church year with gratitude and hope.   GRAHAM FRANK, Minister.

❦ ❦

Bethany College and the Brotherhood.

The present healthy condition of the institution founded by Alexander Campbell is a matter of congratulation with every member of the body known as Disciples of Christ. Five years ago the trustees and faculty felt a crisis had come and were fearful that the college must close. Those entrusted with its management had done heroic and self-sacrificing service for a number of years and were greatly discouraged. Thomas E. Cramblet was called to the presidency, and under his vigorous and wise direction, with the co-operation of the faculty and trustees, and the generous support of the alumni and friends of the institution, the college has once more been put upon its feet and is doing to-day as excellent work in the cause of education as at any period in its history. The work of the college has been of a character to commend itself to the brotherhood during all these sixty-five years of its existence. What would our cause be if Bethany and its work were blotted out?

There is much yet to be done if we discharge our obligation to this school of the

The new church home of the Lansdowne (Ill.) congregation was dedicated July 1. Geo. L. Snively, of THE CHRISTIAN-EVANGELIST, assisted Pastor C. O. Reynard through the day's services. Fifteen hundred dollars were needed to pay the indebtedness on the building and for an adjoining parsonage plat; $1,630 were given and three valuable members added to the membership. Lansdowne is a beautiful and rapidly growing suburb of East St. Louis. Ours is the only church there and members of other religious bodies are co-operating with our brethren in the work of the Lord, several having already taken membership and others will. This bids fair to soon be a strong church. Its success should encourage our brethren in other cities to be first to establish missions in suburbs and rapidly growing communities. Great credit is due Brother Reynard and his talented young wife for the rapid and superb development of this church. Brother Snively has been asked to further assist in a meeting during October.

A fine brick church was dedicated at Poplar Hill, Ontario, on Lord's day, July 1 and 2, free of debt. The edifice is a model of neatness and up-to-dateness, and shows what high aspirations this congregation has for the cause of Christ in this locality. It cost a little over $8,000, and over $3,000 were pledged during the day. J. M. Van Horn, of Toronto, preached morning and evening and Principal F. E. Lumley, assisted by the Sinclair College Band, had charge of the afternoon service and the Monday evening service.

Brother Van Horn preached excellent sermons and the close attention given by the closely packed audience showed how interested all were in the great day. He has made many friends at this place and his general enthusiasm for the work proves how invaluable he is as a worker in Ontario.

Let this be an inspiration to many another church to get alive and experience the joy that comes from dedicating a church free from debt.

prophets. We would commend it to our people as a nourishing mother for their sons and daughters, and urge upon them to remember its claims with their substance and aid us in making it every way worthy of a great memory and a great cause.

           T. W. PHILLIPS,
           W. H. GRAHAM,
           F. D. POWER,
           For the Trustees.

❦ ❦

Changes.

Bush, A. J.—Grand Prairie, to 70 Crawford street, Station A, Dallas, Tex.
Lessig, Ray—Canton, Mo., to Herington, Kan.
Trainum, W. H.—Evanston, to 6024 Ellis avenue, Chicago, Ill.
Bassett, G. H.—Canton, to Box 484, Boonville, Mo.
Chapman, Robert B.—Grafton, Ohio, to Butler, Indiana.
Pegrum, Robert—Charlottetown, P. E. I., to Swampscott, Mass.
Fisher, Lewis P.—Eureka, to Clinton, Ill.
Spafford, C. N.—Meriden, to Larrabee, Ia.
Zeran, John—Sulphur Springs, to Plano, Tex.
Harris, W. L.—Lincoln, to Bethany, Neb.
Schultz, Ferd D.—Ellwood City, Pa., to Bealls ville, Ohio.
Moore, Robert W.—Sioux City, to Adel, Ia.
Smith, Raymond A.—Wilson, N. C., to 1119 Ashland avenue, Indianapolis, Ind.
Clifford, A.—Indianapolis, Ind., to Petoskey, Michigan.
Yeuell, Herbert—Washington, D. C., to Manchester, N. H.
Keene, C. M.—Paw Paw, to Owosso, Mich, 425 Abbott street.
Boyle, D. D.—Laredo, to Cactus, Tex.
Bates, Miner Lee—East Orange, N. J., to 323 West Fifty-sixth street, New York City.
Honeywell, A. A.—Hiram, to McConnelsville, O.
Lanham, W. J.—Washington, Pa., to Cincinnati (Evanston), Ohio, 1921 Clarion avenue.
Simpson, A. N.—Des Moines, Ia., to Box 172 Toronto Junction, Ontario, Canada.
Cook, Garry V.—Hiram, Ohio, to 900 Sheridan street, Monongahela, Pa.

Church Dedications.

C. O. Reynard.

To the Churches of Tidewater District.

Dear Brethren—The annual meeting of the Tidewater District Convention will meet this year at Jerusalem Church, King William county, Va., August 7-9. We request that all churches in the district send delegates, and we extend to them and to all preaching brethren a cordial invitation. They will come to Lestor Manor, and there be met by stage or private conveyance. Trains reach Lestor Manor at 9 a. m. going south and 4 p. m. and 5:30 p. m. going north. Delegates will be met at 9 a. m. and 4 p. m. only.

L. D. ROBINSON, Clerk.

❀ ❀

Modern Religious Persecution.

(Continued from page 879.)

book. Such was not the case in the days when the persecutor was respected, and his judgment heeded; when the books as well as the person of the heretic could be, by law, consigned to the flames. Yet these are those who deprecate the mild measures of the present time against false teaching.

There are those among the Disciples who have even gone so far as to charge these faithful defenders of "our plea" with dishonesty and insincerity. They have asked: How could they charge such ugly things against men who are known to be kind in their families and devout and pure in their personal and religious lives? The answer is very easy. It is all the greater evidence of the fidelity and sincerity of the persecutor that, knowing the personal life and character of the heretic, and the esteem in which he is held by those who know him, in spite of it and of almost probable misconstruction of his motives, he should go faithfully on to warn the unsophisticated and unwary against him. Such courage does not fear the face of man, and is given to but few, and they, the chosen of God.

❀ ❀

Our Plea Among Scandinavians.

(Continued from page 878.)

of God on earth, his one and only family, the true, the real, the genuine Church of Christ universal!

Money can nowhere be spent with greater advantage than in this field, so ripe for the harvest of God. It is the most blessed foreign mission work I know of, and it is right at our own doors. We do not have to cross the ocean for it, nor labor under the deadly equatorial sun in carrying it on. We all ought to co-operate together and utilize to its fullest extent this God-given opportunity right in our own midst, in our homeland, among the best citizens of any land on earth.

It is by earnest request from others that I submit this sketch of my life and this work to the readers of THE CHRISTIAN-EVANGELIST, and I do it with most humble heart, feeling my utter dependency upon God in so great an undertaking. I earnestly ask your prayers, one and all, for wisdom, grace and strength, and all things needed. I rejoice to know that I am in the fullest possible fellowship with every true Disciple of Christ throughout the world, who may be reading these lines. I say from the heart, God bless you all!

Some of My Likings.

(Continued from page 880.)

must bear in mind that the political Puritans passed away. The disciplinary Puritans are no more, for they are not needed. But the doctrinal Puritans live and flourish, for they represent the purity and simplicity of faith as opposed to formalism and sacerdotalism, while they stand for reliance on the Word of God alone with liberty of conscience to interpret and practise it.

Back to the Puritans.

Luther, Wiclif, Calvin, Latimer, Ridley, Wesley, Howe, Charnock, Toplady, Whitefield, Rowland Hill, Alexander Campbell, Spurgeon, all were Puritans. All differed, but all called the people back to the Bible. All made some mistakes, but each in his way and according to the emphasis which he felt impelled to place on some vital element of truth that had been forgotten or perverted was an exponent of apostolic doctrine. These men were all massive Bible scholars and masterly Bible teachers. I think that the chief lack in the theological colleges to-day is the neglect of the works of the Puritan divines and expositors. The very names of Sibbes, Brooks, Owen, Caryl, Charnock and Adams are unknown to large numbers of students and graduates. Who could study Owen's great treatise on "The Holy Spirit" without becoming conscious of a new power of understanding the New Testament? When I came as a novice under the care of the late C. H. Spurgeon one of his first items of counsel was that I should master Charnock on "The Divine Attributes," a profoundly spiritual work. I was by no means advised to plunge solely into the treasures of the Tudor period for Spurgeon at the same time put into my hands a beautiful volume then just out, "The Synonyms of the Greek Testament," by Archbishop Trench. And as years have rolled on I have discovered that the preachers who have most potently shaped the character of the people and have established churches which live and influence society around them, are the men who have drunk closely at the fountain of pure Puritanism.

If they have also quaffed of the Parnassian stream or the classic springs of Helicon, then their literary culture is of no small additional value. The most acceptable preacher is the man of blended classic scholarship and Puritan learning, of course allowing that he is endowed with the power of persuasive appeal.

Conventions.

Iowa Christian Convention.

The Athens of Iowa—Iowa City—entertained the convention this year. The sessions lasted two days and were presided over by President T. J. Dow and Vice President J. H. Ingraham. The reports of corresponding secretary and treasurer showed substantial increase in additions to the churches and offerings for the work. The general fund receipts amounted to $12,102.12, and the reported additions were 6,513. Drake University reports showed a steady progress in every department. The year's enrollment of students was 1,634. President Hill M. Bell spoke with justifiable pride of the "Era of Good Feeling" inaugurated three years ago by the students voluntarily giving up "class rushes" and doing away with fraternities. The plan of work committees of the I. C. C. and the Bible School Association recommended in their reports that the Bible school work be done under the direction of the I. C. C. board of managers, the I. C. C. to receive all sums raised for state Bible school work and be responsible for all bills. The discussion of this recommendation was protracted. Finally the assembly disposed of the matter by referring it to the I. C. C. and Bible school boards. The members of these boards will thrash the matter out at a meeting in Des Moines later on and the result will be made known to the brotherhood of the state. At the opening session Monday evening, June 25, Percy Leach, minister of the entertaining church, welcomed the delegates in behalf of the Christian people of the city, and Mayor Ball, in behalf of the citizens. D. R. Dungan responded to the greetings and words of welcome in a very felicitous way. The opening address was by Bro. H. D. Williams, of Ames, on "The Relation of Our Movement to Other Religious Bodies." I send you separately, for publication, a synopsis of this address. The convention address the day following, by Bro. G. B. Van Arsdall, of Cedar Rapids, was, simply expressed, grand. A resolution presented by Hill M. Bell that the address be taken by the secretary of the Centennial committee, W. R. Warren, and that it be printed in pamphlet form and widely distributed throughout the country, was unanimously passed.

W. J. Wright and S. J. Corey represented the Home and Foreign Missionary Societies, respectively. They delivered admirable addresses. Other speakers were: I. N. McCash, in the interests of temperance work; Chaplain C. S. Medbury, Joel Brown. J. B. Buxton, A. M. Haggard and D. R. Dungan, for Drake; W. B. Clemmer, for Endeavor Society; S. H. Zendt and J. H. Bryan, for Bible school work; also J. H. Hardin, of Missouri, Eugene Curless, E. F. Leake, D. B. Allen, Carl C. Davis, H. E. Van Horn and R. W. Lilly. A few of the speakers who were to talk for "twenty minutes only" took from forty minutes to sixty-five to get rid of their productions, to the great inconvenience of "business," and to the exclusion of other listed speakers. Mrs. Arthur J. Fawcett and Mrs. J. M. Vankirk rendered acceptable singing. Lawyer C. L. Hays, of Eldora, a member of the committee on "Plan of Work," presented the following resolution, which was unanimously and heartily adopted by the convention:

"Resolved, That we again express our approval of the temperance work carried on by the Anti-Saloon League and our full sympathy with and confidence in the superintendent of the Iowa League, Dr. I. N. McCash, in his consecrated work, and we commend to the Christian citizens everywhere their full support of this efficient means of combatting the evils of the saloon and the glory of the rising tide setting toward personal temperance in America."

The devotional meetings of the conven-

tion were led by Arthur Long, Burlington; Milton H. H. Lee, Fort Dodge; W. B. Clemmer, Council Bluffs; B. W. Pettitt, Avery; and S. M. Perkins, Albia. The attendance at the convention was about 200 from outside the city. But the enthusiasm over the grand reports of progress and the bright outlook for the current year, made every session interesting and profitable. The convention next year goes to Des Moines, the Christian bodies there to determine where the meetings shall be held. W. J. Wright so interested the delegates in a simultaneous evangelistic campaign for Iowa that a resolution of President T. J. Dow to hold such a campaign the coming winter was heartily endorsed.

The I. C. C. officers elected were:

State Board—President, J. Madison Williams, Des Moines; vice president, F. L. Moffitt, Centerville; recording secretary, J. J. Grove, Ames; corresponding secretary, B. S. Denney, Des Moines; treasurer, J. M. Lucas, Des Moines.

Assembly Officers—President D. R. Dungan, Des Moines; vice president, F. D. Ferrell, Bloomfield; second vice president, E. F. Leake, Newton; first secretary, T. J. O'Connor, Eldora; second secretary, M. H. H. Lee, Ft. Dodge; superintendent Christian Endeavor, W. B. Clemmer, Council Bluffs.

University Trustees—J. W. Hill, Des Moines, one year; H. M. Whennery, Des Moines, two years.

Other officers named by the convention were the trustees of the anti-saloon league, they being, Hill M. Bell, president of the university, and D. H. Buxton.

The delegates to the American convention of the anti-saloon league to be held next November at St. Louis will be Dr. I. N. McCash and John T. Houser, of Des Moines; F. D. Ferrell, of Bloomfield; R. W, Lilly, of Corydon and Arthur Long, of Burlington.   T. J. O'CONNOR, Sec.

Eldora, Ia.

⁂

Minnesota State Convention.

The fortieth annual convention of the Minnesota Christian Missionary Society was held at the First Christian Church, St. Paul, Minn., June 19-22, 1906. The first session was that of "The Ministerial Association," Tuesday afternoon, June 19. Subject, "The Christian Minister in Min-

nesota." The convention proper opened on Tuesday evening with an address of welcome by A. D. Harmon, and the convention address by M. B. Ainsworth, on the subject, "The Integrity of the Scriptures or the Unity of the Word." State Evangelist C. R. Neel followed with an address on "Minnesota as a Mission Field." Wednesday morning was devoted entirely to the interests of the Christian Endeavor, and Wednesday afternoon to the work of the Bible school. Helpful addresses were given at the morning services by Miss Mildreth Haggard, of Minneapolis, and Wm. H. Knotts, of Howard Lake, and in the afternoon by E. W. Van Aken, president of Parker College (Freewill Baptist), Rochester Irwin, of Rochester; Baxter Waters, of Duluth; Fred M. Lindenmeyer, of Willow Creek; Mrs. D. W. Ham and Mrs. M. H. Towner, of Minneapolis.

Wednesday evening the work of the A. C. M. S. and the church extension society were presented by W. J. Wright, of Cincinnati, O., and G. W. Muckley, of Kansas City. Both addresses were well received.

Thursday morning was an evangelistic session. Addresses were given by E. C.

Nicholson, of Redwood Falls, and B. V. Black, of Mankato. C. S. Osterhus, of Ossian, Ia., presented "The Unity Movement Amongst Norwegians," to a large and interested audience.

Thursday afternoon and evening was devoted to the work of the C. W. B. M. The principal speakers were Miss Mary Kingsbury, of Bilaspur, India, and Mrs. Louise Kelley, of Emporia, Kan. Miss Kelley gave a splendid address on Wednesday evening. Brother Corey of Cincinnati, also presented the cause of world-wide missions on behalf of the F. C. M. S., at this service.

On Friday morning after the business of the convention was concluded we listened to an address by Bro. J. H. Mohorter, on the "Work of the Benevolent Association;" also to an address by Brother Henry, representing the Business Men's Association. The convention closed Friday noon.

The following is a condensed report of the corresponding secretary, J. H. Bicknell: Number of churches, 41; present membership, 3,274; baptized during the past year, 345; otherwise received, 185. Total additions, 530. Total losses, 175. Net gain in membership, 355. Scholars in Bible schools, 2,217; C. E., 491; Juniors, 213. Money raised for local work, $28,411.81; for home missions, $673.89; foreign missions, $948.01; state missions, $1,070.82; church extension society, $170.37; C. W. B. M., $780.35; for other purposes, $9,198.43. Grand total money raised for all purposes, $40,280.68.

Three new churches have been organized during the year—Fairmount, Simpson and Cresco. During the year the state board has had the state evangelist, C. R. Neel, in the field constantly evangelizing. Under his splendid ministry the work has been greatly strengthened.

Most of the churches show a good year's work. The crying need of this field is men—consecrated men to do the work of the ministry. No less than eighteen churches are without pastors. C. R. Neel was re-employed as state evangelist.

The following officers were elected for the coming year: President, M. R. Waters; vice president, A. D. Harmon; treasurer, Charles Oliver; recording secretary, Baxter Waters; corresponding secretary, J. H. Bicknell; superintendent of Bible school, C. B. Osgood; superintendent of C. E., B. V. Black.   J. H. BICKNELL.

The Dakota Convention.

The convention of the churches of South Dakota and North Dakota was held at Carthage, June 21-24, with about seventy delegates enrolled. The program compared favorably wih those of older states. The National Boards were all represented.

The addresses of William J. Wright, of the Home Board, and Stephen J. Corey, of the Foreign Society, were both of a high order and heartily received. Dean A. M. Haggard, of Drake University, was also present and delivered a stirring address on Education, in which a strong and appealing ʟlea was maʋe for the broadest and most thorough training under Christian influences, that the student may attain adequate equipment to meet the demands of the age.

The earnestness and inspiration of all the visiting speʋkers will have a lasting influence for good in the development of the work in the Dakotas. All regret that C. C. Smith could not fill his place on the program, he being called to Jamaica. Also G. W. Muckley, the apostle of Church Extension, was obliged to be absent in order to respond to an urgent call elsewhere. The writer delivered addresses in behalf of the Board of Church Extension and the National Benevolent Association. About $140 were pledged for state work, and over $200 for Carthage and Lead. The following will compose the Board for the coming year: President, A. H. Seymour, Arlington; Vice President, E. E. Headley, Bradley; Treasurer, J. B. Moore, Aberdeen; Recording Secretary, William Carry, Tyndall; Corresponding Secretary, F. B. Sapp, Aberdeen; Members at large, C. P. Gregory, Aberdeen, and J. B. Meharg, Verdon. The state officers for the C. W. B. M. will be: President, Mrs. F. B. Cannon, Aberdeen; Vice President, Mrs. Hackman, Sioux Falls; Treasurer, Mrs. Minnie Branson, Platte; Recording Secretary, Miss Verna Dahlstrom, Clark; Corresponding Secretary, Mrs. Edith White, Lead.

The next convention will be held at Parker, S. D. G. W. Elliott, editor of the "Oracle" at Brookings, made a good report on Literature, as chairman of that committee. He is doing good service in the distribution of tracts and other literature. The work is looking up and the future is full of hope. Two families drove over 100 miles to the convention. The South Dakota brethren are not floating with the current, but rowing up stream. Success is sure to come to them in the heroic work being done.

Aberdeen.   F. B. SAPP, Cor. Sec.

West Kentucky.

The erection of the new $25,000 church building at Mayfield, Ky., will begin soon. —West Kentucky College will add a course in Bible study for the coming year, tuition will be free for all Bible students, and scholarships including board and tuition have been provided for several— J. W. Hudspeth, South Kentucky evangelist, will begin a meeting soon at Shelton's chapel, a congregation recently established by J. C. Shelton under the auspices of the South Kentucky work and of the Mayfield congregation.—The South Kentucky evangelistic work intends soon to locate an evangelist for all his time in the eight counties of West Kentucky, known as "The Jackson Purchase." Such a man is greatly needed in this field.—West Kentucky College will soon begin the erection of a new dormitory for young men. This will give the college three good buildings. Abut $20,000 will be raised and expended for the college.—D. W. Campbell, of Wickliffe, will begin a meeting in a few days at Cuba assisting L. M. Hammonds, and J. W. Holsapple, of Texas, will begin a meeting with the writer at Benton. —The trustees of the Smallwood fund have given $5,000 each to West Kentucky College at Mayfield, and South Kentucky College at Hopkinsville, to be used in each case for the education of young ministers. —The meeting of the South Kentucky Sunday-school conference will meet in the West Kentucky College buildings, Mayfield, Ky., July 30. The conference will be under the supervision of Robert M. Hopkins, state Sunday-school evangelist, and E. O. Fox, general organizer, of Louisville, Ky.—G. A. Lewellen, Mayfield, Ky.

NEWS FROM MANY FIELDS

India Notes.

The Bible college commencement in Jubbulpore took place on May 8. This year there were two graduates, one of whom goes to Mahoba and one to Hatta. During the past year there were twenty students. Brother Adams came over from Bilaspur to deliver the commencement address, and we also had with us Mr. R. Burges, the general secretary of the India Sunday-school Union, who made some very appropriate remarks. The students took a great deal of interest in the exercises and decorated the building with plants and flowers. The closing meetings developed a spiritual interest which they will no doubt carry with them for some time. After commencement the students scattered, going to various stations where they will preach and sell books and engage in other works until work begins again in the Bible college in July.

We are planning this year to have a two weeks' summer school for the mission helpers. Several of our missionaries will be present and deliver lectures on various themes, all calculated to freshen up the minds of those who have been out of school for some time, and hence are beginning to rust, as it were. Considerable interest is taken in this and we are sure it will be a success.

Death has once more invaded our mission ranks. On May 28 Miss Lyda Gertrude Archer died of diabetes, at Landour, Mussoorie. She was the daughter of Mr. and Mrs. G. W. Brown. She had been ill for some time, but of late had not suffered particularly. When the time came for a six weeks' vacation at Landour she rejoiced greatly, feeling that by going to the mountains she would become free from disease and have a happy time. Her hopes were indeed fulfilled, but in a different way from what she had anticipated. A pure, sweet, simple-minded girl, she was greatly loved by all who knew her, and will be greatly missed by many.

Sickness has laid his hand on another station. Brother Stubbin's two children in Hatta, have both been attacked with smallpox, but have recovered. One of them had a very severe case. We have just heard that the mother, too, is now afflicted with the disease. There has been an epidemic of smallpox in this and several other localities. Brother Stubbin tried to have his family vaccinated, but it was impossible to obtain the necessary virus. Living, as they do, twenty-two miles from a railroad, with no Europeans near them, their trial has been doubly severe. Dr. Mary McGavran, from Damoh, however, stayed with them throughout the time of illness.

India is now full of disease and suffering. Famine and pestilence are scattered far and wide. Half a million people are receiving aid from the government in some way or other. Usually they are employed on what are called "relief works." These usually take of the form of constructing roads, railways, reservoirs and sometimes public buildings, in the localities where there is scarcity. Thousands of other people have left their homes and are wandering in other localities in search of work. Had it not been for the prompt action taken by the government there is no doubt but that we should have had a severe famine

No Stomach Trouble

After you take Drake's Palmetto Wine one week. Cures to stay cured all forms of Stomach Trouble. A test bottle free if you write to Drake Co., Wheeling, W. Va.

with much suffering and death. Disease often visits these relief camps. Near Maudaha, 26,000 were employed. Cholera broke out among them, the camp had to be broken up, and the disease was scattered far and wide. Rath is now suffering from it. Jubbulpore has had it, though not as an epidemic, for some time. Smallpox is in numerous places. All are praying for seasonable rains this year, so that there may not be so much distress and illness.

Lately three deaths occurred among the native Christians in Harda. Two were of native helpers, and one the child of a helper. Yet in spite of all these things the missionaries are hopeful. Here and there conversions are occurring and everywhere the work seems to be growing. We believe the hand of God is with us.

❋ ❋

Minnesota as a Mission Field.

The hosts of Disciples gathered in annual convention with the First Church, St. Paul, June 19-22.

We are not great in numbers in Minnesota—only 43 churches, with a membership of 3,000, with a net increase of 355 in the past year. But while our gathering was not so large, the meetings and fellowship were very precious and cordial, and highly appreciated. There were many "scattered Disciples" who came up to this annual feast, and many preachers to whom this was their only opportunity during the year to look into the faces of their comrades. The convention was characterized by warmth of fellowship, brotherhood and reverence for the Lord's work and by faithful attendance at all sessions of the convention.

Minnesota is a great state; in area 80,000 square miles, rich in agriculture, commerce and mines. Its population is rapidly increasing. There are one million and a quarter Scandinavians in the state, 75,000 people who cannot speak the English tongue—in fact every other man you meet is a foreigner. The twin cities are Scandinavian headquarters in this country, and also the citadel of Roman Catholicism in the Northwest. The mining regions of the Range country are filled with foreigners of low type, morally and religiously.

C. S. Osterhus, of Ossian, Iowa, made an address before the convention on "Unity Work Among Scandinavians." He says there is a great "coming out" among these people. They are breaking away from creeddom and are now as sheep having no shepherd. He says they are coming together in groups, some partly organized for religious work, and that now there are as many as 200 of these groups holding meetings and seeking religious light and freedom; they are ready for a pure Gospel. There are 76,000 Scandinavians in Minneapolis alone, and 56,000 of these are not identified with any church whatsoever. Here is a great mission field. Brother Osterhus needs a paper to augment his work.

Our convention program was good, in fact capital. We were favored with the presence of Wright, Muckley, Corey and Mchorter, Mrs. Louise Kelly and Miss Mary Kingsbury, of Bilaspur, India, and others who made noble impressions on our people and blessed us with streams of enthusiasm, and the larger vision. To J. H. Bicknell, corresponding secretary, much praise is due for his zealous efforts and for the splendidly prepared report. A. D. Harmon presided over the convention in the absence of the president. Brother and Sister A. P. Frost, who now live at Winona, were present and gave many a word of cheer at the needed moment.

There is a note of optimism and faith

among the Minnesota workers and preachers. With all its difficulties and discouragements, there are signs of growth. In the past year C. R. Neel, state evangelist, has held some good meetings; among them, Winona, Mankato, Howard Lake, Garden City, and others. He will continue this year under the state board. C. B. Osgood is doing a strong, manly work at Winona. E. C. Nicholson is in the midst of building a fine church at Redwood Falls. The work at Fairmont has made rapid growth under J. P. Child. B. V. Black has recently located at Mankato and is pushing things with vigor. Among the new preachers are: P. J. Rice, at Portland avenue, Minneapolis; Fred. M. Lindenmeyer, at Willow Creek; Rochester Irwin, at Rochester; W. D. Baumer, at Pleasant Grove; A. J. Wilson, at Plainview.

The church at Duluth has just held their annual meeting. Reports show decided gains in all departments. The church is harmonious and hopeful. With a membership of only 150 they raised over $2,500 in the past year.

BAXTER WATERS, Rec. Sec.

❋ ❋

To College this Fall.

Ask for our new illustrated catalogue of "Iowa Christian College." Resident and correspondence courses. Board and tuition $30 per term. Progressive normal methods. Write Pres. Chas. J. Burton, Oskaloosa, Iowa.

Ohio.

Ohio to-day sits in mourning for her dead governor. John M. Pattison, soldier, high grade citizen, clean business man, unspotted politician, governor, Christian gentleman, is dead, and another rules. He never saw the state house from the day of his inauguration. But his manly dignity and high ideals in his campaign last fall and while in office, has made a lasting impression for good. May the Lord of his life lead us who live after him.——Three Ohio preachers have resigned since the last letter. O. D. Maple has done what seemed the impossible at Marion. But he has decided to turn the reins over to another.—— J. J. Cole has fixed the day for his final sermon at Millersburg. E. J. Meacham will preach a farewell at Wilmington July 29. These are three good fields with plenty of hard work for some devoted and wise men.——Collinwood will have the novelty of a union meeting following the Buffalo convention with J. M. Rudy, of Missouri, as evangelist. This will be the first effort of that kind in Ohio and it will be watched with peculiar interest. Three churches—Congregational, M. E. and "ours," will unite.——T. L. Fowler has very wisely yielded to the overtures of the people at Minerva and has withdrawn his resignation. We want to keep such men in Ohio. Minerva is to be congratulated.——The Congregational preachers of Cleveland and the Presbyterian preachers of the same city played a game of ball at League Park June 25. The gate receipts went to the Y. M. C. A. The query is, what was it, Christian union, federation or foolishness?——On the same day and time the preachers who are simply Christians held their annual picnic at Euclid Beach, to which the wives, children and sweethearts were invited. It was a very enjoyable occasion and all voted it more profitable than a ball game.—— Robert Chapman, of North Eaton, goes to Butler, Ind., July 1. He has been at North Eaton for nearly five years and has done a substantial work. We are sorry to lose him from Ohio, but commend him heartily to the Hoosiers.——Rushsylvania is beginning a new church building. It has been long needed. S. L. Lyons is pushing the project.——All the churches of Columbus joined in a union picnic June 20. About 1,000 people were in attendance.—C. A. Freer, Painesville, O.

Southeast Nebraska.

E. D. Price, pastor of the church at Bedford, Ia., stopped at Beatrice for a brief visit with relatives and friends, on his way home from Kansas, where he had been making commencement addresses.—— Chas. E. Cobbey, who recently took charge of the church at Wymore, is doing a very successful work. He has only been at work there three months and twenty have already been added to the Lord at regular services. Keep your eyes on Wymore. Brother Cobbey is a child of the Beatrice church, and just now we can announce that his brother, Jean Cobbey, has entered the ministry.——H. C. Holmes, pastor at Fairbury, is very busy caring for the increase of his flock. The writer went down to his church a short time ago and addressed the business men's club. The visit was an enjoyable one.——The church here at Beatrice is building. We are having fine audiences and feel that we are doing good work. There have been thirty-seven added to the church locally since my coming here, January 1, a great many of whom have been conversions.——Charles Reign Scoville is to hold a meeting for us in our new church in 1907.——Mrs. Princess Long recently completed a tour of Nebraska towns in concert work. Her last date was at Beatrice, where she greatly delighted, during

the evening, a house of 400 people. Mrs. Long's work is very different from any evening's entertainment the writer ever heard. There was a unanimous demand that she come back to the Chautauqua next season. She will always be greeted with a full house at Beatrice.——H. S. Souders, of Beatrice, has begun work at Lawn. He has been a faithful member of the church here.——M. B. Baumer is expecting to enter the active ministry again. On account of sickness in his family and the failure of his own health he has been teaching for the past year. These last two mentioned are good men and I presume will be kept busy.—J. E. Davis, Beatrice, Neb.

Memorial Buildings for Our Centennial.

(Continued from page 871.)

ful works wrought by our God since those heroic days when "our fathers," almost single-handed, planted amidst the confusion, discord and strife of a divided church, the banner of the primitive Gospel. What a forceful impulse would be given to this reformation by the erecting of such memorial structures. Plant them by the rolling rivers, on whose banks our immortal pioneers preached the unpolluted Word and beneath whose glancing wavelets they buried in baptism the confessors of fifty years ago. Plant them in the rural haunts, where the dear old country church has kept pure the spiritual atmosphere and is training a multitude of young men and women who afterwards drift to the cities and make the blood and sinew of our strongest congregations. Plant them where a handful of determined and dauntless disciples have kept the faith and kept the ordinances, when all the city ignored or all the neighborhood despised. Any of these places—all of them—are suitable for such memorial buildings. What matter whether it be in sequestered nook, by running brooks and sunny hay fields and fruitful orchards; or on western plains, fanned by the perfumed breezes of summer and swept by the fierce winter blasts; or in the prosperous county seat, that center of irresistible influence; or in the crowded city, on the busiest thoroughfares of human life? Every place belongs to Christ, and in every place, as we push forward the interests of his church there is the thrill of those who stand on hallowed ground;

"Brothers, we are treading
Where the saints have trod."

Oh, that the heart of our brotherhood may be moved to make such gifts to God,

sacred and permanent, to bless the generations to come. Here the princely gift of one who consecrates his wealth to the Savior, and here the combined gifts of others of lesser means. And every memorial building, with the "century mark" upon it, will be sacred to the highest purposes, as in humility of heart and gladness of gift and joy of service the builders shall say:

"Oh Thou whose own vast temple stands,
Built over earth and sea;
Accept the walls that human hands
Have raised to worship Thee."
St. Louis.

Evangelistic

We invite ministers and others to send reports of meetings, additions and other news of the churches. It is especially requested that additions be reported as "by confession, baptism" or "by letter."

Hot from the Wire.

Special to THE CHRISTIAN-EVANGELIST.

Portland, Ore., July 8.—Rains here to-day. First Church enthusiastically becomes living link in Foreign Society immediately.—E. S. Muckley.

Special to THE CHRISTIAN-EVANGELIST.

Pentwater, Mich., July 9.—Yeuell's meeting in Manchester starts hopefully. Twice the amount of money raised will be needed. Let us stand loyally by him. I call for additional pledges.—J. H. Garrison.

Colorado.

La Junta.—One added by confession since last report and one by statement. More than $20.00 raised Children's Day. We are also making payments on our debt. J. F. Stivers and his singer, Arthur Wake, assisted in services here July first and will help in the meeting in October. Prospects most favorable.—A. L. Ferguson.

Illinois.

West Village.—Three baptized since last report —all young people; one received by letter. For foreign missions, $40.00. Church in prosperous condition.—James Franklin King, minister.

Hindsboro.—One more added; work moves along nicely. We may need an evangelistic singer for two meetings this fall and winter.—Henry B. Easterling.

Quincy.—Our report June 30 shows 29 auditions at regular services—12 by baptism, 11 by letter, 6 by statement.—Walter M. Jordan.

Sullivan.—Six additions at regular services today. We organized C. W. B. M. with 22 members in afternoon. President of state organization spoke in morning.—J. G. McNutt.

Princeton.—One added by baptism at prayer-meeting last Wednesday. We have engaged Harlow and son for February.—Cecil C. Carpenter.

Japan.

Tokio.—I baptized two men this morning. We are establishing another station. The Yotsuya mission expects to employ three evangelists next year. The work is prospering.—W. D. Cunningham.

Kansas.

Mendon.—Three added this month—2 by baptism.—C. C. Atwood, Topeka.

Shaw.—Since our meeting began here we have had 8 additions from other religious bodies, 1 reclamation and 12 by confession and baptism. I begin work at Peabody, Kan., August 1.—George Carter.

Kentucky.

Grayson.—Three additions by letter, one by baptism, to this congregation recently.—Wm. Sumpter.

Minnesota.

Rochester.—One addition lately; went beyond our apportionment Children's day; am called to remain another year.—Rochester Irwin.

Michigan.

Saginaw.—Five additions yesterday, 3 by statement, 2 by confession; one Methodist preacher among the number, a young man of good ability. There were only 189 present in Bible school, but the contribution was $93. There were 34 graduated from the primary department. We are laboring to pay an $1,800 indebtedness on our property this year.—J. Murray Taylor.

Missouri.

Arrow Rock.—One confession yesterday at Arrow Rock.—C. E. Burgess.

Billings.—Four additions and 3 baptisms today in our meeting.—T. S. Vance.

Bell.—We closed a one week's meeting here last Sunday. Three young men made confession. Brother Brewster, of Macedonia, assisted.—E. M. Romine.

Silver City.—Closed our meeting with an organization of 21 members. L. Sewall, of Washington, was called to the work. He takes charge the first of August. Silver City is a hard field, but with Brother Sewall I believe a strong church can be built. The other churches are doing nothing. Jno. T. Stivers, Memphis, Mo.

Mountain Grove.—Two more additions at Mount View yesterday, 1 reclamation, 1 by confession; additions at nearly every service. I begin meeting at Elkland at once; assist A. C. Yoakum; meeting in September at my Illinois birthplace.—E. W. Yoakum.

Nebraska.

Red Cloud—Nine added during June; 6 by confession and baptism.—E. C. Davis.

New York.

Buffalo.—Four added (Jefferson Street) during the past two weeks, 1 by primary obedience. Lowell McPherson and family are here from Havana and are enjoying the reunion of old friends. We start for Lake James, Ind., to-day for an outing of three or four weeks.—P. S. Ferrall.

Ohio.

I just closed a two weeks' meeting at Macon, Ohio, with 58 additions—22 former disciples from the Finecastle church and 27 by confession and from denominations and 21 by baptism. The church was organized, and a building project is now on foot. Macon is a small village and has no church organization or house of worship. The prospects for fruitage is good.—J. D. Garrison, Lawrenceburg, Ind.

Deerfield.—One came to us from the Congregationalists last Lord's day. The outlook is encouraging.—Charles E. Taylor.

South Carolina.

Bonneau.—We have organized a new congregation here with 24 charter members; 11 baptisms and meeting is two weeks' old. This is a small but growing town and prospects are good for a new house of worship before winter. Bro. S. L. Crawford, a prosperous planter, is the Nestor of the work here. W. H. Brunson will probably preach at this point.—Chas. E. Smith.

Texas.

Odessa.—Closed a ten days' meeting; added 5 by confession, 1 reclaimed. Organized with 21 members. Volney Johnson, of Midland, will serve. We had almost doubled the attendance and interest ever known in Odessa.—S. W. Jackson and Wife.

Royse City.—We are with you heart and soul in the four years' campaign. Closed a short meeting at Faste with 14 additions—12 by baptism. E. P. Shannon, whom we baptized last Lord's day, leading the singing. He is not only a good choir leader but very helpful in conducting devotional exercises, etc. Any church desiring his services may secure him after second Lord's day, August. We begin meeting at Caddo Mills next Thursday.—Graham McMurray.

Sulphur Springs.—A three weeks' protracted meeting held here by H. A. Northcutt and Prof. Zeran and wife closed this morning. There were 41 additions—30 by confession and baptism. There were 16 heads of families, 9 men of high standing and influence; 14 families represented; 1 came from the Roman Catholic Church; 1 had formerly been a saloon keeper. Brother Northcutt moved many to tears by his sacred eloquence. Prof. Zeran and Mrs. Zeran are very helpful indeed. The meeting is a great victory for the cause of religion, as there has been but little manifestation of the revival spirit for some time. There were 6 additions the last night of the meeting.— J. W. Faulkner.

Llano.—One addition by confession yesterday; 101 at Sunday-school; Bible school's attendance has almost doubled since January 1, the result of faithful work by officers and teachers.—J. J. Crane.

Virginia.

Monroe.—Seven baptisms last Lord's day. We are arranging now for a protracted meeting; will have electric lights in our building soon.—J. B. Givens.

Washington.

Starbuck.—Closed short meeting here with 16 added. This is our second meeting with this church in five months. Bro. G. A. Butler, of Mound City, Mo., led the singing.—Ellis B. Harris and Wife.

❀ ❀

Third Report of Relief Fund of Christian Churches of San Francisco.

Previously reported	$2,366 32
Receipts for month:	
Christian Church, Pt. Marion, Pa.	20 37
Mrs. T. E. Jones, Sanger, Cal.	2 00
Central Christian Church, Anderson, Ind.	82 34
Christian Church, Dodge City, Kan.	21 12
Redlands Christian Church.	100 00
Sunday-school, Broadway Christian Church, Louisville, Ky.	30 00
E. C. Nelson, Toledo, Ore.	5 00
C. E. Society, Zillah, Wash.	34 65
Christian Church, Lake City, Ia.	11 45
S. S. Cole, Straughn, Ind.	5 00
Central Christian Church, Walla Walla, Wash.	127 48
First Christian Church, Portland, Ore.	51 63
Christian Church, Philadelphia, Pa.	30 00
Christian Church, Dinuba, Cal.	11 00
Christian Church, San Luis Del Rey, Cal.	15 00
Ladies, Christian Church, Woodland, Cal	57 50
Forest Ave. Christian Church, Buffalo, N. Y.	3 50
Christian Church, Kent, Ohio	2 25
J. M. Read, San Francisco, Cal.	5 00
Christian Church, Roseburg, Ore.	7 50
Chinese of Sunday-school, First Christian Church, New York	25 00
Alva C. Brown, Peoria, Ill.	2 00
A. C. M. S.	1,000 00
E. L. Brown, Ex-Treasurer City Board of Evangelization	133 25
Total to date (June 25, 1906).	$4,152 16

HIRAM VAN KIRK,
Financial Secretary.

2230 Dana St., Berkeley, Cal.

Sunday-School
July 22, 1906.

JESUS TEACHING HOW TO PRAY.
—Luke II:1-13.

Memory verses, 9, 10.

Golden Text.—Lord, teach us to pray.
—Luke II:I.

Having left Galilee for the last time,
Jesus had made a visit to the vicinity of
Jerusalem and had then gone across Jordan to the east, to the place where
John had first baptized (John 10:40).
Here it was that the disciples asked
him to teach them. His answer was substantially that contained in the Sermon
on the Mount (Matt. 6). According to
Matthew, it appears that the Sermon on
the Mount was a connected discourse delivered immediately after the calling of
the Twelve, but many parts of it are repeated by the other evangelists in different settings. Such is the case with the
Lord's Prayer and the other instructions
about prayer. Perhaps Matthew meant
merely to collect a number of the sayings
of Jesus and not to indicate that they
were all spoken on one occasion.

The petition that the name of God
may be revered and his kingdom advanced. This precedes all personal requests. After this there are petitions
for provision for temporal wants, for forgiveness of sins and for freedom from
undue temptation. A simpler or a more
comprehensive prayer was never composed. It is simple enough for the child,
and profound enough for the philosopher.

The parable of the importunate friend
is not meant to illustrate the spirit in
which God answers prayer, but the certainty of his doing so. When one makes
an inconvenient request of a friend, the
power of friendship may fail, but even
in such a case importunity may win. How
much more will God give to him who
earnestly and patiently asks, for his love
can not fail as human friendship may.
"Ask—seek—knock." Here is a great
principle of all life, true alike in temporal
and spiritual things. It is only the asker
who receives. It is only the seeker who
finds. It is only when one knocks that
the doors of success are opened. Enlargement and success do not happen in
the spiritual any more than in the financial field. Effort, energy and aggression

Christian Endeavor
By GEO. L. SNIVELY

July 22, 1906.

THE PRAYER OF CHRIST—Matt.
14:23; 26:36-44.

DAILY READINGS.

M.	Prayer and Praise.	Rev. 4:8-11.
T.	Intercession.	Exod. 32:30-35.
W.	Confession.	Lev. 26:38-42.
T.	Thanksgiving.	Mark 8:6-9.
F.	In the Name of Christ.	Eph. 5:14-21.
S.	Earnestness.	Gen. 32:24-28.
S.	Submission.	Matt. 26:36-44.

While our Savior drank the bitter cup
of human guilt that he prayed might pass
by him, the prayer availed for such an increase of strength and fortitude as to minimize or neutralize its baleful effects upon
him. Likewise our own prayers will either
divide our burden or double our strength.

God hears and answers every prayer of
his children—"Yes" or "No." We should be
as grateful for the nays as the yeas. Often-
times it is afterward given us to see the
folly of what we have sought, and the refusal of which brought us low with grief.
Rest assured every disposition of our prayers is as wise and loving whether or not we
ever see the sequel.

Prayer means more than mere personal
petition; it is the true confessional and in-
tercessional; it is the best time and place for
praise, thanksgiving and adoration; its intimate communion possibilities if fully realized will send us forth with face lights
glowing like those of Moses. Recall the
spirit of our former prayers and if we can
detect selfishness there, let us protect our
future prayers from this blight by truer
harmony with "Thy will not mine be done."

Jesus was in prayer seeking deliverance
rather from contact with the moral iniquity
of the race than from the burden or the
torture of the cross. It was necessary that
he bear the weight of our sins and guilt
upon Golgotha and his pure nature shrank
from this sinful infusion and moral pollu-
tion. Just what heaven did for him we do
not know, but he underwent the ordeal, the
sacrifice availed for the sins of the race,
the law is annulled and millions are rejoicing in the liberty wherewith Christ
would make all free.

Midweek Prayer-Meeting

July 18, 1906.

LOVE AND FELLOWSHIP.—Epistle to Philemon:

Christ's so loving his enemies as to die for them should safeguard us against the deadly sin of carrying through life hearts empty of love for his brethren. For Christ's sweet sake fill them with a love that will not fail, though they seem to have no love for us, and apparently walk not with us, nor glorify our King before men.

Paul loved Onesimus more than the slave loved him for the apostle's heart was the larger. Paul, the liberator, did more for the bondman than the object of his love could do for him, for his heart was the larger, and the apostle derived infinitely greater joy from this historic commerce, for his heart was the larger. O, this world and the next belongs not to the great purses, arms or minds, but to the great hearts.

Constituted as we are, it is infinitely preferable to live in poverty and obscurity with a friend who loves us and can and will have fellowship with us in our anxieties and sorrows than to reign as absolute monarch over earth's greatest fortune or empire, but isolated from human sympathy and love and fellowship. Cultivate those qualities that will secure you at least one friend who will live or die for you, and you have a new possession next in value to God.

There is a grace in seeking love's favors that makes their bestowal a pleasure more than compensating for the sacrifice of the gift. Note well Paul's loving overture to Philemon, his gentle pleading for rather than demanding the liberty of his brother, and the expressions of confidence in the true nobility of his friend and the Christian courtesy of his conclusion. Let us attune our intercourse with our friends to this symphony of practical love and half the asperities of life will wing themselves away.

Evidently Onesimus was a bond servant or slave who fled from Philemon to Paul in quest of liberty and protection. Paul returns him to his master, not as a slave, but as a brother beloved. While the apostle can see that he has blessed the slave Onesimus by this liberation, he can but express the belief that he has blessed Philemon even more. As a slave, no matter how much Philemon received for his services, Onesimus was "unprofitable," but as a brother in the Lord, and so regarded and treated by his former master, he became "profitable," as all sacrificed objects, whether liv-

ing or inanimate, are that help to the exaltation of the spirit over the flesh.

There is no lack of meaningless platitudes recited to the unfortunate, but they are as empty of comfort as of real earnestness. It was different with Jesus. Paul and all who have really assuaged earth's sorrows. "Jesus touched the bier," and by that act involved himself in ceremonial and real partnership with the widow whose only son is being borne to the tomb. So with the apostle in our lesson. He would put himself in bonds to Philemon to free Onesimus—"If he hath wronged thee or oweth thee ought, put that on mine account. I will repay it." It is this bearing of one another's burdens that gives the helper the joy of sacrifice, and the beneficiary the comfort and inspiration of human fellowship.

Loving thy neighbor as thyself is half the old law; "Do good unto all men, especially unto them who are of the household of faith," is an apostolic injunction unto us who are under the dispensation of grace. A study of the doctrine reveals that we are to love the members of the body of Christ not simply because through the discipline of the Gospel they have become morally high toned and delectable and lovely, but we are to love them because of the fraternal relation we sustain to them in the household of faith, and in the family of God. We know nothing of the culture of Onesimus, nor of his disposition and temperament,

but Paul loved him because he was his child in the faith as parents love children regardless of personal traits, and he confidently relies on Philemon's loving him because he was a child of the common faith. Many of us base our attitude toward our acquaintance wholly on our estimate of their merits; the Scriptures would largely modify that by the attitude of us all toward God. "Be kindly affectioned one to another in brotherly love."

Unsweetened Condensed Milk.

Peerless Brand Evaporated Cream is ideal milk, collected under perfect sanitary conditions, condensed in vacuo to the consistency of cream, preserved by sterilization only. Suitable for any modification and adapted to all purposes where milk or cream is required.

Books by Disciples of Ch|

The Scriptural Foundation for Christian Liberality.

I have read with pleasure the work of R. H. Lampkin, published by The Christian Publishing Company, St. Louis, Mo. It is an attempt to study the foundations and trust of finance as related to the kingdom of God; it lays deep foundations in the knowledge of God's ownership of ourselves and of what we are, and attempts to find some principle that will regulate our conduct in the matter of our giving to the kingdom.

It is a very earnest study of this whole matter, and brings us to the tithe as simply one of the measures of Jewish giving. He develops the fact that beyond question Jews were required to pay two tithes, or one-fifth, of their entire income, with possibly a third tithe every third year for the work. The New Testament doctrine of giving is developed very fully indeed.

This is one of the most practical problems that is before the Church of Christ to-day. The cause of God could go forward with leaps and bounds if God's children would only deal as liberally with his cause to-day as did the Jews with their religion in the olden times.

I commend this book as a careful study and an earnest appeal to the consecrated of God's people. In the intense commercialism of this age, God's cause seems to be overlooked. This nation is wealthy beyond all precedent, and is growing wealthier each day. The question as to whether our wealth should be sanctified and God's cause advanced by it, or whether it should be used selfishly and thus to our condemnation as a nation, is one that ought to weigh heavily on the conscience of all who love God and his cause. I commend this book as a study of this great problem of financial obligation.

BENJ. L. SMITH.

The Literature of the Disciples.

This dainty little volume by J. W. Monser, from the press of The Christian Publishing Company, St. Louis, will be enjoyed by all who are sufficiently interested in the literature of our people to inquire into its character and influence. It ought to be read by everybody. Brother Monser is qualified in unusual degree to discuss this subject, for he has from the beginning of his long and busy ministry been emphatically a man of books. Those who have conversed with him on the subject know what an omnivorous, yet thorough and discriminating student he is. He is appreciative, yet frankly critical; literary, but not finicky. He who picks up this monograph will not want to lay it down till he has reached its last page. The first three chapters deal with the origin, formation and classification of the publications that have been issued from the pages of "our own" writers. If any criticism is deserved here, it would be that Brother Monser has been too anxious to name every book that has appeared in the catalogs of our publishing houses, or at least every writer who has put pen to paper; even though, in some instances, it may be questioned if he has not spoilt both pen and paper in the process without sufficient compensation in the product. It would have been better, it seems to the writer, if Brother Monser had treated more fully in the body of his work of the really meritorious works which our brethren have produced (which are ample in number to fill the long chapter devoted to that purpose),

and added a few pages of Bibliography at the end of the volume. This might not satisfy every ambitious scribe among us, but it would have comported better with the aim of such a work. The succeeding chapters, which are the critical portion of the work, are in Brother Monser's best vein, and will be read with increasing delight for their vigorous thought, epigrammatic language and intensely graphic style. On the whole, Brother Monser and The Christian Publishing Company are to be congratulated on bringing out so readable, timely and fair a treatment of the literature of a people whose efforts in book-making are yet to bring their noblest results.

W. F. RICHARDSON.

Kansas City, Mo.

Ten Plagues of Modern Life.

This is the title of a book of more than 200 pages, by I. N. McCash, for many years pastor of the University Place Christian Church, Des Moines, Ia., at present superintendent of the Iowa Anti-Saloon League and president of Iowa Children's Home Society, Des Moines, Ia. The book bears the imprint of The Personal Help Publishing Company, Des Moines. The volume is made up of addresses on "Divorce," "Amusements," "Municipal Misrule," "Corrupt Journalism," "Lynching," "Social Impurity," "Our City Carnival," "Murder—Self and Others," "Gambling," "Intemperance" and "The Civic Conscience," these eleven, but the best of all is the last. The author lives in the twentieth century. He has a keen interest in the things of to-day. Dr. McCash is neither "a mossback" nor "a back number." He is not a growling pessimist. He is full of faith and courage. He believes in God and in men. There is a tone of courage in this earnest book. No one can read even a single address without realizing that the man who speaks is a person of earnest conviction.

I find some things in the book that I do not believe. This feature of the volume commends itself to me. I like to read things that are not in accord with "my views." Such books awaken thought, the result may be a modification of opinions, preferences, convictions. The "Ten Plagues of Modern Life" is a book worth reading. It is a pleasure to speak in this way of Dr. McCash's lectures.

Denver, Colo.   B. B. TYLER.

The Greatest Work in the World: or the Mission of Christ's Disciples.

This work, by Charles B. Titus, for seven years a missionary in China, is written from the missionary's point of view. The author has had to deal with sin and unbelief as he found it in pagan lands, and his effort in this book is to show that the claims of what was once called "natural theology" are delusive, and that nothing short of the revelation of God in Christ will answer the demands of the human soul. We do not understand the author to teach that there is nothing to be learned of God in nature, for this would be contrary both to Scripture and to reason; but his contention is that without the revelation which is given in Christ, men are still without a saving knowledge of God, and an adequate revelation of his truth and grace. He points out the fact that the teachings of Confucius do not rise above the ethical, and do not constitute a religion. The author is no doubt right in contending that nature can only teach us its greatest lessons when we have come to know God as revealed in Christ.

The object of th[e] the necessity of pagan lands, see stitute for the t[ained] in Christ.

My Friend and [I.]

The Christian has published m[any] poor ones. So[me] duly heralded a[nd] to the ends of [the earth] had scant praise only to a select[ion] of the brain and a monument w[ith] mental and mor[al] author than ca[n] other kind of m[onument] read with intens[e interest] "Jehovah's War[riors."] Other Addresses have only seen publication. Per[haps] has been said of[?] down without a first chapter in [it] gives title to th[e] book of sermons good preaching i[s] of addresses, th[e] of most exceller[?] acter; it is not [an] outlines," thoug[h] that will bear ins[pection] of biographical d[?] raphy in it is lo[ng] biography of En[?] of thoughts, well and characteristi[c] heart of its auth[or] the beginning of he was my fello[w] friend. Our wa[ys] tered into our pa[?] ship never abat[ed] friend worth hav[ing] gan in the schoo[l] in 1854. He bec[ame a] good teacher, a[nd] and a true man. which he was ca[?] faithful in his ef[?] ligation. He [was] rather than as [a] of thoughts, wel[l] was a man of a his methods of a[d] tion of affairs. addresses and se[?] administrative [?] He was an excee[dingly] sparing himself i[?] ers. He once w[?] in one incessant, mands upon my [?] man in heart, in tenacious in his border of stubbo[rn] friends thought, suade than the o[?] tify, and yet his most conscientio[us] His mental forc[e] had them under goodness he was combined he full great man. The referred is fair[ly] method as teache[?] the book was p[?] "In Memoriam" fined in its inter[est?] family. It is wor[thy?] who are interest[ed] cussed and in th[e] illustration and i[?] judgment.

Kent, O.

SUMMER IS HERE

People must have inducements during such weather to either buy or read, especially good books, and we are determined to offer the inducements. For the month of July we will make the following prices, CASH with order. All books are prepaid. All books are cloth bound where not specified as paper.

	Regular Price	Cut-Rate Price
Life a Flower. By Errett	$1 50	75c
Plain Talks to Young Men	60c	30c
Thirteen and Twelve Others	1 00	50c
Life of Knowles Shaw	1 00	50c
Problem of Problems	1 50	75c
Kaskey's Last Book	1 00	50c
The Form of Baptism. By Briney	1 00	60c
The Temptation of Christ	75c	40c
How Understand and Use Bible	50c	35c
Riverside, or Winning a Soul	75c	35c
Grandma's Patience	20c	15c
After Pentecost, What?	1 00	60c
Know Thyself	1 00	50c
Memorial of J. K. Rogers and Christian College	60c	30c
Koinonia, or the Weekly Contribution	15c	10c
The Juvenile Revival	60c	35c
The Master Key, paper	25c	13c
The Remedial System, 436 pages	2 00	75c
Duke Christopher, Young Hero of Wurttemberg	50c	20c
Bartholet Milan	25c	10c
Remedial System (very badly damaged)	2 00	1 00
Gems from Franklin (very badly damaged)	1 00	50c
Revelation Read	1 00	35c
Trip Around the World	1 00	50c
The Simple Life	50c	35c
Saintly Workers	1 00	50c
Christology of Jesus, one of Stalker's best	1 50	1 00
Origin of the Disciples	1 00	50c
Bible or No Bible, paper	50c	25c
Contradictions of Orthodoxy, paper	25c	15c
A Knight Templar Abroad, 547 pages	2 00	50c
The Story of an Infidel's Family (very interesting)	1 00	50c
Patmos	1 00	35c
Queen Esther. By M. M. Davis	75c	45c
Elijah. By Davis	75c	45c
The Story of an Earnest Life	1 00	60c
Missouri Lectures and Discussions	1 00	30c
Autobiography of Jacob Creath	1 00	50c
Edna Carlisle	75c	45c
King Saul	1 00	60c
In the Days of Jehu	1 00	60c
Prohibition vs. Personal Liberty, paper	25c	10c
Walks About Jerusalem. By Errett	1 00	60c
Talks to Bereans. By Errett	1 00	50c
Science and Pedagogy of Ethics. Fine for teachers	1 50	75c
Sermons and Song	1 00	50c
The Exiled Prophet	1 25	50c
Spiritualism on Trial	1 50	50c
Dictionary of Scripture Proper Names		50c
Organic Evolution Considered	1 50	75c
My Good Poems. By Fairhurst	1 00	50c
Ideals for Young People	50c	30c
Life and Times of Benjamin Franklin	1 00	60c
Reformation of the Nineteenth Century (one of the best)	2 00	1 00
Our First Congress	1 00	35c
Wheeling Through Europe	1 00	60c
Garfield's Great Speeches	1 50	75c
Class Book of Oratory. Fine for elocution	1 50	95c
Christian Missions	75c	40c
The Baptismal Controversy	75c	45c
The Divinity of Christ and Duality of Man	75c	35c
Otto's Good Recitations, paper	25c	15c
The Life of Jesus	1 00	50c
The Young Man from Middlefield	1 00	50c
Leaves from Mission Fields	1 00	50c
The Moberly Pulpit	1 00	25c
Communings in the Sanctuary	50c	25c
Nehushtan	1 00	35c
Bible vs. Materialism, paper	35c	20c

	Regular Price	Cut-Rate Price
Wonders of the Sky	50c	25c
Altar Stairs, splendid fiction	1 50	1 00
June, a Class History	50c	15c
Prison Life in Dixie	1 00	25c
Across the Gulf	1 00	50c
Moral Evil	75c	25c
The Wondrous Works of Christ	75c	25c
Rosa Emerson	1 00	50c
Ecclesiastical Tradition	75c	35c
Facts About China, paper	25c	15c
The Spiritual Side of Our Plea	1 50	75c
Lessons in Soul Winning	75c	45c
The Plan of Salvation for Sinners and Saints	1 00	25c
The Man in the Book	1 00	60c
Missionary Addresses	1 00	35c
Commentary on Matthew. By F. N. Peloubet	1 25	50c
Types and Metaphors of Bible	1 00	50c
An Encyclopedia on the Evidences	2 00	1 00
The Gospel for an Age of Doubt. By Henry VanDyke	1 50	75c
The Making of an American. By Jacob Riis	1 50	75c
Social Evolution. By Benjamin Kidd	1 50	75c
Jesus Christ and the Social Question. By Francis Greenwood Peabody	1 50	75c
The Little Shepherd of Kingdom Come	1 50	75c
The Quest of Happiness. By Newell D. Hillis	1 50	75c
Happiness. By Carl Hilty	1 50	75c
The Women of the Bible. By Mrs. S. T. Martin	1 50	75c
The Conqueror. By Gertrude Atherton	1 50	75c
The Celebrity. By Winston Churchill	1 50	75c
The Choir Invisible. By James Lane Allen	1 50	75c
Sant' Ilario. By F. Marion Crawford	1 50	75c
The Master of Warlock. By Edward Eggleston	1 50	75c
The Customs of the Country. By Mrs. Hugh Fraser	1 50	75c
The Knitting of the Souls. By Maude Clark Gay	1 50	75c
The Law of the Land. By Emerson Hough	1 50	75c
Black Friday. By Frederic S. Isham	1 50	75c
The Medal of Honor. By Capt Charles King	1 50	75c
The Four Feathers. By A. E. W. Mason	1 50	75c
My Lady Peggy Goes to Town. By Frances Aymar Mathews	1 50	75c
Zelda Dameron. By Meredith Nicholson	1 50	75c
The Cost: By David Graham Philips	1 50	75c
On the Face of the Waters. By Flora Annie Steel	1 50	75c
The Pillar of Light. By Louis Tracy	1 50	75c
Marcella; The History of David Grieve. By Mrs. Humphry Ward	1 50	75c
Daughters of Nijo. By Onoto Watanna	1 50	75c
The Magic Forest. By Steward Edward White	1 50	75c
The Yellow Van. By Edward Whiteing	1 50	75c
Children of the Ghetto. By Israel Zangwill	1 50	75c
Lourdes; The Downfall. By Emile Zola	1 50	75c

SONG BOOKS—PREPAID.

Pearly Gates (board binding, 90 pages), per doz	$1 00
Apostolic Hymns (board binding, 112 pages), per doz	1 00
Twilight Zephyrs (board binding, 96 pages), per doz	1 00
New Fount of Blessing (board binding, 190 pages), per dozen	1 00
Tidings of Salvation (board binding, 117 songs), per doz	1 25
Tidings of Salvation (manila, 117 songs), per doz	75c
Tidings of Salvation (limp, 117 songs), per doz	50c

NEW TESTAMENTS.

	Regular	Cut-Rate
Revised to 1881 (silk cloth binding)	30c	15c
Revised to 1881 (larger type, cloth)	60c	25c
Revised to 1881, one page common version, opposite page revised (bourgeois type), cloth)	50c	25c
Revised and common, page for page (long primer type, Morocco binding)	1 00	35c
Reference New Testament (long primer type)	1 25	60c

CHRISTIAN PUBLISHING COMPANY. 2712 Pine Street, St. Louis, Mo.

People's Forum

To the Editor of THE CHRISTIAN-EVANGELIST:

One of the features of a recent union Sunday-school picnic in one of our suburban parks was an "egg hunt," in which hundreds of boiled · eggs were hid upon the grounds, and various prizes, including cash, given to those finding the "lucky" eggs; a large number of children, 10 to 14 years of age, participating. Would you say that this proceeding was calculated to foster in the boys and girls the gambling spirit?   W. P. KEELER.

Chicago.

[While these prizes probably differ so generically from gambling receipts as to prevent the tracing of any cause and effect relationship between them, yet, that the question is raised suggests the prudence of applying to all church and Bible school entertainments principles involved in, "Avoid the very appearance of evil"; and, "If eating meat cause my brother to offend I will eat no more meat while the world stands."—S.]

❀ ❀

OBITUARIES.

[Notices of Deaths, not more than four lines, inserted free. Obituary memoirs, one cent per word. Send the money with the copy.]

PAYNE.

Georgia A. Payne, born at Spring Creek, Ill., in 1865, died April 27, 1906, at her home, 3078 Ferry street, Denver, Colo. She moved with the family, when a child, to Macomb, Ill., where she lived until she was 9 years old, when Columbus, Mo., became her home. Here she united with the Christian Church. She came to Colorado in 1892. For fifteen years she taught school. In this occupation she contracted her mortal disease. She was a true Christian in word and deed. When told that she must die, she said she had no fear. She had suffered intensely for the last two months of the three years of her illness, but was cheerful and resigned.

"We sorrow not as those who have no hope."   FLOURNOY PAYNE.

SAMUEL COBELL HUMPHREY.

It is due to the memory of this good man and able preacher that more than the simple notice of his death should be given to the public. Samuel C. Humphrey was born in Madison, Ind., November 13, 1832, and died in Akron, Ohio, May 27, 1906. He was buried on the nation's Memorial day, May 30, 1906. The funeral services were conducted from the Broad Street Church of Christ in Akron, over whose congregation he was pastor for the years 1890-1892, by F. M. Green, assisted by I. H. Durfee, George Darsie and A. F. Stahl, pastors of churches of Christ in Akron. If "Memorial days are Love's holy days" nothing could have been more satisfactory to him if he could have chosen the time of his departure, than to begin his journey to "the city that hath foundations whose builder and maker is God" on the Lord's memorial day, and to have his burial service on the day when the funeral notes for a nation's dead were sounding in a myriad graveyards, and over which sweet flowers had fallen, like showers of summer rain.

Samuel was the fifth child in a family of seven children—five sons and two daughters. His father's name was Love S. Humphrey, who was born in 1790, and lived to a good old age. His mother's name was Mary Ramsey who was born in 1798, and lived well into the nineteenth century. When Samuel was 2 years old his parents moved to Petersburg, Ill., where many of his boyhood and manhood years were spent. As Petersburg is not far from the old home of Abraham Lincoln, he became one of the boyhood friends of Lincoln, a friendship which he highly prized, and the memories of which he cherished to the last. His boyhood was spent like thousands of others of his generation, amid surroundings of the days of the pioneers. About 1854 he entered Bethany College as a student, graduating from that institution in 1848, to enter into his public life with Robert Moffett and others who have risen high as preachers of the Gospel of Christ. After his graduation he taught in the public schools of Illinois, and for a time in Abingdon College, and preached as occasion presented until 1861, when he located at Charleston, Ill. This was the beginning of his long ministry of forty-five years. During his ministry he was pastor and preacher at Charleston, Tallula, Petersburg, Little Grove Schoolhouse, Lincoln and Cambridge, in Illinois; Abilene and Celina, Kansas; Tonawanda,

N. Y.; East Smithfield, Pa., and Akron, Ohio. He was not a pulpit orator, only so far as clear thinking and earnest and faithful proclamation of the Word are elements of true oratory. As a Scripturian he held a high rank, and his ability to analyze the Scriptures and generalize their teaching was unquestioned. He was a lover of good literature, and a good book to him was a delight. He was a discriminating reader of books, and his judgment was rarely at fault.

February 21, 1861, he was married to Emma Simpson Regnier, at Petersburg, Ill. His wife died May 27, 1876. Just thirty years later, on the same day of the same month he passed into the "great beyond" into which his wife had gone so long ago. At the death of his wife he was left with five children, two daughters and three sons—Mary E., Harry H., C. Victoria, Leroy B. and Samuel C. Jr. To educate and care for these children was the supreme anxiety of his life for several of the succeeding years. June 28, 1893, he was married to Miss Mattie Peckham, of Akron, Ohio. To them was born a daughter, Cornelia M., who, with her mother and the five children by the first marriage, survive him. By his marriage to Miss Peckham he became the brother-in-law of Prof. George A. Peckham, of Hiram College. He closed his active work as a preacher with the congregation at Celina, Kan., preaching only occasionally, and as opportunity offered, up to the time of his death. In 1902 he removed to Akron, which was thereafter his home. Here he lived the quiet life of one whose strenuous labor for more than half a century made rest imperative. He held the love of his brethren until the last, and did what he could among them to build up the house of the Lord.

He was my appreciative friend for more than a quarter of a century. During my service for the American Christian Missionary Society as corresponding secretary I made a tour among the churches of Illinois, near Springfield, and met him in 1898 for the first time, near his old home at Petersburg. Since that time I have known him well, and our fellowship always been in the intimacy of kindred spirits. Though his mental equipment was of a superior character, his natural modesty forbade him "to think of himself more highly than he ought to think," and in the judgment of those who knew him best his appreciation of himself was less than it ought to have been. He had the characteristics of the student and the instincts of the scholar. He took not only what he could find on the surface, but he also dug for the hidden treasure. His sermons were always well prepared and full of "sound meat." His words were well chosen and abounded in wholesome instruction. Some elements which enter into what is called "popular oratory" he

did not possess, and hence he did not command the applause of the multitude, as many with far less · mental and moral strength do. But he was a good and faithful and successful preacher, and in his long ministry he turned many to righteousness, and I fondly believe he will "shine as the stars forever and ever." · His life was well spent and he will be remembered by family and friends and brethren by what he has done.

     F. M. GREEN.

The Home Department

The Little Farmhouse.

It stands afar midst happy, sunlit fields,
A little farmhouse, brown and old,
With ancient, ivy-covered, buttressed walls,
And straw-thatched roof of gold;
And I a wanderer from the dusty town,
Grown weary of its heavy ways,
Wistful, from off the hot, white road, look down
And long for the old days.

For there the nights were blessed with quiet sleep,
The days were filled with happy cares,
And there the skies seemed ever blue, and there
Was time for peace and prayers;
While youth and laughter, Jo'' and hope, and love
Sang in my heart a happy song.
Ah me! a song that's hushed forevermore,
The crowded streets among.

And now I stand and gaze, with heavy heart,
Across dear fields in longing sore,
To where another woman, happier far,
Looks from the low half-door.
Oh, little farmhouse, old and brown, and sweet,
I wane when all the world's at rest
And think of you, and long for the old peace
And the untroubled breast!
—*Pall Mall Gazette.*

The Bronze Vase.

BY J. BRECKENRIDGE ELLIS.

PART III.

CHAPTER II.

As Raymund followed Rhoda from the three-story brick building on Pennsylvania avenue, he was too astounded to find words. That Rhoda, no matter how poor she might be, could have allowed herself to become so unkempt and streaked with coal-soot, was beyond comprehension. How different this was from the meeting he had so often fondly imagined! After three years he met his sister to find her in rags, and wretchedly untidy. He did not believe she was good looking any more, and while that was, of course, to be regretted, it was not so important as her uncleanliness. Dazed by his city experiences and now oppressed by Rhoda's condition, he followed her down the street at a rapid pace. She had said she did not know where they were going; and when she stopped under an electric light and looked at him piteously, he stared back, dumb.

"Oh, it seemed you would *never* come!" she whispered, drawing a long breath. "Now I think we are safe from the house."

"Do you know any place where we can go?" Raymund faltered.

"How much money have you?"

"Nearly a hundred dollars."

"*Goodness!*" exclaimed Rhoda. "Let's find a lodging house. You see where that street car track turns? It runs into Thirteenth street. Let's try that. I know there are lots of rooms to let on that street. Don't be afraid; I know the way."

As they passed from the light into heavy gloom—for the street lights were far apart —Rhoda threw her arm about Raymund and said, "I *knew* you'd come! But if you hadn't, what would have become of me? It's a good thing you came at night; nobody was at home!"

"Ought you to have left the house, then?" inquired Raymund.

"The door locked when I closed it," said Rhoda wearily. "Don't be uneasy about that house. Listen, Raymund; the woman I have worked for, is a shop-lifter!"

"What is that?" inquired Raymund, thrilled by the strange accusation.

"I'll tell you, when we can talk together," said Rhoda. "I'm afraid to speak of it even out here. Listen! Isn't somebody following us?"

Raymund looked about hastily. "A man is standing over yonder on the corner," he said, "but he isn't looking our way."

"Let's us hurry on!" said Rhoda. It was now about 8:30. They tried one of the lodging houses, and were abruptly refused, no doubt on account of Rhoda's disreputable appearance. Undismayed, they tried another, and with the same result. A third failure, however, made them uneasy, and a fourth brought them face to face with despair.

"It won't do," Rhoda whispered, "for us to ask a policeman to help us. We would be taken to a police station, and they would inquire all about it. I can't prove a thing against the woman we've run away from, and it would all fall on me. She might throw everything on me, and I'd be sent to jail!"

Raymund shivered. He suggested, "Why not go to the orphan home?"

"It is full; and they would think I had made up the story against the woman, in order to get back to the home. Anyway, you've helped me; for I remember a lady now, who keeps a lodging house, and I met her at the orphan home. Maybe she will take us in."

They went on for several blocks, and every time they passed an electric arc Raymund stared at Rhoda, saying to himself, "Can this be my sister?" Finally they came to a row of three-story bricks with half-buried basements under the buildings. There was an entrance going down several steps to the basements, and another up several steps to the front door. Rhoda stopped before one of these houses and rang the bell. A middle-aged lady came to the door. The light of the hall streamed over Rhoda and the lady started back. "Mrs. Bannerton," said Rhoda hastily, "my brother and I want to get a room for the night, and I will explain why I am dressed this way, if you will only give me a chance. If you don't take us in, I don't know what we shall do."

"Who are you?" asked the kind-faced lady, peering through her spectacles in the absorbed manner of near-sighted people who are not ashamed to have people see that they *are* near-sighted.

"You saw me sewing at the orphan home," said Rhoda eagerly, "and we got to talking about different things—the ocean— and I said I had never seen the ocean, and I made you a little poem about sweet violets."

"Why, yes, yes," said the lady. "But you do not look like my little poetess."

"I will look like her when I have decent clothes, and have washed up," said Rhoda, "and my brother, who has come to the city after me, has money enough to buy me what I need."

With the light of the hall full upon Rhoda's face, Raymund saw that in spite of her disreputable appearance, her face was very much as he had known it, only more mature, and unsullied purity looked from her deep blue eyes. He put his arm about her, and said, "I don't know why my sister is in this condition; I found her this way about an hour ago, and we've been trying to get a place to stay all night ever since. I haven't the least doubt she can explain everything—not the least doubt."

Mrs. Bannerton hesitated. Then . she said, "I can not promise you a room, but if you want to you may come with me and explain as you best can. I have never taken any one off the street in your condition—and so young—I have forgotten your name—"

"Rhoda Revore. And this is my brother, Raymund."

"I remember the poem," said Mrs. Bannerton, "and I remember our conversation about the ocean. But you seem so changed —I don't mind your rags and bare feet, so much as your untidiness. As for your brother," she peered at the youth, but his face was so frank and open, and he was so unmistakably from the country that the landlady smiled in spite of herself. She went the length of the hall and led them into a room which proved to be the kitchen and dining room, both in one. "Sit down," she said, kindly, "and let me hear, Rhoda, what you have to say."

Rhoda and Raymund sat down side by side, and Rhoda took Raymund's hand and held it, after drawing her dress forward to hide, if possible, her feet. She looked Mrs. Bannerton in the eyes and said, "At last, when I had thought nobody would ever come for me, and when I knew they wouldn't let me stay much longer at the orphan home—for I am 15 and 6 months— one day there came a woman named Mrs. Van Estry—and offered me a place as servant at $1.50 a week."

"Oh, Rhoda!" exclaimed Raymund.

"I went," said Rhoda. "It was the first chance I had had. I didn't write to Raymund because I knew he would feel bad. But I thought if I liked Mrs. Van Estry, that would be a way of having a home and

independent, and I could
keep from ever falling back
want Raymund to go ahead
ication; that's what mother
w can he go to college if he
me? It makes me misera-
nk that I am just a burden
vorking on a farm for three
me he has not quite a hun-
And now I am making him
t !"
.d Raymund, staring up,
r say that again as long as
looked angry, and his blue
t it wasn't anger that moved
iddenly stooped toward her
rom the chair and folded his
r. "She's as ragged as a
Bannerton," he cried, "but
ist the same !"
ted him, and went on talking
i Raymund's embrace. "Peo-
g to Mrs. Van Estry's, and
ke bad people. One night
the house was stolen, every
iat could be carried away—
my shoes—everything. Mrs.
ned so sorry. She said she
e got me this ragged dress,
shoes. I found out after-
: had been one of the chief
robbery. I found out that
ond-hand store down town,
to keep it supplied. She is
She comes home with the
goods, satins and laces, and
elry. She was always tell-
try to explain how she got
erheard her talking to some
There was one young man
o—to marry me. He never
it when he was in the house,
looking at me and saying
iow pretty I was, and that
like I am. Mrs. Van Estry
y, but I tried to make myself
isible, and at last the young
lone, but I found out from
s, Van Estry said to some
: he was determined to have
eant to carry me off, some
s a dreadful looking young
as often drunk. It was like
itmare all the time. But I
accuse Mrs. Van Estry, be-
hey would all band together
irt that it was I who stole
efore I learned the truth,
y managed it so that I was
bundles to different places,
ow it was stolen goods, and
id on me. So you see how
If I go anywhere and tell
ill be between me and Mrs.
to which one tells the truth.
ess girl, and she has a great
I haven't a single witness.
she can make swear falsely.
y accusing her would make
urn against me. All Ray-
ant is a place to stay till he
ings and I can look differ-

Rhoda had been speaking,
his arm about her, had been
indignation and burning
it against those who had
's life miserable; and all the
erton had been watching the
with her most intent gaze.
and said, "There is a little
rd story and another in the
are vacant. You can have
ir a week, apiece; they are
the house and quite small.
ioda has said, and when she
the bathroom no doubt she
ny little poetess. She shall
' old dresses till to-morrow,
I can go and buy what is

BE CONTINUED.)

Advance Society Letters.

BY J. BRECKENRIDGE ELLIS.

This article is to me, at least, just like
a continued story whose ending is unknown. In fact, I don't know how it
will turn out. I will explain. You know,
of course, that we have invited little
orphan Charlie to our house to stay, to
visit our Chautauqua and shoo the chicks
away. Well, last week came a letter
from an old friend of mine, the very
Mrs. Bessie Tracy Ryman who with her
friends kept our Advance Society orphan
a whole month last summer. Perhaps
you read about it in this page. Well,
Mrs. Ryman invites Charlie to come there
again, and right away, and she says that
Terrell Marshall, the boy Charlie visited
and liked so much last summer, wants
him to stay with him, too. They live
near each other, but far away from me.
If Charlie goes to see them I don't see
how we can afford to pay his way down
here to Bentonville. Yet, if he comes to
see me, his vacation will last only about
two weeks, while if he goes to Missouri
it will last two months. Besides, if he
goes to Missouri, he will get to be with
Terrell, his friend of about his own age.
That would be more fun for him. I am
some older than Charlie, and while I
would play marbles or ball with him to
help make him have a good time, I don't
like harnessing up dogs, and catching
lightning bugs, and pulling off grasshop-
pers' legs, and a thousand other pleasures that make a boy want to be a boy.
On the other hand, if Charlie goes to
Missouri he won't get to see his little
sister whom he hasn't seen for nearly
three years. Well, you can see yourself
that this is too difficult a problem for
me to decide, so I just wrote and told
Charlie to choose for himself which trip
he would take. I'm looking for his
answer this morning, and will not finish
this elegant composition until the mail
is in.

In the meantime, do you imagine that
nobody is keeping our Advance Society
rules merely because you are not? On
the contrary some of us are determined
to read five pages of history and thirty
lines of poetry every week; we are steadfast in reading a Bible verse every day;
we will not let anybody keep us from

memorizing : a good c
standard author once
keep an account of our
book. Here is our
Grace Everest, Oklaho
her fifth quarterly repo
a little book, the page
with threads of blue a
society colors. One c
she sends is "The I
Thine," which is true
company comes. Dor
Medaryville, Ind., is he
and sixth reports. He
tion begins, "Truth C
Will Rise Again." Earl
forward with his fourtl
Davis has drawn up h
in neat columns. She a
Salt of Conversation."
why so much talk is flat

ɔ the farm is named. Cliff
s a wide veranda around it
of a long ridge that 'jumps'
k of Cliff House and forms
I wish the Advance Society
s fine view! Little patches
ɡrain and vegetables all
more clumps of trees than
r count; and sheltered with-
ɔ of trees is a little village.
to be seen by the aid of a
he Wei River, on which we
: glimpses of little sailboats
ɪts. The birds are singing
is blue. Sometimes there
ɪrage over the river—beau-
ɔf water and trees, or a vil-
ɔlace makes me feel that I
can again—the elevation, the
ɪ, the river mist, the islands
: blue sky, the bracing but
ɪzes." I must save the rest
for two weeks. As to Char-
n fund, I invite advice from
rs. I will have more to say
two weeks. We must edu-
t we haven't enough money
ɔard and tuition six months.
e an ice cream social? How
for me to give the social,
: a saucer? Of course, you
n't come, but you could send
c and I could eat the ice
ather has returned from the
ɪnd there wasn't a thing in
ɪpt a postal card. But as luck
it that card is from our

orphan Charlie! It comes so conveniently to hand that it almost looks as if
it had heard me talking about it! Here
is Charlie's solution of the problem that
troubled me: "St. Louis, Mo.—I will
start from here the 5th, bound for Bentonville. I could not go on both trips,
because the Orphan Home can't pay any
money for the ticket. I would like to see
Terrell, but I believe I would rather be
with you, and on the way back see my
sister; because I have not seen her for a
long time. Tell Mrs. Ryman I thank her
very much for inviting me, and would
like very much to pay her a visit. Give
Felix a gentle stroke for me. Goodby."
I do not know if this choice cost Charlie
an effort, but I do know that I feel a
higher esteem for him on account of his
decision. Don't you? So, when you read

this, Charlie will doubtless be in Benton-ville. This past week I sent Drusie an-other $5; that made the fifteenth draft the Advance Society has forwarded her. Are you not proud of it? Miss Nana Wood's Sunday-school, of this city, donates 25c for our orphan. I am still thinking about that ice cream idea. I'll tell you what let's do: Let's have a social for Charlie's educational fund, on August 3. The social will be here, and if you can't come (in fact you are not at all expected), send me your 10c. Some of you might get up a little social on that day and send in the combined proceeds. Every one who reads these words or hears about them is invited. Remember, it's August 3; that will be on Friday—just the day for ice cream. You will pour in your dimes. I will go downtown and get me a saucer of ice cream, paying for it, of course. No; now I tell you what: I'll send Charlie a dime and let him get the ice cream. Won't that be a funny social? Who can get up a home social on that day? We will have something more to say about this in two weeks. You see, the idea has just come my way.
Bentonville, Ark.

$12.85 Chicago to Marquette, Mich., and Return.

Via the North-Western Line.

$14.25 Ashland, Wis., and return. These special low round trip rates are in effect every Tuesday, with return limit 21 days. For tickets and reservation apply to your nearest ticket agent or address W. B. Kniskern, P. T. M., C. & N. W. R'y Co., Chicago.

Christian Publishing Company

2712 Pine St., St. Louis, Mo.

J. H. GARRISON, - - - - President
W. W. DOWLING, - - - Vice-President
GEO. L. SNIVELY, - - Sec. and Gen. Supt
R. P. CROW, - - Treas. and Bus. Manager

The picture of Editor J. H. Garrison we are mailing free to all sending in $3 for a renewal and one new subscription to THE CHRISTIAN-EVANGELIST is a fine trophy of the engraver's art, and a possession to be highly prized. The next edition may not be so satisfac-tory. Send at once.

W. W. Dowling's Bible school helps and papers for our youth and chil-dren justly stand first in the estima-tion of the discriminating. We glad ly submit samples to your own im-partial judgment. Our prices are as low as other houses ask for very in-ferior supplies. Order from here and get the best.

If you are contemplating a revival one of the preliminaries should be to order 500 copies of THE CHRISTIAN-EVANGELIST for free distribution a few weeks before and during the meeting. This will guarantee a house full of eager, earnest listeners at the first and every serv-ice of the series. Write us for special rates.

Read the advertisement on page 895 of our annual summer bargain book sale. These are not "bindery seconds" or soiled

volumes or *passe* goods, bu[t] gains designed chiefly for th[e] patrons and in part to more their good will and fellow company. We want to be lers so long as we can do a you than other houses.

Undoubtedly it will be t[o your advan]tage to go to Buffalo over t[he line of] THE CHRISTIAN-EVANGELIST

Over Niagara.

out extra charge you may and Canada or via Toledo Every possible service will our guests and on the l[ine] terms. Soon as you deter[m]us, write that the Wabash [will make] provisions to make.

Picture of War Engine

A beautiful colored [print, ___] inches, of the historic old [Gen-] eral" which was stolen a [near Big Shanty,] Ga., by the Andrew's Raid[ers in the] Civil War, and which is r[__ on exhibi-] tion in the Union Depot, [Nashville,] Tenn., has been gotten out [by the NASH-] VILLE, CHATTANOOGA & ST[. LOUIS R'Y—] The "Battlefields Route." The picture is ready for fr[aming and will] be mailed for 25c. The [picture of "The] General" sent free. W. L. [DANLEY, G.] Pass. Agent, Nashville, Te[nn.]

CHURCH FEDERATION

The Inter-Church Conferenc[e on Fed-] eration, 700 pages, prepa[red by]

THE
CHRISTIAN-EVANGELIST

A WEEKLY RELIGIOUS NEWSPAPER.

Volume XLIII.   No. 29.

ST. LOUIS, JULY 19, 1906.

HERBERT YEUELL,
Now in a Great Meeting at Manchester, New Hampshire.   At this time there is no Church of
this Reformation in that State.

The Christian-Evangelist.

J. H. GARRISON, Editor

PAUL MOORE, Assistant Editor

F. D. POWER, }
B. B. TYLER, } Staff Correspondents.
W. DURBAN, }

Subscription Price, $1.50 a Year.

For foreign countries add $1.04 for postage.

Remittances should be made by money order, draft, or registered letter; *not* by local cheque, unless 10 cents is added to cover cost of collection.

In Ordering Change of Post Office give both old and new address.

Matter for Publication should be addressed to THE CHRISTIAN-EVANGELIST. Subscriptions and remittances should be addressed to the Christian Publishing Company, 2712 Pine Street, St. Louis, Mo.

Unused Manuscripts will be returned only if accompanied by stamps.

News Items, evangelistic and other rise, are solicited, and should be sent on a post card, if possible.

Published by the Christian Publishing Company, 2712 Pine Street, St. Louis, Mo.

Entered at St. Louis P. O. as Second Class Matter

WHAT WE STAND FOR.

For the Christ of Galilee,
For the truth which makes men free,
For the bond of unity
  Which makes God's children one;

For the love which shines in deeds,
For the life which this world needs,
For the church whose triumph speeds
  The prayer: "Thy will be done."

For the right against the wrong,
For the weak against the strong,
For the poor who've waited long
  For the brighter age to be.

For the faith against tradition,
For the truth 'gainst superstition,
For the hope whose glad fruition
  Our waiting eyes shall see.

For the city God is rearing,
For the New Earth now appearing,
For the heaven above us clearing,
  And the song of victory.

J. H. Garrison.

CONTENTS.

Current Events...................... 904
Editorial—
  Christian Union: A Historical Study 905
  Our Reformation in the East........ 906
  Notes and Comments.............. 906
  Current Religious Thought........ 907
  Editor's Easy Chair.............. 908
Contributed Articles—
  As Seen from the Dome. F. D.
    Power 909
  The Manchester Meeting. Herbert
    Yeuell 910
  Bridgeport, Conn., as a Mission Field 911
  The Needs of the East............ 911
Our Budget 913
Dedications 917
News From Many Fields 919
People's Forum 922
Evangelistic 923
Sunday-school 924
Midweek Prayer-meeting 924
Christian Endeavor 925
Current Literature 926
Marriages and Obituaries 926
The Home Department 928

… THE

CHRISTIAN-EVANGELIST

"IN FAITH, UNITY; IN OPINION AND METHODS, LIBERTY; IN ALL THINGS, CHARITY."

| Vol. XLIII. | July 19, 1906 | No. 29 |

1809   CENTENNIAL PROPAGANDA   1909
CHURCHES OF CHRIST
: : : GEO. L. SNIVELY : : :

Looking Toward Pittsburg.

Secretary B. L. Smith was wont to say that we Disciples have four frontiers in the United States. For us New England is still beyond the Eastern frontier, though geographically so much nearer Brush Run and other historic cradle lands of this Restoration than the present day center of our power and influence. We do not forget Roxbury, Worcester, Danbury and even Lubec, but they are simply heralds too long isolated from their comrades. It is time for the army of occupation to appear. While planning for Pittsburg in 1909, we ought to look thoughtfully where the sun and the immigrant first touch our shores. We are pleased to present in Brother Aldrich's paper which follows and in other columns of this issue many interesting facts relating to the history and the plea of the Disciples in New England. Bro. J. H. Garrison together with others who are contributing to the meeting Brother Yeuell is holding in Manchester is making an earnest and self-sacrificing effort to establish a church in the only New England State in which we have no congregation. But before 1909 we ought to have a church in every capital and county seat in that rich and populous part of our country. We commend to our readers the practicability of lengthening our cords over this territory, as well as strengthening our stakes there, as one of our pre-centennial enterprises. We suggest a campaign as long as may be necessary at Manchester as the beginning of this new conquest. Communications from our brethren with reference to this enterprise will be helpful and welcomed. Would that some one to whom the Lord has committed enough money would materialize in word and stone in some of New England's flourishing cities Brother Ireland's idea of Centennial Memorial Churches!

❋ ❋

Our New England Churches.

BY A. B. ALDRICH.

Any consideration of our churches in New England requires some attention to their history, since their condition is the result of their historical development.

Our movement here is mostly an importation from the British Provinces of New Brunswick, Nova Scotia and Prince Edward Island.

In an early day Alexander Campbell visited Boston and delivered addresses on various topics, but I think no trace of the influence of his visit is to be found in the history of our churches.

In the early decades of the last century there was a widespread movement in New England and the Provinces for the establishment of independent congregations organized according to the Scriptural plan, and for the rejection of human creeds. It was one form of the reaction from extreme Calvinistic theology. It was also to some extent a protest against the condition of low spiritual life that then prevailed in the

churches, and took the form of enthusiastic revivalism. Some of the churches that came under this influence went into the Methodist fold, some back into the Baptist, some went to make up the Christian Church or as it is sometimes called the Christian Connection, others were organized as the Free Baptist Church, many went into the various Advent branches and other small denominations while some remained and still remain independent.

I think it is in this movement that we are to find the origin of our oldest churches and of the churches in the Provinces now numbered with our people. It is well known that the strong church at Danbury, Conn., had such an origin. An old record states that the church at River John, Nova Scotia, was planted as early as 1815, when the Campbells were still members of the Baptist Church. Before the middle of the last century we had a flourishing church at Salem, which has long since disappeared. Out of this church came the Worcester church, which in turn has been the mother of most of our present churches.

A church was established in Boston in 1843. It was composed almost entirely of immigrants from the Provinces. Its record, which has happily been recovered, discloses that the paramount idea in that church was the restoration of the ancient order of things. The recorder, after alluding to a church in Baltimore which had three bishops, all engaged in business, this gave vent to his sentiments: "Yes, hireling clergymen, look and be ashamed. Oh, may the churches of Jesus Christ always retain bishops who are workingmen and then the church will remain pure." This church died and the fact of its existence has only been discovered recently. But it is a type of most of our churches here in their early years, and of some as they exist to-day. The church at River John was and still is a thorough-going "anti" church, and through the ninety years of its history it has been the prolific source of that blighting influence among our churches. From that church came most of the churches in the Provinces, and they are either distinctly "anti" churches or of the most conservative type of missionary churches. Such has been the principal source of the Disciple movement as it exists in New England.

Our work in New England has, therefore, been handicapped in two ways. First, the churches represented ideas altogether out of sympathy with the progressive and liberal sentiment of New England. Second, they were made up mostly of foreigners who could not possibly come into close touch with the dominant New England element.

The people of the Provinces are splendid people, descendants of common ancestors with the people of New England. The Provinces were settled largely by emigrants from Massachusetts. But common blood and language do not bridge over the chasm caused by allegiance to different governments. A large and discouraging de-

gree of clannishness is inevitable under such conditions, hardly modified at all by the artificial process of naturalization.

Of the two hindrances, however, the extreme conservatism has probably been the most harmful. Many of our churches in New England have died and are scarcely remembered. Quite a number of those still in existence are likely to succumb to the deadening influence of the modified "antiism" that has prevailed. For in New England, as probably in the whole country, the thorough-going "anti" spirit is capable of far less harm than the modified form seen in many of our churches.

I am glad to be able to say that some of our churches, and they are prosperous churches, are outgrowing the conservatism of their earlier years, and give promise of coming into such full sympathy with prevailing New England sentiment that they may receive fair attention and consideration and be more attractive to the people. One other serious hindrance to our work has been the failing of the national missionary boards to attempt serious work in New England. But we are all so familiar with this fact that I will not discuss it at length at this time.

I am inclined to think that the discouragement we feel at times is due in part to the fact that we are expecting more rapid growth than the conditions justify. The matters to which I have alluded make it inevitable that our growth here should be slow. And there are other facts that tend to the same conclusion. First, the growth of our people in the country at large is not as rapid as it once was. In recent years the increase in our numbers in America has been about three and one-half per cent a year, slightly greater than the increase of other large Protestant denominations. Time was when our growth was justly considered phenomenal, but that time has passed. At present I am sure our growth in New England compares favorably with our growth in the country at large.

Second, it is well known that hardly any religious bodies are making any substantial progress in New England. The time of successful revivals here seems to have passed. I have been told of a certain large denomination which in a recent year held a revival meeting in Boston, conducted by two of the largest and most favorably situated churches in the city, and led by two of the ablest evangelists of that denomination in the country. It is said that the meetings cost over $2,000, and the result was two conversions. To any one who has observed recent attempts of the kind in Boston, the story does not seem incredible. If there is something in the times and in this region that causes such unfortunate failures, we can not expect to escape its influence entirely, and we ought not be discouraged if our growth seems to be slow.

This consideration of the history, characteristics, hindrances and reasonable expectations of our work leads to the practical (Continued on Page 912.)

Current Events

Secretary Root has started on a three-months' tour of the South American republics. The first and greatest object of his trip is to attend the Pan-American Congress at Rio Janeiro, beginning July 21. This will be the third gathering of this character, not counting the Panama congress which was held during John Quincy Adams' administration in 1826, and was attended by Henry Clay, then secretary of state. Of these more recent congresses, the first was held in Washington in 1889, at which time the Bureau of American Republics was organized; the second in Mexico City in 1901. Secretary Root's purpose in connection with the present conference is to improve the diplomatic relations between the United States and our southern neighbors. Many of them have, in recent years, conceived an unreasonable hostility toward our government. Most of these Latin-American republics have an inordinate sense of their rights and dignities and a very inadequate conception of their duties and responsibilities as sovereign states. The United States government has been inclined on occasion to remind them of the latter, and this has not made for popularity. Secretary Root's participation in the conference and his visits to the several republics will be part of the general educational process by which we are trying to teach these young republics how to behave as nations in the family of nations. It is both a large and a delicate enterprise, and Mr. Root will have need for all his sagacity and diplomatic acumen.

The Rio Janeiro Conference.

❦

That was really a great Fourth-of-July speech that Mr. Bryan made in London. It matches up quite well even beside Mr. Roosevelt's address on the same day to his fellow townsmen at Oyster Bay.

❦

One of the most fertile sources of trouble between the South American States and the European governments has been the collection of debts owed by the former to citizens of the latter. If Venezuela owes money to subjects of the Kaiser and refuses to pay the same, the Kaiser sends war ships to blockade the ports of Venezuela until the account is settled. And the modern interpretation of the Monroe doctrine is that we have no ground to interfere with this strenuous process of collection, so long as there is no permanent seizure of territory or other invasion of sovereignty. But while there seems no just ground to stretch the Monroe Doctrine to protect defaulting republics from the just demands of their creditors, there is still apparent justice in the theory which was announced by M. Drogo of Argentine a few years ago. This Drogo Doctrine is that no power should use force to collect the debts of another power to its citizens. Among the first-class powers, this is already established usage. The contrary practise would be far too expensive and dangerous. But the great powers still use force in collecting debts from the small ones. Often there is no other way to do it, for some of these small states, especially the South American republics, exhibit a la-

The Drogo Doctrine.

mentable failure to take their obligations seriously until war ships appear in port. But, then there are citizens in the most enlightened states who do not take their obligations seriously, who put their property in their wives' names and let their creditors whistle. It used to be possible to get at such persons by having them imprisoned for debt, but that has been abolished. The lender now has to take his chances, and in doing so he adjusts the interest to the risk. The war ship method of collecting debts is closely akin to imprisonment for debt. It is applying to a foreign power a degree of compulsion which no civilized state exercises upon its own citizens. The better way—and this is in accordance with the Drogo Doctrine—is for foreign investors to keep their capital out of places where it is notoriously unsafe, or when they do lend money to insolvent or irresponsible governments to make the interest pay for the risk.

❦

One sometimes wonders whether some of the magnificent achievements of engineering and construction which are now under way are in line with legitimate economic demands or are mere freaks of creative enterprise whose chief value is that they will be talked about. There is the Flagler railroad along the Florida Keys to Key West, a marvelous structure, more than half of which will be built on concrete arches in the open sea. There is the "cut-off" built on a vast embankment across Salt Lake in Utah. The Pennsylvania terminals in New York City, now being built at a cost of $30,000,000, will be a great addition to the city and will doubtless draw business for that road, but it will take a lot of new business to pay 5 per cent on that investment. In the building of sky-scrapers, there seems to be no limit. The Singer Sewing Machine Company is erecting a building 593 feet high in New York; and the Metropolitan Life Insurance Company (perhaps to get above the winds of scandal) will begin one this fall on the site of Dr. Parkhurst's church on Madison avenue, which will be 700 feet high. The newest and biggest thing in steamships is the new cunarder "Lusitania," recently launched on the Clyde. It is of the new turbine type with four independent propellors turned by engines developing 75,000 horse-power. The vessel is 790 feet long, 88 feet beam, and is expected to jerk 2,000 passengers across the Atlantic in four days. It is impossible not to admire the daring enterprise of those who are making these great investments and even more the skill of the men who are doing the work. The plain citizen, who does not claim to know much about such matters, wonders whether the building of 700-foot office buildings and $30,000,000 railway terminals is a response to a genuine economic demand or something else.

Freaks?

❦

It is time for Thomas Taggart to retire to very private life. The Democratic party is not in a position to accept the handicap which he gives it by his chairmanship of the national committee. His appointment to that position was a monumental mistake from the first. It was made on the theory that he was a wonderfully astute politician, that he was possessed of an amazing degree of popularity which would swing Indiana into the Democratic

The National Chairmen.

column, and (presumably) that he had at least the minimum amount of character which public opinion expects in a national chairman. All of these turned out to be erroneous assumptions. The recent raiding of the gambling resort of which he is proprietor adds the last touch of disqualification for any public service.

Mr. Cortelyou is, according to report, about to send in his long-deferred resignation as chairman of the Republican national committee. He will be succeeded by Harry S. New, the present vice chairman. Mr. New's grandfather was a famous pioneer preacher in the Christian church. His father, the late John C. New, recently deceased, was a graduate of Bethany College and a man of national prominence. Harry S. New is a Butler College man and a member of the Christian Church. His ability as a political organizer on the largest scale is yet to be put to the proof, but his promise is good. If New gets in before Taggart is gotten out, Indianapolis will for a time be the home of both national chairmen.

❦

The advance of civilization in Africa is indicated by a movement, headed by Lord Curzon, for the protection of the game of that continent against hunters. What would Livingstone or Stanley think of that?

❦

The reorganization of the consular service, which the recent session of congress authorized, has already been mentioned in these columns. It is not all that Secretary Root desired, but if wisely administered, as it will be under the present regime, it will go far to redeem that branch of the service from the unhappy disrepute into which it had fallen. The consuls are arranged in classes and there will be systematic inspection of their work by five consuls-general at large. All consular fees are to be paid into the public treasury. Consular officers who receive a salary of $1,000 or more will be required to devote their whole time to the work, to the exclusion of any other business or profession. Secretary Root was especially anxious to secure a provision that the higher places in the service should be filled only by the promotion of experienced men. This was too strong doctrine for congress, but the same result was secured by an executive order issued by the President on the day before congress adjourned. Under these new regulations, admission to the lower ranks of the consular service will be based upon the merit system, with thorough examination of applicants and promotions to higher positions will be only for meritorious service. It is particularly specified that no applicant's political connections will either help or hinder his appointment. This will be a sad blow to congressmen who have outstanding promises to their henchmen at home and to that class of political handymen who have been in the habit of taking their pay in consulates. But it will help to raise the consular service from something midway between a graft and a game of chance to a dignified and useful profession.

Consular Reform.

❦

President Roosevelt has written a letter to the secretary of the Arizona statehood committee, which is in effect an exhortation to the people of Arizona, urging them to accept joint statehood and warning them that if they reject it they will "condemn themselves to an indefinite continuance in a condition of tutelage."

Christian Union: A Historical Study.

IV. THE PROTESTANT ERA; THE PERIOD OF REUNION.

15. When Christ's Prayer for Unity is Fulfilled.

It is not given to mortals to know with certainty the results of events which lie yet in the future. And yet in the light of reason and of revelation we may forecast, with reasonable certainty, some of the results which would follow the fulfillment of our Lord's prayer for the oneness of his followers. We shall undertake, in this concluding article of the present series, to state some of the probable results which would follow the realization of this much to be desired consummation.

1. It would enrich every part of the now divided church by bringing all into the possession of a common inheritance of truth and of historic experience, which belongs to the several parts. No longer would men say, "I am of Luther," or "I am of Calvin," or "I am of Wesley," or "I am of Campbell," but all of us would realize that "all things" are ours, whether Paul or Apollos or Cephas or Luther or Calvin or Wesley or Campbell—all are ours and that we are Christ's and Christ is God's. It is scarcely possible to exaggerate the value of this larger and better equipment which would come from each part of the church sharing in the truth and experience of the whole Church. It would round out, and render more symmetrical, our uneven development, remedy, to a good degree at least, our religious lopsidedness, bring into use a great many neglected texts of Scripture, and give us a feeling of catholicity and breadth of fellowship which would mightily strengthen and quicken the zeal of the entire Church.

2. It would enrich every part of the Church in the wider circle of Christian fellowship and acquaintanceship. How our denominational barriers separate us from each other and make us strangers one to another! How many noble spirits there are in the religious bodies all about us, to come in contact with whom, in Christian fellowship and service, would be an inspiration to our lives! How comforting and strengthening would be the thought that these pure and noble men and women are our brothers and sisters, fighting under the same banner with us and following the same Leader! How sectarianism has impoverished the Church by erecting unauthorized barriers between its members, and thus robbing each part of the intellectual and spiritual wealth which belongs to the entire body!

3. It would give a mighty and irresistible impulse to all the missionary movements of the Church. Freed from the task of building up denominational walls and carrying on a denominational propaganda, the united Church could devote itself, with singleness of aim and with concentrated power and resources, to the evangelization of the world. How our missionaries in foreign lands, and even in the outposts

of our own country, would rejoice to know that the Church had healed its divisions and that they were all representatives of a united Church, and could work together as brothers without any sense of competition or denominational jealousy! How much more effective would their message be to the heathen world, if the foreign missionaries could say to pagan peoples, "We all represent the one Church of Jesus Christ on earth, and all we ask of you is to become followers of the meek and lowly Nazarene." No longer would these heathen converts be confused by our denominational titles and tenets, nor discouraged by divisions among Christians the meaning of which they cannot understand. A zeal for world-wide evangelization would sweep over the Church, and men and means would be furnished in abundance to supply the needs of pagan lands. How the heart of Christ would rejoice to see His Church rising at last to a conception of the magnitude and urgency of the great task he has laid upon it! Upon the Church thus awakened and thus undertaking in earnest at last the work which he has committed to it. He would pour out the fullness of his blessing and fulfill his ancient promise in a measure that we now little dream of, "Lo I am with you alway, even to the end of the world."

4. The influence of such a moral miracle as the reunion of a divided Church would be incalculable. It would stop the mouths of infidels and gainsayers. It would set at naught the wisdom of the agnostic. It would silence the scoffer and the religious pessimist. It would remove the chief stumbling-block that is keeping thousands of thoughtful men and women out of the Church. It would prevent that pitiable and pathetic spectacle of divided families—husbands and wives, parents and children, belonging to different churches and separated from each other in the highest and most sacred things of life. It would unite thousands of weak churches, in small towns, now competing with each other, fill the prayer-meeting room with earnest and enthusiastic workers, where now only a few discouraged ones meet to lament the spiritual leanness of the Church, and all departments of the church work would feel the thrill of a new life and new strength.

5. In the new strength, and enthusiasm born of union, the Church would resume its lost leadership in the great moral and social reforms of the times, and undertake, as it has never undertaken before, to heal many of our social ills, care more systematically and wisely for the poor and the needy, devote its attention to the rescue of the submerged part of the population of our great cities, concentrate its forces against the legalized saloon, gambling houses and other demoralizing agencies, lend its influence to the settlement of disputes between labor and capital, put a check upon inordinate greed, and inculcate rational methods of living, safe forms of amusement, wiser methods of punishment, and whatever else relates to the moral and material welfare of the people. No more

would it be said to the scandal of the Church that it is so engrossed with its theological dogmas and its ecclesiastical millinery and ritualism, as to be oblivious to the practical needs of suffering and toiling men and women all about them.

6. Engaged in the practical work of helping humanity, the Church would get closer to its Master, formalism would give place to real personal piety, and devotion to human good would absorb the energies erstwhile devoted to theological disputes and denominational strifes. Under this sort of *regime* the Church would recruit its ranks from a class of people who now stand aloof from its fellowship, and would receive from them the very kind of service which it would need to fit it for its new vocation.

7. The daily press of the world, together with all other forms of literature, would give vastly more attention to religious subjects and to the great enterprises of the Church when once the Church has become a united body, working for the redemption of humanity. Every one knows that it is the spirit of jealousy among different denominations that keeps the press from giving as great publicity to religious gatherings and their actions, as to other kinds of meetings in which all the people are interested. This aid of the press would be a powerful adjunct in carrying forward the interests of the kingdom.

8. Finally, who can doubt for a moment that there would be joy in the presence of God and among the angels of heaven and all celestial intelligences, over the blessed consummation of a united Church? The father-heart of God would thrill with joy to see all his children loving one another and working unitedly together to lift the world to a higher moral and spiritual level. The angels, who, we are told, rejoice "over one sinner that repenteth," so deeply are they interested in human affairs, would sing a new hallelujah chorus over a united Church, making possible the repentance of the whole world. That part of the Church which has "crossed the flood" and is glorified, would join in the general jubilation. How deep and pure would be the joy of these redeemed saints, to see the Church militant close its divided ranks for a concerted movement to bring in the reign of the Church triumphant! We know what joy would thrill the hearts of tens of thousands of devout souls on earth who are praying, with their Master, that our sectarian divisions may be healed, and the Church become one in spirit, faith and obedience, if this splendid victory were achieved. A new note of triumph and optimism would enter into all our sermons, our songs, and our prayers, and we should begin to have here on earth a blessed foretaste of the fellowship of heaven. Surely an achievement that would bring joy to the heart of God, to the angels, and to all the good of earth, is worthy of our labors, our prayers, our sacrifices and our tears. That it will one day be realized, no more admits of doubt, as it seems to us, than the ultimate success of the divine purpose of God in sending Christ into the world. In-

deed, these are not separate things, but parts of the same great purpose. He who said, "And I, if I be lifted up from the earth, will draw all men unto me," will fulfill his mission. Blessed are all they who are now working with him for the accomplishment of this sublime end!

Note. Here ends this series of Studies on Christian Union, which has run continuously in these editorial pages for more than six months. It is the Editor's purpose to revise and publish these articles, in a booklet of, perhaps, 100 pages or less, which may later, and in still more condensed form appear, as a part of a larger contemplated work.

❀ ❀

Our Reformation in the East.

It has often been a matter of speculation as to what would have been the result had Mr. Campbell and his co-laborers begun the work of their religious reformation in New England instead of in Western Pennsylvania and Virginia. No doubt it would have gained something from having a New England origin, for ideas seem to travel from east to west more rapidly than from west to east. Whether this fact is to be accounted for on the ground that the east has had more ideas worthy of propagation than the west, or whether the west has been more receptive of new ideas than the east, is a question about which the east and west would no doubt differ. Probably there is some truth in both these hypotheses. The east being the older section of the country, has always had the advantage in its educational facilities and, perhaps, its closer contact with the Old World has also given it a certain advantage, and education is a powerful factor in developing the intellectual power and leadership of a people.

There are other reasons, however, which would probably more than offset any advantages which the east may have had over the west as the starting-point of a new religious reformation. No doubt the soil of the great middle west was better prepared for the reception of the seeds of reformation than that of the east; first, because it was less preoccupied and, second, because the religious conditions made more manifest the need of the plea for Christian union—the cardinal feature of the new movement. In any event, there is good reason for believing that there was providential guidance in the place of the origin of the movement. This matter was, no doubt, settled by divine providence rather than by human wisdom. The rapid growth of the reformation has certainly far exceeded all human expectations, but, perhaps, by far the greater and more enduring work accomplished has been in leavening and molding the thought of the religious world.

We are now, however, face to face with a much more practical problem than that suggested above, namely: How can this cause we are pleading be more strongly established in the east? If we have a fraternal and helpful message for the religious world, as well as for the unconverted world, there is no place where it ought to be more cordially received and more highly appreciated than in the east. It is generally claimed that the churches in the east are more liberal in spirit, and less hampered by denominational prejudices, than elsewhere. There is no reason why their catholicity of spirit and breadth of culture should not make them appreciative of, and sympathetic with, a religious movement that has for its general purpose the unification of the divided forces of Christendom, by a return to Christ and his simple and original gospel. Wherever this message has been wisely presented in the east, it has met with hearty appreciation. For obvious reasons our churches have not multiplied as rapidly in that section as elsewhere. One of the chief reasons for this is that we have done far less work there than elsewhere, and another is, the ground has been more fully occupied by older churches.

In view of the fact that we have a message which we believe the religious people of this country should hear, there is nothing contrary to the spirit of utmost fraternity and co-operation, in our seeking to establish representative churches in the east where we may emphasize those truths which we feel need emphasis to-day, and co-operate with our brethren of other religious folds in the furtherance of the kingdom of God. Indeed, if these brethren in the east be as liberal-minded and catholic-spirited as they are reputed to be, there is no reason why they should not co-operate with our evangelists in establishing churches which may afterwards co-operate with them in a very helpful manner in doing the work of God in their respective communities. The motive which underlies the desire to extend the influence of our cause in the east is not sectarian, unless our whole movement be sectarian in spirit and aim, instead of the very opposite.

Why, for instance, should not Brother Yeuell have the sympathy and co-operation of the churches in Manchester, New Hampshire, in the meeting which he is now holding there? If the gospel, as he preaches it and as his brethren would present it, reaches a class of people there which the churches have not reached, or reaches them more effectively, why should not they rejoice in this fact and seek to aid in the establishment of another local church that would be a potent factor with them in saving the people of that city and sounding out the gospel in all the region round about? If all the people of Manchester were already in the churches which now exist, and these churches were adequate for meeting all the religious needs of the people, there would certainly be no excuse for our entering the field; but the conditions are very different from that. And even in the present situation there would be no reason for our entrance into

adopted the following resolution which the secretary has communicated to us:

"Resolved, That in the opinion of this association it is not wise to urge the consideration of the church federation question at our national convention at Buffalo."

The resolution is a little ambiguous, but it probably means that in the judgment of the Association the basis of federation adopted at the New York conference, last fall, should not come up for consideration before the regular convention of the American Christian Missionary Society, to be held in Buffalo next October. If this be the meaning of the resolution, it is in perfect harmony with what we have advised editorially, months ago, provided there was at the time any difference of opinion among the brethren that would likely jeopardize our missionary interests by its discussion. These New York ministers, however, do not indicate, in their resolution, whether, in their judgment, we should ignore entirely this request for action on the part of the Inter-church Conference of New York, or whether we should postpone action until some indefinite future time, or whether there should be a separate, independent convention, not under the auspices of any missionary society, for the purpose of acting on this important proposition looking to a closer unification of the divided forces of Protestantism. Only one thing is clear from the resolution, and that is that a majority of the preachers which met at Elmira in their Ministerial Association, do not wish to have the Convention which is to be held in their state marred by what they fear will be a heated discussion. This could be avoided, however, in two ways, whether the matter was brought before our general convention or an independent body: First, there might be an agreement on both sides to omit all discussion, since the matter has been pretty thoroughly discussed, and let the vote be taken without any speech-making on either side; or, second, by all who are to take part in the discussion agreeing beforehand to be Christian gentlemen, and to behave themselves as such. If there is any doubt as to the practicability of the latter plan being carried out, the former one would be the safer. So far as we are concerned, however, we are perfectly willing to trust our brethren to discuss, in open parliament, any question of vital concern to the interests of the cause, and to trust their sense of justice and fairness, for a wise decision. The situation suggests a problem which confronts us that is much broader than church federation, and with this problem we shall attempt to deal editorially in an early issue of THE CHRISTIAN-EVANGELIST.

❧

Since the foregoing was written we have received from the Secretary of the Ministerial Association of Oregon a copy of a resolution passed by that body at its recent meeting, as follows:

"Resolved, That because we are not a legislative body and can not and would not bind any action

upon local churches and can, therefore, sustain only an advisory relation upon the question of federation of churches, we recommend that the matter of federation be left to local churches and communities and that we show a spirit of fraternalism and co-operation. We also advise that a committee of three be appointed to report the action of this association to the inter-church committee on federation of churches in Oregon."

If we were inclined to be critical, which we are not, we might ask the brethren of these ministerial associations, how they felt authorized to adopt a resolution relating to church federation, in relation to the national or state convention. We are not denying that they had authority to express their judgment on this or any other question relating to the welfare of the cause, but we would like to point out to them that the National Convention, at Buffalo or the Oregon State Missionary Convention, has exactly the same right to express its opinion on this subject as these brethren have. We desire, however, especially to call attention to the logic of this resolution of the Oregon Ministerial Association. It says, "Because we are not a legislative body, and cannot and would not bind any action upon local churches, and can, therefore, sustain only an advisory relation upon the question of federation of churches, we recommend that the matter of federation be left to local churches." etc. Why not then resolve that all action in relation to missionary work, such as the taking of offerings on special days, and all other action taken at our missionary conventions, be left to the local churches, since, in these matters no less than on the question of federation, the action is only advisory? The same reason that remands this question to local churches, on the ground that we are not a legislative body would remand every other question voted upon at our conventions, to the local churches. And since the churches have no authority over the individual members, to bind them to any given course of action, why not leave the whole matter to the individual conscience? This is the disintegrating logic of the resolution. The fact that our conventions are not legislative bodies, is no reason whatever why they could not express their judgment and advice on any question, just as the brethren. There may be good reasons for any convention refusing to express its judgment or advice on any given subject, but that reason cannot be that our conventions are not legislative bodies, since that is an equally good reason for refusing to take any action on any subject. Let us keep clear heads and steady nerves.

❧ ❧

Current Religious Thought.

Doubtless the "Central Baptist" will undertake to prove the miraculousness of faith thus acquired, but it truthfully says:

"A man must believe the New Testament record about Jesus before he can believe in Jesus. It is a poor sort of logic and a poor sort of faith that professes to hold on to Christ while it discredits the truthfulness of that record. It is readily admitted that it is faith in Christ which saves, but faith in Christ is based upon faith in the Scriptures. 'Faith comes by hearing and hearing by the Word of God.' "

The recent legislation consolidating the Presbyterian and Cumberland Presbyterian churches met with the approval of all friends of Christian union. We note with pleasure in the "Herald and Presbyter" this evidence of its early consummation.

"In many places the Presbyterian and Cumberland Presbyterian churches are arranging for consolidation in advance of the changes in presbyterial organizations. These churches realize that they are now one and they are trying to get the most possible and the speediest good out of consolidation. In many communities two weak churches will combine to form a strong one, with regular services and with well-consummated plans for forward evangelistic efforts. A spirit of goodwill is widely prevalent between the people of the two churches. There are some exceptions which we are sorry to note. It is along the lines of least resistance to stir up strife and bitterness in our poor human nature. It is along the ascending lines of divine grace to promote concord, confidence and love. We hope that just so far as is possible all tendency to friction will be suppressed and that we shall hear from the local churches, ministers, elders, and people, as well as from Presbyteries, that the things are being done and the words being spoken that make for peace."

❧

The "United Presbyterian Witness" probably realizing that Christianity is being strengthened by the union movements now in process among Presbyterian bodies, thus intimates that its Methodist brethren might lend a hand, and suggests the way:

The Gospel of Jesus Christ is the man's religion. It knows no color but white. Whoever embraces it with all his heart becomes white in God's sight at once, whatsoever the color of his skin may be. He is white and clean who is clothed with the white robe of the Redeemer's righteousness. In Christ Jesus there is no distinction of race or nationality. He is the white man who does the will of our Father in heaven and he will sit in one of the seats around the throne of God. We have such distinctions now as the M. E. Church and then the African M. E. Church. Why on this principle should we not say: The Gospel of Jesus Christ for white people, the Gospel of Jesus Christ for black people, the Gospel of Jesus Christ for red men? Jesus Christ did not live in our day and he evidently made no provision for accommodating human prejudice. He just gave one Gospel and organized one church for his whole family and not one is to be excluded from that one communion table who accepts in very deed his one Gospel. Jews and Greeks, Barbarians and Scythians and all are his children and must sit side by side.

❧

How the "fathers" of this Restoration would have rejoiced to hear the "Western Christian Advocate" pleading thus for Christian union.

According to all signs our English brethren are rapidly approaching union. The Methodist New Connection Conference, just adjourned, has passed a plan for church union that presages similar action on the part of other branches of the Methodist denominational family of that country, and though it may be many years before union is consummated, all signs point to that condition ultimately. We believe that in this respect they are making more rapid strides than we in America, due, perhaps, partially to the fact that their country is small and the people of their churches and congregations more in touch with each other. We are glad to note this trend in Methodism for union. The federation of churches is something more than a mere dream and is fast approaching. When that day comes and denomination after denomination is merged and the religious forces of the world moving forward in related bodies, we trust that our Methodism will be able to look back on the history of the movement and feel that they were not secondary in bringing to pass the glorious consummation.

Editor's Easy Chair.

Alexander Selkirk, in his lonely island, is supposed by some one to have felt in his heart, if he did not actually sing:

'O Solitude, where are the charms
That sages have seen in thy face?
Better dwell in the midst of alarms
Than to reign in this horrible place."

Solitude, long protracted, is not good for man. That was a decision announced away back in Eden. But he who has not learned the charms of solitude, for a brief time at least, at frequent intervals in his busy life, has missed one of the fine arts of living. The charm of the vacation period to the Easy Chair is the opportunity it furnishes for quietness, for repose of mind, and for meditation, and that too in the midst of nature's handiwork. A gentleman and his family came from Chicago to this place the other day, and stopped at the Club House. We saw them sitting one day on the broad veranda with the Lake spread out before them in all its beauty, while they were fanned by the breezes that swept over its bosom, and we thought how much they must be enjoying this scene in contrast with the hubbub and everlasting roar of traffic in Chicago. But we learned the same evening that they complained it was "too quiet" for them here, and that they had passed on hunting a gayer and, perhaps, a more fashionable resort. This shows that people differ in their tastes about summer resorts just as they do about everything else. If one likes either the Coney Island or the Newport style of resort, this is no place for him. But to him who is weary of the conventionalities, the noise, and the rush of city life, and desires for a season to seek the quietness of the woods and the fascination of the great Lake whose companionship is an unceasing source of interest and, where, not in utter solitude, but with a few congenial spirits, he may rest his body, soul and spirit, take his reckonings, and gird himself for new tasks and duties, this place offers superior inducements.

❁

We have established a camp in a grove near the house close by the shore-line, but protected from too strong breezes by the upward slope of the hill, where we stretch our hammock, do most of our literary work, and where, on last Sunday afternoon, we received a company of our friends from Pentwater. This camp serves a most useful purpose just now from the fact that the carpenters are at work completing the cottage, which was only partly built last year. The weather has ben ideal for the past week, and this grove has made an excellent addition to our limited quarters. If these Easy Chair paragraphs should have in them any of the odor of the pines and hemlocks, and something of the freedom and breadth of the great Lake, our readers must charge it up to environment! As we write these lines the carol of a song-bird comes floating to us through the tree-tops, and we hope it is but the prophecy of the coming full choir of feathered songsters that are to make their homes in these groves and entertain us with their minstrelsy. We shall try to form their acquaintance, and live on good terms with them and

with the squirrels that build their nests and raise their young in these trees. One of the changes which we have experienced with the passing years is an increasing interest in all living things, and especially in our little brothers and sisters of the woods, whose intelligence and whose feelings the world is coming to understand better now than in former years. We must confess that this love of birds and animals has destroyed very largely our fondness for hunting and is making serious inroads on our enthusiasm in the nne art of angling, as a mere sport. Whereunto this will end we do not know, but we cannot believe it is right to needlessly cause pain to any living creature or to rob it of its life which brings it some measure of joy, for mere sport or entertainment. What is necessary for man's support may properly be taken, with the least possible cruelty or pain, but more than this—well, let every man be his own judge, and be true to his own conscience.

The Pentwater "News" quotes a statement by Dr. Hutchins, who has just returned from a trip through California, and who is now a resident of this beach, that "Pentwater is by nature, the most beautiful resort place, so far as I have seen, on earth." The "News" adds that "the statement is not different from many of those made by visitors who come to Pentwater for the first time, many of whom for the first time actually come in contact with the real beauties of Nature as manifested in the pure air, blue skies, sparkling waters, natural woods, shady retreats, and where there is perfect liberty to enjoy one's self as he pleases. At Pentwater, a half-hour's walk will take you away from humanity, with all its frivolities, into the heart of nature where you can camp at ease and forget that business worries and cares ever existed. And a half hour will bring you back to the village where you can obtain every necessity or luxury of life. * * * When you get out into the hills and woods of Pentwater you are apparently forty miles from nowhere, and yet you are only a few minutes call from the village." "Another desirable feature of Pentwater resort," the "News" adds, "is the high class of people that frequent it. The lawless element common to resorts near large cities is never seen. Among the visitors here are several officials and ex-officials of state, professors of schools and colleges, university students, prominent business men and women, journalists, and others of similar walks of life. All these are men and women of culture and refinement, and are a valuable addition to the local society." We can add our testimony to the high class of people who make this their summer resort. It is sufficiently removed from the large cities to prevent it from being a resort for roughs and rowdies. This feature, together with its natural attractiveness, was a determining factor in our choice of the place for a quiet, restful resort for ourself and such friends as had similar tastes about their outing place for the summer.

❁

There must be some excitement going on somewhere in the brotherhood of which we are not apprised here in our northern resort. We have received a few letters and some resolutions, commented on elsewhere, which indicate a sort of nervousness about our forthcoming National Conven-

As Seen From the Dome   By F. D. Power

Every one in thinking of Egypt thinks of the pyramids. Along a beautiful road shaded by acacia trees, one may go by carriage from Cairo or by trolley to the Sphinx and the great Pyramid. In the clear atmosphere they seem very near, but they are six miles from the city. What a world of speculation these piles of stone have occasioned! Pyramidology is the word, and "Myths and Marvels," "Miracles of Stone," "Gospel in the Stars" are some of the titles the wise men give their books when they write about them. One of our greatest preachers had a lecture on the Pyramids, for the preparation of which he told me he purchased more than a hundred books. Egypt has more buried people than any land on the globe, and these are tombs of its dead, and that is about all there is to it. The Pyramids of Gizeh are one of five groups in the range of the burial places of ancient Memphis. Herodotus says it took 100,000 men twenty years to build Cheops. So the Pyramid seems to answer two purposes: to give employment to the living and a monument to the dead. Of course, the third purpose, to afford a show place to the nations, never occurred to these worthies. Pyramids are grouped always and are only to be found in the center of the necropolis, as in our modern cemeteries a family lot is marked often by a central shaft and the graves are grouped about it. The tombs of great officials called "Mastabas," and other funeral monuments, are found spread around the pyramid. One of the first things a king seemed to do when he ascended the throne was to build himself a tomb pyramid and a new coating of stone was built around it every year that he reigned. The door was walled after his body had been laid in it, and thus it remained a finished tomb. Different sizes in these structures of different kings can be understood on this theory. I did not climb Cheops. Of what use the wear and tear of clothing, and muscle, and nerves, and patience, simply to say you have done a thing? I did not enter Cheops. Of what use the struggle with dust and dirt, and candle grease, and the smell of dead bats, and the pestiferous cries for "backshish," and contact with unclean Arabs and other living things, to see where once a dead Pharaoh was laid? These monuments are wonderfully impressive. I am quite content to gaze upon them and call up the memories of 6,000 years. On one side the Nile the fertile fields and villages, and the great city; at my feet death, ancient death, the sleeping place of millions; beyond the desert the great sterile, pathless desert. It is a great place to think if you can get away from the quarrels of dragomen and the chaffer of donkey and camel boys, and the nuisance of dealers in "antiques."

There are three Pyramids of Gizeh, all built about 3,700 B. C. Khufu, or Cheops,

built the first; Kephren, his successor, the second; Meukaura, the third. Most travelers confine themselves to the great one. The second has some of the outer smooth coating toward the top and is dangerous to climb. The third is easy and so nobody bothers to get to the top. We all want to hitch our wagons to stars. Cheops is 451 feet high and has a length on each side of 750 feet, and covers 13 acres. The second is 447 feet high and 690 feet long. The little one is 204 feet high; and so we pass it with a glance. The great Sphinx, after all, is the object of greatest fascination in this cluster of monuments. Nothing made by man has been the source of so much speculation and confusion of thought. According to the Greek myth the Sphinx was a female monster who propounded the riddle: "A being with four feet, has two feet and three feet, and only one voice; but its feet vary; and when it has most it is weakest." Those who failed to solve the riddle she devoured, and they deserved to be. Oedipus solved it by the answer—"Man," and the Sphinx threw herself from the rock and perished, as many another dealer in conundrums should do. The Egyptian Sphinx is a male deity, with the body of a lion and head of a man. One calls it "the emblem of immobility." That is easy. Another says: "It represents the union of intelligence and power." That is plain also. Still another declares it "the symbol of inorganic nature." That is somewhat confusing and Eddystic. A fellow in one of the pictures is represented with his ear at the sattered lips of the figure listening and asking "What is it?"—a curious Yankee, no doubt. The Sphinx was a solar deity. It symbolizes life; not a dead sun, but the living, rising, benevolent, majestic, everlasting sun, coming each morning out of the east—a symbol of life, of immortality. The Egyptians called it "Hu," and it represents the god, "Harmachis," Horus on the horizon; and while it is the riddle of Egyptologists it really has no secret. This great and noble figure, hewn out of solid rock, is 66 feet high. Between its paws is an altar; and on its breast, a memorial stone of Thothmes IV, 1533 B. C., telling how he freed it from the drifting sands. Below it is a temple built of enormous granite blocks put together in a marvellous way. It was a great privilege to visit these wonders; and turning homeward we drove through the long lane of acacias, meeting by the way the beauty and wealth and fashion of Cairo out for an evening drive under the glow of the setting sun. Time mocks all, but the Pyramids mock time.

Taking the steamer on the Nile and passing through the forest of Giassas, the picturesque Nile boats, we journeyed to Memphis. Memphis was the greatest city in Egypt and of the world, eight miles in diameter; a city that vied with

Babylon, that worshiped Apio, that is associated with Menes; the Noph of the Bible, the city of the Pyramids and of Ramses the Great. Here is the hoary "step pyramid," the oldest of these tombs which points back 5,000 years. Memphis lived 5,000 years, according to some authorities, and had an average population of 500,000; and they figure that under its sands sleep 75,000,000 of people. There is little left of the great metropolis. We mounted our donkeys. My donkey boy, Hassan, said: "Good donkey, little, but good; good Hassan; good American gentleman: good backshish!" and every little way he wanted money to buy clover for the donkey. "Donkey very hungry;" and money to buy oranges for himself, "Hassan hungry;" and money for his family, "three ladies" and "four boys!" A Moslem, he had an extensive household.

We rode through beautiful groves of palms and I found "Moses" a sure-footed little beast and Hassan a good driver. We came first to the two colossal statues of Ramses II, one 25 and the other 42 feet in length, that stood at the entrance of the Temple of Ptah. They are massive and of wonderful workmanship, and conform to the figures given by Herodotus. "The Father of History" has sometimes been charged with a wild fancy, but here he was right. Egypt has always held the worship of cats as a high and holy service, and even to-day homeless mouse catchers and roof musicians are tenderly cared for. Herodotus

(Continued on Page 921.)

❀ ❀

"FEED UP"

Is the Way to Make Old Men Young.

One of the most remarkable evidences of the power of proper food is found in the following interesting story by a Canadian:

"I am now 71 years of age and have been ailing more or less ever since I was 16 years old, part of the time an invalid suffering with stomach and bowel troubles.

"About two years ago, having learned of the good Grape-Nuts food was doing for some friends of ours, I resolved to try it myself and I immediately found help—more vigor and power of endurance.

"That summer the heat did not affect me as it did before I used Grape-Nuts and after about four months constant use I began to realize what it was to be well and found my bowels adjusting themselves so that I am now free from the old troubles. I had long despaired of such results and can safely say I am enjoying better health today than for many years past, for this wonderful food has literally made a new man of me." Name given by Postum Co., Battle Creek, Mich.

There is nothing wonderful about it, only sound, scientific reason that anyone can prove by trial.

Look in pkgs. for a copy of the famous little book, "The Road to Wellville."

The Manchester Meeting   By Herbei

Now that I am on the field I can give my impressions of a few days in the largest city of New Hampshire, this busy city of 65,000 population. I may say before writing this article, which is at tl e request of the Editor of THE CHRIS-TIAN-EVANGELIST, that while I duly appreciate the honor conferred upon me in being selected for this inexpressibly difficult work, that it was with much fear and trembling, thought and prayer, that I consented to lay aside several tempting offers for promising meetings to take up this work and attempt to put at least one spot indicating a work on New Hampshire's map for the convention at Buffalo.

With this end in view Brother Garrison consulted with Bro. W. J. Wright, whose work in the east stamped him as one of the few men who had done effective work in this conservative section. Mrs. Helen Moses wrote to Bro. A. L. Ward, of Boston, with a view to learning to what extent the C. W. B. M. would be justified in aiding in the support of a church if one could be established. Bro. Ward visited Concord and Manchester and favored Manchester. I copy from his letter to Mrs. Moses:

"Manchester is a city of 65,000 population. Twenty-five thousand of this are not Roman Catholics. About 57 per cent o. the population are natives, 42 per cent foreign and about 73 per cent either are foreign born or have foreign parents. There are 20,000 French Catholics and 10,000 Irish. There are about 31,000 young men in the city, but only 765 are church members, and not more than 1,200 attend church. In all Protestant churches, there are about 7,000 members, i. e., 7,000 members out of a Protestant population of 25,000. In all there are 25 churches, including Catholic; 4 Baptist, 4 Congregational, 5 Methodist, 1 Christian Advent, 1 Free Baptist, 1 Unitarian and 1 Christian (connection). Three of these Protestant churches have no pastors. This the secretary of the Y. M. C. A. argues is because of insufficient support. He says there is little or no evangelistic spirit in the churches. He feels that they need us, but said he did not see that we could become self-supporting, as this is the problem all th churches seem to be facing.

After going over this whole matter very carefully, Mr. Hunt and I feel that Manchester is the better place in which to begin the work. I know that this was the decision of the New England board some time ago, but when they made this decision they knew nothing of the real conditions of either city. But I must add, that this is a most difficult field.

Now as to a meeting place in Manchester. We were unable to find a suitable hall. The Y. M. C. A. building is a poor thing, indeed, and looks more like a skating rink than a Y. M. C. A. build-

ing. There is no hall in this building. Private halls are very scarce."

At Bro. Garrison's suggestion I visited Concord, Dover, Portsmouth, Nashua, Laconia and Manchester, and while I saw that Manchester was in all probability the most difficult place, yet I felt that as it was by far the most active city that it should be the most strategic point.

However, after several delays, I am here. The only available meeting place is the Park Theater, the best public hall and central, several car lines passing the door. In many respects it is a good place, but in many others not so good,

A. L. Ward, Boston. One of our ablest
New England Preachers.

because the best attractions have failed to attract audiences in the town theaters, there being several fine lakes and park resorts with innumerable attractions to be enjoyed for the cost of the street car fare, and the city is practically emptied every night.

Having no one on the field who could attend to the previous advertising, I came into the city a comparative stranger last Thursday, and quickly got out some bills and cards, and by the kindness of Mr. Russell Barnes, pension examiner and a member of our home church, Vermont avenue, Washington, D. C., I was favorably introduced to the editors of t.e two leading papers, who, when they were assured that I would take advertising space in their columns, gave me prominent mention in the Saturday issue. Sunday night brought a very representative audience of about 700. We have been hampered by the Fourth festivities, having no service on the Fourth. This is the day after, and I am anxiously waiting to see what to-night may bring forth. I am told that the people may attend well on Sunday, but not during the week for any one.

The price of lumber and work, and poor location, and the excess of foreign and rowdy population, put the tabernacle idea out of the question. It will require time to get the ear of New England's best people, and it is better to wait long enough than to cater to an

irresponsible element.
tended that this is a...
tinction. It would b...
eral evangelistic effort...
work in view we can...
We are trying to ge...
England and through...
evangelize the foreig...
used only for big occa...
one of the most cons...
New England to a...
meetings conducted...
man, without prestige...
in the city. Fully $1...
pended on the first ad...
him as a man with s...
whose? In cold curi...
being too cool for pa...
people gather to se...
speculate on the outco...
bard, a splendid youn...
hill, Mass., is at the p...
stage. Mrs. Susan B...
of Uniontown, Pa., is...
Exactly on time the pre...

(Continued on]

Bridgeport, Conn., as a Mission Field By M. L. Streator

Among the New England states Connecticut occupies a prominent place in geography, history, politics and religion. Bridgeport is conspicuous among its manufacturing centers, and has a fair prospect of becoming its largest city. According to the president of the Board of Trade its population has increased 5,000 during the last year, and now numbers 90,000. Within fifty-seven miles of New York City, it is largely under the influence of the chief American metropolis. Many of the business firms of that city have their factories in this one. The population is mixed, embracing many races and nationalities.

Do you inquire, What has been attempted and accomplished? Something has been done in various parts of New England in which I rejoice. Because of its present and urgent needs, let me speak briefly of my own work in Bridgeport. This is the day of small things with us. But do not despise it. God is quietly planting here the seed of divine truth, which has the power of regenerating the soul and the life. Man is but a feeble agent. God alone is great. The power that saves is his own power. He will accomplish his work although we may perish in the attempt to do what he has entrusted to us. All is well if his will be done.

About the end of March, 1905, I was sent by S. M. Hunt, of Springfield, Mass., from Boston to Bridgeport to "size up the situation" and see what might be accomplished. After six weeks of investigation I wrote to Brother Muckley, the corresponding secretary of the Church Extension Board, reporting the condition of affairs and appealing for aid. I told him that if they would help us buy a lot and build a house of worship here the work could succeed, but that otherwise it must fail. He expressed delight in hearing from me, and at once promised that they would help us to the extent of their ability. We made diligent investigation, and selected and purchased a choice lot in a fine location at a cost of $1,100. The Church Extension Board advanced half of this money. We raised the other half, largely among friends outside of Bridgeport.

To succeed in establishing a church in a large city we need to select an unoccupied portion of it. This we have done. Our lot is on the west side, the largest section of the city, in the residence portion, on Maplewood avenue, at the corner of Iranistan avenue. It is within a mile of the center at the. City Hall, and yet on the border of a new section that is rapidly building up with good homes. The community is largely native Americans, with a sprinkling of foreigners, nearly all of whom are Scandinavians, people of the same race as the Saxons and the Normans. The Lutherans have a church within four blocks of our lot where the preaching is in the Swedish language. Churches with English preaching are six, seven, eight or more blocks away. We have twenty-five members who are scattered in various parts of the city. The Board of Education granted us the free use of an unoccupied school house opposite our lot till we could erect our own building.

We found it impossible to transfer our Sunday-school from the hall where we had met on the east side to the new place of meeting in the school house. To gather a new Sunday-school where we had a few members was a serious problem. The Congregationalists had a mission school in the school house, meeting at 3 o'clock in the afternoon. One Sun-

day evening I found a note from the superintendent awaiting me on the table, requesting me to call and see him the next day at his store, which I did. He congratulated us on our success, stated that they were about to lose four of their best workers by removal, and requested me to furnish them with three teachers and an organist. Their school had been running for eight years. It had been their purpose to build a chapel and to plant a church there. He said, "It is a fine location. But as you have entered the field and are about to buy a lot on which to build, we will not attempt it. The school gradually will come under your influence. When you are ready to go into your new building we will turn it over to you." He told me also that this was in accordance with the official action of the Broad Street Congregational Church, which is one of the best in the city. This proposition, unsolicited, coming unexpectedly in such a gracious manner, and evincing such a Christian spirit moved me to tears. I gratefully accepted it. We had not sufficient officers and teachers to man a Sunday-school. It was a gradually flowing together of two churches in one department of Christian work, where we could work together without the sacrifice of any Christian principle. It has been carried on without any friction. We now have five of the teachers. One of these frequently attends our night services with her husband. She recently said to me, "We like your preaching. You mean every thing you say—some preachers don't—and it is according to the book." The school numbers about ninety. We have had eighty present at one time.

The great task to be accomplished is to raise the means to build the house of worship. Our purpose is to reproduce the building which the Disciples have in Everett, a suburb of Boston. It will cost about $6,000 to do it. I have made repeated appeals to persons of means to build here a memorial church. As yet I have received no favorable response. Possibly some of the readers of this article may be willing to do it. If so, do notify me at once. I am sure the Lord will send you his blessing.

The Church Extension Board have promised us a loan sufficient to cover half of the cost of the building. But they will not furnish the money till the house is built and all debts paid except what their loan will cover. Hence we are under the necessity of raising $3,000 in order to get our church home. As our members here have but little financial strength we must rely on our great brotherhood outside of Bridgeport to supply the means.

My plan is to raise $3,000, or if possible, $4,000. I wish to find ten persons who will give one hundred dollars each. Brother Hunt paid one hundred dollars toward the purchase of the lot, and has promised another hundred for the building. We are but stewards of the manifold blessings of God. Who will join him in making up a thousand dollars? Will you be one of ten to give a hundred dollars?

I wish to find forty persons who will give twenty-five dollars each. Two men in Bridgeport who paid $25 each for the lot have promised $25 apiece for the building. Will you be one of forty to give $25?

I wish to find a hundred persons who will give $10 apiece, and two hundred who will give $5 each. Surely in a membership of 1,125,000 in the United States this ought to be accomplished. Not only individuals, but churches, Sunday-schools and Endeavor societies can aid us in this work, if they will. "A cheerful giver God loves."

It is impossible for us to reach all our members scattered throughout the nation with this appeal. I request that each one reading it will present it to his brethren and sisters, the church, Sunday-school or Endeavor society as he may deem best, or to all of them, if advisable. We need a great co-operative effort for the sake of the Church of Christ in Bridgeport. Being in the employ of the New England Christian Missionary Society, I am responsible to them for every dollar received and disbursed. The American Christian Missionary Society is aiding our New England Board in supporting their evangelists. Help us win New England to the primitive faith. "Remember the words of the Lord Jesus, that he himself said, 'It is more blessed to give than to receive.'"

At the conclusion of a sermon on "What think ye of the Christ? whose Son is he?" which I gave in the Temperance Hall of this city, a woman, dressed in black, arose, and with outstretched arm said with emphasis, "That is God's truth, and I don't hear it anywhere else." Do help us to give the people of Bridgeport God's truth concerning Christ and his Sonship.

Precious truth and genuine beauty pervade the gracious words of Whittier, the beloved Quaker poet, in this gem of his concerning the blessedness of giving:

"All hearts grow warmer in the presence
    Of one who, seeking not his own,
Gives freely for the love of giving,
    Nor reaps for self the harvest sown."

Send pledges or offerings to M. L. Streator, Box 777, Bridgeport, Connecticut.

The Needs of the East

After sixteen years' work here in the east I am convinced that we can not "possess this goodly land" until our people realize the importance of New England as a key to the entire country. The citizens of the east are no more cultured than those of other sections of the land. But there is no portion of our country in greater need of the Gospel of Christ.

New England contains six millions population, or one-fourteenth of our entire population. We have more than seventy cities of over 10,000 each. In all this vast field we have but twenty-one organized churches with about three thousand members.

For many years the east has been the hotbed of new cults; the seat of Unitarian thought; the stronghold of Roman Cath-

olicism; the field of declining faith. Yet our people are migrating by thousands to the West and carrying these conditions wherever they go. For the sake of the safety of the entire country we are duty-bound to put forth our best efforts here in the east.

The foreign population of this section is so vast that our foreign society could spend every dollar of its income right here and yet leave many fields uncultivated.

To-day the swing of the pendulum is away from the higher criticism. The day of investigation has passed and the day of action is upon us. This is the time and here is the place to strike. There is a reaching out after and a longing for the Christ of the New Testament. The plea which we are presenting will put life into the thousands of dead churches. We have towns of 500 population with six protestant churches, averaging only sixty members each. We alone can swing these churches into line and lead them to a common interest. But this work will require time. New England moves slowly. No spasmodic effort will avail. We need substantial aid from A. C. M. S. every year for a long period of years. We need a host of our strongest men—men who are Christian optimists, who will locate in our important centers and stand by the work until it succeeds. We are so few here in New England that the minister locating here buries himself out of sight as completely as does the man who enters central China or the Congo. We need men who are willing to lose themselves for Christ's sake. And our entire brotherhood ought to back the men who are willing to be used of God in planting primitive Christianity in this virgin soil.

To-day we are rejoicing in the prospect of larger things. The A. C. M. S. has promised to aid us this year by the amount of $2,000, or four times more than this society has been putting into this field. But even this depends upon our contributing one-third of this amount directly to the society. This we mean to do, for it will mean larger things for New England.

For the sake of the east I appeal to the brotherhood to sustain the A. C. M. S. An increased May offering will mean greater effort put forth here in New England.

E. JAY TEAGARDEN.

Our New England Churches

(Continued from Page 903.)

question, how may our churches most effectively carry on our work? It would be presumptuous in me to attempt to answer that question in any degree of fullness of detail. But there are some observations bearing more or less directly upon the question which I will offer.

What is the proper work of the church of God? And what relation does it bear to the propagation of what we call "our plea," or the distinctive truths for which we as a people stand? My observation of some other denominations convinces me that their churches cripple their usefulness, and therefore their success, very much because they do not seem to understand the real purpose of the churches, and the place of the doctrines for which they stand. For instance, our Adventist brethren are very devout Christians, but it seems to me that they make a hobby of the doctrines of the advent, which may be true but belief in which is not essential to salvation or to the successful work of the church, and they seem to think the mission of their churches is to preach their conception of the advent rather than to do any other kind of Christian work. And their usefulness and success is hindered by that fact. The same is true of other denominations. In fact the difference between the denominations consists not so much in their belief in different doctrines as in their emphasis of different doctrines which they hold in common.

We as a people hold that we have a mission to seek the unification of the divided church of God and to bring Christians back to the primitive Gospel as a means to such unification. That is our plea. But after all is the propagation of such views the primary function of our churches? Brother A. McLean, of the Foreign Missionary Society, says the primary function of the churches is to carry on foreign missions, because the command was given to the church to carry the Gospel to all parts of the world. It seems to me, however, that the work of missions and the propagation of our plea must both be regarded as incidental functions of our

churches. The local churches are intended to serve the religious needs of their communities above everything else. The primary function of our churches may not easily be defined, but it is to be found in the local work, by which it helps to make the city and community in which it is located a moral and orderly place in which to live, and meets the spiritual needs of those who come under its influence.

If this view be correct, then, since the way to usefulness is the way to success, our attention should be directed chiefly toward making our churches powers for good in their respective communities. I dare say this has been overlooked too much in the past. We have been so very zealous in the peculiar doctrines for which we stand, that we may have made somewhat of a hobby of them, like some of our religious neighbors. And in doing so we may not have been as careful about the spiritual condition of our churches and our members as we might have been. I am sure that is what many in other churches think of us. The fact is, the most effective work we can do in behalf of our peculiar plea is that which is done indirectly. In most things indirect influence is more effective than direct influence. If our views and practices are more correct than those of other churches, it ought to be apparent that our churches are more spiritual and have a more potent influence for good on the lives of their members than other churches. Unless we can make that fact apparent it will be difficult to convince others that ours is the better way. And if we can make that fact apparent we will be doing the most effective work for our plea that can be done.

The aim that of our churches should be to so fully meet the needs of the community that observers will say that this part of your city is more orderly and has a better moral tone because of the work of the faithful band worshiping in this church. That is the surest and I think the only way to success. And the result will be that our plea for union and the primitive Gospel will receive a sympathetic hearing.

It is hardly necessary to add that a hearty co-operation with other churches and worthy organizations in all that tends to civic righteousness and personal morality will be essential to success on these lines of activity.

Just how this work of influencing your community for good can be done, is a problem for the workers at each place to solve. It is a work in which every member of the church ought to be glad to engage in some manner or other. But the ones in authority over the church must seek opportunities to do all that can be done, and to drift along thoughtlessly missing our opportunities, both as individuals and as churches. Opportunities must be sought as well as embraced.

Brockton, Mass.

This is the charm of sages often told.
Converting all it touches into gold;
Content can soothe, where'er by fortune placed,
Can rear a garden in a desert place,
—Henry Kirke White.

The Manchester Meeting

(Continued from Page 909.)

for an hour and a half a simple Gospel service proceeds. Gradually the stolid conservatism gives way to intense interest, and soon the audience is singing heartily, and all through the sermon punctuates the speaker's remarks with nod of approval, or a smile in relish of a piece of humor in illustration of a point, and at the close crowd to the front to take the preacher's hand to bid him God speed. Four local preachers come forward and wish the meeting success. Even the collection was taken by a Baptist preacher and one of his deacons. Whatever of unresponsiveness may be attributed to New Englanders can not be charged to them in this service. Such a crowd at the New England gathering. The attendance at the Monday and Tuesday services was good, although not so large as on Sunday. I was told that New Englanders could not be made to laugh, but these New Eng-

Highland Street Church of Christ, Worcester, Mass.

landers laugh right out whenever a humorous point is scored.

Advertising must be done according to law through the licensed pastor and distributor, consequently this will be a very costly feature of these meetings. It will take so long to develop conditions for the general introduction of our plea and its final acceptance that I fear, with this heavy rent and other expenses and proverbially small collections, that Bro. Wright's prediction of $1,000 falls short by $250.

Even with a small nucleus it is difficult to get life into a movement; but with nothing, absolutely nothing, not even a man to take up a collection, you will see how we need your prayers. Pray for New England!

For a Church in New Hampshire.

Already acknowledged $545 10
W. H. Bates........................... 25 00

Total $570 10

With great power Herbert Yeuell is preaching "the old Jerusalem Gospel" in Manchester, N. H. At present we have no church in that state and no Disciples have yet been found in that city; $700 or more than half have been received are necessary to give this able evangelist a fair chance to establish a New Testament church under such circumstances. Will not some of the brethren and sisters at once send contributions for his support? A victory here will mean many new churches before centennial in cities on our four frontiers.

Our Budget

—Our New England issue.

—There is room for and need of 1,000 new Churches of Christ in New England.

—No better place for beginning their institution could be found, after painstaking investigation, than Manchester, N. H.—a state in which we have not a single congregation.

—Herbert Yeuell with all his great powers of evangelism fully enlisted is making an earnest effort to determine for us whether a Church of Christ can be built from the ground up in a New England city where there is not already existing a strong nucleus for the organization of a church. He is entitled to our help. Will not the friends of primitive Chistianity rally to his support by sending contributions to this office for his maintenance while this experiment is given fair trial?

—Few outside the office know how greatly the thousands of readers of THE CHRISTIAN-EVANGELIST are indebted to Paul Moore, Assistant-Editor, for the good things they enjoy in their favorite paper. Too close application to duty has so impaired Brother Moore's health that physi-

Paul Moore.

cians and friends have driven him into Yellowstone Park for a two months' recuperation. All who have enjoyed his weekly contributions to this journal will unite with us in our earnest desire that he may at the end of that period return to his post greatly improved.

—Read Bro. John S. Stevens' letter in another column. This is also a land and a time of missionary heroism.

—W. L. St. John, who is now at Brownsville, Ore., writes that the children's day apportionment there was five dollars and the collection twelve.

—Brother J. H. Garrison is acting as "summer shepherd" for the little flock at Pentwater, Mich. He preaches to the congregation each Lord's day and will until the minister comes.

—Sister John Hazelwood, of Payson (Ill.) church reports a Children's Day apportionment of $20, but $25 raised. Also two recent additions to the church by confession and baptism.

—James and John Encell recently gave illustrated stereopticon lectures at Marion, Ia., on "Lincoln and His Achieve-

ments." The local G. A. R. post adopted resolutions very highly commending the lectures.

—Bro. J. C. B. Stivers and wife, of Cleveland, O., propose to spend next autumn and winter in the south. Any church desiring the services of an able and consecrated husband and wife would do well to write to them.

—J. A. L. Romig has organized several new churches in the British northwest, and has spied out the land so that he knows where to organize a goodly number more. This is one of the most promising mission fields in America.

—Bro. F. F. Guyman, 1620 Walnut street, Toledo, O., proposes entering the field as a singing evangelist in the autumn. Bros. J. O. Shelburne, C. H. Bass, R. A. Omer and C. R. Oakley all commend him as to character and ability.

—Helping maintain Herbert Yeuell at Manchester should not interfere with generous support of M. L. Streator's great undertaking at Bridgeport. Let us go over into New England and help these men of God.

—Our church at Moberly, Mo., has installed a new pipe organ at a cost of $1,800, and the Chillicothe, Mo., brethren have just placed an order for one to cost $2,000. Both of these organs are from the factory of Geo. Kilgen & Son, of this city.

—The brethren in Delta, O., are planning an evangelistic campaign for next autumn and desire the services of a first-class man as evangelist. They also desire a first-class singer. Some evangelistic team doing regular work should apply for this meeting.

—The genial B. B. Tyler has contracted the "Jerusalem habit." He conducts another party to the Holy Land next February. A year in Bible college would not be more helpful than a four months' pilgrimage through Bible lands with this distinctively Bible man.

—Bro. J. S. Raum, of Yale, Mich., has resigned the pastorate of the church at Saginaw, and has entered the field as an evangelist. He has held a number of good meetings, and is well spoken of by those who know him. His terms are $25 per week. He may be addressed at Yale.

—Bro. W. W. Harris, of New Holland, O., has just published a number of brief tracts on "Our Plea," "Two Laws of Pardons," "Honor Bright," "Two Queries," "The Safe Side" and "The Design of Baptism." These sell at 25 cents per hundred and may be obtained from the author.

—Brother James Egbert has closed his ministry at St. Thomas, Ont., expecting to enter Oberlin (O.) Seminary, August 1. A recent St. Thomas evening journal contains an account of a farewell reception given Brother and Sister Egbert and bears witness of their great popularity in that city.

—J. J. Cole has resigned his work at Millersburg, O. The local paper speaks very highly of his ministry and contains commendatory resolutions adopted by the Millersburg Ministerial Association. Brother Cole is open to an engagement with a church affording opportunities for a large work.

—W. H. Harding, of Blue Mound, Ill, is a minister who has come down from "Our Lady of the Snows" with good purpose and the elements of real success. We congratulate this good friend of THE CHRISTIAN-EVANGELIST over the successful dedication of the beautiful new church home for his people.

—J. G. Shaw, of Francisville, Ind., announces that the second district convention meets at Fountain Park Assembly,

August 9 and 10. Special rates at hotels have been secured for delegates. Those intending to attend should write Brother Shaw in advance. An excellent program has been arranged.

—Bro. E. B. Bagby, Vermont Avenue Church, Washington, D. C., sends us a copy of an exceedingly interesting program to be rendered at the Bethany Beach (Del.) Assembly from July 29 to August 26. The names of very able speakers appear on the program and all who attend are to be congratulated.

—A recent issue of the Atlanta (Ga.) Journal contains a picture of the First Christian church, now being erected in that city, corner South Prior Street and Trinity Avenue. The paper highly eulogizes Brother H. K. Pendleton, the pastor, as a man of large ideas, lofty aims and very scholarly attainments.

—Bro. W. S. Houchins, in charge of our mission in Montreal, has adopted a novel way of advertising his Sunday meetings. He sends printed postal cards announcing his subjects and various meetings of the church through the mail to a large number of persons. This method is rapidly building up an attendance at all the meetings.

—A new star is rising in the constellation evangelistic. This one is named E. E. Violett. He may be addressed at either 2712 Pine Street, St. Louis, Mo., or Shelbyville, Tenn. Brother Violett's marvelous success as a pastor-evangelist has led him

E. E. Violett.

and his friends to believe his opportunities for usefulness will be greatly increased by devoting himself exclusively to this ministry. He has already made a number of engagements, but most churches can well afford to wait a long time for his coming.

—Texas Christian University is to be congratulated on securing Colby D. Hall for its general secretary. The university is now splendidly equipped with buildings, paraphernalia and faculty. Brother Hall will doubtless prove himself a great factor in the educational problems of the Lone Star State. He may be addressed at North Waco, Texas.

—During his continental tour, Hon. W. J. Bryan was invited to a dinner to be given in his honor on the Lord's day. He declined, saying "I am sorry, but this is Sunday and I go to church; won't you go with me?" Here this man who is regarded by most as pre-eminently a politician, has given an example that could be profitably followed by myriads of churchmen.

—J. L. Haddock sends us program of the ninth annual camp meeting of the churches of Christ of Northwest Texas to begin at Benjamin, Texas, August 18, and continuing sixteen days. The preaching will be done principally by Bros. J. L. Haddock and Chalmer McPherson. The place is beautiful for situation, and all will be greatly helped who attend.

—An efficient minister is wanted for a church in southern Missouri, salary $600 or $700 per year. Address L. J. Marshall, 900 South Main Street, Independence, Mo.

—J. F. Grissom has concluded his work at Mulkeytown, Ill., and assumed the pastorate of Bonne Terre (Mo.) church. He will also help some of the neighboring country churches.

—Bro. H. K. Shields, of Rochester, Ind., will soon begin a meeting at Elwood, Ind. He would like to engage evangelistic work in Kentucky and Tennessee. He will be found very helpful.

—From the Daily "News" of Denver, Col., we learn that Jesse B. Haston has accepted a call to the pastorate of the East Side church and that his people are hopeful of great achievements under his leadership.

—Geo. W. Maxwell, of Ute, Iowa, reports the work there greatly prospering. Substantial improvements are being made in the building, helpful additions are coming, and the Sunday-school growth is very gratifying.

—Evangelist S. W. Jackson and wife are in a meeting at Pecos, Tex. The church there wishes to engage a minister. Brother Jackson writes a good strong man will receive a liberal salary and will do well to write J. H. Wilhite immediately.

—Thomas Martin, of California, Pa., has been lecturing on the "Jerusalem Tragedy" in towns near his home. Brother Martin reports a prosperous state of affairs in the California church, and that it will meet all of its missionary apportionments.

—F. G. Tyrrell, formerly pastor of Mt. Cabanne Church, of this city, but now practicing law in Los Angeles, Cal., delivered a "Monologue on Fun" last Monday before the Men's Club of Bro. Jesse T. Mc-Knight's church in Los Angeles.

—Our good friend, Owen Livengood, is supplying the pulpit of the Central, Cincinnati, during the vacation absence of Pastor J. L. Hill. We are pleased to report to Brother Livengood's friends that his health has been fully regained.

—The Charlottesville, Va., Daily "Progress" gives prominence to Bro. C. R. Sines' reconsideration of his resignation as pastor of the Charlottesville church. Great pressure was brought to bear on him to continue with his people and he has decided to do so.

—A witty brother began a paper on "How to Reach the Masses," with this sentence: "There are no masses." So in answer to the question, "Why has there been a slump in our missionary offerings?" we would remark, "There has been no slump." When the returns are all in, this fact will be apparent.

—We are pleased to print elsewhere a communication from Bro. H. C. Kendrick, of Hagerstown, Md. It was a great pleasure to note during a recent visit to Hagerstown the love and affection in which this consecrated and gifted man and his equally capable companion are held by the entire membership of that noble church. We hope they will realize all their aspirations before centennial time.

NERVOUS WOMEN

Take Horsford's Acid Phosphate

It quiets the nerves, relieves nausea and sick headache and induces refreshing sleep.

—F. L. Moffett, for many years pastor at Centerville, Iowa (Gen. F. N. Drake's home church), has accepted a call to the South Side Church at Springfield, Mo. This change will cost Iowa one of her ablest men, but it is a loss that some of our younger ministers there will quickly supply.

—The handsome catalogues of Christian University are from the presses of the Christian Publishing Company. We are pleased to learn from President Johann that Christian University is entering upon what seems to be the most prosperous era in its history. We earnestly desire this may be more than mere seeming.

—J. M. Settle, of New Franklin, writes that Arthur N. Lindsey recently resigned his work in Howard County but the New Franklin and neighboring churches for which he was working rejected his resignation. During his six years' residence there he has added 1,600 to the churches and built three new church homes.

—G. E. Trone, of Bay Field, Col., says if a Christian minister desires to visit that part of Colorado through the summer and will hold meetings in the Bay Field Church for the freewill offerings and his entertainment, the church will be glad to hear from him. There is no organized body of Disciples in that county.

J. H. O. Smith has resigned from the great church at Valparaiso, Ind., to enter the evangelistic field. He will begin at Jacksonville, Ill., September 1. While Brother Smith's great value as pastor is universally recognized, we believe that even greater success will crown his labors in this special field for which he has demonstrated peculiar fitness.

—A Watts (Cal.) brother writes he will not renew his subscription to THE CHRISTIAN-EVANGELIST because of its advocacy to the tithing system which is Judaistic rather than Christian. THE CHRISTIAN-EVANGELIST will not plead guilty, but if this brother will convince us he is giving one-half as much as one-tenth of his income to the Lord we will send him the paper gratuitously.

—After a nine years' pastorate at Clinton, Ill., E. A. Gilliland has tendered his resignation, to become effective in the early autumn. The official board voted not to accept it but against the protests of the board and membership generally, Brother Gilliland will soon close his labors there to enter the evangelistic field. He is highly commended to the churches by those whom he has most faithfully served.

—R. C. Ogburn will close his two years' work with the church at Flora, Ill., about August 1. During his pastorate one hundred have been added to the membership, $2,000 paid off on the debt, while the missionary activities of the church have been greater than ever before, and all the organizations strengthened. It is Brother Ogburn's intention to continue in the pastorate either in Illinois or farther east.

—E. D. Anthony, writing of the meeting Pastor R. O. Rogers recently concluded at Fredericktown, Mo., says it is the most helpful meeting held in that part of the state for many years. There were seventy additions; among the number several from the Catholic, Baptist, Episcopalian, Methodist and Presbyterian churches. A new era of Bible study and church enthusiasm and consecrated living has been inaugurated.

—The Indiana Christian Ministerial Association recently met with the Bethany Park Assembly from July 30 to August 1. An exceptionally able program is provided. Among the men from out the state we note that W. F. Richardson, of Kansas City, delivers three lectures. The brethren will be greatly benefited who at-

tend. President L. L. Carpenter, of the assembly, is making every possible effort to make the summer session profitable.

—We are pleased to learn of the approaching marriage of Miss Tena Williamson to Frank Allen, of Columbia, Mo. Brother Allen is one of our most useful preachers and well deserves his happy future. Miss Williamson will long be remembered as the extraordinarily successful matron of the Christian Orphan's Home of this city. Lives of long continued happiness and usefulness for them will be the wish of all who read this announcement.

—O. D. Maple, of Marion, O., planned for a revival at Delaware, O. Sectarian opposition has so far delayed the meeting. The opposition was so malignant as to awaken the sympathy of the members of the churches of the opposing preachers for the evangelist, and the probabilities are that the meeting Brother Maple will yet hold there will be fully as successful as if he had not to overcome these seeming barriers to success.

—Thomas J. Shuey has been trying to encourage some of our earnest preachers who are laboring faithfully in smaller parishes neighboring his own. He has visited a number of the churches in the interest of home missions, with more than forty additions as a result. His own work at Abingdon, Ill., goes forward. He is now well along in his third year as pastor and the church has given about $500 each year to benevolences and missions.

—Bro. John M. Alexander, of Cropper, Ky., has gone among the churches in his own and adjoining counties at his own expense in the interest of the American Christian Missionary Society seeking to secure an offering from every church. It is only as the brethren will give time to getting the non-contributing churches into line that any of our missionary organizations can hope for large increases. We thank this good man for the hearty help he has given.

—The First Church at Bloomington, Ill., has extended a unanimous call to Bro. Edgar D. Jones, of the Franklin Circle Church of Cleveland, O. Brother Jones has achieved remarkable success at Cleveland, but on account of an incipient throat trouble, will have to leave the city of raw lake winds. We heartily congratulate our Bloomington brethren. Brother Jones is one of THE CHRISTIAN-EVANGELIST'S ablest contributors, and we wish him well in all his enterprises.

—A debate will be held at Lynchburg, Va., August 20 to 23 between H. J. Farmer, a Seventh Day Adventist, and W. G. Johnson, one of our ministers. Question: "Resolved, That the seventh day is the Sabbath of perpetual obligation." Farmer affirms, Johnson denies. Bro. A. C. Kimball reports that both are very able men and that the church is expecting a profitable time and a glorious triumph for the truth. Visitors will be pleasantly entertained for 50 cents or 75 cents per day.

—Bro. J. L. Thompson, of the Tabernacle Church, and F. J. Burnham, of the Central of Decatur, Ill., have recently organized a mission Bible school in that city, with an initial enrollment of 106. This is in a rapidly growing district of the city, and it is believed that ere long a new church may be established with fine prospects of becoming one of the strongest organizations in Central Illinois. We commend this example to other preachers living in rapidly growing cities.

—We have just learned through a note from Bro. J. T. Boone of the sudden death of Bro. T. H. Blenus, of Jacksonville, Fla. He died suddenly on last Sunday morning. Brother Blenus, was pastor of the Church Street Christian Church in that city. It was only recently that we had a very pleasant letter from him from which we made extracts in THE CHRISTIAN-EVANGELIST. Our Christian sympathies are extended to the bereaved wife and congregation. Further notice will, no doubt, be sent us later.

—The call of the Acting Board of the American Christian Missionary Society to W. J. Wright to become corresponding secretary, will meet with universal approval. The great successes characterizing Brother Wright's various ministries, his Christian integrity, and sanctified progressiveness give him great prestige, and his great abilities as an organizer and propagandist will surely make our home society a greater power in the future even than it has been in the past for the extension of primitive Christianity throughout America.

❦ ❦

Young People of Small Means

will be helped in securing an education at "Iowa Christian College." Board and tuition $30 per term. Correspondence courses also. Write Pres. Chas. J. Burton, Oskaloosa, Iowa. Free catalogue.

—Bro. W. H. Bagby, of Missoula, Mont., in a very able article concerning the fluctuation of missionary offerings expresses the opinion that the falling off in the year's receipts from the Home Missionary Society may be readily accounted for without referring it to any discussions in our religious journals. These rising and falling tides are incidents in the history of all missionary societies and are especially liable to follow any high pressure methods of securing funds. He advises more natural and systematic methods of giving as a cure for these reactions.

—Faithful T. M. Kincaid, of Hot Springs, Ark, writes that work on his church is progressing favorably A serious problem now is the support of regular preaching while payments are being made on the new building. Hot Springs is one of the most cosmopolitan cities in the world. There is no more advantageous point for the location of a Church of Christ. Help there is worthily bestowed. He writes further that the prosecuting attorney has eradicated the pool-rooms from the city and it is believed that very soon all forms of gambling will be banished.

—G. K. Berry, of Portland, reports the following lectures recently delivered before his people: Monday evening, "The History and Teaching of the Greek Catholic Church"; Tuesday evening, "The History and Teaching of the Roman Catholic"; Wednesday evening, "The History and Teaching of Martin Luther"; Thursday evening, "The History and Teaching of the Church of England"; Friday evening, "The History and Teaching of John Calvin"; Saturday evening, "The History and Teaching of John Wesley"; Sunday morning, "The History and Teaching of the Baptists"; Sunday evening, "The History and Teaching of the Disciples of Christ." We believe great good will be accomplished by having Brother Berry deliver this course of lectures to all our coast churches.

—George Ringo, writing from Ocean Park, Cal., beside the sun-down sea," earnestly pleads for financial assistance in building a church home for the Disciples in that "Atlantic City of the Pacific Coast." The present opportunity for establishing a Church of Christ there is peculiarly favorable. It is not pre-empted by the denominations, nor is there any existing prejudice against Disciples. The membership in the church has doubled within the past six months, and the attendance at the Bible school has more than doubled in the same time. A local mill has offered to make the pews for cost of material and a Los Angeles firm will glaze the windows without profit. Write Brother Ringo a word of encouragement, backed up with a gift for the new church home.

—George F. Cirtes, Barnesville, O., is working for six months in West Virginia under the joint support of the A. C. M. S. and the West Virginia state society. His first work is in connection with the state-wide simultaneous evangelistic campaign, which will be held next October and November. He is interesting every possible congregation in this movement. He is holding some evangelistic meeetings, has already organized one church, and perhaps by the time this appears will have organized a second. He is securing preachers for the churches needing them and speaking a good word everywhere in behalf of our colleges and missionary enterprises. No man among us has a more important work or in a place which promises greater returns.

—A communication received some time ago from Phil A. Parsons explains some of the difficulties of our cause at Plainfield, N. J. It seems that an old disputed claim against the property of the church, which had been in the courts off and on for ten

years, was decided in favor of the claimants for the sum of $3,100 and costs, which made the brethren liable for about $3,600. For several weeks the situation seemed hopeless, but the Board of Church Extension agreeing to make a loan of $2,000, a compromise with the claimants was effected which necessitated the brethren raising only about $600, immediately. In a little over thirty days the money was raised, since which the work has been prospering as never before. Brother Parsons wishes publicly to express gratitude to many friends who have sympathized with our brethren at Plainfield in their trying hours.

❦ ❦

Picture of War Engine "General."

A beautiful colored picture, 18x25 inches, of the historic old engine "General" which was stolen at Big Shanty, Ga., by the Andrew's Raiders during the Civil War, and which is now on exhibition in the Union Depot, Chattanooga, Tenn., has been gotten out by the NASHVILLE, CHATTANOOGA & ST. LOUIS RY. The "Battlefields Route" to the South. The picture is ready for framing and will be mailed for 25c. The "Story of the General" sent free. W. L. Danley, Gen'l Pass. Agent, Nashville, Tenn.

—The twentieth anniversary of the Howell Street Church of Christ, at Rochester, N. Y., was an occasion of much rejoicing. This congregation has worshiped in the present building about fifteen years, and at its anniversary enough was made to clear off some $300 indebtedness. There was a suggestion of novelty in the method of raising the money. Three hundred shares of stock at $1 each were issued. These were subscribed for by the church members, Sunday-school classes, etc. William D. Ryan, late of Syracuse, in presenting whom F. Richard Eaton introduced as his "spiritual father," said that there are many people who spend more money in two months on theaters than they do in two years on that church. These seem to regard the church as a sort of peanut stand—a place where only nickels are required.

—Geo. A. Kinley, of Wilkinsburg, Pa., writes that L. N. D. Wells surprised his people July 1 by resigning his pastorate there, to take effect September 1. His work has been very successful and has earned for him a foremost position among the able ministers of Western Pennsylvania. Coming to Wilkinsburg less than five years ago, he found not more than 125 Disciples, a mission church receiving $300 aid yearly from the Western Pennsylvania board, and struggling with a heavy mortgage. In the five years of his pastorate he has received into the fellowship of the Disciples of Christ over 500 laborers for the Master. The church is now self-supporting and the mortgage has been reduced several thousands of dollars; besides his people have contributed splendidly for home and foreign missions, until now the church occupies a commanding position in Western Pennsylvania, and is one of the foremost in Wilkinsburg. Brother Wells has also achieved great success in evangelistic work in Western Pennsylvania and Ohio. He is also a strong Prohibition worker and prominent in Christian Endeavor work, and as a teacher of young men's classes in the Bible school. September 1 he will take up his studies in Columbia University, New York City, and at the same time preach for the Christian Church of East Orange, N. J. His earnest preaching, his kind and sympathetic disposition, his helping hand to those in distress, have awakened the respect and love of all, and his leaving is deeply regretted by his own flock, his fellow ministers, the press and hundreds of his fellow townsmen.

—Bro. T. W. Grafton writes us about an interesting contest which was held during May and June between the Sunday-schools of the Central Christian Church, Anderson, Ind., and the Christian Church at Canton, O. Three points were contested—total attendance, new scholars and collections. It will be seen by the tabulated report that Canton sur-

passed Anderson by 2,496 in total attendance, while the Anderson Sunday-school collected $13.51 more than Canton, and gained 287 more new scholars, thus making the Anderson school the winner of the contest. We print the figures as one indication of the values of such contests. We shall be glad to hear from Sunday-school superintendents all over the country as to the permanent value not only in point of figures but in what we regard as even more important, namely, the educational and moral standards to a Bible school of these contests.

CANTON.

	New Scholars.	Total Attendance.	Total Col'ns.
May 6	23	1,144	$27 69
May 13	22	1,161	13 03
May 20	41	1,172	30 88
May 27	52	1,533	34 01
June 3	35	1,322	34 54
June 10	54	1,550	172 50
June 17	39	1,108	51 35
June 24	118	1,644	591 25
	384	10,434	$975 25
		7,938	....
		2,496	....

ANDERSON.

	New Scholars.	Total Attendance.	Total Col'ns.
May 6	32	336	$17 87
May 13	72	792	20 13
May 20	77	886	26 13
May 27	60	1,005	28 14
June 3	91	1,001	31 60
June 10	84	1,089	263 79
June 17	74	1,044	86 95
June 24	211	1,285	520 15
	671	7,938	988 76
	384	....	975 25
	287	....	$13 51

❋ ❋

Nebraska State Convention.

The Nebraska state convention will be held this year at the Bethany Assembly Park, near Lincoln, July 31-August 5. The arrangements are nearing completion and will be the most perfect for the care of the convention goers that we have ever made. Over two thousand were enrolled last year and the indications seem to point to an increase this year. Improvements are making in the grounds and the floor of the tabernacle is being graded. This will make it high and dry and help in the matter of seeing the speakers. It is being painted and the roof stained which will add greatly to its appearance. The dining hall service will be improved as largely as possible.

The program has been carefully arranged and includes some of the great men outside the state, as well as some of the best of our own. W. J. Lhamon will deliver the Bible lectures. Professor Sutton will deliver another series of his splendid missionary addresses. Stephen J. Corey, Geo. B. Ranshaw, R. H. Waggener, Miss Annette Newcomer and I. N. McCash, are among the outstate speakers. State Evangelist Robert F. Whiston will deliver the evangelistic sermons in the evening. They will be short, crisp, full of the old Gospel.

discussed: The Personal Element in Evangelism, The Teaching Element in Evangelism, The Spirit of Evangelism, Constant Evangelism, The Evangelist, The Evangelistic Sermon, The Evangelist for the Twentieth Century, Prayer in Evangelism.

There will be conferences on many subjects, and a question box open daily.

It is expected that many of our prominent evangelists will be present and partake in the proceedings. Those who were present last year will not soon forget the great uplift which they received, and certainly they will be ready for the proposed school this year. It is desired that every preacher within hundreds of miles shall attend in order that his presence may be an inspiration and in order that the speakers may prove an inspiration to him.

Buy a ticket to Indianapolis and go to Bethany Park on the trolley which leaves the interurban station hourly.

❦ ❦

Congratulations to Drake.

Drake University is the happy recipient of another gift of $1,000, on which the University pays an annuity of six per cent. This is the best form of investment. The income is sure every six months, and the money is doing good in educating young men and women. If the reader desires to investigate concerning annuities, write Joel Brown, or President Hill M. Bell, Drake University.

❦ ❦

Annuity News.

The American Christian Missionary Society has just issued its one hundred and thirty-sixth annuity bond to Mrs. Emily J. Alden, Washington, D. C. The amount is $500.

Interest is paid promptly twice per year without asking for it. Donors are conscious that at least this portion of their goods will be used to further the Lord's work. No wills to break. The money is already ours.

AMERICAN CHRISTIAN MISSIONARY SOCIETY, Cincinnati, O.   Y. M. C. A. Bldg.

❦ ❦

Convention in China.

The annual convention of the Central China Christian Mission was held in Nankin in the last week of May. The attendance was very good indeed, every member of the mission now on the field being present with two exceptions. We feel very much pleased with the results of the meeting. A spirit of harmony prevailed throughout. There was indeed almost perfect unanimity as to the policy to be followed out in the future. We feel now that we have passed the experimental stage in our work. There seems to be no reason now for a repetition of some of the mistakes made by new men in a new mission. Our force has been recently depleted by the inval-

iding home of some and the furloughs of others of our mission, making it necessary to readjust and change around a considerable; and there has been no little loss as a consequence. There has been, during the last several years, an abnormal demand from home for spreading out on the mission field. We have yielded to this, really against our better judgment and because there seemed to be no other alternative and as a result got ourselves into such a condition of dilution that the unexpected depletions seriously affected us. We have now come to our senses, and I do not think we will do so any more. It will be a great day for the success of mission work, when the church and the society come to realize that the missionaries on the field know more about what should be the policy in practical details of mission work, than it is possible for any one else to know. If there is one policy more disastrous than another on the mission field it is the policy of scatteration. This, I think, we thoroughly understand now, and if we are allowed to order our work accordingly we can promise great results in the future. Miss Dale is at Wuhu alone, owing to the home-going of Brother Arnold, and Chu Cheo is not much better off on account of the furlough of Dr. Osgood and the serious illness of Willie Hunt, which makes it necessary for Brother Hunt to be away from his station most of his time. Dr. Layton will not return to Bodjou because he has no one to go with him, and the mission does not think he should return, and so the depletion has gone on. These disappointments could not have occurred so much to our detriment had we been wiser and located a sufficient number of workers at these places in the first place to enable us to tide over in such emergencies.

We have now decided that we will open no more new stations as centers which are not of sufficient importance to admit of three resident families and that at least two of these families must be on the field and ready to enter these places, before they are occupied. Further we have determined that the field already occupied must be supplied before we push on into new fields. I have mentioned these points because I think the brethren at home ought to know just what is going on and then they will understand better how to account for some things that transpire which they see in the reports of our work.

But in spite of all our mistakes we have much cause for rejoicing and we are in no measure discouraged. The work has gone steadily on. There has been no going back. There has been increase of interest in every department. The spirit of Christian union has obtained foothold with leaps and bounds during the last year, revivals in the churches have deepened the spiritual life of the members of the churches, and we are in most ways stronger and better prepared for a vigorous campaign than we were at the beginning of last year. Our school work is more prosperous than we had reason to hope it would be. The great strides made by the Chinese government in the opening of schools on modern lines, has tended to create an increasing desire for the kind of work we are doing, and there has been a consequent increase in the number of applicants we have received. Our schools are all full and many have been turned away.

The move on foot now to establish a great Christian University in Nankin promises great things for Christian education in China. It is likely known al-

ready at home that Christian College has arranged for union with the Presbyterian school in Nanking. The two schools will be united in the coming autumn. Then it is hoped that by the first of the next year the larger scheme will be consummated. It is more than federation, it is actual union in school work. There is no manner of compromise. God is in the movement. Its history will be most interesting reading. As the revival spirit goes abroad, we are able, under the pressure of the great work before us of saving China, to forget our differences and work together for the accomplishment of this great purpose. We have no time to quarrel. If some of our brethren who have so much to say about the cause going back, they would get well of their anxiety. The church may split at home, but we shall unite out here. There will be one Church of Christ in China.

We are greatly disappointed because of the home-going of Professor Paul. We had hoped for great things from him on the mission field, but he thinks he ought to go home, and we bow to the inevitable. There is a great opening for men in the school work, and we need some one right away to take Professor Paul's place. I wish some good man would go to see Professor Paul at Hiram and learn of the need and decide to come out forthwith. I should be glad to correspond with any man who will consider the matter of being a missionary teacher in the new university. Pray for us.   F. E. MEIGS.

CHURCH FEDERATION READY.

CHURCH DEDICATIONS.

At Blue Mound, Ill.

The church was organized over fifty years ago by Elder Andrew Northcott, who was its first preacher and is one of the oldest organizations in Macon county. The first meetings were in a schoolhouse at Randallville, as Blue Mound was not then laid out. The little band grew stronger in the face of many difficulties and had much to contend with from the stern sectarianism of the time. About thirty years ago the present old building was purchased from the United Brethren

W. H. Harding, Blue Mound, Ill.

and has been in constant use until the dedication of the present beautiful brick structure on July 8. Many eminent preachers and evangelists have preached and held special meetings in the old building and although the church has had many drawbacks and hindrances it has made steady progress and at the present time is in the best condition in its history with good prospects of greater growth and strength. On May 1, 1905, the present minister, W. H. Harding,

came to the work at the earnest request of the church, and conditions were such that they seemed to need a level head to lead them. At once the present new building enterprise was started and on July 4, 1905, the cornerstone was laid with Bro. B. L. Smith making the address, and the work has gone steadily forward to completion. The building is of Decatur brick and the accompanying cut will show the design. The interior is finished in oak and natural wood. The auditorium will seat 350 and when all the rooms are thrown into one, the full seating capacity will be about 600. The beautiful cathedral glass windows are rich in their design and in harmony with the rest of the building. A large furnace will heat the different rooms and it is lighted throughout with electricity. The basement extends under the entire building, and when finished it will be used for social purposes. The entire cost of the building was $12,000, and on dedication day $8,000 were called for. Bro. L. L. Carpenter came to us and during the day $7,000 in cash and pledges were secured and the other $1,000 easily provided for.

During the day there were visitors from Decatur, Harristown, Taylorville, Mt. Auburn and other places; fully 800 people were packed in the building, the seating capacity of which is only 600. A great victory has been won for the cause of Christ in this community. Brother Carpenter is one of God's noblemen and his visit to Blue Mound will long be remembered.   W. H. HARDING.

Bisbee, Ariz.

Last evening, July 3, we had an informal opening of our new church. With drop curtain partitions for two rooms it is an eight-room building. Three of them are for pastor's home, five for church and Sunday-school. By getting some materials from the old high school building across the street we saved about $1,500. We have the best church building in town. It is beautiful to win out,

to climb up to the top, get a home, domestic or spiritual; that is what the brethren have done. No debt; no lien; pledges will be all in within six months. Some of our difficulties: carpenters struck, agreed to $4 a day, but must have $5 for nine hours. Then plasterers must have $7 a day! The earthquake raised price of some of the materials for us. Oh, well, why should we complain when it is over?

I start for Southern California with Mrs. Trundle July 5.   DAN TRUNDLE.

[We most heartily congratulate our Bisbee brethren on this triumphant conclusion of their efforts to secure a church home.]

✸ ✸

Mahommed Asheroff.

On July 6, 1906, there arrived at the School of the Evangelists a young Arabian having an unusual story to tell. He was born in Beirut, Syria, about twenty-five years ago. His father and mother died when he was 12 years old. He was brought up under the strict and cruel tutelage of Mohammedanism. He was sent to a military training school in Macedonia, and finally became a lieutenant in the Turkish army. He was detailed to escort pilgrims visiting Palestine. In this way he came in contact with many English-speaking people. He speaks English remarkably well. I asked him, "When did you first hear of Jesus?" He answered that he had heard of him for a long time, but it is dangerous to even mention his name in the Turkish army. In the course of time some one gave him a copy of the New Testament in his native tongue. He read until the light began to break. He finally met a traveler named Nichols or Nicholson or Nicoson, who explained the way of salvation to him. Whoever the traveler was, he told the young man the truth. He knows but little, but he knows it straight. He finally asked the traveler where he could go and learn more about the Bible. The traveler drew from his pocket a copy of our catalogue and tore off my address and gave to him, and the young man promptly deserted the army, and with his savings (about $500), started for Kimberlin Heights!

When he got to Liverpool his troubles began. He went to the ticket office of the steamship company; the agent asked him his Christian name. He replied, "I have no Christian name; my name is Mahommed Asheroff, but I want to be a Christian man, agent."

They booked him for passage under the name John Jameson!

In New York the thing grew worse. They wanted to know if he were an anarchist. He did not know what they meant. They asked how many wives he had, and he told them none. Finally he showed them the address, told them he wanted to be a Christian, and they let him land. After many trials he reached his destination.

To-day he heard his first sermon. He even now wishes to be baptized! I believe he is a sincere searcher after the truth.

To us it is remarkable that the little ragged piece of paper so far from Kimberlin Heights, should be his only transport, from darkness to light. It makes us think of the Star of Bethlehem, for it is certain that whatever glory shines from the name on the "transport" it is borrowed from Him whose star it was that guided the wise men to the cradle of the new-born King! He shows a willingness to work. Soon after his arrival he said: "I want to do like the others." He wanted to work. We are gratifying his desire.   ASHLEY S. JOHNSON.

Christian Church, Blue Mound, Ill.

NEWS FROM MANY FIELDS

Hagerstown, Md.

I began my sixth year as pastor of the First Christian Church of Hagerstown, Sunday, July 8. It may be that some of your readers will be interested in the following brief statement of some things that this good church has accomplished during the five years of my ministry.

Total money contributed for all purposes during the five years, $18,450; total for missions, benevolences, etc., $3,822; average per year for missions, etc., $764.00. The church is entirely out of debt. One hundred and forty have been added to the church. In these five years we placed an elegant pipe organ in the church, put new furnaces in the basement, made most pleasing changes to our auditorium, including a new Brussels carpet; beloved friends presented a fine piano for the lecture room, our Sunday-school room is now undergoing a complete change, and in another week we will have one of the most attractive lecture rooms in the city.

There is a shadow to cast on the bright picture. We have had our sorrows, our sad losses, some, it may be, have departed from the faith, and others have departed to be with the loved ones on the other side. We have our regrets. We regret some things that we have done, but possibly the most saddening thought is that to what we have left undone. "Of all sad words of tongue or pen, the saddest are these, it might have been." This report might be better; we might have done more. Comparing ourselves with others, there are few churches that have so much of brightness and so little of shadow; so little to discourage and so much to encourage. With faith, hope, love and courage we have another year, another five years, if God keeps us so long for his work on earth.

The following are some of our aims. At least 100, added to our church this year. We are now in correspondence with some of our strong evangelists with the view of securing their services in a revival. We seek an average attendance in our Sunday-school of 300; our average now is over 200. Our ambition is to become a Living-Link in both home and foreign missions by our Centennial year, 1909. We hope to have a large number of THE CHRISTIAN-EVANGELISTS to aid us in the realization of our aims. May the Lord bless this good paper. Every Disciple needs it above all other papers.   H. C. KENDRICK.

Kentucky Work and Workers.

Morehead congregation has enjoyed the preaching of W. F. Smith every Lord's day during June and the work progresses about as usual.—L. N. Early has closed his work at Chatham, Bracken county, where we have helped in his support. Considerable growth has been made there during his ministry. He leaves Augusta where he has lived and where he has labored the greater part of his time during the past year. He ought to be kept in Kentucky by some one of our congregations and he can be reached at Petersburg, Ky.—J. W. Masters has been laying siege to Harlan Court House. He has gathered together 18 people there, has a lot given and some money pledged. He thinks that he can build a house without getting help outside of the county. He regards that place a fine opening for a school and thinks that our people could do much for that region by establishing one. Nine additions.—D. G. Combs, the tireless, was at work in the counties of Bath, Lewis and

Fleming 27 days, added 62, organized a new congregation in Lewis county and thinks a house will be built at once.—C. M. Summers is in Pike county doing his best to get the work at Pikeville well in hand. The outlook is excellent.—Edw. B. Richey has been at South Louisville all the month. Two added. The new house is well on the way to completion—at least it looks as if the house will be ready for dedication in September, prior to the state convention. It is going to be a beauty and one of the best built houses of its class I ever saw.—W. H. Cord is now in a meeting at Cannel City, E. J. Willis doing the preaching. A fine meeting is expected.—The new house at Springville was dedicated during the month. L. L. Carpenter officiated and raised the money needed to pay the debt on the house, $1,200. G. T. Thomason has been helped for six months in his work there and in that section. This closes our agreement to render such help. He had a good meeting in Greenup county, with 34 added.—Jas. E. Thomas has closed his work at Beattyville and started for Australia. There were additions at the last service and he goes to his far-away home with the love and gratitude of the people where he has labored so self sacrificingly and earnestly for the Master's cause. J. S. Mills will succeed him at that point.—T. S. Buckingham is trying to arrange a meeting for Edmont, in Metcalfe county, where he preaches one Sunday per month, and in which work our board has fellowship.—Bromley has the services of H. C. Runyon in a meeting, six added and much other good done. Earl B. Barr regards the meeting as being very helpful.—The Springfield work goes on about as usual and W. P. Walden reports that the expected meeting is deferred until W. J. Cooke can be had to help in the effort to reach the people of that community with the message of the Gospel.—A meeting will be held at Belleview next month where we help to support E. C. Riley for a part of his time.—Wellsburg enjoyed the services of E. T. Wells and two were added by baptism and two by letter. A meeting will be held next month.—S. J. Short added eight in the Big Sandy Valley and visited four places.—The meeting at Jackson closed with ten added by letter or statement and one by confession. Nine officers were selected and are to be ordained soon. A Sunday-school was organized with 28 in attendance and $3.62 collection.—C. A. Van Winkle was at work 28 days in Jackson and Estill counties. Nineteen additions constitute a part of the results of his work. This closes his work in the field and he will take up the Berea work. He wants to go back into the field and raise money for support of his successor.—H. W. Elliott was engaged all the month at home and abroad in the interest of the work. The collections amounted to $384.42—that is gifts from churches and individuals. This pays only about one-half the month's expenses. The board was compelled to borrow money that the men might be paid. We are getting deeper in debt each month. We appeal to the churches that have not made a gift to this work to do so at the earliest possible moment. We urge all friends of the great work we are seeking to do in the needy fields of Kentucky to lend a hand. This is our time of great need. Hundreds of our brethren and sisters can help up in these trying weeks. Gifts of from $1 to $1,000 could be received from our friends if they would give heed to the calls for support of the Gospel work in our own state.   H. W. ELLIOTT, Sec.

Sulphur, Ky.

New Zealand Items.

Notwithstanding my being so far removed from the seat of war, I am deeply interested in the very lively tilt some of our papers in the home land are having over the federation movement; and take this opportunity to say that I most heartily endorse both the position taken by THE CHRISTIAN-EVANGELIST and the very excellent spirit in which it is defending that position. Brother Garrison's course in this matter must in the end result, not only in great good to the brotherhood, but to the cause of Christian union at large. One of the most amazing things in the controversy is the unkind spirit of passion that some of the opposers of federation have worked themselves into, and that seems to govern them so fully in their writings. Men who are led to such extremes must feel in their own conscience that they have a weak cause. Oh, for a greater measure of that meek and kindly spirit that so fully dominated the Master.

Since commencing this short letter the sad news has been flashed all over the colony that Richard Seddon, the premier of New Zealand, is dead. He died very suddenly on board a steamer, a few hours out from Australia, which was bringing him home from a tour he had been making in that country. Mr. Seddon has been the leader of the liberal government here for the last fifteen years, and was elected a few months ago for another term. He was just 61 years of age. He came up from the ranks of the working men, having at one time labored with his own hands in the mines of this colony.—We have recently had fourteen additions to the church in this city, all by baptism except one. A few weeks ago Evangelist Hamilton and his singer landed in New Zealand from America, and passed on to the south where they were to hold some meetings. I feel that I should not close without saying that I have lately read Brother Garrison's work on the Holy Spirit, and most heartily enjoyed it. I wish it could be read and studied by the whole brotherhood. Our people are greatly lacking in many places in their knowledge of the indwelling of the Spirit.   HUGH T. MORRISON, Sr.

Wellington, Australia.

❦ ❦

Board of Ministerial Relief of the Church of Christ.

Aid in the support of worthy, needy, disabled ministers of the Christian Church and their widows.

THIRD LORD'S DAY IN DECEMBER is the day set apart in all the churches for the offering to this work. If you make individual offerings, send direct to the Board. Wills and Deeds should be made to "BOARD OF MINISTERIAL RELIEF OF THE CHURCH OF CHRIST, a corporation under the laws of the State of Indiana." Money received on the Annuity Plan.

Address all communications and make all checks, drafts, etc., payable to BOARD OF MINISTERIAL RELIEF, 120 E. Market St., Indianapolis, Indiana.

Nebraska Secretary's Letter.

Evon Forell has been called for a seventh year of service at Aurora. He is now the dean of the college of pastors in Nebraska.——D. A. Youtzy has located with the churches at Gering and Mitchell. His long service at Plattsmouth endeared him to the people there.——Nebraska city is repairing their house of worship under the leadership of John T. Smith. The work is in healthy condition.——Lou A. Hussong is supplying for Greenwood and this will doubtless be a permanent arrangement for the coming year. Brother Hussong will take at least another year in the state university.——Austin and McVey were at Esbon, Kan., in a tent meeting when last heard from.——The latest new church to be organized in the state is the one at Oak, in Nuckolls county. Melvin Putman and Miss Egbert held a short meeting and perfected an organization on June 29.——Four baptisms at Auburn in June. Four added at Minden in two weeks. They are occupying the state tent while rebuilding.——R. A. Schell closed his long pastorate at Hebron the last Lord's day in June. Large audiences greeted him. A reception was tendered him and his family on Tuesday following, with substantial remembrances. On Wednesday evening five baptisms completed the closing ceremonies. He has moved to Hastings and is now at work on his new field.——Excavating has begun for the new church at Beatrice, and is probably finished by this writing. Contract let for the brick, and the work is progressing. J. E. Davis is the pastor.——John L. Stine, who was formerly a preacher in active work among us at Schuyler and Auburn, has again entered the ministry and has taken work at Wakefield and Norfolk. He will live at Wakefield. Brother Stine has been teaching for several years. Geo. Light has been preaching at Takamah trying to revive that work.——Burton H. Whiston's wife died suddenly, and the body was taken back to Lowell, Mass., for burial.——J. W. Sapp has moved to Shubert from Nemaha. He still preaches half time at Nemaha. T. B. McDonald has closed his work at Bradshaw and is now visiting with relatives at Cozad. Expects to spend the summer in a tent for the health of both himself and wife.—— The annual report of the Fairbury church. H. C. Holmes, pastor, shows the following: Eighty-six sermons, 27 funerals, 21 weddings. 1,227 visits. Net increase of membership 292. Moneys raised, $3,392.92; for missions and benevolences, $508.52, which does not include about $100 for foreign missions. Increase of membership during Brother Holmes' pastorate is 513.——H. H. Harmon began his work with the first church at Lincoln July 1. The work opens up well and the outlook for a great work is flattering.——N. T. Harmon is supplying at Valparaiso while that church is looking for a preacher.——W. W. Harris has moved to Bethany, and is available for a supply for some church during the summer. Address him there.——J. W. Hilton was re-elected as pastor of the University church at Bethany, for another year. The last year's work has been most profitable and helpful. The church has grown in every way.——Jean Cobbey supplied at Hooker schoolhouse recently and will go again.—— Oscar Sweeney and wife, of Ord, are taking care of Burwell and also Palmer temporarily.——W. A. Baldwin.

North Carolina Notes.

After leaving Winston-Salem, Brother Yeuell held a meeting in Madison, N. C., a town about thirty miles from here. There are only about half a dozen Disciples there. He was invited by a Baptist brother to come. The Baptist brother's pastor happened to be holding a meeting at a Baptist church here. He wrote to his parishioner to have nothing to do with that Campbellite evangelist. Likewise, did the doctor of the M. E. Church South, write to his brother minister in Madison, and like Sanballat with Nehemiah, the ministers there wrote to Winston, some of them to the Presbyterian minister who had preached in Frankfort, Ky., and who came to the meetings here and heard Brother Yeuell, and he wrote to Madison that Brother Yeuell was a credited evangelist of his church, and he knew nothing against him. The other preachers who wrote had not heard him preach. The people of Madison, of all denominations there, participated in the meetings. The preachers did not. Brother Yeuell preached about ten days. I was present the last two nights. He preached a number of the sermons preached there. He explained the place of baptism. He did not emphasize immersion, but did combat false doctrines of conversion. I never remember seeing people of all religious bodies in a town, including the Disciples, more unanimous in their appreciation of a preacher's work. They showed it by a generous purse. He left with an urgent invitation to return at another time and hold a meeting, and some of the people said they never wanted to hear their preachers again on account of their actions in turning down a union meeting because held by a Campbellite (?) evangelist. Brethren, don't be alarmed about federation coming here very soon. The greatest opposition to such a move may come from others beside Disciples.

Many of the churches and Bible schools in our state hold union or co-operation meetings over fifth Lord's days. There will be several the last of July.

Dr. J. C. Coggins, president of the new Holman Christian University at Black Mountain, recently was united in marriage to Miss Kate Penn DeVore. Miss DeVore spent some days in Winston last summer, and was much liked by those who met her.

The Middleton church had a good meeting in June, with thirty-one added. Dennis Davis, evangelist. An elder,

Brother Davenport preaches an average of fifteen sermons a month and drives all over Hyde county and part of Tyrrell.—J. A. Hopkins.

❦ ❦

Ohio Letter.

J. H. Miller has resigned at Ada, Ohio. He has been with this church for some three or four years and has done well. Some church will do well to secure his services.——W. L. VanVoorhis has given up the work at East Toledo. He is in poor health and will spend two or three months on the farm in Licking county. The West Side Church in Dayton has secured a pastor in the person of one of our bachelor preachers, Asa McDaniel, of Zanesville. He will "lay hold" the first of September.——The Alliance Church was not long pastorless after A. B. Moore left. They have called Fred A. Nichols. Brother Nichols has not been preaching regularly for a few years, but we are glad to see him again assume this place.——The Christian Endeavor mission at Clyde will be properly shepherded after July 15 by C. T. Fredenburg, late of Gloversville, N. Y. This is a very hopeful mission, and we look for a new congregation of strength within a short time.——The preachers' retreat at Hiram, August 5-12, promises to be a very interesting and helpful affair. There is no finer place on earth to "rest awhile" than Hiram. The fellowship will be the very finest. The speaking will be from the "best people on earth"—Christian preachers, go to Hiram.——C. J. Tanner, of Detroit, has to come back to Ohio soil each summer for a new supply of inspiration. He is now living at his summer cottage on Lake Erie, at Madison.——Norwalk had a great union revival, under the leadership of Evangelist Williams. He defined sin in plain English and stirred up the natives quite vigorously. Our bishop, J. L. Deming, did not sit back and discuss federation and "cuss" the evangelist for not preaching the whole Gospel, but took off his coat and went to work, and as a result has baptized and churched more people than anybody in town. Whenever you have an opportunity go into a union meeting with a kind heart and a New Testament, and you will get the big end of the results.——Five churches of Painesville are holding union meetings at 4:30 on Sunday afternoon in the park. The city band gives a sacred concert preceeding the sermon. Last Sunday this scribe preached to about 600 people, many of whom never go to church. Try it.—C. A. Freer, Painesville, Ohio.

❦ ❦

Ruston, La.

We are in the ninth week of the battle for God in the pioneer city. We still hold our audience and the interest is unabated. We expect to baptize seven more Sunday night. The opposition has been sullen and strong from the start, but we attended to our own business and battled on. We have had no "revival," for we had no church to revive. We started by preaching the first sermon ever preached by one of our men in this city. We have run the meeting on information, not inflammation. We never have had any excitement. You can't run a meeting in this climate on the excitement plan for nine weeks. The rebound will strike you in about the fourth week and kill the meeting. A meeting on information may be continued six months very safely if the preacher has a "barrel" large enough. We ran here at Ruston for six weeks and organized a church of over forty, and called the state convention to meet with us, which it did

June 26-29. We had about 100 delegates and entertained them free of charge without a hitch. The convention helped us to $500 on our lot. We now have our lot paid for and are making an effort to build us a house. The way this young church gives to this enterprise is something pathetic. There seems to be no end to what they are willing to do. A sight of our national men and women at the convention, such as George B. Ranshaw, H. F. Davis, of The Christian Publishing Company, A. E. Dubber, Mattie Pounds and Lelia Jordan, along with practically the entire ministerial force of Louisiana, seemed to nerve our young church to do its utmost. Then again, the mails continue to bring in dollars from all over the country. Three small contributions have come from saints of 80 years and older. These remembrances, with the letters that come with them, written with old tremulous hands, fire our hearts to do more and more. We have been a long time getting fifty members, but they are the right kind. May God help us to build a modest brick veneer building on our lot by Christmas. Will keep my postoffice at Ruston for sixty days. Faithfully, but well worn.   John A. Stevens.
Ruston, La., July 6, 1906.

❦ ❦

As Seen From the Dome.

(Continued from Page 909.)

said 700,000 men went to Bubastis yearly and brought dead cats for burial; and this statement has been completely authenticated by the discovery of a cat cemetery there containing innumerable bones of this sacred animal. Now 70,000 Moslems must make the pilgrimage to Mecca, and along goes with the caravan the Father of Cats, or "Shech of Cats," who carries in baskets on either side of his saddle as many cats as he can accommodate; and the great Sultan Bebars bequeathed a garden in Cairo for the entertainment of cats!

But Memphis is more than the two Colossi and a mound of ruins where rested the ancient temple. Riding through a native village where ropemakers were at work, and throngs of dirty children cried, "Backshish," and across the fertile plain and through picturesque groves of lofty palms, we came to the desert, and then the great Necropolis of Sakkara, which covers miles and has numerous sepulchral monuments. The Step Pyramid here is the oldest of the Pyramids, so called because it has six steps, or stages, with a combined height of 196 feet. The tombs of Apis, the sacred bulls, form the most magnificent structure of old Memphis. Here the sacred beast of the god Ptah was embalmed and

interred with great ceremony. The galleries extend for 1,040 feet, all hewn out of solid rock, and all along the corridors and recesses are the huge sarcophagi of these mummied bulls, the coffins averaging thirteen feet long, seven wide, and eleven in height, and weighing sixty-five tons. Some of the tombs here are beautifully decorated, representing the life of the buried king or priest. He is at his toilet or a banquet; he is receiving gifts or tribute; he is in the chase or overseeing his workmen; he is in his poultry yard or watching his people building ships, or engaged in pastoral labors, caring for his flocks, or his gardens, or playing chess. There are long processions passing before us of men and women with offerings. There are everywhere the sacred boat and the lotus. All these panels are clearly seen and read, after millenniums in the sands.

Riding homeward over the desert and through the green asters and palm groves, McKinley and Roosevelt, Mary Anderson and Moses, Roosevelt and Ramses II, and the rest of the donkeys, made excellent time. Th venerable man from the Wabash, though an orthodox prohibitionist, was soberly mounted on "Whiskey and Soda," and made good time. The trip on the river back to the city was refreshing indeed after our sixteen mile donkey ride in a broiling sun. The Nile is rich in scenery. The women filling their water jugs at its banks, the shadoof lifting the water for the irrigating ditches with the old-fashioned well-sweep, worked by the fellaheen at ten or twenty cents a day wages; the sakiyeh with its endless chain of earthen jars connected, with a toothed upright wheel and turned by a horizontal wheel lifting the water, and run by a bullock or camel or donkey blindfolded to keep off the flies and impress the animal with the idea that he is moving straight ahead instead of in a circle; the picturesque Nile boats; the palms with tall and slender trunks and lofty, bushy crowns, clusters of blossoms hanging under the long leaves which change by and by to clusters of dates; gardens with oranges, lemons and figs, and fields of rich green, with peasants at work and animals feeding; and beyond, the brown hills and the fiery desert; villages as primitive as a thousand years ago, and the gay and beautiful city in the distance—all go to make up a charming picture. It was an experience long to be remembered—the day in Sakkara—the evening on tne Nile. The camel says, There are three: the Pyramid, the date palm, and myself. Go to!

People's Forum

Rising Tide of Spiritual Ir..erest.
To the Editor of THE CHRISTIAN-EVANGELIST:

Let us grant, men do receive the Holy Spirit according to the terms of salvation laid down by Peter (Acts 2:38); but may we not by earnest and frequent prayer enjoy in a fuller measure the divine benedictions, and glorious revelations of God's power and love, which it is expressly his office to perform, constantly and increasingly?

As for me, I have sustained far graver fears of grieving the holy spirit of God through harsh, unjust and inflexible demands for absolute orthodoxy along these lines, than I have ever realized through humble and earnest prayer for a positive and real increase of the measure of the fulness of the spirit of God. It seems to me almost sacriligious to handle so lightly and hold so peremptorily that concerning which Jesus said God holds so sacred as to grant forgiveness to none who are guilty of blasphemy regarding it.

I suppose if any can be found who received at the time they complied with the terms of salvation an infilling of the Holy Spirit, so complete and abiding, they have never been conscious of lack in meeting the duties of life, they could not be reasonably expected to recognize the interise yearning for a deeper and wider manifestation. I did not so find it. I have found verified the promise, "Blessed is he that hungereth and thirsteth." Not once, but many times, have I been driven to ask for a greater "anointing" by the overwhelming conviction that in this alone depended my strength for service. And in faith I have plead the declaration of Christ, "If we being evil know how to give good gifts, shall not our Heavenly Father give the Holy Spirit to them that ask him," and through believing this very positive declaration I have received.

I rejoice to see the tide rising among us of giving or rather acknowledging the place and purpose of the Holy Spirit as an essential in every Christian life.

Valparaiso, Neb.　　　J. E. Chase.

❁

"The Cause" in Missouri.
To the Editor of THE CHRISTIAN-EVANGELIST:

It has been cause for humiliation for a dozen or more years that from 1,200 to 1,800 churches have been reported—and from 150,000 to 180,000 members claimed, while the conventions all told have numbered less than half a thousand, and the entire fund coming through the co-operation for state work has amounted to $5,000 or $8,000 or less. It is not claimed that these figures are absolutely correct, but they are approximately so.

Many have felt that the figures were certainly exaggerated, or else the means employed to secure the co-operation of the churches have been woefully inefficient.

It is therefore a source of gratification to read the report of the recent convention; and yet it appears from the thinning out as the convention progressed the state convention of the churches was by far the least important of the interests which brought the preachers and the people together. It would be interesting to know how many of the thousand persons present were delegates from the churches, bearing certificates of appointment, and clothed with authority to speak for the churches and especially to vote for them.

There is, of course, no way to ascertain this information, since for years the so-called conventions have been simply mass meetings. One delegate from each church in the state would make a larger convention that has ever been held. The churches would then be committed to the work planned by the convention and larger results would come with far less labor to the secretary.

Would it not be worth a year's work to secure this result? It can be done if the proper effort be made. Even if it shall require a half dozen years. All the interests of the church could in such case be adequately considered by the churches, and preachers and people would find co-operation easy—and the results satisfactory. It is, therefore, moved that at the next convention every member be required to present his credentials.

Kansas City.　　　T. P. Haley.

❁

A Timely Issue.
To the Editor of THE CHRISTIAN-EVANGELIST:

I have been more profoundly interested in the late discussion of the question of Federation in our papers than in the discussion of any religious question for a long time. The issue and its discussion by our people is not only timely, but will form an important historic period in the current reformation. It constitutes a necessary and natural development of our history and the aims and desires of the fathers and founders of the greatest movement of the age, back to apostolic teaching and practice. It is incredible that we could accept or indorse every union movement that may be formulated and introduced by the denominations; but it is equally incredible that we should hesitate to hail with pleasure such movements or to seriously discuss the same. I have had no uneasiness as to the ultimate results of this discussion. No earthly power can stay the progress of a movement which has challenged the world to produce its equal or to paralyze the hand and invisible power behind it. Let no man, be he editor, preacher, writer or what not, regard himself able to turn the course of a religious reformation that is surely and grandly pushing its way

"ACTINA"

Possesses Wonderful Curative Powers

For nearly twenty years that little instrument with the trade-mark name of "Actina" has been accomplishing wonderful results in the relief and cure of ailments and diseases of the Eye, Ear, Head and Throat, caused by poor circulation, catarrh, etc. The vapor emanating from the powerful, yet harmless, chemicals with which this wonderful instrument is charged, is said to be a remarkable specific for catarrh, a powerful astringent and a sure promoter of circulation. When applied to the eyes it not only relieves but cures most eye diseases. Note the announcement in another column.

throughout the world. Out of the million and more men and women forming the membership of the Christian Church, no living man could draw away more than a few thousand into the wilderness as in days of yore, and this would not make a ripple upon the great stream that is coursing its way around the world. THE CHRISTIAN-EVANGELIST may have made some mistakes, and surely it would have been more than human had it not, under its incarnate, but been more than human, been incarnate strain through which it has gone. But THE CHRISTIAN-EVANGELIST may seek consolation in the fact that it has opened to the world a medium of communication for the discussion of one of the most important questions since the days of the fathers. It has also contributed far more to the growth of Christian union and free and dignified discussion of religious subjects than any paper could possibly accomplish, by an uncompromising and sometimes unintelligible opposition to the discussion of a grave and vitally important question. I have been a silent, but deeply interested, reader of all sides of this question, and pencil these lines out of purest motives and to say to my brethren that I can not conceive it possible for any harm to come from federation, or anything else that we can encourage without any violation of our religious conceptions. May God be with you and many subscriptions added to THE CHRISTIAN-EVANGELIST, and a glorious celebration mark the close of our first century.　　　Joseph Lowe.

Oakland, Kan.

Evangelistic

We invite ministers and others to send reports of meetings, additions and other news of the churches. It is especially requested that additions be reported as "by confession and baptism" or "by letter."

Hot from the Wire.

Special to THE CHRISTIAN-EVANGELIST.

Cincinnati, July 16.—Wright accepts as corresponding secretary. Formal announcement follows.—Geo. B. Ranshaw.

Special to THE CHRISTIAN-EVANGELIST.

Atchison, Kan., July 15.—Forty-five today, 116 to date. Tabernacle overcrowded; whole city stirred; Scoville here five days. Smith and the Kendalls direct music.—W. T. Hilton, pastor.

Special to THE CHRISTIAN-EVANGELIST.

Manchester, N. H., July 15.—Meeting two weeks old; audiences and interest growing steadily. Preached in leading Baptist Church Sunday. Audience last night nearly filled the Park Theater. Weather sweltering, people listen sympathetically, although avowedly opposed to introduction of new church. Not one Disciple here, no help of any sort. Going it alone with Mrs. Rutherford, singer, and James Hubbard, pianist. Best people attending now; they know I do not represent a freak religion. Expenses unavoidably frightful, costs city prices to even get tickets distributed; require long campaign. Bad time account people leaving for mountains.—Herbert Yeuell.

Arkansas.

Bentonville, July 16.—Two additions to the church, Sunday, 24.—I. W. Ellis.

California.

Winters, July 9.—There were recently six additions by baptism.—G. A. Ragan.

Idaho.

Rupert, July 11.—I commenced a meeting here last night with four added, two by letter and two by statement. This is a new town a little over a year old, with no church building, but six saloons. The Methodists have an organization of probably twenty-five or thirty. We have one of eighteen. Expect to have a good meeting and leave a church of between fifty and one hundred. The Bible school has an attendance of fifty or sixty and, the Christian Endeavor has twenty-eight members. I expected to begin at Nampa July 6, but the new tabernacle for the meeting was not finished, so I preached in it as it was Lord's day morning and evening, with three additions. Final result at Meridian, church of 63, Bible school of 45 and Christian Endeavor 25. Lots purchased, pastor called for one-half time and good building committee appointed to begin work at once.—Geo. C. Ritchey.

Illinois.

Sullivan, July 8.—Four additions at regular services today. Baptized twelve, one letter. Exchanged pulpits with Brother Lyon, of Newman, Ill., last Sunday.—J. G. McNutt.

Albion (West Village) July 9.—Two united with us by letter yesterday. Foreign missionary offering, $40.—J. F King.

Eureka, July 9.—One by confession yesterday at Emden, Ill.—C. A. Sitther.

Roseville, July 10.—Four confessions here last Lord's day morning at the regular services. I am now entering my second year with the church here. During the year just closed the church received 29 additions, the majority were by confession and baptism. One hundred and sixty dollars were give for missionary purposes. The outlook is good.—C. R. Wo..ord.

Waverly, July 10.—We have been here six months. Have added to the church by commendation eight, and by baptism eleven, and others are expected. The church co-operated with the other churches in the city in a union tent meeting, and I think we gained much by this little spell of "confederation." An excellent feeling exists among the people, a good trend of morals in civic government is set in motion so

Indiana.

Hammond, July 11.—Two confessions at Hammond Sunday and one at Whiting. We recently held a tent meeting at Hammond. The pastor did the preaching and Miss Mary Bailey of Angola sang for us. Audiences large, reaching nearly 1,000. Results of meeting, six by letter; thirty-six confessions.—C. J. Sharp.

Plainfield, July 1.—There were five confessions and baptisms at the morning service. We are planning for a great meeting in October.—I. N. Grisso.

Eaton, July 10.—T. ... Lawrence, living link evangelist of the Christian Publishing Company, on Sunday morning, July 8, filled the pulpit here very acceptably.—L. O. Newcomer.

Indianapolis, July 10.—Six additions to the Olive Branch Christian Church, of this city, recently. Two by letter, four by confession and baptism.—J. M. Canfield.

Ligonier, July 9.—Since last report there have been nine additions to the church here; seven by primary obedience and two by commendation.—I. N. Aldrich.

Indian Territory.

Okmulgee, July 10.—Accessions the last three Lord's days: letters seven, confessions sixteen, from M. E. one. More to follow. This makes forty-five since beginning of year. All but twelve at regular services. One hundred and forty-two since the beginning of the present ministration. Brother Hawkins, our corresponding secretary, was with us last Lord's day. We were all delighted to have him with us. We made an offering of $76.80 to territorial work. We are entering into greater things. I have been granted a vacation of thirty days. I will enter upon it in a short time, but as yet don't know where or how. I am indeed grateful for this much needed rest.—Frank L. Van Voorhis.

Iowa.

Riverton, July 15.—We are building a new church here. We need a man for at least half time. Sidney, Thurman and Bartlett, all in this county, are without a pastor.—T. A. McKenzie, I. C. C. evangelist.

Kansas.

Louisburg, July 9.—We are in a great meeting here. Four added by statement and three by confession and baptism, seven the first day. All grown people but one. Large crowds are attending and we are praying for a great victory.—Clyde Lee Fife.

Moline, July 11.—Received five new members in last two weeks. Work moving on nicely.—J. A. W. Brown.

Marion, July 9.—Five additions here last Lord's day, three by confession and baptism, two from the sects.—W. M. Berkeley.

Wellington, July 9.—Four additions here yesterday. This makes fourteen not previously reported.—L. T. Faulders.

Michigan.

Saginaw, July 9.—Four additions yesterday by statement, two from another communion, making thirty-three at regular services in two months.—J. Murray Taylor.

Missouri.

Dexter, July 15.—The church here will give their minister, R. H. Lampkin, the fifth Sunday for missionary work, and the faithful few at Piggott, Ark., will get the benefit of the time. R. Clyde Tucker, one of the former members of the Dexter congregation, has been working hard to secure a working force and has succeeded so far as to organize with sixteen members and they have purchased a lot and have some money in hand for a building fund.

Trenton, July 10.—We are making commendable progress. Eight additions. The offerings to missions this year will be the largest in the history of the church. Dean W. J. Lhamon, of the Bible College, Columbia, was with us recently during our Chautauqua. He delivered six Bible lectures, and preached on Lord's day to three thousand people. The churches of Grundy county are all doing good work. A new Bible school was organized recently at the Berry church.—B. J. White.

New York.

Brooklyn, July 9.—Since our special meeting closed April 29, there have been eleven added to the Humboldt Street Church, eight by baptism,

that the "lid is on the joints and slot machines." I do not think we sacrifice a single principle that our fathers fought for, and we gained a reputation of favorableness not bad before. Since we came here we have preached the baccalaureate and memorial sermons.—J. A. Clemens.

one by letter, two by statement. Forty-five added to church since April 1, 1906. Church in excellent condition.—Jos. Keevil.

Oregon.

Brownsville, July 9.—One baptized here yesterday and one received the Sunday before by statement. This makes two since our work began in December. We are planning for an advanced movement all along the line.—A. H. Mulkey.

Texas.

Fort Worth, July 9.—There were five additions at the Tabernacle Church yesterday.—A. E. Dubber.

Dalhart, July 10.—Just closed a two weeks' meeting with the minister, John Mullen, at this place with two accessions. This is a very difficult field, being a new railroad town. Closed with a full house and good interest.—Charles E. McVey, song evangelist.

Washington.

Waitsburg, July 6.—After three years of hard work in this field I have resigned, to take effect on or before October 1. The visible results of our labors here are one hundred and fifty additions to the church, over one hundred confessions, and a fine $12,000 church building. My successor will have one of the very best equipped buildings in the west. We will locate elsewhere in September or else take up evangelistic work.—W. T. Adams.

SUBSCRIBERS' WANTS.

society whose members should be bound together by a common and unselfish interest in each other's welfare.

Sunday-School

July 29, 1906.

JESUS DINES WITH A PHARISEE.
—Luke 14:1-14.

Memory verses: 13, 14.

GOLDEN TEXT.—He that humbleth himself shall be exalted.—Luke 14:11.

Jesus felt free to go to the houses of publicans and sinners, but he also accepted the hospitality of Pharisees. As he showed no sense of superiority in the presence of the lowly, so he showed no sense of inferiority in the presence of men of high rank.

The old question of the method and spirit of Sabbath observance came up during this dinner at the Pharisee's house. Is it lawful to heal a sick man on the Sabbath. Early in his ministry (Luke 5, 6) Jesus had made a sharp issue with the Pharisaic legalism with reference to fasting and Sabbath keeping. Their view was that the whole duty of man was to keep the law as it was laid down in the book. His view was that man is worth more than law, and when the literal requirements of the law conflict with the demands of man's welfare the former must give way. It was not Jesus's purpose to set forth a new law in place of the old, but to show the inadequacy of the very concept of law for the purposes of religion. Nothing can be more inaccurate and misleading than the familiar statement that the Bible is primarily a law-book. The religion of Jesus can not be expressed in terms of law.

On another occasion, when about to heal a man on the Sabbath, Jesus reminded his hearers that they would consider it lawful to extricate a mired sheep on the Sabbath, and exclaimed, "How much more is a man worth than a sheep!" That is the principle fundamental to all his teaching and living—that man has a vast and incalculable value, and that the conservation of this value, both in himself and in others, is the chief business of man.

This feast also gave occasion for teaching two other lessons—one on humility and one on unselfish hospitality. At an Oriental feast, as at a modern court dinner, the order of precedence was carefully considered and each guest was anxious to get a position which would properly represent his own rank. But scrambling for preferment, says Jesus, is the poorest way to get it. To assert constantly one's claim to honor and precedence, is to invite rebuffs and consequent embarrassment. The road to honor is through humility.

As to hospitality, the words of Jesus suggest that the word needs to be redeemed to nobler uses. A mere exchange of social favors and courtesies, in which each party expects to get as much as he gives, is not hospitality. In many cases it is merely a pleasant and profitable device for self-advancement, or a method of purchasing entertainment for oneself by furnishing entertainment to others. This may be all right, so far as it goes. But it is not the discharge of one's "social duties." The real social duty involves the loving care of the unfortunate, the generous use of one's possessions for the good of other members of society. Without such consideration of the common good, there can be no society in the true sense, but only an aggregate of selfish individuals. Nineteen centuries of Christian civilization have brought only a very imperfect realization of the Master's ideal of a true

Midweek Prayer-Meeting

July 25, 1906.

THE NEW LIFE IN CHRIST.—
Col. 3:1-4.

"Go up, go up, my heart,
    Dwell with thy God above;
For here thou canst not rest,
    Nor here give out thy love.

"Let not thy love flow out
    To things so soiled and dim;
Go up to heaven and God,
    Take up thy love to Him."

No matter how highly one really be risen with Christ, he may still and will practice the Gospel of the helping hand. When one is too far removed to wreathe men's faces with smiles and improve the general condition of society he is exalted in pride rather than in Christ.

To be risen with Christ it is not only necessary we should first loose ourselves from the controlling love of things that have to do only with earth, but under the compelling power of a genuine new affection for our Savior we must begin seeking after the mercy, gentleness, helpfulness, love and all heavenly idealism that prevail without opposition when Christ is at the right hand of God.

There are no short cuts to the higher spiritual altitudes, or new processes of becoming risen with Christ. That is an estate attained unto by faith, repentance, confession and baptism; it is a region into which we unconsciously enter through growth in grace and the knowledge of the Lord Jesus Christ. It is the result of adding to our faith virtue, knowledge, temperance, patience, godliness, brotherly kindness and love.

As a man thinketh in his heart so is he. Our thoughts are weight or wings. "Brethren, whatsoever things are true, whatsoever things are honest, whatsoever things are just, whatsoever things are lovely, whatsoever things are of good report, if there be any virtue and if there be any praise, think on these things." Such thoughts will help us up into the new and higher life where Christ holds special audience with all his beloved who will enter in.

That we have merely come up from a submersion in water is no proof we have "risen with Christ." That we have buried the old nature together with all its grovelling proclivities and unhallowed idealism, and changed our affections from things on the earth, and are illustrating in our lives the principles of Christ's charity, benevolence, loving kindness, and holiness is far more satisfactory proof of our having risen. The formal doing of things enjoined in the Scriptures is but one wing by which we rise; the other is the inner possession of the spirit of which these formal procedures ought to be the natural expressions.

It is well that in all seriousness we ask ourselves whether we are dead to sin, that is, have wholly separated ourselves from sin. Lot's desire for city life led him to remonstrate with the angel that told him to flee from the plain and into the mountain. He said: "Behold now, this city is near to flee unto and it is a little one: Oh let me escape thither (is it not a little one?) and my soul shall live." He evidently thought the guilt of disobedience would be mini-

Christian Endeavor

By GEO. L. SNIVELY

July 29, 1906.

GARDINER AND MISSIONS TO LATIN AMERICA.—2 Cor. 11:23-30.

DAILY READINGS.

M. The Blessings of the Gospel.   Isa. 40:1-11.
T. The Needs of the Gospel.   Rom. 10: 1-10.
W. Preaching the Gospel.   Mark 1:35-39.
T. Power of the Gospel.   Mark 5:1-10.
F. Privileges of the Gospel.   Luke 10:17-24.
S. Mission of the Twelve.   Mark 6:11-13.
S. Prayer for Missions.   1 Tim. 2:1-8.

"If you can not be the watchman,
Standing high on Zion's wall,
Pointing out the path to heaven,
Offering life and peace to all;
With your prayers and your bounties
You can do what heaven demands.
You can be like faithful Aaron,
Holding up the prophet's hands."

Heaven is represented as a walled city that lieth four square, and on either side are three gates. Those southern gates are constant invitations to the inhabitants of Cape Colony, Tierra del Fuego, and all the Antarctic islands to come home. They are sure prophecies, too, that by the millions they will yet enter into the better land.

While trying to establish a mission in Tierra del Fuego in 1851, Gardiner lost this life to find another and a heavenly one, while about him was not the splendid staging of a death on his ship just as the enemy had lowered their flag and the boundaries of empire were hinging on the result, yet angels noted when he fell and there posterity will rear a monument above the last resting place of one of humanity's great liberators, and the story told at its base be inspiration to more universal liberty in Christ and the regeneration of a world.

It is said Lieutenant Gardiner, the South American missionary in labors most abundant of all, was converted by the reading of a narrative of the beautiful life of his mother written by his father. Here there is another splendid trophy for the diadem of Christian motherhood. The hand that rocked that cradle rocked South America into a sweet sleep after the nightmare of heathen superstition and catholic oppression and from which she is awakening into a new world of privilege, happiness, usefulness and glory. If the Southern continent lays tribute in heaven at the feet of the son, rest assured the mother will not be forgotten who bore him and inspired him to Christian nobility.

Lieutenant Gardiner was of truly knightly character. He resigned from a desirable position in the English navy for the life of a missionary, not to win renown or even the crown of martyrdom, but, seeing the degradation and sufferings of the inhabitants, the spirit of true chivalry he sought to bring to the Southern hemisphere the enlightenment and help and cheer of the Gospel. His object was not to get but to give. He gave years of sacrifice and finally his life, but his was the joy of seeing the true light begin to shine, and now from the heavens he can look down on a continent being redeemed, and seeing the travail of soul rest satisfied.

Not even in old Spain was catholicism so despotic and corrupt as it has long been south of the Rio Grande, but Latin America is now in the dawn of a better day. Notwithstanding the machinations of the priesthood legislation providing for religious toleration has been adopted in every land. This gives missionaries and mission houses the protection of law and guarantees to those people, who have long been in darkness almost as dense as that of heathenism, regenerative influences that will wonderfully bless them and make of them a blessing. Now is the day of great opportunity for Protestantism under the Southern cross.

The progress of Mexico under the presidency of Maximo Diaz is one of the marvels of modern times. It really seems to be "Americanized", in its business enterprise and ethics, in its social development and political idealism. This republic is grandly emerging from gross superstition and the weakness of ignorance and priestly cruelty and oppression up on to the higher levels of national life and usefulness. If the true God of Protestantism be coronated as her God, and primitive Christianity be the religion of her people, the land of the Montezumas will yet justify her enduement with such genial climate, rich mountains of metals and gems, such fertile soil, and a race of men with latent powers truly great. Mexico is a mission field whose conquest is one of the greatest prizes earth affords.

❧ ❧

End-of-the-Week Rates.

Chicago and North-Western Railway.

From Chicago to near-by summer resorts. Tickets at special low rates on sale Friday, Saturday and Sunday, good until the following Monday to return. Other low rates in effect daily. For tickets, rates and booklets giving full information, apply to nearest ticket agent or address W. B. Kniskern, P. T. M., C. & N. W. R'y Co., Chicago.

Current Literature

LETTERS AND SERMONS OF T. B. LARIMORE, Edited by Emma Page. McQuiddy Printing Company, 1904. Nashville, Tenn. Price $1.50.

This volume consists of 450 very solidly printed pages, with illustrations, about equally divided between sermons and letters by Brother Larimore, a well known evangelist of the south. The volume will be of especial interest to Brother Larimore's friends in the large number of churches where he has held meetings. A man of acknowledged piety, and good evangelistic ability, both his sermons and his letters breathe a healthy religious spirit. One chapter is devoted to the children, with illustrations. A good deal of space is given to correspondence between Brother Larimore and Brother F. D. Srygley, a personal friend, who published a former volume relating to Brother Larimore, and contains matter which would have no special interest except to the personal friends of these two men.

✦

THE BOYS' LIFE OF CHRIST, by William B. Forbush, Ph.D. Funk and Wagnalls, New York. 326 pages. Price, $1.25 net.

A new study of the life of Christ is being engaged in by thousands of Christians all over the country this year, for that life of lives has become the topic around which the Sunday school lessons for 1906 center. This book deals simply with Jesus as the boys' hero. His life is presented in the form of one telling a story and the author has achieved great success in his effort. Of course, it does not go into too great details, does not touch the theology or the philosophy of Jesus' life, nor emphasize the miraculous. It rather concerns itself with what he did do, the purpose of the author being to create a liking for the character of Christ with the hope that this will interest young people in their other story of his life narrated in the Gospels, especially by Mark. The author has been eminently successful, though his task was not an easy one.

NOTHING BETTER

NEWLY REVISED TO 1906

MISSIONARY ADDRESSES

By ARCHIBALD McLEAN

TABLE OF CONTENTS.

1. The Supreme Mission of the Church.
2. The Gospel for All Nations.
3. Encouragement in Missions.
4. The Success of Modern Missions.
5. The Heroism of Missions.
6. The Transforming Power of the Gospel.
7. Woman and the Gospel.
8. Missions in the Life of Christ.
9. Missions in the Early Church.
10. Missions in the Middle Ages.
11. Modern Missions.
12. Missions Among the Disciples of Christ.
13. Medical Missions.
14. "This Grace Also."
Appendix: Names and Brief Accounts of those Who Have Labored for the Foreign Christian Missionary Society.
Biography: Selected List of Best Books on Missions, Mission Lands and Missionaries.

Nothing Needed with this book in Your Library. In fine silk cloth binding, 300 pages, postpaid, $1.00.

CHRISTIAN PUBLISHING COMPANY, 2712 Pine Street, St. Louis, Mo.

CHURCH FEDERATION READY.

The Inter-Church Conference on Federation, 700 pages, prepaid.....$2 00

MARRIAGES.

Notices of marriages inserted under this heading at the rate of fifty cents for three lines or less (seven words to a line). Additional words at five cents per word. Cash must be in each case accompany order.

SAUNDERS—HASS.—Miss Lottie M. Saunders to Theodore T. Hass, June 28, 1906. Both of Moorland, O., C. C. Maple of Fredericksburg officiating.

BRISCOE—BLEDSOE.—Miss Jennie Briscoe to A. C. Bledsoe, June 28, 1906. Both of Abilene, Kan. Ceremony performed at the Christian church by Granville Snell. They alsve will be useful and happy.

HARTMAN—GALE.—Miss Martha S. Hartman to Charles Gale, June 28, 1906, at the home of the bride's parents, Cumberland, Ind. W. W. Cunningham pronounced the ceremony.

DOWNEY—TAYLOR.—Miss Oralyn Downey to Alfred Taylor, of Mt. Carmel, Ill., June 30, 1906, at the bride's home in Chandler, Okla. Oscar Ingold, minister.

FORD—BROADHURST.—Miss Alma Ford, of Bentonville, Ark., to R. S. Broadhurst, of Pea Ridge, Ark., June 23, 1906, J. W. Ellis, Bentonville, Officiating.

❀ ❀

OBITUARIES.

[Notices of Deaths, not more than four lines, inserted free. Obituary memoirs, one cent per word. Send the money with the copy.]

ANDREWS.

Hiram Andrews was born at Bucyrus, O., September 27, 1831, and died at Windsor, Mo. June 23, 1906. Removed to Iowa in 1855. Married Miss Lucina Standsfield in 1858. Was a faithful husband and father. First was deacon and then elder in the church. He has lived in Bentonville, Ark., twenty-one years, was elder in this church, useful, true and good. Two children with his bereaved wife mourn his loss. The church will sadly miss him. Bro. J. W. Ellis preached the funeral sermon.

COFFMAN.

Adella Coffman, at her late home, near Fredericksburg, O., June 25, after one week's illness. Burial at Smithville. C. C. MAPLE.

JOHNSON.

Bro. T. M. Johnson died here in Quincy, Ill., on June 30, at the age of 58 years 10 months and 7 days. His widow, who for the past five years has been in the asylum at Jacksonville, and five children, Norman, now at Atlanta, Ga.; Thomas, Cresey, Dayton and Joe, all of Quincy, are the members of his immediate family to survive him. Brother Johnson graduated at Christian University, Canton, Mo., twenty-seven years ago. He held pastorates at Clayton and Payson and other Illinois places. He was an earnest student of the Scriptures. He was buried at Clayton, Ill., near by the graves of three children. The writer conducted the services here. Brother Vandervort at Clayton. WALTER M. JORDAN.

DR. J. R. LUCAS.

Peace, peace, he is not dead, he doth not sleep; he hath awakened from the dream of life.—Shelley. This tribute of love from a grateful heart is written in sacred memory of Dr. J. R. Lucas, who a while ago passed from the toils of earth to the rest of heaven. The last hour of his long and useful life came upon him in the home of his daughter, Mrs. S. H. Wooten, in the city of Chicago. His work was done and he was patiently waiting for the pale messenger with the inverted torch.

Dr. Lucas was born in Pennsylvania seventy-five years ago. He belonged to a good family with a beautiful name, and one which has given to the world many distinguished preachers, teachers and physicians. Our brother—like his namesake, the companion of the Apostle Paul—was both a minister of the Gospel and a beloved physician whose praise was in all the churches. His labors reached over many of the states of the middle west. He had a genius for work. In personal appearance he was as handsome as Absalom. In statue rather below the medium, graceful, with a short body, a classic face set in a framework of long curly hair, and a head denoting a strong intellect, he had also a splendid voice and a good command of language. He had versatility of talents and varied accomplishments. In evangelistic work and in the public discussions which used to be in vogue he had few equals. He met in debate many able and distinguished men. In such discussions he was inimicable. He always remembered the old saying, that "whom the gods would destroy they first make mad." He never allowed himself to be betrayed into showing ill temper or saying unkind things. No greater man ever broke bread at the table of a court. To say or to do a harsh thing gave him nights of solitude and sorrow. The writer of this tribute was an inmate of his home during the two beautiful years spent as a student in Christian University. It was in this way that he came to know Dr. Lucas, both as a father and a friend. The memories of his home linger in his heart as a star in the sky. The one event which contributed more than any other earthly influence to the good doctor's happiness and usefulness was his marriage to Miss Margaret Lowe, a woman whose disposition is as rosy as the morning and as gentle as the dawn. Her children rise up and call her blessed. Her husband also praised her. Great will be her reward in heaven when out of every ingredient of bitterness and sorrow she comes at last to reach the ends to receive the crown.

"How'er it be, it seems to me
'Tis only noble to be good.
Kind hearts are more than coronets,
And simple faith than Norman blood."
Fayetteville, Ark. N. M. RAGLAND.

McPHERSON.

Herman E., son of Taylor and Eliza McPherson, born near Modesto, Ill., obeyed the Gospel at 17; enlisted in army, at 20; served in Spanish-American war, against the Boxer uprising in China; was corporal, sergeant and master-at-arms and legation guard in Peking. Died on board the Baltimore December 21, 1905. Body returned and buried at Modesto, Ill., July 2, 1906.
Eureka, Ill. J. G. WAGGONER.

MOTLEY.

At Montague, Prince Edward Island, May 3, 1906, Virginia Catherine, infant daughter of Mr. and Mrs. W. R. Motley, age 6 days.

❀ ❀

HOW'S THIS?

We offer One Hundred Dollars Reward for any case of Catarrh that cannot be cured by Hall's Catarrh Cure. F. J. CHENEY & CO., Toledo, O.

We, the undersigned, have known F. J. Cheney for the last 15 years, and believe him perfectly honorable in all business transactions and financially able to carry out any obligations made by his firm. WALDING, KINNAN & MARVIN, Wholesale Druggists, Toledo, O.

Hall's Catarrh Cure is taken internally, acting directly upon the blood and mucous surfaces of the system. Testimonials sent free. Price 75c per bottle. Sold by all Druggists.

Take Hall's Family Pills for constipation.

SUMMER IS HERE

People must have inducements during such weather to either buy or read, especially good books, and we are determined to offer the inducements. For the month of July we will make the following prices, CASH with order. All books are prepaid. All books are cloth bound where not specified as paper.

	Regular Price	Cut-Rate Price
Life a Flower. By Errett	$1 50	75c
Plain Talks to Young Men	60c	30c
Thirteen and Twelve Others	1 00	50c
Life of Knowles Shaw	1 00	50c
Problem of Problems	1 50	75c
Kaskey's Last Book	1 00	50c
The Form of Baptism. By Briney	1 00	60c
The Temptation of Christ	75c	40c
How Understand and Use Bible	50c	35c
Riverside, or Winning a Soul	75c	35c
Grandma's Patience	20c	15c
After Pentecost, What?	1 00	60c
Know Thyself	1 00	50c
Memorial of J. K. Rogers and Christian College	60c	30c
Koinonia, or the Weekly Contribution	15c	10c
The Juvenile Revival	60c	35c
The Master Key, paper	25c	13c
The Remedial System, 436 pages	2 00	75c
Duke Christopher, Young Hero of Wurttemberg	50c	20c
Bartholet Milan	25c	10c
Gems from Franklin (very badly damaged)	1 00	50c
Revelation Read	1 00	35c
Trip Around the World	1 00	50c
The Simple Life	50c	35c
Saintly Workers	1 00	50c
Christology of Jesus, one of Stalker's best	1 50	1 00
Origin of the Disciples	1 00	60c
Bible or No Bible, paper	50c	25c
Contradictions of Orthodoxy, paper	25c	15c
A Knight Templar Abroad, 547 pages	2 00	35c
The Story of an Infidel's Family (very interesting)	1 00	50c
Patmos	1 00	35c
Queen Esther. By M. M. Davis	75c	45c
Elijah. By Davis	75c	45c
The Story of an Earnest Life	1 00	60c
Missouri Lectures and Discussions	1 00	30c
Autobiography of Jacob Creath	1 00	30c
Edna Carlisle	75c	45c
King Saul	1 00	60c
In the Days of Jehu	1 00	60c
Prohibition vs. Personal Liberty, paper	25c	10c
Walks About Jerusalem. By Errett	1 00	60c
Talks to Bereans. By Errett	1 00	60c
Science and Pedagogy of Ethics. Fine for teachers	1 50	75c
Sermons and Song	1 25	50c
The Exiled Prophet	1 25	50c
Spiritualism on Trial	1 50	50c
Dictionary of Scripture Proper Names	..	50c
Organic Evolution Considered	1 50	75c
My Good Poems. By Fairhurst	1 00	50c
Ideals for Young People	50c	30c
Life and Times of Benjamin Franklin	1 00	60c
Reformation of the Nineteenth Century (one of the best)	2 00	1 00
Our First Congress	1 00	35c
Wheeling Through Europe	1 00	60c
Garfield's Great Speeches	1 50	75c
Class Book of Oratory. Fine for elocution	1 50	95c
Christian Missions	75c	40c
The Baptismal Controversy	75c	45c
The Divinity of Christ and Duality of Man	75c	35c
Otto's Good Recitations, paper	50c	25c
The Life of Jesus	1 00	50c
The Young Man from Middlefield	1 00	50c
Leaves from Mission Fields	1 00	60c
The Moberly Pulpit	50c	25c
Communings in the Sanctuary	50c	25c
Nehushtan	1 00	35c
Bible vs. Materialism, paper	35c	20c
Wonders of the Sky	50c	25c

	Regular Price	Cut-Rate Price
Altar Stairs, splendid fiction	1 50	1 00
June, a Class History	50c	15c
Prison Life in Dixie	1 00	25c
Across the Gulf	1 00	50c
Moral Evil	75c	25c
The Wondrous Works of Christ	75c	25c
Rosa Emerson	1 00	50c
Ecclesiastical Tradition	75c	35c
Facts About China, paper	25c	15c
The Spiritual Side of Our Plea	1 50	75c
Lessons in Soul Winning	75c	45c
The Plan of Salvation for Sinners and Saints	1 00	25c
The Man in the Book	1 00	60c
Missionary Addresses	1 00	35c
Commentary on Matthew. By F. N. Peloubet	1 25	50c
Types and Metaphors of Bible	1 00	50c
An Encyclopedia on the Evidences	2 00	1 00
The Gospel for an Age of Doubt. By Henry VanDyke	1 50	75c
The Making of an American. By Jacob Riis	1 50	75c
Social Evolution. By Benjamin Kidd	1 50	75c
Jesus Christ and the Social Question. By Francis Greenwood Peabody	1 50	75c
The Little Shepherd of Kingdom Come	1 50	75c
The Quest of Happiness. By Newell D. Hillis	1 50	75c
Happiness. By Carl Hilty	1 50	75c
The Women of the Bible. By Mrs. S. T. Martin	1 50	75c
The Conqueror. By Gertrude Atherton	1 50	75c
The Celebrity. By Winston Churchill	1 50	75c
The Choir Invisible. By James Lane Allen	1 50	75c
Sant' Ilario. By F. Marion Crawford	1 50	75c
The Master of Warlock. By Edward Eggleston	1 50	75c
The Customs of the Country. By Mrs. Hugh Fraser	1 50	75c
The Knitting of the Souls. By Maude Clark Gay	1 50	75c
The Law of the Land. By Emerson Hough	1 50	75c
Black Friday. By Frederic S. Isham	1 50	75c
The Medal of Honor. By Capt Charles King	1 50	75c
The Four Feathers. By A. E. W. Mason	1 50	75c
My Lady Peggy Goes to Town. By Frances Aymar Mathews	1 50	75c
Zelda Dameron. By Meredith Nicholson	1 50	75c
The Cost. By David Graham Philips	1 50	75c
On the Face of the Waters. By Flora Annie Steel	1 50	75c
The Pillar of Light. By Louis Tracy	1 50	75c
Marcella; The History of David Grieve. By Mrs. Humphry Ward	1 50	75c
Daughters of Nijo. By Onoto Watanna	1 50	75c
The Magic Forest. By Steward Edward White	1 50	75c
The Yellow Van. By Edward Whiteing	1 50	75c
Children of the Ghetto. By Israel Zangwill	1 50	75c
Lourdes; The Downfall. By Emile Zola	1 50	75c

SONG BOOKS—PREPAID.

	Regular Price	Cut-Rate Price
Pearly Gates (board binding, 90 pages), per doz	$1 00	
Apostolic Hymns (board binding, 112 pages), per doz	1 00	
Twilight Zephyrs (board binding, 96 pages), per doz	1 00	
New Fount of Blessing (board binding, 190 pages), per dozen	1 00	
Tidings of Salvation (board binding, 117 songs), per doz	1 25	
Tidings of Salvation (manilla, 117 songs), per doz	1 00	
Tidings of Salvation (limp, 117 songs), per doz	1 00	

NEW TESTAMENTS.

	Regular Price	Cut-Rate Price
Revised to 1881 (silk cloth binding)	30c	15c
Revised to 1881 (larger type, cloth)	60c	25c
Revised to 1881, one page common version, opposite page revised (bourgeois type), cloth)	50c	25c
Revised and common, page for page (long primer type, Morocco binding)	1 00	35c
Reference New Testament (long primer type)	1 25	60c

CHRISTIAN PUBLISHING COMPANY. 2712 Pine Street, St. Louis, Mo.

The Home Department

The Old Home Church.

MAURICE F. PLACE.

The old home church? Ah, memory,
No brighter picture dwells in thee,
Than of the humble house of God,
Where as a child my feet hath trod,
     In love secure!
Methinks I see the old spire rise,
A finger, beckoning toward the skies;
No pretext here toward great nor grand,
But just a humble, helping hand,
     To lives more pure.
Old friends I see pass through the door,
With hearty handshakes as of yore.
I feel a warmth and welcome here,
The sweet and sacred atmosphere
     Of other days.
I dream of those who were fed,
With Jesus Christ, the living bread;
Tarrying awhile, and one by one,
To other fields—with duties done,
     They went their ways.
How many hearts, no man can say,
Ofttimes look back, as I to-day,
With retrospection, sweet and glad,
For that rare part this church has had,
     In lives of men.
And when I reach my journey's end,
With none but Jesus to befriend;
How precious then the place and hour,
That Jesus came in love and power,
     Te be my friend.

North Manchester, Ind.

❖ ❖

The Bronze Vase.

BY J. BRECKENRIDGE ELLIS.

PART III.

CHAPTER III.

Mrs. Bannerton showed Rhoda to the bath room on the second floor, and, having provided her with one of her own dresses, told Raymund to wait for his sister in the kitchen. "You will want to have a talk before you go to bed," she said. "I will come to you at 10 o'clock and show you both to your different rooms." Mrs. Bannerton went to get the rooms ready. She was a widow and made her living by keeping lodgers. When the rooms were ready she came back and had a pleasant talk with Raymund while he was waiting for Rhoda. Mrs. Bannerton told him that she had a son at West Point and a daughter at the Boston Conservatory. She had worked very hard to give her son the education necessary to enable him to enter the examination contest, and she was now obliged to save every penny to keep her daughter in the conservatory. "Never any rest for me," said Mrs. Bannerton, smiling, "but my daughter has great musical talent, and I am only too glad that I am strong and can give her the advantages I never had myself. As for my son, if he had gone out to earn his living he could have made nothing of himself but a common workman. But you see, such as I am, I am already made; so I could work and give him his opportunity. One can not work for one's living and polish one's self at the same time."

"It seems very hard to be poor," sighed Raymund.

"It is harder to be rich," said Mrs. Bannerton, laughing out in enjoyment of her quick thought. Raymund laughed too, and presently, although Raymund had not one 5-cent piece more than before, he began to feel more hopeful.

Mrs. Bannerton, hearing Rhoda's bare feet slipping through the hall, left the kitchen that the two might be alone. Raymund was startled by the transformation which the gaslight revealed. Rhoda was herself again. The light, silken hair with its gleam of silver swung down her back to dry. Her splendid blue eyes looked from a face whose soft, creamy complexion well suited the quaint hair.

Mrs. Bannerton's long dress made the girl of 15 look like a woman; she was as tall as Mrs. Bannerton, and her form had a suppleness and grace that did not belong to the landlady. She beamed upon Raymund, and holding up the dress ran at him with a little coo.

"Why, Rhoda!" cried Raymund, holding her off and gazing upon her, "how old you look, and how pretty!" Then he let her slip her arms about him. "Your hair is darker," she said. "Oh, you poor boy! how you have had to work!" Then she discovered the green umbrella. "Why, Raymund! all the time I never once saw that." She snatched it up and buried her face in the faded folds. "But I haven't mother's Bible," she said, looking up. "I was in such a hurry to leave that dreadful house, I was afraid to go back for it."

"I am sorry," said Raymund.

"Yes," said Rhoda, "it had Uncle William's address written in it."

"Oh, but we know that by heart," said the other, disposed to make her think as lightly as possible of her loss.

"Yes," we know it," said Rhoda, "but I don't like for Mrs. Van Estry and those people to see it. It makes me think that it might get us into trouble for them to know anything about us!"

"Don't you worry about those people," said Raymund. "You'll never hear of them again. I've been thinking while I sat here waiting for you; I believe I'll try to find some kind of work here in the city. Now that we're here, and nobody wants us anywhere else, I might as well see what's to be done in this quarter."

"It might be a good thing," said Rhoda, doubtfully, "but let's talk about the to-morrow. Now, the first thing is to get me some clothes. Although it's June and so very warm, it wouldn't do to go barefooted in the house, and I couldn't go on the street in this dress of Mrs. Bannerton's."

"Oh, of course not," said Raymund, easily. "I've got lots of money; you leave everything to me; I'll trick you out, don't you fear!"

"You are the dearest boy!" cried his sister, giving him a squeeze. "But do tell me what you mean to buy!"

"I think it had better be a surprise," said Raymund.

"Well, just tell me about the shoes."

"I'll get you good, serviceable shoes," was the answer; "the kind you can walk in, the kind that won't wear out or split; I am very particular to get the kind that don't hurt a person's feet."

"What number, for instance, Raymund?"

"Well, I reckon about fours will do."

"Oh, Raymund!" cried Rhoda, remonstrating.

"Well," said Raymund, quickly, "I'll get four and a half."

Rhoda laughed and said: "What kind of a dress?"

"A ready-made dress," was the prompt answer.

"I think that would be wise, too," remarked Rhoda, "but I was asking about the material."

"Oh, I was thinking about one of these thin blue kind, you know, that show your arm through the goods and don't look slick, and a white underskirt, for I don't like colored underskirts at all, Rhoda; not at all!"

"What kind of a hat, Raymund?"

"I don't like feathers, do you?" said

indeed, in high glee over the room. It was his first experience of the sort, and he felt that he had gained a distinctly advantageous experience. It could no longer be said that he was unused to city ways, and that he had never rented a room. For the present, all this was his own property—the nondescript, soiled wall paper, the linty carpet, the iron bedstead, the white lead pipe that came in through the ceiling in one corner, then stopped abruptly as if it had entered by mistake, and so came to nothing, the gas jet which could be doubled up or stretched out three joints, and which had a little piece of cotton cloth jammed into one of the joints, a tin matchbox nailed to the wall just over the cracked mirror, the drab-colored door which smelled like soap, though it had apparently never used any, the open window, the dirty shutters and, above all, the view of the outside world. A long time after he had turned out the gas, and even after he had gotten out of bed to stand on a chair with his nose to each joint to be sure there was no leaking, Raymund looked out the window as he lay on the bed.

Directly below the window was the basement yard, and he knew that one of the windows looking into that damp, littered oblong was from Rhoda's room. Beyond the basement yard and about to feet above its blackened brick floor, was a wide, green sward, running up to a residence which stood with its back to Raymund's window. And beyond that were high brick buildings from whose windows lights shone steadily. And beyond them swung higher lights. Far, far away, many streets removed, was a house at least ten stories high; and although so remote, its lights showed Raymund men working in their shirt sleeves. He wondered what they were doing, and if they stayed up all night, and wondering, he fell asleep.

When he woke up it was strange not to hear Tom and Fred stirring about in the Hands' House; it was strange not to have to leap from bed at early dawn and hurry on his clothes; it was strange to hear men calling "Ra-a-a-aspberries!" when at home strawberries were hardly ripe. When Raymund went below, he did not have long to wait before Rhoda came up from the basement. He told her to go to his room and he would bring something to eat. When he reached the street he stared hard at the house to be sure of knowing it again, and he copied the number in his notebook. Luckily there was a store in sight, and he went thither. When he joined Rhoda in his room he held several parcels. There was no place to put them except upon the chair, so he and Rhoda sat on the edge of the bed and opened the crackers, dried beef and bananas. "It was all I could find," said Raymund, "except cheese and crackers, and I thought it too early for that."

"Much too early," said Rhoda, fingering a piece of the clammy dried beef and then popping it into her mouth for fear she might change her mind. Raymund imitated her example. They chewed and chewed, but the dried beef did not give an inch. "We don't have to do this, do we?" said Rhoda, suddenly.

"Of course not!" cried Raymund; taking out his tough morsel and casting it from the window. He proffered the bananas.

"Isn't it funny," said Rhoda, "this long, hard rib that runs through the banana? You ought to have got some boneless bananas, Ray!"

Raymund laughed and nibbled on a musty cracker. As he leaned back to throw it out the window after his dried beef, he saw a man in the yard beyond the basement, watching him. It was a

very disagreeable looking man of middle age, and his stare was so intent and so evil that Raymund could not but believe that the watcher was spying upon him. Why should anybody do that? Could it be that this man had followed Rhoda from Mrs. Van Estry's? As soon as the watcher found that Raymund had discovered him he slunk behind the residence and was seen no more. Raymund became very grave, but Rhoda thought his gravity was occasioned by the light breakfast, and her brother did not reveal what he had seen. There was no need, he thought, of frightening his companion.

(TO BE CONTINUED.)

❦ ❦

"Dat candidate was a gre't disap-intment to me," said the old colored man. "I dunno when I has been so took down."

"Why, he greeted you cordially and took you by the hand."

"Yessuh, he tuck me by han', but when he leggo my han' agin dar wasn' nuffin' in it."

❦ ❦

Two laborers set out from Wexford to walk to Dublin. By the time they reached Bray they were very much tired with their journey, and the more so when they were still twelve miles from Dublin. "Be me sowl," said one, after a little thought; "sure it's but six miles apiece; let us walk on!"

❦ ❦

One Won.

"Tom, I learn you're quite a church worker, would you mind telling me what started you in this direction?" said a friend to a young Canadian, who was in business in New York, and just home for a holiday.

"Well," said Tom, "it was only a little thing that seemed to start me, and yet I suppose that it wasn't a little thing, after all.

"Soon after I went to New York I wandered out one Sunday morning for a stroll. I knew nobody, and knew nothing at all about any of the churches. In passing one of the churches I saw an usher standing in the door. He gave me a pleasant bow, and, as it was not far from church time, I walked in. I had nowhere else to go.

"The singing was good, and the preaching was quite interesting. But nothing specially struck me till I was passing out—the pastor shook hands with me, and asked me to stay a few minutes; he wanted to see me. An usher took me to the parlor. In a few minutes the pastor came in, and asked me my name, and where I boarded, and what I worked at. He took it all down in his note-book.

"At the evening service I didn't go to church, but in the 11 o'clock mail the next morning I received a card from the pastor, saying he had missed me at the evening service, and that he would call on me the same evening at 8 o'clock.

"I stayed in, and he came round and stayed half an hour, and got me to promise to be at prayer-meeting Wednesday night. I went partly against my inclination, but he was so kind I felt obliged to go. He invited me to service and his Bible class next Sunday.

"Well, it went on from that. In a few Sundays the superintendent asked me to take a class, and I've settled down into an old church-worker now."

This young man is now a trusted worker in one of New York's "people's churches," and a heavy contributor to it. He is a success from a business standpoint, but of much greater value to the moral life of the city.

The pastor who found him was doing

what many a faithful pastor is doing in his community—adding to the strength and stability of society in developing young people in Christian character and usefulness.

My Father's World.

This is my Father's world.
O let me ne'er forget
That tho' the wrong seems oft' so strong,
God is the ruler yet.
This is my Father's world.
The battle is not done.
Jesus who died shall be satisfied,
And earth and Heaven be one.
This is my Father's world.
Should my heart be ever sad?
The Lord is King—let the heavens ring.
God reigns——let the earth be glad.
—*Maltbie D. Babcock.*

❀ ❀

Nature's Little Things.

BY REV. FRANCIS L. STRICKLAND, PH. D.

From the day when the Florentine Galileo with his first rude telescope bestowed the gift of a new vision upon his fellows, to the present, men have not ceased to wonder at the infinite reaches of space beyond this world of ours—distances quite beyond our ability to conceive. The telescope sweeps the heavens, and brings within our sight new worlds and new systems of worlds in the universe of unknown vastness about us.

The compound microscope in its humbler sphere reveals a no less wonderful world of beauty and perfection beneath us. This instrument has done a noble work for truth. Not only has it revealed many of the secrets of disease, and thus enabled us to fight more successfully to alleviate pain and prolong human life, but it has also helped some of us to grasp more firmly the great truth of God's power, wisdom, and care. It is strange that men who have looked down the wonder-revealing tube, and have studied the absolute perfection of detail, and the marvelous delicacy of adjustment in the world of organic life, could ever have doubted that there exists a Supreme Thinker and Worker who guides and rules in the realm of nature.

But my present purpose is to tell something of the profit and delight to be gotten from amateur microscopy. There is no scientific recreation that quite equals it. To begin with, it carries its devotees out of doors. In order to secure materials for the stage of the microscope we must explore the ponds and ditches, and find our way to the gardens, woods, and fields. And the revelations of the microscope from the world of nature are more stimulating to the nonprofessional student of nature.

Yes, you say, this may be quite true, but a compound microscope is a very expensive affair, and so the delights of microscopical study and diversion are shut off from many young people who might be glad to enter the fairy gardens of the microscopic world. But, fortunately for you, you are wrong. A plain but serviceable compound microscope is not very expensive in these days. If one wishes to study the starry heavens as an amateur astronomer, he can not do very much without a small telescope, the cost of which is far beyond the capacity of moderate purses. But to explore the almost infinite realms of that world whose wonders are too small for our unaided eyes, requires only an instrument which may be bought for twenty dollars, or even less. While a student in college my father gave me a substantial microscope costing $25. To this I have added a couple of higher power lenses, and a few simple accessories, acquired from time to time as I was able. Thus the expense of my instrument has been hardly felt during the ten years in which I have enjoyed its possession. And my equipment, simple as it is, is more elaborate than is really necessary for the fullest enjoyment of microscopical study and diversion. But the moderate sum invested has brought a great many times its value in healthful recreation and profitable diversion.

We often hear it said that people whose work confines them should cultivate a "hobby" which will take them out of doors and engage the thoughts in ways entirely different from those of the regular occupation. Of the several hobbies I have tried, the microscope is the most lasting.

Every year, when the warm days of early summer come, the blood of the amateur microscopist begins to tingle, and he watches his chance to get away with his collecting bottles and pocket magnifier, to wander along the edge of pond or stream. And then, after the outdoor ramble, comes the joy of sitting down quietly at home with the microscope, and exploring the new worlds contained in a few drops of pond water or a speck of green slime. And here is diversion for hours, if one has the time to spend, and profit, too, for the microscope not only enlarges our powers of physical vision, but broadens our mental outlook, affording a culture which the appreciative study of nature always gives.

And through this wonder-working tube what new and undreamed of beauties open up in every direction! There is no object made in the great laboratory of the Creator which, when properly placed and lighted on the stage of the microscope, will not repay careful study and reveal its wonders. Common insects and their various parts, the tiniest of the garden seeds, very thin sections of various woods and stems, the parts of wild and cultivated flowers; the myriad organisms, both animal and vegetable, which inhabit pond water; feathers of birds, scales of butterflies, hairs, leaves—these and a thousand other objects afford a realm whose mysteries can never be fully explored.

And what lessons are to be learned by the way! Showing a friend a specimen through the microscope recently, he said enthusiastically, "It's great!" and it was great, though it measured only one two hundred and fiftieth of an inch. Greatness is not a matter of size or linear dimensions. We gain some idea of the extent of the half-way point with respect to size between the elephant, the largest animal now existing, and the smallest organism, is the red ant! In other words, the microscope shows us living organisms as much smaller than the ant as the ant is smaller than the elephant. This may seem incredible, but it is true.

But I must tell you in a few words of some of the better known people of the invisible world to whom the microscope serves as an introduction. Let us begin with the smallest.

We take a half tumbler of pure water, into which a few scraps of raw meat have been thrown, and set it in the sun for a few hours. Examining with a moderately high power of the microscope a drop of the water which has become a little cloudy, we find it teeming with myriads of strange looking beings that look like animated corkscrews, sticks, and strings of beads. These are "bacteria," whose name means sticks. Where did they come from? From the air. When we put the meat into the water we formed what the scientific men call a "culture," that is, a medium in which the bacteria will quickly multiply. That these little creatures came from the air is easily proved. If we boil the water in a glass test-tube, and then plug the end tightly with cotton batting, no bacteria will appear. These little beings, which are classed as vegetable rather than animal, are very minute. It would take nearly six thousand of the larger kinds placed end to end to make an inch in length. Many people fancy that all bacteria are harmful, but this is not so; most of the brood are harmless. Only a comparatively small number are the causes of disease; and most of these are harmful only when they get a chance to multiply in our tissues because of a weakened condition of the system.

WASHINGTON CHRISTIAN COLLEGE

WASHINGTON, D. C.

LIBERTY LADIES' COLLEGE

Virginia Christian College

But there are organisms more interesting to us than the bacteria, and more easy to look at. We go to a stagnant pond, and take a little water, a few leaves of duckweed, and a little green slime. Now we have the material for many hours of instructive diversion.

Here is a water flea. He is a giant in the microscopical world for we can see him with the naked eye, as a tiny, jumping speck in the water. But with a low power of the microscope we see right through him, for he is transparent, and we need no X-rays. His lungs are at work, and his stomach is digesting some unfortunate little creature that he ate for breakfast.

He is interesting, but not more so than the green hydra. This individual can change his size and shape at every turn. Now he is spread out with eight long tentacles or arms, ready to grab his prey. But a tap on the glass slide frightens him, and quicker than thought he has become a mere mass of greenish-brown jelly.

Here is a rotifer, who, instead of having a mouth and jaws, has a circular series of long thin fins, with which he creates a current down his throat, thus sucking in many helpless little fellows who begin to digest before they know where they are! This crown of fins looks like a wheel when in operation, and hence the name of these creatures—the "rotifers," or wheel-bearers.

The water contains a host of things which we cannot examine in detail. Here is a green globe beautifully netted, and containing bright spots of red, rolling about in the jolliest fashion. He is the famous volvox. Here is a red spot with a wiggling tail, rushing about in the wildest way, never getting anywhere, but always in a great hurry. His name is monad. Here is a snake-like creature twisting in and out among the debris, and making his dinner out of the garbage of the microscopical world. Here are strange creatures that look like felt hats with a string tied to them. They are the vorticellids. Here also is a great dragon—a terrible beast with fearful jaws. He will be a mosquito some day. He is only an eighth of an inch long, but through the microscope he looks as big as an alligator.

I would like to have you see through the microscope the spider and his web, the strands of which are not simple threads, but tiny ropes, made up of a great many threads stuck together—more than you would believe, I am afraid. But enough has been said to suggest the vastness and wonder of that world we cannot see with the unaided eye. And if some one after reading these words resolves to save up for a microscope, and study Nature's kingdom of minute greatness, some good will have been accomplished by what is here set forth.

The microscope gives us new revelations of God. We find out how beautiful God's work always is. His power and wisdom are seen in the perfect little organisms whose world is a drop of water, just as surely as in the distant worlds that swing through boundless space—

It costs Omnipotence to build a world, [for no more
And set a sun amidst the firmament,
Than mould a dewdrop, and light up its gems."
—*Epworth Herald.*

❦ ❦

"But, ma, Uncle John eats with his knife."

"Hush, dear. Uncle John is rich enough to eat with a fire shovel if he prefers to."

❦ ❦

"The chimney is smoking," he said.

"Yes," she retorted; "that's the effect of bad example. Usually the chimney has consideration enough to do its smoking out-doors."

Thus it came about that he finished his cigar on the back porch.

What Became of Them?

Fifty years ago a gentleman of Ohio noted down ten drinkers, six young men and four boys. "I saw the boys," he says, "drink beer and buy cigars in what was then called a 'grocery' or 'doggery.' I expressed my disapprobation and the seller gave a coarse reply. He continued the business, and in fifteen years he died of delirium tremens, not leaving five dollars.

"I never lost sight of these ten, only as the clods of the valley hid their bodies from human vision. Of the six young men, one died of delirium tremens and one in a drunken fit; two died of disease produced by their excesses before they reached the meridian of life; two of them left families not provided for, and two sons are drunkards. Of the remaining, one is a miserable wreck, and the other a drinker in some better condition.

"Of the four boys, one, who had a good mother, grew up a sober man; one was killed by a club in a drunken brawl; one has served two terms in the penitentiary; and one has drunk himself into an inoffensive dole whose family has to provide for him."—*National Advocate.*

Christian Publishing Company

2712 Pine St., St. Louis, Mo.

H. GARRISON,   -   -   -   President
. W. DOWLING,   -   -   -   Vice-President
     L. SNIVELY.   -   -   Sec. and Gen. Supt
. P. CROW.   -   Treas. and Bus. Manager

Unless you use "Gloria in Excelsis," makes little difference what song book you select. This imperial song book may be bought of us for $5, $6.50, $8, $9.50 or $12 per dozen, or at $40, $50, $65, $75 or $95 per 100—owing to the bindings selected and whether the unabridged or abridged form is ordered.

We have just taken from the press a new edition of A. McLean's Missionary

Bridge Across Niagara.

Addresses, with statistics and other interesting missionary facts and features of the world's progress brought down to date. With this, too, is a compilation of the world's best missionary literature, as viewed by Bro. McLean. $1.00 postpaid.

"Enclosed find $50 for balance on Gloria in Excelsis Hymnal.' The books are giving the best of satisfaction."—George H. Brown (minister), Charleston, Ill. This is one of many tributes paid to this imperial song book. We have a large variety of smaller and cheaper, but excellent, song books for Bible schools, revivals and missions.

"To-day I received the picture of Bro. Garrison you sent me the 10th inst. Thanks. I assure you I appreciate it. With Christian regards."—Andrew Scott,

minister, Danville, Ill. This excellent 11x12½ likeness of our beloved Editor we are sending as a premium for one renewal and a new subscriber to THE CHRISTIAN-EVANGELIST, accompanied by $3.

Of course we sell The Twentieth Century New Testament—$1.00 postpaid. A tentative edition of this translation into the vernacular of the people was printed in 1902. The criticisms and suggestions were studied and with their aid a permanent edition was printed last year and is now being sold by thousands. Its indices and paragraphing, as well as the popular translation itself, are very valuable.

The Buffalo convention promises to be the largest and most interesting held or to be held between the Cincinnati jubilee in 1900 and the Pittsburg centennial in 1909. THE CHRISTIAN-EVANGELIST Special will take a great and happy throng over the Wabash. If you are not incorrigibly despondent, come with us. Write us at once to tell you how to secure free transportation to this great assembly.

Why experiment with sectarian and often untried paragraphers when at no greater cost you can secure the W. W. Dowling series of Bible-school Helps and papers for Children and Youth. After passing by the Dowling there seems to be little choice, but why pass by the best? For thirty years they have been used by most of our schools and with growing approbation. Here you may safely trust the judgment of the majority. Samples sent on application.

The steady but rapid growth of our circulation has not yet yielded to summer fatigue. While the vast majority of our new subscribers are sent singly by pleased patrons, we note the following clubs of new readers received last week: Port Jefferson, Ohio, 11 (William Wagoner, minister); Versailles, Ill., 14 (A. J. Campbell, minister); Girard, Ill., 7 (J. Winbigler, pastor); Decatur, Ill., 14 (J. L. Thompson, minister); East St. Louis, Ill., 28 (W. H. Jones, minister); Bethel, Conn., 3; Denver, Ill., 3; Rushville, Ill., 4 (Walter E. Harmon, pastor); Ruston, La., 3 (John A. Stevens, minister); Worcester, Mass., 3 (Harry Minnick, pastor); Winston-Salem, N. C., 3 (J. A. Hopkins, pastor).

A popular and exceptionally successful evangelist whose fall and winter campaigns begin September 1, writes requisition for 500 CHRISTIAN-EVANGELIST per week for distribution in the homes of the people in the various communities where he will labor. This will not only insure him a house full of hearers but prepare listeners as well. Here, too, those who have not known of us as people will learn the real motives and true genius of this Restoration as they could not be learned from papers that do not love to tell them or that delight more in controversy and litigiousness than preaching the old Jerusalem Gospel. We commend his example to all evangelists.

THE
CHRISTIAN-
EVANGELIST

A WEEKLY RELIGIOUS NEWSPAPER.

Volume XLIII.　　　　　No. 30.

ST. LOUIS, JULY 26, 1906.

WHAT HAST THOU DONE?

BY FLORENCE YARRELL

WHERE is the product of thy brain or hand?
　　Hast thou sown good seed in this great, broad
　　　land?
Hast lightened the burden of any one?
Answer to God before the setting sun—
　　What hast thou done?

As the sun goes down in the gilded west,
Ere a busy world has taken its rest,
Ask thy conscience ere the night has begun—
And the day its eternal course has run—
　　What hast thou done?

Answer this truly and make no mistake;
Didst add to sad heart one joy, or an ache?
The higher walk—hast thou ever begun?
Answer quickly—for thy race is most run—
　　What hast thou done?

Christian-Evangelist.

J. H. GARRISON, Editor

AUL MOORE, Assistant Editor

D. POWER, } Staff Correspondents.
B. TYLER, }
DURBAN, }

bscription Price, $1.50 a Year.

or foreign countries add $1.54 for postage.

tances should be made by money order,
r registered letter; not by local cheque, un-
ents is added to cover cost of collection
iering Change of Post Office give br .n old
address.
for Publication should be addresse , to THE
AN-EVANGELIST. Subscriptions as i remit-
hould be addressed to the Christian Publish-
pany, 2712 Pine Street, St. Louis. M i.
d Manuscripts will be returned nly if so-
ed by stamps.
Items, evangelistic and other rise, are
l, and should be sent on a post 1 card, if

hed by the Christian Publishing Company,
Street, St. Louis, Mo.

at St. Louis P. O. as Second C ass Matter

HAT WE STAND F)R.

or the Christ of Galilee,
or the truth which makes men b ie,
or the bond of unity
Which makes God's children on t.

or the love which shines in deeds
or the life which this world need ,
or the church whose triumph spee is
The prayer: "Thy will be done. '

or the right against the wrong,
or the weak against the strong,
or the poor who've waited long
For the brighter age to be.

or the faith against tradition,
or the truth 'gainst superstition,
or the hope whose glad fruition
Our waiting eyes shall see.

or the city God is rearing,
or the New Earth now appearing,
or the heaven above us clearing,
And the song of victory.

J. H. Garrison.

CONTENTS.

t Events 936
al—
Function and Value of National
nventions 937
Quest of Peace. 938
ent Religious Thought......... 938
r's Easy Chair................. 939
uted Articles—
Seen from the Dome. F. D.
wer 940
rn Religious Persecution—a De-
se. B. L. Chase............. 941
Manchester Meeting. Herbert
uell 942
Newest Evangelism. George
milton Combs 942
Jacksonville-Paris Contest...... 944
ral Bible School, Denver. Geo.
Perrin 945
Pastor and the Sunday-school.
has Shelburne 945
Pastor's Relation to the Sunday-
ool. Josie Ballou Sherman.,.. 946
idget 947
From Many Fields............. 951
s Forum 953
res, Obituaries 953
listic 954
un Endeavor 956
-school 956
sk Prayer-meeting 957
t Literature 958
me Department 959

THE
CHRISTIAN=EVANGELIST

"IN FAITH, UNITY; IN OPINION AND METHODS, LIBERTY, IN ALL THINGS, CHARITY."

Vol. XLIII. July 26, 1906 No. 30

1809 CENTENNIAL PROPAGANDA 1909
CHURCHES OF CHRIST

: : : GEO. L. SNIVELY : : :

Looking Toward Pittsburg.

The leaven is working. Not only are our state and national secretaries doing all in their power to make the best possible showing by 1909, but our ministers are evolving many ingenious plans for enlarging and ennobling our local Zions. The method devised by Bro. Charles Fillmore and outlined below, is both novel and suggestive. We commend it to the consideration of pastors, Bible school superintendents and the officers of our Endeavor societies.

We shall be pleased to print other suggestions having the same end in view, particularly if they have been tried and proven successful by their authors. Any plan is better than aimlessness. A good plan well worked is preferable to a better one allowed to fall into "innocuous desuetude." The first bell was rung at Omaha, the second one is ringing, the time remaining is comparatively brief. Awake sleepers, work dreamers, let us all enthusiastically enter upon what our hands find to do; let every congregation be a hive of industry; let every man be a hero in the struggle against indifference, lethargy and opposition, and the extension of the church, the salvation of men, the honors thus won for the King will invest us all with glory giving us entree to the highest spiritual privileges on earth and before which heaven's gates will swing at last.

The Kentucky Centennial.

The Christian Bible schools of Kentucky and their friends propose to endow a new department of Bible school pedagogy in the College of the Bible at Lexington, Ky., as their centennial enterprise. To do this it will be necessary for the sum of $25,000 to be raised, which is to be added to the permanent endowment of the College of the Bible. The college proposes in return for this to employ a man who is to teach the work of the Sunday school to every student who receives a diploma. In addition to this a special two years' course is to be arranged which teachers and superintendents in the Bible schools may take and for the satisfactory completion of which a certificate will be issued by the college. This course will include sacred history as it is now taught, the public reading of the scripture, vocal music and the art of teaching it in the Bible schools, and the new course on the organization, management and instruction of Bible schools. The college also proposes to furnish such additional courses as may be found necessary or expedient as the demand arises.

This matter has been under advisement for some time. A letter of inquiry was addressed to many prominent preachers, Bible school workers and educators in the state, to which replies have been received which exhibit almost perfect unanimity with regard to the proposed enterprise.

Among those favorably responding are Geo. A. Miller, Covington; J. W. Morrison,

Burris A. Jenkins, Lexington; E. T. Lafferty, Cynthiana; E. L. Powell, J. B. Briney, Louisville; Mary A. Finch, Helena Station; C. R. Hudson, Frankfort; R. H. Crossfield, Owensboro; Geo. C. Long, Hopkinsville; Carey E. Morgan, Paris; J. T. Kackley, Maysville. Certainly this is a step forward which will be welcomed by all who are interested in the cause of Bible study and particularly by those engaged in the service of the Bible schools.

Louisville. ROBERT M. HOPKINS.

Centennial Centurion Bands.

BY CHAS. M. FILLMORE.

The church at Carthage, O., a suburb of Cincinnati, in order to be in line for the centennial celebration in 1909, is preparing for an unusually vigorous campaign for the fall and winter. This is one of the historic churches of the brotherhood, having been organized by Walter Scott in 1832, and having under consideration plans for the celebration of its diamond anniversary in June, 1907.

The plans for the coming fall and winter campaign are being organized along ancient Roman army lines. The primary purpose is the enlistment of a "Centurion Band" or one hundred new members of the Lord's army. Along with this, efforts will be made to enroll a "Centurion Band" of one hundred new pupils in the Bible school.

Then, in order to make these new members an integral part of the present army of the Lord, efforts will be put forth to enroll a "Centurion Band" of one hundred new regular attendants at the Sunday morning service, a "Centurion Band" of one hundred new attendants at the Sunday evening service; a "Centurion Band" of one hundred new attendants at the midweek prayer-meeting.

In addition to these, there will be raised a special fund of $100 in $1 pledges for general expenses; and $100 in $1 pledges for the new building fund.

For the accomplishment of this work there will be organized a "Centurion Band" of one hundred "Whatsoevers"—men, women, boys and girls, who will pledge themselves to do whatsoever they can to make the campaign a complete success.

To recapitulate, the plan contemplates:

CENTURION BANDS.

100 Whatsoeverers.
100 New Recruits.
100 New Bible School Scholars.
100 New Sunday Morning Attendants.
100 New Sunday Evening Attendants.
100 New Prayer-meeting Attendants.
$100 For Current Expenses.
$100 For Building Fund.

All during or before the last one hundred days of the year, beginning September 23, 1906.

SOME MEANS AND METHODS.

Organization: Commander in-chief, the pastor.

Captain of "Centurion Band of Whatsoevers."
Captain of "Centurion Band of New Recruits."
Captain of "Centurion Band of Sunday Morning Attendants."
Captain of "Centurion Band of Sunday Evening Attendants."
Captain of "Centurion Band of Prayer-meeting."
Captain of "Centurion Band of Bible School."
Captain of "Centurion Band of Current Expense Fund."
Captain of "Centurion Band of Building Fund."

Subordinate officers under each of these captains.

A company of scouts composed of boys of Bible School.

A company of Red Cross composed of girls of Sunday-school.

The town to be platted and districted, and certain persons chosen to thoroughly work each district throughout the campaign.

PLANS OF CAMPAIGN.

House to house canvass on Sept. 2.

Sunday-school rally with the aim of having 250 present Sept. 23.

A week's rally, addresses by different preachers, Sept. 24-28.

Sunday morning rally of church, Sept. 30.

Cottage prayer-meetings, October 1-5.

Sunday night rally, October 7.

Prayer-meeting rally, with 100 new attendants, October 10.

All day services and beginning of evangelistic meetings, October 21.

The use of an entire page in the local paper for sixteen weeks during and just preceding the campaign. See that this paper is put into the hands of every family of the entire community each week.

General motto for the campaign: "Attempt great things for God; expect great things from God."

Special motto for "Whatsoeverers":

"I am only one, but I am one;
I can not do everything, but I can do something;
What I can do, I ought to do;
What I ought to do, with the help of God I will do."

Centennial Propagandists.

THE CHRISTIAN-EVANGELIST has ever been a great paper, and just now it seems to be destined to stand first among religious journals. Let it hold fast and consistently to the sublime and inspiring truths of the restoration of New Testament Christianity, and as a consequence Christian unity will come, and it will not be long until it will grow in numbers and influence by leaps and bounds. Holding as in a grip of steel these fundamentals and propagating them in terms that are Christian and practicing what we preach, we shall soon take this world for Christ. I want to see if I can not introduce the paper into a number of our homes.—H. C. Kendrick, minister.

Current Events

When Congress, by the act of June 7, 1897, declared it to be "the settled policy

Indian Schools.

of the government hereafter to make no appropriation for education in any sectarian school," it might have been expected to put an end to the practice of subsidizing Catholic Indian schools. Most of the Protestant schools had already ceased to ask aid. But the obvious intention of this act has not been completely carried out. The government has entered into a contract with the St. Francis Roman Catholic Boarding School to care for 250 children on the Sioux Indians of the Rosebud agency, South Dakota, for $27,000 a year. A petition signed by 212 members of the tribe requested this appropriation of their money. A counter petition signed by 921 members opposes it. The government will be very blind if, in opposition to the will of a large majority of the Indians themselves, in opposition to the general sentiment of the people at large, and in opposition to the expressed will of Congress, it persists in this appropriation. It is not a question of whether, in this particular case, better educational results can be obtained by giving the money to a sectarian school. It is a question of whether or not we want church and state separated or united. Most of the founders of this republic were pious men; and certainly they must have foreseen that, if the church were not supported by the state, the offices of religion must cease in many communities. Yet they thought it better for the church to languish in some places than for it to be supported by the state. And it will be better for Indian education to languish for a time in some places than for the state to support sectarian schools. All this, we admit, has been said a great many times before. We have said it ourselves, in substance, more than once. But it will not be a dead issue so long as any branch of the government forgets that it has already been settled the other way and acts in opposition to the will of the people and the dictates of good policy.

❀

Dreyfus has been acquitted, restored to his rank in the French army and as,

Dreyfus Again.

signed to active duty. Here, let us hope, the incident finally ends. First he was condemned on a charge of treason for betraying military secrets to Germany, and sent to solitary confinement on Devil's Island for life. After five years, he was brought back to France for re-trial. Although the case against him utterly broke down political considerations and "the honor of the army" demanded his conviction. He was found guilty of "treason but with extenuating circumstances," but was pardoned. The conviction and the pardon were alike a confession of the farcical nature of the proceedings. Where there is treason there can be no extenuating circumstances. Now after six years the case is re-opened, Dreyfus is acquitted and restored to his rank. But who shall restore to him the twelve years lost in shame and suffering under a false charge? But if he is a lover of his country he

should not grudge the price he has paid, for he has helped to teach France that, in an affair of justice there is no safety except in rendering justice, and that nothing is ever settled until it is settled right.

❀

Mr. Bonaparte is an admirable man and an excellent secretary of the navy,

A Curious Contract.

but we think he has made a very curious contract for armor-plate for the two new battleships. When the bids were opened, it was found that the Midvale company (independent) bid $345 per ton; the Carnegie company (a branch of the steel trust) $370; and the Bethlehem company (another branch of the same) $380. Since the Midvale is a reliable firm which has done satisfactory government work before, the natural course would have been to give the contract to it as the lowest bidder. Then Mr. Schwab comes to Washington and, after conferences, the trust companies decide that they can afford to meet the price of their competitor and the contract is divided: one-half to the Midvale, the other half divided between the Carnegie and Bethlehem companies. Mr. Schwab said his companies needed the business. But why this anxiety to give the latter companies a share in the business when they were confessedly trying to get thirty or forty dollars a ton more than the job is really worth? Why should the bidders on any future contracts try to put their figures as low as possible if it is understood to be the government's policy to give the high bidders a chance to meet the low bidders' price and then give everybody a slice of the contract? Finally, when did any independent company ever get a chance to put in a second bid and get a share of the business when the trust was the lowest bidder? We fear that Secretary Bonaparte has inadvertently confused the functions of the different departments of this government. The protection of infant industries and full-fed trusts is cared for by the tariff law enacted by Congress and administered by the Treasury Department. The function of the secretary of the navy, so far as this job is concerned, is to buy armor-plate on the best terms as a business man would.

❀

It appears that the Holy Land is enjoying something of a commercial boom.

The Prosperity of Palestine.

A recent consular report suggests that the land is again enjoying a period of milk and honey. More specifically we observe that the district about Gaza exported two million bushels of barley last year, and over one-half a million dollars worth of oranges, the latter chiefly to Scotland; that the region of Jaffa (Joppa) raised nearly $100,000 worth of watermelons more than it needed for home use; that the Jewish colonies (think of "Jewish colonies" in Judea) are pushing the wine business; that the Jerusalem-Jaffa railroad is doing much to stimulate trade and custom-house receipts are steadily increasing. We note an increase in the importation of structural iron and other building materials, and woven goods and in the exportation of "religious goods." It is sad to note a falling off in the exports of sesame and colocynth. At the present writing, with no dictionary within reach, we do not know what colocynth is, but the combination sounds

The Function and Value of National Conventions.

The religious convention is an organ of religious freedom. It has no place in the scheme of ecclesiastical despotism. A Church with an infallible head from whose decision there is no appeal needs only a college of cardinals and a descending scale of an ecclesiastic hierarchy, to carry out its plans and accomplish its purposes. If at long intervals ecumenical councils are convened by a decree of the Pope, they are called to register decisions which have already been made, and to formally ratify dogmas which have already been agreed upon. It has no place for a representative body of delegates representing the churches to deliberate on matters of interest relating to the church and its work, and to express its own conclusions concerning these matters. The religious convention, in its modern sense, we repeat, is an adjunct, and an essential adjunct, of religious freedom.

Why do we say that the religious convention is an *essential* adjunct of religious liberty? Simply because, in the absence of any authoritative head or group of ecclesiastic officials, who have the authority to decide matters of practical interest, this work devolves upon the free churches themselves. Whatever is purely local can be decided upon by the local church, but there are many questions of great moment that interest a large number of local churches which have in them a common interest. Religious freedom and equality require that all the churches having an interest in such questions should have an opportunity to act upon them, either as churches or through chosen representatives who shall act for them. Experience has taught that where a large number of churches within a given district or state are interested in some question of importance to their welfare, the most practical method of dealing with such a question is through conventions or assemblies in which the churches, through their chosen representatives, have a voice. When the whole group of churches having common interests and common enterprises, is so great that a mass meeting of all the churches is impossible, then such a representative body becomes a necessity, if the principles of freedom and equality are to be maintained. Our form of government in this country is based upon the theory of representation in state and national legislatures.

Now, what is the theory as to the function of a religious convention among the Disciples of Christ? We have a number of interests which we generally group under the heads of Missions, Education, and Benevolence, which, in their very nature, require the co-operation of the churches. These conventions are county, state and national, as we have generally adopted the political divisions of the country as convenient boundary lines for these separate conventions. While the same principle holds good in all, we are to consider here the function of the national convention among us. Besides the group of interests mentioned, missionary, education, and benevolent, there are certain moral and social reforms concerning which it has been customary for us to give an expression of judgment with the view of influencing public sentiment in what we believe to be the right direction. It has never been the theory, from the beginning of this Reformation, that these conventions possessed any legislative or disciplinary power. No creed has been formulated by any convention among us, and no man has been tried for alleged heresy. Our conventions have been neither law-making bodies nor courts of judicature. In this respect they differ from many of the national representative bodies, of our religious neighbors. Their action on all subjects is only advisory, never mandatory.

But let no one suppose that because the action of these conventions is enforced only by the moral power and influence of the men composing the convention and of the inherent rightness of the things they recommend, their function is, therefore, unimportant. Without interfering in the least with the freedom of the churches, and appealing only to their sense of duty and of brotherhood, large numbers have been brought into harmonious co-operation along many lines of general interest. Whatever progress we have made in missionary work, and in all our co-operative enterprises, is due very largely to these conventions. They have exerted a mighty unifying, educational, and inspirational influence without which our position and influence in the religious world would have been vastly different from what they are at present.

Hitherto, it has been the practice of these conventions under the direction of our great leaders to consider every question that was regarded as having an important bearing upon the welfare and progress of the cause for which we stand. There was a little shyness at first in admitting education and benevolence into the circle of subjects worthy to be entertained by these national conventions, but at present we believe there is none who disputes their just claim to a place on our national program. From the beginning, however, there has been no dissent from the policy of bringing before such conventions overtures from various religious bodies looking toward Christian union, and nothing has created greater enthusiasm in these conventions than the report of conferences with other Protestant bodies having for their purpose the unification of Christians. Recently, however, for the first time in our history, objections have been raised against the consideration of this class of subjects in our national convention. This position has been taken by the opponents of church federation, who hold that the introduction of this question in our national convention is barred by the fact that our conventions

✦✦✦✦✦

AFFECTION can withstand very severe storms of rigor, but not a long polar frost of downright indifference. Love will subsist on wonderfully little hope, but not altogether without it.

are not legislative bodies. Others, however, not necessarily opposed to federation, are opposed to bringing the matter before what they call our *missionary* conventions, on the ground that they are not "germane" to the purposes of such conventions.

Neither of these objections seems to us well taken, for, as we have before pointed out, if the fact that our conventions are not legislative bodies makes it inadvisable for them to pass a resolution expressing its sentiment on the subject of federation as a method of co-operation, then the same fact would prevent them from passing any resolution expressing its sentiments on any other subject. As to germaneness, all precedents are against the objection. Our conventions are not simply *missionary* conventions and never have been, unless we interpret the word *missionary* in a very liberal way. That our colleges and our benevolent work do have a very close connection with our mission work cannot be denied; but they are not parts of it. And surely any action looking toward Christian union has a very important bearing upon the evangelization of the world. There is only one ground on which reasonable objection can be made against the consideration of the proposed basis of federation at our national conventions, and that is, that it would be *inexpedient*, at present, owing to the misunderstanding that prevails among brethren on this subject, and the injury that might accrue to our missionary interests through the unreasonable course of some brethren who hold our missionary societies, particularly the Home Society, responsible for any action taken by the convention!

As this situation exists, and especially if we are to grant the contention that nothing hereafter should be brought before our conventions but what is *strictly* missionary, we are face-to-face with a condition that calls for immediate action. If our present annual national conventions are to be understood as meetings of the missionary societies to transact only such business as is conducted by these organizations, then it does not need to be argued, that we must have a national convention, other than the missionary conventions, to consider other interests of vital importance to the brotherhood. This is the problem which we are now facing: We must either make our present national convocation the organ and instrument of expressing the collective thought of the brotherhood, on living questions which demand our attention, or we must organize a national council, or assembly or convention, broad enough in its scope and spirit, to deliberate upon every question and interest requiring the action of a deliberative body, and to adopt such recommendations and advisory measures, as may seem wise to such a body. It should be added, however, that this national council should be a strictly representative body in which every church caring to do so should have a voice.

We have simply stated the issue. Every thoughtful man among us knows that one or the other of the two alternatives which we have mentioned must be taken. Which shall it be?

The Quest of Peace.

One of the supreme needs of the human soul, and, indeed, one of the supreme desires of the human heart, is peace. Who of us does not long for it, amid the tumult and strife of life, even as the "hart panteth after the water brooks"? What is peace? How can we define it when the Apostle tells us that it "passeth all understanding"? We may describe it, however, or mention some of its characteristics. It is repose of mind; rest of soul; freedom from carking cares and anxieties; satisfaction of heart; quietness of spirit. Peace is oneness with God; it is the correlation of the human spirit with the divine; it is undisturbed fellowship with God; it is the enfoldment of our trembling, fearful hearts, by the infinite love of God.

Whence cometh this peace? The world can not give it. Wealth can not purchase it. Earthly position and honor do not confer it. It is not a product of physical or intellectual struggle. How many, alas, are seeking it, unconsciously, perhaps, in all these ways, and are the same restless, unsatisfied mortals. Continents have been traversed, oceans crossed, long and weary pilgrimages made, in search of this precious boon, without finding it. Missionaries tell us of pilgrims in the far east traveling long distances on foot, in weariness of body and spirit, to find some sacred place or shrine where they may find peace. Poor, blind, deluded souls! But not more so than those in so-called Christian lands who are seeking satisfaction of soul in the struggle for earthly possessions, or in the race for earthly position or renown. Peace is the gift of God. Like the kingdom of God, of which it is a part, it is "not of this world." The best things of life are not purchasable; they are the free gifts of God.

When Jesus was about to leave the world he wished to make a bequest to his disciples. He had no houses or lands, no silver or gold, no wealth in any material form, to bequeath them. But he had something infinitely better than all material wealth to leave them, and so he said: "Peace I leave with you; my peace I give unto you: not as the world giveth, give I unto you." What a precious legacy! . No, indeed, the world does not give that way. It gives material wealth and worldly honor, but these do not bring rest to the soul. Only Christ can give us that. "My peace," said Jesus. This was the one possession that made his life serene and calm, through all the tumult and conflict which marked his earthly ministry. He wishes his disciples to share that peace with him. He desires to confer it upon them.

But this gift is not unconditional. God can not give to us any good thing until we are ready to receive it. We must believe in God, as he is revealed to us in Christ, and thoroughly commit ourselves to him in loving obedience to his will. In other words, we must trust him. The Psalmist had found the secret of this peace when he said, "Thou wilt keep him in perfect peace whose heart is stayed in thee." Living in conscious disobedience to the will of God forever bars the soul from this peace. Like every good thing, peace must be sought for. "Seek peace and pursue it." Seek it in obedience; in taking Christ's yoke and learning of him; in prayer and communion with God; in doing good to all men as you have opportunity; in walking humbly before God, in loving mercy, and doing justice.

Reader, have you found this peace? If not, search for it as for hidden treasures. But search in God's way, and not in the way of the world. It is a fruit of the Spirit. It will be found only as that divine Guest is admitted into your heart. Open your heart to his incoming, with all earnest longing and loving obedience and he will come in and thou shalt have peace. "And may the peace . of God which passeth all understanding keep thy mind and heart through Jesus Christ."

Notes and Comments.

We are glad to give some space this week to the consideration of our Bible school interests. We feel it to be impossible to exaggerate the value of this part of our work. The new emphasis it is receiving within the last few years is a most hopeful sign. It stands to reason that our men and women in the church of to-morrow are to be just what the training of the boys and girls in our Bible school to-day will make them. We are, therefore, deciding the character of the future membership of the church and, therefore, the future destiny of the church, so far as human hands can shape it, by the manner in which we are fulfilling our duty to the children of to-day. The revival in Bible study which is so much needed as a factor in missionary, evangelistic, educational, and all other branches of our work, can only come through the Sunday or Bible school or, at least, its most effective work must be done there. It is the realization of this fact that is lending new interest to this subject, and it is for this reason that we devote this number of THE CHRISTIAN-EVANGELIST especially to that interest.

⁂

Bro. Herbert Yeuell's meeting in Manchester goes bravely on. Bravely is the right word. It is a heroic thing for a young man to enter a city like Manchester, without brethren, without friends, without acquaintances, under suspicion that he represents some freak religion, to hold a series of religious services in the hot month of July in a down-town theater. And yet these meetings have grown in power from the beginning. Brother Yeuell has sent us clippings from a daily paper, and we have rarely seen as discriminating and well-written notices of a meeting in the daily press. Brother Yeuell's meeting is

Editor's Easy Chair.

PENTWATER MUSINGS.

"The Pioneer" is rapidly assuming the form of a house. The carpenters are at work on the roof to-day. Its broad verandas opening out westward, northward, southward, and each one commanding a view of the lake, have an inviting appearance. What a place for writing, reading, or resting according to one's mood! Meantime, however, we are using the trees about the cottage a good deal for shade and shelter. A few minutes ago a little bird lighted upon the limb of a tree within a few feet of us, and sat there contentedly for a minute or two, until it saw us, and then it flew away. Of course, this flight grew out of its ignorance as to our feeling of friendliness towards it. Had it known our fondness for birds, it would have lighted upon our hand, and we should have had a billing and cooing time of it. They tell us that in parts of the world where man has not intruded, that the birds and animals are perfectly tame with visitors who go there. They have not learned to distrust man and give him credit for harmlessness until he proves himself unworthy of it. What a pity that this primitive basis of social unity and friendship should have been broken up by man's cruelty! Birds are not different from man in this: that mutual confidence is the basis of friendship. The great social and religious union of men awaits a better acquaintanceship, and a more intimate knowledge among men of each other. The process which we call "taming" of animals, is simply a matter of getting their confidence and friendship, by showing them kindness. Even savages have been "tamed" in the same way, and we wouldn't wonder that after while, as our civilization advances, that laboring men and capitalists, and even members of different churches, would learn to adopt this method of "taming" each other! That would be a great gain over war between nations, industrial strife between labor and capital, and religious strife between brother and brother.

❧

The amount of mail that reaches us here shows that Pentwater is very accessible by mail! The variety of an editor's mail makes his life anything but monotonous. Some letters complain, some criticise, some ask for information, many ask for assistance in one way and another, and now and then a royal soul just sits down and writes a word of encouragement, having no favors to ask nor faults to find. We read in a religious paper, the other day, the statement of a man who said he had been preparing the Sunday-school lesson sixteen years for a certain religious journal, and he had never received a word of appreciation of any help he had given, from the readers of that paper, during all these years! And yet if this faithful worker had made a slip in his theology, he would probably have heard from a great many, so prone are people to take for granted what pleases them, and to speak out only when their views are crossed. One of the very

best letters we have received during the past week came from the prison. You can't judge of the quality of a letter by the place it comes from. This man's imprisonment, like that of many another man, has proved a blessing to him, for he has learned to know God in the state prison, as he had not known him while he was at liberty. It is vastly better to be a Christian in prison than a willful sinner at liberty. How little we know what environment is best for us! We are indebted to Paul's imprisonment for some of his greatest epistles, and but for Bedford jail we probably should never have heard of "Bunyan's Pilgrim's Progress." But we were speaking about letters, and what a great variety of them one receives. How much they mean, too, in the way of burdening or brightening one's life! Some days wear a somber hue through all its hours of sunshine, because the morning mail brought letters which have excited anxiety. Some time, of course, such letters are necessary, but let each of us think well before we add an ounce of burden to any man whose load may already be as much as he can carry.

❧

The past week has been a succession of glorious summer days with the exception of one rainy day, which was the most needed of all. The bathing in Lake Michigan has been such as to tempt one to become an aquatic animal, and live in the lake! The sunsets have vied with each other in magnificence and grandeur. One of these was exceptionally fine. It was as if the sun and the lake and the clouds and the atmosphere had held a council and had said, "Go to, now; let us present a scene at this evening's sunset that will hold a place in the memory of all who shall behold it.". And they did. It was a glorious picture, consisting of many parts. There were long strata of clouds on fire, and there were opalescent lakes and golden waterfalls, and rivers of molten lava, flowing down dark mountain sides, and leaping into the abyss. In the midst of the picture, and the center of attraction, was the great sun, belted here and there with dark clouds dividing it into zones, now peeping with his blazing eye through a rift in the vapor, and the while sending up golden shafts of light to paint in crimson and gold the clouds which constituted his retinue. What a scene for a painter! But no; no painter would attempt to put on canvas a scene like that. It was one of the masterpieces of the divine Artist. Such a sunset scene reminds one of the words of the psalmist: "In them (the heavens) hath He set a tabernacle for the sun." Surely no tabernacle ever erected by man could equal the gorgeous splendor and magnificent proportions of that one reared in the heavens as if by magic on that glorious evening.

❧

Pentwater has a young Christian church organized since our last summer's sojourn here, and we have had the privilege of meeting with it and speaking for it since our coming, in its Lord's day morning services, held in the G. A. R. hall of the town. These services have increased in attendance as the visitors from abroad are gathering here for the

summer. Last Lord's day we had with us L. C. Stow and wife of Grand Rapids, who were with us on a transient visit. We hope they will come again and stay longer. Brother Alderman of Pentwater, brother of our missionary who laid down his life for the cause in Mexico, is the leader of the little band of Disciples here who are waiting now the arrival of their preacher, Brother Shonts. We are hoping, as the number of visitors increases here, to have an evening beach service. The morning boat, "The Kansas," which makes tri-weekly trips from Chicago, brought Bro. A. H. Duncan and wife and daughter from St. Louis, who have joined their other married daughter and son-in-law, Mr. and Mrs. Rogers, at the club house. Like everybody else who comes here they are charmed with the beauty and quietness of the place. In thinking over the future of this park we have thought how desirable it would be to have a number of our ministers and business men gather here each summer, not only for rest and physical recuperation, but to counsel together over matters of interest to the brotherhood and to hold some devotional religious services, and to have some Bible studies, in a quiet informal way, that would be wonderfully stimulating and helpful. We have felt the need, sorely, during the past week, of just such wise counselors with whom we could talk over some of the current questions that involve our present and future welfare. This is the ideal which we have in mind, and which led us to this place of peace and quiet.

❧

In a letter a few days ago from a very dear friend who is himself now enjoying a vacation in the east, he says: "Has not the time come in your life when you can have some absolute rest—a real vacation?" We used to dream of such a time, in the long ago, but we hardly expect it now, until it is forced upon us by inability to work. Never in the Editor's whole history has he ever had the luxury of such a vacation. We have often wondered how it would feel to be free from any sense of obligation to perform daily stints of editorial work—to grind out the necessary "copy." The summer vacation, with us, means the removal of our editorial office from St. Louis to the lakeside. But we advise all who can do so to leave their work at home and take a full vacation. The intensity of our American life makes a vacation a real necessity in the lives of most men. The summer resort is really a beneficent institution, and to get people away from their ruts and routine of daily toil and drudgery, to a summer resort, where Nature presents some of her noblest aspects, and where scenes and associations are all new, is to confer upon them a benefit which will be life-long in its influence. It is a blessed arrangement that Memory stores up and carries with us these pictures that delight the eye and fascinate the soul, and they become permanent assets, and we live over again, by means of these pictures, the pleasant experiences of the past. The prospect is that August will be a very full month on this beach. Among other visitors we are expecting within the next few days Mr. and Mrs. W. T. Moore, of Columbia. Of course, we will settle a good many difficult theological problems during the summer!

As Seen From the Dome   By F. D. Power

It is a thousand miles across the Mediterranean in a northwesterly direction from Alexandria to Naples, but a pleasant journey after the summer heat and dust of Egypt. Passing through the straits of Messina we had excellent views of Mt. Etna towering 10,742 feet, the loftiest volcano in Europe. It has not been active since 1892, but generally has an eruption every four or five years, and in one case destroyed forty towns and between 600,000 and 100,000 lives. At the northern end of the straits we steamed between Scylla and Charybdis. According to Homer the rock of Scylla was a roaring and voracious sea-monster, a beautiful virgin above, a monster with a wolf's body and a dolphin's tail below, and in connection with Charybdis opposite, fraught with imminent danger to mariners. Currents and eddies here are very rapid and, the channel very narrow and it is easy to see the origin of the proverb: *"Incidis in Scyllum, cupiens vitare Charybdis."* A little farther on we looked upon the dark form of Stromboli—Stromboli where Aeolus had his home, and from whose crater the crusaders claimed they could hear the lamentations of the lost in Purgatory.

The traveller who approaches Naples by sea may well be excused for any extravagance of language. As the ship enters the bay, passing between the beautiful isles of Ischia and Capri placed like twin outposts to guard the entrance of this watery Paradise, the scene is one that cannot fade from memory. All around stretches the bay in its azure immensity, its sweeping curves bounded on the right by the rocky promontory of Sorrento with its towns and villages, olive-clad precipices, orange groves and vineyards. Then Vesuvius, the genius of the scene, with its vine clad slopes below and dark cone above, belching out fire and smoke. Farther along, the great city of 600,000, a white mass in the distance like a marble quarry, and far beyond a range of snowy peaks of the Abruzzi mountains in the purple haze of the horizon. It is a panorama for beauty and extent which one sees nowhere else, an unequaled combination of sea, mountain, and island scenery. *Vedi Napoli e poi mori!* they say, "see Naples and die," and Goethe declares a man can never be utterly miserable who retains the recollection of it.

The city has its history. The Romans loved it. Lucullus had his gardens here and Virgil wrote his poetry here and has his resting place near by; and Augustus often resided at Naples, and Sallust had his home at the foot of Vesuvius. The modern city is not attractive. One is soon disillusionized by filth and dirt, vulgarities and indecencies, beggars and noise, drivers, street vendors, and guides. The poetry vanished with the vision of maccaroni eaters. Men and women make their toilet in the street, and one sees many things to justify the proverb, "Naples is a paradise inhabited by devils." There are many interesting street scenes. There is the fried-fish stall, where the oil cooks the trout, prepared while you wait. There is the snail soup shop where present day Neopolitans devour these little creatures as did their Roman ancestors. There are the perambulant living dairies—the cow or the goat, driven to your door, or mounting your steps to deliver the goods. There are the lemonade sellers with the barrels on their backs and lemons strung to their waists, dispensing drink to the thirsty at two cents a glass. There are the long bodied wagons with the richly-decorated pad or saddle of the harness having a brilliant array of gaudy brass flags and shining *repousse* plates with figures of the Madonna and the saints, which, with the pagan symbols of horns and crescents are supposed to protect the horses from harm. These ornaments, however, do not seem to save them from the brutality of their masters. Nowhere does one see such loads put upon the teams. The carrying power of a horse seems only limited by the number of passengers that can hang on to a vehicle, and the whip is used unmercifully.

The sights in Naples are not notable. The museum is most frequented. People who do not care for an aquarium, and the "galleria" where women buy coral and Mosaics and cameos at big prices, find great comfort in the collections of statuary and treasures from the buried city of Pompeii. The ancient frescoes from Pompeii, Herculaneum, and other cities and the collection of marbles and bronzes of terra cottas and papyri, of gems and vases gathered from the excavations of the disinterred cities are exceedingly rich and instructive. One sees bread baked since the year 79, and fruit, and even the forms of men and animals, buried under the ashes of Vesuvius over eighteen centuries ago. Among the treasures of the museum is the famous Farnese bull and Hercules. The first is the most celebrated. It is a marvelous group of figures hewn out of a single block of marble. It was found in the Thermae of Caracella at Rome. The two sons of Antiope, Amphion and Zethus, avenge their mother by binding Dirce, who had treated her with greatest cruelty for many years, to the horns of a wild bull. Antiope in the background exhorts them to forgiveness. The group is unrivalled. It has wonderful boldness and life. Its figures are all life size and tell their story in most vivid manner.

After all, the best things in Naples are outside. Capri is here with its famous blue grotto which everybody goes to see, and too often fails to be realized as the narrow entrance cannot be entered, or the visitor is slushed and half drowned by the sea. Entering the portal on your back, "you find yourself transported to a world of wavering subaqueous sheen. The grotto is domed in many chambers; and the water is so clear that you can see the bottom, silvery, with black-finned fishes diapered upon the blue-white sand. All around the spray leaps up with living fire, and when the oars strike the surface it is as if a phosphorescent sea had been smitten and the drops ran from the blades in blue pearls. The spectators seem bathed in liquid sapphire." Many, however, take the trip, get sea sick, and never get in, or, if they do, come home drenched in very prosaic fashion.

The event of my visit to Naples was the ascension of Vesuvius. The mountain is now in eruption. Volumes of smoke and flame, of scoriae and red hot lava are issuing from its cone. Many feared to make the ascent. It looks angry enough and might at any time do something unusual, but the only time to ascend Vesuvius is when it "works." When it is "working" it is most interesting. The hoary old mountain is a majestic figure on the landscape.

(Continued on Page 953.)

❀ ❀
BACK TO PULPIT
What Food Did for a Clergyman.

A minister of Elizabethtown tells how Grape-Nuts food brought him back to his pulpit: "Some 5 years ago I had an attack of what seemed to be La Grippe which left me in a complete state of collapse and I suffered for some time with nervous prostration. My appetite failed, I lost flesh till I was a mere skeleton, life was a burden to me, I lost interest in everything and almost in every body save my precious wife.

"Then on the recommendation of some friends I began to use Grape-Nuts food. At that time I was a miserable skeleton, without appetite and hardly able to walk across the room; had ugly dreams at night, no disposition to entertain or be entertained and began to shun society.

"I finally gave up the regular ministry, indeed I could not collect my thoughts on any subject, and became almost a hermit. After I had been using the Grape-Nuts food for a short time I discovered that I was taking on new life and my appetite began to improve; I began to sleep better and my weight increased steadily; I had lost some 50 pounds but under the new food regime I have gained almost my former weight and have greatly improved in every way.

"I feel that I owe much to Grape-Nuts and can truly recommend the food to all who require a powerful rebuilding agent, delicious to taste and always welcome." Name given by Postum Co., Battle Creek, Mich. A true natural road to regain health, or hold it, is by use of a dish of Grape Nuts and cream morning and night. Do have the food made into some of the many delicious dishes given in the little recipe book found in pkgs.

Ten days' trial of Grape-Nuts helps many. "There's a reason."

Look in pkgs. for a copy of the famous little book, "The Road to Wellville."

us Persecution---A Defense

By B. L. Chase

ı scattered and propagated to the de-
ction of many souls. Some of the
ıg men contemplating the ministry
ld thus be shown how dangerous
fatal error is, and would be deterred
ı 'entering the ministry with such
s. It would be better to have no
istry than to have one that thinks
rary to the way the "rank and file" of
brethren think. Who pays young men
preaching? Are they paid to preach
t they think, or what most of the
hren think the Bible teaches? By
sacrifice of one professor many
ng men are warned away from the
istry, who would enter it to their
:ow with ideas of their own.
s evidence that God is well pleased
h the newspaper method of persecu-
ı, he prospers the newspapers that
pt it. All things work together for
d to those that love God's truth, and
willing to risk their all in defence
it. No one has better claim to the
ine favor than those who persecute
enemies of God's truth. If any one
'e wanting further proof of the divine
roval upon the modern method of
secution, let it be known that all col-
es, missionary societies and papers
t have condoned the infidelities op-
ed in the persecution by refusing to
ı in it, or by giving aid and comfort
the accused, have had a struggle for
stence, while others have prospered
ond all past experience. The most faith-
and zealous newspaper persecutor ıs
d to· have had its subscription list
abled in the five or more years of its
ısade against heresy; while its Sunday-
ıool supplies have increased in use in
corresponding degree. The unselfish
votion of this newspaper to the faith
ce for all delivered to the saints,
ın the sympathy and co-operation of
ıny advertisers of patent medicines—
catarrh, pile, rheumatism, cancer, dys-
psia, kidney, stomach, consumption,
er, bowel, heart, headache, eye, ear,
se and throat, female complaint, blad-
r, anti-fat and nerve cures and reme-

they all subscribed for it and urged their
members to subscribe for it. Evangelists and pastors of town and country
churches preached against the infidel and
the critic. A great cloud of witnesses
rose up from the farms and fields and
said with a loud voice: "Go on;" "you
are right;" "hit it on the head;" "cry
aloud and spare not;" "fire the big
guns;" "stand pat;" "you are flat-footed
and square-toed upon the Word of God;"
"send it (the paper) across the sea; the
heathen need it;" "my eyes have been
opened;" "send me some sample copies." I copy these words from the paper
itself.

These are but a few of the many
words of commendation that fairly burdened the mail bags. After reading these
commendations of persecution from
"brethren tried and true," who can long-
e' doubt that God is on the side of the

(Continued on Page 953.)

❀ ❀

DIDN'T BELIEVE
That Coffee Was the Real Trouble.

Some people flounder around and take
everything that's recommended but finally
find that coffee is the real cause of their
troubles. An Oregon man says:

"For 25 years I was troubled with my
stomach. I was a steady coffee drinker
but didn't suspect that as the cause. I
took almost anything which someone else
had been cured with but to no good. I
was very bad last summer and could not
work at times.

"On Dec. 2, 1902, I was taken so bad the
doctor said I could not live over 24 hours
at the most and I made all preparations to
die. I could hardly eat anything, everything distressed me and I was weak and
sick all over. When in that condition coffee was abandoned and I was put on Postum, the change in my feelings came quickly after the drink that was poisoning me
was removed.

"The pain and sickness fell away from
me and I began to get well day by day so
I stuck to it until now I am well and
strong again, can eat heartily, with no

The Manchester Meeting   By Herbert Yeuell

For two weeks I have borne the critical scrutiny of these oft-deceived people and they are only just beginning to take me seriously as a minister of our common Lord, instead of some religious eccentric. To have said on the start that I had come to organize a new church would have killed the movement outright.

The ministers have been attentive and frequent in their attendance and have resorted to many legitimate schemes to discover my purpose. The leading Baptist minister invited me to preach in his, the largest church of that denomination in the state, and in introducing me at considerable length told his people that I am a Disciple of Christ, here for what purpose he knew not, whether to organize a new church he knew not, but he was glad to say that my people are orthodox and evangelical and that so far my preaching was eminently evangelical and straightforward. Not having myself informed the people of my religious standing this reverend gentleman, perhaps fearing that I might do so blunderingly, relieved me of that sometime necessity.

In some states my position would not be peculiar but here it is exceedingly unique and delicate. This is New England and we have not a Disciple in the city that has come to light yet. This is a city with other New England cities where men of international reputation have utterly failed. Dr. John Robertson, the famous Scotch preacher, who was backed by all the evangelical churches, closed a two weeks' campaign with an almost empty house, and not a convert. The people here are opposed violently to evangelists and revivals.

Observing this feature of New England religious thought, I have "lectured" each night and so far have not extended an invitation. Consequently the curiosity of the city is aroused and my audiences, small at first, have grown steadily, and last night I addressed over one thousand of Manchester's representative people.

I have no choir. My soloist is Mrs. Susan Brooke Rutherford of Pittsburg, and our pianist Mr. James Hubbard of Haverhill, Mass.

I have preached our plea of the New Testament in every address, but always refrained from giving it a denominational flavor, consequently scores of people are studying the Bible, as, I believe, never before. It will require a long campaign to win these slow New Englanders even after they are convinced.

One condition which, while a reason for rejoicing will make it the more difficult to establish our cause, is the general good feeling among the preachers and the churches. So little sectarian sentiment is there that they do not in many instances designate their churches by denomination other than the street or district of their location. This will make it exceedingly difficult in drawing distinctions and teaching the gospel systematically to avoid the appearance of a narrow sectarianism in ourselves and plea.

At this point let me say that the pastor of the leading Congregational church in New Hampshire and by far the leading church in Manchester, was formerly one of our ministers. Before I arrived he informed one of the leading preachers that he left us because we are "a narrow sectarian body always harping on baptism and teaching baptismal regeneration." This, of course, coming from such a source makes it exceedingly difficult to preach the plea without being misunderstood and also keeps the preachers on their guard and suspicious.

This is really the most difficult situation before us in establishing the work. A disputatious or polemical meeting at this time would, I believe, forever ruin our plea for Christian union. Such a meeting might appeal to certain of the baser sort of the Holy Roller type, but it would never touch the real New England.

I am therefore inclined to the idea, and more to on studying the methods of Christian Scientists and Unitarians who are plentiful here, that the only really successful way to establish a church here will be to continue my present method and have an organizer follow up the work.

It is my purpose, however, to draw the net at the proper time and discover all who may be inclined to accept "this way," and before leaving to be satisfied in my own mind as to the prospects of a permanent work here.

This campaign led by the writer will have to be conducted on a high and broad plane, distinctively irenic and entirely minus that quality so common among us, the tone evangelistic. It is well known to the brethren generally that the writer has tackled several very knotty problems in conservative places but he is free to state at this stage that this New England problem presents the very opposite of all the problems and more difficult than all the others combined. It is like starting inside out, or upside down. Everything is different, demanding a reversal of the usual evangelistic traditions among us.

It is very well to say that meetings of the usual type have been held in the east, but they have not been in New England. It is one thing to hold a meeting with a live church and a live pastor with two or three thousand dollars at disposal and scores of workers, but it is another thing to hold a meeting in a stuffy, hot theatre, too hot for successful theatricals, without an usher, no one but volunteers each night from the audience to lift the offering, no choir and every bit of advertising done by the licensed man, because first, there are no workers, and second, because the law forbids promiscuous advertising.

A tent or a tabernacle here would be torn to pieces by the foreign element or else be the legitimate stamping ground for every sort of religious idiot of which New England is full.

Our audiences are remarkable and I am full of hope that many will embrace the plea for Christian unity. So long as we can keep the campaign on a broad plan it will attract the thinking people, but if from lack of funds we have to take small quarters I fear we may fail of our object. New England collections are proverbially small.

Let it be remembered that I have not one person to call upon for the smallest service. Your prayers and your subscriptions are sadly needed.

The Newest Evangelism[*]   By George Hamilton Combs

The evangelization of the world is the supreme business of the church.

The church is an army; its buildings barracks; its preaching words of command; its Bibles swords; its music battle-music. We are soldiers, Christian soldiers, marching as to war.

"One army of the living God,
To his commands we bow."

And that command is, "Go everywhere and evangelize all."

Yet how often have we missed the meaning of it all. He was walking, a plain American, through a great cathedral, a noble pile, pride of a church, that, in Emerson's tooth-sharp words, declares that not by works nor yet by grace but by taste are we saved. Crushed and humbled by its splendors, its immensities, a great awe possessed his soul. Turning to the guide he innocently asked "Do they have many conversions in this church?" "Conversion" —the guide haughtily drew himself up—"Conversions, do you think this is a Wesleyan chapel?" Yet this is the viewpoint of many. The church finds its end in the erection of a beautiful temple. The end of the army is the barracks!

Or it may be the centrality of meaning is found in the preacher. He is eloquent.

[*]Read at the Bible school session Missouri state convention. (Greatly abbreviated.)

Song birds nest in his throat and his speech is the witchery of cadenced music. "Have you heard Dr. Black?" asks the awe struck multitude. The mission of the church is the exploitation of the preacher. The army is called into being that it may hear a speech! Now, I do not underrate the orator. He has his place. The church waits upon his words. But his words must be words that rouse to action, words with the thrill of fife and trumpet, hammerwords, that on conscience anvils pound to shape and use the solemn vows of men. The eloquence that lulls to slumber is a prostituted gift.

Nor does the church exist for the sake of music and the splendor of form and ritual. Outward and spectacular exhibits should never blind us to the real meaning and mission of the church. That mission is the evangelization of the world. All Christian agencies are means to this end. For this all prayers, all sermons, all books, all newspapers, for this all assemblies and conventions.

But what as to procedure, method, agency?

The Old Evangelism.

This term stands for a certain definite well known religious force and method. It is the evangelism of Finney, of Whitfield, of Moody. It is the evangelism associated with great crowds, stirring songs and spiritual raptures and exhilarations. It is the evangelism with the well known machinery and expedients of decision cards, enquiry meetings and strenuous altar-appeal. It is the evangelism with strong insistence upon verbal and mechanical inspiration of the scriptures, the sovereignty of God, the passivity of man in soul transformations, the work of special and supernatural agencies in conversion, hard and forensic interpretations of the atonement. What shall we say of it? That as a system of truth it has been outgrown, and as a method, outworn. It does not dovetail into the needs of to-day. In a word the old evangelism is wholly out of accord with the modern temper (and even in its transformation of content and presentation by our own preachers leaves much still to be desired.)

And yet this in justice ought to be said: with all its limitations, artificialities and truth obscurations this old evangelism has been the life of the church and that the growth of the church has been in exact correspondence with the emphasis laid upon evangelistic enterprise. With all its imperfections this discredited evangelism cannot be sneered out of court. The growth of any denomination can be determined by its evangelistic zeal.

But is there not a better agency and method? The need has been met, we are told. We have

The New Evangelism

The term is freshly minted. It is attractive. What shall we think of it? Frankly at the very outset I wish to confess my disappointment in this large sounding term. Much there is of good in the so-called new evangelism, but the good is the old; the new is the untrue. That which is said to specially characterize it does not commend itself to my judgment. What are its distinguishing marks?

1. It is sociological, rather than theological. This word sociological is quite imposing and of Goliath bulk. But what is the meaning of this utterance? Does it mean that man should consider man? If so it is no new thing. It has been preached from the beginning. Love for one's neighbor has been declared from all pulpits. Does it mean more—as we suspect—that man's duties all relate to man and that the Godward side of obligation is of no great concern? Then it is both shallow and false. Man must look Godward as well as manward, must look up as well as out. Indeed the quickening sense of brotherly obligation and responsibility must come from communion with the invisible God and our hands will never go out in helpfulness to our brother until they have first gone up in prayer to our Father. The sociology of the new evangelism may have the breadth of the earth but it needs also the depth of the sea and the heights of the heavens.

2. It is not only sociological but it is ethical, we are told, ethical rather than emotional.

Pray tell when was evangelism other than ethical? Who could more earnestly plead for a true life than Finney? What doctor of the new school has ever more strongly insisted on the need of a changed life than Dwight L. Moody?

3. The new evangelism we are told is the salvation of the whole man and not the salvation of his soul. This sounds well and for its emphasis upon the need of right environment for the individual and the need of a ministry both to body and to the mind is to be commended and yet again there comes the inevitable conclusion that this is not new and that we are simply dealing with new terminiologies rather than with new truths.

So far I repeat as I understand the new evangelism I am not greatly enamored of it. I object to it.

1. For its indefiniteness. What the old evangelism is you know, what the new is, you can only guess. We meet with new names and old faces and lose ourselves in the glitter of generalities.

2. I object to it because of its would-be substitution of cultural for conversion agencies. It shies at the word salvation; it makes much of the word culture. Now we cannot get rid of that word salvation. We are sinners all and our great need is not that we shall be cultured but that we shall be saved. When you can sweeten the Atlantic with rosewater you may save the world through culture, when the culturist can change the leopard's spots then may he change the human heart.

3. The new evangelism lacks earnestness. It is dilettanteism in pulpit and in pew; it lives and moves and has its being in the realm of the aesthetic. Its boast is that the old time enthusiast, the barnstormer in religion is gone. Gone? The enthusiast gone? Then the church is gone or going. Heat is life. The frozen stream turns no mill, the frozen earth grows no grain. The men who have profoundly moved the world have been men of burning enthusiasm, of lava words and heart. Such a one was Xavier with his cry "more,

more," more souls for the Lord Christ.

4. I object to the new evangelism because it is an evangelism that does not evangelize. Its record is a record of nonaccomplishment. Its sweet placidities can never stir the world. The advocates of the new evangelism preach to no mighty throngs, they minister at no crowded altars, they turn no cities upside down. As well expect an arc light to wake to harvest the seeds that slumber in the cold as the occupant of this velvety throne of aestheticism to come to the sovereignty of human hearts.

The Newest Evangelism.

There is a more excellent way: The way of the newest which is also the oldest evangelism. And this way? The gathering of the children into our Bible schools and through the instrumentality of decision days, never less frequent than monthly, winning them to the acknowledgment of Christ as Lord. Do you say all this we have known and tried? We have not tried it. We have never as yet come to any adequate realization of the boundless possibilities of this evangelism. We think nothing of expending a thousand dollars in a revival that revives for a month, but what churches among us have put a like sum in the upbuilding of its Bible school with the direct purpose of winning the children to Christ? Not one!

1. Consider first of all the effects of this newest evangelism upon the contens of our glorious evangel. What will be the character of the preaching in our Bible schools and how will this method affect the gospel thus declared? The audience is half creator of every sermon. What then will be the effect of this child-audience upon the preacher and his message? Broadly it will be to create a preached theology that missing alike the hardness and the unloveliness of the old theology on the one hand and the vagueness and the shallowness of a new theology on the other shall be temperate, scriptural, wholesome, true.

2. It will insure an affirmative gospel. No man comes before such hearers with guess and hypothesis, doubt and the frippery of dream. Here is no place for conjectures but for certainties. No man who is half a man will weave a mist of doubt around a boy or girl.

2. It would be simple. When the preacher stands before boys and girls he will find himself inevitably emphasizing the few great elementary truths of that gospel. What pulpit, pray, would venture to air his learning and his speculations before such an audience? May I say this? That which cannot be preached to children ought not to be preached to adults.

3. It will be pictorial. This was the way of Christ. His sermons are pictures. In all his recorded utterances you will look in vain for the barrenness of abstractions. Everywhere is the glory of color and movement of life. The profoundest truths of heaven are presented in simple stories of heaven are presented in simple stories easy to the apprehension of children. Let us follow him. Stand before young people and you will learn his method. You must not argue, you must paint.

4. It will be an evangel of light and love. No other evangel fits into the Bible school hour. All hard doctrines veil their faces in the presence of the child. There is not a living man who could preach the doctrine of unconditional election before a Bible school. The picture of an angry God would scorch the fingers of any man who should attempt to bring it before children. There and then it must be as it was at the beginning, the evangel of life and hope and love. Good news to the child mind is good news and not the terrifying pictures of hell. Now that this must profoundly influence our preaching is unquestioned. What radical changes would be wrought!

How lonesome our theological gladiators and heresy hunters would feel in a Bible school.

II. Consider its effect upon the Bible school. This newest evangelism solves all the problems of the school.

1. It solves the initial problem how to increase the attendance of the Bible school. There is no magnet so powerful as evangelism both for the old and the young. How to have a big school? The answer is not in card and banners and orchestras and machinery—the answer is in evangelization.

2. It solves the problem of how to hold. Children by the thousands drop out of our schools every year; we get but do not keep. Why? There is no fervor and stir of evangelism. No school that is not a recruiting station for Christ can ever hold a child. Thousands of boys and girls drift into our schools every year. We make no special effort to have them decide for Christ; in a little while they drift into other schools or more likely out of the reach of all Christian influences. But convert them, then it is our church and our Bible school and they stay. Bad as it is, awful as it is, I can but believe that even so great a heretic as J. H. Garrison may federate with whomsoever he will and yet through the great mercies of God be saved—though as by fire; it is the heresy of indifference to the youth of our land. Eighty per cent of young men and women from our Protestant families have at some time in their lives been in our Bible schools. The majority of these have drifted away; they are no longer in our Bible schools or our churches. Why? In the critical time when they were in our schools we failed to take advantage of a heaven-sent opportunity to induce them to decide for Christ.

3. It solves the problem of how to unify the school. There is a painful lack of unity in our schools. They are lacking in coherence, in orderliness, in esprit de corps. We have sought to bring this about through the use of uniform lessons. This is a step but it is not a long one. Help it grows in attaining a mild type of general unity but locally is does little. A longer step and a wiser is the establishment of the teachers training department. This is foundational and absolutely necessary. All teacher training and all drill and all method is for the sake of (1) making Christians of all who are not Christians; (2) making better Christians of those who are Christians and that not simply for their own sakes, but that they may preach the gospel to others.

4. It will solve the problem of how to spiritualize your school. How sore this problem is! The most discouraging lack in our schools is the lack of the one essential thing—spirituality. Enlist them in evangelism and out of that kindled zeal and out of that deepening consecration will they put away unworthy things as surely as the awakened life in the tree pushes off the old dead leaf with the growing life of the leaf to be. Better than the dynamite of rebuke is the flame of love.

III. Consider this newest evangelism solely as an evangelistic agency and method.

1. It commends itself to us in that it augments the number of evangelists. This is our great need—the need of workers. Evangelistic forces are pitiably inadequate for the task. It is now as in the olden times, the harvest is great but—oh the shame of it and the pity of it—the laborers are few. This newest, which is, as I said at the beginning, the oldest evangelism, increases the number of workers. The curse of the church of to-day is professionalism. The preacher is the evangelist—be alone. But this newest evangelism restores the so-called laity to its place of

(Continued on Page 950.)

The Jacksonville-Paris Contest

From Jacksonville View Point.
C. L. Depew, Superintendent.

The Bible schools of the churches at Jacksonville and Paris, Ill., held a friendly contest in attendance and offerings for six months, ending the last Sunday in June.

The Paris school had an average attendance during the entire six months of about forty-eight more than Jacksonville. The average offering at Jacksonville was about $8.50 larger than at Paris.

In 1905 our average attendance was 300 and our offerings were $900. During the second quarter the average was 350. During the second quarter of 1906 our average attendance was 706, and our average offering was $60.95. Our highest attendance prior to January 1, 1906, was 513.

We had planned to make 1906 a great year, as the equipment for Bible school work was complete in our new building, giving ample room for a school of 1,000, and we had already determined to do our best to fill the new church, when the challenge came from the Paris school asking us to meet them in the six months' contest. We accepted the challenge at once, and will ever be grateful to the Paris school and its workers for the new life which came to us through the contest.

The first efforts were made to increase the interest and attendance at our teachers' meetings. We were having an attendance of from 15 to 20. After adopting the angle method the attendance increased to 35 and up. We were having few occasions to call for substitutes, as in four months, we did not have more than two teachers absent on any one Sunday and many times every teacher was present. Needless to say this splendid work on the part of the teachers had its effect on the rest of the school, and on February 18 we had an attendance of 516.

On the first Sunday of 1906 the announcement was made that we would have an attendance of 600 on dedication day, and an offering of $200, and we surpassed both of these in the old building.

We determined to have our missionary rally on the first Lord's day in March, and although March 4 was cold and stormy we had an attendance of 421 with an offering of $200.10.

April 8 we had a building fund rally, 488 present, offering $129.68. We were now making our plans for dedication day, April 29. We prepared a card for members of the school to get their friends to fill out and sign and to return to the secretary. The card stated that the signer promised to attend our rally at Bible school on dedication day, having a blank space for name and address of signer. Three thousand of these were distributed, and over 1,200 were signed and brought in. We also had plenty of

notices in the daily papers of the city inviting all interested to attend our rally, which was to begin at 8:45. In all of this advertising matter we announced we expected an attendance of over 1,000 and an offering over $200, and that each person present would receive a souvenir button, nearly two inches in diameter, on which was a picture of the church, date of dedication, etc.

April 15, attendance 564, we announced that on the following Sunday, our last in the old church, we would hold a farewell rally, and tickets would be given to every one present on that day to admit bearer to the new Sunday-school room on the afternoon of April 22, to assign classes to their permanent places in the new rooms. Our attendance in the old building the last day was 780, and the offering $90.66. There were over 750 present at the new church in the afternoon, and a short service was held. On dedication day we were all ready for the supreme effort. Our attendance was 1,682, offering $261.71. Our total offerings in April were $551.51.

For the last two months of the contest, our time was largely occupied in getting classes and work properly planned and arranged for the new building. We found the organized class to be an excellent plan to promote interest and attendance. We have 32 of such classes now, varying all from simply adopting a name and badge to the thoroughly organized class, with a full corps of officers and committees.

Our primary department, under Miss Hattie Hayden, superintendent, and 14 teachers, is being properly graded and organized with all the modern divisions. A home department has been organized with Guy B. Williamson as superintendent. New methods and ideas are watched and studied, and the ones that appear to be suited to our needs are tried. In this way we endeavor to keep up with the times and have something new to interest our scholars. Beginning July 1 we will use the star system to help a regular attendance.

As a result of the work being done by our teachers, many of our scholars have confessed Christ, and been received into the church; scarcely a Sunday passes without one or more going forward. On Easter Sunday 15 of them made the good confession, and on June 10 out of 31 received into the church on that day 27 were young people of our school.

From the Paris View Point.
Geo. W. Brown, Superintendent.

The Paris-Jacksonville contest was the result of the tact and foresight of our pastor, Brother Ideman. During the first part of December, 1905, the pastor and superintendent were discussing plans to bring a more complete attendance of the church membership into the Sunday-school. We determined to challenge that Christian Sunday-school of the state, which was nearest us in attendance and membership. We consulted Brother Marion Stevenson, who informed us that the church at Jacksonville was about "our size." We sent the Jacksonville school a formal friendly challenge to a contest as to attendance and offering, which was to continue to and close with the last Sunday in June, 1906. To stimulate our schools to more vigorous work, we agreed to exchange letters each week, stating the result of the contest for the previous Sunday.

When interest was at fever heat we exchanged telegrams.

We organized our teachers with much care, and directed their persistent canvass for new scholars. The Pastor's Aid Society gave much valuable service. Each worker was strictly instructed to solicit no person who attended other schools. "Our own church membership into our own Sunday-school," was the watchword.

As the contest proceeded we could feel ourselves growing permanently stronger. New members were easier to secure. We have at this time almost succeeded in making it popular to attend Sunday-school. Our adult classes grew with unparalleled rapidity. We arranged a series of banners to recognize classes reaching certain goals. One banner was designated "Win One," which was given to the class showing the greatest number of new members enrolled. "Average givers" was awarded the class making the best average offering. We also had another banner, "Perfect Attendance." We soon found that we did not have enough "Perfect Attendance" banners. Six more banners marked "Perfect Attendance" were made. We have had several days when we did not have enough "Perfect Attendance" banners with this addition.

Our average attendance for last year was 302, with an enrollment of 595. For the first six months of this year our enrollment of over 800. We have had only two "big days." Children's day our attendance reached 1,002, while on the closing day we had present in the classes at roll call 924. For the past six months our aggregate attendance has been 15,164 with offerings amounting to $943.57.

All the results of this contest can not be stated in this brief article. Some of them are:

1. We have succeeded in interesting our entire membership in the dynamic power of the Sunday-school.

2. We have become a Sunday-school with a greater missionary activity. Our school now supports by its own efforts a home missionary, amounting to $300 per year. Our Sunday-school gives annually $100 to Christian benevolences.

3. We have had pressed home to us the needs of the membership in our own congregation. We are not loudly proclaiming it, yet for more than a year our church has not permitted one of its members to be supported by the county, nor be buried at public expense.

4. Our teachers have been brought nearer to each other and to Him. Each teacher now more fully recognizes that upon her or him depends largely the salvation of each member of the class. Our teachers have become indeed pastoral helpers, and are welcomed into the sick room with almost as much appreciation as a visit from our pastor.

5. The growth of our own school has stimulated every Sunday-school in the county to renewed efforts, especially those of our own brotherhood.

In conclusion, let us say if your school is waning in interest, you can give it the breath of eternal life in no more helpful way than to wage a friendly contest with a Sunday-school of our own brotherhood. A friendship has been developed between the contesting schools which has been beneficial in its influence. The superintendent of the Paris school visited the Jacksonville school on their dedication day, and was loyally received and entertained.

Central Bible School, Denver

By GEO. W. PERRIN,
Superintendent.

We have been asked what we consider the leading factors in our successful rally for missions at the Central Bible school, Denver.

We have but one grand rally for missions during each year. With this end in view we appoint a missionary committee a year ahead whose duty is to "boost" missions, carry on a definite education of the school, select a definite amount and make that the watchword for the year. Make an apportionment of the school by classes, taking due care to have the amounts low enough so they can go over or meet the amount. We have three very strong adult Bible classes with complete organization. They serve to promote Bible study, sociability, loyalty to class and school and actually apply the principles of Christianity to the every day walks of life as it should be, showing a Christlike spirit toward the stranger out of the kingdom, bringing them first into the class then to Christ as saved souls. We have had more confessions from the Sunday-school this year than during any previous year, showing that it is easy to get money for missions if the souls are first converted to Christ.

Some of the classes gave out little clay pigs months ahead of children's day for catching all stray dimes. A month before the eventful day they were weighed. Another class took pledges of varying amounts, another raised $1 per member and gave a social, each telling how they raised the money; another gave a good measure entertainment for a small silver offering each. The primary and intermediate classes were given the boxes three weeks ahead with the request that they bring $1 on children's day. The superintendent hearing of the success some of the classes were having stimulated others not making good progress by offering them a small cash prize, to be added to the amounts of the three largest gifts in a certain department. There was a good natured rivalry which added to the interest and good results.

Take it all in all it was Bible school day and everybody felt the thrill of their enthusiasm and achievement. We are indebted to Bro. C. M. Morris for bringing into the school the idea of large gifts for missions. He taught his class and the whole school that it is as easy to think in dollars for missions as it is to think and give cents. His class with an attendance of seventy young ladies gave $210, the largest amount for any one class. The Dallas J. Osborne Bible class of about twenty-five young men gave $157, the largest amount per capita. Dr. C. C. Reid's young people's Bible class, with a regular attendance of more than 100, gave $140.58. The primary gave $24.92. All the others exceeded their apportionment with the total amount as given above. It must be said that it did not interfere with the weekly offering of the school, but increased them seventy chairs and other school equipment, such as blackboards, maps, music stands and music for the orchestra. Two hundred new song books and a large flag now grace the walls of our Sunday-school room and teaches a silent lesson of Christian patriotism.

The most delightful feature of the offering is the happy, loving spirit which has dominated from the beginning. It was an offering for the Lord's work, not any special mission, but for all, and to be apportioned as wisdom and love might dictate. Colorado, because the Central is a mother church, and because of its great need, will get more than half, but no selfish motive was used to inspire generosity in giving.

The Pastor and the Sunday School

By Cephas Shelburne

Every pastor ought to be vitally and enthusiastically connected with the Sunday-school of his church. Talking with a pastor, he said, "I believe the Sunday-school is an institution that is very much overrated." That pastor is simply ignorant of the history, achievements, place and possibilities of the Sunday-school. The pastor who is fearful that the great and splendid cause of the Sunday-school is losing ground should read the report of the Eleventh International Sunday-school convention held at Toronto last June. The report and addresses on the work and development of the Sunday-school make a book of 700 pages that will go down into history. There are fourteen hundred thousand officers and teachers, twelve millions of scholars, tens of thousands of libraries containing millions of books in the Sunday-schools of the United States. And the best is yet to be; for this young Atlanta among the religious forces in the church is just now beginning to realize its strength and possibilities. Isaac Errett said in 1884: "Here our money, and toil will yield larger and more beneficial results than in any other field of benevolent activity." President Roosevelt in a late address on the Sunday-school said: "The modern Sunday-school, in my judgment, is the preparatory school for the church. It is the corner stone of the church of the future." The Sunday-school is a "world power" of great significance; an important factor in the extension of the Master's Kingdom. A really great church, great in numbers, in service, growth and possibilities, is impossible without a great Bible training school. The pastor must learn one thing, that as goes the Sunday-school, so goes the church; for here he is to get his converts and workers. This is the church's soul-winning equipment; and if not already such, it is destined to be the greatest evangelistic agency in the world. I believe the time will come when every congregation that builds a church, and every church that is working and every pastor that is preaching to save men will place the supreme emphasis on the Sunday-school. I believe the time will come when the superintendent will be considered holding as honorable place and will draw as large salary as the preacher; and when teachers will be specially trained for their work and will consider it an honor to volunteer their services in so noble a calling. The ultimate end of the Sunday-school is co-ordinate with that of the pastor, namely, to preach the Gospel and save men. Statistics tell us that nine-tenths of all those who come into the church of all denominations, do so before they are twenty-one years of age, and that fully 83 per cent of all who come into the churches come from the Sunday-school. Let the pastor remember that he is one preacher reaching a very few of the young, while he has as many sowers of the good seed, which is the word of God, into mellow, fruitful soil as he has faithful teachers in his Sunday-school. You are dealing with hard, unbending steel in your sad and hardened audiences; the children of the school are pliant clay in the hands of the potter.

But many of our preachers do not appreciate the Sunday-school. On every point in the Sunday-school the pastor ought to be master. As a piece of machinery he ought to know every wheel, pulley and band; as a business he ought to know its organization, methods and finances; as an institution he ought to know its history, work and equipment; as a school he ought to know its teaching force, wants and sources of supply.

We do not say that the pastor should be the superintendent. This responsibility should be assigned to other hands and talents. But every pastor should be the general overseer of his school. Every pastor should be a teacher, not necessarily in the school, but wherever practicable, a teacher of the teachers. He must be mighty in the Scripture, apt to teach. Here he should be authority, and reign without a rival. I do not say that the pastor must be, or at all times can be, in the school during every minute of its progress. But the pastor should be "on the inside," in the very heart of its activities. It is not too much to claim that a pastor's presence and prayer at the opening of the school, an occasional visit to the classes, and on the platform at its close, carries a meaning and benediction with it that he knows not how to estimate.

As God's word does not return unto him void, we are not surprised that the Sunday-school is an evangelistic power, accomplishing marvels; and, if not already such, it is destined to be the greatest evangelistic agency and soul-winning equipment in the world.

Huntington, Ind.

The Pastor's Relation to the Sunday School

By Josie Ballou Sherman

We have a profound respect for those of God's anointed who break to us the bread of life and while this subject was chosen for me, we do not presume, for one moment, to be able to instruct these in righteousness. What we may say is what we would like our pastor to be.

The primary work of the church is to make Jesus Christ known and obeyed and loved throughout the whole world.

The Sunday-school is the great feeder of the church. From it comes its educated, trained, spiritual workers. In these days of progress it would seem strange indeed if there had been no advance made in methods of work in the Sunday-school.

The secret of enabling any organized body to obtain an advantage is one of leadership. The people do not go beyond their leaders in knowledge and zeal, nor surpass them in consecration and sacrifice.

Therefore the pastor's relation to the Sunday-school is second to none. The Christian pastor holds the divinely appointed office for inspiring and guiding the thought and activities of the church. By virtue of his position he can be a mighty factor in the Sunday-school.

He is the general of the young army of boys and girls about to be Christian soldiers.

Wherever you find a pastor with overflowing earnestness, zeal and knowledge, you will find a church earnest and responsive. There is no way to get the ear of the whole church save through him. Any idea which he persistently preaches and prays for in the pulpit will be gradually accepted as a rule of conduct by the church. We want more preachers to work for the Sunday-school through the pulpit, so every father and mother, Christian and non-Christian, will feel the responsibility of being members of the Sunday-school along with the children.

To make this paper practical and fit the place for which the time is given it, we will look at the subject.

First. As an educational factor in the Sunday-school.

We have already said the Sunday-school should be talked through the pulpit. It should be urged upon members of the church to attend. The preacher should then teach a class. His presence in the Sunday-school alone is an inspiration.

He should make a study of progressive methods and plans of teaching, and when he meets with his superintendent and teachers, propose and urge them.

He should visit the homes of the cradle roll members and should know the home department pupils.

In keeping the holidays of the Sunday-school the pastor's influence is unbounded. Often these programs for Easter, Christmas, Rally Day, etc., are placed in charge of young and inexperienced persons which is all right if they have the guiding hand of their director general. He should help choose the program. For instance, at Easter he should see to it that no child is asked to commit to memory one line or stanza or poem that is not worth a place in the memory. No song or recitation should be a part of the Easter program unless it interprets or emphasizes some part of the Easter message.

We have in mind a minister who requested a class of little children to sing the piece,

"Mary to the Savior's tomb,
Hastened at the early dawn,
Spice she brought and sweet perfume,
But the Lord she loved had gone,"

to the tune Martyn and it was indeed charming to listen how simply and sweetly a hymn could tell a chapter of the Easter story.

The same pastor asked his superintendent to admit no song or recitation unless it had some seed of Easter truth.

Tested by the same rule, every special program should be sifted by the pastor. Then the pupils gain that truth for which the service is held.

We have in mind another instance in a made up program for Christmas, where a young Miss recited a poem about "The death of a cow-boy on the western plains" and this was sandwiched between "The Shepherds abiding in the fields" and "The birth of the babe at Bethlehem," two beautiful sections of the Christmas story. Not very appropriate?

A pastor should use as many of the Sunday-school members as is possible, to assist him in his church work. There is a bond of union thus formed between pastor and pupil which will bring forth good.

Second. As a financial force, the pastor's influence is paramount.

Dr. Theodore T. Munger the "Congregationalist" says, "There is no better test of a minister's character and ability to carry on and lead a parish than the way in which he manages its giving. A preacher should preach giving, should teach giving and should be persistent in it and persevering."

There is no better place for the education of systematic giving than in the Sunday-school. Let the pastor use his every power to instruct children along this line. It will then become a habit. Habit forms life.

Let pastors preach more and more on God's will concerning the acquiring, holding and using of money and sound out warnings about the sin of covetousness and the abuse of money.

A pastor should preach from the pulpit and teach in the Sunday-school and talk in the homes against the raising of money by side routes, fairs and festivals. We know this sounds a discordant note in the ears of some, but friends, all honest hearted Christians could be influenced to drop these methods entirely and give outright, because it is right. Then our children will learn to give outright, because it is right. Such things are all right from a social standpoint, but let the pastor preach that such doings to raise money belittle the dignity of the giving enterprises in the minds of Christians, provoke scorn among unbelievers, and dishonor Jesus Christ.

Every pastor should say with Dr. A. J. Gordon, whose church in Boston was such a missionary force, "I am tempted never to beg a cent for God again, but rather to spend my energy in getting Christians spiritualized, assured that they will then become liberalized." One day he came before his people and told them on a certain day a free will offering would be asked and he wished all members of the church, young people's societies, and the Sunday-school, would pray that the offering might be according to the will of God. When the day came around $10,000 was raised instead of $5,000 raised the year before.

Third. As a recruiting force. Bishop Taylor Smith says the needs of the church is to know, to grow, to glow, to go. When the church cannot send forth her members to propagate the gospel, she has reached a state in which she has nothing worth propagating. While it is impossible for a home pastor to be at the same time a foreign soldier in the army of the Lord, it is possible for him to be a recruiting officer for the war for world-wide conquest.

Why are English boys so eager to enter the army and navy? One very important reason is because Wellington and Nelson are held before them so much as heroes.

Then see what grand and noble sentiments might be instilled into the minds of Sunday-school students from babyhood; the sacrifice made that we might enjoy freedom from sin—the study of the lives of the heroes of the cross, the love of doing good for good's sake. The pastor should seek to create in the minds of the people a true conception of the nobility and exalted privilege of the missionary career.

Keep before them the thought that the greatest honor which can come to a Sunday-school is to have some of its members become missionaries. Hold up more frequently the missionary life as an ideal. Draw illustrations of heroism from the lives of missionaries.

Fourth. As a spiritual force.

The pastor, a praying man must make his church a praying church. Prayer and spirituality are as inseparable as faith and works. Jesus Christ by precept, by command and by example has shown with great clearness and force that he recognizes the greatest need of the Sunday-school and all other enterprises of the world-wide evangelization to be prayer. Are more Sunday-school workers needed? Preachers, pray for more workers from the pulpit. Pray ye therefore the Lord of the harvest, that he send forth laborers. Is it money that we need? If so, in prayer lies the deepest secret. We have said and repeat—any idea which a pastor persistently preaches and prays for in the pulpit will be gradually accepted as a rule of conduct by the church. So pastors must pray for the Sunday-school and ask the parents to pray.

Pastors should see that the Sunday-school has more time given to prayer. We believe it to be the thing to teach children to pray to a Father in Heaven—a prayer of thankfulness for blessings given, for protection and care, even before they have arrived at the years of accountability. It is the pastor's work not only to urge the Sunday-school workers to prayer and convince them of its wonderful possibilities, but he must make them realize the urgent need for prayer. With all we have said carried out, the pastor as a spiritual force in the Sunday-school is pre-eminent. The spirituality of his church, the sacredness of the house of God, the salvation of the Sunday-school pupils hinges on the development of spirituality in the Sunday-school. That is the kindergarten of the church, the place for formation of habit, and the wise pastor will make the Sunday-school his constant care.

Keosauqua, Ia.

Our Budget

—Christianity is the only religion with temples for children.

—We cheerfully devote most of our space this week to Bible school interests.

—Preachers no longer loftily relegate such matters to women and children. What seed wheat is to harvests, Bible schools are to churches.

—It is but natural that our Bible schools should become of greater consequence when men like J. H. Hardin of Missouri, Marion Stevenson of Illinois, Howard Rash of Kansas, and J. H. Bryan of Iowa, devote their lives to increasing the efficiency of our schools and demonstrating their importance as factors in world redemption.

—J. Will Walters, Niantic, Ill., is planning for a great meeting in October. Church work there is progressing very favorably.

—I. J. Cahill, of Dayton, O., spent part of Monday at this office, en route to the Howard county (Mo.) annual Christian church rally.

—T. M. Myers is in a meeting at Fordyce, Ark. There have been fourteen added to the church thus far, all of whom are among the best-citizens of the town.

—O. M. Thomason has met with great success during his Washington ministry, but desires to resume evangelistic work farther east. At present he may be addressed at Davenport, Washington.

—D. F. Sellard's congregation at Leon, Iowa, recently gave him a surprise party—the entire resident membership went to prayer meeting. Naturally he would like to be so surprised every Wednesday evening.

—F. E. Truckels, principal of the West Lafayette (Ind.) high school, has determined to offer his services to the churches as a singing evangelist. E. B. Scofield, of Indianapolis, very highly recommends him.

—The Boone county (Mo.) Christian churches, 16 in number, will hold their annual rally and convention at the Red Top Church, from July 30 to Aug. 1. The names of very able men and women grace the program.

—W. A. Parker, minister at Emporia, Kan., writes that his church will sell its old pews at half first cost. They are ash, trimmed in walnut, gothic end blocks. It is hoped this offer will prove helpful to some other congregation.

—John Logan, 733 Ferry St., Eugene, Ore., knows of a middle-aged minister, scholarly, eloquent, and successful who wishes to locate where there is a prospect of building up a strong church and continuing for a number of years.

—W. T. Clarkson, of Lawrence, Kan., is spending his vacation in Birmingham and other points in Alabama. He occupied the pulpit of the First Church at Birmingham July 18, in the absence of A. R: Moore, the regular pastor.

—Albert Shaw has proven so helpful as minister to the church at Fairfield, Ill., that at the last meeting of the official board, he was called to that pastorate so long as the church and pastor are satisfied with present arrangements.

—L. M. D. Wells, formerly of Wilkinsburg, and under whose ministrations that church has become one of the strongest in western Pennsylvania, has accepted a call to East Orange, N. J. He will do graduate work in Columbia University in conjunction with his church duties.

—The Newton county (Mo.) Chautauqua has recently concluded a twelve-day session at Neosho. It is said to have been the most successful yet held in the county. For this much credit is due F. F. Walters, our resident minister.

—N. B. McGhee of the Gage (Okla.) church is in great demand for popular addresses and so fulfills his engagements as to give great delight to his hearers and increase the prestige and helpfulness of the church for which he ministers.

—George W. Kneffer, of Somerset, Pa., has accepted a unanimous call to the Wilkinsburg, Pa., church. He will prove a worthy successor to L. M. D. Wells and contribute a hero's part to the upbuilding of that promising church.

—Evangelist Clara H. Haselrigg recently concluded a meeting at Atwood, Kan., with more than sixty received into the church by confession and baptism, and is now in a meeting at St. Francis with flattering prospects of success.

—The Ralls county (Mo.) convention will meet this year at Prairie View, August 27-29. H. F. Davis, of the Christian Publishing Company, formerly state Bible school superintendent, will make the principal address of the Bible school session.

—Mrs. W. F. Phelps, of Bland, Mo., writes that R. B. Havener has just completed a brief meeting there with six additions to the church—five by confession and baptism. During the meeting the indebtedness of the church was entirely liquidated.

—C. A. Ashton's ministry at St. Francis and Atwood, Kan., is very highly commended. Other preachers are greatly needed in northwestern Kansas. Doubtless Brother Ashton will gladly place those who would go in correspondence with the churches.

—J. D. Lawrence, Christian evangelist supported chiefly by this company, is engaged in a meeting at Rayerton, Ind. Weak churches he can probably aid up to the point of having regular preaching services receive his attention first. Address him at Muncie, Ind.

—Our profoundest sympathy goes to th. bereft N. J. Aylsworth in this hour of his great affliction. Be brave as always, dear brother, it will not be long at the longest, till with all the loved and lost awhile you will be rejoicing in those spiritual realms of which you have written so helpfully.

—C. S. Osterhus, whose splendid article on our Scandinavian brotherhood was one of the chief features of last week's CHRISTIAN-EVANGELIST, resides at Ossian, Ia. He will highly appreciate letters of inquiry concerning his mission and of fraternal greeting and fellowship.

—H. G. Hill will speak at the Rockford, Ill., Chautauqua, August 31. After three weeks' vacation he begins a six months' lecture tour under the management of the Redpath bureau. We are pleased to note Brother Hill's enlarging sphere of usefulness in this new ministry.

—Guy L. Zerby reports a most excellent meeting held at Alexis, Ill., by evangelists Buchanan and Gardner, during which time 42 were added to the church. Brother Zerby soon relinquishes the work there. The church will need a creditable successor. May he soon be found.

—We are in receipt of note that Marion Hunter Garrard, pastor of the Second Christian Church, Syracuse, N. Y., and Miss Marie Antoinette Ziechmann, Cleveland, were recently married by R. Moffett. We wish this young couple lives

of ever-increasing usefulness and consequent growing happiness as the years go on.

—By reason of newspaper reports many have received the impression that Bro. W. D. McCulley was called to the pastorate of Cameron (Mo.) church. Brother McCulley will make his home in Cameron, but L. O. Bricker continues as efficient and beloved pastor of the church in Cameron.

—One of the saddest of editorial tasks is to reduce such a splendid piece of writing as George Combs read before the Missouri State Sunday-school convention to the limitations of our space. Every word taken away was a gem, every sentence a sunburst. Read it, for even its outline is beauty.

—The Lincoln county (Mo.) convention will be held in the New Galileo church beginning the evening of August 13, and holding over August 15. Those going to the convention via Winfield will notify Olin J. Gary, of Moscow Mills, who will have conveyances ready to take them to the assembly.

—Bro. Richard Bagby, of Scranton, Pa., writes that the Dunsmore church is greatly rejoicing over the last payment having been made on its old indebtedness. The Bible school having outgrown its present quarters, the church has contracted for additional rooms to be added to the church at a cost of $3,000.

—E. L. Powell, of Louisville, Ky., has just sent us from his summer vacation grounds in the Old Dominion State an inspiring article that will soon appear in the Centennial department of this paper. All wish this genial pastor and brilliant pulpiteer a restful summer and renewed strength for the great demands the future will make upon him.

—M. W. Harkins, of Union City, Ind., will spend his August vacation on the

Pacific coast supplying J. V. Coombs' pulpit at San Jose, Cal., while the latter is in the east seeking help for the California churches suffering loss by the recent earthquake disaster. Brother Harkins will gladly answer inquiries concerning our cause on the "Golden Slopes."

—J. T. Webb, of the Kearney (Neb.) church, announces that the Clay county convention will meet with the Kearney church July 28 and 29. An excellent program has been arranged and sessions of deep spiritual interest and instruction are expected. His generous, hospitable people extend a cordial invitation to all who possibly can to attend the convention.

—During H. E. Wilhite's two years' pastorate at San Bernardino, Cal., there were 300 additions at regular services. During that time also he organized the churches at Colton and Rialto. Brother Wilhite is now visiting relatives in Kansas and Missouri. He will enter the general evangelistic field in August. He may be addressed at Stafford, Kan.

—After all that is said about "the new evangelism," "the new thought," and "wider views of God's mercy," the Bible still teaches that if a man would be saved he must exercise faith in Jesus as the Son of God, repent of his sins, confess Christ before men, and be baptized into the name of Father, Son and Holy Spirit.

—It also teaches that if one would keep saved, he must to his faith add virtue, knowledge, temperance, patience, godliness, love of the brethren and love for all; that he must grow in grace and in the knowledge of the Lord Jesus Christ, forgetting the things which are behind, stretching forward to the things which are before.

—J. A. Cunningham, the "preacher drummer," of Tupelo, Miss., preached a two hours' sermon before the Baptist congregation at Emma, Miss., on the subject of "The Three Dispensations of the One Plan of Salvation." He tried to impress upon the brethren the necessity of abandoning their teaching that regeneration is complete before baptism.

—After a pastorate of nearly four years at Virginia, Ill., J. W. Carpenter has resigned and accepted the work at Neodesha, Kan. Brother Carpenter and the writer were baptized together in Cuba, Ill., and were room-mates at Eureka and Lexington Bible colleges. We wish for him all the success in his new pastorate that his splendid abilities promise.

—Secretaries Wright and Ranshaw request every preacher to send his name and correct address, together with the name and location of the church to which he ministers to his state corresponding secretary, and not to the Cincinnati office, except where there is no state corresponding secretary. Preachers are requested to give immediate attention to this as the 1907 year book is now in course of preparation.

—The Dexter (Mo.) Chautauqua, under the mangament of Chas. E. Stokes, will be held the first and second week of August. Several men and women of national reputation will address the week day and evening audiences. Geo. L. Snively, of THE CHRISTIAN-EVANGELIST, will be the preacher for Lord's day, August 5. He is eagerly anticipating meeting many Disciples from southeast Missouri.

—"There are only about 300 hymns in the English language that deserve a place in a Christian church hymnal. I think that nearly all these hymns are in Gloria in Excelsis." J. W. McGarvey (president Bible College), Lexington, Ky. There are really more than 300 hymns in the English language that ought to live and all are

found in this book that this company will distribute wherever wanted at lowest possible cost.

—S. E. Thompson, of Hillsburg, Ont., sends an interesting account of the tenth annual convention of the Churches of Christ of the Wellington district, held in Grand Valley, Ont., the 5th and 6th inst. Besides the actual attendance by those living in the district, R. W. Stevenson, "provincial evangelist" for Ontario, and J. Trickey, of the Orangeville Baptist Church, greatly helped make the convention interesting and inspiring.

—We greatly deplore the seemingly untimely decease of Bro. J. G. Creason, pastor of the Lathrop, Mo., church. W. F. Richardson conducted his funeral July 18. Brother Creason was one of our ablest, most devout and successful preachers. We trust the sympathy of a brotherhood her husband so faithfully served and the comfort of the Holy Spirit may sweetly and fully sustain Sister Creason through these sad hours.

—Hiram College has just conferred the degree of Master of Arts on Sherman B. Moore, of Oklahoma City. Accompanying the diploma was the following message from the secretary, "You may regard this action as a personal compliment of a high order but one that all felt was fully deserved in your case in view of your attainments." We can testify from personal observation that Brother Moore is doing the work of an evangelist in a "masterly" way in Oklahoma City.

—J. C. Blanchard, of Smith Centre, dedicated a new union church near Portis, Kan., July 8. The building was erected by citizens of the community as a house of worship and is to be controlled by a board of trustees, no two of whom are allowed to be members of the same religious organization. This is Brother Blanchard's first dedicatory service, but his success was such as to lead his friends to believe he can be helpful to other congregations at dedication time.

—J. T. Ferguson and wife have resigned their pastorate with the East Side church, Moberly, Mo., to re-enter the State University and Bible college at Columbia, Mo. During their eighteen months' stay in Moberly a new church board, an auxiliary to the C. W. B. M., Young Ladies' Circle, Junior Endeavor Society and the prayer meeting were organized, the membership increased more than one-fourth, and a new spirit of union and good will between the two Christian churches in the city created.

—F. D. Power sweetly plaints that the vitals were blue-penciled out of his recent Bethany College article. The piece was universally regarded as interesting and helpful, even if it did fail to state there are now $100,000 in Bethany's Permanent Endowment Fund; that a new library is being built at a cost of $20,000, and a new gymnasium erected and a large dormitory for boys opened. We rejoice in the new era of usefulness dawning upon dear Bethany—the mother of them all.

—Through Wm. L. Hipsley, Table Grove, Ill., we learn the church there recently celebrated its fortieth anniversary by remodeling and rebuilding its house of worship. Appropriate services were conducted by the pastor, E. J. Stanley, assisted by J. E. Parker, of Galesburg, Ill. Thirty have been added to the church during the past year, eighteen by confession and baptism. The church now has prospering full time and begins evangelistic meetings November 1.

—L. G. Batman, of the First Church, Philadelphia, sends us copy of the interesting programme of the seventy-third annual convention of the Christian Missionary So-

church has been greatly strengthened during his ten years' pastorate and the cause of religion mightily advanced. The Centerville church hopes to have a man begin October 1, immediately after Brother Moffett's removal to Springfield.

—Editor J. H. Garrison, commenting upon chairman S. M. Cooper's formal announcement to the churches of W. J. Wright's finally accepting his third call to become Corresponding Secretary of the American Christian Missionary Society, and Brother Cooper's congratulations to the brotherhood over securing such a leader, writes: "THE CHRISTIAN-EVANGELIST also congratulates the brotherhood on brother Wright's acceptance of this most responsible position, and it congratulates Brother Wright also on his manifestation of the qualities which have caused his brethren to call him to this important post. Let him now lead on to greater things, and the rest of us will hold up his hands."

—The congregation at Lebanon, Mo., Harold Bell Wright, minister, has placed THE CHRISTIAN-EVANGELIST in the home of every member of the church. No other expression of fraternity could be so helpful to the membership. There should be a Christian paper in every Christian home everywhere. Every interest of the church, the church itself, and all the ideals of primitive Christianity would be quickly and tremendously advanced if all our congregations would follow the example set by Lebanon. We suggest to all our evangelists the advisability of distributing 300, 500 or 1,000 CHRISTIAN-EVANGELISTS per week in the communities where they are holding meetings. This will not only fill the churches with hearers, but with prepared listeners. It has been proven an exceedingly helpful factor in meetings wherever tried.

—Our general superintendent was born and schooled in Illinois, and has missed preaching in that state comparatively few Lord's days in twenty years, and is to-day ministering to two of her congregations. While Secretary of our Benevolences he saw that state become the largest contributor to that ministry—membership considered. It was his pleasure to receive his first $1,000, $2,500 and $10,000 gifts to the Association from his native state. In his present position he has seen THE CHRISTIAN-EVANGELIST welcomed into more than one thousand new homes and its circulation increasing in that state more rapidly than ever before. Naturally he feels under profound obligations to Illinois Disciples for this continued fellowship and helpful co-operation in the great ministries of the church. Any service he can render the preachers and others of the brotherhood in that grand commonwealth is most cheerfully performed.

—The book on "The Holy Spirit," by the Editor of this paper, has received many remarkable commendations, but none, we think, more remarkable than the following: "I have lately been reading with intense pleasure your remarkable book, "The Holy Spirit." I have never viewed Christianity in the broadly transfigured light you have thrown upon it. I have been studying carefully the four Gospels and comparing them with the theories in your book. The result has been a complete and happy change in my idea of religion, and I feel now as if I had, like a leper of old, touched the robe of Christ and been healed of a long standing infirmity. I thought the New Testament was old and familiar to me; but you have made it a new and marvelous book, full of most precious meaning, and I hope I may be able to impart to those whom it is my duty to instruct, something of the great consolation and hope with which your writing has

filled me." What compensation can come to an author of a book comparable to a testimony like that, and it is only one of hundreds which the author has received orally and by letter.

California State Meeting.

California extends a cordial invitation to the great brotherhood of Disciples to attend the state meeting at Santa Cruz, July 24 to August 5, inclusive. The earthquake shook us up pretty badly, but California to-day, with its mountains and valleys, rivers, lakes and sea, is as beautiful and serene as ever. In addition to scenery we now have ruins that rival those of the coliseum and Karnak. But greater than scenery or ruins is the stalwart faith of our people. Come and be with us.

A. RUSSELL, Cor. Sec.

Palo Alto, Cal.

For a Church in New Hampshire.

Already acknowledged	$570.10
Hon. W. H. Graham, M. C.	25.00
L. C. Stow	10.00
Ora McDonald	1.00
	$606.10

We have no church in the state. "Our plea" was never before preached in Manchester. Brother Yeuell preached to more than 700 last Lord's day and received 7 confessions. If he can be kept there three months, a New Testament church will be established in that important city. Help is needed *right now*. Contributions from $1.00 up will be acknowledged here. Endorse drafts to J. H. Garrison for New Hampshire church.

Another Five Thousand Dollar Fund for Church Extension.

Fred Doeller and family of Columbus, Ind., have agreed to establish a named fund of $5,000 in our church extension work, to be known as "The Ruth M. Doeller Memorial Fund," in memory of their daughter and sister, Ruth M. Doeller. This is the 16th named fund established in our church extension work.

The $5,000 is to be paid into the fund at the rate of $500 or more annually and this named fund is to be loaned in such state or states where Brother Doeller and family maintain an evangelist.

To help erect the new building at Ruston, Louisiana, where the first church has been organized by John A. Stevens, state evangelist, who is supported by Brother Doeller and family. One year ago the Louisiana State Convention was appointed to meet in June, 1906, in Ruston before our brethren in Louisiana knew a church would be organized there. The success of the Louisiana work is more than pleasing—it is an inspiration. It is little wonder that a practical business man and manufacturer like Mr. Doeller should choose a field like this for his named fund to work in.

Of Ruston Brother Stevens writes:

"Well, we are proceeding on the old plan here at Ruston.; that is to buy our own lot and pay for it, get a good title, raise all we are able to on a subscription and then ask the church extension board to loan us $1,000. We have the best church lot in town, just 300 feet from the center of the city. There is but one church on the south side of the railroad and it a small "holiness" church. There are 3,500 people on the south side. On the north side of the railroad there are but 2,000 people and three of the large churches on that side. So you see we pre-empted the larger part of the town. It seems that nothing can keep us from having an audience. There is just one bridge that spans

all the railroad tracks in the business part of the town and our church will stand at the south abutment of that bridge and will be an everlasting advertisement of itself, as it is the only church in the city in full view of the stores and hotels and the entire business part of the town. The lot is worth $1,000, but the man who owned it either thought at the time that it would be an easy way to pick up $50 forfeit money, or else he wanted a church on that side to enhance the value of other property he owns there. So he let me have it for $700. He told me when I bought the option in these words, "I want you to understand that I know that it is worth $1,000 of any man's money, but I said in order to get a church over there you could have it for $700." We will pay every dollar of this money day after to-morrow, for we have it all on hand. Now we hope to be able to have $1,700 worth of property to mortgage to the church extension board, and we want but $1,000.

JOHN A. STEVENS.

What a satisfaction Bro. Doeller and family will have in watching their memorial fund work in this productive field of Louisiana! New prosperous towns are springing up in this state as they are in our western states and the soil is virgin for our plea. Bro. Doeller's money makes it possible to go into these towns early and shape the religious thought of these new communities with the truth that makes us free in Christ Jesus.

Our F. M. Drake fund, started Feb. 1st, 1889, has built 58 churches and has done the work of $22,191 and his fund has been increased by $3,070 of interest at four per cent. There is every inducement to persuade men and women to create named funds in our church extension work.—G. W. MUCKLEY, Cor. Sec.

Board of Ministerial Relief of the Church of Christ.

Aid in the support of worthy, needy, disabled ministers of the Christian Church and their widows.

THIRD LORD'S DAY IN DECEMBER is the day set apart in all the churches for the offering to this work. If you make individual offerings, send direct to the Board. Wills and Deeds should be made to "BOARD OF MINISTERIAL RELIEF OF THE CHURCH OF CHRIST," a corporation under the laws of the State of Indiana." Money received on the Annuity Plan.

Address all communications and make all checks, drafts, etc., payable to
BOARD OF MINISTERIAL RELIEF,
120 E. Market St., Indianapolis, Indiana.

Changes.

Barnes, E. B.—Noblesville, Ind., to Bowmanville, Ontario.
Callahan, J. F.—Noble to Euclid, Ohio, R. D.
Coultard, J. H.—Owosso, to Paw Paw, Mich.
Drake, D. H.—Kirksville, Mo., to Hiawatha, Kan.
Haywood, W. J.—Fort Worth, to Anna, Tex.
Hanna, J. C.—Arlington, to North English, Ia.
Harris, Ellis B.—Starbuck, to Winlock, Wash.
Johnstone, H. M.—Bethany, Neb., to Fredonia, Kansas.
Krahl, P. W.—Clayton, to Folsom, N. M.
Limmerick, J. J.—Wheatland, to Corning, Cal.
McCulley, W. W.—Salisbury, to Cameron, Mo.
Mayfield, Wm. M.—Lansing, to Dighton, Kan.
Millsap, H. E.—Kirksville, to Knox City, Mo.
Pallister, H. A.—Delta, to Extra, Ia.
Stout, J. A.—Marceline, to 2455 Wabash avenue, Kansas City, Mo.
Van Voorhis, W. D.—Toledo to Martinsburg, O. R. F. D. No. 1.

The Newest Evangelism.

(Continued from Page 943.)

original importance and effectiveness. All are priests, all are preachers. In the old way the evangelist battles with his own strength, in the newest way, he has become a multitude. Under the old procedure the success or failure of a meeting hinged almost solely on the evangelist—if he were strong and earnest and eloquent, well; if he were weak and halting in speech then ill. In this newest way it is not so. Any stick of a preacher will do it if the school is on fire with evangelistic zeal.

2. It commends itself to us in that it makes possible a perennial revival. This I take it is a great desideratum. When a boy in the country I used to hear in the conventions of Sunday-school workers the discussion of this topic: "How to Have an Evergreen Sunday-school." It is a worthy aim—a school that runs through the winter as through the summer months—an evergreen school. Now we also want and need an evergreen revival—not a revival of start and spasm but of stand and stay. The church passes through all temperatures and the facility of the upward climb of the mercury is equalled only by the velocity of the downward slide. Now it is a furnace, now an ice house. The new-born soul is cradled in flowers then flung into a snow drift. All this is against reason and against religion. How have a revival that shall be evergreen? By the way of the newest evangelism. Instead of the hiss and crackle of flame followed by a heap of lifeless ashes you may have an equable heat. The way of the newest evangelism is the way into the land of perpetual summer. It is the Florida of the church of God.

3. The newest evangelism commends itself in that it is both scientific and scriptural. Solomon's injunction to begin life culture with the child finds a hearty amen in Starbuck, in James, in King, in Hall—in all the voices of the new psychology. Common sense has not failed to see that the chosen time to combat disease is in its inception, the new physiology and the new psychology bring largeness of confirmatory data. The moist and fertile soil beneath the quickening rays of the spring sun no more strongly invites the sowing of seed than the open heart of childhood the gospel of Jesus Christ. And this child before whom science bows in wonder is the child whom Jesus held in his arms.

4. This newest evangelism is all permeating and all inclusive. Unify your Bible school and you unify the church as a whole. Spiritualize your Bible school and you have spiritualized every department of Christian activity. It is the only way. Heat ascends, not descends. If you would warm your house you do not build a fire in the attic, but in the basement. Nor should the divine fires be kindled in the attic chambers of age, but in the basement chambers of youth. Age is isolation, youth is communication. By so much as the sun is a better evangelist than the snow mountain is the conversion of children better than the conversion of the aged. Get the man or the woman and you have gotten one; get the child and you have gotten both, man and woman.

5. It commends itself by its marvellous results. It is an evangelism that evangelizes. It is no theory but an actuality. It works. It secures largest yields. In no other way will a like expenditure of time and effort count for so much. It invites us by the breadth of its accomplishments. May I be pardoned for a personal word? I speak of what I know. For more than a year the church I have the honor to serve has laid special stress upon this evangelism. Our decision days are the notable days in the calendar and on these days I

have been made glad by such triumphs of the gospel of grace as I had not even dared to dream of. On one of these decision days in response to the invitation twelve came forward—upon another twenty-one—upon another, thirty-two—upon another, forty-eight.

We are approaching our centennial. We would double our membership to two and a half million members by 1909. Along the present lines of effort we shall not even come within sight of such accomplishments. We are but trying with a battle cry. We have no confidence in our undertaking. And yet it is practicable. We can if we will double our membership by that centennial hour. If every church in our great brotherhood shall concentrate its efforts on our Bible schools, putting time into them, putting work into them, putting money into them, striving earnestly and heroically to double their membership and convert them into fire-hot evangelistic forces and agencies—if every church would but do this there would arise to us such Pentecostal awakenings as this old world has never seen before and when that memorable year should have rolled around, we should turn a mighty host two and a half million strong toward the gates of Pittsburg and with jubilation and with song praising God for his wonderful works among the children of men.

I have failed, I know, in giving any adequate expression to the importance and to the promise of this—God's evangelism. May our brotherhood be aroused to this great opportunity. Surely, surely, we cannot fail to read and heed this heaven-sent message. May flaming heralds go up and down among us crying, "Make way, make way for the Bible schools and the evangelism that is in wisdom and in love.

God's blessings upon this mighty host, and may he hasten that at last to reign with him in glory forever and forever.

❖ ❖

Milk That Is Wholesome.

Since the scientific handling and preservation of milk, originated by Gail Borden in the early '50s, the use of Eagle Brand Condensed Milk has become general; but for those purposes where an unsweetened milk is preferred, Borden's Peerless Brand Evaporated-Cream fills every requirement.

NEWS FROM MANY FIELDS

Illinois Notes.

The churches at Emden and Bethel have just joined in support of Bro. C. A. Sittser, who recently came to Eureka College from Wisconsin. He will continue his work in college and serve the two churches. Such a combination would save many weak churches. The churches at Delevan and the Malone church ought to combine. They might include another small church in this circle. There are many such unions or "federations" that would be unquestionable, for good. Try it. At Bethel, our efficient evangelist, W. H. Kindred, grew to manhood, and here our own beloved president, R. E. Hieronymus, obeyed the Gospel of Christ.——At Lincoln, W. H. Cannon and his splendid congregation are doing fine business in their beautiful new house. The membership has about doubled in the last two years and the greater enterprises of the church will feel its warm impulses more in the future than in the past. Education Day was prominent in the church's calendar last year and will doubless ever be in the future.—D. A. Lindsey and the church at Mt. Pulaski have the plans for a new church and are securing subscriptions. They expect it to cost $8,000. The present pastorate has lasted nearly three years and few places in the state have shown more marked improvement. The church numbers 300, with a Sunday-school of 125 and Christian Endeavor of 30. The building spirit is all over the state and at no time in our history have the brethren responded more liberally to this enterprise. It is a very rare instance for a church to be dedicated without all indebtedness being provided for. A number of additions have been received recently by the Cornland church where John Lemmon, one of our valued trustees of Eureka college, preaches half time.

The Texas church, near Clinton, is taking on new life under the ministry of L. P. Fisher, who visits them half time while attending Eureka college. It is a country church with a splendid field and is practically responsible for the spiritual teaching and life of a large territory.

At Moroa W. H. Applegate is just getting settled in his new pastorate. The church feels greatly encouraged to get a minister after waiting so long. The Sunday-school is already greatly increased. From the splendid class of young people there, Eureka college ought to be training some of them for the churches' larger life.

J. F. Smith has recently taken up the work at Waynesville with prospects of large usefulness, with a willing and industrious people. One of its best young men in attending Eureka College. The family consists of mother and son, so mother came also so they could be together. This is a good plan. If others would like to try it we will tell you about property here if you will ask us.

At Clinton, E. A. Gilliland is finishing

Cause of Sick Headache.

Severe attacks of Sick Headache are due to a Torpid, Congested Liver and a Disordered Stomach. No one can enjoy good health when the stomach refuses to do its necessary work. One bottle of Drake's Palmetto Wine, a purely vegetable compound, has often brought complete health to persons suffering with the above named symptoms, and in many cases pronounced incurable by some of the best physicians in the country.

A large bottle, usual dollar size, can be obtained at drug stores for 75 cents, but a trial bottle with full instructions will be sent free to every reader of this paper who needs it.

Address your letter or postal card to The Drake Co., Wheeling, W. Va.

---

nine years of a pastorate; how much is to follow is not yet written. Long pastorates make strong churches and strong preachers if both do their best. The Clinton church has a large membership with all activities hard at work.

At Hallsville, where our ever beloved T. T. Holton ministers to the people, we found things in good order. It is really a country church. Here Harry M. Barnett, one of our strong ministers of Kansas City, Mo., and his cousin, J. A. Barnett, our valuable preacher at Pekin, grew to manhood, graduated at Eureka college, and are great servants of the churches. If more churches would look after the boys, more would enter the ministry.

The strong church at Atlanta, where I. W. Agee, ministers, is doing good work, as it always does. It has had some of our best preachers, among whom are R. F. Thrapp and S. S. Lappin. It is no easy task to follow such men, but we hope that the ministry just begun by Brother Agee will exceed them all. The church numbers 250, with a Sunday-school of 175, for which Sister Tuttle has furnished a splendid library. The auxiliary to the C. W. B. M. numbers 25.

The Pekin church perhaps takes the largest number of CHRISTIAN-EVANGELISTS of any church in the state, the number is 87; if others can beat it let them speak out. The offerings during the last half year for missions and other outside work amounts to $190. This for a young church of 300 members, most of them young, is a fine record for the young pastor, J. A. Barnett to make. Membership, offerings and size of various departments have about doubled during his two and a half years of ministry.

Bro. D. W. Conner is getting the work in fine condition, and is much loved at Edinburg. The church is strong, active, united, and in a good house. They recently royally entertained the convention of the fifth district.

Bro. Moses Hughes is preaching half time at Rochester. This is a fine field, with an excellent preacher and good people. We ought to grow under such conditions.

The good old church at Taylorville is moving forward under the able and delightful ministry of Bro. Z. Moore. This church is able for great things, and is beginning to do them. When it knows its power it will be felt more in all our great enterprises.

At Blue Mound, Bro. W. H. Harding is leading the church in building a new $12,000 house. It is a beauty as well as one of the most substantial buildings we have. We will expect great things from this strong church when it gets into its splendid home.

Bro. J. M. Morgan has just moved to Raymond to serve the church and also to give part time to Harvel. This is a fine combination and both fields, weak in the past, will doubtless grow under the guidance of such a minister.

Litchfield has begun a $5,000 addition to their comparatively new house which proved inadequate to the growing conditions and large audiences that gather under the able preaching of M. S. Johnson. We like to see the walls bursting out to give room for the people to come and worship and hear the gospel. May the houses rapidly become too small. Brethren, fads and sensations have their day, but if you want the churches full of people preach the gospel.   J. G. WAGGONER.

Eureka, Ill.

Iowa Notes.

First: Our state convention. The year 1905-6, was the greatest missionary year in our history. Eighteen churches were assisted in supporting preaching by the I. C. C. paying from $50.00 to $300.00 on the pastor's salary. These missionary pastors added to the churches 284 by confession and baptism and 261 from other sources. The I. C. C. employed ten evangelists for all or part of the year. These ten men held forty-eight meetings, baptized 831 and received 470 from other sources. Besides the above, 26 volunteer missionary meetings were held without expense to the missionary society, in which 322 were baptized and 129 were added from other sources. Twenty-two men were engaged in this work. Here is a summary of the missionary work of the year: I. C. C. evangelists and pastors, 24; pastors holding volunteer meetings, 22; total number of men, 46; number of churches assisted, 90; number of days of labor, 6,494; number of sermons, 3,474; number of baptisms, 1,447; number added from other sources, 860; total number of additions, 2,307; money raised for state missions, $9,405.18.

In addition to the above Secretary Denny raised $13,384.87, that is not included in the above.

Number of churches giving to the I. C. C. year before last, 198; number of churches

giving last year, 264; gain over the year before, 66.

Ninety-one per cent of the churches that have sent in their statistics report gains. The average gain to the church is 23 members for each congregation, 14 by confession and baptism, 3 from the denominations and 6 from other sources. If this average holds good throughout the state there were 10,000 disciples added to the churches last year in Iowa.

The convention was royally entertained by Percy Leach and his church at Iowa City, but the poor railroad facilities and the location of Iowa City at one side of the state made the attendance below our standard. Two hundred sixty-two out-of-town delegates registered. Every session was brim full of interest and the convention was counted one of the best.

We are losing two of our good preachers from Iowa. T. J. Dow who for five years has served the East Des Moines church so well, goes to Minnesota. F. L. Moffett, for ten years pastor of the church at Centerville goes to Springfield, Mo. For two years brother Moffett has been vice-president of our state board and was one of the best of men in counsel. We regret to see these good men go from us but we are sure that they will give a good account of themselves wherever they are.

We are to have a state wide simultaneous evangelistic campaign in Iowa beginning the second Sunday in January, 1907, and continuing until April first. Keep Iowa in mind, there will be something doing here this year.

The executive committee to have the campaign in charge consists of G. B. Van Arsdall for Northwest Iowa, Loren Howe for the northwest, S. H. Zendt for the southeast, W. T. Fisher, southwest, C. S. Medbury, central district, B. S. Denny, general superintendent and H. O. Breeden, chairman. A subcommittee will be appointed for each district with the ones named as chairmen.

F. L. Moffett resigned as vice-president on account of his going out of the state and S. H. Zendt was appointed in his stead.

Our series of district conventions begin August 21.—B. S. Denny, Cor. Sec., Des Moines, Iowa.

Kentucky Notes.

On July 9 there was organized in the First Christian Church, The Louisville Christian Bible School Association. It is composed of representatives of the various Christian churches in and about the city, and its object is to establish new schools in such places as the executive committee may determine. The following officers were elected T. S. Tinsley, president; E. L. Williams, vice-president; G. E. Fisher, secretary, and T. E. Basham, treasurer.—A conference for the Bible school workers of South Kentucky will be held at Mayfield, August 1, 2 and 3. The faculty is composed of R. M. Hopkins, E. A. Fox, R. H. Crossfield, H. D. Smith, G. H. C. Stoney, S. F. Fowler and other prominent Bible school workers. There will be five hours every day devoted to the discussion of Bible Study, Child Study, Methods of Teaching, Methods of Management and the Work of the Pastor. The conference promises to be one of unusual interest to Bible school workers. Cheap railroad rates have been secured and the Mayfield church extends hospitality to all who attend. The names are requested to be sent at once to R. L. Clark, Mayfield, Ky.—The state convention for all departments of church work will be held at the First Christian Church, September 24-27. A most interesting program is announced and a large attendance is expected. All delegates will be provided with lodging and breakfast by the churches of the city. Let us plan now

to make this state convention the greatest in the history of state work.—R. M. Hopkins, Louisville, Ky.

Virginia Items.

Norfolk is enjoying the greatest boom in her existence; I am not saying whether this is enviable or not. All that I can say is, that the majority are making the most out of it possible. The Jamestown Exposition, known as the Tricentennial anniversary of the first white settlement in Virginia, and the first English settlement in America, will open its doors to the world, on April 26, '07. Among those who come—and many will come from every quarter of the globe—we expect to see numbers of our own brethren, and to you we desire to say, bring your religion with you and use it to good purpose, whether you are a visitor on pleasure bent, or seeking an investment and home with us. You can do much to increase the usefulness of the church, and to enlighten those who are in ignorance of us as a people, as to numbers and what we are doing in helping to evangelize the world, but also in bringing God's people into the union for which Jesus prayed. In this section, Norfolk and Portsmouth and adjacent towns, there is a population of considerably more than one hundred thousand souls. We have three churches of not over four hundred members. One, Portsmouth, an infant, not yet a year old, keeping house in a rented hall; another, the Second Park Place, Norfolk, just about two years old, keeping house in a rented hall. You see we need you; come, prepared to work with a people little known, and weak in finance, and you will be rewarded here as well as hereafter. On May 18th we closed an eleven-days' meeting at the Second church, held by R. E. Elmore of Portsmouth, Va.; while there was only one addition, and he reclaimed, the result visible would have justified the outlay and effort. Still we know the invisible results are far-reaching and will not be measured here, when I say the preaching was good, old Jerusalem doctrine, I put it mildly; I join with the good people with whom he has been laboring in regretting the necessity for his leaving here. The little band of the Second church, is com-

posed of noble men and women, who know what it means to labor for the Lord, and to sacrifice too; I have never met nobler people anywhere. Sunday was children's day, and at night the children rendered the program splendidly. It speaks well for the three ladies who had it in charge. Results of birthday box and offering, $14.58, which may seem small to many of you, kind readers, but if you knew them and what else they are doing, you would say, "splendid."—W. C. Wade, Norfolk, Va.

Summer Normal Term

of "Iowa Christian College" opens June 11. Arrange to attend. Send for announcements. If you can not come, take the course by mail. Write Pres. Chas. J. Burton, Oskaloosa, Iowa.

CHURCH FEDERATION READY.

The Inter-Church Conference on Federation. 700 pages, prepaid.....$2.00

People's Forum

To the Editor of The Christian-Evangelist:

Which shall it be—the editors or the secretaries? A little while since a certain editor advised the secretaries that if they—the secretaries—endorsed certain men and certain views—said editor would withdraw support from them and their societies. Under such pressure was constrained to make a declaration of the principles and policies of his society; but even this did not save him.

The tables are now turned and one secretary proclaims in a "fearful parable" that the thief is robbing the society, said thief being the editors who dare to discuss certain questions in which the whole protestant church is interested. Shall the churches be governed by the editors or secretaries? Will the churches speak out.—H.

[We permit the foregoing to go in without note or comment at present, further than to say that "H." is one of our veteran preachers who wears a historic name in the annals of our brotherhood, and whose devotion to its interests no one doubts who knows him.—Editor.]

❧ ❧

Modern Religious Persecution.

(Continued from Page 941.)

persecutor? Does any one wonder that the editor and owners of such a paper are brave and fearless? Why should they respect persons? The God whom they serve is "no respecter of persons," and should they be less faithful than God? When God is for you, who can be against you? God and one true defender of the faith make a majority.

❧ ❧

As Seen From the Dome.

(Continued from Page 940.)

It seems utterly indifferent to the human creatures which move like ants about its base. It rises 4,300 feet above the beautiful bay. Anciently it was very decent. Strabo writes of it: "Mount Vesuvius is covered with beautiful meadows with the exception of the summit;" but fifty years later came a terrible earthquake, A. D. 63, and seriously damaged all the region round about, especially Herculaneum and Pompeii. This was repeated in 64 and August 24, 79, during the reign of Titus, came the appalling disaster to the cities at the base when Pliny perished, and 2,000 were buried at Pompeii, the whole city covered with a layer of ashes and then of pumice stones, twenty feet in depth. Many eruptions have been recorded since, 59 in all, and thousands of lives lost. The last severe one was in 1895. There are premonitory earthquakes, day is turned into night, extraordinary agitation of the sea, dense clouds riven by incessant flashes of lightning, the emission of fire and ashes, rivers of streams of lava, and clouds of smoke, ashes and stones, and of sulphurous fumes. Stones have been thrown fifteen miles, and

---

JOSEPH REILLY
ATTORNEY-AT-LAW
Is prepared to give all legal matters skillful attention. Correspondence solicited.
Office, Room 320 Granite Bldg., St. Louis.

---

hurled 2,000 feet in the air, showers of ashes carried as far as Constantinople. No doubt there is some connection between the mountain and sea, and water temporarily admitted to the burning liquids of the interior of the earth causes the earthquake and vapours and gases that force out the red hot fluid called lava, which reaches 2,000 degrees of heat.

It was a great experience to ascend the mountain and come within a short distance of the blazing crater and these fiery streams of lava. It is, indeed, a vision of the bottomless pit. Along the sides as we go up are at first luxuriant vineyards, gardens and orchards. The famous "Lacrimæ Christi" wine is made here. Higher up we reach huge dark lava streams of past eruptions and magnificent prospects open on every hand. The last 1,300 feet is accomplished by a wire rope railway, which seems to go up almost perpendicularly. The gradient is from 43:100 to 63:100. From this great elevation, 3,900 feet, one gets a great sweep of vision. The mighty mountain at his feet; the great streams and floods of the dark lava of different centuries, with all manner of twisted and contorted forms, serpents and dragons and billows and cataracts, as they have poured red hot down the mountain side and then hardened in myriads of grotesque shapes; the glorious panorama, with Capri, where the deified beast Tiberius stamped the foot prints of illustrious crime, and Sorrento, the birthplace of Torquato Tasso, "village of flowers and flower of villages"; and the buried cities, and long line of white towns clustering about the base of the mountain and clinging to the hills; and the great city with its steeples and domes; the towering island of Ischia on the right, and whole magnificent coast line and broad expanse of water stretching away to the far horizon; and back of us, the smoking crater and hot

John R. Baxter.

lava streams; and away beyond, the Campanian Plain merging into the purple haze of the snow capped Apennines. As we gazed on this radiant picture by a curious atmospheric effect a form of Fata Morgana was seen—the islands seemed lifted out of the water and suspended between earth and sky; and as the sun became lower, through the slight cloud, it formed lakes of molten silver here and there on the blue surface of the matchless bay; and then, later, lakes of molten gold. It was a great day, my day on Vesuvius and I turned with regret from the vision of the red glare on its summit at night to seek my steamer bunk.

P. S.—This was April 2. April 3 we left Naples. April 4 began the most awful eruption known for centuries. F. D. P.

Evangelistic

We invite ministers and others to send reports of meetings, additions and other news of the churches. It is especially requested that additions be reported as "by confession and baptism" or "by letter."

Hot from the Wires.

Special to THE CHRISTIAN-EVANGELIST.

Tacoma, Wash., July 22.—F. M. Rains here to-day. First church becomes a living link in foreign society.—W. A. Moore, pastor.

Special to THE CHRISTIAN-EVANGELIST.

Atchison, Kan., July 21.—Fifty added today, 220 to date. I have been here ten days; best of helpers in Hilton. Smith and Kendalls.—Chas. Reign Scoville.

Special to THE CHRISTIAN-EVANGELIST.

Manchester, N. H., July 22.—Meeting progressing; weather too hot for theater, but 700 to-night. Seven confessions. People beginning to see daylight. Plea never heard here before. Conditions require three months campaign.—Herbert Yeuell.

Special to THE CHRISTIAN-EVANGELIST.

Lima, Ohio, July 21.—Clarence Mitchell, our former minister, preached here and delivered Odd Fellows' memorial address. He just closed short meeting at Auglaize chapel with fifty additions. He is universally loved here in his home city.—H. W. Pears, Elder.

Arkansas.

Bentonville, July 16.—Two additions at regular morning service yesterday. The good work is moving on.—J. W. Ellis.

California.

Bakerfield, July 22.—Two additions last Sunday, seven since last report. The church increases my salary $15 per month and gives me a month's vacation "on pay."—R. E. McKnight.

Eureka, July 14.—One added by statement recently. On the eve of extensive repairs on our building the church contributed liberally to state missions and San Francisco relief.—I. H. Teel.

Illinois.

Fairfield, July 19.—The past year's work here eminently successful. W. W. Yocom, Martinsville, Ind., will assist in a meeting in November.—Mrs. Mary Edith Shaw.

Sullivan, July 15.—Four confessions at the morning service to-day. Union service at night at M. E. church. All departments of the church doing good work. Sunday-school has trebled since the first of the year.—J. G. McNutt.

Pekin, July 19.—Three added by baptism this week, two of them at prayer meeting last night. All departments of the church in good condition.—J. A. Barnett.

Greenville, July 16.—One addition at evening services yesterday, two since last report.—Tallie Defrees.

Indiana.

Indianapolis, July 17.—Ten additions at the Fourth Church since last report, one by letter, one from Congregationalism, two from the Methodists, six by confession and baptism.—Chas. E. Underwood.

Fort Wayne, July 9.—Five confessions June 24, four confessions July 8, one from Methodists and one from United Brethren at Danquo, Ind.—P.

Kansas.

Smith Center, July 16.—Two additions to the Smith Center church yesterday, one by statement and one by confession.—F. E. Blanchard.

Lebo, July 19.—Have preached here six months. Began with a membership of twenty-four. Have had forty additions. I begin a meeting with the church at Galesburg, Kan., on August 6. Will be open for engagements in evangelistic work from September 1. Will supply singer when wanted.—W. M. Stuckey.

Louisburg, July 16.—Six came to-day, four confessions and two by letter. Seven last Sunday, thirteen the past week. Meetings largely attended by men.—Clyde Lee Fife.

Asherville, July 16.—Two added last night from Methodists. The work on the new addition is progressing rapidly. Will rededicate about August 12.—G. P. Clark.

Iowa.

Altoona, July 16.—Good services yesterday; seven additions. Work starting off nicely.—J. Windslgler.

Vinton, July 18.—Three additions not heretofore reported—two by letter, one by primary

obedience. E. G. Stout, of Des Moines, will assist in meeting through December.—A. D. Elliott.

Massachusetts.

Everett, July 16.—Since last writing we have had three additions, three confessions and two baptisms, making thirty-one additions since the beginning of this year.—A. T. June.

Michigan.

Saginaw, July 16.—Three additions yesterday—one by statement, one by letter and one by confession. We have confessions and other additions every Lord's day.—J. Murray Taylor.

Allenville, July. 19.—Since last report have had one by baptism at Lamotte, and two living near Otter Lake were also baptized. At Merkey a new church was organized with twenty-five members, of which twelve were by baptism. Also an aid society of sixteen members, a building committee appointed and the promise of material secured, and a lot donated for house of worship.—R. Bruce Brown.

Missouri.

Eldon, July 19.—Just beginning a meeting here with S. D. Dutcher, of Omaha, as evangelist. J. F. Bickel is the minister. Prospects favorable for a good meeting. Dalhart (Tex.) meeting closed with ten accessions, instead of two, as reported.—Charles E. McVay.

Kansas City, July 19.—Nine additions yesterday, twelve during the month. Work in excellent condition.—I. L. Wray.

St. Joseph, July 19.—Since March 11 we have had forty additions to the King's Hill Church at regular services. The church is progressing in every department.—Clay Baird.

Carthage, July 15.—Two weeks ago I closed a short meeting at Billings, Mo., with ten additions. I returned to-day. At the morning service there were three confessions, three baptisms at the water's edge. I begin a meeting next Lord's day under the auspices of the missionary boards of Sullivan and Putnam counties, in the north part of the state.—S. J. Vance.

Montana.

Helena, July 7.—Have just closed a meeting at Plains, Mont., where our plea had never been heard before. There were in all sixteen added during the two weeks—six by baptism and ten otherwise. Organized a congregation, secured a lot and the building is now in course of construction. We expect to locate a pastor with them soon. Plains is a promising town in the new county of Sanders and the new organization bids fair to become one of the best in that section of the state.—F. A. Groom, state evangelist.

Ohio.

Cincinnati, July 19.—Eight added to the Walnut Hills church, three by confession and baptism, remainder by letter.—R. H. Abberley.

Killbuck, July 19.—Closed a tent meeting recently at Spring Mountain, O., which resulted in a church of thirty-five members and a Sunday-school with sixty enrolled. The church now meets in a tent but is planning for a building. So far as known, none of our ministers had ever preached in the town before and the hospitable reception of our plea was a pleasing surprise. Seven have been added at Killbuck recently in our regular services. Offering on children's day at Killbuck, $92.18, and Glenmonte $72.35.—W. R. Walker.

Oklahoma.

Hobart, July 16.—Four additions at Mangum yesterday. A merchant and his wife came by statement and two young ladies by confession. I locate with some church in Oklahoma or will hold meetings and furnish a singer. My address is Gueda Springs, Kan.—B. F. Stallings.

Gage, July 17.—Three added by letter this week, one by statement and one by baptism. The Sunday-school gave $3.99 children's day. This church is not yet six months old.—N. B. McGhee.

Ontario.

St. Thomas, July 16.—Two accessions yesterday, one by letter, the other by statement. The recommendation of the board for the building of a new $12,000 church was unanimously adopted by the congregation. The building will begin at once.—Jas. Egbert.

Pennsylvania.

Scranton, July 19.—Four additions to the church by baptism in the past two weeks.—Richard Bagby.

Meyersdale, July 19.—A two-weeks' meeting was held at New Centerville, closing July 15. Large audiences every service; sixteen added by confessions, five of them adults. George Knepper, of Somerset, greatly assisted. This congregation learnt its mortgage one month ago.—Chas. E. Geis.

Texas.

Garland, July 19.—Closed my meeting at

Sachse last Tuesday night with thirty-five additions to the church. A large number of them were heads of families. Two were from the Methodist and the others from the world.—Chas. Charteen.

Amarillo, July 19.—Have just closed a two-weeks' meeting at Canyon City, with sixteen additions, seven by baptism, one reclaimed and eight by letter. The church has a fine pastor in J. L. Stockard. His salary was increased $15 per month in appreciation of his good work. Many of his members are readers of THE CHRISTIAN-EVANGELIST, which they feel is a great factor in their Christian growth.—Jewell Howard.

[It is always a great factor wherever read.—ED.]

Devine, July 16.—A fine and growing interest. Four confessions. Move out on the church lawn to-night.—D. D. Boyle, evangelist.

Greenville, July 16.—Our meeting with J. L. Haddock and Frank C. Houston, evangelists, closed last night with thirty-nine additions.—J. W. Holsapple.

Austin, July 15.—During this month twenty-two have been added to the Central Christian Church, of this city, twelve by confession and baptism, two restored and the rest by letter. It is a mistake to suppose that Christian work can not be carried on in southern cities during the hot weather.—J. W. Lowber.

Lampasas, July 19.—Have just closed an encouraging meeting at Kerrville, Tex. There were nineteen additions, over one-half being conversions. Miss Grace Plummer conducted the singing in an able manner. Members in this lovely summer resort are moving forward hopefully for larger things.—W. A. Boggess.

SUBSCRIBERS' WANTS.

E CHURCH OF C|

BY A DISTINGUISHED LAYMAN

FUNK & WAGNALLS COMPANY, Publishers, NEW YORK an

A BRIEF OUTLINE OF THE CONTENTS.

INTRODUCTION—BOOK FIRST. The History of Pardon

Christianity	*The Church*	*Saul and His Conversion*	
of Heaven	*The Day of Pentecost*	*Work of the Apostle Paul*	
Manifestations	*The New Testament Scriptures*	*Call of the Gentiles*	
Teacher	*The Great Salvation*	*What Shall I Do to be Saved?*	
Word of God	*The Apostles Preaching*	*Operations of the Spirit*	
of Christ	*The Seven Chosen*	*Missionary Work of the*	
Revelations	*Miracles*	*Church*	
	Conversions		

BOOK SECOND. The Evidence of Pardon, and the Church as an Organization

e of Pardon	*Church Ordinances*	*Christian Unity*
Pardon	*The Church Complete*	*What is Implied by Unity*
of Christ	*The Apostasy*	*Nature of Division*

WHAT THE PUBLISHERS SAY.

nd original plea for the Simple is unencumbered by the artifi- made creeds and denominational ich simply adopts Christ and His their original clearness, compre and purity.

For the Clergyman, a book full of stimulat- ing and suggestive thought on the fundamental doctrines of Christianity. The reasoning is clear, logical, forceful; the whole work is in- tensely Biblical, and reverently loyal to Chris- tian doctrine throughout; a help and strength to every minister.

For the Layn thought on the ject before the ent generation. simple fact an practical man c experience.

WHAT INDIVIDUALS SAY.

h of Christ, by a layman, con- clear statement on the Bible, teacher and trainer of the young iould * * * consider. * * * In a rceful way he unfolds the great Sacred Volume. R. S. Latimer, Western Pennsylvania Christian ociety, Pittsburg, Pa.

Intelligent, candid, earnest, and study of the most vital subject age a rational mind. There are he discussion in which the writer eloquence. I hail such a work source with grateful satisfaction." LEAVER WILKINSON, Professor of Criticism, University of Chicago.

greatest religious book so far the twentieth century."—M. M. torney at Law, Uniontown, Pa.

nt Message to the Churches st read 'The Church of Christ' by I am delighted and elated with it. n author has served all Christen- f all faiths will hail with enthu- olume and its messages to men. as placed the world's religions be- many pebbles, and after showing

the utter imbecility of all save one he takes up the pearl of great price and with a stroke recounts the triumphs of Christ and the cross through His church. Any Christian living a thousand miles from any church could take this book and with its description of the church and its references to the Bible or- ganize the Church of Christ and invite men of any faith to meet in Him. It is a timely vol- ume. May the dear Lord bless the Layman and his heaven-sent message to the churches."— *Charles Reign Scoville, A. M., LL. D., Evan- gelist, Chicago, Ill.*

All in All to Me·It Is·a Great Book

" 'The Church of Christ' is like a pearl of great price in a setting of gold. We have nothing in our literature in my judgment at all comparable to it. For a clear, logical, com- prehensive, and Scriptural exposition of the New Testament revelation of the origin, princi- ples, purposes, and organization of the Church of Christ as God's agency in this world for the redemption of lost men it fills a place pecul- iarly its own and from which, in my judg- ment, it will not soon be removed. . . . It is timely. It is a book greatly needed at this particular juncture when the truly good and

religious people be feeling dar upon which to if it can secu its worth merit factor in bring Savior's prayer pious hearts. lofty in though attractive in with brevity of quent peroratic commands the reader from c in all to me i liam F. Cowde

"This book i trust it may b *A. McLean, P* sionary Society

"The perusa tion akin to th eler, who had but suddenly meets the imp *Thomes C. Da* Barre, Pa.

WORDS OF PRAISE FROM FAR-OFF COUNTRIES.

Scarcely Be Excelled

read with deep interest 'The 'hrist.' The author's exegesis is lear and satisfactory. Some pass- icely be excelled for strength and y in the English language."—*J. M. D. D.*, Corresponding Secretary e Tract Society, Shanghai, China.

Pure Sunlight of God's Saving Truth

er of this every way admirable are informed by the publisher, 'A Layman.' But that this author hed for something more than ind 'politics,' all who read the be quick to perceive. He is dis r his simple yet robust faith in,

and thorough grasp of, the truth as it is in Jesus; for his splendid powers of generaliza- tion, and for his conspicuous ability to im- part what he knows in plain and forcible Anglo-Saxon, so that all may understand and appreciate it. The book is precisely what is needed at the present juncture, not only un- der the Stars and Stripes, but away here in the land of 'The Golden Fleece,' under the Southern Cross. It is the finest compendium of the matters relating to Salvation, both on its Godward and manward sides, that we have seen. We venture to predict for it a great future—not alone in circulation—but in the work it will be destined to accomplish. This book will, more than any Volume that has ap- peared in our language, tend to break up the fog-banks of theological mysticism, and let in

the pure sunlig a darkened m brimful of pos who makes a will never be effective Gos Auckland, Nev

A Pleasan

"That 'A theme and ha prise and pron book has beer attractively pr turn the atten inal sources of *Coebrane, Asi*

WHAT THE RELIGIOUS PAPERS SAY.

Christian Endeavor

By GEO. L. SNIVELY

August 5, 1906.

DUTY, PRIVILEGE AND EXCUSES.

—Luke 14:15-24.

(*Consecration Meeting.*)

DAILY READINGS.

M.	The Great Supper.	Luke 14:15-24.
T.	A Privileged Class.	Matt. 3:1-10.
W.	A Weak Excuse.	Matt. 8:18-22.
T.	First and Last.	Matt. 19:27-30.
F.	Duty of Obedience.	Acts 5:25-29.
S.	An Obligation.	2 Peter 3:1-12.
S.	Paying Vows.	Psa. 116:12-19.

"Swift fly the hours, and brief the time,
  For action or repose;
Fast flits this scene of woe and crime,
  And soon the whole shall close.
The evening shadows deeper fall,
  The daylight dies away.
Wake slumberer, at thy Master's call,
  And work while it is day!"

It is easy for us to see the self-deception in the excuses others frame for evasion of duty, but wily old Satan usually blinds us to that in our own which is very apparent to our neighbors. Let us realize that we are being *victimized* into any turning aside from the commands of our Father.

The Christian in whose lexicon is found neither "excuse" nor any of its synonyms, but who does his whole duty as he is given light to see it, is the one daily deriving supreme delight from earthly privileges and is joyfully looking forward to their higher consummations in heaven.

The man who would rather prove his oxen than to banquet with his Lord is one whom business is destroying. The man who would rather survey his fields than commune with Jesus has let riches bar him out of the kingdom. The one who plead his marriage as a reason for spurning the Son of God will never know the sweetest meaning of home here on earth, and will have no mansion up yonder.

Physical healing at the hands of the Great Physician is unquestionably one of the boons peculiar to the children of God. It is a blessing, too, we should seek within the Church of Christ, rather than within any semisecular organization that has attached "church" to its title simply because of the hold the name has on the affections of the people, or within the membership of any ethical cult. It is our privilege to pray for health, as it is the delight of angels to bring it in their wings.

Bishop Usher, whose sacred chronology is printed in the margin of most of our Bibles, was one time preaching to a great audience in London, when a messenger from the despotic king James commanded his immmediately coming to the palace. The preacher replied: "I am engaged in the more important business of the greater King. When I have finished my duty to him, then I shall come." This same spirit, even in attenuated form, applied now would send us to many a prayer-meeting on evenings when we regard an invitation to a social as more imperative. Which is greater, God or our society leaders?

Lord Horatio Nelson, who "flamed amazement on the world by a series of noble deeds in the lustre of which all other naval glory looks pale," won his crowning victory at Trafalgar, where the French and Spanish naval power was broken and their hopes of invading England became merely a dream of departed greatness, largely through this appeal quietly signaled from ship to ship—"England expects every man to do his duty to-day." The performance of duty is a constitutional impulse in all right natures. As religious teachers and exemplars we are acting most wisely when kindly making known their duty to men and bringing them to a square decision as to whether they will accept or reject it. If we will look to our great Captain's flagship we can easily discern angels signaling to us through these present day conflicts. "Heaven expects every soldier of the cross to do his duty to-day."

Sunday-School

August 5, 1906.

FALSE EXCUSES—Luke 14:15-24.

Memory Verses, 23-24.

GOLDEN TEXT.—And they all with one consent began to make excuse.—Luke 14:18.

It was at the same dinner at the Pharisee's house where the preceding discourse about humility was spoken, that Jesus gave this parable about the unwilling guests. The figure, in this case, was drawn directly from the situation before him. He was at a feast. The occasion suggested to one of the guests the pious thought that even the best of earthly banquets in the most congenial company, is nothing as compared to the joys of that day when the righteous shall sit down to the banquet of eternal glory in the Kingdom of God. "Blessed he that shall eat bread in the Kingdom of God."

Jesus took up the figure and elaborated it into a parable. Blessed indeed shall it be to sit down at that heavenly feast. But strangely enough, many of those who are invited will not come. There is a strange contrast between the eternal advantages of seeking the things of the Kingdom of God, and the reluctance of men to accept these advantages. John Bunyan expressed the same fact in his story of the man with the muck-rake, so busy with the foul things in which he had learned to take pleasure that he had no time to lift his eyes to see the angel holding over his head a glittering crown which would be his for looking up and reaching up.

So these people who were bidden to the feast lost the greater blessedness in the too eager pursuit of lesser things. It was not that the things which they did were bad.

In fact, they were all good things to do. It is good to buy fields and to go to see them. It is good to buy oxen and to work them. It is certainly good to marry a wife. There are some temptations which, to people of decent inclinations, are more subtle and dangerous than the temptation to indulge in vice. Things good in themselves but misused; activities which in themselves are commendable, but which are allowed to crowd out more important concerns—these are the most potent dangers of our time. The engrossing demands of business, the requirements of social life, the things which are good and important but not best and most important, are a snare to many souls. At another time Jesus said, "Seek first the Kingdom of God and his righteousness, and all these things (food, clothing and other temporal goods) shall be added to you." The lesson is the same as that of this parable of the feast and the unwilling guests. Do not imagine that the pursuit of good things is a valid excuse for failure to seek the best.

PARABLE OF THE VINEYARD.—
Luke 20:9-16.

"Kind Father, look with pity now
  On one by sin defiled;
While at thy mercy-seat I bow,
  O bless thine erring child!

"My struggles, Lord, to do thy will,
  How poor and weak they are!
But thou art gracious to me still,
  Then hear my humble prayer."

Those men were not profited by their wicked withholding of tribute and their murdering the servants and heir. Had they first dealt honestly with the owner, all things would have been added unto them. That principle obtains today. In rejecting God's overtures to us for some returns in goodness and love and helpfulness in redeeming the earth as compensation for what he gives us, we are preparing for our own expulsion from the vineyard here and barring ourselves from the Canaan above.

In the remark that the proprietor went into another country for a long time, Jesus refers to the withholding of visible manifestations of God's presence and power in the midst of the people in order that they might not be consciously overawed by them, but have opportunity for the development of faith and moral responsibility. He never did really withdraw from Israel or any other nation. The Godless nations have all withdrawn from him. He is never far from any of us who will have to do with him.

It is well to note that by killing the servants, these husbandmen so inured themselves to crime that when it seemed to their advantage, they scrupled not to murder the son and heir. So with us. Now there are sanctities we would not violate but neglecting giving, Bible reading, and fraternal solicitude today, tomorrow we absent ourselves from worship, neglect prayer, forget heaven, and soon we are found scoffing at the judgment, trampling the blood of Jesus under our feet, and crucifying anew the Lord of Glory.

Our Judge is not capricious and cruel. Not only do men anticipate his judgments, but approve them. "What therefore shall the lord of the vineyard do unto them?" asked Jesus. Matthew (21:41) tells us they replied: "He will miserably destroy

WILLIAM WOODS COLLEGE

FOR YOUNG LADIES

A college home of the best moral and Christian influences.
Just the place for your daughter.
Courses in literature, science, art, elocution, vocal and instrumental music, domestic science and domestic art, book-keeping and shorthand and typewriting.
A progressive institution with an efficient faculty.
Handsome buildings, beautiful campus.
New chapel in course of erection.
Articulates with the Missouri State University.
Educates daughters of foreign missionaries.
Endowment solicited. Healthful location.
For catalogue or information, address
J. B. JONES, President, Fulton, Mo.

CHURCH FEDERATION READY.
The Inter-Church Conference on Federation, 700 pages, prepaid.....$2 00

those miserable husbandmen and will let out the vineyard unto other husbandmen, who shall render him the fruits in their seasons." All will recognize the justice in the findings of the last day. Sinners will not be driven to their doom; constitutional, inherent, powers of the souls will impel them there.

The servants sent to collect just tribute from the husbandmen were the prophets who at different periods of the nation's history went forth to restore right relations between God and his people. Their coming was not gladly welcomed by the lords of the vineyard nor were they returned fullhanded to their master. Their reception is indicated in the Savior's sad apostrophe, O, Jerusalem. Jerusalem, that killeth the prophets and stoneth them that are sent unto her! Had these messengers been received in manner befitting their mission, like all the angels of God, whether of life or death, they would have left blessings infinitely more valuable than any treasure they would bear away.

The vineyard of our parable is the truths of God and righteousness ,which Jehovah implanted in the hearts of ancient Israel. Under the culture of kings and judges, priests and Levites and the influence of the temple service he instituted he had a right to expect a fruitage of goodness and brotherly love and nobility of character that would soon have peopled the earth with his worshippers. If the great Husbandman could be said to have cherished such expectations they were doomed to cruel disappointment. The bigotry of their leaders isolated the Jews from other nations and prevented the knowledge of their God from filling the earth, while hypocrisy and cant in high places blighted holiness and true worship all over the land. Never was rich sowing rewarded with poorer harvest.

Christian Endeavor

By GEO. L. SNIVELY

August 5, 1906.

DUTY, PRIVILEGE AND EXCUSES.
—Luke 14:15-24.

(Consecration Meeting.)

DAILY READINGS.

M. The Great Supper. Luke 14:15-24.
T. A Privileged Class. Matt. 3:1-10.
W. A Weak Excuse. Matt. 8:18-22.
T. First and Last. Matt. 19:27-30.
F. Duty of Obedience. Acts 5:25-29.
S. An Obligation. 2 Peter 3:1-12.
S. Paying Vows. Psa. 116:12-19.

"Swift fly the hours, and brief the time,
　For action or repose:
Fast flits this scene of woe and crime,
　And soon the whole shall close.'
The evening shadows deeper fall,
　The daylight dies away,
Wake slumberer, at thy Master's call,
　And work while it is day!"

It is easy for us to see the self-deception in the excuses others frame for evasion of duty, but wily old Satan usually blinds us to that in our own which is very apparent to our neighbors. Let us realize that we are being *victimized* into any turning aside from the commands of our Father.

The Christian in whose lexicon is found neither "excuse" nor any of its synonyms, but who does his whole duty as he is given light to see it, is the one daily deriving supreme delight from earthly privileges and is joyfully looking forward to their higher consummations in heaven.

The man who would rather prove his oxen than to banquet with his Lord 's one whom business is destroying. The man who would rather survey his fields than commune with Jesus has let riches bar him out of the kingdom. The one who plead his marriage as a reason for spurning the Son of God will never know the sweetest meaning of home here on earth, and will have no mansion up yonder.

Physical healing at the hands of the Great Physician is unquestionably one of the bonus peculiar to the children of God. It is a blessing, too, we should seek within the Church of Christ, rather than within any semisecular organization that has attached "church" to its title simply because of the hold the name has on the affections of the people, or within the membership of any ethical cult. It is our privilege to pray for health, as it is the delight of angels to bring it in their wings.

Bishop Usher, whose sacred chronology is printed in the margin of most of our Bibles, was one time preaching to a great audience in London, when a messenger from the despotic king James commanded his immmediately coming to the palace. The preacher replied: "I am engaged in the more important business of the greater King. When I have finished my duty to him, then I shall come." This same spirit, even in attenuated form, applied now would send us to many a prayer-meeting on evenings when we regard an invitation to a social as more imperative. Which is greater, God or our society leaders?

Lord Horatio Nelson, who "flamed amazement on the world by a series of noble deeds in the lustre of which all other naval glory looks pale," won his crowning victory at Trafalgar, where the French and Spanish naval power was broken and their hopes of invading England became merely a dream of departed greatness, largely through this appeal quietly signaled from ship to ship—"England expects every man to do his duty today." The performance of duty is a constitutional impulse in all right natures. As religious teachers and exemplars we are acting most wisely when kindly making known their duty to men and bringing them to a square decision as to whether they will accept or reject it. If we will look to our great Captain's flagship we can easily discern angels signaling to us through these present day conflicts. "Heaven expects every soldier of the cross to do his duty to-day."

Sunday-School

August 5, 1906.

FALSE EXCUSES—Luke 14:15-24.

Memory Verses, 23-24.

GOLDEN TEXT.—And they all with one consent began to make excuse.—Luke 14:18.

It was at the same dinner at the Pharisee's house, where the preceding discourse about humility was spoken, that Jesus gave this parable about the unwilling guests. The figure, in this case, was drawn directly from the situation before him. He was at a feast. The occasion suggested to one of the guests the pious thought that even the best of earthly banquets in the most congenial company, is nothing as compared to the joys of that day when the righteous shall sit down to the banquet of eternal glory in the Kingdom of God. "Blessed is he that shall eat bread in the Kingdom of God."

Jesus took up the figure and elaborated it into a parable. Blessed indeed shall it be to sit down at that heavenly feast. But strangely enough, many of those who are invited will not come. There is a strange contrast between the eternal advantages of seeking the things of the Kingdom of God, and the reluctance of men to accept these advantages. John Bunyan expressed the same fact in his story of the man with the muck-rake, so busy with the foul things in which he had learned to take pleasure that he had no time to lift his eyes to see the angel holding over his head a glittering crown which would be his for looking up and reaching up.

So these people who were bidden to the feast lost the greater blessedness in the too eager pursuit of lesser things. It was not that the things which they did were bad.

In fact, they were all good things to do. It is good to buy fields and to go to see them. It is good to buy oxen and to work them. It is certainly good to marry a wife. There are some temptations which, to people of decent inclinations, are more subtle and dangerous than the temptation to indulge in vice. Things good in themselves but misused; activities which in themselves are commendable, but which are allowed to crowd out more important concerns—these are the most potent dangers of our time. The engrossing demands of business, the requirements of social life, the things which are good and important but not best and most important, are a snare to many souls. At another time Jesus said, "Seek first the Kingdom of God and his righteousness, and all these things (food, clothing and other temporal goods) shall be added to you." The lesson is the same as that of this parable of the feast and the unwilling guests. Do not imagine that the pursuit of good things is a valid excuse for failure to seek the best.

❀ ❀

HORSFORD'S ACID PHOSPHATE

Relieves Headache

caused by summer heat, overwork, nervous disorders or impaired digestion. Relieves quickly.

Midweek Prayer-Meeting

August 1, 1906.

PARABLE OF THE VINEYARD.—
Luke 20:9-16.

"Kind Father, look with pity now
  On one by sin defiled;
While at thy mercy-seat I bow,
  O bless thine erring child!

"My struggles, Lord, to do thy will,
  How poor and weak they are!
But thou art gracious to me still,
  Then hear my humble prayer."

Those men were not profited by their wicked withholding of tribute and their murdering the servants and heir. Had they first dealt honestly with the owner, all things would have been added unto them. That principle obtains today. In rejecting God's overtures to us for some returns in goodness and love and helpfulness in redeeming the earth as compensation for what he gives us, we are preparing for our own expulsion from the vineyard here and barring ourselves from the Canaan above.

In the remark that the proprietor went into another country for a long time, Jesus refers to the withholding of visible manifestations of God's presence and power in the midst of the people in order that they might not be consciously overawed by them, but have opportunity for the development of faith and moral responsibility. He never did really withdraw from Israel or any other nation. The Godless nations have all withdrawn from him. He is never far from any of us who will have to do with him.

It is well to note that by killing the servants, these husbandmen so inured themselves to crime that when it seemed to their advantage, they scrupled not to murder the son and heir. So with us. Now there are sanctities we would not violate but neglecting giving, Bible reading, and fraternal solicitude today, tomorrow we absent ourselves from worship, neglect prayer, forget heaven, and soon we are found scoffing at the judgment, trampling the blood of Jesus under our feet, and crucifying anew the Lord of Glory.

Our Judge is not capricious and cruel. Not only do men anticipate his judgments, but approve them. "What therefore shall the lord of the vineyard do unto them?" asked Jesus. Matthew (21:41) tells us they replied: "He will miserably destroy

WILLIAM WOODS COLLEGE

FOR YOUNG LADIES

A college home of the best moral and Christian influences.

Just the place for your daughter.

Courses in literature, science, art, elocution, vocal and instrumental music, domestic science and domestic art, book-keeping and shorthand and typewriting.

A progressive institution with an efficient faculty.

Handsome buildings, beautiful campus.

New chapel in course of erection.

Articulates with the Missouri State University.

Educates daughters of foreign missionaries.
Endowment solicited. Healthful location.
For catalogue or information, address ·
J. B. JONES, President, Fulton, Mo.

CHURCH FEDERATION READY.

The Inter-Church Conference on Federation, 700 pages, prepaid.....$2.00

those miserable husbandmen and will let out the vineyard unto other husbandmen, who shall render him the fruits in their seasons." All will recognize the justice in the findings of the last day. Sinners will not be driven to their doom; constitutional, inherent, powers of the souls will impel them there.

The servants sent to collect just tribute from the husbandmen were the prophets who at different periods of the nation's history went forth to restore right relations between God and his people. Their coming was not gladly welcomed by the lords of the vineyard nor were they returned fullhanded to their master. Their reception is indicated in the Savior's sad apostrophe, O, Jerusalem, Jerusalem, that killeth the prophets and stoneth them that are sent unto her! Had these messengers been received in manner befitting their mission, like all the angels of God, whether of life or death, they would have left blessings infinitely more valuable than any treasure they would bear away.

The vineyard of our parable is the truths of God and righteousness which Jehovah implanted in the hearts of ancient Israel. Under the culture of kings and judges, priests and Levites and the influence of the temple service he instituted he had a right to expect a fruitage of goodness and brotherly love and nobility of character that would soon have peopled the earth with his worshippers. If the great Husbandman could be said to have cherished such expectations they were doomed to cruel dis-

appointment. The bigotry of their leaders isolated the Jews from other nations and prevented the knowledge of their God from filling the earth, while hypocrisy and cant in high places blighted holiness and true worship all over the land. Never was rich sowing rewarded with poorer harvest.

Current Literature

TABLE TALKS OF JESUS. By L. G. Broughton. (Fleming H. Revell Company, Chicago. 50 cts. net.)

As the title indicates the book consists of expositions of the sayings of Jesus as he sat "at meat" and as he "broke bread" with personal friends and others when he dwelt among men. There are eleven of these talks extending from the marriage feast past the memorial supper and on to the promise of the Father.

THE DISCIPLES OF CHRIST.

The reading of this little volume by Errett Gates, Ph. D., has been a distinct inspiration to me as a preacher. It is a good thing for one immersed in the details of pastoral duties to get the larger view and the general trend of our history here set forth. It gives an uplift, a thrill, a power, to our present duties to be had in no other way. The volume gives a clear and satisfactory account of our early history and of the fundamental principles which guided the fathers of our church. It would be difficult to improve on this part of the narrative. Dr. Gates has been a careful student of our history and is familiar with his theme. He has the historical spirit and method which makes it a pleasure to follow him. He has, too, in a pre-eminent degree the spirit of fairness. He does not write as a partisan, but as an unbiased historian. To be sure, part of the book is not pleasant reading, but this is not altogether the author's fault. He has given the facts. But the true historian must also give a proper interpretation of facts. Too much emphasis is here put upon controversial matters. Every religious movement has had its full share of this. It is simply the "gnawing pains" incident to all development. In spite of all controversies we have never ceased to be practically one body—and this can be affirmed of very few denominations now in existence. A glowing chapter might be written on the constructive work we have done as a people, the positive contribution we have made to the religious life of our time and the grand men of God who have been produced by the creative ideal for which we stand. The author groups our history into three divisions, under three prominent leaders: (1) Alexander Campbell. This was the period of laying the foundations. Mr. Campbell was not an organizer like John Wesley, not an evangelist like Whitefield; he was a great Christian statesman, logician and orator. A clear conception of the fundamentals

of religion, a masterly statement and an invincible logic were the elements of his power. This was the period of discussion and gradual separation into a distinct organization. (2) Isaac Errett. In this period the missionary spirit was developed and missionary organization perfected. It represents a distinct advance over the first period and marks our entrance as a great factor among the forces making for the evangelization of the world. (3) This period under the leadership of such men as J. H. Garrison, shows a deepening of the spiritual life of our churches and the development of a spirit of co-operation with other religious bodies for the carrying of the Gospel to the ends of the earth. It marks the passing from the discussion to the practice of Christian union. As the author says: "There has come to some of the best spirits of the denomination a new and intense appreciation of its mission as a Christian union movement. They feel that its chief justification for existence as a separate body lies in what it can contribute toward the union of Christians in this generation. They are not content to wait for the consummation of a far-off, ideal union in some future generation, but desire to prepare the way for it by a larger co-operation and freedom of relationship with other bodies, in the present generation." The book is worthy of a wide and careful reading.   JAMES M. PHILPUTT.

St. Louis.

The Home Department

Sunset at Pentwater.

BY BERTHA M. BRAY, A LITTLE GIRL. *

When the busy day is ended,
And the shades of eve draw near,
When all Nature's voices, blended,
Fall like music on the ear,
Then we love to cross the sand hills,
Stroll along the sandy shore,
Gaze out o'er the lake's wide vista,
Listen to its billows roar.

Then we love to watch the sunset,
As it slowly sinks to rest,
Painting all the clouds with glory,
Hov'ring round the golden west.
Having run its race with patience,
Now it sinks beneath the waves,
Sending back its farewell glances,
And a golden pathway paves.

So may we, our life-work finished,
Close as gently our brief day,
Leaving rays of light behind us,
Showing other souls the way.
From the sun we learn this lesson:
Let us shine our journey through,
And departing leave behind us
Light to guide our neighbors, too.

*Revised by Editor.
Pentwater, Mich.

The Bronze Vase.

BY J. BRECKENRIDGE ELLIS.

PART III.

CHAPTER IV.

Mrs. Bannerton kindly consented to buy the garments essential to Rhoda, and in the evening, Raymund, accompanied by his sister, left the lodging house to seek a restaurant. Raymund was eager in his desire to find employment in the city. "There are so very many stores in Kansas City," he reasoned, "that some of them must need a boy." Rhoda was not very hopeful. She said, "I don't think there is much hope of your getting a place, Ray, as long as you show that you are from the country."

"How do I show it?" he asked.

"It is perfectly dear to me," said Rhoda, smiling at him as they passed along Thirteenth Street, "but business men look at everything in a businesslike way. No, we mustn't stop to look at those boys"—in a high yard three boys were playing ball and a girl, evidently their sister was trying to make them miss a catch, and all were laughing delightedly—"and you mustn't stop to look in the store window."

"I sometimes see the city people stop, to look in the store windows," said Raymund.

"I know it," said Rhoda, "but they are looking for something, and you are just looking because everything is strange to you. It makes a different kind of look, somehow. I don't know how to explain it. And now—no, Raymund, you must not look so friendly at these poor old creatures we meet, and you must not take off your hat if a person looks at you!"

"Very well," said Raymund, "I guess I can learn this just as I learned Latin."

"You must look all the time as if you were going somewhere, as if it were important for you not to be late, and as if you took no interest whatever in the sights about you. These people we meet, pass along these same pavements day after day, year after year. They know how everything looks till they are sick of it all, or anyway, bored by it, and nothing can interest them in it again. And when they see you smiling at what is all monotony to them, and taking interest in things that they consider just the necessary evils of a city's routine, they know you are from a place where people don't see things; and that place is the country!"

"Thank you," said Raymund. "Go right on, Rhoda."

"You will find another thing, Ray," said Rhoda gently; "the walks are so built, that they are level, and you don't have to plant your feet so securely. You won't stumble over any clods, you know." She laughed up at him, and Raymund, taking all this in jolly spirits, laughed aloud, and some men turned around to see what was the matter. When they saw Raymund, although he had left the green umbrella at the lodging-house, they knew instantly that he was from the distant prairie-lands of Missouri.

Rhoda had as little experience of city-restaurants as Raymund, and when their meal was ended, the youth was rather aghast at the bill; but he did not betray his feelings to Rhoda. "It's all right," he assured her, as they returned to the lodging-house, "we'll stick it out this week, for I believe I can get a good position here; and I don't see any use of going back to Crawley; everybody knows there's no work to be had in Crawley. There's one thing I want you to promise me, Rhoda, and that is, never to leave Mrs. Bannerton's lodging-house, unless you go out with me, or with Mrs. Bannerton." Rhoda promised this readily enough, for she had a fear of the people who had threatened her at Mrs. Van Estry's, and particularly of the young man whose brutal, drunken face she could not drive from her memory.

The next few days taught Raymund more about seeking employment in the city, than he could have learned from half-a-dozen magazine articles, illustrations and all. It was not the worst feature about the occupation, that he was invariably refused a position; it was the rude unkindness with which he was treated. There was always the hope ahead that at last some business house might accept his services. But the insulting rejections, the gruff surliness, the supercilious scorn, the sneering politeness, bowed his healthful spirit. He and Rhoda tried one restaurant after another, seeking one where reasonable rates were combined with good cooking, and at their little table, he would take over his failures, never dismally, or complainingly, but quite frankly. At night the tall narrow walls of his little bedroom looked down upon him as if to say, "No luck, hey?" And the meaningless end of lead pipe would seem to squint at him through the ceiling, and the lights as seen from his bed would give a sense of remoteness as if to say, "You do not belong to our world. Why do you not go back to clover fields and rippling brooks?" But in the morning, the sunlight would speak of cheer. So Raymund would cautiously pour from his wire-bound pitcher and set it gently down, and wash away a night's uneasiness. But each day told the same story—tramp, tramp, tramp over hard pavements—blistered feet—unkind refusals—a heavy heart—and back to Rhoda. One interview with an employer went to the length of Raymund's being asked, "Well, what can you do?" That was his crowning success of the week.

On the last afternoon, Raymund was on the east of Main street going from one crowded place of business to another, when he came face to face with the man whom he had discovered watching his bed-room window. Seen so near, the middle-aged man was much more repulsive. The story of a bad life, was to be read in his eyes. Raymund instinctively paused.

"Raymund," said the man abruptly, "I want to talk business with you a few minutes. Come over here." He jerked his thumb in the direction of a vacant lot at the back of a small drygoods store.

"I am busy," said Raymund, amazed that his name should be known to the other.

"So am I," said the man with a grin. "Boggs is my name. Glad to meet you. I've heard your sister speak of you, and you two look so much alike, I couldn't help knowing you. It's to your interest to talk to me a little while. I know you're both staying at Mrs. Bannerton's, and I can give you considerable trouble, both of you."

"You can give us no trouble," said Raymund, but his heart sank. "and if you do not leave us alone, I will turn you over to the police."

"All right," said Boggs, "there's one now. Do you want me to call him for you?"

"I will hear what you have to say," said

NOTHING BETTER

NEWLY REVISED TO 1906

MISSIONARY ADDRESSES

By ARCHIBALD McLEAN

TABLE OF CONTENTS.

1. The Supreme Mission of the Church.
2. The Gospel for All Nations.
3. Encouragement in Missions.
4. The Success of Modern Missions.
5. The Heroism of Missions.
6. The Transferring Power of the Gospel.
7. Woman and the Gospel.
8. Missions in the Life of Christ.
9. Missions in the Early Church.
10. Missions in the Middle Ages.
11. Modern Missions.
12. Missions Among the Disciples of Christ.
13 Medical Missions.
14. "This Grace Also."
Appendix: Names and Brief Accounts of those Who Have Labored for the Foreign Christian Missionary Society.
Biography: Selected List of Best Books on Missions, Mission Lands and Missionaries.

Nothing Needed with this book in Your Library. In fine silk cloth binding, 300 pages, postpaid, $1.00.

CHRISTIAN PUBLISHING COMPANY,
2712 Pine Street, St. Louis, Mo.

REGIMENTAL REUNIONS AND FORTY-THIRD ANNIVERSARY BATTLE CHICKAMAUGA,

CHATTANOOGA, SEPTEMBER 18-20, 1906.

On September 18, 1906, will occur the forty-third anniversary of the Battle of Chickamauga. It is proposed to celebrate this memorable event with a reunion of the various regiments that participated in this memorable battle and the various battles fought around Chattanooga. This reunion will be held at Chickamauga National Park, September 18, 19 and 20, and the present indications are that it will be the largest and most notable gathering ever held in the South. On the above dates, the remnants from the armies of twelve states, comprising the following: Pennsylvania, Ohio, Michigan, Indiana, Illinois, Wisconsin, Minnesota, Iowa, Nebraska, Missouri, Kansas and Kentucky, will assemble, many for the first and last time since they marched from its blood-stained fields, forty-three years ago.

Here is one of the great opportunities for the education of the youth. Don't fail to take your children and show them historic Chattanooga, with all its historical connections. It is the opportunity of a lifetime. Go and see the old war generals and other officers point out the places of interest on the battlefield; let them show you and explain, in person, the maneuvers on the battlefield showing the positions of the opposing armies at the time of battle. It will not be long until none will be left to do this noble work.

It will be many years, if ever again, that such an opportunity will present itself. See that your ticket read via the Louisville & Nashville R. R., the Battlefield Route. Call on your nearest railroad agent for rates and advertising matter pertaining to the reunion, or write nearest representative of the Louisville & Nashville R. R.

J. H. MILLIKEN, D. P. A., Louisville, Ky.
F. D. BUSH, D. P. A., Cincinnati, Ohio.
H. E. DAVENPORT, D. P. A., St. Louis, Mo.
H. C. BAILEY, N. W. P. A., Chicago, Ill.

Raymund, and they walked to the vacant lot.

"It's this," said Boggs. "Your sister made it a steady thing to steal laces and silks from three of the biggest stores in the city. She sold them to a second-hand store on Ninth street. That store finally got uneasy about the goods she kept bringing and they sent word to Mrs. Van Estry—that's where Rhoda worked—to ask how the girl came by all that rich stuff. Some of Mrs. Van Estry's friends were there at the time. I was, for one. Mrs. Van Estry sent for Rhoda and asked her about it right there before us all. Rhoda burst into tears and confessed that she had been stealing for over a year. Well, we all felt so sorry for the girl that we didn't know what to do. We didn't want her sent to jail, so Mrs. Van Estry took back the last things that had been stolen, to the store, and begged the proprietor not to prosecute Rhoda. But he was so mad, he sent the police right to our house; and then we found out that Rhoda had run away. The police are looking everywhere for her, but she is so different since she got new clothes and fixed herself up, that one of them saw you and her going into a restaurant yesterday, and didn't recognize her from Mrs. Van Estry's description. But I know her, and can give her up in a minute. Now to business. I want some money from you, to keep mum about where she is. You've got some in your shoes, and you needn't deny it. I can tell because I've watched how you walk and how you, every now and then, look down to see if they ain't leaking. So pony up. Here is a nice respectable vacant lot, and you can take off your shoes without bringing a blush to the cheek of the most fastidious."

"I know very well," said Raymund, "and I believe you know, that my sister never stole anything in her life, and that she is the kind of girl that couldn't do that sort of thing. You are trying to put on her what others have done."

"It don't matter what you think, or what I think," said Boggs gently, persuasively, even kindly. "It's what will the district station do, when you and Rhoda are dragged before it and we all troop down there as witnesses. I don't care what kind of a girl Rhoda is, but I do care about the money in your shoes. So shell it out, Raymund, my boy, and luck to you, and the stars and stripes over all!" We cannot, of course, know what the reader would have done in Raymund's position, though we have our opinion. What Raymund did, was to sit down upon the edge of the embankment, extract a ten-dollar bill from his right shoe and another from his left, and hand them to Mr. Boggs. "Now," said the evil-browed fellow, pocketing the money, "I will say farewell; and should we ever meet again, old chap, try to make it convenient to have a few more bills in your shoes or there'll be trouble. What a boy you are, carrying ten-dollar bills in your shoes! How odd! Odd, but handy!" He chuckled, squinted his eyes at Raymund with a vile narrowing of the lids, and slouched away. Raymund made all haste to Mrs. Bannerton's and told Rhoda in breathless phrases what had happened. "We must leave the city immediately," he panted. "Back to Crawley—anywhere to get away from that villain!" Rhoda shared his panic. There was a hasty parting with Mrs. Bannerton who was sympathetic, but helpless in their behalf. Their belongings were hastily placed in a small bundle, and once more the green umbrella set forth upon its adventures. Their hurrying feet passed Convention Hall, huge, barnlike, meaningless to Raymund, and later the Grace Episcopal church, whose Norman beauty never failed to impress the youth no matter how heavy of heart. They turned into Washington street, neither real sure of the way, but confident of the general direction toward the Union Station. They hurried down the Twelfth street incline, whence they could see innumerable trains from among which, one might be then on its way to Crawley. From the state line the street car track brought them to their destination, exhausted, frightened, but determined to put themselves out of the power of Mrs. Van Estry, Boggs and the other conspirators. They learned with dismay that there was no train for Crawley till the next morning. It was now half-past-seven, and although still light in the streets, the station was in a glaze of electric lights. "We will have to stay here all night," said Rhoda piteously, to the official whom she had questioned.

"There will be plenty of people here all night," said the official. "Go over yonder in the end, and get a rocking-chair as soon as somebody gets up out of one, and you'll be all right."

Just then a heavy man with white hair entered the door and bawled out in a stentorian voice a long string of cities familiar to a student of geography, adding, "Train on the third track!" As soon as his voice ceased, there was a wild scramble toward the glass doors opening upon the platform.

Rhoda and Raymund were jostled to one side. "I guess we'll have to wait here," said Raymund. "There's such a crowd, I don't believe Boggs could find us, if he were here looking for us." And they made their way toward the far end of the spacious waiting-room.

(To be Continued.)

❋ ❋

Picture of War Engine "General."

A beautiful colored picture, 18x29 inches, of the historic old engine "General" which was stolen at Big Shanty, Ga., by the Andrew's Raiders during the Civil War, and which is now on exhibition in the Union Depot, Chattanooga, Tenn., has been gotten out by the NASHVILLE, CHATTANOOGA & ST. LOUIS RY.— The "Battlefields Route" to the South. The picture is ready for framing and will be mailed for 25c. The "Story of the General" sent free. W. L. Danley, Gen'l Pass. Agent, Nashville, Tenn.

CHURCH FEDERATION READY.
The Inter-Church Conference on Federation, 700 pages, prepaid.....$2 00

Advance Society Letters.

BY J. BRECKENRIDGE ELLIS.

Come to our ice cream social, August 3rd!

But I must tell you about my Fourth of July. That has always been a big holiday with me, but on the Fourth just past, I expected little special enjoyment because I live so far away from the friends with whom I used to shoot off firecrackers. In the morning I started down town and it seemed that everybody was going away on a picnic—except one. Bentonville didn't celebrate, and it was so quiet in town that you could almost hear the weeds growing along the sidewalks. I went to the postoffice and there is a store in the same building, of course; but all the firecrackers were sold out. You couldn't get a thing in town to make a noise with. Even the mail hadn't come in. Nothing was happening except young people climbing into picnic wagons with big baskets. So I went home; and of a sudden here came a special messenger boy bringing me a package just expressed from Moberly, Mo. It was full of flowers,—pansies, oh! so many, many beautiful pansies, and mignonette and fern—they crowded a big bowl. They had been sent me by a person I had never seen; and when I went down to the postoffice again, there was a letter for me; it was as beautiful as the flowers. It, too, was from some one I have never seen. I just sat there feeling good. I liked it better than fireworks. So I had a big Fourth of July, after all. Reader, did you give somebody a good Fourth of July—I don't mean a kinsman or intimate friend, but somebody who had no special claim upon you? The letter—but I can't give it to you, for its perfume would all be dissipated in print. And right there where I was reading this letter, a man came up and invited me to his picnic. We ate on the ground in the shade of the forest trees, and there was laughter and fried chicken. When I came back to town I saw them putting up the big tent for the Chautauqua Assembly. I felt like they were putting up that tent principally for me and orphan Charlie; for you will remember Charlie was invited to visit me during the Chautauqua, the first day of which was July 6th.

I wish all of you who have ever sent me money for Charlie's support, could have been at the station to have welcomed him when he came in from St. Louis the morning of the 6th! Wouldn't we have waved our handkerchiefs and shouted and shaken hands? Nearly every state in the Union would have been represented, besides various divisions of Canada, Japan, China, England, Constantinople, South America, Mexico, and if I've left out any country that should be named, I hope it won't feel bad. So Charlie came 10 hours before I was expecting him, and I find him much improved. We have been going to the Chautauqua three times a day; it ended last night and I am tired. We heard Champ Clark and Gov. Hoch, and Lieut. Hobson, and Geo. Bain and Col. Ham, and Dixon, to say nothing of the moving pictures and illustrated lectures. Now some people don't know how to get the most good out of an illustrated lecture. They sit there in the darkness and they realize that the pictures are beautiful. Yet, somehow, they are always tired when it is over. And this is the secret of coming away from such an entertainment rested and pleased; always carry some cotton with you, and when the lecturer begins with "Now, come with me," stuff it in your ears.

You want to hear about the Av. S. orphan, I am sure. Well, he is quite tall, and looks like the picture that appeared in this paper not so very long ago. As he has lived in St. Louis so many years, right in the heart of the city, he of course thinks that a town like Bentonville is a very small place indeed, and I suspect he imagines that we might blow out the gas if we went to the city, or get run over by a street car, or turn pale in an elevator. He is very kind, however, about keeping all this to himself, and does not make a show of his immense city experience. I find, too, that he is rather strong in his political convictions, and is inclined to believe that those who belong to the *other party* do not like the country quite so well as he does, and that if they get the man in for president next time that you hear a good deal about, there would be a long dry spell in Kansas; but while he thinks these things, he doesn't say them, and as it will be seven years before he can vote, I think by that time he will have learned what many an older head does not understand; that our great political parties were not made for the purpose of fighting each other, but because each thinks its plan of blessing America is the best plan. Charlie is fond of music and I am sorry to say he has not had any music lessons the past year because we couldn't afford to pay for his lessons, and the lady who formerly gave him lessons free, has moved away. If he could have more lessons he could learn to play. He can already pick out the hymns by note, and considering his disadvantages, does well. He can play homemade accompaniments to my violin. We also play chess together. As I write these words, Charlie is lying in the hammock in our back yard. There is a plum tree to the right of him and a different variety to the left. The big ripe plums lie in the grass in great number, but Charlie doesn't even look at them. In fact he has seen as many as he wants to see, for the present.

He has been pushing the lawn mower. It is remarkable how he can get that lawn mower over the ground till all the back yard is mowed, when so many boys with *ever* so many legs cannot be connected with

the handle of a lawn mower. So, as I was saying, Charlie is lying in the hammock under the shade of the old apple tree between the two plum trees. Felix sits near solemnly waving his tail at the extreme tip of it, but holding the main stem motionless. He seems to say, "I have a few more loose hairs about me, whenever you get ready to play with me again." Charlie says that Felix recognized him as soon as he came. I have little more to tell you about Charlie's visit; it was mainly going to the big tent. Charlie might tell you that two of my own compositions were sung by gifted singers to the audiences, and that I, myself, sang one of my songs to an immense crowd and reaped enthusiastic encores. But, alas! Charlie cannot get to speak to you, and as I am too modest to mention my own triumphs, and as there is nobody else to tell you, this is something you can never know. You will remember I wanted to give Charlie a trip to Missouri after leaving me, but we concluded it was too expensive; so we bought him a suit of clothes, a hat, collars, etc., instead. When he arrived he wore the same suit in which he had visited me last August; so I know you are glad he has his new clothes. He will leave here on the 19th to visit his sister Bessie, for the people who adopted her live in a town on the way back to St. Louis. After going to St. Louis, he will go to Dorsey, Ill.—round trip only $1.68. Here is what Mrs. N. C. Skinner of Dorsey writes: "I am glad I wrote for Charlie to come to Dorsey. One who used to preach for us while my father lived, saw my name in the Av. S. notes, and wrote me a beautiful letter. I hadn't heard from him directly in twenty years—J. B. Corwine. Three of my neighbors say they will take Charlie a week, so if you wish, that

will make a month for him here." Isn't that splendid? So he will get his whole summer's outing, after all. While writing this (and being interrupted by company) Charlie went to the postoffice. And what do you think he got? Try to guess! But you *never* could! I wish you could see it! The prettiest little gold locket you ever saw with a blue ribbon through the gold ring, and the face of the locket adorned with an opal, an amethyst and two diamonds. The locket opens, of course, and within is a place for Charlie's picture. On the back of the locket is engraved the word "Felix." No letter came with this locket, but this was written on a sheet of paper: "For Bessie, from Charlie and Felix." You understand? The locket is given to Charlie that he may give it to his sister. Don't you know that that makes Charlie happier than if it were something for *himself?* When will people learn that happiness comes by giving it away? The reason the sun is bright is because it is giving away all its light all the time. Well, it looks like something sweet is always happening in this world. But that doesn't surprise us; isn't it God's world? Now about our ice cream social of August. Can't you give a little social of some kind where you live, and send the proceeds for Charlie's education, and all have their socials on or about August 3, or some other time? I have an idea, partly due to a letter just at hand from Mrs. Carrie P. Johnston, Stewartsville, Mo. I am going to write an invitation in poetry. Please cut it out of this page, and give it to a friend; and consider that you, in reading it, are specially mentioned:

> You're invited by this poetic word
> To our Icecream Social, Aug. 3rd.
> TEN CENTS or more be your donation
> To ORPHAN CHARLIE'S EDUCATION.
> The icecream will not chill your blood,
> It's not expressed but understood.
> Come (in the spirit) shine or rain,
> But send your money by the train.
> You nothing get, save by love's law.
> At BENTONVILLE, in ARK.

❦ ❦

Lake Geneva Summer Train Service.

Via the Chicago & North-Western R'y is now in effect including Saturday afternoon train leaving Chicago 1:00 p. m. and Sunday Train leaving 8:00 a. m. For tickets, rates and full information apply to your nearest ticket agent or address W. B. Kniskern, P. T. M., C. & N. W. R'y Co., Chicago.

ristian Publishing Company

2712 Pine St., St. Louis, Mo.

. GARRISON,	-	-	-	-	President
V. DOWLING,	-	-	-	Vice-President
L. SNIVELY.	-	-	Sec. and Gen. Supt
. CROW.	-	-	Treas. and Bus. Manager

/. W. Dowling's Sunday-school supplies
so growing in popularity that notwith-
ⱨding the first edition for the present
ⱨter was made very large, we were soon
ⱨpelled to issue the second. Samples of
e best supplies sent free on application.

he new church Hymnal "Gloria in Ex-
is," is *par excellence* the hymn book
ⱨe Christian church. It has no equal
it will be a long time before it has its
ⱨrior. The church, choir, and preacher
: are delighted with it. J. H. McNeil
nister) Kokomo, Ind.

ⱨarold Bell Wright of Lebanon, Mo.,
er the direction of his official board, has
ed the CHRISTIAN-EVANGELIST in every
ⱨe represented in his congregation. This

arrangement in combination with such a
minister as Bro. Wright, insures a glorious
future for that fruitful church.

We certainly are taking our preachers
and other readers into partnership and on
most liberal terms in submitting to them
the price list of our summer book bargains
found in last week's issue and to reappear
in the next. These are not defective
copies or unsalable books, but are taken
from our selected stock for the purpose of
rewarding our patrons for their faithfulness and to prevent that "summer slump"
that is the dread of so many publishing
houses. Our helpers are employed and we
purpose keeping them busy.

The accompanying picture is but one of
many beautiful scenic features that will
make delightful the trip to the Buffalo convention in October with the CHRISTIAN-
EVANGELIST special over the Wabash. This
will be the most interesting convention since
the Jubilee in 1900. Every Disciple who
possibly can, should attend. Write us for
particulars. Those wishing to earn transportation by selling the various publications

of this
perinte

The
sufferiⱨ
cess is
neighⱨ
note sⱨ
last wⱨ
son, K
bion, 1
Lansdⱨ
Taylor
ister;
tor; D
tor; Sⱨ
ister;
Wrighⱨ

The Ⱨ
pages,

Drake University College of the Bi[ble]

HILL McCLELLAND BELL, A. M., LL. D., President of the University

LOCATED AT DES MOINES, THE CAPITAL CITY OF THE STATE OF IOWA

===FALL TERM OPENS SEPTEMBER 17, 1906.===

THE FACULTY

ALFRED MARTIN HAGGARD Graduate of Oskaloosa College, 1879, A. M., 1889. Took graduate work in Harvard University, 1900. In. pulpit and pastoral work since 1876. President Oskaloosa College, 1889-92. Secretary Iowa Christian Convention, 1893-98. Dean of Bible College of Drake University, 1899—.

DAVID ROBERTS DUNGAN Student Kentucky University, 1865-6. Graduate Drake University, 1884. LL. D. University of Nebraska, 1891. Minister Christian Church since 1861. Six years missionary in Nebraska. Dean of Bible College, Drake University, 1882-1890. President Cotner University, 1890-96. Professor of Church History in Drake University, 1905—. Author of "On the Rock," "Modern Phases of Skepticism," and numerous other books.

AMBROSE DUDLEY VEATCH Minister since 1895. A. B., Christian University. B. D., Drake University, 1901. A. M., Drake University, 1904. Graduate student Chicago University, 1904-5. Instructor in Bible College, Drake University, 1900-1904. Professor Semitic Languages and Literature Drake University, 1906.

FREDERICK OWEN NORTON Student in Prince College and the Normal School, Prince Edward Island, for two years. Taught public schools of P. E. Island for four years. Graduated course from Kentucky University with highest honors in 18 the Classical Course of the College of the Bible, Lexingt 1895, with highest honors, delivering the valedictory of th both instances. A. M., Kentucky University, 1895. Associat of Western College, Missouri, for three years, and princip year. Professor of Latin and Regent of Christian Univers Graduate student in the University of Chicago, 1900-02. In classics in the South Side Academy of the University p 1902-3. Fellow in Biblical Greek in the University of Chic Professor of Biblical Greek in Drake University, 1906—.

Others doing special work in the Bible College of Drake are Prof. Sherman Kirk, Prof. Frank Brown, H. O. Breed S. Medbury, J. M. Williams, I. N. McCash, J. D. Bryan an Garst. No Bible College in the brotherhood has a larger or ulty of instructors.

UNIVERSITY ADVANTAGES

Drake University, with its many colleges and special schools, affords rare privileges of varied courses of study to the Bible student. The Bible College courses present almost every branch of Biblical learning that Christian workers need, such as Exegesis, History of Missions, Hermeneutics. Old Testament History, New Testament History, and the like. The College of Liberal Arts is one of the strongest in the country. The Normal School and Academy are available to students of this school without extra charge for tuition, and offer the usual branches of preparatory work. The College of Music affords as fine musical training as can be found any place in the West, and this is supplemented by special instruction in church music. The Business College offers Stenography and Typewriting, or any other branch of business training that might seem desirable to pastors' students.

The many churches of Des Moines illustrate every phase of religious activity, and afford opportunities for practical work of every kind. A large number of charitable institutions, missions, rescue stations, social settlements and other enterprises of a similar character are located in and around Des Moines, and are accessible for the instruction of students in the Bible College.

SCOPE OF INSTRUCTION

By a combination of studies which have been taught in the University, and the addition of various courses directly suited to workers of every kind in the church, and especially in the cities and on mission fields, opportunities for special training are offered to the following classes of workers: (1) Preachers' wives, assistant ministers and others, whether men or women, who wish to be efficient promoters of local church work; (2) Christian women who wish to prepare for acceptable service in the churches as pastoral clerks and amanuenses; (3) Preachers who desire special practical training, sermonic, pastoral, or any other kind not leading to thorough theological scholarship; (4) Evangelistic singers, church choristers, sacred soloists, and church organists; (5) Teachers of Sunday schools, leaders of Endeavor societies, secretaries of Young Men's and Young Women's Christian Associations, and organizers of religious societies of any kind.

The growth of this Bible College has been rapid from the first. Th[e] sons for this.

More than 500 ministers and missionaries in the field received their Bible College of Drake University.

MEMORIAL HALL

Memorial Hall, especially constructed for the Bible Colleg Drake University, is in every way admirably arranged and equ This splendid structure contains twelve large recitation rooms, a sembly room, a well equipped dining room and kitchen, and num offices and cloak rooms.

Students are assisted in various ways:

1. Scholarships of the value of $50.00 each have been provided for a number of students.
2. A scholarship established for the benefit of young women preparing for the mission field has been provided.
3. The Phillips and other loan funds make it possible for worthy students to borrow the funds necessary to pay a part of their school expenses, the same to be returned after the student has completed his course and has a chance to earn enough to reimburse the loan fund.
4. Opportunities for young men to preach for churches near Des Moines are abundant and remunerative. Many earn their entire school expense in this way.
5. Those not yet prepared to preach find many opportunities to work and earn all, or a portion of their expense while in school.

Some things you will find out if you attend the Bible Colle[ge]

1. Scholarly, broad-minded men on the faculty who have Christ for creed.
2. A corps of instructors that know how to develop true men into su preachers of the Word.
3. Thorough, practical courses of study arranged to help men to the a ment of the fundamentals of religious truth.
4. An excellent library of books specially selected for the use of mi students.
5. Memorial Hall, the home of the Bible College, the best building campus of the University.
6. A splendidly equipped Bible College that challenges the admiration cures the patronage of a great Brotherhood in this and other lands.
7. One of the most self-respecting, aggressive bands of students ever in any Bible College.
8. An institution whose graduates are filling many of the most import pits in this country, and whose trained missionaries may be found i foreign field.
9. That the Bible College is but one of several prosperous colleges th stitute Drake University, viz: Liberal Arts, Bible, Law, Medical, Music, and Normal.
10. A Bible College that has sent a representative to the mission field fo year of its history.

The expenses are low—so low that no ambitious young man or woman should find it impossible to attend school here. Th tunities offered in Des Moines for students to work for a portion of their expenses are numerous and remunerative. Fully one-h a portion of their expenses while attending the University.

Drake University always has been and still is a school pre-eminently for the poor man or woman who is willing to work for an ed[ucation]

We are anxious to correspond with every young man and woman in the Church of Christ. that desires to prepare for the or the mission field. It will be a great accommodation to us and to this paper if, when writing you will state that you read this a ment in The Christian-Evangelist. We gladly answer correspondence and willingly send announcements of any of the various col the University. Let us send to you our complete Bible College Announcement.

Address all Letters to DRAKE UNIVERSITY, Des Moines, I[owa]

THE
CHRISTIAN-
EVANGELIST

A WEEKLY RELIGIOUS NEWSPAPER.

| Volume XLIII. | No. 31. |

ST. LOUIS, AUGUST 2, 1906.

The fields are white now, but the night cometh.

Harvest Time

The Christian-Evangelist.

J. H. GARRISON, Editor

PAUL MOORE, Assistant Editor

F. D. POWER,
B. B. TYLER, } Staff Correspondents.
W. DURBAN,

Subscription Price, $1.50 a Year.

For foreign countries add $1.54 for postage.

Remittances should be made by money order, draft, or registered letter; not by local cheque, unless 15 cents is added to cover cost of collection.

In Ordering Change of Post Office give both old and new address.

Matter for Publication should be addressed to THE CHRISTIAN-EVANGELIST. Subscriptions and remittances should be addressed to the Christian Publishing Company, 2712 Pine Street, St. Louis. Mo.

Unused Manuscripts will be returned only if accompanied by stamps.

News Items, evangelistic and other also, are solicited, and should be sent on a Post card, if possible.

Published by the Christian Publishing Company, 2712 Pine Street, St. Louis, Mo.

Entered at St. Louis P. O. as Second Class Matter

WHAT WE STAND FOR.

For the Christ of Galilee,
For the truth which makes men free,
For the bond of unity
Which makes God's children one.

For the love which shines in deeds,
For the life which this world needs,
For the church whose triumph speeds
The prayer: "Thy will be done."

For the right against the wrong,
For the weak against the strong,
For the poor who've waited long
For the brighter age to be.

For the faith against tradition,
For the truth 'gainst superstition,
For the hope whose glad fruition
Our waiting eyes shall see.

For the city God is rearing,
For the New Earth now appearing,
For the heaven above us clearing,
And the song of victory.

J. H. Garrison.

CONTENTS.

Centennial Propaganda 967
Current Events 968
Editorial—
  Congregationalists or Individualists—Which? 969
  Temples of God 969
  Notes and Comments............. 970
  Current Religious Thought....... 970
  Editor's Easy Chair............. 971
Contributed Articles—
  Some of My Likings. William Durban 972
  As Seen from the Dome. F. D. Power 973
  What the Brethren are Saying and Doing. B. B. Tyler 974
  Modern Religious Persecution—A Defense. B. L. Chase........ 975
  An India Convention. Adelaide Gail Frost 975
Our Budget 977
News From Many Fields............. 982
The Present Status of the Union Question and Our Attitude Toward It. E. S. Muckley................. 985
Marriages and Obituaries 986
Evangelistic 987
Midweek Prayer-meeting 988
Sunday-school 988
Christian Endeavor 989
People's Forum 990
Current Literature 990
The Home Department 993

THE
CHRISTIAN-EVAN(

"IN FAITH, UNITY; IN OPINION AND METHODS, LIBERTY, IN ALL"

XLIII.   August 2, 1906

809 CENTENNIAL PROPAGANI
CHURCHES OF CHR

: : : GEO. L. SNIVELY : : :

Looking Toward Pittsburg.

L. Powell's article, following, is a
il contribution to the great Cen-
if propaganda. It is commended to
onsideration of those delegates to
uffalo convention who will attend
isiness sessions and help determine
olicy of the churches toward the
urg celebration. Admiring the pa-
s we do, we yet feel constrained to
"amplius" over the face of it. Ful-
either of his suggestions would
been a creditable achievement for us
ears ago but now if our hearts were
lame with love for God and man
vith zeal for the dissemination of
recious truth heaven has commit-
) us for the use of the world, we
f build the memorial in Chicago,
n or New York, fittingly endow old
ny, and after placing these gifts on
ltar, have remaining sufficient re-
es and vitality to write the names
)oo,ooo Disciples on the rosters of
hes of Christ before 1909. All
ness should cease after our next
ntion or we shall not accomplish
ach as one memorial church or en-
ient. Space will be given in this
tment or People's Forum for the
ssion of Brother Powell's sugges-
We urge earnest attention to these
ibutions and trust that they will
our leaders to definiteness of pur-
and ultimately to achievements that
make our Centennial a great bless-
o all mankind.

New Education Society; Its Plans
and Aims.

education than has heretofore been manifested among our people.

In order to meet the demands of present
necessities, the membership fee has been
placed at $2.00 a year, and it is hoped a
large number of friends of this movement
will send contributions at once to Pres. R.
E. Hieronymous of Eureka, the secretary-
treasurer of the new organization.

Our colleges and all our educational institutions must join in a united effort to
make our centennial celebration a worthy
one. To educate our ministry, and to educate our young people for active Christian
service whether they are ministers or not,
is the object of our colleges. If there have
been failures in the past, it has been largely due to the fact that our people have refused to properly equip our educational institutions. If there are to be large results
in the future of any of the great movements of the church, it will be due chiefly
to the fact that our people have realized
the needs of our colleges and have supplied
them.

Hiram, O.

Centennial Aims.

BY E. L. POWELL.

In thinking of a proper observance of
our Centennial as a religious movement,
I am persuaded that to concentrate on
some one definite enterprise and to
achieve it will be far more significant
than to attempt a dozen or a hundred
things—none of which will be conspicuous or commanding, and few of which
will be brought to a successful consummation. Is there not some one thing
upon which we can unite our brotherhood and which shall be possible of ac-

cities
equip
ple r
effec
the t
In a
the
grou
icate
Chris
locat
these
nial
woul
for t
have
of a
nobl
York
whil
pend
as tl
sion
atter
effor
lege
let t
men
such
start
caus
whil
ing
othe
not
to s
one
stan
we l
cogt

Current Events

The Czar's ukase dissolving the Russian parliament marks the culmination of a constant and in-

The Fall of the Douma.

creasing friction between this new legislative body and the old bureaucracy and autocracy which is still spoken of as "the government." The Douma precipitated the crisis by issuing an address to the country on the agrarian question, which the government forbade the newspapers to publish, and passing a resolution of lack of confidence in the ministry and calling for its resignation. The Czar, in his edict, expresses the high hopes which he had at the convocation of the Douma and his disappointment at its performance. "The representatives of the nation, instead of applying themselves to the work of productive legislation, strayed into a field beyond their competence, and have been making comments on the imperfections of the fundamental laws, which can only be modified by our imperial will." The autocratic idea is still too strong to permit comments on its imperfections. The Czar will find that the dissolution of parliament is easier than the solution of the problems now confronting him. Many members of the Douma fled across the border to Viborg, Finland, where they held a session and adopted a protest against the dissolution. This assembly was broken up by a threat of force. The Czar asserts that the acts of the Douma had encouraged disorder throughout the country. This may be true, but its adjournment under these circumstances is a much greater incentive to revolutionary uprisings. Only severe repressive measures can maintain a superficial appearance of internal quiet. St. Petersburg is under martial law and almost anything can be expected. Another election will be held and the new Douma will meet on March 5, 1907.

There have been few careers of stranger contrasts than that of Lady Curzon who died last week at her home in England. The daughter of a Chicago merchant, Levi Leiter, she married a young English nobleman of small fortune who later became Viceroy of India. To live in more than regal magnificence as virtually the empress over three hundred million orientals, does not usually fall within the experience of a Chicago tradesman's daughter.

The death of Russell Sage at the age of ninety years is something of a surprise. It did not seem likely

Russell Sage.

that he would ever die—at least not so long as there was anyone left who wanted to borrow money at good interest on gilt-edged security. As an apostle of thrift and economy, Mr. Sage has perhaps never had an equal. He came very near to putting into practice the familiar directions for getting rich: "Work hard, make all the money you can and never spend a cent." In early life he was interested in politics and served two terms in Congress. Later all other interests were swallowed up in the joy of making money. Perhaps it was habit as much as greed which kept him at it to

his ninetieth year, for he was a very methodical man. He early developed the habits of making much, spending little and giving none, and to these habits he adhered as rigidly as any clerk adheres to the habits which necessity forces upon him. He collected money as others collect rare postage stamps, or Chinese pottery, or Egyptian scarabs—because the collecting gave him pleasure and because he had nothing else to do.

The railroads charge shippers a dollar a day demurrage for every car that is not loaded or unloaded within 48 hours after its delivery. Why should not the railroads pay an equal sum for delay in furnishing cars? Certain Indiana manufacturers are arguing before the state railroad commission for the adoption of such a rule.

Japan is contemplating the nationalization of all her industries, according to a report received by

Japan's Experiment.

the Bureau of Manufactures. This means the biggest experiment in government ownership that has ever been attempted. The first step will be the taking over of the railroads. This in itself is no novelty. Several European governments operate part or all of their railroads and they are not in all cases the most progressive countries which do so. Russia, for example, has government railroads. But Japan's experiment will be much farther reaching and will be conducted under circumstances which will give it great value either as an example or as a warning to the rest of the world. The scheme, if it succeeds, will be an approach to a working socialism. But it does not follow that the result will be that at which the socialists aim. It may be the very opposite. If the government controls the industries, and a small clique controls the government, the last state will be worse than the first.

A brilliant and highly educated physician in Colorado, who for nine years has made a deep study of criminology, has been convicted of forgery. He says that he is a "natural criminal" and that for men so constituted crime is a constitutional necessity. In so far as this theory of crime is true, perhaps it is only a re-statement of the very old doctrine that the "natural man" needs reinforcement and regeneration from a higher source to conquer his downward tendencies.

Pennsylvania has chosen a queer group of men to immortalize on the bronze doors of the new state cap-

The Truly Great.

itol. There are, among others, the features of Quay, Penrose, Pennypacker, Durham and Senator Clark of Montana—all in imperishable bronze to represent the ideals of Pennsylvania statesmanship and citizenship. Benjamin Franklin may think himself lucky not to have been included in this assembly of notables. William Penn would seem, to the average mind, to have had some claim to a place, but he would doubtless gladly waive it, considering the company. And there are those (not members of the late Pennsylvania capitol commission, of course), who might have chosen Robert Morris as a more suitable example

Congregationalists or Individualists—Which?

Following up some of the thoughts in our last week's editorial we raise the above inquiry. We have reached a stage in the development of our organic life as a religious movement when this question seems to us very pertinent. We have been accustomed to say of our form of church government that we are congregationalists; that is, we believe in and practice the autonomy and independence of the local church which is the real unit in the associational life of the Church as a whole. The Baptists, the Congregationalists, and the Disciples of Christ, or Christian churches, are the best representatives of this form of government. The theory of congregationalism does not exclude the fellowship and co-operation of sister churches in the furtherance of common interests.

Let us suppose two local congregations holding essentially the same faith, doctrines and worship. Each is adequate to the carrying on of its own life and work; but a neighboring city has no church and needs one. Neither of the two churches, alone, is able to undertake this enterprise, but jointly they agree to establish a church at this point. The churches still remain free and autonomous as relates to their own local work, but in this common work they co-operate, and each has its voice in the management. Of course, when the number of churches co-operating becomes great, a wise economy requires that certain persons representing all the churches be designated to collect and disburse the funds and have direct supervision of the mission work. This, in a nutshell, is the theory and method of missionary organization.

This has been the theory rather than the practice among the Disciples of Christ in their missionary work. In practice the individual rather than the congregation has become the unit in our organized missionary work. This came about in a natural way. At first there were many congregations opposed to co-operative missionary work through missionary organizations. Local churches, as such, therefore, did not enter into this kind of co-operation, but individual members exercised their right in so doing. This made it necessary in the beginning to establish what was known as life memberships and life directorships, in which individual Christians entered into co-operation for the spread of the Gospel. While this feature of the work has well nigh dropped out of sight, and local churches with their Sunday-schools, are contributing very largely the funds for missionary work, the theory of individual representation in conventions yet prevails, and the local church is practically lost sight of, so far as having a voice through our conventions in the management and policy of our missionary work. We do not hear anything more now about delegates from the churches, or from state conventions

which are supposed to represent groups of churches, but our national conventions, as well as our state conventions, are simply mass meetings of individual members.

While this was probably inevitable under the conditions which prevailed in the past, and while great good has been accomplished in the development of the missionary spirit and in the unification of our membership throughout the country by these mass meetings, has not the time come when our conventions, both state and national, should be based on the idea of representatives from the congregations or local churches? In other words, if we believe in the free, democratic management of the affairs of the church by the churches themselves, instead of by a hierarchy, or by editors or secretaries, ought we not to establish representative conventions which shall voice the sentiment of the brotherhood on the great moral and religious movements of the times? If it be objected that this might lead to an oppressive form of ecclesiasticism, our reply is, that it would be a strange phenomenon in religious history if the local churches, acting through their own chosen representatives, should bind upon themselves a galling and oppressive yoke of tyranny! We may trust the churches to take care of their freedom when they have a voice in the councils of the brotherhood.

If, then, the congregational idea rather than the individualistic idea, is the ideal we have set before us, we ought at once to set about realizing it through a representative gathering in which the local churches are fairly represented. There are great questions, and they are constantly growing greater with our growth—relating to policies and measures in connection with our missionary, educational and benevolent work, and our relation to other Christian bodies, which are seeking the same great ends that we are seeking to accomplish, which require the deliberation and considerate action of a great representative body made up of chosen delegates, acting under parliamentary rules and under the higher motive of Christian love and fellowship. We owe it to ourselves, and to the great cause we represent, to establish as speedily as possible, such a representative body for the transaction of the Master's business, in connection with the on-going of his kingdom.

This, as we have said, has been our theory from the beginning. It is incorporated in the constitution and by-laws which are supposed to govern the convention of the American Christian Missionary Society, but which, as a matter of fact, have, in this respect, become a dead letter. No constitutional changes would be required to realize the kind of convention we are pleading for. It simply requires carrying out, in an orderly and systematic way, the provision of the constitution relating to representation, as it now exists. We can no longer

plead youthfulness, immaturity, and inexperience as excuses for the unmethodical way in which we have been carrying on the Lord's business. We are old enough, large enough, experienced enough, and have wisdom enough, we are sure, to have respect to the apostolic admonition, "Let all things be done decently and in order." Nothing would be more timely, just now, than a circular letter from our Home Mission Board to the various state boards, calling attention to this provision of the constitution, and urging compliance therewith in the selection of delegates to the Buffalo convention, either through the state conventions, or by the boards themselves in cases where the conventions have been held and no such action taken. If it shall be found that any modifications are demanded by changed conditions, let such modifications be made as early as possible. We trust our Home Board will take the initiative in bringing about this needed reform.

❋ ❋

Temples of God.

Every people in every age and in every land have had their sacred places dedicated to the worship of the Supreme Being. That of the Jews at Jerusalem was, perhaps, the most splendid and certainly the most celebrated of all the temples where God's presence was supposed to dwell. But God dwells not in temples made with hands. Even the heaven of heavens can not contain him. He dwells in the humble and contrite heart, forgiven and purified from sin.

In his letter to the church at Corinth the Apostle Paul says: "Know ye not that ye are the temple of God and that the Spirit of God dwelleth in you?" Here the local church is designated as a temple of God. The church was acting, in some respects, as if it were ignorant of this fact. The divisions that were growing up in it were the outgrowth of carnality, and not of the Holy Spirit. The thought of the apostle evidently is, that, as the temple in Jerusalem was the seat and center of the invisible manifestation of God, so each local church, as well as each individual member, is a place where God's presence is to be so manifested that the world may know that God is present with his people molding their character, shaping their policies, and controlling their lives.

Does the average local church realize its responsibility in making manifest the presence of God to the community in which it exists? Does it not need some one to remind it, as Paul did the Corinthians, that it is a temple of God indwelt by the Spirit of God, and that if any man defile the temple of God him will God destroy? Local churches are greatly concerned about their buildings, their location, their material equipment, and these are by no means unimportant, but they are subordinate to the chief thing, which is the manifestation of the life of God in the community. The world is judging the church to-day not by the kind of houses it worships in, nor by the music it furnishes, nor yet by its creed or ritual, but by the kind of character it produces in its members and by its collective life and influence in the community.

Is it asked how the local church may show that it is a temple of God? The answer is very plain. God is holy, and his temple must be holy. The church that would manifest God's presence must put away all evil practices, all selfish and sectarian aims and ambitions, and seek only the glory of God and the good of men. The life of Jesus Christ which is the supreme manifestation of God in history, must be manifest in the lives of such a church. All worldliness of spirit, sordidness of aim, and covetousness, which is idolatry, must be put away by the church that would be a temple of God—a fit dwelling place for the Holy Spirit.

Again the local church that would be a temple of God must be a united church. It was the spirit of strife and division in the Corinthian church that caused Paul to remind it that such a course was inconsistent with the very purpose of the church which was to be a temple of God. The people instinctively know that a church marked by strife and contention is not a temple of God. Such a course grieves away the Spirit of God. A united church whose members love each other and bear each other's burdens, which is united in its councils, working together harmoniously gives a strong evidence that it is indeed a temple of God. Not only will a church in which God's Spirit dwells be united among its own members, but it will be ready to co-operate in every good work with every church seeking to accomplish the same end.

Another way in which the local church may show that God dwells in it by his Spirit and that it is, therefore, a temple of God is that it is doing the work of God in the community and in the world. Such a church puts itself into harmony with the great purposes of God in the evangelization of the world and in ministering to the manifold needs of man. No church that is satisfied with caring for its own local interests and that has no care for the great world lying in sin and ignorance, can justly claim to be a temple of God. Christ's vision was world-wide and the church in which his Spirit dwells will see the world's needs through his eyes and feel its suffering with his heart.

The only true and worthy aim of the local church to make itself worthy to be a temple of God, the dwelling place of his Spirit, and a center of holy influence and religious activity which have for their aim and end the redemption of the world. No church, perhaps, can attain to that ideal in a perfect degree; all can approximate it. Paul, writing to the Ephesians, said: "In whom each several building fitly framed together groweth unto a holy temple in the Lord; in whom ye also are builded together for a habitation of God in the Spirit." It is only by growth in the direction indicated that "each several building," or each local church, can become, in the full sense, "a habitation of God in the Spirit."

Notes and Comments.

Our Baptist brethren know a good thing, when vouched for by this paper, and we are glad to see them recommend it to the brotherhood.

The Disciples are discussing having a department of evangelism in each of their denominational colleges. A Mr. Wm. J. Wright, their national superintendent of evangelism, closes an able article on "Our Colleges and Evangelism" in The Christian-Evangelist, with these words: "Let this be the program in our colleges; make our young preachers evangelistic. Our national board of evangelism, in order to bring this to pass, extends herein to all our colleges a helping hand. The evangelistic institutes and schools of evangelism which we conduct will give your students new ideas of the ministry, and will influence their preaching for many years." We are sure the home board at Atlanta could use our seminary money and well for evangelistic work even as does our Nashville board for Sunday-school work.—*Baptist Argus.*

In another place will be found an address by Bro. E. S. Muckley of Portland, Oregon, delivered before the State Ministerial association at the Oregon State convention at Turner, June 22d, on "The present status of the union question and our attitude toward it." Our readers will not fail to see its harmony with the position advocated by the Christian-Evangelist. It is gratifying that the convention in Oregon requested, by unanimous vote, the publication of this address. We pointed out, recently, what we thought was an illogical inference in a resolution which they passed, but their endorsement of this address shows that their heads and hearts are pointing in the right direction. Referring to the subject of federation, the address says: "I say federate, if we can secure a basis of federation that will not morally bind us to stay out of any community where we feel we ought to preach the gospel." So far as heard from not a man among us favors any other kind of federation. The phrase "as far as possible," in the proposed basis, is intended to cover exactly that point. It ought to be self-evident that no method of co-operation is practicable, to-day, that does not allow that liberty. When the time comes, as we believe it will come, when the gospel will be preached and practiced substantially alike—that is, in all its fundamental doctrines and ordinances—then we may talk about a division of territory, but the best that can be done at present is that this question of overlapping and unnecessary multiplication of churches be made the subject of fraternal conference, leaving the ultimate decision to each co-operating body as to what action it shall take. We have not believed, and do not believe yet, that there is any serious disagreement among the Disciples of Christ on this subject, if we could ever get a fair statement of what we mean by federation before the brethren. We bespeak a careful reading of Brother Muckley's address.

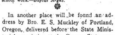

Current Religious Thought.

The following from the "Interior" may not ring just orthodox according to Calvinistic standards, but its truthfulness is very apparent:

"There is enough wickedness in every man to make a demon out of him, if Satan can get the job. There is a possibility in every man of making a saint out of him, if he puts himself in the hands of Christ. We are transformed into the image of the one we serve. It is not so much a question what faculties we possess as it is what we are going to make out of them. It is not so much a question where we are as the direction we are traveling."

In the following extract from an address delivered by Pres. E. Y. Mullins of the Southern Baptist Theological Seminary at Louisville before the Baptist Educational Society of Kentucky, recently, we find some things which we think will be of interest and of profit to our readers. Baptists and Disciples are not only alike in many of their strong points but, also, in many of their weaknesses, as the following extract will indicate:

In Kentucky one of our chief denominational difficulties is, as is so often the case, the exaggeration and abuse of a good thing. It is abnormal doctrinal sensitiveness. The skin of the human body ought to be sensitive up to a certain point. Nature so intended it. But when diseased and inflamed, it may become so sensitive that the slighting of a fly upon it will cause excruciating agony. It becomes abnormally sensitive. It is diseased.

Now I yield to none in my advocacy of sound doctrine, but I am very certain that it is possible for abnormal sensitiveness on the subject to defeat its own ends and open the door to all kinds of heresies. I am ready to prove this from history if necessary.

A does not agree with B on the doctrine of the universal church. This means conversely that B does not agree with A. C does not agree with D on alien immersion, i. e., D does not agree with C. One brother thinks he can trace a succession of Baptist churches back to the apostles; another finds that he can not so trace it. One brother opposes inviting any other than a Baptist into a Baptist pulpit or to the platform of a Baptist school; another does not oppose. Kentucky was once riven on the subject of a strange proceeding, a question of ordination, and missions were sidetracked for a year or two. At another time we had a long controversy over a plan for raising money, and from time to time one or another of the above subjects has been the storm center. Then we have had controversies between Board-ites and Anti-boardites, as if any man could coerce any Baptist to work through a board if he chooses not to, or on the contrary as if any Baptist could prevent any other from working with boards if he sees fit. So of healing without medicine and by faith alone. And lastly came 1841 and the deluge.

Now what I maintain is that all these are questions upon which Baptists differ and will continue to differ doubtless for some time to come. They are questions, moreover, on which they have a right to differ so long as they understand the Scriptures differently on these subjects.

I am not here expressing any opinion regarding any of the above issues. If I were to do so I would be doing the very thing which I think here and now is uncalled for. What I maintain is that there is room within the limits of Baptist orthodoxy for much difference of opinion on subordinate matters. I maintain that I have no right to refuse to call a Baptist my brother merely because he does not happen to be a twin brother, and I also maintain that another Baptist has no right to refuse to call me brother and nag and torment me because I am not his twin. I can love him and co-operate with him and do all I can to advance the kingdom with him, provided only he will let me.

Editor's Easy Chair.

PENTWATER MUSINGS.

We have come again to the most august month of the year. August with her golden days and her calm, clear, starlit nights, sits queenlike on her summer throne, while around her lie in abundance the harvests of sun and soil. It is high noon of the summer season, and one begins to look wistfully back over the summer that is rapidly going, and hopefully forward to the autumn that is coming. How swiftly the summers fly away into the irrevocable past! And what a golden chain of memories they make connecting the past with the present!

"Far away where the summers are sleeping
Lie the beautiful dreams of the past."

True, but, thank God, the present has its dreams too, and they are no less beautiful than those of the summers of the long ago. But they are different. The lights and shadows blend differently from what they did in the earlier dreams, and the scene of their realization lies farther on. But, after all, it is not a question of how rapidly the summers go and the seasons revolve, as it is of what we are doing with life and what we are making out of it. The poet is right:

"We live in deeds, not years; in thoughts, not
'breath;
In feelings, not in figures on the dial.
We should count time by heart-throbs when they
beat
For God, for man, for duty. He most lives,
Who thinks most, feels the noblest, acts the best.
Life is but a means unto an end—that end,
Beginning, mean, and end to all things, God."

❧

To-day thick clouds mantle the sky and cast a somber shadow over land and lake. The trees stand in solemn stillness, as if they were holding out their leaves for the expected rain. Such days have a beauty and charm of their own. It is not good to always have the glare of the bright sunshine. There is a quietness in the woods, in these still, quiet days, and the very trees seem to be at worship. Nature is in a reverent mood, and the lover of nature soon enters into sympathy with this spirit. Part of the beauty of such a day, it is true, comes from the fact that it is not continuous. As we gaze yonder into the gray sky we know that beyond the clouds the sun is shining, and that very soon it will drive the mists away or send them down in refreshing showers, and the earth will once more bask in his radiance. There are some souls whose lives are always cloud-shadowed. This is not normal nor healthy. Better sing with James Whitcomb Riley:

"O, heart of mine, we shouldn't
Worry so.
What we've missed of calm we couldn't
Have, you know!
What we've met of stormy pain
And of sorrow's driving rain,
We can better meet again
If it blow.

For we know, not every morrow
Can be sad;
So, forgetting all the sorrow
We have had,
Let us fold away our fears,
And put by our foolish tears,
And through all the coming years
. . . Just be glad."

❧

It is difficult to convey an accurate mental picture of this place to one who has not been here and who is unacquainted with the peculiar formation of land along the east shore of Lake Michigan. During the past centuries and millenniums the wind and the waves have thrown up vast bulwarks of sand to mark the eastern boundaries of the lake saying to this great, unsalted sea:

"Thus far shalt thou come and no farther,
And here shall thy proud waves be stayed."

The soul, however, that can "just be glad" all the days must send its roots down into deeper sources of happiness than earthly sunshine or shadow or any material condition of life. On the stormiest day that blows when great waves are rolling over the surface of the lake there is down beneath the tumult of waves a deep calm, undisturbed by the storm that rages above it. So, down in the depths of the human heart, there should lie evermore a calm, untroubled peace, undisturbed by the changing fortunes of this mortal life. This is what faith can do for us, when it is triumphant over doubts and fears.

❧

We are receiving many inquiries from friends in different sections of the country about this park, and they are coming from a class of people that we would like to see here. They ask, among other questions, if it is our purpose to maintain the present quiet and restful character of the place, or whether there is danger of it becoming the scene of popular excursions and crowds of pleasure-seekers. There is no danger whatever from these latter disturbances, as our location insures us freedom from such crowds. There is plenty of room here, however, for a summer colony of several hundred people who without crowding each other in the least, may form a congenial society and yet maintain all the exclusion and quietness needful for complete rest. We are asked, again, if we have native woods here. That is exactly what we do have, and in great variety. The window from which we look, as we write these lines, presents a view of a primeval forest. There are enough of the larger and older trees to give dignity to the scene, while the large majority are the younger growth whose best days are yet to come. These woods if cared for will be much finer a quarter of a century hence than they are to-day. Some writers have the idea that we are living a sort of hermit life here, far removed from the haunts of civilization! This is because we have spoken of "The Pioneer," as the only cottage in "Garrison Park." But "Garrison Park" is joined hard by on the north with Oceana Beach, a settlement of choice people who are seeking there exactly what we are seeking here, and their club house is connected with "The Pioneer" cottage by a plank walk running along the hillside, five minutes distant, and this again joins onto Pentwater village with a little lake intervening, only a few minutes distant. So we are not out of touch with our fellow men. We can live all day in the woods alone, if we wish to, or we can meet our friends at the club house for a social time when we desire to do that. At the present time the club house is well nigh filled with St. Louis people.

On these sand dunes thus reared by the forces of nature have been sown the seeds of a great variety of trees and these grow luxuriantly and have cast their foliage on the sand through so many generations that a surface soil has been formed in many places concealing the sand. Down through this range of sand hills, thus forest-mantled, run winding ravines, some of which come through to the lake, but more of them have been obstructed at the mouth by these sand-dunes and have no outlet to the lake. This is the formation at Pentwater, along the beach at "Garrison Park." On the summit of these hills commanding wide ranges of the lake or along the edges of the ravines, or on smaller ridges farther back with glimpses of the lake through the trees, cottages are built and more are to be built, forming ideal summer homes for those who would escape the heat and noise of the cities for the coolness and quiet of the woods and the lake. In a level space between two of these higher sand dunes with a lofty ridge in the rear, and a grove of hemlocks in front of it between it and the lake the "Pioneer" cottage is located, with woods to the right of it, woods to the left of it, woods to the rear of it, and the lake in front of it—another "Edgewood-on-the-Lake," but with more elbow room. We shall present our readers a picture of it soon which will give them a better idea than any verbal description we can give.

❧

Our readers have, no doubt, been much interested as we have been, in watching the outcome of the meeting held in Park Theater, Manchester, New Hampshire, by our Brother Herbert Yeuell. Whatever may be the immediate outcome of that meeting, we predict that it is the forerunner of a church not only in Manchester but in many another New England city, built after the pattern furnished us in the New Testament. The meeting has served to emphasize, as nothing else could have done, the need of an aggressive, evangelistic campaign in the New England cities by the Disciples of Christ. The amount of ignorance and misinformation concerning the Spirit, teaching, and aim of this Reformation which Brother Yeuell has had to contend with in the heart of New England, is a challenge to our whole brotherhood to show these people of the east who we are and what are here for. Of course this should be done in a broad unsectarian way and with the sole motive of advancing the kingdom of God. We have some things to teach our friends in the east, and they, doubtless, have some things which we can learn from them with profit. We believe, therefore, in a campaign that shall be both aggressive and fraternal. This meeting emphasizes, also, what we had learned before; that progress in the east must be made by quiet and persistent effort, time being an essential factor in the success of the work. These hard-headed Yankees do not move as rapidly nor as easily as the people of the south and west; but the plea for a united church by a return to Christ and his simple gospel, and the clear, straightforward evangelistic methods of the New Testament—this is bound to prevail ultimately in every section of our land and in all lands. Oh, that we might worthily preach it, live it, and illustrate it in our church life!

Some of My Likings---4. Why I Like the Disciples of Christ.

By WILLIAM DURBAN

The late beloved Hugh Price Hughes, the popular English Methodist leader of our times, not long before his death expressed the opinion that the progress of the Disciples of Christ in the United States was "the most amazing religious phenomenon of the age." He at the same time said that he wondered whether they could possibly live up to their beautiful name. The Disciples of Christ in America have many great advantages beside "the beautiful name whereby they are called." They constitute the only great body of Christians which had its origin on American soil. Therefore they must always sustain a peculiar claim on the people of the great republic. But this nationalist advantage places them at something of a disadvantage when they enthusiastically seek to claim the sympathy for their views from people of other lands. Their plea is apt to be regarded as something American rather than cosmopolitan. In reality it is, the latter.

Of No Nationality.

F. W. Robertson, of Brighton, said that "Jesus Christ was of no nationality." I like the Disciples because they are in their principles of no nationality, notwithstanding that the magnificent movement which they represent had its genesis in America. They stand for Christianity in its perfect adaptation to humanity without respect to geographical or racial limitations. This explains the remarkable growth in a few years of their foreign missionary society. I have carefully examined the comparative statistics of the great foreign missions, and I find that the work of the Disciples of Christ in this direction is greater than that of any other religious body, in proportion to age. No other organization has shown such a ratio of missionary increase, in resources, in staff, in results. Other societies started far earlier and had greater numbers at their back when the Disciples of Christ had not yet sprung into existence. Indeed, other great Christian communions were commencing their foreign field organization at about the period when these modern Disciples of Christ were about to be heard of for the first time. The rapid success of the Disciples as soon as they were able to launch forth on missionary enterprise amongst various nations is in itself a proof of the universal adaptability of their plea. The Disciple movement as a missionary agency will in the days to come astonish the Disciples themselves. And it will astonish the world.

Good Congregationalists.

I love the Disciples of Christ because they are such excellent congregationalists. Perhaps it is because I was cradled and trained under the auspices of Anglicanism in the old country that therefore I am attached to the congregational form of ecclesiastical polity, by way of reaction from the prelatic exclusiveness of the Church of England. It is perfectly true that in some quarters Congregationalism has long since run to seed and that Congregationalists themselves often admit that they have tended to make of their system a rope of sand. But the principle of polity is soundly scriptural and is in accord with the noblest instincts of the human mind in its love of liberty of conscience, its passion for the assertion of individualism, and its correlative tendency, at the same time, to a spiritual fellowship of all, which is the genesis of true socialism. I have never seen a Church of Disciples of Christ come into being which did not quickly display a desire for co-operation with other churches. Our Churches of Christ in England are all very youthful. I saw them all spring up as the results of efforts on the part of American missionaries (whom may God bless and multiply!). And it has been my delight to mark how, while each of these young churches has enjoyed fullest independence, it has welcomed the affiliating fellowship of its sister communions already established with alacrity. Thus, when only four of the infant interests had come into being, twenty years ago, these formed themselves into a fraternal—or sororal—co-operation, whichever we may call it.

Good Baptists.

I like the Disciples of Christ because they are excellent baptists. As they are not congregationalists in any sectarian sense, but simply according to the style of the apostolic churches, so they are not sectarian Baptists, but are immersionists because the consensus of Christendom admits the apostolicity of immersion, and because the scholarship of the world endorses the interpretation of Hellenist terms on which immersion is founded. I long since came to understand that on points where Congregationalists and Anglicans differ, the former are right and the latter are wrong; on all points where Congregationalists and Baptists differ, the latter are right, and the former are wrong; on all points where Baptists differ from Disciples, the Baptists are wrong, the Disciples right. It may be that we also can be raised up who can set us right.

In Relation to Communion.

I like the position of the Disciples with regard to fellowship and membership. The generally accepted rule is that which C. H. Spurgeon as a Baptist so strenuously advocated and so consistently practiced. Many of his brethren in his own denomination stoutly contended against him, and the Baptists in Britain are to-day deeply divided on this communion controversy. Of late years the practice of open membership, without respect to baptism, has spread extensively, and very large numbers of so-called Baptist churches are union churches, though on no account would they accept any minister as pastor excepting a Baptist. He must be an immersionist, but the officers and members generally may be pedobaptists, to any extent. There are now many Baptist churches in the United Kingdom which are only nominally so. It may be alleged that this system is indicative of the love of Christian unity. Doubtless the motive is right. The spirit is good. But there is something else to be considered. I have found during long observation that our Congregationalist brethren, who have fought heroic battles for freedom of conscience and for truth and righteousness, as well as our splendid Methodist brethren, are by no means pleased with these union churches. They consider that the Baptist churches which definitely call themselves such, and yet fling aside their principles to a sufficient extent to enable them to capture Congregationalists and Methodists and Presbyterians and Episcopalians as members are taking unfair advantage. There is justice in the complaint. On the other hand the strict communion churches, which deny the fellowship in the Lord's Supper to all who have not been immersed, are steadily perishing throughout the United Kingdom. The method which works most happily is that which practices close membership with open communion.

Declarations of Faith.

I like the Disciples of Christ because they fearlessly leave the truth to the care of divine providence and refuse to construct a lot of petty shanty little forts round the Gibraltar rock of Christ's own creed. There is a creed; Jesus himself committed it to his apostles; the church needs no other. It is massive, simple, sublime, impregnable. It is embodied in the immortal formula that "Jesus the Christ is the son of the living God." It is inscribed in Matt. 16:16. That is the creed of the disciples of Christ. It is my creed; because I am a disciple of Christ. It enables me to rejoice in sympathy with Christians of all evangelical bodies alike, instead of limiting my predilections preferentially. I have wandered in the streets of Augsburg, and have there thought over the Augsburg confession of faith. I have pondered over the two Helvetic confessions when standing in Constance where Huss was martyred; and at Ulm, Paris, Berlin, Edinburgh, Oxford, Gloucester, Smithfield have with deeply solemnized feelings reflected on the words of Calvin, Luther, Knox, Latimer, Cranmer, Zwingle, Hooper, Ridley and other makers of great and venerated creeds, symbols and confessions. These had their use and are precious historic relics. Even in Moscow I have felt the power over vast populations of the Russo-Greek spiritual formularies. But the various enunciations of the convictions of good and consecrated leaders have inextricably confused Christendom. They are parts of the jarring theology which has created the religious Babel that fails to scale the heights above our poor divisions, and to soar into the glory of Christian unity.

As Seen From the Dome   By F. D. Power

While our ship lay at Naples we visited the eternal city. It is no easy task for any man to write of Rome, the "city of infinite riches in a little room," a great world-center of conquest, religion and art for three millenniums. It is appalling to undertake to do Rome in three days, and rash beyond description to venture to write up Rome in one or two, or even twenty letters; but while the Pope has a dome 435 feet from the pavement to the summit of the cross, a few feet higher than ours, he can not see as far, nor look upon so fair a city, nor so great a land as we are accustomed to; so we proceed with some degree of assurance to view his domain and speak of its sights. First, one remembers that "this is Rome which sat on its seven hills and from its throne of beauty ruled the world," and we cross the Tiber, to which I lift my hat, and ascend the Janiculum two hundred and seventy-five feet and fix the range, the Aventine and Esquiline, the Palatine and Celian, the Capitoline and Quirinal and Viminal. Here is the eternal city where under the emperors a million and a half people dwelt, now less than 400,000, with a great history and with prospects of rare and ever varying beauty as we look away to the snow capped Apennines, and off to the blue Mediterranean and along the wooded hills, and over villas and olive gardens, parks and palaces, clustering villages and towns, hoary walls and towers and columns and ruins. It is a great sight. We don't wonder that the artist loves it; nor that the pope is willing to play prisoner within its walls.

Our hotel was near the Pantheon, now one of the eighty churches in Rome, dedicated to the Virgin Mary, the only ancient edifice in the city which is still in perfect preservation as to its walls and vaulting. It is a huge circular structure with a vast colonnade. Its portico, thirty-six yards wide is borne by sixteen Corinthian columns of granite, about forty feet in height. The interior is lighted by a single aperture in the center of the dome which produces so beautiful an effect that it was believed at one time the name "Pantheon" was applied to it from its resemblance to the vault of heaven. Here Rome was hospitable to all the gods. Here is the tomb of Victor Immanuel II, and to the left of the altar rest the bones of Raphael, 1483-1520, dying at that fatal age of 37.

Not far from here I strolled into the Corso, the great street of Rome, corresponding to the ancient Via Flaminia, leading from the capitol. It is gay with shops, and with carriages and pedestrians, and runs for a mile through the city. Along this street and across the Tiber I easily found my way to St. Peter's. The Ponte St. Angelo and Hadrian's tomb or the castle of St. Angelo, are readily recognized. The tomb is a great cylinder 80 yards in diameter, 160 feet high, and from Hadrian to Caracella all the emperors were interred here. It is a striking monument of ancient Rome used now as a fortress. St.

Peter's does not disappoint me. The square on which it is built is entered through an elliptical space, enclosed in imposing colonnades, each with four series of Doric columns. It is a fitting aproach to the greatest church in the world. An obelisk brought from Heliopolis by Caligula is in the center, on either side of which is a splendid fountain. The church is said to have been founded by Constantine and erected on the site of the Circus of Nero where Peter is supposed to have suffered martyrdom. About 1450 the present structure was begun and Michael Angelo is the architect of the great dome so marvelously airy and symmetrical, 1546. The new church was consecrated 1626, and cost over $50,000,000 and takes about $40,000 a year to maintain it. It covers 18,000 square yards. It is a perfect museum of statues, paintings, mosaics, bronzes and marbles; and while its exterior is somewhat disappointing, the effect Michael Angelo intended to produce in this dome being seriously injured by the great portico, the interior with arch upon arch, and dome upon dome, with its superb decorations, is wonderfully impressive. We pass the round slab of porphyry where Charlemagne and other emperors were crowned, between massive Corinthian pillars. On the right is the celebrated "Pieta" by Michael Angelo, a masterpiece, the mother holding the dead body of the son. The group has an ideal beauty. Opposite is the monument of Clement XIII by Canova, with two great marble lions. Farther on by one of the columns is the bronze statue of St. Peter whose toe is worn smooth by a million million kisses. One cannot recognize our old friend of Pentecost in this bronze idol. Still farther, under the bronze canopy beneath the dome, is the tomb of St. Peter, though nobody knows that Peter ever saw Rome or suffered in Rome. The great temple has 55 chapels and services are held in all of them daily. I attended a Sunday service in one of them and heard magnificent music and an eloquent sermon in Italian from Father Gretano Zoreti, a noted Jesuit. Eighty thousand people may gather in St. Peter's.

The Vatican palace, the largest palace in the world, with twenty courts and 11,000 halls, chapels, saloons and apartments is here and the Vatican gardens, library and galleries. Passing the gorgeously decorated Swiss guards, whose garments Michael Angelo invented for the world's admiration, we enter the famous Sistine chapel. Here the masters exhausted themselves. The place is literally crammed with artistic wonders—too crowded by far to be effective. It is supposed to represent the culminating effort of modern art, but I confess even Angelo's "Last Judgment" wearies me. It is too studied. His Christ here, and his prophets and Sibyls in the vaulting of the chapel are triumphs of art. In the Sistine chapel the great services are held and Pius officiates. The sculpture in the Vatican and the Raphael pictures are the center of interest. One needs a month here to take in

the exceeding embarrassment of riches. Think of the Transfiguration and the Laocoon, the Apollo Belvedere and Torso of Hercules, the Grecian, Roman, Egyptian and Etruscan treasures. I did not call on "the prisoner of the vatican." In the great dome one reads in Latin around it, painted in letters six feet in length, the words of the great Teacher: *"Tu es Petrus, et super hanc petram aedificabo ecclesiam meam et tibi dabo claves regni caelorum;"* but this was said to the fisherman, and he has no successor.

From these modern things it was good to get away to the Forum and Colosseum. Here we see the unspeakable glory of ancient Rome. The first lies between the capitol and Palatine. This hollow was the scene of the conflict between the Romans under Romulus and the Sabines after the rape of their women, and here later was the center of the republic. Here the great popular assemblies were held and along its Sacra Via the triumphant processions ascended to the capitol. Here were the Temple of Vesta with its eternal fire and the dwelling of the Pontifex Maximus, the temples of Jupiter and of Saturn, of Castor and Pollux, of Concord, of Vespasian, of Cæsar, and of Faustina. Here were the great basilicas, quadrangular courts surrounded by colonnades, the Porcia, Aemilia, Sempronia, and Julia. Here were gilded bronzes and rare marbles, columns, triumphal arches, statues, and works of art and great gatherings when Rome was greatest. Now one surveys the ruins. It is still wonderful. The Arch of Severus is here; and the Column of Phocas; and three splendid columns of the Temple of Castor and Pollux where the Roman Senate met; a part of the Temple of Vespasian and of the Sacra Via; and eight columns of the Temple of Saturn, and the remains of the Rostra or orator's tribune; and the ruins of the Temple of Cæsar in front of which was the rostrum where Mark Antony made his great speech March 20, B. C. 44; and three colossal arches of the Basilica of Constantine erected by Maxentius from which Michael Angelo modelled the vaulting of St. Peter's—acres and acres of majestic ruins!

I passed through the Arch of Titus, commemorating his triumph over the Jews, and dedicated to him by Domitian in 81, as the inscription reads: *Senatus Populusque Romanus divo Tito divi Vespasiani filio Vespasiano Augusto.* I saw clearly the triumphal procession within with captive Jews, the table with shew-bread, and seven-branched candle-stick. It is all there. Farther on is the triumphal Arch of Constantine, perhaps the most impressive in Rome, erected after his victory over Maxentius when he embraced Christianity. It has three passages, the Central, over the Appian Way. And beside this splendid arch, which should have its imitations in our great Capitol on the Potomac, is the

(Continued on Page 974.)

What the Brethren Are Saying and D

By B. B. Tyler

The Young Men's Christian Association began and prosecuted a wonderfully successful work in the Japanese army during the recent war with Russia. The readers of THE CHRISTIAN-EVANGELIST, I am sure, will be pleased to receive information as to the attitude of the emperor and minister of war in respect to this work. Two years ago, and more, the war department granted permission to three Young Men's Christian Association secretaries to pitch their tents on the banks of the Yalu River, in the rear of General Kuroki's army. The army at the time was considered closed to Christian workers. The allied Christian bodies had failed to get their representatives to the front, and it was only by most fortunate circumstances that the Young Men's Christian Association was permitted to give a practical exhibition of the nature and value of its work. The beginning was difficult, but once in the field the work spread from the one post on the banks of the Yalu River to eleven bases of the army, so covering the field that at least three-quarters of a million different soldiers were ministered to before the army returned to Japan. To these men were given 3,385,000 pieces of stationery and 416,000 pieces of religious literature. Supplies of buttons, thread, soap, etc., were furnished to 88,000 men, books were loaned to 26,000, and barbers' supplies to more than 152,000. The association secretaries made 764 visits to hospitals and isolated posts, gave 1,752 graphophone concerts and entertainments, and held 613 religious meetings. About 1,566,000 soldiers entered the different branches. This work cost about $30,000 in gold. The emperor and empress gave $5,000. This contribution testifies in an unmistakable and most emphatic way their appreciation of the work of the Young Men's Christian Association with the soldiers of the Japanese army.

Major General Kamio, formerly chief of staff at Dalny, in a public address made the following statements:

"Though I venture to say that everything was completely provided for the prosecution of war, yet I must frankly acknowledge that there was no provision made for the field recreation of the Japanese soldiers; it was entirely outside the Japanese army system.

"In all eleven places where work was definitely organized, the Young Men's Christian Association provided suitable buildings, divided into meeting and music halls, library, reading room, tea room, barber shop, letter writing room, etc. To these rooms soldiers were given free access day and night. The men who had charge of the association received the innumerable soldiers with untiring zeal and kindness. They give the soldiers healthy recreation and everything else they needed, which made them almost forget that they were in the field of war.

"At the same time, the association secretaries visited the military hospitals and distributed newspapers, magazines and pictures among the sick and wounded and comforted them by preaching and lecturing. When the transportation of soldiers to Japan commenced after the restoration of peace, the association provided music and at the principal railway stations and distributed newspapers and magazines among the soldiers thus making them forget the tediousness of the journey.

"I firmly believe that the many-sided work done by the Y. M. C. A. enabled innumerable soldiers to pass their time in the most wholesome and agreeable ways and prevented their being tempted into harmful habits and dissipation. Thus the hundreds of thousands of soldiers made their triumphant return deeply grateful for the warm-hearted service rendered by the association. I believe that the officers of the association as well as those who contributed money and various articles for the work should feel well satisfied that their object was successfully accomplished.

"Let me remark that I can discover two results from the successful work of the association: First, hundreds of thousands of Japanese society, were made acquainted with the Gospel of Christ; secondly, when these hundreds of thousands returned home, they told their parents, brothers and friends about the kind ministry of the Young Men's Christian Association, and thus many millions more have been made somewhat acquainted with the spirit of the Christian religion."

From beginning to end, the secretaries report the military authorities enthusiastically co-operated in making the work practical, effective, successful. For instance, free transportation for secretaries and supplies and the use of good buildings at the various points were given. Some of the officers gave both time and money to the work. General Oshima, the military governor of Manchuria, recently contributed $500 to continue the work of the associations.

General Terauchi, the minister of war, has sent the following remarkable letter to the president of the national committee of the association:

"The Young Men's Christian Association, moved by the desire to minister to the welfare and comfort of our officers and soldiers at the front, carried on its beneficent work throughout the Russo-Japanese war of 1904-1905. Beginning at Chinampho early in September, pace with the northward progress forces for nearly twenty long March, 1906, establishing its wor posts in Manchuria and Korea. At of money and labor and by a gre means, it filled the leisure of our soldiers, far from home, with whol tion. The completeness of the equip success of the enterprise were univ and recognized by our troops in the fully assured that the recipients of erous service are filled with dee pressible gratitude.

"Now, simultaneously with the t turn of our armies, as I learn of termination of your enterprise, I portunity to express my heartfelt tha noble services, and at the same time appreciation of the generosity of a have either by gifts or by persons ported the work.

(Signed) "M. T
"Minist
"Tokyo, 28th May, 39th Meiji
"To Yoichi Honda, Esq.,
"President, The Japanese Young tian Association Union."

One of my favorite religio has a department entitled, "Th of the Kingdom." The report making comes most appropria this head. Surely the successf the Young Men's Christian / is a bit of information concer Progress of the Kingdom of ness, peace and joy, in which p loyal to the Christ will rejoice.

✸ ✸

As Seen From the D

(Continued from Page 9

Colosseum, the crowning ruin o nal city.

The Colosseum is to me the posing structure in the world. it was the *Amphitheatrum Fla* pleted by Titus A. D. 80. At 5,000 wild animals were killed gladiatorial combats lasted 100 seated 87,000 spectators. It is of travertine blocks. The cir measures 576 yards or nearly o a mile, and its diameter is 205 the height is 156 feet. Above which is 93 by 58 yards, rise tiers of seats. Next the Esqui a well preserved portion four st the first being formed of arcade lars of which are adorned wit of the Doric, Ionic and Corinti There are four great entrances, t emperor and the others for t processions at the games. Th arcades came the spectators the arena were the chambers for wild beasts, and through t ways came the Christian marty one-third of the gigantic structu but it is indescribable in its maj Colosseum was the symbol c greatness.

"While stands the Colosseum, Rome
When falls the Colosseum, Rome shal
And when Rome falls, the world!"

Modern Religious Persecution---A Defense

3. The Amiableness of Persecutors.

By B. L. Chase

I have often heard men express their surprise at the courage, perseverance and confidence of the persecutor when he is called upon to expose the false teaching of men about whom there is a universal atmosphere of sanctity and integrity. To be able to deal impartially with old and young, learned and unlearned, obscure and illustrious men who are corrupters of the faith, requires a calmness of judgment, a courage of conviction, a forgetfulness of self. and of all consequences, possessed by few men. It seems that God calls upon only the most highly and peculiarly endowed men to carry out such delicate, perilous and thankless tasks. No man would consent to act the part of persecutor without long study and preparation, long prayer and fasting.

When one considers the infinite variety of heresies, their subtlety, their cunning elaboration, their profundity, their embodiment in learned language, their tortuous syllogisms, their connection with philosophies hoary with age, one is almost appalled at the learning and skill which are required to understand them, explain them to the "rank and file" of the brethren, and refute them. Take the learned infidelities connected with the modern study of the Old Testament. What knowledge of the Semitic languages, history and ideas it requires—what hours of reading and study to master the scholarly output of German and French scholars, to be able with confidence to pronounce as false a conclusion which has been agreed upon by the majority of learned scholars! And yet the Disciples have defenders of the faith who are putting to silence every week the most learned scholars of the world. They have repeatedly challenged the propagators of false teachings to come to the defense of their mongrel intellectual progeny in the pages of the weekly newspaper; but not one of the great scholars of Europe or America has ever dared to cross swords with our bravest dialecticians. They have called upon Harnack and Wellhausen to reply to them; but they have maintained a discreet silence. They have asked Harper and Briggs to debate the question with them; but they have been too busy to answer their letters. They have, metaphorically speaking, shot the ideas of these men full of holes, but they have let the poor things die without aid, and have not given them so much attention as to offer them a decent burial. The silence of these men when they are being attacked as infidels is sufficient evidence that they have been put to confusion, and know from reading the unanswerable refutations of their ideas that their positions are weak and untenable. They don't believe their own ideas; if they did they would come to their defense.

The Disciples scarcely realize what a few brainy men among them are doing to save the Christian religion from annihilation. The Disciples themselves would have disappeared as a brotherhood about three years ago if it had not been for them. For their signal services ou behalf of the "old Jerusalem Gospel," they are deserving of a warmer reception than they are receiving in some quarters. My heart is pained at the thankless way the pictures of one of these men were received in some places when they were offered free of charge beautifully mounted upon a button to be worn upon the coat. It has been reported that copies of that paper which has done more than all other papers put together among the Disciples to hunt out the heretic from his hiding place, were actually taken out and kindled into a bonfire! It would seem that every home among the Disciples would be glad to have the faces of these men hanging upon the wall looking down benignantly upon the little children and the household pets. They are deserving better at our hands than they are receiving. Subscriptions to their newspapers and books are well enough; the use of their Sunday-school helps is well enough; but what they desire above all other things is the unutterable blessedness of being helpful to the brethren. They are here to minister, not to be ministered unto. If any church should desire a minister, nothing would give them greater pleasure than to recommend a man for the place who is known to be "sound." If one of the colleges should be in need of a president or professor, they would count it a pleasure to have the selection of such officers turned over to them. They would even pay the postage on their own letter of appointment. Or if one of the colleges desired an opinion on the soundness of a text book, they would count it no inconvenience to read such a book and pass judgment on it; they would even write one for the purpose. If any of the missionary boards were at a loss for a man as secretary, they would count it no imposition to be asked to nominate a man for the place. I have reason to believe that they would even consent to make up the programs of the various district, state and national conventions, if any of the secretaries should not have time to do so. They desire, above everything else to be useful to the brethren. Let all who desire to reward them as they desire, follow the above suggestions, which I am making without their knowledge.

An India Convention

By Adelaide Gail Frost.

I have had such a grand uplift which, more than anything else, seemed like this to me: The curtain of a panorama just beginning to uproll, just far enough for us to catch a glimpse of India To-Be, the wonderful day when the church of Jesus Christ in India shall be ready to meet the bridegroom. Imagine yourselves in a long audience room. Looking up you see the cream colored tiles of the roof, about the walls are blackboards, on which our convention's daily program is written in Hindi and the special song of the convention, a translation of the Glory Song. Above the speaker's stand is the motto of the Christian Woman's Board of Missions in Hindi —"The Love of Christ Constraineth Us,"— "Masih ka prem namen bash kar leta hai." The two side rooms like alcoves are filled with the smaller children of the orphanage, and mothers who are not too certain of the behavior of their own "small fry." I must say here that the tiny folk of Miss Burgess' family and David Livingstone Menzies are the prize church babies for model deportment. The front part of the main room is filled with the orphanage girls sitting on mats. Back of them are rows of benches where I looked most often with thankful eyes. There sat the adult Christians of the Hamirpur District, about sixty in all, and we had beside fifteen visitors from outside the district, such earnest faces, cleanly and sufficiently clothed persons, India's own, but more, Christ's own. They sang, some translated hymns, some songs of praise to Jesus written for their own native airs. The latter they sing with such giesto as to almost make the tiles rattle! I am going to copy some of the notes I took on that occasion that you may have some idea of the way our native brethren and sisters speak. Yakub Ali of Maudha (Ya- koob A le, the first name means Jacob), who was once a Mohammedan religious teacher, said: "We should have our hearts so filled with the love of Christ that there shall be room for nothing else"— and then it thrilled me to hear that some time Mohammedan leader tell of the difference between the works of Jesus and that of other prophets. "We find no selfishness in him," he said.

One of our young men school teachers said: "We must work to give the gospel to every one of our brothers and sisters."

One young Christian woman said of her work with women: "When we speak lovingly to them then their love turns toward us. Sometimes at first they will close the door and say, 'There is no one to hear,' but later they insist on our words with their hearts, and call us to come back and teach them. We should listen to their tales of joy or sorrow and tell them of One who always understands."

Another young Christian man said: "There are thousands of villages where the Word of the Lord has never been spoken, there shall yet be witnesses who shall speak clearly, but so many are needed now."

Still another said: "When we are one in spirit and prayer and endeavor then it will not be so hard to overcome the great strength of idolatry around us."

A teacher from Rath said (pronounced rot), "Asia should more fully than any other continent in the world understand and follow the teachings of Jesus whose birthplace upon earth was in Asia."

You can imagine the sensations such words from the lips of those, most of whom had been born into heathenism, would awake in us. Beginnings of great days are dawning.

This meeting was presided over by Yakub Ali, the secretary was also a native brother. I am sure our men missionaries enjoyed being audience most of the time.

It is beginning to grow quite warm. Soon our school will begin at six in the morning.   ADELAIDE GAIL FROST.

Reconstruction in Alameda

A good illustration of church extension is found at Alameda, Cal. In 1893 the secretary was on the Pacific coast seeking to know for the board what could be done to aid our people to get good church homes. At that time a corner church lot was selected in Alameda facing the city park. It was the best lot in town. At a cost of $1900 the board purchased it a little later and a church building seating 150 people was erected by the Alameda brethren. After a few reverses the church paid off its debt and grew and was about to build when the terrible fire and earthquake broke up all their plans. But the earthquake also increased their opportunities. Alameda became a refuge city across the bay and at once they must build. A loan was needed and though our board could not see the money coming except by faith, the $5,000 was granted at the earnest solicitation of all the churches and preachers around the Bay. We believe the brotherhood will give this money. We *must* do some work in faith.

It is an inspiration to read the letters of Bro. Macfarlane. We give one herewith after the loan was granted and also one

board has saved the situation. I have always believed in church extension, but never realized before what it meant to have a great solid institution; such as it is, ready to step into the breach and take up the work which our hands were rendered unable to support.

The lessons of the California earthquake and the San Francisco fire ought to insure an offering of $100,000 for church extension in September.

That you may receive it is the fervent prayer of the Alameda church. Yours faithfully,
Alameda, Col.   P. C. MACFARLANE.

DEAR BROTHER MUCKLEY—Only those who are confronted with unspeakable devastation and unparalleled opportunity as is conjoined in this bay district of California, can in anywise appreciate the timeliness of your loan of $5,000 to the Alameda brethren. Whatever builds up one of our churches strengthens us all. Whatever help the brethren in need receive from the brotherhood fills all of us with the thrills of renewed courage and determination.

P. C. Macfarlane has been focalizing the moral sense of Alameda for a long time. His well tempered and masterful leadership in civic righteousness has won to our church there a prestige which makes their pitiably inadequate facilities stand out in sharp contrast. Even without the need multiplied manifold by the fire across the bay, that church deserves generous recognition from our people at large. And now that you have granted this timely loan, based on your faith in our brotherly sentiments we applaud your board unstintedly.

Bear with one further word. Some of our

Our New Church Building at Alameda, Cal.

from Bro. Shepherd. These letters should be read carefully. The extension fund is a great emergency fund. Will our brethren soon get it through their minds—it is an emergency fund to snatch victory from the jaws of defeat. This Alameda case is accentuated by earthquake and by fire. We now have 97 other worthy appeals that have accumulated since March when our board ceased granting loans and it will take $125,000 to answer them. Read the letters and digest them.
                         G. W. MUCKLEY, Cor. Sec.

DEAR BROTHER MUCKLEY—Words can hardly express our gratitude at the receipt of your telegram announcing the granting of a loan of $5,000. The clouds rolled away and enthusiasm kindled immediately. We asked for $5,000 for a Sunday-school room, not hoping to do more than furnish it ourselves; but the prospect of receiving $5,000 from your board led us to plan larger things, and while we felt hardly able to raise a dollar, we are now planning at least an $8,000 building, and the money is coming in so rapidly that we will possibly go to $10,000. Our architect is planning a building which is a marvel at that figure. It will be in the mission style, shingled outside, with wood finish within, and provides for a church auditorium for 400, a Sunday-school room for 400, with nine separate class rooms, a combined auditorium seating 800, and a basement under the Sunday-school room. It will be the most unique and practical church building in the city.

Twelve hundred of the $3,000 we have to raise was subscribed on the day the announcement of your loan was made; $900 of this $1,200 came from people injured financially by the fire. One lady, who made the confession that morning, subscribed $50 before leaving the church; and a gentleman, who is not a member, but whose wife was recently baptized from the Catholic church, and whose entire business was in ruins, voluntarily subscribed $100.

The work in Alameda was just entering upon larger things when the fire crushed our prospects and increased our needs. The church extension

belated brethren, for whatever reason, withhold support from our church extension work. This loan to Alameda is but another instance added to the already long list of providential helps you have been able to minister to the growing needs of our church. Keep up the good work, as you can not fail to do, and gradually you will force into the open the actual basis of opposition and neglect of church extension work, timid faith in a penurious Christ or a penurious faith in a Christ who is not alive nowadays. The dear Lord forgive our misrepresentations of his bountiful care for his children and his bountiful care for his children and his bountiful care for his children and his bountiful. Get that $1,000,000 fund as quickly as possible. Future emergencies may not rise from fire and quaking earth, but emergencies are rising all about us all the time. Loyally yours,
                              R. P. SHEPHERD.
Berkeley, Cal.

❁ ❁

The Passing of a Veteran.
By F. D. Power.

Dexter A. Snow, eldest son of Asiel Snow, was born in Staunton, Va., May 20, 1819. His father and mother, Mary Snow (nee Mary Bullard) were both from Massachusetts and emigrated to Virginia about the year 1818. They moved from Staunton, Va., to Christiansburg, Va., when their first born was an infant, where they lived until the death of his mother in 1830, leaving three children, Dexter, Harriet and Stillman. His mother was the eldest daughter of Daniel Bullard and his wife, Mary Bullard, and was a devout Christian woman. It was the early teaching of his mother and the later influence of his grandmother Bullard, and that of his uncle Chester C. Bullard, that gave the religious direction to the mind and life of this boy. The prayers of the mother for the child, kneeling at his bedside with her hands on his head, had a restraining effect upon his tendency to sin; and in the after years of his life, the sudden memory of those prayers often checked a wicked impulse and arrested a sinful act.

At the age of 16 he obeyed the Gospel under the preaching of Dr. Chester Bullard and was the first convert to the Christian religion, as he preached it, west of New River. To obey the

Our Budget

—Where is the "boy preacher"?

—He certainly is not in print as he used to be.

—It can not be said he is older. We rejoice that the *genus* is perennial.

—He is as ambitious now and is working as earnestly as ever but is not so much in the lime light to-day because ——

—Our churches are manifesting greater appreciation of Christian experience and mature wisdom and are lengthening the period of their usefulness for studious, devoted ministers.

—Observation unmistakably reveals that the ministerial dead line is changed. If it is anywhere, it is ten years further west than it used to be. Ben Tyler has reached the Rockies but has not seen it yet. None of our preachers do who read the CHRISTIAN-EVANGELIST, the latest books and prepare new sermons.

—Tell this to the boys. Many of them are restrained from entering the ministry through fear that doors of opportunity close to all preachers soon as even the earlier frosts of the years fall on their hair. We have learned it is age rather than years before which the doors swing inward. The power inherent in a long life of consecrated ability is now at a premium and will continue to be. This should cheer every preacher and form a new tie between him and his study. It is rich with significance to the church of the next decade.

—Arthur N. Lindsey, New Brooklin, Mo., was elected chaplain of the Missouri Drummers' Association at their late Booneville convention.

—H. F. McLane, of Hiram, O., has some open time for meetings after September 1. He will give prompt attention to any calls for help.

—Evangelists Fife and Saunders are in a meeting at Converse, Mo. We hope for reports showing this excellent church greatly increased numerically and otherwise.

—James A. Brown, who graduated from Hiram last June, began with the Hartford (Mich.) church, July 8. He reports excellent prospects for the growth of the Hartford congregation.

—L. E. Sellers reports that the Pisgah, Ill., congregation has recently purchased a lot for their new church home. Walter Carpenter will give his time to financing the building enterprise.

—Dr. J. G. M. Luttenberger sailed on the Kron-Prinz Wilhelm, on the 31st ult., for Berlin, where he will devote several months to special hospital work, further fitting himself for his professional career.

—With most appropriate services the corner stone of the Broad Street Church of Christ, Columbus, O., was laid, June 29. W. S. Priest's ministry with that people is being greatly blessed.

—W. W. Wharton, Jacksonville, Ill., can place inquirers in communication with a worthy brother who is employed half time with one church and wishes to assist another congregation with the balance.

—O. B. Clark, of the department of history, Drake University, reports an attendance of over 600 through the summer sessions. Brother Clark will spend the balance of the summer at his old Illinois home near Bloomington.

—Roseberry, Idaho, offers good inducements to a first-class creamery man and to a physician who will bring with him or buy a stock of drugs. Members of the Christian Church preferred. Write Bro. H. C. Varner.

—J. W. Lowber, of Austin, delivered a lecture before the Texas Chautauqua, Mineral Wells, on the "Evolution of Democracy and the Future of Our Country," which was published in full in the Austin "Tribune."

—The Miami (Mo.) church gave $30 for foreign missions in March, and $20 for American missions on Children's day. An Endeavor society of twenty members was recently organized. Evangelistic meetings will begin in October.

—Miss Madge L. Kent, who has served the Central Christian church at Terre Haute (Ind.) as assistant pastor for the past three years, resigned her position July 1, and is now at her home in Chagrin Falls, Ohio, taking a much needed rest.

—G. A. Gordon, a Lexington Bible student, has just closed a very successful meeting at McKinney, Ky. A church of 45 members, and a very promising Bible school were organized. W. L. Ewers was selected as pastor of this young flock.

—Frank M. Dowling has returned to his beloved Pasadena, Cal. We hope this move signifies his restoration to health, and that his unusual gifts of learning and eloquence will hereafter be more exclusively devoted to preaching and writing the Word.

—W. M. Semones, Nampa, Idaho, informs us the church there met for the first time in its new home last Lord's day. Three were added to the membership, by letter. A minister will soon be called to the pastorate of the churches at Nampa and Meridian.

—Louis S. Cupp has not yet completed his first year with the Hyde Park Church, Kansas City, but has had 76 additions to the membership. The growth of our Kansas City congregations is an inspiration to the entire brotherhood.

—W. J. Lhamon was chief lecturer at the preachers' institute held in conjunction with the recent Nebraska state meeting at Bethany. He held the same office there three years ago. It is needless to say that Brother Lhamon's lectures were an invaluable feature of the assembly.

—The new church building at Sapulpa, I. T., was dedicated by the pastor, A. M. Harral, and his people June 22. Brother Randolph, of Tulsa, is assisting in a brief meeting, which has had a good start. The Bible school attendance has doubled during the year.

—H. A. Northcutt, evangelist, and John S. Zeran and wife, singers, are helping E. H. Holmes in a meeting at Plano, Texas. There have been 40 additions to date. Brother Northcutt's next meeting will be with his home church, at Knox City, Mo.

—E. B. Bagby will spend the next month at Bethany, recuperating for his winter's campaign in the capital of the nation. Like all preachers, he must have his favorite paper during vacation time. THE CHRISTIAN-EVANGELIST will follow him, and our other readers to their summer vacations on notification.

—W. A. Haynes, of Skidmore, Mo., begins general evangelistic work as soon as opportunity comes. Though but 32 years of age, he has been in the ministry 17 years. He is completing his fourth year at Skidmore, his first and only pastorate. His services should be called into immediate requisition.

—A Charlottesville (Va.) daily gives an extended account of the final payments being made on all indebtedness against our church in that city, and of the great success attending the ministry of C. R. Sine with our people there. It is a pleasure to know that Brother Sine will continue

his pastorate in that important religious and educational center.

—Charles M. Farnham, of Newberry, Ind., offers his services to the churches as a general evangelist. Brother Farnham holds degrees from two universities, and is otherwise well equipped for this ministry. He has no fixed charges, but depends on voluntary contributions for his support.

—Braymer, Mo., is prospering under the pastorate of S. W. Crutcher. On June 22 the last mortgage note owing the board of church extension was burned. The church is but five years old, has the best building in the town, and is rapidly growing in numbers and influence.

—Erwin Taylor LeBaron recently resigned his pastorate at Macon, Mo., to re-enter the evangelistic field September 1. He desires the help of a brother singing evangelist, who can play the instrument when necessary. Brother LeBaron's past ministry gives promise of his helping multitudes into the kingdom.

—One of the elders of the Mechanicsburg (Ill.) church writes that L. A. Chapman, who has labored there the past few years, is leaving the church much stronger financially and better equipped in every way for aggressive work than it has ever been in his knowledge of the church.

—We very much regret to read in Sec. W. L. Lowe's Kansas letter, that he has resigned the office which he has so capably filled the last nine years. We can easily read in his successes a call to continue for many years. We hope Brother Lowe will also read it clear and not insist on his resignation being accepted.

—Herb. Lewis, of Gravette, Ark., writes that the local congregation has pledged $350 for the salary of a resident minister half time. There are good opportunities for his engaging the other half within easy access of Gravette. A significant line is "a middle-aged man, nonantagonistic, preferred."

—Herman P. Williams, of Vigan, Philippine Islands, reports ten baptisms recently at Santo Domingo. The Bible college has opened for its second year's work, with seven students. This sounds like the day of small things, but there are those living who will yet see the full corn in the ear in those far-away islands.

—The beautiful new church at Acampo, Cal., recently erected for the Christian Colony Church, of Acampo, has been dedicated free of indebtedness. J. V. Coombs conducted the services. Brother Coombs writes that J. P. Dargitz has been the moving spirit in establishing that promising congregation.

—F. E. Giles, Haverhill, Mass., informs us that his church board unanimously voted to let the pastor, W. C. Crerie, go to Manchester to assist Herbert Yeuell in the attempt to establish a church of Christ in that city. A fellow feeling makes the New England brethren wonderfully kind to one another.

—E. T. Wise, East Liverpool, Ohio, reports his audiences holding up remarkably well during the summer. A great Endeavor and Bible school rally will be begun September 1. The churches of East Liverpool and Wellsville have arranged jointly to become a Living Link. Two were recently added to the East Liverpool membership.

—S. J. Vance is in a meeting at Reger, Mo. Since we have no building there, the meeting will be held in the Methodist church house. Brother Vance thinks he has a fine opportunity of trying federation, co-operation, and union, all at once and expresses a willingness to undertake the experiment. He hopes soon to report good results.

—A. H. Brown, Greenwood, Ind., informs us the church there is in a very prosperous condition and is greatly enjoying the ministry of Geo. W. Winfrey. During the month two were added to the church by letter and three by primary obedience.

—T. P. Reid has been called to the pastorate of the Acampo (Cal.) church. With their new building and an enthusiastic and consecrated congregation, he may expect great progressiveness in the extension of the kingdom in that part of the Lord's vineyard, which is literally "a vineyard."

—The ninth annual session of the Piedmont assembly will meet with the Gordonsville (Va.) church from July 27 to August 5. Among the names of those on the program from without that district, we note C. A. Young, Chicago; E. L. Powell, Louisville; P. A. Cave, Maysville, Ky., and B. P. Smith, Atlanta, Ga.

—Cephas Shelburne writes that the church at Hunting, Ind., closes a year's work in the theatre and will move into their new church home first Sunday in September. This will be one of the most complete church buildings in the brotherhood. Brother Shelburne will spend the month of August at Long Lake, Mich.

—For the first time the work of our Bible Chair at Charlottesville, Va., under the superintendency of William Forrest, will be affiliated with the university, and due credit be given for work done in the Bible department. It is a pleasure to note this evidence of appreciation of Brother Forrest's work by the university trustees.

—Our Oklahoma brethren will meet in their fifteenth and last territorial convention at El Reno, September 3-6. A strong program has been prepared. The largest attendance in the history of our missionary work in that land of wonders is expected. Pastor O. L. Smith and his hospitable people extend a cordial welcome to all.

—Earl M. Todd sends the sad news that W. C. Hull, for five years pastor of the North Tonawanda (N. Y.) church, lies in a Brooklyn hospital with a fractured skull, caused by falling from a moving train. It was first thought to be a fatal accident, but a successful operation gives hopes of ultimate recovery.

—George P. Rutledge, of the Third Church, Philadelphia, was recently elected vice president of the Pennsylvania Christian Endeavor Union, and Clarence H. Chain, one of the trustees of his church, was elected president of the Philadelphia Endeavor Union. It is gratifying to see our brethren assuming leadership in this great movement.

—J. M. Bailey has been called by the Pettis county (Mo.) missionary board to act as county evangelist for the ensuing year. The Lamont church has given liberally for missions and is now sending its pastor, I. H. Fuller, to a country church for afternoon and evening services once each month. Chas. H, Altheide, of Bloomfield, Ia., is now assisting him in a protracted meeting at this mission.

—Evangelist E. E. Violett and wife paid the office force a very enjoyable visit en route to Winchester, Ill., where they began revival services June 29. They will have THE CHRISTIAN-EVANGELIST placed in every home in the town and sent far into the country. This will not only insure a big tent full of people, but will prepare listeners for Brother Violett's earnest preaching of the cross.

—J. H. Brooks, of Blytheville, secretary of northeast Arkansas missionary district,

sends an appeal for preachers of ability and sterling character to come there and help develop the religious opportunities of that rapidly growing part of the new south. He commends it, too, as a place in which our brethren can most advantageously make investments and locate homes. He will gladly answer all letters containing return postage.

—Bro. J. Durham, Irvington, Cal., reports having recently baptized an excellent business woman of Clay, Cal., who listened to him preach on "Objections to Baptism Removed." She stated that all her objections were removed. It is thought her example will have many followers. At Elliott, Cal., he recently baptized a deaf, mute, student of Berkley. The scene at her confession and baptism is reported as being most beautiful and affecting.

—E. F. Henderson, the colored evangelist, is engaged in a very promising work with his people in Los Angeles, Cal. There are more than 12,000 negroes in the city and the number is rapidly increasing. A mission for their benefit was recently started by the philanthropic B. F. Coulter and his Broadway congregation. He has just presented them with a commodious new church home and will help sustain Brother Henderson till the church becomes self-supporting.

—I. H. Fuller has convicted the Sedalia preachers of being "federationists." The entire band took their families and suppers and a bag of horseshoes to the park last Friday evening and spent the time in merry-making and planning for the advancement of their common Christianity. One said of them, "Behold, how they love one another." While it is not in the indictment, we are led to believe that our own J. M. Rudy and W. F. Hamann were among the chief conspirators.

—"The Martin family" will soon make an experiment that is unique even in these days of resourceful evangelism. Brother Martin has purchased a large portable steel tabernacle, in which to hold meetings after October 1. While this will be an added expense, he feels that it will be justified by giving him opportunity to preach to more people than can be accommodated in the ordinary church building. During his recent meetings in Kentucky over 300 were added to the churches.

—G. Lyle Smith, whose work at the Central in Waco, Texas, has been characterized by great success, has tendered his resignation as pastor and, though it was rejected by a practically unanimous vote of the church, he yet feels it is best for him to change his field of labor. After September 1 he will be open to engagement elsewhere. Brother Smith is an able, devoted, minister and will prove a great blessing to any church where his lines may be cast.

—Joseph Utterback reports the Christian colony congregation east of Acampo, Cal., is in the enjoyment of great spiritual blessedness. A band of forty-six have been gathered into a New Testament church, dwelling together in brotherly love. A Christian Endeavor society of forty members and a Bible school of fifty-five have been organized. The well furnished church house is as good as paid for and there are bright prospects of greatly increased usefulness before the church.

—George C. Ritchey has concluded a very successful meeting at Rupert, Idaho. A young preacher and his wife are needed there at once. The church can pay a salary of $600. Bro. Ritchey writes that Rupert is desert now, but in a short time will blossom like a rose. Water from the mighty Snake will be turned on the land in a few months, then homesteads will assume

joins the long list of those who are entering the distinctively evangelistic field. An authorized statement from the official board is to the effect that the congregation reluctantly accepted Brother Brundige's resignation, and only because of the physician's advice that he must make his home in a drier climate. He is highly commended to the churches by the people among whom he has labored.

—T. M. Mayers, of Eureka Springs, recently concluded a very successful meeting at Fordyce, Ark. E. M. Berry, the beloved pastor of the Fordyce church, is dangerously ill and his people have united in a request that brethren everywhere unite with them in prayers for his recovery. We request every reader to comply with their desire for fellowship before the throne of grace.

—E. B. Scofield writes that the opening of Bethany assembly was the most auspicious of any in its history. President L. L. Carpenter's lecture based on his recent tour of the Holy Land, was very entertaining and instructive. A. L. Crim made one of the best temperance addresses ever heard at the park. Brother Scofield was re-elected president of the State Sunday-school convention, and T. J. Legg was called to his fifteenth year's work as State Sunday-school evangelist. The assembly continues to August 12. All who attend will doubtless be greatly benefited.

—J. H. Mohorter, secretary of our National Benevolences, has just returned from a tour among eastern churches that embraced Poestenkill, Troy, Gloversville, Eagle Mills, Syracuse, East Aurora and Buffalo, N. Y., West Rupert, Vt., Danbury, Conn., and Jefferson, Ravena and Ashland, O., in its scope. He attended the dedication of the new Cleveland Orphanage, and the New York convention of Disciples while swinging this circle. Everywhere he found great encouragement for "the Gospel of the Helping Hand." Bro. Mohorter is justifying the fondest expectations of those who rejoiced over his acceptance of his position in this holy ministry.

—William J. Russell, of Frankfort, Ind., writes: "Gloria in Excelsis" is the most progressive and up-to-date church hymnal of the twentieth century. Its value has been tested in the First Christian Church of Frankfort, Ind. It is superb in its binding, and it is the first hymn book published by the Disciples of Christ that has size enough to make it worthy to be called a Church Hymnal. Its responsive readings are rich in variety, and these are essential to the enrichment of the Lord's day morning service. It contains the best of all that is found in the old and the new hymnologies. It is a delight to my people, and has given dignity and spiritual tone to our services."

—The Board of Church Extension has recently been the recipient of six gifts on the Annuity Plan, aggregating $7,200. $5,000 of this amount is from a friend in Illinois 89 years old; $1,000 is from a friend in Missouri; two $500 gifts came from friends in Iowa; $100 from Arkansas; and the other $100 from Kansas. This last is the 171st gift to the Annuity Fund. This makes, including the Church Extension Annuity fund, nearly $185,000 in the Church Extension Annuity fund. There is no safer place to put annuity money, because we have over $565,000 in our Church Extension fund which is increasing from day to day, as security for our annuity bonds. Address G. W. Muckley, Kansas City, Mo., for information.

—I. H. Fuller, our enterprising Lamont (Mo.) minister, utilized all his church delegates to the Hannibal convention in reporting that inspiring assembly to his townsmen. At a meeting held in the church the following Monday evening all the delegates gave their impressions of the C. W. B. M. sessions of the convention. Tuesday

night all reported the Christian Endeavor convention, each of the delegates emphasizing some special feature of the Endeavor sessions. On Wednesday and Thursday evenings other departments of the convention were considered in the same manner. The delegates gave five minute reports and Brother Fuller would conclude the meeting with a twenty minute address on the great interests considered. He highly recommends the plan to other ministers.

—It is difficult to repress a protest against conditions that drive little children into the rounds of toil at such tender ages in our great cities. On the car this morning were three little girls not yet in their teens carrying lunches to one of the great mills. Though clean they could not be said to have "bright morning faces;" they were nervous, careworn and almost uncanny in their premature age. They have had no childhood. O, that they could have been sent to the nursery rather than to the pitiless mill. Drink, corporate greed, poverty drive them there. Possibly extravagance, lack of paternal love, or shiftlessness let them go, at least they are there and ought not be. Christianity is their only deliverer. O Church of Christ, emancipate these little white slaves, unfurl the roses where lilies pale in their faces, and give them all the liberties he would have them enjoy who took them in his arms and blessed them!

—Read Herbert Yeuell's inspiring telegram on page 987. That this intense interest in the plea of this Restoration could be created in one summer month amidst such conservatism as prevails in Manchester is complete justification of Editor J. H. Garrison's attempt to establish a New Testament church in New Hampshire before our next national convention. Though compelled by local conditions to desist for a few weeks, Brother Crerie, of Haverhill, Mass., is on the ground and will fully conserve all the good accomplished so that the meeting can be resumed with a nucleus of local support entirely wanting at the beginning. It is now clearly demonstrated that where we determine to do so, there we can establish a church. With victory so nearly assured it would be sinning against a great opportunity not to complete this enterprise and bejewel that part of New England with a church patterned in every particular after the Jerusalem model. Let contributions for this special work continue. They will be acknowledged through these columns and economically applied to this pious design. Soon the hearts of the givers will be gladened by reports of the institution of the new church.

—Evangelist Charles Reign Scoville has received more than 500 calls for evangelistic meetings within a single year. This shows the great demand for evangelistic work. Dozens of more evangelists of character and ability are needed in our ranks. We have plenty of some kinds, too many of others, but not enough real men in this work. Appreciating the very great need in this direction, Brother Scoville has come forward with a liberal offer. He proposes to put into the hands of the National Secretary of Evangelism during this year $300 to be used in supporting an evangelist in some needy field under direction of the Board of Evangelism. This contribution, in itself, will constitute Brother Scoville the supporter of a living link evangelist under our board. It is thought that a capable man can raise the remainder of his salary on the field, even though he occasionally be sent to a place which could not pay him for his services. We have very few evangelists or preachers who could make such a liberal offer as this, but those of our

brethren who are abundantly able to give $300 per year are legion. We call upon others for similar gifts in order that hundreds of calls for evangelists may be answered within the next year.

❋ ❋

Buffalo Railroad Rates.

Concerning the rates to the International convention, we are authorized to state that the Trunk Line association, which covers the territory east of Buffalo, has granted a rate of a fare and one-third on the certificate plan; that the Western Passenger association, covering the territory west of Chicago and St. Louis, has granted a rate of one lowest regular first-class tariff fare plus two dollars from points in the territory to Buffalo and return, date of sale October 10-12, inclusive, tickets good for return from Buffalo until (including) the 19th; Central Passenger association, one fare plus one dollar, covering territory east of the Mississippi, west of Buffalo, north of the Ohio river, tickets to be sold October 11, 12, and 13, with return limit of October 19. The New England Passenger association has advised us that they have authorized the rate of one fare and one-third on the certificate plan. The Southwestern Association has granted a rate of one fare plus two dollars for the round trip. We confidently expect the Southeastern association to make equally as good a rate.

The Trunk Line association has made a special authorization of one and one-half cents per mile per capita between points visited for guaranteed party of one hundred or more going via New York, Philadelphia, and Baltimore to Washington returning direct to Buffalo within limit of ticket to Buffalo. Those desiring to take this trip should communicate with Brother George L. Snively of St. Louis, who has been instrumental in organizing. These rates ought to insure us the largest attendance that has ever been recorded at any of our conventions.

Buffalo is just on the border of the territory wherein our great strength lies. This year the convention is held on eastern territory and in the state of New York, where we have long sought to make an impression. This ought to be another incentive to our people to assemble upon this rich home missionary territory.

Many people will avail themselves of the opportunity to take a trip to Niagara Falls, which is about an hour's ride above the city. Many will want to go to Canada; some will want to proceed to New York or Washington or Baltimore. Provision is being made for all these trips and we hope to announce arrangements for parties later.

We have reason to believe that this will be a year of great advancement in all departments of our co-operative work. The convention program has been completed, and we confidently believe that the program which the home society will present this year has never been excelled.

If anyone desires information upon particular matters let him write to R. H. Miller, 255 West Utica Street, Buffalo, who will refer his letter to the proper committee chairman for reply.

W. J. WRIGHT, Cor. Sec.
GEO. B. RANSHAW, Field Sec.

For a Church in New Hampshire.

Already acknowledged $606.10
Mrs. C. H. King 1.00

Total $607.10

If Herbert Yeuell's efforts to establish a church in New Hampshire modeled perfectly after the New Testament pattern should fail for lack of financial support, many able to give would deeply regret their having wasted this opportunity for coming to the help of the Lord against the mighty. But $1 was received last week, while expenses are $240. Register your desire for the advancement for this Restoration in New England by sending a draft to J. H. Garrison, "for New Hampshire Fund."

District Meeting.

The Seventh District (Mo.) convention was held at Camden Point July 23-25. Delightful weather and the hospitality of the Disciples of that prosperous section of Platte county, together with the fellowship of kindred souls, made it a season of great refreshing to the thirty preachers and other workers in attendance. Among the speakers and topics were: E. B. Bourland, "The Preacher and His Relation to Social Problems;" J. P. Pinkerton, "The Preacher and His Spiritual Life;" C. M. Chilton, "Raising Money for Missions;" J. H. Hardin, "Bible School Work;" A. E. Corey, "The Trail of the Dragon;" E. L. Barham, "Our Schools and Colleges;" M. M. Goode, "Does the New Testament Furnish a Sufficient Basis for the Union of all Christians?" These addresses were followed by discussions that were very helpful.

A practical work of the conference was the adoption of a plan of co-operation for the association, with the hope that other

churches will accept it, and join in an effort to advance the cause of Christ in Northwest Missouri. A plan of co-operation will soon be presented through our papers, and details will not be given here. The following officers were elected for the ensuing year: C. M. Chilton, president; T. H. Capp, E. C. Whitaker and George C. McGee, vice-presidents; C. A. Lowe, of St. Joseph, secretary and treasurer. The above officers constitute the executive committee. The plan contemplates co-operation with the state board, which will be asked to locate a district secretary or evangelist at St. Joseph, the state board and district board acting together in directing his work. The next convention will meet at Chillicothe, Mo., July 22-24, 1907.

C. A. LOWE.

Missouri State Bible School Work.

Missouri Bible school work has been advancing satisfactorily since our great convention at Hannibal. We hope for one of the most effective years in the history of the association.

The state superintendent held institutes at Joplin and Windsor, July 13-15 and 20-22, respectively. These were well attended and proved effective. Teacher-training classes were organized at both places. At Joplin, addresses were made in both the First and Second churches. Great work is being done in that region.

District conventions were attended at Sweet Springs and Camden Point, districts Nos. 2 and 7, and at both of these places the superintendent made addresses and assisted in the organization of the districts.

SOME OF OUR CHURCHES RECENTLY

One of the unexplained "postal mysteries" is our delay in getting J. Len Keevil's beautiful description of the dedication of the Johnson City (Tenn.) Church. This modern structure was dedicated by Z. T. Sweeney, June 10. Brother Keevil says that while Tennessee may be conservative in some respects she is not one whit behind our most progressive states in adding new church buildings to our Centennial list, and raising money for the payment of church debts. Brother Sweeney asked for $10,000; in a short time $15,000—$5,000 more than enough to meet all obligations—were secured. The new church has the best location in the city. The foundations are of native blue limestone, laid in cement; the tower rises 86 feet; the walls up to the windows are of dressed stone; the upper walls are of gray granite brick, with arches of red pressed brick; the roof is of the best Virginia slate. The auditorium has the bowled floor, and is seated with circular pews; seating capacity is about 1,200. It has numerous class rooms and other facilities for Bible school, Endeavor and institutional work. Brother Keevil pays an eloquent tribute to the generosity and faithfulness of his official board and other members of the church, and with his characteristic self-forgetfulness, gives them all the credit of this splendid achievement.

Harrison, Ark.

The Christian congregation of Harrison, Ark., was organized by W. B. Flippin soon after the civil war, and with many trials and difficulties has continued a faithful band of Disciples. From its organization

Christian Church, John...

its growth has been ing the "anti" ele had to contend. becoming too small gregation the pres but on account of not finished till J. year. The buildin modern in all its ec The building was July 22. All other sisted with their Brother Deatherage sermon. We canno talented pastor wh lofty eloquence has people here to so i

Much is to be he
organizations.
County, conventi
Pickering and F
tions were largel
and quite effective
sionary intelligenc
forces in the Lord
On the evening
graduating exercis

teacher-training class, the first of our classes to finish their course and receive their diplomas. There were eleven graduates. The pastor, L. P. Kopp, is one of the most effective teachers to be found anywhere.

Now that we are well started for the present year, it remains for every superintendent, teacher, and pastor in the state, to give their earnest and prompt support to the Bible school work to insure gratifying results. Notices regarding the first quarter of the pledges made at Hannibal have been sent out and every one should make it a point to respond at once. Remember that the pledges are due quarterly, the 1st of July, October, January, and April. It will be much easier to pay these pledges in quarterly installments than to wait until the end of the year and have all to pay at once.   J. H. HARDIN, State Supt.
311 Century Bldg, Kansas City, Mo.

❁ ❁

The Churches to Blame.

In reply to your request to say something concerning the supply of preachers for our churches, I may say briefly that the chief difficulty lies with the churches. Time was when the churches were active in seeking out among its members worthy young men for the ministry, and these young men were encouraged to enter some college and prepare themselves for the great work to which they aspired. In short, the churches really furnished the material, and often helped to educate these young men. The case now is very different. Very few churches seem to feel any special interest in the education of their young men for the ministry. If a young man goes to college from any of our churches, it is probable that very few in the church know anything about his movements, and most of them care even less. This compels the young man to go, if he goes at all, without feeling that he has the church behind him, or any sympathy from the church as a whole, even if a few members should take an interest in him. But very generally, no one seems to care when or where he goes or what he may do. I do not charge this as wilful indifference upon the part of the churches. It seems to have become a habit, and now no one feels that there is any wrong in it, or even want of sympathy with the young man. Churches act upon the principle that "What is everybody's business is nobody's business," and as there is no organized effort to find and en-

courage young men to enter the ministry, the whole matter is left to take care of itself without any help whatever from the church.

Of course, there are other reasons why it is difficult to find young men willing to enter the ministry, but I believe the one I have given is the most fundamental and is really working very great evil at the present time.
Columbia, Mo.   W. T. MOORE.

❁ ❁

South Kentucky's Secretary Reminiscent.

Fifty-one to-day. What a wonderful thing it is to live—yes even in the flesh—and meet the realities of life. What great problems to solve! What wonderful obligations to confront! Fifty-one years old to-day, June 28, 1906. More of this life passed away than there is to come. Fifty-one years old to-day. Not so many mistakes in the future as have been made in the past, let us hope and trust. Fifty-one years old to-day, and how is it with me? Not many of the family left—only one sister out of a large family of five boys and six girls—somewhat lonesome do you say? No! No! not much after all, for "Thou art with me," saith David. "I will never leave thee nor forsake thee," saith the Lord.

Fifty-one years old to-day, and out of a family of our own of six children, only one precious boy remains in the flesh with us, while the others are our "guardian angels," may we not believe?

Fifty-one years old to-day, and what are the prospects for the future of this life? Very hopeful indeed. God is blessing us as never before and crowning our labors in South Kentucky with abundant success. Two months of our missionary year gone and nearly $1,500 of the $4,000 we are going to raise for South Kentucky missions this missionary year, already raised in cash and good pledges. That will do very well, don't you think? I do. Besides the summer campaign is just now on. Two days from this date we enter the evangelistic field for the entire summer and fall, reaching to December 15. Let us all work to one great end—that of saving the lost around us. We are every day one day's march nearer home than ever before, when a day's work for the Lord is done.

Fifty-one years old this 28th day of June,

in the year of our Lord, 1906, and what are the prospects for the joys of the life to come? Growing brighter every day, thank you. The higher we climb, the brighter the way becomes, until we can almost see the loved ones, and feel their touch and hear their voice. Blessed hope. Praise God.—W. J. Hudspeth, Hopkinsville, Ky.

NEWS FROM MANY

Louisiana.

May 10 we began a meeting at Ruston, La., my wife directing the music and myself doing the preaching. We had one man and five women to start with. Others showed up when we went on for a few days; but there were only a few who had been members before that were heard from. However, it happened that the few we found in Ruston were of good quality. We held the meeting against a most stubborn opposition for eight weeks and three days. Result: A church of 46 members, a beautiful lot bought and paid for, which cost $700 cash, and a good subscription on a stone-cement block church, with preaching twice a month. We, in the midst of the meeting, entertained the state convention of about 100 delegates free of charge to them, without a hitch. The convention contributed $500 to the Ruston house and lot. Our Louisiana brotherhood regard the Ruston meeting as another victory for New Testament Christianity.——Wife and I begin next Wednesday night at Calhoun, La. Like Ruston, Calhoun has never had a sermon by one of our preachers. We have but one member in or about Calhoun that we know of, but I feel delighted to have the honor of joining this one member, and opening fire on the forts of sin in that town. I will preach the Gospel in Calhoun with as much force as a badly jaded man can, till the forts give way and we establish a church.—John A. Stevens.

Indian Territory Letter.

We are making some notable advances in the Indian Territory. Last week we arranged with the Chickasaw church to become a living link. Already we have engaged Bro. R. E. Rosenstein, the popular and successful minister at Bartlesville. He will evangelize throughout the Chickasaw Nation. He is ready to lend a helping hand to any small band of Disciples within his field. We hope to establish a church in every neighborhood in the Chickasaw. We ask that the brethren throughout the Chickasaw receive him kindly and co-operate with him heartily. Those wishing to secure him should write him for the present at Bartlesville, or to S. R. Hawkins, South McAlester, I. T. A good friend of our Indian Territory work, who lives in Indiana, has notified me that he is having a fine new tent made in Kansas City, and will ship it to me in a few days. He does not give us this tent, but lends it to us until he sees fit to call for it, which will be not for nearly a year, if at all. We are planning to hold our greatest convention the last week in August. It will be held with the church in South McAlester. The C. W. B. M. convention will immediately precede that of the Indian Territory Missionary Co-operation. It will begin on Monday afternoon. August 27, and continue until noon the following day. The I. T. M. C. will begin the afternoon of Tuesday, August

28, and continue until Thursday night following. We wil have the strongest program ever presented by one of our conventions in the I. T. The location is a central one, the railroad facilities are the best afforded by the Territory, the program will be a feast of good things from end to end, the season the most opportune of the whole year, the rate of travel the lowest obtainable, and the cause paramount. All this being true, we have a right to expect a great and enthusiastic gathering. Reader, if you reside in the I. T., we want you to come and be with us in this convention, for it will do you good, and through you will bless the cause.   H.

Southwest Missouri.

While this section has been receiving some of our finest workers we have been called on to lose some of our best. D. W. Moore, so long at South St. Springfield, has succeeded J. H. Mohorter at the Central, Pueblo, Colo. And now O. W. Jones, for four years at Jasper, goes to Milan, this state. In the course of time, however, we expect to kill the fatted calf as we welcome them home again.

The church at Marionville is seeking to secure J. R. Blunt, of Richland; Pierce City has eyes on R. H. Tanksley, of Neodasha, Kan., and Diamond is working hard for Jas. M. Miller, all as pastors. Our churches thus are coming to seek men instead of men seeking them. And nothing but the best will do either. These are fine young men. Brother Miller has just finished school at Kentucky University, and has many opportunities, but southwest Missouri claims him.

J. W. Baker, our tireless Jasper County evangelist, has been doing some work outside the county by urgent solicitation. At Monett he assisted Robert Simons and the church to wipe out their debt of many years standing. Pierce City, near there, then wanted him and he has just concluded a meeting there with a number of additions and money raised to employ a pastor for all the time. Joseph Gaylor, who had been supplying for them prepared the way. Now they have the "vision." Brother Baker's plan is to locate a pastor wherever he holds a meeting with a pastorless church. This is the fourth time he has succeeded. We hear that W. C. Willey, of Carl Junction, has just closed a great meeting at Waco, this county, with 50 additions.

Neosho, under the energetic leadership of F. F. Walters, is going to build a new house. The lot is already purchased. The Webb City church has just enlarged their building with galleries ready for a meeting, with Lockhart and Garmong. Carterville, their neighbor, talks a new building.

The South Joplin church, under the leadership of Geo. L. Peters, is making steady progress. They have a fine mission Bible school in Blendville, the southwest section of Joplin, with an attendance of 50. He will hold his own meeting this September.

At the First, Joplin, we are in a campaign to increase our Bible school. J. H. Hardin, state secretary, was with us last week in an institute. We propose to have a modern school in every sense of the word. Last Sunday in the rain we organized a fine mission at Villa Heights, in the east part of the city. We will at once erect a good building seating 200 and hope to follow with a meeting and possibly organize our third church before the end of the year. J. W. Baker will oversee the

A Free Bottle.

Indian Territory Letter.

We have just returned from a short vacation in the Indian Territory, and while there held a short meeting at Roff. There were 18 additions to the church. They had held a very successful meeting only a few months before, and had a large ingathering. The purpose of our meeting was to present a special series of doctrinal sermons setting forth our plea for a restoration of the New Testament church, and gather in, if possible, some who were not reached by the former meeting. The congregation was greatly strengthened and another harvest will be gathered in the early future.

The Roff church is one of the best in the territory. Its success so far is largely due to its faithful minister, Bro. E. S. Allhands. He is one of God's noblemen and is loved and respected by everybody in the town. It is a matter of general regret that he has decided to give up his pastorate there in the early future to re-enter the evangelistic field. This looks like a mistake on the part of both pastor and church.

We were surprised to see so many evidences of the material growth and prosperity of the country.

There are plenty of Indians yet, but they are being civilized and Christianized, and are becoming good farmers and citizens. The per cent of church members among them is about as large as it is among the white people.

Our visit and experiences there were the most pleasant and profitable.

We begin next Sunday at Converse, Mo.—Fife and Saunders, evangelists, Kansas City, Mo.

❧ ❧

Illinois Notes.

The Davidson reunion, lasting a fortnight, was one of the summer events of Eureka. Mrs. Dr. Crawford, president of the I. C. E. A., the youngest of ten children, with her brother, W. A. Davidson, planned and carried it to successful completion. All the children are living, and were present. There were 88 descendants of father and mother, who settled near Eureka in 1831, where they raised their family, made their record and died. The relatives are widely scattered, New York and Arkansas being represented as well as other states. There were three great public days. One on the Fourth of July, when a picnic was held in the old home pasture. A sumptuous dinner was enjoyed by about 300 kindred and friends. A number of addresses were made, the opening one fittingly by Hon. Ben Davidson, of Fayetteville, Ark., another by Frank Davidson, a Missouri state legislator. Others spoke and others sang. Another important occasion was the reception at Dr. Crawford's residence, which was beautifully decorated, where some 250 people met the Davidsons and tendered their congratulations and good wishes to the ten children, all more than three-score years old. The other and chief event was the spiritual services on the Lord's day. Prof. B. J. Radford, a life long friend, delivered a powerful sermon. The choir was chosen from the family. All Davidsons came in a body and sat together. Their father's barn was the early sanctuary to the pioneer preaching of the Gospel. So it is not surprising that the children, and children's children, to the fourth generation, should look forward as the climax of their family reunion, to this time when they should gather at the Lord's table together once more, and doubtless for the last time on earth. May it be the happy lot of every one so to live that he shall sit down

in the larger family, in the "sweet by and by."

At Barnett, we had a pleasant call with William Barnett, a former trustee of Eureka College, who moved to Eureka to educate his boys. He regards this as one of the best investments that he ever made, for both his boys now are active officers in the church. Better give more attention to the boys and girls, even if we do not have quite so many hogs and horses.

The little church at Gillespie is having a hard struggle, as nearly all new churches do, in their earlier years. It is not far from St. Louis, and has been supplied by Dr. Lettenberger part of the time.

The Carlinville church is prospering under the ministry of A. L. West and his faithful wife. They have a good house, good field and good prospects. United, vigorous effort will soon make the church the leading spiritual power of the city.

T. R. Hodkinson is getting well into the work at Palmyra, where we have one of the good old churches of the state. The large audience that came to hear about Christian education showed a deep interest in one of the vital forces of the kingdom of God, the Christian college. Such evidence is not always visible. Is it still a question whether we really believe very much in the moral and spiritual culture of our young people? Do we believe much in the training and education of young men for the ministry? But we will grow into these larger enterprises, as we have already grown in missionary and benevolent work. It will some day be a great pleasure to see young men consecrating themselves to the ministry and being trained for the world's life. Palmyra gave us the McPherson boys, one our missionary in Havana, Cuba, the other preaching at Dunkirk, N. Y.

Modesto is about arranging for a minister. They have a good house and a good membership, in a good field. United effort and personal sacrifices will win a great victory for the Master here.

At Sheldon I found Fred Nichols spending the summer trying to build up the church. He will still visit the church after school opens and he returns to Eureka College. With such preaching and pastoral care as Brother Nichols can give, the church will prosper.

At Donovan J. N. Cloe has just entered the new elegant parsonage with his splendid bride, and they are already well enshrined in the hearts of the people. His work is divided among the churches at Donovan, Prairie Dell and Iroquoise, certainly field enough for his holiest ambi-

tion, and we predict prosperity to the work in his hands. At Donovan Ellia Gish preaches half time, and at Pitwood the other half. He is resting from his school studies and spending the summer with the churches for which he preaches. Not only is he looking up the spiritual interests of the churches, in visiting the people, enlarging the Sunday-schools, the Christian Endeavor Societies, and harmonizing the church forces but he is superintending the repairing of both churches of worship. Several hundred dollars will be used in this way. We are looking for a large increase in the attendance of young preachers, that have had some experience, in September. Churches without preachers in reach, would do well to write us early, so as to secure a good man. By good management, a little time, sacrifice and co-operation all churches in reach of Eureka can have good ministers.

M. G. O'Brien has just finished his first year's service at Kankakee. He has baptized about 40 people and materially improved the house of worship. The church numbers some 250 members, with an Endeavor Society of about 75 as fine young people as we have in any church. The Sunday-school has about 200 enrolled and has been a great power for good in carrying forward the church's work, as it always will, when properly managed. Kankakee is a good city and the church ought to be a great power in its moral and spiritual life, but it suffers much from removals, and being out of the territory where we are numerous, few move in.—J. G. Wagoner, Eureka, Ill.

:r.

reather in the
corn is being
an race should
ongregation at
enlarged house
The writer has
G. P. Clark
f this thriving
meeting at
te wide atten-
ers are attend-
hods of Brother
d everything in
——J. M. Lowe
angelist after a
at Blue Rapids
s has been try-
t Eskridge dur-
The bones are
y. Bert Bentley
ice.——W. M.
ary meeting at
W. H. Nation
g at Kanopolis,
es have recent-
orado, Hartford,
One is scheduled
ing to-morrow,
e ground where
en. These coun-
sionary nature,
siderable utility
ple who seldom
conventions.——
ion meets with
tember 17 to 20,
be given by the
. on Thursday
rates have been
ounced in a few
g to make this
history of our
esigned his po-
of missions, to
intention is to
Seven years of
one to a line of
y, and more
W. S. Lowe

n Letter.

ot seriously af-
Yakima Valley
st keep up well
ent.——Wapalo
riter last Janu-
expects to be
in three weeks.
y this work an.
uring the sum-
Des Moines, Ia.,
advantages at
I wish to speak
Bro. and Sister

Lands

eral Colonisation
ilway Exchange,
folder, telling all
y the Santa Fe in
do, New Mexico,
ct to homestead

inoccupied acres.
gated, or crops
em of "dry farm-
al card to find out

and in

rnia

Green. They give one of the best concerts
that it has been my privilege to hear and
have received highest praise from the most
critical musical people of the Pacific coast
cities. Our churches and societies need have
no hesitancy in securing them when they go
east, as they will be sure to please.——Our
state work in Washington under the direction of the East and West Washington
Boards of Missions show gains for the
year and it is to be hoped that with the new
experience they have had under the new
order a much larger work may be done in
this year.——North Yakima church is prospering. The fund for the new building is
growing satisfactorily. The church has
kindly granted the pastor a three months'
leave and he with his family will start east
about August 8th for a rest and recreation, and to visit the "home folks."——Ellensburg church is building and the work is
going forward. Another year will show
all of our churches in Central Washington
well housed. There is vast opportunity for
securing good homes and paying investments here in the Yakima Valley and I
shall be pleased to answer any inquiries
from brethren who propose coming if they
will enclose stamp for reply.——Why is the
CHRISTIAN-EVANGELIST like a Yakima Valley orchard? Because it bears more and
better fruit each year and leaves no bitter taste.—Morton L., Rose.

From the Old Dominion.

The Lord's work in the Old Dominion
has been displaying greater vigor than
usual recently. The prospects for a successful summer and fall campaign are particularly bright.——C. O. Woodward is
preaching in a tabernacle seating 800 people, while the Manchester church is being
enlarged. He has been having great congregations.——F. W. Berry is erecting two
new church buildings this summer. One
at Trix and the other near Finneywood.
——The new house at Blackstone is nearing completion." It is a beauty, and a
credit to the Blackstone brethren and to
the cause at large.——After so long a time
of planning the Petersburg brethren have
the roof on their new house, and will get
into it this fall. With the completion of
this splendid house the Petersburg church
should be self-supporting at a very early
date. It is now a V. C. M. S. mission.——
W. R. Jinnett has made a good beginning
at Newport News.——At the very beginning of the ministry of C. N. Williams, the
Sunday-school room of the Hampton
church was destroyed by fire, the main auditorium was only slightly damaged.——D.
S. Henkel, and Bro. Blick have recently
held a meeting at a mission place in East
End Newport News in which there were
more than forty added. J. T. Watson and
W. I. Burner added forty-seven at Chestnut Grove in Craig county. W. G. Johnston added forty-five at Level Green, and
organized a congregation of fifty at Lucas
Memorial. This latter congregation worships in the house erected on the Lucas
homestead, near the burial place of the
sainted C. S. Lucas.——Brother Adams, of
Bluefield and Stephen Davis of Tazewell,
added forty-five at Falls Mills.——J. S.
Meadows added twenty-four at Grassy
Spur.——H. D. Coffey erected a permanent
tabernacle on the best lot in East Roanoke
in the month of June. He is now holding
the first meeting ever held by white Disciples in Floyd county. We have a colored church in the county.——Jas. P. Licht-

---

enberger of New York, and Miss Wambaugh of Angola, Ind., are in a promising
meeting with the Tazewell church.——The
Piedmont assembly will be held July 20
to August 8. This is a great event
among Virginia Disciples, and the present
meeting promises to be as good as any of
its predecessors.—H. C. Combs.

CHURCH FEDERATION READY.

The Inter-Church Conference on Federation, 700 pages, prepaid.....$4.00

The Present Status of the Union Question and our Attitude Toward It.*

The age in which we are living may be called an age of rapid transitions. Old philosophies are being rapidly supplanted. Psychology is an entirely different study from what it was fifteen years ago. All the data of science can by no means be said to be established beyond a doubt. We are rapidly taking on and in new ideas of civil polity. The science of government is undergoing such rapid changes that the old politicians are standing aghast at the transformation. Sociology is a new science to-day. So is economics. Political economists are walking in a much brighter light than did Adam Smith a century and a quarter ago. Things that were legally right are getting to be legally wrong. Systems are nothing; truth is everything. Everything to-day must prove its right to exist by some other claim than that it has existed for some time. Ability to cope with the present and the future is the clincher. Men are willing to see the old systems crumble provided the rubbish is cleared away for better ones to arise. To certain schools of thought this seems almost sacrilegious. But it will not seem so when we comprehend the fact that it is the function of truth to establish righteousness at any cost. Truth comes with a sword and peace can not be established without its use. So Christ said: "I am not come to bring peace but a sword."

Theological systems are put to the same tests as others. Wherever error is found or wrong conditions prevail, there truth must get in its work. And in no age of the world has truth been so active and potent as in this. So rapid are its strides that we can hardly keep apace with the world's progress. Some are getting behind trying to defend their systems, trying to keep their little systems of truth and human speculations from expanding and breaking their credal boundaries to let out the human and let in the divine. But others are catching the spirit of the day and are trying to let God and truth sweep grandly on, and do not lose their faith amidst the crumbling ruins. If this is an age of doubt, it is doubt in the permanency of existing institutions and forms rather than doubt in God or Christ. Some are making the mistake of waiting to actively identify themselves with truth until it takes permanent form. But this it will not do unless it becomes crystallized, and it can not become crystallized for it is living.

The age, then, in which we are living demands conscientious thinking, candid spirits, and Christian charity; for the gravest problems of to-day are those that vitally concern the church. It seems to me that we are in one of the most important transition periods in the history of the church. The movements are rapid, the strides are long, the direction right. In all this we have a part to play, the most important in my judgment of all the religious bodies.

The one question whose solution involves the solution of all others is the question of Christian unity. We have not laid too much stress upon this vital question. And I am most profoundly convinced that there is more need to-day than at any previous time in our history, to preach Christian unity. Not church unity, for no such unity is contemplated in the New Testament.

But in our treatment of the question to-day, it is necessary to raise the congressman's question, "Where are we at?" In other words, have we made any progress in its solution? Is the Christian world where it was a hundred years ago? I answer, and you will agree with the answer, we have made progress in its solution, and the Christian world is long stages ahead of where it was a hundred years ago.

The Christian unity problem is a complex one. We know what the answer should be, or we think we do. Toward that answer we have taken some steps. Were this not the case we would have existed almost a century in vain. This none of us will admit. We have impressed ourselves most remarkably upon the Christian thought of the world, and the problem is in part solved, in fact the major part. For have we not seen a divided church, once wholly inimical to the idea of Christian unity as chimerical and undesirable, change until almost every denomination now regards it as both practicable and desirable? How has this come about? Simply by the idea inaugurated by the Campbells, and advocated by their co-workers (not followers), both contemporaries and successors, with such persistency and persuasion, that it gradually percolated through the various religious bodies so quietly and yet effectually, that it seemed to many of them that it originated with them. The idea as yet is largely in the formative period with them, and therefore looks very imperfect to us who have lived in it and grown up with it.

Now, it seems to me that the very imperfection of the idea of Christian unity as an ultimate consummation, held by our religious neighbors, demands two things of us.

1. That we continue to emphasize the scriptural conception of ultimate union, because we are in a better position than any other body to be teachers on this subject, having been drilled for nigh a century in the art of teaching it. And let me emphasize, we should approach the task with becoming humility and Christian patience, not only because we are no more intelligent than those we would teach, but also because we have had better advantages than they to comprehend the Scriptural idea, having made it the theme of special study.

2. We should hail with profound gratitude every opportunity of closer approach to those we would teach. All Christian truth held in common should be made a bond of unity in love. In the realm of honest differences the utmost deference should be shown those who do not agree with us. We should aim to supplant controversy with conference on points of difference; not that controversy does not have its merits at certain stages in any propagandism; but, that after we have gained our place among the religious forces and established our right to exist, aye more, have created a demand for the very thing that was once rejected as useless and worthless, then the time has come for conference, for in free and fraternal conference there is the best opportunity to show the merits of our ware.

Now I have said all these things to emphasize the one need of getting where we can do the most effective teaching along the line of our specialty. Where is that position? The full answer must await until I have said a few other things. But in passing let me say that I believe the time is ripe for the most effective presentation of our plea to the teachers of the

E. S. Muckley.

other religious bodies. We have never yet been able to get at the rank and file of what some of us are pleased to call the denominations. I am convinced that the only way to reach the masses of the other churches with our plea of Christian unity is to get at them through their teachers, the ministry. For the people generally have confidence in their leaders. Denominations are not dead. They do not even seem to be dying. They continue to show an increase every year. To compass Christian unity, does it mean that we must win all these into our church fellowship, by having them come into formal fellowship with our local churches? If Christian unity can come only by this program, it will never come in my humble judgment. The program I am wont to think has been prepared by a higher power than man. God is working now as surely and irresistably as ever in the evolution of things. I am as sure that Christian unity will be acomplished as I am that Christ reigns. And I am equally sure that it will be accomplished in God's way in spite of human prejudices. The condition of denominationalism existing to-day was not contemplated in New Testament times. Therefore the steps from denominationalism to unity are not marked out in the New Testament. If they were the problem would be easy. But the condition being extra-apostolic, the program will be extra-apostolic.

But to guard myself at this point from being misunderstood, I want to say that the picture of the united church is distinct in the New Testament. So perfect is it that we do not want to fail to bring our religious neighbors where they can get the same clear view we have, so they may fall in love with the picture. But apart from that, all we have to help us is certain guiding principles. The distinct steps are not marked out for us. Now I insist that any step that does not compromise the Gospel, that will bring the divided church to a nearer view of the apostolic church, is a step that can be taken by our people with the confidence that God in his overruling providence is guiding it. Now, if the masses of the religious bodies can only be brought to see the perfect New Testament church through the instrumentality of their teachers, we should hail with delight any movement that will put us in closer touch with these teachers. Any assumption of pharisaical superiority will not do it. Any disposition to reject proper overtures for closer Christian fellowship will create the impression that we are not sincere in our desire for unity, and will discredit our plea not only before the Christians in other churches, but before the world as well. We would thus lose our grip and influence alike upon the church and world. The only thing necessary for us to guard is that we do not compromise our position.

While the subject of this paper does not involve a historical statement of Christian unity, showing how schisms occurred in the church, and how the idea of unity had its inception and growth, there is a philosophy of that history that is vitally connected with, and in measure explanatory of, the present status of the union question and what should be our attitude towards it. To this phase of the question I invite your most earnest attention and most conscientious consideration; for the facts I now propose to set forth and what seem to me to be the logical deductions from them, are of most vital importance in relation in this all-absorbing theme.

Denominationalism was the only and inevitable pathway by which God could lead his church out of the anti-Scriptural unity of medieval ages into the Scriptural unity for which we have been praying. The distance from unity under a pope to unity under Christ was too great for one step. The very age in which Luther lived made it impossible for him to see what we see to-day, and achieve what we are trying to achieve to-day. In the first place, he did not get into all the light himself; and second, if he had he could not have gotten the church into it. And it was but natural, in an age when the doctrines of the church were comprehended in forms of human symbols and creeds, that Luther and his followers should put in credal form the doctrines that differentiated them from Rome, out of whose bondage they had been delivered at so great a cost. Then besides, it was but natural that the author of the memorable ninety-five theses should be the dominating personality in the forming of a creed and a party, though he did not intend that his name should be the symbol of that party; and in fact, it was his hope that a new party would not be necessary. However, other new parties did spring up to correct errors and appropriate unemphasized truths. And it was unavoidable, too, that nonessentials should be made the basis of new propagandisms, because of the imperfect vision of men. So Protestantism had its attendant evils, for no other reason than that all evils can not be eradicated at once. But it likewise had its attendant good; for a divided Protestantism was infinitely preferable to a united Catholicism.

We are wont to speak of denominationalism as the state of Babel, the confusion of tongues. But was not this confusion of tongues, this scattering of the people, necessary to defeat the purposes and overthrow the ambitions of men?

I believe that God made Babel out of Rome, by the confusion of tongues in denominationalism, to break up a unity that was not in harmony with his purposes for his church, in order that he might bring about a desire for that unity that would achieve his own purposes in his own way. Not that God endorsed human weaknesses that produced denominations, or the errors that made them necessary; but that he used them in spite of these weaknesses and errors.

But from another standpoint denominationalism was a necessary concomitant of Protestantism. It resulted from the application of the fundamental principle of the reformation, the principle of religious liberty and private judgment; the very principle, the working out of which, made the restoration movement of the last century possible. If one man had the right to exercise private judgment in the interpretation of Scripture and gather about him those whose private judgment led them toward him, another had the same right, and still another and another, until men abused it as every good thing has been abused.

Still again. The very forms of state government of the reformation period, in which one or a very few held the reins of national affairs, was conducive to denominationalism. The fact that the few assumed, without being questioned, the right to guide in the affairs of state, made it easy and natural for one strong character or a few to assume the right to guide in religious affairs. And in fact, while it was the principle of private judgment that made the reformation popular as a bold and original idea, yet so timid were the masses in applying it, and so easy was it for them by habit, both in state and religious affairs, to let others do their thinking for them, that they did not question the right of their leaders to determine what the Bible taught and formulate its doctrines into creeds for them. And the very protestant spirit would produce other strong leaders who would gather their followers into parties.

I have said this much to show that denominationalism was a necessary condition of Protestantism and a result of the spirit of the times. That God was in the Protestant movement I think none of us question. The great religious bodies have been used of him for the conservation of truth. They had a right to exist. So few were the evils of divided Protestantism compared with those of united Catholicism, that they were not seen at first. But the right of yesterday becomes the wrong of to-day, through the law of progress. God used denominationalism as an expedient, not a finality. The time was to come when he would be done with it. Has that time come? We have been saying yes for nearly a hundred years. Louder and louder we have been

*A paper read by E. S. Muckley, of Portland, before the State Ministerial Association of the Oregon State Convention at Turner, June 22.

sounding it forth, other isolated voices joining us in the cry, until well nigh the whole religious world is making it echo through the land.

Now what are the deductions from these facts, and what our logical attitude toward these bodies taking up the cry for unity but seeing with an imperfect vision. The work they did before, our restoration movement made it possible. It can not be proven that if Alexander Campbell had lived in Luther's day he would have seen with any clearer vision than Luther did. The only safe inference is that he would not. Luther, Zwingli, Calvin, the Wesleys, sowed; he reaped. They labored; he entered into their labors and wrought more largely.

Now if these things be so, and I think no one will dissent from these statements, we can not afford to take any attitude toward the other religious bodies that would seem to ignore the great work they have done for Christianity. This is my first deduction, and one previously hinted. Second: We are bound, by the very fact that God has placed the seal of his approval upon their work despite their errors, and by the fact that we are under obligations to them for working out the Protestant idea and problem to the point where our movement was made possible, to enter into the closest possible co-operative fellowship with them consistent with loyalty to the apostolic conception of unity.

The question is: Shall we co-operate in a haphazard, accidental sort of way, or shall we enter into a methodized co-operation after a plan mutually agreed upon? To federate or not to federate, that is the question? I say federate, if we can secure a basis of federation that will not morally bind us to stay out of any community where we feel we ought to preach the Gospel. From this on let us look at some of the objections and difficulties in the way of federation.

The objection is filed against it that it contemplates a handicap upon our people, that it is a deliberate plan conceived in the hearts of our enemies to greatly limit our freedom. To think that the great body of Christian gentlemen who gathered in New York city last November had laid awake nights concocting a scheme to entrap a million and a quarter people into an irretrievable loss of their liberty in the land of the free and the twentieth century, is too ridiculous to seriously consider were it not for the suspicion it casts upon earnest Christian men seeking a way to union. Brethren, "Love thinketh no evil," and we are a New Testament church, you know. We have no right to treat our religious neighbors with suspicion. Suspicion will not promote unity. Sow suspicion and we will reap suspicion. Sow confidence and the seed will be true to its kind.

Objection second. We can not federate, because to do so would be to recognize the denominational churches as churches of Christ. Though you will allow me to confess that it is difficult for me to see why a Methodist church that gave $1,700 for foreign missions as the Taylor Street Church of Portland did last year, is not as worthy of being called a Christian church, as is one of ours, that does not contribute a dollar for any mission in the light of the command to go into all the world. But still I am willing to waive the claim that the denominational churches are churches of Christ, and insist that we should federate with them anyhow, because we all admit that there are Christians among them. I insist that federation, which is nothing more than methodized co-operation after some mutually agreed upon plan, involves neither the endorsement nor the extenuation of that which is censurable in the creeds, names and practices of the other religious bodies. Does the fact that God used the reformers and the denominations they led, mean that he endorsed the errors they brought out of Rome and their failure to appropriate their full New Testament privileges? Not at all. If God has worked with the great religious bodies in spite of their errors in his effort to lead us away from our errors into the truth, then I, who am nor infallible though I may stand in a little larger light than my neighbors, can not afford to refuse to associate in the most intimate way possible with the great bodies

with whom God has worked for centuries. But you say: "To federate means to"—but hold on; it doesn't matter what federation means in some other connection. What meaning has it as applied to the closer affiliation of the parts of the divided church? Let us not have a war over words; the principle is what we are after. If the principle is right it matters little what word is the vehicle of its meaning. Nearly all the war in the church anyhow has been over terminology. Let us escape that blunder. It may be well to emphasize the fact that no federation has ever demanded exact likeness on the part of the federation bodies. A common interest was all that was ever demanded. If federation with the religious bodies meant the endorsement of their errors, I would be its deadliest enemy.

The one question is, can we work with Christian people in other religious bodies in a closer, more fraternal way? Will we ignore their approaches to us in an I-am-more-holy-than-thou air, or will we take these religious neighbors by the hand in Christian love, and work with them in a federation which is imperfect that we may help them realize the perfect union for which they are looking? By the federation plan the spirit of co-operation would be encouraged and extended by reason of the fact that a plan has been mutually agreed upon. It would result ultimately in great economy in administering the affairs of the kingdom. For churches that are essentially alike would not attempt to cover the same territory in neglected communities. Working together thus in the spirit of Christ, because of frequent conferences that would thus be made possible and necessary, would emphasize the points of agreement and lead to a strong desire to eliminate, in harmony with the truth, all differences that are keeping us from complete unity.

As I view this question, it is not so much a question as to whether we will lose by federating, as it is one of how much we will lose by not federating; for in refusing to federate, we could prove neither to God nor man the sincerity of our plea for Christian unity. And God will simply allow us to crystallize our notions of how unity ought to be brought about into a narrow unwritten creed that will be more binding and demoralizing than the written creeds of our neighbors; and then we will become a disappearing brotherhood sure, as sure as truth has power to burst all creeds and lead their narrow devotees out of their narrow confines and make them disappear into the great company of unfettered souls in Christ.

Before the great naval battle of Trafalgar, Admiral Nelson called to his flag ship Captain Collingwood and Captain Hardy who had been deadly enemies, and commanded them to shake hands as he pointed to the French fleet and said: "Gentlemen, there's your enemy." Brethren, as I understand it, in the plan of federation I can shake hands with my brethren of the other religious bodies without the sacrifice of a single conviction or the compromise of a single essential position, while I see my Master pointing with pierced hands to the hosts of Satan emboldened by the fact of a divided church, and hear him say with trumpet tones: "Brethren, there's your enemy." Yes, and I can see him point to the whitening harvest fields and hear him say: "There's your harvest. Together cast in your sickles, for I have called you to labor together as brethren and in its reaping."

❈ ❈

The Passing of a Veteran.

(Continued from Page 976.)

would be safe to say from 1,000 to 1,200 persons have been baptized since the beginning of this work in Wythe county.

During these twenty years Brother Snow preached monthly for eleven years for the church at Bell Spring, Va., often preaching twice a day and sometimes holding protracted meetings. He was also pastor of the church at Bristol, Tenn., for some time and had appointments from time to time in the counties of Pulaski, Bland, Tazewell, Floyd, Patrick and Henry in Virginia, and occasional calls to North Carolina and Tennessee. For this work he was content to have his expenses paid, which was not always done, however.

After the loss of his sight he ceased to travel but continued to preach for the Wythe county congregations until he removed to Washington, D. C., in 1884. Here he often preached for us and his life for over twenty years among us has been a holy benediction. Seventy years and over a Christian; nearly three score and ten, a preacher of the Gospel; for a score of years groping in physical night, he has grown and grown, and ripened and ripened, and his path, as the path of the just, has been brighter and brighter until it has come to the perfect day. Thursday, July 18, our aged and sightless pilgrim reached the city that hath foundations whose builder and maker is God, and opened his eyes to behold the God whom he served and the Savior who redeemed him. He has preached great sermons in these later years. Sermons on trust, on patience, on godliness. As he has grown in years he has grown in spiritual-mindedness, in trustfulness, in gentleness and loving kindness, in largeness and clearness of vision, in all the gifts and graces of the Spirit of God. A priceless heritage he has left to the church and to his loved ones in his long and useful life and lofty Christian character. "Mark the perfect man and behold the upright for the end of that man is peace."

Evangelistic

We invite ministers and others to send reports of meetings, additions and other news of the churches. It is especially requested that additions be reported as "by confession and baptism" or "by letter."

HOT FROM THE WIRE.

Special to THE CHRISTIAN-EVANGELIST.

Atchison, Kan., July 30.—Fifty-three to-day, 185 in seven days, 355 to date. Continue.—Scoville, Evangelist, W. T. Hilton, Pastor.

Special to THE CHRISTIAN-EVANGELIST.

Bethany Park, Ind., July 29.—Ten thousand people to-day. Largest attendance past week ever recorded. Program universally approved. Concerts under Hackleman enthusiastically received. Ground lighted with electricity, finest mineral water, interurban facilities every hour, $1,500 in cement walks, fine fishing and bathing, many new cottages, debts paid, are some things in which we rejoice. Ministerial and evangelistic schools this week. Come.—L. L. Carpenter.

Special to THE CHRISTIAN-EVANGELIST.

Manchester, N. H., July 30.—Over one thousand at Park Theatre last night at closing service. Theatre contract for July filled. No place for continuance. Meeting suspended over August for local reasons. Not ready for organization though over three hundred came forward to endorse the plea for unity and about one hundred promised to stand by mission, although not leaving their church. Situation cannot be appreciated by our people generally who know not New England. Newspapers say last night's demonstration remarkable for Manchester. Brother Crerie of Haverhill, Mass., will preach during the interval and prepare for final campaign. Have great hopes of good organization.—Herbert Yeuell.

Canada.

St. Thomas, Ont., July 26.—One added by baptism last night at the last service in the old church building.—James Egbert, pastor.

Illinois.

Farmer City, July 24.—Preached for church at Le Roy, July 22. Two baptisms as result.—A. Immanuel Zeller.

Sullivan, July 21.—Baptized 8 to-night, 7 additions at regular services to-day, 6 confessions. Forty-one since Jan. 1.—J. G. McNutt.

Greenville, July 22.—Two additions last Lord's day, one by baptism, one from another communion.—Tallie Defrees.

Sullivan, July 29.—Two additions at morning service to-day; union services at night; 2 baptisms during day.—J. G. McNutt.

Clinton, July 30.—Two were baptized, a husband and wife, and 3 others made confession at our evening service yesterday.—E. A. Gilliland.

Indiana.

Rushville, July 23.—Seven additions recently, two baptisms, three by letter and statement, two from another communion.—W. C. Sniff.

Brazil, July 19.—Six baptisms and 5 otherwise added here, not yet reported.—E. L. Day.

Indian Territory.

Roff, July 27.—Meeting closed last night with 18 additions under preaching of Evangelists Fife and Saunders. During my service here for two years and eight months the congregation has grown from 32 to 160, and a $3,000 church house has been built.—E. S. Allhands.

Kansas.

Asherville, July 24.—Two confessions last Lord's day.—G. F. Clark.

Mayetta, July 25.—Two confessions last Lord's day.—Nelson Gardner.

Kentucky.

Burgin, July 23.—Three weeks' meeting closed Friday night; result, 43 added, 31 by baptism,

4 from other communion, 8 by letter or statement. The church has not had such an awakening in years, if ever. O. W. Darnold, minister; J. T. McKissick, evangelist; C. W. Daniels, singer.—E. W. Reeves.

Michigan.

Allenville, July 19.—Since last report have had 1 addition at Lamont and 2 at Otter Lake, both by baptism. At Markey a new church was organized with 25 members of which 12 were baptized. An Aid, also was organized with 26 members. Building committee appointed and material promised and lot donated for new house of worship.—R. Bruce Brown.

Saginaw, July 23.—Two confessions at prayer-meeting Thursday. Are getting ready to paint building.—J. Murray Taylor.

Missouri.

Higbee, July 21.—Twenty-eight additions to church here Sunday, indirect result of union meeting.—A. N. Lindsey.

Macon, July 23.—Six more additions Sunday, making 24 since last report.

Butler, July 23.—One added yesterday by confession at Elizabeth Chapel. Immense audience for summer.—Henry W. Hunter.

Lamonte, July 25.—Am in meeting seven miles in the country.—I. H. Fuller.

Troy, July 25.—One addition by letter at Elsberry, July 22.—E. G. Merrill.

Unionville, July 25.—Began meeting here July 23. No Christian church here. Are using M. E. South house. Great prejudice, but audience doubled second night. W. L. Harris, of Lincoln, Neb., will assist us in meeting beginning August 16.—J. B. Lockhart.

Calhoun, July 24.—Good meeting here, with 7. J. Head as evangelist. Seven added so far, 3 confessions, 4 by statement. Meeting week old. Expect many more.—S. E. Hendrickson.

Ohio.

Beallsville, July 27.—Two additions last Lord's day at Belmont Ridge Church. Plans have been made for our fall meeting.—Ferd F. Schultz, minister.

Ontario.

Grand Valley, July 20.—Four baptisms and 2 by statement since last report.—J. Munro.

South Carolina.

St. Stephens, July 16.—Bonneau meeting resulted in the organization of a church and Bible school, and money raised to employ a preacher regularly. Two confessions at Russellville.—Charles E. Smith, state evangelist.

Texas.

Piano, July 24.—Fine meeting here. Twenty additions so far, 18 by confession; E. H. Holmes, minister.—John S. Zeran.

Mabank, July 23.—Closed missionary meeting here Saturday night. Fine growing town of 800 or 1,000 people. This first meeting held here by our people, except by an extremely "loyal" brother. Fourteen came forward, others will latter. Plans drawn up for new church building.—Ward Russell.

Fort Worth, July 23.—Five additions at the Tabernacle church yesterday.—A. E. Dubber.

Greenville, July 23.—Two baptisms at prayer-meeting. Two by letter yesterday, one by statement.—J. W. Holsapple.

Llano, July 23.—Meeting closed with 12 accessions, seven of them by confession and baptism. Bro. Arthur W. Jones, of Dallas, did the preaching. One young lady made the confession yesterday morning, and another this afternoon; both were baptized this afternoon.—J. J. Cramer.

Washington.

Rockford, July 24.—Work at this place in splendid condition; audiences nearly fill the house. Two additions last Lord's day.—A. J. Adams, pastor.

Changes.

Egbert, Jas.—St. Thomas, Ont., to Kipton, O.
Jones, O. W.—Jasper, to Milan, Mo.
Youtzy, D. A.—Plattsmouth, to Gering, Neb.
Trainum, W. H.—Chicago, to 823, Foster street, Evanston, Ill.
Bedall, W.—Acampo, to Garfield Park, Santa Cruz, Cal.
Parker, L. G.—Galesburg, Ill., to University Place Station, Des Moines, Ia.
Sloan, J. F.—Pleasant Hill, O., to 722 West Eighth Street, Topeka, Kan.
Hedges, Chas. P.—Bethany, to Follansbee, W. Va.
Black, B. V.—Garden City, Ia., to 201 Byron street, Mankato, Minn.
Wells, C. E.—Keota, to Griswold, Ia.
Morgans, Morgan—Indianapolis, Okla, to Atlanta, Texas.
Nichols, Fred A.—Auburndale, Fla., to Alliance, O.
Jackson, G. D.—Eustis, to Riverside avenue, Jacksonville, Fla.
Weste, Otto L.—Flat River to Boss, Mo.
Mahoney, J. Franklin—Toledo, to Niles, O.
Schmidt, C. F.—Mason City, to Plymouth, Ia.
Rogers, W. H.—Swampscott, to P. O. box 139, Lynn, Mass.
Longanecker, F. M.—Bethany, W. Va., to 429 West Walnut street, Kalamazoo, Mich.

Midweek Prayer-Meeting
August 8, 1906.

SINS OF THE TONGUE.—1 Pet. 3:10.

The crowning infamy of the tongue is blasphemy, and by this is meant profanity, and all speech that impairs men's faith in God or that in anywise detracts from his influence over the lives and hopes of men and his glory in the world.

They consist in evasion of responsibility, vid. Adam and Eve, Gen. 3:12, 13; half truths, vid. Gen. 20:2-7; deception, vid. Gen. 27:1-36; false promises, vid. Ex. 8:8, and the story of other plagues; insincerity, vid. 1 Sam. 24:8-22, and 26:1-5; lying, Acts 5:1-11; misrepresentation, Acts 24:1-8.

Flattery may not be the greatest sin of the tongue, but it is one of the commonest and most debasing. It is hard to tell which is most victimized—the one on its throne or the fawner at its base. There may be thrift in fawning but there is debasement. Honest praise for real merit is commendable, but to degrade ourselves by insincere expressions of approval or praise is an abdication of real manhood and womanhood.

"Words are things of little cost,
Quickly spoken, quickly lost;
We forget them, but they stand
Witnesses at God's right hand,
And their testimony bear,
For us or against us there.

"Oh, how oft our words have been
Idle words and words of sin;
Words of anger, scorn and pride,
Or desire our thoughts to hide;
Envious tales, or strife unkind,
Leaving bitter thoughts behind!"

One may soon forget the impatient word spoken as he hastens to his morning task, but in the heart of wife or child it may rankle all day and more painfully than if a brutal driver had lashed them with a heavy whip. We would have risked our lives to protect them from the ruffian, but love ourselves too much to make the sacrifice involved in so controlling ourselves as to leave a gentle instead of a turbulent word for our farewell.

Deception—mendacity is one of the commonest sins of the tongue. This is often practiced where we should least expect it—in the death chamber. We approach one already unconsciously embarking for that bourne whence no traveler returneth and say "Why, how well you look, how greatly you have improved!" when we are conscious that the lilies in their faces are more pallid and their cheeks are frailer. To no purpose we have diverted their thoughts from God when they should be thinking of little else. We have chained their attention to earth that should be riveted upon the gates of pearl. We have deceived them and wronged ourselves.

The tongue of the soothsayer often involves its owner in blood guiltiness. If one should say to the pleasure party drifting down the river, "I know there are no rapids below, sing joyfully and without concern," ought not a measure of responsibility devolve on him when amid shrieks of horror they are fatally engulfed in the waiting cataract? Who, then, can compute the guilt of those who say to our youth, "Go on in your thoughtlessness. The judgment is a priestly fable, hell is an exploded myth, the present is supreme." In equal peril, too, are those who teach that the mercy of God makes unnecessary any reparation or contrition for our wrong doing or minimize the heinousness or fatality of sin.

Sunday-School
August 12, 1906.

THE PARABLE OF THE TWO SONS.—Luke 15:11-32.

Memory Verses: 17, 18.

GOLDEN TEXT.—Return unto me and I will return unto you.—Mat. 3:7.

This lesson would have been better named, "The parable of the Father and Son." The chief point of it is the relation of the father to his wandering boy rather than the relation between the prodigal and his elder brother. The latter element, however, is not lacking. The Pharisees were grumbling because Jesus associated with sinners. (Luke 15:1.) To silence them, Jesus spoke three parables—sometimes called the "three parables of grace"—showing how lost things are sought and how they are appreciated when found. The contrast between the two brothers shows that a wayward and despised wanderer may be more worthy of consideration than a selfish, sullen and respectable saint.

In studying parables it must be borne in mind that no one parable can be made the vehicle for the conveyance of all truth, not even the whole truth about one subject. It is usually an illustration of some one great principle. This group of parables will illustrate this. The occasion for them, as already stated, was the Pharisees' criticism of Jesus for his friendly attitude to sinners. His defense was that the divine grace reaches out to sinners, that they are capable of restoration, and consequently that good men ought to be friendly and helpful to them.

The lost sheep, the lost coin and the lost son all illustrate this splendid principle—the very corner stone of all religion. But as to how the return of the lost is effected, one might draw very different theories from the different parables. The lost coin was wholly passive. It was lost through no fault of its own; it must patiently remain lost until a power above itself seized it and brought it back. This is a Calvinistic parable. The lost sheep strayed through its own wilfulness or carelessness and perhaps even resisted the grace which sought to save it, but it was saved in spite of itself. Hyper-Calvinism here. The prodigal son went away from home by the free act of his own will, and he came back by his own free act. The father awaited his return but did nothing to expedite it. With no need of "enabling grace," the prodigal came back when his own experiences taught him the wisdom and propriety of so doing. This can be cited in support of Arminianism.

But the fact is that the parables support neither Calvinism nor Arminianism, because they were not designed to show just how sinful man gets back to God, but only the great fact of the universal love of God and the salvability of man.

These are the great truths which Jesus seemed always most anxious to impress upon his followers and hearers; that man is worth saving, that he can be saved, that God wants to save him, that the true and natural relation between God and man is so intimate that it is no exaggeration to speak of them as father and son, and that the present sinful condition of any man is not a destruction of this relationship but only a sad interruption of its enjoyment.

Without pressing the details of the parable too far, note the significance of the following expressions in the parable: "Give me the portion of goods that falleth to me." This was a presumptuous demand. The boy had no claims yet to his father's estate. Sin begins with a demand for a kind and degree of liberty to which one has no right.

"Wasted his substance." Sin is wasteful. It is a misuse of resources, a foolish squandering of powers designed for higher uses. "He went and joined himself to a citizen of that country." The rejection of the easy ties of sonship and the demand for utter freedom from all constraint ends in slavery of the most degrading type.

"He came to himself." The sinner is abnormal. He is beside himself. His first need is to come to his true self. People often think of religion as something abnormal, a departure from the natural life of man. It is a return to true and sane and complete manhood.

"My son was lost and is found." The sinner is still a son. He has abandoned the privileges of sonship, but in the fact that he is still a son lies the ground of his worth and of the possibility of his return.

Christian Endeavor

By GEO. L. SNIDELY

August 12, 1906.

FAVORITE PARABLES.—Matt. 13:10-17; Psa. 119:97-104.

DAILY READINGS.

M.	The Sower.	Matt. 13:1-17.
T.	The Marriage Feast.	Matt. 22:1-14.
W.	The Gospel Net.	Matt. 13:47-50.
T.	The Vineyard.	Matt. 20:1-10.
F.	The Two Servants.	Matt. 18:28-32.
S.	The Good Samaritan.	Luke 10:25-37.
S.	The Prodigal Son.	Luke 15:11-23.

"Return, return! Why any longer linger?
There are sandals for your feet,
And a ring to deck your finger.
Your Father reconciled
With loving heart will you behold.
In his arms he will enfold you;
Come back, come back, my child."

Would that the marriage guest presumptuously entering the palace without the wedding garment, though speechless, might deliver a message that would save us all from condemnation to the outer darkness with its weeping and gnashing of teeth. Before the King we all shall stand. If unprepared, no other fate awaits us. O why will men forever die!

In the parable of the two servants, we may easily read our censure if not our doom. We have all appealed to God to forgive our transgression against him and he has done so, but when a frail mortal has trespassed against us in kind but only to an infinitesimally small degree we mercilessly insist that only as we forgive are we forgiven.

The parable of the lost sheep is a marvelously realistic portrayal of the Good Shepherd himself. As under shepherds let us emulate his example and seek for the lost till we find them. There is still joy among the angels when we restore the lost and wounded, and in finding them we assure ourselves of joy when we also appear pear among the angels.

Jesus does not mean he is speaking to the multitudes in an incomprehensible manner to punish them for their grossly materialistic lives; but simply states that as a result of this gross materialism what he says is to them as a speaking in parables beyond their powers of comprehension. Had they been more spiritually minded, they would have understood all the significance of the spoken word. As our thoughts become purified and the eyes of our faith become brighter through holy living new meaning is constantly breaking forth from the written word so that what was formerly "parable" becomes plain command, promise, or exhortation.

The "Prodigal Son" will remain the world's favorite parable as long as so many of us are alienated by sin from our Father's house and, out in the far country, are longing for pardon and home. Sin may not geographically separate us from sacred places, but it does place a chasm between us and peace that only divine love can bridge. Fear not. Christ would not represent an earthly father as being more forgiving than his own Father. The parable teaches that when we come to ourselves and return to our Father's house there await us a welcome, forgiveness, the robe and ring and great joy.

No other preacher in literature is a more eloquent exponent of the grace of pure, uncalculating, philanthrophy than the good Samaritan. Racial prejudice, intense as it becomes in the Orient, personal danger, great as it was between Jerusalem and Jericho, nor anything else could overcome his love of fellow man or hinder his helping an unfortunate. This love exalted him sublimely above priest and Levite. The garb is an outward sign of what ought to be within, but the hand in the heart is proof of one's belonging to the true nobility of earth and sky. This good Samaritan has saved the name from odium. Such chivalry on our part will atone for serious errors of doctrines and help redeem a loveless past.

❁ ❁

THE WORLD'S FAVORITE

For Skin, Scalp, Hair, and Hands is Cuticura Soap, Medicinal, Emollient, Antiseptic.

For preserving, purifying and beautifying the skin, for cleansing the scalp of crusts, scales, and dandruff, and the stopping of falling hair, for softening, whitening, and soothing red, rough, and sore hands, for baby rashes, itchings, and chaffings, for annoying irritations and ulcerative weaknesses, and many sanative, antiseptic purposes which readily suggest themselve to mothers, as well as for all the purposes of the toilet, bath, and nursery, Cuticura Soap, assisted by Cuticura Ointment, the great Skin Cure, is invaluable. The purity and sweetness, the certainty of immediate and grateful relief, the great economy and simplicity of treatment, have made Cuticura Soap, Ointment, and Pills, the favorite mother remedies.

People's Forum

To the Editor of THE CHRISTIAN-EVANGELIST:

"I would like to have your opinion," says one, "as to whether it is right to raise money for church purposes by giving picnics, suppers, entertainments, etc."

There is no specific Bible prohibition of money raising for church purposes by picnics, suppers or entertainments. But it would require a freak of the imagination to picture the men of the early church—men like Peter and Paul—urging the followers of the meek and lowly Jesus to sell tickets for a musical and literary entertainment for the benefit of any church organization. Those clear headed leaders would have known, as the wise leaders of to-day know with profound conviction, that the buying of a ticket to an entertainment is not giving to the church. Any plan that offers a substitute for genuine giving sets a lower standard for God's people than a plan which leads to giving without any thought of return to the giver. And just so far as it is wrong to replace a high standard with a lower, at least so far it is wrong to replace free giving with a mercantile transaction in which a buyer, who is falsely supposed to be a giver, gets a good percentage of earthly return for his money. Not only is this fact becoming more and more apparent to the Christian of to-day, but he is learning that, from the standpoint of economy of time and strength, as compared with the result in money, an organized effort to secure actual giving is far more profitable than the ofttimes desperate struggle to make an entertainment "pay." Men and women and children ought to be asked to give. It is good for them to be asked, and better yet for them to give when they are asked, and to do so with no thought of what they will get for their money.

F. E. Mallory.

About Conventions and Resolutions.

To the Editor of THE CHRISTIAN-EVANGELIST:

I have never been in sympathy with the idea that these gatherings should not make pronouncement on the great social and religious movements of the day; and even political movements when moral questions are involved. Such a position is unworthy of us. We are here. We can't help being here; and would not help it if we could. World movements are here too. We can't help them being here. What are we as a religious body (and it is hoped an aggressive and sane and spirit-filled body) to do? Take to the woods when brought face to face with world movements that involve the interests of the kingdom of God?

I should regret to think that the brotherhood had not brains and heart enough to make a ringing pronouncement on any of the great questions of the day. Why should we not have the manhood to stand up and be counted? The world knows where to find the great religious bodies on the great movements of the time; why should we be forever and forever a nonentity? Brethren, when there is anything "doing" in the moral and religious world I want to stand up and be counted; and I want the church in which my life is wrapped up to stand up and be counted. It is folly for a great and aggressive body to be in the world and not take part in the issues that are abroad. Let us have forever done with a provincialism that is too timid to meet world movements face to face and bear its share of the world's work. If I mistake not the temper of our people is such that they are not willing longer to be held nack by outgrown traditions and unreasonable timidities.

Little Rock, Ark. J. N. Jessup.

[The above is an illustration of the spirit and stamina that under the leadership of the author are transforming the Church of Christ in Little Rock from weakness into the greatest power for righteousness in that capital city.]

The Panama Conference.

To the Editor of THE CHRISTIAN-EVANGELIST:

Permit me to say just a word on your editorial on "The Rio Janeiro Conference," or one phase of it—your reference to the "Panama Congress" of 1826. Let me say first, though, that the "Current Events" editorials are uniformly interesting, sane and true to fact, and it is not in the spirit of fault-finding that I refer to the above topic, but simply to make a correction in your historical facts concerning the old "Panama Congress," thinking you would welcome such correction.

This is what you say: "* * * the Panama Congress which was held during John Quincy Adams' administration in 1826, and was attended by Henry Clay, then secretary of state."

Now, as a matter of fact, Henry Clay did not attend that congress, nor was he to attend it; nor did any one from the United States attend it. The United States senate wrestled long and hard with the question of accepting the invitation to send representatives—this when the president sent the names of Richard C. Anderson, John Sergeant as representatives, and William B. Rochester as secretary, but finally confirmed the president's nominations. The delegation was then delayed because of the opposition in the house to making the necessary appropriations to defray the expenses of the representatives. It was not until late in April of that year that the necessary appropriations were finally passed, and later still, in the summer, that our delegates started for Panama. Mr. Anderson sickened and died on the way and Sergeant and his secretary reached Panama, only to find that the congress had adjourned to convene again later at Tocubaya, Mexico. This later meeting never took place, owing to domestic disturbances among some of the republics. Sergeant was compelled to return therefore without having accomplished anything. See Annals of Congress and Journals of Senate for 1826; McMaster's History of the People of the United States. vol. v. pp. 440-59.

Des Moines, Iowa. O. B. Clark.

50 More Young People

Fifty More Young People can get special rates for room, board and tuition at Iowa Christian College. Home study courses also. New illustrated catalog ready. Write Pres. Chas. J. Burton, Oskaloosa, Iowa.

How to Succ by R. A. T Toronto, Fl cloth, 25 cts

This little b to young Chri character. Its Right;" "The "Assurance of Holy Spirit;' "Church Me "Difficulties i "Working for "Companions;' tion," and "Gu in the devout Torrey, and w converts in se tian life.

Raising the New York, H. Revell C

This small v cis E. Clark, fo and two of the in the "Christi author's well w phasize the va days of our li highest by hol highest ideals, nothing less th hardly fail to ; liever who wis life.

The Universai Moore, instru Manual Train Chicago, Cha:

The thesis of that man is kin having develope and spirit, cons tion, from an c are no doubt a mentioned in th contention that greater regard life is an entit with which we But the amazir that one whose scientific habits the most stupei in human life such facts to In the author's he feels it nece to make him mi who is to retur no more. Of s lies behind all which he descr carrying forwar ation, developin tiny, the autho nothing. And y the work is that no defect in this lly believes that bow down to to pass away, and claim their alle expects "the tim ments of these ; two or three, a the rest; they w and law." This reached a finalit human frailty ar trained only in science!

SUMMER IS HERE

People must have inducements during such weather to either buy or read, especially good books, and we are determined to offer the inducements. For the month of July we will make the following prices, CASH with order. All books are prepaid. All books are cloth bound where not specified as paper.

CHRISTIAN PUBLISHING COMPANY. 2712 Pine Street, St. Louis, Mo.

The Home Department

lothing Lost.

R. HORNISH.

the universe that's lost.
1 the water tossed,
gain.

not be expressed,
lover's breast;
ot die.

ded but to fade.
s of the glade,
again.

did not gain,
and the shame,
ir reward.

subtle grace,
m the once fair face,
ma' in memory.

ildhood grown
e once its own,
in old folklore.

enith rose,
rate, finds repose;
has its reward.

ume of all;
rise and fall,
its recompense.

f His hand,
by Time's sand,
held for good alway.

※ ※

onze Vase.

KENRIDGE ELLIS.

RT III.

PTER V.

, the end of the vast
h Raymund and Rhoda
artitioned off from the
dies' waiting room. In-
een several very large
nes for the ladies, the
emigrants, besides the
ing room. All these were
ne long chamber, and it
om one end to the other
ght it most unlikely that
should glance through
ors, could see them. He
the extreme end, where
leads up to a more ex-
om. The young people
ther the steps led, and
ll enough, for later in
avy board was placed
ides bearing the words,
ight." Although Rhoda
nual fear of discovering
face in the throng, and
not improbable that the
d so terrified her might
till, the moving crowd
ation that deadened her
teresting to see streams
at the cry of the floor-
eresting to note the dif-
ange baggage, the family
ches out of pasteboard
rds and even cats, borne
as like free moving pic-
g of freight-engines re-
he car shed—those en-
mot the polished hissing
g of passenger engines,
rasping, as if they had
p in the best society. It
r the crier call the names
e young people's minds
by a sort of mythical
ton and New York and
Denver and Seattle and
d it was like hearing of
ces to listen to the call
s, Quincy, Springfield,

Memphis, Little Rock, Chattanooga, Peoria, and Ottawa. But when they heard
Moberly, Sedalia, Mexico and St. Louis,
they felt like rising and exclaiming, "These
we know. They are our old friends."

At first they had been unable to find two
vacant seats together, so Rhoda had taken
one and Raymund had stood by her, waiting for the departure of the fleshy lady
who sat next to her with four valises about
her feet and a bird cage in her ample lap.
The fleshy lady was anxious for her train
to come, and, with no faith in the clock,
stopped every official that came within hail,
to ask how long it would be now?"
But the children were almost as anxious
for her train to come, and when it did,
Raymund had her seat. They made a
strikingly picturesque little scene, the little
bundle on Rhoda's knee, and the green umbrella in Raymund's hand, their eyes blue
and interested, and very alert for the always possible Mr. Boggs, or Mrs. Van Estry, and their hair gleaming duskily silver
in the shadow of the high back of their
bench. Every uniformed man that passed
stopped to ask them, "And where are you
going?"

When they answered, "Crawley," the response came invariably, "Six-thirty." After
the day forces had been relieved by the
night officials, each of the new-comers
paused to say, "And where are you going?"
And being told, they answered, "Six-thirty;" so there could be no doubt about it.
When the clock showed the way from ten
to eleven, the atmosphere of the Union Station changed; it was no longer pre-eminently practical, rushed, heedless. The lunch-
counter began to show empty stools, the
arrivals found family groups waiting to receive them, there were affectionate greetings; more and more the element of romance permeated the scene. There was
something like adventure in getting off the
trains so late, and eyes sparkled brighter
than by day. At twelve, the trains did not
come in so often, and at one, the faces that
entered the glass doors began to look tired
and even wan, and some of them even
cross. At two, the business seemed over.
There were perhaps fifty in the vast chamber, the men at the remote end smoking
cigars, and a few mothers slowly walking
from one wall to the other, leading a hopelessly awake young child.

At last Raymund pounced upon an empty
rocking chair that had not ceased to vibrate
from its occupant, and Rhoda was installed
in it. Raymund tried to take a nap on the
bench at her side, but the iron arm-rests
that portioned off the bench were much in
the way. He tried curling up like a cat
with his nose between his knees; he tried
lying across the arm-rest in the vain hope
that its sharp edges might be softened by
unconsciousness; he tried dangling his legs
over the side and bowing out, his back to
fit the bench-back. but his head—there was
no place to put his head! The girls had all
gone from the lunch counters and when an
engineer came in at three for a cup of
coffee—the coffee that was always smoking
in the beautiful polished tanks, the man
who "ran the stand" had to be roused from
heavy sleep—he had stretched himself out
upon one of his counters. The lights at
the bookstand had all been turned off that
the proprietor might then better sleep
among his books, and the baggage room
just beyond the men smoking their cigars,
was closed.

Sometimes Raymund would start out of
a minute's sleep, feeling that one of his
limbs was being cut off by an executioner,

and he would see Rho
ing in her rocking-chair
peace and purity! Rayn
high in brotherly pride
had stopped, but there
saloons across the stre
never came to an end.
rusty snores sounded f
where men slept in spit
rests. Long ago the bla
mop had sent a flood
benches, making the
move to another part c
before that, men had r
about the floor, gather
and discarded bones of
unbuttered scraps of l
longer the lusty-lunged
of geographical interest
bench to bench, giving
muttering some destin
half-whisper. Between h
Raymund stared at his
was his sister and grate
could sleep, and dro
Boggs would try to sto
could get on the Cra
times his thoughts wo
the length of "And wh
Crawley? What do yo
in Crawley? There's
you!" But even this
awake.

It was nearly five whe
to the duties of the d
yards came the first pa
was still a long time
Early twilight came qu

NOTHING
NEWLY REVISI

MISSIONARY
By ARCHIBAL

TABLE OF CON
1. The Supreme Mission
2. The Gospel for All
3. Encouragement in M
4. The Success of Mode
5. The Heroism of Mis
6. The Transforming Po
7. Woman and the Gospe
8. Missions in the Life
9. Missions in the Early
10. Missions in the Midd
11 Modern Missions.
12. Missions Among the
13 Medical Missions.
14. "This Grace Also."
Appendix: Names and B
Who Have Labored for the
sionary Society.
Biography: Selected List
sions, Mission Lands and
Nothing Needed with this
In fine silk cloth bind
paid, $1.00.

CHRISTIAN PUBLIS
2712 Pine Street,

CANCER
WITH SOOTHIN
Cancer, Tumor, Catarrh,
Eczema and all Skin and I
for Illustrated Book. Ser
DR. BYE, Cor. 9th &
Broadway,

CHURCH FEDER

The Inter-Church Cor
eration, 700 pages

lights were turned out and a cool dusk stole over the reddish brown floor. Raymund rose stiffly. Rhoda was still sleeping. The youth placed his umbrella in his seat in lieu of a reserve ticket, and walked to one of the doors and looked out upon the car tracks. High in the iron roof a glass globed electric arc still sent out its spangled rays, and directly under it was Boggs. Raymund for a moment wondered if the villain had been standing there all night, or if he had just come to see that Rhoda did not escape on the Crawley train; and if the latter were true, why he had come so long before train-time, and why he did not come into the waiting room and pounce upon his intended victim. Coupled with this vague wonder was the idea that perhaps Boggs did not know of their presence or intentions, and was there on some secret business that had no connection with them. All this was deadened, indistinct, unemotional. But, of a sudden, Raymund, as it were, woke up. He came to the fearful danger of the situation. It mattered not why Boggs was there. He was there, and they could not go to Crawley—at least not this morning; but it was possible that they might escape their enemy.

The youth darted to Rhoda's side and drew her to her feet before she was half-awake. "Has the train come?" she asked, bewildered, as she grabbed for the little bundle.

"We must run for our lives," said Raymund, seizing her arm. She was wide awake now, and hurried by his side without a question. When they were in the street, Raymund said briefly, "I saw Boggs on the platform." The hack drivers stared at them curiously as they crossed over to the saloons. They almost ran past the little bookstores where the impure books in the display-booths—those beggars of the literary world—seemed to implore the passers-by for charity. They crossed the bridge over which heavy vans were already beginning to lumber, and with hardly a glimpse for the river rolling away in mist, and with no thought of the long lines of freight cars groaning beneath their feet, they sped into the advancing day. Was Boggs following? Was Mrs. Van Estry waiting at the next corner to cry, "Stop thief!" Were the police on their track? Whither turn? Whither direct their way?

"We must not go back to Mrs. Bannerton's," Rhoda panted, "or to the orphan home. We mustn't go where I have ever been seen. Let's hunt out a little hotel somewhere and stay till the afternoon train for Crawley, and try it again."

"But Boggs will be waiting," said Raymund fearfully.

"Yes," said Rhoda in despair, "Oh! what shall we do? If I had any friends in this city—anybody who had known us for years we could go to them. But we are just orphans, Raymund, and nobody is sure of us, nobody really knows us or cares about us. If Mrs. Van Estry has me taken to the police-station, there wouldn't be anybody to contradict her witnesses. Even at the orphan home they could only say that while I have been there, I haven't done anything wrong, as far as they know. And Mrs. Bannerton is really a stranger to us. But even if they didn't send me to jail, just to be taken to the police-courts, and maybe locked up till my case could be heard, would kill me! Raymund, you are my protector," cried Rhoda wildly "and you must take care of your poor Rose!"

"And I will!" cried Raymund stoutly, though in truth he was at his wits' end. They hastily turned a corner and almost

---

CHURCH FEDERATION READY.

The Inter-Church Conference on Federation, 700 pages, prepaid.....$2 00

---

ran into a short, spare man with a dry, wrinkled face, though it was not an old face; a stubbly beard ran unevenly over the chin and lean cheeks. The man was in his shirt sleeves, and the part of his lower figure was clothed in a very tight pair of blue cotton trowsers. He started back to avoid the collision, and looking up sharply from under the glazed tip of his cap, said, "Which it is Rhoda and Raymund!"

"O Wizzen!" they cried out in a breath.

(TO BE CONTINUED.)

✿ ✿

"Father Does It."

Behold the one clear gage of the boy's endeavor—what father does. Mothers' clubs may make motions divine in wisdom and in goodness; mothers' congresses may form all elements of virtue into laws; mothers individually in the home may talk, work, struggle, to make their sons models by which to shape a new heaven and a new earth. But the boy's world is in the man who is his father, and the boy believes that, whatever may be right on Sundays or at prayer time, the things that are really good, that really count in life, are what father does. Moreover, it is what father does which defines the means with which the boy shall work, the sphere wherein his efforts shall be shaped. In a word, what father does is the beginning as it is the end of the boy's achievements. This is not a menace, either, to the mother's higher aims or to the boy's best endeavor. It is simply one of the rather neglected facts of human experience.—*Harper's Bazar*.

The Bestest Time.

I'll tell you what's the very best
Of all the things I know;
It's when I get a dreful cold,
So ma says, "You can't go
Outdoors a-tall, ner off t' school;
You stay 'ith me to-day."
'Nen she looks around and says,
"Less see, what shall we play?"

"Injuns," I yell, good and loud,
'Cause injuns' mostest fun;
"Dear me, no," says ma, "if we play that
I won't' get nothin' done."
"I'll be a great big nelefent,
An' you're jest awful 'fraid."
"All right," says ma, "you rant an' roar
Till I get my cookies made."

An' when she gets her work all done,
An' we get tired o' play,
She pulls her chair up to th' fire,
An' holds me, this-a-way.
Most times she says 'at I'm too big,
She won't hold me a-tall,
But when I'm sick she says 'at I'm
Her baby, after all.

'Nen she gives me hoarhoun' drops,
M-m, hoarhoun's goodes' stuff!
An' lemonade, all nice an' hot,
Till I'm just ful enuff.
'Nen she lays me on th' lounge,
An' tucks her shawl aroun',
An' pats me till, firs' thing i know,
I'm sleepin' jes's soun'.
—*Lippincott's.*

Two Thorns.

It hurt. Every minute it seemed to hurt
worse—worser, Elizabeth said. She kept
uncrumpling her palm and looking at it,
and touching it to make sure it hurt very
much—and groaning softly under her
breath. There was nobody in the world
Elizabeth pitied so much as Elizabeth, for
probably there wasn't any other little girl
with a cruel thorn in her hand.

Mademoiselle looked sorry, but Elizabeth
would not look at Mademoiselle. You don't
look at folks that keep you a whole hour
away from your play to learn your spelling
all over again, or that say: "What, what!"
at you when you say your three table.
Folks like that you—'spise.

"Gov'nesses are dreadful folks," sighed
Elizabeth. "I wish my mother'd let me go
to school instead of having me governed."
But she could not wish anything very long,
except that the thorn would come out of
her hand. It certainly did ache worser
than ever—there now, didn't it! Hadn't she
pinched it to see, and didn't it?

"Elizabeth"—the voice was quite gentle,
but firm. Elizabeth did not turn round.
Her little white forehead above the tan-
line was wrinkled with real pain.

"There is still the spelling"—

As if she could learn her spelling with
a thorn in her hand! But she opened the
book again and whispered "A-ch-e—
a-ch-e" over and over to herself.

Why! Why! That was what she was doing now, this minute—a-ch-e-ing! Elizabeth laughed softly, in spite of herself.
After that the word was easy enough to
spell. Elizabeth was eight; but as long as
she lived, even when she was eighty, she
would know how to spell a-ch-e.

Some one was talking to Mademoiselle
at the door.

"No," Mademoiselle was sighing, "I can
not yet come." Some words Elizabeth lost
there, then, "She is my little—what you
call?—thorn in the flesh."

Elizabeth sat up straighter. The speller
slid to the floor.

It was rather a startling idea. She's
got one in her flesh, too, and it's—me!"

"She means me," she thought. It had
never been clear like that before—what her
naughtiness was like to Mademoiselle. How
much it must hurt if it was like a thorn
in her hand! It must burn and sting and
ache-a-ch-e. How much it must a-ch-e!

Elizabeth found herself beginning to be
sorry for Mademoiselle on account of that
thorn. If some one would take it out!
Nobody in the world could take it out except Elizabeth. And Elizabeth—she turned
suddenly and ran to Mademoiselle.

"I'll take it out!" laughed Elizabeth,
softly. "I've got one in my hand, too, an'
I know how it hurts. I never s'posed before that thorns and—and bad little girls
hurt just alike. I can spell a-ch-e now,
an' my tables. Don't you think it will come
out of your flesh then?"

Mademoiselle understood. With a little
cry she caught Elizabeth up and kissed her.
Then as gently as she could she uncrumpled
the little aching hand and drew out Elizabeth's thorn. They were both laughing
when it was over, so Mademoiselle's thorn
must have come out, too.—Annie Hamilton
Donnell, in "Zion's Herald."

Our Funnies.

He—"You've got to have a pull to get
ahead."
She—"Yes, and you've got to have a
head to get a pull."

"You are an hour late this morning,
Sam."
"Yes, sah; I know it, sah."
"Well, what excuse have you?"
"Well, when we got rich enough to have
here, sah."
"That ought not to have detained you
an hour, Sam."
"Well, you see, it wouldn't if he'd only
kicked me in dis direction, but he kicked
me the other way!"

"When we were poor," remarked the
prosperous man, reflectively, "we looked
forward to the time when we could have a
summer home."
"Well?"
"Well, when we got rich enough to have
one we didn't like going to the same place
every summer, because it was monotonous,
and we looked forward to the time when
we could have another variety."
"Well?"
"Well, we got another, and then we began to long for a winter place, so that we
wouldn't have to be so much in the big
house in the city."
"Well?"
"Well, we've got them all now."
"And are you happy?"
"I suppose so. At least, I suppose my
wife is. She keeps them all shut up and
spends most of her time in Europe, but she
knows she has them."

The Sin of Omission.

BY MARGARET SANGSTER.

'Tis not only the thing you do, dear,
    It's the thing you've left undone,
Which gives you a bit of heartache,
    At the setting of the sun.
The tender word forgotten,
    The letter you did not write,
The flower you might have sent, dear,
    Are your haunting ghosts to-night.

The stone you might have lifted
    Out of a brother's way,
The bit of heartsome counsel
    You were hurried too much to say;
The loving touch of the hand, dear,
    The gentle and winsome tone
That you had no time nor thought for,
    With troubles enough of your own.

The little acts of kindness,
    So easily out of mind;
These chances to be angels
    Which every mortal finds—
They come in light and silence—
    Each chill, reproachful wrath,
When hope is faint and flagging,
    And a blight has dropped on faith.

For life is all too short, dear,
    And sorrow is all too great,
To suffer our slow compassion
    That tarries until too late;
And it's not the thing you do, dear,
    It's the thing you leave undone,
Which gives you the bit of heartache
    At the setting of the sun.

❖ ❖

Eternity, Where Shall I Spend It?

BY DR. R. A. TORREY.

Many years ago, when the elder Forbes Winslow was living—the most eminent pathologist in diseases of the mind that England ever produced—there came over from France a young Frenchman. He brought letters of recommendation from many eminent men in France, among them one from Napoleon III., at that time Emperor of France. Dr. Winslow read the letters, and said:

"What is your trouble?"
He said: "I don't know."
"Have you lost money?"
"No, not lately."
"Have you suffered in honor or reputation?"
"No, not so far as I know."
"Have you lost friends?"
"No, not recently."
"Then what keeps you awake?"
"Well, my trouble is I am an infidel, and my father was an infidel before me. But strangely enough, every night when I lie down to sleep this question rises before me. 'Eternity, and where shall I spend it?' During the night I can think of but that one thing, and I can't sleep."
Dr. Winslow said: "I can't help you, but I can tell you a physician that can." He took his Bible from a table, and turned to Isaiah liii, 5, and read: "He was wounded for our transgressions; he was bruised for our iniquities; the chastisement of our peace was upon him; and by his stripes we are healed." There was a curl of scorn upon the Frenchman's lip. He said:
"Dr. Winslow, do you mean to tell me that a man in your eminent scientific position believes that effete superstition of Christianity?"
"Yes," said Dr. Forbes Winslow, "I believe in Jesus Christ, and I believe in the Bible; and believing in Christ and the Bible has saved me from becoming what you are."
The man dropped his head for a moment. The he said:
"If I am an honest man I ought at least to be willing to consider it, ought I not? Will you teach me?"
Dr. Winslow consented, and the physician of the mind became the physician of the soul. He showed the young man from the Bible the way of darkness into light. In three or four days his doubts were all gone, and he went back to France with his mind at rest, for he had settled the ques-

tion of "Eternity, and where shall I spend it?" He would spend it with Christ, in glory.

"Eternity, and where shall I spend it?"
Thank God I know where I shall spend eternity. Do you?—Exchange.

Doors That Are Closed Against Cigarette Users.

Athletic clubs.
A business college.
Union Pacific Railroad.
Omaha schools.
Swift & Company, Packing House, Chicago.
Marshall Field, dry goods, Chicago.
Life insurance companies (some).
Lehigh Valley Railroad.
United States army positions.
United States naval schools.
Carson, Pirie & Scott, Chicago.
Chicago, Rock Island & Pacific Railroad.
Central Railroad, Georgia.
Three high schools, and more.
Ayer's Sarsaparilla Co., Lowell.
Wanamaker's, Philadelphia.
Morgan & Wright Tire Co., Chicago.
Western Union Telegraph Company (in message service).
Burlington Railroad.
United States Weather Bureau (Willis M. Moore, chief).
Heath & Milligan.
Montgomery, Ward & Co.
Academy of Northwestern University, Chicago.
Telephone Company (Cumberland).
New York, New Haven & Hartford Railroad.
Pittsburgh & Western Railroad.
West Superior (Wisconsin) Railroad.

❖ ❖

Picture of War Engine "General."

A beautiful colored picture, 18x25 inches, of the historic old engine "General" which was stolen at Big Shanty, Ga., by the Andrew's Raiders during the Civil War, and which is now on exhibition in the Union Depot, Chattanooga, Tenn., has been gotten out by the NASHVILLE, CHATTANOOGA & ST. LOUIS RY.—The "Battlefields Route" to the South. The picture is ready for framing and will be mailed for 25c. The "Story of the General" sent free. W. L. Danley, Gen'l Pass. Agent, Nashville, Tenn.

Christian Publishing Company
2712 Pine St., St. Louis, Mo.

J. H. GARRISON, - - - President
W. W. DOWLING, - - - Vice-President
GEO. L. SNIVELY, - - Sec. and Gen. Supt
R. P. CROW. - - Treas. and Bus. Manager

Our rubber baptismal suits are the best made, and we sell them lower than the advertised prices of other houses for the same grade.

"The Garrison Library" is attractive enough in itself, to wit: Alone with God, 75 cents; Heavenward Way, 75 cents; Half-Hour Studies at the Cross, 75 cents; Helps to Faith, $1.00; The Holy Spirit, $1.00, and THE CHRISTIAN-EVANGELIST, $1.50, all pre-

paid, for $5.00. But during the summer we shall give as a premium an excellent 11x24½-inch picture of the author.

This is an excellent time to buy Christmas books. Read our list of special offerings on page 991. If ordered now, we will hold till Christmas-gift time and mail as directed. It means a saving of 50, 75 and even 100 per cent.

We are always pleased to submit our Bible school literature to committees for comparison with supplies sent out by other publishers. When the verdict is based on merit the order invariably comes to us to send the W. W. Dowling series.

THE CHRISTIAN-EVANGELIST special over the Wabash gives our friends the privilege of a lake ride from Detroit to Buffalo. A staunch steamer has been secured that will make "a night on the deep" safe as in a Pullman. A multitude of our readers may earn free transportation while rendering the church a helpful ministry. Write us for the plan.

Evidently the conviction is everywhere prevailing that THE CHRISTIAN-EVANGELIST is the truest exponent of the doctrines and aspirations of the "fathers" of this Restoration, that it best represents and expresses the real genius of our movement toward Christian unity and the extension of primitive Christianity throughout the earth, and that in conjunction with the preaching of the word it is the greatest force among us for enlisting men in the Lord's army and making better soldiers even of the veterans. Recall the long lists of new subscriptions published in each of many past issues. In addition to new ones received by one's and two's last week we note these clubs: Madison, N. C., 3; Hamilton, Ill., 18, W. H. Waggoner, pastor; Carthage, Ill., 35; J. M. Elam,

minister; Dallas, Ill., 7, C. L. minister; Monmouth, Ill., 61, Hughes, pastor; Rayerton, Ind., Lawrence, evangelist; Atchison, W. T. Hilton, pastor; Fayettesv 3, N. M. Ragland, minister; East Ill., 11, W. H. Jones, minister.

* *

HAVE YOU READ

The Holy Spirit, by J. H. Garr
pages, in silk cloth, postpaid $1.0
Christian Publishing Com
2712 Pine St., St. L

By Courtesy of the "Wabash" that draws "The Christian-Evangelist Special" to the Buffalo Convention, October 12-18.

THE
CHRISTIAN-
EVANGELIST

A WEEKLY RELIGIOUS NEWSPAPER.

Volume XLIII.	No. 32.

ST. LOUIS, AUGUST 9, 1906.

WHILE THE EARTH REMAINETH, SEED TIME AND HARVEST SHALL NOT CEASE.
—Genesis.

The Christian-Evangelist.

J. H. GARRISON, Editor

PAUL MOORE, Assistant Editor

F. D. POWER,
B. B. TYLER, } Staff Correspondents.
W. DURBAN,

Subscription Price, $1.50 a Year.

For foreign countries add $1.04 for postage.

Remittances should be made by money order, draft, or registered letter; not by local cheque, unless 15 cents is added to cover cost of collection.

In Ordering Change of Post Office give both old and new address.

Matter for Publication should be addressed to THE CHRISTIAN-EVANGELIST. Subscriptions and remittances should be addressed to the Christian Publishing Company, 2712 Pine Street, St. Louis, Mo.

Unused Manuscripts will be returned only if accompanied by stamps.

News Items, evangelistic and other rise, are solicited, and should be sent on a postal card, if possible.

Published by the Christian Publishing Company, 2712 Pine Street, St. Louis, Mo.

Entered at St. Louis P. O. as Second Class Matter

WHAT WE STAND FOR.

For the Christ of Galilee,
For the truth which makes men free,
For the bond of unity
  Which makes God's children one.

For the love which shines in deeds,
For the life which this world needs,
For the church whose triumph speeds
  The prayer: "Thy will be done."

For the right against the wrong,
For the weak against the strong,
For the poor who've waited long
  For the brighter age to be.

For the faith against tradition,
For the truth 'gainst superstition,
For the hope whose glad fruition
  Our waiting eyes shall see.

For the city God is rearing,
For the New Earth now appearing,
For the heaven above us clearing,
  And the song of victory.

                                    J. H. Garrison.

CONTENTS.

Centennial Propaganda............ 999
Current Events.................... 1000
Editorial—
  Our National Convention and
    Our History 1001
  A Timely Sermon 1001
  Notes and Comments 1002
  Current Religious Thought....... 1002
  Editor's Easy Chair............. 1003
Contributed Articles—
  As Seen from the Dome. F. D.
    Power 1004
  Modern Religious Persecution—A
    Defense. B. L. Chase.......... 1005
  The Content of the Evangelistic
    Sermon. J. N. Scholes........ 1006
  The Unity of Christians. Alexander Whyte.................... 1007
  Who is a Christian in the Twentieth
    Century? E. L. Frazier....... 1008
  Reports from California. Charles
    Reign Scoville 1009
Our Budget 1011
Evangelistic 1019
Sunday-school 1020
Christian Endeavor.............. 1020
Midweek Prayer-meeting 1021
People's Forum 1022
Current Literature 1022
Marriages, Obituaries 1022
The Home Department 1024

THE
CHRISTIAN-EVANGELIST

"IN FAITH, UNITY, IN OPINION AND METHODS, LIBERTY, IN ALL THINGS, CHARITY."

| Vol. XLIII. | August 9, 1906 | No. 32 |

1809   CENTENNIAL PROPAGANDA   1909
CHURCHES OF CHRIST
: : : GEO. L. SNIVELY : : :

Looking Toward Pittsburg.

None of the many able advocates who have appeared in this forum has come to the very heart of the matter better than does Brother Macfarlane in the following article. "Pittsburg and Pentecost" may not be truly alliterative, but if we attain unto the spirit of this article, they will be terms prophetically, historically and most intimately associated. Let us adopt "practizo" as one of our slogans. Let us rely on doing more than others as the chief proof of our being more nearly theologically correct than others. Let us make our adornment of the doctrines of the Lord Jesus through lives of peculiar usefulness and holiness one of the irresistible appeals to men to surge into the kingdom, bringing with them all they have and are, before Centennial.

Conscious that it is without thought of personal interest, we follow Brother Macfarlane's article with testimonials of appreciation many wish to express for THE CHRISTIAN-EVANGELIST. Years of travel and observation have made known to us that it is closely read by those preachers who are baptizing converts and leading the masses onward and upward; that it is found in most all the homes that are as springs refreshing our great church enterprises and commending the true faith to their neighbors, and that its sentiments largely prevail in those churches that are redeeming this world. All who have had experience will testify there is little financial profit in publishing a religious paper, but to be of large helpfulness to the brotherhood is a rich reward, and this privilege all can share who will help us to place this inspirational journal in 100,000 homes before Centennial. The sooner this is done, the more glorious will be Pittsburg's Pentecostal and the greater the spiritual reward of our co-laborers. This attempt for 100,000 CHRISTIAN-EVANGELISTS by 1909 is a truly altruistic enterprise. Let us all lend a hand and immediately.

Centennial Goals and Preaching Aims.
BY P. C. MACFARLANE.

Good preaching will per se abound in good teaching, but it will not reat there. Its mark is beyond. The sublime aim of preaching is not to teach what a good life is, but to persuade men to live the good life. A sermon is not a sermon when it is theological only; it must be biological and ontological and spiritually pomological. The true preacher sways by the power of his own life as well as by his words. The true prophet and his message are one. Why did Jesus write not? Because he wrote always. His life was his message. It is good to be sound in preaching; it is equally good to be sound in living. Some sound preaching sounds hollow.

Again, it is good to be right about the way into the Kingdom, and we preach it with unfailing insistency, but our greater need just now is preaching on the way within the Kingdom. If a better plea does not produce better character, wherein is it better? A keen critic has said of us that our preaching is almost wholly soteriological. This is hardly just, I think. Our aim may be soteriological, but our end is surely sociological which is Christological. Saved! but for what? Service! The ultimate test of salvation is not a form but a service. Certain are upon the left at the judgment day not because they are uncircumcised, but because they are unchristianized; not because they are goats, but because they are not sheep. The test of a man's salvation is the service he renders; and yet this is no doctrine of salvation by works. He works because he is saved; and is not saved because he works.

Why does not the religious world hearken with more humility to our plea? In part because of pride and sectarianism; but in part also because the badge of superior character is the only badge of authority for the Christian. When we have to debate to prove our apostolicity or apostleship is vain. When one comes asking, 'Art thou he that should come or look we for another?' It is better to be able to answer 'Go tell the things which ye see and hear.' The next four years is a good time for less debating and more demonstrating; less talk about *baptizo* and more thoughts about *practizo*, (Sic.)

Let every preacher aim to double his spiritual power and that of his church. Let the elders resolve to double their graces and the manifestations thereof. Let the deacons minister twice as faithfully. Let the teachers prepare their lessons twice as carefully and thrice as prayerfully. And let every worker and every humblest member be twice as loyal, and the Centennial campaign will close with such an outpouring of the Spirit as will remind Pittsburg of Pentecost.

I often wonder if our evangelism does not put the vehicle before the motive power. It is not the voice of Jesus uplifted in preaching or prayer, but the body of him uplifted on the cross, that draws men to him. It is the life and not the letter, the love and not the law, the vim and not the voice of Jesus that gives him power over the hearts of men. It is not a legend but a life that moulds character and appeals to the affections of the race. The mightiest demonstration of the truths of the gospel and the integrity of Jesus and the authority of his person is not contained in syllogisms or wrought out in theologies, nor forged in dogmas nor boomed out in ecclesiastical gunnery. It is in a body of loyal believers in Jesus Christ, no matter how ignorant or humble or poor or uncouth or obscure, whose souls are on fire with the love of God and whose daily walk shows them to have been with Jesus. The sarcasms of an infidel, the shafts of the destructive critic, the thunderbolts of logic and the chilling snow-balls of agnosticism, dash themselves in vain against such breastworks of faith as this.

We wish to be evangelical. True Christianity is excessively evangelical. "Go ye," is the first article of its creed. Query: Would we be more evangelical if we were less so? Would we not divert more people from sin if we converted more nominal Christians to real Christian living? If we made it harder to get in and more worth while to be in? If we talked less about the blessedness of life over there and revealed more of the blessedness of life over here? Quacks advertise; good physicians are sought after. When I look at the quantity of Christians in my town I am puffed up; when I look at the quality of them I feel like Sheba's Queen the day after.

And yet, mind you, I am hurrying along with the rest of the pack in full cry after numbers. I agonize to make converts. I draw the net as eagerly as any. I rejoice when it is full to bursting; I mourn when it is empty. And yet, I cannot help thinking that the surest way to get converts is to make what we have better. The world has a notion we are trying to get it into the church; some people who are not pessimists have a notion we have got a good bit of the world into the church. Perhaps if we should covet numbers less and turn to and multiply our graces and rejoice in them, the world would pause to look and turn to follow. To the infirm of Bethesda Jesus said, "Wouldst thou be made whole?" He never spent a moment urging himself upon any. He stands and knocks but he never tries a door. He caused many men to hesitate upon the threshold; he never dragged one over.

To consider as I have above may seem to some to consider very curiously; I may even grant as much; yet, nevertheless, I record my solemn conviction that to double our numbers in four years is a trivial aim, but to double the sway of Christ over the hearts and lives of our brotherhood is a mark worthy the blood of a hundred thousand martyrs.

Rather than aim to be twice as large numerically, let us aim to be twice as large charismatically, and it will follow as the light the dark that our statisticians will grow stale with idleness.

Alameda, Cal.

❀ ❀

Centennial Propaganda.

I always hope to have such a worthy Christian paper as THE CHRISTIAN-EVANGELIST in my home.—W. S. Fuqua, Hannibal, Mo.

I shall do all I can for THE CHRISTIAN-EVANGELIST, and hope to be able to send you quite a number of subscribers. I am wonderfully pleased with it. It easily distances any other paper among us. Am sending it to my brother, who is a Methodist minister.—H. L. Walthan, Bloomingdale, Mich.

ent Events

adjournment of Congress
pon the defenseless public
a large number of
l　congressmen, most
of whom at once
to their respective dis-
semination of the law-
the general mass of the
oes no harm to the public
ellent thing for the law-
ables them to correct their
that movements the people
heart and what issues will
he coming congressional
r example, we think most
:an members will find that
proposition is not one
use the enthusiasm of the
districts. Some of these
g will have to be done
ff. There are two meth-
that issue and they have
:rnately about as long as
. One is to admit that
ded but to argue that the
an auspicious moment to
The other is the stand-
d to let well enough alone.
>rizing attitudes toward an
>n. The less said about
he better it will be for
:cess.

⁂

mmins, of Iowa, has been
ter a brisk contest in the
on. Iowa Republicans
idea" and its chief spokes-
stand-patism.

⁂

on, in being interviewed
about the issues of the
campaign, said:
he　　　"What can the
Republican party
on its records?" That is
In fact, that is about all
nybody can do in solicit-
ion of public confidence.
his true of the party in
isks continuance in office.
the Republican party so
resent Congress has been
ianks chiefly to constant
ie White House. Many
en uncovered and with
Congress has grappled.
lar word in the political
now is "Reform." Al-
r admits that Roosevelt
But does his spirit ex-
y in Congress and else-
an extent that the party
usted as the exponent
of reform? Or is it
ias been dragged by the
tram of reform for which
and from which it has
escape on account of the
igor of the executive, but

from which it will escape at the first opportunity? As to the Democratic party,
most people would admit that it represents the spirit and impulse of reform
(as opposition parties usually do), but
reform must not end in impulse. Has
the party the ability and discretion to do
constructive reformatory work? These
are the questions which we must answer
for ourselves. The Republican party in
Congress can show achievements in reform, but one is tempted to suspect that
it had no great heart in them. The
Democratic party's heart is in the right
place, but it has no recent achievements,
to exhibit in token of its ability. We
must take our choice.

⁂

Russia's troubles multiply. To financial embarrassment, civil strife and the
crash of falling cabinets, is added the
menace of a concerted mutiny (now apparently a failure) in the Baltic fortresses. The douma is gone but the
doom remains impending over the empire. It is saved from overturning only
by its vast mass and the sheer force of
political gravity which holds great and
inert masses in their place.

⁂

A Philadelphia judge has asserted the
proposition that the proper agency for
　　　　　　　　　investigating
Newspaper　　　abuses in govern-
Juries.　　　　　ment, including
misconduct of public officials, is not the
grand jury but the newspaper. The
newspaper is an institution having a
large force of men who are trained to
find out everything that is interesting or
important, and complete liberty to tell
everything it finds out. The newspaper
has a continuity, and therefore a degree
of efficiency, which the grand jury can
not have. It also has facilities for bringing the facts which it may discover to
the attention of the proper responsible
authorities and of the people themselves.
There is a good deal of truth in all this.
The ideal newspaper not only has the
power of diagnosing the ills of the body
politic, but also has facilities for administering the publicity cure in the most
effective way. If the people govern in
this country—and there is a tradition to
the effect that they do—then a general
notification regarding any discovered
abuse ought to be the proper step toward
remedying it. One is reminded of the
familiar saying of a great American
statesman that he would rather live in a
country with newspapers and no government than in one with a government
and no newspapers. But this high definition of the function of the newspaper
holds good only of the impartial and independent newspaper. The "organ" has
but little governmental utility. So long
as partisanship obtains in the majority
of newspaper offices it will be necessary
at least to supplement their efforts by
other instruments of justice which are
less seriously complicated with personal
and political considerations.

Slower music will be used when the
veterans of the G. A. R. march in parade
　　　　　　　　　at their annual en-
Slow Music.　　campment at Min-
　　　　　　　　　neapolis this
month. Commander-in-Chief Tanner has
issued a circular ordering that the time
of the music shall be reduced from 120 to
90 beats to the minute. The latter figure
indicates the tempo of the music to
which the armies of the civil war
marched, and it was fast enough to bring
them to victory. The quicker step of
these modern days is too fatiguing for
the veterans. Give them slower music.
The army thins as it advances. The
spirit is still blythe and brave but the feet
are faltering. Many are dropping by the
roadside while their comrades march on
a little farther. For thousands who
were in line last year the slowest music
is now too fast. They have fought their
fight. They have almost finished their
course. Let there be slow music.

⁂

The race of the "Robert E. Lee" and
the "Natchez" from New Orleans to St.
Louis is famous in the annals of the old
Mississippi steamboat traffic. The pilot
of the victorious "Lee" in that race,
Capt. J. W. Connor, died last week. It
was thirty-six years ago that the great
race occurred.

⁂

Mr. Rockefeller returned from Europe
last week. His welcome was not as
　　　　　　　　　warm as that which
Standard Oil.　　Mr. Bryan will re-
　　　　　　　　　ceive at the end of
this month. Still his arrival was not un-
observed. There were officers ready to
serve papers on him to secure his appearance in Ohio courts to answer
charges which are pending against the
Standard Oil Company. He has promised to appear. Several Standard Oil
men have been cited to appear before
the grand jury, but Mr. Rockefeller has
not been called. It is feared that if he
is required to give testimony against the
company, and incidentally against himself, before the grand jury, he might be
able to claim immunity when later proceedings are instituted. The war on
Standard Oil is to be carried on with
vigor. The octopus may yet find some
way of escape through the jungle of
technicalities, but it will have the fight
of its life. Meanwhile, there is ground
to wonder whether cheap alcohol, made
possible by the recently passed free alcohol bill, will not furnish a way of escape from bondage to the oil trust. Great
things are claimed for alcohol as a fuel,
and nobody can monopolize it unless he
can control all the potatoes, corn (both
grain and stalks), beets and most of the
other farm products raised in this country.

⁂

At the primary election held in Illinois
August 4, Shelby M. Cullom, the man
who looks like Lincoln, defeated former
Governor Yates for the United States Senate by a very decisive majority. This will
make Senator Cullom's fifth term. In 50
years of political life he has never been defeated.

Our National Convention and Our History.

If one should attempt to write a history of the Disciples of Christ as a distinct religious movement, leaving out the historic events which have transpired in connection with our conventions and all the interests and enterprises which have originated in them, it would make a very lean and barren historical narrative. Our national conventions have been the highest expression of the life, aims, and aspirations of our religious movement. They have been the Mount Pisgahs from which we have caught glimpses of the Promised Land before us. They have been the Mount Hermons from whose glowing summits we have caught visions of the transfigured Christ, and have heard again his great command to disciple the nations. Every national enterprise among us which has given us character and standing, as a religious force in Christendom, has had its origin in and been nourished by, our national conventions. There has always been among us, as there has always been in every religious movement in Christendom, certain divisive influences at work, but the greatest unifying human agency among us has been our national conventions.

It is because of such considerations as these that we should guard jealously the function and freedom of our national conventions, and resist any tendency to diminish their power and influence for good. There remains much to be done to make them more effective instruments for carrying out the aspirations and aims of the brotherhood. As we have already pointed out in a previous article, they should be made more representative in character, and should be brought into more vital touch with the churches, as their agents for carrying forward their work and giving expression to their sentiments in a spirit and manner perfectly in accord with the genius and aim of our movement.

And then, in the arrangement of the programs of these conventions, in giving each interest its proper place, and in providing for the free discussion of all questions relating to the welfare of the cause, the greatest care and consideration are necessary. The freer and more democratic these conventions can be made, and the closer they can be brought to the churches and to the individual delegates from the churches, the more effectively will they serve their purpose and be a worthy instrument of carrying out the purposes of the brotherhood. Nothing would be more surely destructive of the influence and value of these conventions than the feeling, on the part of the people generally, that they were managed by a few men whose decisions and plans the convention is expected to approve without discussion. We are sure that no such desire or purpose exists on the part of any of our leaders, but it is important to avoid any semblance of such method of conducting our conventions. The welfare of the church, no less than of the state and of the nation, depends on freedom of discussion in which all stand upon an equal platform having equal rights with perfect freedom to express their individual convictions.

There is no more interesting and inspiring spectacle in the life of a free church than a great deliberative body, marked by order and parliamentary decorum, facing some great and living issue of the times in free, fraternal and dignified discussion. There is no better test of the real Christian culture of a people than their ability to conduct such a discussion in a manner worthy of Christianity and of the great interests at stake. One man presents one aspect of a great question, clearly, cogently and courteously. Another rises and presents a still different view of the same theme, or it may be tests the relevancy or bearing of some argument presented. Still another sees and emphasizes the common truth underlying these differences, and when all have spoken the whole convention has a wider, clearer and more symmetrical view of the question at issue than it could possibly have had without such discussion.

To carry out these ends in our national conventions due prominence should be given to the hours for devotional service, and they should be made seasons of preparation for the tasks of the convention. Most of our conventions fail here. The devotional hour comes at a time when most of the delegates have not arrived at the place of meeting, and on account of the pressure of business only a few moments are devoted to waiting on the Lord, seeking wisdom and strength from him to do his work. We can not cherish too highly nor guard too jealously the place and the value of our national conventions in the promotion of the common aims and enterprises of the brotherhood.

❋ ❋

A Timely Sermon.

We take great pleasure in reprinting from the "British Weekly" the sermon found elsewhere on "The Unity of Christians," by Dr. Alexander Whyte. Its spirit and sentiment seem to us exceedingly timely just now for our own people. If any of our readers should miss a careful perusal of this sermon they will be the losers for such omission.

Notice, first of all, in the letter preceding the sermon, the four statements or truths which these distinguished leaders of the various religious forces in England assert that "all Christians can make their own." Note what vast progress that indicates in religious sentiment on the subject of Christian union. If the Christian leaders of this country have reached, with equal unanimity, these same conclusions—and we believe most of them have—then indeed we who have made the plea for union our specialty have reason to thank God and take courage.

The most vital and timely part of the sermon itself, in our judgment, is that which relates to the fitness of any man, or of any religious people, to advocate Christian unity. "Before the apostle will permit any man, leader or led, to open a mouth or to take up a pen concerning the reunion of Christians, he first demands of that man whether he himself is a truly Christian man or no; whether he himself is truly united to Christ or no; whether or no he has himself received any consolation from Christ amid the disunions of his own soul and amid the alienations and the enmities of his own life."

These statements try us like fire. It is only the calloused mind and heart that does not realize their incisiveness. They strike at the very heart and center of the whole problem. Many of us of late have felt this very thing to be true, but we have not said it perhaps in the same forceful and cogent way. After a careful reading and re-reading of this sermon we felt like kneeling in the presence of God and saying, "Lord, who am I that I should be an advocate of that deeper spiritual life, which is involved in Christian unity? Is my own spirit sufficiently imbued with Thy spirit, to enable me to lead others in the path of closer union and fellowship with Thee? Have I the humility and meekness of spirit, the disinterested zeal for the kingdom of God, to enable me to speak for Thee in behalf of unity?" That such will be the effect of the reading of this sermon on thousands of others of our readers we cannot doubt. The danger is that many of us will think and say that this applies to Brother So and So, and forget to apply it to ourselves. We have made a personal application of this lesson to our own heart, and we advise all our readers to do the same.

Perhaps none of us have ever realized, as we should have done, what great honor and responsibility God has placed upon us in permitting us to be advocates of Christian union. We have not been sufficiently humbled by it, and have not been made to feel our unworthiness for so holy a task. If recent experiences shall serve to humble us all, and make us feel our unfitness for the task that God has laid upon us, and shall lead us to such severe and honest self-examination and self-criticism, as will result in a better preparation for this great work, then God's purpose in such experiences will, no doubt, be realized. God teaches us by our failures no less than by our successes.

Nothing can be plainer than that the spirit which Dr. Whyte describes as the preparation for leadership in Christian union, is the very spirit in which this great problem must be approached. In so far as we have gone about it in any spirit of strife or vain glory, with the knowledge that puffs up rather than with the love that edifies, we have been in error, and we can not too soon correct that error. Christian union belongs to the holy of holies in Christianity. It lies at the heart of things, not on the surface. It belongs to the deeper and profounder things of the kingdom of God. No one can wisely lead in such a matter who has not himself known something of the deeper life with God, and whose soul has not been cleansed from all pride of opinion and obstinacy of spirit, and self-sufficiency and unchar-itableness, and has been clothed with humility as with a garment. Our prayer to God for this whole brotherhood of Disciples who have rendered such heroic service in behalf of Christian unity in spite of our own imperfections is that we all may come into such vital union with the Lord Jesus, and be so filled with his spirit that we may be worthy advocates of the holy cause of Christian unity.

Notes and Comments.

Dr. Henry A. Stimson tells in the New York "Observer" of a conversation he had with Dr. R. S. Storrs, the famous Brook-lyn pastor, just before his death. Dr. Stimson had referred to the many churches in Brooklyn which owed their origin to him. The great preacher and pastor re-plied: "They succeeded because my best men went into them. I would never give encouragement to any new movement un-less my best people living in that neigh-borhood would join it." That is the kind of unselfishness which only a great-heart-ed, broad-minded man can feel. Some-times, of course, it is unwise to organize a new church in a given community, but if it is determined by those interested that a church is needed there, then the mother church and its pastor should be willing to give up such of its members as would be necessary to make it a success.

A part of our centennial task as origin-ally outlined, it must be remembered, is the building of centennial memorial churches and the paying off of old church debts. In the building of new churches special atten-tion should be given to the most approved forms of church architecture. The new conception of church work, and especially the new prominence given to the Sunday-school idea, must find embodiment in our church architecture. Church buildings ought to be architecturally graceful and beautiful, and they *must* be adapted to the work of the church or they are practically useless. We hope soon to give special attention to this subject in a special issue of THE CHRISTIAN-EVANGELIST.

It is hard to overcome a popular mis-conception. Brother Yeuell reports that in his New England meeting he found the preachers had the idea pretty well fixed in their minds that the Disciples of Christ are baptismal regenerationists! It is not necessary to suppose any special depravity underlying this misconception since we have learned how easy it is for us to mis-understand and utterly misrepresent each other on matters much less complicated

than this. The lesson which this fact im-poses upon the representatives of our re-formatory movement is special care in guarding against any such misconception and in taking pains to remove it where it exists. That preacher who leaves in any community the impression he thinks that Christianity or the kingdom of God con-sists mainly in the proper observance of ordinances has certainly been at fault in his method of preaching. Christianity is pre-eminently a spiritual religion, and the *inwardness* of Christ's teaching is what distinguishes him chiefly from all other religious teachers.

Wm. H. Cord, principal Hazel Green Academy at Hazel Green, Ky., describes a situation in a mountain mining town in that state of twelve hundred people, where there are groups of Presbyterians, Episcopalians, Catholics, Northern and Southern Methodists, Missionary and Hard-shell Baptists, and several Chris-tians or Disciples of Christ. They meet in a union church, each of the four lead-ing bodies occupying one Lord's day in each month. The Sunday-school is made up of representatives from all these churches, both in its teaching force and constituency. Brother Cord asks how we would apply the principle of federa-tion to a situation like that. The prin-ciple of federation is already being ap-plied in that town. It is only a question of how much further, if any, they can apply it. If, for instance, they could all meet together each Lord's day and the ministers alternate in preaching; that would, perhaps, be an advance on what they are now doing. If they are not al-ready co-operating in efforts looking to the moral welfare of the people of the town, they could do that. If they could see their way clear to hold union evan-gelistic services by mutual concessions that would sacrifice no principle, they should also do that. In a word, the prin-ciple of federation would require that they work together just so far as they can do so, freely and conscientiously, for the promotion of the kingdom of God in that town, each respecting the con-scientious convictions of others, and all remaining true to their own convictions.

An Urgent Call.

The total expenses of the Yeuell meet-ing at Manchester, N. H., were $1,142.23. I am in receipt of vouchers in the form of receipted bills, for all these expenses save balance due the evangelist for per-sonal expenses and salary. On closing the meeting he wired for $250 to meet outstanding bills, which I authorized to be sent to him at once, though there were only $62 on hand. The total amount contributed for this fund up to date is $713.75, leaving a deficit of $428.48. Brother Yeuell, who needed rest very much, was about to start to Bethany, Beach for a two weeks' rest when he was suddenly called to England by the precarious condition of his mother's

health. He sailed at one try, asking that balance to an address which he f don, at once. He will have it. I have, therefor brethren, authorized th due him be sent as di the labor and expense of tracted correspondence, i telegrams, I will freely of this deficit, and I earn the remaining amount, tributed at once.

The meeting has beer wide and far-reaching result in a church in Man to the principles of this F sides a broad-casting of ligious reformation throu ment. May I trust to contribute promptly the to liquidate this indebted

J.

Current Religious

"The Standard" (Baptis ly realize that Christian u pressed only in its hea variations on its "inter comity" it will one day s er mote of absolute oneness never vary far from it ag editorial advocacy of ur Protestants to secure bet superannuated ministers, it sense of the need of a cl all the children of the Ki

We are emphasizing these practical co-operation among re hence have reason to feel that spirit exists than once was kno service is done for humanity. account of William Quayles p fund of millions for ministers out of service, such as the C school teachers.] Some method commensurate with the material as well as with the equity of it. are giving vast fortunes for ad anthropic work, the proposal not only timely but fruitful! Protestant denominations could long enough to see the wisdom character of such a movement long before some men of weal movement and the denomination practical co-operation. Such tainly could not make a less it would unquestionably prod happier men in the ministry one of the problems of the chu

This editorial on a Resta trines in last week's St. I Advocate" would be quite we not believe our friend is in error. We believe t ferred to are due to a chan ments of Methodists rather ing significance of words:

There seems in some quarti taken idea regarding the pro by members of the general c appointment of a committee statement of Methodist faith. lar papers seem to be of the Methodists have fallen behind learned that they must keep u be further from the truth. The ciples of Methodism have not odistic faith in its cardinalities always has been. But words significance; in the popular un do not now mean what they di century; and a half ago, and to Methodistic faith to the com hearers, the conference propose such a form as to render it m the men of to-day. The faith founded on Biblical doctrine ar terpreted by Wesley, and his e purpose of the revision of restat than to present in the langua fundamental truths on which Met

Editor's Easy Chair.

PENTWATER MUSINGS.

Last evening as we sat upon the western veranda watching through the branches of the hemlocks the red sun sinking to rest beneath the waves, it was observed that the crimson path over the lake ran directly to each of the observers. This, said the Easy Chair, is a parable. Yon glowing orb of day stands for the Sun of Righteousness who is the effulgence, the outshining of God. Each one sees this divine effulgence of God for himself, and no two, perhaps, see it exactly alike. But to each believing soul who looks steadfastly on him who is the light of the world, he sends forth his beams of light which make a shining pathway of duty reaching from God to each believing heart. What does God require of any man but to walk in the light as he is able to see the light? Why should we quarrel with each other because we chance to see the light from a different angle of vision? For after all the chief trouble with all of us is not so much in the lack of sufficient light as in our failure to walk in the light we have. As we gazed at that crimson pathway that lay across the lake, far out to the setting sun, there came to us that comforting passage: "The path of the just groweth brighter unto the perfect day." To him who uses the light he has, God giveth more light until his pathway, once dim and uncertain, widens and brightens into a shining highway. And so all nature is a parable teaching us the ways of God with men, when we cause to understand it. This material universe is but the outward investiture of him whose Spirit fills all worlds and all time, even that measureless time, which we call eternity. This is why it is that

"The heavens declare the glory of God.
And the firmament showeth his handiwork."

⚘

Perhaps more people are seeking rest during this month of August than in any other month of the year. It is not simply rest from either physical or mental toil which men seek when they leave their homes in the summer season for some quiet nook far from the city's maddening crowd. It is the rest that comes from change of scenery and occupation and therefore a change of thought and method of living. Often there is an indefinable longing of soul for a deeper rest underlying this habit of leaving the shop, the office, and the counting room for a season to get closer to the heart of nature. So much is man a unit and so intimately are the different parts of his nature blended that it is often difficult to know where this longing for rest takes on a religious quality. When David wrote: "Oh, that I had wings like a dove, then I would fly away and be at rest," he was thinking, no doubt, of something higher and deeper than absence of the cares of state and the responsibilities of kingship. A celebrated picture exhibited once in the Royal Academy represented King David seated upon the broad, flat roof of his palace surrounded by the symbols of his high office, but wearing a careworn expression on his face, his

brow furrowed with lines of care and his eyes looking away from the glitter and pomp of his royal surroundings and gazing into the infinite space, where, in a storm-swept sky, care-free and buoyant several white winged doves were flying. This was the artist's comment on the passage we have quoted above. Sooner or later the soul learns the lesson perceived by Augustine long ago—that our souls come from God and are restless until they rest in him.

⚘

The noise and confusion incident to building are not conducive to quiet reading, but we have read four or five books thus far—scientific, religious and theological—and these in connection with our regular literary work, and the preparation of a volume for the press has been quite sufficient to keep us busy. It was during one of our summer vacations that we prepared the volume of sermons by Alexander Proctor for publication. This was a labor of love which we greatly enjoyed, although there was a great deal of labor in it. We loved Alexander Proctor and admired his genius, and to seek to put some of his noble thoughts into permanent literary form was a real pleasure. The book has had a good sale but there are thousands of our ministers who would be greatly quickened intellectually and spiritually by coming in contact with the inspiring thoughts of these sermons. There ought to have been a volume of sermons from George W. Longan. Each of these great men richly deserves a well written biography. We do not believe the State of Missouri has produced two nobler types of manhood, nor two abler preachers of the Gospel, than Alexander Proctor and George W. Longan. To have enjoyed their love and confidence during their lifetime is an inspiration to us even yet. It was their misfortune, if it may be called such, to live somewhat in advance of their own time and to apprehend certain great truths and principles which even yet are hidden to many of their brethren. But time will vindicate the general correctness of their view, and some day, let us hope, some biographer of our great men will do justice to the memory of these great Missouri preachers who lived and wrought nobly and have passed on to the higher and holier fellowships and activities of the life unseen. To us earth is poorer since they left it and heaven is richer for their going thither.

⚘

On the north veranda of "The Pioneer" two thrifty young oaks were standing just in a line east and west, and instead of cutting them down we built the veranda around them and they are just the right distance apart to swing a hammock between them. In this hammock the Easy Chair is located this morning facing the lake which lies before us in broad ribbons of green and purple and orange. Now some readers will think that is a luxurious position, even for an Easy Chair. And so it is, but we are sure none of our readers will begrudge a toilsome editor an occasional moment

of luxurious repose amid such surroundings. Of course, there are people, on the other hand, who would smile at the idea of anything so primitive as that we have described being luxurious. But that is all a matter of taste. The Easy Chair prefers it to a king's palace with all its luxurious appointments. With Pastor Wagner we believe in the "Simple Life," and that is what we are trying to live here in these Michigan woods by the lake shore. Let Newport and Atlantic City and other popular, fashionable seaside resorts frolic and carouse and put on society airs if they wish. But as for us give us the society of the trees, the music of the waves, and for a canopy the over-arching blue of the heavens, and for perfumes the odors of the pine and the hemlock, and quiet to think of God and duty and destiny, and we will be content. So many people prefer this kind of a resort that the problem before us just now is to prepare for their accommodation. The steamer "Kansas," which arrived this morning from Chicago, brought a dozen souls seeking rest here upon this beach. Some of these will have to lodge in the village of Pentwater for the present. That is a cool and delightful spot for people coming from the south and west. By another season we hope to have more ample accommodations, both in the way of cottages and increased hotel facilities, on this beach.

⚘

The Buffalo convention is little more than two months away. Great interest should attach to this annual convocation of our hosts. For the first time in our history our national convention enters the Empire State. It will reach a number of people who have never before had the opportunity of attending one of our national conventions. We meet in one of the great and beautiful cities of that state where a national convention of such dimensions as ours can not fail to attract wide attention. Special effort should be made for a good attendance but more particularly, as we have before urged, for a representative attendance of the important business which comes before these annual conventions. It is an exceedingly interesting time in our own history when our movement is aggressive, hopeful and moving on toward its centennial celebration which is near at hand. Every public utterance on that convention should be carefully considered and every set address should be the subject of earnest prayer as well as of earnest study. Let us make it a great convention in the high ideals we shall place before ourselves, in the spirit of consecration and of unity which shall mark every session, and in the large plans we may devise for advancing Christ's kingdom in the world. We are sure many eager eyes will be turned toward that convention to see what shall be its great keynotes and key-words for the coming campaign. In all our plans for the convention, let us not forget to ask and to plan for the Lord Jesus to be with us and guide our deliberations to his own glory.

As Seen From the Dome

There is a world of art in Rome beside the Vatican treasures. The Capitol Museum, for example, has a fine collection of statuary. The Capitol is the smallest, but historically the most important of Rome's hills. The great temple of Jupiter was here, the most sacred shrine of ancient Rome. In the center of the piazza before the museum is an admirable statue of Marcus Aurelius on horseback in bronze. It would be a fine model for the men that build the innumerable equestrian statues for our city of Washington. Owing to its moderate height the head is distinctly visible while our multitudinous bronze soldiers are so high as to be almost indistinguishable. In the museum are some wonderful works. Here is the world-famed Dying Gladiator, found at Rome in the sixteenth century. The dying warrior, recognized as a Gaul by his twisted collar, short hair and mustache, is sitting on his shield while the blood pours from his wounded breast. He has evidently inflicted the blow himself, having previously broken the crooked horn which lies on his shield. He prefers death to captivity. It is a great figure cut in a masterful way. Read Childe Harold, Canto 4:140. Another interesting figure is the Satyr of Praxiteles, which suggested Nathaniel Hawthorne's "Marble Faun." The busts of the philosophers, and of the emperors are probably the finest in the world. And here also we saw the Capitoline Venus, a perfect type of feminine grace; and the "Doves on a Fountain Basin" found in Hadrian's villa, a simple but perfectly beautiful mosaic. One never tires of these rare objects of the highest art.

Near the museum, on the Capitol Hill, is "the Church of the Altar of Heaven," with the famous Bambino. Who has not heard of the Bambino? and what is the Bambino? Il Santo Bambino or, Holy Child, is an image believed to protect persons in imminent danger and is frequently invoked and revered and worshiped, and sometimes borne to the houses of the sick, on such occasions passers-by kneeling at its approach. During Christmas week children come and address their petitions to the Bambino. The whole figure is covered with watches, diamond ornaments and jewels of every description which are placed upon it by devotees. Is this idolatry, or is it not? A prayer to the Bambino repeated a certain number of times secures certain benefits for the living and for the dead.

The Forum of Trajan is one of the ancient places which every one sees. It was formerly an aggregate of splendid edifices, and was considered the most magnificent in Rome. All that is left today is Trajan's column, constructed entirely of marble, 147 feet including the statue of St. Peter which supplants that of the emperor. The column is 11 feet

in diameter at the bottom and 10 at the top. Around it runs a spiral band, 3 feet wide, and 660 long, covered with admirable reliefs from Trajan's wars with the Dacians, animals, machines, etc., over 2,500 human figures. Beneath this column Trajan was buried and on top was his statue. It was excavated to the depth of 100 feet and the ruins at its base, broken columns and pavement, show what a Forum once existed there in the great days of the city.

Guido Reni's Aurora in the Rospigliosi Palace, is one of the world's great pictures. It is a ceiling painting and is best studied in a mirror. Aurora is strewing flowers before the chariot of the god of the sun who is surrounded by the dancing hours. The coloring is a marvel. The strongest light is thrown upon the figure of Apollo whose hair and flesh are of a golden hue, and of corresponding tint are the yellowish red robes of the nymphs nearest Apollo. The colors are then gradually shaded off from blue to white and from green to white, while the dun-colored horses accord with the clouds in the background. It is a perfect picture. I enjoyed it more than any other in Rome. To show how people take in such things, however, I said to a very intelligent man, "Did you get to the Rospigliosi?" "O, yes," was the answer, "and I saw the chariot race!" Two other pictures in this gallery are great: Guido Reni's "Andromeda" and Domenichino's "Triumph of David." Near this palace they show you one of those horrible collections of human skeletons such as one sees in Malta and Cologne, the bones of 4,000 monks displayed in all sorts of cunning mosaic work in the church of the Capuchins. It is a ghastly array. Each vault contains a tomb with earth from Jerusalem. In case of a new interment the bones which have longest been undisturbed are used in the decorations. Chicago people, and some others, ornament the skulls with their names in pencil. The Lord deliver us from the fate of these poor fellows. In the church is a picture, Guido Reni's "St. Michael," which is worth the vision of all the bones in Christendom.

Rome has many great churches beside St. Peter's. She has about 365, or one for every day in the year; and some of them are perfect wonders for beauty and treasure. St. John in Lateran, the Cathedral of Rome, is one of the richest. It is a basilica, "Omnium urbis et orbis ecclesiarum mater et caput," and was the principal church of Rome after the time of Constantine. Five great councils have been held here. It has an imposing portico and five entrances. The Porte Santa is walled up and opened only in the year of jubilee. The principal entrance has great bronze doors and on the left is an ancient statue of Constantine. It has many fine statues and paintings, columns and mosaics and claims the heads

popes It contains what is claimed to be the sarcophagus of Paul who, according to tradition, was interred by a pious woman named Lucina, on her property here. Columns, mosaics, statues, decorations and paintings in this church positively overwhelm you with their magnificence. The interior is 130 long, 65 in width and 75 feet high. The alabaster columns and malachite altars, colossal statues and glowing mosaics of Peter and Paul, portrait medallions of popes and splendid frescoes and paintings, and the vast colonnades are worthy of the great name with which men associate them. Not far away, it is said, three miles out from the Ostian gate, Paul suffered martyrdom.

Another place associated with the great apostle is the Appian Way. This is the military road constructed by Appius Claudius, B. C. 312. It is still a queen of roads, and is the nearest excursion to the Campagna. It affords fine prospects of the country, ruins of aque-

ducts, mountains and ancient tombs, We passed out the St. Sebastian gate and stopped at the little church, "Domine Quo Vadis," so named from the legend that Peter, fleeing from the death of a martyr, here met his Master and enquired: "Domine, Quo vadis?" to which he received reply, "Venio iterum crucifigi"; whereupon the apostle ashamed of his weakness, returned. They pretend to show the foot print of Christ. Farther on we entered the catacombs. These subterranean passages where the Christian dead were interred are wonderfully interesting. They extend around the city in a great circle, upwards of forty different ones, covering an area of 615 acres as far as discovered, a total length of 545 miles. The highest are 22-25 feet below the surface, and lowest 40-50 feet. The passages are one above the other, two and a half feet wide with niches one above the other where the bodies were laid, and closed with tablets of marble or terra cotta, usually in-

scribed in pace, with earthen lamps and symbols of the resurrection; the bodies wrapped in cloth and with various ornaments and memorials. At intervals are large chambers and small chapels; and often statues and pottery, and paintings of the Lord's supper and of his baptism, of the Good Shepherd, and the raising of Lazarus, of Old Testament scenes and the miracles of Christ, of the fish, the special Christian symbol, as the Greek Ichthus consists of the initial letters of the words "Jesus, Christ the Savior, Son of God.". These burying places of the martyrs have largely been robbed for relics.

Along this Appian Way Paul entered Rome A. D. 62° and in the month of June. His ship entered Puteoli Bay. Acts 28:11. He met brethren at Tres Tabernae, and "took courage." The Jews show an ancient building of Roman construction in the Ghetto as his "hired house." Here he wrote and here he suffered in the imperial city. It is easy to prove an alibi for Peter. 2 Tim 4:11.

Modern Religious Persecution---A Defense

By B. L. Chase

4. Secret of Persecutor's Power.

What is the secret of the marvelous constancy and fearlessness shown by persecutors? We wonder how in medieval times councils and courts of inquisition could carry out sentences of banishment and death against good men whose only crime was that they did not agree with the persecutors. One would think that their consciences would shrink from the awful business. How unusual, rather unnatural, must have been the souls of those men who could contemplate the suffering of the condemned man or woman at the stake or on the gallows, the agony of the bereft family—the children left without a father and protector, the wife without a husband and companion—and yet obtain the consent of their consciences to carry out the sentence. What gave them such strength of will? It was the courage of their convictions. What gave them such courage of conviction? It was the will of God which they were carrying out. They were sure they were right.

It is this courage of conviction, this intimacy with the will of God, that makes the prophet and the persecutor so much alike. The persecutor, like the prophet, does not go forth in his own strength. He is not trusting his own wisdom, but God's; he is not fighting his own battle, but God's. His judgments against his brethren are righteous judgments, because they are God's judgments. They are done in truth and equity. Right makes might in any cause. This is the secret of the persecutor's strength, for whose business few men have either the courage or the liking. It is this rare quality of character which is possessed by all great leaders—this courage of conviction, this certainty of having God on one's side. It belonged to Mohammed, to Huss, to Loyola, to Luther, to Joseph Smith and to Dowie. No one can question the courage of conviction, on the success of these men.

We do not need to go so far from the ranks of the Disciples for illustrations of the success that attends courage of conviction and certainty of being right. The people like it and rally around those that have it. It has made Dowie a multimillionaire in 10 years, and doubled the circulation of one newspaper in five years. People will pay money for strong convictions, for the same convictions that they hold. It simply shows the business blindness of some editors who fail to see that the people will pay for only that which they want. They will support loyally the paper or pulpit or college—any institution —that is true to their convictions. How foolish to disagree with the people when they are right. If you stick to the people they will stick to you. We all like people who think as we do. The trouble with Savonarola and other prophets who have been put to death for their convictions was that they were not careful enough to agree with the convictions of others. You will always get into trouble if you do not agree with the majority.

The motto of all successful persecutors has been: "Be sure you are right, then go ahead." God is always on the side of right; while God and the right make a majority. But you wonder how a persecutor can be so sure he is right, when he starts out to put a man to death, as in mediaeval times, or to drive a man from the college, the missionary secretaryship or pulpit, as in modern times. That is so simple a matter that the wayfaring man should not be in doubt. Did not the ancient persecutor have an infallible Pope to tell him the will of God; and does not the modern persecutor have an infallible book to tell him the will of God? But you say he is likely to misinterpret and misunderstand the letter and spirit of the

book; while it would be a dreadful thing for him to call a man an "infidel" or a "skeptic," and find out later that he was mistaken as to what the man believed. Then there are so many different interpretations of the Bible, and no one would want to risk the possibility of doing a positive wrong by basing a persecution of a brother upon his private interpretation of the Bible.

In reply to this objection I would remind the objector that he is entirely ignorant of one of the cardinal principles of the Disciples, and shows by his ignorance that he has not been with them long; or else, ought not to remain among them long. Have the Disciples not always taught that one should not interpret the Bible, but simply read it, and

❧ ❧

"NO TROUBLE"

To Change from Coffee to Postum.

"Postum has done a world of good for me," writes an Ills. man.

"I've had indigestion nearly all my life but never dreamed coffee was the cause of my trouble until last Spring I got so bad I was in misery all the time.

"A coffee drinker for 30 years, it irritated my stomach and nerves, yet I was just crazy for it. After drinking it with my meals, I would leave the table, go out and lose my meal and the coffee too. Then I'd be as hungry as ever.

'A friend advised me to quit coffee and use Postum—said it cured him. Since taking his advice I retain my food and get all the good out of it, and don't have those awful hungry spells.

"I changed from coffee to Postum without any trouble whatever; felt better from the first day I drank it. I am well now and give the credit to Postum." Name given by Postum Co., Battle Creek, Mich. Read the little book, "The Road to Wellville," in pkgs. "There's a reason."

plain literal sense? It is this prin-
hich has preserved their unity, while
eligious bodies have divided. It is
iple which helps them to see eye
and heart to heart, upon so many
ns; and enables the conservative to
id speak kindly of the progressive,
er critic of the higher critic, the
lerationist of the federationist.
is the principle that gives the perse-
is courage of conviction and of exe-
with this sense of certainty and
cy in his heart, he can go straight
rrow to the mark. He sets an ex-
of assurance which should be the
on and envy of every Disciple. It
mission to weed out error, treason,
pocrisy, from our midst, and to pre-
a peculiar people among whom there is
ion—a people among whom there is
rence of opinion. Every one knows
ference of opinion among Christians,
ause of division; and that there is

but one way to have unity, and that is for
every one to think and believe alike. This
is the high and noble aim of our persecutors—to compel every one among the
Disciples to think alike, by thinking as they
do. If we pay no heed to their earnest appeals the time will come among the Disciples when there will be disputes, controversies, heart-burnings, and possible division; we might better part with a few men
who believe in the higher criticism or federation, than be divided among ourselves.
We would become the laughing stock of
the religious world when we, a people born
with Christian union upon our lips, dispute
and wrangle among ourselves. We must
never let it come. We must let our leading persecutors save us from it. They are
the only ones among us who have convictions and are perfectly sure they are
right. Why not let them lead? They are
the only ones who have the courage or
nerve to carry out persecuting programs.

Let us be grateful to them. If every one
could think God's thoughts after him, and
be sure of it, I would not urge this matter upon the brotherhood. But since we
have such men, let us use them; let us
honor them with our silver and our gold,
and the first fruits of all our increase; let
us cease to doubt their infallability, and
their right to put away from among us all
difference of opinion. Who will look after
the heretic, the infidel, the traitor, the federationist, and the higher critic, if they do
not? It ought to disqualify a man forever,
especially if he be a young man, from holding a position in one of our pulpits, or missionary societies, or colleges, for daring to
become an antagonist of one of the chosen
persecutors. They are our "leading men."
Disagreement with one of them is proof
enough that a man is a destructive teacher,
an infidel, and a blasphemer. He ought to
be cut off from among his brethren, that
he may go to "his own place." Let all
such copy the example of Judas.

The Content of the Evangelistic Sermon

By J. N. Scholes

Savior's purpose is to save. "The
man came to seek and to save
hich was lost." The sinner needs
saved. "Lord, save me or I per-
The Gospel is the Lord's means.
he power of God unto salvation."
inner's fundamental means is
"Believe on the Lord Jesus
" The Lord's chosen method is
ing. "Preach the Word." The
i is but the method and it must.
n to the Savior's purpose and to
ner's need.
nished sermon has form, filling,
s and application. My chief
t is filling—content, the others
idental.

I.

I.—That which is important to
i also necessary—beginning, con-
, and, not too remote, discontinu-
sing.)
said, "Ye men of Athens, I per-
at in all things ye are very re-
For as I passed by and beheld
vations I found an altar with this
ion, To the Unknown God. Whom
re ye ignorantly worship, him de-
unto you." These sentences intro-
e of the mightiest sermons of the
While we rightly suspect that
ot fully reported, yet we gather
y, two things: the introduction
ef—it introduced the theme.
nuing and discontinuing.—Heed
voice that says, "Why did you
soon?" It is not the voice of the
Neither consider seriously the
says, "You weary me." It is not
of authority. Your appointment
to exhibit the endurance of the
nor to compromise with the car-
lard, but to preach Christ. Let
rmons be like that man who falls
tenith of his power: like that
river, which, rising beyond no
able obstacles sweeps on and on,
into its course every legitimate

tributary and pours into the sea the volume of its greatest strength.

II.

Filling.—The gospels contain partial
reports of forty-five sermons by the Savior touching an infinite variety of subject matter. The Acts contains about
half as many sermons and sermonettes
conforming closely to the Master's. By
these examples present day preaching is
limited to the Bible for subject matter,
but liberated to the universe for illustration and application. Paul preached his
first sermon in Damascus. His theme
was, "Jesus is the Christ." Until the
fight was finished he knew nothing but
Christ and him crucified, and dying,
bequeathed his richest legacy in a single
sentence, "Preach the Word."

Man's ignorance of self and God are
the divine reasons for preaching. Our unceasing obligation proceeds from the fact
that Christ hath declared the Father
unto men. Entertainment can not excuse, evangelism can not license the
omission of these main features. Man
does not know God until he knows
righteousness, and he does not know
righteousness until he sees it in Jesus.
Man does not know self until he knows
sin, and then his knowledge is to no purpose until he knows that he may be
reconciled to God.

All preaching is to one purpose.
Evangelism is to make Christians. Pas-
toralism is to make better Christians, or
to make Christians better. One is to
make God known, the other is to complete and perfect the acquaintance.
Evangelism is proclaiming the Gospel
and drawing men to its acceptance. It
is the saved soul telling the lost soul of
its salvation and of its Savior. Evangelism is more than moving men—it is saving men. Multitudes are moved in div-

ers directions, preacherward, society-
ward, churchward, waterward, who are
not moved Christward. Christ must be
the center of all evangelistic themes—
and his love, his mercy, his power, his
judgment, his suffering, his word, his authority and his Spirit must reach every
point of the circumference.

III.

Features.—Brother Grant Lewis said
that he learned homiletics in his father's
generously large dooryard. "But how?"
said I. "Making snow men," said he. "I
just roll up a big one and place it, and
then I put one on top, and another on
top of that. Then I dig through and it
stands on legs. I dig out a little there
and a little there, and a little more there,
and it has two eyes and a mouth; I
pack a little on here, and there, and
there, and it has ears and a nose. A roll
for an arm on this side and on that and
I have a snow man. But it was not a
snow man until he added the features.
Neither is that pile of promiscuous
thought a sermon. The Bible and the
world of life are inexhaustible fields of
illustration. They both belong to God,
and his servant may glorify Jesus Christ
by a legitimate use of them in the em-
bellishment of divine thought. Knowledge must have proper conveyance—vehicles of thought-wheels. It can not get
to you nor from you without them.

Do not be afraid of being called unscriptural. Some sermons are so scripturally unscriptural as to miss the time
by nineteen hundred years and the place
by four thousand miles. Remember that
you are in America—not in Asia. You
are talking to Americans living under the
strenuous and pacific administration of
Theodore Roosevelt—not to Jews under
Herodian dominion: men, multitudes of
whom know little beyond the experiences
of their own generation. Jesus said,
"Preach the Gospel to all creation." Do
not leave the impression that it has not

taken its departure from Jerusalem but carefully mold it into American thought.

IV.

Application.—Take time to apply. Eliminate, if needful, the introduction, economize on filling that you may have time for application. David Burrell with a fine sense of grace, says, "Preaching is not fencing. The sword must not only be unsheathed and brandished, but it must be driven home." A sermon is a thrust. The nail is driven—it must be clinched. To Paul's experience with God and men Felix listened with respectful official dignity, but when he reasoned of justice, self-control and impending judgment he was terrified.

This is where preaching rises to its truest art. The message is from God, and, to give it authority, the messenger must ever bear the imprint of recent communion with him—for he must not leave his audience looking at any man, but seeing Jesus only. When the saintly Summerfield was dying, he said: "Oh! Now if I might return to my pulpit for an hour, how I could preach! For I have looked into eternity: I have seen God face to face."

Lima, Ohio.

The Unity of Christians* By Dr. Alexander Whyte
In British Weekly.

In common with my brethren I have received this letter, which I will now read:

A UNITED EFFORT OF PRAYER.

Sir—We, who subscribe this letter, represent widely different Christian communities. We agree in deprecating at present any large schemes of corporate reunion, which seem to us premature, or any attempts to treat our existing religious divergences as unimportant; but we agree, also, in believing profoundly that our Lord Jesus Christ meant us to be one in visible fellowship; we feel profoundly the paralyzing effect upon the moral forces of Christianity which our divisions inevitably produce, and we recognize with the fullest conviction that it is the duty of all Christians, who desire in this respect the fulfillment of the Divine purpose, to give themselves to penitence and prayer—to penitence, because we have all, in various ways, as bodies and as individuals, contributed to produce and perpetuate differences; and to prayer, because what we all alike need is that God should open our minds and hearts to receive without prejudice the gradual revelation of his will as to the ways by which we are to be drawn together.

Being so far agreed, we are venturing, not we believe without the guidance of the Holy Spirit, to approach as far as we can, all the Christian ministers of religion in England to ask them to prepare their congregations for a united effort of prayer on Whitsunday next, at the principal morning service, for the reunion of Christians—special care being taken that such prayer should be entirely uncontroversial, and should involve no assumptions except those which all Christians can make, their own, viz.:

That our Lord meant us to be one in visible fellowship:

That our existing divisions hinder or even paralyze his work;

That we all deserve chastisement, and need penitence, for the various ways in which we have contributed to produce or promote division;

That we all need open and candid minds to receive light and yet more light, so that, in ways we perhaps as yet can hardly imagine, we may be led back towards unity.

We believe that by these solemn exercises of penitential devotion dispositions may be created and nourished which will do much to remove the needless embitterment so frequently pervading our differences of judgment and creed; and, that a freer way may be prepared for the Divine purpose to realize itself. RANDALL CANTUAR,
T. J. DICKENSON,
President of the United Methodist Free Churches.
J. H. JOWETT.
WILLIAM EBOR,
Chairman of the Congregational Union of England and Wales.
C. H. KELLY,
President of the Wesleyan Methodist Conference,
J. B. MEHARRY,
Moderator-Elect of the English Presbyterian Church.
F. B. MEYER,
President of the Baptist Union.
A. J. MILNE,
Moderator of the General Assembly of the Church of Scotland.
ROBERT RAINY,
Moderator of the General Assembly of the United Free Church of Scotland.
E. J. ROBINSON,
President of the Methodist New Connexion Church.
GEORGE ST. ANDREWS.
Primus of the Scottish Church.

*A Whitsunday Reunion Sermon.
(Phil. ii. 1-4.)

Along with that so influentially signed letter let this still more influentially signed letter be read, which was addressed to the church at Philippi, and which was brought to Philippi from Rome by Epaphroditus. And especially let this peacemaking passage in this apostolic epistle be well pondered in our day and by ourselves. "If there be therefore any consolation in Christ, if any comfort of love, if any fellowship of the Spirit, if any bowels and mercies, fulfill ye my joy, that ye be likeminded, having the same love, being of one accord, of one mind." The apostle as good as says: "You write a letter to promote the reunion of your churches and you urge your people to pray and to work for that reunion, and you do well in that. But be sure that you make clear to yourselves and to your people who are the proper persons to propose such a reunion and to pray for it and to work for it. As also make it absolutely clear to yourselves and to them what manner of persons they must be who will ever be employed by God to bring about such a reunion." Let a man examine himself is a fundamental and a universal rule with the apostle. And he applies this fundamental and universal rule of his to all the advocates and to all the promoters of reunion, as well as to all the candidates for the Lord's Supper. And this self-scrutinizing rule of his is not laid down for the leaders and the people of the Philippian church alone; it is laid down for the leaders and the people of the Churches of England and of Scotland, as well as for the leaders and the people of the Greek Church and the Church of Rome. Before the apostle will permit any man, leader or led, to open a mouth or to take up a pen concerning the reunion of Christians, he first demands of that man whether he himself is a truly Christian man or no; whether he himself is truly united to Christ or no; whether or no he has himself received any consolation from Christ amid the dissensions of his own soul and amid the alienations and the enmities of his own life. Because, if a man's own soul is not at peace with God, how can that man be a mediator of peace and reunion in the Church of Christ? He cannot. The thing is impossible. Then, again, let every man examine himself as to this—has he any of the comforts of love in his own soul? For it is the lack of love, and it is the lack of comforts of love, that has been the chief cause of all the disunions and all the divisions in the Church of Christ, as well as in the whole world of mankind. Then, again, there is what Paul here calls the fellowship of the Spirit. That is to say, does the very Spirit of Christ dwell in your heart? Does the very Spirit of Christ really hold his holy temple, with all its spiritual services, in your hidden heart? Because, it is in the communion of the Holy Spirit alone that we are made capable of any true communion with one another. And, then, as the sure result of all that, have you any bowels and mercies? the apostle demands. That is to say, have you any yearning, tenderness of heart, and any true brokenness of heart, over the divisions and the distresses of the Church of Christ? As well as over those multitudes of men who are wholly outside of the Church of Christ, and are aliens from the commonwealth of Israel, and strangers to the covenants of promise? Be it known unto you, says the apostle, that these are the only men who are eligible of God either for prayer, or for proposing plans, or for carrying out plans in connection with the re-uniting of the Church of Christ. Let all other men see to themselves first.

And, then, the proper promoters of reunion being thus tested and selected, there follows the apostolical program of church principles, as we would say, and the true articles of reunion for the whole of Christendom, east and west, north and south. And first: Be ye likeminded, having the same love, being of one accord, of one mind. Likeminded is a great word with Paul. I cannot tell you how often the word likeminded occurs all up and down his pastoral and his homiletical epistles. But how is that likemindedness to be brought about among men? it may well be asked. Many men many minds, is true of the Church of Christ, as well as of the world without. With so many doubtful and dubious matters agitating the minds of men; with so many difficult matters at once in the doctrine, and in the worship, and in the government, and in the manifold life of the Church of Christ; with the facial differences of the nations of the earth, and of the peoples of mankind among whom the Church of Christ has been planted; and with men's education, and enlightenment, and temperament, and religious experiences, and moral and spiritual attainments so very different, how is the same mind at all possible among so many men? Love will do it, replies Paul. Love will do all that needs to be done. Christian men, the very best, will never to the end of time see eye to eye in everything. But they will more and more bear with one another, where they do not see eye to eye. They will more and more accommodate themselves to one another. They will more and more leave many matters open and undetermined; open and undetermined and waiting for more light and more experience and more maturity of mind; but especially open and undetermined and waiting for more love. Paul is a great man for love. John gets more praise for love than Paul gets, but I doubt if he deserves it. John deserves all the praise that he gets, and more; but Paul is not one whit behind John in his doctrine and practice of love; to my mind he is far before him. Having the same love, says Paul, will produce the same mind. Let love be your overruling principle in all your prayers, and in all your negotiations for reunion, says Paul; a real love, a deep love, a self-suppressing, and a self-obliterating love of all the other negotiators, and you will be astonished how the most dividing and difficult matters will begin to clear up and to give way. And, where they do not clear up and give way all at once, continue your attempts at the good work of reunion, still contributing more and more love to one another all round the table of the committee, and all your difficulties are bound to clear up and to give way at last. Nothing can resist love. Just try enough love on the reunion of Christendom and see.

And, in all your debates that tend toward disunion, and then, in all your deliberations and negotiations for reunion, says the apostle, let nothing be done through strife or vainglory. Now, we must all take that rebuke home to ourselves and say, I am the man. The truth is Paul here puts his finger on the real plague-spot in us all, and in all our churches. For it is beyond all dispute that strife and vainglory were largely, if not wholly, the cause of all our original and all our aggravated divisions in past days. There has always been so much strife and vainglory in the Church of Christ that the wonder is she has not been blown into a thousand pieces, and blown out of existence. The wonder is that there is one really united and harmonious body of believers in all the world. As indeed there is not. I alone am wholly in the right in this and in that, and you all are wholly in the wrong. And I will fight against you for my own way with my bitter tongue and with my poisoned pen. And if I cannot silence you with these weapons, then if I have the power I will silence you with the boot, and with the rack, and with the stake, and with the scaffold. A cruel and a persecuting strife like that has in all ages made the Church of Christ to be a very synagogue of Satan, wherever the sword has been grafted on the crook; and wherever the state church could hand over her rebellious children to the civil magistrate. And the same strife and vainglory continue to this very day, and they invade every company even of Christian men. You cannot sit in the most friendly deliberation and discussion for an hour in any company even of sincerely Christian men, without seeing vainglory intruding itself and strife and intolerance beginning to show themselves. So unlike their Master are the best of his disciples; so vain of themselves are the humblest of his disciples; and so full of an

ill-suppressed strife are of his disciples. "Natu all a love of our own Hooker in his "Ecclesiast the contradiction of othe flame our self-love. Our to maintain that which o and done sharpeneth ou and to argue, and by all i what we have said and Hooker himself is not alw and vainglory, as Coleric honestly and so boldly in vines."

When you come togeth debate towards disunion; and to work for reunion, ceeds, let it be in such a l that you will honestly est men, both friends and fo men than yourselves. A mand, you will say. For man and a good man, as such a man with his eye other men whatsoever to than himself? How can of himself and of all other simple truth and with sob An able and honest and man cannot surely shut simple fact that he is a far that fool and that sluggar around him. Certainly n not at all the apostle apostle's point is this. the apostle would have all matters of debate and reunion must be men from head to foot with h to say, they must be men more at their own lapses fi from love than at all the v folly and all the self-seekin

(Continued on Pag

Who Is a Christian in the Twentieth Cen

By E. L. Frazier

There can be but one answer to this question. The same party who was a Christian in the first century. In heaven a plan for the redemption and salvation of man was devised. In the fullness of time the Son of God wrought out that plan.

When he had said on the cross "it is finished," he, after giving instruction and promise and commission to his apostles, went back to heaven. To the apostles he gave the keys of the kingdom and the promise of the Holy Spirit who should guide them into all truth. Note 'all truth."

The Holy Spirit came. By the Holy Spirit the apostles were guided. They spake as the Holy Spirit directed. These apostles thus guided told the people how to become Christians. They have had no successors, will have none. They told the people what was required to make Christians in the first century. Their word was final. God has added nothing to it and taken nothing from it.

Who was a Christian in the first century?

The one who believed on Jesus Christ as the Son of God, with all his heart, repented of the wrongs in his past life, and was "baptized into Christ," was a Christian. None others. They were in the kingdom. None others could be. John 3:5 fixes that forever. Baptism was a "burial," a birth of water. That also is fixed.

All knew what faith was. All understood repentance. All knew what baptism was. No man has presumed to change the faith or repentance, but baptism has been tampered with. Many in the twentieth century are honestly mistaken about this point and think sprinkling is baptism. Is sprinkling baptism? Can their honesty and sincerity change what the Holy Spirit taught through the apostles—Spirit guided "into all truth" twenty centuries ago?

It is not a question of what God will do with these sincerely honest people. The question is, are they Christians? About one hundred years ago a church was projected which made Christian character the condition of membership. Many in other religious bodies do so. Some of our people and among them some editors and preachers, are disposed to do so. There is a great difference between a Christian character and a non- or anti-Christian character. All know this and feel drawn to the one showing Christian character. But is he a Christian because he is a Christian in character?

A Masonic character does not make one a Mason. Every Mason knows what makes one a Mason.

An American character does not make one foreign born an American citizen. Every American citizen knows what is required in addition to character to make one an American citizen, and no man thinks his foreign born brother is an American citizen before he takes

the oath of allegiance, on government has a right and to prescribe the oath. oath be administered ar sincere applicant for citize he is an American citizen, is, he is mistaken. That

All the character in the make a man a husband try. The most devoted make him a husband. He fixed. The proper autho nounce him a husband.

We have no quarrel v lodge or with the governi submit. One may be Ch and in heart and in charac this and "baptized into C him a Christian in fact.

I dare not and will no is a Christian who is not liever. I dare say no ma believer who has not b The time has come in o experience as a people v essary to take a positive all important matter.

The logic of the sit that we admit every Chr bership in the church. I I will receive any first tian into the church.

I have been a close o movements for some yea as my opinion that just we need most of all is to and open stand on this m the world know that we Christian character and those who give signs of it world know that we do n world know that we do n into Christ.' Here I stan

Morristown, Ind.

Reports From California   By Charles Reign Scoville

Jessie Williams,
Press Reporter, Long Beach, Cal.

Charles Reign Scoville.

Mrs. W. C. Reynolds,
President Home Department, Long
Beach, Cal.

I have just spent a most delightful season of two months on the Pacific coast. I was there "on business for the King." Brother DeLoss Smith was with me in the last meeting at Long Beach and Brother and Sister Percy M. Kendall were with me through both meetings.

I began in San Bernardino and was only there two weeks and three days with 190 added in all. The pastor, Bro. H. E. Wilhite, resigned just before I reached there. Another pastor was chosen, who resigned before he began his work, and the church was not ready for a great ingathering under the circumstances, and I decided that it was not best to stay and gather in a host of souls with no shepherd to look after them, so went on to Long Beach. We have some noble souls at San Bernardino, and some man can do a great work there. Brother Wilhite entered the evan-

gelistic field and has the ability to hold great meetings.

I reached Long Beach on decoration day, just after the soldiers had cast hun-

First Christian Church,
Long Beach, Cal.

dreds of California's most beautiful flowers on the waves of the Pacific, thus decorating the graves of those who died at sea while in defense of their country. Our Long Beach pastor and Bro. S. A. Sanderson had visited the former meeting and I had a vivid recollection of Brother Sanderson, for it was he who cornered me at the San Francisco convention and refused to be refused a meeting.

I told him that if he would be as persistent in personal work for sinners as he was to get the evangelist there we would have a great meeting, and he promised he would. He kept this promise, even giving up his business for a time to push the advertising work, of which committee he was chairman. Arthur Everts, of Dallas, Texas; R. E. Carpenter, of

W. L. Porterfield,
Sunday-School Superintendent and President State Sunday-School Association,
Long Beach, Cal.

E. W. Thornton,
Pastor, Long Beach, Cal.

S. A. Sanderson,
Chairman Advertising Committee, Long
Beach, Cal.

New York city, and S. A. Sanderson, of Long Beach, are the three greatest men I have ever had at the head of the most important committee of a gospel meeting.

The Long Beach church rented a tabernacle at a cost of $300. They did the work as though they meant business from start to finish. The city was full of visitors for it is the Atlantic City of the Pacific, except that it is a saner, nobler, better city. Although two great skating rinks, a vast auditorium, a Beach City band with all other attractions were running full blast all the time, the meeting was a grand success. Two hundred and fifty-five souls accepted Christ, and many people of talent and influence were among the converts.

When we came to the close they paid me the largest salary I have ever received, except from one other church, which paid me the same. This church was only organized eleven years ago with twelve charter members. The city then had only one thousand inhabitants, and now numbers 20,000. Bro. Grant K. Lewis, whom I knew in college days, and who is now general secretary of Southern California and Arizona, took charge of the church in 1902. The church then had only seventy-five members, with a Sunday-school of thirty members. Brother Lewis resigned one year ago to take the above named position: Bro. E. H. Keller acted as pastor until November, 1905, doing a splendid work for so short a period, and then E. W. Thornton was chosen pastor. Brother Thornton, like Brother Lewis, is a grand wholesouled man of faith and was a mighty inspiration to the writer in all the work. He is greatly beloved by all the membership and has has all the sunshine of his "Old Kentucky Home" in his make-up. Mrs. Thornton is a most excellent woman, who fills her place at church and in her home like a queen.

The membership of the church is now about 600, and with an average midsummer Sunday-school attendance of 325. The Long Beach church is one of our best California churches. W. L. Porterfield, Sunday-school superintendent, is also state superintendent of Sunday-schools, and one of the grandest Christian business men in the brotherhood. He will be heard from in more ways than one if the Lord spares his life to us. The sacrifice he made for the meeting was enough to stir an evangelist even if the whole church had been asleep. But the church was awake.

Mrs. Grant K. Lewis is one of the best primary superintendents on the Pacific coast, and she has great influence with the Christian Endeavor in directing its missionary work. Mrs. Wiley, formerly president of District C. W. B. M., is president of the society at Long Beach. which only has seventy members, but much new material.

Carle Ridenour and Miss Elizabeth Venable are president of the Senior and Intermediate Christian Endeavorers. Mrs. M. S. Julian is president of Ladies' Aid. Mrs. W. C. Reynolds is superintendent of the home department of the Sunday-school and is a woman of ability and consecration and a soul-winner. The pity is that some people get into office who neither do anything themselves nor will they permit others to go ahead in gleaning for the Master. C. J. Hargis is chairman of the official board, and an elder of the church. Miss Nellie Gunder is president of the Young Ladies' Missionary Circle, and it is a live society.

Miss Jessie Williams, formerly of New York city, and whose father is one of the strong men in Dr. Breeden's church, Des Moines, where we won a mighty victory in 1901, was our reporter, and we never

had better or more spicy reports. They read as if a reporter of years experience had written them. Although Miss Williams is assistant cashier of one of the best banks in Long Beach, she is worthy of a larger field. I was most excellently entertained by Brother and Sister Fry, formerly of my old home state, Indiana. The church is remarkable for its stability and foresight. The property is worth $45,000 and did not cost one-half that. A lot has been bought on the west side for the establishing of a second church. This lot has practically doubled in value since it was purchased. Brother Windham, formerly of Central America, is also a great worker in the church and, like Brother Porterfield, one of the large promoters of the coast. It was really a privilege to work with such a church and I shall hail with the greatest pleasure the moment when time permits me to turn my face toward Long Beach.

The pastors of that part of the state

were often at the meetii our splendid church at Monday night and crowded. The Sout churches will hold sir ings in May and June invited me to become the entire movement, not be able to do that nestly requested, yet I main over and give them and start the movement o thus on time, I came as cisco with the state Ch train en route to the sta Berkeley. Brother Sand of our delegation and I assistant state superin Christian Endeavor.

I am sorry that I do Beach, that's all.

We have reached 2,914 so far in 1906.

"Baptism Unto Remiss
By J. WILL WALTERS.

President Mullins' paper at the congress of Disciples of Christ at Indianapolis upon the subject, "What is the New Testament Teaching on the Relation of Baptism to the Remission of Sins and the New Birth?" is as strong and as succinct a defense of the theory that baptism is for "ceremonial cleansing" and not "actual cleansing" (or forgiveness) as it has been my privilege to hear. The spirit of the article is also gracious and admirable. But I think its fallacy must be apparent to every one who has learned to rightly divide the word of truth and whose views have not been too greatly distorted by preconceived ideas regarding the subject. But many have not so learned. And while I consider Bro. I. J. Spencer's "Review" (in THE CHRISTIAN-EVANGELIST, May 10) an able exposition of its fallacy, yet a few additional lines may not be amiss.

President Mullins presents two "closed circles," as he terms them. One, in which are found certain Scriptures connecting baptism and remission of sins, and another circle "vitally connecting faith and repentance with remission"—without any reference whatever to baptism.

He therefore endeavors to harmonize the two circles by concluding that faith and repentance are conditions of actual forgiveness, while baptism is simply a condition of ceremonial forgiveness. Hear his own words:

"It is that in one closed circle of teachings, the ceremonial, we find a distinct ceremonial principle in Christianity; that

The Unseen Shore.

A few who have watched me sail away
Will miss my craft from the busy bay:
Some friendly barks I anchored near,
Some loving souls that my heart held dear,
  In silent sorrow will drop a tear.
But I shall have peacefully furled my sail
In mornings sheltered from storm or gale,
And greeted the friends who have called before
O'er the Unknown Sea to the Unseen Shore.

in the other closed circ we find a distinct spiritu there is no union or a these two principles on th there is no conflict betwe other."

That there is no confl readily agree, but is not and harmony found in a not do violence to the w make void that law by I would call attention to rule of interpretation "Where salvation is pred word upon any one thing ascribed to less than th it is predicated. It may upon more, but never upo

We find salvation is re dependent upon baptism, 16:16; Acts 22:16, etc. S can be conditioned upon violence to the word of Evidently not, without vic and also the word of Go

If we teach that bapt actual, but only for "("symbolical remission" of say: "It matters not whe emonially cleansed' or 'sy given,' just so I am ass forgiveness.'"

Peter did not say (Acts and be baptized for the mission of your sins," b mission of your sins." I baptism looked forward t ject. If baptism was for mission, so was repentan Faith and love are not and quibble over human t er baptism for remission actual, but only "ceremo but desiring to know the ing but the truth, will as wilt thou have me to d shall faithfully proclaim recorded in his word the fied to do his will and cl promise of sins forgiven. *Niantic, Ill.*

Our Budget

—"For web begun God sends thread."

—This means: That God loves and crowns a venturesome faith.

—That if the membership will earnestly try to pay its indebtedness, he will supply the wherewithall for church debts.

—That a congregation needing more commodious quarters, a more creditable temple, can have material in proportion to its constructive faith.

—That if in life's stresses, we go cheerfully as far as to-day's courage 'enableth, we shall receive such new enduements that we may attempt all our tasks with cheerful courage—one of life's real victories.

—That the union of his people for which Jesus prayed and that is the fundamental purpose of this Restoration will be quickly accomplished, if we will use all that the various religious bodies now hold in common as grafting boughs, for he gives life and vitality to "threads" like these.

—That while we have our limitations, are bounded by who our father is, by what our mother thought when a girl, by the scenes of childhood, the bent of our nationality, and all our physical and moral environment, yet there are no hedges above us, and he will give us inspiration and power to rise for our loom, if we begin weaving the heavenly impulses we now have for a tie to the stars or the throne.

—Thomas J. Easterwood, of Temple, Tex., offers his services to evangelists and churches as a helper in song.

—H. A. Pallister, of Delta, Ia., is located with the church at Exira, same state, and desires correspondents to note change.

—The South Idaho state board wishes two evangelistic pastors to work amid real hardships. Volunteers may write to Dr. Semones, of Nampa, Idaho.

—J. W. Reynolds, of Saunemin, Ill., was an office visitor last week. In him some church desiring a minister will find a faithful and capable helper.

—The Fredericksburg, Ohio, church will sell for $15 two large chandeliers costing $65 when new. The church there is now lighted with gas and offers this bargain to some of our poor congregations.

—M. B. Ingle, assisted by H. A. Easton, recently organized a church of seventeen members at Lipscomb, Texas. Five of these were baptized during the progress of a union meeting in the neighborhood.

—C. C. Atwood, of Topeka, Kan., and Mrs. Atwood began their "fall campaign" this year in mid-summer. They are now in a meeting at Circleville, Kan. Sister Atwood directs a great chorus through these services.

—E. J. Church, of Seneca, Mo., is in a meeting at Newtonia, with thirty-one additions to date and more sure to follow. This reminds us that never in our memory have summer meetings been so successful as those of 1906.

—W. A. Wherry has been instrumental in adding 23 to the membership of the Commerce, Tex., church recently. He is now in a meeting at South Sulphur Mission. Brother Wherry is being greatly blessed in his ministry.

—Eugene H. Holmes, in reporting the recent meeting at Plano, Texas, in which there were 46 accessions to the church,

says H. A. Northcutt grows in power as he grows in years, and that the Zerans are most efficient workers in revival services.

—J. W. Holsapple, of Greenville, Tex., is visiting his aged mother in the old Kentucky home. While there he will hold a brief meeting at Benton. He reports two added to the Greenville church by confession and baptism the past week.

—Louis S. Cupp and wife, of the Hyde Park Church, Kansas City, will spend a month's vacation along the St. Lawrence river. His pulpit will be supplied in his absence. Brother and Sister Cupp have fairly earned this vacation granted by their church.

—This office has been favored with an announcement of the marriage of Harriett Hyatt Parker, of Mitchell, Ind., to Charles Rollin Hudson, pastor of the Frankfort (Ky.) church. We wish these young people long lives of ever-increasing happiness and usefulness.

—Wallace M. Stuckey is in a meeting at Galesburg, Kan. Among other helps employed he uses 300 CHRISTIAN-EVANGELISTS each week. This not only fills his house with auditors, but with pre-

Wallace M. Stuckey.

pared listeners. All who have adopted this plan most highly commend it to others. Any church will be greatly blessed that secures the services of this talented servant of the Master.

—A Red and Blue contest in the Mendon, Mo., church was won by the Reds. Among other results of the contest was the addition of 48 to the membership. The minister, D. Millar, beautifully commends the work of Superintendent Foster Windell.

—G. P. Coler, dean of our Bible chair at Ann Arbor, Mich., knows a good teacher of Latin and psychology, whom he will recommend to any of our colleges needing such faculty help. This man is a loyal Disciple, well trained in Bible study and a preacher of ability.

—W. J. Lockhart, of Des Moines, and C. H. Altheide, of Bloomfield, Ia., will assist Frank L. Bowen, city evangelist of Kansas City, in a meeting with the Jackson avenue church, beginning September 2. This combination ought to produce great results.

—J. O. Heddleston, of East Liverpool, O., recently preached to a great audience at Chester, W. Va. He reports a Bible-study class that meets every Lord's day evening, which is one of the most effective helps to the church that he has ever seen.

—President W. W. Herold sends a copy of the Pettis county Christian

church convention program. From the names on the program and the topics assigned, this should be a very helpful gathering. The sessions will be held at Green Ridge August 20 and 21.

—"Fragments," a local paper published by the Union Church in Christ, Monroe, Wis., announces that Charles Reign Scoville is to begin a union revival meeting at the armory in that place the first week in August. He is to be assisted by DeLoss Smith, singing evangelist.

—Miss Mayme Eisenbarger will lead the singing in a revival G. A. Reynolds will begin with the Dyersburg, Tenn., church September 12. After September 1 Sister Eisenbarger will be open for other engagements in this special work to which she is devoting herself.

—THE CHRISTIAN-EVANGELIST wishes to acknowledge many courtesies by W. P. Keeler, of the Englewood congregation, Chicago. Though a member of the great Marshall Field Dry Goods Company he devotes much time to matters pertaining to the kingdom. He is prospering. "Haec fabula docet," etc.

—We are pleased to note that the Commissioners of the Jamestown Exposition, which opens April 26, 1907, have decided that the grounds shall be closed against all visitors on Lord's days, and that the influence of this great fair will be exerted altogether in favor of the American Lord's day, instead of the European Sunday.

—Our beloved Bro. N. J. Aylsworth, of Auburn, N. Y., writes concerning the editorial series on Christian Union, recently closed, and now undergoing revision, as follows: "Nothing more valuable and timely has appeared in our literature for a long time, and I am glad it is to appear in more permanent form."

—The new church building at Armington, Ill., will be dedicated the first Lord's day in September. L. E. Chase, the minister, has just accepted a call to serve the LeRoy, Ill., church, for the ensuing three years. Brother Chase's pastorate at Armington was an epoch-making period in the history of that congregation.

—F. H. Lemon reports 89 additions to the Boise (Idaho) church since beginning there, January 14. We wonder if the alleged discouragements to our cause in the great northwest are not to some extent the spectres of lack of faith in the power of the Gospel to reach and save men and build up churches. Brother Lemon sees no signs of failure.

—Edward O. Tilburn is rejoicing over arrangements made for liquidating the indebtedness of $900 against his Mishawaka (Ind.) church by the first of the new year. In appreciation of Brother Tilburn's faithful services his church has granted him a month's vacation, during which time he will visit his former congregations at Tohawanda and Buffalo, N. Y.

—Jewell Howard, of Amarillo, Texas, orders 18 sets of the Bethany Reading Courses for the benefit of the Ladies' Aid Society of his church. It is a very happy thought to have these faithful women thus growing in knowledge of the Lord and his church, while with skillful fingers they are helping in the material development of the local congregation. We commend Brother Howard's idea to others.

—For the last two months Edward O. Tilburn, Mishawaka, Ind., has been lecturing to large audiences at the Thursday night services on the "Plea of the Christian Church and How to Make It Successful." This will be followed by an evangelistic campaign later, when he will be assisted by W. E. M. Hackelman, of Indianapolis, as musical director. A great victory for righteousness is expected.

—John . Neighbor, of Greenup, Ill., a singing evangelist, offers to assist evangelists and churches needing his services.

—H. K. Shields, singing evangelist, is helping J. W. Witkämper in a meeting at Elwood, Ind. A great ingathering is confidently expected.

—T. P. Reid, formerly pastor of the Nicolaus, Cal., church, has been called to the work at Acampo. We believe this means great growth to this congregation.

—Evangelist W. L. Harris, of Bethany, Neb., wishes to join with him in an evangelistic team a good Gospel singer. Brother Harris now has engagements carrying him over until 1907.

—The new church at Heyworth, Ill., will be dedicated September 9. The ministry of John P. Givens, always successful, has been eminently so with that congregation.

—The Disciples of Christ of Wayne and Holmes counties, Ohio, will hold their yearly meeting at Fredericksburg August 24-27. A cordial invitation is extended all Disciples to attend this meeting.

—Dinger and Gardner begin a meeting with Neel Overman at Lincoln, Kan., next Lord's day. There is a combination that should make this an epoch-making meeting in the history of that church.

—Evangelist E. M. Romine visited the office Monday. Brother Romine belongs to that untiring, hard-working band of evangelists who, without much personal celebrity, accomplish great things for the kingdom.

—Charles E. McVay, song evangelist, of Benkelman, Neb., has an open date through September. Brother McVay sings the Gospel with the spirit and understanding and we cheerfully commend him to the churches.

—We regret to learn that W. A. Haynes, of Skidmore, Mo., lost over $500 worth of books by fire on August 2. The loss of the preacher's library, with its references and loved passages and volumes, can not be estimated in terms of dollars.

—It is with pleasure we hear many tributes of admiration paid to Mrs. H. A. Denton, president of the Missouri C. W. B. M. This is a great cause, it now has great opportunity, and Sister Denton is proving herself to be eminently the woman for the hour.

—E. S. Allhands, whose work at Roff gives one of the brightest pages in our history in Indian Territory, has resigned to become a general evangelist. His first meeting will be at Arkadelphia. This able preacher should be kept busy among the churches.

—V. E. Ridenour will assist George L. Peters in a meeting at South Joplin, Mo., in September. This is Brother Ridenour's third meeting in Joplin. He will also assist W. T. Turner at Hamilton Ave. during the St. Louis simultaneous meetings in November.

—Charles E. Smith, of St. Stephen, state evangelist of South Carolina, wants a good preacher to act as pastor-evangelist for a district of churches in South Carolina. Only an energetic man thoroughly acquainted with the Word need apply. Correspondents must enclose postage.

❀ ❀

—Those on the ground are the best judges of the success of the Manchester meeting. Wm. C. Crerie, pastor of the Haverhill, Mass., church of Christ, will preach in Manchester every two weeks until the meeting is resumed. Read his letter in another column.

—Since Governor Folk has enforced the Sunday closing ordinances in this city it is reliably reported that emergency cases in the city hospital have decreased fully 66 2-3 per cent. This is only one of the countless blessings following in the wake of one who is strong in the right.

—W. H. Rust, formerly of Humboldt, Kan., has entered upon his ministry at Burlington Junction, Mo., and is greatly delighted with his prospects of accomplishing a notable work there. Though he has been in ill health several months he is encouraged to believe that complete restoration is near at hand.

—A clipping from a Sapulpa, I. T., paper contains the account of the dedication of the new Christian church there July 22. The dedication sermon was preached by S. R. Hawkins. The account contains a glowing tribute of the ability of Bro. Randolph Cook, who is holding revival services in the new church.

—Our summer meetings are phenomenally successful, and will be more general hereafter. The evangelists, too, who are adding most to the saved, are those who uncompromisingly preach the old Gospel of faith, repentance, confession, baptism and good works, death to the old life and a rising up to a new life in Christ.

—At the recent Santa Cruz convention Thomas G. Picton, R. E. Jape and Otho Wilkison were for the third time selected to constitute the state Sunday-school board in Northern California. We believe our work generally will be more honored by continuing faithful servants in office than by passing around the honors to inexperienced men.

—W. A. McCausland, of Coffeyville, Kan., practices law through the week and preaches most helpfully to the Deering congregation five miles in the country on Lord's days. Our great dearth of preachers would be somewhat atoned for, if more of our brethren gifted in the Word as Brother McCausland is, would follow his example.

—Brother A. R. Moore, of Seneca, Mo., informs us the Newton county convention will be held in that town the first week in October, and that it will be followed with a three weeks' meeting, if an evangelist and singer can be secured for that time. Evangelists may write him. He reports fifteen additions to the Seneca church during the year.

—A note from P. A. Dickson, of the City Temple Christian Church, Sidney, Australia, informs us that our 10 churches in that city are all prospering. It is the expectation to organize others in the near future. The City Temple hopes, as a result of its recent protracted meeting, to build anew in a better part of the city. The congregation now numbers about 500.

—John T. Brown, of Louisville, has just concluded a meeting in the City Temple Church of Christ, Sidney, Australia, which is said to have been the greatest revival ever held on the island. There were 185 confessions and baptisms. Hundreds of people in that city of 500,000 heard our plea for the first time, and it is thought the meeting will bear fruit for years to come.

—From Lewis O. Lehman, minister, we learn that Harold E. Monser recently closed a tent meeting in Havana, Ill., resulting in ten immediate additions to

fice force, en route to their Texas home. Brother Smith graduated from the Lexington Bible school last spring and has met with gratifying success in his first pastorate. We trust this young couple will realize their highest ideals of happiness and usefulness and worth.

—A. T. June, of Everett, Mass., reports two recent additions to his congregation and all departments of his church prospering. America has no truer heroes than these brethren who, amidst discouragements at home, and many allurements elsewhere, are tarrying by the stuff in our New England stations. But we are coming, brethren, we are coming, and soon your few will be transformed into hosts.

—Hon. W. A. McCausland writes that the Coffeyville, Kan., church has called Ellis Purlee, who for four years has so acceptably served the church, to an indefinite pastorate, the fond hope being that he will continue with them many years. Evangelist Thomas Cooksey, of Ohio, will assist Brother Purlee in a meeting beginning September 1. This should be a very successful revival.

—A great camp meeting, under the auspices of the Wichita County Camp Meeting Association, will be held at Hyars Hole, on Medicine Creek, seven miles northwest of Lawton, Okla., August 27-29. W. A. Merrill, of Hobart, and O. L. Smith, of El Reno, will do the preaching. C. M. Bliss, of El Reno, will conduct the musical services. We advise all our readers who can to attend.

—H. M. Allen, of Elyria, Ohio, father of our Edgar W. Allen, of the West Jefferson Street Church, Ft. Wayne, Ind., is at Hope Hospital, in the latter place, preparing to undergo a surgical operation. The elder Brother Allen has preached in Ohio and Michigan for more than a generation. He asks the prayers of the brotherhood to the end that he may be fully restored to his place in the ministry.

—We are indebted to H. F. Barstow, the faithful corresponding secretary of our Wisconsin Missionary Board, for items of interest relating to the convention of our churches to be held at Ladysmith, September 20-23. All expecting to attend should notify F. L. Dean, of Ladysmith, that entertainment may be provided. A very strong program has been provided, and all who possibly can should attend.

—R. H. Bolton, of Boston, Mass., secretary of the New England Missionary Society, is entitled to the credit of the authorship of the splendid article on "Our Cause in New England" which appeared in the issue of July 19. We hope for further communications from Brother Bolton. The Christian-Evangelist's circulation is rapidly increasing in New England, and we wish our news service to at least keep pace therewith.

—Mrs. J. E. Smith, of Royerton, Ind., writes an expression of the profound gratitude that congregation entertains for the Christian Publishing Company for sending its evangelist, J. D. Lawrence, for the meeting that so greatly revived the church. Brother Lawrence is ready to assist other churches that can only partly pay for the services of an evangelist. Parties wishing such meetings may either address this company or J. D. Lawrence, Muncie, Ind.

—J. N. Armstrong, president of the Christian Bible school at Odessa, Mo., will begin a series of meetings in the

vicinity of Marcus and Easton avenue, this city, August 12. A large tent has been secured for the use of this meeting. Bro. J. W. Atkinson gives us this information. We bespeak the prayers of thousands of St. Louis Disciples that the Church of Christ may be greatly strengthened and unbuilded by these meetings.

—The Christian Endeavor Society of the First Church, East Liverpool, O., has elected the following officers: President, Okey Heddleston; Vice-president, Chas. Aley; Sec., Mary Stanley; Cor. Sec., Margaret Hague; Treas., Isaac Connolly. These youg people are holding positions with opportunities for doing a greater and more lasting good than is accomplished by many Governors and other executive officers of states. May they magnify their offices.

—The "Wilkes-Barre Times" gives generous space to a report of the convention of the Eastern Pennsylvania Disciples that has just closed its sessions in that city. This is said to be the largest, most enthusiastic yet practical convention our people have yet held in that territory. The paper gives great praise to E. E. Cowperthwaite for the development of this religious movement into a power with which sin and sectarianism in Eastern Pennsylvania have to reckon.

—The Webster City (Ia.) church held a mortgage burning service August 7. Milton H. Lee, of Ft. Dodge, and W. C. Cole, of Jewell Junction, greatly encouraged the congregation by their addresses. R. M. Dungan, the happy minister, writes that the membership caught glimpses of a new and more glorious era about to dawn upon that congregation. The church is free from indebtedness, the first time in thirteen years. Brother Dungan has been called to continue as minister at a substantial increase in salary.

—The Illinois Christian Missionary Convention will meet with the Paris church September 10 to 13. Among those from out the state whose names appear on the program we note Dr. Mary Longdon, Deoghur, India; Mesdames Anna R. Atwater and Helen E. Moses, of Indianapolis; Mrs. Ida W. Harrison, Lexington, Ky.; J. W. Henry, Mobile, Ala; J. H. Garrison, St. Louis; G. W. Muckley, Kansas City, and E. L. Powell, Louisville. In addition to these is an equally brilliant galaxy of Illinois speakers, both men and women.

—Frank L. Bowen has made splendid proof of his ministry as city evangelist of Kansas City. He is just entering upon his tenth year. When he began there were seven pastors in that metropolis of the Missouri valley; to-day there are twelve, with four mission stations at present and others to be instituted in the autumn. The city missions have added 1,000 to the membership and have acquired $25,000 in property. In a letter Brother Bowen highly commends his faithful co-laborers in that city, both of the pulpit and pew.

—G. M. Read, minister; L. A. Lowry, elder, and E. M. Shelley, treasurer, of the Weiser, Idaho, church, make an earnest appeal to the brotherhood for financial assistance. The church there was involved in an indebtedness by parties who have now removed from the city, which the present membership is unable to pay. Weiser is a growing city where we ought to have a strong church. If this indebtedness is removed this will be one of our most hopeful fields in the west. Contributions to the debt fund may be sent to Treasurer E. M. Shelley.

—Mrs. H. S. Hubbard, Haverhill, Mass., too late for publication, sends us observations of the great Manchester meeting. This sentiment taken from her

letter shows the opinion of one on the ground: "Now that the good work has been so grandly started in New Hampshire, I trust every Disciple preacher in New England will exert himself to keep it alive until Brother Yeuell can return." Surely all who have contributed to this success will rejoice in the part they have had. Let us proceed without any abatement of enthusiasm in the collection of funds for the establishment of the church in the near future.

—A. B. Jones, writing from Colorado where he is summering with his children, says: "Every few years some one suggests that we (the Disciples) are passing a 'crisis' and I think we have passed several. At times the outlook has appeared stormy and doubtful, but the old ship of Zion has somehow always weathered the storm and she is yet seaworthy." Brother Jones heartily approves the attitude of THE CHRISTIAN-EVANGELIST in recent discussions and says its position is "invulnerable." He is enjoying his Colorado outing, of course, but it is easy to see that he is longing for the lakeside once more, his fishing rod, and that electric thrill which only a "good bite" can give.

❋ ❋

Young People of Small Means

will be helped in securing an education at "Iowa Christian College." Board and tuition $30 per term. Correspondence courses also. Write Pres. Chas. J. Burton, Oskaloosa, Iowa. Free catalogue.

—We regret to learn that Herbert Yeuell has been summoned to England to see his mother, whose health is very precarious. Brother and Sister Yeuell and son, Donovan, sailed August 3. He will return in time to assist J. J. Castleburg at Union City through a revival in the early autumn. W. E. M. Hackleman will have charge of the music through this meeting. Correspondents are requested to address Brother Yeuell at Washington, D. C., where their mail will be cared for. We hope to hear of Mother Yeuell's improvement in health, and that her two evangelist sons may long be blessed with the inspiration of her earthly presence.

—The veteran John S. Sweeney, of Paris, Ky., paid the office force a visit last Monday that was greatly enjoyed. For thirty years he served the church at Paris as pastor. His earlier ministry was in Illinois. He is now visiting amidst the scenes of his first triumphs in the Gospel. He will soon preach in the church where he held his first debate (he certainly can not remember where all the others were held), and will preach again where his first sermon was delivered. Though past the three score years and ten, he preaches and lectures with great power. Long may he live to witness the prosperity of the Cause he so greatly helped to establish in the middle West.

—Church Extension has a hearing on another page. The case is stated carefully; contains information the churches ought to have and should be read by all. If Brother Muckley does not in this appeal awaken our churches, only Gabriel can blow the trumpet call that will arouse them to the needs and opportunities of the hour. The board has a great work on its hands. It ought to be enabled by our churches to do that work creditably to our brotherhood. We have no right to elect our boards as trustees for us and then desert them on the one day of the offering. See that your church is in line. This is not too early to begin preparations, for the annual offering commences the first Sunday in September.

—None among us loves more than our Editor to meet with the brethren in our conventions and other summer assemblies. None other has done more to make them popular and helpful, but it is denied to him to participate in them this summer. The family physician has ordered this veteran of the civil war, and this soldier whose service in the Lord's army antedates the harrowing sixties, that until frost comes he must not descend far from 44 degrees latitude N. Since he so reluctantly admits any abatement of his remarkable physical stamina of war times it is only just to Brother Garrison and program committees all over the land that this decision of Aesculapius (from which we permit no appeal) should be made known.

—In "Gloria in Excelsis" you have given us a book worthy of our great brotherhood. It is the peer of any hymn book on the market. It has many excellent features. The responsive readings are well chosen. They fill a great need. The classification is complete, placing its wealth of material at the easy command of the user. It is just the right size. It is large enough to cause the singer to feel that it is generous. It is not large enough to make it awkward to handle. The hymns contain

the best thought, theology and poetry in use to-day. It contains the best old tunes and the best new tunes. The best tunes abound. It is stately, dignified, worshipful in spirit. I pronounce it *par excellance*. Our churches will not be long in discovering its worth.—James H. Mohorter.

Order direct from this house.

❦ ❦

Sidelights on a Successful Pastorate.

The church at Fort Smith, Ark., has enjoyed the ministrations of the present pastor, E. T. Edmonds, since 1891, excepting two years of this time, when Brother Edmonds served as pastor for the church at Boston, Mass. The church at Fort Smith at the time Brother Edmonds began his labors there had a membership of about 100, but they represented in a degree quite unusual for such a small membership many of the best families in the community, and more than a proportionate part of the social and financial strength of the community. Gradually the church has grown until now the membership is close

E. T. Edmonds,
Fort Smith, Ark.

to the 500 mark. The church supports its own Living Link missionary in the northwest part of the state of Arkansas, and contributes to all the missionary interests of the church. The present church building is one of the best in all the southwest. It is built of Eureka Springs (Ark.) stone, and the tower is considered by competent judges to be an architectural gem. Indeed, all the visitors to the city of Fort Smith are surprised to find so splendid an edifice in a town that for many years was one of the border towns of the southwest. The auditorium will seat about 800 people. The present cost of the church and lot would be about $35,000. It is on one of the finest streets in the city, and, excepting the Catholic church, occupies the finest site in the town.

The pastor recently lectured to the Jews of Fort Smith in the local synagogue, and preached to them in his church. Brother Edmonds has thoroughly identified himself with the city in which he lives, and speaks at public meetings on such questions as civic improvements, etc. Recently he has taken into the church an Advent minister, and not long ago baptized a Congregational minister.

Brother Edmonds has been for many years the president of the Fort Smith Chautauqua Association and is now the superintendent.

C. A. Young, of Chicago, last spring

held an interesting meeting for the church, and quite a number were gathered into the fold. Brother Young was delighted at the culture of the audiences he addressed, and the fact that his Bible studies, prepared for Bible chair work, were well received and heard with uncommon pleasure. There is no doubt that a great future awaits the Fort Smith church. The officers are a fine body of men and aggressive in the business life of the community, and no finer body of women can be found in any church than in the church at Fort Smith, Ark.

Fort Smith has a population of 30,000 and is rapidly growing. To show its enterprise, a contract was recently let for paving over 50 miles of streets and for the sewering of the entire city now outside of the sewer district. A great jobbing business is carried on in this city, and large manufacturing plants are already at work. Fort Smith is the great eastern gateway into the new state of Oklahoma, and expects to reap great results from this strategic situation.

The brethren at Fort Smith are now getting ready to begin a second church, and a rural work a few miles south of the city seems to have a promising outlook. An assistant pastor is also one of the pressing needs of the church, which it is hoped will soon be provided.

❦ ❦

For a Church in New Hampshire.

Already acknowledged $607 10
"A Cincinnati Friend" 1 00
Mrs. G. W. Weir 2 00
H. F. Bland and wife 2 00
Phebe Benedict 5 00
F. L. Benedict 5 00
C W. Bisbee 5 00
Woodson (Tex.) church 11 65
Niles (O.) Christian church ... 20 00
I. H. Shaver 25 00
"A California Sister" 30 00

Total $713 75

It must not be taken that the enterprise of establishing a New Testament church in Manchester has been abandoned. The great daily meetings have temporarily concluded, but Brother Crerie, of Haverhill, Mass., is in Manchester safeguarding all that was gained during the past month, and soon as conditions warrant Brother Yeuell will return for a continuation of the meeting and, we doubt not, the organization of a church. We ought to have $1,250 by September 1 for this purpose. We appeal to the chivalry of our friends to help in the establishment of this first church in New Hampshire.

❦ ❦

Their Works Do Follow Them.

Among the faithful and consecrated members of the old historic church at Ravenna, O., were Brother Charles Judd and wife and their daughter, Mrs. Alvira Williamson. Last week the trustee of their estates, according to the terms of their wills, turned over to Hiram College the sum of $8,651; to the A. C. M. S. the sum of $2,133; to the Southern Christian Institute the sum of $734, and to the Ravenna Church of Christ six acres of land and the sum of $2,133.—M. E. Chatley, pastor.

A Call to the Churches from the Church Extension Board.

As the September offering for Church Extension is approaching, the churches should be preparing for it both in heart and purse. This offering is the chief source of income for the enlargement of our General Church Extension Fund.

No missionary society has a right to appeal to the brotherhood unless, first, it needs money to carry on its work, and, second, unless it is proving a worthy steward of the trust committed to its hands.

First—As to the need of funds. At the regular meeting of the Board of Extension on March 6 of this year it was decided to cease promising new loans until such time as the condition of our treasury would warrant it. After the terrible calamity at San Francisco a resolution was passed by our board to first help churches in and around San Francisco to rebuild, because we believed that was the wish of our brotherhood. Accordingly we granted $5,000 to help build a $10,000 church in Alameda, where many refugees are being cared for.

Another loan of $150 was granted Gladstone, N. D., because our board had never aided a church in North Dakota. Also a $2,500 annuity loan at 6 per cent. was granted Vinita, I. T. These are all the loans granted since our April meeting, and we now have requests on hand from 96 worthy churches, aggregating more than $125,000, distributed through 28 states and Canada, 10 of them being in California. Never before in the history of our church extension work have there been so many appeals for aid as are now accumulated, just on the eve of our annual offering. Our receipts to July 31 show a gain of $12,393.10 over the same time last year. Over $5,000 of this gain is from the churches. In spite of this gain we cannot keep pace with the demands. We have never had such an era of church building among our missions as we have had this year, all of which is very hopeful for the permanency of our mission congregations. Our missions must build or they cannot hold what they have gained.

This exhibit of needs constituting 96 specific appeals for aid from March 6 to July 31 should be sufficient inspiration for churches to do their best in the forthcoming annual offering.

Second—Has your Board of Church Extension been a worthy steward? There is now something over $565,000 in the Church Extension Fund. Over $510,000 has been returned on loans and interest. This makes over $1,075,000 which the board has handled with the slight loss of only $563. This is greatly to the credit of the mission churches who have borrowed this money and your board deserves credit for wise business methods. The fund has built 10 July 31, 1906, 1,005 churches. Of this number over 470 have paid their loans in full. The Church Extension Fund has certainly made good, and deserves a liberal offering to help build these 96 churches at once.

One record we are not proud of. Last year only 1,108 churches as churches contributed to this work. One in 11. Is not this record a burning shame? We are now claiming to be a missionary people, and yet only one church in 11 sent an offering to church extension last year, and the amount the churches sent was only $18,516.96. This is an average of a little less than $17 per congregation contributing. Thus far the churches this year have sent over $5,000 more than last year. This is encouraging. It being the first of our four years' centennial campaign for the million dollars, it behooves the churches to stir themselves, because we must raise at least $100,000 a year if we are to reach the million by 1909. Forgetting the things that are behind, let us press forward and make a better record both in the number of contributing churches and the amount contributed.

Faithfully yours,
in behalf of the board,
G. W. MUCKLEY, Cor. Sec.

Kentucky Convention.

The Kentucky state convention of the Christian Church will be held in the First Church, Fourth and Walnut streets, Louisville, September 24 to 27, and it promises to be a convention of unusual interest. A railroad rate of one fare plus 25 cents for the round trip from all points in Kentucky has been secured and fully 2,000 delegates are expected to be in attendance. Some of the speakers are to be Miss Belle Bennett, president of the Methodist Home Missionary Society; Mrs. Helen E. Moses, Miss Ada Boyd, Bilaspur, India; President E. Y. Mullins, of the Baptist Theological Seminary; Marion Lawrance, secretary of the International Sunday-school Association; President B. A. Jenkins, of Kentucky University; President J. W. McGarvey, of the College of the Bible; H. D. Smith, of Hopkinsville; R. H. Crossfield, of Owensboro; Carey E. Morgan, of Paris; Miss Mary Finch, of Maysville, and H. D. Clark, of Mount Sterling. A general committee has been appointed representing the Christian churches of Louisville, with Robert M. Hopkins as chairman. Further information may be had by addressing him at the Keller building, Louisville. All persons who send in their names in advance will be furnished with lodging and breakfast free.

The Homeless Church.

The congregation without its own place of meeting is a family out in the street; a school without a building; a disembodied spirit; an egg without a shell. We have become so accustomed to the anomalous state in which two or three thousand of our congregations are constantly struggling to exist, that we are in danger of becoming indifferent to it. We are touched to the point of tears by the sight or even the story of an orphan child, and the feeling is a credit to our human nature, and an indication of the spark of divinity that abides within our hearts; but if we are moved by the homelessness of a human child—mere physical homelessness, how much more should we be stirred by the homeless condition of that spiritual child—a church of Christ! In its sad plight are involved the destinies of countless chil-

STATECRAFT AND STATEHOOD.

John Sharp Williams contributes an article in September SOUTHWEST upon the "Admission of the New State: Its Political and Commercial Significance."

September SOUTHWEST is devoted exclusively to the New State.

FIVE CENTS A COPY—FIFTY CENTS A YEAR

SOUTHWEST,
1037 Frisco Building,
St. Louis, Mo.

dren. It is not a matter of comfort or happiness! it is a matter of life itself, and of life not for a few years but for eternity. Nothing more vital or fundamental is being undertaken in the centennial campaign than the increase of the church extension fund to $1,000,000 by 1909. This will not be sufficient to house all the homeless, but it will care for hundreds of the most desperate cases and will be a pledge to our Redeemer of our concern for the rest and our purpose to have fellowship with them in their need and to foster them into the strength that will glorify his name.
W. R. WARREN,
Centennial Secretary.

Board of Ministerial Relief of the Church of Christ.

Aid in the support of worthy, needy, disabled ministers of the Christian Church and their widows.

THIRD LORD'S DAY IN DECEMBER is the day set apart in all the churches for the offering to this work. If you make individual offerings, send direct to the Board.

Wills and Deeds should be made to "BOARD OF MINISTERIAL RELIEF OF THE CHURCH OF CHRIST, a corporation under the laws of the State of Indiana." Money received on the Annuity Plan.

Address all communications and make all checks, drafts, etc., payable to BOARD OF MINISTERIAL RELIEF, 120 E. Market St., Indianapolis, Indiana.

NEWS FROM MANY FIELDS

Illinois Notes.

The church at Watseka is taking on new life under the active ministry of W. S. Gamboe. He is recently from Kentucky, but seems to assimilate easily to his new conditions and the enterprises of his adopted state. This is most commendable. It is unfair for our churches to have to wait a year or two on a slow preacher to get into sympathy and co-operation with the great work which each state has in hand, simply because the preacher comes from another state. A bright future seems to be before the preacher and people at the beautiful town of Watseka.——Milford is a great field and P. Baker is filling the pulpit ably as he always does, and is justly loved for his consecration and wise counsel for the best and highest interests of the kingdom of God. Consecration to the work of the Master by its large and influential membership, would soon make a church of great power in the kingdom of God. This is the home of Brother Harmon, whose wife for a time was connected with the Orphans' Home in St. Louis. It is useless to say that they are fervent in the Lord's work. We regretted to miss Dr. Gillum, who had passed away this spring. He and Brother Harmon were valuable patrons and friends of Eureka College.——H. H. Peters has just resigned at Rossville to take up the work at Dixon. The Rossville church appreciate most highly his valuable services for the last eighteen months, during which time the church has rapidly grown and the Sunday-school has doubled. They have chosen his successor, who, we hope, will be able to carry forward the work without break, as but one Lord's day intervenes between the pastorates.——At Alvin the church is improving in various departments, under the six months' ministry of our young Bro. T. Z. Cummins. The church is comparatively young, has about one hundred members, with a Sunday-school enrollment of as many. This is a hard age on our young people. Sunday ball games and social functions are destroying their thousands. Endeavor work is often left out of the program, even by young people who would like to be counted for something in the community. But we trust a wiser spirit will prevail and that the better things will help to make such character, as will produce worthy and great men for the greatest age the world has ever seen.——I chanced to spend the night recently in the home of a young banker, who had married a rich man's daughter. On their center table were two Testaments, a Bible and the Sunday-school quarterlies. The family altar was a part of each day's program. I said in my heart, how blessed the people, and the day, when the children, whom the Lord has blest with means, shall consecrate themselves and theirs unto him.—— At Danville our three strong men are at their post pushing the claims of the Master upon the hearts of the people. S. S. Jones, the veteran preacher of Danville, is strongly and justly intrenched in the hearts of the third church.—— A. Scott is having some valuable additions to his flock in the Second church. His young people are proving a source of great strength as they always can, when they devote themselves properly to the Master's service.——Sorry to learn that J. H. Smart had resigned his work in Danville, where the church has grown so splendidly during his two years' ministry, more than 200 having been added.

His talented wife is a most valuable aid to any church. He closes his work with September and should immediately be located where his unabated strength and large experience could have their full force. It is a great mistake to pass by our learned, vigorous and valuable men simply because a few "gray hairs their temples adorn."——The little church at Chrisman has the valuable services of J. A. Lytle one-fourth of the time. This is a fine field and we can build up a strong church here by united and consecrated service.——A. H. Harrell, living at Tuscola, preaches at Metcalf, Hume and Brockton. What possibilities there are in such a wide-spread pastorate in three splendid places. This is a very rich, fertile country, in which are situated these little cities. What a splendid field to start young preachers, to stir out young people for college out of which to make leaders of the world's life. We shall be disappointed if Brother Harrell does not discover some fine material in his territory.——Oakland is another preaching place of J. A. Lytle. It has It has 100 Disciples and 90 in Sunday-school. A fine field with a good preacher.——Another similar town is Hindsboro, where H. B. Easterling preaches half time and lives at Decatur. It has 10 Disciples and ninety in Sunday-school.——As these churches are samples of perhaps more than half the churches in the state I may be pardoned if I venture a few suggestions. The brethren would greatly enjoy a little more pastoral care. If the preachers could stay a day or two at each visit besides Sunday and visit among the people, get acquainted with the young people and strangers, and aliens and work up the Sunday-school and the young people's meeting, would it not be a great investment? The Lord's day when the preacher is absent may be most valuably used to develop the church's active ability. The trouble usually is that nobody makes any particular preparation. No program is prepared. Nobody is expected in particular to lead, so everything is spontaneous, haphazard, accidental, but not much to edification. Can not the preacher appoint a program committee, or at least leader; let him select persons to fill various parts in the program and give them time to prepare? Occasionally a sermon can be read, or selections, that would be instructive if some one was appointed to do it, who reads well and would take time to prepare well. Third, churches are suffering all over the state for want of fellowship in all the great enterprises of the church. The preacher visiting a church but once a month apologizes for not taking general offerings, by saying that half his visits would then be devoted to general offerings. The church apologizes by saying it is poor and has all it can do at home. What is to be done? What is the right thing to do? With what course will the Lord be pleased? What course would tend to the prosperity of the church? What course would make the church worthy of the Lord's blessing and promotion? The liberal soul shall be made fat; he that watereth himself shall be watered again." "Give and it shall be given to you," etc. Do we believe these statements? Then practice them. Let every day of our offerings to public enterprises be faithfully observed. If they happen to come at the time of the regular visits of the minister, make the most of the day with his help. If it is not on his

day let a program be prepared by the church. The various boards will furnish the necessary literature for a great program. Then the people according to their knowledge, generosity and ability will give and grow "fat" and the world will be blest with the Gospel. Lastly, go to church and attend to business. So many churches are nothing, if they have no preacher, no memorial of the Savior's love, no meeting for his praise and for the edifying of each other, no offering for his work. It is made a day of visiting, loafing, excursions. No wonder so many churches never grow strong. Come, brethren, the time is short, let us honor our high calling and do our duty while it is day, for the night cometh. Determine now to turn over a new leaf, and if a few will do this we will have a wonderful awakening in hundreds of churches. These are legitimate Illinois notes, for I am in Illinois, with Illinois conditions.   J. G. WAGGONER.

Eureka, Ill.

Free Test Bottle.

Bethany College.

The new interurban railway from Wellsburg to Bethany is an assured fact. President Cramblet has secured the necessary amount of money for its construction and service. Students may go home for the Christmas holidays on the "Wellsburg, Bethany, and Pittsburgh" traction line. This road has been needed for years, and will mean many more students in the coming year.

More rooms have been engaged for next year than ever before at this time of the year. Last year marked Bethany's highest enrollment, but this year's work will doubtless go far beyond it. The special expense proposition of the college should prove attractive to prospective students; $136 pays all expenses for the regular college student, while only $124 is charged for the ministerial students and the children of ministers and missionaries. This secures good comfortable quarters, good, wholesome food and all tuition and fees. Those desiring better service can secure the same at a reasonable rate. Many students from our well-to-do families are always in attendance.

Professor Johnson goes to Washington, D. C., and Old Virginia for his vacation. Professor Bourne is on the fifth tour of Europe. Professor Longanecker is in Ann Arbor and will spend the summer in Michigan. . Professor Moos is in Canada. Professor Ellis is in Knoxville, Professor McEvoy in Pittsburg and President Cramblet is everywhere. It seems that Bethany college faculty is on wheels already.

The Sunday-school closed last week and all pronounced it a decided success. At the closing church service last Sunday evening three came forward to make the good confession, and Monday evening, "On the Banks of the Old Buffalo" at the baptismal service, a noble young man made the good confession. Our revival has begun, or rather, continues.

Mrs. Frank H. Main and family go to Atlantic City this week where they will be joined by Brother Main. Later they will go to Bethany Beach.

E. Lee Perry, of Pennsylvania, has been chosen financial secretary. He begins the campaign for the $100,000 endowment fund as a Centennial offering from the brotherhood for the mother college, founded by Alexander Campbell, aided by his father. This really should be made $250,000 before 1909, the Centennial of the "Declaration and Address," which marks the beginning of our movement for Christian union. Bethany College has done more for this, the greatest of all religious movements, than any other institution; why should it not be honored? If Bethany and the men she has trained were taken out of this movement little would remain. One hundred thousand dollars is a small expression of our gratitude. The endowment has now reached $200,000, counting productive property. Two hundred and fifty thousand dollars more would enable her to continue her noble work for all time to come. I repeat this statement recently made about Bethany's work: "No institution in America for the same number of matriculates has turned out so many men of prominence."

A new addition to the town of Bethany has recently been laid out, and at least six new houses are building and will be

erected this fall. Bethany is moving. We have other important news for the near future.—W .B. Taylor.

Ohio Letter.

Homer Sala, a recent graduate of Bethany and a brother of our well-known John Sala, of Elyria, has taken the pastorate of the church at Sebering. His brother, John, has set a good pace for him and we fully expect that he will make good."—W. A. Brundige has resigned at Marietta. The river fogs were too much for his constitution and the doctor advised him that he must leave. He will move to Columbus and again enter evangelistic work. He has made a fine record at Marietta. A good man will be needed for that field.—E. J. Meacham withdrew his resignation at Wilmington and will stay and build the new house. In this all rejoice, but Wilmington church most of all.—The three churches composing the parish of Chester Sprague, East Liberty, Middleburg and Mill Creek, will join in a tabernacle meeting at East Liberty beginning August 19. John E. Pounds and wife of Cleveland will hold the meeting.—The Collinwood union meeting will be held earlier than was expected. It will be in September and held under a tent.—Franklin Mahoney, of Toledo, Norwood avenue, has accepted a call to work at Niles, where Herbert Yeuell held the successful meeting last January. He will find plenty of work at Niles.—I. J.

Cahill preached for the annual county meeting at Fayette, Mo., Sunday, July 29. He spent about ten days with the brethren there and gave them some excellent pabulum from the Word.—G. W. Watson, of Pittsburg, found favor in the sight of the good people of Van Wert and they asked him to become their bishop, which he will do at once. Ohio extends a cordial hand to Brother Watson.—The time for the fall conventions in Ohio districts is on. They begin as usual in District No. 8, meeting this year at Bellefontaine. The date is August 15-17. They have made a good program and will work hard for a fine convention.— Whatever may be your conviction on the question of federation, it will be a paying investment for you to put $2 into the volume that gives an account of the New York conference. There is a marvelous diversity of subjects treated by some of the best men of the country. It is very valuable as a book of reference. Every preacher ought to have it. The Christian Publishing Company will send it to you for a two dollar bill.——J. M. Vanhorn has been back to Ohio for his annual vacation and supply of inspiration from his old parishioners at Warren. He preached in Warren July 29.—J. E. Lynn, the pastor at Warren, is taking a part of his vacation at Chautauqua.—The Cedar Avenue Church at Cleveland has decided to move their location. They will sell where they are and go further east and buy a new lot and build a new plant. J. J. Tisdall is leading this move. —Any church wanting a good preacher and pastor at a moderate salary can be put in touch with a young man of good record by addressing the undersigned. —C. A. Freer, Painesville, O.

❦ ❦

The Manchester Meeting.

To those who are accustomed to measure a meeting by the number of additions, this meeting may appear small; and, because the meeting closed without an organization being established, some might infer that the effort has been a failure. Nevertheless, it has been both a great and successful meeting. When Brother Yeuell arrived in Manchester he found that we were practically unknown, except by a few who counted us as a "narrow bigoted sect, always harping on baptism." Accordingly he was first treated with suspicion. Different means were employed to break up the meeting before it was a week old.

One minister chose for his text John 10:10, laying particular stress on that part which reads, "The thief cometh not but for to steal." But such opposition served only as seed to promote deeper interest in the meeting. The entire city began to feel the influence of the simple

Gospel. They were amazed at the simplicity of the plea. Their interest increased with each service. They sat as one bewildered when their long cherished doctrines were brought under the light of the New Testament and proven false. Even then their sympathy was with the evangelist and the next service found them in the theater to learn still more about the perfect way.

One young school teacher deferred her trip to Denver, Col., so as to hear the truth as preached by Brother Yeuell. The newspapers caught the spirit of the meeting and often published a column or more about it.

It is said by those who know that Mr. Yeuell is the greatest evangelist ever seen or heard in Manchester and his influence the best ever manifested. That don't look like a small meeting.

But why was there no church established during this meeting? It should be remembered that this meeting has not really closed. It has been thought best to discontinue the services for a while for several reasons. In the first place, the theater could not be rented and there was not a church that would open the doors for the meeting. It is out of the question to expect to organize a church in a theater in Manchester.

However, the first great thing has been done. The plea of the Disciples of Christ has gone deep into the hearts of scores of people. It is there to stay. In a hundred breasts this night in Manchester the grand old plea is throbbing with life. Who then shall say that an organization has not been started? Remember the 'law of growth, "first the blade, then the ear, after that the full corn in the ear."

The good work will go on; plans will be made whereby to keep our plea before the people, and then as soon as expedient we will have another great meeting in a building of our own. We may then expect to establish a representative church in Manchester. The churches there are dying under their worn out doctrines. Give them the bread of life and behold the results! Brethren, pray for New England.—Wm. C. Crerie, Haverhill, Mass.

❦ ❦

Imported Japanese Fans.

A set of four very attractive Japanese fans, issued by the Chicago & Northwestern Railway, will be sent to any address, securely packed, on receipt of 10 cents to pay postage. Address W. B. Kniskern, Pass. Traffic Manager, 215 Jackson Blvd., Chicago.

Evangelistic

We invite ministers and others to send reports of meetings, additions and other news of the churches. It is especially requested that additions be reported as "by confession and baptism" or "by letter."

HOT FROM THE WIRE.

Special to THE CHRISTIAN-EVANGELIST.

Atchison, Kan., Aug. 5.—Thirty-nine to-day. Closed with 496. Many more coming.—W. T. Hilton, Pastor.

California.

Ukiah, Aug. 1.—Ten added to Ukiah recently —8 by confession and baptism. Am coming east on a short vacation.—Otho Wilkison.

Illinois.

Moline.—Just closed a three weeks' tent meeting with J. Fred Jones doing the preaching. The membership was doubled about already in the membership greatly strengthened. Brother Jones is second to none in his presentation of the simple gospel story.—Robert E. Henry, minister.

Keysport, Aug. 6.—Two baptisms at regular service last night.

Princeton, Aug. 6.—One added yesterday.— Cecil C. Carpenter.

Indiana.

Marion, July 30.—The Bible school of Tabernacle church is enjoying a splendid growth. Right now in the mid-summer season the attendance and influence are the best yet, and this too without any sort of prize button contest plan. During our first six months' labor, here there have been 31 additions at regular services—11 since last report.—Milo Atkinson.

Iowa.

Webster City, Aug. 3.—Four additions last week and three by baptism. Church is being greatly blessed. We thank God and take courage.—R. M. Dungan.

Ohio.

Shawnee, Aug. 2.—We closed a two weeks' meeting July 29, with 26 additions—18 by confession, 4 by statement and 6 re-instated. C. N. Filson, the West Virginia evangelist, was with us 12 days. He is a great worker and an excellent speaker. Everything is in good condition. —R. J. Bennett.

Fredericksburg.—There were four baptisms at the regular morning service July 15.—C. C. Maple, minister.

Kansas.

Manhattan, July 30.—One by statement yesterday.—W. T. McLain.

Asherville, July 30.—Last Saturday we met at the river to baptize two who had previously been converted. At the services two more witnessed the good confession and were baptized "the same hour."—G. F. Clark.

Missouri.

Eagleville, July 30.—One confession yesterday. —Thos. H. Popplewell.

Galmey, July 30.—Meeting one week old. Good interest; 2 confessions.—Pleasant Clark, minister.

Eidon, Aug. 1.—We are having a splendid meeting. Many turned away every night. Excellent preaching by S. D. Dutcher, J. F. Bickel, the minister, is a good mixer; 17 accessions to date. Large chorus with piano, organ and cornet accompaniment.—Chas. E. McVay.

Warrensburg, Aug. 1.—Just closed a short meeting at Kingsville, Mo., where my brother, Phil Stark, is pastor. There were 10 additions by confession, 1 by baptism; 1 by statement. The church is in excellent condition.—King Stark.

St. Louis, Aug. 1.—Five added at Macedonia church recently. There are many good people in this church.—W. H. Kern, 518 Garrison Ave.

Rolla, Aug. 3.—Closed one week's meeting at Bridge School House near Rolla, with 11 added—9 by confession and baptism.—E. M. Romine.

Belle, August 3.—Had 38 additions to the church here since October 1 last—31 by confession and baptism. Am compelled to relinquish this good field.—E. M. Romine.

Schell City, Aug. 4.—We have just closed a two weeks' meeting with the Schell City brethren; 11 additions. Pastor Funderburk will continue the meeting over Sunday. This is a great victory for Schell City, as the community is divided into factions over saloon and anti-saloon issues and old church difficulties. Through Brother Funderburk's untiring efforts better conditions are prevailing. Clara Garten, Moundville, assisted in the singing.—J. D. Pontius.

Nebraska.

Fairfield, July 31.—We have had 8 additions by confession and baptism during the month.— H. C. Williams, pastor.

Oklahoma.

Chandler, Aug. 3.—Our meeting is now five

days old with five added to date. Immense crowds and great interest. We have a tabernacle pitched in a public place, and are expecting a great meeting.—Oscar Ingold.

The Unity of Christians.

(Continued from Page 1008.)

They are bitterly alive to their own levity, and rashness, and indiscretion, and precipitancy. With all honesty they dwell upon the excellent things that they are continually finding but in their rivals, and even in their enemies. And they are cold, and sceptical, and suspicious about the flattering things that are said concerning themselves among their too indulgent friends. They know better. Luther thus describes them: "They are of such true humility," says the Reformer, "that they never know that they have any humility themselves at all." Their humility is so tender and so exquisite that it cannot endure the sight of itself. Their humility, and their lowliness of mind are hidden with Christ in God." Let all those men who would put out a hand to bind up the long-standing wounds of the church be lowly-minded men, says the apostle. Let them be men of this measure of humility, that they esteem all other men to be better fitted for such a holy work than they are themselves.

"And, then, as if all that were not enough, and as if to make such a universal reunion impossible in this world, the apostle still proceeds with his immense and his irreducible demands on all the proposers and all the promoters of union. "Look not every man on his own things," he insists, "but every man also on the things of others." An impossible demand again. For it is not in the Vatican, neither is it in Lambeth, and far less is it among ourselves in Scotland that such an assemblage of unearthly virtues and evangelical graces are to be found. We shall not see such a Union Committee of Churchmen constituted and co-operating for reunion, or for anything else, on this side the New Jerusalem. At the same time, let these tremendous tests of mind and heart and character continue to be applied to us, till we are driven desperate with pain and with shame at ourselves. And, then, when by his grace to us, we are at last brought to that, the God of truth and love and peace will begin to get his work of truth and love and peace wrought by us. Let this heavenly legend then be written in letters of gold every convocation and general assembly, and Episcopal and Presbyterian synod in this world. And then, when they his grace enly legend in letters of the purest gold. "Look not every man on his own things, but every man also on the things of others." "With all the fervor of his honest heart," writes Gardiner in his "Civil War," "Edmund Verney might pray for peace; but there was nothing in his conception of the situation which was at all like to hasten peace. To be a peacemaker, in any real sense of the word, requires the highest powers of the imagination. A peacemaker must have a clear and a sympathetic perception of that which is best and noblest on either side. And it was just in the perception of anything good or noble in Puritanism that Falkland and his associates were entirely lacking." * * * When we look not so much at our own short history, however brilliant to our own eyes that history may be; nor so much at our own peculiar attainments and possessions as Protestants and as evangelical believers, however precious and inalienable those attainments and possessions may be; but when we look more at the antiquity, and the nobility, and the grandeur, and the stateliness of those other churches, as over against the too great provincialism and rusticity and indecorum of speech and action that have often far too much characterized ourselves; when we have humbled ourselves to admit that some

other churches have things of no small moment to teach us and to share with us, and things it will greatly enrich us to receive and to assimilate; when we are of a Christian mind enough to admit and even to welcome thoughts and views and feelings like these—then the day of a reconstructed Christendom will have begun to dawn, at least for ourselves. For then Ephraim shall not any more envy Judah, nor Judah any more vex Ephraim. Who is this that looketh forth as the morning, fair as the moon, clear as the sun, and terrible as an army with banners? Enlarge the place of thy tent, and let them stretch forth the curtains of thine habitation; lengthen thy cords, and strengthen thy stakes. For thy seed shall inherit the Gentiles, and shall make the desolate cities to be inhabited. Amen; in God's good time it shall be seen!

[See editorial in this sermon.]

Deafness Cannot be Cured

by local applications, as they can not reach the diseased portion of the ear. There is only one way to cure deafness, and that is by constitutional remedies. Deafness is caused by an inflamed condition of the mucous lining of the Eustachian Tube. When this tube is inflamed you have a rumbling sound or imperfect hearing, and when it is entirely closed, Deafness is the result, and unless the inflammation can be taken out and this tube restored to its normal condition, hearing will be destroyed forever; nine cases out of ten are caused by Catarrh, which is nothing but an inflamed condition of the mucous surfaces.

We will give One Hundred Dollars for any case of Deafness (caused by catarrh) that can not be cured by Hall's Catarrh Cure. Send for circulars free.   F. J. CHENEY & CO., Toledo, O.

Sold by Druggists, 75c.

Take Hall's Family Pills for constipation.

THE JUDGE, THE PHARISEE AND THE PUBLICAN.—Luke 18:1-14.

Memory Verses, 13, 14.

GOLDEN TEXT.—God be merciful to me a sinner.—Luke 18:13.

The kingdom of God was a central conception in the teaching of Jesus. Probably the term always carried with it, to his less intimate hearers, a sense of the spectacular and political triumph of righteousness which he never intended. To the Jews of that time, the triumph of righteousness meant, in a very vivid and personal sense, the triumph of the righteous, and that meant the triumph of the Jews. So they were always ready to hear about the kingdom of God.

Some of the Pharisees had been asking when it would come. Perhaps they thought it too much trouble to be in a state of continual preparedness, but were willing to be on the lookout for the advent of the kingdom if they knew just when it would arrive. The substance of Jesus' answer to this question (Luke 17: 27-37) was that no advantage was to be gained by knowing the hour of the supposed sudden advent of the kingdom, for it was an internal and spiritual matter. "The kingdom of God is within you." The only way into the kingdom is by the possession of spiritual qualifications. It will not help to be at a given place at a given time. When the spiritual criterion is applied, persons closely allied, and alike in all external respects (two men in one bed, or two women grinding at one mill) may be separated, one in the kingdom and one out of it.

In this same connection Jesus spoke the parable of the judge and the widow. The judge was a poor representative of his profession. He cared for neither law nor equity. But the persistence of the widow finally wore him out and she gained her cause. Such is to be the perseverance in prayer of those who seek the kingdom, and a wise and loving father will certainly be no harder to entreat than was the harsh judge.

In all matters pertaining to the spiritual life—in prayer and in seeking entrance to the kingdom of God, it is the steady and constant effort that counts. Jerks and spurts have little value in religion. Religion is so truly vital, that it can flourish only through the vital processes of nurture and growth. These processes take time, and whatever takes time requires patience and persistence.

The parable of the Pharisee and the publican, the arrogance and conceit of the one and the humility of the other, is one of the most precious things in the New Testament. The parable was spoken to Pharisees. It was not only about these religious aristocrats, but was actually spoken "unto certain which trusted in themselves that they were righteous." Jesus always delivered his teaching to the people most nearly concerned.

The characters of these two men represent the contrast between a regime of law and a dispensation of grace. Dependence solely upon obedience to law in overt acts for salvation has for its natural product the hard, cold, correct and self-satisfied individual who keeps the law as the price which he must pay for salvation, as the rogue may pay his debts to keep out of jail. It means formally correct conduct without character. Law, as a means for saving the human race, was weak and unsatisfactory not only because perfect obedience was humanly impossible, but because the nearer one came to perfect obedience the greater was his danger of falling into a loveless egotism which is ruinous to character.

It was not the publican's sins, but his humility and contrition that won commendation. Humility without sin is better. But the sin which leaves a man penitent and humble and conscious of his need of grace, has not been without its saving influence.

Christian Endeavor

By GEO. L. SNIVELY

August 19, 1906.

WHAT IS THE SIN OF PHARISEEISM.—Luke 11:42-44.

DAILY READINGS.

M.	Seekers of Signs.	Matt. 16:1-12.
T.	Hypocrites.	Matt. 21:23-46.
W.	Covetousness.	Luke 12:13-15.
T.	Self-Righteousness.	Luke 15:1-10.
F.	Presumption.	Luke 18:10-14.
S.	Rejectors of Christ.	Matt. 21:33-46.
S.	Divers Sins.	Luke 11:42-44.

"God beholds thee, wretch, though wrapped in prayer,
A wolf disguised, a painted sepulchre;
Regards no more thy cant, and godly whine,
Than yon dumb statue, on the marble shrine,
Whose hands are seen, in holy rapture closed
And steadfast eyes, to heaven alone disposed,
Prayer's senseless image, where no soul within
Speaks through the form and animates the mien."

In this "woe" Jesus is not decreeing a penalty on Phariseism, but predicting it. In the very nature of things the denouement of their scrupulous attention to cleansing the outside of the platter and neglecting the inside, of tithing anise and ignoring the moralities of the law would be disaster to their happiness, fatality to their worth, and involve them in woes innumerable.

Self-justification is a prominent trait of Phariseeism. It is a bar to righteousness—a state unattainable save through repentance. The Pharisee can not be penitent, for seen through his eyes of spiritual pride he has done no wrong. Let us pray that our motives and actions may appear to us as they do to God, and that with penitential tears we may keep our lives white as they were once made in Jesus' blood.

The rewards of Phariseeism are not full compensation for its pains. It requires an effort to affect Christian character. If that effort to counterfeit were directed toward becoming a genuine Christian, it might not make one a very illustrious Christian, but it would be a positive step in the right direction, it would be an acquisition having real, even though small, value. All that tempts us into Pharisaical attempts to seem better than we are are Satan's promises—made to be broken, apples of Sodom that turn to dust at our eager touch.

A vast majority of those really desiring to be good get their ideals of God and goodness from what they see the reputed religious doing rather than from studying Christ and meditating on "what would Jesus do?" Here is a measure of the responsibility devolving upon sharers in the faith of God. Phariseeism, with its shoddy, hollowness and conceit and its pretensions of knowledge and piety designed to deceive the unlearned conveys very imperfect and distorted conceptions of these themes. For these

THE OLD LIFE AND THE NEW.— Romans 6:3-7.

"Rise, my soul, and stretch thy wings;
Thy better portion trace;
Rise, from transitory things,
Toward heaven thy native place."

"Sun and moon, and stars decay;
Time shall soon this earth remove;
Rise, my soul, and haste away
To realms prepared above!'"

The old life was of the earth and earthy, the new life is come down from heaven and is heavenly. The muck-rake is symbolic of one, the telescope of the other. If there is not much of heavenliness in us let us re-examine the foundations of our faith, the sincerity of our repentance, the reality of our fellowship in the death and life of our Redeemer. The trouble is with the man, and not with the divine plan.

The fourth verse is a grave in which we may bury, and ought to deeply bury, all incertitudes and disputations concerning the form of Christian baptism. Submersion in water, immersion alone meets the requirements of this portrayal and of the beautiful, instructive and prophetic symbolism of the rite. If the energy devoted to polemics about baptism were devoted to create desire and make preparation for it, more would be saved. Some day all disputation concerning this will give place to the voice of exhortation.

Christ died unto sin once. He took our sins upon himself once and then disposed of them forever. Having died unto sin, that is, having separated himself from it, "he liveth unto God." It should be so with us. The trouble with us is we do not extirpate sin from our lives, root and branch. Enough remains after our frequent reconsecrations to get another start. Of us it ought to be said, "Having died unto sin once, he liveth unto God." Let us cease blending these livings and dyings. Let us henceforth live only.

We really lost nothing in relinquishing the old life. None that has lived for it alone believes its games are worth their candles; what seems like roses are thick-set with thorns; and portentous clouds veil all but glimpses of the blue empyrean. But we no sooner begin cultivating the higher affinities of the new life than they whisper of a paradise without a tempter, of songs having no weeping tremolo, of hillsides never cleft by the sexton's spade, of an eternity through which we live in an ever-ascending scale, till in a sense earth can not conceive we become God-like.

One may undergo burial in water and yet not be dead to sin nor rise to walk in newness of life with Christ. But if one is prepared for baptism—if he has heard and learned of Christ and attained unto vital faith in him as the Son of God, and has in all sincerity repented of his sins, renounced them and made restitution for them so far as he could, and has honestly confessed Jesus before men to be his Savior, then he will leave his sins and sinful nature in the grave and come forth a new man in Christ, and sin will no more have dominion over him. If we were not so prepared for baptism let us do again the first works, and the blessing of freedom from the old man

of sin will come to us even years this side of the grave where we should have been separated from his service.

Before we were risen with Christ it was fitting we should be largely concerned about our adjustment to conditions affecting our physical welfare—food, clothing, shelter, sanitation. We were deeply interested in our social relations, too—good neighbors, schools, entertainment, and laws securing equity and protecting life and property. But now that we are risen with Christ, they seem like inferior relations. We are more concerned now to harmonize our lives with higher relationships—to have our souls fed with the "bread of life," to keep in tune with the infinite, to feel ourselves preparing for the companionship of angels and the redeemed forever. When adjusting our physical and social selves to their best environment we are tuning the bass and tenor of our lives to the universal concord, but not till we come to these spiritual relations are we harmonizing the soprano and all the highest and sweetest notes of our music.

* * *

People's Forum

That New York Resolution.

To the Editor of THE CHRISTIAN-EVANGELIST:

Although not a member of the New York Ministerial association, I was present at its last annual meeting held in Elmira and listened to the temperate discussion that preceded the adoption of the resolution sent you for publication, and found on page 907 of the July 19 issue of your most excellent paper. I therefore confidently believe I am capable of rightly judging the situation. I frankly admit that I am utterly unable to perceive any "ambiguity" in the resolution. On the contrary, it seems to be clear and positive in its meaning, and expressed in language easily comprehended, containing no subtle or hidden purpose. What you think it "probably" means is precisely what it does mean. The ministers of the Empire state are unquestionably sound on the federation question, and when they find it necessary to do so, are abundantly able to give their beliefs an expression that will be equally as clear as their resolution, which seems to have been a disturbing element in your editorial shop.

Your comments on the resolution seems to imply that the claimed "ambiguity" consists in what the resolution does not state rather than what it *does* express. If this be true, it must be a new species of "higher criticism" that has strayed beyond all reasonable bounds, and needs to be called home, effectively spanked, poulticed and sent to bed, there to remain until a suit of swaddling clothes can be prepared for its next appearance. Something is likely to happen that will damage its anatomy if this is not done.

And you err in declaring that "only one thing is clear from the resolution," and that is the fear of "heated discussion." You have no more right to read that into the resolution than the assertion that these good ministers see the folly of not giving God a chance to adjust and settle a few questions in his own righteous way, unaided by, and independent of his restless, impatient, frail and recalcitrant children.

There is as much faith in God and trust in the brethren in New York state as in any other locality, but appearances would seem to justify the conclusion that the quality of the former is slightly superior because of the willingness of the Empire state brethren to supplement their faith and confidence in God with a liberal use of wisdom, prudence and consecrated common sense. Let us indeed keep clear heads and steady nerves, not forgetting the wisdom dispensed by that Jerusalem Doctor of Law which has not up to the present suffered any improvement.

Buffalo, N. Y.   A. B. KELLOGG.

[The foregoing requires only a brief word of comment.

1. We must not allow our correspondent to place us in seeming opposition to the Ministerial Association of New York. What we understood them to mean by their resolution—and Brother Kellogg says we were right in our understanding—we had previously recommended, so that brings us into substantial unity. The only "ambiguity" attached to the resolution was in the use of the word "Convention," since a proposition had been made to have a separate convention for the consideration of some matters which it was not considered expedient to bring before the regular convention. We inferred they meant the regular convention, and had no thought of any "subtle or hidden purpose" in the resolution.

2. We have no doubt that the New York ministers, in common with all the brethren, "see the folly of not giving God a chance to adjust and settle a few questions in his own righteous way," but we should not charge them with holding to the view that we were excluding God from any problem by seeking, as far as we know, to do his will. On the contrary we are justified by our critic himself in inferring rather that the brethren of the empire state believe in "supplementing their faith and confidence in God, with a liberal use of wisdom, prudence and consecrated common sense." This was what, in our weak and stumbling way, we were trying to do.

Dr. Gamaliel's advice, it should be remembered, was given not to the friends but to the opponents of Christianity, and it is very wise advice now for those who oppose federation, or the systematic co-operation, as far as possible, of all Christians; but it does not apply to the believers in Christ and Christianity, nor to the advocates of Christian union and of co-operation as a step thereto, as respects their duty to a cause which they have no doubt is "of God." It is the duty, however, of the advocates of every righteous cause to use wisdom in its advocacy, and to exercise great patience with those who are mistakenly opposed to it. In this, we need not say, we are in perfect agreement with our esteemed correspondent. We depend too little upon God and too much upon ourselves in settling aright the great questions which have to do with the progress of his kingdom.—EDITOR.]

Current Literature

POEMS. By Henry W. Longfellow. Chicago. W. B. Conkey Company.

This edition occupies 192 octavo pages, and is well bound. It answers very well for a reasonably cheap edition of this popular American poet.

MARRIAGE. By Jane Dearborn Mills. Philadelphia, The Nunc Licet Press. Pages 82. Price 50c.

This book is written from the woman's standpoint and is due to the demand for a previously written book circulated privately. The present work has been entirely rewritten and added to. It holds up a high ideal of the marriage relationship and has a word on its purity, its service, "the marriage of the unmarried," and marriage laws.

THE AWAKENING OF HELENA RICHIE. By Margaret Deland. Illustrated by Walter Appleton Clark. (Harper Brothers, publishers, New York. ($1.50.)

Helena Richie is a new arrival among the delightful Old Chester people of Mrs. Deland's earlier stories. About her young widowhood there is mystery for Old Chester, but there is a loneliness for her and self centeredness blighting a splendid quality of mind and heart. Her redemption comes through the adoption of little David, who to the end of the story fairly divides the reader's interest with the heroine. Affection for her ward overcomes self love and makes of her a true priestess in the great temple of humanity.

DEMOCRACY IN THE CHURCH. By Edgar L. Heermance (The Pilgrim Press, Chicago. $1.25 net.

As intimated in the title, this is a discussion of church polity. It ranges from the sentiment, "We must become more compact, if we are to do our work in the kingdom. Consolidation is the tendency of the age,"—to that other and apparently equally popular clamor, "Centralization is the sale of our birthright. What is wanted is not a change of system but a change of heart." The author's apology for writing at this time is the world-wide desire for Christian unity, and he regards the book as particularly opportune in view of moves recently made toward union between Congregationalists, United Brethren and Methodist Protestants. It is an analytical study of the organization and government of the apostolic church and a strong protest against departure from the Jerusalem model. Among the prominent assertions stoutly maintained is that the ancient democracy in the church (as opposed to ecclesiasticism) means the continuous leadership of the Spirit.

SUMMER IS HERE

People must have inducements during such weather to either buy or read, especially good books, and we are determined to offer the inducements. For the month of July we will make the following prices, CASH with order. All books are prepaid. All books are cloth bound where not specified as paper.

	Regular Price	Cut-Rate Price		Regular Price	Cut-Rate Price
Life a Flower. By Errett	$1 50	75c	Altar Stairs, splendid fiction	1 50	1 00
Plain Talks to Young Men	60c	30c	June, a Class History	50c	15c
Thirteen and Twelve Others	1 00	50c	Prison Life in Dixie	1 00	25c
Life of Knowles Shaw	1 00	50c	Across the Gulf	1 00	50c
Problem of Problems	1 50	75c	Moral Evil	75c	25c
Kaskey's Last Book	1 00	50c	The Wondrous Works of Christ	75c	25c
The Form of Baptism. By Briney	1 00	60c	Rosa Emerson	1 00	50c
The Temptation of Christ	75c	40c	Ecclesiastical Tradition	75c	35c
How Understand and Use Bible	50c	35c	Facts About China, paper	25c	15c
Riverside, or Winning a Soul	75c	35c	The Spiritual Side of Our Plea	1 50	75c
Grandma's Patience	20c	15c	Lessons in Soul Winning	75c	45c
After Pentecost, What?	1 00	60c	The Plan of Salvation for Sinners and Saints	1 00	25c
Know Thyself	1 00	50c	The Man in the Book	1 00	60c
Memorial of J. K. Rogers and Christian			Missionary Addresses	1 00	35c
College	60c	30c	Commentary on Matthew. By F. N. Peloubet	1 25	50c
Koinonia. or the Weekly Contribution	15c	10c	Types and Metaphors of Bible	1 00	50c
The Juvenile Revival	60c	35c	An Encyclopedia on the Evidences	2 00	1 00
The Master Key, paper	25c	13c	The Gospel for an Age of Doubt. By Henry		
The Remedial System, 436 pages	2 00	75c	VanDyke	1 50	75c
Duke Christopher, Young Hero of Württemberg			The Making of an American. By Jacob Riis.	1 50	75c
berg	50c	20c	Social Evolution. By Benjamin Kidd	1 50	75c
Bartholet Milan	25c	10c	Jesus Christ and the Social Question. ⸻Francis Greenwood Peabody	1 50	75c
Gems from Franklin (very badly damaged)	1 00	50c	The Little Shepherd of Kingdom Com⸻	1 50	75c
Revelation Read	1 00	35c	The Quest of Happiness. By Newell Hillis.	1 50	75c
Trip Around the World	1 00	50c	Happiness. By Carl Hilty	1 50	75c
The Simple Life	50c	35c	The Women of the Bible. By Mrs. S. 1. Martin	1 50	75c
Saintly Workers	1 00	50c	The Conqueror. By Gertrude Atherton	1 50	75c
Christology of Jesus, one of Stalker's best	1 50	1 00	The Celebrity. By Winston Churchill	1 50	75c
Origin of the Disciples	1 00	50c	The Choir Invisible. By James Lane Allen	1 50	75c
Bible or No Bible, paper	50c	25c	Sant' Ilario. By F. Marion Crawford	1 50	75c
Contradictions of Orthodoxy, paper	25c	15c	The Master of Warlock. By Edward Eggleston	1 50	75c
A Knight Templar Abroad, 547 pages	2 00	35c	The Customs of the Country. By Mrs. Hugh		
The Story of an Infidel's Family (very			Fraser	1 50	75c
interesting)	1 00	50c	The Knitting of the Souls. By Maude Clark		
Patmos	1 00	35c	Gay	1 50	75c
Queen Esther. By M. M. Davis	75c	45c	The Law of the Land. By Emerson Hough	1 50	75c
Elijah. By Davis	75c	45c	Black Friday. By Frederic S. Isham	1 50	75c
The Story of an Earnest Life	1 00	60c	The Medal of Honor. By Capt Charles King	1 50	75c
Missouri Lectures and Discussions	1 00	30c	The Four Feathers. By A. E. W. Mason	1 50	75c
Autobiography of Jacob Creath	1 00	50c	My Lady Peggy Goes to Town. By Frances		
Edna Carlisle	75c	45c	Aymar Mathews	1 50	75c
King Saul	1 00	60c	Zelda Dameron. By Meredith Nicholson	1 50	75c
In the Days of Jehu	1 00	60c	The Cost. By David Graham Philips	1 50	75c
Prohibition vs. Personal Liberty, paper	25c	10c	On the Face of the Waters. By Flora Annie		
Walks About Jerusalem. By Errett	1 00	60c	Steel	1 50	75c
Talks to Bereans. By Errett	1 00	60c	The Pillar of Light. By Louis Tracy	1 50	75c
Science and Pedagogy of Ethics. Fine for			Marcella; The History of David Grieve. By		
teachers	1 50	75c	Mrs. Humphry Ward	1 50	75c
Sermons and Song	1 00	50c	Daughters of Nijo. By Onoto Watanna	1 50	75c
The Exiled Prophet	1 25	50c	The Magic Forest. By Steward Edward White	1 50	75c
Spiritualism on Trial	1 50	50c	The Yellow Van. By Edward Whiteing	1 50	75c
Dictionary of Scripture Proper Names		50c	Children of the Ghetto. By Israel Zangwill	1 50	75c
Organic Evolution Considered	1 50	75c	Lourdes; The Downfall. By Emile Zola	1 50	75c
My Good Poems. By Fairhurst	1 00	50c			
Ideals for Young People	50c	30c	**SONG BOOKS—PREPAID.**		
Life and Times of Benjamin Franklin	1 00	60c	Pearly Gates (board binding, 90 pages), per doz		$1 00
An Endeavorer's Working Journey Around the			Apostolic Hymns (board binding, 112 pages), per doz		1 00
World	1 50	75c	Twilight Zephyrs (board binding, 96 pages), per doz		1 00
Our First Congress	1 00	60c	New Fount of Blessing (board binding, 190 pages), per		
Wheeling Through Europe	1 00	60c	dozen		1 00
Garfield's Great Speeches	1 50	75c	Tidings of Salvation (board binding, 117 songs), per doz		1 25
Class Book of Oratory. Fine for elocution	1 50	95c	Tidings of Salvation (manila, 117 songs), per doz		1 00
Christian Missions	75c	40c	Tidings of Salvation (limp, 117 songs), per doz		1 00
The Baptismal Controversy	75c	45c			
The Divinity of Christ and Duality of Man	75c	35c	**NEW TESTAMENTS.**		
Otto's Good Recitations, paper	50c	25c	Revised to 1881 (silk cloth binding)	30c	15c
The Life of Jesus	1 00	50c	Revised to 1881 (larger type, cloth)	60c	25c
The Young Man from Middlefield	1 00	50c	Revised to 1881, one page common version,		
Leaves from Mission Fields	1 00	50c	opposite page revised (bourgeois type),		
The Moberly Pulpit	50c	25c	cloth)	50c	25c
Communings in the Sanctuary	50c	25c	Revised and common, page for page (long		
Nehushtan	1 00	35c	primer type, Morocco binding)	1 00	35c
Bible vs. Materialism, paper	35c	20c	Reference New Testament (long primer type)	1 25	60c
Wonders of the Sky	50c	25c			

CHRISTIAN PUBLISHING COMPANY, 2712 Pine Street, St. Louis, Mo.

The Home Department

The Stepmother.

BY KATHLEEN KAVANAUGH.

Within a fortnight of my birth
My fair young mother passed from earth,
And Memory left to me no trace
Of her dear form or face.
In time another took her place:·

The one who led me down the years,
Who kissed away all fret and tears,
Upon whose warm, responsive breast,
Whenever care oppressed,
I·always found relief and·rest.

It is my hope I'll see them stand
At heaven's gate, clasped hand in hand,
The mother sweet I never knew,
The one tried, noble, true,
Who filled her place—my mother, too.
—*Good Housekeeping.*

❦ ❦

The Bronze Vase.

BY J. BRECKENRIDGE ELLIS.

PART III.

CHAPTER VI.

'Never as at that moment had Wizzen's dry, wrinkled face seemed so friendly, or his black shirt and blue cotton trowsers so homelike, or his glazed cap so grateful. Raymund and Rhoda could almost have embraced him upon the spot; they were in such desperate strait and he had such an air of helpfulness. "This is certainly a surprise to me," said Wizzen, who was chewing tobacco, and while having his own ideas about the propriety in the presence of ladies, sought to conceal the fact.

"Wizzen," said Raymund, speaking rapidly, "some wicked people have invented a story about Rhoda to get her in their power, and they are hunting us at this minute. We are running away, but we don't know where to run to! Help us, Wizzen, we are in dreadful trouble."

"Come on," said Wizzen briskly, and without waiting for another word, he bolted down an alley, brought them upon a rough road that skirted a high bluff, and held his quid in his cheek with the resolute determination of a man who would run over and drown himself before he would afflict the feelings of a lady who could have no sympathy in his tobacco. Rhoda, seeing his danger, ostensibly turned her head to gaze at the shanties perched on the summit of the bluff; when she turned about Wizzen had gotten rid of his quid and was himself again. "I want to show you something mighty pretty," he said pursing up his mouth and wrinkling his eyes hard. At the first turning he pointed out a mover's wagon, to which were hitched its two hard-worked horses. The horses did not seem so feeble as when the young people had known them, but they had no extra strength to boast of. "Pile right into that there wagon," said Wizzen heartily, "and they won't nobody find you; and I'll git on the front seat and take you where it will be as safe as an ant in an anthill!" They obeyed with spirits of thanksgiving. The canvas covering was drawn tight on all four sides, and as Wizzen sat on the front seat, outside of this roofing and walls of white security, they could see him only as a vague blur as he drove along.

"How delightful this is!" said Rhoda, staring about her, as the wagon slowly moved forward, creaking and rattling and grinding in a complaining tone about its axles. "Why don't you grease us?" the axles inquired, and with reason enough. Raymund and Rhoda found themselves in a romantic room of cloth which in a way reminded the youth of the labyrinth in the Hands' House, the night of his thirteenth birthday. Ah, what would Nelsie Loraine have thought of this canvas-apartment? How common and ridiculous such a chamber must appear to the millionaire's daughter, now about to start upon her European tour! No matter. It was neither common nor ridiculous to Raymund.

At the end of the wagon farthest from the driver's seat, was a little erect coal stove, which took up but small space; the pipe ran from it up through the canvas, where one of the oaken arches spanned from side to side. There was just room between the back of the stove, and the sideboard, for a coalbucket, and there the coalbucket stood. Fortunately there was no fire in the stove, for the June morning was already oppressively warm. Next the stove was placed a spring wagonseat, with a quantity of straw all about it, for one's feet. There were cushions on the low seat, and the jarring of the wagon was partly counterbalanced by the give of the springs. In one corner was piled a quantity of bedclothes, in another, several large pine boxes, and opposite the spring wagon seat, which ran lengthwise of the wagonbed, was a little gasoline stove, and a tall metal trunk. In the corner opposite the stove was a plain but substantial table, and fastened upon it in an inverted position was another table, its legs in the air. Everything was tied to its place by ropes, except the stove, which was heavily wired. By cautiously drawing up the canvas in the rear, they could look into a long narrow box, nailed to the end of the wagon, and covered by a sloping lid to keep out the rain. In this box, Rhoda divined, were the cooking vessels; beneath the box swung a wooden bucket, and a large tin basin. Rhoda was so enthusiastic over the moving palace, that she climbed to the front and drew aside the flap to compliment Wizzen; but finding him enjoying his tobacco in a hearty, open-mouth way that spoke of a sense of utmost security, she gave up her intention.

The mover's wagon traveled along roads that grew rougher and rougher. The wheels no longer ground over uneven pavements, and there was all the time a downward slant that showed the advantage of having the stove wired to its place. On each side were little flaps which could be opened to serve as windows; but the young people, not caring to expose their faces to the enemy, should Boggs be in pursuit, did not often take advantage of this privilege. They saw enough, however, to tell them that they were leaving the city and advancing along the grassless, sandy wastes of the river bottom. At last the wagon stopped. It had frequently done this before on account of the unwillingness of the horses to keep to their business. As Wizzen once called back through the canvas, "These here hosses is like me; they don't keer for no unbroken work." But now the wagon stooped because it had reached the end of the journey. Wizzen dismounted and drew up the end-flap, assuring his passengers that it was quite safe for them to dismount.

They found themselves in the midst of a wild and desolate scene. Not very far away ran the muddy Missouri, and all about, stretched the flat sandy waste, littered with wreckage from the last overflow. Broken doors, decayed window-casings, rusty wheels, rotting planks, tangled wire, discolored telephone poles were all jumbled together in different heaps. Here and there stood a stranded houseboat, its flat deck converted into a porch. Wizzen had checked his horses before a passenger-coach which the river had swept from a submerged track and had hurled hither in its mad fury. The coach was half buried in the sand. Only the top and one side was visible.

"Here's home," said Wizzen. "Me and Mrs. Weed has been living here nigh on a month, till I could git ready for our overland voyage."

Even as he spoke, the door of the coach opened and Mrs. Weed, now seventy-eight years old, but still active, looked out at them. She recognized Rhoda and Raymund at once and waved her knitting genially. "Come right in," she cried. "The house is mighty high but you won't mind that, I reckon."

"She means low," said Wizzen admiringly. "I tell you, my mother-in-law gets sprier ever' day. And I don't keer what words she lays hold on, I kin gineral...

grapple onto what she means. It's a sorter gift on my part I reckon."

"Come right in!" urged the old lady, who could not hear a word they said.

"We'll go in," said Wizzen. "I'll just leave my hosses standing which they wouldn't move nohow, unless the river riz an' washed 'em away. I found this here pazzenger-coach buried out here in the sand, an' not wanting to pay no rent which it is only fair to say I never do, for I feel that as to paying rent, you ain't gitting nothing as to say it is your own which is what I want when paying out. So I taken my shovel and dug away the windows on one side, and cleaned out this hole to git to the door, and I plunked old Mrs. Weed down there where what with the June sun a' brilling down on the iron roof so stiddy, she ain't never onct called for a fire. But now I've bought ever-thing I want for our trip, and only to-night it is my mind to pull out."

"O Wizzen!" cried Rhoda as they bowed their heads to enter, "do take us with you! Where are you going?"

"Bee-line for St. Louis," said Wizzen. They seated themselves upon seats which had once been splendid in blue velvet upholstery, but which had long since lost their form and color.

"How romantic!" Rhoda could not help exclaiming, as she looked down the aisle, dusty and forlorn and read above the wrecked door the warning, "NO SMOKING!"

Raymund said eagerly, "Wizzen, let us go with you! Our uncle is in St. Louis, and maybe if we come face to face with him, he won't send us away. Anyway, we might as well be there as anywhere, and if we try to leave Kansas City by the train, we are afraid Boggs will arrest Rhoda. I have some money with me, and can help pay for our expense. And oh, Rhoda, and I always wanted to go across the country in a covered-wagon, didn't we, Rhoda!"

His appealing to her was so like his childhood way that Rhoda beamed upon him with tender affection. "Of course we always did. Don't you remember, Wizzen, how we stole off to your house to beg you once to help us?"

"And don't you remember," said Wizzen, "how I told you that a dozen years from then, you'd forget all about your present troubles. Well, three years only has passed and now you've forgot them troubles, and is bothering over new ones! I tell you life is a strange thing which the more of it I git the more it seems so to me."

"Henry," said Mrs. Weed, "don't you

think it is time for us to sleep?"

"She means to *eat*," said Wizzen, "for we ain't had no breakfast yet; and as to her calling me Henry, that is just her vagary." Then taking the old lady's ear-trumpet, he bawled into it, "I'll go and git breakfast now. These children—" Wizzen added in a lower voice, "no need to tell her your names, young folks, for if they went into one of her ears, which it is only fair to say is more than unlikely, it wouldn't git ketched in her brain long enough for her to use 'em onct." Wizzen then raised his voice: "These is my friends, Mrs. Weed, friends—do you hear?"

"Yes," said the old lady, nodding and smiling. "If that's so, they're my friends, too."

"They want to go with us along to St. Louis. Any objection, Mrs. Weed?"

"Reflection?" said Mrs. Weed.

"No, Mrs. Weed, objection, ob—jection?"

"Do they shun *me*?" asked the old lady in a pained voice. "Why young people, I am very glad to have you here, as you are Henry's friends!"

"She never called me Henry before," said Wizzen, nodding to Rhoda. "It's wonderful where she gets all these names and words. He raised his voice and explained to Mrs. Weed, who heartily seconded Wiz-

zen's permission ; so it was decided upon the spot that the orphans should make the "overland voyage," from Kansas City to St. Louis."

(TO BE CONTINUED.)

❋ ❋

Picture of War Engine "General."

A beautiful colored picture, 18x25 inches, of the historic old engine "General" which was stolen at Big Shanty, Ga., by the Andrew's Raiders during the Civil War, and which is now on exhibition in the Union Depot, Chattanooga, Tenn., has been gotten out by the NASHVILLE, CHATTANOOGA & ST. LOUIS RY.—The "Battlefields Route" to the South. The picture is ready for framing and will be mailed for 25c. The "Story of the General" sent free. W. L. Danley, Gen'l Pass. Agent, Nashville, Tenn.

A Morning Prayer.

Father, we thank thee for the night,
And for the pleasant morning light;
For rest, and food, and perfect care,
And all that makes the day so fair.

Help us to do the things we should,
To be to others kind and good,
In all our work and all our play,
To love thee, better, every day.
—*Exchange.*

Advance Society Letters.

BY J. BRECKENRIDGE ELLIS.

But I was telling you about our orphan Charlie's vacation, and didn't get through. During the Chautauqua we were invited to eat dinner with Mr. and Mrs. Burris, who had brought their dinner to the tent. We decided to eat on the platform, where there was a small speaker's table, so we spread out the picnic dinner on the table—or rather, we doubled it up, as the table wasn't large enough for spreading. It was fun to eat on the great rostrum in the big deserted tent, knowing that in about two hours Sam Jones would be speaking in that very spot to a great multitude. I greatly regret to have to tell you that orphan Charlie dropped his plate on the floor with his chicken under the plate. Perhaps I might have spoken a friendly word of caution and advice to him about it, had I not dropped my own plate about that time. I dropped my plate because the table was so small, but don't know why Charlie was so careless. When the dinner was ended, there were marks on the floor where we had sopped our chicken, and a little later you ought to have seen the flies! Sam Jones had to stand right amongst them to lecture, and if he said some pretty hard things about Arkansas, maybe the flies were partly to blame. . . Charlie had a buggy ride while in Bentonville. There were ever and ever so many nice people with buggies who might have taken him, but Miss Nana Wood is the young lady who did take him. He also went to the Endeavor society and read his Bible verses clearly and correctly and without having to be begged. . . . . He went on two picnics while here. The crowd on both occasions consisted of the same dramatis personae (I trust I am spelling my Latin in Roman form); it consisted of my young friend, Roy Dixon and myself. That only seems to be two, yet I am sure there were three—why, bless me! yes: there was Charlie himself. Of course that makes three. Our first picnic consisted of going a mile afoot to Park Springs over torn-up sidewalks and under very hot Arkansas sun, throwing rocks (of which there was an abundance) at trees, pecans (very old pecans) and almonds (very dry almonds). The way you do is this: You take a marshmallow, stick a pecan kernel in each corner, stick a large chocolate-drop on top of the kernels, stick an almond-kernel on top of the building, for a chimney (by this time it is quite sticky) open your mouth very wide, not as if you were going to say "o," but as if you were going to cry double-o, and then, what? Put it in your mouth, of course: not just sit there looking at it. Then you throw a rock at a tree. It was a very good picnic. . . The second picnic, however, was perhaps more enjoyed. True we did not go so far and did not get so hot, but there were enough other troubles to make it seem picnicky. You go along a certain street as if you were not expecting to get any place in particular, when of a sudden you come to the mouth of a walled-in alley that runs dark and narrow, and seems to stop at a board fence and try to get back; but when you

reach the board fence you find a mysterious turn, and the alley runs away and never stops till it reaches a wood with soft grass and forest trees and a cow that somebody has staked out for supper. So orphan Charlie and Roy and I took dominoes and peanuts and cheap, very cheap, candy that smelt like the clothes of the young man who clerks in the drugstore, and also some real expensive candy, some perfectly extravagant chocolate-drops, the five for a nickel variety in a small town. But wait, you haven't heard the climax. We took Iron Brew, Lemon Sour and Dr. Pepper. In this park there were no water works, and feeling sure we'd get thirsty after the candy course, we took three soda pops, whose names were as given. After we had almost played the spots off pop. As we did not know the relative merits of Iron Brew, Lemon Sour or Dr. Pepper, we wrote the initials of each pop on separate slips of paper and cast them in the air, with the understanding that the man must take the pop whose name fell closest to him. Well, "L. S." fluttered closest; to me; "I. B." fell to the lot of Roy Dixon, and Charlie swooped upon "D. P." The next thing was to open our bottles. They weren't the kind you slap down to make fizz, but the flat silver (likely enough only plated) smooth mouthed bottles that need a twister. We didn't have a twister, but there was a barbed-wire fence near, which we pounded at with our bottles. Finally Roy got off his top before he thought it was coming, and his Iron Brew shot into his eye. We cried to him to clap the neck of his bottle into his mouth, but it was throwing Iron Brew in such a steady stream that he was blinded and couldn't find his mouth. About that time Charlie whacked off his top triumphantly and drank his Dr. Pepper with a bleeding hand. I had no other mishap than to drink my Lemon Sour to the last drop. Lest any one think this an advertise-

ment, I will add that, judging from my internal sensation and the pallid faces of my friends as we filed down the alley homeward, these three pops are equally to be avoided. Does some one ask, "What is all this about Lemon Sour and Iron Brew in my religious paper?" But consider, friend, which is more religious—to make a speech about brotherly love at a prayer-meeting, or to scatter a little Lemon Sour and Dr. Pepper into some life that needs a friend?

I am writing this on the last day of July, but when you read it, you will be bowling along through the hot, dusty highway of August. Just now I am all excitement. My ice cream social, to which every one of you is invited, comes off August 3—only three more days. I wonder if we will take in much money for Charlie's education? If any of you forgot about it, you might send on for a dish of our ice cream—it hasn't melted yet. Now, what dress shall I wear? I am sure I would not look right all in white. By the way, I have received some advance orders for reserved seats at the table. Since Charlie left here for his sister's, I have heard from him. He writes: "I got here all right yesterday, at about two o'clock. Bessie was delighted with the locket." (This is the gold locket Mrs. Rothwell, of Moberly, Mo., gave Charlie to give his little sister. It contains Charlie's photograph, taken here, and a real good one.) "It has been raining here ever since I came. Bessie has a very nice home here. Could you send me the last CHRISTIAN-EVANGELIST? I don't want to miss any of 'The Bronze Vase.' How are 'L. S.,' 'I. B.,' and 'D. P.?' Tell Roy I said 'Hello.' " I have received a beautiful illustrated post-card which informs me that our Grace Everest is at Grand Lake, Col.: "I came here Sunday and will stay about a month. This picture of Moffat Line above Bowlder Park represents one of the beautiful places we have seen. I have not forgotten the Av. S." From M. T. D., Hannibal, Mo., comes this: "To help make Mrs. Shryock's prayer come true, I send $5 for Drusie, $5 for Charlie. I have just cut out the Evening Prayer at the head of the Av. S. Letters of May 21, and shall send it to my daughter, who, I hope, will receive it in the steamer on which, God willing, she will shortly sail home from Europe. I have watched with interest for years the work of the Av. S. and its supplemental work, that of supporting an orphan and missionary. God alone knows the great results that may come of it all." (It seems good to hear a friendly voice from the city in whose shadow I was born. The letter contains a prayer for me, too personal for print, and I wouldn't mention it at all except to point my remark. The remark is this: Every now and then a letter comes with the sweetest wishes and the dearest prayers, from grandmothers and grand-children—people I've never seen. Now suppose I had spent my life making money, buying cattle, let us say, or controlling railroads and saving, saving. Hannibal wouldn't care whether I'd been born or not. I wouldn't be anything to anybody except just to kinfolks and myself. So let's be happy and poor, and give away something of the little that's left.)

Ruth Day, Sparta, Mo.: "I intended naming July 4th as the day for the fried chicken eating, but put it off till too late. But come any time; there will be plenty of chickens later on." (Yes, but a chicken that's "later on" has to be boiled instead of fried.) "I would have been glad to celebrate with Donnie Swift, down at Billings, but it is most too far from home. I am glad Charlie is getting to stay and see his sister Bessie on his way home. I hope he will have as nice a time from the city as I do when I visit my aunt in the city. I hope those orphans in the 'Bronze Vase' can manage somehow so they can live together. I enclose 20 cents for Charlie and Drusie and wish it could be as many dollars. I must go feed my chickens." (Don't forget to put some water in that pan.) B. Roth, Ness City, Kan.: "I want to ask your opinion on chain letters as a means of collecting money for benevolent purposes. I received one from Neptune, Kansas. They are unpopular among my friends, so I took some names I found in the Advance Society. Do you think it was an imposition, especially as some of them were from Missouri? I become more and more interested in

the Av. S. My son is a Christian preacher." (When my opinion is solicited, I tell exactly what I think, and what I think about chain letters is that they ought not to be. I used to feel differently about them. I used to get a chain letter in a big stack of mail, when I would have to write till my eyes were burning and my tongue dry and my hands tired. Then I would open the chain letter. It would begin, "Dear Mr. Breck—I have been asked to write," etc.; and then it would go on, "Please make 10 copies of this letter to your friends, requesting each to write ten, that no link may be broken." Incidentally it would ask me to send a dime, and to ask my ten unsuspecting friends to send each a dime, and for them to ask their poor acquaintances to send their hundred dimes, etc. When I was a babe to chain letters, I was so afraid a link would be broken that I would toil over those ten copies when I could have been using my time in a useful and pleasant manner. And I am confident my friends, if they read those copies, had a grudge against me when they saw my name signed. I got to thinking, "This chain will be broken in the course of time; why not snap a link right here?" So I did, but I felt bad about it. Not so, now. Now, I love to break chain letters. I feel I am doing the world a good turn. I say boldly that I am a Chain Letter Smasher. Look here: If any chain letter remained unbroken, and if it only called for a two-cent stamp, in a short time it would capture all the stamps in the world. It's asking too much. It's selfish to want millions of dollars for one particular cause. It doesn't leave anything for other causes. Some chain letters ask for prayers instead of money. Then it's "Write to 10 of your friends to pray for a certain thing, and ask each of them to write to 10 more, but if you can not do this, kindly return this letter so no link will be broken." I believe in prayer; but I think the 20 cents I'd spend in mailing my 10 copies would do the certain thing more good than putting 10 people out of patience because you've asked them to write 10 letters. So I put that request

in my waste basket, and I break my link and feel good about it, and I think of my 10 friends to whom I have NOT written, and I am happy. Now, that is my opinion of chain letters. It may not be worth anything to other people, but it's mighty handy to me.) Bertha Beesley, Moselle, Mo.: "I wish some of the Av. S. would try this plan mamma and I have adopted: We keep an account of all the eggs we get on Sundays and place their cash values in our missionary box. Sometimes we get but a few cents, again, quite a sum. In this way we are sure our fund will grow a little each week." (I think a plan like that is fine. Hens will work on Sunday, they refuse to be idle. Then why not make them be missionary hens? Who else will have missionary hens besides Bertha? In two weeks I will tell you all about the great Ice Cream Social for our orphan, and who sat at the table, and what we had and did, and didn't do. I have a letter from Drusie also, and by the way, I sent her another $5 yesterday from us, the sixteenth draft from you and me since we began her support. Bentonville, Ark.

End-of-the-Week Rates.

Chicago and North-Western Railway.

From Chicago to near-by summer resorts. Tickets at special low rates on sale Friday, Saturday and Sunday, good until the following Monday to return. Other low rates in effect daily. For tickets, rates and booklets giving full information, apply to nearest ticket agent or address W. B. Kniskern, P. T. M., C. & N. W. R'y Co., Chicago.

Christian Publishing Company

While "Gloria in Excelsis" is the premier among our church music-books we publish and sell many others. We have lower priced books that will be invaluable helps to Bible-schools and protracted meetings. Price list sent on application.

We are filling numerous orders for the picture of Editor Garrison. This is a fine photogravure, 11x12½. This is a work of art all may have for sending us a renewal and one new subscription to THE CHRISTIAN-EVANGELIST and the necessary $3.00.

In preparing for a protracted meeting, add a few dollars to the expense budget and order a few hundred CHRISTIAN-EVANGELISTS for distribution each week. We will furnish them at a surprisingly low price and they will prove to be of greatest

helpfulness next to Bible study and the preached Word in bringing men to Christ.

We hardly expected such responses to our Summer Bargain Sale advertised on page 1023 as are making our book room a scene of busy industry. The hundreds of dollars worth of orders filled now may injure Fall trade but the book-men say these prices will be maintained through August regardless of consequences. Cut out the adv., check books wanted, return to us and we will ship promptly.

We sell our Bible-school supplies wholly on their merits and not by disparaging the work of others. We send the Dowling series with the statement that they are the best. If on examination you are not convinced they are the best, place your order elsewhere. Nothing else does more to affect a child's future relations with the church than the Bible-school helps. Don't lightly pass by the Dowling series.

THE CHRISTIAN-EVANGELIST Special over the Wabash leaves St. Louis at noon Oct. 11. Connecting trains will come in from

Tennessee, Arkansas, Oklahoma, Kansas City, Omaha and Des Moin, best of train service assured. P vides at Detroit. Those preferr water route will proceed by one best of lake steamers, the others over the Wabash through Canada us soon as you determine positivel that we may make abundant reser

The circulation of THE CH EVANGELIST is growing rapidly b oaken solidity. The clubs we a as well as individual subscriptions a ing at the regular $1.50 rate. Th continue with us. The majority c singles. Here are last week's clubs don, Mo., 3; D. Millar, pastor; Brad Ont., 3; Allerton, Ia., 5, R. H. Ingra ister; Irving, Ill., 10, L. Hadway, Gage, Okla., 17; N. B. McGhee, m Litchfield, Ill., 19, W. S. Johnson, Knoxville, Ill., 19, Albert Schwartz, Eureka, Ill., 20, A. W. Taylor, pastor chester, N. H., 21, Herbert Yeuell gelist; Galesburg, Ill., 24, N. G. pastor; Abington, Ill., 27, T. J. minister,

A View of Niagara Our "Special" Friends Will See.

THE
CHRISTIAN-
EVANGELIST
A WEEKLY RELIGIOUS NEWSPAPER.

Volume XLIII. No. 33.

ST. LOUIS, AUGUST 16, 1906.

A MOTTO

By W. T. Moore

W HAT'S the use of crying?—Fight it!
If for wrong you're sighing—Right it!
Go to work and do not slight it,
    Then brighter hope will dawn to-morrow.

Make each day a step up higher,
Every step will bring you nigher
Where at work you will not tire,
    And where joy takes place of sorrow.

What's the use of fretting?—Shoot it!
Spend no time regretting—Boot it!
Trouble needs no petting—Loot it!
    Life will then be worth the living.

Stand for truth and do not blunder,
That which kills is not the thunder,
Bluster is not normal wonder,
    Power comes through quiet giving.

What's the use of pining?—Cheer up!
There's nothing made by whining—Stir up!
The sun will soon be shining—Clear up!
    Then do not sickly troubles borrow.

Fight each battle for the better,
Make each day a great red letter,
And trust the right to break each fetter
    Binding now the hands of sorrow.

The Christian-Evangelist.

J. H. GARRISON, Editor

PAUL MOORE, Assistant Editor

F. D. POWER,
B. B. TYLER, } Staff Correspondents.
W. DURBAN,

Subscription Price, $1.50 a Year.

For foreign countries add $1.04 for postage.

Remittances should be made by money order, draft, or registered letter; not by local cheque, unless 15 cents is added to cover cost of collection.

In Ordering Change of Post Office give both old and new address.

Matter for Publication should be addressed to THE CHRISTIAN-EVANGELIST. Subscriptions and remittances should be addressed to the Christian Publishing Company, 2712 Pine Street, St. Louis, Mo.

Unused Manuscripts will be returned only if accompanied by stamps.

News Items, evangelistic and other, are solicited, and should be sent on a postal card, if possible.

Published by the Christian Publishing Company, 2712 Pine Street, St. Louis, Mo.

Entered at St. Louis P. O. as Second Class Matter

WHAT WE STAND FOR.

For the Christ of Galilee,
For the truth which makes men free,
For the bond of unity
　　Which makes God's children one.

For the love which shines in deeds
For the life which this world needs
For the church whose triumph speed is
　　The prayer: "Thy will be done."

For the right against the wrong,
For the weak against the strong,
For the poor who've waited long
　　For the brighter age to be.

For the faith against tradition,
For the truth 'gainst superstition,
For the hope whose glad fruition
　　Our waiting eyes shall see.

For the city God is rearing,
For the New Earth now appearing,
For the heaven above us clearing,
　　And the song of victory.

　　　　　　　　　　J. H. Garrison.

CONTENTS.

Centennial Propaganda 1031
Current Events 1032
Editorial—
　Progress of Peace 1033
　Business Side of Christian Union... 1033
　Close of the Manchester Meeting... 1033
　Current Religious Thought........ 1034
　Notes and Comments............ 1034
　Editor's Easy Chair.............. 1035
Contributed Articles—
　As Seen from the Dome. F. D.
　Power 1036
　Religious Bosses. William Durban. 1037
　What the Brethren are Saying and
　　Doing. B. B. Tyler............. 1038
　Modern Religious Persecution—A
　　Defense. B. L. Chase.......... 1039
　Our Great Agreements. G. L.
　　Wharton 1040
　The Field of Sport. Andrew Scott. 1040
Our Budget 1041
News from Many Fields............ 1047
Evangelistic 1050
People's Forum 1051
Mid-week Prayer-meeting 1052
Christian Endeavor 1052
Sunday-school 1053
Current Literature 1054
Marriages, Obituaries 1054
The Home Department 1055

ved
THE
CHRISTIAN=EVANGELIST

"IN FAITH, UNITY, IN OPINION AND METHODS, LIBERTY, IN ALL THINGS, CHARITY."

| Vol. XLIII. | August 16, 1906 | No. 33 |

1809 CENTENNIAL PROPAGANDA CHURCHES OF CHRIST 1909
: : : GEO. L. SNIVELY : : :

Looking Toward Pittsburg.

Geo. W. Muckley, known to some of our people as secretary of our Board of Church Extension, and who has been heard in some quarters to admit that church extension is one of the really important interests of the Churches of Christ, will contribute a few articles in this Centennial Propaganda, the first of which is presented below. God grant him the million by 1909!

There is not a week but at least a few more hundred Disciples begin looking toward Pittsburg. One sure index to the number is THE CHRISTIAN-EVANGELIST'S new subscription lists. All our readers are looking toward Pittsburg. They are not overlooking intervening conventions, county, district, state and national; they are not ignoring our missionary claims and days nor other opportunities for service and privilege, but they are looking forward to the centennial as the consummation of high hopes. If THE CHRISTIAN-EVANGELIST goes regularly to 100,000 homes a year before 1909, that convention will celebrate achievements far beyond our most sanguine expectations. Below is the testimony of a few friends as to its Christian helpfulness. You are helping a home and a great cause wherever you make it a family fixture.

OUR CENTENNIAL CELEBRATION AND CHURCH EXTENSION.
BY G. W. MUCKLEY.
An Announcement.

Great interest is already being manifested in our centennial celebration of this Restoration movement which is to be held at Pittsburg in 1909. This interest is growing daily. Wherever your Secretary of Church Extension goes to address churches the preachers and the people are asking "What does this centennial celebration mean?" We ought to be asking ourselves, "What can we make it mean to the religious world?" Can we deepen our spiritual life and increase the number of those who pray "that they all may be one," to the number of two million during the next four years? Can we become more liberal toward all missionary enterprises; increase our college endowments and benevolences and erect the family altar in thousands of homes? Can we put a Christian paper in every Christian home to fire our hearts and to nourish our enthusiasm for the tasks before us? All of this is possible, and much more. An announcements of the Centennial Committee's plans have already been made and approved by an alert and eager brotherhood. Our religious papers are filling pages with information and a most capable, devoted man, W. R. Warren, of Pittsburg, Pa., has been chosen as our leader, and is the secretary of the committee. It remains now for our brethren everywhere to follow the leadership. In his own congregation every pastor will be the main source of information and inspiration for his people regarding the work to be done preparatory to a fitting celebration.

The Centennial Committee reporting first to our national convention in Omaha in October, 1902, recommended: "That our Church Extension Fund, that splendid feature of home missions, should be increased to $1,000,000 by the time of our one hundredth anniversary at Pittsburg in October, 1909."

Can we reach the million for church extension?

An apportionment has been sent to each congregation in the United States and Canada, the raising of which will insure the million dollars for church extension by October, 1909. The amount asked of each church is not beyond what might reasonably be expected. Many will not raise their apportionments but just as many will go far beyond the amount asked. It is certainly worth while to make the effort since raising the apportionments insures the million. Letters of confidence and good cheer have been coming almost daily since our books closed last September, saying, "Don't lower the standard. We can raise the million by 1909!" This board asked the Centennial Committee at its recent meeting in Pittsburg: "Is the million dollar standard too high?" The answer came in a chorus, "No! Push for the million. Anything less would be unworthy." Let us reason soberly in the light of church extension's history since 1888:

The first watchword was a quarter of a million by 1900, with which to begin the twentieth century. The mark was reached by September 30 that year, and more. Then a half million was called for by 1905. On December 30, 1905, the fund amounted to over $540,-000. The mark had been passed and over $40,000 besides as an advance toward the million dollars.

The outlook is bright for reaching a million dollar fund by October, 1909. On November 21, 1888, $10,662.80 was turned over, by the home board of Cincinnati, to T. R. Bryan, treasurer of the Board of Church Extension, which had been elected by the national convention in October of the same year at Springfield, Ill. We were twelve years reaching the quarter of a million, which we secured by the close of 1900. In four years we raised the second $250,000. Why should it be thought a thing impossible to add a second half million within the next four years? With over $565,000 in the fund on August 1, 1906, we have only $435,000 to raise, or $110,-000 annually. This is reasonable, for our receipts last year were $96,654.82, including the $50,000 Logan gift. We have put our hands to the plow, and can not look back. Forward is the word! It means that the churches now giving must treble their offerings, and those not yet co-operating must fall into line in this work so vital to our home field. Individuals must give large amounts, the annuity fund must grow. With God and a consecrated brotherhood all things are possible. The million dollars for church extension must be reached by 1909!

Centennial Propaganda.

I have been a reader of the CHRISTIAN-EVANGELIST since its beginning and we cannot do without it. I shall do all I can to increase the subscription list in this congregation.—Mrs. S. L. McLeese, Denver, Colo.

Sometimes THE CHRISTIAN-EVANGELIST doesn't suit me, but sometimes I don't suit my wife exactly, but she continues to stand by me in spite of my faults. That is what I have done for THE CHRISTIAN-EVANGELIST for years.—W. T. Henson, Slater, Mo.

I am very much in love with THE CHRISTIAN-EVANGELIST, its Editor and most of its writers. It is doing more to clear away preconceived ideas on the Bible than any other agency among us. I have only good wishes for its success. —A. N. Woodson.

We have no organization here, and I know of none within forty or fifty miles. I take great comfort in THE CHRISTIAN-EVANGELIST which comes to me every week with such good sermons and other help. It is a pleasure to read it, and learn our people are doing so much for the advancement of Christian union and are not afraid to accept the overtures of the divided Christians.—Mrs. C. S. Crane, Russell, Kas.

I have been a subscriber to "The Christian" and to "The Evangelist" and to THE CHRISTIAN-EVANGELIST. It is my highly esteemed helper. Its arrival is always welcome. For its Editor-in-chief I have great respect and sincere affection. He is rendering the plea of the Disciples an inestimable service. I desire to see THE CHRISTIAN-EVANGELIST introduced into more of our homes, and I hope soon to send some subscriptions.—John C. Hay, Hollywood, Cal.

It has been with growing interest that I have followed your discussion of federation. I desire to express to you my heartiest approval of your course. You would not for one moment assume to be saving this Restoration, but, in my judgment, this is what you are doing. If the spirit manifested by another of our papers is to prevail, then the Restoration movement of the Disciples will prove a monumental failure. These words are written by one who thoroughly believes in the plea of the Disciples of Christ.—A. L. Ward, Christian minister, Roxbury, Mass.

Current Events

The physician who sent in a bill of $25,000 against the estate of the late Marshall Field for one week of unsuccessful professional services in the millionaire's last illness, has come in for a good deal of criticism. The old practice was to bleed the patients. The modern way, it seems, is to bleed their estates. There can be no doubt but that this was a greedy doctor. He saw a chance to grab, and he grabbed. In extenuation it may be said that he asked no more than the services were worth to the man who received them. At a time of mortal peril, a man with a hundred millions might be quite willing to pay twenty-five thousand dollars for the attendance of the physician who, in his opinion, would be more likely than any other to save his life. The charge, in other words, was proportioned to the value of the service to the man who received it and not to the cost of the service to the man that rendered it. This is simply "charging what the traffic will bear"—a system which was in vogue long before Mr. C. P. Huntington defined it in this trenchant phrase. In general, the maximum possible price of any commodity is its value to the consumer and the minimum is the cost to the producer. The actual price tends to approximate the maximum, except as competition and the prospect of increasing the volume of business and the total profit by reducing prices tend to draw it toward the minimum. In the case of Mr. Field and his physician, the latter influences were not at work—so up went the price. The competitive principle can never operate freely with reference to professional services, and it is therefore the more needful that the intangible influence known as "the honor of the profession" shall exercise an equivalent restraint. If the ethics of the medical profession condemn a doctor for advertising but permit him to practice extortion, the code needs revision.

Medical Fees.

❦

One of the Paris dailies complains bitterly because the European governments have failed to utilize the opportunity of which Secretary Root is making such splendid use at Rio Janeiro. The Latin countries of Europe have been (characteristically) asleep while the Pan-American congress has been in session. Secretary Root, though only an unofficial visitor, has been by all odds the most influential person at the conference. The warm reception which he has received there has evidently reminded at least one Parisian editor that South America has almost broken the ties which formerly bound it to Europe and is rapidly making new alliances. It will not be many years before the entire western hemisphere will have definitely ceased, as Mr. Root says, to be considered as ground for European colonization.

Europe and South America.

For a sunny-hearted optimist, with a genuine Mark Tapley brand of unadulterated cheerfulness, commend us to Mr. John D. Rockefeller. The following words, spoken shortly after his recent return from Europe to a reporter whose persistence had secured an interview, may seem to the scoffer to contain a certain element of platitude, but when one remembers that Mr. Rockefeller's specialty is not literature but oil, one will not be disposed to make much of that trifling defect. He says:

An Optimist.

"I never despair. Sometimes things that are said of me are cruel and they hurt, but I am never a pessimist. I believe in man and in the brotherhood of man, and am confident that everything will come out for the good of all in the end. You can always believe in real men. I bear no ill to any man. I am confident that there is more good than bad in the world, and I am full of the joy of living. I believe in men. Do that and the world is bound to seem a good world to you."

We are gratified to learn that Mr. Rockefeller does not despair. And since he admits a certain sensitiveness regarding the things that are said about him, perhaps the rest of us need not yet despair either. While it hurts, there is hope. A year or two ago there was a general impression that none of the Standard Oil people cared what was said about them. If they really do care, it is worth while to go on saying the true and unpleasant things which need to be said. Our philosophy of life, like Mr. Rockefeller's, includes a firm conviction that "there is more good than bad in the world," and that everything will come out for the good of all in the end." Mr. Rockefeller has occupied a position in which he could, with complacency and entire comfort, await the tardy arrival of this epoch of universal justice. But we wonder if he will recognize it when it comes. Perhaps the Ohio and federal courts which are now after him will help to usher it in. Meanwhile (again like Mr. Rockefeller) we will go on believing in real men, and defining real men as those whom we can believe in.

❦

Mr. H. G. Wells is an English literary man who deals largely in futures. Just now he is contributing to "Harper's Weekly," an excellent series of articles on "The Future of America." His comments on Niagara are exceedingly good. He saw the beauty of the falls, of course, but he saw also the beauty of the tunnels and turbines and dynamos by which a portion of Niagara's energy is made available for human use. They impressed him, he says, far more profoundly than the Cave of the Winds. They "are greater and more beautiful than that accidental eddying of air beside a downpour. They are will made visible, thought translated into easy and commanding things." It is not hard to see the beauty of a great cataract. There has been a chorus of "ohs" and "ahs" going up beside Niagara for generations. But in the course of time there come economic necessities which demand that the beautiful thing be put to practical uses. In their first stages, practical uses are likely to be ugly. But this should never be accepted as ultimate. The practical must be made

Niagara.

Progress of Peace.

One who is interested in the extension of the kingdom of God on earth should keep his eyes open to those wider movements of the world which make for peace and righteousness. These are no less the result of the influence of Christ's teaching than the additions to our churches under the preaching of the Gospel. It is a fault common among Christians not to look for the evidences of the growth of the kingdom outside of church circles; but we should remember that God is moving upon this world through every avenue of influence open to him, and both by direct and indirect efforts is seeking to bring in the "new heavens and the new earth wherein dwelleth righteousness."

At the present time there is in session in the royal gallery of Westminster Palace at London the Interparliamentary Union, consisting of more than 500 members, representing twenty-three national parliaments. It is composed of some of the ablest and most progressive men of these various parliaments. This is the fourteenth session of this union, the twelfth of which was held in St. Louis during the World's Fair. It is interesting to know that America's representatives are among the leaders in this important movement for the peace of the world. Some of their ideas were objected to at first as too advanced for European nations, but gradually these principles are being endorsed. Some of the important measures taken by this body are: (1) Converting the conference at The Hague into a permanent body with power to assemble periodically and on its own initiative, thus making it a permanent council whose special object is to study the best ways of promoting the peace of nations; (2) widening the scope of this peace council by referring to it certain causes of misunderstanding between nations which had hitherto been excluded; (3) the paying of a salary to the members of The Hague court, and instructing them to begin work at once upon the codification of the law of nations so that there can be a body of international law ready to be applied to international disputes.

Mr. Bryan has just addressed this peace conference in London urging an amendment to the effect that in those questions which are reserved for settlement upon the battle field, force shall not be resorted to until after an investigation by the international court. This amendment, though proposed at a previous session and defeated, was unanimously adopted in London under the strong presentation of Mr. Bryan. It is pleasing to notice that the representatives of the two leading parties in this country are working harmoniously together in this conference in the interest of peace. The prime mover among Americans in this interparliamentary union, was the Hon. Richard Bartholdt, member of Congress from St. Louis, and a Republican, whose action is strongly endorsed by Mr. Bry-

an. The strong influence which has been brought to bear in behalf of this peace movement by President Roosevelt is well known.

All this looks as if the time were surely coming, and is not so far away, when Tennyson's vision shall be fulfilled:

"When the war-drum throbs no longer and the
    battle flags are furled
In the parliament of man, the federation of the
    world."

The ultimate union of nations for the promotion of the peace of mankind is as inevitable as the ultimate union of Christians for the advancement of the kingdom of God.

❁ ❁

Business Side of Christian Union.

Christianity like man has a body as well as a spirit. Some people ignore this fact and preach a sort of disembodied Christianity. True, as in the case of man, the spirit is more important than the body, but, as in the case of man again, the body is quite essential for doing business here in the world. Christianity embodies itself, first of all, in living, regenerated human beings, who reproduce in some measure the life of Christ. It embodies itself in ordinances which set forth, symbolically, the fundamental facts of the Gospel. It embodies itself, also, in external organization, as in local congregations and other forms of organized and co-operative activities. Furthermore, it tends continually to embody its spirit in laws, customs, institutions, and constitutions; in a word, in Christian civilization.

But in order to these forms of self-expression, Christianity has a business side. This is a fact that is frequently forgotten. The erection of suitable buildings in which local congregations of Christians may carry on the Lord's work is a necessary part of this business side of Christianity. No church in our day and time can accomplish the best results for itself and the community without a suitable meeting-place adapted to the kind of work which it desires to do. Since church buildings are, therefore, a necessity in order to the successful carrying on of Christianity, it is a part of wisdom, or what we sometimes call "sanctified common sense," to do this work in the most businesslike way. The methods of church extension, by which limited sums of money are loaned at a low rate of interest to local congregations, on strictly business principles, to supplement what they can do on the ground, toward the erection of a building, and to be paid back in easy installments, has been found, by long experience, to be the most effective way of assisting young churches in housing themselves and thus in making permanent and practical the results of evangelization. The work as conducted by our own board of church extension has been wonderfully successful and has justified itself in the eyes of business men who have investigated it. It is the privilege of the churches once each year, namely: on

the first Lord's day in September, to make an offering to the cause of church extension. As that time is near approaching we call the attention of the churches to this opportunity which is coming to them to assist all their brethren who are without church buildings, in the most businesslike way, to provide themselves houses of worship. This is such an improvement over the old haphazard method of responding to local appeals for churches here and there that it is a wonder that any church among us can be found that is not a willing and regular contributor to this businesslike and systematic method of extending aid to needy churches.

The board of church extension has set for its mark a million dollars by our centennial anniversary in October, 1909. This would be an achievement worthy of celebration within itself. As over $400,000 of this amount yet remains to be raised it will be seen that something over $100,000 a year should be contributed by the churches during the next four years to realize this aim. This can be easily accomplished if all the churches will bear a part and each one do its duty. May we not hope that wherever THE CHRISTIAN-EVANGELIST circulates, which is very largely throughout the brotherhood, the churches will see to it that this offering is regularly and conscientiously taken? Remember that every dollar thus contributed goes into a permanent fund to be used for building churches through all future time.

❁ ❁

Close of the Manchester Meeting.

The meeting which was conducted during the month of July in the Park Theater, Manchester, N. H., must be set down as one of the notable meetings of the year. All the conditions surrounding the meeting served to test, most severely, both the tact and ability of the evangelist and the message which he had for the people. The evangelist has succeeded, beyond doubt, in making a deep impression, and a most favorable one, on the best people of Manchester concerning the nature and the plea of the Disciples of Christ for the unity of Christians and a return to simple New Testament Christianity. This impression is reflected by the daily press, as shown by the following extract from the Manchester Union, commenting on the close of the meeting:

After a month of special meetings at the Park Theater, Dr. Herbert Yeuell closed his engagement Sunday night with an audience of over a thousand, which, considering the hot weather, was a most remarkable crowd to attend an indoor attraction of any sort. The influence of Mr. Yeuell's preaching has been felt throughout the entire city, and large numbers have come in from neighboring towns to hear him.

The undenominational character of his work has won the sympathy of all classes. Besides being a speaker of unusual eloquence, his personality has stood the severest test that a New England audience could give it. It is many years since an evangelist has held the attention of Manchester audiences so continuously. Some of the most famous evangelists have been brought here, out they have gone away in some instances before the time expired, without creating a ripple.

Mr. Yeuell has talked to his audiences as few men would dare to address any people. He has laughed at their foibles as well as praised their virtues, and they have laughed back good-naturedly and seemingly thanked him for his frankness. He is eminently endowed with the saving grace of humor. His evident sincerity and naturalness disarm whatever of criticism might be aroused by his frequent attacks on what he terms "ecclesiastical mossbackism." He says the people he represents, known as the Disciples of Christ, renounce ecclesiasticism and church bossism and creedal entanglements of all kinds and stand apart from all denominationalism and modern fads, demanding of their converts faith in Christ and an observance of the ordinances of baptism and the Lord's Supper, as in the days of the apostles.

Following this, the article gives quite a full statement of the basis of unity advocated by Bro. Yeuell, which is familiar to our readers. After this statement the article closes with a description of the closing incidents of the last meeting, as follows:

At the close of the sermon Mr. Yeuell asked all those who endorsed the sermon to come forward and take his hand. Fully half the audience crowded to the front. Mr. Yeuell then said if they could thus endorse that sermon they should be willing to advocate its teachings, and asked all who would to signify in some way. There was a loud response of amens and a liberal show of hands. He last of all pressed the matter still closer and asked all who would stand by such a movement in Manchester to indicate it in some way. The response was not so prompt. The evangelist then, with a peculiar smile and remarkable tact, said, "Ah, it is one thing to endorse a generality, but will you stand by your convictions? Don't tell me you believe what I preach and come forward to take my hand and cry 'Amen,' and then act unworthy of New England, the home of liberty, political and religious." At this about a hundred hands were raised and several audible responses were made. Mr. Yeuell said it is the intention to disseminate throughout New Hampshire this broad platform of Christian unity based simply on Christ and the New Testament.

There was great demonstration of feeling while the large audience sang "Blest Be the Tie That Binds." There was general rejoicing when Mr. Yeuell said he would return and carry on the work started so auspiciously.

We submit that this was a rather remarkable demonstration when one considers that it was in a New England audience, among people who had hitherto been in ignorance of our position. Among other evidences of the widespread influence of the meeting is a letter which we have in our possession from a Baptist pastor at Nashua, N. H., who, having read the reports of the meeting in the daily papers of Manchester, writes an urgent letter to Bro. Yeuell to come to that city and conduct a union meeting there. Another letter from a lady of one of the first families of the city asks Bro. Yeuell to have THE CHRISTIAN-EVANGELIST sent her, and expresses the sincere hope that some time he may return to Manchester, and wishes him success where-ever he goes.

It would be a great mistake not to follow up such an auspicious beginning as has been made in that New England city, and our readers will be pleased to know that the intention is to follow it up vigorously with another meeting, the results of the present being con-

served, meantime, by frequent visits of Bro. W. C. Crerie, pastor of the Haverhill church, whose congregation has generously permitted this arrangement.

We submitted a financial statement last week showing a considerable shortage in the fund which had been contributed to defray the expenses of this meeting. We trust it is only necessary to state this fact to call forth from our generous readers a sufficient sum to liquidate this indebtedness and to insure the carrying on of the work.

The real significance of this New England meeting is and ought to be that it is the beginning of a more aggressive campaign in the east. Bro. W. J. Wright, the new corresponding secretary, is well acquainted with the conditions in the east, and we are sure will give his hearty sympathy to this movement for giving New England the benefit of a clear presentation of the principles of the Reformation we plead by our most capable evangelists.

❀ ❀

Current Religious Thought.

For a century nearly "our plea" has been for Christian unity. We have faithfully preached Christian unity, we rejoice in seeing even our denominational brethren cheerfully practice it. From the last "Western Christian Advocate" we learn of this beautiful fruitage in far Japan:

The Joint Commission of the Union of Methodism in Japan, composed of representatives of the Methodist Episcopal Church, North, the Methodist Episcopal Church, South, and the Methodist Church of Canada, met in the city of Buffalo, N. Y., July 18, 1906. After two days of patient and prayerful consideration, articles of union were unanimously adopted and provision made for the organization of the Methodist Church of Japan. This action, authorized by the general conferences of the said churches in the United States and Canada, was in response to the practically unanimous conviction of the pastors and members of the churches in Japan, as well as the foreign missionaries working among them. The name of the United Church will be "Nippon Methodist Kyokwai"—the Methodist Church of Japan."

The new church will begin its independent existence with a membership of over 11,650, and a native ministry of over 100. The churches in the United States and Canada will continue their active support of the work in Japan as heretofore, co-operating with the "Nippon Methodist Kyokwai."

❀

Our own history abounds in ingenious opposition to the progress of the kingdom, but nowhere does it surpass this from the "Religious Telescope" (United Brethren) opposing the proposed merger of the United Brethren, Congregational and Methodist Protestant bodies. Partly for the comfort it may give our own sorely pressed "anti" we submit this specimen of reasoning "how not to."

Is our church a child of providence? If so, then God had a special purpose in not only permitting it to be born, but in directing that birth so as to give it a distinct personality and identity, that it might, in that distinct form, serve the purpose of its birth. Is the United Brethren Church a child of providence? This is what we were taught to believe, and it is what we have taught our children to believe. When we take into consideration the peculiar circumstances connected with the founding of the church, and its subsequent success and prosperity, I think the hand of God is clearly seen. Doctor Berger

recognized this fact when he says, on page 19 of our Church History: "The founders of the Church for a long time had little thought of forming an independent church organization, and when once Providence so clearly marked out their course that they could not do otherwise, then they took those steps which must lead to a separate denominational life."

The above being true, have we a right to say and feel that the United Brethren Church, in her distinctive identity, is not a child of providence?

If she is a child of providence, then God created her for a noble purpose and mission. Is that mission performed, and has God subserved his purpose with her as a distinct organization? If so, then let her be merged into something else, and let her be no more as an independent organization. I would rather, however, see her die a natural death than have her killed by our own hands. I don't wish to stain my hands with her blood.

But what are the evidences that her mission is completed and that her work as a distinct organization is done? Has God closed the field to her? Has he ceased to bless her efforts to bring souls to Christ and build up God's kingdom? For over a century God's hand has been leading her into battle and to victory, and through her efforts hundreds of thousands of souls have been won to Christ and saved. At no time in her history has she been more wonderfully blessed than now. At no time has she done a greater work than she is doing to-day. At no time in her history has the field been open to her so wide as it is to-day. At no time has she been so competent to enter and gather the harvest as now. With her colleges and seminary, and with her well-equipped ministry and her well-trained and benevolent laity, she is competent to enter any field and compete with any foe. She is bringing more souls to Christ than ever before. In all this conclusive evidence that God's hand is still guiding, that her mission is not finished, and her work not done? In the face of all this, shall we, by forming an organic union with the above-named churches, blot her out of existence as a distinct organization?

❀ ❀

Notes and Comments.

Referring to the subject of our recent editorials on our national conventions, Bro. T. P. Haley, of Kansas City, writes: "There are certain tendencies and certain assumptions of some among us that need attention. What we need, I think, is not another convention, but a delegate convention authorized to speak for the churches. In the denominations it is esteemed an honor to be chosen a delegate to their deliberative bodies. No adequate effort has ever been made to secure such a convention among us. I have faith in our people and in our preachers and believe they can be trusted in a convention to discuss any question that concerns the welfare of our cause." President C. C. Rowlison, of Hiram College, writes: "I have read with much interest your article in last week's CHRISTIAN-EVANGELIST on "The Function and Value of National Conventions." It seems to me that you have spoken a very true word, and that there is no reason why our national conventions should become merely missionary conventions. To insist that they shall be such, will do more than anything I can conceive of, to destroy the unity and high purpose of our brotherhood. The Disciples of Christ owe their origin to freedom of speech and intelligent discussion of the great questions of religious experience and clear teaching about God and his Word. We will commit suicide if we refuse to stand upon these principles. We ought to emphatically express ourselves as opposed to all such narrowing of the purpose and character of our national conventions." There is no mistaking the sentiment of the leading men among us on this question.

Editor's Easy Chair.

PENTWATER MUSINGS.

A pine-knot fire in an open fire-place on a rainy day is worth more as a promoter of comfort and good cheer than the most costly furniture and richest upholsterings and tapestries. An open fire-place is an open sesame to happiness and peace. No family should be without one. It is Charles Dudley Warner, we believe, that speaks of the absurdity of the family group gathered about the hole in the wall, called a register! What an intrusion civilization has made upon domestic happiness by the invention of stoves, furnaces and steam coils! It is necessary, perhaps, in the present state of things, but so much the worse for the city. But think of building a summer cottage without an open fire-place! And yet some people do it, and substitute a hole in the flue for a stove pipe! As for us, we decided on the fire-place with its hearth and chimney, the first thing, and then built the remainder of the cottage around that idea! And thus it is that the Easy Chair sits to-day before a fire of glowing and crackling pine chunks, and under the magic spell of the yellow flame and red coals, is unmindful of veiled skies and dripping clouds. How the glowing embers kindle the imagination! It would be interesting to know how many poems, books and great works of art have received their primal impulse from the magic influence of the open fire with its curling flames and its radiant coals. It is associated in memory with childhood, youth and old age, all of which acknowledge its influence and yield to its spell. Blessings on the head of Prometheus, who drew the fire down from heaven, according to the ancient legend, and peace to all its votaries who offer the incense of gratitude on its glowing altars!

⚹

Every phase of life has a joy of its own when we once learn how to extract it from the outward shell of circumstances. There is a satisfaction, for instance, in the sense of completeness, as when one's house is finished and furnished, and every room is fitted up with conveniences that adapt it to the use for which it was intended. But there is another kind of joy and satisfaction in the process of bringing order out of chaos, and completeness out of incompleteness. This has been the kind of joy with which we, who make up "The Pioneer" household, have had to content ourselves during the present summer. For a month we have been witnessing the transformation of a pile of lumber into a house, until it has reached that stage in its development in which the carpenters have practically finished their work, and we have taken up the work of the smaller details, which, after all have so much to do with making a house a real dwelling place. "Every house is built by some one," says the author of the Hebrew letter, "but he who built all things is God." Right. Houses do not grow by "resident forces," nor are they

the results of accident or chance. Every house, even though it be a summer cottage, that is to be a human dwelling place, must be carefully thought out in its general plan and in all its details, if it is to serve well the purpose for which it is intended. It is a real pleasure, however, to see one's plans taking tangible form, and coming to completion. But the supreme Architect and Builder, as the inspired writer quoted above states, is God himself. What a magnificent structure is this material universe! How even this planet upon which we live showeth his handiwork! And yet this world is only in the making. What must it be when he shall put upon it the last finishing touch? Meanwhile, his is the joy of seeing the cosmos come out of chaos, and all his moral creation growing slowly, but steadily, into conformity to his divine plan.

⚹

Speaking of the joy that is associated with imperfection and incompleteness, is this not about the only kind of joy that human beings can have in this world? Who of us is not impressed, increasingly with the passing years, with the incompleteness and imperfection of his own life? Who of us ever realizes his ideals here in this life? How slowly our characters develop into the Christlikeness! As we grow older in Christian life and experience, our imperfections seem to be more apparent and our faults more glaring, than they once seemed to us. The best people who have ever lived in the world have been compelled to exclaim, with the Apostle Paul, "I have not yet attained; I am not yet perfect!" It is not this sense of imperfection that gives us any joy, but the belief that, with the help of God, we are gradually growing out of our imperfections, and that one day we shall see him as he is, and be like him. Even our life-work here must remain incomplete. None of us can hope to realize here on earth all our plans and accomplish all our purposes. When the evening time comes and our sun is setting, unfinished work will lie all about us. But we need not repine at this fact. Our Master knoweth best. Perhaps he has some higher and better work for us to do elsewhere. Perhaps those who come after us can carry out, much better than we, our unfinished plans. In any event, we can not doubt that somewhere, under better conditions, we grow into that completeness and perfection which the soul craves and which are denied us here. And so, with Paul, we "press on toward the goal, for the prize of our high calling in Christ Jesus," not knowing, as John tells us, "what we shall be," but knowing that when Christ shall be manifested we shall see him and be like him. Surely that is enough!

⚹

Our little colony here at Pentwater grows steadily. The Stows from Grand Rapids, the Denholmes from New Orleans, and Mrs. W. T. Moore from Columbia, are among the latest arrivals. Mrs. R. B. Moore, of Indianapolis, is expected to-morrow and W. F. Richardson and wife, of Kansas City, are coming about the 22d instant. Those who

come once, they say, get the Pentwater habit and come ever afterward. We have had refreshing rains of late which will bring out later vegetables and small fruits. The peach season is on here now. And this county (Oceana) is the banner fruit county of the state. We have never known the flavor of peaches to be better than it is this year. Even the fish have a good flavor, this year! If our old confirmed anglers who read the Easy Chair, could have seen the brace or pair of black bass we carried home last night it would have made their mouths water! Brother Stow was witness and *particeps criminis* to the transaction which occurred right in the channel near where the little ferry crosses. With characteristic unselfishness he was doing the rowing, while the Easy Chair sat in the rear of the boat, trolling with an artificial minnow. Suddenly there was a yank on the line, and then a large Tiger bass (smallmouthed) leaped from the water fifty or seventy-five feet in rear of the boat, and the tug began! Brother Stow in his excitement, advised us to abandon the rod and reel and pull him in hand over hand, but of course we took no chances of that kind. When he was safely landed in the boat, the experience was so delightful we turned about and repeated it with the same result. Like true sportsmen having caught enough for one day, we desisted. When Judge Montgomery, of the supreme court of Michigan, saw us carrying those bass home he said he could readily do the same thing but he was afraid it would make him proud! Is there anything quite so cruel as envy?

⚹

Looking out over the brotherhood from this our northern perch by the lake side, there seems to be a great deal going on among us in the way of religious activity. Even the summer resorts are becoming centers of religious interest, while great meetings are being reported in different sections of the country. This is as it should be. Rest does not mean laziness, nor idleness. The next offering on the calendar is that for church extension, and we imagine the churches—the real live churches—everywhere are rolling up their sleeves in preparation for a great offering. The indomitable secretary learned through the Easy Chair that a few Disciples were meeting here in an upper room "to break bread," after the manner of primitive Christians, and he has sent us a notice of our apportionment for church extension. Think of a faith like that, not to call it by another name! A homeless, preacherless church give to church extension? We venture the prediction that his faith will be rewarded by the receipt of the sum for which he asks. Because this little band wants to grow into a strong Church of Christ, and it doesn't know of any other way to make such growth, than by joining heartily with the brethren in doing the Lord's work. We are to have an interesting union meeting here next Lord's day, of which we will give report later. Grace, mercy and peace be multiplied to the churches everywhere through the knowledge and service of our Lord Jesus Christ, to whom be glory and dominion forever and ever! Amen.

As Seen From the Dome   By F. D. Powel

From Naples to Nice is not a long journey. We said good-bye to the beautiful bay, and the threatening old monster that dominates all this fair region, at 11 o'clock in the day, and early next morning, were in sight of the Maritime Alps. We passed Elba and Corsica on the way—islands so intimately associated with the world's champion butcher. Nice is a city of 90,000, the Queen of the Riviera. In front the blue Mediterranean smiles with myriad dimples to the clear-cut horizon; on every side a vast semi-circle of mountains. It is the cosmopolitan winter capital of fashionable seekers after health and pleasure. Garibaldi was born here, and Massena and Gambetta are buried here. It dates from the fifth century B. C. and was Nicaea, "Victory." It shows such a panorama of sea and mountain, such flowers and waves and soft air and sunshine; such orange and lemon groves and olive and fig orchards, such gardens and villas, as one seldom sees on earth. It is not given over wholly to "the fitful and fearsome joys of the Casino." Nature has made it beautiful, and for its rare loveliness of scenery every one is enraptured by it. Mediterranean color, Mediterranean sunshine, Mediterranean romance and poetry, lend it enchantment. A river runs through it, the Paillon, which is nearly dry, and thronged with washerwomen, and miles of garments hung up to dry. It looks as if all the great multitude of the unwashed came to Nice to get washed up for Sunday. It is a paradise for consumptives, and has an endless array of sun worshippers gathered together to this temple of the sun from all the four quarters of the habitable globe. For us, however, it was a raw atmosphere, and while we had the vision of palms and blossoming trees, of rich geraniums and mignonette, and banksia roses falling in cataracts over the walls, of luxuriant festoons of honeysuckle and mimosa draping the trellis-work arcades, and beds of pansies and anemones, and tropical gardens in villa courts, of olive and lemon and orange trees laden with fruit, we had to button our overcoats up to the throat and face a snow shower. Still, Nice is known as the gay and rose-wreathed queen of the smiling Riviera, as the Riviera is known as the garden of Europe, and away from frost and cold, away from the fogs and bronchitis of northern climes come the poor winter exiles to the visions of gray olives shimmering silvery in the breeze on its mountain slopes, and the cataracts of Marechal Niels falling over its gray limestone walls, and aloes and cactuses on its sun-smitten rocks; and its deep blue waters playing under cloudless blue skies. It is the smiling coast from Marseilles to Genoa that is known as "the Riviera." Nice, Monte Carlo and Mentone are the best known resorts. The Maritime Alps cut off the sharp northerly winds, and here at their feet is a sort of Eden of beauty and delight.

It is a wonderful, little principality, this of Monaco, at the corner where France and Italy come together, a little independent kingdom in itself, hemmed in between high mountains and the assailing sea. It has its prince and its individuality, and its world-wide fame. Monte Carlo is its center of power, and all the world knows it. We took the upper Corniche road for 15 miles from Nice. No one who has ever passed over that route has forgotten it or will forget it. There is no road in the world like the road from Nice to Monte Carlo, unless it be that from Monte Carlo to Nice. The famous Corniche route runs along a ledge high up on the beetling side of the promontory, and looks down from a height of 1,500 feet upon the sea and its ships riding at anchor. Its windings unfold on either side charming views of the Mediterranean. It is a triumph of engineering built on the mountain side. It affords constant and ever-varying pictures of the quaint ridge of land crowned by the strange capital of the tiny principality which shelters one of the plague spots of the world. As you look down on Monte Carlo from the heights of the Corniche you see without a doubt the most picturesque town site in all Europe, and feel that the devil has chosen for his little hell a veritable Eden of beauty. On every side save seaward great mountains gird it; then the blue, smiling Mediterranean, its rippling waves breaking in soft lace-like foam on the rocks, and beyond streaked with many colors in its many beautiful bays; at your feet the red-tiled houses and white palaces, with their blooming gardens, all lie spread out, like some perfect picture painted in the bright blue of Mediterranean seas, the dazzling gray of Mediterranean sunshine and the brilliant russet of Mediterranean roofs. So winding about, seemingly so near and yet so far, getting at every turn a finer prospect than before, the marvelous road at last leads you down into the streets of the little city, and then one wonders more and more at the picturesqueness of the buildings, often perched high up on the bold, rocky elevations. It is a surpassingly lovely spot. And the center of Monte Carlo is the Casino. With all the charm of the surroundings, it is to many a man and woman a gaping mouth to the bottomless pit. It is a fair representation of the fabled Isle of the Syrens. Lovely by nature, the grounds of the great gambling hell are made still more lovely by art. From the water's edge terraces of tropical vegetation succeed each other in gradual steps toward the grand facade of the gaming house, clusters of palms and aloes, beds of exotic flowers and beautiful lawns, and trees arranged skilfully to bring bay and mountains to view in most artistic vistas, and then the glare of lights and the dazzle of brilliantly gowned and jewelled women, and glare of exquisite music and fine painting and sculpture. Entering the great palace, you pass under the eye of numerous liveried attendants, and, if acceptable, receive your ticket of admission, remove your wraps and pass in and mingle with the great throngs of men and women. One is struck at once by the exceeding seriousness of the groups about the gambling machines. Crowds gather about every table, pressing upon each other in their eagerness to stake their money, and all quiet and terribly in earnest. One can see on their faces how strained and tense, and yet fearfully excited and swayed by fierce passion, many of the gamblers are. Women are as infatuated as men. Some have piles of gold before them and play with the utmost skill and desperate hazard. It is a mistake to suppose they are played against each other—they are pitted against the machine. In the principal game there is a wheel of fortune which is turned on a long table by the managers of the bank and a tiny ball goes whirling around a disk marked with numbers. The silver and gold are placed by the gamblers on corresponding numbers on a diagram on the table. When the ball stops on a number corresponding to yours on the table you win, and a certain sum goes into your pocket and all the rest on the table goes to the bank. It is a skin game where the bank has 35 chances to the player's one, and only an idiot would ever risk his money on it; yet thousands are drawn into this awful whirlpool and swallowed up. A million of dollars changing hands daily and a score of suicides every month will tell the story. Many who venture their money and their reputations on the remorseless and certain rock of destruction are professed Christians. It is a terrible spot which the nations should unite in wiping out. Its baneful work affects not only French and Italian young men and women, but Germany, England, America and all the nations suffer from this iniquity. The whole town of Monte Carlo is kept up by this accursed thing. The Prince of Monaco leases the Casino to the company managing it. The church, even is called "the Church of Our Lady of the Roulette." The gold and silver which is relentlessly raked in at these tables every hour would seem enough to enrich a kingdom. One looks on in astonishment at this perfect illustration of the wise man's word that "the fool and his money are soon parted," and one wonders at the cool and unblushing legalized robbery going on before his very eyes. It was not without a feeling of relief we turned away from this place of exquisite beauty and gilded yet hellish sin. A drive along the Lower Corniche road, and we found ourselves again on the good ship Arabic, and were soon steaming away toward Liverpool. The journey through the Western Mediterranean, along the coast of France, through the Balearic Islands, and the Spanish waters, brings us again to the Straits of Gibraltar; and then northward, in all a seven days' sea voyage before we reach our starting point for America. This season, we understand, Monte Carlo has broken its record, hundreds of thousands more than last year to the credit of "the bank." Sometimes the public wins. A young Polish count, Jean Sobansky, recently, late in the evening, gathered in $70,000. With its printers and its croupiers and all its gold and glory it is a moral Vesuvius in eruption.

Religious Bosses   By William Durban

For many years I have been impressed with the conviction that the valuable influence involved in gifted personality is habitually so sadly abused that the overshadowing ascendency of great individuals is for, the most part an evil. I used to think it a blessing. I have come to consider that it is generally a bane.

The Universal Popery.

After Martin Luther had achieved his emancipation from Romanist superstition he thought for a time that he had absolutely done with popery. So indeed he had, in the ecclesiastical sense. But before long he exclaimed, "Alas! every man is born with a pope in his own stomach." It does not appear to be realized, even by the acutest observers, that the papistical bacteria swarm everywhere, so that on all sides men spring up, in church and in state alike, who pose as miniature autocrats. In my own country, the masters who are most cordially detested by their workmen are those who have risen from the ranks of the employes. For they too often become tyrants of industry, expecting those beneath them to grovel at their feet. The reason is simple. The native pope in the stomach has found scope for his development; that is all!

The Tyranny of the Individual.

My topic has nothing whatever to do with individualism and socialism. I make this proviso lest the mention of "the individual" might raise a suspicion that I am going to drag the kind reader into a very familiar quagmire. I like to avoid bottomless bogs. Those can flounder there who will. I look up with deference and admiration to every individual better and greater than myself. And I revere those who are within the right spirit seeking to work out some brighter social ideal than any yet attained. So I am a socialist-individualist, as the New Testament teaches us that Jesus and the apostles were. The Gospel for those who really apprehend its beauty and its truth contains the exact principles of perfect economics. But individualism and socialism alike encounter a crucial difficulty. That obstacle lies in human nature. Godet reminds us that wherever Paul planted any church he invariably found that very soon his work was marred by the perversity or malignity of some obtrusive spirit. All who attempt apostolic enterprise make the same melancholy discovery.

My point, however, is that even great and noble souls have wrought irrepressible harm by their attitude of domination and their autocratic sway. The political world has abounded in records which demonstrate the force of my proposition. As long as Lord Palmerston lived no other statesman had any chance of becoming premier. He was the uncrowned secondary king of England. But he became a puppet in the hands of Napoleon III. and was foolish enough to plunge Europe into the awful Crimean War, under the miserable auspices of that "Napoleon the Little." Mr. Gladstone was the greatest statesman Britain ever knew, and was a shining Christian. But his influence became so overmastering that he unconsciously played the political despot, provoked a rupture in his Cabinet and in Parliament, and flung the nation into political chaos. Still more infatuated did the nation become with the "Cecilian legend" under the power of the late Marquis of Salisbury. Till he in failing health gave up his sceptre, he could and did wield it as a rod of iron. The people are suffering to-day most keenly from the effects of the obscurantist Toryism, which under Salisbury brought back mediaevalism, feudalism and utter contempt for the common people. But strangest of all was the influence of Salisbury's predecessor and master, Lord Beaconsfield, who as Benjamin D'Israeli has been the brilliant rival of Gladstone when both were young. The nation grovelled abjectly at Beaconsfield's feet. He made the good and wise Victoria Empress of India, and his blandishments even infatuated her, so that she seemed to lean decidedly towards the Tory party, in spite of her loyalty to constitutionalism. And thus there are always men who seem by their commanding attributes able to bewitch others and to hypnotize the vast majority of those around them. Such men become the sovereigns of "the sovereign people." Bismarck, Cavour, Ignatieff, Thiers, Parnell, Gambetta, have in their days of domination shown what one man of transcendent capacity could do. With few exceptions, such influence has wrought evil issues in the end.

Despots of Divinity.

How many careers have been blighted and how many hearts have been broken in ministerial circles by those who have been born with the insatiable lust for power, and have found scope for its exercise will never be known. But everybody of protracted experience too well knows that in all the religious bodies sad suffering has resulted from the personal predominance of certain men who have secured great influence, as well as from the abuse of authority by many officials. Some of the saddest of all quiet martyrdoms have been endured at the hands of inquisitors who strange to say, were never weary of proclaiming themselves the elect upraised champions of spiritual freedom from the tyranny of the sects. I happened years ago to make acquaintance with John Nelson Darby, the famous nephew of Lord Nelson, and the founder of the peculiar clique of earnest Christians popularly known as Strict Plymouth Brethren, in contradistinction from the section split off from them under George Muller and Benjamin Wills Newton, known as the Open Plymouth Brethren. Wherever you meet any members of the various

❖ ❖

bodies of "Brethren," for there are now many splits of the original splits, and splits are being born yet, you will always find that they vehemently denounce sectism, boast of their mission to restore the unity of the Christian church, and deny that they belong to any kind of sect or denomination. But always in each congregation of these good people some boss springs up. In time he finds other bosses competing with him, and there is generally a conflict with clamorous protests about the authority of the Holy Spirit alone. The Brethren began well. There was good cause for their origin. But Darby and Newton spoilt the whole movement. It was bossed to death. And wherever we look there are parallels. I turn to the Anglican Church. The high churchmen have their aristocratic autocrat in Earl Nelson. His personal ascendancy vitiates the plea made by his followers for a revival of spiritual life in the Church of England. And no sooner was the estimable Canon Gore elevated to the Episcopal bench than he forgot all his broad church confessions and began to persecute a parish clergyman for alleged heresy. In America the secretary of the Baptist annual congress, Dr. Gessler, has been telling me, in talking of his reminiscences, how a learned and beloved university professor, who was his tutor, was relentlessly persecuted and at length expelled by the authorities, dying soon afterwards broken-hearted.

Whence Proceeds the Autocracy?

My younger readers can, I suppose, hardly appreciate the importance of the topic I have chosen for this article. But older men can. They know that the producing cause of the boss, and of bossism is composite. It proceeds primarily from the individual spirit of Diotrephes, and secondarily from the tendency of sectarians to develop a zeal amounting to fanaticism in the interests of their own opinions. I remember how in my youth many an English Congregationalist minister and deacon was smarting at the memory of the overbearing dealings of Dr. Campbell, who edited for some years a paper called "The Standard," and used his position with remorseless cruelty whenever he felt constrained to differ from preachers of broader views than himself. That poet preacher, T. T. Lynch, suffered many things at the hands of this Congregationalist boss. During the last years of his life the beloved C. H. Spurgeon was betrayed into playing the theological boss. He attempted to straighten out the theology of the whole of the Baptist denomination, broke up his great annual conference and remodeled it on narrow evangelical lines, with a Calvinistic creed which all must sign, and only suffered acutely himself from the rebellion of a large contingent of his young followers, some of whom were amongst the ablest preachers who had gone forth from his college. The noblest leaders commit errors of procedure. I have just received a letter from the most brilliant young Wesleyan minister I know in England. He draws very large congregations. But he is being bitterly pursued by certain casehardened old leaders in his own circuit and some circuits adjoining. He has preached fearlessly along lines of thought not always strictly according to Methodist tradition. He has been made to smart for his individuality. He complains that, excellent though Methodism is in many features of its organization, its theology is of a cast-iron type. He was recently cordially invited to a very fine new district, but certain powers behind the scenes intervened and nullified the overtures. Enough! I might proceed, but this time desist.

What the Brethren Are Saying and Doing

By B. B. Tyler

Herbert Yeuell's reports of his work at Manchester, N. H., have awakened my interest and excited my enthusiasm from the beginning. The climacteric report is that in THE CHRISTIAN-EVANGELIST of August 2. It is certainly a great thing to have an audience of 1,000 interested people the last Lord's day evening in the month of July. To call together such a congregation at such a time, to have almost one-third of those present formally endorse the preaching and express sympathy with the new movement, while 100 express a readiness to become members of the to-be-organized church, is a most extraordinary achievement, especially under the circumstances existing in the city of Manchester. How many ministers of the Word in the United States, suppose you, preached to a thousand men and women Sunday evening, July 29? It will be interesting to see their names in print. I thank God for young men who can assemble such audiences and excite their interest in the things of the kingdom.

But the writer of "Our Budget," in what he says about this effort to organize a church in Manchester, did not, it seems to me, express himself clearly, or say exactly what he meant, when he spoke of the potential congregation as a church "patterned in every particular after the Jerusalem model."

It is to be hoped that the church which will be organized in Manchester will be a better congregation than was the church in Jerusalem. In some respects the congregation in Jerusalem was a model—in other respects it was not. It had the right creed and the right ordinances. The foundation of the church was exactly right. It rested on the Christ as the chief corner stone. The people of which the church was composed faced in the right direction. This is the best that one can say for the church in Jerusalem. It is true that it was an example of liberality in caring for its own poor. But that to the credit of the Jerusalem congregation; but, its charity was not dignified and orderly. The members meant well, but, in a short time were in a snarl because some were, as they thought, neglected in the distribution of alms. "Lessons from the Jerusalem church" would be a good subject for a sermon. Try it!

This church was not a missionary congregation. It made no attempt, so far as the record furnishes information, to obey the command of the Christ to herald the good news to the whole creation. It is more than probable that an uncircumcised Gentile believer would not have been cordially received into its fellowship nor have been given a welcome to the Lord's table. The Jerusalem congregation was an anti-missionary, close communion, Hebrew Christian church. The most conspicuous member of this church did not, for a long time, understand that in every nation he who fears God and works righteousness is acceptable to him; and it required a miracle thrice times repeated, before he was able to grasp this fundamental principle of Christianity, and this was years after the beginning of the church. This good man scorned to associate with men of Gentile birth and breeding. The Jerusalem church was pretty narrow. Don't you think so? It is not referred to by any writer in the New Testament as a "model." Paul spoke of the congregation in Thessalonica as an "example"— but not the church in Jerusalem. Paul did not stand well in that church. But for the influence of Barnabas he would not have been recognized by it as a Disciple of Christ. See how, years after his conversion, the members of the Jerusalem church felt toward him, and how they treated him, on account of the catholicity of his spirit. Do not fail as you study this "model" (?) church to note the kind of teachers who went out from it, the doctrine they taught, and the serious trouble of which they were the occasion. Collect all that is said in the New Testament about the Jerusalem congregation and you will join with me, I am sure, in the wish that the church to be organized in Manchester, N. H., may be more like the head of the body, even our Lord Jesus Christ, than was "the Jerusalem model."

When my mail came in this morning I found in a paper DEVOTED TO THE RESTORATION OF PRIMITIVE CHRISTIANITY, ITS DOCTRINES, ITS ORDINANCES AND ITS FRUITS, a picture of a meeting-house around which was a multitude of people, and under which were the following words:

"An independent Church of Christ near Minden, Neb. These are mostly Danes. This church is only partially organized, but as far as I know, these are all IMMERSED BELIEVERS WHO PRACTICE NOTHING ELSE."

This is good. "Immersed believers who practice nothing else."

Such believers are numerous in Colorado. There is an indefinite number of "immersed believers" in the middle west, and even in the district east, "who practice nothing else."

Immersed men and women, who believe in Jesus Christ our Lord, ought to practice, habitually, many other things. To stop with immersion is to make a fatal mistake. Immersed believers ought to practice self control, patience, godliness and brotherly kindness. They ought to practice prayer and the forgiveness of injuries. They ought to take the Lord into partnership in the making and in the spending of money. Out of every dollar that the immersed believer earns, or makes, he ought to lay by at least 10 cents to be used in helping all men, especially those who are members of the household of the faith, and in the promotion of righteousness among men. There are altogether too many immersed believers in our churches "who practice nothing else."

But this, of course, is not what the brother meant. He did not mean that the baptized Danes, of whom he wrote, do not practice the virtues named. He meant to say that when they baptized folks they immerse them in water, they do not sprinkle water on believers and call it baptism. They do not pour water on men and women who believe in the Christ and call it baptism. When persons believe in their hearts that Jesus is the Christ, the Son of God, when they repent of their sins, and openly confess Christ, they are immersed in water, into the name of the Father, and of the Son, and of the Holy Spirit. And this

these Danes call baptism. In this they are indisputably right. Their position is invulnerable. No one calls it in question; the man does not live who will say that penitent believers immersed in water, with the accompanying formula, have not been baptized.

And this baptism is, on the part of the baptized, a solemn agreement entered into with the Head of the Body that they will endeavor to be and to do, at all times, in all places, and under all circumstances, whatever the Lord Jesus desires them to be and to do. This is what baptism means. There is no step more solemn; none more important.

Denver, Colo.

Modern Religious Persecution---A Defense
By B. L. Chase

5. Instructions to Persecutors.

In carrying on your arduous, delicate and ill-reputed business, among an independent and free people like the Disciples, perhaps the experience of one who has been a long and careful observer of persecuting methods and their effects will be helpful to you.

First of all, I would say, read the Scriptures, especially the Old Testament. You will need mental and spiritual preparation to brace you for your work; you must remember that the heretic and his friends do not see the malignity of his crime as you do. They are at first, likely to resent your interference with his work, and will inquire who appointed you a judge over him. They think you are a man of like passions with themselves—as likely to be mistaken, to be biased, and to be mercenary, as themselves. But they do not realize the purity and unselfishness of your motives, the infallibility of your discernment, the universality of your learning.

I would especially recommend for your reading, parts of the books of Joshua and the Judges, Judges 4:21, would be especially strengthening just before you are about to open a professor's head and show his college trustees and supporters its diseased contents. The passage reads: "Then Joel, Heber's wife took a tent-pin, and took a hammer in her hand, and went softly unto him, and smote the pin into his temples, and it pierced through into the ground; for he was in a deep sleep." Be sure to catch the professor when he is asleep, as most of them are when they need your services. Be careful, however, to show to the brethren who contribute money to the college, only the diseased parts of his brain. If you should find, on opening, that it was only slightly diseased, have near by you the diseased brains of famous infidels, and stealthily substitute them for the sound parts of the professor's brain, so that his brain will appear completely diseased. It will be immaterial what infidel's brains you have ready, whether Celsus, Voltaire, Paine or Ingersoll. Make sure that they look bad and emit a very disagreeable odor. What you want is a clear case at any cost.

Of course I am speaking figuratively, you know what I mean. It would certainly be embarrassing to attach the name "infidel" to a man and then let him get away and disprove it to the people. A few such mistakes have happened in our recent history. It is rather hurtful to your business. Better wait until you have a decisive case worked up against him. Two or three more failures may discredit your sanctity and infallibility. Above all things you must carry the people with you, for they support both the persecutors and professors. It would be disastrous to turn away the support from yourself to the accused. But in such a case the very best thing to do is to acknowledge your mistake, for what you lose of infallibility in the one case, you get back in the repute for fairness in the latter case. Then you can remind the people that you were imposed upon by the witnesses, and they will take out their contempt on the rascally witnesses. The people easily forget such things any way, especially if you keep right on preaching their convictions. A cause so holy as the exposure of heresy is sure to find support.

Another group of Old Testament passages which it would be helpful to read, would be the "imprecatory Psalms." Let me caution you against reading the New Testament while you have a man on trial. Don't read the Sermon on the Mount, or the 13th chapter of I. Corinthians, for experience has shown that they are very debilitating to the persecutor. Men will rise up in defense of the heretic and will talk senseless things about love, brotherliness and freedom. Don't listen to their siren voices. Liberty has always been the plea of the accused heretic. He desires to be free to poison the streams of life, and to deny you the freedom to prevent it. Luther desired to be free to change the constitution of the church to suit his fancy. His strike for liberty filled all Europe with war. How gloriously our New England fathers beat back the encroachments of liberty. They understood what a foul thing it was. One wrote:

"Let men of God in courts and churches watch,
O'er such as do a toleration hatch,
Lest that ill egg bring forth a cocatrice,
To poison all with heresy and vice."

They banished the so-called "apostle of religious liberty," Roger Williams; hung the Quakers who died with a plea for liberty upon their lips, and strangled all dissent. They are said to have cultivated familiarity with Old Testment history.

If objections to your persecutions remind you of the claims of love and brotherhood, remind them of what God's faithful servants of olden time did with the enemies of Jehovah, how Joshua put the people of Jericho to death, "both man and woman, both young and old;" how

❀

AN OLD TIMER
Has Had Experiences.

A woman who has used Postum Food Coffee since it came upon the market 8 years ago knows from experience the necessity of using Postum in place of coffee if one values health and a steady brain.

She says: "At the time Postum was first put on the market I was suffering from nervous dyspepsia and my physician had repeatedly told me not to use tea or coffee. Finally I decided to take his advice and try Postum, and got a sample and had it carefully prepared, finding it delicious to the taste. So I continued its use and very soon its beneficial effects convinced me of its value for I got well of my nervousness and dyspepsia.

"My husband had been drinking coffee all his life until it had affected his nerves terribly. I persuaded him to shift to Postum and it was easy to get him to make the change for the Postum is so delicious. It certainly worked wonders for him.

"We soon learned that Postum does not exhilarate or depress and does not stimulate, but steadily and honestly strengthens the nerves and the stomach. To make a long story short our entire family have now used Postum for eight years with completely satisfying results as shown in our fine condition of health and we have noticed a rather unexpected improvement in brain and nerve power." Name given by Postum Co., Battle Creek, Mich.

Increased brain and nerve power always follow the use of Postum in place of coffee, sometimes in a very marked manner.

Look in pkgs. for "The Road to Wellville."

the people of Israel under the direction of the prophets slaughtered the Canaanites, the Amalekites and the Philistines; how Elijah commanded the prophets of Baal, more than four hundred in number, to be slain; then ask the objectors how they could possibly object to so mild and kind a treatment of a heretic among the Disciples as to cut off his living and his usefulness. You do not forbid him to live, but simply to get a living by preaching or teaching among the Disciples.

Under the specious pretense of charity or liberty a brood of errors might creep into the teaching of our colleges and churches. The people of the churches and the students of the colleges need protection. They are ignorant of the fine points of heresy and infidelity. Students and people alike are as helpless in the hands of preachers and teachers as David would have been if he had met Goliath without a sling. We need preachers to watch the people; we need persecutors to watch the preachers and professors; but the persecutors give account directly to God. There is nobody above them but God.

In case you single out for exposure a professor with a large family of little children to care for, I would recommend that you prepare yourself by reading, in addition to the "Wars of Israel," the story of "French and Indian Wars." It will have a tendency to allay all foolish compunctions of conscience. I have said nothing of the histories of the "Inquisition of the Middle Ages," by Lea, or of his later work, the first volume of which has just come out on "The Spanish Inquisition." I took for granted your familiarity with them, and with the story of your illustrious predecessors in office, Torquemada and the Duke of Alva.

Our Great Agreements

An Illustration From the Himalaya Mountains
By G. L. WHARTON

It was on the Himalaya mountains over 7,000 feet above sea level. A Christian Endeavor Society had been organized composed of the missionaries and their families and friends who were thrown together for a time. It was composed of different kinds of Presbyterians, Baptists, Methodists, Disciples and several Church of England young people. At one of our meetings it was proposed that we try to get the Church of England chaplain to join us. Some thought it would be useless, for he was known to be a high ritualist. The society, however, appointed your correspondent to visit the reverend gentleman and invite him to join us.

I called at his residence one morning before breakfast and sent in my card. He received me coolly but with courtesy. I at once made known my purpose, saying that I had come to see if he would not join our society. He remarked that it could hardly be for, he said, "I am a high churchman, you know."

"Yes," I replied, "and I am no churchman at all; yet I believe that we agree in many more things than we differ."

"I hardly know," he replied doubtfully.

I had made some preparation for this part of our conversation, so I said, "Let us see in how many things we do agree," taking out a paper from my pocket. I suggested that we write down our agreements first and then our disagreements and then compare them. With this he seemed pleased and interested. I began:

1. "We agree that there is one God and that he is our Heavenly Father."

"Oh, certainly," he replied.

2. "We agree that Jesus is the Christ the Son of God and our Savior."

"Most surely," he said.

3. "We agree that the Holy Spirit is given to all God's people as a guide and comfort in all times of trouble."

"Yes, I do," he said.

4. "We agree that the Bible is the Word of God, and is the only sure and perfect rule of faith and practice."

To this he gave most hearty assent.

5. "We agree that salvation is through the atoning sacrifice and grace of our Lord and Savior Jesus Christ and not from any merit in human works."

"Most certainly," he replied.

6. "We agree that it is the duty of all Christians to live a holy, righteous and godly life after the pattern of our Master, Christ."

"Yes," he said.

7. "We agree that the Gospel is the power of God unto salvation and that it must be preached in all the world according to the Great Commission."

To this he replied with a hearty affirmative.

8. "We agree that it is the desire and prayer of Jesus our Lord that all who believe on him should be one that the world may believe."

"Yes."

9. "We agree that Christ will come again in glory to judge the world in righteousness."

"Certainly," he affirmed.

10. "We agree that there will be a resurrection of the dead—both the just and the unjust—at his appearing, and that he will give a crown of life to all who love his appearing."

To this he gave assent as usual.

(Cotinued on Page 1053.)

The Field of Sport By Andrew Scott

A time for everything. A time to make merry and a time for prayer. A time to work and a time for play. It is not our purpose to argue the necessity or the helpfulness of legitimate sport. Recreation follows creation and many so-called sports are regarded by people in a position to know, as the best means, under proper conditions, of recreation known to them. We concede then the right of men to fish, boat, run, jump, play ball, hunt, etc. We are now concerned simply with the time of these things. I admit that the kind and character of sport; its place and environment are questions worthy of our attention. The time of it is the question of the hour. I am aware of the fact that this question touches other questions which might properly be considered with it. The abnormal interest taken in sport by many at this time is having much to do in fixing the time of it, but we must, for fear of diverting attention from the main issue, refrain from going into these things now.

Our fathers had a Lord's day of quiet worship and rest. Our Lord's day is desecrated. We are greatly disturbed on every hand. Excursions, picnics, ball games and resorts galore interfere with the quiet and rest of the day most sacred of all. The shriek of the locomotive and the cheer from the ball game disturb the worship of the sanctuary. This is not all. The day set apart to the memory of the departed loved ones, May 30, has already become the greatest of all the days of the year for games and sport of all kinds. The day set apart for thanksgiving and family reunions is perverted in the same way. The time would fail me to tell of labor day, Washington and Lincoln's birthdays, etc., when the spirit of sport takes possesion and holds high carnival regardless of the importance or sacredness of the day. If things keep on in this way we shall soon be unable to have a funeral without a picnic-basket, a ball-bat or a fire cracker bobbing up to claim the right of way. I protest against this usurpation. While conceding the legitimacy of healthful, helpful sport we object to its encroachment on sacred days and hours set apart for purposes high as heaven and holy as our God. Let a day be set apart for recreation when proper and helpful sports may be indulged in to the pleasure and satisfaction of all. Such day may be annual or monthly, or even weekly, if thought best. Many who indulge in recreation on the Lord's day violate their conscience in so doing. The temptation is set before them and their love of sport causes them to yield. Their conscience is violated. It becomes seared as with a hot iron and ceases to trouble them. This is dangerous. Recreation thus becomes dissipation and not only religion but good morals are damaged and wrecked. The nation is in danger. History is repeating itself. Remember Rome. Our civilization and government are founded on Christianity. Let us not desecrate its institutions and laws. Let ministers and editors cry aloud and spare not and let all good citizens aid in rescuing our sacred days from desecration and thus help save our people and nation.

Danville, Ill.

Our Budget

—"One thing thou lackest!"

—Let us frankly concede its universal application.

—We sweetly admit lack of perfection in our friends and our wives' relatives.

—But how about me?—aye there's the rub,—

"O wad some power the giftie gie us
To see oursilves as ithers see us."

—There is no virtue in merely confessing shortcomings and in meek resignation to lack of even one thing needful to make men or congregations better and more useful.

—Schedule, inventory, take stock, probe, hammer, drop the plummett, use the microscope and mirror, learn your lack. It is generally discovered when on one's knees, or standing in the white light raying forth from the immediate presence of the immaculate Son of God.

—If the lack is courage, go with Moses to Egypt's throneroom; if optimism, read THE CHRISTIAN-EVANGELIST; if faith, walk with Abraham; if brotherly love, scan one of our contemporaries and experience *similia similibus curantur*; if patience, remember heaven's long sufferance of you; if it is a sense of direction, stand with Isaiah on mountains of hope as divine purposes unfurl; if zeal, go forth one day with the apostles preaching the everlasting Gospel. In some way quickly complete your equipment and work for the night cometh.

—Let every pledge for foreign missions be redeemed before September 30. Please send your offerings at once.

—H. J. Reynolds, Camp Point, Ill., wishes the services of a good gospel singer for a meeting with his home church beginning November 18.

—Ernest H. Wylie is in a good meeting at Enterprise, Texas. Brother Wylie is an able Gospel preacher and will doubtless greatly edify that enterprising church.

—Our general superintendent will preach next Lord's day morning at the Mexico (Mo.) Chautauqua. He hopes while there to meet many of the central Missouri preachers and other disciples.

—The handsome new $6,000 church building at Jellico, Tenn., will be dedicated early in October. Tennessee is making many handsome contributions of late to our church architecture.

—The foreign society is sending forth a splendid body of new missionaries to foreign lands next month. This step will involve an increased outlay. The friends of the work must bear this in mind.

—We regret to learn of the dangerous illness of the wife of our Missouri state corresponding secretary. The prayers of all her friends are solicited, to the end that Sister Abbott's health may be completely restored to her.

—In the two weeks' meeting recently closed at Lebanon, Texas, J. P. Adcock added 13 to the membership of the church. Of these six were by confession and baptism, three from Baptists and one from Methodists.

—R. B. Havener, of Windsor, Mo., dedicated the Alder Springs, Mo., church the 5th instant. All indebtedness was fully paid, and better than that, during the services five dedicated their lives to the Master's service.

—Robert B. Chapman, of the Butler, Ind., church, informs us the Disciples of DeKalb county will hold their yearly meeting with his church August 25 and 26. Wallace Tharp, of Allegheny City, has been secured as chief lecturer.

—J. F. Sloan is supplying C. A. Finch's pulpit at Topeka, Kan., during the latter's vacation. The middle of September Brother Sloan will take his departure for Los Angeles, Cal. He will greatly help any church in which he ministers.

—Wren J. Grinstead, of Jellico, Tenn., knows of five excellent fields of usefulness, with salaries ranging from $800 to $1,000, to which he would like to recommend suitable ministers, if applicants will send him good recommendations as to fitness.

—We are pleased to again welcome to our desk the "Pacific Christian," that has emerged from its baptism of fire bright, newsy, consecrated to the extension of primitive Christianity and most helpful. We bespeak for it the generous patronage of all Disciples on the coast.

—Wren J. Grinstead has resigned the pastorate of the Jellico, Tenn., church to accept the chair of languages in the Eastern Kentucky State Normal at Richmond. Such leisure as he may have from school duties will be devoted to the study of religious pedagogy.

—L. D. Hill has resigned as evangelist for the Seventh Illinois Missionary District and located with the church at Benton, Ill. Brother Hill is one of our best young preachers, and we are sure he and his wife will prove great helpers to the Benton church and community.

—W. H. Scott is in a meeting at Russellville, Mo. It is a very difficult field, but there have been four additions to the membership. He wishes the address of E. E. Davidson. Any one knowing the whereabouts of this brother write Brother Scott at Eldon, Mo., R. F. D. No. 1.

—Remember the books of the foreign society close for the current missionary year September 30. All offerings should be sent to F. M. Rains, secretary, box 884, Cincinnati, O., before that date. The time is now short and immediate attention should be given to this important matter.

—O. D. Maple, of Marion, O., has united with him J. Ross Miller in an evangelistic team. Their first meeting will be at Gas City, Ind., beginning September 10. Brother Maple is a workman of whom none needs to be ashamed. We predict a most successful evangelistic career.

—Andrew Scott's "Field of Sport," in another column, is worth serious consideration by all Disciples. Desecration of the Lord's day is bound to end in a very serious lowering of the moral tone of any community, if indeed it does not impair the foundations of all government.

—Wallace M. Stuckey is now engaged in his Galesburg, Kan., meeting. Rains and mud have interfered with attendance, but have not dampened the ardor of this enthusiastic evangelist. He is assisted by 300 CHRISTIAN-EVANGELISTS each week. We hope for splendid results.

—B. L. Wray reports 54 additions at regular services during his eleven months' pastorate at the Budd Park Church, Kansas City, Mo. The church is planning for a great evangelistic campaign during September. We rejoice in Brother Wray's success in our sister city at the mouth of the Kaw.

—Heartiest congratulations, A. E. Dubber, over the action of the Tabernacle church in Fort Worth, Tex., in unanimously increasing your salary $500 per annum. But preachers who, like you, seek first the kingdom of God and his righteousness usually have an abundance of worldly things added unto them.

—Daniel George Cole, 5031 Page avenue, St. Louis, received a young woman, who is both deaf and dumb, into the membership of the Festus, Mo., church, August 5. Through an interpreter the convert, in sign language, expressed great joy in having found her Savior and the helpfulness of brothers and sisters in Christ.

—R. H. Lampkin writes that the sermon of George L. Snively, of this paper, "delivered before the Dexter, Mo., Chautauqua August 5 was a masterful presentation of the fundamentals of Christian faith, and many were the words of favorable comment heard on every hand. Our cause received a great uplift by reason of his visit here."

—Evangelist S. J. Vance is meeting with gratifying success at Reger, Mo. Eighteen have signified their intention of uniting with the Church of Christ. This new church will be founded at once and regular preaching services provided for before the meeting concludes. Brother Vance soon begins another meeting at Sorrell, Mo.

—The fifteenth annual state convention of the Christian churches of Oklahoma will be held in El Reno September 3-6. This will be the last territorial convention. A most excellent program has been prepared and a large attendance is confidently expected and greatly desired. O. L. Smith and his local congregation will be most delightful hosts.

—"The Daily Herald," of Columbia, Mo., announces that Prof. Chas. M. Sharpe will deliver a series of popular Bible lectures through the Columbia Mo., Chautauqua Assembly. Among the topics we note, "Prehistoric Origins," "Moses the Creator of Israel;" "Samuel the Israelitish Warwick;" "The Wonderful Book;" "The Everlasting Jew."

—J. R. Crank concludes his Paragould, Ark., pastorate September 16. He writes: "This is a good field for an energetic man of God, but it will be a disappointment to any one who loves a nice place and a good salary more than the work of the Master." Any church is to be congratulated that secures the services of Brother and Sister Crank.

—Brother Garrison seems to think he is resting in his lake shore home among the Pentwater pines, but most of us would think we were working if we, like him, were preaching every Lord's day, writing several pages for THE CHRISTIAN EVANGELIST, attending to an immense personal and editorial correspondence and preparing a book on "The History of Christian Unity" for publication.

—The "Dallas News" reports the death of George E. Walk, son of David Walk. In the beginning of his ministry he was a member of the Christian Church, but later in life united with the Episcopalians, and at the time of his death was dean of St. Matthew's Cathedral, the largest Episcopal parish in Texas. Our sympathy goes out to his venerable father and all his relatives and friends.

—Senator B. F. Wirt, of Youngstown, who is a candidate for the Republican nomination for the office of secretary of state of Ohio, is a zealous member of the Third Christian Church of that city. He is of the third generation of his family to be actively identified with this Restoration movement in the Western Reserve. Naturally, the members of our churches in Ohio are very desirous the convention will honor itself by making him the nominee.

—A minister is needed for half time at Newtonia, Mo. Inquirers may address C. C. Graves, of Newtonia, or E. J. Church, Seneca, Mo.

—C. L. McKim has resigned at Dallas City, Ill., to accept the pastorate of the Oelwein (Ia.) church. Iowa thus adds another to the long list of able preachers she has recently taken from Illinois.

—Alice Long, of Cravity, Ia., writes that the church there wishes a minister. Salary $700 to $800. We hope regular services will soon be resumed in that congregation.

—All desiring the minutes of the South Kentucky Christian Missionary and Sunday-school Association may receive one by applying to W. J. Hudspeth, Hopkinsville, Ky.

—His hosts of friends will rejoice to know that Assistant Editor Moore is rapidly regaining health and strength among the heights, thermal springs and other wonders of the Yellowstone.

—C. W. Comstock, of King City, Mo., assisted by G. A. Butler, leader of song is in a meeting at Orrick, Mo. We hope soon to hear that the Orrick church has greatly increased in membership and been edified in the faith.

—T. D. Secrest reports a meeting just closed at Marfa, Texas, conducted by B. B. Sanders, assisted by Mrs. Edith Steinbrook. There were six additions at Marfa and four at Valentine as the visible results of the meeting.

—S. B. Moore, of the Hammett Place Church, St. Louis, is visiting in his boyhood home at Madison, Ind. Very few veterans of the civil war are blessed like Brother Moore with the presence of their parents in the old home.

—R. E. Rosenstein's first meeting as Living Link evangelist continued ten days at Banner school house, near Chickasha, I. T. There were thirty-three additions, nineteen being by confession and baptism. He is now in a meeting at China Springs, Texas.

—Correspondents of F. G. Fisher will please take note that he is no longer at Adel, Ia., but at 43 Leicester Court, Detroit, Mich. He is being greatly blessed in his ministry at the Woodward Avenue Church. There have been eight additions since last report.

—Evangelist S. M. Martin is in a meeting at Sturgis, Ky., with twenty additions to date. Within the past few months more than 350 have been added to the Kentucky churches during his meetings. Brother Martin is assisted by several members of his family.

—George L. Bush, whose ministry at McKinney, Texas, has been one of the most successful of all those that are making us so strong in the Lone Star State, has accepted a call to the Gainesville (Tex.) church. May his characteristic successes and manifest blessings from on high continue with him.

—Robert H. Newton's church at Normal, Ill., will hold special revival meetings through October. To help insure success S. E. Fisher, of Champaign, and H. A. Easton, of Chicago, have been engaged to assist. More than eighty of the homes represented in the membership now take a church paper.

—R. B. Havener, of Windsor, Mo., has closed an eighteen days' meeting with the Adler Springs church, Atwell, Mo. There were thirty-eight additions, thirty being by primary obedience. The church now has 117 members, a new church home, is free of indebtedness and will hereafter have preaching half time.

—M. G. Mershon reports a meeting held by E. S. Baker, of Jackson, Tenn.,

with the Milan, Tenn., church. There were thirteen additions, ten being by confession and baptism. The official board of the Milan church wishes to correspond with a minister with a view of calling him to the Milan pastorate.

—M. J. Nicoson is proving a most worthy successor of J. W. Kilbourne, at Keokuk, Ia. He has returned from his vacation in Indiana, and will enter upon the fall and winter campaign with renewed strength and enthusiasm. He ministers to one of the most delectable congregations in our brotherhood.

—R. O. Rogers, of Fredericktown, Mo., sends us a booklet by T. P. Matthews— "Which? Are you a Christian or a Campbellite?" The young Endeavorer author makes the privilege of bearing the name of Christ seem very precious, and his writings should be widely distributed among our people and others.

—From the "Christian Observer" (Presbyterian), of Louisville, Ky., we learn that J. P. Lichtenberger, of New York, assisted by Miss Wambaugh, of Indiana, is holding a very successful revival at Tazewell, Va. It is an indication of better things to be to have this denominational paper speak so kindly of this meeting.

—F. M. Rains is returning to Cincinnati after an exceedingly successful tour through the west. He developed four Living Links in the foreign missionary society, dedicated the church at Ocean Park, Cal., and addressed four state conventions. This zealous secretary may be fully relied on to do his full part toward making our Pittsburg Centennial splendid.

—The ninth and last territorial convention of the Disciples of the Indian Territory will be held in McAlester August 28-30. The C. W. B. M. will hold its annual convention at the same place August 27-28. An exceedingly interesting program has been arranged and a large attendance is expected. Those expecting to attend should address T. R. Dean, South McAlester, I. T.

—Corresponding Secretary John H. Brooks sends an appeal for more good preachers for Northeast Arkansas. He has recently closed a meeting of five days at Blythedale with three confessions. The people are hungering and thirsting for the knowledge of the truth as it is in Jesus. Are there not ministerial volunteers for this rapidly growing section of our country?

—F. H. Groom, Whitehall, Mont., reports great encouragement in his revival services. There have perhaps been more evangelistic meetings held in Montana this summer in proportion to the number of our congregations than in any other part of the land. Soon we shall hear no more of the "godless northwest." Heartiest good wishes, Brother Groom, and to all your co-laborers in that mountain empire.

—Your next week's CHRISTIAN-EVANGELIST will contain a pink subscription blank. The intention of this is not to remind you of any subscription delinquencies, but to solicit your co-operation in doubling the circulation of THE CHRISTIAN-EVANGELIST. If you find it impossible to return this blank with the name of a friend who is not now reading THE CHRISTIAN-EVANGELIST, you may use it for your own renewal.

—Evangelist C. O. McFarland held a very successful meeting at Green Ridge, Mo., the last three weeks in July. Though there was much opposition to the meeting manifested by certain sectarians, seven united with the church by confession and baptism, three came from

—Chas. L. Beal reports that the Palo Alto, Cal., church building is the first of those severely damaged by the earthquake to be thoroughly repaired. Great credit for this is due the National C. W. B. M., that sent money for the repairs immediately after being notified of the amount required to restore the building. Two young people were baptized at prayer-meeting recently. The church is in a prosperous condition.

—George C. Ritchey, state evangelist of Idaho, closed a 27 days' meeting at Rupert, the 6th. Visible results, the organization of a church of 46 members, a Bible school of 70 pupils and a Christian Endeavor of 28 members. Of the new membership one came from the Catholic, three from the Mormons and three from the Baptists. Five came by confession and baptism. He is now in a meeting at Emmett, Idaho.

—H. D. Smith, of Kentucky, will assist Pastor N. M. Ragland in a meeting at Fayetteville, Ark., beginning October 15. Brother Ragland wishes to secure the services of a capable leader of song for these meetings. With such men as Ragland and Smith in the lead and the co-operation of such a church as the former has trained in Fayetteville for the past twenty years we will expect a great ingathering.

—H. Gale Spencer, of Morgantown, W. Va., has recently closed brief meetings at Friendly, Wick and Buffalo churches, W. Va. One result was to effect a co-operation between these congregations enabling them to call Thos. Knox, a recent graduate of the Lexington Bible College, into that field to serve as pastor. Brother Spencer received several into the churches and greatly emphasized "second principles."

—Henry F. Davis, of the committee on denominational co-operation, is circularizing the brotherhood in the interest of the State Interdenominational Sunday-school convention, to be held in Sedalia, Mo., August 28-30. It is earnestly desired that all our churches send the largest possible delegations to this convention. Since there are more members of the Churches of Christ in Missouri than of any other religious body we ought to excel all others in representation at gatherings like this.

—I. H. Fuller, of La Monte, closed a meeting in the Primitive Baptist church near La Monte, on the 12th. There were two confessions, two by statement, two from the Baptist and one reclaimed. He was assisted by Charles H. Altheide, of Bloomfield, Ia., whom he recommends very highly to the churches. It is hoped there will soon be enough Disciples in that community for the organization of a church. Brother Fuller will continue preaching in that vicinity until the church is established.

—Evangelist E. E. Violett is in a meeting that promises to become truly great, in his boyhood home at Winchester, Ill., assisting Pastor E. O. Sharpe. The latter writes: "Brother Violett is preaching magnificent sermons replete with learning, eloquence and persuasive power. I regard him the peer of any man in the evangelistic field, and if he wins twenty-five to Christ here, it will equal two hundred at almost any other place, for it is his home town and has elsewhere as the Nazarene spirit." Two additions last week.

—Charles E. Smith, state evangelist of South Carolina, held a meeting recently at Walterboro, at which two were added by primary obedience. The congregation was so encouraged as to re-establish the regular observance of the Lord's supper. During the meeting Brother Smith was challenged for a debate by an Adventist, but after a friendly discussion all acrimony ceased and the challenger publicly wished our evangelist God-speed in his ministry of love and helpfulness. It is still true that a kind answer turneth away wrath.

—On the occasion of the laying of the corner stone for the new church edifice of the Central Church of Christ, Columbus, O., the pastor, Walter Scott Priest, delivered an address on "The One and Only Foundation," which the Editor has had the privilege of reading. He recently preached on the same subject in the Wesley Chapel of the M. E. Church of that city and the Methodist brethren were very hearty in their commendation of the sermon. It is a glorious fact that when it comes to Christ, as the one foundation, all Christians are in substantial accord.

—F. F. Walters, of Neosho, Mo., has concluded a very helpful meeting at Newtonia, Mo. There were sixty additions to the church, twenty-three by primary obedience, ten from the denominations and the balance restored fellowship. Brother Walters states that great credit for the success of this revival is due to E. J. Church, of Seneca, who holds services twice each month at Newtonia. The evangelist was a guest of Prof. S. C. Graves and family during the meeting. Brother Graves graduated from Bethany college during the presidency of Alexander Campbell and is a very ardent admirer of the great reformer.

—Edgar W. Allen has concluded his pastorate of nearly seven years with the West Jefferson Street Church, Fort Wayne, Ind., and accepted a call to the Central, of Wichita, Kan. While at Fort Wayne he received 593 additions to the church. Thirty thousand dollars were raised for various purposes, $5,000 of which went to benevolences and missions. Two valuable and promising missions, having more than 100 members, were established in the county outside of the city. Brother Allen writes that Jefferson street church has a splendid past, but he modestly adds, "It has a more glorious immediate future."

—Prof. W. P. Howe, of Mt. Pleasant, Ia., sends us an account, taken from the "Daily Journal," of the golden wedding of Mr. and Mrs. S. C. Toof, Memphis, Tenn. Brother Toof is president of one of the largest lithograph and printing establishments in the United States and a very zealous member of the Mississippi Avenue Christian Church. Sister Toof is a daughter of the late Daniel Bates, "who founded THE CHRISTIAN EVANGELIST, the chief exponent of the Christian Church in the United States and one of the ablest religious publications in the world." We trust the future will be full of golden days for these venerable and useful disciples of our Lord.

—R. H. Crossfield, of Owensboro, Ky., has just closed a meeting with the church at Chaplin, Ky., with forty-eight additions. Thirty-six were by confession and baptism, the others being added by letter and from the denominations. T. W. Harrison is the minister of the flock and is held in highest esteem. A bright future awaits such a capable and righteously ambitious young man. The music was in charge of Mrs. Beulah Barrick Steen, of Glasgow, Ky. Of her Brother Crossfield writes: "Much of the success of the meeting was due to her direction of the chorus and sympathetic solo work. Having known Mrs. Steen for fifteen years, I can unhesitatingly commend her Christian character and ability as a musician and director of revival music."

—The annual convention of our western Pennsylvania churches will be held at Homestead September 25-27. The morning and afternoon sessions will be held in the church, the evening meetings in Carnegie Hall. It has a seating capacity of over 1,200. It is confidently expected that with the growing interest in our churches in western Pennsylvania and the exceptionally strong program to be presented this hall's seating capacity will be taxed to its utmost. Wednesday evening will be "Pioneer Night," with addresses of Walter Carpenter, F. M. Gordon, and President Cramblet, of Bethany College, on "Walter Scott," "Barton W. Stone" and "Alexander Campbell," respectively. Pastor E. D. Salkald gives a hearty invitation to all Disciples who possibly can to attend this convention.

❋ ❋

Board of Ministerial Relief of the Church of Christ.

Aid in the support of worthy, needy, disabled ministers of the Christian Church and their widows.

THIRD LORD'S DAY IN DECEMBER is the day set apart in all the churches for the offering to this work. If you make individual offerings, send direct to the Board. Wills and Deeds should be made to "BOARD OF MINISTERIAL RELIEF OF THE CHURCH OF CHRIST, a corporation under the laws of the State of Indiana." Money received on the Annuity Plan.

Address all communications and make all checks, drafts, etc., payable to BOARD OF MINISTERIAL RELIEF, 120 E. Market St., Indianapolis, Indiana.

—Reduced railway rates have been secured for the Buffalo convention. Hotels now offer room and meals on the American plan for $2 per day and up; on the European plan, rooms for 50 cents, 75 cents, $1 and up. Boarding houses offer rooms for 50 cents and 75 cents; rooms and breakfast $1 and $1.50. Private houses offer rooms for 50 cents and 75 cents; room and breakfast 75 cents to $1. Special rates are offered to large parties stopping at one hotel. These low rates, together with those offered by the railways, will make it possible for thousands to attend, who would be barred by the usual prices. The splendid program and inspiration always derived from these great national gatherings will perhaps bring to Buffalo the largest convention attendance since the jubilee of 1900.

—Brother B. B. Tyler, always happy and hopeful, is now dwelling somewhere in the region of the third heaven, because of the steady and growing prosperity of the work under his charge. In a personal letter to the Editor under date of August 7, he writes: "Three months have passed since I returned to Denver from the Orient. During this time twenty-two persons have united with the South Broadway church—six by baptism, four by statement (almost more important than original conversions), and twelve by letter. These additions to the church were gained at our regular meetings. There has been no revival pressure. For May, June and July this is not bad. During this time the free-will offerings of the people, as the plates have been passed, Sunday after Sunday, have exceeded the amount needed to defray expenses, $419.95. I do not count contributions for other purposes. Is not this great? This surpasses any previous experience in my life! Where is the dead line? The congregations that I have served in the past, some at least, have borrowed money to tide over the summer. The summer is not ended, and the South Broadway church pays current expenses, gains twenty-two members, and accumulates a surplus of $419.95. Now, the next things are repairing the house of worship, the purchase of an organ and becoming a living link church. praise the Lord!" There is no dead line, for either preacher or church that believes in Christ and *keeps growing*.

The Northern California Convention.

Our convention has left an afterglow that will ever be a beacon light to our sunny hills and verdant vales. The earthquake seemed to have loosened an extra number of brethren and sisters from their moorings, for there were more delegates representing churches than we have ever had before. The quantity of good all carried home with them depended on the size of the pitcher each one brought to the fountain. Every address was well prepared and as well delivered. The reports were the best in every respect.

The most noteworthy feature of the convention was the series of lectures by Prof. H. L. Willett, of Chicago University. He gave two lectures each day to large audiences, and from start to finish they were uplifting and inspiring. Every hearer ascended with him into the "Mountain of the Lord's House," there to feast on the good things, the Father and his Son has prepared for those that love him. Our Presbyterian brethren have secured a large parcel of land about ten miles from Santa Cruz, in the mountains, and christened it "Mount Hermon." They called Brother Willett to their as-

sembly each day to lecture for them. During his lectures for us, there were a hundred times more Bible readings than ever before. His good work and words were as bread cast upon the waters.

Sister Bertha Mason, the evangelist from Mexico, and national officer of our C. W. B. M., was another godsend to the brethren as well as the sisters of our coast.

Our C. W. B. M. of California north are making a record that will tell in volumes in eternity.

It was a delight to see so many Christian Endeavorers stringing down Garfield avenue at the ringing of the old Jerusalem bell to meet on Endeavor Rock for the sunrise prayer-meeting. Old and young met as young people, sang and prayed and talked together amid the chorus of the sea and acclaim from the rocks.

The Endeavorers will take scholarships in Berkeley Bible Seminary and help educate young men for the ministry. The last year has been another prosperous one for our Bible Seminary, and applications are being made from beyond the Rockies, and plans are being formulated for much more extended work for the coming year.

The Bible school sessions were presided over by Brother Picton, of Woodland, in a masterly manner. The devotional service each day was directed by Professor Van Kirk. So that the day opened with prayer and praise. It is enough to say that the music was directed by Prof. E. T. Nesbit and every one knows that it was a success.

Professor Elston, of Berkeley, is a most excellent chairman, and you would say the right man in the right place. It was a pleasure to see so many new men from the east panoplied for the California work and filled with enthusiasm to help us carry California for "Christ and the church." The writer has attended more California state meetings than any other living person, and I must say that as the moon waxed in brightness and the ocean waves swelled for high tide so did the sweet spirit, sympathy, love and enthusiasm rise to the highest. Every day you would feel that you were on the mountain of transfiguration.

Great improvements have been made about the park. Every lot has been sold, new cottages built, and two new railroads just outside our park on opposite sides. The reconstruction of the churches about the bay is a very anxious matter and we are in a shape to "go up and possess the land" if the good people of the east will help us. Everything is so favorable. Other religious bodies seeing this are on the alert and are responding liberally.—J. Durham.

Vancouver's War of the Roses.

Unbroken success is scarcely known in the progress of any one method of conduct. The contest revival in Sunday-school or Christian Endeavor has not always met with ready approval. It has not succeeded everywhere. In some societies it has ended in general disorder and scatterment rather than marshaling of forces. But this does not argue that the "War of Roses" is of no value anywhere if properly conducted. I have gone through several such conflicts and have, in every instance, witnessed splendid results, but no harm. Our last closed July 27 with a grand banquet in honor of the victorious side. For three months the "Silver" and the "Gold" worked earnestly and effectively. They saw a weak, dragging little society of twenty-seven irregular members rise to an enthusias-

For a Church in New Hampshire.

Already acknowledged $713 75
S. W. Birch 1 00
Miss M. G. Watson 1 50
J. H. Garrison (supplemental) ... 50 00

Total $766 25

The Herbert Yeuell meeting, made possible by Brother Garrison's standing sponsor for the brotherhood's desire to have at least one church in New Hampshire patterned after the New Testament order, and for their generosity in supporting it, is perhaps the most memorable event in the religious annals of Manchester.

We are learning that our evangelist's modesty really prevented its being known here in the west what intense interest was created in the plea of this Restoration and how far reaching were the results of these preliminary services.

When he first entered the city it was a question whether he could secure a hearing and then whether his message would find any favor with the class of people who would make possible an enduring church.

These "whethers" are now cancelled out of the problem and "how great a start shall we give the new church" has taken their place.

Soon as the necessary funds are secured and some satisfactory local conditions are effected the present pastoral labors of Wm. C. Crerie will be supplemented by another great evangelistic campaign that will make the new church one of the prominent religious institutions of the city. The great need now is money. Each issue of this paper ought to contain a half column of donors to this sacred fund. Will not some double former gifts? Let all have part in this extension of the kingdom. Enroll your name on this scroll of honor. He gives double who gives quickly.

A New Christian College.

E. V. Zollars, former president of Hiram College, also of Texas Christian University, has been invited by the home missionary boards of Oklahoma and Indian Territory to visit the larger towns of the two territories and present to the brethren the necessity of establishing a school for the Christian church in the soon to be new state. President Zollars was greeted by a joint board at Woodward. The brethren here unanimously indorse his plans for establishing the school. President Zollars is the right man to take the great work placed upon him by the boards of the two territories. He is a profound scholar, a bringer of things to pass. His twenty-five years' experience in college and university work will be of help in this important undertaking. We of Oklahoma who know Professor Zollars believe that the hand of God led him here to direct us. Whenever God has a great work to be done he always sends the right man.—Ed. S. McKinney.

Imported Japanese Fans.

A set of four very attractive Japanese fans, issued by the Chicago & Northwestern Railway, will be sent to any address, securely packed, on receipt of 10 cents to pay postage. Address W. B. Kniskern, Pass. Traffic Manager, 215 Jackson Blvd., Chicago.

Illinois Notes.

The Newman church is one of the few in small cities, which by energy and wisdom, coupled with public spirit and liberality has forged to the front and holds its proper place of usefulness and religious power in the community. It built a new modern commodious brick house of worship which it greatly enjoyed by all from the least unto the greatest. It has been peculiarly fortunate in its history is our devoted L. R. Thomas and his talented wife. Then came the energetic J. G. McNutt, now doing such splendid work at Sullivan. Now they have the scholarly and talented O. L. Lyon, whose excellent ministry is greatly enjoyed by all. The church has been liberal in giving the minister the best possible evangelistic help. There seems to be an unusual proportion of active able helpers in the church. I have found few places with such a fine combination for success in full use. It is not surprising, therefore, that the church numbers nearly 400 members, with a Sunday-school enrolling about 250, a C. E. of 70, a Junior C. E. of 40, a strong C. W. B. M., and observes all public calls for offerings "Education Day," of course, among the rest.

At Charleston. This is one of our old churches. Here Alexander Campbell preached in an early day. Here B. B. Tyler held one of his first pastorates. Other strong men followed. F. W. Burnham, W. F. Shaw and Brother Brown bringing the work up-to-date. They have a good house, a large, influential membership with all the auxiliaries well developed and in fine working order. Every great enterprise of the church should thrill with the magnificent power of this church which has been so wonderfully blest.

At Mattoon D. N. Wetzel, one of our choice men has labored four months with several additions, and ever increasing popularity with the people. The church numbers more than 300 souls, has a S. S. of 300, a C. E. of more than 100 and a Junior of 70, and a large C. W. B. M. The final $2,000 of indebtedness on their excellent church edifice has been provided for since Brother Wetzel took charge of the work, and all are looking forward to still larger things for the Master. The policy of the church is to keep in live and efficient touch with all our great enterprises by having sermons and offerings for them all.

The convention of the Seventh District of Illinois was held with the splendid church at Carmi, Aug. 7-9. The district includes 22 counties reaching across the state from East St. Louis to the Wabash, containing 200 churches with 18,000 members and with about 77 preachers. It is the largest district in the state and has more disciples in it than any other district except the Sixth.

The C. W. B. M. has 21 auxiliaries in it which raised $500 the past year for the general treasury and for state development. Mrs. Minnie M. Daily of Olney, is district secretary and presided over the meetings with dignity and in a business-like way. Miss Anna E. Davidson of Eureka, state president, Miss Lura V. Thompson, state secretary, and Miss Clara B. Griffin, superintendent of children's work, were all present, which insured a splendid convention. Reports were encouraging, addresses optimistic and plans for future vigorous. The chief address was by Miss Davidson on "Our Centennial." She has already the just reputation of being one of the best speakers in all the ranks of the C. W. B. M. and this address was one of the best. Her clear voice and accurate articulation make her clearly heard to the remotest corner.

The regular missionary work of the District was done chiefly by Lew D. Hill who gave some ten months to the work, who added about 75 to the churches and did much other work. About 75 churches made offerings to state work, aggregating about $700.

The convention was attended by about twenty preachers and fifty other delegates all of whom had free entertainment by the generous Carmi church.

The chief addresses all meritorious and carefully prepared were delivered by W. H. Boles, Marion Stevenson, J. W. Kilburn, L. D. Hill, C. C. Garrigues, H. H. Peters, W. Henry Jones, J. Fred Jones, E. U. Smith, R. Leland Brown and Jesse Story. It is hard to leave these efficient speakers with this simple announcement, but want of space demands it. J. K. Dickinson, a business man from Lawrenceville, was president, who also gave a most practical address and led the convention with promptness and wisdom. We ought to have more of our business men in all our conventions.

"Christian Education" also very properly had a place on the program. Indeed the college in Illinois is coming to be recognized as a most radical and essential necessity for the growth of our work. The convention unanimously voted that the churches encourage their young people to attend Eureka College and also observe "Education Day" January 20, 1907. Southern Illinois has sent to Eureka College a large number of splendid young men. J. T. Alsup and R. L. Beshers, David Husband, S. S. Lappin and his two brothers, J. C. and W. O., K. C. Ventress, J. C. Hall, H. H. Peters, Finis Idleman, E. J. Hart and many others. Several are now in college from Southern Illinois and more are coming. Brother Hart brought into the churches about 4,000 souls. How many a young man wastes what might be a great life because he fails to put himself under proper environments and training in his youth.

The officers for the Seventh District for the coming year are Pres. J. F. Rosborough, Vice-Pres. C. C. Garrigues, Sec. C. M. Smithson and Treas. J. W. Kilburn. A vice-president was also selected in each county to co-operate with the board and form a part of it. The next convention goes to Mt. Vernon. This is central and ought to be a great convention. If all the churches in the district would take offerings, every preacher be active in co-operation, what a great work a year would mean. Brethren, we look to you for great things for Christ and his cause.—J. G. Waggoner, Eureka, Ill.

A Good Report.

On last Sunday L. J. Marshall closed his fourth year of work with the church at this place. During the last eleven months there have been fifty-eight additions to the church. The Bible school has increased about one-third; all missionary interests have been remembered, the church giving in all about $1,800 to missions. A lot has been purchased costing over $8,000, and money will be raised during the year for the erection of a new church house. Brother Marshall is now on his annual vacation and will return about September 1. We are planning greater things.

M. C. MASTERS, Clerk.
Independence, Mo.

※ ※

An Improved College Property.

Toward the end of last autumn the main building of South Kentucky College was destroyed by fire. It is now being rebuilt and is nearing completion. It is greatly improved in architecture both interior and exterior. A new dormitory for young ladies is also nearing completion.

The school has new plans of interest. Most notable among these is its plan to give board and tuition each year to two young men preparing for the ministry. Those scholarly Christian gentlemen, Pres. A. C. Kuy Krudall and Vice-Pres. H. Clay Smith, are to continue in their respective positions. A full faculty of other teachers will assist them. The fall term will open on Sept. 11, at which time the builders have promised that the new buildings will be ready for occupancy.
Hopkinsville Ky. H. D. SMITH.

※ ※

Walden's Meetings.

There is still unspoken for enough of G. T. Walden's time, while he will be in America, for two meetings—one to begin September 9, the other immediately after the general convention. Brother Walden is one of our best preachers, a man of pleasing manners, and a most earnest and tactful worker. After graduating at Lexington in 1888, where he took the honors of his class, he went to Lygon St., Melbourne, then our largest church in Australia; in 1892 he succeeded W. T. Moore at the West London Tabernacle; in 1896 he was compelled to go to Australia on account of the health of one of his children, and took the work at Enmore, Sydney, where he has been ten years. During this time the church has been enlarged twice to accommodate the growing congregation. He is president of the C. E. Union of Australia with a membership of 85,000; as such he has attended this summer the British convention at Leeds, and the World's C. E. convention at Geneva, Switzerland. During his visit in England he has had an audience with King Edward and has presented him with a boomerang from his loyal aboriginal subjects in New South Wales. Altogether Brother Walden is a man of rare qualities. He loves to preach and is very successful in winning souls. He devotes much of his time to protracted meeting work in Australia—mission work as it is called there. He will have reached New York about August 9. I shall be glad to hear from any churches desiring his services. He may be addressed personally in my care.
Lexington, Ky. MARK COLLIS.

NEWS FROM MANY FIELDS

Western Pennsylvania Letter.

Work in western Pennsylvania is moving steadily forward, despite the extreme heat and the fact of vacation season being upon us. Brother Tharp with Bro. Z. T. Sweeney is fishing in Michigan. We expect considerable "ictheology" when vacation season ends.——T. A. Bright, of Waynesburg, Pa., is looking after the Allegheny work during August.——Brother Slater and family are spending the month in central Ohio, and President Cramblet, of Bethany, is holding forth in the East End during his absence.——Brother and Sister Place, of Bellevue, are in Bowling Green, O.—— Bro. Jean Duty, a ministerial boy from the Wilkensburg church, supplied in Bellevue Sunday.——Grant E. Pike, of Shady avenue, Albany, is raising money to clear the mortgage and preparing for publication a large work on baptism—good substantial work for this season.——The Thurgoods, of Central church, are just home from their vacation.——Brother Manley is booming things in Belmar.——F. M. Gordon preaches all summer in his new church in Knoxville.——Bro. Garnett Wynne has just taken up his work in Hazelwood. Five accessions are reported for last Sunday. The work is in a hopeful and most promising condition.——S. E. Brewster, of McKees Rocks, with his family leave next week for a visit in the east. The mission bee is buzzing in his bonnet and he is investigating a point of great promise near his own church.——McKeesport under Brother Howard Cramblet is making preparations for a great meeting this fall.——Brother Pitman has just gotten hold of the reins at Dravosburg and we look for great things there.——Of course Homestead is booming. Ed. Salkeld makes everything go. He is very busy preparing for the entertainment of our fall convention.——J. A. Joyce recently preached a few evenings at "Nadine," a new point on the Allegheny River. Seven disciples were found and two responded to the gospel invitation. Brother Joyce is pushing that most estimable book,

"The Church of Christ," by "A Layman." Don't fail to read it.——They are talking parsonage in Scottdale, where Bro. M. C. Frick, though no longer a young man, is pushing the work enthusiastically. His son, C. H. Frick, who has just graduated from Hiram, is now on the field as Western Pennsylvania evangelist. He is at present prospecting among the most promising mission fields. He is strong, earnest and enthusiastic and will be a great accession to our Western Pennsylvania work.——J. D. Dabney is closing his second and most successful year on Herron Hill.——R. S. Lattimer, our Western Pennsylvania veteran president, is enjoying the surf at Bethany Beach, and helping all visitors to enjoy themselves.——Time and space will not permit what I should like to say of E. A. Hibler and his splendid work in Johnstown. He has just dedicated a most beautiful and perfectly equipped building, the best one among our people in the state. Brother Hibler is among our oldest (in point of service) pastors in the state and few, if any, have done a greater work than he.——O. H. Philips, the veteran pastor of Braddock, has just refused a most tempting call from one of Ohio's best churches. We all rejoice in his loyalty to West Pennsylvania. He will be one of our leaders in preparation for the centennial meeting here.——The writer has just returned from a ten days' visit in Canada. He recently addressed the Ohio Valley Endeavor rally at Bellaire, O., and will be present to address at the international Christian Endeavor rally in Columbia county, O., on August 24. After five years' service we have resigned our work in Wilkinsburg, and accepted a call to East Orange, N. J., where we begin September 1. Will also do graduate work in Columbia University, New York city. Bro. George W. Knepper, of Somerset, has been called as my successor and will be on the field October 1.— L. N. D. Wells.

North Carolina Notes.

W. G. Walker, state evangelist, had a long, hard siege at Durham, where he held the fort for about seven weeks. He knew of only three Disciples when he went there. There were many hindrances, but they organized a congregation of 22 members. McKinney was his singing evangelist, and Brother Walker speaks highly of him and his work.

W. G. Johnson, late of Roanoke, Va., was to hold a meeting at Stoneville in July. Have not heard results.——The writer held a meeting at Mathews Chapel, seven miles from Winston, beginning July 22 and closing July 29. We have but about half a dozen members in this congregation, a good many having moved away. No additions, but the interest seemed revived.——On Lord's day, July 29, had five additions at Winston. Two were baptized, one from Louisville, Ky., a grand nephew of Isaac Errett. One sister came by letter. Her husband, a Baptist, came with her. A very cheering announcement was made, that the last note on our debt to the Church Extension Board was paid. The debt was $900 at Christmas, 1905. That with interest has been paid within the year. We will have a mortgage burning later.——The district co-operation meeting in this section will be held at Winston beginning Friday before fifth Lord's day in August.——The church at

Winston has granted me, without asking for it, a vacation during August. Part of the time is being spent at my mother's home, Bellaire, O. While here I read in a Steubenville, O., paper that "a contract has been let for the construction and equipment of the road ready to turn over to the company for operation." That is, the electric road from Wellsburg to Bethany. This will be a great advantage to Bethany College.—J. A. Hopkins.

July State Mission Work in Kentucky.

The month of July found L. B. Haskins at work half his time at Erlanger, with well sustained interest in the work. A meeting is expected the last of September, in which W. J. Cocke will assist.——Professor W. H. Cord was helped at Cannel City in a meeting by E. J. Willis and there were eight baptisms. The people enjoyed the preaching very much and the cause was helped.——S. J. Short spent twenty-three days in the Big Sandy valley, added five and visited four places.——W. J. Cocke preached twenty-five sermons during July, added nine, raised in cash and pledges for Kentucky missions, $216.10.——D. G. Combs was in Fleming and Carter counties, added 41 and did much general work.——W. J. Dodge reports the work at Jackson as moving on in the usual way. He is making special effort now to raise the balance he pledged to raise on dedication day.——W. C. McCallum says that the Valley View mission is encouraging. He gives half time to this field.——Latonia continues to give H. C. Runyon audiences that overtax the capacity of house. One added. Effort being made to get a larger lot and plans on foot to enlarge house or build new one.——Leslie county had the services of J. W. Masters for a meeting in July; twenty-three added; $19 for Kentucky missions. He expects to go to Hyden, the county seat for a meeting in October. We have a number of people in that remote county; but if we have any house of worship it is unknown to the writer.——South Louisville has had the services of Edw. B. Richey nearly all the past month. He was in a meeting at West Point for several days. Building progressing well.——The pews for Jellico house of worship are ordered for October, and Wren J. Grinstead thinks that the house will be dedicated soon after that.——G. W. Adkins baptized one and added one otherwise. He is out for a summer campaign in eastern Kentucky.——C. M. Summers reports work at Fikeville as doing well. He helped H. H. Thomson in a meeting out in the county and there were twenty-three baptized.——There were seven added in the work of H. L. Morgan in southeastern Kentucky and other general work reported.——F. M. Stamper reports eighteen added during the past four months in Morgan and Wolfe counties. He is helped by the Hubble church, through the state board.——H. W. Elliott was at work all the month in the interest of state missions. He collected $298.59—just about one-half enough to pay the expenses of the month. We had just such a shortage in June and hence we are more than a month behind. We trust that this month will witness a general coming up on the part of many churches and individuals. To close the year as we ought we must have about $4,000. If all the churches that have not done so will pay their apportionments in full we can compass this and go to Louisville September 24-27 with a smile on our faces and joy in our hearts.——Our plan of entertainment is different this year from any convention in our history. The Louisville people will give us lodging and breakfast and we will pay for our dinner and supper. This will give our brethren with whom we meet a better opportunity to enjoy and profit by the convention.——A rate of one fare plus

25 cents, on the round trip ticket plan has been secured on all except two railroad lines. It is confidently expected by the Louisville brethren having this matter in charge that these will also give same plan and rate.——R. M. Hopkins will be largely in charge of affairs and will be helped by a thorough organization for taking care of the great crowd that we confidently expect to see gathered at Louisville September 24-27.

Sulphur, Ky.   H. W. ELLIOTT, Sec.

A Wonderful Machine.

So many and varied have been the wonders produced by the inventive genius of man that, as an Irishman would say, there are no wonders.

That which would have been regarded as marvelous a generation ago, is only common-place now. And yet it is remarkable how the mechanical knowledge of the race has kept pace (and at times seemingly, led) the needs of a growing civilization. No sooner has a want announced itself to the world than genius responds with that which satisfies.

One of the most interesting and practical devices for economizing energy and securing accuracy is called to the attention of the readers of this journal, in this issue of THE CHRISTIAN-EVANGELIST. We refer to the advertisement of the Standard Adding Machine in another part of the paper. This device, scarcely as large as a typewriter, enables one to add from the smallest to the largest amounts with great rapidity and absolute and unfailing accuracy. It is valuable, not only in banks and large offices, but in the accounting department of the ordinary merchant. The Standard Adding Machine has a peculiar interest for readers of THE CHRISTIAN-EVANGELIST, because it was invented by W. W. Hopkins, a minister of the Christian Church, and at one time office editor of this paper. The president of the company which makes the machine is F. M. Call, formerly business manager and treasurer of the Christian Publishing Company. E. J. Ganz, another of our well known brothers from the preaching ranks, has charge of the sales department, and in the office force, the salesmen and the stock-holders the membership of the Christian Church is well represented. The Christian Publishing Company has used a Standard Adding Machine for ten months, with no need for repairs, and has found it almost indispensable, although it doubted that it had need at all for it when first induced to try it.

Readers who are engaged in business of any kind will obtain very full information concerning the way in which the machine can be of help to them by writing for booklet. As may be judged from what has been written above, mention of the fact that they are readers of this paper will secure for their communications especial attention.

Good Music is of Supreme Importance

When we say *good* we mean both in sentiment and melody.

LIVING PRAISE

By CHAS. H. GABRIEL and W. W. DOWLING.

Is that kind of a Song Book.

Drop us a postal card request and we will tell you all about this superb collection of 281 pieces of sacred music. Three styles of binding.

Christian Publishing Co.,   St. Louis, Mo.

Callaway County (Mo.) Convention.

Owing to rain the convention convened August 8 instead of 7, and continued to the 10th. The opening sermon was preached by C. H. Caton, of Columbia, Mo. Among the preachers and church workers participating were H. N. McKee, W. J. Lhamon and C. H. Caton of Columbia, Pastor Ainsworth, of Dixie church, County Evangelist Cunningham, Dr. F. J. Nichols, president of the convention, Egan Herndon, of Centralia, and the writer.

It was a good convention. Dr. F. J. Nichols, C. O. Adkinson and S. T. Moore were elected to constitute the county board for the ensuing year. The next convention will be held with the Hickory Grove church in the northwest part of the county, about August 1, 1907.

The cause in Callaway county is in a healthy condition, with a few symptoms of disorder in spots. Co-operation between churches occupying contiguous territory was discussed and recommended. It has been tried in the county, and has much in its favor.

A vigorous administration by the county board during the year will mean much for our people in the county. The next convention, in my humble judgment, should be planned for months ahead. It should be a convention of Callaway churches. Every church should send several delegates, with full reports of the work. The work of the churches should be the burden of the convention. Plans should be presented by competent workers, every department of the church should be studied, missions should be emphasized, and less time should be consumed by sermons. The people enjoy sermons; but they need other things as well. If outside speakers are invited they ought to be assigned subjects that relate to the needs of the county. The Disciples of the Kingdom have a right to expect the county board to plan carefully and vigorously for the best convention the county ever had for next year.—C. A. Lowe, St. Joseph Mo.

❧ ❧

India Notes.

July 9th was the 300th anniversary of the beginning of Protestant missions in India. The Danes at that time arrived in the port of Tranquebar, but apparently did not land until the 11th. Then they met with a rebuff from the native king and were compelled to stand outside his gates until afternoon. All over India this anniversary was celebrated, in some places on the 9th and in others on the 11th. Our celebration was on the 11th. The station theater was engaged for the event. The stage was occupied by the missionaries, the speakers, and a few invited guests. The auditorium was filled with native Christians, of whom 500 or 600 were present. All the missions in Jubbulpore were represented on the program. Several of the missionaries made brief addresses, and five minute speeches were made by four native Christians; one a convert from Mohammedanism, one a convert from Hinduism, one a famine waif brought up in an orphanage, and one born, as he expressed it, into the Church of England. The most interesting speech made by any of these was that made by the Hindu convert, who, in an enthusiastic address, declared that the power of caste, which is the back bone of heathenism, was broken, and that the system was failing to the ground, and that in numerous respects, some of which he illustrated, Hindus and Mohammedans were imitating Christians, by establishing prayer-meetings and publication societies, and opening schools

STATECRAFT AND STATEHOOD.

John Sharp Williams contributes an article in September Southwest upon the "Admission of the New State: Its Political and Commercial Significance."

September Southwest is devoted exclusively to the New State.

FIVE CENTS A COPY—FIFTY CENTS A YEAR

SOUTHWEST,
1037 Frisco Building,
St. Louis, Mo.

---

and orphanages. But none of these, he thought, could stop the advance of Christianity. We are having a summer school for our mission helpers, in connection with the Bible college. Those assisting in giving instruction, in addition to the writer, are Messrs. Grainger, McGavran, Adams, and Menzies. Twenty evangelists are present from our several stations, and four lectures are delivered daily. We are doing all we can to emphasize the great text, "Preach the Word." We feel, from the interest manifested that much good is being accomplished. The Bible college will begin its regular work on the 23d. We look for an increase of students over last year's number. Our little Hindi paper, started with four and then eight pages, has proved so useful that we are now enlarging it to twelve pages weekly. The readers are much pleased with it, and are crying for its enlargement. It is the only periodical that most of our subscribers get.—Geo. W. Brown, Jubbulpore.

❧ ❧

Deafness Cannot be Cured

by local applications, as they can not reach the diseased portion of the ear. There is only one way to cure deafness, and that is by constitutional remedies. Deafness is caused by an inflamed condition of the mucous lining of the Eustachian Tube. When this tube is inflamed you have a rumbling sound or imperfect hearing, and when it is entirely closed, Deafness is the result, and unless the inflammation can be taken out and this tube restored to its normal condition, hearing will be destroyed forever; nine cases out of ten are caused by Catarrh, which is nothing but an inflamed condition of the mucous surfaces.

We will give One Hundred Dollars for any case of Deafness (caused by catarrh) that can not be cured by Hall's Catarrh Cure. Send for circulars free.
F. J. CHENEY & CO., Toledo, O.
Sold by Druggists, 75c.
Take Hall's Family Pills for constipation.

Evangelistic

We invite ministers and others to send reports of meetings, additions and other news of the churches. It is especially requested that additions be reported as "by confession and baptism" or "by letter."

HOT FROM THE WIRE.

Special to THE CHRISTIAN-EVANGELIST.

Ennis, Texas, August 12.—Harlow and Harlow opening fall campaign here with largest crowds and best interest ever had in this city. Twenty to date.—C. B. Knight, pastor.

Special to THE CHRISTIAN-EVANGELIST.

Monroe, Wis., August 13.—Charles Reign Scoville and De Loss Smith are here. in a union meeting with five churches. City has 5,000 inhabitants and twenty-six saloons. Have been here six days; gave first invitation last night; fifty-one confessions.—J. H. Berkey.

Special to THE CHRISTIAN-EVANGELIST.

Kansas City, Mo., August 11.—Fife and Saunders spent ten days with me at Converse, Mo. Thirty-six added to the saved. The house was too small to hold any night audience. We had great preaching and singing. We regret that we could not keep them one more week. They begin their campaign at Holden, Mo., August 12.—Clyde Lee Fife.

California.

Long Beach, Aug. 6.—Eleven added a week ago. Five yesterday. Average Sunday-school attendance during July, 330; in August, 377.—E. W. Thornton.

Illinois.

Clinton, Aug. 7.—On July 29 the Mt. Olivet church near Clarence, Ill., took up a good offering for foreign missions. One confession at the

SUNDAY-SCHOOL SUPPLIES

Edited by W. W. DOWLING.

Our Series of Sunday-School Helps Consists of the Following Graded Quarterlies and Weeklies.

QUARTERLIES

The Beginners' Quarterly
The Primary Quarterly
The Youths' Quarterly
The Scholars' Quarterly
The Bible Student
The Bible Lesson Picture Roll

WEEKLIES

The Little Ones
The Young Evangelist
The Round Table
Our Young Folks
Bible Lesson Leaves
Bible Lesson Picture Cards

If you are not using these excellent supplies in your Sunday-School send for **FREE SAMPLES**, to

Christian Publishing Co., - St. Louis, Mo.

Texas church, near Clinton, last Lord's day.—Lewis P. Fisher.

Mason City, Aug. 6.—Four added here in July, all baptisms. Two of them from another communion.—O. C. Bolman, Sec.

St. Elmo, Aug. 4.—Two baptisms, and two by baptism last week; expect two more to-night.—S. A. Walker.

Sullivan, Aug. 12.—Two young men, ages 21 and 24, made the confession this morning.—J. T. McNutt.

Indiana.

Elwood, Aug. 1.—Have 25 in chorus in meeting here. Good preaching by J. W. Wittkamper. Meeting starting off lively.—H. K. Shields.

Indian Territory.

Tulsa, Aug. 6.—Two additions here since last report. Have added 98 members the past year, an increase of 100 per cent.—Randolph Cook.

Sapulpa, Aug. 6.—Have just closed meeting with Brother Harral here, resulting in 9 additions to church. Brother Harral has done fine work here, recently dedicating a neat house of worship.—Randolph Cook.

Missouri.

Isadore, Aug. 6.—Two additions last night. One by confession, 1 from another communion. Begin our meeting first Lord's day in September.—Challie E. Graham.

Rosendale, Aug. 8.—Began meeting July 22, closing Aug. 3, at Christian Chapel, DeKalb county, with 11 baptisms. Three reclaimed and 1 from another communion.—W. A. Chapman.

Mayview, Aug. 8.—This church has recently spent about $100 on improvements. Are hoping for great revival under the leadership of W. C. Cole, of Jewell, Ia., who begins with us Aug. 12.—Arthur Downs.

Butler, Aug. 13.—Another addition by confession at Elizabeth chapel, Sunday.—Henry W. Hunter, pastor.

Elkland, Aug. 13.—Our meeting here closed last night. Eight additions, 5 by confession, 3 by statement.—E. W. Yocum.

Ohio.

Ballsville, Aug. 6.—Six additions since last service held here. Are planning for the greatest fall campaign ever carried on at this place. A hundred present at Endeavor meeting, 30 per cent taking part.—Ferd H. Schultz, minister.

Oklahoma.

Chandler, Aug. 5.—Meeting one week old, with 10 added to date. We continue.—Oscar Ingold, pastor.

Texas.

Commerce, Aug. 10.—Meeting at South Sulphur mission closed on the 9th. Twenty-five additions, seven by baptism, eighteen by statement. One confession at Commerce, August 5.—W. A. Wherry, minister.

Virginia.

Clifton Forge, Aug. 6.—In meeting with our church at Millboro, had 20 additions.—Gerald Culbertson.

CHURCH FEDERATION READY.

The Inter-Church Conference on Federation, 700 pages, prepaid....$2 00

People's Forum

Ten Per Cent Off.

To the Editor of THE CHRISTIAN-EVANGELIST:

In your issue of June 21st is an excellent article by Brother Cupp on Ministerial Dignity. He is strongly opposed to a minister accepting the usual 10 per cent discount on his purchases. I am unable to see anything wrong in a preacher accepting a courtesy of this kind. Of course, a preacher ought not to ask for a discount. But if a discount is offered I see no impropriety in accepting it. Nearly all of us accept fifty per cent off on our purchases of railroad tickets and we even make application for our clergy certificates. I admit that a preacher ought not to ask for a ten per cent discount on purchases, but I contend that there is nothing undignified in accepting it when offered. It would be improper for me to ask a man whom I meet on the street to give me $5. But should he hand me $5, I see no impropriety in accepting it. Brother Cupp says that the world calls it graft. Probably some of them do so call it. But I have not heard it called graft except by people who call the minister's salary graft. I have heard ten times more objection to taking an incidental collection than I have heard to a preacher accepting a per cent on his purchases. Is it inconsistent to accept 10 per cent off of our purchases from our merchants and at the same time consistent to accept fifty per cent off from a railroad corporation? Some of the best Christian business men whom I know offer a per cent off to ministers, and I see no impropriety in accepting it.　T. D. SECREST.
Marfa, Tex.

"De gustibus non est disputandum."—S.

Procrastination.

To the Editor of THE CHRISTIAN-EVANGELIST:

We have two more confessions to report since our meeting closed. On Elder very sad circumstances. A young man of exceptionally good habits who attended our meetings some but did not confess the Savior at that time. He complained some on Tuesday, a physician was called on Wednesday, an operation was deemed necessary on Thursday, and he died in Atlanta about midnight of Friday. Before his death he asked for me, but it was not possible to reach him.

Another minister was called, with whom he talked, saying that he had known his duty for years, but his stubborn will had kept him from making the good confession. He repeated the twenty-third Psalm, prayed for himself and those about him and went into eternity asking that his name be placed among the list of those who had accepted Christ during our meeting. A large and very attentive audience listened to a talk by the writer from Rom. 8:35. We tried to show that while the love of Christ was inexhaustible, there was danger in delay. Many wept and many said that it was the most impressive moment in their lives. May the God and Father of us all help that we may profit by this sad lesson.
Elliott, Iowa.　　　SAM B. ROSS.

The question raised is a very delicate one and can rarely be discussed at a funeral without lacerating sad hearts. But may this inspire us to preach with new fervor that now is the accepted time.—S.

Midweek Prayer-Meeting

August 22, 1906.

FINDING OUR LIFE CALLING—
Acts 9:6-20.

"To the work, to the work,
We are servants of God,
We will follow the path
That our Saviour hath trod;
With the balm of his counsel
Our strength to renew,
We will do with our might
What our hands find to do."

Saul no sooner learned his life calling
than he entered upon it. He obeyed the
voice,: "And straightway in the syna-
gogues he proclaimed Jesus that he is the
Son of God." All altruistic impulses in
harmony with the Word may safely be interpreted as life callings, and our disposition of them is their acceptance or rejection. Let us be Sauls rather than Jonahs,
good soldiers and not renegades.

Persistency is an essential to the
achievement of success in any calling.
One man abandons a mine when just
another stroke of the pick would have
uncovered a wealth of gold. Had the
patriots made one more charge, the invaders had been routed and liberty won.
Through lack of patient continuance in
well-doing many a life that otherwise
would have become nobly distinguished
has fallen back to the commonplace.

We have found our life calling when
we see the field of greatest usefulness
for which our natural endowments qualify us. That calling is not only to be
good and do good, but to be the best
and do the greatest good we can. It
should be remembered, too that true
honor consists not so much in what good
work we engage as in the character of our
work. In doing well the humblest tasks
we have fellowship with the greatest works
of God.

James and John, Peter and Andrew
heard the call and left their nets.
Matthew heard it at the receipt of custom
and quitted his office. Saul heard it before the gates of Damascus, and at its
command entered the way of martyrdom and glory, and they all are among
the nobility of the church. Demas heard
and forsook the way. Felix listened and
trembled. It came to Agrippa, and he
was almost persuaded. The priest and
Levite were called, but turned and passed
by on the other side. May we not only
hear the calling to a life of service, but
in all things obey it.

We are all called to be Christians, and
being a Christian should be our chief employ. Music is the vocation of the musician. He may devote some time to
gardening or painting as avocations, but
if he ever excels as a musician, he must
give himself chiefly to that art. Our
vocation is being Christians. As avocations we may sell goods or peg shoes,
but if we win divine approval we will
be known in the community as Christians rather than merchants or cobblers,
nor will we at any time more faithfully
illustrate our high calling than when engaged in our avocations.

Miracles never supplant the more usual
processes in the fulfillment of God's
plans; they merely supplement them. The
miracle brought Saul who wanted to
know, into touch with Ananias, who
could inform him. Rarely is such a
miracle needed now, for men have
learned not to expect special revelations

from the skies when they wish to learn
of their religious duties and privileges,
but to confer with modern saintly Ana-
niases, who can instruct them in the
ways of the Lord more perfectly. It is
something to be greatly encouraged. We
ought to talk more about the Kingdom.
How rarely do we have our conversation
in heaven!

Christian Endeavor

By GEO. L. SNIVELY

August 26, 1906.

OUR ISLAND POSSESSIONS — Is.
42:1-12.

DAILY READINGS.

M.	The Example of Jesus.	Matt. 4:17-25.
T.	The Command of Jesus.	Mark 16:15-18.
W.	The Example of Philip.	Acts 8:5-13.
T.	The Example of Peter.	Acts 8:32-45.
F.	The Example of Antioch.	Acts 11:21-26.
S.	The Example of Paul.	Acts 14:20-28.
S.	The Ambition of Paul.	Rom. 15:23-32.

While Spanish is the language spoken
by all save the lowest tribes of our insular wards, they readily learn English
in the public schools. Their labor is
more valuable, they are faring better
than before, our merchants are teaching
them to get, our missionaries are inspiring them to be. They are not of the
dying races. Those helping in their development are having part in the making
of nations that will yet prove important
factors in the destiny of the earth for
good or evil.

In the Philippines the various churches
have recognized "spheres of influence,"
having divided the territory among themselves so there would be no confusion
of doctrines among the natives or any denominational clashes. There is less difference in denominational teachings on
the mission fields than at home, however. The heathen take little interest
in theology; they hunger for the Bread
of Life. The Christian unity we all so
desire will probably come to us via our
island missions.

Our Bro. G. D. Edwards, of Honolulu, writes letters full of hope for the
future of the churches of Christ in Hawaii. The natives are naturally religious
and those won to the Saviour love him
with their whole heart. But this is rapidly becoming a modern and metropolitan city, and there he is preaching the
old Gospel to men of many nations. A
gracious courtesy would be for many
Endeavorers to write Brother and Sister
Edwards messages of Christian sympathy and cheer.

The justification of our seizure of the
Spanish islands will not be produced in
commercial circles or political councils,
but by the churches. The merchant will
try to sell them more than he buys; the
politician's services in governing them
will not be gratuitous; only the church
will give to them, asking nothing. Public sentiment may have supported traders
and office-seekers in this conquest, but
this sentiment is wrong unless we confer
on those islanders greater spiritual
blessings than they could otherwise have
enjoyed.

Protestantism has 29 preaching stations in Porto Rico, and 11 organized
churches. There are 1,089 members affiliated with the different churches. Of
the 15 Protestant ministers on the island,
two are supported by churches of Christ.
This may not seem like much progress
during the past five years, but these

Sunday-School

August 26, 1906.

THE RICH YOUNG RULER.—Mark 10:17-31.

Memory verses: 23, 24.

GOLDEN TEXT.—If any man will come after me, let him deny himself and take up his cross and follow me.—Matt. 16:24.

This story of the rich young ruler has all the pathos of a great opportunity lost, of a great talent wasted, of a great gain missed by a narrow margin. The key-word of it, perhaps, is "almost."

If we may read between the lines, we will say that this young man was sincerely interested in the great Teacher and sincerely desirous of bettering his own moral and spiritual condition if possible. He was fully aware of his own virtues, however. His inquiry of Jesus was made quite respectfully and sincerely, perhaps a trifle condescendingly, as from one already sure of his own excellence and expecting rather approval than any advice radically at variance with his established mode of life. Certainly it was made in a cautious and tentative way. He was not putting himself without reserve under the guidance of Jesus, but was proposing to get his advice and then use it in so far as it agreed with his own views. This last point was one of his chief failings. One can not profitably consult a physician or a lawyer in that spirit. Much less can one get the blessing which Christ has to give by approaching him in that hesitant and untrusting manner.

He was a good young man. He may have been conceited, but he was evidently virtuous and there was about him a winsomeness which made the Master love him. His virtue and the lovable qualities of his character were a solid asset of great value. They were not final values, but they constituted a great opportunity. The possession of them did not (to use the common phrase) "save" him, but it gave him an opportunity to be saved.

The advice which Jesus gave him—to sell his great possessions and give the proceeds to the poor—discovered the lurking defect of his character. He clung to his goods with the grip of avarice. More than that, he showed himself unwilling to pay the price required for companionship with Jesus. He wanted to enter the kingdom of God—if it could be done without serious inconvenience. He had never yet come to the cross-roads where virtue and prosperity part company. So when the alternative was presented, to continue in the enjoyment of his wealth or to gain the fellowship of the Master, he chose his wealth.

It does not follow that Jesus meant this advice for a general command to all his followers. Different persons need different tests, as different patients need different prescriptions. Jesus was not laying down a universal command in these words. But he indicated a general moral principle, which was that trusting in wealth makes wealth a barrier to the kingdom of God.

The young man "went away sorrowful." Why? Not at giving up his riches, for he did not give them up. But at giving up Jesus. He had come within the magic circle of his influence and had caught some glimpse of the glory of the better life that he might have with the Master. He had heard the call, but it did not quite command his obedience. He had lost his old content of possession and failed to gain the new joy of sacrifice and service. Such is ever the fate of those who see and do not follow the heavenly vision.

⁂

Our Great Agreements.

(Continued from Page 1040.)

Here I stopped and remarked that the list was getting to be a long one, and yet we had not by any means exhausted our agreements. I suggested that we write down some of our disagreements. He gave his assent and we began:

1. "We disagree on apostolic succession."

2. "We disagree on the subject of baptism." I said to him that as I understood it he believed in baptismal regeneration, pouring and sprinkling and infant baptism. He replied that I had stated it correctly.

3. "We disagree about the name of the church." He thought that the name "Church of England" was all right.

4. "We disagree in regard to the priestly function of the ministry, the rubric and ritual of the church."

Here I hesitated and said, "I am about to run out of disagreements." I asked him to name some of the things about which we were not likely to agree. He replied that he did not think of any other.

"Now," I said, "let us look at our two lists and compare them. In the first place we see that in actual count there is a two-thirds majority in favor of our agreements. In the second place we must weigh and measure as well as count. Here are ten agreements to four disagreements. If we put all four of these disagreements together, they are not to be compared in weight or importance to any one of the ten on the other side where we agree."

The chaplain very pleasantly replied, "I never looked at it in that way before." "But," he said, "tell me about this Endeavor society. What is it? What does it mean? What does it do?" I explained something of its nature and history and handed him a copy of the constitution and a tract by Dr. Clark. Before leaving he consented for me to propose his name, and in two weeks he lead one of the meetings beautifully, being the first chaplain of the Church of England in India to become a member of the Christian Endeavor Society.

I think this chaplain learned something from our conference that morning. I believe, however, that I learned more than he did. Among the important lessons I learned anew were these:

1. The importance of the great agreements among Protestants.

Many a time I had said that Protestant agreements were greater and more important than their disagreements, but I had not realized what that meant. Here was a high churchman and a no churchman at all discovering that they were one in all the great essentials of the Christian faith. We had looked each other in the face in front of our ten great agreements. Supposing such a conference had been held with a Presbyterian or Methodist or Baptist. The agreements would have been much increased and the disagreements greatly lessened.

2. The great sin of divisions in the church.

"Let there be no divisions among you," comes with a new force as we study the meaning of our great agreements. Let us make real to ourselves the great fact even as Abraham stated, "We are brethren." In the mind of Jesus this is fundamental, "One is your Master; all ye are brethren." There is no justification for sectarianism. There is no sane reason for division. Refusing to unite with all who believe in Jesus notwithstanding some disagreements on other items is treason to the prayer of Jesus and shows blindness of vision and cruelty of heart. When the earthquake and fire came, San Francisco could easily federate. When Christians have vision and heart, when they see and feel things as they are, they also can and will unite, co-operate, federate, anything else but separate. In view of our great agreements and the great danger and destruction of sin and Satan, we must work and fight together under the same Leader and overcome our common enemy.

3. The great agreements are the highways of approach to perfect union.

"Can two walk together except they be agreed?" By the recognition of our agreements, not only as respects the great fundamental facts of Christianity, but also our agreements in the heart experiences of salvation and spiritual life, the way will be paved for a profitable discussion of any disagreements we may have as brethren in the same church or between separate churches. May it not be that Christian union will come from traversing lovingly this highway of truth and love which leads to life and heaven? We can never argue down or overcome our disagreements by ignoring or being false to our great agreements. Christian love is the first and greatest step towards Christian union.

Current Literature

THE MAN AND THE MASTER, by James E. Freeman. (Thomas Whittaker, Bible House, N. Y. 75 cents.)

This is a valuable blending of the life of Jesus —the Son of God and the Son of David. The studies relate to His Boyhood and Home, to Jesus the Workman, Teacher, Reformer, Friend, Liberator, Savior. While there is no compromise of his sovereignty and divinity, his humanness is vividly exploited, his experiences become most inspirational and a walk with him one of our sweetest privileges. It is an inexpensive but valuable book of 127 pages.

EVANGELISM, by G. Campbell Morgan, 99 pages; price not given.

Five addresses delivered to students in theological seminaries. Morgan is a prophet of God. He is at his best in these addresses, and like a good scribe brings from his spiritual storehouse things both new and old. He discusses "The Evangel," "The Church Evangelistic," "The Evangelistic Service," and "The Present Opportunity." The New Evangelism is thus disposed of: "Why not pray for an old fashioned revival? Because I want God's next new thing. Then why not forecast the lines of a new evangelism? Because one evangel is enough for all time." The work of the evangelist is thus described: "The business of the evangelist is to get an immediate verdict for Jesus Christ." I repeat, it is the message of a prophet. Let every preacher buy and read this booklet.

THE PASSION FOR SOULS, by J. H. Jowett, 128 pages, 50 cents net.

The strong spiritual element which marks all Dr. Jowett's other books is prominent in this one. The book treats "The Disciple's Theme," which is soul-winning; "The Disciple's Sacrifice," which is in behalf of soul-winning; "The Disciple's Tenderness," which should be characteristic of his manner in soul-winning, and "The Disciple Watching for Souls," which ought to be his attitude and employment. The Scriptures upon which he bases his discussions are such as these: "Unto me, who am less than the least of all saints, was this grace given, to preach

---

REGIMENTAL REUNIONS AND FORTY-THIRD ANNIVERSARY BATTLE CHICKAMAUGA.

CHATTANOOGA, SEPTEMBER 18-20, 1906.

On September 18, 1906, will occur the forty-third anniversary of the Battle of Chickamauga. It is proposed to celebrate this memorable event with a reunion of the various regiments that participated in this memorable battle and the various battles fought around Chattanooga. This reunion will be held at Chickamauga National Park, September 18, 19 and 20, and the present indications are that it will be the largest and most notable gathering ever held in the South. On the above dates, the remnants from the armies of twelve states, comprising the following: Pennsylvania, Ohio, Michigan, Indiana, Illinois, Wisconsin, Minnesota, Iowa, Nebraska, Missouri, Kansas and Kentucky, will assemble, many for the first and last time since they marched, from its blood-stained fields, forty-three years ago.

Here is one of the great opportunities for the education of the youth. Don't fail to take your children and show them historic Chattanooga, with all its historical connections. It is the opportunity of a lifetime. Go and see the old war generals and other officers; point out the places of interest on the battlefield; let them show you and explain, in person, the markers erected on the battlefield showing the positions of the opposing armies at the time of battle. It will not be long until none will be left to do this noble work.

It will be many years, if ever again, that such an opportunity will present itself. See that your tickets read via the Louisville & Nashville R. R., the Battlefield Route. Call on your nearest railroad agent for rates and advertising matter pertaining to the reunion, or write nearest representative of the Louisville & Nashville R. R.

J. H. MILLIKEN, D. P. A., Louisville, Ky.
J. D. BUSH, D. P. A., Cincinnati, Ohio.
J. E. DAVENPORT, D. P. A., St. Louis, Mo.
H. C. BAILEY, N. W. P. A., Chicago, Ill.

---

unto the Gentiles the unsearchable riches of Christ;" and, "I fill up that which is behind of the afflictions of Christ." Nowhere else in the Book could better passages be found to set forth the fact that the Christian should have a passion for souls. That preacher has missed his calling who can read this little book without the embers of soul-winning being fanned into a flame.

MARRIAGES.

Notices of marriages inserted under this heading at the rate of fifty cents for three lines or less (seven words to a line). Additional words at five cents per word. Cash must in each case accompany order.

ALLEN—WILLIAMSON.—At Lebanon, Mo., on July 30, 1906, at the residence of J. F. Williamson, the marriage of Frank W. Allen of Columbia, Mo., and Miss Tena Williamson, of Lebanon, Mo., was celebrated. The ceremony was performed by E. B. Redd, of St. Louis, Mo., in the presence of the family and relatives. Bro. Allen is as widely and favorably known as any minister of the Christian church in the state. His long and successful pastorates, at Hannibal, Chillicothe, Fulton and other places, as well as his successful work, as president of the church schools at Camden Point and Fulton, Mo., have greatly endeared him to the brotherhood of the entire state. The bride, Miss Tena Williamson, is also widely and favorably known through her successful self-sacrificing work as matron of the Christian Orphans' Home of St. Louis, Mo., which won for her a place in the esteem and affection of all who love the gospel of the helping hand.

Their hosts of friends wish for them long lives of happy usefulness in the service of him whom they both delight to honor. After a short bridal trip, they will be at home to their friends at their residence in Columbia, Mo. — E. B. REDD.

OBITUARIES.

[Notices of Deaths, not more than four lines, inserted free. Obituary memoirs, one cent per word. Send the money with the copy.]

MERRIDITH

Bro. Charles M. Merridith died at Taylorville, Ill., July 24, in his sixty-seventh year. He had been a member of the church for years. He leaves a widow, two daughters, brother and sisters. He was buried from the church July 27th. His old soldier comrade and pastor, Elder W. W. Weeden, preaching the funeral sermon. — L. MOORE.

ROBERTS.

Died, in Moberly, Mo., July 30, 1906, Mrs. Julia D. Roberts, daughter of Thomas P. Coats, deceased. She leaves one son and four daughters. Sister Roberts had been a member of the church of God in Christ for sixty-eight years. The funeral sermon was preached by the writer in Central Christian church of Moberly, Mo., Wednesday, August 1. — E. J. LAMPTON.

DYSON.

James H. Dyson, an elder in the church at Thomson, Ill., died Monday, August 6, aged 67 years. He was as consecrated and earnest as it is possible for man to be and the chief purpose of his life was to do his Master's will. For twenty years he served as elder of the church, and was faithful to his trust. The funeral was held Wednesday, August 8, from the church and in charge of the minister at Thomson.

MISS MYRTLE E. VERY,
CECIL C. CARPENTER.

Princeton, Ill.

MARSH.

Joseph M. Marsh was born near Keytesville, Mo., Jan. 7, 1835, and died suddenly of heart

---

INDIVIDUAL COMMUNION SERVICE.

The THOMAS SYSTEM is the simplest and best. 3000 churches now use this service. Our "Self-Collecting" tray has no equal, besides, it saves ONE FOURTH of what other systems cost. Our Filler places the wine in 150 glasses per minute. Write for catalogue and our *liberal offer*. Address Thomas Communion Service Co., Box 45, Lima, O.

failure at his home in Triplett, Mo., June 14, 1906, aged 71 years, 6 months and 12 days. He was married to Miss Margaret Hampton, of Charlton county, June 5, 1859. The union was blessed with four children, three of whom, one son and two daughters survive, with their invalid mother and a large community of relatives and friends, to mourn an irreparable loss.

Judge Marsh, as he was widely and familiarly known in central and northern Missouri, was a man of unusual attainments. Physically, morally, intellectually and spiritually, his was "A combination and a form indeed, Where every god did seem to set his seal, To give the world assurance of a man."

Passing through the dark days of the civil war as an officer in the Confederate army, he emerged a staunch believer in the cause of the Federal government, to which subsequently he gave his most loyal support. For many years he was cashier of the Farmer's Bank of Triplett, an honored and useful Elder in the church, a Mason of high rank, a prominent Odd Fellow, and a leading citizen of Charlton county, which distinction he bore to the day of his demise. He read the CHRISTIAN-EVANGELIST from its founding as "The Pioneer" without missing a copy, and his devotion to the great cause which it pleads was the ruling passion of his life.

Extensive reading and wide experience, through an active life of more than fifty years, gave him a knowledge almost encyclopaedic. There was scarce a subject you could bring before him, that you had not cause to wonder at the richness and fullness of the information he had somehow gathered, and so reliable was this that it was almost perilous to encounter him in controversy. Yet there lay his power, for he was broad, cheerful, magnanimous, employing his talents as a sacred trust for the benefit of others, who, knowing his sterling integrity, trusted him implicitly, and profited by that which most men would have used as an increased facility for promoting their own selfish ambitions and gain. It was thus that Judge Marsh the influential man that he was first in his home, first in the church, then ever where and in all things where duty seemed to call, and where opportunity could be clothed with the dignity and privilege of genuine Christian citizenship.

The writer conducted the funeral service in the presence of the largest concourse of people that has ever seen on such an occasion, and the remains were tenderly laid to rest mourned by the whole community. Blessed are the dead which die in the Lord from henceforth; yea, saith the Spirit, that they may rest from their labors; and their works do follow them. — C. P. SMITH.

Mason City, Iowa.

Send for Our Complete Catalog
Christian Publishing Co.,
2712 Pine St.,   St. Louis, Mo.

☜ The Home Department ☞

The Aftermath.

His children talked apart from her, nor learned
  To care for her as they had loved another;
Though much she tried to draw anear, and yearned
  To be to them in very truth a mother.

And he, with saddened face and hair grown gray,
  Saw that she came and went without repining,
Though oft he dreamed of her who went away
  While still the radiant suns of spring were
    shining.

So passed the years; and if she ever thought
  Of her who went before, the rich field robbing,
None ever knew the lonely fight she fought,
  Nor ever heard her in the long nights sobbing.
         —Louis Dodge.

✸ ✸

The Bronze Vase.

BY J. BRECKENRIDGE ELLIS.

PART III.

CHAPTER VII.

Wizzen cooked breakfast over a fire built upon the flat, sandy waste. He was rich in kindling and other inflammable wood, thanks to the generosity of the river. In recent floods it had brought all kinds of refuse. It had even carried heavy articles of iron and brass, and had battered them out of shape in its terrible but brief power. From a distance Kansas City was to be seen clinging to its rugged cliffs and peeping over high embankments at the swift river. The steamboat ferry passed and repassed the line of vision, and many skiffs and rafts floated under the bridges. Closer at hand were the huge piers of a bridge that had hoped to be great in the world, but had never gotten itself finished, and now looked as if it might be flat on its back with only its white legs sticking up in the air.

When the meal was ready, Wizzen unstrapped the upper table from his mover's wagon and set it in the shade of the wagon, for already the sun was hot on the desert. Mrs. Weed came from the clammy, earthy-smelling passenger coach, and a box was brought for her to sit upon. The rest stood up. Wizzen had fried bacon on an iron prong, and the young people had never before tasted bacon so good. On the table were various ready-made dishes, and when Mrs. Weed called for anything, they waited for her to point, for she always named something she didn't want. Raymund watched to see if she would ever call anything by its proper name, but she never did. Sometimes she could not tell what she wanted by even a wrong name, because no name at all would come to her, and then she would wear a surprised look as if she thought something amiss with the English language, and would merely say, "Please hand me—" and nod her head in a certain direction. All this was a source of great admiration to Wizzen. "Surprising how the old lady can eat," he would murmur, "which she sometimes can do better than me!"

During the heat of that day, Rhoda remained with the old lady inside the coach, and Raymund and Wizzen gasped for air in the shade of the wagon, and sat in the car by turns. The air rang with the shouts of bare-legged children at play about the stranded houseboats—children in miserable rags and squalid filth who made nothing of the blazing heat, and who dodged the blows of their drunken parents, and set out upon begging expeditions to the city, as happy as kings and with far less responsibility. In the evening the covered wagon set forth upon its journey to St. Louis, and Raymund sat beside Wizzen on the front seat, while the canvas was tucked up all about, to admit the air.

"And how long do you think it will take, Wizzen?" asked Raymund when the city was lost from sight and the cool perfume of country fields was wafted to them on twilight breezes.

"It always depends on the hosses," said Wizzen.

"How long does it take your horses, Wizzen?"

"That depends," said Wizzen. He said it as if he considered the subject disposed of, so the other asked no more. Rhoda and old Mrs. Weed sat on the spring seat with their feet in the straw and their backs resting against pillows. Rhoda noticed that at each heavy jar the old lady swayed toward the end of the bench with some danger of falling upon the stove, so at last she put her arm about her companion and nestled close to her. Mrs. Weed was greatly startled, and trembled as with a chill. Rhoda, afraid her protection was undesired, started to draw away, but the old lady, divining her intention, caught her hand and held her arm in its place. It was now so dark in the wagon that they could not see each other's faces, but Rhoda knew that it was a tear that fell upon her hand. Was Mrs. Weed thinking about her daughter who had married Wizzen and then had deserted both husband and mother? Had there once been a time when that daughter, now wandering somewhere in a world of vice, had been a pure affectionate girl like Rhoda, ready to offer her embrace in protecting care? On the front seat, Raymund grew drowsy. He found himself nodding beside the driver, while Wizzen, secure in the darkness, chewed his tobacco safe from any eyes but the winking stars. When the wagon stopped, it was about 10 o'clock. The horses were hastily unhitched. The spring wagon seat was taken out that there might be room for Rhoda and Mrs. Weed to undress and go to bed. Wizzen and Raymund rolled up in comforts and slept under the wagon. May be the earth made a hard bed; the youth did not know. He had not slept much the night before in the Union Station and now he made up for it. When he awoke, the sun was sending long inquiring beams right under the wagon. They had passed the night at the hedgeside. There was the double-noted cry of the meadow lark from every side, and the air, cool with fragrant dew, made one want to nestle into the very heart of the comfort. But no; one must get up! Not far away was a pond, and thence water was brought for the toilette, after which the bucket was carried to a farmhouse beyond the pond, for drinking water. Wizzen had brought some driftwood from the river—not much for fear of tiring the horses. A fire was built and coffee was boiled. "This is great!" cried Wizzen as he sat at the roots of the hedge, a huge tin can of coffee in one hand, and a hunk of baker's bread in the other. "Boys, they's nothing like just keeping a-moving!" It was evident that he included Mrs. Weed under his generic term of "boys," for he added, "and nothing ain't more satisfying to me than to know how the old lady delights in it!" He nodded toward Mrs. Weed, to let her know he was talking about her, and the old lady smiling cheerfully, asked him if his tea was too hot. After breakfast the journey was resumed. "By rights," Wizzen told Raymund, "we ought to rest in the heat of the day, and travel early and late. But you can't have no set rules with my hosses. You've got to take 'em when they kin go, and not strain them too hard." Which gave prospects of a very long "overland voyage," for the animals had the look of being easily strained. That night Rhoda was much astonished when Mrs. Weed whispered to her in the privacy of the wagon, "Oh, if we could only get some place and stay there!" Rhoda would have returned that she thought Mrs. Weed liked moving about, but the ear-trumpet was lost, as usual, and even if it had been at hand, the girl would not have cared to shout so long a sentence. Perhaps Mrs. Weed suspected her thought for she added in a low voice, "It has been my dream ever since my marriage, to settle down some place and have a little home of my own. Just to know my own pump and go to it every day—and my own dear henhouse, and a garden, and know it was mine, and

I was fixed to it!" She sighed plaintively. "But Wizzen loves to go from one place to another. He's as much at home in this wagon as if the wheels were stone foundations. He doesn't care for earth at all, or chickens, or cats. It would never do for him to know how I pine to stop somewhere and stay there. He is so good to me—better than many an own son, much better—and he thinks I like travelling around, like a letter. I do not, Rhoda, but this is a deep secret. I know I can trust you."

Rhoda squeezed her hand assuringly and Mrs. Weed said, "You are so good to me, I wanted you to know my little secret. I am so glad to open my heart to you. Wizzen tells me you are an orphan and have no home of your own, and I know just how you feel. I feel the same way. I don't care how humble a spot you may pick out, or if the hut on it is cold in summer and damp in winter, just so it is home—just so you can stay there and feel that nobody can get tired of you there—nobody can wonder how long you are going to stay; because you are at home. And you love the look of the bare ground or weeds or grass, as the case may be, for it is your bare ground, or weeds or what not. You say 'The world is wide and crowded with millions of people who do not know me, and who wouldn't care for me if they did; but this spot knows me and cares for me—these chickens come when I beat the tin pan—this cat expects its milk from my hands—these birds are in my trees, like enough waiting to rob me of my berries or peck my tomatoes—ah, dear, sometimes my words may be mixed up, though perhaps you haven't noticed it; but when I get to talking about home, everything comes to my tongue that it needs."

There was a pause, then Mrs. Weed said, "But don't think I complain. Wizzen loves changing about, and we must pretend to like it too or he will be unhappy." Day after day, the wagon traveled eastward, till Booneville was reached. "Now, we'll go some out of the way," Wizzen announced, "but you won't keer for that as it will make the voyage last all the longer." The truth is that Rhoda had begun to find a striking monotony in the journey, but she imitated Mrs. Weed's prudence. Instead of crossing the river, they kept along the northern shore, passing various towns and villages. At last they reached Cole county and came to Jefferson City. "We'll not cross the river here," said Wizzen, "and so not have to cross her at all, thanks to our coming this far out of our way." Raymund had often wished that they might have come to some town with a cheap book store, and now his desire was gratified. He would be able, no doubt, to get the school books he needed, at a price somewhat in proportion to his needs. He still had over $60, and while there was that much wealth at his disposal, his mind ought not to suffer for lack of proper food. When they drove into Jefferson City it was raining hard, and everything looked as dismal as possible, and that is saying a good deal when you remember that we are speaking of the state capital. The wagon was driven upon a vacant lot, of which there were a plenty, and when the horses had been tied to the wheel—a needless ceremony—Wizzen informed the party that he had business in the city. Raymund, protected by his green umbrella set forth with him, but Wizzen presently contrived to give him the slip; perhaps he was not interested in books. When Raymund at last saw in the distance a book store, he hastened thither with a wildly beating heart, for books excited him as much as spring bonnets or fast horses do some others.

Just as he reached the door his foot slipped, for the pavement was streaming with the downpour, and in recovering his balance he was hurled into the bosom of a man advancing from the other direction—a short, very fleshy man past fifty, with a bald head and a heavy white mustache, as if all the hair of his head had been washed downhill by the rain.

"What do you mean, sir?" cried the man staggering back and almost falling. He was very angry and glared at Raymund crying, "Why don't you look where you are going, sir?" Then his eyes grew wider and his face redder, and his breath more labored, as he cried, "What! if it isn't the young fellow with the green umbrella! Do you know, sir, that my leg you gave it in Kansas City? Have you followed me all the way to the capitol to destroy me with that vile weapon?"

Raymund now recognized the passenger who had denounced him so fiercely on his first arrival at the Union Station. "I beg your pardon," he said earnestly. "I am very sorry indeed. And— and I can't help saying that I'm glad to see you again, for it's like meeting an old acquaintance!" And he bestowed his winning smile upon the storm-tossed fat man.

"Oh, you are, hey?" growled the other looking at him from under his shaggy eyebrows. "I make no doubt you are glad! What are you doing here? Did you follow me up?"

"I am looking for some cheap school books," said Raymund, still smiling, for the other, in spite of his angry voice, did not look at all dangerous.

"Then come in here," the fat man snapped. "I expect I can be of service to you."

(TO BE CONTINUED.)

❄ ❄

Picture of War Engine "General."

A beautiful colored picture, 18x25 inches of the historic old engine "General" which was stolen at Big Shanty, Ga., by the Andrew's Raiders during the Civil War, and which is now on exhibition in the Union Depot, Chattanooga, Tenn., has been gotten out by the NASHVILLE, CHATTANOOGA & ST. LOUIS RY.—The "Battlefields Route to the South. The picture is ready for framing and will be mailed for 25c. The "Story of the General" sent free. W. Danley, Gen'l Pass. Agent, Nashville, Tenn.

My Mamma's Lap.

I like t' play wif dollies an' I like t' go t'
　　school;
I like t' jump my skippin' rope in mornings when
　　it's cool;
I like t' play go visitun while dolly takes her
　　nap,
But sometimes nuffin' else'll do 'but sit in mam-
　　ma's lap.

I like t' climb th' peach tree an' I like 't' make
　　mud pies;
I like t' play wif puppy an' I like a birfday
　　s'prise;
I like t' go out ridin' an' lst wear my little
　　cap,
But when I'm tired an' sleepy, w'y, I want my
　　mamma's lap.

I like t' tend my playhouse—is th' finest place
　　in town;
I like t' play big lady wif long skirts a-hangin'
　　down;
I like t' go t' Sabbath school an' wear my new
　　silk wrap—
But when a lump gets in my 'froat I lst want
　　mamma's lap.
—Strickland W. Gilliland, in Leslie's Weekly.

❁　❁

"Boy Wanted."

People laughed when they saw the sign
again. It seemed to be always in Mr.
Peter's window. For a day or two—
sometimes only for an hour or two—it
would be missing, and passers-by would
wonder whether Mr. Peters had at last
fcund a boy to suit him; but sooner or
later it was sure to appear again.

"What sort of a boy does he want,
anyway?", one and another would ask;
and then they would say to one another
that they supposed he was looking for a
perfect boy, and, in their opinion, he
would look a great while before he found
one. Not that there were not plenty of
boys— as many as a dozen used sometimes to appear in the course of a morning, trying for the situation. Mr. Peters
was said to be rich and queer, and for
one or both of these reasons, boys were
anxious to try to suit him.

"All he wants is for a fellow to run
on errands; it must be easy work and
sure pay"—this was the way they talked
to one another; but Mr. Peters wanted
something more than a boy to run errands. John Simmons found it out, and
this is the way he did it. He had been
engaged that very morning, and had been
kept busy all the forenoon at pleasant
enough work; and although he was a
lazy fellow, he rather enjoyed the place.
It was toward the middle of the afternoon that he was sent up to the attic, a
dark, dirty place, inhabited by mice and
cobwebs.

"You will find a long, deep box there,"
said Mr. Peters, "which I want you to
have put in order. It stands right in the
middle of the room—you can't miss it."
John looked doleful. "A long, deep
box! I should think it was!" he said to
himself as the attic door closed after
him. It will weigh a ton, I guess; and
what is there in it? Nothing in the
world but old nails and screws, and
pieces of iron, and broken keys, and
things—rubbish, the whole of it. Nothing worth touching. And it is as dark
as a pocket up here, and cold besides.
How the wind blows in through those
knotholes! There's a mouse! If there is
anything I hate, it's mice! I'll tell you
what it is, if old Peters thinks I'm going
to stay up here and tumble over his old
rusty nails, he's much mistaken. I wasn't
hired for that kind of work."

Whereupon John bounced down the attic stairs three at a time, and was found
lounging in the show-window an hour
afterwards when Mr. Peters appeared.

"Have you put the box in order already?" was the gentleman's question.

"I didn't find anything to put in order;
there was nothing in it but old nails and
things."

"Exactly. It was the nails and things

that I wanted put in order. Did you do
it?"

"No, sir, it was dark up there and cold;
and I didn't see anything worth doing.
Besides, I thought I was hired to run
errands."

"Oh," said Mr. Peters, "I thought you
were hired to do as you were told."

But he smiled pleasantly enough and
at once gave John an errand to go down
town; and the boy went off chuckling,
declaring to himself that he knew how
to manage the old man; all it needed was
a little standing up for his rights.

Precisely at six o'clock John was
called and paid the sum promised him
for a day's work; and then, to his dismay,
was told that his services would not be
needed any more. He asked no questions. Indeed, he had time for none, as
Mr. Peters immediately closed the door.

The next morning the old sign, "Boy
Wanted," appeared in its usual place.
But before noon it was taken down and
Charles Jones was the fortunate boy.
Errands—plenty of them! He was kept
busy until within an hour of closing.
Then, behold!—he was sent up to the
attic to put the long box in order. He
was not afraid of a mouse nor of the
cold but he grumbled much over the box.
Nothing in it worthy his attention. However, he tumbled over the things, grumbling all the time, picked out a few
straight nails, a key or two, and finally
appeared with this message:

"Here's all there is worth keeping in
that box. The rest of the nails are rusty,
and the hooks are bent, or something."

"Very well," said Mr. Peters, and he
sent him to the postoffice.

What do you think! By the close of
the next day Charlie had been paid and
discharged, and the old sign hung in the
window.

"I've no kind of a notion why I was

discharged," grumbled Charlie to his
mother. "He said that wouldn't suit.
It's my opinion that he doesn't want a
boy at all, and takes that way to cheat.
Mean old fellow!"

It was Crawford Mills who was hired
next. He knew neither of the other boys,
and so did his errands in blissful ignorance of the long box until the second
morning of his stay, when in a leisure
hour he was sent to put it in order. The
morning passed, dinner time came, and
still Crawford had not appeared from
the attic. At last Mr. Peters called him,
"Got through?"

"No, sir, there is ever so much more
to do."

"All right. It is dinner time now. You
may go back to it after dinner."

After dinner he went back. All the

short afternoon he was not heard from, but just as Mr. Peters was deciding to call him again he appeared.

"I've done my best, sir," he said, "and down at the very bottom of the box I found this."

"This" was a five-dollar gold piece.

"That's a queer place for gold," said Mr. Peters. "It's good you found it. Well, sir, I suppose you will be on hand to-morrow morning?"

This he said as he was putting the gold piece in his pocketbook.

After Crawford had said good-night and gone, Mr. Peters took the lantern and went slowly up the attic stairs. There was the long, deep box in which the rub-b:sh of twenty-five years had gathered. Crawford had evidently been to the bot-tom. He had fitted shingles to make compartments, and in these different rooms he had placed the articles with bits of shingle laid on top, and labeled thus: "Good Screws," "Picture Nails." "Small Keys, Somewhat Bent." "Picture Hooks." "Pieces of Iron whose use I don't know." And so, on through the long box. In perfect order it was at least, and very little that really could be called useful could be found within it.

But Mr. Peters, as he bent over and read the labels, laughed gleefully, and murmured to the mice: "If we are not both mistaken, I have found a boy; and he has found a fortune."

Sure enough, the sign disappeared from the window, and was seen no more.

Crawford became the well-known er-rand boy of the firm of Peters & Co. He had a little room neatly fitted up next to the attic, where he spent the evenings, and at the foot of the bed hangs a motto which Mr. Peters gave him. "It tells your fortune for you, don't forget it," he said, when he handed it to Crawford; and the boy laughed and read it curiously: "He that is faithful in that which is least, is faithful in much." I'll try to be, sir," and he never once thought of the long box over which he had been "faithful."

All this happened years ago. Craw-ford Mills is errand boy no more, but the firm is Peters, Mills & Co.—a young man and a rich man.

"He found his fortune in the long box of rubbish," Mr. Peters said once, laugh-ing. "Never was a five-dollar gold piece so successful in business as that one of his has been; it is good he found it."

Then, after a moment of silence, he said, gravely: "No, he didn't; he found it in his mother's Bible; 'He that is faithful in that which is least, is faithful also in much.' It is true; Mills the boy was 'faithful,' and Mills the man we trust."—*Exchange*.

❀ ❀

Lake Geneva Summer Train Service.

Via the Chicago & North-Western R'y is now in effect including Saturday after-noon train leaving Chicago 1:00 p. m. and Sunday Train leaving 8:00 a. m. For tickets, rates and full information apply to your nearest ticket agent or address W. B. Kniskern, P. T. M., C. & N. W. R'y Co., Chicago.

Who Is She?

I know the dearest little girl,
　About as big as you.
Her eyes are black or brown or gray,
　Or maybe they are blue;
But, anyway, her hands are clean;
　Her teeth are white as snow;
Her little dress is always neat;
　She goes to school, you know.
This little girl—I love her well,
　And see her often, too—
If I to-day her name should tell—
　She—might—be—you. —*Little Folks.*

❀ ❀

How Is It With You?

Bessie had been told about Jesus when she was a tiny girl, and she can not re-member a time when she did not love him. Her teacher once asked her: "Bes-sie, have you found the Saviour yet?" "Why, I have never lost him," was the sweet reply. Can you say you have never lost the Saviour, but have always felt that he was with you?—*Ex.*

❀ ❀

My Master Is Always In.

"Johnny," said a man, looking at a boy who was taking care of a shop while his master was out, "you must give me an extra measure; your master is not in."

Johnny looked up into the man's face very seriously and said: "My master is always in."

Johnny's Master was the all-seeing God. Let us all, when tempted to do wrong, adopt Johnny's motto: "My Mas-ter is always in." It will save us from many a sin and much sorrow.—*Selected.*

❀ ❀

"You're a Brick."

When Tom says admiringly to Harry, "You're a brick!"—I wonder if he knows how the saying originated.

In the golden days of Greece, an am-bassador once came from Epirus to Sparta, and was shown by the king over his capital. He was surprised to find no walls around the city.

"Sire!" he exclaimed, "I have visited nearly all the towns in Greece, but I find no walls for their defense. Why is this?"

"Indeed!" the king replied, "you can-not have looked carefully. Come with me to-morrow and I will show you the walls of Sparta."

On the following morning the king led his guest out upon the plains where his army was drawing up in battle array, and pointing proudly to the valiant sol-diers, he said:

"There you behold the walls of Sparta —every man a brick!"

❀ ❀

50 More Young People

Fifty More Young People can get spe-cial rates for room, board and tuition at *Iowa Christian College*. Home study courses also. New illustrated catalog ready. Write Pres. Chas. J. Burton, Os-kaloosa, Iowa.

Christian Publishing Company
2712 Pine St., St. Louis, Mo.

Alexander Campbell's "Popular Lectures and Addresses" sold until recently for $3. This summer we will sell the book and THE CHRISTIAN-EVANGELIST for that price.

In the name of helpless children we protest against imposing inferior literature upon them that helps drive them from our Bible schools as soon as they get old enough to have initiative, when the W. W. Dowling supplies can be bought at prices no higher.

People of refined sensibilities who object to drinking from a common communion cup are entitled to some consideration, even if the "ruling elder" says there is no danger of spreading tubercular or other diseases in that way. Our individual communion service lends a new charm to this beautiful part of the worship. Write us for illustrations and price list.

I have received the picture of Brother Garrison. It is an excellent likeness of a splendid man that after generations will say lived ahead of his time. But he has helped us of his own day onward.—Harry Bower, Albion, Ill.

Brother Bower sent more than is required, but we will send the picture for one new subscription and one renewal, accompanied by $3.

We have found a pen we can recommend. It is a self-filling fountain pen. Regular price $2.50. We have arranged to sell pen and CHRISTIAN-EVANGELIST for $2.75. The manufacturers are Christian men. They are financially reliable. If through ordinary use it becomes unsatisfactory within ten years, it may be returned to the manufacturers and a new one will be given on application. A description of pen sent on application.

Dog days are here, but dull days have not come to us as yet. A gratifying feature of our rapidly increasing circulation is the great number of new subscriptions coming one and two at a time from congregations in all parts of the land. These scattered legions of friends becoming keenly interested in introducing this best of literature in more homes is our confidence for the future. The following clubs of new subscribers have come since last week: Alameda, Cal., 5, P. C. Macfarlane, minister; Payson, Ill., 4, Gilbert Ellis, pastor; Fredericktown, Mo., 17, R. O. Rog-

---

EVERY BIBLE SCHOOL SHOULD HAVE IT
ALL GOOD ONES WILL

Map of Palestine in the Time of Christ, 36x48 inches. Latest and best. Paper, Mounted on cloth, with Rollers. Prepaid - - - - - $2.00
Linen finish cloth, prepaid - - - $1.00

Map C. Palestine in the Time of Christ, with Map of Jerusalem, 48x72 inches. Has all the known places and localities so marked, all the conjectural ones likewise. Has a system of concentric circles showing distances from Jerusalem. Has table of mountains, heights, etc. Is complete. Price, on Map paper, cloth back, mounted on Rollers - - - - - $6.00
On linen finish cloth, unmounted, prepaid - - - - - $4.00
With patent spring rollers, complete, prepaid - - - - - $7.50

CHRISTIAN PUBLISHING COMPANY, St. Louis, Mo.

---

ers, minister; San Angelo, Tex., 3, S. T. Shore, pastor; Rowlett, Texas, 3; Sachse, Texas, 10; Dayton, O., 20, I. J. Cahill, pastor; Moberly, Mo., 13, W. B. Taylor, minister; Atchison, Kan., 11, W. S. Hilton, pastor; Circleville, Kan., 3.

In my judgment, the coming hymnal for Christian churches has arrived in "Gloria in Excelsis." My people are not simply pleased, they are immensely gratified with its introduction. Beauty and dignity in its appearance—a scope of variety in its songs to meet any demand in worship—with responsive readings on which the people lay hold with pleasure—the Wabash congregation believes it has the 'ne plus ultra' of hymnals.—E. F. Daugherty, Wabash, Ind.

In going to the Buffalo convention October 12-18 get to the Wabash as soon as possible. Start from everywhere so as to connect with THE CHRISTIAN-EVANGELIST Special, which leaves St. Louis Thursday noon, October 11. Come via St. Louis from Omaha, Des Moines and all points west, south and southwest. You will have your choice from Detroit by lake or through Canada without extra charge. We shall secure you the best of hotel service in Buffalo at the lowest rates and with congenial friends.

After carefully examining "Gloria in Excelsis," I am fully convinced that the ed-

---

itor-in-chief and his associates have splendidly succeeded in making this book just what they designed it to be—"a high-grade dignified hymnal for the use of the churches." Its arrangement is faultless. The choice selections of Scripture are so abundant, and so well adapted to the different phases of church service, that every possible demand seems to be supplied. The distinct and careful classification of hymns, with the thorough indexing of subjects, is a feature of great practical value. The hymns selected are the very best, including practically all the old standard hymns of real worth, and many of the excellent modern hymns that have become an essential part of our best hymnology. The mechanical feature of the book in every sense could not well be excelled.— P. H. Duncan, Latonia, Ky.

✸ ✸

The other night a street evangelist was preaching what might be called an "excited" sermon on a corner a couple of blocks east of the union depot. In his audience was a small newsboy. The preacher waved his arms and shook his head. Suddenly he quieted down and asked:

"My friends, who is it that watches over us; saves us from harm; frowns on wickedness; wants us to be gentle, and wishes to see not brutality?"

"I know," came from the newsboy. "It's President Roosevelt."—Denver Post.

By Courtesy of "The Wabash." Write us about free tickets to the Convention. Let us all see the Falls together.

THE
CHRISTIAN-
EVANGELIST

A WEEKLY RELIGIOUS NEWSPAPER.

Volume XLIII.	No. 34.

ST. LOUIS, AUGUST 23, 1906.

FORGIVENESS

By John Greenleaf Whittier

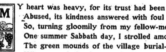

MY heart was heavy, for its trust had been
Abused, its kindness answered with foul wrong;
So, turning gloomily from my fellow-men,
One summer Sabbath day, I strolled among
The green mounds of the village burial-place;
Where, pondering how all human love and hate
Find one sad level; and how, soon or late,
Wronged and wrong-doer, each with meekened
    face
And cold hands folded over a still heart,
Pass the green threshold of our common grave,
Whither all footsteps tend, and none depart.
Awed for myself, and pitying my race,
Our common sorrow, like a mighty wave,
Swept all my pride away, and trembling I forgave.

The Christian-Evangelist.

J. H. GARRISON, Editor

PAUL MOORE, Assistant Editor

F. D. POWER,
B. B. TYLER, } Staff Correspondents.
W. DURBAN,

Subscription Price, $1.50 a Year.

For foreign countries add $1.04 for postage.

Remittances should be made by money order, draft, or registered-letter; not by local cheque, unless 10 cents is added to cover cost of collection

In Ordering Change of Post Office give both old and new address.

Matter for Publication should be addressed to THE CHRISTIAN-EVANGELIST. Subscriptions and remittances should be addressed to the Christian Publishing Company, 2712 Pine Street, St. Louis, Mo.

Unused Manuscripts will be returned only if accompanied by stamps.

News items, evangelistic and other fise, are solicited, and should be sent on a postal card, if possible.

Published by the Christian Publishing Company, 2712 Pine Street, St. Louis, Mo.

Entered at St. Louis P. O. as Second Class Matter.

WHAT WE STAND FOR.

For the Christ of Galilee,
For the truth which makes men free,
For the bond of unity
Which makes God's children one.

For the love which shines in deeds
For the life which this world need,
For the church whose triumph speeds
The prayer: "Thy will be done."

For the right against the wrong,
For the weak against the strong,
For the poor who've waited long
For the brighter age to be.

For the faith against tradition,
For the truth 'gainst superstition,
For the hope whose glad fruition
Our waiting eyes shall see.

For the city God is rearing,
For the New Earth now appearing,
For the heaven above us clearing,
And the song of victory.

             J. H. Garrison.

CONTENTS.

Centennial Propaganda 1063
Current Events 1064
Editorial—
  Where Jesus Placed the Emphasis . 1065
  An Estimate of the Manchester
    Meeting 1065
  Notes and Comments 1066
  Current Religious Thought 1066
  Editor's Easy Chair 1067
Contributed Articles—
  As Seen from the Dome. F. D.
    Power 1068
  Modern Religious Persecution—A
    Defense. B. L. Chase 1069
  From Presbyterian to Christian
    Church, by Way of Baptist.
    David Millar 1070
  Religious Atavism. W. T. Moore . 1071
  The Practice of Immortality.
    Cephas Shelburne 1072
  Some Helps to a Study of the Holy
    Spirit. Edgar D. Jones 1073
Our Budget 1074
News from Many Fields 1081
Evangelistic 1083
Sunday-school 1084
Midweek Prayer-meeting 1084
Christian Endeavor 1085
People's Forum 1086
Current Literature 1086
The Home Department 1087

THE
CHRISTIAN-EVANGELIST

"IN FAITH, UNITY, IN OPINION AND METHODS, LIBERTY, IN ALL THINGS, CHARITY."

| Vol. XLIII. | August 23, 1906 | No. 34 |

1809 — CENTENNIAL PROPAGANDA — CHURCHES OF CHRIST — 1909

: : : GEO. L. SNIVELY.

Looking Toward Pittsburg.

It is not likely that even Brother Muck-ley could make a more eloquent appeal for an offering from every church for church extension than is contained in correspondence printed below. Thousands are looking hopefully to the directors of this fund for "help to a foothold." They have the truth and convictions and, courage and knowledge to nobly do when doing at all is made possible. An offering by every church the first Lord's day in September will mean the establishment of a multitude of new, strong churches by 1909.

We gladly give coveted Centennial Propaganda page space to Sister Harrison's report of Mrs. Maud D. Ferris' queenly memorial to her mother. How pleasing such Christian chivalry must be to Him who did not forget his dear mother even amidst the cares of establishing his kingdom and the anguish of the cross. May we not hope that many other dear departed ones than our saintly Sister Davis may thus be memorialized by loved ones lingering here who feel their names ought to be perpetuated on earth as an inspiration to all good works.

We most heartily congratulate the president and secretary of our national C. W. B. M., Sisters Garrison, of Louisville, and Harrison, of Louisville, and all their helpers over this splendid fruitage of their labors, which we hope is simply the first fruits of a greater harvest.

Memorial Gift to the Christian Woman's Centennial Offering.

A beautiful gift is beautiful at any season; but it is altogether lovely when it comes at an appropriate time, and the grace of fitness is added to the grace of giving. The memorial idea is the very heart of our centennial movement, for our plans for celebrating this birthday of our church are all memorials to our great principles to which we have borne witness for one hundred years, and to the fathers of our faith who first voiced them. The Christian Woman's Board of Missions is bearing its part in this anniversary by establishing and strengthening memorial missions at eleven points in seven different countries. How fitting a season then is this for making memorial gifts!

It has come into the heart of a loving daughter to do this gracious deed—Mrs. Maud D. Ferris of Detroit, Mich., has given $25,000 to our new missionary training school at Indianapolis, in memory of her mother, Mrs. Sarah A. Davis, and it will be called in her honor, "The Sarah A. Davis Memorial Training School."

This gift will be a beginning in many ways. It is the largest gift ever received by the Christian Woman's Board of Missions, and may be an inspiration to others to do great things for God. It gives assurance of starting the first missionary

training school among the Disciples of Christ on a scale worthy of the enterprise. And it is the first memorial offering to our centennial fund. May others claim a like beautiful ministry in the name and for the sake of their dear dead!—Ida W. Harrison, Centennial Sec. C. W. B. M.

Good Reasons for the Church Extension Offering.

There are 107 reasons why the church extension offering should be taken similar to the three we are giving by printing some letters forwarded to us by our corresponding secretary. These churches are our neighbors because our neighbor is the one in need. If every congregation among us could be a Board of Church Extension for just one week and make answer to the appeals as does the board at Kansas City, saying "we cannot help you until the churches send the money," it may be stated truly that no church in our brotherhood would be classed as a noncontributor to the September offering. Our extension board needs $130,000 now to answer appeals that have come since last March.

Fair Oak, Ind., Aug. 11, 1906.
Dear Brother Muckley:—I don't know whether it will be worth while, but I am going to write you to see if there will be any chance to secure a loan. Our house is small but good and insured for $800, but we have a debt of $355 and pay 8 per cent interest and the party is crowding us. We are few in members and poor in purse, but striving to build up, having secured regular preaching for half time. We feel fearful of losing our property unless we can secure a loan from you. The cause has always had a strong fight with the denominations here from the first, but now our minister gets a good hearing and we are in the road to a permanent footing if we can only hold our house. Hoping we can secure help from the Extension Fund, I remain.—W. F. Wilson.

Plains, Mont., June 19, 1906.
Dear Brother Muckley:—I am here in a meeting which is certain to result in a permanent organization. Am the first of our preachers to ever visit the town. Population about 500, and only four miles from the Flathead Indian Reservation soon to be opened. Sure to be a good town. Our people here are progressive, loyal and thoroughly acquainted with our plan of work. Emigrated here from Missouri several years ago. A lot has been donated and we will likely build this summer. In that event, is it your opinion that we could get a loan of $600 or $900, or even less? I should like to have your idea in the matter so as to formulate plans before closing the meeting July 1st. Our lot is centrally located, and for trustees we expect to put in good responsible persons.—F. H. Groom.

Ocean Park, Cal., April 28, 1906.
Dear Brother Muckley:—A choice tract, 213 lots in the heart of a city, has just been put on the market, and the Christian church secures, option on a choice corner 103x125 at $3,000. This is a concession of $800 by the owners. The next corner north of us is held at $100 a foot, and the one just opposite us at $80 a foot. You can see what I have accomplished for the church in this. We want to erect a building for present use worth $2,500 to $3,000, and enlarge it in about two years. After raising all we can locally we shall need a loan of about $1,500. Can our church grant it? This is a beach town of high class, 17 miles from heart of Los Angeles and only nine miles from city limits. It has grown from nothing to 10,000 population in five years. Our location is central, two blocks from postoffice. Three blocks from the ocean. We will commence building as soon as plans can be pre-

pared. I am on the Southern California Board which endorses our work. Please let me hear from you soon and favorably.—Geo. Ringo.

OUR CENTENNIAL HELPERS.

Find enclosed $1.50 for subscription to CHRISTIAN-EVANGELIST. We cannot do without it.—Melvin Hobbs, Smith Center, Kas.

Many good things have been appearing in THE CHRISTIAN-EVANGELIST. "Our Budget" is refreshing and stimulating.—D. R. Bebout, Effingham, Ill.

I should not like to have to get along without THE CHRISTIAN-EVANGELIST. Whenever opportunity offers, I will help increase its circulation.—Mary Nichels, Murray, Neb.

Enclosed find $1.50 to apply on my subscription. I thank you for sending the paper after my time was out. I do not wish to miss a number.—Mrs. E. Beem, Tacoma, Wash.

I am a very enthusiastic friend of THE CHRISTIAN-EVANGELIST. In my judgment it represents a type of journalism that must and will inevitably prevail in our brotherhood.—C. A. Polson, minister, Topeka, Kas.

I enjoy the visits of THE CHRISTIAN-EVANGELIST and hope it will live—well, I was going to say forever, but will say so long as time, accomplishing a noble work for the cause.—E. J. Allen, Homestead, Pa.

Enclosed find payment of my subscription to THE CHRISTIAN-EVANGELIST to February, 1908. Where a man's money goes his heart surely is. My heart is surely with THE CHRISTIAN-EVANGELIST in the brave, truthful, gentle and sane spirit continuously in evidence.—G. D. Edwards, Honolulu, Hawaii.

I am sending you a few names to whom I wish you to send THE CHRISTIAN-EVANGELIST for a few issues, and I will do my best to secure their subscriptions. I feel free to tell them that, according to my judgment it is the best paper published in the brotherhood. I am much pleased with the catholic spirit of THE CHRISTIAN-EVANGELIST, and will do what I can to assist in promoting the interest of the cause so dear to all our hearts through its wider circulation.—T. L. Read.

I notice in last week's CHRISTIAN-EVANGELIST that for two subscriptions and $3 you will give the picture of Bro. J. H. Garrison. Now, I want this picture and will prize it very much, for I dearly love Brother Garrison, though I have never met him. I would go farther to meet him and shake hands with him than any other man in the nation, even our Chief Executive. For 25 years I have so much enjoyed his writings as to form a great attachment for him. Send me 20 sample copies of THE CHRISTIAN-EVANGELIST. I would like to have the paper in every home of my brethren for its gracious ministry.—A. M. Noel.

Current Events

It really seems that the courts mean business with the Standard Oil Company.

Indictment of Standard Oil.
The tidings as they come through the press seem almost too good to be true. We have been in the habit of taking it for granted that there is always a way for an evil-doer to escape punishment, provided he is a big enough evil-doer. We have never believed this theory very implicitly and we hope that the public's faith in it is in a fair way to be destroyed. A federal grand jury at Chicago, and another at Jamestown, N. Y., have indicted the Standard for illegally receiving railroad rebates. The New York jury has also indicted the Pennsylvania railroad, and the Vacuum Oil Company. The Chicago jury has not yet indicted any railroads, but it may be taken for granted that, if the Standard is guilty of receiving rebates, somebody must be guilty of giving them. The interesting fact about all this is that the action has been taken under the old law which has been on the statute books for many years. The occurrence strongly confirms the position of those who have been asserting that what we need is more enforcement rather than more law. The new railroad rate bill will go into effect the latter part of this month, and then perhaps, we shall have both more law and more enforcement, which will be better than an increased supply of either element alone.

Ex-Senator James K. Jones, of Arkansas, is now figuring as attorney for the

A Fallen Angel.
Standard Oil Company, and is especially interested in helping to evade the regulations of the Department of the Interior and enable the Standard to get control of all the oil wells in the Indian Territory. It will be remembered—and the cynical will smile as they remember it—that Senator Jones was chairman of the Democratic national committee in 1896 and 1900, and led in two whirlwind campaigns whose chief strength was in their opposition to plutocracy. The senator has either suffered a change of heart or enjoyed a raise of salary.

One of the most striking results of the new railroad rate law will be the separation of the railroad

Railroads and Coal.
business from the coal business. The law makes it compulsory for railroads to dispose of their holdings in coal mines and coal lands before January 1, 1908. It is a matter of common knowledge that the coal situation in the east has been completely controlled by certain railroads. As common carriers they have been compelled to serve both themselves (in the capacity of coal producers) and their competitors. The temptation to down the competitors by withholding cars and raising freight rates has been too great for them. There is scarcely any section of the country in which coal is found in large quantities where one will not find abandoned coal mines or mines which have been sold at sacrifice for this reason. The separation of railroad interests and coal-producing interests will not only give the independent operators a chance, but will give the public at least half a chance to get coal at a fair rate.

Mr. Bryan is undertaking an enterprise of most tremendous difficulty when he

Mr. Bryan.
starts upon a two years' campaign for the presidential nomination. To be sure he has, perhaps, not deliberately launched himself upon any such campaign, but the thing has been done for him by his best friends and without his disapproval. One of two things is true: either he is confident that he can make a two years' race without losing his wind, or laying himself open to fatal criticism in the press; or else he feels that his party needs the kind of exhortation and agitation which he alone can give and is not notably anxious as to the results for his own personal career. While we do not doubt that Mr. Bryan shares with nearly all the rest of the male population of this country the desire to be president, we are inclined to think that the latter hypothesis is the correct one. He is too good a politician to enter on a two years' campaign if getting the nomination were the only end in view. Within such a period there is too much time to make mistakes, say foolish things and make enemies. If he proceeds in other cases as he has with Mr. Sullivan, of Illinois, the process of making enemies will go on apace, and yet, it seems that even in this episode he has gained more than he has lost. Mr. Sullivan refuses to resign from the national committee, refuses even to get mad at the attack upon himself, and proposes to make the Illinois convention, which he will probably dominate, declare in favor of Bryan.

That reminds us that our very good friend Ashley J. Elliott, manager of the

A Criticism.
Illinois Car Service Association, criticises our recent suggestion that railroads ought to pay demurrage for failure to furnish cars if they require shippers to pay it for failure to load or unload them promptly. He says:

"The incentives of the two parties are diametrically opposed to each other. It is always to the railroad's interest to furnish cars promptly, while it is not always to the shipper's interest to unload them promptly. Of the railroad's sins of omission, failure to furnish cars to the extent of their ability is not one."

It might, to be sure, be assumed that, if furnishing and hauling cars is the business of a corporation, it will be to its interest to furnish them as promptly as possible, just as it is to a grocer's interest to wait on his customers as promptly as possible. But the case is not quite so simple. As we have said, railroads are sometimes competitors with their patrons, as in the coal business. Sometimes they have alliances with one patron which make it advisable not to serve others in the same line, as in the oil business. Some of the independent coal operators who have been ruined be-

Where Jesus Placed the Emphasis.

The cry "Back to Christ" has become a very popular one and there are but few theological back numbers left who would not agree that all our theologies and religious teachings should be tested by the mind of Christ. It is one thing, however, to accept a popular slogan, and another thing to be true to all that is involved in it. It is one thing to repeat the cry, "Back to Christ," and a very different thing to apply Christ's teaching to the problems of our own time. It is scarcely too much to say that the supreme need of the present time is that the church should adopt Christ's point of view, so far as possible, put into practical use his teaching, and emphasize those truths and duties which he emphasized. In a few articles we propose to call attention to some of the important things which Jesus emphasized in his life and teaching, hoping this may serve, in some measure, as a corrective of any wrong tendencies either in teaching or practice, but especially to incite to a forward movement along sane and safe lines of spiritual development.

I. *The nature of God.* It was doubtless one of the supreme aims of Jesus to reveal to men the true nature of God. This is fundamental in all true religion. Many false ideas had cursed the world for ages, and other ideas there were which were inadequate and unsatisfactory. What the world needed was a true knowledge of God. "And this is life eternal that they should know the only true God, and him whom thou didst send, even Jesus Christ" (John 17:3). The great and characteristic teaching of Jesus concerning God is his truth. Concerning this fundamental truth Jesus himself said, "Neither doth any know the Father, save the Son and he to whomsoever the Son willeth to reveal him" (Matt. 11:27). He also said to Philip who had asked him to "show us the Father"; "Have I been so long time with you and dost thou not know me, Philip? He that hath seen me hath seen the Father; how saith thou, Show us the Father? Believest thou not that I am in John 14:9,10). To Thomas he had just said: "No one cometh unto the Father but by me" (John 14:6). He taught his disciples when they prayed to say, "Our Father who art in heaven" (Matt. 6:9).

This is at once the most informing and comforting view of God which has ever been revealed to men. We have only yet begun to understand what is involved in this sublime truth. The religious world has been slow to grasp its significance. It has already destroyed many erroneous doctrines concerning the atonement, the method of God's government, the spirit of our worship, and future rewards and punishments. We can not here enter into the matter of how far and in what direction the fatherhood of God has modified, and, in some cases

destroyed once popular doctrines on this subject. It must suffice here to say that no doctrine can long survive that antagonizes, or is inconsistent with, the idea that God is our Father. Take a single illustration: The once popular theory that God sent his Son into the world to die for the elect few whom he had foreordained to be saved, while passing by all others because they had been foreordained to eternal damnation—how utterly inconsistent this doctrine is with the fatherhood of God! Would an earthly father treat his children thus? If we being evil know how to treat our children impartially, how much more will our heavenly Father be equally kind and merciful to all his children?

It is a strange fact that men often charge God with doing what would be a crime in an earthly father. No just and kind-hearted earthly parent would think of punishing a child for mistaking the meaning of a command, and honestly and lovingly doing what he thought was his father's will; and yet many Christians hold it to be very unsound and unsafe doctrine to teach that God is as good and just as an earthly father in this respect! If we would only be loyal to the instincts of our own heart, we would in many respects be better theologians than when we seek to construct our theology on purely logical and intellectual grounds.

The truth of God's fatherhood has implications in the direction of sociology which the church is only beginning to apprehend. Even yet the great mass of Christians are indifferent to the claims which the outcasts and the neglected portions of society have upon them. If God is the Father of all men in a very true and real sense, having created them and endowed them with a moral nature and a will like his own, does he not care for the sufferings and the mental, moral and physical poverty of these great wretched masses of humanity which are without God and without hope in the world? Does not his heart go out in loving and fatherly sympathy toward all these prodigal sons and daughters of his who are in the far country? How then can the church be indifferent to what is a matter of deep concern to the heart of God? One would think, judging from the vast tomes of theology which have been written, and the comparatively small attention that has been given to the subject of how to alleviate human suffering and sorrow and carry light and life to the "submerged tenth," that God was more concerned about our having correct philosophical and theological conceptions of the Trinity, than about how we treated our brother man. But John thoroughly represents the mind of Jesus in saying, "If a man say, I love God, and hateth his brother, he is a liar; for he that loveth not his brother whom he hath seen, can not love God whom he hath not seen" (1 John 4:20). The church that is not concerning itself with the work of caring for the poor, the infirm, and even the criminal and out-

cast classes of society, has a new lesson to learn from the teaching of Jesus concerning the fatherhood of God.

This truth, too, has an important bearing in our evangelistic work which, hitherto, has been too largely confined to respectable and well-to-do classes of people. We have yet to carry our evangelism into the slums and seek to save drunkards, thieves and libertines, the victims of lust and of evil habits. And yet Jesus said he "came not to call the righteous but sinners to repentance," meaning, thereby, the very outcasts of society. If there be more joy in heaven over one of these prodigal souls recovered from sin and Satan, than over ninety and nine respectable, moral people, it would seem that we ought to make more effort to bring this class of people to repentance. This is surely one of the implications of the truth of God's fatherhood.

❀ ❀

An Estimate of the Manchester Meeting.

In response to a letter from the Editor asking Brother Crerie of Haverhill, Mass., his impression of the Manchester meeting, after referring to some of the opposition and misconceptions which had to be overcome, Brother Crerie says:

But this misrepresentation, opposition, etc., was met with and overcome. The people soon learned that a "Holy Roller" or "Holy Jumper" was not preaching to them, but one with the open Bible, rightly dividing the Word. Naturally, they regarded the teaching at first with suspicion. It was altogether new. The appeal to their intelligence was one which they could not at once appreciate. However, the plea was attractive and audiences increased. Men and women brought their Bibles. It was evident that the Book was being searched as never before. Questions were asked and were promptly answered. Confidence in the evangelist was manifest, and the truth was admitted by many who acknowledged that never before had they understood God's word in its true light. This was not done with smiling faces, but with tears in their eyes. How could they help it? Were they not being torn away from the faith of their mothers and fathers, the faith of their childhood? All that was dear to them seemed to be vanishing away, but nevertheless they saw the way to the Father's home more perfectly and were constrained to admit it.

When the meeting closed there were quite a number who said they would stand by a work if we established one there. Therefore, it is necessary that the work continue until Brother Yeuell returns for a big campaign. The prospects look encouraging to me; yet, I am aware that it means hard work and undaunted faith and hope in New England to accomplish a respectable organization in Manchester. It can be done and it will be done.

The building of the Christian church (connection) has not been secured as yet; however, if we cannot get it we may be able to secure the city hall, which is not too large, for a very reasonable amount of money. By preaching twice a month and visiting those who are interested and distributing some of our tracts I believe that a solid foundation can be laid for a great meeting, which will result in a live church.

This work should be started without delay as there are opportunities now which later will be harder to realize. It will be wise to strike while the iron is hot.

We quite agree with Brother Crerie as to the wisdom of "striking while the iron is hot." This splendid meeting should be followed up, as soon as possible, by another which shall carry on to completion the work which has been so well begun. If the contributions from the brethren for this work shall indicate their approval, no doubt it will be promptly and vigorously followed up.

Notes and Comments.

Under this caption we are requested to assume the role of school master this week. We comply, hoping to receive and throw at least a little light on these problems grown familiar perhaps to our older readers, but of interest to those waves of younger Disciples ever riding into positions of responsibility in the churches.

❋

Where is the authority for a woman to preach?
—M. D. Burner.

See Galatians 3:28; Acts 21:9; Philippians 4:3. This liberty, however, should not be exercised whenever it would come in conflict with any other teaching of the Word of God.

❋

1. Was the apostle Paul eligible to the office of bishop or elder?
2. Is a single man possessing all the other qualifications eligible to the office of deacon?
3. If a man who has used the office of elder almost continually for forty years, possessing all the qualifications, should unfortunately lose his wife by death, would the church for this reason be justified in demanding his resignation?
ENQUIRER.

1. He was a bishop, or elder, of the church, though more of the church at large than of any local congregation. He had "the care of all the churches."
2. We think so; though other things being equal a man with a wife would be preferable. It is not, as we understand, the absence of a wife but a plurality of wives that is a bar to the eldership.
3. Certainly not.

❋

1. Give chapter and Verse in Bible for the expression, "Church of Christ," singular number.
2. Is "Christian Church" when applied to one of our local churches any more sectarian than "Church of Christ?"
3. When the deed of one of our churches has read "Christian Church" for 25 years are we justified in having it changed to "Church of Christ?"
4. If it happens to be in Tennessee where "Church of Christ" stands for warfare on the organ, would one of our congregations do well to change from "Christian Church" to "Church of Christ" and thus be branded as exceedingly sectarian in pushing non-essentials to the point of tests of fellowship?
5. Is not "Church of God" (Acts 20:28) the actual Scriptural name for the local church?
6. Does not "Church of God" include in its meaning a recognition of Father, Son and Holy Spirit, and thus give a fuller meaning to the real name of the church?
Boulder, Col.   S. M. BERNARD.

1. Christ's statement, "On this rock I will build my church" (Matt. 16:18), is sufficient authority, if there were no other, for the name "Church of Christ." The use of this name in the plural, however, for local congregations (Rom. 16:16) implies the correctness of its use for the church universal.
2. No. It is just as Scriptural in its

meaning, we think, if not in its form, as "Church of Christ."
3. We think not. We can see no justification for such change.
4. We think not. We would not allow a monopoly of the name "Church of Christ" to those who would sectarianize it and make it equivalent to an "anti-organ" or "anti-missionary" church.
5. It is one "actual Scriptural name," but has no monopoly since other names are used.
6. We think not, since the name "Church of Christ" carries with it the teaching of Christ concerning the Father, Son and Holy Spirit.
It will be an excellent indication of real progress among us when we cease to contend about which of these Scriptural names we shall be known by, and become far more concerned that our churches shall be worthy of any one of these names.

❋ ❋

Current Religious Thought.

"The Baptist Argus," in the following editorial on "A New Baptist Literature," recognizes the necessity of a constructive literature based on the positive elements of Baptist faith that Baptists might have confidence in the sufficiency of the Baptist message, initiative, inspiration, doctrines, graces, culture and power to win this world for Christ.

Too great a proportion of our own literature is suggestive rather of the forum and tournament than of the temple. Our books should be illumined with love and positive teaching rather than with scintillations from Damascan blades. A demand for this literature will soon create it. We shall make better progress when going toward the gates of the city that lieth four square instead of up against our "religious adversaries."

Very much of the contents of the shelves in our Baptist libraries necessarily belong to limited periods in our history. Controversies, like those involved with the Hardshell and Disciple movements, threw off quite a number of books and tracts, which we have done wisely to preserve, but it is well for us to recognize the fact that such publications can hardly be called literature. Like the rings in a tree, they make record of what happened at the time, but they live not, and, like the rings in the tree are covered up with new growth and left behind. Such publications are valuable in their way. With much zeal have we recently been studying the ring made in the seventeenth century, sending experts to the dusty vaults of Europe where lie buried the publications of that time.

But Baptists cannot content themselves with the kind of publications which are thrown off in times of controversy. Dr. J. B. Gambrell strikingly says that, "It is a mighty poor theology which is pitted up against some other theology." The truths of God are great enough to stand alone. Our weakness and ignorance need in quiet hours to feed upon the complete things of heaven. Our ultimate work is to join as co-workers with the Father and the Son in building a mighty kingdom on earth, in turning this world into heaven. Here and there and now and then we may have to tear down some structure in the way, cast out of the land some opposers of the King, but our great work is construction. Some few of us may need to be chosen as sheriffs and executioners, whom we should pray for and pity as

Editor's Easy Chair.

PENTWATER MUSINGS.

Summer has never seemed more queenly, nor has her reign been more mild and beneficent than during the present season in this latitude. The beautiful days and star-lit nights following each other in succession have been linked together by golden sunsets, making a chain of bright memories which will bind the hearts of many to the quiet woodland ways, winding ravines and commanding heights of "Garrison Park," at Pentwater. If at intervals the blue skies have been veiled with clouds, these clouds have been the chariots of God with which he waters the hills and vales and refreshes all living things. Michigan is rapidly becoming the greatest summer resort state in the Union. The shores of her inland lakes, as well as those of the great "unsalted sea" which bears her name, are dotted with summer cottages, some stately and beautiful, some humble and cozy, in which tens of thousands of people from the great cities of the south and middle west find refuge from the heat of summer. The east shore of Lake Michigan possesses, we believe, the finest summer climate in the United States. But only those favored spots along its shore line where an inland lake, connecting with the great lake, provides a channel and a harbor for the steamers, combine the advantages necessary for an ideal resort. Professor E. S. Ames, of the University of Chicago, recently visited the east shore of Lake Michigan, stopping off at the various resorts from Michigan City as far north as Pentwater, where we had the pleasure of a visit with him during one day. He came as a committee representing the Campbell Institute, made up of a large number of our young ministers, and some others that are older, to spy out a place where its membership could have fellowship together in a cool, healthful, quiet restful resort. On his return to Chicago he reported unanimously, in favor of Pentwater. This is the class of people that Pentwater appeals to, and this is the kind she is drawing to her shores.

❀

A few weeks ago the Editor had a letter from the Baptist minister at Spring Lake, near Grand Haven, Mich., Rev. Wm. A. Alleyn, asking us to stop off and preach for him in passing, if possible, expressing at the same time a special interest in the position of the Disciples. We invited him to Pentwater and proposed a union meeting between the Baptists and the Disciples in the Baptist church here, which was arranged for last Lord's day. At his request we preached in the morning on "Christian Union," to a good audience made up of representatives of different religious bodies. The sermon seems to have been heartily approved by all and particularly by our ministerial visitor. Brother Alleyn spoke at night on "Conditions of Discipleship," from the text, "If ye abide in my word then are ye truly my disciples; and ye shall know the truth and

the truth shall make you free." He was heard with interest and approval by both Baptists and Disciples of Christ. As the Baptists have no minister at present, and the Disciples no house nor settled pastor either, it would seem they might co-operate with profit in sustaining religious services until such time as they could see their way to unite more fully, or, if that is impracticable, to at least work together as far as possible for the religious welfare of the community, in which an aggressive type of Christianity is greatly lacking. There are many other communities in a similar condition where the Baptists and Disciples would be mutually benefited by getting closer together. The matter of organic union need not be pushed. That will take care of itself if the conditions are made favorable for the cultivation of brotherly love.

❀

One of the most pleasant incidents of the season thus far was a picnic of a few friends up Lake Pentwater on Monday following the meeting mentioned above. The Stows of Grand Rapids, the Denholmes of New Orleans, the Garrisons and their guest, Brother Alleyn, made up the party. Brother Stow chartered one of those combination boats which have a double motor power of engine and sail, which afforded ample room for the party and the generous cargo of provisions which is necessary to a successful picnic. On a shady knoll fronting a bayou on the lake, about two miles up from Lake Michigan, we camped and spent a delightful afternoon in social fellowship and in such pastimes as young people enjoy, and everybody is young at a picnic. At 6 o'clock a bountiful repast was served and relished as only picnickers can relish such a meal. The day was ideal for such an occasion. Back in the country further it would have been called warm, but under the shade of the trees and fanned by the breeze which came up over the lake, it was delightful. At 6:30 our boat returned for us, coming as near the shore as the depth of water would permit, while the two row boats which we had towed up served to transport the passengers and baggage out to it. The ride back down the lake on that quiet evening, with the great red sun in front just sinking behind the sand dunes of Lake Michigan, the crimson and purple ripples of the lake behind us and the green hills on either side, made a charming picture which memory will long cherish. Such familiar hymns as "Shall we gather at the River?" "Homeward Bound" and "Throw out the Lifeline," sung by the party on the return trip, made us think of the old days at Macatawa and the friends with whom we were wont to gather there on similar occasions.

❀

Last night all the resorters on Lake Michigan south of the channel, including those of Oceana Beach and "Garrison Park," were the guests of Judge Montgomery and wife at a corn-roast down on the beach. A great bonfire was built in

the early twilight, and by the time night's candles were lighted in the heavens, the entire population of these resorts were gathered by the shore of the rippling lake and around the bonfire enjoying a very happy social. The corn and butter and salt were furnished by our hosts, and each one had the privilege of roasting his corn by holding it over the coals at the end of a long stick or by covering it up in the shuck in the hot embers. The corn thus cooked was delicious but not more so than the good fellowship which prevailed among all the people present. One other judge of the supreme court of Michigan was present besides our host, and we understand a third one is coming. There is no doubt but what we shall have good order at this resort! Among other things proposed was a suggestion by the Easy Chair for a Sunday evening vesper service on the beach, such as has been held for years at Macatawa Park. The idea met with enthusiastic approval and we shall probably hold the first service of the kind on August 26. Our suggestion that this corn-roast be made a perpetual annual institution was also heartily approved. A vote of thanks was given Judge and Mrs. Montgomery for their hospitality and the pleasure they had afforded the company, and after a number of songs the resorters quietly dispersed to their cottages. It will be seen by the foregoing incidents that we are not without enough of the social life here on this shore to prevent us from becoming barbarians!

❀

From some letters which have reached us we infer that the recent paragraph in the Budget, referring to the Editor's health and the doctor's advice for him to stick to his "reservation" during the heated term, and not attend the conventions, has been interpreted more seriously than was intended by the office editor, pro tem, who, in the kindness of his heart, thought to protect us from being pressed into service in the torrid belt during the hay-fever season. One widely known brother writes expressing his deep regret that we are not to attend the national convention at Buffalo. We are glad to say that, although for a few weeks we have hardly been in our usual health, there is no cause whatever for serious apprehension on the part of our friends. We are able to keep up our regular work with some extra work thrown in, and it is our full purpose at present to attend the Buffalo convention. We are hoping that it will be one of the great milestones in our religious progress toward higher and better things. We are praying that the spirit of unity, of brotherly love, of humbleness of mind, and consecration of heart, may so pervade that convention that it shall become a real Mount of Vision from which we shall get a clearer view of the work to which God has called us and of the mighty possibilities within our reach. It will require much prayer, as well as wise planning, to make such a convention possible. But is not the object worth the effort?

As Seen From the Dome   By F. D. Pow

It is a two thousand mile journey from Nice to Liverpool through the western Mediterranean, the Straits of Gibraltar, the Atlantic, Bay of Biscay and St. George's Channel. It was restful enough after our somewhat strenuous life in the east. On reaching England we learned of the frightful eruption of Vesuvius which I had ascended only four days before it wrought such ruin. We could not but regret we missed the startling scenes of April 7-14, though we were no doubt safer at sea. England received us coldly after dealing with the Syrian, Egyptian and Italian suns. The signs of spring were everywhere, but the change was most noticeable. Hedges were turning green and flowers blooming, and fruit trees in full blossom by the roadways. England's delightful rural scenery is approaching its ideal beauty. Our journey was first to Oxford, the seat of the great university. It is a city of 60,000, charmingly situated on the Thames, an hour and a half from London. It is the center of conservative England. When I purchased my first newspaper, the question was "what is your politics, Conservative or Liberal?" "Liberal," I answered. Oxford is a part of old England. It is beautiful and restful, and that was what I wanted. The Easter holiday was on which, strangely enough, lasts five weeks. So we had the colleges to ourselves. We pitched our tent near Carfax. "Carfax" is simply a place where four roads meet, a center, *quadrifurcus*, "four-forked." So our English friends work wonders in words, as the famous St. Mary Magdalen college here becomes "Mandlen." Turning to the right here I found myself at once in Christ Church college. At its entrance is the "Tom Tower," so called because an 18,000-pound bell called "Great Tom" hangs here. Nothing seemed so sweet and musical in Oxford as its bells. Every night at 9.05 we would listen to Tom toll 101 strokes a curfew and signal for the closing of the college gates. The gates were erected by Cardinal Wolsey and the bell tower was added by Sir Christopher Wren. We passed through into the great quadrangle, 264x261 feet. All the twenty-six colleges which constitute the university are built this way. There may be several of these "quads" and they differ in size, but about them in one continuous pile are the dormitories, lecture rooms, and three most important structures, library, chapel and dining hall. Passing through this quadrangle we entered the chapel which is also the "Cathedral Church of Christ" of Oxford. This goes back to Saxon times to the religious house founded in 740 by St. Frideswide. The present church is 800 years old. It has curious old tombs, splendid windows, and fan-traceried roof with beautiful vistas. Wolsey founded Christ Church college and it has graduated such men as Mansfield and John Locke, Sir Robert Peel and Canning, Ben Johnson and Sir Philip Sydney, Gladstone, Salisbury and Rosebery, John and Charles Wesley, and

others who have made England illustrious. Across from Christ church a little ways one enters Pembroke college, a plainer group of buildings. What most interested me here was the association with Dr. Johnson. The old fellow's rooms were just over the entrance way. The care-taker showed me his desks, his portrait by Sir Joshua Reynolds, which is preserved most sacredly, his teapot and cup. He is credited with drinking twenty cups of his favorite beverage at the time; this cup holds at least a pint! Boswell should rise and explain. Along the same way I passed to the Folly bridge which crosses the Thames and I was on the "Isis," as this part of the river is classically known at Oxford. Here were the college barges and boat houses, and numberless craft from "Canaders" to eight-oars and here the great races are rowed. It is a charming spot with its meadows and waters. One notices strange old streets and signs "rows" and "yards" as he walks about Oxford. Here are old time taverns "The Dolphin and the Anchor," the "Three Cups," the "Lamb and the Flag," and the "Bull and the Mouth."

Turning to the left from Carfax along "Corn-market street," I came to a cross in the pavement marking the spot where Latimer and Ridley were burned, as every child once read about in Fox's "Book of Martyrs." Near the spot is a monument with statues of the three great ones, Latimer, Ridley and Cranmer, "who yielded their bodies to be burned bearing witness to the sacred truths which they had affirmed and maintained against the errors of the Church of Rome, and refusing but to them it was given not only to believe in Christ, but also to suffer for his sake."

Balliol college is near the Martyrs' Memorial. This is Robert Browning's college and the "Old Yellow Book" which suggested the "Ring and the Book," is shown you, and some of his original manuscripts. The college was founded in 1260. John Wycliffe was fellow and master of Balliol, Adam Smith and Lockhart, Sir William Hamilton and Southey, Benjamin Jowett, Lord Milner and Lord Curzon were among its distinguished sons. I read this tribute to Netbeship, for thirty years tutor here: "He loved great things and thought little of himself. Desiring neither fame nor influence he won the devotion of men and was a power in their lives, and seeking no disciples he taught to many the greatness of the world and of man's mind."

All of the colleges are of great interest to the visitor, each having its special features. Trinity, with its gardens and famous "Lime walk," grass plots and ancient yews; Exeter, founded in 1314, with its magnificent chapel and wonderful piece of tapestry by Burne-Jones, "The Adoration of the Magi;" Lincoln, the plainest and cheapest of the great schools, where I looked into the little room of John Wesley about 8x7, and the small meeting place of "The Holy Club," where Methodism was born; All Souls, with its great Codrington library

of 80,000 volumes, its memories of Jer Taylor, Christopher Wren, Bishop H and the poet Young, and Sir Wil Blackstone whom every lawyer is supp to know and the announcement of w lectures one sees framed and hung in library—all have a great history. Per the most beautiful of this great cluste institutions is Magdalen. In All Souls I one of the tutors who for thirty years taught history. As illustrating the con vatism of Oxford he was a good one spoke of Mr. Gladstone, an honorary low of All Souls. "A very remarkable son," said the tutor. "Did a good m bad things. Miserable foreign policy, a remarkable person!" In Magdalen I a bright student who showed me aro "Magdalen," wrote Macaulay, "is one the most remarkable of our academical stitutions. Its graceful tower catches off the eye of the traveler who comes road from London. As he approaches finds that this tower arises from an battled pile, low and irregular, yet sir larly venerable, which embowered in dure, overhangs the sluggish waters of Cherwell." It is indeed an ideal spot, on side the botanic gardens, and on the of "The Water Walks of Magdalen." It d from 1458. The buildings form four qu rangles covering twelve acres. The walks" were specially loved by Addi and its grove has a large herd of d quietly browsing under huge old elms, cawing rooks as though the haunts of i were distant and forgotten. One obser curious old customs in these colleges. H at "Mandlen" for example, in one cor of the old "quad" is a little canopied pu John the Baptist day to a congregation sembled in the quadrangle, the ground ing strewn with rushes and grass, and buildings dressed with green boughs commemoration of the preaching of J. in the wilderness. Another custom is sing on every May day morning at o'clock on the summit of the tower a L hymn to the Trinity by the choir hab in their surplices. Still another quaint c monial is observed at Queen's coll where, on New Year's Day, the Bursar sents to each member or guest a nee and thread with the words, "Take this be thrifty," derived, it is said, from a fa ful rebus on the name of the founder, lesfield—*aiguille et fil.*

The Bodleian library is one of the g things of Oxford, called for Sir Tho Bodley, the tercentenary of which was k October 8, 1902. It has 700,000 volu and vast literary treasures. I saw h Queen Elizabeth's exercise books whe child and a wonderful Shelley collecti and this letter written on papyrus by Egyptian boy of the second century sh ing that boys are everywhere and in ages boys: "Theon to his father The Greeting: It was a fine thing of you to take me with you to Alexandria. S me a lyre, I implore you. If you don' won't eat; I won't drink, there. now!" I saw here also the famous "Logia" fragment words of Jesus found by the Egyptian Exploration Fund.

The Clarendon Press is another wonder of Oxford. Here the famous Bibles are printed, 40,000 a year. There are 700 persons employed and 247 machines. I saw them printing Bibles in all tongues, and the process from the setting of type to the finishing of the complete Bible and their great Oxford "Dictionary on Historical Principles," nine parts of which are issued and

only four letters published, though begun in 1882. They are past masters in the art of printing. It is still a question whether the first book published in England was issued from Oxford or from the Caxton's. In the infancy of the art preservative of arts a book appeared having i'. Colophon Oxonic 1468. They print here the "finger Testament" and "finger prayer-book" and "thumb prayer-book," the Brilliant Text Bible which is the smallest ever published, weighing three ounces, and the Folio Bible, which is the largest.

Who are now some of the great men of Oxford? Well, of the 400 and over of teachers instructing 4,000 students, are such men as Robinson Ellis in Latin and Bywater in Greek, Pelham in Roman History, Firth in Modern History, Bigg and Cheyne and Driver, Dicey and Sayce, and our man Osler. Oxford is a great place. "It is a despair to see such a place and ever to leave it; for it would take a lifetime and more than one, to comprehend and enjoy it satisfactorily," as Hawthorne said.

Modern Religious Persecution---A Defense

By B. L. Chase

6. Instructions to Persecutors.

I would always recommend that you use the regular weekly religious newspaper as your method of persecution. It is very much better than going in person to the supporters of a college or the members of a church. It is both sober and cheaper.

Calculate how much it would cost in time, car-fare and hotel bills to go in person, for instance, to California to visit every trustee and friend and supporter of Berkeley Bible Seminary, if there were some teacher in the school against whom you had collected proof of heresy. Then, too, it would look mean and disreputable for a venerable persecutor to go around the state from town to town, and from house to house, explaining and elaborating the charges of heresy to the various churches and contributors toward the seminary. It would be undignified. Even the printing of circulars containing the charges would be costly, and their circulation through the mails would be costly.

The very best, the neatest, cheapest, and most respectable plan, would be to go to the newspaper that had the widest circulation in the state and give your material to the editor. Be sure, of course, that he is in favor of persecution in general, or of this case in particular. He will print the charges, with all the evidence, direct and indirect, without any cost to you, and the mails will carry it at newspaper rates, to every Disciple in the state. It is easy and desirable in such a case to send sample copies of that issue to many persons in the state who do not take the paper. There is no extra expense, and some persons might be induced to subscribe for the paper when they see the profound interest which it takes in the religious and educational affairs of the state. You see how simply and how clearly it is all done by the newspaper method. You can speak in the newspaper exactly as you would in person, while few object to it.

Your difficulty, however, will be in persuading the management of the paper to surrender its columns and influence to your cause. You should make it appear how advantageous it would be to the cause of Christ, and how profitable to the newspaper. Not every newspaper among the Disciples can be swung around to such a proposition. They have silly scruples and false notions about the function of a re-

ligious journal, and those impossible ideals of a broad, sweet, and Christian-spirited journalism that they will tell you about. The facts in the case show that such papers do not prosper as others. They are not ready to sacrifice themselves for the purity of religious doctrine, and in defense of the "Old Jerusalem Gospel." The people like a good, clean fight against heresy, and they will put up for it.

As for the various words in the English language which you should use as instruments of persecution (since the law and public opinion limit you to the use of language) I would recommend that you use the most suggestive and general terms of reproach. Use such general terms as "infidel," "Unitarian," and "heretic." They cover a great many meanings, so that you can bring a great many charges under them. If you can not make one charge stick, you can try another—all under the same general charge of "infidelity." The infidelity is of different degrees of seriousness. You have the convenience of several effective synonyms, "unbelief," "skepticism," "doubt," "agnosticism," "atheism," "deism," etc. You will need to change your instruments from time to time, to avoid depriving them of edge and effectiveness. I fear that you have over-used some of your instruments in the past. They seem to have lost their edge in certain quarters.

One of the terms which seems to me to have been overworked by the profession is the term "higher critic;" the fact is that by a too loose and free and indiscriminate use of the term, people seem to have come to like him. At least they no longer seem to fear him. They invite him into their churches to preach and lecture, and into their homes to eat. You over-drew his picture when you gave him those horns and hoofs. The pictures you sent out in advance did not agree with the person himself when he appeared. The people saw the difference when they looked upon his fair face and listened to his fine words, and concluded that you had been trying to scare them. The better they got acquainted with him the better they liked him, and the less they feared to fear in him. You let one or two of the cleverest of them get loose among the brethren, and I regret to say, they have seriously injured your business.

I have heard a few say they would not believe you now, if you told them that quinine was bitter. They would sure have believed you if you had told them that quinine was sweet.

But such has been the history of very many names that were at first given in reproach. The names "Methodist" and "Baptist" were once names of reproach; but a man's standing would not be seriously injured in Protestant communities to-day if he were called a "Methodist" or "Baptist." It is coming to be so of "higher critic." There are still places where the person and the thing have been disowned; but there are other places where they could not get along without them. The

❀ ❀

MORE THAN MONEY
A Minister Talks About Grape-Nuts.

"My first stomach trouble began back in 1895," writes a minister in Nebr., resulting from hasty eating and eating too much. I found no relief from medicine and grew so bad that all food gave me a great distress.

"It was that sore, gnawing, hungry feeling in my stomach that was so distressing and I became a sick man. Grape-Nuts was recommended as a food that could be easily digested.

"Leaving the old diet that had given me so much trouble, I began to eat Grape-Nuts with a little cream and sugar. The change effected in 24 hours was truly remarkable, and in a few weeks I was back to health again.

"My work as a minister calls me away from home a great deal, and recently I drifted back to fat meat and indigestible foods, which put me again on the sick list.

"So I went back to Grape-Nuts and cream and in four days I was put right again. The old dull headaches are gone, stomach comfortable, head clear, and it is a delight to pursue my studies and work.

"Grape-Nuts food is worth more than money to me and I hope this may induce some sufferer to follow the same course I have."

Name given by Postum Co., Battle Creek, Mich.

"There's a reason."

Read the little book, "The Road to Wellville," in pkgs.

word is unfortunate for your purposes, for persecutors are not agreed among themselves that it is "always, everywhere, and by all," a bad thing. One of your own venerable company declared once in print, that it was "a legitimate art and has been employed by biblical scholars ever since the need of such investigations began to be realized." You ought to have coached him better. That statement has been used against you a great deal by the friends of persecuted critics. They say: "If it is a legitimate art, why do you anathematize a man for employing it?" Of course, they do not understand that it is an art which only two or three men among the Disciples can safely practice; and that no young man should be permitted to use it. I cite these facts as warnings against an ill-advised use of epithets. There is danger of the \
of its awful
could name
the question
classed as in
grams of ou
advise one o
men off futu
demonstratic
not be circu
mistake.

From Presbyterian to Christian Church, by W

By DAVID MILLAR

I am of Scotch birth, my parents being Presbyterians of the Old School, descended from Covenanters. No wonder then they were strict and severe in the upbringing of their children and very pronounced in their religious views, which were Calvinistic in the extreme.

When I remember the "Sabbath days" of youthful years I almost expire, and feel thankful that children to-day are not called upon to grunt and sweat under the burden of Mosaic law; on the other hand I fear that Christian parents are sliding to the other extreme and becoming too lax in the use of the strap and in the observance of the Lord's day.

When I think of the minister and his sermon, I wonder what kind of a congregation he could pick up to-day. He was supposed to be a powerful preacher and the old beadle would point out with pride the evidences of the assertion to visitors, showing them several old pulpit Bibles that had been knocked to pieces by his fist (fine days for publishing houses). Nevertheless, I would sleep for the hour and a half that he exploited himself and only awoke when the hammering conclusion took place. I remember being as much afraid of the minister as I was of old Nick himself. I guess it was because I was a bad little rascal. (Totally depraved?)

Morning sermon began at 10 o'clock; ended at 2. Afternoon services, after kail dinner, began at 2; ended at 4. Sabbath school, 4 to 5. After tea about 7 o'clock, the "books" would be brought and all who could read would do so, verse about, four or five chapters being read.

I became a Christian the first time I heard the Gospel preached. Let me explain that in church, Sunday-school and home the teaching of early years was, be a good boy and you will go to heaven when you die. That was no "good news" to me. I knew I was anything but good, always in some mischief, a regular little Jonah always bringing trouble to myself and others, but as for dying I never thought of it, and so the promise of heaven at some time in the future was a very unsatisfactory thing, even if I was good enough to get there. But I heard the good news of Jesus, the Savior from sin, from the penalty, love and power of it, and I was told to believe and confess, and I did.

At midnight on the last day of a week, I knelt before God, reviewed my past life, realized my need of a Savior, determined upon complete submission and obedience to Christ, was reconciled to God and appropriated pardon of past sins on the ground that Christ had paid my debt on the cross of Calvary, and I enjoyed the peace that comes through pardon, and I began to live by the power that came after pardon. I united with the only church I knew anything of, the old blue stocking Presbyterian.

I immediately began to prepare for the ministry, and in due time began the work in the Presbyterian church.

In a few years I became interested in the "Second coming of the Lord Jesus Christ." In my study I entered the book of Acts of the Apostles and while reading it my thoughts were arrested and transferred from the Second coming of Christ to that of Pentecost with its wonders. I soon discovered how erroneous were my views regarding the Church of Christ and the first principles of Christianity.

I readily saw that in agreement with the promise made by Jesus, "I will build my church," that the establishment of the church upon earth was officially effected when the Holy Spirit was given on Pentecost, and that baptism was the initiatory rite whereby membership with all its privileges was obtained, and that baptism was immersion. As baptism was to be preceded by the "hearing of the Word" and belief of its facts, and by repentance of the mind, and confession of faith by the mouth, the logical conclusion was that only they who could hear the Word by which faith was created, only those who had need to repent and could exercise their will to determine and mouth to confess were the subjects of baptism.

Believe me, when I got this far I felt bad, and wanted to get rid of the whole thing. It was all new and strange, for at this time I had never seen a baptism (immersion). I was a Presbyterian of the Presbyterians, and seldom had been in any other church service until this time, and so one day I started out to get one of the most respected and scholarly divines of the Presbyterian church to put me back right. All the satisfaction I got was, "Do you think it is becoming in you to set yourself up in judgment against the scholarly and pious fathers of the church who have gone to their reward?"

Personal responsibility was one of the new though
time. It wa
scholarly ar
tuted sprink
the answer

I placed
Baptist min
pendent mar
it was not ,
ing things,
baptize me (
baptism), on
And this he
until it becar
"gee" and I

The quest
I seek Christ
answer was,

S/
Often Cat

How many
so disturbs c
muddy, yellов
A ten days'
has proven a
of clearing u
A Washn.
rience:

"All of us
brother—had
years until 1
trouble more

"We were
pimples, breat
the mouth, ar
bundles of ne

"We didn't
cause of the 1
out of coffee
from a neig
Postum and t

"Although
all felt sure w
our strong co
try Postum a:
delicious.

"We read
got more and
wouldn't have
able to dige
trouble, each
tongues clean
condition. W
but Postum.
Name given b
Mich. Read
to Wellville."

tered the Baptist fold, knowing nothing of its customs. After doing evangelistic work for some time, I began an effort under the direction of the city missionary board of the Baptist church to organize a church in one of the needy fields of the city. After several weeks' work I had a goodly number who had made the confession of faith in Christ, and were waiting to be baptized. I asked the city missionary secretary where I would baptize the converts and got my medicine in the shape of Baptist usage. I was told that the converts would require to be baptized into the fellowship of a nearby Baptist church and then after a council had decided as to the advisability of the establishment of a church they would be granted letters. I asked this question of the Baptist ministers, "Did Paul after he preached and made converts in the city of Corinth, require to take them over to Ephesus and baptize them into the fellowship of that church before he could organize a

church at Corinth?" The answer was of course in the negative. I concluded then that what Paul did was right and that it was the right thing for me to follow the apostle's method and I called together seven baptized believers and organized a Baptist church.

Now the puzzle was, where would I baptize the converts? I asked several Baptist ministers (whole souled men) for the use of their baptistries, but while all of them said they would be glad personally to grant my request, the deacons, they said, would object.

At this time I was told something about the Disciples of Christ. The Presbyterian minister who told me of them, said that he had lately met some members of the Christian church and they had explained their position to him and he thought that what I was teaching and preaching agreed with their teachings and preaching. He advised me to look up one of their ministers and have a talk with him. This I did the fol-

lowing day. Getting the address of the pastor of the Third Christian church from the city directory, I called upon him and after a morning's conversation, in which I stated my doctrinal position and experiences, the brother, George P. Rutledge, one of the grandest of men and a princely preacher, said, "Why, you belong to us," and invited me to use his baptistry. Next day he called upon me, accompanied by the pastor of the First Christian church, J. S. Myers, of Sedalia fame, who also kindly proffered the use of his baptistry, with the result that I baptized half the converts in each church pool.

Soon afterward, at a joint meeting of the Disciples of the city, I was extended the right hand of fellowship by Dr. E. E. Montgomery, on behalf of the Disciples and became a Christian in name, as well as in fact, and my "Baptist church" was henceforth known as a Christian church.

Thus I became identified with the brotherhood of believers called Disciples of Christ.

Religious　Atavism　　By W. T. Moore

Reversion to an ancestral type is a well known fact in physiology. Sometimes this reversion does not take place until two or three generations have passed. But no matter how long the time intervening may be, no one can doubt the striking resemblance to the ancestor whose type is reproduced. It is not strange that this law holds good in religious movements as well as in other things. Indeed, this tendency to revert to original conditions is so powerful that nearly every religious movement which has been inaugurated, in the history of the Christian Church, has ultimately reproduced in its development practically the same characteristics against which it stoutly protested when the movement was first started. As an illustration, it may be said that the Protestant reformation under Luther and those associated with him was mainly a plea for religious liberty, but after this liberty had been achieved there was a constant tendency to return to the original type from which the movement sprang, and it was not very long until the very liberty for which the movement contended was practically stranded in human creeds, thereby returning to the ancestral type from which the movement had its origin. It sometimes happens that these reversions give us even a worse type than that from which it originated. There is often an added increment of evil which seems to have developed in its proportions during the years wherein it was quietly sleeping, and when no one suspected that this evil would ever again become a controlling force in the religious world.

It may be well just now for the Disciples of Christ to study carefully this remarkable law. Their own religious movement, when considered from an historical point of view, had its origin in a

condition of things which may not be very difficult to reproduce by the very law to which attention has been called. At this very time it seems to me that religious atavism is in the air. The great philosopher, Emanuel Kant, contended that there were just three things that must be postulated in order to explain man's present and eternal destiny. These three are God, liberty and immortality. These three were fundamental in the religious movement of the Disciples, with an immense emphasis on the second. Religious liberty, with the pioneers of our movement, was a priceless boon, and whoever will study carefully the history of the movement can not fail to notice that liberty was intensified in its importance by the remembrance of the slavery out of which the liberty came. Its ancestral religious type was religious despotism. Its plea was to break the bonds of human creeds and give to the world freedom of thought, freedom of speech and the right of individual interpretation. This, indeed, was the main thing for which our fathers contended. Everything else was in some respects subordinate to this great plea for liberty in the highest and best sense.

Will the movement now revert to the type out of which it came? This may easily result. When a movement becomes stereotyped in its principles, so that its growth is no longer possible, it is almost certain to revert back to the original type. Life requires movement of some kind. If we can not go forward, we must go backward. To stand still is death. Our religious movement has reached a point where some have written upon it "Ne plus ultra." This means death to the movement unless we begin to go backward, and this is precisely what some seem to be doing. They are not equal to meeting the demands of the

new day in which we live, nor are they willing to regard our religious movement as capable of development in certain directions which are necessary to give it vitality and adaptation in the present state of the religious world, and consequently, if these Disciples move at all they must move backward, and that means a reversion to the type of Christianity which was prevalent when our movement had its beginning.

It is not necessary to manifest an ugly spirit about this fact. It is an inexorable law which many can not resist. Indeed, they are strengthened in their tendency by the conviction that they are doing God's service when they refuse to go forward in answer to the call of legitimate progress. They believe that progress means innovation. They have never gone further in their religious life than the Episcopal prayer book, which says: "As it was in the beginning, is now, and ever shall be." This is the rock on which some most excellent Christians are stranded. They are as conscientious as Saul of Tarsus was when he was persecuting the church of God. Their whole idea is to be consistent with the past, but there is a sense in which this consistency is, as Emerson declares, "The hob-goblin of fools." To be consistent with the past is to go back to the time when the Campbells began their religious movement, and then seek to reproduce the very religious condition out of which that movement came. The Campbells were themselves most inconsistent, as men generally understand consistency. Theirs was really a forward movement. It claimed to be a movement for the restoration of the ancient order of things, but it was this only so far as its principles are concerned. Its methods were alive with the new-born conditions of the world at that time. Its methods must still keep pace with the march of events. Its watchword must be "forward," and when we say that it is a movement "back to Christ," we must understand that this means back to his principles, to his teaching, to his great and virile life, while at the same time it means that our movement must go forward in its methods, in its adaptation to the age in which we live, in its enthusiasm and sacrifice for souls, and in its power of expansion and development in the great work of converting the world to Christ. Reproduction of the ancestral type may be our shame, and the only way to prevent this is to keep our faces forward and our movements toward the goal for which it is set, and our eyes steadily fixed upon him who is the same yesterday, to-day and forever, and consequently in whom there is neither past, present nor future, but only from everlasting to everlasting.

Columbia, Mo.

The Practice of Immortality   By Cephas Shelburne

Aristotle, long before the coming of Christ, with not a page of Revelation to guide him, depending wholly upon the light of reason, said to his disciples: "Live as nearly as you can the immortal life. There is a such a thing as the practice of immortality, living the immortal life—the life that cannot die. I believe that man can create an immortal atmosphere for himself to live in, that he can seek the immortal things. Paul says we look for the things which are eternal, and he promises eternal life "to them who by patient continuance in well-doing seek for glory, and honor and immortality." He tells us that if we would have this immortality we must strive for it, practice it "if by any means we may attain to the resurrection of the dead." He would say to us, "Lay hold on eternal life."

Immortality is not something to be conferred upon one hereafter, it is here; you may be here and now living the immortal life. Jesus exhorts men to enter into life, eternal life, here; "to make the great hereafter a glorious here." This is the great thought that he brought to light, that he would have us believe and vitalize, that we are immortal, and being immortal that we should live accordingly; that our heredity is from God and we should therefore live as the sons of God. As David Gregg has truly said: "Cherish this truth, that you are immortal. Have no anxiety as to this fact, for that is settled. But let your anxiety be that you build into yourselves the things that are worthy your immortality and the things that you would like to see immortal."

Let this hope that is in you purify you, vitalize you, enrich all your life with great thoughts and interests, services and ends. Train all your powers, desires, emotions, acts into things that are divine, and that build up the heaven-life here and make you worthy of it there; the things that are meet for the inheritance of the saints in light. "Let your anxiety be to have a white soul for the white robes, and a spirit of praise for the harps of gold, and a thoroughly loyal personality for the everlasting crown."

What was it that gave Christ power over the grave, by which he was not holden of death? Not a power acting on the outside of him, not a power conferred upon him after the resurrection. He was the resurrection and the life. He had in himself the immortal life; like Victor Hugo, he was rising he knew toward the skies. There was power in him to rise again; there was no power in the grave to hold him and prevent him from rising. "Destroy this temple and in three days I will raise it up again." "I have power to lay it down, and I have power to take it again." From the very beginning he was conscious of eternal life abiding in him. And this power was not conferred upon him by the Holy Spirit. It was a conscious element of his own nature and personality—he had it from childhood. He knew the grave had no victory and death no sting. The potter hath power over the clay, but clay hath no power over the maker and molder of clay. When Christ anointed the eyes of the blind man, he put his power and divinity into clay, and the clay made dead eyes to see. And so his divine personality gave resurrection power to the Arimathean tomb, and when the women came to see the sepulcher, the angel said: "He is not here; he is risen as he said."

The sublime truth of the resurrection does not rest on the resurrection; but the fact of the resurrection rests on the sublime truth of immortal life abiding in him. There was a current in his life that bore him onward, not toward a grave in the grass, not to Calvary simply but his life was moving toward resurrection, ascension and glorification. Of this he was conscious from the beginning. It was embodied in the angel's song at his birth; in the temple at the age of twelve, and before the descent of the Holy Spirit at his baptism. Every great event in Christ's life, every culminating point, was prophesied in his personality. He seemed always to be touching the future, pointing ahead, moving toward some far-off divine event. Great events issued out of his life, from the very springs of his being, and revealed his relations to the beyond. There is not a great event in the life of the Savior that can be explained, save as we see it in the declaration of the angel at the open tomb on the morning of the resurrection, saying to the women: "He is risen as he said."

Christ visibly put on immortality. There beamed from his very presence the immortal life; he lived it. When they would throw him over the cliff at Nazareth, without a stroke he passed through the midst of them unharmed. When they came to arrest him with swords and staves there went from his very presence a power that caused them to fall to the ground. The transfiguration was the manifestation of the glory in him. His face was set toward the radiant beyond, and was radiant with the beyond. Such a life was not confined to the narrow limits of space and time. There is a law that we reap what we sow. Christ literally reaped the life that he sowed. His goodness, character, nature and soul was not subject to the law of death.

And what is true of Christ is true of the followers of Christ. Their life, death and resurrection is like his. They have the power of an endless life within. He who lives the immortal life must reap life everlasting. You carry immortality in you here and now. The prophetic quality in life, in any life, has its source within, in the very structure of things—the divine principle, given within. You cannot kill love, pure mind and thought, goodness has no principle of death in it. These are the image of God in us. Let us see that the God-element remain not dormant in us; but let us develop it, bring it out, give it wings, aspiration, room to range, clearness of vision, the perspective of eternity. My conviction is that we live below ourselves, on the lower levels and we do not dwell on the summits. We undervalue and under-rate ourselves. We are wont to call ourselves poor, miserable, worms of the dust; we despise and neglect that which is within, and which is "so noble that it can be called the image of God." Let us accept the truth of the divine indwelling, believe in the highest, trust all these finer impulses of the soul, and live in accordance with them.

It is said of Robert Louis Stevenson that he was always hungry for the greater world; not the sham world of cities, clubs, commercialism, steam cars and all that, but the great world out of doors; the vast heavens above and the wide expanse of the seas; the world of mind, and spirit, heart and God. There is such a thing as the spirit's opening to the consciousness of who and what we are, whither and whence, and entering the larger life—the life of an immortal. We have only to look up at the sky; watch the rising and falling of the tides; the movement of the planets in their orbits; the floating of a luminous cloud "across the loveliness of a summer's day;" the opening of a flower—to realize that we and they are citizens of the immeasurable universe, affected by other worlds, and remote influences, and surrounded by the depths, the greatness and the splendor of God. And it is the spiritual side of man's nature, the image of God there, the immortal within—greater than our vocabulary, wider than the range of our bodies, more far-reaching and far-seeing than the natural eye and ear—that reaches out after the divine, that leaps up to catch this splendor, that lifts us out of the ordinary and into a region above time and space and dismal despair, and "floods all life with glory, helpfulness, hope and beauty"—the immortal soul in league with light. Keyed to its harmonies, responsive to its influences, living the life of an immortal.

Huntington, Ind.

Some Helps to a Study of the Holy Spirit

By Edgar D. Jones

Perhaps at no time in the history of the Disciples of Christ has there been so much interest manifested in the doctrine of the Holy Spirit as there is just now. Nor is this interest confined by any means to the Disciples. The convention programs and publications of the various religious bodies afford evidence that this subject is receiving general attention. For a full year the writer's special readings have been on this theme and he wishes to make acknowledgment of four books that have helped him in the study of the Spirit's ministry.

There isn't, by the way, very much literature on the Holy Spirit, and what there is is of recent date. One author says that the past nineteen years have seen more literature on this subject than all the rest of the nineteen hundred years together. And yet the bulk is not large. A casual scanning of catalogues would seem to convince one that there are less than fifty books of recognized merit on the subject. So far as the writer has been able to learn there have been but three widely read books on the Holy Spirit published by the Disciples of Christ, viz., Dr. Richardson's excellent work; "A Symposium on the Holy Spirit," with chapters by A. B. Jones, Thos. Munnell, G. W. Longan, J. Z. Taylor and A. Campbell, published by John Burns, in 1879, and the recent volume by J. H. Garrison.

Now for the four helpful books referred to above.

1. "The Ministry of the Spirit," by Dr. A. J. Gordon. This is doubtless the most popular book ever written on the subject. It is so well known that extended comment on it is unnecessary. Its author was a choice character. His was a spirit-filled life. For many years this beloved pastor sought with success to impress on his congregation the fact that the Holy Spirit dwells literally in the Christian and that he is ready if he finds a willing people, to oversee and administer all that pertains to the affairs of the body of Christ. There have been wealthier churches than Dr. Gordon's, churches larger numerically and with statelier edifices perhaps, but it is doubtful if there has been anywhere in modern times a church so intensely spiritual, so genuinely worshipful, and so free from occasions of criticisms as was his.

The secret of it all was simply this. Dr. Gordon and his congregation looked to God not only for salvation, but also for *power* through his Spirit. Such a man and such a church commend the book to say nothing of the intrinsic worth of its ten chapters.

2. "The Indwelling Christ," by James M. Campbell, author of "Saved to the Uttermost," "After Pentecost What?" etc. The introduction to the little volume is written by Professor A. B. Bruce, of the Free Church College, Glasgow. There are eighteen chapters,

all worth one's while to read. The one on "The Abiding Presence" is especially good. The author heads it with Whittier's well known lines:

"No fable old, no mythic lore,
    Nor charms of bards or seers,
No dread fact stranded on the shores
    Of the oblivious years;

But warm, sweet, tender, even yet
    A present life is He,
And faith hath yet its Olivet
    And love its Galilee!"

Then he says:

"The familiar refrain 'Jesus of Nazareth passeth by,' ought to be changed into 'Jesus of Nazareth standeth by.' He is not here to-day and away to-morrow. He is perpetually present. He lives and moves in the midst of us. He is nearer to us than any one else, nearer to us than we are to ourselves. * * * * * * * * He is something more than the Christ of history—a blessed memory; or the Christ of prophecy—a sublime hope. He is the Christ of to-day, and of every day, a living reality in our lives, a very present help in time of need. * * * * * * * An absent Lord! Think of it; and yet he has said, 'Lo, I am with you all the days, even unto the consummation of the ages!' A friendless stranger! Think of it; and yet he says, 'I will not leave you orphans, I will come unto you.' Why should the church keep mourning the absence of her Lord when she has the assurance of his abiding presence? Why should the spouse of the ever living Christ sit down in the dust, clad in the weeds of widowhood, bewailing the loss of the Lord when he is really present with her? Why should believers in a risen Christ dolefully sing, 'Down life's dark vale we wander till Jesus comes,' when they ought rapturously to sing 'Joy to the world the Lord is come?'"

Both of these books are published by Revell. Neither book is very new, the former having been published in 1894; the latter in 1895.

3. "A Help to the Study of the Holy Spirit," by William E. Biederwolf. This volume differs in toto from the two just mentioned in so far as the method of treating the subject is concerned. The book is in a way a compilation of many works on the subject. The author evidently read everything on the subject he could find besides making a careful study of the New Testament references

to the Spirit. In his thirteenth chapter, besides some independent studies, Mr. Biederwolf gives the views of distinguished preachers and exegetes on controverted points such as "The Baptism of the Spirit," and then endeavors to decide the issue by an appeal to the Scriptures as the arbiter and final test. It can scarcely be said that the results are always satisfactory but the work is reverent and in many places instructive. A most excellent feature of this book is the bibliography it contains. Nearly everything that has been published on the Holy Spirit since John Owen issued his book in 1674, is in the list and the volumes especially helpful are starred. The Winona Company, of Chicago, is the publisher of this work.

And last, but by no means least, "The Holy Spirit," by J. H. Garrison. Its twelve chapters are all good. The writer has read them again and again and he has turned oftenest to and lingered longest over the one on "Blessings from the Holy Spirit."

Leaving out of consideration for the present all controverted points and differences here is a book with a message for every follower of the Christ. It is so wholesome, so sane, so devotional in its treatment of the subject that one could wish the volume were twice as thick. The timeliness of this book must be apparent to many. For nearly two thousand years we have been saying, "I believe in the Holy Spirit." Surely it were time for us to say what we believe about him and how much we believe in him.

Finally the writer wishes to say that he has received encouragement in his study of this subject from his older brethren in the ministry. Not long ago a well known elderly minister among the Disciples of Christ came across the writer in a book store. The elderly preacher looked at the book which the writer was examining, and on seeing it was a work on the Holy Spirit, he said:

"Few things give me more pleasure these days than the fact that our young ministers are giving time to the study of the Holy Spirit. It augurs well for the future of our people."

"As the marsh-hen secretly builds on the watery
        sod,
Behold I will build me a nest on the greatness of
        God.
I will fly in the greatness of God as the marsh-
        hen flies,
In the freedom that fills all the space 'twixt the
        marsh and the skies.
By so many roots as the marsh-grass sends in the
        sod
I will heartily lay me a hold on the greatness of
        God."

Bloomington, Ill.

What can I give him,
    Poor as I am?
If I were a shepherd,
    I would bring a lamb,
If I were a wise man,
    I would do my part—
Yet what I can, I give him,
    Give my heart.
                —*Christina Rossetti.*

[Another able, recent work on the subject, entitled, "The Teaching of Christ Concerning the Holy Spirit," has just come to our notice, by Professor Crane, and published by the American Tract Society, Nassau street, New York. — Editor.]

Our Budget

—Church Extension Day September second!

—Church extension has right of way through August and September—

—Naturally the most unfavorable season of the year. Let us chivalrously "overcome nature with grace."

—Do not preach last year's Church Extension sermon. Prepare a new one; make it glitter with latest statistics, make it ring with, "Thou shalt love thy neighbor as thyself;" make it effective by putting your soul into the weaving of it, and all your strength into its presentation.

—Other mission funds are like bread—consumed by use. Church extension funds, like love or power, continually increase by use. What prestige we will have when it is said: "The Churches of Christ have $1,000,000 in one of their funds"! A little more than $100,000 annually will place $1,000,000 with our Board of Church Extension by 1909. We can get it. We will.

—R. W. Mills, of Bartley, Neb., will give churches needing an efficient minister helpful information.

—The new church at Ocean Park, Cal., was dedicated August 5, F. M. Rains assisting the pastor, Geo. Ringo.

—C. C. Atwood is in the midst of a great meeting at Circleville, Kan. Seven additions at last report and large audiences.

—The Greeley, Colo., church will begin revival meeting September 2. Evangelist Charles E. McVay will have charge of the music.

—The church building at Salem, Ind., W. G. Allen, minister, has been enlarged and remodeled. Dedicatory services will be held August 26, F. T. Porter, of New Albany, assisting the pastor.

—W. H. Wilson, of Texmo, Okla., assisted by O. C. Otis as singer, is holding revival services with fine prospects of establishing a thriving congregation there.

—The Forrest, Ill., congregation under the leadership of pastor J. W. Reynolds has outgrown half-time preaching and wishes to locate a minister for full time.

—M. J. Thompson has been called to the Dayton, Ore., church. Brother Thompson's record is in itself a prediction of a day of larger things for Dayton.

—C. F. Kimball, assisted by F. M. O'Neal and wife as singers, has just closed a two weeks' meeting at Selling, Okla., resulting in 26 additions to the church.

—The pulpit of the Rowland street church, Syracuse, N. Y., is vacant. An able energetic preacher is desired by the membership. Address Geo. H. Doust, 208 Richmond Ave.

—N. M. Baker, of Meridian, Miss., will be assisted in an evangelistic campaign through November by R. H. Crossfield, of Owensboro, Ky., and J. E. Harris, singing evangelist.

—The venerable N. A. Walker, of St. Elmo, Ill., whose zeal has never waned with the flight of years, is in a meeting at Douglass, Ill., with excellent prospects for a most helpful revival.

—James A. Challener has resigned his ministry at the Ross Avenue Church, Dallas, Texas, and accepted the work at Artesia, New Mexico. We wish Brother Challener and his new church great

usefulness and abundant evidences of success.

—A. R. Spicer, assisted by E. A. Gilliland, of Clinton, Ill., is holding revival services at Moweaqua, Ill. He writes: "Meeting moves with power; in the second week, twenty-two added."

—J. R. Perkins, of Huntsville, assisted B. F. Goslin in a two weeks' meeting at New Hope, near Columbia, Mo. Twelve were added to the membership and the church greatly edified.

—A letter from Mrs. A. J. Alderman, of Monterey, Mexico, states that the work of the mission with which she is identified is greatly prospering, notwithstanding the intense tropical heat.

—E. O. Sharpe, of Winchester, one of our most successful Illinois pastors and an able preacher, is compelled to seek a warmer clime. This is a good opportunity for one of our southern churches to secure a very successful minister.

—C. W. Comstock, assisted by Professor Butler and wife, of Mound City, Mo., as singing evangelists, is in a meeting at Orrick, Mo. Large audiences are in attendance and a good interest is manifested.

—J. H. Hardin, with his faithful companion, is in the enjoyment of his beloved Macatawa. No one among us is more entitled to a few weeks' free hearted playtime than Missouri's able Bible school superintendent.

—Lew C. Harris, who began work with the Logan, Ia., church last April, writes that his "work is progressing very acceptably. The audiences are increasing in spite of the hot weather and everything looks prosperous."

—At the last reports thirty-four had been added to the Ennis, Tex., church during a revival in which pastor R. D. Shults is being assisted by W. E. and Clyde Harlow, evangelists. Brother Harlow begins a meeting at Sharon, Pa., in September.

—As we go to press the Audrain county (Mo.) convention is in session at Vandalia and the Pike county convention at Bowling Green. We hope for encouraging reports from these gatherings for our readers in next week's issue.

—Eugene McFarland, of the Fourth Church, this city, is in a very promising meeting at Elvins, Mo. Brother McFarland uniformly preaches the Gospel with a simplicity and earnestness most helpful to church and community wherever he goes.

—Evangelist H. E. Wilhite is in a good meeting at Belpre, Kan., that has already outgrown the seating capacity of the building where it began. The church has been organized during the meeting. Money is being gathered to house the new church.

—Alfred Munyon is in a meeting at Bucklin, Mo., assisted by home forces, and also 100 copies per week of THE CHRISTIAN-EVANGELIST, that are being distributed into the homes of the people whom it is especially desired should be interested in the services.

—The new church building at Rensselaer, Ind., will be dedicated the first Lord's day in September. G. H. Clarke, minister, will be assisted by Evangelist J. H. O. Smith. A cordial invitation is extended all Disciples who can to attend these ceremonies.

—Secretary J. H. Mohorter reports the Benevolent Association has just come into possession of $1,581.83 from the estate of Richard C. Weirick, deceased, late of St. Louis. This good man, "though dead yet speaketh," his benevolent spirit lingers in the world to bless.

—Robert H. Newton, of Normal, Ill., has almost guaranteed a great meeting

in his church for October him S. E. Fisher, of preacher, and H. A. Eas as singer. The church for this evangelistic can

—Evangelist H. A. No ing Pastor Pierce in a n City, Mo. Prophet N without honor even in hi splendid audiences are in ance and a number of the friends have already co vior.

—Isom Roberts, railro the Oklahoma conventic at El Reno September 3-the roads have granted o fare for round trip on the Ministers are requested gates they must secure o the starting point.

—R. S. Smedley is a heroic southwestern pre last five years he has or four congregations and thirty-one church homes. great many meetings and from the active ministry.

—C. E. Swartz, assistec Call, in a meeting at F that resulted in thirty a church. Brother McCall celebrated his last birthd his first converts. This w ful tie between him and assisted into the new life

—W. M. Baker, of Meri cently concluded a 12 day the church at Tupelo, Mis eight additions, four being and baptism. Brother Bal is great need of preachers but that it is not a great fi ers unwilling to serve for

—A. Sterling, of Warren three weeks' meeting for at Metz, Mo., with twenty so far regained his health in the home land under the C. W. B. M. The board will first be direct a hospital in San Franc teaching Christ to the Ch at the University of Calif

—E. O. Sharpe, minister, Ill., meeting says, "On on with gathering force a believe we will yet crack th under God bring things to learned to love and admir lets as I have but few men of all praise for his fidelity Christ and the beauty of hi

—The official board of Okla., church sends a stat ing Bro. Oscar Ingold, highly eulogistic of his It sets forth that "B preaching is clear and log the spirit of love. He dc preach the whole Gospel, plead for Christian unio the primitive plan."

—Friends and admirers of John L. Brandt, of the First Church of this city, will regret to learn he is suffering from another very serious attack of appendicitis.

—We are pleased to learn that Sister Stahl, of Kansas City, is recovering from her long and dangerous illness. Bro. W. L. Stahl of 318 Temple block, can be secured by some church or churches adjacent to Kansas City, for Lord's day preaching.

—C. R. Noe, of Kansas, has just added another $100 to his $600 previously given to the National Benevolent Association on the annuity plan. J. H. Mohorter, 903 Aubert avenue, St. Louis, will answer all inquiries concerning the annuity plan and the work of the association.

—H. F. Davis, of this House, is temporarily supplying the pulpit at High Hill, Mo., and reports the work there in a most encouraging state. R. B. Havener will begin a meeting early in October, at which time it is hoped sufficient money will be secured to build a new church home.

—S. D. Dutcher, of Omaha, assisted by Charles E. McVay, singer, concluded a brief meeting at Eldon, Mo., me 15th, resulting in 38 additions, principally by primary obedience. Pastor J. F. Bickel has done excellent work with this congregation and his personal efforts had much to do with the success of the meet-

ing. Brother Dutcher's preaching is very greatly commended.

—Evangelist O. P. Spiegel, of Birmingham, Ala., and Baxter Golightly conducted the religious exercises of the west central Texas camp meeting at Caddo, extending from July 19 to August 5. These brethren are already planning for the greatest meeting of their lives in the same place next year.

—This sad intelligence was taken from a Monday's daily:

Danville, Ill., August 19.—Last Friday the Christian Church at Wallace, Ind., an inland town, nine miles south of Hillsboro, was struck by lightning. Mrs. Lulu Belles was killed and Ura Shoaff and Tessie Philpott were injured. The church was struck early in the afternoon while sixteen women members of a church society were rehearsing for an entertainment. The church caught fire and was badly damaged.

—Wm. J. Lockhart, of Des Moines, will assist W. E. Reavis, of Webb City, Mo., in an evangelistic campaign through November. The Webb City brethren have completed a new gallery in their church increasing the seating capacity to 700. W. E. M. Hackleman will assist in the meeting as musical director. We predict a Pentecostal blessing to this church.

—Mrs. J. D. Richards, formerly of the Hammett Place church, St. Louis, now of El Campo, Tex., writes there is a great dearth of faithful preachers in that part of Texas. Men able to give a reason for the hope that is within them and who will

preach by example as well as precept are much needed. Sister Richards will gladly assist any such brethren to locate in Texas.

—W. B. Clemmer, of Council Bluffs, Ia., is spending his vacation with the mission church at Sterling, Colo. Arthur Wake, of La Junta, is leading the singing. There are good audiences and 13 additions the first ten days, 11 being by confession and baptism. Brother Clemmer writes that the Sterling and Atwood churches (six miles distant) will need a pastor September 1.

—J. W. Reynolds has just closed a successful year's work with the churches at Saunemin and Forrest, Ill., and is open for engagement with some active church. During the year the two congregations raised for all purposes $4,200, $350 of which went for missions. Brother Reynolds is a Hiram graduate, has been preaching for eight years and has been successful both as pastor and evangelist.

—W. H. Wilson, of Texmo, Okla., is another of our preachers "of whom this world is not worthy." For many years he has labored without material compensation in the great Southwest for the upbuilding of the cause of primitive Christianity. He is growing old and pleads for younger preachers to come to take the place of himself and other veterans almost worn out in the service. We trust many young preachers will write him volunteering their lives for kingdom come in that country.

—J. F. Callahan is contemplating a reprint of the Millennial Harbinger of 1863. Those interested may address him at Euclid, O.

—J. J. Limerick, Corning, Cal., may be secured for protracted meetings this fall and winter, in northern California, Oregon and Washington.

—A most cordial welcome home, John J. Handsaker. It is a far cry from Kingston, Jamaica, to Hoquiam, Wash., but such men as you are greatly needed in our northwest—and everywhere.

—There is great need of pastoral work in the church at Lenora, Okla. The salary will be small but quick and most helpful results may be achieved by a man of consecrated ability. Such a one may write R. H. Manning.

—The indefatigable F. E. Day, of Nelson, Neb., has appointed October 7 next as the time at which all his church's indebtedness must be paid in full. He is sanguine of success. He is greeted with large audiences each Lord's day and additions are frequent.

—J. D. Babb will assist Pastor S. E. Hendrickson in a meeting at Hermitage, Mo., beginning August 27. The Hickory county, Mo., convention will be held at Wheatland September 12 and 13. We are hoping our people will take greater interest in the county and district conventions. They should be to our state and national conventions what the families are to our congregation.

—Use the pink circular found in this paper to send us the name of a new subscriber to THE CHRISTIAN-EVANGELIST. You may be placing the paper in a home where for twenty-five years it will be second only to the Bible as a lamp to the feet of friends and a light to their pathway. The salvation of immortal souls may be largely due to your ministry.

—Henry J. Lunger concluded his meeting at Tallapoosa, Ga., July 12· There were four additions by confession and baptism and one from the Baptists. The prayer-meetings which had been neglected were resumed, and the Christian Endeavor, which had had no meetings for three years, was reorganized. The church wishes to engage a minister at once. If the right man comes, the future of the church seems very bright.

—H. J. Lunger's last revival conducted as evangelist for the Western District of Georgia was at Carrollton, and closed July 30. There were five additions to the church by confession and baptism. Our people had held no services for the last three years and part of the time denominationalists were using the building. Brother Bellomby paved the way for this reorganization by his faithful ministry for a few months preceding the revival. A Bible school has been organized and the work of the church begun in real earnest.

✿ ✿ A Free Gift.

A trial bottle of Drake's Palmetto Wine is sent prepaid, free of charge to every reader of this paper who has chronic Stomach Trouble, Flatulency, Constipation, Catarrh of the Mucous Membranes, Congestion of Liver or Kitneys, or Inflammation of Bladder. One dose a day relieves immediately, cures absolutely, builds up the nervous system and promotes a larger, purer and richer blood supply; 75 cents at drug stores for usual $1.00 size bottle. For a free test bottle write Drake Co., Wheeling, W. Va.

—George Gowen, formerly of Vine Street Church, Nashville, the last few months of whose life have been so pathetic, writes us that he is entering a private sanitarium in New York where he will probably remain for one year for rest and treatment.

—E. E. Faris, former missionary to South Africa, later of the "Texas Courier," and now called to a chair in Texas Christian University, paid a visit to this office Monday while returning to Dallas from attendance on lectures at Chicago University. Brother Faris' usefulness to the churches bids fair to measure up to that of his father's, the veteran preacher and editor, G. A. Faris, and that is honor enough for any man.

—A stenographic error made the second editorial in last week's issue "Business Side of Christian Union," instead of "Business Side of Christianity," as intended by its author, but it was a ringing and helpful advocacy of Church Extension even under its strange title. After all, Church Extension may perhaps do as much for Christian union as any other means we are employing, and the terms be more nearly synonymous than appears at first glance.

—Harry D. Smith, of Hopkinsville, Ky., writes that the South Kentucky Missionary Association owns "two board and tuition scholarships" in South Kentucky College, which it wishes to exchange for preaching in the vicinity of Hopkinsville. Any young preacher wishing additional school advantages under these conditions may write President A. C. Kuykendall, W. J. Hudspeth or H. D. Smith, at Hopkinsville, Ky.

—Bros. R. S. Harvey and Franklin, of Eldon, Mo., have just presented the local congregation with an excellent modern parsonage. Would that their example were emulated all over the country! Many ministers are greatly embarrassed to find homes in our smaller cities and towns at all creditable to the membership they represent. Let us seek to inaugurate a parsonage building era in the material development of our churches.

—The secular press reports a gift of $40,000 from the venerable A. B. Teachout, of Cleveland, O., to Cotner University. While this report has not been verified to us by either the alleged donor or President Aylsworth, of Cotner, it is so characteristic of the Christlike generosity of Brother Teachout that we give the report for what it is worth. Surely we are entering into an era of princely giving by Disciples for the cause of Christ.

—J. F. Stevens, of La Junta, Colo., organized a church of 27 members at Silver City, New Mexico, last spring. The congregation desires a minister to locate with them. The church can pay but a small salary at the beginning, but prospects are good for upbuilding the church and increasing the salary. Silver City is described as a delightful place of residence. Ministerial volunteers for this field are requested to write Miss Lizzie Young.

—W. B. Blakemore, of Lexington, assisted Pastor Aden Bristow in a two weeks' meeting at Connersville, Ky., resulting in 32 additions—25 by confession and baptism. This church was organized one year ago with 15 members and now has 81. It has a Bible readers' union and a normal training class and is in a healthy, growing condition. The pastor speaks very highly of the evangelist's ability to effectively preach the old Jerusalem Gospel.

—Percy G. Cross, of Hope, Ark., is in a brief meeting at Okolona, Ark., with seven additions to date. He writes, "THE CHRIS-

—The Central Church, Columbus, O., was among the very first, if not the first, to place an order for the new hymnal, "Gloria in Excelsis." Our people are delighted with it. It looks like a "hymnal." There is a character, there is dignity about it. Its arrangement is wellnigh perfect. The good music, the stately music, the great hymns are all there. Its mechanical get-up reflects credit upon its publishers. We expect to order 150 more copies for our new church building.—Walter Scott Priest, Columbus, O.

—The Kansas State Missionary Society will meet at Parsons September 17-20. The Parsons brethren are making preparations to entertain at least 500 delegates. Lodging and breakfast will be free, dinners and suppers served in the basement of the church for 20 cents and 25 cents. A flat rate of one and onethird fare has been granted by the railroads. No certificates are necessary. Tickets on sale September 16-18 going, and up to and including September 23 returning.

—Wallace M. Stuckey, assisted by his daughter, Ethel, as singing evangelist, is having great success at Galesburg, Kan. Two-thirds of his large audiences consist of young folk. The people are earnestly reading THE CHRISTIAN-EVANGELIST that he distributes among the audiences in order to learn our position and as an inspiration unto all righteousness. There are bright hopes of a large ingathering to the church in addition to the confirmation of the faith of the saints and the interest aroused in the breasts of sinners.

—During Brother Garrison's sojourn at Pentwater he unfolds the Word of Life to assembled Disciples each Lord's day. In part, at least, through his efforts there are now excellent prospects of a perfect union of the Christian and Baptist congregations. If this is effected it will be another beautiful illustration of the sunshine of brotherly love's doing more than the blustering winds of debate and party pride in causing those who truly love the Lord to discard the mantle of sectarianism and walk arm in arm toward the beautiful gate.

—The secretary of the Wholesale Liquor Dealers' Association of Missouri has sent circulars broadcast over the state advising citizens that 17 senators and 144 representatives in the next state legislature will be elected in November. The circular states "It is not less essential for us to prevent

any one from taking a seat in our legislature disposed to ruin the business we are engaged in. Prohibitionists are fanatics. It is important that every citizen of this state vote against a candidate who is backed by the anti-saloon league or the prohibition party. It is your duty to interview your candidates and let them declare how they stand on the liquor question. Vote and work for those that are with you irrespective of your political affiliations." When, oh when, will "the children of light" be as wise in their day and generation as the children of this present world?

—We are greatly surprised to learn that E. B. Bagby has resigned the pastorate of the Ninth Street Church, Washington, D. C., to accept the pastorate of the Franklin Circle Church, Cleveland. For the past fifteen years Brother Bagby has preached for the Ninth Street Church, and it was generally understood that, like his illustrious mentor, F. D. Power, he had received a life sentence to the Nation's capital. Under his influence the church has grown from a little mission of sixty-five members to a membership of more than 1,100, and he is become one of the most popular and able ministers of the city. We most heartily congratulate Ohio over this accession to her ministerial ranks and particularly the Franklin Circle Church in securing the services of one so endued with evangelistic fervor, so gifted as a pastor, and helpful as counselor and friend.

—One of the finest things said recently about THE CHRISTIAN-EVANGELIST comes from a preacher in the far west, who, on his way to Kentucky for a visit, stopped off at the Grand Canyon of Arizona and writing from the sublimities of that place says: "I could not help but think of the good work being done by THE CHRISTIAN-EVANGELIST. You know there are individuals and papers that deal with small truths. I am glad that THE CHRISTIAN-EVANGELIST emphasizes Grand Canyon truths." The sublime truths and facts of God in revelation are worthy to be compared with the sublimest things in nature, and THE CHRISTIAN-EVANGELIST has tried to concern itself with some of the deepest and most vital truths of Christianity. That there are men and women by the thousand that appreciate our efforts in this direction is no small compensation for our labor. Don Quixote never tilted a lance to less purpose than did the white plumed

knight of the Rockies in his cheerful demolition of the Budget paragraph that would have our new church at Manchester "patterned in every particular after the Jerusalem model." The Jerusalem brethren may not have been as enthusiastic for world wide missions, or as dignified in their worship as Brother Tyler wishes they had been, but we confidently maintain that the church Christ had in mind when he said: "And on this rock I will build my church" was builded in Jerusalem, and notwithstanding all opposition was builded just as Christ wished it to be. The life and spirit of that church may not have found perfect expression through its early membership, nevertheless all the ages will continue going back to Jerusalem for a divine pattern of the model Church of Christ or the gates of Hades will prevail against it.

❋ ❋

Announcement.

I desire to announce that the "Hughes Key to the Revelation of Jesus Christ Which God Gave Unto Him to Show to His Servants," is now in the hands of the printer.

"Blessed is he that readeth and they that hear the words of prophecy and keep the things which are written therein."

"Let him that hath an ear hear what the Spirit saith to the churches."

"And the angel said to me: these are the true words of God and faithful."

"Here is wisdom: He that hath understanding let him consider the number of the beast for it is the number of man."

"I will tell thee the mystery. Here is the meaning which hath wisdom, the seven heads of the beast are the seven mountains."—JASPER S. HUGHES.

Macatawa Park, Mich.

❋ ❋

A Home in Decatur, Ill.

My pastorate with the First Church of Christ, Danville, Ill., will close September 30, 1906. I expected to remain with this church longer, but I find it best to terminate my work here as above stated. A report of the work will be given about October 1.

I have made no request for another pastorate, though I am as able for such work as I have been for the past fifteen years. I have bought a home in Decatur, Ill., to which I expect to move early in October. The Lord willing Decatur

—The Young People's Bible Class of the First Christian Church, St. Louis, Mo., has an enrollment of 234, and has had an average attendance during the summer months of more than 100. The attendance is much larger during the school period, when students from all parts of the country are in the city attending the various colleges. The class is well organized, with officers and committees, and has regular monthly business meetings. The social feature is manifested in the class picnics, trolley rides, boat excursions, lawn fetes, banquets, etc. These are conducted with a dignity that becometh Christians. The members of this class have raised during the past twelve months, by personal and class offerings, more than $3,000 for church, missionary and benevolent work. These offerings are made cheerfully, and many with great sacrifice. The class has sent out many well trained church workers for the Master. The three superintendents of the Sundayschool and ten of the fourteen teachers, the presidents and most of the committeemen in the Christian Endeavor societies, and the superintendent and most of the teachers in the Chinese mission have been trained in this Bible class. Best of all, out of this class has gone forth twenty-one young men for the ministry and two young ladies for the missionary field. Nine of these are now in the field preaching, and the others will enter college this fall to make a more thorough preparation for the ministry. The class is made up of consecrated soul winners who have caught the spirit and enthusiasm of their pastor and teacher, John L. Brandt.

will be our permanent home. Whatever
work may come to me in Decatur, or the
neighboring churches, I shall cheerfully
accept and do as unto the Lord. Any
church or churches within easy reach of
Decatur needing such services as I can
give, and desiring it, can address me till
the last of September as below.

J. H. SMART,

309 W. Seminary St., Danville, Ill.

❀　❀

Missouri Missions and Church Extension.

We have just closed a four weeks meeting here with J. Clarence Read, of Fulton,
Ky., doing the preaching. There were 12
additions, 2 by confession and 10 by letter. One of the greatest blessings of the
meeting came from a member of the
Methodist church in the shape of the
best lot in town for a church building. Brother Read is a great worker,
and held the attention of a large tent
full every night. People who have never
heard the plea of our people have become interested in it. Hundreds of people in this part of the state have never
heard our cause preached and knew nothing about us nor what we stood for.
There is no use of hunting places where
our plea is unknown. We have thousands in the state of Missouri that know
nothing whatever of it. We have not a
church building in Scott county, and only
this one organization. All wishing to
help the Cause can help us build on the
lot we had given to us here. Think of it,
a town of 3,000 people in the great state
of Missouri and not a church of the
brotherhood in the entire county, in
which this town is situated. Can you
find a more inviting field in the entire
country? That is not all, this is the
richest town in dollars and cents in the
world, size considered. Money is their
god.

We want a preacher now that is a good
hustler and a good preacher as well. One
that can preach the love of Christ, and
present our cause in a loving way to this
people. We can and will have a congregation of several hundred in a few years
if we can but get a building, and we are
going to get it; for we have several hundred dollars pledged already.

Have the brethren in the state to look
this way for a while, and get this part of
Missouri under the banner of our Cause.

We meet now in the opera house, but
will later get a better building for our
place of worship. Pray that the Lord
may be with the people in this part of
Missouri, and especially to help the
church at Sikeston.

Sikeston, Mo. CLARENCE F. BRUTON.

❀　❀

Board of Ministerial Relief of the Church of Christ.

Aid in the support of worthy, needy, disabled ministers of the Christian Church
and their widows.

THIRD LORD'S DAY IN DECEMBER
is the day set apart in all the churches for
the offering to this work. If you make individual offerings, send direct to the Board.
Wills and Deeds should be made to
"BOARD OF MINISTERIAL RELIEF
OF THE CHURCH OF CHRIST, a corporation under the laws of the State of Indiana." Money received on the Annuity
Plan.

Address all communications and make
all checks, drafts, etc., payable to
BOARD OF MINISTERIAL RELIEF,
120 E. Market St., Indianapolis, Indiana.

HAVE YOU OUR CATALOG?

If not, send us your name and it will
be sent you.
CHRISTIAN PUBLISHING CO.,
2712 Pine Street, St. Louis, Mo.

Struck Twelve.

I refer to Herbert Yeuell in his recent
evangelistic campaign in Manchester,
N. H. I doubt that any man among us
in pioneer work ever left a better first
impression. The many favorable newspaper reports indicate that he "struck
twelve." He is to return in the near future and prosecute the work until he organizes a strong Christian church. The
meeting cost more than $1,200, the ren-
tal of the opera house being the heaviest
item of expense. I have known single
meetings to cost one of our congregations from $2,000 to $2,500, so the cost of
this meeting was not excessive. Indeed,
in view of what promises to come of it,
the cost is light.

But it is unjust and ungenerous in us
to permit the deficit of $400 or $500 to
fall on one man, Bro. J. H. Garrison.
Will our great, strong, wealthy brotherhood permit it? The work is ours, not
his. Let a hundred more have immediate fellowship in it. Send a generous offering to Brother Garrison at once, or
if sent to me and marked for the Manchester, N. H. meeting, I will forward
it. Let us receive $500 within two
weeks. WM. J. WRIGHT,

Cor. Sec., A. C. M. S.

❀　❀

For a Church in New Hampshire.

Already acknowledged............$766 25
Vermont Avenue C. C. Sunday-
school 25 00
Missionary Society, Washington,
D. C. 20 00
George T. Smith............... 1 00
　　　　　　　　　　　　　　　　——————
Total $812 25

For years Brother Smith labored for
the establishment of the kingdom in the
Orient. He now gives of his means for the
institution of a New Testament church
in a neglected portion of the home land.
The new church will not be suffered to
languish and perish. One of our missionary societies that never fails in bringing its enterprises to successful consummations will care for the young organization till its own resources are sufficient
to make it strong, enabling it to keep the
lamp of truth gleaming afar, and its
membership to be a rugged crew saving
the lives of multitudes engulfed in indifference and error more dangerous than
Atlantic's tides that beat against Manchester's rocky portals.

We appeal to our brethren for an additional $500, enabling us to resume the
meeting and found the church. Act at
once on the noblest impulse of your heart
and send Brother Garrison a check or
draft for the amount of fellowship you
wish in establishing a church in New
Hampshire.

❀　❀

Adding Machines.

Would it not be well to urge our
brethren in the colleges not to permit any
"short cuts" in mathematics? Who
knows just who, of all the students in
our colleges, will become evangelists
after the flight of a few years? And
what success will ever attend their efforts if they do not know how to "figure." For it is the figures that seem to
bulk large in modern evangelism. When
I try to wade through the bewildering
figures in the Monday telegrams in our
papers, I am led to wonder as to how
many were received without the courtesy
of a letter, how many came who had
the "jining habit," how many were
scared in, and how many will become regular attendants at the Lord's table, how
many will place their names on the lists
of regular contributors to the benevo-

STATECRAFT AND STATEHOOD.

John Sharp Williams contributes an article in September SOUTHWEST upon the "Admission of the New State: Its Political and Commercial Significance."

September SOUTHWEST is devoted exclusively to the New State.

FIVE CENTS A COPY—FIFTY CENTS A YEAR

SOUTHWEST,
1037 Frisco Building,
St. Louis, Mo.

"What Shall I Do To Be Saved?"

We have been blessed in the use of copies of Acts of Apostles as a tract on "What shall I do to be saved?" We buy them from the American Bible Society, New York, at two cents per copy, plus express. The booklets are first given into the hands of our Christian Endeavors, who mark in red ink the passages that relate to conversion. In the marking, they are directed by an experienced leader. This is an education to our young people and also makes the plan of salvation plain to the hurried reader.

We have given these booklets out by the hundreds and nothing done by us this year has made the impression that this work has done. The copies of Acts make a neat appearance and are much prized by the recipients. They are read by workmen in the shops, by women in the kitchen, by all sorts of people, everywhere. Our own members are wonderfully helped in doing personal work. The fact that this tract speaks with the authority of the Scripture carries great weight. Our success makes us think that many congregations ought to be distributing Acts of Apostles as a tract on "What shall I do to be saved?" Ten or twenty dollars spent in this way will be a most profitable investment.   CHARLES DARSIE.

Uhrichsville, Ohio.

Song Books

...FOR...

The Church, Sunday-School

...AND...

Endeavor Societies.

GLORIA IN EXCELSIS, The New Church Hymnal.

GOSPEL CALL, Published in Combined Edition, and Part One and Part Two.

CHRISTIAN HYMNAL Revised

GOSPEL MELODIES.

POPULAR HYMNS No. 2.

LIVING PRAISE.

SILVER AND GOLD.

PRAISES TO THE PRINCE.

CHRISTIAN SUNDAY-SCHOOL HYMNAL, Shape Note Edition Only.

Write us the kind of Song Book you are needing and we will take pleasure in giving you full particulars concerning our Music Books.

Christian Publishing Co., St. Louis, Mo.

Southern California Convention.

The annual state meeting of the Disciples of Christ at Santa Cruz, Cal., July 24-August 5, was up to the high standard of previous conventions, even excelling them in some particulars. First the attendance was larger than usual. Nearly 1,500 attendants registered and 233 official delegates, representing forty-seven churches, reported. All the business of the state convention was transacted by these delegates. Hence the convention was congregational, not only in theory but in practice.

The different departments of the convention, C. W. B. M., Y. P. S. C. E., Bible school and Berkeley Bible Seminary, furnished good reports and splendid programs.

Much of the business of the convention concerned itself with the problems of reconstruction of the churches in the stricken district and in re-establishing the "Pacific Christian."

A reconstruction commission was chosen, which plans large things for the cause in the bay cities. They ask for $200,000, one-half of which shall be raised by the local churches and the other half from outside sources. The brethren in California believe in large undertakings worthy of a great purpose and brotherhood.

The Berkeley Bible Seminary reported nearly $4,000 new funds and three new instructors added to her teaching force— A. M. Elston to the department of public speaking, W. P. Bentley as lecturer on missions, and R. P. Shepherd, pastor of the Berkeley church, to the department of religious pedagogics. President McInerney, with his high ideals for the seminary and his popularity with the coast brethren, is doing a great work for the seminary on the outside which is ably seconded by Dean Van Kirk and his collaborers on the inside. All this means ultimately a well endowed and thoroughly equipped Bible college equal to any in our brotherhood.

Plans were formulated for putting the "Pacific Christian" on a more substantial basis and increasing its circulation.

A committee on a Pacific coast congress was appointed. D. A. Russell was re-elected state secretary.

Dr. H. O. Breden, of Des Moines, visited the convention and contributed an excellent sermon to its program.

Miss Bertha Mason, national organizer for the C. W. B. M., was present and addressed the convention and conducted very helpful conferences with the sisters.

The chief attraction of the convention was Prof. H. L. Willett, who preached the first Sunday morning sermon, gave a series of lectures on "The Beginning of Christianity," and conducted three informal discussions on "Modern Methods of Bible Study," "Evangelism" and "Christian Union." Large and appreciative audiences greeted him on all these occasions. Everybody was charmed, pleased and edified by his Christian culture, loyalty to Christ and aptness as a religious teacher. Many expressed themselves as hoping that he would return next year.

A sweet Christian spirit prevailed throughout the convention which was not disturbed by an informal discussion of church federation.

This state meeting may be fittingly characterized by the words enthusiasm, enlargement and unity.

    G. A. RAGAN.

Conference at Hiram.

There has just terminated at Hiram College a conference of ministers having for its object the deepening and quickening of spiritual life. Away from the rush and turmoil of the world the brethren came with one mind and heart to the verdant quietude of the college hill with its beautiful campus, to commune with one another and with God, to drink deeper draughts at the springs of spiritual power, to seek to enter into the great things which God has prepared for those who love him.

Although the attendance was small the services were fraught with much blessing. Much time was spent in meditation and prayer. Strong, searching personal messages came to all hearts from the Word, and there were helpful discussions of the great problems of the religious life.

Surely a great spiritual hunger is manifesting itself among our people—a hunger in which there is divine purpose, in which there is divine satisfaction. Our ministers feel the call to a larger consecration and to deeper experiences of divine things, that they

---

may more effectually lead their congregations in "the blessed life and the blessed service."

The conference sermons were preached by Bros. J. H. Goldner, of Cleveland and J. E. Lynn, of Warren. Bro. E. M. Todd, of North Tonawanda, led us to the mount of vision in his discourses on the Theology of the Apostle John. Helpful devotional services were conducted by Bros. J. E. Pounds, J. E. Lynn, President Rowlison and others. Sub-conferences were led as follows: On Evangelism, by Bros. W. J. Wright and C. A. Freer; on Christian Education, by President Rowlison; On Missions, by Professor Paul and Dr. Osgood, just returned from China. Bro. I. J. Cahill, of Dayton, spoke on "The Perfect Life," and Bro. J. L. Hill, of Cincinnati, preached the closing sermon.

The results of the conference were so satisfactory that a committee was appointed to arrange for its perpetuation as an "annual retreat." Why should we not have our own Northfield or Keswick? "The Spiritualization of our Plea" must begin with the spiritualization of our own lives. Arrangements are already going forward toward the conference at Hiram next year. It is part of the plan of the committee to secure some man of great spiritual power to be present several days. The committee will meet during the Buffalo convention.

CHARLES T. PAUL, Chairman.

❧ ❧

Mexico, Mo.

August 19 was delightfully spent with Pastors Kokendoffer and Harding. The chief purpose of the visit was to preach to the Mexico Chautauqua. This was a great pleasure, both on account of the large and appreciative audience, the courtesies of the able manager and his wife, Charles E. Stokes, of Kansas City, and the fellowship of our editorial friend, W. B. Palmore, of the "St. Louis Christian Advocate." The latter caused much merriment in the course of a very kind

James Small, Evangelist.

introduction of the preacher, by delivering a eulogy on THE CHRISTIAN-EVANGELIST, in which he declared it to be the ablest religious paper published, and that it was the duty of all who wished to keep in touch with the progress of the kingdom, and who truly love the Lord to read its every issue. Suddenly remembering the ablest of the "Advocate family," amid the laughter of hundreds, he tried to limit his eulogium to the bounds of the Churches of Christ.

It was a sweet privilege to address our

Bible school which, under the leadership of Dr. W. F. Traughber, was one of the most helpful friends the writer had while secretary of our national benevolences.

The new church home at Mexico is a marvel of beauty, convenience and durability achieved at the cost of $35,000. Rarely does the large auditorium seat

A. W. Kokendoffer, Pastor.

Brother Kokendoffer's audiences, but the overflow is satisfactorily cared for in the lecture room annex. Many of our faithful preachers have greatly endeared themselves to their congregations, but none more so than this true man of God.

Next Lord's day Evangelists James Small and LeRoy St. John begin meetings with this historic church. A stronger combination than Pastors, Kokendoffer and Harding and Evangelists Small and St. John would be difficult to find. They will be temporarily aided, too, by W. B. Taylor, of Moberly, Mo., a former and greatly beloved pastor, who is spending his vacation in Mexico. Here "Raccoon" John Smith spent his last days, here many of our strongest men have lived and labored; a membership of finer spiritual timbre and one more thoroughly imbued with the genius of this Restoration can nowhere be found. We predict a great meeting. Five hundred CHRISTIAN-EVANGELISTS per week will assist in the enterprise.

For a preacher's paradise give us a church like Kokendoffer's—the strongest one in a county seat of between 5,000 and 20,000, free of faction, intelligent, missionary, enterprising, neither exceeding rich or poor, and thoroughly in love with the Lord and his churches.   S.

❧ ❧

"Charles Carlton Memorial."

T. F. Weaver, pastor of Central Christian church, Whitewright, Texas, has been secured to represent Texas Christian University, Waco, Tex., and Carlton College, Bonham, Tex.

Brother Weaver is well known in Texas and Illinois as a Christian preacher of ability and an experienced college professor, and an excellent business man.

Besides soliciting students for the above institutions, Brother Weaver will solicit donations for "Charles Carlton Memorial" $30,000 building, to be erected in 1907.

By the blessing of God, and the liberality of the alumni, friends and Christian brotherhood of Texas and adjoining states, success is assured.

Are you interested in the success of this enterprise? Do not wait to see our representative, but write at once to T. F. Weaver, Whitewright, Texas, Pres. C. T. Carlton, Bonham, Texas.

Bethany Park Assembly.

To the Editor of THE CHRISTIAN-EVANGELIST:

It was my pleasure to spend a few days with the Indiana brethren, in their state assembly at Bethany Park, recently. I had not visited this place for many years, and the changes were very marked. The trees have grown into a splendid forest; cottages in large numbers have been erected, and the lake has been enlarged and its shores beautified by the generous growths of trees and grasses. The same Hoosier hospitality made my stay a constant delight, while the happy face of Bro. L. L. Carpenter shone more brightly than ever. And well it might; for Bethany is out of debt, for the first time in its history; some needed improvements are now in sight, and the outlook for this center of our work in Indiana is brighter than ever. In honor of the years of service given to Bethany by Brother Carpenter, the hotel building, formerly known as the sanitarium, was christened Carpenter Hotel, and a free room voted to Brother Carpenter for life. This was a merited honor, and much more fitting than tardy resolutions of respect adopted after his life work had ended. Would that we would always distribute some of our flowers to the living. With the improvements that are being projected for Bethany Park realized, it should become one of the most attractive resorts for Disciples for the summer season, combining rest and worship, pleasure and instruction.   W. F. RICHARDSON.

Kansas City, Mo.

❧ ❧

SUPERIOR TRAIN SERVICE

via the Michigan Central, "The Niagara Falls Route," between Chicago, Detroit, Niagara Falls, Buffalo, New York, Boston, and New England points. For information as to trains, rates, etc., ask any ticket agent or address H. I. Newton, Pass. Agent, 257 Main St., Dallas, Texas; W. J. Lynch, Pass. Traffic Manager, Chicago.

NEWS FROM MANY FIELDS

Chandler (Okla.) Christian Church.

Like all the congregations organized in new countries the faithful here had a long and hard struggle. Emigrants were coming and going, and in that unsettled condition of affairs, the less faithful would have given up in despair. The church of Chandler today is a monument to remind the world that "where there is a will there is a way."

The writer was called to this pastorate May 6, last, and has found it a congenial home. There are 355 enrolled at present. I never saw brethren and sisters more devoted to the church than those with whom I now labor.

This church has had a remarkable growth of late. Two years ago this August E. L. Frazier began a meeting which was continued seven weeks and resulted in the addition of seventy-two new members. Good seed had been sowed for several years preceding, and at that time a revival began which has never since languished; the church has actually been in a state of revival ever since. Bro. J. E. Dinger was called to the pastorate here to begin March 28, 1905, and served the congregation one year, during which time ninety-two were added. Though Brother Dinger had engaged to enter the evangelistic field at once, the church here persuaded him to remain one week longer for a short "revival." He then preached for them eleven nights and added forty-five more.

Since I came here we have added 16. July 29, we commenced a protracted effort which will continue as long as interest demands. We have a large tent pitched in a public place, and immense crowds are now hearing the primitive plea. Pray for our success.   OSCAR INGOLD,
Chandler, Okla.

A New Church.

We closed our Reger (Mo.) meeting August 17, with an organization of twenty-one members. This is the first effort at organization in this place. It gives us a nucleus around which we hope to build a strong congregation. In this work we have received many Christian courtesies from our religious neighbors. They tendered us their (M. E.) house in which to hold our services, furnishing a good share of the congregations and helping us materially in song service and prayer. We came mighty close to federation with a strong case of co-operation and I talked union on the "Bible and the Bible alone," from the beginning to the close of the meeting. I had a splendid opportunity to get the true teachings of God before the people and I did not fail the opportunity. As a result of this meeting the people have a better understanding of our teachings and a kindlier feeling for us.

Desiring to continue the work that the board began here the brethren have arranged for preaching once a month. O. W. Jones, one of the strong preachers of this county, will have the spiritual oversight of this congregation. He is now the pastor at Milan, Mo.

As an appreciation of the board's work here, the brethren have arranged for a monthly contribution for the ensuing year to the missionary work in Sullivan and Putnam counties.

Under the direction of the board we begin our next meeting at Sorrell, the fourth Lord's day in this month.   S. J. VANCE, Evangelist,
Carthage, Mo.

Ohio Letter.

The daily press brings the intelligence that the Franklin Circle church of Cleveland has extended a call to E. B. Bagby of Washington, D. C., and that he has accepted it. We wish to congratulate Franklin Circle church most heartily and extend a very cordial hand from the Ohio disciples to Brother Bagby. It is our prayer that his ministry may be long and prosperous.——The convocation at Hiram, August 5-12, was not so very largely attended at any one session, yet quite a company was there all together. Most of the preachers attended only a part of the sessions. The conferences were very helpful indeed. Earl M. Todd of Tonawanda, N. Y., gave two Bible studies that were of rare interest. The Ohio man also enjoyed a two-hour car ride conversation with Brother Todd that was equally as helpful. W. J. Wright added much to the program, making a great address on evangelism.——The Eastern Ohio ministerial association had a business session and elected officers and received candidates. R. Moffett and F. M. Green are the only charter members left.——The brethren at Pauld.ing will let the contract on September 1 for a new $15,000 synagogue and also a new manse for the parson. J. P. Meyers is making a fine record with these people.——C. A. Freer will be.gin a meeting at North Royalton September 9. Chas. Ford is the regular pastor. Any church wanting a short meeting beginning December 2, can "get next" by writing the above-named evangelist.——Are you going to Buffalo? It is only a short time ahead. Let the nickel-saving start at once. Make up your mind early and the money will be found.——Bowling Green has the foundation for a $25,000 meetin' house about completed. It is built on the same lot as the old house. Bishop Darsie spent his vacation at Hiram with his father and mother. Where on earth could a better place be found for a vacation? A fort.night with father and mother beats all the summer resorts in creation.——C. A. Kleeberger has spent six weeks treeing students for Bethany. He reports several finds.——Don't forget that Geo. W. Muckley wants you to pass the hat for church extension September 2. Fill the hat full.——C. A. Freer, Painesville, O.

The Scandinavians and Our Plea.

I am glad the Scandinavians are to hear our plea for a united church. They are religious, devout, reverent. Those who regard the Lutheran faith as the one true religion see but little difference in the many hued denominational flags of their adopted country, while others, finding themselves in a community without a church of their own become inquirers and seekers for truth going from this church to that wondering which is "the right church," or the "nearest right." The perplexity of such inquirers only increases upon learning that most of the churches recognize each other as Christians and that the services and sermons in the different places of worship do not differ materially. Faith in Christ, Christian worship, Christian missions, Christian living, is not only endorsed, but urged on every hand. Why then all this division, these many churches, evangelists, schools, church papers and unseemly rivalries? That is what the uninitiated Scandinavian cannot understand and I honestly believe that we, the Disciples of Christ, are the only people who can give a satisfactory answer to this riddle, and we ought to do it.

I need not here restate the A, B, C's of the Gospel—the supremacy of Christ—and love the greatest thing in the world without which the union for which Christ prayed is an impossibility. Suffice it to say, we much teach the Scandinavian

as we are seeking to teach all others, what are the first principles of the Oracles of God and be at peace among ourselves. We need the Scandinavians in our churches. Their faith in the first principles of success would act as a valuable tonic in very many places. The Northman believes in hard work, rigid economy and honest service. His creed is that whatever is right is bound to win and he is perfectly willing to earn his success. This reminds me that with the exception of the president of the United States, about all my interests are being looked after by Scandinavians, from Senator Knute Nelson and Congressman Volstad to our own Governor Johnson, state senator and representative, superintendent of public instruction, nearly all county, town and school officers are Scandinavians, all of which leads me to believe that not only are the Scandinavians capable of understanding and appreciating our plea, but the same force of character which has made them the recognized leaders in opening up the great Northwest, would make them powerful allies in bringing our matchless plea before their countrymen. A few suggestions as to how this is to be done is reserved for another article.—P. S. Olson.

Niagara Falls.

Outside of the big convention itself Niagara Falls will be a chief point of interest to those who come to Buffalo in October.

A fifty minutes' ride by the New York Central, or an hour and a quarter by the yellow electric car brings one from the convention city, north, to Niagara, the "thunder of water." The city of Niagara Falls itself is of interest. Known to many, at a distance as only a place for tourists on a closer observation it is seen to be a great railroad center and the electric power city of the world. Its population now 27,000 has doubled in the last ten years, and will probably do as much in the next year. It is a city of great factories most of which have located here by reason of the cheap electric power by which they are run.

Across on the Canadian side is Niagara Falls, Ont., a city of about 8000 people. Here, just recently completed at a cost of millions, are to be found three immense power plants. These will distribute electric power to Toronto and other points of Ontario.

But to most visitors the river itself and the scenes connected therewith will be of the most interest. Three-quarters of a mile above the falls the river by its steep descent and rocky bottom is broken into white-capped rapids. It is divided by Goat Island into the American and Canadian Falls. The American side has a width of about 920 yards and the water falls 175 feet. The Horseshoe or Canadian side has a width of 600 yards and a fall of about 160 feet. The water dashing down to the great rocks below is churned into white foam from which arises continually a spray white like steam.

One of the beautiful parks around the falls is Prospect park, on the American side, belonging to the New York State government. This has a $20,000 shelter house, seats for tourists and other conveniences free. On the Canadian side is Victoria park made beautiful with flowers and inviting to visitors. Between the two cataracts and belonging to New York is Goat Island, a park of 75 acres, on which stand the original forest trees.

If desired one may walk around Goat Island, seeing all points of interest in an hour. Those who prefer to ride may take a government carriage in Prospect park and go around the island for 15 cents, stopping at any point of interest and waiting for another carriage without extra charge. From Goat Island for $1 one may obtain a rubber coat and an experienced guide, and by passing over great rocks through the spray go back a short way behind the falling sheet of water into the Cave of the Winds.

From Prospect park an inclined plane railway leads to the foot of the American falls. By all means go down and look up. The ride will cost ten cents the round trip. If one likes walking he may take the 252 steps on the stairway free, but if will take more than ten cents worth of St. Jacob's oil the next day to relieve stiffness. While down this incline take the little boat, "The Maid of the Mist," which for 50 cents will furnish a rubber coat and hood, take you a half hour's ride through the mist and rainbows past the face of the American falls and up to where the water boils before the Horseshoe falls. No better view can be obtained of the falls than from the deck of this little steamer, which has carried its thousands and never yet had an accident.

It is 14 miles from the falls to where the river empties into lake Ontario. Seven miles of this distance is so full of interest that it has no dull points. The descent in the first seven miles is 104 feet, and most of the way are rapids which must be seen to have their grandeur appreciated. Many things of interest in and about the falls must be passed by in this short article. Suffice it to say, we have here enough to bring you across the continent even if there was to be no great convention. And here will be found a sufficient variety to charm or suit the inclination of any.

For the unmarried brothers, the Three Sister Islands and The Maid of the Mist. With these you may flirt to your heart's content. For those who had no chance to be heard on the conven-

tion platform the Cave of the Winds is a safe place for the explosives. The inclined plane railway will accommodate the backsliding, while the "Great Gorge route" will be attractive to those who like to eat. The shady minded may stop at the "Devil's Hole." Come, brethren, to the convention, and see Niagara ere you pass over Jordan.　　J. A. WHARTON.

Niagara Falls, N. Y.

❀ ❀ Australian Notes.

The first Sunday in July we took the offering for Foreign Missions, at the tabernacle, and the result was nearly four times as much as was received last year. My Bible class, which averages one hundred and thirty, gave $25. I have been in Sydney ten weeks, and more than seventy have come into the church by primary obedience. The building seats eight hundred, but extra chairs have to be brought in every Sunday night. The Tabernacle church is the largest church we have in Australia, and is probably the most enthusiastic. I go to Brisbane, Queensland, the 9th of September, will remain there, in a tent meeting, until October 12, at which time I sail for Japan, China, etc.—Jno. T. Brown.

❀ Changes.

Braden, Arthur—Newcastle, Pa., to 38 North Division street, Auburn, N. Y.
Carter, Geo.—Shaw, to Peabody, Kan.
Carter, M. O.—Freedom Sta., O., to Hazel Green, Ky.
Cook, Eldon E.—Lufkin, Tex., to Rolla, Mo.
Crerie, Wm. C.—Somerville to 29 Ninth avenue, Haverhill, Mass.
Dunkleberger, C. E.—Flat River, Mo., to Cumberland, Iowa.
Forrest, W. M.—Ann Arbor, Mich., to The University, Charlottesville, Va.
German, W. C.—Atwood, Colo., to 821 South Second street, St. Louis, Mo.
Hall, Colby D.—Hillsboro to North Waco, Texas.
Hill, Roscoe A.—Bloomington, Ill., tp Manzano, at Mantuasa, Cuba.
Harris, Ellis B.—Santa Cruz, to 201 Kipling street, Palo Alto, Cal.
Hayden, W. A.—Lowellville, O., to 331 Burgess avenue, Indianapolis, Ind.
Luggna, M. C.—Shoals to Bicknell, Ind.
Jones, Edgar D.—Cleveland, O., to First Christian church, Bloomington, Ill.
Krahl, P. W.—Folsoni, to Corrumpa, N. Mex.
Martin, Richard S.—Chicago, Ill., to "Martin Family," Sturgis, Ky.
McCreary, L. W.—(For August only) St. Louis, Mo., to R. F. D. No. 3, Fredericktown, O.
Myers, T. M.—Lexington, Ky., to 48 Spruce street, Asheville, N. C.
Peters, H. M.—Rossville to Dixon, Ill.
Quisenberry, J. F.—Lockhart to 703 North Thirteenth street, Waco, Tex.
Reid, T. P.—Nicolaus, to Acampo, San Joaquin county, Cal.
Smith, J. N.—3114 Downing avenue, Los Angeles, Cal., to 215 North Sichel street.
Stevens, John A.—Sulphur Springs, Tex., to Calhoun, La.
Swift, Chas. H.—Syracuse, N. Y., to Minden Mines, Mo., Box 29.
Winter, T. E.—Irvington to 2614 Dana street, Berkeley, Cal.

Evangelistic

We invite ministers and others to send reports of meetings, additions and other news of the churches. It is especially requested that additions be reported as "by confession and baptism" or "by letter."

Special to THE CHRISTIAN-EVANGELIST.

Ennis, Texas, August 19.—Immense interest and great crowds at Harlow and Harlow meeting, 72 added in 15 days. We continue.—C. B. Knight.

Special to THE CHRISTIAN-EVANGELIST.

Monroe, Wis., August 20.—One hundred and forty-eight added in first seven invitations. Am in union meetings with five churches here; 3,225 so far this year.—Scoville and Smith.

Special to THE CHRISTIAN-EVANGELIST.

Sturgis, Ky., August 20.—Twenty-three additions already. Immense crowds yesterday. Seven confessions Sunday. Twelve baptisms Monday. Continue. Nearly four hundred added since "Martin family" Kentucky campaign commenced.—J. W. Ligon.

Illinois.

Princeton, Aug. 14.—One confession last Sunday.—Cecil C. Carpenter.

Armington, Aug. 17.—Two confessions last Lord's day.—L. E. Chase.

Pekin, Aug. 13.—A choice young lady obeyed her Lord in baptism last night.—J. A. Barnett.

St. Elmo, Aug. 16.—Two confessions, two by letter following our grand meeting.—N. A. Walker.

Indiana.

Scottsburg, Aug. 23.—E. F. Crawford, an elder of this congregation, recently closed a twelve days meeting at Bridgeport in Clark county. Fourteen additions.—C. O. Burton.

Hartford City, Aug. 17.—Four additions since last report, two by letter and two confessions. We have engaged Dinger and Gardner for our revival and will enter the simultaneous campaign October 28.—Wm. Elmer Payne.

Scottsburg, Aug. 13.—The Christian churches of Scott county held their annual meeting August

ALL WILL WANT

QUIET TALKS ABOUT JESUS

BY S. D. GORDON

The author of "Quiet Talks on Prayer" (now in its 38th thousand), and "Quiet Talks on Power" (now in its 26th thousand).

Cloth, 12mo. 288 pages. Net 75c.

"QUIET TALKS ABOUT JESUS" is an attempt to group up in simplest Anglo-Saxon English the statements of the entire Bible regarding Jesus. The purpose is wholly practical, that one may get at a glance, for his own thought and heart, the swing of the Bible from end to end on its central theme. Mr. Gordon's life work has been leading up to the theme of his new book.

TOPICAL ARRANGEMENT

FIRST—The purpose of Jesus' coming: the plan of his coming; the tragic break that occurred in the plan; the surprises that worked out of that break.

SECOND—The Person of Jesus from three points of view: the human; the divine; the winsomeness of his personality.

THIRD—The seven great outstanding experiences which reveal Jesus: the Jordan Baptism; the Wilderness Temptation; the Transfiguration as an emergency triumph; the Gethsemane struggle; the Victory of Calvary.

FOURTH—Study Notes. One of the most important features of the book, making it possible for the earnest reader to follow for himself Mr. Gordon's analytical methods.

CHRISTIAN PUBLISHING COMPANY
ST. LOUIS. MO.

10-12. Reports showed substantial gain during the year. I began meeting with the Zoah congregation last Saturday evening. Four added on Sunday. Will continue.—C. O. Burton.

Kentucky.

Wilmora, Aug. 8.—Just closed a two weeks' meeting at New Liberty, Anderson county. There were thirty-six additions, nineteen by baptism. C. C. Allen, the minister, was with me in the work.—Wm. Lowen.

Minnesota.

Amboy, Aug. 10.—One addution at Willow Creek recently. Bro. C. R. Neel begins meeting with us Aug. 26.—Fred M. Lindenmeyer.

Missouri.

Festus, Aug. 20.—One addition by letter yesterday.—Daniel C. Cole, pastor.

Kansas City, Aug. 16.—Three more baptisms at Louisburg Sunday. Beginning meeting at West Line Sunday with good prospects.—Clyde Lee Fife.

Trenton, Aug. 14.—Four additions recently. The Bible school is growing. Have recently organized home department and cradle roll. The church has pledged $100 to the permanent fund of State Missionary Association.—S. J. White, minister.

Cox, Aug. 9.—Closed sixteen days' meeting at Fairview, Macon county, last night. Twenty-three additions, sixteen by obedience, five from other communions.—W. A. Dameron.

Farmington, Aug. 17.—At a meeting of the Farmington Ministerial Alliance, held Aug. 16, it was decided to commence simultaneous meetings in the five churches in the city in November.—Edward Owers, president.

Orrick, Aug. 19.—Two added by letter and four by confession and baptism.—Prof. G. A. Butler and wife, singing evangelists, C. W. Comstock, minister.

Grayson, Aug. 19.—Two confessions at Wallace, one of them Bro. Lewis Johnson, for many years always at church and foremost in its support, but still refusing to confess.—W. A. Oldham.

Norborne, Aug. 18.—I baptized two at Methodist camp-meeting in this county Thursday last. We will begin a meeting at Mt. Carmel September 2, with G. A. Butler and wife as singing evangelists.—C. E. Taylor.

Weaubleau, Aug. 20.—Two additions at Hermitage last Sunday. Both from denominations. There were fourteen added at Calhoun in one meeting, ten baptisms. J. H. Jones is kept in meeting with eight added first week, seven baptisms, six young men.—S. E. Hendrickson.

New York.

Buffalo, Aug. 15.—One added Sunday from another communion.—B. S. Ferrall.

Washington.

Hoquiam, Aug. 15.—D. E. Olson and G. A. Webb and wife closed a five weeks' meeting Aug. 5, with 64 additions. Brother and Sister Webb are now at Chehalis, Wash., where N. L. Brooks is beginning a meeting, with eight added the first week. The Chehalis brethren are building. John J. Handsaker has been called to Hoquiam and began work August 12.—R.

❀ ❀

Ministerial Exchange.

Singing Evangelists F. M. O'Neal and wife can be engaged for meetings in September and October. Permanent address, 842 W. Florida street, Springfield, Mo.

❀ ❀

OBITUARIES.

[Notices of Deaths, not more than four lines, inserted free. Obituary memoirs, one cent per word. Send the money with the copy.]

MARGERY.

Alexander T. Margery, aged 57 years, a graduate of Bethany college, but who has for many years resided in Australia, died in Adelaide, South Australia, June 20, 1906.

HERRON.

Mrs. Rose Marmaduke Herron, who had been living for the past two years in Urbana, Ill., died very unexpectedly in Mexico, Mo., on July 21, 1906. Mrs. Herron was the daughter of the late Morgan B. White of Montgomery county, Mo., and was born February 14, 1836. In 1865 she was married to John F. Herron of Pittsburg, Pa., who died in 1870. She leaves in her immediate family a daughter, Miss BelVa M. Herron, a sister, Mrs. F. W. Gatewood and three brothers. Mrs. Herron was an active member of the Christian church, of the Woman's Christian Temperance Union, and of various literary and social clubs in the places where she had resided, but of more significance than her work in these organizations, were her individual efforts for the betterment of the world about her. Early deprived of the comfort and care of family life, she devoted herself to help-

---

ing the sick, and the afflicted. Mrs. Herron possessed unusual physical and mental vigor, unfailing cheerfulness, quick Wit, and a keen sense of humor. These qualities, together with a deep religious faith, made her a most unusual character, one whose memory is a blessing.

Sunday-School

September 2, 1906.

BARTIMAEUS AND ZACCHAEUS.—
Luke 18:35-19:10.

Memory Verses, 42, 43.

GOLDEN TEXT.—The Son of Man is come to seek and to save that which was lost.—Luke 19:10.

The golden text of this lesson is one of the many statements of Jesus's attitude toward sinners. No reader of the gospels can fail to notice how large a part of them is occupied with discourses, parables and incidents whose chief point and purpose was to teach the principle that sinful men are worth caring for, and that outward respectability and conformity to religious conventionalities are no proper criterion for judging the real worth of men. We have already had half a dozen or more lessons embodying this principle. It might almost be said that this was the most conspicuous and important element of the teaching of Jesus.

The episode of blind Bartimaeus (and the other blind man, according to Matthew) is a typical miracle. It was a beneficent work of healing, wrought under the impulse of pity upon a needy and friendless man who exhibited both faith and persistence in his petition, and resulting in a confirmation of faith both in the beneficiary of the miracle and in the witnesses. "Thy faith hath made thee whole," is the keynote of this incident. There are those who say it makes no difference what a man believes. It made a great deal of difference to Bartimaeus. He believed that Jesus could give him his sight, and he acted accordingly. His belief (if he had any) as to how Jesus would heal him, was a matter of small consequence. Probably he had no theory about it. But his faith in the person of Jesus was fundamental.

This incident occurred when Jesus was nearing Jericho as he was on his last journey to Jerusalem. The stories of Bartimaeus and Zacchaeus both indicate that Jesus was at this time a widely known personage who had a great crowd of more or less sympathetic followers and whose actions were being carefully watched by all classes. His popularity and renown made his condescension in the case of Zacchaeus the more notable—surprising to the publican himself and inexplicable to the Pharisees.

What sort of man was Zacchaeus? Probably the best hated man in Jericho. To be a publican was to be a tool of Rome in collecting extortionate taxes from his own people. Under the Roman system of "farming the taxes"—that is, selling the privilege of collecting taxes—extortion was inevitable. To be a rich publican was to be a successful extortioner. Publicans were always the objects of hatred and contempt, and they generally deserved it.

Why did Jesus go to the house of Zacchaeus? Because Zacchaeus needed him. Jesus went not to those who could help him but to those whom he could help. And because Zacchaeus wanted him. He did not invite him, had never dreamed that the great and popular rabbi whom all men thronged to see would condescend to visit his house, but he received him joyfully. Jesus knocks at doors, but does not break them down. To this day, he comes only where he is wanted. And again, Jesus went to the house of Zacchaeus because he saw the worth of the man beneath all his sins and meanness. The others saw only the sinner and the publican; Jesus saw the man. Even the most sinful man is more than a sinner. He is primarily and essen-

tially a man. His sinnerhood debases and defiles, but does not destroy or supersede his manhood.

The result of the visit was that by the power of friendship Zacchaeus conceived a new respect for himself and a new desire for righteousness. And in the light of silent and uncriticising purity he saw his own sinfulness as no amount of Pharisaic denunciation had ever shown it to him.

Midweek Prayer-Meeting

August 29, 1906.

THE LIFE-GIVING STREAM.—Ezek. 47:1-12.

"While in the slippery paths of youth
  I run secure and free,
Oh, let thy blessed Word of Truth
  My Guide and Counsel be!

"Thus o'er my life let mercy move,
  And guide my feet the way
That leads me to thy throne above—
  To everlasting day!"

Well may this river represent the ideal development of Christian character, and be another presentation of first the seed of the kingdom in the heart, then the blade, followed by the corn, and then the full corn in the ear.

These streams originated in the temple, but proceeded out over the land refreshing, beautifying, and blessing far and away. It should be so with us. In the church and in our homes we gain knowledge and power and grace but they are not to be confined there. Out into society and a thirsty, needy world we are to go expanding in sympathies, deepening in love and power, and more quickly hastening to cheer and restore and prosper.

The life-giving stream is made wide and deep and perennial by the confluence of many tributaries. Here blend in one great swelling tide food and raiment, home and its sanctities, friends and social amenities, forgiveness and long suffering, the indwelling of the Holy Spirit and the companionship of Jesus, resurrection and coronation. O that all the hot and feverish of earth would drink of its cooling waters and regale themselves in the verdure and beauty of its shores.

In the contents of the books are many unstudied evidences that the Bible was written by its reputed authors and in the land of its alleged nativity. There waters are particularly appreciated. The land is stony and hilly. The streams run quickly from the mountains to the sunken seas and the fears of drouths are unending nightmares. In every picture of bliss unfailing streams abound naturally as in the poor man's dream he is owner of vast estates. The blessings of the temple could not otherwise be so effectively portrayed to Ezekiel's first-hearers and readers as flowing forth in streams of waters that not only were not stanched by summer but deepened and widened with its onward flight.

This river ever increasing in volume may be likened to the resources of the Church of Christ through the ages. In the first century its visible strength consisted of a few fishermen, the peasant apostles, the stream was ankle deep. In the fourth century Constantine invested it with the political power and military prestige of the empire and it was knee deep. By the sixteenth century Europe had been evangelized, scholarship dedicated its greatest gifts to the church, and ecclesiastical dignity and splendor had

Christian Endeavor

By GEO. L. SNIVELY

September 2, 1906.

SPIRITUAL BLINDNESS.—Jno. 9:35-41; Acts 26:12-19.

DAILY READINGS.

M. Blindness of the Pharisees. John 9:35-41.
T. Blindness of the Jews. Acts 26:12-19.
W. Seeing Without Perceiving. Isa. 6:10-13.
T. Lovers of Darkness. John 3:16-21.
F. Knowledge and Sin. John 15:18-25.
S. Blind Guides. Matt. 23:16-26.
S. Light for All. Isa. 42:13-17.

Let us cultivate a vision enabling us to see defects rather than graces in our own characters, and good rather than ill in others.

Color blindness is a great calamity, but spiritual blindness is more deplorable. The former is a serious misfortune, but in America the latter is a crime. The one can not be helped by the victim but the other is almost always a matter of choice.

That Great Physician who opened the eyes of the blind when he was on earth among men has power to give us visions of fairer worlds and nobler careers and more splendid goals. No matter how great the darkness we will be guided "with mine eye" to the foot of the cross, if we wish to go, and find healing.

The Jews said to Jesus, "We never have been in bondage to any man, how sayest thou, ye shall be made free?" There is none so blind as those who will not see. They said, "We never have been in bondage," yet all around them were evidences of their subjugation by Rome's galling bondage. So with us: we deny bondage to Satan and yet we are unkind, impatient, intemperate, unprayerful and despairing.

We have known naturally severe and rheumatic old dames to demand that some young people be summarily dismissed from the church on account of their alleged "inconsistent amusements." We would not encourage young people to indulge in amusements inconsistent with their church vows or that grieve good people, but we wish those censors could so overcome their spiritual blindness as to see their uncharitableness and harshness toward those young people is more heinous in the sight of the Master than the other "inconsistencies" about which they are so concerned.

On artists' easels are frequently found stones or cards in the deep primary colors. They are used to retone the painters' eyes that frequently become fatigued and lose their power of nice distinction in colors and shadings. So in morals we sometimes lose the fine sense of distinguishing between things permitted and things harmful and need the immediate presence of some of the rugged old spiritual maxims that never vary with the capricious moral sense of ages and nations. Among these are "God is and a rewarder of them that serve him." "The soul that sinneth it shall die." "And these shall go away into eternal punishment, but the righteous into eternal life."

How differently we see! The laborer sees in the rose a thing of beauty lending a charm to his happy home. The poet sees it not in its relation to that home; to him it is a part of the world, a smile on the face of nature expressive of its jubilant spirit. The botanist views it in ways purely scientific, he traces its harmony with the rest of the universe; it awakens no sentiment in his heart; its address is wholly to his mind. How fortunate if each could see in the rose all that they separately behold! One may be fuller visioned than another but each is partly blind. It is so with God. To one he is a Nemesis, to another simply Creator, to another a heavenly Father. One may be fuller visioned, but each is partly blind. Gazing steadfastly into the heavens heals the spiritual eyes. There let us look till we can behold the King in all his beauty.

❀ ❀

FOR BABY RASHES,

Itchings and Chafings, Cuticura Soap and Cuticura Ointment are Worth Their Weight in Gold.

The suffering which Cuticura Soap and Ointment have alleviated among the young, and the comfort they have afforded worn-out and worried parents, have led to their adoption in countless homes as priceless curatives for the skin and scalp. Infantile and birth humors, milk-crust, scald-head, eczemas, rashes, itching, chafings, and every form of itching, scaly, pimply skin and scalp humors, with loss of hair, are speedily, permanently, and economically cured when all other remedies suitable for children, and even the best physicians, fail.

People's Forum

"Centennial Aims."

To the Editor of THE CHRISTIAN-EVANGELIST:

I have read Bro. E. L. Powell's article in THE CHRISTIAN-EVANGELIST, of August 9, on "Centennial Aims." Though Brother Powell is a man of brilliant brain and fine spirit, I do not agree with his "one-idea" monument plan—especially not with that of some tremendous edifice. I have already felt that perhaps too much of our centennial energy is spent in a material way, urging fine church edifices and college buildings. The "aim" and sum of the centennial energy should be spent in preaching the truth of the Almighty God directly to sinners to convert them to Jesus Christ, and to Christians to make them more pure in spirit and higher in conceptions. And it makes no special difference if much of this preaching and thousands of converts made are never even mentioned in the papers.

The leading mind and spirit of the age has passed beyond the brick and mortar stage. These impress not the best thought of the age. This statement has no reference whatever to neat and serviceable buildings. Let us not spend the principal part of our centennial energy in a material way.

Washington, D. C. DANIEL E. MOTLEY.

So long as thinking men are interested in the kingdom there will be differences of opinion as to how best glorify God and save men. We favor the suggestions of both these able brethren. We ought to preach Christ more generally and more fervently, but we need not fall short of Brother Powell's splendid ideals in order to preach him acceptably.

What Do We Stand For?

DEAR BROTHER GARRISON—I feel pressed in spirit to ask, through THE CHRISTIAN-EVANGELIST, a few suggestive questions in relation to your position upon Christian union. I am only an humble elder in the Church of Christ, but in my mind the most important crisis of the restorative movement is upon us. If our plea was and is right, it will fail or be successful according to the attitude we take towards this desirable achievement. I have no words to express my deep anxiety upon this vital question, and thousands who are of like precious faith are equally interested, and are praying that this matter may be adjusted so as to please him who gave himself for the Church.

We all are exceedingly pleased with the spirit manifested toward those with whom you differ, but are sorry to say that we—or rather I—am somewhat at a loss to understand how you would have Christian union practically consummated. That may be because I am "slow to understand," or because I have not read all you have said or written upon the subject. Pardon me for being somewhat personal.

In the past I was connected with a religious body who alleged that they took "the Scriptures for their rule of faith and practice," and "Christian character as their test of fellowship." They would receive any one into full fellowship who came to them expressing a desire to live a Christian, whose range of "private" belief was anywhere from the Quaker to the Unitarian. Baptism in no case was required of them. However, if, after being received into the church (by a vote of the same), they "felt" it to be their "duty," they were ordinarily immersed. After listening to the "plea" of the Disciples of Christ, and thoughtfully reading God's Word, I became convinced that I was wrong, and united with the Church of Christ because I thought they were right, and the more I read and think and observe I am confirmed in the belief that they stand for the Gospel of Christ,

and on the only ground of permanent Christian union.

I have much to learn. I would not be stubborn, I would not be wrong, but if the church from which I came, and others like it, with their mourners' bench religion, and their sprinkling, and infant baptism, "ordinances" and so on—if they are churches of Christ *because* they are "honest" in their views, and seem to have as good "a spirit as we have," then I and many others have made a great mistake, and should make a hasty retreat back to the church of our first love, and by confessing our sins perchance they will again take us into their fold. Does the New Testament church consist of immersed believers or not? Are we only a church among other churches? What do we stand for? How much must we compromise? Wherein have we been wrong? We love your spirit; we acknowledge your ability. Lead us out of the depths into the true light. D. H. HARRINGTON.

Columbus, Ohio.

We commend the spirit of the foregoing, but we hope our brother will be able to see, on reflection, the inconsistency of the position that, if any other churches than our own may be classed as Christian in spite of grave errors, then we ought to go back and join these churches out of which we have come, because of the better knowledge we obtained as we believe, of the truth as it is in Jesus. A one-eyed man, or a one-armed man, or a one-legged man, is a *man*, nevertheless, in spite of his defects. Does this fact tempt any one who has two eyes, two arms, and two legs, to destroy one of these members, because he can be a *man* without it? Besides, it does not follow, by any means, that if those may be regarded as Christians who live up to the best light of Christ's will which they have, that we, who have learned that will better, may be so classed if we be disobedient to the light, as it has shined upon us.

We favor no compromise of the truth, and we believe in the correctness of our position, or we would not advocate it; but that the correctness of our position involves the condemnation of all who do not stand with us, to everlasting perdition, or to the realms of the unsaved, is what we emphatically deny. The Editor of this paper, like our correspondent, came from another religious body, and he has no disposition whatever to return to it, not because he does not believe that it is a Christian body, but because he believes that the position we occupy is broader, truer, freer, and better adapted to people pleading for Christian union. We sincerely hope that our brother, whose article manifests a good spirit, will be able to see a distinction so plain and so vital as this.—EDITOR.

Current Literature

THE MOSAIC LAW IN MODERN LIFE. By Cleland B. McAfee. (Fleming H. Revell Company, Chicago. $1.00 net.)

The author is Dr. Cuyler's successor at the Lafayette Avenue Presbyterian church, Brooklyn, both have made famous. The book is an exposition of the Ten Commandments, in which sound thinking is garbed in the raiment of beautiful language. The first chapter treats of the relation of the law to life. Each of the remaining ten chapters is given to one of the commandments—Singleness in Worship, Spirituality in Worship, Present Day Reverence, Present Day Sabbath Observance, Present Day Family Life, Present Day Regard for Life; Present Day Purity, Present Day Honesty, Present Day Veracity, Present Day Contentment. The ways of God all are made to appear because of love to man.

❖

MISSIONARY ADDRESSES. By A. McLean, President Foreign Christian Missionary Society. (Christian Publishing Company, St. Louis.)

The first book presented to me after I entered the ministry was a copy of the above-named work. That copy is now much thumbed and the margin of its pages plentifully penciled. Little wonder! For seven years it has been the birthplace of my missionary sermons and rally addresses. The other day I saw an item in THE CHRISTIAN-EVANGELIST to the effect that a new edition of these addresses had come from the press. I ordered a new volume at once. It has come and lies before me now. An excellent likeness of the author, our beloved president, beams out from the frontispiece. The body of each address is unchanged, but the statistics and data are brought down to 1905. In my opinion the market does not afford a better single volume on the subject than this one. It is brimful of missionary information. Its fund of scriptural citations is striking. There isn't a dull line in it. W. F. Turner, of Joplin, once said to me that this was one of the few books that had moved him to tears. The author has imparted to the printed page somewhat of the warmth and magnificent enthusiasm for world-wide missions that characterizes his platform and pulpit utterances, and makes him a "God-intoxicated man." Whether the preacher's missionary library be large or small, it should contain this book. The price is $1 and the place to obtain it The Christian Publishing Company, St. Louis, Mo.

EDGAR D. JONES.

First Church, Bloomington, Ill.

The Home Department

Then Comes the Rainy Day.

I.

W'en no trouble in de sunshine
Is waitin' on de way,
'Long come de trouble
Of de rainy day!
You lissen, en you lissen
Ter what de raindraps say,
En Jedgment seems ter find you
On de rainy day!

II.

De ol' ha'nts fum de churchyard
'Come wid de shadders gray;
Dey lead you ter de pas' time—
Dar, whar yo' conscience stay;
Hit's lak' de dead come back ter life
W'en come de rainy day!

III.

I wish dem li'l' chilluns
Would be louder wid dey playin'!
De noise would drown de lonesomeness—
De drip-drip er de rain!
I wish de thunder'd break de spell—
De lightnin' ease my pain!
—*Frank L. Stanton in Atlanta Constitution.*

The Bronze Vase.

BY J. BRECKENRIDGE ELLIS.

PART III.

CHAPTER VIII.

Raymund closed his umbrella at the door and entered the bookstore with the fleshy gentleman. "Stick that vile thing in a corner," said the bald-headed man, still breathing heavily, and mopping his brow. "If I ever meet you again I'm going to take out an accident policy against green umbrellas. What kind of books do you want?"

"I want Cicero for one, and an advanced Latin grammar, and something in French—I think a French history in that language will be a good thing; and a trigonometry, and a psychology and a logic, and a—"

"How old are you, sir?" the man interrupted, staring hard.

"Fifteen; and a botany. I can use the botany well for I am traveling across the country." He started toward the counter but the other said, "Wait. I know that man, and I can get you bargains. But you tell me this; what are these books for?"

"For me; I can study them as we drive on to St. Louis. We are in a covered wagon."

"I would have judged so," said the other with a disparaging glance at Raymund's clothes. "The straw is still sticking to you!" There chanced to be a bit of straw lodged on the youth's shoulder. He brushed it off, laughing, for the other was so oddly frank and so childlike in his very anger, that Raymund could not but like him. "My name is Willby," said the fleshy gentleman. "Now, what's yours?"

This being told, the fleshy gentleman said, "Why are you driving to. St. Louis?"

"My sister and I are on our way there to our uncle's, and as we are poor, a friend is taking us in his wagon. My sister's name is Rhoda."

"How old is she?" snapped Mr. Willby.

"Fifteen; we are twins."

"Have you no father or mother? And if not, how did you get so far advanced in your studies? Where do you go to school? Can you read Cicero? Have you already finished Caesar?"

"We are orphans," said Raymund, when the other had paused for breath. "My sister has been kept in an orphan home until now, but I have been working on a farm; and at night I would study; I studied very hard. I went to the country school house one term, but it wasn't much use, because I was ahead of all the classes. I got it by just digging away when everybody else was asleep. Caesar was real easy, I thought. I read all the eight books. I finished all the books I had. I liked geometry splendidly." Raymund was anxious to give as many details as possible to spare Mr. Willby from asking any more questions.

"Here, John," called Mr. Willby, to the book dealer, "get us these books at once—and we want 'em cheap. We don't care how worn or battered they are, if every page is there—hey, Raymund?"

"Certainly not," said Raymund. The bookseller climbed his ladder to look at his most faded collection, and Mr. Willby said, "Whose farm was it? and what did you do on it? and why did you leave it? and what do you expect to do in St. Louis?" So, as there was really no need to conceal a thing, except about Boggs and Mrs. Van Estry, Raymund told his story. When the books were done up in a parcel and the fat gentleman could think of no more questions, he said, "If you've no objection, I'll go home with you—meaning to your wagon—when the rain has stopped." Raymund explained that the house on wheels was not in a condition to receive visitors of state, but added that if the other could make allowances, he would be received gladly.

"I know all about movers' wagons," said Mr. Willby, "though I am glad to say, I have never ridden in one. I know what to expect, and I'm expecting it, so don't you bother!" Until the rain ceased, he talked about the books, and showed himself on familiar terms with their contents. He passed Raymund through a rather rigid examination and finished by patting the youth upon the back. "You're all right!" he cried, beaming delightedly. "And if you learned all that alone, the right stuff is in you!"

"A French governess gave me a start," said Raymund. "I owe a great deal to her."

"What's her name?"

"Mrs. De Fer."

"Well, my lad, since you owe her a debt, I'm glad to hear you paying it. Be grateful! That's the most neglected branch known to mortals, gratitude is. I'm glad to hear you speak of her in that way. Now the rain has let up." He led the way out with a side glance at the green umbrella, but presently darted into a shop from which he emerged with a bundle. When they came to the vacant lot, the wet canvas walls had been spread outward to dry. The seat, over which Wizzen had spread a waterproof cloth, was occupied by Rhoda and Mrs. Wizzen. The latter was knitting.

Raymund introduced Mr. Willby, who placed his bundle in Rhoda's lap. It proved to be candy, oranges and bananas. Rhoda was a good deal surprised by this offering from a stranger, but her brother hastened to explain that Mr. Willby knew almost as much about them as they knew themselves.

Mr. Willby, seated upon the tongue of the wagon, addressed Mrs. Wizzen with, "And how old are *you*, madam?"

"She is very hard of hearing," said Rhoda, shaking her head.

The fat gentleman immediately raised his voice and bawled his question.

"Sold?" said Mrs. Wizzen, laying down her knitting. "Has Wizzen sold the horses?" There was a hopeful note in her tone.

"Madam," shouted Mr. Willby, standing upon the tongue to bring his face closer to the old lady, "I say, how old are you?"

"Yes," Mrs. Weed admitted, "they *are* rather old, but they are good for some years yet, I assure you, sir."

"Mr. Willby," said Raymund, "I think she is about seventy-eight. She is very active for her age."

"I want to know her age," said Mr. Willby, "without any surmises. I do not think she is seventy-eight. Has she no ear-trumpet?"

"Yes, sir," said Rhoda, "but it has been

ice yesterday. We know it is in
ron, but there are so many things
e, that when anything is lost, we
look for it any more. Wizzen
saves time, that way."

o is Wizzen?" the other immedi-
emanded. "And where is he? Is
g with you to St. Louis?" In the
of an hour Mr. Willby's curiosity
en as fully gratified as it could
rout the employment of an ear-
t. "I must leave you, now," he
gretfully, "but I have this to say:
n Frog Bend, a town not far from
n the river. You'll pass near it.
to say, that if you orphans ever
friend, look me up. I can't in-
Mrs. Weed in this invitation; I
t have anybody about me who is
ng or unable to answer my re-
But you, Raymund and Rhoda,
: welcome guests at my house.
ive entertained me, and I will en-
you."

will never forget you," said
"But I wish we could invite you
to dinner; and we do invite you
would be willing to take your part
."

ppreciate that," said Mr. Willby,
mean no offence when I say that
ot think it likely that your board
satisfy my needs. I am a well-
ed man, and I owe my good
and cheerfulness to a careful diet.
very particular about the kind of
eat. So if you will pardon me, I
save without meeting Wizzen,
there are a hundred questions I
like to ask him."

n it was past noon and Wizzen
t returned, Rhoda suggested that
rt the gasoline stove and put on
fee. Of course while they were in
irt of the capital they would cook
t in the privacy of the covered
While she and Raymund were
ing the point, a black man, wear-
hite apron entered the vacant lot,
g a very large tray. It proved to
inner, sent from the restaurant, at
illby's orders. Judging from the
d repast, Mr. Willby must have
when he spoke of being careful
his diet, that he was careful to get
good things his money could buy.
was some excitement in transfer-
e various dainties into plates and
o the tray and its dishes could be
away. Still, Wizzen did not re-
nd they were obliged to eat with-
n. When he did come, he looked
ike the ordinary Wizzen, that he
despondent spell upon all. He
not eat, and he did not seem to
o hear about Mr. Willby. It was
tly evident that he was trying to
himself interested in the strange
and at last he worked himself up
point of going off to a convenient
e to chew his tobacco. But he
reatly depressed. Raymund once
y inquired if he had heard or seen
ng of Boggs or Mrs. Van Estry,
izzen shook his head impatiently.
he took Rhoda to one side.
here, Rhoda, I'm in trouble, and
you can help me. I've been to
nitentiary."

la did not know if this was said in
iy of reminiscence, or if he had
iis visit with a free will, but she
iite startled at his words.

ten drew his cap farther over his
id pulled up a stone to look under
opened his pocketknife to feel the
and then said, "She is in there,
ow."

la did not know, and Wizzen was
that she didn't, but he found it
explain. "Now it all comes down
," said Wizzen, "which they is no
ving any sentiment or moonshine,

for I'm a plain moving man and don't
know nothing about this thing of brooding over a trouble as if you was trying
to hatch something out of it. Nothing
won't hatch out of a trouble but another
trouble, so I don't brood over it, but
just leave it there to git cold. But as I
say, she is in there; in the pen, Rhoda,
in the pen. And Mrs. Weed don't
know it."

"O, Wizzen!" exclaimed Rhoda suddenly, "do you mean her daughter?"

"Yap. That's who I mean. I've been
to see her and we talked quite a spell.
It ain't that she keered anything about
my coming, for she never keered for me
though once I thought she did. But me
knowing her to be in the pen, and her ma
thinking her loose was the point. And
she don't want her mother to know which
it ain't so much of importance what she
wants done, but what do you think
about it?"

"I don't understand, Wizzen, at all."

"Well, it looks plain to me," said Wizzen in a dry and difficult voice. "Which
would please her mother most; to think
her gal was free to come and go, or to
know that she's clapped up in prison for
five year or more?"

"Why, Wizzen! how could it make her
happier to know her daughter is in
prison?"

"It's this way," said Wizzen: "Her being in the pen, we know she will lead a
good honest life for as long as she is in
there, but if she was free we would know,
if we knowed her, that all the time she

would be up to mischie
kind."

"Of course I can't b
said Rhoda thoughtfully,
carefully hid their pity
a new situation to me.
was a mother, I'd rather
ter free to do most anyt
think of her behind i
bread and water."

"I reckon you're righ
"I believe the old lady
of her, as if she hac
throwed off by her. Wc
no more about it. But
of this town as quick as
ing wouldn't hire me tc
not if I was elected a

(TO BE CONTII

Sunset and Evening Star.

BY ALFRED TENNYSON.

Sunset and evening star,
  And one clear call for me!
And may there be no moaning of the bar
  When I put out to sea,
But such a tide as moving seems asleep,
  Too full for sound and foam,
When that which drew from out the boundless deep
  Turns again home.

Twilight and evening bell
  And after that the dark,
And may there be no sadness of farewell
  When I embark;
For though from out our bourne of time and place
  The flood may bear me far,
I hope to see my Pilot face to face
  When I have crossed the bar.

❋ ❋

Some Chautauqua Notes.

I mean the first, the great Chautauqua, not one of the 325 satellites that glow in various parts of the world this summer, the harvest of the seed planted at Chautauqua Lake in 1874.

Every year on the night of August 7 Chautauqua celebrates with enthusiasm and spirit the beginning of this great movement, and calls it "Old First Night." This season, on this occasion, the amphitheatre, which is built in a natural ravine and seats between six and seven thousand, and when the aisles are filled with camp chairs a couple of thousand more, was crowded until it became a solid mass of nearly ten thousand human beings, a wonderful sight, indeed.

At this meeting Chancellor Vincent, who presided, announced a gift of $20,000 for the building of a new organ in the amphitheatre, from a donor whose name was withheld.

At the close the Chautauqua roll was called, when those belonging to the various classes of the Chautauqua Literary Circle rose or waved their handkerchiefs as the year was called. Every year was represented, and as the roll call went back year by year, and the "old guard" responded, the enthusiasm waxed high. This was followed by the roll call of states, which served to show the cosmopolitan character of Chautauquan life, as it was answered by representatives from the south, from Canada and from the wide world. The number of the C. L. S. C. now number one-half million with a million and a half readers.

One of the most popular lecturers this year was Dr. Dawson of London. It was a privilege to enjoy a week of such teaching as his in the devotional hour and to hear his masterly literary lectures. Prof. S. C. Schmucker and Dr. Edward Howard Griggs are always fine, but never better than this season.

When you have visited a place like Chautauqua your life is enriched by the memory of the rare souls you have met. Among these was Miss Christina Butler, daughter of the pioneer Methodist missionaries to India, Dr. and Mrs. Wm. Butler. She is her father's biographer, and this autumn expects to return to India with her mother, now over eighty years of age, to attend the jubilee of Methodist missions in that country.

One thing that adds much to the Chautauqua life for Disciples is that we have a pleasant, centrally located headquarters, a general place for meetings and gatherings. This is due, largely, to the efforts of Mr. and Mrs. W. J. Ford who have worked faithfully for the past nine years to accomplish this end. The Disciples, few in number in those days, first met in the "upper room" of the Congregational house. The next step was a hut which was occupied for two seasons, when in 1896 the present house was bought. It was remodeled and dedicated in 1904, and has all these years been presided over by Brother and Sister Ford, who welcome the coming and speed the departing guest with genuine Christian hospitality, and who take a pardonable pride in the fact that we have as good a headquarters as any, if not the best on the grounds. It is spacious and attractive, and has a hall that will seat about 200. The quiet communion hour on Lord's day morning is one of the most delightful memories you carry away from Chautauqua. August 5 165 sat down to the Lord's supper together, the services being conducted by Bros. F. W. Brown, of Chagrin Falls, O., and Stevens, of Cleveland.   EMMA R. WHARTON.

❋ ❋

It Did Not Matter.

Booker T. Washington tells the following story of a member of the "po'h" white trash who endeavored to cross a stream by a ferry owned by a negro.

"Uncle Mose," said the white man, "I want to cross, but I hain't got no money."

Uncle Mose scratched his head. "Doan you got no money't all?" he queried.

"No," said the wayfaring stranger, "I haven't a cent."

"But hit done cost you but free cents ter cross de fery."

"I know, but I haven't the money," insisted the white man.

Uncle Mose was in a quandary, and after a few moments' thought, said:

"Boss, I done tole you what. 'Er man what ain't got no free cents am jes' ez well off on dis side of der ribber as on der odder."

❋ ❋

$12.85 Chicago to Marquette, Mich., and Return.

Via the North-Western Line.

$14.25 Ashland, Wis., and return. These special low round trip rates are in effect every Tuesday, with return limit 21 days. For tickets and reservation apply to your nearest ticket agent or address W. B. Kniskern, P. T. M., C. & N. W. R'y Co., Chicago.

The Service of Grief.

Christ's heart was wrung for me if mine is sore;
And if my feet are weary, his have bled;
He had no place wherein to lay his head;
If I am burdened, he was burdened more!

The cup I drink, he drank of long before,
He felt the unuttered anguish which I dread;
He hungered, who the hungry thousands fed,
And thirsted, who the world's refreshment bore.

If grief be such a looking-glass as shows
Christ's face and man's in some sort made alike,
Then grief is pleasure with a subtle taste;
Wherefore should any fret or faint, or haste?
Grief is not grievous to a soul that knows
Christ comes and listens for that hour to strike.
—*Christina Rossetti.*

❧ ❧

Advance Society Letters.

BY J. BRECKENRIDGE ELLIS.

You are now to hear about the great ice cream social at Bentonville, Ark., of August 3. It was the strangest social I ever heard of. Everybody was invited to stay at home and send 10 cents for a saucer of imaginary ice cream, and all the proceeds were to be saved up to help in our orphan Charlie's education. The usual inducements of going to a social were all absent. Nobody expected, as usually happens, to get in exchange for his dime, about 5 cents worth of ice cream and the rest in religion. Nobody could show her pretty clothes or look at other people's, or play out in the church-yard while the older people sat on benches waiting for it to be over. Nobody sat in a corner lonesomely looking as if having a good time, on purpose. And when it was over, there were no dishes to clean, no room to be swept, no lights to be paid for, nobody going home sleepy and cross, and best of all, no deductions to be made from the collection for "necessary" expenses." You ask, why should anybody send money to stay at home, for ice cream that was all air? The answer is simple: to help educate an orphan who has only one leg and who can never make a man of himself unless helped in his education. You say, "Oh, yes, of course it's a good thing, but there are so many other good causes that need money, I doubt if many went to your queer ice cream social!" Reader, if the names of all who came were printed on this page, the three columns would be a solid mass of names! We were here from fifteen different states, and you can see, yourself, that if all these names were printed, nobody would want to read our department. I suppose the best way is to make a dive into this stack of letters on my table, without picking for best or shortest; so here goes, and you can imagine you hear our ice cream guests chatting in merry voices as they wend their mental way to Bentonville.

Mabel E. Nicholas, Burlington Jct., Mo.: "I have never seen any Av. S. letters from Burlington Junction. 'The Bronze Vase' is interesting. Papa, mamma, brother and I spent last winter in Colorado for mamma's health, but this summer brother and I are visiting our aunt and uncle here in the country. We have a nice time eating apples and peaches, taking care of little chickens and, best of all, eating fried chicken." (I suppose your apples and peaches were shipped from Arkansas, as I am under the impression that they are raised only in this state). "Papa and mamma write us a nice long letter each week. We like our new pastor, W. H. Rust, very much. It was thoughtful to have an ice cream social for Charlie's educational fund. Uncle, aunt, brother and I each send 10 cents." Myrtle Searcy, Springfield, Ill.: "Mamma, sister Margaret and I send 30 cents for Charlie's education. We hope Felix will get his share of ice cream at your expense." (He has just had more than

his share of mouse at my expense, for I found some of the remains of my study-chair cushion and there has been great cleaning going on, and some excitement). "My sister had a yellow cat, named Felix, and he was so much like a preacher, he caught a number of chickens. When we found it out he died. If you don't want to be bothered with neighbors' chickens, teach Felix to catch them." (I trust none of my neighbors will see this; however, nobody in Bentonville came to the social except the Wood girls [25 cents], and as they live on the other side of town, I know of no safer place to talk about my neighbors than on this page.) Laura Hutchinson, Anderson, Mo.: "Here is a dime for Charlie's education. I hope the social may prove remunerative." Jenny Bagby, Plattsburg, Mo.: "In response to the invitation to the social, I send 50 cents from Marvin Sherwood in memory of the pleasant afternoon he spent in the woods with you and Tom Capp, Robert and Prince Thompson. My mother is the only mother he remembers and since she died, he sympathizes with all orphans. As five of you went to the woods that happy day this will treat each one to a dish of cream. Read Matt. 6:3, which means, I would rather not sign my name, but that would be impolite." (How well I remember that afternoon at the falls, crawling under the barbed-wire fence, and rolling big stones down the baby mountain! The pleasure of the day all lives again in getting 50 cents from it for our orphan.) Beulah Shortridge, Greenwood, Ind.: "I could not get up a social for our orphan, but I went around among my friends and told them about Charlie and the Av. S. I send $1.50 and names of the contributors." (Not room to give them here, but every guest's name is entered in my Av. S. account book.) Mrs. W. C. Merrill, Long Beach, Cal.: "Here it is 3 o'clock and I've not started to the social! Won't you and Charlie rest out in the shade till I come? Since I'm here, I must tell you that Mr. Merrill and myself and the five little Merrills enjoy the Av. S. stories very much. All who come to our social treat the very happy to feel that they are doing good in the world and giving pleasure to Charlie and others. I wish you had been here in June to hear Brother Scoville. Our S. S. now numbers over 300. We all love Brother Thornton and his family. We had 255 additions, and since the Scoville meeting have had one or more every Sunday since. This is not for the paper, only for yourself and Felix." (The paper will please keep its hands off.) Mrs. Edith Slightam, Spokane, Wash.: "I send for 10 dishes of cream at 10 cents each." (And that makes Felix purr.) "A

Friend". (Quaker?) "Philadelphia: 25 cents for Charlie's education." Mrs. Lucy Marrer, Wabash, Ind.: "After reading your kind invitation to attend the ice cream social at Bentonville, I told the ladies of the Christian church about it, and they were all willing to sample the cream to compare it with Hoosier cream. I am glad to send you $2. I hope Charlie will never forget his true friends, and that in after days his earlier years will be pleasant memories. Rev. Edgar Daugherty is our pastor." Donnie Swift, Billings, Mo.: "I send 10 cents for my dish of ice cream. I suppose the social will be over when this reaches you." (No, just on time.) Mr. and Mrs. F. A. Allen, Los Angeles, Cal.: "It is with much elation that we accept your invitation to be present at that social August 3. We are coming—in the spirit—at that time or somewhere near it, to help swell that worthy fund of which we've heard. Please reserve then, ice cream plenty, enough, in fact, for a crowd of 20, the price of which we're sending by this mail. May all respond in this like manner, then success will perch on Charlie's banner." (Charlie, get your banner ready) "and in life's future conflicts he'll not fail. We are growing poetical, too, you see." (I had to print the stanzas as prose to economize space, but it's all right, for everybody must see it's poetry, it is just swelling and bursting through the lines.) Zoe C. Moller, San Francisco, Cal.: "My husband and I enjoy the Av. S. stories and send 25 cents for Charlie's ice cream. If he likes it as well as I do, he will have no trouble in eating that

Next session opens September 10.

much, and more!" (You have heard of churches who couldn't help mission or orphan homes because they were in debt; but, reader, what do you think of San Francisco sending money for orphan Charlie's education— and sending it not with a look of conscious heroism, but with a jolly laugh and a word of sunshine? When I cast my mite upon the waters of popular sympathy and help that not long since flowed toward the Golden Gate, I little dreamed that in so short a time my bread would be returned.) Harry Buckley, Lawrenceburg, Ky.: "I heartily endorse the ice cream social for Charlie's education. That's the kind of a social that suits me, a social with the *quid pro quo* left out" (this is not Latin for tobacco but is put into English by Harry's next words) "where every dime taken in, represents a solid dime" (and no ice cream is taken in). "Put me down for 10 tickets in the front row where I hope to see Ruth Sampsel, Donnie Swift, Bertha Beesley, Grace Everest and the other faithful ones. I am yours for a jolly crowd and a good time." Bertha Beesley, Moselle, Mo.; "I send $2 for our missionary Drusie. I made a collection for Charlie's social and took up $1.30. I enclose list of contributors" (all of whom are recorded in my book.) Mrs. Thos. G. V8, Plainview, Texas: "I am sending a package of cards for Drusie, saved up by my S. S. class, that she may share them with the little ones in China, also $2 from the S. S. for Drusie, and 50 cents from myself for Charlie. May God bless them both is my prayer." M. J. O'Dell, Fayette, Idaho: "I send $1 for our Charlie with a hope and prayer that dimes and dollars may be plentiful at the social. Tell Charlie it is as hot here in Fayette valley as I ever felt in St. Louis, but it is cool enough after midnight to sleep comfortably under a blanket. Tell Felix when he goes out hunting to be careful not to catch malaria. It might spoil his complexion." (Who said there was any malaria in Arkansas?) Harriet McCausland, Coffeyville, Kan.: "I send my 2 quarterly reports beginning with February 11. I have begun over again because it was so long since I sent in any that I have forgotten how many I did send before. Papa, mamma and I want to come to the social so we send 30 cents and wish it were $30. I am glad Charlie has his vacation. I think 'Bronze Vase' is fine and I think you are splendid." (Now, good for you, Harriet, I feel that you understand me as I am!) "What do you do with all these reports? How long do you keep them? You must have a pile!" (They are piled up until each February 11; then the prize reports are decided; then all except the best are solemnly burned and their ashes scattered to the four quarters [one for each quarterly report.)

Charlie, Dorsey, Ill. (you see that Charlie has finished his visit with his sister Bessie, from his new address): "I had a pleasant time with my sister. Ethel Orr said she was going to give Bessie a chain for her locket. I came here to Mrs. Skinner's last night. I reached Dorsey about 9, and as Mrs. Skinner didn't know when I would come, there was no one to meet me. I telephoned and they had just got in bed. They hitched up the horse and came after me. It was a two-and-a-half-mile drive. It was cool and pleasant so I enjoyed it." (It must have also been cool getting out of bed and I hope was equally enjoyed.) "You won't have to send me THE CHRISTIAN-EVANGELIST, because 'Mrs. Skinner takes it.' I think Arkansas people ought to share up their rains with us, for the farmers here need them." (They can have 'em. It has rained every day here

for the past nine days and it's just stopped now to get ready to do it again.) Mrs. N. C. Skinner, Dorsey, Ill.: "The Ridgely Sunday-school accepts the invitation to Charlie's social, and sends $2.40. Ours is a small school. I send $1, half for Drusie. My four-year-old grandson, Clarke Forman, sends 11 pennies for Charlie." Mrs. B. R. Brown, Orphan Home, St. Louis, Mo.: "Some of the ladies followed your suggestion and had an ice cream social for Charlie's education. I am sending money order for $18. We regret that you, Charlie and Felix, could not be present. I am so grateful to hear that you noticed an improvement in Charlie. I do so trust that he may grow up to be a good, noble man. Tell Charlie I am so anxious to see him in his new suit. We thank those who have given Charlie the lovely vacation he so much needed." (I am sorry I can't tell about every guest to our social in one number of the paper. In two weeks we will go on with the story. I can't tell you just how much the social made us, because people are still buying our ice cream. As soon as we sell out all that's left, we can announce the sum. Up to the present our receipts are $64.90, but I am hoping somebody will send for another saucer, so we can have it $65. I am sure that two weeks from now, all money will be in, and then we can tell exactly what the social brought Charlie. As far as I am concerned, I think $64.90 for an ice cream social at which there was no ice cream is doing pretty well! In two weeks we will try to print all the letters that are left over this time.)

Bentonville, Ark.

❀ ❀

Picture of War Engine "General."

A beautiful colored picture, 18x25 inches, of the historic old engine "General" which was stolen at Big Shanty, Ga., by the Andrew's Raiders during the Civil War, and which is now on exhibition in the Union Depot, Chattanooga, Tenn., has been gotten out by the NASHVILLE, CHATTANOOGA & ST. LOUIS RY.—The "Battlefields Route" to the South. The picture is ready for framing and will be mailed for 25c. The "Story of the General" sent free. W. L. Danley, Gen'l Pass. Agent, Nashville, Tenn.

Christian Publishing Company

2712 Pine St., St. Louis, Mo.

J. H. GARRISON, - - - - President
W. W. DOWLING, - - - Vice-President
GEO. L. SNIVELY, - - Sec. and Gen. Supt
R. P. CROW. - - Tress. and Bus. Manager

We are filling many orders for Baptismal suits. We sell but one grade and that is the best. We sell these cheaper than the same quality is advertised by other firms.

S. D. Gordon's "Quiet Talks" is a famous series. Two new ones have been added—"Quiet Talks About Jesus" and "Quiet Talks on Service." These books are more fully described in other columns. We sell them at 75c. each, net.

The pink circular in this paper does not have to do with your subscription. We trust you will use it in securing a subscription from a friend who does not now enjoy your privilege of reading THE CHRISTIAN-EVANGELIST.

Go with us to the great Buffalo convention via the Wabash. Join our train at the nearest cross roads, if you do not

Over Niagara via "Wabash."

start with us from St. Louis at noon October 11. Without extra cost you may go from Detroit either by lake or through Canada.

For one new subscription sent us at $1.50 we will send you a "diamond point"

pen "warranted by the manufacturers" and that could not be purchased at retail for less than $1.00. For $2.75 we will send you THE CHRISTIAN-EVANGELIST and an automatically filling fountain pen warranted for ten years.

When we get older we select our own literature, while children it is selected for us, but in childhood it is usually determined whether we shall continue Bible readers all our lives or whether we shall "throw off this yoke of bondage" when no longer under direct parental control. By all means use the W. W. Dowling Bible School series that the children may cultivate a liking for religious literature. They cost no more than inferior and alienating sorts.

Matters of tremendous consequence to this Restoration movement are to be considered at Buffalo, which promises to be the greatest convention since our Cincinnati Jubilee. You ought to be a witness to its procedures and have a voice in its councils. Those willing to secure subscriptions for THE CHRISTIAN-EVANGELIST can earn transportation. Write us for particulars. You will enjoy the convention the more because the expense does not all come from your regular income. You will bless every home you visit while earning transportation.

While not so many clubs have been received this week as usual, yet a great many have sent the subscriptions of friends they have solicited to become member of THE CHRISTIAN-EVANGELIST family. That is the most substantial growth, but we are pleased to have received the following clubs of new subscriptions at $1.50 each, to-wit: Millville, Pa., 4; Moulton, Ia., 7, W. D. Endree, minister; Cynthiana, Ky., 30, W. E. Ellis, minister; Washington, O., 12, Wm. Boden, pastor; Jamestown, O., 6, W. J. Loos, pastor; Moberly, Mo., 23, W. B. Taylor, pastor; Farmington, Mo., 3, Edward Owers, pastor; Granger, Ia., 4; Woodward, Ia., 6.

A Western Kansas postmaster wanted to inform the public that the location of the postoffice had been changed, so he inserted this notice in the local paper: "The postoffice has been moved from where it was to where it is now."

The Waiter's Rebuke.

Secretary Taft said of a certain domineering statesman:

"He fills men with dread. They quu before him. They can't call their so their own in his presence. Altogether, makes me think of a waiter I once m in the west.

"In a small western town many yea ago I put up at the Palace Hotel.

"I was assigned to a room. There w no water or towels in the room, and ring.

"There was no reply.

"I rang again.

"Still no reply.

"And again and again and yet again rang, and finally a waiter appeared.

"This waiter was a robust man stern and forbidding aspect.

"'Did you ring?' he said in a rumblir bass voice.

"'I did,' I answered.

"'Well, don't do it again,' said tl waiter with a menacing scowl, as I withdrew.'"

※ ※

A small boy sat quietly and patient in a railway car on a hot, dusty day. A old lady, leaning forward, asked symp "Aren't you tired of the lor ride, dear, and the dust and the heat The lad looked up brightly, and repli with a smile: "Yes, ma'am, a littl But I don't mind it much ,because n father is going to meet me when I g to the end of it."—W. F. Crafts, Ph.

THE
CHRISTIAN-
EVANGELIST

A WEEKLY RELIGIOUS NEWSPAPER.

Volume XLIII. No. 35.

ST. LOUIS, AUGUST 30, 1906.

THE AGES COME AND GO

By H. W. Longfellow.

THE Ages come and go,
The Centuries pass as years;
The life of man is a gleam
Of light, that comes and goes
Like the course of the Holy Stream,
The cityless river that flows
From fountains no one knows,
Through the Lake of Galilee,
And Him evermore I behold
Walking in Galilee,
Through the cornfield's waving gold,
In hamlet, in wood, and in wold,
By the shores of the Beautiful Sea,
He toucheth the sightless eyes;
Before Him the demons flee;
To the dead He sayeth: Arise!
To the living: Follow Me!
And that voice still soundeth on
From the centuries that are gone,
To the centuries that shall be.

From all vain pomps and shows,
From the pride that overflows,
And the false conceits of men;
From all the narrow rules
And subtleties of Schools
And the craft of tongue and pen;
Bewildered in its search,
Bewildered with the cry:
Lo, here! lo there, the Church!
Poor, sad Humanity
Through all the dust and heat
Turns back with bleeding feet,
By the weary road it came,
Unto the simple thought
By the great Master taught,
And that remaineth still:
Not he that repeateth the name,
But he that doeth the will!

From "The Golden Legend."

THE CHRISTIAN-EVANGELIST.

The Christian-Evangelist.

J. H. GARRISON, Editor

PAUL MOORE, Assistant Editor

F. D. POWER,
B. B. TYLER, } Staff Correspondents.
W. DURBAN,

Subscription Price, $1.50 a Year.

For foreign countries add $1.04 for postage.

Remittances should be made by money order, draft, or registered letter; not by local cheque, unless 10 cents is added to cover cost of collection

In Ordering Change of Post Office give both old and new address.

Matter for Publication should be addresse : to THE CHRISTIAN-EVANGELIST. Subscriptions and remittances should be addressed to the Christian Publishing Company, 2712 Pine Street, St. Louis, Mo.

Unused Manuscripts will be returned only if accompanied by stamps.

News Items, evangelistic and other rise, are solicited, and should be sent on a postal card, if possible.

Published by the Christian Publishing Company, 2712 Pine Street, St. Louis, Mo.

Entered at St. Louis P. O. as Second Class Matter

WHAT WE STAND FOR.

For the Christ of Galilee,
For the truth which makes men free,
For the bond of unity
Which makes God's children one.

For the love which shines in deeds,
For the life which this world need,
For the church whose triumph speeds
The prayer "Thy will be done."

For the right against the wrong,
For the weak against the strong,
For the poor who've waited long
For the brighter age to be.

For the faith against tradition,
For the truth 'gainst superstition,
For the hope whose glad fruition
Our waiting eyes shall see.

For the city God is rearing,
For the New Earth now appearing,
For the heaven above us clearing,
And the song of victory.

J. H. Garrison.

CONTENTS.

Centennial Propaganda 1095
Current Events 1096
Editorial—
Where Jesus Placed the Emphasis—II. 1097
A Situation and a Remedy...... 1097
Notes and Comments 1098
Current Religious Thought...... 1098
Editor's Easy Chair 1099
Contributed Articles—
As Seen from the Dome. F. D. Power 1100
B. B. Tyler on the Jerusalem Church. J. W. McGarvey...... 1101
Modern Religious Persecution—A Defense. B. L. Chase......... 1102
What the Brethren are Saying and Doing. B. B. Tyler........... 1103
Why I Became a Christian Preacher. S. R. Maxwell...... 1104
The Waning Sense of Sin. James Norvel Crutcher 1104
African Missions and the Uncompleted Chain. Eben Creighton.. 1105
The Problem of the Country Church. J. F. Rosborough... 1106
Our Budget 1107
News from Many Fields............ 1112
Evangelistic 1115
Midweek Prayer-meeting 1116
Sunday-school 1116
Christian Endeavor 1117
People's Forum 1118
Obituaries 1119
The Home Department............. 1120

THE
CHRISTIAN=EVANGELIST

"IN FAITH, UNITY; IN OPINION AND METHODS, LIBERTY; IN ALL THINGS· CHARITY."

| Vol. XLIII. | August 30, 1906 | No. 35 |

1809 CENTENNIAL PROPAGANDA CHURCHES OF CHRIST 1909
: : : GEO. L. SNIVELY : : :

Looking Toward Pittsburg.

Read A. L. Ward's earnest second to the motion recently made by E. L. Powell, in these columns, for a memorial church in Boston. We bear personal testimony to the unfortunate location of our present church and to the heroism of Boston Disciples, and particularly to that of Brother and Sister Ward.

We call particular attention to our centennial secretary's article following. A great many goals are set before us for 1909. One of the brightest and most certainly attainable is "One Million Dollars for Church Extension." We plead for a generous offering from every congregation of Disciples in the land next Lord's day, and for large individual gifts. We pray for a great revival of church extension, enthusiasm and consecration. One million dollars in this fund will give heartening and hope and victory to thousands of our struggling congregations and make them sources of strength to our brotherhood in their communities instead of objects of charity and pity. We hope next week's CHRISTIAN-EVANGELIST will contain columns of telegraphic announcements of congregations having gone far beyond the "Extension Apportionment."

Dr. E. T. Davis, of Kansas City, makes a very helpful Centennial suggestion to our churches and preachers. He deeply deplores our brief pastorates, the frequent changes, occasioned by restlessness of the preachers and the caprice of congregations. Among the evils of this practice is failure to plan wisely and whole-heartedly for the continuous development of the churches, providing for the payment of church debts and new buildings, the acquirement and right use of social and religious prestige and other achievements possible, only where there are long-continued pastorates. He calls on all Disciples to help overcome this crying evil and suggests that plans be laid for having regular preaching every Lord's day in all our churches between this and the Centennial, and that every church in the brotherhood begin now to plan for a great revival during the last few months of this first century, and to have them all to conclude in time for the statistics to be part of our first Centennial reports.

Stopping Leaks.
BY W. R. WARREN.

If all of the leaks about our churches could be stopped, we should be well on the way to the attainment of most of the Centennial aims. Ever since its organization, the Board of Church Extension has been constantly and consistently stopping leaks. Every one of the thousand churches that it has helped has been saved from the leaks of fire, defective title and unsafe construction. The brotherhood of churches has been saved from the loss of money given to help one church in stopping them. Over half a million dollars that would otherwise have ceased from their labors long ago are now in the fund and devoted to perpetual beneficence. Without church extension there would be a constant succession of solicitors before our churches. Among those an occasional impostor would slip in and not only rob the cause but discredit the worthy; so springing a double leak. Few honest men are as cautious in handling the funds of others as they are when dealing with their own. In the old hap-hazard way of every needy church going out to seek its own help, many churches were erected in ill-chosen locations, many were unwisely planned and extravagantly built, some were sold for debt after they were finished. All these leaks church extension has effectually stopped. Next to the first mentioned leak the heaviest was from the amount expended in traveling expenses by the solicitors for local churches. And it was more serious than the other, for nothing remained to show for it. The other was a "sinking fund," being entirely absorbed by the one point; but this was sheer waste. If the financial leakage of the old, irregular way of helping young churches to build was serious, still more fearful was the moral loss. Churches, like individuals, should have self-reliance, business integrity and respect for the rights of others. These things were apt to go at loose ends in the old days. The Church Extension Board has been a wise, kind and firm schoolmaster, training up young churches to wise and just administration of their affairs and saving untold loss in the vital elements of church life. Every dollar given to church extension is not only perpetually safe for good work, but incidentally it will be forever saving both money and character.

Why Not a Memorial Church in Boston?
BY A. L. WARD.

A Church of Christ was organized in Boston July 23, 1843. This church continued to meet for about one year, after which there were no meetings of our brethren until November 11, 1866. From this time regular meetings were held for about the period of ten years, and then after another interruption of three years, they began to meet regularly again. In 1880 the scattered Disciples of the city were brought together into a more efficient organization; in 1882 they met in old Horticultural hall; in 1885 in the South End tabernacle; in 1899 in the present building on St. James street, Roxbury.

The work began, of course, with the meeting of a very few people to "break bread," and to talk over the possibility of a church building of their own. The numbers grew until in the South End tabernacle there were about seven hundred members. With the move to the present location the number was reduced to about 350. One of the reasons for this was the fact that the church had moved and that too from a locality where many of the members lived; but another reason, and to my mind the chief one, the church was unfortunately located on a side street. This street is frequented only by the few people who live upon it, and by a few others who have business dealings with those who live there. While the street is near a great thoroughfare it is itself little traveled.

My ministry has been of sufficient length here to convince me that the church which hopes for success must be on a street that is used by the people. If we are to continue in the city, and make the success which our cause is worthy of, we must have a more public location. I am certain that I have the support in this position of such men among our brethren as the successful minister here, Bro. J. H. Mohorter, and the former equally successful secretary of the American Society, Bro. B. L. Smith. These men know this field and also know how illy prepared we are to cope with the situation. There is just now an opportunity for us to get a church property ideally located at the head of St. James street, and on the great thoroughfare leading to the best residential section of the city. Thousands of people go over this street each day. But the one thing we lack is the money with which to secure this splendid property. The congregation is liberal. It has done its share in the past for missions, and that too when the money was badly needed to push the local work. The people spend about $50 each year in car fare in coming to the church services. This, I dare say, can not be duplicated in the entire brotherhood.

This is an opportunity for the Boston church, and an opening for the extension of primitive Christianity. Who will come to the help of this worthy people? It will take not less than $12,000 in addition to our present property, which is worth about $16,000. It would be a noble report for the Centennial convention, and one second to none that will be made there, if it could be reported that its Boston church has secured this splendid property. Will not some of our brethren with means investigate this? It is a call of God.

＊ ＊

We college men certainly appreciate your deep interest in education, and the space your paper so readily gives to education. We are highly pleased with THE CHRISTIAN-EVANGELIST in mechanical make-up and in its spirit.—Daniel E. Motley, Washington, D. C.

Current Events

Mr. Shontz and Mr. Gompers have
locked horns on the question of Chinese
Chinese on labor and the
the Isthmus. eight-hour law on
the Isthmus of
Panama. Mr. Shontz has announced
that it is the intention of the Canal Commission to import Chinese coolies under
contract, and, if the experiment proves
successful, to use their labor exclusively
in constructing the canal; he also announces that the eight-hour law will not
be considered as binding in the isthmus.
Mr. Gompers, as president of the Federation of Labor, denounces both of these
propositions as illegal and unwise. He is
afraid that the introduction of Chinese
labor on the canal strip of the Isthmus
of Panama will be but an entering wedge
for its introduction in the United States
proper; and he argues that if eight hours
is enough for a man to work in our temperate climate, common humanity forbids requiring any one to labor nine or
ten hours a day in a tropical climate. At
the bottom of the opposition to the use
of Chinese labor on the canal, seems to
be the vague feeling that it is some way
an injustice to American labor. We are
so much in the habit of thinking of
Chinese laborers as undesirable competitors in the home market that the familiar
arguments for Chinese exclusion get
themselves transferred to Panama, although the conditions are wholly different. American laborers will not go to the
Isthmus. At the present time Jamaica
negroes are being employed. The introduction of the Chinese will displace no
one except the Jamaicans. It is not easy
to see just what harm can come to the
American laboring man through the introduction of coolies to do work which
he refuses to do. As to the legal right
to bring Chinese contract labor into the
canal zone, Mr. Shontz is acting upon
the opinion of the attorney general of
the United States that the Chinese exclusion law does not apply to that territory. To a layman in law, it would seem
tolerably obvious that the Chinese exclusion law can not be expected to follow the flag if the constitution itself does
not. The same is true of the eight-hour
law. On the legal phase of the subject,
we should say that Mr. Shontz has the
long end of the argument. Moreover,
it seems that the only way to get the
canal dug is to have the Chinese dig it.
The Americans will not, and the Jamaicans can not do the work. If the
Chinese can and will, why not let them
have the job?

❋

Speaker Cannon's Presidential boom
broke the silence last week at Danville,
Cannon's Ill., at the district
Boom. convention. Mr.
Cannon was re-
nominated for Congress and was very
pointedly designated as the choice of his
district for the next Republican Presidential nomination. The speech which
Mr. Cannon delivered on that occasion
was the keynote speech for the convention, and may fairly be taken to indicate
the keynote of any presidential campaign
or administration which he might have
the opportunity of conducting. The beginning, middle and end of his argument
for the continuance of Republican rule
was prosperity. In the history of this
country, he said, high tariff, Republican

rule and prosperity have always been
coincident, while financial depression has
always been the corollary of free trade
and Democratic domination. We are not
at present interested in either affirming
or denying that the Republican party
ought to be kept in power, but we have
no hesitancy in saying that Speaker Cannon's arguments on the proposition
seem to us seriously inconclusive. To begin with, his assertion of the unfailing
relation between high tariff and prosperity is not historically true, as the hasti-
est survey of our financial history will
indicate. In the second place, we have
never tried free trade, and so have no
experimental knowledge of its results.
It is true, however, that at least once in
our history a tariff which was virtually
for revenue only was in operation at a
time of great prosperity, namely, in 1844
and the years immediately thereafter.
In the third place, the prosperity argument assumes, though it dare not assert, that sunshine and rain, bumper corn
crops and great gold discoveries, are the
direct result of a wise and beneficent administration. There are a good many
people in this country who call themselves Republicans and will vote the Republican ticket if they have a fair chance,
who would nevertheless be grievously
disappointed if the party were to enter
upon the next presidential campaign
with no more honorable issue than the
full belly and the big corn crop.

❋

The impression of prosperity is usually created rather by the aggregate of
Wages and business and the
Prices. height of prices
than by the consid-
eration of the actual purchasing power
of the average man's wages. During the
past decade this country has, as all must
admit, been enjoying a period of extraordinary prosperity. A recent bulletin of
the Bureau of Labor, however, indicates
that the cost of living has more than kept
pace with the advance in wages. Basing
the estimate upon the average retail price
of 30 food staples taken in quantities proportioned to the amounts used by an average family, it appears that the cost of
food has increased 17.7 per cent during
the past 10 years, while the average rate
of wages has increased only 14.6 per cent.
The chief advantage so far as the wage-
earner is concerned, is that fewer men
are out of employment now than 10
years ago. Merchants, manufacturers
and others to whom the increase in
prices means an increase in income are
doing exceedingly well, but wage-earners and salaried people who find the
purchasing power of their dollars diminished, while there is no corresponding increase in the number of their dollars, have reason to feel that they are
scarcely getting their share of the general prosperity which is so widely advertised.

❋

The free seed graft seems to be almost
at an end. The appropriation of $290,-
Free Seeds. 000 for the distribution of seed next
spring had a nar-
row escape in a recent session of Congress, and it seems probable that the
ancient custom will not survive another
winter. It would have perished long
ago, as it deserved to perish, had there
not been among the congressmen of
both parties a superstitious notion that
opposition to it would lose the farmer
vote. And yet it was a good scheme
when it was first introduced. The original theory was that, since it was the

Editorial

Where Jesus Placed the Emphasis.—II.

There yet remain a few practical applications of the teaching of Jesus concerning the fatherhood of God to which we wish to call attention.

One of the great evils of our time is the spirit of unrest, disquietude and anxiety, among professed Christians, even as among others. Men and women grow prematurely old by fretting and worrying over matters which they can not control. This, in its last analysis, springs from a distrust either in the wisdom or goodness of God. Jesus saw this evil in his own day and sought to remedy it. This was one reason, at least, why he laid emphasis upon the fatherhood of God. His specific for the evil which is causing so much unhappiness in our day, is set forth in the following passage, than which there is nothing more beautiful and comforting in all the literature of the world:

"Therefore I say unto you, be not anxious for your life, what ye shall eat, or what ye shall drink; nor yet for your body, what ye shall put on. Is not the life more than food, and the body than the raiment? Behold the birds of the heaven, they sow not, neither do they reap, nor gather into barns; and your heavenly Father feedeth them. Are not ye of much more value than they? And which of you by being anxious can add one cubit unto the measure of his life? And why are ye anxious concerning raiment? Consider the lilies of the field, how they grow; they toil not, neither do they spin: yet I say unto you, that even Solomon in all his glory was not arrayed like one of these. But if God doth so clothe the grass of the field which to-day is, and to-morrow is cast into the oven, shall he not much more clothe you, O ye of little faith! Be not therefore anxious saying, what shall we eat? or, what shall we drink? or, wherewithal shall we be clothed? For after all these things do the Gentiles seek; for your heavenly Father knoweth that ye have need of all these things." (Matt. 6:25-32).

The chief secret of the growth of Christian Science will, we believe, be found in the emphasis which it puts upon this part of the teaching of Jesus. It affects the daily life of the people vastly more than many of the theological doctrines on which stress is laid. If God is indeed our Father, why should we be anxious about those things which lie outside the sphere of our will, but under the general superintendence of his providence? Why not trust his father-heart? If he feeds the birds of the air and notes the sparrow's fall, will he not care for his children? A man lay tossing upon his bed at night, unable to

sleep because of the care and anxiety that filled his mind, when his little child, sleeping near him, wakened in a fright and called, "father!" Reaching out his hand and taking the hand of his little child, the little one, whose fears were at once quieted, was soon sound asleep again. This lesson of trust was not lost. The care-ridden man asked himself, Why can not I, also, trust my heavenly Father? and casting all his care upon him, he turned over and fell asleep.

"Let not your heart be troubled: believe in God, believe also in me." To believe "also" in Christ is to believe in God, as Father, and that is Jesus' remedy for troubled hearts. Why should our hearts be troubled over the departure of our loved ones, if they are only going into another apartment of our Father's house? Has the reader ever observed the significant connection in which that beautiful and familiar passage of Jesus occurs—"Come unto me, all ye that labor and are heavy laden and I will give you rest"? It immediately follows the statement, "Neither doth any know the Father save the Son and he to whom the Son willeth to reveal him." (Matt. 11:27). Is not the lesson obvious, that Jesus will give rest to the weary by revealing to them God as Father; and this truth must be "revealed" to every man in his own religious experience before he finds rest unto his soul.

What zest this teaching of Jesus concerning God should give to prayer! "When ye pray," said Jesus to his disciples, "say, Our Father who art in heaven." He has never really prayed as Jesus prayed who does not have some realizing sense of God as Father. When the Holy Spirit within the heart of the believer enables him to cry "Abba, Father," then he can truly pray. How strange it is, after all, that any believer can be neglectful of the privilege of prayer, when he has a heavenly Father who takes delight in giving him all the good things needful for him, including even his Holy Spirit! Does this neglect not spring from a failure to realize God's fatherliness? Is it not a question which the pulpit of to-day may well put to itself, whether it places the emphasis upon the truth that God is our Father that Jesus placed upon it?

The obligation of holiness of life grows out of the fact that God is our Father. "Be ye perfect even as your heavenly Father is perfect." Children are supposed to resemble their father, and the fact that we are children of God ought to be a mighty stimulus for holy living.

This truth should strengthen us also in enduring chastening, seeing that "God chasteneth every son whom he receiveth." The chastening of a wise and good father is for the child's good. This is certainly true of all God's chastening.

Other lessons from God's fatherhood might be drawn, but we leave our read-

ers to do this for themselves and pass on to notice other truths on which Jesus placed emphasis.

❦　❦

A Situation and a Remedy.

One of our most thoughtful ministers preaching in a town in one of our western cities describes the following local condition, which, we opine, is duplicated in many another town east, west, north and south.

DEAR BROTHER GARRISON:—A town of 1,500 inhabitants, a county seat, amidst almost untold prosperity. We have six churches, including our own. All of them are struggling hard to maintain ministers of very common ability, not one of them having a man of commanding strength. This condition has existed for many years. As a result public sentiment has come to count churches as a matter of course, but not seriously to be reckoned with, when it comes to the powers that be in the town. There is a large proportion of the membership in all churches that neither works nor pays nor attends church regularly. Fraternities claim the bulk of the sympathy of the people, many belonging to from two to six of them. This is true of some church members. The saloon element, races, baseball, Sunday fishing and Sunday target practice by the Volunteers; Sunday visiting in the country; low theaters and shows and dances; Wednesday evening band concerts at the prayer-meeting hour, in spite of kindly protests of all the ministers; toleration of vice and open adultery; the mayor a sportsman who measures his obligations to religion by a $5 or so to each of the churches, a man who is "all things to all men" for the sake of political ambition; a county attorney who is the son of a sot, a partial drunkard himself and a willing cat's-paw to the baser element; a city marshal whose highest philosophy for the removal of vice, which is blighting our young people, is to license it. These are some of the conditions that give complexion to our society. I know of but one devout man in the town, and he has recently come here, and his righteous soul is vexed because of the discountenance to which he is subjected because of his refusal to join in riotous living.

This is indeed a dark picture but the minister assures me that it is not at all overdrawn. He compassionates the people more than he blames them. "They have not had Christ presented to them as a rule as much above the sniveling sentimentalist, interpreted with as many crotchets as there are sectarian preachers. I can not but believe that the better element among unbelievers are bewildered or mistaken. By so much I believe that they would listen, and some of them would accept, if the Christ were held up to them as the 'one among ten thousand, the one altogether lovely.' They are waiting to see that the Gospel is really the power of God and to be asked to give expression to the very best they are capable of in yielding obedience to Christ." The minister so writing is trying to so present Christ, but the great mass of people do not know it, and hence are not profited by his ministry. This is the situation. What is the remedy?

In such a situation we should call the ministers and other godly people of the town together to talk over the condition and see if some plan could not be agreed upon for united action in bringing about a better state of things. The man who sees and feels the unsatisfactoriness of this condition of things is the man to take the initiative in seeking the remedy for it. The first thing that is generally thought of in a case of this kind, is a union revival service. But it seems to us there is a good deal to be done before such a service can accomplish its best results. If the remnant of godly members in all the churches would come together and pray over the situation and take counsel together, they might agree upon a program of concerted action that would put their churches in better condition for an aggressive movement on the vice and iniquity of the town. Church members themselves must put away iniquity and religious indifference before they are prepared to take any part in an aggressive movement.

But suppose the other ministers and churches are content with the situation and refuse to take any concerted action? In that case let the minister and church that feel the need of a better state of things put themselves in readiness and send for a good evangelist and plan for such a meeting as will attract the attention of the town. Nothing but a bold, aggressive gospel that condemns vice and exalts righteousness, that presents Christ as the remedy for all our human ills, can meet the demands of the situation. Our ministers and churches should take the lead, where others are not taking it, in seeking to remedy such a condition of things as that described above. Quiet acquiescence in it would be a crime.

❋ ❋ ❋

Notes and Comments.

The church at Jerusalem, like all the primitive churches whose names are mentioned in the New Testament, had both its strong points and its weak points. In its original unity, liberality and brotherly love, and in its steadfast devotion to apostolic teaching and to worship, it is a model for all time. Its weak points were its failure to sympathize with the larger meaning of Christianity which came to such prophetic souls as Stephen and Paul, and its consequent failure to make the most of its opportunity as the mother church. It is the *ideal* which the New Testament furnishes of what a church should be that is our model, rather than any actual church which existed in the apostolic age.

❋

Something or other, no matter what it is, has reminded us to say that the matter of being *politic* may be easily overdone. We have known many a good case spoiled by it. Somehow we learn to suspect the sincerity of a man who is controlled very largely by policy. The word *politic* is used in both a good and bad sense. In its good sense it means *wise, prudent, sagacious;* in its bad sense it means *artful, unscrupulous, cunning.* It is a nice thing to draw the line between the two, but an honest-hearted, courageous man is not likely to allow his prudence to lead him into mere artfulness in concealing his real position, nor his policy to degenerate into *timorousness* and *duplicity.* After all, the "shirt

sleeve" type of diplomacy, which strikes straight at its point, is apt, in the long run, to win the respect of most people whose respect is worth having.

❋

The department of "Sidelights on Current Events" in the "Globe-Democrat," contains a good deal of sense, as well as a good deal of humor, and not infrequently it expresses a religious sentiment that would do credit to the pulpit. In a recent number commenting upon a sermon on the subject of "Worldly Malaria" in the church in which the preacher had advised his congregation to "climb up to the hills of God" and escape the pestilence, the "Sidelights" fears that a good many people and many churches, even, will misconstrue this advice, and interpret it to mean "climbing to the hills of aristocratic localities and abandoning the fruitful fields of endeavor in the low slums." The following suggestions to the churches coming from the secular press, might well be taken to heart and put into practice. We have often felt that if men had a little more heroic work to do in the church they would have a great deal more interest in it, and their own spiritual life would thrive much better. The writer says:

"Instead of draining these noxious moral swamps, and making them wholesome and fit, they leave them to their fate. And the miasma and poisonous vapors will rise and follow and overwhelm them.

"They need to return, take off their coats and do a little ditch digging. Most of us would enjoy such labor. The churches complain of us that we do not attend services, but that may be because they give us nothing to do but to listen to platitudes.

"The artifices of the Sunday-school picnic and the church fair may draw us out on their occasion, but it is for a worldly 'good time,' and not to seriously consider our obligations to God and man.

"We like obstacles. We want work to do and difficulties to surmount. We want to fight the devil, not make a truce with him. Show us the swamps and where this moral malaria originates and let us clean them out."

❋

The acting assistant editor is taking some liberties in the absence of editorial authority in quoting from a letter intended for the editor alone, but silences his scruples by suppressing the name of the author. He assumes responsibility for publishing the following excerpt because he believes it voices the sentiments of thousands of Disciples rising into fuller liberty and more splendid vision and who are becoming the stay and hope of this Restoration:

"I am beginning the second year of my first pastorate after six years in one of our own universities. Among the many formative influences of my ministerial life and work, I count not the least the broad and sweet spirit of THE CHRISTIAN-EVANGELIST. I am one of the rising hosts of young men who have been with you in seeing the dawning of a better day for our cause and in thinking that its best interests lay in keeping abreast of the times and in watching for the leadership of the spirit of God in the movements of the day. You have been charged with being unsound in faith and with leading young men astray in the principles which you advocate; but I think you are saving the faith of many. Some years ago, when I began to think

Editor's Easy Chair.

PENTWATER MUSINGS.

At this early morning hour, when no one about "The Pioneer" is stirring, profound quiet reigns, save the low swish of the lake. Scarcely a leaf trembles on the trees. Out yonder on the lake the fishermen's red boat with its white sails, on its way to the nets, is about the only sign of life that is visible. With almost the regularity of clockwork, does that fishermen's boat make its trip to the nets to gather in the night's harvest of fish. These hardy, stolid men in calm and storm pursue their craft, never elated, apparently, with success nor discouraged by failure. The best "catch" is only "tolerable" or "fair," and the biggest failure is only, fishermen's luck. No doubt they possess some of the same traits which characterized those fishermen of Galilee whom Jesus called to be fishers of men. Now the sun, climbing above the hilltops east of us is lifting the mists from the lake and touching the thin clouds here and there with saffron and gold. The magic morning hour, the miracle of the dawn, with its stillness and the suggestion of mystery, is giving way to the glory of the day. A special charm attaches to all beginnings, whether it be the dawn of day, the opening rosebud, childhood, or the earliest premonitions of a higher and better civilization. He who slumbers away the hour of early dawn and sunrise, robs himself of the best hour of the day and one that may be made to tell most on the failure or success of the day. The "Morning Watch" should put all the sentinels of the soul on guard and kindle the fires of devotion to God and to duty.

❀

We have not told our readers about our new office here on the lakeside. As a matter of fact, it has only been ready for use within the past few days. Unlike the editorial office at "Edgewood-on-the-Lake," this is an integral part of "The Pioneer" cottage. It is on the south side of the cottage, and has two windows, one facing south and the other west, both of them commanding a view of the lake, but the southern one of the woods as well. One who is fond of both the water and the trees is sometimes at a loss in choosing a location, as to whether he will go to the forest, or to the seaside or lakeside. But here we have the combination of lake and forest, and one may, without changing his seat, look out upon the one or the other as inclination may suggest. We have found it a distinct advantage to have a study window overlooking the lake and commanding a wide range of vision. It prevents one from being too provincial and circumscribed in his thoughts and sympathies. And then we like to gaze far out to the horizon line in the southwest toward St. Louis and the home office, and to think of all the interests which center there. The evening star, as it shines out in the western sky at this season, seems to direct the eye homeward, and to stand over the city which for a third of

a century has been our home and the center of all our activities. THE CHRISTIAN-EVANGELIST has become so thoroughly identified with St. Louis that the very name of the city has become a synonym among us for a certain type of religious thought and influence, distinguished from others by its well known characteristics. The relation of this type of thought to the kingdom of God and to the permanent progress of our cause, is a matter we are willing to leave to the future historian.

❀

Speaking of history, who of us cares to be judged by the passions and prejudices of the little hour in which he lives and labors. How small a matter is it if one should be misjudged and misunderstood, during the brief span of his active life, if his labor and influence should be able to stand the calm, judicial test of history! It was, no doubt, a painful experience for Paul to be estranged from his extremely conservative brethren because of the freedom and breadth of the Gospel which he preached, but how insignificant it was, after all, compared with the honor and affection which all Christendom has accorded him since his day! "His day," did we say? All the subsequent days since he lived and wrought have been his, because his life and teaching have contributed mightily for whatever glory and triumph they have achieved. Whoever links himself with God and truth, regardless of present consequences, and works unselfishly for the betterment of mankind, enters so largely into the life of the future that all the coming times are his. If we could all live and labor under the inspiration of this idea, truth would make more rapid progress in the world, and the kingdom of God would go forward by leaps and bounds. Yonder steamer, which has just hove into view, and which will soon reach its port, little heeds the winds and waves which may have retarded its progress, if only it but reach its desired haven, bringing with it its precious cargo of human life. What will it matter to us, a thousand years from now, what the men of our time have said or thought about us, if only we have given the best there was in us for the good of humanity and the glory of God? One "well done" from the Master himself will more than offset the reproaches of a thousand critics who, like ourselves, have no power to discern the real motives which have controlled our lives.

❀

This will be our last opportunity, before the offering for church extension, the first Lord's day in September, to urge upon our churches everywhere the importance of having a part in this offering. It is the union of effort that tells. That great lake that stretches out before us as we write, is but a vast combination of drops of water. In the long ago it was decreed that there should assemble together, in co-operative union, an infinite number of kindred drops of water, in this great basin; and Lake Michigan is the result! Great ships, carrying the commerce of the great states

surrounding it, float upon its bosom, and innumerable tribes of fish swim beneath its surface, furnishing food for countless thousands. How different would have been the result if the various particles forming this great inland sea had declined to enter into the wider co-operation, because of their individual weakness! A thousand green, stagnant ponds, breeding mosquitoes and malaria, might thus have taken the place of the one great, sublime, life-giving and health-promoting Lake Michigan! Thus nature itself is teaching us the necessity of co-operation in every good work. How many poor, struggling churches might be floated out of the shallows of their present poverty and neglect, into the full sea of prosperity and usefulness if all the churches of the brotherhood were to unite their contributions in this church extension fund, which reaches out its brotherly hand to every struggling church within its reach! We can see many motives why the churches should unite in this offering, but we can not think of one, that is at all worthy and honorable, for refusing to do so. One of the special things to aim at this year, as it seems to us, is the enlistment of a much larger number of churches in this form of Christian benevolence. We trust that our ministers and church officials everywhere will interest themselves in seeing that this offering is made, and that their church has a part in the enlargement of the fund to a million dollars by the coming of our centennial.

❀

Our summer colony here at Pentwater grows steadily, and the problem for the coming season will be to accommodate with cottages those who wish to come. Brother and Sister Richardson of Kansas City have arrived for a short stay and are guests at "The Pioneer." Brother Richardson has already tackled a fish that was too much for him, and lost part of his tackle and his fish, too, after a gallant fight in which the great fish led. Bro. C. M. Fillmore, of Cincinnati, who had just arrived, was with us in the boat and watched the encounter. Brother Fillmore is suffering from overwork and is here under his physician's order to rest. Brother Idleman, pastor at Paris, Ill., and a party of friends are expected next week seeking a summer resort for future use. Several members of the Campbell Institute expect to hold a "retreat" here at the club house the first week in September. Bro. J. H. Hardin, our Missouri superintendent of Bible schools, with his wife, are expected here to-day to spend Sunday with us. Bro. R. M. Denholme, manager "New Orleans Item," is expected here next week to join his family, who have taken a cottage in Pentwater. We have had several calls during the present week from readers of "Pentwater Musings" in different parts of the country, who could not resist the temptation to come and see for themselves. We have had a busy week, but it has been relieved by the faces of friends and by association with some of God's elect spirits. All together, now, for church extension and the Buffalo convention!

We are once more in London—London the pride and the problem of the race, a stone forest of houses, a rushing stream of faces, a metropolis covering 693 square miles, with 7,000 miles of streets, 900,000 houses, and 6,581,402 people. Of course it is big. It is the capital of a vast empire. The United Kingdom has 43,000,000 souls, and, including India, the empire has 385,348,000. London is the great city of the United Kingdom. Then come Glasgow, with 761,709; Liverpool, with 584,958; Manchester, with 543,872, and Birmingham, with 522,204. Next to London in the empire would be Calcutta, with 847,796, and Bombay, with 776,006. In the United Kingdom, that is the British Isles alone, they consume 256,000,000 bushels of wheat yearly, or six bushels per head, and 1,234 million gallons of beer, or 28.8 gallons per head, and 256½ million pounds of tea, or six pounds per head. Their coal production the past year was 232,428,272 tons, iron ore, 13,-774,282 tons, and wool, 132 million pounds. Their shipping showed a tonnage—sailing vessels for these islands alone, 1,802,667, and steam vessels, 8,751,853. Such is England, and London is its capital.

There are many Americans here—over 30,000 live and do business in the city. If Americans do not feel a pride in the mother country they are not true Americans. Landing at Plymouth their feet touch the figures "1620"; at the dock at Gravesend they drop a tear on the tomb of Pocahontas, the Indian princess, in St. George's Church; in Warwickshire they see on the gravestones the names of the ancestors of Virginia colonists, and in London the memorials and associations of William Rogers and Sir Henry Vane, Washington and Franklin and Benjamin West, John Harvard and George Peabody, Lincoln and Lowell and Longfellow and Phillips Brooks. And have they not a common heritage, a common Bible, a common language, a common work and a common destiny?

A cleaner or better governed city than London can not be found. It has many features which might be copied with advantage by us. There are 28 boroughs, each borough with its mayor, annually elected, with aldermen and councillors, the boroughs varying in population from 26,968 to 334,928. The mayor of Shoreditch, Mr. Thomas Burnell, is a Disciple of 35 years' experience in the metropolis, and to him I was indebted

to office by proceeding in state on November 9 to the Royal Courts of Justice to be sworn in, and then by giving a banquet the same evening at Guildhall which costs him, with the "show," $20,000, so his salary of $50,000 for the year of his incumbency easily goes. In "the city" the lord mayor takes precedence of everybody save the king. The city has two sheriffs, 25 aldermen and 206 members of the council, elected annually by the taxpayers, and a police force of 1,000 men, while all London has a force of 17,000. It costs $75,000,000 annually to run the government of London, and it has a debt of $229,000,000. The last 10 years it added 600,000 people. It has 166,670 paupers, and its voluntary offerings for charity exceed $25,000,000. It is blessed with more hospitals than any city on earth, and on "Hospital Sunday" all the churches take offerings, and ladies station themselves at the street corners to receive gifts, $225,000 being the receipts of the day.

Guildhall is the stately civic palace associated in the popular mind with the great banquet of Lord Mayor's Day, when the members of the government make their political pronouncements. It has been the scene of some of the most stirring episodes in English history. Nearly every crowned head in Europe has been feted here, and all the leading statesmen, soldiers and sailors and men who have been honored with "the freedom of the city." In the great hall elections are held, and the great feasts are given and the famous deliverances made. Gog and Magog, two huge wooden figures, stand near the entrance. Its council chamber and aldermanic court room are most sumptuously decorated. There is a library, with 115,000 volumes, and a museum of great interest, with antiquities and curiosities, old Roman remains and shop and tavern signs, such as the "Boar's Head," connected with Falstaff and Bluff Prince Hal, Goldsmith and many others of England's characters.

A history of Guildhall would be a history of the nation. Here we see Richard Coeur-de-Lion in Crusader times, and Fitz Walter, when the citizens lend aid to the barons in wresting from John the charter of England's liberties. Here, in 1529, is the first banquet on Lord Mayor's Day, and here Charles I is feted, and Cromwell, the first Englishman of his time. Here it looks forth upon the great plague in 1665, which carried off one-

up "respectful but solemn warning against the fatal policy pursued by the king's ministers toward the American colonies," and again petitioning King George "to suspend hostilities and adopt such conciliatory measures as might restore union and confidence and peace to the whole empire." Here we see the Duke of Wellington, Peel, Russell, Livingstone, Gladstone, Disraeli, Salisbury, Shaftsbury, Nelson, Colin Campbell, Wolsely, Roberts and Kitchener; Victoria, in 1837, and again with Albert in 1851, and again the splendors of the jubilee. Over its front we may read the words, *Domina Dirige Nos*—"the Lord direct us"—as we see over the Royal Exchange, "The Earth is the Lord's and the fulness thereof," and over the very drinking fountains, "The Fear of the Lord is the Fountain of Life"; and while statues are here of Nelson and Wellington and other great Englishmen, one observes over the entrance images of stone representing Law, Learning, Dis-

❋ ❋

GOOD NIGHT'S SLEEP

No Medicine so Beneficial to Brain and Nerves.

Lying awake nights makes it hard to keep awake and do things in day time. To take "tonics and stimulants" under such circumstances is like setting the house on fire to see if you can put it out.

The right kind of food promotes refreshing sleep at night and a wide awake individual during the day.

A lady changed from her old way of eating, to Grape-Nuts, and says:

"For about three years I had been a great sufferer from indigestion. After trying several kinds of medicine, the doctor would ask me to drop off potatoes, then meat, and so on, but in a few days that craving, gnawing feeling would start up, and I would vomit everything I ate and drank.

"When I started on Grape-Nuts, vomiting stopped, and the bloating feeling which was so distressing disappeared entirely.

"My mother was very much bothered with diarrhea before commencing the Grape-Nuts, because her stomach was so weak she could not digest her food. Since using Grape-Nuts she is well, and says she don't think she could live without it.

"It is a great brain restorer and nerve

cipline, Justice, Fortitude, Temperance, with the figure of Christ surmounting the whole, which will set forth the spirit of the city and of the nation.

My friend Mr. Burnell showed me through the public buildings of his borough. Nothing interested me so much in London as the municipal provisions for the people. I went through the public baths and wash houses. Hundreds of thousands are invested in a single plant. Shoreditch, for example, has two of these institutions. Accommodations are provided for hundreds of men and women. A first-class bath for 12½ cents, hot water, soap, towels and every comfort. A second-class, quite as good, with all necessaries, for five cents. Connected with each class is a large swimming pool, and in winter these are covered over, furnishing large halls for gatherings of every kind. Wash houses are fitted up with modern machinery, and poor women come and for three cents an hour are provided with hot water, tubs, machines operated by steam for drying and pressing, and every essential to the care of the week's washing. A free library and reading room belong to the plant. Another feature we may well imitate is the public lavatories in the streets at convenient locations all over London. They are built under the pavement at the chief crossings, cost from $2,000 to $3,000, have conveniences for both men and women, free for those who have no money, and private, with soap, towels, hot water and even bath, for those who prefer to pay a few pennies. They pay the boroughs and are a blessing to the people. Think of our good city of Washington without even one such public convenience along the whole of Pennsylvania avenue, thronged as it is every four years by half a million people! Another thing is the "safeties"—little reserved elevated places around the street lamps in the great thoroughfares to which men and women and children may stop for security in the rush of traffic. Who does not bless the city fathers of London for this little contrivance! Everything about London seems for the people—schools, thousands of acres in parks and gardens for their enjoyment, crime reduced to a minimum, sanitation as near perfect as can be, 'busses taking you everywhere for two cents, and the best police force and safest streets in the world.

B. B. Tyler on the Jerusalem Church   By J. W. McGarvey

I am one of those who regard the original church in Jerusalem as a model, as "the mother of us all," and my wrath was naturally kindled by Brother Tyler's criticisms upon her in The Christian-Evangelist of August 16. For fear that the faults which this genial and talented writer finds with her shall be accepted by many as real faults, I come to her defense.

The first fault found is that, while she was an example in caring for her poor, her charity "was not dignified and orderly. The members meant well, but in a short time they were in a snarl because some were, as they thought, neglected in the distribution of alms." Now, it is unjust to say that the church was in a snarl; for this murmuring came from only a small minority, and the church immediately prevented a snarl by appointing seven men of the dissatisfied party to take charge of the whole business, as much as to say, You think your widows are comparatively neglected; now, we turn over the whole business, including the care of our widows, into your hands. This was the action of the church, and was it not a model in this particular? It buried the murmuring under an avalanche of generosity and hushed it forever.

The second fault found is that this church was anti-missionary. This charge has become quite common with brethren who have more zeal for missions than discretion in their advocacy of them. "It made no attempt," says Brother Tyler, "to herald the good news to the whole creation." This is true up to the death of Stephen. And why? The apostles had been commanded to begin at Jerusalem; and such was their success in that city that the number of their converts was daily increasing and multiplying up to the very day in which Stephen was stoned, and the disciples, all except the apostles, were compelled to flee to save their lives. Up to that moment it had appeared as if the whole city would be won to Christ in a short time. Was that a time for any of the apostles to leave Jerusalem and go to Samaria? He who thinks so would have interrupted Scoville in the midst of his great meeting in Anderson, when sinners were confessing the Lord by the score every day, and have said to him, "See here, my brother, they need the gospel down here on Goose creek more than they do in Anderson; leave here and go down there." And when this church was dispersed by the persecution did the members prove themselves anti-missionary? Everybody answers, No; for "they went everywhere preaching the gospel. Though they had lost their homes and all their earthly possessions, they persevered in the good work which had brought all this upon them.

But Brother Tyler says: "It is more than probable that an uncircumcised Gentile believer would not have been given a welcome to the Lord's table." This is not only probable, but it is certain; and for the very good reason that in the wisdom of Christ the time had not yet come for uncircumcised Gentiles to be thus received. The model church is one that follows her Lord; not one who runs ahead of him.

Again, Brother Tyler says: "The most conspicuous member of this church did not, for a long time, understand that in every nation he who fears God and works righteousness is acceptable to him." This was because the question who is acceptable to God is, with true believers, a subject of revelation, and God had not yet made the revelation. Peter did not understand that he that believeth and is baptized shall be saved, until it was revealed to him. The model church hearkens to its Lord and leans not upon its own understanding.

"The Jerusalem church was pretty narrow. Don't you think so?" This, with many, is the severest charge of all. With some persons to be narrow is the worst of faults in a church. They run on the broad gauge themselves—broad enough to take in the world, the flesh and a good deal of the devil. They toss their caps and shout because they are in the broad way, not seeing to what gate it leads, and they sneer at those who are so narrow as to keep within the narrow way that leads to the other gate. Call a man narrow, and you have got him down. There is an excess of boldness in applying this epithet to the church founded and guided by the inspired apostles. If it was narrow, the Lord save the rest of us from being broad.

But finally Brother Tyler finds that Paul thought too little of this church to call it a model, and that it thought very little of Paul. But while Paul nowhere

❋ ❋

DUBIOUS

About What Her Husband Would Say.

calls the Jerusalem church a model, he does say of it that though the literal Jerusalem was in bondage with her children, "The Jerusalem that is above is free, which is our mother," and by this Jerusalem he means the Jerusalem church. Paul could never severely criticize his mother; and he never did. But, says Brother Tyler, "Paul did not stand

well in that church." It is true that when he returned from his persecuting trip to Damascus the apostles were slow to believe that he had become a disciple; it is true that certain men from that church came to Antioch and contended that his Gentile converts must be circumcised and keep the law; and it is true that many members of that church,

at a later period, were prejudiced against him because of a false report which had come to them; but in every instance, on being properly informed the church sustained and honored him. Is not this the way for a model church?

Brother Tyler is too good-humored a man to be laying violent hands on "the mother of us all."

Modern Religious Persecution---A Defense

By B. L. Chase

7. **Sorrows of Persecutors.**

Do not think that the persecutor is void of feeling when he shows no sympathy for the suffering of the condemned heretic, or refuses to bestow a kind word upon his afflicted and humiliated family. He knows that these things must be; and that these light afflictions, which are for the moment, work out a far more exceeding and eternal weight of glory for the brotherhood and the venerable company of persecutors. He knows that by the divine law the sins of the fathers must be visited upon the children to the third and fourth generation. Why should these things move him? The persecutor has troubles of his own, contrary to the popular opinion. Is it no pain to him, think you, when a heretic escapes by the breaking down of the case against him? When the brethren of the leading churches continue him in good standing and full fellowship after being pronounced unworthy of fellowship? When he is given a place on a national convention program after being called a "Unitarian" and an "Alien"? When those who take no stock in the infallibility of persecutors and have no fear of them, are called "leading men among us"? When the very condemned are appointed by the brotherhood to represent them in interdenominational meetings? When missionary and educational enterprises prosper after they have been condemned by the persecutor? Has he no feeling? Such things are enough to bring tears from a heart of stone! No, the persecutor is human, if he is infallible; he can suffer for some things, if he can not suffer for the accused.

It has been said that one peculiarly sensitive and tender-hearted persecutor lay awake all one night because a college continued to use in its classes a book which he condemned as "infidel." Another has steadily lost flesh because the Disciples refuse to make his "convictions" a test of fellowship among their churches. It has been a continual sorrow to all persecutors that the leading pastors and churches do not join heartily in the various persecutions and they stand hourly in dread lest the Disciples will oppose all persecution as contrary to the Spirit of Christ.

Another thing that gives the persecutor sorrow is the enmity of the man he has condemned to punishment as a heretic. The ill will of any man is a sorrow to him, much more that of a man

whose soul he seeks to save. Very few heretics ever recognize the motive that lies back of their persecution. They will not endure correction. Their pride of opinion; their love of liberty and fairness stand in the way of their souls' health. They do not realize that the persecutor loves the one he chastens; and that his fatherly hand applies the rod because it is needed. What child ever did receive the rod as it was given? A part of the test which the persecutor applies to the heretic is the way in which he treats his correction. If he repents of his errors and accepts the "convictions" of the persecutor he is forgiven and received back into favor. If he rebels and resents it, that alone is sufficient evidence that his heart is not right. Every persecutor knows how liable to be wrong in the heart is every man who is wrong in the head. The justness of their persecution on account of his opinions is frequently confirmed by the indifference of the persecuted to the words of Christ. The persecutors always admonish them to receive their persecution as becometh the sons of God. Jesus said: "Love your enemies and pray for them that persecute you." How many persecuted heretics ever do? They entertain hard feelings toward their persecutors, and call them "popish" and "bigoted." How ungrateful toward their benefactors who have sought only their good and that of the truth! When they are smitten by their persecutor they smite back; whereas Christ taught that his disciples should not resist evil, but when smitten upon one cheek should turn the other. What sorrow it must give a persecutor to see one who professes to be a follower of Christ smite back! That is evidence enough that such a one is unworthy of fellowship. But worst of all it frequently happens that churches among the Disciples keep such persons in their membership.

Another thing that gives the persecutor sorrow is his temptation to pay heed to his humane impulses. He would flee from his task with horror if he did not view it as the surgeon views his work. Human sympathy and the moral consciousness would drive him to despair if he were to forget the missionary and benevolent purpose of his work. It is a horrible thing to go suddenly to a man who is happily, earnestly and

acceptably carrying on his work as a teacher in a college, and say to him, "You must resign your place here and cease forever to be a teacher among the Disciples." It is like the coming of a death summons to a man in the bloom of health. Many a man loves his teaching, his college, and his scholars so devotedly that he could almost as easily give up his life as give up his work. It is enough to make a persecutor pause before blasting such a man's happiness and usefulness. No small offense could tempt a good man to ruin another man's usefulness. It is the last depth of malignity of nature to do so under cover of zeal for the "truth," "our plea," or "the good of the cause." No "cause" or institution is more important than common fairness or humanity. No cause can long survive at the expense of them.

And yet the persecutor's duty calls upon him to take away that which is as sweet as life itself. His humanity often revolts at it. He would listen to the voices of his humanity and conscience if there were not other voices in his soul more imperative and commanding. Another voice in his soul says: "There is a professor in a certain college who is reported to be teaching the higher criticism to his students. The students, in their simplicity, like it, and will carry it among the churches, and the people, in their simplicity, will like it too. And then we will disappear as a brotherhood." I must get that teacher out of that school or we will disappear as a brotherhood." Such is his unanswerable logic.

It is the superior, long look ahead that characterizes the persecutor, as well as the certainty of his conviction. It is this that nerves the surgeon for his work. He can remove the arm, leg or eye of a patient with real pleasure because he knows it will be for the health of the whole body. He is thinking of the rest of the body that is imperiled by the diseased member. He follows his medical conviction, just as the persecutor follows his religious conviction. The only difference is that in most cases the sick man gives himself willingly into the hands of the surgeon, knowing himself to be in danger; while the heretic, not knowing himself to be diseased and to be endangering the health of the whole body of Disciples, objects to being put into the hands of his persecutors.

The persecutor does for the whole body of Disciples what each Christian is commanded to do for himself. "If thine eye cause thee to stumble, pluck it out, and cast it from thee; it is good for thee to enter into life with one eye, rather than having two eyes, to be cast into hell fire." There are men among the Disciples who seem as precious to them as an eye to the body; but if we

are likely to disappear as a brotherhood on account of their teaching, better drive them from us than pass into extinction. Who is going to perform the doctrinal surgery for the Disciples if not our persecutors? It must be done; the bad

doctrine must be exposed and the teacher of it removed. If he will not remove himself, it must be done for him, and against his will. Let us sympathize with our persecutors in their troubles and sorrows.

What the Brethren Are Saying and Doing

By B. B. Tyler

Does prohibition prohibit? If the prohibition of the liquor traffic does not prohibit, if as much intoxicating liquor is sold where there is a prohibitory law as where there is a license law, why are men who are interested in the sale of liquor universally opposed to prohibition? Facts show, however, beyond a peradventure, that prohibition prohibits. San Francisco from the 20th of April until the Fourth of July was under prohibition. It is said that so strictly was prohibition enforced during this period of time that a man caught with a bottle of liquor in his pocket was shot down dead. This statement seems to me to be an exaggeration. Let it pass as such. This, however, is a fact that from April 18th to July 4th, with thousands of homeless people in the city, and thousands of visitors from north, south, east and west, in San Francisco, to see the sights, the arrests of the evil doers were only from two to six a day. In all the turmoil and confusion of the tens of thousands of homeless people, and the influx of uncounted thousands of visitors, such order prevailed that the police force, according to its own statement, had nothing to do.

San Francisco is now granting licenses to sell intoxicating liquors, the license fee is now $500, as against $85 prior to the earthquake. What is the result in the *immediate and visible* result? *The first Monday after the opening of the saloons there were seventy-four cases before the police courts as against five the preceding Monday. Seventy-two on Friday, as against two on the previous Friday, and the second Monday one hundred and thirteen as against three or four the second Monday before reopening the saloons.* Let these facts stand out before the eyes of our readers in majestic capitals.

Why did San Francisco decide to reopen the liquor saloons? The standing argument everywhere is, "the city needs and must have the revenue from the saloons." It is said that before the disastrous earthquake and fire in the month of April there were 3,400 saloons in the Golden Gate City. It cost the people of the municipality, so it is said, and the statement is not unreasonable, $737,160 more to pay for police protection alone than the amount of revenue received by the city from the saloons: And this is business!! A company of ordinary preachers could do better than that!!!

"The Commerce Monthly" is "a chronicle of banking and financial news," published in St. Louis. In its issue of August 14, it contained the following on the editorial page:

BUSINESS AND "THE LID."

The awakening of the public conscience, as is evidenced by the so-called putting on of "the lid" in numerous places in the land, is certainly a mat-

ter for congratulation by law-abiding citizens. It is a matter of congratulation, not so much because it has made a large reduction in a certain class of crime, as because people who have for years considered a "wide open" town necessary for prosperous business conditions have come out differently.

Business—and by business is meant finance as well as trade—is in no wise allied with riotous living. For a time, to be sure, a "wide open" town may seem to be the most prosperous and thriving, but when the real test is made it will be found that the law-abiding and conservative community makes the best showing.

Furthermore a city which "puts on the lid" and stands by, it comes to be well spoken of abroad, as not note by the following in the "Indianapolis Star," which says:

"The lid" is on in St. Louis tighter to-day than it has ever been. There is no back door, no side door, no slipping in. And what is the result? In the first place, they have quit killing people on Sunday to make a St. Louis holiday. The coroner has far less work to do, and the morgue keeper has a chance to read the newspapers. There are now fewer than one hundred prisoners in the city jail—a state of affairs not paralleled in years—and a recent report of the police department record shows that crime has fallen off something like 70 per cent in twelve months. The facts are eloquent. St. Louis has come to know "the lid" and likes it.

The same condition exists in other cities where the experiment has been given a fair trial. And can any one say that from a business standpoint St. Louis isn't as prosperous now and doing as great business and growing as rapidly or more so than ever before? Sobriety and a strict observance of all laws is the best plan for any city.

Do not fail, please, to note that this quotation is *not* from a "cranky" temperance publication. "The Commerce Monthly" is a strictly *business* paper. It claims to number "among its subscribers nearly every progressive banking institution in the country," the copy from which I quote I picked up in the United States National Bank in Denver. It is a sign of the times when such papers as "The Commerce Monthly" and "The Indianapolis Star" use such language as is here recited.

"The Denver Republican" this morning, announces that "Reorganized Church of Jesus Christ of Latter Day Saints" are holding a ten days' meeting in one of our city parks. This meeting represents the church with the long name in the eastern part of Colorado. The announcement explains that "this church has no affiliation with 'the Latter Day Saints of Utah,' or 'Mormons,' as they are better known, and repudiates their polygamous teachings and

many of their other doctrines." The headquarters of "the Reorganized church" is at Lamoni, Iowa.

"Mormonism" is an "issue" and "a live question in this part of the world." I smile when I read in eastern papers that "the Church of Jesus Christ of Latter Day Saints," of the Utah variety, has given up the doctrine of plural marriages and the practice of polygamy. There is not a word of truth in this statement—not a word. Their missionaries in Denver go from house to house teaching the doctrine of polygamy. This is their specialty. I met two of their "elders" in a home in this city, in which they insisted on setting forth the doctrine of plural marriage. They are contemptible sneaks. When you have an opportunity to meet them, do so. When you meet them, do not treat them as gentlemen. If you do so you will make a mistake. Proceed to wipe the earth with them. This is what I did and I have not been able to meet one of them since. This was a private seance, the "elders" were so sure of their position that they expressed a desire to meet me in the home of the lady where they had insisted on talking up polygamy. They said to her: "We will be delighted to meet your pastor and discuss matters with him in your presence. We do not desire anything better. You will at once see the superiority of the Church of Jesus Christ of Latter Day Saints in its doctrine, to the church of which you are a member." The scoundrels will not meet me again. You think the word "scoundrel" is too strong. That is because you are not acquainted with the doctrines, the methods, the practices, of the Mormons.

In the political field, they hold the balance of power in a number of states in this great Rocky Mountain empire. Reed Smoot has recently been in Idaho and here are some of the things that he is reported to have said:

The Mormons can dictate their own terms in Idaho this fall, and this I can declare to you officially.

Our colonization of certain counties is full and complete to assure the right returns. I have personally made the canvass. In the next legislature in that state the balance of power will be held by the Mormons and the Democrats and Republicans alike will find a futility of effort without Mormon support.

We are a great power and our power will grow and our enemies must reckon with us.

There is much more of the same kind for which there is not space in this letter. There is "a Mormon menace." Believe me, my brother, this statement is more than a mere alliteration.

Denver, Colorado.

I am tired of planning and toiling
  In the crowded hives of men;
Heart-weary of building and spoiling,
  And spoiling and building again.
And I long for the dear old river,
  Where I dreamed my youth away;
For a dreamer lives forever,
  And a toiler dies in a day.
      —John Boyle O'Reilly.

Why I Became a Christian Preacher By S. R. Maxwell

Ships are turned by helms, horses are turned by rein and bit, and men, if they have any brains, are turned by the power of ideas.

I was a Methodist preacher for nine years, and I am now and have been for the past eight years a preacher in the ranks of the current Reformation. I was induced to leave Methodism and champion the plea of the Christian church on account of the compelling power of new ideas.

To begin with, I believed in Christian union and I was convinced that Christians could not get together on any sectarian basis. "Whatsoever a man soweth that shall he also reap." Sow the Methodist discipline and you grow Methodists. Sow the Augsburg confession and you grow Lutherans. Sow the Thirty-nine Articles and the prayer book and you grow Episcopalians. Sow the Westminster confession and you grow Presbyterians. Ideas are seeds and they have an inveterate tendency to produce their kind. It became clear to me that if you want a uniform crop, you must sow uniform seed; *uni form*, that is seed of *one form*. Now, I had read in the New Testament that "We are born not of corruptible seed but of incorruptible, even the Word of God which liveth and abideth forever." Then it became clear to my mind that the only way to bring about union was on the Word of God alone, divorced from all human opinions whatsoever. When I arrived at this conclusion I was living in the city of Wilmington, Del., and I went to

Washington, D. C., and had an interview with Bro. W. J. Wright, who is now corresponding secretary of the A. C. M. S., and in my opinion splendidly

S. R. Maxwell.

equipped for the position. I related my experience to him and stated my views. He smiled, and when I had finished he said: "My good brother, you stand exactly where we as a people stand. We stand for union on a platform that can never be brought into the realm of debate amongst Protestants. We stand for union (1) on the creed of the New Tes-

tament church, "Thou art the Christ the Son of the living God; (2) on the ordinances of the New Testament church, baptism and the Lord's supper; (3) on the life of the New Testament church, that of love expressing itself in self-sacrifice, the salvation of others.

I consider it fortunate for me that I came into contact with the plea of the Christian Church incarnated in the person of such a broad, deep, intelligent man as Brother Wright is. Ideas influence men but men also influence ideas. An idea is a compressible thing and sometimes it gets into a small man. The broad, universal, reconciling, harmonizing principles in the platform of the Christian church become narrow and sectarian when they pass through the mental processes of some men. "It is easier for a camel to go through the eye of a needle" than it is for the great ideas presented to the religious world by Alexander Campbell to pass through the narrow passages of some men's brains without becoming narrow and savagely sectarian.

What won me was not that the Christian church is the only church that is infallibly right, but that the Christian church is the only organization amongst Protestants anywhere else that presents a platform for union composed of principles that never have been in dispute, are not now in dispute and never can be brought into dispute amongst Protestants. The plea is well expressed in THE CHRISTIAN-EVANGELIST:

"In faith, unity; in opinions and methods, liberty; in all things, charity." I rest on this platform, and if any one can show me one that is superior, I will move instantly.

The Waning Sense of Sin By JAMES NORVEL CRUTCHER

Is sin, after all, so sinful? With the "new theology," the "new happiness," and "the new faith," have we not a new sense of sin? And is not this new sense the warp and woof of present-day waywardness and disobedience? Sin was once said to be garbed in flaming apparel and preachers sought new and frightful words to tell the depths of despair into which a sinner would fall. Sin was thought to sear men's hearts, wither their hopes, blight their lives and destroy them eternally. Sin was pictured as a "hideous monster, of so terrible a mien that to be hated was but to be

and unrepentant souls. Exhorters waxed eloquent in their descriptions of "sinners in the hands of an angry God." From these things the religious world has drifted to the extreme of excusing sin, of silence on many of the popular sins of the times. After all, the devil is not so bad—if there is a devil! He has laid aside the crimson cowl of Mephisto and is now a "jolly good fellow," companion for saints, all garbed in the pale winding sheets of self esteem and appreciation. "Boys will be boys, you know," and there is always virgin soil for wild oats. The prophet declared that the time

eternity; they look at the human heart from the human standpoint and measure life by the human standard. It is not what sinful men think of themselves but what God thinks about them. It is not fair to measure ourselves by ourselves. Men are as unwise to-day, with all of the conceit of the times, as they were when the apostles preached against sin. To become wise they must now, as then, lay their lives once more against the law of God, and learn, from the fearful discrepancy which such a course reveals, that God can not look upon sin with the least degree of allowance. Sin is a fearful, tragic reality. We see its rav-

African Missions and the Uncompleted Chain[*]

Swift movements of Divine Providence mark the Africa of to-day. What was, until recently the ancient continent of weirdness and strange mysteries, is now the modern land of keen effort and intelligent study. Here the maker of states and the maker of money alike contend, flanked by the missionary, the anthropologist, and the student of flora and fauna. The statesman, the speculator, the missionary and the scientist all find in this gaunt and giant stretch of blackness a real and rugged field for endeavor and achievement.

This land the statesman has parcelled and colonized and is fast Europeanizing, the speculator has exploited and opened, and is fast commercializing, the scientist has traversed and observed, and is fast classifying. At last this slow-going continent of the ages moves with modern alertness. A new Africa is thus emerging from the mist and darkness that so long enveloped the old.

But what of the missionary and his labors? The statesman has his chain of colonies, protectorates and dependencies; the speculator has his traffic chain of rail, caravan and waterways, and along these the scientist pushes his observation and study.

Is the missionary left behind in this grand march of new Africa progress? Not so. To learn the contrary, one has but to note the white dots on the black surface of Africa's missionary map. These mission stations now skirt the entire coastline and are penetrating the tropics from all sides—from Egypt up the Nile into the Soudan, from the east into Uganda and around the great lakes; from the south, up beyond the Zambezi River, and from the west coast, up the waterways of the great Congo and its tributaries. Missionary progress in Africa is indeed the striking chapter in recent church history. But not to be carried away by the enthusiasm of accomplishment, a sober facing of these great reaches of unevangelized background sometimes suggests that phrase applied to the church, viz., "Playing at Missions."

Beginning at the Cape-end of the great continent, the traveler, considering the long residence in that section of the two European peoples, expects to find the largest and best result of Christian missions in Africa. But territory rather than teaching has mostly occupied the European, the securing of the one to himself, not the imparting of the other to the native. But the first may be the best and necessary way to get at the other. And then "gold" rather than "gospel" is in the ascendancy in South Africa. The Christian (and he is in bonds to give the gospel to primitive as to all races) can not but wish that there had been, and even now was, less strife to get and more striving to give, less eagerness to secure land and wealth, and more eagerness to save life and soil.

However, despite these serious adverse circumstances in South Africa of political and gold greed, the Lord's work is not without large marks of blessing. Thousands of Zulus and Basutos are regularly hearing the Gospel of Christ. In addition to the activities of the missionary societies of the different churches, there are the labors of the South African general mission with centers at Capetown, Durban and Johannesburg, and with work in Zululand, Pondoland, Basutoland, Gazaland, and extending north into Portuguese territory.

[*] As seen by Eben Creighton on a journey through South and Central Africa.

It is a cause for great thanksgiving that large sections of the Boer Church are taking new and fresh interest in the work of giving the Gospel to the natives. The founding of the missionary training school by the Dutch Church, was necessitated by a remarkable movement of the Holy Spirit among the young Boers, who at the time were prisoners of war at such places as St. Helena and Ceylon. This movement, while not of the same range and scope as the Welsh revival, was, in its true inwardness, most like to that work of Christ. These Boer volunteers for country, for the time captives of war, at once became volunteers for God and missions. "Het Boren Gesunden Institute," known as "de Drostdy" (Worcester Cape-colony) came into being with this new missionary life, generated by the Spirit of God, and thus captive volunteers became "student volunteers." Such men as Abram Louw, Mr. Murray and Pastor DeVilliers, have occasion "to thank God and take courage" in view of his movement of the Holy Spirit with which God has honored and used them. The missionary work of the Boer church is to-day a telling one in British Central Africa. One is sure to read with quickening interest that book by the Boer missionary secretary, "Thousand Miles in the Heart of Africa."

But there is no more striking or remarkable work in any section than that of the equatorial regions. Entering the tropics from the east coast, the traveler at once learns of the C. M. S. work with its bishop and new cathedral, and scattered missionaries.

The recently organized American work, known as the Africa Inland Mission, has its six or more stations along the general direction of the railroad through British East Africa. Some of their mission stations are situated a few miles back of the line and are doing a work in populous and quite neglected districts.

The American Society of Friends less than three years ago established a station known as Kaimosi, situated about twenty-five miles north of Kavirondo gulf (in Victoria Nyanza). This is the only Protestant mission to the large Kavirondo tribe—a people friendly to the government, quite industrious, and although walking about in their native nudity, they are an exceptionally moral tribe. It is to be hoped that the friends will multiply stations among these people.

Doubtless the C. M. S. whose aggressive bishop in Uganda has already itinerated there will soon be pushing work up the slopes of Mount Elgon and take the story of grace to the neglected, and in some parts, hostile peoples there. This mountain, over 14,000 feet high, has an active volcanic crater some eight miles in diameter and seven hundred feet deep. The cave dwellers are there, and it is to be hoped that the Gospel will be carried to them and to all the environing peoples, and their spoken languages reduced to writing.

The Nandi tribe adjoins the Kavirondo on the east. They are a fierce and warlike people. Against them the British government has recently completed a considerable and successful expedition. No mission exists among these savages. May the evangel of the missionary soon come to them and lead them from the warfare of cruelty and destruction to the warfare of faith and holiness.

To the south lies German East Africa

which, despite what has already been done, has yet remaining vast tracts of unevangelized land.

The C. M. S. work, which, as already stated, begins at Mombasa on the east coast, continues with increasing intensity and influence in Uganda. This aggressive work, with its well equipped quota of missionaries, its many native Christians and church buildings, its excellent Uganda Bible and literature, its native pastors and teachers, is all too well known for detailed description here. Pushing westward from Uganda's port, on the great Nyanza, the traveler, during sixteen days of marching, sees more of this work as he continues into the country of Toro.

Here on the slopes of proud snow-crowned Ruwenzori, is another strong center of C. M. S. work, of the same policy and stamp as that of Uganda, and connected therewith. With its native pastor, teachers, churches and schools, this work is fast giving to the country, as we think should be the aim always, a native church, which could in any event of wisdom or necessity become self-perpetuating. As in Uganda, this Toro work evidently began, and certainly continues, with the patronage, so to speak, of the upper class, king, queen, big chiefs and leaders coming to daily Bible class.

The striking success of all the C. M. S. work in these parts is due, we think, first, to the fact that the advent of the missionary was prior to that of either the official or merchant; second, to the emphasis on the Word of God, and the making of that the one text-book of the land; third, to the fact that Christian and spiritual culture occupies the place given in other lands to general education; fourth, to the influence of the rulers, chiefs and leaders, who became the first converts; and perhaps more than all other causes, fifth, to that of the reliance upon, and blessing of the Holy Spirit; and sixth, lack of all division and sectarian strife in the church of God, since the existence even of a divided church is unknown to the Baganda Christians.

But still westward the caravan moves, the Baganda Christian has tucked away his hymn book and Scriptures which he carries; and you should see him as he picks up a sixty or seventy-pound box of goods, puts its on his head and goes off on a trot with a shout and a song. The traveler bids a reluctant farewell to the missionaries and native Christians at Toro, nestling so quietly and beautifully on the eastern slopes of towering Ruwenzori. He is awed as he goes away from this last mission out-post on the east, knowing that a long journey of weeks awaits him before he sees another missionary, which will not be until he reaches the great Congo river. Thus with sad heart he journeys, knowing that he is traversing the dark gap which marks the uncompleted chain of Africa's equatorial mission stations.

As the mission stations entering from the east coast end at Toro, so the stations entering from the west coast end at Yakusu, the English Baptist Missionary Society, three hours' river travel below Stanley Falls. To cover this intervening gap one tramps for eight weeks of six days of six hours each. He will pass through more than 100 towns and villages. These are clearings made in the great 300,000 square mile forest. In these settlements are people numbering from one hundred to a thousand. During the last days of the march, in the approach to Stanley Falls, these clearings greatly amplify and multiply. Besides these native village clearings, through which the traveler passes, there are in the deeper forest, villages of those interesting little people, the timid, shrinking pygmies. During all these eight weeks of travel, one sees not a single herald of the Gospel of God's grace and Christian love. Aside from out-and-out heathenism and its sad accompaniments, the religion of these forest peoples is a heathenized Mohammedanism. This has been disseminated, as in so many other parts of Africa

The Problem of the Country Churc

Abraham Lincoln said: "The Lord surely loves the common people, he made so many of them." Evidently the Lord loves the country churches, he has so many of them. Let us remember that "Christ loved the church and gave himself for it." May his infinite love for the weak churches inspire our hearts with a corresponding love. The pioneers of the movement for the restoration of primitive Christianity were generally plain men, many of them without liberal education, but learned in the Scriptures. These earnest preachers, very naturally, found strong affinity and hearty response in the rural places. These faithful servants of God were Christ-commissioned, and went into the field without any guarantee of compensation, and independent of any society or congregation. This fact, together with the emphasis on the doctrine of "liberty in Christ," and the excellency of being the 'Lord's free men," led to complete isolation of congregations, or what we may well call ultra-congregationalism. This congregational independence was inevitable under the circumstances, and its continuance might not be so disastrous if each congregation were able to keep and support a competent leader, but the fact that the church had been planted without any mention of money, the inability to give and a prejudice against a "hireling ministry" made it impossible in many places to maintain regular preaching. Consequently many a promising sowing came to nothing because of neglect to cultivate the field and gather the harvest. The little band failed to catch the spirit of sacrifice from the faithful minister and soon assumed the spirit of humility born of supposed poverty. Nothing is easier to cultivate than modesty and humility when church finances are being considered. Another discouraging feature with many country churches is the emigration to the cities often of their best workers or leaders. This entails loss and discouragement to the weak and struggling country church, and unless encouragement or help come soon it results in cessation of work, loss of interest and decay.

Many a church has died for want of leadership in business management as well as for want of a shepherd to feed the flock. Whether the method of our fathers was the wisest, or whether it would have been better to plant the cause first in the towns, so the church might grow with the town's growth, and become a radiating center of Gospel influence, is an open question. But on this, we agree, we must set ourselves to the task of solving the problem. A large per cent of our churches are in the country and villages. Each year witnesses the constituting of many new ones, and the loss of others. On the whole the net gain is not proportionate to the importance of the plea and our resources. This lack of increase is due, mainly, to losses. This is a calamity. The country must continue to be a base of supply in morals and Christian character, as well as in material products. I have in mind several churches that have ceased to meet, except when some one drops in and temporarily resuscitates the church. In some cases the unknown preacher victimizes the church and leaves it in a state of convulsion. Some churches having been admonished against unknown preachers, have settled down to an undisturbed rest, which may be the sleep of death. Our complacency amid this appalling death is sinful. Our motto should be: "Every church and every member shepherded and kept for aggressive service." The commission requires this. Perishing souls demand it. The principles of utility and economy compel it. Let us settle the conviction among the preachers and boards that these churches *must* be saved to the cause. But *how* can it be done? The Gospel is the *means* in saving men and advancing the king-

dom, but consecrated judgment must decide on *methods* of work. We must win through sane methods, consecrated effort and patience. We can not speak out of large experience; therefore we can not be dogmatic. We are feeling our way. I submit a few propositions:

First. Success or failure of churches is largely a question of leadership.

Second. Every congregation should have a competent minister who can preach the Word and lead in other matters pertaining to the church's welfare.

Third. If a church is able, it should sustain a minister full time.

Fourth. Churches not able individually to provide preaching full time should be grouped with other churches to maintain regular preaching.

Fifth. The grouping should be regarded as permanent, or until something better is possible.

Sixth. The minister for a group of churches should, if possible, live in their midst.

Seventh. State and district evangelists should superintend the fundamental teaching and grouping of churches.

I now proceed to sustain the seven propositions:

First—There is in every congregation enough native, latent ability to make the church aggressive and successful. Yet in the very presence of such possibilities and power churches wane and die. It is simply a question of leadership, of directing the power. It is safe to say that our country churches are not doing the half of what would be possible with good leadership.

Second—The Minister and Leader. There are few born leaders. Even *these* must study *how* to lead. Most of us are followers. The trained minister is a necessity. Our schools will more and more train the minister not only to fill the pulpit, but to lead the church into aggressive service. We must have ministers with *constructive ability* for these country churches.

Third—Preaching Full Time by Resident Minister. There are many advantages in a minister devoting full time to one church. Many country churches could easily install and support a minister, and, by so doing, quadruple their power for good and increase their own joy.

Fourth—Uniting Churches in Groups. It is simply a business proposition that a church unable to support preaching full time should join with others to provide regular preaching. A church can not live to itself, but it *can die* to itself. Manifestly two neighboring churches uniting for services represent more power than the two working separately. "One shall chase a thousand, and two shall put ten thousand to flight."

Fifth—Permanency. Temporary and changing plans, or the constant danger of dissolution of plans is enervating. Permanency gives strength

Fret Not Thyself.

The little sharp vexations,
  And the briars that sting and fret,
Why not take all to the Helper
  Who has never failed us yet?
Tell him about the heartache
  And tell him the longings too;
Tell him the baffled purpose,
  When we scarce knew what to do;
Then, leaving all our weakness
  With the One divinely strong,
Forget that we bore the burden,
  And carry away the song.
            —*Phillips Brooks.*

Our Budget

—Send us a "wire" Monday—

—If you exceed your apportionment.

—Church Extension should be the theme till a gift has been sent Brother Muckley.

—But little more than $100,000 per annum is required to give us $1,000,000 in this fund by 1909.

—Take the offering Sunday if possible. Church Extension will be in the air. You will get telepathic assistance from hundreds of surrounding churches denied you the next Lord's day.

—But if for any reason the offering is postponed, Church Extension should have right of way in press and pulpit, in plans and prayers till every congregation has met its obligations to those thousands of our brethren struggling for a church home.

—The next turn of the wheel may transfer many of us preachers to a charge where we shall need Church Extension money to house our mission, or to modernize the antiquated building in which our people will be meeting. Let us all plead so earnestly through September for the Church Extension fund that in all good conscience we can call on our brethren for assistance when the Board must intervene between us and barren years of waiting.

—Charles E. Schultz and wife, of Newcastle, Ind., are entering the evangelistic field. Their first meeting will be with Cecil Franklin, at Yorkton, Ind.

—King Stark, assisted by singer R. T. McRae is in a most encouraging meeting at Dover, Mo. There have been 36 additions to date, 31 being by confession and baptism.

—We regret to learn of the decease of J. M. Carwell, of Pocahontas, Ark. He was a faithful friend of THE CHRISTIAN-EVANGELIST whom we hope to meet in the better land.

—Irving Taylor Le Baron, assisted by Singer L. Byron Conrad, of Illinois is in a meeting at Mt. Olive, Mo. Other congregations desiring the services of this evangelistic team may address Bro. I. T. Le Baron at Macon, Mo.

—There are now 109 appeals that have come to our Board of Church Extension since March 1, when the board ceased granting loans for lack of funds. Inspiration enough for a great offering.

—F. Ellsworth Day, of Nelson, Neb., offers his services to the churches for two meetings between September and March. Brother Day is a good preacher and will pro e of e I help to the churches calling him.

—H. L. Veach reports that the Pike county convention of the churches of Christ, held at Barry, Ill., August 13 and 14, was well attended and all those present departed greatly strengthened for future usefulness.

—Irving Taylor Le Baron, evangelist, gave a stereopticon lecture on "From Cause to Effect," before the Union Sunday-school convention at New Cambria, Mo., August 23, that was reported as being very interesting and instructive.

—Everything has been done from the office at Kansas City that could be done for the church extension offering. The success of church extension day is now in the hands of the preachers and churches. Will the preachers lead the way?

—Last week the Foreign Society received a gift of $1,000 on the annuity plan from a friend in Ohio. This was the second gift from this source and the number of the bond was 274. Also a gift of $50 came in from a brother in Montana.

—G. A. Reynolds, of Dyersburg, Tenn., is holding protracted meetings, assisted by Evangelists Sheldon and Eisenbarger Although it is August in Tennes-

Do By

see, their very large tent is filled to overflowing every night, and profound interest prevails.

—Anson G. Chester writes that the Richmond Avenue Church, at Buffalo, sustains a real loss through the removal of Dr. W. A. B. Clarke and family to New Rochelle, N. Y It is a beautiful testimonial to so live in a church that our departure is sincerely mourned by the faithful.

—W. S. Johnson, of Litchfield, Ill., was a welcome visitor last week. His church during his ministry has advanced from one of the weakest to the strongest

Church Extension

in the city. In a few weeks his people will rejoice in the dedication of a beautiful new house of worship.

—Frank W. Allen, of Odessa, Mo., closed a two weeks' meeting at the Midway church in Audrain county, August 19. There were seven additions, six by confession and baptism. The brethren speak in high terms of the splendid preaching of this young man.

—In next week's CHRISTIAN-EVANGELIST will be a very interesting reply by E. S. Muckley of Portland, Ore., to E. L. Frazier's "Who is a Christian in the Twentieth

As Christ

Century." We believe kindly discussions of these important things will be most helpful and gladly give room to them.

—Our Bentonville (Ark.) brethren recognize their blessings while in possession, and have given J. W. Ellis, their able minister, an unanimous call to the pastorate for an indefinite time. The congregation is harmonious and enthusiastic for the Master in all good works.

—This office greatly enjoyed a visit last Thursday from Charles A. Young, editor, evangelist and college lecturer. Brother Young seems to lose none of his youth, geniality and righteous ambi-

Would Have You

tion with the flight of years, but to grow in grace and power. Come again, Brother Young.

—J. H. Mohorter, secretary of our National Benevolent Association, is arranging for a tour among the strong churches of the southwest in behalf of the Juliet Fowler Home at Dallas. Brother Mohorter's work in the interest of orphans, helpless old people, and the friendless sick, is being greatly blessed.

—J. B. Lockhart has been unanimously called by the church at Unionville, Mo., to continue his pastorate there for his third year. W. L. Harris, of Lincoln, Neb., and L. W. Mailey, of Greensburg, Ind., are assisting him in a revival meet-

ing. Two additions to date, and interest rapidly growing.

—Evangelist Richard Martin, together with six of his family, are in a very successful meeting at Sturgis, Ky. These various members assist as violinists, soloists and personal workers. There have been nearly 1,500 added to the churches in Brother Martin's meetings since beginning his southern tour.

—Evangelist M. L. Anthony is in a meeting at Glasgow, Ill., where he first became a member of the body of Christ under the ministry of John H. Coates. He is free for other engagements after his October meeting in Scottville, Ill. We cheerfully commend Brother Anthony to the brotherhood as an able and successful evangelist.

—There is always room in this paper for brief, reverent, articles instructive in the plan of salvation, confirming faith in the inspiration of the Word and the sovereignty of Christ, and whose tendency is to convert sinners and edify saints. Such contributions by brethren really adding to the number of the saved are thankfully received.

—Lura V. Thompson, Carthage, Ill., C. W. B. M. organizer for Illinois, visited with us last Thursday, returning home from a very successful tour through southern Illinois. Sister Thompson is not only an able official, but greatly endears the C. W. B. M. to all through her own personification of the graces it would inculcate in the home and foreign lands.

—Dan Trundle and wife, of Bisbee, Ariz., are spending their summer vacation at Long Beach. Brother Trundle writes that on August 7 he baptized a young man in the Pacific Ocean "because there was much water there." He also bears testimony to the great enthusiasm and helpfulness of the recent Southern California convention.

—Evangelist Small's meeting in the Mexico (Mo.) church, announced to begin September 2, has been postponed one week on account of Brother Small's being detained elsewhere. We can not censure the churches for holding on to Brother Small as long as possible. We predict he will have no "small" meeting with Bros. Kokendoffer and Harding at Mexico.

—Hugh C. Gresham, of Trenton, Neb., is meeting with fine success in his union Bible school revival work. That he is appreciated is proven by the executive committee's enlarging his field from two to five counties. Brother Gresham writes that Nebraska is a fine field for our ministers to enter. The people are appreciative and eager to hear the truth.

—O. D. Maple and J. Ross Miller, evangelists, will begin meetings at Gas City, Ind., September 10, and Cairo, Ill., October 1. Three hundred copies of THE CHRISTIAN-EVANGELIST will be among their helpers. This is a strong evangelistic team, and we trust they will be constantly engaged by the churches to preach and sing the old story of Christ's redeeming love.

—It is source of satisfaction to the Budget paragrapher to hear President McGarvey put the seal of approval on his observation relative to the new Manchester church being patterned after the old Jerusalem model. This also tends to confirm our hope that our scholarly brother will yet attain unto perfect harmony with the sentiments and aspirations of THE CHRISTIAN-EVANGELIST.

❋ ❋

For Loss of Appetite

—Alonzo B. Aldrich, of Brockton, Mass., writes: "The Manchester (N. H.) work is a great blessing to us in New England, and we owe the same to the CHRISTIAN-EVANGELIST and those connected therewith. May God bless you all and add his special blessing upon the lines sent out each week."

—D. Wesley Campbell and L. E. Swigert as singer, are helping D. W. Conner, of Edinburg, Ill., in a meeting that promises to be one of the greatest in the history of that congregation. Brother Conner recently baptized Miss Margaret Cole, who goes to Porto Rico in a few days as teacher by government appointment.

—J. S. Dabney has just received a unanimous call to continue as pastor of the Herron Hill congregation, Pittsburgh, for three years longer. There were three additions last Lord's day and the church is greatly prospering. This paragrapher dedicated the new church building two years ago and greatly rejoices in the popularity of "Brother Joe" and the prosperity of his church.

—President Hill M. Bell, of Drake University, visited St. Louis recently for conference with a number of young men contemplating entering the university. The result is that six of them will enter that great school in September and five others will follow later. The development of this institution of learning under President Bell's administration is a generous part of our centennial glory.

—Ferd F. Schultz, Beallsville, Ohio, is preparing now for a great evangelistic campaign to be inaugurated there in the near future. As one aid, he will place a copy of THE CHRISTIAN-EVANGELIST in each home in town and countryside every week of the meeting. Brother Schultz is one of those able, consecrated, unassuming ministers whose labors with our churches are always fraught with blessing.

—J. D. Williams, of the Eldara and New Hartford (Ill.) churches, is very happy in his ministry. He was assisted by W. H. Cannon, of Lincoln, in securing $415 at a basket picnic on August 19, for the payment of all indebtedness on the New Hartford church. He is having frequent additions to both churches, and is very hopeful for their great upbuilding numerically, financially and spiritually.

—R. O. Rogers, the enterprising and tireless pastor at Fredericktown, Mo., is the first of our ministers to complete the list of subscriptions necessary to secure free transportation to Buffalo. This was so easily done he will begin at once to secure another ticket. This will injure no pastor's prestige with his people, but help it rather. Congregations are glad to thus co-operate with preachers they love. Let all our ministers attempt this enterprise.

—How seldom are our evangelists called to conduct union meetings! But how successfully they could do so is being illustrated by Charles Reign Scoville at Monroe, Wis.—see "Hot from the Wire." Brother Scoville has promised us an early account of this unique revival. We are interested in learning how this most orthodox evangelist is co-operating with our denominational neighbors in saving the lost.

—J. B. Hunley, of Canyon City, ably seconds Brother Garrison's recent editorial suggestion that the importance of the devotional part of our state and national conventions should be greatly emphasized. He expresses the fear that we fall behind the great missionary and Bible school conventions of some of our denominational brethren in this important matter. If this has been true in the

past, let us see that it will be true no longer.

—Edward Keller is in a meeting at the Plainview church, near Memphis, Neb., assisting Harry G. Knowles, minister. We hope for an early and inspiring report.

—James G. Causler is in an excellent meeting at Payson, Okla. There were 26 accessions the first fourteen nights. Great interest is manifested by the large audiences that wait nightly upon the services.

—Chas. H. Caton, one of our unusually able preachers, writes us that he has completed a number of summer engagements and is now resting at Columbia, Mo. We hope our churches will keep him busily engaged.

—After a few weeks' vacation spent with his family in this city, S. R. Maxwell has returned to his Kennet (Mo.) pastorate. On account of old and invalid parents he is compelled to forego the pleasure of having his loved ones with him always.

—President Carl Johann, of Christian University, was among the week's callers. We are happy to report he is making rapid progress in freeing from all indebtedness this school that has had such a creditable part in building up our cause in these great valley states.

—Notice in another column Wallace Stuckey's testimonial to the efficiency of the CHRISTIAN-EVANGELIST as an evangelistic assistant in protracted meetings.

We furnish them to the churches at a price so low all can have the benefit of their silent advocacy of Christ and the church.

—Cephas Shelburne has just closed his fourth year with the Huntington, Ind., church. During the time 400 have been added to the membership, the Sunday-school has reached 450, the C. W. B. M. 100, the old building outgrown, and on next Sunday, September 2, they dedicate the best church edifice in northern Indiana and one of the best equipped in the brotherhood.

—L. L. Carpenter, of Wabash, Ind., assisted M. M. Ammunson in the dedication of a new church home for the Independence (Ind.) congregation August 12. What might seem unnecessary to add to an account of one of Brother Carpenter's dedications is that the necessary money was raised for the payment of all indebtedness. Brother Ammunson is greatly beloved in the community where he labors.

—Perry James Rice, whose long ministry at South Bend is one of the most illustrious in our Indiana annals, appears to be accompanied by his characteristic success in his new pastorate with the Portland Avenue Church at Minneapolis. In him our "northern frontier" has an able sentinel and oracle. We wish Brother and Sister Rice great happiness and many evidences of a successful ministry in their new home.

—With sorrow we report the death of T. J. Arnold, one of our missionaries to China since 1889. He came to Santa Cruz, Cal., some months ago upon the

—J. Ross Miller, O. D. Maple's singer, is training the chorus choir at Gas City, Ind., for the meeting which the Maple-Miller team will begin September 10. These preliminary services are invaluable aids to meetings, and we recommend that the people meet in song and prayer services for weeks preceding the coming of our evangelists. This will enable them to visit many more congregations each year and multiply the number of the saved.

—Pastor G. A. Reynolds, of Dyersburg, Tenn., assisted by Evangelist W. J. Shelburne and Miss Mayme Eisenbarger, singer, is in a tent meeting. During the first two weeks there have been fourteen additions by confession and baptism and five otherwise. It is reported that Brother Reynolds has greatly endeared himself to the community in which he is laboring and that his personal influence is a large factor in the success of this meeting.

—A. W. Kokendoffer reports the Audrain county convention held at Vandalia last week to have been one of the best in the history of the county. One of the results of this gathering will be the establishment of a new mission church in Audrain county in the immediate future. Summer seems to be losing its terrors for conventions and protracted meetings among the Disciples. The tendency now is to give all twelve of the months to the advancement of the kingdom.

—From the "Kansas City Star" we learn that Bro. T. P. Haley will continue as pastor of the South Side Christian Church another year. Bro. Haley resigned, thinking a younger and more active man would be of greater benefit to the church. The church, however, disagreed with him and unanimously called him to another year's work. Brother Haley has accepted this call and will enter actively upon his ministry as soon as he returns from Macatawa.

—A. C. Parker, of Ladonia, Texas, writes the meeting there in which he was assisted by R. R. Hamlin, of Fort Worth, and F. C. Huston, of Indianapolis, was the most successful ever held in Ladonia. There were 107 additions, ninety being by confession and baptism. Some of the most wicked men in the community turned to the Lord. Every one in the Bible school old enough to obey the Savior, came into the church. The whole city was moved. He very highly commends this evangelistic team.

—Corresponding Secretary H. W. Elliott sends the final announcement of the seventy-fourth annual convention of the Kentucky Disciples that will meet at the First Church, Louisville, September 24-27. All delegates sending their names in advance to R. M. Hopkins, 218 Keller building, will be provided with free entertainment for lodging and breakfast. Reduced rates have been secured without the necessity of getting certificates. A very instructive program has been provided and a large attendance of Kentucky Disciples is greatly desired.

—While C. V. Allison and wife, of Mound City, Mo., were attending the county convention at Maitland, Mo., Sister Allison was stricken with appendicitis and was compelled to undergo an immediate operation. Brother Allison writes that after two weeks the indications are for her recovery. His letter overflows with expressions of gratitude to the kind friends of Mound City and Maitland, and especially the family of Mrs. C. C. Phillips, at whose home they were being entertained during the convention and where Sister Allison still is. We join hosts of other friends in hoping for Sister Allison's early and complete restoration.

—J. A. Cunningham, the "drummer preacher" of Tupelo, Miss., preached Lord's day morning and evening at Una, Miss., August 12. We commend the example of this brother to all other traveling men and tourists gifted with the power to interpret the Scriptures. In the early days the disciples "went everywhere preaching the Word." Whether specially called to the ministry or engaged in secular pursuits through the week, wherever a Disciple of Christ goes he ought to tell men of his Saviour and win them into his fold.

—S. S. Smith, Eldorado, Kan., sends a beautiful tribute to his mother, Mary Margaret Smith, who entered into the better land July 10, 1906. In his letter accompanying the booklet he states: "There was nothing to her like her dear old Bible and THE CHRISTIAN-EVANGELIST, of which she had been a careful reader for years." While more people are reading THE CHRISTIAN-EVANGELIST than ever before in its history, we doubt not it has a greater host of friends on the other side of the river and among the dearest of them is Sister Smith.

—The Dallas county (Mo.) Christian churches will hold their convention at Buffalo, September 14-16. Every effort is being made by the committee to have an interesting convention and it is hoped the attendance will be large. J. Q. Biggs, of the Buffalo (Mo.) church, writes that there is great development in his local Christian Endeavor society and that the Bible school will soon have a rally. The church is planning for a revival in November. Brother Biggs may always be depended upon to give all he has and is for the advancement of the kingdom.

—One of the ablest, most faithful and successful evangelists now winning the mighty northwest to Christ is George C. Ritchey, of Roseburg, Ore., and now in a meeting at Nampa, Idaho. Brother Ritchey has organized several new churches in his territory and greatly added to the membership of older congregations. He has engaged 300 CHRISTIAN-EVANGELISTS per week to preach in Nampa homes while he tells the story of redeeming love from the pulpit and illustrates it in his daily walk.

—The following communication, printed verbatim et literatim et fly speckum, was recently received in answer to a business communication. Is it not in itself a vindication of our claim that THE CHRISTIAN-EVANGELIST has a mission in this world?

Nary Sunday school hear, sitch things is onskripteral. wee rede our bibels and don't talk nobody's word. No humen explanashun in owern wee don't want none of ole merely literachure. wee jest eat this bibel hear. wee have alredy got a bibel class and ax one and other bibel questions and the breathren ancer up and wee don't hafter take no human explaning. Mr. Garrisown, please put this ancer in your paper.—Cheerman Bibel class, which means no litratour of man. Arkansaa.

—Dr. J. G. M. Luttenberger is attending hospital lectures in Berlin. He writes that there are great opportunities for the dissemination of the principles of the churches of Christ in that capital city of the empire, if Americans of means would endow the enterprise. He says the tendency of Lutheranism is towards rationalism; that the people would gladly hear the more spiritual doctrines of our churches. The Baptists are well established there, having six

churches with a membership of 7,000. We hope ere long some movement will be made for the preaching of primitive Christianity throughout that great German land.

—S. R. Reynolds, Des Moines, Ia., asks "What would be the influence of church federation on organic unity and on the organized activities of the church?" It is believed by the friends of federation that it would be a powerful influence working for Christian union, but whether organic unity or not, would depend on the meaning we attach to the term "organic." The organized activities of the church would go on, much the same, but should be quickened by this closer conformity to the will of Christ concerning the union and co-operation of his disciples. Whatever the church does in harmony with Christ's will ought to help it in all its work done in Christ's name.

—Charles Reign Scoville, evangelist, writing from his great union meeting at Monroe, Wis., says: "I want to thank you ten thousand times for THE CHRISTIAN-EVANGELIST two weeks ago with that most excellent editorial and Dr. Whyte's article on Christian Union. That is the first time that I have ever been able to see how union could be brought about. I positively believe it is possible through love—love of God, love of the truth, love of all people. When we look not to the things of ourselves but the things of others, loving our neighbors as ourselves, we will see many things from their standpoint, and also they will be made to see many things from our point of view, and how much for which he prayed is possible. I am showing that article to every one of these pastors."

—How easily we may alienate ourselves from Christ, and how frequently we do! The inspired dictum is, "If any man hath not the spirit of Christ, he is none of his." With most of the great CHRISTIAN-EVANGELIST family the paramount question need not be, "Have I entered the kingdom in the divinely appointed way," for most of us have with scrupulous care, but it is, "Is the spirit of Christ prevailing in me"? "Am I still of his or has this ill temper, litigiousness, vengefulness, suspiciousness, censoriousness, this lack of brotherly love made me other than his this hour"?

—We urge all our readers who possibly can to attend the great international convention of Disciples at Buffalo, beginning October 12. The provisional program appearing in another column does in itself constitute an almost unanswerable reason for our going. We should remember, too, that while Buffalo is not far from the scene amid which this Restoration had its origin, Disciples are comparatively few along and east of the "Niagara frontier." The effect of a convention of great magnitude in impressing a sense of our mighty numerical strength and social consequence upon the children of the east will be almost magical, and forward through a week's demonstration our cause there as much as has been gained during the past decade. In addition to the personal pleasure and help you will receive, considerations of loyalty and help to the church should be thrown into the scale when determining whether or not you will muster with us at the convention.

—The Editor is in receipt of a letter from Brother Herbert Yeuell dated August 11, and written from the steamship as it was nearing Ireland, saying: "After nine days of stormless voyage from Boston we are beginning to look for the Irish coast." Very few of the passengers, he writes, had been ill and his wife, who feared the voyage, had stood it remarkably well. He writes that there are two ministers besides himself and several typical Scotch Presbyterians on board. He distributed Bro. W. J. Wright's tract among them and had an interesting time with them. He says: "I find that the old country people are less inclined to criticise our attitude than are Americans. They seem to be in advance of Americans as regards union sentiments. One very intelligent Scotchman said, after I had outlined our position, 'Why, we believe that in Scotland, already, but the failure of the Plymouth brethren to teach their ideal along those lines would make it difficult for you to succeed in our country with that plea! Besides,' said he, 'we have Disciples of Christ in Glasgow, and they hold to your views on baptism and the Lord's supper, but they are exclusive, and no one takes them seriously, and they will fraternize with none but their kind. You seem to be of a broader school and more acceptable to my way of thinking.' I told him that we had some of that same sort in America, but that did not destroy our ideal, although, in many places, it woefully hindered our progress. I told him of our hosts of men and churches co-operating with Christians of all sects so far as a practical application of Christ could be made, but that we still held to our ideal, earnestly praying for the entire unity of God's people." Brother Yeuell did not expect to reach London before August 13, and was anxious to reach his mother's beside and know how she was.

A. C. M. S. Convention Program.

The following is an outline of the program of the American Christian Missionary Society for the national convention, Buffalo, N. Y., October 12-18, 1906:

Saturday, October 13—2:30 a. m., general board meeting of A. C. M. S.; night, Christian Endeavor session (program supplied by R. H. Waggoner, Nat'l Supt.).

Sunday, October 14—11 a. m., preaching in offered pulpits (all preachers are requested to preach missionary sermons); 3 p. m., union communion service, S. M. Cooper and R. H. Miller, presiding (convention hall and nearby churches if necessary); 7:30 p. m., preaching in all offered pulpits.

Monday, October 15—sessions of the Foreign Christian Missionary Society.

Tuesday, October 16—the American Christian Missionary Society, S. M. Cooper, presiding; 9:30 a. m., prayer and praise service; appointment of committees; report of Board of Church Extension; report of Acting Board of American Christian Missionary Society; report of Standing Committee on Evangelism; address, "God's Purpose and Plan in Home Missions," B. F. Daugherty, Wabash, Ind.; introduction of home missionaries, by Geo. B. Ranshaw, field secretary; address, "Higher Ideals in Christian Stewardship," by H. D. Smith, Hopkinsville, Ky.; address, "The Oughtness of Ministerial Relief," by C. J. Tanar, Detroit, Mich.; address, "Evangelism," by J. P. Lichtenberger, New York City; business session; adjournment. 7:30 p. m., song and prayer service. 8:00 p. m., church extension address. S. M. Cooper; adjournment. Wednesday, October 17—9:30 a. m., prayer and praise service; address, "The Challenge of the Canadian Northwest," by Alex McMillan, Winnipeg, Man.; address, "The Greatest Mission Field in the World," by S. T. Willis, New York City; business session; address, "The America of the Future and our Contribution to it," by W. H. Sheffer, Memphis, Tenn.; final adjournment; afternoon and night sessions by the affiliated interests. Thursday, October 18—excursions and outings.

All meetings of the American Christian Missionary Society to be held in Convention Hall.

The Galesburg (Kan.) Meeting.

Still the crowds come. Three additions last night. The whole country is being stirred by the meeting. Everybody reading THE CHRISTIAN-EVANGELIST and learning they have misunderstood our plea in the past. THE CHRISTIAN-EVANGELIST has helped in getting our plea before the people in the right light.

We have been assisted by Bros. J. H. Stuckey and Duncan McFarland. Many are "almost persuaded" to accept the Lord. Another religious body in the town whose attitude is not just what it should be, but their members attend largely.

We continue for a few days but must soon go home for my own meeting which is postponed till September 9. Miss Snowie Ditch will sing for us at Libo. Will baptize Monday evening and shall perhaps close Tuesday to get home.—Wallace M. and Ethel Stuckey.

A Good Revival and Fellowship.

During the 17 days' meeting which closed August 15 at South Elkhorn, 83 were added, 56 of whom were baptized. Prof. H. L. Calhoun, of the College of the Bible, did the preaching. The house was full at every meeting, and it was frequently filled to overflowing. The interest in listening to the old Jerusalem gospel was great from the beginning. The speaker's style was so plain and truthful that no one who heard him could fail to understand the truth of the Gospel. The spirit of love and fellowship prevailed among all Christian people who attended the meeting.

On the last Lord's day 69 of those who had joined during the meeting stood in line while, in the old-time way, the congregation extended to them the hand of fellowship. This hearty welcome did

much good. More handshaking would help most of our congregations.

Lexington, Ky. A. FAIRHURST.

For a Church in New Hampshire.

Already acknowledged	$812 25
Mary F. Holbrook	50 00
D. O. Smart	25 00
American Christian Missionary Society	25 00
"A Sister" (Oakland, Cal.)	10 00
Total	$922 25

The above is the second contribution the president of our Board of Church Extension has made for this New Hampshire fund. Are there not others who, having learned of the unexpectedly large expense of establishing a new church in a wealthy eastern city without one resident Disciple, wish for larger fellowship in this purely missionary enterprise? It is not a question of whether God wishes this Restoration represented in New Hampshire or whether it is possible at this time to found a church there. It is simply a question of whether we can secure enough money to rent an auditorium in a desirable part of the city and maintain an evangelist long enough to win people to our plea. Let us quickly double our present receipts and our reproach of coming to our first centennial without a single church in one of our oldest commonwealths will soon be removed.

A Modern Miracle.

Mrs. S. T. Roberts, Clinton, La., sent a postal card request for a trial bottle of Drake's Palmetto Wine to Drake Co., Drake Bldg., and received it promptly by return mail without expense to her. Mrs. Roberts writes that a bottle of this wonderful Palmetto Medicine proved quite sufficient to completely cure her. She says: "One bottle of Drake's Palmetto Wine has cured me after months of intense suffering. My trouble was Inflammation of Bladder and serious condition of Urinary organs. Drake's Palmetto Wine gave me quick and entire relief, and I have had no trouble since using the one bottle."

Drake's Palmetto Wine cures every such case to stay cured. It is a true, unfailing specific for Liver, Kidney, Bladder and Prostate Troubles caused by Inflammation, Congestion or Catarrh. When there is Constipation, Drake's Palmetto Wine produces a gentle and natural action of the bowels and cures Constipation immediately to stay cured. One small dose a day does all this splendid work, and any reader of this paper may prove it by writing to Drake Co., Wheeling, W. Va., for a test bottle of Drake's Palmetto Wine. A letter or postal card is your only expense.

Changes.

E. H. Kellar, Covina to 2509 S. Hope street, Los Angeles, Cal.
Chas. Seign Scoville, Atchison, Kan., to Monroe, Wis.
F. L. Moffett, Austerville, Ia., to 512 South street, Springfield, Mo.
A. Lyle De Jarnette, Saratoga, Cal., to Santa Cruz, Cal.
F. M. Longanecker, Kalamazoo, Mich., to Charleston, W. Va.
R. E. Stevens, Shiloh, Ore., to R. F. D. 4, Greenwich, Ohio.
Ralph V. Calloway, Des Moines, Ia., to North Waco, Tex.
M. F. Thompson, Eugene to Dayton, Ore.
F. L. Atkinson, California, Pa., to Flushing, Ohio.
S. M. Conner, Burlington to Greenwood, Ind.
Chalmers McPherson, Eureka Springs, Ark., to Waxahachie, Tex.
H. G. Bennett, Westport, Ky., to Monroe, Wis.

Resorts Near Buffalo.

Buffalo is situated in the midst of many and beautiful resorts—probably the most beautiful in the United States.

Twenty-one miles to the north is Niagara Falls, one of the scenic wonders of the world. This resort attracts to it, annually many thousands of visitors from all parts of the world, and has been admired by the princes and nobility of almost every nation. The scenery along Niagara River is extremely beautiful. The river is about 33 miles in length, and descends 328 feet in its course from Lake Erie to Lake Ontario. Where the river leaves Lake Erie it is less than a mile wide, but in its course expands to several miles, and is dotted with several islands, the largest of which is Grand Island, 11 miles long, and which extends to within a mile and a half of the great cataract. The narrowing of the channel and the rapid descent, at the rate of 60 feet to the mile, produce the Upper Rapids, in which the leaping river presents the most beautiful expanse of foam and spray. It is quite impossible to describe the beauty and grandeur of the cataract. The river, at this point 4,750 feet wide, leaps over a cliff nearly 150 feet high, and discharges its thundering waters into a channel 180 feet deep below. It is estimated the river discharges about 18,000,000 cubic feet of water every minute. The American Falls, being shallower, present a most beautiful white, lace-like appearance as they leap over the higher elevation. The Canadian Falls, being very deep, preserve their rich green color until they have dropped far out from the crest. The spirit of the wild things pervades the place, and the deep roar of the waters, from which the Indians gave the falls their name, fills one with a sublime sense of awe and wonder. Many beautiful Indian traditions linger in this enchanted spot. Dickens said of this wonderful scene: "I heard the mighty rush of water, and felt the ground tremble underneath my feet. I could see an immense torrent of water tearing down from some great height, but had no idea of shape or situation, but great immensity. I was in a manner stunned, and unable to comprehend the vastness of the scene. Then, when I felt how near to my Creator I was standing, the first effect and the enduring one—instant and lasting—of the tremendous spectacle, was peace. Niagara was at once stamped upon my heart, an image of beauty; to remain there, changeless and indelible, until its pulses ceased to beat, forever. I think in every quiet season now, still do these waters roll and leap and roar and tumble, all day long; still are the rainbows spanning them, a hundred feet below. Still, when the day is gloomy, do they fall like snow, or seem to crumble away like the front of a great chalk cliff, or roll down the rock like dense white smoke. But always does the mighty stream appear to die as it comes down, and always from its unfathomable grave arises that tremendous ghost of spray and mist which is never laid."

Not less interesting is the river below. For a mile the startled waters flow deeply and quietly on. Then the deep channel narrows to a few rods and the pent-up waters surge and foam in the mad rush of the Lower Rapids. These discharge into a basin of rock, where the river turns upon itself at right angles, forming the famous Whirlpool, the depth and power of which no man can measure. The river pursues its mad way through this narrow channel until it reaches Lewiston, where the torrent expands into a deep and swift-flowing river. On either side of this channel, the banks rise almost perpendicularly to a height of nearly 200 feet. Through this distance of seven miles the river descends 104 feet. This is the Great Gorge. The International Traction Co. has placed a trolley at the foot of the cliff, at the edge of the rushing torrent, on the American side, and on the brink of the cliff on the Canadian side. This trip is one of the most interesting and inspiring in the world.

The falls are surrounded by places of great historic interest. At the end of the gorge, looking out over the expanse of the river below and the receding hills, to Lake Ontario, is Brock's monument, the scene of a famous battle between the American and British forces in the war of 1812, when the American forces were pressed over the steep embankment into the mad waters below. Here are still to be seen the breast-works. Bayard Taylor said of this emminence that it was the moost beautiful view in the United States.

A most delightful trip is that across Lake Ontario, in the large steamers, to Toronto, the leading city of Canada. The steamers leave from Lewiston, at the end of the gorge, pass downward through seven miles of the lower river, past Niagara-on-the-lake, Queenstown, Youngstown and out into the lake, to Toronto—a distance of about 45 miles, and a ride of about two hours.

Buffalo has two beautiful beaches within easy reach. One of these is Crystal Beach, on the Canadian shore of Lake Erie, and within an hour's ride by steamer of the city. This is a fine bathing resort, and the summer home of many cottagers. It is patronized by many of Buffalo's best citizens. No liquors are sold on the place. The other is Olcott Beach, on the southern shore of Lake Ontario, reached by a two hours' ride by trolley, through a picturesque country, through the Tonawandas, the largest lumber port in the United States, and through Lockport where are located the locks of the famous Erie Canal.

Niagara river is a part of the St. Lawrence system, leading to the Thousand Islands, and from thence, past Montreal and Quebec, to the sea. This is considered a particularly attractive trip by thousands of people annually.

Buffalo is within easy access of all the famous resorts of the east. Not more than a hundred miles to the southwest of Buffalo is Chautauqua lake, with its famous Chautauqua Assembly. In the eastern part of the state are the Berkshire Hills and the Adirondack mountains. Here are the Catskill mountains, the scene of the famous story of Rip Van Winkle. The central part of the state is dotted with large and beautiful lakes. To the east is Lake George, nestled among the clouds, one of the favorite resorts of the east, and the seat of the Silver Bay conference. Here also is Lake Champlain. There is the beautiful Hudson, flowing past West Point, Sleepy Hollow and the country residences of the wealth of New York City, down past the metropolis of the nation, and out into the sea. Pleasure seekers take the day ride up or down the Hudson by steamer, on which their railroad tickets are honored.

Buffalo is the gateway from the west to the historical ground of New England, and such centers as Boston, Philadelphia and a score of other localities, made sacred to every American heart by the history of the past.

It would be difficult, if not possible, to find a finer aggregation of interesting places and pleasant resorts than are to be found in the vicinity of Buffalo. Doubtless many will plan their vacations so as to attend the convention, and then spend a period of sight-seeing or recreation at some of these famous resorts in New York.

N. Tonawanda, N. Y. W. C. Bower.

Sixteen Hundred Acres in Texas.

For sale—1,600 acres of land in the famous Texas oil field, surrounded by the Humble, Cleveland, Myrtle Hill, Dayton, Davis Hill, Batson and Saratoga fields. Has gas well on one corner of tract and another on adjoining tract. This is a proven oil field and other lands joining this have been selling at from $40 to $60 per acre. This is offered at $40 per acre for the entire tract. The owner is not an oil man and has authorized me to say that if we can make a sale he will give $10,000 of the proceeds to Carlton College, of Bonham, Texas, a part of Texas Christian University. Here is an opportunity for some one to make a fine investment and at the same time help one of our most worthy institutions. For further particulars address Clement Few, Paris, Texas.

Brother Few is secretary of the State Bible school committee of Texas.

Board of Ministerial Relief of the Church of Christ.

Aid in the support of worthy, needy, disabled ministers of the Christian Church and their widows.

THIRD LORD'S DAY IN DECEMBER is the day set apart in all the churches for the offering to this work. If you make individual offerings, send direct to the Board. Wills and Deeds should be made to "BOARD OF MINISTERIAL RELIEF OF THE CHURCH OF CHRIST, a corporation under the laws of the State of Indiana." Money reecived on the Annuity Plan.

Address all communications and make all checks, drafts, etc., payable to
BOARD OF MINISTERIAL RELIEF,
120 E. Market St., Indianapolis, Indiana.

Scoville at Atchison.

Atchison, Kansas, has just closed the most successful meeting ever held in that state. The meeting was conducted by Charles Reign Scoville, assisted by De Loss Smith and Mr. and Mrs. P. M. Kendall. The meeting continued four weeks under Brother Scoville, and resulted in 503 additions. Mr. and Mrs. Kendall came two weeks in advance of Brother Scoville, and they with the pastor began the meeting. When Brother Scoville arrived the interest was thoroughly aroused, and there had been eleven additions. Upon the first invitation by Brother Scoville, eight stepped out and from that time to the close, there were confessions at every invitation save one, and that was a rainy Sunday morning when the congregation was made up almost wholly of members of the church. The least nunmber that came upon any invitation was five. The largest number upon a single invitation was 36.

The meeting was a remarkable one in many respects. It was held in midsummer. The weather at times was hot, very hot. It was thought by many that at such a time we could not hold a successful meeting.

As our church building will seat but 400 people, it was necessary to build a tabernacle. The tabernacle seated 1,500 and cost $350. There were many who said to the pastor when the building was under construction, "You do not expect to fill this, do you?" It was filled night after night and proved to be far too small for the crowds. Hundreds stood on the outside during the entire service. People came from all the surrounding country. Topeka sent up a delegation of 80 on one trip. The meeting has contributed members to nearly all the churches in the surrounding country.

People in the church and out of it, when they heard of Scoville's meeting in other cities, would say, "You might hold a great meeting in some places but it can't be done in Atchison." Of course, this is an old story and just what you will hear in any city when a great meeting is proposed.

A real hindrance to us in Atchison was the fact that we have just one daily paper and its editor is an unbeliever. Anything going on in church circles is not considered by him news at all, and finds no place in his columns. We had to pay five cents a line for every news item that went into the paper. If the editor or his staff made any reference to the meeting it was to cast some slur or to reflect on the sincerity of the workers, or the value, or the permanence of the work. By the way, if you know of a good man with brains or money enough to run a first-class daily paper, send him to Atchison. I know of no better opening for such an enterprise than right here.

But in spite of doubts and hindrances the meeting proved a great victory. Atchison had its eyes opened. It has been demonstrated that Christianity is not dead, that the Gospel is still the power of God unto salvation. Five hundred added to the church does not tell the whole story of this meeting. All the churches of Atchison have been benefited and thousands of lives have been made better. The saloon power has been shaken and multitudes of men who did not come into the church have resolved to let whisky alone.

What shall I say of Brother Scoville? Little need be said, for his fame has gone abroad. In persuading men to take a stand for Christ, and do it *now*, he is without a peer. He is downright in earnest and everybody knows it. He builds up the membership of the church. He strengthens the pastor. The membership of our church love and appreciate me now more than before Brother Scoville came. He never lost an opportunity both in public and in private to speak well of the pastor.

DeLoss Smith is a great soloist. His songs touch the heart. Often Brother Scoville would call for a song in the midst of a sermon. It seems that Brother Smith was most effective at such a time and many more sung into the kingdom.

We had a great chorus of 100 voices, directed by P. M. Kendall. As a chorus director, Brother Kendall is superb. He is good natured, always sweet, and never sour. He never scolds nor finds fault. The people love him and would like to keep him here all the time.

Mrs. Kendall works with the children, and we appreciate what she did just as much as we appreciate Brother Scoville, or any of the other members. Her work can not be praised too highly. The Bible drills which she gave our children will never be forgotten by them, or by us. She is rejoicing that every member in her class that was not in the church has confessed Christ during the meeting.

We have no regrets over this meeting. Everybody is happy and everybody is ready for work.

The Atchison congregation is now the largest in the state. We have a membership of 1,082. Our Bible school is the largest of the Christian churches of the state. Our midweek prayer meeting is so large that we have taken it to the main auditorium. Ever since the close of the meeting we have used new members altogether as ushers and for the handling of the offerings and the Lord's Supper.

W. T. Hilton, pastor.

NEWS FROM MANY FIELDS

The Growth of the Disciples in the Lone Star.

The closing year has been our most prosperous year. Harmony has prevailed and a substantial growth in all directions has been made. 100,-000 additions to our ranks in the United States indicate a healthy growth. Texas has supplied one-twentieth of these. Ten per cent of the new churches started in the United States by our missionaries in the past year were planted by our Texas missionaries. For exact figures reporting work done see appended report. Note that this report is only of work done by workers in part supported from our Texas mission fund and does not include the work of the self-sustaining churches.

The rapid growth of Texas in material things calls for increased liberality and effort upon our part. No part of our great country is adding to its population more rapidly than Texas. They are coming from the older states in great numbers. Our cheap, though broad and fertile lands, are inviting. Nowhere except in Texas can there be found such lands and prices, with modern conveniences and advanced civilization. Our stalwart Americanism, our splendid public school fund, with its resultant educational institutions, with churches quite the equal of those found in the older states, are immensely attractive, and that to the best class of people in the northern and eastern states. We must enlarge our borders and strengthen our stakes, in order to properly receive and care for our own coming to us.

Foreign immigration is coming—1,026,499, last year—these in a short time, to become citizens, must be trained for Christian citizenship, or become a menace to our peace and happiness, and a powerful force in the demoralization of our sacred religion, the very foundation and bulwark of our American freedom and prosperity. Great herds of foreigners, together with American youth, are gathering in the cities where ignorance and crime grow rampant, and with the saloon added, they become veritable hotbeds, breeding every form of vice, corrupting the main arteries of our civilization, until municipal misgovernment has given our entire country a bad odor abroad. True, we have our Roosevelt, Joe Folk, Hanley and Pattison. The growing popularity of such men is a splendid omen, and the history of the early training of such men, an unmistakable index, pointing us the way to success. Christian homes, schools, and churches must supply us the men and women who will save our country from the inevitable ruin which would follow the rule of the un-American, un-Christian foreigner, with his brewery and beer-joint. We are glad to testify that a large number of foreigners do not belong to this class, but in many communities in Texas, a lower grade, led by vicious men of our own blood, hold the balance of power. We will find it infinitely more economical and better, from every view point, to train these men and their children for a better citizenship than to meet the inevitable clash which must come with their increased numbers and intensified habits, if not tempered by Christian training—aye, if they are not saved by the Christ who has saved our own Anglo-Saxon race from barbarism.

With this object in view, we must give larger endowment to our Christian schools. We should make it possible for every youth in the land to secure a Christian education. We should be looking out from among the children of the foreigner, intelligent boys and girls, who are willing to become the trained teachers of their own people. It has been demonstrated that the sturdy German, already well educated in the German way, can be trained into a splendid American Christian citizenship. The best teacher of the Mexicans is a true, trained and faithful Mexican. Look ye out, such youth and furnish the means for their education if you would convert the foreigner at

home or abroad. There is a great need for the translation of our best Christian books and tracts. That which has been so potent a power in bringing light and liberty to the Disciples of Christ, will find a responsive chord in the hearts of all as they shall come to appreciate the freedom with which Christ has set us free. We need training schools for ministers and for missionaries, who are not popularly regarded as ministers of the Gospel—though we are all ministers if we serve. "Let him that would be great among you, become your servant," said the Master to His wrangling disciples.

A genuine conversion to Christ is the first and greatest essential to efficient service in the salvation of men. This will stop our quibbling about plans, and give impetus to a forward movement that will find us succeeding in the

J. C. Mason.

Lord's work. In the presence of the enemy of souls, and with opportunities all about us, imploring us forward, we must not stop to split hairs about far-fetched questions, and allow the prizes almost within our grasp to pass us by never more to return.

One result of a thorough conversion to Christ must be united brotherhood, not in opinion or doctrine, as men count doctrine, but united in an effort to so preach Christ as to win men to him. This is the union for which Christ prayed, John, 17th chapter, "That the world may believe that thou has sent me." Faith comes by hearing the word of God. Let us then preach Christ crucified and rejoice that we may be partakers of his sufferings, that the burden of the world's ignorance and sin may be borne by us while we lean upon his promise. "Lo, I am with you always, even unto the end of the ages." Genuine conversion will lead to larger liberality. A Spirit-filled man counts naught that he possesses his own.

We should give especial attention to the call of the weak churches. To that end the annual offering should be made much of. City evangelism demands larger liberality and consecration. United effort, concert of action all point the way to success.

We have a very few who are doing nobly. The number must be increased by ten fold. Sunday-schools are the greatest factors in leading to a useful Christian life. We should unite with the Inter-denominational Bible school effort in order to avail ourselves of the benefit of the experience of experts and carefully import to all our

Concentration is a lesson that we are slow to learn. These districts which are working in closest harmony with the state board are becoming more systematic and reliable, and therefore more certainly successful in the work.

While pointing with gratitude to the advance we have been able to make, as shown by the figures in the appended report, I cannot forbear repeating that we must enlarge the work. Crying calls are coming to us from every quarter, "Come over and help us." In many instances a very little help to start a mission or aid a weak church will develop unexpected but latent ability. Men of Israel, help! Our pleas must be heard. The old, old story in its purity must be told. Shall we begin now to do, by God's help, the greatest year's work in the history of Texas? Our Master commands us to go forward and assures us that his word shall not return unto him void.

Report of the work of Texas Missionaries for the year ending May 31, 1906:

Number of men employed	34
Days	7755
Sermons	3825
Additions by confessions and baptism	910
By letters and reclaimed	690
From the denominations	220
Total added by missionaries	1820
Cash by and for missionaries	$17,660.00
Cash for missions, houses, lots, pastors, etc.	13,272.31
Cash raised by our missionaries for all purposes	30,932.31
Pledges	15,396.00
Total cash and pledges	$46,328.31

❀ ❀ Deafness Cannot be Cured

by local applications, as they can not reach the diseased portion of the ear. There is only one way to cure deafness, and that is by constitutional remedies. Deafness is caused by an inflamed condition of the mucous lining of the Eustachian Tube. When this tube is inflamed you have a rumbling sound or imperfect hearing, and when it is entirely closed, Deafness is the result, and unless the inflammation can be taken out and this tube restored to its normal condition, hearing will be destroyed forever; nine cases out of ten are caused by Catarrh, which is nothing but an inflamed condition of the mucous surfaces.

We will give One Hundred Dollars for any case of Deafness (caused by catarrh) that can not be cured by Hall's Catarrh Cure. Send for circulars free.　F. J. CHENEY & CO., Toledo, O.

Sold by Druggists, 75c.

Take Hall's Family Pills for constipation.

Illinois Notes.

The comparatively new congregation at St. Elmo has built a splendid house of worship, and when the debt is lifted the church will be in condition to do large service for the Master. They need a good preacher located with them to lead and develop the work.

Made a short call at Vandalia with Judge B. W. Henry, whose father was my father in the Gospel and a charter trustee of Eureka College and a pioneer preacher of great power in Central Illinois. The judge is a true, loyal Disciple of Christ.

The church at Flora, with its splendid new, modern church and good parsonage, is moving forward. The minister, R. G. Ogburn, has resigned, and C. M. Smithson, of Mt. Vernon, will be his successor September 1. This is an unusually strong church, whose enterprise and sacrifice have won for it a leading place. It will soon be ready to fall in line of liberal support of all the great enterprises of the church. Near here E. J. Hart grew to manhood, graduated in Eureka College in '72, devoted himself to the Christian ministry, brought about 4,000 souls into the kingdom of God and has now passed on to his reward. Are there not other such boys, whose life might be full of great results, if they were encouraged to devote themselves to the ministry? Do our preachers and churches realize our great need of more efficient men?

The church at Sumner is without a preacher, but is keeping up regular worship and the Sunday-school.

The Lawrenceville church is one of the strongest on the Wabash. Brother McDonald has been with it only a short time, but is making a good start. The Sunday-school is one of the most active and vigorous of any that I have seen in Illinois. Hot weather seems to have cooled the ardor of many of our schools and churches, but not of this one. If the Lawrenceville church carries out the large influence and power which our good Father has given it, it will truly be a great and shining light for the life of many.

West Salem has one of the oldest churches of Central Illinois. It numbers 360 members, with 100 in Sunday-school and a Young People's Society of 25. G. W. Ford is the efficient minister, dividing his time with the Shiloh and Marion churches. He is a very useful man and fully alive to the cause of the Master.

The church at Carmi, under the leadership of Frank Thompson, is about completing a beautiful modern church, costing about $15,000. It is built entirely of cement blocks, and makes a beautiful house. It will be dedicated in the early fall. I do not know of a more heroic effort in church building than is manifested by the Carmi people. What can not faith and work, with God's blessing, do?

The Enfield church seems to be in good condition under the half-time ministry of B. S. Kello. It numbers 100 members, with nearly as many in Sunday-school and a C. E. of 20.

McLeansboro has about doubled its church membership in the two years' ministry of E. U. Smith. It has a fine company of young people, and we shall be surprised if from among them some do not enter Eureka College to prepare for, large and useful lives. I was sorry to hear any intimation looking towards a change of pastorates. Churches and preachers sometimes are not content to let well enough alone. I could see no reason why another two years of good solid work should not be as useful as the past.

Mt. Vernon is one of the cleverest, brightest, best-improved cities of Southern Illinois. Although a city approaching 10,000 people, it has no saloons nor places where liquor is sold. Its only route to drunkenness is by the express

companies, and these are not very happy in their debauching business. C. M. Smithson for two years has led the church to almost double membership and a greatly improved property, free from debt. But he has resigned his work to take the pastorate at Flora.

L. D. Hill becomes the minister of the Benton church September 1. This is a fine field, and we shall expect good results from this happy combination. Sister Hill knows well how to tell the story of the cross, and will be happy to cooperate with the women in enlarging the public spirit and larger usefulness of the church. "Enlargement" is a splendid watchword for us all until missions home and abroad and Christian education shall all feel the warm blood of our liberality.

Metropolis, on the banks of the Ohio, is growing in spirit and numbers under the energetic leadership of T. F. Hall. This is one of the good old churches that is always heard from when the Macedonian call comes. The minister here who does not preach missions holds a very uncertain tenure to his pulpit. Jesus preached "Go"; why should any preacher hold a ministry who does not preach "Go"? This is the home of J. B. McCartney, a sterling business man whose heart is large enough to retain interest and to make investments in the King's business as well as in stocks and bonds. This church has just royally entertained the Eighth District convention. It is composed of 14 counties in the south end of the state. There are in it 71 churches, 31 preachers and nearly 6,000 members. The C. W. B. M. had an excellent program. Miss Osteene, of Herrin, is district secretary, and presided over the C. W. B. M. sessions and was re-elected to serve another year. There are but nine auxiliaries and one Young Ladies' Circle in the district. Miss Osteene will try very hard to increase the number, and if she meets proper co-operation she will succeed. The spiritual interest and enterprise that comes into the church far outweighs the few dollars that go to the world-wide of the C. W. B. M. W. W. Weeden gave a strong C. W. B. M. sermon. Miss Clara Griffin gave an excellent address on "Children's Work." Mrs. John Duncan's paper on "Ambassadors for Christ" stirred all hearts. Miss Anna E. Davidson, state president, gave the leading address in her happy, clear and powerful way.

The program in the other departments was strong and vigorous. The patriarch of the convention was W. L. Crim, who gave a great address on the "Attractions of the Cross." A district with such men in it as W. W. Weeden, J. J. Harris, A. M. Growden, T. F. Hall, R. H. Roberson, E. C. Stark, T. J. Holloman, F. L. Davis, D. A. Hunter and others whose names are well worthy of mention will surely do some business for the Master. Already R. L. Cartwright has labored five months in the district as evangelist. His services are continued, and give promise of

large usefulness. He deserves the cordial support of every preacher and church in the district.

J. F. Alsup, L. D. Hill and R. L. Beshers grew to manhood in this district. A. L. Huff, H. G. Burgess and S. T. Fanon, now in Eureka College, are from this district. We expect others when college opens September 18. Any of our young friends wanting to know more of the college please write us.   J. G. WAGGONER.

Eureka, Ill.

❀ ❀

Important Notice to Illinois Sunday-Schools.

Illinois Sunday-schools are requested to observe Children's Day for Home Missions on September 30 this year, and not November 25.

Last year only 83 of our schools gave the boys and girls a chance to have fellowship in home missions as they had in foreign missions. Four hundred and twenty-six schools observed Children's Day for Foreign Missions. At least the same number ought to put the home mission opportunity within reach of the children who are to grow up to possess this country.

The reason most frequently given for the non-observance of home mission day in November was, "It is too near Christmas. Impossible to

arrange for the day and Christmas Day in so short a time."

In conversation with Secretary W. J. Wright, I suggested that our Illinois schools be permitted to observe September 30 as Children's Day for Home Missions. He agreed heartily. Let us redeem Illinois from the reproach of only 83 schools.

In connection with the day the annual fall Sunday-school rally may be observed also. This will make it a high day. Rally all the school and community. Send to the Cincinnati office now for supplies, musical exercises, envelopes and money banks.

Will the Illinois ministers lend their enthusiasm to making this day notable? September 30, 1906, Children's Day for Home Missions for Illinois!

State Superintendent Bible Schools for Illinois.

MARION STEVENSON.

❦ ❦

To the Foreign Field.

The Foreign Society sends out a splendid body of new missionaries to the foreign field in September. The are as follows: Miss Genevieve Perkins, of Des Moines, Ia., a graduate of Drake University, goes to Lu Cheo fu, China; Miss Rose Johnson, of Warrensburg, Mo., a graduate of William Woods College, Fulton, Mo., goes to Japan; Dr. G. E. Miller, of Mowrystown, Ohio, a graduate of the Medical College, Cincinnati, Ohio, and who also attended the Bible College, Lexington, Ky., goes to Damoh, India. Miss Ella Ewing, of Jacksonville, Ill., goes to Africa. She is a graduate of Eureka College, Ill. George B. Baird, of Shelbyville, Ind., who attended the Bible College, Lexington, Ky., and takes the degree of A. B. from Butler College, Indianapolis, Ind., goes to China; John Lord, of Deer Island, N. B., who spent some time in Acadia University and also in the College of the Bible, Lexington, Ky., goes to the Philippines; Dr. W. C. Widdowson, of Indiana, Pa., a graduate of the medical college at Louisville, Ky., goes to Africa; Miss Mary Frances Lediard, of Owen Sound, Ont., goes to Japan; Raymond A. McCorkle and wife, graduates of Hiram College, Ohio, go to Osaka, Japan. F. L. Mendenhall, graduate of Auburn Theological Seminary, Auburn, N. Y., and wife go to China.

❦ ❦

Union Work in China.

I want to let you know how I appreciate THE CHRISTIAN-EVANGELIST. It is indeed a welcome visitor in this land, or rather a friend that I should miss very much if it failed to come each week.

Please permit me personally to express my joy and thankfulness for the stand you have taken in the various discussions that have claimed attention, especially in regard to "Christian union" and "federation" and the receiving of the Holy Spirit. My heart echoes a cordial "amen" to what I have read from your pen in THE CHRISTIAN-EVANGELIST. While I have not yet seen a copy of your book on the Holy Spirit, I praise God

for what has been read in your paper. I am glad to know from experience what it means to have the Holy Spirit dwelling within, as Comforter, Guide, Teacher, Keeper. He is very real to me, and since receiving him the Word has become wonderfully living, precious, helpful to me. Oh, if I only had words to tell what he has done for me! And of the marvelous way in which Jesus has led and kept and *answered prayer*, especially since I came to China. If there are any of our people who do not know what it is to be "filled with the Spirit" in "all his fulness" (and there are many lukewarm and lifeless professing Christians who are in that condition), my prayer is that their eyes may be opened and that they may see their blessed privilege, and "go up" and "take possession" of their full inheritance in Christ Jesus.

The "federation" movement is being watched with deep interest. Dr. Mullins' excellent paper gave me much joy. How we praise God for this spirit of union that is in the air everywhere. I always feel at home among the Baptists; I worked in a Baptist mission in Louisville, Ky., for several years. Brother Haley's paper caused another "hallelujah" (May 17, 24). If the homeland people only realized what union would mean to our work among the heathen! We have tried it here in a way no other mission has ever tried it. We have in our mission missionaries from 13 different denominations, and—would you believe it?—*without a word being said by any one*. Every one of the pedobaptist brethren, one by one, asked to be immersed, some before leaving Los Angeles, some after arriving in China, the last one being immersed about seven months after arriving here. And there are 42 missionaries in our mission. It is so blessed to see all of us together, partaking of the Lord's Supper—Friends, Baptists, Presbyterians, Methodists, Moravians, and all. Really, if we represented these different denominations, these heathen would think we were representing that many different gods.

To Brother Colby I should like to say: "Yes, the Word of God is more powerful than any two-edged sword, and God has promised that his Word shall not return void, but accomplish his purpose, but we here have *seen the quickening power of the Spirit* in converting heathen and strengthening or raising up these weak, stumbling, tempted babes in Christ."

Fifty-two applicants for one pulpit! Oh, my Father, how can these things be when *thousands* are dying in this land not having so much as heard that there is such a being as Jesus or the true God? Lord, open the eyes of thy people, give them a glimpse of our waiting Jesus, who can not return until we have witnessed in every nation; give them a vision of souls, lost souls, all over this world, going to a Christless grave and a hopeless eternity! Pray! He will answer.

In his glad service, "till he come," your sister South Chih-li Mission, Taiming-fu, North China, in Jesus, DRUSIE R. MALOTT.

❦ ❦

Texas Notes.

Your Texas Notes man has been too busy since the Waxahachie convention to make many notes. At the state convention a special campaign fund was subscribed and a stirring campaign has been on since. We have engaged such earnest and successful workers as A. D. Rogers, W. A. Boggess, V. L. Graves, E. C. Boynton, J. W. Marshall, E. O. Beyer, G. H. Morrison, B. F. Hall, S. D. Perkinson, J. R. Hodges, J. P. Holmes, J. C. Eubank, R. V. Small, J. R. Kelley, A. M. Shelton, C. C. Scitern and others, and no less than 40 "mission revivals" have been held. Success of the permanent kind has attended these efforts, for our evangelists are encouraged to "set in order the things that are wanting in the churches" where they labor; also to provide for regular teaching

Evangelistic

We invite ministers and others to send reports of meetings, additions and other news of the churches. It is especially requested that additions be reported as "by confession and baptism," or "by letter."

Special to THE CHRISTIAN-EVANGELIST.

Carney, Okla., August 27.—C. F. Trimble is holding meetings. Twenty-one additions in ten days. Ten last night. Trimble is great.—James Cage.

Special to THE CHRISTIAN-EVANGELIST.

Monroe, Wis., August 27.—Fifty-five added to-day in union meetings conducted by Scoville and Smith; 238 in two weeks. Whole community is stirred. United Christian work is a success. Praise God!—J. S. Berkey.

Special to THE CHRISTIAN-EVANGELIST.

California, Mo., August 26.—Forty-two additions to-night; 168 in meeting; all adults but three. Eighty-eight grown men. Country congregation of eighty joins here, making church of 248. Money being raised to build. Neither church nor Sunday-school when we began. H. J. Corwine, pastor California, inaugurated the work. Begin at Central, Toledo, O., September 2.—Allen Wilson and Linnt brothers, evangelists.

Illinois.

Greenville, Aug. 27.—One young lady added to our forces by primary obedience yesterday.—Tallie Defrees.

Cairo, Aug. 20.—O. D. Maple preached here August 19 when one was added by letter.

Tallula, Aug. 22.—We will begin a revival September 2, with Bro. Harold E. Monser at the helm. We solicit the prayers of God's people everywhere that we may have a great meeting. One baptism since last report. Work moving along well.—J. H. Henderson.

Indiana.

Elwood, Aug. 20.—Great interest in meeting at Harmony church and miles north of here. Brother Wittkamper is doing splendid work. He was assisted by Bros. Sellers, of Elwood, and C. H. DeVoe, of Peru, last Friday night. Twenty-eight added in 22 days. Will continue through Fair week, something unknown before.—H. B. Shields, Singer and helper.

Indian Territory.

Duncan, Aug. 21.—Closed meeting at Marlow Sunday night with 14 additions. Began here last night in large pavilion. Prospects for a good meeting are good. Plenty of antham in this country.—Charles Chasteen.

Kansas.

Manhattan, Aug. 20.—One by confession yesterday.—W. T. McLain.

Smith Center, Aug. 20.—Three added to the congregation at this place since last report; two by letter and one by baptism.—F. E. Blanchard.

Logan, Aug. 19.—We are just beginning a meeting here, with large audiences. Otha Wilkison is the evangelist. There is only a small band of Disciples here, but they are anxious to build up a strong congregation. This is Brother Wilkison's old home and people are flocking to hear him.

Hoisington, Aug. 24.—One added by statement and one by baptism this week. Three churches—M. E., W. B. and Christian—here held three Sunday night union services in August. The young peoples' societies also held union services. The meetings promoted a good feeling among the congregations.—F. M. McHale.

Kentucky.

Orangeburg, Aug. 20.—Two weeks' meeting closed last night. Geo. A. Miller, Covington, Ky., has done a great work for us. Thirty-three additions. Over $1,700 raised to repair church. Strong sentiment in favor of new church building.—H. M. Stansifer.

Germantown, Aug. 20.—Mark Collis of Lexington, Ky., recently closed a meeting of 18 days here with 73 additions; 48 by confession, the others by letter and statement. The success of this meeting was largely due to the efficient labors of the minister.—C. E. Miller.

Michigan.

Sault Sainte Marie, Aug. 22.—Two confessed their faith in Christ at the close of the service last Lord's day and were baptized the same hour. So far as I know these were the first baptized by the Disciples here. I go to Calumet, about 273 miles farther north, to hold a meeting for three weeks and will then return to this place to remain for some time.—R. Bruce Brown.

Missouri.

Festus, Aug. 20.—One addition by letter last Lord's day.—Daniel George Cole.

Festus, Aug. 27.—Two baptized into Christ yesterday. One sister much comforted by poem on last week's cover page.—Geo. G. Cole, minister.

Mayview, Aug. 23.—The meeting here is progressing very nicely. One confession Aug. 21. Three confessions Aug. 22. W. C. Cole, Jewell, Ia., doing the preaching.—Arthur Downs.

Dover, Aug. 26.—Meeting continues with unabated interest. Ten additions last night; 9 by confession and 1 reclaimed. Have been here 15 days and have had 49 additions; 43 by confession.—Stark and McRay.

Brunswick, Aug. 27.—Three added by letter since last report. Bro. R. E. L. Prunty, of Brookfield, will assist us in a series of gospel meetings beginning Sunday, September 2. We believe the field is white unto harvest.—E. H. Williamson.

Mt. Vernon, Aug. 23.—A splendid meeting with the Elm Branch church four miles north of Aurora is in progress under the direction of the Lawrence County Board. Bro. George Prewitt of the Aurora Church is doing the preaching. Twenty have made the good confession and the meeting only 8 days old. Our annual county convention will be held at Pierce City in October and prospects are good for an enthusiastic gathering, and a consequent larger work for the coming year.—H. A. Carpenter.

St. Joseph, Aug. 25.—Closed a two weeks' meeting with the second Creek Church, Platte county on last Monday night. The attendance and interest were fine. Three were baptized. A few weeks before the meeting began I baptized a man 79 years old. I preach for them twice a month. The church gave $7.88 to Home Missions and the Bible School, by the help of the church, gave over $30 to Foreign Missions.—N. R. Davis.

Oklahoma.

Chandler, Aug. 27.—Twenty-four added to date. Nine in the last three days. We continue.—Oscar Ingold.

Gage, Aug. 24.—Audiences fine notwithstanding the hot weather. Two added by statement last Sunday.—N. B. McGhee.

Sterling, Aug. 25.—I dedicated the new chapel of the Church of Christ here August 19 in presence of large audience and raised nearly $100 above all indebtedness. Preached a few nights and added ten to the congregation. Next meeting begins at Carnegie, O. T., September 1.—James W. Zachary.

Mulhall, Aug. 20.—Just closed a successful meeting at the Antioch Christian Church. My wife did the preaching and did it so well that the church was strengthened in faith. Twenty souls were added to its membership; 15 by baptism and five by statement. Our meeting is in progress here. Crowds and interest increasing.—James Mason and wife.

Cushing, Aug. 24.—I closed a three weeks' meeting at Friendship, Anderson county, on the 13th inst., with 30 additions; 19 by baptism, 11 otherwise. This church sent me out to preach the gospel over twelve years ago. It was a delightful vacation and privilege to be with these dear people again. Bro. C. F. McCall, of Columbia, Mo., is their efficient pastor.—C. E. Smootz.

Philippine Islands.

Vigan, June 27.—Three baptisms the last week here—one our first Turguian—a student in Bible College. Twenty-five preachers have found missionary association for this "Bulagaw district."—Hermon P. Williams.

Texas.

Harper, Aug. 24.—One baptism at Lipscomb, and Bible School organized.—M. B. Ingle.

Midweek Prayer-Meeting

September 5, 1906.

SIN AND THE WAY FROM IT.—
1 John 1:7-10.

"God of mercy, God of love,
  Hear our sad, repentant songs;
Listen to thy suppliant ones;
  Thou to whom all grace belongs.

"Deep regret for follies past,
  Talents wasted, time misspent;
Hearts debased by worldly cares,
  Thankless for the blessings sent."

The "new thought," the "later evangelism," nor anything else can supplant the old Gospel formula of escaping the practice and doom of sin, to-wit: Learning of Christ, faith, repentance, confession, baptism, and then to faith adding virtue, knowledge, temperance, patience, godliness, charity, love, and all the graces inculcated in the Bible.

We may differ in race, fortune, learning, ambition, ideals and character, but in one particular we are all alike—we all have sinned and come short of the glory of God. We may expect to be regarded as rich, learned or popular men who happen to be sinners, but he with whom we all have to do will treat us all alike—just as sinners who happen to be rich or poor, popular or obscure.

The sun-lit side of the planet is righteousness, the reverse side is sin. From this figure we must not infer we are of necessity half sinful and half righteous, for if we will have Father, Son and Holy Spirit come and abide in us they will, and our nature becomes changed from satellite to star, and we need be in no darkness at all, but altogether in the light of the glory of God as seen in the face of Jesus.

Not in restitution, penances, conformation to human codes of ethics, or the most approved asceticism is there forgiveness of sin or atonement for the transgressor. Either of these and all of them are inadequate without the addition of Jesus' blood. There could be no general remission of sin without the shedding of the blood of the Lamb of God, and there can be no special instance of it save by the application of the blood of Christ by the individual sinner and to his own needs.

Appeals to family love, pride of name, to avarice or ambition, are not the strongest inducement to one to enter upon the "white life." If all these have failed, then tell and retell of Jesus and his love for sinners so intense that even the death dew on Golgotha could not extinguish it. Tell and illustrate of a beauty and joy and helpfulness of a close walk with him, and soon love for Christ born in the heart of the sinner will expel the love of sin from the transgressor's heart and stay its practice.

Boys will rarely eat green apples if ripe ones are at hand. Few would be continually reaping the wages of sin if familiar with the peaceable fruits of righteousness. We may each keep multitudes from sin by illustrating in our lives the joy and contentment and power that comes from the daily exercise of faith and practice of Christianity. One uncured patient will deter many from the hospital, and halting disciples keep many from the Great Physician. One sensational cure will fill the doctor's waiting rooms, and a notable triumph of grace wrought in us will effect the release of many from the thrall of sin.

Sunday-School

September 9, 1906.

JESUS ENTERS IN TRIUMPH.—
Matt. 21:1-17.

Memory verses, 9-11.

Golden Text.—Blessed is he that cometh in the name of the Lord.—Matt. 21:9.

Passing through Jericho, where the incidents of the healing of blind Bartimaeus and the visit of Zacchaeus occurred, Jesus came at once into the vicinity of Jerusalem and stopped over the Sabbath at Bethany, where he had warm friends. This was the last Sabbath before the crucifixion. On that day he dined at the house of Simon "the leper" —perhaps a man whom Jesus had cured of leprosy and who had, therefore, like his fellow-townsman Lazarus, a lively sense of friendship and gratitude toward him. And it was at that dinner that Judas Iscariot protested agains the wicked waste of good ointment which was poured out upon the head of Jesus.

Lazarus also was present at this feast and John notes the fact that he was an object of great interest to the other guests, and that the priests planned to put him out of the way because his very existence, after his known death, was a piece of evidence which led many Jews to believe on Jesus. (Read Browning's poem entitled, "An Epistle Containing the Strange Medical Experience of Karshish the Arab Physician." It is an account of the supposed impression produced by Lazarus and his story upon a wandering physician many years after).

We come now to Passion Week. Before taking up the opening incident of it, note how the days of this week were spent—the greatest week of all human history.

Sunday—Triumph, the entry into Jerusalem.

Monday—Authority, cleansing the temple.

Tuesday—Conflict, argument with scribes and warning to disciples.

Wednesday—Retirement, no incidents recorded.

Thursday—The farewell, last supper.

Friday—Suffering, the crucifixion.

Saturday—The day in the tomb.

Sunday—The resurrection.

It was the week of the Passover and multitudes were coming to the feast. John says there was much speculation as to whether Jesus would come to the feast. People were eager to see him. Perhaps, too, they suspected the enmity of the priests and wondered whether he would dare to come.

The entry into Jerusalem was not an organized triumphal procession. It was a wholly spontaneous and impromptu demonstration. Jesus sent two disciples to bring an ass from a neighboring village. Probably the owner was a follower or a friend of Jesus, and the phrase "The Lord hath need of them" was meant for an explanation which would be entirely satisfactory to him and not as any magic to silence his objection.

It was no lapse into human vanity when Jesus consented for an hour to receive the acclamations of the populace. The day of his humiliation was at hand. The faith of his followers would be sorely tried. He wanted to give them every possible memory and association which would help them to be faithful through the dark hours. To have heard their Master hailed as king, to have seen the crowds spreading garments and garlands in his way as he entered Jerusalem

Christian Endeavor
By GEO. L. SNIVELY

September 9, 1906.

THE TRIUMPH OF CHRISTIANITY.
John, 12:32; 1 Cor. 15:20-28.

DAILY READINGS.

M. Triumphs of Grace. Eph. 2:1-9.
T. Triumph Over Death. John 10:17, 18.
W. Triumph Over Enemies. Psa. 110:1-7.
T. The Crowning Triumph. Zech. 14:3-11.
F. The Glory of God. Phil. 1:19-30.
S. The World's Homage. Isa. 45:20-25.
S. Triumph of Christianity. John .12:32.

"Hearken to him as he comes in his might,
Monarch of monarchs, victorious in fight;
Speaks he in anger, the sinner to blame?
Speaks he in sorrow, the dastard to shame?
With no reproach for blindness
He meets his own to-day,
In perfect loving-kindness
Thus only will he say."

When one given to equivocation and exaggeration becomes truthful, when the impatient becomes forbearing, and the bibulous and gluttonous, temperate, and charitable, we witness a triumph of Christianity more pleasing to the King than when a parliament adopts a resolution declaring a nation is no longer heathen, but Christian.

Seventy years ago John Williams was killed and eaten by New Hebrides cannibals. The recent religious conference held at Erromanga was opened with prayer by his murderer's son, who for years has been an elder in a Presbyterian church in that locality. Romance can not exceed in sensationalism these daily events in the conquest of this world by the Son of God.

The world's admiration for the man who in the rounds of humble usefulness is too pure to think evil, too kind to injure another, too honest to covet, too truthful to doubt that the golden age of man is in the future, even though he is sans wealth, learning, official ancestry, or social prestige, is a triumph of Christianity over worldliness great as that won by the sun over Boreas when genial rays unlock the frozen streams, fashion foliage in the trees, and cover the earth with verdure.

Christianity never won greater victories over heathenism in ancient times than the Associated Press dispatches report to us almost daily. The governor of Hunan recently gave $13,000 to the Christian Mission Hospital at Changsha. The first missionary entered the city 19 years ago, and was driven out by officials and priests. The change in this conservative people implied in this gift is almost incredible save by those who realize that it is in Christ's program to win this world to himself.

When Jesus triumphantly declared, "The gates of hades shall never prevail against my kingdom," perhaps he knew there would be 500,000 Christians in the world he came to redeem by the end of the first century, and 15,000,000 by the fifth, and 50,000,000 by the tenth, and 100,000,000 by the fifteenth, and 200,000,000 at the close of the eighteenth, and 350,000,000 now who have crowned him "Lord of all." Skepticism may never have blustered more than now, but it has never been more ineffectual.

One whose thoughts dwell constantly upon the humiliations in the palace of

Caiaphas, of the Praetorium, and Golgotha, is apt to become spiritually as they are physically who dwell in darkness and whose only light is that of a lamp. To be strong, buoyant and conquering we must also breathe the sunny atmosphere of victory. We must pursue the stricken temple traders, shout with those strewing garments and olive branches for the triumphal entry into Jerusalem, and above the tumult of the crucifixion hear the dying thief say, "Remember me when thou comest into thy kingdom"; and the Centurion's "Surely this is a son of the gods."

❋ ❋

End-of-the-Week Rates.
Chicago and North-Western Railway.

From Chicago to near-by summer resorts. Tickets at special low rates on sale Friday, Saturday and Sunday, good until the following Monday to return. Other low rates in effect daily. For tickets, rates and booklets giving full information, apply to nearest ticket agent or address W. B. Kniskern, P. T. M., C. & N. W. R'y Co., Chicago.

People's Forum

Concerning Preparation for the Ministry.

The following correspondence has come into our hands, and we venture to publish it in the interest both of our Bible colleges and of young men who are seeking to prepare themselves for the ministry of the Word:

W. J. Lhamon, Columbia, Mo.

Dear Brother:—Will you please send to my address one of your catalogs? I am contemplating going to school somewhere next September. I am undecided yet as to where I shall attend. I will continue my preaching. I will have to have a position with a salary of $800. And I am going to investigate the matter. I have done fine work at this place. My regular pastoral work has added 25 to our church roll, besides those taken in at the time of our meeting. I have been here 10 months. Hope to gain others before the close of the year. Trusting that I may be able to hear from you soon, I am yours in his name. Yours fraternally,

X. Y. Z.

REPLY TO THE ABOVE.

Dear Brother X. Y. Z.:—Your favor is in hand and noted. I am sending you a catalog and some circulars.

As to position, allow me to say that a number of churches within reach of Columbia are in need of good men, but I fear it would be some time before you could reach $800 as a student. If you go to these churches and take care of them they will, as a rule, I believe, support you as well as they can, and that is all a man ought to ask while he is in school. A young man in the ministry who has the spirit of the Master will not rate himself by the salary he gets. If you are unmarried you can get through a year in Columbia on $200 to $300. Many get through on much less than $200. We have more than a thousand men in Columbia preparing for law and medicine and engineering and agriculture, etc., who do not dream of earning a cent in their professions till they have graduated and are really ready for work. Why, then, should a young minister expect to go to school and receive practically a full salary at the same time? If you really want an education more than you want money, we have from four to twenty years of work for you in Columbia. Meanwhile, if you are worth anything to the surrounding churches, you can live while you are studying, and if you are unusually able and fortunate you can save something. In either case you will be better off than hundreds of men who are preparing for other lines of work. That you have succeeded in your present work is to your credit, and I rejoice with you. But it argues nothing with respect to your accomplishments in academic and Biblical studies. Many a man succeeds in spite of his limitations. If so it is one of the best reasons why he should seek to be a "finished" man, and scholar, and preacher. I have spoken plainly but kindly, and I am sure you will appreciate it. I shall hope to hear from you again, and we shall rejoice if you decide to come to Columbia in the spirit of an earnest and self-sacrificing man of God. Very truly and fraternally,

Dean W. J. Lhamon.

News From Many Fields.

(Continued from Page 1114.)

started to tell your readers about the camp meeting. The meeting was held under the district tent, seating comfortably 800 people, and it was often crowded to overflowing. J. N. Wooten is pastor of the Christian Church. J. W. Marshall and E. O. Beyer were the evangelists. H. E. Luck and the writer took part of the burden of teaching and preaching. Three of the ministers of Hereford preached each one or more times. No agreement was entered into. We invited the ministers of the denominations to preach, and feel at liberty to choose their own way. The best of feeling prevailed; not an adverse criticism was heard. All worked and prayed for the salvation of souls. It was clearly demonstrated that brethren with widely differing views can work harmoniously together; also that the one-man pull on the congregation is not essential to success. It was universally conceded that this was the most successful meeting held here for years.

Bro. B. B. Sanders, former corresponding secretary of Texas, is in constant demand as an evangelist, and seldom fails of a successful meeting. At our state convention 25 new preachers were introduced to the convention, and half as many more have come into the state within the last year. Still there is room for faithful, God-fearing, industrious ministers who have succeeded elsewhere and can afford to do hard work for $600 to $1,000 per annum. The large places are easily filled. We need some ordinary men.

Our receipts for Texas missions so far this summer are above the receipts for the same time last summer. We want our people to do their duty by church extension, and then get ready for the largest offering for state missions in November ever made in Texas, or for that matter in any other state. We confidently expect this to be the case. Our people are unusually prosperous. There is no finer field for the old Gospel than Texas. Now is the time to meet the great growth of the state and give newcomers a Gospel welcome.

Quite a number of Texas people are expecting to go to Buffalo. We leave Texas via the Missouri, Kansas & Texas Railroad, and hope to go out of St. Louis on The Christian-Evangelist Special over the Wabash route. The writer will take pleasure in securing accommodations en route, if the request is made in time. The churches should each send a delegate, and if your pastor is a married man, send two. Write me to-day if you think of going.

J. C. Mason.

Station A, Dallas, Texas.

Northeast Arkansas Calls You.

Still we need men for giving the Gospel to this part of our great state. How many? Well, we have four county-seats where we have lots paid for, and a faithful band needing a capable leader; there are two places where men are needed for full time where we have good buildings; there are several towns where we have good buildings, that need a minister for part time, with other good towns near them that ought to co-operate that they may mutually assist each other in the support of a preacher so that no congregation be left without care and time and money be not wasted by unnecessary traveling. In our Northeast Arkansas Missionary district of twenty-one counties, we have but eight preachers of the co-operative class that give themselves wholly to this holy ministry. We need so much men who come determined by his grace and the forbearance of the faithful to stay. We need princely men; men who can endure hardness, as a good stoldier of our Christ. Brothers Browning, State Cor. Sec., Jessup of Little Rock, Ballard at Texarkana, Ragland at Fayettesville, Edmondson, of Fort Smith—these all came years ago, and they have remained, and the work is established in their towns. By faithful continuance in well-doing in hope Brothers Creel, Crank, Pedrick, Kincaid, Ellis, Cross and others in the State may do similar work and accomplish the same kind of results. There is no co-operative minister now laboring in this district that has been in his present charge quite one year. I have been in the state over six years, and during that time no preacher has continued in one charge as long as two years. We need permanency in the ministerial supply in this country. Arkansas is not educating her young men for the ministry, and so we have to look to other places for our supply. Salaries for our work here are not large. Perhaps if we had better preaching we might have better pay. The "laborer is worthy of his hire;" but his salary often needs to be higher than it is. This state is one of wonderful natural resources, *the most resourceful*, I think, in the Union. Land that sold for $5 or $10 per acre a few years ago, this season will *net* from $25 to $45 per acre; and this mainly on raw prairie sod. Corn will yield 50 to 75 bushels per acre. Cotton on bottom land produces from three-fourths to one and a half bales per acre. The ground that grows it rents for from $5 to $7 per acre, cash. Market-gardening, dairying, fruit and berry raising, can all be made very profitable. Live stock, such as cattle, sheep, Angora goats are profitable investments. Our summers are pleasant, the winters are mild, and the health of *all temperate people* is good. I have been here over six years, and our health is as good as it ever was back in our dear "old Kentucky home." Everything considered, good homes can be had cheap. This is a land of fine timber. The mills have helped to make it easy to clear up a good farm for cultivation. Much overcut lands are for sale; partially improved lands are easily obtained; well improved farms can be bought at fair prices. The country is settling up rapidly. Homeseekers and investors come chiefly from Missouri, Illinois, Indiana, Ohio, Iowa, Kentucky and Tennessee.

What we need and are longing for now are pastor-evangelists to help us take this district for our Christ, and to enlarge our population from a good class of citizens to strengthen our present membership, and to share in the rapidly increasing prosperity now on.

Preaching brethren who want to consider this call, will please get a letter from their home congregation, and also from their state or district corresponding secretary, or board, and sent to me or bring along with them any time they decide to come to look the country over. Any who write me, will please send stamp for reply.—James H. Brooks, Cor. Sec., Blytheville, Ark., Box 24.

Stock Ranch

1285 ACRES IN COLORADO

ONLY $21 AN ACRE.

Miles of wire fencing and 10,000 acres of adjacent wild grazing land (5,000 acres additional can be bought—good colony proposition). Great opportunity for a stockman. Occupied as a CATTLE AND HAY RANCH the past seven years by the owner. By reason of health of family must be sold for less than value. 300 ACRES UNDER IRRIGATION (own ditch); grows all sorts of grain, alfalfa, sugar beets, vegetables. Well improved, residence, reservoir, stables; 800 acres fenced pasture. For whole land and improvements only $27,000. Two and four miles from railway stations; 500 miles from Kansas City. Other improved small farms and large ranches—20 acres to 2,000 acres—at $10 to $100 an acre; both irrigated and grazing land. Settled neighborhood, with schools, churches, etc. Address R. A. MATHEWS, 134 Monroe street, Chicago.

Some Missouri Notes.

The Pettis county convention was held at Green Ridge, August 20-21. It was a grand good convention, well attended, good work done, and a brighter future for us.

We preached at Atlantic, Ia., August 19. They have a beautiful new house in which to worship. They are still without a pastor. They extended me a call, but we have not yet decided to accept. They are a grand people there. We enjoyed our visit with them.

B. F. Hill, as preacher, with L. D. Sprague as singer, both of California, Mo., have been engaged to hold us a meeting in October. We are praying for and expecting a great meeting.

D. L. Ammons, of Plattsburg, Mo., preached at Lamonte, Mo., August 19, and attended the county convention at Green Ridge. Brother Ammons can be secured as pastor of some good church in Missouri. Write him.

Revival meetings at Houstonia in progress now. Brother Briney, of Lexington, is doing the preaching.

W. A. Fite delivered a masterly address on Federation at our county convention. We wish all Missouri could have heard it. I hope he will publish it.

Word has reached us that Brother Abbott, our corresponding secretary, is very ill. We pray God to bless and restore him to health, and to us.

Hope to secure a number of new subscribers for The Christian-Evangelist soon as I can get around to see the parties. The hope is to place a good paper in every home. I have The Christian-Evangelist, "The Standard" and "The Century," also "The Union" of Des Moines. I would sooner have them than four preachers, for they do not eat, nor sleep, and they speak so many good things to us. Try one or two and see.—I. H. Fuller, Lamonte, Mo.

Current Literature

LIVING IN THE SUNSHINE. By Hannah Whitall Smith. (Fleming H. Revell Company, New York. Price, $1 net. Pages, 254.)

The silver-haired author of this book has made a study and a practice of the Christian's secret of a happy life. The object of her new book is to help those who have, as D. L. Moody used to say, "just enough religion to make them miserable." Mrs. Smith has for years lived close to God. She has had a wide experience of the world and its people. She has been a worker on behalf of her sex and in the temperance cause. Her own assurance can not but be helpful to one in doubt, and we therefore cordially commend this book.

✦

FAULTY DICTION; or Errors in the Use of the English Language and How to Correct Them. By Thomas H. Russell, LL. B. (George W. Ogilvie & Co., publishers. Price, 25c, cloth bound; 50c Russia leather.)

The best of us make occasional slips in the use of the English language. Some of us who know better constantly make errors that have perhaps been acquired by mere habit or environment. "If I were her"; "Was it him?"; "Who war it by?"; "Let you and I go"; "You are younger than me"; "Between you and I," and such phrases are heard constantly and are passed as slips of the tongue, and yet so common are they that many people look upon these improper forms as being the correct ones. Mr. Russell has done a needed service in producing this little book. It can be carried in the vest pocket, and will help the best educated of us to a better knowledge of a language which is, at its easiest, difficult in its grammatical construction and hopeless in its spelling. There are over a thousand headings treated in the book, under some of which—plurals, for instance—over 50 errors that are not at all unusual will be found illustrated and corrected.

✦

THE PAROCHIAL SCHOOL: A CURSE TO THE CHURCH, A MENACE TO THE NATION. By Rev. Jeremiah H. Crowley, author and publisher, 1113 Shiller Building, 103-109 East Randolph street, Chicago, Ill.

This is the fourth edition of this most remarkable work—remarkable from the fact that it is not written by an "ex-priest," but by one who maintains his position in the Roman Catholic Church and declares himself as a thorough believer in the divine mission of that church. He writes, as "a Catholic priest and an Ameri-

can citizen," warning the people of the United States against the dangerous encroachments of Roman Catholics on our public schools, and warning the church especially against the immorality, not to say the moral rottenness, of a part of the Catholic priesthood of America. The revelations in this volume would be incredible did they not come from one whose character and aim are vouched for by men of high rank and standing in the Roman Catholic Church. The information contained in this volume ought to be in possession of the American people, and yet it is difficult to see how it is to get there except through the circulation of this volume, for the daily press and public officials, generally, are very chary about any public utterance that antagonizes so powerful a political force in this country as the Roman Catholic Church. And yet why should this be so, in the case of a book of this kind, which is not antagonizing the church, in which the author thoroughly believes, but is opposing its flagrant corruptions and abuses? Referring to his charges, he says: "If I have falsified, why do they not investigate and prove me false? But I have not. My charges are supplemented by willing and credible witnesses, names and dates. I am not fighting my church, and never will. I am fighting the evil men who, in this diocese at least, are sapping her power, dishonoring her sanctuaries, and blaspheming the God of all Christians. If that be a crime I do not understand what loyalty, decency, and virtue mean." But Father Crowley has had no trial, and will not be given an opportunity of proving the truth of his charges. His efforts in exposing these abuses in the Roman Church, especially as they relate to our public school system and free government, should receive the sympathy and aid of all good American citizens, regardless of creed or party.

✦

JESUS: AN UNFINISHED PORTRAIT. By Charles Van Norden. (Funk & Wagnalls, publishers. Pages, 295. Price, $1 net.)

We find ourselves unable to agree with this Unitarian author in some of his conclusions, but we must readily accord to him the gift of a pleasant style, a simple treatment and a high ideal. Dr. Van Norden has produced a readable book, and we are glad that he has called his picture an unfinished one. This makes us hopeful that he may some day come to see in the Man of Nazareth the real divinity that is of the Father. He accepts almost all that the trinitarian might say of Jesus, except that he was the Son of God. This book is the summing up of 35 years of study, and is an effort to present the real Man—his actual teachings and the bearing of his life upon present religious problems. He explains the miraculous on the modern ground of telepathy, hypnotism, clairvoyance and other psychic powers which he believes Jesus had to an unusual degree. Of course this necessitates attributing many of the wonderful things that are associated with Christ to a combination of credulity and devotion on the part of his followers. The spirit of the writer may be seen in the following paragraphs from his last chapter:

"It is easy to cut the Gordian knot by saying that he was God incarnate; that would begin and end the matter, and there would be nothing to wonder at and nothing to explain; then, superlative qualities of mind and heart would be matter of course, quite to have been expected, and this book an impertinence, a folly stupendous, and nothing short of blasphemy.

"But assuming him to be a veritable man, inbreathed of the Spirit of God, yet still himself, humanity appears in him expanding in sublime possibilities, and in our very failure satisfactorily to analyze, we take courage, aspire and strive."

OBITUARIES.

[Notices of Deaths, not more than four lines, inserted free. Obituary memoirs, one cent per word. Send the money with the copy.]

LOWTHER.

Little Jewel Lowther was called to be one of the gems in her Savior's crown August 21, 1906. She was a faithful member of the Bible school and Junior C. E. of the Fourth Christian Church, St. Louis, Mo. Funeral service by pastor E. J. McFarland.

The Home Department

The Sunset Limited.

Oh, Hush-a-bye Land is a beautiful place
For sleepy small people to go,
And the Rock-a-bye Route is the favorite one
With a certain wee laddie I know.

The track lies on sleepers of feathers and down,
No accidents ever take place;
Though there's only one track, and there's only
one train,
But it runs at a wonderful pace.

There are beautiful things to be seen, on this
route,
If you're good you may take just a peep;
But strange as it seems, they are seen best in
dreams;
Be sure that you soon go to sleep.

Say good-night to the Sun, for he's off to bed,
too—
He can't hear you, so just wave your hand;
The Moon and the Stars they will light up the
cars
As you travel to Hush-a-bye Land.

So, quck, jump aboard, it is time to be off,
You have nothing to pay, you young elf;
Just think of the luxury, laddie, you'll have—
A whole sleeping-car to yourself!
—*Booklovers' Magazine.*

The Bronze Vase.

BY J. BRECKENRIDGE ELLIS.

PART III.

CHAPTER IX.

It was the first rain since the covered wagon had left Kansas City. It had begun heavily in Jefferson City, and the respite of a few hours only emphasized its renewed attack. As the horses plodded eastward, the wheels began to sink in the yielding earth. The air grew chilly—cold enough for Mrs. Weed to have a fire, but not cold enough for the others to enjoy the heated coal stove. Darkness came early, but Wizzen drove on; he knew the way. Night came. At last several lights were to be seen far away to their left. "The river's over there," said Wizzen to Raymund, who sat beside him; "that there's the town that them which lives in it call it Frog Bend, though that ain't its proper name. It's a nickname, that's what I call it; that's my expression for it, a nickname." Wizzen almost chuckled as if he had just invented a word; but the chuckle did not come to perfection because he was so unusually despondent. Wizzen had so arranged the canvas that it projected over the front seat and kept the rain out at the sides, and Raymond felt that if it didn't matter about Wizzen's legs, it didn't about his own. He called to Rhoda that over yonder were the lights of Frog Bend. "The place where Mr. Willby lives?" said Rhoda. "I wonder if we will ever go there?"

"Mr. Willby meant it when he invited us," said Raymund. "If uncle William won't let us stay with him, we'll try Frog Bend and see how we like it."

Wizzen spoke up, trying to be cheerful; " that's what I love in moving about. You have the pick of the hull earth, and if you don't like one locality, you kin hike out—which I am taking for granted that you have some way of doing your hiking—and go to another place. That's what I like about the old lady. She don't keer where I take her, her mind is a regular variety, just like mine." Rhoda might have told him of Mrs. Weed's longing for a spot she could call home, but the girl was too loyal to the old lady to betray her confidence. She stared hard at the distant lights of Frog Bend, and when they were out of sight, drew back into

the wagon. When they stopped at last, it was still raining and all four were obliged to sleep in the wagon. Wizzen showed great skill in piling up the many objects in the wagon to get them out of the way. He made a partition dividing the wagon into two chambers; the partition was formed of the goods boxes, the gasoline stove, the tables and the spring wagon seat. The tank was taken off the gasoline stove and put in the end box of the wagon, for the coal stove threatened a conflagration. Then Wizzen and Raymund curled up in their clothes in the end next the front, and Rhoda and Mrs. Weed lay at the back end. Mrs. Weed had put too much coal in the stove (Wizzen remarked that her eyes had been too big for her stomach) and all four lay sweltering in torrid heat, while the rain beat upon their canvas-ceiling. Occasionally Wizzen would cautiously raise a flag for air, whereupon Mrs. Weed would sneeze just as if a spring had been touched. Rhoda, unable to sleep, lay thinking about Mrs. Weed's having a daughter in the penitentiary, and about Wizzen being the husband of that confined lady. The penitentiary had never entered Rhoda's life before in the most remote manner, and it made her think that she had fallen in with very low people, indeed. While she appreciated Wizzen's kindness, and Mrs. Weed's good heart, it seemed very pathetic that she and Raymund so far removed from the other two in training and experience, should be thus spending their days in such intimate proximity. To Raymund it was different, because he looked upon the "overland voyage" as a sort of camping out expedition, a species of adventure. To Rhoda it seemed a piece of their real lives. Wizzen could not sleep, and in his tossings, rendered more violent because he lay quite still as long as he could, then plunged for relief, he endangered the barricade. More than once his foot rattled the gasoline stove and made the tables threaten to fall down upon somebody. Rhoda thought, "No doubt he's thinking about his wife in prison!" and the very thought made her shrink from the nearness of Wizzen.

Suddenly Mrs. Weed grasped Rhoda's arm and said. "Light the lantern!" Rhoda was frightened, but there was no use asking the deaf old lady for a reason, so she hastened to obey. Mrs. Weed sat up in her night cap, then sank down and said hurriedly, "Rhoda, go over there to the bureau and get me that—" She paused for the word. Of course there was no bureau, and Rhoda looked about blankly.

"That—that—" Mrs. Weed was still struggling for the word, and it was evident to the girl that she was suffering greatly. Mrs. Weed nodded her nightcap faintly toward the spot where one of the goods boxes had stood. "That—that—" she said feebly. "Oh, what do you call it—the colorless liquid that smells—in the little box-bottle—Rhoda, call Wizzen—he will know what I want!"

"Camphor!" cried Wizzen, who was already upon his feet. "Mrs. Weed has one of her sinking spells," he went on in a hurried voice. "She gits powerful low, and the camphor is in this lowest box." He indicated one of the goods boxes at the bottom of the temporary partition. "Here, Raymond, git ready to ketch the table if it starts to fall! Rhoda, put on some water to heat, as quick as

you kin, and the flat iron to heat the fire!" Wizzen tugg and the table fell. Ra and that turned over and smashed into the Wizzen plunged over th tition and applied the Weed's nose. Mrs. We voice, "It is the dinne sent us to-day." She Willby. She whispered Oh, Wizzen, put som rag and hold it to n you've been mighty go "Shuck!" said Wizzen "Here, Rhoda, you sit Rhoda, frightened and down beside the pal sprang to the stove iron. It was not h shook the little stove, another box. Almost turned, saying, "Rhoda how to clap on me Rhoda shook her head out of the way. I'm knows how to be a lady according as circum either gender. It can't s ute, the old lady is so but something has to

time he was talking, Wizzen was rapidly at work. Mrs. Weed, as pale as death, lay quite motionless. "I know where to put my finger right on the heart of the trouble," muttered Wizzen, never stopping an instant, "which it is only fair to say there is that in her stomach which had of rights best be elsewhere, but strength will not always permit a discarding of what is not necessary. Now, we'll take off the plaster, and if the iron is het—" He had plunged the iron into the burning coals. As it gave forth a grateful little sigh when tested by moisture Wizzen wrapped it up in newspapers and applied it to Mrs. Weed's person.

"If we only had a doctor!" murmured Raymund.

"Don't be wishing the old lady no harm," said Wizzen. "When the water's het it will bring her round. This is one of her worst spells and we'll have to use it inside and outside. You say water is just a part of nature. Well, what of it? They is no doctor like nature. Nature never had to go to school, for what is knowed, it knowed." Wizzen was excited and seemed disposed to be quarrelsome, but that was only because he was uneasy. When the iron grew cool the water was "ready," so he saturated a cloth in it and having wrapped it in a newspaper, brought it to bear upon the afflicted portion of Mrs. Weed. At last the old lady sighed and said, "I am just a speck better, Wizzen—dear Wizzen! I am so much trouble to you."

"Trouble nothing!" said Wizzen rudely. "Got that pain?"

"Awful—it's awful," said Mrs. Weed, who could not hear, but who understood well enough what he had said.

"I'll fix you," muttered Wizzen, and darting to the medicine chest, as such the goods box was proving to be, he brought forth a small pill box. He held up his mother-in-law's head and the pill was swallowed by means of the hot water. "Get down as much of this water as you can," said Wizzen, as he held the cup to the blue lips. It was not long after that before color stole to the shriveled cheeks, and Mrs. Weed became strong and began to talk. Her eyes were very bright, and seeing Rhoda beside her, she took the girl's hand in a hot clasp saying, "Why, Lizzie! It's you, Lizzie, it's you! I didn't know it was Lizzie!" Her voice sounded indescribably pathetic, it was so joyous, yet afraid. "Can it be Lizzie? I know it is Lizzie!" Rhoda sat quite still.

"You won't go away again, will you, Lizzie?" said Mrs. Weed, beseechingly. "Tell me you won't go away again! We've looked for you day after day. The police have hunted. The newspapers have advertised. Oh we don't care where you've been, if you'll only stay. Won't you stay?" The large, beseeching eyes turned upon Rhoda, made her chill with fear.

"Don't you mind," Wizzen muttered. "She'll go to sleep pretty soon, and if you move it'll spoil her chances. Nod your head to her."

"Lizzie, he's the best man that ever lived," the eager voice went on. "He hasn't ever said a word against you, not a word. He just hunts, hunts, his face looking so full of pain—"

Wizzen muttered, "She's talking about one of her old neighbors. Simmons, his name is. Mighty active he was, when Lizzie run off."

"If you knew him like I do, Lizzie," said Mrs. Weed, still grasping Rhoda's hand, "you wouldn't ever want to go anywhere but to kneel at his feet to be forgiven. But he would lift you up. He loves you so much that he has taken me in as if I were his own mother."

"Yes," muttered Wizzen, "Simmons was a mighty fine sort of chap."

"Won't you stay, Lizzie?" Rhoda nodded her head emphatically. "God bless you, my child! There's not another man in th world would treat you as he will. I used to think you had married out of your station, but although he isn't educated, his heart is pure gold, and I want you to stay with me, 'May the good Lord bless Wizzen!' Won't you say that, darling?"

Rhoda looked over at the man, tears shining in her blue eyes, and she said softly, "May the good Lord bless Wizzen!" Wizzen turned hastily away and seen the movement of Rhoda's lips, and quite content, she fell asleep. They watched beside her through the night, taking turn about. At break of day she woke up, and her pain and fever were gone. Wizzen hovered over her, the ear-trumpet in his hand.

"Ah, Wizzen," sighed the old lady, "I am as good as new now, but I have been dreadful trouble to you-all!"

Wizzen put the trumpet to her ear and said, "Well, mother, it's trouble taking care of you, but it's just as it would be trouble taking care of a gold mine if I had it. I ain't got one, which I needn't say, but I've got you, which I would rether!"

The old lady's eyes filled with grateful tears, and she patted the puckered and dry, stubby face of Wizzen. It was the first time Rhoda or Raymund had ever heard him call her "mother," and it was evident that he had worked hard in stringing himself up to the necessary ten-

sion in order to sound out that note of tenderness, for he immediately, as it were, let go of the peg, and unslacked. "We'll lay by here a day," he said through the trumpet, "till you are completely fixed over which the horses is almost as tuckered out as you, and then we'll travel. And I want to say right now, old lady, that as long as I live and have strength,' I'll keep a-moving and a-carrying you from place to place, and giving you variety continual and everlasting." And he slapped his blue-trowsered leg with the air of a man who means every word he says.

(TO BE CONTINUED.)

❀ ❀ ❀

50 More Young People

Fifty More Young People can get special rates for room, board and tuition at *Iowa Christian College.* Home study courses also. New illustrated catalog ready. Write Pres. Chas. J. Burton, Oskaloosa, Iowa.

June in India.

BY ADELAIDE GAIL FROST.

The standard coin of India is a silver piece called the rupee; it is worth about one-third of our dollar. There are sixteen annas in a rupee and proportionate comparisons are generally expressed in terms of this coin, for instance "an eight anna crop" is a half crop, a "twelve anna" one, a yield of three-fourths. Kipling says: "No man can toil eighteen annas in the rupee in June without suffering,'" which is to say a man should not overwork in the last hot days before the rains and the first stressful ones waiting for the clouds to come with refreshing for "the used up, over handled earth under foot." We long for the days when "the rain among the trees says, 'Hush, hush, hush,'" and now the clouds are rolling up and we hope and hope. Our epidemic of smallpox is over in the Orphanage with only one death and that of a weak little child, measles reign in the place of smallpox and one of our dear, young girls has "slipped away" with that disease and the sick room is full. One of our best girls was laid away day before yesterday after a struggle of less than six hours with the dread cholera. She was taken sick on the morning side of midnight and was unconscious and dying before six o'clock. This disease is epidemic in the town, of an unusually fatal type it seems, but we pray it may not spread in our large family and with one good doctor and unusually good sanitation—for India—we try to "trust and not be afraid." We had a June wedding on the first anniversary of Mr. and Mrs. Gordon's wedding far away in Des Moines. Jangi, one of the first graduates from the Bible College in Jubbulpore and Biti, one of our girls whom he has known a long time as he is a Mahoba boy, were the happy pair. Mr. and Mrs. Gordon gave a dinner *on the floor* of our dining room to the grown Christians. White table cloths were spread upon the carpet and we sat about and partook of good Indian dishes with our respectable fingers, sitting on our own respectable feet, if not occasionally on the same members of others, for space was limited, but it was a merry dinner and the "fragments" fed the hungrier afterwards. The bride was a fashionable Hindu bride to the extent of partaking of nothing whatever; she simply sat and looked pretty and shy in her soft white mull draperies.

We had a singing practice in our dining room last night and there were three "*dhols*," or native drums and Mr. Gordon's concertina upon which he plays the native airs very well. They sang with spirit enough to *almost* increase the vibration of the punkah swinging overhead. This is an attempt at translating one of the songs with a tune that is very popular with both us and the natives. It has such a thrilling swing, and spite of its plain talk does not seem to be offensive to native audiences.

Refrain: My heart falls at the feet of Jesus.

    Some wear the rosaries of prayer,
    Some in their foreheads place the sacred sign,
    Some wind about them ropes of hair,
    And some, the cord of Brahman line.

    Some smear with ashes all their limbs,
    Some are with deer skin ever found,
    Some wear the blanket coarse and black,
    Some crawl as snakes do on the ground.

    Some worship gods and goddesses,
    Some bathe where Ganges' water flows,
    Some sprinkle water by the peepul tree,
    Some call and feed the hungry crows.

    Some wander in the jungles wild,
    Some hold their arms as sticks held out,
    Some sit where burn five fires,
    I flee, I flee, from things of doubt.

    The servants of the Lord beseech,
    Hear men and women, young and old,
    Jesus Christ has saved us all,
    No longer shall doubt's dreams enfold!

I will try to explain some of the references. The prayer beads, usually of wood, are used to count the "vain repetitions" of the names of their gods. What habit does it suggest which now exists in Christian lands in the Church of Rome? The "sacred signs," or tilak, in the forehead of idolaters indicates the special god chosen as patron; there are different symbols for different gods. Some of these "marks of the beast" are brilliantly red and sanguinary looking, giving a ferocious cast to the face. The ropes of hair, called the seli (sa-lie) are usually made from the tail of the sacred cow, and are repulsive looking. The Brahminical cord is worn by that caste, and at the time of the investiture of a Brahman lad there are special ceremonies. It is worn next the skin and is often the only clothing of the upper part of the body of that sacred (?) caste. How ghastly the holy (?) men look, smeared with ashes. Thousands of men are wandering over India in this hideous state, their bodies quite naked, except for the loin cloth, and rubbed in ashes. The deer skin is a sure sign of a Hindu devotee, and they sit upon them while worshiping. The black blanket adds to the terrible appearance of the ash-covered sadhus. Sometimes in the cool season we often see men measuring their length in the dust en route to some place of idolatry. This snake-like movement is often seen in Deogarh.

The first two lines of the third stanza are plain. The peepul tree, my teacher explained to me, is the Brahman among trees. It is worshiped by circumambulation. They usually go around it seven times, sprinkling water from a brass jar. Brass and gold are sacred metals.

Many sadhus, or holy men, live in wild, jungley places, on rocky hills and in the desert. I have seen devotees who have held their arms straight up until they are quite stiff and can not be changed; the nails are allowed to grow. Often up on our lake front I see some pilgrim sadhu sitting surrounded by his five smoky fires in the burning heat of the day! This is to "mortify the flesh." Through a hideous wilderness of lies and corruption so many of our brothers are crawling like dumb beasts, and the day hastes away in which we may help

them. You will be glad to know that a young man who had started to be a sadhu is now a member of the church in Mahoba. He became a Christian only a few months ago, since Mr. Gordan came, and seems to have very thoroughly left old things behind him.

Picture of War Engine "General."

A beautiful colored picture, 18x25 inches, of the historic old engine "General" which was stolen at Big Shanty, Ga., by the Andrew's Raiders during the Civil War, and which is now on exhibition in the Union Depot, Chattanooga, Tenn., has been gotten out by the NASHVILLE, CHATTANOOGA & ST. LOUIS RY.—The "Battlefields Route" to the South. The picture is ready for framing and will be mailed for 25c. The "Story of the General" sent free. W. L. Danley, Gen'l Pass. Agent, Nashville, Tenn.

Forgive Me, Dear.

BY MARY HEWITT STURDEVANT.

If ever I were cold to you
　(Sometimes I think you thought me so),
Or if in all you tried to do
　Full sympathy I did not show;
If quick to blame and slow to praise,
　Or if I teased one bitter tear,
Oh, in these clearer visioned days,
　My heart cries out, "Forgive me, dear."

Life's lesson learning year by year
　My soul has gained a wider view
Of what I might have been to you,
　The tenderer words I did not say,
The smiles you looked for but in vain—
　They haunt me with regretful pain,
And from a contrite heart I pray
　"Forgive me, dear! Forgive me, dear!"

Happiness.

BY J. M. LOWE.

Her house was little and old. It was innocent of paint or style or ornament. The surroundings were unattractive. But within, neatness and order reigned supreme. Her face was bright, her person neatly gowned and her laugh was natural and free. Her two children were bright and well behaved. She was a good mother. She was a child with them. It was refreshing to hear her prattle as she told them of the pictures and provoked them to wild and happy laughter by her cute and childish antics. She loved them and showed her love by kindly word and helpful deed. They were in her heart.

She was industrious and cheerful. Her well papered walls, well swept floors and tidy, kitchen, told how well she used the broom and scrub brush. Her industry kept the cobwebs out of her house and her cheerfulness kept them out of her mind.

It was a singular example of overcoming conditions. It showed clearly that happiness is from within, not without, and may reign everywhere. I wondered how many people of mansion and palace might learn from this busy little woman the lesson of joy and contentment. Not all the joy is behind palace walls nor all the misery in the cot. Both are from within and come at the bidding of the glad or gloomy soul. It all depends upon whether we are slaves to conditions or masters of them.

The secret of her happiness was her love which forgot self in the service of others. I am afraid those who are pining for better conditions will still be pining when the better conditions have come. Be happy now or never.

An Incomplete Story.

"Goin' far, mister?"

They were in a third-class compartment of one of the expresses running from London to Liverpool. The question was asked by a long-nosed, thin-lipped man with pointed chin, scanty whiskers, a slouch hat, and a hungry expression of countenance. He was resting his feet on the opposite seat of the carriage, which seat was partly occupied by a passenger in a gray check suit. The passenger addressed turned partly round, and took a look at his questioner.

"Yes, I am going to Crewe," he replied. "My business there is to sell four shares of bank stock, dispose of my interest in a farm of 80 acres, 10 miles from the town, and invest the proceeds in a clothing establishment. I am from St. Albans, in Hertfordshire. I got into the train there at 9:32 o'clock this morning. It was 49 minutes behind time. My ticket from Euston cost me 13s 6d. Had my breakfast about an hour ago.

Paid 1s 6d for it. This cigar cost me 3d, or five a shilling. I have been a smoker for about 13 years. My name is Thomas Williams. I am 39 years old, have a wife and four children, and am a member of the Congregational Church. I was formerly a chemist, but sold out to a man named Treadway, and I am not in business now. I am worth perhaps 2,000 pounds. My father was a cooper, and my grandfather was a sea-captain. My wife's name was Carr before I married her. Her father was a surveyor. The children have all had the mumps, chicken-pox and measles. When I reach Crewe I expect to put up at a hotel."

He stopped. The long-nosed man regarded him a moment with interest, and then asked in a dissatisfied way:

"What did your great-grandfather do for a livin'?"

The most beautiful object in Windsor Castle is the thumb-worn and marked Bible which General Gordon had used for years, and was with him when he was killed at Khartoum, and has been presented by his sister to the queen. It now rests in a little cabinet in a hall through which every visitor to the castle must pass, and is a perpetual reminder of the value of one copy of the Bible to the devout Christian.—J. M. Beckley.

SUPERIOR TRAIN SERVICE

via the Michigan Central, "The Niagara Falls Route," between Chicago, Detroit, Niagara Falls, Buffalo, New York, Boston, and New England points. For information as to trains, rates, etc., ask any ticket agent or address H. J. Newton, Pass. Agent, 257 Main St., Dallas, Texas, W. J. Lynch, Pass. Traffic Manager, Chicago.

Christian Publishing Company
2712 Pine St., St. Louis, Mo.

J. H. GARRISON, - - - - President
W. W. DOWLING, - - - Vice-President
GEO. L. SNIVELY, - - Sec. and Gen. Supt
R. P. CROW, - - Treas. and Bus. Manager

THE CHRISTIAN-EVANGELIST and a fountain pen to a new subscriber for $1.75. THE CHRISTIAN-EVANGELIST and a $2.50 self-filling fountain pen guaranteed for ten years for $2.75.

A new volume—The History of Christian Unity—will soon be added to the famous "Garrison Library." This will be uniform in size with the "Helps to Faith" and "Holy Spirit" series. Advance orders for the first edition will be received at any time.

It used to be contemptuously asked, "Who reads an American book?" and that spirit hurts American literature. Many of our preachers as unreasonably seem to be soliloquizing, who reads a book written by a Disciple. That spirit hurts this Restoration.

One of our representatives took 24 new subscriptions at $1.50 each in a five hours' canvass of a small Missouri town last week. The people are glad to subscribe when told of the merits of THE CHRISTIAN-EVANGELIST. One thousand other friends can do as well in 1000 other towns. Volunteers, write us for samples and blanks.

Desiring something better than your present Sunday-school supplies? Send to us for samples of the W. W. Dowling series and price lists. It is a mistake to use the insipid and colorless interdenominational publications. The children should be taught the plan of salvation as it is understood by the leaders of this Restoration movement. This and other vital truths are taught by Brother Dowling and so impressed on the minds of the young as never to be forgotten.

Make good use of the pink subscription blank found in your last week's CHRISTIAN-EVANGELIST. Religious papers depend for their life and augmented power upon the personal work of their readers as much as churches do on that of their members. Secure the subscription of a friend, and a quarter of a century later some man trembling on the brink of ruin may be saved by the reawakening of religious sentiment fostered by this paper in his old home. Thus may you have a part in the salvation of an immortal soul.

August is not usually considered a very favorable month for church paper subscriptions yet we have recorded a handsome net increase. Aside from the many subscriptions coming in by ones and twos, we are pleased to report the following clubs taken at the uniform price of $1.50 each, to-wit: Billings, Mont., 3; Farmington, Mo., 3; Edward Owers, minister; Greenville, O., 5, Aldinus Baker, pastor; Montpelier, Ind., 5, D. F. Harris, minister; Hartford City, Ind., 16, W. E. Payne, pastor; Marion, Ind., 23, Milo Atkinson, minister; Macon, Mo., 23, Irvin T. Le Baron, minister; Barger's Springs, W. Va., 3; Newport, Ark., 7; Callao, Mo., 5; Bevier, Mo., 28, W. E. Reavis, minister.

THE CHRISTIAN-EVANGELIST's Special to Buffalo goes over the Wabash. It leaves St. Louis at noon, October 11. There will be standard Pullmans, also new tourist, and reclining chair cars. The rates are one fare plus $1 for round trip from all points east of the Mississippi. One fare plus $2 for all points west of the river. We are arranging for the best train service en route and hotel accommodations after reaching the convention city. As soon as you determine to go with us, advise us, that we may engage enough cars. A great many preachers and other Disciples will earn transportation to the Buffalo convention by securing subscribers for The Christian-Evangelist. Other things being equal, the y will enjoy the convention more than others because of the great blessings they are bringing into multitudes of homes while making possible this trip to themselves at very little expense.

A woman hurried up to a policeman the corner of Twenty-third street.
"Does the crosstown car take y down to the bridge toward Brooklyn she demanded.
"Why, madam," returned the poli man, "do you want to go to Brooklyn
"No, I don't want to," the woman plied, "but I have to."—*New York Sun.*

A New York woman tells of an experience which she had recently in o of the large department stores. S was looking for some house furnishin and, walking up to one of the floo walkers, asked where she could see t candelabra.
"All canned goods two counters to t left," answered the official guide, briefly *Harper's Weekly.*

What "Christian-Evangelist" Special tourists will se from below the Falls.

THE CHRISTIAN-EVANGELIST

A WEEKLY RELIGIOUS NEWSPAPER.

Volume XLIII.	No. 36.

ST. LOUIS, SEPTEMBER 6, 1906.

A CONQUERING FAITH

William H. Bathurst.

FOR a faith that will not shrink,
  Though pressed by every foe,
That will not tremble on the brink
  Of any earthly woe!

That will not murmur nor complain
  Beneath the chastening rod,
But, in the hour of grief or pain,
  Will lean upon its God,

A faith that shines more bright and clear
  When tempests rage without,
That when in danger knows no fear,
  In darkness feels no doubt;

Lord, give me such a faith as this,
  And then, whate'er may come,
I'll taste, e'en now, the hallowed bliss
  Of an eternal home.

The Christian-Evangelist.

J. H. GARRISON, Editor

PAUL MOORE, Assistant Editor

F. D. POWER,
B. B. TYLER,   } Staff Correspondents.
W. DURBAN,

Subscription Price, $1.50 a Year.

For foreign countries add $1.04 for postage.

Remittances should be made by money order, draft, or registered letter; not by local cheque, unless 15 cents is added to cover cost of collection.

In Ordering Change of Post Office give both old and new address.

Matter for Publication should be addresse to THE CHRISTIAN-EVANGELIST. Subscriptions and remittances should be addressed to the Christian Publishing Company, 2712 Pine Street, St. Louis, Mo.

Unused Manuscripts will be returned only if accompanied by stamps.

News Items, evangelistic and other rise, are solicited, and should be sent on a post card, if possible.

Published by the Christian Publishing Company, 2712 Pine Street, St. Louis, Mo.

Entered at St. Louis P. O. as Second Class Matter

WHAT WE STAND FOR.

For the Christ of Galilee,
For the truth which makes men free,
For the bond of unity
Which makes God's children one.

For the love which shines in deeds
For the life which this world need,
For the church whose triumph speed is
The prayer: "Thy will be done."

For the right against the wrong,
For the weak against the strong,
For the poor who've waited long
For the brighter age to be.

For the faith against tradition,
For the truth 'gainst superstition,
For the hope whose glad fruition
Our waiting eyes shall see.

For the city God is rearing,
For the New Earth now appearing,
For the heaven above us clearing,
And the song of victory.

J. H. Garrison.

CONTENTS.

Centennial Propaganda 1127
Current Events 1128
Editorial—
    Where Jesus Placed the Emphasis—III. 1129
    The Country Church Problem....1129
    Notes and Comments 1130
    Current Religious Thought......1130
    Editor's Easy Chair.............1131
Contributed Articles—
    As Seen from the Dome. F. D. Power 1132
    Modern Religious Persecution—A Defense. B. L. Chase..........1133
    Back to the Great Apostasy. William Durban 1134
    The Joy of Soul Winning. R. H. Crossfield 1135
    African Missions and the Uncompleted Task 1136
    E. L. Frazier's Dilemma. E. S. Muckley 1137
Our Budget 1138
News from Many Fields.........1143
Evangelistic 1147
Midweek Prayer-meeting 1148
Christian Endeavor 1148
Sunday-school 1149
People's Forum 1150
Church Dedications 1151
The Home Department 1152

THE
CHRISTIAN-EVANGELIST

"IN FAITH, UNITY; IN OPINION AND METHODS, LIBERTY; IN ALL THINGS, CHARITY."

Vol. XLIII.　　　　　　September 6, 1906　　　　　　No. 36

1809　CENTENNIAL PROPAGANDA
CHURCHES OF CHRIST　1909
: : : GEO. L. SNIVELY : : :

Looking Toward Pittsburg.

Church Extension still has the right-of-way and should have all through September unless every Disciple has earlier fellowship in this great ministry.

For this reason, and also because of the intrinsic merits of the piece, we give our Centennial Secretary's following article publication on this page and bespeak for it a careful reading. Doubtless many of our Centennial aspirations will not be realized, but we can have "$1,000,-000 in our Church Extension fund by 2909" if we all faithfully strive to place it there.

How glorious it is that our people are thinking in the higher denominations now! Two weeks ago this page was freighted with Sister Harrison's report of a gift of $25,000 for a missionary training school in Indianapolis, and here comes Chancellor Aylsworth with the glad tidings of $20,000 having been given by the saintly A. B. Teachout for the enlargement of Cotner University's usefulness to this Restoration.

Our larger liberty in Christ, our passing beyond the distinctively controversial stage of our existence, our seeking earnestly after the best gifts of the grace of God is bearing this precious fruitage, in which we shall more and more abound. How others of greater fortunes than are possessed by these generous donors can pass by on the other side of imperial opportunities for doing good we know not.

Meanwhile our hopes of a great centennial are not centered upon the few large gifts the rich will make to our church interests, but rather upon the almost countless offerings of the poor and middle classes.

Universal Relief.

BY W. R. WARREN.

A great Centennial Church Extension Fund of a million dollars will minister relief in one way or another, or both, to every church in the brotherhood. A place of meeting is a church's prime necessity. Universal recognition of this truth is found in the fact that more money can be raised for a church building than for any other purpose. Every member reaches his highest standard of single offerings when giving to the meeting house. Members of other churches and of no church will help in this when they will ignore every other appeal. When its members and neighbors are together unequal to the undertaking, it has a recognized claim upon other congregations to the end of the land. But if its minister is sent out to present its appeal, the loss of his time from his proper work and the dead waste in traveling expenses work a double injury to the cause. So the Church Extension Board was constituted to serve as a clearing house be-

tween needy churches and those that should help them.

It effects universal relief. It relieves the minister from heart-breaking, peripatetic soliciting; it relieves all the churches of frequent and unseasonable appeals; it relieves both the needy and the strong of imposition from unwise and unworthy enterprises; it relieves the homeless church in a self-respecting way with funds that it will send back as it is able, to go out again to the relief of other churches in like helpless state. And the helped church, when the day of its strength arrives, is relieved of numerous appeals for assistance.

There is not a church in the brotherhood that can not be reached by the direst appeal of some needy point. Surely, then, all should make common cause in responding to all these calls through this common agency that has proved its efficiency in over a thousand cases. Let every church become a partner in its beneficent service. It does not speak well for our sense, for our humanity or our consecration when the churches contributing outnumber only slightly those that have been helped. Universal relief should have universal support.

OUR CENTENNIAL PROGRAM FOR CHURCH EXTENSION.

First—To have every minister, that believes in organized missionary work, enlisted to secure an offering from his congregation, or congregations, during the next four years, that the churches may have their part in raising the Million Dollar Church Extension Fund by October, 1909. We had $365,399.22 in the Fund August 1, 1906.

Second—To have every Endeavor Society contribute something each year in order to the creation of a large "Y. P. S. C. E. Named Loan Fund for Church Extension." All Endeavor offerings from societies, as such, will go into this special fund.

Third—To increase our Annuity Fund to at least $300,000 by October, 1909. It is now $186,-704.

Fourth—To increase the number of our Named Loan Funds to at least fifty. We now have fifteen.

Fifth—To secure at least $100,000 by individual gifts, aside from annuities.

Sixth—To house every homeless mission by October, 1909.

A Magnificent Gift.

BY CHANCELLOR W. P. AYLSWORTH.

It will be a pleasure to the readers of THE EVANGELIST, so many of whom are interested in our work at Cotner, to know that we have recently received from Bro. Abram Teachout, of Cleveland, Ohio, a contribution to the endowment of Cotner University of productive securities of $20,000. By his consent this splendid gift has been devoted to the establishment of a department of education and a chair at the head of this department will be known as the Teachout Chair of Education. Prof. J. A. Beattie, for four years head of the State Normal School of Nebraska, and a specialist in this department of education, has been chosen to fill this important place. This opens new avenues of influence and usefulness heretofore impossible to reach. It is all the more ap-

preciated as the gift came almost as a surprise, and was accompanied by expressions of encouragement and good will.

It is our wish, as never before, to press on to greater things in the enlargement of the possibilities of our work in this center of education. I bespeak the prayers and aid of THE EVANGELIST family in this effort to place the institution upon a larger foundation.

Our Centennial Helpers.

THE CHRISTIAN-EVANGELIST is increasingly newsy which, with its desirable Christian spirit, will make friends wherever read.—Earl P. Kempher, Hebron, Ohio.

Enclosed find $1.50 that moves my date up to July, 1907. I can not do without THE CHRISTIAN-EVANGELIST, wish it were in every home.—Mrs. Jessie W. Pierce, Belton, Texas.

I am glad to see the signs of prosperity on the weekly issues of THE CHRISTIAN-EVANGELIST. I have had it from the beginning and am glad to renew my allegiance to it.—F. M. Green, Akron, Ohio.

Enclosed find $1.50 for my CHRISTIAN-EVANGELIST. I have only taken it one year but expect to continue it as long as I live. May God bless you in your work.—Mrs. W. R. Thompson, Bluefield, Va.

I will do what I can for THE CHRISTIAN-EVANGELIST. I am very anxious for its success. I know it is right on federation. Brother Garrison is a grand, good man. I wish every member of the Church of Christ had more of his spirit.—Wm. Irelan, Monterey, Mex.

Sickness and death compelled me to give up THE CHRISTIAN-EVANGELIST, but when the dear old paper came to me to-day it seemed like the face of a dear friend and I must again receive it into my home. It gives me such great comfort to read its messages of love and hope.—Mrs. W. P. Boyd, New York City.

I feel I could not get along without THE CHRISTIAN-EVANGELIST. It is a great help to me in every way and I hope it will continue to reach out and get into every home in the brotherhood, and may its noble editor be spared many years to carry out the grand work he is doing.—T. R. Shawin, Morelos, Mexico.

I have been a subscriber to THE CHRISTIAN-EVANGELIST back in the '60s even before it was merged into your hands. I have watched its progress with much interest and read its pages with pleasure, benefit and comfort. It has helped me grow strong spiritually. I want it to abide with me still.—Mrs. M. E. Craig, Anacortis, Wash.

I bid our grand, veteran editor God speed in delivering his messages of Christian fellowship and brotherly love. I regard THE CHRISTIAN-EVANGELIST as one of the Master's finger-boards pointing out the way leading to the fulfillment of his prayer that all may be one. I have been a constant reader of the paper since 1874. It grows better every week.—J. N. Springer, Los Angeles, Cal.

I have long wanted to express my high appreciation of the Easy Chair. Your words on "Prayer" three weeks ago fitted me exactly. I have from personal experience your deductions are correct. I also fully agree with you in your attitude on higher criticism and church union. I have lately hoped I might be in the vicinity of your "lodge" on Lake Michigan, when I would certainly invite myself to meet you and tell you personally my appreciation of the comfort your writings give the son of the man (Daniel Bates) that established THE CHRISTIAN-EVANGELIST in January, 1850, and at the same time "wet a line" with you.—W. H. Bates, Memphis, Tenn.

THE CHRISTIAN-EVANGELIST.

Current Events

The home-coming of Mr. Bryan was the great event of last week. Welcomed by Democrats who had gathered from all parts of the country—a reception committee that looked more like a mass meeting—he appeared Thursday evening before an audience of nearly 20,000 people in Madison Square Garden and delivered his long-anticipated address. The speech covered almost as many topics as a president's message to congress usually does. Perhaps he was practicing. He spoke of the growth of the sentiment and practice of international arbitration; declared that our experiment in "colonial government" was a failure and had lowered our national prestige; said his observations in the Philippines confirmed him in the belief that we should give them immediate independence; urged election of senators by popular vote; defended the income tax; encouraged arbitration in disputes between capital and labor; criticized government by injunction; upheld the eight-hour working day; renewed his declaration of allegiance to bi-metallism, though admitting that the increased production of gold had removed the urgent necessity for bimetallism by increasing the quantity of money; denounced the practice of receiving campaign contributions from corporations; declared the trusts to be the paramount issue; asserted that tariff reform was an essential part of the anti-trust program; and defended public ownership of railroads, trunk lines to be owned by the federal government, local lines by the several states. This is a good deal of ground to get over in one speech. From New York Mr. Bryan starts immediately on a circuitous tour which will occupy about three weeks, terminating at his home at Lincoln, Neb. This period will be crowded as full of speeches as possible.

Mr. Bryan's Home-Coming.

The Illinois Democratic convention endorsed Mr. Bryan for president and refused to endorse his demand for Roger Sullivan's retirement, without which Mr. Bryan said he did not want Illinois' endorsement.

One hundred and thirty-one million and eighty thousand dollars is the sum which the Standard Oil Company will be called upon to pay in fines if it is found guilty on all the counts for which it is now under indictment and is given the maximum penalty in each case. The federal grand jury in Chicago last week returned indictments against it on 6,424 counts, each of which represents a tank-car on which a freight rebate was received. Add to this 126 counts from the James-

Millions in Fines.

town (N. Y.) grand jury. The fine is fixed by law at not less than $1,000 and not more than $20,000 on each count. Even at the minimum the fine would be something more than six and a half millions. But it is one thing to get an indictment and another thing to get a conviction. We await the latter with interest. And there is a good deal more chance of it than anybody supposed a year or two ago. Meanwhile the Standard continues to do business, however. It is said to have gotten control of the new oil fields in eastern Illinois in the vicinity of Casey and Robinson, where a tremendous oil boom is in progress and scenes not unlike those at Beaumont are being enacted.

The gubernatorial fight in Georgia between Hoke Smith and Clark Howell, of the "Atlanta Constitution," is virtually ended by the endorsement of Smith at the Democratic primaries. It was a lively fight while it lasted. Smith accused Howell of being a railroad candidate, and Howell accused Smith of favoring negro education. Smith explained this serious charge away, however, by showing how unalterably opposed he was to negro suffrage, whatever the educational status of the negro might be. This explanation seemed to be satisfactory to the people.

Senator Beveridge, in a political speech in Maine, says that the issue of the present congressional campaign is not economic but moral. It is a long way from Maine to Danville, Ill., but not farther than from this sentiment to the one which prevailed in Speaker Cannon's recent keynote speech. The speaker's position is that Republican rule is right because it is profitable. The senator's is that it is desirable because it is right—and incidentally profitable. The president's letter to Mr. Watson leans apparently to the former doctrine. It is a very poor exposition of his policy as he has been actually working it out. As a campaign document the president's record is much better than his letter.

Moral or Economic.

The failure of the Milwaukee Republicans to endorse Speaker Cannon's candidacy is an indication, says the Chicago "Tribune," that the speaker's boom does not extend quite from Danville to Beersheba.

The street car strike in San Francisco has become so serious that strikebreakers are being imported from New York by the train load.

A representative of the internal revenue service has just returned after two months spent in studying the manufacture and use of denatured alcohol in Europe. He finds that it is much used for fuel but not to any extent for the production of power. Apparently not even a beginning has been made in running automo-

The Use of Alcohol.

Editorial

Where Jesus Placed the Emphasis.—III.

The Nature and Consequences of Sin.

When Jesus came into the world He found sin to be a universal fact. It is one of the most obvious facts in human experience. Death itself is not more universal and scarcely less manifest than the prevalence of sin among men. If the existence of sin be thus obvious to ordinary eyes, much more so must it have been to the pure eyes of the only sinless One who has entered into and shared the lot of our common humanity. Indeed it was this moral disorder that brought Jesus into the world. Sin was the one dark blot on the fair face of God's creation which He came to remove. He saw it as a dark shadow projecting itself across all the pages of human history and as a foul pestilential breath scattering the seeds of disease and death everywhere. It is a remarkable fact that Jesus propounded no theory of the origin of sin, nor of its relation to the Adamic fall. He concerned himself rather with its nature, its source in the human heart, and its remedy.

Jesus taught no theory of sin that interfered with human responsibility. He said nothing about "total hereditary depravity." He taught rather that every man born into the world possessed a moral nature capable of distinguishing between right and wrong. "The lamp of the body is the eye; if therefore thine eye be single, thy whole body shall be full of light. But if thine eye be evil, thy whole body shall be full of darkness. If therefore the light that is in thee be darkness, how great is the darkness!" (Matt. 6:22, 23). As the eye is the lamp of the body, so the human conscience is the light of the soul, lighted by Him who "lighteth every man, coming into the world." If this light be obscured through fleshly desires and lusts, until it ceases to shine, how great is the darkness! In the view of Jesus sin is abnormal; it is a disease. When He taught as a whole," He taught, "need not a physician but they that are sick." He was the great Physician of souls. Holiness with Jesus is wholeness; it is moral sanity. To recover man from sin is to bring him back into his normal relation to God.

This idea of the abnormality of sin in the teaching of Jesus is shown by His speaking of the sinner as one that is "lost." The parables of the lost sheep, the lost coin, and the lost son, show that He conceived of the sinner as one who had gotten out of his rightful place, had wandered from the Father's house, and as such was subject to privations and perils. He "came to seek and to save the lost"—those who had wandered from

the path of right and truth, and were straying and stumbling upon the dark mountains of sin and disobedience. Nothing is more tender and touching than His picture of the good shepherd bringing back on his shoulder the lost sheep that had strayed from the fold. So, He tells us, He came to seek "the lost sheep of the house of Israel."

"But none of the ransomed ever knew
 How deep were the waters crossed,
Nor how dark was the night that the Lord
     passed through
Ere He found His sheep that was lost."

With Jesus sin had its origin in the human heart. When He told the Pharisees and Scribes who came from Jerusalem that "Not that which entereth into the mouth defileth a man; but that which proceedeth out of the mouth this defileth the man," even his disciples were astonished at His teaching, while the Pharisees were greatly offended at it. But Jesus had to explain to His disciples that "the things which proceed out of the mouth come forth out of the heart, and they defile the man. For out of the heart come forth evil thoughts, murders, adulteries, fornication, thefts, false witness, railings: these are the things which defile the man." (Matt. 15:17-19.) This teaching was in marked contrast with that of the Scribes and Pharisees. It located sin within the heart and shows that *purification of the heart* is the only cure for sin. To His disciples He said, "Except your righteousness shall exceed the righteousness of the Scribes and Pharisees ye shall in no wise enter into the kingdom of heaven." (Matt. 5:20.)

This is where Jesus placed the emphasis on sin. No external remedy can cure it. Those who think a change in environment will cure sin, need to sit at the feet of Jesus and learn that it is too deep-seated to be eradicated by a change of surroundings. Nothing is more characteristic of the teaching of Jesus than this view of sin as having its seat in the heart in the form of evil thoughts, desires and purposes, and proceeding thence in the form of evil words and deeds. This fact underlies all His teaching about sin, and indeed underlies His sacrificial death for sin. Sin, with Jesus, is not a mistake of the intellect; it is vastly more fundamental than that. It is a *wrong purpose of the heart*, a yielding to the lower and baser motives against the moral sense and in violation of conscience.

Jesus' estimate of the awful consequences of sin may be seen also from such passages as the following: "And if thy right eye causeth thee to stumble, pluck it out and cast it from thee; for it is profitable for thee that one of thy members should perish and not thy whole body be cast into hell. And if thy right hand causeth thee to stumble, cut it off and cast it from thee: for it is profitable for thee that one of thy members should perish and not thy whole body go into hell." (Matt. 5:29, 30), No matter how highly cher-

ished may be the thing that causes thee to sin, put it away, for nothing can compensate for the loss of one's soul by sin. Again, He taught His disciples to "Be not afraid of them that kill the body, but are not able to kill the soul; but rather fear him who is able to destroy both soul and body in hell." (Matt. 10:28.) In what more graphic way could our divine Teacher indicate the awful consequences of sin than He has done in this language?

Since sin is the great disturbing force in the world producing all the disorder and conflict which exist among men, poisoning the fountains of our individual, domestic, social and political life, how important it is that we emphasize the teaching of Jesus on this subject, locate sin where He locates it, regard it as He regarded it, as the one thing to be feared and avoided, if we would carry forward successfully the great work of redeeming the world from sin. If the sinner is, indeed, lost, alienated from God—the source of life and all peace—and, therefore, morally dead, subject to all the destructive ravages of sin, ending in everlasting "banishment from the presence of God and from the glory of His power," what sacrifice is too great on our part to effect the recovery of men from sin for whom Christ laid down his life?

The Country Church Problem.

Just now the perennial country church problem is to the fore. While the matter is being discussed it may be well to consider some of the features which are not usually regarded as factors of the problem. Very few well-informed men among us will seriously contend that our country churches, taken as a whole, are in a healthy condition. A few of them are doing fairly well, but it is perhaps true that the majority are far from prosperous, and not a few are practically dying or are already dead. This surely ought not to be the case. Much of our prosperity in the past, as a religious people, was owing to the vigorous life of our country churches. There are no insuperable reasons why this same kind of life should not be manifested at the present time. It is freely granted that conditions have somewhat changed since the early days of our religious movement, and that these conditions require a change in our methods in some respects. Still it remains true that some of the changes that have been made have not been productive of the best results. At any rate it will not be unprofitable if we look candidly at some of the causes which seem, at least, to operate against the success of our country churches. But in taking a candid look at the present situation it is not our purpose to find fault with any one for the state of things which really exists. It is probably true that in most cases every one has tried to do the very best that could be done under the circumstances. However, some general statements may be helpful at particular points where we think improvement might be made.

In some instances, at least, the management of our country churches is entirely too autocratic. Everything seems to be in the hands of two or three men. These men, are generally men of excellent character and are most anxious for the church to succeed. They do everything in their power to make success. They are, for the most part, liberal with their means, and in some cases they are practically the main reliance in sustaining the cause. But we fear they do not always act wisely. It is well known that very many of our country churches are so entirely managed by a few men that even the calling of a preacher is done without consulting the church as a whole. The preacher is "hired" by the elders, and then the congregation is informed as to what has been done, but in no real sense have the people been consulted in the matter. As a result many of the members will feel little sympathy with the preacher and less perhaps with the work which is to be done. Apart entirely from this unscriptural way of doing things, it is well to consider the matter from a practical point of view. This is emphatically the day of the people. Any method of church government which ignores this fact will probably come to grief. It may succeed for a time, but it is certain to finally end in failure. This is especially true where the financial question is involved. There is always a financial element in the calling of the preacher, and yet in many of our country churches the preacher is hired (to use the term usually employed) without consulting the congregation at all; and yet the congregation is expected to contribute largely to the financial support of the man who has been "hired" by the elders, or by those who are specially managing things. This, in our judgment, is an unwise way of meeting the case. Doubtless it is generally better that the elders should do the preliminary correspondence with men whose services are being sought, but there comes a time when the church itself should be informed as to the facts of the case and asked to participate in the invitation which is to be extended; and the final decision with respect to the matter should be the act of the church at a meeting specially called for that purpose. Then if things do not turn out satisfactorily the church can not lay the blame upon a few men who would certainly be blamed if the whole church should not be consulted. Taxation without representation is un-American.

Not the least advantage of taking the course suggested would be the united sympathy which it would secure for the man who comes to minister to the people. The church would regard him as their own minister and not simply the minister of a few men who had hired him without the consent of the church.

It is readily conceded that the problem of church management everywhere has its difficulties and these difficulties are perhaps greater in our country churches than anywhere else; and yet this problem is certainly not simplified by placing the whole management in the hands of a few men, however well qualified they may be for their difficult task. But it happens sometimes that these men have very few qualifications for the work, though they may be worthy of all praise for the sacrifices which they make. Even the highest Christian character and the noblest consecration can not always compensate for a lack of wisdom in the management of a church. In any case it must be emphatically affirmed that no permanent success can be assured in the present day without recognizing the democratic element which is so prominently characteristic of the age. At another sitting we may take a look at some other features of the problem under consideration.

Notes and Comments.

Bro. T. P. Haley, of Kansas City, is not a prophet without honor in his own city. His recent call to another year's pastorate of the South Side Church in that city was made the occasion by the local press of most honorable mention of his long and useful service in the cause of the Master. "The Kansas City Journal" gives quite a lengthy account of his life and labors, and a highly complimentary editorial notice, found elsewhere, which shows the high place which our distinguished brother holds among the people of the city in which he has so long lived and labored. So far as the brotherhood itself is concerned, Brother Haley's place has long been secure as one of the ablest of our ministers and pastors, as among the manliest of men, the truest of friends, and a Christian gentleman without reproach. In honoring such a man the city of his adoption honors itself.

It was kind of the president to issue his spelling reform order just in the middle of August, when the newspapers were needing a new topic interesting enough and light enough for the hot weather. The substance of the order was that the public printer, in printing executive messages, should follow the spelling recommended by the spelling reform committee, of which Professor Brander Matthews, of Columbia University, is chairman, in a list of 300 words which that committee has put forth. The president's stenographers have received a similar order. Many of the comments which this action has elicited are based on a misunderstanding of it. Two facts are to be remembered. First, the order relates only to the spelling of the president's own messages and correspondence. It is not an attempt to reform the spelling of the world. Doubtless the president would be glad to see other people, including publishers and school teachers, take the same action that he has taken, but he is exercising no au-

thority in the matter. In the second place, the order has reference to the spelling of only 300 words, more than half of which are already commonly spelled in the new way. The following include all the changes in the list: e for œ, as in esthetic; o for œ, as in honor; er for re, as in theater; t for final ed, as in dropt; single for double letters in a few cases, as in fulfil; the dropping of final silent letters as in program; dropping silent medial e, as in judgment; dropping silent gh or ugh, as in tho, thru, and thoro. The only changes which can be considered at all radical are the last mentioned group and the final t in place of ed. Of these, the former was adopted years ago by one great publishing house, and the latter is directly in line with the natural development of the language as illustrated by such universally recognized words as blest, burnt, gilt (for gilded) and many others. A well-known literary man comments that "it serves us right" to have our spelling reform undertaken by energetic but amateur hands since the experts will not undertake it. But the experts have undertaken it. This list of 300 revised words is their work. The president is not reforming the English language, but is simply reforming his own English according to recommendations made by a committee of experts headed by Professor Matthews.

Current Religious Thought.

Let us not think we alone are advocating Christian unity The following taken from the "Central Christian Advocate" (Methodist), is evidence that others are also longing for the day in which all God's people shall be one.

Without a doubt union is in the air. That which was apparently insolvable a few years ago is now being gradually brought to a point of convergence. It will be conceded by every thoughtful mind that the union of two or more churches is a splendid thing when no principle is sacrificed for the good of humanity and the glory of God. This question of church federation is probably the most vexed and the most important problem in the ecclesiastical world. Whether men wish it or no, the question will be discussed and thoroughly aired. There are those who earnestly desire organic union of all the branches of the Christian Church, while, on the other hand, there are those who stringently oppose any such movement. In all the unions that have ever taken place, there has been considerable opposition. The union of the new school and old school branches of the Presbyterian Church in the United States was consummated only after years of discussion and negotiation.

Then the union of the Presbyterian bodies in Canada in 1875 was not completed until a great deal of opposition had been given. The union of the Methodist Churches in 1884 met with similar opposition, a number of both ministers and laymen feeling very keenly the position into which they were thrown. The opposition in Scotland to the amalgamation of the Free and United Presbyterian Churches is still fresh in our memory. When we consider the opposition which marked almost every union in the past, we are surprised to find how little antagonism has accompanied this prospective union thus far. This condition of things indicates a very general conviction that union is not only desirable but practicable and should be reached as soon as possible. It is one of the signs of the times that the old spirit of rivalry is passing away and that the churches are thinking more about the great fundamentals of Christianity and the problem of saving souls than about doctrinal differences or even ecclesiastical polity. If the mind of the church is fixed upon the great central truths of Christianity, the outlook for evangelism is infinitely brighter than though the denominations were wrangling over theological doctrines or hurling deadly catapults at one another in the battle for supremacy.

Editor's Easy Chair.

PENTWATER MUSINGS.

The half-full moon has turned the night into a softer day, and its beams of light have converted the lake into a silver sea. The sun went to his rest, this evening, in a cloudless sky from which the quiet stars are now shedding their mild radiance. The wind did not lay with the setting sun, as usual, and the lake is sending up its deep monotone, filling the night with its solemn music. The night wind, sighing through the pines and hemlocks, makes a fit accompaniment for the anthem of the waves. Perhaps it was not wholly from fear of the Jews that Nicodemus came to Jesus by night. There is a solemnity in its very stillness, and in the quiet ministry of the stars which look down upon us like angels' eyes, which fits the soul for religious meditation. Perhaps it was in some such mood as this that the Jewish Rabbi sought the great Teacher to hear from him the words of eternal life. Then, as now, the night wind moaned through the trees, and Jesus used it to illustrate the great fact of the birth from above. With what freedom it sweeps to-night across the lake out of the west, and who can tell its starting-place or prophesy its destination? There will always be mystery connected with the movements of the divine Spirit upon the spirit of man, and he who imagines that he has mastered all the secrets of that Spirit, in his method of reaching, convicting, illuminating, comforting, and guiding the human soul, has most to learn of his ways with men. The Jewish doctor learned from the Master that night that his participation in the kingdom of God was not a thing of descent from Abraham, nor yet a matter of the acceptance of John's baptism, but a question of life from the life-giving Spirit. This is the distinctive difference between Judaism and Christianity. To be a Christian is to possess the new life which Jesus came to give to men. "He that hath the Son hath life."

❁

On last Sunday evening just at the going down of the sun, and while all the west was crimson and gold as painted by his farewell beams, a group of more than fifty people gathered on the sand to hold the first beach service of this resort. A brisk wind was blowing from the northwest, the great lake was sending up a resounding anthem, and so the wind and the waves joined their music with ours as we sang some of the sweet old songs of redeeming love. An Episcopal rector from Chicago, Dr. Gardner, W. F. Richardson of Kansas City, and C. M. Fillmore of Cincinnati, were the ministers present, besides the writer. After a few of the old hymns the little company recited together the twenty-third Psalm and the rector led our hearts in prayer. In a brief introductory talk we stated what the beach meeting seemed to us to stand for: (1) For that conception of religion which connects it with all life, outdoors as well as indoors, and every day of the week as well as Sunday; which makes it the

great, regulative principle of all our conduct, and makes all life holier and sweeter. (2) For Christian fraternity and unity. No denominational lines are drawn in these meetings on the sand. We are all of one faith and of one church here, and no sectarianism is allowed to poison or embitter the cup of our common fellowship. No narrow, circumscribed ideas of fellowship would comport with this broad lake on whose sands we meet, nor with the infinite heavens that bend above us. (3) For mutual acquaintanceship and good neighborhood. In these meetings we learn to know each other better and to love each other more, and so to become mutual helpers while we are sojourning together in our summer homes. Brief addresses were also made by Dr. Gardner and W. F. Richardson, and when we had sung "Blest be the tie that binds" and "God be with you till we meet again" and the benediction had been pronounced, the people greeted each other cordially, and said how good it was to have such a service and how much they had enjoyed it.

❁

After an unusually warm spell of weather for this region, we have been favored with copious rains and cooler breezes. One of these culminating down-pours of rain took the form of a terrific thunder-storm which occurred just after we had retired at night. Flash after flash of lightning was followed by peal after peal of detonating thunder, whose reverberations over the lake and through the forest were truly awe-inspiring. The last of these lightning-bolts and thunder-peals were simultaneous, and we knew by the deafening crash that the bolt had descended to the earth not very far from us. It was not until morning, however, while we sat at the breakfast table that it was discovered that the lightning had struck one of the tall pine trees standing not more than twenty feet from the cottage, following its trunk from the very top down to the earth and making its pathway very distinct by the bark which it threw off. Not till then did we realize how near the death-dealing stroke had come to us, and we felt truly grateful for our preservation from danger. Another storm came in the early morning. As we waked and looked out of our west bedroom window the storm was advancing over the lake when suddenly the sun, rising above the hill-top on the east, shot the clouds and rain through with its rosy light, presenting a scene of surpassing beauty. So may the Sun of Righteousness, shining upon our earth-lives make beautiful the clouds which encompass us. For several days the air has been cool, the skies very blue, and the atmosphere so crystal clear that distant objects along the shore or out on the lake seem near by. To-day a stiff breeze blows from the northwest and Neptune is again pasturing his white flocks on the green meadows of the deep. These glorious days have in them a hint of autumn, and the closing, not many days hence, of our sojourn by the lakeside for the present season.

❁

Already the population of "Garrison Park" and of the Oceana Beach Company is thinning out for the season.

The Duncans and the Moores have left us, and the coming week will witness the departure of most of those that remain. These cooler days create a desire in those who can do so to return to their homes and to their work. A few of us are compelled to linger until as near the frost-line as possible to make it safe to return. No season of the year, however, is more enjoyable on this shore than these early autumn days. The clubhouse here keeps open next week for the coming of the young men of the Campbell Institute, who are coming to enjoy a little fellowship together, and with Nature and with the God of Nature. This, we trust, will be but the beginning of an annual meeting of not less than a week, not limited to the Campbell Institute, but held, perhaps, under its auspices, for devotional Bible study, the deepening of the spiritual life, and the consideration of those things which have to do with the best interests of our cause. A month earlier, perhaps, would be the best time, say the first week in August; for such a meeting. Such a meeting of devout spirits waiting upon God and seeking his spirit of counsel, would be far-reaching in its influence for good. This organization embraces a large number of the most scholarly young men in our ranks, together with a number of middle-aged ministers and a few others that are "older grown and gray," and whose aim in thus associating themselves together is their own mutual improvement, and the advancement, in all that is highest and best, of the cause to which they have consecrated their lives.

❁

One of the sweetest things which comes to us in this life of mingled joys and sorrows is our human friendships which have been sanctified by Christian fellowship. For more than a week we have been enjoying here in our summer home the most delightful Christian intercourse with Brother and Sister Richardson of Kansas City. Brother Richardson has been known to the Editor of this paper from his boyhood, when he was associated in the office where "The Christian," as the paper was then called, was published, and we have watched with deepest interest his growth in power and influence until he stands to-day in the foremost rank of our preachers and pastors, seeking not his own advancement, but that of the cause, standing firm on the old truths, while his mind open for whatever new light God may be giving to his church. He has grown in intellectual breadth and in spiritual depth, through all the years of his ministry. Sister Richardson is entirely like-minded with her husband, sharing in his labors and triumphs, an efficient helpmate in his pastoral work as well as in their home, and their two sons and two daughters who have now grown to young manhood and young womanhood are worthy of such parents. It has been a delight to have these two faithful friends and servants of God in our home for a while. Brother Richardson kindly preached for us here at Pentwater last Lord's day and is to do so next Lord's day before they return to their home. They both seem to have greatly enjoyed their visit here, and we are sure their coming has proved a blessing not only to our household but to the church and the people of Pentwater.

As Seen From the Dome

One can never fully see London. Every day there are a thousand new things to look up in the great city and from the top of a bus the vision is kaleidoscopic and never ending. We were near the British Museum and so spent our first day among its treasures. Weeks and even years might be given profitably to these collections alone. A million people visit it yearly. Here is a library of 2,000,000 as one thing. One of the first collections has a most fascinating interest; manuscripts and old books. You read original autograph letters of England's kings and queens: Elizabeth and Victoria, George III, and Cromwell; and of such men as Pitt, Burke and Walpole, Nelson and Wellington, Dickens, Carlyle, Kant, Schiller, Gibbon, manuscripts of Keats, Browning, Burns, Pope, Tasso, Defoe and others; a letter from Tennyson "Penny-post maddened;" a letter from John Wesley saying "I still think when the Methodists leave the church of England God will leave them," and exhorting brother Jackson to "advise Ridel not to please the devil by preaching himself to death." One sees the Bible in the earlier English version of Wicliff and the Codex Alexandrinus which with the Vaticanus and Sinaiticus ranks as the oldest, the original bull of Leo X conferring on Henry VIII the title of "Defender of the Faith;" and first editions of "Paradise Lost" and "Pilgrim's Progress" and Shakespeare's first folios, 1623. Here are the great Elgin marbles from Athens, figures executed by Phidias, the greatest sculptor the world has known; and the fragments of the Temple of Diana at Ephesus; and remains of the magnificent Mausoleum of Halicarnassus; and Assyrian and Egyptian, Etruscan and Babylonian antiquities of untold value and interest. Here are ancient gold ornaments and gems, the finest collection in the world, with the celebrated Portland vase and a single gold enameled cup 550 years old that cost the museum $40,000. Here is the famous Rosetta stone, a slab of black basalt with three inscriptions in Greek, Demotic and Egyptian, a decree of the priests of Memphis conferring divine honors on Ptolemy Epiphanes, which furnished the key to the decipherment of the Egytian hieroglyphs.

From the museum it is an easy stroll to the national gallery. First one gets among the portraits, twelve hundred of them, representing eminent men and women of all ranks and ages, from 1134 down to 1906, kings, statesmen, poets, judges, writers, warriors, actors, scientists, divines, pictures by all the great artists from Van Dyck, Kneller, Gainsborough, Reynolds and Watts down, of all the great people, that have made England great. I saw here Washington, a Stuart portrait, Franklin, and "Charles, first Marquess Cornwallis, who distinguished himself bravely in the American war." The national gallery proper has many great pictures. Here first of all are the Turners; his "Sun Rising in a Mist," and "Dido Building

Carthage" compared with Claude Lorraine's "Isaac and Rebecca," and "Embarkation of the Queen of Sheba"; his "Death of Nelson," "Childe Harold's Pilgrimage," and "Burial at Sea." Gorgeous dreams they are by the greatest landscape painter that ever lived. Here are Raphael's "Vision of a Knight" and his "Virgin and Child," known as the "Ansidei Madonna," which cost $350,000; and Titian's "Bacchus and Ariadne" one of the best of the works of the old man who lived to be 99 and painted and worked to the end; and Paul Veronese's great picture, "The Family of Darius at the Feet of Alexander the Great,"—"the most precious Veronese in the world," said John Ruskin, and "The Money Changers," and Murillo's "Holy Family," and Reni's "Holy Family" with John playing with the cat, and Landseer's "Shoeing" and "Dignity and Impudence" and "Sleeping Hound," and Reynolds' "Age of Innocence" and "Heads of Angels" and "Dr. Samuel Johnson," the best conception of the philosopher in the brown coat and metal buttons, and hundreds of others in the twenty-two rooms under the "pepper box turret."

There are other collections in London that one greatly enjoys. The Tate gallery has the modern pictures, twenty-five by Watts; for example, the most impressive being his "Dray Horses"; then "Her Mother's Voice," "The Doctor," "Uncle Tom and His Wife for Sale," and "Life's Illusions," and "The Equestrian Portrait," by different masters 'specially pleased me. The Wallace is another choice collection. Pictures, furniture, porcelain, minatures, enamels and arms and armour worth twenty millions are brought together in the old Hartford House. Wonderful portraits by Rembrandt; canvasses by Meissonier that may be examined with a microscope; perfect heads by Greuze, such as "Innocence," "Sorrow," "Fidelity"; portraits by Gainsborough and Reynolds, works of Rubens and Murillo and Velasquez that are things of beauty and a joy forever are here. One wearies of the embarrassment of riches.

I strolled about this neighborhood and found Henry Hallam's home and the house where Gibbon lived and wrote the "Decline and Fall," and the home of Mrs. Browning and Barry Cornwall and Adelaide Proctor; where Turner painted and Wilkie Collins and Anthony Trollope died and Herschel lived and where Dickens wrote from 1839-51 "The Old Curiosity Shop," "Martin Chuzzlewit," "Dombey and Son" and "David Copperfield." All these are near Cavendish square, and where I roomed, Russell square, both Thackeray and Dickens lived and F. D. Maurice and Justice Mansfield, Thomas Hughes, author of "Tom Brown's School-days," Henry Cavendish and Isaac D'Israeli. The square figures in "Vanity Fair." So all

When I read the epitaphs of the beautiful every inordinate desire goes out. When I see kings lying by those who deposed them; when I consider rival wits placed side by side, or the holy men who divided the world with their contests and disputes I reflect with sorrow and astonishment on the little competitions, factions and debates of mankind," said one who sleeps here with crowned heads.

Walking on, I came to St. Paul's, colossal and majestic, completed by Wren in 1710, who was building at the same time thirty other city churches, no two of which are alike, and all of which are to-day the pride of London, and for which he was receiving the princely salary of a thousand dollars a year! When an old man he was taken once every year to a spot beneath the dome where he could contemplate the work of his hands. He died at 91, and we read here on his tombstone the famous words, *"Lector, Si monumentum requiris, Circumspice"*—"Reader, if thou seekest his monument, look around"— and it is declared, *"Non sibi, sed pro bono publico"*—"he lived not for himself but for the public good."

Nelson and Wellington are both buried here, but John Howard's tomb and Chinese Gordon's most impressed me. The inscription on the latter reads: "At all times and everywhere he gave his strength to the weak, his substance to the poor, his sympathy to the suffering, his heart to God," and on the former, "He trod an open but unfrequented path in the ardent and unintermitted exercise of Christian charity and from the throne to the dungeon his name was mentioned with great respect, gratitude and admiration."

Modern Religious Persecution---A Defense

By B. L. Chase

8. Advice to the Disciples.

First of all I would advise the Disciples to put the glorious institution of persecution upon a solid basis, by officially organizing it, and commending it to the favor of the brotherhood. Unless something of this sort is done it is likely to languish in the atmosphere of this truth-seeking and liberty-loving age. We have fallen upon degenerate days. Every one thinks that it is his duty to find the truth and be made free; whereas there are only one or two who can find the truth, or who know it when they find it, and be made free. We ought to put these men in charge of our faith and practice to keep them sound and pure. Only a few men in a religious body can be safe judges of what is true and right. We must have our judges in the church as in the state. Only a few men, not all citizens, are elected to be judges over us.

Nothing would so completely distinguish the Disciples as a "peculiar people" as the revival of that ancient office of Inquisitor, called the "Holy Office." It has been in more or less successful operation among the Disciples for 15 years, but it has never received the official sanction as a body. A few learned and peculiarly endowed men among us have carried it on as a purely personal enterprise. One editor and one professor have been the most active in its operation. They have given their time and strength to the work without compensation except what resulted in the way of increased circulation of the newspaper and Sunday-school supplies in the one case, and increased endowment and attendance in the college in the other case. It is not fair that a few men should bear the brunt of this work, and be responsible for it.

We forget what they have had to do. They have defined and fixed the faith and practice of the Disciples. Think what that means for one or two men to do for a million people. No other religious body, except the Roman Catholic Church, permits one man to fix its faith and practice. But the Pope is handsomely paid for it. What have the Disciples ever paid these men? Has the American Christian Missionary Society, or Church Extension, or Foreign Society, or any other society ever paid these men anything for keeping them straight? Think of the trouble they have had to keep the home society out of trouble. They have saved to the home board treasury thousands of dollars that would have gone to pay the salaries of heretics. How much more would have been saved if our other newspapers had been as zealous to expose heresy. They might also have doubled the circulation of their papers in five years if they had been as active. If other college presidents had come out openly and declared that they would have nothing to do with the "higher criticism," they might also have increased their student attendance and endowment.

It ought to be perfectly apparent to the Disciples that here is a rich gold mine for their development. If they would just enter heartily upon a crusade of persecution they could double the attendance and endowment of their colleges, the circulation of their papers and the income of their missionary societies.

Since the Disciples have so much to gain or lose by carrying on persecutions it is time that a board was organized to take care of the work. It would be a worthy celebration of the first hundred years of our history to inaugurate the "Holy Office" at Pittsburg in 1909. The work has been left too long to private initiative. It is a matter that concerns the Disciples as a body. By taking it out of private hands we can rescue it from certain evils and weaknesses that are likely to afflict it. It has been carried on in a desultory and half-hearted way in the past, and only one heretic a year, on an average, has been tried and convicted in the newspapers. The Disciples have enough heretics to furnish a trial every week. What a magnificent stimulus to our educational and missionary work to try one heretic a week. Our people are famishing for the spiritual nourishment and inspiration that it would afford. Why do our colleges and missionary societies have such a struggle for money to carry on their work? Because we have so few heresy trials. Why are there so few conversions in some of the churches? Because there are no heresy trials to refresh the souls of the lukewarm and wavering. If every church in the brotherhood could have a heresy trial once a year in the dull season, it would be as good as a protracted meeting. Evangelism and persecution go together. Did not the church thrive and grow in the days of the great Roman persecutions? Did not one of the great fathers of the church say that the "blood of martyrs is the seed of the church"? Do we not read that the Apostle Paul "took pleasure in persecutions and distresses," and was made strong by them? The church grows lazy, luxurious and self-satisfied in times of peace and prosperity. She needs seasons of persecution

❀ ❀

BODY BUILDING

Right Food Makes Fine Boys.

Many people have questioned the truthfulness of the statement that the brain can be readily nourished and built up from some particular kind of food.

Experience is better than any kind of theory.

The wife of a prominent legislator in Kentucky says: "A woman of my acquaintance was in a badly run down condition at the time she became a mother, and at three months of age the child was a mite of humanity pitiful to look upon, with no more brain development than a monkey.

"About the time I speak of when the child was three months old the mother began feeding him Grape-Nuts.

"In ten days it was plain that a change was taking place and in a few weeks the boy became rosy, healthy and rounded out.

"He is now five years old and his food this entire time has been Grape-Nuts and cream. He seldom ever takes any other kind of food.

"It is a splendid illustration of the fact that selected food can produce results, for this boy is perfectly formed, has a beautiful body and arms and legs of a young athlete, while his head and brain development appears perfect, and he is as bright and intelligent as can be.

"I cannot comprehend a better illustration of the truth of the claim made for Grape-Nuts, that it is a brain and body builder." Name given by Postum Co., Battle Creek, Mich.

to arouse her from her sleep of contentment, to purify her from dross and error. Did not Jesus say he came to send, not peace, but a sword, and to set a man at variance against his father, and the daughter against her mother"? When have we so nearly fulfilled the promise of Christ as when the organ and anti-organ parties were at each other's throats; as when the brotherhood was divided between the critics and the anti-critics, the federationists and the anti-federationists? The largest protracted meeting in the history of the Disciples was held during the last winter, when the discussion of federation was at its height. If the church at Anderson could have had a splendid heresy trial just before or just after the great meeting the number of converts would have been 2,500 instead of 1,250. What we need is more persecutions. We are going to stagnate and disappear as a brotherhood if we do not have more heresy trials. Every pastor ought to start one in his church, and get all the members stirred up. They would come to church, to the prayer-meeting and even the Sunday-school. They would talk about the church, religion and their brethren in their homes, upon the streets, and in the shops. We need a revival of

interest in religious things. Persecution is the way to have it. It would double the membership of our churches, as it doubled the circulation of a newspaper in five years.

Then again a board of persecution would furnish employment to a great many men. Men are walking the streets of our cities looking for employment. We could give many of our unemployed preachers work to do. It has been demonstrated that preachers who have not been acceptable to the churches, and have failed in everything else, can succeed as spies and informers on their brethren. Many of them enjoy it and find it congenial. We would need a great many spies, informers and evidence hunters. We would require one for each of our schools to live incognito upon the ground to watch the professors. A level-headed student might sometimes be obtained more economically for the place. We would also want a spotter for each of our missionary societies and state boards. It would be a good thing to place a spy with each of our mission stations on the foreign field to see that the missionaries did not betray our plea by fraternizing or co-operating with the Presbyterians and Baptists on the field. The board of persecution could be made

self-supporting by levying the expenses of each heresy trial upon the college or church that furnished the heretic. That alone would make the colleges careful in their selection of men.

Another reason why the Disciples should officially take charge of persecution of heretics is because of the abuses to which it is liable in the hands of men. As it stands now anybody who thinks he scents heresy can start a persecution. It is possible to-day as in mediaeval times for designing men to make use of it to satisfy private ambitions or personal grudges. Men who desired to wreak vengeance upon their enemies, husbands who wanted to get rid of their wives, or suitors who desired to put their rivals out of their way, denounced them as heretics to the Inquisition. So to-day when a newspaper editor desires to cripple a competitor newspaper, or when a college president desires to build up his school at the expense of another school he makes out a case of heresy and lodges it against a teacher in the rival school, that furnishes a chance for all private enemies of the accused to join together to injure him. This has never happened among the Disciples, for our persecutors are above human weaknesses and debasements of that sort.

Back to the Great Apostasy   By William Durban

Prelude.

Home again! After three months of further observation and experience in America I have once more touched my native shore. I find that European history is being rapidly made. The religious kaleidoscope especially is quickly shifting. The people of London have been watching the sessions of the International Parliamentary Conference, have been hearing the utterances of seven men from the Russian Duma, and have been undoubtedly charmed by the various speeches on tour of Mr. W. J. Bryan. I am always impressed by the fact that an eminent man from America who visits Britain is the subject of much greater attention than is a noted Britisher presenting himself in the United States. The American papers afford scanty space to what an English visitor may say, even if he is a really celebrated character. The London papers have reported every word that Mr. Bryan has publicly uttered, together with various interviews with the famous Nebraskan. I am of opinion that this somewhat airy and supercilious treatment of Europeans who deserve a display of real interest involves intellectual loss to the national American mind. In reading many of the best American papers I have noticed a tendency to narrowness of outlook and an accent of contempt for the doings of the vast world outside the United States. Should not the British empire, with its enormous area, its colossal possibilities, and its rapidly growing power in every portion of the globe, count for some-

thing? America is, of course, a very great country, but, after all, it is not the whole universe. I hope that the topic which this article will treat may secure the interest of my kind American readers, even though it relates primarily to British affairs. Before I finish it may be apparent that this subject indirectly concerns Americans most seriously.

The Real Enemy.

"Voila l'ennemi," exclaimed a popular Frenchman, pointing to a priest. And the Gallican church has recently dealt drastically with the Gallican church, French disestablishment and disendowment being entirely caused by the attitude of the church, which posed as the enemy of the liberties of the nation. In like manner the English people are just now realizing very vividly that the priest is the enemy. For priestcraft has been preparing ambuscades on a vast scale from which to assail the constitution. The two most sensational events of July in England have been the passing through the house of commons of the famous education bill and the report of the royal commission on ecclesiastical discipline. Unfortunately, although the house of commons has splendidly fulfilled its duty, passing the liberal education bill by the entire progressive majority at the command of the prime minister, the real danger will be encountered at the autumn session, in the house of lords, during the committee stage of the third reading. It is always during this stage that every great measure of legislative reform is imperiled. The lords, espe-

cially the bishops, those lordliest of the lords, will find their opportunity in committee of mutilating and mangling the bill. The religious hotheads amongst the Tories may be curbed by more prudent statesmen of their party, or they may prove infatuated. Should the lords attempt to defy the commons over this matter, and to force sectarian education on the nation, the cry of disestablishment will at once be raised in multitudinous volume.

Traitors to the Reformation.

An immense sensation is being created by the publication of the report of the royal commission, for it affords a most lurid picture of the extent to which ritualists in the Church of England are endeavoring to teach practices condemned by the commissioners. Two noble ladies, the Countess of Lindsey and Lady Wimborne, who are ardent Protestants and devoted members of the Anglican church, made it their duty to investigate matters and give evidence before the commission. And many other highly competent and intelligent persons gave their testimony, all in the same direction. Lady Wimborne has been visiting various churches. She emphatically described the children's mass celebrated in several different sanctuaries, and some of the clergy who added their testimony dwelt indignantly on this children's eucharist. A priest leads the boys and girls in acts of adoration of the sacrament. Thousands of children in different parts of the land are being taught the doctrine of trans-substantiation and the adoration of the Virgin. Such teaching in professedly Protestant churches is naturally considered by true Protestants an intolerable abomination. The great aim of the Pseudo-Protestants otherwise styled Anglo-Catholics, is to capture the young people, and to a large extent they are succeeding. But the most audacious moves are being made in other directions. The "Monks of Plaistow" are an illustration. These are Anglican clergymen who have established an order which is in all essential characteristics really Romanist. They call their organization, planted on the edge of London, not far from my own suburb, "The Society of the Divine Compassion." Now, these Romanizing priests are all members of the Church of England, the Church of the Reforma-

tion and the boasted bulwark of the nation against popery; nevertheless, they defy all the regulations and enactments of the church as an evangelical institution, and go coolly on their insidious course, wearing vestments fearfully and wonderfully made, burning lights on the altar, reserving the sacrament for the sick, hearing the confessions, while performing devout work amongst the very poor. The members of this order wear black monastic habits, with cowls and girdles, and their bare feet are shod in sandals. These remarkable men gain their living by watchmaking and printing.

Cradled at Oxford.

This curious order sprang up at that "nidus" of ritualism, the University of

Oxford. It was founded twelve years ago at Oxford by three young men of good family—Father Adderley, Father Chappell and Father Andrew. Such an order grows slowly. The bishop of St. Albans "professed" the members and blessed their habits. His successor, the present bishop, is known sternly to disapprove the ways of these Romanizers in the Anglican church, but they laugh at the thought of his interference, and have been openly deriding the condemnation passed on the ritualists by the report. The order to-day consists of five fathers, all of whom are priests of the Church of England, three brothers, and ten novices—one of whom, a parish clergyman with a good appointment, gave up his living to join the society.

(Continued on Page 1149.)

The Joy of Soul Winning[*]   By R. H. Crossfield

"If a man is unhappy, this must be his own fault; for God intended all men to be happy." Thus spake Epictetus, the Roman slave philosopher, and he spake the truth.

The reason that we are not happy frequently lies in the fact that we are not looking for happiness in the right place. The rich man sought it in great accumulation, and when he thought he had found great joy his soul took wings and flew down to hell. The younger son sought it in riotous living with courtesans, and the moment he drained the cup of dissipation to the lees, he found the direst shame and destitution awaiting him. Napoleon sought joy on the field of glory, but when about to stride three continents like a mighty colossus, he found his sun that arose in marvelous splendor at Austerlitz ingloriously setting at Waterloo. Mark Anthony sought this *summum bonum* in love, but when Cleopatra became the goddess of his idolatry, when "content with her to live, content with her to die," he discovered that human love lasts but a day, and he paid the price of his blood for thus loving.

God wants you to have the joy that Christ experienced in the three dimensions. Have you been in the habit of looking on Christ as the man of sorrow and acquainted with grief? True, his babyhood and manhood were hotly pursued by malice and hatred. His friends were few, means he had none, and, what was worse, he was despised and rejected of men. Yet, these were but the incidents of his life. His *real* life from beginning to end was full of joy—a gladness not dependent on the thermometer, appetite, property, friends, home or social standing, but derived from serving his Father by doing good. This is his meaning when he says, "I have meat to eat ye know not of." Again, he rejoices because God had revealed his plan of redemption to the ignorant, poor and burdened, through him.

Do you want the most characteristic portraiture of Christ? Go not to Raphael's *Transfiguration*, or Rubens' *Descent From the Cross* or Munkacsy's *Christ Before Pi-*

late, or Hoffman's *Christ in Gethsemane*, or Titian's *Redeemer*, or Holman Hunt's *Light of The World*, but turn to his own delineation of himself in the parable of the Shepherd and the Lost Sheep. The ninety and nine were safe in the fold, but one had wandered "out on the mountains wild and bare, far from the tender shepherd's care," and immediately he goes to seek the lost. When he finds it he lays it on his shoulder, *rejoicing*. When he returns home he calls his friends and neighbors to rejoice with him, saying, "I have found the lost sheep."

Did Christ ever rejoice? I answer, did he ever find the lost? Passing by the custom house one day, he found a publican, Matthew by name, and Christ rejoiced for a lost sheep was found. In a sycamore tree he found Zacchaeus, in the land of Zarepta he found the widow, at Capernaum he found the woman with an issue of blood and the Centurion, at Bethany, the family of Lazarus, and in the Sanhedrim at Jerusalem, Nicodemus and Joseph of Arimathea. Great rejoicing always, for in the short period of his ministry he found at least five hundred men and women who were lost.

Now Christ came to give that joy to you and to me, the happiness that comes to the redeemed as a result of being saved and of saving others. Any man may very seriously question his claim to Christianity whose life is barren of the joys of the gospel. However genuine may have been your conversion, you should know that the joyless life is not now Christian. Such should pray to God, "Restore unto me the joy of thy salvation."

The joys of a saved life do not depend upon physical or moral environment. The Christian is not exempt from suffering, trouble and death. The hot breath of disease may consume the body. Pale death may knock at your door and take away the idol of your home. Temptation may aim his arrows at your heart. To render the Christian incapable of suffering, trouble and death would be to render him incapable of joy. But these things are merely on the surface and do not extend to the deep things of life. In a mighty storm at

sea one thinks that the whole ocean must be troubled to its bottom by Neptune's trident. But not so; the great ocean never knows a storm. The waves do not extend more than 40 or 50 feet below the surface. Go down 100 feet and the disturbance is not enough to break a rope of sand. At the bottom, no evidence is found of recent or even remote fury, save the wrecks that have quietly taken their place with the dead. So Christ prayed that his disciples might have a joy that this world can

❦ ❦

GOOD AND HARD

Results of Excessive Coffee Drinking.

It is remarkable what suffering some persons put up with just to satisfy an appetite for something.

A Mich. woman says: "I had been using coffee since I was old enough to have a cup of my own at the table, and from it I have suffered agony hundreds of times in the years past.

"My trouble first began in the form of bilious colic, coming on every few weeks and almost ending my life. At every attack for 8 years I suffered in this way. I used to pray for death to relieve me from my suffering. I had also attacks of sick headache, and began to suffer from catarrh of the stomach, and of course awful dyspepsia.

"For about a year I lived on crackers and water. Believing that coffee was the cause of all this suffering, I finally quit it and began to use Postum Food Coffee. It agreed with my stomach, my troubles have left me and I am fast gaining my health under its use.

"No wonder I condemn coffee and tea. No one could be in a much more critical condition than I was from the use of coffee. Some doctors pronounced it cancer, others ulceration, but none gave me any relief. But since I stopped coffee and began Postum I am getting well so fast I can heartily recommend it for all who suffer as I did." Name given by Postum Co., Battle Creek, Mich. Read the little book, "The Road to Wellville." "There's a reason."

*Address delivered at the State Sunday-school Association convention at Ashland, Ky., August 23.

ay. If you are a genuine Chris-
you have a joy in your life.
: seventy returned to Jesus they
ing because of the overthrow
plans and the grace manifested
After the beginning of the re-
amaria, Luke observes, "And
nuch joy in that city." When
s believed at Antioch the dis-
filled with joy, and when the
ed Jerusalem there was great
the brethren. Paul addresses
ans as "my joy and my crown."
lonians are likewise praised as
and joy."
e mother of the Gracchi was
her jewels she answered, point-
boys, "These are my jewels."
tand before the throne of grace
t point to wealth, fame or real-
on, but to those we have
Christ, saying, "These are my
joy and crown."

we have brought to the foot of the

b we have lead to the fold,
as bright jewels, our crown to adorn,
autiful city of gold."

ds, do not pray for joy. It is
f cause and effect rather than
ix two parts of hydrogen and
oxygen and the result will be
s is invariably the result in all

worlds and eras. Now, put a Christian
and a loving effort to save souls together
and the result will be just as invariably,
a joy-filled life. You need not have the
accessories of wealth, influence, environment, learning, friends—this is a sure recipe for joy.

Hear Theodore Cuyler after forty-four
years' experience as a preacher: "To serve
Him in saving men gives me so much delight that I would not stoop down to pick
up a monarch's crown."

Sunday-school teachers, if your life is
more or less cheerless and disconsolate, go
to work in dead earnest to save that bad
boy or uninterested girl in your class. Such
work will transfigure your present life.

"Would you know earth's highest happiness,
Would you know its greatest blessedness,
Would you know its truest joyfulness,
Make some other heart rejoice."

I often wonder why it is that Sunday-
school teachers do not bring more of their
pupils to Christ without the assistance of
the evangelist. May I venture to give some
reasons for this condition? First of all,
frequently Christ is obscured in our lives.
Men and women do not read the Bible
from the cold page of the canon. They
read it as translated by our words and
deeds. They do not know Christ as Matthew, Mark, Luke and John have characterized him, but as you have reproduced

him in your professed Christia
is pre-eminently true of the
such especially are we unwritt
yet known and read accurately.

The second cause of the fail
the boy or girl of accountable
to a lack of zeal. Why not a
plan? At Corinth, Ephesus and
he *persuaded* both Jews and G
cerning Jesus." In the presen
to become a Christian. Writ
Church of Corinth he said, "K
fear of the Lord we persuade n
not become so zealous for the s
our boys and girls that we will
the burden of our hearts and
persuade them to accept Christ?
Finally, we fail frequently f
faith. Blessed is the Sunday-sc
er that expects the salvation of
Never give up. Sink self, ex
believe that God will give you
in the lives of those he has
teach, and sooner or later the v
be won.

Covet earnestly the joy of seei
saved come to salvation. P
trust, to this end, and God will
the desire of thy heart and a
teous and exquisite!

Owensboro, Ky.

can Missions and the Uncompleted Ch

uded from Last Week.)

be stated that gifts have been
to the English B. M. S. and
attempts put forth, chiefly
enfel, the veteran missionary
iety, for the express purpose
connecting the eastern and
ains of stations, and thus
ca one great trans-continental
issionary activity.

k intervening gap lies quite
the territory of the Congo
in its great eastern section.
arrest of missionary prog-
s as well as in other tracts,
nost unpardonable and crim-
te" only in pushing the das-
k of self-enrichment and na-
rement. This state has no
or the Gospel than the devil
ow sharp a contrast between
: and actual practices of this
ation to the Lord's work and
es, professed and theoretical,
ding! We should not expect
quests for mission sites along
ai, made to the State by the
n the hope of lessening the
ch between the eastern and
ains of stations should be, as
wholly ignored, and now for
years. The one site that was
em by the State was with-
a Catholic mission is now lo-
The gifts, prayers and ef-
od's children will some day
Heaven for the completion of

ler "thanks God and takes
s he reaches the chain of
tions from the west coast,
) English societies, B. M. S
B. M., and the two American
e A. B. M. U. and the F. C.
stands on Christian soil, is
by a Gospel meeting, and
greets not only European
: native Christians.

tual conditions of the upper
r with its mission stations,
hools, native evangelists and
orkers, is in strong contrast
f the dark gap which marks
real central Africa.

r Eben Creighton on a journey
and Central Africa.

The genius of the work both at Yakusu on the west and of Toro on the east
is that of pushing on and on into Africa's
central heart-blackness untill together
they close in, the gap vanishing, and the
work and workers touching heart and
hand for God and the native race. In
this region the problem of the evangel
would at once be that of leading the
Mohammedan to the true worship of
God and his Christ; for even the heathen is swayed by his influence. Because of other conditions he is not likely
to repeat the experience of the C. M. S.
at the Mombasa coast and labor on for
thirty years without a single convert to
Christianity from that rock of Mohammedanism. With a working knowledge
of Ki-Swahili (to be obtained from the
valuable C. M. S. grammar, and from
one's porter carriers as he proceeds
westward to and through the forest) one,
it is believed, could preach to the hearing
and salvation of the Mohammedan-
heathen peoples, stretching from the
western slopes of Mount Ruwenzori to
the Congo River. One can not think
that this gap will divide the C. M. S. on
the one side and the B. M. S. on the
other, or that these missions will have
the realization of their prayers and aims
long deferred.

The story of Christian missions on
the Congo is not a new one. The large
and rapid multiplication of schools by
the B. M. S. is reaching many out of the
vicinity of the mission station.

The Congo Balolo Mission is interdenominational in character and is doing
most remarkable work in penetrating
the great unevangelized interior along
the Lolanga River and its tributaries.

The work of the American Baptist
Missionary Union, formerly the Livingstone Inland Mission, is for the most
part confined to the Lower Congo; the
two stations on the Upper Congo are
Bwemba and Ikoko. Bwemba Station
is now taking up work among the long-
neglected Bateke. The Ikoko Station
founded by those pioneers, Mr. and Mrs.
Joseph Clark, is the one missionary post
on Lake Mantumba, which is some fifty
miles south from the main river. The
training and teaching of girls, together
with industrial work, are the striking

features of the Ikoko Station.
the largest churches of Cong
in the A. B. M. U. work. Ba
ka and the name of that vetera
Henry Richards, at once bring
the large and sweeping work of
Spirit in that revival there, wh
is an outstanding fact in missic
tory.

After the refreshing Christ
at Stanley Falls with the Yakı
ers, the traveler, happily exch
weary land journey for the rest
er descent on the great Con;
way, calls on the ninth day o
at Bolengi, the American F.
station on the equator, the
of which work he had not eve
until reaching the Congo River.

The traveler's purpose wa
willed, to push up the
River and traverse in the ir
the Lord's work the great unev
tract extending into the So
on to Lake Chad. But the cert
idence attending the traveler,
welcome at this Christian sett
a great wilderness of woe and
a vital point in his own life.
of the accompanying Provide
also a sense that greater fi
might attend a settled work.
the wide reaches of Bolengi's b
try, and the traveler's own con
feeling, all combined welcome
home-like, hospitable welcome
warm, generous invitation of
Mrs. Dye, to induce the missio
eler, stranger that he was, to :
Bolengi and help if he may in
the work, for which this mi
tion stands.

The youngest work of all, th
Foreign Christian Missionary
is conducted by the Disciples
and is located at Bolengi, at
where the equator crosses th
on the west. This work, with
church of 126 members, suppor
and 13 native evangelists, is pl
emphasis where is found Afric
set need, and the chief retur
sionary labor, viz., on having
of itinerating evangelists trave
back and unevangelized tracts
sands of square miles of unev

territory to the east and south await the labor of the F. C. M. S.

Friends at home who have not already done so, may be interested in tracing upon the map the outline of the parish of the Bolengi station. You will not forget that this one mission station of the F. C. M. S. in Africa is located close to the place where the great Congo River crosses the equator on the west.

The spacious parish which looks to Bolengi for the Gospel forms an immense triangle, whose apex falls upon the basis station itself. Practically all of this vast country lies either on or south of this line. But first let us look at the one section of the parish in which lies the upper side of the Congo River. From the Mobangi River stretching eastward on to the main river is a "V"-shaped section of territory. This entire district is untouched by the Gospel save as the Bolengi evangelists visit it. This section is inhabited by the fierce cannibal "Balois." It is a fact for thanksgiving that Bolengi's native evangelists have already opened up the work in this needy country. It is the plan and purpose of the mission that a periodical itinerary of the missionary himself be made in these countries, and thus enforce, supplement and superintend the work of the native evangelists. The presence of the white teacher is necessary to the influence, growth and stability of the work in every section, however often the visits of the native worker may be.

Returning to the field which lies on the lower side of the river, we take our position at Bolengi, the apex of the triangular section of country with its thousands of square miles of territory, with its people numbering into the millions. Northwards the parish of Bolengi is limited by the Lolanga River. Eastward the field yet to be evangelized extends to the watershed of the Lemani River, seven degrees east of Bolengi. To the south the parish may be said to extend to the great Kassai River, four degrees south of Bolengi.

In pushing work through this great section of territory the evangelist will follow the waterways, not only of the Ikelemba and Bosira Rivers, but also along the Juapa and Momboyo Rivers, large, navigable branches of the Bosira. Along the Bosira the itinerary of the evangelist lies to the southeast, and along the Juapa his journey will be eastward towards the watershed of the Lemami. The evangelists have made successive preaching trips up the Bosira and the Momboyo for a distance of 150 miles. The country around the Bolengi station to a radius of 50 miles has been thoroughly evangelized.

In the Bosira district the Catholic work is firmly entrenched, having the aid and favor of the state, while the Bolengi evangelists meet with constant difficulty, and recently have been repeatedly sent back to the station with scarce a hearing for the Gospel of life they preached. Bolengi evangelists were compelled to sleep on the sandbars of the river during their last trip, because the natives did not dare to let them stay or land in their towns. Thus a real setback has come to the aggressive work since the place where, formerly, the evangelists of Bolengi were freely received is now closed to them. Yet we are happy to state that three Christian young men, the first fruits of that country, have returned home, and are now holding services in their own and neighboring towns. In spite of concealed interference by the Catholic government to the Protestant mission and the interest kindled in past days is not entirely dying out, and the spark of Chris-

tian faith and life still stays on, and will, we trust, soon be fanned to burning flames.

The white teacher, as the natives love to call him, as soon as he is able to travel, hopes to itinerate in these new closed sections.

Real church unity prevails on the Congo, the natives passing freely by letter from the communion of their own to that of another church. In times of sickness or need, the members of one society hasten to the side of a fellow missionary of another mission and a healthy Scriptural fellowship is thus maintained. Evidently the native Christians know nothing of the denominational divisions of the homelands.

Africa, with the in-rush of new Europeanism, has a peculiar present, pressing need. This should rest heavily upon the heart of the Church. The incoming of government agents, promoters, speculators and traders is affecting already the proverbial native degeneration, the resultant of the contract of complex with primitive peoples. To the moral depravity of heathen degradation, with its witchcraft, polygamy and slavery, is added the rottenness of licentious Europeans; and this is the standard of enlightenment that so-called civilization gives to benighted Africa.

And then to this add the fact that ag-

gressive missionary work has been so curtailed to the present by the refusal of the state to give permanent sites, that the trader and government official, with their baneful influences, are far in advance of the missionary firing line. All the advance work is practically restricted to the few itinerating journeys that the busy missionary and his native evangelists can make. And things have come to such a pass that even the itinerating of the native evangelists is obstructed.

The traveler, in the long, silent marches of Africa's caravan file, often recalls that sure prophetic promise accorded by Scripture to the dark land, viz.: "Ethiopia shall yet stretch forth her hands unto God." This land which sheltered not only the ancient people of God's chosen race, but even the threatened infancy of the Redeemer himself; this land which gave a cross-bearer to the weary Saviour, dropping on his march to the world's redemption, and which received the Christian Ethiopian on his classic journey from Palestine; this land which has received so choice a cluster of life-offerings—a Livingstone, a Mackay, a Gordon—will one day, the curse lifting, the blessing descending, enter upon that life of fullness, emancipation and victory that our Father in heaven purposes for all his children on earth.

E. L. Frazier's Dilemma
By E. S. MUCKLEY.

In his article in THE CHRISTIAN-EVANGELIST of August 9, under the question, "Who is a Christian in the Twentieth Century?" E. L. Frazier unconsciously reveals himself in the situation of a dilemma. The fact that there are "pious, unimmersed" gets him there. On the one hand he discovers that the people, who honestly, in the spirit of submission to their chosen Master, were sprinkled believing they were obeying him in the ordinance of baptism, seem to manifest a Christian character fully as high in grade, judging by the New Testament requirements of Christian character, as is manifest in those who have been immersed. On the other hand he discovers that the New Testament demands faith, repentance and immersion of those who want to be Christians.

Brother Frazier recognizes that the faith and repentance of those who have honestly thought their sprinkling baptism are as genuine as the faith and repentance of the immersed, and their characters as good; but he hinges their right to be called Christians on the act of immersion. And as they have not been immersed they are not Christians. But he does not want to just deliberately disown them, or intimate that God disowns them, and his Christian courtesy prevents him from wanting to hurt their feelings, so he admits that they have Christian characters. To admit that they are Christians would be to validate their faith and repentance, for these and not baptism are the steps that determine Christian character. Their bodies have not been immersed, therefore they are not Christians; their characters are all right, therefore they (their characters) are Christian. You may not call them Christians, but you may call their characters Christian.

Now, it seems to me that it is sufficient to state this position of Brother Frazier's in this extended form to display its fallacy. However, I want to show that his attempt to seize both horns of the dilem-

ma is both illogical and unscriptural. I am sure that neither good logic nor the New Testament will sustain his attempt to show that a man can have a Christian character without being a Christian. He says:

"There is a great difference between a Christian character and a non- or anti-Christian character. All know this and feel drawn to the one showing Christian character. But is he a Christian because he is a Christian in character?"

Now, what I want to show is, that the only way to answer this question logically or Scripturally is in the affirmative.

In the first place Brother Frazier's logic goes limping in the illustrations he uses. The fallacy may not be apparent at first glance. If I did not know Brother Frazier's contempt for trickery in logic, I would accuse him of working off a shrewd bit of sophistry on his brethren. The fallacy is in the double use of the word "character," which implies that there is as much of a change from the non-Masonic to the Masonic character, or from the non-American to the American character, as there is from the non-Christian to the Christian character. Now, Brother Frazier would not admit that the change is as great, or of the same nature, in the one case as in the other. Therefore he will have to admit that his illustrations are not only inapt but fallacious in point of logic.

The change from the non-Christian to a Christian character is essentially a moral and spiritual change, an inward transformation that not only makes one unlike his former self, but also distinguishes him from his fellows who are Christian in character. But no such change, or similar change, is necessary in becoming a Mason or an American. The morals of a man are not supposed to be effected at all in becoming a Mason or an American. If a change of character is necessary at all it must occur before a man becomes a Mason. That is, the process of making a Mason does not

(Continued on Page 1150.)

Our Budget

—Our International Convention!—

—Now has the center of the stage and the lime light glow.

—October 12-18 are the magic days, Buffalo the place. Your presence essential to greatest success.

—Sacrifice some where else if need be (not from amounts allotted church and benevolences) and attend this convention. Go in the spirit of ancient Israel ascending to Jerusalem in the days of her glory.

—Matters of infinitely greater moment to the Republic than will come before the great national political convention, will be considered and largely determined at this assembly. You are entitled to a seat in its deliberations. This, like other Christian privileges, ought to be lived up to.

—Our general superintendent was prospecting over the Wabash and in the convention city last week and was greatly pleased with the car service and provisions being made by the Buffalo brethren for the entertainment of the convention. If a 30-day extension of our tickets is secured everything will have been done that could be to prove their hospitality, enterprise and sagacity.

—Every congregation, aye, every Christian household ought to have a delegate in the convention going determined to do and receive good, who will get surcharged with the convention spirit while there, and make an enthusiastic and intelligible report after returning home. There are others than preachers who can do this but churches never invest money more profitably than when sending their ministers up to our great convocations.

—CHRISTIAN-EVANGELIST headquarters will be at the Buckingham, within two blocks of convention hall. So long as there is room (but it is limited) we shall welcome our friends there. We have secured the remarkably low rate of $2 per diem, American plan. The hall is not in the hotel district, so we have secured hundreds of rooms in nearby homes having all modern conveniences, at the rate of $1 per room and breakfast. Other meals may be taken at the Buckingham or with the convention caterer. This will be found a considerable saving in time and car fare. Friends will be assigned rapidly as their names are sent us. Our services freely and gladly accorded our patrons.

—A. M. Hooton, of Lowell, Ind., resigned his pastorate there August 27 to take effect at once.

—B. S. Edwards is in a meeting at Amen Chapel, Ralls county, Mo., with four added at last report and growing interest.

—W. J. Dodge, of Jackson, is in Minnesota on account of his health. His friends are hoping he will soon be restored to his Kentucky ministry and with renewed strength.

—Wren J. Grinstead closed his work at Jellico, Ky., September 1, and has accepted a position in the State Normal at Richmond. R. G. Sherer succeeds him at once at Jellico.

—Churches needing an educated and experienced minister after next December will be placed in communication with one by addressing J. F. King, Box 75, R. R. No. 2, Albion, Ill.

—The churches at Canton and Galva, Kan., are in need of a pastor, each being a "half-time" point. Salary $700. Fay Finkle, Galva, Kan., will advise with applicants for the position.

—The affable H. R. Murphy, of the Soldier, Kan., church, visited us Tuesday, returning to his work from vacation visits at Fulton, Ky., and Jackson, Tenn., and other haunts of his earlier days.

—G. W. Terrell, of Stanberry, is in a meeting at Amity, Mo. Neighboring preachers are earnestly invited to attend the meeting when possible and assist in the strengthening of our cause at Amity.

—Secretary J. H. Mohorter was most enthusiastically received by the Indian Territory convention and received three life memberships for the organization to which he is giving such splendid service.

—We were favored Thursday with visits from E. M. Smith, of Centralia, Mo., and Daniel Stewart, of Selma, Cal. These are two of the ablest young men from their respective states. Their kindling enthusiasm for the Master is infectious and helpful.

—Remember that the reason for a great offering for Church Extension lies in the great need. The ambition of our Board of Church Extension is to house every one of our homeless missions by October, 1909. That is one feature of the Centennial program.

—C. F. Trimble, assisted by F. M. O'Neal and wife, of Springfield, Mo., closed a two weeks' meeting at Seiling, Okla., August 12, with 26 additions. Thence they went to Carnev, Okla., and are now in meeting at Ada, I. T.

—L. C. Howe, of New Castle, Ind., advises us that Charles Schults and wife, of that city, are ready to hold evangelistic meetings. He writes that Brother Schults holds very successful meetings and preaches a strong, clear and pure gospel, and that his wife is an excellent singer and leader.

—E. W. Allen's welcome to the Central Church at Wichita has been most cordial and whole-hearted. While Brother Allen relinquished a great church in Indiana, he has found material for one equally great among his new people. There were six additions at his first Lord's day service and two since.

—D. G. Combs, in a recent brief evangelistic tour through Carter, Mercer and Madison counties, Kentucky, added 61 to the membership of the churches. He was in the midst of a promising meeting when compelled to conclude on account of the serious illness of his daughter.

—E. J. Meacham is in a meeting at Murfreesboro, Tenn. This means our church there will be greatly strengthened numerically, educationally and spiritually. J. H. Mohorter, secretary of our National Benevolent Association, will preach in Brother Meacham's Wilmington (Ohio) church September 9.

—The yearly meeting of the Fredericksburg (Ohio) church, recently held, was a great success. C. C. Maple, minister, writes that "the preaching was of the old order, and was well received, even by the denominations, who gave us the best of attention." The meeting will be held next year in October.

—R. H. Lampkin, of Dexter, preached in Charleston, Mo., August 29. He found four tithers there and five others pledged themselves to the tithing system after hearing his sermon. The church is without regular preaching, but is building a substantial brick house at a cost of $3,200 on a $1,400 lot.

great city will be greatly helped by them through the fall and winter campaigns.

—J. W. Masters has been evangelizing in Clay county, Mo., during August. He organized a new country congregation of 23 members.

—H. H. Hubbell, of Lewiston, Idaho, has resigned the pastorate of the church there to accept the work at Grangeville, same state.

—G. L. Bush, formerly of McKinney, Texas, has begun his new pastorate at Gainesville under most favorable omens. McKinney has not yet called his successor.

—The Martin family have concluded their meeting at Sturgis, Ky., with eighteen additions, and are now assisting C. A. Donelson in a meeting at Muncie, Ind.

—A. P. Aten, one of our able Indian Territory preachers, has resigned his pastorate at Holdenville and accepted a position as teacher in the high school at Oklahoma City.

—Any congregation desiring the services of a young man of wide experience, whose character and reputation are O. K., will hear something to their advantage by addressing B. B. Tyler, 156 South Pennsylvania avenue Denver.

—B. W. Rice, of Caldwell, Ida., has just launched "The Actual Doer" on the sea of journalism. It is in advocacy of the Gospel of a kind-heart and helping hand. We wish our brother great success in preaching through its columns.

—The books of the American Christian Missionary Society close September 30. Let all remittances designed to enter into this year's reports be forwarded immediately to the society at the Y. M. C. A. building, Cincinnati, O.

—The fifth annual meeting of the West Virginia Ministerial Association will be held at Sistersville, W. Va., September 12-16. A very interesting and helpful program has been arranged and which it is hoped a host of attendants will enjoy.

—J. C. Mullens, of Hartshorne, I. T., has begun his new pastorate at South McAlester. He was delayed in making the change several weeks on account of the serious illness of Sister Mullens. We are glad to report she is now greatly improved in health.

—O. C. Smith, San Bernardino, Cal., informs us that after a "pastorless summer," E. E. Lowe, of Arkansas City, Kan., has begun his ministry with that church. Great results with Brother Lowe as pastor are anticipated by the San Bernardino congregation, " as he knows no other than success."

—C. W. Comstock, of Miami, Mo., closed a twenty-day meeting at Orrick, Friday, with fifteen additions, eleven by confession and baptism. He was assisted by Prof. J. A. Butler and wife, of Mound City, Mo. Brother Comstock adds, "It is a great thing to win souls."

—Professor Zollars has been in Oklahoma and the Indian Territory for the past 30 days in the interest of a new college. Disciples are thoroughly aroused as to the needs of such an institution. The recent South McAlester convention voted to act in co-operation with Oklahoma in establishing a Bible school. The present indications are that the enterprise will soon be launched.

❧❧

For the Nursery—For the Table.

Whether as an ideal food for infants or for general household use, Borden's Eagle Brand Condensed Milk has no equal; of no other food product can this be truthfully said.

—Following the example set by numerous other congregations of late, the Sturgis, Ky., church has purchased a beautiful parsonage costing $1,400. One of our Centennial efforts should be complementing every possible church building with a home for the minister.

—A. H. Mulkey, of Brownsville, Ore., is the recipient of two surprises; one was a two-weeks' vacation, granted by his church board, and the second was to find his church house beautifully painted on his return. Such amenities are among the delights of Christian fellowship.

—Wilford Field, of Effingham, Ill., writes that D. K. Bebout will soon remove from that city. Brother Bebout is a graduate of Bethany College and a post-graduate student of Butler. Not only has he splendid educational training but an untarnished Christian character.

—John N. Talley, of Manor, Texas, recently concluded a meeting with home forces with fifteen added by confession and baptism. He will resume the meeting in November. Brother Talley's Mississippi ministry was crowned with great success, as his work in Texas will also doubtless be.

—J. V. Coombs has again heard "the cry of the wild." He has resigned at San Jose, Cal., and enters the evangelistic field, beginning at Kent, O., September 9. J. Walter Wilson will conduct the singing. Brother Coombs' permanent address will be 413 Majestic building, Indianapolis, Ind.

—We call attention to the dedication of the new building at Kimberlin Heights, Tenn. President Johnson is doing a noble, self-sacrificing work in behalf of indigent young Disciples who would become preachers of the Word. We wish for him the help of the brotherhood and bright visions of achievements growing more splendid with the flight of years.

—The New England Christian Missionary Society will hold its September convention at Marion, R. I., October 4-7. In the printed program confidence is expressed in the early establishment of a prosperous church at Manchester as a result of Brother Yeuell's evangelistic campaign, followed as it is by W. C. Crerie's faithful pastoral work.

—J. I. Orrison, of Sedalia, recently concluded two good meetings, one at Montrose, Mo., resulting in sixteen additions; the other at Sheldon with twenty additions. He reports eighteen additions in his regular work since last report. What a proselyter Brother Orrison is getting to be; seventeen of these fifty-four were from the denominations.

—F. F. Walters preached the concluding sermon of the summer Sunday evening union meetings at Neosho, Mo. It is described as a masterful review of Acts 2: 1-40. One of the city school teachers made the good confession at the conclusion of the sermon. There have been 103 additions to the church during Brother Walters' nine months' pastorate. He begins meeting with W. F. Turner at the First Church, Joplin, next Lord's day.

—F. E. Blanchard, our able minister at Smith Centre, Kan., is in a meeting with the nearby Stuart church. He writes that the Dewey Christian Endeavor Society has recently issued a unique and beautiful souvenir of their church. He will supply Endeavorers with samples for 15 cents, and suggests they can not only be used as beautiful souvenirs but also as a source of profit to any Endeavor society or church.

—G Lyle Smith, whose pastorate at Waco, Texas, has been successful beyond most sanguine expectations, has been called to Texarkana to succeed

W. S. Bullard. It seemed Brother Bullard's enforced abandonment would prove almost ruinous to our Texarkana church, but under Brother Smith's leadership it will have a bright future. A host of friends hope for Brother Bullard's early restoration to health.

—Secretary J. H. Mohorter reports the Indian Territory convention at South McAlester was the greatest in the history of territorial co-operation. The largest offerings were made during the year of any preceding 12 months. There were more additions to the churches and the largest number of new churches established. We may rest assured the east end of the new state of Oklahoma will lose none of its enthusiasm for Christ and the missions after the merger.

—I. L. Burgess, of the Grayville, Ill., Christian church begins a revival meeting next Lord's day. After the 16th he will be assisted by Evangelist T. J. Head, of Missouri. Brother Burgess wishes to "colonize" Disciples around his work in Grayville. He writes there is a good opening for general merchandising, also for one who would care to purchase a printing establishment, together with a weekly paper having a circulation of 1,000.

—E. S. Allhands, of Arkadelphia, Ark., has just concluded a sixteen-day meeting with his brother, Charles A., with the Bethesda church, near Amity, Ark. Visible results were eighteen additions, ten being by primary obedience. A Sunday-school was organized and the preliminary steps taken for the formation of an Endeavor society. Our congratulations to every church securing the services of these consecrated and gifted evangelists.

—The twenty-third annual convention of the churches of Christ in Mississippi meets in McComb City September 10-

13. Every church is urged to send representatives to this convention. Those attending must secure certificates from their railroad agents. This will guarantee a return rate of one cent per mile plus 25 cents. The notice is signed by M. F. Harmon, president convention; Will A. Sessions, president board, and W. W. Phares, corresponding secretary.

—A letter from Brother Kokendoffer informs us that the Small-St. John meeting for which such extensive preparations have been made at Mexico, Mo., is started with excellent prospects of great success. The prayer-meeting of the preceding Wednesday evening was intense in prayerful thought and exhortation. One young lady made the good confession and was buried with her Lord in baptism the next morn-

P. W. Harding.

ing. On the preceding Lord's day great sermons were preached by W. B. Taylor, former pastor, now of Moberly, Mo., and A. E. Cory, of China. Brother Kokendoffer is relying a great deal on the help of his assistant, P. W. Harding, to whose fidelity and general effectiveness he pays a beautiful tribute. Brother Harding was for a number of years traveling representative of THE CHRISTIAN-EVANGELIST and is kindly remembered by thousands all over the land. Faithful reports of this meeting will be made in these columns every week. Five hundred CHRISTIAN-EVANGELISTS each week will aid Brother Kokendoffer and his other assistants through this meeting.

—The annual gathering of the Disciples of DeKalb county, Ind., convened with the Butler church August 25 and 26. The pastor, Robert B. Chapman, writes that the success of the meeting was due to the fact that Bro. Wallace Tharp was the speaker of the occasion, delivering four masterful discourses in his eloquent way. Brother Tharp left a most favorable impression, and the entire community hope for another visit from him.

—Evangelists Spicer and Douthit closed a revival meeting at Troy, Texas, August 9 with thirteen additions; another at Elgin, Texas, August 26, with twenty-two additions. They are now in Johnson City, Texas, with fine prospects for a good meeting with Brother Hardin Welsh's congregation. Brother Welsh has made such excellent preparation for this meeting that the evangelists will gladly attribute to him the largest meed of success.

—George E. Dew, minister of the church at Holden, Mo., reports R. H. Fife's meeting, concluding there August 31, as one

of the best in the history of that church for years. It was of 19 days' duration, with 29 additions, 23 by confession and baptism. The church is greatly strengthened and in fine condition for aggressive work for the Master. Brother Dew thus concludes: "Brethren Fife and Saunders are both good men and true, and make a strong Gospel team. May God bless them!"

—J. J. Cole, of Millersburg, Ohio, is unable to accept a pastorate at present that will involve his moving on account of the serious illness of his wife, who will probably have to undergo a second surgical operation. He would, however, like to assist some churches in protracted meetings until November, after which time he hopes to again enter a settled pastorate. Brother Cole is a man of ability and will be of great assistance to any church calling him into a revival meeting.

—J. D. Lawrence, of Muncie, Ind., Living-Link evangelist of this company, recently concluded a brief meeting at the Elm Grove Church, Geneva, Ind. A letter just received from J. L. Aspy, elder, informs us that the congregation tendered a unanimous vote of thanks to this company for sending Brother Lawrence to them. It was very gratifying to this House to know it is helping in the re-establishment of worship in many of our poor congregations. In this work Brother Lawrence has been phenomenally successful.

—The Kentucky state convention is assuming large proportions. Those asking for homes are sending in their names early and everything indicates that fully two thousand persons will attend. The railroads have granted half fare rates from all points, and as the Bible school work in central and southern Kentucky is united, the attendance promises to be good from both sections of the state. All names for entertainment should be sent to R. M. Hopkins, 218 Keller building, Louisville.

—The University of Missouri will hereafter grant credits for specified courses of work done in the Bible college of Missouri. This will enable our young men and women who come to Columbia for university work to take as a part of their work the courses specified in the Bible college. Pastors and parents should encourage them to do this. Dean W. J. Lhamon will consider it a favor if names and addresses are sent to him of young men and women who expect to attend the university the coming semester.

—Thomas Penn Ullom, Traverse City, Mich., sends an account of a visit to Monroe, Wis., where Chas. Reign Scoville is holding a great union revival meeting, to which we would gladly give publication save that Brother Scoville will send an illustrated report of the meeting at its conclusion, and we fear Brother Ullom has anticipated many features that would be duplicated in the evangelist's report. Brother Ullom pays eloquent tribute to Brother Scoville's ability and does some very fine writing in portraying ideal evangelism.

—An excellent article on "Repentance," by J. W. Kilborn, of Mt. Carmel, Ill., will appear next week. Thousands of CHRISTIAN-EVANGELISTS are now used each week by evangelists, and articles such as this are especially valuable to our readers. No other contributions will be more highly prized by the CHRISTIAN-EVANGELIST'S constituency than expositions of the great doctrines of faith, repentance and baptism and of the terms of forgiveness, inspiration of the Bible, the divinity of Christ, the laws of holiness and all that prepares us for Zion and helps us on the way.

Forty Places Left

Lynchburg, Va., Aug., 28' 1906.

DEAR EVANGELIST:

Randolph-Macon Woman's College has added this year, besides four other buildings, a new dormitory to accommodate another hundred students— giving homes for nearly four hundred students in residence. This is the reason that we have now forty places open for engagement. We shall be glad to hear from forty more well prepared students who want the best facilities.

WM. W. SMITH,
President.

—In our comments of Mrs. Maud D. Ferris's gift of $25,000 to our Christian Woman's Board of Missions for the establishment of a missionary training school as a memorial of her mother, Sarah A. Davis, Mrs. J. H. Garrison was reported as president of the Centennial Committee of the C. W. B. M. Sister Garrison's position is that of Centennial Secretary for the Missouri Auxiliaries. She, too, will be pleased to acknowledge the receipt of any sum of money for the realization of the C. W. B. M. Centennial hopes and purposes.

—Geo. A. Meek, secretary of the board of elders, favors us with a copy of the 21st anniversary programme of the Englewood Christian Church, Chicago, which will be rendered September 16-18. Among other interesting features will be a reception tendered to Editor J. H. Garrison at 4 p. m., Tuesday, September 18. Brother Garrison will lecture on Christian' Union at eight o'clock that evening. The program is replete with addresses by some of the ablest men and women of our brotherhood. The rapid growth of the Englewood church into a great power for righteousness in that mighty city during the pastorate of Bro. Charles G. Kindred is one of the happiest pages in the history of this Restoration movement in Chicago.

—Evangelist George C. Ritchey has served the South Idaho State Board since May 1, and in thirteen weeks' work has established three new churches, at Meridian, Emmett and Rupert. At Rupert the brethren had gotten together and selected officers, but the meeting added thirty-three of their membership, making forty-six in all. The church at Emmett starts with eighteen and the Meridian church with sixty-three. Rupert and Meridian have good Bible schools and Christian Endeavor societies. Emmett expects to organize a school soon. Brother Ritchey is in a meeting now at Nampa (aided by 300 CHRISTIAN-EVANGELISTS each week), which will be the last for the Idaho board at present. His time is taken until February. 1, 1907. After that date he will have associated with him his brother, Arthur F. Ritchey, a trained singing evangelist. They will accept calls anywhere after February 1, 1907, but prefer the Pacific coast and northwest. Address George C. Ritchey, Monmouth, Ore., box 166.

—There were 172 additions in the recent revival at Latham, Mo., in which H. J. Corwine, of California, Mo., was assisted by evangelists Allen Wilson and W. F. Lintt. Of these additions, 144 were by confession and baptism. The local paper

says: "H. J. Corwine, pastor of the California church, was the moving spirit in this great meeting, and to him should be given the credit for the inception and much of the success of the meeting. He planned the organization of the Christian churches of the county, and selected Latham as the most available point for the meeting. For months he has labored, advertising, and organizing for the meetings, and during the services he was the great power behind the wheel and is the happiest man in the county as a result." But Brother Corwine himself writes of the evangelists: "Brother Allen's sermons are replete with thought and enthusiasm. He is noticeably consistent and free from graft and sectarian bigotry. He presents the Christianity of Christ in a strictly modern way. His sermons on Christian evidences are especially strong. There is more of Christ in his sermons than in any other I ever heard. If he preaches you a sermon on baptism, you will see more Christ than water." Of W. F. Lintt he says: 'His personality, his ability and disposition to do personal work, his amiable disposition and character will make him a mighty power for God and good in any community." With such a combination of evangelists and pastor, what else can we expect but great meetings like this?

❦ ❦

The Maple-Miller Meeting, Gas City, Indiana.

The Maple-Miller evangelistic team begins their meeting with the Christian church, Gas City, Ind., next Monday evening. The first part of August Evangelist Maple was at Gas City preparing the way, organizing, appointing committees, etc., and the membership of the church have worked hard to have a great meeting. A report from there indicates that everything is ready for an ingathering.

Gas City is one of the boom towns, but now has the stability of a permanent, growing city in which we should

O. D. Maple.

have a strong church. It will now become a solid growing one. They have a good building paid for and located well, a good Bible school and Endeavor, and the church has a future.

J. Ross Miller, the singer, is one of their own young men. Nothing speaks better for a preacher or singer just en-

Catarrh Cured at Home.

Dr. Blosser Offers to Mail a Liberal Trial Treatment of His Catarrh Remedy Free to Sufferers.

If you have catarrh of the nose, throat or lungs, if you are constantly spitting, blowing the nose, have stopped up feeling, head noises, deafness, asthma, bronchitis or weak lungs, you can cure yourself at home by a remedy so simple that even a child can use it.

It will cost you only a postal card to get a liberal free trial package of Dr. Blosser's wonderful remedy. He sends it by mail to every interested sufferer. Certainly no offer could be more liberal, but he has such confidence in the remedy that he is willing to submit it to an actual test in your home. The full treatment is not expensive. A package containing enough to last one whole month will be sent by mail for $1.00.

A postal card with your name and address sent to Dr. J. W. Blosser, 475 Walton St., Atlanta, Ga., will bring you by return mail the free trial treatment and an interesting booklet, so that you can at once begin to cure yourself privately at home.

tering the work than for his own home congregation not only to endorse him but to employ him. Brother Miller is an exemplary Christian, and sings understandingly from the heart and sings to save souls.

It is to be hoped that in next week's CHRISTIAN-EVANGELIST, the report from Gas City will be inspiring. They will be helped by 300 CHRISTIAN-EVANGELISTS each week. The Maple-Miller team goes from Gas City to Cairo, Ill., where they begin a meeting October 1, and then Princeton, Ind., October 29.

❦ ❦

For a Church in New Hampshire.

Already acknowledged $922 25
J. F. Callahan ....　1 00
Oscar W. Riley ....　1 00
J. A. Hopkins ....　1 00
Mary E. Brown................　1 00
C. B. Spalding ....　2 00
W. F. Richardson ....　10 00
L. C. Stow ....　10 00

Total $948 25

There are hundreds of Disciples who would have fellowship in the Manchester church if they knew it would be a success. Brother and Sister, this enterprise is already a success. The degree of success depends upon the contributions of Disciples who desire a church of our own "faith and order" there sufficiently to pay out of their means for it. The people are ready for it, we have evangelists capable of doing their part well, and the Lord's approval of the undertaking is very manifest.

Now, while times are so prosperous nearly any of us can get some money for the church, and while there is so much interest in Manchester let us double the present subscription, maintain Brother Crerie for at least half time during this interim and soon have one of our best evangelists in Manchester to build up a Church of Christ there that will be creditable to us, inspiring to all New England Disciples, and a means unto the salvation of myriads.

Bringing the Children to Jesus.

BY FERD F. SCHULTZ.

Children are sadly neglected by many parents as regards their spiritual training. We underestimate their ability to understand the simple truths of the Word of God. It is often said that under certain ages, children are too young to learn these truths. This is wrong. The sooner the seed is planted, the sooner it will take root and grow, if we will only take the time and patience to properly prepare the ground for the receiving of the precious seed. But this is not all; there must be continued care and patience exercised in the cultivation of this seed that has been planted in the young hearts. It has been truly said that no other form of Christian effort will bring forth such immediate, large and lasting results as the work that is spent for the conversion of children.

Some children understand at an earlier age than others, hence no definite time can be set for the beginning of an understanding of spiritual truths. The writer remembers a boy just past his sixth year who has as clear a conception of the truth as regards his relation to the Savior as many an older person and upon his confession he was admitted into the membership of the church.

Now where shall the children be taught this spiritual truth? I would say, in the Bible school. This is the nursery of the church, and is thus the proper place for the children of the families of the church to be brought up in the knowledge of God and the Scriptures. Early Bible school service is the greatest stimulus in the young life for continuous service and ultimately coming into the kingdom. It is also the best safeguard in keeping children away from places of sin into which those who are neglected so easily fall. Children are more readily led to Christ than adults, hence the parents should redouble their efforts to make these good impressions early. It is important that parents accompany their children to divine services for the influence of their so doing is never forgotten.

A child's mind is very plastic, "like clay to impress and like marble to retain." Again, early conversions stand the test of years better than those made at a later period. Then, too, those who enter the church early have not so much to unlearn as those who have grown old in sin. Dr. Torrey very tritely remarks that "a man converted at sixty is a soul saved plus ten years, but a child saved at ten is a soul saved plus sixty years of service."

Beallsville, Ohio.

A Noble Offer.

Drake's Palmetto Wine, a purely vegetable compound gives vigor and energy to the whole body, soothes, heals and invigorates stomachs that are weakened by injurious living, or when the mucous lining of the stomach is impaired by hurtful medicines or food. Drake's Palmetto Wine will clear the Liver and Kidneys from congestion, cause them to perform their necessary work thoroughly and insure their healthy condition. Drake's Palmetto Wine cures every form of Stomach distress, such as indigestion, distress after eating, shortness of breath and heart trouble caused by indigestion. Drake's Palmetto Wine cures you permanently of that bad taste in the mouth, offensive breath, loss of appetite, heartburn, inflamed catarrhal or ulcerated Stomach and constipated or flatulent Bowels. The Drake Co., Wheeling, W. Va., proves all this to you by sending you free and prepaid a test bottle. For sale by all druggists. *Seventy-five cents* a bottle, usual dollar size.

Beautifying the Church House.

Nothing can be more fitting, appropriate, helpful in every way or important to a congregation than a good church house built and furnished for both convenience and beauty. Both of these qualities are everywhere evident in the natural world directly ordered and created by the great ruler of the universe. Love for them is a divine attribute that was planted in the very beginning in the heart of man.

As man is gradually brought from the darkness into which sin has led him, into the light where he may gaze upon the things which are pure, good and lovely, his admiration for order, convenience and beauty grows. If it is considered of prime importance for our homes and our cities to be built with these things in view, how very much more important for us to give our most thoughtful attention to the building and furnishing of our church homes in such a manner as will please the properly cultivated taste. This does not necessarily mean an expensive and imposing establishment any more than it can be claimed that only the mansion can be made an attractive home. Cottages may be made both convenient and beautiful—indeed, there are not lacking who will prefer them to the mansion, especially where the show of magnificence is the principal feature of the latter. We have passed our pioneer days and if we are to lead people to higher things spiritually we can not afford to offend against the law of order and beauty which is one of our God's laws. If humanity loves the beauty of the parks, and it does, why not consider it wise and helpful to make of the church lawn a thing of beauty? If the symmetrical lines of a well designed building attract attention and cultivate the artistic in man, why not have this fact in mind when planning the church building?

In this issue of THE CHRISTIAN-EVANGELIST we inaugurate a department of advertising under the head of "Church Architecture, Furniture and Ornamentation," where the cards of houses engaged in the lines indicated will be found. Only such establishments as we can recommend our readers to patronize will be permitted to have a place in this column, and we will be glad to answer any inquiries concerning plans in the direction pointed out by this article.

In this issue we present the following list of reliable houses: The Cincinnati Bell Foundry, Church Bells, Cincinnati, O. The Jacoby Art Glass Co., Art Glass and Memorial Windows, St. Louis. Geo. H. Springer, Individual Communion Service Ware, Boston. Thomas Communion Service Co., Communion Service Ware, Lima, O. Geo. Kilgen & Son, Pipe Organs, St. Louis. Hinners Organ Co., Pipe Organs, Pekin, Ill. Burlington Pipe Organ Co., Pipe Organs, Burlington, Ia.

We expect to add others to this list until it shall contain the names of one or more firms in every branch of this important and helpful line of business. It is earnestly requested that our readers who are commissioned by their congregations to look after such matters of improvement write to the houses represented in this column, and when you write please mention the fact that you saw the announcement in THE CHRISTIAN-EVANGELIST.

Fifty Years a Minister.

Such a life as has been lived in this community by Rev. T. P. Haley is noteworthy in many respects. For fifty years he has been a minister of the gospel and for twenty-five years he has been laboring quietly and unostentatiously in Kansas City. So far as we recall there is no other clergy-

NEWS FROM MANY FIELDS

Illinois Notes.

Few times of greater interest ever come to the young, than when they leave the parental roof, the home, Sunday-school and the old church to go to college. Here and now, by the choice of the college and the conduct in it, is as largely determined the destiny of the individual. It is the hour of crisis, dangers threaten, allure, persist, destroy, possibilities; helpful influences, unfolding powers, lead on and upward with holy inspiration the youth whose face is set in the right direction. Illinois is said to have more schools of higher learning, in proportion to population, than any other state in the Union, except one. The qualities are as wide in range as the number, and the results as various. A state that furnished the nation's president in time of its greatest peril, the army's general in the nation's greatest struggle and the spiritual leader to organize a uniform Bible study for 20,000,000 Sunday-school people will constantly be called upon for great men, leaders in all affairs of human good. Men and communities are constantly being tested. It requires moral and spiritual character as well as intellectual culture to meet the pressure in this day of strenuous life. The preparation, therefore, should be comprehensive, thorough and radical. As the day approaches for the doors of learning to swing open, interests, of both parents and children, center upon the where and with what possible, probable results? Will the son or daughter return home to love it better, to lend to his community a stronger helping hand in all its intellectual, moral and spiritual forces? Is he going to college where there are matters of concern? It is needless to say that hundreds of young people every years lose, rather than gain in the highest elements of character and consequently in chances for larger and more permanent success, because their college surroundings were bad. Every parent and child is therefore deeply and vitally interested, in looking into the character, environments, and influences of the college chosen, especially for his earlier years of higher education. Eureka College has been provided and supported by the Church of Christ, as nearly ideal as possible for the thorough all-round education and culture of well-disposed young people. The eminence attained by a vast company of her students and alumnae in all honorable vocations, shows it to be a college of unusual power and usefulness. The Savior has furnished us the best standard of judgment, "Fruits." It is an honor and high recommendation for any young man or woman to have been a student of Eureka College. Illinois Disciples can do no better than to thoroughly patronize their own great school.——The church at Mt. Zion, three miles from Eureka, where about 150 young ministers have preached among their first sermons, still lives and prospers. It was here that A. P. Cobb, tried to preach his first sermon, utterly failed, broke down and almost vowed to abandon his purpose as a preacher, but kind hearts and the generous church saved him to the ministry. It was in this church that J. T. Stivers, now evangelist of Colorado, grew to manhood and began his ministry. The church has always been a loyal helper to the college and has more members in the Illinois Christian Educational Association in proportion to membership, than any other church in the state. Prof. B. J. Radford preaches for them regularly and is justly very highly esteemed.——The church at Rock Island has many years of hard struggle, but through the long ministry of T. W. Grafton, and the building of the church by Mrs. M. H. Wadsworth, a memorial to her honored father, P. L. Mitchell, in 1894, prosperity and large strength have come. The building is a beautiful, commodious house in the heart of the city, with equipments and rooms, for various activities of the church. All our great enterprises are represented, all receive offerings. Paris, Bloomington and Eureka were the only churches in the state that made larger offerings on Education Day, than Rock Island. O. W. Lawrence was away on his vacation at my visit, but I heard only words of apprecia-

tion and praise for his efficient work. I had the pleasure of being guest in the delightful home of G. C. Sanderson, whom I had not seen for 20 years, but who was one of my most reliable helpers among the young people during my pastorate at Pittsfield. I was glad to find him a faithful, trusted officer at Rock Island.——The Kewanee church has not gotten through the days of struggle that come as a kind of selection and seasoning in most all churches. It has been about 6 years since a few members were banded together for the Lord's work. They have all the usual auxiliaries to church life, and has an enrolled membership of 280, and a Sunday-school of 150. Its young people have already learned where Eureka College is, and have enjoyed some of its blessings. The state board has done much for this church and made a good investment. As soon as they can get free from debt they expect to plan for a better house. W. A. Green has preached for them since November, 21 have been added to the church, and $800 have been paid on debts. Preacher and people seem happy in their struggles and both have bright futures before them.——The Washburn church of 42 years has steadily held up the banner of the cross. It has been especially wise in its selection of ministers, and has now an enrollment of about 325, with 250 in Sunday-school, 35 in Christian Endeavor, 35 in Junior, 63 in C. W. B. M. W. H. Jenner has been here two years and a half; during his ministry 77 have been added to the church. He is a most active and aggressive man in pulpit, church business and pastoral care. The missionary and benevolent offerings the past year were $925 for interests beyond the church's local borders. What a power in the world the church would be if all our congregations would live and give like Washburn! Besides this manner of effort; four preachers have grown up in this congregation, Gilbert Gish, L. R. Pickerill, C. E. Richards, and last but not least, S. E. Fisher, our minister in Champaign.

T. L. Read, our preacher from South Chicago, has just moved his family to Eureka for educational purposes. A. R. Finnell, from East Side church, Springfield, has moved to Eureka to be in college. Several other good men are coming and by September 18 it appears now that a very fine company of young people will be ready to enter college.   J. G. WAGGONER.

Southern California Convention.

Another annual encampment by the sea by the Disciples of Christ in Southern California has come and gone. From August 9 to 19 Long Beach entertained the largest number of Disciples that ever attended our conventions. For those ten days our brethren enjoyed a "feast of reason and flow of soul." The attendance was by far the largest in our history. The enthusiasm ran at high tide from the first service in the Long Beach church till the last amen was said in the great auditorium where people sat spellbound under the magic powers of Prof. Willett. The reports for last year's work as given by Secretary Lewis were most encouraging. Financial aid was given to 30 mission points. Those missions reported 150 conversions and 432 added otherwise. These 30 mission churches have a membership of 1,375 souls and gave $1,212 for missions. In this bishopic there are 60 churches with 10,000 members and they gave last year for missions $15,000, for current expenses $55,000 and for church property $55,000, making a grand total of $125,000. Their increase in membership was 25 per cent. This was largely due to the large influx of population from the east. The treasurer of the convention reported that $8,042.70 had passed through his hands and had been distributed into the various channels of work carried on by the convention. A number of eastern workers made distinct contributions to our work. The sisters had Mrs. Louise Kelley and Miss Bertha Mason as helpers and they rendered great service. George Ranshaw made a great appeal in behalf of home missions. F. M. Rains overflowed when, at the end of a great

speech on foreign mission four Living Links for foreign missions were given. It was all an illustration of the wisdom and benefit of keeping well trained men among the churches in behalf of this greatest work of the church. H. L. Willett was the chief speaker of the convention. It is putting it mildly to say that he captured the convention. He is surely a prince among Christian gentlemen, among scholars, lecturers and preachers. Some came to doubt and all went away from his lectures to praise. He is surely one of the sons of genius. One of the unique features of the convention were the steps taken to consolidate our educational interests in Southern California with those of Pomona College. This institution of learning was established by the Congregationalists and is largely under their control at present. They own a plant with a property and endowment worth $500,000. Last June they had 35 graduates in regular college courses. They expended for current expenses last session $50,000. George A. Gates is their president. They recently made an offer to the Baptists and Disciples to merge their educational interests in Southern California. The terms and conditions of this union were so favorable that it was accepted absolutely unanimously by the convention and henceforth Pomona College is to be our college. The Baptists will decide upon their relation to the college at their Southern California convention in December, 1906. We feel this to be a great step in advance not only in the interest of the cause of the Disciples of Christ, but also of the wide fellowship of all the children of God and a very distinct step toward that Christian union for which we so distinctly pray and preach. It is our custom at these conventions to take pledges for our work the following year. This year the pledges were as follows: for Southern California work, $7,500; for church building league, $750; for C. W. B. M. interests, $1,200; four Living Links for Foreign Society, $2,400, and Christian Endeavor $350. Grand total, $12,200. For the 8,000 Disciples in Southern California affiliating with this organized work this makes a commendable showing. It is peculiarly gratifying to the writer to see this great growth in the cause so dear to him. He has seen it grow from infancy, when it was largely the creature of the noble church for which he has ministered these sixteen years, to its present commanding power and influence and finds in its growth and power one of his chief joys. May the Lord nurture and prosper this great work.
Los Angeles.   A. C. SMITHER.

Kentucky State Convention Matters.

We are almost at the threshold of the time honored gatherings of our people. Lacking one year we have gone up to these meetings for three quarters of a century.——The writer does not intimate that he has been going that long, but that Kentucky Disciples may in 1907 celebrate the diamond jubilee of state missions.——We are confidently expecting the greatest gathering in the history of our Kentucky people at Louisville, September 24-27, in the First Christian Church. Reduced rates have been granted on all railroads. We are promised a rate of one fare plus 25 cts. You need to buy a round trip ticket from starting point. No certificate. You are thankful for this, and so am I. Better ask your ticket agent if he has received instructions and if he has not, tell your troubles at once to R. M. Hopkins, No. 218 Keller Building, Louisville, Ky.——Entertainment. —While you are writing to the genial Sunday-school man, if the above matter demands it, tell him that you will be there. If you do not have to write about railroad matters, you must tell him that you expect to go to the convention and that you would like to be provided with a home where you will be furnished lodging and breakfast. You must carry enough money to pay for dinner and supper each day. If you do not tell Hopkins about your intentions you will not expect him to see that you are lodged and breakfasted—will you? Tell him now. The Delinquent List.—If by any means your congregation belongs to this list you want to have it transferred to the list of churches paying their apportionment, or at least making a creditable contribution, for Kentucky missions. Some of the churches on this list now would amaze the brethren; but when the report is read September 26, many of these will be reported as in line. Prompt action is indispensable to avert a defeat and a financial report of which our people will not be proud. Delay invites defeat. Procrastination is not only the thief of time; but the fruitful cause of failure. Prompt, vigorous, hearty, determined action is imperative. Yours in great anxiety.   H. W. ELLIOTT, Sec.

❀ ❀

North Carolina Notes.

At last meeting your correspondent was visiting his home people at Bellaire, O. August 12, preached for the congregation at Smithfield, O., in the community where I was born. At that church I was received into the fellowship, having been baptized at fourteen years of age by Cyrus McNeeley at Hopedale, O., at the annual meeting the third Lord's day in August. We had no regular preaching at Smithfield then. Nobody gave the invitation, and I had to go away from home to hear much preaching. Smithfield now has a modern house and a resident preacher. Hopedale still continues the annual meeting. I would have been glad to attend after many years' absence from the place of my spiritual birth, but my face was set toward Bethany Beach, Del., the eastern resort of Disciples. If the Editor of THE CHRISTIAN-EVANGELIST will forsake for one season his park at Pentwater, and come down there to the broad Atlantic's shores, he can enjoy a dip in the ocean that will give as much pleasure as the one he enjoyed in the pool at San Bernardino, Cal., a year ago, and he can go out over the breakers and dip his line in the ocean and catch more than two fish in one forenoon. Then he can enjoy the fellowship of Power and Bagby and Cramblet and Batman and Tharp and many more. Mr. Editor, if you want to have a good time, come to Bethany Beach next year.—There were numerous good things on the program. Mrs. Princess Long and the Nitz sisters delighted the people with their music. The editor of "The Christian Standard" gave an address of breadth and strength on liberty. Brother Power gave an interesting address for the children on "A Night in Palestine." Brother Batman of Philadelphia, gave a strong sermon on a restatement of the way of salvation, and there were other good things we have not room to mention. The service on Lord's day

morning, August 19, was one of the best we ever attended at the beach. The Vesper services are enjoyable.——E. B. Bagby, C. M. Watson, of Connelsville, Pa., and Dr. McMains, of Baltimore, and others were displaying their skill on the tennis court.—Ex-Governor Tunnel, of Delaware, who has a cottage at another resort, enjoys the breezes and the fellowship, stopping at "The Sussex." The Atlantic hotels and other cottages were well patronized.——Mrs. B. C. Hagerman, of Lexington, Ky., is building a nice cottage on the beach next to Congressman Graham's.—— Brother Drexler and family, of Braddock, Pa., spent last winter on the beach.——August 26, I preached for Brother Power at Vermont avenue, 11 a. m. and for Brother Bagby at Ninth street, 8 p. m.——Ere September 1, Providence permitting, I will be home with my brethren in Winston-Salem, N. C.   J. A. HOPKINS.

❀ ❀

Chicago Letter.

I have now served two months as city evangelist and superintendent of missions in Chicago. I begin to have some fair idea of the general situation. We have in this second city of America 26 churches and missions—a very small representation among her two million souls. Since coming I have spoken in the Jackson Boulevard, Metropolitan, Austin, Harvey, Irving Park, Maywood, and West End churches. Besides I have visited the South Chicago, Monroe Street, and Hyde Park fields. Most of my time has been spent in a tent meeting with the West End Mission. There were 20 in all came forward. About half of them may be counted as additions to our force. The rest went to other churches, or were prevented from being baptized. For two years Bro. E. A. Henry, a student in Chicago University, has been the minister. In that time not one addition has been made. This fact will give some hint of the difficulty of the field. For the present I am to serve them in the hope of adding further to their members, and soon securing a regular and suitable meeting place. We have rented the Presbyterian Church of Sunday afternoons. They will enter their fine new house of worship about October 1. After that we hope to buy their old church. It is offered us at a fair price. It is well located and is a good building, and will serve all our purposes well for some years. Within one year you may expect to learn of a church of at least 100 members—there are 30 now—with a Sunday-school of over 100. Our next pressing work is to provide a meeting for the Maywood and South Chicago Missions, both of which must also have help in getting suitable meeting places before the work can grow or promise permanency. For all this our Church Extension Fund must be our chief reliance. I never realized before as I do since coming to Chicago how essential to our growth and property in the cities this fund is. I am hoping so earnestly that the September offering will be far the largest ever received for this all-important work. Some features of the Chicago situation strike the observer as very strange. Here after more than a half century of effort the Disciples have not a single church of the first rank. True the Jackson Boulevard and Metropolitan churches are good, active congregations, but do not rank with our strong churches in many of the smaller cities. I trust that by the time another decade has passed some better things can be said.

Another thing. No one of our Chicago preachers has been long on the field, except Geo. A. Campbell at Austin, and Ed. S. Ames, of Hyde Park. Parker Stockdale has been with the Jackson Boulevard church but a few months. The same is true of Rothenberger at Irving Park. Willett and Handley at the First, Moffett at Ashland, Buckner at Harvey, Lockhart at Chicago Heights, Fortune at Garfield Boulevard, Adlinger at Douglass Park, Campbell at the Metropolitan, Cummings at Logan Square, Hoover at Pullman, Shaw at Sheffield Avenue, Ward at Evanston, and Read at South Chicago. Kindred has been several years with the Englewood church, and Scoville several years with the Metropolitan.

Conditions of religious work are peculiarly difficult in Chicago, and no place calls for more wisdom and consecration. These qualities, happily, are found in the group of noble, educated,

Buffalo—Where You Are Coming.

BY B. H. HAYDEN.

The Mecca of the Churches of Christ changes annually. This year it is Buffalo, N. Y., October 12-18. The same religious thrill attends every pilgrimage. By request I attempt to delineate some minor attractions. We desire to know about a place to which we are going. Before starting to the Orient I read all I could of places to heighten the joy when there.

"In 1804 Joseph Ellicott surveyed out the 'village plot of Buffalo.'" (Records.) In 1809 Thomas Campbell surveyed out the plot of primitive Christianity in his notable "Declaration and Address."

"When we mean to build we first survey the plot." (Shakespeare.) It is fitting that the people of a religious movement meet in a city whose growth has so nearly paralleled it.

Jerusalem is the site of the Salem of King Melchisedec that preceded it, the Salem of the wild tribes of the Jebusites. Buffalo is the site of a village of the Seneca Indians of the Kahkwa nation. Long and painful race wars filled the early years, mingling human cries with the sounds of the troubled waters of Niagara.

But struggles centering in Buffalo, old Fort Erie and Niagara Falls were not all with the "poor Indian," forests primeval or resistless waters. The years circling about 1812 tell their own sad story of near of kin in combat along an imaginary national line out in the middle of river and lake. The Pyramids of Egypt derive part of their interest from the fact that they will never be repeated, human energies being turned now to better purposes; so the three years beginning 1812 derive interest from the fact that the people on different sides of this imaginary line are so on the same side of all right and higher issues and have been made to know and appreciate each other, that busy as the Evil Spirit of War still is, he can never again stir up such strife between such peoples. Hence now in the spirit of peace and fraternity we use the words of a message of those days summoning to War; "Come in companies, half companies, pairs or singly; come any way, but come." The convention thus can be claimed as a Victory by the subjects of the crown and states alike, as by some was the battle of Lundy's Lane at Niagara Falls.

Well, now that we have come and have been true to the higher objects of our coming, what about your hundred years old city? Well, first, 375,000 inhabitants—all sorts. Two hundred and fifty daily passenger trains. (Look out to take the right one); a fine harbor that "harbors" 4,000 lake craft annually, some of which are like great ocean steamers. Grain elevators with capacity of 21,140,000 bushels, and 125,000,000 bushels came into the city in 1905. Lumber yards that handle 175,000,000 feet every year. Stock yards of 100 acres and an annual business of $100,000,000, second largest in the world; a pocket which if filled with gold would ruin the world; but it is a coal pocket, the Lackawanna, 5,000 feet long.

Then here is the Lackawanna Steel Plant that doesn't steal, as so many banks are doing lately, and it has a capital of $60,000,000.

The banks of Buffalo number 16 with an aggregate capital and surplus of $15,245,732 and deposits of $28,259,506.

Buffalo has 237 miles of asphalt pavement, surpassing Washington and Paris in this respect. Many of the business blocks and buildings will compare favorably with those of older and greater cities, one of which, the Ellicott Square building, has a floor area of 9 acres, and 16 elevators distribute the people to heights and directions sought.

But Buffalo has things of higher significance. The Public Library, housed in a fine building, has 220,000 volumes. The University of Buffalo, 60 years old, 3,000 alumni, 150 professors and teachers, and had 700 students the last year.

The Y. M. C. A. of Buffalo has one of the best buildings, if not the best in the world; 10 stories high, with every desirable feauture and equipment. There are 3,200 members, with a very large number of boys. The secretary and assistant join in extending hearty courtesies to the convention comers, not only to look through the building but to make it a rest. The press of

Buffalo ranks high in tone and enterprise, and is hospitable to the coming of these great multitudes.

Buffalo is exceptional in its beautiful avenues and streets, pure atmosphere and elegant homes. Delaware avenue is the Euclid avenue of Cleveland or the Michigan avenue of Chicago, and the Delaware Park at its terminus is one of the most delightful. On Delaware avenue is the Milburn residence, where McKinley died, and the Wilcox residence where Roosevelt took the oath of office. On the west border of Delaware Park, and overlooking lakelets reminding of Como and Lucerne, is the Albright Art Gallery, most elegant architecturally, and containing treasures admired by art critics of the world. In sight of this is the marble building of the historical society, cost $200,000, where one might spend weeks in profitable study. An Indian inscription attracted my attention as a fitting reminder during our coming conventions, reading as follows: "Neh-Ko, Cah-gis-dah-yen-duk," viz.: "Other council fires were here before ours."

✾ ✾

A Word to Oregon Disciples.

Our state convention for 1906 is now a matter of history, but its plans and inspiration shall abide as an inspiration for the year upon which we have entered. We are all delighted that the old debt has been provided for, in pledges, some of which are already in, and that all our efforts for this year are to be given advancement in our mission work. This year should be very fruitful in results.

The convention re-districted the state and so adjusted the official representation as to make each district superintendent a Vice-president of the state board. This will properly link together the work throughout the state and give a representative on the state board from every section of the state. The minutes of the convention are now in the hands of the printer. We hope to

get a copy into each one of our homes that all may know what has been planned for the future. Knowledge concerning the work to be done will beget interest in its advancement.

It is the plan of the convention to send your secretary to every church in the state, to get acquainted with the workers and to interest the entire membership in the great work to be done.

Three of the new districts will hold conventions in October, the northwest, central and southwest. The northeast district already has Bro. N. H. Brooks in the field. The central district is helping the church at Woodburn in the erection of a house of worship. This work is under the able direction of Bro. L. F. Stephens, and will be dedicated next Lord's day. This district will have the services of Bro. J. N. McConnell after October 1.

The outlook for our work is very bright. We should make this the greatest year in our history. The convention adopted the motto: "Two thousand conversions and $6,000 for Oregon missions." This means only one conversion for every five members, and but an average of 57 cents each for Oregon missions. Several churches did better than that last year. One gave $1.45 per member and reported one conversion for every two old members.

Remember, we are to gain 100 per cent, in all lines by 1909. "Oregon for Christ." Let us pray for it, work for it, expect it. Jehovah is our God and Christ Jesus is our Captain, our Saviour, our Strength. Mark November 4 and surprise pastor and the church by the generosity of your provision for this great work.

While you are planning for greater things for Oregon, do not forget children's day for home missions. Every Bible school in Oregon should be enlisted. May we not have it so on September 2? Yours in his name,

F. E. BILLINGTON, Cor. Sec. O. C. M. C.

Cottage Grove, Ore., August 20, 1906.

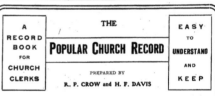

Mexico, Mo.

Small and St. John began with us yesterday. Between 800 and 900 people attended both morning and night services. Everybody delighted with the music and preaching. Lowell C. McPherson spoke in the afternoon on Cuba to a good sized audience, and thus our meeting opened under the most inspiring influences. Two were received into the fellowship of the church at the morning service, but just as the evening sermon was closing thunder and lightning excited the audience and broke the deep feeling that was prevailing, under which some souls might have been won for Christ. The whole church is ready for a great meeting and we are confidently expecting great results.
A. W. KOKENDOFFER.

Mexico, Mo.

Redeem West Virginia from Her Reproach.

The reproach of West Virginia must be removed, and the forces now at work are determined to accomplish this result before 1909, when the hosts gathering during an even hundred years, shall surprise the religious world by their achievements. West Virginia was the nursery of this great movement and through Bethany College has continued that work throughout the years. The Campbells evangelized very little throughout the state, and while the ministerial graduates of Bethany have blessed all nations with the result of their labors, until about ten years ago West Virginia knew none of them. The Mountain State, like the old home place after the children are grown and gone, has been left without up-to-date cultivation, and is overrun with weeds and decay; anti-ism flourished like a green bay tree, till now the tree is brown and sear, bearing no fruit, tossed to and fro by every ism that has ever disturbed our people. Our preachers and churches have even been ready to lend themselves to any leader with mob-leading proclivites. Through it all there has resulted a lack of union that amounts to a divisive spirit, an indifference, a lethargy, that have been hard to overcome. West Virginia like Jerusalem

REGIMENTAL REUNIONS AND FORTY-THIRD ANNIVERSARY BATTLE CHICKAMAUGA,

CHATTANOOGA, SEPTEMBER 18-20, 1906.

On September 18, 1906, will occur the forty-third anniversary of the Battle of Chickamauga. It is proposed to celebrate this memorable event with a reunion of the various regiments that participated in this memorable battle and the various battles fought around Chattanooga. This reunion will be held at Chickamauga National Park, September 18, 19 and 20, and the present indications are that it will be the largest and most notable gathering ever held in the South. On the above dates, the remnants from the armies of twelve states, comprising the following: Pennsylvania, Ohio, Michigan, Indiana, Illinois, Wisconsin, Minnesota, Iowa, Nebraska, Missouri, Kansas and Kentucky, will assemble, many for the first and last time since they marched from its bloodstained fields, forty-three years ago.

Here is one of the great opportunities for the education of the youth. Don't fail to take your children and show them historic Chattanooga, with all its historical connections. It is the opportunity of a lifetime. Go and see the old war generals and other officers; point out the places of interest on the battlefield; let them show you and explain, in person, the markers erected on the battlefield showing the positions of the opposing armies at the time of battle. It will not be long until none will be left to do this noble work.

It will be many years, if ever again, that such an opportunity will present itself. See that your tickets read via the Louisville & Nashville R. R., the Battlefield Route. Call on your nearest railroad agent for rates and advertising matter pertaining to the reunion, or write nearest representative of the Louisville & Nashville R. R.
J. H. MILLIKEN, D. P. A., Louisville, Ky.
J. D. BUSH, D. P. A., Cincinnati, Ohio.
J. E. DAVENPORT, D. P. A., St. Louis, Mo.
H. C. BAILEY, N. W. P. A., Chicago, Ill.

of old gave up her fires to warm other localities, and the world has been profited by the dispersed energy, but coldness and reproach come upon the givers in each case. The reproach of West Virginia consists in this, that instead of being first among the states which carry on this great movement, a position is occupied among those which do the least. This reproach has been intensified by the indifference and division. Has been, yes, but shall be no more, so say the consecrated ministers who now occupy the leading pulpits, and the churches under their influence. The West Virginia Christian Missionary Society is to be the instrument of action. This conviction is not the sentiment of an hour, but is the conviction developed by the history of the last ten years. These years have really been wonderful years, as practically all the larger cities save those in the region of Bethany have been entered during that time. The work has been done with only a struggling state organization, which has been without money and with only a few of the churches backing it up. The work is a monument to A. Linkletter who has struggled to support himself, and who has done that very thing during the twelve years of his ministry as corresponding secretary of the society. His work has largely consisted in keeping the pastoral question before the people and in inducing Bethany men and other college men to locate with the churches. One considers with regret what could have been done during this time if there had been back of him a strong financial support so that there would have been money to revive and strengthen the weak churches and to support missions, as has been done by other state organizations. The time has now come when the churches may be drawn closer together by state and district organizations. To forward this and to find out and to know each other, a simultaneous revival has been inaugurated to begin at once after the convention at Buffalo. To forward the revival and to enlist as many churches as possible in the initial movement the committee, of which Percy H. Wilson of Moundsville, is chairman, secured the services of George F. Crites, of Ohio, from the Ohio Missionary Society for six months, as special field agent. Brother Crites has organized two missions during this time, one for the Huntington church with a membership of sixty-five, and one at Williamson with some fifty members. He has also stirred up many churches to the need of the work and enlisted many in the revival. There never has been the interest we now find in our state work and the coming convention at Sistersville will no doubt strengthen the society, and send us all back to the coming year's work with new plans, new hopes and new zeal for the conquest of West Virginia. The impure preacher and the division maker will soon find that West Virginia is no longer a haven of rest for all who would disturb, nor for those who would propagate ism nor lead mobs against some brother departed from the faith."

Jesus is coming into West Virginia with his purity and with his peace-making power, while the hosts gather to greet and follow wheresoever He may lead.
ORILAS G. WHITE.

Huntington, W. Va.

Palmyra, Illinois.

Nearly a score of years ago, when the writer was disentangling himself from the meshes of sectism, a tract of Brother Garrison's did much towards his liberation; but Bro. A. Martin, then of Liverpool, Eng., now of Davenport, Ia., was the man to cut the last strands of inherited error. It was therefore a happy coincidence that timed Brother Martin's vacation just when his friend needed an experienced evangelist to conduct a meeting for him. The "vacation" has been filled with unstinted effort to convert sinners and uplift saints. Fourteen new members may seem a small result to some, but not to those who know the limitations of the field, and the combination of extraordinary hindrances. Storms, heat, picnics (a matter of consequence to rural communities), funerals, etc., but the preacher ever cheery; arousing slumbering "beloog-ers," refreshing the faithful, comforting the sorrowing and greatly strengthening the hands of his "auld acquaintance."
T. R. HODKINSON, Pastor.

Evangelistic

We invite ministers and others to send reports of meetings, additions and other news of the churches. It is especially requested that additions be reported as "by confession and baptism," or "by letter."

Hot from the Wire.

Special to THE CHRISTIAN-EVANGELIST.

Charleston, S. C., Sept. 3.—Church extension $35 plus. Apportioned $10. —Marcellus R. Ely.

Special to THE CHRISTIAN-EVANGELIST.

Carthage, Mo., Sept. 3.—Church extension offering $175; apportionment $100. —Newel Sims.

Special to THE CHRISTIAN-EVANGELIST.

Chicago, Ill., Sept. 3.—Big day at Saginaw church yesterday; $400 raised on debt; am on vacation.—J. Murray Taylor.

Special to THE CHRISTIAN-EVANGELIST.

Farmington, Mo., Sept. 2.—Apportionment for Church Extension $10. Offering this morning $20.90. More to follow.—Edward Owers.

Special to THE CHRISTIAN-EVANGELIST.

Hillsboro, Texas, Sept. 2.—Church Extension offering not all in, but we have raised more than our apportionment, which was $30.—Ernest J. Bradley.

Special to THE CHRISTIAN-EVANGELIST.

Huntington, Ind., Sept. 2.—Zach T. Sweeney dedicated Central Christian Church here to-day. Twenty-five thousand dollars raised. Building seats 1,500. Rain but crowds. Cephas Shelburne, pastor.—H. S. Butler.

Special to THE CHRISTIAN-EVANGELIST.

Kansas City, Mo., Sept. 3.—Fall campaign opened yesterday with fifteen added at Jackson Avenue Church. Splendid preparation by Pastor Frank L. Bowen. Charles H. Altheide, singer. —Wm. J. Lockhart.

Special to THE CHRISTIAN-EVANGELIST.

Oklahoma City, Okla., Sept. 3.— Church Extension offerings yesterday, South Side Kansas City, $203; First Joplin (Mo.), over $100, more to follow; Webb City, Mo., $43; Oklahoma City, Okla., $22.—G. W. Muckley.

Special to THE CHRISTIAN-EVANGELIST.

Ennis, Texas, August 28.—Closed to-night. Ninety-eight additions in 24 days. Rain 11 days of the 24. Pastor C. B. Knight an excellent organizer and untiring worker. Oklahoma City our next engagement.—Harlow and Harlow.

Illinois.

Carbondale, Aug. 31.—One baptized Aug. 26.— A. M. Growden.

Gurnee, Aug. 24.—Have had 1 confession during my visit here.—John S. Zeran.

Indiana.

Montpelier, Aug. 29.—We began a tent meeting here September 2, with Clarence Mitchell, of Lima, O., as evangelist, and Prof. Arthur Haley as singer.—D. F. Harris.

Elwood, Aug. 27.—Closed meeting with Harmony Church of Christ, 6 miles north of Elwood, with Bro. J. W. Wittkamper—result 39 were added, 33 of these were baptized, 92.3 per cent. Next meeting is with Bro. I. N. Grisso; have December open.—H. K. Shields, Rochester, Ind., Singer and Helper.

Kansas.

Circleville, Aug. 31.—Twenty-eight added, 20 confessions.—C. C. Atwood.

Galesburg, Aug. 31.—Nine additions in the meeting, seven baptized. Had to bring meeting to close on account of my own work at Lebo. Ethel Stuckey, singer.—Wallace M. Stuckey.

Logan, Aug. 27.—Otha Wilkison and Charles E. McVay, just closed a short meeting. Brother Wilkison is pastor of the Christian church at Ukiah, Cal.

Brickenmdy, Aug. 30.—O. P. Spiegel of Birmingham, Ala., and T. F. Odeneal have just closed a good meeting. Brother Spiegel is now holding a meeting in Cincinnati with A. M. Harvuot.

Louisiana.

Leesville, Aug. 27.—One lady made the good confession last night and was baptized. One other addition by statement since last report.—G. Washington Wise, pastor.

Michigan.

Owosso, Aug. 27.—There have been 6 added to the church in this place since beginning the work in July, and every department is improving. —C. M. Keene.

Missouri.

Piedmont, Aug. 31.—Fine meeting Lord's day. One accession from M. E. church.—John A. Allen, minister.

Granite City, Aug. 31.—Four additions since last report. One by letter, one from the M. E.'s and two from other connections.—W. A. Shullenberger.

Kansas City, Aug. 27.—Twelve added in August and the interest fine. Lockhart and Altheide begin next Lord's day.—Frank L. Bowen, City Evangelist.

Fredericktown, Sept. 3.—Had fine services yesterday with three good accessions. We will soon begin to break the earth for the foundation for our new church house.—R. O. Rogers, minister.

Moberly, Aug. 8.—Closed at High Point and at Salem with five baptisms. Am here at Antioch in a meeting. Will hold at Corinth, Davis and Houck Point, Lincoln county, Missouri.—S. J. Copher.

Gorin, Aug. 31.—Meeting closed Sunday night with 15 additions—the second meeting in nine months. Sunday-school membership doubled, and 67 added to the church.—A. C. Biggs, elder; Cecil V. Pearce, minister.

Knox City, Aug. 30.—We are having a great meeting in my home town (Knox City), Thirty-eight confessions and baptisms to date. The pastor of this church (Brother Pierce), was called away to conduct a meeting in Millport, Mo.—H. A. Northcutt.

Nebraska.

Danbury, Aug. 29.—John T. Smith, of Nebraska City, commenced a 4 weeks' meeting at this place on Sept. 2.—W. R. Burbridge.

Ohio.

Fredericksburg, Aug. 27.—One confession and baptism Sunday evening.—Elder C. C. Maple, pastor.

Norwood, Aug. 29.—Three added by letter and 1 confession. Preached recently at Mulbury, O. where 1 was added by confession.—Joseph Armistead, minister.

Oklahoma.

Chandler, Aug. 30.—Thirty-nine added to date. Expect to double over next Lord's day.—Oscar Ingold.

Watonga, August 27.—Three accessions since last report—one confession last Sunday, and also one two weeks ago, and one by letter. We are making preparation for our revival meeting, which we hope to begin about October 1.—F. Douglas Wharton.

Texas.

Commerce, Aug. 27.—Three additions at services yesterday; 2 by confession and baptism, 1 by statement.—W. A. Wherry, minister.

Dalhart, Aug. 28.—Four additions to the church here last Sunday: 2 by confession, 1 by letter, 1 by statement.—John Mullen, minister.

Midweek Prayer-Meeting

September 12, 1906.

CHRIST AS A WORKMAN.—
Mark 6:3.

If Christ's enemies could have held before him one imperfect plow-beam that would have been a serious reflection on his divinity. There is a moral obliquity in the slovenly doing of even the humblest tasks that the world is beginning to recognize and that God always has. Another phase of pure religion and undefiled is always doing our best.

Any yardstick Jesus, the carpenter, may have made would be fully thirty-six inches long. For the sake of a wage he would not have debased his skill to assist an employer in defrauding. Indignant rebellion in workshops, to-day would help many a haughty employer to repentance.

With toiled-stained and callous hands, Jesus, the workingman, has invested labor with a dignity of which tyranny, oppression, and poverty have never been able to despoil it.

It is encouraging to know Christ's works are always complete. The blind he healed saw perfectly; the lame he cured leaped as a hart; the leprous he cleansed were made every whit whole; the dead he revived were lusty and strong. This gives us assurance that when he forgives our sins, they will be entirely obliterated; that when we are resurrected, we will come forth in beauty and power, and when coronated, we shall be completely endued with all the prerogatives of prophets, priests and kings unto God.

Had Jesus the carpenter made poor gates and chests in Nazareth we might have expected Bartimaeus to have seen men as trees walking, Lazarus, the Ruler's daughter, and the widow's son to have been invalids following their resuscitation, the grave but half robbed of its terrors, and the plan of salvation at the best an uncertain way of escape from sin. In the seeming inconsequentials we should form habits of exactness. They will serve us well when the great works are assigned us.

One can not think of carpenter Jesus hanging a door and leaving it till it swung evenly and fitted exactly. Just to the extent that the farmer throws an uneven furrow, and the maid is untidy, and the tailor's garment is ill-fitting, and the painter's work is defective, and the lawyer's brief is not germane, and the physician's diagnosis is not scientific, do they all fall short of Christlikeness. Not till we attach ethical significance to handiwork and braincraft as well as to thought and worship do we apprehend the mind of the Master.

The microscope reveals that in the pointing of a thorn there is a perfectness unapproachable by human mechanics, and that in the arrangement and tinting of the scales on the butterfly's wing the perfection is the despair of artists. This same painstaking care is manifest not only in the minutiae but also in the magnitudes. Centripetal and centrifugal forces among the stars exactly balance or constellations would be wrecked and the universe changed into chaos. The bee's instinct must build the honey cell with exact precision or all the works of God would not be perfect and human confidence in his omniscience and **omnipresence** would waver. One test of

our godliness is the doing well of all our tasks, great or small, and whether they be public as the door plate or a piece of hidden frieze.

Christian Endeavor

By GEO. L. SNIVELY

September 16, 1906.

HOW JESUS MET HIS ENEMIES AND HOW WE SHOULD MEET OURS.—Luke   4:28-30;   11:37-44;   23:33-34.

DAILY READINGS.

M.	The Great Conflict.	Matt. 4:1-11.
T.	Meeting Hatred.	Psa. 37:1-10.
W.	Meeting Afflictions.	Isa. 38:1-8, 21.
T.	Meeting Hinderers.	Acts 21:8-14.
F.	Meeting Scorn.	Luke 23:6-11.
S.	Meeting Prejudice.	Luke 9:51-56.
S.	A Great Triumph.	Luke 4:28-30.

The mandates still apply, "Let not the sun go down on thy wrath." "If thou art offering thy gift on the altar and rememberest that thy brother hath ought against thee, leave thy gift beside the altar, go, be reconciled to thy brother, and then return and offer thy gift."

An open enemy is more helpful than most of our friends. An indulgent friend would palliate many wrongs to which we are tempted, while many have been restrained from evil by thoughts of the pitiless exposure enemies would make if the transgression were detected. This may not be a lofty motive to righteousness, but it at least saves us from forming the habit of sin and bringing down upon us the destructiveness of actual commission.

The Pharisees were Christ's recognized foes, but it must not be imagined that as their enemy he pronounced the woes upon them. In love and forgiveness he told them their sins and their accompanying doom. It may require more grace than we have yet attained unto, but sufficient grace we should possess to warn our enemies of a sinner's doom. And we ought to so live that our enemies would know that not in malice but in love we have spoken.

The best possible disposition to make of an enemy is to convert him into a friend.

There will be no enmities in heaven. There are two parties to all animosities on earth, and it is unlikely they will meet in the world of peace beyond. It is certain the gates will be barred against the one most at fault, and possibly against both. In view of this let us be very sure we have our quarrels just. Possibly much of the torment of the lost will be caused by the eternal waging of fierce feuds not amicably settled on earth when they began.

It is not enjoined upon us to supinely submit to the machinations of our enemies. Had David surrendered to Saul Israel had been deprived of her most illustrious reign. Christ's enemies took him to a precipice intending to hurl him headlong down, "but he passing through the midst of them went his way." Likewise with us. We should protect our lives, vindicate our good names, not with vindictiveness, but in simple justice to ourselves and all the good we may do in after years; we must defend ourselves and prevent any curtailment of our prerogatives and power of service. Most of all should we resist Satan even unto

Sunday-School
September 16, 1906

JESUS SILENCES THE PHARISEES AND SADDUCEES.—Mark 12:13-27.

Memory Verse, 27.

Golden Text.—Render to Caesar the things that are Caesar's, and to God the things that are God's—Mark 12:17.

Tuesday of Passion Week was marked by arguments and conflicts with the Pharisees and Sadducees. There was a double purpose in these arguments. The members of these two sects were not only trying to entrap Jesus, but were also trying to entrap each other and to draw from Jesus arguments against the other's position. In the three questions which were asked him (Mark 12:13-34) we can see the play of these motives.

"Is it lawful to give tribute to Caesar?" the Pharisees asked. The Sadducees held that it was. They complaisantly accepted Roman rule and tried to get what advantage they could from it. The Pharisees were the party of perpetual protest against the profanation of Judah by Roman domination. They knew that Jesus had been looked to by many people as a possible leader of revolt against Rome. If he said it was not lawful to give tribute to Caesar and give a reason for it, he would be helping them to confute the Sadducees. If he said that it was lawful, he would estrange many of his own followers who were perhaps still expecting him to issue a declaration of independence for Israel.

His reply was not a mere verbal quibble. It was more than a verbal "silencing" of the Pharisees. It was the statement of a great principle. The Jews of Jesus' day thought that their religion could not flourish unless it had a political government back of it. They blamed Rome for the decadence of their religion, just as the Pope blames the French government for the decay of religion in France. Jesus' statement meant that religion is a thing of the Spirit; that it can not be bound by political ties; that under any political conditions it is still possible to serve God. This position transcended the teaching of both Pharisees and Sadducees. It was this principle that rendered possible a non-political Messiahship and which renders possible a church not "established" by the state.

The Sadducees, encouraged perhaps by the appearance of agreement with their position in "render unto Caesar the things that are Caesar's," come now with a question directed against the Pharisees' doctrine of the resurrection, which the Sadducees denied. There is almost no doctrine of a future life in the Old Testament, so the Sadducees were not so far from the traditions as it may seem to us.

The question of the Sadducees assumed that if there is a future life its conditions and institutions must be like those of this life—for example, the institution of marriage. Jesus destroyed their argument by destroying this assumption. Exactly what the future life may be like we may not know. But it is a spiritual existence in which marriage plays no part.

The answer to this question was the complete discomfiture of the Sadducees and the assertion of the doctrine of immortality.

Back to the Great Apostasy.

(Continued from Page 1135.)

One of the novices was a lawyer with a fine practice; another was an accomplished artist. The discipline is strict. Every day in the private chapel in the garden the members say lauds, prime, terce, sext, nones, vespers and compline. They have a church shop in which habited in their cowls, they supply various goods. One of them works as a tailor, making all the habits. These men in their little band form only one of the different companies of Romanizers who are bewitching large numbers of the people. They are silently and insidiously toiling to undo the Reformation. This could never be done by papist agencies outside, but the enemy is inside the pale of the Protestant church and unless the movement can be effectively checked in a few years the Church of England will be simply the Anglican branch of the Roman church. Large numbers of its clergy are sworn to drag this magnificent, historic communion back to the mediaeval apostasy. They are rapidly becoming the dominant element in the Church of England. The bishops are either in occult sympathy, or are powerless in face of this appalling prospect. But the great body of the nation is soundly Protestant at heart. That is the awkward fact for the ritualists. They know that their great difficulty will be the coming clamor for the disestablishment of the church. And in order to forestall this as a Protestant movement they are themselves declaring in favor of freedom of the church from the state. It is a curious development that we are witnessing in England. The nonconformists and the ultra high churchmen are irreconcilably antagonistic, yet they both favor disestablishment. Thus strangely do extremes meet in the motives of parties hostile to each other. The Romanizing ritualists want to be free to transform the church into an appanage of the Vatican. The free churchmen wish to see the Anglican church set free to purge itself from worldliness and superstition alike. We have lively times ahead. And they are very near at hand.

* * *

Board of Ministerial Relief of the Church of Christ.

Aid in the support of worthy, needy, disabled ministers of the Christian Church and their widows. THIRD LORD'S DAY IN DECEMBER is the day set apart in all the churches for the offering to this work. If you make individual offerings, send direct to the Board. Wills and Deeds should be made to "BOARD OF MINISTERIAL RELIEF OF THE CHURCH OF CHRIST, a corporation under the laws of the State of Indiana." Money received on the Annuity Plan.

Address all communications and make all checks, drafts, etc., payable to

People's Forum

"Here I Stand"

(E. L. F. et al.)

And see the grand procession go by.

There are some stations where standing is at a premium, others where it is perilous. Then, brethren, have you not observed that frequent standing, even upon good ground, begets a *mulishness* in us so that we become confused and *stand* more than go *ahead* in the luminous future of revealed truths and opening fields of thought and investigation.

I often wanted to *cut the breeching* in the harness of a valuable ·horse, when a boy. The very choice blooded Kentucky animal *drew the lines* (balked) between single and double work. Is it not so, often with us, brethren? And may not some brighter intelligence want to *cut the breeching?* Let us discriminate and go ahead.

Euclid, O.   J. F. CALLAHAN.

E. L. Frazier's Dilemma.

(Continued from Page 1137.)

involve at all a change in moral character. More than that, the Masons seek to recruit their· ranks from among those who are as good as they are. The better the ·man before he becomes a Mason the greater· the victory. The mark ·or character of ·the Mason is external, a badge· on the· lapel of· the· coat which in no sense· stands· for a great moral change.

But it is ·not ·so in the· making· of a Christian. The morals of the man are supposed to be affected. We do not ·ask that ·a man's character be changed before we begin to put him through the process that makes him a Christian; but we seek to change ·it in the process of making him a Christian. The ·worse a man is before he becomes a Christian the greater the· victory. The ·mark or character of the Christian is internal and stands for a great renovating transformation. Now, what is that mark? The answer to this question brings up to the second point of criticism, namely: That Brother Frazier's position is unscriptural.

The reason "There is a great difference between the Christian character and the non- or anti-Christian character," is because the Holy Spirit plays an important part in producing the marvelous transformation that justifies us in saying a man has a Christian character. But the Holy Spirit has nothing to do with making a man a Mason or an American. The change from the non-Christian to the Christian character is not only a moral change, which ·in· itself would be sufficient to distinguish the change to the Christian character from that to the Masonic character, but it is spiritual as well. The Christian has been Spirit-taught, Spirit-led, Spirit-impressed, Spirit-filled; and because he has received the gift of the Holy Spirit is now a Spirit-led man. This fact and this alone is what gives us a right to affirm that any one has a Christian character. The possession of the Holy Spirit is the distinguishing character of the Christian, or that which gives him his distinguishing character. Paul ·says in Eph. 1:13, "In whom, having also believed,· ye· were sealed with the Holy Spirit of promise." (Compare Eph. 4:30· and 2 Cor. 1:22). Paul thus clearly teaches that God, by the gift of the Holy Spirit, sets a seal, or

mark, ·or a· character upon Christians· by which he indicates who are his. Baptism is not the seal. Brother· Frazier would almost· have us think so. A man is ·not a Christian because he has been ·immersed, ·for that may be a hypocritical act which God alone can discern; but he is a Christian ·because God has given him the Holy Spirit. Baptism in one· phase of it is an overt act of obedience which gives expression to· a new· disposition ·which has been ·planted,· and a spirit or character of obedience which is being formed, in the subject requesting baptism. But the final proof ·that any baptism is genuine is the giving ·of the Holy Spirit.

Now, how can Brother ·Frazier or any. body else know that a man possesses the Holy Spirit? By his bearing the fruit of the Spirit and giving expression in service to the new character planted in him. A man is not a Christian in character unless ·he is. giving Christian service and bearing the fruit of the Spirit. He can not bear the fruit of the Spirit unless he possesses the Spirit. And ·if he has the Holy Spirit he is a Christian in· fact. It is illogical and unscriptural, therefore, to affirm ·that a man can ·be a "Christian in character·' ·and not be a "Christian in fact." ·And· as Christ's purpose in· the Gospel is to produce Christian character, Brother ·Frazier's position compels him to acknowledge that the ultimate purpose of Christ to effect the individual's salvation by· planting his own character in him, can be accomplished without ·making·'a man a Christian in· fact. It seems to me that Brother Frazier is either compelled to· affirm· 'that· those who have been conscientiously sprinkled for baptism are Christians if they· have Christian characters, or else deny that they have Christian characters. The readers of THE CHRISTIAN-EVANGELIST will be glad to know what Brother Frazier will have to say further about this.

· *Portland*, Ore.

Picture of War Engine "General."

A beautiful colored picture, 18x25 inches, of ·the historic old engine "General" which was stolen at Big Shanty, Ga., by the Andrew's Raiders during the Civil War, and which is now on exhibition in the Union Depot, Chattanooga, Tenn., has·been gotten out· by the NASHVILLE, CHATTANOOGA & ST. LOUIS RY.—The "Battlefields Route" to the South. The picture is ready for framing· and will be mailed for 25c. The "Story of the General" sent free. W. L. Danley, Gen'l Pass. Agent, Nashville, Tenn.

CHURCH DEDICATIONS.

Asherville, Kan.

Lord's day. August 26, was a field day for our people. Our church was dedicated by W. S. Lowe, of Topeka, after raising the $400 lacking to meet all bills. After the morning service we went to the groves—God's first temple—and there was provided stacks of good things to eat. They were attended to by a large audience. At 3 p. m. the church was again crowded to its full capacity, and Bro. W. H. Scrivner, pastor of the Christian Church of Beloit, gave us a masterly sermon. After this service we found that Brother Lowe would be unable to preach any more that day, so we arranged for our pastor, Brother Clark, to supply for Brother Scrivner at Beloit, and Brother Scrivner gave us another great sermon at 8 p. m. to a packed house. The Baptist brethren dismissed their services and came with us, their pastor assisting in every service, and we all felt how blessed it was for brethren to dwell together in unity. It was an ideal day—cool and pleasant. The gracious blessing of our dear Lord was all about us, and we greatly rejoiced together.

A. N. NOELL.

Kimberlin Heights, Tenn.

It is now 22 months since our main building was totally destroyed by fire. About 120 young preachers were turned out on a cold and unresponsive world. It was a sad ending to ten years of toil and sacrifice. We began the work of restoration and enlargements the day after the fire and we had proved one thing sure: God, our Father, still hears and answers the prayer of faith. Thirty-three hundred and fifty ($3350) people, congregations and societies have contributed to the building fund. Many of them have given repeatedly. In all we have raised about $30000 and we need yet about $1,800. We have a magnificent equipment and we hope to dedicate it free from debt. This institution has solved the question of getting an edcation and keeping out of debt. Thirty dollars ($30) and three half hours a day, and four half hours on Mondays will pay all college fees for one year, including board. We have room for any young man who is free from the tobacco and other bad habits, and who is willing to help himself. The boat will leave Knoxville for Kimberlin Heights September 19, 1906, at 10 o'clock. Bring plenty bedding.
Dedication September 20, 1906.

ASHLEY S. JOHNSON.

Huntington, Ind.

The first Lord's day in September was a great day and triumph for the Huntington, (Ind.) church. It was the day on which their great new building was dedicated. Z. T. Sweeney did the preaching and securing of pledges masterfully. Although the day was stormy and rainy, there were four great services: great services, great sermons, splendid music, free fellowships, sweet communion and consecrated giving. During the day $26,000 was raised, and the building dedicated with all the cost—$36,000—provided for. The building is the best church edifice in the city and in Northern Indiana, and one of the best equipped in the entire brotherhood. The church is of the combination type, the auditorium and Sunday-school department being separated by massive sliding doors bearing decorations that conform to the entire walls. The auditorium has cowled floor, amphitheatrical seating, and with a convenient terraced gallery, has a seating capacity of 750. The pews are of golden oak, to correspond with the panel and wood work of the balconies and choir loft and the handsome pipe organ.

The Sunday-school department is a triumph of the skill of the architect, George W. Kramer. It is without question the most modern structure of the kind in Indiana, and is capable of accommodating a completely graded school of 800. There are 16 class rooms. Provision is made for a Sunday-school orchestra, library and secretary's rooms and for stereopticon. The main auditorium and Sunday-school room, when thrown together, form one room with a seating capacity of 1,500.

The basement is arranged for all the social functions and work of the church. A completely equipped kitchen and pantry, dining-room seating 200, lecture hall seating 400, parlors, toilets, robing rooms, choir waiting room, janitor's office and stores.

The decorations are subdued and simple, but rich and artistic, and the windows are of rich stained glass, without figures. The building itself is of modified Gothic architecture in design, and is an exemplification of the modern tendency to get away from the tower, the spire and all useless appendages. This church is built for use and equipped for service; is constructed of white sand-lime brick, with heavy Bedford stone trimmings.

The church dates back in its history to about 1845, when a little band, faithful to the cause they espoused, met from house to house to break bread. At times preaching was heard from visiting preachers, and an occasional evangelist held a week's meeting in the court house. Believers made the good confession and were baptized in the Wabash River and added to the flock. Thus the original 13 grew and multiplied, and in 1851 a plain frame chapel was erected. In 1886 L. Berry

Smith was called to the pastorate, and the good man labored with them for 21 years and was followed in a seven-years' pastorate by H. C. Kendrick. A brick church was erected in 1881, greatly added to and remodeled in 1898. Short pastorates were held by O. S. Reed, W. T. Wells, and C. A. Hill. In September, 1902, Cephas Shelburne was called to the work. In a pastorate of four years the work has been greatly strengthened and built up. The best feeling exists between pastor and people, the finest harmony prevails and all departments of the work are growing and prospering. During that time 400 have been added to the membership, the Sunday-school has grown to 500, the C. W. B. M. numbers about 100, there is an excellent ladies' society, and the church is splendidly organized and finely officered and is a power for good in the community. The chief triumph of these four years is the building and dedication to the service of the Master this splendid church edifice. Twelve columns were given to the dedication by each of our daily papers. The church is planning for larger things.

RALLY DAY SOUVENIRS

Why not have a Rally Day in your Sunday School? It is a grand opportunity to bring scholars to church. A school can prepare any form of a service desired and announce that all who attend will be given a pretty souvenir. The extra collection derived from such an announcement will more than pay the expense. We offer three attractive novelties, as described below.

THE ANCHOR.

A most artistic design in the shape of an anchor, with beautiful harvest leaves in the form of a wreath, all printed in three colors. The words "Rally Day" are prominently printed out in red letters in the centre, and a scripture selection from Hebrews, "Which hope we have as an anchor of the soul," is neatly printed on the prong part of the anchor. The souvenirs are cut in above shape and are the exact size of the illustration, only far more beautiful by reason of their being in colors. Each one has a silk ribbon (assorted colors) attached to hang or be pinned to coat or dress. Price $1.50 per 100. Delivered anywhere when cash accompanies the order. Less than 100 supplied at 2c each. Samples mailed for 5c in stamps.

THE TREE STUMP.

An attractive novelty in three colors, combining all the beauties of Rally Day and Harvest Time. The old tree stump, filled with chestnut burrs, cones and acorns, and hanging over the sides the beautiful maple leaves in the natural harvest colors, together with a pretty red squirrel eating a nut just outside his home in the hollow of the tree. A most pleasing and attractive souvenir in every way. Printed in three colors with assorted silk ribbons to attach to the coat or dress. The souvenirs are the exact size of the illustration, but far more handsome on account of being in colors. Price $1.50 per 100. Delivered anywhere when cash accompanies the order. Less than 100 supplied at 2c each. Sample mailed for 5c in stamps.

THE STAR.

A pretty design in the shape of a star, indicating "The Star of Hope," "The Star of Promise," etc. Printed in three colors, with a selection from John 6:51, reading "Gather together in one the children of God." Has the sheaf of wheat, oak tree, fruit, Vegetables, etc., in each of the six corners or points of the star. Each star has a silk ribbon (assorted colors) attached, to hang or be pinned to the coat or dress. Price $1.50 per 100. Delivered anywhere when cash accompanies the order. Less than 100 supplied at 2c each. Sample mailed for 5c in stamps. Stars are exact size of illustration.

RALLY DAY POST CARD

An invitation, well worded, inviting members or others to the Rally Day gathering. Can be sent by mail for 1c. each. Price of Rally Day Post Cards, 50c. per hundred, postpaid.

CHRISTIAN PUBLISHING COMPANY,
2712 Pine Street,   St. Louis, Mo.

The Home Departmen

The Creed of Ethan Allen.

BY FRANK HONEYWELL.

Beside his daughter's death-bed Ethan Allen sat
　　　one day!
He knew that ere another morn her soul must
　　　pass away
And leave alone with him a form of stillness
　　　and decay.

Upon his brow and in his eyes a hopeless look
　　　was set;
He gazed into his daughter's face, and as their
　　　gazes met,
Both pairs of eyes were dry, for naught had
　　　burst the tear-fount yet.

"O father," said the dying child, "pray tell me,
　　　tell me, now—
Shall I reject my mother's God, before him cease
　　　to bow?
What did it mean when you to mother made that
　　　sacred vow?

"When mother left you vowed to keep me near
　　　the faith until
I grew of age to follow my own conscience-
　　　governed will.
Oh, tell me, is that vow to mother firm and
　　　earnest still?

"Or is there naught in Calvary, no Christ-ruled
　　　Heaven-place?
But where the hope in such belief?—I see none
　　　in your face!
I see but lines of stern-checked grief, all hope-
　　　less to erase."

The father, well-night overcome, braced all the
　　　nerve he had;
He felt the tear-fount full to burst, a bursting
　　　that makes glad;
And in his inmost soul he screamed, "Mad infi-
　　　del, you're mad!"

The fountain burst, nor in advance of bursting
　　　gave a sign,
And thus he sobbed, a conquered soul, "My
　　　daughter, choice is thine:
Keep, if you will, your mother's faith—there
　　　is no hope in mine."

Next day he bowed him o'er a form bereft of
　　　life and will,
And wondered at the peace that beautified her
　　　face, until
He felt an unwarned shudder at the doubt that
　　　bound him still.

The Bronze Vase.

BY J. BRECKENRIDGE ELLIS.

PART III.

CHAPTER X.

When the "overland voyage" was resumed, Mrs. Weed was herself again,
and the horses were themselves, too—
that is saying more for Mrs. Weed than
for the horses. After the night of Mrs.
Weed's illness, Rhoda never thought of
her or of Wizzen as she had before.
Somehow all of their peculiarities were
softened, and in a way made sacred.
Wizzen's grammar was as peculiar as
ever, and his devotion to the use of
"which" as pronounced; and Mrs. Weed
was still groping blindly among the difficult recesses of the English language.
But whatever they said or did, Rhoda
knew that back of everything were their
faithful hearts. As Wizzen once remarked, "I tell you, young folks, in
speaking of the old lady, or of anybody else for that matter, when goodness is at the roots of the tongue it
ain't of so much signification what
trickles off the end of it. You two are
digging and delving into them books
hour after hour, and that's all right, I
reckon. As long as they is books in the
world, they ought to be some of a mind
for 'em. But books alone makes a
mighty pore specimen of humans. As I
look at it, if they ain't a foundation, it
don't matter what kind of a house you
build. You may make it out of a ency-
clopedia of a hundred volumes, but it

won't stick in a big windstorm. But
the Bible puts it better than I can, to
which I refer you, as to say a house built
on rock or sand."

Wizzen's words about the young people
studying from hour to hour were not
unwarranted. It is true that Raymond's
books were far beyond the place of
Rhoda's studies. "But that doesn't
matter," said Raymond, finding her eager
to learn. "Cicero is easier than Caesar
anyhow, and one grammar is as much
grammar as another. It will do me good
to teach you what I know, and it's so
fine for us to be together!" And he
smiled at her with affectionate enthusiasm. The botany proved one of their
keenest delights. Often they walked
to ease poor Wizzen's horses, and as they
passed along the country roads they were
continually calling to each other to look
at some weed or wild flower or leaf.
They made books of pressed leaves and
grasses, and analyzed them with loving
care. It was just like a holiday. Before the studies were taken up, Rhoda
had found the journey pretty monotonous and tiresome; now it grew delightful. One no longer sat dully counting
the mileposts or looking at the figures
on the telephone-poles; one learned
conjugations and declensions; one dived
into intuitions, abstractions and subjec-
tivity; one conned over the words in the
dictionaries; one was always busy! And
it was all in the open air, with the sunshine about them and the quails darting
from the road, and the rabbits frisking
their stubs of tails as if they knew they
would not be good to eat till cold weather. So they traveled on and on, fitting
themselves day by day for future positions of usefulness, and at last the goal
of their ambition—St. Louis—smoked
before them like one great chimney. The
trip from Kansas City had taken them
six weeks because the horses had been
treated with unusual consideration. "I'm
going to sell these beasts before they
die," said Wizzen, driving into the straggling suburbs, "and if so, it will have to
be did mighty quick! I 'low to git more
enterprising beasts than these before I
start back with the old lady to Crawley."
"When will you be going back?" asked
Raymund, but he was so excited by the
entrance into the great city that he
hardly heeded the answer.
"Don't know," said Wizzen; "they is
no profit in moving when it's all cut and
dried beforehand. Where does your uncle
live?"
In a chorus Raymund and Rhoda gave
the direction. "You'd best walk there,"
said Wizzen, with decision. "I'll drive
along till I hit a vacant lot and we'll take
possession and there stay till we are
made to get out. But you two will walk
to the place, for your uncle will think
more of you which he don't see you
making your grand entry into the city
in a mover's wagon."
"I'm not ashamed of the wagon, or
of you," cried Rhoda, her eyes flashing.
"Then you can just be ashamed of
human nature," returned Wizzen, un-
yieldingly, "for such is the case." I
ended as Wizzen proposed. Mrs. Weed
was left to take care of the wagon in a
frowsy vacant lot which was scooped out
in the center, presenting somewhat the
appearance of an amphitheater. Down
in the bottom of this great hole the
wagon and horses looked unnaturally
small. As the others looked down from
the street, Mrs. Weed waved a handker-

than you," said Raymund, with hesitation. "We'd better go in and ask."

So they went in the door, and as they passed under the number on the transom—that number which they had so often seen in their mother's Bible—it was like venturing into a world of childhood's vague imagining. A counter faced the door, upon which objects of widely different natures were displayed, and to the right of the counter were piles of old clothes. To the left was a gate which led behind the counter, and beyond that was a door to the rear of the little shop. Behind the counter sat a woman of about 30, exceedingly tall and thin, with such an aggressive display of bone in her presentment that it was easy to imagine that she had an extra rib from Mother Eve. Her hair was coiled in a tangled twist at the back of her head, and she wore her dress low, as if to show the world how very long a lady's neck could be. She smiled at the children, thereby revealing one black tooth, which at first seemed a gap. The smile was not at all pleasant, though it meant to be so, for the lady was so used to exercising unyielding authority that she was utterly unable to relax even when smiling.

"Well, children," she said, "what can I do for you to-day?"

"Does Mr. William Hodges live here?" inquired Raymund, stepping up to the counter.

"I am keeping the shop now," said the lady, rather sternly. She still showed the black tooth, because her lips never came together on ordinary occasions. The black tooth now showed it was not a gap, but appeared to be a sort of danger-signal, meaning, "Better keep away!" The other teeth appeared to be taking the air with easy freedom on account of having this black guard always on the outlook.

"Is this Mr. William Hodges's shop?" asked Rhoda.

"If you want anything here," said the lady, abruptly, "just consider this shop mine. And if you must have names, my name is Miss Pinns."

Raymund, now believing that she was trying to put them off, put on a bold front, and said: "We have come all the way from Kansas City to see Mr. William Hodges."

Miss Pinns looked at them with a dart of amazing sharpness and considered. Then she said, "Who are you?"

"Mr. Hodges is our uncle William," said Rhoda, flushing. "Please tell him we are here."

"He is your uncle!" cried Miss Pinns, turning pale and looking more disagreeable than ever; "that is a likely story, indeed!"

"It is the truth," said Raymund, "and we can prove it. Where is he?"

Miss Pinns again relapsed into meditation, her narrow forehead wrinkling in perplexity. At last she rose from the high stool which seemed only too short for her long proportions; and said, in a begrudging voice, "I will call him."

She accordingly walked to the rear door and opened it. "Mr. Hodges," she said, "come here!" Her voice was milder than when she had addressed the children, but it still showed the muffled note of authority, as if she owned Mr. Hodges about as absolutely as she controlled the shop. A little, stooped man of anywhere from 60 to 80 came to the door, leaning upon two canes. He looked at Raymund and Rhoda through large spectacles of divided lenses. They made him duck his head lower than his bent shoulders, that he might look through the top of the lenses. "Well?" he said, briefly.

(To be Continued.)

Serving.

The sweetest lives are those to duty wed,
    Whose deeds, both great and small,
Are close-knit strands of unbroken thread,
    Where love ennobles all.
The world may mend no trumpets, ring no bells;
    The book of life the shining record tells.

Thy love shall chant its own beautitudes
After its own life-working. A child's kiss
Set on the sighing lips shall make thee glad,
A sick man helped by thee shall make thee strong.
Thou shalt be served thyself by every sense
Of service which thou rendereth.
                    —*Elizabeth Barrett Browning.*

Advance Society Letters.

BY J. BRECKENRIDGE ELLIS.

Now, some more about the Ice Cream Social given for Charlie's Educational Fund. At the last report we had received $64.90. I felt quite sure there would be some after-orders for ice cream, at least enough to make it $65. I was right. This is certainly the most successful social I ever heard of. And it is a real social, not a make-believe social; for though none of us were together in the same place, were not our thoughts touching hands with each other? were not our wishes for orphan Charlie sitting side by side? and did not our prayers for his future nobility and success come together here, and go on to God in company? Let us hear more from those who attended in spirit the social where the ice cream was doing good to the helpless, and the cake was just one big angel-food of love and service. Grace Everest, Oklahoma City: "My brother says he will escort me to your ice cream social, so we will want two dishes. I was wondering the other day how many members there are in the Av. S. An easy way to keep the reports is to put down the Bible-references each day in the note-book you will receive. Then you can mail it the day the quarter is finished. I was glad to see a letter from Beulah Shortridge. Why don't some of the older members write oftener? Harry Buckley made me feel very good by naming me as one of the 'faithful ones.' Maybe he is like my uncle—always saying something *pleasant* about somebody." (That's the very nicest habit I know of, that a person can fall into. I wish every Av. S. member or friend would fall in so deep he could never get out of it. I am sure I don't know how many members we have. I used to keep count till they grew so many. And yet, of all our members, very few ever keep our simple little rules for twelve weeks, although they must know that to keep them will make them stronger of mind and heart, and so, of more use to the world. Why is it? Of course it isn't because they are lazy; it is because they are so industrious about doing something else.) Mrs. Virgil D. Brown, Los Angeles, Cal.: "Am I in time? Mr. Brown and I will take two dishes of cream. We hope Charlie will grow to be a useful man. We came from Plattsburg last October, and though we like Los Angeles fine, we can't get over the habit of peeping over Old Baldy Mountain, at Plattsburg, in Clinton county, on the other side." (Just as you spoke, I was peeping over the northern edge of the Ozarks in the same direction.) "It is very warm here, which the Californians tell us is unusual. We had a fine rain here last night." (We had a fine rain here, too, last night; but why do I particularize? we've had a rain every day for the past 19 days; that's as far back as I began keeping count. The Arkansawyers say it's unusual, too. Do you know, I think that's a habit of speech that natives acquire unconsciously?) "We are enjoying the Bronze Vase very much" (the reader will kindly observe that it is not *I* who am now speaking) "and the Av. S. Letters. Terrell Marshall is my nephew; I am sorry orphan Charlie couldn't spend his vacation with him. My sister and family enjoyed him so much last summer. I hope the social will be a success in every way." Mrs. E. F. S. Kelso, Putnam, Ill.: "I enclose 10 dishes of ice cream for Charlie's education. I enjoy the Av. S. page; especially the remarks by—" (Oh, thank you!) Mrs. S., Bronaugh, Mo.: "Fifty cents to be used for little Charlie." Greenfield, Tenn.: "We read your very original invitation to the ice cream supper and gladly accept, wishing Charlie many happy returns of the day." (Fifty cents in that letter.) Clinton, Ia.: "Your invitation here on time. I send to you this little dime. Sorry the ice cream is understood, for the day's so hot, it would be good. I hope you'll get a lot of money, though your plan does seem a little funny." (We got eighty-five dollars, honey!) Mrs. L. Porter, Jacobs, Ky.: "I send 25 cents for Charlie's ice cream supper. I enjoy the Av. S. Letters so much. I saw you and your father at Pertle Springs 19 or 20 years ago." (Not me surely! What, 20 years ago? Wasn't I too little to go to the springs 20 years ago? I must have been awfully young!) Oklahoma City: "I send 10 cents for Charlie's picnic, and I wish it were dollars, but I send this out of my poverty and hope to send Drusie something before long; God bless them both. What a chase poor Raymond and Rhoda are having to avoid that ubiquitous Mr. Boggs! Please do not let him find them." (If I were only there, I'd show Mr. Boggs. But you see, I couldn't put myself into the story.) Some one from Moberly, Mo., sends a dime for the ice cream supper, and another sends $5, and there is a heart of love and a prayer in faith behind each gift. Belton, Mo.: "I think this a splendid idea to have a social for Charlie's education. Good evening, Brother Ellis." (Why, howd'y, Belton; I'm pleased to see you're still on the map.) "I have come for my saucer of ice cream and will pay my dime." (Yes, I'll relieve you of it, as it's probably heavy.) "No, I don't like to do that. I think it a selfish old maid or bachelor who spends only one dime at a social and just on himself. I've brought a dollar and will treat you and Charlie. I am glad Charlie made his decision to visit you and Felix this summer. Once I visited the St. Louis orphan home. The first thing I asked Miss Tena was to show me Charlie. I like his appearance very much. I hope we may have a large crowd this evening." (We have received orders for eight hundred and fifty saucers.) Ala A. Russell, Greenfield, Mo.: "I could not serve ice cream for Charlie's benefit, as I have three motherless children to care for, so I took them all in a buggy and drove around to a few of the sisters and collected $1.25; and my grandchildren add I add $1. Little John, four years old, kept asking where you lived and would you have the cream ready, and baby said, 'He wants some team, too!' The other one is six, so you see I have my hands full." (May heaven bless all three and the hands that minister to them. The name of each donor is inscribed in my account book.)

One of the sweetest things about the Advance Society is the way we get acquainted with noble souls whom in the visible world we would doubtless never have met, or at least learned as they are. Who of us does not at once feel acquainted with the writer of the last letter? We see the buggy going down the road with the children in it, all bent on soliciting something for the orphan boy known to them only through our page. The baby is doubtless holding the tip end of the lines, imagining him-

self the driver. You will remember that when Charlie ended his visit with his sister, he went to Mrs. Skinner. I have a personal letter from her, part of which is not to be printed. Indeed she would rather none of it were, but I want you to have a little heart-glimpse of this friend of orphans. Mrs. N. C. Skinner, Dorsey, Ill.: "When Charlie came on his visit, there was no one to meet him. He got to Dorsey at nine, Sunday night. We got a telephone message saying he was at Dorsey. We were all in bed. Charlie said if we could direct him, maybe he could walk over—two and a half miles. Mr. Skinner said he would go right over to Dorsey. I felt so sorry for Charlie that I had to kiss him, and we took him right to our hearts. He is a love-boy. He and my great-nephew, 12 years old, have a good time, and Charlie and 'Houndpup' do, too." And here is something from Charlie himself: "I am surprised to hear the social took in so much money. I thank you so very much. I hope I will soon get to go to business school, for I am anxious to get an education. I don't know how I can ever repay the friends who take such an interest in me." (By becoming a good man; that is all the reward they ask.) "This is a farm; it is such a pleasant place. From Mrs. Skinner's I will go to Mrs. Thornton Stahl. I have gone hunting several times. I helped turn the washing machine yesterday. I get all the apples and grapes I can eat. The Ridgely Sunday-school is not very large, but it is all O. K. There is a threshing machine just across the road panting like its little heart would break. I have sure had a fine vacation so far. But I did hate to part with Bessie. Give your mother and father my love." (When Charlie's vacation ends, we will print every item of his expense; for it is your money that he is spending, and you ought to know all about its use.) Kathryn Lammert, McKirk, Mo.: "A little early, but yet I've eaten

my cream and forward my money immediately. My! but it was good, so pure and sweet! I could have eaten a dollar's worth. It's not because it makes my head hurt that I only took one saucer, but because I just had a dime. I inclose as many good wishes, though, as if it were $10. 'Tis not what we give, you know; 'tis what we share; for the gift without the giver is bare.' The Av. S. Letters are grand. All the family read them. 'Bronze Vase' is all right. Do you know, I was in a city once and a lady pointed out to me a gentleman sitting on a porch, and she told me how he counted everything he saw; in fact, he was just like the Mr. Merlin Agency you described in the 'Bronze Vase.' We live in the country on pretty Clover Dale Farm, and mamma says we'll invite Charlie here some time. Papa, mamma, brothers and sisters have all gone to a big revival, and I am here at home looking after things and trying to write with the meanest pen on earth." (I have one I'd like to enter against yours in a state competition.) "So don't you print this letter under any consideration, hear me?" (Too bad, but I didn't hear you until it was too late, and I had copied off your letter. But I ask all the contributors, please not to read the letter. Now, then, hear me?) Jacksonville, Ill.: "One dollar for Drusie. May her work never suffer for lack of funds, and may the Av. S. be faithful to the trust committed to its care." Drusie

Malott, South Chih-li Mission, Tai Ming-fu, North China (please remember the direction; first you go south, then you go north): "Well, well! Two foreign mails within the last eight days, and you should have seen me when the mailman came! The delightful pile of packages and papers could hardly be carried in my arms. Friends came running to my room to see if Christmas hadn't made a mistake at the wrong end! We were soon examining the lovely books that some kind heart had sent. Nine books and two bundles of papers! Please always let me have the pleasure of knowing the names of the senders of these much-appreciated gifts. But I hope friends wil not use for me money needed in so many places in the Master's service. Indeed, I put it as a request. From THE CHRISTIAN-EVANGELIST I find that Elizabeth M. Rothwell, Moberly, Mo., is one who so kindly sent me a number of books. To her I extend sincerest thanks. And when I found that your own dear mother tied them up for mailing, I said, 'God bless her kind, motherly heart.' They were tied up just right for the long voyage. 'Daily Strength for Daily Needs' was especially appreciated—in fact, was an answer to a prayer of several months previous. Does anybody know where I can get a 'Birthday Edition of Daily Light'? About books: I am not hard to please. I enjoy all books worth reading. I brought very few to China because I came so suddenly, so unexpectedly; there were no duplicates in the packages sent. THE CHRISTIAN-EVANGELIST grows more interesting each week. My own letters when printed are so old that they seem new to me. Tell Mrs. Shryock that a dollar with such a prayer is worth more than $25 without a prayer. God does answer prayer. Some of the answers have been marvelous—so marked. But, young people, the Father desires you above all other gifts. You, your life, body and spirit, wherever he chooses for you to serve him. It is worth all. It is the only true living, the only real happiness. Do you doubt it? Try it and see! * * * July 26: Since beginning this letter, I have received another package of books and a package of papers. Also precious letters from Mrs. Romwebber and Ataline Stokes and Mrs. Damarell and her two daughters, the first inclosing $7 and $1 respectively, and the latter saying they were making their offering to you. Best of all, each assured me of her prayers. That is more than anything else, for I know an answer will come, and I am strengthened and encouraged." (Drusie acknowledges receipt of the monthly $5 from the Av. S. But, indeed, we may claim the $8 she mentions; since the Av. S. was no doubt the cause of their being sent. Another $5 from you goes to her from Bentonville this week. By the way, speaking of Bentonville, I am proud to say that it turned out to be the social after all; it was rather late, but there was plenty of ice cream to be scraped out of the freezers; pretty hard, you know, but just as good as any, Plattsburg, too, my old home, came in great numbers. Why, dear me! I will have to devote another week to finishing up this story of the social. Mrs. Johnston, of Stewartsville, and even the ladies of Detroit, Mich.—just think of that! And while you're thinking, I'll slip away.
Bentonville, Ark.

⁂

Young People of Small Means will be helped in securing an education at "Iowa Christian College." Board and tuition $30 per term. Correspondence courses also, Write Pres. Chas. J. Burton, Oskaloosa, Iowa. Free catalogue.

Over the River.

"Over the River"—the old, sweet song!
The road to the rest there is not so long;
A song and a sigh, and a brief good-bye
And we meet with the dreams 'neath a stormless
sky.

"Over the River"—the song that thrills
In music down from the heavenly hills;
The pain and peril of Life's time past,
And the rest that is given of God at last!

"Over the River"—so sweet it seems
To drift away to the starlit dreams!
To fear no more the fall o' the Night
"Over the River" where "Love is Light!"
—Frank L. Stanton in Atlanta Constitution.

❋ ❋

A Dreadful Dilemma.

A capital story is told of Governor Van Sant, of Minnesota, in connection with a recent visit of his to New York.

Soon after the governor had been assigned to a hotel room, a former resident of Minnesota called and found him gazing with gloomy countenance at his trunk.

After an exchange of salutations, Mr. Van Sant said: "John, I'm in a tremendous fix. I want a suit of clothes out of that trunk. Oh, yes, I've got the key all right, but my wife packed the trunk. She was to come along, but was prevented at the last moment. To my certain knowledge she put in enough to fill three trunks the way a man would pack them. If I open it, the things will boil all over the room, and I could never get half of them back. Now, what I'm

wondering about is whether it would be cheaper to go out and buy a new suit of clothes or two additional trunks."

A young Japanese compositor, employed on a Japanese paper in New York, was riding down town in a City Hall train the other morning. He was engrossed in his morning paper, and paid little attention to the other passengers.

But a fresh looking young man who sat next to him, and who had been eyeing him all along, suddenly asked:

"What sort of 'nese' are you, anyway; a Chinese or a Japanese?"

The little Jap was not caught napping. Quick as a wink he replied:

"What sort of a key are you, anyway; a monkey, a donkey, or a Yankee?"

The fresh young man had no more to say, and left the train quickly when City Hall station was reached.—The Crown, Newark, N. J.

❋ ❋

Lake Geneva Summer Train Service.

Via the Chicago & North-Western R'y is now in effect including Saturday afternoon train leaving Chicago 1:00 p. m. and Sunday Train leaving 8:00 a. m. For tickets, rates and full information apply to your nearest ticket agent or address W. B. Kniskern, P. T. M., C. & N. W. R'y Co., Chicago.

Christian Publishing Company

2712 Pine St., St. Louis, Mo.

J. H. GARRISON, - - - - President
W. W. DOWLING, - - - Vice-President
GEO. L. SNIVELY, - - Sec. and Gen. Supt
R. P. CROW, - - Treas. and Bus. Manager

The picture of our Editor for one renewal and one new subscription accompanied by the $3 has proven a very popular premium, and we are sending his "lineaments" to many a home and study.

Again we advise all our readers to get to the Wabash in time to catch the train leaving St. Louis at noon, October 11. We will gladly secure you accommodations in the city and will do all in our power to make your attendance upon the convention a most pleasing memory,

A representative of this House has just gone over the route of "THE CHRISTIAN-EVANGELIST" Special to Buffalo. He "followed the flag over the Wabash." The service is of the very safest, best and most courteous. Arrangements were made for housing the party at the very best and most economical hotels and close to the convention hall.

It is a great surprise to the writer that many of our preachers known to have large libraries order their books through secular agencies exclusively. Unconsciously, they are paying more than is necessary for the books and at the same time are failing to have part in the building up of a publishing house most creditable to our brotherhood and helpful to our preachers and other book-reading disciples.

About the most extravagant eulogium pronounced upon other Bible school literature is that "it is as good as Dowling's." We publish all of W. W. Dowling's contributions to our Bible school literature and charge no more for it than others ask for their productions. Why not get the best and rejoice in the assurance that you are doing in this particular all that can be done for the young folk.

Three hundred, five hundred, one thousand CHRISTIAN-EVANGELISTS per week will cost comparatively little during your protracted meeting but their contribution to the success of the services will be only second to that of the evangelist and pastor, and the Bible. Write or wire us for terms, and your orders, and the papers will be sent promptly. Preachers and evangelists give striking testimony to the efficiency of the voiceless eloquence of these papers in urging men to wait upon the preaching and preparing them for the unfolding of the

Word and helping them to go forward when the invitation is given.

Hundreds of congratulatory letters are received from well-wishers over the manifestly rapid growth of the circulation of THE CHRISTIAN-EVANGELIST. These are profoundly appreciated especially when accompanied by a subscription list. In addition to the large number of ones and twos, we are pleased to report the follow clubs of new subscriptions received during the past week at the regular $1.50 rate, to-wit.: Rockwell City, Ia., 3, H. Brown, pastor; Swayzee, Ind., 6, A. McKown, minister; Alexandria, Ind., 47, H. A. Wingard, pastor; Elwood, Ind., 18, Robt. Sellers, minister; Independence, Mo., 3, A. J. Marshall, pastor; Marceline, Mo., 39, W. D. Bolton, minister; Mobile, Ala., 8, Claude E. Hill, pastor; Citronelle, Ala., 3; Fairhope, Ala., 4; Brookfield, Mo., 26; Bucklin, Mo., 7; Allerton, Ia., 3, R. H. Ingram, minister.

Assurances come to us from every source that the vast majority of our preachers are in perfect sympathy with the aspirations of THE CHRISTIAN-EVANGELIST for our brotherhood. If these brethren will only co-operate with us persistently, aggressively and lovingly, they can introduce THE CHRISTIAN-EVANGELIST into 100,000 homes long before the 1909 Centennial and yet not injure the business of any other of our publishing houses. Not one household in five in which we have members is taking any religious paper. Will not thousands of our

preachers give practical expression of their interest in the propaganda of THE CHRISTIAN-EVANGELIST by enrolling the names tens of thousands of this non-reading class on our subscription lists? It will be wonderful impetus to our churches and American Christianity.

THE
CHRISTIAN·EVANGELIST

A WEEKLY RELIGIOUS NEWSPAPER.

Volume XLIII.   No. 37.

ST. LOUIS, SEPTEMBER 13, 1906.

HOLDING FAST

Washington Gladden

IN the bitter waves of woe,
　Beaten and tossed about
By the sullen winds that blew
　From the desolate shores of doubt.

Where the anchors that Faith has cast
　Are dragging in the gale,
I am quietly holding fast
　To the things that can not fail.

I know that right is right,
　That it is not good to lie;
That love is better than spite
　And a neighbor than a spy.

I know that passion needs
　The leash of a sober mind;
I know that generous deeds
　Some sure reward shall find;

That the rulers must obey,
　That the givers shall increase;
That Duty lights the way
　For the beautiful feet of Peace;

In the darkest of the year,
　When the stars have all gone out,
That courage is better than fear,
　That faith is better than doubt.

And fierce though the friends may fight,
　And long though the angels hide,
I know that truth and right
　Have the universe on their side.

The Christian-Evangelist.

J. H. GARRISON, Editor

PAUL MOORE, Assistant Editor

F. D. POWER,
B. B. TYLER, } Staff Correspondents.
W. DURBAN,

Subscription Price, $1.50 a Year.

For foreign countries add $1.04 for postage.

Remittances should be made by money order, draft, or registered letter; not by local cheque, unless 15 cents is added to cover cost of collection

In Ordering Change of Post Office give both old and new address.

Matter for Publication should be addressed to THE CHRISTIAN-EVANGELIST. Subscriptions and remittances should be addressed to the Christian Publishing Company, 2712 Pine Street, St. Louis, Mo.

Unused Manuscripts will be returned only if accompanied by stamps.

News Items, evangelistic and other rise, are solicited, and should be sent on a postal card, if possible.

Published by the Christian Publishing Company, 2712 Pine Street, St. Louis, Mo.

Entered at St. Louis P. O. as Second Class Matter.

WHAT WE STAND FOR.

For the Christ of Galilee,
For the truth which makes men free,
For the bond of unity
Which makes God's children one.

For the love which shines in deeds,
For the life which this world needs,
For the church whose triumph speeds
The prayer: "Thy will be done."

For the right against the wrong,
For the weak against the strong,
For the poor who've waited long
For the brighter age to be.

For the faith against tradition,
For the truth 'gainst superstition,
For the hope whose glad fruition
Our waiting eyes shall see.

For the city God is rearing,
For the New Earth now appearing,
For the heaven above us clearing,
And the song of victory.

J. H. Garrison.

CONTENTS.

Centennial Propaganda: 1159
Current Events 1160
Editorial—
  Where Jesus Placed the Emphasis—IV. 1161
  A Scientist's Creed 1161
  Notes and Comments 1162
  Current Religious Thought 1162
  Editor's Easy Chair 1163
Contributed Articles—
  As Seen from the Dome. F. D. Power 1164
  What the Brethren are Saying and Doing. B. B. Tyler 1165
  Modern Religious Persecution. B. L. Chase 1166
  Why I Am a Christian Only and not a Denominationalist. J. K. Ballou. 1167
  Repentance. J. W. Kilborn 1167
  The Man With the Ax. Edward O. Sharpe 1168
Our Budget 1169
News from Many Fields 1175
Evangelistic 1178
Christian Endeavor 1178
Midweek Prayer-meeting 1179
Sunday-school 1180
Current Literature 1181
People's Forum 1182
The Home Department 1183

THE
CHRISTIAN-EVANGELIST

"IN FAITH, UNITY, IN OPINION AND METHODS, LIBERTY, IN ALL THINGS, CHARITY."

| Vol. XLIII. | September 13, 1906 | No. 37 |

1809 — CENTENNIAL PROPAGANDA CHURCHES OF CHRIST — 1909
: : : GEO. L. SNIVELY : : :

Looking Toward Pittsburg.

Robert Hopkins writes: "I covet a little of your Centennial page in behalf of the Kentucky Centennial." It is granted. Nowhere else do we look more hopefully for "the what-ought-to-be" than to our Bible schools. What public schools are to the future America so these Lord's day schools are to the church of to-morrow. No press space is too precious, no time too valuable, no abilities too great, no sacrifice too costly, to devote to the upbuilding of these schools, securing for them merited consideration in the councils of the church, and the preparation of their membership for all the responsibilities of Christian husbandmen, soldiers and priests.

It is a prophecy of a glorious "second century" when men like J. W. McGarvey, E. L. Powell, R. H. Crossfield and Robert M. Hopkins devote themselves to the solution of the problem of the betterment of our schools and the inspiration of the workers.

A prosperous Illinois congregation is seeking a pastor. Notwithstanding THE CHRISTIAN-EVANGELIST is largely circulated among its membership, the official board adopted a resolution barring any minister from their consideration who has passed his fortieth year. One fallacy in such action may be better illustrated than argued. That resolution would bar Jas. H. Gilliland of Bloomington and perhaps R. F. Thrapp of Jacksonville, two of the ablest and most successful preachers the state has produced. No one knowing these two men believes they have accomplished nearly so much during the past score of years as they will during the next twenty of their ministry.

We so deeply regret this action that we would not give it this publicity were not the practice of relegating our middle-aged preachers to inactivity rapidly dying out, and we wish to help in the obsequies. These officers would doubtless explain their action by saying "We favor long pastorates and wish a young man to come who will continue with us for the next quarter century." But observation shows that pastorates of our younger preachers are much briefer than those held by men in the fifties and sixties. After this "young preacher" is gone, this church will possibly call some man of fifty or sixty years of age, now rejected on account of his years, to a prosperous pastorate of ten or fifteen years. We do not disparage the calling of young men, but protest against a cast-iron resolution barring preachers who have passed a stipulated age milestone. Nothing is doing more to drive preachers into business, to induce them to go where the immediate salary is largest, to refrain from devoting themselves exclusively to the ministry of the Word, to discourage the most thorough ministerial preparation for life-time service beside the altar. Let us have other criteria of usefulness. Sanguineness, hopefulness, enthusiasm, buoyancy of spirit, genius for soul-saving, adaptation, the habit of success, are each far more important factors than mere matter of years in determining one's fitness for the pastorate. Our second century will be characterized by many old men eloquent in our pulpits whose wisdom, venerableness and holiness will impart additional lustre to the glory of the church. In the meantime let us use every soldier of the cross both young and old in extending to the utmost limits the boundaries of the kingdom and making it delectible as possible within those bounds before Pittsburg and 1909.

The Kentucky Centennial.

BY ROBERT M. HOPKINS.

"A Bible school chair in the Bible College" is the slogan by which Kentucky Bible schools are being rallied to the Centennial cause. It is proposed to raise $25,000 from the Bible schools and their friends to endow this new department in the College of the Bible. The college in turn will offer a course of study in Bible school methods and principles which will be obligatory upon all students, and also form a special two-year department where Bible school teachers and workers may be trained for their duties, giving a diploma for the satisfactory completion of this department. Additional work will be provided as may be demanded. "Full of good promises for both the college and the Bible schools," says Brother McGarvey. "It would be a great matter if Kentucky should be able to point to this one thing as having been actually done as a lasting monument in commemoration of our centenary as a religious body," is Bro. E. L. Powell's comment.

The Bible College Centennial session of the state convention in Louisville, September 27, bids fair to be the greatest service in this great convention. The speakers will be Marion Lawrance, J. W. McGarvey, E. Y. Mullins, E. L. Powell and R. H. Crossfield.

Our Centennial Helpers.

Enclosed find $1.50 for THE CHRISTIAN-EVANGELIST. Yours in sympathy with federation. Have been praying for it for sixty years.—H. B. Osborn.

Enclosed is $1.50 for THE CHRISTIAN-EVANGELIST. I greatly enjoy reading it more especially since I can seldom get to church on account of inability to walk.—Mrs. L. A. Campbell.

Send me missing numbers of THE CHRISTIAN-EVANGELIST with bill. I have been a constant reader for thirty-two years and I find I am daily hankering for the good things I know I have missed.—Mrs. M. G. Heard.

By the kindness of Mr. Carpenter, of the Church of the Disciples, a graduate of last year from Yale Divinity School, I have had the privilege of reading THE CHRISTIAN-EVANGELIST during the past year. I wish to express my satisfaction with the general tone of the paper. The discussion of important questions has seemed to me eminently intelligent and fair. My knowledge of those things for which the Church of the Disciples stands has been enlarged and my appreciation of the significance of the movement with which it is identified has been intensified.—Louis O. Brocton, Yale University.

I believe THE CHRISTIAN-EVANGELIST is the ablest and most interesting paper published by our brethren, and should be in every Christian home. I believe its editorials on federation of Christians unanswerable and so convincing the whole world should read. I endorse its views of the Holy Spirit and other vital topics.—William Frazier.

I enclose $1.50 for my CHRISTIAN-EVANGELIST, and wish to say that the sweet Christian spirit you manifest, and the broad, intelligent view you take of things, makes your paper not only helpful, but perfectly charming to me. I can not do without it. May our dear Lord spare you many years to represent our people in your great work!—Jennie Woodruff, Little Rock, Ark.

Please send me the subscription of ——. She was formerly a Presbyterian. I sent her THE CHRISTIAN-EVANGELIST, and now she expects to become a Disciple, or a Christian only.—W. E. Beckler.

Aside from the preaching of the Word, there is no greater recruiting agency for the Disciples of Christ than THE CHRISTIAN-EVANGELIST.

When your paper is regularly read by one in our community it does the work of an assistant pastor, and down in this district where the anti is yet untamed I need the help of your Christian literature. Like THE CHRISTIAN-EVANGELIST it causes them to think of the things that are lovely and enters the home as material for the building of fifty framed Christian characters.—Andrew Jay Jones, minister.

I have been a constant reader of THE CHRISTIAN-EVANGELIST since it was published at Quincy, Ill. I thought it good at first, but it has continued to improve ever since. I do not think it can get much better as it is one of the best religious papers published. If a copy fails to come I can not content myself until I get one and have it read to me. I hope you will continue to publish as good a paper in the future as in the past.—Mrs. J. H. Suddeth, La Grange, Mo.

Mrs. John Hazlewood, Payson, Ill., writes of a beautiful illustration of the practical application of church federation to the good of that community. The Congregationalists, Baptists and Church of Christ united in a revival meeting. Our pastor was asked to invite one of his brethren to hold the meeting. Not being able to secure the one he wished, a Congregational minister from Kansas City was called. Our minister and young men labored earnestly to lead the people into the better way with the result that the larger number of converts became members of the Christian Church, and a feeling of brotherly love kindled that greatly benefited all the congregations. She writes that the time was when such a course could not have been employed because our minister would have refused to participate in the meeting. Behold, how beautiful and helpful it is for the brethren to dwell together in love!

I have been more deeply interested in the issue on federation which has occupied so much space in our papers of late than in any other feature of religious discussion for a long time. I have had no uneasiness as to the outcome, as it is impossible for any earthly opposition to seriously interfere with the advancement and final consummation of the aims of the current Reformation. Neither life nor death, loyalty nor disloyalty nor any editor or preacher can stay the progress the Church of Christ is making throughout the world. THE CHRISTIAN-EVANGELIST may have made some mistakes—it would be more than mortal if it had not, under the immense strain it has gone through—but its attitude on this important issue will open the way to larger growth of real Christian union than any paper could possibly have done by an uncompromising and sometimes unintelligible opposition to a discussion of a vital, religious question. No harm can come to the cause by federation or anything else we can do without sacrifice of conception.—Joseph Lowe, Evangelist.

Current Events

A good deal of superfluous excitement has been generated in the minds of some Democratic statesmen and in the editorial columns of some Democratic journals by Mr. Bryan's pronouncement in favor of federal and state ownership of railroads.

Mr. Bryan on Public Ownership.

As we understand it, he was not formulating a plan for immediate action, but was dealing with the topic in a wholly academic and theoretical manner. He was not defining the policy which he would pursue if elected to the presidency, but was defining himself. He was saying to his fellow-Democrats, and to his fellow-countrymen at large: "I am the sort of man who believes in government ownership of railroads. If you elect me to the presidency, it must be with the understanding that I am that sort of a man. But whether or not I would try to put such a policy into effect at a given time, would depend upon circumstances." Such a declaration, entirely creditable to the frankness of the man who made it, need not cause alarm to the most sensitive and timid capitalist. We may be tolerably certain, whatever may be Mr. Bryan's abstract theories about public ownership, he will not be hasty about trying to put them into operation and that he would not be able to do so even if he tried. If public ownership is the worst, no one is in the slightest degree justified in considering the Bryan boom to be a Bryan menace.

❈

Mr. Hearst says positively that he will not be a candidate for the presidency or the vice-presidency in 1908. We believe his prediction is quite correct. He is, however, a very lively and troublesome candidate for the governorship of New York this year.

The New York Muddle.

The wide-open spirit of the New York Republicans and the auto-nominations of Hearst and Jerome, either of whom will run independently if the Democrats nominate the other, makes the political situation in the empire state about as complicated and uncertain as it could well be. No prognostication at present can safely go beyond the point of saying that probably somebody will be elected governor, but as to his person or party, only time can tell.

❈

Who ought to pay for the enforcement of the law? The public, whose representatives enacted the law; or the much smaller group of those who really want it enforced? At Fort Harrison, in Marion county, Ind., after much urgency on the part of the temperance people and the reform forces generally, the "blind tigers" and illegal liquor shops in the vicinity of the barracks were cleaned out. This was simply an enforcement of the law. But when the sheriff presents to the county

Who Ought To Pay?

commissioners the bill for the expense of doing the job, they refuse to pay it and tell him to try to collect from the temperance societies who were so anxious to have the joints closed. Seldom does a country board put itself in a more undignified and undefensible position than that. It is a virtual repudiation of the law after it has been enforced, and an assertion that the cleaning out of the dens was merely an accommodation to a group of temperance enthusiasts, rather than an enforcement of public law for the public welfare.

❈

The National Irrigation Congress met last week in Boise, Idaho. The congress is composed of representatives appointed by the governors, mayors and chambers of commerce throughout the arid and semi-arid states. At Boise it had opportunity to see one of the greatest irrigation works now under construction by the government's reclamation service.

The Last Report From San Francisco.

The San Francisco death list, according to the final report, totals 452, including five who were shot and two who were poisoned by eating unwholesome emergency rations. The number of murders avoided by closing the saloons for some months after the fire and the number of suicides prevented by the peculiar psychological influence of the disaster, would almost equal the number of fatalities. Of those killed by the earthquake and fire, only eighteen were Chinese. Almost all the remainder were whites.

Mr. Bryan has issued a reply to the "Letters of a Chinese Official." The letters were a glorification of oriental and a criticism of occidental civilization. It is generally believed that no Chinaman, official or otherwise, had anything to do with the writing of them. The writer was assured by an eminent Chinese diplomat a year or two ago that the letters were actually written by a Chinese official who had long been a resident of England, but that he had been assisted in matters of style by a well known English literary woman.

The Fugitive Banker.

The runaway banker, Stensland, whose misdeeds wrecked the Chicago bank, of which he was president, has been found in Tangier, Morocco. He does not deny his guilt but insists that he never meant to do wrong. He never deliberately planned to rob his bank. He did not wish any person to lose his savings on his account. But when he was needing money once, about ten years ago, he borrowed money from the bank and put his own notes in their place. Then, because it would look bad to have the bank holding so much of his paper, he forged notes and cashed them—always fully intending to pay back the money. Finally he found that he could not pay it back, so he ran away. He proves his good intentions by saying that when he went away he might have taken a very

large amount of the bank's money with him, but did not. It would be hard to preach the appropriate sermon from this text without falling into platitude. It is only the old truth that good intentions pave the way to—Tangier or bankruptcy or dishonor, or some other sort of calamity unless they are backed up by good sense, good judgment and good morals; and that the beginning of dishonesty is not in some overt act of obvious and palpable villainy, but in the hair's breadth transgression of the line between mine and his, in the taking of a risk with another's property. The solid virtue of honesty needs to be hedged about by the grace of honor.

❈

The Labor Famine.

Mr. James J. Hill points out in a recent speech, that the great need of the country is for more workers. He means especially what we call unskilled labor and the cheaper grades of workmen. The railroads depend almost entirely upon foreigners and can not get enough of them, and the farmers are at their wit's end to get any sort of laborers. This demand for labor in excess of the supply is a result of prosperity. The condition insures every able-bodied man against starvation, for he can earn a dollar or a dollar and a half a day by manual labor. But it does not add much to the prosperity and comfort of the salaried man who finds that the expense of living increases while his salary stands still.

❈

The History of Language.

The usual and expected protest against spelling reform is that it ignores the history and development of language. The London papers have come nobly to the rescue of the king's English against the Roosevelt and Carnegie reform, and accuse these eminent gentlemen and all others who write "tho" for "though" and spell honor with only five letters, of "sacrificing the history and meaning of the language." How Shakespeare's conservative contemporaries must have bewailed the sacrifice of the history and meaning of the language because the great Elizabethans, departing from Chaucer's usage wrote "very" for "verry," "had" for "hadde," and "said" for "sayde." Even as late as Spencer, a knight could be described as "Ycladd in mightie armies and silver shields." Even since the death of Shakespeare the language has traveled far and even those who stand so stoutly for the "history and meaning of the language" would not ask us to return to the spelling of his epitaph:

"Good frend, for Jesus sake forbeare
To digg the dust encloased heare;
Blese be ye man yt spares thes stones,
Aud curst be he yt moves my bones."

No, the argument from history is all on the side of reform. It has required a long process of development to make the English language and the process is not yet completed. The next step is no more sacrilegious than the last one was. The vast amount of literature which has been printed in English as at present spelled and the prevalence of dictionaries have given to the present spelling a degree of stability never attained by any previous form of the language, but have not made it necessarily the final or perfect stage.

Where Jesus Placed the Emphasis.—IV.

His Remedy for Sin.

As previously intimated, Jesus was vastly more concerned about the cure for sin, than about how it entered into the world. He saw that it was the one destructive influence that was marring the wellbeing and happiness of humanity, and he sought to eradicate it from the human heart, where he located it. According to Jesus sin resides in the *intention*, in the moral purposes of men. In opposition to this teaching of Jesus preachers have been known to illustrate the workings of the moral law by those of physical law. Who of us has not heard it stated in this manner: If a man walking in the darkness, or by mistake, steps over a precipice, the fact that he does it ignorantly and without intention does not save him from being killed by the fall. So, it is argued, if a man mistakes the meaning of a moral law, or a command of God without intending to disobey God, his good intention avails nothing. This is to ignore the distinction between moral and physical law, and to wholly misunderstand the nature of salvation by grace. Sin, with Jesus, as we have seen, means the corruption of the heart; it is wrong desires, wrong purposes, and evil thoughts. Hence his remedy for sin was the purification of the heart.

Jesus' method of bringing about this purification of the heart is unique among religions. With a sublime confidence in the good, and the godly element in humanity, he believed that men were to be won from sin by showing them its opposite—incarnate goodness and purity. The horribleness of a sinful life was to be revealed to men by the exhibition of a sinless life. What the world needed was a practical embodiment of the divine ideal of purity, of righteousness and of truth, and this was furnished to men in the life and teaching of Jesus of Nazareth. But this sinless and holy personality must win the hearts of men by loving them, and the higher the manifestation of love the more effective it is in winning men from sin to holiness. Does God love men in spite of their sins, and is he willing to accept them if they come to him confessing their sins? It was not easy for men to believe that a holy and just God could love and save sinners. Jesus came to demonstrate that fact, and by his life, his teaching, his deeds of mercy among men, and especially by his death for the sins of the world, he manifested the love of God for lost men.

There is no more astonishing fact in all the gospels than the confidence which Jesus expressed in humanity when he said, "And I, if I be lifted up from the earth, will draw all men unto me." It is as if he had said, Men may misunderstand my motives and my mission in the world; but when they see the supreme manifestation of my love for them in my death on their behalf, they will all be drawn to me. The saddest thing about the impenitent sinner, who has learned of Christ's death and remains impenitent, is the fact that he has disappointed Christ, and has failed to be worthy of the confidence which he reposed in him.

Christ's remedy for sin, then, was to point out to men its awful consequences, to show them the beauty of holiness as exhibited in his own life, and to convince them of his own and his Father's love for men, by his death on the cross. This, he believed, would bring men to repentance, which he did not fail to enjoin upon all as essential to forgiveness and to life everlasting. Jesus laid profound emphasis upon repentance. So important was it that even one sinner repenting caused joy among the angels of heaven. Repentance with Jesus was the inward change of mind and heart, resulting in turning away from sin in its outward manifestations. His life, his teaching, his death, all looked to this end—bringing men to repentance and therefore to God. God can forgive a penitent, but not an impenitent sinner. Hence Christ's death, in his own language, was "for the remission of sins." This is the supreme place which the cross of Christ holds in the Christian system, as a revelation of the terrible consequences of sin, and of the infinite love of God, and his willingness to save the sinner. Trust in Jesus Christ who revealed him, otherwise called faith or believing, would also result from this Gospel of Christ, and in the effort to conform the life to his teaching. Jesus taught that sin was an obstacle to faith, and he told the Jews to repent that they might believe the Gospel. By putting away such gross sins as they were already conscious of, they would be able to believe on Christ, which faith would lead them to a still further repentance.

But let it be definitely understood that Jesus Christ offered *himself* to men as the only remedy for sin. Not his church, nor his moral teaching, no, not even faith, repentance, or baptism, or any "plan" or "scheme" of salvation is the divine remedy for sin. These are only helps to bring men to the true remedy which is Jesus Christ himself. He is the light of the world, and he is the life of the world. He came that men might have life and that more abundantly. "Ye will not come to me," said Jesus to the Jews, "that ye may have life." (John 5:40.) "Come unto me all ye that labor and are heavy laden, and I will give you rest." (Matt. 11:28.) Faith, repentance and baptism are valuable just as they aid in bringing the sinner to Christ himself for healing and for forgiveness. That is their meaning and purpose. They have no efficacy in themselves. To claim deliverance from sin on compliance with any outward conditions when there is no experience of Christ's redeeming power in the heart and life is to be self-deceived. "He that hath the Son hath life."

The chief emphasis to-day, as it seems to us, should be laid upon these facts concerning the nature of sin, and Christ as the remedy, with a view of bringing men to repentance and thus to forgiveness.

A Scientist's Creed.

None of us objects to his own creed. Even he who speaks most loudly about "the old Jerusalem gospel" has a creed. Hence we need not regard it as a strange thing that a scientist should have a creed. Much depends upon what a creed is as to whether we object to it or not. When by means of a long set of theological formulas we seek to bind men to one system of belief we may expect trouble. Sir Oliver Lodge, one of the greatest physicists, believes this, and yet he sees the value, too, in having something reasonably definite for the average man to grasp and feel that his own belief is shared by thousands of other humans.

Professor Lodge has written an article for the "Hibbert Journal" in which he suggests a method for inculcating the "First Principles of Faith," in a reasonable and scientific way into the minds of children and young folks at school. "A creed," he says, "or catechism should not be regarded as something superhuman, infallible, and immutable; it should be considered to be what it really is—a careful statement of what, in the best light of the time, can be regarded as true and important about matters partially beyond the range of scientific knowledge."

Prof. Lodge's belief is not what would be termed orthodox. He submits a "scientific catchism," drawn up for the purpose of avoiding matters of sectarian controversy, and based upon the current thought of natural and psychological science. But the following creed or expression of faith is what this scientist proposes:

"I believe in one Infinite and Eternal Being, a guiding and loving Father, in whom all things consist. I believe that the Divine Nature is specially revealed to man through Jesus Christ, our Lord, who lived and taught and suffered in Palestine 1900 years ago, and has since been worshiped by the Christian Church as the Immortal Son of God, the Savior of the world.

"I believe that man is privileged to understand and assist the Divine purpose on this earth, that prayer is a means of communion between man and God, and that the Holy Spirit is ever ready to help us along the Way towards Goodness and Truth, so that by unselfish service we may gradually enter into the Life Eternal, the Communion of Saints, and the Peace of God.

The niceties of this creed we will not now discuss but it is a beacon light pointing to a harbor where many a mind unsettled by the wisdom of this world may yet find a way to the feet of Him who said "If I do not the works of my father, believe me not."

Notes and Comments.

Can a man be a Prohibitionist and work with the Anti-Saloon League at the same time? This question was raised recently in a conversation between one of our evangelists and an Episcopal canon, who said that prohibition is right but is too ideal, therefore he thought the Anti-Saloon League is better. The evangelist told him he could see no reason why he could not be a Prohibitionist and an Anti-Saloon man at the same time, holding on to his ideal as the right one, and working with the Anti-Saloon League as one of the ways of realizing that ideal. The Episcopal brother acknowledged that he could. Then the evangelist made the application that he could hold his ideal of a perfect, visible organic Christian union, while co-operating with the brethren of other churches through church federation, for the realization of that ideal. The canon acknowledged himself handsomely trapped by this view of things, and good naturedly, surrendered to the argument.

Idealism is a good thing. No great work is accomplished without a high ideal. But if we make our ideals a substitute for practical measures leading thereto, instead of an inspiration and guide in the use of practical measures, then we become idle and inefficient dreamers instead of successful doers of things. It is this mistake that has brought idealism into disrepute. We can not immediately have the ideal state, the ideal church, the ideal civilization, the ideal society, or the ideal unity of religious forces; shall we, therefore, have no government, no church, no civilization, no society, or no form or degree of Christian unity? That would be folly. Let us hold to our ideals and be content to take all the intermediate steps leading to their realization.

A brother who has had opportunity recently of meeting a large number of ministers representing different religious bodies writes: "I am surprised to find that nearly all these ministers agree with our plea 'in the main.'" This has always been the strength of our position—that in its chief points, at least, it challenges the approval of all. How could it be otherwise? Christian men cannot well express themselves against loyalty to the word of God, the exaltation of Christ above all human authority, the unity of all Christians in him, brotherliness and co-operation, instead of sectarianism and strife, and the effort to restore the New Testament ideal church in its creed, its ordinances, and its life. To stand for these principles and to seek to exemplify them both in our teaching and conduct is the highest vocation one can have in this life.

Ambassador Whitelaw Reid has just given utterance to sentiments that are vital. In a remarkable address before one of the British universities he showed how much more widespread were the higher institutions of learning in our own country than

in any other. But what we are most interested in is his declaration that from the feeble beginnings at Jamestown and Plymouth to the present, the two essentials in every settlement and in every isolated pioneer outpost in the wilderness were a church and a school-house. These two, working on the race history and the race instinct, have molded the people. Here is a strong endorsement of church extension. It is worth while taking note, too, of the fact that so keen an observer as Mr. Reid believes that the present tendency in the American educational system is to shift the emphasis from the purely practical and scientific to the intellectual and spiritual.

Current Religious Thought.

The passion for Christian union is burning hopefully in the hearts of those who truly love the Lord regardless of "faiths and orders." Many are approaching this through the medium of federation. At the recent conference at Carrollton of the Missouri Southern Methodists the following among other proceedings were held. (Culled from the "St. Louis Christian Advocate.")

REPORT OF COMMITTEE ON FEDERATION.

We, your committee on federation beg leave to submit the following report:

We met in joint session with commission from the Methodist Episcopal Church, in Cameron, August 27, 1906, and transacted the following business:

It was recommended that the Methodist Episcopal church discontinue its organization in Shelbina, and also at Wesley Church in the Edina circuit, and that the membership of these churches be requested to unite with the Methodist Episcopal Church South; and also that the church in Queen City and Bethel on the Edina circuit, of the Methodist Episcopal Church South, and the membership of the same be requested to unite with the Methodist Episcopal church. In each case the presiding bishop ratified the work of the commission.

We are gratified to know that the bishops of the Methodist Episcopal Church in their annual meeting commended Federation to their conferences and adopted what is known as the "Missouri Plan" which was inaugurated by the commission of the Missouri conferences.

We note also with pleasure that the presiding elders and pastors of our conferences have in the main been ready to render your committee any assistance needed in their most delicate work.

We have faith in the wisdom and piety of the two greatest Methodist churches and believe that the day is not far distant when many struggling congregations, maintained by missionary boards in the Missouri conferences will be consolidated and that there will be a great saving of men and money to the Kingdom of our common Lord.

A. C. Browning, R. H. Cooper, C. Grimes, B. J. Casteel and S. P. Emmons, Committee.

Doubtless in many communities where Christian and Baptist congregations are struggling for bare existence, if proper overtures were made, the latter could be induced to come with us and be one in Christ and stronger. The experiment is worth trying.

Robert J. Burdette, whose chief reputation formerly was that of a humorous writer, but who has been for some years the pastor of a Baptist church in Los Angeles, has been objecting to the length of the form of service for the

presentation of children. We think are some Methodist ministers whose have been, such when they have bapti as to sympathize with Mr. Burdette says: "There may be some fathers stand and hold a baby through that service, and there may be some babies be sweet as cherubs from 'Dearly l 'Amen,' but as a rule I think the 'serv not be longer than the baby." We are of the opinion that there ought to be a form of the present baptismal service.

Here is the old confusion th controversy. If the "Western Advocate" would be content wit cation or "presentation of chil might be worth while to consider t of such a service. But when it c things that are different we ar opinion that there ought not only abridged form of the present service," but that this should be with entirely. Then there woul need for the fathers to get nervo babies to cry. And the child cou more mature, with some understa legiance to the Lord Jesus Christ, the act of immersion, so full of ligious bodies.

We commend the following—an in the "Congregationalist"—to ever of "our own" papers:

How fine a revelation of character made by the light, unguarded word, penciled scrap of writing, the unplanne These were the last written words of was suddenly called higher—"this dear One who loved him found them and l reverently, away among her treasur seemed but the natural, sweet outbrea his daily life. His feet, like his Mast often been "tired with going afoot," I had scorned no roughest lowliest duty, b and pen had been simply and unreser the church's service. Is the church so near to all our hearts as that—so dear? Our lives must say many thing people will believe much what our lips ing. Can we stand up in church witho ing and sing the hymn that says, "For tears shall fall, for her our prayers sh Or are we often careful already that no light on us nor any heat that we can avoid by slipping out of her services rands? The day comes fast when all us as an open book. Even now to one other come swift, unforeseen revealit rose's perfume steals out unaware; so sweetness of a consistent Christian life.

"The Central Christian Advocate,' ca the minimum on which a country pastor supporting wife and two children, figure yearly total at $700... And the minimun from going higher still only by such me culations as $90 for all the clothes that tl requires, $25 for household furnishings, like. And there isn't a cent set aside The calculation doesn't even allow the to give away a tithe; the portion for be is only $50. In thousands of churches, i sponsible officers would only sit down and count up what it costs them to lo own families going, they would quickl that their pastors have not enough to Instead, however, of this businesslike wa mating the pastor's needs, the average trustees begins at the other end of the and proceeds to ascertain what the Varic bers of the church feel like giving. preacher puts up with what they happen t The Interior.

Editor's Easy Chair.

PENTWATER MUSINGS.

Summer has fled. The days are perceptibly shorter. Last night the sun went down over the lake several degrees south of where he made his exit when we first came to the Park. There is a September haze over the lake and over the land, a September nip in the air, and a suggestion of autumn in the home-going of our resorters and in the quietness which reigns along the lake shore and in the still woods. The fishermen, in anticipation of equinoctial gales, are lifting their nets which have brought them rich harvests of fish during the summer months. Across the channel, however, in the little village, the signs of life and activity are abundant. It is the height of the peach season, and the canning factories are running day and night, and vessels are coming and going, ladened with the ripened fruit which they bear away to market. No more beautiful days have come during the whole summer than these early September days have been. In these quiet days, when nearly all the resorters have gone, one has opportunity to look at the summer in retrospect. Has it been used to the best advantage? Have we availed ourselves of all the opportunities which it has brought to us in the new scenes and associations which we have enjoyed? Have we opened our minds and hearts to the wider vision of truth which God is continually seeking to impart to us? Have we carried with us through the vacation season the sense of God's presence, and cultivated a closer fellowship with him? None of us, we suppose, feels that he has quite come up to what he had hoped in these respects, but many, no doubt, will return or have returned, to their homes and to their accustomed labors, feeling richer in spirit and in closer sympathy with their fellowmen for the hours of quiet meditation which they have been permitted to enjoy amid the scenes of nature in its varied manifestations.

❧

While nearly all the regular resorters have closed their cottages on the beach and returned to their homes, we have just now an interesting group of visitors made up of a number of young men from the Campbell Institute and some of their wives and children. The club house had just closed for the season, but they have secured the privilege of rooming there, and will take their meals across the channel in the village. The arrivals of this group at present are E. S. Ames and family, Errett Gates and Mrs. George A. Campbell and their little son, of Chicago, C. C. Morrison, of Springfield, Ill. Others will come later. They are having the club house down on the beach all by themselves and if they do not have a good time, they will have only themselves to blame. Some of them, at least, will remain a week or two, and we have already pressed Brother Gates into service for a sermon next Sunday. We

have notified these young brethren of the University of Chicago that no seeds of heresy are to be sown along this shore! They acknowedge that this resort is within the jurisdiction of our diocese, and have promised to "be good"—that is, as far as it is possible for men to be—coming out of the atmosphere of that institution! It has been one of the happiest circumstances of our editorial career to keep in close touch and sympathy with the young men who have entered our ministry, having availed themselves of the best opportunities of the times in preparing themselves for their high calling. We have not been able always, of course, to endorse all their theories and opinions, many of which, no doubt, they themselves will not be able to endorse in later years. But we thoroughly believe in their essential soundness in the faith, the sincerity of their motives, their high and noble ideals, the purity of their lives, and their future usefulness to our cause. The latch-string at "Garrison Park" hangs out for all lovers and seekers after truth and a higher life.

❧

Among the departures of our friends during the past week were W. F. Richardson and wife of Kansas City, of whom we have spoken, and C. M. Fillmore of Carthage, Ohio, a suburb of Cincinnati. These friends were greatly enjoyed while here and greatly missed now that they have gone. The Fillmore Bros., worthy sons of a noble sire, we have loved these many years. They have always stood for the highest and best aspirations of our own movement, and for temperance and social reform. Their music publishing house, after having passed through the usual experiences of such enterprises, has reached a basis of what seems to be a growing and enduring prosperity at which we rejoice. At our last Sunday's service Brother Fillmore sang for us his far-famed solo, sung round the world, the music and words of which he is the author, "Tell mother I'll be there," which was greatly enjoyed by the audience. He came in a very weakened, nervous condition, and made great improvement during his two weeks' stay, and should, in our judgment, have remained longer, but he felt that the work in his congregation demanded his return. The problem of harmonizing the interest of a pastor's health with the demands of his work in the church, is a very perplexing one, and deserves the sympathetic co-operation of the church in its solution. Many a conscientious man is the victim of his own sense of duty to the cause and people he loves.

❧

An anxious brother writes to know what action, if any, will be taken at Buffalo concerning the proposed Basis of Federation which has been submitted to the various religious bodies by the Inter-Church Conference in New York. Nobody is authorized to answer that question. It is for the Convention itself to determine whether

it will take any action at that time and, if so, what. In a convention of free people which acknowledges no "boss" it remains for the body itself to determine its course on all the great questions which arise. One thing is reasonably certain, and that is that Christian love and Christian courtesy will prevail and will decide, in due time, the proper course to pursue in reference to the great and important matter which has been submitted to us. Of course, we cannot afford to ignore a matter of such commanding importance, and relating so directly to one of the chief objects and aims of our movement. No one acquainted with public sentiment among us, perhaps, will question the possibility of passing a safe and conservative resolution, expressing our sympathy with the movement for closer co-operation, but whether it were wiser to do so by a majority vote, while there is a considerable dissenting minority, resulting wholly from a misunderstanding of the matter, or whether it would be better to postpone action until there is time for the removal of such misunderstanding, is a question for the brethren to decide. We are sure, now that there has been time for sober reflection, that nothing will be done "through strife or vainglory," or in any factious spirit. We are none of us going to Buffalo in any mood for such action as that, but looking to God for his counsel and the guidance of His Spirit, we shall be led in the way of unity and of brotherliness.

❧

To the victims of hay-fever those lines of James Whitcomb Riley,

"When the frost is on the pumpkin
And the fodder's in the shock,"

have a peculiar charm. Frost is the only effective remedy, so far as we have learned, for the annoying malady. There are many alleged preventives of sea-sickness, but lying under the shade of a tree is about the only effective one we know of. So there are many preventives and cures of hay-fever advertised, but as yet the average victim looks forward to the season of the year celebrated by Whitcomb's lines as the only sure cure. Strange the doctors of the world don't appoint a commission to chase down the particular bacillus that is at the bottom of all this trouble, and capture it and provide a destroyer for it, and thus become the benefactors of that part of the human race that spends at least one month of the year in a kind of misery known only to the unfortunate victims of hay-fever. Autumn has many other attractions when she clothes the forests in robes of more than regal splendor and spreads her thin veil of haze over all the landscape, but its chief attraction to the hay-fever sufferer is that its biting frosts destroy the pollen of those flowers and weeds which are at the bottom of his suffering. This fact is only referred to here as an apology for not fulfilling some conditional promises to deliver addresses at some conventions and other meetings during the month of September.

As Seen From the Dome   By F. D.

Dead London is interesting, but one finds vastly more in living London. The bank is a good place to study it, and the Exchange hard by. The bank is the hub of things. When "the old lady of Threadneedle street" speaks the world generally listens. It is a large one-story structure covering four acres, without any windows. It is the government agent in dealing with its debt of $3,250,-000,000, though a private corporation. It is the busiest spot in London, both above and below ground. Seven of the most important thoroughfares converge here, omnibuses alone averaging 700 an hour passing it. Ground at this point is worth $16,250,000 an acre, or $150 a square inch. People pour along the streets by the million and there is a subway under the street through which scores of thousands pass to avoid the rush of traffic. This institution issues 50,000 bank notes daily, from $25 to $5,000, and one is shown for $5,000,000. These are immediately canceled when paid in, so the life of a note may be only a day. Weighing machines they use which weigh thirty-three gold sovereigns a minute, which throw those of full weight into one compartment and light ones into another. I bought here a hundred farthings and they were as careful of them as of the gold to give the exact weight. George Peabody's statue stands at the bank, as well as that of Wellington. Peabody, the American merchant, who gave half a million for better houses for the working classes, which accommodate 20,000 people at an average weekly rent of $1.30. The queen offered him a baronetcy, but he declined it and asked her picture instead.

Not far from the bank one finds the tower of London, and I was fortunate enough to strike upon a day when a hundred thousand north country people were in the metropolis to see a football match, and they surged through the tower—40,000 of them—and I could see them and hear their peculiar dialect. The tower covers eighteen acres in the heart of London, and has been fortress, palace and prison. As Macaulay said "there is no sadder place on earth than this." Its moat and its walls and its history are interesting. Its "Beef-eaters," or guards, whose uniform has not been changed since Henry VII, after the battle of Bosworth; its armory with figures of men on foot and horseback, clad in steel; its display of the crown jewels, blazing sceptres, swords, orbs and crowns, orders and insignia, the king's crown with its 3,000 diamonds, its pearls and other precious stones on top, enclosed in an iron cage; all challenge attention, but its instruments of torture, its block and axe, and its spot where Sir Thomas More, Anne Boleyn, Lady Jane Grey, Guilford Dudley, Somerset, Strafford and Laud, Catherine Howard,

the Earl of Essex and many others had their heads chopped off, thrill us with horror. And it is only a little over 150 years since the last person beheaded in England, Lord Lovat, lost his head here, 1747!

Another good place to see London life is on the bridges. Just beyond this place I crossed the tower bridge. Ten thousand vehicles were coming and going. It cost over seven millions in our money, and has a footway 142 feet above, and leaves, which are raised to allow the passage of large vessels. A bell is rung, the leaves go up, and in three minutes the tide of humanity surges on. I crossed and saw St. Savior's Church, seven hundred years old, the Cathedral of South London, where Edmund Shakespeare, brother of the poet, is buried, and Massinger and Fletcher, and Gower, Chaucer's friend, and the Protestant martyrs under Queen Mary were tried, and John Harvard, the founder of Harvard University, was baptized in 1607, to whom a beautiful American window was unveiled by Mr. Choate. Then I took my way back across London bridge. This famous structure, by Rennie, built in 1831 is of granite with five arches, having a length of 928 feet; 30,-000 vehicles and 120,000 pedestrians cross it daily. It looks down on the busy pool. The Celtic *Llyn*, "a pool," and *dun*, "a hill," is the origin of the name London, and "the pool" is the busiest spot on the Thames. At the other end of the bridge is Billingsgate, the great fish market, and one may find near by Whitechapel and the great docks, the Peoples' Palace and Toynbee Hall, and Dr. Barnardo's Homes. Still another place to see living London is in the zoo. There are elephants, rhinoceroses, hippopotami, giraffes, bears, lions and monkeys in great numbers, and human animals by the thousand. We were three of American species, and there were 43,000 English the same day, as the turnstiles said. Another place to see people is in the churches. I sat on the pedestal of Lord Mansfield's monument at Westminster and listened to Canon Henson, and again at Shakespeare's in the poet's corner, and heard charming music, and the people were there. I went to the city temple to a Thursday service and heard R. J. Campbell. He had an audience of 1,200. Dr. Joseph Parker kept up this service over thirty years. A memorial window commemorates the one thousandth meeting. "When mammon is at white heat," he said, "midweek noon hour" and here it is. Mr. Campbell has kept it going four years. One of his men told me the congregations were from 1,200 to 1,800. The church is down town and has only about 600 members. Fourteen meetings were announced for the week. I spoke to Mr. Campbell, having met him in Amer-

ica, and asked him about ditions in London. "Not he said. I congratulated sermon as "straight good midweek audience. He s women come though, a seats, and the men are rear; and I don't like it if Christian Endeavor was London, reminding him of convention which he atte: not know. "But you hav ciety?" "Yes," he said, preacher, and it ends there bell, I believe, has not health, and it was agreed charge of the temple th simply fill the pulpit. I at ice at Westbourne Park ch Clifford's, and found here t attendance and the same meetings announced, conf ers' and Dorcas meetings, Christian Endeavor, temp of Hope, missionary, club cle, and P. S. A. services.

The May meetings are begin in April and end in all called "May meetings them are held in Exeter a list of 236 missionary a societies announced. I opening session of the which met in the city tem 2,500 were present from United Kingdom. I never enthusiastic assembly. Th inspired. In the opening much politics as we put i ment. The brother, Hugh Dublin, cried: "Lord, save craft and catechisms," an many "amens." "Lord, George's day. We don't k George did for this count know the dragon is still he of sin and superstition, of and of bigotry." He allud cation bill which is causin all over Great Britain. F. B. Meyer, delivered the pronouncement on all qu the British public I ever educational contention was out gloves. He maintaine cleavage should be "ben blood; character, not cas not gold." He paid his r landlords; the sweatshops, and the bishops and othe there were cries of "Hea much approval. By the w is a Baptist, preaches for tional Church, and employ tional assistant who baptiz while he immerses the adu one of the Baptist preach lows have a strange mix-t London has more hospitals benevolent organizations on earth. There are 10 various charitable and religious, temperance and missionary servi e in the city, some with an income of many thousands and scores of workers. I dropped in upon the British and Foreign Bible Society, seeing Matt. 24:35 over the door, and was shown through their great Bible house. They send out 70,000 copies every working day, translate the Bible into 390 distinct forms of speech, added ten last year, and have issued since, the

beginning in 1804, 192,000,000 copies of the Scriptures. London has 2,700 places of worship: only six classified as "Disciples of Christ." I found the West London Tabernacle well attended and received many courtesies from Mark Wayne Williams and Leslie Morgan. A day with these brethren at Hampton Court and in the Museum of Natural History at Kensington will be long remembered. We were met in Liverpool by a full

congregation in Upper Parliament street of members from that church and Chester, Saltney, Birkenhead and Southport, and Brethren Hughes, Moss, Coop, Wrathall, Pratley, and the rest gave us a greeting and farewell which greatly cheered us on our journey. Taking the Baltic, the largest steamship afloat, 24,000 tons, 725 feet long, 76 wide and 49 deep, we, with 2,700 others, sailed April 25, reaching New York May 4, safely, after nearly 16,000 miles' travel.

What the Brethren Are Saying and Doing

By B. B. Tyler

Is faith in Christ as the Son of God necessary to salvation? If so, why?

A man may be virtuous, have knowledge, temperance, patience, kindness, charity, honesty, etc., and believe in God as a good lord and ruler of the universe; yet believe in Jesus, only as a great teacher or moralist of high ideals. He may believe conscientiously after wide study and investigation that the great miracles surrounding his life story are myths or fables coming from tradition as did many Grecian and Roman myths.

Suppose a person can't help but look at in something of that light, yet is seeking honestly the highest and best way of living and a hope for a future life. He studies Christ, Ingersoll, Buddha, Confucius, Mohammed, Darwin and everything he can get bearing on the great problem of life and destiny. He finds some good in all, many things reasonable, beautiful and good. Some more than others. In all he finds ideas, teachings and stories which are absurd to all reason and absolutely incapable of proof or demonstration at present. He accepts and embodies in his character all the good he can from all teachers.

Will he be saved? Does the Bible offer any hope to a person of that kind?

The foregoing inquiry came to me some days ago. I pass it on to the readers of THE CHRISTIAN-EVANGELIST. What is your answer to the question, "Is faith in Christ, as the Son of God, necessary to salvation?" Will the man be saved who can not believe that Jesus of Nazareth is the Son of God? Does the Bible offer any hope to a person of that kind?

1. The work of the minister of the Word is the preaching of the Gospel, "Preach the Word," "Do the work of an evangelist," "This one thing I do." "I determined to know nothing among you save Jesus Christ and him crucified." This was the determination of Paul when he entered Corinth after his experience in Athens. Hence I make emphatic the pronoun.

2. Faith in Jesus, as the Son of God, is not necessary to salvation in the case of infants, insane persons and idiots. Faith in Christ is not necessary to salvation in the case of those who are unable to believe. Our Father does not require the impossible of his children under pain of eternal damnation. "If there be first a willing mind, it is accepted according to that a man hath

and not according to that he hath not." This is the statement of a fundamental principle in the Christian religion. The Master said: "Unto whomsoever much is given, of him much shall be required." Reasonable men act on this principle. "To whom men have committed much, of him they will ask the more."

3. To such as are capable of believing in Jesus, as the Son of God, the Scriptures teach that faith is a necessary condition of salvation. The prison keeper in Philippi could believe. Hence Paul, as an ambassador of Jesus Christ, commanded him to believe on the Lord Jesus and assured him that if he would do so he would be saved. This instruction was given and this command was issued in answer to the question: "What *must* I do to be saved?" This then was what the pagan prison keeper *must* do to be saved. "Without faith it is impossible" for such a person "to please God."

4. The person described in the foregoing is a very foolish man. "He studies Christ, Ingersoll, Buddha, Confucius, Mohammed, Darwin and everything he can get." If the seeker after truth was mentally sound in the beginning such a hodge podge would, it seems to me, in a little while, cause him to become daft. This man knows not how to study. The issue relates to Jesus. "Who is he?" This is the question. What light does Darwin, or Mohammed, or Confucius, or Buddha, or Ingersoll, throw on this question? None whatever! There is a great difference between this wide and indiscriminate reading and earnest investigation. It is safe to say that, as a matter of fact, this individual does not study Christ, Ingersoll, Buddha, Confucius, Mohammed, and Darwin. It is probable that he reads quotations from them. It is also probable that he gives more time and attention to Ingersoll than to all the others.

5. Jesus himself suggested a method which, if pursued, will bring most gratifying results. "If any man willeth to do his will, he shall know of the teaching, whether it is of God or whether I speak from myself" (John 7:17). If this man really desires to know, let him begin at once to practice in his daily life, both toward God and toward his fellow men, the doctrine or teaching of Jesus. Knowledge will come by doing.

Experience in doing what the Christ requires will result in certainty as to the divine wisdom and power of Mary's Son. Any person pursuing this course will be saved beyond a peradventure. His salvation is absolutely certain.

6. *How can the Bible bring hope to a man who does not believe what it says?*

A man promises to give me a thousand dollars. My honest opinion is that he is a liar. While I entertain this opinion of him his words can not beget hope. This man thinks that the Bible—its story of Jesus and all the rest—is a collection of fables, or myths, or something of the kind. This collection of untruths can not generate hope. Impossible! Does the Bible hope to a man of this kind? Not a bit.

Denver, Colo.

✦ ✦

HOW MANY OF US?

Fail to Select Food Nature Demands to Ward Off Ailments.

A Ky. lady, speaking about food, says: "I was accustomed to eating all kinds of ordinary food until, for some reason, indigestion and nervous prostration set in.

"After I had run down seriously my attention was called to the necessity of some change in my diet, and I discontinued my ordinary breakfast and began using Grape-Nuts with a good quantity of rich cream.

"In a few days my condition changed in a remarkable way, and I began to have a strength that I had never been possessed of before, a vigor of body and a poise of mind that amazed me. It was entirely new in my experience.

"My former attacks of indigestion had been accompanied by heat flashes, and many times my condition was distressing with blind spells of dizziness, rush of blood to the head and neuralgia pains in the chest.

"Since using Grape-Nuts alone for breakfast I have been free from these troubles, except at times when I have indulged in rich, greasy foods in quantity, then I would be warned by a pain under the left shoulder blade, and unless I heeded the warning the old trouble would come back, but when I finally got to know where these troubles originated I returned to my Grape-Nuts and cream and the pain and disturbance left very quickly.

"I am now in prime of health as a result of my use of Grape-Nuts." Name given by Postum Co., Battle Creek, Mich.

Modern Religious Persecution---A De:

By B. L. Chase

9. Some Deadly Heresies.

The most deadly heresy that has sprung up among the Disciples—the most alarming because so widespread and dangerous—is the teaching that other religious bodies are Christian and churches of Christ. It is appalling how deep-seated this heresy has become among the Disciples. The majority of our editors and our leading pastors in the large city churches have fallen into this error, but the "rank and file" are against it. To my knowledge there is just one editor who is sound on this question, and he it was who saved us from disappearing as a brotherhood about three years ago. I need not speak his name; it is a household word. In another generation he will be known as the Restorer of the Restoration Movement. His name will be linked with the beloved name of Benjamin Franklin, as Joshua's was linked with that of Moses. He has taken up the work where Franklin laid it down, and upon him has fallen the intellectual and doctrinal mantle of that great leader. He is the only man left among us in these apostate times who knows perfectly the mind and reproduces exactly the spirit of the great Franklin. He is the only one who has been strong enough to resist the flatteries and bewitching advances of the denominations. All others are speaking kindly of the sects, and are mixing with them—are even saying that there are Christians among them. They are even quoting the words of Alexander Campbell, who fell away from the true faith in his later years. He said in 1837, just before his great apostasy, that a Christian was "one that believes in his heart that Jesus of Nazareth is the Messiah, the Son of God; repents of his sins, and obeys him in all things, according to his measure of knowledge of his will." He was so bold as to say he believed there were Christians among the sects. From the time of this utterance his decline toward Babylon was rapid.

Our ministry to-day is not what it once was. We used to have strong men who were not afraid to denounce the Methodists and Baptists and call upon those who desired to be saved to come out from among them. But where do we now hear preachers bear strong testimony against the sects? They can not resist their smiles, and are so bewitched that many of them are ready to fall into the "federation trap" which the sects have spread for the Disciples. We used to have debates going on against the faith and practices of the sects, but now where do we hear of debates? Instead of fighting them, we are trying to get our arms around them. We used to have plenty of preachers who were not afraid to stand up and say: "We are right and everybody else is wrong." We have but a few now. Who can say we do not need the Inquisition?

The alarming thing is that we will have to summon many of our very best men before the awful tribunal for holding this deadly heresy. On the list of men to be tried first, I regret to place such honored names as Garrison, Tyler, Power, Philputt, Powell, Breeden, Combs, Craig, Tyrrell, Richardson, Moore, Haley and a host of others who have been misled by them. But why should we pause before an honored name? Did the church in medieval times hesitate before the name of a Huss, a Latimer, or a Galileo? We should be unworthy successors of the great persecutors who have gone before us if we did not purge the Church of these heretics.

Such heretics actually believe that Luther, Knox, Calvin and Wesley were Christians; that Carey, Judson and Livingstone were saved; while none of these men were members of the true, apostolic Christian Church. They believe that Thomas and Alexander Campbell were Christians before they were immersed in 1812. If that is so, then our plea for primitive Christianity has had no meaning. They were just as well off without baptism for the remission of sins as we are who have been baptized. Then a person is just as likely to be saved in the Methodist as in the Christian Church. No wonder the Disciples are disappearing where such things are being taught. If we are going to live and grow as a people we must have preachers who will preach that we are the only true Church; that Jesus spoke of the Disciples when he said, "Upon this rock I will build my Church"; that we have "the truth, the whole truth and nothing but the truth."

The Gospel was lost from the time of the apostles until it was discovered by the Campbells. There was no Christian church in the world from the first century until 1812, when one was organized at Brush Run, Pa. There were no Christians until then. In the year 1900 there were a little over one million Christians in the world, according to the year book of the Disciples. There were many millions of Methodists, Jews, Hindoos, Buddhists, Baptists, Roman Catholics, Mohammedans, Atheists and Pagans, but just 1,118,000 Christians.

The Disciples have before them a tremendous task to evangelize all the rest of the world—Pagan, Protestant and Catholic. But if we let some of our heretics go on teaching that the Baptists and Methodists are Christians then we shall have to federate with them in saving the world. If we federate, we must disappear as a brotherhood. The only way we can save ourselves from annihilation is to start a persecution against every man that recognizes the denominations as churches of Christ. This is our only hope of holding our own against them, and of continued growth. Would a Methodist leave his church and join us if he felt he was just as safe in that church? If we do not keep on telling the members of the denominations they will be lost if they remain with them we shall cut off a very large annual increase in our membership from these churches.

What if the Disciples of disappear? There would be of Christ on earth to teach salem Gospel" to immerse remission of sins, to preach of no one who could teach the baptism, the true nature of science, or the correct doctr of the Holy Spirit; none wh how to organize true churc how often to celebrate the I how to take a confession of or how rightly to divide the It would be a dark world, in one left in it to save the M Baptists and the heathen. sects would go on blindly pou money to build hospitals, churches; to send the "Gospe

❀ ❀

CAN DRINK TROI
That's One Way to (

Although the many won't admit ple who suffer from sick h other ails get them straigl coffee they drink and it is if they're not afraid to leav as in the case of a lady in

"I had been a sufferer fro: aches for twenty-five years who has ever had a bad s knows what I suffered. Son days in the week I would ha in bed, at other times I coulc the pain would be so great. a torture and if I went away for a day I always came bac than alive.

"One day I was telling a troubles and she told me sh it was probably coffee caused she had been cured by stoppir using Postum Food Coffee an to try this food drink.

"That's how I came to send some Postum and from th: never been without it for it s: and I have been entirely cure old troubles. All I did was to coffee and tea and drink Postum in its place. This cha: me more good than everyth: together.

"Our house was like a dr: my husband bought everythi: of to help me without doing s when I began on the Postum n ceased and the other troubles appeared. I have a friend ' experience just like mine coffee and using Postum cu: as it did me.

"The headaches left and health has been improved and stronger than before. I now cious Postum more than I ever Name given by Postum Co., 1 Mich.

"There's a reason" and it's ing out.

derstand it" to the heathen; supporting missionaries, hospitals and schools in foreign lands; but the work would all have to be done over again, if God ever sent his true church into the world. These Protestant sects are all building upon the wrong foundation, and their work will come to naught.

Since the Disciples are the only ones who have the truth, they ought to go into every place where there is a Methodist or Presbyterian church and try to convert the members to Christ. They are following Wesley, Calvin and other human leaders; the Disciples alone are following Christ. We have the right name, the right baptism, the right organization and the right creed; and if we have all these things right, our spirit and life will be right. I have always noticed how much better lives the Disciples lead, how much better spirit they manifest toward each other, how much

more sacrificing and unselfish they are, than the members of other churches. That is because they were baptized correctly, and celebrate the Lord's Supper with proper frequency, and have the proper form of church government, and write "Disciples" with a little d. These are the marks of the true church of Christ. If Jesus or Paul should visit the earth in person they would come straight to a church of the Disciples. They might pass right by a Methodist church and not know what it was, because it would not have the right name painted on the signboard or chiseled into the corner-stone. The first questions Jesus would ask a church of the Disciples would be: "How were you baptized? How often do you celebrate the Lord's Supper? How is your church organized? Do you believe in federation? Do you write Disciples with a big D or a little d? Do you think you are a denomination? Do you believe Moses

wrote every word of the Penteteuch? Are there one or two Isaiahs? When was the book of Daniel written? Did the whale swallow Jonah?"

The answer to these questions would determine whether Jesus remained with that church or passed on to another, looking for the church that he founded upon the rock. Yet in the face of these unanswerable facts there are preachers tolerated among the Disciples who say that the true church is known, not by the name or organization that it bears, but by the spirit and life of the members; that if a man lives like Christ in all love and purity, though he may be called a Methodist and belong to that church, yet he is a Christian! Such teaching is enough to make Benjamin Franklin and J. F. Rowe turn over in their graves. The Disciples should drive every preacher and church member out of their ranks who holds such soul-destroying doctrine. Better a thousand times that the brotherhood be torn to fragments than harbor such poisonous teaching.

Why I Am a Christian Only and Not a Denominationalist

By J. K. BALLOU.

I am a Christian only because that is all Christ asks; it is all the Bible teaches one should be; it is all the apostles and first Christians were; it is all that is compatible with Christ's teaching and the spirit of the New Testament.

I am not a denominationalist, for that would make me a divisionalist, and divisions are classed as fruits of the flesh ("idolatry, sorcery, enmities, strife, jealousies, wraths, factions, divisions, heresies." Gal. 5:20. R. V.)

All denominations cause divisions and divisions are condemned by the Bible. ("Now I beseech you, brethren, through the name of our Lord Jesus Christ, that ye all speak the same thing, and that there be no divisions among you." I Cor. 1:10.)

Denominationalism defeats the purpose and spirit of Christ's prayer ("Neither for these only do I pray, but for them also, that believe on me through their word; that they may all be one; even as thou Father art in me, and I in thee, that they also may be one in us; that the world may believe that thou didst send me." John 17:20, 21.)

Denominations prevent Christian union, retard missionary activity and furnish an excuse for not accepting and believing on Christ. It is something in addition to Christianity, and is not necessary to salvation, but plainly antagonistic to the teaching of the New Testament. Denominations exalt opinions into tests of fellowship. They are not divided on faith, but opinion. It is positively wrong to divide the church of God on opinion. The New Testament alone will never make a denomination, but added to this a prayer-book, a confession of faith, a book of discipline, an arbitrary test of fellowship, and we have a denomination. The Christian world will not unite on any denomination. It must unite on Christ, for Christ and in Christ. Hence to belong to any denomination prevents Christian union.

What must one give up to be simply a Christian without being a denominationalist? He must give up nothing divine—nothing required by Christ or taught by the Bible. He must give up all denominational names, such as Methodist, Baptist, Presbyterian, etc., for none of these are in the Bible, but are of

human origin and foster divisions, then for the sake of unity can not we all drop them? He must give up all arbitrary creeds and confessions. Christ is the Christian's creed and a confession of faith in him is all inclusive. ("Thou art the Christ the son of the living God." Matt. 16:16.) To be a Christian only is to wear Christ's name only—to honor him by wearing his name. The names in the Bible are not denominational or party names; all others are.

To be simply a Christian one must give up a sectarian spirit, man-made creeds, artificial tests of fellowship, human names and ordinances and displace them by the Christian spirit, the divine creed, which is Christ, faith in him as a sufficient test of fellowship, the name Christian or any name in the Bible, and the ordinances as observed and kept by the apostles. Denominationalism is very expensive; it is a great waste of the Lord's money to build and maintain churches where a few will serve much better.

Denominationalists are Christians and as good people as are to be found, but that is in spite of the fact that they are denominationalists, and because they are Christians. They are not living up to their highest privilege and enjoying the liberty they might have in Christ as long as their energies are directed in maintaining a denomination, which is of necessity more or less antagonistic to every other denomination. It is not complimentary to other denominations to belong to a certain one.

Since there is nothing to lose but much to gain by parting company with all sectarian and denominational parties, and since it is antagonistic to the plain teaching of the Bible, and an impediment in the way of Christian union, why do so many still hold on to it? The sad answer is because they do not know how to get away fom it; in too many the love for the denomination is too strong and Christ's will is too little known in this particular to induce them to stand fast in that liberty wherewith Christ has made them free.

Repentance　By J. W. Kilborn

"I tell you, Nay; but except ye repent, ye shall all likewise perish."—Luke 13:3.

Some sinners had come to tell Jesus about the death of some other sinners, about which they seemed deeply concerned. We are not to understand from the manner of Jesus' reply that he treated the matter in the least degree flippantly, but he saw at once, and tried to make the sinners see, that the affair so far as those Galileans was concerned was a "closed incident," while "live issues" confronted those to whom he was speaking and whom he had been trying to teach. "Do you think those Galileans whose blood Pilate mingled in one of his ghastly orgies, or those upon whom the tower of Siloam fell, were viler sinners than all the rest of mankind, that such awful calamities should have fallen upon them? No; sinners doubtless they were, but that matter was passed beyond recall. And now except you repent, except you get right with God, except you likewise learn that God is not the God of the dead, but of the living, you shall also in like manner

be eternally lost." God is no respecter of persons. God has one law. God will not suffer that one man, because of hypocritical observance of the letter of the law, should pass into the enjoyment of the "rest that remaineth," but except each shall for himself and by himself make his life clean and pure and holy, except he shall bow down before the Master in loving, contrite repentance, ready to pray with another sinner, "Depart from me, O Lord, for I am a sinful man," God can not find himself a home in the heart and life. Like these Galileans, how much time we waste in concern for the sins of the other, and how little we are concerned over the shame we hide under our own cloaks. A great company stood before a man who "spake as the Holy Spirit gave him utterance." They heard his masterful array of evidences; they listened to his scathing, blistering indictment of their own crime in murdering their Christ; the arrow of conviction sank to the very depths of their hearts; they believed themselves sinners in the sight of the God whom blindly, gropingly, they had tried to find that they might worship him. The very foundations of their faith in the old life, the old self, the old system, crumbled

ind they cried out, "Men and breth-
hat *shall* we do?" What a thrilling
it all was. Hear the dignified an-
)f the Spirit-filled man, "Repent ye;
ye; repent ye." May we not well
: that each one of these preachers
o the waiting, anxious inquirers that
g command, "Repent ye?" Yes, I
the rest of it, too, but my theme is
ance, for this we need before the
f the command. Establish the vital

principle of repentance and the rest inevitably follows. No man who repents in the
sense in which Jesus used the term, or in
that in which the apostles used it on Pentecost and similar occasions, will stop at any
command the word of inspiration lays upon
him. He can not—*he dare not*. What is
it, then? Need I pursue the case further?
Do we not all know that the subtle, mysterious change that makes the thief make restitution, that causes the libertine to cease

from his sensuality, the drunks
open his hand and spend his
God, the scarlet woman to anoil
of Jesus and bathe them even it
—this is the repentance that "bi
fruits", and brings the whole bei
jection to God. May God bring
repentance, for "Except *ye repen*
all likewise perish."
Mt. Carmel, Ill.

he Man with the Ax   By Edward O. Sh

re was a great reformer in the
igo who thus spoke:
en now the ax also lieth at the root
: trees; every tree, therefore, that
th not forth good fruit is hewn down
ast into the fire."
is, with prophetic solemnity, is de-
| the doom of every evil thing and
i that curses the human race.
: who work out their cruel
ies are strangely obtuse to this
ng. They go on planting evil trees
:ulturing them, heedless of the un-
r ax of retributive justice and the
ming fires of an oppressed people's
There is to-day a vast forest
:h growth which must be cut down,
ierely because of evil fruition, but
because the space is needed for
lanting of orchards and grain for
hildren of our One Father.
: broad and fertile fields of a con-
t, or hemisphere, unite to form
tate, wherein the homes are pillars
ength and beauty. In an evil hour
isidious seeds of industrial and so-
yranny are planted and for a time
unseen but at length, lofty and
ageous, they spread their branches
nd wide over a whole people and
all space for their own. Time-
red, moss-covered conservatism,
g in the soft places of luxury and
r, seeks selfish and unjust rule over
to whom Jehovah gave, not only
y but dominion. When the hour
eming triumph for the evil thing
s then comes the Man with the Ax.
: battle between radical and con-
tive has been age-long, and concur-
with racial development. There
been victories that eclipse the glo-
f Austerlitz and Marengo, and de-
sadder than French tears at Water-
The victories endure; the defeats
ut eddies in the mighty, onward
The Man with the Ax never sur-
rs; he has battered down the dun-
of wrong, and, with ringing tools,
the temples of national weal and
He has ever been a revolutionist
ways hated till his heroic endeavor
wned with success—then hailed as
ii-god. He knows he is not a fa-
with his contemporaries. and
ts will come with floral praise on
nib.

This is, O Truth, the deepest woe
  Of him thou biddest to protest,
With men no kinship may be know,
  Thy mission hems from worst and best.

The wolf that gauntly prowled the wood
  From human-kind more mercy got
Than he who warns men to be good,
  And stands alone and finches not."

'ultra-conservative is the apothe-
f inertia. He esteems all desire
orm, as unreasonable and vision-
he had his way there would be
e season for him—a continual har-
me. If evils are pointed out to
: calmly replies: "Such things
have been and always will be—
or you always have with you,' you.
The radical protests against
paralysis of philanthropy and
Ith confidence; "The ax is laid at
t of the tree." This is the divine

sanction upon radicalism, God's benediction on the Man with the Ax.
Conservatism does but "skin and film
the ulcerous place" while radicalism applies the keen edge and removes all the
diseased tissue, even to the very roots,
for radicalism is root-work, etymologi-
cally and rationally considered.
The Man with the Ax is the prime
minister of progress; he pleads the emancipation of the slaves of evil circumstance. He is hooted by the reactionaries in the parliament of man. Then

Edward O. Sharpe.

the ax swings swiftly, surely, and the
old order is gone.
It is charged that the radical injures
the good in his violent efforts to destroy evil. Even if this were true it would
not justify a policy of *laissez faire* or
folded arms and paralysis of social conscience. But it is not true except in a
far-fetched sense. "Destroy in order
to save," is quite a philosophic admonition; the flower fails and the seed is
found; the seed perishes that the blossoms of a new springtime may be born.
The present generation can not be clad
in the out-worn garments of the social
and industrial past, however highly we
may regard them as heirlooms. Every
upward movement of the race has been
purchased with treasures of love and
blood. In war for the liberty of a people many hearts must ache in lonely woe
for loved ones fallen on the crimson
field. Desolation lies ever in the wake
of an army clad in righteous armor.
The radical is far removed from the
nihilist. He holds to the reign of law
in the administration of a government
that shall prevent the action of a powerful and sinful individualism. He is
socialistic, in that he demands the application of principles that guarantee
every man an equal opportunity and
where none shall injure or overreach
by superior mental talents or shrewd-
ness. He does not propose a vacuum
in which moral and social rights and relations can not exist. If, in the read-

justment of economic conditio
injury is done to vested right:
trenched privileges, it is bec
stand in the way of the grea
to the greater number. The M
the Ax is nobler in his heritage
ship than the conservative in h
itary purple and fine linen. T
leaves the world as he finds it—
—while the former clears the
the progress of generations yet
hither.
There is ever a returning cris
age has its own problems wit
it must grapple. The lines of
now drawn up in America; migh
are in process of alignment and
sition to each other. The appeal
to reason and conscience. Th
ing to move brutality and covet
there must come the arbitramen
thority. A regnant voice must
terance to the imperial mand
righteousness. In the final a
tion *vox populi, vox Dei*. If as
iniquity and oppression can mai
sway in this great western
heaven help the race! The peo
only to swing the ax and sm
gods of the market place.
The first and worst enemy of
man that must perish is *ignoranc*
the most valuable auxiliary of
would enslave their fellow-men
itual or social degradation. S
tion and degeneracy will flee bef
education as bats before the
light. As the hands of angels
from mortal view shift the sce
the heavens and dissolve n
shade with the glory of dawn,
the heralds of intellectual day
the light of knowledge from b
lip and pen until a blinded ra
see and claim its dower right,
The mass of our American (
is honestly desirous of making o
try truly great, but there has
much commercial and political
ery in the past few decades
patriotic heart grows sick an
There is, to-day, a fight on betwe
cenery Capitalism and the Arm
Common Good. Vast corpori
tems that owe their existence
concession and unpopular taxa
on plundering the many and e
the few until it bewilders and d
ery conception of popular sov
Never satisfied, these corporate
besiege legislatures and courts
vor and further opportunity to |
bones of the poor. The Man
Ax is on their trail and he will |
if they don't watch out.
Let us not be pessimistic; th
day is coming and not very f:
Every evil that lays the victim
finally be relegated to the g
with Herod, Judas, Caligula, Bc
Von Plehve. Let the people
and advance with caution upon th
works of Satan's fortresses, but
as

"Right is right and God is Go
  Then Right the day must w
  To doubt would be disloyalty,
    To falter would be sin,"

Our Budget

"O do not pray for easy lives;
Pray to be stronger men!—
Do not pray for tasks equal to your powers,
Pray for power equal to your tasks!"

—Let us make this our greatest year.

—"Love thyself last" is a good motto to help us do this.

—Remember that all Church Extension offerings should be sent promptly to G. W. Muckley, 600 Water Works Bldg., Kansas City, Mo.

—Union Avenue Christian Church begins a Named Loan Fund in our Church Extension work. Let others of our strong churches do the same. $300 annually creates a Named Fund.

Special to THE CHRISTIAN-EVANGELIST.

—The Kansas special railroad rate to the Kansas convention at Parsons has been reduced to one fare plus 50c for the round trip.—W. S. Lowe.

—John L. Brandt, pastor of the First Christian Church, St. Louis, who has been ailing for some time, has just undergone an operation for a pronounced case of appendicitis. We are glad to report that the indications point to a rapid recovery. Brother Brandt has been working too hard. Geo. L. Snively will preach at the First Christian until the pastor is able to take charge.

—Lewis P. Fisher has accepted a unanimous call to continue his ministry with the Texas (Ill.) church.

—Edward Clutter is in a meeting at Plainview, Neb., with nine additions at the time of the last report.

—Harlow and Harlow are assisting S. B. Moore in what promises to be a great meeting in Oklahoma City, Okla.

—Hugh C. Gresham, of Trenton, Neb., wishes to engage a singing evangelist to assist in the country school house meetings.

—J. B. Lockhart reports that J. L. Harris and L. Wood Mailey have concluded a very helpful three weeks' meeting at Unionville, Mo.

—E. A. Child, of Eugene, Ore., has closed out his college interests at Sodaville and offers his services to the churches as general evangelist.

—Percy T. Carnes, of La Plata, Mo., is assisting W. F. McCormack in a revival meeting at Lenox, Iowa. We hope for good reports soon.

—William Lowen just closed a two-weeks' meeting with the Fairview (Ky.) church. There were 13 additions, seven by confession and baptism.

—W. A. Haynes preached at North Bend, Neb., September 2. He speaks very highly of the work being accomplished there by Pastor J. E. Chase.

—Nellie B. McGhee wife of N. B. McGhee, pastor of the Gage (Oklahoma) church, was formally ordained for the ministry of the Word at Gage, August 29, 1906.

—Nellie Pollock, who has been assisting Harold E. Monser, has a vacant date through October. Brother Monser very highly recommends her as a singing evangelist.

—O. L. Adams recently concluded a three weeks' meeting at Craig, Ill., with five baptisms, four of which were young men. He was assisted by C. A. Adams and John G. Olmsted, singers.

—Allen T. Shaw celebrated his first anniversary with the Fairfield (Ill.) church last Lord's day. More than $1,500 was raised during the year. The church is harmonious, aggressive and prosperous. Princess Long assists in the serv-

ices next Lord's day, going under the auspices of the C. W. B. M.

—Irving Taylor LeBaron's meeting at Mt. Olive, near Macon, Mo., continues with 11 added the first week. Among the baptized is one lady of 77 years. The meeting is largely attended.

—W. D. Baker has concluded his ministry at Cameron and accepted a call at Sterling, Ill. He reports the Cameron church, with its membership of 285, as an almost ideal pastorate for an able, energetic man.

—L. H. Humphrey, of Greeley, Co., is in a meeting with good prospects of a great ingathering. His church has been organized but little over two years, but his membership is 142, with a very flourishing Bible school.

—The August "Eagle" contains an extended account of the resignation of N. E. Cory, of Augusta, together with a resume of his splendid ministry in that place. We hope to hear of Brother Cory's early call to some of our larger churches.

—Brother LeRoy St. John, whose picture adorns our pages this week, is teaming with Brother Small and they love each other like brothers. Brother St. John three years ago was a Methodist, but was won to the plea by H. A. Northcutt and has since had his

LeRoy St. John.

membership at Terre Haute, where L. E. Sellers ministers. He is, beyond question, among the very best leaders and soloists in the land. His work is of a high grade, and his presence has the right kind of influence in the meeting. He is of a hopeful disposition and never fails to make friends and wins the large choruses, which he leads to him at the beginning. His whole heart and soul are in his work.

—In answer to inquiries we wish to say that THE CHRISTIAN-EVANGELIST special train to the Buffalo convention will be supplied with baggage cars, also with a diner and a commissary car that will supply sandwiches and coffee at much cheaper rates than the regular diner. In fact, nothing is being left undone to serve the convenience of our traveling companions and minister to their entertainment during the trip.

—C. R. L. Vawter, of the First Church of Christ, Shelby, Ohio, is in a meeting with the Mill Hall (Pa.) church. Brother Vawter held some very successful tent meetings in Pennsylvania last summer, and has had numerous calls for meetings since, but he has accepted none till the one came from Mill Hall, preferring to stay with his own church.

The Avis (Pa.) church, which he organized last summer in a tent, is now in the toils of a building enterprise.

—James S. Beem, of Bethany, Neb., has had 24 additions to the Low Centre church during his three months' pulpit supply there. He now offers his services to the churches as general evangelist.

—T. L. Fox and family, which includes Mrs. J. T. Toof and daughter, have removed from Quincy, Ill., to Englewood, N. J. Of course the indispensable CHRISTIAN-EVANGELIST will follow them to their new home.

—Evangelist James T. McKissick recently assisted J. W. McGarvey, Jr., in a meeting at Mount Zion, Ky., with 64 additions, 50 being by primary obedience. Brother McKissick has helped to add 166 to our churches since July 1.

—B. H. Morris, Watervalley, Miss., has begun the publication of "The Christian Worker," an excellent four-page Christian paper. We wish for Brother Morris better material success than is the portion of most of us editors.

—State Evangelist Joseph Gaylor sends an interesting report of the reception accorded their new minister, F. L. Moffett, and wife by the South Side Church at Springfield, Mo. We congratulate pastor and people on what seems to be a very fortunate union.

—Albert Nichols of Winfield, Kan., will be assisted in revival services through November by J. B. Bowen and Leonard Dougherty. Brother Nichols is anticipating the greatest revival ever held in Winfield. We hope he will not be disappointed.

—J. H. O. Smith is in a protracted meeting at Jacksonville, Ill., with R. F. Thrapp, and an enthusiastic host of Disciples accustomed to undertake and accomplish great things for the Master. Assistant Guy B. Williams will have charge of the music.

—W. E. M. Hackelman, of Indianapolis, visited with us last Friday en route to Union City, Tenn., where he will assist Herbert Yeuell through a revival in J. J. Castleberry's church. This is an exceptionally strong combination, and we anticipate a great meeting.

—Mary A. Lyons, the indefatigable corresponding secretary of the Ohio C. W. B. M., has changed her headquarters from Hiram to 9726 Logan Court, N. E., Cleveland, Ohio. We trust the labors of Sister Lyons may long be blessed with the success that has attended her hitherto.

—W. W. Burks has recently returned from a vacation spent in the southwest. He reports E. S. Bullard happily located with the Las Vegas (New Mexico) church; that his people are greatly pleased with their new pastor, and that prospects for the great upbuilding of the congregation are most excellent.

—The railroad rates to the Kentucky convention at Louisville, September 24 to 27, will be one fare plus 25 cents, instead of one and one-third fare plus 25 cents, as erroneously stated by the corresponding secretary in former announcements. No certificates are needed.

—What May is to the farmer September is to the preacher. It is a time of quickening kindling enthusiasm, preparing for the great spiritual harvests of November and midwinter. Let us all enter enthusiastically upon our work and give to the world some astonishing church statistics.

—R. R. Hamlin, who is having remarkable success as evangelist since his resignation at Fort Worth, Texas, will begin a meeting in Nevada, Mo., early in November. We welcome him into these more northern latitudes. We expect the Nevada church soon to be one of the strongest in our Missouri brotherhood.

—The annual convention of the Western Pennsylvania Christian Missionary Society will be held at Homestead September 25-27. An excellent program has been arranged.

—The American Christian Missionary Society would notify its friends that the books for this year close September 30. Churches, Bible schools, Endeavor societies, ladies' aid societies and all other organizations, as well as individuals, wishing to contribute to this year's receipts must make remittances at once.

—R. W. Tanksley, who was compelled by throat trouble to relinquish a very successful pastorate at Neodesha, Kan., after a three months' sojourn at Eureka Springs, is enabled to resume his labors with the churches. His address is Neodesha, but we hope to learn of his early call to one of our churches.

—In a letter from Mrs. H. A. Wheeldon we learn that the Missoula (Mont.) church, under the leadership of Brother and Sister W. H. Bagby, is growing rapidly in numbers, prestige and usefulness. In the letter THE CHRISTIAN-EVANGELIST, which is circulating largely in this church, comes in for a generous meed of praise.

—Evangelist John T. Stivers holds meetings nearly all the year. During his vacation he just "holds meetings." During his vacation for three weeks at Memphis, Mo., assisted by J. T. Shreves, resulting in twenty-one additions. Brother Stivers speaks very highly of Brother Shreves' pastoral and pulpit abilities.

—H. A. Northcutt is in a meeting in his old home town, Knox City, Mo., with 83 additions at last report. More than half of these are men. Roy Westcott, a young local merchant, has charge of the singing; Brother Northcutt says that he serves God in the store as well as in the church. Verily, such men are the hope of the church of the future.

—The office has been favored with an announcement of the marriage of Lura Margaret Wallace to Leslie Garfield Parker, of Des Moines, Ia. These young people will be at home to their friends in Des Moines after September 24. We wish them great happiness and usefulness as they go down through the years together.

—If one of our young men of the Student Volunteer Band who has in view the dedication of his life to either foreign or frontier work would like to have the advantage of a year's exercise in one of our large cities, he might communicate with George L. Snively, president of the City Mission Board, Christian Publishing Company, St. Louis.

—O. L. Hull, of Randolph, Ohio, concluded a meeting last Lord's day with his home church of one week's duration, with 14 additions by confession and baptism. He has closed his work with the church there to accept the pastorate of the Garrett (Ind.) congregation, where he will assist in the building of a new church home.

—In a communication from Charles Reign Scoville, of September 6, he reports 353 additions in his union meeting at Monroe, Wis. This totals 4,330 additions to the churches through Brother Scoville's meeting for 1906. Among the great contributions this Restoration has made to the religious world is this remarkably successful evangelist.

—The resourceful pastor of our Amarillo (Texas) congregation adds in a note enclosing subscriptions to THE CHRISTIAN-EVANGELIST that his church

surpassed its Church Extension apportionment. We naturally expect CHRISTIAN-EVANGELIST churches to do this, especially when such a consecrated minister as Howard Jewell is at the prow.

—Evangelist Chas. W. Mahin is in a meeting with Rock church ten miles from Huntington, Ind. He writes there is every kind of "ism" represented there; that sinners are confused by them and there is difficulty even in teaching them the truth. There were two additions at last report with prospects for a good increase. He begins with the Ambia (Ind.) church September 15.

—Evangelist W. A. Haynes, Skidmore, Mo., will begin a meeting in Doniphan, same state, the first Lord's day in October. He orders 500 copies of THE CHRISTIAN-EVANGELIST to his assistance through the meeting. Brother Haynes has been highly recommended to us as a soul winner, and we delight in having this fellowship with him in revival services.

—W. B. Blakemore is having a very happy time at Mill Creek, Ky. Over $800 worth of improvements have been made to the church property during the past year. The Twelfth district Sunday-school and the C. W. B. M. conventions held very successful sessions in his church August 15 and 16. His people recently gave $110 for Kentucky state missions.

—Children's day for home missions is the first Lord's day before Thanksgiving. A beautiful exercise, "Soldiers of the Cross," has been prepared by this society, and will be sent free wherever requested. Attractive boxes in which to collect money for this important ministry have been prepared, and will be distributed gratuitously among the Bible schools applying.

—John S. Sweeney, of Paris, Ky., was an office visitor last week. He recently held a brief meeting with 11 additions at Old Union, Green county, Ill., where he preached his first sermon 50 years ago. He visited other scenes of his earlier ministry with great pleasure to himself and help to the churches. There is many a good sermon and lecture and even debate in the old hero yet.

—Chas. E. Smith, state evangelist, has just closed a short meeting at Versailles, S. C., with five added to the membership during the meeting and a very substantial payment made on the church extension loan owed by that congregation. Some sectarian and bitter opposition at St. Stephens was changed into admiration and love for our plea before the meeting concluded. Brother Smith is now at Merrit's Bridge.

—W. J. Cocke recently conducted a two weeks' meeting with the Mill Creek (Ky.) church, with 37 additions—23 by confession and baptism. The successes that characterized his Georgia ministry are following him to a marked degree into his new field of labor in Kentucky. Together with his other schoolmates, this paragrapher greatly rejoices in Brother Cocke's victories for the truth.

—J. A. L. Romig, Portage La Prairie, Manitoba, corresponding secretary of the Western Canada Missionary Association, has prepared a twenty-page booklet reporting his work and the general development of the cause of primitive Christianity in his territory. It abounds in encouragement to Disciples living in the land of "Our Lady of the Snows." We hope many of our Canadian brethren will attend our Buffalo Convention next month.

—F. M. Rogers concluded his first two years' service with the West Side Church, Springfield, Ill., August 31; and was immediately re-engaged until January 1, 1910. The membership of that new church is 522. Its growth in all the elements of church

strength has been almost Brother Rogers' continual a guarantee there will be r tor Dorris and C. H. Al him in revival meeting, b be it.

—W. W. Burks, of Ne us the subscription of H. tor of the Presbyterian ch He had expressed admira ings of the paper. This opportunity to those who plea fully understood by ou brethren. Several thousa from denominational mini be secured by our prea plishment that would great extension of this Restorati

—Sumner T. Martin, street, Chicago, city evan all persons knowing of Christian church movin send him their names dresses. The importance realized when it is nath ed there are more membe tian church in Chicago, York, Kansas City, Pueb other large cities not aff churches than are identi

—The Kentucky sta meets September 24. A men and women on th note President C. L. Lo H. D. Clark, J. T. Kackl kins, R. L. Clark, P. A. Ewers, Mark Collis, W. Buckner, Carey E. Morg son, J. W. McGarvey, F. A. Finch, R. H. Crossfiel rance, E. L. Powell, P Mullins, R. M. Simpson H. W. Elliott.

—James H. Henderson his church, writes that field, at present minis church at Chambersburg,

to Texas in a few weeks. He has not decided on any location yet. Our correspondent writes that Brother Battonfield has been successful in every field where he has labored and that he will undoubtedly prove helpful to any Texas church engaging his services.

—O. C. Moomaw, after a three years' faithful and successful pastorate at Clay Center, Kan., has resigned and the church wishes a new minister to begin October 1. The church is free of indebtedness, alive to missions, has a good building, well located in a city of 4,000. Otha Wilkison, of Ukiah, Cal., will conduct revival meetings there through September. Ministers considering this pastorate may address L. M. Householder, Clay Center, Kan.

—The missionaries of the Foreign Society in the Philippine Islands report 540 additions during the past year. When it is remembered that there are only three men there giving themselves wholly to evangelistic work, it will be seen that these are most encouraging figures. The society has recently expended $16,000 in ground and a building in Manila. This work was begun only five years ago and there are already 17 organized churches.

—We very much regret to state that Brother Garrison is so severely afflicted with hay fever as to make it impossible for him to attend the Paris convention of Illinois Disciples. This is as great a disappointment to him, as it will be to those who expected to hear and meet him. His place on the Endeavor program, however, will be supplied, and a great convention will be edified by splendid reports of work done and inspirational addresses by some of our ablest and noblest men and women.

—Hiram Van Kirk, of 2230 Dana street, Berkeley, Cal., has been requested to secure delegates for the national convention at Buffalo. The rates will be one fare plus $2. As this is the first opportunity to secure half fares east since the World's Fair, it is hoped many will avail themselves of the opportunity. Let those intending to come from California wire Brother Van Kirk at once. We hope these California delegates will come over the Wabash from St. Louis joining THE CHRISTIAN-EVANGELIST Special at noon, October 11.

—Lynn R. Hornish, in a letter containing remittance for the New Hampshire fund, says: "I had intended to give my little for a long time, but have neglected to do so. I am afraid there are thousands who have delayed even as I have. If we only would do and not delay." Would that these "thousands" would "do" at once that a sufficient fund mighty quickly be compounded for holding this meeting and the first month's salary of a located preacher, that we might go on to other victories.

—W. E. Garrison, who was compelled by threatened pulmonary complications to relinquish the presidency of Butler College in the dawn of what promised to be an unusually brilliant career, has just been selected principal of the High School of Santa Fe, N. M. One significance of this that will delight hosts of friends is that all who are considered for this responsible position must first undergo a rigid examination and be found absolutely free from all traces of tuberculosis.

No Stomach Trouble.

After you take Drake's Palmetto Wine one week. Cures to stay cured all forms of Stomach Trouble. A test bottle free if you write to Drake Co., Wheeling, W. Va.

—Secretary W. J. Wright stopped with us part of a day on his way to the Indian Territory convention at South McAlester. He is quite sanguine that offerings for home missions will aggregate as much for 1906 as for the previous year, notwithstanding the interregnum following the resignation of Secretary B. L. Smith before his own recent acceptance of this important portfolio. Our hearts and prayers are with Brothers Wright and Ranshaw in their heroic undertaking for the evangelization of the home-land.

—Next Sunday afternoon at three o'clock the officers of the Teachers' Union of the Christian Bible school of this city will hold a rally at the Hamilton Avenue Church to consider ways and means of advancing Sunday-school interests. All interested in Sunday-school work and the upbuilding of the cause of Christ are invited to attend regardless of denominational lines. Among others on the program other than our own workers are S. J. Lindsay and P. M. Hammon. Governor Folk has been invited and has signified his intention of being present if circumstances permit.

—The company of Disciples that will leave New York to visit Palestine next February will include Mrs. Dessie Campbell Barclay, daughter of Alexander Campbell, who spent three years at one time in the Holy Land; J. P. Lichtenberger and wife, of New York and A. C. Smither and wife, of Los Angeles. If these are fair samples of the character of the company the Disciple pilgrims will constitute a select group on the steamship Arabic. From Bro. B. B. Tyler we learn that the next cruise promises to be unusually popular.

—Herbert H. Saunders, of Noblesville, Ind., writes a beautifully worded letter commending the evangelistic methods, aspirations and successes of R. H. Fife, of Kansas City, whom he heard through a revival meeting at Holden, Mo. "I heard Brother Fife say many times, 'Unless you want to accept Christ in determination to work for him for the extension of his kingdom, no matter what that sacrifice may entail, you would better stay where you are.'" Brother Fife is known to this office as a man of faith, purity, ability and success.

—We will gladly serve our friends by securing entertainment for them at Buffalo. We have secured options on a multitude of homes equipped with all modern conveniences and within easy walking distance of the convention hall. The convention hall is not located in the hotel district. Entertainment in private homes is preferable to hotel service. Rates 75 cents and $1 for room and breakfast. Our services are absolutely gratuitous. If names are sent us soon enough the Buffalo entertainment committee will mail assignments with directions for finding them to applicants.

—W. E. M. Hackleman has been selected by the Buffalo convention committee to conduct the music for the national convention October 12-18. This is the fourth time Brother Hackleman has been selected for this important position. The music of the program will be taken from "Gloria In Excelsis," that best of all church hymnals. In Indiana, alone, this hymnal has been adopted by such county seat churches as Brazil, Rushville, Frankfort, Lafayette, Anderson, Noblesville, Kokomo, Central, Indianapolis, Fourth, Indianapolis, Jeffersonville, Wabash, Huntington, Crawfordsville, etc.

—On Sunday, August 26, L. N. D. Wells preached his farewell sermons—to his congregation in the morning, and to the public in the evening. At both services the house was crowded, the evening audience overtax-

ing the capacity of the house. Three confessed Christ in the morning and were baptized in the evening when still another made the good confession. At the close of the evening service Bro. Wells was presented with a beautiful gold watch, and Mrs. Wells was the recipient of a splendid silver set as a token of the love of the members of the Wilkinsburg church. This popular preacher has taken up his new work in East Orange, N. J.

—Evangelist S. J. Vance, of Carthage, Mo., held a meeting at Sorrell, Mo., in the Baptist church, under the auspices of the Missouri Christian Missionary Society. There were 11 additions at the first Lord's day service. "The Baptists very kindly granted us the privilege of organizing a congregation of Christians only, but not the only Christians, in their church, which we will do during the progress of this meeting. This is another great opportunity for preaching Christian union, which I am not neglecting to do. I preached yesterday on 'The Divine Plea,' with many colorings of Bible union."

—There were five additions the first two days of Evangelist George C. Ritchey's meeting at Nampa, Idaho, where he is being assisted by 300 CHRISTIAN-EVANGELISTS each week. He was at Emmett, Idaho, 10 days, and organized a church of 17 members that has since been added to. This church is now negotiating for a church building. A new church building will be dedicated at Rupert in October, where he closed a meeting August 5. Meridian, Idaho, expects to have a new building completed in December, when Brother Ritchey begins his second meeting there. Each of these congregations needs a good pastor.

—Referring to a brief personal notice of himself in this department of the paper in connection with his relation to the Marshall Field Dry Goods Company, Bro. W. P. Keeler, of Chicago, writes: "Be it understood that your humble servant is but an employe of Marshall Field & Co., now in his thirty-fifth year of service." While Brother Keeler thus disclaims the honor of being "a member of the great Marshall Field Dry Goods Company," his long connection with that firm in a responsible position is high testimony to his ability and integrity.

—Parties going with THE CHRISTIAN-EVANGELIST special over the Wabash to the Buffalo convention will have their choice of going from Detroit on to the convention city either by rail through Canada or over the full length of Lake Erie on a staunch, safe ship. We advise our friends to go one way and return the other. There is no extra charge for the ship ride. The rate from your home will be one fare plus $1 east of the Mississippi and plus $2 west of the river. From wherever you start get to the Wabash as soon as possible. Lowest possible rates will be secured for side trips to Niagara and elsewhere, and best entertainment provided for while at the convention.

—A letter has been received by the Editor from Evangelist Herbert Yeuell, dated London, August 25, in which he announces that he was to sail from Liverpool in the steamer "Coronia" on Tuesday, August 28, and that he expected to be able to start his meeting at Union City, Tenn., September 9. He reports that his mother's health is improved somewhat though she is still ill. He was to preach at the West London Tabernacle on Lord's day evening, August 26. He will probably be in his meeting before this reaches our readers. On account of the crowded condition of the steamships coming this way his wife and son who accompanied him to England will not return until a few weeks later.

—During his recent vacation, Percy T. Carnes, of La Plata, Mo., held a three weeks' meeting in Bayfield, Colo. There were but two members in the town, and a few in the surrounding country when he arrived, nor had there ever been a sermon by a Christian minister in the county. Notwithstanding there was much prejudice and misunderstanding to be removed, the people heard "the new doctrine" gladly. He preached to the largest audiences ever assembled in Bayfield. "We closed the meeting with a great baptismal and union service, the reception of scattered disciples and members from the denominations, and the organization of the first church simply Christian in the county. Bro. G. E. Trone, elder and "fireside preacher," will lead the work for awhile."

—The "Daily Vidette" contains more than a two-column account of the farewell reception given Brother and Sister J. H. O. Smith by their Valparaiso (Ind.) church, together with the pulpit committee's very reluctant acceptance of their resignation and a tribute to the real worth of the pastor and his wife— or rather these joint pastors, we are justified in saying. Brother Smith's resignation abounds in expressions of profound appreciation of the tender and sacred relationships existing between him and his church for so many years. The kindly interest of all Valparaiso as well as Disciples everywhere will fol-

low honest-hearted, consecrated and eloquent J. H. O. Smith through his evangelistic career.

—"Arrangements have been made and the money raised for securing the services of a pastor at the Christian Church. Wallace Stuckey, of Lebo, who has so successfully managed the big revival that has been in progress for some time, is responsible for the great religious wave that has swept over Galesburg and vicinity. This organization has been at a standstill for several years, but new life and vigor have been infused, and it promises to be one of the strongest organizations in this section of the country. It seems that every citizen is more than pleased that its door will be opened again soon for regular services, and the people of the town have responded nicely to the call for financial support."
—Thayer (Mo.) News.

—Charles Frederick Trimble, Oklahoma state evangelist, began a campaign for the restoration of primitive Christianity at Ada, I. T., September 7, under the direction of the state board. Brother Trimble is being loaned by the Oklahoma Christian Missionary Society for this meeting on account of the great importance of that field. He is spoken of by his board as the "Apostle of

Charles Frederick Trimble.

Love." So successful have been his evangelistic labors for the past twelve years that he has earned a front rank position among our evangelists. More than half the baptisms reported by Irving link evangelists at the recent El Reno convention were the results of his work. Of his 400 additions to Oklahoma churches during the year 235 were by confession and baptism. Three hundred CHRISTIAN-EVANGELISTS will be among the aids to Brother Trimble in this meeting to which the brethren are looking forward with so much hopefulness.

—During Pastor J. M. Philputt's vacation from Union Avenue Church, this city, Irving S. Chenoweth, his assistant, had full charge, preaching twice every Sunday and keeping up a large amount of pastoral work, besides speaking every Thursday night at a downtown mission. It was a great responsibility for one of his years to assume, but he discharged his duties to the increasing satisfaction of the church, and showed himself to be a man of unusual natural and spiritual resources. He is now at his home in Illinois enjoying a well-earned vacation. The problem before the Union Avenue Church this year is the erection of the main auditorium. They are plan-

ning to let the contrac and hope to begin wor spring.

—In advance of a ful El Reno (Okla.) conv pleased to state on go that it was the largest thusiastic of any ever held

—The members and First Christian Church c W. Va., gave a receptic their retiring pastor, G. Monday night, that was event. Ministers of the v were present and the se local Y. M. C. A. who m plimentary addresses, wh spersed with music. B was then called to the pla sentations of silver and made to him and wife o church and his Sunday-s the close refreshments w large company. J. M. F boro, O., succeeds Brothe goes to Rogersville, Pa.

—In a letter from B. B of the office force he stat whelmed with work and happy. Received ten Lord's day and two since; tize three to-morrow; wr the work of the ministry 1861. This one thing I ing all these years. I h gaged in business or even er. I have served either evangelist forty-five full now doing the best and ha my life. Have never h sickness; my health now an ache nor a pain; not dread. I am simply boili morning with joy, and he Praise the Lord. The j the burden is light.

—We have received fro Neal, of Grayson, Ky., t anti-Mormonism, a cop Cowdery's Defence and which is No. 9 in his s Mormon tracts. This is important document in of the fraudulent claims o Oliver Cowdery, it will be was one of the three orig who saw the wonderful "I scribe who wrote down of these "plates" dictated b through "the Urim and T was also the first person the "Latter Day Saints C baptized by the hands of Jr., the prophet. This tra light on the inside of Mo should be in the hands of in contact with this mod tion. Address the publis and help him to scatter tl among those in need of su Ten cents per copy. Writ quantities.

❦ ❦

Board of Ministerial Relief of Christ.

Aid in the support of wort abled ministers of the Ch and their widows.
THIRD LORD'S DAY IN is the day set apart in all th the offering to this work. I dividual offerings, send direc Wills and Deeds should "BOARD OF MINISTER OF THE CHURCH OF C poration under the laws of t diana." Money received o Plan.
Address all communicati all checks, drafts, etc., paya

—The following Disciples have been in attendance at University of Chicago during the summer quarter: F. C. Aldinger, Prof. M. A. Ben Kori, E. E. Faris, A. W. Fortune, R. W. Gentry, E. A. Henry, Guy M. Hoover, O. F. Jordan, C. R. Hudson, Guy E. Killie, H. B. Robison, L. P. Schooling, Prof. Walter M. Stairs, G. B. Stewart, W. H. Trainum, Prof. A. D. Veatch, R. L. Handley, Miss Virginia K. Hearne, Mrs. Ethel O. McCormick, C. H. Winders, Prof. Albert Buxton, F. D. Butchart, Asa McDaniel, E. M. Smith, W. F. Hamann and Miss Laura Gentry.

—One of our ministers in the south sends us a copy of a tract published by the publishing house of the Methodist Episcopal Church, South, Nashville, Tenn., entitled "Divine Precedent for Baptism by Affusion," and asks us to publish a refutation of the same in THE CHRISTIAN-EVANGELIST. Fortunately the readers of THE CHRISTIAN-EVANGELIST do not need any refutation of the author's arguments. The author relies chiefly on the account of the baptism in the Holy Spirit in the second chapter of Acts for his argument in favor of affusion. The Holy Spirit was poured out or shed forth upon the disciples; therefore baptism is by pouring. The author is oblivious, apparently, to the fact that baptism in the Holy Spirit was not

the *pouring out* of the Spirit, but a result of that pouring out, by reason of which the disciples were "filled with the Holy Spirit." It was their spirits, not their bodies, that were submerged in the Holy Spirit, just as the body is submerged in water in literal baptism. But we refer our brother who sends the tract to the book on "The Form of Baptism," published by the Christian Publishing Company, which answers these arguments and many others in a most thorough manner.

—The home-coming of Paul Moore, our assistant editor, to which we are all looking forward with great pleasure, came nearly being terminated by a tragedy deep as a maelstrom and dark as the shadow of death. On September 1 Brother Moore was fishing in the Yellowstone, and was so carried away with the sport he failed to see that the sun was sinking and was no longer lighting his pathway in the shallows of the river. When he realized that darkness was coming on his path was utterly obliterated. The waters were deep and the current like a millrace. A misstep precipitated him beyond his depth and he was swirled down to what seemed certain death, but fortunately he was borne to a huge rock rising above the surface. Calls for help brought others to the shore, and after hours of trial a rope was floated to his perilous retreat. Fastening this about him, he threw himself out into the current and was swept to the shallows and finally rescued more nearly dead than alive. Fire was soon built on the shore, and he was resuscitated and able to return to camp about midnight after the most hazardous experience of his many adventures by land and sea. Thousands will join with us in thanksgiving that one so capable and devoted to the good and true has been spared to further service to the church and all humanity.

✿　✿

Church Extension Offerings.

Special to THE CHRISTIAN-EVANGELIST.

Charleston, S. C., Sept. 10.—The Church Extension offering reaches $50.—Marcellus R. Ely.

Special to THE CHRISTIAN-EVANGELIST.

Central Church, Wichita, Kas., raised $100 for Church Extension.—E. W. Allen, pastor.

Special to THE CHRISTIAN-EVANGELIST.

Oklahoma City, First Church gives over $100 to Church Extension this year. —Sherman Moore, pastor.

Special to THE CHRISTIAN-EVANGELIST.

Independence Boulevard Church, Kansas City, gives over $400 to Church Extension.—Geo. H. Combs, pastor.

Special to THE CHRISTIAN-EVANGELIST.

Hamilton Avenue, St, Louis, gives $100 to Church Extension. Apportionment seventy-five.—L. W. McCreary.

✿　✿

For a Church in New Hampshire.

Already acknowledged $948.25
Miss Mary Kingsbury................ 1.00
Lynn R. Hornish................... 1.00
Mrs. M. S. Wagner, Alameda, Cal.. 2.50
Mary B. Culver 5.00
　　　　　　　　　　　　　　　　　　————
Total $955.75

An Elijah Dowie can go to most any of our great cities and establish a congregation and found a church. When Elijah II. went to Chicago he had over $100,000, it is true, to make trumpets blare, and street cars blaze, and the press heralded his sayings, and with which to secure famous auditoriums for the comfortable seating of his hearers, but every body in Chicago

knew that "the prophet" was in the city.

It may be said it ought not require $100,-000 to establish a true church in one of our cities. It will not, but how comes it that men will give $100,000 for the founding of a false church while we so reluctantly or at least so slowly give $3,000 for the institution of a true Church of Christ in another American city?

Conditions are such that we must have an able evangelist preach in a prominent place widely advertised. There are no brethren to act as hosts. All is hired service. These difficulties ought to inspire us rather than daunt us. We WILL win. Let us quickly double our present gifts and then happily tell of our new church in Manchester.

REGIMENTAL REUNIONS AND FORTY-THIRD ANNIVERSARY BATTLE CHICKAMAUGA,
CHATTANOOGA, SEPTEMBER 18-20, 1906.

On September 18, 1906, will occur the forty-third anniversary of the Battle of Chickamauga. It is proposed to celebrate this memorable event with a reunion of the various regiments that participated in this memorable battle and the various battles fought around Chattanooga. This reunion will be held at Chickamauga National Park, September 18, 19 and 20, and the present indications are that it will be the largest and most notable gathering ever held in the South. On the above dates, the remnants from the armies of twelve states, comprising the following: Pennsylvania, Ohio, Michigan, Indiana, Illinois, Wisconsin, Minnesota, Iowa, Nebraska, Missouri, Kansas and Kentucky, will assemble, many for the first and last time since they marched from its blood-stained fields, forty-three years ago.

Here is one of the great opportunities for the education of the youth. Don't fail to take your children and show them historic Chattanooga, with all its historical connections. It is the opportunity of a lifetime. Go and see the old war generals and other officers; point out the places of interest on the battlefield; let them show you and explain, in person, the markers erected on the battlefield showing the positions of the opposing armies at the time of battle. It will not be long until none will be left to do this noble work.

It will be many years, if ever again, that such an opportunity will present itself. See that your tickets read via the Louisville & Nashville R. R., the Battlefield Route. Call on your nearest railroad agent for rates and advertising matter pertaining to the reunion, or write nearest representative of the Louisville & Nashville R. R.

J. H. MILLIKEN, D. P. A., Louisville, Ky.
F. D. BUSH, D. P. A., Cincinnati, Ohio.
E. E. DAVENPORT, D. P. A., St. Louis, Mo.
H. C. BAILEY, N. W. P. A., Chicago, Ill.

Candor.

I found this in the Harbinger and as a specimen of brotherly candor it stands alone.

"Elder ———— made us a short visit to Bethany, and while here, by request, delivered to us a discourse. He has been laboring amongst us and the Baptists for many years. He was not popular amongst the Baptists and he is not popular amongst our brethren; and I presume, as he is constituted and as other men are constituted, never can be popular in any community.

"Which are to blame I will not presume to guess. But the world is large enough for all its inhabitants, and if Brother ———— has his eccentricities and peculiarities, other men have something of their own that they had better not have; and, therefore, some forbearance is necessary.

"I, therefore, think that those who approve Brother ———— should hear him and assist him, and that he ought not to offer his services to any people who neither solicit them nor appreciate them. In so doing, he and the brethren will get along more satisfactorily.　　A. C."

After reading this I am sure that no one could accuse Brother Campbell of favoritism nor of a desire to puff up his brethren.　　　　　　F. P. ARTHUR.

Grand Rapids, Mich.

❋ ❋

Small-St. John at Mexico, Mo.

The Small-St. John meeting is now six days old with six added. The meeting came upon us with but one week's preparation. Last fall seventy-five were added, with baptisms regularly since. Hence, the field has been somewhat gleaned, and the material of that more difficult class to reach. Brother Small is preaching great sermons, the congregations are large and the whole town is pleased and talking the meeting. Men are becoming interested who seldom attend church, and we are confident of splendid results.

St. John is a singer of great power, a fine soloist and chorus leader and above all a sweet spirited Christian. His work among the boys and girls organizing them into a chorus here has been of a very pleasing character. Out of town visitors have been W. T. Moore, W. B. Taylor, Lowell C. McPherson, H. A. Northcutt and J. N. Coil. The additions have included one from another religious body. The meeting will continue at least two weeks longer.

A. W. KOKENDOFFER.

We are here in a meeting with Brother Kokendoffer and the congregation at Mexico, and unless all signs fail we will have a good meeting. Brother St. John is my constant companion in labor. Already we have heard Christ's name confessed and we expect a good day tomorrow (Sunday). The congregations are large and especially attentive and we are hoping that "times of refreshing may come to us all" in the meeting.

Brother Kokendoffer is much beloved by the church and by the citizens of the town. He is surely living to serve the people. He freely offers his services to all who may need them, and esteems it a favor to be informed by any one whom he can help. He will visit the aged and sick, the discouraged and unfortunate, read and pray with them, bury the dead and marry the lovers, whenever and wherever called without respect to church or creed. This week he married two couples on the same day and two of the contracting parties were members of another church. He is really the servant of the community and he is known only to be trusted and loved. His work in Mexico in the past five years has been good and only good. He has built up a congregation which now numbers 800, and they have a church building which I have seldom seen excelled anywhere. When our ministers and Christian workers are praying for the evangelists we ask kindly and sincerely to be remembered. Our next meeting will be with R. H. Crossfield, of Owensboro, Ky. We begin there September 23. All the people in Mexico are reading THE CHRISTIAN-EVANGELIST while the meeting continues. We are scattering them judiciously through the audiences and at each home with the evangelist's themes on for the week.

Mexico, Mo.　　　　　JAMES SMALL.

❋ ❋

Primary Superintendent Appointed.

It is with great pleasure that I announce that Mrs. Leonora L. Buxton, 3001 East Sixth street, Kansas City, Mo., has been appointed the primary superintendent of the Christian Church Bible schools in Missouri. Mrs. Buxton will soon be in communication with our primary workers in the Sunday-schools of Missouri, and also will be available for certain field work in conventions and institutes, under the direction of the state superintendent. All who desire to consult her in regard to primary work will write her at the above address, and those who desire to secure her services in conventions and institutes will please write to J. H. Hardin, state superintendent, 311 Century building, Kansas City, Mo.

J. H. HARDIN.

❋ ❋

Kentucky Bible Schools.

There are a few items to which we wish to call the attention of our Kentucky Bible schools.

1. We are heavily in debt this year. Unless prompt remittance is made on the part of all delinquent schools, both large and small, we shall come to the state convention in debt for the first time in our history.

2. The program for the Bible school sections of the state convention embraces the names of Marion Lawrence, J. W. McGarvey, E. L. Powell, R. H. Crossfield, Miss Mary A. Finch and President E. Y. Mullins. No finer array of talent has ever been announced. These will speak on Thursday, September 27.

3. The chief topic for discussion in the convention will be our centennial enterprise, "A Bible School Chair in the Bible College." We must raise $25,000 to endow this chair by October 1, 1909. All schools are asked to come prepared to state what share they will assume in the making of this centennial enterprise possible.

This is the most far-reaching step in the interest of Bible school work that has been contemplated by our people. Its accomplishment will insure that every preacher who is educated at the

Charcoal Kills Bad Breath.

Disagreeable Odor Arising From Indigestion or From Any Habit or Indulgence, Can Be Instantly Stopped.

Sample Package Mailed Free.

Other people notice your bad breath where you would not notice it at all. It is nauseating to other people to stand before them and while you are talking, give them a whiff or two of your bad breath. It usually comes from food fermenting on your stomach. Sometimes you have it in the morning—that awful sour, bilious, bad breath. You can stop that at once by swallowing one or two Stuart Charcoal Lozenges, the most powerful gas and odor absorbers ever prepared.

Sometimes your meals will reveal themselves in your breath to those who talk with you. "You've had onions," or "You've been eating cabbage," and all of a sudden you belch in the face of your friend. Charcoal is a wonderful absorber of odors, as every one knows. That is why Stuart's Charcoal Lozenges are so quick to stop all gases and odors of odorous foods, or gas from indigestion.

Don't use breath perfumes. They never conceal the odor, and never absorb the gas that causes the odor. Besides, the very fact of using them reveals the reason for their use. Stuart's Charcoal Lozenges in the first place stop that all sour brash and belching of gas, and make your breath pure, fresh and sweet, just after you've eaten. Then no one will turn his face away from you when you breathe or talk; your breath will be pure and fresh, and besides, your food will taste so much better to you at your next meal. Just try it.

Charcoal does other wonderful things, too. It carries away from your stomach and intestines, all the impurities there massed together and which cause the bad breath. Charcoal is a purifier as well as an absorber.

Charcoal is now by far the best, most easy and mild laxative known. A whole boxful will do no harm; in fact, the more you take the better. Stuart's Charcoal Lozenges are made of pure willow charcoal and mixed with just a faint flavor of honey to make them palatable for you, but not too sweet. You just chew them like candy. They are absolutely harmless.

Get a new, pure, sweet breath, freshen your stomach for your next meal, and keep the intestines in good working order. These two things are the secret of good health and long life. You can get all the charcoal necessary to do these wonderful but simple things by getting Stuart's Charcoal Lozenges. We want you to test these little wonder workers yourself before you buy them. So send us your full name and address for a free sample of Stuart's Charcoal Lozenges. Then after you have tried the sample, and been convinced, go to your druggist and get a 25c box of them. You'll feel better all over, more comfortable, and "cleaner" inside.

Send us your name and address to-day and we will at once send you by mail a sample package, free. Address F. A. Stuart Co., 60 Stuart Bldg., Marshall, Mich.

College of the Bible will be trained for efficient Bible school work, and also superintendents and Bible school workers may educate themselves for their special lines of work.　　ROBT. M. HOPKINS.

Louisville, Ky.

NEWS FROM MANY FIELDS

San Francisco's Relief.

Ninth report of H. Van Kirk, financial secretary of City Board of Evangelization, acting as relief committee, is as follows:

Previously reported	$4,152 16
Christian Church, Mellot, Ind.	3 75
Christian Church, Independence, Mo.	32 80
C. E. Anaconda, Mont.	33 20
C. W. B. M.	250 00
A. C. M. S.	500 00
S. S., Zenith, Os.	7 50
S. S., Charleston, Wash.	3 00
Mrs. M. A. Van Matre, Mineral Point, Wis.	2 00
F. S. Brown, Fruitvale, Cal.	15 00
A. T. Marsh, Fruitvale, Cal.	9 00

Total received to date..............$5,028 31
August 30, 1906.

A Great Rally.

On August 26 we had a great rally at Owensboro, consisting of many of the churches in Daviess county and vicinity, in order to secure a better co-operation between all of them in securing preachers to labor with and for them. The meeting was held in the great tabernacle located on the Chautauqua grounds, and is an ideal place for such a meeting. Fully 1,500 people were in attendance. Bro. Walter M. White, of Lexington, was present and preached a splendid sermon. R. H. Crossfield, the ever ready minister of the Owensboro church, presided with grace and dignity. Dinner was served on the ground in great abundance. All present were happy while there and went away happy.

We have a much better prospect for a more united effort in that section than ever before, and we believe it will result in great good. Brother White preached at night in the Christian church house in Owensboro to the delight of a large audience. W. J. Hudspeth.
Hopkinsville, Ky.

A Successful Campmeeting.

The first annual encampment of the Wichita Mountain Assembly is now a matter of history. The first effort of the kind ever attempted in this new country by any religious people has come and gone and is pronounced a success.

The meeting was held in the military reservation, on Medicine creek, seven miles northwest of Lawton, Okla. The location was ideal in every way, nature having bestowed her richest gifts upon it. Being near five miles from any white settlement, the majority of those who attended the services were encamped on the grounds.

The preaching was done by two of our ablest Oklahoma ministers, O. L. Smith, of El Reno, and W. A. Merrill, of Hobart. To those who know these brethren it is needless for me to say that the work was well done. Being of a widely different type of men, they were able to present the Gospel from different standpoints. Both men are fully imbued with the spirit of Christ and preach the Word with power.

Prof. C. M. Bliss, of El Reno, conducted the song service. Professor Bliss is an artist in his profession. Much of the success of the meeting was due to the excellent song service under his leadership.

The meeting was a success from two standpoints. In the first place the Gospel was preached, the good seed were sown, and in time the harvest must come. In the second place, the meeting resulted in a permanent organization which will mean much to the Disciples in this new country. The association aims to combine some Chautauqua features with the camp-meeting idea which will enlist many who would not otherwise be interested. Once enlisted, they will get the benefit of the teaching which is to be a special feature of the association, and thus the end will be reached.

The officers for the ensuing year are: C. M. Barnes, of Lawton, president; C. M. Bliss of El Reno, vice-president; H. C. Stubblefield of Lawton, secretary, and Charles L. Thornton of Faxon, treasurer. These officers, together with three other members to be chosen later, constitute the executive committee. The next encampment will be held during the summer of 1907 somewhere in the Wichita mountains. H. C. Stubblefield, Secretary.

Colorado Assembly.

My month's vacation was spent at Gato, on the "Moffat road," thirty-six miles from Denver. This is indeed in the "lap of the Rockies," and is the place selected by the Disciples of Colorado for their summer assembly. At this place that marvelous feat of engineering, the Moffat road, reaches the height of 8,000 feet, and the canyon through which dashes the beautiful South Boulder creek opens a little and the tops of the sometimes perpendicular walls fall back giving an ideal location for the encampment.

Already more than a hundred acres of pines, rocks and quicken asps have been surveyed off into large lots and a half dozen permanent cottages have been built. A system of waterworks is being completed and by next season a hotel and a store will be added to the accommodations of the place. It is hard to imagine a more ideal place for vacations and summer homes, and for a religious assembly of Christian people; situated as it is so close to Denver, and yet in the midst of the wildest and most beautiful mountain scenery where intense summer heat is not known, and where a ride of an hour and a half on the train brings one to the top of the continental divide, the region of perpetual snow.

The assembly proper lasted this year two weeks. Sessions were held in the forenoons and evenings, the afternoons being given over to rest and recreation. An effort will be made to have the permanent tabernacle ready for the sessions next year, and no pains will be spared to make the program the very best. Among those who helped make the program a success this year were B. B. Tyler, W. B. Craig, Mrs. Cornelia Miles, Hon. Ben C. Hilliard, Crayton S. Brooks, O. W. Lawrence, Chaplain J. P. Lucas, Dr. Oliva Baldwin, Jesse B. Hasten, L. C. Thompson, Miss Mary Carpenter, Mrs. Sudie E. Flint, E. F. Harris and many others. Too much praise can not be given to J. E. Pickett, the president, for the success of this assembly; so far. On his shoulders has been the burden of arranging the program.

D. B. Titus.

Northwest Kansas Notes.

A. R. Poe, of Colby, comes to Dresden to live and preach half time for this worthy congregation. They have a building recently dedicated and nicely furnished and are hoping for splendid things during Brother Poe's ministry, as he is a worker and has a strong hold on the community already.——M. J. Hibbs is doing a fine work at Hill City and Roscoe, in spite of a long siege of sickness in his family, which has hindered him much.——Brother Gilpin and wife are at Agra, and though they have been there but a short time, have already formed a strong feeling of fellowship, having won the confidence and love of the people. They are young, energetic workers and have an enthusiastic church membership, composed largely of young people whose sterling worth is of great value to the cause in that community. Agra church will prosper.——We hear that Bro. F. U. Harmon is doing some good work in and around Norcatur, and that a church building at Kanona is now assured.——The first service was recently held in our new church building at Lenora. They hope to have a meeting this fall. Brother Mulkey has worked faithfully to accomplish what has been done in this neglected field.——The writer and wife spent two weeks at Logan, presenting Christian evidences and the plea of the Christian church to the people of that community. Large audiences attended and splendid interest was manifested. Charles McVay was present the last week of the meeting and his solos were enjoyed by all.

No organization was effected on account of having to give up the opera house before any permanent work could be accomplished, but they hope to reap from this sowing not many days hence, for the people with one accord gave heed to things which were taught.——We begin at Clay Center on the 9th and will likely be there two weeks or longer, before returning to our work at Ukiah, Cal. Otha Wilkison.

August in Oregon.

Although the month has furnished its share of hot weather, the work in Oregon has forged ahead. One Victory that will cause all to rejoice is the payment of the remaining $450 held against our state work by the Salem State Bank. This is one fruit of the Turner convention and of Brother Rains' visit to Oregon. There remain yet $400 to be paid on the old debt, but there are pledges outstanding to fully cover this amount. If all those making pledges at the state convention and to the secretary prior to the convention, will send in the amounts pledged, the whole debt may be canceled by October 1. If these pledges are not sent in soon they will interfere with the November offering for our missionary enterprises, planned in convention. Remember, brethren, "2,000 conVersions and $6,000 for Oregon missions."

Another Victory was marked by the dedication of a neat and commodious chapel in the town of Woodburn. This is also a fruit of Turner plans. The building was erected by the help of the central district, and is largely the work of our beloved and efficient "church builder," Bro. L. F. Stephens. The writer and two other preachers had the privilege of helping a few days—long enough to testify to the efficiency of Brother Stephens' work. This work is not only a Victory for the central district, but also for the whole brotherhood. Our people now have a suitable home in this important but difficult field. The dedication took place August 26. The dedicatory sermon was preached by our president, J. W. Jenkins, and the evening sermon by Brother Stephens. Everything went off well, and those present pledged more than was asked for on the occasion. Let us have more work like this; it will do us good.

All will regret to learn of the burning of the church at Phoenix, where a little band of Disciples has been unholding the banner of the Christ. They will likely need aid in rebuilding. We are all "one in Christ Jesus." Don't forget November 4.   F. E. BILLINGTON, Cor. Sec.

Cottage Grove, Ore.

The Madison (Mo.) Meeting.

The gifted A. N. Lindsey, New Franklin, Mo., left for his home to-day, after a continuous service here of over four weeks. Seventy-nine, for the most part by baptism, were added. The most remarkable feature was that two-thirds or more were men. There was no unusual excitement, but the whole community was stirred to a permanent betterment. Lindsey is a power in both public and private work, and can do a better work next year than this even. After nineteen months of quiet work on the part of the church and the writer, during which time about 25 were added, and for half-time preaching, repairs, missions and benevolence about $1,700 raised and expended, we were ready for a Victory, but the most sanguine did not anticipate such a great one. Fourteen were added last night, and auditorium and Sunday-school rooms crowded to the doors. This gives us a membership of over 400 and otherwise increases our endowments and possibilities. Lindsey, with a cheerfulness that graciously commends him, took all the burden he could from my shoulders in deference to my physical ailments, and made it one of the most pleasant meetings of my life. He does not count himself a professional evangelist, but has the native and acquired ability to make him a most successful one. Except the regular evening offering, no special calls were made for funds, but by the quiet plan inaugurated by one of the best boards with which I ever labored we will have a surplus in the treasury. Bro. P. Hales, with the chorus he has led for several years, even surpassed himself by the efficient aid of Miss Sinnie Frank at the piano.   I. B. CORWINE,
September 8.   Minister.

HOME DEPARTMENT AND CRADLE ROLL SUPPLIES.

Buttons, Cards, Booklets, and everything else that is helpful in a Sunday-school.

Christian Publishing Co., St. Louis, Mo.

Buffalo Guides.

The following-named brethren have been appointed district excursion managers for the Buffalo convention, to work in connection with the local convention committees. They are in position to give any needed information:

Alabama.—See Georgia.
Arizona.—See California.
Arkansas.—Rev. J. N. Jessup, 1005 Louisiana street, Little Rock.
California.—Rev. W. E. Crabtree, 770 Twenty-first street, San Diego. (Arizona, New Mexico).
Colorado.—Rev. L. C. Thompson, 71 West Byers place, Denver.
Connecticut.—See New England.
District of Columbia.—See Pennsylvania, (Eastern).
Florida.—See Georgia.
Georgia.—Rev. E. L. Shellnut, 27 East Hunter street, Atlanta. (Alabama, Florida).
Idaho.—See Oregon.
Illinois (State).—Rev. F. M. Rogers, 800 S. West Grand avenue, Springfield; Chicago, Rev. A. W. Fortune, 995 W. Congress street, Chicago.
Iowa.—Rev. G. B. Van Arsdall, 1207 Fifth avenue, Cedar Rapids.
Indiana.—Rev. T. J. Legg, 1202 Pleasant street, Indianapolis.
Indian Territory.—See Kansas.
Kansas.—Rev. G. W. Muckley, 600 Waterworks building, Kansas City, Mo.; (Western Missouri, Oklahoma, Indian Territory); Rev. T. A. Abbott and Rev. J. H. Hardin, 311 Century building, Kansas City, Mo.
Kentucky.—Rev. H. W. Elliott, Sulphur.
Louisiana.—Rev. G. Washington Wise, Leesville.
Maryland.—See Pennsylvania, Eastern.
Massachusetts.—See New England.
Michigan.—Rev. C. J. Tanner, 650 Second avenue, Detroit.
Minnesota.—Mr. M. R. Waters, 707 Phoenix building, Minneapolis. (North and South Dakota, Wisconsin).
Mississippi.—Rev. W. W. Phares, McComb City.
Missouri, Eastern—Rev. G. A. Hoffman, Maplewood.
Missouri, Western.—See Kansas.
Montana.—See Oregon.
Nebraska.—Rev. W. A. Baldwin, 541 North Twenty-eighth street, Lincoln.
New England.—Rev. G. A. Reinel, 812 Main street, Worcester, Mass.
New Mexico.—See California.
New York.—City, Rev. S. T. Willis, 1281 Union avenue, New York City; state, Rev. G. B. Townsend, 155 Sixth avenue, Troy.
North Carolina.—Rev. J. Boyd Jones, Wilson. (South Carolina).
North Dakota.—See Minnesota.
Ohio.—State, Rev. S. H. Bartlett, 300 Beckman building, Cleveland; Cincinnati, Mr. R. H. Waggener, southeast corner Ninth and Cutter streets.
Oklahoma.—See Kansas.
Oregon.—Rev. F. E. Billington, Cottage Grove, box 145. (Washington, Idaho, Montana).
Pennsylvania.—Western, Mr. Robert Latimer, 644 Grant street, Pittsburgh. Eastern (New Jersey, Maryland, D. C.), Rev. L. O. Knipp, Plymouth.
South Carolina.—See North Carolina.
South Dakota.—See Minnesota.
Tennessee.—Mr. F. C. McFarland, Chattanooga.
Texas.—Rev. J. C. Mason, box 280, Station A, Dallas.
Virginia.—Rev. H. C. Combs, 104 South Fifth street, Richmond.
Washington.—See Oregon.
West Virginia.—Rev. O. G. White, Huntington.
Wisconsin.—See Minnesota.
Ontario.—Rev. J. M. Van Horn, 35 1-2 Major street, Toronto.
Nova Scotia.—Rev. John Waugh, Milton, N. S. (New Brunswick, P. E. I.).
N. B.—States enclosed in parenthesis are included in district with the state named immediately before.   ELI H. LONG,
Chairman Transportation Committee.

1905 G. H. Clarke became pastor. The contract was let and the work of construction and the raising of funds went steadily on until it was ready to be dedicated to the Lord.

The building is 89x66, and has a basement under the entire structure. It is of pressed brick laid in red mortar, with stone and white mortar trimmings. The foundation is of stone and cement blocks. It is heated by a double furnace. The floor of the main audience room is bowled and seated with circular pews. The Sunday-school room is provided with chairs and can be thrown into the main room. The two will seat about 800 people.

There are three beautiful memorial windows filling the north end of the main audience room. One of the smaller ones is in memory of Mr. and Mrs. George N. Brown, and is a reproduction of "Christ in the Garden." The main window is in honor of Dr. and Mrs. I. B. Washburn, and is a reproduction of "Christ in the Temple." The third is in memory of Jessie Bartoo, and represents "Christ Risen." There are three large rose windows in the gables.

This church was dedicated last Sunday by J. H. O. Smith, of Valparaiso, Ind. Four thousand dollars was called for and almost the entire amount was raised and the house dedicated to God. The building and furnishings cost $11,000. Brother Smith proved himself a master of assemblies, a prince at raising money, an eloquent and faithful preacher of the Gospel. On Monday evening he delivered a practical lecture on "Gumption," to a crowded house. The day will long be remembered by the church as one of the high days in its history.

G. H. CLARKE.

Salem, Ind.

On August 26, after a year of hard labor, the good people of Salem, Ind., gathered to dedicate their beautiful new church. It was certainly a beautiful sight, the house complete to the minutest details, the grounds beautiful with green and flowers and the interior abloom from choir loft to entrance. Everywhere seemed to be gladness.

The house was full when services began, and through the intense heat every one remained deeply interested in every part of the program. The music was fine, the grand new vocalion adding greatly to the inspiration of all the services.

After the communion service F. T. Porter, of New Albany, preached the dedicatory sermon.

The afternoon was filled with music and short, bright addresses by local ministers. The Presbyterian minister said one thing he noticed was that we (the Church of Christ) were everywhere in evidence, and nothing could put us down or put us out of sight. All seemed anxious to forget they were anything but Christians.

The treasurer's report was an especially interesting part of the program. We learned that about $4,500 had been spent, and every cent of indebtedness was paid and money in the treasury.

The dedication by the membership in concert was long to be remembered. In the evening watchwords were called for, and out of a large number of very suggestive ones the church voted to adopt "This church a magnet to draw and hold all classes to Christ and Christian living." Under this it was expected to make use of many suggested plans for growth and work.

Then came the evening sermon by F. T. Porter, which was given fine attention.

The new church at Salem is a fact because Bro. W. Y. Allen, the minister for the past five years, had the will, executive ability and untiring energy to make it so. He alone thought it possible, but all stood loyally by him in his plans, and now a brick building that has aid society, C. E., prayer-meeting and study rooms, besides the main auditorium, takes the place of the old brick of one room. The aid society, as usual, was most useful. The young ladies and Sunday-school also shared in the burdens. This is the sixth church Brother Allen has built. May it ever be spiritually as materially a monument to him. May the love of his people and community ever, as now, be his.

MRS. F. T. PORTER.

Evangelistic

We invite ministers and others to send reports of meetings, additions and other news of the churches. It is especially requested that additions be reported as "by confession and baptism," or "by letter."

Special to THE CHRISTIAN-EVANGELIST.

Coffeyville, Kan., Sept. 10.—Meeting one week old; twenty-eight additions. Ellis Purlee is pastor.—Cooksey and Parks.

Special to THE CHRISTIAN-EVANGELIST.

Belpre, Kan., Sept. 5.—Meeting closed; 50 additions, $2,700 raised for new building. Expect to dedicate $4,000 house in four months; then we return for another meeting. Chicago next.—H. E. Wilhite.

Special to THE CHRISTIAN-EVANGELIST.

Mexico, Mo., Sept. 9.—Seven confessions to-day, 13 added to date, in the Small-St John meeting. Brother Small is preaching some great sermons and the whole town is hearing the Gospel. The Christian church was packed on Sunday night with 1,000 people who sat for over one and one-half hours through song and sermon in heat of 90 degrees. His sermon on "Beauty and Basis of Christian Union" is great. To indicate the temper of our fellowship in Mexico the pastor of the Christian church preached in the Baptist church to a large audience Sunday morning. We believe in fellowship. The field is great and difficult, but we believe victory will be ours.—A. W. Kokendoffer.

Arkansas.

Evadale, Sept. 3.—One baptism. Work is in progress on our new church buildings at Osceola and Blytheville. The outlook is fine for crops of all kinds in northeast Arkansas this year.—James H. Brooks.

California.

Ventura, Sept. 4.—Two additions, one by confession and baptism; one reclaimed.—Dan Trundle.

District of Columbia.

Washington, Sept. 4.—Present at ministers' meeting; F. D. Power, E. B. Bagby, Walter F. Smith, J. E. Stuart, W. T. Laprade and the writer. Reports: Vermont Avenue (F. D. Power), 1 baptism, 1 by statement, and 2 by letter; Vier na, Va. (W. T. Laprade), 4 by letter; Ninth Street (E. B. Bagby), 3 baptisms and 1 restored; Thirty-fourth Street (Claude C. Jones), 3 by letter. W. F. Smith had a baptism in a meeting at Luray, Va. C. C. Jones had 1 baptism and received 1 by letter in a meeting at Hyattstown, Md. Total additions reported 19, 7 baptisms, 7 restored, 1 by statement and 10 by letter.—Claude C. Jones, Sec.

Idaho.

Nampa, Sept. 7.—Nine accessions in five days, all by letter and statement.—Geo. C. Ritchey.

Weiser, Sept. 6.—One confession. Our work is growing in interest and we are hopeful of the future.—G. M. Read.

Illinois.

Princeton, Sept. 3.—One added by letter.—Cecil C. Carpenter.

Walshville, Aug. 30.—I just closed a ten days' meeting with 27 additions; 24 baptisms, 3 otherwise.—J. E. Story.

Litchfield, Aug. 28.—Work on the new church progressing finely. One from the Baptists two weeks ago.—M. S. Johnson.

Indiana.

Ligonier, Sept. 1.—Three added here recently. H. F. MacLane, of Hiram, O., is to hold a meeting.—I. N. A.

Indianapolis, Sept. 4.—At our regular service at Plum Creek Church, Rush county, yesterday, there was one confession and baptism—a man 80 years old and prominent in the affairs of the county. We begin a protracted meeting there September 27.—L. E. Murray.

Bluff Creek, Sept. 5.—We have just closed a

nineteen days' meeting with 23 additions—18 by confession, 5 by letter. There were seven heads of families in the number. The church is doing well.—Clay Trusty.

Indian Territory.

Tuttle, Sept. 7.—During my first month as Living Link evangelist for the Chickasaw nation I visited seven places and attended the territorial convention. Held one short meeting resulting in the organization of a congregation with 35 members, 19 of whom were by primary obedience. Would like to hear from churches or communities in my territory desiring my services during the fall or winter. Write me at Norman, Okla.—Robert E. Rosenstein.

Iowa.

Altoona, Sept. 3.—One confession last night. Work going on nicely.—J. Windbigler.

Des Moines.—Evangelist C. L. Organ is in a great tent meeting at Luther, with fine interest.—Will H. Betts.

Burlington, Sept. 4.—By confession 4, reclaimed 3, letter 1, statement 1. From Methodist church 1 by letter.—F. D. Eisenhart.

Kansas.

Plainville, Sept. 2.—Two added here. One man, 76 years of age, was baptized yesterday.—N. Ferd Engle.

Louisiana.

New Orleans.—Our work here is prospering, though many members are on vacation.—W. M. Taylor.

Michigan.

Petersburg, Sept. 4.—Two additions by baptism since last report.—V. Hayes Miller.

Missouri.

Braymer.—We more than raised our apportionment.—S. W. Crutcher.

St. Joseph, Sept. 3.—One confession at King Hill Christian Church, making 43 accessions since February at regular services.—Clay Baird.

Wallace, Aug. 29.—Including two already reported, 12 additions in a two weeks' meeting at Wallace. All were immersed.—W. A. Oldham.

King City, Sept. 3.—One from the Presbyterians at Miami Sept. 2.—Evangelist C. O. McFarland begins a meeting for us there the first Sunday in November.—C. W. Comstock.

Canton, Sept. 3.—We just closed a two weeks' meeting at Ariel, Ralls Co., with 14 additions—2 from the Catholics, 2 from the Methodists, 1 from the Baptists, 2 restored.—John E. Gorton, minister.

Tuxedo, Sept. 1.—There have been 22 additions to the church since my return from California, June 10, 20 of them by primary obedience. All departments of the work growing.—J. A. Bennett, minister.

Bucklin.—The meeting conducted by Alfred Munyon and home forces is two weeks old with 25 additions, 19 by confession and baptism. The meeting will continue another week. The distribution of THE CHRISTIAN-EVANGELIST is proving very helpful.

Sweet Springs, Sept. 8.—We have just concluded what is said to have been the best meeting in the history of the Christian church in Houstonia. There were 33 added to the church, 30 by baptism and 3 by statement. The whole church was edified by the earnest preaching of R. B. Briney, of Lexington, Mo.—F. B. Elmore.

St. Joseph, Sept. 3.—Three confessions and one addition by statement to Mitchell Park congregation during August. J. L. Harris, representing the Christian Publishing Company, was here Sept. 3, and with our assistance secured about thirty subscriptions to THE CHRISTIAN-EVANGELIST. More subscriptions will follow.—C. A. Lowe.

Trenton, Mo., September 8.—We are driving through Missouri in our gospel wagon and are having good opportunities to preach the Gospel. We have closed a meeting at Topsy, where we preached in the Christian Union Church, with interest unabated to the close. At present we are preaching in the Church of Christ.—W. H. and E. B. Van Deusen.

Braymer, Sept. 3.—Two confessions at Cowgill yesterday. Preached 10 days at Pee Dee Church, a mission point in Chariton Co., and left the meeting in the hands of J. S. Wolf, of Keytesville. The house is owned by Baptists, Christians and Holiness people. T. A. Abbott dedicated the house a few years ago, and while we have only 5 members I think we will succeed at Pee Dee.—S. W. Crutcher.

Ohio.

Collinwood, Sept. 3.—J. M. Rudy, of Sedalia, Mo., will begin a union tent meeting here September 9. M. L. Buckley is pastor of the Church of Christ there, which is the largest church in that town of 7,000 population. Collinwood is a railroad town.—M. L. Buckley.

Texas.

Dallart, Sept. 6.—Two additions.—John Mullen.

Denison, Sept. 3.—Five additions during the

month of August, 2 by letter and by confession and baptism.—George W. Lee.

Greenville, Sept. 3.—Two additions by baptism and two by letter.—J. W. Holsapple.

Commerce, Sept. 3.—One addition by statement yesterday; 119 additions in 17 months to the church at Commerce. Offering for church extension yesterday will be nearly double our apportionment.—W. A. Wherry, minister.

Hillsboro, Sept. 1.—Closed a nine days' meeting with J. P. Howard at Frost, August 30. In all there were 18 additions—11 by confession and baptism, one from the Baptist, two reclaimed, and four by letter.—Ernest J. Bradley.

Santa Anna, Sept. 8.—The Hamlin-Huston meeting here is now 15 days old with 45 additions. Four services almost entirely rained out by the unusually heavy rains. Best audiences in the history of our work in this town.—J. A. Arnold, pastor.

Washington.

Davenport, Sept. 3.—Doubled our apportionment for church extension. Prospects brightening up.—O. M. Thomason, pastor.

Ellensburg.—Two confessions and one by letter here yesterday. One of the converts was the editor of our daily. Two other confessions not reported; 133 added since January 1. Outlook good.—C. H. Hilton.

Waitsburg, Sept. 3.—Since last report there have been seven additions to the church—four by confession and baptism and three by letter. Also three additions at Prescott, where I preached a few evenings—two confessions and 1 by letter. We close our three years' work here September 30.—W. T. Adams.

❖ ❖

Ministerial Exchange.

C. C. Maple, minister at Fredericksburg, Wayne county, Ohio, would like to correspond with an evangelist who will hold a meeting for free-will offering. He will furnish tent and assist in the meeting.

J. J. Limerick, of Corning, Cal., will be ready to engage in evangelistic meetings in the near future.

C. R. L. Vawter, minister of the First Christian Church, Shelby, Ohio, can recommend two ministers to churches needing pastors if they will address him enclosing stamp for reply. One is a middle-aged, experienced worker, the other a bright young Bethany College graduate.

The church at Fairhope, Ala., across the bay from Mobile, desires a preacher to begin October 1. The church can pay $600. There is a daily boat service to Mobile, a good building and the church is well organized. The church prefers a young, active married man. No brokendown preacher need apply. Parties desiring to know more of this field write Claude E. Hill, Mobile, or A. H. Mershon, Fairhope, Ala.

Christian Endeavor

By GEO. L. SNIVELY.

September 23, 1906.

A STRONG WILL.—1 Peter 4:1-11.

(A Temperance Service.)

DAILY READINGS.

M. A Strong Will.	1 Peter 4:1-11.
T. Against Temptation.	Psa. 141:1-10.
W. For the Right.	Psa. 144:1-11.
T. Against Appetite.	Mark 5:1-6.
F. Against Custom.	Acts 15:1-11.
S. To Help Another.	Philemon 8-19.
S. A Will to Abstain.	Num. 6:1-5.

"Vice is a monster of such horrid mien,
To be dreaded, needs but to be seen.
But, seen too oft, familiar with her face,
We first endure, then pity, then embrace."

There is that so suggestive of omnipotence in a dauntless "No" as to establish the divine origin of the one who pronounces it. All the future belongs to the man who will make a "No" ring out over the multitude and then not waver before lions' dens, fiery furnaces, or contemptuous sneers.

To one with God's sense of proportion he that governeth himself is greater than he that governeth a city but is subject to his own caprices and the inbreathings of Satan. The consciousness of self-mastery under Bible directions is a most superb and satisfactory possession. The feeling of true royalty and sovereignty over the empire of one's own life is worth more than it costs of self-restriction and denial.

In all the realm of diplomacy there is no other art equal to that of saying "Yes" and "No" honestly. When one whose honesty has been proven takes refuge in either of these fortresses the batteries of the evil one are trained elsewhere—he knows they are invulnerable. When an irresolute man says either, the enemy has located him in fragile defenses, concentrates his artillery on this one point and soon receives his capitulation.

The invaders' ammunition was almost exhausted. Another charge and they would have fled in confusion across the border. Alas, the patriot defenders knew it not; they were disheartened, they rested on their arms, and that land is a vassal that might have been a new star in the constellation of freedom. So with those withstanding wine. Perhaps the last thirst pang has been endured. Resist longer, assume the offensive, and perchance this time the fiend of the still will flee.

Intelligence will save the strong-willed from the weakness of obstinacy. Resoluteness has to do with principles rather than specific acts. The stubborn man may say, "I will never enter a saloon," and will see a tempted man stand before the bar and will not enter to lead him away because of his vow. Another equally resolute would vow, "I will not patronize the saloon," and is free to rescue the unfortunate. A will of steel adaptable to circumstances is better than one of unadjustable cast iron.

In knightly tournaments determination, stamina, persistency were often more potent factors in the winning of the victory than length of blade or strength of arm. In the tempted's conflicts with Bacchus these same qualities are much more availing than high-sounding declarations of independence or scathing denunciation. In these contests between men and the rum demon choose as victors not the men of handsome form, stately carriage, brilliancy of mind and eloquence of tongue, but rather those of courage, grit, indomitable will.

Midweek Prayer-Meeting

September 19, 1906.

THE VALUE OF TEMPTATION.—
James 1:12.

"Yield not to temptation,
For yielding is sin;
Each victory will help you
Some other to win;
Press valiantly onward,
Dark passions subdue;
Look ever to Jesus;
He'll carry you through."

It never has been satisfactorily proven that there is value in briars, diseases and temptations. In themselves they are part of the primal curse. The world would be happier and better without them. It is our duty to eradicate them from the earth and try to make of land and sea a paradise without a thorn, pain, pest or tempter. God is not the author of temptations. They spring from Satan's baleful influence among men.

God sends us the good angels—opportunities to do good and become better—and it is our joy to receive them. Satan sends the bad angels—temptations to do wrong—and it is our salvation to reject them. Many treat temptations as if they were heavenly emissaries to be cherished and reluctantly relinquished, if at all—folly as great as warming the dormant viper in one's bosom. No matter how luring they are, they are demoniacal and the wise will treat them as deadly foes.

Temptations are not necessary to the development of sterling characters. That the youth is temperate can be otherwise determined than by beguiling him into the saloon. Many sins that haunt the memories of men and taint many a beautiful ideal would never have been known to them nor injured them had they not been deceived into believing that they were not really virtuous till they had come into ungloved contact with sin and vanquished it. Scars may show we have been through the flames, but why burn tinsel in our faces for the sake of having scars?

There is a sinful temptation to put one's self in the way of temptation. Men have gone into the lion's cage to see what the lion would do. The lion did according to the lion nature, but the inquisitive adventurer never told of it. Men have gone all the way to hell just to see what is along the route and to determine whether they could resist the fascinations. Amidst flames and wailings they learned they were baubles in Satan's hands, who leered as he tossed them toward the iron gates.

If there is value in temptation it lies in revealing to us our weakness and sinfulness and absolute need of a Father's love and an elder Brother's ceaseless vigils and companionship. For there is nothing really beautiful or attractive in any article of temptation Satan fabricates or in any staging, sylvan, astronomical, commercial, social or political, he may set. It is not outer charms so much as inner depravity that lures, affects our judgment, paralyzes our moral sensibilities and destroys us. May

all temptations drive us only closer to our sources of strength and grace.

That God made the elements of which temptations are composed in no wise makes him responsible for the wicked combinations men have made of them. God never built a still nor inspired others to. As well hold him responsible for every murderous bullet as for a compounded narcotic. There is grace acquired by resisting invading temptations, but guilt involved in helping one into being, or setting it in the way, or in any wise subjecting others to its influence.

※ ※ ※

Sunday-School

September 23, 1906.

THIRD QUARTERLY REVIEW.

Memory Verse, Matt. 16:25.

GOLDEN TEXT.—And they were astonished at his doctrine; for his word was with power.—Luke 4:32.

The lessons of the past quarter are from the latter part of the ministry of Jesus, beginning about the time of his final departure from Galilee and ending in Tuesday of Passion Week. Most of the lessons are from the period known as the Perean ministry.

In every one of the lessons we find presented some important items of the teaching of Jesus. In these final months of his ministry we would certainly expect that he would be dealing with no trivial matter but giving the last touch of emphasis to the teaching which he considered most vitally important. The passages chosen for the lessons are fairly representative of the body of his teaching during this period.

For the review, therefore, especially with adult classes, it will be profitable to disregard the historical incidents and to summarize and systematize the teachings of Jesus as found in these lessons. Every teacher and student should go over the lessons and make out such a list as the following (only fuller, if possible), giving the important teachings of the several lessons:

1. Jesus and the Children.—Humility and forgiveness; the need of sacrifice for salvation; God's care for the lost.

2. The Duty of Forgiveness.—Divine forgiveness granted only to the forgiving; the efficacy of prayer.

3. The Good Samaritan.—Helpfulness to the poor; obligation to help all needy persons, regardless of race or condition.

4. Jesus Teaching How to Pray.—God is a loving Father; men are God's children; therefore pray with confidence.

5. Jesus Dines with a Pharisee.—The supreme value of man as compared with things or institutions; humility.

6. False Excuses.—Contrast between God's willingness to save and man's unwillingness to be saved; the Gospel for the poor and despised.

7. The Parable of the Two Sons.—God's love for the lost; the sonship even of sinners; the salvability of man; duty toward the lowly and outcast.

8. The Judge, Pharisee and Publican.—Persistence in prayer; humility, even with sin, better than self-sufficient righteousness.

9. The Rich Young Ruler.—Insufficiency of legal righteousness; necessity of entire surrender; danger of riches.

10. Bartimaeus and Zaccheus.—Mercy on the poor; kindness to the despised; a hated sinner saved by friendship.

11. Jesus Enters Jerusalem in Triumph.—A peaceful triumph; rebuke to unholy traffic in the name of religion; pity for the poor and halt.

12. Jesus Silences Pharisees and Sadducees.—Political loyalty consistent with religious liberty; the resurrection and a spiritual state.

Make a topical grouping of these and any other moral and spiritual principles that Jesus taught in these lessons. What did he teach about God? About man? About the duty of man to man? About the relation of man to God? Are any principles much emphasized in the teaching of Jesus which are usually neglected at this day? Does Jesus seem to omit or touch lightly upon any things which the church has been in the habit of emphasizing?

❊ ❊

SKINS ON FIRE WITH ECZEMA

Instantly Relieved by a Single Application of Cuticura Ointment.

The Great Skin Cure, preceded by a warm bath with Cuticura Soap. This treatment, when followed in the severer forms with mild doses of Cuticura Resolvent Pills, affords instant relief, permits rest and sleep, and points to a speedy cure in the most torturing and disfiguring of itching, burning and scaly humors, eczemas, rashes and inflammations, from infancy to age. A single set (costing $1.00) is often sufficient to cure when the usual remedies fail.

Current Literature

THE RELIGION OF THE NEW TESTAMENT. By Prof. Weiss. Funk and Wagnalls Company, New York. Pages 440. Price $2.00 net.

It was fifty years ago that the author of this volume began his academic career with a lecture on "The Relation of Exegesis to Biblical Theology." In that address was emphasized the fact that a purely historical account of the different types of doctrine furnished by the theology of the New Testament must be supplemented by a work giving the underlying unity of this diversity. This book is the outcome of this idea. It is a summary of dogmatic conclusions, the author's answer as to what the religion of the New Testament really is. His aim is to permit the Scriptures to speak for themselves. We may have more to say about the book later. Though we think the distinguished professor makes some mistakes, his book is one that has to be reckoned with as that of a scholar and a man who speaks out of long experience.

❖

QUESTIONS OF FAITH. A Series of Lectures on the Creed. New York. A. C. Armstrong and Son. Pages 212; price $1.50.

Here we have some of the best thought, by some of the foremost theologians, on some of the greatest questions of our religion. The book appeals to every thinking man for any one of the three reasons we have suggested. The writers are all Scotchmen and holding front rank in that country where theology is almost as much discussed as oatmeal is eaten. "What is God?" is treated by Prof. James Orr. Prof. H. R. Mackintosh discusses "Is Christ the Son of God?" Dr. Marcus Dods considers the question, "Did Christ Rise from the Dead?" Prof. John Laidlaw gives his answer to the question, "What do We Mean by the Holy Spirit?" Principal Lindsay writes on "What is the Catholic Church?" Prof. James Denney answers the question, "Can Sin be Forgiven?" and P. Carnegie Simson considers the problem, "Is There Life After Death?" These various themes were presented in seven lectures to enormous British audiences. They form a fine apologetic, and the fact that they were cast for popular presentation and go straight to the heart of the matters of which they treat is their greatest merit.

❖

THE LIFE AND WORK OF THE REV. E. J. PECK AMONG THE ESKIMOS. By the Rev. Arthur Lewis, New York. A. C. Armstrong and Son. Pages 350, price $1.75.

From time to time heralds of the gospel have worked on the Greenland, Labrador, and other northern coasts, but to Edmund James Peck belongs the distinction of being the first missionary who has devoted his whole life to the Eskimos. As a lad he entered the British navy in which he served for ten years. During this time his heart and mind were being prepared for the conviction which came to him that he could be useful as a Christian worker in the polar regions. After a few months spent in the training school of the Church Missionary Society of London, he went to his chosen field in 1876, so that for about thirty years he has been breaking the word to "that people whose native name, 'Innuet,' means 'The people', and who have the belief that they really are the salt of the earth and the highest type of humanity." This book is as interesting as a novel, and we wish we had the space to give many excerpts or a lengthy summary of its contents. The ordinary life of the native is graphically set forth, and we glean here what we do not get from most books written about the northern seas. How brave a man is this England missionary may be

seen from the fact that but one ship each year reaches the station on the Little Whale River, and that only once in six months does the overland mail come to him.

What Principles Are Involved?

J. H. Garrison, Editor CHRISTIAN-EVANGELIST:

I am interested in your paper and am in love with the spirit of charity and co-operation with other Christian bodies, but as to federation, I do not understand and would like to be informed: as to what extent so-called federation put in practice might involve the foundation principles for which the Church of Christ stands. I wish information that I may know myself and also give answer when asked.   MRS. M. C. PETERSON.
Beaver City, Neb.

While we feel that the question asked in the foregoing has been sufficiently answered in the discussion in our columns, we have no disposition to refuse answer to the courteous and evidently sincere question which our sister asks. Federation as it is proposed and advocated by many leaders in all the religious bodies, is simply a method of co-operation among Christian people to the extent that is possible, under present conditions, without any sacrifice of conscience or principle. It, therefore, involves the principle of brother love, of the charity that thinketh no evil, and of the unity of the spirit—principles which are

vital and fundamental in our religious movement. It does not involve the violation of any of these "foundation principles," but it involves the putting into practice of these principles, just as far as can be done. Of course no one among us is opposed to this kind of Federation, when he understands what it is. Nothing different is proposed.—EDITOR.

To the Editor of THE CHRISTIAN-EVANGELIST:

How much we need divine guidance in all the walks of life, the many pitfalls for unwary feet, the great strength of will power needed to overcome the evil. When we are happy we think the world a good place and think little of the future, but when sorrow comes and the heart is sad everything seems to say, "Look higher." I would like to hear from others on this subject. Personally I do not believe it was intended for us mortals to be perfectly happy on this earth. If so, we would set our hearts too much on "things that perish with the using." This subject is an old one but much could yet be said upon it, and as I write, these words come to me—

"Must I be carried to the skies
On flowery beds of ease,
While others fought to win the prize
And sail through bloody seas."
Shelbina, Mo.   MRS. SHERMAN SMITH.

Local Federation a Blessing.

To the Editor of THE CHRISTIAN-EVANGELIST:

For seven consecutive Lord's day evenings we have tested "Federation" in union services, and we arise to say that, so far as Ponca City is concerned, federation will work, and it has worked here without the sacrifice of a single Gospel declaration, and hence nobody sacrificed any conscience in the federation. Our audiences were large and all the churches engaged,—Methodists, Baptists, Presbyterians and Christians greatly enjoyed the services. We are all now making preparations for big revival meeting. Our work in the Christian church moves along nicely.
                              R. H. LOVE, pastor.
Ponca City, Okla.

Diocesan Bishops.

To the Editor of THE CHRISTIAN-EVANGELIST:

Does the New Testament teach that there are bishops or elders other than those of the local congregation?

Did not the Apostle Paul's "care of all the churches" grow out of his office as apostle, instead of out of his office as bishop or elder. Yours for truth,   J. H. BOYD.

No, there are no bishops or elders known to the New Testament except those for local churches. The apostles, no doubt, had a sort of general supervision of all the churches, at least within certain districts where they labored, but, as indicated, this oversight was by virtue of their apostolic office. The Diocesan Bishop came in later than New Testament time though the advocates of "the Historic Episcopate" hold that the seeds of this new order of things were sown by the apostles, yet, as it seems to us, without sufficient evidence.—EDITOR.

Home Study College Courses,

leading to degrees. History, Evidences, Science, Languages, the Bible and sacred Literature. Over a thousand students enrolled. Full particulars free. Write Pres. Chas. J. Burton, Christian College, Oskaloosa, Iowa.

The Home Department

"Step Lively, Please!"

As up and down this world I fare,
And try to get to anywhere,
This startling cry assaults the air:
　"Step lively, please!"

If on the trolley car I seek
My way to find by question meek,
With strident voice conductors shriek:
　Step lively, please!"

If from the ferryboat I go
To pick my way through mud or snow,
Loud the policeman shouts his "Ho!
　Step lively, please!"

Then into upper air I fly,
To take the "L," and with it try
To flee from that pursuing cry:
　"Step lively, please!"

At last I turn my weary feet
Down subway stairs beneath the street—
To hear, alas! the guard repeat:
　"Step lively, please!"

I wonder will it be my fate
To hear, St. Peter at the gate
Say: "Come, you are a little late.
　Step lively, please!"　　—The Century.

❧ ❧

The Bronze Vase.

BY J. BRECKENRIDGE ELLIS.

PART III.

CHAPTER XI.

There was an awkward silence as Raymund and Rhoda stared at the uncle, now seen for the first time; then Mr. William Hodges turned to Miss Pinns inquiringly. "What is wanted?" he asked. "Whatever you do, Miss Pinns, is approved by me."

"These young people," said Miss Pinns, showing her black tooth at the twins in her most hostile manner, "claim that you are their uncle."

"Nonsense," said the old man, leaning heavily upon his two canes, and staring hard through the upper division of his divided lenses.

"That's what I told them," cried Miss Pinns, triumphantly. "Of course, in a sense you are everybody's uncle," and she nodded her head toward the sign of the three golden balls. Mr. Hodges looked rather displeased at this, and said to Raymund, "Now, sir, what do you want?"

"I am Raymund Revore, and this is my sister Rhoda. Our mother is dead— she was your sister—and we come here, hoping you can help us, for we have nothing."

Miss Pinns looked inquiringly at the old man. He said: "What was your mother's name?"

"Susie Revore. We lived here till Rhoda and I were six years old, then we moved to Crawley. Mother wrote to you from time to time, but you never answered."

"Well!" cried Miss Pinns, "that ought to have told you it was no use coming here!"

"Your mother was my half-sister," said the old man, begrudgingly.

"And so," cried Miss Pinns, "he is only your half-uncle, and that doesn't count!"

"I had nothing to answer your mother," continued Mr. Hodges. "I was sorry for her, but I am poor myself. Sometimes I thought I would write just to tell her I was sorry, but somehow I didn't. When you don't see a person, you neglect such things. I am a poor man to-day. I don't know what I can do for you."

"Are you a pawnbroker, Uncle William?" asked Raymund, doubtfully.

"No," said Mr. Hodges, turning red. "My business is second-hand clothes and other odds and ends. In connection with the clothing department it is true I conduct what you might call a pawnshop; but it is purely a side issue. I should never call myself a pawnbroker, or allow any one else to do so."

"I should think not!" cried Miss Pinns.

"Uncle William," said Rhoda, walking up to him, "can't you take us in, and let us help you? We have no other relation in the world; you are our only chance; don't send us away, when we have no place to go!"

"Don't stand so close to Mr. Hodges," exclaimed Miss Pinns, "you will strike one of his canes."

The bowed old man looked at Rhoda uneasily. "As I said, I am a poor man. How can I afford to keep two healthy young appetites?"

"We do not eat very much," said Raymund, hopefully, "and we are in such trouble!"

"We have troubles that belong to us," said Miss Pinns, "and they are enough for us to nurse without borrowing other people's offsprings."

"Uncle William!" said Rhoda, laying her hand on his arm, "I can cook for you and clean your house and do as much as a woman. And Raymund is strong and always ready to help."

"The room over this shop," said Mr. Hodges, "is just filled with goods. You might sleep there."

"No beds!" cried Miss Pinns.

"Those second-hand beds," said Mr. Hodges, in a conciliatory voice.

"Poof!" cried Miss Pinns, impatiently plumping herself down upon the high stool and striking the leg with an impatient heel. "Poof!" Mr. Hodges looked at Miss Pinns as if he hardly dared meet her eyes, then gazed upon the eager blue eyes and the silken hair of Rhoda. Oh, what a difference. No wonder Rhoda won the day! Presently she and Raymund went out to the lamppost to tell Wizzen they were to stay, and Wizzen agreed to notify them, should he move Mrs. Weed from the vacant lot. That night the brother and sister slept in the barn-like space above the shop. It was only a half-story, and the roof came down to the floor on three sides. In the highest place there was barely room to stand up. There was a variety of bedsteads, from which they selected two, and any number of quilts and spreads and pillows. They had no light in the room to go to bed by, but through the one low window came the rays from the street. Mr. Hodges was a miser, and would not allow them the use of a lamp. The attic, for such the place really was, was cumbered with broken and mended furniture, and it was easy enough to partition off Rhoda's corner and give her perfect privacy. She felt strange in the gloomy place with the roof so low she might have reached up from her bed to touch the ceiling. Although furniture was stacked all about her, she did not feel that she was alone, and presently to test her walls, she whispered, "Raymund!"

Then Raymund from his bed whispered, "What is it?"

"Good night," whispered Rhoda, smiling in the darkness, and knowing he could hear, she fell asleep. The days passed with their uncle William were uneventful. Most of the housekeeping was thrust upon the girl. Raymund was taught to clean and press old clothes. He and his uncle spent most of the day in the back room at this work. Miss Pinns managed the shop and its owner. She had originally been employed as Mr. Hodges's housekeeper, and while he attended to customers, she had kept the house clean and had done the cooking. Gradually she had risen in the world, and as she rose Mr. Hodges fell. Miss Pinns had known how to play upon his emotions, all of which were directly connected with his own personal money-question. Though the old man had no kindred except the orphans, he toiled from early dawn till night in making all he could and trying to save all he had. Miss Pinns encouraged him as nobody else ever had. She made him think that she admired his stinginess, that she considered his miserliness a noble quality; and to the degree that she made his conscience easy, Mr. Hodges felt the need of Miss Pinns. She may have had a great deal of heart, but it never appeared in her business relations. When some poor wretch entered the shop to pawn his last piece of jewelry, Miss Pinns would beat him down to the last penny, and then send him away with a generous display of her black tooth that said: "I have half a mind to give you up to the police!" Mr. Hodges never attended to the work of the pawnshop. He despised it, and would have despised himself for having it run, if Miss Pinns had not known how to ease the burden of his conscience. It was not from philanthropy or pity that the lady was so careful of the old gentleman, or that she made herself so necessary to him. She had not been his housekeeper longer than a week before she had made up her mind to marry him in spite of himself. The old bach-

---

A Noted Minister and Doctor of Atlanta, Ga., is Meeting with Wonderful Success.

Those who have long doubted whether there really is a permanent cure for catarrh will be glad to learn that a southern physician, Rev. J. W. Blosser, M. D., of Atlanta, Ga., has discovered a method whereby catarrh can be cured to the very last symptom without regard to climate or condition. So that there may be no misgivings about it, he will send a free sample to any man or woman without expecting payment. The regular price of the remedy is $1.00 for a box containing one month's treatment.

The Doctor's remedy is radically different from all others, and the results he has achieved seem to mark a new era in the scientific cure of catarrh, foul breath, hawking and spitting, stopped-up feeling in nose and throat, coughing spells, difficult breathing, catarrhal deafness, asthma, bronchitis and the many other symptoms of a bad case of catarrh.

If you wish to see for yourself what this remarkable remedy will do, send your name and address to Dr. J. W. Blosser, 475 Walton St., Atlanta, Ga., and you will receive the free package and an illustrated book.

elor had held her at bay thus long, but Miss Pinns could afford to bide her time, because she was so much younger; she felt sure she would have him at last, and what was a good deal more important, as she regarded it, she would have the shop, too. Mr. Hodges might talk as much as he pleased about being a poor man. Miss Pinns knew better, and she knew he had not only a snug sum of money in the bank, but a larger amount buried somewhere about the place. Where it was buried she had never been able to discover, but she was watching.

Of course, the busy life of the orphans interfered somewhat with their studies, but not fatally. Raymund bought coal oil out of his own money, and he worked so diligently that Mr. Hodges could not begrudge his using it in one of his second-hand lamps. To one looking for an excuse to keep from having to study, the stay at the pawnshop would have seemed a perfect gold mine. There were enough excuses to have supplied a hundred high school students. Rhoda cooked, scrubbed, swept, dusted, marketed, and, thanks to the second-hand dresses that were given her as a reward, kept herself neat. Raymund ironed, stamped, applied gasoline and various other liquids to discolored fabrics with a skill that constantly grew finer and surer, and even sewed. But study they would. There was no other way for them to ever become the man and woman they were resolved to become, and, fortunately, they realized this truth. On Mr. Omer's farm, while acting as nurse to Baby, Raymund had started out as he meant to continue. In the orphan home, Rhoda, though busily pressed by cares and surrounded by many noisy children, had entered upon her career. Her first success in that career came while living with her uncle. Behold! In one of the great St. Louis dailies there appeared one Sunday morning, almost engulfed in a mass of special articles and colored illustrations, the following:

"A CROWN OF OTHER HALVES.
"By RHODA REVOEL.

"When but a child, so many deeds
　Of good I longed to do;
But strength was wanting my young hands—
　Was it not so with you?

"Good works I started many times
　While earth and heaven smiled,
Then had to leave them half undone
　Because I was a child.

"Now in old age among the wreck
　Of hopes deferred I stand,
I find the cloak of good I weave
　Half finished in my hand.

"Last night I dreamt myself beyond
　The storms of life's wild sea.
An angel came and brought the Crown
　Of Other Halves to me,—

"The other halves of deeds half wrought;
　The second word of kindness
The aid that should have followed thought,
　The chance lost in our blindness.

"And when I woke, I said, 'Henceforth
　No doubt shall make me shirk.
Where'er, whene'er I can, I will
　Begin some loving work.

"And if to finish it, the power
　Should never here be given,
Perhaps the Other Half may help
　To gild my crown in heaven."

"Why, Rhoda!" exclaimed Raymund, with a surprised smile, as he came down stairs to go with her to church and found her poring over this article, "you have bought a Sunday paper. How reckless!" For he knew nothing of her plot.

"Come here, Ray," said Rhoda, and she tried hard to keep her voice from quavering. "I want to show you something!" Raymund peeped over her shoulder and caught sight of her name. He grabbed the paper out of her hand. The shop was shut up for the day. Miss Pinns was in her room at the back of the house, and the twins were alone. Suddenly Raymund turned and took Rhoda in his arms and, Rhoda began to sob—but she was very happy. "Doesn't it look handsome!" she murmured. "And right on the same page with an extract from Kipling and another from Oliver Wendell Holmes! And it is all set up right, except it says, 'The cloak of good I grieve."

"Does it?" exclaimed Raymund, looking at the line. "I didn't notice that; I read it weave from the jump. I don't believe anybody will notice it."

"And if they do," said Rhoda, hopefully, "they will be sure to know what I meant, won't they?"

"Of course they will, if they aren't idiots. Oh, Rhoda, how proud I am of you! Why, that's as good as any poetry I ever read! I never read much," he added, truthfully; "I haven't had time. How could you ever get a chance to make this up?"

"It was when I was scrubbing the floors," said Rhoda, softly. "The work was so hateful to me, and so mean and—and unworthy of me, it seemed, that I wondered if I couldn't ennoble it by making up poetry while I scrubbed. So I made up 'A Crown of Other Halves.' I am glad you like it, Ray. If you hadn't I—I don't know what I would have done!"

"You would have cut my head off—or you ought to have done so. How could I help like it? We won't be able to listen to the sermon, I'm afraid. And in the afternoon we'll visit Wizzen and Mrs. Weed and take that paper along."

"But," said Rhoda, as with a beaming face she watched her brother out of the darkened shop, "do you think we would care for that kind of thing?" izz

"Well," said Raymund, his enthusiasm a little checked, "well, you know," he said, with sudden hope, "Wizzen will enjoy looking at the pictures."
(To be Continued.)

❋ ❋ ❋

An Irishman wooed and won a Jewess. When the first-born was to be baptized the contentions waxed stout between the two families as to the proper name for the babe, his family insisting that it should be Patrick, and hers that it should be Moses. Neither side would yield, until in desperation they said to a clergyman, "We can't agree; you give him a name, sir; only let it be a Bible name." And instantly he proceeded with the service—"Pat-mos, I baptize thee," etc.

❋ ❋ ❋

"To live content with small means; to study hard, think quietly, talk gently, act frankly; to listen to stars and birds, to babes and sages, with open heart; to bear all cheerfully, do all bravely—in a word, to let the spiritual, unbidden and unconscious, grow up through the common—this is to be my symphony."—Dr. Channing.

❋ ❋ ❋

There Are Others.

There was an old darky preacher down in Georgia who refused to become ordained, but was content to remain simply an exhorter. This dissent appeared strange to some of his congregation, and one day one of his flock asked about it.

"Well, it am dis way," he replied; "when you's a real preacher you's gotter have a text and stick right close to it; but if you is only a exhorter, you kin branch."

❋ ❋ ❋

Picture of War Engine "General."

The Evolving of a Woman.

The house smelled of new pine boards—pitchy knots, oozing in the hot July sun. Isabel hurried through her dusting. The pungent odors sickened her. She arranged her few vases and bric-a-brac, and her easels, holding pictures of her old-time friends, along the mantel impatiently. She once had pronounced it "such a pretty mantel!" in its white drapings of tissue paper, caught tastefully here and there with gilt tacks; and the cheap little easels had pleased her. They had seemed in harmony; but now—now she herself was out of harmony, and therefore all things were discord.

She hated the plain glass vases that reproved her so with their emptiness. At first she had not wearied of searching diligently for flowers sufficiently sweet and dainty to deck so fine a setting; now she said that even flowers could not hide their ugliness.

The little plaster shepherdess, with her placid face, angered her. She hid her perpetual smile from sight behind a portrait of her stern great-aunt Roxana, who she usually kept with her face to the wall in memory of the many times when she, Isabel, had been kept in a like position by this same good great-aunt in the flesh. Everything displeased her. The curious and delicate shells that had been George's addition to the decorations, she spurned from sight with the very tip of her duster. They were horrid, disgusting things. She let the unique wooden fan, unfurled from a single piece of pine by one of the mill hands, so George said, fall to the floor, and splinter the delicate carvings. They had thought it odd, colored as it was with red squaw berries and green snake's grass; but now she crushed it together ruthlessly as she picked it up. The sight of the crude things nettled her beyond endurance.

She dusted her pictures without looking at them. She had no heart to look in the faces of old college chums; some were friends from her home town, closer yet.

She dusted the cheap, varnished table, and a bitter tear fell upon the centerpiece she had done when she was a girl. She said now it was the one really nice thing she possessed; she said too that it was out of place. George had promised to buy a better table. They had said when they placed the centerpiece there that it should be a nucleus, drawing all things in harmony to it; that they would gradually cull out things accepted through necessity, till their little home pleased them. The cotton velour furniture and the varnishy chairs would have to go. They had been the best obtainable in the little town where they had been obliged to get their "things." It was fresh and bright. George liked it. But of course it was only a "makeshift." This morning Isabel felt almost above dusting the "tawdry stuff."

The gaudy brass and pink lamp that George had won with tickets had never looked so cheap before. She meant to have it changed at once. It seemed now that she could not endure seeing it lit another night. The bright rugs on the floor antagonized her, and the one that was George's favorite, with a huge dog portrayed in its center, became positively hideous. She didn't see why he had ever consented to the buying of the thing. She dragged a vallenced rocker over it to hide part of its ugliness.

Her pretty cushions, spread along the chintz cosy corner, were already becoming faded and dingy, she noticed, in the too bright light. The one she valued most, her precious poppy pillow, was quite ruined. She looped back the chintz curtains above into the smallest possible compass, and wondered how she ever could have chosen such a combination of colors;

then she remembered that George was fond of pink and green.

In the process of dusting, a fancy picture fell from the screen to the floor. She picked it up and stood holding it; but her eyes did not soften. She did not stop to conjecture who it looked like—whose mouth, whose eyes—as she had done so many, many times. It was the picture of a baby, dimpling with irresistible baby sweetness. It linked a sacred sentiment between her and George; but now she thrust it cruelly into a stock of old magazines that were going into the attic. She was

tired and out of patience; and it was nothing but a cheap little print after all.

Out on the stifling front porch, facing south, dazzling and pitchy in the sun, she sat and thought about her old home and all the luxuries thereof. She pictured her white-haired mother, sitting in quiet refinement in the cool, shadowy front sitting-room—a piece of fine embroidery in her lap, maybe, or a bit of thread lace. She pictured her young sister, in immaculate linen, lounging in from a game of croquet to "cool off" in father's dim old library among the treasured books, or perhaps

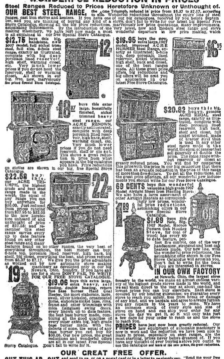

running through an exercise on the piano. Grace was fitting herself for a career. In a vision Isabel saw her, white, shapely hands touching the keys. They would never have coarse, unsightly tasks to do. The little home parlor smelled of lavender.

Isabel's eyes wandered across the hand's breadth of scorched sawdust street to the row of yellow pine cottages, identically the same—the same little porch patched on in front, the same sloping kitchen clinging to the rear. She counted the front windows, two by two, as far as she could see. She wondered if the woman on the other side was doing the same.

In the dry tufts of grass along the fence a miserable cricket begged her for succor. A nesting swallow, flying to the eaves with mud, upbraided her harshly. She seemed to have no sympathy with home-making. Her eyes seemed fixed on the wavering heat rays rising from the unpainted fence boards.

Far away was a modest brown house shaded by vines, looking out upon a quiet avenue lined on either side by aged maples. Through them one could see a church spire rising, and catching glimpses of well-bred lawn plants in neighboring dooryards—cannas and geraniums and stately palms. Her eyes despised the one solitary stunted plant struggling through the rocks at her feet. Long since she had ceased watering and tending it. The sickly yellow hue creeping up its stalk pleaded with her mightily, but she ignored it.

A little front dooryard with old-fashioned sweet posies had been one of her dreams, and she had spent days digging places in the hard soil for her seeds. There had been pinks and asters and bachelor's buttons and sweet phlox and verbenas. The one puny spot was the fruit of her labors. Flowers did not thrive in Higginsville. What sweetness or beauty could thrive within sight of the great belching stacks and smoking waste pits—within sound of the screeching saws and thudding, grinding engines that rested neither day nor night? Would a flower dare to lift its head along the drifting sawdust roads? She remembered shady village streets where many a blue violet bloomed its life out unmolested in the luxuriant borders. Here everything was so yellow and so hot. She put her aching forehead in her hands miserably. It had been not quite a year yet, and how tired she was of it all!

Her mind went back to the time when they had set out. Of course she had known it would be hard leaving home and all her dear friends, and going into a strange land. She never had had any experience in this sort of life; but it had seemed like a good chance, and they had planned how they would make it a stepping stone. George was foreman, and it was one of the largest plants in the state; but of course things were not as she had expected. She did not bother to figure out in just what way they were different. Her head ached, and the gnawing sound of the saws kept on.

True, George had secured the best house in Higginsville. She had a well in her own back yard, and the walls inside were papered with a very handsome paper for Higginsville—a great deal of gilt in scrolls and fancy medallion figures. At first she had been proud, it had looked so fine amongst its dull neighbors; but now the gold was vulgar, the medallions ugly. She thouht longingly of the genteel sage walls at home, decorated with well-bred photographs and genuine bits of water color and oil from the hands of friends. The large autumn scene that George had borne home so proudly, thinking he had such a fine thing, became only a daub in comparison. The cheap prints that had seemed within their means became unendurable.

She thought of all her friends who had gathered after the wedding to wish her well. It had sounded fine to tell them that George was foreman of a big lumber plant in Minnesota, and that they were going to begin life in the woods. With George there, beside her, immaculate in his black suit and white front, well groomed and confident (he had been handsome and imposing to look at then), and she in a stunning gown with bride's roses, anything would have sounded well then. She wondered what any of her friends would say if they could see her now in these surroundings.

When George came home at noon, she had been crying. He missed her from the little front gate where she usually waited with a greeting. "I'm going home, George," she told him when he tried to comfort her. "I can't stand it any longer. I'm going home." He reached out his strong brown arms for her, but she drew away.

"It isn't any use, George. I've made up my mind. I can't stand it any longer."

"All right, little woman," he said, cheerfully. "When you going?"

"I believe I'll start to-morrow," she decided, nerved to sudden decision by his calmness. "You can shut things up here. There's the boarding house, you know," she suggested.

"Oh, don't worry about me! Want me to lay off and help you pack?" He was magnanimous.

"No, never mind! I shan't need much. You know," she said, as she went about dishing up the dinner, "things aren't as I expected they would be—they're worse—they're horrid!" George came up from a noisy splash in the wash basin.

"Well, I should say they were! It's beastly hot. It's like an oven in the mill."

"You know, I'm just as disappointed as I can be," persisted Isabel. "Everything here is so—so coarse—so common. I'm not used to it." She looked at him reproachfully from across the table. He seemed vulgarly engrossed in the steaming viands before him. The sleeves of his blue shirt were rolled to the elbows, showing arms burned to a leathery hue. There were pitch stains that soap and water would not remove. His low collar did not hide a burned and weather-beaten neck. His hair clung in damp, uncomely locks. Isabel's lip curled.

"At home things are different," she continued, petulantly. "I don't know how I ever thought I could stand it. I just can't, that's all."

"It will be a lovely trip. Wish I was going with you!" George remarked between huge mouthfuls of food.

"I don't know what I'll tell them, George. They'll ask about—about everything; how I like it—and if—and if I'm happy. I couldn't tell them the truth; it's too horrid."

"You go home and rest a while, little girl, and things won't look so bad to you," he told her, as he pulled on his old slouch hat and hurried back to work. Isabel watched him from the front window. In his loose work clothes his gait seemed slouching. His long arms swung to keep pace with his ungainly strides. She turned away with a sigh.

The afternoon and evening were filled with preparations for the journey, and on the morrow there was time for only a hurried good-bye. "Have a good time and don't worry about me," George told her. "Tell all the folks hello." Then the train started and shut the sight of him from her eyes, and from her ears the sound of buzzing saws. She bought a well-bred magazine and settled down in the luxurious car seat to enjoy herself.

She got off at the familiar home station, and a group of her old-time friends were waiting there to greet her. She went up the street with them, laughing and chatting, and said she was "Oh, so glad to get back!" She sat in the quiet home parlor and told them how tired she was of the puny green thing· struggling up· through rocks. She wished she had remembered to water it before she started. She thought of the swallow, and how she might have protected the nest in the eaves from possible storms. Some realization· of the woe of washed-out nests swept over her. There were birds in the maple trees outside, but their full notes of satisfaction seemed to need nothing from her. She even remembered the distressed cricket by the fence, whose cries she had not heeded.

Everything was still—oppressively still. She took down· some of the old favorites from her father's library, but they lay· in her lap unopened. She could not keep her eyes from the· street, and she found herself listening intently for a footstep that did not come. She wondered what ailed her, till they called her in to dinner; then she knew that· she had missed· the whistle, and George coming home to· his evening meal. She lay awake in her still, lavender-scented sleeping room and listened for the sound of saws.

The house . swarmed .with gay. young friends eager to visit, and yet she felt miserably· alone in their midst. "Poor Isabel is so changed," they said. "She doesn't seem like herself!"

She came down to breakfast one morn·i·g·more wan than usual. Her mother was alarmed. "Why, child! What is the matter?" she cried. "I know, though; it's that horrid life you've been living. It has been too much for you. It's a shame ! I··· ·bel w.s always such·a .fresh-looking gi··," she lamented.

They got her to· tell again about the lit·'e ·backwoods town," with its sawdust stre·ts nd unpainted cottages. They spoke of them as "shanties," though Isabel acknowledged with inward shame that she was to blame for the title. Memory of the really .neat little house, grown suddenly dear, filled her with remorse.

They heaped dainty dishes upon her. "Try to eat," they said. "You must make up .now for all.the good things you have missed. Those berries are lovely. Try some, dear! I don't suppose you can get fresh fruit in Higginsville. Just think! The poor. child can't get a bit of ice, and they use condensed milk . Isn't it a shame! I should think George could manage to have some shipped in!"

Isabel's · cheeks ·flamed ·as she heard George's shortcomings discussed in detail. "I don't see ·how· poor Issie gets along withouc ice cream; she used to be so fond of it," put in Grace, languidly. "It's no ·· nder Isabel is getting thin! Don't you know, father, she said it was next to im-.ossible· to get fresh meat? Think of it, no meat and no cream!"

"Don't talk·of impossible to me!" sen·re·ced her father, harshly. "I haven't any patience." Isabel was conscience-stricken. A mental picture of the little board where she and George shared their ideals, would come. She acknowledged to herself now that .it never .had lacked for anything—that there had even been luxuries—and that George· had· spared ·neither effort. nor money. There was the consciousness, too, that she had created the false impression; this filled her with a growing remorse.

"I had a long talk with George when you were married," her father was saying. "I told him that you· were not fit for a rough life. You had been babied and pampered. He promised·to take care of you. I thought he was a man of his word."

"George has been· good to me," Isabel ventured, desperately.

"Oh, yes! Of course!" Her father folded his napkin decisively. "He hasn't beaten you, or anything of that sort; but I don't think much of a .man who drags his wife through every discomfort and subjects her to all sorts of privations. I never had to do that. Your mother always had things comfortable. I saw to that."

Isabel would have spoken, but he mo-

---

tioned her to silence. "Don't excuse him, my dear! I understand! I wouldn't have thought it of George Barton!"

Isabel's breath came in sobs as she fled to the seclusion of her own room. There on the window ledge, with her head in the honeysuckle vine, she wept all the crisp freshness out of her white sleeves. "Oh, my dear, my dear!" she sobbed in an agony of contrition. Then she went about putting things into her trunk. Her mother came seeking her before· she had finished.

"Why, Isabel ! What ails you, dear? Are you ill? Why, my child!" Isabel was holding a bit of lace fichu to her· cheek, passionately. "What made you slip away, child? We missed you. Father was wanting you to play one of your old ·pieces. You musn't miss a moment, now you are where you can take a little comfort, my poor Isabel!"

"Don't, mother." Isabel lifted her head, desperately. "I can't bear it. It isn't true. I've led you to believe it, but it's false, every word of it. Oh, I can never forgive myself, never! See here! He gave me this; he· gave me this, ·and this." She piled her treasures from the trunk to the floor. "They're beautiful. I never half appreciated them—only now that I haven't got him, they're dearer than anything. I'm going back to-morrow, because—because I can't be away from him another minute." Her breath caught in a passion of sobs.

"It's all true that father said," she went ·n, bitterly. "I've been babied and pampered till I'm no mate for a ·man like George Barton. He is always giving and I am always taking. The truth of the matter is, he has taken too good care of me—he has finished spoiling me.

"Oh, mother!" she said, with sudden eagerness, "I wish you could see our little home; it's the dearest place—so cosy and cheerful. I never knew how much I—I thought of it before. Oh, mother!" her head dropped in contrition. "The sweetest little cosies! George made them—the cunningest rose bowl—and, oh, mother! I do wish you could see my little, stewpans!" And then she sat down and wept again from pure homesickness.

* * * * * * * * *

"I thought the train would never get here, never!" she said, with a deep sigh of satisfaction as she went about touching

---

her treasures to make sure of their safety. "Oh, George! I'm never going away again; I'm so glad to be home. My! but this does me good. Oh, dear, dear things!" she said, with motherly pats here and there. "You're mine, and that's everything. What do I smell?" She sniffed about, hungrily. "Oh, I know! It's pine. Don't it smell homey! And do you know, I believe I'm actually glad to hear those saws, they sound so jolly." Then she pounced upon a little picture; reinstated in its old place on the screen. "My baby! Where did you find it? Oh, George! I've lain awake nights thinking of it up in the attic alone."

"I couldn't spare all my little family, could I?" he questioned her, softly, as he held them both.—*The Interior.*

We have recently prepared a "Popular Church Record" that surpasses any other made. We send it "on approval" at $2.50 postpaid.

We are happy to announce that with the new year we will have "Teachers' Quarterlies" for the various grades of the Dowling Bible School series.

Our "Bargain Book Sale" is closed. We still sell many of the best $1.50 works of fiction like "The Man from Glengarry" and "Little Shepherd of Kingdom Come" at 75c postpaid.

See advertisement of Rally Day souvenirs on page 1151. Rally Day comes this month. It would be better not to delay ordering as we were barely able to fill all requisitions last year.

B. W. Johnson's "Peoples' New Testament with Notes" is having a great sale among those wishing a perfectly accurate commentary on the New Testament. It is in two volumes, $2.00 postpaid.

The Christian-Evangelist and a fountain pen to either a new subscriber or a renewal for $2. The Christian-Evangelist and a self-filling fountain pen guaranteed by the manufacturers for ten years to a new subscriber for $2.50—the retail price of the pen.

We offer our readers this heretofore unheard-of proposition, to-wit: The Christian-Evangelist and the "Review of Reviews" for $3. You can not secure the latter alone from the New York office for less than $3. This offer gives you the best religious paper and the best literary review published for the price of the magazine.

Many pastors and evangelists are using 300 or 500 copies of The Christian-Evangelists per week through evangelistic meetings and with splendid results. We send with them for insertion in the papers colored circulars containing the pictures of pastors and evangelists and local announcements. These are valuable helpers. Write us for terms.

Multitudes of Disciples have realized the inconsistency of purchasing books elsewhere, thus building up secular and denom-inational publishing houses at the expense of one in their own brotherhood, and are properly sending their orders to us. Hence our book trade is flourishing as never before, enabling us to make book offers of ever-increasing advantage to our patrons. Write us before purchasing, no matter what the book you wish.

We can say no more for our W. W. Dowling's series of Sunday-school supplies than that for the new year they will be a little better than ever before. Samples sent gratuitously on application. Do not use those undenominational series that fail to interpret the scriptures and unfold the plan of salvation according to the doctrines of this Restoration movement. Do not use any inferior sorts while the Dowling series is so inexpensive.

The Armory building in which the Buffalo Convention will be held is not in the hotel district. The Christian-Evangelist headquarters will be at the Buckingham, the only hotel near the convention hall. This is within two blocks of it. Around this hotel and within easy walking distance, we have secured a great many rooms in good homes at 75c and $1 per day for room and breakfast. This is much better than going to a down-town hotel where rooms will be higher priced and table service quite expensive.

The Christian-Evangelist special over the Wabash leaves St. Louis, October 11, at noon. The cost of the tickets will be one fare plus $2 for round trip west of the Mississippi and one fare plus $1 east of the river. From Detroit our friends have their choice of going either by rail through Canada or by steamship across Lake Erie without additional expense. Our special train will consist of standard Pullmans, bright new tourist and reclining chair-cars. Every possible care will be given those going with this party and our services are absolutely gratuitous. Get to the Wabash and the "Christian-Evangelist Special" as quickly as possible if you do not live on this line.

The Christian-Evangelist's remarkable growth in circulation is not ephemeral as our published list in each issue for several months shows. While the great majority comes by ones and twos we are pleased to note the following clubs received during the week, to-wit: Brunswick, Mo., E. H. Williamson, pastor, 12; Stanberry, Mo., G. W. Terrell, pastor, 27; Hagerstown, Md., H. C. Kendrick, minister, 6; Butler, Ind., Robt. B. Chapman, minister, 30; Huntington, Ind., Cephas Shelburne, pastor, 17; St. Joseph, Mo., A. C. Lowe, pastor, 27; Bucklin, Mo., A. Munyon, minister, 4; Amarillo, Texas, Jewell Howard, minister, 7; Savannah, Mo., Geo. McGee, pastor, 25; Grant City, Mo., W. A. Shullenberger, pastor, 23; Lincoln, Neb., 26, G. H. Exley, Agt.; Belpre, Kan., 7. We pledge ourselves to make every copy of The Christian-Evangelist a light bearer and life giver. Again we call on our friends to rally around us in our efforts to place The Christian-Evangelist in 100,000 homes before the Centennial.

By Courtesy of "The Wabash." Write us about free tickets to the Convention. Let us all see the Falls together.

THE
CHRISTIAN-
EVANGELIST

A WEEKLY RELIGIOUS NEWSPAPER.

Volume XLIII.   No. 38.

ST. LOUIS, SEPTEMBER 20, 1906.

BUFFALO EN ROUTE TO THE NEW JERUSALEM

By W. R. Warren, Centennial Secretary.

HY ARE YOU endeavoring to get to heaven? Among the chief delights in that "city that hath foundations" is the reunion with those you have loved long since and lost awhile, fellowship with the great and good whose words and lives have been an inspiration to you and the enlargement of your being by acquaintance and friendship with other choice spirits whom time and chance have thus far not allowed you to meet. Well, Buffalo is en route to the New Jerusalem. There will be such reunions as will make your heart glad for many days to come. The great men are not all dead. Even the heroic pioneers of the current reformation have not all passed beyond. The call of the convention appeals only to the best. While its gates stand open as do those of the New Jerusalem, none enter there except those for whom it has been prepared, and it is worth while to know them. Sometimes you are lonely and discouraged in your work. Here your heart will sing for joy as you behold seven thousand of those who have not bowed the knee to Baal.

In the round of the year time and strength and money are demanded by many sordid interests, the world that now is presses hard upon you every day, the multitude about you run headlong in the broad way. Come aside with the Disciples of your Lord and give your soul a rest, a feast and a chance. It is but once in a year, and it is necessary.

The Christian-Evangelist.

J. H. GARRISON, Editor

PAUL MOORE, Assistant Editor

F. D. POWER,
B. B. TYLER, } Staff Correspondents.
W. DURBAN,

Subscription Price, $1.50 a Year.

For foreign countries add $1.04 for postage.

Remittances should be made by money order, draft, or registered letter; *not* by local cheque, unless 10 cents is added to cover cost of collection.
In Ordering Change of Post Office give both old and new address.
Matter for Publication should be addressed to THE CHRISTIAN-EVANGELIST. Subscriptions and remittances should be addressed to the Christian Publishing Company, 2712 Pine Street, St. Louis, Mo.
Unused Manuscripts will be returned only if accompanied by stamps.
News Items, evangelistic and otherwise, are solicited, and should be sent on a postal card, if possible.
Published by the Christian Publishing Company, 2712 Pine Street, St. Louis, Mo.

Entered at St. Louis P. O. as Second Class Matter

WHAT WE STAND FOR.

For the Christ of Galilee,
For the truth which makes men free,
For the bond of unity
Which makes God's children on :

For the love which shines in deed,
For the life which this world needs,
For the church whose triumph speed is
The prayer: "Thy will be done."

For the right against the wrong,
For the weak against the strong,
For the poor who've waited long
For the brighter age to be.

For the faith against tradition,
For the truth 'gainst superstition,
For the hope whose glad fruition
Our waiting eyes shall see.

For the city God is rearing,
For the New Earth now appearing,
For the heaven above us clearing,
And the song of victory.

         J. H. Garrison.

CONTENTS.

Centennial Propaganda 1191
Current Events 1192
Editorial—
  Where Jesus Placed the Emphasis V:......1193
  Some Key-Words for the Buffalo Convention 1193
  Notes and Comments...................1194
  Editor's Easy Chair 1195
Contributed Articles—
  The Devotional Feature of the Convention.
  James M. Philput.....................1196
  The Scope of Our National Convention.
  W. F. Richardson.....................1196
  Shall We Have a Delegate Convention?
  T. P. Haley..........................1197
  The Business Side of the Convention.
  F. M. Rains 1197
  Educational Value of the Great Convention.
  Herbert L. Willett...................1198
  Local Arrangements at Buffalo. R. H.
  Miller 1198
As Seen from the Dome. F. D. Power....1199
Buffalo Churches and Preachers...........1200
Convention Program 1202
Convention Pointers 1203
Our Budget 1204
News from Many Fields 1208
Evangelistic 1210
Sunday-school 1211
Christian Endeavor 1211
Midweek Prayer-meeting 1212
Current Literature 1214
The Home Department....................1215

THE
CHRISTIAN=EVANGELIST

"IN FAITH, UNITY; IN OPINION AND METHODS, LIBERTY; IN ALL THINGS, CHARITY."

Vol. XLIII. September 20, 1906. No. 38

1809 — CENTENNIAL PROPAGANDA — CHURCHES OF CHRIST — 1909
: : : GEO. L. SNIVELY : : :

Buffalo 1906 and Pittsburg 1909.

W. R. WARREN.

Two great states, side by side since their settlement and step by step in their progress, have led America in her advance toward world primacy. Each has an eastern and western metropolis. New York's western city gathers the commerce of the great lakes to its docks; Pittsburg's harbor, where the Allegheny and the Monongehela rivers combine to form the Ohio, floats more coal than any other water in the world; each is a converging point for railroads between the east and the middle west; one draws upon a vast field of coal for power, the other lays Niagara herself under tribute, and both reach out to the rich ore fields on the lake's shore for raw materials.

The four years of the centennial campaign culminate in four conventions—Buffalo is the first and Pittsburg is the last. How will the various and vast interests of the brotherhood come up to this first quarter-pole? What is the record of the Christian Woman's Board of Missions, whose splendid and ready organization enabled it to get away first in the race? What report, in spite of its handicap, comes from the American Christian Missionary Society and its new secretary? How far towards the goal is the Foreign Christian Missionary Society and its world-wide task? How grows the million dollar fund for Church Extension? What progress have we made in the pure and undefiled religion that cares for the widow and the orphan? Have we quite forgotten the aged preacher? How many are we educating to succeed him? Call the roll of the states; what is each doing for liberty in Christ and union under him? Call out the men and women from the thin, white line of missionaries with which we face the world! Let us see their faces and hear their voices! Let us grasp their hands and enter into sympathy with their heroism.

Office of Centennial Secretary.

The Centennial and Pre-Conventions.

There ought to be 100,000 Disciples in Pittsburg during our Centennial. To secure this attendance, which will be a sensational feature of the close of our first cycle, our pre-conventions must be such as to cause many to form the "convention habit." Programs alone, though largely, are not to be solely instrumental in this. The physical comfort of attendants both while at the convention and en route there and returning will be a large factor in securing the numbers, so essential to the visible success of the Pittsburg ceremonials.

THE CHRISTIAN-EVANGELIST is doing all in its power to make those going up to

Buffalo enjoy their entourage and sojourn in the city.

We have arranged for a special train over the Wabash to leave St. Louis at noon October 11. This train will be equipped with standard Pullman, tourist sleeper, reclining chair, baggage, commissary and dining cars. The commissary car will serve inexpensive but wholesome lunches along the way, and prevent the necessity of patronizing the more expensive diner. The tourist cars will be new and clean and substitutes for the more costly berths none need hesitate to employ. The rate will be one fare plus $1 for the round trip. Passengers will have choice, without extra expense of going from Detroit either by rail through Canada or by ship across Lake Erie. On account of reaching Buffalo in time to receive assignments and attend the first session of the convention we strongly urge all of THE CHRISTIAN-EVANGELIST Special patrons to go by rail and return by water. There will be the same privilege of returning from Buffalo by water as in going. Every possible concession for the comfort of our friends will be secured. We urge all going from west of this city to plan to be here in time to join with us. Parties coming in special cars may arrange to have their cars attached to our "Special" over the Wabash.

The convention hall is not in the business and hotel district of the city. The Buckingham is the only hotel very near the Armory building. This is within two blocks of the convention and all the delegates it receives will be assigned by the manager of THE CHRISTIAN-EVANGELIST Special. The rates are $2 per day for room and meals for the limited number that can be entertained there. Hundreds of homes in the immediate neighborhood of the convention hall will receive those going with us for 75 cents and $1 per diem for room and breakfast. Other meals may be secured at the Buckingham or of the convention caterer. This is infinitely preferable to stopping at the distant hotels where rooms are higher and meals much more expensive to say nothing of the saving in car fare and time. These homes are equipped with all modern conveniences and the guests will receive therein a cordial "welcome home". Those intending to go with us may write us and we will secure their assignments and mail to them at once. Guides will meet THE CHRISTIAN-EVANGELIST Special at the Buffalo Wabash station and conduct them safely to their stopping places. Specially conducted parties to Niagara Falls and elsewhere are also on our program.

Our services are entirely gratuitous. No other reward is expected than the grateful appreciation of those whom we serve.

THE CHRISTIAN-EVANGELIST will in like manner minister to all our other convention assemblies preceding the great conven-

tion at Pittsburg fondly hoping in this capacity it may have at least a small part in pressing six figures into requisition in order to tell the number present at Pittsburg in 1909.

❊

OUR CENTENNIAL HELPERS.

Such a grand paper as THE CHRISTIAN-EVANGELIST should be in every home.—Mrs. H. A. Wheeldon.

I cannot tell you how much good the paper has done me. I cannot do without it.—A. M. Gates, Hiram, Ohio.

I shall be only too glad to do all I can to increase the circulation of THE CHRISTIAN-EVANGELIST in this great city.—E. A. Long, New York.

I have been a reader of THE CHRISTIAN-EVANGELIST for thirty years and I would rather give up all my other papers than it.—F. H. Symonds, Admire, Kan.

I admire the spirit and appreciate the broad and forward view of the present day topics in THE CHRISTIAN-EVANGELIST.—B. E. Utz, Spokane Bridge, Wash.

I would that THE CHRISTIAN-EVANGELIST might go weekly into every home in Christendom not only among our own people but all the Lord's people however perfect or imperfect they may be. —Jas. H. Brooks, (evangelist.)

I have been a reader of THE CHRISTIAN-EVANGELIST the most of my natural life. My present subscription does not expire until January, 1907, then I shall renew. THE CHRISTIAN-EVANGELIST is all right.—P. H. Duncan, Latonia, Ky.

I wish I could get one hundred names for THE CHRISTIAN-EVANGELIST. The dear old paper ought to be in every home and I wish we could place it not only in Christian homes but in those where they know not God and his goodness. It is surely a great preacher. I will do all in my power to get a list of names.—Anna Garner.

Our members after being taught that federation —the union of God's children—means the life of God and man together and the very foundation of a Christian's hope will believe that they cannot live as they ought on sectarianism. I cannot see how our contemporary can live with a clear conscience after printing what it did about Brother Garrison, a man that has given, over forty years of his life to the cause of our Master. It must have been done for subscription's sake. It is not right. I have been taking the CHRISTIAN-EVANGELIST for thirty years and shall continue.—W. A. Dodson, Denison, Kan.

Why, bless you, I would not be without THE CHRISTIAN-EVANGELIST a week for anything. You were a small chap when I began to read THE CHRISTIAN-EVANGELIST, George. I used to help mail it when Brother Hickey owned and edited it at Oskaloosa, Iowa. I know all about how THE CHRISTIAN-EVANGELIST came to its present high estate and prominence. I have gotten more than a world of good out of it. Really now as to helpfulness to me as a minister, THE CHRISTIAN-EVANGELIST has stood for many years next to the Bible. Yes, I am for THE CHRISTIAN-EVANGELIST, federation and all.—A. C. Corbin, Ashland, Oregon, (minister.)

I want to record it now, while soft beating in my heart, that THE CHRISTIAN-EVANGELIST, as one visible expression of the even flowing, thankful, sweet-spirited soul of the Editor-in-chief, comes to us in this remote part of the world as a choice benediction. As I follow the Easy Chair, I can recall even the intonations of the speaker as he uttered similar expressions of peace and hope more than twenty years ago. Many readers will not know, but Brother Garrison will recall the scene when the writer as a lad made the confession of his faith in Christ—the first visible fruits of his gospel ministry in New England. I want to thank my first pastor and my father in the faith for his most helpful influence through these years.—Edwin Carey Davis, Maotha, Hamirpur, India.

Current Events

Roosevelt Again? The president has said, as clearly and as positively as any man could say it, that he will not, under any circumstances, be a candidate for re-election in 1908. He said so on the night of his election in 1904. He has said so several times since. And his friends have repeatedly said so on his authority. However, he said not merely that he would not seek the nomination, but that he would not accept it. Still there are many persons not notably obtuse who assert that he will probably be renominated, and many others whose moral sense is at least as good as the average declare that he is under no obligation to refuse if the nomination is offered. It must be admitted that there are numerous precedents for statesmen changing their mind and accepting nominations which they said they would not accept. Mr. Roosevelt himself, when he was governor of New York, said that he would not accept the vice-presidential nomination. But he did. He was convinced that the welfare of the party demanded it. There is so little surplus honor in politics that we should regret to see any system of sophistry established which would further weaken the binding force of promises. We hope Mr. Roosevelt will not subject himself to criticism by changing his mind. If, when the time for nomination arrives, it shall appear that no other Republican candidate would have a fair chance of being elected and that Democratic success would seriously interfere with the country's welfare, we believe Mr. Roosevelt would be morally justified in accepting a nomination. It would be manifestly improper and immoral for him to seek or to accept the nomination in the absence of such an emergency. And for the party to nominate him would, as it seems to us, be a confession of weakness.

❦

Taft on the Tariff. In a campaign speech at Bath, Me., Secretary Taft expressed sentiments which aroused the drooping spirits of the tariff reformers and encouraged them to believe that the Watson letter did not sound the death knell of their hopes. If Secretary Taft in public speaks favorably of tariff reform, it is a fair indication that the president thinks favorably of it. The personal and official relations existing between Mr. Taft and the president are such that the former would scarcely speak on such a vital topic without being sure that his sentiments were in accordance with the views of the administration. So, all at once, the air is full of rumors of a possible special session of congress to be called for the purpose of revising the tariff immediately after the congressional election. It would be an excellent time to do something which very much needs to be done.

❦

The Naval Review. Every great naval review—such as the one at Oyster Bay week before last, which was the greatest in all our naval history—gives the critics an opportunity. We hear it said that an expense of tens of thousands of dollars was incurred simply to give the president a pleasant day at his summer home and gratify his pride. It is pointed out that Lincoln never treated himself to a naval parade. Certainly he did not. But Lincoln's task was to keep the country's fighting forces at their best in a time of war. Roosevelt's is to keep them from getting rusty and useless in a time of peace. Reviews are profitable for the latter but not for the former purpose. Besides, given a navy already in commission, it does not cost much more to have a review at Oyster Bay than to have the vessels steaming about individually. Rear Admiral Evans says this review did not cost more than $300, which we suppose was expended on powder for firing salutes. One who objects to the costliness of a review must begin farther back and criticize the whole policy of maintaining a navy. Such an argument, whether convincing or not, may at least be consistent.

❦

Howells on Spelling. The "little folk of little soul," who are industriously trying to discredit the advocates of spelling reform and to pose as the only people who hold history and literature sacred, ought to be (if they are not) considerably embarrassed by the presence of great and scholarly names among the reformers. Professor Skeat, who knows more about Anglo-Saxon than the Anglo-Saxons themselves knew, and who is the highest authority on the history of the English language, is for spelling reform. So is Professor Murray, who is editing the monumental Oxford dictionary which will be the greatest and most scholarly of all dictionaries. So is Professor Lounsbury, who says that the only thing more contemptible than English spelling is the arguments by which it is defended. Mr. W. D. Howells, the high-priest of letters on this side of the Atlantic, expressed himself at large on the subject before the recent controversy arose. He says:

"It is held creditable to spell in the fashion of lexicographers, but it is really discreditable, if to defy law and order is infamy. A child is punished if it obeys its instinct and spells phonetically, but it ought to be rewarded, and its instinctive orthography reverently studied in the hope of some hint for the amelioration of the abuse under which we all suffer. The actual English spelling does not spell anything, really; it is a kind of picture-writing, in which certain groups of letters symbolize certain sounds without representing them. The difference between our spelling and our speech is such that the lexicographer finds his burden divided between orthography and orthoepy, and yet doubled in the failure to show how the printed word shall be spoken. For the literary artist, who wishes to

indicate variations, the system is worse than useless; he must frame a convention and trust the reader's intelligence for its acceptance before he can hope to suggest the accents he has in mind. Nothing worse could be said of our spelling than that it does not spell; that is quite enough to condemn it. If it fulfilled its office, one might not repine at its manifold difficulties; but it breaks down at the first step and at every step. It is a failure which nothing but the immense power of the race which suffers it could repair."

❦

The Anglo-American Boat Race. The great Harvard-Cambridge boat race which was rowed on the Thames a couple of weeks ago, resulted in a victory for the English crew. Three times in recent years American crews have tried to beat the English oarsmen in their own waters: the Cornell crew in (or about) 1895, the Yale crew in 1896, and now the Harvard crew. Each time the Englishmen won. While the races have in each case been simply between two universities, they have been accepted and properly, as genuine international contests. While all good Americans want to see their own team win in such an event, the opposite outcome affords some satisfaction to those who believe that the English system of athletics in institutions of learning is superior to our own. The English can still show the world its finest examples of the spirit of pure sportsmanship.

❦

An Extension of Jury Trial. A writer in a current magazine, claiming to be himself a millionaire, proposes that all wills involving property worth more than $50,000 should be submitted to the approval of a jury of twelve men before being admitted to probate. This jury should have power to disapprove and annul any parts of the will which it considers unjust, unwise, or malicious, and to add new provisions if sufficient sums have not been left to charities and other public causes or to persons who had a proper expectation of being remembered. It is said that a large proportion of the wills which dispose of great estates are brought into courts anyway by the efforts of relatives to have the provisions altered, and that the proposed plan would be no serious extension of the government's function. It would, however, be a very serious and radical extension. The present theory is that a man has a right to dispose of his property as selfishly or unwisely as he pleases, and when a will is set aside or altered it is on the ground that it does not really represent the testator's wishes. If this theory were to be given up, it would be simpler to go the whole length and say that a man's property at his death reverts to the state to be disposed of as the state shall decide. It is not likely that such a principle will be adopted in other than a thoroughly socialistic state. Meanwhile, in spite of the occasional appearance of bad wills, it is gratifying to notice that few men dispose of large estates without showing some consciousness of a moral obligation to the community and of a duty extending beyond the limits of the family.

Editorial

Where Jesus Placed the Emphasis.—V.

The Kingdom of God.

No reader of the Gospels, particularly of the three synoptic Gospels, can fail to be impressed with the prominence which Jesus gives to the kingdom of God or the kingdom of heaven. It is the first of the promised blessings in the Beatitudes: "Blessed are the poor in spirit, for theirs is the kingdom of heaven" (Matt. 5:3). In teaching his disciples to pray, the first formal petition is: "Thy kingdom come. Thy will be done, as in heaven so in earth" (Matt. 6:10). When he would solve for his disciples and for all the world the age-long problem of what is the greatest good, he said: "But seek ye first the kingdom of God and his righteousness" (Matt. 6:33). In later chapters he devotes a series of parables to explaining the methods and principles of that kingdom. It is evident, therefore, that the kingdom of God held the place of chief importance in the mind and in the teaching of Jesus.

What meaning does the kingdom of God or the kingdom of heaven have in the thought of Jesus? There is a wide sense in which the kingdom of God is sometimes used to signify God's over-ruling providence over all nations and over all the universe; but Jesus is using the phrase in a more limited and in a deeper sense. He evidently means by it that divine sway which God was to exert and is now exerting over the human heart and life by the revelation of himself and of his power, through Jesus Christ. It was in this sense only that the kingdom of God was "at hand," or near by. In the wider sense God's kingdom has always existed. With Jesus the kingdom of God is not some external organization which comes with observation, but an internal spiritual force renovating and ruling human lives, though ultimately objectifying itself in many ways, but notably in the Church, for the promotion of human welfare. It is "not of this world," according to the teaching of Jesus, and is not extended by force. It has no weapon but truth, no law but love, and no object but the salvation of men and the redemption of the earth from the dominion of sin. It aims to regulate all life, to control and perfect human society, to bring all men under its dominion, and to pervade and purify all the relationships and activities of human life, claiming all time, all places and all that relates to human welfare as the legitimate fields of its operations. The Parable of the Sower indicates the methods of its operation; that of the Mustard Seed, its progressive development in the world; that of the Leaven and the Measures of Meal, its contagious and aggressive nature; that of the Wheat and Tares, the obstacles which oppose it and its ultimate triumph.

The kingdom of God is not the Church, much less any denomination or section of the Church. It is coterminous with the Church at some points, but it is wider in its scope than any or all organizations. Many are in our churches who are not in the kingdom of God, and many are more or less under the influence of the kingdom of God who are not in any of the churches. To identify the Church, as an external organization, with the kingdom of God, has been a source of much error and of much intolerance and persecution. No doubt every true and loyal disciple of Jesus Christ, where opportunity affords, is both a member of Christ's church and a citizen of his kingdom. The Church is

A Snap-shot of the Editor of The Christian-Evangelist Cleaning Fish, Taken by his Wife.

God's chief agency for the extension of his kingdom throughout all the world. When any local church or any religious movement consisting of a group of churches loses sight of this fact and seeks its own glory and enlargement *as an end* instead of the advancement of the kingdom of God, it becomes sectarian in aim and character, and is likely to become a hindrance rather than a help in the extension of the kingdom.

As God's kingdom, contrary to the expectation of the Jews of Christ's time, is a spiritual kingdom, entrance into it is only by a spiritual birth. The characteristics of citizens in the kingdom of God are described in the Beatitudes, which antagonized all the prevailing notions of blessedness in Jesus' day, and many ideas and traits still prevalent in the Church. No man can be said to be in the kingdom of God who does not possess, in some measure, the Spirit of Christ and bring forth the fruits thereof in his life. The formal and open surrender to Christ's reign in the ordinance of baptism, important as it is, as an act of obedience, is not to be substituted for that newness of life which is the essence of the birth from above.

To restore God's rule over the lives of men, and to bring back the earth, which had become a revolted province, under the divine government, was the great mission of Christ to the world. That work is steadily going on. One has but to look back at the beginning, when the kingdom of God consisted of Christ and a few disciples unknown to the world and unrecognized by the powers that then were, and contrast that situation with the kingdom of God as it exists to-day, to see what vast strides it has made in the world, and to feel assured of its ultimate triumph. Tyrannous governments have been and are being overthrown; cruel customs and laws have been abolished; womanhood lifted up and coronated; childhood honored and protected; slavery overthrown; despotism undermined and human rights everywhere asserted; warring nations are studying the arts of peace and forming international courts to prevent war; while the despised and rejected Prophet of Galilee, who in his own day "had not where to lay his head," is the most potential personality and the chief controlling factor in the world's civilization. Surely these are evidences of the speedy coming of that time when all the kingdoms and governments of this world shall become the kingdom of Christ, and his dominion shall be from sea to sea and from the rivers to the end of the earth.

❀ ❀

Some Key-words for the Buffalo Convention.

The greatness of a man does not consist in the amount of his avoirdupois, but in the greatness of his spirit. Even so a great convention is not one having a large attendance, though it may have, and ought to have that, but in the quality of spirit that pervades it. A mere aggregation of numbers, unless fused into unity by the divine Spirit, and lifted to heights of holy enthusiasm by great ideas and aims, is not a great convention. What are some of the great ideas and aims that should mark the coming conventions at Buffalo? These may be indicated by certain key-words which stand for ideas that make a convention great in the quality of its work and in its far-reaching consequences.

Consecration.—If we could think of a less conventional and less abused term that would express the same idea we would use it. What we mean by it, and what we would put into it, is the utter surrender of ourselves with all that we possess, to the will of Christ, to be used by him in the furtherance of his kingdom. It is the true and literal acceptance of Christ's Word that it is our first and supreme duty to seek the kingdom of God and his righteousness. What could a body such as the Disciples of

Christ not accomplish, if it were to put itself wholly at the service of Christ, to be used by him for his purposes? This is what Jesus meant when he said, "For this purpose I sanctify myself, that they also may be sanctified." That is, he devoted, he dedicated, he consecrated himself to the salvation of the world, that his disciples might do the same thing. Has the church ever risen to the height of this great conception of its duty? Can it ever triumph over the forces of evil in the world until it does thus lay itself on the altar of Christian service? Is there anything else which the Disciples of Christ need more in order to succeed in their great mission, than this complete consecration of themselves—their talents, their knowledge of God's will, their means, and their influence—to Christ and the interests of his kingdom?

Unification.—This must follow our *consecration*, and can not extend any further than it extends. We need to "study the things that make for peace," both among ourselves and with all those who love our Lord Jesus Christ in sincerity. Division is a source of confusion and weakness. It is carnal, and is evidence of carnality where it exists. The existence of bitter controversies and uncharitable criticisms argues the need of a deeper spirituality. That is only saying that it shows the need of a larger measure of the Holy Spirit, who alone can bring about "the unity of the Spirit." No people in the world need so much the guidance and influence of the Holy Spirit as those who are pleading for Christian union, and who should therefore furnish a practical illustration of its beauty and its utility. By *unification* we do not mean *uniformity* of opinion, but "the unity of the Spirit," which is consistent with diversity of opinions and methods. What we *need* is to learn to love one another in spite of those little differences growing out of our temperaments, education and environments. Let the note of brotherly love, of "forbearing one another in love," of the need of cementing the bonds of unity among ourselves, while pleading for a wider union, be sounded clear and strong at Buffalo, and we are sure it will find a hearty response in the hearts of those who shall be gathered there. Better to leave undone some things that some of us feel ought to be done, than attempt to do them at the expense of brotherly love and unity. And then, let the great certainties of religion to which all believers hold, be duly accentuated.

Evangelization.—A consecrated and unified people are prepared for the work of evangelization. God can use such a people in the evangelization of the world with the best results. Their work of conversion will be thorough for they will convert to Christ, and not proselyte to a party. They will sow the seeds of unity broadcast among the people, and not those of strife and division. The evangelization of our great home field with its rapidly-increasing foreign populations, and carrying the light of Christ's Gospel to pagan lands—what an enterprise is that to call forth the enthusiasm and energies of a great people who have surrendered themselves to the will and authority of Christ! No doubt this note will be sounded oft and with power. We have not been wanting in zeal for evangelism, but with many of us the idea needs deepening and widening. Let us give it increased breadth and depth at Buffalo, until it shall be broad enough to include the whole world, and deep enough to meet the needs of the vilest sinner.

Education.—This must follow hard on the heels of evangelization. "Teaching them to observe all things whatsoever I have commanded you," is an essential part of the commission under which we labor. It is the part, however, that has been much neglected. On that account it needs special emphasis. The training of converts in the knowledge of God's Word, and in methods of Christian service, and the development of their spiritual life is one of the most sacred responsibilities the church has laid upon it. It involves the establishment of schools for the training of ministers and other Christian workers, and the endowment and equipment of these schools. Herein, too, we have been deficient. Our educational needs to-day are among the most pressing. We can not longer ignore them without suffering severe loss. We are now, in fact, suffering greatly from this neglect. Whoever stresses the need of our struggling colleges at Buffalo will be doing real service for our cause. The consecration of our means to Christ's cause, to which we have already adverted, will be sure to result in larger college endowments, and in a larger number of trained ministers and business-men for service in Christ's kingdom. Benevolence, too, would go forth with full hands to minister to the fatherless and the widow, and to all the needy servants of God.

If these great keywords, or the things for which they stand, be emphasized at the Buffalo convention, and if the beautiful and Christly spirit of humility shall banish all unseemly denominational pride and braggadocio, so that we shall be humbled at how little we have accomplished, with such a cause to plead, and yet grateful that he has so richly blessed our unworthy labors, the great convocation of Disciples who will gather there, will separate, feeling that they have been upon the very mount of God and have caught a fresh vision of his glory and a wider vision of our duty and obligation.

✿ ✿

Notes and Comments.

It is the way of the world. The children are nearly always more progressive than the old folks. Great Britain has advanced as far as to have considerable measure of federation, and a "Free Church Council" was an estab-

Editor's Easy Chair.

PENTWATER MUSINGS.

"Break! break! break!"
O waves of an inland sea!
"And would that I could utter
The thoughts that arise in me."

With apologies to Tennyson for the adaptation, we quote the above lines as fitly expressing the situation here this morning, and the feeling which it awakens. All night long the wind has blown a stiff gale from the southwest until the early dawn, when it changed to the west and northwest, and now the waves are tumbling over each other in wild confusion, for they can not change their direction as speedily as the wind. This is the break of a long warm spell, and the change is welcome. Looking out across the wide waste of waters, and listening to the tumultuous roar of the waves as they break on the shore, one indeed feels his soul stirred with thoughts which can not well be uttered. It is in the power of a sublime scene like this, or the sweet and tender strains of music, or a great painting, to lift the soul out of its narrow limitations which inhere in the body, into the wider and illimitable ranges of the spirit which, while under its spell, knows not time, nor place, nor environment, but is swallowed up in communion with the invisible and the eternal. It is deep answering unto deep. It is the divinity within man, responding to the manifestations of the divine in the world about us. But who is capable of conveying in intelligible speech the thoughts which at times sweep over the soul, as the great waves this morning are sweeping over the surface of the lake! Perhaps not till the soul attains to perfection will its expression be equal to its impression, and its utterance be a complete revelation of its inward thoughts and feelings.

❦

Looking far out toward the sky-line over the movable hillocks which the wind has thrown up from the bosom of the lake, one gets the impression of a vast, primitive, western prairie, where the tall grass is swayed by the breeze, except there is a touch of wildness and sublimity in the water-scene that does not belong to the landscape. Sitting here by the fire this morning and gazing out through the windows on these wild and tumultuous waves, one can but congratulate himself that he is on shore rather than being tossed about on those noisy billows. And yet far out on the lake and lifting up its masts against the sky is a sailing vessel wrestling with the waves and pushing on bravely toward its destination. It might have turned its course toward this port and soon have found anchorage in a quiet harbor, but instead its sails are set steadily for its more distant port. And, no doubt, these jolly sailors, accustomed to "life on the ocean wave" on the great lakes, enjoy these adventurous experiences of the stormy weather far more than being becalmed on quiet, listless days, when the soft, languorous breeze is scarcely sufficient to keep their sails from idly flapping. The lesson these hardy sailors teach is that he who would

reach some distant, difficult port across life's stormy sea must not turn aside because of wind or wave to find some quiet harbor, but must push on to the desired haven. One is reminded of those heroic lines of Joaquin Miller on Columbus:

Behind him lay the gray Azores,
Behind the Gates of Hercules;
Behind him not the ghost of shores;
Before him only shoreless seas.
The good mate said: "Now must we pray,
For, lo! the very stars are gone.
Brave Adm'r'l, speak; what shall I say?"
"Why, say: 'Sail on! sail on! and on!'"

These gray skies, northern winds and boisterous lake bespeak the demise of the summer season on this shore. The loud anthem which the waves are sending up to-day is a fitting funeral dirge in memory of the dead summer. We are always glad to witness these tokens of the change of season before we leave these shores, for, while we enjoy these wilder moods of the lake, and welcome the cooler breeze which sweeps down from the north, they make us the more willing to forsake the beach, with all its pleasant summer memories and enjoyments, to take up the routine of duties in the crowded city again. We have had, however, a number of visitors to this park since September. Bro. R. M. Denholme, manager of the New Orleans "Item," has joined his family here and equally with them is charmed with the beauty of this place and will build here a tabernacle for a refuge from southern heat. The Campbell Institute colony at the club-house have been reinforced by several fresh arrivals and have been having a most restful and enjoyable season of fellowship and recreation. They, too, have decided that somewhere on the heights of "Garrison Park" they will pitch their tents hereafter for a few weeks of midsummer rest and fellowship together. A few evenings since, while the weather was yet summerlike, we built a council fire down upon the beach and all of us who yet remain on this shore gathered about it in a function known as a "marshmallow roast." It was a goodly company of friends whose faces glowed with the light of the bonfire on that balmy evening. When the marshmallows had been duly roasted on long sticks over the glowing embers and all had partaken, there were songs and conundrums and stories until the logs had been reduced to coals. Forming a circle about the fire and joining hands, we sang a verse of "Auld lang syne" and parted with happy "goodnights," closing what will probably be the last bonfire gathering on the beach for the season of 1906.

❦

We are awakened from these autumnal reveries here by the lakeside—the last of our Pentwater Musings for the year—by remembering the near approach of the Buffalo convention and the great autumnal convocation of the brotherhood of Disciples yonder by another lakeside at Buffalo. We are giving special prominence to that convention in our columns, this week, hoping thereby not only to stimulate attendance, but to awaken a deeper interest on the part of the brotherhood in these annual gath-

erings, and to help us make the best possible use of them. The articles which appear on different aspects of the convention in this number, have been written at our request and we bespeak for them the careful perusal of our readers. To use wisely the opportunities of life is the great secret of success. This is equally true of religious movements as of individuals. A national convention of Christian workers, having in view the same great ends, is a great opportunity, and to fail to make the best possible use of it would be a serious blunder. These conventions are opportunities for social acquaintanceship; for hearing and for learning; for inspiration and for high resolve; for spiritual illumination and for deeper consecration; for a wider vision of the world's needs and a clearer grasp of great spiritual realities; for fraternal counsel; for cementing the bonds of fellowship and of unity; and for forming larger plans for the development of the Redeemer's kingdom. No one who fails to go to Buffalo with an open mind and heart, seeking a divine blessing for himself and his brethren, can get out of it the enduring good that is possible for one to receive from such an assembly. It is only when our souls are attuned to the Infinite that we are prepared to have joyful and profitable fellowship with each other, in worship and in service.

❦

One night has intervened since the foregoing was written, and this morning calm has succeeded the storm, and quietness rests upon the lake and woods. The clouds have rolled by, and the sun is shining once more out of a clear sky. The air, however, is autumnal rather than vernal, and out in the still woods already the leaves of the maple and the hickory are putting on their autumnal tints. The latest visitor to the park is our active, energetic superintendent of the Christian Publishing Company, George L. Snively, who blew in upon us yesterday, in the midst of the storm, and who purposes to cross the lake to-night on his return home. Brother Snively has borne what would be a pretty heavy burden to the average man during the summer season, in the absence from the office of both the Editor and his Assistant, but work with him is what play is to most people—his joy and recreation. Brother Snively has climbed some of the heights of "Garrison Park" and had the magnificent view of lakes and woods, and confesses, as did the queen of old, that the half had not been told. By the time this paragraph reaches the eyes of our readers we expect to be in St. Louis, and with this paragraph, therefore, we close our "musings" at Pentwater for the season. If anything herein recorded during the summer months has given any pleasure or feeling of restfulness to our readers, as many have indicated, we are grateful for the privilege of having ministered to their enjoyment. If anything of the contrary sort has appeared, we would gladly cancel it. Trusting we shall have the joy of meeting and greeting many of our Easy Chair readers in this beautiful resting place beside the lake in future summers. If God shall give them to us, we close this chapter of our summer "musings" and resume our accustomed place and duties yonder in that great metropolis that sits like a queen on the banks of the Father of Waters.

The Devotional Feature of t

By James M. Philputt

It is of the highest importance that a more prominent place be given in our national conventions to the devotional feature. The paltry fifteen minutes for "prayer and praise" at the opening of each day's session, while most of the delegates are taking their seats, is a poor apology for what this service ought to be. Not only, should more time be given to it, but it should come at a time when the great throng would get the benefit of it. Some hour in the afternoon would be more appropriate. A practical difficulty in the way is the fact that the program is always overcrowded. There is not time enough, as it is, for all the things that press for utterance. Luther used to say that some days were so full of work he had to take three hours for prayer instead of one—the more work the more time needed for prayer. The time spent in devotion is not

lost, but gained. The mental poise and greater clearness of spiritual vision which come from devout waiting upon God will give increased facility and expedition to all other duties.

Let there be the opening song and prayer at the beginning of the day as at present, but in addition on at least two days of the convention there should be an hour given up wholly to quiet, heart-searching devotion, prayer and testimony and meditation, listening for the voice of the Master who ever calls to a deeper spirituality and a more consecrated service. Better curtail some of the addresses and cut down the reports than to miss the inspiration which would certainly come to the great assembly from such an exercise as this. At a

re
di
to
ch.
wi
ho
wil
tha
wh
wil
pe:
Bu
kn
hea
of
roc
\
sin
giv
fau

The Scope of Our National

By W. F. Richardson

This is perhaps a fitting time for us to inquire as to the extent to which our national convention can go, in the consideration of questions that relate to the common judgment or concerted action of our people, where these questions do not have to do directly with the work of preaching the Gospel to the unsaved world. Space will allow of only the briefest treatment, and that rather suggestive than argumentative.

The constitution of the American Christian Missionary Society, in article II, states its object to be as follows: "Its object shall be the spreading of the Gospel in this and other lands." Nothing in this article of the constitution determines how much is included in this brief statement, but they treat of methods of securing and administering funds, and the like. Nothing is said as to what questions may come before the annual meetings of the society, but common sense, and the usages of such gatherings would indicate that such matters as have to do vitally with the carrying out of the specific object of the society would properly come before them.

Some questions, it is plain, could not receive consideration there. The Gospel that is to be proclaimed, the conditions to be imposed upon those who seek fellowship with the church and salvation from their sins, the rules that are to determine the spiritual lives of the children of God, and the names they are to wear—all such questions are settled for us by the New Testament, and our very plea for the restoration of primitive Christianity forbids that we should follow the example of those religious bodies that settle questions of doctrine and discipline in their ecclesiastic assemblies. Happily we have had little trouble along these lines, and have kept our annual gathering true to its primal purpose.

Yet there have been many matters, not immediately connected with preaching

of the Gospel to the unsaved that we have felt not only free, but impelled to consider in our conventions. The building of church houses, the care of disabled and aged ministers, the relief of the widow and orphan, the cause of Christian and ministerial education, the Bible school and Christian Endeavor work, have all received consideration. For some of these interests we have organized separate boards, directed by the society and fostered through their agencies. None of them has been counted alien to our great purpose of spreading the Gospel throughout the world.

Questions of a somewhat different character have found a place in our deliberations, without protest from any friends of the society. At different times, the work of the Bible societies, the Evangelical Alliance and similar Christian organizations, has been given a cordial hearing and hearty approval, so far as they have commended themselves to our judgment. Christian union has been a question of unfailing interest in these assemblies, and standing committees to further this holy cause have acted in the name and by the authority of the convention for many years. All these have been recognized as legitimate, though indirect adjuncts to the primary object of the society. It would have been folly for us to organize a separate convention for the consideration of each of these questions, and we have never considered it necessary. Why should it be needed now, when we are asked simply to say whether we are willing to co-operate with other Christian people in such aims for social and spiritual betterment as will not require any sacrifice of conscience, or surrender of our plea for Christian union?

Let us not forget two facts. First,

tha
rea
con
tur
but
cor
fut
pre
ters
sion
that
atte
any
ber
tion
exp:
chu
ther
stru
tion
tion
vidu
carr
vent
beer
of t
weir
con
crat
bod:
to :
righ
acti:
so i
ing
gath
que:
with
worl
co-c
no :
com
van
erat
for
God
bret
it m
with
prej
but
we
to t
the

Shall We Have a Delegate Convention?

By T. P. Haley

Our national conventions have become the pride of our people, and the wonder of our contemporaries. The large attendance, the admirable addresses, and the apparent harmony of the proceedings are a constant surprise to the ecclesiastic bodies of the country.

That such diversified interests and so many of them should be considered and disposed of in less than a week is indeed most remarkable. That the several societies are able to so divide the time that there is apparently no friction is still more remarkable. They are in many respects very great meetings, and yet many of our most thoughtful brethren are wondering if there is not still a better way. This feeling is wide-spread and begins to find expression in many parts of the country. Is it not the part of wisdom to give heed?

The American Christian Missionary under different names is "the mother of us all." It has under its general management and control "Home Missions," "Church Extension," Benevolences, Ministerial Relief, the Educational Society. It has considered the question of federation and at times civic, state and national questions. In a word it stands for the general interests of our Zion throughout the country.

The Foreign society was at the beginning composed of life directors, life members, and annual members. It was hoped that its funds would be secured from these sources, but in its history it became necessary to appeal directly to the churches. The C. W. B. M. Society is composed of its auxiliaries, its life members, and theirs is more nearly a delegate convention than any of the societies, but they are not delegates from the churches. All the conventions representing these various interests have become essentially mass meetings. They are not representative bodies in any correct sense of the word. They are composed of all who can be induced to attend. Cheap rates, cheap entertainment, special trains over attractive routes are invoked by different agencies for all they are worth to swell the attendance.

The business for the most part is transacted by the different boards of the various interests and their action is generally ratified without discussion, by the votes of the masses—the churches that give the money, and that are supposed to be interested, are only indirectly represented.

It is not strange that many feel that the time is come for a closer touch of the churches with these conventions. While these societies are accomplishing great results, it is a matter of profound regret that up to this date we have not been able to secure the co-operation of a majority of our congregations, perhaps not a majority of our preachers.

The writer confidently believes that in order to secure this end and in order to the highest efficiency of the conventions, they should be made strictly delegate bodies; that no one should be recognized as a part of the convention who does not bear from some church or some association of churches certificates of appointment as delegates with authority to speak and vote for the churches.

This would secure, sooner or later, representation from all the churches among us.

It is considered a high honor, sought and coveted, among our religious neighbors to be chosen to represent their churches in their assemblies, conferences and associations. Why not among us? Perhaps even one delegate from each church would make the conventions cumbersome, but county and districts and state could easily arrange the matter of representation. The first great gain would be to give every church a voice in the deliberations of the convention. The second gain would be to keep all the preachers and churches in intelligent touch with all our enterprises. In the third place a majority vote in the convention on any question would determine every question of interest and go far toward the reconciliation of that element called the Anti. In the fourth place, the churches and not the editors nor the secretaries would decide the questions to be considered, for such a delegation could be trusted to consider and decide any and all questions that come before a growing people. All power resides in the people, and the people rather than the clergy can be trusted. It requires no prophet to see that the breach between the co-operating churches and noncontributing churches will continue to widen unless in some way we can be brought into common counsel. It would be wise to make it the chief concern of all agencies of the societies to secure increasing representation in our meetings. Only in this way can the unity which we have so earnestly commended to others be preserved among us. Let there be the utmost freedom in all our discussions, in conventions and trust the inevitable law of "the survival of the fittest." As this great country could not survive "half free and half slaves," so be assured that the unity of our great brotherhood can not be preserved half co-operating and half opposing or indifferent.

The Business Side of the Convention

By F. M. Rains

The business transacted in our national conventions is all important. Indeed, this is the chief reason for the convention. Most of the business, however, is necessarily done in committees. The time required would be too great and the process too tedious to conduct all the business in open convention. Hence the careful selection of well-equipped men and women to go over every phase and detail of the work. This is done in the quiet of the committee room, with most thoughtful attention. Results are reported and recommendations are offered. Such a report after due consideration by a competent and painstaking committee should command, and usually does command, great respect by the whole body. Amendments and substitutes will be offered for such a report after careful reflection and with due caution. The convention is no parlimentary gymnasium. To expedite real business is the constant aim. However, the reports of the committees are the property of the conventions to be disposed of as the combined wisdom of the great body may suggest.

It goes without saying that when one accepts a position on a committee he should serve faithfully. No personal inconvenience should be permitted to in any way prevent. This may involve the loss of a part of the program, even some of the very best addresses. No matter. Certain important work has been accepted and must be looked into carefully and from every possible angle of view. Neglect will retard and frustrate the objects of the convention.

Another matter. Due attention should be given to the annual meeting of the Board of Managers of the different societies. Every really interested member of such board will be present when possible. The work of a whole year is reviewed and plans are adopted or proposed for future activities. Sometimes the attendance upon such meetings is altogether too small. It is important that each member acquaint himself as far as possible before the meeting with the scope of the report to be reviewed. This implies, of course, investigation and preparation before the annual gathering. Of course, the boards will inquire diligently into the condition of the treasuries and learn all about the financial strength of the work, the obligations assumed, and the probable resources, etc. Business caution will also learn the exact facts as to the safety of trust funds and other invested funds, the bonds of treasurers and other safeguards as to permanency and absolute public confidence.

As our work in all departments grows, the conventions should be more and more on the alert in the selection of officers and boards of the various societies. As far as possible every such member should be thoroughly interested in the work and his efficiency should be above question. The importance of a live, up-to-date, wide-awake board or executive committee can hardly be overstated. No department of work will go beyond the intelligent interest and enterprising efficiency of the board having it in hand. The convention as a whole can hardly make wise selections, and hence the responsibilities of the various nominating committees.

The convention addresses are important, the social enjoyment is most delightful, the spiritual awakening and experience will be remembered with inexpressible joy, but the conventions must give due emphasis to the business side if they are altogether successful.

I believe this great international gathering will prove one of the most useful in our splendid history.

Cincinnati, Ohio.

Educational Value of the Great Conventions
By HERBERT L. WILLETT.

There is no school in which the spirit and purpose of the Disciples of Christ may be so accurately learned as in the annual conventions which gather to consider the great interests of the brotherhood. Up to this central place representatives from all sections of the land and from beyond the sea come to bring their offerings of money and testimony and to exchange information regarding the progress of the cause.

The educational value of the convention is foremost that of affording knowledge of our missionary work. The reports of the board, the addresses of the leaders in our Israel, the recital of missionary experiences by those who have returned from their fields of service give the listener new and expanded horizons and reveal the opportunities set before the Disciples for larger things.

The social side of the convention is not without distinct educational value. The give and take of conversation during the intervals of the sessions, the revival of old associations, the forming of new acquaintances and the perception of the spirit of and personnel of the brotherhood are among the best experiences of the occasion.

One goes back to his home with a new sense of the greatness of the people with which he is associated, and a new consciousness of the opportunities confronting him. If he lives in a region where the Disciples are numerous he has the privilege of bringing to them the inspiration of a great gathering; if he is an isolated Disciple, he gains courage to bear an urgent and more vital testimony regarding Christian union on the New Testament platform.

The conventions are our greatest educational force.

The Local Arrangements at Buffalo
By R. H. MILLER,
Chairman of the Executive Committee.

The Entertainment Committee for the Buffalo convention has spared no pains to secure the convenience and comfort of the delegates. Buffalo is a great convention city. Conventions follow one upon the other without intermission. The hotels and boarding houses are crowded the year around. It is therefore difficult to secure reduced rates or to reserve accommodations in advance.

Nevertheless, the committee has secured reduced rates at nearly all hotels and also a limited number of advance reservations. Only first-class hotels and boarding houses have been selected.

It is well to keep in mind that Convention Hall, where all sessions of the convention will be held, is on the border of the residence section of the city. It is removed from the commercial hotels and the cafes and restaurants. The committee has tried, therefore, to get rates at the hotels near Convention Hall on the American plan, i. e., lodging and meals. Delegates are advised to take hotels where offered on the American plan. Considering the location of the hall, it has been necessary for the committee to make provision for the noonday and the evening meals near the place of meeting. Excellent cafes may be found in the downtown section within three-quarters of a mile of Convention Hall. But many will prefer to be accommodated within easy walking distance of the hall. We have provided for a lunch counter on the second floor of Convention Hall, where a nicely prepared box lunch will be served with tea, coffee, lemonade, ice cream and fruits at the lowest possible rate. This lunch counter will be open from 10 a. m. to 8 p. m., so that light refreshments may be had at any hour. On the second floor, with this lunch counter, will be the exhibit room for the missionary societies and the newspaper room, where will be the booths of our brotherhood papers. Both these rooms will be provided with abundance of chairs and divans. On this floor also will be a fine room for the ladies. This will be furnished as a drawing room, with every comfort and convenience. A room for the men, with spacious halls connecting all, will furnish place for all who will avail themselves of this kind of noonday rest and refreshment. For the more fastidious, who are not accommodated at the nearby hotes or the downtown restaurants, we have arranged for a temporary cafe, under the management of one of the best caterers in the city. This will be located within two or three blocks of the hall. Here a first-class meal can be secured at a reasonable rate.

A committee of 200 women have canvassed the residence section of the city to secure homes for the entertainment of delegates. This canvass has been conducted only in the better section of the city and within one mile and a half of the convention. The accommodations offered to the delegates to the Buffalo Convention will be exceptional in the class of homes opened to them.

A rate of one dollar for lodging and breakfast, and from 40 to 75 cents for lodging will prevail. A stub will be torn from the registration card at the registration desk at convention hall, stating the assignment and giving directions how to reach the place. When necessary pages will be provided to escort to the place of entertainment. All cars leading to Convention Hall will be marked "Convention Hall." A special folder explaining the mission and position of the Disciples of Christ will be furnished in numbers to each delegate to use in answering questions of the curious, and to leave upon the cars and in the streets.

Buffalo is not like other cities in climatic

As Seen From the Dome　By F. D. Power

That cruise ended I am at liberty to see things at home. Those letters were all written on shipboard and for nearly five months my pen has been resting. Meantime much has been going on in sight of my lofty perch. Federation still worries some folks; Mr. Roosevelt's spelling reform disturbs others; Mr. Bryan's views on government ownership of railroads are not without their elements of vexation and annoyance; the packing industry, the oil octopus, the dissolution of the Douma, Russell Sage's $60,000,000, Philadelphia's trust company and Chicago's Milwaukee avenue bank; the Thaw & Corey nastiness, the $50,000,-000 being spent at the nation's capitol in improvements, and many other matters of interest have been passing in review. The nation has even paused to read millions of extras announcing a bloody prize fight, and telling how in the presence of 10,000 howling American savages a negro pounded a white man out in Nevada! The very dome hides its diminished head in shame.

In our little religious world there have been movements. Bethany Beach has had another season—the best in its history. The attendance was the largest and the assembly the most successful. E. B. Bagby was in charge of the program, and such names as Wallace Tharp, I. J. Spencer, J. A. Lord, J. W. Carpenter, Peter Ainslie, L. G. Batman, Mrs. Princess Long, the Netz sisters, H. Lookabill, H. H. Moninger, J. A. Hopkins, Charles M. Watson, W. R. Warren, J. E. Stuart, W. H. Graham, Walter F. Smith, Philip Johnson and H. P. Atkins will give some idea of the excellence of the bill of fare. Visitors were with us from fifteen states, as far north as Michigan and west as Missouri and south as Kentucky and North Carolina. Some new cottages have gone up and others are planned, and among new improvements a large hotel, electric lights, and ice plant.

The removal of E. B. Bagby from our midst is greatly regretted. The Franklin avenue church has done well to secure him. He has rendered splendid service here and built up a reputation that any man might well covet. The Ninth street church can ill afford to give him up. It is grieving over its great loss, and in all the throes of the choice of his successor. In the fifteen years of its life it has known no other pastor. It has

E. B. Bagby.

been a great hive of young people, and our brother has been an elder brother to them. He has been an unusually devoted pastor as well as a faithful and efficient teacher, and naturally his people are deeply attached to him. And not only in the church but in the city Mr. Bagby has a large following. The influence of his life has been felt far and wide. His service as chaplain of the house brought him in contact with many of the leading men in government circles. His zeal for the work of Christian Endeavor gave him a wide acquaintance with the young people of all the churches. His evangelical fervor and success made him felt in all the general missionary operations of our Christian forces. His sound judgment, fervent piety, and genuine humanity made him popular with all classes. So the work under his stewardship grew steadily and the church to-day enrolls over one thousand souls. It is an excellent field for a consecrated man. The retiring pastor goes with the prayers and good wishes of all our churches. We feel assured that his success in his new field will be every way in keeping with his honorable achievements at the nation's capital.

Still I am old fashioned enough to believe in long pastorates. Yesterday I preached my thirty-first anniversary sermon. The text was Acts 9:31. Take it up in your regular ministry some time and see how fruitful it is. Rest, edification, practical religion, joy of spiritual life, multiplication. We have had a profitable year notwithstanding the preacher's absence during the winter. Fifty-four have been added at our regular meetings and over $8,000 have been contributed for the various causes that have appealed to us. Our Sunday-school has been larger than ever before in our history, and our people have grown in the graces and fruits of the Spirit. Some of our best beloved have fallen asleep in Christ, and others have removed to other parts of the Lord's vineyard, but the work in all departments has steadily advanced. Ten thousand causes of thanksgiving are ours for past blessing and ten thousand thousand causes of encouragement as we look to the future.

One of the best things this summer has been the improvements in our house of worship. It is one of the most attractive now in the city. Newly frescoed and lighted, with new cushions and carpet, and a new baptistry with white tiling and marble coping transformed into a thing of beauty and a joy forever, the whole church appears as a new sanctuary. Our people are happy and ready for such a year of service as we have never before known. Only four persons were present at this anniversary who were with us at the beginning. In this period the church has changed perhaps three times and it has been possible three times for the preacher to turn the barrel. Vermont avenue may need a change, but the pastor anchors here—a new state of things would appall him.

❧ ❧

WELL PEOPLE TOO

Wise Doctor Gives Postum to Convalescents.

BUFFALO ·CHURCHES AND PREACHERS

Richmond Avenue Church, Buffalo.

Church of Christ, Niagara Falls.

The first mission of the Church of Christ that was established in Buffalo was in 1867, and at the instance of interested brethren in western New York. Services were held in the Protestant French church at the corner of Tupper and Ellicott streets. In 1870 a regular church organization was effected with thirty-one charter members. Within a few years the body had attained strength enough to build a comfortable though plain house of worship at the corner of Cottage and Maryland streets. This building was occupied till 1887, when the beautiful stone church at the corner of Richmond avenue and Bryant street was dedicated to the worship of God, and has been up to the present the home of the mother church in the city. Early in the '90s a mission was opened on Jefferson street near Utica, and this has outgrown the mother church in membership and is known as the Jefferson Street Church of Christ. Another mission point was established at Forest avenue and Danforth street some years later, and a church was soon after organized, the membership of which is now in the neighborhood of two hundred. The membership in the city has grown from 31 in 1870 to about 1,200 in 1906.

There are churches of the New Testament faith and practice in the suburbs of Buffalo and near-by cities. In the Tonawandas we are represented by three buildings. Niagara Falls, East Aurora, Williamsville, Clarence and North Lancaster have each one church.

Jefferson Street Church, Buffalo, N. Y.

The Jefferson street mission school in Buffalo was started under the superintendency of Bro. Geo. R. Godfrey, in the third story over a grocery. A building was erected before the church was organized, so the new congregation started at once with a church home. Among the charter members are noted the names of Bartholomew, Williamson and Samuel W. Beeson, with their families, and Richard Bulgin.

Located in a rapidly growing section, the field presented for the labors of the church was an unsurpassed one. Its responsiveness was shown in a growth of membership to 278 in five years. The present membership is over 600. The congregation has been fortunate in its pastors, all of whom have been faithful servants of the Lord and efficient leaders of men. The following have served up to the present time: Hiram Van Kirk, D. W. Besaw, Lowell C. McPherson, J. P. Lichtenberger, J. M. Rudy, Benjamin S. Ferrall. Also in 1906, Mrs. Nettie H. McCorkle served as pastoral helper for six and one-half months.

From the first the church has been actively evangelistic and missionary. Meetings with large results have been held by the following brethren: J. H. O. Smith, Roland A. Nichols, J. P. Lichtenberger and Allen Wilson. Besides these, the pastors and other brethren have held excellent meetings.

In 1899 the pastor, Lowell McPherson and wife were given up to become missionaries to Havana, Cuba; and in 1904 the church became a living link by sending one of its own young ladies, Miss Meldrum, to Cuba. B. S. Ferrall is the present pastor.

The Church at North Lancaster, N. Y.

In November, 1833, Brother Jasper Moss came to Lancaster to proclaim

W. C. Bower, Pastor of the Christian Tabernacle, N. Tonawanda.

R. H. Miller, Chairman of the Buffalo Convention Executive Committee, and Pastor of the Richmond Avenue Church of Christ.

Edward F. Randall, Pastor of the Tonawanda Church.

Christian Tabernacle, North Tonawanda.   Church of Christ, Tonawanda.

the ancient Gospel. He preached two evenings at the stone schoolhouse, after which he and Brother Porter Thomas and Brother Yearnshaw preached at different intervals of time at the same place until April 3, 1834, when a three days' meeting was held. Many were baptized and began to meet on the first day of the week to search the Scriptures. Thomas Hutchinson was appointed to open the meeting and presided. During the summer many were added to the church, notwithstanding the opposition from sectarianism was very great. The number of additions was 84. Christian Vinecke was appointed bishop of the church. In 1848 a meeting was held and a building committtee appointed. One-fourth of an acre of land was purchased, a meeting house, dimensions 47 feet long and 32 feet wide, was built and completed, and is still in use by the congregation at the present time.

The congregation has ever since kept up its organization. During the fall of 1855 a meeting was held by William Hayes, and a large number were added to the church. Milton Bartlett was the minister for a number of years. J. C. Goodrich held a meeting about the year 1866 or 1867; many were added. Since then, James Encell, W. O. Moore, McKay, A. M. Harvuot, Sinclair, Simon Rohrer, E. C. Wells, Smootz Sutton have ministered to the church. L. B. Withee is the present minister. Being a country church, its membership is greatly diminished by removals.

Clarence Church.

Prior to the year 1834 Alexander

Campbell traveled through Western New York preaching a few sermons at different points, Clarence being one of them. In 1834 Brethren Moss, Thomas and Yearnshaw visited Clarence and established a congregation numbering about 20, who met from house to house, but principally at the home of Jacob Strickler. In 1844 Daniel Strickler and Peleg Stranahan appeared before Emanuel Herr, justice of the peace, making affidavit to an article setting forth the facts that a society had been organized to be known as the First Congregation of Disciples of Christ, in Clarence. In 1844 the first meeting house was built at the west end of the village, on a lot given by Bro. Abram Shope. Many soul-stirring sermons were afterwards preached in the old stone meeting house on the hill by J. J. Moss, A. B. Green, Isaac Errett, Dr. Belden and others. In 1876 the church property was sold and a lot bought near the center of the village, and a substantial brick building erected, where the congregation still worships. The membership numbers about 50, about 35 being active workers.

The Church at Niagara Falls, N. Y.

On December 6, 1868, the Church of Christ located at Niagara Falls was organized by Tobias Witmer, David Greybiel and Joshua Goodrich. It began life in a school house in the country about three miles east of what was then the village of Suspension Bridge. The next year a small building was purchased in the city at the present location,, Niagara avenue and Tenth street, and the first meeting was held

in this building April 11, 1869. The new building, modern and commodious, was dedicated in September, 1898, by E. V. Zollars during the pastorate of F. W. Norton. The present membership numbers about 300. The property is valued at $15,000. The church holds a place of respect and influence among the other religious bodies of the community. It is progressive and missionary. Among those who have served as regular pastors are E. A. Pardee, J. H. Gordenier, John C. Encell, O. G. Hertzog, Dr. W. A. Belding, Andrew Scott, B. C. Black and F. W. Norton. The present minister, J. A. Wharton, has been in charge of the work for the past six years.

The Tonawanda Church.

The Church of Christ at Tonawanda, N. Y., was organized in March, 1853. This church was practically the pioneer among the churches known as "the Church of Christ" in Western New York. It has been instrumental in assisting to establish the work in Buffalo, Niagara Falls and North Tonawanda. It has been served by such men as Jasper J. Moss, J. M. Bartlett, J. D. Benedict, C. L. Straight; H. C. Parsons, J. C. Goodrich, George Lobingier, Levi Osborne, Frank Talmage, S. C. Humphrey and others of more recent years. The present membership roll comprises 420 names. The church is active in carrying forward the local work, and is a contributor to the missionary enterprises of the brotherhood.

Edward F. Randall, who is now the

J A. Wharton, Pastor at Niagara Falls.   Earle Marion Todd, Pastor of the North Tonawanda Church.   R. P. McPherson, Pastor of the Dunkirk Mission.

pastor, began his work as a Christian minister in October, 1892, at Cato, Cayuga county, N. Y. Four years were spent with that congregation. After 15 months' pastorate at Waterloo, N. Y., he removed to Swampscott, Mass., where an exceedingly difficult work was undertaken. After a brief interim, during which time he served the church at Troy, Pa., the work was again taken up at Swampscott and continued until January, 1904, at which time he was called to the work at Tonawanda, N. Y.

The Central Church of Christ at North Tonawanda was the outgrowth of a mission Sunday-school which was organized in a growing section of that city in February, 1899. It is situated in what is known as the Ironton District. There is no other English-speaking Protestant church within a half mile of this site, and previously to its organization little direct religious influence was being exerted on that part of the city. From the first the Bible-school has had a prosperous growth, the numbers of the school increasing until it was crowded out of the first quarters, which was a remodeled store building. From its organization Mr. George F.

Rand, president of the Columbia National and the Central National Banks of Buffalo, and the First National, of Tonawanda, has been its efficient superintendent. The school now has an enrollment of more than 500, and its average attendance last year was 334.

To answer the needs of this growing work, a church was organized in March of 1901, with 40 charter members. The church has steadily grown, until at the present time it has a membership of 300. It is active in evangelistic, missionary and philanthropic enterprises, and has a bright future. Plans were early laid for a large and modern building. In 1903 the present Bible school portion of the Christian Tabernacle was completed. This is a thoroughly modern structure, built upon the most modern school architecture, and erected at a cost of about $20,000. The church is planning to build the remainder of the tabernacle in the near future. When completed, the tabernacle will have a capacity of 1,500, and will cost about $40,000. The church has had two pastors. The first was J. H. Hughes, of California, and the present one W. C. Bower, formerly of Indiana.

Convention Program---Buffalo,

Christian Woman's Board of Missions.

Friday Evening, October 11.

7:45—Devotional Service, Mrs. Anna R. Atwater, Indiana.
President's Address, Mrs. N. E. Atkinson.
Music.
Address, "Our Centennial," Mrs. A. M. Atkinson, Kentucky.

Saturday Morning, October 13.

9:30—Devotional Service, Mrs. M. M. Wiseman, Iowa.
Report of the Board, the treasurer, Literature Committee and Superintendent of Young Peoples' Work.
Address, Miss Mary Graybiel, Mahoba, India.
Music.
Address, "Jamaica," W. F. Richardson, Missouri.
Introduction of Missionaries.

Saturday Afternoon.

2:00—Devotional Service, Mrs. Ella F. McConnell, Ohio.
Talks by Missionaries, Miss Graybiel, Miss Boyd, Dr. Longdon, Miss Maddock, India, Mr. and Mrs. Ireland and Miss Siler, Porto Rico.
Address, "Twenty Years of Educational Work in the Kentucky Highlands," H. J. Derthick, Kentucky.
Music.
Report of Nominating Committee.
Report of Committee on Watchword and Aim.
Closing Address, Mrs. W. W. Wharton, Illinois.

Foreign Christian Missionary Society.

Monday Morning, October 15.

9:30, Prayer and Praise, led by Miner Lee Bates.
9:45—Appointment of Committees.
10:00—Annual Reports.
10:30—Address, "The Lord Working With Them," Wallace Tharp.
10:45—Address, "Our New Responsibilities," M. A. Denton.
11:00—Introduction of Missionaries.
12:00—Adjournment.

Monday Afternoon.

2:30—Devotional Exercises, led by Amos Tovell.
2:40—Reports of Committees.
3:00—Address, "Completing Christ's Suffering," J. M. Philputt.
3:35—Address, "The Missionary Bump," C. J. Armstrong.
3:50—Symposium on "Taking the Offering," led by F. M. Rains.

Monday Evening.

7:30—Song and Prayer Service, led by A. D. Harmon.

8:00—Address, "Grounds for Encouragement," W. W. Sniff.
8:15—Address, "Christ, the Inspiration of Missions," W. F. Turner.
8:30—Address, "The Dignity of the Missionary Enterprise," J. A. Lord.

American Christian Missionary Society.

CONVENTION HALL.

Saturday Afternoon, October 13.

2:30—General Board Meeting, A. C. M. S.

Saturday Evening.

7:30—Christian Endeavor Session, R. H. Wagener, National Superintendent, presiding.

Sunday Morning, October 14.

11:00—Preaching in all offered pulpits (all preachers requested to preach missionary sermons).

Sunday Afternoon.

3:00—Union Communion Service (Convention Hall and nearby churches if necessary), S. M. Cooper, R. H. Miller, presiding.

Sunday Evening.

7:30—Preaching in all offered pulpits. (Preachers are requested to preach missionary sermons.)

Monday, October 15.

(Sessions of Foreign Christian Missionary Society in Convention Hall.)

Tuesday Morning, October 16.

American Christian Missionary Society.
9:30—Prayer and Praise, E. A. Cole, C. M. Kreidler.
9:45—Appointment of Committees.
9:55—Report of Board of Church Extension, Geo. W. Muckley, Cor. Sec.
10:15—Report of Statistician—G. A. Hoffmann.
10:25—Report of Acting Board, American Christian Missionary Society and Standing Committee on Evangelism, Wm. J. Wright, Cor. Sec.
10:30—Address, "God's Purpose and Plan in Home Missions," E. F. Daugherty, Wabash, Ind.
11:10—Introduction of Home Missionaries, by Geo. B. Ranshaw, Field Sec.
11:40—Address, "Higher Ideals in Christian Stewardship," H. D. Smith, Hopkinsville, Ky.

Tuesday Afternoon.

2:30—Prayer and Praise—H. H. Saunders.
2:45—Ministerial Relief—Report, A. L. Orcutt, president.
Address, "The Oughtness of Ministerial Relief," C. J. Tanner, Detroit, Mich.

Convention Pointers.

Buffalo is the second city of New York state.

It offers exceptional attractions and conveniences to delegates.

It has an ideal October climate; bright, cool and invigorating.

The convention will be held in Convention Hall, by courtesy of the city of Buffalo.

The sessions of the C. W. B. M. will be held in the beautiful Delaware Avenue Methodist Church, by courtesy of the trustees.

Convention Hall is on the corner of Virginia street and Elmwood avenue.

The Methodist church is on the corner of Delaware avenue and Tupper street.

The Elmwood avenue cars proceed directly from the union depot to Convention Hall.

The universal transfer system prevails in Buffalo. One transfer from any boat dock or depot will deliver you at the door of Convention Hall.

All cars leading to Convention Hall will be marked.

The reception committee will meet all trains and boats.

The entertainment committee will furnish minute instructions to delegates to find places of entertainment as assigned or send escort.

Go directly to Convention Hall on arrival and receive assignment and the beautiful souvenir program and badge.

A special agent has been appointed to attend to the convenience and comfort of the delegates at the hall.

Attendants will be on duty at all hours to give delegates information and assistance.

An agent of the railroads and excursion will be present during the convention.

Rest rooms will be comfortably furnished.

Postoffice, telegraphs, telephones are installed in Convention Hall.

The Christian Woman's Board of Missions will have in several particulars the best report in the history of its work. This has been for it a year of building, and in the United States, Jamaica, India, Mexico and Porto Rico its equipment has been materially bettered.

H. A. Denton is one of the most successful and energetic of our Missouri preachers. He is well known to convention goers in our state as he is a ready debater. He is especially identified with Christian Endeavor work.

Miss Ada Boyd, for twenty-four years a worker in India's zenanas, will tell of her work in and about Bilaspur. Miss Boyd is one of the pioneer missionaries of the Christian Woman's Board of Missions in India, and one of its most efficient workers.

Porto Rico will be represented by Mr. and Mrs. Elmer Ireland and Miss Nora Siler. These workers are all from Bayamon, which is the center of the work in Porto Rico. They have all been connected with the educational work of the mission, and will speak of their experiences.

The Christian Woman's Board of Missions will hold its annual board meeting in the Delaware Avenue Methodist Church, Buffalo, N. Y., Friday, October 12, beginning at 10 o'clock in the morning. All state presidents and state secretaries are urged to be present.

Miss Mary Graybiel, who opened the work in Mahoba, India, will speak of the history of the work in the Hamirpur

district. Miss Graybiel has been identified with our forward workers in India and will be heard with deep interest.

The Christian Woman's Board of Missions urges all its friends and acquaintances to meet with it in the national convention in Buffalo, N. Y., October 12, 1906. The first meeting will be held Friday evening, opening at 7:45 o'clock. The work will continue through Saturday, morning and afternoon. Come and rejoice with this organization in the work of the year.

The Foreign Missionary Society, whose session will be held on Monday, has arranged an excellent program. Some men well known to the brotherhood, like J. A. Lord, of "The Christian Standard," and J. M. Philputt, of St. Louis, will take prominent part. The latter will be welcomed by the New York people as he spent many years of his ministry in that state. One of the speakers will be Wallace Tharp, who has charge of a great church at Allegheny City, Pa.

Miner Lee Bates is one of our young men who has undertaken the very difficult work of the pastorate so long held by B. B. Tyler in New York city. He is on the program of the Foreign Society.

S. M. Cooper, who has been the president of the American Christian Missionary Society since the convention at San Francisco, will be general chairman of the Buffalo convention. Brother Cooper is a business man, but has long shown a devoted interest in the organized work of our churches.

Harry D. Smith, one of the most popular of Kentucky preachers, will, we are sure, give us some "straight talk" in his address on "Higher Ideals in Christian Stewardship," which is on the program of the A. C. M. S.

W. E. M. Hackleman will have charge of the music and into no hands could it be committed with more assurance. The selected hymns have been chosen from "Gloria in Excelsis," the new hymnal published by the Christian Publishing Company.

Miss Ella Maddock, Deoghur, India, who has had charge of our leper station since the death of Miss Jane Adam, will tell of her work for these unfortunates.

W. F. Richardson, of Kansas City, Mo., who will speak of Jamaica has had unusually good opportunities for becoming acquainted with the people of that beautiful island. Some of his adventures, while there but a few months ago, were most interesting. We are sure he will take his audience into his confidence, telling his hearers not only of the churches of Jamaica, but how to ford its swift rushing streams, to climb its steep mountains, and to quote its pointed proverbs.

Prof. H. J. Derthick, of Hazel Green, Ky., who addressed the national convention on the subject of educational work in the Kentucky Highlands, has long been an earnest worker among the mountain people. He knows the mountains and will open a most fascinating chapter in their history.

Dr. and Mrs. Rioch.

Missionaries under the Foreign Society who will be present at the convention are A. E. Cory and wife, of Wuwu, China, who are soon to return to their field; David Rioch and wife, of India, and Ray Eldred and wife, of Bolengi, Africa.

Dr. Mary Longdon.

Our Budget

—Ho, for Buffalo!

—A convention city without a peer!

—October 12-18 is the date.

—In other columns of THE CHRISTIAN-EVANGELIST you will find much about this great international gathering of the Christian churches.

—How will you go? If you would like to enjoy the fellowship of the party in the "CHRISTIAN-EVANGELIST Special" we will try to give you a place, if you will write us at once. See further particulars on page 1191.

—The church at Ozark, Mo., is still without a pastor.

—There is in hand one more article of the series, "Modern Religious Persecution."

—Grant A. Waller, of Utica, Ohio, has been called to the pastorate at Zanesville, Ohio.

—C. A. Hill has been called to fill the pulpit of the Island Church, Wheeling, W. Va., until January 1.

—The work of the First Church, of Springfield, Mo., is prospering under the leadership of A. S. Morrison.

—The Foreign Society has received a gift on the annuity plan from a friend in Missouri. This is the second gift by this donor.

—W. O. Breeden writes that with two more payments the church at DeQueen, Ark., will be out of debt. They have just called a pastor.

—The office force is eagerly awaiting the return of its Chief, who, all being well, will, with Mrs. Garrison, be back in St. Louis before these lines reach our readers.

—We had a pleasant call from C. C. Peck, who was for some time located at Arkansas City, Kan. Brother Peck was on his way to the state meeting and may again locate in Kansas.

—Cecil J. Armstrong has been pastor of the church at Winchester, Ky., since his graduation from college. His suc-

—J. R. Blunt will leave Richland, Mo., to take up the work at Marionville about October 1. Richland is a good field for the right man. Brother Blunt speaks very highly of the brethren there.

—A. R. Wallace, of Seligman, has been added to the state forces in Southwest Missouri. He will be sent to help county boards where they are not strong enough to employ a man during the year.

—Charles W. Mahin writes that the church at Rock Creek Centre needs a minister for one-fourth time. Write him at Angola, Ind., if you desire to be put into correspondence with the proper parties.

—Alfred Munyon has just entered upon his tenth year's pastorate of the church at Kirksville, Mo. That speaks well both for the church and the preacher. We need more of these more permanent pastorates.

—T. M. Myers, Lexington, Ky., writes that a new church has just been dedicated at Charlotte Furnace, Ky., where he has been holding a meeting with a large attendance, and 10 additions up to date.

—Dr. Luttenberger sends us a picture post-card from Munich, containing a representation of the Frauenkirche—one of the finest churches in Europe. Dr. Luttenberger may attend the Buffalo convention.

—C. A. Burkhardt, one of the young men of the South Joplin church, was recently set apart for the ministry, this being the third ordination in that congregation since it was organized less than three years ago.

—We are glad to learn that the board of the church at Bethany, Mo., has just recommended to that church that it become a living link in the Foreign Society. The average attendance at the Bible school has been increased through the summer months and a contest is to be begun with the schools at Albany and Bethany. T. J. Golightly is the pastor.

where A. A. Doak is pastor manent address is 413 Maj Indianapolis, Ind.

—The new church at Wash., which will cost $40,0 pleted, has been opened for

—J. J. Bare will take up Sumner, Ill., September 16 of his time to Bridgeport Hill.

—Secretary F. M. Rains d churches as follows: Arr September 2, L. E. Chase, worth, Ill., September 9, Joh pastor; South Louisville, ber 16, E. B. Richey, pastor

—The Junior Christian E ciety of Armington, Ill., is society of that state, it hav larger amount per member than any society in Illinois. Chase is superintendent.

—Ralph McCorkle, who g der the Foreign Missiona was a visitor at THE CHRIST 1ST office last week. He to let our readers have the b experiences in the foreign fie

—We are glad to hear tha Newton, who has been laid time with an attack of appen last on the mend and he able to be at the convention "THE CHRISTIAN-EVANGELIS party.

—Evangelist H. F. MacL ram, Ohio, has been speakir Trumbull, Ohio, and Sandy He will begin at Ladonia, Ir ber 23. He is also to take simultaneous meeting at the last of October.

—Thursday, September 27 College Centennial Day" in th state convention. The colle ington will go on a special large attendance is expected Sunday-schools in the state. tist and Presbyterian semin been invited, and a strong pr being arranged, President E. being among the speakers.

—W. F. Turner is a man of souri is proud. He has done

Cecil J. Armstrong, a Convention Speaker.

cess there has made other churches wonder whether they could not persuade him to leave. We believe that Missouri has its eye on him at the present moment.

—Victor Dorris is to help F. M. Rogers with a meeting in Springfield, Ill., and 500 copies of THE CHRISTIAN-EVANGELIST will be used by this strong evangelistic force as aids.

B. H. Hayden, Pastor of the Forest Avenue Church, Buffalo.

—All offerings for the Board of Church Extension should be sent to G. W. Muckley, corresponding secretary, 600 Waterworks building, Kansas City, Mo. Remember that the books close at noon September 29.

—J. V. Coombs and J. Walter Wilson have united their work in the evangelistic field and are now holding a meeting in the large tabernacle at Kent, O.,

W. F. Turner, a Convention

work at Joplin—the great min of our southwest.

—We have not received the thoritatively, but a newspape announces that C. C. Morris signed his pastorate at Sprin and it has been accepted. It is stated that he will take unto wife soon.

—H. W. Milner has resigne

at Harrison, Ohio, and will be ready soon for a new field of labor. He enjoyed recently the helpful association of Joseph Armistead, of Norwood, Ohio, and R. W. Abberley, of Walnut Hills, in a fine rally day service.

—D. T. Stanley has accepted a call from the Kensington Christian Church, Philadelphia, Pa., and has already entered upon the work. He writes that he has been given a royal welcome. A reception was tendered him on Thursday evening in which all the churches of the city took part.

—S. M. Bernard, who is located at Boulder, Colo., which is the site of the State University, has just taken what we believe a very excellent step in giving four Sunday evening addresses for the new student. He discusses him "Away from home, among friends, spending money and laying a solid foundation."

—The church at Salem, Ind., is enjoying happy times. Every dollar of the $4,500 that have just been spent on the building has been paid. A $1,200 organ has been installed, Mr. Carnegie paying one-half of it while the other half has already been raised by the church. W. Y. Allen, the pastor, has been called for his sixth year.

—The First Christian Church of Bloomington, Ill., has just given a reception for their new pastor, Edgar D. Jones, and his wife. Special invitations were issued to the members of the Second Christian Church and the resident pastors and their wives. It was a very happy occasion and the indications are that under the leadership of Brother Jones this church will accomplish much for its city and our cause.

—Dr. Jennie Fleming, of Columbia, Mo., has just been appointed a missionary to India by the Foreign Society. She sails from New York in company with Dr. C. C. Drummond and family, October 13. She will do the work of a trained nurse in the Christian Hospital at Harda, India. The church at Columbia, Mo., of which she is a member, and C. H. Winders is pastor, will provide her support after this year.

safely back from the midst of danger and we thank friends who have expressed their interest in our narrow escape from going where some of our belongings probably went—over the great falls of the Yellowstone.

—Robert E. Henry, writing of the work at Moline, Kan., where he is pastor, says the church is prospering and he asks the co-operation of any one who knows of members of the Christian church who have moved to Moline or neighborhood, to notify him of this fact. The church is but five months old and its Church Extension offering is nearly $10. Among those who recently joined the membership are two of the leading citizens, one of them being the postmaster as well as the editor of the largest city daily.

—Bernard W. Bass, who recently resigned the pastorate of the Tenth Street Church, at Paducah, Ky., made us a pleasant call on his way to take up work at Prineville, Ore. This is a small but growing community in the northwest and Brother Bass believes that it offers a fine field for an energetic Christian worker. He will be the only minister of the simple New Testament plea within a radius of 100 miles. Both the churches at Paducah are now without preachers.

—Efforts are being made looking towards the establishment of a high grade college or university for our brotherhood within the new state of Oklahoma. E. V. Zollars, late president of Texas Christian University, for so long identified with Hiram College, has been selected as the head of this movement. The location of the university has not been determined and bids are asked to be sent in before October 1 to W. A. Humphrey, Guthrie, Okla., at which time the Board will meet.

—Talk is crystalizing into a definite plan at Versailles, Ky. R. J. Bamber, the energetic pastor of the Christian church, is leading a movement to erect a handsome, modern $25,000 house of worship. It is proposed to raise a fund of $15,000 to be added to the material in the present building and the value of that site, should it be deemed necessary

"Help us to get into our own church home."

DID YOU TAKE

a Church Extension Offering the first Sunday of September?

The Offering began then but it should not end until every church sends an Offering. Select the best Sunday to suit local conditions, but

SEND AN OFFERING

to G. W. Muckley, Cor. Sec., 600 Water Works Bldg., Kansas City, Mo.

The Annuity feature of Church Extension is profitable to you and the Board. You receive 6 per cent and the Board builds churches with your money.

Voorhis and family. Words of kindly greeting came from every department of the church, and representatives of the Pastors' Union added their words of welcome. The brethren are planning to send a strong delegation to Buffalo, and are hoping to get I. J. Spencer to lead them in their fall campaign for soul winning.

—The Board of Church Extension received the following annuity gifts during August: One hundred dollars from a friend in Kansas; $500 from friends in Montana; $100 from a friend in Lodi, Cal.; $50 from a brother in Oklahoma, and $166.66 from a sister in Michigan. All remittances on the annuity plan should be sent to G. W. Muckley, cor-

Convention Hall.

Ray Eldred, African Missionary Who Will Speak at the Convention.

—The Assistant Editor is back at his desk, with steadier nerves and some color in his cheeks. He is grateful to all who have made it possible for him to take a needed rest, and would make especial mention of his co-laborer, George L. Snively, who so willingly took up the burden of the office work and handled it so admirably. We are grateful, of course, to the Protector who brought us

Mrs. Ray Eldred.

to secure a new location. This matter has not been decided. Five thousand dollars have already been raised, and, according to the local newspaper, there is little doubt that the entire amount will be secured this year.

—We are glad to hear a good word from the old church at Bellaire, Ohio, which is just starting out under a new pastorate. The good people have just given a royal welcome to W. D. Van

responding secretary, 600 Waterworks building, Kansas City, Mo.

—Ellis Purlee writes us very enthusiastically about the meeting that is being held at Coffeyville, Kan., by Thomas L. Cooksey, who is assisted by Sister Lucille Park, a member of the congregation there, and one of our best evangelistic singers. About forty-two additions are reported after twelve days of service. Brother Cooksey is a good preacher and an indefatigable worker and as the town is a live and growing one and the people have the spirit to pay heed to what is good and right, we have no doubt that our cause will be greatly advanced when the meeting closes.

—As we go to press there comes the sad news from W. O. Stephens of the death of B. B. Sanders, the pioneer evangelist of the Texas field. He died at his home in Austin September 14, of apoplexy. He was in the midst of a most successful meeting when the stroke came. Brother Sanders was 66 years old and had been an indefatigable worker. Brother Stephens writes: "He was the most successful, the most widely known and the best beloved of all our Texas preachers. He left not an enemy behind, for he was a good man. There are thousands of homes in Texas to-day that are filled with weeping because 'Daddy' as we loved to call him, has passed away. His life and work have made a permanent impression upon our cause in this great state." We hope to receive a fuller account of the life work of this good man.

How the Foreign Society Stands.

The receipts of the Foreign Society for the first eleven months of the missionary year, or to September 1, amounted to $221,333, a gain over the corresponding eleven months last year of $848. The gain in regular receipts amounted to $7,623. Let it be borne in mind that the books close September 30. The receipts must amount to about $35,000 during September or there will be a loss.

This Testimony

Will surely interest many readers of this paper.

James G. Gray, Gibson, Mo., writes about Drake's Palmetto Wine as follows: "I live in the Missouri Swamps in Dunklin County and have been sick with Malarial fever, and for fifteen months a walking skeleton. One bottle of Drake's Palmetto Wine has done me more good than all the medicine I have taken in that fifteen months. I am buying two more bottles to stay cured. Drake's Palmetto Wine is the best medicine and tonic for Malaria, Kidney and Liver ailments I ever used or heard of. I feel well now after using one bottle."

A. A. Felding, Knoxville, Tenn., writes: "I had a bad case of sour Stomach and Indigestion. I could eat so little that I was 'falling to bones' and could not sleep nor attend to my business. I used the test bottle and two large seventy-five cent bottles, and can truthfully say I am entirely cured. I have advised many to write for a free test bottle."

J. W. Moore, Monticello, Minn., makes the following statement about himself and a neighbor. He says: "Four bottles of Drake's Palmetto Wine have cured me of Catarrh of Bladder and Kidney Trouble. I suffered ten years and spent hundreds of dollars with the best doctors and specialists without benefit. Drake's Palmetto Wine has made me a well man. A young woman here was given up to die by a Minneapolis specialist, and he and our local doctor said they could do no more for her. She has been taking Drake's Palmetto Wine one week and is rapidly recovering."

The Drake Co., Wheeling, W. Va., will send a test bottle of Drake's Palmetto Wine, a purely vegetable compound, free and prepaid to any reader of this paper. A letter or postal card is your only expense to get this free bottle.

—A church of fifty members with plenty of life in them is the result of the work of H. E. Wilhite and wife, of San Bernardino, Cal. They have recently been at Belpre, Kan., where their efforts have been greatly blessed. Several thousand dollars have been subscribed towards a building and Elder T. F. Clarke is ready to correspond with some young minister who would like to undertake to enlarge this work. Orville D. Clarke writes that the little town has now two churches—one Bapist and one Catholic—and that in the last two years the Disciples of Christ have erected four beautiful churches of worship within the county, which is in the heart of the wheat belt. The brethren are anxious to have a permanent pastor just as soon as possible.

—The Hammett Place Christian Church of St. Louis will celebrate the thirteenth anniversary of the formation of the congregation on Friday evening, September 28, in a social gathering, and on Sunday evening, September 30, with a more elaborate program suitable to the day and appropriate to the occasion. Former members of the congregation are now settled in every section of the nation and an invitation is extended to them to arrange to be present, if possible. The congregation was formed under the name of Beulah Christian Church, September 29, 1893, under the guidance of O. A. Bartholomew. E. M. Smith, now of Centralia, Mo., was the first pastor, followed by W. A. Moore, now of Tacoma, Wash., and Samuel B. Moore, the present pastor.

—William J. Russell is in continual demand for platform work. The reason for this is not far to see. Brother Russell is a cultured speaker, has a fine presence and always has something to say. It is a pleasure to know that he is not too dignified to do pastoral work nor even to help on the canvass of a religious newspaper. A representative of THE CHRISTIAN-EVANGELIST was recently in Frankfort, Ind., and received not only the cordial well wishes of Brother Russell but his active co-operation in the two days of canvass, when some 52 copies of THE CHRISTIAN-EVANGELIST were put in the homes. Brother Russell writes in the following terms of our representative: "It was a blessing to me to be associated with this quiet and unassuming man. He is courteous to all other religious publications. He is a perfect Christian gentleman. The educational value coming from these fifty-two copies of THE CHRISTIAN-EVANGELIST can not be estimated in words." This is the kind of spirit we like to meet. The universal testimony is that where a good religious paper is circulated extensively in a congregation, that congregation is the one where the best fruits of the Christian life are manifested.

—We hear with deepest regret of the great affliction that has come to W. B. Clemmer and wife. Their only son, Clyde, aged 17, was drowned while Brother and Sister Clemmer were in a vacation meeting at Sterling, Colo. The youth was spending a few weeks with friends near Noble's Lake, Iowa, where his death occurred. He was a junior in the high school and of special promise. We do not wonder that Brother Clemmer writes: "Our loss seems greater than we can bear," but he adds—and here is one of the great facts of our religious experience—"strength is being given day by day." THE CHRISTIAN-EVANGELIST voices the feeling of a great brotherhood when it expresses its sympathy with our brother and sister in their great loss. We got to know something of the worth of W. B. Clemmer aboard "THE

For a Church in New Hampshire.

Already acknowledged $955 75
A friend (Lawson, Mo.) 2 00
O. F. Rakestraw 1 00

Total $958 75

A Good Letter.

L. O. Knipp, pastor of our church at Plymouth, Pa., has prepared a letter which we commend to the brotherhood generally. Other churches should find a suggestion in it. While we have no objections to congregations presenting their pastors with fancy clocks, walking sticks or even easy chairs in token of appreciation, we believe it would be a wise policy where these gifts can not be made in addition to the sending of the pastor to our national conventions that personal gifts be omitted in favor of a railroad ticket and convention expenses. The Plymouth church has sent its pastor regularly to these national gatherings. They even paid his expenses all the way to San Francisco. Brother Knipp is very appreciative of these courtesies and the congregation has discovered that the church is the gainer in the end. We append Brother Knipp's letter:

To the Official Board of the Christian Church:

DEAR BRETHREN—In a few weeks, October 12 to 18, we expect a large attendance at our International Convention at Buffalo. This is the first time it has been so close to our doors; for this reason we expect the largest attendance of delegates we have ever had from this section at any of our conventions.

Will you please encourage the members of your church to attend?

It is also desired that every preacher in my section attend, and to accomplish this, I ask you, as I am asking all the other churches, to please send your pastor as a delegate and tell him your church will pay his expenses. It will not cost you very much, and in this way you will show him your appreciation of his labors.

Earnestness, consecration and eagerness for souls will be characteristic of this convention, which he will enjoy, and your church will be the gainer many times over.

Trusting a favorable reply be received from you very soon, I am, sincerely yours, L. O. KNIPP.

"The Church of Christ."

Special attention is called to the page advertisement in this issue of THE CHRISTIAN-EVANGELIST of the book entitled, "The Church of Christ."

This work of a layman in the church is presented strictly on the merits of the book itself, and for this reason the name of the author is not given. It is a remarkably strong, clear and logical presentation of the origin, doctrines, purposes and problems of the church and is finding its way into the hands of an ever-increasing circle of readers.

Concerning this very lucid and helpful book, F. D. Power, of Washington, D. C., has written as follows:

"It will be seen the book covers a wide scope. It is written in a very succinct and satisfactory style, however, its positions well buttressed by scripture texts and illustrated with apt examples. Some of its teaching will, no doubt, meet with criticism, but its clearness and candor and eminent Christian spirit must commend it to most readers of every school of religious thought as a suggestive and valuable contribution to the literature on this subject. Whoever its author may be, it is evident at once that he is a devout student of the Holy Scriptures and a genuine lover of his kind. An impartial and serious examination of this volume will, we are satisfied, aid in the solution of the most trying and tremendous problems which confront our modern church. The claim that the Church of Christ should be one and identical in organization, teaching and practice with the New Testament church before the beginning of a creed, sect, or party; and that such unity, according to Christ's own word, is essential to its complete and final triumph; and must bring in the glad day when the kingdoms of the world shall become our Lord's kingdom, is surely a mighty one and worthy of the prayerful consideration of all lovers of the Christ. Our unknown author has done a good service, and we trust he will meet with a wide reading."

—W. W. Sniff, of Rushville, Ind., is one of the progressive young preachers who will help the foreign society. Brother Sniff was once located in St. Louis and also served the Franklin Circle Church at Cleveland, O.

—R. H. Bacon, who has been at Verdon and South Elrod, S. D., during the summer, is returning to Drake University to finish the liberal arts course. Brother Kerr, of Ohio, is to take up the work at Verdon on September 23.

—During the recent revival meeting at the Christian Church, Winchester, Ill., much interest was aroused on the subject of baptism. The Presbyterian preacher delivered a discourse on one Lord's day in defense of his church's views, and the pastor of the Christian Church and many of his people were present. The following Sunday night, Pastor Sharpe reviewed this sermon and very completely demolished, we should think, the contention of Mr. Gibson, who declared that immersion was not the Scriptural mode of baptism. Brother Sharpe's address was given the extent of over three columns in the county paper, and it was a very succinct and clear statement of Scriptural baptism.

—F. D. Eisenhart writes us about the work of Arthur Long, who has completed five years in the pastorate at Burlington, Iowa. He went there from Canton University, and during his charge has had 543 additions, that the membership of the church now being 560. In every way there has been progress, and at the present moment a new building is under process of construction, with the expectation that it will be dedicated in November. The membership, enthusiastic and working in harmony, is accomplishing much for the church and the city. Brother Long was not only appreciated by his own church, but he is president of the City Ministerial Association. We re-echo Brother Eisenhart's wish that Brother Long may have another five years of just as successful work in Burlington.

Help, Men of God!

With your help home missions will win a great victory this year. Gifts from individuals and churches generally contributing, but not having sent an offering this year, will put our receipts far in advance of those for last year. Just now we have about the same amount as for the same time a year ago. But hundreds of our friends are yet to be heard from. A little from each will make the grand total one of which to be proud.

Help, men of God! Send the offering without fail before September 30. Make checks payable to The American Christian Missionary Society, and send to Y. M. C. A. building, Cincinnati, O.

Wm. J. Wright,
Corresponding Secretary.

The New Jersey Federation of Labor protests against the quiet Sunday because union musicians lose their jobs at the beer gardens, union barkeepers lose the day's pay, and the sale of union-made cigars is curtailed. Anything for the union. Morals? Away with them. Fortunately, all organized labor does not take this attitude.

Stockholders' Meeting.

Notice is hereby given that the annual meeting of the stockholders of the Christian Publishing Company will be held at the company's office, 2712 Pine street, St. Louis, Mo., on Tuesday, October 2, 1906, at 10 o'clock a. m., for the election of directors and for the transaction of such other business as may legally come before said meeting.   J. H. GARRISON, Pres.,
GEO. L. SNIVELY, Sec'y.

St. Louis, Aug. 27, 1906.

REV. J. W. BLOSSER, M. D.

A Noted Minister and Doctor of Atlanta, Ga., is Meeting with Wonderful Success.

Those who have long doubted whether there really is a permanent cure for catarrh will be glad to learn that a southern physician, Rev. J. W. Blosser, M. D., of Atlanta, Ga., has discovered a method whereby catarrh can be cured to the very last symptom without regard to climate or condition. So that there may be no misgivings about it, he will send a free sample to any man or woman without expecting payment. The regular price of the remedy is $1.00 for a box containing one month's treatment.

The Doctor's remedy is radically different from all others, and the results he has achieved seem to mark a new era in the scientific cure of catarrh, foul breath, hawking and spitting, stopped-up feeling in nose and throat, coughing spells, difficult breathing, catarrhal deafness, asthma, bronchitis, and the many other symptoms of a bad case of catarrh.

If you wish to see for yourself what this remarkable remedy will do, send your name and address to Dr. J. W. Blosser, 475 Walnut St., Atlanta, Ga., and you will receive the free package and an illustrated book.

NEWS FROM MANY FIEI

Ohio.

The church at Bellefontaine will begin a meeting Sunday, September 16, with Pastor Roy L. Brown in the pulpit and Frank C. Huston as leader of song. The church is in good condition for a meeting, and this team ought to bring good results. S. L. Lyons has resigned at Rushsylvania to take some post-graduate work at Oberlin Seminary. He will preach for some church nearby if it can be so arranged. The Central Church, at Marion, has called as its pastor B. C. Piatt, who was until a short time ago pastor at Ashland. The Ohio letter man preached at Marion on the Sunday the call was extended and found a very energetic and enthusiastic body of Disciples who are perfectly united in their work. There are great possibilities for the Marion church. They have a fine new plant that is modern in every way. This union of preacher and people ought to mean much for the kingdom. Secretary Bartlett, with helpers, is now on the tour of the state in the interest of the fall offering for Ohio missions. J. J. Tisdall, of Cleveland, goes along to lead the singing. L J. Cahill, of Dayton, and T. W. Pinkerton, of Kenton, have been lending assistance in the arguments for Ohio missions. The response thus far has been very encouraging, and with a pull all together Ohio will free herself from debt by January. W. E. Adams is getting acquainted with his new field at Perry by holding an August meeting. A soloist from Wellsville, N. Y., added to the interest. The meeting was developing a good interest when last heard from. W. L. Neal, who has always been an Ohio man up to two years ago, but is now of California, has been visiting in Ohio with his children and his old parishioners at Wooster and Marion. Of course we all know that he would like to be back in Ohio permanently, even if he does not admit it. There will be a large number of Ohio people at the Buffalo convention. On every hand we hear people talking of the trip. We shall be very greatly disappointed personally in not being there. A meeting in Pawnee City, Neb., will make it impossible. The church at Canton has a new assistant. H. E. Parker, of Cleveland, has been employed as leader of all music and financial secretary of the church. Thus the church supports three paid workers—Pastor Welsheimer, Miss Staub, assistant, and Musical Director, Parker. They will hold a meeting with home forces in October. We were all shocked to see the news in the daily papers of the death of C. Manly Rice, pastor of the Island Church, Wheeling, W. Va. Brother Rice died August 29 at the home of relatives in Lorain of typhoid fever. He has been among the Ohio brethren for several years, serving as pastor at Greenwich, Wooster, Lisbon and then to Wheeling. He was a man of much ability and great energy. He was called in the prime of life. Our sympathies go out to the bereaved family and the Wheeling church. The funeral service was held at Lorain, Brother Fields, of the First Church, Wheeling, preaching the sermon, and the pastors at Lorain acting as pallbearers. The church at Painesville has extended a unanimous call to S. H. Bartlett to again become its pastor, and he has accepted. Brother Bartlett left the Painesville church to take the Ohio secretaryship. He will preach on Sundays after the Ohio offering is taken November 1, but will not give all his time to the church till next May, when he gives up the Ohio work. There is perhaps no man who will be better able to take hold of the work at Painesville and push it on successfully than Brother Bartlett can do. The church has Herbert Yeuell for a meeting in January. The Third Church in Youngstown had a corner-stone laying Sunday, September 16. John E. Pounds, of Cleveland, was the speaker. They are erecting a $10,000 building, or rather additional building. Frank D. Draper is bishop of this diocese. John Mullen writes that he has regained his strength by a sojourn in the balmy breezes of Texas, and will return to Ohio about November 1. Brother Mullen

is a splendid, capable man, and some Ohio church will do well to be on the lookout for him. He has served the church at Dalhart, Texas, temporarily while there. Hiram College will open the year's work September 25. The outlook for the year is reported to be very good. They expect too in the freshman class. The contract has been let for a $10,000 house on the west side at Warren. This means a second church in that city.   C. A. Freer.

Painesville, Ohio.

Western Pennsylvania.

Changes in the Pittsburg ministry have come rapidly. L. W. D. Wells resigned at Wilkinsburg and took the work at East Orange, N. I., September 1. George W. Knepper, of Somerset, will succeed him October 1. George Watson resigned at Squirrel Hill to accept the call to Van Wert, Ohio. G. E. Jones will enter Bethany College this fall to more fully fit himself for his work. E. E. Manley, of Belmar, has given a 90 days' notice that he will leave that field. He lately dedicated a $15,880.06 church, and has done fine work there. John A. Jayne has resigned at Observatory Hill to enter the lecture field and do journalistic work, in which he has already been very successful. These men will be missed from their fields and from our fellowship. Brother Knissef has entered upon his work among the foreigners of our district. Thirty languages are spoken in Allegheny and two adjoining counties. A special train will leave Pittsburg at 10 a. m. on October 12 to carry the delegates to Buffalo via the Pittsburg & Lake Erie. Arrangements will be completed this week for one of the best hotels for headquarters. The ministers meet every week at our headquarters in the Bissell block. Disciples passing through the city or visiting here will find a rest room and a place to meet friends at any time. It is near the depots and in the shopping district. Visit us. The officers for the year are: President, John G. Slater; vice-president, A. W. Place; secretary, J. D. Dabney; treasurer, Grant E. Pike. Our annual convention will be held in Homestead September 24 to 26. Carnegie Hall, which seats 1,200 people, has been secured for the night sessions. We expect to fill it.

                                           Howard Cramblet.

Cincinnati.

After a vacation of two months the Cincinnati Ministerial Association is again running in full blast with R. W. Abberley, J. W. Hagin and A. A. Sebastian at the head. Under the leadership of these faithful brethren we are expecting great things.——An evangelistic wave has struck our city. O. P. Spiegel and J. E. Sturgis are in a fine meeting with A. M. Harvuot at Evanston. Central. J. L. Hill, pastor, began a meeting Sept. 16, with W. H. Pinkerton as evangelist. Madisonville, W. H. Sallier, pastor, will begin Oct. 17 with G. W. Thompson and W. C. Smith evangelists. Northside, J. N. Green, pastor, will begin in October, with W. H. C. Runyan, evangelist. Walnut Hills, R. W. Abberley, pastor, will begin in October, with Herbert Yeuell and Leroy St. John. Other churches are planning for meetings, but the dates are not yet announced. J. I. Irwin has accepted a call to the church at Bellevue, and is already at work. This church has been without a minister for several months, but at last has secured the right man, and an abundant work will be looked for. George A. Miller spent his vacation holding two meetings in which there were about 15 additions. W. H. Dickerson, pastor of the Maple Street Church (colored), Lockland, has been engaged by the C. W. B. M. to take charge of the buildings and also to teach in the Bible school at Louisville. He is a man worthy of the position, and the school is to be congratulated in being able to secure him for this work. C. C. Smith is home after summering in Jamaica, and he came into the association meeeting September 9

with an interesting [...] H. W. Milner has resi[...] take up work elsewhere[...] has had a successful [...] sixth annual family S[...] First Church, Lockla[...] laters, September 9[...] speaker for the occasi[...] served in the interests [...] A local Sunday-school [...] state association will n[...] result of this day's ser[...] Brother Moninger for [...] ly benefited.

Station R.

The Annual Convention of the Indian Territory.

The ninth annual convention of the Indian Territory Missionary Co-operation was held with the church in South McAlester August 27-30.

The Christian Woman's Board of Missions occupied the first day. They had a fine meeting. Sister Atwater, national representative, was present throughout the session and rendered valuable assistance.

Prof. E. V. Zollars conducted Bible study each morning and afternoon, which was very much enjoyed by the delegates.

J. H. Mohorter, of St. Louis, gave an earnest and helpful address in the interest of our benevolent institutions. R. H. Waggoner, national superintendent of Y. P. S. C. E., spoke in the interest of Christian Endeavor work. George W. Muckley, of St. Louis, presented Church Extension in his most fascinating style, while W. J. Wright, in two great addresses, represented American Missions and Evangelism. L. B. Grogan, of Chickasha, read an historical paper dealing with the origin and history of the organized missionary work in the Indian Territory. In addition to the Bible lessons, E. V. Zollars delivered an address on the matter of a school in the central west. The convention unanimously endorsed the idea, and appointed a committee to act jointly with a like committee to be appointed by the Oklahoma convention, in taking immediate steps looking to the founding of such an institution.

F. L. Van Voorhis reported for the board. Among other things he said: "The advance of the past year over any previous year is almost incredible." The report of the corresponding secretary, S. R. Hawkins, showed a threefold increase over any previous year, in the amount of money raised for the support of the work, nearly six hundred additions, ten churches organized, about one dozen housed, twenty-eight meetings held under the auspices of the board and much other work accomplished.

Others who took part on the program and added to its interest and effectiveness were as follows: A. B. Carpenter, Atoka; George H. Farley, Muskogee; Randolph Cook, Tulsa; J. C. Mullens, Hartshorne; J. S. Hawkins, Pryor Creek; E. M. Harris, Wagoner; A. M. Harrol, Sapulpa; A. P. Aton, Holdenville; J. J. Stobaugh, Tichomingo; J. H. Crutcher, Middle Grove, Mo.; George Wolfe, Mattoon, Ill.; R. E. Rosenstein, Norman, Okla.; C. C. Ayers, Muskogee; W. H. Ligon, Broken Arrow.

It was a great convention. A history-making convention.

The writer has been re-employed to serve as corresponding secretary. Already I have plunged into the work, determined to do not only as well the coming year, but better. Brethren, pray for us, and help us.

End-of-the-Week Rates.

Chicago and North-Western Railway.

From Chicago to near-by summer resorts. Tickets at special low rates on sale Friday, Saturday and Sunday, good until the following Monday to return. Other low rates in effect daily. For tickets, rates and booklets giving full information, apply to nearest ticket agent or address W. B. Kniskern, P. T. M., C. & N. W. R'y Co., Chicago.

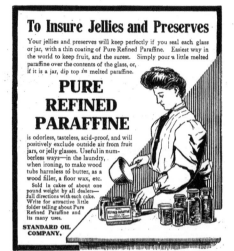

The Nebraska Institute and State Meeting.

It is the rule with our Nebraska preachers to spend two weeks in study and fellowship together just before the Nebraska state meeting. Their institute is held in Bethany, in one of the rooms of the Cotner University building. Chancellor Aylsworth gives each year a series of lectures. This year Prof. H. T. Sutton also gave a series of missionary studies. Both are able men and their work was highly profitable. Each year an out-of-state lecturer is secured, and I have twice had the pleasure of serving in this capacity. This year, besides a number of evening lectures of a general nature, I gave two courses of studies, one on comparative religion and one on the literature of the Bible. The names of 37 Nebraska preachers have been handed me as having been members of the classes. They are, I feel, the most earnest, reverent, open-minded men that one may meet. They are Christians and students, and it is a benediction to know them. Bro. H. C. Holmes, of Fairbury, is secretary, and I believe Brother Schell is president of the institute.

Following the institute, the Nebraska people have their state convention in Bethany. They own a beautiful piece of land, sheltered by great trees, on which they have erected a handsome pavilion at a cost of about $2,000. On the ground there were a hundred tents occupied by Disciples who came to spend the week and get and give in a great convention way. In spite of the almost continual rain, there were great audiences, and the people abounded in a spirit of joy and hope.

President E. V. Zollars was elected as the out-of-state lecturer and state meeting preacher for the coming year.

This Nebraska movement should be studied by other states in which it might prove feasible. Without disparagement to other states, I may say that I have seen nothing that answers the needs of a state convention so well as this, and there are few state conventions that are so largely attended.   W. J. LHAMON.

Columbia, Mo.

A Conspicuous Seccess.

Sunday afternoon, September 16, at 3 o'clock, there was held in the Hamilton Avenue Christian Church in this city, a large and enthusiastic meeting of the Bible-school workers of greater St. Louis, under the auspices of the Officers' and Teachers' Union, of this city. This organization is one of the results of the series of institutes held by State Superintendent J. H. Hardin in St. Louis last winter. The purpose of this organization is to foster closer co-operation on the part of Christian Bible school workers in St. Louis. It has done much in this direction, and last Sunday afternoon's meeting was an expression of its work so far. State Superintendent J. H. Hardin made the first address on the program on the subject, "What Our People are Doing Throughout the State." Other addresses were made by Dr. Chaffant, Dr. Lindsay (of the Anti-Saloon League), President Hanson (of the Union State Sunday-school Convention), and by Pastor McCreary (of the Hamilton Avenue Church). Reports were tabulated on a sheet, and this tabulation will be published and circulated in large numbers. The reports were, in the main, encouraging, but showed a great deal yet to be done.

Evangelistic

We invite ministers and others to send reports of meetings, additions and other news of the churches. It is especially requested that additions be reported as "by confession and baptism," or "by letter."

Special to THE CHRISTIAN-EVANGELIST.

Coffeyville, Kan., Sept. 17.—Fifty-four additions in fifteen days.—Cooksey and Park.

Special to THE CHRISTIAN-EVANGELIST.

Jacksonville, Ill.—Twenty additions in meeting with J. H. O. Smith.—R. H. Thrapp.

Special to THE CHRISTIAN-EVANGELIST.

Kansas City, Mo., Sept. 16.—Twenty-two to-day; one hundred and four to date in fifteen days; continue.—Wm. J. Lockhart, Altheide, Bowen.

Special to THE CHRISTIAN-EVANGELIST.

Oskaloosa, Ia., Sept. 17.—Meeting one week old; 21 added; splendid audiences, in spite of intense heat. A. E. Cory, former pastor, preaching; Mrs. Collins, of Keokuk, singing.—S. H. Zendt, pastor.

Special to THE CHRISTIAN-EVANGELIST.

Sullivan, Ill., Sept. 17.—Closed at Monroe, Wis., Monday with four sixty-one added. I gave first invitation here last night and had six confessions.—Charles Reign Scoville.

Special to THE CHRISTIAN-EVANGELIST.

Bloomington, Ill., Sept. 16.—We are in a most promising revival with the united forces of J. H. Gilliland and Edgar Jones. Fifty-three to date. Twenty-three to-day.—Brooks Bros.

Special to THE CHRISTIAN-EVANGELIST.

Arkansas.

DeQueen.—One addition by baptism.—W. O. Breeden.

Arkadelphia, Sept. 11.—A meeting of 9 days at Hebron church gave us 10 additions—6 conversions and 3 from other religious bodies and 1 by statement.—E. S. Allhands.

California.

Dinuba, Sept. 10.—One addition and others coming.—R. A. Staley.

Colorado.

Greeley, Sept. 11.—Meeting one week old, with 9 additions. L. H. Humphreys, pastor, is preaching. There is the greatest interest. I am leading a large chorus.—Charles E. McVay.

Illinois.

Princeton, Sept. 10.—Two by letter.—Cecil C. Carpenter.

St. Elmo, Aug. 24.—Two by confession and baptism, two by renewals.—Alfred T. Tucker.

Golden Point.—Seven baptisms not reported and a good Christian Endeavor Society started.—F. J. Yokley, Canton, Mo.

Douglas, Sept. 9.—Meeting still in progress. Five baptisms to-day; among them chief physician of the town.—N. A. Walker.

Edinburg.—Our big tent is crowded and the interest is intense. There has been a number of accessions. Brother Campbell is preaching.—D. W. Conner.

Niantic, Sept. 14.—We are preparing for a meeting in October. J. Will Walters, pastor, will do the preaching. Chas. E. McVay will have charge of the music.

Chicago, Sept. 13.—I wish to give a brief account of our meeting at Belpre, Kan., which closed September 2. We had no organization there when we went and but few members. These few were anxious for a meeting, and we began August 1. The interest increased until the Baptist Church building was quite well filled, and on special occasions standing room taken. The result of the meeting was 50 additions, many of these the most prominent people of the town. The mayor and his wife, as well as nearly half of the business people of the little city, united with the Church during the meeting. Several of these people are well to do financially. We raised $2,700 toward a building, which they begin at once, to cost not less than $4,000. Our church is the strongest in Belpre now and will grow. As soon as the new building is dedicated we are to return and hold another month's meeting. The church has a strong official board and is anxious to employ an able man as pastor. They will give the right man $1,000 salary. None but successful men need apply. S. G. Clark will answer all communications. A telegram from Brother Martin calling us to Chicago for a meeting hastened the close. We are here in South Chicago in a big tent meeting, with fairly good prospects. The audiences are increasing, with three additions the last three nights. It will require a long effort to accomplish results here. We must have a successful meeting this time, as they have never had a big meeting from the standpoint of additions. The church is weak in numbers, but willing to do all it can. The brethren are very hopeful of this meeting resulting in great strength to their ranks. There are 50,000 people in this section of the city, and this one small congregation of Disciples to represent our idea.—H. E. Wilhite.

Indiana.

Trafalgar, Johnson county.—I. N. Grisso and I began a meeting last Lord's day.—H. B. Shields.

Salem, Sept. 10.—Seven additions since last report.—W. Y. Allen.

Palestine.—One more added by confession, making nine since I have been supplying their pulpit.—Willis N. Cunningham.

Angola, Sept. 10—We held a short meeting at Rock Creek Centre Church, with 12 additions—ten by confession, all over 15 years of age, nine men. The church has heavy odds against it for different reasons, but the membership is faithful and energetic. Our next work is at Ambia.—Charles W. Mahin and Wife.

Indian Territory.

Tulsa, Sept. 10.—Four additions yesterday and one not reported. Our work prospers all over the territory.—Randolph Cook.

Buffalo, Sept. 10.—Five by letter since last report. I have just completed my first year's work here and have had 89 additions for this church and at other points where I have preached.—A. M. Harrall.

Davis, Sept. 12.—A. C. Parker, of Ladonia, Texas, assisted by Brother Cooper, of the same place, as song leader, has just closed his successful meetings in spite of great hindrance from stormy weather. We had 36 additions, 19 by confession and baptism and nine by statement and letter. Last year Brother Parker added 75 to his congregation in two weeks. Thus in five weeks 111 have become members of the Davis church through his influence.—J. R. Clemmons, Elder.

Iowa.

Oskaloosa, Sept. 14.—In a short meeting at Pulaski there were 7 additions—3 baptisms.—D. Dunkleberger.

Sioux Rapids.—Julius Stone reports 10 baptisms. Fifteen have been added in a few months.—E. F. Christian.

Jefferson.—The Putman-Egbert meeting of three weeks closed with seventeen additions and the church greatly strengthened.—Samuel Gregg, pastor.

Bloomfield.—Thirty-three baptisms and 5 by transfer in an eighteen days' meeting at Stiles, Ia. Bro. Dan Hastings ministers one-fourth time there, but was hindered from being present at this meeting, taking my place at Bloomfield while I was with his congregation. We organized a Christian Endeavor Society for the new converts, and started a subscription list to pay for half-time preaching.—F. D. Ferrell.

Kansas.

Manhattan, Sept. 10.—Two confessions since last report.—W. T. McLain.

Plainville, Sept. 14.—Work is on the up-grade here; audiences growing. We are planning for a meeting to begin October 28. Neal Overman, of Lincoln, will do the preaching.—N. Ferd. Engle.

Clay Center, Sept. 15.—Bro. Otha Wilkison and wife are with us in a meeting. The interest is increasing and the crowds come regardless of the inclement weather. Brother and Sister Wilkison are spending their summer vacation in the Lord's work. When this meeting closes they will return to Ukiah, Cal., where they have held pastorate for three years.—O. C. Moomaw, minister.

Kentucky.

Alton.—I have just closed a splendid meeting, lasting 2 weeks with 32 additions. Clarence E. Miller is pastor.—R. J. Bamber.

Charlotte Furnace, Sept. 13.—We have had 10 additions, and the attendance is large. I will ordain officers. Ruby Huffman is singing for me. I have promised three other meetings in this part of the state.—T. M. Myers.

Michigan.

Fremont, Sept. 11.—Five confessions lately and five baptisms at the Lake on September 9. We are having large audiences.—T. W. Bellingham.

Missouri.

Higdon, Sept. 10.—There were two additions at Whitewater yesterday.—I. B. Dodson.

Azen.—Eight additions not reported; 6 baptisms and 2 by statement.—F. J. Yokley, Canton, Mo.

Festus, Sept. 10.—Five added—2 by letter, 2 by statement, and 1 from another religious body.—Daniel G. Cole.

Duenweg, Sept. 13.—Closed a twelve days' meeting here with Simpson Ely; 29 added—17 by confession, 11 by statement, 1 by letter, 1 reclaimed.—Samuel D. Smith.

Lexington.—I have just closed a seventeen days' meeting for F. B. Ellmore, of Houstonia, Mo., with 30 baptisms, 3 received otherwise, and the church thoroughly aroused.—R. B. Briney.

Unionville, Sept. 11.—We had 6 additions in our three weeks' meeting here. The town is one where a strong man like J. B. Lockhart is needed, for evil influences abound.—W. L. Harris, evangelist.

Kansas City, Sept. 10.—Our meeting at the West Line Church closed Wednesday night with 34 added—30 by baptism. I preached at Lewisburg yesterday, and 2 were added by letter.—Clyde Lee Fife.

Sorrell, Sept. 10.—Our meeting in the Baptist church grows in interest, with 21 additions to date—12 baptisms Sunday afternoon. Meeting continues indefinitely.—S. J. Vance, evangelist, Carthage, Mo.

Pittsburg, Sept. 9.—Three by confession, 1 by letter, at Dooly Bend not reported. Our meeting at Antioch closed August 27 with 9 additions—7 by baptism. T. J. Head did the preaching.—Pleasant Clarke, minister.

Kirksville, Sept. 10.—Our ninth revival at Bucklin, conducted by home forces, closed with 30 additions—22 by baptism and confession. The church will have preaching two Sundays in the month next year.—Alfred Munyon, minister.

Holden.—Our meeting continued for three weeks, with 29 additions—23 by primary obedience. The meeting should have continued longer. The attendance at the Bible school was trebled. Every department of the church took on new life. George E. Drew and his family are doing a great work. Our next meeting is at Union Star, and after the convention we will begin at Huntington, W. Va.—Fife and Saunders.

Knox City, Sept. 7.—We closed our meeting with 96 additions in all—80 by confession and baptism; 47 of these are men—44 of them heads of families. It was a great pleasure to me to see many men and women whom I had known all my life take their stand with the church. I am glad my Christian life has been such as to command the respect of people I have known so well. I am a stronger and better man because of this meeting. There are ten Christian churches in this county, and not a resident pastor.—H. A. Northcutt.

Nebraska.

Kearney.—Our work is prospering. Seventy-one persons have been received into the fellowship in sixteen and one-half months, 25 of them being by baptism. We began our second year April 16, since which time 9 have been baptized and 16 received into fellowship. We have had no revival meeting, but expect to hold one this fall.—F. D. Hobson.

Craig.—Closed a five months' supply at Craig with 3 by statement and the baptism of a man who was within a few days of being 80 years of age. This was his first public profession of faith. There were 11 baptisms and 8 otherwise added during the five months. I will do student work this year while attending Cotner University, Bethany.—O. L. Adams.

Ohio.

Hamilton, Sept. 10.—Successful rally day at the Lindenwalk Sunday-school yesterday, with the largest attendance we ever had, in spite of the rain. One confession; 3 young men added since last report—2 by baptism and 1 by statement.—W. H. Hedges.

Harrison, Sept. 7.—Closed a two weeks' meeting at Bright, Ind. Rainy weather, but good interest, and 4 additions. Miss Vera Sigur, of Angola, Ind., who had charge of the music, showed herself a capable singing evangelist.—H. W. Milner.

Oklahoma Territory.

Carnegie, Sept. 15.—Nineteen added to date; will close Sunday and go to Lexington, Ky. Return to Oklahoma in October.—James W. Zachary.

Perkins, Sept. 15.—We have just closed an arbor meeting eight miles west of Perkins. Results, 14 immersed, 5 otherwise; total, 19. We will try to build a church in that neighborhood.—J. W. Garner.

Philippine Islands.

Vigon, Aug. 24.—Seven baptisms the past week. Belesario reports 3 more; Lara reports 4 more in Badoc.—Hermon P. Williams.

Texas.

Garland, Sept. 10.—Sixteen additions at Sachse yesterday—12 by primary obendience. This church, with preaching once a month and two meetings, has in the last thirteen months had 116 additions, and I have been privileged to serve them during this time as pastor and evangelist.—Chas. Chasteen.

Wisconsin.

Ladysmith, Sept. 15.—Twenty-one additions to date in the meeting at Chippewa Falls, by J. W. Street, of Mackinaw, Ill. Will close Sunday.—H. F. Barstow.

Sunday-School

September 30, 1906.

TEMPERANCE LESSON.—Gal.
5:15-26; 6:7, 8.

Memory verses, 7, 8.

Golden Text.—Wine is a worker; strong drink is raging. Prov. 20:1.

In the epistle to the Galatians Paul devotes himself to pointing out the contrast between the law and the gospel. As in the epistle to the Romans, where the same topic is argued and developed more elaborately, he shows not simply that the Jewish law has been superseded because it was inadequate, but that the whole conception of law is inadequate for the guidance of life. The Jewish law was inferior to the Gospel, not because its specific commands were ill ordered, but because it was law.

It is sometimes said that the Bible is essentially a law book: This is exactly the opposite of the truth so far as the New Testament is concerned. The Gospel was not given as a new and improved law, but as a new and higher system based on wholly different principles.

There was always danger—as there still is—that the abrogation of law would be considered by some as an opening of the way for all sorts of evil and injurious conduct. So, while Paul warns his hearers to "stand fast in their freedom," he must also warn them not to "use their freedom for an occasion to the flesh."

The contest between the flesh and the spirit, is the theme of this passage. A certain duality in man's nature has been recognized by nearly all moralists. The classic expression of this "war in the members" is given in Romans 7:15-24. Tennyson states it in "The Two Voices."

The root of all intemperance is giving way to the rule of the baser of these two elements, being guided only by the impulses and desires of the flesh and disregarding the contrary influences of the spirit. For one man, this lawless and uncurbed leading of the flesh may be in the direction of alcoholic indulgence. For another, toward sensuality. For another, covetousness. For another, anger or resentment or undue pride. All are alike intemperance.

Let us beware of thinking that our temperance lessons are directed only against the sin of drunkenness. They are aimed against all of those sins into which we may fall—and into which most of us do fall from time to time—through failure to allow the higher and more spiritual motives which are embodied in the Gospel to have full force and effect in directing our lives.

❀ ❀

SKIN-TORTURED BABIES

Instantly Relieved by Warm Baths with Cuticura Soap and Anointings with Cuticura.

The suffering which Cuticura Soap and Ointment have alleviated among the young, and the comfort they have afforded worn-out and worried parents, have led to their adoption in countless homes as priceless curatives for the skin and scalp. Infantile and birth humors, milk-crust, scald-head, eczemas, rashes, and every form of itching, scaly, pimply skin and scalp humors, with loss of hair, are speedily, permanently and economically cured when all other remedies suitable for children, and even the best physicians, in most cases, fail.

Christian Endeavor

By GEO. L. SNIVELY

September 26, 1906.

MISSIONS IN CHINA, AND JAMES GILMOUR.—Is. 49:6-12.

DAILY READINGS.

M. God's Word a Light.	Psa. 119:105.
T. God's Word a Hammer.	Jer. 23:29.
W. God's Word Illuminating.	Psa. 119:130.
T. God's Word Cleansing.	John 15:3.
F. God's Word Abiding.	Isa. 40:8.
S. God's Word Complete.	2 Tim. 3:16.
S. God's Word a Sword.	Heb. 4:12,13.

"Like sunrise lances through the wood,
So through our hearts, through nations, climes,
Flash, till the clash of heavenly chimes
Shall hail o'er earth and dawn of good.
  Rise, orbed in glory! Saviour! King!
Jehovah! Jesus! Truth! Light! Love!
  Lion of Judah! Lamb and Dove!
Reign thou, till earth like heaven shall sing!"

The atrocities of the Boxer uprising, infanticide, the debasement of China's motherhood, the oppression of the poor, punitive fiendishness, and all the exposures made of China's interior life show that the pall of darkest Africa is no blacker than hangs over central China.

While our churches do not have one missionary to each ten million of China's population we are making notable gains. The college at Nankin presided over by our Bro. F. E. Meigs, is a lamp at which thousands of young Celestials will light their torches for the dispelling of pagan gloom and chill.

Confucianism, the moral stay of China, is a philosophy rather than a religion. Its heart is "Whatsoever ye would men should not do unto you, do ye not unto them." But men need more than negatives to inspire them to righteousness and salvation. Those who know of Christianity, even if they have not embraced it, feel the need of its positive affirmation, and long for its warmth and love. Virtue will no more flourish under it than will roses under an electric light. Both need the sunlight of the true and living God.

Buddhism is the purest and most nearly spiritual religion of the Orient, but the good in it is not sufficiently virile to maintain itself against the destructiveness of heathenism. It has lost its power with the people. Its edifices are falling into decay, and few new ones are reared. It long served as a trellis for the religious impulses of the people. Naturally the best that is in them would cling to Christianity if an opportunity were given, and to give that opportunity is one thing for which Christian Endeavor exists.

In encyclopedias, if you have no better facilities, read the story of James Gilmour, the Scotch lad who gave twenty years to the regeneration of China and whose biography is a missionary romance delighting the very angels. He cured the foul diseases of the people and pointed them to the Great Physician. He helped them to better homes on earth and led them toward the heavenly home. Notwithstanding all he did he owes more to China than the empire does to him.

Taonism that once had millions of devotees now has lost its hold on thoughtful Chinese. They disdainfully regard it as a superstition and its priests as mountebanks and parasites. They laugh at its intercourse with de-

Pimples Stopped In 5 Days

Every Possible Skin Eruption Cured In Marvelously Quick Time by the New Calcium Treatment.

Send for Free Sample Package Today.

Boys have been cured in 3 days, and some of the worst cases of skin diseases have been cured in a week, by the wonderful action of Stuart's Calcium Wafers. These wafers contain as their main ingredient, the most thorough, quick and effective blood-cleanser known, calcium sulphide.

Most treatments for the blood and for the skin eruptions are miserably slow in their results, and besides, many of them are poisonous. Stuart's Calcium Wafers contain no poison or drug of any kind; they are absolutely harmless, and yet do work which cannot fail to surprise you. They are the most powerful blood purifier and skin clearer ever discovered; and they never derange the system.

No matter what you suffer from, pimples, blackheads, acme, red rash, spots, blotches, rash, tetter or any other skin eruption, you can get rid of them long before other treatments can even begin to show results.

Don't go around with a humiliating, disgusting mass of pimples and blackheads on your face. A face covered over with these disgusting things makes people turn away from you, and breeds failure in your life work. Stop it. Read what an Iowa man said when he woke up one morning and found he had a new face:

"By George, I never saw anything like it. There I've been for three years trying to get rid of pimples and blackheads, and guess I used everything under the sun. I used your Calcium Wafers for just seven days. This morning every blessed pimple is gone and I can't find a blackhead. I could write you a volume of thanks, I am so grateful to you."

You can depend upon this treatment being a never-failing cure.

Just send us your name and address in full, today, and we will send you a trial package of Stuart's Calcium Wafers, free to test. After you have tried the sample and been convinced that all we say is true, you will go to your nearest druggist and get a 25c box and be cured of your facial trouble. They are in tablet form, and no trouble whatever to take. You go about your work as usual, and there you are,—cured and happy.

Send us your name and address today and we will at once send yo by mail a sample package free. Address F. A. Stuart Co., 55 Stuart Bldg., Marshall, Mich.

parted spirits and defy its incantations. Yet the people fondly follow in thought and love their dead, and would gladly believe in a power greater than human to so manipulate the great forces as to bless mankind. When Christianity is made known to them the Taonists will build its temples and flock into them by millions.

❀ ❀

WHEN SLEEP FAILS

Take Horsford's Acid Phosphate

Half a teaspoon in half a glass of water just before retiring brings refreshing sleep.

A SUM IN ADDITION.—

2 Peter 1:1-11.

"Purer yet and purer
I would be in mind,
Dearer yet and dearer
Every duty find;

"Hoping still, and trusting
God without a fear,
Patiently believing
He will make all clear;

"Calmer yet and calmer
Trial bear and pain,
Surer yet and surer
Peace at last to gain."

Let us add to the number who will say, "you have helped me"; to the sad whose hearts we have lightened; to the uncertain we have guided through the mists; to those we have exalted from lower to higher levels of thought and idealism; to those who in heaven will say, "I dare not hope I should have been here had you not applied the blood of the Lamb to my guilty soul."

A sum in addition as far beyond the power of human imagination as the incomprehensible distances of astronomy is, "How many would be added to the saved if for the next decade every disciple of Jesus should lead a convert to the foot of the cross." But something more profitable than this computation is a resolution in every disciple's heart to bring the greatest possible number to the Master.

We should add hundreds of missionaries to our present force before Centennial and many provinces in many zones to our present "spheres of influence." "Go" has not been subtracted from the great commission. Possibly, "or send" has not been wrongfully added, but "go or send" must be added to the practice of many churches and individuals to save them from confusion at last.

We have but two hospitals in the United States under the auspices of our church. Some of the denominations have more in a single city. To these should be added enough to have one conducted in every considerable town before we have done "more than others" to prove our loyalty to the Great Physician who came to save men from hunger and poverty and cold and sickness and disease as well as from sin and an adverse judgment and doom at last.

It is by accretion rather than by addition we increase in spiritual stature and possessions. We grow as a flower or tree rather than as a wall or a fabric. In us is a principle of life that must increase uniformly and in entirety in order to advantageous growth. We must develop arm, limb and body uniformly or there is physical distortion. The same is true if we increase in one moral virtue to the neglect of others. Let us earnestly seek to develop in all the graces of the Christian life.

Adding repentance to faith, and confession to repentance and baptism to confession is not a mere mechanical process. They are as vitally connected as the succeeding years of a child's stature. Faith does not cease growth when repentance is produced, nor does repentance wane when the subject is baptized. Faith ought to increase with the years and that spirit that leads one into the baptismal

Current Literature

WHAT A YOUNG BOY OUGHT TO KNOW. By Sylvanus Stall, D. D., and WHAT A YOUNG GIRL OUGHT TO KNOW, by Mrs. Mary Wood-Allen, M. D. Virginia Publishing Co., Philadelphia. $1 each, net.

Questions concerning the origin of life should always reach the child through its parents. The writers of these books, realising how few parents know just the best way to present this difficult and delicate subject to the mind of an inquiring child, have set themselves to this task. The whole subject of the perpetuation of life among plants, fishes, birds, and animals is set forth in a manner as delicate and pure as it is scientific and satisfactory to both parent and child. These books have been used and are highly prized by thousands of parents in this country and Europe, and we can cordially commend them as of the greatest value. Many a girl and boy will be saved from wretchedness and ill-health by having these books put into their hands at the right time, with a word of friendly counsel from the parent.

THE DUTY OF IMPERIAL THINKING. By Wm. L. Watkinson, D. D., LL. D. Fleming H. Revell Company, New York. Pages 270. Price $1.00 net.

Dr. Watkinson is himself an imperial thinker. He has one of the brightest minds in the British pulpit to-day. He is one of the few men in the Methodist pulpit who have the real literary touch, but he makes up by genius for a great deal that is commonplace. He is fresh, sane, full of the sweetest sap, is always worth reading, and these chapters on "things worth while" can be cordially commended for their helpfulness and their charm.

STUDIES IN THE GOSPEL ACCORDING TO MARK. By Ernest DeWitt Burton. University of Chicago Press. Pages 248. Price $1.00.

This book is for the use of classes in secondary schools and the secondary division of the Sunday-school, and it is one of the "Constructive Bible Studies" published by the University of Chicago. It is written from the standpoint of the modern, Biblical scholar with two purposes in view: first, to bring a knowledge of the life of Jesus to the student, and to help him to form the habit of coming to each of the books of the Bible with the question, "What does it mean?" The prefaces to the pupil and to the teacher are themselves extremely valuable helps in the way of Gospel study, to say nothing of the light thrown on the text. There are a large number of review questions and an analysis of the Gospel, as well as a dictionary of words used in the Gospel.

THE WOMAN IN THE ALCOVE. By Anna Katherine Green. Bobbs-Merrill Company, Indianapolis. Pages 372.

This is a good story of mysteries. Those who are fond of the detective style of novel will get all they care for. People who really have no connection with the murder are plunged into compromising positions by their own carelessness, while the person who did the deed is hidden until the very end of the narrative. We find nothing particularly elevating in the book, though it has an interest of its own. One would not class it with great fiction.

THE GARDEN OF NUTS. By W. Robertson Nicoll. A. C. Armstrong and Son, New York. Pages 152. Price $1.25.

Dr. Nicoll is one of the best known editors in the field of religious literature. He commands a widely circulated religious newspaper and is the literary advisor of one of the largest religious publishing houses in the world. The present volume consists of two parts, the first being a lecture at the Glasgow Summer School of Theology, and the second consists of expositions reprinted from the British Weekly. It was in this paper that Dr. Nicoll developed his own mystical writing. He has evidently been a close student of mysticism that in this utilitarian, rushing age we may well pause to consider. The literature of the subject is not easy of access. The very heart

of mysticism is the sense of the necessity of the divine union, the realization of Christ on earth, the true, certain, and absolute knowledge of God the supreme. Dr. Nicoll disavows all intention of expounding all the dangers which inhere in mysticism. He leaves that to the individual student. The mystical interpreters expounded the phrase, "The Garden of Nuts," as pointing to the prophecies, allegories, parables and poetry of the Old Testament. He uses the words as a convenient title for the brief series of articles on what he believes to be the true, precious, and divinely sanctioned method of interpretation. It is an appeal for the illustration of the Scriptures from the Scriptures. While many will rebel at the fanciful interpretations which mystical writers have given to the Scriptures, we can say that Dr. Nicoll, both in his style and in his expositions, will be found full of charm and suggestion.

HELPS AND HINTS IN NURSING. By J. Quintin Griffith, M. D., Ph. D. The John C. Winston Company, Philadelphia. Pages 482.

Three points are specially emphasized in this book: first, it seeks to be a guide for times of sickness; second, for caring for infants and children; third, for preserving health. It is not intended to tell you how to prescribe medicines. That is the province of a physician, but it gives a great deal of practical information and good advice such as will prove valuable in any home.

OBITUARIES.

[Notices of Deaths, not more than four lines, inserted free. Obituary memoirs, one cent per word. Send the money with the copy.]

BEERS.

Thomas W. Beers was born in a log cabin in the town of Wells, Bradford county, Pa., on Jan. 15, 1821. On October 24, 1844, he married Miss Amy Carr, and he brought his family to Warren county, Ill., in 1850. He lived upon a farm there for more than a third of a century, but settled at Monmouth in 1885, where his death has just occurred. After the death of his first wife he married Mrs. Cyrena Means in November, 1884. Besides the widow, there remain five daughters by his first marriage: Mrs. W. W. Pease, of Kirkwood; Mrs. H. C. Calvin, of Roseville; Mrs. Sanford Delong, Mrs. John Allison and Mrs. Ad Rankin, of Monmouth. There are nineteen grandchildren living. Three brothers and three sisters survive in the east. Mr. Beers' life of four score and five years was full of activity. Some years ago he united with the Christian church, and was a deacon of the congregation. He was thought to be one of the oldest Odd Fellows in Illinois.

KICKER.

Oscar C. Kicker was born in Chilton county, Okla., Sept. 23, 1874, and died at his residence in Bentonville, Ark., Sept. 5, 1906. He was an earnest Christian and led a life to inspire and encourage others. June 9, 1900, he married Miss Mary A. Howard, of Brownwood, Tex. Besides Sister Kicker and two children, deceased leaves his father and mother, five brothers and three sisters to mourn his loss.   J. W. ELLIS.
Bentonville, Ark.

The Home Department

At the Grave.

It is a world of seeming:
The changeless moon seems changing ever,
The sun sets daily, but sets never,
So near the stars and yet so far;
So small they seem, so large they are!
It is a world of seeming.

And so it seems that she is dead;
Yet so seems only; for, instead,
Her life is just begun; and this—
Is but an empty chrysalis;
While she, unseen to mortal eyes,
Now wins her way in brighter skies—
Beyond this world of seeming.
—*Henry Ames Blood.*

The Bronze Vase.

PART III.

CHAPTER XII.

Of course Rhoda had not beeen paid anything for her poem, except with the pleasure of seeing it in print. But she would not have exchanged the bliss resulting from that experience for a good many dollars. One's thoughts seem so much more distant and beautiful when in printed lines, even if some of the lines are dim and even if advertisements are jostling them with one elbow. The thoughts in our brain are like people who have not yet dressed themselves, and though there is as much flesh and blood in them while in their night dresses, they are not presentable until clothed for the public eye. And there is the thought that thousands are reading what you have imagined in your solitude, though likely enough thousands are skipping your effusion, especially if it be poetry. And there is the hope, perhaps not boldly acknowledge by yourself, that here is the first step toward fame and fortune—but always fame *first;* and that you have seen thousands of your words printed that you begin to realize that the world is going ahead as if you were not in it. As for me, I can look at this printed chapter with a soul quite unmoved. But Rhoda was all fresh and innocent and hopeful. Thrilled with her first success, she sat through a long sermon and thought it short. This alone will reveal somewhat her exalted condition. In the evening they visited Warren and Mrs. Weed. The wagon still stood in the depths of the excavated vacant lot. The twins climbed down the winding path which led among frowsy weeds and broken bricks and heaps of ashes and gravel. They were received joyously by Mrs. Weed, whom Rhoda embraced with true affection; but Wizzen, though glad to see them, was very much preoccupied.

"Oh, Wizzen," said Raymund, "what do you think? Rhoda has had a poem published in the biggest daily in St. Louis!"

"Has she?" said Wizzen. "Look here, Raymund, you have come at a good time. I've sold the off horse and the fellow is coming for him pretty soon." Wizzen stood beside the off horse, which looked very despondent, as if grieving over the approaching separation.

"It's in seven stanzas," said Raymund, "and printed at the very top of the column."

"Yes," said Wizzen. "Now, the trouble is to keep this off horse on its legs and able to follow the feller that's bought it."

As he spoke the off horse tried to lie down, but Wizzen grappled it by the head, crying, "No, you don't! Here, Raymund, reach me that liniment."

Raymund handed him the bucket indicated, and Wizzen dipped his cloth in it and began to rub the off horse's legs. "I've put in some whisky," he confided to Raymund, "and I hope it will hearten up the beast till the feller can git here. He bought it with his eyes open, and givet me ten dollars, which may be its value and may not, depending if it can be kept on its legs." The horse tried to lie down again. "Hand me that bottle," cried Wizzen. "Now, I'll get it into his mouth. Look out; he is pretty active when he's first swallowed! Run up to the road, Raymund, and see if you kin see that feller coming. He ought to be here."

Raymund obligingly climbed the hill and looked about for a man whose eye betokened a horse buyer. "How is it?" shouted Wizzen. Raymund shook his head. "Well, hail me if you see him," cried Wizzen, and he thrust the long-necked bottle in his pocket ready to use it at the proper moment. The off horse lay down.

"Poor horse!" said Rhoda, peeping from the wagon. "Is it suffering?"

"It ain't suffering," said Wizzen, judiciously, "except as you may say that any person suffers which he knows he has got old and feeble and will never be the boy he oncet was. Git up from here, you varmint!"

Raymund came running down the hill, waving his hat.

"Git up, I tell you," shouted Wizzen, angrily. "Stir your rusty old bones, you long-lived patriarch! I *would* be a giving up at my time of life if I was you! Here, take this bottle back of your jaw teeth. Be lively, now!"

When the purchaser had led the off horse away with exceeding difficulty, Wizzen said: "Now, where is that there poetry?" It was taken from Mrs. Weed, who had read it with much appreciation, and handed to Wizzen. He carried it to the wagon tongue, seated himself, and bowed over it. They could see him laboriously spelling out the words, and trying various pronunciations after each spelling. At the end of half an hour or so he rose and handed Rhoda the paper. "It's a great piece," he said. "That's what I call genius. If you ever get out a book of that sort let me know. I'm in the market to buy. I like poetry."

"I didn't know that," said Rhoda, much gratified and a good deal surprised.

"Oh, yes," said Wizzen, "I've made up a lot of it, myself. When I was younger I used to amuse myself by them rhymes. It come handy to me—sorter born in me, I reckon, which they say a poet such should be by nature." Mrs. Weed, showing a curiosity to know what was being said, it was communicated to her through the ear trumpet. "I don't know of his being a poet," she said, nodding toward Wizzen, "but of course he could be if he set his mind on it."

So Rhoda began to see that what she had known it was not so uncommon after all. When it was time to leave, Rhoda ostensibly drew forth the huge silver watch, Wizzen's gift of three years ago. Wizzen never saw it without looking upon the ground in an embarrassed way and picking up something for critical examination. Rhoda had never mentioned the watch to Wizzen, for his manner forbade such a daring trespass upon his sensitive nature, but she liked for him to know it was constantly in use. After leaving the vacant lot, the twins went to Washington Park, where "A Crown of Other Halves" was read several times over, and then the young author and her admirer looked at the rest of the pa-

per. And that is how they suddenly learned that both Boggs and Mrs. Van Estry had been arrested in Kansas City. There was a long article about them with big pictures that were made up of long lines and white space in the crevices. It appeared that both had been discovered stealing goods from a big department store in order to convey the same to a second-hand store of evil reputation. This had brought out other circumstances in the lives of the thieves, that proved them guilty of many evil deeds, and seemed to connect them with a murder of some years past. Had Boggs and Mrs. Van Estry simply stolen forks and rings they might have been sent to the penitentiary for a number of years without great loss of time. But because they had done so many wicked deeds, and it seemed almost sure that they must have killed the man whose murderers had thus far escaped detection, it would be necessary to have a very long trial with a great many witnesses; and as both criminals had money to appeal the case should it go against them, it would necessarily be years before they could be imprisoned at Jefferson City, and likely enough they would finally get off free. "But I am glad they are arrested," said Raymund, "for whatever becomes of them, they can't ever bother *us* again. Now, let's read your poem once more. I will look at it, while you read it."

* * * * * * * * *

The weeks spent with their Uncle William were not without many bright hours for Raymund and Rhoda. They regularly attended a church near enough to save carfare, and they found friends in the Sunday-school teachers, as well as in the minister. The latter even called at the shop, but he was not encouraged by Miss Pinns, and as for Mr. Hodges, he had less and less to say about what should be done on his premises. Miss Pinns took in a good deal of money at the pawn shop, and the old man made considerable out of his renovated clothes. What became of the money was not clear, for Mr. Hodges was always complaining of being poor. One day as Raymund stood in the dingy street taking some of the coal soot, but thinking that he was taking the air, a young man in a cadet's uniform slowly approached, his bloodshot eyes fixed upon the sign of the three golden balls. Raymund thought he had surely seen him before, but could not remember where. The young man drew a handsome gold watch from his pocket and looked at it and then at the show window where other watches were displayed. He hesitated. Raymund could plainly smell whisky on the other's breath, and he understood the feverish glow of the cadet's eyes. At the corner of the street stood some young fellows waiting, and they cried to the uniformed young man to hurry up, that he would have no trouble winning his money back. So Raymund knew he wanted to pawn the watch to gamble. Suddenly he remembered what his lady in Kansas City had said about her son being at West Point, and then he knew why the face had looked familiar; it was strikingly like Mrs. Bannerton's.

"Excuse me," said Raymund, stepping up; "I work at this place. Is there something you would like? Are you Mr. Bannerton?"

The cadet started violently and colored to the roots of his hair. "No, I'm not," he said, so angrily that Raymund knew he was. "Then excuse me," said Raymund. "You look so very much like a lady in Kansas City, whose son is studying at West Point, that I thought you might be the one. She keeps a lodging house."

"When did you see her?" asked the young man, looking at his watch and then at the window, and then at the half-drunken men who were waiting.

"It has been over two months," said Raymund. "I stopped there about a week. She told me about her daughter being at a Boston conservatory, and how willing she was to work and save and endure most anything if she could keep the daughter there. She said she had kept lodgers to support her son until he had been educated enough to get into West Point. She was so hard-working

my heart used to ache to see how tired she was, but whenever she thought of her children it gave her extra strength. She didn't keep any servants—cleaned the rooms herself, washed off the front stone steps on her knees real early in the morning before the others were awake. I was raised on the farm, and used to get up pretty early—that's how I know."

The young man thrust his watch in his pocket. "I'm off on a month's furlough," he muttered.

"Are you?" said Raymund, brightly. "Going home, I suppose, to the old folks?"

"Yes, I am," cried the young man. "I won't have another vacation for two years."

"Well, that's fine, to have the month," said Raymund. "You don't want to lose a minute of it from your kinfolks, I suppose?"

"I just struck St. Louis this morning," said the other. "I'm going to pull out on the first train. He reached out his hand and grasped Raymund's in a manner half ashamed. "Say, old man," he said, hurriedly, "er—ah—God bless you!" Then he hurried in an opposite direction from that of his former companions.

(To be Continued.)

❀ ❀

Newly-Hatched Americans.

The humors of citizen-making are described by a New York Sun reporter who paid a visit to the Federal court to see the naturalization of a contingent from Italy who had been coached as to the answers they should make. Whenever the commissioner suspects a candidate is unworthy, he does not show it in his demeanor. He first puts the question:

"Do you renounce allegiance to the king of Italy?"

"Sure," answers the Italian.

"Will you take up arms against our president?"

"Sure," comes the reply with promptness and a note of sincerity indicating long practice.

"Will you trample upon the American flag?"

"Sure."

"Will you sack and burn Washington?"

"Sure."

"Will you gloat over the nation's ruin?"

"Sure."

At this point, when the candidate thinks all is well, the commissioner puts a sudden and definite end to his hopes.

A Queer Little Hen.

There was once a little brown hen,
A dear little, queer little hen,
    Her work was to lay
    Her one egg every day,
And she did it, this good little hen.

She'd fly up in a tree, and right then,
Seated high on a branch, this queer hen,
    Her egg she would lay,
    Just one egg every day,
This good little, queer little hen.

'I was a strange thing to do, I must say,
Lay an egg from a tree every day,
    And what good was the egg?—
    Just tell that, I beg—
That fell from a tree in that way?

But some people do things just as queer;
I know it; I've seen it, my dear.
    They have a good thought,
    But it just comes to naught;
From the wrong place they drop it, my dear.

There's a lesson for you and for me
From a hen that laid eggs in a tree.
    If we do a right thing,
    If a good thought we bring,
Let's not choose a wrong place, you and me.
                        —*Independent.*

❀ ❀

Advance Society Letters.

BY J. BRECKENRIDGE ELLIS.

This is our third number devoted to
the story of orphan Charlie's ice cream social. I hope we may find time this week
to finish with the letters of our guests.
By the way, I saw articles in two papers
last week telling about this social; how
everybody was invited to stay at home
and send a dime for a dish of imaginary
ice cream, all money to be used toward
Charlie's education. The social
is really over; the last spoonful of ice
cream has been scraped out of the freez-
er. It has been so successful that I think
perhaps we will make it an annual affair
and hold another next August 3. Mrs.
J. O. Johnston, Stewartsville, Mo.: "I
have gathered up a little party to bring
to the social. I kept it in mind during
my visits, and spoke of it publicly at
Sunday-school with the inclosed result—
$3. Had we been rich, I suppose we
should have written you a good big
check." (Oh, no, in that case I should
have expected but a dime. Mrs. Johnston
sends names of all who contributed, and
amount of each, all of which is recorded
in my Av. S. account book. Among them
I note an old schoolmate of mine, Harvey Loller, who promised us, when we
were boys, that he would one day write
a history of the world that all the world
would read. He hasn't got to it yet, so
many other things have been crowded
upon him, but, bless his heart! he got
to our orphan's ice cream social, which
is more than could be said of those who
used to remark [with irony] that they'd
buy Harvey's history when he wrote it.)
Bessie Tracy Ryman, Liberty, Mo. (who
entertained Charlie a month last summer): "I send $1.40. It is so hard to in-
terest people in such things. I collected
30 cents outside my own relatives, and
have talked $30 worth at least. Ha! ha!
I value my speeches pretty high. We had
pineapple ice August 3 and collected at
home. I will send the names, so you can see
who responded. I do not write this for publication; my pen is poor.'" A Grandmother, Modesto, Cal.: "Inclosed find 10 cents.
I wish I had the ice cream here this warm
morning. I wish I could send enough
money to educate the dear boy, but am glad
I can send even this. I pray the richest
blessings upon the Av. S. for the good it is
doing the young folks and the old folks as
well. I hope you may not get sick from
eating too much ice cream." (Well, they
say you won't drown if you don't go near
the water.) "I wish Charlie a glorious
visit with you and Felix." Ruth Peters,
Joplin, Mo.: "I thought I would send some
Sunday-school papers to you to be forwarded to Drusie. You may expect some
more. I am a daughter of Ella J. Dun-
ham and a great granddaughter of Lawson
Moore, who lived near you in Plattsburg.
Papa preaches for the South Joplin Christian Church." (We loved Bro. Lawson
Moore, who lived just across the street
from us. He died when I was a boy, but
I always think of the old brick house as
"Brother Moore's house," though many a
year has slipped by since he crossed the
railed front porch for the last time, his
witty tongue stilled.) Inez E. Humphrey,
Palmyra, Ill.: "The Juniors of the Palmyra Christian Church, Mrs. Annie Mahan,
superintendent, send $1 for Charlie and $1
for Drusie. Since its beginning I have
been interested in the Av. S., and though I
have never succeeded in keeping its rules
12 weeks, have read a number of poems
and pages of history through trying. Primary teachers have many, many things to
do. May our Heavenly Father bless the
Av. S." Mrs. S. A. Penn, Wellsville, Mo.:
"We are delighted that we can attend (in
the spirit) Charlie's social. Our family
consists of papa, mamma and four little
boys, and we are all present, with prayers
and best wishes" (and a dollar). L. B.
Miller, Detroit, Mich.: "As a result of the
self-denial social for Charlie at my home,
I am sending $6.30. It is not nearly so
much as might have been wished, but the
night was hot, threatening a storm, and, as
you say, 10 cents is 10 cents, and it takes
a good many to educate a boy. This is
chiefly from the Woodward Avenue Christian Church, and we are not very strong
yet; were organized last March. NOT for
publication." (Couldn't help it, but hope
I left out all the part you wouldn't want
printed.) Mrs. Sallie Riding, Meadville,
Mo.: "I have read the Av. S. letters from
the beginning and have often thought I
would help, so when you got up that ice
cream social I thought 'Now is my time.'
So this afternoon I had company and told
them about it; as they were all friends of
the Av. S., I raised 85 cents. I hope
you won't make yourself sick eating ice
cream." (People are mighty uneasy about
me! When have I had any ice cream?)
"My prayer is that Charlie may receive a
good education and grow up to be an
honor to the Av. S." Evelyn Hord, Excelsior Springs, Mo.: "Mrs. A. E. Watson
and I send our dimes. The 40 cents is for
Drusie. I had to stop keeping the Av. S.
rules, as my eyes were weak, but they are
all right now, and I may begin again. I
will have the pleasure of teaching 60 pupils
this winter. I taught last year and like it."
Clarence and Carl Per Lee, Grand Rapids,
Mich.: "We send $3, half for Drusie, half
for Charlie. We are still alive, you see,
earning money for your missionary and orphan." (Are you still selling newspapers?) "We still take interest in the Av.
S. and think the Bronze Vase fine. We
hope Rhoda and Raymund will some day
escape the sharp eye of Mr. Boggs. We
have heard from Drusie twice. Once she
sent a sample of Chinese writing, which,
however, we were unable to read. We
have received a wrapper which had apparently been around a three-cornered box.
It reached us empty. Can any one inform
us what was in it?" Jean Chambers, Kensington, Ky.: "I finished my fourteenth
quarter long ago, and was nearly through
with the fifteenth when I got disgusted at
the way I was reading—waiting until Saturday night every time, and then of course
not having time to read much—so I
wouldn't count it. We are a little late
getting to the social, but there was plenty
of ice cream left. It was very good, although the saucers were small, but that's
to be expected at a social." (I don't think
I would talk, if I were you, as I helped
you to ice cream three times!) "This dollar includes all the family, including grandma." Nannie D. Chambers, same state:
"We enjoyed Charlie's ice cream supper
very much and I send you in this the
money due him for our part. I wish I

could have eaten mine in Bentonville, but perhaps ours tasted just as well here." (If it was made out of Kentucky cream I feel quite sure it did.) "A few minutes ago I heard Jean singing your new song, 'Fishing in the Ozarks.' We think it is fine. We learned it as soon as it came out, and have sung it a good many times." (The general reader will note my opportunity for a little advertising along here.) Antoinette Thompson, Pittstown, N. Y.: "Are we too late for the social? Mrs. Harriet A. Cook, of Troy, N. Y., wants a saucer of ice cream, so do I; so we send a dime each. If you were in that picture of your house that was printed in THE CHRISTIAN-EVANGELIST, somebody would have to have sharper eyes than I to discover it. I think after all that airing you gave me in the paper I deserve to have a good picture of you—don't you think so?" (We have recently had a picture struck of Felix. Incidentally, I was in it, too. Perhaps we can produce it on this page in about a month. Then you can feast your eyes.) "I am much interested in "The Bronze Vase." I wish all the ministers and the otherwise great men who go to the Buffalo convention would wear placards so we could know them. I wonder if you are going?" (Am I an otherwise great man?) M. M. Limbry, Salt Lake City, Utah: "I am heartily in sympathy with the work of the Av. S. It is a great education along the lines of missions and good works. I send $1, half for Charlie, half for Drusie. I am glad the ice cream social was such a success. I have known you through THE CHRISTIAN-EVANGELIST for years." Des Moines, Iowa: "It is very warm here, and I feel that a dish of ice cream is just what I need. Here is my dime and may it help Charlie, though ever so little." Mrs. V. L. Gallaher, Danville, Ill.: "Here are six dimes for Charlie's social, with names of donors. I wish it were many more." Elenora Ross, Commerce, Mo.; "Accept the inclosed dime for

the social. It was a happy thought." Mr. and Mrs. W. H. Ewin, Burdett, Kan.: "We are a little late, but we had threshers on September 3, so know you will excuse the delay." Nellie F. Hawes, Atlanta, Ill.: "I send $2 from Mrs. S. A. Boruff, and the same from myself, equally for Charlie and Drusie; also another dollar from a friend for Charlie." May E. Parker, Marine, Ill.: "I send my dime hoping that at Charlie's social there may be a great meeting of dimes." C. M. Reynolds, Latah, Wash.: "We three send 30 cents for Charlie's social." Denver, Col.: "Two dishes, please!" Kinsley, Kan.: "Ten cents for a dish of ice cream, as it is very hot here this evening." Exline, Iowa: "Fifty cents for Drusie and Charlie." E. J. P., Fern Acres, Vashon, Wash.: "God bless the Av. S. work! This is our first contribution; 50 cents for Charlie, same for Drusie." Mrs. Hattie V. Welton, Iowa City: "It is a little late, but I must have a dish of ice cream. May God bless the social, the givers and the receiver! I read THE CHRISTIAN-EVANGELIST, you see!" Winifred C. Welton, same locality: "Mamma's dish of ice cream was so good that I want one, too!" Mrs. Fannie Newman, Lexington, Mo.: "That social is a fine one-sided affair, but think I can afford the price for three saucers." Mrs. C. A. Walker, Denver, Col.: "As I can't come to the social, I send 50 cents. I am glad Charlie had a splendid visit." Mrs. Amie Chapman, Wilton, Iowa: "I send $1.10 for the social for Orphan Charlie's education, and may God bless you and him." Sallie Huffaker, Holt, Mo.: "We are coming, sister Mary, my cousin, Mrs. Garrett and myself. This is the strangest social I ever heard of—no cake! I suppose you have the headache and can not cook it. Well, I guess we will have to hurry or our ticket will expire." Mrs. W. A. Mason, Nevada, Mo.: "Two dishes of ice cream, please, for my husband and me. Glad Charlie spent part of his vacation with you." Mrs. J. W. Penn, Shelbyville, Mo.: "I send $1 for Charlie's social. You may eat the cream. May God's richest blessings be upon all engaged in the noble work of the Av. S."

And now the story of the social is told. Have I left out any name except my kinfolks? To be sure, 36 people from Plattsburg, Mo., attended our celebration, but they are almost kinfolks, for you see that is the home of my childhood. Dora Thompson, who graduated there at the high school last May, chaperoned a big crowd of my old neighbors down to the Ozarks. Miss Jenny Bagby's letter has already been printed. Here at Bentonville, the Endeavor Society gave $2.30, and several gave individually. Emma Simpson Bland used to be a regular keeper of our rules. Her grandmother sent $1 for Charlie and Drusie. Susie Scearce kept the rules for ever so many quarters; she and family sent $1.10 for Charlie. A cousin down in Oklahoma made her presents felt. As for my own immediate family, we found Arkansas soil pretty hard and thin, but we scratched up a little. Utah was the eighteenth state to come to the social. From New York to California the dimes came trooping in to Charlie's ice cream social. Now, the last penny is in, and the books are closed. We took in $91.50, which means that we sold 950 dishes of imaginary ice cream for our orphan's education. Don't you feel like crying "Hurrah"? I do! Then, why not? HURRAH! New Honor List in two weeks.

Bentonville, Ark.

❀ ❀ ❀

Over a Thousand Enrolled

for fall and winter work in our Bible correspondence courses. Let us tell you about it. Catalogue free. Write Pres. Chas. J. Burton, Christian College, Oskaloosa, Iowa.

Christian Publishing Company
2712 Pine St., St. Louis, Mo.

J. H. GARRISON,	President
W. W. DOWLING,	Vice-President
GEO. L. SNIVELY,	Sec. and Gen. Supt
R. P. CROW,	Treas. and Bus. Manager

J. W. Monser's "The Literature of the Disciples" at 35 cents is one of our best book propositions.

It is universally conceded that E. L. Powell is one of the greatest orators of our church. His volume of magnificent addresses, "The Victory of Faith," is published by this House and being sold at $1.00.

You will search in vain through THE CHRISTIAN-EVANGELIST for those fake cancer cures, speculative and other questionable advertisements appearing without apology in the columns of our contemporaries. Will not our readers who appreciate this recommend the paper to a neighbor?

Advance orders are being taken for Editor Garrison's new book—"The History of Christian Union." This is uniform in size with his other works on the "Holy Spirit" and "Helps to Faith," and sells for the same price, $1.00. It is an invaluable addition to every library. We hope many editions will be required to supply the demand.

While for church services Gloria in Excelsis is a peerless collection of church music and is as low-priced as it is possible to make it, we sell cheaper books—Living Praise, Popular Hymns No. 2, Silver and Gold, Praises to the Prince, Gospel Call, sold in limp cloth, $2.00 per dozen; in boards, $2.50; in cloth, $3.00; purchaser to pay shipping.

To other incomparable features of the Dowling series of Bible school supplies there will be added a Teacher's Quarterly for each grade. Many schools grown weary of other publications have signified their intention of sending to us for the best next quarter. Start in the new year aright by supplying your young people with the Dowling Lesson helps and papers.

Many will write in great haste, "Reserve Pullman berth lower six for me

without fail," but it will be too late. Immediately notify us whether you are going on the reclining chair car, tourist or Pullman sleeper that we may make your reservation at once. Everything possible will be done for the comfort and entertainment of our friends going up to the great convention via THE CHRISTIAN-EVANGELIST special over the Wabash.

Thousands of copies of THE CHRISTIAN-EVANGELIST are being used each week by pastors and evangelists in protracted meetings and all testify to their efficiency as soul savers. These are furnished at a price so low as to place them within the reach of every congregation seeking through special meetings to exalt Christ and greatly up-build the church. Write us for terms and instructions about the "pink circulars" furnished gratuitously for general distribution.

For months we have published each week clubs of new subscriptions to THE CHRISTIAN-EVANGELIST at the regular price of $1.50. There has been no diminution in the number published each week through the summer. While THE CHRISTIAN-EVANGELIST's peculiar organization and standing with the people brings most of our new subscribers by ones and twos as friends interest their neighbors, we are pleased to submit the following clubs received last week: Rockwell City, Iowa, H. Brown, pastor, 3; Mobile, Ala., Claude Hill, minister, 4; Trenton, Mo., S. J. White, minister, 5; Peru, Ind., C. H. Devoe, pastor 17; Eaton, Ind., L. O. Newcomer, minister, 17; Portland, Ore., E. S. Muckley, pastor, 23; Bethany, Mo., T. J. Golightly, minister, 23; Maryville, Mo., H. A. Denton, pastor, 27; Frankfort, Ind., W. J. Russell, pastor, 53. This is gratifying to a House that is trying to make every number a light giver and a life saver, and our joy is that it is equally gratifying to thousands of friends endued with the true missionary spirit.

※ ※

The difficulties of the English language are well illustrated in a story recently told of three French boys who were doing Shakespeare into English from their French versions. When they came to the line from "Hamlet," "To be, or not to be," the three translations came out as follows: "To was or not to am," "To were or is to not," "To should or not to will."

The fallacy of asking too many questions is generally followed by much embarrassment.

I was stopping at a large hotel, and one day as I came out and took my hat from the hands of the hat keeper I said to him:

"How do you know that is my hat?"

"I don't know it, suh," said the boy.

"Then why do you give it to me?" I insisted.

"Because," replied the boy, "you gave it to me."—Lippincott's.

"Is it necessary to enclose stamps?" asked the poet.

"More necessary, even, than to enclose poetry," responded the editor.—St. Joseph News-Press.

※ ※

Picture of War Engine "General."

A beautiful colored picture, 18x25 inches, of the historic old engine "General" which was stolen at Big Shanty, Ga., by the Andrew's Raiders during the Civil War, and which is now on exhibition in the Union Depot, Chattanooga, Tenn., has been gotten out by the NASHVILLE, CHATTANOOGA & ST. LOUIS RY.—The "Battlefields Route" to the South. The picture is ready for framing and will be mailed for 25c. The "Story of the General" sent free. W. L. Danley, Gen'l Pass. Agent, Nashville, Tenn.

A View of Niagara Our "Special" Friends Will See.

THE
CHRISTIAN-EVANGELIST

A WEEKLY RELIGIOUS NEWSPAPER.

Volume XLIII.	No. 39

ST. LOUIS, SEPTEMBER 27, 1906.

Missionaries of the Foreign Christian Missionary Society recently assembled at Cincinnati, O. (See page 1245.) Reading from left to right the above are:

Rear Row—Frederic Mendenhall, John Lord, Ray McCorkle, Dr. E. T. Osgood, Secretary S. J. Corey, A. E. Cory, Ray Eldred.

Ladies Standing—Miss Genevieve Perkins, Miss Mary Lediard, Miss Jessie Ashbury, Mrs. C. C. Drummond, Miss Mary Rioch, Miss Jennie Fleming.

Ladies Seated—Mrs. Frederic Mendenhall, Miss Rose Johnson, Miss Ella Ewing, Miss Alice Ferrin, Mrs. Ray McCorkle.

Gentlemen Seated—Geo. B. Baird, Dr. Geo. E. Miller, David Rioch, Dr. C. C. Drummond, Dr. W. C. Widdowson.

The Christian-Evangelist.

J. H. GARRISON, Editor

PAUL MOORE, Assistant Editor

F. D. POWER,
B. B. TYLER, } Staff Correspondents.
W. DURBAN,

Subscription Price, $1.50 a Year.

For foreign countries add $1.04 for postage.

Remittances should be made by money order, draft, or registered letter) not by local cheque, unless 15 cents is added to cover cost of collection.
In Ordering Change of Post Office give both old and new address.
Matter for Publication should be addressed to THE CHRISTIAN-EVANGELIST. Subscriptions and remittances should be addressed to the Christian Publishing Company, 2712 Pine Street, St. Louis, Mo.
Unused Manuscripts will be returned only if accompanied by stamps.
News Items, evangelistic and otherwise, are solicited, and should be sent on a postal card, if possible.
Published by the Christian Publishing Company, 2712 Pine Street, St. Louis, Mo.

Entered at St. Louis P. O. as Second Class Matte

WHAT WE STAND FOR.

For the Christ of Galilee,
For the truth which makes men fire,
For the bond of unity
Which makes God's children one :

For the love which shines in deeds
For the life which this world needs,
For the church whose triumph speeds
The prayer "Thy will be done."

For the right against the wrong,
For the weak against the strong,
For the poor who've waited long
For the brighter age to be.

For the faith against tradition,
For the truth 'gainst superstition,
For the hope whose glad fruition
Our waiting eyes shall see,

For the city God is rearing,
For the New Earth now appearing,
For the heaven above us clearing,
And the song of victory.

J. H. Garrison.

CONTENTS.

Centennial Propaganda..............1223
Current Events.....................1224
Editorial—
Where Jesus Placed the Emphasis—VI 1225
Greetings to Our New Readers..1225
The Churches and Religious Journalism 1226
Notes and Comments 1226
Editor's Easy Chair...............1227
Contributed Articles—
Hebrew Poetry—Illustrating Nature Treatment in the Psalms.
James Egbert.................1228
The Epidemic of Backsliding. William Durban........ 1229
Modern Religious Persecution—
A Defense. B. L. Chase..........1230
As Seen from the Dome. F. D.
Power 1231
What the Brethren Are Saying
and Doing. B. B. Tyler........1232
Our Budget 1234
Illinois State Convention.........1238
Oklahoma's Fifteenth and History
Making Convention.............1239
News from Many Fields..........1240
Evangelistic 1242
Sunday-school 1243
Midweek Prayer-meeting.........1243
Christian Endeavor..............1244
People's Forum 1245
Obituaries 1245
The Home Department 1246

THE
CHRISTIAN-EVANGELIST

"IN FAITH, UNITY; IN OPINION AND METHODS, LIBERTY, IN ALL THINGS, CHARITY."

| Vol. XLIII. | September 27, 1906 | No. 39 |

1809 — CENTENNIAL PROPAGANDA CHURCHES OF CHRIST — 1909
: : : GEO. L. SNIVELY : : :

Looking Toward Pittsburg.

General expectancy in itself would almost send us such articles as follows from A. W. Taylor. The world is more concerned about what we as a people are doing through this close of our first century than about what we are believing and teaching. There were times when a great deal of heterodoxy of living and doing could be atoned for in public estimation by orthodoxy of belief, but they are gone. These days will pardon many whims and heresies of doctrine if the life lies in the direction of the great Philanthropist. Men now care little whether the wheels of the clock move by weights or springs so the hands on the dial plate point to the true hour of the day, when they inquire the time.

We are the Church of Christ, not by claiming to be such, but by being it, doing its work, reproducing its ministries and continuing its life as they were in the days of the personal presence of the holy apostles and their immediate successors. A glaring omission in our reproduction of primitive Christianity is observed in respect to church benevolences. We are not keeping pace with many of the great Protestant denominations in this regard, while the Catholics have far surpassed us all. The Baptists are doing more in St. Louis alone to reproduce the healing ministries of the great Physician than we Disciples are in all the United States.

We shall not long be under this reproach. Preachers like A. W. Taylor and givers like Joseph H. Parker will not permit it. But the most heroic expressions of persistent agitation and exhortation and liberality will be required to enable us to make a creditable showing of Christian benevolence by Centennial time.

We would deeply regret, however, to see this Pontiac sanitarium enterprise launched under any other auspices than of our National Benevolent Association. The multiplication of boards and sources of appeal must for the highest interest of the great cause of this Restoration itself be firmly restricted.

We hope Brothers Taylor and Mohorter may soon have the white banner of Immanuel and the purple insignia of our church benevolences waving forth an invitation in the name of the Lord to all indigent sufferers from over a wide area to come to the Master's cure for healing.

We have received numerous letters approving a recent protest on this page because of an Illinois church's discrimination against ministers beyond their fortieth year in calling a new pastor. But without exception they have been written by ministers beyond that outlawed age. We fondly hoped for many letters from Disciples enjoying the ministry of men of mature years testifying to their acceptance to the church and the good work they are doing and the preference of congregations for the riper rather than the callow ministerial years.

We invite readers whose pastors are between fifty and seventy years to testify whether they believe them incapacitated by reason of such age from rendering helpful service. We believe testimony can thus be secured convincing our church boards and committees on receiving preacher resignations that in the ministry as in medicine, law, merchandise and other professional and commercial vocations, a man's best services are beyond rather than under fifty. We trust the outcome of this discussion will be a higher valuation of the labors of our older brethren and their longer retention in places of usefulness, and thus an actual doubling of our ministerial forces be accomplished as we enter upon the second century of our history. Let the communications relating to this theme be brief and consist rather of the testimony of facts than of arguments based thereon.

We confess some alarm and disappointment as we note the absence of men of hoary heads in our conventions. It means that many have gone from the ministry to commercial and industrial pursuits preventing their attendance on the conventions. Many absenteeisms are due to the erroneous belief of our elderly brethren that their presence and constitutional conservatism are not appreciated nor their help in carrying on the work of the Lord greatly desired by their younger conferees. Let us set in motion influences that will recall many of these veterans, prematurely mustered out of the ranks, back into service, and that will overcome a prejudice we believe to be groundless against preachers who have passed into the youth of old age, that is driving hosts of boys who would otherwise grace our ministry into other callings, so that Pittsburg, 1909, will rejoice in seeing thousands of men whose heads may indeed be whitened by the frosts of years, but whose enthusiasm for righteousness is as fervent as at forty, and whose fruitful services will be profoundly appreciated by a great and ever growing constituency.

These discussions must be free from disparagements of our young preachers. They who, resisting the blandishments of this materialistic age, enter upon the ministry of the Word, are worthy of all praise. If arrows pierce their souls let them be sped by demons rather than by Disciples.

To make our Centennial great and our second century more glorious than this God needs them all—youth and his zeal and strength, and age with its experience, wisdom and power.

That Centennial Monument.
BY ALVA W. TAYLOR.

A rare opportunity presents itself to us for a Centennial monument, in line with Brother Powell's recent suggestion, in the Freeport Sanitarium. Dr. White, who is the founder of this institution, is an ardent Disciple as well as an eminent surgeon and general practitioner. He has built up at Freeport this splendid institution with a property and equipment of between $50,000 and $60,000. It pays him 30 per cent on the investment each year, yet this benevolent physician offers to turn the whole property over to the church for a nominal return on his actually invested capital and receive only a salary as its manager, a much less salary than his income and the growth of the institution would justify commercially. He has recently associated with him Dr. Kost, of the Dixon Church, an eminent surgeon in north Illinois, and these two men propose to devote themselves to the philanthropy of building up a national institution under the auspices of the Disciples of Christ; to build up for us, in other words, an institution that will become our Battle Creek if proper support is received. The property is being put into the hands of a board of trustees and is to be managed like our other benevolent institutions. Expert treatment will make it largely self supporting and the aim will be to make a sanitarium for chronic diseases especially.

Here is the opportunity for the church for a great Centennial monument. What could better mark the close of a century's work and inaugurate that of a second than the endowing of a great ministry of the helping hand like this? To it any church could send its poor who need medical skill at the mere cost of their railroad fare. There societies can furnish rooms and support beds for those upon whom the Master had such compassion, to the healing of whom he gave so much of his time. Indeed he was the great Physician to the world of his day so much did his ministry become one of healing. Here is our one, neglected ministry in his name. We could fittingly set our whole Gospel forth to the world at a time when all eyes will be turned our way by setting forth the Master thus in such a ministry of healing. The world looks askance at the Christian people to-day who practice not Christ's charity among men. Let us justify ourselves in this and convince men of mercy and love even, as did he who was the Great Physician.

OUR CENTENNIAL HELPERS.

I am now in my second year with THE CHRISTIAN-EVANGELIST. I am well pleased with it, and with God's help I will try to keep it in my home.—Arthur W. Inabinett, Charleston, S. C.

I consider THE CHRISTIAN-EVANGELIST a broad but quite orthodox paper. It is up with the times, but not beyond the unchangeable truth. It is a paper full of great thoughts for a great people.—Rochester Erwin (minister), Rochester, Minn.

I trust I shall be able to get many permanent subscribers here in Pomona for THE CHRISTIAN-EVANGELIST. I count it a privilege to do what I can to extend the circulation of such a worthy paper. The message is clear, convincing and essentially, vitally Christian.—Madison A. Hart (minister), Pomona, Cal.

Current Events

The president has taken hold of the Cuban trouble with his usual vigor and,

The President and Cuba. we may say—so far as his actions up to date are concerned—with his usual wisdom. In sending Secretary Taft to Cuba to look into the matter he gave an argument for peace, the force of which was at once felt by both parties to the quarrel. The Cuban government and the insurrectionary leaders both gave orders for their respective forces to maintain an attitude of defense and refrain from aggressive warfare for a time. The president's letter to Senor Quesada, the Cuban minister at Washington, which was sent simultaneously with the announcement of Secretary Taft's mission, assures the Cuban people of his interest in their welfare and his hope to see them continue in the enjoyment of independence; but it assures them also that he will not hesitate to perform his duty under the treaty, and intervene if a stable government is not maintained and if life and property are not protected. These conditions of peace and order, he says, have already ceased to exist in Cuba and unless they are speedily restored intervention will be inevitable. Since both parties in Cuba are far more afraid of American intervention than they are of each other, it was natural that the publication of this letter should have a very pacifying effect upon them.

❀

We sincerely hope that intervention will not be necessary and we believe that

The Right to Fight. it will take much more than the present disturbances (so far as we are informed of their character and extent) to justify intervention. During the seven years of her independence Cuba has been reasonably free from discord and dissension. Indeed, she has, all things considered, done much better than we did during the seven years following the Revolutionary war. At the present time Cuba seems to be in the throes of a civil war as real, though not on as large a scale, as our own civil war. A civil war nearly always produces conditions more or less dangerous to life and property. It was so in the case of our own war. But the existence of a civil war with its necessary attendant injuries to noncombatants, does not prove that a nation is incapable of self-government. That would be indicated only by an indefinite continuance of such disturbances, or by the obvious indifference of the nominal government to the rights of foreigners, or by what the president calls the "insurrectionary habit." Among the inalienable rights of every nation, especially of every young and small nation which is trying to find itself, is the right to fight a little once in a while by way of learning how to settle differences without fighting.

❀

Mr. Pierce, of the Waters-Pierce Oil Company, has admitted in court that the

The Oil Business. Standard Oil Company owns a majority of the stock of his concern and that the profits of the business are between 600 and 700 per cent per annum. We have had a suspicion all along that there was money in the oil business, if carefully managed. The percentage of profit is partly accounted for by the fact that it is estimated on the basis of the capital stock, $400,000, while the actual assets of the concern are thirty times that amount. Even so, it must be admitted that the business is lucrative. Otherwise how did the company increase its assets thirtyfold without increasing its capital stock?

❀

The election in Maine was chiefly interesting to outsiders by reason of the

Gompers vs. Littlefield. attempt of Mr. Gompers, representing the Federation of Labor, to defeat Mr. Littlefield on account of the latter's vote against the eight-hour law as applied to all government works. It was the first battle in the political campaign which the labor unions have announced their intention to wage in behalf of what they consider their rights. The outcome will doubtless be encouraging to the labor forces for, either through their efforts or from other causes or both, the Republican plurality throughout the state was much reduced. There will be many contests and the Democrats are claiming the legislature on joint ballot, which would mean a Democratic senator when Mr. Frye's term expires. Mr. Littlefield's plurality was reduced from about 8,000 to an uncomfortably narrow margin. The fight on the prohibition feature of the Republican program undoubtedly had much to do with the outcome. We are glad Mr. Littlefield was re-elected. He is a good congressman and has contributed more than most of his fellows to the advancement of reform movements by legislation. If the unions are going to make their fight on men of his quality they will not better their standing in the eyes of the disinterested observer.

❀

Agnes Repplier and Madame Hunt, the former a brilliant essayist and the latter

Hats. the president of the National Milliners' Association, have joined, by either design or coincidence, in a simultaneous campaign against the prevailing style of masculine head-gear. We suspect that these ladies have been moved to envy on contemplating the ease with which a man buys his spring or fall hat. Five minutes is

Editorial

Where Jesus Placed the Emphasis.—VI.

Our Human Relationships.

The kingdom of God, as we have seen, contemplates not simply the renovation of the individual man and bringing him into right relations with God, but its ultimate aim is the renovation and reconstruction of human society, The petition, "Thy kingdom come" is elaborated in the phrase, "Thy will be done, as in heaven so on earth." The kingdom will not have come in its fullest sense until this sublime end is reached. But this involves, of course, the bringing of men into right relations with each other—the relationship of fraternity and of mutual helpfulness. The "great commandment," according to Jesus, is to love God with all the mind, heart, and strength, and the second which is "like unto it" is to "love thy neighbor as thyself."

Everywhere in the teaching of Jesus this matter of our human relationships is emphasized. He would not have his disciples be content with loving one another. "Ye have heard that it was said, Thou shalt love thy neighbor, and hate thine enemy; but I say unto you, Love your enemies, and pray for them that persecute you; that ye may be sons of your Father who is in heaven; for he maketh the sun to rise on the evil and the good, and sendeth rain on the just and the unjust. For if ye love them that love you what reward have you? Do not even the Publicans the same? And if ye salute your brethren only, what do ye more than others? Do not even the Gentiles the same?" (Matt. 5:43-48.) So highly does he prize the restoration of fraternal relations between men that he places the restoration of such relationship, when it is broken up, even before worship. "If therefore thou art offering thy gifts at the altar, and there rememberest that thy brother hast aught against thee, leave there thy gift before the altar, and go thy way, first be reconciled to thy brother, and then come and offer thy gift." (Matt. 5:23, 24.) It is in harmony with this teaching that he says, "Blessed are the peacemakers; for they shall be called the sons of God" (Matt. 5:9). What shall they be called who sow seeds of strife and discord among people, and array neighbor against neighbor, and brother against brother?

We have not attained Christ's point of view concerning our human relationships, until we are prepared to accept this teaching of Jesus fully and without reserve. How often is the peace of a church disturbed, and its usefulness in a community neutralized, by alienations and strifes between its members. Sometimes the peace of a whole brotherhood is marred, its influence greatly lessened, and its progress retarded, by unseemly controversies which are void of the spirit of forbearance and brotherly love. How little is said or

thought about the heresy of hating one's brother or of fomenting strife among brethren! And, yet, with Jesus, this was one of the gravest offenses which one could commit against the principles and spirit of His kingdom. When Jesus placed love, Godward and manward, above all other requirements as fulfilling all the law and the prophets, he gave us the solution of a thousand human problems. It will solve the question of war between nations, of conflict between labor and capital, of strife and jealousy between section and section, and it points the way, unmistakably, to the realization of His own prayer for the unity of His disciples.

His "new commandment" which He gave to His disciples is that they should love one another as He had loved them. When this commandment is obeyed, the difficulties which lie in the way of Christian union will dissolve like the mists before the rising sun, for when we love each other as Christ loved us, we will allow no differences of opinion to disturb our fraternal relationship, and as to faith and duty, love will find the way to unity where logic and argument have failed. Jesus made love the badge of our discipleship to Him. "By this shall all men know that ye are my disciples, if ye have love one to another" (Matt. 13:35).

Let the teachers of the Church universal begin to place the emphasis where Jesus placed it, on love as the great regulative principle of human relationships, and as the supreme force of the kingdom of God, and we shall soon see our mutual misconceptions, alienations, and prejudices, giving way to the irresistible power of love, and all our divisions giving place to "the unity of the Spirit" held secure in "the bond of peace." But not only so. Such emphasis would mean much for the home. It would exalt right relations between husband and wife, and parents and children, as vastly more important, in the sight of God, as an expression of true religion, than correctness of ritual in worship, and soundness in doctrinal creed. It would unmask the hypocrisy of church members who make long prayers and are exceedingly zealous for soundness in the faith, who, in their avarice, devour widows' houses, underpay and otherwise mistreat their employees and steel their hearts against the cry of the poor. It would make apparent the absurdity of any profession of religion by men who, in their eagerness to make money, ignore their civic duties when the welfare of the people is at stake.

The church that manifests a deep interest in whatever relates to human welfare in the community and in the world, is acting in line with Christ's teaching, and is placing the emphasis where He placed it. The "common people," too, will hear the message of such a church as it gladly heard that of the Master. It would vastly increase the influence and popularity of local churches, if in addition to a faithful and loving proclamation of the gospel, they

would give greater heed to the conditions and principles which affect human relationships and seek to apply to them the teaching of Christ. While the church, like the kingdom, is "not of this world," it is in the world, and its business is to help men and women bear their burdens, perform their duties and resist the temptations which come upon them here in the world. Right living consists in discharging the obligations of our various relationships in life. Christ came to help men do that. Blessed is the church that echoes Christ's teaching on this subject and illustrates it in its life!

❀ ❀

Greetings to Our New Readers.

The large influx of new subscribers to THE CHRISTIAN-EVANGELIST which has come in during the summer months, and which continues with each mail, justifies us in extending this word of hearty welcome to these new additions to our CHRISTIAN-EVANGELIST family. We would like to write you each a personal letter, but you are too many for that; so we ask each of you to consider yourself as personally addressed in this greeting.

We welcome you to the feast we weekly spread. You may not relish everything on the table. Do not reject other dishes, however, because of that. Eat what agrees with you. Read articles on subjects in which you are not interested, and see if you do not become interested. A religious paper worth reading at all, is worth reading pretty thoroughly. Those who read it most get most good out of it and are sure to become regular readers. Read with open mind and heart, not necessarily to accept all you read, but to give the writer a fair show to present his thought.

When an article specially impresses you as helpful, speak of it to others. When you have finshed your paper hand it to a neighbor to read, pointing out something you think will interest him or her. In this way you may sow seeds that will bear fruit that you little dream of. A single article has often changed a life. If the paper helps you, try to get another to read it, and you will help him. We hope you will like us. If you stay with us long enough we are sure you will. You will soon come to understand that THE CHRISTIAN-EVANGELIST stands for loyalty to Christ —his teaching, his Spirit, his example; for Christian brotherhood and fraternity; for Christian union, and all the steps that lead thitherward; for education, for progress in knowledge and character; for a deeper spiritual life; for applied Christianity; for joining forces to fight the devil and all his agencies, and to help humanity up to a higher and happier life. If you favor these things you will like the paper.

Again, we welcome you to our circle of readers. Help yourselves to what you see, and if you do not see what you wish, call for it. May our relationship as Editors and readers be mutually pleasant and helpful, and therefore enduring. The peace of God be with you and rest upon your homes, and the light of his countenance cheer you all life's journey through!

The Churches and Religious Journalism.

There are many indisputable signs of an awakening interest on the part of ministers and the most intelligent members in our churches as to the value of a good religious journal in the homes of their members. We have felt sure for years that such an awakening was bound to come. The relation of religious journalism to the successful on-going of all departments of work in the kingdom of God is so vital that it is strange that this revival of interest in the circulation of our religious journals has not come sooner. It is only just, perhaps, to admit that we who control the character of our religious journals are, in part, responsible for this delay and for the apparent indifference of our ministry and church officials in the past on this subject. We have not made our papers as free from objectionable matter as they ought to be, to make them most helpful in the promotion of religious interest and brotherly love and unity, on the part of their readers. We are persuaded, however, that the chief cause for this indifference is deeper seated than this. There has been too little thoughtful study, on the part of pastors and other church leaders, of the causes which would deepen the religious interest of their members, and increase their interest and activity in the various lines of Christian work. They have not watched closely the effects, on the families of their churches, of the reading of a good, religious journal, and noted how efficient a pastoral helper it may become. This is being seen and felt now as never before, and we believe our editors are also making an honest effort to respond to this demand and to make their journals sources of strength and of unity among the churches, rather than of discouragement, suspicion and division.

As one expression among many of this awakening interest in the circulation of a good, religious journal, we take the liberty to quote from a letter we have just received from Dr. E. T. Davis. After congratulating THE CHRISTIAN-EVANGELIST on its policy of omitting objectionable advertisements and on its general policy, it says: "I believe the next great move to be for all the churches to supply THE CHRISTIAN-EVANGELIST for all the families in the congregation, just as we now supply seats, song books and preaching for all. At —— city we have 197 members, about one-third of whom attend church regularly. The church as a body pays for preaching to all the church, yet nearly two-thirds of the members fail to hear it regularly. Now suppose we have sixty families in the church and twenty take the paper themselves. That would leave forty copies to be paid for by the church. It will preach to them every week, even if they do not come to church. It would be a small expense to preach to all the church through our paper, and I don't see how an intelligent Disciple could read THE CHRISTIAN-EVANGELIST every week and be contented to stay out from the fellowship and regular work of the church. I don't believe one-third of them would do it. One year of such teaching would be of more benefit to the congregation than the average yearly meetings which costs much more than the copies of the paper would. I hope THE CHRISTIAN-EVANGELIST will soon be as much a part of our church provision as preaching is now."

We believe the wisdom of this suggestion will commend itself to many of our churches. But whatever method may be adopted, we are sure that our best churches henceforth will see to it that their members receive and read at least one or more of our religious journals, that one being selected which, in the judgment of the pastor and his most intelligent members, will best promote the spiritual edification and growth of the church. When this policy shall be generally adopted its quickening effect on all departments of our work and on the spiritual status of the churches themselves, will be quickly noticed, and our cause will receive an additional impetus to go on its conquering way.

We shall be glad to take this matter up with such churches as may regard THE CHRISTIAN-EVANGELIST as an important agency for developing the religious life of their members.

Notes and Comments.

We are concluding the series of articles this week by B. L. Chase under the title. "Modern Religious Persecution— A Defense." The articles were admitted on the ground that they were intended to be a mild satire on the spirit of intolerance which now and then crops out among us, and from which none of us are, perhaps, at all times, exempt. The liberal can be as dogmatic in his way as the conservative, and so far as the articles have served as a rebuke to intolerance, regardless of where it manifests itself, they have served the cause of truth. Luther was perhaps right in saying that every man had a little pope in him, and each of us would do well to look after the pope that is within him as well as the popes that are without. Some of our readers have misunderstood the intent of the articles, regarding them as serious rather than satirical. This suggests that our writers who deal with that dangerous weapon, satire, should be careful to label their articles so distinctly that none will misunderstand them. Others, again, have interpreted the articles as being aimed specifically against certain men and papers. In so far as these articles give countenance to this interpretation, we think they frustrate the real aim of the author which was to rebuke a certain *tendency* and not certain specific individuals. At any rate, this has been our aim in giving space to the articles. We would not like to say that satire is never, under any circumstances, admissible in religious journalism, but we are free to say that we believe love to be a far more potent weapon with which to correct errors.

We print elsewhere an interesting statement by Brother Zollars concerning the plans for inaugurating a school in the soon-to-be new state of Oklahoma. It is encouraging to contrast this method of consultation and co-operation with the haphazard and independent style of procedure once in vogue. It has in it the promise of success from the beginning. Referring to the question as to whether the brethren in Oklahoma should attempt to build up and endow a college to compete with the State University, in its scientific and academic features, or, utilizing the State University for these departments, should concentrate their efforts in building up a great Bible college, and so endowing it as to secure the ablest teaching talent in the brotherhood, that would influence the whole student community with the great facts, truths and principles of the Bible, we can not refrain from saying that the latter policy seems to be reinforced by so many reasons that it is difficult to see why a different course would commend itself to the brethren in that region. If they had a million dollars with which to endow an independent school, we could see how there might be an argument for that policy; but given the fact, that all the money that is likely to be raised in a quarter of a century will be needed to properly equip and sustain a Bible college, why should this money be spent in providing rooms and teachers for the teaching of such branches as are equally well taught by the state and offered to them without additional cost? This is the economic reason, but it is by no means the only one. The value to a cause like ours that makes its appeal to the reason of intelligent people, of having its Bible college located at the seat of the State University where it would come in contact with the largest number of educated and ambitious young men and women in the state, is incalculable. Our specialty is Bible teaching. That is what we are here to do. Let us give ourselves to that work with a singleness of aim and an intensity of zeal that will command the attention and respect of the people. In states where we have independent schools already well established, it is wise to support them and carry them on; but in new states the brethren ought to avail themselves of the opportunities offered, by our state universities for concentrating their means and efforts on those things which others can not do for us, and which God will hold us responsible for doing up to the full measure of our ability.

Editor's Easy Chair.

Our last Sunday at Pentwater was a strenuous one, both in labor and in anxiety. For several days previous a forest fire had been slowly aproaching us from the south, and on Sunday morning a favorable south wind caused it to make rapid progress toward "Garrison Park." We had agreed to preach at the Methodist church, in the absence of the pastor, and at the hour appointed we directed our steps thither, but met on the way a number of men carrying spades and buckets, going down to fight the fire. On reaching the church we found a good audience, but made up mostly of women. After a short sermon the men were urged to join their fellow-townsmen in fighting the fire, when the people were dismissed. Soon after reaching home, and while we were eating dinner, a party returning from the fire advised all the cottagers to pack their goods and have them ready to be carried to the beach in case the fire reached the Park, which then seemed probable. We immediately set about getting our household goods in shape for carrying to the beach. Parties of people were coming and going, bringing contradictory reports of the progress of the fire. As we were assured that there were more people down at the fire than could be used, we made such preparation as we could to fight it when it reached our premises, and waited with anxiety the coming of the night and of the morning. J. M. Ford and wife, of St. Louis, and R. M. Denholme and family, of New Orleans, who occupied cottages north of us, pledged assistance in moving our household goods in case the fire reached us before morning. A favorable change of wind gave us hope, and so we retired and slept the greater part of the night, not knowing, however, what the morning might bring forth.

In the early dawn of Monday morning the Easy Chair Editor walked down the beach about two miles to the point where the fire had reached near the beach and where it had been stopped by a small stream which flowed into the lake. Walking inland through the burnt district, we found that the fire had crossed the little stream and had made its way farther north. Going still to the east we came to a plowed strip of ground running nearly east and west and found that this had stopped the fire and, aside from burning logs here and there, the fire had died out and danger for the present was averted. And so, returning to the cottage, we put our house in order and departed on the afternoon train. Credit is due the authorities of the village and the fire department for the heroic services they rendered in avoiding what might have proved a very destructive fire to the resort property, about Pentwater. This warning, we are sure, will not be lost and measures will

be adopted hereafter by which it will be impossible for a forest fire to approach the Park from any direction. The beautiful groves of pines and oaks and hemlocks which crown these hills and ravines are its glory, and their destruction would have been a loss which it would have taken years to retrieve. We left the place feeling grateful that the threatened danger had been averted and that thousands of others in the years to come are to enjoy the beauty and shade of these trees and the quiet restfulness of these hills, as we have done during the three summers past.

❧

After a few hours' rest in the hospitable home of the Stows at Grand Rapids, the night train brought us to Chicago, where our arrival had been timed to participate in the closing meeting of a three days' celebration by the Englewood church of its twenty-first anniversary. A recent write-up of this church in our columns, showing its splendid progress, renders it unnecessary here to go into any details. It is a good thing for a church to observe its anniversary. A church that is conscious of serving the community in which it lives, and the kingdom of God of which it is a part, is likely to mark, by some appropriate service, the passing of its more important anniversaries. This church at Englewood has good reason to celebrate its twenty-first anniversary. It has come up through difficulties, conquered them successfully, has secured a splendid habitation for itself, is practically out of debt, has the prestige of success, and has achieved an honorable reputation. For seven years, or about one-third of the life of the church, the present pastor, C. G. Kindred, has been at the helm and to him much credit is due for the position which the church holds to-day. It was our privilege to address a large audience of people on Tuesday evening on "The Present Phase of the Christian Union Problem." There were several representatives of our ministers in the city present, and several ministers of neighboring Protestant churches of Englewood. The spirit of brotherhood seemed to exist between this congregation and its neighbor churches, and between Brother Kindred and his brother ministers about him. The singing was hearty, the spirit was that of gratitude for the past and hopefulness for the future. Our hearty congratulations are extended to both pastor and people on their splendid record and still brighter outlook.

❧

And now here we are in old St. Louis and the Easy Chair is once more on its native heath. It is a good thing, occasionally, to go way off on the edge of the brotherhood and its activities, and look at them from a distance. But for the most part it is better to be at the center where you can look out along all the

radiating lines into the great field of activities, and where one can feel the pulse-beats of the brotherhood in its labors, conflicts, hopes and aspirations. Sometimes when there are fluttering sensations in the region of the heart, and there is fear of organic trouble, the careful physician puts his ear to the patient's heart and, distinguishing between muscular pains or nervous disorder, and genuine organic heart trouble, says, "Your heart is all right." That sentence removes a great load of anxiety. If one puts his ear close to the beating of the heart of the brotherhood, distinguishing between mental perturbations and misconceptions and the real desires and aspirations of the great mass of the brotherhood, he is bound to say, "There is no organic heart trouble; the brethren, as a whole, love the truth and desire to see it triumph, and what *seems* to the contrary is, unless in exceptional cases, only apparent. We believe in the moral sanity, spiritual soundness and clear-mindedness of the great mass of the brotherhood when they have time and opportunity of judging the great issues that come before us. It is this fact that gives us heart and hope.

❧

After all, this optimism in the final outcome of things; this confidence that the great body of the brotherhood will ultimately settle these questions the right way, is only faith in the principle of democracy as applied to religion. We all believe in that principle in this country as applied to politics. Our form of government is based on that idea. Why should we hesitate to apply the same principle in matters religious? Of course this is contrary to the belief and practice of the Roman Catholic Church, and perhaps of some others which claim the right to do the thinking for the great mass of people, and require them to accept these ready-made doctrines and opinions. This, however, is inconsistent with Protestantism, however much some Protestants may indulge in it. The Disciples of Christ, however, claim to have carried the Protestant principle of the right of private judgment to its logical results, and they have, therefore, rejected all ready-made standards of doctrine, and insist that the people shall think for themselves, believing that ultimately they are more apt to think about right, than would a limited number. In other words, we believe that *all* the people are wiser than *part* of the people. It was Lincoln's democracy that made him believe that you couldn't "fool all the people all the time." Religious editors ought to have the same confidence in the common sense and insight of the masses of their brethren, and it would

"From many a blunder free us,
And foolish notion."

Whatever renewal of strength and of vitality we have gained by our summer's sojourn by the lakeside we now dedicate to the service of Him whose favor is life and peace.

Hebrew Poetry---Illustrating Nature Tre

By JAMES EGBERT

Matthew Arnold said twenty-five years ago, "The future of poetry is immense, because in poetry, where it is worthy of its high destinies, our race, as time goes on, will find an ever surer and surer stay. There is not a creed which is not shaken, not an accredited dogma which is not shown to be questionable, not a received tradition which does not threaten to dissolve. Our religion has materialized itself in the fact, in the supposed fact; it has attached its emotion to the fact, and now the fact is failing it. But for poetry the idea is everything; the rest is a world of illusion, of divine illusion. Poetry attaches its emotion to the idea; the idea is the fact. The strongest part of our religion to-day is its unconscious poetry."

The truth of this is to-day evident wherever the river of poetic song has flowed. The Hebrew stream has cut its channel deep and has well fertilized its banks. It commends itself to the world as both poetry and religion. From the recognition of Arnold's statement Hebrew poetry takes its place well to the front in the body of the world's literature.

Of course, Hellenic genius is pre-eminent. But it is art for art's sake. If the poet is a great teacher, and an inspirer of truer and nobler ideals, then Hebrew poetry must take first place. The "Sepher Tehillim," book of praises, is the perfect flower of Israel's song. The Psalter is a collection of religious lyrics. Lyric poetry is defined as "that which directly expresses the individual emotions of the poet." The Hebrew heart was large and finely tuned to the Divine Key. In the Psalms we hear the varied strains responsive to the touch of God. We fail to find the polish of Tennyson and the skill and labor of Arnold and Wordsworth. In fact there is no nature description as such. We have but to compare modern versified translations with the Psalms to feel that power has been sacrificed to beauty of descrption.

Take Addison's

"The spacious firmament on high,
With all the blue ethereal sky
And spangled heavens, a shining frame,
Their Great Original proclaim."

Here is conscious effort to make a fine picture. The emotions that swept across the Hebrew poet's soul lifted him at once into the "grand style"—

"The heavens declare the glory of God;
And the firmament showeth his handiwork."

The Hebrew poet had a genuine love for nature. His is the poetry of the heart rather than of the intellect. His poetry is his experience put into song. What he saw, heard and felt found place in his verse. There is no philosophizing or cold logical reasoning. He sings only because he must sing—because he feels so deeply. His song is direct, simple,

natural, spontaneous. Israel's heart is found not in its law or its history, but in its poetry. To the Hebrew the soul was everything. Mrs. Browning wrote in the true Hebrew spirit when she said of form:

"Let me think of forms less, and the external,
Trust the spirit, as sovereign nature does, to
make the form;
For otherwise, we only imprison spirit, and not
embody."

Form is used by the Hebrew poet only as a means to present life and action. If Arnold's principle be true that poetry is a criticism of life and that the greatness of the poet lies in his powerful and beautiful applications to ideas of life—how to live, then the Hebrews wrote genuine poetry. Life and action characterize all their poetry. Dean Church said: "The Vedic hymns are dead remains, known in their real spirit and meaning to few students. The Psalms are as much alive to-day as when they were written. They were composed in an age at least as immature as that of the singers of the Veda, but they are now what they have been for centuries, the very life of spiritual religion—they suit the needs they express, as nothing else can express, the deepest religious truths, ideals of "the foremost in the files of time."

The form of Hebrew poetry is rather obscure, yet John Milton, that master of lyric poetry, said: "Not in their divine argument alone, but in the very critical art of composition, the Psalms may be easily made to appear over all kinds of lyric poetry, incomparable." Meter, as we understand it, was unknown to the Hebrews. They used a method of parallelism or balanced structure. Herder describes it "the systole and diastole of heart and breath." Phrase is set over against phrase, clause against clause, verse against vesse, thought against thought. We may call it thought-rhyme. This was learned from nature in the rise and fall of the tide, the ebb and flow of the tide, the sound followed by its echo. It is much like the heaving and sinking of the troubled heart. The Hebrew poets having the noblest truths to express, went to nature to learn the art of expression. Great things engrossed the Hebrew mind. Impressively did he express because so naturally. To illustrate see in Ps. 33:5, 6:

"Oh Jehovah, thy love is in the heavens,
Thy faithfulness reacheth unto the skies,
Thy righteousness is like the mountain of God,
Thy judgments are a great deep."

The great things that absorb his mind are Jehovah, his faithfulness, his righteousness and his judgments. To express them he simply points the beholder to the four greatest things in nature, i. e., the heavens, the mountains, the great deep. No coloring is needed. Adjectives add nothing

The Epidemic of Backsliding By William Durban

Prelude.

"Keswick" has come and gone. To a vast number of people "Keswick" has come to be a term of theologic symbolism. Mr. Albert Head, the chairman of the great gathering in our romantic Westmoreland Lakeland, when speaking in one of the tents, expressed his deep regret that "Keswick" had become a technical term. That is a fact. For to be in sympathy with this annual Keswick conclave is indicative of a certain ultra-Evangelical trend of mind, looked on by the majority of the churches as narrow, Puritanic and exclusive. But it is nevertheless remarkable how profoundly impressed with a sense of intense spirituality are all who attend Keswick. Many people who go with a strong tincture of prejudice find this speedily eliminated. The idea of narrowness is forgotten. The atmosphere is purely Biblical. And there is truly something in Keswick, with its 6,000 earnest souls attending meetings for a whole week, that defies criticism and answers to the deepest need of Christian hearts.

The Contemporary Apostasy.

There is heard just now in many quarters a lament which suggests that the deepening of individual Christian life, and the consolidation of Christian character is one of the chief needs of the times. And this quickening and deepening of spiritual life all who know the Keswick convention just alluded to well understand as being the main aim of that institution.

"We are witnessing an epidemic of backsliding," was the melancholy statement of a popular preacher in a recent meeting in London. I fear that facts are only too seriously in accord with this sad declaration. All through my own long ministry I can not remember a single great revival which was not followed by much disappointment. No preacher could ever have been more enthusiastically sympathetic with revivalists than I have always been and am at this hour. Such workers as revivalists needed. They command an indispensable function. Often they fulfill it nobly. I do not believe in "the passing of the evangelist," so very cleverly descanted on at times by certain writers. But I have noted constant records of the sweeping and wonderful results immediately following evangelistic campaigns. I have never through the years of my experience seen any record of the numbers of converts who have quickly tumbled into the world. Now, what is the use of converts who make a conspicuous confession only to be hurled back by Satan into the vile pit of worldliness from which they suddenly sprang?

Candid Congregationalists.

I note that this bitter cry from ministers and leaders of religious thought and work is being made most loudly and emphatically echoed by certain excellent Congregationalists at the present juncture. I have at times heard it from Methodists and Presbyterians. I am bound to say that less is heard from Baptists concerning grievous and numerous cases of backsliding. Also, there seems to be in proportion less of this lamentable kind of easy apostasy amongst our own people, the Disciples of Christ. Of course Baptists and Disciples are by no means unfamiliar with the evil and with the disappointment experienced in consequence. I can not help inquiring why amongst pedobaptists the facile and fatal backsliding should be specially rife. I do not think the answer is difficult to formulate. It was recently supplied very succinctly by a Congregational minister when he bluntly said, "We lose many converts easily because we gain them so easily." This simple statement is deeply significant and abundantly suggestive.

A Kindly Suggestion.

I have often felt disposed to reason out certain considerations with my pedobaptist friends, who, I am glad to say, are not few. On some occasions I have been indulged by their forbearance and their patience, when I have tried to dwell with them on the chief point involved in the exceeding facility of entrance into any church where the ancient mode of admission into Christian fellowship has been modified. Without doubt there has been in modern days a general tendency to make it easier and easier for any professing Christian to become incorporated with the visible and local church. And modern revivalism of the feverish and most popular type knocks down all barriers whatever. The rushing "pacemaking" of certain evangelists sweeps so-called converts into the fellowship in hundreds. There are many revivalists who despise units, although the Holy Spirit saves us all one by one. They even look with contempt on batches of a dozen or a score, and are unhappy or ashamed if they can not score success by recording hundreds of conversions every season. I have never forgotten how my old friend in Liverpool, the sainted W. P. Lockhart, said some months after a great revival campaign in that city, "We had a wonderful number of additions, but we have been turning out squads of those converts every month since. Mr. A. B. brought them in." And yet the evangelist to whom he referred was one with whose name all England and all America was still ringing. May we not imagine that large numbers of the "converts" went back easily because they were brought in easily?

A Point of Philosophy.

Christianity is beautifully and profoundly philosophic. And I have long felt that its divinely metaphysical character is nowhere more conspicuously evidenced than in its ordinances, when we accept them in their original purity. The church of God was never intended to be open like a bleak wilderness. It is the garden of the Lord. It is a refuge for the wanderer. It is a shelter from the blast. But surely when we strip the fold of all fences, when we remove the protecting barriers from the harbor, when we take the door of the home from its hinges, when we fling down the gate of the garden, we then simply turn all into open desert, we let in the storm, we invite the wolf or the pirate, and we have improved all protection, privilege and special provision out of existence. The ordinances as instituted by Jesus and reverently practiced in the apostolic churches were simple indeed, but their meaning was manifold and their purpose was far-reaching. They have largely become misunderstood as to their original significance. When these institutions are rightly practiced they explain themselves, and they impart a

❀ ❀

THE WAY OUT.

Change of Food Brought Success and Happiness.

An ambitious but delicate girl, after failing to go through school on account of nervousness and hysteria, found in Grape-Nuts the only thing that seemed to build her up and furnish her the peace of health.

"From infancy," she says, "I have not been strong. Being ambitious to learn at any cost, I finally got to the high school, but soon had to abandon my studies on account of nervous prostration and hysteria.

"My food did not agree with me, I grew thin and despondent. I could not enjoy the simplest social affair for I suffered constantly from nervousness in spite of all sorts of medicine.

"This wretched condition continued until I was 25, when I became interested in the letters of those who had cases like mine and who were being cured by eating Grape-Nuts.

"I had little faith but procured a box and after the first dish I experienced a peculiar satisfied feeling that I had never gained from any ordinary food. I slept and rested better that night and in a few days began to grow stronger.

"I had a new feeling of peace and restfulness. In a few weeks, to my great joy, the headaches and nervousness left me and life became bright and hopeful. I resumed my studies and later taught ten months with ease—of course using Grape-Nuts every day. It is now four years since I began to use Grape-Nuts. I am the mistress of a happy home and the old weakness has never returned." Name given by Postum Co., Battle Creek, Mich.

"There's a reason." Read the little book, "The Road to Wellville," in pkgs.

mingled dignity, majesty, solemnity, power and sweetness to the Christian religion. The popular modes of admitting converts to the churches involve so much trifling with the original institution that many go on to trifle the whole system away soon after they have cooled down. They are subjects of the religion of excitement, rather than of the excite-

ment of religion. The great plea of the Disciples of Christ is bound as time goes on to meet with an increasingly kind and favorable consideration from other Christians. Gradually these will come to see that one great cause of the epidemic of backsliding lies in the too easy methods of sweeping recruits into the army. There surely would be fewer

deserters were the initiation more serious. What after all is there to instill reverence in connection with the popular style of becoming a professed Christian? We should respectfully urge this question on our fellow-Christians in season and out of season, for it is concerned with vital issues.

London, England.

Modern Religious Persecution---A Defense

By B. L. Chase

10. Deadly Heresies; Federation.

Closely connected with the recognition of other religious bodies as churches of Christ is another deadly heresy which now threatens to entrap a large part of the Disciples. It is federation. The one is the principle of which the other is the practice. Our wisest persecutors and keenest observers have recognized the scheme of federation as a trick on the part of the sects to prolong their life. They see that Christian union is coming just as the Disciples have preached it and planned it; which would mean their unconditional surrender to our position. They see that if union comes they will have to give up their creeds, their organizations and their names, and be absorbed as a part of the Disciples. They have simply got scared, and a clever group of their leaders got together in New York to devise ways and means for preventing the Disciples from carrying out their plan.

They saw how humiliating it would be for them to have to come on their knees begging the Disciples to allow them to take the right name, the right interpretation of Acts 2:38, and the right system of church organization. How humbling for them to have to say to the Disciples: "You are right and always have been; we are wrong and always have been. The whole Christian world has walked in darkness until the Disciples appeared, bringing a great light. None of the millions of Christians who have lived before the appearance of the Disciples had the perfect light—neither the Fathers, nor the martyrs, nor the theologians, nor Aquinas, nor Wyclif, nor Luther, nor Cranmer, nor Wesley; for none of these could answer the question, 'What must I do to be saved?' " In order to save themselves this humiliating confession and submission, they invented this federation trap, by which they hoped to lure the Disciples off the track of sectarianism and prevent the union of all Christians. They wanted to perpetuate their names—Lutheran, Wesleyan, Presbyterian, etc. How would it make Luther and Wesley and Calvin and other great denomination builders feel to awake on the morning of resurrection and find none but Disciples of Christ who write their name with a little d!

They come now offering to work with us on the plan that each be left free to preach the Gospel as he understands it, and plant churches wherever there is room for one. No loyal Disciple will

ever fall into this trap. It means that we will have to let the Methodists preach their doctrine and establish churches wherever they want to—the very thing we have come into the world to prevent. If we are right, the Methodists are wrong; if they are wrong, we should not eat or sleep until we have destroyed them root and branch. We ought to curse them in season and out of season, ridicule their teaching, and steal their members. We ought to refuse to have anything to do with the sects until they accept "our position"—until they accept our name, "Disciples of Christ," and write it with a little d, and preach our interpretation of Acts 2:38. It would be useless for them to try to work harmoniously with us, much less unite with us, until they agreed with our persecutors, who have determined that Moses wrote all the Pentateuch, that Isaiah wrote all the book of Isaiah, that Daniel was written before the Maccabean period, that the whale actually swallowed Jonah, that the name "Disciple" should be written with a little d, and that no preacher should call himself "pastor." Any man who can not compress his faith in the foregoing articles of faith should not come among the Disciples who write their name with a little d; for until he can accept these great essential truths, our persecutors will treat him as a "destructive critic," "an infidel," and "an alien."

We should have nothing to do with the sects until they come to the Disciples and say: "We will do, whatever you want us to do; we will believe all you teach, and practice all you suggest. We will turn over our organizations for you to destroy or remodel as you may choose." Not until they do this can we federate with them, and then what light can federate with darkness, or truth with error. Any other federation would be treason. It is the other kind of federation that has captivated the most of our leading heretics and traitors. All the worst and most dangerous elements among the Disciples have gone into it—all but two editors—the "leading men" of our city churches, the college presidents and professors, the convention speakers and the prophets of the new era. But the "rank and file" are against it—those who subscribe for the newspapers, boom the subscription lists in the churches, plead for "sound" Sunday-

school supplies, hate the denominations, persecute the critics, and preach the "old Jerusalem Gospel."

The sects have been looking up the statistics of our growth; they have been watching the reports of our evangelists for the numbers of persons added "from the sects"; they see that if we keep on getting their members and growing faster than any religious body, in about one

❀ ❀

billion years our growth will overtake the increase of population on the globe, and then there will be no one on earth but the Disciples. No wonder they are scared and are already looking around for plans to avert the awful catastrophe. They see that we mean business, and that we will wind up the affairs of every ecclesiastical and religious establishment in the resistless onrush of our growth.

The first thing we will do, they see, is to get possession of the government and make it a criminal offense not to subscribe for the official organ of persecution. We will get control of the legislative, judicial and executive branches of our city, county, state and national governments. We would then legalize persecution, and banish those who persisted in writing the name Disciple with a big D; put out the eyes of those who could see two Isaiahs; hang those who disagreed with the persecutors; put in the insane asylum those who preached federation or Christian union after the Dis-

ciples had absorbed all other denominations, and any one who said a soul could be saved without immersion would be drowned.

After a universal absorption of the denominations in the home field—after all the sects had either been converted or translated—we would march upon the foreign field and follow the same plan. We would treat the heathen more leniently than the sects, because their light being less their guilt would be less. In lands where we had never sent missionaries the heathen would not know how wicked it would be to write Disciples with a big D, or eat the bodies of their enemies slain in battle. We would first call upon all sectarians to accept "our position," or take the consequences. When we had rid the country of Methodist and Presbyterian missionaries we would then open the jails and pardon every cannibal condemned to death for eating the bodies of Methodist missionaries, and put into his hands a copy of

"McGarvey on the Acts." If after twenty-four hours he did not know what to do to be saved, we would give him up as a hopeless case.

In due course of time, with the sword of the Spirit in one hand and the sword of the persecutor in the other hand, we would girdle the earth with our plea, and bring in the glorious unity prayed for by Christ and his apostles. Where would the Methodists and Presbyterians be then? There would not be any. There would be only Disciples of Christ who wrote the word "Disciples" with a little d. No wonder the sects fear us and are planning to escape their doom. Every one who accepts federation now and begins to love the sects and regard them as Christian is a traitor. The sects are on the run before us, and if we are only faithful to the plea of the Disciples who write their name with a little d, we will take them, bag and baggage, at six o'clock on the evening of December 31, A. D. 999999990. God speed the time!

As Seen From the Dome   By F. D. Power

The anniversaries come next. Buffalo awaits the hosts of our Israel. For every one of our churches and preachers there is a call to prayer for the October meetings. For every one that can go up to the feast there is a special blessing. For every great cause represented in Buffalo there is upon our hearts a burden of solicitude. We should remember in our pulpits and in our prayer-meetings and in our closets these interests of our Lord's kingdom. The coming conventions mark the high tide in our missionary offerings and work, and of our spiritual development as well. They are not to be a mere aggregation of people, a display of numbers and of material force. God forbid there should be aught of boasting or glorying in our achievements. In the fear of God and in humble thanksgiving for his great grace to us, in the spirit of confession and of consecration, in hungering and hoping and planning for larger things, in prayer, in a sense of our deep unworthiness, and yet of the unspeakable exaltation to which our Lord has brought us, in devout and heartfelt recognition of the fact that it is "not by might, nor by power, but by my Spirit, saith the Lord of hosts," and in love and loyalty and lowly reliance upon our God for his blessing, we should come up to our Jerusalem to our annual feast.

For such a season then we should prepare our churches and our hearts religiously. From the pulpit and in the prayer-meeting supplication should be made unto the Lord for his presence and the guidance of his Spirit. Mention should be made of God's goodness to us, of our failures as well as of our successes, and of our sincere desire to be worthy of the great trust imposed in us. Earnest prayer should be offered, not

only for our missionaries and their converts, for our givers and helpers, but especially for the multitudes that have no part in the work, for those who oppose themselves, for the many who fail to see clearly their duty to the cause of world-wide evangelization. What a blessed meeting indeed if all our Zion could come up as one man with the prayer: "Thy kingdom come, Thy will be done in earth as it is in heaven!" What a triumph if this season of rejoicing and reconsecration could witness the thorough union and co-operation in every good word and work of all those who are pleading for the union of all God's people on the basis of New Testament Christianity! I am not so sure but that a day of fasting and prayer should be set apart in the midst of these occasions of rejoicing to invoke the divine favor on all who fail to measure up to their responsibility and privilege. Careful self-examination might reveal the fact that we dare not distinguish between missionary and anti-missionary for we are all guilty before God.

Whatever we make of this October gathering on the lake let it be one of spiritual power. Let every delegate and every visitor see that for him it is a mount of communion and transfiguration. Let prayer be supreme. Let this above all things be our petition: "Father, glorify thyself!" Standing by the grave of Gossner one said of him: "He prayed up the walls of a hospital and the hearts of the nurses; he prayed mission stations into being and missionaries into faith; he prayed open the hearts of the rich and gold from distant lands." We need such praying men. We have not yet learned the relation of prayer to missions. The significant word of the Master; "Pray ye the Lord of the harvest that he may

send forth laborers into his harvest." To Buffalo then on our knees.

The Jewish Passover, the first and greatest of the three annual feasts instituted by Moses, was "a holy convocation." With devout and humble service Israel assembled to glorify God for their deliverance. In the same spirit let us assemble. Let this be a holy convocation. With one great purpose to glorify God let his people prepare themselves and come to the feast. Let every report, every address, every song breathe the spirit of devotion. Let Christ and him crucified be first with every man and woman who participates in this solemn yet joyous assembly. Let the disciples of the Master show to all the great city that they have been with Jesus and learned of him. In the churches, in the sessions of the convention, in the hotels and on the streets, to all classes, let this spirit be manifest. This is our first great convention in the Empire State, let it be our best, noblest, worthiest.

Our general conventions are our mountain tops of vision; our milestones of progress. We have but to go back a few years and note the advancement. My first convention was in 1874. The meeting was held in Cincinnati and R. M. Bishop was president. My wife and I were entertained at No. 95, corner of College and Seventh, the president's home, over whose front seemed written, "Given to Hospitality." That was the convention that gave birth to the C. W. B. M. It was a great mass meeting. Little work was reported and for all general causes about $6,000 was raised. Thomas Munnell was heroically laying foundations. From $6,000 we have grown to $528,000 in 1905, counting merely the offerings of the foreign and home societies, C. W. B. M. and Church Extension, to say nothing of state missions, Christian Benevolence, Education and Ministerial 'Relief. What a step forward in less than a third of a century! My next convention was in 1876 at Richmond, where Isaac Errett made his great address on Foreign Missions. This society had been organized the previous year and came in with its report of $1,760. Last year its offering was $255,923. Who shall say this is not a worthy record in three decades? In those days, which are, after all, not far away from every one of us, most of the annual income was secured by persistent appeals at the convention itself and in the Richmond meeting after Errett's masterly presentation of the cause of world-wide evangelization, and one of his unequalled appeals for subscriptions to increase the paltry $1,960, one of our leading preachers took the floor saying: "You have been talking about foreign missions, now let us see what you will do for home missions," and made a tearful and strenuous call for aid for a little mission church in North Carolina! It was a curious jumble of big things and little, the sublime and ridiculous.

The steady march forward and upward is seen and known to all men. And the growth in our general work has inspired all our enterprises and made every state and district organization and every local church stronger and broader and richer in good works. At that time, for example, there was no state organization in Maryland and the District of Columbia. I called a few of our brethren together in convention, and we organized, and have accomplished a great service in this missionary territory, raising thousands of dollars and establishing a score or more of churches. Let us be thankful. We have laid some beautiful foundations, let us go on with the superstructure. There can be no true Christianity without the missionary spirit. Let us be men of one idea and that idea the conversion of the whole world to the Christ.

What the Brethren Are Saying and Doing

By B. B. Tyler

The Very Reverend H. Martyn Hart, D. D., dean of St. John's Cathedral (Protestant Episcopal), Denver, is a character. The dean takes himself seriously, but few others do. He has spells, the dean has. He had one on a recent Sunday. He discoursed, in the Chapter House, on "The Immorality of Colorado." He thinks that Colorado is one of the most immoral of the American states. Colorado is bad—Missouri, Illinois, Ohio, Kentucky, Indiana, etc., etc., are worse. The dean has been in pursuit of statistics showing how very, very wicked Colorado and all the states in the North American Republic are. The divorce evil is the greatest of the plague spots in the body politic. There are, the dean says, one-fourth as many divorces in this state as there are marriages. This is a bad showing, on the face of the returns, for the Centennial state.

The dean is an Englishman. He gets his daily news, it is said, from the London "Times." In his discourse, on the Lord's day, he contrasted the morals of the United States with the morals of Great Britain, to the disadvantage, of course, of the Republic. England is bad; the United States is worse. The doom of our experiment in a government of the people, by the people, for the people, is inevitable if we continue to move in the direction in which we are, at present, going, is the decision of this good man. The contention of the dean may be correct. I do not, in this place, join issue with him. Grant that his allegations rest on a bed rock of facts, that they are indisputable. What then? Is this the kind of preaching that will introduce a better order? The huge interrogation point is my reply, for the present.

Here is a letter from another good man, also born on the other side of the Atlantic Ocean, in which he says:

"Can't we get our editors reconciled, and let us all set about preaching the Gospel, which is God's power to save, in dead earnest, and begin to practice Christian union as never before?"

Good! If I were editor of the "Christian Standard" and he were editor of THE CHRISTIAN-EVANGELIST, we would be "reconciled," and both papers would be thoroughly Christian. This is the way out of this Wilderness of Sin. Plain as anything can be!

But the editors we now have are not as bad as they might be. There is a bit of comfort in this thought. They are not infallible. Sometimes they seem to think that they are, but, in this opinion, they err. Let us be patient. "All things are working together for good." Even our editors will come out all right!

The suggestion that we "all set about preaching the Gospel" ought to be unanimously adopted, by a rising vote, and reduced to practice without delay. The brother from whom I quote is doing this with wonderful success. As he preaches the Gospel it is the power of God unto salvation." There are ways and ways of preaching the Gospel.

In the above suggestion is found the divine panacea for Dean Hart's troubles, "Preach the word." The Christ is the power of God and the Wisdom of God. Enthrone the Christ in the thoughts, hearts, consciences, lives of men, by a faithful, constant, loving presentation of him to the people, and he will himself right the wrongs which we all lament. Jesus is our example. He did not spend his time in lamentations over the degeneracy of men. What says the record? He went about doing good and preaching the Gospel of the kingdom. He commanded the twelve to do the same when he sent them to the lost sheep of the house of Israel, on a tentative mission, throughout the province of Galilee. When he was on the eve of his departure from earth to heaven he commanded those whom he had carefully trained for this great work to go into all the world and preach the glad tidings to the whole creation. "So they went forth and preached everywhere." Read the sermons in the book of Acts. There are no statistics showing how bad men were. Men were wicked then; men are sinful now. They know it. In their hearts they are conscious of their evil estate. Assume the sinfulness of human nature and preach the Gospel of love, sympathy, courage, hope. Declare the joyful message as the great evangelists have ever told the story of God's love, and men by the score, by the hundred, by the thousand, will pass out of slavery into liberty. Give us a thousand James Smalls in these United States and God alone knows what the glorious result would be.

Jesus "began both to do and to teach." Doing and teaching go hand in hand. Doctrine and deeds; this is the Christian way. It is the Christian way because it was, and is, and ever more will be, Christ's way. Teaching and life are joined together in a holy wedlock. Divine wisdom, grace and authority have united them, and no man may lawfully put them asunder.

The Young Men's Christian Association in Denver owns a health farm. This is an effort on the part of this great organization to apply the teaching of Jesus. The Association Health Farm is a concrete illustration of "applied Christianity." The two-fold object of the Health Farm is (1) to offer "open-air treatment" to consumptive young men sent to Colorado by their home physicians, and unable to afford the privileges of a regular sanitarium, and (2) to provide the most needy of these with employment capable of helping them financially during their stay, and at the same time suited to their physical condition. For information address Mr. W. M. Danner, 1119 Ogden street, Denver, Colo.

About three years ago there appeared from the press of McClure, Phillips & Co. a booklet of 75 pages entitled "Letters from a Chinese Official." These letters set forth in a racy style what claimed to be an eastern view of our western civilization. The same house now gives to the public a volume of 97 pages entitled "Letters to a Chinese Official," by William Jennings Bryan—of whom you may have heard. Mr. Bryan replies definitely and effectively to the Chinese arraignment of our civilization. He contrasts, among other things, Confucianism and Christianity. This booklet ought to be read by those who are afflicted as was Dean Hart last Sunday. Mr. Bryan speaks eloquently of the "growth of Christianity from its beginning on the banks of the Jordan, until to-day, when its converts are baptized in all the rivers of the earth."

"Baptized in all the rivers of the earth" is good for a dyed-in-the-wool Presbyterian as is William Jennings Bryan. His brief account of the progress of the Christian religion is thrillingly interesting. Read these two little books.

Denver, Colo.

❀ ❀

What Conventions Are Doing For Me?

By DAVID H. SHIELDS.
Mayor of Salina, Kan.

The mere magnitude of our national conventions has greatly enlarged my view of what God is doing in the world. The earth is never quite the same to a man who has once stood on the summit of the mountains.

The unity of purpose of this vast throng has assured me that the prayer of Jesus shall be answered and that God will finally win. This assurance has sent me back home from time to time girded for fuller service.

The fellowship of these great gatherings has enriched my life. Having met the men who are leading us onward, life is a finer thing since, and the sense of isolation has passed away. If a man attends one of these conventions in the right spirit he will never get the idea that he is the only righteous man left, and that they are seeking to kill him.

❀ ❀

The night has a thousand eyes,
 The day but one;
Yet the light of the whole world dies
 With the setting of the sun;
 The mind has a thousand eyes;
 The heart but one;
Yet the light of a whole life dies
 When love is done!

Why Attend the Convention in Buffalo?

By THOMAS PENN ULLOM.

1. It seems to me to be the duty of every minister to attend our national convention in Buffalo. Here in a very short time the best thoughts and the best ways of doing things by our best men and women will be brought to a focus, so that the impression made upon the delegates is nothing less than reconstructive.

2. A change of environment if for only a few days will give vigor of intellect, sweetness of spirit and recreate the physical organism.

3. The necessity of an annual submergence in such an atmosphere as is generated in our national gatherings is absolute to every one who desires to keep on the front line and out of the rut. Some one has said that a "rut" is the grave with both ends knocked out. I am not ready for it, so I'm going to Buffalo, N. Y.

Traverse City, Mich.

❀ ❀

"It is only by thinking about great and good things that we come to love them, and it is only by loving them that we come to long for them, and it is only by longing for them that we are impelled to seek after them, and it is only by seeking after them that they become ours and we enter into vital experience of their beauty and blessedness."—Henry Van Dyke.

Minister's Reply.

Quite a time ago a statement appeared in the papers regarding a minister's experience in rebuilding his lost health by correcting his diet, and without drugs.

The original statement is here reprinted followed by some extracts from a letter he wrote to another minister who made inquiry of him.

(Original Statement.)

FOLLOWING SCRIPTURE
He Proved the Good Thing and Holds Fast To It.

A young preacher found the change from life on the home farm to the city and college very trying, especially the transition from the wholesome country food to the boarding-house fare. How he solved the food question is interesting.

"I soon came to face a serious problem," he says, "I began to decline in health, grew thin in flesh and weak in body and mind. The doctor diagnosed my trouble as 'indigestion,' but was unable to give me relief. I tried patent medicines with the same result. I was weak and growing weaker, and had no capacity for study. For 4 years I fought a hard battle—fought it poorly, because of my physical and mental condition.

"A Postum Cereal calendar fell into my hands. I hung it over my study table. It bore the inscription 'Brains Repaired' cross the face. I used to lean back and gaze at it when weary with study, till at last it occurred to me that my brains needed repairing. Why not try Grape-Nuts food and see what it would do for me? I acted on the thought, beginning a few months ago.

"Gradually I found that it was making me stronger and better. Then I decided that as Grape-Nuts was helping me I would stop coffee and take on Postum. This I did, and the two are simply working wonders! And while the improvement has been only gradual, it is permanent. I do not gain a little for a few days and then lapse back—I keep what I gain.

"From the use of the two, Grape-Nuts and Postum Coffee, I have acquired a quickened vitality, capacity for harder work, clearer and more energetic mentality and can study better. My flesh has become firm and healthy and to-day I weigh more than for years before. I am a new man. As pastor of the Christian Church I preach Christ from the pulpit and in my pastoral work, as a man among men, I also preach Grape-Nuts and Postum. I have proved them to be good, and am holding fast to them.'" Name given by Postum Co., Battle Creek, Mich.

A 10-days' trial is easy.

Box 244, Metropole, Ill., Apr. 19, '06.
Rev.——,

Dear Sir and Brother:

"Your letter at hand and contents noted. Yes, a minister's life is very busy, but his duty is to 'do good' and no man in real need should be considered by him as a stranger. Therefore I take pleasure in writing you the facts as I know them, in hopes they may be suggestive and place you in a better position to understand my troubles and the blessing derived from Grape-Nuts and Postum, for I honestly believe these were the "black-winged ravens" that brought, or induced the return of the natural activities of the body which condition we call "health."

"Until I was 25 years of age I could and did eat anything I wanted at any time day or night. I entered the "College of the Bible" at Lexington, Ky., and after three months took the measles which settled in my stomach, and in a short time was com-

pelled to give up my work. I re-entered College the next September but bad stomach and hard study kept me torn up. I fought along for over a year taking pepsin, and several other preparations besides medicine from the doctors. I was a sufferer, did poor work and did it at all times in the face of the aggravated condition of my 'stomach which made me so very nervous. I starved myself, eating very little but soup and this was even painful to me.

"One day a calendar came to my study which was placed over my table and it bore a peculiar message—'Brains Repaired.' Mine were gone and my nerves gone. I doubted whether they could be properly restored. At last my wife urged me or rather sent and purchased two packages under protest (if I remember well). I began eating. I had been drinking coffee but had given that up and was taking water. As coffee was injuring my wife's health I proposed she try Postum which she did to her relief and my surprise. I soon began taking Postum also. I had been eating Grape-Nuts and drinking Postum but a few days until I was feeling better. Even then I did not think of giving Grape-Nuts the credit. I kept eating and still grew stronger in mind, nervous condition improved. I was taking no medicine, working harder, with much more ease and comfort, from the growing sensation in my stomach. Before, I got hungry but dared not eat, now I did not get hungry as before. I finished that year's work (9 months) and came out in far better condition than I began. September came again, it found me in my place for my fourth and last year. I had missed two-thirds of my first year by measles, now if I finished I must do the fourth year's work and two-thirds of the first. I had discovered my weapons the year before. They were Grape-Nuts and Postum. That year's work was the most satisfactory to me, also to my professors as same told me.

"I did not take Grape-Nuts as a medicine but a natural food. I still keep it up. My wife and two little school girls find in it a nourishing morsel which guards against fatigue. It is our meat.

"I have tried many of the breakfast foods on the market now, as a change, but invariably I flee to Grape-Nuts and Postum as the Old Reliables.

"I am glad you wrote me and I will be pleased to answer any question which I have not made perfectly clear. My praise of Grape-Nuts and Postum is given not in the interest of the Company, but simply my honest conviction of what they have done for me and can do for others. Hoping for your speedy recovery, I am,

Your Bro.,"

Pastor Christian Church.

Ministers owe to themselves and to their noble cause, that they keep "the machine," (the body, which they use to carry out their work), in fine working order, and naturally they feel a certain responsibility for the physical welfare of their people, for the man or woman who is consciously or unconsciously crippling the "beautiful human temple" by the use of harmful food, drink, or drug habits cannot express the intent of the Creator, until those habits are eliminated and the body again assumes its proper condition, the reward comes when a clean soul dwells in a well ordered house. A minister can consistently guide for physical well-being while seeking to influence towards the higher life.

❀ ❀

"Why stand ye here all the day idle?" (Matt. 20:6).
1. Why? The vineyard is so large.
2. Why? The Master is so kind.
3. Why? The reward is so liberal.
4. Why? The time for working is so short.—Rev. G. B. F. Hallock, D. D.

Our Budget

—October approaches, and Buffalo looms high above the horizon.

—Send in all the offerings promptly to the various secretaries that they may close their books before the 30th inst.

—After Buffalo, where next? Why not the Jamestown Exposition? The next convention will be invited there, and we hold over till next week a communication from Virginia urging strong reasons why our next convention should be held there.

—In another place will be found an editorial welcome to our new readers who, breaking all records, have continued coming right on through the summer months. Not the least gratifying feature of this increase is the fact that they are coming at our regular price, which means that most of them have come to stay.

—We wish state secretaries and others having convention announcements to make would get them to this office in good time for us to give them such a position as we would like to give them. Frequently they reach us just as we are going to press and it is impossible, under these circumstances, to give anything more than the briefest announcement. News matter should, if possible, be sent as early in the week previous to the appearance of THE CHRISTIAN-EVANGELIST as possible. We can handle brief telegraph or telephone dispatches as late as the first thing Tuesday morning, but brethren must not expect us to crowd out news already in type for the sake of their communications. We can only get so much type into the paper, and it requires careful thought how to give the just proportion to the different articles and news matter that we receive.

—Our friends can go with us to Buffalo in "THE CHRISTIAN-EVANGELIST Special" over the Wabash from St. Louis without a change of cars. They may go from Detroit by rail or water, though we advise that they go by rail and return from Buffalo to Detroit by ship. Prompt response will be made from this office to all inquiries concerning transportation and entertainment at the convention city and side trips to Niagara Falls, Toronto and elsewhere.

—A fine new church is nearly completed at Chehalis, Wash.

—A. A. Burr, who has been preaching, has just moved to Eureka, Ill., to attend college.

—J. W. Walters, of Niantic, Ill., has been suffering much from hay fever and asthma.

—We regret to learn that William Ireland has been quite ill for four weeks at Monterey, Mexico.

—Thomas Martin, of California, Pa., is, we regret to learn, confined to his room with a sprained ankle.

—J. M. Monroe has dedicated a church at Apache, Okla., with $982 raised and an indebtedness of $450.

—John G. Cropper has been doing some evangelistic work in Colorado. He writes that he likes the people and the country. His wife is assisting him.

—J. A. Napper, of Earle, S. C., writes that one young man has been ordained to the ministry and three others are in school preparing for the work.

—We regret to learn that owing to the sudden illness of Brother Couch, a good meeting at Tipton, Mo., under the leadership of H. A. Northcutt, had to be abandoned.

—The brethren of Greenridge, Mo.,

have just paid about all their debt on their new building. This will gratify them and the news will please the brethren in general.

—Thomas Shuey reports that his church at Abingdon, Ill., will this year give $100 to the Church Extension fund, which is twice as much as the church has ever given before.

—President R. E. Hieronymous, of Eureka College, is home from his trip through Europe, where he was benefited physically and his life enriched for his high calling.

—Frank E. Janes has taken up the pastorate at Pendleton, Ind. Brother Janes did good work at Freemont, Neb., and has had considerable success in the evangelistic field.

—A personal note from G. Kevorkian indicates that he is compelled to leave Turkey, after many years' of work and return to the United States. No reasons are assigned.

—W. T. Clarkson, formerly of the North Side Church, Lawrence, Kan., will enter Columbia University and Union Theological Seminary this fall for post-graduate work.

—King Stark, who is employed by the county board, has begun a meeting at Woodlaw Church in Clay county, Mo., and is being assisted by R. T. McCray, of Warrensburg, Mo.

—The church extension offering at Pomona, Cal., where Madison A. Hart recently entered upon the pastorate, was $185, and it is expected that the amount will be raised to at least $200.

—We have received cards announcing the marriage of Alda Louise, daughter of Mrs. Nancy Rowley, of Ashtabula, O., to Mr. Albert Teachout, Jr. We extend our congratulations.

—Herbert Yeuell, now in a meeting at Union City, Tenn., writes that his wife and boy will remain in England until spring when he is to return for a meeting at Cheltenham, Gloucestershire.

—A. E. Dubber has just closed his first year's association with the Tabernacle Church, Fort Worth, Texas. The $6,000 debt has been paid off and 102 additions gained during the regular services.

—The church extension offering of the Woodward Avenue Christian Church, at Detroit, Mich., which is only six months old, and which has sixty members, has reached $180. S. G. Fisher is the minister.

—H. M. Barnett will close his work with the Forest Avenue Church of Kansas City, Mo., next Lord's day, after which he will be ready to hold evangelistic meetings. He may be addressed at 1500 Harrison street.

—N. J. Wright has resigned the pastorate of the First Christian Church, Terrell, Texas, and will remove to Artesia, a pioneer point where there is no church of any kind. He has already helped to organize a Sunday-school there.

—William M. Thomas and C. V. Allison have arranged an exchange of meetings. Brother Allison will begin the first meeting at Frederick Avenue Church, St. Joseph, Mo., October 1, and the Mound City meeting will be held later.

—The work at Valdosta, Ga., is encouraging. A recent Church Extension offering amounted to $52.65 where the apportionment was only $35. Richard W. Wallace is the minister. This church is to entertain the state convention which meets on November 19-22.

—On the occasion of his delivering the

"Help us to get into our own church home."

DID YOU TAKE

a Church Extension Offering the first Sunday of September?

The Offering began then but it should not end until every church sends an Offering. Select the best Sunday to suit local conditions, but

SEND AN OFFERING

to G. W. Muckley, Cor. Sec., 600 Water Works Bldg., Kansas City, Mo.

The Annuity feature of Church Extension is profitable to you and the Board. You receive 6 per cent and the Board builds churches with your money.

address at the laying of the corner-stone of the Odd Fellows' temple at Carlsbad, New Mexico, C. C. Hill preached in the evening at an open air union service, at which all the preachers of the town participated.

—D. D. Boyle, who is now in the ranch country near Cactus, Texas, hopes later on to organize churches at Laredo, Cottula and Pearsall. Brother Boyle expects to be in a meeting during part of October at Watunga, Okla., where Douglass Horton is the efficient pastor.

—Ernest Reed has just located at Agra, Okla., for full time. The church has been lately without any preaching, but is now well filled and a good feeling prevails. An effort is being made to secure the services of Oscar Ingold, Chandler, Okla., to hold a meeting at once.

—T. L. Read and family have removed from South Chicago to Eureka for the purpose of putting their daughter in school there. Brother Read, who has had large experience as an efficient minister, can devote all his time to one or two congregations within one hundred miles of Eureka.

—Clay Center, Church, Nebraska, becomes a living link in the Nebraska Christian Missionary Society, and will support E. von Forrell as its evangelist. The $300 necessary were raised in a very few minutes in response to a single appeal. A. D. Smith is the pastor of this church, for which Melvin Putnam is to begin an evangelistic campaign at the end of this month.

❋ ❋

—I. H. Fuller writes that this meeting at La Monte, Mo., in which B. F. Hill, of California, is to do the preaching, will begin October 7. Phil Stark is to hold a meeting at Knobnoster, October 14. John Jones, the Pettis county evangelist, will hold a meeting at Dresden some time in the same month.

—We just learn of the resignation of H. R. Trickett at Monroe City, Mo. Brother Trickett is a man of considerable ability and is known to many as the author of "On what are you building, my brother?" and other hymns. We hope he may soon find another field of work suited to his brilliant attainments.

—The congregation at the Antioch church, near Hillsboro, Ind., has experienced a newness of life under the ministry of Elmer Williams, of Crawfordsville. This is the old home congregation of Will H. Newlin, of Jamestown, Ind., where a revival meeting with home forces was begun last Lord's day.

—The Tennessee state convention will be held at Paris, October 1-4. The program arranged is a good one, and while it has nothing that is novel, all the subjects are vital. Among the speakers are State Secretary A. I. Myhr, W. J. Shelburne, W. F. Crouch, J. E. Gorsuch, Robert Stewart and others, including well known national leaders.

—E. J. Fenstermacher, of Poplar Bluff, will assist Frank W. Allen in a meeting at Odessa, Mo., soon. Three hundred copies of THE CHRISTIAN-EVANGELIST will also bear their silent but resistless testimony each week to the immanence of God in this world and the power of the Gospel to save men from sin.

—Percy Leach has begun his sixth year as pastor in Iowa City, where there are now 405 names on the church roll. A two months' evangelistic campaign has just been inaugurated, at the present time a tent in the country being used. C. C. Morrison will hold a three weeks' meeting about the middle of October.

—The church at Hunter, Okla., sent their minister, W. L. Dalton, and his wife to the convention at El Reno. Upon their return the ladies of the church acknowledged Brother Dalton's birthday with a handsome gold watch. Arrangements are being made for Evangelist Trimble to begin a meeting there November 1.

—H. E. Van Horn will close four years' of work with the church at Osceola, Ia., October 1, and will remove to Des Moines to take charge of the East Side Church. The church at Osceola is one of the best fields in southern Iowa, and a strong man is needed to take oversight of it. Applicants should write R. M. Lewis for information.

❄ ❄

Cause of Sick Headache.

Severe attacks of Sick Headache are due to a Torpid, Congested Liver and a Disordered Stomach. No one can enjoy good health when the stomach refuses to do its necessary work. One bottle of Drake's Palmetto Wine, a purely vegetable compound, has often brought complete health to persons suffering with the above named symptoms, and in many cases pronounced incurable by some of the best physicians in the country.

A large bottle, usual dollar size, can be obtained at drug stores for 75 cents, but a trial bottle with full Instructions will be sent free to every reader of this paper who needs it.

Address your letter or postal card to The Drake Co., Wheeling, W. Va.

—F. M. Rogers writes us that the pulpit at Stewart Street Church, Springfield, Ill., is still vacant. C. C. Morrison will close his pastorate at the First Church next Lord's day. The brethren are hoping to secure two good men for these churches at an early date. Brother Morrison, we believe, will take charge of the Monroe Street Church, Chicago, Ill.

—E. S. Allhands has taken steps towards the organization of an Endeavor society at Arkadelphia, Ark. For some time this church was strongly anti, but Charles A. Allhands, of Pike City, Ark., has been preaching for them for the past two years and has just been called for his third year. With a Sunday-school and a Y. P. S. C. E. organized we may hope for considerable progress.

—James A. Brown, a Warren boy, and recently graduated from Hiram, will be ordained to the ministry at his home church where J. E. Lynn ministers, next Lord's day. He has been doing excellent work at Hartford, Mich. This will be the second of her young men ordained at the Warren church within a little over a year.

—The St. Francois County Christian Church co-operation will hold their annual convention at Libertyville, Mo., October 5, 6. A strong and helpful program is being prepared. Some of the speakers are E. J. Fenstermacher, T. A. Abbott, W. A. Kokendoffer, Mrs. Bantz, Judge G. O. Nations, G. T. McFarland, Edward Owers, George B. Smith and R. O. Rogers.

—Charles M. Fillmore, writing to the office since his return from a brief vacation, says that he is now able to preach twice on Sunday and is slowly improving. He says: "It almost pays to be sick to find how many good, kind people there are in the world. I am more anxious than ever to get well so as to pay back for all I have received." How many of us have had this same experience and this same feeling!

—There was a printer's error in the article by E. S. Muckley entitled "T. L. Frazier's Dilemma." The compositor omitted the word "not" before the word "Christian" in the ninth line from the bottom of page 1137. The clause "who are Christian in character" should have read "who are not Christian in character." We regret the oversight, but feel sure that nearly every one who read Brother Muckley's interesting article understood his meaning.

—"I have found THE CHRISTIAN-EVANGELIST a very great help," writes Charles Frederick Trimble, who is engaged in a meeting at Ada, I. T. Notwithstanding the unfavorable conditions, success is being achieved. The daily paper of the town has published Brother Trimble's sermons and this, with the wide field he covers with the 300 CHRISTIAN-EVANGELISTS which he is using is greatly extending his influence for good.

—A brother wishes to know our opinion of one who has been baptized in the Christian Church and who claims to know "that the Christian ministers have a discipline among themselves, and that it is a sworn secret among them to keep it among the ministry." Our opinion is that this brother is very ignorant and needs teaching or else is exceedingly careless about handling the truth and needs the New Testament discipline.

—E. B. Barnes recently preached at the invitation of the minister of the Methodist Episcopal Church, at Noblesville, Ind., on the subject of "Lodges." The three points he emphasized were that lodges are not charitable institutions, that they are hindrances to church progress, and that the lodges will not save the souls of men. The editor of

the local paper wrote an editorial on the subject supporting Brother Barnes' position.

—John Ewers has been asked by a unanimous vote to remain as pastor of the First Christian Church, Youngstown, O., for a period of two years. Brother Ewers has done a good work for this church during a comparatively brief service. He is secretary of the ministerial association. His salary has been increased by $300, and now the church is ready to enter into an aggressive campaign of religious work during the winter.

—The Colorado convention will meet with Central Christian Church, Pueblo, October 2-4. A good program will be presented. All who pay full fare going will be entitled to one-fifth fare returning, provided they take receipt for fare paid to Pueblo and present this receipt to the secretary of the convention. There is no doubt that the necessary number will be secured. Those expecting to attend should advise D. W. Moore, 711 Summit street, Pueblo.

—Clarence Mitchell, of Lima, O., is to be the evangelist who will assist Pastor G. Hubert Steed in the evangelistic meeting at the Second Christian Church at Johnstown, Pa. A large choir under the direction of W. Z. Replogle, a well known singer, will be one of the features of the meeting which the congregation is working to make the most successful in its history. The conclusion of this meeting will mark the completion of a three years' work under the leadership of the present minister, and a splendid advance is being confidently expected.

—In another column is an account of a very enjoyable and helpful conference that was recently held under the auspices of our F. M. C. S., at Cincinnati, and on our front page will be found a portrait group of the missionaries who were present on that occasion. Fourteen of the number are new missionaries who go out this fall. The other ten are missionaries who are at home on furlough. Secretary Stephen A. Corey is one of the figures in the group.

—A new house of worship has just been completed at Ladonia, Texas, where E. V. Spicer and E. M. Douthit have just closed a good meeting with the organization of a Sunday-school in addition to many conversions. We are hopeful that they may be able to secure preaching more than once a month. Hardin Walsh, of Austin, preaches for them at present, and if they can have more of the pastoral care of such a faithful leader, they can accomplish a great deal more.

—The Maryland, District of Columbia, and Delaware convention will be held with the church at Antioch near Vienna, Va., October 1-5. Cars leave the Virginia side of Aqueduct Bridge, Wash., on the Washington, Arlington and Falls Church Electric Railway every hour. A special rate of 40 cents round trip is made for those who have identification slips from their pastors. Seventy-five cents per day is the cost of entertainment. J. A. Dyer, Vienna, Va., has charge of this arrangement. The Antioch church, of which W. T. Laprade is pastor, will welcome you.

—Miss Carrie May McFarland and Mr. Clyde Everett Handley were recently united in marriage by E. T. McFarland, pastor of the Fourth Christian Church, St. Louis, assisted by C. O. McFarland, state evangelist of Missouri, brothers of the bride, and R. L. Handley, assistant pastor of the First Christian Church, Chicago, brother of the groom. Miss McFarland has, for some years, been associated with our publishing house and THE CHRISTIAN-EVANGELIST extends its congratulations and well wishes to the young couple.

—E. J. Church, pastor at Seneca, Mo., writes us that the churches of Newton county are moving on to victory. During the past year there has been an increase in membership of about 400 Brother Walters, of Neosho, has fitted that place admirably and has done a fine work. James Miller is starting out with promise at Diamond. The county cooperative meeting will be held at Seneca October 2, 3, and at the same time a meeting is to be begun with the assistance of Brother and Sister O. G. Blackwell, of New Vienna, Ind., as evangelists.

—The Southeast Minnesota missionary convention met last week at Winona. At this writing we have not received any report of the proceedings. Immediately following the convention an evangelistic meeting was begun, M. D. Banner, of Pleasant Grove, and Rochester Irwin, of Rochester, co-operating with the resident pastor, C. B. Osgood. At the close of this meeting a similar effort will be made at Rochester and following that, perhaps, at Pleasant Grove. Minnesota is a great field for missionary effort, and earnest, capable men for this purpose are in demand.

—The Board of Church Extension is just in receipt of an annuity gift of $2,000 from a friend in Illinois. Others should remember Church Extension by annuity gifts during the months of September and October, thus helping us to raise our $100,000 for this year. Up to

Wednesday, the 19th, the receipts for September were $1,631.58 ahead of last year's. Remember that offerings should be taken in October if they can not be sent in September. Remittance should be promptly made to George W. Muckley, corresponding secretary, 600 Waterworks building, Kansas City, Mo.

—D. Wesley Campbell, who has just been holding a good meeting at Edinburg, Ill., with Pastor D. W. Conner, speaks very highly of that preacher and his wife: "He is deeply in earnest about missions, as he is about everything else. He is well backed up by an excellent membership." In this meeting E. E. Nelms led the music and proved very efficient. Brother Campbell writes that

D. WESLEY CAMPBELL.

"THE CHRISTIAN-EVANGELIST has contributed very largely to the general interest. Three hundred copies of THE CHRISTIAN-EVANGELIST wisely distributed in the homes can not do otherwise than aid the evangelist and pastor in a meeting." Brother Campbell's next meeting will be at Oakland, Ky.

—We very gladly call attention to a request from V. L. Parker, minister of our church at New Decatur, Ala. He is planning for a meeting this fall. Brother Parker would like to hear from some brother minister who could help the church immediately after the Buffalo convention. The pay would be small but, as he says, God will richly repay any man who will go there and help get the church on its feet, for the possibilities are great and it will be one of the strongest churches in the state in a few years. Anti-ism is very strong there and that, of course, makes it difficult for those who are under the ministrations of Brother Parker to make great progress.

—On Lord's day next F. N. Calvin will complete three years' of service with the Compton Heights Church of St. Louis. During this pastorate the membership has nearly doubled in spite of many removals. The Bible school has increased to an attendance of over 500 and every department is quite thoroughly organized. Perfect harmony exists in the church, and at a meeting of the board of officers Brother Calvin was asked to continue indefinitely, while another increase in his salary was voted. This is the third time the salary has been increased which is, in itself, an evidence of appreciation which the brethren have for the hard, honest work which Brother Calvin has done.

For a Church in New Hampshire.

Previously acknowledged $958 75
Caroline Greene 2 00
Hon. J. M. McBeath............. 2 50
E. J. Jeffress 5 00

Total $968 25

One of the hoped for amenities of the Buffalo convention is the interchange of greetings with our first church in New Hampshire—the new congregation at Manchester. But $232.75 stands between us and the consummation of this hope. Twelve hundred dollars will not only defray the expenses of the great Yeuell meeting, but will leave a small balance to provide emergency expenses incident to the location of the pastor. This will enable us to make over this work free of indebtedness to our National C. W. B. M., who will assume the responsibility for the future of the church. This great organization never fails in its enterprises and their patronage assures the perpetual burning of this new lamp of hope in New England. Will not many follow the good examples of President D. O. Smart, of our Church Extension Board, and L. C. Stow in making a second contribution to this sacred purpose? No other appeal will be made to our readers for the support of this church after this $1,200 is raised. Let all who wish to have first or second fellowship with us in this work of the Lord, respond at once. Let us quickly dispose of this matter aright and pass on to new ministries.

The Last Call.

Heed this call or you are too late for this missionary year. The books of the American Christian Missionary Society close September 30. Our receipts lack a little of being equal to those for a like period last year. However, nine hundred churches which contributed liberally last year have not sent a dollar this year. If they rally to our support in these last few days, we can report at Buffalo the greatest amount of our history. Send the offering at once. Or telegraph us by the night of September 30 the amount you will send the next day. You can help us win a glorious victory.

Send all money to the American Christian Missionary Society, Y. M. C. A. building, Cincinnati, O.

As We Go to Press.

St. Stephen, S. C., Sept. 24.—Merritt's Bridge country church dedicated without debt, a young man ordained and thirty-one added.—Charles E. Smith, state evangelist.
Special to THE CHRISTIAN-EVANGELIST.

Jacksonville, Ill., Sept. 24.—Sixty-two added in two weeks; two thousand attended last night.—Thrapp and Smith.
Special to THE CHRISTIAN-EVANGELIST.

Oskaloosa, Ia., Sept. 24.—Meeting two weeks old; 102 added; sixty-five yesterday; overflowing audiences.—Corey, Evangelist; Bendt, Pastor.
Special to THE CHRISTIAN-EVANGELIST.

Jeffersonville, Ind., Sept. 24.—Closed in Cincinnati with thirty-five additions and three-fourths of the debt raised. Sturgis directed the music; much enthusiasm; good beginning here.—O. P. Spiegel.
Special to THE CHRISTIAN-EVANGELIST.

Tuscola, Ill., Sept. 24.—We had 46, instead of 6 as you reported, last Sunday and have had exactly 200 in the first six invitations, as follows: Forty-six, fourteen, fifty, twenty-four, sixteen and fifty. Smith and Kendal, singers; McNutt, pastor.—Charles Reign Scoville.
Special to THE CHRISTIAN-EVANGELIST.

Bloomington, Ill., Sept. 23.—Brooks Brothers leading us in a great revival; thirty-seven to-day, 131 to date. Sunday audiences are so large that services are divided; seven separate services today. J. H. Gilliland's nineteen years' ministry here has been a power for good.—Edgar D. Jones, pastor.

Ministerial Exchange.

W. A. Stullenberger, pastor of the Christian church at Grant City, Mo., desires a first class evangelistic male singer to assist in a meeting to begin October 14. Applicants please send terms and references.

The church at Osceola, Iowa, will need from October 1 a strong man as its pastor. The church is in excellent condition. For information address R. M. Lewis.

S. J. Vance, evangelist, Carthage, Mo., can hold meetings after December.

N. E. Cory, one of our oldest preachers, but still strong, would like to locate again and churches may correspond with him at Augusta, Ill.

John A. Stephens, state corresponding secretary for Louisiana, located at Alexandria, wants to get into communication with an energetic, young preacher for a town of 2500 people. No debt on the church. Salary $65, but if married, $60 and parsonage. Also, an elderly preacher wanted for an old church. Salary $300. Another preacher wanted to take four or five small churches. Salary about $600, which can be increased with the growth of the work. Good references required.

An Educational Enterprise for the Middle Southwest.

At the invitation of the missionary secretaries of the Oklahoma and Indian Territories, and through the co-operation and support of Bro. T. W. Phillips, of New Castle, Pa., I began a tour of the two territories named in the interests of a school for the Disciples of Christ in the middle southwest. I have visited twenty-nine different places and have made thirty-eight addresses. There is but one voice in this matter, and that is in favor of the school. Both conventions have voted unanimously for the school, and an educational board of twelve men was appointed. This board has called me to the presidency of the school, and I have accepted the position. Six or eight different points are competing for the location of the school. October 1 has been appointed as the date when the bids will be canvassed and the location settled upon. Already bids closely approximating $100,000 have been made.

Two principal ideas prevail. Some hold that it will be wisest to plant the school by the side of the state university, where a very liberal offer has been made to us. The university authorities offer us very satisfactory concessions, as to credits, etc., for our work. If we should go there the school will be strictly a Bible college, or Bible university. On the other hand, there are some who are strongly in favor of an independent school similar to the other colleges of our brotherhood, and some very liberal propositions are being made to us for the location of this school. This question will also be decided by the board on October 1.

The school will occupy a strategic position. Four great states and several territories will be immediately tributary to the school, in which we have no school of our brotherhood.

This country is destined to hold a tremendous population in the very near future. The Disciples of Christ are said to be the strongest religious body in Oklahoma, and they rank well up in the Indian Territory. There is, however, one great lack, namely, preachers. Scores and even hundreds of preachers are wanted for this rapidly developing region. This makes the planting of a Bible college of great importance. If the college is well located, one hundred young men preparing for the ministry will be able to find by they will be enabled to defray part or all of their school expenses. The board has also decided to have one hundred and sixty acres of land, more or less, close to the school, where earnest young men may assist themselves in defraying expenses by working one or more hours per day. E. V. ZOLLARS.

Lake Geneva Summer Train Service.

Via the Chicago & North-Western R'y is now in effect including Saturday afternoon train leaving Chicago 1:00 p. m. and Sunday Train leaving 8:30 a. m. For tickets, rates and full information apply to your nearest ticket agent or address W. B. Kniskern, P. T. M., C. & N. W. R'y Co., Chicago.

ILLINOIS STATE CONVENTION.

About 500 choice people have just been to the beautiful city of Paris to consider the work of the Master. They came from every part of the state, from Chicago to Metropolis and from St. Louis to Danville. It was not a meeting to nominate great officers, nor to provide large salaries, but to promote a work sufficiently important that delegates were willing to pay their own way and considerable expenses while there that they might participate in it. And it is doubtful if there is one that regrets his investment. Finis Idleman and his great congregation of 1500 people are a royal host, and right royally did they serve. The $40,000 stone church afforded ample facilities for all purposes.

The C. W. B. M. opened the convention, a report of whose proceedings follows, prepared by Mrs. Lillis Watson Hall.

The session was very successful. The state officers had the work carefully planned. It was a matter of congratulation that the program was carried out exactly as printed.

The convention was fortunate in the presence of Mrs. Moses and Mrs. Atwater of Indianapolis, Mrs. Harrison of Kentucky, and Dr. Mary Longdon of Deoghur, India. Mrs. Atwater gave an address on Monday evening and Dr. Longdon Tuesday afternoon. Mrs. Moses, whose sweet presence was in itself a benediction, closed the convention with a short talk on Harvest Sheaves.

Mrs. Ida W. Harrison presented the Centennial plan. She sketched briefly the events commemorated by the Centennial, explained the plans of the C. W. B. M. and earnestly presented a plea for its success. Following her address the report of the Centennial Committee was presented by Miss Annie E. Davidson and adopted. The Centennial aim is "A Doubled Membership (4,500 *new* members)" a Centennial thank offering of $15,000 by 1909. The committee recommended in part: 1. That every auxiliary appoint a Centennial secretary. 2. That preachers, where we have no auxiliaries, be asked to co-operate with Miss Thompson, the state secretary. 3. That local auxiliaries adopt the suggestions sent out by Miss Thompson, particularly the holding of Centennial rallies. 4. That it be aimed to secure 1,500 new members and $5,000 by September, 1907.

Every report submitted during the convention showed pleasing gains. Miss Davidson, state president; Mrs. Crawford, state treasurer, and Miss Griffin, superintendent of young people's work, had reports showing satisfactory progress in their work. Miss Davidson laid especial emphasis on "Mission Leaves," the state paper of which she is editor. Miss Griffin reported a gain of twenty-three young people's societies. The state banner was presented to the Junior Endeavorers at Armington.

The committee on future work submitted a report full of plans for active future work. The state aim is to be: National, $14,000; state, $2,500; Illinois Special, $4,600, and 2,500 copies of "Missionary Tidings" and "Mission Leaves." Illinois this year will support Mrs. Lohr in India, Miss Westrup in Mexico, Mrs. Burner in South America, Professor Button at Morehead, Ky., and will give $2,000 to Chicago city missions.

Will F. Shaw, of Chicago, delivered the C. W. B. M. sermon, and it was one of the best things of the convention. Much of the effectiveness of the organization comes from the co-operation of pastors, and their sympathy and help is prized. This appreciation of the high aims of these women was never more tenderly or beautifully expressed than in the address by Brother Shaw.

The C. W. B. M. sessions were model in every respect. A great deal of business was accomplished. The women were inspired and impressed by the counsels of our national officers and our noble missionary, Dr. Longdon. The state workers were especially pleased with the interest and enthusiasm shown. The whole convention seemed a prophecy of a fruitful and happy year's work to follow.

The State Missionary Society convention was introduced by a great address by its president, F. W. Burnham, of Decatur, on Tuesday evening. It was a vigorous rallying address to go forward, illustrated by an incident in Israel's life, when God said, "Long enough have ye compassed this mountain, turn ye northward." It was full of instruction and prophetic in hope.

Wednesday morning was the leading business session. Field Secretary J. F. Jones shows that there has been steady progress during the eleven years of his service. The past year, in the 237 churches that reported, there were 4,287 conversions, 2,096 other additions, making a total growth of 6,083 additions. There were 154 meetings held. In the state we have 814 churches, 97,038 members, 711 Bible schools, 62,853 pupils, 360 Endeavor societies, with 11,168 members. Junior societies 113, with 4,150 members. There are 388 ministers. Brother Jones had a busy and fruitful year. There were 58 men who did some state work; they visited 183 churches, in 4,183 days, held 51 meetings, delivered 2,291 sermons, baptized 1,044 people, had 577 other additions, organized six churches, aided 46. The total money raised for missionary purposes was $12,008.81. This truly is a great year's work, but after all there is so much more that ought to be done. "Enlargement" ought to be the word until every church in the state is a partner in this holy fellowship in saving Illinois.

The report of Marion Stevenson, Sunday-school evangelist, was full of interest and help. Schools by the score ought to invite him to spend from one to five days with them in the interest of the Sunday-school. Write him at Bloomington about it. He gave three fine courses of lectures to the students in Eureka college last session and is engaged to deliver others during the present session.

The society is fortunate in having such an office secretary as W. D. Deweese. His report shows care and economy. It was a matter of universal regret to lose P. Whitmer, of Bloomington, from the board, and especially from the committee on the permanent fund which now amounts to $24,634.42. He really has handled this fund from the beginning. His place was filled by J. P. Darst, of Peoria. A resolution of gratitude for Brother Whitmer's valuable services was gladly passed.

J. P. Darst presented the treasurer's report, also the report on the permanent fund, as above. Also the student's aid fund report, showing that $635 were used by students last year, with a balance to begin with this year, $287.82. The entire fund contains about $6,000 and is loaned to worthy needy young men preparing for the ministry.

The addresses of the convention were of a very superior character. The speakers seemed to feel that to them was committed a duty and trust to put their best thought and plenty of time to solve the hard problems involved in their themes. The addresses had the clear tone of faith in God, in Christ, in the Scriptures and that it is our particular business to preach Christ, preach the Word, in order to save men.

R. F. Thrapp, of Jacksonville, discussed the "Relation of Church and Pastor." There was a straightforward directness

Oklahoma's Fifteenth and History Making Convention

The last convention, which met at El Reno, was marked as the largest in attendance and interest e er held in this great territory. By the close of the first session the railroad secretary, Isom Roberts, could turn back certificates, although the regulations forbid any minister using any certificate. This shows the large attendance of business men and women. It indicates the attendance of C. W. B. M, Bible school, Christian Endeavor and other workers.

Another great feature was the music of the convention, under the direction of Prof. C. M. Bliss, of El Reno. People from the east, and secretaries from Indianapolis, Cincinnati, St. Louis, and Kansas City, as well as religious newspaper n n, pronounced it as high grade as they had ever heard in any convention. One secretary said it was the best he had heard since he left Boston.

Still another feature is to be commended, was the fact that every session began promptly on time, and outside the noted brethren from without the territory, each speaker was true to his time allotted on the program.

It was a historic convention in the work of helping to unite the two missionary organizations of Indian Territory and Oklahoma into one organization to begin its new life with next year; and in launching a college enterprise to be worked out at once.

The first session began at 2:30 p. m., on Monday, September 3. "Our Centennial" was discussed by J. M. Morris, of Perkins, as leader, W. P. Maupin, of Hennessey, C. M. Barnes, of Lawton, K. C. Ventrees, of Guthrie, and a number of other brethren from all parts of the territory. The social feature of this first session was good and beneficial to all, since each convention in this new southwest brings so many new faces to get acquainted with.

W. F. Turner, of Joplin, Mo., spoke for foreign missions. He had a trying position to fill when speaking as the representative of A. McLean on the subject of world-wide evangelism. We can express nothing better than to say, he gave entire satisfaction. His plea was spiritual and stimulating intellectually. His heart is big, with a sympathy for lost humanity.

J. H. Mohorter also made his initial appearance as the new secretary of benevolence. His plea for this work of applied Christianity was ably presented, and established confidence in the minds of all Oklahoma in the ability of Brother Mohorter to successfully carry on the work so well begun by his successful predecessor, G. L. Snively. A. J. Bush, of Dallas, Texas, was also present as a representative of this vitally essential work of the church.

Hon. Dick T. Morgan delivered his fourteenth annual address as president on Tuesday morning. He predicted that the new state of Oklahoma would have 100,000 Disciples by 1916, or in the next ten years. And the convention accepted this as a commonplace matter, sure of fulfillment, in the course of coming events. The committees were duly appointed after this address. Scott Anderson, of Enid, became chairman of the nominating committee; W. B. Young, of resolutions, and K. C. Ventrees, of ways and means.

The next period attracted close attention since it was to discuss the possibilities of the union of Indian Territory and Oklahoma into one organization in the one state soon to be. For a number of years these have been separated. Each had its history and its ties of work that were dear to each. S. R. Hawkins, corresponding secretary of Indianapolis, spoke in a candid, direct manner on "How to

Unite the Two Territories," Brother Hawkins pointed out some of the difficulties that stood in the way of union. J. B. Boen, of Chickasha, I. T., followed in the discussion. His was an enthusiastic speech in favor of union. At the close of the discussion a committee of five, consisting of O. L. Smith, J. M. Monroe, Isom Roberts, W. F. Ross and Ed. S. McKinney, was appointed to meet a like committee from Indian Territory, to treat diplomatically on the question. The Indian Territory committee consisted of S. R. Hawkins, Randolph Cook, G. H. Farley, C. R. Sadler and another brother who did not attend nor send a proxy for another to act in his place. After meetings had been held and plans discussed it was finally agreed that each territory should continue as now constituted, until next convention time, when each organization should go out of existence, and in a joint convention a new organization should be formed. To provide for the next convention, it was agreed that three members from each territorial board should be appointed by each to prepare and submit a constitution and by-laws, and prepare a program for the joint convention. All this was duly signed, and the protocol of religious treaty passed into history.

W. J. Wright addressed the convention on the "Home Mission Problem." It was a great address which reached the hearts of the delegates. We learned to honor his judgment and prize his ability. We believe him to be a man of great sympathy, and a general of no mean ability.

Prof. E. V. Zollars spoke on "Ministerial Training." It became a plea for more ministers, and the means to supply them, which must be found in more schools of our own people. He declared we had passed through the periods of agitation and organization. We are now compelled, by reason of our success, to enter upon an era of education.

The C. W. B. M. session on Tuesday afternoon was another epoch-making session. Mrs. W. W. Storms, of Oklahoma City, presided with dignity and carried on the work with method and dispatch. The reports of Mrs. M. A. Lucy, corresponding secretary, and C. S. Kennedy, superintendent young people's work, showed a year of steady advancement.

Mrs. Alice Starry, the treasurer, showed a growing condition in the C. W. B. M. finance. Strong papers on various lines of the work were presented by Mrs. W. B. Young, of Grantop; Mrs. Ella Bass, of Lawton, Mrs. A. P. Aten, of Oklahoma City, and Mrs. W. H. Downs, of Luther. Any of these papers would have been well received in any convention. They were well prepared, and each handled her subject in a strong and invigorating manner. Mrs. Bass proved to be a poetess, whose bright wit attracted close attention. The presence in the convention and the evening address of Mrs. Atwater added much to the spirit and enthusiasm of the C. W. B. M. session.

The Tuesday evening audience was large, and the evening exceedingly warm for this country, yet G. W. Muckley came on with his perpetual story of church extension, with some new features thrown in, and held the large audience with a rapt attention. He called forth laughter and applause. He made friends for his worthy cause. Oklahoma owes much to church extension. She is in duty bound to respond to her appeals.

This was also the evening of excursion announcements to Buffalo and other special interests that desired to present their interests in personal interviews.

Wednesday morning was devoted to Oklahoma missions. J. M. Monroe submitted a report that was large with facts and figures. We now have 408 congrega-

tions in Oklahoma alone, with 26,000 brethren. Over 200 of these are housed in their own buildings; 41 new buildings have been built this year. Six field workers have been kept busy during the past year. Five of these were sustained by the living link plan. These were sustained as follows: J. W. Cameron, in Northeast Oklahoma and C. M. Barnes in Southeast Oklahoma by the C. W. B. M.; Geo. T. Thomas and C. F. Trimble by the El Reno and Guthrie churches, and Brother Smedley by Brother and Sister J. M. Monroe. During the year a brother from Bellaire, Ohio, supported an evangelist and during the latter period Brother and Sister Beach were supported by this fund. Also the Christian Publishing Company supported a man in Northwest Oklahoma a part of the year. All this will be continued, and the Oklahoma city church and Brother and Sister W. A. Wright came up to add themselves to the living link list for Oklahoma missions. Each of the workers present at the convention spoke during this session. These were Cameron, Beach, Trimble Barnes and W. B. Young for Woods county. The secretary's report will be printed and distributed.

The afternoon session was devoted to the Bible school interest. Brother H. S. Gilliam, our new superintendent, and wife, were the leading spirits in this session, which was practical and stimulating. Especial help was given this session by H. F. Davis, of Missouri; William Rogers, general secretary for Oklahoma, and Brother Dowes, of Muskogee, I. T.; R. E. McKorkle, of Norman; D. F. Solliday, of Oklahoma City, and Oscar Ingold, of Chandler, took part in this session with prepared addresses. Steps were taken leading to a state Bible school organization. Prof. C. M. Bliss, of El Reno, was elected president, and H. S. Gilliam, secretary.

The evening session attracted intense interest on account of the report of the standing committee on education. Brother Gilliam delivered the Bible school address. He clearly showed this work to be the church carrying out its teaching function. He spoke with earnestness. Brother Gilliam grew in the estimation of the brotherhood during the entire convention. The educational committee now reported through W. A. Humphrey, of Guthrie, a set of three resolutions which favored the launching of an educational enterprise at this time, and recommending that six trustees be elected to act with a like number already appointed from Indian Territory. This was carried and Dick T. Morgan, W. A. Humphrey, J. M. Monroe, O. L. Smith, Ed Johnson and C. M. Jackman were then duly elected as the educational board for Oklahoma. Prof. E. V. Zollars again addressed the convention on "Christianity and Education." The nominating committee also reported at the evening session, and Dick T. Morgan was again elected president; W. A. Humphrey, vice-president; G. W. McQuiddy, secretary;

(Continued on Page 1244.)

NEWS FROM MANY FIELDS

Bible School Matters in Missouri.

The Union State Sunday-school Convention at Sedalia, Sept. 28-30, was thought to be one of the best held in recent years. A number of leading instructors and platform speakers, from this and other states, were present and addressed the people. Strong ground was taken on the subject of the Bible in the public schools, on the temperance question and other reforms. State Secretary Lacey made a splendid report and the convention laid out liberal plans for the current year. The writer delivered two addresses.—— The Lewis County Convention was held at Williamstown, and the long distance from any railroad prevented as large an attendance as would otherwise have been present, but there were many people and most, if not all, of the churches were represented. It had been 17 years since the writer had spoken at Williamstown and yet found one brother who remembered the occasion and the text of the sermon. It was a great pleasure to meet with the friends of the Lord in dear old Lewis, in which county we fought such a strenuous battle for Christian education and for local option in the days long ago. We had the pleasure of shaking hands with a number of friends on the streets and at the station in Canton as we were passing through. Professors in Christian University and other friends of the institution assured us of the bright prospects of the college for this year.——The convention of Sullivan and Putnam counties, held at Green City, was largely attended and a splendid success in every way. The state superintendent arrived in time to make an address on state missions, representing T. A. Abbott, who was prevented from being present by other engagements, and the following day he delivered an address on the state Bible school work before a large and sympathetic audience. The plan of uniting these two counties in one organization for co-operative purposes is proving a good one. It might be a good plan for other counties which lie favorably in point of railroads, etc., to unite in co-operative work, if it is impracticable for either county to work alone. Try it.——Sunday morning, Sept. 16, found the writer at the Sunday-school of the Union Avenue church of St. Louis. It was rally day with J. J. Searcy and his large school, and they were using it for all it was worth for the reorganization of the work for the coming fall and winter. There were 531 present at Sunday-school. The report showed only ten per cent of adult church members present at the school. Union Avenue is not behind other churches in this regard. The fact is mentioned, not as a criticism, but to show that here is yet a large work for us to do to enlist all those in the church who ought to be in the Bible studying service. Minister J. M. Philputt preached an interesting and instructive sermon on the study of the Bible. The purpose of this visit to St. Louis was to be present to make an address at a meeting of the Officers' and Teachers' Union of Greater St. Louis, at the Hamilton Avenue Church, an account of which has appeared in THE CHRISTIAN-EVANGELIST. The reports were tabulated before the audience on a large sheet and this tabulation will be published for wide circulation.——Sunday afternoon, September 16, there was held in the First Christian Church a meeting of the Officers' and Teachers' Union of Greater Kansas City, which was addressed by Howard C. Rash, of Salina, Kan. These city unions, such as the ones alluded to above, in St. Louis, and the one that met the same afternoon in Kansas City, are proving splendid centers around which organization for better things will soon be gathered. The state superintendent goes to St. Joseph after the National Convention to visit all of the schools and churches of that city, and hopes to organize an Officers' and Teachers' Union there. Good reports come to the office from the union formed in Springfield in June and it is hoped the workers there will keep it alive and going. There has been altogether too little co-operation among our churches in our cities. These organizations of our Bible school

workers will prove of great help to our groups of city churches in all lines of effort.——The services of Mrs. Buxton, our state primary superintendent, are being called for from different directions and the prospects are that she will be kept as busy as the time for which we can compensate her will allow.——Let every Missouri Bible school prepare to send in the second quarterly installment of all pledges and apportionments promptly, as the second quarter falls due October 1. Do not neglect this.——Watch out for Children's Day for home missions to be observed by our Bible schools everywhere on November 25. Send to W. J. Wright, corresponding secretary, Y. M. C. A. Building, Cincinnati, O., for a delightful exercise, collection blanks, and other necessary literature for the proper recognition of the day.

For all matters concerning Missouri Bible school work, address,   J. H. HARDIN,
311 Century Bldg., Kansas City, Mo.

✸ ✸

Southern California.

The August convention left as its heritage an unusual amount of work to undertake. Though the secretary had been granted a short vacation, the board was obliged to call it off, and send him immediately into the field. The record of his labors appears in part in these notes: A visit to the Ventura-Oxnard field indicates, plainly how well the new pastor, Dan Trundle, formerly of Bisbee, Ariz., is getting things into hand. He lives at Ventura and serves both that church and the one at Oxnard, ten miles distant. This is one of our hardest fields. We have arranged for a more permanent ministry there. Our brethren are greatly encouraged in both places. The arrangement with Brother Trundle is such that the Church Extension debt at Oxnard will be whittled down by regular monthly payments. We have no more loyal people anywhere than in this difficult field.——Oscar Sweeney, of Nebraska, has been called to take charge of the work in Rialto and Colton. This is another joint pastorate. The work at Rialto is especially bright with promise. They are expecting to build this fall. The Colton situation is somewhat discouraging. For divers reasons "the bottom seems to have dropped out" of things there. Many have moved away. The heat of the summer and the absence of a pastor did the rest. Negotiations had been nearly affected whereby our property was to pass to other hands. The secretary succeeded in saving the situation only by the prompt payment of some money to stay the proceedings. No greater opportunity presents itself to our people on the coast than this which will confront Oscar Sweeney. We expect him October 1.——The Downey church, after a pastoral interim of nearly four months, has welcomed to its work R. M. Bailey, of Colorado. His first Sunday was September 9.——In a new community, on the Los Angeles Pacific railroad some seven miles from the center of the city, known as Sunny Side Park addition, live about sixty families. This place is growing. There are no religious services within a mile. They offer a lot and the work for a building to any religious body that will inaugurate a work. This is only one of a number of open doors.——Redondo presents a very difficult field for religious work. The churches already there feel that the situation is theirs. The sentiment prevails that the town is already overchurched, yet an urgent appeal comes from a portion of its people to us to enter and preach the Gospel. A meeting, doubtless, will be held soon. The Baptists and Disciples ought to join forces here, as everywhere else.——W. J. Adams, of Waitsburg, Wash., has accepted an urgent call to serve the churches at Arlington and Corona under a joint pastorate. He will live at Corona. We congratulate the field and the man. Our work is opening auspiciously for our small churches, chiefly because of this willingness to co-operate. They are thus enabled to secure stronger men for their work.——A recent Sunday with the First Church, Los

Angeles, indicates great activity, and did faith of the noble First, in its field. Their newly equipped Sunday-school put them in line with the very best for city for Christian work. Under the leadership of Leon Shaw theirs will doubtless be a day-school. The church that spends its forces in behalf of its Bible school work is the church of most promise for the future. Hollingsworth has resigned at Holtville. A congregation in the famous imperial. They need a good minister. They are building a house of worship.——J. F. Tout, ily, after a summer spent at Long Beach for the relief from the heat, has returned to work at Imperial.——R. H. Bateman, of splendid service at Whittier, has resigned church has called W. H. Martin of Santa Barbara, as his successor. It is understood he will accept.——Frank G. Tyrrell, who is one of the leading attorneys in Los Angeles, has been supplying the pulpit at San Bernardino this summer. This church welcomes this work of pastor E. E. Love, of Arkansas City, who has been making a great fight to hold the work during these summer months. Though he respects a difficult work made the most of the circumstances in the church, yet Brother Love comes to a field of great promise. The people in his church, together with the hopeful opportunities presented by the field, able him to do the greatest work of his life. San Bernardino.——J. R. Jolly has removed to Ontario, where he begins a pastorate of great promise.——Leander Lane terminates his pastor at Santa Anna October 1. His work has been very sick this summer but removed to Canada, a few miles northeast of Los Angeles, is bringing back her accustomed health. Lane's wide experience and splendid ability as a preacher will doubtless command a place with him among some of our good churches.—— Lewis, Secretary.

✸ ✸

The St. Louis Letter.

The St. Louis ministers have all returned to their vacations, and are taking hold of work with renewed interest.——We regret that Moore has resigned at the Hammett Place church. Brother Moore is one of our most faithful ministers, and will be missed from the work of the city. We have not been informed of his future plans.——All are very busy getting ready for the great simultaneous campaign to be inaugurated in this city November 4. Our workers so far as learned are: Brother Yeuell at First, Brother Chilton at the Union church, Brother Turner at the Hamilton Avenue church, Hoffman at Granite City, and Harlow at Compton Heights. The Fourth will secure other forces.——John L. Brandt has just passed through a very severe and dangerous operation for appendicitis. We rejoice that he is now out of danger, and hope for his speedy recovery.——Our Bible schools all held their Lord's day. The schools make excellent records. So far as heard from, Compton led the list in attendance, having 301 with $28.11 collection. Carondelet and wood led in the collections, Carondelet over $45 and Maplewood over $50.——The Men's Association of the Compton church had a delightful opening of work on Tuesday evening, September 1, in the form of a luncheon at the church for a luncheon was served by the Woman's church. The toast theme was "Our Revival." Addresses were made on several phases of the subject, and all seemed to be present that evening very much. We feel sure the were present will feel a greater interest in the revival than was felt before.——The churches never had a more hopeful outlook a great work than at present. Bro. G. L. of Carondelet, has been chosen city pastor. We all know Brother Ireland to be a good and his extended acquaintance with the city will enable him to do the right work from the very first.——F. N. Calvin.

DO YOU WANT A CHURCH

North Carolina.

Atlantic Christian College, Wilson, N. C., of which J. J. Harper is president, opened on September 4. President Harper wishes they aim at first-class work, and the rates are low.——Walker and McKinney, evangelists, organized another congregation at Windsor with 17 members. The church established this year by our State Evangelist Walker at Fremont has secured a lot and has plans for a house of worship. McKinney and Walker also closed a meeting at Belhaven August 12 with 26 additions. About 18 of these, who were living in the community without a church home, came by statement. J. R. Tingle is the minister there. Their next meeting was at Dunn. There were 11 accessions at last report. We are sorry Brother McKinney had to leave for other work. Brother Walker needs a singer. The state convention will be at Dunn the last week in October.——A. B. Cunningham, of Washington, N. C., preached a week at Richlands and five days at Union Chapel, where he reports three baptisms. He is holding a meeting with his own church at Washington. The Colored Christian Church of Washington reports about 150 members. J. L. Gregory, of Greenville, is the minister, and visits them twice a month, and makes but few trips without baptizing some one.——The work of the Colored Christian Church in Winston seems to be improving. R. L. Peters still ministers for them, and last Lord's day I preached for them in the afternoon. They seemed to appreciate the visit and discourse. It is said there are about 10,000 colored Disciples in North Carolina.——Prof. J. C. Coggins preached four sermons at Dover, N. C., and the result was 12 baptisms.——W. F. Shinall, the blind evangelist from Virginia, recently preached at Spray in a meeting with Dr. B. T. Bitting. There were about 28 added.——J. B. Jones, state secretary, has been busy. He held a week's meeting at Salem in August. He has been visiting Wilmington looking up the prospects of starting a church there. The state board and the Pamlico Union will co-operate in establishing a church there. Our Piedmont Union will meet at Winston-Salem September 28 and 29. We hope the State Board will cast its eyes in this direction, and plan some co-operation, as this is one of the needy sections of the state. The state secretary also visited Rocky Mount, assisting the congregation in selecting the plans for their new house. His church at Wilson will have a new pipe organ by November 1, and other improvements will be made.——Others of our preaching brethren have been holding short meetings, and our readers will see that North Carolina is pushing forward in many points old and new. The reports at too many places are: "If the preacher only could have staid longer much could have been done." We ought to plan for longer meetings, and not such hurried ones. We will have our mortgage burning the last of October, when we can have H. C. Bowen, a former pastor, with us. J. A. HOPKINS, Winston-Salem, N. C.

※

Cairo's Campaign for Christ.

O. D. Maple and J. Ross Miller, evangelists, will lay siege to sinful Cairo, Ill., October 1. Christians of all churches are invited to join in the soul-saving work. ConVerts will be given the privilege of going to any church. Meetings will be held in a tent on the corner of Seventeenth and Washington. The evangelist will speak the first evening on "A United Army: Means Victory." These evangelists are continually holding meetings, have engagements for all of this year and a part of next. They are now closing a meeting at Gas City, Ind., and will from here go to Princeton, Ind., where they enter the simultaneous meeting, which means that about 500 churches will hold revivals at the same time.

Of the Gas City (Ind.) meeting, "The Journal" says, among other things:

"The meetings at the Christian church under the leadership of O. D. Maple and J. Ross Miller are creating unusual interest. Gospel truths are being presented in a clear and forcible manner, and people seem anxious to hear the plan of salvation as taught in the Scriptures. Sunday services were unusually well attended. The special feature of the day was the children's hour, when Mr. Maple gave an object lesson illustrating the effects of sin upon a life and the restoration of that life through the gospel of Christ. Practical themes are on the program and the aim will be to make these services as helpful as possible. These occasions with their themes are fraught with too much interest to be missed by any one."

The Christian church in Cairo, that leads in the united effort, is an old organization and has an old building. No church in a city of 18,000 is better located than this one, but the building is too old in which to do much for Christ. Plans for a modern, up-to-date building have been selected and some money has been subscribed toward its erection.

Cairo has 18,000 population, and its natural advantages make it destined to be one of the greatest manufacturing centers in the southwest. The great Singer works and many other large manufacturing plants are here, four elevators and two large flour mills, large export market for lumber, grain and flour, a city whose business is never interrupted by floods. There are many saloons. These make all the more needful a city campaign for Christ in Cairo, Ill.

※

DEDICATIONS.

Charlotte Furnace, Ky.

The new church here was dedicated Sept. 9. An excellent meeting followed conducted by T. M. Myers.   RUBY HUFFMAN.

※

Philippine Islands.

Our chapel dedicated and three baptisms at Magsingal last Wednesday.—Hermon P. Williams, Vigan.

※

Armington, Ill.

A very successful dedication service marked the close of our two years service with the Armington congregation. We had planned long and well for this service, and thanks to the brethren who gave us their hearty co-operation, everything was in splendid shape. Additions at our regular services were frequent; a Bible school contest with a much stronger sister congregation, resulting in a great victory for Armington in all interests; the contested points, brought our school to its highest attendance and efficiency, with an enrollment of over 400 and a home department of 66. The last Lord's day in the old building was one that will be long remembered; the Bible school was the largest in the history of the congregation. The morning preaching hour was given over to a "Farewell Service" for the retiring minister and wife at the close of which three were received into the church. The "Farewell Service" for the old building in the evening was a great success.

Dedication day found us with a debt of $6,500 staring us in the face. The morning was as disagreeable as possible, but a good audience greeted Brother Rains and answered his appeal by pledges amounting to $5,800; the remainder was raised at the afternoon service. In the evening service a handsome purse was presented to the retiring minister and wife.

After eighty years of tears, toil, sacrifice and trust this congregation finds itself one of the strongest of our great brotherhood, and fully equipped for doing the work of the Lord. There is no doubt that she will make the most of her opportunities to sound forth the name of Jesus to the ends of the earth. Bro. John C. Lappin, a young man of great spirituality, takes up the work at once, and will carry it on to a

greater success than it has yet attained. After a month of much needed rest I will take up the work at LeRoy.   L. E. CRASE.

※

Pasadena, Cal.

Lord's day, Sept. 16, was observed as church building day. C. C. Chapman, of Fullerton, was with us as master of ceremonies. After a splendid address on "The Church," he called for pledges. The amount raised was $13,000. We now have $25,000 with which to begin work on our $50,000 house.   FRANK M. DOWLING.

※

Stockholders' Meeting.

Notice is hereby given that the annual meeting of the stockholders of the Christian Publishing Company will be held at the company's office, 2712 Pine street, St. Louis, Mo., on Tuesday, October 2, 1906, at 10 o'clock a. m., for the election of directors and for the transaction of such other business as may legally come before said meeting.   J. H. GARRISON, Pres.
                              GEO. L. SNIVELY, Sec'y.

St. Louis, Aug. 27, 1906.

Evangelistic

We invite ministers and others to send reports of meetings, additions and other news of the churches. It is especially requested that additions be reported as "by confession and baptism," or "by letter."

Special to THE CHRISTIAN-EVANGELIST.

Kansas City, Mo., Sept. 23.—Twenty-four to-day, one hundred and sixty-eight to date; continuing.—Altheide and Bowen.

Special to THE CHRISTIAN-EVANGELIST.

Roodhouse, Ill., Sept. 23.—Burned mortgage here to-day; two additions; big rally this week.—W. W. Wharton, Evangelist.

Special to THE CHRISTIAN-EVANGELIST.

Kirksville, Mo., Sept. 23.—Meeting fourteen days old; seventy-one additions, sixteen to-day; will continue.—R. Bruce Brown, Evangelist.

Special to THE CHRISTIAN-EVANGELIST.

Jacksonville, Ill., Sept. 21.—Forty-three additions in our meeting here with Evangelist J. H. O. Smith.—R. F. Thrapp, pastor; Guy B. Williamson, assistant.

Alabama.

New Decatur, Sept. 3.—We have had 5 additions recently, making 16 in four months. We are planning for a meeting this fall. I would like to put THE CHRISTIAN-EVANGELIST in 50 homes. Anti-ism is very strong here.—V. L. Parker.

District of Columbia.

Washington, Sept. 19.—Present at ministers' meeting: President Walter F. Smith, F. D. Power, E. B. Bagby, W. F Laprade, J. E. Stuart, Daniel E. Motley, and the writer. Reports: Vermont Avenue (F. D. Power), 2 by letter and 3 by confession and baptism; Ninth Street (E. B. Bagby), 1 by letter and 1 by confession and baptism; Fifteenth Street (J. E. Stuart), 1 by baptism; Whitney Avenue (W. F. Smith), 3 by confession and baptism. Total 11—3 by letter and 8 by confession and baptism.—Claude C. Jones, secretary.

Indiana.

Sullivan, Sept. 17.—We are now in a most difficult field; 2 confessions and 1 reclaimed.— E. W. Brickert.

Brook, Sept. 17.—Two added in our meeting. Sister Lola Calvert, of Indianapolis, is assisting me as singing evangelist. We are having good audiences.—A. Walter Gehres, pastor.

Muncie, Sept. 17.—The Central Church is enjoying a meeting under the direction of the Martin family. The outlook is very promising. Last Lord's day witnessed the largest audience that was ever in the church.—Richard Martin.

Indian Territory.

Tulsa, Sept. 16.—One addition.—Randolph Cook.

Ada, Sept. 17.—Eighteen additions in 10 days. The prospect is very good. We have found THE CHRISTIAN-EVANGELIST a very great help.—Charles Frederick Trimble.

Stillwell, Sept. 12.—Last Lord's day, the first in the new pastorate of H. S. Kline at this place, we had 3 confessions and 2 baptisms. Brother Kline also baptized 2 at Westville, 15 miles north of here. We begin a protracted effort at once, with A. M. Harral and wife, of Sapulpa.—J. C. Holleman.

Illinois.

Litchfield, Sept. 18.—One confession Sunday morning.—M. S. Johnson.

Springfield, Sept. 21.—West Side Church has had seven baptisms at regular services since last report.—F. M. Rogers.

Grayville, Sept. 19.—Meeting here four days old, with 1 addition. Our meeting at Calhoun, Mo., closed with 14 additions—10 baptisms. "Antioch" meeting in Hickory county, Mo., 9 additions, all by primary obedience. Our 10 days' meeting at Mountain View closed with 32 additions—10 baptisms, 21 by statement—T. J. Head.

Iowa.

Des Moines, Sept. 22.—Just closed a meeting at Sheridan, Mo., with 23 additions—Homer L. Lewis.

Sioux Rapids, Sept. 20.—Julius Stone reports meeting closed Sunday night with 27 addition. Baptized 10 last night and gave reception to new members. Goes to Ladysmith to state convention this week.—E. F. Christian.

Kentucky.

Pleasant Valley, Sept. 20.—Just closed a two weeks' meeting here resulting in 41 additions.— J. T. Bays.

Erlanger, Sept. 13.—The best meeting in which it has ever been my privilege to engage closed Sunday evening, September 9, at Stringtown (Elizabeth), Grant county. This was my first charge, when a student in the College of the Bible. Consequently it was a delight to return and hold a meeting after three years of absence. We labored together for two weeks, with 68 additions, 30 baptisms, 11 from other religious bodies, two reclaimed and the remainder by statement. There is now preaching twice a month instead of once, or weekly observance of the Lord's Supper in lieu of monthly, and the congregation is interested in the education of one of its young men for the ministry who has already spent two years in the School of the Evangelists. For a two weeks' meeting in a country congregation, with more than 50 years' history and with preaching but once a month, this was considered a most remarkable ingathering. The interest was intense. There were 13 additions the last night. Of the 30 baptisms, 30 were men aged 20 women. Three grandfathers, one grandmother, and 13 heads of families. The character of the converts is such as will add strength and dignity to the congregation. John Thomas Brown, of Lexington, is the faithful, tireless, consecrated minister. I see before him and this congregation a great future.—L. B. Harkins.

Kansas.

Windsor.—Just closed a meeting at Cloverdale with 4 confessions.—W. M. Mundell.

Salina, Sept. 18.—Fourteen by baptism and 21 by letter at our regular services since last report. —David H. Shields.

Argentine, Sept. 15.—Closed a short missionary meeting at Powhattan September 9, with 6 additions by baptism. The church is very much encouraged. We are ready to make dates elsewhere for fall and winter.—James E. Stebbins and wife, Argentine, Kan.

Missouri.

Warrensburg, Sept. 17.—One addition by statement last night. One confession at Dover.—King Stark.

Kansas City, Sept. 17.—Three more added at West Line, 1 by confession, 1 by letter.—Clyde Lee Fife.

Lewistown, Sept. 17.—C. F. Rose, of Canton, Mo., has closed a three weeks' meeting here with 48 additions.—F. M. Day.

St. Louis, Sept. 18.—Three additions at Festus last Lord's day—one by letter and 2 by statement.—Daniel George Cole.

Lamonte, Sept. 14.—Two added at Walnut Branch Chapel last Sunday. We will soon organize there.—I. H. Fuller.

Kirksville, Sept. 17.—Meeting one week old, with 30 additions; 26 yesterday.—R. Bruce Brown, evangelist; D. A. Wickiser, pastor.

Windsor, Sept. 17.—Three conversions at Ionia. Concluded a meeting begun by Brother Allen, resulting in 5 additions.—W. A. Fite.

Seneca, Sept. 17.—Five added yesterday at regular services, making a total of 90 additions in our work the past year.—E. J. Church.

Mendon, Sept. 16.—Closed a meeting at Mike, Mo., with 18 additions—9 by statement and 9 by baptism. Brother Cornelius, of Canton, Mo., will preach one-fourth time for them.—D. Millar.

St. Louis, Sept. 24.—The Old Orchard Church has just concluded a meeting with State Evangelist C. O. McFarland and wife. There were 22 additions—9 by baptism.—R. L. Wilson.

Hale, Sept. 20.—W. I. Harris, who has his headquarters at Bethany, Neb., is in a great meeting here, where C. C. Taylor ministers; a addition the first day; large audiences and deep interest.

Plattsburg, Sept. 20.—Closed a meeting at Bethany, Clinton county, last night with 5 baptisms and 1 reclaimed. We were much pleased and greatly edified by the preaching of E. B. Bousland.—D. A. Ammons.

Tipton, Sept. 17.—Our meeting here closed last night on account of the serious illness of the pastor, Brother Couch. We expect to begin a meeting at Keytesville, Mo., to-night.—H. A. Northcutt.

Norborne, Sept. 20.—I close to-night a 19 days' meeting at Mt. Carmel with 17 additions, 13 of which are baptisms. Geo. A. Butler and wife, of Mound City, were with us 12 days and did us great good.—C. C. Taylor.

Sheldon, Sept. 16.—We have just closed a meeting at Rinehart, Mo., with 22 additions—3 by statement, 2 reclaimed and 13 by confession; 17 of the 24 were baptized. R. A. Blalock did the preaching.—H. E. Carpenter.

Sorrell, Sept. 17.—Twenty-six additions to date, with 17 confessions and 3 from other religious bodies. Raised $60. at our services yesterday to apply on the building. We hope to be able to dedicate soon. This has been rather a remarkable meeting, from the fact that we had but four women and a girl when we came here who claimed to be Christians only, and without a church organization or a single Christian man, to

Sunday-School

October 7, 1906.

THE TWO GREAT COMMAND-MENTS.—Mark 12:28-34, 38-44.

Memory verses, 30, 31.

Golden Text.—Thou shalt love the Lord thy God with all thy heart.—Mark 12:30.

It was on Tuesday of Passion week, in the course of the same conversation with the Pharisees and Sadducees which we were studying three weeks ago, that the question was put to Jesus about the greatest commandment. The scribes, who were the specialists in Judaic law and were often pettifogging ecclesiastical lawyers, were in the habit of believing that all laws were of equal importance. Any given injunction derived its importance and value from the fact that it was in the code, that it had been commanded. Theirs was the appeal to outward authority alone. To such a mind there can be no greatest commandment for none was less than any other.

Although the question was perhaps meant for a trap, to lead Jesus into some expression about the law which could be used against him, he answered it boldly and straightforwardly. The first commandment is to love God completely. The second is to love man serviceably. He does not say that either of these is greater than the other, but love to God comes logically first, since belief in God and love to him and in understanding of his character and of his relation to men afford a basis for love to men as children of God.

"Love thy neighbor as thyself." Perhaps this means manner as well as quality of love. There are times when a man must love his neighbor much more than himself. All heroic deeds of self-sacrifice mean that, when it came to a choice, the doer of the deed chose to serve others rather than self, and service is the measure of love.

We are told then to love our neighbor not only as much as we love ourselves but in the same way. How is that? Sentimentally? No, in sane minds, self-love is not a gush of affectionate feeling for one's self. It is the settled habit of looking after our own interests, of serving ourselves. In such a way we are to love our neighbors—by being as careful of their welfare as we are of our own.

The scribe who asked this question was stirred by the answer into a realization of the truth that principle is greater than law and that love is more important than any amount of fidelity to ritual requirements.

But, though this scribe was "not far from the kingdom of God," most of the scribes were very far from it. The machinery of religion was, with them, an impediment to religion. They made of the whole formal system of religion a cloak for their sins, a means of self-deception and an occasion for hypocrisy. Jesus was never severe except against formalists and hypocrites. He was always tender toward the honest sinner, even to the thief who was openly a thief. But he had no mercy on meanness in the guise of virtue. So he drove from the temple those who under pretense of furnishing animals for sacrifice for the accommodation of worshippers, were really seeking only their own profit and that by unfair laws, and he constantly and sometimes fiercely condemns the Pharisees who held themselves up as the patterns of religion and virtue without in reality having either.

Midweek Prayer-Meeting

October 3, 1906.

A COLD CHURCH.—Rev. 2:1-7.

"O for a closer walk with God!
A calm and heavenly frame!
A light to shine upon the road
That leads me to the Lamb!

"Where is the blessedness I knew
When first I saw the Lord?
Where is the soul-refreshing view
Of Jesus and his word?

"Return, O holy Dove, return,
Sweet messenger of rest!
I hate the sins that made thee mourn,
And drove thee from my breast."

Be alarmed by the first abatement of your devotion to the King. That unrepented and unatoned may be the first slight rifting of the lute that will make all the after music of your life discordant with the songs of redeeming love the angels sing. Pray more fervently, give more generously, live more hollly.

A few with hearts all aflame with zeal for benevolences, missions and evangelism can raise the spiritual temperature of any church. Readers, try it. Even a mighty iceberg is at the mercy of a small torch if the latter is kept constantly burning. The melting down of a cold, passionless church may be the work to which you have been specially ordained of God.

A cold church is as much a misnomer as hot ice cream would be. A congregation is a mere assembly; it can not be a church if the element of fervor is lacking. There God and man must be loved and served with a heartiness expelling all coldness that represses life and growth and generating an atmosphere in which all the graces of life and spirit will flourish and flower.

Factionalism is one of the best of Satan's devices for changing a church into a cold storage. He succeeds in this by persuading each to esteem himself better than others, and to make the acknowledgment of his own importance and the vindication of his own contentions of far more consequence than the upbuilding of the church, the honoring of God or the saving of souls. From this deadly sin O Lord deliver us.

Better far profuse handshakings and lusty amens and effusive sociability in the church than chill greetings and repression of all emotions of good will toward God and man. "Dignity of worship" and "church decorum" are too often used as masks to conceal loveless hearts and natures that have become the graves of any religious sentiments that may ever have thrilled them. Our church life should so glow with warmth, sociability and cheer as to supply a congenial atmosphere for the development of all the social graces and every fraternal and filial virtue of our higher natures.

When a patriot risks his life to save an army from ambuscade or in defense of his country he expects burning testimonials of gratitude and love from his countrymen. The world would regard them as ingrates if they did not bestow them. They themselves would sink in the scale of manhood if they were withheld and incentive to altruistic devotion would largely cease. Even so with God, whose impulses are not totally unlike our own. In the person of his Son he died to redeem us from death. That

any church with unimpassioned complacency can contemplate him who gave his life for it is inconsistent with a nature whose ardor and nobility have not been marred by the evil one. That coldness is a herald of death that can only be overcome by warmth of affection, devotion to good works and an ardor of worship akin to that arising from around the great white throne.

Christian Endeavor

By GEO. L. SNIVELY

October 7, 1906.

CHRIST'S COMMANDMENTS.—Jno.
15:1-17.

DAILY READINGS.

M. Obedience to Christ. John 15:1-17.
T. Hearing and Doing. Luke 6:46-49.
W. Knowing and Doing. Rom. 2:7-13.
T. Watching and Obeying. Luke 12:35-40.
F. Obedient and Fruitful. Matt. 13:18-23.
S. Following and Serving. John 12:20-26.
S. Promise to the Oebident. Rev. 22:14.

It is better to obey: "Blessed are they
that do his commandments, that they may
have right to the tree of life, and may enter
in through the gates into the city."

"I have chosen you and ordained you
that ye should go and bring forth fruit."
What have we brought to the Master at all
worthy his cross, the Father's love that
sent him, the institution of the church, the
lives of holy apostles, the blood of the
martyrs, our hopes in Christ, our inheritance among the angels? If empty handed
yet, even now let us go forth and labor
earnestly for the night cometh.

A good intention has a value similar to
that of a blossom. The latter is essential
to the fruit, but has no value unless it progresses into golden grain or horticultural
lusciousness. Likewise good intentions are
prerequisites to noble deeds, but are void of
value simply as good intentions. Indeed,
unless they are translated into deeds they
militate against us, for they are proofs
that we know better than we do.

As authoritatively as Christ commanded
us to go forth teaching and baptizing, he
commands us to love one another as he
loved us all. Can we who have found
heterodoxy in the doctrines and methods of
others concerning baptism prove our own
orthodoxy with respect to the Master's
teachings about love? Let us love one another with that love that permits no malice,
overcomes casuistry, that defends, comforts
and inspires.

Modern assumption should carefully heed
the solemn words of Samuel to Israel's
haughty king: "Hath the Lord as great delight in burnt offerings and sacrifices, as in
obeying the voice of the Lord? Behold to
obey is better than sacrifice, and to hearken
than the fat of rams. For rebellion is as
the sin of witchcraft and stubbornness is as
iniquity and idolatry. Because thou hast
rejected the word of the Lord, he hath
rejected thee from being king.

Unless we through obedience abide fruit-
fully in Christ we become separated from
him. No one visibly comes and hews us
away, we die away. We receive less and
less from him and because of the disappear-
ance of these vitalizing currents atrophyca-
tion begins. The connection between us
and him who is our life is dead and shatters
and is gone. Our only hope of continued
life and fruitfulness is close commerce with
him through prayer for instruction and
obedience in complying to his will.

"Without me ye can do nothing," and yet
Cicero spoke immortal words, and Homer
sang songs the world will not let die, and
Raphael painted pictures whose voiceless
eloquence still inspires to lofty conceptions
of beauty and privilege, and Augustus
changed Rome from a city of bricks to one
of marble. But Jesus' word still is "Without me ye can do nothing." Reconciliation
is found only in our knowing that art and
sculpture, eloquence and conquest are all

as nothing in comparison with those
achievements in goodness and spirituality
possible to us with Christ's aid, but that
can not be accomplished without him.

Illinois State Convention.

(Continued from Page 1238.)

leadership. There were many shorter addresses which merit large mention, if space
permitted.

It was a solemn memorial, when for a
few moments business paused, while we
remembered the victors of the cross who
had entered into their rest. Such names
as J. C. Reynolds, G. W. Tate and D. R.
Howe were included. "Precious in the
sight of the Lord is the death of his saints."

The convention goes to Jacksonville,
where R. F. Thrapp and his congregation
of some 1,200 members will (D. V.) entertain us September 9-12, in the largest
church owned by our people in our state.
Finis Idleman is president; O. W. Lawrence, vice-president; J. W. Kilborn and
W. E. Spicer, secretaries.

The propriety of establishing a sanitarium, owned by the church, and located at
Rockford, was presented to the convention.

The interests of the church are many
and diversified. It is a strenuous school—
such a convention, as has just closed. He
is, indeed, narrow who sees but one department and neglects all else.

It was inspiring to see the class of young
men, strong, scholarly and loyal that are
to carry forward the great work of the
Master. The Lord bless and guide them.
In every department of the convention
C. W. B. M., foreign missions, general and
state church extension there was a strong
and just plea for money. There never was
a day when the rich man had such an opportunity to help make the world rich in
the unfading glory of God. But there was
not a plea for money that did not equally
appeal for men. If a church is built it
is useless if there is no preacher to be in
it. Money for the foreign and home fields
will be effective only as they command the
talent of missionaries. If we plant a
church in New Hampshire it means either
to plant a new man in the ministry or
empty a pulpit now filled. Who is looking
after the supply of the ever increasing
army of young men to take their places
in the ministry? The college, the West
Point of the army of Christ, is looked
to from every direction to supply the men.
Shall it be able to do it?

J. G. WAGGONER.

Eureka, Ill.

Oklahoma's Fifteenth and His-
tory Making Convention.

(Continued from Page 1239.)

C. H. Everest, treasurer, and K. C. Ventrees, O. L. Smith, J. P. Park, E. B. Johnson, Mrs. M. A. Lucy, W. P. Maupin and
George Rainey were elected members of
the territorial board. This gives a widely
distributed membership to the board for
the new year.

The Thursday morning session was
given to the Christian Endeavor work. All
declared this to be one of the most practical and spiritual sessions of the entire convention. Miss Mabel Fry, of Yukon, presided with dignity, and kept the convention
on time throughout a closely crowded program.

Scott Anderson spoke on "Twenty-five
Years of Christian Endeavor"; G. J. Chap-
man on "Christian Endeavorers as Young
Evangelists"; Miss Ora Van Vorhees,
"Christian Endeavor as a Spreader of Mis-
sionary Intelligence"; Oscar Ingold,
"Christian Endeavorers as Systematic and
Proportionate Givers," while "Christian
Endeavor as a Factor in Uniting God's

People's Forum

E. L. Frazier's Dilemma.

To the Editor of THE CHRISTIAN-EVANGELIST:

The CHRISTIAN-EVANGELIST of September 6 has some words from Bro. E. S. Muckley on the above, and after what he has to say about it concludes with the challenge: "The readers of THE CHRISTIAN-EVANGELIST will be glad to know what Brother Frazier will have to say further about this." Brother Frazier has nothing further to say about "Who is a Christian in the Twentieth Century." He is sure that he is understood on that matter. The "further" about it must be about what Brother Muckley has said. I am ready to say it.

Before saying it, however, I will notice what my kind Christian, courteous brother, J. F. Callahan, the man from Euclid, O., has said about my "mulishness," etc. To my words, "Here I stand," he has added: "And see the grand procession go by." I accept it. I have been watching the grand procession. Some of the names of the grand men who form the grand procession would bring to mind the grandeur and glory of the procession and show where it is bound for as it goes by. Head that procession with the illustrious name of Sidney Rigdon of Mormon memory and add as the last name so far added from among our preachers, Voliva of Zion City, follower of that pretender, John Alexander Dowie, and usurper of his throne. One who has watched the grand procession go by can easily fill in with the names of those who have turned back to denominationalism and found place in the Episcopal and other "branches of the church," and in the ranks of the followers of Mrs. Eddy.

I am watching the procession and am young enough in years to join it as do others join that procession, and it is my purpose to "stand" firm in the faith and true to my Master Christ and our great mission—Restoration.

Now about that dilemma. My Brother Muckley is mistaken if he thinks I am in a dilemma. There are no two horns for me. The same process that made one a Christian in the first century makes one a Christian in the twentieth century. "That process was 'Christian character' expressed in faith in Jesus Christ, repentance and being baptized into Christ. The man who thinks that part of this process in the twentieth century makes a Christian is the one who finds himself in a dilemma. Choose your horn, Brother Muckley. "That last, *and this alone*, (italics mine) is what gives us a right to affirm that any one has a Christian character." This centers it. Now what is this alone thing? "The Christian has been Spirit-taught, Spirit-led, Spirit-impressed, Spirit-filled and because he has received the gift of the Holy Spirit is now a Spirit-led man." Put this also to this: "But he is a Christian because God has given him the Holy Spirit." Now add also this: "But the final proof that any baptism is genuine is the giving of the Holy Spirit." All this is very familiar language to those who have been about the mourner's bench.

Now, Brother Muckley, I find you in a dilemma. The final proof of any baptism, you say, to be genuine is the giving of the Holy Spirit. I am led to think that you think God gives the Holy Spirit before baptism, but whether before or after, you think those who are sprinkled receive the Holy Spirit; therefore, this being "the final

JOSEPH REILLY,
ATTORNEY·AT·LAW

I▸ prepared to give all legal matters skillful attention. Correspondence solicited.
Office 320 Room, Granite Bldg., St. Louis.

proof of the genuineness of the baptism," sprinkling is genuine baptism. Take them into the church, then; you can not consistently or logically or reasonably do otherwise.

Must I begin to teach a preacher in our ranks that the Holy Spirit approaches the sinner or alien through "the power of God unto salvation," the gospel? That the Holy Spirit teaches and influences and leads the man to accept and surrender to Jesus Christ and to "put on Christ" and walk in him, and he does this through the power of God unto salvation—the gospel?

Your reference to Eph. 1:13, reveals to me the fact that you have not caught the evident thought that when Paul said, "In whom having also believed, ye were sealed with the Holy Spirit of promise." We used, the word "believed" as it was then used, meaning having become a Christian. And Paul never could make a Christian without baptizing him into Christ.

I wish now, my dear brother, to put some matters before you. I will ask my good brother Callahan to stand by, knife in hand, ready to "cut the breeching" if you balk. When Paul said that he and the Christians at Rome were baptized into Christ, and that the Galatian Christians were baptized into Christ, and by this means "put on Christ" (first century process), did he mean they were not in Christ before they were baptized into Christ? Can one be a Christian and not be in Christ?

When Jesus said (John 3:5), "Except a man be born of the water and of the Spirit he can not enter into the Kingdom of God," did he speak a truth for the twentieth century people? Can one be a Christian who is not in the Kingdom of God? When Peter said (Ac. 2:38), "Repent and be baptized every one of you in the name of Jesus Christ, for the remission of sins and you shall receive the gift of the Holy Spirit," did he speak for twentieth century people? Is a man a Christian whose sins have not been forgiven? Did these people receive the gift of the Holy Spirit before they became Christians? Why was Cornelius baptized? Was he not a Christian in character, especially after he had "believed on Christ"?

Pull out of this dilemma now, Brother Muckley. Cut his breeching, Brother Callahan, if he does not pull.

I will receive into the fellowship of the local congregation any one whom I recognize as a Christian. Will you?

Here I *stand*? Where is the procession going to?   E. L. FRAZIER.

Morristown, Ind.

❊ ❊

God Speed the Missionaries.

One of the great events of the year is the conference of missionaries at the rooms of the Foreign Society, Cincinnati, just before the sailing of the newly appointed workers. The meeting for this year was held September 5 and 6. There were present fourteen new missionaries and nine of the older ones who are home on furlough.

Seven of these return this fall. This makes twenty-one workers who will sail for their respective fields during this month and the first of October.

The sessions of this conference marked the high tide of enthusiasm and spiritual fellowship. Most of the returned missionaries made addresses. Their words were of keenest interest to the new ones just going out. They spoke on their experiences and of the things that the younger people need especially to know. There were also addresses by members of the official board. We were all inspired by brief addresses from Bishop Waldron and Bishop Hartzell of the Methodist church, who happened to be in the city at the time. Bishop Hartzell is missionary bishop of Africa.

Through all the addresses ran the spirit

"Dinner's Coming —I Smell It"

Does Your Stomach Feel Happy When Meal-Time Comes?

When you sniffle in the air the appetizing aroma of something cooking, do you feel that you could sit down, open your mouth, pin back your ears and eat with a delicious gusto, everything set before you, and not feel any bad effects from it?

In other words, can your poor stomach take care of everything and anything you put into it? There are thousands and thousands of people who do not know what it is to have a good, strong, healthy stomach, nor do they realize what it is to have a good appetite.

You can have an all-powerful stomach and a fetching appetite for every meal, and every day, if you give your stomach a rest, and let something else take hold of your food for you and digest it as it comes into the stomach, something that is harmless but that really does the work of digesting, quickly and thoroughly.

This "something" is Stuart's Dyspepsia Tablets, the most effective little tablets in the world for curing anything that may be wrong with your stomach. One ingredient of these precious little workers digests 3,000 grains of the coarsest or richest food put into the stomach. Think of it, 3,000 grains! They are really an artificial stomach, because they act just like the stomach in rest, digest your food, just as though you didn't have a stomach at all. It supplies the stomach with the digestive juices which have become weak and scanty.

Then your indigestion, dyspepsia, sour risings, brash, belchings, acidity, fermentation, loss of appetite, aversion to food, bloaty feeling, heartburn and nausea, will be no more. You can then eat anything you want, all you want, whenever you want, and your stomach will feel fine before and after your meals. Your appetite will be a thing of pleasure to have, your meals will be a pleasure to eat and relish, and your digestion will be thorough and soothing to the whole body.

You can't do your work well, or be cheerful, or have energy or vim or ambition, when your stomach is bad. Make yourself feel good after a hearty meal, feel good all over, clear your mind and make you enjoy life, by taking Stuart's Dyspepsia Tablets.

Give your stomach a rest, so it can right itself, then you need fear nothing. Send us your name and address today and get a free sample package of Stuart's Dyspepsia Tablets by return mail. After you have tried the sample, you will be thoroughly convinced of what they can do for you that you will go to your nearest druggist and get a 50c box of them.

Send us your name and address today and we will at once send you by mail a sample package free. Address F. A. Stuart Co., 53 Stuart Bldg., Marshall, Mich.

of hope and confidence in the ultimate conquest of the world for Christ. Every new missionary is anxious to get out to the field, every old missionary anxious to return. There is something about the devotion of these people to their great work that stirs the heart.

The new missionaries and their respective fields are as follows: Mr. and Mrs. Ray McCorkle, Miss Ledyard and Miss Rose Johnson, Japan; Mr. and Mrs. Mendenhall, Geo. Baird and Miss Genevieve Perkins, China; Dr. Miller and Miss Fleming to India; John Lord to the Philippines; and Dr. Widdowson, Miss Ella Ewing and Miss Ferrin to Africa. Dr. Widdowson started directly from the conference to Bolengi, Africa, to relieve Dr. Royal J. Dye. Mrs. Dye has been stricken with the African fever for over six months.

The older missionaries who sail soon are Dr. and Mrs. Drummond to India; A. E. Cory and wife and Mrs. Molland to China, Miss Rioch to Japan and Ray Eldred to Africa.

The closing session in which each departing missionary told why he or she was going out was very impressive. These new recruits will make strong reinforcements for our grand army of workers in heathen lands. They will be welcomed with great delight and thanksgiving by the workers on the field. Let the prayers of a whole brotherhood follow them as they go.

❀ ❀

Board of Ministerial Relief of the Church of Christ.

Aid in the support of worthy, needy, disabled ministers of the Christian Church and their widows.

THIRD LORD'S DAY IN DECEMBER is the day set apart in all the churches for the offering to this work. If you make individual offerings, send direct to the Board. Wills and Deeds should be made to "BOARD OF MINISTERIAL RELIEF OF THE CHURCH OF CHRIST, a corporation under the laws of the State of Indiana." Money received on the Annuity Plan.

Address all communications and make all checks, drafts, etc., payable to
BOARD OF MINISTERIAL RELIEF, 120 E. Market St., Indianapolis, Indiana.

OBITUARIES.

[Notices of Deaths, not more than four lines, inserted free. Obituary memoirs, one cent per word. Send the money with the copy.]

BYRAM.

Bertha Celia Byram, daughter of William W. and Margaret D. Byram, now of Abingdon, Ill., is gone to her reward. Her three brothers, Claude D., Belt and Claire are thus left to mourn. Her life was mostly spent at the farm house of her parents, where her bright and cheery ways enlivened the family circle. At the age of 16 she confessed her Savior before men and put him in his own appointed way, ever after following in his steps to the end of her brief career which terminated so suddenly, and cast a mantle of deepest gloom over the entire community on Lord's day, July 22.

DITTEMORE.

Nancy A. Dittemore was born in Owen county, Ind., December 29, 1832, and departed this life June 9, 1906, near De Kalb, Mo. Survivors are the husband, J. C. T. Dittemore; a son, A. P. Dittemore, and daughter, Roxie Thompson. She is gone—the preacher's home at Bethel is changed. In this home the emblems of the communion were prepared for thirty years. She was a charter member here and only eight survive her. John W. Sandy, her brother, is among the mourners. She was strong in faith, well prepared, and dear to all.   H. E. BALLOU.

FLEMING.

Samuel P. Fleming, son of Dr. N. and Martha H. Fleming, was born in Farmington, Mo., November 29, 1838, and fell on sleep at Aurora, Mo., September 4, 1906, where he had gone for a short visit to his son, Dr. Bart Fleming. At the age of 17 he confessed Christ, and united with the church at Libertyville, Mo. He was a charter member of the church at Farmington, of which church he has been an elder for many years, and also chairman of the official board. Through the whole of his life, he was in the highest sense one of the best citizens in this community, combining all the elements of genuine manhood and faithful Christian character.

His life has been and the world in that life. He lea daughter, all memb

The funeral s Christian church, tember 6, by the text, "After he h by the will of God

The Home Department

The Remorseful Cakes.

A little boy named Thomas ate
  Hot buckwheat cakes for tea—
A very rash proceeding, as
  We presently shall see.

He went to bed at eight o'clock,
  As all good children do,
But scarce had closed his little eyes,
  When he most restless grew.

He dreamt a great big lion came
  And ripped and raved and roared
While on his breast two furious bulls
  In mortal combat gored.

He dreamt he heard the flap of wings
  Within the chimney flue—
And down there crawled, to gnaw his ears,
  An awful bugaboo!

When Thomas rose next morn his face
  Was pallid as a sheet;
"I never more," he firmly said,
  "Will cakes for supper eat!"
       —*Eugene Field.*

❦ ❦

The Bronze Vase.

BY J. BRECKENRIDGE ELLIS.

PART III.

CHAPTER XIII.

When Raymund entered the shop, he found Miss Pinns and Mr. Hodges standing just within the little counter-gate. "I saw him," said Miss Pinns, pointing at Raymund. "He drove away a customer, a young man who had already taken out a fine gold watch to pawn. He was half-drunk, and would never have come back for the watch—that-kind never do—a young soldier, too!"

Rhoda entered and overhearing the last words, looked at Raymund with a frightened face.

"What's this?" said Mr. Hodges to his nephew. "How dare you send away our customers? What do you mean by it, after I've taken the bread out of my own mouth to put into yours?"

"Uncle William," said Raymund, "it was the son of a lady who had been very kind to Rhoda and me. He was half-drunk at first, but when I let him know about his mother, it sobered him up."

"He'll pawn it somewhere else," cried Miss Pinns, "and we might as well have the money as anybody. Besides, he'd have had a ticket for it."

"Oh, Raymund!" cried Rhoda, "was it Mrs. Bannerton's son?"

"Yes, Rhoda, and when I reminded him how she was working herself old and stiff, and half-starved herself to keep his sister at a conservatory, as she had done to send him to West Point, he said he would go home at once—he has a month's furlough."

"I am so glad!" cried Rhoda, "so glad! Isn't it nice to think we could do something for Mrs. Bannerton?"

"Yes it is," said Mr. Hodges suddenly, and he straightened himself till he had to lean on only one cane. "Yes it is, Rhoda, and I am proud of Raymund for saving the young fool!" Then he marched back into his repair-shop, and Miss Pinns sent a look at Raymund that made Rhoda shiver. But Rhoda did not despair. She had set herself the task of winning over her uncle William from the influence of Miss Pinns. It was often hard to decide which had the advantage. Mr. Hodges grew fond of the faithful girl who hesitated from no work, and who received begrudged favors with a thankful smile. But Miss Pinns was a money-maker, and the money that she made all went to him. "I am not working here for wages," Miss Pinns once remarked at the dreadfully frugal dinner-table. "Mr. Hodges took me in when I

had no home, and he has given me a roof and this good food, ever since. And I'll stay with him till I die—I don't expect to live long. But while I'm here, I don't work for wages, but for love." And she cast a glance at Mr. Hodges that made him drop his knife in embarrassed perturbation.

Raymund could have secured a position at the dark, little grocery on the corner, but Mr. Hodges objected. "You won't get but two dollars a week there," he said, "and you couldn't pay your board out of that. You stay here for nothing. You're too young to think of earning money, yet. You are at home, boy!" Mr. Hodges liked Raymund as well as Rhoda. And he liked the work he got out of both, for it was a saving of labor and money. Visits to Wizzen and Mrs. Weed were not infrequent. On one occasion they found that the second horse had been sold, and that there was a negotiation in the air touching the covered wagon. "And then I don't know what we will do," said Wizzen, "for pay rent I wont. But they's always one solution to every trouble, which it is to move, and I reckon nothing else wouldn't satisfy the old lady, no how." It was in September, and St. Louis, after a prostration of breathless heat and mosquitoes was taking its first breath of relief, when Wizzen appeared at the shop door. Miss Pinns tried to transfix him with a glance, but Wizzen made nothing of her keen eyes or of her black tooth. He called for Rhoda and Raymund, and told them "if they wanted to tell Mrs. Weed goodby, to come ahead!"

"Oh!" cried Rhoda. "I hope she isn't going to leave the city!"

"We're going to pull out," said Wizzen. "Come on." When they were at a safe distance down the gloomy, narrow street, Wizzen remarked, "Miss Pinns is well named which there don't seem nothing to the long leanness of her but a head and a point to stick with." He chuckled in much enjoyment over this comparison, and screwed his eyes and stuck his tongue in his cheek and pulled his cap lower over his towseled hair; and as they went on he muttered, "A head and a point to stick with. I must remember to tell that to the old lady."

At last they reached a steep paved street up and down which heavy vans and wagons loaded with huge pyramids of barrels and bales of goods were crawling. He descended to the river. Wizzen led the way to a house-boat which was chained to a whitewashed post at the margin of a pier. There on the deck, seated in a splint-bottom chair, was old Mrs. Weed, her ear-trumpet in hand; and at the cabin door stood a very disreputable-looking man with an enormous quantity of hair all over his face and down his neck. He was barefooted and his feet were wide and flat and set far apart.

They went aboard, and Rhoda talked to Mrs. Weed through the ear trumpet, but she was rather nervous on account of the wild-looking creature who poised a long pole in his hands with the air of a pirate. Wizzen, observing her sidelong glances, said, by way of introduction, "That there is the man that owns this here boat."

"Yap, it is," said the man, staring at Rhoda.

"We're goin' to float with him down to New Orleans," said Wizzen. "What a picnic for the old lady! Don't mind how he looks, Rhoda." This in an apologetic tone which the owner of the boat seemed to take in excellent part. "He's untootered, as I may say, but back of all that there hair is a warm heart."

"Ahoy!" cried the waterman, by way of confirmation.

"Don't be skeered of him," said Wizzen. "Come right by him and I'll show you our boat. It's great." So all went to look at the little flat cabins, and then they climbed the short ladder to the level top—"Our upper deck," said Wizzen. "Me and that character is devising to set out a block and tickle, and whenever the old lady wants a wider view, we'll histe her amidships, so to say, and set her right up here, which as yet she says she prefers the low deck."

The hairy owner of the boat jumped off the roof to the lower deck without troubling himself about the ladder, and having spread his bare feet wider apart than before grinned at Rhoda.

Rhoda whispered to Wizzen, "How very awful! I am afraid Mrs. Weed won't want to be with such a man, Wizzen."

"Oh, she don't keer," said Wizzen aloud. "He's all right, jest untootered, which now, if Mrs. Weed wasn't so old as she is, I might say, 'Let us consider;' but being in her advanced state she is as safe as me. Been writing any more poetry lately, Rhoda?"

"Yes, a little, Wizzen."

"I used to make it up whenever I had nothing else to do," said Wizzen. "It was just play, you know. It wasn't no study to me, it just come. Rhymes is easier to me than just straightforrid talking. You take *cow* which it naturally suggests *now* and *thou* and *how*, too. But in straightforrid talking you say *cow* and that seems to end the subject as to knowing what to say for to make conversation."

"I would say," growled the hairy boat-owner, "What petty-gree?"

"Don't pay no 'tention to him," said Wizzen disparagingly. "Come on down and walk right past him, he won't do nothing." When farewells had been spoken, Rhoda and Raymund stood on the dusty pier till the flat boat dropped down the river out of sight. Then they went back to the shop, feeling they had parted from true friends.

Autumn congealed to winter, and the or-

phans found it bitterly cold in the attic without a fire. There was no studying up there at night, but after the shop was closed they sat behind the counter with their books till the heat had all died away from the stove. On no account were they to put in another lump of coal after Miss Pinns had "fixed it for the night." One December night as they sat thus in the silent room, with the lamplight making bright spots on the watches and rings in the showcase, Rhoda looked up suddenly and saw Raymund with a dreamy look on his face, staring into space. She spoke to him and he started, and turned red. "O Raymund!" cried Rhoda, "I believe you were thinking about Nelsie Loraine!"

"Well," said Raymund smiling, "I was."

"Oh, Raymund!" cried Rhoda reproachfully.

"Well, what of it?" said Raymund. "I tell you, Rhoda, in spite of everything, Nelsie Loraine was mighty good to me. And she is a good-hearted girl. And as pretty as I can think!"

"O Raymund!" cried Rhoda, her blue eyes accusing and her hands clenched.

"Well," said Raymund stoutly, "she liked me and I liked her. That's all about it."

"I know what it means when you sit there with your eyes seeing nothing!" said Rhoda. "I've noticed it before!"

"Of course I'll marry some day," said Raymund grandly, as he snapped to his trigonometry.

"You are rather young to talk about it now," Rhoda taunted, with something like tears in her eyes.

"Oh, because you never saw anybody you cared for, you don't understand," said Raymund a trifle severely. "I like Nelsie Loraine better than when I saw her every day. I didn't think much about her when we were studying French and Latin together. But I get to wondering how she is spending her time in Europe, and if she ever thinks of me, and if I'll ever see her again, and that's what it means when you see my eyes just staring at nothing; its that. I'm seeing the dream of Nelsie Loraine. I wish I could see her!"

"Maybe I have seen somebody I could like," said Rhoda, coloring. "And if you want to know who, it was Jack Bellfield."

"Why, Rhoda!" cried Raymund, frowning. "Jack Bellfield isn't half good enough for you to ever think of."

"I thought he was your friend. You get letters from him sometimes. And he gave you the clothes off his own back!"

"Of course, he's my friend, but he isn't good enough for you. I have thought I'd marry some day, and you would live with us. You wouldn't ever marry, but just stay in our house and be happy that way."

"Who is we and us?" cried Rhoda. "No, sir, if you marry, I'll marry. And if you don't, I won't. Now, then! Jack Bellfield is as good for me as Nelsie Loraine is for you!"

"Rhoda," said Raymund almost angrily, "I never want to hear you speak of marrying Jack Bellfield, as long as you live!" He rose.

"Then you quit looking at the dream of Nelsie Loraine," cried Rhoda, her blue eyes burning, and her cheeks very red. And they went to bed with a little cloud between them.

But Christmas morning, when they got up very early, and Rhoda came out of her barricaded corner to look at her stocking, and Raymund, only half dressed, went to look into his sock, the cloud passed away. They had shouted "Christmas gift!" simultaneously, and now in the pale light of a smoky lamp they examined the treasures that each had given the other. At the bottom of Raymund's sock he found a slip of paper on which was written, "Jack." When he opened and read the slip, Rhoda smiled and said, "That's my Christmas gift to you; I've given up Jack for good!" Then she

emptied her stocking and gave a little cry of joy; for on a slip of paper was written, "N. L."

"Yes," said Raymund, "I saw what you wrote on your slip, and I guessed what you meant. So I'm giving you Nelsie Loraine for my Christmas gift!" Rhoda in her nightdress rushed at her brother and flung her arms about him and they began to laugh very hard. "Neither of us will ever marry!" cried Rhoda, who felt quite old in virtue of having become sixteen the day before. "Never, never, never, as long as we live!"

"But Rhoda," said Raymund, examining his treasures, "where did you ever find the money to buy all these things I've wanted so bad?"

"Well, I'll tell you," said Rhoda, nestling closer, for it was cold and clammy in the half-lighted attic. "I hired a little boy to bring my watch to the shop—the one Wizzen gave me,—and I took the money from that!"

"Oh, Rhoda! Would you part from Wizzen's gift?"

"Why of course not, boy!" cried Rhoda. "I knew you'd redeem it out of your money and give it back to me!" Then Raymund shouted with laughter and Rhoda pealed out her merriest, and Miss Pinns poked her head in the door to say, in her sourest tone and with the widest display of the black tooth, "I've got a morsel of news for you that will stop that hollering, I dare say!" And I dare say, he had. For it's usually when you are laughing hardest that bad news is coming around the corner.

(To be Continued.)

✿ ✿

Our Crosses.

BY MARY CARY BLACKBURN.

How human it is when sorrow comes to us to let it fill our hearts with bitterness and our eyes with tears.

Yet, in a measure, a great measure, it is possible for us to live above these things which hurt and annoy.

If we look at them in the right spirit they are a blessing to us. It is when the flower is crushed that it gives us the sweetest perfume. When the tree is pruned it yields the finest fruit. And so when our hearts bleed we are a little more tender, more charitable, not so prone to condemn our weak brothers and sisters, in short, as God wants us to be, and sent the suffering to us for that purpose, we are more like the divine pattern, Christ.

If we fill our minds and hearts with pure, beautiful thoughts, the discontent, the impure, will be crowded out. "For

as a man thinketh in his heart so is he." With these higher minds we shall be able to look down upon our sorrow, our temptation, our suffering of whatever kind, and bear it with patience and resignation. And because of our cross we can be a blessing to others.

✿ ✿

"I Love You."

BY J. EDGAR RUSSELL.

A mother holds her babe against her breast,
Kisses the dimples on its rosy cheeks,
Lisps to the prattle of its childish tongue,
And then she slowly, softly to it speaks,
"I love you."

With snowy hair, and trembling hand and step,
Behold that mother after many years,
With figure bent, she gazes at her son,
And these, the joyful words she gladly hears,
"I love you."

❦ ❦

THE HISTORY OF A
HEART TRAGEDY.

BY OLIVE A. SMITH.

If I had not committed my few remaining days to the cause of literary art, I certainly would not write this story, for the writing of it will add many bitter drops to a cup of anguish already overflowing. But I know Dorothy will never write it. Dorothy is so mundane at times; so prone to lose sight of those heights, which another poet, fully as great as either of us, has called "the Alpine summits overhead." And she is several months my senior, too. She is nearly 15, and I am only fourteen and a half.

The cause of art demands that I write the story, and I shall strive to write it truthfully, because the editors of the great magazines all desire truth in their stories, and I intend that this story shall be published in the very greatest of the great magazines.

But I must now begin the real story. The above paragraphs form the introduction and these same editors who want truth in a story, have said, very emphatically that the writer should plunge into the story in the first few sentences of the introduction. That is the reason I mentioned Dorothy in the very first paragraph. Dorothy is one of the characters in the story. In fact, she is the only important character besides myself and Professor Ramey.

Another editor has said that "Telling a story in the first person is open to serious objections." I considered that saying very carefully before beginning my story, but I reasoned the matter over calmly and decided that, if I told the truth, I must tell the story in the first person, for the story is the history of the heart-tragedy that has overshadowed Dorothy's life and mine. Furthermore, editors all desire truth, and I never heard of more than one who objected to the first person. So I determined not to sacrifice moral integrity, even to the great cause of art, and I will proceed with my story in the first person.

Dorothy and I live within a block of one another, and we were always the dearest of earthly friends until that friendship was wrecked by the tempest of sorrow which I will soon describe.

The trouble all came from this erroneous idea that Dorothy and I are children, when we are not children. It is a long time since we both of us took a firm hold of the serious problems of human life and destiny. I make this explanation here, in deference to another editor, who has said that "every sentence in the story should be an unfolding and a development of the plot."

Well, "on the morning of that eventful day," as a fellow-novelist has said, Dorothy and I walked to the academy as usual. We received our history lessons for practice, just as usual, and then, just as usual, we talked about Professor Ramey. He is our history teacher, and I can't remember a single morning last term when we didn't talk about him. Sometimes we spoke of his kindness and goodness; of his beautiful ideals of life,

and his vast knowledge of things. We wondered how he had accumulated those vast stores of wisdom. We often spoke of his eyes. He has such eyes! So dark, and deep, and often "sparkling with merriment," as one of our minor poets has said. Sometimes we wondered how he could be so big and broadshouldered, and not look at all awkward. Dorothy said it was because he was so "exquisitely proportioned," and I was amused at her use of a borrowed expression. I always use original language myself, even if it is not quite so effective.

That morning we mentioned the professor's peculiar habit of twisting his mustache with great violence when he is excited or very much amused about anything. Then we wondered why he is not married. All the other professors are married, and we know that he is much older than some of them. I said: "Perhaps he will marry some time. I guess he isn't so very old."

"Why, Bessie Merwin!" exclaimed Dorothy. "Professor Ramey is far past the meridian of life. Yesterday, when I stood by his desk, I saw four gray hairs, two on each side of his forehead.

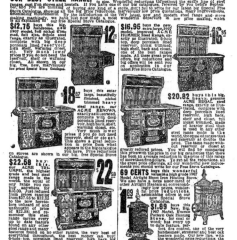

and they matched beautifully! He must be nearly forty. Just think of it!"

"Well, what if he is forty," I answered. "In these days of culture it is only the crude and unformed mind that makes so much of a few years. Professor Ramey is no ordinary man, and his years can not be measured by an ordinary standard."

Dorothy and I have never quarreled and made up after the manner of frivolous girlhood; but she turned up her nose and sniffed at those words. Then she said, in a sarcastic tone, "Oh, of course not! Neither is Miss Bessie Merwin an ordinary girl, and her years can not be measured by an ordinary standard. Perhaps she is almost as old as professor Ramey." I gazed at her in gentle dignity; for I was disgusted with her childishness. I do not think it necessary to the development or unfolding of the plot of this story, that I relate, in detail, the further incidents of that walk. I will say, however, that there was a slight unpleasantness of feeling between us. During the chapel, and algebra, and study hours we never looked at each other, and once, when Miss Herrington stepped out of the room, Rob Reynolds nudged Charley Wilson, and they winked and grinned in our direction. Rob whispered, loud enough for us to hear, "Them dearest friends been quarreling again, I guess. Ain't it funny watchin' girls try to be chums!"

I frowned severely at Rob. So did Dorothy. I can not endure the youth. He is so lacking in culture and ideals! And his conversation is shockingly provincial and ungrammatical.

When we passed into Professor Ramey's room he stood near the door, looking handsome and noble as usual, yet kind of sad and dreamy, as if he were thinking of something far away. I was at the head of the line, and when he saw me that far-off expression instantly left his face, and he smiled at me. He has such a sweet smile, and I had never seen it so radiant and beautiful before.

I fairly danced along to my seat, and I could not resist the temptation to turn and look at Dorothy. Oh, gentle reader, you should have seen her! The expression of her face was fairly murderous! "Our eyes met in one quick, comprehensive glance," as another fellow-novelist has remarked, and the whole tragic truth, which will be suddenly revealed in the denouement of the story, forced itself upon our minds.

I was positively brilliant in my recitation that day, and Dorothy made almost a complete failure. Her mother had sent her to bed the day before, because she had a sore throat. So she hadn't studied much. She was terribly humiliated over her failure, and I was quite sorry for her. The minute the class was dismissed she ran to the music room, where she was to take her lesson in 15 minutes. The Graham girls and Madge Benedict came to my desk, and while we were talking about what we would do during vacation, Professor Ramey went whistling about the room, collecting test papers and clearing up his desk. When we started to go, he looked up and said: "That was a first-class lesson to-day, Miss Bessie. I wish we had a few more like it."

I said: "Thank you, professor," and he smiled again, very sweetly, and I ran down to the cloak room to tell Dorothy. I had to wait a long time, and when I told her she turned up her nose, just as she had in the morning, and said: "That's nothing compared with some of the compliments I have received from Professor Ramey. He told me the oth-

er day that he didn't know how they could get along in the history class without me." Again we exchanged a few unpleasant words, but we became reconciled so far that we walked home together. On the way home, another incident occurred which has a great deal to do with the development of the plot. Some boys gave us great big hand-bills, announcing a lecture to be given by a Madam Luvaney, who had traveled clear around the earth three times. The subject of the lecture was "The Emancipation of Women from Conventionality." Dorothy and I, being young women inclined to progressive thought in all things, were enthusiastic about it from the first. Our mothers do not approve of our going out to lectures and things when we have lessons to study, so we arranged a little plan of our own. We were to get permission to take our drawing books over to Madge Benedict's, and work all together. Then we were to slip quietly over to the East Side Hall and hear the lecture. Of course we were sorry to make use of a plan that involved a little deceit, still we felt justified, because the emancipation of woman from anything is a very great cause. We felt it was our duty to be thoroughly informed on so important a subject.

(To be Concluded.)

In Evanston the other evening the parents of a bright little girl had some of their friends in to dinner, and a number of toasts were given. After the older ones had finished, the young lady stood up, held her glass of water high—water is always used for toasting purposes in Evanston—and said: "Here's to the auto. May we hear its toot in time to scoot."

Too Curious Tourist.

"Have you nothing else?" inquired Mrs. Schoppen, who was looking at half-hose for her husband.

"No, ma'am," replied the shopman. "I've shown you every pair in stock."

"Are you sure," she persisted, leaning

over the counter, "there are none there I have not seen?"

"Yes'm," stammered the shopman, "except—er—the pair I'm wearing."

Picture of War Engine "General."

A beautiful colored picture, 18x25 inches, of the historic old engine "General" which was stolen at Big Shanty, Ga., by the Andrew's Raiders during the Civil War, and which is now on exhibition in the Union Depot, Chattanooga, Tenn., has been gotten out by the NASHVILLE, CHATTANOOGA & ST. LOUIS RY.—The "Battlefields Route" to the South. The picture is ready for framing and will be mailed for 25c. The "Story of the General" sent free. W. L. Danley, Gen'l Pass. Agent, Nashville, Tenn.

At the Stamp Window.

Just before 12 o'clock yesterday forenoon there were thirteen men and one woman at the stamp window of the postoffice. Most of the men had letters to post for the outgoing trains. The woman had something tied up in a blue matchbox. She got there first, and she held the position with her head in the window and both elbows on the shelf.

"Is there such a place in this country as Cleveland?" she began.

"Oh, yes."

"Do you send mail there?"

"Yes."

"Well, a woman living next door asked me to mail this box for her. I guess it is directed all right. She said it ought to go for a cent."

"Takes two cents," said the clerk, after weighing it. "If there is writing inside it will be twelve cents."

"Mercy on me, but how you do charge." Here the thirteen men began to push up and hustle around and talk about one old match-box delaying two dozen business letters; but the woman had lots of time.

"Then it will be two cents, eh?"

She's sending some flower seeds to her sister, and I presume she has told her how to plant 'em."

"Two threes," called out one of the crowd, as he tried to get to the window.

"Hurry up," cried another.

"If there is no writing inside."

"Well, there may be. I know she is a great hand to write."

"There ought to be a separate window for women," growled a third.

"Then it will take twelve cents?" she calmly queried, as she fumbled around for her purse.

"Yes."

"Well, I'd better pay it, I guess."

From one pocket she took two coppers. From her reticule she took a three-cent piece. From her purse she fished out a nickel; and it was only after a hunt of eighty seconds that she got the twelve cents together. She then consumed four minutes in licking on the stamps, asking where to post the box, and wondering if there really was any writing inside—but woman proposes and man disposes. Twenty thousand dollars' worth of business was being detained by a twelve-cent woman, and a tidal wave suddenly took her away from the window. In sixty seconds the thirteen men had been waited on and gone their ways, and the woman returned to the window, handed in the box and said:

"Them stamps are licked on kind o' crooked, but it won't make any difference, will it?"—*Bee Hive.*

❖ ❖

"You're a Brick."

When Tom says admiringly to Harry, "You're a brick!" I wonder if he knows how the saving originated.

In the golden days of Greece, an ambassador once came from Epirus to Sparta, and was shown by the king over his capital. He was surprised to find no walls around the city.

"Sire!" he exclaimed. "I have visited nearly all the towns in Greece, but I find no walls for their defense. Why is this?"

"Indeed!" the king replied, "you cannot have looked carefully. Come with me to-morrow and I will show you the walls of Sparta."

On the following morning the king led his guest out upon the plains where his army was drawing up in battle array, and pointing proudly to the valiant soldiers, he said:

"There you behold the walls of Sparta —every man a brick!"—*Exchange.*

❖ ❖

Spicy Sayings.

Harold ran back from the lion in the museum.

"Don't be afraid, dear," grandmother said. "That lion is stuffed."

"Yes," said Harold, "but mebbe he isn't stuffed so full that he couldn't find room for a little boy like me."

❖

"Mamma, which star is yours?" asked Kitty.

"What do you mean?"

"Well, we were looking at the stars last night, and Mary pointed to one and said, 'That is Mars,' and I thought that if her mother owned one, you must have one too."—*Little Chronicle.*

❖

A little Topeka girl came home from church the other day and was asked what the minister's text was.

"I know it all right," she asserted.

"Well, repeat it," her questioner demanded.

"Don't be afraid and I will get you a bed-quilt," was the astounding answer.

Investigation proved that the central thought of the sermon had been, "Fear not, and I will send you a comforter."—*Kansas City Journal.*

❖ ❖

Sauce for the Goose.

The old saying that "Chickens come home to roost," has many a good application. It is also true that the good we would do is often outdone by our own mistakes. The following needs no further comment:

"She was dressed smartly, and when she met a little urchin carrying a bird's nest with eggs in it, she said: 'You are a wicked boy; how could you rob that nest! No doubt the poor mother is now grieving for the loss of her eggs.'

"'Oh, she don't care,' answered the boy, edging away, 'she's on your hat.'"—*Selected.*

❖ ❖

"Remember that there is one thing better than making a living—making a life."
Gov. Russell.

g Company
ouis, Mo.

- President
Vice-President
Sec. and Gen. Supt
and Bus. Manager

iospel for an
patrons for 75
ess" goes for
t.

n honor to the
t to all connect-
J. H. Garrison,
st, St. Louis.

other reporters
copy" to this
NGELIST'S great
require crisp,
ibutions to our

ian 5,000 song
hat we do not
this is due to
ithout sending
e the best, and

iany preachers
o secure trans-
convention by
IAN-EVANGELIST
t once for our
is.

st and Review
HE CHRISTIAN-
in pen for $2.
T and a self-
inteed for ten
ber) for $2.50.
IST and The
i for $2.25.

ney, Texas, in
opular Church
very highly.
every church
ing old records
its classified

the "Garrison
tory of Chris-
be published
tional conven-
t series, Alone
es at the Cross,
elps to Faith,
tory of Chris-
HRISTIAN-EVAN-

r Bible school
the Dowling."
best. We sell
ple prices. An
ar's series will
er's Quarterly
sent on appli-

IST headquar-
ckingham, the
ention hall. A
riends will be
day, American'
once. It will
re lodging and
ts in comfort-
e armory at 75

r power to tell
have examined
I now look
ect. Style, the

---

order of arrangement, mechanical construction, in fact the whole book is a
joy and a delight to the soul. You have
placed the entire brotherhood under
everlasting obligation to you for the excellent Hymnal you have given to us."—
W. M. White, Kentucky University, Lexington, Ky.

The tourist car on THE CHRISTIAN-
EVANGELIST Special will cost $2, the
standard Pullman $4, excellent reclining
chair car service free. The fare from St.
Louis and return will be $19.25. Reser-
vations should be made at once. Those
not living along the line of the Wabash
should insist on their agents routing
them over that line, and leave home in
time to catch this Special leaving St.
Louis at high noon, Thursday, October 11.

The circulation of THE CHRISTIAN-
EVANGELIST has increased 30½ per cent
since October 1, 1905. We question
whether this has been paralleled in the
history of our church journalism. This
is due not only to the superior excellence of the journal itself, but in large
part also to the increasing aggressive
loyalty and devotion of thousands of
its friends. While scores of new subscriptions come by ones and twos, we
have this week received the following
new clubs at $1.50 each: Hoquiam,
Wash., John J. Handsaker, minister,
4; Cameron, Mo., I. O. Bricker, minister, 5; Jefferson, Ia., Samuel Gregg, pas-

---

tor, 5; Woodward, Ia., 6; Fort Dodge
Ia., 9; Webster City, Ia., R. M. Dur
gan, pastor, 9; Tipton, Ind., L. H. Stine
minister, 11; Windsor, Mo., W. A. Fitt
pastor, 12; Niantic, Ill., J. Will Walter
minister, 14; Kansas City, Mo., T. F
Haley, pastor, 16; St. Joseph, Mo
C. A. Lowe, minister, 19; Noble
ville, Ind., R. W. Clymer, pastor, 19
Flora, Ind., A. B. Houze, pastor, 19
Houston, Mo., J. D. Lawrence, evange
ist, 23.

An occasional gleam of sunshine
bright scintillations from the great realm
of delicious sentiment—occasionally fa
over the pens, statistical tables, circu
lation reports and other grim evidence
of a business age, littering our Superin
tendent's desk. This is the latest, writte
on the reverse side of an important busi
ness communication, escaping the attentio
of the author, whose name we would no
surrender for weighty gold: "My ow
owniest—Just sent you a letter but this jus
came and I want to send it on, also your
of Tuesday night. Oh, I need you—if
wrote all day I could only give the cry o
my heart. I need you, I want you. R."

❋ ❋

The Day After the Fourth.

Mrs. De Style—That pin-wheel
bought here yesterday had no powder i
it.

Storekeeper—I know dot, lady; id' vo
a safety pin-wheel.—Woman's Home Com
panion for July.

THE CHRISTIAN-EVANGELIST

A WEEKLY RELIGIOUS NEWSPAPER

| Volume XLIII. | No. 40. |

ST. LOUIS, OCTOBER 4, 1906.

WHAT A NATIONAL CONVENTION MEANS

WHO CAN sum up a national convention? It is condensed history. It is Hope rising on triumphant wing for a loftier flight. It is Faith, seeing visions and planning campaigns. It is Love, greeting old comrades, cementing new friendships, forming higher resolves, and getting a foretaste of heaven. It is Memory opening her books and showing us half-forgotten faces and chapters lying back in the dim past, as long sundered friends meet and greet each other. It is college days lived over again as the gray-headed boys and girls meet and revive the incidents of those distant, by-gone days. It is a spur of the Delectable Mountain, from whose summit we catch glimpses of the city which hath foundations. It is a river of holy enthusiasm in which we bathe our weary spirits and are refreshed for the journey. It is a school of the Master in which he gathers his disciples about him once more to repeat to them his last command, "Go teach all nations." It is a Jerusalem in which the disciples tarry awhile for a fresh enduement of power from on high. It is an Antioch from which the missionaries, separated from their fellows by the Holy Spirit, are sent forth to new conquests in the mission field, and to which, returning, they report what the Lord hath wrought through them. It is a Patmos from which the beloved disciples see, in bold outline, the future struggles of the Church with her foes, and her glorious triumph. Blessed fellowship! Hallowed associations! Our hearts shall know nothing sweeter or holier until our feet shall stand within thy gates, O Jerusalem the golden, the redeemed city of God!

—Easy Chair, on San Francisco Convention.

The Christian-Evangelist.

J. H. GARRISON, Editor

PAUL MOORE, Assistant Editor

F. D. POWER,
B. B. TYLER, } Staff Correspondents.
W. DURBAN, }

Subscription Price, $1.50 a Year.

For foreign countries add $1.04 for postage.

Remittances should be made by money order, draft, or registered letter; not by local cheque, unless 15 cents is added to cover cost of collection.

In Ordering Change of Post Office give both old and new address.

Matter for Publication should be addressed to THE CHRISTIAN-EVANGELIST. Subscriptions and remittances should be addressed to the Christian Publishing Company, 2712 Pine Street, St. Louis, Mo.

Unused Manuscripts will be returned only if accompanied by stamps.

News Items, evangelistic and otherwise, are solicited, and should be sent on a postal card, if possible.

Published by the Christian Publishing Company, 2712 Pine Street, St. Louis, Mo.

Entered at St. Louis P. O. as Second Class Matter

WHAT WE STAND FOR.

For the Christ of Galilee,
For the truth which makes men free,
For the bond of unity
Which makes God's children one.

For the love which shines in deeds,
For the life which this world needs,
For the church whose triumph speeds
The prayer: "Thy will be done."

For the right against the wrong,
For the weak against the strong,
For the poor who've waited long
For the brighter age to be.

For the faith against tradition,
For the truth 'gainst superstition,
For the hope whose glad fruition
Our waiting eyes shall see.

For the city God is rearing,
For the New Earth now appearing,
For the heaven above us clearing,
And the song of victory,

J. H. Garrison.

CONTENTS.

Centennial Propaganda 1255
Current Events 1256
Editorial—
  Where Jesus Placed the Emphasis—VII. 1257
  Bearing Witness to the Truth....1258
  Rules of Church Order.........1258
  Notes and Comments..........1258
  Editor's Easy Chair............1259
Contributed Articles—
  Our Cause in Arkansas. J. N. Jessup 1260
  Hebrew Poetry—Illustrating Nature Treatment in the Psalms. James Egbert 1262
  In the Abyss. William Durban..1263
  As Seen from the Dome. F. D. Power 1264
Our Budget 1265
News from Many Fields.....,....1270
Evangelistic ....,...1273
Sunday-school 1274
Midweek Prayer-meeting 1274
Christian Endeavor .....,.........1275
People's Forum 1276
Current Literature 1277
The Home Department 1278

THE
CHRISTIAN-EVANGELIST

"IN FAITH, UNITY, IN OPINION AND METHODS, LIBERTY, IN ALL THINGS, CHARITY."

| Vol. XLIII. | October 4, 1906 | No. 40 |

1809 CENTENNIAL PROPAGANDA CHURCHES OF CHRIST 1909
: : : GEO. L. SNIVELY : : :

Looking Toward Pittsburg.

A. L. Orcutt, of the Board of Ministerial Relief, advises our readers this year's report by the custodians of the funds , so piously given for the care of our aged ministers and their wives through their declining years to be presented at Buffalo will be the best in the history of that organization. May Bro. A. M. Atkinson see in it the travail of his soul and be satisfied, may the dear beneficiaries of the brotherhood's gratitude have less concern about food, raiment and shelter while this winter's wild winds howl around them, but amid peace and plenty with happiness review their past years and with the sweetest anticipations of joy look forward to their home-going and coronation.

It is well to supplement Brother Mohorter's "Program" which follows with the remark that among the most interesting features of the convention will be his own activities as secretary of our National Benevolent Association. Though he has been secretary but a few months, his former identification with the ministry through his membership on the Central Board has given him complete mastery of the details as well as full comprehension of the sublime part this Association is to have in the Centennial triumphs and all the future of this Restoration. The wisdom of his selection for his present position is receiving daily confirmation through the work of his hands and heart.

A communication received from Secretary Muckley as we are almost ready for press, states Church Extension receipts for the current year are $60,-113.80, a gain of $13,439.05 over last year. The interest from investment funds bring the receipts up to over $80,000. This is indeed gratifying evidence that Church Extension has moved well out into the Centennial current of progress and triumph. We congratulate our Board of Church Extension, its indomitable secretary and above all, all who are engaged in this great movement for the restoration of apostolic Christianity to the faith and practice of men over the almost assured consummation of our Centennial aim to have $1,000,000 at the disposal of the Board of Church Extension by Pittsburg, 1909.

Churches from their treasury supply their membership with communion emblems, hymn books and Bible school helps. Why not with a Christian paper? The sanctifying influence of religious journals is unknown to half our people. Florists, horticulturists, agriculturists, mechanics, tradesmen, merchants, scientists, professionals, all regard an organ of their own craft indispensable to the higher development of their vocations and their own preparedness for them. The constituency of no other great interest so needs such help

as that of the church. The great commission of the church—"Go Teach"—is powerfully supplemented by knowledge of the field. From no other source can this information be secured in attractive form save from the religious press. Few church members have the proper conception of the importance of many things pastors deem very consequential unless he sees them dignified with newspaper advocacy and himself importuned into active alliance therewith by the agency of the press. His own enthusiasm as a soul saver will be tremendously enhanced by glowing reports from many fields found in every issue of a paper like THE CHRISTIAN-EVANGELIST. Proper pride in his own church will be inculcated by learning in these columns what is making other churches strong, prosperous and useful. A large circulation won by its own initiative might be more profitable to our publishing houses than one given them in the method we now suggest; but relieved of the expense of solicitors' charges and helped by an increased circulation of tens of thousands, any of them would doubtless furnish the papers in clubs of fifty and one hundred much cheaper than they can be sold under the present system. A few months ago, Lebanon, Mo., introduced one of our church papers into every home represented in the membership. Just what that has meant to the church may be learned by addressing the pastor—Harold Bell Wright. We believe nothing else the churches could do would contribute more to a great Centennial or inaugurate our second Centennial movement with greater enthusiasm or brighter hopes of success than for the church officiary to place a Christian paper in every home. With respect to this, we welcome the opinions of the brethren.

❦ ❦

The Program of the Buffalo Convention.
BY J. H. MOHORTER.

Much has been said about the physical beauties of the city of Buffalo and the might and majesty of Niagara Falls. While these may contribute to the profit or a visit to our National Convention, the real profit, however, must be found in the program. In this particular the Buffalo Convention offers a rare attraction. The program for this year is the peer of any of its great predecessors. It insures a rare intellectual and spiritual uplift. The men and women who are to speak on this occasion are all specialists, who have learned the secret of success in the Lord's work, and who are abundantly endowed to feed our minds and set our hearts aflame with the fire of a holy enthusiasm.

As a people, we are engaged in a great work, in enterprises that are worldwide in their influence and age-lasting in their endurance. Every member of our great brotherhood should know about plans, purposes, and conquest of our united effort to bring in the universal reign of Christ. If all our brethren were fully informed about our triumphs

at home and abroad they would begin to experience the real joy of Christian service, and all our work, missionary, educational and benevolent would feel the impulse of divine optimism. The program of our coming convention will carry us to the mount of vision where we may behold our Lord in the midst of his loyal followers as he triumphantly leads on to victory. It will take us into the sweetest and most intimate fellowship with him, for it will, as to his "friends," uncover to us the secret yearning of his great heart over a lost and ruined world.

Then the fellowship of this occasion will be one of the rare treats of a lifetime. The great religious activities in which we are engaged are borne forward under the leadership of some of the noblest men and women of God in the religious world. They are of the purest character, the largest vision, the deepest consecration to God and humanity. Who can measure the value of a personal acquaintance with these men and women whose lives have been so richly fruitful? To meet them face to face and mingle with them in sympathetic fellowship is to secure for ourselves a fuller, richer appreciation of them and the appeals they bring to our hearts and to place ourselves in touch with a heroic band of the friends of Christ and humanity. To look into the faces of the battle-scarred soldiers of the cross from the firing line far out on the frontier of heathen darkness, to hear the messages of these men and women who will have laid all upon the altar of service will be a holy benediction. Then to sit down with the multitudes as they gather in loving memory around the Lord's table will remove all feeling of isolation and will make more real the brotherhood we have in the Church of Christ. The sense of partnership we have in Christ with an almost countless multitude of sainted spirits, both in heaven and upon earth, will gird us with strength to climb to the very summit of Christian service and experience. We owe it to ourselves to go to the Buffalo convention that we may rejoice in the splendid victories of the year, that we may receive new courage for the larger service through our sense of partnership with a multitude of the choicest spirits in the religious world, that from its lofty summit we may view the thrilling magnitude of the work into which our God has called us, that we may be brought into the most intimate nearness to the heart of our Savior as he opens to us his glorious will.

St. Louis, Mo.

❦ ❦

We like THE CHRISTIAN-EVANGELIST and "Our Young Folks," and feel as if we could not get along without them in our home very well.—Edgar Teghtmeyer, Langdon, Kas.

I am thoroughly enjoying THE CHRISTIAN-EVANGELIST, and believe that it will accomplish much good here if I can succeed in placing it in several homes.—V. L. Parker, minister, New Decatur, Ala.

Current Events

It is reported that the Russian grand dukes are fleeing from Russia into other parts of Europe. Assassinations have become too frequent for their peace of mind. The sudden death of General Trepoff, which is suspected of having been an assassination by poison, was a particularly discouraging event for the grand dukes. Trepoff was supposed to be the policeman-in-chief for the protection of all the privileged ones against the indignation of the oppressed. It was his business to ward off the bombs of the anarchists from the dukes and others in high place. But if he could not even protect himself, surely it is time for the others to escape while they can. So they think, apparently, for they are putting their estates in the hands of agents, packing their portable wealth and hastening to Germany and France.

The Flight of the Dukes.

❦

The special commission which is preparing the rules under which the pure food and pure drug law is to be enforced is now in session in New York. It has prepared some tentative rules governing the sale of drugs and medical preparations. According to these it is required that the label shall state all the ingredients of the preparation (using the English names), the name of the manufacturer and the place of production. It is also provided that geographical names shall not be used unless the articles so labelled actually come from the places mentioned. For example, nothing shall be sold as Jamaica ginger that does not come from Jamaica, and Peruvian bark must come from Peru. The times are changing. When this law goes into effect it will be impossible for the man who regularly takes his stimulants in the form of patent medicines which are 20 to 30 per cent alcohol, to delude himself with the belief that he is a strict temperance man.

Pure Drugs.

❦

James T. Smith was inaugurated governor-general of the Philippines on Tuesday of last week, in place of Governor-General Ide. In his inaugural address he said that his policy would be that which has already been established, namely, to prepare the people by education for the exercise and enjoyment of independence. But he added that independence is no guarantee of happiness and prosperity, and cited the case of Cuba as proving that independence is not always a blessing. As a general proposition it is, of course, true that independence is no guarantee of felicity. Some men are really better off in jail than at large. But men in

In the Philippines.

jail will wish for liberty and political communities will desire independence. Nothing as yet has convinced us—not even Mr. Bryan's statement—that the Filipinos are capable of self-government. We still believe, and hope, that when they are they will get it. And we trust that Governor Smith's administration will be directed to that end.

❦

The agents of the special interests which seek governmental subsidy or protection and labor to avert unfriendly legislation, have long been known as the "third house" of congress. No one doubts the right of any group of business men to maintain agents in Washington to see that members of congress are duly informed and properly argued with touching proposed legislation which affects their interests. But there is a well-grounded suspicion that, while various groups of special interests are thus ably taking care of themselves, some not less important general interests are in danger of being overlooked. The things that are everybody's business always stand a chance of being neglected. Bad legislation gets through because somebody urges it and nobody opposes it until it is too late. The "Success" Magazine has been developing a plan for the establishment of what it calls "the people's lobby," to be composed of a group of well-known and public-spirited citizens who, with the aid of competent legal advisers, shall look after the interests of the public when congress is in session as the present lobby looks after the interests of the railroads, and the other great corporations. Some of the men who have already agreed to serve on this committee are Lincoln Steffens, Mark Twain, Benjamin Ide Wheeler, John Mitchell and William Allen White. We wish success to the scheme. The most serious difficulty which we apprehend is that these are all busy men. A man who is running a great university in California or editing a newspaper in Kansas can not keep an eye on congress by day and by night as one does who has no other interest in life but to see that the oil business or the railroad business gets the most generous possible treatment. Still, it is worth trying. It will at least serve as a reminder that the special interests are not the only interests which are to be considered in legislation. In congress, as in the insurance companies, it may be worth while to have a policy-holders' committee.

The People's Lobby.

❦

What is virtually a new magazine begins this month with the first issue of the "American Magazine" under its new management. A defection from the staff of McClure's and the addition of other able writers gives the "American," as its owners, editors and chief contributors,

Magazines.

Mr. Phillips, of McClure and Phillips, Ida M. Tarbell, Steffens, White, Baker and Dunne. Their magazine will apparently be devoted largely to good government and social, political and economic reform. The publishers of "Everybody's" have announced a unique weekly which will be at once national and local, to be issued simultaneously at ten cities from New York to San Francisco with identical treatment of general topics and separate treatment of local topics. It will attempt, by a liberal use of telegraph and fast presses, to solve the problem of getting the news of the week into a paper of late circulation before it becomes stale. The "North American Review," which began life nearly a century ago as a quarterly, and became in succession a bi-monthly and a monthly, is now issued fortnightly. It will attempt to present a serious and deliberate study of current topics, as it has always done, and to keep a little nearer to the events than it was possible to do in a monthly.

❦

A common sailor in the United States Navy has brought suit against an amusement company for excluding him from a place of public entertainment because he wore his uniform. The president has expressed his opinion of the matter by contributing $100 to the expense of the suit. Considering the recent decision of the New York courts in the Metcalf case it is doubtful whether he will win. In that case it was held that the manager of a theater may exclude an undesirable dramatic critic or any other person. It is not bound, like a common carrier, to serve the whole public. Still we hope the sailor will win. The men who are good enough to fight our battles in time of war are good enough to share our amusements in time of peace. Several years ago Kipling wrote a poem in which he voices the complaint of "Tommy Atkins" (the English common soldier) against a similar discrimination. Some of the lines of that poem apply to this present case as pat as Scripture. These lines are taken somewhat at random from the poem:

The Honor of the Service.

> I went into a public 'ouse to get a pint o' beer,
> The publican 'e up and sey, "we serve no red-
>   coats here."
> The girls behind the bar they laughed an' giggled
>   fit to die;
> I out into the street again an' to myself sey I:
>
> O, it's Tommy this, and Tommy that,
>   And "Tommy go away;"
> But it's thank you, mister Atkins,
>   When the band begins to play.
>
> I went into a theatre as sober as could be,
> They gave a drunk civilian room, but 'adn't none
>   for me;
>
> For it's Tommy this, and Tommy that and
>   "Tommy, wait outside;"
> But it's "special train for Atkins," when
>   The trooper's on the tide.
>
> Yes, makin' mock o' uniforms that guard you
>   while you sleep,
> Is cheaper than them uniforms, and thy're star-
>   vation cheap.
>
> For it's Tommy this and Tommy that,
>   And "chuck him out, the brute,"
> But it's "Savior of 'is country," when
>   The guns begin to shoot.

Editorial

Where Jesus Placed the Emphasis.—VII.

Prayer.

A foolish question is sometimes raised as to the value of prayer. "Does not God know all things?" it is asked. "What is the use, then, of our telling him our needs?" Another objection is based on the unvarying nature of God's laws. "How can our prayer affect these unchanging laws of God on whose continuity all scientific calculations are based?" This is the objection of the skeptical scientist. It would be easy to answer these questions on philosophic grounds, and to show that they arise out of false and inadequate conceptions of what prayer is, and out of ignorance of some of God's spiritual laws. But the short-cut method of answering these and all other objections to prayer is the undisputed and significant fact that Jesus himself who, whatever men may think of his deity, stands without a peer as a teacher of God and of spiritual things, himself often prayed. How often we read of his going apart from his disciples and from the multitude to pray! Sometimes he seems to have spent all night in prayer. At his baptism in the Jordan, at Capernaum when crowds of sick gathered about him for healing, on the night before choosing his apostles, on the Mount of Transfiguration, at the raising of Lazarus, in the Garden of Gethsemane, and even upon the cross, our Savior prayed. Who that reverences his name and reveres his example can doubt the efficacy of prayer?

Not only did Jesus himself pray, but he taught his disciples to pray, also. Does not this involve the value of prayer? Once when he was praying in their presence, his disciples requested him to teach them to pray. No doubt there was something in his manner of prayer so reverent, so simple, so trustful, so sublime, so uplifting, and so different from what they had been accustomed to hear, it created in them a strong desire to pray like that. In response to their request he gave them that model prayer. The more one studies it, the more he is impressed with its marvelous depth and breadth. Who but the Son of God himself who knew perfectly the mind and character of God on the one hand, and human nature and its needs on the other, could teach such a prayer?

"Our Father!" Here is the deepest meaning of his revelation. He came to show us the Father. How we thank him for the unspeakable privilege of saying, when we pray, "Our Father"! How near that brings him to our hearts! How it encourages the soul to pour into his sympathetic ear the story of its sins, of its needs! How we love to turn away from all the subtle, metaphysical definitions and descriptions of the Almighty, in which theologians have indulged, and come back to the dear, tender, childlike words, "Our Father"! And notice that it is our Father, therefore, we be brethren and must so regard and treat each other.

"Who art in heaven." What matters it where heaven is? It is enough that our Father is there, and our "Father's house" is there. It is the "home of the soul." It is freedom from sin and sorrow and pain and death. With Browning we can all say:

"But deep within my heart of heart there hid
Ever the confidence, amends for all,
That heaven repairs what wrongs earth's journey did."

"Hallowed be Thy name." This is the spirit of devout reverence which recognizes the infinite holiness and righteousness of God. Name, in Bible language, means character.

"Thy kingdom come. Thy will be done on earth as it is in heaven." A petition for the reign of God over our own hearts and lives, and over all the earth, bringing men in subjection to the will of God, even as are the angels of heaven. Who can breathe that petition meaningfully, without being enlarged and purified by it? How vast the program it suggests! How sublime the end that it contemplates!

"Give us this day our daily bread." Feed us as the father feeds his children, and we will receive it as from God.

"Forgive us our debts as we also have forgiven our debtors." Surely "our Father" will forgive our sins, if we will forgive the wrongs and injuries which others have done us. But we must forgive, to be forgiven. So God links our filial relationship to him with our fraternal relationship with our fellowmen.

"And bring us not into temptation but deliver us from the evil one." A recognition of our own human weakness, and of our trust in God for deliverance from the power of the evil one.

We are persuaded that one great hindrance to prayer, as Jesus saw it, is the cherishing of wrong feelings in our heart toward others. To make that lesson emphatic, he adds to the prayer above this encouragement and caution: "For if ye forgive men their trespasses, your heavenly Father will also forgive you. But if ye forgive not men their trespasses, neither will your Father forgive your trespasses." (Matt. 6:14, 15.) Another hindrance to prayer is our lack of persistence. Jesus emphasized the importance of that in two or three parables in which he taught that "Men ought always to pray and not to faint." This importunity is not to overcome God's reluctance, but to prepare our own hearts for the blessings we ask. Nor must we think that the failure to receive the special thing we ask in the manner in which we expected to receive it, is proof that our prayer has not been answered. Jesus taught us by his own example that our prayers should be in the spirit of submission to the will of God—"Not my will, but Thine be done"! He oft-

en gives us much greater blessings than those we ask for, but some times they come in disguise and we do not recognize them.

Again Jesus taught that faith is essential to all prevailing prayer. His most remarkable saying on this point is that in connection with the withered fig tree at which the disciples wondered. "Have faith in God. Verily I say unto you, whosoever shall say unto this mountain, Be thou taken up and cast into the sea; and shall not doubt in his heart, but shall believe that what he saith cometh to pass; he shall have it. Therefore I say unto you, All things whatsoever ye pray and ask for, believe that ye receive them, and ye shall have them." (Mark 11:22-24.) No doubt we lose many precious blessings because we do not appropriate them by faith. Here, for instance, is some burden or anxiety which we feel is too heavy for us to carry. We avail ourselves of the divine promise and "cast our burden on the Lord." We do so in our prayer, and ask him to take the burden from our hearts. Then, instead of thanking him for having done so, and rejoicing in the fact that he has done so, we go on worrying over it, just as before, not believing that he has fulfilled his promise to us! Jesus knew this weakness of our human natures when he said, "What ye ask for believe that ye receive it, and ye shall have it."

Prayer can only live and thrive in the atmosphere of trust in God and of good will toward all our fellowmen. Distrust in God and all feelings of malice, or envy, or hatred toward others, stifle prayer and rob it of its power. One can not, therefore, live a life of prayer except he cultivate the spirit of trust in his heavenly Father, and of kindly feelings toward all his fellowmen, and seek to put away all known sin from his heart and life.

To preach well is a great achievement; but to pray well is a much greater one. "Have you heard our minister preach?" we were once asked when visiting a church. "No," we replied, "but what is a much better test, we have heard him pray." Spurgeon once asked a visiting preacher to pray, saying: "I never feel that I know a man till I hear him pray." How many preachers prepare their hearts for that most important part of their service, the public prayer?

In view of this teaching of Jesus, and of his own example, we may well doubt if there is sufficient emphasis laid today on the value of prayer, and what prayer is, and its essential conditions. If prayer is the only atmosphere in which men can attain their true spiritual development and accomplish most successfully the great tasks of life, then surely it should have a most prominent place in our pulpits and religious journals, in our church services, in our conventions, and in our daily lives.

Bearing Witness to the Truth.

Jesus told the Roman governor before whose tribunal he had been called, that his mission to this world was to "bear witness to the truth." This, too, is the mission of the Church and of each individual follower of Christ. In this re- spect each Christian must be like his Master—loyal to the truth as God has given him to see the truth. There is this difference, however, which must always be borne in mind: Jesus saw the truth full-orbed, while we only "know in part and prophesy in part." He saw truth in its proper relation and proportion; we often emphasize one phase of it at the expense of another. What is true of each individual is true of the Church as a whole and of the several groups of Christians, separated from each other by their differences, but claiming the leadership of a common Lord.

Not one of these groups, and no indi- vidual member of any of them, sees the truth as a whole, as Jesus saw it, and gives due emphasis to each part of it as he gave. Nevertheless, he expects each individual follower of his to "bear witness to the truth," as he is able to see the truth. He expects his Church to be like its Founder in this respect, and to "bear witness to the truth" as he has given it to see the truth, through evil report as well as through good report. He knows that his disciples do not all see the truth just alike, and he knew that they would not thus see it, from the be- ginning. Nevertheless, he taught them to be one in him, and prayed that they all might be one, even as he and the Father are one. This means that he ex- pects them to be one in the things that are vital and essential—the things with- out which one can not be a Christian— and to have sufficient charity, not to be alienated from each other by unavoida- ble differences in matters not vital. In other words, he expects each of us to give others credit for being true to their own consciences as we are trying to be true to ours. This mutual confidence in each other's sincerity and honesty of conviction in spite of differences of opin- ion is the basis for mutual fellowship. But this is the element that is lacking in the genuine sectarian and bigot. It is hard for him to believe that other people can be honest and differ from him! It is quite impossible for him to believe that others can be Christian while hav- ing a different understanding of some of Christ's teaching. It is just here that the logic-chopper gets in his work, and proves to his own satisfaction that all those who do not interpret Christ's or- dinances, as he does, are non-Christian. That the spirit of Christ is too large to be confined to the grooves of his logic, has never dawned upon him. That Christianity is broader than a syllogism, with a human content in the premises, is a fact he has not yet discovered.

What then? If one may be a Chris- tian with a faulty view; let us say, of the ordinances; if he is a Christian, as Mr. Campbell said, who believes on Christ with his whole heart and obeys him to the full measure of his knowledge of Christ's will, even though that knowl- edge be imperfect, shall we then aban- don our practice of insisting on New Testament conditions of membership in our local churches, as we understand those conditions? That would not be bearing witness to the truth as God has given us to see the truth. If we be- lieve, for instance, that the two ordi- nances bear distinct testimony to great fundamental Gospel facts, and that this testimony is needed to-day and will be needed while the church lasts, we must, so far as in us lies, see that this testi- mony is perpetuated in the Church. God expects us to bear this witness, but he does not expect us to un-Christianize all who do not see these truths as we see them, but rather that we should, in Chris- tian love and forbearance, seek to in- struct them in the way of the Lord more perfectly as respects these matters, while we, on our part, hold ourselves in an attitude to receive instruction from others in those things wherein they may be bearing witness to truths that we have not fully seen nor realized.

In this way, as it seems to us, we may bear witness to the truth as God has given us to see the truth, while "forbear- ing one another in love," as God has given us to know the supreme power and excellence of love. In this way we may be loyal to the truth which Christ taught, and at the same time loyal to the spirit which Christ manifested, and to the prin- ciple of unity for which we plead. To be "sound in faith" is well; to be "sound in charity" is even better. To know the will of Christ is vastly important; but to have the mind of Christ—the spirit of Christ—without which we are none of his—that is vital; that is essential.

❀ ❀

Rules of Church Order.

We are continually receiving inquiries about the proper method of procedure in cases of friction relating to the call- ing or resignation of a minister, or the election or resignation of some officer in the church. There are a few plain, sim- ple, scriptural rules that will meet all these cases, and prevent friction, if they are strictly adhered to. We mention a few of these:

(1) "Do nothing through faction or through vainglory, but in lowliness of mind each counting other better than himself."—Phil. 2:3. . . .

(2) "Let all things be done decently and in order." 1 Cor. 14:40.

(3) "Whatsoever ye do, in word or in deed, do all in the name of the Lord Jesus." Col. 3:17.

(4) "Let all things be done unto edifying." 1 Cor. 14:26.

(5) "Neither as lording it over the charge al- lotted to you, but making yourselves ensamples to the flock." 1 Pet. 5:3.

We guarantee that a faithful observ- ance of these rules of church order will solve all our local church problems re- lating to the calling and dismissal of pas-

Editor's Easy Chair.

When a baby makes his first effort to walk and falls, the parental hand near by catches it, steadies it, and encourages it to try again, until the little fellow has learned to use his legs, and has mastered the art of walking. It is in this spirit that Uncle Sam seems to be dealing with the infant republic of Cuba in its first effort at self-government. The infant has fallen down, it would seem, and failed in its first attempt at independent government. But the beneficent hand of Uncle Sam was there to catch it, and prevent it from self-destruction. He will coach it a little more, help it to get on its feet, and give it a second trial. A very beneficent old gentleman is Uncle Samuel, but he will not hesitate to use a switch if necessary to correct this Antillean youngster, if he shows himself to be obstreperous and inclined to disturb the peace of his neighbors.

The art of self-government is not half so easy as it may seem to an onlooker. It requires the development, in a good degree, of the sterling qualities of courage, self-restraint, love of liberty, and the love of justice which underlies liberty, respect for law, and reliance upon constitutional processes for righting wrongs rather than upon force. Our forefathers had to go to school for many years to develop these virtues, and it may be that Cuba will have to take a few more lessons in the school of experience, before she can acquit herself creditably in the eyes of the world as a self-governing people. We of this great republic have many things yet to learn and to practice before our government, the freest and best on earth, as we believe, shall satisfactorily accomplish all the ends for which government was instituted among men.

If any one thinks we have reached perfection as a government, let him stop to think of how often justice miscarries while the guilty goes unpunished and the innocent suffer; how many good laws are not enforced, and how many bad laws are not repealed; how all legislation hitherto has proved ineffectual in preventing human greed and avarice, acting through corporations and private monopolies, from trampling under their feet the principles of equity and of righteousness, and preying upon the public and especially the helpless classes; let him think of the anomaly of a government, established to insure justice and promote domestic tranquility, legalizing and protecting a traffic like that in intoxicating drinks, which tends continually and only to public demoralization, to domestic brawls and unhappiness, to individual degradation and ruin, to the multiplication of widows and orphans, to poverty and to wretchedness. Some day, please God, we shall get be-

yond all this and look back upon it as we now look back upon the awful cruelties and atrocities which marked the history of the Roman empire.

Welcome October with its brown, russet, yellow, and crimson leaves, its cooler and more bracing atmosphere, with the home-coming of the wanderers and the resumption of activities in church and business circles! This latitude has no more glorious month in all the year than October. There is that in its air which causes the blood to tingle in the veins, quickens the step, intensifies the energy and banishes pessimism from all but the hopeless. To our readers it is always a welcome month because it brings around our great national convocation— the reunion of a mighty host of those committed to the program of Christian union in order to the world's conversion. Many eager eyes are now turned to that queenly city yonder by the lakeside, almost within hearing of the thunder of Niagara, whither our tribes will soon be wending their way to strike glad hands of Christian fellowship, to sit down together in brotherly counsel, and to listen to inspiring reports of progress in the Master's work in this and other lands. Those who by reason of untoward circumstances or indifference, shall fail to attend this great gathering of Disciples at Buffalo, will miss one of the best and most inspiring things which October brings to us.

One of the "songs of ascent" which the Jews used to sing on their way up to Jerusalem to attend their great annual feasts, was:

"I was glad when they said unto me,
Let us go unto the house of Jehovah.
Our feet are standing
Within thy gates, O Jerusalem.

Whither the tribes go up, even the tribes of Jehovah,
For an ordinance for Israel,
To give thanks unto the name of Jehovah."

Another of these songs ran:
"Except Jehovah build the house,
They labor in vain that build it:
Except Jehovah keep the city,
The watchman waketh but in vain."

This was the secret of Israel's strength among the nations—their trust in Jehovah. Let us go up to our Jerusalem leaning on the divine strength and feeling that it is only as God shall build us up that we can grow into a holy temple, a place for his indwelling. I am sure we can all say of our Zion,

"Peace be within thy walls,
And prosperity within thy palaces."

The strength of any people is to make their cause identical with the cause of

God, and thus to feel that his strength is their strength, and his victory is their victory. This is why Jesus said, "Without me ye can do nothing." And this is why Paul said, "I can do all things through Christ who strengtheneth me."

In his tender, reverent prayer the pastor said: "Teach us, O God, that our daily duties are the very altar-stairs that lead up to Thee." Is not this the very lesson that many of us need to learn? We pray for a sense of nearness to God; that he will be with us continually; and this is the desire, no doubt, of every sincere, pious heart. And yet, is it sometimes forgotten that our daily duties, faithfully and conscientiously performed, are the very steps—the "altar stairs"— that lead up to God, and to the sweetest fellowship with him? There are, of course, moments of quiet meditation and prayer in every earnest life, and these can not be dispensed with by one who would know God and enjoy the comfort of his abiding presence. But these periods of repose, and quiet communion with God, need to be supplemented by active toil in meeting the daily duties, and in bearing what would otherwise be the drudgery of our daily tasks, if they are to mean to us all that they are intended to mean. Even prayer soon ceases to be profitable if there be no earnest effort of the soul to do the will of God as that will comes to us in the manifold duties of life. Prayer ceases to be vital when it is no longer an inspiration to sacrifice and labor for human good and for the advancement of the kingdom of God.

We ran across a little anonymous poem the other day that caused some heart-searching. Perhaps it may have that effect upon our Easy Chair readers. It follows:

There is a faith unmixed with doubt,
A love all free from fear;
A walk with Jesus, where is felt
His presence always near.
There is a rest that God bestows,
Transcending pardon's peace,
A lowly, sweet simplicity;
Where inward conflicts cease.

There is a service God-inspired,
A zeal that tireless grows,
Where self is crucified with Christ,
And joy unceasing flows.
There is a being "right with God,"
That yields to His commands
Unswerving, true fidelity,
A loyalty that stands.

There is a meekness free from pride,
That feels no anger rise
At slights, or hate, or ridicule,
But crosses count a prize.
There is a patience that endures
Without a fret or care,
But joyful sings, "His will be done,"
"My Lord's sweet grace I share."

There is a purity of heart,
A cleanness of desire,
Wrought by the Holy Comforter
With sanctifying fire.
There is a glory that awaits
Each blood-washed soul on high,
When Christ returns to take his bride,
With him beyond the sky.

My God! I thank thee who has made
The earth so bright—
So full of splendor and of joy,
Beauty and light;
So many glorious things are here
Noble and right.   —A. A. Proctor.

Our Cause in Arkansas   By J. N. Jessu

A LITTLE HISTORY AS EXPLANATION.

Some time ago I wrote to G. A. Hoffman, our statistician, on behalf of our state board, requesting him to change the representation of Arkansas in our statistical tables from 425 churches to 300, and from 36,000 members to 20,000. I said there were not now and never had been 435 churches and 35,000 members in Arkansas; that figures from this state had always been an exaggerated guess; that no satisfactory count had ever been made; that even the revised figures were probably largely in excess of the actual facts; that the large figures put us in an unfavorable light before the brotherhood, etc., etc.

Brother Hoffman requested me to write an explanation of this state of affairs as it seemed to me. He asked, "Why is this true? Our cause was planted in Little Rock and Fayetteville and other important towns as early as in many other towns." He said: "Give the reasons for our losing growth and why we are not gaining in membership."

I undertake to answer these questions as best I can. The phrase, "reasons for our losing growth" is misleading. We have not lost anything. We simply never had the figures attributed to us. In giving the causes of our slow growth I will name first, the lack of leadership. It is true that our cause was preached here at an early date. Dr. R. F. Hall, of Kentucky, preached in Little Rock and organized a church as early as 1832. J. T. Johnson and R. T. Ricketts, both of Kentucky, preached in Little Rock and Fayetteville in 1845 and 1848. Charles Carlton did some preaching in the state. Robert Graham established a school in Fayetteville just before the war. His school went down in the wreck of the civil war and Brother Graham left the state. Not one of these men who were capable of leadership remained in the state. Arkansas has not a single great name among its pioneers. Arkansas has no Nestor. In this respect the state has been irretrievably impoverished. For twenty-five years after the war there is not a single name of note. Brother N. M. Ragland, of Fayetteville, although he has been in the state twenty years, can not be called a pioneer. Compare this situation with Missouri, Kentucky, Indiana or Ohio. A single name like

Alexander Procter would have immeasurably enriched the pioneer days of Arkansas.

Second, the lack of progressive and aggressive methods, or the prevalence of anti-ism. No states of the union have suffered at the hands of the non-progressive or "anti" element like Tennessee and Arkansas. Tennessee is the fountain head of the most blighting spirit that ever touched our church. Arkansas is next door neighbor to the high apostolic oracle of anti-ism. It was inevitable that Arkansas should suffer the blight of its contagion. Practically all the early preachers of the state took their cue from Nashville and reiterated the Gospel of stagnation throughout this state. The results are sorely manifest. Our cause in nearly every community has been kept in the death valley. Our church in hundreds of places has become a hiss and a byword among the intelligent, cultured and spiritually minded people. It could be said in truth that the spirit of this restoration movement was never preached in this state from the days of Robert Graham (1860) until recent years. Between these dates there is a long stretch of years that, in the history of the Christian church in this state, ought to be known as the "Dark Ages." Two-thirds of the preachers in the state now are the Nashville type of men. To this very good day, when these disintegrating spirits are forced out of Kentucky and Missouri they take refuge in Arkansas, and the small bands of believers that, with the right kind of preachers, would soon make themselves felt for good, become a prey of these men whose touch is death. I have known these men, unable to get support among their own kind, hold their scruples in abeyance and accept work with a progressive church, under the specious plea of reforming that church! The end can easily be forecast. In estimating church statistics these "antis" are put in at full value, when in truth they do not consider themselves of us and in reality have nothing in common with us. This restoration movement has been immeasurably hindered, and in no wise helped by these people.

Third, the lack of a church school.

What Bethany has done for Virginia and the entire east; Kentucky University and the Bible College for Kentucky; Hira for Ohio; Butler for Indiana; Drake for Iowa; Christian and Columbia for Missouri; Texas Christian for Texas Eureka for Illinois—that thing no school or college has done for Arkansas. We have not the slightest sign of a school or college. Who can say what our cause in this state would have been if Robert Graham and his seminary, that was the real beginning of what is now our State University, had remained in Fayetteville? Truly the situation would have been different. This would have been the antidote to all littleness and ignorant, bigoted sectarianism. This school would have sent out scores of young men in this state to preach the spirit of the Master as conceived in the greatest religious movement of the last century. A different story would have been told. I would not now be writing on "the slowness of our growth in Arkansas."

There is one other consideration that should have a place here, and that is the lack of people. Arkansas is a thinly populated state. We have only 900,000 white population. This in 53,850 square miles makes only 16 people to a square mile. Compare this average with Kentucky, 53, or Missouri, 44, and you will see that we have not had the people to work on. Until very recent years Arkansas was an almost unknown land. Migration westward and southward passed over Arkansas as an uninviting land. The immigrant was lured by the vast plains of Texas and Oklahoma and Indian Territory. Consequently the population changed but little and ideas and habits of thought did not change. It can readily be seen that anti-ism, once rooted in the soil here, would long abide. Very few immigrants came in to teach the native people a more excellent way. Anti-ism has been driven from Texas and the territories by northern immigration. If we could have had the immigration into this state that Texas and the territories have had the nonprogressive element would have seen the light and we would have had in every community a nucleus for a live,

J. N. Jessup, Little Rock.   First Christian Church, Little Rock.   E. T. Edmonds, Fort Smith.

progressive and aggressive church. Compared with other states Arkansas, with all its hindrances, has not done so badly. In Indiana, one of the six strong states, we have 5 per cent of the population; in Missouri, another one of the six, we have 6 per cent; in Georgia, less than 1 per cent of white population; in Texas 4½ per cent of white population; in Colorado 1 per cent; in Arkansas 2 per cent white population.

What of the outlook? Better things, far better things are in store for Arkansas. We have now a better body of preachers than ever before; and more are coming all the time. E. C. Browning is now at the head of the state work.

First Christian Church, Fayetteville.

The nonprogressive element is in retreat everywhere. The preachers who train with that crowd are speaking their sentiments "softly." A great transition is coming over the people. The light is shining in the dark places. People have found out the more excellent way. They are demanding progress. Railroads are being built. Anti-ism can not stand the coming of railroads. Railroads bring a more modern type of life, and when a modern type of life appears the antis take to the woods.

Steps are being taken for the establishment of a Bible chair. This seems most feasible now. No school has heretofore been established because we have been a "poor folk." A great transition is coming over the people. We have had no people of large means. That has been true in the past. We lacked both the spirit and the means of building a school. That is true no longer. We have now, the spirit, the enterprise, the money to do worthy things. It will be done.

Arkansas is going to have the people. She is awaking from her sleep of ages. In five years she has become famous. We have just found out that she is one of the richest of states in natural resources. Her vast mineral wealth, her almost boundless tracts of timber, her agricultural possibilities—these have only been touched. And the people are coming; thousands are pouring into the state from the north and east. Our church is sharing the benefits of this incoming multitude. In less than ten years Arkansas will report astonishing things.

Little Rock, Ark.

✿ ✿

—T. N. Kincaid paid THE CHRISTIAN-EVANGELIST force a visit while on his way from Cincinnati where the Clark fund, under control of the Richmond Street Church, has been renewed for two years for the benefit of the work at Hot Springs, Ark.

On the same pages with Brother Jessup's article we place a few illustrations that we have been able to obtain.

E. T. Edmonds, of Fort Smith, Ark., has been pastor of the church there since 1891, with the exception of two years when he served the church at Boston, Mass. From a membership of 100 the church at Fort Smith is now close to the 500 mark. We regret that we have not a photograph of the church building which is one of the best in the state, costing about $35,000, with the lot. The brethren are contemplating the formation of a second church, and the prospects for our cause are good.

Little Rock has the distinction of probably being the first place in Arkansas where preaching was done by any of our pioneers. There was a small church of Baptists meeting in a log house at Little Rock in 1832. Dr. F. R. Hall, of Kentucky, did some preaching for them. After awhile they abandoned the name of Baptist and the Philadelphia Confession of Faith as an authorized statement of doctrine, and determined to call themselves simply Christians, and the church a Church of God or a Church of Christ. An account of this work may be found in the Millennial Harbinger for 1832. The present pastor of the church there, J. Newton Jessup, took up the work in 1898. He is a graduate of Butler University and was pastor at three important points in Indiana prior to entering upon his successful work in Arkansas. The chapel of a new Christian church erected by the congregation of the First Christian church has just been opened, and we give on these pages illustrations of the existing church and of the new chapel. This latter will be occupied for church services, Sunday-school, and auxiliary services while the main auditorium is under construction. The chapel is built of solid brick walls, faced with St. Louis brick of a red granite shade. It is elaborately trimmed with white granite from Carthage, Mo., and its cost has been $15,000. The assembly room on the second floor will accommodate 300 people. The first floor is the Sunday-school department proper. In the basement there

is a large dining hall. The building is thoroughly modern in its appointments and is equipped for all the purposes of a church home.

N. M. Ragland, of Fayetteville, Ark., though not an early pioneer, is one of the preachers most intimately identified with

N. M. Ragland, Fayetteville.

the Church of Christ in Arkansas. E. C. Browning, the corresponding secretary and state evangelist, says of Brother Ragland that "the mantle of Robert Graham could scarcely have fallen on more worthy shoulders." That sweet character established a college at Fayetteville which went down in the wreck of the Civil War. Bro. Ragland was called to the church in 1885 from the pastorate at Carthage, Mo. The fruits of a score of years have more than justified the wisdom of the choice made. The work so well begun by Robert Graham, whose ministry lasted 14 years there, was revived. Beginning with a membership of 80 when Brother Ragland preached his anniversary sermon last November he was able to report to this number had been added 930, the majority of them confessions, during the twenty years, with an enrollment at that time of 300; to this may be added, in part at least, the membership at the Second Church and at Farmington, children of the First Church.

Chapel Just Dedicated at Little Rock.

Hebrew Poetry---Illustrating Nature Treatment in the Psalms

(Concluded from Last Week.)

By JAMES EGBERT

The usual Hebrew method of treating nature is as a chamber of Jahve's Presence or as his garment, his veil through which he ever breaks to reveal himself. Never is nature beautiful in itself. Jehovah makes it resplendent by his shining through. It is beautiful that it may be fitting. They treat nature just as it appears to them—as they see it. At once does the poet pass to God, the great reality. In his brevity he leaves much for the beholder to discover. Rapidly does he pass from image to image. Often does he use concealed imagery.

The ninetieth Psalm is generally known as a service for the burial of the dead. A casual glance suggests gloom. A careful study in view of concealed imagery shows it to be a hymn of mountain sunrise. It is vision that rises from the setting of the concealed image of a mountain sunrise to the climax,

"So teach us to number our days,
That we may get us an heart of wisdom."

No unity in nature treatment is evident. No unity in style. The only unity displayed in the Psalter is true in Jehovah under all circumstances. In battle song or nature lyric, in plant or reverie or national hymn, in pilgrim march or dirge, the one key note is praise to Jehovah who keeps Israel and is faithful forever.

Their treatment of nature is best illustrated in the Psalms themselves. Psalm 29 describes a thunder storm such as one may see in Palestine as it comes down out of the Lebanons and travels the entire land to the south. This storm first disturbs the heavens then falls to earth. The poet at once reads the message across the face of the storm. It is the soul trembling under divine judgment. Men become insensible of God as he comes in graciousness. He must come in a strong way that all may feel him. As the storm raised in heaven crashes to earth's remotest bounds, the highest heights as well as the lowest depths experience the power of Jehovah. In what different ways the different parts of the earth feels this is briefly but vividly portrayed. On the heights the sons of God, the heavenly spirits, experience joy and become jubilant. The dark storm cloud brings to them a new revelation of divine power. On earth there is failure to understand the angry God and there is resistance. On earth the storm prevails. Vast forests and great mountains are swept away before the storm. Even man falls before its terror. Yet the poet is not dismayed. This awful manifestation is but an expression of Jehovah's nearness. He sings,

"Hark, Jahve is on the waters,
The God of Glory thunders,
Jahve is on many waters,
Hark, Jahve, is in his strength."

It is he that rides upon those storm clouds. The terror brings him near. His power is on exhibition, 'tis Jahve that thunders. But he controls the forces of nature. The poet hears from the heights, the palace above, all speaking, "Glory." So may earth be glad. Jahve is King. He rules. Right will triumph. Blessing is secured to earth in the very character of its King—he is all powerful. The poem closes with peace. The poet has a feeling of relief because Jehovah does not always come thus; it is only occasional; he calls it Jahve coming in his holiday attire.

In Psalms 19 we have a calm. The usual Palestinian sky shines. Yet the natural beauty fails to captivate the poet's heart. Beyond this is Jahve. The clear, shining, silent firmament speaks the glory of God. It unveils the divine mind. From the seen to the unseen. From the particulars to the universal, soars the Hebrew mind. This order, splendor, tranquillity—ever in unbroken succession, day unto day and night unto night, tell of the unchangeableness of God.

Psalm 8 is a night-song. The poet under the midnight sky is overwhelmed in the face of the glory of the noon and the myriads of stars. He is made to feel as a child under its splendor. As one in despair he cries out "What is man, frail child of the earth, that thou thinkest of him?" But nature is controlled and ordered by Jehovah. He has made it for man and made man lord over it. So from his quiet contemplation of nature, he feels that man is the crowning work and that glorious is Jahve.

The sixty-fifth is a sweet psalm. It falls in three parts. In the first, history stands as a witness to Jehovah's goodness. In the second, nature joins voices with history in his praise. Here are pictured the mountains, the sea with its billows. The third part carries one along banks of full rivers, through fields of corn growing under the showers, into pastures and meadows, upon heights and into valleys. It is a song of springtime for it is the annual visit of Jehovah. Softness and tenderness combine to make this a beautiful prayer of thanksgiving to Jehovah for his loving kindness.

The one hundred twenty-first Psalm well illustrates how nature appealed to the Hebrews.

"I will lift up mine eyes unto the hills—
From whence cometh my help?"

Not from the hills would the help come. No true Israelite ever got the needed help from the hills. But there was a help beyond the hills. The hills but cut the skyline for the appearance of Jahve. Upon the background of the skyline the poet saw him as the helper and keeper of Israel moving about the sky the clouds as a shield that the sun might not smite.

Psalm 104 is a creation psalm. It is replete with vivid nature pictures. It is no scientific view of creation that he gets, but just as it would appear to one looking out upon the world with the creation story of Genesis as a basis. The universe as the garment of God and he shining through all his attributes is the one sublime thought that underlies the poem. True to the Genesis idea, he begins with light. Jehovah has clothed himself with it. Thus he moves about the heavens, stretching them out like a curtain. The clouds are his chariots, He walks on the wings of the wind. He busies himself in dispatching his servants, wind and fire. Above it all is the thunder—his voice. The waters flee at its sound. Up rise mountains; down sink the valleys. Jehovah is now at work on the earth. Then the poet in order presents picture upon picture of Jehovah adjusting and peopling the earth. To the poet even all nature must look to God for food and renewal—else it would expire and return to the dust. He hears the roar of the lion as a prayer for meat. The completed inhabited earth is all a beauty and a joy save one blot to mar—sin. He closes this magnificent psalm with the customary Jewish feeling, "Be the sinners consumed from the earth, and the wicked be no more." The cause of this sin-blighted earth is man's failure to know God. Israel's inspired poets were ever singing of the time when

"The earth shall be full of the knowledge of
the Lord as the waters cover the sea."

St. Thomas, Ontario.

❀ ❀

CAREFUL DOCTOR

Prescribed Change of Food Instead of Drugs.

It takes considerable courage for a doctor to deliberately prescribe only food for a despairing patient, instead of resorting to the usual list of medicines.

There are some truly scientific physicians among the present generation who recognize and treat conditions as they are and should be treated regardless of the value to their pockets. Here's an instance:

"Four years ago I was taken with severe gastritis and nothing would stay on my stomach, so that I was on the verge of starvation.

"I heard of a doctor who had a summer cottage near me—a specialist from N. Y.—and as a last hope, sent for him.

"After he examined me carefully he advised me to try a small quantity of Grape-Nuts at first, then as my stomach became stronger to eat more.

"I kept at it and gradually got so I could eat and digest three teaspoonfuls. Then I began to have color in my face, memory became clear, where before everything seemed a blank. My limbs got stronger and I could walk. So I steadily recovered.

"Now after a year on Grape-Nuts I weigh 153 lbs. My people were surprised at the way I grew fleshy and strong on this food." Name given by Postum Co., Battle Creek, Mich. Read the little book, "The Road to Wellville," in pkgs.

"There's a reason."

In the Abyss By William Durban

Prelude.

Scotland is mourning the loss of her most refined preacher, Rev. Dr. George Matheson. This renowned Presbyterian has just died suddenly at North Berwick. He was the prince of poet-preachers since the death some years ago of John Pulsford. George Matheson lost his eyesight at the age of 20, yet such were his intellectual and oratorical gifts that he rose to be recognized as one of the most eloquent preachers in the Scottish pulpit. In 1886 he became a minister in the large city congregation of St. Bernard's, Edinburgh, and remained there till his retirement a few years ago. Dr. Matheson was the author of one of the best-known hymns in the Scottish hymnal, "O love that will not let me go," which, set to music by the late Dr. Peace, of Glasgow, is known all the world over. The little "Meditations," which for many years appeared weekly from Dr. Matheson's pen in the London "Christian World," were lyrical gems of prose poetry, each being a cut-gem of thought of purest ray serene. There is no one to fill the place of the blind Scottish preacher as a thinker.

The Bitter Cry of Poor Respectables.

Perhaps my American readers can hardly appreciate what I mean by "poor respectables." Unfortunately, in any European country the expression would be anywhere comprehended with painful and mournful facility. In England, which is far richer than any other country next to the United States (now leading the world in wealth), we are face to face with an appalling problem. Whatever may be the real producing cause, or causes, the vast majority of the British people are struggling with economic conditions of a cruel character. It is true that the vast masses of the working classes are not plunged into the abject penury and the actual want of decent food that they suffered in the days after the Battle of Waterloo, and before the famous repeal of the corn laws by Sir Robert Peel 70 years since. But though the standard of living for the great working class has risen yet the greater part of these are toiling even now for very little more than a bare subsistence, and one in every seventeen of our population is a pauper dependent on charity, while incalculable numbers are always on the verge of becoming such. But there is a very large section more to be pitied. Education is now practically universal and millions of the people are really cultured. I rarely meet any fellow citizen of either sex who could be called ignorant or illiterate. The generaly intelligence of the people, indeed, astonishes me. I knew that when I was a lad it was needful for preachers, if they had sympathy with the common people and were anxious to be understood by them, to use the simplest diction in the pulpit, and to refrain from indulging in elaborate or profound thought. But the conditions have altogether changed. Multitudes of our mechanics and poor laborers are capable of writing, when they feel impelled, letters to the newspapers in their grievances. These appear in great numbers, and many of them would do credit to a professor of political economy. But at this moment an agonizing correspondence is in full blast. It relates to the sad conditions of many thousands of well educated people who can find no way of gaining a livelihood.

Before the Abyss.

Hundreds of lurid and tragic letters have been appearing in the London "Daily News" during the past few weeks, disclosing the position in which the writers find themselves. They all proclaim themselves just about to fall into the abyss of want and despair, unless some extraordinary interposition of Providence should save them from the threatened doom. All are highly respectable. All have lived in good society. All have behaved well. They are victims of misfortune, owing to our social conditions. And no one seems to know what to advise them to do. The editors confess themselves puzzled. Here then we have in old England, with all its vast wealth, a cataract of humanity tumbling over into the black gulf from the depths of which very few ever emerge. The victims fall out of sight, wither and perish, uncared for and unknown. This is a condition of things unknown in America and other new countries. But new countries will become old. The United States will fill up. Then the crucial social problems which challenge solution there also, if the same social system is to continue. Is that system of God's ordinance? This is, I make bold to say, the paramount question which will call for answer in the near future. Are countless numbers of people who are willing to work, and are capable of doing useful work in various directions, to be condemned to failure and to misery through no fault of their own?

The Churches Indicted.

Of course a loud outcry is being raised and re-echoed against the churches and against Christianity, because religion seems helpless in face of the dire needs of myriads who only need timely aid and find none to succor them. In this country the rich are growing richer, and the poor are growing poorer. Here is the reason why I write this article. A great responsibility lies on the aggregate Christian Church today. Humanity is beginning everywhere to murmur impatiently at a state of society which can not possibly be in accordance with the mind of the Son of Man. The socialist dream is of course a delusion; but increasing numbers of the people in Germany, France and Britain are becoming dreamers in that direction. I am aware of the splendid efforts of the various institutional churches, but your American Dr. Dixon, of Boston, who has just resigned the pastorate of such a church in Boston, declares that from a spiritual point of view that kind of church is a failure. He found that the employment agency, etc., was "a millstone round the neck of the church." Moreover, he holds that the institutional church, besides helping to pauperize some, repels the self-respecting poor who are not in need of assistance. This is a very serious conclusion, because in Britain the institutional church is in many quarters imagined to be a short cut to the millennium, and there is to-day a tendency rapidly growing to look on all ordinary churches as antiquated cumberers of the ground, or as religious drawing-rooms and social clubs, where comfortable, selfish and luxurious folk enjoy themselves during a good time on earth while passing on to the celestial drawing-rooms reserved for them in the mansions of the blessed. That is the sort of sentiment cherished and now being sullenly expressed amongst large and growing members of the British proletariat. I can not say that I wonder at it. In another early communication I may say why.

❀ ❀

RIGHT HOME
Doctor Recommends Postum from Personal Test.

No one is better able to realize the injurious action of caffeine—the drug in coffee—on the heart, than the doctor.

When the doctor himself has been relieved by simply leaving off coffee and using Postum, he can refer with full conviction to his own case.

A Mo. physician prescribes Postum for many of his patients because he was benefited by it. He says:

"I wish to add my testimony in regard to that excellent preparation—Postum. I have had functional or nervous heart trouble for over 15 years, and part of the time was unable to attend to my business.

"I was a moderate user of coffee and did not think drinking it hurt me. But on stopping it and using Postum instead, my heart has got all right, and I ascribe it to the change from coffee to Postum.

"I am prescribing it now in cases of sickness, especially when coffee does not agree, or affects the heart, nerves or stomach.

"When made right it has a much better flavor than coffee, and is a vital sustainer of the system. I shall continue to recommend it to our people, and I have my own case to refer to." Name given by Postum Co., Battle Creek, Mich. Read the little book, "The Road to Wellville," in pkgs. "There's a reason."

As Seen From the Dome By F. D. Pow[ell]

I do not know that I can define religion. The word occurs but five times in the Bible. Some derive it from a Latin word to "reconsider," others from a word signifying "to bind fast." The first is Cicero's and it is the reasonable origin. So religion would denote diligent study of whatever pertains to the worship of God, and those who show great zeal in this were called *religiosi*, and their conduct *religio*. The foundation of all religion rests upon belief in the existence of God, and the work of religion deals with man's duty to God. There is such a thing as the science of religion. Science has three steps: Observation of facts, induction of laws, verification of these laws by experiment. Facts of conscience, faith, hope, love, are real; moral laws are real; the verification of these laws is real; spiritual experiences are real. Nothing is more real than religion. In my recent travels I observed this fact, that everywhere we came face to face with religion. In Egypt before Christ, before the Trojan war, before the time of Homer or the commonwealth of Israel there was religion. Go up the Nile. One sees what was once splendid buildings with walls covered with carved figures and hieroglyphic inscriptions; groups of pyramids; old Memphis, Thebes, Karnak, Luxor; temples, palaces, obelisks, majestic tombs; every town its. Gods, every day its festival, every street its temple; priests, prayers, incense, processions, festivals, hymns and rituals; even dogs, cats and crocodiles worshiped, and over all, one supreme being.

We are in Athens. It is the time of the Pan-Athenaic festival. All Greece comes to do homage to the Virgin Goddess. It is the age of Pericles, Phidias, Sophocles, Euripides, Socrates. Anaxagoras has first taught the doctrine of one Supreme being and Aspasia has the same thought. There they go. We can picture the scene. Old men carrying green granches of olive, soldiers with shields and spears, strangers with boats showing they came from afar, women with pots of sacred water, young men singing hymns, virgins of noble families carrying in baskets implements of sacrifice. So they wind up the Acropolis, covered with temples of polished marble, on to the Parthenon, the one structure in all the world to-day of unsurpassed majesty. Egyptian worship was somber, mysterious; that of the Greeks bright and joyous.

We may go farther into Asia. Another race, speaking a different language, we shall find, worshiping other gods; a vast priesthood, temples, sacrifices, prayers; hymns to the sun, the heavens, the dawn, fire, air, the elements. Time disappears; Eternity is in the heart. To be absolved in God is their thought. In Persia, another great race and religion. The supreme being is worshiped under symbol of fire. Without the Egyptian idea of transmigration, or the Greek thought of festivity, but the mighty battle between good and evil—Ormazd and Ahriman. In the deserts of Arabia among its wandering peoples, a man comes forth with a great religious conviction—faith in a supreme being and abhorrence of all inferior worship, and soon all the world of his time is aflame with his idea.

So everywhere, from the earliest times, among Assyrians, Babylonians, Phoenicians, Carthaginians, Druids, Astecs—in China, Japan, Burmah, Thibet—religion, religion, religion! Where did they come from? What is their value? Wherein do they differ? Wherein do they agree? What is the great lesson we draw from this universal acknowledgment of man's need of God and man's relation to God?

Take up the great names which give evidence of this universal condition. Here is Job, greatest of all the men of the East, who wrote the greatest poem in human history on the greatest problem of human experience. Here is Solomon, one of the most extraordinary characters named in the Holy Scriptures, the wisest of men. "Thou Solomon, my son, know thou the God of thy father, and serve him with a perfect heart and willing mind, for the Lord searcheth all hearts. If thou seek him he will be found of thee, but if thou forsake him he will cast thee off forever." And Solomon sums up all wisdom in one word: "Fear God and keep his commandments, for this is the whole of man"—not the whole duty, nor the whole interest, but "the whole of man"! Here is Cyrus, the most accomplished prince of profane history. "He is my shepherd and shall perform my pleasure." Dying, he calls his children about him: "Fear the Deity who never dies; who sees all things; whose power is infinite. Fear him and let that fear prevent you from ever doing or deliberating to do anything contrary to religion and virtue." Here is Socrates, greatest of heathen, whose life and death are full of religious spirit and beauty and power; and here is Confucius, the Chinese philosopher, of exalted piety, dying lamented by an empire. Here is Paul. "Behold, I go bound in the spirit to Jerusalem, not knowing the things that shall befall me there; save that in every city bonds and afflictions abide me. But none of these things move me, neither count I my life dear unto myself, so that I might finish my course with joy and the ministry which I have received of the Lord Jesus, to testify the Gospel of the grace of God. I am ready to be offered up and the time of my departure is at hand. I have fought a good fight, I have finished my course, I have kept the faith: henceforth there is laid up for me a crown of righteous-

ness which the Lord, the righte[ous] judge, shall give me at that day." H[ere] is Ignatius, facing the wild beasts. H[ere] is Polycarp in the flame. Here is Louis IX of France, and Charles V [of] Germany, Jane, Queen of Navarre, Lady Jane Gray, Walter Raleigh, Ba[con] and Oxenstiern, Grotius, John Sel[den,] "the glory of the English nation," I[s]masius, Dante, Pascal, Sir Isaac N[ew]ton, Victoria, Gladstone. Here is [the] supreme court of the United States, greatest, the most powerful tribunal on earth; the body which sets aside decr[ees] of presidents and congresses, and wh[ich] is supposed to be made up of the gre[at]est masters in the matter of weigh[ing] evidence; and from the foundation [of] the government, made up of Christ[ian] men, religious men; not a skeptic e[ver] on the bench!

What a power religion has over minds and hearts and lives of men! W[ith] an impossible thing to root out and dest[roy] that which is so woven into histo[ry]. Society, literature, government—all [is] warp and woof of the life of man w[hich] is always and everywhere a religious [an]imal! What folly to think of religi[on] as so many sermons, as so many de[vo]tions, as so many church meetin[gs,] when religion means habitual recoll[ec]tion of God and service to man; and far from being something for dyspe[p]tics, and invalids, nervous people a[nd] women, finds its highest expression [in] men and women of robust bodies a[nd] lofty intellects and divine spirits. T[he] world's greatest bear this testimony. Now the test of any religion is [its] fruits. This is true of a nation, an a[ge,] an individual, a religion. What is t[he] story of Mohammedism? Let Turk[ey] answer. What is the record of Bud[d]hism? Let India bear witness. What [is] the merit of Confucianism? Let Chi[na] say. What is the fruit of Christianit[y?] Let England speak. Let America g[ive] its testimony. "Ye shall know them [by] their fruits." An infidel was lecturi[ng] in a village in the north of England, a[nd] at the close, challenged discussion. W[ho] should accept the challenge but a be[nt] old woman, in most antiquated atti[re] who arose and said: "Sir, I have a question to put to you." "Well, [my] good woman, what is it?" "Ten ye[ars] ago I was left a widow, with eight ch[il]dren, utterly unprovided for, and nothi[ng] to call my own but this Bible. By [its] direction and looking to God for stren[gth] I have been enabled to feed myself a[nd] my family. I am now tottering to [the] grave, but I am perfectly happy [be]cause I look forward to a life of imm[or]tality with Jesus in heaven. That [is] what my religion has done for me. W[hat] has your way of thinking done [for] you?" "Well, my good lady," sta[m]mered the lecturer, "I don't want to di[s]turb your comfort, but"—"O, that [is] not the question! Keep to the poi[nt,] sir. What has your way of thinki[ng] done for you?" The infidel endeavor[ed] again to shirk. The feeling of the me[eting] gave way to uproarious applau[se] and the lecturer had to slink away d[is]comfited by an old woman. "You sh[all] know them by their fruits. Do m[en] gather grapes of thorns or figs of th[is]tles?"

Our Budget

—Buffalo next week!

—Have you made your arrangements?

—See page 1284 for some particulars.

—If you can not go on "THE CHRISTIAN-EVANGELIST Special" train, go on another. But be sure to go. The convention is the main thing, not the train.

—See "Editorial Notes" for news from the societies.

—Col. Alexander Campbell, the oldest son of Alexander Campbell, founder of Bethany College, died last week at his home in Bethany, Brook county, W. Va., after a painful illness extending over a period of several months. Death was due to heart trouble and paralysis. He was in his seventy-fifth year. Colonel Campbell was perhaps best known in the south, where he served with distinction throughout the civil war in the Confederate army, and he was, at one time, prominent in political circles. We must reserve until our next issue a fuller account of his life.

—Next week we shall publish what we may call an "Alexander Campbell Pictorial Number." We have had this in view for some time, and it is something of a coincidence that the death of the oldest living son of Alexander Campbell should have occurred just about the time we had set for the production of this number. It will contain articles by some of our best-known writers who, through special familiarity with Alexander Campbell and his life and work, are peculiarly fitted for such service. This issue will be illustrated by a great many valuable pictures, many of which have not before been published. Every member of the Christian churches who has any interest in the history and the progress of the Campbellian movement will wish to have a copy of this number. As we can print only a limited number beyond our regular circulation, those who wish extra copies should write at once to our subscription department, placing their order and enclosing stamps for the same. The price will be 5 cents per copy, 25 cents per dozen and $4 per hundred. We believe that a great many preachers will see the value of every member of their churches having a copy of this issue.

—We have received an account of the recent twenty-first anniversary of the Englewood Church, Chicago, but too late for any consideration in our columns this week. We wish brethren would favor us with their reports immediately after the occurrence of any important event. We value it far more when it is fresh news, and much prefer brevity and promptness rather than detailed reports that reach us late and after they have been, perhaps, published elsewhere. This is the time of year when the pressure on our columns is greatest.

—Charles Reign Scoville is still holding great meetings. At present he is at Sullivan, Ill., from which point he has sent us an article which we requested from him, on the union meetings recently held at Monroe, Wis. We hope to find space for this in our next week's issue.

—J. R. Sparks has located at Raven, Va.

—After November 1 D. F. Sellards gives up the work at Leon, Ia.

—The new pipe organ just installed at the Jefferson Street Church of Christ, Buffalo, is to be formally opened this evening.

—The new church building is rapidly nearing completion at Ottumwa, Ia.

—A. C. Corbin, late of Ashland, has just entered upon the pastorate at Dallas, Ore.

—The beautiful new church building at Lohrville, Ia., is nearing completion.

—G. L. Bush is now at work with the Dixon Street Church, Gainesville, Tex.

—Lee Tinsley has closed his work at Olney, Ill., to take up the pastorate at Nineveh, Ind.

—J. A. Barnett is arranging to leave Pekin, Ill., soon to take up the work in Freeport.

—E. E. Lowe has taken charge of the First Christian Church at San Bernardino, California.

—J. W. McGarvey, Jr., Lexington, Ky., contemplates entering the evangelistic field.

—Texas Christian University has opened with the largest enrollment in its history.

—I. N. McCash is suffering from inflammatory rheumatism and is unable to leave his bed.

—W. D. Endres has entered Chicago

W. W. Sniff, of Rushville, Ind., a Convention Speaker.

University where he expects to remain for a couple of years.

—We regret to record the death of E. W. Miller, who was well known in northwest Iowa.

—The brethren at Lacona, Ia., have purchased a lot and moved their church building onto it.

—F. F. Guyman, singing evangelist, is with Geo. L. Peters, of South Joplin, Mo., in a good meeting.

—C. H. Strawn, of Prairie City, Ia., has been elected president of the central district of that state.

—Horace Pearce has resigned at Mt. Vernon, Mo., and may be secured as pastor by some good church.

—G. Lyle Smith has for the second time entered upon the pastorate of the church at Terrell, Texas.

—The state of the cause is advancing at Mt. Ayr, Ia., where O. M. Johnson has recently taken charge.

—A. N. Cooper, late of Muir, Mich., is expected to take up the pastorate at Laurens, Ia., October 6.

—We regret to lose J. D. Babb from Missouri. He has gone to Burlington, Colo., to make this his future home.

—James W. Zachary has just dedicated a church near Sterling, O. T. He is tired of roaming and would like to locate.

—We are glad to announce that W. F. Hamann has just been chosen president of the Ministers' Alliance, Sedalia, Mo.

—John S. Sweeney recently held a short meeting at Old Union, Ill., where he preached his first sermon fifty years ago.

—E. W. Bowers, who has for some time been temporary pastor at Marshalltown, Ia., will enter the evangelistic field.

—The Church Extension offering of the church at Niantic, Ill., J. W. Walters, pastor, was nearly double its apportionment of $25.

—Oren Orahood who has been supplying at Covington, Ind., his home town, during the summer, has located at Martinsburg, W. Va.

—Claude E. Miller will serve the church at Tiffin, Ia. This engagement was entered into as a result of one Sunday's service.

—M. M. Davis recently dedicated a remodeled and enlarged church at Charlotte, Kan., where G. W. Kitchen is the popular pastor.

—J. A. Erwin, late missionary to Porto Rico, has entered upon the pastorate of the Christian church at Dayton-Belvue, Ky.

—W. W. Burks, of Nevada, Mo., has been enjoying a vacation at Las Vegas, New Mexico. His church is planning for a big meeting in November.

—L. B. Haskins, of Erlanger, Ky., will retire from that pastorate not later than the end of the year and desires to give his whole time to one church.

—The Foreign Society his just received a direct gift of $5,000 from a friend of the work. This is a source of great encouragement to the managers of the society.

—It is at the church at Bethsaida, Ark., and not at Arkadelphia, as reported in "Our Budget" last week, that E. S. Allhands has organized an Endeavor society.

—H. E. Wilhite has just entered upon the hardest field that he has ever found, so far as immediate results are concerned—South Chicago—but he feels encouraged.

—S. L. Lyon writes that he did resign, as announced in our Ohio notes, but that his people will not let him leave them this year. So he will not go to Oberlin, but remain at Rushsylvania.

—As a result of a good meeting at Luther, Ia., held by C. L. Organ, $1,200 were raised on the last night, for a building, and a plow was procured and ground broken that night.

—C. J. Sharpe, minister at Hammond, Ind., is one of the preachers who preaches during his vacation. As a result of his efforts in a tent meeting at Whiting, Ind., we will now have a good church.

—The Baptist church at Polo, Ill., was recently purchased by our brethren and has just been dedicated. F. A. Sword, the recently called pastor, is following the dedication with a meeting.

—Boyd White writes us that the work at Mount Healthy, O., is opening up with fine prospects. It is expected that a mission work at New Burlington, a rural field of great promise, will be opened soon.

—The new building of the First Christian Church, Atlanta, Ga., which, when completed, will be one of the best equipped church buildings in the city, will be ready for use before many weeks.

—C. F. Ward has just taken the work at Boone, Iowa. He feels that the outlook there is very good. Our church has an $18,000 building. Brother Ward speaks well of his late field and the people he has left.

—As an immediate result of an excellent meeting held by A. R. Spicer at Loraine, Ill., the church will call a minister for all time and will remodel and enlarge what is already the best church in town.

—F. F. Walters, of Neosho, is assisting W. F. Turner and the First Church of Joplin, Mo., in a fine meeting. Brother Walters has ten calls for meetings now which he can not answer. He is a strong preacher and worker.

—President Hill, of Drake University, reports that that institution has opened the most auspicious year in its history. One hundred more have enrolled than the same period in any other year. The enrollment of the Bible College is unusually large.

—Extensive improvements have been made on the lot and house of worship at Eureka, Cal., where I. H. Teel is pastor. A sermon just preached on "Fallacious Claims of Modern Divine Healers," was published in full in the city daily paper.

—W. T. Clarkson, formerly of Lawrence, Kan., is now doing graduate work in the Columbia University and Union Theological Seminary, New York. He was invited to preach on a recent Sunday in a Presbyterian church at Huntington, Long Island.

—J. W. Baker, of Joplin, is in a good meeting at Sarcoxie, Mo. He will later hold meetings at Villa Heights, Joplin and Granby. He has so many calls for meetings that he has about decided to enter the general evangelistic field after November.

—A movement has been on foot to send Allen Hickey to the Buffalo convention at the expense of the Iowa brethren, but Brother Hickey has already arranged to go to Washington where he would like to engage in missionary work.

—We regret to learn of the death of Mrs. Grace Hugh, wife of Louie Hugh, the Chinese missionary under the employ of the C. W. B. M., at Portland, Ore. She was a very effective worker and thoroughly devoted to the ministry of the Christian church.

—The board of officers at Albany, Ind., have voted to send B. F. Cato, their pastor, to the Buffalo Convention. J. H. O. Smith is to be with them in a meeting in January. During Brother Cato's recent vacation he preached thirty-seven times and had twenty-seven additions to the churches.

—We regret to learn of the death of Mrs. Matthew Small. She was a most effective helper to her good husband, who is the brother of the better known James Small, one of our leading evangelists. We have received no information other than the fact of this good woman's death.

—J. E. Davis, of Beatrice, Neb., was a pleasant visitor at THE CHRISTIAN-EVANGELIST office last week. Brother Davis was about the business of the brethren who are arranging to erect at once a $30,000 church building. We congratulate pastor and people on this sign of Christian zeal and life.

—Roland A. Nichols has preached his farewell sermon in the Highland Street Church of Christ, Worcester, Mass. Austin P. Finley will be his successor and take up the work October 21. He is to make his first appearance in New England, October 7, when he will preach before the convention at Manton, R. I., after which

he goes to the National Convention at Buffalo.

—W. A. Dameron, who has been studying at Christian University, Canton, Mo., has just been invited to succeed C. E. Wagner in the pastorate at Shelbyville, Mo. Brother Wagner, who leaves the church there in a fine condition will enter upon the pastorate at Yates Center, Kan., early in this month.

—F. F. Grim has just closed his work at Leaday, Texas. On account of the death of Mrs. Lea the plans for the building of a school have been suspended for the present. Brother Grim goes to San Angelo, Texas, for a rest before accepting work elsewhere. We trust there will be soon a good opening for so faithful a man.

—The veteran N. A. Walker finds that total indifference is the greatest obstacle to successful work at Douglas, Ill. There was no church to help him, but at the close of the meeting, in which he preached four weeks and Alfred Tucker two, twenty-seven names were taken to form a church, some of them among the best people of the town.

—B. S. Ferrall, chairman of the pulpit supply of the Buffalo convention, has arranged for 115 different services with eleven different religious bodies, for Sunday, October 14. A great Y. M. C. A. mass meeting and a Y. W. C. A. vesper service on the same day will be addressed by well known representatives in attendance upon the convention.

—D. Millar is in a very successful meeting at Grove, Ind. From there he goes to Mendon, Mo., where he will have the assistance of 300 CHRISTIAN-EVANGELISTS each week. Brother Millar has open dates through November and December. Churches will be entitled to congratulations that secure his services for these weeks.

—W. F. Turner, pastor of the First Church, Joplin, Mo., spoke for the Foreign Christian Missionary Society recently at the Oklahoma Convention at El Reno, and at the Kansas Convention at Parsons. He also made the address for the American Missionary Society at Parsons. Brother Mohorter and others testify as to the worth of Brother Turner's address.

—A. E. Cory, our missionary to China, who returns to his field November 20, is now in a meeting with the church at Oskaloosa, Iowa. He was formerly pastor of that church. He hopes to make it a living link in the Foreign Society before the meeting closes. He will be stationed in China at Wuhu, the city formerly occupied by T. J. Arnold, who recently died.

—Horace Siberell expects to begin a meeting at Moorehouse, Mo., about the 15th of this month. This is a new place where the people know very little about our plea. Brother Siberell realizes the help that a good religious paper can give him under these conditions and will make use of THE CHRISTIAN-EVANGELIST. Brother Siberell is now in a meeting at Naylor, Mo.

—L. L. Carpenter, of Wabash, Ind., dedicated during the month of September churches at the following places: Auburn, Ind.; Forest City, Ark.; Olive Branch, Ind.; New Palestine, Ind., and Fayette, O. At each place he raised money enough to provide for all indebtedness, and at Forest City, Ark., $500 additional to apply on a new personage.

—W. J. Frost, writing from Houston, Mo., says he is just home from the joint convention of the churches of Texas and Wright counties, held at Mountain Grove. It was a good convention for a first one. The preachers present included Brothers Hicks, Morris, Hunt, Frost, Gaylor and Abbott. Mrs. Hooten organized an auxiliary to the C. W. B. M. Towards start-

ing an evan[...] scribed. All [...]

—John L. [...] recovered fr[...] expects to b[...] future.

—Owen I. [...] pastorate la[...] at Spartanb[...] has hitherto [...] preaching. [...] made possib[...] winter by M. [...] Ind. Brothe[...] gin a meetin[...] Willard Guy, [...] versity, mini[...] with C. C. S[...] tinsville, O. [...] nizes the val[...] one aim of [...] put a CHR[...] home connec[...]

—O. M. [...] Wash., has re[...] enter the eva[...] ing will be at [...] ris is minister [...] Waterville, [...] Chelan, Cash[...] er Thomason [...] position of st[...] kota.

—The Ma[...] City, Ind., is [...] most success[...] munity. The [...] night; the c[...] thusiastic as [...] meeting of th[...] at Cairo, Ill. [...] til March 10, [...] Clarinda, Ia. [...] that their ne[...] vicinity.

—The offeri[...] eign and home [...] en by the ch[...] amount was [...] among these [...] best the churc[...] able it to sta[...] the Church I[...] Darsie has jus[...] the church. D[...] been added to [...] Jennie Jenkin[...] of pastoral he [...] The Bible sch[...] between six na[...]

—"Christian [...] church, to whi[...] EVANGELIST c[...] of our reader[...] the new churc[...] pletion and w[...] the pews can [...] the pastor, h[...] meeting at Br[...] son, the pasto[...] "We all fell i[...] and think it [...] able to do s[...] Brookfield. S[...] intending to g[...] church buildin[...]

Drake's Pal[...] etable compo[...] tite, assist di[...] er and Kidn[...] ache, Dyspe[...] ness and cons[...] er of this pa[...] secure a tea[...] you quick rel[...] and cost you [...] day to The D[...]

—O. G. Blackwell, the. Indiana evangelist, accompanied by his singer, is helping E. J. Church in a meeting at Seneca, Mo. These brethren are aided also by 300 CHRISTIAN-EVANGELISTS per week. Brother Church's high standing with the Seneca public, together with the talent he has rallied to his support, almost insures a splendid meeting.

—H. O. Breeden has resigned the pastorate of the Central Christian Church, Des Moines, Iowa, after twenty-one years of service. This has been a great pastorate and we have asked Brother Breeden to favor us with some of the lessons that he has gleaned from it. The resignation is to take effect January 1. Brother Breeden's main reason is his desire to engage in evangelistic work.

—We are glad to report that the thirteenth anniversary services of the Hammett Place Christian Church, St. Louis, were very enjoyable. On Lord's day evening the Editor of THE CHRISTIAN-EVANGELIST preached, and at the conclusion of the sermon made an appeal for the clearing off of the debt of the building. This amounted to $1,800 and before the meeting adjourned two dollars more than this sum were pledged to be paid during the coming year.

—Two hundred rigs in a parade and over 5,000 people at the rally speak well for the interest in Sunday-school work in Mitchell county, Kan. David H. Shields, who is the minister of the Christian Church, as well as the mayor, at Salina, Kan., recently gave the annual address at this rally, and he has been engaged as a speaker for next year. Brother Shields also made two of the addresses at the simultaneous temperance rally which the churches of Hutchinson, Kan., had last Lord's day.

—J. H. Mohorter, General Secretary of the Benevolent Association, is having a round of conventions. He reports the one in Kansas as being fine. At its close a collection was taken to pay for the admission of Brother Bell, an old Kansas preacher, to one of our homes. In West Virginia enthusiasm was great. Brother Mohorter spent one Sunday with the church at Wilmington, Ohio, and another with Vernon Stauffer at Angola, Ind., where he had a great day. He has just been at Ladysmith attending the Wisconsin convention. All reports go to show that Brother Mohorter is heart and soul in his work for benevolence, and his efforts are being recognized by the brotherhood.

—We have just received the following pathetic, yet inspiring, letter. It is addressed to the general superintendent, and is in reply to a communication from him:

DEAR BROTHER: Your favor of Aug. 7 is before me and communications received before from your loving hand. But I could not answer for I could not write, and now I have a lap-board and hold my pencil with both hands with the end against my breast to try to write these lines. I have been unable to feed myself for nearly two years. I cannot travel any more. I will be 70 years old Jan 9 and I have preached 56 years. My work is done for this life and it pains my heart to think of laying down the sword while there is so much to do. Tell the young brethren to fight on till the victory is won for Christ. I can only pray for victory while others fight. My good wife has to feed me. Pray for me in my affliction.—Wm. Judd, Tivoli, Oklahoma.

—We hear a good report of the church at Maplewood, Mo. F. A. Mayhall has recently entered upon the pastorate there and seems to have done much in reconciling the interests that have not always worked harmoniously. The regular collections are the best in the history of the church. There were nineteen additions during the months of July and August and the most encouraging feature of the work is the deepening of the spiritual life. On September 16 it was reported that $1,200 had been raised in cash to wipe out the present indebtedness of the church, and this day the Bible school brought forth the largest collection and the largest attendance that the school has known, the 210 present giving a collection of $55.23 as against the previous high water mark of 103 attendance and $15.35 collection. We rejoice to hear of this forward step and the unity now prevailing without which there can be no successful work in such a place as Maplewood.

—"I am beginning to think 'Put me off at Buffalo.'" So writes W. A. Fite, who certainly deserves to enjoy the pleasure a visit to the convention city will have. He is doing good work for the church at Windsor, Mo. The church extension offering just taken there amounts to $60, about three times what was given last year. Of the value of a religious paper Brother Fite writes: "It is possible for a church to have several preachers at once when its members are reading our religious papers." He highly commends the lectureship course recently given by W. J. Lhamon. The following report of the work at Windsor speaks for itself: "We have recently installed the individual communion cups with which we are very much pleased; put in a fine granitoid walk and steps. We have been using 'Gloria in Excelsis' for almost a year and pronounce it par excellence. We have put in a Sunday-school teachers' library and propose to have an up-to-date Sunday-school. We have the teacher training course, in which much interest is being taken. This church undertakes to give the Gospel to Bowen, a church four miles from Windsor, which has no organization or house of any faith. We have rented a tent and began the work of evangelization yesterday. We shall be missionary at home and remember the missionary enterprises away from home.". Yes, we believe W. A. Fite has a good right to say "Put me off at Buffalo."

—Bro. Charles C. Chapman, Fullerton, Cal., responding to our appeal for funds to assist in establishing our cause in Manchester, N. H., by enclosing us a cheque for $50 and expressing his interest in the work in New England, adds this important word of news concerning the wonderful progress of the cause in southern California, in which he himself has borne so honorable a part:

"Our work is progressing splendidly in southern California. In Los Angeles alone in just one year closing yesterday I have assisted in dedicating four new church buildings, and there was one more built. Our people in southern California are very active, and the demands are great on all those who have funds to give, yet I feel it is an opportune time, and we should make a splendid effort to establish as many churches as possible. Yesterday we dedicated the Naomi Street Church, Los Angeles, a beautiful, artistic building costing something like $15,000. The Sunday before I assisted in Pasadena in raising funds for their new $50,000 building. The congregation has a magnificent lot and over half the amount for the building and equipment. All honor to our business

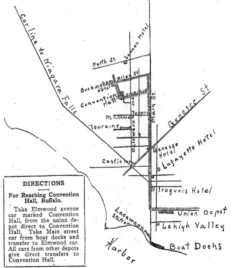

DIRECTIONS

For Reaching Convention Hall, Buffalo.

Take Elmwood avenue car marked Convention Hall, from the union depot direct to Convention Hall. Take Main street car from boat docks and transfer to Elmwood car. All cars from other points give direct transfers to Convention Hall.

men who are putting their time and means at the service of Christ.

—"LeBaron and Conrad" is a new evangelistic combination. The first meeting these brethren have held together was at the Mount Olive church, Macon county, Mo., where 35 were added to the church. They are now at Laplata, Mo. Irving Taylor LeBaron has had 18 years' experience in the field and the results of his work both in additions and church build-

Irving Taylor Le Baron, Evangelist.

ings that have followed his meetings testify to his fitness for this kind of service. Brother LeBaron makes use of canvas illustrations and for special work a fine stereopticon. L. Byron Conrad, who is asso-

L. Byron Conrad, Singer.

ciated with him as leader of music, is the possessor of several medals won for his ability as a vocalist and conductor, and, what is better, he can use his gift for the advancement of the cause of Christ. Macon, Mo., is the headquarters of these brethren.

❀ ❀

If extremely low colonist rates to California, Oregon, Washington and all points west will interest you, write L. E. Townsley, G. A. Union Pacific R. R. Co., 903 Olive, St. Louis.

—Frank L. Van Voorhis has resigned at Okmulgee, I. T., though against the wishes of the congregation and the community. The work is well established there and a new building has recently been dedicated. During the twenty-six months that Brother Van Voorhis has been there, our brethren, from being merely recognized, have grown to be the leading congregation in the community. While going through the laborious trials of building, 150 were added to the church roll and 65 other additions were won through the labors of Brother Van Voorhis at other places. He has been called to Shawnee and believes that the work there needs what he feels himself capable of doing, with the Divine help.

—"Vacation is over. Now let us devote ourselves diligently to our vocation," writes J. P. Litchenberger in his little church paper. Brother Litchenberger's vacation was passed in holding two meetings, one at Tazewell and the other at Graham, Va., which resulted in ninety-nine additions to the churches. Brother Lichtenberger thus did not forget his vocation. He is on the conven-

J. P. Lichtenberger.

tion program of the American Christian Missionary Society and his address on the subject of "Evangelism" will be listened to with great interest, especially by ministers of city churches.

❀ ❀

For a Church in New Hampshire.

Previously acknowledged .....$ 968 25
Mrs. E. M. Griffis............. 3 50
C. C. Chapman................ 50 00

Total $1,021 75

Bro. J. H. Garrison's San Francisco pledge to the brotherhood to make every possible effort for the establishment of a church in New England before the Buffalo convention has been grandly redeemed. He has given more money to the enterprise than one in his circumstances and subject to his countless calls for help ought to be permitted to give; he used rare discrimination in sending thither an evangelist especially adapted to that peculiar field; from a sanguine heart overflowing with sympathy and courage he sustained the preacher through the early discouragements; he has arranged with our National C. W. B. M. for the early location of a pastor there and the thorough organization and nurturing of the young church until it comes into its inheritance of self-maintaining resources and power for the extension of primitive Christianity over a wide area of densely populated New England.

It seems wonderful that such a work could be established for $1,200. But such is the inherent strength of our plea

that the stated sum will launch the new church free from all "entangling alliances" and with enough ready money in the treasury for a few weeks home keeping free from the embarrassment of an empty exchequer. In the confidence of their interest in this great work we appeal to our brothers and sisters in Christ for the remainder of this required amount. Kindly remit as soon as possible and as generously.—S.

❀ ❀

—George W. Wise, who is about to take charge of our work at Alton, Ill., is a Tennessee boy who has held successful pastorates at Hampton, in that state, Plainview and Rochester, Minn., and at Leesville, La. Of his work at the latter place John A. Stephens, the state evangelist, speaks very highly. Of his departure Brother Stephens writes: "Personally, I feel that the loss

G. W. Wise.

will be a severe one to me and our work." Brother Wise set a pace for state missions which others were induced to follow. He has conducted two or three evangelistic meetings each year of his ministry and has baptized more than a thousand converts.

❀ ❀

Buffalo Expected Blessing.

The convention was wanted in Buffalo because it was felt it would be such a help to the cause here. A word as to how this may most be realized may not be amiss, and I am sure it will be well received. I believe each one who comes will be happier to feel that he is contributing to this end.

I am led to these reflections by what came up in conversation in a home where I dined recently. I was impressed with the way they spoke of some people who were in their home only a few days during the Pan-American Fair. They came as total strangers and won a place as abiding friends. After those people returned they sent back pictures of themselves and their houses, thus showing the friendship was not a transient one on their part.

Whatever impression may be made in Buffalo by the sight of great multitudes and badges, or by addresses and newspaper accounts will pass away with the coming of the next excitement; but these personal touches, courtesies and friendships will be the abiding influences favorable to the great end we all have in view.

You who come to this convention have the opportunity to do in a week for the cause you all love what all your brethren in Buffalo can not possibly do in years. It will not be by what you say so much as by what you are seen to be in spirit and bearing. The most of you will be guests in homes. Homes are sanctuaries which we enter only by permission; and although pay is to be received usually, yet it is more for the favor than the pay in most cases that the homes are thrown open.

Somehow I have a notion that a Christian should enter a home not with the thought of how much comfort he is to get out of it, but how much of the Christ he is to bring into it. Would it not be good for us all to read and ponder what Jesus said about, "And into whatsoever house ye shall enter?" B. H. HAYDEN.

Buffalo, N. Y.

Death of Mrs. W. B. Craig.

We are deeply grieved to learn of the death of Sister William Bayard Craig, of Denver, who passed away on September 20. In a letter from Bro. B. B. Tyler, written on that date, he says:

"We are in deep grief. Mrs. Emma Pickerell Craig, wife of William Bayard Craig, pastor of the Central Christian Church, passed to the other side a few minutes ago. For some time Sister Craig has been in ill health. This morning, as a last resort, she came under the surgeon's knife. The result was as indicated.

"In the decease of Sister Craig our churches in Denver, and the Central Church, especially, sustain an irreparable loss. Mrs. Craig was a queenly woman. There was a royal dignity in her bearing. She was sweet-spirited, intelligent and earnest, wise, enthusiastic, in the service of our Lord. All Denver is poorer by reason of her departure. In her sympathies and efforts she was truly catholic. As I trace these lines tears come unbidden and blind my eyes in deepest sympathy with Brother Craig. He is, as you well know, one of God's noblemen. The loss to him no tongue can tell, no pen describe. He and his wife were so truly joined together that there was the most perfect harmony and unity. They were one couple in a thousand.

"South Broadway will feel the loss of Sister Craig next to the Central Church. Brother and Sister Craig were under God, the founders of this great church. They served the infant congregation two or three years without salary, and superintended the erection of our splendid house of worship. Only one week ago this afternoon Brother Craig spoke in the South Broadway Church at the funeral of one of the older members. I have never known better work than the service rendered by Brother and Sister Craig in the organization and building of the South Broadway Church. In all of Brother Craig's work, both in the pastoral office and in the office of chancellor of Drake University, his wife was a loyal and effective helpmeet. We mourn, but not as those who are destitute of hope."

To these true and appreciative words of Brother Tyler, the Editor wishes to add his personal testimony to the high character, great ability and supreme devotion to the cause of Christ of Sister Craig. Having known her personally in her home life, in the work of the church, and in the social circle, we can testify cheerfully to her extraordinary worth. Brother Craig always spoke of their joint work in the pastorate, for she was, indeed, a most valuable helper, and never, perhaps, were two hearts more closely united in their love and loyalty to each other and to their common Master. To Brother Craig, whose loss is unspeakable, and to the church whose interests she

carried on her heart equally with her husband, we tender our sincerest sympathy. The earth is better for her having lived in it, and heaven will be richer to many because of her departure from this earth.

As We Go to Press.

Special to THE CHRISTIAN-EVANGELIST.

Cincinnati, O., Oct. 1.—Foreign Christian Missionary Society's receipts $268,000; a gain of about $13,000.—F. M. Rains.

Special to THE CHRISTIAN-EVANGELIST.

Canton, Mo., Oct. 1.—Debt on Christian University cleared. Nearly $16,000 raised.

Special to THE CHRISTIAN-EVANGELIST.

Oskaloosa, Ia., Oct. 1.—Twenty-three yesterday, 165 in three weeks. Must close Thursday on account of Cory leaving for China. Mrs. Collin, splendid leader of song, can be secured for October and November meetings.—S. H. Zendt, minister.

Special to THE CHRISTIAN-EVANGELIST.

Quincy, Ill., Oct. 1.—Sister Jordan, wife of Walter M. Jordan, pastor, and only daughter of D. R. Dungan, died from typhoid fever this morning, after six weeks' sickness.—Edgar S. Potter.

Special to THE CHRISTIAN-EVANGELIST.

Sullivan, Ill., Oct. 1.—Scoville, Smith and Kendall in union meeting; forty-six added to-day, 306 in ten days; 11 of 14 to-day were men. We are reaching the best citizens; the whole country is stirred; delegations here from Decatur, Mattoon and Charleston.—J. G. McNutt.

Special to THE CHRISTIAN-EVANGELIST.

Muncie, Ind., Oct. 1.—Martin family, evangelists, had three great audiences yesterday; 35 already added collections yesterday $65. Richard Martin lectures on Cuba.—C. A. Donnelson.

Special to THE CHRISTIAN-EVANGELIST.

Kansas City, Mo., Sept. 30.—Wm. J. Lockhart leads us in a great victory; 33 to-day, 229 to date. Altheide is the singer. We continue.—Frank L. Bowen, pastor.

Special to THE CHRISTIAN-EVANGELIST.

Bloomington, Ill., Sept. 30.—Revival growing in crowds and interest; 197 to date; 30 to-day; many are adults. We continue.—W. T. Brooks.

Special to THE CHRISTIAN-EVANGELIST.

Wichita, Kan., Sept. 30.—Six hundred and nineteen at Sunday-school at the Central Church to-day. Ninety-one dollars for home missions; half a dozen new classes organized.—E. W. Allen; pastor.

Special to THE CHRISTIAN-EVANGELIST.

Kirksville, Mo., Oct. 1.—One hundred and five in three weeks, 25 yesterday. Wickizer is the pastor and had field well gleaned.—Bruce Brown.

Jellico's Church Wrecked by Dynamite.

On September 21, the Christian church, newly erected, was wrecked in the terrible dynamite explosion that took place in Jellico, Tenn. We have received a lengthy appeal signed by the present pastor of the church there, Raymond G. Sherrer, but it reaches us at a time when our columns are already crowded, so we must necessarily condense the statement.

In 1899 there were less than a dozen members of our brotherhood at Jellico. As a result of a meeting held by J. W. Masters an organization was perfected with 23 members. In 1900 D. G. Combs held a meeting in the Congregational church, but the effort to secure funds for the erection of a building for our own brethren was unsuccessful. A. I.

Myhr, the state secretary, after a visit in 1902 arranged for Wm. Burleigh to hold a meeting. In 1904 E. J. Fenstermacher assisted in a meeting, and the church was reorganized. In October of the same year Milo Atkinson added to the membership. The following January W. J. Shelburne increased the interest so much that a lot was purchased for $1,000, and E. B. Barnes and H. H. Saunders held a meeting which added to the membership and led to the securing of a minister. Up to this time the congregation had been meeting in vacant stores and halls and in the city school building. For a time the brethren met in a coal office to hold Sunday-school and observe the Lord's Supper. But finally in October, 1905, a contract for a $6,000 building was let, and by much self-sacrifice and devotion on the part of a few, this building was completed just eight days before the 21st of September, 1906. Early in the morning of that day the entire town was damaged by the explosion of a car load of dynamite in the railroad yards, and the Christian church was so badly wrecked that it has been condemned and must be rebuilt. The brethren in Jellico can not do this without outside help. They have no place in which they can hold services, and they have asked Brother Sherrer, their minister, to go into the field and endeavor to secure help to rebuild their house of worship. Contributions may be sent directly to Dr. L. M. Scott, chairman of the building committee, Box 305, Jellico, Tenn. We are sure that the sympathy of the entire brotherhood goes out to the members at Jellico and that this will be demonstrated in a practical manner.

Changes.

Allin, B. L.—Harriman, to Tullahoma, Tenn.
Bush, G. L.—McKinney, to Gainesville, Texas.
Buckner, George W.—Macomb, Ill., to Canton, Mo.
Bacon, R. H.—Verdon, S. D., to University Place Station, DesMoines, Ia.
Breaker, D. M.—Ringgold, Ga., to Kissimmee, Fla.
Beshers, R. L.—El Paso, to Walnut, Ill.
Betts, Will H.—1409 Twenty-ninth street, to 1333 Twenty-ninth street, DesMoines, Ia.
Cline, C. C.—Little Rock, to Pine Bluff, Ark.
Combs, George H.—Macatawa, Mich., to 3026 East Sixth, Kansas City, Mo.
Chapman, L. A.—Mechanicsburg, Ill., to Mt. Pleasant, Ia.
Comstock, C. W.—King City, to Columbia, Mo.
Council, Mrs. J. W.—Hico, to El Paso, Texas.
Cole, J. J.—Millersburg, O., to Jackson, Ky., cafe of O. A. Myers.
Chase, L. R.—Armington, to Le Roy, Ill.
Dow, T. J.—Cutler, to 3317 Stephens avenue, South Minneapolis, Minn.
Encell, J. G.—Marion, Ia., to Lake City, Ia.
Gerdineer, John H.—Troy, Pa., to Scio, N. Y.
Gentry, Richard W., 6633 Kimbark avenue, to 7239 Wilcox avenue, Chicago, Ill.
Grinstead, Wren J.—Jellico, Tenn., to Richmond, Ky.
Hull, O. L.—Randolph, to Garrett, Ind.
Hardin, J. H.—Macatawa, Mich., to 923 Prospect avenue, Kansas City, Mo.
Jones, A. E.—Denver, Colo., to Liberty, Mo.
Janes, Frank R.—Fremont, Neb., to Pendleton, Ind.
Jackson, G. D.—343 Riverside avenue, Jacksonville, to box 358, DeLand, Fla.
Jewett, Frank L.—Horton, Kan., to 2009 University avenue, Austin, Tex.
Kershner, Frederic D.—Martinsburg, W. Va., to Harriman, Tenn.
Lunger, E. C.—Lungerville, Pa., to 434 Walnut street, Lexington, Ky.
Lobdell, G. L.—Dallas, Ore., to Chico, Cal.
Martin, Richard—Sturgis, Ky., to Muncie, Ind.
Myers, H. A.—Marion, Ky., to 509 West Third street, Lexington, Ky.
Murray, L. E.—Indianapolis, to Middletown, Ind.
Morro, W. C.—Rectorville, Ky., to 332 Blackburn avenue, Lexington, Ky.
Maple, O. D.—Marion, O., to Gas City, Ind.
Millsap, H. F.—Knox City, to Hunnewell, Mo.
Rehorn, W. S.—Lowell, to Waukomis, Okla.
Read, T. J.—Chicago, to Eureka, Ills.
Stivers, John T.—Memphis, Mo., to Dodge City, Kan.
Sloan, J. F.—Topeka, Kan., to 3271 Arroyo Seco avenue, Los Angeles, Cal.
Stanley, D. T.—Birmingham, Ala., to 2754 Emerald street, Philadelphia, Pa.

NEWS FROM MANY FIELDS

Illinois Notes.

The Illinois Christian Educational Association held its annual meeting with the State Missionary Society at Paris. While its work is in support of the college, the men trained in the school became at once the earnest supporters of state missions as well as all other great enterprises, so it is justly and wisely reckoned among the missionary forces of the state and most appropriately welcomed to a good place on the program. The 2,200 people who have been enrolled as members of the association, as well as thousands of friends of Eureka College will be glad to have a fairly full report of the past, and plans for future work.—— The large attendance at the educational session, which came late in the convention, showed a live, earnest interest in Christian education. This interest is not only in the production of well trained and thoroughly educated ministers and missionaries but in the thorough education also of all our young people under good moral and spiritual conditions.—— The Educational association has been at work about nine years and has raised about $25,000. Its purpose is to secure the co-operation of the Disciples of Christ in Illinois, in the enlargement and maintenance of Eureka College, by disseminating a knowledge of its work and needs by increasing the attendance and by providing financial support. Its departments are: (1) A regular membership, paying $1 annually; (2) An Attendance League, pledging to secure, if possible, one or more students; (3) A Gift League, pledging to give the college something each year; (4) A life membership by the payment of $25. The annual convention added two other departments; (5) A life directorship, on the payment of $50, entitling to a place on the advisory board; (6) A Living Link, by either an individual or church on the payment of $100, entitling the donor to send a worthy indigent young person to college free of tuition, as long as the living link is continued. Its broad scope enables every friend of Christian education to do something. Very few are unable to give a dollar a year, to produce such a ministry as the Church of Christ deserves, and to thoroughly equip the college for the fullest training, highest and noblest culture of all our young people. If too poor to do this, he can become a recruiting officer in the Attendance League. But many can give the larger sums, thus adding more rapidly to the growth of the college. Beyond all this we hope for many to give on the annuity plan and others remember the college liberally in their wills.—— The treasurers' report showed balance on hand, $307.64; from various membership dues, $4,176; education day and improvement funds, $892.12; Coleman fund, $2,800; other receipts, $168.89; total receipts, $6,344.45. This was expended as follows: General college fund, $5,083.22; field secretary's salary and expenses, $583.99; treasurer, $200. The rest was spent on repairs and furniture in "Lida's Wood," printing, postage, envelopes, etc., except $320.68, left in the treasury. Printed detailed statement from the treasurer can be had for the asking, Miss Clara L. Davidson, Eureka. The field secretary reported having visited 293 places, delivered eighty-seven addresses on Christian education, enrolled 103 I. C. E. A. members, and 41 life members, received in cash, $1,034.88, and in pledges, conditional and otherwise, $5,050. That the college had received from our good friend, William Britt, $2,000 on endowment.——Education day was observed by 74 churches with sermons on Christian Education and an offering of $1,405.57. This in many cases included regular dues. We are indebted much to the press, with the earnest co-operation of our editors, and to the worthy pastors and churches whose public spirit and unselfish enterprise led them to this noble and fundamental service which underlies the growth and prosperity of all departments of work.——The college people and their friends held twenty-four conferences for information in as many places, which were attended by 90 preachers and 3,765 others.——The proposition of present effort is to find thirty men who will each give $100, when 500 new names are added to the membership of

the I. C. E. A. About 200 are secured and eleven men to give $100 each.——Mrs. S. J. Crawford, president of the association, gave a full outline of the persons and work of the association into which she has put so much of her life and for the large usefulness of which she is profoundly grateful.——S. E. Fisher, Champaign, gave the educational address, which was a stirring appeal to the state to put Eureka College in condition for larger usefulness. The demands of business require men of character, society demands women of true Christian refinement. The church is suffering for want of ministers, well trained and thoroughly equipped for their responsible work. The reports of the committee on future work was enthusiastically adopted. It recommended (1) that all the churches be urged to observe Education Day, January 20; (2) that the educational conferences be continued; (3) that life directorships on the payment of $50 be constituted; (4) that living links on the payment of $100 be established; (5) that the churches be urged to make provision for a definite stated offering each year to be applied on current expenses; (6) that our ministers be urged to press upon their congregations the necessity and work of the Christian college until every church is thoroughly enlisted both in patronage and support; (7) that our centennial aims be (a) to increase the I. C. E. A. membership to 5,000; (b) to raise $150,000 endowment and (c) to increase the attendance to 400 students; (8) that the executive committee consider the selection of a centennial secretary. In harmony with this report, the session of the missionary convention recommended that this convention assume the responsibility, by and with the consent and advice of the board of trustees, of raising an endowment of $250,000, and that the presidents of the convention, the college and the educational association, select a committee to raise the amount, and that the state missionary board be asked to devote $100 for the use of said committee. Now for one strong pull altogether and do what ought to have been done long ago. Seventy-six preachers already pledged to observe Education day. The centennial committee will be selected as soon as possible and a centennial secretary put in the field. This all looks forward to a better day for Christian education in our great state, which ought to lead in all these great enterprises for the world's betterment. The officers of the association are as follows: Mrs. S. J. Crawford, Pres.; R. E. Hieronymus and Mrs. A. T. Ross, Vice-pres.; Mrs. M. M. Conklin, Cor. Sec.; Mrs. Ada H. McGuire, Rec. Sec.; Mrs. Clara L. Davidson, Treas.; Prof. Silas Jones, Auditor. The advisory board additional, Mrs. B. J. Radford, Mrs. R. D. Smith, Mrs. Mary Major, Mrs. Jane C. Davidson, Mrs. Sue M. Elkin, Mrs. Anna Hieronymus, Mrs. Emma Darst, L. O. Lehman and W. F. Shaw.   J. G. WAGGONER.
Eureka, Ill.

Arkansas' Many Good People Rejoice.

"Amendment No. 8" carried by a large majority. Our secretary of state has announced the official vote on the constitutional amendment, increasing the state and district school tax from the present maximum of seven (7) mills to ten "(10) mills on the dollar. It appears that a total of 152,827 votes were cast. Those voting for the amendment number 93,237. The number necessary for adoption is 76,414, so that the amendment is decidedly adopted, and will become a part of the state constitution next January. Arkansas already has many excellent public schools, some splendid colleges, and one of the largest and best southern state universities. The enrollment for the ensuing session is anticipated to be 1,200 students.——We hope to see the day not far in the future when the C. W. B. M. will have endowed a Bible chair at this important center of education in Arkansas.——This year the vote against license in the state, taken by counties, breaks all records. As county option prevails, the big majority against license will have no effect upon the counties that have voted for license.

It is very likely, however, that a few counties that have voted wet, will become dry by petition; we had six cases of this kind two years ago. It is very probable that more than one county that is reported wet will be contested and shown to be dry; this is almost certain in Mississippi county. Two years ago the majority in the state against license was only 1,953, and this was the first majority ever given by the state against license. This year the total vote against license is 82,250, being a majority against license of 14,273, the largest prohibition vote ever cast in the state. The vote breaks the record, and no doubt will forever keep the forces of temperance in the front. Fifty-three counties in this state are officially reported dry by vote. This year we gain several dry counties, and lose two only that went dry two years ago. Furthermore it is known that the full vote against license was not cast, many not voting. Still the increase in the anti-license majority over that of two years ago is 12,320.—The good people all over the state are greatly rejoicing over this great victory for temperance, and amendment No. 8, which means better education for the masses.—The writer, with others of "the true faith," are glad of good prospects to get some good preacher to join in our work; and those who come, we hope will be glad to remain, and make us glad for them to remain. Any one who desires to come, can save time by always sending a letter from his home congregation, and one also from his state or district secretary. This will enable me to put your case in the most favorable light before the brethren; and as this corresponding secretary does this work gratis, you will kindly enclose stamp for reply. Will you come over and rejoice with those who are now rejoicing over recent victories and who hope to achieve others for temperance, education and Christian culture?

JAMES H. BROOKS, Cor. Sec.
Blytheville, Ark.

From "A Swamp Angel."

August was vacation month and was spent far from these sylvan scenes of Southeast Missouri. August 5 I preached for the Jeffersonville (Ind.) congregation, J. M. Vawter, an ex-Missourian, pastor. I found pastor and people in joyous relationship. August. 12-19 I was at the "old home," Mulberry, Ohio; here I joined Brother Hays, pastor, and Bro. Jos. Armistead, of Norwood, in triple preaching, four making the good confession. August 20 and September 3, I renewed my fellowship with Henry Dodson, a brother beloved, at New Antioch, O. Three precious ones were here obedient to the faith. Our own meeting begins October 7. A. W. Kokendoffer, of Mexico, Mo., to do the preaching.

Poplar Bluff, Mo.   E. J. FENSTERMACHER.

❀ ❀ ❀

West Kentucky.

W. J. Hudspeth, South Kentucky evangelist, who recently visited Mayfield, reports over $2,000 already raised for the new year's work.——The trustees of the Smallwood fund have recently endowed two scholarships in West Kentucky College for able Students. These scholarships are worth $125 for four years.——W. J. Hudspeth recently closed an excellent meeting with the Murray congregation and is now visiting the churches of West Kentucky and raising funds to locate a special evangelist in the eight counties of the Jackson's purchase.——The congregation at Lynville has lately reorganized and is building a new house of worship. They were recently greatly revived and strengthened by a meeting held by W. J. Hudspeth. L. M. Hammonds, a student in West Kentucky College, preaches for them once a month.——"Ground-breaking exercises" were recently held at Mayfield, marking with appropriate ceremonies and worship, the beginning of the erection of the new house of worship. This is to cost by contract $27,000, exclusive of glass, carpets, pews, heating, lighting, and organ—the whole costing not less than $30,000.——West Kentucky College has just begun its new year with fine attendance and bright prospects.

Mayfield, Ky.   G. A. LINCOLN.

❀ ❀ ❀

Great Camp Meeting.

The ninth annual camp meeting of the Churches of Christ in Northwest Texas was held near Benjamin, Tex., for sixteen days. I was assisted in the preaching by J. A. Minton, of Erick, O. T. Brother Minton did a great work and pleased the people. This was the best meeting in the history of the organization. There were 73 additions, nearly all by baptism. Many of the number were cattle men of large means, some came hundreds of miles and have gone back home to establish the Church of Christ in their home towns.

In order that the brotherhood may understand something of the magnitude of the camp meeting I give the following facts: The organization has a regular evangelist employed; there have been about 2,500 additions; $70,000 expended; twelve churches organized; six houses built; $1,000 presented to Texas Christian University, thousands of dollars presented to other schools, orphan homes and charitable institutions. Brother A. J. Bush visited our camp-meeting at Benjamin, made an appeal in the interest of the orphans' home, and raised over $250 in a few minutes. Hence, you can see that the brethren are heartily in sympathy with every good work. For five years the writer has been working with these good people, and, if the Lord will, I am to assist again in 1907, and I frankly admit that this is one of the greatest opportunities for doing good that I ever saw. The next camp meeting will be near Haskell, where I am now trying to advance our cause in the growing little city.

Our church house here is small, hence we rented the "skating rink," which can accommodate more people than any other building in town. We have no regular preacher at Benjamin nor here; We need a good preacher at both places. Any one who is willing to begin on rather a small salary and work up a strong church, please send name if you can come recommended by the state corresponding secretary of your state.

Haskell, Tex.   J. L. HODNOX.

A Good Meeting.

The meeting just held by Thomas L. Cooksey, and Miss Park with the church at Coffeyville, Kan., and its pastor Ellis Purlee, resulted in 56 additions, all of these adults except four. Weather conditions were unfavorable and there were outside attractions to draw the people. Brother McKinney will lead the singing for Brother Cooksey in a meeting just begun at Holton. At the conclusion of this meeting Brother Cooksey goes to the West Side Church in Indianapolis to hold the simultaneous meeting to be held in that city. The evangelists have open dates for December. The meeting just held shows that they have power to preach and sing the gospel with effect.

❀ ❀

Empire State.

The brethren of the whole state of New York join with Buffalo in inviting the brotherhood to our International Missionary Convention. To have you within our borders is a privilege that we prize. You will do us much good. The fellowship of your presence will encourage us. We are comparatively few in number in the limitless field of the Empire state and our efforts will be greatly aided by the impression that a large missionary gathering will make upon the people of the past. They will be forced to see we are a great people.

It is a great mistake to suppose that the people of the east are not responsive to our plea; for our growth in this state will average up well with that of the whole country. New York City alone made a net increase of 14.6 per cent this year.

The most that we can do for you in this convention is to convince you of the unlimited field which the east presents. We can not show large numbers; but we can show a steady growth and a solid front for all missionary enterprises of our people. And we want to have you understand that New York and Massachusetts constitutes today our greatest and most important fields for Home Missions. You will be surprised at the large number of cities in these two states, that are not occupied by us. Come to the convention. Buffalo is a beautiful city and we shall try to match the hospitality of other sections.

Our state work promises well this year under the leadership of D. C. Tremaine, who fills the position of corresponding secretary-evangelist. As are obliged to be contented with only one man in the field for the present. The open doors would employ half a dozen if we had the money to enter them. Several new pastors have come into the state since our state convention. Miner Lee Bates has taken up the work at West Fifty-sixth street, New York City. J. A. Serena has become pastor of the First Church, Syracuse. T. F. Burger is pastor at Brewerton. We look for good results in these important places.

It has just been learned that Bro. Lowell C.

Columbia Normal Academy

Columbia, Missouri. For Young Men and Women. 545 enrolled last year. Four departments—Academic, Normal, Music, Elocution. **HAMILTON HALL.** A refined home for 10 boys. Model sanitation.

LINN HALL. A home for 28 young ladies. Every convenience necessary for health and comfort.

McPherson has resigned the work in Havana, Cuba, in order to afford his children the educational advantages of this country. We rejoice to know that he has accepted a call to become pastor at Wellsville. The brethren of New York love Brother and Sister McPherson for their sterling qualities and their work of love both upon the mission field and in Buffalo. The six and one-half years of their leadership at Jefferson street, Buffalo, were attended by probably the most signal advances that any church in the east has ever made, all things being considered. We welcome them back to the state with open arms, feeling assured that the Lord will bless their labors in the new field as he has done in the past.

Our state day occurs November 4. We expect the largest offering ever made in the state. Brethren of the state, come to the Buffalo convention. This is your opportunity to attend one of our great conventions near home.

ELI H. LOWE.

❀

MARRIAGES.

Notices of marriages inserted under this heading at the rate of fifty cents for three lines or less (seven, words to a line). Additional words at five cents per word. Cash must in each case accompany order.

HARLAN—CARDINET—Wm. C. Harlan and Elva Cardinet, of Santa Rosa, Cal., at Petoluma, Cal., September 16, 1906, J. E. Denton, officiating.

STULL-THOMPSON.—Samuel L. Stull and Miss Urso Thompson, both of California, Pa.

❀

OBITUARIES.

[Notices of Deaths, not more than four lines, inserted free. Obituary memoirs, one cent per word. Send the money with the copy.]

ZUMWALT.

Brother Zumwalt died in Topeka, Kan., September 7, 1906, after a long sickness and terrible suffering, at the age of 78 years. He had been a faithful member of the Christian church over fifty years. He was twice married; by the last union there were two sons—Clarin and Irwin, both in the Christian University. He was born in St. Charles county, Mo., and left an orphan at the age of five years. He leaves three sons and one daughter by his first wife and the two by his last, with Sister Zumwalt to mourn the loss of a kind, Christian husband and father. His work of faith and labor of love deserves a far more extended notice. B. MATCHETT.

WINTERMOTE.

In the death of Bro. Joseph F. Wintermote, the First Christian Church of Kansas City, Mo., has lost one of its most faithful members, and his household a most devoted and honored husband and father. Brother Wintermote was born in Darke county, Ohio, January 1, 1832, and died in Kansas City, Mo., August 19, 1906 aged 74 years, 7 months, 19 days. He was married in Lexington, Ky., February 16, 1859, to Miss Maria J. Van Pelt, with whom he lived in most happy union until his death. He joined the Christian church at the age of 24, and lived in most cor-

Columbia Business College

a separate school, but under same management. Complete business course. Shorthand and typewriting course, and penmanship course.

Catalogue and special circular mailed free to anyone on application. Address Department B. Mention the course in which you are interested.

College of the Bible,

Lexington, Ky.

Our oldest, most thorough and most numerously attended College for preachers.

Six Professors. Two hundred and eighteen students.

Next session opens September 10.

For catalogue and other information address

J. W. McGARVEY, Pres

SUBSCRIBERS' WANTS.

dial fellowship with the people of God wherever his home chanced to be. He lived in Clarksville, Tenn., during the war, after which he moved to Versailles, Ky. In 1888 he came to Kansas City, which has been his home ever since. Besides his widow, he leaves five sons and three daughters, all of whom are members of the Christian church. His life was a benediction to the world, and his memory will be an inspiration unto righteousness to all who knew him. W. F. RICHARDSON.

Ellis Purlee, Pastor of the Christian Church, Coffeyville, Kan.

Miss Lucille Park, Singer, Coffeyville, Kan.

Thomas L. Cooksey, Evangelist.

Evangelistic

We invite ministers and others to send reports of meetings, additions and other news of the churches. It is especially requested that additions be reported as "by confession and baptism," or "by letter."

California.

Eureka, Sept. 17.—Four additions.—I. H. Teel, pastor.

Los Angeles, Sept. 25.—I have been with the church at Sawtelle (a suburb of Los Angeles) two Lord's days with five additions to the church. The outlook is hopeful. I have been here a little over a week.—J. F. Sloan.

Colorado.

Greeley, Sept. 24.—Closed a good meeting here last night with the pastor, L. H. Humphreys. Thirteen were added to the church.—Charles E. McVay, song evangelist.

Illinois.

Normal, Sept. 23.—Three university students added—two by confession.—R. H. Newon.

Pekin, Sept. 24.—One confession, a mother, at our services yesterday.—J. A. Barnett.

Williamsville, Sept. 23.—One addition by baptism September 23.—C. D. Haskell, minister.

Normal, Sept. 24.—We rejoice over three added to the church yesterday, all university students—two by confession, one by statement.—R. H. Newton.

Chicago, Sept. 26.—Our meeting in this difficult field is largely attended. The largest audience last. Five added. No evangelist ever had great results here.—H. E. Wilhite.

Rutland, Sept. 27.—I closed at Luther, Iowa, September 18, with 16 added. This makes 322 added to Iowa churches in the last few months under my preaching as state evangelist. I am assisting R. B. Doan in a meeting here. Meeting four days days old with four confessions.—C. L. Organ, evangelist.

Loraine, Sept. 28.—Evangelist A. R. Spicer, of Moweaqua, closed a four weeks' meeting with us Monday, resulting in 75 additions, most of them heads of families and adults; 56 baptisms. This is Brother Spicer's old home; he had 87 additions here last winter in two and a half weeks' time. H. A. Davis assisted in song service. The large tent, seating more than a thousand, was filled from night to night. The meeting aroused this section of the county. People came from 15 to 25 miles and some additions from that distance.—J. O. Wade.

Indiana.

Indiana Harbor.—A meeting conducted by the Snodgrass brothers has resulted in 17 additions to date.

New Castle, Sept. 28.—Closed a three weeks' meeting with Brother Franklin at Yorktown, 18 added.—Chas. E. Shultz and wife, evangelists.

Irvington, Sept. 24.—Just closed a three weeks' meeting at Bargersville with 26 added—19 by confession, five by letter; 13 men.—Clay Trusty.

Gas City, Sept. 30.—Meeting closed last night with 18 added. Audiences large. The meeting goes on with another man. Gas City was a pastorless church and hence a difficult field.—Maple and Miller.

Huntington, Sept. 24.—We are having fine audiences, the large auditorium being filled in the evening, and a large Sunday-school. Two additions yesterday.—Cephas Shelburne.

Hammond, Sept. 24.—Held tent meeting at Hammond this summer with 42 additions. Have had 111 additions in the past 12 months. Held a tent meeting in Whiting in August with 64 additions.—C. J. Sharp, minister.

Indian Territory.

Okmulgee, Sept. 25.—There were five accessions to the church here last Lord's day—three by letter, one reclaimed, and one confession.—Frank L. Van Voorhis.

Iowa.

Maxwell, Sept. 21.—Twenty-one added at regular services.—G. E. Roberts.

Vinton, Sept. 26.—Two by baptism, two from denomination, two by statement. We are preparing for a revival here in December.—E. B. Elliott.

Minburn, Sept. 20.—My meeting at Minburn closed September 23. In the 22 days there were 22 additions. Fourteen were baptisms.—Roy E. Deadman.

Bayard, Sept. 24.—Evangelist Stout closed a 28 days' meeting with the church at Bayard, with 14 additions—nine by baptism, two reclaimed, and one by statement. We begin a campaign at Bagley with Brother Stout next week.—F. W. Mutchler, minister.

Des Moines, Sept. 29.—Our tent meeting at Luther closed September 18 with 16 additions, 15 by baptism. C. L. Organ, of Des Moines, was selected to herald the truth, and the brethren at Luther feel that a better evangelist could not be secured. We advertised every way and everywhere: On fences for five miles around, in surrounding villages, and on the team that we drove we had fly-nets with an invitation to come to the meetings. We drove from 15 to 25 miles per day, from house to house, posted banners on all the threshing machines in the surrounding country. This meeting is the contribution of the Meadow Grove congregation, 2½ miles out from Luther, to the Centennial crusade, "each church build one."—Will H. Betts, minister.

Idaho.

Weiser, Sept. 25.—One more confession and baptism last Sunday.—G. M. Read.

Kansas.

Manhattan, Sept. 24.—Eight added since last report.—W. T. McLain.

Caldwell, Sept. 28.—Sister Hazelrigg has been with us four weeks, preaching every evening; by letter and statements, 14; confession and baptism, 5; from another organization, 2; total, 20.—Lee H. Barnum.

Arkansas City, Sept. 20.—I closed a 17 days' meeting at Geuda Springs, Kan. on September 5. There were 20 added. Miss Ruby Clark of Fredonia, Kan., assisted the last ten days. She is an excellent singing evangelist.—M. Lee Sorey.

Mayetta, Sept. 27.—Closed here with Nelson Gardner; second meeting within two months; 17 added, and money left in the treasury. Gardner, one of our best young men. I begin pastoral work at Meriden and Circleville.—C. C. Atwood, Topeka, Kan.

Clay Center, Sept. 28.—Otha Wilkison and wife, of Ukiah, Cal., closed a two weeks' meeting; four additions—all grown people. These two noble people served this church as pastors eight years ago, and have many friends in the town. I am closing a three years' pastorate at Clay Center with a noble band of workers. They will want a minister immediately.—Otha C. Moomaw.

Lebo, Sept. 26.—Having a great meeting with home forces under a large tent. Many go home for lack of standing room near the tent. Baptized two, and expect a great harvest before the meetings close. Brother Donaldson, of Iola, assisted three evenings and we are expecting other help next week. The M. E. pastor preached for me one evening, and the presiding elder was with us in one service; the very best spirit prevails in the meetings and people are beginning to know they have misunderstood the attitude of the Christian church on many points and acknowledging the same.—Wallace M. Stuckey, pastor.

Kentucky.

Lexington, Sept. 27.—I closed meeting at Carnegie, O. T., a mission point, with 22 added last week. The brethren go forward to build a house of worship. Ten added.—James Zachery, evangelist.

Missouri.

Festus, Sept. 25.—Two were added by letter last Sunday.—Daniel George Cole.

Canton, Sept. 25.—We close a short meeting at Plevna, Mo., with six baptisms.—W. A. Dameron.

Brunswick, Sept. 24.—Meeting closed last night with 16 additions—five confessions.—E. H. Williamson, pastor.

Chillicothe, Sept. 24.—Seven added yesterday, three one week ago, one baptized at prayer-meeting last week. Our audiences are large.—James N. Crutcher.

Triplett, Sept. 29.—Our meeting at Mike closed with 17 additions, just doubling our numbers. David Millar of Meridan, assisted us in the meeting.—H. Eubank.

Sedalia, Sept. 24.—At our regular service at Eldorado, our country church where I preach once a month, I baptized three.—E. L. Cunningham.

Hale, Sept. 25.—W. L. Harris of Lincoln, Neb., is conducting a revival for us here. Meeting nine days old with eight additions, large audiences, fine interest. Church is enthused and we are sure to have a great meeting.—C. C. Taylor.

Houston, Sept. 21.—J. D. Lawrence, THE CHRISTIAN-EVANGELIST living link evangelist, closed a two weeks' meeting here September 16 with 14 additions—seven were baptized and seven were received by statement or letter. A Christian Endeavor Society was organized. It was a splendid meeting.—W. J. Frost.

Canton, Sept. 28.—We closed an 18 days meeting at Neeper, Mo., which resulted in 19 additions—4 from other bodies, one reclaimed, 14 confessions. Oscar Marks, of Canton, had charge of the song service. Brother Marks is one of the most promising young men in the singing evangelist field. He is a student of Christian University.—E. M. Carr, minister.

Nebraska.

Fremont, Sept. 24.—Took three confessions on the 18th, and baptized four persons.—T. W. Billingham.

Alma, Sept. 21.—Eight additions by letter and two by baptism since last report.—W. E. Rambo.

Danbury, Sept. 23.—Eight added to date. Brother Smith has been doing the preaching.—W. R. Bushbridge.

New York.

Buffalo, Sept. 24.—Two added—one by primary obedience.—B. S. Ferrall.

Throopsville, Sept. 24.—We have recently received four by baptism at our regular services.—A. B. Chamberlain.

Ohio.

Minerva, Sept. 25.—One hundred and one additions. Great crowds continue.—Violett and Clarkson.

Mount Healthy, Sept. 25.—Two added since our last report.—Boyd White.

Belmont Ridge, Sept. 29.—Our meeting opened under very bright auspices. We are aided in our work with 300 CHRISTIAN-EVANGELISTS which we have endeavored to place in every home within a radius of many miles; this is quite a difficult work when one considers this as a farming community. Four confessions and baptisms and one by statement. There are more to follow.—Ferd. F. Schultz.

Oklahoma Territory.

Oklahoma City, Sept. 27.—Our meeting of 24 days with Harlow and son on the 25th inst., with 107 additions, 41 of whom were from the world, a few from the denominations and the rest by letter or statement. The next engagement of Harlow and Harlow will be Wheeling, W. Va.—S. B. Moore.

Texas.

Greenville, Sept. 24.—I preached a few days between Sundays, recently, at Lone Oak. There were 18 additions.—J. W. Holsapple.

Virginia.

Clifton Forge, Sept. 28.—Two additions at Millsboro, Va., by confession and baptism.—Gerald Culberson.

J. P. Lichtenberger of New York City, spent a few weeks of his vacation in Virginia holding two meetings. One at Tazewell with 35 added, another at Graham with 64, making 99 in the two short meetings. At Graham 14 came forward at the last invitation, 14 of them men.

Washington.

Davenport, Sept. 24.—One added yesterday by letter. Interest increasing.—O. M. Thomason, evangelist.

Waitsburg, Sept. 19.—One confession and one baptism a week ago last Sunday.—W. T. Adams.

Ministerial Exchange.

The old pews of the church at Salina, Kan., are for sale.

Thomas L. Cooksey's address is 138 Dillon Ave., Irvington, Ind.

Charles C. Shultz and wife desire to arrange a meeting for December.

The brethren at Prescott, Iowa, are in need of a pastor. Applicants may address S. E. Fackler, elder.

Charles E. McVay, singing evangelist, of Benkleman, Neb., can be secured for a meeting in December.

The pulpit at La Porte, Ind., is vacant. A college graduate is desired. Salary $800 to $900. Write F. R. Liddell.

F. M. O'Neal can be engaged as song leader during October and November. Address 842 West Florida street, Springfield, Mo.

Miss Catherine Graves is available as singing evangelist and leader during October, November and December. Address Topeka, Kan.

The church at Lamar, Colo., will want a preacher November 1. Can pay $800. Address, with references, J. A. Downing, Lamar, Colo.

W. B. Ingle writes that his time is all taken for meetings for this year, and that he is now making engagements for 1907. Churches desiring meetings should write him at once at Harper, Kan.

J. B. Mayfield, recently of Winchester, Kan., but now located near Clarksville, Mo., is open to engagements for meetings, or for regular appointments within a hundred miles of Clarksville. Permanent address, Clarksville, Mo., R. F. D. 2.

The church of Gravity, Iowa, wants a pastor. Salary $750. Applicants will please give in first letter church board reference of congregation served, and any others they may desire, and brief sketch of themselves and family. Address J. R. Lorimer, Gravity, Iowa.

J. B. Lockhart will have the privilege of making two or three dates with churches for meetings, beginning with November before taking up regular work as minister for a church. He has resigned the work at Unionville, and his time is taken with meetings until November.

The church at Moorhead, Iowa, is in need of a minister at once. They have an $8,000 building paid for. The work is in splendid condition and the church harmonious. About $800 will be paid. Address E. E. Richards, clerk, Moorhead, Iowa.

Sunday-School

October 14, 1906.

THE TEN VIRGINS.—Matt. 25:1-13.

Memory verses, 1, 2.

Golden Text.—Watch, therefore, for ye know neither the day nor the hour wherein the Son of man cometh.—Matt. 25:13.

We are still dealing with the events and discourses of Tuesday of Passion week, the "day of conflict," which was occupied largely with controversies with the Scribes and Pharisees, denunciations of them, and discourses concerning the destruction of Jerusalem and the end of the world.

Matthew 24 has furnished much trouble for the commentators. Just how much of it refers to the destruction of Jerusalem by the Romans and how much (if any) to the end of the world and the coming of Christ at that time, is not always clear. It is clear, however, that the disciples understood Jesus to tell them that he would come again and set up his kingdom with glory before many years. This is indicated not only by the report of this discourse of Jesus as given by Matthew, Mark and John, but also by the history of the first generation after Pentecost and by many allusions in Paul's epistles.

Doubtless the expectation of the apostles and their interpretation of Jesus' words was colored largely by the Jewish apocalyptic literature with which they were familiar. This literature dealt largely with sudden and spectacular manifestations of power and glory, the discomfiture of the enemies of the faith and the visible triumph of the faithful. When such an expectation was prevalent, evidently the duty and necessity of watchfulness would be emphasized. It is equally important even though the method and circumstances of the final triumph and judgment be quite different from the apocalyptic picture.

The parable of the wise and foolish virgins illustrates the duty of watchfulness. Although the kingdom of heaven is like a seed in its gradual growth, as other parables declare, yet there are in every man's experience certain crises and times of special opportunity. The life of the soul, like political, social or financial life, is not a dead level of equally important moments.

To be preparing for the crisis during the quiet hours when there seems nothing to do but wait, and, with the strength gained in these dull times of standing still, to go forward swiftly when the hour for going forward arrives—this is the true method of spiritual progress as inculcated by this parable. "The unlit lamp and the ungirt loin" are among the most common and the most fatal of failings.

❋ ❋

SKIN TORTURES.

Itching, Burning, Crusted and Scaly Humors Instantly Relieved By Cuticura.

Bathe the affected parts with hot water and Cuticura Soap, to cleanse the skin of crusts and scales and soften the thickened cuticle. Dry, without hard rubbing, and apply Cuticura Ointment to allay itching, irritation, and inflammation, and soothe and heal, and lastly take Cuticura Resolvent Pills to cool and cleanse the blood. This pure, sweet, and wholesome treatment affords instant relief, permits rest and sleep in the severest forms of eczema and other itching, burning, scaly humors, and points to a speedy cure when all else fails.

Midweek Prayer-Meeting

October 10, 1906.

A CHURCH IN TRIBULATION.—Rev. 2:8-4.

Be strong!
We are not here to play, to dream, to drift;
We have hard work to do and loads to lift.
Shun not the struggle—face it, 'tis God's gift.

Be strong!
Say not, "The days are evil, who's to blame?"
And fold the hands and acquiesce. Oh, Shame!
Stand up, speak out and bravely, in God's name.

Be strong!
It matters not how deep intrenched the wrong
How hard the battle goes, the day how long.
Faint not, fight on! To-morrow comes the song.

O, the consolation of the assurance that God knows it all!—the outer provocations and the inner repressions; if our failures, no less truly our aspiration; our contrition as well as our transgression; our love for him notwithstanding our contradictions before men; our passion for Jerusalem even if our outer life is of Babylon.

Most of the tribulations in which our churches are involved spring from within rather than destroy from without. When a church fails in its loyalty to Christ's manifest program of Christian benevolence, evangelism, and the cultivation of the higher life it at once becomes the victim of legalism, factionalism, worldliness, and its light is as dark as if its candle were removed.

With a church as with an individual, persistent faithfulness is a great desideratum. Good they did in earlier years is no justification for half-heartedness now. Resting on laurels, idleness begets the self-satisfaction and vainglory from which spring troubles, as did dragons from ancient Greek soil, but encompass the destruction of men and congregations. Few churches take cognizance of hindrances, clouds, threatenings, or mustering foes while faithfully performing the work God committed unto them.

There was a great difference between Smyrna and Jerusalem. Abounding peace and prosperity were tokens to the latter of Jehovah's approval; while drouth and siege were proofs their sins were known and God displeased. But with the church in Smyrna trials and tribulations indicated the malignancy of Satan and not God's wrath. They became rather means of grace, for God helped them to bear their crosses and through them revealed himself as their Father, loving, sympathetic, sustaining.

"Be thou faithful until death and I will give thee a crown of life," is heaven's recognition of the fact that most of the visible fruitage of the Christian life is beyond the Jordan of death. But, there were anticipations of happiness in Canaan that gave joy to Israel even in the wilderness. Likewise there are visions of peace and plenty, of usefulness and nobleness coming to the faithful in even the most troubled church that thrills the Christian's heart with rapture. If we will look up toward God more, rather than around upon our vexations, the earthly happiness of us all will be greatly increased.

A vivid distinction should always be made between our spiritual and physical estates. Poverty may point threateningly toward the almshouse, but we

can not say we are poor if good angels are pointing to the gates of paradise. The higher denomination should control the lower and we are to reckon our standing and lot in life not from the lower but the higher conditions. We are rich or poor, beatific or pitiable according as we are rich or poor toward God, whether we can look unflinchingly up into his face or whether we shield ourselves from his glance as the inflamed eye blinks in the sunlight. Lazarus in tatters, sores and hunger was richer than Dives though few would have supposed it.

❋ ❋

Christian Endeavor

By GEO. L. SNIVELY

October 14, 1906.

THE FOOLISH AND THE WISE.—
Matt. 25:11-13.

DAILY READINGS.

M. The Parable..................Matt. 25:1-13.
T. Watchful and Prayerful.......Mark 13:34-37.
W. Oil for the Lamps............Zech. 4:1-6.
T. The Sleeping Church..........Rom. 13:11-14.
F. The Name that Saves..........Acts 4:5-12.
S. The Bridegroom...............Rev. 19:5-9.
S. The Closed Door..............John 10:1-9.

"'Almost persuaded,' harvest is past!
Almost persuaded,' doom comes at last!
Almost can not avail;
Almost is but to fail!
Sad, sad the bitter avail—
Almost, but lost."

The Lord is long suffering now but his character is symmetrical, full orbed, and justice is one of his attributes. An unprepared spirit in the celestial Eden would despoil it and justice to those who have entered in requires the alien nature should be barred out. Therefore the heavenly Bridegroom will say to those too unappreciative to take oil in their vessels, when they stand knocking, "Depart, I know you not."

It is not enough to be prayerful. We must also be prepared. Prayerfulness is a going to school, but the actual performance of duties revealed to us in the visions of our season of prayer is largely the justification of our devoting time to prayer. To pray for forgiveness without ceasing that "easily besetting sin" is mockery. To pray to be more like Christ without struggling to overcome an evil disposition, and to abound more in love and holiness is sealing our own doom. Let preparedness be our quest.

Had the bridegroom come at the expected time those foolish virgins had passed as wise as the others. The difference between them, wide as the eternities, consisted in part of them making provision for emergencies. When the unexpected happened, they were ready. Here is seen the wisdom of our cultivating a faith that will weather all the storms of doubt; of our making a repentance that needeth not be repented of; of our developing a spiritual vitality that will sustain us through fiery and unexpected trials. The over soul is the wise soul.

Many doubtless thought the virgins who not only filled their lamps but also carried an additional vessel of oil were foolishly over-cautious. There are not lacking those to-day who smile pityingly on brethren very zealous in religious activities, very ardent in their devotion, very self-sacrificing in their giving. But the decision of judgment day will be none ever made too much preparation against the coming of the bridegroom. That day consecration will receive its crown and dalliance its doom. Let the world pronounce your course foolishness, if only God will call it wise.

Heaven's gates open not to receive those who were wanton all through life, but who after death and at sight thereof are in terror fleeing the horrors of hell. They swing wide ajar rather at the approach of those who honor the Lord and serve him and are drawn after him by the affinity of love and holiness. Had the celebration of the marriage been the supreme desire of the hearts of those maidens, they would have neglected other things rather than the most minute preparation for the coming of the bridegroom. The doors were opened to the wise maidens who desired above all

things else that day to honor the bridegroom and enjoy the wedding festival. Where one's heart is there is his eternity also.

What will in our experience correspond with the coming of the bridegroom of our parable is the coming of the death angel to bear us to judgment and on to our eternal destiny. At his coming all our tasks will be left finished or incomplete. We can make no further preparation after it is announced. We can not "go to them that sell." The time of his coming is so uncertain that there is only wisdom in being always ready. Could we enter in with him into the heavenly marriage were he to come now with the suddenness of an earthquake or of the lightning's flash?

❋ ❋

For the Nursery—For the Table.

For all ages, in all climates, under all conditions, Borden's Eagle Brand Condensed milk and Peerless Brand Evaporated-Cream fill every milk requirement. Superior for ice cream.

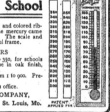

People's Forum

Significant Signs.

To the Editor of THE CHRISTIAN-EVANGELIST:

In addition to many various and even variant signs of the progressive trend toward the unity in mind and spirit of the Christian thinker in the many membered family of Christendom, I think it exceedingly important that we note the constantly converging lines in what we call secular learning.

It was my instructive pleasure to be present at the opening services of the University of Missouri. I have spent most of the summer in and about Columbia, the Athens of Missouri, preaching during July for Brother Winders' great congregation, and having myself domiciled, by the courtesy of Brethren Lhamon and Sharpe, in the Columbia Bible college building, from which vantage position I might read and look around. I have been much impressed with the wisdom and enterprise of the projectors of the Bible college in such close touch with the State University.

I have been a silent witness of the battle raging with more or less heat around the phrase, "Higher Criticism," and I have not been thrown into any straining panic over the apprehensions of some of our Jeremiahs. It seems there is a widespread feeling that the higher institutions of learning are taking the bit into their teeth and are running away with our religion. While it may be true that "much learning doth make some people mad," I am of the impression that we are in more danger from the lack of learning. I was impressed with the very evident religious center through the whole opening program of Missouri State University. In truth, the dominant note of the entire service was religious. The convocation opened with a musical number by the director of the musical department and it was that highly devotional Aria from St. Paul by Mendelssohn, "I praise thee, O Lord." The only other musical contribution was of the same spirit, "The Heavens are Telling the Glory of God," by Beethoven. The great student body in reverential attention followed these musical outreachings toward God as if they had never been questioned by critics high or low.

President Jesse made a simple straightforward address in which he was searchingly insistent on character as the central significance in the business of a university training. He thanked God that he had the gracious good fortune to be president of an institution that belongs to God. He disclaimed being anxious about a large enrollment, but "we want quality rather than many." A university to succeed must have a faculty competently trained and animated with high purpose; students with the well intentioned purpose of the completest manhood and womanhood. Not a word was uttered as to how to succeed in life. How different this from the burden of our magazine literature! It was a plea for complete men and women, and that plea was accentuated in every utterance with the religious note. It was the insistence that even in the so-called secular studies, the successful teacher is he who leads his students into methods of "thinking God's thoughts after him." If this initial announcement argues anything as to class work, and I think it does, the sons and daughters of Missouri will find here a sane and safe atmosphere for academic training.

I wanted to call attention to at least one state university that is helping the real cause of unity among all religionists without directly applying itself to what we call

Christian union. May not this way be quite as effectual as many of our most direct attacks on the question of divisions? After all that has been said for and against "Higher Criticism" may we not be lacking in proper viewpoint? Might it not help much if we stop to see that criticism high or low is simply an affair of the intellect? And the lower or obstructive critic is just as much an intellectualist as is the higher critic. Even this so-called secular institution recognizes that transcendent quality that sings a faith it can not prove.

I can not overestimate the auspicious opportunity to the Christian church of Missouri our Columbia Bible College affords, with free access to the university with its faculty of university trained men. Our church never, to my thinking, cried so loud for pulpit men, trained not only in the Bible, but equipped with academic training. The larger conception of unity is the growing feeling that the nature world is God's world, controlled by God's laws, and any scientific study is a part of any real religious study, each is complementary to the other. The University of Missouri now grants credit for Bible study here and what an unspeakable opportunity for our people, first on the ground with an institution where the candidate for the pulpit may go out with university training, able to undergird the pedantry of "science falsely so-called" with a learning broader and deeper.

CHAS. H. CATON.

The Dead Line at Forty.

To the Editor of THE CHRISTIAN-EVANGELIST:

I want to thank you for the timely words you have given us on the Centennial page in THE CHRISTIAN-EVANGELIST concerning the action of the board of one of our Illinois congregations barring from the pastorate of their church all preachers above forty years of age. Do these brethren realize that if such action should become general among our churches that it would result in barring all young men of brains and energy from our ministry. What young man that possesses real talent would feel that he could afford to spend the time and means necessary to prepare himself for this great work with such a rule, or even such a sentiment as this, staring him in the face? One of the deplorable things in the church to-day is the fact that so many of our ministers are forsaking the pulpit and embarking in business to make a living, and that too many of these are pushing these land and mining schemes as a means of filling up their depleted pocket-books. Every church that passes such a resolution as this should follow it immediately with another binding the church to pay a sufficient salary that the preacher may be able to lay by something to support him when the evil day comes and the fortieth birthday arrives. If the young preachers can only realize what a blow such resolutions are to the sacred calling of the ministry, they would avoid pulpits that are hedged by such unwise resolutions, unless perchance they may hope to turn the official boards away from such unwise action. I can well remember that the ministers who influenced my life most were such men as Elijah Goodwin, J. M. Mathes, A. I. Hobbs, John O. Miller, H. R. Pritchard, Love H. Jameson, and men of like character and ability and at a time when all would have been barred by this rule. Let this sentiment become common among our churches and we will have no more men to compare with them in our ministry. Fraternally,

T. J. CLARK.

[These timely words from Brother Clark, in a letter addressed to Brother Snively, are well worth serious consideration. We do not believe the sentiment that would limit the period of a preacher's usefulness to forty years of age, is very widespread. No doubt, however, there is a tendency to make an artificial age limit, which is not wise or healthy. It is not a question of age, but a question of physical, intellectual and spiritual strength and vitality. We doubt if many men in normal health reach the period of their greatest useful-

ness as preachers much under sixty years, and still fewer is the number that reach the zenith of their powers before fifty. The church needs both its young men and its gray-haired veterans in the ministry. Each of these classes can do a work which the other can not well do. They supplement each other, and neither class should ever feel that the other is in its way. As a purely economic question it is easy to see that the longer we protract the period of a preacher's service up to the limit of his usefulness, the more we conserve and utilize the forces of the church and the greater will be the results. Then there is the consideration Brother C. suggests of its effect on young men entering the ministry. The tendency, therefore, should be to lengthen rather than to shorten the period of active service of our ministers.—EDITOR.]

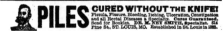

Current Literature

SCIENCE AND IDEALISM. By Hugo Munsterberg. Houghton, Mifflin & Co. 85 cents, net.

A year ago Yale University received a gift from a Harvard graduate and it was decided to use the money for the establishment of a series of lectures to be delivered every year at Yale by members of the Harvard faculty. In the first year of that lectureship Harvard was represented by President Eliot and Professors Palmar and Munsterberg. This small volume contains Professor Munsterberg's address on "Science and Idealism." The task which the philosopher set himself in this lecture was to find in the world as defined by modern science, both physical and psychological, an abiding basis for the fixed and universal values of truth, beauty and right which give life its significance. On the other hand, individualistic idealism and current pragmatism would destroy all permanent and universal values by referring all judgments and estimates to the irresponsible whim or fancy of the individual. If the individual creates his own world, unhelped and unhindered by any external realities, then there is no ground for the affirmation of any principle or value as having universal validity. The author, as an idealist, is interested in finding a basis for a belief in logical, ethical, aesthetic and metaphysical principles which shall be independent of individual fancy and free from the relativity and mutability of mere pleasure-and-pain concepts. He does it by finding in the external world—that chaos of raw material for experiences out of which each of us must construct his own orderly world—certain established and immutable demands which condition all experience. The universe is not ready-made, finished and dead. It becomes, in fact, truly a universe only as each observer for himself exercises upon it a constructive process. But it does impose upon us certain requirements which we must observe if "we want the world to be a world for us," and not merely a dream or a chaos. The conclusion is that "science falls asunder if we disbelieve in absolute ideals."

IN QUEST OF LIGHT. By Goldwin Smith. The Macmillan Co. $1.00.

This is a collection of letters written to the "New York Sun" during five or six years past. They are short, disconnected and repetitious. The attitude of Goldwin Smith toward religion illustrates the familiar dictum that man is incurably religious. In spite of his lack of faith he could not help considering religion as a matter of primary concern. He was an agnostic not satisfied with his acknowledged inability to answer the questions about God and immortality, and therefore always honestly and earnestly, in quest of light. While he accepts, as assumed results of science, many conclusions which most orthodox persons would regard as destructive of Christian and even of theistic belief, he can use the expression "a Christian of my way of thinking," and he represents himself as chiefly interested in "challenging the extreme assumptions of the materialist school." While he asserts that he has no theory—which of course is not true of any man—he defines his position by saying that he is "one of many who in these days of perplexity and doubt are trying to find some secure foundation for belief in the moral government of the universe, in the authority of conscience, and in the more hopeful view of the change which is to take place at death." While on the negative side he defines himself as "one who, though he has by no means renounced theistic belief, has lost faith in the evidences of a miraculous revelation and in the authority of dogma." While most of us would be compelled to call such a man an "unbeliever," if forced to classify him, his letters contain many suggestions which are helpful to faith. His constant insistence that there is something in man

which rises above the world of sense, that science and the senses can not exhaust the universe, that evolution, while it may show us whence man came as a physical being, can set us bounds to his development and worth as a spiritual being—these are all helpful considerations coming from a man of science. It is rather extraordinary to see a man of Professor Smith's erudition refer to the "immaculate conception" (page 127) when he evidently means the miraculous birth of Jesus. The immaculate conception is the recent Roman Catholic dogma of the birth of the Virgin Mary free from the taint of original sin and has nothing to do with the birth of Jesus. Another unwarrantable statement, which is six times repeated almost verbatim in as many letters, is to the effect that our belief in the Incarnation and Redemption, hinges on our acceptance of the Mosaic account of the Creation and the Fall.

Professor Smith is a seeker after religious truth—an unsuccessful one in the main, but it is worth a great deal to see a man honestly seeking and honestly stating what he thinks he finds. There is tonic in reading such a man's writings, though one were compelled to disagree with him on every point. He is orthodox at least in this final statement: "Nor is there any way of salvation for us but unwavering and untrammeled pursuit of truth."

THE CONQUEST OF ARID AMERICA. By William E. Smythe. Revised Edition. Macmillan. $1.50 net.

This is an elaboration and amplification of Greeley's famous advice, "Go west, young man." It tells what sort of young men should go west, why they should go, and what they may do when they get there. "Arid America is that half of our country lying west of the ninety-seventh meridian of longitude. West of this line there is, in general, not enough rainfall for general agriculture." But here, according to Mr. Smythe is incomparably the better half of the country. Its aridity is a blessing because it means irrigation and irrigation means scientific and accurate control of those conditions which make crops certain; because aridity always means richness of soil; because irrigation farming encourages intensive cultivation of small areas, resulting in relative density of rural population and consequent social advantages; and because of the climate. So great is Mr. Smythe's faith in the west that he says "if the Pilgrim Fathers had landed at San Diego rather than at Plymouth, that half of the country which now contains over 90 per cent of the total population should be regarded as comparatively worthless.

However, that may be, arid America is well worthy of being conquered and transformed from desert to garden, and the process is being carried forward on a scale which is beyond comprehension of those who have not seen it and with results almost beyond the belief of easterners even when they have seen it. The book is divided into four parts. The first, "Colonial Expansion at Home," discusses the general question of the development of the west and the "miracle of irrigation." The second describes certain "real Utopias of the west," where wonderful results have already been achieved. The third, on "undeveloped America," gives a series of chapters descriptive of the resources and present development of each of the so-called arid states and territories. The fourth tells of irrigation as a national movement and of the work now being done by the federal reclamation service.

OUTLINES OF THE LIFE OF CHRIST. By W. Sanday, D. D. LL. D., New York. Charles Scribner's Sons. Price $1.25 net.

This book is a reprint of the article "Jesus Christ," in the second volume of Dr. Hasting's dictionary of the Bible. The publishers feel that the time has arrived when it would be right to accede to the wish that has been expressed in various quarters for a separate issue of this article by the distinguished Lady Margaret Professor and Canon of Christ Church, Oxford, England. We agree with the publishers and are glad to have this able treatment put into a form which is more readily accessible than it was in the larger and expensive book. The article has been reprinted much as it stood, with such change as is necessary to carry out the principle of *mutatis mutandus* and to convert it into a book. As Dr.

Sanday has in preparation a larger work on the same subject he has thought it best not to attempt to bring his first experiment more strictly up to date, but to leave it as an expression of his own mind in the year 1899, when it was written. The probabilities are that he will not have any serious alteration to make in the general treatment of the life of Christ. A map, however, which forms an important addition to this volume embodies the writer's changed opinion as to the site of Capernaum. The author, at the start, makes a survey of conditions treating those external laws as government, sects, and parties, and the internal ones, such as the state of religious thought and life, and passes to the early ministry, the teaching, and miracles, the later ministry, the Messianic crisis; and, as supplemental chapters, he discusses the nativity, infancy, and the verdict of history. Dr. Sanday does not make any great concessions to negative criticism. His book is a scholarly and dispassionate review, and it will be very interesting to compare it with the book that is promised in some years to come.

EGOISM: a Study in the Social Premises of Religion, By Louis Wallis. The University of Chicago Press. $1.00 net.

The thesis of this interesting little volume is, that Egoism is the basic principle or force in all human activity. The recognition of this fact lends illumination to historical biblical study. The inability of higher criticism to make any advance to-day is due, the author believes, to its failure to employ this sociological principle. This is the bond that is to unite the cold facts of a mere historical study and to transmute them into the constituted elements of a practical popular faith. The thesis is developed upon a basis of biblical history. Our sacred literature is an expression of social progress, whose value depends upon its fidelity to that egoistic or social principle. The concluding chapter applies this principle to present social problems.

The Home Department

What Answer?*

BY MRS. P. R. GIBSON.

Summer has passed away—what has it taken,
With all its beauty and its bloom, from me?
Has there been in my life one sin forsaken?
Have I from secret error been set free?

Have I, dear Lord and Master, drawn still nearer
To thee, to walk more closely by thy side?
O, has thy love to me seemed ever dearer?
Am I content in that dear love to abide?

And do I trust thee with a faith unshaken,
As autumn follows summer, and life's flowers
Like blossoms in the frost's chill fingers taken,
Wither and die with summer's passing hours?

O, is my life with richer beauty glowing,
In this its golden autumn afternoon?
Are love and trust their brightest hues bestow-
ing?
And am I ready if the night come soon?

Dear Master, be my help in each endeavor
To follow on, as thou shalt lead the way,
Till I may come to dwell with thee forever,
Where is no night, but everlasting day.

The Bronze Vase.

BY J. BRECKENRIDGE ELLIS.

PART III.

CHAPTER XIV.

During that Christmas breakfast—which was just as frugal as any other breakfast—Rhoda and Raymund wondered what the bad news could be with which Miss Pinns had threatened them. They were soon to know. As soon as the meal ended, Mr. William Hodges asked his niece to go with him into the repair-room; and as they passed through the door and closed it after them, Miss Pinns gave Raymund a triumphant look which seemed to say, "Now she's going to catch it!"

When Rhoda and her uncle were alone, she found the old man unusually embarrassed and bowed over upon his two canes. "Rhoda," he said, "I have something to tell you." But instead of telling her, he sat down and nervously knocked the canes together. He took off his spectacles and looked at them, then put them on and ducked his head to peer through the upper lenses at the girl. "Rhoda, I-er-Miss Pinns-er-we are going to get married, to-day."

"O, Uncle William!" cried Rhoda, turning pale.

"And you and Raymund will have to find another home," continued the other hurriedly. "Miranda says we can not afford to keep you any longer."

"Who is Miranda?" asked Rhoda rather sharply.

"That's Miss Pinns." said her uncle William, knocking the canes together louder than before.

Rhoda began to cry. "I just couldn't help it," she explained afterwards to Raymund.

"I'm awfully sorry," said the old man with a quaver of distress, "it tears my heart. Rhoda, you can't imagine how dear you and Raymund have grown to me. I often reproach myself that when your mother lived here I didn't go to see her or have anything to do with her. Once she came to the shop, just after her husband's death, and she had you twins with her—you weren't more than four at the most, and I would hardly give her civil words. It's this way with me, child; I've never felt like falling down before a person just because kin to me. I never cared for relations on the ground that they were relations. I'd never known Susie Revore, and she was no more to me, although my half-

*Suggested by a question in "Pentwater Mus-ings" on the passing of the summer.

sister, than any other stranger. Of course I'd known her as a little girl, but that wasn't knowing the woman. And as to you twins, you were entire strangers, of course; as I may say, she hardly knew you herself. But you've lived with me now over five months, and you've been good and faithful in helping me to save, poor as I am." Rhoda believed the old man spoke at such length to hide his nervousness, but she was sure he felt kindly toward her.

"Oh, Uncle William," she cried, "if you like us and think we've done our part, will you send us out into the world when there's no place to go? If you don't care for us because we are kin, can't you give us a roof till we are a little older just for our work?"

"Miss Pinns won't hear to it," said the other. "I want you to believe, Rhoda, that I've urged your case."

"But why must you do what she says?"

"Because she is Miss Pinns, I suppose," said the old man glancing timidly toward the door. "Don't speak so loud, Rhoda."

Rhoda came nearer. "Uncle William, I don't believe you can be happy with her. Don't let her come between us! She can never love you as we can."

"She is very saving," said Mr. Hodges slowly. "She is a money-maker. I could not do without her. She knows just what I need, and what I like. She saves. I tell you, child, that woman's a miser. She is a great character. I can't do without her, and I suppose it's best to make everything rounded up and agreeable to feelings that we should marry."

Rhoda seized his hand and said in an urgent whisper, "Uncle William, break away from her influence!"

"Child, I can't!" murmured the other, trembling.

"Run away," whispered Rhoda. "Come with me and Raymund. Run from her. We'll hide somewhere."

"Where?" asked Mr. Hodges, a gleam of hope showing for a moment in his eyes. "Do you know of any retreat?"

Rhoda could not answer.

"No," said Mr. Hodges with a sigh, "it's not to be thought of. Look at me, on my two canes. Do I look like running away?" And then there's this to consider: Miss Pinns would come after me! No, the only way to do for her is to marry her. And I'll marry her!" he added somewhat bitterly. "Oh, yes, I'll do it! And then we'll see which of the two of us is the biggest saver and tightest squeezer!" He thumped his canes on the floor and looked defiant. "Let her come on!" he muttered, still afraid to speak aloud lest Miss Pinns be listening at the door. "Hist, now, Rhoda, here"—He made a sudden motion and thrust some bank notes into her hand. "I'm not going to send you out helpless and penniless, that is! Be careful of it; turn it over and over, and you'll be rich one day. S-h-h! hush! Don't say a word. She's awful sharp. Go on out before she begins to suspicion. Hide those bills in your bosom."

As Rhoda started away, the old man said softly, "Come back, child!" She returned. The old man put his hand in his pocket, kept it there a good while, and drew it out apparently with the greatest effort, as if it were partially paralyzed. "Here!" He handed her

some more notes. "That's another seventy-five. I meant to give you a hundred and fifty from the first, but I-er-I-a-ah-I forgot."

"Uncle William," said Rhoda, laying her hand upon his bowed shoulder, "I'd rather have your love and protection than all the money you have."

"It isn't worth that much," said Uncle William, shaking his head. "But I'm a poor man. Run on, Rhoda, get that money put somewhere quick, it makes me nervous."

So Miss Pinns married Mr. William Hodges on Christmas day, and Raymund and Rhoda were the melancholy witnesses. That day Raymund wrote a letter to Mr. Willby, of Frog Bend. It was as follows:

"Dear Mr. Willby—"We have been with Uncle William five months and two weeks. He married to-day, and they can not let us stay here any longer. Do you remember once telling me that if Rhoda and I ever needed a friend to call on you? We do indeed need a friend now, that our only relation in the world (but he was only mamma's half-brother) will not let us stay with him. Is there any work I could do in Frog Bend? I am willing to do any honest work, I don't care how hard it is. Yesterday Rhoda and I were sixteen. A few more years I will be a man. We can stay here till we hear from you, if an answer comes within the week. Maybe you could get me a place on a farm as a farm-hand—I've had experience in that, as I told you; or I could help in a second-hand clothing store, or could clerk, or do anything that just depends on perseverance and strength."

Two days after the mailing of this letter, a boy appeared at the pawnshop.

with a yellow envelope addressed to Raymund Revore. It contained a telegram to this effect: "Come immediately, green umbrella and all. Big surprise for you.—Nathaniel Willby."

Two days later Raymund and Rhoda got off the train at Frog Bend and had no difficulty in finding Mr. Willby's big brick house. He seemed as much delighted over their coming as if they had not been orphans, discarded by their sole surviving relative. His wife, a gentle refined lady, with snowy hair and a face of peace and beauty, made them feel at home as soon as she entered the room, for an atmosphere of home enveloped her. She was not really old, and the young people learned in the course of the day that her hair had turned white after the death of an only child, a young man of talent and promise. Perhaps it was to take her mind from the grave overlooking the Missouri that her husband had grown eccentric, abrupt and somewhat childlike. When her face settled in its most pensive calm, he would burst forth impetuously about some trifle, quarreling about the merchant who had not given him quite as much for his money as he would have given had he been the merchant and had the merchant been the purchaser—or quarreling because the neighbors let their cows roam the town and their chickens inundate his front yard—or, in short, railing about any trifle—but never a harsh word for Mrs. Willby.

When the first bloom of the meeting had been rubbed off by the friction of Mr. Willby's many questions, he said, "And now I want you to tell me how old that old woman is!"

"Who—Mrs. Weed?" said Rhoda. "I think she is seventy-eight."

"But you never asked? Didn't you ever find the ear-trumpet?"

"We found the ear-trumpet, but—"

"Amazing!" cried Mr. Willby, starting up. "Amazing! Have you no interest in your fellow-men? But come! I wired you that I had a big surprise in store for you. Come! Follow me!"

He led the way across the street to a one-story cottage perched upon a bluff that skirted the river shore.

"Go up there," said Mr. Willby, pointing his finger at the cottage, "and ring at that door!"

Rhoda would have felt some hesitation about ringing at a strange door, had she not detected Mr. Willby with a triumphant smile, digging his elbow into Raymund's side. Rhoda timidly passed up the walk and rang the doorbell. As soon as she did so, she caught sight, through a transparent square in the frosted glass, of a gray-haired man, with a long blue-checked apron fastened about his waist, wielding a broom upon the hall carpet. At the first sound of the bell, the gentleman wildly snatched at his apron and fled, swinging the broom over his shoulder. Rhoda could not help smiling at the panic she had produced. The figure of the fugitive seemed familiar.

"Ring again," called Mr. Willby impatiently, as he and Raymund came upon the porch. "Stamp hard, Raymund! Let's make him think a houseful of company has come. They're always coming here, as it is. They will kill his wife some day, this prowling, dressed-up, count-your-calls everlasting company. Ugh! how I hate it!"

Rhoda rang again. She was beginning to understand the big surprise in store for her. So when the door presently opened, and Brother Bellfield confronted her she was not quite as surprised as Mr. Willby had expected.

(To be Continued.)

THE HISTORY OF A HEART TRAGEDY.

BY OLIVE A. SMITH.

(Concluded from last week.)

Well, the plan worked beautifully, and at 8 o'clock that evening we were sitting in front seats at the hall. It is not the most elegant and refined auditorium in our town, and, after looking around, Dorothy whispered: "Bess, I don't know anybody here. The people don't seem to belong to our set. I'm kind of frightened; aren't you?"

"Nonsense!" I replied. "What if the audience is composed of persons belonging to a social stratum somewhat beneath our own? It is an evidence of a small nature to notice such trifles. See, there comes Madam Luvaney. O, look at those diamonds! And that dress!"

The costume was of pale blue silk, trimmed with perfectly elegant lace. The upper end of it was very greatly abridged and abbreviated. The lower end was as greatly extended and expanded. It (the lower end) expanded almost over the entire hall platform. Dorothy giggled and whispered: "That's a decolete toilette, and you know, Bess Merwin, it isn't proper to wear it to lecture in! They only belong at balls and dinners, and such things. I'm going right home, I am!"

My own nerves were a bit tremulous, but I had committed myself to the cause of emancipation, and I would not turn back. So I said, bravely: "Nonsense! Who cares about such trifles? She's going to lecture on the subject, and it's proper for her to ignore conventionalities herself. Sit still now and listen. She's going to begin."

If it were not that editors all object to the use of time-worn phrases, I would say that Dorothy and I were spell-bound by Madam Luvaney's beautiful lecture. It was grand! I can see her yet, as she raised her tall, graceful figure to its full height, and hurled from her charming red lips the following impassioned appeal:

"Why, O why, my sisters, will ye not rise in your might and break the shackles of conventionality with which the despot man hath bound ye? Why will ye who know the divine fire of human love sit passive, hiding your bruised and bleeding hearts from the world, and from the object of your affection, while man woes forth, free as the birds of the air, to seek his mate? Why, O why, my sisters, will ye bow down to tradition? O be free! Be free!"

At those words Dorothy got so excited that she stood right up. I took hold of her sash to pull her down, but the bow just untied and dangled down, looking so funny that, deeply moved as I was by the cause of emancipation, I giggled just like a silly school-girl. That made her cross, and she turned around and slapped my hand. But the audience was all applauding and shouting so that they didn't notice us. I tied her sash, and she sat down, and our eyes met, just as they did in the morning, and we understood each other. But to say more on that subject now would ruin the delicate unfolding of the plot that the editors are so fond of.

On the way home, we heard a woman say: "She's pretty well fixed, so she might have got along without taking up a collection. She's got six divorced husbands, and they averaged thirty thousand apiece in alimony."

"O!" whispered Dorothy, "just listen!" But I was not in the least excited. "What if she has made six uncongenial matrimonial alliances?" I answered. "She is a woman of lofty ideals, and it

Charcoal Kills Bad Breath.

would naturally be difficult for her to discover her true soul-affinity. Perseverence is much to be admired in matrimony, as in any other realm of life."

I am now rapidly approaching the climax to my story. Some editors say that it is the most important of all the parts. Others insist that the introduction is the most important. I do not wish to take sides either way, for I understand that editors are very sensitive men, and that their feelings are easily wounded, especially by their contributors. Only a few days ago I read in a magazine that "The editor experiences an acute pang every time he is forced to return an unsuccessful manuscript to its owner." That statement impressed me, gentle reader, because I saw, in another magazine, that some editors return 25 manuscripts every day. Just think of a poor editor experiencing 25 "acute pangs" every day in the year except Sunday! I used to think, in my childish ignorance, that editors lived an easy, luxurious life. Perhaps they do, with the exception of those "acute pangs," but they must be dreadfully wearing on the constitution.

I pass by the soul-stirring events of the next few days, not because they are unworthy of narration, but because the principles of art demand that I make the denouement of the story a complete surprise to you and the editor. I will proceed at once to the denouement.

On Tuesday afternoon, the door of Professor Ramey's room was burst open with great violence, and two suffering heroines, with tear-dimmed eyes and dishevelled locks, stood, hand in hand, before their hearts' idol.

"We have come," sobbed Dorothy, "because we can no longer hide from the world our bruised and bleeding hearts."

"We can not!" I echoed, from the folds of the handkerchief where my swollen face was hidden.

"We have risen in our might—and broken—the shacks—of conven—tion—ality," gasped Dorothy. She is so excitable! She should have said "shackles," but I thought it was no time to be exacting about trifles, so I moaned faintly, for I was very weak, "We have."

"Pray choose one of us," I wailed, "and the other—will go—forth to—her fate."

We could stand no longer, gentle reader, and we sank exhausted on the front seats. At the same time we were conscious of a peculiar, spasmodic sort of a noise that came from the region of Professor Ramey's desk. So great is the power of tradition over the feminine soul that we had kept our faces hidden. But the silence became so oppressive that I finally peeped out with my right eye, just as Dorothy peeped out with her left eye. The north window was open, and Professor Ramey stood there, his back turned toward us, and his broad shoulders heaving with emotion. Presently he turned around and walked to his desk. His eyes were red and watery, and he looked so grave and tragic! He stood there, twisting his mustache violently for some minutes. Then he looked at us as if he were going to speak. Then—O so suddenly!—he dropped his face into his hands and laughed! Such a great, hearty laugh as it was! I never heard anything like it from a professor before.

I will not attempt to describe our emotions. I will simply say that our womanly pride came to our rescue, and that we arose and walked haughtily and

rapidly down the aisle. I had grasped the handle of the door, when I heard the professor's voice. It had a ring of authority in it. We had heard that ring before. "Girls," he said, "come here."

We went.

"Sit down there," he said; "I want to talk to you a few moments."

We sat. I hope, gentle reader, that you and the editor do not expect Dorothy and me to remember every detail of that conversation. Our minds were in too great a tumult for that. But the professor talked nicely. He said that he appreciated our excellent work in history, and he feared he had encouraged us to confine ourselves too closely to books. He said that we must romp around during vacation, and not be in too much of a hurry to get hold of the lives of other people.

"In regard to the madam's cause," he continued, twisting his mustache again, and looking very grave, "you know we learn in history that reform is always of slow and difficult growth. You may live to see the day when the lady's ideals are realized, but I do not expect to. I shall probably have passed on to a higher plane of life. Personally I derive great comfort from that thought."

Then he said he must finish grading the "C" class papers, and asked us if we would like to help. Dorothy brightened right up, and said yes. We spread our wet handkerchiefs on the desk to dry, and, strange as it may seem, we were soon actually smiling over the limited knowledge of history revealed by those "C" class papers.

School closed the next week, and the professor made a lovely speech. He said he was going to travel during vacation, but was glad that he would have us all again next term. I have thought that perhaps we ought to be brave and cheerful, and wear smiling faces when we can. So we girls are going for a picnic tomorrow. I'm going to wear my new white dress, and—O, but we'll have a time!

———

EPILOGUE.

There is one point in my story that has worried me. It is the moral. Dorothy and I read up on the subject, and one editor said that "the moral should not stick out like the sting of a wasp." Another editor intimated that the custom of introducing any kind of morals in stories is an obsolete custom. We decided to adopt that view, so you will find no moral in the story.

After settling that question, we hunted up a book entitled "Hints to Young Writers." One of the hints was, "Stamps for the return of a manuscript should be enclosed in case it should be unavailable." Dorothy got out her dictionary to see what "unavailable" means, but the word wasn't there. Then I knew, as soon as I thought about it, that editors need dictionaries of their own, somewhat different from the dictionaries used by the masses. I told Dorothy that they would need words of their own in which to give adequate expression to their emotions when suffering from those "acute pangs" heretofore mentioned. I shall not enclose any stamps, for I know that my story will not be unavailable, no matter what that may mean.

Another hint was: "Letters of advice should be enclosed with the manuscript, not sent in separate envelopes." I shall not advise the editor very much, for men often resent advice given by females, even their own beloved partners. I shall merely advise him to publish my story in the very next number of his magazine, and to begin it on the first

❀ ❀

An old woman who entered a country savings bank not long ago was asked whether she wanted to draw or deposit.

"Nayther; I wants to put some money in," was the reply.

The clerk entered the amount and pushed the slip toward her to sign.

"Sign on this line, please," he said.

"Above or below it?"

"Just above it."

"Me whole name?"

"Yes."

"Before I was married?"

"No; just as it is now."

"Oi can't write."—*Harper's Weekly.*

❀ ❀

Gleanings from Magazines.

Secret of Woman's Health.

If the woman of the twentieth century is going to give the greater part of her waking hours to unnecessary care of her body, she sinks to the level of the Indian squaws, who were the pets of the great chiefs hundreds of years ago. The squaws were oiled and painted and overhung with sharks' teeth and wampum—they had rings on their fingers and bells on their toes. What real differences are there between those fine ladies of the Choctaws and the Iroquois and the fine ladies of to-day? And yet there echo in the ears of the modern woman the cry of the tenement house, the cry of the child laborer, the cry of all the pressing, unsolved problems of the home and of the world—the cry of her own immortal soul—the while she dawdles over her silly face, and grimaces before a mirror! The squaw was the nobler woman of the two. At least, she "lived up to her lights."

The whole "beautification" enterprise is delusive. The woman who scrupulously regards neatness, who observes the laws of health, who does the duty of each day as thought it might be her last, and then gives her best efforts to making her world better and happier, without much considering her own complexion—that woman is not only admirable for her character, but she is also likely to be far better looking than her be-laced, over-dressed, powdered, roughed, "cerated," massaged, and over-manipulated sister.—*Kate Upson Clark in Leslie's Weekly.*

How to be Very, Very Popular!

Never hesitate to talk about yourself and your affairs. This will interest everybody.

Do not fail to throw cold water on other people's plans and to discourage their ambitions. Nobody is sensitive about this.

Be sure to dwell upon the defects and failings of others, and call everybody's attention to them. Everybody likes gossip.

Always be on the watch for slights and insults. Remember, most people are your social superiors and are trying to cut you.

Always take the best seat wherever you go, and, after you are well seated, offer your seat to others without the slightest intention of getting up.

Just look out for your own comforts. Let other people do the same.

Never do anything that you do not feel like doing.

Never try to force your moods. Let them take care of themselves. Nobody will mind if you get into a rage, or nag or scold, or if you have the "blues." It is pleasant to have gloomy, moody people with long faces around the house; it is so uplifting to everybody.

Never hesitate to show it when your feelings are hurt, or to indicate your jealousy when others receive more attention or are better dressed than you.

If things do not suit you, slam things around the house. Be just as disagreeable as possible. Never mind if you break a thing or two now and then. It will relieve the blood pressure on the brain.

Always remember that praise is a splendid thing for you, but very bad for others. It encourages vanity, and people who are praised get so "puffed up" and "big headed" that there is no living with them.—*Success.*

Bees that Burrow in the Ground.

The burrowing-bees are commonly ranked with solitary insects. Certainly they are not "social," living in organized communities, like honey-bees. But one might venture to call them "neighborly insects," for they love to make their cavernous hermitages in well-peopled neighborhoods. Their burrow sites are preferably upon hard, dry spots, with a bit of slope, maybe. Therein the mother will sink a shaft eight or ten inches deep and about three-eighths of an inch wide. On either side she will dig out small ovate cells, five or six in all, which she duly provisions and supplies with an egg apiece.

The burrows are about the bigness of the occupant and extend inward for a foot or so with sundry enlargements, after the fashion of their kind, wherein the young are bred. In the height of the season these bee neighborhoods are the scene of a busy life. The air resounds with the hum of wings as the insects fly to and fro on parental duties bent, plenishing their nurseries with pollen and honey-of-the-flowers. But just inside each burrow-gate an interesting phase of insect life goes on. Beyond the gateway, which is about the length of the bee, there rises a vestibule—a tiny expansion of the burrow—whose use soon appears. Just within the gateway, with face toward the opening, one of the housekeepers, now the male and now the female, but oftener the former, keeps constantly on guard. And great need there is for such sentry duty; for insect rogues and thieves besiege the doors to plunder the contents of the nurseries or infect them with parasitic eggs.

Here, then, we see the male on sentry duty, his body blocking up the gateway and his rounded head closing up the entrance. When his mate comes home with her bee-basket full, the guard backs into the vestibule, which is large enough to allow the passing of the female, and returns to his post. A loving welcome awaits the incomer; for the doorkeeper with open mandibles and waving antennæ, the apian style of embrace, greets his partner right joyously. Thus the good mistresses of our homes and their maids at the back gate are not the only order of housekeeping creatures that exchange kisses at one's doorways!—*A. C. McCook, in Harper's Magazine for September.*

Graduate Courses at Home,

leading to degrees. If you can not come to the college, the college can go to you. Let us send you particulars. Write Pres. Chas. J. Burton, Christian College, Oskaloosa, Iowa.

Twenty Times a Day.

BY W. R. RAMBO.

Twenty times a day, dear,
  Twenty times a day,
Your mother thinks about you,
  At school, or else at play.
She's busy in the kitchen,
  Or she's busy up the stairs;
But like a song her heart within,
  Her love for you is there.

There's just a little thing, dear,
  She wishes you would do,
I'll whisper, 'tis a secret;
  Now, mind, I'll tell it you;
Twenty times a day, dear,
  And more, I've heard you say,
"I'm coming in a minute,"
  When you should at once obey."

At once, as soldiers instant
  At the motion of command;
At once, as sailors seeing
  The captain's warning hand,
You could make the mother happy
  By minding in that way,
Twenty times a day, dear,
  Twenty times a day.
     —Margaret E. Sangster.

❀ ❀

Advance Society Letters.

BY J. BRECKENRIDGE ELLIS.

I announced two weeks ago that our ice cream social was closed, but since then I have been obliged to send out and get more ice cream, for the orders have kept coming in right along. At that time we had taken in, you will remember, $91.50, which we thought pretty well, considering that the ice cream was all imaginary and you had to stay at home to eat it. So we cried "Hurrah!" But this week I think we will all have to throw up our hats, for we have inched our way above the $100 line. Here's a note from Mrs. V. F. Johnson and her children, Everest and Majorie, Clinton, Ia.: "We have become very much interested in orphan Charlie. Everest and Majorie are two little Clinton residents; each wants to send 10 cents for the educational fund. Count it in your ice cream social. What is required of the members of the Av. S.? We think we would like to join. We pray that Charlie may grow to be a good and useful man." (We mustn't forget that THE CHRISTIAN-EVANGELIST is getting new subscribers all the time, and though we know so much about the Av. S., others may not. The Advance Society was founded for the purpose of leading people to read good literature regularly; primarily for young people and secondarily for anybody. The rules are: Read 5 pp. history and 30 lines of poetry every week, memorize a good quotation weekly, read at least one verse in the Bible every day, and keep an account of work done in a notebook; at the end of 12 weeks, a "quarter," send me your report. Every time you keep a "quarter" it entitles you to be printed on our honor list. Our new honor list is as follows: Beulah Shrotridge, Glenwood, Ind. (10th quarter); Ruth E. Day, Sparta, Mo. (5th); Harriet M. Causland, Coffeyville, Kan. (the number of quarter is not marked on this report); Edna Bear, Iberia, Mo. (11th and 12th); Walter S. Whitacre, Mt. Vernon, Ill. (9th); Flossie Davis, Des Moines, Ia. (9th); Mrs. F. A. Potts, Chattanooga, Tenn. (22d); Grace Everest, Oklahoma, Okla. (7th); Jean Chambers, Richwood, Ky. (14th); Nannie D. Chambers, Richwood, Ky. (30th and 31st). While I am still in this parenthesis I will thank Edith Slightman, of Spokane, Wash., for a picture card entitled, "On the Stump." The illustration is a white-and-gray cat, lying upon a stump. It is not nearly so handsome and graceful a cat as my Felix, but I presume it was the best feline they could find up in Washington. I certainly appreciated the remembrance, though this may not sound as if I did. Had it been anything but a cat I

wouldn't have said a word, but of course any cat instinctively invites comparison with Felix. I also have an illustrated post card from our old-time Av. S. member, Susie Scearce, from Colorado Springs. She writes: "We took the trip through the Garden of the Gods Friday. It is certainly wonderful. Wednesday I walked up to the Halfway House. It is a steep walk of three miles. The mountains are wonderful. We leave for Salt Lake City to-morrow." The picture on this card of the Balanced Rock is novel and pretty; there is no cat on it. Also I have a picture card from Bessie Tracy Ryman, Liberty, Mo., of the Smithville High School. The building, I observe, is of two stories, and the telephone pole of four, which is about all I can say for this picture. I suspect there are cats in that basement. I will crawl out of the open where there is more air, though it does look as if it were "fixing" to rain— and a church social at our house this very night!)

Mrs. Ella G. Parker, Hannibal, Mo.: "Here we are, the Junior Christian Endeavorers of the First Christian Church, with the proceeds of our literal ice cream social. Last summer we sewed and made many things for the Babies' Home, St. Louis, but this summer sickness prevented—my boys sew beautifully. As superintendents, we promised our Juniors an interesting social. We had 1,300 tickets struck—sold every one, and some paid 20 cents for a ticket just to help along. We told everybody about Charlie, and that we also wanted to send part of our proceeds to the other orphans at the Orphans' Home, St. Louis. Mrs. T. G. Delaney offered us the use of her lawn; she thinks so much of the Av. S." (And we think so much of her.) "So Mrs. Delaney, Mrs. Arnold, Miss Austin and I met with the children and prepared to make a fine appearance. We had beautiful Chinese lanterns, etc. So many people came that we sold all our cream and had to send for more," (just as I had to do.) "And such fine home-made cake as our mothers made for us!" (Um-mm-mmh!) "We inclose $15 for Charlie's education; that is half of what we cleared. We wish you could visit our Junior meeting some time." (And so do I.) "Our attendance has been 25 to 50 every Sunday during the summer, though many of our too members were out of town. Mrs. V. Arnold is assistant. We wish Charlie a pleasant winter's work, and all success this life can afford." Mrs. N. C. Skinner, Dorsey, Ill.: "While Charlie was visiting us we noticed his crutches were rather short, and a few interested friends send you this little donation ($3.30) to get him new ones. We wanted Charlie to stay to our basket meeting September 1. Brother Groner has preached for this church 26 years to-morrow, and we celebrate each anniversary with a basket dinner, free to all. Please come and take dinner with us." (I am thoroughly in sympathy with that basket dinner, and appreciate your kind invitation so much, but am sorry to say that I have already had my dinner of September 1 and feel that I could not take another bite during that day.) Manie Bayless, Mulkeytown, Ill.: "Have been wishing I could help with the social ever since you proposed it. A friend has given me a little money to use, so I send a dime for a dish of Charlie's ice cream. Hope you are not sold out yet." (I would have been sold out if I hadn't heard from faithful old comrades like yourself.) "May God shower his richest blessings on you and Charlie and Drusie." Sarah Ann Gibbs,

Fresno, Cal.: "I have just got home from San Francisco for the first time. I struck the strike. From there I went to Santa Clara Valley, visited Aunt Abby on her prune ranch; went to San Jose to the ice cream social at the Woman's Exchange, gave Aunt Allie the ice cream and now send you the 20 cents for Charlie. I hope Charlie will meet Rhoda and Rayntund in St. Louis and have a good chat with them." Flossie Davis, Des Moines: "Have been visiting all summer and have had company ever since I got home. I almost forgot to read my history last week. I neglected to send to the library so I had to hustle around on Saturday and borrow one. I've read all we have. I got 3 books of poetry Christmas and am almost through the last one. I guess I am too late for the social, but will send my little dime anyhow. I must close and get some dinner for my company." (Yes, that's the trouble with company. Nobody cares about their being around except at meal time. Oh, give me company who do not eat! Your dime was on time. They always are. I smile inwardly when people meet me and say, "I am so sorry I didn't know about your social, so I could have given something." What's to keep 'em from doing it yet? The laws of Arkansas may not be all they should be, but they don't forbid that.) "We are going out to Ft. Des Moines this afternoon to see the soldiers' quarters. It is very pretty out there." Edna Bear, Iberia, Mo.: "It has been 4 years since I began keeping the Av. S. rules. I inclose $1.15; 15 for Charlie's education, 10 for Drusie, and for the 90 cents, send me a gold Av. S. pin." (I have ordered the pin to be sent you from N. Y. Let me know when you receive it.) "I attended the picnic of the Farmers' Institute one day. It was held Sept. 14, 15. In the morning was the parade, headed by the Iberia cornet band, followed by the M. W. A. and the farmers with their display of corn, also dairying. Then came the flower display and lastly the young women riding white horses. I visited the new dormitory built for the young ladies of Iberia Academy. In the evening I heard some very able speaking, also music by the band." Mrs. A. B. Cornelius, Humboldt, Neb.: "I look forward to the time when my little daughters will become interested in the Av. S. work. It is a relief to turn from theology and sectarian discussions to children who do not talk so much, but are doing things. Thanks for introducing me to Felix. Like yourself I like cats,—at a respectful distance; then Felix always amuses and never annoys me." (Yes, in other words, for let us be plain about this matter, you don't have to feed him.) "Here is a dollar each for Charlie and Drusie. I thank you for your words about chain letters. You said what I have long wanted to say; you gave me much moral encouragement." Reader of THE CHRISTIAN-EVANGELIST: "I inclose money order for $25 for orphan Charlie's educational fund. From all accounts I judge him a promising lad, one who will make good use of any advantages given him. Am much interested in the aim, work and progress of the Av. S." (This note, brief and eminently to the point hails from Riverside, Cal.) Walter S., Whitacre, Mt. Vernon, Ill.: "I have about two more quarters finished now, and will copy and mail them as soon as I can. I send my 9th quarter anyway, because my ability to do anything is so uncertain that I must wait no longer. I was greatly surprised and pleased to receive your novel, 'Garcilaso,' as an Av. S. premium, but was unable at the time to sit up to write my acknowledgement. I am very sorry I could not attend the ice cream social. That's just the kind I like—a social where I can't get hold of the cream or anything to eat." (At some socials you don't hold much when you are given sure enough things.) "I attended this one in spirit but for certain legitimate reasons failed to order my cream. I am proud of the Av. S., proud to be a member of it. If I were president of such an organization I fear I would be too proud for anything. But you have too much to think about to be affected that way; writing books and stories and letters, and reading letters and counting money and watching it rain, and looking after Felix is enough to keep any one in an humble frame of mind. I have been thinking of going to Eureka Springs for my health; that's in an adjoining county to yours. They claim to average 300 clear days there per year." (If you could secure a claim like that and settle on it, you would be rich before the year was out. Seriously, though, my county stays dry from the first of January to the end of those wornout, listless, unsatisfactory days that follow Christmas; yes, we've just voted it.) "When I go to Eureka and fatten on spring water I'll make it a point to climb the mountains and call on you and Felix." (Good! You'd better lay in a supply of alpenstocks, though, before you try to reach Bentonville. It is needless to caution any one who has followed me through these pages to fetch an umbrella.) Mrs. Mary S. Lemar, Rich Hill, Mo.: "Here is a dollar for Charlie's educational fund; hope I am not too late for a dish of ice cream." (We have sent the boys to bring in some empty benches from the old church; plenty of room yet.) Nelle Northcutt, Knox City, Mo.: "Our ice cream social is a little late. It came off some time ago, but on account of illness have been unable to send the money before, $2.05. I am so glad you have been so successful. I send the names of those who contributed." (Among which I note with pleasure that of my old friend Brother H. A. Northcutt.) Anna P. Smith, Howard, Kan.: "Am I too late for the social? If the freezer is empty and the angel food all gone, give me 15 big red Arkansas apples—here is $1.50 for myself and S. S. class. I had one of those apples at the World's Fair and know they are good. I pray the Lord's richest blessings upon all members of the Av. S. for their noble work, and I pray that Charlie may live to be noble and good." Mrs. F. A. Potts, Chattanooga: "I congratulate you on the success of the ice cream social. It is very encouraging. It seems there should be enough

to start Charlie in school. How long do you expect it to take him to finish the course? If I have anything encouraging to tell you a little later I will write you again." (Mrs. Potts tells me that she collected $1.30 for the social and has placed it in the bank at Chattanooga to our credit. I do not count it in with our receipts because I have made it a rule of my life and of the Av. S., never to count any money till my eye has gazed upon its honest face. All the same, we will remember it is down south for us, for Mrs. Potts has put it with a little sum which is drawing interest at the bank for Charlie. I have several letters from Charlie and from Drusie, but must wait two weeks to hand them out; at which time we will discuss Charlie's educational prospects. Oh, here is a post script to Walter Whitacre's letter which I overlooked): "When it came to getting this letter and Av. S. report ready for the mail, I just kept wishing a dish of Charlie's ice cream worse and worse, and so my partner and I hunted around till we found a couple of dimes and here they are for our two dishes. I could eat a dozen or two of that kind of cream if I had dimes enough. I am a little older than Charlie and I remember when I was about his age, how badly I wanted money to go to school on. I owe Drusie a letter and now that I am able to write I must write to her the very next one. By the way, is the South Chih-li Mission a union mission?" (It is union in the sense that when its missionaries left this country they laid aside all denominational differences, and went simply on the Bible, without any creeds, or under any organizations. These missionaries among whom Drusie is so happy, find the natives wholly ignorant of predestination, original sin and close communion; but as they are equally ignorant of the story of our Savior, they think it best to devote all their time to teaching the heathen about the Blessed One of Bethlehem. A last word about our ice cream social; it has brought in, up to date, $138.15!

Bentonville, Ark.

The Right Kind of Hearts.

BY MRS. L. MEALEY.

'Twas only a little dead baby lying there so pale and cold, its little form like sculptured marble. The little dimpled hands were meekly crossed above the quiet breast. The golden curls were brushed from off the broad, white brow, and the long, silken lashes swept the rounded cheek. 'Twas just a pale little rosebud broken from off the parent stem. Its little life ended almost before it had begun. The pure soul had escaped from its tenement of clay, and gone to live with God.

> Sweetly it rests and on dream wings flies
> To play with the angels of paradise.

Its mission on earth was ended. No more would the silent rooms echo with its childish laughter and the pattering of little feet. But the baby hands are now reaching down from above to draw the hearts of the grief-stricken parents heavenward. There lay the little casket in all its snowy loveliness, fit emblem of purity. We, too, must become pure in heart like little children if we would enter the kingdom of heaven, and behold its glories. For nothing unclean, or tarnished may enter there. We must have our robes washed white in the blood of the Lamb. We must live pure lives day by day, and do nothing that is displeasing to the Master. Let us not be desirous of vain glory, provoking one another, envying one another. We must also be careful in little things as well as in great things.

It is the little things sometimes that tell. I once knew a dear old Christian woman who was poor in this world's goods, but who had treasures untold laid up above. Well, this dear old mother in Zion wove carpets for a living, and one day a customer accused her of keeping back some of her carpet rags. "Why, my dear woman," she said, "I wouldn't do a thing like that for the whole world, for what would it profit me if I gained the carpet rags but lost my immortal soul?"

And so the little things count as well as the great things. We should also have a spiritual housecleaning occasionally; in fact, we should have one every day. We must not only sweep out the middle of the room, but we must dig out the corners and sweep down all of the spiritual cobwebs, such as roots of bitterness, wicked thoughts, jealousies, etc., that may be lurking there awaiting a favorable opportunity to spring forth some unlucky day to confound us. A friend of mine one time asked her minister how she could obtain a pure heart and keep it pure. She had made a profession of religion and united with the church, but she was not satisfied. She feared her religion was mere empty form. She attended church regularly, but she feared her devotion lacked the life and spirit that they should have; besides, she realized that she was proud and vain, easily puffed up, and was conscious of cherishing roots of bitterness towards a friend. She felt that she was wrong in every way. She was in the slough of despondency and was not spiritually strong enough to climb out. And so she carried her troubles to her pastor. He told her that in the first place she must humble herself and become as a little child; carry her griefs to her heavenly Father, just as she would to her own earthly parent; and make a complete surrender. She must not keep back anything. If the gift was complete, and she was truly sincere, God would pour out his richest blessings upon her. She took the advice and made the surrender, and she became a power for good both in her home and in the church.

Perhaps some of us are not living as close to the Master as we should. Only God and our own hearts know.

Lyons, Kan.

Christian Publishing Company

2712 Pine St., St. Louis, Mo.

J. H. GARRISON,	- - - -	President
W. W. DOWLING,	- - -	Vice-President
GEO. L. SNIVELY,	- -	Sec. and Gen. Supt
R. P. CROW,	- -	Treas. and Bus. Manager

Our first supply of rally day souvenirs was quickly exhausted. We have a new shipment and can now fill all orders promptly.

This sentiment is expressed in scores of letters—"Having examined several church hymnals, our committee has decided to purchase 'Gloria in Excelsis.' Send them at your earliest convenience."

We are receiving many orders for the picture of Editor J. H. Garrison that we are giving as a premium for one new subscription and one renewal accompanied by the necessary $3. This picture should be in home, study and church library.

Though not conspicuously advertised of late, the "Holy Spirit" by J. H. Garrison, and "Victory of Faith," by E. L. Powell, have been great sellers through the summer. Only $1 each, or either in combination with THE CHRISTIAN-EVANGELIST for $2.25.

Below we present a cut of the "Buckingham," THE CHRISTIAN-EVANGELIST's headquarters in Buffalo. We can get the management to agree to receive only a limited number of our guests, as this popular resort is usually full to its utmost capacity. Two dollars per day, American plan, will be the rate. It is within two blocks of the convention hall.

When told other Bible school literature is "just as good as the Dowling," a tribute is being paid our Bible school supplies that we highly appreciate. Such testimonials have their part in securing for this house orders from thousands of our schools for lesson helps, juvenile papers and song books. Samples always sent on application. We court comparison of quality and prices.

THE CHRISTIAN-EVANGELIST and a fountain pen for $2. THE CHRISTIAN-EVANGELIST and the "Ladies' Home Companion"

"The Buckingham"— Headquarters in Buffalo for "Christian-Evangelist Special" Tourists.

$2.25. THE CHRISTIAN-EVANGELIST (to a new subscriber) and a self-filling fountain pen warranted ten years, $2.50. THE CHRISTIAN-EVANGELIST and the "Review of Reviews" to either a new subscriber or a renewal, $3—the latter alone will cost you $3 if ordered from the Review office.

"I am glad you have taken hold of this method of supplying preachers with the best books published on the greatest themes of our times and on such favorable terms that many of us could not buy on any other conditions. You keep abreast of the times as a publishing house and an appreciative ministry will doubtless reward you by their gratitude and patronage.—Joseph Lowe, Oakland, Kan.

Write us for the installment plan of buying the best books at the lowest prices.

THE CHRISTIAN-EVANGELIST Special over the Wabash leaves St. Louis at noon, Thursday, October 11. We will have a specially conducted party, and will gladly welcome all disciples who wish to go with us up to the convention city. Officers of the Wabash company will be in attendance and every accommodation possible will be granted our companions in travel. Remember you have the choice of a lake trip without added expense.

Arrangements have been made in the interest of our Foreign Missionary Society to sell regular $1.50 books like Mrs. Susie Rijnhart's "With the Tibetans in Tent and Temple," at 60c. Bishop Thoburn's "Conquest of India," John H. DeForest's "Sunrise in the Sunrise Kingdom," Wilson S. Naylor's "Daybreak in the Dark Continent," and Ralph E. Dif-

fendorfer's "Child Life in Mission Lands" at 50c. Cloth bound.

Adding new galleys to our mailing list is a prominent feature of our composing room. Our constituency and even those who were not formerly our constituents, but who realize as never before the need of journalistic leadership surcharged with the sentiment "In faith, unity; in opinion and methods, liberty; in all things, charity," have thrown themselves in uncalculating devotion and enthusiasm into the enterprise of placing THE CHRISTIAN-EVANGELIST in 100,000 homes. They bid fair to succeed before 1909. Every mail brings multitudes of subscriptions by ones and twos accompanied by the regular $1.50 fee. We are happy to report the following clubs also, during the week:

Lima, Ohio, J. N. Scholes, pastor	3
Cimmaron, Kan., L. E. Minton, agent	3
Denison, Tex., G. W. Lee, minister	4
Thorntown, Ind., E. P. Lane, minister	4
Collinwood, Ont., John Williams, pastor	5
Beaver Creek, Md., W. S. Hade, pastor	5
Laplata, Mo., Percy J. Carnes, pastor	7
Sheridan, Ind., W. D. Bartle, pastor	7
Ladoga, Ind., S. W. Sumner, minister	7
Elvins, Mo., J. F. Grissom, pastor	8
Havana, Ill., Louis O. Lehman	10
Moline, Kan., J. A. M. Brown, pastor	12
Jamestown, Ind., W. H. Newlin, pastor	12
Lincoln, Neb., G. H. Exley, agent	14
Danville, Ind., E. E. Moorman, pastor	17
Crawfordsville, Ind., Earl Wilfley, pastor	24
Lafayette, Ind., Una Dell Berry, assistant pastor	49

THE
CHRISTIAN-
EVANGELIST

A WEEKLY RELIGIOUS NEWSPAPER.

Volume XLIII.	No. 41.

ST. LOUIS, OCTOBER 11, 1906.

From an oil painting made by Bogle in 1859. See page 1294.

ALEXANDER CAMPBELL, AGE 72.

Copyright by Mrs. Decima Campbell Barclay. Bethany, W. Va.

"Light is certainly increasing, charity enlarging the circle of its activities, the mountains of discord diminishing, and the deep valleys which separated Christians, are filling up."

The Christian-Evangelist.

J. H. GARRISON, Editor

PAUL MOORE, Assistant Editor

F. D. POWER,
B. B. TYLER, } Staff Correspondents.
W. DURBAN,

Subscription Price, $1.50 a Year.

For foreign countries add $1.04 for postage.

Remittances should be made by money order, draft, or registered letter; not by local cheque, unless 15 cents is added to cover cost of collection.

In Ordering Change of Post Office give both old and new address.

Matter for Publication should be addressed to THE CHRISTIAN-EVANGELIST. Subscriptions and remittances should be addressed to the Christian Publishing Company, 2712 Pine Street, St. Louis, Mo. Unused Manuscripts will be returned only if accompanied by stamps.

News Items, evangelistic and otherwise, are solicited, and should be sent on a postal card, if possible.

Published by the Christian Publishing Company, 2712 Pine Street, St. Louis, Mo.

Entered at St. Louis P. O. as Second Class Matter

WHAT WE STAND FOR.

For the Christ of Galilee,
For the truth which makes men free,
For the bond of unity
Which makes God's children one.

For the love which shines in deeds,
For the life which this world need,
For the church whose triumph speeds
The prayer: "Thy will be done."

For the right against the wrong,
For the weak against the strong,
For the poor who've waited long
For the brighter age to be.

For the faith against tradition,
For the truth 'gainst superstition,
For the hope whose glad fruition
Our waiting eyes shall see.

For the city God is rearing,
For the New Earth now appearing,
For the heaven above us clearing,
And the song of victory.

— J. H. Garrison.

CHRISTIAN=EVANGELIST

"IN FAITH, UNITY, IN OPINION AND METHODS, LIBERTY, IN ALL THINGS, CHARITY."

Vol. XLIII.   October 11, 1906   No. 41

1809 CENTENNIAL PROPAGANDA CHURCHES OF CHRIST 1909

: : : GEO. L. SNIVELY : : :

Marching to Victory.

BY O. M. THOMASON.

Tune—"Marching Through Georgia."

Let us tune our voices for the great triumphant song,
Let us glean the golden sheaves as we march along,
Let the Pittsburg meeting be fifty thousand strong,
As we go marching to Victory.

Chorus—

Hurrah! hurrah! we'll make the music ring;
Hurrah! hurrah! the gospel we will sing,
And many a weary soul to Christ in triumph we will bring,
As we go marching to Victory.

From the land where heathen souls are in the greatest need,
There will be the sowers who have sown the gospel seed,
Telling of the precious souls from bondage they have freed,
While they were marching to Victory.

There will be the reapers from the islands of the sea,
Telling of the joy there is in making sinners free,
Telling of the work that yet remains for you and me,
As we go marching to victory.

There will be rejoicing by the workers gathered there,
Telling of their fields of labor scatter'd far and near,
Don't you want to do your part and in the glory share?
When we accomplish the victory?

There we'll get encouragement to press on evermore,
And gather inspiration for the work that lies before,
Till our ship will anchor on the happy golden shore,
And we've accomplished the victory..
Davenport, Wash.

LOOKING TOWARD PITTSBURG.

It is not surprising that under the inspiration of our Centennial's appeals for heroic initiative and achievements sublime our poets whose hearts are full should break forth into song.

During that great festival there will be triumphal odes read to applauding thousands, and afterward commemorative ones will find way into our literature. But doubtless the songs angels will most approve are those sung along the way, helping us past discouragements, cheering us under the clouds and through the dust of the conflict, and bringing us victory beaming into the Centennial Assembly in 1909. We shall sing your song, Brother Thomason, and thank you for its pictures and sentiments of sacred conquest.

Congratulations, Brothers Gates and Johann. We rejoice in the rising tide of interest in our Bible colleges. Christian missions, Christian benevolence and Christian education constitute a trinity of interests embracing most of the best incentives and activities of our churches. There should be a proportional development of these. The greatest good to our common Christianity will be conserved by their being builded up together. Let us closely scrutinize the statistical tables and rally to the help of the weakest while

rejoicing in the progress of the more prosperous.

A Large (Conditional) Gift.

Mrs. E. L. Ford and daughters, Estelle and Nell B., have agreed to give to the Disciples' Divinity House the sum of $10,000 to establish an endowed scholarship fund, on condition that a like sum be added to it from other sources.

The interest from this gift of the Fords will be used to aid young men to study

THOMAS CAMPBELL,

Father of Alexander Campbell. (See Easy Chair.)

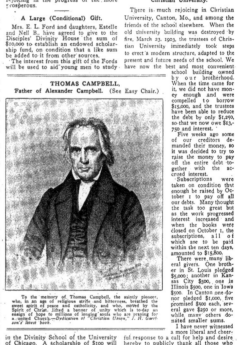

To the memory of Thomas Campbell, the saintly pioneer, who, in an age of religious strife and bitterness, breathed the sweet spirit of peace and catholicity, and who, moved by the Spirit of Christ, lifted a banner of unity which is to-day an ensign of hope to millions of longing souls who are praying for a united Church.—*Dedication of "Christian Union," I. H. Garrison's latest book.*

in the Divinity School of the University of Chicago. A scholarship of $100 will be offered annually to the graduating classes of each of the colleges. They will be assigned by a committee of the college faculty to the students best qualified by character and scholarship, for the ministry of the Gospel. The ultimate end in view is to raise the average of ministerial qualification and equipment among the Disciples. Each $100 of revenue from the fund will bring one new student annually to the university.

ERRETT GATES.

Christian University.

There is much rejoicing in Christian University, Canton, Mo., and among the friends of the school elsewhere. When the old university building was destroyed by fire, March 23, 1903, the trustees of Christian University immediately took steps to erect a modern structure, adapted to the present and future needs of the school. We have now the best and most convenient school building owned by our brotherhood. When the time came for it, we did not have money enough and were compelled to borrow $15,000, and the trustees have been able to reduce the debt by only $1,250, so that we now owe $13,750 and interest.

Five weeks ago some of our creditors demanded their money, so it was decided to try to raise the money to pay off the entire debt together with the accrued interest.

Subscriptions were taken on condition that enough be raised by October 1 to pay off all our debts. Many thought the task too great but as the work progressed interest increased and when the books were closed on October 1, the subscriptions, all of which are to be paid within the next ten days, amounted to $15,800.

There were many liberal givers. One brother in St. Louis pledged $5,000; another in Kansas City $500, one in Illinois $500, one in Iowa $500. In Canton one donor pledged $1,000, five promised $500 each, several gave $250 or more, while many others donated smaller sums.

I have never witnessed a more liberal and cheerful response to a call for help and desire hereby to publicly thank all those who have assisted us in word or deed.

Within the next two weeks Christian University will be entirely out of debt. The new building with its furniture and apparatus is worth $60,000 and we shall be glad to present it to the, brotherhood, free of all incumbrance.

It is now our purpose to work for additional endowment and expect to report an increase of no less than $100,000, when we come to the Centennial in 1909. CARL JOHANN, President C. U.

election held after the withdrawal of our troops. The weak point of the South American republics has always been the unwillingness of the party in power to retire from office when its time is up and the unwillingness of the party out of power to stay out patiently when it is the victim of an unfair election. From the most reliable indications, it seems that the election by which Palma was made president for a second term was not much more honest than the elections in St. Louis and Philadelphia used to be a few years ago, and that the Liberals had very little chance of voting. The Cuban Liberals, moreover, were not nearly so patient as the St. Louis Republicans and the Philadelphia Democrats used to be, and they tried to get their rights by fighting for them. That started the trouble which ended in the resignation of Palma and the setting up of the new provisional American government in Cuba. Taft is just the man for such an emergency. He has been through the same sort of thing in the Philippines, and he is big and strong and wise enough to manage the matter. It is lucky for us that we had him to send and lucky for Cuba that we sent him. One failure does not prove incapacity for self-government, and the president is determined that Cuba shall have another chance. Most babies fall at least once while they are learning to walk. When they do, it is a kindness to them to pick them up—that is intervention— but it is not necessary to strap them back in their go-carts forever.

❀

The New York Republicans have nominated Hughes for governor and the

Hearst and Hughes. Democrats have put Hearst at the head of their ticket. Jerome says he will stump the state for Hughes "for the good of the Democratic party." This means, clearly enough, that he will withdraw from the independent candidacy to which he had seemed committed. Hearst's nomination splits the Democratic party as wide open as the Republican party was before the recent reconciliation of its factions. Mayor McClellan of New York says he is too good a Democrat to vote for Hearst. Numerous other prominent Democrats declare that they will bolt Hearst. Bourke Cockran makes a lame apology for the nomination by saying that the only choice open to the convention, as between Hearst and his rivals, was the alternative between "rottenness and riot." As between these two evils, he prefers riot—that is, Hearst. This definition of Hearst may or may not be just. We are inclined to believe that he is really not so bad as his own papers would lead one to suppose. But at any rate it represents the opinion of many both in and out of his party, and there will be a good many thousands of Democrats and independents who, when it comes to choosing at the polls between

Hearst and Hughes, who stands for neither rottenness nor riot, will vote for Hughes. Mr. Hughes is known to the public only as the man who conducted the insurance investigation before the legislative committee with conspicuous ability and therein showed himself immune to the baleful effects of corporate influence. There is no reason why he should not get a tolerably full vote from his own party and he will certainly get a large number of independent and Democratic votes.

❀

Five new and conflicting prophets have arisen in Zion City, we are told, each

Rival Prophets. with his separate scheme for reforming and redeeming that religio-medico-financial enterprise, and most of them proposing to lead the faithful away from the flesh-pots of Dowie's and Voliva's commercialism into a Canaan flowing with purely spiritual milk and honey. At the same time it is announced that Dowie himself has decided to remain in Zion City and take his chances of recovering his health there. No wonder he feels it necessary to remain and stay the tide of such dangerous and destructive reformation. Zion City without its commercialism and Dowieism without its abundant rake-offs for the "General Overseer" and its glittering prospect of fat dividends for pious investors, would be like the play of Hamlet with Hamlet and Polonius and Ophelia and the King and Queen and everybody else left out— except the grave-digger.

❀

On Thursday of last week occurred one of the most imposing civic parades which

The St. Louis Parade. the city of St. Louis accustomed to pageants of this kind, ever witnessed. The occasion was the unveiling of the statue "St. Louis", in front of the Art Building, on Art Hill, in Forest Park, the scene of the recent World's Fair. The presentation speech was made by ex-Governor D. R. Francis, and the response thereto was made by Mayor Wells, whose little daughter, at the close of his address, pulled the rope that unveiled to the gaze of cheering thousands this splendid statue symbolizing St. Louis on her onward march. Governor Francis took occasion to urge a subscription of at least $500,000 to renovate and enlarge Art Hall and put it in condition for receiving the finest works of art, and of throwing it open to the public as a free art museum. Later he subscribed $50,000 to the enterprise, and others joining him have insured the raising of that amount. The various departments of the city—its postoffice clerks, its fire department, its water department, the street-cleaning department, together with the representatives of the different kinds of business and the military organizations, marching under a bright October sun, made an imposing pageant for the immense throngs of citizens and visitors that witnessed it.

Editorial

Where Jesus Placed the Emphasis.—VIII.

Obedience.

One of the cardinal principles which Jesus taught and exemplified in his own life was that of obedience to the will of God. At the beginning of his ministry he went from Galilee to the Jordan unto John to be baptized of him, and John, recognizing his sinless character, would have hindered him, saying "I have need to be baptized of thee, and comest thou to me?" The sufficient reply of Jesus was, "Thus it becometh us to fulfill all righteousness." It was, in his thought, then, a "righteous" thing to submit to an ordinance which had been instituted under divine direction and which would place him at once in touch and fellowship with those who were seeking to honor God and to separate from sinners. In the light of this example of Jesus it is difficult to understand the attitude of some toward the ordinance of Christian baptism. If Jesus felt it becoming to him to submit to baptism, why should any one seeking to follow in his footsteps hesitate in rendering obedience to an ordinance which still stands as the line of separation between the church and the world, and obedience to which is a token of surrender to him in whose name we are baptized?

But we are not to think of baptism as exhausting the meaning of obedience, or even of constituting its most essential feature. Obedience is conforming to the will of God, both inwardly and outwardly. All the beatitudes indicate the obedience of the heart and mind to the will of God. But it is no token of our loyalty in spirit, to be neglectful of any command of God. Jesus said, "Whosoever therefore shall break one of these least commandments, and shall teach men so, shall be called least in the kingdom of heaven; but whosoever shall do and teach them, he shall be called great in the kingdom of heaven." (Matt. 5:19.) Jesus taught that men's characters are to be judged by their lives. "By their fruits ye shall know them. Do men gather grapes of thorns, or figs of thistles?" (Matt. 7:16.) Again he said, "Not every one that saith 'unto me, Lord, Lord, shall enter into the kingdom of heaven; but he that doeth the will of my Father who is in heaven." (Matt. 7:21.) By doing the will of the Father, we must understand general conformity to the will of God, as far as we understand it. The close of Jesus' Sermon on the Mount, it will be remembered, likens the man who hears his words and doeth them, "unto a wise man who built his house upon a rock," while he who hears and does not obey his sayings, is likened unto "a foolish man who built his house upon the sand." Human destiny is here

clearly involved in our doing or not doing what Jesus requires of us. If any one doubts whether the obedience which Jesus enjoins is internal as well as external, let him recall the "woe" which he pronounced against the Scribes and Pharisees, whom he denounced as "hypocrites" and "like unto whited sepulchres which outwardly appear beautiful, but inwardly are full of dead men's bones, and of all uncleanness, even so ye also outwardly appear righteous unto men, but inwardly ye are full of hypocrisy and iniquity." All tendency to limit our thought of obedience to a few external requirements, is a tendency to that outward formalism which Jesus so severely condemned in the Pharisees of his day.

Jesus not only taught the necessity of obedience to God in order to acceptance by him, but he emphasized the value of obedience as a means of distinguishing between what is the will of God and the will of man. He said: "If any man willeth to do his will, he shall know of the teaching, whether it is of God, or whether I speak for myself." (John 7:17.) Here the obedient spirit, or a sincere purpose to do the will of God, which is inward obedience, is made the very organ of knowledge by which we come to a clearer understanding of the will of God. Few sayings of Jesus indicate more clearly than this his profound knowledge of human nature, and of the art of teaching. Given the will to do God's will, we can safely predict a clear knowledge of what God's will is. Jesus would, therefore, say, and have his ministers say, to all who are in doubt concerning certain parts of the divine teaching, "Be sure that you have willed to do the will of God, and are obedient to that will, as far as you understand it, for it is in such obedience that you will be led to a clear knowledge of what the will of God is, in other matters."

The supreme test of the obedience of Jesus was in his becoming "obedient unto death, even the death of the cross." There is no picture in all literature so profoundly impressive and touching as that scene in the Garden, where, on the night of his betrayal, the shadow and agony of the cross were upon him. "Father, all things are possible with thee; remove this cup from me; howbeit not what I will, but what thou wilt!" This thrice-repeated prayer, in which he was consenting to drink the bitter cup of suffering and humiliation if it were the will of his Father, touches the profoundest depths of obedience. Had he failed here, all would have been lost. It is comparatively easy to obey God in his external requirements, but when it comes to meekness, patience, forgiveness, long-suffering under persecution and in the face of an excruciating death, this is far more difficult. Sometimes it is easier even to suffer martyrdom than to endure patiently the temptations, sorrows, afflictions and adversities of life, and yet the latter is obedience as well

as the former. What Jesus emphasized as vitally important is the submergence of our will into the will of God, and seeking daily and continually, in season and out of season, to conform our lives, our characters, our tempers and dispositions, to the will of our heavenly Father. Only thus can we enjoy citizenship in the everlasting kingdom of God, and be sharers in the life everlasting.

❧ ❧

Alexander Campbell as a Reformer.

In certain polite circles the term reformer is one of reproach. He is considered a vulgar disturber of the peace by this easy-going class of people whose governing principle is that of laisser-faire, or letting things alone as they are. He who attempts to disturb the existing order of things in politics or religion is sure to be the target for many a poison arrow from those who prefer to be in error, and to have other people in error, than to have their mental furniture disarranged by the introduction of new ideas, or to have their ease disturbed. But the world needs reformers, and has never made any progress without them. Not every man, even though he be true and loyal-hearted, is fitted to be a reformer. God chooses the man whom he would have lead his church forward out of its errors and false practices into a larger and better life.

Alexander Campbell was a reformer. Like Luther and Wesley, he had a message from God for the church and for the world. The times in which he lived demanded a reformation, just as the times of Luther and Wesley demanded the reformations which they inaugurated. In each of these cases there was the conjunction of the man and the occasion. This is not accidental. It is God's method in history. When he has a special work to accomplish he raises up the man to do it, and fits him for the work. The men whom God has chosen for the work of reformation, besides the pre-requisites of intellectual ability and mental discipline, have had unfaltering faith in God and in the omnipotence of truth, high courage to speak and act in harmony with their deepest convictions, and a love for humanity so intense that they are willing to be counted "of no reputation" if only they may benefit their fellowmen and extend the kingdom of God.

Such a man was Alexander Campbell. He was born to be a reformer. Endowed by nature with a remarkable physical and mental constitution, he had that religious training and intellectual culture which fitted him for the important work he was called to do. One of his most striking characteristics was his mental independence. Once convinced by his own investigation of what God's Word teaches, he hesitated not to declare that truth, no matter how many great names or high ecclesiastical councils were arrayed against him. He acknowledged himself indebted to all the world's great reformers and thinkers, both in philosophy and religion, who had gone before him, but he ventured to test all their conclusions by what was to him the ultimate standard of truth—the revealed will of God. Nor was he ever troubled by statistics, as if God were dependent upon numbers for the success of his truth! He loved truth, as all noble souls do. His mind was open to the truth, as all true souls are.

Given a man with these qualifications, and let him stand, untrammeled, in the presence of religious error and ecclesiastical corruption, and you have 'a reformer. What Mr. Campbell saw, as he looked out upon the religious world with a heart yearning to serve God and humanity, was a divided church, split up into denominations and making war with each other over their respective creeds, instead of the ideal church of the New Testament, united under the leadership of Jesus Christ and moving forward against a common foe. He saw that the resources of the church were being wasted in fratricidal strife, and in sectarian propagandism. His father, Thomas Campbell, a man of equal spiritual vision and insight, if less gifted in some other respects, had seen it before him and had issued a most remarkable appeal to his fellow Christians to surrender their party names, their party creeds, and party spirit, and come and sit together at the feet of Jesus to learn of him, and to be led by him alone. Alexander took up this appeal, and, possessed of a religious genius and commanding ability which would have made him a marked man in any age and in any country, he made the world hear it. It may be said that Mr. Campbell was an idealist, a dreamer, an advocate of an impracticable reform. True, the ideal for which he contended is not yet realized, but it is in process of realization and the church is stronger, purer, and more united to-day because of his life and labors. The religious world does not yet know Alexander Campbell. His time has not yet come. Some day when the church has outgrown its rankling prejudices and forgotten its old time strifes, and shall have entered into a new era of unity and catholicity, his name will be written with the great reformers in the church, who, with prophetic vision were the heralds of better days yet to be. It is sometimes said that Mr. Campbell was a *restorer* rather than a *reformer*. But restoration was only a part of his work. There were errors in faith and practice to be removed as well as neglected truths and practices to be restored. Reformation covers both these phases of his work.

What would be the attitude of Alexander Campbell to the questions of our time, were he now living in the full prime of his vigorous manhood? This, of course, can only be surmised. Those who know him best would, we are sure,

say that he would be open-minded and open-hearted to all the truth shining out of the history of the past, out of science and philosophy, out of the great religious movements of our time, and out of the sacred volume. He would not be afraid of any investigation. He would welcome truth from every source. His heart would rejoice at all the movements looking in the direction of Christian union. His voice would be heard in all the great councils of Christian men, called to promote the unity of Chrisians and the triumph of Christianity in the world. But every move that tends to compromise the glory, dignity, and supreme authority of Christ, or to subordinate his teaching to the philosophy of men, would meet with his stern and unfaltering opposition. But, standing immovable upon the sure foundation which has been laid in Zion, how gladly he would co-operate with all kindred spirits in seeking to bring about the fulfillment of Christ's prayer for the union of his followers! His voice would be lifted for education, for enlightenment, for the diffusion of Bible knowledge, for healing our own petty divisions and alienations in order to the success of our plea and the evangelization of the world.

We shall best honor his memory and the memory of those who stood by him and who came after him, by maintaining the same open-mindedness, the same loyalty to truth, and the same adaptation of our message to the needs of our day, which characterized these great men of God. May we have grace and wisdom to be loyal to the inheritance of truth which we have received from them, while seeking to enlarge that inheritance for transmission to those who shall come after us.

❊ ❊

Notes and Comments.

Rev. W. H. Smith, of Richmond, Va., writing to the "Central Baptist," says:

"The carnal Christian is a 'regenerate' man, a babe in Christ, in whom the flesh is still predominant. A spiritual Christian is one in whom the spirit is predominant.'"

Paul divided Christians into two classes as "spiritual" and "carnal," the latter being "babes in Christ." There is a constant tendency to ignore this distinction, and to think and speak of all who may rightly claim the name Christian as occupying the same plane of spiritual development. There are degrees in Christianity as in everything else. But whoever is satisfied to remain always a babe in Christ, can know nothing of the deeper experiences which belong to Christian manhood and womanhood. They are "spiritual" who are dominated by the Spirit; they are "carnal" who are dominated by the flesh. In every life one or the other of these is the dominant factor.

❊

Dr. James Mudge, writing on "Fifty Years of Christian Experience," in the "Western Christian Advocate," in urging

Editor's Easy Chair.

Never did ancient Jew, with his heart overflowing with patriotic pride and religious devotion, turn his face toward Jerusalem, to attend one of their great annual feasts, with more eagerness than the Easy Chair this week turns its face toward Buffalo—our Jerusalem for the present year, whither the tribes go up for counsel, for fellowship, for information and for inspiration. There is no legal enactment compelling attendance at these annual conventions, but there is a force mightier than law which is turning the feet of thousands toward Buffalo this week. It is the impulse of love—love for God, love for the truth, love for the brotherhood, love for humanity. The impulse which is drawing thousands of the Disciples of Christ from various states of the Union and from the Canadian provinces to the city of Buffalo, this week, comes from heaven. There are no rewards to be distributed, no honors to be conferred, no offices to be gained, no personal ends to be served. We are engaged, as we believe, in a divine enterprise, co-operating with Jesus Christ for the extension of his reign over the hearts and lives of men. As this is his work, pre-eminently, we expect him to meet with us in spirit and to be the unifying power of the convention. Those who gather there will be drawn thither by his spirit, to do his work in his name. Can any one doubt that it will be a great convention? If where two or three are met together in his name he is in the midst of them, surely we may rely upon his presence at Buffalo and feel sure that he will be the inspiration of every prayer that is offered, every song that is sung, every report that is made, every address and sermon that is delivered, and of every motion that is passed.

❧

We are giving our readers this week a number of articles and pictures relating to Alexander Campbell and his work, which we hope will serve to renew in the hearts of our readers the fire of devotion to the great reformation with which we are connected and to the aims and ideals which our fathers had before them in the inauguration of this work. We are no worshipers of Mr. Campbell. We do not regard his statements as possessing any final authority. We feel at perfect liberty to differ from any conclusion of his just as we do from the conclusion of any other reformer. He wrote no creed for those who were to carry on the work which he began. He left them as free, as he claimed himself to be, to accept truth from every source, and nothing but the truth. We regard him as an eminent servant of God, chosen to be the leader in a movement for a return to the sim-

plicity and purity of the religion of Jesus Christ, and for the union of all Christians upon the original foundation upon which the church was built. It was a movement conceived in the broad spirit of Christian brotherhood, and of utmost loyalty to the New Testament ideal of the church. We need to be on our guard continually against all the narrowing influences and partisan tendencies which would divert a great Christian union movement into sectarian channels and toward sectarian aims. Nothing, we think, aside from the presence and guidance of the divine Spirit, will help us to avoid this danger more than the keeping alive in the memories and hearts of the brotherhood the beginnings of the movement and the great men who under God had most to do with its inception, and in giving it that character which has been the source of its strength and success.

❧

There is one saintly man whose personality has always stood in the background, in the history of this reformation, who, we believe, in the days to come will be given his rightful place at the very front of that heroic band who in the early part of the previous century consecrated their lives to the work of religious reform. We refer to Thomas Campbell. No one can read his famous "Declaration and Address" without seeing therein not only a splendid statement of the principles for which we plead, but the manifestation of a spirit which is eminently in harmony with his plea for unity. We have always felt that the movement has lost something very essential to its success in losing, as so many of us have, the spirit of catholicity, of brotherly love, and of profound piety, which breathes throughout that Address. Without questioning the superior fitness of Alexander Campbell for leadership in a movement that antagonized to such a degree prevailing customs and conceptions, we may still regret that, in connection with his fearless assault upon error, and his brave defense of the truth, there could not have been maintained, among all those who succeeded these great leaders, the same gentleness of spirit, the same breadth of fellowship and spiritual power, which marked the writings of Thomas Campbell. These are no less vital than the truths and principles themselves in order to draw together and cement in bonds of unity the severed and alienated people of God. We believe it would be well, therefore, for our cause if we had a revival of interest in the life and writings of Thomas Campbell, and if his spirit were carried into the advocacy of the great principles which he was the first to formulate.

❧

It is sometimes said that Protestantism has passed through the Petrine and

Pauline stages of its development and is just entering upon the Johannine period. It would be truer, perhaps, to say that the church of to-day is adding to the Petrine and Pauline teaching that of John, as he is understood to be the apostle of love. It is doubtful, however, whether John had any pre-eminence over Paul in his emphasis of love. Of one thing, however, we are sure, and that is, whether in the case of Protestantism in general, or of our own religious movement, there is a manifest tendency to grow away from the period of polemics into that of irenics, and this growth or transition is being effected under the increasing dominancy of love as the law of the Christian life. The more Christian people love each other, the more they can afford to differ from each other without forfeiting mutual respect and confidence, or severing the bonds of fellowship. That Christian people must all think alike and feel alike and act alike in order to be brothers, and to recognize each other as such, is a delusion that is rapidly passing away and giving place to a manlier and saner conception of Christianity. In such a time it seems to us, a spirit like that of Thomas Campbell must come into his due inheritance of honor as one of the great leaders in the Church Universal, who opposed sectarianism without becoming sectarian, and who advocated union in the broad spirit which alone makes union possible.

❧

It has always seemed to us that one of the first meetings in our great annual gatherings should be a prayer and praise service. Coming together from fields remotely separated, and many meeting each other for the first time, face to face in the flesh, how delightful it would be to spend an hour together in the atmosphere of praise and thanksgiving in which our spirits would be attuned to the Infinite! It is not so much the great addresses or the great reports that will make the Buffalo Convention a real Bethel to many a heart, as the glimpses of the celestial world, that will come to them in moments when all hearts are kindled into a flame of devotion. All that is retained distinctly in our memory of the first national convention we ever attended, is a prayer which was offered by one of the old veterans of the cross, which lifted us to the very gate of heaven. Who preached, who made addresses, what motions were passed—these are all forgotten, but the memory of that prayer and the inspiration of it remain with us. Those moments in the convention in which we come in closest touch with God and catch a glimpse of heaven on earth will be the most memorable. May there be many such at Buffalo!

Alexander Campbell

Born Sept. 12, 1788, near Ballymena, Antrim, Ireland.

Died at Bethany, W. Va., March 6, 1866.

A Brief Sketch by
T. W. Grafton

In a storm off the coast of Scotland a vessel was stranded. On its deck, on the stump of a broken mast, sat a young man in meditation. In the near prospect of death, he awoke to an appreciation of the purpose of earthly existence. Life came to him with new meaning. Its true object appeared as he had never before conceived it. On the one hand was the folly of earthly aim and ambition. On the other only one motive seemed worthy of human effort and that the salvation and everlasting happiness of mankind.

That young man was Alexander Campbell, and it was there that he formed the resolution that, if saved from the threatening peril, he would give himself wholly to God and his service, and spend his entire life in the ministry of his Word. From that time onward he never faltered in his purpose. Immediately following his rescue he bent all his energy in fitting himself as best he could for his life work.

A few months were spent in the University of Glasgow. They were important months, but more important because of new religious impressions received than for anything learned in the class room. He had entered the university with no other purpose than the newly-formed one of preparing himself for the ministry of the Presbyterian church. But the religious atmosphere of Glasgow began at once to exert a modifying influence upon his views and was destined to work an entire revolution in his convictions and feelings with respect to existing denominations. A religious ferment was going on at that time stimulated by the influence of Robert and James Haldane who were pleading for a return to some neglected primitive practices. While Mr. Campbell was in the midst of his studies, he was brought in contact with this new movement and its chief promoters. Cherishing as he did the feeling of religious unrest he listened the more readily to men, who like himself were longing for some better way than the old beaten paths of tradition. Though not as yet accepting their peculiar views, a profound impression was made upon his mind and the defense of the principles which they advocated, in a modified form, was destined to become the ruling passion of his life and ministry. In after years, in explaining his course, he declared that he had "imbibed disgust at the popular schemes, chiefly while a student at Glasgow."

At last his doubts led him to question his right to continue in the fellowship of the Presbyterian church. At the semiannual communion service he entered the church with the required metallic token as a guarantee of his religious fitness, but his scruples overcame him and instead of taking his place among the communicants, he cast his token into the plate that was passed around and declined to partake with the rest. The ring of that token as it fell from his hands, like the ring of Martin Luther's hammer on the door of the Wittenberg cathedral, announced his renunciation of the old church ties, and marks the moment at which he forever ceased to recognize the claims of authority of a human creed to bind upon men the conditions of their acceptance with God. Henceforth, he resolved, with the help of God, to stand for the defense of "the faith which was once delivered unto the saints."

With the sublime purpose of breaking the shackles of religious tradition and of starting upon an independent search for truth as revealed in the word of God, Alexander Campbell came to America in 1809. To his surprise he found a soil already prepared for the planting. His father, Thomas Campbell, who had preceded him by two years, had inaugurated a movement leading in the direction toward which the young man had resolutely set his face. A company of rugged pioneers in Western Pennsylvania had adopted as a Magna Charta of religious freedom a few resolutions written by the pen of Thomas Campbell, which closed with these words: "Nothing is to be received as a matter of faith or duty for which there can not be expressly provided a 'thus saith the Lord,' either in express terms or approved precedent." Upon this platform after months of deliberation a church was organized, now famous as the Brush Run church, and Alexander Campbell, though but in his twenty-third year, was, in recognition of his great talent, chosen as its preacher.

Here began the real life-work of Alexander Campbell and throughout his splendid career it never shifted its center. At first he felt his way cautiously. But having adopted the famous maxim of his father, "where the Scriptures speak we speak, and where the Scriptures are silent, we are silent—" he did not shrink from the logical consequences of his new position. but determined to follow wherever it led him. Having resolved to accept nothing on the tradition of the fathers the whole realm of accepted faith came upon him afresh for investigation. He determined that each step should be taken under Scriptural guidance and not until he was clearly convinced that he was following in the Master's footsteps. This accounts for the gradual unfolding of the new reformation covering a period of some sixteen years, from 1811 to 1827.

The first question to force itself upon his attention was that of Scriptural baptism, a subject to which he had hitherto given but little thought. But now he must know the mind of the Master. A careful study of the whole subject followed. Abandoning all uninspired authorities, he applied himself afresh to the study of the Bible, with the result that he and the larger part of his little congregation were driven into the waters of baptism, holding that immersion in water upon a true profession of faith in Christ alone constituted Christian baptism.

From this point onward Mr. Campbell's natural affiliation was with the Baptists, and he with his congregation, were received into the Red Stone Association of the Baptist churches. Here his growing talent and originality in dealing with Scriptural themes won him widespread reputation and at the same time awakened the bitter opposition of the clergy who branded his disregard of time-honored customs as heresy. Finally their hostility led to open attack, and to his arraignment before a religious tribunal of the association, to escape which, and for the sake of peace he and thirty of his friends withdrew from the old Brush Run church and organized a new church at Wellsburg, Va., and upon application was admitted into the Mahoning Association of Ohio, an association of Baptist churches characterized by greater liberality of feeling and a readier disposition to follow the Scriptures.

From this point onward Mr. Campbell gave himself to the wider advocacy of the principles he had adopted. This was in the autumn of 1823, and for the first time, he cherished the hope that something might be done on a more extended scale to restore religious society to its primitive simplicity. Travelling up and down the country on his trusted horse, he rode preached, wherever he could get men to listen, a crusade against religious corruption with all the fire and zeal of a Peter the Hermit. These early excursions took him through portions of Pennsylvania, Virginia, Ohio and Kentucky, and wherever he went his plea was for a new order of things, or rather a return to the faith, customs and practices of the apostolic church. But the old horse was too slow a vehicle for the transportation of such a plea, so he called to his aid the press.

The first number of the "Christian Baptist" was issued July 4, 1823. Its appearance marks a new era in religious literature. It was a veritable John the Baptist in religious journalism. Its continuous message was a call to repentance to erring ecclesiasts. It at once fearlessly attacked whatever was conceived to be a departure from New Testament standards, and it felt like a fire-brand onto hundreds of widely scattered communities.

The effect of the "Christian Baptist" was magical. First it provoked everywhere a new spirit of inquiry and won to the movement for the restoration of primitive Christianity thousands of loyal supporters. But on the other hand it awakened the bitter opposition to those whose authority it attacked, and made impossible longer fellowship in the Baptist fold for those who shared Mr. Campbell's views and urged the cause of reformation. Unable to check the spirit of discord and intolerance that now swept the church, the great leader calmly awaited the result, at the same time disavowing any responsibility for the dissensions he lamented. Between 1827 and 1830 the work of separation went on, and from this point dates the separate existence of the religious body known as the Disciples of Christ.

From 1830 onward Mr. Campbell's energies were spent in training and organizing this new force. This was no small task. Heterogeneous elements representing the various schools of religious thought were brought together in many communities. There were questions of expedience, and

forms of administration to settle, and but for the leadership of a commanding genius, sound and sane, broad and rugged like that presented in the mind and heart of Mr. Campbell, the cause would have been shipwrecked in the first decade of its history.

Recollections By James O. Carson

Realizing how wholly incompetent I am for the task I comply with your request to note some recollections of the early days of the religious movement in western Pennsylvania known as the "Campbell movement;" the men who were in it from the first and the condition of the religious world in that district of country at the time. It was my good fortune to have been familiar with this great work since it began to take form, and to have been personally acquainted with the greater number of the men who were in it from the first, as well as with many who were their immediate successors. Of the first there is, perhaps, but one living—John Schaffer—who recently celebrated his one hundredth anniversary.

The religious condition of the people was pitiable, and fitly described as "a people sitting in a valley overhung with death shades." They knew God only as the great *avenger*, who visited the sins of the parents on the children to the third and fourth generation." Every vicissitude of life was looked upon as a *punishment* sent by God for sins committed by the affected one or his parents. Their conception of religion was to propitiate God and "make gracious." The great converting power was the *wrath* of God and the effective "means of grace" the "mourners' bench." Here the struggle was made to "reconcile God to the sinner." Here both saint and sinner wrestled with God for a blessing as did Jacob of old. The unsuccessful sinner was exhorted to persevere, and told that in "his own good time the Holy Ghost would come and speak peace to his soul." They were strangers to the "obedience of faith," and to the assurance of acceptance with God which this gives, and hence were subject to seasons of trust and of doubt; seasons of hope and seasons of fear. These were favorite subjects for recitation in "experience meeting."

Among the denominations party spirit dominated, and each denomination was as separate from another as were the political parties. Sound doctrine—which meant "our creed"—was the gospel preached, and served well to foster the party spirit and embitter it.

These, briefly outlined, were the religious conditions existing at the time this movement began. As soon, however, as the new religion began to spread, these conditions, as respected parties, changed. A truce was called and an alliance, offensive and defensive, was entered into by the heretofore belligerent

forces, and a crusade began on the "new religion" that in bitterness of feeling and expression, can not be conceived as possible by Christians of the present day.

An actual occurrence will give some idea of the state of feeling that existed. An old man—a "Campbellite"—who sometimes preached, was walking up the aisle of an orthodox church where services were to be held, and was discovered by an alert sister who at once began to sing:

"Jesus, great shepherd of thy sheep,
To their for help we fly,
Thy little flock in safety keep,
For lo, the *wolf* is nigh."

The vigilance of the sister was perhaps commendable for it is quite probable the *wolf* was out foraging for material for a sermon, and deserved the shot.

This conflict was kept up for a long time, but, under the influence of the conservative element on both sides, began to soften and disappear. The first formal challenge of the "orthodoxy" of the "Disciples" was made in St. Louis. At the solicitation of personal friends, members of the society, several members of the Disciples' church made application for membership in the society of "Evangelical Alliance," then in its infancy here. Their acceptance was opposed by the ultra orthodox element in the society, led by Rev. N. L. Rice, of "Campbell and Rice debate" notoriety, on the ground that they were not "orthodox." The applicants for admission were represented by Alexander Proctor, then quite a young man and pastor of the only Disciples' church in the city. The meeting to determine the question was held in a public hall, and after a full discussion of the question the applicants were received, much to the discomfiture of the reverend doctor, and probably leaving him feeling somewhat as the boy who had been apprenticed to a blacksmith, who, after two days' experience, said he wish't he hadn't learn't the trade; that he'd been blow'en cold wind into that fire for two days and the harder he blowed the hotter the blasted thing got."

In the early days of this movement, few, if any of the churches could support a minister his entire time and the preacher's work was purely evangelistic, he going from village to village, and from district to district, wherever a courthouse or schoolhouse could be obtained in which services could be held. In their eagerness to hear the people would often follow the minister from the public service to the private residence where he was staying, and there sit and listen

the entire interim between early and late services. Under the inspiration of such conditions these men preached with an earnestness and pathos seldom heard in the present day. This may be regarded as extravagant, but I appeal to the fact that audiences, packed beyond comfort in a room, would sit for two hours and more, and listen to an address without the least evidence of impatience or fatigue. It has been said of Thomas Campbell that after speaking an hour he would say, "and now dearly beloved, with these introductory remarks we are prepared to enter upon the investigation of this very interesting and important subject;" yet no one grew impatient or weary, no one quitted his seat. Under like conditions during like period of time I have listened to Alexander Campbell, when the entire audience would become wholly unconscious of the passing of time. An incident will give some idea of Mr. Campbell's power. On one occasion he was addressing a large audience; an old gentleman was sitting near and immediately in front of the platform, his elbow on his knee and his head on his hand, intently gazing into the face of the speaker. Straightening himself up he gave a yawn that was heard in every part of the large room; changed from one hand and knee to the other, wholly unconscious of his action, and, moreover, without the least perceptible effect on the audience. Nor were these alone and singular—as much may be said of a host of others. Under the inspiration of an expectant waiting audience, Walter Scott would stand on the mount of transfiguration, talk of the sufferings of Christ and the glory to come after, lead his hearers up to the New Jerusalem, through the gates into the city, and over the golden streets up to the dwelling place of the "blessed Father," and there in the divine presence, as it were, appeal to his hearers in irresistible eloquence and pathos to accept the great salvation.

But among the remarkable men of that remarkable period John Smith—"Raccoon John Smith"—stands alone in his own unique personality. In intellectual strength he had few, if any, superiors; as a minister of the Gospel he was a great power, and to "orthodoxy" a terror. With the dexterity of an expert anatomist he would dissect the old body; with the cold indifference of an experienced undertaker prepare it for "the last look of friends;" and then bury it under an unmerciful avalanche of denunciation, sarcasm and ridicule.

(Continued on Page 1296.)

PORTRAITS OF ALEXANDER CAMPBELL

We have made an effort to secure copies of the different photographs and paintings that were made of Alexander Campbell, and we present in this issue of THE CHRISTIAN-EVANGELIST such as we have been able to obtain. If any readers of the paper have other pictures that are not represented in our pages this week, we shall be glad to hear from them. The picture which we have used on our frontispiece was painted from life when Mr. Campbell was seventy-two years of age, six years before he died. It is considered by his relations as a most striking likeness. The photograph was made from an oil painting by Bogle in 1859, and has been copyrighted by his daughter, Mrs. Decima Campbell Barclay, of Bethany, W. Va. In sending it to us for reproduction she says it is by far

the finest picture of him in existence." It represents Mr. Campbell as he often appeared before the students in Bethany College pulpit. Mrs. Barclay says the attitude portrayed by the artist was quite characteristic of her father, who would stand with his eye-glasses in one hand while the other rested on the Bible, the fingers indicating a purpose to turn to further citations from the Book of books. The picture of Mr. and Mrs. Campbell found on page 1298 is, also, a very good one and is in the possession of Mrs. Barclay. It was taken in Cincinnati in 1861 while her father and mother were attending the annual missionary meeting and were the guests of R. M. Bishop and wife. The mother of the Assistant Editor of THE CHRISTIAN-EVANGELIST went with them to the photographer's when it was taken.

Of some of the portraits we are unable to give particulars. The first one on the previous page is the earliest one of which we have any traces. Mr. Campbell was probably about thirty years of age. The one representing him at the age of about thirty-five was painted by the artist Cooper in Nashville, Tenn. There is another picture made from a steel

engraving representing him at the age of forty-one. The rather rough looking portrait on the lower left hand corner of the other page was taken just after his arrival in Philadelphia on the boat, and about the time he was arrested for libel. It is in the possession of C. C. Redgrave, as is also the next one taken from a daguerreotype made when he was in his prime and at the height of his great power. This daguerreotype was owned by Dr. A. M. Collins, but is now the property of Russell Errett, of Cincinnati. Bro. James O. Carson possesses a very fine daguerreotype from which we have made the picture presented next. The other portraits we are not able to date, with the exception of the one with the beard on the page before, made by J. Perry Elliott in 1864.

Recollections.

(Continued from Page 1293.)

I would gladly go on and speak of others of the mighty men of these bygone days, of their individual peculiarities and rowth—of Challen and Church; of Burnett and Darsie; Creath and Anderson and Pendleton and Errett and others. But there are others unnamed but not less worthy whose unmarked graves I can not pass without a tribute of grateful remembrance, however weak and imperfect it may be. These are they who, in response to the emergency call of the Master, went out "without scrip or purse or two coats," into the byways and highways to carry the bread of life to his helpless, famishing children, going on foot or as best they might; from village to village; from log cabin to log cabin, on the way posting at cross roads their own appointments to preach the next

Lord's day at the nearest school house, and receiving, for the most part—all the recipients had to give—the warm hospitality always found in a log cabin, a cake of corn bread, a shuck mattress bed, made vacant for the stranger, and at parting a grateful tear-moistened "God bless you, won't you come again?" It would have been strange—more than strange—if at times, to the weary, sore-footed one, the way had not seemed hard and dreary; the sun to shine with a sombre hue; the leaves seem listless on the trees; the songs of the birds dull and discordant, and stranger still, if in moments like these the tempter had not come with the proffer of the easier life, the larger compensation, the greater opportunities that were waiting over in the settlements. But from the wilderness beyond the Jordan there always came the voice of the Master, "Get thee behind

me, Satan. Man shall not live for bread alone, but for every duty that comes to him from God." And the dusty feet were washed, the dreary way made cheerful, leaves danced with delight, and mingling with the song of the birds, a strong, clear voice was heard;

"Jesus, I my cross have taken,
All to leave and follow thee.

Go then earthly fame and treasure,
Come disaster, scorn and pain,
In thy service pain is pleasure,
With thy favor loss is gain."

The sacrifices and self-denials of these men, like their names, have not been recorded, and when it is asked in heaven, "Who are these?" the angels will bow their heads and answer, "These are they who came up through great tribulation, and who have washed their robes white, in the blood of the Lamb."

St. Louis.

The Personality of Mr. Campbell   By W. T. Moore

Personality is the biggest word in the English language. No matter from what point of view we regard it, it must always occupy the chief place. This is why biography is the best of all history. The history of wars, battlefields, governments and empires may be interesting and even instructive, but these have no real meaning until they reach personality. Things are important in their place, but they were made to serve persons. A world without personality would be a body without life and mere framework without potentiality. Personality must therefore be regarded as the sublime end of the whole physical universe.

But what is personality? We need not now consider this question from a psychological point of view. This point of view is important, but it need not enter prominently into our present discussion. Nevertheless, it is difficult to treat the subject under consideration without reckoning with certain differentia which distinguish individuals from one another. Some of these differentia are easily perceived; others are only dimly indicated by certain phenomena in character which can not be readily defined, and yet these phenomena are among the most determining factors in what we call the character of a man.

During the last half century, it has been my good fortune to know some of the most distinguished men of both Europe and America, and also to have come into contact with many others in a way that gave me a knowledge of their characters; and I can say, without hesitation, that Alexander Campbell possessed the most striking and interesting personality with which I was acquainted during all that time. I do not now refer to his superior intellect, nor again to his fine physical development, but rather to that indefinable something we call personal influence, without which a man may be a giant in other respects and yet practically fail

to make a very decided impression upon those with whom he comes in contact. Mr. Campbell was richly endowed with that indefinable quality which gives power to its possessor, though no one is able to tell precisely what this quality is or where it specially resides. Carlyle was a man of great intellectual endowments, but he was personally almost disagreeable, and certainly not attractive to many people. Bismarck was the impersonification of intellectual force, but he had not a single quality that attracted to him personally those by whom he was surrounded. Mr. Gladstone was a very different kind of a man. He possessed to a large degree the quality which I have seen him arise to speak in the British parliament, during a somewhat stormy session, and immediately all eyes were fixed upon him, while perfect silence reigned among his hearers during the time of his address. Mr. Campbell possessed this personal magnetism in even a greater degree than that possessed by Mr. Gladstone. When he arose to speak in an assembly he did not have to win the attention of his hearers by his introductory remarks; immediately every one was attentive, and often he almost annihilated time by the intense interest he created in his hearers, so that an hour and a half speech seemed really only a few minutes.

This same quality was constantly manifested in the social circle. He was remarkably companionable, and never seemingly attempted to monopolize the time in conversation, and yet unconsciously, on his part, as well as on the part of the entire social circle, he became the center of that circle and usually did most of the talking. Nor did this show in this the slightest degree of egotism. Every one seemed to assign cordially to him the chief place in conversation and this was so decidedly the case that sometimes he practically lectured while every one else became lis-

teners. Nor was this privilege granted him simply because of his superior intellectual power. It was rather owing to that indefinable quality which distinguished his personality, and to which attention has already been called. Well do I remember a visit he made to me while I was in Bethany College. I had preached the night before at the church. I had always said I would not preach in his pulpit when he was present. F had given special instruction to his daughter, Virginia, to keep him at home when I was announced to preach at night. On the night referred to, I had just gone into the pulpit with a friend of mine who was to open the meeting with the reading of the Scriptures and prayer. The congregation was singing the introductory hymn, when Mr. Campbell came in and took his seat in the front pew. I immediately walked down to him and told him that he must preach, as I could not. He answered by saying that he had no appointment to preach and therefore could not do so. I then urged him to go home, as I felt my utter inability to preach in his pulpit when he was present. He took hold of my hand and drew me down by his side, and in a few words he both shamed me and encouraged me in such an effective manner that I went back into the pulpit and implicitly threw myself on the pulpit and implicitly threw myself on my Heavenly Father for help, and if ever I prayed in my life, I prayed that night that I might have strength for the service and overcome all difficulties in my way to accomplish some good in my Master's cause. Perhaps I never preached a more effective sermon. A protracted meeting was held in the church a little time after this, and a number of the converts dated their conversion to that evening's service.

The day following Mr. Campbell called at my room in my boarding house and spent nearly an hour with me questioning me with respect to my plan of life. I do not now remember much that he said, but I shall never forget the impression his great personality made upon me. Indeed, I owe much of whatever success I have made in life to that remarkable visit. His fatherly advice would have been very effective if that had been the only influence wrought upon me; but there was something indescribable in Mr. Campbell's personality that told more upon my future life than anything he specially said, however important this may have been. In after years I was with him frequently, and often in the most intimate relationship, and I never failed to realize the curious, magnetic power which he seemed always to possess in a remarkable degree.

Perhaps this magnetic power was augmented because Mr. Campbell seemed always to live in the sunshine. I have never known a brighter nature than his. He could weep with those that weep, but it was his supreme delight to

rejoice with those that rejoice. There was not a particle of pessimism in his nature. Hope reigned supremely over every day of his life. Whoever will read his writings will be impressed with the hopeful spirit which breathes in every line. He knew no such thing as discouragement. His strong faith in the Son of God gave him an assurance doubly sure that victory would ultimately crown every worthy effort made in the interest of Christ's great cause; and so thoroughly was Mr. Campbell convinced that he was pleading for Christ's cause that nothing seemed to permanently cloud his vision or create a doubt in his mind as to the ultimate triumph of the principles he advocated.

It is also worthy of notice that the single, definite purpose of Mr. Campbell's life must have had a powerful influence in giving his personality the charm it possessed. He lived with a definite aim before him to the end of his

life. It was this *terminus ad quem*, or aim in view, which gave to his character a power almost irresistible. Perhaps no one has ever become great who did not live for some supreme end. Our divine Lord himself had just one aim in view during the whole of his personal ministry. He came to *do the will* of his Father. This was the beginning and end of his earthly mission, and this fact gave a power to his personality which nothing else could have done. The moment Alexander Campbell became convinced he had a special mission, from that moment he gave himself up supremely to that mission, and it dominated his whole life, and subordinated every faculty of his being to the accomplishment of the great work he undertook to do. This singleness of purpose impressed itself upon his personal life and made that life one of sunshine, beauty, fellowship and power. Perhaps it is too early for any one to take his true measure, but I do not hesitate to predict that the time will come when he will be reckoned as one of the greatest men who lived during the nineteenth century.

Alexander Campbell and Bethany College

I take pleasure in complying with the request of THE CHRISTIAN-EVANGELIST for a short article on the subject announced above. I do so the more willingly because the recent death of Alexander Campbell, Jr., whom I have known intimately for fifty-nine years and more, has carried me back to the early days of Bethany, and brought afresh into my memory many of the scenes in which he and I mingled in boyhood. He and his four younger brothers and sisters, of whom only two of the latter survive him, were then but children. Mrs. Barclay, the younger of the two sisters, was a little girl of 8 or 9 years, and frequently followed

By J. W. McGarvey

on his staff, too dim of sight to walk abroad without a guide. I was myself just rounding out my seventeenth year, but was prepared to enter the Freshmen class.

The chief work of Mr. Campbell in the college consisted in delivering a lecture on the Bible to the whole college every morning. He alternated between the Old Testament and the New; but he seldom went farther in the former than the Pentateuch, and in the latter, than the Gospels and Acts. He did not comment on these portions exhaustively, chapter after chapter, but he selected in consecutive order such subjects in each as enabled him to set forth the great themes which they suggest, and the distinctive features of the several dispensations which they represent. His remarks were very discursive, as was his habit in preaching, and by pursuing this method he not only threw light on the particular passages in hand, but on all the leading themes of divine revelation. His lecture room was one of the class-rooms of the old college building, about 20 by 30 feet in dimensions, seated with rude benches, which were whittled with all manner of devices by idle students while pretending to hear the lectures. He sat in a plain chair on a small platform about six inches high in

one corner of the room, with a plain unvarnished desk before him. His career was near its close when the new and splendid college edifice was completed.

All students of the college, without exception, were required to attend these lectures. Usually there were not more of them than could be conveniently seated in the room. No study was required except to listen to the lectures and to answer a few general questions propounded about once a week. Under this system of instruction, thoughtful students who were careful to take notes and study them in the light of the Scripture text, gained much invaluable information; but the idle and irreligious young men gathered only a few crumbs of Scripture knowledge. I well remember an incident that illustrates the manner in which some of these received the great addresses. After having lectured for several days on the events connected with the valley of Mesopotamia, Mr. Campbell put this question: "Mr. B, will you tell us some of the remarkable events connected with Mesopotamia?" After a little hesitation and scratching his head, B. answered: "I believe, sir, that that is the place where God made the world." Many in the room who joined in the roar of laughter could not have given a much better answer. But little as idle students learned from these great lectures in the way of facts laid up in the memory, they were every one deeply impressed by the eloquence and power of the lecturer, and in very many instances these impressions led to earnest religious lives in later years. Some, indeed, who were careless and idle while in college, were so impressed that they afterward became preachers. The educational power of a great personality has been exaggerated, I think, by some writers in recent years, but it is undoubtedly one of the chief factors in de-

Bethany in the 'Forties.

her father into the cheap little pulpit at the church, and sat there during the sermon. She occupies and owns the old homestead. Mrs. Thompson, now of Washington City, was a half grown girl in short dresses, not yet receiving the attention of beaux. Alec was yet in the primary department; and as frolicsome as a boy could well be. Their venerable father was entering the last decade of his wonderful career, and the grandfather, Thomas Campbell, was leaning

veloping the mental and moral powers of the young. Parents and young persons who choose for themselves should think of this in selecting their teachers. It was only in this that Alexander Campbell was a teacher of extraordinary merit; but in this he was pre-eminent. Every student who sat many months before him in that humble chapel can recall bursts of eloquence the equal in thrill-

Alexander Campbell and wife in 1861.

ing power of the grandest which fell from his lips in his great orations.

I think it was for a time almost universal among younger colleges founded by our brethren, to follow the example of Bethany in morning lectures on the Bible; but the lecturers did not prove to be Campbells; and in every instance, I think, even in Bethany, the custom has been discontinued. I am not sure that the discontinuance has been wise; for a daily lesson in the Scriptures, even if feebly presented, keeps the conscience aroused and prevents the young mind from forgetting God. It is now the custom to require of all who graduate a small amount of Bible study; but this is escaped by those who do not aim at graduation, and a large majority of college students who suspend their studies without graduating go out into the world almost as ignorant as horses about the Bible. These are the victims of all the fads and fancies in the name of religion, and the readiest victims of every new phase of skepticism. When young men are once made familiar with Abraham and the prophets, Christ and the apos-

tles, they can afterward no more doubt the reality of their existence than that of their classmates and professors.

In closing this brief sketch I venture the suggestion to the managers of all of our colleges, that they should put their heads together at once and provide more instruction in the Bible. Their Bible courses should include more of the book and Bible study should be required, not only of all who graduate, but of all who matriculate. The question of religious instruction in the public schools is now undergoing fresh discussion throughout the country; why not a movement for more of it in the colleges? I said, religious instruction; but the best religious instruction, and the only kind that can possibly hope for introduction into public schools and state universities, is the study of the Bible. Especially ought this feature of higher education to characterize all so-called denominational colleges. No youth can now graduate from a college with a full curriculum without a knowledge of Greek and Roman history. The reputable college graduate can speak freely of all the great names of heathen an-

tiquity; but he knows nothing of the early history of God's ancient people, or of those mighty men whose example has done more to uplift our race than that of all other men combined. This ought not to be so; and it will not be when believers in the Bible get their eyes open to the interests involved. It will not do to say that we have not room in our curriculum for more Bible study; we must make room. Some years ago I spent an hour in the class room of a theological professor in Vanderbilt University. The recitation was in the Greek New Testament, and somehow both students and professor got to questioning me about the College of the Bible. When I informed them that the most characteristic course in that college was a careful study of all the historical matter in the Bible, running through four years of daily recitations, the professor expressed admiration for such a course, but asked me, "How in the world do you find it possible to get that much Bible study into your curriculum?" I answered, "We put this in because we regard it as indispensable, and then we put in just so much of other studies as there is room for." This, the experience of more than forty years, has convinced me, is the most effective way to prepare men for preaching the Gospel, and for living a right life. To Alexander Campbell is due the credit of leading American colleges into the way of rightly appreciating this, the greatest theme of human study. All honor to his great name!

❋ ❋

"My being wrong in saying there never was a grey swan, will not prove that I am in an error when I allege that there is not in this land a white crow. Our opponents too often seem to proceed upon such a principle. We would wish to see them discriminate with more accuracy, and examine with more candor."
—Alexander Campbell.

Mr. Campbell's Study at Bethany.

Mr. Campbell's Descendants.
As Seen From the Dome
By F. D. POWER

On March 4, 1866, Alexander Campbell died. We are soon to celebrate our Centennial, which is only a brief period of forty-three years from the death of the great leader and preacher. Everything connected with him has a fresh interest as we approach the great assembly in Pittsburg in 1909. It will do no harm to revive the memories of our heroic days; and in all our literature, and all our conventions, state as well as national, we should be awakening the attention of our people to the great principles and history of our movement. It is not too early to begin to prepare for this great event. There will be pilgrimages to Bethany as one of the special features of our Centennial celebration, and the story of the reformer, of his home and his college, of his family and his associates, of his work and his teachings, will be of thrilling interest to scores of thousands to whom his life has been a benediction.

The recent death of his oldest son, Col. Alexander Campbell, at Bethany, has called forth many expressions of sympathy and kindness. He passed away September 25, after an illness of two months. It was my pleasure to visit him in June, and he was then evidently declining. He was 75 years of age, and a severe attack of pneumonia hastened the end. Surrounded by his beloved ones, he fell asleep peacefully. The funeral service was conducted by Prof. R. H. Wynne, of the College, and his remains were laid to rest on the hill near those of his revered father. Old students will remember his genial nature, generous hospitality, fine social gifts, and kindly interest in the boys. He had been since 1870 one of the trustees, had attended every commencement with, I believe, one exception, since the institution was founded, was himself a graduate, and always deeply interested in the work of the college. He was a man of unquestioned ability, and filled many positions of honor and trust. Always with a taste for politics, he served twelve years as a member of the Democratic National Committee. He was also a member of the West Virginia Constitutional Convention of 1872. President Pendleton, who served in that body, said of him: "Mr. Campbell is deservedly one of the most popular members of the convention, and has been a true and untiring worker for the interests of our people. The citizens of Brooke, I am satisfied, could not have found in the county, a more influential and watchful guardian of their interests." During his first term President Cleveland appointed Col. Campbell one of three Commissioners to the Melbourne Exposition, and he spent a year in Australia. He was very useful in this office to the Government, and subsequently was sent to Australia to work up the interests of the Chicago Exposition, and with excellent results. Mr. Campbell married Miss Mary Anna

Purvis, of Louisiana, a gracious Christian woman, who survives him, and whose aged mother, Mrs. Elizabeth Rose Miller, passed away at 93 years of age in his home at Bethany the week before his death. He leaves seven children—Virginia, who married Alexander T. Magarey of Australia, and has two children; Mary, who is the wife of B. C. Hagerman of Lexington, Ky., and has one child; Robert M., who is our pastor in Owingsville, Ky., and has one child; Archie, who lives in San Francisco; Ewing, whose home is in Nevada, and Alexander and William, who live at Bethany.

Mr. Magarey, who married Col. Campbell's oldest daughter, Virginia, died sud-

The Campbell Home at Bethany, W. Va.

denly at his home in Adelaide June 20. He had recently visited the United States and was with us here, and preached for me in the Vermont Avenue Church. While not regularly in the Christian ministry, he often rendered such service. He was able and consecrated, a man of large influence in his own country, and was sincerely mourned. He was one of the founders and honorable secretaries of the Royal Geographical Society, and a gifted naturalist. He was a man of beautiful character, of strong religious convictions, and of varied learning, a member of the Church of Christ at Stirling East in Adelaide, and preached frequently there. Mr. and Mrs. Magarey's only daughter married Julian Barclay, son of J. J. and Mrs. Decima Campbell Barclay. His son, Archibald Campbell Magarey, is a student of medicine at Adelaide University.

Mrs. Virginia Campbell Thompson has been for nine years a resident of Washington, and has a position in the Congressional Library. She was for thirteen years Postmaster at Louisville, Ky.

She married William R. Thompson, of Louisville, a prominent lawyer, and her children are A. C. Thompson of Pittsburg, Robert Thompson of Wilmington, N. C., and Virginia Campbell Thompson of this city. We have had Mrs. Thompson, Robert and Virginia in our Vermont Avenue fellowship, and hold them in high esteem.

Mr. Campbell's tenth child was Mrs. Decima Barclay, now of Bethany, wife of J. J. Barclay, son of Dr. J. T. Barclay, missionary to Jerusalem and United States Consul there, and author of "The City of the Great King." Mr. Barclay served as United States Consul at Taagier. The children of Mr. and Mrs. Barclay are Dr. Judson Barclay of Topeka, Kans.; Alexander C. of Portland, Ore., and Julian T., who married Miss Mary Magarey, now professor of modern languages in the University of Louisiana. The Barclays occupy the Old Mansion, Bishop Campbell's old home at Bethany, where they dispense a gracious hospitality, and will welcome the Centennial pilgrims. Mrs. Barclay will this winter take the cruise of the Arabic to the Orient.

William Pendleton Campbell, Mr. Campbell's youngest son, lives in Wellsburg, W. Va., and is engaged in the real estate business. He married Miss Nannie Cochran of Louisville, Ky., and has four children—Patrick C. of Joplin, Mo.; Argyle, of Chicago, and Jeannette and Alice, who reside with their parents.

The descendants of Alexander Campbell by his first wife are not numerous. His oldest daughter, Jane Caroline, married Albert Gallatin Ewing. Her daughter, Margaret, became the wife of Joseph Pendleton, a cousin of W. K. Pendleton, and a successful lawyer of Wheeling. John O. Pendleton of Wheeling, who served in Congress, Mrs. Virginia Wilson, Miss Lizzie and Miss Maggie Pendleton are her children. Sarah Ewing married John W. Bush of Texas, and nine children were born to them. Maria Louise Campbell became the wife of Robert Y. Henley of Virginia, and their

(Continued on Page 1314.)

Alexander Campbell---A Master of Assemblies

By Archibald McLean

Alexander Campbell was ordained on January 1, 1812. It is safe to say that he was one of the most effective preachers of all time. While he lived in Bethany, he traveled much and preached everywhere. The announcement that he was to speak called together a throng too great for any building. When the weather permitted he spoke in the open air to the thousands that assembled from near and from far. Much of his preaching was done in what was then the frontier. The people were hungry for the bread of life. No man in a metropolitan pulpit spoke to more intelligent or responsive audiences. Like most of the preachers of the wilderness, Mr. Campbell was an extemporaneous speaker. The pioneers liked men who "could shoot without a rest." While he made the most careful preparation for the pulpit, he wrote but little. Because of this, few of his sermons have been preserved, and even these are not verbatim reports.

Mr. Campbell's sermons can not be placed in evidence. The most one can do is to gather up the testimonies of some of those who heard him. Judge Black said: "As a great preacher, he will be remembered with unqualified admiration by all who had the good fortune to hear him in the prime of his life. The first sentence drew the audience still as death, and every word was heard with rapt attention to the close. It did not appear to be eloquence; it was logic, explanation and argument, so clear that everybody followed without an effort, and all felt that it was raising them to the level of a superior mind." Robert Graham said: "He charmed all alike, the old and the young, the educated and the uneducated. No one could listen to him and not confess him to be one of the greatest men of his age. He had a style of his own, and always elicited the admiration of his hearers." J. S. Lamar spoke of the way the people followed him and quoted him and hung enchained upon his lips, and how they spread his name and fame wide and far. He adds: "He did not belong to that class that is commonly meant when we speak of popular preachers. He did not preach like them. He filled and moved in a sphere of his own. He seemed to have, and deeply to feel that he had, a special mission, an appointment from his Lord, to do a peculiar and world-wide work." He spoke of him as a great man, God-appointed and God-inspired. He represented him as a figure statuesque, colossal, mighty, a grand and masterful man, worthy of his sacred mission, worthy of the great brotherhood he led into the light and liberty of the gospel, and worthy of the large place he will one day be given in the history of the Church. President Humphrey spoke thus of Mr. Campbell: "In listening to him you feel that you are in the presence of a great man. He speaks like a master of assem-

blies, one who has entire confidence in the mastery of his subject and his powers, and who expects to carry conviction without any of the adventitious aids on which ordinary men find it necessary to rely. There were many fine and truly eloquent passages in the two discourses I heard, but they seemed to cost him no effort, and to betray no consciousness that they were fine." President Madison said: "It was my pleasure to hear him very often as a preacher of the Gospel, and I regard him as the ablest and most original expounder of the Scriptures I have ever heard." One Baptist preacher said what many felt, "I once thought I could preach, but since I heard this man; I do not seem any larger in my own estimation than my little finger." The people heard with delight. Not only so, but the truth was retained and treasured up in their hearts to be solemnly reconsidered and pondered, changing in very many cases the very currents of life, and leading to a blessed and glorious destiny.

Mr. Campbell's style was his own. He did not aim to copy any of the famous orators of ancient or modern times. Strangers were surprised to find in him an entire want of gesture or mannerism; that he talked as men commonly talk. Leaning on a cane, he often spoke in a true conversational style for two or three hours. He rarely made a gesture of any sort. "There was no attitudinizing; no pointing upward to the stars; no stretching forth of outspread arms, as if to embrace mountains." He was seldom tender or pathetic. His style reminded some of the Apostle as he opened the Scriptures and alleged that the Jesus he preached was the Christ. At rare intervals he spoke with the utmost fervor. Then he was like a living fire or a sweeping tornado, forcing the hearer to forget all idea of logical connection, and impressing him only with the idea of power. President Pendleton said of him: "His ideas flowed on a perpetual stream, majestic for its stately volume, and grand for its width and sweeping magnificence of its current. With a voice that thrilled with the magnetism of great thoughts, and a person imposing and majestic as his mind was vigorous and commanding, no one could hear and see him and fail to discover that he was in the presence of one on whom nature had set the seal of transcendent greatness."

Robert Richardson called attention to Mr. Campbell's singular ability to interest the hearer in the subject he treated. While his voice was heard nothing could dissolve the charm. Minutes became seconds, and hours became minutes, so that the auditor became unconscious of the lapse of time, and his attention during the longest discourse never

flagged. One minister complained that he rode thirty miles to hear a man speak thirty minutes. On looking at his watch he found it had been two hours and thirty minutes. Two hours had gone, and he knew not how, though he had been awake all the time.

His style of sermonizing was as peculiar as his delivery. Mr. Campbell did not believe in textual preaching. He spoke on the themes that run like rivers through all Scripture. In all his preaching his one aim was to set forth the mind of the Spirit. One man went to hear him to learn if he were a Calvinist or an Arminian. On being asked if he discovered where Mr. Campbell stood, he said: "No, I know nothing about him; but be he devil or be he saint, he has thrown more light on that Epistle and on the whole Scriptures than all the preaching to which I have ever listened." Mr. Campbell went back of Calvin and Arminius and Athanasius to Christ and his apostles. He saw in Christ, and in Christ alone, the one true rallying point for all believers. Christ was the core of all his preaching, his character, his offices, his perfection, and his supremacy. No other preacher ever held more consistently and more firmly to the essen-

❀ ❀

tial deity of our Lord.' He saw in him the only hope of men and of nations.

Mr. Campbell's preaching may be summarized as follows: Christ, the only teacher; the Bible, the only authoritative book; the Church, the only institution for spiritual ends; faith in Jesus as the Christ, and repentance towards God the only prerequisites to baptism; obedience to the divine commands, the test of Christian standing; the gospel, the essential channel of spiritual influence in conversion; the truth of the gospel to enlighten; the love of God as seen in the gospel to persuade; the ordinances of the gospel as tests of submission to the divine will; the promises of the gospel, as the evidence of pardon and acceptance; and the Holy Spirit in and through all these accomplishing his work of enlightening, convincing of sin, guiding the penitent soul to pardon, and bearing witness to the obedient believer of his adoption into the family of God.

In his youth Mr. Campbell preached a sermon in which he contrasted the gospel with the law of Moses. He combated the idea, then so common, that in every conversion there must be a work of the law. The sinner must hear the thunders of Sinai before he could hear the pardoning voice of the Son of God. Mr. Campbell held that Mosaism was provisional and local. It was for one people and for one age. It had no glory because of the more excellent glory of the Christian system. He never denied or doubted the value or the permanency of the ethical element in Mosaism. That was taken up and incorporated in the Christian system. But as a system, Mosaism waxed old, and long since passed away. Mr. Campbell distinguished between the dispensations. He spoke of the patriarchal as starlight, of the Jewish as moonlight, of the mission of John the Baptist as twilight, and the Christian dispensation as the sunlight of the world. The patriarchs had the bud, the Jews had the blossom, we have the mature fruit of divine grace. The sermon was thoroughly evangelical. But because of it as author was tried for heresy. He put his accusers to flight. Thirty years after the sermon was preached it was published. So great had been the change in public sentiment in that time that no intelligent man could be found who took exceptions to its teaching.

The preaching of Mr. Campbell would not have had the influence it had if he had not been a great and good man. The man behind the sermon is as important as the man behind the message. It was said of him by one of his pupils that nature was in a fertile mood when she molded his large and sinewy body. "Material was abundant and bestowed with no grudging hand. There was not a pound of flesh too much, nor a pound too little. As to the resources of the mind, no word but opulent will describe him. Here he was pre-eminent. His head was faultless, the finest I ever

A Poem by Mr. Campbell.

The following lines were written by Mr. Campbell to his wife one Sunday morning in 1858, when travelling on the Cumberland River:

Serene the morn, and bright the sky;
  I walked the deck alone;
The morning-star with silvery rays
  In all its splendor shone.

❖ ❖ ❖

Some golden streaks of brightest hue
  Were trembling on the sky;
The forest leaves with drops of dew
  Gave hope that Spring was nigh.

❖ ❖ ❖

It was, indeed, the Lord's-day morn,
  And soon my thoughts were turned
To those bright scenes of hope and joy
  With which our hearts have burned.

❖ ❖ ❖

How soon shall all the toils of earth
  Give place to Heavenly rest;
And those who live for God and Christ
  Shall be forever blest!

❖ ❖ ❖

Hold on thy way, my sister wife,
  In faith, and hope, and love;
And when our toils on earth are past,
  We'll meet in Heaven above.

❖ ❖ ❖

Be this our aim, our happy choice,
  Till all our toils are o'er,
Then we shall meet among the blest,
  And part again no more."

saw." No one ever called his character in question. He had enemies. All sorts of charges were made against him for the views he held and for those he was supposed to hold. He ever wore the white flower of a blameless life. No father could wish for an only son a career more splendid or more stainless. He lived in constant and conscious fellowship with Jesus Christ. He was filled with the Holy Spirit. His piety was nourished and instructed by the daily study of the Word of God, and by a perpetual habit of prayer.

This article may fitly conclude with the testimony of four men of renown. Judge Black, speaking of Mr. Campbell's life and work, said this: "To effect a great reformation in such circumstances, to convince large numbers against their will, to organize the believers into a compact and powerful body, to conquer the respect of the world—these are proofs of intellectuality and moral force with which few of the children of men have been gifted. To these qualities were added an unfailing courage, a fortitude that nothing could shake, a chivalrous sense of justice to his opponents and affection for his friends, second only to his love for the cause to which he devoted his life. What greater claim can any man give to the character of a hero?" George D. Prentice spoke of Mr. Campbell as being unquestionably one of the most extraordinary men of his time. "His intellect is among the clearest, richest, profoundest ever vouchsafed to men. He grasps and handles the highest, subtlest, and most comprehensive princi-

ples as if they were the liveliest impressions of the senses. No poet's soul is more crowded with imagery than his is with the ripest forms of thought. Surely the life of a man thus excellent and gifted is a part of the common treasure of society. In his essential character he belongs to no sect or party, but to the world."

Bishop Hurst has said that few men have impressed themselves more profoundly on the religious life of their age than Alexander Campbell. His personality was of the most vigorous type, and for over a generation his name was a tower of strength over the whole United States. He was a man of the purest character and the highest consecration. He leavened the whole country with his views. Few men have exerted a wider influence. General Lee said that if Mr. Campbell had been delegated as a representative of his species to any one of the many superior worlds, he would have suggested a grand idea of the human race. The New York "Independent" has said that there is not a religious body in Christendom that, whether it will confess it or not, has not been profoundly affected by his life and work. His influence and fame have increased rather than diminished since his death. Many competent judges believe that they will continue to increase till that for which he pleaded so long and so earnestly and so ably will be accomplished, and there will be one flock as there is one Shepherd. Coming generations will rank Mr. Campbell among the greatest of the God-given men who have blessed earth.

❖ ❖

DOCTOR'S WORDS
Talks About the Analysis of Postum Food Coffee.

To the Doubting Thomases, the endorsement of a physician as to the wholesomeness of Postum Food Coffee may be comforting.

When coffee causes nervousness and dyspepsia, it's time to stop it. And there is where Postum is a true comforter. It is a warm, palatable and wholesome beverage and at the same time is a liquid food.

Coffee does harm, not because it's well or poorly made—not because it's high or low priced—but because of the alkaloid —drug—caffeine, it contains. The habitual use of coffee, therefore, forms a drug habit.

A Buffalo physician said recently, "I have used Postum Food Coffee in my family and find it to be all that is claimed for it—a most wholesome, delicious beverage. When made and served according to directions it is certainly delightful and refreshing.

"I have read carefully Dr. Davenport's analysis of Postum Food Coffee, as printed on the pkg, which I most heartily endorse. I have been prescribing it to my patients."

The Dr. is right and there's a reason. Read the little book, "The Road to Wellville" in pkgs.

Alexander Campbell's Imprisonment

By C. C. REDGRAVE.

The Edinburgh poster and the picture of the South Prison in Glasgow, presented with this article, introduce us to a chapter in the life of the sage of Bethany full of painful memories. Having in the month of August, 1847, reached the city of Edinburgh, on his European tour, Mr. Campbell was interviewed by the Rev. James Robertson and two other deputies of the "Scotch Anti-Slavery Society," to whom he frankly confided his Views of American slavery and of the abolitionists in Great Britain and America.

These ostensibly friendly visitors, however,

of character, and the plea that flight from Scotland was premeditated, Mr. Robertson secured a warrant for Mr. Campbell's arrest in Glasgow.

In the firm belief that he was being persecuted for righteousness sake, Mr. Campbell refused to accept bail and was committed to the common prison to await his trial. After ten days the case was brought before Lord Murray, who declared the warrant illegal and ordered the prisoner's discharge.

That the "South Prison" (see illustration) was the place of Mr. Campbell's confinement in Glas-

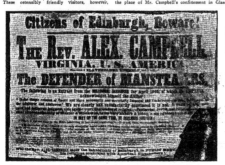

A Remarkable Edinburgh Poster.

proved to be enemies in disguise. For they proceeded immediately, in the most public manner and in a spirit of virulence, to defame their distinguished guest and erstwhile fellow-citizen. Large posters (see photographic copy with this sketch) were displayed all over the city, and men were employed to parade in front of the buildings, where Mr. Campbell was announced to speak, carrying the huge bills on boards in front of them and on their backs. The same tactics were employed in other cities, so that Mr. Campbell was everywhere heralded by these defamatory reports. The excitement was intense, threats were frequently heard, and grave fears were entertained regarding Mr. Campbell's safety. Leaving to his biographers, the full discussion of the events of this exciting period, we content ourselves with just a word or two with regard to his Views on American slavery and the immediate cause of his imprisonment.

Mr. Campbell looked upon American slavery as the darkest blot on the national escutcheon. He manumitted his own slaves—the slaves found on the farm so generously given him by his father-in-law, and even bought slaves and gave them their liberty. He contended earnestly for the God-given rights which the negro inherited in common with the white man. Yet believing as he did that the New Testament did not condemn the simple relation of master and servant, as such, his remedy for the blighting curse was the inculcation of Christian duty, and the dissemination of Bible truth. Moreover, he strenuously maintained that the full enfranchisement of the negro should come by proper constitutional means and not by cannon and the sword.

Meanwhile Mr. Campbell was the subject of much evil report. Replying to Mr. Robertson's challenge to publicly discuss the question at issue, Mr. Campbell said he would debate "provided only that he be not that *Reverend James Robertson*, who was publicly censured and excluded from the Baptist church for violating the fifth commandment in reference to his mother, of which I have heard something in Dundee."

On the strength of this supposed defamation

gow is evident. There were but two prisons in the city in 1847. The "North Prison," which prior to 1841, was designated "Bridewell," is now named, "Her Majesty's Prison, Duke street, Glasgow." In the records of this prison for 1847, which were carefully examined, at my request, by the governor of the jail no mention is made of A. Campbell, though particulars are given of one by that name, who was confined there in 1846, and described as twenty-six years' old, a hammerman by trade, charged with breach of peace, and sentenced to twenty days imprisonment.

The records of the "South Prison" are lost,

and have not been available for more than fifty years. Still, with this lack of official certification, it is pertinent to ask, if Mr. Campbell was not committed to "South Prison," was he imprisoned in Glasgow at all?

The cell in which the great reformer was placed was "small, with little light and no comforts save a stool and a small table and a piece of carpet two feet by four on the cold stone floor." A bed was improvised by hanging a hammock from two hooks driven into the walls. "South Prison" is a massive building with a superb Grecian portico and is altogether a splendid specimen of the Greek style of architecture. It is located at the foot of Saltmarket facing Glasgow Green and was built in 1810 at a cost of $175,000. The cells, or prison proper constitutes the rear of the Justiciary Court House, seen in the illustration, but it is in so cramped a space that it can not be photographed. C. C. REDGRAVE.

P. S.—The Edinburgh poster is in the possession of Mrs. D. C. Barclay. It was brought over by Mr. Campbell to let his wife see by what means he obtained his unenviable notoriety. The poster is much the worse for age and wear, and the lower right hand corner is lost.

❋ ❋

A Campbell Incident.

In an early day in the Campbell movement an appointment was made for Alexander Campbell to deliver an address in one of the largest towns in the district. Religiously, the Presbyterians largely predominated in the town, and, besides, a strong prejudice existed against Mr. Campbell on account of a belief entertained by the people that (being a citizen of Virginia), he was a slave owner. However, when the evening came for delivery of the address, the large court room where it was delivered, was crowded with an audience of more than average intelligence. For considerably more than an hour Mr. Campbell held his audience in profoundest attention, which was only broken by the announcement of the usual invitation hymn. During the singing of the hymn an old and well known negro man was discovered pressing his way to the platform where the speaker was standing. As soon as the old man's purpose became known, a smile passed over the faces of the audience, partly in contempt for the old negro, but more in anticipation of the disappointment and chagrin, which his coming would bring to the speaker. For a moment Mr. Campbell was perplexed, but so soon as he discovered the old negro coming, he divined the cause of the smile, promptly stepped forward and cordially took him by the hand, and then, for a moment surveying the audience, in a clear, calm voice, that reached every one in the room, said: "I thank God that he has made of one blood all peoples who dwell upon the earth; and that whosoever will obey him and work righteousness is accepted by him." At once the entire audience was in a tremor of suppressed emotion, in the midst of which Mr. Campbell proceeded to take the old man's confession.

JAMES O. CARSON.

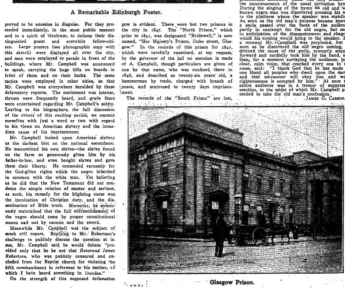

Glasgow Prison.

he scene of many bloody battles. No thier part of America is richer in history and no place more suitable for a reat international historic celebration han on the shores of Hampton Roads, here the Jamestown Exposition is to be eld.

Aside from the interesting historical and steamship lines leading to Norfolk have assured the exposition company that especially low rates will be made for the exposition visitors.

The massive auditorium, or Hall of Congresses, near the center of the exposition grounds will be placed at the disposal of the Disciples of Christ for and no other for their con ments offered same at all ti offer such an town Expositi ment can be no other peri

Our Budget

—"Put me off at Buffalo!"

—All aboard for the great National Convention!

—If you have decided not to go, when you see this, think it over and reverse your decision.

—It is still time for you to take in the Lord's day communion service and the Home and Foreign Missionary Conventions.

—Here's a unique and pressing invitation from Buffalo which came too late, even though flashed over the wires, for our last week's issue:

"Buffalo, Oct. 2, 1906.
"Side-track everything for the convention. Specials October 11-12. World-wide missions. Christian fellowship and higher individual spirituality have the right-of-way. Stop over in Buffalo for sightseeing from the top of convention mountain. Unsurpassed views of world-wide fields and inspiring visions of celestial glory. Stamp all tickets 'Enthusiasm and Devotion.' Jesus Christ will personally conduct all parties. Secure travelers' insurance against pessimism, hobbyism, criticism and sectarianism. All things are ready. Come!
"R. H. MILLER,
"International Missionary Convention."

—If that does not bring you, no added word of ours would reach your case. Even if you are unable to secure the kind of insurance suggested, you would be reasonably safe from any of the diseases mentioned in an assembly like that convening this week in Buffalo, where they seldom break out, and are soon cured when they do. The atmosphere of our conventions soon destroys the germs of these moral disorders.

—We regret that we are unable to include either all the articles or all the pictures relating to the life of Alexander Campbell which we had planned to appear in this number of THE CHRISTIAN-EVANGELIST. We shall publish other articles and photographs just as soon as we can find space for them in our crowded columns.

—The work at Belle Plain, Ill., has grown under the four months' ministration of F. A. Scott.

—The Christian Woman's Board of Missions has raised $206,553.12. The aim was $200,000.

—A good Bible institute has just been held at Chester, Neb., by Knox B. Taylor of Bloomington, Ill.

—The Foreign Society has received $500 on the annuity plan from a friend in Ohio 87 years of age.

—J. E. Couch will close his work at Minier, Ill., next Lord's day and begin at Pauls Valley, I. T., the following Sunday.

—We regret to hear of the death of A. H. Smith of Mataura, Southland, New Zealand. He had been attending Christian University at Canton, Mo.

—"Watch for Texas at Buffalo." So writes C. C. Bearden, of Clarendon. We know that Texas is all right and that J. C. Mason is "a good general."

—An organization has been completed at Arlington, Ky., with E. H. Rayther, who is attending the College of the Bible, in charge.

—O. E. Hamilton and J. P. Garmong are having successful meetings in Australia. Later they may make a trip to the Orient and Palestine.

—George E. Lyon, of Lyons, has been chosen as superintendent of Kansas Missions, the position held for the last seven years by W. S. Lowe. The first Sunday in November, it will be remembered, is State Mission Sunday, to be observed in all the states by a collection for the benefit of a forward work in the states.

—W. E. Harlow and son paid THE CHRISTIAN-EVANGELIST a brief visit on their way to Wheeling, W. Va., where they open the evangelistic campaign at the First Church.

—The balance of the church debt at Norwood, Ohio, will be paid this week. Joseph Armistead is the happy minister. Walter M. White will begin a meeting October 21.

—The corner-stone of a new church has just been laid at Coshocton, Ohio, the Masons having charge of part of the ceremonies. P. H. Welshimer, of Canton, delivered the oration. J. N. Johnston is the successful pastor.

—The new building at Uniontown, Pa., will soon be ready for its roof. The accommodation will provide for an audience of 1,500 people at least. J. Walter Carpenter is the pastor.

—A. M. Growden has accepted a call to Osceola, Ia. He commends the church at Carbondale, Ill., which he leaves at an early date because compelled to seek a drier climate.

—Harold E. Monser, of Champaign, Ill., has been compelled on account of the continued illness of his wife, to cancel his engagement with the church at Stillwater, Okla., and will be home for a while.

—Mrs. Lily W. Molland, with her children and Miss Genevieve Perkins, missionaries of the Foreign Society, sail from San Francisco, for China on the steamship "Nippon Maru," October 12.

—W. E. M. Hackleman, who is to lead the music at the National Convention at Buffalo this week, will help Evangelist W. J. Lockhart in two campaigns to be held at Lincoln, Ill., and Webb City, Mo., in November and December.

—We have only space in this issue to announce the fact that F. M. Green has just celebrated his seventieth birthday. THE CHRISTIAN-EVANGELIST extends its congratulations and wishes this veteran continued usefulness to the cause he has served for so many years.

—E. B. Bagby has preached his farewell sermon to a great congregation at Washington, D. C., and taken up his work at Cleveland, O. "We shall miss him greatly," writes Claude E. Jones, secretary of the Washington Ministerial Association.

—A. E. Cory, missionary of the Foreign Society to Wuhu, China, who recently closed a splendid meeting at Oskaloosa, Ia., where he was formerly pastor of the church, sails with his family on the steamship "Korea" from San Francisco November 20.

—The church at Angola, Ind., where Vernon Stauffer is pastor, has just made the greatest offering for home missions and related interests in its history, a total of $531 being given. Some twenty of this congregation will attend the Buffalo Convention.

—J. Q. Biggs, of Buffalo, Mo., writes us that the county convention held there was a great success. One of the greatest meetings of the kind ever held in the county was the Sunday-school rally with 247 in attendance, and a good collection for state missions.

—F. F. Walters, of Neosho, Mo., says: "The Newton County (Mo.) convention in Seneca was a success—the best in its history. The devotional and aggressive spirit was high throughout the session of two days, October 2-3. The addresses were all of the strongest and inspiring."

—Charles Reign Scoville has good word to say for the union meetings. Brother Scoville is now in a big meet-

A Rare Investment
A Sane Investment
A Safe Investment
SECURED BY REAL ESTATE

Six per cent interest guaranteed up to dividend paying period. Large, certain and annually increasing dividends thereafter. This is a very unusual opportunity.

For particulars address,
THOMAS KANE & COMPANY,
64-66 Wabash Ave.,
Chicago, Ill.

—Evangelist Charles Reign Scoville is to hold another union meeting soon, in which the union is expected to be permanent. His marriage to Miss Arlene Cornelia Dux, daughter of Mr. and Mrs. Joseph Dux, 4 Campbell Park Boulevard, Chicago, is announced to take place October 17, 1906. THE CHRISTIAN-EVANGELIST extends both hands in congratulations and good wishes.

—THE CHRISTIAN-EVANGELIST is indebted to L. H. Stine, minister of the West Side Church, Tipton, Ind., for his recent hearty co-operation with us in greatly increasing the circulation of our paper in this congregation. Many of our preachers are bringing us under obligations of gratitude to them for similar courtesies.

—B. N. Mitchell, who has recently spent three years as pastor at Liverpool, England, doing a substantial work there, and who is at present at Joliet, Ill., doing some temporary work with the church there, can be secured as pastor of some church needing a strong preacher, or for evangelistic work in which he has also had great success. Address him at 108 Macomber avenue, Joliet, Ill.

—J. S. Edwards, late pastor of the Christian Church at Amarillo, Texas, has returned to Colorado Springs, his former home. He was at Amarillo for four years and on departing received the highest encomiums from the officers of the church for his Christian life and genial disposition, and a liberal purse was presented to him and his wife in token of the church's love and fellowship.

—Hiram College will have a banquet at the Buffalo Convention on Monday evening. It will be held at the University Club at $1 per plate. Those who expect to attend may reserve accommodations by addressing the Secretary of the College, J. O. Newcomb, Hiram, Ohio, or Convention Hall, Buffalo. There will, of course, be other college banquets, but we have had no announcements as to when or where these will take place.

—E. L. Day's work at Brazil, Ind., goes on in good shape. It will be remembered that the brethren there, in face of great difficulty, erected another handsome building after the destruction of their church by fire. It is a great satisfaction to see such confidence. We are glad to report, too, that Brother Day and his congregation are seeking to keep abreast with the general work of the brotherhood, and many of them are reading THE CHRISTIAN-EVANGELIST.

—J. B. Boen, who has just preached his farewell sermon at Chickasha, I. T., was presented with a handsome gold watch as a token of the regard of the congregation, while the devoted Christian life of his wife was also acknowledged. Texas is to be their future home, and J. E. Dinger, who recently entered upon evangelistic work, was called by long distance telephone, while in a meet-

ing at Lincoln, Kans., and entered upon the pastorate last Lord's day.

—Thomas P. Ullom, who has for nearly six years been the pastor of our church at Traverse City, Mich., has just tendered his resignation, to take effect November 1. He will take up evangelistic work. Brother Ullom's work has been a good one, and he speaks to the largest congregations in the city, while he has a church membership of 450. Two years ago a handsome new building was dedicated.

—Brother Medbury is no doubt very happy. He writes from his great church in Des Moines, Ia.: "We have just made final remittances to the different boards, from our splendid Home Missionary offering of September 16. The amount was $628, which has been proportioned among the different boards doing work in the national field. This offering does not include state missions. We are now happy in having two living links in the foreign field, one in the general home field, and another in the state."

❀ ❀

Board of Ministerial Relief of the Church of Christ.

Aid in the support of worthy, needy, disabled ministers of the Christian Church and their widows.

THIRD LORD'S DAY IN DECEMBER is the day set apart in all the churches for the offering to this work. If you make individual offerings, send direct to the Board. Wills and Deeds should be made to "BOARD OF MINISTERIAL RELIEF OF THE CHURCH OF CHRIST, a corporation under the laws of the State of Indiana." Money received on the Annuity Plan.

Address all communications and make all checks, drafts, etc., payable to

BOARD OF MINISTERIAL RELIEF, 120 E. Market St., Indianapolis, Indiana.

—W. M. Stuckey has just closed a fine meeting with his home church under a tent, unifying the Christians of Lebo as they never were before, and opening their eyes to the follies of sectarianism. As a relief from pastoral labors, he will enter the evangelistic field for a time, and is now in a meeting at Williamsburg, Kans. He will be open for other duties in December.

—We are glad to be able to print in this issue an article from the pen of Bro. James O. Carson who will celebrate his eighty-seventh birthday on the seventeenth of this month. Brother Carson was personally acquainted with the Campbells and most of the leaders of our movement. He entertained many of these at his home in St. Louis in the early days. Brother Carson has a desire to live long enough and to have strength enough to be present at the Centennial celebration in Pittsburg, and we will all pray that he may be spared to participate in that happy event.

—We are glad to note that H. C. Kendrick, who recently resigned at Hagerstown, Md., has been called to the great church at Georgetown, Ky., which is within twenty-five miles of his birthplace. This church has a membership of 700, and was erected recently at a cost of $40,000. Brother Kendrick, in writing about this change, says: "There are sad hearts in Hagerstown, and the saddest are the minister and family. The splendid church by many tokens of its love is making it very hard for us to leave. It is like breaking of home ties. I hope the move will redound to the great good of all parties especially concerned and to the honor and glory of the "Name that is above every name." The official board, after offering inducements in the way of increase of salary to retain Brother Kendrick, finally passed resolutions commending him and assuring him of the friendship of the congregation. We went to Hagerstown about five years ago. During his pastorate the church has been freed from debt and renovated and about 150 have been added to the membership.

—The Christian church at Fayette, Mo., traces its organization back to the pioneer days of 1830. It has had its periods of struggle, but through each has risen triumphant. Among its

W. F. Shearer, Evangelist, of Angola, Ind.

early preachers of note were T. M. Allen, Dr. Hopson and John W. McGarvey. The building used at present was dedicated in 1886. The membership to-day is something over 400, and of the usual

church organizations the C. W. B. M. Auxiliary is deserving of special notice for the efficient work it has done in recent years. F. M. Grimes, Sr., Solon Smith and J. R. Callemore are now the elders of the church, while R. B. Helser has served it as pastor during the past two years, during which time there has been a net gain of 140 members. A meeting is now being held with Evangelist W. F. Shearer, of Angola, Ind., as-

R. B. Helser, Pastor at Fayette, Mo.

sisting Brother Helser, and Bro. Ben Hill, the local choir leader, in charge of the music. Brother Shearer is a man of faith and evangelistic power, while Brother Helser has good executive and pastoral ability. This combination ought to make for a forward movement in the church.

—The fine new church building just opened at Walla Walla, Wash., will accommodate about 900 people and will cost in the neighborhood of $40,000. When occasion requires, folding doors may be thrown open so that some twelve or fifteen hundred people can hear the preacher's voice. We congratulate Morton Gregory and his congregation on their admirable new equipment. The dedicatory ceremony will be postponed until the arrival of a large pipe organ and the entire completion of the interior of the building.

—It is quite a good sized directory that has been published by the First Church of Christ, Akron, O., no less than 1,154 names being found in it. Of this number 132 are non-residents of Akron and 55 are those whose addresses are unknown leaving a resident membership of 967. We note that not only is there an alphabetical list of the membership but there is a street directory as well wherein may quickly be found the names of the families that are members of the church. George Darsie is the minister of this church and Miss Jennie Jenkinson his pastoral helper. THE CHRISTIAN-EVANGELIST extends congratulations and wishes that this great church, with its accomplished leaders, may have another year of great prosperity.

—A member of the church at Indiana Harbor, Ind., a city of 6,000 inhabitants and 70 saloons, writes that two young brothers by the name of Snodgrass have been conducting a meeting of great power in a tent there. We make the following quotation from our sister's letter: "On

Sunday afternoon as the writer trudged behind, being late, a beautiful picture rose before me. Looking far along the shores of Lake Michigan, with many people following to witness the sacred ordinance of baptism, I thought of the days of long ago when many followed after Jesus. What a beautiful thought to know that to-day they were still following him. As the breakers rose up and sometimes crossed over my pathway, I cried out, 'O Galilee, blue Galilee, where Jesus loved so much to be.' An old lady 70 years old was baptized that afternoon."

—On our Centennial page we record some good news from some of our colleges. We are glad to note that all schools that have reported to us show signs of growth. Cotner University has just opened, with the largest enrollment in its history, an increase of 28 per cent over last year. Eleven states are represented in the student body, and there is a representative of Japan, China, Korea, and one student from Tarsus, in Asia Minor. The College of the Bible, at Lexington, has about the same number of students as they began with last year. About half of the $25,000 being sought for a chair of Bible-school pedagogy was secured at the state convention recently held at Louisville. A venerable resident of Lexington, who has known the college from the time of its organization, has just died, leaving an unsolicited bequest of $7,000 out of a moderate esta .

❦ ❦

Don't Fool Your System.

—During the meeting of Bruce Brown with the church at Kirksville, Mo., he received news of the sudden death of his aged father. Brother Brown writes: "He was much more to me than a father—my constant adviser and helper. I never undertook any task without conferring with him. His faith in Christ and his devoted life have made me what-ever I am." While we sympathize with our brother in his bereavement, we congratulate him also on the heritage of a noble and blessed memory which his father leaves to him.

—No question comes to our desk more frequently than whether the board of officers of any congregation has the right to withdraw fellowship from any member of the church without the consent of the church. It ought to be thoroughly understood that the officers of the church are the agents or organs through which the church acts, and that the authority they possess they derive from the congregation that appoints them. They can recommend withdrawal of fellowship from an unworthy member, or the name of a preacher to be called, or any other measure, but the validity of such measure depends upon the approval of the congregation.

—We have received an interesting travel letter from J. N. Smith, for which we would like to have space. Granted a two months' vacation by his congregation at Los Angeles, he went to Helena, Mont., where one of his sons resides. He had the pleasure of spending some time in the Montana Association which was in session at our church, and met many of the ministers. Passing on to Billings, he preached there on the Lord's day, and later went to visit his only living brother at Hebron, Neb. He had not seen him for sixteen years. Brother Smith is due in Missouri about this time and will visit several of the towns in the state. H. A. Denton, of Maryville, is a son-in-law and, of course, he will have a royal visit there. His son, C. P., ministers at Mason City, where he is to deliver an address on the fifteenth anniversary of that church in October. The Buffalo convention will be attended in company with a Missouri delegation. Brother Smith first visited Hebron some thirty years ago when, it is said, one-half of the adult population of the county were present to hear him preach. Now

they have a good church with a membership of about 300. At present, however, there is no pastor, R. A. Schell, who ministered to them for eight years, having gone early in July to take the work at Hastings, to the deep regret of the Hebron congregation. Any one interested in this pastorate should address F. A. Powell, one of the elders, and give references.

❀ ❀

The Manchester (N. H.) Meeting—Account Closed.

Amount previously acknowledged $1,021 75
Received since then—
L. E. Murray................. 5 00
F. F. Grim 5 00
E. G. Aftermath............ 10 00
C. G. and J. S. Munro......... 2 00

Total $1,043 75

At our San Francisco convention the Editor of THE CHRISTIAN-EVANGELIST assumed the financial responsibility of raising a sufficient amount of funds for sustaining an evangelist to hold a meeting somewhere in New Hampshire, with a view of organizing our first church in that state. As it is now known, the city of Manchester was selected and Bro. Herbert Yeuell was chosen as evangelist. The meeting lasted a month, costing something less that $1,200 for all expenses. The response to our appeals through THE CHRISTIAN-EVANGELIST and to personal letters which the Editor sent to a number of our business men, has been very gratifying as indicating the interest which the brethren everywhere feel in that work. Counting the collections taken during the meeting a sufficient sum has been received to cancel all obligations. Those who have generously responded to our call for assistance have our sincere thanks for their co-operation.

It gives us pleasure to report that the Christian Woman's Board of Missions, which had agreed before the meeting began to support a pastor for the church when it was organized, has magnanimously consented to undertake the work at its present stage, sustain an evangelist there to gather the fruits of Brother Yeuell's meeting in the organization of a church, and then to support a permanent pastor there. This means

that not a dollar that has been paid to this undertaking will be lost, but that the fruits of the meeting will be conserved and the work carried on to permanent success. A small balance on hand will be turned over to the C. W. B. M. for that work.

We congratulate all the parties concerned on this successful issue of our enterprise, and on the prospect that hereafter New Hampshire will have a place on our religious map along with the other states of the union.

❀ ❀

Babies To Be Cared For.

The Mothers' and Babies' Home of the Christian Church, 2821 Lawton avenue, St. Louis, Mo., has for adoption several baby boys and girls under one year of age, a pair of twin boys 2 years of age and twin girls 1 year old, besides a number of boys about 3 years old. We will be glad to find good homes for these children.

Let me say, too, that we are really in urgent need of funds for our institution.
MRS. T. R. AYARS.

❀ ❀

As We Go to Press.

Special to THE CHRISTIAN-EVANGELIST.

Oklahoma City, Okt. 9.—The general college idea carried. Enid gives $100,000 and wins the location.—O. L. Smith.

Special to THE CHRISTIAN-EVANGELIST.

Kansas City, Mo., Oct. 7.—Jackson avenue continues with Wm. J. Lockhart, and Charles Altheide leading. Splendid men and a great church.—Frank L. Bowen, pastor.

Special to THE CHRISTIAN-EVANGELIST.

Ethel, Mo., Oct. 8.—Thirty-five at Mount Olive; six at the last service; twenty here yesterday.—LeBaron & Conrad.

Special to THE CHRISTIAN-EVANGELIST.

Sullivan, Ill., Oct. 7.—Seventy-eight tonight; eighty-six to-day! four hundred and seventy to date; four thousand and eight since January 1.—Scoville, Smith and the Kendalls.

❀ ❀

Ernest J. Bradley, minister of the Central Christian church at Hillsboro, Texas, desires to exchange meetings with some member of THE CHRISTIAN-EVANGELIST family. Hillsboro is a town of 7,000, and the Central church has a membership of more than 200. Brother Bradley desires the meeting in Hillsboro to begin about October 20-25. He will give return meeting to meet the need of the church exchanging meetings.

NEWS FROM MANY FIELDS.

Kansas State Convention.

The state convention of the Christian churches of Kansas met at Parsons, September 17-20. To try to describe it by adjectives would exhaust the vocabulary. Every arrangement was made by the church at Parsons to entertain the convention. There was no "address of welcome," but committees met every one at the train and gave them a personal welcome. Then we were taken to the church where every modern accommodation was provided. Postoffice, check-room, dining-room—where dinner and supper were served—and assignment made. We had lodging and breakfast in the splendid homes of Parsons. The program embraced every department of the work, with specialists in each department, from this and other states. At the start the Y. P. S. C. E. department gave life to the whole convention.

The first address was by F. E. Mallory, of Topeka, on "The Essence of Christianity," which he gave in these words, and which rang through the whole convention, "Thou shalt love the Lord, thy God, with all thy heart and thy neighbor as thyself," dwelling on the "neighbor."

In the church period we had many good things. I make special mention of the address by Chas. A. Finch, of Topeka, on "Walled Cities," which was eloquent and helpful, and that of H. A. Orchard, of Ft. Scott, on "The Country Preacher," which was ordered to be published by the convention. The two addresses of W. F. Turner, of Joplin, Mo., on "Home and Foreign Missions" were masterpieces, and worthy of the man that he is.

The reports from the workers showed substantial gains in the work. The sad feature of this period was the announcement that W. S. Lowe would no longer serve as a field secretary. He has filled this responsible position seven years, with great satisfaction to the board and brotherhood. The specialist in the Bible school department was Robert M. Hopkins, of Louisville, Ky., who was very helpful to us all. In the C. W. B. M. period we had special treats in the addresses of Mrs. J. E. McDaniel, of Newton, and Mrs. W. C. Payne, of Lawrence, and Miss Nora Siler, missionary in Porto Rico. The junior period was opened by prayer by Grandma Curry, of Parsons, who is 96 years old, and followed by a program by the children, thus combining childhood and age in the service of him who loves all alike.

DeLoss Smith had charge of the music, which is all we need to say on that subject. There were 267 enrolled delegates and that with the great church at Parsons made a great convention. The Parsons C. W. B. M. auxiliary referred to as the Kansas wonder, in having 165 members.

G. W. KITCHEN.

Wisconsin Convention.

The churches of the state met in their annual missionary convention at Ladysmith, September 20-23. Brother Thurman, our president, owing to the serious illness of his mother-in-law, and sister was unable to be with us. C. W. Dean, of Grand Rapids, acted as chairman. Themes for discussion were well chosen and the speakers were of the best. Mrs. Mettie Monroe presided during the C. W. B. M. sessions. These were made interesting by the presence of Mrs. Louise Kelly, Emporia, Kan., national organizer and Miss Boyd of India. G. W. Muckley, Stephen J. Corey and J. H. Mohorter, each representing their respective boards, were with us at one or more of our sessions and gave us inspiring addresses. Especial mention should be made of the scholarly paper read by Chas. W. Dean on "The Present Status of Christian Union." So worthy was the paper that it was recommended by the convention that it should appear in print. Music by Mrs. Chas.

W. Dean, of Oakland, Cal., added to the pleasure of the convention. Brother Street, of Eureka College, led in song. One was impressed with the Christian fellowship made manifest during the convention not only among our brethren, but with the other churches of Ladysmith. This fellowship is largely due to the Christian character and liberal mind of Brother Barstow. Reports from the mission churches show a steady growth, and with Brother Barstow in the field as state evangelist and Bro. C. W. Dean as our state secretary, we see no reason why we can not achieve greater success in the year to come. The Ladysmith people gave us a cordial entertainment and the memory of their hospitality will long remain as will the spiritual uplift we each received.

Rib Lake, Wis.   P. A. SHERMAN.

Ohio.

H. M. Garn has offered his resignation at Lakewood and will seek knowledge and culture for a year at least in Chicago University. Lakewood has recently sold the old church house and lot and is now building a new house further east. They already have an eye on a successor to Brother Garn.——C. C. Cunningham has been holding a good meeting with his congregation at Garrettsville, assisted by E. T. Robinson as song leader. The word "Disciple" has recently been chiseled off of the meeting house at Garrettsville and it is now a plain Church of Christ. Good. Let others do likewise.——Bellaire is to be congratulated on securing the services of W. D. VanVoorhis. He is of the salt of the earth and Mrs. Vanvoorhis is a fine worker and brilliant writer. We hope this union will be lasting and very fruitful.——F. M. Green celebrated his 70th birthday September 28. He has been in public service for 52 years and is as vigorous as ever, and preaches almost every Sunday. He has recently been elected a member of the American Academy of Political and Social Science of Philadelphia. The Ohio letter extends congratulations to Brother Green on his "three score and ten" and also the honor that has come to him.——L. O. Newcomer is welcomed to Ohio as bishop at Mt. Vernon. He has accepted a call from this excellent church and begun his ministry. May it, too, be long and prosperous.——E. B. Bagby begins his labors at Franklin Circle, Cleveland, Sunday, October 7. They will have a rally day on that date and are working for 500 in the Bible school. A most cordial welcome, Brother Bagby, for all the "Buckeyes." The Cleveland preachers' meetings for the year began September 24 with "Vacation experiences." The meeting was well attended and very interesting.——The cornerstone of the new house of worship at Coshocton was laid September 30; Pastor Johnson is leading with a steady but sure hand at Coshocton and the result will be a splendid, substantial church. Secretary Bartlett is still touring the state in the interest of Ohio missions. Lowe, Sala, Shelborne, Mansel, et al., have been lending a hand in the speech-making. But after all remember that November 4 is the judgment day. Let all the enthusiasm be crystallized on that day in dollars and dimes.——The Ohio scribe has been at North Royalton for three weeks in a very interesting meeting. This church is 77 years old. It is a country church but an exceedingly good one as country churches go in these days. The membership is about 100 and they are of the purest blood of Western Reserve Yankee extraction. If you want to live on the fat of the land, hold a meeting in the country in September! It has been a rare treat to be here. The church is in fine condition and going ahead under the leadership of Bro. Chas. Ford, who is loved by everybody in and out of the church. He has done an excellent year's work with this people. Over half of this township is owned by Bohemians. They are good farmers, too. The American born and reared are excellent citizens. The name of Christ has been confessed in this meeting by Bohemian lips. We are looking for others. The scenery hereabouts

is superb. The very point where writing is next to the highest in Ohio logical survey tablet is in the walls of this house that says I am now 1238 feet [above] sea. Two books have greatly interested here. I am a little behind hand in "F Authority" by Sabatier, but that does my delight in it and profit accruing there one book if you have not yet read have been reading a new book of the D. W. Forrest on "The Authority of This book is published by T. and T. London, but can now be had from The Publishing Company of St. Louis at $1 great book. No book of the year will You see I am storing up on the authority. It is always well to know are at."   C. A

Painesville, Ohio.

Cozy Homes.

The discovery of a new wick [is] effective and yet so simple that it's a one thought of it before—has so revolutionized the manufacture of oil heaters and explosions, smoke and smell, caused as things of the past.

This new wick attachment is to be the Perfection Oil Heater. Interest show that, although the heater gives heat, the wick can not be turned on too low—absolute safety thus being assured other feature which is worthy of mention smokeless device which prevents all odor. The portability of the heater mends it for general household use is very light and can be easily carried. Its simple operation, usefulness in heat and warming cold rooms make it a really useful article in any home. It is so far superior to other oil heaters, such fair price that its universal [use] but a matter of time.

The Rayo Lamp, which is made by manufacturers of the Perfection Oil Heater out doubt the best lamp for all-round use. It is equipped with the latest improvements and gives a bright, steady light at small able for any room, whether library, dining parlor, or bed-room.

The Perfection Oil Heater and the Rayo form a combination that for real comfort can not be equalled. When one is taken of the simple operation of the Rayo lamp, their absolute safety, the light generated by the one, and the bright light given by the other—all without smell—their value in any home, large or small, can be somewhat appreciated. Sold by dealers.

Texas.

Two interesting conventions have recently been attended by your scribe at the First Mexican Christian Church Convention held in Monterey. The attendance was good and the spirit was Christian. The addresses were of a high grade and manifested a grasp of the problems before the Mexican missionaries and a disposition toward a united effort that was refreshing. Father Westrup who has been working and praying for such a day as this for many years was delighted. His reminiscenses if he could be persuaded to commit them to writing would be read with deep interest and should be preserved as a most interesting chapter in the history of Mexico Missions. We had a delightful welcome from our missionaries and it was my privilege to deliver four addresses. Mr. Enrique Westrup was my interpreter and it is said that he did his work well though it was amusing when he translated "visionary" by "crazy" in the following sentence: "Some people think me visionary." I was indulging in what my friends call a characteristic prophecy, about the future of the work in Mexico. We have the Mexican Christian Institute, with some 400 pupils with Jasper T. Moses at its head, who seems to be the right man in the right place. He has a capable and devoted corps of teachers. The evangelistic work is conducted with zeal and prudence by Brother Inman and his helpers. Four out stations are maintained in Monterey, besides the missions at Saltillo, Fuentes and other points. We have also in Texas four Mexican missions conducted under the direction of our state board. We are doing both native and foreign mission work in Texas and would be glad to double the home and foreign mission spirit in Texas and multiply both by a larger liberality and put the sum into our November offering for state missions. According to the title, "The

Twenty-fourth Annual Texas Christian Missionary Convention," on the program, four years before the white Disciples were organized for Texas mission work, the negro Disciples were holding state conventions. There are probably 15,000 of the negro Disciples in Texas. Not far from 200 were present at Dangerfield where the convention was held. There seemed to be a single purpose that of "saving and developing in the Christian life our people." J. B. Lehman, of the Southern Christian Institute of Edwards, Miss., was present and gave daily Bible lessons which were greatly appreciated. Brother Lehman is well equipped for the great and good work which he is doing. The Christian Industrial school is destined to be a factor in the solution of the "race problem." The addresses and spirit of this convention showed commendable progress and most earnest devotion to the work of giving to the negroes of Texas the Christianity of the New Testament. J. C. MASON.

❀ ❀ ❀

The First Conference of the Mexican Mission.

We have just held in Monterey what to us on the field has been a wonderful gathering. Not that large delegations came, but for a week the mission force in Monterey, along with a good part of the church of the same city, and representatives from our churches at Saltillo, Fuente, Sabinas, and Las Esperanzas met together four times daily to study about things of the Kingdom and means of more swiftly causing it to come upon the whole earth. The plan of the conference was to make it about half work between a convention and a school of methods. An early morning devotional meeting was held at 6 o'clock every day, at 9 and at 3, in one of the class rooms of the school; with note books and pencils.

RIBBED-FLEECE UNDERWEAR
A New Idea in Underwear Attended by Tremendous Success.

This new underwear, known as Vellastic Utica Ribbed Fleece Underwear, was first put upon the market two years ago. The hygienic value and comfort-giving properties of this new weave in undergarments have made such a strong appeal to the public that the mills can hardly keep up with the demand.

Vellastic Underwear is a ribbed fabric with fleece lining. This means the warmth, comfort and softness of a fleece-lined garment, with the elasticity of a ribbed garment.

Vellastic Utica Ribbed Fleece Underwear always retains its shape and elasticity in washing, and the fleece its downy softness.

Another very attractive feature of this new underwear is its low price. Its extreme softness and pliability commend it to those who are accustomed to garments of finest texture.

Men's and women's garments, at 50c each; Ladies' union Suits, $1.00; children's sizes in union suits, 50c; in two piece suits, 25c the garment.

The trade mark, Vellastic Utica Ribbed-Fleece, is sewed on every garment. If not at your dealer's, write us, giving his name. Booklet and sample of fabric free.

Utica Knitting Company, Utica, New York.

we studied practical methods of work. At night a popular meeting, with special music and a soul-stirring address, was held in the chapel. The motto of the week was "To get God's man in God's place, doing God's work, in God's way, for God's glory." Each day had its special theme. Monday night the delegates told why they had come. Tuesday the theme was "The Church in History;" Wednesday, "The Church at Work— Her Ministers;" Thursday, "Her Auxiliaries;" Friday, "Her Organization and Problems;" "Saturday, "Our Aim—Mexico for Christ." The two chief instructors were J. C. Mason from Texas, who gave us most helpful addresses on such themes as "Christian Union," "Our Position," "How to deliver Sermons," "Pastoral Work," "Church Organization," and E. M. Sein, the National Secretary, of the Mexican Sunday-school Association, who was a power with his message, not only on his special work but also in such discourses as those he gave on "The Preparation of Sermons," "The Influencing of Young Men for the Ministry," and "Not a Drone in the Hive." ——The early morning quiet hours were among the most helpful meetings. The Mexican Christians know how to pray and are not ashamed to do so in public. The closing meeting was one of consecration, and it consisted almost entirely of prayer. There were few dry eyes in the audience at its close. On another morning, Brother Jimenez, pastor at Sabinas, gave us a talk on "The Holy Spirit's Guidance," which I never heard surpassed in one of our National Endeavor Conventions.——The reports from the field showed a remarkable progress; from a local work in Monterey and Saltillo, we have grown to be a recognized power in the evangelization of northern Mexico. Fourteen months ago we had three preaching points in Mexico. Now we have twenty, six of which are organized congregations. There have been eighty-nine baptisms during the year. Not counting the contributions of the American congregation, there has been raised on the field over $600 gold, six times what it was last year. The publication of Brother Wharton's tract in Spanish has contributed in no small degree to this. Five converts to the tithe system were made at the conference.——The other pastors of the city attended the sessions as regularly as did our own delegates, and throughout the week the spirit of union was notable. Thursday noon the city pastors and visiting preachers were invited to a dinner given in the private dining room of the Iturbide Hotel, by a layman member of the Presbyterian church. The delegates were also entertained at dinner by Brother Moses, and by one of our Mexican members. Altogether the spirit of fellowship, enthusiasm, and consecration, that ruled at all times gives us great hope for our work of making the saving health of God known to this benighted land. And for this encouragement we thank our God. For the deeper we go into our problem, the more difficult we perceive it to be. S. G. INMAN.

Scoville's Union Meeting.

The Scoville union revival in Monroe, Wis., came to a close on September 10. A greater victory was never won against conditions apparently insurmountable. I do not say that there are not other evangelists who are just as consecrated and able as Scoville, but I doubt if there can be found another man possessing the peculiar personal qualities to carry by storm a position that to all appearances seemed invulnerable. From a spiritual standpoint Monroe has for many years been completely overwhelmed with worldliness. The influence of twenty-six saloons and a brewery, to a great extent, has dominated the city. Open violation of both local and state laws has not only been tolerated, but approved by the majority of the city council.

Five churches united in the movement as follows: Methodist, United Brethren, English Lutheran, German Evangelical and the Union Church in Christ. The Armory, seating about 1,500 people, was hired for four weeks. Many church people shook their heads and said, "What folly; when one of the churches would accommodate all that would attend a religious meeting." Others said, "You can't get sixty converts in six months."

Brother Scoville and De Loss Smith came and opened a campaign that, at the last was reinforced by Brother and Sister Kendall. For about a week Scoville preached the straight gospel without giving an invitation, and then he opened the door and fifty-one souls responded. The meetings continued for five weeks, at the end of which time four hundred and sixty-one souls had stepped out for Christ, and the city and the adjacent country for miles had received a spiritual "uplift" that will bless for ages to come. The free will offerings at the close was a telling mark of the deep interest of the people. It goes without saying that the hosts of sin, including the saloons, are furious.

We thank God, and rejoice that he sent us Charles Reign Scoville, and his consecrated helpers, De Loss Smith and the Kendalls. May the blessings of God be with them wherever they may go, in the great battle for the establishment of his kingdom.   J. H. BERKEY.
Pastor "Union Church in Christ."

From the Evangelist.

I have received many letters from nearly all directions inquiring as to my opinion of the union meetings, and these have come from both evangelists and pastors, and I wish to add a word to the report of Brother Berkey, who is a pastor of the Union Church of Christ at Monroe, and through whom I was invited to conduct the union meetings in that city.

Personally, I feel that I have verified the passage of Scripture, "Upon this rock I will build my church, and the gates of hell shall not prevail against it." If there is any town of four thousand inhabitants this side of hell that needed the gospel any worse than Monroe, I have never seen it. I am sure my brethren will not misunderstand me. I am not in the habit of speaking of cities in this way, as you all well know.

Brother Berkey's report names the five churches united in the meeting. It would be well to say two of these churches were very small, and the combined membership of the five would not give as many Christians as I have had in one single congregation of our own brotherhood. Also the churches of Monroe were weak. This victory gained through union, makes me more enthusiastic and to desire Christian union more than ever before. I have had a taste. I have seen the arm of the Lord upraised by the united churches and even if those forces appeared to be few in number, we found that in union there was strength.

If the churches of America were united, all the ends of the earth would be praising God in this generation; the union of all the Christian forces of the city, together with consecrated earnestness of the pastors united in one purpose; the fact that all the Christian merchants, and all the country people, bankers and business men, and Christian clerks and stenographers, and greater still the papers backing these meetings, means more than these lines can tell.

Somebody is saying, "What about the preaching?" I am sorry somebody else did not write about this, but since they did not, I will say that I have preached many of the very same sermons; in fact, nearly all that I have preached in the meetings held for our home churches and that without changing them in the least. Scripture lessons on the divine name, Christian union, faith, conversion, repentance, conversion, prayer and the Holy Spirit, were read continuously, and no one found any fault whatever. The good confession was taken every night, and the only difference was the fact that there was no bap-

tistry, and no baptizing at the ice; otherwise, anybody dropp could not have told the diff union meeting and a meeting of Christ anywhere.

I was there to receive as have never been supported pastors than I was by seven denominational churches. which were begun by Brothe homes and carried on, and spread to other churches, sho a living example to our breth WheneVer, as a people, we we can feel that it is more to receive, and give in the s man, or other church will be Wherever the man or cheer when he can look on the thin on the things of himself; w from the other man's stand spirit in which that man or of and works, I am sure that will cry out "Behold, how bl ren to dwell together in unit to sanction division, far fr mean to recognize all that is nominations, and to thank of the many, and in recogniz prominent the things wherein we shall actually fall in lo The things in which we disa to be small grievances, and will constrain us and we will run with patience, th us, looking unto Jesus, the of our faith, and not looki formists or creed differences.
CHA

Catarrh Cannot

Evangelistic

We invite ministers and others to send reports of meetings, additions and other news of the churches. It is especially requested that additions be reported as "by confession and baptism," or "by letter."

Colorado.

Boulder.—Four added.—S. M. Bernard.

District of Columbia.

Washington, Oct. 1.—Vermont Avenue (F. D. Power), 6 by letter and 1 confession; Fifteenth Street (I. E. Stuart), 2 by letter; Ninth Street (E. B. Bagby), 1 by statement and 5 by confession and baptism; Thirty-fourth Street (Claude E. Jones), one by statement and three by confession and baptism.—Claude E. Jones, Sec.

Iowa.

Oskaloosa, Oct. 5.—Meeting closed last night. There were 25 added in 16 days. Twenty-seven added last service, 14 men. Cory, evangelist; Mrs. Collins, singer.—S. H. Zendt, pastor.

Oskaloosa, Oct. 6.—A. E. Cory has just closed a great meeting here. Under his leadership, ably aided by our pastor, Brother Zendt, and Mrs. Collins, of Keokuk, as singer, 232 were added to our membership. The hearty moral support of the other religious bodies of the city was a delightful feature, savoring of a genuine Christian unity.—John M. Stoke.

Illinois.

Blue Mound, Oct. 1.—Two additions yesterday—1 by letter and 1 by baptism.—W. H. Harding.

Newman.—Six added to the church during September at the regular services. W. E. Harlow will be with us in December.—O. L. Lyon, minister.

Jacksonville, Oct. 5.—Meeting with J. H. O. Smith continued 25 days with 115 added. A fine meeting.—E. F. Thrapp.

Heyworth, Oct. 6.—Heyworth church closed a meeting of four weeks, led by W. F. Shearer with 24 additions.—J. P. Givens, pastor.

Washburn, Oct. 4.—F. A. Scott, minister at Belle Plain, recently closed a meeting there with 32 added by baptism and three otherwise.—H. H. Jenner.

Catlin, Oct. 5.—Have received 105 persons into the church since January 14, 1906, 27 into the church here and 28 into the church at West Lebanon.—Lewis R. Hotaling.

Rutland, Oct. 5.—Our meeting is only 12 days old with 18 added, all by baptism but three. C. L. Organ, state evangelist of Iowa, is leading the forces.—R. B. Doan, minister.

Virden, Oct. 7.—Thirty-eight additions to date. Fine interest. Edward O. Beyer is my helper. H. J. Hostetler is the successful pastor. We continue.—John W. Marshall.

Tallula, Oct. —Our meeting, in which Brother Monser and Sister Pollock led us so effectively, closed last Sunday night, resulting in 39 additions—18 by baptism and 18 by letter or statement. A Christian Endeavor Society was organized with about 20 members.—J. H. Henderson.

Indiana.

Angola, Oct. 4.—Three confessions Sunday evening. The work prospers.—Vernon Stauffer.

Plainfield.—I baptized 6 in a days' meeting at Trafalgar, Ind., and 2 added otherwise.—I. N. Grisso.

Brook, Oct. 3.—Closed our meeting here last Lord's day evening with 23 added. Sister Lola Calvert did efficient work as chorus leader and personal worker.

Angola, Oct. 7.—We left our meeting at Ambia owing to the expiration of our time there, in the hands of Brother Mercer, of Hoopeston, Ill., who will continue this week. We had 11 additions, 5 by confession. As the pastor, Warner King, will close his work there January 1, the church will need a hustling, consecrated man for half time, and he will find a good field for work. We began at Montrovia, Ind., yesterday with crowded house and splendid interest.—Chas. W. Mahin and wife, evangelists.

Indian Territory.

Tuttle, Oct. 5.—In spite of difficulties meeting here resulted in an organization of 34 and the assurance of a house of worship. This church will grow.—Robt. E. Rosenstein.

Kansas.

Manhattan, Oct. 1.—Five added yesterday—1

confession and 4 by letter.—W. T. McLain.

Kentucky.

Lexington, Sept. 27.—Have had 6 additions to our Arlington Church in last six weeks, as follows: Two by confession and baptism, 3 by statement and 1 from another denomination.—E. H. Rayner.

Michigan.

Adrian, Oct. 2.—Two additions by confession and baptism.—B. W. Huntsman.

Missouri.

Fredericktown.—Had another confession yesterday, making 73 additions in five months.—R. O. Rogers.

Keytesville, Oct. 5.—A good meeting. I. F. Wolfe is the pastor. We expect to be with Hugh McLellan in Richmond, Ky., October 10.—H. A. Northcutt, evangelist, J. S. Zeran and wife, singers.

LemonVille.—The writer closed a meeting of one week at LemonVille with 9 additions—6 by confession.—J. B. Lookhart.

Kansas City, Oct. 2.—Three additions recently —2 by baptism and 1 by letter—at the Budd Park Church.—B. L. Wray, pastor.

Adrian, Oct. 3.—Recently closed a very successful meeting at Gunn City, assisted by J. S. Clements, with 16 additions.—Leslie M. Lucas, pastor.

Maitland, Oct. 1.—Just closed a meeting conducted by D. L. Dunkleburger, at Graham, with 19 additions. Great good has been done.—B. F. Baker, pastor.

Festus, Oct. 8.—Two additions by letter yesterday. We organized a Young Ladies' Aid Society with twelve members. Had the best audience during the past year.—Daniel George Cole.

Milan, Sept. 28.—I began my third meeting last Sunday under the auspices of the Missionary Board in the M. E. Church of Zion. Good audiences, good interest and one addition last night.—S. J. Vance.

Joplin, Oct. 5.—F. F. Walters, of Neosho, Mo., has just closed a splendid meeting for the First Church here, lasting over four Lord's days. There were 39 additions, 17 of them being by confession and baptism.—W. F. Turner.

Triplett, Oct. 6.—Our meeting here with home forces, is said by the members to be the greatest in the history of the church. There were 40 accessions at the four services, making 48 additions up to the present.—W. D. McCulley, pastor.

Kansas City, Oct. 5.—Three added by confession and baptism at Lisle, Mo. Ten added in two nights at Everett, Mo., 5 by confession and baptism. I went to close a meeting well begun by the pastor, Bro. Shelton, who was stricken with pneumonia.—Clyde Lee Fife.

Seneca.—A meeting, following a most enthusiastic county convention, is being held here by F. J. Church, of Seneca, and Blackwell and Blackwell, of New Vienna, Ohio. Brother Church had the congregation well prepared and is aided each week by 300 CHRISTIAN-EVANGELISTS. Brother Blackwell supplements strong preaching with chalk talks to the children and chart sermons. His wife also speaks with much ability, as well as leads the singing.—A. R. Moore.

Montana.

Helena, Sept. 24.—Two added by baptism at Deer Lodge, Mont., recently.—F. H. Groom.

Nebraska.

Chester, Oct. 4.—After a three weeks' Bible institute led by Knox P. Taylor, there were seven additions to the church here—five by confession.—D. G. Wagner.

Beaver Crossing, Sept. 30.—I am in a fine meeting here—39 added to date, nearly all adults and several husbands and wives. We continue this week.—DeForest Austin, evangelist.

New Zealand.

Dunedin, Sept. 6.—Meetings closed here with 230 additions. This is the greatest campaign for Christ in point of visible results ever held by the church in New Zealand.—Hamilton and Garmong.

Ohio.

Minerva, Oct. 3.—Closed here with 114 added. Begin at Lorain, Ohio, Sunday after convention.—Violett and Clarkson.

Norwood, Oct. 1.—Grand Sunday-school rally yesterday. House crowded. New graded system for the Bible school will be inaugurated next Lord's day. One added by letter.—Joseph Armistead, minister.

Bellmont Ridge, Oct. 6.—Our meeting was one of the best short meetings ever held. In thirteen days there were 16 additions, 13 by confession and baptism. Weather conditions were unfavorable. The CHRISTIAN-EVANGELISTS which we cir-

culated were a great help.—Ferd F. Shultz, pastor-evangelist.

Oklahoma.

Chandler, Oct. 1.—Last week I preached a few nights at a school house three miles in the country, resulting in 10 additions.—Oscar Ingold.

Stroud, Oct. 4.—I have just closed a short meeting here, with 67 additions. Charles M. Ashmore is the much-beloved minister there.—W. Mark Sexson, Cleveland, Okla.

Pennsylvania.

Uniontown, Sept. 29.—Three were baptized into Christ at the Uniontown (Pa.) church recently.—J. Walter Carpenter.

South Carolina.

St. Stephen, Oct. 7.—S. D. Colyer is in a splendid meeting here with 12 additions to date, mostly baptisms.—Charles E. Smith, state evangelist.

Tennessee.

Union City, Oct. 5.—We recently held a short meeting assisted by Brethren Yeuell and Hackleman, which resulted in 22 accessions. Two more came forward at our regular service last Sunday.—J. J. Castleberry, minister.

Texas.

Ft. Worth, Oct. 1.—There were 5 additions at the Tabernacle church yesterday.—B. B. Dubber.

Denison, Oct. 2.—Four additions during September—3 by letter and 1 by confession.—George W. Lee.

Clarendon, Oct. 1.—Had two additions yesterday which makes 12 since our last report.—C. C. Beardon.

Junction City, Oct. 5.—Evangelist S. S. McGill closed a ten days' meeting last night with 7 additions, 5 by confession.—W. L. Garrison, minister.

❀ ❀

If extremely low colonist rates to California, Oregon, Washington and all points west will interest you, write L. E. Townsley, G. A. Union Pacific R. R. Co., 903 Olive, St. Louis.

Sunday-School

October 21, 1906.

THE PARABLE OF THE TALENTS.
—Matt. 25:14-30.

Memory verse, 21.

Golden Text.—A faithful man shall abound with blessings.—Prov. 28:20.

Jesus is continuing the discourse about the end of the world, the second coming of Christ, the final judgment and the end of the world. The time is probably late on Tuesday of Passion week. The time of his departure is at hand. The parable of the man leaving his servants and going into a far country gains force when we remember that it was spoken when Jesus was about to leave his disciples, entrusting to them a certain message and certain powers, and that he was urging them to make good use of these powers in view of his certain return.

The twelve—or the eleven who were faithful—made industrious use of the talents which their lord left with them. Some apparently had a greater talent than others but the work of each was in proportion to his ability and the total result was that the Gospel was preached to the ends of the Roman empire in little more than a generation. They have their reward.

But the parable was not alone to the twelve. It teaches that all possession is stewardship; that opportunity means responsibility; and that, though the reckoning may be long uncalled for, the account which every man owes to his maker, is not cancelled.

The self-made man is one of the chief glories of America. But there are no self-made men. Men are born into a world enriched with all the thoughts, the discoveries, the achievements of the past. These are indispensable to the life of civilized man. They are our inheritance as truly as the million-dollar legacy may be an inheritance of the rich man's son. Moreover, man is born with certain senses, certain physical and mental capacities which are the capital with which he begins business and without which he could not begin it. Let us be very humble, and very careful how we boast of our independence. We are as workmen who have received their tools and their raw materials as a loan, or have bought them on credit. What we make may reflect credit upon our industry and skill and may earn the Master's praise, but it is not ours to use without regard to our first indebtedness.

To owe service to God is to owe service to all his children. For Paul, the term "steward" seemed too honorable. He said: "I am the bond-servant of Jesus Christ," and it was because of that fact that he was also ready to say, "I am debtor both to the Greeks and to the barbarians."

❋ ❋

HER FACE HER FORTUNE.

Facial Beauty Preserved By Cuticura Soap, Assisted By Cuticura Ointment, the Great Skin Cure.

Because of its delicate, medicinal, emollient, sanative, and antiseptic properties, derived from, Cuticura Ointment, the great Skin Cure, Cuticura Soap is not only the most effective skin purifying and beautifying soap ever compounded, but it is also the purest and sweetest for toilet, bath, and nursery. For facial eruptions, skin irritations, scalp affections, falling hair, baby rashes and chafings, red, rough hands, and sanative, antiseptic cleansing, Cuticura Soap, assisted by Cuticura Ointment, the great Skin Cure, is priceless.

Christian Endeavor

By GEO. L. SNIVELY

October 21, 1906.

FAITHFULNESS. Luke 16:10; 1 Cor. 4:1-5; Rev. 2:10.

(Honorary Members' Service.)

DAILY READINGS.

M.	Faithful in All Things.	Luke 16-10.
T.	Faithfulness in Practice.	Titus 2:1-15.
W.	Faithfulness Against Error.	Jude 1:4-22.
T.	Faithful Thessalonians.	1 Thess. 1:11-10.
F.	Faithful Colossians.	Col. 1:11-8.
S.	Paul's Faithfulness.	Acts 20:18-21.
S.	Reward of Faithfulness.	Rev. 2-10.

Faith is that by which we look up; by hope we reach up; by love we climb up.

The cruelest of persecutors never devised afflictions harder to bear than are the natural results of sin. Neither have philanthropists nor appreciative kings nor grateful republics compounded compensations and rewards so rich and delectable as the fruitage of a life of faithfulness toward God and man.

Christ knows the value of wealth to the establishment of the Kingdom, and Barnabas was called; he appreciates learning and Paul became an apostle; impulsiveness has important uses, and Peter was among the chosen three; affection is an attribute he has always prized and he leaned upon John's bosom, and yet we must remember to but one he said, "Well done, thou good and *faithful* servant."

With many faith is become a term almost meaningless. That its scope is high as the heavens and wide as the eternities, and that its tensile strength is greater than that of steel is beyond their comprehension and they fail to use this faculty for self-ennoblement and the conquest of the future. Faith is a faculty of the soul we may each develop till we can hear and see and know and utilize countless realities to us now as though they were not.

> "All ages dead and splendid,
>   All masters that are past,
>   All hero figures vast—
> By hate and scorn attended,
> By Death and Time defended—,
>   As with a bugle blast
>   Cry out to us, 'Stand fast!'
> All's well when all is ended!
>
> Across the gulf of ages
>   We send our answering hail:
> "O poets, heroes, sages,
>   We lift to you a beaker
>   Filled to the very brim;
>   The Lord's cause is no weaker
>   Than when you died for him;
> Though long the battle rages
>   The victory shall not fail—
> Right shall at last prevail!"

Faith is chiefly a mental state. It is the effect of intellectual conviction, the result of a succession of judgments. Faithfulness is a life in harmony with our convictions. We have faith that God is and that he is a rewarder of righteousness and yet we live as if there were no God and judgment. That is an unfaithful life. We know that through self-sacrifice and love and service and holiness we are to reach our highest destiny. When we practice thus we are faithful; at other times disloyal to ourselves and God.

Though man be unfaithful God never is. He faithfully administers to every transgression its just recompense of reward that no one be deluded into the folly of sin through the belief that he might es-

Midweek Prayer-Meeting

October 17. 1906.

AN IMPERFECT CHURCH.
—Rev. 2:12-17.

"My soul, be on thy guard;
  Ten thousand foes arise;
The hosts of sin are pressing hard
  To draw thee from the skies.

"O, watch, and fight, and pray;
  The battle ne'er give o'er!
Renew it boldly every day,
  And help Divine implore."

Among the Jews the maxim was current that, where the Word of God is not studied, there Satan has his seat. Among the shortcomings of that ancient church was one sin of which we are all guilty who neglect the study of the book. Dwight L. Moody once said, "Had I devoted part of the time I have given to prayer to the study of the Bible I would be a better man."

It is possible for one to lash himself fast to the throne even if he is near where Satan's seat is. One may there exemplify a life beautiful as the lily that rises in loveliness above the black swamp mud, but it is not a place of residence to be commended. One would better surrender half his living than to abide in the vicinity of iniquities; it would be better to lose eyesight than to have it and with it read Satan's writings. If near Satan's seat in residence, in reading, musing, or aspiration, move out, move up, escape, to the heights, be free!

Balaam stands for compromise between Israel and surrounding heathen tribes. That Balaam sentiment was the destruction of Pergamos and is a peril to-day. In a sense we would be God's "peculiar people," but we do not care to be so peculiar as to attract attention. We wish to be good—not too good but just good enough to escape being under condemnation. But when we prize gold more than sacred knowledge, and secular society more than the assemblies of the saints we are so compromising with idolatry as to merit the seal of Balaam on our brows.

It is said friends in olden times would exchange vows of perpetual hospitality and fellowship and a token of the compact was their names written in durable stones and then sawn asunder in such form that each had half of both autographs. Their descendants would receive each other with unreserved hospitality whenever the corresponding parts of the stone could be produced. This was a great boon to them, if misfortune should come to one party or his descendants. The Savior promises the half stone "to him that overcometh." The hospitality accorded the possessor will be such as we may expect the king of heaven to give his loyal brethren.

Holding fast the name of the Lord and refusing to deny the faith in former times was almost inevitably accompanied by martyrdom. "Art thou a Christian?" the Roman inquisitor asked the early disciples. If the answer was "Christianus sum"—I am a Christian—they were hurried to the amphitheater or the flames. The Mahometan zealots cried, "Who says God has an equal in a Son or any other, let him die," and in their fury against those having faith in Jesus they threatened the extermina-

tion of Christianity in Asia and Africa. In the face of our lesser perils—rarely greater than a sneer—let us keep the faith and honor the name of our Savior.

It may be an open question whether the church at Pergamos is being reproved by the Spirit for retaining in its membership those holding to the doctrine of Balaam notwithstanding its immorality, or for the church's failure to convert them from their errors of faith and practice. Paul had already written, "Now we command you, brethren, in the name of our Lord Jesus Christ that ye withdraw yourselves from every brother that walketh disorderly, and not after the tradition which he received of us." The Pergamites were also familiar with "Brethren, if a man be overtaken in a fault, ye which are spiritual, restore such an one in the spirit of meekness; considering thyself, lest thou also be tempted." One thing very apparent is that heresy of life or doctrine is not to be ignored by the churches. Transgressors are to be redeemed or removed.

As Seen From the Dome.
(Continued from Page 1299.)
son, Dr. T. M. Henley, has four daughters living. He married Miss P. B. Bagby, who survives him, and his children were Roberta, Maria Louise, Thomasina and Caroline, all of whom were members of my first church in Virginia, and later of the Vermont Avenue Church, Washington.

Two of Mr. Campbell's daughters by the first marriage became wives of W. K. Pendleton. The beloved "Miss Cammie," professor of modern languages in Bethany College, is the daughter of Lavinia, and William Campbell Pendleton of Warren, O., is the son of Clarinda. He married the daughter of the late Harmon Austin, of blessed memory, and has several children. Miss Cammie was named Alexandria Campbellina, after her grandfather. She has been closer perhaps to his great work at Bethany than any one of his descendants. She has given her life unreservedly to its interests. The family of the great reformer, however, are all identified with the cause for which he gave himself.

The Home Department

October.

Blue are the skies these fair October days,
Bright as Spring flowers are all the woodland ways,
Their gala robes glow in the unclouded sun.
Purple and gold, crimson and brown and dun.

Ah, how the passing seasons come and go!
Springtime and summer, autumn, winter's snow.
Each brings its pleasures, yet no joy I trace
Like the glad smile on fair October's face.

She leads us back with her to other days,
We walk once more in memory's gladsome ways,
And smiles that made the hours so golden bright
Come back again with all their olden light.

Dear friends, departed to the other shore,
Come in her light to walk with us once more.
And sorrows, seen through memory's sunlight haze
But quicken faith and hope, these autumn days.
MRS. P. R. GIBSON, St. Louis, Mo.

The Bronze Vase.

PART III.

CHAPTER XV.

After Brother Bellfield had opened the front door he stood blinking at Rhoda and Raymund, so taken by surprise—for Mr. Willby had not told him a word about the letter they had written from St. Louis, or about his telegram to them—that he did not know the twins, and hardly knew himself. He was breathing heavy from his exertion of sweeping, and as he gasped confusedly, "Haven't I seen you before?" the dust which was rolling toward the porch to get out of the hall, made him sneeze. The next moment he exclaimed, "It's Rhoda Revore! It's Raymund! Bless your hearts, children! where have you come from?" And without the least ceremony he took Rhoda in his arms; then, looking over her shoulder at her brother, he shouted delightedly, "Your turn'll come in a minute, boy." So he kissed Raymund, too; and Mr. Willby was so excited over the suddenness of his surprise, that he cried in ecstasy, "Brother Bellfield, how old are you?" If Brother Bellfield heard he had no time to answer, for Rhoda exclaimed, "I saw you sweeping, Brother Bellfield. Now, where is that broom and apron? I'm going to finish it myself!"

"You're going to do nothing of the kind!" returned the minister, grasping an arm of each of the twins. "You're going to come into the parlor and tell me all about yourselves." He raised his voice—"Wife! come down! company!" Then he dragged the young people into the parlor.

"This is the cause of it all!" said Mr. Willby, holding up the faded old green umbrella. "It made me acquainted with Raymund and Rhoda, and I spent a long time with them, finding out everything about their lives; and they told me about Brother Bellfield. Everything was Brother Bellfield this, and Brother Bellfield that. When I came home I said to my wife that the man who took in orphans when his own house was overrunning with people was the preacher for me; so I had him called here to Frog Bend. They were willing to let him go at Crawley, for he'd been there three years, and you take a little Missouri town—it don't take longer than that for it to get sick and tired of any preacher that ever preached. How old are you, Brother Bellfield?"

"I'm over fifty," said the minister; "but here's my wife," he added with relief as at that moment his hard-worked delicate little wife entered. She was flushed from recent exercise, but cordial. Raymund asked about Jack, and was informed that the youngest son had started to the state university.

"And Mr. Morton?" asked Rhoda, remembering the heart-broken romanticist and his autumn confidences about sweetheart Lily.

"He's with us now," said Brother Bellfield. "Morton's married and has two of the finest babies you ever saw. He married soon after you left us, Rhoda."

"Did he marry a young lady named Lily?" inquired Rhoda eagerly.

"Lily?" asked the minister. No, her name is Jane. She was a Butts; Jane Butts was her name. They are staying with us now. Morton is looking about for some kind of business to go into. He is thinking a little of the real estate business. He would like to boom Frog Bend and make it a shipping point, and have the boats land here regularly. The river is quite navigable."

This reminded Rhoda of the oldest son, and she asked about Mr. Jasper and his three children.

"There are five now," said Brother Bellfield. "Well, Jasper is doing fairly well—fairly well. They have moved to Oklahoma to see how they like it, but from the wife's letters, I think they will be back soon. They don't like Oklahoma."

"Did Mr. Jasper ever find any business to go into?" asked Raymund, wishing to appear interested; he had been on the eve of remarking that perhaps Mrs. Jasper Bellfield did not like Oklahoma climate, but decided upon his question.

"Well, no," said Brother Bellfield, a little wearily, "I can't say that he has, Raymund; at least, nothing congenial. He has tried several things, but they were not suitable. He is merely looking about down there, as Morton is up here."

Everybody seemed a little depressed at this point, and Rhoda asked about the invalid sister of the minister. "She's doing fine," said the minister, brightening up. "She's just as eager as ever to read aloud the pieces she finds in the papers and magazines. You are just the thing for her, Rhoda! Unfortunately, though, I have another plan for you." He turned to Mr. Willby. "Remember that scholarship?"

"Of course," said Mr. Willby. "I knew as soon as I brought on these folks, you'd decide on Rhoda."

"Oh, what is it?" cried Rhoda, trembling with a hope she dared not utter.

"I have a scholarship to a school in Fulton," said Brother Bellfield, "and I'm going to give it to you, Rhoda, my child!"

"That's why I telegraphed to come at once," said Mr. Willby, triumphantly. "I knew he'd offer it to you, Rhoda, and I wanted to put you in the school as soon as the Christmas holidays are over."

"Oh, Brother Bellfield!" cried Rhoda, rushing at him.

"Board and all!" cried the minister, delightedly. "Board and all! And during the summers Willby and I will see that you get along; hey, Willby?"

"When Brother Bellfield told me he could keep a girl in school, I began looking about for a worthy victim," said Mr. Willby. "Just about that time here came a letter from Raymund. I said to my wife, 'Rhoda is the girl! I didn't say a word to Brother Bellfield—did I?"

"Not a word!" cried the minister.

"I just sat down and telegraphed for you to come immediately. He didn't know you were coming—did you, Brother Bellfield?"

"Never dreamed of it!" returned the other.

"As for Raymund, here," said Mr. Willby, "he's to go to the university; he's to work his way through, and I'll see that he's kept above the water at the start. If he's any 'count—I think he is—he'll swim after he's been thrown into the water. Hey, Raymund?"

"It's glorious!" cried Raymund. "And I have some money of my own to start on; and now that Rhoda is to be taken care of, I can afford to spend it. Besides, Uncle William gave her something when he sent us away."

"Bless your hearts!" cried Brother Bellfield. "It seems that you are both money-holders! I expect you've got more than I have, right now." And he laughed heartily.

So Rhoda was sent to the Fulton school and Raymund went to the university at Columbia. Thanks to the dogged perseverance he had manifested in his solitary studies, he knew thoroughly what he knew at all, and he was able to pass the examinations, that stand like grim iron-heatred monsters between Outsiders and Freshmen. I wonder if you will think any less of Raymund when you learn how he "worked his way through"? He rented a larger room than those usually taken by the poor students; and he occupied it alone, instead of sharing the expenses with a schoolmate. A cheap calico curtain divided the room into two chambers. The one opening upon the hall was his renovating room. Here he received the garments of the young men and removed spots, patched and darned holes and "snags," pressed trousers, and sewed on buttons. He was among the first in his classes, but he realized from the beginning that it was not for him to strive for honors. That privilege was for those who could give all their time to study. With a difficult lesson but half-learned, many a time he laid aside his book to go to work at once upon a suit; and when the menial task was done, though it might be far into the night, the lesson would be taken up anew.

He was liked at the university. The teachers were proud of his industry and of his independence. So were the boys, in a way. Of course, he did not go with the fashionable set, or indeed, with any "set." He had no time. And, of course, the young fellows who brought him clothes to be renewed that they might attend balls and parties to which he was never invited, could not but in a sense look down upon him. If at times, they found him poring over his Greek, they were as liable to come upon him needle in hand, sewing away as if he had been a tailor from his earliest youth.

Three years passed by, and at nineteen Raymund graduated, without honors, but with great credit. During that time, Jack Bellfield had been his only intimate friend. Though Jack went with the "highest-toned" fellows, he was never ashamed of his friendship for Raymund, and was the means of getting the younger man all the trade he could handle. "You know," Jack would say to his chums, "Ray will drop all that when he's on his feet."

I wish I could tell you about Raymund's university days, and about Rhoda's experience at the young women's college in Fulton; but this story must really be finished before 1906 laps over into 1907, and the only way to finish it is to take up the twins in their nineteenth year, when both are done with school, and have not yet made up their

minds about the future. There is one thing you must know about the school years. Raymund had not been at the university quite a year when he found that a change had come over Rhoda's letters. At first, the change was so gradual that he did not perceive it, and even later it was not very tangible; but he realized at last that she did not write as had been her wont. There was no more poetry in her letters, but that was not so much what he minded. They seemed to have lost their old affectionate ring. During the summer vacations they were in Frog Bend, and Raymund was able to pay for their board at Brother Bellfield's, and thus really be of service to the minister. The latter would not take the board until Raymund declared he would not stay upon other conditions; but the minister really needed the money, for one son or another was always with him, to say nothing of the son's relations—by marriage. Raymund was proud to find that he could make enough by tailoring to support not only himself, but Rhoda.

But Rhoda was indeed changed. Every summer when they met, the difference shocked him—it was a difference she sought to conceal. It appeared to him that she had ceased to care for him. She avoided being alone with him for any great length of time, and finding that she shrank from his impetuous kisses and embraces, he demanded an explanation, but Rhoda assured him with a face of distress that there was nothing to explain.

"Aren't you glad to see me?" he asked when she shrank from him on his return from graduation.

"Of course, I am glad, Raymund! What a question!" said Rhoda, turning red and pale.

"Then why don't you let a fellow kiss you?" he retorted, half displeased and deeply hurt.

"I just don't like to be kissed," said Rhoda, desperately.

"Oh, very well," said Raymund, turning away, stiffly. He would not let her see how the change in her manner had saddened his last year at the university, and how it now threw a heavy chill upon him. He was too proud to plead for the love that seemed gone. Could it be that his humble work with needle and thread and flatiron had lowered him in her esteem? Or was it that she had become acquainted with some young man who had taught her another kind of love? Surely, she had not begun to care for Jack Bellfield? Raymund was too proud to try to force Rhoda to reveal her secret, if she had a secret, or to try to coax back the affection his sister had always—until two years ago—lavishly bestowed upon him. It was strange to feel that now that he had graduated, that consummation once so far ahead, and with such difficulty wrought, found him unhappy! He could not see Rhoda steal from the room at his approach, or feel her hand quickly withdrawn when it touched his, without experiencing a bitter pain. But he steeled himself, that she might not know how she was making him suffer, and he began to make plans for the future of both.

(End of Part Three.)

❋ ❋

Of the Home Brand.

The hall-mark of exclusiveness just now is to be "home-made." The gown cost a pretty penny—what could you expect? It was all hand-work—home-made. You have to pay for that! Well, there are other things worth having of the home brand—boys and girls, for instance. The home-made girl, the boy

An Old Poem Revised.

[The poem "Twenty Times A Day," which appeared in our issue last week was attributed wrongfully to W. E. Rambo. The following is Mr. Rambo's production.—EDITOR.]

"Twinkle, twinkle, little star,
How I wonder what you are,
Up above the world so high,
Like a diamond in the sky!"

"Twinkle, twinkle, little star,"
Science tells me what you are.
You're a planet, held in space
By Gravitation's mighty mace.

You're composed of mineral ore—
Dust of elements a score—
And you with a borrowed light
"Twinkle, twinkle all the night."

Or, perchance, you are a sun!
'Round you other planets run!
In your composition prove
By the fires that in you move.

This I know, and more beside,
Since the school has been my guide.
"Now that I'm a man," I say,
"Childish things are put away."

But even now, when twilight gray
Darkens at the closing day,
I 'look into the deepening sky
And watch the dome-lights multiply.

And see so much I do not know—
So little I have proved as so—
I cry with child-like awe once more
The mystery I felt of yore:

"Twinkle, twinkle, little star,
How I wonder what you are,
Up above the world so high,
Like a diamond in the sky!"
Alma, Neb.   —W. E. RAMBO.

❀ ❀

A mother asked her little girl what she was drawing, and the little one replied: "Little black devils, mummy!"
"But," said the mother, "you should not draw devils; you should draw angels."
"How can I, mummy," replied the child, "when I've only got a black pencil?"—*Gossip.*

❀ ❀

Zigzagging.

"The poor dog is tired out," said Mary, as the wagon drove into the yard and Towser, covered with the dust of the road, dropped lolling and panting upon the green grass.
"'Tain't the journey he had to take that's tired him," laughed the farmer.
"He's used himself up by zigzagging from one side of the road to the other

---

VERY LOW RATES

via

Louisville & Nashville R. R.

TO NEW ORLEANS

account

BIENNIAL MEETING

Knights of Pythias

October 15-25, 1906

For rates, information as to dates of sale and limits on tickets or for illustrated booklet descriptive of New Orleans and points of interest to be seen en route address.

F. D. BUSH,   H. C. BAILEY,
D. P. A., Cincinnati.   N. W. P. A., Chicago
J. E DAVENPORT,   J. H. MILLIKEN,
D. P. A., St. Louis.   D. P. A., Louisville

C. L. STONE, Gen'l Passenger Agent,
LOUISVILLE, KY.

---

and tendin' to everything that didn't concern him. He couldn't pass a gate without runnin' through to see what was on the other side, nor see a hen anywhere along the road without feelin' called on to chase her. Every dog that barked started him to barkin', and everything that moved took him out of his way to find out what it was and where it was goin'. No wonder he's tired! But you'll find plenty of human bein's that are travelin' their lives through in just that same way. They ain't satisfied with the bit of road that's marked out for their feet, but they try to oversee all their neighbor's goin's and doin's, and take charge of no end of things that they can't either help or hinder. They're like old Towser; it wears 'em all out. If they'd follow straight after the Master themselves, the way wouldn't be nigh so long nor hard."

❀ ❀

The Greatest of Fools.

Is he who imposes on himself, and in his greatest concern thinks certainly he knows that which he has least studied, and of which he is most profoundly ignorant.

❀ ❀

Buster Brown's Resolve.

Resolved, That to-day is the whole thing. Yesterday gave me all it can ever give me. I'll get what's coming from the future; but if I want any good things now I've got to keep my eye on to-day. Some people spend all their time in thinking over the pleasures they had last week or what pleasures they are going to have next week. This minute is only down once in the calendar, and I'd better get sixty seconds' worth of real, true living out of it while I've got it, too, if I use every second.

❀ ❀

Due to Drink.

Of the 33,000 men passed into Wandsworth (England) poorhouse since 1886 by Dr. A. E. Dodson, there were only fifteen abstainers. Of the fifteen at least seven were mentally or physically unfit to maintain themselves. This makes the proportion of needy (ablebodied) drinkers to needy (ablebodied) abstainers practically 33,000 to eight, and affords new evidence for the old contention, "But for drink the poorhouse might be closed." The proportion of inmates brought by drink to the poorhouses of America would not be nearly so large, yet it is enormous.

❀ ❀

Money From Weeds.

The people of Norway neglect no opportunity to turn an honest penny. On the southeast coast a profitable industry has been built up in burning seaweed, which grows in great profusion, some of the plants being four and five feet high. When the crop is harvested during burn like beacon lights along the coast. The ashes are shipped to England, where their valuable chemical properties are utilized in manufacturing. So profitable is the industry that many have grown rich at it, and now the cultivation is being improved by scientific methods.

❀ ❀

Doing Things to the Language.

The proprietors of a Siamese newspaper have distributed handbills containing the following notice:

"The news of English we tell the latest. Writ in perfectly style and most earliest. Do a murder, git commit, we hear of and

---

Piles Cured
Quickly at Home

Without Pain, Cutting or Surgery. Instant Relief.

We Prove It. Sample Package Free.

Seven people out of ten are said to have Piles. Not one man in a million need have them and we are proving it every day at our own expense. We send a sample package of the wonderful Pyramid Pile Cure to any person absolutely free.

We don't do this as a matter of amusement or philanthropy, but because it is to our interest to do so. We know that the sufferer from piles, tormented and driven almost crazy by this wretched trouble, will find such immediate relief that he will go at once to his druggist and buy a box and get well.

We know that we have got the greatest remedy in the world for piles, and we are ready and willing to stand or fall by the verdict of those who make the trial. We have been doing this for some years now and we never yet have had occasion to regret it.

And the remedy at the drug store is exactly the same as the sample we send out. As, for instance, here is a man who got such immediate relief from the sample that he at once bought a box. Was it just the same? Undoubtedly, since it cured him after all sorts and kinds of things had failed.

Here is a sample of the kind of letters we get every day and we don't have to ask for them:

"Received your sample of Pile Cure and have given it a fair trial and it has proven the best I ever tried and effected a complete cure. I can recommend you highly in this vicinity. Have used your sample and one box and it has been a complete cure. It has been worth $100 to me.

"Thanking you for the sample and the cure, I will recommend you to everybody. Yours respectfully, Julius Mayer, Dealer in Feathers, Ginseng and Hides, Bedford, Ind."

Pyramid Pile Cure is for sale at every druggist's at 50 cents a box or, if you would like to try a sample first, you will receive one by return mail by sending your name and address to The Pyramid Drug Company, 59 Pyramid Building, Marshall, Mich.

---

tell it. Do a mighty chief die, we publish it, and in borders of sombre. Staff has each on been colleged, and write like Kippling and the Dickens. We circle every town and extortionate not for advertisements. Buy it. Buy it. Tell each of you its greatness for good. Ready on Friday. Number first."—*Bangkok (Siam) Times.*

❀ ❀

Whyte.—Don't you think Brown is a good descriptive writer? Black—Yes, generally; but he makes mistakes sometimes. "For instance?" "Well, he was writing a naval battle once, and he said that three hundred brave sailors on the defeated vessel bit the dust!"

❀ ❀

Home Study College Courses,

leading to degrees. History, Evidences, Science, Languages, the Bible and sacred Literature. Over a thousand students enrolled. Full particulars free. Write Pres. Chas. J. Burton, Christian College, Oskaloosa, Iowa.

The Gardener's Soliloquy.

BY METTIE CRANE-NEWTON.

Oh, would I were a squirrel!
I'd roam the wide earth o'er;
And gather heaps of treasure
And lay them up in store

For future use and comfort,
When winter breezes blow;
And young life's hopes and pleasures,
Lie buried 'neath the snow.

I'd climb the tree of knowledge,
And nibble rarest fruit;
Appease my soul's deep longings
And be no more a brute.

I'd seek the wise and learned
And follow in their track
Many tomes of modern lore—
And find new nuts to crack.

I see among religions,
That truth and error clash;
Too oft the false's exalted
The good falls 'neath the lash.

I'd mount the stump and give them
The truth, whate'er it be;
God hates the moral coward;
God loves the nobly free.

So in the wordy contests,
'Twixt man and man and me,
I'd push my way to vict'ry,
And riot run up a tree!
tral Park, N. Y. City.

The Wood Procession.

BY HILDA RICHMOND.

"ow, children, you'll have to clear out
tis," said the head carpenter briskly.
too bad to rob you of your play-
nd, but we're going to set fire to this
of trash, and it would be too dan-
us to have you near it."

te little folks reluctantly gathered up
shovels and pails. For a whole
th they had a lovely playground in
big sand pile, and now they were to
it. Every day during that time an
r boy or girl sat on an old stool in
shade keeping an eye on the happy
tren, and all the mothers rejoiced to
k they were safe and having a good
. A row of old buildings had been
down, and a large new brick house
to be built as soon as the trash and
oards could be disposed of.

re you going to burn all these
ls, Mr. Gray?" asked Margaret
y, who was looking after the little
that morning. "It seems too

ou see, Miss Margaret, no one
d buy that stuff, and it costs too
1 to get it cut up into kindlings. I'd
agly give it away, but no one wants
ituff."

hildren," said Margaret suddenly,
many of you have little wagons?"
I! I!" cried a chorus of voices.
ow, Mr. Gray, if I get some big boys
lp, and the little children haul this
l to Mrs. McGuire's house, may we
1at?"

es, if you can get it done to-day,"
Mr. Gray. "The children will soon
red of the task, but I'll give you till
ing to dispose of the old wood."
less than two minutes Mr. Gray was
e in the big yard. The children were
pering for their wagons and Mar-
t was getting together all the big
in the neighborhood. The first
g old Mrs. McGuire knew of the plan
when a procession of little wagons
ed into her yard all loaded with
es of old boards and shingles.
he saints be praised!" cried the old
, hurrying out with two pairs of
ses on. "Whatever is the meanin' of
?"

Ne are bringing you a little wood,"
ained Margaret. "They were going
nake a bonfire of it to get rid of it,
the children will bring it to you."

thought the children would soon
up, said Mr. Gray, coming out to

see the little wagons still making trips
to the yard and back again. "These boys
and girls deserve a whole lot of praise."
The big boys broke up the long boards
and loaded the wagons, while the girls
helped the children all morning. It was
a very busy time, but a very happy one,
and by noon every trace of the pile of
wood was gone. Mrs. McGuire was
crying over the wood house full of dry
wood and telling the children they had
made her very happy.

"I have another house to tear down
on Summit street next week and"—began
Mr. Gray, and all the children shouted,
"May we have another wood proces-
sion? We can give the wood to 'Mrs.
Kelton?'

And what do you think Mr. Gray did?
He made a large box out of old boards
and filled it with sand for the little people to play in whenever they want to,
for he says they save him a great deal
of trouble, and the wood keeps some
poor person warm a long time. Don't
you think it paid them to give up one
morning's pleasure to carry wood to po, r
people?—*United Presbyterian.*

The editor

The editor decided to try the White
House-Carnegie brand of spelling in his
paper and the experiment seemed a success.
until he got the following:

"Dere Sur—I hav tuk yure paper fur
leven yeres, butt ef yow kant spell eny beter
than hev bin doin' fer last to weeks yew
ma jest stoppit."—*American Spectator.*

Father Knows.

A gentleman was one day opening a
box of goods. His little son was standing near, and as the father took the packages from the box, he laid them on the
arm of the boy. A young playmate was
standing and looking on. As parcel
after parcel was laid on the arm of the
boy, his friend began to fear that the
load was becoming too heavy, and said:

"Don't you think you have
as you can carry?"
"Never mind," said the boy
py tone, "father knows how n
carry."

He Was Ready.

"Now," said Freddy's motl
got him ready for a visit to
"be sure you are not late to
That won't do when you are
On her son's return his anx
er inquired if he was ready in t
"Yes'm!" responded Freddy
antly. "I was down every
soon's any of 'em."
"I am so glad: hope you'll k
"You won't let me."
"Won't let you? Why not
"Well, you see, I just put
on and slept in my clothes,
nice and ready in the morn
York Tribune.

Christian Publishing Company

2712 Pine St., St. Louis, Mo.

J. H. GARRISON,	· · ·	President
W. W. DOWLING,	· · ·	Vice-President
GEO. L. SNIVELY,	· · ·	Sec. and Gen. Supt
R. P. CROW.	· · ·	Treas. and Bus. Manager

—Read the best of the latest books.

—They are the bread of life to long pastorates and continued usefulness anywhere.

—More devotedly than ever before we wish to serve our patrons in the capacity of book sellers. Write us before purchasing elsewhere and learn whether we can save you time and money.

—We are favorably disposed toward opening accounts with brethren whom we can accommodate by sending them desired books at once and waiting for our pay. Many are finding our instalment plan very serviceable.

—Read in another column E. E. Moorman's estimate of THE CHRISTIAN-EVANGELIST to the pastors when placed in the homes of our people. THE CHRISTIAN-EVANGELIST will surely be an "untold help" both to minister and reader wherever circulated.

—While reading this Campbell number of your favorite paper remember that at an almost incredibly small sum you can purchase the great "Campbell Library." We will make Christian System, Popular Lectures and Addresses, Lectures on the Pen-

tateuch, Evidences of Christianity, Christian Baptism, Campbell-Purcell Debate, Sermon on the Law and other of his matchless productions yours on receipt of $8.

—Multitudes of schools that have tried other Sunday-school supplies recommended to them as being "as good as the Dowling series," have learned by experience that the "Dowling" is the best and signify their intention of returning to their first love with the new quarter. Write us for samples and prices.

—It is a pleasure to us to assist churches in getting pastors, and to help our preachers into pastorates. Whatever we can do to promote the general interests of all our people is our mission. To the extent that circulating THE CHRISTIAN-EVANGELIST will accomplish this well, but in all ways we wish to serve.

—"The Responsive Readings in 'Gloria in Excelsis' are a feature I have long believed should be in our hymnals. What especially pleases me is the size and style of the book. It is such a book as the other religious bodies have been publishing for years. It is a fine book to take into the hands."—C. J. Tanner, pastor, Detroit, Mich.

—The indications are that Editor Garrison's new book on "Christian Union" will be fully as popular as "The Holy Spirit." It will be uniform in size and price with "The Holy Spirit" and "Helps to Faith"—$1. Orders will now be received and the book mailed at once. Reviews will soon be published but get your first impressions from the book itself.

—"Our Young Folks" and THE CHRISTIAN-EVANGELIST, $1.75; a fountain pen and THE CHRISTIAN-EVANGELIST, $2.00; "The American Boy" and THE CHRISTIAN-EVANGELIST, $2.00; "The Ladies' Home Companion" and THE CHRISTIAN-EVANGELIST, $2.25; a self-filling fountain pen warranted ten years and THE CHRISTIAN-EVANGELIST (to a new subscriber), $2.50; "The Review of Reviews" and THE CHRISTIAN-EVANGELIST, $3.00. These liberal discounts should receive immediate consideration. Any of these would make most desirable Christmas gifts. They can be ordered now and the premiums will be sent at Christmas time.

—Readers of this page are convinced that the remarkable increase of the circulation of THE CHRISTIAN-EVANGELIST is not of spasmodic or mushroom growth. Examination of its records for many months past will reveal in addition to the numerous subscriptions coming each day, singly and in pairs, new club lists similar to the following:

Havana, Ill., L. O. Lehman, minister.........	3
Camp Point, Ill., H. J. Reynolds, pastor.....	4
Owensboro, Ky., R.__, Crossfield, pastor......	4
Homewood, Kan.	4
Star, Mo., R. H. Fife, pastor.................	5
Greencastle, Ind., C. W. Cauble, pastor......	5
Kansas City, Mo., Nancy Gordon, asst. pastor..	5
Fortville, Ind., S. M. Hawthorne, pastor......	5
Atlanta, Ind., E. B. Long, pastor.............	5
Denison, Tex., G. W. Lee, minister...........	6
Augusta, Ill.	8
Columbia, Mo.	12
Lincoln, Neb., G. H. Exley, pastor...........	17
Everette, Mass., A. T. June, pastor..........	20
Shelbyville, Ky., Hugh MacLachlin, pastor....	21
Louisville, Ky., E. L. Powell, minister......	50
Brasil, E. L. Day, pastor....................	64

—This company's fiscal year closed September 30. The volume of business transacted during the year was the largest by far of any year in our history. For this, we are grateful, and more particularly, because of thousands of letters received expressing the hearty good will of the brethren and their manifest interest in our building up a publishing house creditable to our great brotherhood and of ever-increasing usefulness to the Disciples of Christ. The financial significance of this to those responsible for the publication of our papers is too small for self-gratula-

tions, but the love and appreciation of our constituents is a great inspiration to attempt and accomplish greater things for the common weal through this new year.

Christian Papers in Christian Homes.

The more than doubling of our CHRISTIAN-EVANGELIST subscription list through a day's visit of your courteous and successful representative, caused me to make some inquiries as to THE CHRISTIAN-EVANGELIST's circulation. I was pleased to discover that it had increased 30½ per cent. since October 1, 1905. This means much to the brotherhood. It means a corresponding increase in zeal and enthusiasm in church work and in the support given to our missionary enterprises. It will mean a kindlier feeling among brethren and a broader, saner view of what we stand for as a people. The spirit and the view point of THE CHRISTIAN-EVANGELIST are indispensable to the brotherhood at the present time. Its introduction into our homes will be an educational force for the spiritual side of our plea. It will create an atmosphere in which the pastor will be untrammeled in leading on to second principles and in working toward the spirit as well as the form of our contentions as a people. The advantages of having a Christian paper such as THE CHRISTIAN-EVANGELIST in every Christian home are obvious. Every pastor should work toward that end. It will be an untold help in his work.

Danville, Ind.   E. E. MOORMAN.

❋

Not what we give, but what we share—
(For the gift without the giver is bare;)
Who gives himself with his alms feeds three—
Himself—his hungering neighbor, and me.
—*Lowell.*

❋❋❋

A bright little girl asked to be absent from school half a day on the plea that company was coming.

"It is my father's half sister and her three boys," said the girl anxiously, "and mother doesn't see how she can do without me, because those boys act dreadfully."

The teacher referred her to the printed list of reasons which justified absence, and asked her if her case came under any of them.

"O yes, Miss Smith," said the girl eagerly, "it comes under this head," and she pointed to the words, "Domestic Affliction."

THE

CHRISTIAN-EVANGELIST

A WEEKLY RELIGIOUS NEWSPAPER.

Volume XLIII.   No. 42.

ST. LOUIS, OCTOBER 18, 1906.

THE WORLD'S APPEAL TO THE CHURCH.

By Thomas Curtis Clark.

 E weary of your forms and creeds,
  Your soulless psalms and prayers;
O tell of Him whose words and deeds
  Show forth the love He bears!

We ask to hear of Him who taught
  In blessed Galilee;
We long to know the deeds He wrought
  Beside the silvery sea.

Teach us of Him by children loved,
  Close to His bosom pressed;
Tell how He sought, where'er He moved,
  To give the weary rest!

Tell how He suffered for our gain
  In dark Gethsemane;
Tell of the cross He bore, the pain
  Endured on Calvary!

Sin-weary, we would lean upon
  His arm, who knew no sin;
In darkness, we would know His dawn;
  O let His light shine in!

Teach us no more vain words, we plead,
  But to our sad hearts bring
The words of Him who knows our need,
  Our Brother—and our King!

The Christian-Evangelist.

J. H. GARRISON, Editor

PAUL MOORE, Assistant Editor

F. D. POWER, B. B. TYLER, W. DURBAN, } Staff Correspondents.

Subscription Price, $1.50 a Year.

For foreign countries add $1.04 for postage.

Remittances should be made by money order, draft, or registered letter; not by local cheque, un-less 15 cents is added to cover cost of collection.
In Ordering Change of Post Office give both old and new address.
Matter for Publication should be addressed to THE CHRISTIAN-EVANGELIST. Subscriptions and remit-tances should be addressed to the Christian Publish-ing Company, 2712 Pine Street, St. Louis, Mo.
Unused Manuscripts will be returned only if ac-companied by stamps.
News Items, evangelistic and otherwise, are solicited, and should be sent on a postal card, if possible.
Published by the Christian Publishing Company, 2712 Pine Street, St. Louis, Mo.

Entered at St. Louis P. O. as Second Class Matter

CONTENTS.

Centennial Propaganda...............1323
Current Events.................. 1324
Editorial.
Where Jesus Placed the Emphasis—
   IX. 1325
Christian Union in Australia.....1325
Notes and Comments...............1326
Current Religious Thought.........1326
Editor's Easy Chair...............1327
Contributed Articles.
Baptists and Disciples. By the Editor
   of the "Southern Baptist".........1328
As Seen From the Dome. F. D.
   Power 1329
Our English Conference. William
   Durban 1330
What the Brethren are Saying and
   Doing. B. B. Tyler..............1331
Two Great Debates. C. C. Redgrave..1332
International Missionary Convention..1333
Our Budget 1336
The Kentucky State Convention.....1339
Western Pennsylvania Convention...1340
Tennessee State Convention....
News From Many Fields:....
Evangelistic ....
Sunday-school ....
Mid-week Prayer-meeting .....
Christian Endeavor ....
People's Forum ....
Obituaries : ,.................
The Home Department ..:....

THE
CHRISTIAN-EVANGELIST

"IN FAITH, UNITY; IN OPINION AND METHODS, LIBERTY, IN ALL THINGS, CHARITY."

| Vol. XLIII. | October 18, 1906 | No. 42 |

1809 CENTENNIAL PROPAGANDA 1909
CHURCHES OF CHRIST
::: GEO. L. SNIVELY :::

LOOKING TOWARD PITTSBURG.

There is no other Centennial achievement in which the brethren seem more deeply interested nor in which they are more enthusiastically enlisted than in placing a Christian paper in every Christian home.

The rapidity of the increase in the circulation of THE CHRISTIAN-EVANGELIST is exciting a great deal of favorable comment, the general trend of which appears in the following communications from Brothers Smither and Russell.

It is our desire that all our other papers gain thousands of new readers, too, and we believe they are. It would diminish the pleasure with which we view our own lengthening lists if we thought it was done to the injury of our editorial colleagues of other papers instead of signifying that myriads of hitherto unread Disciples were weekly gaining that information concerning the meaning and progress of the kingdom and the inspiration heavenward that the people have a right to expect from our religious press.

A source of deep gratification to us in this movement is the manifestly growing popularity of all for which THE CHRISTIAN-EVANGELIST stands. "In faith, unity; in opinions and methods, liberty; in all things, charity," Bible research, ceaseless evangelism, growth in grace and the knowledge of the Lord Jesus and the unification of all God's people.

There are numerous gratifying features in the report of our Foreign Missionary Society. Two hundred and sixty-eight thousand seven hundred and twenty-six dollars this year shows we are over the quarter million mark to stay. The growing interest manifested by our Bible schools is a prophecy that in our second century we shall sweep far beyond the achievements of the first in world-wide evangelization. Like apples of gold is the statement of a gain of 344 contributing churches. Our people are now ready to believe that the best way of evangelizing the world is perfectly scriptural and a little longer demonstration of the economy and expedition of our Foreign Society will enlist in its support practically all our congregations having more than a name to live.

A Sanguine Convert.

BY WILLIAM J. RUSSELL.

We are stepping upon the wave of a new religious era. It is a joy and an inspiration to be permitted to live at the present time. The throbbing heart of even our own great religious brotherhood is anxiously and longingly waiting and working for the evangelization of the world. Forces that work for righteousness are being utilized as never before. Among these forces is the religious press. In my own ministry I find the people are more eager to get a religious paper than at any previous time. They want to know what the people are doing who are pleading for the Restoration of Primitive Christianity. The Centennial Propaganda has been announced with much fervor, and the people have caught a vision of 100,000 Disciples marching up to Pittsburg in 1909. They want to know what is being done preparatory to that great convocation. This is an incentive to take the paper, which, when once introduced into the home, is going to be read. This is going to mean much to the church in the future. It will increase the interest in all departments of the local work, and cause to be multiplied many fold our general benevolences. As ministers of the Gospel, I fear that heretofore we have been too indifferent toward the work of increasing the circulation of our religious papers. I know of one true and genuine conversion toward this work. The writer has been more than compensated in the part he took in placing fifty-three annual subscriptions to THE CHRISTIAN-EVANGELIST in that many homes of the Frankfort Christian Church. In the future he does not propose to hold second place in this department of our educational work.

THE CHRISTIAN-EVANGELIST as a religious paper, either for the family, or the student of current and religious thought, is unsurpassed. It is dignified in its dress, gentle and optimistic in its spirit, deep and steady in its thinking. It does not move with fits and starts. There is nothing spasmodic about it. Where you find it to-day, there you will find it to-morrow. The writer has read every copy for more than twenty years. To him it has been equal to a course in any theological seminary. Its beloved Editor stands without a peer. His name has come to be a household word; familiar to all, from the youngest to the oldest. The future generations will rise up and call him blessed for the splendid service he has rendered.

The careful observer can not help but notice the wave of interest that is pointing toward THE CHRISTIAN-EVANGELIST. The paper, what it is in itself, has created this interest. The people know a good thing when they see it. The writer found many families dissatisfied with the paper they were taking. Gladly did they substitute THE CHRISTIAN-EVANGELIST. Let controversy continue when it is necessary to make clear our intellectual thinking. But the heart craves for something else besides controversy. It wants a clearer vision of God. It longs for more of that life that was exemplified in the person of Jesus Christ, the Incarnate Son of God. THE CHRISTIAN-EVANGELIST in its entire history has given much attention to heart culture, and the edification of the home life. This has made it a power for righteousness. It will continue to grow in favor. It is the truest and best exponent of the Disciples of Christ, and its loyalty to the fundamental principles of the Restoration Movement will win for it permanent and lasting praise.

Frankfort, Ind.

Increasing Circulation of Christian-Evangelist.

BY A. G. SMITHER.

I am delighted to be apprised that THE CHRISTIAN-EVANGELIST has increased its circulation 30 per cent within the last year. This is remarkable and is a tribute to the sanity and discrimination of the Disciples of Christ with regard to a religious newspaper. The general spirit of THE CHRISTIAN-EVANGELIST, its sensible attitude on the Church Federation question, its avoidance of yellow journal methods, its Christian and catholic spirit must commend it to the approval of the intelligence of our rapidly increasing brotherhood. It is reported of Lincoln that he said: "You can fool some of the people all the time; you can fool all the people some of the time, but you can not fool all the people all the time." This is surely applicable to newspapers, though we must confess that with humiliation many of the people are deceived much of the time in this matter as in many others. One strong feature of THE CHRISTIAN-EVANGELIST is that you need never apologize to strangers for it. It does its work quietly but effectively. Let its circulation go on increasing. Enlarge its borders and lengthen its territory that Christ may be magnified as a result of its mighty service.

Los Angeles, Cal.

OUR CENTENNIAL HELPERS.

I am well pleased with THE CHRISTIAN-EVANGELIST. Its contents are of high order; its spirit amiable; its editorials are able. I admire Brother Garrison as I do but few men.—J. E. Ballou, minister, Sioux City, Ia.

I have taken your paper since the very beginning. Am now in eighty-third year and want to take it as long as I live. I recommend it to every Christian family, as well as those who are not.—V. B. Butler, Denver, Ill.

I am very grateful to be in receipt of THE CHRISTIAN-EVANGELIST every week. It is a great factor in religious life and work. I hope through the new subscriptions I am sending you to introduce it into many homes.—J. N. Scholes (minister), Lima, Ohio.

I enclose $1.50 to renew my subscription for your valuable paper. I trust that success will follow all your endeavors. God speed the good work you are doing and may your years be so lengthened as to see the fulfillment of your ardent labors.—E. G. Naylor, Louisville, Ky.

We are proud of THE CHRISTIAN-EVANGELIST as a Christian paper. It has been a constant source of pleasure and education to us for many years. We have been with you in your discussions and leading. May God give you many years of editorial life.—J. H. Fillmore (minister), Cincinnati, Ohio.

I want to thank you for the help I have received from your new book on "The Holy Spirit." It has confirmed former convictions in some things, while in others it has been a revelation to me, being associated on one side by the holiness, on the other by our own extreme legalists. It has helped me "to attain a clearer vision, a decided conviction and a largeness of comprehension."—C. E. Burgess (minister), Columbia, Mo.

THE CHRISTIAN-EVANGELIST.

Current Events

In his speech at the dedication of the new Pennsylvania capitol building at Harrisburg, President Roosevelt said some things which may be taken as pointing toward his next great legislative effort. The theme is the control of corporate wealth. No particular plan is yet outlined except that it must be done by the federal government. There must be "adequate supervision and control over the business use of the swollen fortunes of to-day"; and some power must "wisely determine the conditions upon which these fortunes are to be transmitted and the percentage that they shall pay to the government." Here is a program whose magnitude and daring dwarf the railroad rate bill into insignificance. And it is the program which the country needs far more than it needs any particular legislation touching currency or tariff schedules. We do not believe that the country is going to ruin, or that the existence of rich men, even of extremely rich men, is a proof of national decay. But that the peril of plutocracy confronts us, as it must ever confront every prosperous people, admits of no doubt. It is easy to generalize on this theme, but it is not easy to frame wise legislation which will accomplish the ends which the president defines, and it will be, perhaps, hardest of all to get such legislation enacted after it has been framed. The machine men of Mr. Roosevelt's party will feel no enthusiasm over such a measure. But a president in his second term has nothing to fear from the machine, and the present incumbent has never exhibited great deference to machine even in his first term.

The President's Next Move.

It is a part of the president's belief that the control of great fortunes can be accomplished only by the federal government. "Only the nation can do this work," he says. "To relegate it to the states is a farce." And again: "Actual experience has shown that the states are wholly powerless to deal with this subject; and any action or decision that deprives the nation of this power to deal with it simply results in leaving the corporations absolutely free to work without any supervision whatever. . . . I maintain that the national government should have complete power to deal with all this wealth which in any way goes into the commerce between the states—and practically all of it that is employed in the great corporations does thus go in." This, with much more to the same purpose expresses the president's conviction that henceforth in this country great national problems must be dealt with as national problems and not as state problems, and that any degree of loose construction of the constitution which may be necessary to this end is proper and justifiable. No academic doctrine of states rights, framed to

Federal Government.

suit conditions which are now wholly altered, must stand in the way of doing the things that must be done. This increase in the federal power is contrary to the traditional principles of the Democratic party, but the better element of that party is so strongly opposed to the rule of wealth that it should not be expected to offer any very serious opposition to the president's program.

The Republicans of New York are taking the "Hearst peril" very seriously. They fear the power of Hearst's appeal to the labor vote. No man who has nine newspapers of his own is to be despised as an antagonist in this day of the power of the press. Perhaps, too, they affect a nervousness which they do not quite feel in order to guard against the dangers of over-confidence. The Republican chairman has secured the president's promise to take the stump for Hughes if the situation becomes really threatening. Mr. Hearst's letter of acceptance to the Independence League does not exhibit him as a profound political philosopher. His grand panacea for all evils of the body politic seems to be the election of officials for short terms so that every office-holder may be responsible at very short range to the people who elected him. That public officials should be responsible to the people is a principle fundamental to our form of government. But that this end is accomplished by reducing all terms of office to the minimum, is very shallow doctrine. The public is often impatient. A considerable part of it, being influenced by shrieking newspapers like Mr. Hearst's, is apt to be drawn into hasty opinions, from which, upon reflection, it is forced to retreat. It will not do to subject every day's work of an official to a separate scrutiny and keep him in office to-morrow or put him out according as we approve or disapprove of what he did to-day. It is general results that count, and no public official can properly be brought to account until he has had time to form and carry out a policy. It is particularly futile to expect an efficient and independent judiciary if the judges are, as Mr. Hearst recommends, elected by the people for short terms. Moreover, when elections are controlled by political machines and party bosses, the official is not likely to be the better public servant for being frequently called upon to remember who elected him. If by any chance Mr. Hearst should be elected, for example, it is not likely that Tammany will permit him to forget who elected him.

The "Hearst Peril."

The Republican campaign orators are gradually getting it into their heads that it is not good form for them to indulge in spread-eagle talk about the flag going up to stay in Cuba, while the president and the secretary of state and Secretary Taft are busy saying that we are in Cuba only to give her another chance to try self-government. Senator Hemenway, who is an able statesman and ought to know better, has been making public predictions

Taming the Jingos.

that we will keep Cuba, "because we need it," and urges the probability of annexation with the accompanying problems to be solved as a reason for continuing the Republican party in power. If a forcible annexation of Cuba by a Republican administration and congress were in prospect, it would be the best sort of reason for electing a Democratic congress. The published dispatches from Washington regarding the attitude of the administration, and probably private dispatches as well, are having their effect in taming the fiery jingo campaign orators.

Two hundred and ninety-seven miles in two hundred and ninety minutes is the record made by the winner of the recent automobile race for the Vanderbilt cup. The race was won by a French car with a French driver named Wagner. (This is not the Wagner who expounds the simple life. This one is an able exponent of the very rapid life.) Of course a speed of over a mile a minute is no longer considered anything remarkable in a racing automobile. On a short spurt a racer recently covered two miles in fifty-eight seconds and the track was said to be "slow and dangerous." But this achievement of Wagner's was over nearly 300 miles of American road, and his time included the time required to replace a broken tire. There is not an express train in the world whose schedule calls for it to cover an equal distance in an equal time. While the achievement is interesting and wonderful, it is, to a degree, demoralizing to all owners of automobiles. It encourages them to believe that fast time on the road is the great desideratum. The very fast automobile has no legitimate place outside of the race track. At present we have only one set of roads for all sorts of traffic and any vehicle which travels at the rate of a mile a minute; or half of that, on these roads is dangerous to other traffic.

Speed.

The steel trust has purchased a vast body of iron ore from James J. Hill and the Northern Pacific railroad. The amount of ore involved is estimated at 750,000,000 tons, which is a comfortable amount of raw material even for a concern as large as the United States Steel Corporation. It is said to be the largest financial transaction in this country since the buying out of Mr. Carnegie and the organization of the steel trust. It brings the Northern Pacific safely within the provision of the recent law requiring railroads to dispose of their interests in other industries, and it is the first important transaction in which the influence of that law is traceable.

A Big Sale.

The Grand Duke Michael, brother of the czar, and for many years before the birth of the czarevitch, heir apparent to the throne of Russia, has become engaged to the Princess Patricia, daughter of the Duke of Connaught and niece of the king of England. The princess will have to become a member of the Russian orthodox church, but that will be as easy as it was for the English princess who lately became the wife of King Alfonso to become a Catholic.

Editorial

Where Jesus Placed the Emphasis.—IX.

The Right Use of Money.

It is clear that Jesus recognized wealth as constituting a peril to man's moral welfare. Not that wealth in itself is sinful, but that it is a temptation to luxury, to self-indulgence, to pride and arrogance, and to covetousness which is idolatry. We can only examine a few of the passages containing His teaching upon this subject but these will suffice to show how great value He attached to the proper use of money, or earthly treasures in any form. In His sermon on the Mount, containing many fundamental principles of His kingdom, He said to His disciples: "Lay not up for yourselves treasures upon earth where moth and rust consume, and where thieves break through and steal: but lay up for yourselves treasures in heaven, where neither moth nor rust doth consume, and where thieves do not break through nor steal; for where thy treasure is, there will thy heart be also." (Matt. 6:19-21.) How are we to reconcile the possession of wealth by a Christian with this statement of Jesus? We once put this question to a Christian man of large means, widely known for his generous gifts. His answer was, "I have not laid up any treasures for myself, but am trying to administer what means I have in the interest of the kingdom of God." How many other men regard their treasures in this light, we do not know, but we fear that a very much larger number of men and women, whose names are on our church books as Christians, regard their means as wholly and entirely their own, to be used for their own pleasure, with small recognition of any claim which God may have upon their possessions. Nor do they seem to be conscious that in spending their thousands for earthly pleasures and enjoyments and in giving a mere pittance to the Lord's work, they are rejecting the teaching of Christ and dishonoring the name *Christian.* The responsibility for this apparent ignorance of the claims of God upon our substance must rest with those whose duty it is to teach the people their religious obligations.

Again Jesus laid down the fundamental principle—"Ye can not serve God and mammon." (Matt. 6:24.) Mammon was the Syrian god of riches. To serve him is to devote our time, thought, and energies to the accumulation of wealth at the expense of our moral and religious nature, and to the neglect of the claims of God upon us. There can be little doubt that there are thousands of persons in all the churches who are trying this impossible experiment of serving God and mammon at the same time to the wider interests of the kingdom of God." Concerning these conflicting claims Jesus taught, "Seek ye first His kingdom, and His righteousness; and all these things shall be added unto you." Among the causes assigned by Jesus why

the good seed sown in the hearts of men often fails to bring forth fruit is "the care of the world, and the deceitfulness of riches," which "choke the word." (Matt. 13:22.) That phrase, "the deceitfulness of riches," is most suggestive. How they lure the soul on with promises of satisfaction and happiness which are never realized! How the love of riches steals into the heart imperceptibly, deadens the moral sense, engrosses the time and thought and interest, until the victim almost unconsciously becomes a mammon-worshiper.

The story of the rich young man who came to Jesus to know "what good thing" he should do to have eternal life, is full of pathos. His moral life, apparently, was above reproach, but seeing the canker that was eating at the heart of this young man —the love of money—He puts his loyalty to the test by telling him to "Go, sell that which thou hast, and give to the poor, and thou shalt have treasure in heaven: and come, follow me." The young man was unequal to the test and "went away sorrowful." Commenting on the incident Jesus said, "It is hard for a rich man to enter into the kingdom of heaven. And again I say unto you, it is easier for a camel to go through a needle's eye, than for a rich man to enter into the kingdom of God." (Matt. 19:23, 24.) No wonder the disciples of Jesus were "astonished exceedingly," and asked "Who then can be saved?" Jesus' answer was: "With man this is impossible; but with God all things are possible." It is not impossible, therefore, for a rich man to be saved through the mercy of God, but he cannot be saved trusting in his riches nor while serving mammon rather than God.

When a man approached Jesus, saying, "Teacher, bid my brother divide the inheritance with me"—more concerned, evidently, about his earthly, than about his heavenly inheritance—Jesus said unto him, "Man, who made me a judge or a divider over you?" And then, using the incident to teach a lesson He said to His disciples, "Take heed, and keep yourselves from all covetousness: for a man's life consisteth not in the abundance of the things which he possesseth." (Luke 12:13-15.) Then follows the parable of the rich man whose ground brought forth plentifully and who reasoned with himself, saying, "What shall I do, because I have not where to bestow my fruits? And he said, this will I do: I will pull down my barns, and build greater, and there will I bestow all my grain and my goods. And I will say to my soul, Soul, thou hast much goods laid up for many years; take thine ease, eat, drink, be merry. But God said unto him, thou foolish one, this night is thy soul required of thee; and the things which thou hast prepared, whose shall they be? So is he that layeth up treasure for himself, and is not rich toward God." (Luke 12:16-21.) Alas, that such teaching as this should have made so little impression upon the life of the church! How zealous many men of wealth are for their creed, or for the ordinances, who utterly ignore this teaching of Jesus concerning the use of wealth and, apparently, without any twinge of conscience!

No doubt there are hundreds of men in our churches who are congratulating themselves upon their accumulated possessions, thinking only of enlarging their barns and business houses, and who are unmindful of the demands which Christ is making upon them for the right use of the means which have been committed to them.

It will require another article to present even the most prominent passages in the teaching of Jesus on this vital question.

❀ ❀

Christian Union in Australia.

In another place in this issue will be found an article from "The Southern Baptist" of Australia, entitled "Baptists and Disciples," which we are sure our readers will be interested in reading. The editor of "The Southern Baptist" is doubtless correct in stating that the chief differences hitherto existing between Baptists and Disciples of Christ relate to the meaning of baptism, and to the personality and work of the Holy Spirit in the regeneration of the soul." Two things have contributed to lessen greatly these differences. One of these is that the position of the Disciples is being much better understood than it was during the days of debate and conflict, when the smoke of battle interfered with clearness of vision. No really representative man, among the Disciples of Christ ever denied the personality and work of the Holy Spirit in regeneration, nor has any representative teacher among us ever made the ordinance of baptism an indispensable channel of grace without which there is no salvation, as do Roman Catholics and High Churchmen. The position of the Disciples of Christ on this subject is now much more clearly understood than in former days. On the other hand, it is only true to say that there doubtless has been, by many, Disciples at least, an over accentuation, or at least a *disproportionate* emphasis of baptism, growing naturally enough out of the discussions of the times, while, at the same time, there has no doubt been an unauthorized *limitation* of the work of the Holy Spirit, on the part of some, in opposing certain extreme views on that subject held by others. The period of battle having passed away, in the main, and the real constructive work having begun, the position of Disciples on these and other questions is being stated in more irenic spirit and with a wiser distribution of emphasis.

Another fact should be stated, which we are sure no intelligent Baptist will deny, that the Baptists have likewise modified their former teaching on this subject, giving an emphasis to the place of the gospel in relation to faith and to the work of the Spirit that was not given aforetime by many Baptists, and discarding certain extreme views of the Holy Spirit, which were once commonly held. This mutual approach to a saner and more scriptural view of these questions has brought the two bodies into much greater harmony than once existed. There are partisans in both religious bodies, however, who stoutly deny any such approximation and who ring the changes on the old party slogans, and who imagine that in doing so they are manifesting exceptional loyalty to the truth! No doubt these constitute a diminishing number, and sooner or later the irenic spirit will prevail, and the two bodies co-operate, in all practicable ways, in promoting the great principles which they hold in common.

The author of the work on "The Holy Spirit" does not claim that all his brethren endorse every position taken in the book. The truth is, several brethren have taken strong exceptions to some of these positions; but that the main teaching of the book would be endorsed by the great body of representative preachers and teachers among the Disciples of Christ, there can be no reasonable doubt. Any irenic statement from the Baptist point of view of their attitude to-day on these questions would, we believe, receive as much opposition from extreme Baptists as this work on "The Holy Spirit" has received from the Disciples.

❀ ❀ Notes and Comments.

The "Christian Weekly" is grieved that the "Baptist Argus" should have said recently that "Two of their [our] leading papers are week after week sending forth the truth in connection with baptism." THE CHRISTIAN-EVANGELIST is suspected by the "Weekly" of being one of these papers, and the editor says "We have asked these two papers to state plainly and publicly whether the "Argus" is right in this claim." So far as THE CHRISTIAN-EVANGELIST is concerned, we have no disposition to deny the mild impeachment that we are "sending forth the truth in connection with baptism." We are glad the "Argus" thinks so. We regret that the "Christian Weekly" does not rejoice with us. It is not for us to deny that the position we have stated is in harmony with the true Baptist position, if Baptists think so. We believe every statement we have made on the subject is in harmony with the New Testament teaching, and if the "Baptist Argus" and other Baptist authorities agree with our statements, and claim them as a statement of their position, we thank God and take courage.

❀

If one wishes his faith in the Gospel enlarged and his zeal for missions quickened, let him read the Thirty-first Annual Report of the Foreign Christian Missionary Society, as we have just been doing. What faith, what zeal, what courage, what heroism, what joy, these missionaries of the foreign field manifest! And how the work prospers in every land! In dreamy old India, in awakened Japan, in awakening China, in darkest Africa, from the far-off Philippines under the stars and stripes, from Cuba, the Pearl of the Antilles, from staid old England, Scandinavia and the Hawaiian Islands, the work goes bravely and triumphantly on. What a cheering note is that from China, where our own missionaries and those of the Presbyterians and Methodists are uniting in an effort

to build a great university at Nanking! Why not? The Baptists, Congregationalists and Disciples of Christ are uniting in building up a Christian institution in Southern California. Truly "it is daybreak everywhere." Read this report from cover to cover and get a vision of what God is doing through our co-operation in foreign lands.

❀

Scarcely less inspiring, and even more stimulating to our patriotism, is the annual report of the operations of the American Christian Missionary Society. What a mighty base of operations is this magnificent domain for world-wide movements for the betterment of mankind! What unused opportunities and undeveloped resources lie dormant in this land of mighty possibilities! Here, too, in many a city, town and outpost are faithful heralds proclaiming the good news of salvation through Christ and pleading for greater love and unity among Christians. One can not read this report without remembering the Master's words, "Pray ye the Lord of the harvest that he thrust forth more laborers into the field, for truly the harvest is great and the laborers are few." How many places are calling for evangelists to tell "the old, old story of Jesus and his love"! What a mighty work our Home Board could accomplish if it had the funds at its disposal to respond to all these appeals! And yet, even with limited resources, see what splendid results are achieved. If such victories can be won with only a half-awakened church, what might be accomplished if our entire membership were fully awake to their duties and obligations, and were unitedly devoted to the evangelization and Christianization of our home land?

❀

Referring to the union in educational work in China mentioned above, Frank Garrett, of Nanking, says, in a letter to the Editor:

"Our movement here to unite with the Presbyterians and Methodists in educational work is the greatest opportunity of our lives. Every professor is left perfectly free to teach and to preach the truth as he sees it. Our men are not at all afraid our cause will suffer in the open light of the working day on the mission field. There is more desire here among all churches that we present a united front to the foe than there is at home. There is now so much love and sympathy and desire to be mutually helpful in all relations that the possibility of serious internal strife is precluded."

We have always felt that Christian union would receive its greatest impetus

A Petition.

HENRY VAN DYKE.

These are the gifts I ask of thee, Spirit serene;
Strength for the daily task,
Courage to face the road,
Good cheer to help me bear the traveler's load.
And for the hours of rest that come between,
An inward joy in all things heard and seen.
These are the sins I fain
Would have Thee take away:
Malice, and cold disdain,
Hot anger, sullen hate.
Scorn of the lowly, envy of the great.
And discontent that casts a shadow gray,
On all the brightness of the common day.

Editor's Easy Chair.

No sooner had the Wabash train, drawing THE CHRISTIAN-EVANGELIST party, pulled out of the Union Station at St. Louis, on Thursday evening for Buffalo, than the convention was on. No time was lost waiting for the arrival at the convention city. Where a hundred readers of THE CHRISTIAN-EVANGELIST are gathered together representing a dozen states, there you have a general convention. The first order of business was greetings. We soon discovered that there were several on board who were with us on our special train to San Francisco last year. They wanted some more of the same kind of fellowship. After greetings and handshakings were over, then came the second course which, with preachers, is nearly always anecdotes. These followed each other in rapid succession, the chief rivalry being between W. T. Moore, of Missouri, and Jewell Howard, of Texas. Then came the "Quiet Hour" thoughts, the tattoo and dreams of loved ones left behind, and of warm greetings of fellow-workers on ahead. Silence reigned, except the roar of the train, which rushed on through the night, bearing more than two carloads of sleeping delegates, who had committed themselves to Him who neither slumbers nor sleeps, but whose watchful eye guards those who are seeking to advance his kingdom in the world. In spite of numerous accidents people still have faith in the railroads and in the fidelity of the man who holds the throttle-valve, and watches while others sleep. It is well that this is so!

On Friday morning when all had breakfasted, the delegation was crowded into one car by doubling up and standing in the aisle, and a social meeting was conducted. The leader stated that it was the spirit of a convention that made it great, and requested especially that prayers be offered for God's blessing upon the convention now meeting at Buffalo, and that all who gathered there might be actuated by the single purpose of spreading the Redeemer's kingdom. The Twenty-third Psalm was recited in concert, after which there were songs, prayers and short talks by quite a number of delegates, both men and women. Nearly all the states represented in the delegation were represented in these talks. It was one of the best railroad meetings we ever witnessed. There was a spirit of devoutness, of dependence upon God for success, of brotherhood, of unity, that augured well for the convention. Naturally enough there was great unanimity of sentiment in this delegation of convention goers, in behalf of the ideals for which THE CHRISTIAN-EVANGELIST stands. Some of them had come out of their way, as they stated, to enjoy the fellowship of this company of believers en route to the convention. It was a foretaste of the convention and a preliminary part of it. It was a prep-aration of mind and heart for the convention. Above the roar of the train the voices of the enthusiastic singers were heard in the sweet old songs of Zion. "Nearer, my God, to Thee," "All hail the power of Jesus' name," "Blest be the tie that binds," "My faith looks up to thee," were some of our "Songs of Ascent," on our way up to Buffalo to attend our great annual feast. But how much more of God's nature and will do we know than was known to those ancient Hebrews! Let us see to it that this increased knowledge of God, as revealed in Christ, finds expression in lives correspondingly more God-like.

At Detroit, where we arrived Friday morning, our train "took to water," as might have been expected, and we had a ride on the great ferry up the Detroit river to Windsor, Canada, where we passed under the Union Jack. The grass, however, seemed just as green, the crops as bountiful, the woods as beautiful and nature as charming as under the Stars and Stripes. We are glad that our own kith and kin own and control this fertile land so close to us, rather than some other nation more alien to our national traditions and institutions. At the Buffalo convention the geographical and political line between the United States and Canada will be ignored, and we will be one people, under one flag—the banner of the cross. If blood be thicker than water, much more is faith stronger than our geographical and governmental distinctions. When it became evident that our train would arrive at Buffalo too late for most of the evening program, another religious service was conducted, Brother Snively leading, in which the central thought was the Buffalo convention, our immediate Jerusalem, as a preparation for the Jerusalem that is above. In conclusion each one was asked to express a sentiment concerning the convention as to what he would like to have it emphasize and stand for. These sentiments were worthy of the representatives of a great people. At the close of this wonderful meeting we felt moved to say that should the train reverse its course and return to St. Louis at once we would feel well repaid for the two meetings we had enjoyed on the way. It was indeed a convention on wheels, and if the spirit of the delegation shall be the spirit of the entire convention it will be one of the most remarkable gatherings in our history in its spiritual power and consecration. That it should be this was the ardent desire and prayer of this entire company.

Those of our belated delegation who hastened at once to the church where the convention was in progress, without waiting to find hotel accommodations, had the pleasure of hearing Mrs. Ida Harrison, of Kentucky, on the Centennial aims and ideals. If we may judge the whole address by the part we heard, standing in the aisle of the crowded church, holding hat and overcoat, it was a great and timely address, sounding the very keynotes that need emphasis in this convention. This was the verdict concerning it by those who heard it all. The president, Mrs. A. M. Atkinson, had delivered her presidential address earlier in the evening, and we heard it described in highly complimentary terms. It was a great introductory audience that greeted our sisters in this opening session. The Methodist Church, in which the convention met, it is said, seats comfortably fifteen hundred people. It could not seat the audience on Friday evening by several hundred. The great audience was responsive to the sentiments of Mrs. Harrison's address, and we thought there was special zest put into the cheering when the speaker expressed the idea that one of the things to be greatly desired in our advocacy of Christian union was that we should learn to discuss our own differences with much more charity and fraternity. It is to be hoped that all the editors and contributors to our papers heard this sentiment, and its emphatic endorsement, and will govern themselves accordingly. It is a clear case of where vox populi is vox dei. It is scarcely too much to say that one of the greatest hindrances to our own unity and the more rapid progress of our plea for union is the discordant notes struck in our religious journals, and the absence, at times, of that spirit of fraternity without which union is impossible, either among ourselves or with others.

And now we are in the midst of greetings of friends new and old. For a whole generation we have been attending these conventions, and the faces of many of the old convention goers are very familiar to us. Indeed, one of our conventions without the presence of these men would seem very strange. Their heads, for the most part, are hoary, and some of them move about with feeble and cautious step, but their presence is a benediction to our great gatherings. But before long our convention will meet and these familiar faces will not be present. One by one they will be summoned home and we shall have to go on our way without their presence and counsel. But there is a great and growing host of younger men who attend these conventions to meet and greet whom is a great pleasure. They are preparing themselves for that leadership which must be soon laid down by the "Old Guard." Nor do we fear that they will be found wanting either in ability or fidelity to the great principles for which we stand. God bless our young men and give them a double portion of his Spirit for the great work that lies before them! And then, here are the men and women who come up from the ranks of our membership and who are the strength and stay of the local churches where they belong. Many of them are for the first time in one of our great annual conventions. It is a great privilege to these to look into the faces of men and women after whom or about whom they have been reading for many years. And so the social side of these conventions is not only a source of joy, but a means of grace as well, and because of it many come who would otherwise remain away. At the present writing there is every indication of a great convention. May it prove a very Bethel to those who have eyes to see ladders reaching up to heaven and angels ascending and descending!

Baptists and Disciples By the Edito

There are two bodies in Australia who hold and practise believer's immersion—the Disciples of Christ and the Baptists. Their separation has been frequently deplored, and conferences have been occasionally held between their respective leaders, to discover, if possible, some basis of union. Hitherto such conferences have led to no other practical result than a better understanding of our mutual hopes and aims, as it was found that apart altogether from any question of names or polity, there were grave differences of belief that precluded unity.

These differences were mainly with regard to the meaning of baptism, and to the personality and work of the Holy Spirit in the regeneration of the soul. Baptism is regarded by our brethren the Disciples as one of the conditions essential to salvation, as always associated with repentance and faith, while by many of them, possibly not by all, the Holy Spirit's direct operation on the soul was denied. On these two points Baptists greatly disagreed with them, and all hope of union seemed impossible.

Exactly the same difficulties have been experienced in America, where, in 1827, the division between Disciples and Baptists first occurred, and where the hope of reunion has never died out. But latterly some important deliverances by some of the ablest and most representative leaders of the Disciples show a remarkable agreement with Baptist beliefs, so that the question of organic union is brought within the range of practical politics.

We quote the following which appeared in the "Baptist Argus" from the "Christian Century," a leading Disciple

on which he always laid stress as the characteristics of the children of God."

Every word of this would be heartily endorsed by the Baptists of the "Commonwealth," and if the Disciples would only accept this utterance as the authoritative interpretation of the meaning and place of baptism one great obstacle to union would be removed.

Again on the subject of the work of the Holy Spirit, Dr. J. H. Garrison, the Editor of THE CHRISTIAN-EVANGELIST, writes as follows, in his recently published book on "The Holy Spirit," which he says "is written from the general standpoint of the Disciples of Christ":

Page 60: "'The truth' is much broader than the inspired words written in the Bible. That the Holy Spirit in the church and in each individual believer exerts a power for the conversion of men, and that his influence is potent in the living preacher of the Word, whose very tones and gestures may help to convey the truth to the hearts of hearers, is in no way antagonistic to the fundamental position we hold on this subject. . . . Nor should any of these instrumentalities be separated form the agency of that Spirit who breathes where He listeth in His divine eagerness to infuse life into the barren souls of men. . . . It would be difficult, however, to exaggerate the value to the religious world, and to the work of evangelization, of the contention which our fathers have made from the beginning, and which we of to-day hold with the same tenacity, that the Gospel of the grace of God is the supreme and essential power for the conversion of men, and these great facts and truths in bringing men to penitence and faith, and to the

As Seen From the Dome   By F. D. Power

The Christian missionary convention of Maryland, Delaware and District of Columbia met at Vienna, Va., October 1-4. Vienna is the only church we have in northern Virginia and works with our Maryland and District of Columbia co-operation. We take in five states and the District in our missionary territory, as one of our churches, Martinsburg, is in West Virginia and another, Waynesboro, is in Pennsylvania. The Vienna church started with a mission from our Vermont- Avenue Church about fifteen years ago. I first preached in a schoolhouse in the little town which is about eighteen miles from the capital. The leader there, Joel Grayson, I baptized perhaps twenty-five years ago, when a page in the house of representatives. He is now one of the most important functionaries of the house, being a special employe of the document room, paid by special appropriation from the treasury, and probably better known and a greater necessity to the M. C's. than any man at the Capitol. The mission had many ups and downs. Our brother, Philemon Vawter, preached there and died there. Joseph Watson finally took hold of it and gathered in a goodly company of people, and under his leadership a beautiful chapel was erected on a hill among the chestnuts, and the congregation has fifty-four members, and is doing well under the pastoral care of W. T. Laprade. Here, a little out of town, with the goldenrod blooming all about us and the chestnuts falling by thousands out of their burrs, we met in our twenty-ninth annual session.

The first day, as usual, was "Preachers' Day," but the preachers on this program were scattered through the three days' sessions. Papers were read on "Preaching the Chief Work of the Church," H. R. Lookabill; "Spiritual Truths Most Needed by the Times," H. C. Kendrick; "The Normal Development of the Church," J. E. Stuart; "Pastoral Work," Thomas P. Wood; "Mission Planting in Cities," N. Pickering; "What the C. W. B. M. Auxiliary is to the Small Church," Claude C. Jones; "Bible Studies in Our Country Churches," W. E. Powell; "The Bible, the Only Text Book in the Bible School," J. A. Hopkins, and "Business Management of Mission Work," M. A. Collins. B. A. Abbott preached a great sermon on "A Sane Twentieth Century Religious Platform," and also discussed "What the C. W. B M. Auxiliary is to the Large Church." President Peter Ainslie directed the work of the convention with skill and dispatch and was re-elected.

Our visiting brethren did splendid service. It was really a general convention in a nutshell. We have never known the general causes of the brotherhood so well represented. S. T.

Willis spoke for the Church Extension interests; L. G. Batman for the General Home Society; S. J. Corey for Foreign Missions; J. H. Mohorter for the National Benevolent Association; W. R. Warren for "Our Centennial"; Miss Ada Boyd represented our returned missionaries, and R. M. Hopkins did fine work for the Sunday-school and Christian Endeavor cause. Nothing more could be desired in the matter of a full-orbed presentation of all the departments of our work. Federation was not without cordial championship, and the best plea I ever heard for union between Baptists and Disciples was presented in this little chapel among the chestnuts at this little Maryland convention. Dr. Charles H. Dodd, of the Eutaw Place Baptist Church, Baltimore, Md., gave a most fraternal and thoroughly Christian address on this subject, which was received with great enthusiasm by our body. The good doctor is already united, and we voted him in unanimously as a life member of our society. We also, at his invitation, named B. A. Abbott our fraternal delegate to the Maryland Baptist Association. Altogether this was one of the most pleasing incidents I have ever known in one of our conventions; and coming as it did on the sacred soil of Virginia, where the Dover Decrees had ruled us out—one, the great grandfather of our president, and the grandfathers of at least two others of us—we could very heartily appreciate the sentiments so happily expressed by our distinguished visitor. It would be a help toward the cause of union if Dr. Dodd could give his address to the wider circle of THE CHRISTIAN-EVANGELIST family.

The reports from churches and Sunday-schools and women's societies were all most encouraging. There are thirty-five churches and missions, twenty-seven reporting: Membership 5,562, 831 added during the year, $5,233.50 given for missions, and for all purposes contributed $57,120. Sunday-schools show an enrollment of 4,179, and 247 converts. They gave for all purposes the sum of $5,501. The board of managers gave reports from six evangelists in their employ and recommended the employment of a field evangelist, which the convention determined to do. The educational committee reported good work done in preparing young men for the ministry. "Take this, and consecrate it to some good purpose," said Mrs. Julia Reckord, handing W. S. Hoye a five-dollar gold piece found in her husband's pocket at his death. That small sum was the beginning of our educational fund. During the eighteen years of its existence twenty young men have been aided, and among them some of our brightest and brainiest preachers, both on the home and foreign field. Six young men are

now at college receiving help from this source. The sum is now $3,000. The saintly Henry and Julia Reckord are both at rest from their labors, but their works do follow them.

Very similar was the beginning of our woman's work in this section. One of our sisters, Mrs. Clara Schell, came to me some time after the organization of the Woman's Board, and said: "Here is $5 for missions. I thought you might get a few others to give something, and we might send it on to the women." "No," I said, "keep your $5. We will organize an auxiliary and send thousands." So we organized our first auxiliary. Later I called the women together at our convention and Mrs. Schell addressed them, and then for years I served them as president, until they organized for themselves, and now have one of our best sessions. Mrs. Emma Lattimore, of Washington, presided at Vienna and the meeting was the finest we ever had. Last year our women raised $7,673.77, $1,891.42 being contributed through the auxiliaries; $327.62 by Juniors and Mission Bands; the rest by Aid Societies.

When this convention was organized twenty-nine years ago we had 200 members in Washington, one church for missions, and raised all told about $3,500. The past missionary year Vermont Avenue and the seven churches that have sprung out of it, report a membership of 2,331, giving $22,123 for all purposes, $1,986 being for missions; 280 additions, $1,739 in the Sunday-schools. Our church property has increased from $7,000 to over $150,000. Our Baltimore brethren at that time numbered 700 in the one church. They have now seven congregations with a brotherhood of 1,500, and contributed to all causes $20,-266.55.

Joseph A. Scott was continued as "Field Secretary of Bible schools." E. A. Gongwer, superintendent of Vermont Avenue Sunday-school, led a most helpful conference of superintendents. Oren Orahood, the new preacher at Martinsburg, was with us, and Jacob Walters who recently gave up the work at Ocean View, Del.; an excellent man now open for engagements. H. C. Kendrick, to our universal regret, leaves Hagerstown for Georgetown, Ky. Walter F. Smith, after a useful pastorate, has resigned at Whitney Avenue, Washington. E. B. Bagby was greatly missed. George A. Miller, of Covington, Ky., has been called to the Ninth Street Church, Baltimore. We enrolled 146 delegates. The next convention goes to the Temple Church, Baltimore. The only one present who took part in the organization of the society was myself. Seven of my fifteen elders attended this meeting. Come to "Maryland, My Maryland," if you would know what a real live convention is.

Our English Conference   By William Durban

It is once more the season for the gathering of the spiritual clans. The great denominations are preparing forthwith to assemble their unions, their conventions, their annual conclaves to celebrate the triumphs of the past year and to deliberate on the outlook. The Baptist and Congregational unions and the Anglican Church make much more of autumnal sessions than of the spring assemblies, though these are always of very great interest.

Our London Meeting.

I write this article under a sense of deepest disappointment, and a severe personal loss. For the first time in twenty-three years I have been absent from the annual meeting of the Christian conference. My unusually robust health suddenly broke down just for the very week of this delightful assembly. Unaccountably I was during that week flung into the very caldron of the dyspeptic purgatory. This experience was the more trying because this year the conference has gathered in London. It was, as it were, at my own door. But pleasing echoes in the shape of full information reached me through daily visits of beloved brethren. "Our best conference yet!" "Our best year in the English work!" "The happiest time we ever had!" Such were some of the expressions of appreciation on the part of the friends who had attended. The conference met at Tasso Tabernacle, Fulham, the scene of the ministry of E. Brearley.

Real Progress.

During the history of just over a quarter of a century there have been some depressing years. This past year has not been one of these periods. It has been a time of very great encouragement. A real forward movement has evidently begun. Several of our churches have emerged from the wilderness into the land flowing with milk and honey. Most of the pastors are able to indulge in the felicitous outlook of ardent hope. Numbers are steadily growing. There have been no spasmodic revivals, but all along the line the advance has been marked in a degree unknown in any previous year. Best of all, perhaps, is the evidence of increasing strength and confidence shown in the attempt to establish new stations where fresh centers of work will be located. One of these has already been inaugurated at Kentish Town, in northwest London. This new meeting has been inaugurated by the enterprise of Brother Grinsted, son of one of our ministers in the United States. Brother Grinsted's father, though he removed years ago to America, is an Englishman. The son has always resided here in his native London, being engaged in business, while making himself abundantly useful in preaching. Now he will lead a new mission which is already affiliated with our Association. As we specially need more centers in London, it is a matter of gratification also that from "Our Cathedral," West London Tabernacle, branches are likely to be formed in the suburbs which are growing so enormously. Brother Williams and his voluntary preachers contemplate opening a station in the beautiful district of Ealing. And there is a prospect in the north of England of the formation of at least one more interest, probably as an offshoot of our young and promising Church of Christ at Chorley, the scene of the successful labors of our Brother Kennedy.

Financial Emancipation.

Another bright feature is the prospect of liquidation of debt by one church after another. The church at Upper Parliament street, Liverpool, has set a noble example. By a great and determined effort the brethren during the year wiped out their somewhat heavy debt. Brother Mitchell had stimulated them strenuously and they responded splendidly when they once tackled the problem. So that Brother Hughes, his successor, has been able to undertake his ministry under most encouraging auspices.

To speak once more of London, I must make special allusion to a very beautiful mission to which I have referred before in these letters. In the district of Western Suburban London, near Wimbledon,

The Discipline of Life.

FROM THE GERMAN.

I own it. He bruises, he pierces me sore,
But the hammer and chisel affect me no more.
Shall I tell you the reason? It is that I see
The Sculptor will carve out an angel from me.

I shrink from no suffering, how painful so e'er,
When once I can feel that my God's hand is there;
For soft on the anvil the iron shall glow
When the smith with his hammer deals blow
     upon blow.

God presses me hard, but he gives patience, too,
And no tone from the organ can swell in the
     breeze
Till the organist's fingers press down on the
     keys.

So come, then, and welcome the blow and the
     pain;
Without them no mortal can heaven attain.
For what can the sheaves in the barn floor avail
Till the thresher shall put out the chaff with his
     flail?

'Tis only a moment God chastens with pain;
Joy follows on sorrow like sunshine on rain;
Then bear thou what God on thy spirit shall lay,
Be dumb, but when tempted to murmur, then
     pray.

was sprung up a township called Southfields. Two former members of West London Tabernacle, our Brother and Sister Green, settled in this place three years ago, and felt inspired to throw open a room in their house for worship, with the gratifying result that they quickly gathered a permanent little congregation. About once every month it has been my own great privilege to preach in this spot, taking turns with other preachers. And now a young church has been organized, of which Bro. W. R. Green acts as the voluntary pastor, without fee or reward, and which has its officiary regularly elected. Above all—though this is, of course, to begin with one of those "kat'oikon" ecclesias of which we read in the New Testament epistles, a "church in the house"—it will not long remain in this preliminary stage. For Brother Green and his friends have secured a fine plot on which to build a sanctuary. I think it is now clear that I had a right to say that our prospect in London is wonderfully brightening.

A very pleasant episode at the conference in Fulham was the address at the meeting of the C. W. B. M., by Brother McDougall, passing on through London to Calcutta, under appointment by the C. W. B. M. of America. We hope to hear more of this new missionary.

London, England.

❀ ❀

FOND OF PIES

But Had to Give Them Up.

Anyone who has eaten New England pies knows how good they are.

But some things that taste good, don't always agree. A Mass. lady had to leave off pie, but found something far better for her stomach. She writes:

"Six or eight years ago chronic liver trouble was greatly exaggerated by eating too much fat meat, pastry and particularly pies, of which I was very fond.

"Severe headaches, dizziness, nausea followed, and food, even fruit, lay like lead in my stomach accompanied by a dull heavy pain almost unbearable. I had peculiar 'spells'—flashes of light before my sight. I could read half a word and the rest would be invisible.

"A feeling of lassitude and confusion of ideas made me even more miserable. I finally decided to change food altogether and began on Grape-Nuts food which brought me prompt relief—removed the dizziness, headache, confused feeling, and put me on the road to health and happiness. It clears my head, strengthens both brain and nerves.

"Whenever I enter our grocer's store, he usually calls out 'six packages of Grape-Nuts!'—and he's nearly always right." Name given by Postum Co., Battle Creek, Mich. "There's a reason." Read the famous booklet, "The Road to Wellville," in pkgs.

What the Brethren Are Saying and Doing

By B. B. Tyler

I clip from a secular paper the following: "Plans have been made by the Presbyterian evangelistic committee for the continuance, along aggressive lines, of the work which it has been doing for some time under the leadership of Dr. J. Wilbur Chapman. One change in the methods of the committee which took effect last year, and is said to have been most helpful, is expressed by Dr. Chapman to this effect: 'The committee was not successful when it was trying to make Presbyterians, at least not wholly so; success has come since we have been trying to make Christians.'"

Why should any preacher at any time, or in any place, try to persuade men to be anything else, in religion, than Christians? That is good enough. The Christ is pleased with the person who is a Christian, the Head of the Body will be no better pleased if the Christian should decide to be a Presbyterian, Methodist or Baptist, Christian.

The funeral of Sister Craig was conducted in the Central Christian Church Lord's day morning, September 30. The service was as near to perfection as any service of this character that I ever attended. Every detail was arranged by her husband, the congregation was, of course, very large, testing to its utmost the capacity of the audience room. Brother Craig and daughter, with brothers, sisters, other relatives and intimate personal friends, occupied the large parlor back of the pulpit, where they could hear every word without being seen by the great audience. A special edition of the "Weekly Bulletin" was distributed, from which I clip the following beautiful tribute:

Mrs. Emma Pickrell Craig,
Born at Mechanicsburg, Ill., January 11, 1849,
Died September 26, 1906.
Married Wm. Bayard Craig, October 29, 1885.

An ideal wife and mother in the home. A working partner and leader of women's work in the Church. A joy and inspiration in social life. A sympathetic and joyous companion in the mountains. A most winsome and helpful incarnation of the Christian spirit. Never speaking unkindly, never criticizing, she won the love and esteem of every one by a remarkable grace of spirit and manner. She was one among ten thousand. We who knew her best can not think of a fault for fearless candor to set down against her. She was as strong and effective in home, social or church work as she was beautiful. With all her amiability she was wonderful in executive power, both in planning and execution. The highest praise seems inadequate to express the facts. Christian womanhood was glorified in her. Our feeling of loss and loneliness are beyond the power of words to express. Love for her will inspire us to do something more than heretofore to continue her work and influence.

There is not a word of exaggeration in this. Every word here written is true in letter and in spirit of Sister Craig. She was a great and good woman.

"The world do move!" The following is from the paper of a local Presbyterian Christian church:

Next Wednesday evening our study in the "Founding of the Christian church" begins. Read Acts, chapters 1 and 2, then come with us, and bring your friends. The pastor hopes to see every member of the church in this important and interesting study. An earnest invitation is extended to all others to join us also.

The time was, and that, too, easily within the memory of some who are yet in the flesh, when such an announcement as this would have been regarded as downright heresy on the part of the Campbellian variety. Read of the "founding of the Christian church" in Acts of Apostles, chapters 1 and 2! No, indeed, the Christian church began in the days of Abraham! The place in which to read of the beginning of the Church is in "the Book of Genesis." This was the position of our brethren of the Presbyterian brand in the part of the country where, and in the time when, I began to preach. I merely note the above for the encouragement of some brethren who seem to think that we all stand exactly where we stood forty or fifty years ago.

The political pot is boiling in Colorado. Have you heard of it? There are three candidates for governor—all good men—or they were good men until after their nominations! Now they are all bad men—very bad men!! A political campaign in Colorado is unlike a political campaign in any other state. Words can not describe it; at any rate, my words can not. I will, therefore, not attempt a description. There are no good, old-fashioned, unwashed Democrats now in evidence in Colorado. We have *Reform* Democrats, led by United States Senator Patterson, and "Independent" or Reformed Reform Democrats, led by Judge B. B. Lindsey, of the far-famed Juvenile Court. Alva Adams, B. B. Lindsey and Henry R. Buchtel are the candidates for the office of governor. The latter is a Methodist preacher and the chancellor of Denver University. Our next governor of Colorado will, certainly, be a good man! I think that our state is to be congratulated!

Denver, Colo.

❦ ❦
"Onward" is the Word.
BY W. A. HAYNES.

Rome, in her declining days, clung to the worship of her older and more glorious days. She denounced the ingratitude of forsaking the gods under whom she had become empress of the world. She urged the following objection: "If the gods have led us into great blessings when we worshipped them in different form, how may we expect future good without remaining under their guidance"?

The same problem seems to perplex the minds of many even at this late day. "My father was brought to success while believing certain things. Why can not I be successful and study no more questions than were contained in his catechism?"

The ages are advancing. So must man advance. We have the presentation of the gods, and the experience of our fathers. Why will an advance step insult the gods who were followed by our fathers so far as the times would permit human strength to follow? Why would the glory of another star in our sky reveal a lack of respect for our fathers who led us by the hand until their burdens were laid down? When one soldier drops the flag, shall not another take it up and bear it onward to the conflict?

Our fathers dropped the standard before the battle was won, or perfect victory was in view. Shall we not gather up this standard of truth and bear it onward in the face of new enemies our fathers never saw, to new conflicts of which they never dreamed? Shall we not rather disregard the spirits of our fathers if we lift not the burdens that bore down their failing forms, and hasten to plant the standard nearer the eminence towards which they had set their faces?

The law of life is exacting. It demands a continual gathering of interest in order to preserve the principle. No
(Continued on Page 1352.)

❦ ❦
NO DAWDLING
A Man of 70 After Finding Coffee Hurt Him, Stopped Short.

When a man has lived to be 70 years old with a 40-year-old habit grown to him like a knot on a tree, chances are he'll stick to the habit till he dies.

But occasionally the spirit of youth and determination remains in some men to the last day of their lives. When such men do find any habit of life has been doing them harm, they surprise the Oslerites by a degree of will power that is supposed to belong to men under 40, only.

"I had been a user of coffee until three years ago—a period of 40 years—and am now 70," writes a N. Dak. man. "I was extremely nervous and debilitated, and saw plainly that I must make a change.

"I am thankful to say I had the nerve to quit coffee at once and take on Postum without any dawdling, and experienced no ill effects. On the contrary, I commenced to gain, losing my nervousness within two months, also gaining strength and health otherwise.

"For a man of my age, I am very well and hearty. I sometimes meet persons who have not made their Postum right and don't like it. But I tell them to boil it long enough, and call their attention to my looks now, and before I used it, that seems convincing.

"Now, when I have writing to do, or long columns of figures to cast up, I fell equal to it and can get through my work without the fagged out feeling of old." Name given by Postum Co., Battle Creek, Mich. Read the book, "The Road to Wellville," in pkgs. "There's a reason."

Two Great Debates   By C. C. Redgrave

"I come not here to advocate the particular tenets of any sect, but to defend the great cardinal principles of Protestantism." These were the words with which Mr. Campbell opened the historic debate with Bishop Purcell, the Roman Catholic prelate, in Cincinnati, O.

The place of this notable passage of arms was the Sycamore Street Christian

evangelistic efforts of Jeremiah Vardeman, many of the members of the Enon Baptist Church, on Walnut and Baker streets, had accepted the principles of reform advocated by the Campbells and others. The climax was reached when more than a hundred of the members received letters of dismission and immediately constituted themselves the Sycamore Street Baptist Church, with James Challen as pastor. The name "Baptist

Sycamore Street Christian Church, Cincinnati, O., Scene of the Campbell-Purcell Debate.

Church. The debate lasted seven days, beginning January 13, 1837. The occasion was the address of Mr. Campbell on "Moral Culture," delivered before the College of Teachers at Cincinnati, a few months previously, in which the "rapid march of modern improvement was connected with the spirit of inquiry produced by the Protestant reformation." Purcell affirmed that the "Protestant reformation had been the cause of all the contention and infidelity in the world," and he advocated the exclusion of the Bible from the common schools. The satisfaction with which the Protestants of the "Queen City" reviewed the debate may be inferred from the fact that at a mass meeting of representative citizens, the following resolution, among others, was passed with great enthusiasm: "Resolved, that it is the unanimous opinion of this meeting that the cause of Protestantism has been fully sustained throughout this discussion."

The "College of Teachers" endorsed the championship in the following words: "Resolved, that in the judgment of the college, the Bible should be introduced into every high school, from the lowest to the highest, as a text-book."

The Sycamore street meeting house possesses additional historic interest as marking an important era in the "Current Reformation." Under the preaching of James Challen, the pastor, and the

Church" was shortly after discarded and erased from the stone tablet on the front wall, the covenant and creed cast out, and the New Testament adopted as their only rule of faith and practice. The building was sold to the Methodist Church South in 1845, and they in turn sold it to the Roman Catholics, in whose possession it remains to-day. Shades of

Alexander Campbell! How incongruously must the echoes of the great man's victory commingle with the daily chanting of the priests and the confessions of the people!

The Sycamore Street Christian Church has been a "seed church." "In fact all the Disciple congregations in and around Cincinnati are offshoots of this church."

The "Reform Church," or, as it is more generally known, the Main Street Christian Church, Lexington, Ky., will always be remembered as the scene of Alexander Campbell's last and greatest public debate. On this occasion Mr. Campbell was not the champion of Protestantism against Infidelity or Roman Catholicism, as when he met Owen and Purcell in Cincinnati. Rather he was called upon to defend the religion of the New Testament against the "traditions and other baseless tenets of Protestantism. And in the themes discussed, the Holy Spirit, baptism and human creeds, the "whole range of truth for which the Disciples contended was reviewed and defended with consummate skill and ability. The debate lasted sixteen days, beginning November 15, 1843, and was attended by a large concourse of people, and created profound and widespread interest in religious circles. Henry Clay, the noted statesman and orator, presided, manifesting the deepest interest in the proceedings, and he is reported to have said afterward that Mr. Campbell was the "profoundest theologian and most eloquent and able debater of the age."

The Rev. N. L. Rice, of Paris, Ky., represented the Presbyterians in this debate. His friends were so jubilant over what they sincerely considered his great victory over Mr. Campbell, that they eagerly purchased at $2,000 the copyright of the debate, a book of 900 closely printed pages. The reading of the debate, however, made many converts to the principles of the reformation, but none to Presbyterianism, and the copyright was as eagerly resold, this time for a "small sum to a member of the Christian church at Jacksonville, Ill., C. D. Roberts." The work has had a wide and appreciative patronage, and is generally considered one of the ablest debates on

(Continued on Page 1335.)

Main Street Christian Church, Lexington, Ky.—Scene of Campbell-Rice Debate.

International Missionary Convention

Christian Woman's Board of Missions

The women had, as usual, the first part of the program at the Convention assigned to them, and on Friday evening they crowded the Delaware Avenue Methodist Church which had been placed at their disposal. This meeting, as well as the more strictly business sessions, which came next day, were marked by a restrained enthusiasm that means more, perhaps, for the accomplishment of the aim they have set for themselves for the coming year than any excited outbursts such as are sometimes manifested when an aim has been surpassed. For during the past year they have gone beyond their expectations. Mrs. N. E. Atkinson's presidential address was marked by a quiet yet thoroughly optimistic tone; while that of Mrs. Harrison, of Lexington, Ky., was a fuller light thrown on the aims and the prospects ahead. "Our Centennial" was her theme. As Mrs. Harrison will have many calls for this address throughout the country, we will not attempt any report of it here. Her saying that "The Centennial of American missions is coincident with the centenary of our religious truth," was, of course, pleasing to her audience.

On Saturday morning the church was again filled with an expectant throng. Miss Newcomer, of Iowa, led the devotionals instead of Mrs. M. N. Wiseman, who was unable to be present. After greetings from the maritime provinces had been read, the report of the board was epitomized by Mrs. Helen E. Moses. At the outset she explained that the recommendations which she had to read had been passed by the executive committee the day before. She referred to the blessings that had crowned the year, in which there had been an advance in every line of work. There were reported 2,661 auxiliaries and mission circles, a gain of 634 organizations; 47,210 members, a gain of 3,462; 21,233 Tidings sold, a gain of 2,615; receipts $206,553.12, a gain of $31,144.14. Of course applause greeted the announcement of these figures, and there were more good things—16 new buildings erected and 3,607 conversions reported in the churches through which the C. W. B. M. works. The greatest need emphasized in the report was a determined, vigorous personal canvass for members. The recommendations, all of which were accepted, included the sending of A. H. Owen, of New York, to Jamaica as a minister, and Charles Shirley, of Illinois as native missionary; and the erection of a new home, $4,000 more being required for this enlargement than the $13,454 expended last year in the island. It was decided to transfer Mr. and Mrs. Munro to Jhansi and that a married men be sent out to Deoghur. For this work in India $4,500 additional is to be expended. A modest dormitory is to be built in Monterey and property purchased at Sabinas, Mexico, and the forces to be strengthened. In Porto Rico a building is to be erected at Bayamon and another worker is to be sent to aid Brother and Sister Burner in Buenos Ayres. In the homeland the work at Manchester, N. H., and at Reno, Nev., is to be cared for as well as the oriental work carried on by

W. P. Bentley on the coast, and all lines are to be advanced.

The executive meeting held the previous day recommended further that (1) with the beginning of the year the furlough salaries of missionaries be the same as those in the field; (2) with this year the salaries of married missionaries in Mexico, Jamaica, Porto Rico and South America be the same as the salaries of married missionaries in India; (3) the anniversary of the twenty-fifth year of C. W. B. M. work in India be fittingly celebrated; (4) the C. W. B. M. and the National Benevolent Association unite in the observance of Easter day for the benefit of the orphans of all lands, the proceeds to be divided equally and a committee to be appointed to confer with the Benevolent Association representatives. The chair appointed Mrs. Haggard, Mrs. McCleary, Miss Graybiel, Mrs. Davidson and Mrs. Moses. All these suggestions were agreeable to the convention and were unanimously adopted. Indeed in the open convention there was no discussion. A matter was presented and adopted in double-quick time. Women may sometimes be late in getting their bonnets on but the C. W. B. M. at this convention acted with greater dispatch than any convention this scribe has ever attended. Bro. Charles Louis Loos, who was on the front seat; at one time challenged a vote. Mrs. Atkinson's "Don't let it be said that Brother Loos can do a thing with this audience that I can't," brought forth a louder expression to the satisfaction of the veteran convention-goer from Lexington.

Miss Mary Graybiel, sweet of face, gray haired in the service of the C. W. B. M., read a touching address, whose burden was "Save the child and you have saved the woman."

After some music, which was admirably led, by the way, throughout the sessions by W. E. M. Hackleman, came W. F. Richardson's address on Jamaica. It was an interesting survey of Jamaica, touching upon topography, climate, history, people, of this "isle of springs," where there are trees that are likened to women's tongues and where "the smells are all plural." It was a racy speech, such as one would expect of Brother Richardson. He enjoyed himself there on this trip with Mrs. Moses and Mrs. Atwater, notwithstanding he had to be a "pieless American" for five weeks and be fed on "condensed milk and condemned butter." His speech was the expression of a strong belief in the good outcome of Christian work. He instanced many cases of consecration on the part of the native Christians.

The treasurer's report showed a balance on hand October 1, 1905, of $27,-216.04, with actual receipts of $206,553.12 during this year. Loans returned amounted to $22,155, and to the general fund $168.65 were returned, giving a grand total of $256,092.81, against the disbursement account which was $235,-715.43, leaving a balance in bank of $20,-377.38.

The Young People's department report was a good one. The receipts were $27,215, being a gain of $4,341.93. Twelve states and territories exceeded their apportionments, Missouri leading with 30½ per cent gain, Tennessee coming next with 16½ per cent gain. To Missouri, therefore, goes the National Banner. A place upon the roll of honor—the award of those who have increased their offerings—was won by 795 organizations. For the fifth consecutive time

Paris, Ky., won the position of National Banner Organization, Central, Lexington, coming next, with Bluefield, W. Va., third. Others in order were Franklin Circle, Cleveland, O.; First Church, Jacksonville, Ill., and Lockhaven, Pa. The chief building enterprise of the year is the Boys' Orphanage in Porto Rico which is to be dedicated immediately. Chapels destroyed by the tornado in Jamaica have either been replaced or shortly will be. Many of the young folks have joined the Centennial brigade.

At the afternoon session the following missionaries and workers were introduced, each speaking a few words: Miss Graybiel, Miss Boyd, Mrs. Baldwin, M. D.; Miss Maddock, Miss Longdon, M. D.—all representing India; Miss Siler (Porto Rico), Mrs. Fullem, one of the originators of the orphanage work; F. H. Groom (Montana), and J. M. Hoffmann, general evangelist.

The interest was not lessened when the next speaker came to the platform—a mountain boy from East Kentucky, yet "perfectly harmless." Experience after experience he told to impress his hearers with the needs of the mountaineers, their worth and possibilities. There were the boys who came to school with their revolvers. But the preacher's "tune book" wrought where his prayer-meeting would not be tolerated and led to the boys saying, "Ye, can't go until ye promise to come again." Seven out of ten of these boys gave themselves to Jesus Christ and all ten of them voluntarily put aside their revolvers. Then there were six boys who wanted to break up the meeting—every one of them heavily armed. Brother Derthick persuaded them to join the choir on that particular occasion and in this way prevented mischief. He illustrated the good of the educational work of Hazell Green, which has sent out over 400 students, seven-eighths of them Christians, by the effect it had upon a feudist girl, a niece of Hargis, who, from her hatred of another girl, was finally led to say, "I forgive you; let us be sisters in Jesus Christ," and then there was a picture. Taylor and Amanda were sweethearts. Taylor was a bright boy taking an education. But Amanda wanted the marriage to take place and Taylor had agreed. Mr. Derthick tried to persuade him to wait and finish his school, encouraging him with the thought that he might be a professor or represent his county. But the woman had to be satisfied and Brother Derthick finally undertook to talk to her. He drew two pictures—the rough mountain hut and the cosy home in the school town. "It'll be just as you say, Amanda." "It'll be just as you say, Taylor," came the reply. Brother Derthick told the denouement: Five weeks ago Taylor was elected to the state legislature and four weeks ago he led Amanda to the altar.

There was more interest in the election of officers this year than usual, for Mrs. N. E. Atkinson had expressed her intention to retire from the presidential position she has held so long and well. The nominating committee submitted its report, which was immediately adopted. The following were elected:

Mrs. Helen E. Moses, president; Mrs. A. R. Atwater, vice-president; Mrs. M. E. Harlan, corresponding secretary; Mrs. Anna B. Gray, recording secretary; Mrs. Mary Judson, treasurer and Miss Mattie Pounds, superintendent of Young People's Department. The residential members elected were Mrs. N. E. Atkinson, Mrs. Effie Cunningham, Mrs. R. K. Sybers, Mrs. E. M. Duncan, and Mrs. Alice Sedener.

Mrs. Atkinson expressed her gratitude for the kindnesses of the members and for their granting her request for release from active leadership.

The report of the Committee on Watchword and Aim was adopted. The watchword is to be "Pray, Work, Give"—pray for more women, deeper consecration, larger gifts; work for increased member-ship, tidings in every home, special gifts from all; give freely of time, talent, means. The aim is to be 50,000 members, 25,000 Tidings, $215,000 in offerings exclusive of the Centennial offering.

After delightful musical refreshment from the Netz sisters, Mrs. W. W. Wharton, of Jacksonville, Ill., gave the closing address, chaste in its diction, poetic in its conception and tender in its pathos.

The C. W. B. M. has had a great year and a splendid convention.

Foreign Christian Missionary Society

An Abstract of the Thirty-first Annual Report, Presented at Buffalo, October 15, 1906.

Thirty-one years ago we did not have in the wide field destitute of the gospel a single herald of the cross. At the present time, we are represented on all the continents and on many of the islands of the sea. Evangelists, physicians, teachers, colporteurs; Bible women and native helpers are supported by the society. The past year has been one of the very best in our history. The Lord has worked with us and through us to accomplish his own gracious purpose. As we rehearse his dealings we would think and praise his glorious name.

The receipts amounted to $268,726.62. This is an increase of $12,804.11. At the beginning of the year it was hoped that $300,000 would be raised. While this has not been done, the receipts are considerably larger than in any previous year. The churches, as churches, gave $109,018.39, or $13,517.55 more than they gave last year. This is the largest gain ever made in one year. What is equally gratifying is the fact that there was a gain of 344 in the number of contributing churches. The Bible schools gave $66,800.65, or $4,992.05 more than in the year before. There was a gain of 86 in the number of contributing schools. The Christian Endeavor Societies gave $12,007.97, or $1,134.89 more than in 1905. There was a gain of 169 in the number of contributing societies. There was a slight gain in bequests; but a falling off in the number of individual offerings, and in the amount received on the annuity plan. Year after year there is a marked increase in the total receipts of the society. This is an unmistakable proof of the growing interest among our people in the world's evangelization.

Fourteen new names have been added to the list of workers. These have been sent to where the needs were greatest. Some were obliged to retire from the field on account of failing health. It is seldom that one gives up the work for any other reason. One of the faithful workers in China entered into the life that is life indeed. The others have been protected against the pestilence that walks in darkness and the destruction that wastes at noonday.

The missionary force numbers 487. Of this number, 154 are missionaries, and 333 are native evangelists and teachers and helpers. But they all make it their chief business to speak good words for the Lord Jesus. Every other thing done is designed to aid the cause of evangelists, teachers and helpers. But they all make it their chief business to speak good words for the Lord Jesus. Every other thing done is designed to aid the cause of evangelism. In their own homes, in the chapels, along the streets, at the wells, in the temples and theatres, wherever there is a soul to listen they are glad to make known the way of life and salvation. Not only so, but they go on long tours into unoccupied territory and press the claims of the gospel home to the hearts and consciences of all with whom they have to do. Hundreds of thousands are reached every year with the joyful message. The good seed of the Kingdom is scattered far and near. It must be that some of it will fall into good and honest hearts and bring forth fruit an hundred or a thousand fold. God only can foresee what the harvest will be from this sowing.

The youth are gathered into schools and are trained for lives of usefulness and nobleness. Thousands are under instruction in the schools sustained by the society. In the colleges the ablest and most promising young men and women are being educated to serve as pastors, evangelists, teachers, editors and helpers in other capacities. The fact is recognized that a people can be evangelized only by members of their own race. In order to do this the missionaries must educate some of the best of the converts for this service.

Medical work is carried on by our representatives on a large scale. Last year 90,313 patients were treated in our hospitals and dispensaries. The in-patients numbered 1,435. The medical fees amounted to $3,467.40. Patients came from great distances to be healed of their diseases. The medical work breaks down prejudice and opens homes and hearts to the Gospel and its advocates. The cures wrought affect the people very much as the cures wrought by our Lord and his apostles affected the people of their time. A successful operation is a miracle in their estimation; the medical missionary is almost, if not altogether a god. The fame of the mission is carried far beyond the limits of the country traversed and evangelized by the missionaries. Moreover, every patient hears the Gospel at the dispensary or in the hospital. If he can read he is supplied with portions of the Scriptures and with other Christian literature. On his return he tells his family and neighbors the great things he has heard from the man of God while undergoing treatment.

The press has been used on all the large fields. Papers are published and widely circulated. Sunday-school literature is prepared and supplied to teachers and pupils. Books and booklets are published. The printed page is an effective evangelistic agency. It is not a substitute for the living voice, but it is a mighty auxiliary of the living voice. It can go where no missionary agent can go. It can be read at home by those who wish to know more of what is heard in the public gathering.

Rescue and benevolent work is carried on by the missionaries. Orphans are taken in and cared for and taught. They are thus saved from lives of sin and shame. In the famine district in Japan our workers did what they could to save the people alive. They served on committees that appealed for funds, and distributed what they received for this purpose. They visited wounded soldiers and ministered to their bodily and spiritual needs. The missionaries do whatever they can do to help the people among whom they live. The supreme aim in all they do is to win them to Christ.

The reports from the field read in detail of those who wish complete and accurate

The Third Christian Church, Youngstown, O.

—The corner-stone of the Third Christian Church, at Youngstown, O., was laid on the afternoon of Lord's day September 16. It is to be a $10,000 building to replace the old one which was dismantled some time ago. The congregation in the meantime has been holding services temporarily in a tent. The congregation was organized in 1900 and was the outcome of work by Wilcox and Perry Updike. There were about sixty charter members, and the present membership numbers about 200 and is being steadily increased under the excellent leadership of F. D. Draper, who is the present pastor. John E. Pounds, John R. Ewers and W. S. Goode took part.

❀ ❀

TWO GREAT DEBATES.

(Continued from Page 1332.)

the subjects treated. "all debates since then on these subjects having been but an echo of this great contest at Lexington."

The building where the debate was held was built in 1843, at a cost of $15,-000, and was considered at the time one of the finest buildings of the brotherhood in the state. Dr. L. L. Pinkerton was the first pastor of the Main street congregation, serving from 1841 to the fall of 1843. About eight years ago the members moved into their new and handsome building on Walnut street, two blocks away. Since then the old building has been used for political meetings and theatrical performances of a cheap kind. It is expected that it will soon be torn down to make way for a business block.

So the old landmarks of the current reform are passing from human ken. But the good abides and from

"Age to age
Goes down the goodly heritage."

C. C. REDGRAVE.

Our Budget

—Tennessee puts in E. S. Baker, of Jackson, as state evangelist.

—We are glad to report that the church at Mobile, Ala., was only slightly injured in the great storm that did so much damage in the south. Claude E. Hill, the pastor, reports that the brethren there are expecting to entertain the Alabama State Convention beginning November 15. W. T. Moore, J. A. Lord, and J. H. Garrison are among those on the program.

—Lew D. Hill has given up his state work in Illinois, and has located at Benton.

—Every teacher in Christian University, Canton, Mo., is a Christian preacher this year.

—Geo. W. Buckner, who has closed six years' service at Macomb, Ill., is now preaching for the church at Canton, Mo.

—John T. Brown is now holding a meeting at Brisbane, Australia, whence he proceeds to Manila, Japan and other points.

—The revival at Bloomington, Ill., being still in progress, Brothers Gilliland and Jones were unable to attend the convention.

—A. M. Harrall has been assisting H. S. Kline at Stillwell, Ind. Ty., in a short meeting. A building is soon to be completed there.

—W. H. Garrard has resigned his pastorate of the Rowland Street Church, Syracuse, N. Y., and taken charge of the work at LaPorte, Ind.

—The church at Farmington, Mo., has been presented with a very beautiful individual communion set, which was used for the first time on October 14.

—Extensive repairs are about to be made upon the church building at Hazel Green, Ky. H. L. Atkinson, the preacher, reports that the Mountain School has great things in prospect, and is doing a splendid work.

—H. L. Atkinson has been called to the pastorate of the church at Hazel Green, Ky., and is at work there. Already plans are on foot to repair the church building and the outlook for aggressive work is fine.

—B. F. Creason, of Liberal, Mo., has been unanimously called to the pastorate at Lathrop, and will enter upon his work immediately. N. M. Perry writes us that the church is in good working order and the future very promising.

—The church at Nelsonville, O., will begin the erection of a new building to cost not less than $10,000 in the spring. W. S. Cook is the pastor. At the recent rally day 400 were present and the offering was over $41. There is a Bible class of 125 and a young men's class of 32.

—"Medicine shows are passing out of date, especially when they come in contact with more substantial things." This is the editorial comment of a Nebraska paper in speaking of a meeting recently held by Austin and McVey, which drew the crowds and left no one for "the show."

—Sherman B. Moore has a very difficult field, for Oklahoma City has the reputation of being a very worldly place. Despite that fact, Brother S. B. Moore can record a total of 421 additions to the First Church there during the past twenty-five months, with progress in various other ways.

—C. M. Kreidler's church at Baltimore, Md., has just closed its official year. He

has held the pastorate eleven months, during which time there were fifty-three additions and all of the departments strengthened. The building is now being enlarged. E. J. Meacham, of Wilmington, Ohio, began a meeting for the church last Lord's day.

—"We are growing, but I hope have not reached maturity yet." That is a good message which comes from Will A. Harding, Columbus, Ind., where the Bible school raised $35 for Church Extension and the Christian Endeavorers, $50. The Bible school offering goes to help the church in the named loan fund.

—J. R. Stebbins and wife have resigned from the pastorate of the first Christian Church at Argentine, Kan., to take up evangelistic work. During the past year 110 additions to the brotherhood have come through their efforts. They can arrange for a few more meetings and may be addressed at 1016 West Silver avenue, Argentine, Kan.

—"Uncle" Tommy Anderson, who was born in Logan county, Ky., July 21, 1814, came from the Cumberland Presbyterian

"Uncle" Tommy Anderson.

church into the Christian church under the preaching of the first preacher of our brotherhood he ever heard in 1841. He is a cousin of "Bill" Anderson, the celebrated bushwhacker, though "Uncle Tommy," himself, was allied with the Union. The most important feature about this kindly old brother, now in his ninety-third year, is that he is in his class at Bible school almost every Lord's day morning. He is also seldom absent from the morning service of the Christian Church at Odessa, of which he is a loyal member.

—Our church at Collingwood, Ontario, has been having a season of "looking backward and looking forward." That is the title of the sermon its pastor, John Williams, preached on this occasion. It was a helpful discourse and we find a sketch of it printed in the newspaper of the town. The report of the year showed that in addition to good pastoral work, fifteen new members had been received, bringing up

the present membership of the church to eighty-three. All financial obligations were met and $800 expended in improving the house of worship. Both pastor and people address themselves to the work of another year with increasing hope and devotion.

—J. B. Lockhart has closed his ministry at Unionville, Mo., and will be open for engagement about November 1. There have been between sixty and seventy additions in his Unionville pastorate, while the missionary collections have been the largest in the history of the church. He is glad to report that there are many loyal brethren there.

—THE CHRISTIAN-EVANGELIST office had a very pleasant visit from John S. Zeran and wife as they passed through St. Louis. They have been doing good work as evangelistic helpers both in singing and speaking. By reason of the fact, however, that they have a young family, they intend to locate soon, and have accepted a call to Gurney, Ill. They will take part, however, in several meetings first.

—As a result of some planning by H. J. Corwin, a fine meeting was held some time ago which we believe has not been reported in our columns. Brother Corwin is the minister at California, Mo., and he was instrumental in organizing the Moniteau County Co-operative Association for the purpose of evangelizing the county. He enlisted eight churches in the movement and though these were at too remote distance to give much personal help in the meeting they gave it their support. There were, in all, 170 additions, and all adults but three. We trust that Brother Corwin's health may be so established that he can repeat this work at some point next year.

—He who takes up the duties of starting a new paper is a brave man, but we are always glad to commend any effort in this direction that will aid our Christian work. Whether there is a field for a paper, devoted especially to West Texas we can not at this distance say. If it shall prove so, we shall rejoice. J. H. Shepard, pastor of the church at Haskell, has just begun publication of the "West Texas Christian," a religious magazine intended especially for that section of the country; but we warn brethren everywhere that it is not an easy matter to make a success of a local paper, and they should canvass the situation carefully before they attempt to start one.

—We have received the following from Bro. E. S. Ames, pastor of the Hyde Park Church of Disciples, Chicago: "Mr. Frank Noataro Otsuka is now prepared and eager to return to Japan to do missionary work. As it is not the policy of the Foreign Missionary Society to send natives to foreign countries to be in charge of mission work, he must secure his own support. President A. McLean, of this society, has given him hearty endorsement. He has asked me, as his pastor, to receive all money given directly to him or sent to me to defray his traveling expenses to Japan. This I shall gladly do, making proper acknowledgment of the same through the papers. This is a most worthy undertaking and should meet with a ready response of sympathy and money."

—L. L. Carpenter recently dedicated the new church at Palestine, Ind. The building cost $3,500, and is all provided for. Carl H. Barnett is the pastor.

—A. H. Smith, whose death we recorded last week, was attending the Bible college at Canton, Mo. He died at Holliday, Monroe county, Mo., of typhoid fever. He was holding a meeting at Holliday when he was stricken. At his request, he was buried at Holliday, although his home is in New Zealand. The funeral services were in charge of Rolla G. Sears and eleven ministers of the Christian church were present.

—Flourney Payne has resigned the pastorate of the Berkeley church, Denver, Col., where he has done a good work. He is a great grandson of John F. Johnson, one of our pioneer evangelists. Brother Payne is a young man of culture and blameless life and a successful pastor and preacher. Here is an opportunity for a pastorless congregation. Brother Payne's address is 4180 Xavier street, Denver, Colo.

—S. M. Bernard, minister of our church at Boulder, Colo., reports a delightful week of prayer and Bible study just held there. A fine attendance and deep spirituality encouraged those who believe that such subjects as the Holy Spirit, Christian life, conversion, the Church, and kindred themes, are not only of vital interest, but can prove attractive in this day of more sensational things.

—We have seen the plans of the new building which is being erected by our church at Tacoma, Washington. It will be of old Corinthian design and one of the handsomest structures on the coast. Twenty separate rooms will be provided for the Bible school which will occupy the first floor. The building, when complete, will be worth over $40,000, and its location is one of the best in the city. W. A. Moore is the pastor, and we congratulate him and the brethren at Tacoma on their enterprise and faith.

—Bro. L. C. Howe, the successful and greatly beloved pastor of about 500 of God's chosen people at New Castle, Ind., threw THE CHRISTIAN-EVANGELIST force into a flutter of happy excitement last week by sending in a list of 106 new subscribers. It was a list without a blemish —all for one year at $1.50 each; the most substantial list received by THE CHRISTIAN-EVANGELIST in many months. New Castle's list will greatly encourage other churches, and Brother Howe feels that the result of this house-to-house canvass will be a blessing to his people.

—M. E. Harlan, who has been out of his Brooklyn pulpit since June 2 on account of illness, will rest for a year, when he hopes to be as strong as ever. His condition, he feels, will take him from his Brooklyn work and his plan is to live on ranches, farms and quiet places and visit with his kinsfolk in the west. He was recently called to a pastorate in Washington, D. C., but for the reason mentioned could not consider it even had he been desirous of leaving the Sterling Place Christian Church, of which he has been pastor for seven years. Brother Harlan has been a strong personality and has attracted much attention in the east by his advocacy of Christian union. We sincerely regret that he is forced, for a time, from active work.

Get Your Stomach Right.

In one week with Drake's Palmetto Wine. No distress after three days. Cures to stay cured.

If you want a test bottle send your address to Drake Co., 311 Drake Bldg., Wheeling, W. Va.

Special to THE CHRISTIAN-EVANGELIST.

Buffalo, N. Y., Oct. 15.—Four thousand delegates have registered. Sunday an ideal day. Protestant pulpits filled by our preachers morning and evening. Great throng attended church services in the afternoon; five thousand, it is estimated, joined in celebrating the Lord's supper in convention hall. It was a great and impressive service. These splendid sessions of the Christian Woman's Board of Missions were followed by an enthusiastic Christian Endeavor convention on Saturday night. The Foreign Society is now holding one of the best conventions in its history. Buffalo is playing its part as host magnificently. Press of the city is giving fine reports. All Buffalo and the region round about know we are here and what for.

J. H. GARRISON.

—The brethren at Nelson, Neb., are rejoicing. The old debt of the church has just been wiped out, and money raised in cash to repair it, buy new song books, and still a sum in the treasury. There was an enthusiastic all-day meeting, and, best of all, there were confessions. A county convention has been organized for aggressive work. As an expression of their appreciation of the good work of their minister, Elsworth Day, the Ladies' Aid furnished him with the money to go to the International Convention at Buffalo.

—Our esteemed contemporary, the "Christian Courier," of Dallas, Texas, referring to the commission as recorded in Matt. 28:29, says: "The 1881 edition of the Revised Version changed 'in' to 'into,' but the American Standard Revised Bible has returned to 'in.'" This is not the case in the edition of the American Revised Bible which we possess, and which this house sells. There must be some misunderstanding on this point. There can be no excuse for rendering eis by "in" in such connection. The "Courier" must get a new Bible.

—Bro. Joseph Lowe, speaking of a meeting which he closed at Homewood, Kan., says he made the acquaintance while there of Sister Altman, "who has just passed her one hundredth birthday. She has been totally blind for many years, and is very hard of hearing, but her mind is as clear, her faith as strong, and her hope as bright, as those of any one we have ever conversed with. She was immersed sixty-five years ago by the father of W. W. Dowling. I felt that I was listening to the echoes of the century gone while talking to this faithful centenarian."

—The birthday of George H. Brown occurred on the same day as his first anniversary in the pastorate of our church at Charleston, Ill. The occasion was seized upon by the congregation to express their good-will toward their pastor and his family. Among other useful and valuable gifts was a fine sectional book-case, that would delight the heart of a preacher who has some books. During the past year the church has raised more money for missions than ever before in its history for the same period. There have been seventy additions to the church and everything is in the best working condition.

—It is a good report that J. R. Crank can furnish with reference to our church at Paragould, Ark., where he is

---

pastor, and which has just closed one of the best years in its history. Every bill has been settled and there is money in the treasury, and every department is well organized. The additions numbered thirty-eight; H. A. Davis holding a meeting which produced 22, and Mrs. Crank holding another with nine additions, while there were seven in regular pastoral work. The most notable gain was in missionary gifts, which increased from about $40 to more than $300.

—W. Daviess Pittman, of St. Louis, a man of large business affairs, but with a zeal for the church that gives him no rest where there is opportunity of service, conducted services at Eureka Springs, Ark., during his summer vacation. There were twenty-seven additions to the church, and interest in all matters pertaining to the Lord greatly increased. Brother Pittman believes an energetic, capable minister could accomplish great good there and recommends that such a one write to the elders of the church.

—Roger H. Fife has just completed his first year in evangelistic work with a record of 985 additions to the congregations, 890 of these being a net gain to the brotherhood. His largest ingatherings were in the meetings in the larger city churches; yet he has worked among the weaker churches, three of his meetings being with missions and two with country churches. Herbert H. Saunders, a fine singer and helper, has been associated with Brother Fife for the last six months. Their next meeting will be at Huntington, West Va., after the convention.

—Walter Scott Priest has just entered upon his fourth year of service at the Central Church, Columbus, O. During that period bills were first liquidated to the extent of $1,500, then the old property was sold, and a fine location secured for a new building which is now in the course of erection and will be one of the most commodious houses in the city. The total cost will be about $75,000, some $18,000 of which will yet to be raised in subscriptions. Of this amount $6,000 have already been promised. It is suggested that there may be some former members of the Central Church who would like to have a share in this worthy enterprise, and a certain number of windows have been set aside for purchase at from $15 to $25. During the three years 235 have been received into fellowship. About thirty-one others were baptized, but united with the new congregation at Linden Heights and with other churches in the city. The pastor has received the hearty support of the church and has entered upon another term of three years' ministry with every encouragement. It is expected that the new building will be occupied in about four or five months.

Board of Ministerial Relief of the Church of Christ.

Aid in the support of worthy, needy, disabled ministers of the Christian Church and their widows.

THIRD LORD'S DAY IN DECEMBER is the day set apart in all the churches for the offering to this work. If you make individual offerings, send direct to the Board. Wills and Deeds should be made to "BOARD OF MINISTERIAL RELIEF OF THE CHURCH OF CHRIST," a corporation under the laws of the State of Indiana." Money received on the Annuity Plan.

Address all communications and make all checks, drafts, etc., payable to BOARD OF MINISTERIAL RELIEF, 120 E. Market St., Indianapolis, Indiana.

—Dr. D. M. Breaker has just run across a back number of THE CHRISTIAN-EVANGELIST, which he missed, containing a paper read by J. J. Haley at our congress on "The Union of Baptists and Disciples." He suggests that it should be published in tract form and wishes to record himself as in favor of the movement looking to the reunion of these two bodies of Christians. Brother Breaker and others interested in this subject will be pleased to know that a number of brethren were selected at our congress at Indianapolis to have a conference with an equal number of our Baptist brethren with a view of publishing for the information of the two bodies a sort of irenicon setting forth the things in which they agree, and, perhaps, indicating some of the points of divergence. We believe such a statement will serve to show that we hold much more in common than has generally been supposed, and that the points of difference are not so vital as many think.

—Just on the eve of starting to the Buffalo convention we are in receipt of a letter from R. M. Denholme, of New Orleans, minister of the Soniat Avenue Christian Church, in that city, and Brother Charlton have left for the convention "armed with letters from the church, the governor of Louisiana, the mayor and the Progressive Union of this city inviting the National Convention to meet next year at dear old New Orleans. Should the convention decide to visit us, they will meet with no disappointment. A great welcome will be given and the arrangements will be thoroughly attended to." Now, that is pluck, and faith, and enterprise, and hospitality, all combined. Such faith ought to have its reward, but whether it will have it next year, with the Jamestown Exposition, and, no doubt, other cities as competitors, remains to be seen. We are prepared, however, to vouch for these brethren that should the convention decide to go there, no pains will be spared on the part of the New Orleans brethren to make it a great success.

—In a communication from Mrs. Princess Long, intended for last week's issue, but unavoidably crowded out, and which we can only condense here, she urges that some opportunity should be given somewhere, in some time during our national conventions, for the singing-evangelists to meet with evangelists and pastors that they may get acquainted with each other. This, she says, is especially due to the younger and more unknown men and women who are devoting themselves to this branch of evangelistic work—the singing of the gospel. At the same time the older and more experienced singers could give helpful suggestions to the younger ones, who, she is satisfied from the number of letters she is receiving, are anxious for advice and suggestions relative to their work. She believes there must come a larger recognition of the place of song in our evangelism, and believes that those who devote themselves with singleness of heart to this work, having the necessary qualifications, should be encouraged and assisted in every legitimate way. We hope to secure a few articles from Mrs. Long giving some of the results of her experience for the benefit of these younger singers, and perhaps from others, also.

✦ ✦

Unsweetened Condensed Milk.

Peerless Brand Evaporated Cream is ideal milk, collected under perfect sanitary conditions, condensed in vacuo to the consistency of cream, preserved by sterilization only. Suitable for any modification and adapted to all purposes where milk or

As We Go to Press.

Special to THE CHRISTIAN-EVANGELIST.
Kansas City, Mo., Oct. 14.—Closed tonight; 307 additions; Kansas City's greatest meeting. William J. Lockhart, Charles Altheide, Evangelists.—Frank L. Bowen.

Special to THE CHRISTIAN-EVANGELIST.
Union Star, Mo., Oct. 15.—Great co-operation meeting with Union Star and Orchid churches, 55 additions to date, 22 confessions yesterday; Saunders remains to close of meetings. We begin at Huntington, W. Va., Sunday.—R. H. Fife and H. H. Saunders, Evangelists.

Special to THE CHRISTIAN-EVANGELIST.
Bloomington, Ill., Oct. 14.—Two hundred and forty-five additions. Nine different services to-day. W. T. Brooks and J. H. Gilliland conducted meetings at the Second Church, Arthur K. Brooks and Edgar D. Jones at the First Opera house mass meeting for men this afternoon in the interest of good citizenship attended by nearly 1,000 men.—Brooks Bros.

✦ ✦

Children's Day for Home Missions.

About 800 Sunday-schools observed it during the present missionary year, and sent us more than $10,000 for American evangelization. This is a splendid gain. We hope that 1,200 schools will observe it this year, and send us $15,000.

The day generally observed is November 25, but many schools select other days. Some use our new exercise, Soldiers of the Cross, and take the offering on the day of the autumn rally in the Sunday-schools.

Our program and exercise are the best we have ever provided. Send for them. Observe a day in your Sunday-school for home missions. Make it a big day. Send for our exercise. It will cost you nothing.

American Christian Missionary Society, Y. M. C. A. Building, Cincinnati, O.

✦ ✦

Iowa Campaigns.

Two notable campaigns are planned for the coming winter in Iowa beginning in January, 1907, and continuing through three months. There will be the state-wide simultaneous evangelistic campaign, under the leadership of the state board, and a special evangelistic committee. With these is associated W. J. Wright, corresponding secretary of the American board. In preparation for this campaign will be the state-wide Bible school campaign, running through the third quarter of 1906. We have adopted the centennial motto, "All the Church in the Bible School, and as Many More," and believe Centennial Secretary W. R. Warren is right when he says: "To double the church membership we must first double the Bible school membership." The chief aim of the campaign will be, therefore, to increase the Bible school attendance.

The "sinews of war" for this campaign are being gathered in in the first quarterly payments for the current year, and these should all be paid by October 1. Some schools will advance the second quarter, and some will pay their full offering for the year. It is essential to the success of the campaign that we have a general response to this call.

The plans being adopted to stimulate the schools in their work include the red and blue button contest, the house to house canvass, with follow up plan, star systems, the campaign for our folks and their families, etc., etc. Contests between schools are being arranged. The Central Des Moines has challenged the First Church, Kansas City, Mo.

the way for the evangelistic efforts of 1907 and for decision day next February, many school will have decision days during the campaign this fall. All departments will be revived in some schools, new departments added.

Particulars concerning the Bible school campaign and suggestions as to methods will be sent on application to State Superintendent J. H. Bryan, Thirty-first and State streets, Des Moines, Iowa.

✦ ✦

Ministerial Exchange.

J. S. Vance, of Carthage, Mo., is ready to arrange with churches for meetings.

F. F. Guymon is commended as a song leader, worthy of the esteem of the brethren. He can be had for meetings by addressing him at Toledo, Ohio.

M. Lee Sorey, Arkansas City, Kan., knows a man of excellent quality, who has been preaching several years with a good, clean record, who can be had by some church in southern Kansas or Oklahoma at a very reasonable salary.

Churches desiring the services of an evangelist will do well to write S. V. Williams, General Delivery, Brooklyn, N. Y. His terms are most reasonable.

O. L. Adams, of Bethany, Neb., who has been preaching at Craig, Neb., writes that the brethren there desire to locate a preacher.

W. T. Walker, of Salem, Mo., would like work one-half time in reach of Salem, or can hold a few short meetings.

The Kentucky State Convention

The Kentucky C. W. B. M., the Kentucky Bible School Association, and the Kentucky Christian Missionary Convention, held their annual meetings in Louisville, September 24-27. It was the twenty-fourth annual meeting of the first named organization, the sixty-sixth anniversary of the second, and the thirty-fourth annual gathering of the third.

In point of attendance, interest manifested, work reported, work accomplished during the sessions, enthusiasm generated, and plans outlined for the future, this was said by many to have been the most successful convention in the history of our organized work in the state. The churches of the city entertained the delegates for lodging and breakfast. This is the first time this plan of entertainment has been attempted in a Kentucky convention, and it proved eminently satisfactory to all. It is becoming more and more apparent, however, that what is needed in Kentucky is some such place within the state as Bethany Park in Indiana, whither the tribes may annually go up, and, untrammeled by the social obligations which our past methods have imposed, give themselves unreservedly to the work in hand.

From the first session Monday night the interest and enthusiasm steadily increased, culminating in the splendid meetings of the last day. Addresses of welcome were made on behalf of the churches and citizens of Louisville, by Dr. S. S. Waltz, president of the Ministerial Association, and Judge Henry S. Barker of the Court of Appeals. Appropriate responses were made by Mrs. Carey E. Morgan, of Paris; H. D. Clark, of Mt. Sterling; and S. W. Bedford, of Owensboro.

The sessions of the C. W. B. M. were marked by the greatest interest and enthusiasm. The address of the president, Mrs. A. M. Harrison, of Lexington, and the report of the state organizer and secretary, Mrs. S. K. Yancey, of Lexington, showed the work in the state to be in a most prosperous condition. The membership in the state was reported to be 3,081, 141 new members having been added during the year. The amount contributed by these last year was $16,183.97. Forty-six auxiliaries were reported on the honor roll, ten of these gaining the distinction of star auxiliaries, having increased their membership 25 per cent over last year. Twenty-three new auxiliaries were reported. The Missionary Tidings has a circulation in the state of 1,769. Mrs. Sallie Ashbrook, of Cynthiana, reported encouraging progress in raising the $15,000 apportioned to Kentucky auxiliaries on the Centennial fund of $100,000.

The addresses of Miss Belle Bennett and Mrs. Nora Collins Ireland were of a high order. The ormer is president of the Woman's Home Mission Society of the Southern Methodist church, and spoke on "The Training School for Mission Workers." The latter is the living link of the Paris auxiliary, Porto Rico being her field of labor. Mrs. Mary S. Walden, of Danville; Mrs. W. T. Lafferty, of Cynthiana; Prof. F. C. Button and Bro. W. F. Smith, of Morehead, and A. J. Thompson, of Louisville, all made fine reports of their work. A touching memorial service was conducted by Miss Jessie Tandy, of Ghent. A sad incident of the convention was the sudden death of the mother of Mrs. Hattie Moody at Eminence. Mrs. Moody was in attendance at the convention when the sad message summoned her home.

The concluding session of the C. W. B. M. convention on Tuesday night was addressed by Mrs. Helen E. Moses, of Indianapolis; Miss Ada Boyd, living link of the Central Church auxiliary, Lexington, and who is home from Bilaspur, India, on a furlough, and Mrs. Luella St. Clair, president of Hamilton College.

All the sessions of the K. C. M. C. and the Bible School Association were attended by large crowds. This was one of the most orderly and faithfully attended conventions the writer has ever attended. The continual rain, the noise of the busy corner on which the First Church is situated and the many attractions of the city, did not seem to affect the attendance at all. The large auditorium was crowded nearly all the time, and, the interest in the proceedings at no time relaxed.

This report cannot speak in detail of the work of the sessions. Every moment was full of interest. Those presiding at the various periods were C. L. Loos, H. D. Clark, H. C. Garrison, and J. T. Kackley. The report of State Secretary H. W. Elliott showed an encouraging gain in receipts. Forty workers were employed during the year, who preached 4,451 sermons and gained 2,062 additions. Fifty-nine preachers were located, 27 Bible schools organized, and nine churches established. The work of the year closed with a good balance in the treasury.

R. M. Hopkins, reporting for the Bible school association, emphasized the Centennial enterprise of raising $25,000 to establish a chair of Bible school pedagogy in the College of the Bible, Lexington. The air was electric with the thought of this enterprise throughout the convention, and at the Thursday afternoon session, under the influence of the speeches by R. H. Crossfield, Marion Lawrance and E. L. Powell a perfect storm of subscriptions was precipitated, which could scarcely be checked by the chairman. In a short time, in sums ranging from $1,000 to $10 about $11,400 was raised to endow this chair. If the time had sufficed, several thousand dollars more would have been subscribed. When the time arrived for the address of Pres. E. Y. Mullins of the Southern Baptist Theological Seminary, the chairman had to absolutely refuse to receive any more gifts.

The establishment of this chair in the College of the Bible will make the third of its kind in institutions of learning in the country, the other two being in Vanderbilt University, Nashville, and the Southern Baptist Theological Seminary, Louisville. This was one of the most important and far-reaching accomplishments of the convention. The plan is to raise the entire $25,000 by issuing 2,500 shares of stock at $10 per share. The remaining stock will be rapidly taken by schools and churches not represented in the convention. The faculty and students of the College of the Bible attended this session in a body, and lent much to the interest of the proceedings.

Another forward move along educational lines made by the convention was the appointment of a committee to ascertain the attitude of our various schools in the state toward unifying all our educational interests. This committee is to prepare a feasible plan for such action and report to the next convention.

The committee on anti-saloon work reported seventy-four prohibition counties in the state, new local option territory being added almost every week under the operation of the County Unit bill passed by the last legislature.

The addresses were all up to the general high standard of the convention. R. L. Clark, of Mayfield, was fraternal delegate from South Kentucky. M. G. Buckner, of Harrodsburg spoke for the Kentucky Orphan's Home, taking for his subject, "The Slaughter of the Innocents." Carey E. Morgan, of Paris, spoke on "State Work." J. W. McGarvey had for his theme "Daniel in the Critic's Den." Miss Mary Finch, of Mays Lick gave an address on "The Purpose of State Bible School Work," and R. H. Crossfield, of Owensboro, discussed "Our Centennial Enterprise."

The "outside" speakers were Marion Lawrance, of Toledo, Ohio, known to every Bible school worker, and Pres. E. Y. Mullins, of Louisville. The former spoke on "The Sunday-school Star approaching its Zenith," and the latter had for his subject, "The Pastor and the Sunday-school." These addresses were beyond criticism and were listened to by great congregations. The address of Pres. Mullins did not begin till 5 o'clock in the afternoon, and he faced an audience that had been in session since 1:30 o'clock, Yet they seemed unwilling for him to cease after he had spoken nearly an hour.

The Louisville convention was a great convention.   W. N. BRINEY.
Louisville, Ky.

KENTUCKY CONVENTION SNAP SHOTS.

There were 1,033 delegates and visitors present outside of Louisville.

The following officers were elected by the C. W. B. M. convention, viz: President, Mrs. A. M. Harrison; Vice-Presidents, Mesdames Carey Morgan, John Gay, Jr., O. E. Hagerman; Secretary and Organizer, Mrs. S. K. Yancey; Treasurer, Mrs. O. L. Bradley; Superintendent Y. P. department, Mrs. Mary Walden; President South Kentucky department, Mrs. Elizabeth Seargeant.

The K. C. M. C. elected the following officers, viz: President, B. M. Arnett, Nicholasville; Vice-President, C. K. Marshall, Richmond; Secretary, B. M. Trimble, Mt. Sterling; State Evangelist and Treasurer, H. W. Elliott, Sulphur; Executive Committee, C. L. Loos, B. C. Deweese, R. N. Simpson and W. C. Morro, Lexington; C. E. Morgan, Paris; B. W. Trimble, Mt. Sterling and Geo. W. Kemper, Midway.

The Sunday-school convention elected the following officers, viz: President, Hume Logan, Louisville; Vice-Presidents, J. K. Bondurant, Paducah; W. T. Hinton, Paris, and C. E. Tate, Stanford; Secretary, R. N. Simpson, Lexington. The following were also selected to fill vacancies on the state board, viz: J. S. Carpenter, G. L. Sehon, Jos. Burge, J. S. Hilton.

We have never seen a larger gathering of preachers at a state convention. Nearly every preacher in Central Kentucky was on hand. This ought to mean much to the success of our state work the ensuing year.

The Louisville preachers "behaved themselves admirably, under the circumstances." They did their part well, and were here, there and everywhere serving to the comfort of their guests. Their little white caps were especially becoming! We tried to get a glimpse of Brother Powell with "his on," but couldn't.

Too much credit can not be given to Miss Florence Miller, who acted as chairman of the entertainment committee. She was greatly complimented on the graceful manner in which she filled her office.

Several of our staid and tried old bachelor-preachers were on hand, looking as bright and fresh as you please—but to no effect, as yet!

It was indeed a glad sight to see such men as C. L. Loos, J. W. McGarvey, J. B. Briney, and others of the older preachers, in health and strength, taking an active part in the deliberations of the convention.

The largest individual pledge toward the endowment of the proposed chair of Sunday-school pedagogy in the College of the Bible, was made by Brother Thomas, of Shelbyville, who gave $1,000. The Sunday-school at Covington, through its superintendent, Judge Fiske, also pledged $1,000.

The annual reports of Brothers Elliott and Hopkins were very gratifying and showed a splendid work done by them last year.

The work of the state board has been under the general supervision of H. W. Elliott as state evangelist for the past fourteen years, during which time it has greatly increased. He enters upon the present year with increased hopes and courage, and, if the churches support him as they should, this will be our banner year in state mission work.

The time and place of the next convention was left in the hands of the state board.

Midway, Ky.   GEO. W. KEMPER.

Western Pennsylvania Convention

The largest, most enthusiastic and in every way the best convention of this district has adjourned. The enrolled attendance was over three hundred, but as it was known that many came who did not register, the total attendance was probably six hundred. The simultaneous campaign last November interfered with the offering in many places, yet the receipts for the year were the largest in our history.

Nineteen years ago, when the present co-operation was formed, we had scarcely 7,000 members in the district; now we have 19,000. Of these, 4,001 in Allegheny county, and 3,437 in the region beyond, were gained under the fostering care of the board. In this county the property has increased from $70,000 to $400,200, of which $242,000 was gained under the board. In the outside counties the gain has been $185,800 under the co-operation. We have a million dollars in property to-day, and more members in Greater Pittsburg than we had in all Western Pennsylvania then.

Such churches as Central, Pittsburg, Beaver, Knoxville, Greensburg, Uniontown, Wilkinsberg, Observatory Hill, Homestead, and many others have been aided to become sources of strength and centers of influence. We will have nine counties in which we own property, and many cities in which there are from ten to forty Disciples calling for aid.

The program would have done credit to a national convention. Wallace Tharp preached the convention sermon on "Pioneer Night." J. Walter Carpenter, of Uniontown, Fred M. Gordon, of Knoxville, E. A. Cole, of Washington, delivered addresses on "Barton W. Stone," "Walter Scott," and "Alexander Campbell." The convention closed with a lecture by Joseph Clark, secretary of the Ohio Bible School Association. Space forbids the mention of other excellent addresses.

The C. W. B. M. had a half day. The reports showed they had kept pace with the brethren in their work. Five new auxiliaries with 120 members have been organized, and $5,000 sent to the National Board. Five new Junior Societies have been organized, $681 were paid by the auxiliaries for state fund. About $200 also came from special gifts to this fund.

The same officers were elected by both boards for the coming year except that J. Walter Carpenter takes the place of Geo. W. Knepper as superintendent of Christian Endeavor.

Notes.

E. E. Manley goes to Scranton November 1. Frank G. Longdon takes the work at Beech View under the board. The Banksville congregation will be moved to the new location where property has been purchased. Miss Sarah Klippelt leaves Central, after a long and faithful service, to return to her home in Mansfield, O. John A. Jayne takes the work at Belmar. O. H. Philipps has resigned after fourteen years at Braddock, to take charge of the "Christian Worker." Walter S. Rounds goes to Flatbush church, Brooklyn. He will take work in the University. C. H. Frick will go to Franklin and Butler to remain till churches are organized and buildings erected. N. W. Philipps has led the Greensburg church to pay its burden of debt. It was once feared the work would be lost.   HOWARD CRAMBLET.

Tennessee State Convention

Disciples of Christ have just been to the beautiful little city of Paris for their annual meeting, which was as fine a convention as was ever held by the brotherhood in Tennessee. Called to order by President Robert Stewart, of Knoxville, the convention was opened by prayer by R. P. Meeks, of Humboldt, after which the delegates were welcomed to the city by Judge A. B. Lamb. After this we listened to a sermon by President Stewart on "The Heart of Missions"—a fine subject to put all of us in the right spirit for a good missionary convention.

Tuesday morning, promptly on time, the meeting began its work. First was an able sermon on missions by W. H. Shelburne, who has had a number of years' experience in the evangelistic field. This was followed by an address by the Hon. H. M. Meeks, of Nashville, Tenn., on "Tennessee and the Church," and so well pleased was the convention with it that on motion it was ordered put into a tract and distributed throughout the state. Next came the report of A. I. Myhr, state secretary, which was his seventeenth annual report and showed we had made substantial gains all along the line of our work.

During the year ten were in the employ of the churches all the time and fifteen men a portion of the year or sufficient to make the year's work for one man. As a result of their labors about 800 members were added to our membership and sixty places were given help by the board during the year, which shows substantial work done when we consider that the whole number of Disciples in the state who are assisting in this work is not more than 15,000. About $15,000 was raised for this work and the permanent fund was increased until it now amounts to $14,500. There are about 175 preachers in the state who devote all their time to preaching. The amount of moneys raised for educational purposes was $30,000 and for all purposes about $150,000, or about $3 per member. Of course, this does not include moneys raised in Sunday-schools and Endeavor societies, as we have had no one giving his time wholly to Sunday-school work; but it was decided to put a man in the field at once, and E. S. Baker, of Jackson, was selected as our Sunday-school evangelist, and we hope to make a good showing during this year, as it is estimated we have 25,000 scholars in our schools in the state. With the help of our evangelist we hope to raise not less than $1,200 or $1,500 from the schools.

Tuesday afternoon L. D. Riddell, of Memphis, made a strong address on "The Four Years' Crusade and Its Effect on Tennessee."

Tuesday night, W. H. Sheffer, of Memphis, delivered one of the strongest sermons on Christian Union. It was illustrated by large colored charts.

Wednesday morning Brother McKissock, of Nashville, delivered an interesting

NEWS FROM MANY FIELDS

Kansas.

W. S. Lowe has closed seven fruitful years of work for the Kansas Christian Missionary Society as their superintendent, and has located with the church in Paola, Kan. His mantle fell unexpectedly and unsought upon me. It seems at this time to be too long and large, unless the ministers and members of the Church in the state will stand as an aid in every effort to carry out the instructions of the convention.

At this time there is a deficit of over $1,000. The board borrowed the money that the laborers might continue in the most important work entrusted to us.

November 4 is the day sacred to Kansas missions. Every church is urged to secure an offering from all their members. Plan for large things in Kansas this year by a large November offering. Let us work together now that we may rejoice together at the close of the year.

GEORGE E. LYON,
Superintendent of Kansas Missions.

A Happy Coming of Age.

The twenty-first anniversary of the church at Englewood, Chicago, was a very happy occasion. Sunday was Bible school day. Marion Stevenson giving a beautiful address in the morning and the regular Sunday-school hour was devoted to the Annual Poll Rally Day, with C. B. Jackson, superintendent, presiding. A striking incident of this session was when the class of Pastor Kindred rose to their feet seventy-nine strong. W. C. Merritt and Herbert Moninger were to the front in the Sunday-school workers' session, while the latter and W. C. Pearce, the international teachers' training secretary, and Marion Stevenson filled their parts on the program in the afternoon meeting, W. C. Pearce speaking also in the place of W. R. Jacobs, one of the best-known of Sunday-school workers, who was able to be present. A. McLean was one of the speakers on this anniversary, taking for his theme "The Sunday-school and World-wide Missions." Three of the members who have chosen the ministry for their life-work were called to the front—Walter Wright, who goes to Drake, and Charles Adams and William Madison, who are at Eureka. On Monday afternoon, the C. W. B. M. Auxiliary had their meeting, Dr. Mary Longdon and Mrs. A. B. Cole having the floor. In the evening Brother McLean gave his great lecture on Alexander Campbell. On Tuesday the Ladies' Aid was addressed by Brother Kindred and Mrs. C. B. Jackson gave an excellent report of the society, which has made a fine record. One of their contributions was $1,500 toward the purchase of the new church. A miscellaneous program was rendered in the afternoon, and a reception followed to Mr. and Mrs. J. H. Garrison, along with a goodly number of visitors. In the evening came the event of the occasion—Brother Garrison's address on "The Present Phase of the Christian Union Problem." The lay fever, which still held our brother in its grip, seemingly did not in any degree quench the fire which entered into the delivery of this splendid address. Had I space I would like to give some of the thoughts advanced and give some of my own views. The history of the Englewood church was traced in THE CHRISTIAN-EVANGELIST two years ago, when, under the leadership of our minister, C. G. Kindred, we dedicated our present edifice, beautiful for situation and representing a money value of close upon $40,000, with a debt to-day of less than $3,000. Our ideal of the years is at least partially realized—a beautiful church home and a creditable property, practically free of encumbrance, without slighting the chief obligation of every congregation to keep alive its missionary spirit; for while in the process of newly housing ourselves we became a living link in both the home and foreign field. Brother Kindred has just entered his eighth year with us and in the twenty-one years of this church's life B. H. Hayden served four years and N. S. Haynes six and one-

half years. The heart and interest of these former ministers were so interwoven with this church as to inseparably identify them with it. Our present minister is broad visioned and faith filled. Enlargement is always our watchword, and we are moving for the erection on the rear of our lots of the first section of a model Sunday-school building. We are planning for more living links in our chain. W. P. KEELER.

North Carolina.

The Piedmont district of North Carolina held its co-operation meeting with the church in Winston on September 28 and 29. There were about twelve delegates from outside the city. About twenty churches are located in this section of the state. A number of them are small and not very active. Our convention had reports from most of the congregations.—W. C. Walker, state evangelist, was present, and gave a rousing sermon on Friday night. He also was very helpful in the discussions of the convention. Dr. B. T. Bitting, the beloved physician and minister of the church at Spray, gave a stirring discourse on "Evangelization in Our District." The convention determined to endeavor to secure money from the churches and put an evangelist in our field, to "set in order the things that are wanting," and plant new missions as soon as possible. A committee on evangelizing was appointed, consisting of five members. The choir of the Winston Church gave some special music at the night service. We have now fifteen in our chorus and a good male quartette.—We are looking forward to our mortgage burning, October 24. We hope to have with us H. C. Bowen, pastor when the church was built, and W. J. Wright, corresponding secretary, who held a meeting in Winston some years ago.

Winston-Salem, N. C.　　J. A. HOPKINS.

Nebraska.

Knox P. Taylor, of Illinois, held a Bible school institute at Chester, and is now at Belvidere. He can be had for further dates. Write him or G. R. Dill at Belvidere.—One added by baptism and one by statement at Minden, where B. H. Whiston preaches. Two by baptism and one by letter at Stella September 30. A. L. Ogden, minister half time. Five added at Ansley September 23; T. C. McIntire is the regular preacher.—N. T. Harmon is open for evangelistic meetings. Address him at David City.—Bloomington will begin a meeting October 28 with J. Stuart Miller, of Edison, as evangelist. G. C. Johnson is the regular preacher there.—Nine were added to the church at York, where Thomas Maxwell ministers, during September—5 by baptism and 4 by letter. There have been 40 added at regular services during the year ending October 1—18 of these by baptism and 31 by letter and statement. They have a splendid Bible school, with Mrs. E. E. Bradwell superintendent.—Bert Wilson is at Virginia in a meeting. J. G. Olmstead is the singer.—Austin and McVey are at Beaver Crossing in a tent meeting. Had 14 added when last heard from. Medicine show and rainy weather were hindering causes, but good audiences prevailed.—State Evangelist Forell is at Vesta. This is a small place, and our work is new, being just a year old. Two added at last report—Brother Forell is the Living Link evangelist for the church at Clay Center, where A. G. Smith ministers. This congregation took up the suggestion to become a Living Link in state missions very enthusiastically, and pledged the necessary $300 in a short time on Lord's day morning. When it is remembered that this church has built a new church and parsonage in the last three years, it will be seen that they are a missionary people.—State Evangelist Whiston has been and still is in a tent meeting at Norfolk. The cause is new here also, and the problems are hard to solve. The rainy week that prevailed at the very first, with cold weather, was a serious handicap. They

now have a stove in the tent, and are beginning to get a fair hearing. Eight had been added up till October 4. The meeting continues. The church is preparing to build a house on the lots purchased this summer.—O. A. Adams has been called and has accepted the work of state evangelist under the Nebraska board. His work will begin October 30, probably at Mason City, where we have a few brethren.—The meeting at Danbury closed October 1. John T. Smith, of Nebraska City, was the preacher. There were 3 baptisms and 3 by statement.—Last month's report made this letter say that 55 would probably be gathered together in the Adams meeting. This should have read 25. The actual number ing was held the last two weeks by J. D. For is 23, as reported after organization. This meeting, and begun by Charles and Jean Cobbey.—George Light has gone to Trenton, Neb, and writes that he will hold a meeting there and at Cornell. We have an unused house at Trenton, and a small congregation at Cornell.—Samuel Gregg, of Jefferson, Iowa, preached at Fremont October 1, and was expected there again on October 7. He may be called to that field.—L. N. Early has been called to the pastorate at Broken Bow, and is now at work in that field. The church is planning a new house on a new location.—Z. O. Doward, state superintendent of Christian Endeavor for the Christian churches, attended the State Union C. E. convention at Hastings. He reports a very enthusiastic convention.　　W. A. BALDWIN, Cor. Sec.

Lincoln, Neb.

Catarrh Cannot be Cured

with LOCAL APPLICATIONS, as they cannot reach the seat of the disease. Catarrh is a blood or constitutional disease, and in order to cure it you must take internal remedies. Hall's Catarrh Cure is taken internally, and acts directly on the blood and mucous surfaces. Hall's Catarrh Cure is not a quack medicine. It was prescribed by one of the best physicians in this country for years and is a regular prescription. It is composed of the best tonics known, combined with the best blood purifiers, acting directly on the mucous surfaces. The perfect combination of the two ingredients is what produces such wonderful results in curing Catarrh. Send for testimonials free.

F. J. CHENEY & CO., Props., Toledo, O.
Sold by Druggists, price 75c.
Take Hall's Family Pills for constipation.

Advancing the Work in Texas.

At Haskell, Texas, there were 23 additions up to October 3, mostly by letter and statement. Brother Stanley lead the music.——The Haskell people are planning to have a missionary convention in November. J. C. Mason has agreed to be with them. This is a great church.——We go from here to Crowell, Texas, which is a missionary field where we have a few members anxious that the people shall have our plea. Crowell is a fine new town in northwest Texas.

J. L. HADDOCK

Cotner.

A. J. Hollingsworth is doing acceptable work at Tecumseh, while a student at Cotner. Lincoln McConnell began a union meeting there October 14.——J. E. Clutter has closed a year's work at Irvington, while pursuing his course of study. He will probably preach at Bower half time.—— T. B. McDonald has accepted the Waco work and will move there in a few months.——Churches within reach of Bethany could have some good work done by active, earnest preachers who are in Cotner this year. Write Frank Woten, secretary ministerial association, Bethany, Neb.

Bethany, Neb.   O. L. ADAMS.

Not a Superstitious Church.

On October 7, the church at Peru, Ind., observed its thirteenth anniversary. A supply of new "Praise Hymnals" was on hand for the service, as was also a new individual communion set which was used for the first time by this congregation. Eleven persons were added during the day and the cash offerings amounted to $80. The church was organized thirteen years ago by Charles L. Fillmore with thirteen charter members. The first trustees were elected on the thirteenth of the month. There are now thirteen members on the official board, thirteen classes in the Bible school and thirteen teachers. On last Lord's day the contribution of the school was $13 and the pastor lives at No. 113. We are not superstitious, but believe that this is our lucky number, as the church has never had any trouble or friction and has always prospered and is in a good, healthy growing condition with a bright future before it.

Peru, Ind.   C. H. DEVOE.

How the Church was Built at Quinlan, Okla.

A new house of worship of the Disciples at Quinlan, Okla., has been dedicated. J. M. Monroe, Cor. Sec. of Oklahoma, preached the sermon. Brother Monroe knows how to strike silver and gold bearing veins. Five hundred dollars were needed to cover all indebtedness on the church. This was readily pledged. The Church Extension Board let this congregation have $500, but this amount is covered with pledges. Our rapid and healthy growth at Quinlan has strengthened my faith in the success of our plea. Seven months ago there were about a dozen scattered brethren there, and no organization at all. During February of this year J. D. Lawrence, the living-ling evangelist, then supported by THE CHRISTIAN-EVANGELIST, held a meeting. As a result of the meeting a church of over 100 members was organized. The majority of those who came into the church were young people, who after their primary obedience. The brethren at once began to prepare for themselves a church house. The corresponding secretary made a trip to Quinlan and secured $500 in pledges. The town site company donated four lots. But after the building had been started the brethren seemed to lose interest. There was talk of giving up the undertaking of building the house. During March a young man, fresh from Texas Christian University, landed in Quinlan. The text of his first sermon was "So built we the walls." He told the people under what difficulties the walls and temple at Jerusalem were rebuilt. During the week this young man worked with hammer and

saw, and he would then preach three sermons each Sunday in the surrounding school houses. As a result of his leadership the building, with the exception of the tower, was soon completed, chairs and a bell were bought, and the church dedicated free of debt. The young man who brought this about was Theo. Edwards, late of Australia. I predict for Brother Edwards great success in the ministry. The corresponding secretary of Oklahoma said to me last week, "These Australians are pure gold."   ED. S. MCKINNEY.

Woodward, Okla.

Kentucky.

At Berea, Ky., A. Van Winkle is getting matters well in hand for a vigorous winter campaign. From twelve to fifteen hundred students are expected this winter and a great opportunity is presented for preaching the gospel. W. J. Cocke had a good month. There were 20 added. He is now in a meeting at Erlanger with L. B. Haskins. Brother Haskins has resigned to take effect January 1. He is a fine man and we expect to see him give up this field.——A lot has been secured and $605.50 raised to build a house of worship at Harlan Court House. Another county seat will soon be provided with a house that is Christian only.——Harlan C. Runyan had two additions at Latonia, burned the Church Extension notes that had been paid and reports that Mrs. Whipps has given on the annuity plan a house and lot worth $1,600 adjoining the church lot. Either the enlargement of the house of worship or the building of a new house is imperative. Not room for the people who attend the services.——At Bardstown J. B. Briney and the church will be helped in a meeting by Dr. M. Gano Buckner, Harrodsburg.——Valley View had the services of D. C. McCallum half time. A meeting is planned.——H. W. Elliott was at work all September in the interest of state missions. He preached every Sunday at one or more places, attended two conventions aside from the state convention, added two, raised $1,781.56, reported a balance on hand at Louisville of $1,188.84, and we increased the amount given by

the churches over the former year $ made us able to meet our obligations to September and left a balance on ha We enter a new year with greater than ever before. Already insistent being made for help. By the time print letters concerning the Novem will have been mailed. The replies ters must in a large measure gover in arranging the work for 1907. Pr us some idea as to your willingness during the coming year. Let all t and all the churches give us immedia of their plans relative to our work in

Sulphur, Ky.   H. W. ELL

St. Francois Co-operati

The St. Francois County Christian operation convened at Libertyville, I tober 5, Judge G. O. Nations presid one of the best meetings for many key note was struck by E. J. Fenst his sermon on "The teachings of Je Christian Church as the exponent of ing." He was followed by Mrs. I spoke for the C. W. B. M. Judge a masterful way presented the plea ciples of Christ, based on the de Thomas Campbell in 1809, looking This led to the Centennial aims, pre O. Rogers. In the absence of T. A evening session was devoted to a ve round table talk on Bible school wor by Edward Owers. Saturday morning opened with a strong and helpful ac W. Kokendoffer. Geo. T. Smith rep educational feature of our work, a Owers made a very strong plea for paper in every Christian home." 1 lowed by a solution to one of the p lems confronting the church to-day— but by no means least, with a serm to Remove Hindrances" by R. O. R dollars were pledged on condition can be raised to place a good evan county for a year. The officers e Judge G. O. Nations, president; O. president; J. E. Cover, treasurer; E secretary.

Evangelistic

We invite ministers and others to send reports of meetings, additions and other news of the churches. It is especially requested that additions be reported as "by confession and baptism," or "by letter."

Alabama.

Mobile, Oct. 9.—Twelve accessions by letter and statement since last report.—J. H. Robinson, secretary Official Board.

California.

Ocean Park, Oct. 8.—Two confessions yesterday. Eight since last report. Membership doubled since January 1.—George Ringo.

Illinois.

Saybrook, Oct. 9.—Two added—1 by baptism and 1 by letter.—James N. Thomas.

Scottville, Oct. 13.—Am in a good meeting here. Four additions last night. Fine audiences. E. E. Booker- conducts the singing.—M. L. Anthony, evangelist.

Long Point, Oct. 8.—Three weeks' meeting closed yesterday. Thirteen added—10 confessions. W. G. McColley, Pontiac, Ill., did the preaching, and Mrs. J. E. Powell, Bloomington, Ill., led the singing.—F. W. Sutton, pastor.

Indiana.

Russellville, Oct. 8.—Two confessions last night. A splendid meeting here. Have had several confessions already.

New Palestine, Oct. 10.—Seven additions since September 23. Work is taking on a prosperous front.—Carl H. Barnett, pastor.

Monticello, Oct. 8.—Nineteen additions at Cullen Creek—18 baptisms. A. W. Jackman did the preaching, assisted in the singing by F. E. Truckness, of La Fayette, Ind.

Coothersville, Oct. 9.—Closed a meeting at this place last Thursday night which resulted in 13 additions, 10 by confession and baptism and 3 by letter. The music was in charge of Mrs. A. W. Crabb, of Brazil, Ind., and Miss Bertha Short, of Seymour, Ind.—A. W. Crabb.

Indian Territory.

Amber, Oct. 8.—Three confessions last night. Twenty-four added in six days. Good prospects. —Robert E. Rosenstein.

Sapulpa, Sept. 10.—Through the efforts of H. S. Kline and myself, I have added in a few days' meeting at Stilwell, I. T.—A. M. Harral.

Muskogee, Oct. 9.—Closed a two weeks' meeting at Ada with 30 additions. Am now in a meeting at Muskogee with George H. Farley, pastor.—C. F. Trimble.

Iowa.

Cumberland, Oct. 6.—We are holding a meeting with conversions, assisted by Miss Mayme Eisenbarger, of Bethany, Mo.—C. E. Dunkleberger.

Des Moines, Oct. 11.—Had two additions at Salem, Mo., Sunday.—H. L. Lewis.

Mt. Pleasant, Oct. 11.—Work here is opening up nicely. One added recently by statement.—L. A. Chapman.

Idaho.

Nampa, Oct. 1.—Closed Nampa meeting with 12 accessions. Two confessions, 4 letters and 6 by statement. P. R. Burnett did good service as singing evangelist. Have had 128 additions in the four missionary meetings in Idaho this summer.—George C. Ritchey.

Weiser, Oct. 8.—Four additions yesterday.—G. M. Read.

Kansas.

Manhattan, Oct. 8.—Two added yesterday.—W. T. McLain.

Smith Center, Oct. 8.—Closed a meeting at Stuart with 7 additons, 5 baptisms.—F. E. Blanchard.

Pleasanton, Oct. 9.—Closed a three weeks' meeting here resulting in 44 additions, 30 confessions, 14 otherwise. Have been pastor here eight months. All departments of work are doing well.—O. A. Ismand.

Kentucky.

Hazel Green, Oct. 10.—Two added by letter yesterday.—H. L. Atkinson.

Lawrenceburg, Oct. 10.—Closed an interesting meeting of 12 days for the Fox Creek (Ky.) church, with 15 baptisms. The members were so aroused that they meet this week to organize a weekly prayer-meeting, and expect to have preaching twice instead of once a month. The Lawrenceburg church generously gave me the time, and this marks the beginning of mission work in Anderson, in which our churches will give its minister to weak country churches in an effort to revive the work and lead to closer co-operation and fellowship. A Girls' Circle was recently organized with 27 members, and an auxiliary to the C. W. B. M. with 19 members. Have

a club for boys with 19 members. Two recently added by letter, one by confession.—Walter C. Gibbs, minister.

Richmond, October 11.—We begin meeting here to-night. Church had rally last night. Good congregation.—H. A. Northcutt, evangelist, J. S. Zeran and wife, singers.

Missouri.

Flat River, Oct. 7.—One by baptism.—Edward Owers.

Canton, Sept. 30.—Five additions at Holliday since last report.—Rolla G. Sears.

Plattsburg, Oct. 6.—Had eight baptisms in a short meeting at Perrin.—J. P. Pinkerton.

Laplata, Oct. 9.—Three confessions and baptisms last Lord's day.—Percy T. Carnes, minister.

Columbia, Oct. 9.—Five were received into membership at Friendship last Sunday.—Charles E. Robinson.

Knobnoster, Oct. 10.—R. A. Blalock closed a three weeks' meeting at Valley City, October 7, with 39 conversions.—R. H. Benton.

Ethel, Oct. 11.—Twenty-eight added since last Sunday. Five last night. Interest good. Meeting continues.—Irving Taylor LeBaron.

Milan, Oct. 8.—Five confessions yesterday in our meeting in the Zion Methodist Church. We go next to Milan, Mo.—S. J. Vance, evangelist.

Joplin, Oct. 1.—One meeting with home forces resulted in 26 additions. F. F. Guymon, of Toledo, Ohio led the singing.—George L. Peters.

Kansas City, Oct. 8.—Two more additions yesterday to the Budd Park Church; 61 the past 13 months at regular services.—B. L. Wray, pastor.

Bethany, Oct. 11.—A successful meeting at Hale closed with 20 added, 11 by baptism. W. L. Harris of Bethany, Neb., did the preaching.—C. C. Taylor.

Bethany, Oct. 11.—Have just closed a meeting at Bethel church near Cumberland, Iowa, with 24 confessions.—C. E. Dunkleberger is the pastor.—Mayme Eisenbarger.

Madison, Oct. 8.—R. B. Havener closed a two weeks' meeting at Ash last Friday with 11 additions. The church is indebted to the State Board for the loan of its servant.—J. B. Corwine.

Eldon, Oct. 10.—We are in a good meeting at Oleon, Mo. Meeting two weeks old. Ten confessions and 9 by relationship. Meeting continues. C. O. McFarland and wife are our evangelists.—W. H. Scott, minister.

Warrensburg, Oct. 10.—Have closed a meeting at Woodland with 16 additions, 10 by confession. Had been no service in the church for three years. Was assisted by my brother as singer. We begin at Knobnoster next Lord's day.—King Stark.

Crocker, Oct. 10.—I recently assisted Clark Smith in a meeting at Aldrich, resulting in 12 accessions, 7 by obedience, 5 by letter. Am now in a meeting at Crocker. Brother O'Neal and wife are singers for me. Four additions last night.—Joseph Gaylor.

Downing, Oct. 9.—T. A. Hedges, with the aid of home forces, has just closed a two weeks' meeting resulting in 12 additions, 8 by confession and baptism, 2 by letter, and 2 by statement. All departments of church work are greatly strengthened and revived.—W. B. Smith.

Montana.

Billings.—Closed the Jacksonville (Ill.) meeting with 112 additions. Begin here last Lord's day with O. F. McHargue. Howard Saxton and wife have charge of the music.—J. H. O. Smith.

Ohio.

Leipsic, Oct. 9.—Five accessions at regular services last Lord's day evening. One by primary obedience and 4 by letter. One by letter not previously reported.—H. C. Boblitt, minister.

Oklahoma City, Oct. 9.—Six additions to First Church last Sunday.—S. B. Moore.

Oklahoma.

Beaver City, Oct. 9.—Closed a seven days' meeting at Elmwood, resulting in the organization of a church with 25 members.—Walter Renner.

Perry, Oct. 10.—Have just closed a two weeks' meeting at Sumner, with 10 additions—four baptisms, 4 by letter and statement and two from other religious bodies.—L. L. Kirtley.

Philippine Islands.

Vigon, Aug. 27.—Baptized one at Bucay; 12 at San Jose last week. One reported from San Quentin.—Hermon P. Williams.

South Dakota.

Lead, Oct. 8.—Closed a 26 days' meeting with five accessions by statement and letter. J. E. Lintt from Lincoln, Neb., was our song leader.—W. B. Harter.

Tennessee.

Union City, Oct. 9.—Herbert Yeuell and W. E.

M. Hackleman assisted pastor J. J. Castleberry in the Union City Tennessee Annual meeting lasting 12 days with 23 added.

Texas.

Ladonia, Oct. 8.—Closed our meeting at Marble Falls, Texas, with 30 additions in all. Organized a church of aggressive workers. A Sunday-school was also organized. This is a new but very promising work.—V. Spicer and E. M. Douthit, evangelists.

Grand Falls, Oct. 8.—Closed a two weeks' meeting here with 11 added, 10 confessions. We go next to Carlsbad, New Mexico.—S. W. Jackson and wife.

SUBSCRIBERS' WANTS.

Advertisements will be inserted under this head at the rate of two cents a word, each insertion, all words, large or small, to be counted and two initials being counted as a word. Advertisements must be accompanied by remittance, to save bookkeeping.

SEND $1.00 to J. A. Cunningham, Tupelo, Miss., for his twelve sermons pronounced "Masterpieces," and his "Blue and Gray."

SEND for catalog of Christian University, Canton, Mo. Departments—Preparatory, Classical, Scientific, Biblical, Commercial and Music. For ladies and gentlemen. Address Pres. Carl Johann, Canton, Mo.

FOR SALE—General store and fixtures, in Illinois town on Illinois Central. Good country, fine trade. Half interest in private bank goes with the deal, if desired. Owner has business in St. Louis—the reason for selling. Member of the Christian Church preferred. Address B., care CHRISTIAN-EVANGELIST.

Sunday-School

October 28, 1906.

JESUS ANOINTED IN BETHANY.—
Matt. 26:6-16.

Memory verses, 12, 13.

Golden Text.—She hath wrought a
good work upon me. Matt. 26:10.

It is unfortunate that, in giving this
lesson its place in the course, the committee did not put it in its probable
chronological order. While Matthew
records the incident of the anointing in
Bethany immediately before the Last
Supper, both Mark and John put it just
before the Triumphal Entry. John even
tells exactly when it occurred—"six
days before the passover." Since
Matthew is never much interested in
chronological sequence but prefers a
topical arrangement, the harmonists generally agree that the anointing at Bethany occurred on the Sabbath preceding
the Triumphal Entry. It was thus the
last event before the beginning of Passover week.

Simon the leper was probably a man
whom Jesus had, at some earlier time,
cleansed of his leprosy. There is a dramatic force in bringing together in the last
hour before the beginning of the week
of suffering and death, the Great Healer,
Lazarus whom he had raised from the
dead, and Simon, who had been restored
from what was almost equivalent to
death.

The criticism made by the disciples
(John says by Judas alone) against
Mary's lavish outpouring of precious
ointment, is a piece of the perpetual outcry of short-sighted souls against everything which is not palpably and materially useful. They could understand well
enough the virtue of feeding the poor—
truly a most substantial and excellent
virtue. But the virtue and value of a
beautiful act of love, the fragrance of
the spikenard poured out in utter devotion as the precious symbol of the
heart's complete surrender—these were
hidden from them. They smelled the
ointment. It was agreeable—and waste-
fully costly. As their nostrils could not
catch the finer aroma which, going forth
from the spirit of Mary's gracious deed,
has made its sweetness felt through all
the Christian centuries and throughout
the world.

A beautiful act is always worth its
cost—if it is beautiful and perfect
enough. The poor are not robbed by
any outpouring of devotion however extravagant. We do not gain in practical
helpfulness by withholding either time
or money from worship. Whatever
tends to the truest cultivation and the
most eloquent expression of devotion
is thoroughly practical.

❋ ❋

Picture of War Engine "General."

A beautiful colored picture, 18x25 inches,
of the historic old engine "General" which
was stolen at Big Shanty, Ga., by the An-

Midweek Prayer-Meeting

October 24, 1906.

A CHURCH UNDER FALSE TEACH-
ING.—Rev. 2:18-29.

"My God, my Strength, my Hope,
On thee I cast my care,
With humble confidence look up,
And know thou hearest my prayer
Give me on thee to wait.
Till I can all things do—
On thee, almighty to create,
Almighty to renew.

"I want a Godly fear,
A quick-discerning eye,
That looks to thee when sin is near,
And bids the tempter fly;
A spirit still prepared,
And armed with jealous care,
Forever standing on its guard,
And watching unto prayer."

It is not difficult for Bible readers to
know the doctrine whether it be of God.
One of the favoring conditions under which
destructive teachings are propagated is ignorance of the Word of God. To the
book, O Israel! There are knowledge, divine approval and life.

Jezebel is the personification of worldliness. Her lures were promises of pleasure
addressed to physical sensation or the pride
of life. Spiritual joys or the will of God
were not considered. The denouement was
unquenchable thirst, a looking forward to
wrath to come, and will kill her children
with death.

Strong evidence of our divine origin is
that countless men and women are naturally better than their priests and the moral
instruction administered by them. In all
the religious denominations are those of
Christian character notwithstanding serious
errors of teaching and belief. The inherent righteousness is implanted of God and
is stronger than the false teachings of man.

Thyatira was guilty of easy complacency
in the heresies of Jezebel. This lesson is
very significant to church elders whose duty
it is to watch over the flocks and see on
what they are being fed. All teachings
permitted must be tested by Gospel standards and forbidden if deficient in or in
excess of Bible authorization, and followed
simplicitly if in accordance with the Word.

There are errors of teachings atoned for

so far as the teacher is concerned by orthodoxy of life. On the other hand the
pronouncement of the most correct principles is often more than nullified by
heterodoxy of practice. Where there is
perfect consistency between theories of life,
harmonious with the Scriptures and one's
daily life, there is earth's true nobility.

The Spirit's admonition to the seven
churches which were in Asia to hold faithful unto the end were not observed. In
their faithfulness would have been their
glory. In their disloyalty was their doom.
They were in Asia, to-day they are only in
history. Though a forest may become extinct, some of the individual trees may have
beautifully completed their cycle. Thyatira
has only a name, but some of her membership may be glorious in the skies. Though
we be identified with a congregation whose
works are not worth the candle, still, individually, we may win divine approval.

❋ ❋

Christian Endeavor

By Thomas Curtis Clark

October 28, 1906.

MISSIONS TO AFRICANS.—Psalms 68:28-35.

DAILY READINGS.

M.	An Ethiopian Forecast.	2 Chron. 14:9-13.
T.	A Soul Saved.	Psa. 87:1-7.
W.	The Power of God.	Isa. 45:14-16.
T.	An Important Question.	Jer. 13:22-24.
F.	The Ethiopians.	Amos. 9:7-10.
S.	Ethiopia's Appeal.	Psa. 68:28-35.
S.	An Ethiopian Convert.	Acts 8:26-38.

"I know of a land that is sunk in shame,
Of hearts that faint and tire—
And I know of a Name, a Name, a Name,
Can set that land on fire.
Its sound is a band, its letters flame—
I know of a Name, a Name, a Name,
Will set that land on fire."

Twelve hundred missionaries in Africa! Good, we say. But, when we consider the vastness of the field, we are led to say of this body of workers, "What are these among so many?" Africa has a population of 200,000,000. The continent embraces about one-fourth of the land area of the globe. Europe, the United States, India, China and the British Isles could be placed within her borders.

It was Stanley who applied the term "Dark Continent" to Africa. This has a peculiar fitness as applied to this continent: first, because Africa alone, at the beginning of the nineteenth century, lay in unpenetrated darkness; second, because it is the one continent whose population is composed almost entirely of dark peoples; third, it is the one continent whose native religion is without sacred writings and definite systems.

In Africa to-day there are 45 societies at work. They are represented by 1,200 missionaries, 1,000 stations and about 1,000,000 Protestant adherents. The Bible has been translated in whole or in part into 70 languages. Thirty years ago there was not a convert in all Central Africa, to-day there are over 60,000; thirty years ago there were no churches or schools, to-day there are over 2,000 places of worship and instruction; then there were no pupils, to-day there are 300,000; then, no native workers, to-day there are 100 ordained evangelists and over 3,000 helpers among the natives.

The "roll-call of heroes" would certainly not be complete without the names of Moffatt, the dauntless pioneer; Livingstone, the missionary explorer; Mackenzie, the missionary statesman; Mackay, the devoted diplomat and scholar; Johnson, Crowther, Steere, Arnot, Greenfell, the Combers, Hannington, Coillard, Hore—all these were among those who, by faith, "subdued kingdoms, wrought righteousness, turned to flight the armies of the aliens." Like the heroes of old, they "endured as seeing that which is invisible." They "looked for a city, whose builder and maker is God."

Christianity is not alone in her effort to capture Africa for herself. The Moslems are to-day stirred with a genuine missionary zeal and are taking great steps in accomplishing their purpose. The question is, shall Africa be Mohammedan or Christian? With millions of adherents already in the heart of the continent the advantage in numbers is clearly on the side of the "false prophet." The outlook, indeed, would be discouraging, did we not have the prophetic assurance that the time will come

when "the earth shall be full of the knowledge of the Lord, as the waters cover the sea."

That "the blood of the martyrs is the seed of the church" is no mere sentiment, is amply evidenced by the history of missions in Africa. From statistics furnished by the seven leading missionary societies of the United States, it is estimated that the average length of service of the missionaries under their auspices has been eight years, and that since 1833 these seven societies have given 195 lives for Africa. Consider the career of Livingstone, the greatest of African missionaries. He travelled thirty thousand miles through parching thirst or drenching rains. He made graves for his wife and child in the dense forests, and finally in the spring of 1873 was himself found by his faithful black men, kneeling by his bed of grass, his candle still burning, his head resting on both his hands, his spirit gone to Him, in whom he had "lived, moved and had his being" through all those years of physical suffering and defeat.

※ ※

People's Forum

A New Idea.

To the Editor of THE CHRISTIAN-EVANGELIST:

The preacher, in the book of Ecclesiastes, says: "There is no new thing under the sun." Perhaps the preacher was talking about *real* things and not chimeras, about facts and not fiction. For surely a preacher in THE CHRISTIAN-EVANGELIST of recent date has given to the world a new *idea* that a man may have a Christian *character* and not be a *Christian*. I have long thought that there was a popular delusion abroad in ecclesiastical circles that a man may be a Christian and not have a Christian *character*. The way many church members live leads to that conclusion. But that a man can have a Christian character and yet not be a Christian, when it is that very thing that makes him a Christian, is a brand new idea. I have wondered whether such a piece of fancy was ever entertained by any human being before. It may be, but in all my travels in the realm of religious literature I have never met with the vagary.

That a man may have a Christian character and not be a *perfect* Christian, I can easily believe. We are all incomplete in some respects. Who understands Christianity thoroughly, and who complies perfectly with each and every item of its doctrine and its life?

I frequently meet an old soldier minus an arm or a leg. Does this defect outlaw him as a man, or as a citizen, or a patriot? If incompleteness outlaws a man as a Christian, then we are all undone.

The same reasoning applies to churches. Is a church not a Christian church because it is not in complete accord with the New Testament model or ideal of a church of Christ? If so, then there is no ecclesiastical body on earth to-day that can be called the Christian church, or a Christian church. They are all outlawed, all undone.

The Pope of Rome with his claims to infallibility in his interpretations of Scripture is not without his rivals even among Protestants.　　　A. B. JONES.

Liberty, Mo.

❋ ❋

If extremely low colonist rates to California, Oregon, Washington and all points west will interest you, write L. E. Townsley, G. A. Union Pacific R. R. Co., 903 Olive, St. Louis.

OBITUARIES.

[Notices of Deaths, not more than four lines, inserted free. Obituary memoirs, one cent per word. Send the money with the copy.]

ROBERTSON.

The faithful wife of R. S. Robertson, who is now pastor of the Christian Church at Osborn, Kan., departed this life September 26, 1906. She was a good mother and faithful servant of Christ to the end. By her teaching and influence in the home she helped to lead her entire family of seven children into the kingdom of Christ. Funeral services were held at Jewell City, where the remains were laid to rest.　B. A. CHANNER.

WELLS.

Mrs. Jane E. Wells, wife of the late Levi Wells, of Pompey, N. Y., passed away at the "Hill Top" House in that village, September 18. Her sterling qualities of character, combined with a bright and sunny temperament, gave her an interesting and attractive personality, which greatly endeared her to her friends. She went to Pompey from her home in Syracuse, N. Y., for her usual summer outing on August 1. Soon after her arrival she sustained a fracture of the hip, which, while it may not have been the immediate cause of her death, hastened it. Her funeral services were held at the Church of Christ in Pompey September 21. She leaves two sisters—Mrs. Cordelia A. Blinn and Mrs. Adaline S. Rockwell, of 111 Merriman avenue, Syracuse, N. Y.

ARMSTRONG.

Elizabeth Dustin Armstrong, *nee* Holton, was born at Lincoln, Ill., April 3, 1875, and died at Springfield, Ill., September 3, 1906. On March 15, 1905, she was married to W. H. Armstrong, who grieves at her early departure. She was the youngest of six children born to T. T. and Ellen C. Holton. Besides her parents and husband, she is survived by one brother, Campbell Holton, Bloomington, Ill.; Helen Lucas, Osawatomie, Kan.; Pauline Evans, Elkhart, Ill.; Anna McConnell, Lincoln, Ill., and Mary Rue, Tallula, Ill. When she was twelve years old she made the good confession under the preaching of L. M. Robinson, and was baptized by her father. She was a faithful Christian and a beautiful spirit. Her funeral was held at the home of her brother in Bloomington, and her body was laid to rest in the cemetery there.

Lincoln, Ill.　　W. H. CANNON.

TANNER.

James Washington Tanner, son of Joseph and Malinda Tanner, was born October 23, 1835, near Eagle Village, Ind., and died at his home in Stilwell, Ill., September 6, 1906. In 1854 he was married to Elizabeth Weer, and had one son, Francis E. Tanner, of Stilwell. In 1855 he moved to Hancock county, Ill. In 1859 death removed his chosen companion. He was married to Ary J. Short December 19, 1861. Of this union were born five children—Arlie L., Martha L., Everett E., Ada F. and Herbert J.—four on whom survive, Arlie L. having died in 1866. He served one year in the Civil War. He united with the Christian Church in 1846, and served as elder of the Stilwell congregation for over thirty years. His life has been one of earnest devotion to the cause of his Master. In addition to his many friends, he leaves a large number of relatives, almost all of whom are following in his footsteps, as he followed in the footsteps of Christ.

REYNOLDS.

In the death of Sister Elizabeth Stanley Reynolds the Hamilton Ave. Christian church of St. Louis, records its first loss this year, and the family mourns the departure of a devoted Christian mother. Sister Reynolds, whose maiden name was Milton, was born August 23, 1832, and died August 24, 1906, aged 74 years and 1 day. She was married to Mitchell Reynolds at Chaplin, Nelson county, Ky., in 1852, and one year later moved to Union county, Ky., where in 1866 her husband died. In 1867 she united with the Christian church at Old Cyprus, Union county, Ky. She was the mother of four children—two sons, J. M. and C. P. Reynolds, both dead, and two daughters, Mrs. Alice Taylor, of Bardwell, Ky., and Mrs. Anice R. Davis, of this city, with whom she was living at the time of her death. Dying in the triumphs of a beautiful faith which characterized her entire life, we may say all is well.

　　　　　　　　　L. W. McCREARY.

NAYLOR.

Samuel Grafton Naylor, son of Joseph R. and Hester C. Naylor, was born in Brooke county, W. Va., March 13, 1841, and died at the home of his daughter, Mrs. Frank W. Donaldson, West Alexander, Pa., on the morning of July 26. He was married to Addie C. Melvin in 1862, Charles Louis Loos officiating. Six children were born to this union. A son, three daughters and Mrs. Naylor are still living. Brother Naylor's Christian activities cover a little more than half a century. Bro. W. T. Moore, who was so long in London, England, immersed him when he was 13 years of age. He engaged in teaching at Wellsburg, W. Va., and at Wheeling, and later engaged in mercantile pursuits for a period of nearly thirty years. At 53 years of age Brother Naylor entered the ministry, and held three successful pastorates. He spent two years at Mt. Pleasant, Iowa, and three or four years at Frankfort, Ind.

☙ The Home Department ☜

A Goin' Home From Singin'.

BY A KENTUCKY MOUNTAIN BOY.

We walked across the paster field
A-goin' home from singin'.
The good, old, solemn meetin' tunes
In both our ears a-ringin'.

The moon a-hangin' on his end,
He lengthened out our shadders,
While now and then a bull-frog's note
Was fetched across the medders.

The calico that wrapped her form,
The lace that trimmed her bonnet—
I loved it, every thread and stitch,
An' every button on it,

I wished that I'd a been the grass
The dew was beddin' over,
So I could kiss her pretty feet,
As she walked through the clover.

We'd nearly got across the field
When, what should we diskiver,
But Batra's bull, a raisin' sand,
Like death was in his liver.

She jumped; I caught her in my arms
For fear the brute 'ud harm her.
I wish this world was full of bulls
On every side and corner.
—*From the Bibliotheca Sacra.*

❈ ❈

The Bronze Vase.

BY J. BRECKENRIDGE ELLIS.

PART IV.

CHAPTER I.

Now that Raymund had graduated at Columbia, and Rhoda at Fulton, it seemd to them that their lives had opened a new chapter, which must contain experiences, emotions and thoughts entirely distinct from those of the past. There was, indeed, one element running throughout their memories that bound all together in a perfect unity—their poverty. But it seemed the only thing that had remained the same. Once Raymund would have supposed that the love between him and Rhoda would be the only changeless thing in their experience. But he had been mistaken. If Rhoda loved him as she had formerly, he could not see any evidence of it. She was reserved, quiet, uncommunicative in his presence, and at times even cold. The most distressing part about it to Raymund was that Rhoda persisted she had not changed; that he had never offended her; that she was as interested in his career as she had ever been. But he knew she was hiding a secret, a secret which made her treat him at times almost as if he were a stranger.

This summer of their nineteenth year was spent, just as their vacations had been, at Brother Bellfield's. Raymund had saved just fifty dollars over and above his expenses at the university—fifty dollars made by cleaning the clothes of the more prosperous students. During this summer he worked at whatever he could get to do. He came back to Frog Bend after the strawberry season, so he missed that chance to increase his store. But farm hands were scarce in the neighborhood, and he secured engagements of several weeks' duration on different farms, till the "busy time" at those particular farms was over. He spent Saturday night and all of Sunday at Brother Bellfield's, but he never returned to work on Sunday night after services at the church without a heartache over Rhoda's demeanor. One Sunday morning in August he stood with her on the minister's porch, about to start to Sunday-school, but delayed by Jasper Bellfield's wife, who had expressed a desire to go with them. Mrs. Jasper was never able to make herself ready on time, no matter what that time was. Perhaps the climate was to blame. This August it chanced that both Jasper and Morton and their numerous children, as well as Jasper's mother-in-law, were all staying with the minister, who slept on the parlor floor with Raymund. As the young people waited for the dilatory lady Raymund earnestly expressed a regret that he was unable to pay off any of his mother's debts in Crawley. "I am nineteen," he said, "and yet not one cent has been paid Mr. Walker or Mr. Jennings, or any of the others."

"You have done well," said Rhoda, gazing toward the river, "to get a university education and have fifty dollars left over. I think very few young men could have done that," The river, as seen from the minister's house was beautiful. It swept around the point upon which the town was built, forming a graceful arc, much too pretty to have been named after frogs. But pretty as it was, Raymund was discontented. Why did Rhoda no longer look at him when she talked? She used to gaze so delightfully into his blue eyes, while her own blue eyes shone with such eager light. And Raymund could not help but reflect that of the $150 given Rhoda by their Uncle William, never had he seen a cent of it, or been told a word about its disposition. He looked at the river and frowned at it. As they still waited for Mrs. Jasper Bellfield, a short, fleshy man came hurriedly from across the street. It was Mr. Willby.

"News for you, Rhoda," he cried, excitedly. "Saw all the Board of the Prairie Schoolhouse a few minutes ago. The whole gang was in a big wagon, starting off to church. I boarded the wagon and rode with them about half a mile. The upshot of it is that you are to have the Prairie school at forty dollars a month. Hold on!—there's a condition—you've got to stay at my house; do you hear? This Bellfield man is always crowded to the gunwales with company; never any room for you here."

Rhoda was greatly excited. "Oh, my first school!" she cried. "My first school! Forty dollars a month! Three hundred and sixty dollars a year! Think of making that much with my own poor head! Raymund, why don't you congratulate me?"

"It's splendid," said Raymund, "and I'm not a bit jealous, Rhoda," He put his arm about her and drew her to him. He would have kissed her, but she drew away, laughing and blushing.

"This is too public!" she declared. "O, Mr. Willby!" And she grasped both his hands. "But that Board couldn't ever have made a condition of my staying with you. Why should they care where I stay? You know I sleep with Brother Bellfield's invalid sister, and somehow she thinks I am the only one she can sleep with. Nobody else will humor her little ways."

"I'll tell you how it is, Mr. Willby," said Raymund. "After they've gone to bed Miss Bellfield pulls the lamp up to her side and reads aloud the morsels she's been saving up during the day. Think of Rhoda going through that after teaching all day!"

"But it is such a comfort to her," said Rhoda, "and I can go off to sleep."

"No," Mr. Willby declared, positively. "I'll not have it. I've stood it this long because I knew she needed a sympathetic listener. But if you teach school you've got to take care of your nerves. I have thought it all out. I'll come over here every afternoon and sit and let old Miss Bellfield read to me. That will do the business for her. And I want you to know," he added, fiercely, "that my wife needs cheering up, too! Since our boy died she's never known such comfort as comes from your visits. You'll stay right in our house. I'll drive you to the schoolhouse every morning; it's two miles in the country. How'll you get there without me? I'll not take you unless you stay with us!" He snapped his finger. "That for old Miss Bellfield! If she don't want to read aloud to me, let her go dry!"

One afternoon, some two or three weeks later, Raymund and Jack Bellfield were roaming through the woods that looked down upon the Missouri. They had undertaken the exploration at Jack's request. He was full of his plans of going to the University Medical at Kansas City, the next October, to fit himself to become a physician. As he poured out his hopes and plans, with his accustomed gay vivacity, Raymund tried to enter into his enthusiasm. But all the time he was oppressed by wondering if Jack was the cause of Rhoda's change. Perhaps the two young schoolteachers were sweethearts; but if so, why did not Rhoda tell him, and why did not Jack? The mystery was a heavy weight upon his heart. Jack Bellfield went back to Columbia day, reminding Raymund of various adventures which Raymund had witnessed only from the outskirts—adventures of which Jack had formed the center of the whirlwind. The minister's son could not but observe Raymund's silence and despondency, and it occurred to him that Raymund, too, longed for an opening where he might exert his mental powers. He suggested that when he had gone to Kansas City he might find a situation for his friend. It was late when the two returned to Frog Bend. The sun's setting and its mellow glow softened the water and gilded the shores. As they approached Brother Bellfield's they saw the relatives standing about the porch, or perching upon its balustrades. The center of interest was a stranger, who had come during the absence of the young men.

"Just came from the train," said Mr. Willby, who was waiting at his gate for Raymund to come up with Jack. "I'll go over with you, and see what new company the preacher's got aboard now." Charged with curiosity, Mr. Willby crossed the road with them. The newcomer was a little lady with hair-whitening hair. She had a peach complexion, which made her look younger than she was, and bright, alert eyes. Although a stranger to the Bellfields, she was entertaining them greatly to the enjoyment of the minister's ten grandchildren (there were now ten), and even causing at times the fleshy and flabby Mrs. Jasper to rise to the exertion of a smile.

"Oh," cried Raymund, suddenly hurrying his pace, "it is Mrs. De Fer!" He rushed upon the porch and bent over the little French lady.

"Don't you dare kiss me!" cried the lady, drawing back her little white head. But when Raymund, in sudden doubt, paused, she kissed him herself. "O, what a big boy!" she cried. "I have come for you. Go pack your trunk."

"How?" asked Raymund, bewildered. "Go where?"

"Kansas City. No time to lose. Tell all adieu."

Rhoda smiled at Raymund from a distant end of the porch. "Mrs. De Fer has a position for you," she said, proudly. "O Raymund! we will start *together!*"

Raymund cast a quick glance at Jack to discover if he and Rhoda were together in the conspiracy. But Jack was dumb with surprise, and could only stare at the white-haired French lady.

"Yes," said Mrs. De Fer, "one such good position. I was engaged as a governess, to two young fellows, of age nine and fourteen, with parents very rich and grand. I staid but a month—yes! Then I have to do something else. The parents are very kind, they say whoever I recommend shall have the tutoring of the ignorants—oh, so ignorant, but very, very rich! So I apply to my friend the French professor of Columbia University. He says there is one young man so diligent and so recommended by all the teachers for being thorough, and one needing a place. And when I see your name and address I remember our days on the Omer farm, and I cry. But, yes, yes, I will go and see if it is my Raymund! So I talk to Mr. Bellfield here, who says, oh, such dear things about you, and I hear what your sister says. And now I see you. Pack your trunk, Raymund, at once; do not delay at all! For it is sixty dollars a month, and you have still a great deal of time of your own to come and go. So you like the thing I have done, is it not? And you will go, is it not? And you are pleased with your Mrs. De Fer, is it not, Raymund?"

"I am so pleased!" cried Raymund, again grasping both her hands.

"Mrs. De Fer," cried Mr. Willby, quite ecstatic over Raymund's opportunity, "*how* old are you, madam?"

"Ah, ah," cried Mrs. De Fer, smiling, "I do not tell my age, kind sir. That is knowledge which I find too useful to give away."

As she seemed a little embarrassed, Jack came to the rescue by saying: "Mrs. De Fer, do you ever think of the time we took our refreshments in the dining-room-in-the-air?"

The French lady burst forth into a shower of silvery peals. "And Nelsie Loraine," she cried, "she was almost taking the yellow and green candy, when—ah! ah!—the entire table disappeared! By the way," she added, suddenly, "Nelsie Loraine has returned from Europe sooner than she intended. I suppose she found a protracted education too much of ennui. They are all in Kansas City for the year, till the lease on the farm will have expired."

Rhoda suddenly took an interest in the conversation. "She is in Kansas City?" she repeated, with a startled look.

Mr. Willby again came to the front. "Mrs. De Fer, if you don't mind telling something else, since it seems that your age is such a secret, why have you given up the care of these two young ignorant rich fellows, age nine and fourteen?"

"Ah," said Mrs. De Fer, "you ask questions that probe to the heart, kind sir. But you would learn sooner or later, so I tell you that I am to be married."

"Married, madam?" cried Mr. Willby, "and to whom, if you please?"

"To the French professor of the university," said Mrs. De Fer, blushing and looking younger than ever.

"How old is he?" demanded Mr. Willby.

(To Be Continued.)

❀ ❀

Slipping the Cable.

I stood on the wharf at Genoa, watching a great steamer casting itself loose from the pier for its flight across the Atlantic. Dear friends were on the ship, and I was seeing them off on their homeward voyage.

The ten-thousand-ton liner was surrounded by many craft, large and small; and it seemed impossible for her to get free from them and make her way through the narrow and tortuous channel which led from the inner harbor to the open sea.

By enormous cables she was tied to the pier, and I soon saw that inch by inch these cables were being loosened and she was getting free.

Almost imperceptible was her progress at first. For fifteen minutes she seemed scarcely to gain a yard, and I could tell that she moved at all only by comparing one of her masts with a flagstaff on the shore.

But move she did; little by little, an inch at a time, the cables that bound her to the shore were lengthening, and the open water beneath her stern and the pier was increasing.

After half an hour, perhaps, the cables were cast off altogether; and cautiously and very, very slowly, under her own steam, she began to feel her way among the many craft which crowded her on all sides.

At length she reached the comparatively open channel; my friends' faces on the upper deck, and their fluttering handkerchiefs, became more and more indistinct, until at last they were a mere blur, as I suppose my face was to them. At last, under full steam, and, seemingly, with a glad bound, the noble ship pushed

him to the home port—"to depart and
be with Christ is far better."—*Francis E.
Clark, in Christian Endeavor World.*

Gleanings From Magazines.

Paternal Provocation.

I

It is 10 p. m. They are seated in the
parlor.

"No," she says, bowing her head, "Pa
says I am too young to become engaged."

II

It is just 1:30 a. m. They are still
seated in the parlor.

Suddenly, from somewhere upstairs, a
gruff voice shouts: "Henrietta, if that
fellow waits a little longer you'll be old
enough to accept his proposal."—*Woman's
Home Companion.*

A Lay Sermon to Fathers.

Vacation has taught fathers and sons
a good many lessons, but none more
startling than the fact that boys grow up.
And what is stranger, your boy is growing up. Some day he will be a man;
some day he will be where you are, and
life will have pushed off on him the responsibilities you bear to-day.

And yet—God forgive us!—too many
of us fathers are trusting schools and
clubs and haphazard circumstances to
fit our boys for this inevitable usurpation. We are too busy to give them the
companionship we owe them; too tired
and irritable to read the promise of
strength in their restlessness; too indifferent to their unspoken hopes to share
in and shape their ambitions. Life and
work close in upon us and we forget
that they and not we ourselves are to
be our successors.

We have not yet reached the blear-

eyed Utopia in which parents breed
children and society brings them up. Despite the polygamy and polyandry of the
divorce courts we are still a nation of
parents and children. And just because
we are thus settled in families, fathers
and mothers ought to be friends of their
children. The more complicated our social life becomes, the more imperative
does this duty and—as all sermons say—
this privilege become. It is not merely
that such friendships make parents better
parents and children better men and
women; they will make more gentle that
approaching usurpation which for a moment startled us when we saw our boys
could run almost as fast as we, and
could plan almost as wisely and as vigorously as we. For we shall surrender
to friends.

Schools and school teachers are no
substitutes for fathers and mothers. The
winter has its opportunities just as truly
as has the summer. And the home can
have its friendships for Father and Boy
just as truly as have the trail and the
camp and the farm. Happy is the Boy
who knows this. And happier still is
the father.—*The World To-Day.*

Falling of the Leaves.

The leaf-fall only becomes possible
after a long preparation on the part of
the tree, which forms, a peculiar layer
of cells in each leaf stem called the cleavage plate.

This cleavage plate, or separation layer, consists of a section of loosely attached, thin-walled cells with a few
strands of stronger woody fiber in among
them; so, in the early autumn, although
the leaves appear as firmly attached as
ever before, they are really only held on
the tree by these few woody strands and
the outer brittle skin or epidermis of the
stem. Now only a slight shock or wind
flurry is sufficient to break the fragile
support and bring the leaves in showers
to the ground. We may see these woody
strands broken through the leaf-scar of
the horse-chestnut, where they appear as
little rounded projections on the broken
surface and are often spoken of from
their fancied resemblance to the nails of
a horseshoe. The hickory and ash
among other trees have similar markings
on their leaf-scars and from the sarsaparilla which projects just above the
ground a like series of little projections
will be seen upon the ring-like scar
which surrounds the bud where the leaf-
stalk has just separated.

Often the leaves separate and fall
even on the quietest days, for their own
weight is sufficient to break the frail
support. These hushed and supremely
tranquil days we all remember, when our
October walks are accompanied by the
soft, small sounds of falling leaves, by
the rustlings and dry whisperings of their
showering multitudes.—*From "Nature and
Science," in St. Nicholas.*

When Mark Twain Was Reported as
Dying.

This reminds me—nine years ago,
when we were living in Tedworth
Square, London, a report was cabled to
the American journals that I was dying.
I was not the one. It was another
Clemens, a cousin of mine—Dr. J. Ross
Clemens, now of St. Louis—who was
due to die but presently escaped, by some
chicanery or other characteristic of the
tribe of Clemens. The London representative of the American papers began to flock in with American cables in
their hands, to inquire into my condition.
There was nothing the matter with me,

54,600 Meals
Did Him No Good.

How One Wasted 50 Years of His Life.
Thousands Like Him.

"What's the use of eatin', anyhow?"
said the scrawny dyspeptic to his ro-
tund, prosperous-looking friend. "Here
I've been eatin' three times a day, and
sometimes twice a day, for 50 years, and
look at me. I'm rawboned and skinny,
still at the bottom of the ladder, sour on
the world, and a pessimist. I know it,
and I can't help it. If I had it to do over
again, though, I would take care of
my stomach, for I don't believe I ever
really relished a meal in my life, not
even mother's Christmas dinners, and I
firmly believe that my way of eating, or
whatever it was, brought along with it
darkness and impossibility of success."

"You're right," nodded his companion.
"Of course, that isn't always the case.
But in this age we must not only 'Trust
in the Lord and keep our powder dry,'
but we must swallow sunshine with our
food. Cheerfulness, especially while eating, which is the most essential act of
man, is as necessary to him as sunshine
is to the flowers. Nothing normal can be
produced in darkness.

"But this is what you haven't been doing, Mr. Dyspeptic. Your brain and your
stomach, remember, are twins, and you
have to treat them accordingly. Why not
start now and repair the damage you've
done? It is never too late, you know."

"You mean at my age? And suppose
you can't always get the sunshine?"

"Absolutely, yes. Science has made
it possible to get the sunshine, the health
and the strength that your stomach
needs, all put up together in little tablets.
They call them Stuart's Dyspepsia Tablets, the most effective tablets in the
world for this very thing. One ingredient in these tablets digests 3,000 grains
of food without the help of the stomach.
Two tablets after each meal can do more
work, quicker work and better work, in
digesting a heavy meal, than the stomach
can itself. The stomach need not work
at all. Stuart's Dyspepsia Tablets does
all the work, and gives your jaded stomach a rest, the rest it needs. Meanwhile
you cure yourself of brash, irritation,
burning sensation, heartburn, sour stomach, acidity, fermentation, bloat, and the
worst cases of dyspepsia and indigestion. You get rid of these for all time.
And then, besides, you can eat all you
want and whenever you want, and you
will also relish mother's Christmas dinners if you will take Stuart's Dyspepsia
Tablets after eating. That's the sunshine I was talking about. Then your
face will reflect the internal change going on, you'll be more energetic, your
mind will be clearer, you will have more
confidence in yourself, you'll be happier,
and you'll be yourself again.

"Your heart will change and you'll
feel rosy. You'll enjoy your meals—and
live. Let's walk down to the drug store
and let me introduce you to one little
package of the Stuart's Dyspepsia Tablets.
You can get them at any drug store in the
world for only 50c a package. It is worth
it, Mr. Dyspeptic."

and each in his turn was astonished, and
disappointed, to find me reading and
smoking in my study and worth next to
nothing as a text for transatlantic news.
One of these men was a gentle and
kindly and grave and sympathetic Irishman, who hid his sorrow the best he
could, and tried to look glad, and told

tian song, Stephanie's heart softened. After all, her lot was not so hard.

Sweetly the girlish voices sang:

"Spirit of God, descend upon my heart;
  Win it from earth; through all its pulses
    move;
Stoop to my weakness, mighty as Thou art,
  And make me love Thee as I ought to love."

Stephanie's heart was getting in tune once more.

"Teach me to feel that Thou art always nigh;
  Teach me the struggles of the soul to bear,
  To check the rising doubt—"

Ah, she scorned to doubt; she whose father had been a pillar in the church, and his father before; whose mother was a saint. Doubt? She who had generations of stanch Christianity back of her? Ah, never!

"To check the rising doubt, the rebel sigh."

The remainder of the song she did not hear. Her sighing and complaining had been rebellion against God. The pity of it! God, who was so good to her, so full of tender compassion, who had so led her all her days—and now even, in a strange, lonely city, when full of murmuring, had led her to this place, this quiet place where he was. Ah, thank God!

The meeting outwardly was but a commonplace one. There were no great manifestations, no wonderful experiences related, but one girl, at least, went away with new courage, new strength, and a determination to "check the rebel sigh" which was eating away the joy of her Christian life like a canker worm.

With such thoughts, it was not strange that the girls in the boarding house parlor looked at her shining face as she passed the open door, and asked, wonderingly, "Where've you been?"

She saw the shabby parlor and the loud-voiced, thoughtless girls with new eyes. Here was something for her to do. Why should she complain against the surroundings when she did nothing to better them? The days to come should be full; she would no longer sit and complain.

She thanked God that night, though the cold rain still pattered on the tin roof, for the place in which her lot had been cast, and most of all that her eyes had been opened to the blessed privileges awaiting her.

Advance Society Letters.

BY J. BRECKENRIDGE ELLIS.

What is the Advance Society? That is what the new readers of THE CHRISTIAN-EVANGELIST are asking. Thousands of you know; but perhaps none of you are acquainted with the real beginning of this society. I will tell you about it. When I was a little boy, ever and ever so long ago, I was very fond of reading stories; so fond, in fact, that I cared for no other kind of reading. But when I got to be as old as fourteen, I saw something must be done about it, if ever I amounted to anything in the world; and somehow I never doubted but what I should amount to a whole lot, a ten-acre lot, at least. So I said to myself, "Let's start a society that will make every member read solid stuff each week." So I did, and called it the "Advance Society." I was every member there was in it. Sort of lonesome work, sometimes. But every Sunday or the next day, I would write a report of what I had done—a report which nobody ever saw but myself. Some satisfaction just in looking at it, you know. And because I was the only one in it, sometimes interest would flag and the reports would cease. But the next year I would start up the organization with renewed enthusiasm. You see I knew I could never develop my mind unless it had a lot of history and poetry, etc., on board. Here is a report from my seventeenth year: "Read Romeo and Juliet, and began King Lear; resumed third volume of Hume; read Irving's Washington, and finished it in the front yard; began book of Romans, week September 18-25." Here's one from the next year: "Prescott's 'Ferdinand and Isabella,' 5 pp.; 'Boswell's Johnson,' 103 pp.; Latin, 96 lines; botany, 1 pp.; Whittier, 4 poems; Kant, 2 chapters; Bible every day." The next year, the Advance Society was still doing business, thus, a week in the vacation of June: Greek, 4 hours' study; Addison's "Spectator," 3 hours' reading; Cook on "Transcendentalism" (goodness); Lowell's essay on "Dryden" (that was fine); Palmer's "Anthologue" (splendid music in that); "Othello," act 1; New Testament each morning before breakfast.

I noticed as I grew older, how people are, about the kind of books they read. They want novels. Somehow novels never get to them so like one another that they lose their taste. And you can't lend them a history or poem; they laugh when you make such a suggestion. Their brains are stunted because they didn't exercise enough when they were young. So I thought I would try to extend my Advance Society. It had done me good; I wanted it to help others. It was seven years ago, and in this time of the year, that I told about the Advance Society in this very paper. I proposed five simple rules. You were to read five pages of history, not one taught-in your school, every week; thirty lines of poetry not in your schoolbooks; at least one Bible verse daily. Then, you were to memorize a quotation from a standard author each week. Lastly, you were to keep an account of your work in a notebook, and send me a report every twelve weeks. Twelve weeks make one quarter. Well, the young people and the old, liked the idea, and thousands responded. I do not know how many thousands, from New York to California, and from California, and from England and British America to South America and Japan. I wonder what that little boy would have thought, as he sat in his front yard in the bluegrass—for it was not Arkansas —with Irving's "Washington" upon his knee, if he could have known I should be telling on him one day to so many thousands? So that's how the Advance Society started; and that is what it is.

But that isn't all. We were not satisfied simply to improve ourselves; we wanted to help others. We have raised an orphan fund and a mission fund, and another fund which I have not told you about. The orphan fund simply means that children from all over the world are banded together to try to educate an orphan boy, who, having only one leg, needs help until his education is acquired. With the mission fund, we help support a young girl in China who is not supported by any missionary board. And the little boy or girl who sends me a dime for Charlie and Drusie, has as much right to feel that he is a factor in this great work as the man or woman who strains a point and sends a quarter. But we have a third fund of which I will say just a word. Occasionally (not often, alas!) some one sends me some money, say 20 cents or 15, and once $5 with the request that I use it in the way I think it will do most good. Usually I divide such sums between Charlie and Drusie, equally. But sometimes I take it for some great and pressing need that I happen to know of (and I happen to know of so many!); now, some of the work I am able to do with this third fund, is not of the kind that ought to be mentioned in public, for to mention it would be to rob it of all grace. But I am sure you are satisfied or you wouldn't entrust the spending of that money to me; and I am sure I am satisfied, except that there isn't enough of it to go very far!

The ice cream supper given for orphan Charlie is still bringing in returns. In my last report, we had $138.15. If I had needed a text for the opening of this article, the following from Bertha Beesley of Moselle, Mo., would have illustrated every point, namely, the mind-culture and the giving; "Tardy again. My report should have been sent in last month." (But she sends it now; and it is her thirty-first quarter!) "Also you will find inclosed $4 for Drusie and Charlie, equally. Mamma and I pledged ourselves to give $5 for both Charlie and Drusie this year, but we are beating that; this finishes Charlie's $5, and makes $6.50 for Drusie. And the year hasn't gone yet. I wish I could step over with a basket of apples and have an hour's chat with you." (How I wish you could! the good kind of apples that we ship from here but never have for ourselves.) "I am very much interested in 'Bronze Vase.' The children's page and Drusie's letters are a source of great delight to me. I am committing 'The Crown of Other Halves' from 'Bronze Vase,' to memory this week."

Mrs. J. R. Goodwin, Abilene, Kan. "I do love ice cream, but if I am too late for the social, perhaps I can have four oyster stews; they are just as good, so here is $1. And may you just continue having socials! May God bless Charlie. If you will suggest a good book for Drusie, I will have you send her one." (Any by Susan B. Warner. I have read Wych Hazel at least a dozen times.) Mrs. S. B. Gibbons, Garfield, Wash.: "While visiting in the east, that is, Missouri (I trust Missouri is listening and appreciates the compliment),"I saw about your ice cream social for Charlie, August 3; but, being called home unexpectedly, I forgot all about it. Visiting a friend, Sunday, I picked up THE EVANGELIST and turned to the Advance Society page as is my wont to see what the Advance Society was doing, and, O my! what an ice cream social they have been having! And as I was very warm, my mouth got dry for a dish of that ice cream. There were three others present and I suggested that each of us take a dish. We send 40 cents and our names. May God bless and prosper the Advance Society." (The reader will please note one word in Mrs. Gibbons welcome letter; she looked over at the Advance Society page to see what we were doing. And I am proud to say that not one soul was urged to come to Charlie's social. Nobody was scolded or plead with. If they didn't want to come, they didn't; and a good many didn't, I'll say that for them; but look how many did! Emma Schrimsher, Brock, Neb.: "The Charter Oak Church of Christ is a country church five miles from Brock; and the Charter Oak Sunday-school sends, as a little offering, $2 for Charlie's educational fund. We wish Charlie much profit and enjoyment in his school work. May he ever remember his creator." Mrs. Joel M. Fisher, Caldwell, Idaho: "We inclose 50 cents for five dishes of Charlie's ice cream. We were glad to see your social a grand success." Mrs. Smith, Denver, Col.: "I send $1 for our dear boy Charlie. The Lord has blessed this novel way of doing good. I have read the Advance Society page for many years, and would have joined myself, but since I have been a grandmother, I have lost the ability to memorize as I once did." Mrs. Edith Slightam, Spokane, Wash., who sent me the cat picture not long since.: "I am sending $1 for our missionary Drusie, the last for 1906; but I will not forget to come next year." J. D. Dillard (who is the Missouri collector for our orphan's home), St. Louis, Mo.: "On September 16, I spoke in Grandin, in the Congregational church—we have no members in the town. The minister was exceedingly kind to me. The congregation contributed $22.76 for the orphans' home, and the Intermediate Christian Endeavor Society contributed $5 for Charlie's educational fund. Inclosed you will find the $5 for Charlie." Does it not warm your heart to think of these young people of the Congregational church at Grandin, Mo., taking such a strong hand in helping our orphan along? But I know you would like to hear from our orphan boy, for he has not said a word to you since his vacation trip. Charlie, St. Louis, July 29: "I am having a nice time here now with my sister. I have made two windmills. I just love to whittle. I buried that old dime that you saw—the one that was bent—under the bark of an old apple tree. The bark is green and I thing will grow over it. I am going to leave it there and if I get to come back to see Bessie next summer, I will see if it is still there." September 6: "I had no accidents coming back to St. Louis. The schools of Missouri teach vertical writing, but I like Spencerian best. Which would you advise me to take up." (Anything rather than the vertical system.) "I study grammar, geography, spelling, arithmetic, writing, reading. I just had a lovely vacation. My crutches are about four inches too short. Mrs. Skinner

said she sent some money to you to get a new pair with the tops padded." September 15: "When you look at this don't say, I wish he would get tired of writing. It is simply another bill. Crutches and tips cost $2.10 and the carfare was 15 cents. I would like to hear from you. Now, if you are thinking of going out to Tennis Park, or some place else, you must stop and write me a letter." September 24: "I received your letter which inclosed $5.50. The money matters are now all arranged, as this settles for the money Mrs. Hansbrough advanced on my railroad ticket. She hopes the ice cream social will be an annual affair until I am capable of supporting myself. My teacher is Miss Mary Griffetts, Kimberlin Heights College, Tenn., was named after her grandfather. I go to school here in the Orphans' Home. I would go to public school were it not for contagious diseases which frequently break out here in the home. I would lots rather go to public school. I have a public library ticket and can get any book I want to read. This helps pass what time I am not studying and writing letters. I do various things about the house, such as putting doors on hinges, nailing boards on the fence, etc. I received a nice letter from Mrs. Skinner last week. My sister sent me one of her pictures. Goodbye." The matron of the home, Mrs. Bettie R. Brown, St. Louis, writes: "I have thought a good deal about Charlie's future. Charlie would do better at school, if he were out of the home. There is only one other child in the home as far advanced as he. He would have gone to public school before now, but for the feeling in the home against contagious diseases. It will be about two years before Charlie will have grammar education enough to take a business course. If some of the church people are willing to keep him and let him help a little evenings and mornings for his board, he will be able to get along without much expense for the two years. Then you can help him with his business course. Under the circumstances, this is the best that could be done. I would like to hear from the society on this point. Know of anybody who could take Charlie under these conditions? Just at this moment comes the mail with this from Mrs. Brown: "Am sending $5 to be added to Charlie's educational fund; this is given by Mr. J. H. Avery, Hot Springs." That's the way we do things in Arkansas. By the way, should any one ask you from how much our social for Charlie took in, you can tell them $156.55, for such is the case." Look out for our next Advance Society page; it will be a great Missionary Drusie number, just packed and crammed with good things!

Bentonville Ark.

❧ ❧

Over a Thousand Enrolled

for fall and winter work in our Bible correspondence courses. Let us tell you about it. Catalogue free. Write Pres. Chas. J. Burton, Christian College, Oskaloosa, Iowa.

The following new subscriptions for THE
CHRISTIAN-EVANGELIST have been received
during the past week:

❀ ❀

"Onward is the Word."

(Continued from Page 1331.)

blessing can be retained apart from another blessing that preserves the former
one. Life must be a continual advancement in the world of possessions. The
slothful servant gained no interest. The
principal was consumed. He who did
gain the interest profited by the slothful man's principal. Our fathers handed
us a heritage. We are to preserve it and
add the wealth of advancement, or some
other people, who do advance, will take our
principal.

It is no graft for the mind to seek new
territory. Conquest must be the aim.
A mortal conflict is waging. The inactive
must perish, either by invasion, or as Rome
did, by turning on themselves and preying
upon their own life.

The mistake is that men do not seem
to distinguish between theology and religion. The first is the science of doctrines, and with all other sciences it must
of necessity be progressive. Sometimes
it comes near the line of true religion,
but often it is quite foreign to the religion of the Bible.

True religion is love to God and man.
This is not progressive. The reason it
seems to be progressive lies in the fact
that men who possess it must ever explore for new territory wherein they may
plant this principle of life. They must
study man and find better ways of applying its benefits to his needs.

Theology is often out of harmony with
all other sciences and true religion, but
true religion is never out of harmony
with true science or the Bible.

Theology searches for truths. True
religion searches for worthy objects
upon which it may bestow an everlasting principle.

Men think they can not change their
views with reference to theology without changing with reference to religion
itself. This is a very great mistake.

"Why," then you ask, "is it necessary
to pay attention to theology at all?" Because the clearer our theology the greater
and better our vision with reference to
objects upon which to bestow our religion. If our theology is clouded or deficient our opportunities for practical application of love are limited to that extent.

A man may possess true love in
spirit, and yet be dependent upon some
revelation of "truth to make him free"
in its application with reference to his
fellowmen. Would we preserve a true
religion? Let us, then, search for and
receive the truths, from any source, that

THE
CHRISTIAN-EVANGELIST

A WEEKLY RELIGIOUS NEWSPAPER.

| Volume XLIII. | No. 43. |

ST. LOUIS, OCTOBER 25, 1906.

A GROUP OF SECRETARIES, TAKEN AT THE BUFFALO CONVENTION.

In the Front—W. R. Warren, Pres. A. McLean, F. M. Rains, Pres. A. L. Orcutt.
First Row Standing—T. A. Abbott (Mo.), B. S. Denny (Iowa), W. A. Baldwin (Neb.), Geo. R. Ranshaw, Geo. S. Muckley.
In the next row are B. S. Ferrall, E. C. Browning (Ark.), D. Monro, and A. McMillan.
In the rear stand H. C. Combs (Va.), and T. J. Legg (Ind.).

The Christian-Evangelist.

J. H. GARRISON, Editor

PAUL MOORE, Assistant Editor

F. D. POWER,
B. B. TYLER, } Staff Correspondents.
W. DURBAN,

Subscription Price, $1.50 a Year.

For foreign countries add $1.04 for postage.

Remittances should be made by money order, draft, or registered letter; not by local cheque, unless 10 cents is added to cover cost of collection.

In Ordering Change of Post Office give both old and new address.

Matter for Publication should be addressed to THE CHRISTIAN-EVANGELIST. Subscriptions and remittances should be addressed to the Christian Publishing Company, 2712 Pine Street, St. Louis, Mo.

Unused Manuscripts will be returned only if accompanied by stamps.

News Items, evangelistic and otherwise, are solicited, and should be sent on a postal card, if possible.

Published by the Christian Publishing Company, 2712 Pine Street, St. Louis, Mo.

Entered at St. Louis P. O. as Second Class Matter

CONTENTS.

Centennial Propaganda 1355
Current Events 1356
Editorial—
The Buffalo Convention 1357
Convention Incidents and Personals........1358
Editor's Easy Chair 1359
Contributed Articles—
Importance of Christianity to America. S.
  M. Cooper 1360
Christ, the Inspiration of Missions. W. F.
  Turner 1361
God, Yourself and Your Neighbor. Mrs.
  W. W. Wharton 1362
The Missionary Bump. Cecil J. Armstrong.1363
As Seen from the Dome. F. D. Power....1364
The Convention—
Foreign Society 1365
Home Society 1366
Affiliated Interests 1367
Miscellaneous 1368

Our Budget 1371
News from Many Fields.....................1374
Evangelistic 1377
Sunday-school ....
Midweek Prayer-meeting ....
Christian Endeavor ....
The Home Department......................

THE
CHRISTIAN-EVANGELIST

"IN FAITH, UNITY; IN OPINION AND METHODS, LIBERTY; IN ALL THINGS, CHARITY."

Vol. XLIII.   October 25, 1906   No. 43

1809 CENTENNIAL PROPAGANDA CHURCHES OF CHRIST 1909

: : : GEO. L. SNIVELY : : :

THE CENTENNIAL COMMITTEE.

One of the most interesting reports made to the Buffalo convention was that of W. R. Warren, secretary of the Centennial committee, J. H. Garrison being chairman of the general, and T. W. Phillips of the executive committee.

After reference to the general desire for a fitting celebration of our first century's triumphs and the organization of proper committees, he continues:

Pursuant to the San Francisco convention's action, a secretary was employed beginning December 1, 1905. Since that date Centennial headquarters have been maintained in Pittsburg. This is not to promote the Centennial convention of 1909, but to assist in the Centennial campaign of the intervening years. Allegheny county is building a million dollar convention hall, which, with Duquesne Garden and Carnegie Music Hall will afford seating for 20,000 people within a few blocks. The Pittsburg brethren and their neighbors in a metropolis of a million people will care for the convention. But the entire brotherhood must be enlisted in the accomplishment of such things, in the name and by the might of our King, as will justify a Centennial celebration.

To enable immediate inauguration of the campaign, to give it universal scope and at the same time to emphasize the plea for a single and universal Gospel all the organizations and institutions of the churches were asked for financial support. All the general societies, nine colleges and twenty-two state societies have so far made appropriations, thus forming a practical co-operation of co-operations. Most of them are giving out of their deep poverty and some with a truly heroic devotion. There are assurances of early and favorable action by the rest. How can we plead for union, if we can not unite among ourselves for such great and divine ends?

We have commended to individual churches the following Centennial aims, as suggestive of things they should undertake according to their strength.

1. Each one win one.
2. All the church and as many more in the Bible school.
3. Two Christian papers in every home; one local and the other national.
4. To start a young man in the ministry.
5. To get all our people and as many more to read the New Testament through before January 1.
6. To revive and strengthen the midweek prayer-meeting and the young people's services.
7. To erect a new church building.
8. To pay off our debt of $.
9. To start a new Bible school.
10. To organize another church.
11. To have at least one sermon per year on Annuities and Bequests, and one on Systematic Giving.

12. To double our offering for state missions; and thus—
13. To meet the state missionary board's expense in employing a missionary pastor.
14. To surpass our own best offering for home missions in both the church and Bible school, and by so doing—
15. To maintain our own home missionary.
16. To double the membership of our auxiliary to the Christian Woman's Board of Missions, and to make a generous offering to its special Centennial fund.
17. To exceed our apportionment in both the March and Children's Day offerings, and so become a shareholder in a missionary station; or—
18. To support a living link on the foreign field.
19. To increase our offering to the million dollar fund for Church Extension, sufficiently—
20. To establish a named loan fund under the Church Extension Board.
21. To observe ministerial relief day, the third Lord's day in December.
22. To observe education day, the third Lord's day in January.
23. To sustain and educate an orphan, care for some dependent saint or provide a hospital bed under the National Benevolent Association of the Christian Church.
24. To send at least one representative to every national convention, and a large delegation to Pittsburg in 1909.

In General We Recommend:

1. That while urging with increased vigor all the regular work of all the interests of the brotherhood we concentrate attention on an effort to add ten million dollars to the permanent assets of churches and church institutions.
2. This is necessarily an educational movement. We are all disciples of Christ. Let every one make a gift this year to some Christian college, and let our young people enjoy the noble influence of these conservators of light and liberty.
3. That especial emphasis be placed upon tithing of incomes; that the Lord's work may profit by the prosperity which he sends, instead of suffering thereby as it does now, and that reduced earnings may not result in entire cessation of giving.
4. That particular stress be placed upon effort in all directions to increase the supply of ministers and to develop the ministry of all members. Pray ye, therefore, the Lord of the Harvest.
5. That redoubled plans be given to Bible school work. We have nothing to teach but the Bible; and nothing to do but to teach the Bible. Only as we magnify this office can we make our gains permanent.
6. That effort be made to organize through the American Christian Mission-

ary Society, and under the auspices of the several state societies a succession of state-wide simultaneous evangelistic campaigns, sweeping successive zones of the country, until all the upper Mississippi valley be completely covered.

7. That in all our stronger states there be a co-operation of the state societies, the A. C. M. S. and the Church Extension Board to plant a church in every unoccupied county seat.

8. That the effort of the A. C. M. S. and C. W. B. M. to plant the cause in states where we are but slightly represented and particularly in all the principal cities of these states be strongly seconded by the whole brotherhood.

9. That the use of Christian literature be greatly increased particularly in the circulation of our newspapers, state and national, missionary magazines, tracts and books.

10. That we endeavor to interest local philanthropists in the establishment of a broadly Christian hospital in every principal city of the country under the general direction of the N. B. A. C. C.

11. That the Centennial campaign be given a place on the program of every state and district convention and that all these meetings, as well as the services of our local churches, be made to ring with the Centennial aims and mottoes.

12. The quick passing of a hundred years as well as the successive departure of our loved ones must remind us all that we are on a pilgrimage. To-day we are commemorating great deeds and loving hearts; to-morrow we are ourselves subjects of memory. While it is called to-day let us rear, as monuments to those who have gone, chapels, schools, homes and hospitals on the mission fields; churches, hospitals and colleges in the home land, and establish permanent funds for perpetual service in all phases of Christian activity. Thus we shall best remember those who best remembered the Savior, alleviate the pain and lift the darkness of our fellow pilgrims and perpetuate the influence of our own fleeting lives.

13. That not only as many missionaries as possible be enabled to attend the Centennial exercises in 1909, but that representative converts from all lands be brought together that we may have a foretaste of that day when the great multitude which no man can number, out of every nation and of all tribes and peoples and tongues shall stand before the throne and before the Lamb.

14. That all that is undertaken be done, not for success which may be counted ours, but for the glory of the King whom all the world should acknowledge, and that all rejoicing in aims realized and goals attained be with a humbled sense of our own unworthiness and with everywhere recognition of the truth commemorated in the weekly observance of the Lord's Supper, "By grace are we saved, through faith."

Current Events

Many a greater man will be less missed, when he is called away, than will Sam Jones, whose death occurred suddenly last week. While conducting a series of evangelistic meetings, without warning he took the train for his home in Georgia and died in his berth during the night. He was nearly sixty years old and had been in the ministry more than thirty years. His fame as a preacher and lecturer was largely due to the peculiar uncouth and vulgar style of his discourse. His speeches were full of good-natured vituperation, uncomplimentary epithets and striking slang. Abusing his audience was one of his specialties, and the audiences generally seemed to like it, or at least to admit the substantial truth of his charges. But this was merely his method. Back of that there was a large-hearted man who loved men and wanted to help them. He offended outrageously, and doubtless consciously and willingly, against every known law of good taste in order that he might persuade men not to offend against the laws of righteousness. It is a dangerous method, and in the mouths of his multitude of puny imitators it is a nauseating thing. But Sam Jones was big enough and original enough to use the method with a maximum of good and a minimum of evil results.

Sam Jones.

❀

Senator Burton, of Kansas, who was convicted of bribery, must go to prison. The United States Supreme Court has denied the petition for a re-hearing. This leaves his sentence of fine and imprisonment in full effect. When the senate was about to expel him while this appeal was pending, he promised that he would abide by the result of this appeal and that, if the decision were against him, he would not attempt to find any other method of escaping punishment. We have not the least animosity against Mr. Burton, but, considering the overwhelming probability of his guilt, it is to be hoped that he will soon be behind the bars. When a man in high office deliberately sells his official influence, and in consideration of an "attorney's fee," attempts to get concessions from the government for a private (and in this case, fraudulent) concern by the use of the influence which is his only because he is a senator, he is guilty of the grossest corruption. A bribe by any other name—such as attorney's fee—is still a bribe.

Prison for Burton.

❀

Recent experiments in the care of milk, under the direction of the Department of Agriculture, have shown that perfectly clean milk possesses greater keeping qualities than is usually supposed. It was found to be entirely practicable to keep milk sweet and fresh, without artificial preservatives, from two to seven weeks, if it is absolutely clean and if it is promptly cooled and kept cooled.

The Care of Milk.

The secrets are cleanliness and coolness. The milk must be artificially cooled as soon as possible after milking and must be kept at a temperature between 32 and 50 degrees. As to cleanliness, everybody believes in it, but few practice it with sufficient care. Nothing is more easily contaminated than milk. It absorbs odors as a sponge absorbs water. It gathers germs, bacteria, dust and minute particles of filth of any kind that may be in the air. This means that if proper cleanliness is to be obtained there must be a clean milker, a clean cow and a clean stable. Cleanliness in the parlor is a luxury and a grace; in the dairy barn it is a cardinal virtue and a necessity.

❀

The receivership in Cuba is now in full operation. Governor Magoon has succeeded Secretary Taft at the head of the provisional government. The disarmament of the belligerents has been virtually accomplished, though from the antique character of many of the guns turned in by the insurgents it is suspected that they may have more serviceable and modern weapons which they are keeping back. Some documents which have come to light indicate that President Palma's resignation was not precipitated by his resentment of American interference, but that the purpose of it was to necessitate intervention which he saw was the only salvation for the republic since his own administration had utterly failed. In his initial proclamation, Governor Magoon reaffirmed Secretary Taft's declaration that the intervention is in the interests of the Cuban republic whose flag still floats over the island. He says: "I shall seek to bring about the restoration of the ordinary agencies and methods of government under the general provisions of the Cuban constitution;" and he states the general purpose of his administration as: "The preservation of Cuban independence and the protection of life and property."

Cuba.

❀

In general interest the fight between Hearst and Hughes in New York eclipses all other features of the fall political campaign. Mr. Hughes is making the most of his discovery that Mr. Hearst's New York papers are published by "The Star Company," a corporation organized under the laws of New Jersey and having its (nominal) home office in the same building with the (nominal) offices of the sugar trust, the tobacco trust, the steel trust, and some hundreds of other corporations which sought the shelter of New Jersey's favorable corporation laws. For a company whose chief business is in some other state to organize under the laws of New Jersey is equivalent to confession of an attempt to evade legal responsibilities and just burdens of taxation. It is a sad circumstance if the great trust-fighter, who is running for governor on an anti-corporation platform and who can think of nothing worse to say about his competitor than that he is a corporation lawyer, shall turn out to be using in his own business and to his own profit those same tricks of the law of which he is, through his papers, so stern a critic. He has not yet been able to think of anything to say in answer to this charge which Mr. Hughes is making in every speech. If William R.

Under the Laws of New Jersey.

The BUFFALO CONVENTION

Prophecy has been turned into history, anticipation into realization, sowing into reaping, as relates to the Buffalo convention. It fell behind our expectations in no particular. We expected a large, enthusiastic and harmonious convention. It was all that. But it was more than that. It was a spiritual convention. This feature did not find expression so much in devotional meetings for which no adequate time was provided, as in the tone of the addresses and the manner in which these addresses were received. No one could have listened to the addresses and prayers in this convention without feeling that we were passing into an era of deeper spirituality and of wider sympathies.

The absence of unseemly boasting, or of any spirit of vainglory, was very gratifying, marking, as it does, a maturer stage of development. There was not wanting a just appreciation of the position we occupy, and of the responsibility which it imposes, but with this there was the consciousness that we had fallen too far short of our obligations to admit of any feeling of self-righteousness. Denominational braggadocio is a weakness to which religious conventions are peculiarly exposed since it is always popular to flatter people, by telling them their strong points, and concealing their weak ones. One of the convention speakers told of the Japanese official who, when Mr. Bryan, visiting in that country, had praised the Japanese for many good things, thanked him, but said: "Now tell us the worst thing you have noticed in Japan that we may correct it." That is the spirit of progress.

Key Notes.

The key-words which THE CHRISTIAN-EVANGELIST had suggested in its pre-convention number, as those which needed emphasis, are the very ones which received emphasis, namely: *Consecration, unification, evangelization, education.* This was not because we had suggested them, but because we had only interpreted the needs of the hour as these men have done. Consecration, or a more single-hearted devotion of ourselves and our possessions to the furtherance of Christ's kingdom, was the supreme note of the convention, as all else, unity included, would naturally follow. Not only was the need of union emphasized, but the duty of *practicing* union as far as possible with all others who love Christ, was equally stressed, and these sentiments never failed to elicit the popular approval of the convention.

The special features of evangelism which were made emphatic, were individual evangelism, under the motto suggested by THE CHRISTIAN-EVANGELIST early in our Centennial campaign—"Each one win one," and union evangelism, or our co-operation with other Christian workers in converting men to Jesus Christ. These are both healthy signs, the one indicating the rising sense of individual responsibility and the other marking the decadence of sectarian feeling and the growth of catholicity and the union spirit. The thirteenth chapter of First Corinthians had its inning in this convention, and Paul's sentiment—"the greatest of these is love"—had practical demonstration.

The necessity of converting men to Christ, and not to any theory, of making Christians rather than mere partisans, was also properly stressed. No greater mistake can be made than to suppose that, if we have convinced a man that "the plan of salvation" as we present it, is the Scriptural one, he is prepared for baptism! Not until he sees himself a sinner, and is led to such faith in Christ as that he is willing to commit himself to Him for time and eternity, is he a fit subject for baptism. This fact is now appreciated more thoroughly by our evangelists and pastors than ever before. It is vital.

The Centennial note rang clear and strong through all the conventions. The Centennial idea is taking root in all departments of our work, and gives promise of an abundant harvest by 1909. There are no longer doubting Thomases as to the vast advance which has been, and is being made in all the branches of our one work, under the inspiration of our Centennial aims, and the pressure of our various Centennial agencies. The recommendation of the Centennial committee at the San Francisco convention that a secretary be appointed to devote himself wholly to this work, and the action of the convention in authorizing such appointment, have been abundantly vindicated in the increased interest and activity now manifest in our Centennial anniversary. The wisdom of the selection made, of a man to lead us in this great undertaking becomes also increasingly manifest.

Great Speeches.

In no convention we have ever attended was there more evidence of faithful, studious work on the part of those honored with a place on the program. This, of course, is just as it should be. The selection of themes and speakers for one of our national conventions is a most important duty. The value of the short speech was shown at Buffalo, and it might be well to increase the number of these and diminish the number of longer ones. At any rate there should be more time for impressing and explaining the reports and recommendations of boards and committees. This part of our convention proceedings is altogether too perfunctory. The impatience of discussion, and the apparent railroading of measures through with no motive, of course, but to save time or fear of discussion, is to be deprecated and discouraged. When we get afraid to discuss legitimate questions the conventions should adjourn *sine die.* Many feared that federation might come up for discussion, but the friends of Christian co-operation have no purpose or desire to bring that subject before the convention until there is opportunity for disabusing the public mind as to what federation is. But there is no reason why the time of holding our next convention should not have had full and fair discussion.

The official reports speak for themselves. They are the records of a splendid year's work in the several departments. There has been gain all along the line. This shows that the officers in the several organizations are not only faithful but efficient. The note of optimism, sounding in all the reports and addresses, is the sure sign that past progress is only the prophecy of larger things yet to come.

Some Important Measures.

The appointment of a committee by the general board to revise the constitution was a much-needed measure. It should have thorough consideration and revision so as to adjust it to our present needs and conditions. The present one has been outgrown. Another committee was appointed to revise the scheme of days for the various offerings to the end that all our interests may have a fair opportunity to present their claims to the brotherhood. If this committee does its work faithfully and impartially and the representatives of the churches will approve its recommendations an advance step will have been taken in the matter of our offerings. It is difficult for the representatives of any particular work to appreciate, at its full value, other departments of the work, and to recognize their unity, but we must all learn this lesson if we would love our neighbor and our neighbor's work, as we love ourselves and our own work.

The vote on going to Norfolk, Va., next year, in connection with the Jamestown Exposition, was unanimous. Perhaps it was the pleasing and inspiring memory of our great convention in connection with the St. Louis World's Fair that produced such unanimity of sentiment. The Norfolk brethren did their work quietly but effectively. New Orleans, which, through able representatives, presented the claims of that city, gracefully yielded to Norfolk with the understanding that its claims would be recognized later.

On the whole the Buffalo convention is entitled to be reckoned among our greatest conventions. Indeed in its spiritual tone we believe it registered high water mark thus far. If there were something abnormal in its fear of discussion, this can readily be accounted for, and it will readily adjust itself. The Buffalo convention will remain a pleasant memory, and a milestone on the road of progress toward higher and better things which we are yet to see.

Convention Incidents and Personals

The Buffalo weather was on its good behavior during the convention, though there were evidences that only a day or two before it had been playing winter at an alarming rate.

The street car conductors were so courteous and well-bred with their crowded cars that a lady moved a vote of thanks to them in the convention and it was unanimously carried.

The oldest man who attended the convention was Abram Teachout, of Cleveland, who is in his ninetieth year. He was in his place more regularly than some younger delegates, and his large heart went out in sympathy to every righteous cause. His tender talk before the business men's session of the convention was very effective and affecting.

Prof. Charles Louis Loos, of Lexington, Ky., was perhaps the next oldest man in years and one of the youngest in spirit, at the convention. He was a 'forty-niner, being at our first national missionary convention. He has the convention habit permanently fixed.

L. L. Carpenter, "the tall sycamore of the Wabash," was on hand, looming up head and shoulders above his brethren, like Saul the son of Kish. A brother told a story on him that during his recent travels abroad an English brother, desiring to give him a particularly warm reception, introduced him as "Hell Hell Carpenter, double hell D!" He is not that bad!

Among the very youngest in spirit of the older men in years was W. T. Moore, of Columbia, Mo., who was generally seen surrounded by a group of young preachers listening to a story from him, or sitting at his feet for counsel. He has been a prominent figure in our conventions for more than a generation.

S. M. Cooper, chairman of the general convention, is as mild a mannered man as ever wielded a gavel; but he knows how to put "the previous question" and order a too persevering brother to "sit down over there!" He made an excellent presiding officer.

Speaking of "the previous question"—to move it when only one side has been heard, and when the discussion had not lasted fifteen minutes, and the convention was ahead of time, is not the Anglo-Saxon idea of free speech. It is a parliamentary closure that needs to be resorted to very rarely in religious assemblies. Even to cry "question!" "question!" when only one's own side has been heard, is not a manifestation of fairness. We can not too jealously guard the right of free discussion.

J. B. Briney, of "The Christian Weekly," and of "Briney's Monthly," was on hand among his brethren, as usual. Many of our older brethren seem to prize the fellowship of their brethren in convention more than many younger ones who failed to attend, but who could do so with much less physical discomfort. We trust the time may never come when there shall not be a large number of hoary heads in our convention. If the convention could find time to hear a word from these veterans, it would be well to sit at their feet and receive instruction from them.

F. D. Power, the bishop at Washington, and popular staff correspondent of THE CHRISTIAN-EVANGELIST, is often mistaken for an old man because of his white hair, but he seldom misses our national gatherings, and is always heard with profit.

Our leading papers and many of the smaller ones were represented by their editors, as it is proper they should be, and they will all join us this week in reporting the convention for the benefit of the great majority who did not attend.

The Buffalo convention is to be commended for remaining until the convention was completed. The last session on Wednesday evening was perhaps as largely attended as any other of the convention. The plan of having the convention close on Wednesday evening left the people without excuse for leaving before the end.

The careful preparation made by the local committee for the comfort and convenience of the delegates left nothing to be desired. No committee, we think, has ever done more careful or painstaking work and the thanks of the convention was something more than formal.

The vote to go to Norfolk, Va., next year in connection with the Jamestown Exposition, was unanimous. We missed the usual fun and excitement which comes from the contest between different places. Not even a representative from the Old Dominion or from Norfolk was asked to extend a welcome to the convention although a telegram was read from the governor of that state inviting the convention.

The music of the convention was a very prominent feature, and it was much enjoyed. Brother Hackelman, for the most part, led the singing though there were several soloists, quartettes and choruses. The singing of the Netz sisters was perhaps the most popular part of the music. The hymns published in the program, together with pictures and other valuable information, make this a desirable souvenir of the convention and of the city of Buffalo.

Among the men of age and dignity who attended the convention was Hon. T. W. Phillips, of Newcastle, Pa., who is chairman of the executive committee of our Centennial propaganda, and who also acted as chairman of the meeting of the Board of Managers of the American Christian Missionary Society. He not only served his country well as a member of congress, but he has rendered distinguished service to the cause of our common Christianity. His authorship of the now widely known book, "The Church of Christ," is an open secret, at least within a limited circle, and through that work he has reached and is reaching a large number of people who otherwise have not been reached with so clear and lucid a statement of the fundamental principles of Christianity.

Few men have been longer in their service to our missionary societies, and a more regular attendant on our missionary conventions, than W. S. Dickinson, of Cincinnati. Quiet and unobtrusive in manner, but wise in counsel, he has been a rock of strength to our missionary organizations in their days of weakness and struggle, as well as now in their period of greater prosperity.

Mention also should be made of such "honorable women" as Mrs. A. M. Atkinson, whose retirement from the presidency of the Christian Woman's Board of Missions is a matter of general regret; of Mrs. Helen E. Moses, whose return to health and whose succession to the presidency, is a matter of general congratulation; Mrs. Anna R. Atwater, the vice-president and editor of the "Tidings," whose influence is widely felt; Miss Mary Graybiel, whose long and useful service on the foreign field, has endeared her to all our hearts; Mrs. Ida Harrison, whose able Centennial address struck the right key on Christian union, and all that splendid galaxy of women connected with the headquarters of the Christian Woman's Board of Missions at Indianapolis, together with the state officers who were present from other states, made up a group of consecrated Christian women for which any religious body might well feel grateful.

When the Netz Sisters sang at the meeting of the Benevolent Association, "The home of the soul," by Philip Phillips, it was moved that it be adopted as the national song of the Benevolent Association. As the motion was about to be put a friend at our side suggested that he would like to move that the Netz Sisters be adopted as the national singers, not only for the Benevolent Association, but for the whole convention! The amendment, had it been put, would have met with enthusiastic endorsement.

CONVENTION SAYINGS.

"When can we get the church to put this missionary question along with baptism and the Lord's Supper? Until we do this we can not be called an evangelistic people."—F. M. Rains.

"There's no trouble to get *em* in this world; the trouble is to get *up*."—Wallace Tharp.

"The sermons of fifty years ago, if preached *verbatim et literatim* to-day would not be much more effective in transforming the world than a young man's grandfather's love letters in changing the mind of his indifferent girl."—S. M. Cooper.

"The really respectable churches are coming to have a prize in reaching their apportionments."—F. M. Rains.

"There's a small man sitting behind a large woman"—she had a hat—"Friends, do your duty."—Pres. A. McLean.

"We want no sentiment in China; we want business. I'm getting 100 per cent on my investment."—A. E. Cory.

"We have three missionary families at Tung Chow and not a decent place where they can live."—F. M. Rains.

"Were Luther, Wesley, or Knox—or Alexander Campbell to return to earth to-day and preach the same sermons they proclaimed when they passed this way before we would have to take a walk through the halls of memory and see these great men of God when their preaching was more opportune in order to maintain an appreciation of them."—S. M. Cooper.

"Long Beach, Cal., is supporting three living link missionaries. Friends, the sun is rising in the west."—F. M. Rains.

"A living link is a church that supports a missionary atmosphere; it can live only in a missionary atmosphere."—Wallace Tharp.

"Neither shall we compass so glorious an end by assaulting or ignoring those who differ from us in matters of doctrine or policy. The representative of any church whose ministry consists in denouncing other religious bodies as sects, instead of advancing the interests of the kingdom of God, but proves himself, as respects breadth of sympathy and extent of vision, an insect."—S. M. Cooper.

"Don't hurry!' I am mighty glad to hear you say 'don't hurry.' You have been hurrying me for thirteen years."—F. M. Rains to Pres. McLean.

"It is as if the church were taking up the work of world-saving where the apostles left off."—W. W. Sniff, speaking of the new enthusiasm for missions.

"The dignity of some church members is the dignity of a broomstick."—J. A. Lord.

"The ponderous respectability of inherited orthodoxy."—J. A. Lord.

"A man that spends $15,000 or $20,000 a year to live, and run an automobile and get thrown out and get killed some day, ought to support a foreign missionary."—F. M. Rains.

"The progress of the church depends upon the mutual acquaintance and recognition of the moral worth of its adherents and concert of action as divinely warranted under the banner of the Prince of Peace."—S. M. Cooper.

Editor's Easy Chair.

"Let us build here three tabernacles—one for thee, one for Moses and one for Elijah"—cried the impulsive Peter amid the glories of the Transfiguration scene. This he spake out of the first impulse of his heart, without stopping to weigh the proposition in the scales of reason. Is it not an impulse we have all felt amid the sweet fellowship and high inspiration of our great national gatherings, when the transfigured Christ is revealing to us glimpses of his glory? "How good and how pleasant it is for brethren to dwell together in unity," wrote one of the godly men of ancient times. Surely it is a more blessed thing for those who have been made one in Christ to "dwell together" in Christian fellowship and blessed communion. Their faith is one, their aims are one, their hope is one, their work is one. Why shouldn't they feel very close to each other, and why should not the well being of each one be very precious to all the others? They are fellow-pilgrims to a common country. They are fellow-laborers in a common cause. They are fellow-heirs of a common inheritance. Jesus Christ has drawn them together in counsel concerning his work. He meets with them. They feel his presence. Their hearts burn within them, as they hear reports of the triumph of his kingdom. They hear once again the voice coming down out of the excellent glory, "This is my beloved Son; hear ye him." Is it any wonder that amid all these inspiring scenes and experiences there should be felt a loathness to separate and go away to our separate fields to labor, often in loneliness and isolation? "Master, it is good to be here." So far, Peter, you are right. It is indeed good to have these mountain-top experiences, and dwell together in fellowship with each other and receive a wider vision of the world's needs, and a larger enduement of power. But after that it is good to come down to minister to the waiting multitudes in the plain below. For this purpose Christ led us up to the Holy Mount.

And yet there have been certain utilitarians in our day who have asked, "Why this waste of money in attending these annual conventions?" Let him answer who has gone away from one of these conventions with his vision widened, his heart enlarged, his faith strengthened, his zeal for missions at home and abroad, quickened, his love of the brethren intensified, and his whole religious nature enriched by what he has seen and heard and felt. Waste? What sort of investment would yield richer returns, both for the life that now is and that which is to come? It is interesting to watch those members who have come up to one of

these great assemblies for the first time. Their fight out on the frontier has been a hard one, and they have been outnumbered and often despised by their richer and more numerous religious neighbors. Now they stand in the great congregation of their brethren, and here and yonder are the great, strong leaders of whom they have read, but whose faces they have never beheld before. "Coronation" is being sung, and as the great swelling tide of music rolls over their souls, they feel they are close to the gates of the New Jerusalem. "And all these are my brethren and sisters! We are not a feeble folk, but a great, strong, triumphant brotherhood." Tears of holy joy run down their cheeks. They have caught a vision that will never forsake them, not even when they go down to their hard and humble fields of toil. That great sermon, that inspiring address, the talks of the missionaries who were so glad to give their lives for Christ, those prayers that opened to us the gates of heaven, the sweet songs that lifted us above the world and its trifles, and filled the soul with holy aspirations—will the memory and inspiration of these ever be wholly lost? Not so, and the memory of them will be a perpetual benediction. Does it pay to go to our annual conventions?

Five thousand Christians—more or less —sitting down together in holy communion to celebrate the death of One who, "for us men and our salvation," nineteen centuries ago died upon a Roman cross! No wonder the people marvel at it, and ask what it means. It means that love is the greatest thing in the world. Because he loved us and gave himself for us, in the death of the cross, the world will not forget him. He is the magnetic Christ. He is drawing the whole world unto himself. It is love that has drawn that vast multitude of Disciples together, with one accord in one place, to show forth his death, and pledge anew their faith, and his death for our sins is the ground of their hope. As he is the center of the Christian system, so his death is the central fact of the Gospel, and the remembrance of that fact in the observance of the Lord's supper is the central act of worship. How reverently the people sit and wait for the opening word! Softly and sweetly the old songs of Calvary are sung. Many a little meeting house, or upper chamber, with its handful of communicants, rises before the memory of the faithful, as they look out upon this sea of upturned faces radiant with Christian faith, and love. The sweet old hymns, the words of Holy Scripture, the prayers of thanksgiving, and the great audience is quietly, orderly and speedily waited upon with the sacred emblems, an offering is made for aged and destitute ministers and their families, a parting hymn is sung, and the great multitude disperses but not without a foretaste of

what it will be to sit down at the marriage supper of the Lamb.

The highest note of a convention in which there were many high notes, was consecration—more love, more sacrifices, more time, more thought, more money, more of ourselves, for Christ and his kingdom. That was seen to be the antidote for every ill and every evil. Our Centennial aims heighten and brighten, as the time approaches. Everywhere there is a girding of the loins for a nobler effort. What Browning calls "the lit lamp and the girt loin" is now the watchword among us. When, before the Minneapolis convention in 1901 we called attention in THE CHRISTIAN-EVANGELIST, to the approaching Centennial of the Declaration and Address, and suggested the importance of planning for the celebration of that event, and later, brought in a report pointing out a suitable method of marking the completion of the first century of our history, there was more acquiescence than enthusiasm on the subject. It is not so now. Every department of our work is enlisted, vagueness has given place to definiteness, and indifference to enthusiasm. The next three years will witness a remarkable development not only in financial gains but in spiritual power and efficiency. And the best thing about our Centennial when it is past will not be the monuments we have erected in the form of enlarged missionary interest, endowed colleges, equipped homes and hospitals, memorial churches or better and more widely-circulated religious journals, but the enlarged faith, love and consecration which made these possible.

Niagara! It is another name for sublimity. Its ceaseless thunder is the voice of God, calling men to adoration. Its majesty is a rebuke to human pride. Its beauty is a reproof to all forms of ugliness, and especially to moral impurity. Its magnificence is a challenge to all that is noblest and greatest in man. Its unwasting bountifulness condemns and shames our stinginess. Its cloud of incense rising continually, appeals to our reverence and awe. Its rainbow encircling its brow, formed by sunshine and mist, reminds us that the most beautiful things in life come from God's love shining through human tears and suffering. It is Nature's noblest anthem. It is one of the masterpieces of the great Artist. It is a royal gift to humanity. Seen on a bright October day when all the trees of the forest are clothed in crimson, green and gold, it forms a picture of incomparable beauty and sublimity which time can not efface from the tablet of memory. Flow on thy rapid way, O mighty Niagara, and fling thyself with sublime abandon over the lofty precipice that Nature has prepared for thee, until the roar of thy falls shall be lost in the wreck of matter and the crash of worlds!

Importance of Christianity

By S. M. Cooper

To what does American character owe its strength and energy? Our climate, our material resources, our superior educational advantages, have played a prominent part in the formation of the American's character, but much of his strength and energy, much of that which constitutes his chief success and glory is traceable to the stern discipline of Puritan morality practiced by his forefathers.

And that which will guarantee the increase of our strength, and the molding of men of all nationalities into one dominant American type worthy of our noble ancestors, is an increase of faith in God and of love for God and man, expressing themselves in sober, righteous and godly living.

Americans through their government have expressed the highest confidence in one another, for our government practically says to all of us, "Manage your own business affairs, found and direct your own educational institutions, enact and administer your own laws, look after your own religious development." Commensurate with this freedom there must be knowledge and virtue on the part of the people, for otherwise liberty will degenerate into license to do wrong. Americans have been wise enough to recognize this fact, hence all along our pathway we see the establishment of the school and church.

He who is faithful to the church stands for everything that is essential to our free institutions. He stands for purity, strength and courage in the individual; for wisdom and love in the home; for righteousness in our social and industrial life; for intelligence and patriotism in our political life. If any one doubts the value of the church to our free institutions, let him but trace the history of home missions in our northwest territory which has justly been denominated "The Keystone of our American Commonwealth."

Joseph B. Clark says, "Take away this keystone from our national arch with its Yankees from the East, its Hoosiers from the South, its Teutons from Middle Europe, its wealth of agriculture, manufacture and commerce, and above all its men and women with what they have done and what they stand for, and the republic would crumble with its own weight."

When this territory was opened up, and men and women went thither to occupy it, there were those in New England and other parts of our country whose vision was extensive enough, whose faith in God and man was strong enough to prompt them to show rare foresight and courage by helping the people of this new territory to plant churches. With the development of the church there appeared her inseparable companions and most potent allies, the school and the college. Dr. Storrs, referring to their loyalty and its causes, said, "Home missions saved this coun-

*Presidential address delivered before the American Christian Missionary Society at Buffalo, October 16.

try once and if necessary will do it again."

Statistics tell us that there are in the United States 160 cities having in the aggregate a population of 20,000,000—about one-fourth of our entire population. Fifty-three per cent of these 20,000,000 are either foreign-born or are of foreign parentage. Many of them have been men of intellectual freedom, men of faith, of hope and courage, possessing those sturdy qualities needed in our economic and political life. With many of them, however, there have been imported ideas destructive of our free institutions, and being away from the restraining influences of home and native land withal surrounded by many new and strong temptations, the clear vision of their needs compels the recognition of our indebtedness. The unifying influences of the school and the purifying influence of the church must be applied to the millions coming to our shores that the composite man, representing all nationalities may be a true American. If there is any plea suited to the intelligent foreigner, it is that of the Disciples of Christ. Its exaltation of the Christ, its recognition of the worth and authority of the individual, its advocacy of union and its democratic spirit clothe it with great power for this work which not to use is to abuse.

But we must evangelize not simply the foreign population in our cities, but our entire cities irrespective of race or nationality. This must be done because the people are here. It must be done because our cities are the centers of civilization. Here there is manifested the greatest and most general indifference to the duties and responsibilities of citizenship. Here as nowhere else the ignorant and corrupt control politically until it has been justly affirmed of our municipal governments that "They are the worst in Christendom, the most expensive, the most inefficient, and the most corrupt." Here we see the moral overstrain of our modern life disproportionate to our moral strength, and hence account for the fact that the ratio of criminals in this country has risen within the last forty years from one in 3,000 to one in 700. Brethren, if this republic ever fails, the secret of its failure will be found in the ignorance and corruption of our great cities. If the government of our country is losing faith in any class of its subjects to-day, it is in those who dwell in cities; and if it be true that the greatest tragedy that can befall the American government is to lose faith in its subjects who are its authors.

Let us then give more attention to the evangelization of our cities. We have in the main been a country people. For the most part we are still a country people. But this fact, instead of disqualifying us for city work only emphasizes our obligation to capture the cities for Christ. The majority of men in our cities who control our factories, stores and banks, who own and edit our papers, who plead our causes and sit in judgment on our cases, who cure our ills, who occupy our pulpits, who superintend and teach our schools and colleges, are from the country. Emerson says that the city would have died out and rotted long ago had it not been recruited from the country. If our cities are to be redeemed our country churches must help accomplish it. If I wanted to rejuvenate a disinte-

Christ, the Inspiration of Missions*

By W. F. Turner

The discovery has been made that the Bible is a missionary library. It opens with a universal promise and ends with a vision of universal triumph. Starlight promises, moonlight prophecies, sunlight precepts and blazing noonday practice of Spirit-filled apostles, all proclaim the note of jubilee to a lost world. Moreover, this purpose is to be consummated through human instrumentality, the highest expression of which is the Church. "How shall they preach except they be sent?" And to know the Master's will and do it not means many stripes.

We, too, have been warned against the sin of ingratitude. The foundation of present-day civilization has been traced to Christian missions. Whatever we may say of evolution, it is a fact that we came from a heathen ancestry. Our forefathers were fierce savages who practiced free love, idolatry and cannibalism. Going back to Plymouth Rock and Jamestown, we find the Pilgrims and Cavaliers landing on our shores with the Bible and a devout faith. Further back we find Anskar going to Scandinavia. We find Boniface going to Germany. We find Columba going to Scotland. We find Boniface going to Germany. We find St. Patrick going to Ireland. Back of all these we find Augustine, who brought the Gospel to England from Rome. Back yet we find Paul, who brought it to Rome direct from the Lord, who brought it from heaven to earth. Here is at least one line of succession that can not be broken. It is a line of Gospel heroes conquering a line of barbarians, whose work led to Anglo-Saxon culture and liberty. Freely we have received; freely must we give. "This is a day of glad tidings; evil will overtake us if we hold our peace," Were there not ten thousand congregations of Disciples healed? Where are the seven thousand who are failing to come up to the help of the Lord against the mighty?

The example of Christ has been set before us. "He went about doing good." When asked to remain in one place, he said: "I must preach the Gospel in other cities also." "He left us an example that we should follow in his steps." To follow him we must go. A church that is not missionary should not put on its corner-stone, "Church of Christ," whoever be its preacher or whatever be its creed.

The command of Christ has also been emphasized. We say *the* command because it is the last and only command after the resurrection. The Moravians feel that the desire of Christ is sufficient to move every fifty-seven of their number to send the fifty-eighth one to win the travail of Christ's soul that he may be satisfied. But beside the desire we have the command backed with all the authority of heaven and earth. We may as well face the proposition that indifference to this command is treason against God.

Humanitarianism has been presented as a motive. The nations are sick and wounded. Priests and Levites are passing by. As we think of the Good Samaritan we hear the Master's words, "Go, and do thou likewise." Even Charles Darwin, though not a believer in the divine origin of Christianity, when he saw the marvelous results of missions in the islands of Tierra del Fuego, be-

came a life contributor to the London Society. Many preachers and churches among us might well imitate the theology of Darwin on this point. G. L. Wharton, now in Jubbulpore, India, tells of a mother who brought her daughter to worship a hideous idol. The little thing drew back with cries of terror, but she was forced to kneel before it. Just across the way at the mission station the girls were at that very hour at their prayers, saying in Hindu, "Our Father, who art in heaven, hallowed be thy name." That incident alone should convert the whole Church of God to missions.

Our Church pride has been stirred up Our faithful secretaries and editors have

W. F. Turner.

given us line upon line, precept upon precept, here a little and there quite a good deal. They tell us that a great increase of numbers without a corresponding increase in liberality is a humiliating inconsistency. One and a quarter million members does not sound well in the same sentence with a quarter million dollars. And, frankly, brethren, we should be ashamed to preach among the churches of the great brotherhood and have no part in the great missionary activities of our brethren. If love does not constrain us, pride should.

Last, the law of reflex influence has been demonstrated before us from actual experience. To succeed we must have the presence of Jesus. But his presence is conditioned upon obedience to his last command. "Lo" is promised only when we "go." If we would have the barrel of meal never fail, and the cruse of oil always full, we must make God a little cake first.

Yet, with all the mighty array of argument the Church halts and the chariot wheels of Zion drag heavily. Fifty years of marvelous missionary achievement are past. A century has gone since the organization of the American Board. Nineteen hundred years the Church has been the custodian of the priceless message, and as yet we are only playing at the task. We have, like children, picked up a mission station here and there, while the great sea of humanity lives unconquered before us. Rich clusters from Eschol tell of lands flowing with milk and

honey, but Israel waits at the border. Spies report walled cities and giant evils to be overcome, but with one voice say, "We are well able to go up and possess the land." What then is the matter? We have waved the first fruits. Doors are open. The earth is explored. We have the men. We have the money. The whole world can be reached in this generation. Where lies the difficulty?

In this, We have had appeal; we need the inward fire. We have been compelled; we need to be impelled. We have had incentive; we need an inspiration. Appeal is not without its value. "The law was pure, and holy, and good." It was our tutor to bring us to Christ. But we are now no longer under law, but under grace. Has not the hour arrived for us to pass under the new covenant of missions? Incentives are external and temporary, and must be used with increasing frequency. A galvanic battery applied to the legs of a dead frog will induce muscular activity. But life is what is needed. Many churches moved with a fervent appeal or a stinging rebuke will make spasmodic offerings. They will show signs of activity and sometimes indulge in kicking. But that church is dead while it lives. The church that drinks of such waters will thirst again. The one that drinks inspiration from Christ will not thirst, neither require a secretary to come all the way hither to draw. In them will be a fountain springing up evermore.

This principle is in harmony with history. The world's great religions are at a standstill. They are ethnic. Their message is local. They have truth and power, but lack life from which expansion can only come. Hence they have no missions. They are content to hold their own or decline. Enthusiasm is dead. This was true of Judaism. It was local and external. A few reluctant efforts were made to reach others such as Jonah's visit to Nineveh and the presence of Israel in Egypt and Babylon. But here they wept. There was no song. A few proselytes satisfied the most optimistic. There was no world-wide mission till a divine life filled their hearts. Then they went everywhere. Fagot, stake, cross and sword could not stay them. Motley tells us of a Protestant congregation in Brussels that was seized in part with their officers and burned alive in the public square. The pastor and those left continued their devotions in an upper room overlooking that square, reading the Scriptures by the light of their burning brethren at the stake. Where this inbreathing has been experienced such sacrifices have been made clear from Paul to the Armenian and Chinese martyrs of our own day.

On this ground we explain how missionary effort was arrested. After the world was becoming filled with truth the Church ceased to proclaim and began to debate. So doing, the vision of Christ was lost. In these latter days we have heard the cry, "Back to Christ," and as the sun of righteousness is rising to the meridian of our hearts the mercury in the missionary thermometer is also rising. Somehow when Christ gets into the human heart that heart is anxious about others. Philip seeks Andrew, the Samaritan her neighbors, Saul the Gentiles. Our first impulse after confession is to invite others to go with us to the better land. Pity that new convert or newly organized church that is not invited to join the missionary enterprise.

This inspiration is the need of the hour. The worker on the far-away field needs

*An address before the Foreign Christian Missionary Society of the International Convention of the Christian church at Buffalo, slightly abbreviated.

it to hold him to the task. The secretary needs it to help when the hands hang down. The preacher needs it lest he flee from his church to Tarshish. The Church needs it that duty may be done if all others fail. Then our interest will not wane. There will be no spasms of giving. Stormy days will not ruin the offering. Men will not need to become prematurely old to stir up a negligent church. Changing ministries will not affect the missionary programs of any congregation.

Yes, the church has the machinery, the money and the men. Only the power is lacking. When Isaiah had a vision of God, he exclaimed, "Here am I, send me." Oh, for a vision of God in Christ that will impel us now.

May we not join in the prayer of the psalmist, "I will lift up mine eyes to the hills from whence my help cometh." First, we see with uplifted sight the hill of Calvary, where our Savior died. There are many things in the Catholic Church which we can not endorse. But may we not endorse the Golden Litany which Dr. Storrs pronounced the greatest litany ever written? A few of its sentences run thus: "By that cold crib thou layedst in, wrapped in poor clothes, have mercy on us; by thy flight into Egypt and all

the pains thou didst suffer there; by thy thirst, cold, heat and hunger in this vale of misery; by thy wonderful signs and miracles thou wroughtest; by the inward and great heaviness which thou hadst, when praying to thy Father in the garden beside the Mount of Olivet; by the spitting on thee and the scourging of thee; by thy purple garments, and the crown of thorns violently pressed down upon thy head; by the nailing of thy right hand and shedding thy precious blood, cleanse us, Lord, from all sin; by the nailing of thy left hand and thy most holy wound and precious blood, save us, purge us, enlighten us and reconcile us to God the Father; by the lifting up of thy most holy body on the cross and thy sore bruising thereof, that gave to all parts of thy body an incredible pain; by the bitterness of thy death and the intolerable pains wherewith thy heart brake; by thy glorious resurrection in body and soul; by thy wonderful and glorious ascension, comfort us; by thy glory and divine majesty and virtue of thy holy name, save us and govern us now and forever." As we read this marvelous litany may we not endorse the sentiment that "here we touch the flaming heart of all that is best in the Roman Catholic Church. We cease to be

amazed at such heroes as Xavier, Francis of Assissi or Raymond Lully."

We look again and see the mount of Olivet. Near the hill of sacrifice was the hill of ascension. One was the scene of shame; the other of triumph. The heavenly train came to escort him back to that glory he had before the world was. There he lifted his hands of blessing and gave his commission. "Go, make disciples of all nations," and then he went to the Father.

Once more we lift our eyes to the hills. Between the hill of Calvary and the hill of Olivet is the hill of Zion. On this height the little band waited for the promise of the Father. From there was to go forth the new law of love. From there the angel was to fly through the world with the everlasting Gospel to be preached to all nations. After ten days' of waiting the Spirit came and the work began which is to continue till all rule and authority are put under his feet and which if we had not faltered would long ago have been accomplished. Looking to Calvary for pardon, to Olivet for the word of command and to Zion for the Spirit-filled message we are able to go forth from this convention to attempt the task before us.

God, Yourself and Your Neighbor*

By Mrs. W. W. Wharton

There are two forces that must precede all accomplishment—the power to see and the will to do. But the vision must come first. Before the real comes the ideal. Every notable deed has first been a thought, a vision, in some one's mind. To-day we have been upon the mount of vision God has led us up and has given us the power to see. We have seen the army of the Lord upon its onward march. We have heard of its battles, its conquests and have caught a vision of the country yet to be possessed.

And have we not had the vision which shall stir our hearts to their deepest depths, so that mind and heart alike shall force us to action? We have heard the bitter cry of India's millions for light; we have quivered with pity for the darkening doom of the islands of the sea. As I look into the face of my little daughter and think of the sweet heritage of womanhood soon to be hers, I think of that heathen mother who dares not even love her hapless little daughter, that sweet little woman-child whose life, if she be allowed to keep it, must be a nightmare of hopeless misery. And when I think of the little head that was once pillowed on my breast, but now finds a resting place upon the Master's breast—oh, when I think of that little lamb of worldly wisdom undefiled, whose little feet have pattered through the pearl-set gates straight into the outstretched arms of the Good Shepherd, I long to take the comfort I have found to every mother who longs for the touch of a vanished hand, the sound of a voice that is still. Our womanhood and the sacred gift it brings us, motherhood, calls us to carry the peace and comfort God's Son has brought us on to our sisters in every clime.

Linked with this love to God, Christ has joined two other loves—the love to

*Some extracts from the closing address of the C. W. B. M. Convention at Buffalo.

self and love to neighbor. Some one has said that it takes three persons to express the Christian religion—God, yourself and your neighbor. Christ has made our love for our neighbor dependent upon our love for self. So in pleading for a greater love for our brother for whom Christ died, I point you to your heart. There is so much dangerous teaching in regard to the love of self. We are told to empty ourselves of self

Mrs. W. W. Wharton.

and allow the power of the Almighty to flow in—to stand still and wait—that not in striving do things of life come to us, but that what is ours will find us wherever we are. Sly half truths have done more harm in this world than bold untruths. The foremost fact for me in all the universe is that I am. I may add predicates as knowledge comes and life develops, but first I am, and I am myself wholly different from you or any one else, and first of all responsible for what I do with the talents with which God has endowed me.

Does not your heart thrill within you as you witness what God hath done? One hundred years ago missionaries were derided as fanatics, lunatics; to-day they are honored as God's elect. One hundred years ago they met with opposition on every hand, and could scarcely gain an entrance into their field of labor; to-day every land is open. The opening of the doors of opportunity into Africa,

Corea, China and Thibet is a story of love and sacrifice more thrilling than the mind of man can imagine. The greatest heroes are the heroes of the cross, and they have prepared the ground for the harvest we shall reap by the shedding of their own blood. A century ago the great heathen religions seemed to occupy impregnable positions, but to-day their power is waning. They have been gradually undermined, and their followers are losing faith. In India, statistics show that the Hindu population has decreased, while the native Christian population has increased forty per cent in the last decade. The Christian nations are coming more and more into control of the world, so that the Word of God and the Man of God may to-day find entrance into every land and the means of going and the facilities for work have been wondrously improved. The doors are open, the pioneer work done and the laborers are laying aside human opinion and are letting the heathen world see Jesus only, who is the Light which lighteth every man who cometh into the world. John R. Mott, after a tour of the world, says that "few facts on the mission field inspire one with more hope for the immediate future of missionary enterprise than the certainly growing tendency toward practical Christian unity among the organized forces of Protestant Christianity."

We have left the Mount of Vision, we have crossed the Valley of Decision, and have given ourselves, our best, our highest, most exalted selves, to Him. What shall we carry back to those who wait for us, who lean on us for inspiration? Many are striving in this work and in that to satisfy their longing for mental culture, and by this philanthropy and that to still the cry of their hearts and lessen the sum of the world's misery. Can we not make these noble souls, these true hearts, realize the dignity of our cause, the breadth of mental culture, the study of the field brings with its study of the land, its history, its art, its literature—the depth of spiritual culture the effort to give eternal life and a happier earth-life to humanity brings? Heart-hunger, mind-hunger and soul-hunger, all find their satisfaction in our work of love.

The Missionary Bump* By Cecil J. Armstrong

In my boyhood days the subject of phrenology was much discussed. The phrenologist read the character and predicted the future of his subject by feeling the various bumps on his cranium. In the course of the examination such expressions as "the bump of courage," "the bump of memory," "the bump of finance," were frequently heard. It had been many years since I had thought of phrenology. About two years ago an esteemed member of my congregation forced the subject upon my mind in a very startling manner. In speaking of our missionary development at Winchester, he said: "Yes, it is all right, I guess: but, to be perfectly frank, your missionary bump is overdeveloped." Now, I had heard of many different kinds of bumps, but that was the first time I had ever heard of a missionary bump—and an overdeveloped missionary bump at that! I could hardly refrain from feeling my cranium to find out if thereon there was not a knot as large and as prominent as the can that sits so serenely on the head of the renowned Happy Hooligan.

This remark of my esteemed brother was called forth by the fact that the church at Winchester has in the last five years had a great growth in missionary liberality, as the following figures will show: To all missionary causes the church gave in 1902, $687; 1903, $1,637; 1904, $2,985; 1905, $3,600. And all this my worthy brother attributed to an overdeveloped missionary bump!

This remark has suggested to me three questions, viz—(1) Can the missionary zeal of a pastor be too great? (2) By whom is the pastor's zeal to be judged, by man or Christ? (3) Must the pastor slacken in his zeal because of some who oppose great missionary development in his church? These questions I wish briefly to consider in their order.

1. Can the missionary zeal of a pastor be too great? In every church there are those who will answer this question affirmatively. Sometimes pastors, by action, if not by word, thus settle this question. But the pastor who ascends the mount of vision and beholds the world's degradation and need, who really enters into God's purpose in Jesus Christ, who fully appreciates the divine imperative to evangelize the world must answer this question in the negative. The pastor's missionary zeal can not be too great. It was missionary zeal that consumed the Lord. Was there ever such an incarnation of the missionary spirit? Is the disciple above his Lord? Will the faithful pastor forsake the path of sacrifice, the path made sacred by the feet of Jesus? What if it does cost him suffering because his zeal is misunder-

stood, or is not rewarded with a commensurate response from his church? What if it does cost him his pulpit? He will be rewarded with fellowship in the sufferings of Christ, and the sacred joy that comes to those who have done their best.

2. By whom is the pastor to be judged: by man or Christ? We pastors need to have this question thrust upon our attention for so often we are tempted to make our recognition of Christ's judgeship theoretical and the judgeship of man real. Yet in our heart of hearts, in spite of plausible excuses and fallacious reasonings, we know that it is unto Christ that we stand or fall. The judgment means more to the pastor than to the man in the pew. The pastor bears a double responsibility. He is accountable for his life and deeds, and also for the way in which he instructs and leads the people of God. When a pastor really grasps the awful fact that Christ, not man, is his judge he realizes that to preach the Gospel is more than to instruct in first principles, to emphasize Christian unity, and to impress people with the necessity of righteous living. It means to do that, but to do much more. It means to clarify the church's vision that she may see "unto the uttermost part of the earth," to enlarge her heart that she may love the heathen for whom Christ died, to expand her liberality so that, joyfully and lovingly she may give her money to send the Gospel to all men. Well may the pastor, as he faces the responsibility of his office, tremble and exclaim: "Woe is unto me if I am not true to the missionary obligation. Christ is my judge. It is in his presence that I must stand to be judged faithful or unfaithful." Let men judge as they may, the pastor must be faithful to Christ.

3. May the pastor slacken in his missionary zeal because of opposition in his church? This question has virtually been answered, but I discuss it here because it needs great emphasis. When the pastor is confronted with opposition (and every pastor will meet opposition to a missionary propaganda) he is tempted to slacken in missionary zeal. Good friends will sometimes advise it and prominent members sometimes demand it. Caution will whisper "Go fast slowly." But, granting that the pastor is wise in his methods, he must refuse to listen to those cautious ones who advise cessation, or to those who, lacking the spirit of Christ, and being willing for the church at home to languish and the heathen abroad to live in darkness, demand cessation. The call to missionary effort is a "heavenly vision" granted by the risen, radiant Christ to the pastor, and he who is "disobedient unto the heavenly vision" must stultify his soul and betray his trust. While the pastor

is in a true sense the servant of the church, in a much higher sense he is the servant of him who died for all men. The message of the Cross is more than a call to repentance; it is a call to worldwide evangelization. Who is the supreme master of the pastor? Is he the man who says "Be cautious," the man who says "Stop," or the Christ who says "Go"? Faith must never be subservient to caution, nor optimism the bond servant of circumstances. There is a place where faith must refuse the advice of caution, and optimism must break the shackles of bigotry and covetousness that would enslave it. This faith and optimism the pastor must have. Missionary development does not come in a night. It is the result of prayer and anguish on the part of the pastor. It is nurtured amid the struggle with opposition that stops not at the repudiation of the last command of Jesus. The pastor must never slacken in his missionary zeal. In too many pulpits to-

(Continued on Page 1375.)

※ ※

A FOOD CONVERT

Good Food the True Road to Health.

The pernicious habit some persons still have of relying on nauseous drugs to relieve dyspepsia, keeps up the patent medicine business and helps keep up the army of dyspeptics.

Indigestion—dyspepsia—is caused by what is put into the stomach in the way of improper food, the kind that so taxes the strength of the digestive organs they are actually crippled.

When this state is reached, to resort to stimulants is like whipping a tired horse with a big load. Every additional effort he makes under the lash increases his loss of power to move the load.

Try helping the stomach by leaving off heavy, greasy, indigestible food and take on Grape-Nuts—light, easily digested, full of strength for nerves and brain, in every grain of it. There's no waste of time nor energy when Grape-Nuts is the food.

"I am an enthusiastic user of Grape-Nuts and consider it an ideal food", writes a Maine man:

"I had nervous dyspepsia and was all run down and my food seemed to do me but little good. From reading an adv. I tried Grape-Nuts food, and, after a few weeks' steady use of it, felt greatly improved.

"Am much stronger, not nervous now, and can do more work without feeling so tired, and am better every way.

"I relish Grape-Nuts best with cream and use four heaping teaspoonfuls at a meal. I am sure there are thousands of persons with stomach trouble who would be benefited by using Grape-Nuts. Name given by Postum Co., Battle Creek, Mich. Read the little book, "The Road to Wellville", in pkgs. "There's a reason".

*Delivered at the Buffalo National Convention, Monday, October 15, 1906, by Cecil J. Armstrong, pastor First Christian Church, Winchester, Ky.

The Convention

As Seen From the Dome

By F. D. POWER

The journey from Washington to Buffalo, a trip of twelve hours through Maryland, Central Pennsylvania and Southwestern New York, is a delight in October. On the hills the autumn flames are being kindled. In the fields the corn is shocked and the pumpkins lie scattered in careless and rich profusion; while goldenrod and wild asters are blooming everywhere. It is not the richest agricultural region, nor are there pretty cities and towns, but there is a certain ruggedness and picturesque aspect to the country that attracts, even to the quaint stump fences by the roadway. Buffalo itself is a great center of life and activity. It is the eighth city in the world. Its people are called Bisonians and there are 400,000 of them. It has some of the greatest things—the largest coal trestle in the world, the largest flour depot, the largest individual steel plant, the largest office building and the largest art gallery of its kind. It is a city of handsome residences, lovely parks, fine squares and great industries; the terminus of "Clinton's Ditch," and the owner of the biggest waterfall on the continent.

The Churches of Christ on this Niagara frontier are among the best in the brotherhood. They are thoroughly missionary. There are about 2,500 disciples in and about the city. The Whartons and Miss Mary Graybiel went out from these churches. They now support three missionaries. It is a fine atmosphere for a national convention, and they have handled it well. The hall was an excellent one with every convenience and comfort, beautifully decorated; and the homes of the best people were open to our delegates. The papers gave generous notices, though Buffalo can scarcely boast of a first-class press; and the convention impressed the city.

The convention opened as usual with the meetings of our C. W. B. M., which were well attended and full of interest. It was a great report the women rendered of their stewardship. The 2,661 auxiliaries and circles and 47,210 members that constitute the working force of this organization, contributing the past year $206,553, show a great work accomplished for Christ and the church. One can not but feel how much more might be done if our 600,000 women were all enrolled. There were many good things in the program. W. F. Richardson's report for Jamaica, H. J. Derthick's address on the mountain work in Kentucky, and the introduction of missionaries were all excellent features. Mrs. Atkinson, after thirty-two years of official service, retires; Mrs. Moses becomes president, and Mrs. M. E. Harlan, the corresponding secretary, "Work, Pray, Give," makes an inspiring motto for another year.

The preaching on the Lord's day in many pulpits, the great communion service where over 5,000 came together "to break bread," had a most wholesome influence. Eighty churches opened their pulpits and in every case cordial words of welcome were spoken and fervent prayers uttered for the convention and its work. One Presbyterian pastor stated his prayer-meeting for the week would be omitted and exhorted his people to attend the session given to Christian benevolence. The papers spoke of the communion service as "a religious spectacle such as Buffalo had never seen before. The scene was inspiring, yet devotional; spectacular, yet reverent. Hundreds of people seemed deeply affected by the religious significance of their act of loving worship, and tears coursed silently down the cheeks of bowed faces here and there amid the throng of worshipers."

The Foreign Society had a most successful session on Monday, October 15. The thirty-first report shows an income of $268,726, and a gain of 344 churches making offerings. Of 11,110 churches reported by our statistician only 3,178 gave anything for foreign missions, but the growth in the number contributing is surely encouraging. President McLean conducted the sessions in his usual spirited way, using his handkerchief to dust off his speakers with becoming grace and missionary activity. Tharp and Denton, Lord and Armstrong, Turner and Philputt, made trenchant talks on various aspects of this great work. The introduction of missionaries was an inspiring scene and many of the short addresses were very stirring. Secretary Rains is as unique as ever and Secretary Corey is a splendid second. The venerable President Loos was a welcome and impressive figure in the assembly. He shared the patriarchal honors with W. T. Moore, J. B. Briney, L. L. Carpenter, Addison Clark, Abram Teachout and J. H. Gordinier. The home society reported the most successful year in the society's history of fifty-six years. A record of 373 workers, 116 churches organized, 15,013 persons brought into the church, and $103,647 in receipts is no mean work for the year of grace, 1906. Then the two departments: ministerial relief, raising $11,059, and Church Extension, $59,697, and the state organizations raising $186,129; together with $109,090 given by the Woman's Board to work in America, make a total of $469,619 for home work during the year. President Cooper made a worthy presidential utterance, and one does not hear once in a long time such addresses as those of Medbury and Daugherty, Tanner and Smith, Lichtenberger and the rest. In all my experience at national conventions I have never heard a more splendid series taken from first to last. That of E. F. Daugherty deserves the very highest mention. The old men must look to their laurels. This was a young men's convention, and they did

credit to all the traditions of the church for inspiring sacred eloquence. The choice of George H. Combs as president of the American Society for next year, of W. J. Wright as corresponding secretary, and of Norfolk, Va., as the place of meeting, was just the right thing to do in each case. The usual exploitation of the different sections of the country as ripe for the harvest was well done by Alex McMillan, S. T. Willis and W. H. Sheffer, and the cause of education and religion well cared for by President Josephus Hopwood and E. B. Bagby.

The fellowship was great. The college banquets and reunions were delightful. Bethany had over 200 and many turned away for lack of room. Some words like "Holy Writ," "zealot," "pre-

(Continued on Page 1379.)

❀ ❀

HUSBAND DECEIVED

But Thanked His Wife Afterwards.

A man ought not to complain if his wife puts up a little job on him, when he finds out later that it was all on account of her love for him. Mighty few men would.

Sometimes a fellow gets so set in his habits that some sort of a ruse must be employed to get him to change; and if the habit, like excessive coffee drinking, is harmful, the end justifies the means—if not too severe. An Ills. woman says:

"My husband used coffee for 25 years, and almost every day.

"He had a sour stomach (dyspepsia) and a terrible pain across his kidneys a good deal of the time. This would often be so severe he could not straighten up. His complexion was a yellowish-brown color; the doctors said he had liver trouble.

"An awful headache would follow if he did not have his coffee at every meal, because he missed the drug.

"I tried to coax him to quit coffee, but he thought he could not do without it. Our little girl 3 years old sat by him at table and used to reach over and drink coffee from papa's cup. She got like her father—her kidneys began to trouble her.

"On account of the baby, I coaxed my husband to get a package of Postum. After the first time he drank it he had a headache and wanted his coffee. We had some coffee in the house, but I hid it and made Postum as strong as I could and he though was having his coffee and had no headaches.

"In one week after using Postum his color began to improve, his stomach got right, and the little girl's kidney trouble was soon all gone. My husband works hard, eats hearty and has no stomach or kidney trouble any more. After he had used Postum a month, without knowing it, I brought out the coffee. He told me to throw it away." Name given by Postum Co., Battle Creek, Mich. Read the little book, "The Road to Wellville," in pkgs. "There's a reason."

THE CONVENTION---The Home Society

The sessions of the American Missionary Society were held on Tuesday and Wednesday morning. After a devotional service and the appointment of committees, G. A. Hoffman read his statistical report, the substance of which will be found on another page. G. W. Muckley followed with his statement of the work of the Board of Church Extension. This will be found elsewhere.

The fifty-sixth annual report of the Acting Board of Managers of the Home Society was presented by W. J. Wright. It referred to the special difficulties of the work due to the vacancy in the secretaryship for a portion of the time and to the great disaster in California. The total receipts were $103,647.34, surpassing last year's record by $3,324.31, and exceeding the best former year, 1903, by $1,201.24. A summary of the work showed that there were 373 missionaries employed, 100 of whom are supported by direct appropriations from the treasury and 273 by appropriations to the various state boards of missions; 116 churches were organized and 15,013 persons brought into the Church, of whom 8,273 were by baptism and 6,740 by commendation or statement. A summary of the work of all the state boards showed missionaries employed 508, baptisms 14,542, total additions 26,012, churches organized 166; amount raised for state missions $186,129.64. There was a gain of 158 schools remitting from Children's Day, the gain this year being $2,130.65; A number of the missions have become self supporting. Over $5,000 was given to help the brotherhood in San Francisco and towns affected by the earthquake and fire. The report spoke of the good work of Julius Stone among Scandinavians. The standing committee on evangelism expressed its encouragement in the work it is doing in making all churches evangelistic. The Home Board finds many new fields that ought to be entered. The calls for aid are numerous. Now is the formative period in many parts of our country and the needs are as appalling as the opportunities are great. The report referred to the clashing of offerings as the different days are now arranged, and recommended that a committee report upon a new and better scheme. The solution of deciding which places need immediate help, it said, is a five-fold greater fund, and for this fund a call was made to make the present year's offering greater than any that has ever been given.

There was perhaps little difference of opinion about the resolutions presented, as passed in the executive committee, and practically no discussion. It was resolved that a committee of three be appointed to consider a revision of the constitution; that a member of the Acting Board of Managers, removing from Cincinnati may have his traveling expenses paid by the board from points within Ohio, Indiana, and Kentucky, should this be deemed wise; that it be recommended that the Board of Ministerial Relief employ a secretary for all his time, and that such other means be adopted as is necessary to present the work more fully to all the churches, with the hope that not less than $25,000 shall be raised next year; that a committee of three be appointed to ascertain whether the Board of Church Extension can legally contribute its work should it separate itself from the American Christian Missionary Society, and, in the event that this should be found impracticable, ascertain whether the Board of Church Extension can be le-

gally employed to execute all papers required in its work, said committee to report the result of its findings with recommendations to the American Christian Missionary Society Board at its next meeting; and, finally, that a large, impartial, representative and competent committee, whose task it shall be to consider faithfully all our organized interests, report at the next annual convention a new and better scheme of offerings, which, we hope, will hurt none; will, if possible, prove of advantage to all, but will at least help some of those which now suffer because of their poor location.

The first address was a strong one by E. F. Daugherty, of Wabash, Ind., its theme being "God's Purpose and Plan in Home Missions." We shall not attempt to give any outline of this speech, as we shall give it large space in a subsequent issue of THE CHRISTIAN-EVANGELIST. It was, by many, regarded as the speech of the convention. Brother Daugherty surprised those who were not familiar with his delivery by his virility, his magnetism, his fine voice and his dramatic power. The other speech of the morning was by Harry D. Smith, of Hopkinsville, Ky., the theme being "Higher Ideals in Christian Stewardship." This address was a very admirable one, and we shall present it to our readers as soon as we can find space. It was the kind of speech that one styles classic. The report on union with the Free Baptists, which was prepared by Robert Moffett, was read by S. H. Bartlett. This will be found in its essence under Brother Moffett's own signature in our next issue.

S. T. Willis presided at the afternoon session, when the subject of ministerial relief was at the forefront. The report of the board was presented by A. L. Orcutt, its president. This showed us the general fund a total of $11,054.39 receipts, with $5,759.50 expended for ministerial relief, and a balance of $2,861.76. The receipts of the general fund stand at $29,245.07. There were 114 new churches and 72 new individual contributors last year. Eight churches gave $100 or more.

C. J. Tanner, of Detroit, Mich., made a very admirable plea on behalf of the old and sick preachers, under the title "The Oughtness of Ministerial Relief."

"Evangelism" was the theme of J. P. Lichtenberger, of New York City. It was a great address, broad in its scope, keen in its analysis and scintillating with bright and shrewd remarks. We trust that we may be able to present it in somewhat extended form in our columns for the benefit of the readers of THE CHRISTIAN-EVANGELIST.

It was decided that the place of the next meeting should be Norfolk, Va., New Orleans waiving its claims until the following year. The following officers were elected: President, George H. Combs. Kansas City; first vice-president, R. M. Miller, Buffalo; second vice-president, Vernon Stauffer, Angola, Ind.; third vice-president, E. W. Thornton, Long Beach, Cal.; recording secretaries, R. F. Thrapp, Jacksonville, Ill.; C. R. Hudson, Frankfort, Ky.; Charles Watson, Connellsville, Pa.; corresponding secretary, W. J. Wright, Cincinnati; treasurer, C. J. Neare, Cincinnati; field secretary, George B. Ranshaw, Cincinnati; statistician, G. A. Hoffman, St. Louis; superintendent of Christian Endeavor, Claude E. Hill, Mobile, Ala.; Acting Board of Managers, S. M. Cooper, H. T. Loomis, Benjamin Sebastian, Carey Morgan, H. C. Kendrick, R. W. Abberley, P. Y. Pendleton, C. J. Neare, A. M. Harvuot, Joseph Hagin. The su-

perintendent of evangelism is to be chosen by the standing committee on evangelism, constituted as follows: H. O. Breeden, B. S. Denny, I. N. McCash, C. S. Medbury, H. E. Van Horn, G. B. Van Arsdall, Finis Idleman, Charles R. Scoville. Other committees are as last year.

In the evening a great audience listened with intense interest and pleasure to the speeches by C. S. Medbury, who spoke for Church Extension, and S. M. Cooper, who delivered his presidential address. The latter will be found slightly abbreviated in the present issue of THE CHRISTIAN-EVANGELIST. It was a worthy deliverance, and Brother Cooper rose in the estimation of many who have only known him as a business man with a clear head for business matters. A very pleasing and effective part of the program was the singing at this point by the Netz sisters of "O, My America," as they swung the stars and stripes to the time of the music.

"The Challenge of the Canadian Northwest" was the very striking title of a short address the following morning by Alexander McMillan, of Winnipeg, Manitoba. We still have a great west above the forty-ninth parallel, he told us, and Roman and Greek churches are contending for the mastery. Winnipeg, a city of 4,500 people four years ago, now has a population of 100,000. Over 57,000 Americans settled in the Canadian Northwest last year. He urged that home mission work be done there by the Disciples, and he made such an impression that the matter was recommended to the attention of the convention in one of the committee reports. There are, he informed us, about 12,000 Disciples and 50 preachers in that territory.

S. T. Willis, by chart and word of mouth, brought before the convention what he called "the greatest mission field in the world." It was within the Empire State, and the speaker divided his attention between New York and the Imperial City. The speech deserves greater space than we can give to it in this report. It was indeed a great mission field that the speaker presented. What was needed, he said, is sacrificing young men who will plant Sunday-schools and churches, burying themselves, if necessary.

The last address on the Home Society's program was by W. H. Sheffer, of Memphis, Tenn. It was a fine speech on "The America of the Future and Our Contribution to It," delivered in the style of the southern orator. We hope to publish the greater part, at least, of the speech.

The committee on recommendations reported (1) that the acting board should give immediate and favorable consideration to the claims of the Northwest; (2) that the request for a living link evangelist in Mississippi to be supported by offerings in that state be granted and the state work helped from the board's funds, if possible; (3) that the board assume the support of C. S. Osterhus in work among the Scandinavians, extend this as far as possible and inaugurate a work on far broader lines looking toward the evangelization of all foreign peoples within our borders; (4) that the board make effort to secure a special fund in behalf of San Francisco sufferers, and that funds used in building houses of worship be administered through the Board of Church Extension; (5) that a field secretary be employed whose special work it shall be to raise funds for the society.

The committee on the Centennial, through F. D. Power as spokesman, suggested as aims $250,000 for American missions by 1909, 1,000 evangelists in the field, 500 new churches organized and 300,000 converts, a contribution from every church and from every member of every church, and to this end it emphasized the spiritual edification of our people through the faithful proclamation, on the part of all our leaders and workers, not only of the first principles, but of the second principles of the Gospel of Christ.

The committee on time did not find itself unanimous. One member from the south urged that May or June was best. Another member suggested either the last of June, when preachers are leaving for their vacations, or the first week in September, when they are returning to their work. He contended that October is especially bad for business men, for teachers and even for preachers. Two members were satisfied with present conditions. This left it for the chairman of the committee to decide. He recognized the objections to the present month, but believed any other month would be open to objection. After considerable inquiry he found no decided trend of sentiment against October and gave his vote for no change.

The vote of the convention was to hold to October. W. T. Moore immediately moved that the question of time should be referred to the state conventions for careful consideration and that they should instruct the national convention. This was adopted unanimously.

The Foreign Society Session

The opening session of the Foreign Christian Missionary Society began on Monday morning in convention hall with devotions led by Miner Lee Bates, and prayer by Dr. E. I. Osgood, missionary in China. The appointment of committees followed.

This year the presentation of the report was divided between Secretaries Stephen A. Corey and F. M. Rains. It was Brother Corey's first year of work with the Foreign Society and he said it had been a very happy one. As we give this week in some fullness many of the striking points of the annual report, of which an abstract appeared in our last issue, we will not attempt to report here the speeches of Brother Corey or Brother Rains, but we must emphasize what Brother Corey regarded as one of the most noteworthy points in the work, which is the trend toward Christian union. A move is being consummated in union education work in China where it is almost certain that our college will unite with the Presbyterian college in Nanking. It is further proposed that the three missions in Nanking, the Christian, Presbyterian and Methodist, unite in building up a great university, each organization to have equal control in the teaching force. There will be perfect liberty for our instructors to teach as the Bible and conscience dictate. F. M. Rains, in speaking of finances, said that the society was very much encouraged. Yet he could not understand the fact that 700 churches have ceased to contribute. There are now seventy-two living link churches and it is hoped next year there will be 100.

Only one of the Foreign Society's missionaries died during the past year, it being T. J. Arnold, of China. Eleven new missionaries were sent to the field. The greatest need emphasized was buildings for hospitals and homes. Over $25,000 a month is required to meet the expenses of the society.

George H. Combs having offered prayer and the report having been referred to the proper committee, Wallace Tharp made a brief address on "The Lord Working With Them." The part of the text here quoted, he said, was the jewel, while the seven verses were the seven facets. "The go" is the center and circumference of all religious duty. This was the word spoken to Christ's disciples while to all the rest of the world he said "come." Christ worked with his disciples because they worked with him.

H. A. Denton, whose theme was "Our New Responsibilities," argued our new responsibilities from the following considerations: (1) new wealth and numbers; (2) new knowledge of the field; (3) our new constituency; (4) we must hold occupied territory by "helping the army up the hill;" (5) there is much land yet to be possessed; (6) the marvelous success of the Gospel bids us to enter the open doors; (7) homes and schools for the missionaries and their children is another question the church has to face; (8) we can not redeem those who have given their lives on the foreign field, but our responsibility is to make the country where they rest, Christian.

There followed what is usually one of the most interesting hours of the convention, that of the introduction of the men and women who have been on or are going to the foreign fields. President McLean introduced them one by one, stating briefly something of their character or work, and in a paternal kind of way indicating when it was time for them to take their seats. R. Ray Eldred, of Bolengi, Africa, reported that there had been sixteen more baptisms there; that Mrs. Dye had been confined to her bed for more than forty weeks, but still was able to do some effective work. He urged that the missionary work should not be considered as a sacrifice but as a glorious privilege. "People ask me if I am going back," he said. "Of course I am going back. I had rather die and be buried amid the pines of Bolengi than in any spot I have ever seen." Brother Eldred is a graduate of Kentucky University and has spent one term of service on the Congo. He has gone to the forest and cut down trees, and sawn them into boards. He has made brick with his own hands. Brother McLean says he has something of a Livingstone in his nature. David Rioch said that more workers were needed in India and that he knew of no greater miracle than that the Lord had wrought than in the hearts of the orphan boys there. Mrs. Rioch brought a message from 163 of these who were members of the Christian Endeavor Society at Damoh, and sent their greetings. Brother Rioch was born in Canada and was educated in Butler College. He has been seven years in India. Mrs. Rioch was born in England, her maiden name being Minnie Henley. She took her medical degree in Indianapolis and has been most active and helpful in the work in India. Little David Rioch was introduced; though, as President McLean said, he is not on the staff as a paid worker, he is a missionary and speaks to the people by his life and through his lips. Miss Jessie Asbury sang "Now I lay me down to sleep" in Japanese. She hails from Augusta, Ky., but has been in Akita, Japan, for eight years. She teaches in the day and Sunday-school and works in the homes of the people. L. C. McPherson and Mrs. McPherson spoke of their work in

promptly accepted without any discussion whatever. A. McLean, president; B. C. Deweese, J. J. Spencer, G. A. Miller, W. S. Dickinson, J. L. Hill, A. B. Philputt, vice-presidents; Justin N. Green, recorder; M. Y. Cooper, auditor; F. M. Rains and Stephen J. Corey, secretaries; P. I. Kilgore, M. D., medical examiner.

The address of J. M. Philputt, of St. Louis, was, as its title, "Completing Christ's Suffering," would indicate, deeply spiritual, it being a fine plea for a reincarnation of the spirit of Calvary. We shall publish this address, which was listened to with the closest attention and will well repay perusal. On another page in this issue will be found the address of Cecil J. Armstrong, which, though of a different character, was certainly of a kind to help "the bump develop." The young Kentucky preacher captivated his audience.

A cablegram was read expressing the greetings of the Australian churches to the convention and George T. Walden, of Sydney, welcomed to the platform. He spoke of the value to the foreign missionary sentiment in Australia of the visits of the American brethren and said Australia expected to send over a large delegation to our Centennial celebration and would raise $20,000.

After F. M. Rains had explained the retirement of S. M. Cooper from the duties of treasurer he led a symposium on the taking of the March offering. S. E. Fisher said that the sermon before the offering must be well born of faith in God and faith in men. Speaking of the co-operation of the deacon J. E. Lynn said he must be (1) intelligent in missions, (2) enthusiastic, (3) of great boldness. Mark Collis considered the offering as an act of worship. We prepare for it by listening to the call of God through every week, he said, and without gifts, worship is in vain. J. Walter Carpenter was in favor of asking for a definite sum. We must not let the greatest business in the world go at loose ends. G. B. Van Arsdall insisting upon "getting something from every member," told how out of 450 churches in Iowa the 67 who gave to three of our missionary societies averaged 35 cents per member, while those who gave to two averaged 13 cents per member and those who gave to one only averaged 8 cents per member. G. B. Townsend thought that in order to have a worthier offering we must be led to the mountain top of vision, where we can see the great tribes and nations that know not God and through this realize that we must do our part if humanity is to be saved. T. P. Ullom said the preacher must have seen the Lord before he could have his rightful part in the offering. S. T. Willis, speaking for the preacher as a leader, said he must be (1) a student of missionary literature, the field and its needs and the Bible; (2) a man of prayer; (3) he must make an offering himself; (4) he must organize the forces, and bring to bear upon the people all he knows and feels out of his experiences. "No other offering" was the theme of P. H. Welshimer who said "lead all men to give if you can, compel them if you must." C. R. Hudson in suggesting how to take the offering mentioned a few "don'ts." Don't neglect the scattered disciples, don't apologize for the work of missions, don't pass the hat, don't have the organ play, were some of these.

It was a great audience that filled the hall in the evening. When the Foreign Society session was concluded, F. M. Rains made a brief statement about the special Centennial fund that is to be raised for land and buildings. "Let's haunt this brotherhood with that $250,000," he concluded. Round about the hall were banners and streamers with such "aims" as the following: "$10,000,000 Increase in Assets," "Every Preacher Preaching," "Every Preacher His Timothy," "50,000 Pittsburg, 1909," and "Every Church Its Mission. And in the course of the evening Dr. Peck, for the International Reform Bureau, was permitted to present a resolution urging that liquor be kept from the uncivilized races. "We keep out the liquors from this hall, let us enlarge our vision," was a statement that preceded the thunderous "Aye" of approval while one delegate added that he wished the resolution would take in the United States. No one from Cincinnati or representing the "rank and file" was heard to protest against this *missionary* convention 'resoluting" upon the actions of foreign governments! Oh, what a surprise! The first speaker of the evening was W. W. Sniff, of Rushville, Ind., who made an inspiring address upon "Grounds for Encouragement." Delivered without a note, the speech was chaste in its diction, perfectly balanced and admirable in every way. Everywhere throughout the Scriptures, he said, the reign of God upon earth is set forth as sublimely triumphant. The enterprise of world-wide evangelism is sealed and sustained by divine authority and pervaded and guided by the unfailing divine presence. The best commentary on the Great Commission is found in the Acts of Apostles and the record of modern missions. In the last century the church has been returning to the purpose and plan of the Master for the salvation of the world. The church is again hearing above the confusion and distracting sounds of the world the great words on the Galilean Mount. As the Disciples of the Lord have gone forth in obedience, the signs have everywhere followed. All excluding barriers have yielded or are yielding to the message of light and love. The church of to-day has a missionary literature filled with the triumphs of missionary labors, which is bringing inspiration to the hearts of millions at home. Mission study is being taken up systematically in colleges and universities as well as churches. Yale University has established a new department of the theory and practice of missions. Young people as never before in the history of the church are committed and consecrated to the highest and best and many hearts are eager for missionary work. What we lack most of all is the grace of giving. But even in this there has been rapid growth. Encouraging signs are everywhere manifest. The sun is rising upon every dark land and no hand can bar the gates of the morning.

The second address was by W. F. Turner, of Joplin, Mo., and it is printed on another page. Brother Turner was quiet in his delivery, but he said things that reached their mark. J. A. Lord, editor of the "Christian Standard," followed, reading a rather lengthy address on "The Dignity of the Missionary Enterprise," and adding a peroration that was probably of the moment. A text was chosen: "And the word became flesh," etc. The incarnation, said the speaker, was as much a divine as a human necessity. The salvation from sin was the sublime end of God's intention through Christ and the complete ministry of Jesus will result in some way in a new heaven and a new earth. But now the redemption is fully in the hands of men. Every disciple must be a missionary. The hottest fires will be for an anti-missionary and traitorous church. The whole significance of Christ's life is missionary. The missionary enterprise gives true dignity to life; it is beyond all human speech and thought. The dignity of love, unselfishness and consecration is in Calvary.

GOLD NUGGETS.

From the Report of Foreign Christian Missionary Society.

BEST YET.—The thirty-first annual report is the best in history of society. Great advances made in foreign fields, and largest receipts at home.

INCOME.—The receipts amounted to $268,726, a gain of $12,804. The gain in regular receipts was $13,053.

OFFERINGS.—The total number of offerings including those from churches, Sunday-schools, Endeavor Societies and individuals, was 8,979, a gain of 232.

CHURCHES.—Number contributing 3,178, a gain of 344, or more than 12 per cent. They gave $109,018, a gain of $13,517, or more than 14 per cent., the largest gain from the churches, as churches, in history of society. Churches averaged $31.11, and 928 reached their full apportionment. It is unfortunate that 697 churches which contributed in 1905 did not respond in 1906.

LIVING-LINKS.—Seventen new Living-Link churches enlisted past year. Present number Living-Link churches, 74.

SUNDAY-SCHOOLS.—Number observing Children's Day, 3,638, gain of 86. Amount contributed, $66,809, gain of $4,991. Average offering, $18.33, and 1,483 reached Roll of Honor, a gain of 218. Begin preparations now for Children's Day, 1907.

ENDEAVOR SOCIETIES.—Gave $12,007, gain of $1,134; number contributing, 969; gain, 169. They support the great orphanage work at Damoh, India. This orphanage is one of the bright stars in the black night of heathenism. Already 150 mission-study classes have been organized. Christian Endeavor Day is first Sunday in February.

PERSONAL.—Gifts amount to $36,706; number of gifts, 1,198, which averaged $30.66. Received one gift of $10,000, another of $5,000. We ask friends of the work to send direct personal gifts.

BEQUESTS.—Amount from this source, $7,662; gain, $2,563. A larger number of Christian people should remember Foreign Missions in their last will and testament.

ANNUITIES.—About $250,000 has been received on the Annuity Plan since 1897. During the past year $22,012 was received. We are anxious to interest more people in this plan. Its advantages are: 1. Yields a large income. 2. The value of an annuity will not decline. 3. It continues uninterrupted. 4. There is no risk. Illustrated booklet explaining fully, sent on application.

NEW MISSIONARIES.—Fourteen new missionaries were sent out during the past year. Many more are urgently needed.

MISSIONARY FORCE.—The whole missionary force now numbers 487, a gain of 21, including 333 native evangelists and helpers.

MEDICAL.—The society supports nineteen hospitals, and last year 90,333 patients were treated, a gain of 30,530. This is a marvelous work.

EDUCATIONAL.—Forty colleges and schools are supported, and the attendance last year was 2,225, and 79 of this number are preparing for the ministry.

ORPHANS.—The Foreign Society feeds and clothes and houses and educates about 400 orphans. This is a Christly work indeed.

LITERATURE.—Much literature is written and translated and printed and distributed in the different tongues, where work is being done. This branch of the service needs to be enlarged.

MEMBERSHIP.—The membership in all the fields numbers 8,252. The number in the Sunday-schools is 8,831.

CONTRIBUTIONS.—Contributions from all mission fields is $45,827.

FEES.—The medical fees received by our medical staff from natives and others amounted to $3,467, a loss of $756. School fees amounted to $2,836, a loss of $216. Total fees amounted to $6,303.

GREAT WORK.—The above facts indicate that the Foreign Society is doing a great work indeed, in the regions beyond, a greater work than many suppose. The work is worthy of and demands the liberal support of members of the Christian church in all the world.

WHOLE AMOUNT.—Received by this Society since its organization in 1875 is $2,768,799. This comparatively small amount has accomplished wonders in planting the Gospel in fields where it had never before been heard.

ENLARGEMENT.—What is now needed is a great enlargement in every direction—more missionaries more native evangelists, more schools and hospitals, more churches and a large number of new stations. To this end the churches should give larger amounts, more churches and Sunday-schools should be enlisted, and a larger number of personal friends should remember the work.

CENTENNIAL FUND.—We want to raise a special Centennial Fund of $250,000 by personal gifts by 1909, to be used in buying land and erecting buildings on the mission fields. Your personal offering is solicited. With $1,000 or more we can erect memorial building. Correspondence is solicited.

PAYMENTS.—Last year the payments of the Foreign Society reached the great sum of $278,042, the largest by far in our history, and $9,316 more than the receipts.

OFFERINGS.—The time for the offerings is as follows:

Endeavor Societies,	First Sunday in February.
Churches,	First Sunday in March.
Sunday-schools,	First Sunday in June.
Individual gifts,	Every day in the year.

LEADING STATES.—Missouri leads in number of contributing churches, 332; Ohio next, 329; Illinois and Indiana next, 322 each. Kentucky leads in offerings from churches as churches, $14,065; Ohio next, $12,318; Illinois next, $10,875. Illinois leads in number of contributing Sunday-schools, 430; Indiana next, 400; Ohio next, 383. Ohio leads in amount contributed by Sunday-schools, $10,369; Illinois next, $7,701; Indiana next, $6,970. Ohio leads in total amount given from all sources, $34,200; Indiana next, $25,591; Kentucky next, $23,080; Illinois next, $21,577.

Communion Service.

The united communion service was held in convention hall and never before had Buffalo seen its like. About 5,000 people partook of the emblems which were passed by 120 deacons. Favorite devotional and communion hymns were sung by the congregation and large chorus, lead by W. E. M. Hackleman, with fine judgment. R. H. Miller, chairman of the local executive committee, and S. M. Cooper came to the platform promptly at 3 o'clock and the former asked the congregation to unite in repeating the twenty-third Psalm. After a song by the Netz sisters W. T. Moore, who presided at the center table, was called on to give thanks for the loaf. There was no confusion at all and the large concourse was served with celerity and quietness. Prof. C. L. Loos gave thanks for the cup. A. L. Orcutt made the plea for the aged and infirm ministers and the collection amounted to $526.86. J. B. Briney pronounced the benediction.

BUFFALO CONVENTION

PROGRAMS

There has been left over quite a number of these handsome souvenirs of the great Buffalo Convention. They can be had at the following prices:

One copy by mail, 25 cents; twelve copies one dollar, and one hundred copies eight dollars, by express, or freight charges to follow.

Address:

International Missionary Conventions

308 Marine Bank Bldg., BUFFALO, N. Y.

The Affiliated Interests

The Wednesday afternoon sessions were of the most interesting of the entire convention, and the attendance was as large as at any save the night meetings. Charles S. Medbury, of Des Moines, ably presided. The devotional services were conducted by T. E. Cramblet, of Bethany. President W. H. McClain presented the annual report of the National Bible School Association, and E. B. Bagby, of the Franklin Circle Church, Cleveland, delivered an eloquent plea in behalf of the schools. He presented statistics showing that a large percentage of the new additions to the churches come from the Bible schools, and urged the institution of mission schools in city and country as most helpful to the up-building of the churches. During this Bible school period a great and rapidly growing interest in our Sunday-schools throughout the entire brotherhood was very manifest.

General Secretary J. H. Mohorter made the annual report for our Benevolent Association. The receipts were nearly $92,000, being a very substantial increase over any previous year in the history of the association. He presented for the ratification of the convention a resolution adopted by the Central Board of the association looking to the removal of any friction between the Benevolent Association and the C. W. B. M. over their conflicting claims to the celebration of Easter and the accompanying offerings. It provided that the offerings for next Easter collected from the Bible schools and Junior Endeavor societies should be equally divided between the two organizations and that this arrangement should continue until the committee appointed by the American Christian Missionary Society to secure a better adjustment of days between the various interests of the church should make its report. The resolution further provided that the C. W. B. M. should use its influence in securing for the association a regular and generally recognized day for the presentation of its claims to the churches and receiving of gifts for the prosecution of its ministry. This resolution was unanimously adopted by the convention.

President J. Hopwood, of Lynchburg, Va., gave an able address, setting forth the value of Christian education to the proper development of this Restoration movement. He was followed by President C. C. Rowlison, of Hiram, who referred very feelingly to the sacrifices that have been made for the advancement of education among the Disciples of Christ and especially for the sake of an educated ministry. He declared that not all the martyrs were in foreign fields, but that men who, like W. E. Garrison, of Butler, and Burris A. Jenkins, of Lexington, had sacrificed health and strength for the sake of Christian scholarship, were as truly heroic as those practicing self-abnegation in foreign lands. This sentiment was heartily endorsed by his hearers.

In the absence of President J. H. Allen and Secretary J. W. Henry, of the Business Men's Association, George L. Snively directed its part of the program. The following officers were elected for the ensuing year: President, J. H. Allen; vice-president, F. E. Udell; secretary, W. Davis Pittman; treasurer, S. H. Thomson; auditor, S. B. Sala. F. E. Udell, of St. Louis, made a brief but telling appeal to men to be as loyal to heaven as to their business. A general discussion as to the value and ministry of this association was very spirited and helpful; it was the general opinion that

the best interests of the churches of Christ demand a thorough organization of its work and its perpetuation. During this session occurred one of the most touching incidents of the entire convention. The venerable A. B. Teachout, of Cleveland, more than 90 years of age, who has given fortunes to the church, gave a brief address heard throughout the hall, in which he urged all business men to make it an inviolable rule to deal fairly with the Lord in all their business enterprises and to give generously for the extension of the Kingdom and the exaltation of the King. He announced this to be the last convention he would attend, and as he gave the few parting words of counsel and encouragement every eye was suffused with tears.

The convention was brought to a close on Wednesday evening, when there was another fine session, the speakers being F. D. Power, on behalf of benevolence, and W. R. Warren, for the Centennial Committee. The report of this committee will be found on page 1355.

Church Extension

The report presented by George W. Muckley showed that the total receipts were $61,113.87, a gain of $14,459, while the treasurer's receipts were $103,205.55 from returned loans, making a grand total of $164,319.42. The statement showed the total amount, including the Logan fund to be $588,882.28 with 1,022 churches added since the beginning.

The board has paid or closed 92 loans during the year, aggregating $114,840. In addition to this, 59 congregations have been promised help to the amount of $83,100. During the year $99,640.13 has been paid in interest and returned principal. Eighty congregations have paid their loans in full. The total amount which these missions have paid in returned loans and interest since the organization of this work is $577,301.64. Of 190 requests on file Mr. Muckley stated that eight were from one of our oldest states—Kentucky. Seven new named funds were added, making twenty in all, and there have been 178 gifts in the annuity plan, amounting to $194,434.14. In the course of the convention Brother Muckley received a letter from George F. Rand, one of our wealthy brethren at Buffalo, stating that he would pay $5,000 to the name loan fund. Brother Rand was already a contributor to the general funds.

The Church Extension speech was a thrilling one by Charles S. Medbury. His subject was, "Loyalty to the Loyal," and the address was a plea for a recognition of the character worth of congregations who are pleading for the help of the general brotherhood that they may build church homes. It was a great speech, delivered with an abandon that sacrificed no dignity, but thrilled every hearer. He emphasized in the first place, the fact that these scattered Disciples are loyal in general lines of righteousness. New standards of life have not won them from old moorings of faith. In the second place, he spoke of the loyalty of these struggling bands to the distinctive things for which the Church of Christ contest. (Continued on Page 1373.)

(Continued on Page 1373.)

INTERESTING CONTEST
Heavy Cost of Unpaid Postage.

One of the most curious contests ever before the public was conducted by many thousand persons under the offer of the Postum Cereal Co., Ltd., of Battle Creek, Mich., for prizes of 31 boxes of gold and 300 greenbacks to those making the most words out of the letters Y-I-O-Grape-Nuts.

The contest was started in February, 1906, and it was arranged to have the prizes awarded on Apr. 30, 1906.

When the public announcement appeared many persons began to form the words from these letters, sometimes the whole family being occupied evenings, a combination of amusement and education.

After a while the lists began to come in to the Postum Office and before long the volume grew until it required wagons to carry the mail. Many of the contestants were thoughtless enough to send their lists with insufficient postage and for a period it cost the Company from twenty-five to fifty-eight and sixty dollars a day to pay the unpaid postage.

Young ladies, generally those who had graduated from the high school, were employed to examine these lists and count the correct words. Webster's Dictionary was the standard and each list was very carefully corrected except those which fell below 8000 for it soon became clear that nothing below that could win. Some of the lists required the work of a young lady for a solid week on each individual list. The work was done very carefully and accurately but the Company had no idea, at the time the offer was made, that the people would respond so generally and they were compelled to fill every available space in the offices with these young lady examiners, and notwithstanding

they worked steadily, it was impossible to complete the examination until Sept. 29, over six months after the prizes should have been awarded.

This delay caused a great many inquiries and naturally created some dissatisfaction. It has been thought best to make this report in practically all of the newspapers in the United States and many of the magazines in order to make clear to the people the conditions of the contest.

Many lists contained enormous numbers of words which, under the rules, had to be eliminated. "Pegger" would count "Peggers" would not. Some lists contained over 50,000 words, the great majority of which were cut out. The largest lists were checked over two, and in some cases, three times to insure accuracy.

The $100.00 gold prize was won by L. D. Reber, 1227-15th St., Denver, Colo., with 9941 correct words. The highest $10.00 gold prize went to S. K. Fraser, Lincoln, Pa., with 9921 correct words.

A complete list of the 331 winners with their home addresses will be sent to any contestant enquiring on a postal card. Be sure and give name and address clearly.

This contest has cost the Co. many thousand dollars, and probably has not been a profitable advertisement, nevertheless perhaps some who had never before tried Grape Nuts food have been interested in the contest, and from trial of the food have been shown its wonderful rebuilding powers.

It teaches in a practical manner that scientifically gathered food elements can be selected from the field grains, which nature will use for rebuilding the nerve centers and brain in a way that is unmistakable to users of Grape-Nuts.

"There's a reason."

Postal Cereal Co., Ltd., Battle Creek, Mich.

Statistical Report By G. A. Hoffmann

In securing church statistics, we have great difficulties; (1) Because many of our church clerks keep a very poor record of their membership. (2) Many of our church boards are indifferent to the importance of statistical information and therefore do not instruct their church clerks to make the proper reports. (3) There is no pay to anyone for this work. (4) It often requires from five to ten years for a new state secretary to secure sufficient experience to properly supervise the reports he receives from churches, counties, or districts in his state.

Our instructions to state secretaries are, "Where there is no local organization between churches secure statistics direct from the congregation. Where there is city organization secure your reports from this organization for that city. Where there is county or district organization secure your reports through these organizations wherever it is possible, and whenever it can be done have these reports published through these local organizations in connection with their annual minutes. In states where reports are not so published print them in connection with the state minutes." These published reports serve as a correction to any error that may be made. In a number of states these instructions are followed and accurate results are secured.

As there is some question also as to the comparative growth of the Disciples of Christ, I have prepared a table for your perusal on this question. The presentation of our statistical tables has not always satisfied all of our brotherhood at all times, and your secretary is not at all surprised at this. The table that I wish to bring before you shows the number of communicants in the various religious bodies in the years of 1890 and 1905 together with the gain percentage of each body. It must not be forgotten when we compare the Disciples of Christ with others that their gains over and beyond all others are being made without close national organization and with a great lack of funds to aid young men in their preparation for the ministry as well as properly endowed colleges for this purpose. In addition, there is no foreign immigration to swell the ranks of the Disciples of Christ.

As much as is said about the growth of the Universalists and the Unitarians we thought it well to add them although neither have 100,000 members. In fact their membership in 1830, seventy-five years ago, was nearly as large as it is now. The six great bodies which have over a million members each show gains as follows: Disciples of Christ,

94 per cent; Roman Catholics, 73 per cent; Lutherans, 51 per cent; Methodists, 40 per cent; Baptists, 38 per cent; and Presbyterians, 35 per cent. It will be noticed that there is but little difference in the growth of the denominations of Baptists, Methodists, and Presbyterians. The Disciples of Christ show more than double the gains of these bodies. The Lutherans gain more rapidly than the three mentioned above. Their gains have come largely from Germany, Denmark, Sweden, and Norway, together with their children, who remain in the faith. They have but few additions from conversions. The Roman Catholics, of course have their gains from foreign immigration. Nearly two-thirds of the immigrants who land on our shores at the present time are Catholics. If all of these who have landed on the shores of the United States had remained Catholics and their descendants had remained in the faith we should now have at least 30,000,000 inhabitants of the Catholic faith, and possibly more.

In regard to the statistics of the Disciples of Christ I would say that there are thousands of members outside of our church organization and even in the church membership of denominations who were turned to God under the preaching of our ministry and for a time were in fellowship in one of the Churches of Christ who firmly believe in us in all essentials but for various causes, which seem sufficient to them, are now worshiping with others or have become non-affiliated in church work.

The great need is more ministers to shepherd our smaller or weaker churches. Men who will be willing to labor and live in our country and village churches. Our schools are doing well for their opportunities but their financial basis is insufficient to render aid to many young men who would cheerfully preach the Gospel if they could secure the proper training.

Allow me again to present to you our most remarkable growth of the past century, brought down to 1905:

1830	10,000
1840	40,000
1850	118,000
1860	225,000
1870	350,000
1880	473,000
1890	641,000
1900	1,025,000
1905	1,242,000

The growth in some departments of the church has even been more surprising than the gains in members.

	1890	1895	1900	1905
Churches	8,096	9,169	10,101	11,110
Ministers	4,039	4,929	5,737	6,675
Members	641,000	889,019	1,120,000	1,242,690
Students studying for ministry	468	690	807	1,017
Amounts contributed to National Missionary Societies	$146,343	$208,616	$413,641	$628,310
Amounts contributed to State Missionary Societies	$132,155	$148,000	$126,075	$216,019
No. of churches contributing to Nat. Christian Missionary Soc.	1,504	3,151	4,075	4,615
No. of churches contributing to State and not to Nat. Soc.	1,400	1,400	1,400	1,800
Whole No. of churches contributing to missions	2,764	4,764	5,556	6,415
*Partly estimated.				

Bear in mind that this table represents the growth of fifteen years only. Reliable statistics back of 1890 in a good portion of this table could not be secured. There is one thing in connection with this table, the very work, that is, national missionary organization, of which we were most fearful, has prospered and gained most rapidly. Here is a multiplication of nearly 350 per cent in the receipts of the treasury in fifteen years. In these reports we only count funds actually received and expended by the treasury of our national societies.

Another interesting thing is the comparative growth in different parts of our country known as our missionary fields. Frequent appeals come to the American Christian Missionary Society with more or less urgency and all claiming to be the field

which will return the greatest results for our Master's kingdom for the labor expended. I have made three groups of the states in which our cause is not strong and present to you the membership, growth, and gain for ten years. The eastern group includes District of Columbia, Maryland, and West Virginia, thirteen states in all. The South-Eastern group includes Virginia, Tennessee, Louisiana, etc., nine states in all. The western group includes all prairie, mountain, and Pacific states, except Texas, west of the Missouri or Kansas City, seventeen in number. None of the central states, with large memberships, are included.

	1896	1906	Gain.	P.C. Gain.
Eastern Group	42,397	66,090	23,183	55
So. East. (roup)	113,581	132,583	20,101	18
Western (roup)	116,900	162,076	45,176	40

Do not forget that this table represents a ten years' gain in these several sections. Although the gains in Delaware, New Jersey and six New England states are comparatively nothing, the other four, including the District of Columbia, have made very large gains. Our membership and churches in these states, while few in proportion to their immense population, are among the most vigorous in the brotherhood. While the south-eastern states have made only 18 per cent gain in the ten years indicated there is good growth in some parts of them. But taken together these districts show the least activity and the smallest gains of any great district among us. The great western field, comprising over one-third of the territory of the United States, has made a considerable but not nearly so large a gain as the emigration of our people to that part of the country would indicate. Our losses in the far west are simply enormous. Our American Christian Missionary Society is without the means to answer the calls of this great field and in all this immense territory there are but three feeble efforts made as yet to educate young men for the Christian ministry; one in Oregon, one in California, and the other at Bethany, Nebraska. These schools report seventy-one students studying for the Christian ministry where there should be not less than four hundred to properly supply the needs of this great field. It is sad to think that hundreds of inviting opportunities to build up splendid churches are perishing before our eyes on account of lack of means to answer these calls of our Master.

The year just closing has in some respects, made an excellent record. It has been remarkable for the large gains in many larger towns and cities and the quietness in many of the country churches. Could we have gained alike in the country churches as well as the town churches, we could report one of the largest gains in our history. Where large gains are reported we generally find upon examination an efficient and active ministry. Our ministry among and for the country churches is passing away.

Our gain in membership at the present time is a little below three per cent per annum. The increase of the churches is about one and one-half per cent. While this growth is greater than the average Protestant religious body in the United States it is not as large as it might be.

(Continued on Next Page.)

1890	1905	P.C. Gain
Baptists (13 bodies)	3,594,090	4,974,047	—
Catholics, Roman	6,230,979	10,785,466	73
Congregationalists	491,057	687,042	—
Disciples of Christ	641,051	1,242,590	94
Dunkards (4 bodies)	73,795	116,273	—
Evangelical Association	133,313	166,078	—
German Evangelical Synod	187,432	261,611	—
Jewish Congregations	130,496	143,000	—
Lutherans (22 bodies)	1,231,072	1,841,346	51
Methodists (17 bodies)	4,589,284	6,437,339	40
Presbyterians (12 bodies)	1,278,332	1,730,604	35
Protestant Episcopals	540,509	788,783	—
Reformed (3 bodies)	309,458	401,758	—
United Brethren (2 bodies)	225,281	274,158	—
Unitarians	75,000	102,000	—
Universalists	49,290	65,749	—

Our Budget

—Here's a glimpse of the Buffalo convention.

—There will be more' to follow. It was too big to report in one number.

—Read these addresses carefully and catch the spirit of the convention.

—Now begin to get ready to go to Norfolk next year to take in the convention and the Jamestown exposition.

—We are having trouble to get enough CHRISTIAN-EVANGELISTS printed to supply the demand for extra copies.

—All hands around now for the greatest autumn and winter's work in our history. Simultaneous meetings in St. Louis begin November 4.

—State mission offerings November 4.

—We regret very much that we were unable to supply the demand for our "Alexander Campbell Pictorial Number." A large number of copies were printed with the expectation that the brotherhood would want them, but we entirely underestimated the demand. We could easily have used 5,000 or 6,000 more copies than our presses printed. We are still receiving requests for this number. We are very glad to see this interest in things historical that pertain to the origin of our reformatory movement, and we regret that brethren did not pay attention to our warning and order in advance, as we suggested they should. From one quarter alone came a demand for 1,000 copies, when we had not a single copy available. Had this good brother expressed an interest in the matter before we went to press we might have been able to run off the extra number of copies he desired. We have so much printing and so many papers to get out that careful consideration has to be made in order to get out the different editions so as to reach their various destinations on time. It is not possible, therefore, for us to get out second editions or else we would be glad to print copies and to supply the great demand which we have had for this Campbell number. We trust that all who sent money for copies we were not able to supply have received this back again.

—As we have already indicated we have other interesting articles and pictures relating to the life of Mr. Campbell and his associates which we hope to publish as we shall find opportunity.

—The picture of Mr. Campbell at the lower right hand corner of page 1295 in our recent issue is, we learn from W. B. Taylor, of Moberly, Mo., taken from a daguerreotype made in Versailles, Ky., about 1853. Our house of worship there was completed in that year and Mr. Campbell preached the opening sermon. The picture was taken by Brother Benjamin Duvall and his daughter gave it to Brother Taylor a few years ago. It appeared first in F. D. Power's "Life of Pendleton."

—The largest single church delegation was, perhaps, from Uhrichsville, O.—thirty-two all told.

—It was announced during the Christian Endeavor session of the convention that the church at Summerside, Prince Edward Island, which is the home church of President A. McLean and several other preachers, had been burned in a fire that destroyed a large part of the town. A collection was immediately taken amounting to nearly $250, and at a subsequent session it was suggested

that the church should be rebuilt as a memorial to Brother McLean, and that he should receive subscriptions for this purpose. We trust that the necessary money will be forthcoming at once.

—Referring to the article by C. C. Redgrave, in last week's CHRISTIAN-EVANGELIST, I. J. Spencer writes us that it is true that the old church edifice in which was held the Campbell and Rice debate was for a time "used for political meetings and cheap theatrical performances," but two years ago one of the most attractive structures in Lexington was erected on the general location of the old church property. The exact spot where the old church building stood is now the central part of the front yards of the new depot, and it is to be ornamented with grass, flowers and trees, and is to be made a beautiful garden in the heart of the business section, and, as Brother Spencer says, no worthier or more monumental use of the old historic site could be desired.

—A new secretary of Christian Endeavor was elected at the convention, Claude E. Hill, of Mobile, Ala., being chosen. Brother Hill promised to send us a report of this session, but this and

STATISTICAL REPORT.

(Continued from Page 1369.)

At the close of the year on September 30, the reports received indicated that our statistics stand as follows:

	1905	1906
Churches	11,110	11,198
Communicants	1,238,515	1,269,591
Bible schools	8,761	8,952
Enrolled in Bible schools	850,500	870,622
Ministers	6,675	
Gain in membership, for 1906		31,076

The following table shows a gain in missionary receipts of $60,982. This is a most important gain, being about 7 per cent.

MISSIONARY RECEIPTS.

Foreign Christian Missionary Society	$268,747
Christian Women's Board of Missions	206,653
American Christian Missionary Society	193,415
Board of Church Extension	85,597
State and District Missions	241,217
Miscellaneous Missions	30,000
Total	$935,599

EDUCATION AND BENEVOLENCE.

Buildings and Endowments of Schools	$375,000
National Benevolent Association	91,795
Ministerial Relief	22,750
Kentucky Widows' and Orphans' Home	10,000
Total	$499,545

LOCAL CHURCH WORK.

Ministerial Support	$4,475,000
Incidental Church expenses	1,000,000
Church Buildings	750,000
Church and Bible school literature	350,000
Total	$6,575,000
Grand total	$8,010,054

Another year's gain like the present will bring our missionary receipts up to $1,000,000. Our motto, however, should be $1,500,000 for missions and 1,500,000 of Disciples by 1909. Not more than one-half the churches make an offering and not more than one-half of the membership participate where the offering is taken.

Our schools are prospering and gathering strength from year to year. We have sixteen colleges and universities in which young men are being trained for the Christian ministry. We also have seven Bible Chairs or schools doing excellent mission work in connection with state universities.

The future outlook for our Master's kingdom is full of hope. Taking the states of Ohio, Kentucky, Indiana, Illinois, Missouri, Kansas and Oklahoma we find that the Disciples of Christ are the strongest religious force in these states when taken together. This is the heart of the nation, through which the mighty arteries of commerce are flowing.

—It has been a good year with the Hyde Park Church, Kansas City. Louis S. Cupp's first anniversary as pastor has just been celebrated, and on that occasion there were 374 persons in the Bible school. The year closed with eighty-five additions at regular services and about $3,000 raised for all purposes.

—George A. Miller has been wooed away from Covington, Ky., where he has been pastor, to accept a call from the Ninth Street Church, Washington, D. C., which it will be remembered, was the one for which E. B. Bagby preached so long. Brother Miller will enter upon his new field January 1, 1907.

—W. A. Morrison is in a meeting at Potwin, Kan., where Oscar Hunsaker is pastor. The latter will preach on Sunday at McPherson during this meeting. The church at the latter place raised its apportionment for Church Extension. Brother Morrison will hold a meeting at Groveland during November. This is a newly organized church.

—Cephas Shelburne preached at Wabash and Anderson, Ind., while T. W. Grafton and E. F. Daugherty were at the convention. He says: "These are great churches, and audiences of one thousand people, four hundred of them men, greeted me at Anderson. The interest and enthusiasm created by the Scoville meeting still keeps up."

—H. J. Corwine has resigned his work at California, Mo., to accept a call to

Bartlesville, I. T., where he expects to go November 1. Brother Corwine has rendered most useful service for the church in California and the churches thereabouts, and he will be a source of strength to our growing cause in the new state of Oklahoma.

—Otto Shirley, Burton, Kan., will be assisted in a meeting to begin October 28, by Evangelist David Lyon. These brethren see the advantage of using Christian literature as an aid to their pastoral and evangelistic work; and 300 CHRISTIAN-EVANGELISTS will be circulated in the town where they are calculated to do most good. We hear nothing but good reports from preachers who are using a high-toned religious paper to aid their own earnest efforts.

—Alva W. Taylor recently entered upon the fifth year of his pastorate of our church at Eureka, Ill. During the four years there were baptized about 100, while 300 were received into the church. There was a net gain of about fifty, more letters having been granted than received. There was raised for all purposes about $23,000, $8,000 being given to missions. Brother Taylor is a man of lovable character and well fitted for the work of the ministry.

—W. L. Harris, who has just been holding a meeting for C. C. Taylor at Hale, Mo., says he never found a more devoted or heroic band than at this place. There are six preachers living there who do not believe in the use of the organ and the "anti" church is stronger than those who are allied with our own organized efforts; yet harmony and love prevailed during the meeting and a new and beautiful church has been built and paid for by those who believe in a more progressive policy.

—L. C. Howe, Newcastle, Ind., is not only an effective pastor but one who believes in the mission of good literature. He recently took a personal interest in helping THE CHRISTIAN-EVANGELIST's agent in putting 106 copies of our paper into the hands of his church members. Brother Howe will get good returns from this investment for he will have a more intelligent congregation, one who can appreciate the good things he may bring to them, and one that will be alive to the great things that are being done by our brotherhood.

—J. Q. Biggs has been asked by a unanimous vote to remain with our church at Buffalo, Mo. We had the pleasure of visiting this church some time ago and were delighted to find what a hold Brother Biggs has upon the young people. During the past year he has organized a prayer-meeting and Ladies' Aid Society, the Sunday-school has grown from an average of fifty to 100 and collections of the church amounted to $1,700, the amount for missions being four times as much as that given the previous year. A meeting will be held in November, with H. E. Wilhite and wife assisting.

—R. H. Lampkin delivered his sermon on "Tithing" to several of our churches in Buffalo and neighborhood during the convention season. We hear the address very well spoken of and we have not a doubt but that could Brother Lampkin be secured to give this address in our churches all over the country it would be

productive of very much good in the settling of financial questions. Brother Lampkin's address is Dexter, Mo. He has a very admirable book on this subject which is published by the Christian Publishing Company.

—Several weeks ago we made reference to the good work at Maplewood, Mo., since F. A. Mayhall entered upon the pastorate. At the very outset of his work he stated that he hoped to see all the past indebtedness paid, the church decorated and the church membership doubled during the coming year. R. A. Swink, chairman of the board, writes us that in less than three months from that time $1,300 have been raised and all the past indebtedness paid. The Sunday-school pledged itself to decorate the interior of the church and in eleven weeks raised the $140 necessary for this purpose. A resolution was passed by the congregation at a recent Lord's day service, expressing the church's great satisfaction with the work of their new pastor. Surely this is an encouragement to other churches, and an emphatic comment on what can be done when harmony rules in a congregation.

❧ ❧

FROM THE MOMENT OF BIRTH

Mothers Should Use Cuticura Soap, the World's Favorite for Baby's Skin, Scalp, Hair and Hands.

Mothers are assured of the absolute purity and unfailing efficacy of Cuticura Soap and Cuticura Ointment, the great Skin Cure, and purest of emollients, in the preservation and purification of the skin, scalp, hair, and hands of infants and children. For baby humors, eczemas, rashes, itchings, and chafings, as a mother's remedy for annoying irritations and ulcerative weaknesses, and purest, sanative, antiseptic purposes which readily suggest themselves to women, as well as for all the purposes of the toilet, bath, and nursery, Cuticura Soap and Ointment are priceless.

—J. H. Smart closed his pastorate with the First Church of Christ, Danville, Ill., the end of September, having served just twenty-nine months. He reports the field a difficult one, on account of local causes, despite which Brother Smart accomplished some excellent work. All the societies were largely increased, but the prayer-meeting was not a great success. An old indebtedness of more than $600 was paid, a $500 mortgage with interest and taxes were paid, a $2,500 pipe organ installed and paid for, and 206 additions to the church were gained, while the missionary offerings were increased. Brother Smart leaves the church in better shape for aggressive work and hopes his successor, M. B. Ainsworth, will lead the church on to greater success. The address of Brother and Sister Smart is now 2096 North Union street, Decatur, Ill., where they will be pleased to see their friends. We believe that it will give our good brother pleasure to do some evangelistic work or to serve churches in the neighborhood in such ways as he can.

❀ ❀

Constipation—Its Cause and Cure.

—Replying last week to a statement of the "Christian Courier" that while the Revised Version had rendered *eis* by *into,* in Matt. 28:19 (baptizing them *into,* etc.), the American Revised Bible had gone back to *in,* we stated that this was not the case in the American Revised Bible which we were using and which this House was selling. This is true, but we find on examination that an edition of the American Revised Bible in 1900, does contain the rendering *in,* but "the Standard Edition" of 1901 has *into* in the passage mentioned. The former must have been a typographical error. In buying the American Revised Bible see that you get the Standard Edition.

—Edward Tilburn has just begun his second year with the church at Mishawaka, Ind. During the past year there were 121 accessions to the church, with a net increase of 104. Over $3,160 were reported from all departments of the work, $275 being contributed for missions. The Sunday-school has trebled and the Christian Endeavor doubled its membership. Many improvements have been made in the church building and arrangements made to pay the debt which has been hanging for ten years on the church. The annual evangelistic season will commence December 31, with W. E. M. Hackleman conducting the music. Brother Tilburn begins his second year with an increase in salary.

—The congregation at Mt. Sterling, Ill., having outgrown their building, have recently expended some $3,300 for an addition and repairs. This work was accomplished under the enthusiastic leadership of J. L. Lorton. The dedication was held on October 14, and Russell F. Thrapp, of Jacksonville, who spent the day with the Mt. Sterling brethren writes us that enough money was raised to wipe out all indebtedness and have enough left over to finish the basement. The Bible school at Mt. Sterling which is led by Edward E. Clark, is the largest in the country.

—The lot which was purchased for the First Christian Church, Oakland, Cal., about a year ago as a site for a new church home has recently been sold at an advance of more than double the price originally paid, which was $12,250. Another lot has just been purchased for $18,000 just a block to the north of the former one and the

difference of $7,000 is sufficient to practically pay the balance over and above what has been paid in on the subscriptions, so that almost all that may come in on the building fund in the future will go towards the erection of the house.

—As a result of a good meeting held by James C. Burkhardt, pastor at Connersville, Ind., the brethren at the Hennigan Church, Rush county, will have preaching half time, James Teeter dividing his time between that point and Lyons Station, while he is in attendance at Butler College. At Philomath, Wayne county, many people had never seen a sign of organization or building, but as a result of Brother Burkhardt's efforts his nephew, John W. Burkhardt, will now preach at that point once a month in the schoolhouse. The work at Connersville goes forward. The offerings during the year have been over $17,000 and the indebtedness on the new $40,000 building is now less than $10,000. The offerings on a recent Sunday amounted to $1,220.

—During the past year the church at Hope, Ark., employed a pastor for all of his time. This was a decided step in advance. For the first time they supplied their minister with a home to live in. The result has been that more money has been raised and expended than in any two previous years and 130 additions to the church are reported, 89 by baptism, and all through regular services, excepting 29 that came during the meeting with Brother Sanders. The

---

NEW OFFICERS OF THE HOME SOCIETY.

R. H. Miller, First Vice-President.

George H. Combs, President.

Vernon Stauffer, Second Vice-President.

church has become a living link in the Home Society and by November 1 Brother Humphrey, of Kentucky, will be at work in the Hope district. Forty-five other additions are reported and one church organized as a result of the work of the pastor, Percy G. Cross, during his vacation. He will continue at Hope with an increase of salary.

❀ ❀

CHURCH EXTENSION.

(Continued from Page 1363.)

stands. They are unwilling that their identity should be lost, and are willing to get under mortgage for their faith's sake. As a further appeal, the speaker urged the loyalty of these little bands of workers to the ethics of Christ in the business realm. He spoke of the truly wonderful record of the Board of Church Extension in dealing with these churches. In all, 1,022 loans have been made, and in the work over $1,000,000 has been handled, and yet the board has only lost in all its dealings in forty-three states and territories during the past eighteen years the insignificant amount of $563. The churches have maintained their credit in clean cut business life. A fourth mark of loyalty was noted in the missionary activity of 100 representative Church Extension churches. In spite of heavy local obligations these 100 representative churches gave to missionary enterprises during the past year more than $9,000. The last line of emphasis was the loyalty of these churches which the brotherhood had helped to the work of evangelization. Fifty-eight out of 100 representative churches reported 13,771 additions since their Church Extension loan was granted, 3,748 of these additions being during the past year. In closing, the speaker urged an even more generous response on the part of the churches at large to loyal but homeless bands of Disciples still knocking at the doors.

❀ ❀

As We Go to Press.

Special to THE CHRISTIAN-EVANGELIST.

Springfield, Ill., October 21.—Unparalleled audiences at West Side. Church to-day; thirty-five added.—Dorris and Altheide.

Special to THE CHRISTIAN-EVANGELIST.

Huntington, W. Va., Oct. 22.—Beginning here with great interest; thirteen additions first day.—Orilas G. White, pastor; Fife & Saunders, evangelists.

Special to THE CHRISTIAN-EVANGELIST.

Johnstown, Pa., October 20.—Twenty additions. Eleven churches in this ward. Hibler and Steed men of fine influence. Hibler has built two churches, a $55,000 property and $8,000 property; Steed elected president ministerial union.—Clarence Dumont Mitchell.

Special to THE CHRISTIAN-EVANGELIST.

Russellville, Ind., Oct. 22.—Our large, handsome church overpacked yesterday; interest great; Richard Martin, evangelist; twenty additions already; sixteen baptized; nearly two thousand added at Martin family meetings during the past twenty-seven months.—Elder Benjamin Goff.

Special to THE CHRISTIAN-EVANGELIST.

Bloomington, Ill., October 21.—Brooks brothers' revival closed to-night with vast audience and impressive services. Twenty-one added to-day. Total 278. J. V. Updike, who recently purchased a home here; took membership with us to-day. His presence at union communion

service this afternoon a benediction. Evangelists go next to Central Church, Lexington, Ky.—Edgar D. Jones.

Special to THE CHRISTIAN-EVANGELIST.

Kansas City, Mo., Oct. 22.—Immense audiences here yesterday; thirteen additions. Geo. H. Combs among unselfish and spiritual men of earth; Sunday-school nearly thousand, everybody rejoicing.—Small and St. John.

Special to THE CHRISTIAN-EVANGELIST.

Cameron, Mo., October 22.—Great meeting here with Herbert Yeuell; thirty additions to-day, seventy to date; best people of the city; a union meeting running in one of the leading churches.—L. O. Bricker, Minister.

Special to THE CHRISTIAN-EVANGELIST.

Charles R. Scoville has closed a union meeting at Sullivan, Ill., with 732 additions to the churches. Of these 450 will unite with the Christian Church, which is continuing the meeting with home forces, J. G. McNutt being the pastor. There were twenty additions in the first four days after Brother Scoville left. Three hundred have already been baptized. Brother McNutt reports that the other churches are baptizing nearly all their converts.

❀ ❀

Princeton's Evangelistic Campaign.

Princeton, Ind., will enter upon the great state simultaneous campaign on Monday evening, October 29. H. J. Otto, pastor of the church there, will have as his special evangelists O. D. Maple and J. R. Miller. It is probable that this movement will, in some respects, differ from the usual movements employed in evangelistic efforts in that its first endeavor will be to summon all the power at its command towards impressing the public with one text, "That ye love one another as

H. J. Otto, Princeton, Ind.

I have loved you." Like other cities, Princeton does not lack for varied forms of Christian teaching, nor is it without signs of prudence. It has much that commends it in the way of religious activity, but its religious forces need to be united in Christ. The Christian body of Disciples desires to disprove the prevailing impression that salvation is by water only, as well as that it is trying to bring about Christian union by proving that baptism is essential to salvation. Where the "If you love me" is emphasized, we may hope for the matter of ordinances finding its own solution. Brother Otto has been planning, preparing, and praying that souls may be saved and that the local congregation which has assisted so faithfully in the preparation is looking with delightful anticipation to the great work of evangelization. It is hoped that Princeton will catch the spirit of the real Pentecostal love. Evangelist Maple's first sermon—"A United Army Means Victory" is one in which he will urge, first, that the members of the Christian church work as one map for the saving of souls; second, that Christians of all churches aid in the greatest of all Vocations; third, that the intention of our Lord and Master was and is to have only one faith, one fold, one church. Other subjects for the first

week are "The Revival Princeton Needs and Must Have," "To Serve is to be Grand," "The Enthusiasm of Evangelization," "Soul Winning," and "Qualifications of Soul Winners." During the meeting announcements will be made of how the campaign is going throughout the state and in other states as well.

❀ ❀

Board of Ministerial Relief of the Church of Christ.

Aid in the support of worthy, needy, disabled ministers of the Christian Church and their widows.

THIRD LORD'S DAY IN DECEMBER is the day set apart in all the churches for the offering to this work. If you make individual offerings, send direct to the Board. Wills and Deeds should be made to "BOARD OF MINISTERIAL RELIEF OF THE CHURCH OF CHRIST," a corporation under the laws of the State of Indiana." Money received on the Annuity Plan.

Address all communications and make all checks, drafts, etc., payable to

BOARD OF MINISTERIAL RELIEF, 120 E. Market St., Indianapolis, Indiana.

NEWS FROM MANY FIELDS

West Kentucky Notes.

The Sunday-school Convention of the Twenty-third District will meet at Fulton, November 1 and 2. This district is composed of the eight western counties known as "The Jackson Purchase."——The erection of the new church building at Mayfield is being pushed forward with great energy. When completed it will be one of the best in the state.——West Kentucky College has opened up finely with an excellent body of students in attendance. The high grade of the student body is most gratifying. New students are entering every week.——Bro. W. T. Wells, pastor of the Bowling Green church, is assisting R. L. Clark at Mayfield in a protracted meeting with fine prospects of success. Brother Wells is a strong, well-equipped and fearless preacher of the Gospel.——Bro. R. L. Clark has resigned his work with the Mayfield congregation to take effect January 1. Here is an excellent opportunity for some church to secure a strong preacher and a good pastor. During his four years' pastorate, the Mayfield church has increased from a membership of about 400 to 600, and the money has been raised and the contract let for one of the finest houses of worship in West Kentucky.
Mayfield, Ky.   G. A. LEWELLEN.

Illinois Notes.

Bell Plain, or Pattensburg, has one of the oldest churches in the state. It was near here that Mrs. O. A. Burgess grew to womanhood and from which she entered Eureka college. Near here father Palmer, a pioneer preacher of great power, resided a half century ago, whose influence extended to all this region of country, and whose name is dear to all the old people. The church is perhaps smaller and weaker than fifty years ago, because of deaths and removals to railroad towns, but it is still a good church holding forth the word of life and taking liberal offerings for all our enterprises. F. A. Scott is the faithful and devoted minister.——At Bell Ridge, H. M. Brooks preaches, which necessarily means public enterprise and progress. Three years ago a woman, Mrs. O'Hair, determined that the country community, which is ten miles south of Paris, should have a Sunday-school. She organized it in the nearby school house, which was soon filled with people. Preaching was occasionally had, finally a meeting, $5,000; church was built, another meeting by Brothers Brooks and Idleman, with more than 100 additions. In short, a woman's devotion, husband's co-operation, a community's right purpose, all helping, the right preacher, a mind to work and the blessing of God, which always waits to help the willing-hearted, in three short years results in the conversion of nearly 200 people, a church of 220, a $5,000 house, a Sunday-school averaging 100, with one of the finest companies of young people that I have seen anywhere. What cannot the Lord's people do with his gracious help! In how many places is he waiting and longing to be gracious, if only his people would arise in their strength and his, and go forward. There are but few churches now in our state that ought not to be planning a great meeting this fall or winter. Never in our history has the Lord poured out upon us a more fruitful season, nor greater harvests. Shall we liberally honor him by having the Gospel preached? So far as in us is, let us be worthy of his bounty.——J. I. Gunn is getting well into the work as well as into the hearts of the people at Arcola. This is one of our strongest churches, which through several years' ministry of L. T. Faulders took great strides forward. It will be no small task to hold the ground already taken and keep advancing in all lines of church activity at home, and take an increasing interest and part in all the great enterprises of the church. Brother Gunn, with the faithful co-operation of the church, will be able for these things.——At Atlanta, I. W. Agee is devoting his Christian energies. A splendid new parsonage is a valuable acquirement of the church. The Sunday-school, under the leadership of Brother Mountjoy, is full of life and interest. It has the best Sunday-school orchestra that I have seen in Illinois.——The Minier church is enjoying a vastly improved house of worship. The audiences at church and attendance at Sunday-school are fine. J. E. Couch, for several years the minister, has resigned, and expects to go west. The church that secures his services will be fortunate. He is a native of Illinois, and we are sorry to lose him. May his work always be blessed.——The work at Mason City prospers under the splendid ministry of O. C. Bolman. There are additions most every week. The church audiences and Sunday-school are large. The church membership is 145; 55 having been added in the year and a half of Brother Bolman's ministry with the church. The Christian Endeavor and C. W. B. M. are prosperous. This has been the home for about 40 years of J. M. Haughey, whose preaching has blessed many parts of Mason county, as well as of Mason City. He has married about 1,500 couples and buried 1,500 dead. He is now enjoying a quiet and peaceful old age with his wife, who has been a partner truly in all his labors and joys. How beautiful to grow old with a sweet, loving spirit and heart in humble trust and loyal faith in Christ.——The strong church at Petersburg is still doing business in its old house. Occasionally a stir calls for the new and modern, but quiet is soon restored. It is a good time to build while times are prosperous. Petersburg is a good town. Many of its young people go away to college. Some come to Eureka. Some of our former students are among the leaders of the city's life. W. M. Grove, the popular minister of the church is full of enthusiasm and is eminently successful in his work. He led one of the best and most enthusiastic prayer-meetings that I have attended for some time. We miss from the happy faces in the congregation of other years, Judge Blane and father Smoot, but younger people are taking their places, whether as faithful and true, or not time will tell. Bro. L. F. Watson, of Wateska, now lives here and as ever is active in the church.——The Athens church still struggles and succeeds. It numbers about 125, with 100 or more in Sunday-school. Its new, modern house is paid for and makes a splendid spiritual home for young and old and all departments of church work. Their young and active preacher, F. E. Welton, is in his first pastorate, having left a lucrative business in Decatur last spring to preach the gospel. Some forty have been added to the church since he came and all parts of the work seem to prosper. There are many men in business and in the professions who ought to be preaching the gospel and saving the people. We need, so much, more preachers. We have more than twice as many churches in Illinois as preachers, many communities have to suffer. The college in its present support and patronage falls far short of supplying the demand.——J. H. Henderson is getting well into his work at Tallula. This is one of our older churches and it likes its preacher and is doing good service for the Master. H. E. Monser was just closing a meeting with some 35 additions to the church. He is an able evangelist. Miss Nellie Pollock, of Nebo, led the singing and I heard only words of praise of her work. It was here that R. F. Thrapp, now the pastor of the Jacksonville church, grew to manhood and from here entered Eureka college. Here M. O. Breeden, now of the Central church, Des Moines, Iowa, preached his first sermon while a student of Eureka college. Both these men feel much indebted to that godly woman, now gone home, Mrs. J. W. Judy for many wise and helpful suggestions. Her husband, Col. Judy, still resides here to bless the church.——At Literberry, H. G. Vandervort, of Clayton, ministers half time. They have a good house, some 150 members, Sunday-school of 100. All missionary collections are remembered. I was there "Rally day" for Home Missions. The collection was $16.56. The church, Sunday-school and Endeavor society are all thoroughly alive.——Bro. Charles Coleman has been at Chandlerville nine months. There have been 16 additions to the church which numbers 135 with a Sunday-school of 100. All is peace and harmony and a good work is being done. This is the home of Dr. H. B. Boone and wife, both graduates of Eureka college, and are thoroughly alive and active leaders in the church. Whether a Christian college means more to the cause of Christ in training its ministry or its laity is still an open question. Whether it pays for Christian parents to patronize a Christian college or not, depends on the value put on the Christian life, influence and destiny of the child.
Eureka, Ill.   J. G. WAGGONER.

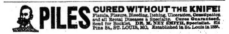

St. Louis Letter.

We are happy to announce that John L. Brandt has nearly recovered from his recent surgical operation. We hear that he has gone to marrying people again.——Sister Princess Long, of Paris, Ky., gave a musical and literary entertainment in the Compton Heights church last week. The audience was delighted. Sister Long's entertainment is of very high grade. It is not only entertaining but helpful and inspiring. Any church or Aid Society that desires a delightful entertainer for an evening, will find it to their advantage to get sister Long, if possible.——The St. Louis preachers are working overtime now. Together with our preparation for the simultaneous meetings we are taking interest in the effort to put other than saloon men into our city and state offices at the next election. We have often heard it said that there is nothing so peculiar as people, we have about decided that politics is.—— The revival interest is already on in the Compton Heights church. We had six additions Sunday of last week; three were baptized on Wednesday evening. One hundred and fifty-five attended the Christian Endeavor meeting, about eighty attend the mid-week prayer-meeting, and the Bible school is crawling toward the four hundred mark in regular attendance.——Good reports from the Buffalo Convention are already coming in. Many of us were deprived the privilege and pleasure of that great meeting, but we are planning to be in Pittsburg in 1909.—F. N. Calvin.

※ ※ ※

Advancing the Cause at Springfield, Ill.

Conspicuous among the younger congregations throughout the brotherhood is the West Side Christian Church of Springfield, Ill. This congregation was organized a little less than five years ago. The First Christian Church, under the leadership of her pastor, J. E. Lynn, now of Warren, Ohio, gave a notable example of unselfishness when she entered heartily into this new movement, releasing one hundred and ten of her own number, to form the charter membership list and contributing, as a body, generously, to the erection of the new house. In this comparatively short time, the West Side Church has made its way up into the ranks of the thoroughly organized churches of the state. Its name is found upon the books of all of her missionary societies with liberal gifts, and its local work is regarded as one of the most successful in the city. The membership has grown rapidly, more than six hundred having been received into its fellowship. The present membership is about five hundred and forty. The Sunday-school enrollment is something over five hundred, the largest attendance at any one session this year being five hundred and five. All departments of church work are thoroughly organized and well supported by the membership. The Sunday-school has one of the largest kindergarten departments and some of the most efficient teachers to be found in the city.

The congregation is, at the present time, engaged in a series of evangelistic meetings, which are being conducted by Victor Dorris, of Pendleton, Ore., and Chas. H. Altheide, of Bloomington, Ia. Under their leadership, the congregation expects to make a most successful campaign. Victor Dorris is too well-known to require any words of introduction. Though his time has been spent largely in pastoral work for the past twenty years, holding a pastorate at Georgetown, Ky., continuously for ten years, he has yet held some of the great meetings of the church. He uses no sensational methods of any kind, but is a strong, persuasive preacher whose messages are enforced by a deeply spiritual life and a winning personality. Chas. H. Altheide is comparatively new in the field of singing evangelists, but has been eminently successful and comes to Springfield at this time for his third meeting. He has just assisted Wm. J. Lockhart in one of his Kansas City churches.

※ ※ ※

The Missionary Bump.

'(Continued from Page 1363.)

day there is a theoretical acknowledgement of the authority of Christ, and a practical acknowledgment of the authority of narrow-minded and stingy brethren. The acknowledgment of the authority of Jesus is valueless unless it is proved by a sincere preaching of the Gospel of giving and a fearless effort to engage the church in her real mission, viz:—the evangelization of the whole world. Let men oppose if they will, let the church be cold and unresponsive if she will, but do thou, O pastor, behold

the towering figure of the Son if God, as, clothed with all authority in heaven and on earth, he points to the regions beyond, to the unnumbered millions who wander beneath the stars vainly wondering if they be the myriad eyes of an avenging deity or the blossoms that mark the footprints of a beneficent God, and do thou hear him as, in a voice that tolerates no disobedience, he commands thee to send to them his Gospel. Dare you disobey? Dare you?

No, brethren, let the missionary bump be developed. It will never become large enough to disfigure the classic contour of your massive craniums. When tempted to turn aside from this sacred duty, this divine privilege, spend a while at the foot of the Cross, fight out the battle in the presence of the agonies of Calvary, and there you will receive inspiration and courage to do the work so dear to the heart of your dying Redeemer. As you gaze into the face of the Crucified One you will hear him gently say:

"I gave, I gave my life for thee:
   What hast thou given for me?"

"What song is sung not of sorrow?
   What triumph well won without pain?
What virtue shall be, and not borrow
   Bright lustre from many a stain?

"What birth has there been without travail?
   What battle well won without blood?
What good shall there be without evil
   Ingarnered as chaff with the good?

"Lo, the Cross set in rocks by the Roman,
   And nourished by blood of the Lamb,
And watered by tears of the woman,
   Has flourished, has spread like the palm;

'Has put forth in the frosts and far regions
   Of snows in the North and South sands,
Where never the tramp of His legions
   Was heard, nor reached forth His red hands.

"Be thankful; the price and the payment,
   The birth, the privations and scorn,
The Cross, and the parting of raiment,
   Are finished. The star brought us morn:

"Look steward; stand far and unearthy,
   Free-soul'd as a banner unfurled,
Be worthy, O brother, be worthy!
   For a God was the price of the world."

※ ※ ※

Catarrh Cannot be Cured

with LOCAL APPLICATIONS, as they cannot reach the seat of the disease. Catarrh is a blood or constitutional disease, and in order to cure it you must take internal remedies. Hall's Catarrh Cure is taken internally, and acts directly on the blood and mucous surfaces. Hall's Catarrh Cure is not a quack medicine. It was prescribed by one of the best physicians in this country for years and is a regular prescription. It is composed of the best tonics known, combined with the best blood purifiers, acting directly on the mucous surfaces. The perfect combination of the two ingredients is what produces such wonderful results in curing Catarrh. Send for testimonials free.

F. J. CHENEY & CO., Props., Toledo, O.
Sold by Druggists, price 75c.
Take Hall's Family Pills for constipation.

Kansas City's Greatest Meeting.

Our splendid meeting, in which the largest number ever won for Christ in any church in Kansas City, closed Sunday night, October 14, with 307 additions. Wm. J. Lockhart and Chas. H. Altheide were the evangelists. I have nothing but words of praise for these splendid men. Brother Altheide is a good leader of song and gave us perfect satisfaction with his chorus of from sixty to seventy members. Brother Lockhart is an ideal evangelist, earnest, clean and true. He has no methods that are objectionable and never said one word that we wished he had not spoken, and is a tireless worker. Our entire church and com-

Frank L. Bowen, Kansas City, Mo.

munity wish to recommend him as a consecrated and noble man of God. We have no wounds to heal, no mistakes to overcome and no actions to cover up.

The meeting lasted six weeks and one day and from the very first service, when 15 came, until the close of the meeting there were additions at every regular service. There had been hard work in preparation for months before the arrival of our men. We talked of the meeting everywhere. The final work was done by sixty of our consecrated women, who canvassed every home within four square miles, ascertaining the religious attitude of the people and leaving an invitation to the meetings. No expense was considered in our advertising. Thousands upon thousands of invitations were given out as the meeting continued and we also used a large bulletin board erected on a prominent corner upon which were the facts of the meeting. Fifty or more young men and women

members. One of the very best results was the securing of fifty-one new subscribers for THE CHRISTIAN-EVANGELIST.

We are a happy church. We must enlarge our building. Jackson Avenue Church is now the third church in the city in size of membership. We shall soon take our offering for missions and hope to move forward in every department. We praise our God for all the influences that helped to gain the Victory. The glory is the Lord's. The blessing is ours. FRANK L. BOWEN, pastor.

From the Evangelist.

In March of this year Frank L. Bowen wrote me saying, "We want you to come and lead us in the greatest meeting Kansas City ever had." Arrangements were made for the meeting. On September 1 I met the pastor and his people in conference. I said; "You may ask what you will, for God is able to do exceeding abundantly above all that we ask or think according to the power that worketh in us."

Brother Bowen's faith was the strongest of all and he said, "I shall not measure this meeting by numbers reached, but I shall hope to see as many as 300 brought into the Kingdom." I mention this that I may again register my conviction that the Church of Christ may have anything asked for when there is a great passionate longing for the thing desired. There was not a service held without additions. There were no wonderful days—33 was the largest number added in one day—but a steady stream of those turning to the Lord or consecrating themselves anew to his services.

Aside from the divine power that enlists into every great meeting the strong factor was the work and influence of Brother Bowen and his faithful wife. Ten years ago the Jackson Avenue Church that now numbers over 700 members was a mission just started by Brother Bowen, who was city evangelist. This was but one of several missions under the supervision and direct pastoral care of Brother Bowen. For seven years he was pastor of all of these missions. During those past years good church buildings were erected Jackson avenue, Budd Park, Ivanhoe Park and Mt. Washington, and during the past three years pastors were located in three of these and they are all growing into strong churches. Brother Bowen is still the general superintendent of city missions, but for three years past he has been pastor also of the Jackson Avenue Church. His has been a great work and he is now enjoying the large fruitage of the ten years of planting.

The people of the Jackson Avenue Church have the spirit of sacrifice and devotion that should mark a true Church of Christ. There was never an objection or a criticism as to the way the work was done. Never have I had more loyal support. Money was no consideration when the object was

With the Church at Odessa, Mo.

The work of the church at Odessa, Mo., under Frank Waller Allen, only son of F. G. Allen, of "Old Path Guide" memory, has been greatly blessed. Some thirty have been baptized, as many added otherwise and the church brought into

C. H. Altheide, Springfield, Ill.

Frank Waller Allen.

E. J. Fensterma

gave us constant service as messengers. Daily visitation by our workers was a feature. Among the converts were 138 married men and women and about 75 young men and young ladies. Twenty-nine came from other religious bodies and almost one hundred from our Sunday-school.

Brother Lockhart closes his meetings with good results. After his sermon to the new converts pledges were taken for the current expenses of the church and $1,500 were pledged by the new

a harmonious fellowship during the present pastorate, beginning May, 1904. The missionary offerings have been doubled each year, and the current expense fund increased from $900 to $1,800. Repairs to the extent of several hundred dollars have been made, and other exterior improvements are contemplated. The present membership is about 275.

This is Brother Allen's first regular pastorate and manifests his ability to fill larger fields to which he has had calls, but the loyalty of his

the reaching of more people for (ple are all a working people, but purposes came without an effort was spent in direct advertising of this was no small factor in the

Chas. H. Altheide, of Bloomfield of song, won the sympathy and people from the start. He is a leader and even stronger as a s lection of music is of the very h he spares no time or money to l self for his chosen work. A spe demands more than a passing not concert planned and executed fo what it was intended to do.

I should do that great body injustice if, in closing, I should faith, courage and devotion of ministers. Never have I met wholesome body of men and I been made much stronger for my the sympathy and fellowship of Kansas City, who stand for th Christ above creed. Would the there might be the same high sta fellowship! The unity of our City makes it entirely correct to u term, "the Church at" Kansas C Des Moines, Iowa. WM.

people and his advocacy of the have thus far held him at Odessa

On November 5 his brother-in termacher, of Poplar Bluff, wit meeting. Brother Fenstermacher in Missouri. Besides his pastor held some good meetings, notabl where about 75 were added. Th the church bears tribute of appr cial letter from which I quot

"Your manner has been un speech eloquent, and your mes and intelligibly delivered as c Master's command 'Go preach' Sister F. G. Allen, who yet siding with her daughter at Po present during the meeting.

Added to this strong combi influence of 360 copies of THE GELIST distributed weekly. A. W

Evangelistic

We invite ministers and others to send reports of meetings, additions and other news of the churches. It is especially requested that additions be reported as "by confession and baptism," or "by letter."

Arkansas.

Bentonville, Oct. 8.—One baptism at the regular Lord's day service.—J. W. Ellis.

California.

Dinuba, Oct. 10.—One added Sunday night.—R. A. Staley.

Bakersfield, Oct. 16.—Five added last Lord's day.—R. E. McKnight.

Pomona.—Am now in a meeting with home forces. Twenty additions in two weeks. Will continue one more week.—M. A. Hart.

Corona, Oct. 12.—Closed my work at Waitsburg, Wash., September 23, with three additions. Commenced work here October 7.—W. T. Adams.

Bakersfield, Oct. 11.—Nine added the last two Sundays. Membership has more than doubled in the last ten months without a protracted meeting. Every department of church work is prospering.—R. E. McKnight.

Colorado.

Ft. Collins, Oct. 16.—The meeting just closed at the First Church resulted in 27 additions, making 71 in our work. All departments of church work are making good progress.—J. F. Findley.

Idaho.

Weiser, Oct. 16.—One more addition last Sunday.—G. M. Read.

Illinois.

Cairo.—Eight added.—O. D. Maple, evangelist.

Putnam.—Closed a splendid meeting October 3, at Putnam, Ill., with no additions.

Scottville, Oct. 15.—Ten added here in two weeks, six yesterday. Meeting will continue a few days.—M. L. Anthony, evangelist.

Blue Mound, Oct. 17.—Our meeting here with W. H. Harding has opened with bright prospects. Five confessions so far, and fine audiences.

Springfield, Oct. 18.—Evangelists Victor Dorris and C. H. Altheide are now in a splendid meeting at the West Church. Twenty-four accessions to date.—F. M. Rogers.

Chicago, Oct. 18.—Thirty-nine accessions have been gained at the West Pullman Church during the past year, 23 by confession and baptism, and 16 by letter and statement.—Guy Hoover, minister.

Niantic, Oct. 18.—Fifteen added here—13 by confession, during first ten days of our meeting. Charles E. McVey is conducting the music. Forty have been added since I began here last March.—J. Will Walters.

Chicago, Oct. 8.—Closed our meeting here with seven confessions the last day. Eighteen additions in all. Had to close too soon. Interest and attendance greatly increased during the last week. I begin in Downs, Kansas, next Sunday.—H. E. Wilhite.

Indiana.

Hartford City, Oct. 16.—Two by letter last Lord's day.—William Elmer Payne.

New Albany, Oct. 15.—Four added since last report.—E. T. Porter, minister Park church.

Connersville, Oct. 12.—Forty-three added to the Central church at Connersville in regular services have not been reported.—James C. Burkhardt.

Rushville, Oct. 13.—Thirty-nine additions, 33 by baptism, at the Harmony church, in a four weeks' meeting held by H. K. Shields and J. W. Wittkamper.

Middletown, Oct. 15.—Eight additions at Plum Creek in a short meeting, all baptisms. Will continue with the church there another year, preaching once a month.—L. E. Murray.

Rensselaer, Oct. 16.—Have just closed a meeting at the Good Hope church, with 18 confessions. Organized an Endeavor Society. They have a good Sunday-school and the church is greatly revived.—G. H. Clarke.

Connersville, Oct. 17.—James C. Burkhardt has held two brief meetings recently. One, of four days at the Hannigan church in Rush county, resulted in 11 additions. The other, a meeting of five nights with seven added, was at Philomath, an entirely new field.

Ambia, Oct. 8.—The meeting at Ambia resulted in 19 additions; nine by obedience. Brother Mahin, of Angola, did the preaching for the first part of the meeting, after which the writer and Brother Mercer of Hoopeston, continued. If Brother Mahin could have remained, there would, we believe, have been more additions.—Warner King.

Indian Territory.

Tulsa, Oct. 19.—Three additions since last report. Work in a prosperous condition.—Randolph Cook.

Amber, Oct. 18.—Had splendid interest here with 28 additions. Heavy rains interfered. Close to-morrow night.—Robert E. Rosenstein.

Iowa.

Marcus, Oct. 18.—Closed a ten days' meeting with the Cleghorn church with 15 additions—14 confessions and one by statement.—William Baier, minister.

Kansas.

Downs, Oct. 16.—Our meeting starts well. Two days old with six additions.—H. E. Wilhite.

Manhattan, Oct. 15.—Four added yesterday. One by confession and baptism, and three by letter.—W. T. McLain.

Fredonia, Oct. 15.—Twelve added last Sunday, seven others since last report, making 19 at regular services in about two and one-half months.—H. M. Johnstone, pastor.

McPherson, Oct. 15.—Five baptized yesterday. Five others added by letter the last three Sundays. Will begin a meeting at Potwin, Kan., October 22.—W. A. Morrison, minister.

Baxter Springs, Oct. 18.—Preached two weeks at Neutral. Had good hearing and baptized five. Brother Patrick, of Duenweg, Mo., preaches for them, and baptized one before our meeting.—C. W. Yard.

Kentucky.

Ashland, Oct. 15.—Have begun a meeting with home forces. Six added yesterday—four of them confessions.—William D. Ryan.

Cherryvale, Oct. 16.—One added by letter and one by baptism October 7. An auxiliary to the C. W. B. M. has been organized.—B. D. Gilliapie.

Erlanger, Oct. 19.—Closed a two weeks' meeting October 14 with 11 additions—five by primary obedience, six by letter and statement. W. J. Cocke did the preaching.—L. D. Haskins, minister.

Lancaster, Oct. 15.—Our meetings closed with 19 additions, but this does not measure the good accomplished. John E. Pounds, of Cleveland, Ohio, did the preaching, and Miss Ida Hanna of Cincinnati, led the singing. Three added since the meeting closed.—F. M. Tinder.

Missouri.

Brunswick, Oct. 15.—Three confessions yesterday.—E. H. Williamson.

Centralia, Oct. 9.—Closed in Green City with 17 additions.—H. G. Bennett.

Hunnewell, Oct. 15.—Our meeting starts nicely. Seven additions to date.—R. B. Havener.

St. Louis, Oct. 15.—Seven additions at Antioch. In Monroe county since last report, and three at AuxVasse.—H. M. Kern.

New Franklin.—Two confessions and baptisms at New Franklin, two at Higbee, two at Armstrong.—A. N. Lindsey.

Kansas City, Oct. 15.—Eight additions to the church October 7—six by letter and two by confession.—Louis S. Cupp.

Canton, Oct. 19.—Have closed a meeting at Newark, Mo., with 13 additions. I begin at Sweet Oak, October 22.—C. F. Rose.

Ridgeway, Oct. 17.—Am in a meeting here with home forces. Meeting two weeks old. Fine interest. Thirty-two additions to date.—W. H. Hobbs.

Warrensburg, Oct. 17.—Have just closed a meeting at Eldorado Springs. No additions, but good audiences. Meeting should have continued but other engagements prevented.—A. Sterling.

Higginsville, Oct. 20.—A meeting at the Cedar Grove church near here with 27 confessions to date; 14 at last two services; 10 young men confessed Christ last night; the meeting will continue.—L. B. Coggins.

Elmira, Oct. 16.—Closed a week's meeting here last Sunday with seven additions—three by confession and baptism. Have commenced at Pleasant View. J. N. Crowther will assist me, a few days.—O. L. Sumner, minister.

Eldorado Springs, Oct. 15.—The Central Christian Church has just closed a three weeks' meeting. R. Sterling, of Warrensburg, did the preaching. While there were but three added, the meeting was a grand success.—W. G. iiearn, pastor.

Moberly, Oct. 20.—Our meeting with Homer T. Wilson as evangelist closed last Monday night. There were 28 additions—23 confessions. The meeting did great good. Six confessions and 23 additions by letter before the meeting.—W. B. Taylor.

Moberly, Oct. 14.—Homer T. Wilson, of San Antonio, is with us for a short meeting at the Central church. There have been 22 additions—19 confessions. Our meeting has been a quiet one, but has steadily grown in interest.—W. B. Taylor.

Atlanta, Oct. 15.—C. L. Harbord, pastor, has just closed a two weeks' meeting with the church here. There were 21 additions—11 by confession and baptism, and ten by statement and letter. This has been the most successful meeting held in Atlanta for years. Bro. Harbord will remain as another year.—W. M. Atterbury.

Union Star.—R. H. Fife and I held a two weeks' meeting with 18 added. Then went to Orchid, a country church, where we had 40 additions, all confessions but two. Twenty decided on Sunday night under the appeals of Brother Fife while I was baptizing. Brother De Val, the pastor, being absent at the convention. The brethren are rejoicing. We will be in the campaign at Huntington, W. Va., next.—Herbert H. Saunders.

Nebraska.

Fairfield, Oct. 15.—Three additions by confession and baptism.—H. C. Williams, pastor.

Grand Island, Oct. 18.—Two additions here September 30 from another church, four on October 7, two by baptism. Thirty-five added at regular services since we came in March.—James R. McIntire.

Norfolk, Oct. 16.—State Evangelist R. F. Whiston closed a four weeks' meeting here Sunday. The meeting was held in a tent. It rained nearly all the first week and the last week it was very cold. It was a good meeting. There were three additions by baptism and 14 by letter, by statement and reclaimed. We now have a membership of 44. We proceed to build at once. Brother Whiston and wife go from here to Guide Rock.—John L. Stine.

Ohio.

North Royalton, Oct. 12.—Evangelist Charles A. Freer conducted a three weeks' meeting for us, resulting in six baptisms and one added by statement.—Charles Ford.

Oregon.

Dallas, Oct. 15.—Seven added here the past two Lord's days—all by letter.—A. C. Corben, pastor.

Texas.

Ft. Worth, Oct. 15.—Eight additions at the Tabernacle church. Six by baptism.—A. E. Dubber.

Houston, Oct. 17.—The first quarter's work with the Second church closed with the following results: Ten added by letter and statement, 13 by confession, three from other religious bodies.—P. B. Scrimsher, minister.

Austin, Oct. 12.—Thirty-two were added to the Central Christian church during July, August and September. Eleven were by confession and baptism, three from other religious bodies, 14 restored, and the others by letter and commendation.—J. W. Lowber.

San Angelo, Oct. 13.—R. R. Hamlin and Leonard Daugherty closed a three weeks' meeting for the church here last Sunday. The meeting was a success. It closed with 34 additions—11 baptisms, 16 by letter and three from other religious bodies.—S. T. Shore, pastor.

Washington.

Tacoma.—Fifteen additions.—W. A. Moore.

Seattle, Oct. 16.—Closed a four weeks' meeting in Everett, Wash., October 14, with 12 additions. N. H. Brooks was the evangelist. George A. Webb and wife, singing evangelists.

Sunday-School

November 4, 1906.

**THE LORD'S SUPPER.—Matt.
26:17-30.**

Golden Text.—This do in remembrance
of me.—1 Cor. 11:24.

Memory verses, 26, 27.

The man who furnished the room in
which the last supper was eaten is one of
the obscure and unnamed contributors to
the Lord's work—like the owner of the
ass used in the triumphal entry, and the
boy whose loaves and fishes fed the five
thousand. These are of that noble company of the humble saints whose names are
written in no earthly record, but who, by
hidden deeds of helpfulness or by small
but timely aid which they alone could give,
have contributed to the advancement of the
kingdom.

This last passover supper had three
meanings. First of all, it was a passover
supper eaten in accordance with the requirements of Jewish law and custom, for
Jesus made no unnecessary and premature
break with the religion of his fathers. Second, it was a friendly meal by which was
symbolized the close brotherly relations of
the group which ate it, for by oriental
usage breaking bread together was a token
of intimate fellowship and alliance.

In the third place, the bread and the cup
were made the symbols of the body and
blood of Christ, and thus of his approaching death, so that the supper became a
symbolical statement of what Jesus had
much earlier expressed in figurative speech
when he said: (John 6:35), "I am the
bread of life." and (John 6:53), "Except
ye eat the flesh of the Son of man and
drink his blood, ye have not life in yourselves."

Did Jesus mean that his disciples should
observe the supper as a perpetual institution? Was he consciously establishing an
ordinance? Or was he merely putting a
new meaning into the common meal and
asking to be remembered with every breaking of bread. The texts do not support
either view with certainty as opposed to
the other. But one thing is clear from the
history of the apostolic church; the disciples who were present at the supper, and
who heard the whole of the discourses and
instructions which are reported to us only
in fragments, were of the opinion that it
was an ordinance for perpetual observance.
Their understanding of the matter must
carry more weight than the interpretation
of any particular text.

So the Lord's supper became an established and recognized institution in the
church. At first it was held in connection
with a real meal, within a century this
meal, called the "love feast" or *agape*, was
discontinued and only the symbolical elements in minimum quantities were retained.
At the very first in the Jerusalem church
the meeting for breaking of bread was
probably daily (but this is a disputed
point), but very soon, in apostolic days, the
weekly observance was the universal rule.

❀ ❀

Midweek Prayer-Meeting

October 31, 1906.

A DEAD CHURCH.—Rev. 3:1-6.

"My soul, it is thy God
Who calls thee by his grace;
Now loose thee from each cumbering load,
And bend thee to the race.

"Make thy salvation sure;
All sloth and slumber shun;
Nor dare a moment rest secure,
Till thou the goal hast won.

"Thy crown of life hold fast;
Thy heart with courage stay;
Nor let one trembling glance be cast
Along the backward way."

Sardis may be destroyed, but even
amid the shadows of her impending desolation the Spirit would still in full-con-
fidence breathe forth: He that overcometh, the same shall be clothed in white
raiment; and I will not blot out his
name out of the book of life, but I will
confess his name before my Father, and
before his angels.

It is well to note that in heavenly par-
lance the clerk of the church is called
"angel." There ought to be some simi-
larity in the characters of clerk and angels as well as in their duties. In selecting this officer there should be closer
scrutiny of his spiritual timbre than of
his penmanship. Indeed every one who
serves in the house of the Lord in any
capacity ought to put on the Lord Jesus
Christ and endeavor as others do not to
live as and be God men and God women.

Many of us have a name to live, for
are not our names on the church register? Were all names transcribed from
the records of the angel of the church at
Sardis to the Lamb's book of life? There
are reasons for believing that he who
sees by all the light of the seven stars
and knew the spirits of those ancients
cherishing the delusion that church membership was a guaranty of immortality
and glory, wrote opposite many names
—"and art dead."

Possibly Sardis had been well instructed in the ways of the Lord, and
knew so well the plan of salvation they
could unerringly give to sinners the formula of redemption, but "I have not
found thy works perfect before God."
O that men would realize that it is not in
statements of belief, nor in the smoke
of burnt offerings, nor in eloquent exhortations to righteousness but in the
doing of the will of God, divine approval and salvation are found.

Through her sins Sardis had not separated herself from God's love or watchfulness. Sardis was dead in the sense
that she was separated from God, was
drawing no strength, warmth, conscience,
courage or hope from him. It was only
through penitence, her melting away with
penitential tears the barrier in sinfulness she had thrown between her and the
sources of her life the old life could be
resumed. It is so with us. The old inheritance of love is still ours if through
repentance, renunciation, restitution and
sanctification we come into vital relationship with it.

Sardis was the capital of ancient
Lydia. It was the home of Croesus, the
richest man of antiquity. The wars of
Saracen and Turk and earthquake shock
have made a ruin of the great and once
splendid city. We know nothing of the
history of the church there save this testimony of Jesus. It was neither the op-

ally bearing up our interests in his pray-ers. Kingdoms and all their glory were they ours would be as baubles to be thrown aside to receive this blessing con-ditioned on our obedience to Christ, "And I will pray the Father, and he shall give you another comforter, that he may abide with you forever."

It would seem the halcyon days of the race were when God walked and talked familiarly with Adam and Eve in Eden, but I doubt not he is nearer to many to-day than to them. They received him in a garden; but the happiest of earth's children have enshrined him in their hearts. His presence there filled our first parents with guilty fears; may it fill ours with peace and joy. After their communings in the garden they saw the flaming sword guarding the way to the tree of life; after ours may we see the throne and the scepter and fadeless glory.

Two men look on the same sunset but it speaks to them a different language. To one it tells how soon the burdens of the day may be laid down and the even-ing's rest begun. To the other it sug-gests the close of life, the end of dynas-ties, the fading glory of days and eras, other worlds eagerly awaiting its com-ing and eternities where there is no need of suns because God is their light. It is even so in communion with Christ. It is a privilege as common as looking into sunsets but for the one prepared for

it there is in each moment of it a bless-edness the crass minded can not com-prehend, nor of which he can become possessed till there is in him more of the mind of the Master.

❀ ❀

As Seen From the Dome.

(Continued from Page 1364.)

miership," "isolated," "truths," "pen-chant," need looking up in the Standard or some other dictionary. "Strategic," "age-long" and "along these lines" were overworked as usual, the last in some form appearing five times in one short report. "Ponderous re-spectability of inherited orthodoxy," "Put your heart into China," "Cubans are good for something else beside rais-ing Cain literally and figuratively," "We can trust the common people with a trust second only to our trust in God," "Your face is similar to me, but I can't recognize you," "We are not ungenerous, only untaught with respect to money," "We give by fits, but the trouble is the fits are neither violent nor protracted," were some of the crumbs swept up. Our old friends "reactionaries," "com-mercialism," and "the strenuous life," were there.

❧ The Home Department ❧

'Member?

BY BURGES JOHNSON.

'Member, awful long ago—
Most a million weeks or so—
How we tried to run away
An' was gone for most a day?
Your Pa found us bofe, and ven
Asked if we'd be bad again,
An' we promised, by-um-by,
Do you 'member? So d' I.

'Member when I tried to crawl
Frough vat hole beneaf your wall,
An' I stuck becuz my head
Was too big? Your Muvver said,
When she came to pull me frough,
S'prised you didn't try it too.
And you did it, by-um-by.
'Member! Do y'? So do I.

'Member once, when you an' me,
Found your Muvver's pantry key?
All ve folks stayed out till late,
An' we ate an'—ate-an' ate!
Ma was s'prised, so she confessed,
Vat we didn't eat vp rest.
An' we did it, by-um-by.
Course you 'member? So d' I.

'Member when your Muvver said
"At she wisht I'd run an' do
All ve mischief in my head
All at once an' get it frough?
S'pose we did, why, maybe ven
We could do it all again!
Guess we could if we should try.
Will y' sometime? So'll I.

❀ ❀

The Bronze Vase.

BY J. BRECKENRIDGE ELLIS.

PART IV.

CHAPTER II.

The train for Kansas City did not leave till the next morning, but Raymund took Mrs. De Fer's advice about packing his trunk. He and Rhoda and Mrs. De Fer spent the night at Mr. Willby's, though the fleshy, irascible old gentleman never entirely forgave the French lady for not telling her age. The next morning, Raymund and Rhoda had a few minutes alone in Mr. Willby's parlor, for their adieus:

"Now that we are starting out in life," said Raymund, "let us shape everything for improvement and advancement. As for me, I shall never rest satisfied with my work, but always be looking ahead toward greater service. And I will save and save till those debts are paid off!"

"You'll go to Mrs. Bannerton's for a room, I know," said Rhoda. "Give her my love, if she is still there. And—and Raymund—" She paused, and looked down.

"Well," said Raymund a little impatiently, "why don't you look at me, Rhoda? Well, what were you going to say?"

"Nelsie Loraine will be there," said Rhoda, "and—"

"It isn't likely that I'll ever see her," said the young man; "she'll go in the society of the rich. She'll know nothing about poor tutors."

"I'm not sure," said Rhoda. "But I want you to remember that once—" she stopped in confusion.

Raymund thought he knew what she was thinking, for he said quickly, "And I remember that you gave me Jack Bellfield in the toe of my stocking, for a Christmas present. Sometimes I think you want it back."

Rhoda blushed brightly and smiled and cried with energy, "I don't want it back, and I never have!"

"Oh, Rhoda!" cried Raymund embracing her, "I thought that was what was the matter!"

"There isn't any thing the matter," exclaimed Rhoda trying to break away. But Raymund kissed her once and then again, before he let her go. "There!" he cried, "I'm going to love you, Rhoda, in spite of yourself! I am going to be the brother to you that mother expected me to be. And no matter how indifferent you grow, or how little you get to caring for me, I mean to be your protector, and I mean to keep you my rose!" Then with a very high head, and a heart wounded and half-angry, he marched from the room, leaving Rhoda in tears. At the station, as she bade him good-by, her face was still pale and his eyes were still accusing. He had never found her so unsatisfactory at parting as now. It seemed even after the train had started, that he must go back and ask her why she was a different Rhoda from the Rhoda of his boyhood. When they reached Kansas City, Mrs. De Fer took him at once to one of those splendid houses on Troost avenue that look so aristocratic and are so new. She introduced him to the Geisthauser family. There were the father and mother, and the two Geisthauser boys of nine and fourteen.

"My father," Mr. Geisthauser explained, "was a saloon-keeper from Germany. He could hardly speak English, and he worked so hard after he came to this country, that he had no time to polish himself. I had to knock around considerable myself, in my young days. But the old man had his eyes open, and he kept me in school and wouldn't let me learn German except the public school course. And now, I'm running a distillery—quite an uplift, hey? Now, my sons here, they're to go a notch higher and get out the whisky business altogether. I want you to make gentlemen out of them. Fix 'em up for Congress. I've got plenty of money and I can control the wards in my district, through the saloon-keepers. I'll get 'em in Congress all right, but I want them to be able to stand on their legs when they get there."

"Me," spoke up Ernest Geisthauser, the older boy, "it's nearly impossible for me to learn. Looks like my head won't respond, somehow. Mrs. De Fer, herself, she says it is awful hard for me!"

"Yes," said Mrs. De Fer, "but as kind hearted a lad as ever lived."

"Yes," said Mr. Geisthauser, "it's going to be uphill work, Mr. Revore, but I'm giving you an uphill salary. You just go to work on 'em, for be educated they must, and if you have to bore a hole into their heads to get it in, I'll help hold the augur!"

"We want to learn," said Ernest, "but it looks like we can't. That's why we've quit the public. Every class slipped away from us at the public. Now, I'll tell you how it was. You've seen a boy standing on a sled, and of a sudden some fellow would sneak up and give the rope a pull, and the sled would go on right out from under the boy. That's the way it was with us—wasn't it, Franz?"

"Just that way," the younger Geisthauser nodded. "It looked like we couldn't do nothing! The teacher he always said so himself, and we knowed it. And you ask Mrs. De Fer, she'll tell you the same story."

"We think," chirruped Mrs. Geisthauser, "that Mrs. De Fer has dropped the work because it was so hard for her that she looks on marrying as easier."

"Yes," said Mr. Geisthauser, "I don't think she'd ever have dreamed of taking a man, if Ernest and Franz hadn't been such pudding-heads."

Mrs. De Fer laughed, and Ernest and Franz beamed with stolid good humor. The elder Geisthausers were highly satisfied. "There's one thing," the father remarked, "if you can't do anything with these boys, they're rich anyhow, and can just buy their way through life, if they've no wits to win out with!"

Having made his arrangements for the first lessons, to be given on the morrow, Raymund parted from Mrs. De Fer and hunted up the three-story lodging house on Thirteenth street where he had spent a week with Rhoda in their fifteenth year. How well he remembered their slight beating hearts with which they had climbed the few stone steps! It all came back to him and when in answer to his ring, a maid opened the door, he felt a little shock of surprise because it was not his former landlady. He asked if Mrs. Bannerton still kept the lodging-house, and being told that she did, asked to see her. He now found that the front room was occupied by Mrs. Bannerton; in the old days it had been leased by one of the high-priced lodgers. He was shown in to her. Mrs. Bannerton, supposing it was a stranger come to engage a room, peered at him intently through her near-sighted glasses.

"I am sorry, sir," she said, "but every room is taken, except a little back room on the third story. There is no flue in it, but if you would be willing to use it till cold weather, you can have it for a dollar a week. I do not think you will find another room in a respectable house on this street any cheaper, though I should tell you before you see it, that it is very small and plainly furnished."

"It is the very room I want," said Raymund, smiling. "I remember how it delighted me when I was in it before;

and I can't afford a high price for lodgings."

"Do you mean that you were once in that room?" asked Mrs. Bannerton, peering harder than ever. Before he could answer she had recognized him. "Raymund!" she cried. "Mr. Raymund," she corrected herself. She grasped his hand warmly.

"Yes, Mrs. Bannerton," he said, greatly pleased. "But I wonder that you remember my name after all this time. I was here only a week, and four years ago."

"Not remember your name?" cried Mrs. Bannerton, smiling at him tenderly, and brushing a sudden tear from her eye, "I owe you a month's visit from my boy! Do you remember? He was about to pawn his watch in St. Louis—you spoke to him. He had fallen in with wild companions. He told me all about it when he came. Do you think I can ever forget your name?" Then they had a long talk. She wanted to know all about his sister, but about him, most of all. He learned that her daughter had graduated in music, and had a class in the city. She lived with Mrs. Bannerton, and from their combined earnings, and from what the young soldier sent, they were enabled to keep help and to live in comparative ease and comfort. "I say comparative ease and comfort," said Mrs. Bannerton, correcting herself; "perhaps the case is only comparative, for my daughter works hard with her class, and I have a good deal of management upon my hands. But such comfort! It is a perfect comfort, Mr. Raymund, because I can be proud both of my daughter and of my son. And I often think that if Mr. Bannerton had lived, he would not have been ashamed of them. And when I go to him, Mr. Raymund, do you not think I can give a good account of my guardianship?"

"Call me Raymund," cried the young man. "We are such good friends that

you ought not to build up a barricade of a 'mister' between us." Presently he was shown to the little back room on the third story. Left alone, he gazed about, with what emotions! How uncertain of the future he had been when last those walls looked down upon him, with their faded paper. How restless his young feet had trod that linty carpet. The piece of lead pipe peeping through the ceiling had watched him planning to escape from Boggs. The iron bedstead had held his form as it tossed in feverish despair because no employment could be found in the city. And yet, in a way, he was not so happy now as in those troubled days! He was sure of a roof, now, sure of a position, sure of a steady and generous salary. But he was not sure of Rhoda. In the old days there had been the terror of Boggs and of Mrs. Van Estry; but there had also been the warm, impulsive, outspoken love of his sister. He found himself looking back upon the past with a sigh of regret. "Everything is so much better, now," he sighed, "and yet . . . And yet, somehow, I wish I had that old cracked pitcher with the wire twisted around it to keep it together! And I'd prefer the broken mirror to this new one! I wonder if anybody is ever satisfied?" He threw himself upon the bed and stared out the window. Below was the basement yard into which had once shone the light from Rhoda's window. Beyond was the green lawn leading to the brick residence. He had seen Boggs, four years ago, dodge behind that residence. "I wish I could see him now," muttered Raymund grimly. "How happy I was in those days! I'd even be glad to see Boggs again!" He laughed at himself, but it was not a happy laugh.

Suddenly he smote the window sill with his fist. "They've even put a fire-escape to this window," he muttered. "Everything is for my convenience and comfort. But it's no use! I'll tell you what I'm going to do," he went on, addressing the piece of pipe whose presence in the room was as much a mystery as ever. "I'll go to Crawley at the first chance —probably Christmas—and ask at the bank for that tin box. Mother said that if a difference ever came between me and Rhoda I could do that. Mother didn't want me to see that box, but the difference has come. Once, I imagined it never could! I will see that box," he went on with renewed determination. "Perhaps this difference in Rhoda is the very difference mother foresaw, or rather, feared would come. I've thought of it for a long time. Now I've made up my mind. I must know the meaning of this secret!"

(To be Continued.)

❖ ❖

Pretty Rancid Cheese.

"Recently I visited a small town in the southern part of Kentucky," says a correspondent of the Denver News, "and called on the only merchant of the place. I found him opening a case of axle-grease. He took off the lid of one of the small boxes of yellow grease and left it uncovered.

"Soon an old colored man came in, and, noticing the axle-grease, said:

"'Good morning; Massa Johnson! What am dem little cheeses worf?'

"'About 15 cents, I reckon, Sam,' said the merchant.

"'S'pose I buys one you will frow in de crackers.'

"'Yes, sam.'

"Sam put his hand into his pocket and fished out fifteen cents, and Mr. Johnson took his scoop and dipped up some crackers.

"Sam picked up the uncovered box and

the crackers and went to the back part of the store. Then he took out his knife and fell to eating.

"Another customer came in, and Mr. Johnson lost sight of his colored friend for a moment. Presently Mr. Johnson went to the back part of the store and said:

"'Well, Sam, how goes it?'

"'Say, Massa Johnson, dem crackers is all right, but dat am de ransomest cheese I eber eat!'"

❖ ❖

Picture of War Engine "General."

A beautiful colored picture, 18x25 inches, of the historic old engine "General" which was stolen at Big Shanty, Ga., by the Andrew's Raiders during the Civil War, and which is now on exhibition in the Union Depot, Chattanooga, Tenn., has been gotten out by the NASHVILLE, CHATTANOOGA & ST. LOUIS RY.—The "Battlefields Route" to the South. The picture is ready for framing and will be mailed for 25c. The "Story of the General" sent free. W. L. Danley, Gen'l Pass. Agent, Nashville, Tenn.

A Short Railway Journey in India.

BY ADELAIDE GAIL FROST.

Two of our friends at the Mahoba railway station, Mr. and Mrs. Higgs, asked me to take a trip with them to Banda, thirty-three miles from Mahoba. When we arrived at our destination the large traveler's bungalow there seemed quite like a home, as Mrs. Higgs had sent on her household servants and "tiffin" or luncheon was ready when we reached the bungalow. Mr. Higgs is called the "Plateer Sahib," as he is the "plate-layer," or permanent way inspector on this branch of the India Midland railway. His work is to see that the road is in perfect repair over a section about sixty miles in length. In the rainy season he must take especial care and inspect or oversee the inspection with great fidelity and accuracy. Heavy and sudden rains make washouts and the ballasting of the road must also be carefully attended to. Through the months of July, August and September, night patrolmen go over every foot of the track lest the great iron road of civilization fail in some spot. Each two men have a patrol of four miles.

Traveler's bungalows are such a convenience in India; we were soon quite at home in the large, airy rooms; though if screens did not partition the dining room one might feel desolate in its great and not elaborately furnished, expanse. Its dimensions are 44x21 feet. We had only finished our luncheon when an ancient native arrived with some boxes tied up in a dirty cloth, not at all inviting looking! Untying these same dingy rags he began to spread out his treasures on them. Soon the topaz and amethyst crystals, beautifully cut and polished shone on the poor cloth in glittering little heaps, then exquisite paper knives of agate and paper weights of a beautiful conglomerate containing a great deal of jasper. There were many lovely cut and polished settings and buttons of moss agate, "grass stone," gold stone and many varieties of chalcedony. Most wonderful of all were the crystals enclosing a few drops of liquid. We saw one most beautiful great agate that must have been five inches in diameter and with so much water in its heart that we could easily hear its sound when the stone was shaken. The price of this sounds large at one hundred rupees, but something less at $33.

We endured considerable temptation, and then came what was to me a real treat. Just at evening Mr. Higgs took us out on his trolley for a ride, this trolley is something like a hand car with a long seat upon which three or four can sit. This was a very exhilarating ride. I was astonished at the agility of the trolley men. When we came to an upgrade or where speed was required, the trolley men jumped off and pushed, running along rapidly on the rails. It was very wonderful to me, they never made a misstep on that narrow surface for the soles of their feet. We glided over the rails in the cool, damp evening air, past the picturesque abrupt hills like mountain spurs which are characteristic of this part of India. Huge pyramids of green and brown and gray, some seemed, and here the rocks furnished foundation for the turrets and bastions of an ancient fort, recalling India's feudal days and there they were crowned by crumbling

old temples and many were the tiny, wayside shrines with freshly painted idols within, telling us of the antiquity and the present day belief in gods of stone. Now we come to fields of cotton, broom corn, rice and grain just springing up, so vividly green in this soft light of evening. The rains have been very much better here than about Mahoba. We are "wearying" for the rain there. Here we are at the great railway bridge which spans the Ken river not far from Banda. This immense bridge has twelve spans of 100 feet each and one of 250 feet. The water is about forty feet deep in the deepest place in the hot, dry season, while it comes up to twice that depth in the rains. The river is not yet high and the great, irregular rocky bottom was disclosed in many places, the great swirls of rock looking to me like a huge, petrified whirlpool. Mr. Higgs told me that once while trolleying across the bridge he saw the dead body of a little native child stretched on those cruel rocks where the current had tossed the light form. One shuddered again thinking of the crocodiles in these waters! Did any one care when the little body was thrown there? Did any one miss the baby? It was probably a little girl and some one felt that death were better than life for her and she was not wanted. Across the bridge we looked away to the sunset, some gleams and bands of crimson rifting the gray clouds, then rose, then ashes of roses, still we sped on until one of the trolley men said: "Your gun, Sahib, hiran!" And there they were, five beautiful deer bounding along on an elevation not far away. In a moment the trolley had stopped and Mr. Higgs was creeping up the embankment, one shot and a beautiful little animal looking so clean and perfect was placed at the back of the trolley. I had never seen a deer bound as I saw what must have been a tame deer near a village, bound along by the trolley. Its graceful little body would spring far into the air, the dainty little feet actually did seem to spurn the ground.

As we came back across the river we saw a ferry boat crossing; there is no bridge for pedestrians and vehicles here and when the rains have been heavy the river is very much wider. There are both low and high water landings for the boats. From this Ken River come the beautiful stones which tempted us earlier in the day.

We passed numbers of villages and as ever a thought went out to those whose lives are so poor in many things we count good and whose few, few wants seem so scantily met, one cloth a year, one full (?) meal a day, for bread—a stone, no comfort in life's tragedies, no shelter in the storms of temptation, no school, no books and these but a few out of the thousands of India's similar villages.

When we returned to the bungalow, one of Mr. Higgs' contractors was there with a huge tray of Indian sweet-meats and another of puris and vegetables, cooked in a most tasty way and brought us in dishes fashioned from leaves, in a beautifully primitive manner, pickles there were, too, made from mangoes, seeds of the bread fruit and many curious fruits, vegetables and seeds.

On Sunday we attended an English vesper service in a very pretty little church, restored since the mutiny. The beautiful stained glass, I am told, was bought with fines the government imposed on the insurrectionists. There is a table in the church to the memory of the young civil officer killed in Banda during the mutiny. He was only 27 years old. The Society for the Propa-

gation of the Gospel whose mission is located here in Banda is a "high church" organization whose ritual does not speak to me as it would shorn of some extra flourishes. I thank God that I was, as Miss Graybiel says, "free-born."

Two Schools.

BY REV. HENRY VAN DYKE, D. D

I put my heart to school,
    In the world where men grew wise.
"Go out," I said, "and learn the rule:
    Come back when you win the prize."

My heart came back again,
    "And where is the prize?" I cried.
"This rule was false, and the prize was pain,
    And the teacher's name was Pride."

I put my heart to school
    In the woods where wild birds sing,
    In the fields where flowers spring,
    Where brooks run cold and clear,
    And the blue heaven bends near.
"Go out," I said, "you are only a fool,
    But perhaps they can teach you here."

And why do you stay so long,
    My heart, and where do you roam?
The answer came with a laugh and a song,
    "I find this school is home."
                    —*Atlantic Monthly.*

Billy and the Wee Pig.

"Bill-y-y! Bill-eee!" This loud shout went after Billy into the land of dreams —beautiful land, where he rode a horse, owned a farm, and was "somebody pretty fine."

"Ye'es, sir," cried Billy, zealous to obey, the burr of sleep yet on his tongue. He tumbled out of bed, rubbing his shut eyes, and staggering on his slim legs to the head of the stairs, where he appeared in his night shirt, again saying, "Ye-es, sir!"

Billy had never seen a night shirt until he had come to Farmer Tracy's, in May, as a "fresh-air boy." He thought that a night shirt of new unbleached cotton, made long, and with a turned-down collar, was pretty nearly full dress. Farmer Tracy stood at the stair-foot; he had his spurs on, and a riding whip in his hand. "Billy! do you suppose you could let out the sheep?"

"Course I could!" cried Billy, getting awake very fast.

"Put them over in the big pasture, beyond the turnip field and the clover meadow."

"Oh, I know," said Billy.

"But they have to be got there, out of the stock yard," said the farmer.

"That's easy," said Billy. "You open the gates, and say, co-ee-ee-ee, and they all run out. They want to; you see."

"Yes; it's easy. You open the gates and call 'em. Then there's the collie in the barn. All you have to do is to open the gates, let out the collie, and he'll herd the sheep. I've got to get to town quicker'n a wink."

Billy was so eager to get out, and be independent shepherd of three hundred sheep, that he very nearly forgot his promise to Mrs. Tracy, that he would not leave his room until he washed his face, neck and hands, combed his hair, and said his morning prayer. However, he remembered at the last minute: "I won't go back on what I promised," said Billy, "and then it does feel nice to start the day kinder clean like inside and out."

At last away, on a sharp run, to the barnyards. The collie was let out, the big gate was thrown open. There was a rush of bleating sheep and barking collie, and ahead of it all a little boy in a red shirt, speeding away to the next gate. The gate was set wide, and Billy mounted the post to watch the sheep come up and go through.

But what was the yellowish red thing, crossing the corner of the clover field, with some pinkish thing on its neck? A lion, or tiger? Not big enough, and none wild here. A wolf for panther? Farmer Tracy said, "None 'round for forty years." A great bushy tail waved up. "A fox! A sure 'nuff fox!" Billy had stood to listen to the men's tales of fox hunts. Great foxes

making for their holes across country. Robber foxes, that plundered poultry yards, and little lambs. Oh, if he could catch a fox! The sheep had a field and a half to cross before they came up to the last gate. Hooray for a fox hunt! Away raced Billy along the edge of the clover field, to meet the red robber. On came the fox and his booty to meet him; along the osage orange hedge ran the boy; up drew the sheep and smelled an enemy; the collie smelled him, too; boy shouted, sheep b-a-a-a-a-ed wildly, collie barked madly, and Mr. Fox dropped his burden, stretched out his tail level, and was off like the wind to his den on the hills, just tinted with the rising sun.

No use trying to catch him; race horses couldn't do it. But what had he dropped? Billy ran to search. He heard pitiful wailings. There lay a wee pink pig of a few days old. Its tail was bitten off, half of an ear was gone, and a large piece was torn out of its soft pink nose. Billy took the pig to a little stream, and washed its wounds. He had a clean handkerchief in his pocket, one of four Mrs. Tracy had made him out of a thin flour sack. He wet that and bound up the pig's wounded head. Then holding it carefully, as if it were a baby, Billy ran home toward breakfast.

But first he must tell his story, and minister to that pig. Mrs. Tracy gave him some old linen. "A pig can spare its tail," she said, "and a piece of an ear, but how that pig can ever root, or eat, with half its nose gone, I don't see."

"I'm going to feed it out of a bottle, like you did the cosset lamb," said Billy.

He made a bed in a basket, fed his pig new milk out of a bottle, wrapped it in flannel, and left it in peace.

At tea time Mrs. Tracy said, "I wonder whose pig that is?"

"Mr. Todd's, I reckon," said the farmer; "he owns a fresh litter of choice breed pigs."

This put a new light on affairs for Billy. He had thought this was his pig.

"That pig Mr. Todd's?" he cried.

"Guess so. Whose pig did you think it was?" said the farmer.

"Why, mine. In the city the boys all said—'finders keepers.'"

"Oh, no," said the farmer. "You must try and find an owner. Suppose a boy found that new hat I gave you, ought he to keep it?"

"I 'spose them city boys don't know everything," sighed Billy. "Well, shall I carry the pig over to Mr. Todd?"

"Better go first and inquire if it is his. No need to carry it half a mile and find it isn't his. If it is his, you can take it to him later."

Off went Billy, too sad to eat his supper. He wanted that little pig. Mr. Todd was by the pig pens. "I say, Mr. Todd, did you lose a tiny baby pig?" asked Billy.

"I should say I did. A varmint of a fox carried one off last night."

"I saw him with it and made him drop it," said Billy. "Its tail is gone, an' piece of its ear, an' half its nose, too."

"Pshaw!" said Mr. Todd.

"I bandaged it up and fed it out of a bottle," said Billy. "I'll fetch it over to you to-morrow mornin'. I'm kinder tired to-night."

"Land!" said Mr. Todd, "I haven't any time to feed pigs out of bottles, and I don't take much stock in a pig with half a nose. You can keep it, Billy, if you want it."

"Have it for mine—have it forever!" cried Billy wildly.

"My, yes, boy—I don't want it."

"That boy beats all for kindness to animals," said Farmer Tracy. "He

oughtn't to live in the city, where he don't have any brutes to see to. The Bible says, good men are merciful to beasts—also good boys, or words very like it. I say, Billy, do you want to go back to the city?"

"No, sir-r, I don't," said Billy.

"Then what's to hinder your staying on here, for my boy? I'll make a farmer of you before you know it."

That was how Billy, the waif, came to stay where he had, as he thought, the nicest little room, the nicest food, the warmest clothes, the best district school, and the kindest people any boy ever had. The next spring he sold his mended pig for $9.

"What you going to do with all that money?" asked the farmer.

"Put it in the bank and add more, till some day I can have a farm—a stock farm. Then here's what I'm going to put over the front gate: 'Everybody on this place has gott to be kind to animiiles.'"—*Ex.*

Christian Publishing Company

2712 Pine St., St. Louis, Mo.

J. H. GARRISON, · · · · President
W. W. DOWLING, · · · Vice-President
GEO. L. SNIVELY, · · Sec. and Gen. Supt
R. P. CROW, · · Tress. and Bus. Manager

—When you secure subscriptions to THE CHRISTIAN-EVANGELIST, you sell a paper the purchaser will actually read. This is different from merely "introducing a religious paper into a home."

—Editor Garrison's books are exceedingly popular to Disciples of every school of thought. "Christian Union" is the latest child of his brain. This scholarly and exceedingly interesting historical work is now ready for distribution. Price $1.

—A representative secured 60 new subscriptions to this paper in one day at Newcastle, Ind., recently. We believe this can easily be duplicated in hundreds of our congregations by Disciples desiring the influence of this earnest advocate of primitive Christianity.

—The men placed on our National programs and who thrill great convention assemblies are readers and thinkers. They get the best books. We correspond with them about books and papers. Let us thus help you into greater usefulness and prominence.

—Numerous letters are received philosophizing over THE CHRISTIAN-EVANGELIST's remarkable increase in circulation. The consensus of opinion is that it is not due to a change in the paper, but to the growing appreciation of a journal that never watches the weather vane of popularity, but is only concerned as to whether it is acceptably doing what Jesus would have it do.

—One of the greatest premiums we have ever offered for new subscribers is either "Helps to Faith," by Editor J. H. Garrison, or "Victory of Faith," by E. L. Powell. The proposition is limited to our preachers and students in our Bible colleges. Immediately on receipt of a new name accompanied by the $1.50, we send you your choice of these imperial books. Preacher: Why not thus secure both?

—It is confessedly difficult to keep our children in Bible school after they have passed their earlier teens. The most efficient aid in accomplishing it is a faithful and interesting teacher. The next best help is a vivacious, accurate, picturesque, instructive literature; both are needed. Our churches must furnish the first. In the Dowling series of Bible school supplies, this house will gladly send the second to all our churches.

—We printed 4,500 extra copies of our "Campbell number" of the 11th inst. These were quickly ordered and we could have sold 5,000 additional copies, but the next week's paper was already crowding our pressmen before the Campbell issue was taken from the press. But really every issue is a number of special value. We wish all Disciples were enjoying the weekly treat our editors and correspondents are giving the brotherhood.

—At a very low price we will furnish churches engaged in protracted meetings, with 300, 500, or 1,000 copies of this paper. With the first shipment we will send pink circulars to be inserted in THE CHRISTIAN-EVANGELIST and distributed throughout the community announcing the meeting, and containing pictures of pastors and evangelists. This not only insures a large audience from the first, but a house full of prepared listeners. Wherever tried, it is a great success. Write us for particulars.

—"Our Young Folks" and THE CHRISTIAN-EVANGELIST $1.75; a fountain pen and

THE CHRISTIAN-EVANGELIST, $2; "The American Boy" (a splendid paper for boys) and THE CHRISTIAN-EVANGELIST, $2; "The Ladies' Home Companion" and THE CHRISTIAN-EVANGELIST, $2.25; a self-filling fountain pen, warranted ten years, and THE CHRISTIAN-EVANGELIST (to a new subscriber) $2.50; "The Review of Reviews" (price $3) and THE CHRISTIAN-EVANGELIST, $3. Any of these premiums makes a most acceptable Christmas gift. They may be ordered now and the premiums held until Christmas time.

—We trust all our church interests will be as greatly blessed by the Centennial *esprit de corps* as is THE CHRISTIAN-EVANGELIST. But blessings coming to this paper are heralds of greater ones coming to our other church interests. At least multitudes of friends believe that a great circulation of THE CHRISTIAN-EVANGELIS. will be a lever lifting all our other enterprises higher up into places of sunlight, usefulness, and glory. Each week for months we have published lists of new subscriptions received at the uniform rate of $1.50 each in addition to multitudes of names coming singly and in pairs. The following were received last week:

King City, Mo., C. O. McFarland, pastor...... 3
Amity, Mo. 4
Wheeling, W. Va., W. H. Fields, pastor...... 4
Morristown, Ind., A. Burris, minister........ 6
Middletown, Ind., L. E. Murray, minister.....12
Seymour, Ind., Harley Jackson, pastor........12
Georgetown, Ky., C. Kendrick, pastor........27
Lexington, Ky. 44
Kansas City, Mo., Frank L. Bowen, minister..54

A Commendation and a Theory.

The American people love independence, and are not slow to recognize and reward a true patriot, whether in politics, religion, or society. The great increase in the circulation of THE CHRISTIAN-EVANGELIST, I think, is attributable to its nonsectarian, non-partisan, and non-commercial stand on recent questions of general interest to the brotherhood. Not that the entire brotherhood endorsed its position in every instance, but that they do endorse its independent non-selfishness, whether right or wrong in the points of contention and argument. Writing to you candidly, in the interest of the cause of Christ from the standpoint of one of the rank and file, I will say that our brotherhood has made

a mistake in not building up a great religious weekly belonging to themselves as a whole, and not to private corporations or individuals. Had this been done, or were it done now, the questions of self-interest and commercialism would be eliminated from its leading editorials and arguments, with no effort whatever on the part of the writers. This must be done before we can ever have a mouthpiece for the entire brotherhood, without favor to its own business interests, or fear of loss of patronage, in publishing the truth, the whole truth and nothing but the truth, as it is in Christ, as it is in the church, and as it is in the world. May God and the brotherhood speed the day!   Yours for the cause,

Mobile, Ala. · J. WALLER HENRY.

THE
CHRISTIAN-EVANGELIST
A WEEKLY RELIGIOUS NEWSPAPER.

Volume XLIII.	No. 4.

ST. LOUIS, NOVEMBER 1, 1906.

A CONVENTION GROUP TAKEN AT BUFFALO.

Seated—J. B. Briney, W. T. Moore, L. L. Carpenter.
First Row, Standing—C. C. Smith, George L. Snively, C. C. Rowlison, F. W. Norton, S. T. Willis, R. H. Miller, A. M. Haevuot.
Rear Row—R. W. Abberley, Lloyd Darsie, S. M. Cooper, Paul Moore, H. O. Breeden, J. G. Waggoner.

The Christian-Evangelist.

J. H. GARRISON, Editor

PAUL MOORE, Assistant Editor

F. D. POWER,
B. B. TYLER, } Staff Correspondents.
W. DURBAN,

Subscription Price, $1.50 a Year.

For foreign countries add $1.04 for postage.

Remittances should be made by money order, draft, or registered letter; not by local cheque, unless 15 cents is added to cover cost of collection.

In Ordering Change of Post Office give both old and new address.

Matter for Publication should be addressed to THE CHRISTIAN-EVANGELIST. Subscriptions and remittances should be addressed to the Christian Publishing Company, 2712 Pine Street, St. Louis, Mo.

Unused Manuscripts will be returned only if accompanied by stamps.

News Items, evangelistic and otherwise, are solicited, and should be sent on a postal card, if possible.

Published by the Christian Publishing Company, 2712 Pine Street, St. Louis, Mo.

Entered at St. Louis P. O. as Second Class Matte

CONTENTS.

Centennial Propaganda...........1387
Current Events....................1388
Editorial—
Where Jesus Placed the Emphasis......1389
"Beginning at Jerusalem.".........1389
Sam Jones 1390
Newspaper Evangelism 1390
Convention Notes and Personals........1390
Editor's Easy Chair...............1391
Contributed Articles—
"And When the Year's End Came." Harry S. Smith 1392
The Two Nations. William Durban......1394
As Seen from the Dome. F. D. Power....1395
State Loyalty. W. R. Warren..........1396
The Call of the States...............1396
Our Budget 1400
Simultaneous Evangelistic Campaigns.......1401
The Christian Church at Lexington, Mo......1404
The Buffalo Convention.............1405
News from Many Fields..............1466
Evangelistic 1469
Midweek Prayer-meeting 1410
Sunday-school 1410
Christian Endeavor 1411
The Home Department...............1412

THE
CHRISTIAN-EVANGELIST

"IN FAITH, UNITY; IN OPINION AND METHODS, LIBERTY; IN ALL THINGS, CHARITY."

| Vol. XLIII. | November 1, 1906 | No. 44 |

1809 CENTENNIAL PROPAGANDA CHURCHES OF CHRIST 1909
: : : GEO. L. SNIVELY : : :

Looking Toward Pittsburg.

—The great Buffalo convention was all athrill with interest in the greater one to be in Pittsburg in 1909. From a full heart THE CHRISTIAN-EVANGELIST acknowledges from many of our men and women who know expressions of appreciation for what it is doing through the dedication of this page and in its editorial columns toward making this Centennial the greatest religious event in American history since the formulation of the Declaration and Address.

—Secretary Rains' "Retrospect and Prospect" is inspirational Centennial Propaganda. The past of this society is glorious and safe. It has received and disbursed nearly $3,000,000. Such is its business standing, that it can any day borrow $50,000 at the banks where it does business, yet it has never closed a year with any indebtedness resting upon it. Our hearts are with McLean, Rains, Corey and all who with them are training heathen voices to blend with ours in Centennial hallelujahs. Let us help them realize the quarter million dollars stipulated on the opposite page.

—W. F. Richardson's article following merits consideration. THE CHRISTIAN-EVANGELIST is no more seeking its "100,-000 by 1909" for financial considerations than preachers seek larger fields of usefulness for increased perquisites. The shores of this Restoration are strewn with so many wrecked publishing houses (and so many others are in troubled waters) that our people surely know the publication of THE CHRISTIAN-EVANGELIST is purely altruistic. It is our way of serving. We wish to render the largest possible service. Will not our friends "adopt some plan, at an early date, whereby THE CHRISTIAN-EVANGELIST can be placed in every home of the church"? Almost any plan is better than none. What is yours? A greater Centennial awaits your answer.

The Minister's Assistant.

BY W. F. RICHARDSON.

I have read with great pleasure the recent statement of the large increase in the circulation of THE CHRISTIAN-EVANGELIST during the year just closing. This is a fact of considerable significance, as it seems to me, and I have been asking myself as to the reason for it. If you had been devoting the columns of your paper, during this time, to pushing your circulation, subordinating every other interest to that of your subscription list, and taking subscribers at greatly reduced rates, it could easily be explained. But you have said little, and that quite modestly, about the matter, and have held steadfastly to your

regular subscription rates. I must therefore interpret the fact of this increase:

1. As an evidence of the merits of THE CHRISTIAN-EVANGELIST, as a religious paper, able to win its way by meeting the higher needs of our families, churches and ministers.

2. As an indication of the growing approval of our brotherhood of the spirit of the paper, as shown during some of the recent discussions, wherein some of our papers I fear fell far short of that frank and kindly disposition that ought ever to mark the utterances of brethren in Christ-Jesus.

3. As a token of the increasing appreciation of the value of a good religious paper as an adjunct to the work of the pastor in his church and community. If we can secure the regular reading of a good religious paper in all the homes of the church, we will vastly augment our power as preachers of the Gospel, and elevate more rapidly the moral and spiritual tone of our Christian life.

I believe that every minister of Christ among us who realizes the value of your excellent paper ought to adopt some plan, at an early date, whereby THE CHRISTIAN-EVANGELIST can be placed in every home of the church. Nothing would tell more powerfully for the upbuilding of our people in spirituality and consecration. Let us have a general movement among our ministers to this end. Write to Brother Snively and he will help you in forming and carrying out your plans. We ought to give THE CHRISTIAN-EVANGELIST a hundred thousand new subscribers within the next year. And what this would mean to our sacred cause only eternity could tell.

Kansas City, Mo.

Retrospect and Prospect.

F. M. RAINS.

Marvelous growth has been made in the foreign missionary operations by the Foreign Christian Missionary Society in the past thirty-one years of its history. The receipts have been doubled in seven years; they have been more than trebled in ten years, and the number of native evangelists has been multiplied by five in ten years and doubled in five.

The chief ground of gratitude for the society, however, is the character and faithfulness of the missionaries. What mighty men and women have come upon the stage of action within less than a third of a century! They are the choicest spirits of our churches. It is an honor to provide for them while they are doing the Lord's work. The glory of our people is not our fine churches, nor our great colleges, nor eloquent preachers, nor a great membership, nor wealth, nor learning; but our chief glory is the army of consecrated men and women who

have buried themselves in the heart of pagan lands on the frontiers of the world that Christ may be known to those who sit in darkness and in death.

What a marvelous work has been done in heathen lands! Its missionaries have preached the Gospel in many cities and towns where the story of redemption was never before proclaimed. These heralds of the cross have baptized penitent believers in waters never before disturbed by the observance of the sacred ordinance. They have spread the table of the Lord in numerous communities for the first time. Tens of thousands of children to whom the story of the cross had never before come have been gathered into churches to learn of him whose cradle was a manger. Hundreds of thousands have received the kindly and healing touch of the medical missionary who before had never so much as heard of such merciful and helpful skill. The society has opened the doors of forty-two schools and colleges in these pagan lands where almost 2,500 are in daily attendance. About 400 orphans are clothed and fed and housed and daily trained in all Christian activities. Their dark minds are flooded with the light of life that comes down from him who is the light of the world. Christian homes have been planted; the opium eater has become the evangelist and church builder; the idolater now worships in spirit and in truth; and the licentious life has been transformed into one of purity and holiness.

No other society in the world has probably made greater growth in the last quarter of a century than this. But we have visions of larger and better things by 1909, the Centennial of the "Declaration and Address." The income should be doubled by the time 50,-000 of our people gather in Pittsburg. To this end we labor.

The larger vision connected with the world's evangelization will do more to enrich and build up a church in its local work than anything else. Such a church stands with Christ on his highest ground, the ground of universality. What many a struggling church needs more than anything else is the inspiration of missions. If you seem to be small at home, annex the world. Have a share in big things. Keep in line with God's eternal purpose. Indeed, this is the need of our papers and our colleges and our pulpits and all who would restore the New Testament church.

The Foreign Society joins heartily in the Centennial campaign. We aim to do our part in celebrating the great event of the publication of the "Declaration and Address by Thomas Campbell.

The fathers of our movement pleaded for the union of the people of God to the end that the world might be evangelized. This is the meaning of our plea. This is our plea. It is primarily and essentially a missionary movement.

Current Events

The "St. Louis Republic" in its issue of the 23rd contains an editorial on the nominations of the two leading par-

St. Louis Nominations.

ties for legislative and judicial officers in state and city, in which it says:

"The citizens of St. Louis are confronted with legislative nominations that are, to say the least, a source of regret. In many instances the nominees are men who are not only without the necessary qualifications to serve in the legislature of a great state, but are, moreover, wholly unfit for any public office. . . . . The citizen who wants to place the welfare of his city and state above considerations of partisan success is left to choose, not between the better of two good men, but between the lesser of two evils. . . . In the list of candidates are to be found seven men who are bartenders, saloon keepers, or employees of breweries. Two others were formerly engaged in the business of selling liquor."

This is the class of men which the p-litical machines of the two parties ask people to vote for. There is no reason why the citizens of St. Louis should be compelled, as the "Republic" says "to choose between the lesser of two evils." A movement was inaugurated by the ministers of the city, and backed up by the Anti-Saloon League, to put a clean ticket in the field, by selecting the few good men on both the party tickets, and supplementing them with independent candidates whose records give assurance that if elected they would serve with credit the interests of their city and state. But they did not get to work early enough to get the proper legal recognition and so the citizens of St. Louis are left in this deplorable situation. But they can at least scratch.

❦

A correspondent in the east, referring to a paragraph in this department con-

Mr. Hearst Commended.

cerning the gubernatorial situation in New York, infers some things concerning our estimate of Mr. Hearst, which we did not state, but he adds: "Mr. Hearst stands for honest count of the people's votes, against corporate greed and its 'baleful influence'; he prevented the present mayor of New York signing over and making a present of the people's money to the gas trust; he has also paid court expenses for about one thousand poor people to fight against corporate gas trust greed, in its attempt to rob them; he is so much like your own present governor of Missouri that the corrupt ones hate him," etc. If these things be true of Mr. Hearst, and we doubt not that he has his good points, they serve at least in part to account for the popularity which has given him the nomination of his party in that state against the protest of many of its leaders. It is no part of our duty or desire to take any partisan side in any purely partisan controversy. Our aim simply is to state facts and to estimate them in the light of moral principles.

The Lake Mohonk conference held its annual session last week under the pres-

Lake Mohonk Conference.

idency of Andrew W. Draper. This conference is a voluntary meeting of a number of distinguished citizens who style themselves "friends of the Indians and other dependent peoples." May their tribe increase! They have for many years shown themselves good friends and true. Like the Indian Rights Association, of which Secretary Bonaparte has long been a moving spirit, the Lake Mohonk conference has achieved a considerable degree of practical helpfulness toward those whom we conventionally call the nation's wards, without falling seriously into the feeble sentimentality to which the Indian question so readily lends itself. At the present time the Indians are, in the main, doing quite well. They are not a disappearing race. Probably there are as many of them in the United States as there were in the same territory when Columbus discovered America, and, in spite of the injuries which they have repeatedly received from the government, they are much better off than their ancestors were. Some of them are rich; most of them are comfortable; and nearly all of them are, through the care of the government, entirely free from those economic anxieties and uncertainties which are the lot of the average wage-worker. President Draper is right in saying that the Indian question is small and easy compared with the problems raised by our thirty-fold greater company of Filipino and Porto Rican dependents. There is opportunity for the patriotic and intelligent gentlemen who compose these nonpartisan associations to do a good service in considering and helping to solve these larger problems. So long as the Filipinos and the rest are exploited either for commercial gain or for political advantage, the real problems can not be seriously approached.

❦

The recent lapse of the Cubans from self-government to temporary wardship gives us a new and more vivid idea of the magnitude and undesirability of our task of uplifting the Filipinos. But it must also be something of a backset to those who argue that the Filipinos are ready for immediate independence.

❦

Senator Beveridge's suggestion, which he made in a political speech last week,

Federal Control of Insurance.

was one which was certain to come from some one about now. It is that the scope of the federal government's jurisdiction must be stretched to include control of the insurance business, both fire and life. This would doubtless come within the generous limits of the president's newly proposed plan to secure federal control of all aggregated wealth which is enjoyed in interstate commerce. The assets of the great insurance companies certainly represent wealth in a highly aggregated form, and there is no doubt about their being engaged in interstate commerce. What the president said about the futility of state control of cor-

Editorial

Where Jesus Placed the Emphasis.—X.

The Right Use of Money.

The parable of the unjust steward (Luke 16:1-15) deserves careful study by those who would know the mind of Jesus concerning the right use of wealth. When this steward knew that he was about to lose his position of trust because he had wasted his master's goods, he hit upon the shrewd scheme of making his master's debtors his own debtors by cutting down their bills and thus placing them under obligations to him, so that when he was put out of the stewardship they might receive him into their houses. Even the master himself, at whose expense this servant had provided for his future comfort, could not but commend his wisdom, and Jesus himself adds that "The sons of this world are, for their own generation, wiser than the sons of the light." That is, they are often wiser in looking after their interests, for this present world, than the children of light frequently are in looking after their interests in the world that is to come. He then gives this admonition to his disciples: "Make to yourself friends by means of the mammon of unrighteousness; that, when it shall fail, they may receive you into eternal tabernacles."

The right use of money, then, according to Jesus, is such use as will make friends who will receive us into their eternal tabernacles. To give money to care for the widow and the orphan, the homeless and the friendless, to send the Gospel to those who are perishing for lack of it, to endow colleges for the training of young men and women to become teachers and leaders of the people, to establish and promote whatever tends to alleviate human sorrow, promote human happiness and develop a truer and better civilization, would surely be to make friends by such use of it who would receive us into everlasting habitations.

In the same connection we have this lesson on the subject from the great Teacher: "He that is faithful in a very little is faithful also in much: and he that is unrighteous in a very little is unrighteous also in much. If therefore ye have not been faithful in the unrighteous mammon, who will commit to your trust the true riches? And if ye have not been faithful in that which is another's who will give you that which is your own?" These are questions which we may well ponder upon our knees. It is no wonder that "the Pharisees, who were lovers of money, heard of these things and scoffed at him." No doubt there are rich men to-day in the church who would scoff at such teaching. But of such Jesus would say as he said of the Pharisees: "Ye are they that justify yourselves in the sight of men; but God knoweth your hearts: for that which is exalted among men is an abomination in the sight of God."

The story of the rich man and Lazarus is too familiar to need reciting. Jesus draws the picture as it is on this side, with the rich man clothed in purple and fine linen and faring sumptuously every day, while Lazarus, a poor beggar, was lying at his gate desiring the crumbs from his table and receiving them not; and then he lifts the curtain and shows us the scene on the other side with Lazarus in Abraham's bosom comforted, and the rich man in torment, and now himself a beggar, begging father Abraham to send Lazarus whom he had despised and neglected in this life, to minister to his relief. Lazarus was not saved because he was poor on earth, nor the rich man tormented in the future world because he was rich in this. The parable is designed to show how human judgments and situations are reversed by God: that a man may be poor and despised here, but accepted of God; and he may be rich and honored here and rejected of God, because of the improper use of the means and opportunities which God hath intrusted him with.

The parable of the pounds which a certain nobleman distributed among his servants to be used in his absence, and his condemnation of the "wicked servant" who made no use of his pound, contains a lesson too plain to be misunderstood. The pound was taken from the unfaithful servant and given to the one that would make better use of it, showing that Jesus intends that we shall make the best possible use of whatever ability we have received. The parable of the talents (Matt. 25) teaches the same lesson with the added thought that our responsibility is in proportion to the amount we have received. Both these parables accentuate the fact that what we have is given to us in trust, and that we will be held to a strict accountability for a wise use of the same.

The spirit in which we are to make our gifts and the standard by which they are measured in the sight of God, Jesus teaches from the incident of the poor widow casting into the treasury her two mites, and who, he said, gave more than all the rich men. Our gifts, then, are measured by our ability and by the spirit of consecration which prompts them. It is a great mistake whereby we can not give but little, we may with impunity neglect giving anything. Giving, it must be remembered, is essential to our own spiritual growth and development. God, does not need our gifts, for "the earth is the Lord's and the fulness thereof," but we need to give for our own salvation and for the salvation of others.

The prominence which this subject has in the teaching of Jesus ought to give it more prominence in all our teaching and practice. We do not here enter upon the matter of tithing which is ably treated by many modern writers, further than to say that no man is likely to flourish in this grace of giving until he adopts some systematic method of giving, and divides his income with the Lord on some fixed basis, the very minimum being a tenth. When we begin to keep books with the Lord, conscientiously, all his work will prosper in our hands, and no righteous cause will be found begging for support.

❋ ❋

"Beginning at Jerusalem."

The national convention has passed, and those of us who attended have come home rejoicing in reports of the success of the Gospel at home and abroad. Those who have read the reports share in this rejoicing. We feel that our labors and sacrifices have not been in vain in the Lord. The blesssed news of salvation from sin and death through Christ is bringing joy and hope to thousands of hearts beyond the seas in pagan lands, while in the general home field the same simple Gospel, untrammeled by human names, creeds and traditions, is winning its thousands to Christ and to our plea for Christian union.

But now we find ourselves confronted with the call for the observance of State Mission Day all over the Union. Is this out of harmony with what we have been hearing and rejoicing in at our national conventions? Not so. We are now to strengthen the base of all our wider missionary activities. At the foundation of all the success we have won in foreign fields, in the new states and territories, and in most of our great cities, is state missions. It was through the co-operation of the churches originally planted within the several states that the cause has been extended, first within those states, and then into the regions beyond and finally into pagan lands. This is a fact we must never forget, though the failure of many churches to observe the first Lord's day in November as State Mission Day shows that many of us are inclined to forget it. The principle involved in "beginning at Jerusalem" is just as true now as it was in the beginning. Let us see if this be not so.

What is the principle involved in the policy of "beginning at Jerusalem"? Was it not to use the most available material at hand out of which to make Christians in order to create a base of operations for carrying the Gospel into Judea, Samaria, and to the uttermost parts of the earth? America is our Jerusalem, and the several states are, in our missionary geography, simply the subdivisions by means of which we are enabled to reach the whole country more effectively. We are strong in America just in proportion as we are strong in the several states of the Union. Or, if we use America in its continental sense, we are strong in America as we are strong within the several states of the Union and within the several provinces of Canada. We can not greatly extend our work either in foreign lands or in the religiously waste places of America, only as we strengthen the base of supplies within the several states and provinces. We can strengthen our base of supplies in two ways: first, by increasing the number of churches, and, second, by strengthening the churches already in existence. This is the twofold purpose of our state co-operations. They seek to plant as many new churches as possible in the most needy fields and at the most strategic points, to enlist as many churches as possible in co-operation in all parts of our missionary work, and through this mutual co-operation to strengthen, both spiritually and numerically, all the churches.

We have said that America is our Jerusalem. It is a very large Jerusalem. Here is to be found the most available material out of which to make Christians to be used in world-wide evangelization. We must continue, therefore, our active operations here while sending out the Gospel abroad, until this wide field has been brought under spiritual cultivation. If it is folly to say, as some do, that we must defer operations abroad as long as we have heathens at home, it would be equally fatal for us to conclude that we may discontinue our evangelistic operations at home in order to push the work in foreign fields. The work at home and abroad must go on, side by side, and the one will prosper as the other prospers, and suffer as the other suffers.

In these days of Centennial preparation there is special need that our offerings for state missions be brought up to a higher figure if we are to reach our Centennial aims. Perhaps the weakest point in our "far-flung battle line" is state missions. Reinforcement at this point, therefore, will send a thrill of renewed confidence and of expectant victory all along the line. May we not hope, therefore, that our churches everywhere will observe the first Lord's day in November as state mission day, with the same conscientiousness and regularity as they observe other fixed days for our missionary offerings?

❧ ❧

Sam Jones.

He was unique. There was only one original, though there were many imitators. He had a zeal for righteousness, having himself been rescued from sin. He believed in the power of God to save the worst of sinners. His career was more like that of John the Baptist, minus the baptism, than that of any man of modern times. He rose to fame in the mountains of the south as John the Baptist rose to fame in the Judean wilderness, by denouncing sin and calling the people to repentance. He feared God, but the fear of man was not before his face. There was not much sectarian-

ism about him. He said he was a Christian, and that Methodism was only the harness in which he worked. He could work with all Christians and did do so. Our ministers worked with him harmoniously. He seemed to like them and they liked many things about him. When one of our ministers took him aside once and explained to him the way of salvation according to the New Testament, he thanked him most heartily and said he had a better understanding of the subject than ever before. Behind a rough exterior he had a tender, loving heart that sympathized with the sinful and the sorrowing. He was capable of rising to the loftiest heights of sacred eloquence, and of making an appeal before which the strongest men trembled. His methods, perhaps, could not all be approved; his speech often offended ears polite; but he stood foursquare against every popular evil that assailed our humankind, and his whole influence was thrown on the side of righteousness and against wrong. We doubt not that many thousands will rise up in the future to call him blessed, because he aroused them from the stupor of sin and brought them to repentance. May he have many successors in spirit, in courage, in faith, if not in method.

❧ ❧

Newspaper Evangelism.

We believe we are entering upon an era of both wider and deeper evangelism —wider, because more workers will engage in it, and a wider scope will be covered; deeper, because of an increasing consciousness that only genuine conversions to Christ strengthen the church. A new force has recently entered into our evangelism. The religious newspaper is being used as never before as an adjunct to the preaching of the evangelist. THE CHRISTIAN-EVANGELIST, true to its name, has entered this field and desires to make itself increasingly useful, both in helping to turn people to Christ, and in building them up in Christian faith and life.

We are asking the co-operation of a large number of our ministers, in sending us short, fresh, pointed articles on the different phases of our holy evangel, which shall make each issue of the paper an able assistant of the pastor or evangelist in soul-winning. The ministers and others thus co-operating with us will greatly extend their ministry, and we shall all be co-workers together in winning men from the service of sin, whose wages is death, to the service of Christ, whose gift is life eternal. Our evangelists are already using the paper in large numbers, and now that we are taking

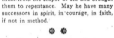

It is easy enough to be pleasant
When joys go by like a song—
But the man worth while
Is the man who will smile
When everything goes dead wrong.

special pains to make THE CHRISTIAN-EVANGELIST serviceable in this direction, we shall expect a still greater demand for it.

❧ ❧

Convention Notes and Personals.

(CONTINUED.)

Our space last week did not permit us to complete all we wished to say concerning our recent convention for the benefit of our readers who were not present. We feel that a religious journal has no higher public function to discharge than to report adequately so great and important a gathering as our national convention.

Considering the proximity of Niagara Falls to Buffalo, it is complimentary to the delegates that so many of them stayed by the sessions of the convention throughout. Any effort to conduct excursions during the regular sessions of our conventions ought to be discountenanced.

One of the best short speeches of the whole convention was a purely extemporaneous one by the chairman of the local committee on arrangements, R. H. Miller, pastor of the Richmond Street church, who, when called out on the last evening, made a most appropriate and effective speech which the convention greatly appreciated. He spoke for the other members of his committee as they were too modest to appear. The last hour of every convention ought to be given to short, extemporaneous, voluntary speeches, summing up the lessons and impressions of the convention.

Few men in our ranks have been more faithful in their attendance at these conventions and have contributed more to their success in the past than the Veteran Robert Moffett, of Cleveland, who for many years was the standard-bearer of the American Christian Missionary Society. His whole life has been a contribution to the cause of missions. He is now rendering good service as secretary of the committee on Christian union.

This leads us to say, in reply to some inquiries, that at a meeting of as many of the delegates to the Interchurch Conference in New York City last November, as could be gotten together in Buffalo, together with a few other brethren of influence, it was decided that the official communication sent by the committee of correspondence in that body to the Disciples of Christ in convention assembled, be turned over to the standing committee on Christian Union for their consideration and future report.

It was pleasant to note in the convention the presence of S. C. Toof, one of the pillars of our cause for many years in the city of Memphis, who, with his wife and daughter, attended the Buffalo convention and greatly enjoyed its proceedings. To secure a larger number of our business men at our conventions is a most desirable consummation.

The report of the committee on registration, which Bro. A. B. Kellogg has kindly furnished us, some facts from which are reported elsewhere, emphasize the need of a more representative body, not in the character of the men who attend, but in a larger number of representatives from churches in all sections of the country. Steps should be taken at once to remedy this defect by providing for a delegate body. The first step in this direction has already been taken in providing for the revision of the constitution. This revision should embody a new basis of representation, and, no doubt, will do so. The churches must be brought into closer contact with our missionary work, as they are furnishing the sinews of war. This, of course, need not interfere with a large miscellaneous attendance upon the proceedings of the convention, but it would secure a delegated body who would feel responsible for the proper dispatch of the business of the convention.

Much greater space might be given to the brief addresses of the missionaries, if they had been stenographically reported. Cory of China, Eldred of Africa, McPherson of Cuba, and his wife, and others, made ringing speeches. When Eldred said, "I would rather be buried under the palms of Bolengi than in any other place in the world," he revealed the spirit of a true missionary.

Editor's Easy Chair.

As one wakes from some pleasant dream regretfully, wishing its bright scenes and associations might have been real and permanent, so we who attended the Buffalo Convention are recalling now the casual meetings of friends, the warm hand-clasps, and then the passing on of the rapid panorama. There come to us mere glimpses of faces that smiled upon us and vanished in the press of people, and we saw them no more. Now that we look back upon it we wish we might have taken the time for a friendly stroll and chat together with these dear friends whom we so seldom meet. But, alas, there was no time to take. We wonder sometimes whether it were not worth while to have a convention without any program or any business, but just for personal intercourse, where heart could commune with heart. It does seem, at least, that we could afford to be less in a hurry in these great gatherings, and take a little more time to get acquainted with each other and to strengthen the tie that binds. This is by no means the least important function of our conventions. Let us arrange next year, and every year, for at least one hour in which we can all come together without a program, and with only some one to preside and introduce each person with name and postoffice, asking it where he does not know it, and where each speaker will have from one to three minutes to say what is on his heart, or to pray, or to sing, as the Spirit might move him. And then if there could be longer intervals between sessions in which friend could meet friend and in which those happy reunions of various kinds could be held, it would add a satisfying element to these conventions which they seem to lack.

❦

One of the happiest little reunions which the Easy Chair has enjoyed for a long while, was the English tea-meeting at Buffalo, and the reunion of some of the men and women who toiled together in old England a quarter of a century ago, concerning which another pen has written elsewhere in this issue. While enjoying the reminiscences of that brief hour, and feeling how strong is the bond of friendship that binds together that surviving band of workers, the thought came to us that one of the sweetest joys of heaven will be for friends who have known each other and have toiled together in the kingdom of God on earth to meet up there, in some fair sequestered nook by the river of the water of life, and talk over the scenes, associations, labors, and triumphs of the earth-life. And then there will be so much time for it! One of the verses of an old hymn which used to strike our youthful imagination, was:

"When we've been there ten thousand years
  Bright shining as the sun;
We've no less days to sing God's praise
  Than when we first begun."

But we do not believe we shall devote all our time to singing, even in heaven. There will be time for association, intercourse,

and for recalling the experiences of the life which we are now living in the flesh. And heaven will be all the sweeter because of the blessed memories which join together the life in this terrestrial body, and the life in the body celestial. No heaven that does not link itself with earth, and the conflicts and experiences of earth can ever satisfy the human heart.

❦

To-day is a typical autumn day. The skies are overcast with scurrying clouds and the great oaks at Rose Hill sway and moan before the wind. One feels to-day as he looks out upon the splendid pageant of autumn, the truth of the poet's lines:

"When spring first breathes on the russet hill
  In her own faint, lovely fashion,
One's pulses stir with a sudden thrill;
But when autumn comes the heart stands still,
  Moved with a deeper passion."

Yes, "with a deeper passion." Somehow these wailing winds and falling leaves do stir up feelings that lie too deep for utterance, and start questions that go down to the very roots of our being. Are these fading and falling leaves one of God's methods of reminding us that all earthly pomp and glory will soon fade away and fall to the ground like these autumn leaves? That God is speaking to the human soul in Nature, as well as in that Sacred Volume in which breathes the Spirit of God, we do not doubt. Every season and every phenomenon in nature has its voice and its message from Him who paints the rose and the lily, and clothes the forests with their autumnal robes. But is it altogether sad—this message from God that "we all do fade as a leaf," and that as the leaves now falling are to be succeeded by other leaves, so others will take the places we now hold, live in the houses we now inhabit, do the work that we are now doing, and enter into the experiences of joy and of sorrow through which we are now passing? Not if we have a heavenly Father whose hand is leading us, and whose love has prepared for us something "far better" beyond, than anything we have known here, glorious as this has been. So we refuse to be saddened by the message of autumn.

❦

Kipling has recently written a verse that is likely to live longer than much he has written. It is a genuine expression of true patriotism which Americans no less than Englishmen can apply to their own land.

"Land of our birth, our faith, our pride,
For whose dear sake our fathers died,
O, Motherland, we pledge to thee,
  Head, heart and hand through years to be!"

It is a good thing to renew this pledge of devotion to our Motherland in these election days, and to see to it that we serve her with head and heart and hand. There is a conjunction of two events just now in both of which we may serve our country and show the quality of our patriotism. In the election now pending, we may serve our country best by voting only

for men known to be honest and capable, no matter if others of a contrary kind have their names upon our party ticket. In this way independent voters will force their party leaders to nominate worthy men, and in no other way. Just preceding the election, on the first Sunday in November, we will have opportunity of showing our patriotism, as well as our Christianity, by an offering for the preaching of the gospel in the several states and the inculcation of those truths and principles which are essential to the perpetuity of all free government. There is no truer patriotism, and none so effective, as that which seeks to evangelize and to bring under the influence of the gospel of Christ, the people of these great commonwealths in whose hands are the destiny of these states and of the nation. Give liberally for missions, and vote for honest men, and you may sing Kipling's verse as quoted above. The gospel of a united Church fits in well with our political gospel of the United States. Our freedom in Christ harmonizes beautifully with liberty under our constitution and flag.

❦

Plea of our faith, our hope, our love,
  For whose dear sake our fathers strove.
  O, blessed Christ, we pledge to thee
  Head, heart and hand through years to be?

With apologies to Mr. Kipling we present the foregoing as a pledge worthy of these great Centennial days among the Disciples of Christ. If there is one word that expresses all that is involved in the great plea which our fathers inaugurated and for which they strove, nearly a century ago, that word is Christ. Christ in faith, in doctrine, in His ordinances, in His church, making it one, and uniting it to Himself in holy wedlock, and using it to convert the world—that is the plea of our fathers and it is our plea. May we not pledge to such a holy cause, the service of our "head, heart and hand, through years to be"? We believe there is almost universal readiness among us to pledge loyalty to this great plea. Not a halting or hesitating note did we hear, in all the great addresses at our recent national convention. Heart, conscience, intellect, all seemed to be enlisted in the plea for the fulfillment of Christ's prayer for the unity of His disciples, according to His own spirit and method. Let this spirit of devotion to the plea of our faith, our hope, our love be universal, and we shall see greater things in the years to come than our fathers were permitted to see. But this requires that we shall be as alert to the opportunities of our times, and as ready to adapt ourselves to them as our fathers were to the opportunities of their day. It is only by continuing to be a growing religious movement, keeping pace with the advancing knowledge and changing needs of the world that we can remain loyal to the spirit of our fathers, and make vital to the people of the present day, the principles which were so potential in their day.

"And When the Year's End Came"

An Address on Higher Ideals in Christian Stewardship, delivered at the Buffalo Convention

By Harry D. Smith
Hopkinsville, Kentucky

In wealth, as increased and endowed through modern invention, is a wonder-working power concerning which let us ask during the next score of minutes two questions:

1. What are we Disciples doing with it? It were easy to answer this question so as to beget and foster self-complacency. For our charity is various, and beautiful and achieves mightily for the help of a needy world. Where it goes, and it is by no means provincial in its travels, "the blind receive their sight, and the lame walk, the lepers are cared for, if not cleansed, and the deaf hear, and the dead in trespasses and in sins are raised up, and even the poor have the good tidings preached to them."

But to answer only so were to blink much more than half of the truth, and so to do ourselves vast harm. For what we need most and indispensably in this, as in every other matter, is not to feel good about it, but to know the truth of it. Indeed there is no deadlier foe of the duty yet to be done in any relation than satisfaction, not to say boastfulness, on account of present attainments. "Brethren, I count not myself to have laid hold," is the voice of a living, growing, battling, conquering soul. Whoever says or thinks the opposite is dead or dying. Recently, while in Japan, Mr. Bryan was praising the enlightenment, loyalty and efficiency which were in evidence everywhere about him. A distinguished leader said to him: "You have praised us; we thank you. Now, tell us the worst thing you have seen in Japan that we may correct it." O, my friends, we wish to know, at least we ought to wish to know, the worst things in the kingdom of Christ and especially among ourselves, that by his grace, we may correct them.

Now, just what are we Disciples doing financially for the kingdom of God?

Our year book for 1905 credits us with gifts to all causes during the year just preceding its issuance which aggregated, in round figures, seven and a half millions of dollars. A vast sum, which tempts one to mention it with unction and think of it with pride. But let us defer our exultation while we ask two or three questions. First, who gave this sum? On the face of the matter it is the gift of the brotherhood, numbering a million and a quarter. And how much is that from each of us, supposing we all gave equally? The year book saves us the trouble of performing the division and answers six dollars and a quarter. These millions that tempt us to be proud of ourselves, they dwindle, do they not, when we cut them up this way? But some one says, "The most of the brethren are sisters." Well, what of that? Have not women money? Do they not spend money? Somewhere I have got an idea that women, some few of them, do sometimes, that is, occasionally, spend money—a little, just a little, of it. But one is told, and seriously, that since their husbands are members of other churches, or of no church, many Christian wives are deterred by feelings of delicacy from asking for money for the support of the Church. That is, one may ask one's husband for the price of silken gowns, Parisian hats, trinkets of gold, diamonds, horses, carriages, houses, and suffer no inconvenience from one's feelings of delicacy; but only let one think of asking him for money for the Lord who bought one, and one has a spasm of delicacy that chokes one into dumbness. Does anybody think $6.25 is other than a trifling gift from the average woman of our churches for a whole year?

I say, then, if we were all women, we should be easily able to give all we now give and much more.

But another tells me that we have many children among us. Again I tell you, if we were all children between 10 and 16 years of age, such as are now in the homes of our people, we should be able to give this average out of our pocket change and still have left to spend upon our pleasures.

Still another reminds me of our poor. Yes, some of us are poor—so poor that a gift of $6.25 would be creditable to us. But we are very few, a really negligible quantity in the present matter.

But the truth concerning the elements which go to make up our numbers is of course that we are not all women who are financially dependent, nor children, nor poor, nor any combination of these. Besides these elements, we have a host of women with their own means, many youths and maidens with considerable incomes, an army of artisans with wages ranging from $1.50 to $6 a day, another army of farmers owning millions of acres of our best lands; another army of merchants, brokers and bankers who have incomes ranging from $1,200 to $12,000, another army of physicians, lawyers and civil engineers of like earning capacity. We have also among us railway officials, cattle kings, coal and iron kings. We have not a few who would regard the largest income just mentioned as small. And it is certain that we add tens of millions to our property yearly.

We are, indeed, not such, as tried by the standards of the new and marvelous prosperity of our own America, would be called rich, but we are vastly well to do. Further, I think it likely that in the average of physical satisfactions enjoyed, no equally numerous religious body ever excelled us; for while we have less than some others, what we have is more equally distributed among us.

Let us ask a second question. For what was this average of $6.25 given? If it was given for some trifling or secondary interest, it was perhaps enough, or even too much, for even the rich may be excused for giving trifles to trifling objects. But what is the fact? The year book says it was given to all our causes. It was our total money gift to make the world more like Christ. Our gifts to our local poor were in it. Fortunately for the poor, as noted a moment ago, they are not very numerous and not very poor. It included our gifts to all our home churches, for preaching, for music, for incidentals and repairing and improving property. Our gifts to schools, colleges and universities were in it. And not one of these is adequately endowed. Many have no endowment at all. Teachers in these institutions, and some of them our greatest teachers, such is my information, are working on meager salaries, insufficient to enable them to do their best work, and dying at last in such poverty as is a shame to us all. In this average were our gifts to negro evangelization and education, to city evangelization and to district, state and general home missions. In all of these departments there is the greatest need of more men, while many an one of those already at work suffers for lack of proper shelter, and sometimes of even fire or food. There is room, my friends, for a supplement to "Fox's Book of Martyrs." The new work would be called "Lives of American Home Missionaries."

And of this average we gave about eight cents to build houses of worship for our new churches, twelve hundred of which have no house of their own. To foreign missions we gave something more than 20 cents. This to evangelize and educate two-thirds of the race! This to give the hope of Christ to those who die, not having known of him, at the rate of an hundred thousand every day!

> "Worthy followers of the prophets we who hold
>   our gold so dear,
> True descendants of the martyrs, Christ held far
>   and coin held near,
> Bold co-workers with the Almighty, with our
>   twenty cents a year.
>
> See the few, our saints, our heroes, battling
>   bravely hand to hand,
> Where the myriad-headed horrors of the pit pos-
>   sess the land,
> Striving one against a million to obey the Lord's
>   command.
>
> Christians, have you heard the story, how the
>   basest man of men
> Flung his foul, accursed silver in abhorrence
>   back again?
> Thirty pieces was the purchase of the world's
>   Redeemer then.
>
> Now, its twenty cents in copper, for the Savior
>   has grown cheap
> Now to sell our Lord and Master, we need only
>   stay asleep.
> Now, the accursed Judas money is the money
>   that we keep."

Let us suspend our pride in our gifts a moment longer, while we ask one more question. To whom did we give this $6.25? We gave it to Jesus Christ. We gathered at the table where he wished us to remember his humiliation, his wounds and his death for us. We did this every week. And whenever we were gathered thus the Master came and held out his right hand and said, "Freely ye have received, freely give," and we covered the nail-print in that gracious hand with our weekly gifts. And when the year's end came this was the total of them.

But we are reminded of the fact that some of us gave liberally, even hundreds and thousands of times this average. For this giving, as it is related to the givers, we rejoice. For it, as it is related to the liberality of the most of us, we must grieve the more, since credit for the few in this case means deeper shame for the many.

2. We have now thought somewhat of our neglect to use our property largely in the maintenance and spread of the Gospel. It is time to think of our duty more positively. How much ought we to give for these mighty purposes? Upon what plan or plans? With what motives?

The beginning of wisdom touching giving is that we have nothing to give—nothing. The Bible resounds with God's claim to all that we have. "The silver and the gold are mine"; "The cattle on a thousand hills are mine," nor is claim laid to all property merely, but to all the world, including those who dwell in it. "Behold, all souls are mine." The tithe, as has been repeatedly pointed out, was simply a part of one's wealth, asked and accepted by God, for specific uses, in token that one's whole wealth was his. In Christ the ancient claim is doubled. In him we are debtors not only for creation and sustenance, but for our redemption also. "Ye are bought with a price."

Why then speak of giving at all? It is a convenient word. It marks a distinction from the use of money or property in trade. The Master used it, and the Biblical writers generally used it. But the Christian, nay, all men, should always read or hear it, remembering that the highest and noblest truth is that they have nothing to give—except in the name of God, whose stewards they are. For property, like

"Merit lives from man to man,
And not from man, O Lord, to Thee."

Hence it follows that one is bound to use all one's property, not one-tenth, or one-half, or nine-tenths of it, for him. How? Shall one pay it all into the Church treasury? No, one must live, even though he recognize his stewardship to God. So must his family. "He who provides not for his own has denied the faith." So must the state "render therefore to Caesar the things that are Caesar's." Nor is there any intimation in Biblical teaching that the demands of taste or culture are to be ignored and neglected. On the contrary, the Bible is the most beautiful of books, not only in respect of the moral ideas which it contains, but also in its literary forms, And this most beautiful of books dwells fondly upon the beauties of earth and sea and sky. It revels here and there in the beauties of great buildings even. It lures us on our earthly way with pictures of a beautiful heaven. The God of the Bible has found beauty very useful, and we shall not do our best for him without it, and without a delicate taste for it.

Now, how shall I distribute my Lord's money, which he has intrusted to me? He has given me no detailed instructions, such as he gave his earlier trustees, the ancient Jews. Instead of all these,

he has given me a single commandment, to love him and humanity for his sake. In the light of this, and of this alone, I must discharge my trust, apportioning to each interest of what he has placed in my hands. He trusts me freely, largely, wondrously, that he may in this way bring me to be worthy of his trust. Therefore none must seek to supply the commands that he has not seen fit to give.

However, one may properly be advised as to the application of this one new commandment. And one needs such advice sorely. In what shall it consist?

Mingled with and mastering all particulars such as would be suitable to our many and various specific cases, these principles, you will agree, should appear:

First—Love must consider what is the supreme concern of the beloved, and make that her own supreme concern. What is the supreme concern of God in Christ? Let our Lord himself answer: "The Son of man is come to seek and to save that which is lost." Saving the world from sin, then, is our supreme affair, if indeed we love God.

Second—Again love must have regard in her distribution of her Lord's bounty, of course, to every need of those for whom he lived and died, but her chief regard should be to their chief need. And what is the world's chief need? Jesus taught that it was salvation from sin.

Third—But love will cause one to spend on oneself what will make one the best possible servant of his Master's interests. As my Lord's servant I owe myself care, not merely to the extent of the bare necessities of physical life, but of preparation and equipment for a larger usefulness.

Fourth—Love will also make one most scrupulous, lest beginning to care for himself, for his Master's sake, he should end with caring for himself for his own sake. "Love seeketh not her own."

Fifth—And when doubt arises, as it must, as to whether one shall spend upon one's self, or upon others, love will give others the benefit of the doubt.

Sixth—Again, he who loves gives cheerfully, gladly, hilariously. He who would learn to love must give as he can.

Seventh—Nor does love ask how much *must* I give to answer the world's need of Christ, but how much *can* I give?

Eighth—And it is safe to say that love will scrutinize with a lynx-eyed scrutiny all its expenditures; it will ask itself such blunt, practical questions as these: "How much of Christ's money shall I spend for tobacco?" "How much for the theater?" "How much for social entertainments?" "How much for excursions of mere pleasure?" "How much for diamonds?" "How much for expensive clothing, seldom worn?" "How much for delicate food?" "How much for houses unused the most of the year?" "How much for needless horses and carriages?" She will arouse her conscience to new alertness and fineness of perception, occasionally demanding sternly, "May I feast while my neighbor starves?" and, "Who is my neighbor?" "Is he not any human being anywhere whom I may help? And have I not then many starving neighbors? Some whose bodies die of hunger, and a world full of neighbors whose souls are hungry?"

But is there no word of the New Testament that so much as hints a plan of giving? In the way of definite sums or fixed percentages there 's none. What then of the tithe? It is not commanded, and as a tax upon us by the Church upon its members, is not therefore allowable. As a tax upon one's self,

imposed by one's self, it is permissible, and in view of our present low ideals of our stewardship, its adoption were a gigantic stride upward. Especially, if it be regarded as a minimum beyond which one will give as much as one can, much can be said for it. First, it had the divine approval for ages. We are nowhere forbidden to use it thus individually and voluntarily. As a minimum below which we are not to permit ourselves to give no one could, of course, imagine that it would displease our Lord. The suggested reflection that a Christian ought to do as a matter of liberality as much as the ancient Jew did from necessity (and the latter paid out not one-tenth, but two or more, for religious purposes), is sound and just, and should stir us as with the trump of God.

But to renew our question. Does the New Testament offer us no word concerning a plan of giving?

The nearest approach to what might properly be called a plan of giving is in these familiar words: "Upon the first day of the week let each one of you lay by him in store as he may prosper." To the reverent and receptive spirit these words are full of guidance. They are resplendent with practical wisdom. Some one has happily called them "the inspired rule of three." "Upon the first day of the week" means give regularly. The most of us give by fits, and the fits, unhappily, are neither violent nor protracted. "Each one of you" means let everybody give. Don't give in spots. We not only give in spots, but often the spots are so microscopic that you can not see them well with the naked eye. "As he may prosper" means give in proportion to what you have and what you make. It means that every gift is justly estimated according to what the giver retains. A fifth of a cent measured against nothing retained is an infinite gift. Any fraction divided by nought gives infinity, while a million divided by a million gives only one.

"The accursed Judas money is the money that we keep."

My friends, every time is a great time, it only there be somewhere a great man or a great people to give practical recognition to the fact. Nevertheless, some times seem more favorable to the accomplishment of desirable ends than others. Such a time is the present to us. It is almost an hundred years since, in the beginnings of our history, liberty in Christ came to a new birth. In view of this, our minds are being renewed in the thoughts and our hearts and wills in the affections and purposes which belonged to our earliest days. As is fitting, we are preparing to give expression to these in a monumental meeting, in the very region where they had their first adequate utterance. With tongue and pen our leaders call upon us to make that meeting worthy of our cause. The period is not long until we shall stand upon that sacred soil. What memories shall throng us there! We shall remember, among other things, that something more than a hundred years before, on the opposite edge of the same state, political liberty was also born again. We shall think of Thomas Jefferson and his Declaration, and of Thomas Campbell and his declaration, in the same moment, and we shall tell one another that in ultimate significance to mankind the latter declaration is not less than the former. We shall add, with conviction: "It is the finger of God that unites thus in their beginnings the freest of churches and the freest of countries." We shall recall and reckon up there what we owe our country, how her liberty has given play and power to our own. It were good to be able to remember there, also, that we had paid this debt in the amplest ministry of the Word possible to us among the people of our own land. We shall also crave there to be able to remember that we made some worthy effort, at least, that the influence of our Lord might be as wide and penetrate to every place as quickly as the influence of our country. In a word, we shall there wish to have done our utmost for Christ.

During the next three years, my friends, we shall look back to the autumn of 1809 and forward to the autumn of 1909. Stirred with the story of the centuries beginning, and expectant of its illustrious ending, we should be capable of high things. There are a million and a quarter of us. Our people are intelligent, and not a few of them have a good degree of sound learning. We have the secret of the most successful evangelism seen in modern times. We are young and full of a mighty hope. The instinct of victory is within us; we have abundant means. We are not ungenerous, merely untaught in respect to money.

Brethren, we shall not have used our opportunity well unless these three years be made to exceed in tangible results any decade of our history thus far. But if we shall achieve thus we must be taught and practice some goodly part of our duty in respect to money; and we who constitute this convention must hold ourselves largely responsible for that teaching.

"Give as the morning flows out of heaven,
Give as the waves when their channel is riven
Give as the free air and sunshine are given
Lavishly, utterly, ceaselessly given.

Not the waste drops of our cup overflowing
Not the faint sparks of our hearts overglowing
not a pale bud from the June roses blowing
But as He gave to thee, who gave thee to live."

The Two Nations By William Durban

As years roll on, and my acquaintance with the great world enlarges, I seem to be more and more deeply impressed with the conviction that our Anglo-Saxon race is destined to control the future. At the outset of these present observations I may observe that the term "Anglo-Saxon" is here used in a large sense which includes a reference to the British and American nations taken collectively. For, although little England and the mighty United States contain exceedingly composite nationalities the Anglo-Saxon element is predominant; and, moreover, this element is welding all others into harmony with itself. I recently, while in the United States, went over some immense cement works. I found that nearly all the workmen were Hungarians. But the descendants of these will be undistinguishable from Anglo-Saxons. So it is with us in the United Kingdom, for though, as Tennyson says, "Saxon and Norman and Dane are we," we entirely forget the two latter categories and only the first counts.

International Rivalry.

Last Saturday masses of spectators swarmed along the banks of the River Thames. It is calculated that the crowd was the biggest that has ever assembled on any occasion in the world's history, for it must have numbered at least half a million people. The occasion was the boat race between an American and a British crew, representing Harvard and Cambridge universities, respectively. The contest was one of the most brilliant and exciting ever witnessed in athletic annals, and though the English crew happened to win, the Harvard crew attracted universal admiration. It matters not which side wins or which loses in such competitions. England has been defeated in the great yacht races, year after year, but the benefit of this kind of international rivalry is independent of victory for this or that side. The spirit evoked was well expressed by a London paper, "The Morning Leader," which said: "We are all glad that Cambridge won—even Oxford men were observed to cheer. We shall all be glad, too, if Harvard wins another time." Most likely Harvard *will* win another time. The British people are proud of being related to a nation which is a match for it, but which it can possibly sometimes excel. Americans and Britishers know that neither nation can in all respects outshine the other. But they can not do better than sustain an amicable rivalry in all directions in which they can show the world that both peoples are indomitably strenuous. The English people are saying to the grand Harvard rowers, "Come again!"

Britannia and the Sea.

As I have so recently landed on English shores after a voyage on the Caronia, I am mindful that I went away on the sister ship, the Carmania, a description of which I wrote some months ago for this paper. These are the two biggest ships on earth, but I can not forbear writing a few words about what appears to me to be a remarkable sign of the stupendous progress of civilization in this age. Before these lines reach America there will be launched two vessels which will be larger than any hitherto built. These will be the Mauretania and the Adriatic. Both will be launched on the same day—one at Newcastle, the other at Belfast. Thus does England still hold primacy on the sea. It is surely not an evil for the world that she should do so. For ours is a maritime empire. Our shipping is of utility to all nations. And wherever the British flag flies it is honestly intended to be the signal of human freedom. I have frequently heard Americans who know both countries say that there is even greater liberty in England than in America; and I have listened with deepest interest to some interesting arguments in which they have tried to prove their statement. I do not presume to decide; nor do I think there is much difference. The Anglo-Saxon race possesses, as no other race does, the instinct for freedom, the genius of liberty and the Anglo-Saxon spirit has decided once and for ever in favor of popular liberty. All our political fights are only struggles for certain preferential phases of that liberty.

The Anglo-American Pulpit Alliance.

I should now like permission to inform my kind American readers why I am so ardently attached to the work of the Disciples of Christ, as represented in the Old Country. Apart from the fundamental principles of the New Testament advocacy and from the movement which is going forward slowly but surely, even in this conservative country, I know of no system which so conspicuously and so continuously plants American preachers before the English public. I wish that a hundred of our American preachers could be sent here for ten years to echo our plea in a hundred different districts of these islands. Scotland has not even one! Ireland has not a single individual of this category! Yet Alexander Campbell was born in Ireland and studied in Scotland. Wales has not one of our own preachers. It is the most spiritual country on earth, but knows nothing whatever of this Reformation, and the great revival only issues in a renewed sectarian activity. I note with much satisfaction that our F. C. M. S. is constantly increasing its staff of missionaries in foreign lands. We shall shortly, according to very promising appearances, have a few fresh stations opened in this country. If to these some of the brightest of our preachers in the United States could be sent, a wonderful forward movement would be the result. The typical American preacher is liked and is heeded in England, but the supply is short. We want what I once heard the late Dr. Norman McLeod pleading for, at a missionary meeting at St. Andrews in Scotland—more men and more money. It is futile to imagine that a great work can be accomplished without the expenditure of a great sum of money. The Lord, I suppose, does not intend that any great work should be achieved without such a sacrifice of means. There is no more magnificent field for evangelization than the United Kingdom, for it is the focus of the earth; the international hub of the world; and the nervous ganglion where all the complex influences of civilization centrally throb and vibrate. Protestantism may indeed have originated in Germany; but England is the real fountain of the great world-current of Protestantism. England is the mother of Puritanism. England is the cradle of liberty. England struck the gong which sounded the signal of emancipation for the slave. England set foreign missions going in their strength, after their sources only a few feeble initial efforts had been made to evangelize the heathen. Even saved humanity from the thrall of a blasting papacy. England has perpetrated errors, blunders, mistakes, and is often blundering and mistaken still. Therefore she needs the strenuous help of her children, especially of her grandest and richest Daughter Offshoot. The mother of empires is nowhere near being decrepit. The statistics of her commerce just issued are startling and magnificent. But spiritually she is hindered and impeded by the incubus of an aristocratic and conservative Erastianism. To abolish this, to aid the Free Churches in a tremendous struggle approaching after the education bill is out of the way, she needs just that aid which America could give—especially the Disciples!

As Seen From the Dome   By F. D. Power

The Buffalo convention closed in splendid shape. The people were loyal to the last. There was the same great audience, the same spirit and enthusiasm to the end. The music, the closing words of the secretaries, the great Centennial speech of Warren, the sweet notes of the Netz sisters and the Pittsburg quartette, the introduction of our royal hosts, R. H. Miller and his helpers, the fine management of Presiding Officer Denton, the last prayer—all made it a memorable session.

The Buffalo churches served us most worthily. It was just what we might have expected of them. They have not been behind in any sense of the saints of any city where our convention hosts have been entertained. In decorations and in the finely selected mottoes on every side, as well as in acoustical properties and arrangements for the comfort and convenience of the guests, the hall was far and away beyond any we have ever used for our assemblies. The eloquence of our speakers reached every ear, the sweet songs of Zion were never heard to better advantage. God gave us beautiful days at Buffalo, and the whole city smiled on us. Not a jarring note was heard. Brotherly love seemed to abound. The spirit of peace and good will, and of a fine optimism, pervaded every session from start to finish. R. H. Miller said the convention had put the cause ten years ahead of anything that could have been reached by the state forces alone. We all owe a debt to the faithful men and women who made this convention.

Of course we all saw Niagara. Piloted by Pastors Miller and Wharton a party of sixty of us enjoyed the day there following the convention. It pours itself over the great wall of rock as majestically as ever. Since 1871 I have been visiting the awful cataract, and I have never wearied of it. One-eighth of its waters we are told is diverted to meet the calls of commercialism; and I fancied in thirty-five years I could see a change in its great volume. I saw its power used in the trolley cars that pulled us around the streets of the city, and in the manufacture of Larkin's soaps. I beheld it harnessed even to make shredded wheat biscuits. Niagara is the home of this sawdust fabric known as "shredded wheat biscuit." They show you a $100,000 plant, which uses from 1,200 to 1,800 bushels of wheat a day, and turns out 115,000 boxes of these curious crinkled crackers, twelve in a box, 1,380,000 daily to feed the breakfast food folks; and Niagara does everything

but put them in the boxes and chew them and many no doubt would be willing for the Falls to complete the process. Still with all the use of Niagara for purposes of gain there is some water left to tumble over the precipice for the delight and amazement of visitors and the profit of the Niagarenes. Uncle Jerry Peebles had seen frequent references in the papers to the necessity of saving Niagara, and was fearful there would be nothing to see if he did not hurry, and so took advantage of cheap excursion rates and went to the falls. "Gosh!" he said, as he looked at the wonderful spectacle for the first time, "what's the use tryin' to save 'em, when they're runnin' as if the devil was after 'em! You can't stop a thing like that!"

The falls are ever an unsurpassed wonder. Sir Edwin Arnold has described the cataract, and Mrs. Sigourney apostrophized it, but no description can ever do it justice. Ever since Joseph Price and Henry Wilmington, the young missionaries, led by the Indian chief Maiook, penetrated the wilderness and discovered the falls they have rolled on, the same magnificent and bewildering spectacle. Awful in its sublimity, one is overwhelmed and speechless in its presence. It is indeed as the redmen named it—Niagara, "the thundering waters." As you watch it rushing, smoking, glittering with green and white rollers and rapids, hurling the waters of a whole continent in splendor and speed over the sharp ledges of rock; the coiling spirals of twisted and furious flood crashing in terrible impulse of descent down, down upon the great boulders and boiling cauldron beneath, and listen to the fearful tumult and view the clouds of water-smoke rising: as you look upon the river winding its way eagerly to its stupendous leap, and see the first breakers forming, and then. the leaping billows where they feel the mighty draw of the cataracts, springing forward as so many living creatures under some fatal and irresistible doom; and then at the brink the apparent pause, "all quiet and glassy and rounded and green as the border of a field of rye" while they turn the fearful ledge, and hurl themselves, a wild chaos of seething, tumbling, waters into the awful gulf of mystery and horrible din; and at that very moment of monstrous uproar and grandeur you view the exquisite and reposeful beauty of lovely rainbows spanning the awe-inspiring chasm, and suspended above all the turmoil and clamor of the great abyss, Niagara loses its terror, and all graceful and beautiful, becomes a picture of the loving kindness of God that overshadows all his works, and the tender mercy of the Father from whom no terror or gloom or mystery can ever separate his children.

While we were here in Buffalo a party of six persons were nearly carried over the falls. Out on the river in a gasoline launch they ran into a bar and broke both propellers. The disabled launch drifted down stream. They threw out a small anchor. It caught, but the rope parted and the boat again raced down stream. A large anchor was thrown out, but it dragged the bottom without catching or retarding the speed of the boat, now in the seventeen-mile current. People along shore attracted by the cries and the flash light of the launch, could render no assistance. Police and firemen from Niagara Falls heard of the boat's peril and started up stream, but were powerless to render aid. The launch was rapidly getting to the point where no human help could avail when the anchor caught back of a big stone and held, and the people were saved. Terror-stricken by their danger the women had fainted and the men had given up in despair. A question for every man: Does your anchor hold? Are you drifting helpless, and hurrying toward the fearful precipice, or does your anchor hold?

Just above Goat Island one can readily see where the waters divide—one side passing over the American and the other over the Horse Shoe Fall. A piece of timber will come to the spot and balance itself for a moment. The slightest influence will determine its course. A moment will decide. It swings one way, or the other, and passes over. So with human destiny. We hurry on. The turning point is reached. We drift away from God, or we find him.

The great cataract has its lessons. It speaks in no uncertain voice of its Creator.

"Flow on forever, in thy glorious robe
Of terror and of beauty. God hath set
His rainbow on thy forehead, and the clouds
Mantled around thy feet; and He doth give
Thy Voice of thunder power to speak of Him
Eternally; bidding the lips of man
Keep silence, and upon thy rocky altar pour
Incense of awe-struck praise."

CHRIST is very patient with our imperfect obedience, if we truly love him. If we are sincerely trying to do what he would have us to do, e,en though we fail and fall far below his standard, he accepts our work, and knowing our intention and seeing the sincerity of our effort, he is pleased.

State Loyalty   By W. R. Warren

In the breast of every worthy man there exists a spirit which for want of a better term we designate self-respect. It is the recognition of the duty which every man owes to himself. It manifests itself in many ways. In some individuals it is lacking to such a degree that the person becomes contemptible. In others it has had such undue development that their arrogance is exasperating. But the happy mean is an indispensable element in every worthy character. In much the same way each individual has his family pride, his civic pride, his state loyalty, his national patriotism, and his humanitarianism. Our religion inevitably expresses itself successively through these concentric circles. Most of us accepted Christ in the first place for our own salvation. We help in the church's maintenance for the sake of family and neighbors. If we have any religious feeling for our state it must express itself through the State Missionary Society just as our religious patriotism is manifested through our support of the American Christian Missionary Society, and our regard for mankind through the Foreign Christian Missionary Society.

State loyalty leads us to contribute of our means through taxation millions of dollars every year for public education and public charities, but the Bible, the foundation of all true education, is excluded from our public schools, and the Gospel, from which all charity springs, can be proclaimed only in places and by persons supported by voluntary gifts. Liberty and love, rather than law, are the fundamental principles of Christianity, but Christians present to the world the anomaly of doing far more under legal taxation than under Gospel impulse. This is most strikingly true in state affairs. If we would worthily celebrate our Centennial, we must redeem our states by generously and universally supporting state missions. The obligation touches every church and every member and they should have fellowship in the annual offering the first Lord's day in November.

The Call of the States

Arkansas.

The most essential condition to be brought about in Arkansas, and I suppose in most parts of the south, is to locate, at central points, efficient men who have the tact to come readily in sympathetic touch with all classes of workers who are willing to help build up the cause. We need men who will stay, men who wish to make a permanent home in this sun-bright clime, and who realize that it will be necessary to work for a time on much less salary than men of the same talent will command where the cause is better established.

There have been not less than twenty churches organized within the last year in this state, in sympathy with co-operative work. One-half of these will not live without help from without. Congregations have been organized during the last two years, in not less than ten county seats and other important towns, of 3,000 population or more, and arrangements are made for building. Four houses have been dedicated in county seats during the year.

The solution of the matter here is sufficient mission funds to enable us to hold efficient preachers for a little while. There are not less than fifteen, among the larger towns, of the states where work can be made successful, that must fail without assistance.

Little Rock, Ark.   E. C. BROWNING.

Colorado's Advance Steps.

Our recent state convention took several advance steps in the work for the year beginning October 1:

1. Recommending that "special attention be given to the strengthening of missions hitherto under the care of the state board; that effort be concentrated upon the more promising of these with a view to making them self-supporting at least by the end of the present year; that new churches be organized wherever it can be done with reasonable promise of permanency."

2. Instructing the state board to employ an evangelist, whose time shall be given wholly to holding meetings, strengthening weak places, helping mission churches toward self-support, and opening new fields wherever the way may be open. The board has already apointed a committee to secure the man for this work.

3. Placing our financial watchword this year at $3,500. In the year just closed we raised $1,831.34, the largest amount ever raised in one year. The new watchword contemplates a great advance over any previous year.

4. Logically following this recommendation was the resolution to enter now and here upon a serious campaign to induce at least 3,000 members in our Colorado churches to become tithers.

5. It was strongly recommended "that unless local conditions render it altogether impracticable, every church observe the first Lord's day of November as state mission day, taking pledges and offerings on that day." If the pledges are made early the board can more intelligently plan the work of the year, besides more money can be secured than if the offering is deferred. If the offering is delayed, other offerings which have a just claim upon our liberality interfere with a good contribution to state work. Again, the time of the corresponding secretary is taken in raising money late in the year when other work should claim his attention. It is hoped that all the churches will try to observe this day.

The area of Colorado is exactly equal to that of the states of Iowa and New York. We have but forty-eight churches; some of them not active. There are fifty-nine county seat towns, and we have congregations in only twenty of them.

This is the time to push the work in Colorado, for the state is very prosperous. E. E. Hill, commissioner of the Colorado Car Service Bureau, has recently said: "There never were such shipments made out of and into the state before. The traffic is simply appalling. The manufactories have made wonderful strides; the state has grown from the size of a child to the stature of a man in almost a day, and the shipments of a few years ago, which we used to consider abnormal, are now but as pygmies when compared to the shipments of this season."

We appeal to all pastors and churches in Colorado to help make this a record-breaking year, and begin it by enthusiastically observing Colorado day, Lord's day, November 4.

Denver, Col.   LEONARD G. THOMPSON, Cor. Sec.

Encouraging Facts from Indiana.

Two years ago I was called by our state convention, through the executive board, to serve the Indiana Christian Missionary Society as corresponding secretary. I began with practically an empty treasury, two large debts and only the incomplete "Year Book" with preachers' names as a correspondence list.

1. Information was necessary. Transient circulars can never do the work. So the "Indiana Christian" was resurrected and is the regular official organ of the state missions, entered at the postoffice at second-class rates and owned and controlled by our state society. A complete reporting system has been put in operation which already has on alphabetical file complete reports of a half dozen counties, and promises as much for all other counties by the new plan. When this is done a complete and authentic "Year Book for Indiana" will give accurate information to every preacher and church.

2. A new organization by counties linked with district and state by co-operation in reports, conventions, offerings and evangelism is being rapidly consummated and looks forward to the complete unification of all state interests soon in co-operative work.

3. This is securing already in several counties complete co-operation by grouping churches by counties, and employing evangelists and preachers where there have been none for months and even years. To do this great work for the great army of 835 churches (last report) there has been incurred a greater expense than the receipts, from the churches would meet. This has brought embarrassment and hardship to this magnificent service which threatens to close the door which is now open wide with the glorious promise of future usefulness.

We ask you to note these facts: A gain in cash receipts has been secured this year over last year of $1,047.32, or 41 per cent. In number of contributing churches, a gain of 22, or 16 per cent. Note also 61 meetings were held with 1,404 accessions, 64 weak churches were helped, 12 new churches were organized and seven reorganized, while fully 200 worthy calls could not be answered for want of funds. W. J. Wright says this is by far the best gain of which he has learned. Please note these facts also: There were 976 churches in Indiana this last fiscal year (reported by our state evangelist). One hundred and fifty-five gave about $3,000. Eight hundred and twenty-one gave not one cent. Five hundred of these could give easily an average of $15 each and no other equal investment could so mightily help world-wide missions and so wonderfully bless and strengthen the churches of Indiana. This is practical and possible if the preachers and officers of our churches say so. If we give $17,000 for heathen missions why should we not give as much for Hoosier missions?

We stand hesitating and trembling with the burden of mighty responsibilities at great open doors of opportunity, awaiting the word of assurance and the offering of necessary help to go in and possess the land. The assurance of the November day offerings, or as soon thereafter as possible is absolutely necessary to our future plans and work. If half of our 140,000 members would give on an average of 20 cents each we would have $14,000 and 25 state evangelists the whole year. Or if half of our 835 churches would give on an average $20 each we would have $9,340 and sixteen evangelists the whole year. Each dollar invested brings, with a representative preacher, two or three more from the field. Over 200 worthy churches are calling.

There were thirty-nine churches built and sixteen churches repaired in Indiana last year by the Disciples of Christ. The money invested amounts to $333,650 and the increased seating capacity aggregates 25,000. This includes a large number of splendid brick and Bedford stone buildings, modern in every respect for work and worship.

J. O. ROSE, Cor. Sec.

From the Late Superintendent of Kansas Missions.

Only those who know by experience the wide contrast between the words "home" and "homeless," can fully sympathize and rejoice with the writer in the change that he has made from the superintendency of Kansas missions to the pastorate; from days and nights on the rail to an uninterrupted period at home with the loved ones; from the care of all the churches" to the care of but one, and from numberless duties and obligations to the simple life of the shepherd of one flock, and yet I was never really homeless. I had many homes during those seven busy years. It is no exaggeration to say that I had hundreds of homes. Many of them the best, the cheeriest, the most delightful the Sunflower State affords, where the welcome was hearty and the feast broad spread with the richest of earth's bounties. But,

"Home's not merely four square walls
Hung with pictures, framed and gilded,
Home is where affection calls,
Filled with shrines the heart hath builded."

The good people of this little city are showing us every consideration. A public reception was given us at the home of Brother and Sister Rossman, which was largely attended. We have a most excellent people with whom to labor. Good men have preceded us here in the pastorate, and Brother and Sister Sherman Hill, our immediate predecessors, were among the best.

Kansas day draws near, and all our Kansas churches should do their part by Kansas missions. We should heed the call of the state board and that of our new superintendent, George E. Lyon.

Paola will do her part cheerfully. Long live and prosper THE CHRISTIAN-EVANGELIST, with its uniform and constant message of liberty, light and love.

Paola, Kan. W. S. LOWE.

Illinois.

The field secretary served 365 days, visited 109 churches, delivered 235 sermons, held 38 missionary rallies, several short meetings, 6 county rallies, 6 district conventions, dedicated 6 churches.

His collections were $1,411.77, and expenses $209.24. The office secretary, W. D. Deweese, served 312 days.

Marion Stevenson, superintendent, served 334 days, visited 199 schools; delivered 303 addresses, attended several conventions, secured pledges from 177 schools amounting to $1,416.39, and collected in the field $291.81. His traveling expenses were $209.81, office expenses $21.33, postage $69.91.

The summary for the year is: Men in the service, 58; churches visited, 183; days' service, 4,183; revival meetings, 51; sermons delivered, 2,291; conversions, 1,044; other additions, 577; total additions, 1,621; churches organized, 6; churches aided, 46; money raised for state and district missions from all sources, $12,088.81.

The summary for eleven years is: Men in the service, 336; days, 23,832; churches visited, 1,603; revival meetings, 616; sermons, 18,037; conversions, 9,117; other additions, 5,802; total additions, 14,919; churches organized, 79; churches aided, 479; houses dedicated, 18; total offerings for state and district missions, $89,731.88.

Iowa's State Campaign.

Our Iowa mission work is state wide in its plan. We have the state divided into five districts, and the secretary of each respective district is a member of the state board, thus linking all sections are represented. The growth of interest and offerings for the state work are very encouraging. Last year we had ten evangelists at work all or part of the year, and fourteen missionary pastors. Twenty-three men held volunteer missionary meetings for our board without cost to our treasury. We held meetings or gave assistance to pastoral support to ninety churches, and more than 100 churches were benefited by our force of workers.

Evangelism is our watch cry for Iowa this year, and we are bending every energy to accomplish the greatest possible results for our God. From January 1 to April 1, 1907, we will wage a state-wide, simultaneous evangelistic campaign, in which we hope to enlist every church in the state.

We have our Central Executive Committee, consisting of general chairman, general superintendent and one member from each of the five districts, to act as superintendents of their respective districts. Each of these men have their territory divided into four or five sections, and a committeeman over each. Our churches are divided into three classes. 1. Those who can arrange their own meetings, select their own evangelists, and pay their own bills. 2. Those able to pay their own bills but in need of assistance in arranging the meeting. 3. Churches able to do little or nothing toward making the plans or financing the meeting. Blanks suitable for each church have been printed and mailed to the churches, and they are asked to fill in the blank report that suits their condition. We have planned an evangelistic institute for each of the sub-districts, from which we hope to gather great inspiration for the state mission offering and for the evangelistic campaign.

The program for the institute is as follows, and will continue two nights and one day: Evening—Devotional, "Under Commission"; sermon, "Our Simultaneous Campaign for Souls." Forenoon—Devotional, "Whitened Harvest Fields"; address, "Organization of the Forces"; discussion; address, "Individual Work for Individuals"; discussion. Afternoon—Devotional, "God's Promises to the Reapers"; address, "What to Preach and How to Preach It"; discussion; conference: 1. "Every Church in Line"—(a) Have you

arranged your meeting? (b) What help do you need? (c) What help can you give? (d) Reporting to headquarters. 2. A day sacred to all this work, Iowa Day, November 4. Evening—Devotional, "The Soul Winner's Joy"; Evangelistic sermon.

Summary of mission work for the year—Number of men engaged, 47; days service, 6,494; sermons, 3,474; baptisms, 1,447; other additions, 860; places assisted, 90. Our missionaries cost $1.25 each per day; additions by our missionaries cost $4 each.

B. S. DENNY, Cor. Sec.

Des Moines, Iowa.

Kentucky Missions for 1906 and 1907.

The year that closed with our recent state convention at Louisville was in many respects the best year we have had in our state work for a dozen years. We had a larger number of additions, 2,062 being the total reported by the men whose support we shared. We built some excellent houses of worship in most important fields. South Louisville, South Portsmouth, Jackson, Jellico and other places were helped in the struggle to build and establish the cause. Aside from the signal success in many of our special fields, our evangelists gave a good account of themselves.

The greatest difficulty was in reaching the fields where they were urgently needed. Many of the worthy appeals had to be passed because we had neither men nor money to meet the needs of the situation. Already the appeals for the next year are coming in thick and fast. On October 6 the board went carefully over the fields that must be helped and considered one by one the men to be employed. No appropriations were made, for as much we hear from the churches before we answer these appeals. We are unable to calculate wisely until the congregations have indicated what they are willing to do for the support of the work. We await the orders of our commander-in-chief—the churches.

Already the appeals for help will require 50 per cent. larger contributions for the evangelistic fund. We made last year an increase in the contributions of the churches of $1,035. This was a good advance, and such an advance another year will enable us to enter more fields and answer more appeals.

The fields already occupied must be held until they can take care of themselves. Other doors are open wide to us and it will be criminal not to enter them. Another strong evangelist ought to be at work in the Big Sandy Valley. We have the man in mind, and only need to have assurance of the funds being furnished to enable us to undertake this larger effort. Some of our most important special mission work is pleading for increased appropriations. Springfield, for instance, wants the board to give three times as much as we have been paying to that field, urging that such help given them for one year will probably enable them to dispense with the aid of the brethren. South Louisville wants more money to help in support of their preacher. They have a heavy load of debt, and urge that now is the day of their salvation. A dollar spent there now in that rapidly-growing section of our metropolis will accomplish more than $5 a year or two later. Jackson thinks that it is indispensable to have preaching every Sunday, and urges more money for 1907.

From every quarter, the demand is made for enlargement. We can meet these demands only as our people enable us to do so. November 4 must be made a high day, and in the month must be consecrated to Kentucky missions by Kentucky churches if we meet worthily the demands that are upon us.

We plead for prompt response to the letters mailed to each congregation, and beg to assure you that nothing is as blighting and withering as cold indifference. Better opposition than that. If you will not help us, say so. If you have good reasons for this, all well and good. If it arises from simple indifference as to whether the Lord's work is done, then the Lord pity you. We are praying that not many may be described by these last words, and that our people in old Kentucky may give fresh proof of an increasing interest in reaching the waste places of our commonwealth that they may be made to blossom as the rose.

H. W. ELLIOTT, Cor. Sec.

Sulphur, Ky.

Missouri Work and Plans.

One of the most successful years in the history of our Missouri mission work was that which closed June 1, 1906. The fear was expressed by some that the effort to raise $12,000 for our permanent fund would seriously cripple the securing of funds for the regular work. The contrary proved too true, for $10,-275 were raised, as against $6,321 in the year before; adding the money secured for the permanent fund of $10,000 and we have over $20,000, three times as much as came to hand the year previous. We take this as a strong indication of a deepening interest in this great work on the part of both ministers and people; people will not give for that in which they are not interested.

But in other ways the forward move was fully as marked as it was in the financial phase. There has been trouble all of the time in some parts of the state; the work and plans of the state board were not heartily endorsed, and there was much friction. This we believe has happily passed away and there is a harmony and unity among our people, a determination to stand heartily by the state board and its plans, that has prophecies of great things for the future. Missouri churches united have a tremendous power; they may dare to do anything, even the seemingly impossible, and accomplish it. There is no power in any other section of our great land comparable to this and our confident belief is that this giant is now arousing himself to the putting forth of his tremendous power.

The policy of the board to assist weak churches at important and strategic points, is to be continued. When we remember that nearly all of the strong churches of St. Louis were planted and came to their strength in this way, that in Kansas City and many of the towns and villages of the state there are churches that have become giants in power through this policy, we are sure this will have hearty endorsement.

The state has been redistricted; there are seven districts now. St. Louis and Kansas City each form one, while two are north of the river and three lie south of it. It is the purpose of the board that each one of these districts shall have an efficient evangelist, not simply a protracted meeting holder, but a man of consecration, of wisdom, of power with God and men, who shall have the care of all the churches on his heart. Such a man we have in Joseph Gaylor in district 3; in G. E. Ireland in St. Louis. Kansas City has one—none better—in F. L. Bowen. C. O. McFarland is serving the two districts north of the river.

We need another man north of the river, one in southeast, or district No. 4, and one in district No. 2. Thus the state will be covered by competent men whose whole-duty, business and joy it shall be to see that the cause we love shall be planted and fostered in each and every part of their own territory.

Brethren, this in mere outline is our purpose, these are our plans. The only thing lacking is the means. Do you like the plans? Has our purpose your endorsement? The best answer is the offering. Mere gush or sentiment counts for but little; what we need is the largest offering ever taken for state missions.

T. A. ABBOTT, Cor. Sec.

Kansas City, Mo.

Ohio Missionary Plans.

The Ohio Christian Missionary Society is planning this year to pay off every dollar of debt. This debt was incurred by the support of missions, the establishing of churches and the saving of souls. Our state board planned for larger things than the people were willing to pay for, and did a larger mission work than the funds in hand warranted. Hence the debt. At the beginning of the Centennial campaign this debt ought to be paid and that promptly.

In the second place we have in Ohio at the present time twenty-five missions, some of them receiving a meager support. This mission work ought to be continued with a stronger hand and new missions added.

Another plan of far-reaching import is our state-wide evangelistic campaign, November 15, 1907, to February 15, 1908. In this campaign we expect to have 500 churches engaged, one-half of them in a strong evangelistic campaign before the holidays and the balance in a vigorous campaign after the holidays. Already the forces are being gathered, the churches are falling into line and vigorous plans for the campaign will be pushed after the Ohio day offering in November, when the secretary can give a little more time and attention to this work.

Another far-reaching plan for Ohio missions is the establishing of a church in every county seat by 1909. There are now twenty-four county seats in which we have no church as yet. We shall have to plant these county seats rapidly if the work is done. Eight each year of the three years remaining will have to be the schedule.

In order to carry on this work we are asking the churches this year for $20,000 for Ohio missions. It is a liberal increase over last year but not one whit too large for the work demanded of us. As the day for the November offering approaches the prospects for a large increase over the offerings of previous years are bright.

Our campaign this fall has been more energetic and has reached more people than ever before. Instead of depending upon our few district conventions we have held aid and are holding forty-five missionary rallies, taking with us a touring party of three or four speakers and devoting an afternoon and evening to Ohio missions. It has created much enthusiasm and we believe will increase the offering for Ohio missions materially. The plan of missionary rallies is taking in the state and next year there will be a larger demand for them than ever before. We believe that the day for larger things in Ohio missions is at hand.

S. H. BARTLETT.

Oklahoma.

Last year the following work was done by an average of seven and a half men, including our corresponding secretary and the living link missionaries. Number of men employed, 7½; days' service, 2,730; sermons, 1,568; baptisms, 492; other accessions, 864; total accessions, 1,356; churches organized, 29; churches assisted, 97; church buildings erected, 44;

meetings held, 56; amount of money raised, $48,400.

To accomplish this work the following amount of money was expended: The A. C. M. S., $1,100; the C. W. B. M. $600; individual pledges and church offerings in Oklahoma, $862.11; living link money raised in Oklahoma, $1,052. Total, $3,612.11.

J. M. MONROE, Cor. Sec.

Oregon Central District.

The central district of the Oregon Christian Missionary Convention has just closed a very successful convention at Albany. The program represented the C. W. B. M. and the regular church work. Every speaker was present except one, and arrangements were made for a year of aggressive work in the central district. This district comprises Lane, Linn, Marion, Benton and Lincoln counties. There are in this district thirty-eight churches and 3,800 Disciples. These churches will support J. N. McConnell as evangelist, and it is hoped that one church or a group of churches of this district will supply $300 for the support of an evangelist in the "unoccupied southeast" section of the state.

Both parts of the program did credit to the causes represented, and will likely be reported by other hands. T. S. Handsaker is superintendent of the church work, and Mrs. Billington, of the C. W. B. M., for the district. We all counted ourselves fortunate to be the guests of J. J. Evans and the Albany church. Our district president, Brother Handsaker, delivered an excellent address, which will be published, by vote of the convention.

The following report of the Committee on Future Work will show the spirit and purpose of the whole convention:

"1. We recommend that the officers and Executive Committee chosen at the Turner convention be continued until the next state convention. 2. We would advise this convention to authorize its delegates to the state convention to nominate a district president while at the convention. 3. We recommend that this convention endorse the action of the Committee on Benevolence appointed by the O. C. M. C. in locating the home for the aged at Eugene, and pledge itself to co-operate in the support of this institution. 4. That we adopt as an evangelistic policy the building up of declining churches and as opportunity offers inaugurating new work. 5. We endorse the action of the Executive Committee in the employment of J. N. McConnell as evangelist for the district, and pledge ourselves to support him in every possible way. 6. That it is the sense of this convention that we are in full accord and sympathy with the work of the O. C. M. C. and regard ourselves as a force auxiliary to it. 7. We recommend that all churches in the district organize dollar leagues in support of the work."

This report was unanimously adopted, and is a sign that the central district intends to do business for Christ and the Church.

The northwest and southwest districts will hold their conventions the latter part of October and the first of November.

F. E. BILLINGTON,

Cor. Sec. O. C. M. C.

Cottage Grove, Ore.

South Idaho's Need.

The maintenance of a state evangelist was made possible by gifts of the American Board. This year's state work in Idaho sums up: Four new churches organized—Emmett, with 18 members, has bought a lot, is purchasing a good building to move to lot; will be served by B. W. Rice. Rupert, with 46 members, bought a lot, are now building, have not yet reported securing a pastor.

Meridian, with 63 members, engaged E. A. Child to begin pastorate Nov. 1, bought a lot and plan to build. Nampa, with 48 members, bought a lot, built a plain, cheap house, engage C. A. Child half time. Besides this we assisted Weiser to support G. M. Redd, and gained 22 members.

Will the American Board be able to give us a state evangelist for next year, or for the next five years, to gather and nurture such as these?

Wm. M. Semones, Cor. Sec.

Texas Missions.

Our summer campaign has been very successful. We report three months' work. We have had 35 different men in the field; days, 2,162; sermons, 1,413; baptisms, 651; from denominations, 55; by letter and statement, 393. Twelve new churches were planted. The cash amount raised by and for those men was $6,257. With this we paid for the 2,162 days' work and traveling expenses and paid for three issues of our monthly "Texas Missions," and other printing, amounting all told to $250. Our missionaries raised for church houses; lots, ttc., $4,448. Total cash raised, therefore, was $10,705. We aided 179 places and took pledges to the amount of $3,800. This gives us the largest results ever reported in Texas mission work for one quarter.

Now, when we consider that in our evangelistic work our aim is to aid only the weak churches and new points and not to leave them until we have put them in condition to go forward with the work; the economy with which this work has been conducted will be more appreciated. It is also true that numbers as such have not been the chief aim but permanency in the work. We give this as a sample of what we have been enabled to do by the liberality of the brethren and would make these facts the basis of an appeal for larger liberality. We would not boast. There is entirely too much land to be possessed for any boasting. Our men have done well, but the Texas Disciples are able to do a much larger work. The population of the state is growing as never before. Appeals are coming to this office that would touch the hearts of all our people if we could find space to give them to you. There has never been a time when the people heard the Word more gladly. Brethren of Texas, let us have grand missionary rallies for Texas missions in November. Give us the means and we will surprise even the sanguine with what God can do through his people when we will.

Dallas, Texas.   J. C. Mason.

The Indian Territory Plan.

1. One territorial and two district conventions are held annually. One district convention is held in the northern part of the territory, the other in the southern part, the territorial convention at some central point.

2. The district conventions are an integral part of the work at large in the territory, and are held under the supervision of the corresponding secretary.

3. The annual territorial convention elects a board of directors, seven of whom are chosen to act as an executive committee. This committee employs a corresponding secretary who also acts as superintendent of missions and financial secretary.

4. All moneys are receipted for and classified in the books according to sources; the corresponding secretary passes the money on to the treasurer, who pays it out as authorized to by vouchers, signed by the corresponding secretary and chairman of the executive committee.

5. The books of the corresponding secretary and treasurer are audited annually by an expert, and he reports his findings to the convention.

6. Appropriations are made to weak and important points for three months at a time, to assist in the support of regular preaching. Appropriations for this purpose are $6.25, $12.50 and $25 per month, according to the necessity of the case. In all these cases we require the point assisted to make a monthly offering to our Indian Territory missions equal to a fraction more than one-half our appropriation. The advantages of this system are many and important.

7. We answer all calls for meetings, provided we are given a reasonable amount of time. To do this we employ "living link" evangelists, where it is convenient to do so, otherwise we get some church to lend us its pastor for a few days, allowing him whatever he may receive. But in case he gets less than a stated amount per week we supplement this, allowing never more than $10 per week supplement.

8. We have a tent that we furnish to missions when it is desired.

9. We assist all the churches to find and locate preachers, and to secure evangelists.

10. We aid the churches and the cause in every proper way that comes to hand.

11. The executive committee meets every three months. The committee hears the report of the corresponding secretary and treasurer, and then plans the work for another three months.

12. This system has worked wonders in the Indian Territory since its inauguration, less than three years ago.

S. R. Hawkins, Cor. Sec.

Virginia.

The Virginia Christian Missionary Society has just closed another successful year. The total receipts were $7,757.03. Our receipts the previous year were $7,310.31. Not a very large increase, but an increase. Our watchword for the new year, will be, $10,000 for Virginia missions. The total number added was 901. Seven churches were organized, and six Sunday-schools were constituted.

We are supporting a number of preachers in mission points. Chief among these are Portsmouth, Blacksburg, Petersburg and Harrisonburg. Portsmouth is a city of 25,000, in which we had not preached in seventy years. We organized a mission last year, and are now supporting it. We hope to have a good church in a short while. This is perhaps our most important point. Blacksburg is the seat of the Virginia Polytechnic Institute, where there are 700 students. Our congregation is three years old and owns its own house and a parsonage. We have a large hearing, and our preacher, E. B. Kemm, supported by the V. C. M. S., is called the most popular minister in the town.

For the last six years, the secretary of the Virginia work has been supported by individual subscriptions made for that purpose, so that all the offerings from the churches and Sunday-schools are used for the real work of missions. The plan works well, and has given Virginia her most successful years.

While the work in the east is slow, and the people conservative, we thank God and take courage.   H. C. Combs,

Financial Sec'y., V. C. M. S.

Wisconsin.

To-day Wisconsin presents a whitened field for the home mission harvest. Priceless forests, untold water power, and productive soil is bringing to her a vast population. Here is a great foreign mission field. But as a problem it must be worked out by the state board. Here in Wisconsin, as in few other states of the Union, is found the frontier, community, with its restless, reckless, disregard of the higher needs of life; and touching it is the old, well established thoroughly orthodox community, with a conservatism that spells senility for religion. How to reach and win for Christ these different yet equally needy millions, is the problem to which the Wisconsin Christian Missionary Association bends its every energy.

Splendid cities are springing up like magic. We must enter them before they have grown too large, or find the field an expensive and difficult one later on. To do this our board must have men, and to secure men we must have money. We believe that "the Lord helps those who help themselves." Hence we are planning an offering to state missions, in which each church will give an amount equal to $1 for each member. Our recent state convention voted first, to put a man in the field as evangelist who shall have the care of all the churches, strengthening the weak and building the new. Second, to plant a new church at Janesville, a thriving city, and hold the convention of 1907 there.

The Scandinavian work is full of promise. The recent meeting at Chippewa Falls, a gift from the splendid church at Mackinaw, Ill., is an object lesson. Thousands of these people are now just where Mr. Campbell and his colaborers were a century ago. The free air of the great northwest has emancipated them from earlier religious affiliations. They have broken with the old. But no voice has as yet sounded out a message that will guide them into the new, sweet reasonableness of Christ—the sublime simplicity of the faith of the apostles as found in the New Testament. I believe that God will raise up men, consecrated men, who will come into Wisconsin fields and come to stay, to preach the primitive Gospel. I believe that God's will in the life of a great brotherhood will pour in money until we can enter a dozen of these new cities and build therein strong missionary churches that will go in the name of Christ to seek and save the lost.

Chas. Wm. Dean, Cor. Sec.
Grand Rapids, Wis.

Work in South Kentucky.

At the convention in May we reported that last year about $2,700 was expended for all purposes, and about $2,500 raised for actual missionary purposes, leaving a balance in our treasury with which to begin the new year's work. The corresponding secretary held twelve meetings during the year besides other duties too numerous to name devolving upon him. Other meetings were held in destitute fields by other faithful helpers under the direction of the association, and all resulted in the organizing of seven new congregations. Not less than $5,000 was raised for local purposes, such as funds to build houses and sustain preaching, pay church debts, etc. We are expecting to raise not less than $4,000 for purely mission purposes this year. We are planning to place more evangelists in the field as soon as funds will justify. Our financial resources in South Kentucky are almost without limit if we could only command them. One of the greatest problems I ever undertook to solve is this problem of liberality. Are we using missionary money in an unwise way? Do our brethren of wealth look upon money expended for missionary purposes as an unwise expenditure?

W. J. Hudspeth.
Hopkinsville, Ky.

Our Budget

—Next Lord's day, November 4, is state mission day.

—If you have not prepared a special sermon, read to your congregation the address by Harry D. Smith, and add your own peroration or application.

—Ohio has some far-reaching plans.

—Those of Indian Territory have been very successful.

—A city in Virginia where our plea had not been presented during seventy years has been entered.

—Kansas now has a woman as its corresponding secretary. A. Rosalea Pendleton is her name. George E. Lyon is the new superintendent.

—Colorado seeks 3,000 tithers.

—You will find other interesting items in the reports from the states on other pages of this issue.

—We have in preparation another special issue of THE CHRISTIAN-EVANGELIST to be devoted to some of the co-workers with Alexander Campbell and the pioneers of our movement. We shall be glad to hear from any of our readers who have photographs, daguerreotypes or anything that would be worth while illustrating, or that will throw any light on the character and work of these worthies.

❖ ❖ ❖

—The Foreign Society missionary rallies begin November 19.

—Fife and Saunders can lead a meeting beginning November 18. Address Huntington, W. Va.

—During the past ten months the membership at Louisburg, Mo., has been doubled, 52 having been added.

—On its recent rally day the Thirty-fourth Street Church, Washington, secured about $600 for a new building.

—The Sunday-school at Delta, O., has trebled during the past ten months. William B. Hendershot is the pastor there.

—Edward O. Sharpe has recently entered upon the pastorate at San Antonio, Texas. He reports six additions and fine prospects.

—James A. Challener reports a good work with the church at Artesia, New Mexico, which has been without a pastor for some time.

—Robert Pegrum has accepted a unanimous call to the church at Milton, Queens county, N. S. He entered upon his pastorate October 7.

—An organization of sixty members has been effected at Davis, Mo., and $1,300 raised for a new building. Brother Taylor is the pastor.

—F. H. Schmitt is now holding a meeting at Le Roy, Kan., where he was born and brought up. His wife has lived in the same community since childhood.

—As a result of a meeting by Clyde Sharp, the church at Fayetteville, Mo., will employ a pastor as soon as possible. Brother Sharp has returned to his home at La Harpe, Kan.

—A new church building has just been dedicated at Carmi, Ill., with Z. T. Sweeney in charge of the exercises. There was a call for $3,500 and $5,300 were raised. Frank Thompson is the pastor.

—At a meeting of the board of directors of the Bethany Assembly W. E. M. Hackleman was elected secretary. New buildings will be erected during the coming year and other important improvements made.

—B. E. Utz, late of Spokane, Wash., is supplying the pulpit of the Ninth Street Church at Washington, which Brother Bagby has vacated and which George Miller, of Covington, Ky., will enter in January.

—As a result of a good meeting just held by J. B. Boen and Leonard Daugherty, the brethren at Winfield, Kan., where Albert Nichols is pastor, are talking of a new church building. More room is needed, there having been liberal gains during the past two years.

—J. M. Bailey will close his ministry at Frankford, Mo., at the end of the year, and will be glad to get into communication with a church in need of a minister. During his two years' pastorate at Frankford some 50 have been added to the church and the brethren are harmonious and ready for a good work.

NEW READERS IN THE SOUTH.

As will be seen from "Georgia Notes," by Bro. E. L. Shelnutt, the "Southern Evangelist," of which he has been the editor and proprietor, has been merged in The Christian-Evangelist, beginning with this number. We welcome the "Southern Evangelist" readers into our great and growing Christian-Evangelist family. The transition ought to be easy from the one Evangelist to the other, and we are sure our new readers from the Sunny Southland will feel quite at home with us. Brother Shelnutt has kindly promised to furnish us the news from the South and in that way he will keep in touch with his old readers and keep our readers in touch with that field. As in union there is strength, we see no reason why this union of forces will not prove helpful to both and, what is more important, helpful to the cause we are seeking to advance. It is the day of union, of joining hands and hearts for the better accomplishment of common ends and aims. We trust the former readers of the "Southern Evangelist" who are now readers of this journal, will feel free to express themselves or report news as freely as in their old paper.

—Uncle Hugh Wilson, who has been a faithful contributor to every missionary movement by the Church of Christ, attended most of the meetings recently held at Russellville, Ind., by the Martin family. He is 92 years of age and his father and mother were baptized by Barton W. Stone during the Cane Ridge revival.

—Herbert J. Corwine, whose resignation of the pastorate at California, Mo., we have announced, writes us that the congregation there is in splendid accord with the truth and is in perfect harmony. Brother Corwine leaves them because of health considerations and is hopeful that they will find a good pastor to work among them.

—George L. Zimmerman, of the congregation of Tillamook, Ore, is in a meeting with Evangelist George C. Ritchey and his singer, A. W. Shaffer. This strong force will be assisted by the circulation of 300 CHRISTIAN-EVANGELISTS, and the brethren feel that our church there will be one of the strongest pow-

—M. S. Johnson, of Litchfield, Ill., has been subjected to some annoyance and some libelous attacks by certain individuals, whose opposition was aroused by Brother Johnson's determined efforts to speak the truth about the saloons and other resorts of ill character. By means of trickery one of the newspapers was misled into publishing an attack upon Brother Johnson, but its withdrawal of the charges and prompt apology did something to atone for the injury the first announcement may have caused in the minds of those who do not know Brother Johnson. The brethren of our own church, of course, would not have been deceived by any such anonymous attacks. The new church at Litchfield is to be dedicated about November 18 or 25.

—J. H. Berkey, Monroe, Wis., says he is receiving letters of inquiry from different parts of th country regarding the effect of the Scoville meeting in the Union Church in Christ in that place. He answers: "There were five churches in the union. There were 450 confessions, of which this church has received in round numbers, 100. During the meeting we built a new baptistry in which I personally baptized 80. In the same baptistry the pastor of the Methodist church baptized eight and the pastor of the United Brethren Church 20. Our Sunday-school jumped from about 60 to 125. Our prayer-meeting from a dozen to about fifty. We are building a small addition to our church to meet present needs of Sunday-school and Endeavor societies. Nearly my entire Sunday-school was converted. Is the spirit of Christian union a success?"

—H. E. Wilhite, who is making quite a success as evangelist, was born at Everett, Cass county, Mo., in 1872. He was educated for the ministry at Cotner University, Lincoln, Neb., and his work has been a very successful one. He has held some of the best pulpits and added hundreds to the membership of the churches. Under his preaching at his last pastorate at San Bernardino, Cal., over 300 joined the church in twenty-six months. He is of the evangelistic type and likes this field best. Two weeks ago Brother Wilhite closed a successful meeting in South Dakota and is, at present, at Downs, Kan., whence is reported 24 additions in two weeks. The audiences are as large as can be accommodated and it is expected that there will be many additions. Brother Wilhite goes next to the Forest Avenue Church at Kansas City, Mo. The evangelist's wife conducts a Bible drill every evening for half an hour before the preaching time.

—E. L. Frazier, of Indianapolis, Ind., calls our attention to the fact that there is before the people of that state, and we may say also of others, an opportunity not for party politics but for righteousness. Brother Frazier points out that a number of the candidates in Indiana are members of the Christian church, "rank high in mentality, are capable as the most capable," are true men, pure, clean and strong. A. L. Crim is candidate for secretary of state, W. O. Bailey is candidate for superintendent of public instruction, D. F. Dailey is candidate for congress. Brother Frazier is personally acquainted with these brethren and with Mr. Charles M. Lemon, candidate for treasurer of state, and says that they are in every way reliable and a vote for them is a vote for righteousness. We need not say that THE CHRISTIAN-EVANGELIST puts the personal character of all candidates for office before any political affiliations. We trust that every Democrat and every Republican in St. Louis

and in Missouri will scratch any man on the ticket who is known to be unworthy, and will vote for the candidate of the other party if he is good and fit for the position. It is only by such action that good citizens can overcome the jugglery of the boss and saloon element.

—Some very interesting figures have been compiled by the brethren at Buffalo. We believe that at no other convention has any such attempt been made to ascertain the makeup of a convention crowd. It appears that the total registration was 4,519. Of these persons 2,748 were women and 1,771 men. Of course, it was expected that New York state would furnish the largest attendance and the record shows that 2,417 people from New York were present. Ohio had the next largest delegation with an attendance of 562, and Pennsylvania came third in order with 351 representatives. The far west sent few delegates, Oregon and North Dakota sending only one, though in proportion to membership North Dakota was perhaps well represented with its solitary delegate. In rank with these came South Carolina and Delaware with one representative each. California, where the convention was held last year, registered fourteen delegates. Missouri had 101 representatives in attendance. It is a matter of very considerable interest to notice that from states other than New York no less than fifty-three registered who belonged to other religious bodies. A striking feature is that nearly every religious body had a representative present from among the citizens of Buffalo. The tabulated results show 31 Episcopalians, 67 Methodist Episcopalians, 133 Presbyterians, 66 Methodists, 121 Baptists, 18 Congregationalists, while there were also present 16 Lutherans, 6 Catholics, 4 United Brethren, 3 Unitarians, 3 Universalists, 2 Christian Scientists, 3 of the Reformed Church, 1 of the Salvation Army, 1 of the Millennial Dawn persuasion, and 56 miscellaneous. All of the larger bodies had representatives from other cities in New York state while there was also a representative of the Mennonites. We commend the registration bureau, which was under the charge of Brother Randall, for the carefulness in the tabulation, bringing before us, so clearly, facts which some people have never suspected.

❦

The Scoville-Dux Wedding.

An event of wide interest throughout our brotherhood was that of the marriage of Charles Reign Scoville to Arlene Cornelia Dux in Chicago October 17. The ceremony was read by Dean W. J. Lhamon, of Columbia, Mo. The entire program of the evening was characterized by a simple yet impressive dignity. His colaborer in many a hard struggle and mighty victory, DeLoss Smith, sang in his own sweet charm "For All Eternity." P. M. Kendall and wife, who are now associated with Brother Scoville, were everywhere present to assist their leader in this his hour of hours. A. W. Fortune, formerly pastor of the Metropolitan Church, and A. T. Campbell, the present pastor, assisted in the services. Friends were there from Michigan and Indiana and Illinois. The delightful home of

Mr. and Mrs. Dux was crowded to its utmost when, at 8 o'clock, Dean Lhamon led the way into the parlors. He was followed by the groom, unattended. Then came the bride, walking alone, the type of queenly womanhood. Thomas P. Ullom, of Traverse City, Mich., bore the wedding ring. The service was worthy of Dean Lhamon, and in keeping with the enviable reputation of the man who that hour was plighting his life's interests. They left for the east that night, followed by the congratulations of the hundred guests who were present and the blessings of the countless thousands everywhere who have been gladdened by Brother Scoville's ministry. All rejoice that his strong and virile soul is to be complemented by the gentle and tender ministry of a cultured woman's love. FINIS IDLEMAN.
Paris, Ill.

❦

As We Go to Press.

Special to THE CHRISTIAN-EVANGELIST.

Downs, Kan., Oct. 29.—Greatest crowd in history of church here; meeting two weeks old. Twenty-four additions, seven yesterday. Evangelist Wilhite.—F. T. Ray, minister.

Special to THE CHRISTIAN-EVANGELIST.

Kansas City, Mo., October 29—Seventy-three added in seven days; best meeting for the time ever seen here; meeting full of power; continue with great prospects; this is a wonderful church.—Small and St. John.

Special to THE CHRISTIAN-EVANGELIST.

Lincoln, Ill., October 28.—Sixteen added to-day, thirty-six first eight days. All in the Sunday-school are Christians and there are few directly in touch with the church to be reached. We are moving on the town. W. H. Cannon has done great work here.—W. E. M. Hackleman, Singer; Wm. J. Lockhart, Evangelist.

Special to THE CHRISTIAN-EVANGELIST.

Springfield, Ill., October 28.—Dorris-Altheide meeting arousing great interest; fifty-two added; continue.—F. M. Rogers.

Special to THE CHRISTIAN-EVANGELIST.

Joplin, Mo., October 28.—Joplin dedicated the Third Church at Villa Heights to-day, free of debt. A centennial rejoicing meeting follows.—W. F. Turner, pastor of First Church; Geo. L. Peters, pastor of South Joplin Church; J. W. Baker, County Evangelist.

Special to THE CHRISTIAN-EVANGELIST.

Indianapolis, Ind., October 29.—Abberley and Mrs. Powell captured our people at Central Church yesterday; huge audiences; twelve additions.—Allan B. Philputt.

Catarrh Cured at Home.

Dr. Blosser Offers to Mail a Liberal Trial Treatment of His Catarrh Remedy Free to Sufferers.

If you have catarrh of the nose, throat or lungs, if you are constantly spitting, blowing the nose, have stopped up feeling, head noises, deafness, asthma, bronchitis or weak lungs, you can cure yourself at home by a remedy so simple that even a child can use it.

It will cost you only a postal card to get a liberal free trial package of Dr. Blosser's wonderful remedy. He sends it by mail to every interested sufferer. Certainly no offer could be more liberal, but he has such confidence in the remedy that he is willing to submit it to an actual test in your home. The full treatment is not expensive. A package containing enough to last one whole month will be sent by mail for $1.00.

A postal card with your name and address sent to Dr. J. W. Blosser, 475 Walton St., Atlanta, Ga., will bring you by return mail the free trial treatment and an interesting booklet, so that you can at once begin to cure yourself privately at home.

The Report of the Committee on Union

By R. MOFFETT

The report made by the committee on union with the Free Baptists at the Buffalo convention embraced the report in THE CHRISTIAN-EVANGELIST of December 28. This gave an account of the joint meeting last November in Brooklyn, at which little was done except to prepare for a subsequent meeting which has not been held. The next week after this meeting the two committees representing the Free Baptists and the regular Baptists, met in Brooklyn, and agreed upon a basis of union which awaits the action of the two bodies in national conferences and conventions. There is a strong probability that the union of these two churches will be effected in the near future.

This action made it quite impracticable for the Disciples' committee to press any further proposition for a joint meeting of the two committees at the present time, and especially since it is well known that the Free Baptists prefer alliance with the regular Baptists. The report of our committee continued as follows:

"The leaven of union is working in this country and in other countries. Not long ago we saw a circular bearing the names of distinguished men of the English and non-conformist churches of England, in which they comment on 'the paralizing effect of division on the moral forces of Christianity,' and say, 'We profoundly feel that our Lord Jesus Christ meant us to be one visible fellowship.' The Wesleyan, Presbyterian and Congregational churches of Canada have been considering the feasibility of uniting in one church, to be called the United Church of Canada, which is 'pronounced by some a movement so extraordinary as to find no parallel for centuries.' The joint committee has published that 'they find, neither in doctrine nor polity, any insuperable obstacles to organic union.' * * * In this country the Congregationalists, United Brethren and Protestant Methodists have nearly completed a visible union. The Free Baptists of New Brunswick and Nova Scotia have united with the Baptists of those provinces, and in this country these two bodies are likely to complete a visible union, as elsewhere stated in this report. Last November 1,500 representatives of thirty Christian bodies, aggregating 18,000,000 of communicants, met in Carnegie Hall, New York, to hold sessions for one week and talk and pray and plan for closer union of the Lord's people. These delegates were among the most distinguished men of the Christian denominations. This fact itself is deeply significant, however much or little we may approve the plan adopted. This great conference has said to Christendom, 'In the Providence of God, the time has come that it seems fitting more fully to manifest the essential oneness of the Christian churches of America * * and to promote the spirit of fellowship and co-operation among them.' There are many brethren on the floor of this convention who remember the time when no such expressions of mutual confidence and fraternal fellowship would have been heard. The Christian people here present who have preached and prayed for union these many years, can not but rejoice in these evidences of growth toward—if not to—the oneness for which Jesus prayed; and the importance of this oneness as the great factor in the world's conversion, was emphasized by the men who delivered the addresses. * * *

"The spirit of love and fellowship among the Lord's hosts is rapidly growing. Good seed is being sown all over the world, and specially among the missionaries in heathen lands, where they feel the need of united work as we can not in America.

"Let us take care to show the grace of a true Christian courtesy toward all who seek to follow our Lord and Savior. Toward our Baptist brethren we should manifest the fullest possible fellowship. Is it not possible for the two union committees, appointed by these bodies, to arrange for holding a joint congress, composed of leading men of each body, to discuss the practicability of union between the two bodies? Such a joint convocation would be one step toward the union for which our Lord prayed. Evidently the organic union of

(Continued on Page 1408.)

THE SIMULTANEOUS CAMPAIGNS

One of the results of the appointment of a Board and Superintendent of Evangelism has been the holding of evangelistic meetings by a number of churches in a district at or near the same time. All Southern California is going into a campaign in the early spring. In January a state-wide campaign will be inaugurated in Iowa. Towards the end of next year Ohio will fall in line. But already other states and cities have begun the good work. We all remember Pittsburg, Kansas City, Cincinnati and other cities. Next week—the First Church, with Herbert Yeuell leading, began last Lord's day—most of the St. Louis churches begin meetings; already the churches of Virginia are in full swing, and many churches of Indianapolis and Indianapolis began last Lord's day or will begin immediately a great simultaneous effort for the conversion of souls and the upbuilding of the church members.

St. Louis.

The churches that will hold the meetings simultaneously are: The First, with Herbert Yeuell; Compton Heights, with Harlow and Harlow; Union Avenue, with C. M. Chilton and C. H. Altheide; Hamilton Avenue, with W. F. Turner and V. E. Ridenour. The Fourth Church will proceed with home forces. Hammett Place will be in line and Maplewood also. J. M. Hoffman will evangelize at Granite City and Lansdowne and East St. Louis will participate. In our next issue we will give further particulars. There were 14 additions to the First last Sunday and 18 at Compton Heights.

Indianapolis and Indiana.

The simultaneous evangelistic campaign in and about Indianapolis began on Sunday, October 28. The fourteen Christian churches of the city, with a membership of above 6,000, are joined in this campaign by about forty churches in the state. Two hundred more churches have pledged to continue the campaign by meetings between this and the state convention in May.

Following is a list of city churches with their leaders:

Central, A. B. Philputt, pastor; R. W. Abberley, evangelist; Percy Parks, chorus leader; Mrs. J. E. Powell, soloist. Second (colored), H. L. Herod, pastor; W. H. Brown, evangelist; E. E. Winston, singer. Third, C. D. Newman, pastor; Chas. Reign Scoville, evangelist; P. M. Kendall, chorus leader; DeLoss Smith, soloist. Fourth, C. E. Underwood, pastor; E. L. Frazier, evangelist; Harry K. Shields, singer. Downey Avenue, F. W. Norton, pastor; Chas. A. Young, evangelist; A. J. Green, singer. Sixth, A. L. Orcutt, pastor; H. F. MacLane, evangelist; C. E. McVey, singer. Seventh, D. K. Lucas, pastor; J. P. Lucas, evangelist; Mrs. Mary Lucas Ade, singer. Hillside, O. K. Tomes, pastor; H. O. Pritchard, evangelist. Morris Street, C. A. Johnson, pastor; Thos. L. Cooksey, evangelist; Mrs. Nona Earhart, singer. Bismarck Avenue, G. F. Powers, pastor; Clay Trusty, evangelist; Carl Barnett, singer. North Park, Austin Hunter, pastor; M. W. Harkins, evangelist. Englewood, no pastor; J. O. Rose, evangelist; Harry Frank, singer. Olive Branch, F. F. Smith, pastor; B. J. Legg, evangelist; Mrs. Lola Calvert, singer.

The general management of the campaign in the city is under the direction of an executive committee of thirteen, of which the writer is chairman, and C. E. Tomes, secretary, having headquarters at room 34, Union Trust Building. The details of the work are cared for by the following sub-committees:

Public Meetings, A. B. Philputt, chairman; Publicity, A. L. Orcutt, chairman; Evangelists, C. B. Newman, chairman; Music, O. K. Tomes, chairman; Literature and methods, Austin Hunter.

FAMOUS MEN
OF THE OLD TESTAMENT

Table of Contents.

ABRAHAM, The Friend of God and Father of the Faithful.
JACOB, The Father of the Twelve Tribes.
JOSEPH, The Savior of His People.
MOSES, The Leader, Lawgiver and Literatus.
JOSHUA, The Father of His Country.
GIDEON, The Mighty Man of Valor.
JEPHTHAH, The Misinterpreted Judge.
ELI, The Pious Priest but Indulgent Parent.
SAUL, The First King of Israel.
DAVID, The Great Theocratic King.
SOLOMON, The Grand Monarch of Israel.
ELIJAH, The Prophet of Fire.
JONAH, The Recreant but Repentant Prophet.
DANIEL, The Daring Statesman and Prophet.
BALAAM, The Corrupt Prophet and Diviner.
ABSALOM, The Reckless and Rebellious Son.
NEHEMIAH, The Jewish Patriot and Reformer.

334 pages, silk cloth, postpaid, $1.50.

Christian Publishing Company,
St. Louis, Mo.

chairman; Canvas, C. B. Coleman, chairman; Finance, Walter Lowe, chairman.

The general expenses of the work will be provided for by the Christian Church Union of the city. Mass meetings are to be held in Tomlinson Hall on three Sunday afternoons beginning November 4. Z. T. Sweeney will speak at the first meeting and John E. Pounds at the second. Arrangements have been perfected for receiving reports from all the meetings every night at headquarters for publication. We are hopeful for a great forward movement in the work.

F. W. NORTON.

West Virginia.

Most of the churches engaged in this state campaign began their meetings on October 21. West Liberty, on account of its pastor, J. W. Underwood being a student at Bethany, began earlier and closed October 14. A. E. Davis being the evangelist. Wheeling First Church began early to enable Harlow and son to come to St. Louis. Montgomery, with F. L. Davis as evangelist, also began early and closed with seven additions. Wayne begins November 8; Fairmont, with E. E. Bates, pastor, and W. F. Shearer, evangelist, begins November 11; Core, with G. H. Ellis as evangelist, starts November 18, and F. A. Bright can not be with Pastor W. E. Pierce at Cameron until December 9. We regret that we have not space in this issue to give a full list of the churches and workers engaged but the early results of the campaign indicate an average attendance at 19 churches of 161 and 123 additions. We have made arrangements to be kept in touch with this campaign and will report it for the benefit of the churches engaged and the inspiration of all our readers.

Ministerial Exchange.

The Christian church at Stuttgart, Ark., wants a preacher, a man of ability; prefer a married man about forty years of age. Salary $1,000 a year.

Robert E. Rosenstein has some time vacant during fall and winter. Any one in the Chickasaw Nation wishing to correspond with him will address him at Norman, Okla.

Miss Mayme Eisenbarger, gospel singer, of Bethany, Mo., is open for engagements.

M. S. Harrison, Neosho, Mo., who has been out of regular work the past year because of sickness in his family, can be secured by some church willing to pay $600 or $700. He is 46 years old, highly commended, and counted both worthy and capable.

H. K. Shields, Rochester, Ind., helper and singer, has February open for engagements.

"After October 15 I will need some one to take charge of the music for my meetings. I want one who has had experience and who can and will take all the work of building up the chorus. One who can sing solos effectively, and can make others sing." Address O. D. Maple, evangelist, Cairo, Ill.

"We have installed electric lights in our church, and one lime acetylene plant, capable of lighting a house of 500, will be sold cheap. It cost $125 and is in good shape. Sale price $30."—R. A. Staley, Dinuba, Cal.

Charles Ford expects to do some evangelistic work this fall and winter. Any one desiring his services can address him at Breckenville, Ohio.

The church at Artesia, N. M., wants a pastor. Can pay the right man $900 to $1,000 per year. Prefer a middle aged man who has no family, and who wants western life and ways. Address D. W. Robertson, Sec. of the Board.

C. F. Rose expects to take up evangelistic work after January 1. Those interested can write him at Canton, Mo.

Esther W. Olive, Greenville, Ill., desires a situation as pastor's assistant.

C. R. L. Vawter, pastor of the First Church of Christ, Shelby, Ohio, can be had for a meeting or two this fall or winter. Brother Vawter has had good success in evangelistic work in several states, some of these meetings being exceedingly difficult pioneer tent work. Write for terms and plans to C. R. L. Vawter, Shelby, Ohio.

"Churches desiring meetings please write me at my permanent address, Bethany, Neb. I raise my own money. Can bring a singer."—Jas. S. Beem, general evangelist.

"I know a strong, fearless, gospel preacher of twelve years' experience in the ministry, whose services can be secured soon by some strong church in eastern Illinois or western Indiana. Any desiring the services of such a minister, write me at once."—G. Halleck Rowe, Sidell, Ill.

Charles W. Mahin and wife, evangelists have

an open date for a meeting in January, and will receive correspondence at Angola, Ind.

"As I shall have some vacant Sundays this fall and winter, I desire to fill pulpits for those who wish to be away in meetings. My limit would be about 100 miles from Kansas City. Ad. dress J. W. Monser, 1316 Broadway, Kansas City, Mo. References: T. P. Haley and W. F. Richardson.

"I have an open date for December and January meetings. Can furnish good song leader, $30 per week, and expenses for self, or the offerings and expenses. Address me at Wickliffe, Ky."—D. Wesley Campbell.

"I wish to commend the work of Miss Bertha Short, of Seymour, Ind. She is an excellent singer of sacred songs, a fine organist and a consecrated personal worker. Any evangelist or church in need of a singing evangelist should communicate with her."—A. W. Crabb.

FAMOUS WOMEN
OF SACRED STORY

Pen Pictures of the most Attractive Characters in All History.

NEW TESTAMENT CHARACTERS

Table of Contents.

MARJAMNE, The Jewess, Wife of Herod the Great.
ELIZABETH, The Mother of John the Baptist.
MARY, The Virgin Mother of Christ.
MARY, The Mother of the God-Man.
ANNA, The Prophetess in the Temple.
HERODIAS, The Wicked Instigator of Her Daughter.
JOANNA, The Wife of Herod's Steward.
WOMAN OF CANAAN, Nameless, but Full of Faith.
WOMAN OF SAMARIA, The Adulteress, But Saved.
DAUGHTER OF JAIRUS, Dead but Raised to Life.
MARY OF BETHANY, The Anointer of Jesus' Feet.
MARY MAGDALENE, The Victim of Seven Demons.
DORCAS, The Disciple Raised to Life by Peter.
SAPPHIRA, The Lying Partner of Her Husband.
LYDIA, Paul's First European Convert.
THE ELECT LADY, Whom John Loved.

In full silk cloth, postpaid..............$1.50

OLD TESTAMENT CHARACTERS

Table of Contents.

EVE, The Mother of the Human Family.
SARAH, The Mother of the Faithful in Every Age.
REBEKAH, The Beautiful but Deceptive Wife.
RACHEL, The Lovely Wife of Jacob.
MIRIAM, The Grand, Patriotic Old Maid.
RUTH, The Lovely, Young and Honored Widow.
DEBORAH, The Strong Minded Woman.
JEPHTHAH'S DAUGHTER, The Consecrated Maiden.
DELILAH, The Fair but Deceitful Wife.
THE WITCH OF ENDOR, The Enchantress of Samuel's Ghost.
HANNAH, The Praying and Devoted Mother.
ABIGAIL, The Wife of the Shepherd-King.
THE QUEEN OF SHEBA, Solomon's Royal Guest.
JEZEBEL, The Bloody Mary of Scripture.
THE WOMAN OF SHUNEM, Elisha's Friend.
ESTHER, The Deliverer of Her People.

318 pages, in full silk cloth, postpaid.....$1.50

Christian Publishing Company,
St. Louis, Mo.

As We Go to Press.

Special to THE CHRISTIAN-EVANGELIST.

Downs, Kan., Oct. 29.—Greatest crowd in history of church here; meeting two weeks old. Twenty-four additions, seven yesterday. Evangelist Wilhite.—F. T. Ray, minister.

Special to THE CHRISTIAN-EVANGELIST.

Kansas City, Mo., October 29.—Seventy-three added in seven days; best meeting for the time ever seen here; meeting full of power; continue with great prospects; this is a wonderful church.—Small and St. John.

Special to THE CHRISTIAN-EVANGELIST.

Lincoln, Ill., October 28.—Sixteen added to-day, thirty-six first eight days. All in the Sunday-school are Christians and there are few directly in touch with the church to be reached. We are moving on the town. W. H. Cannon has done great work here.—W. E. M. Hackleman, Singer; Wm. J. Lockhart, Evangelist.

Special to THE CHRISTIAN-EVANGELIST.

Springfield, Ill., October 28.—Dorris-Altheide meeting arousing great interest; fifty-two added; continue.—F. M. Rogers.

Special to THE CHRISTIAN-EVANGELIST.

Joplin, Mo., October 28.—Joplin dedicated the Third Church at Villa Heights to-day, free of debt. A centennial rejoicing meeting follows.—W. F. Turner, pastor of First Church; Geo. L. Peters, pastor of South Joplin Church; J. W. Baker, County Evangelist.

Special to THE CHRISTIAN-EVANGELIST.

Indianapolis, Ind., October 29.—Abberley and Mrs. Powell captured our people at Central Church yesterday; huge audiences; twelve additions.—Allan B. Philputt.

Catarrh Cured at Home.

Dr. Blosser Offers to Mail a Liberal Trial Treatment of His Catarrh Remedy Free to Sufferers.

If you have catarrh of the nose, throat or lungs, if you are constantly spitting, blowing the nose, have stopped up feeling, head noises, deafness, asthma, bronchitis or weak lungs, you can cure yourself at home by a remedy so simple that even a child can use it.

It will cost you only a postal card to get a liberal free trial package of Dr. Blosser's wonderful remedy. He sends it by mail to every interested sufferer. Certainly no offer could be more liberal, but he has such confidence in the remedy that he is willing to submit it to an actual test in your home. The full treatment is not expensive. A package containing enough to last one whole month will be sent by mail for $1.00.

A postal card with your name and address sent to Dr. J. W. Blosser, 475 Walton St., Atlanta, Ga., will bring you by return mail the free trial treatment and an interesting booklet, so that you can at once begin to cure yourself privately at home.

The Report of the Committee on Union
By R. MOFFETT

The report made by the committee on union with the Free Baptists at the Buffalo convention embraced the report in THE CHRISTIAN-EVANGELIST of December 28. This gave an account of the joint meeting last November in Brooklyn, at which little was done except to prepare for a subsequent meeting which has not been held. The next week after this meeting the two committees representing the Free Baptists and the regular Baptists, met in Brooklyn, and agreed upon a basis of union which awaits the action of the two bodies in national conferences and conventions. There is a strong probability that the union of these two churches will be effected in the near future.

This action made it quite impracticable for the Disciples' committee to press any further proposition for a joint meeting of the two committees at the present time, and especially since it is well known that the Free Baptists prefer alliance with the regular Baptists. The report of our committee continued as follows:

"The leaven of union is working in this country and in other countries. Not long ago we saw a circular bearing the names of distinguished men of the English and non-conformist churches of England, in which they comment on 'the paralizing effect of division on the moral forces of Christianity,' and say, 'We profoundly feel that our Lord Jesus Christ meant us to be one visible fellowship.' The Wesleyan, Presbyterian and Congregational churches of Canada have been considering the feasibility of uniting in one church, to be called the United Church of Canada, which is 'pronounced by some a movement so extraordinary as to find no parallel for centuries.' The joint committee has published that 'they find, neither in doctrine nor polity, any insuperable obstacles to organic union.'
*   *   In this country the Congregationalists, United Brethren and Protestant Methodists have nearly completed a visible union. The Free Baptists of New Brunswick and Nova Scotia have united with the Baptists of those provinces, and in this country these two bodies are likely to complete a visible union, as elsewhere stated in this report. Last November 1,500 representatives of thirty Christian bodies, aggregating 18,000,000 of communicants, met in Carnegie Hall, New York, to hold sessions for one week and talk and pray and plan for closer union of the Lord's people. These delegates were among the most distinguished men of the Christian denominations. This fact itself is deeply significant, however much or little we may approve the plan adopted. This great conference has said to Christendom, 'In the Providence of God, the time has come when it seems fitting more fully to manifest the essential oneness of the Christian churches of America * * and to promote the spirit of fellowship and co-operation among them.' There are many brethren on the floor of this convention who remember the time when no such expressions of mutual confidence and fraternal fellowship would have been heard. The Christian people here present who have preached and prayed for union these many years, can not but rejoice in these evidences of growth toward—if not to—the oneness for which Jesus prayed: and the importance of this oneness as the great factor in the world's conversion, was emphasized by the men who delivered the addresses. * * *

"The spirit of love and fellowship [among the Lord's hosts is rapidly growing. Good seed is being sown all over the world, and specially among the missionaries in heathen lands, where they feel the need of united work as we can not in America.

"Let us take care to show the grace of a true Christian courtesy toward all who seek to follow our Lord and Savior. Toward our Baptist brethren we should manifest the fullest possible fellowship. Is it not possible for the two union committees, appointed by these bodies, to arrange for holding a joint congress, composed of leading men of each body, to discuss the practicability of union between the two bodies? Such a joint convocation would be one step toward the union for which our Lord prayed. Evidently the organic union of

(Continued on Page 1408.)

THE SIMULTANEOUS CAMPAIGNS

One of the results of the appointment of a Board and Superintendent of Evangelism has been the holding of evangelistic meetings by a number of churches in a district at or near the same time. All Southern California is going into a campaign in the early spring. In January a state-wide campaign will be inaugurated in Iowa. Towards the end of next year Ohio will fall in line. But already other states and cities have begun the good work. We all remember Pittsburg, Kansas City, Cincinnati and other cities. Next week—the First Church, with Herbert Yeuell leading, began last Lord's day—most of the St. Louis churches begin meetings; already the churches of Virginia are in full swing, and many churches of Indianapolis and Indianapolis began last Lord's day or will begin immediately a great simultaneous effort for the conversion of souls and the upbuilding of the church members.

St. Louis.

The churches that will hold the meetings simultaneously are: The First, with Herbert Yeuell; Compton Heights, with Harlow and Harlow; Union Avenue, with C. M. Chilton and C. H. Altheide; Hamilton Avenue, with W. F. Turner and V. E. Ridenour. The Fourth Church will proceed with home forces. Hammett Place will be in line and Maplewood also. J. M. Hoffman will evangelize at Granite City, and Lansdowne and East St. Louis will participate. In our next issue, we will give further particulars. There were 14 additions to the First last Sunday and 18 at Compton Heights.

Indianapolis and Indiana.

The simultaneous evangelistic campaign in and about Indianapolis began on Sunday, October 28. The fourteen Christian churches of the city, with a membership of above 6,000, are joined in this campaign by about forty churches in the state. Two hundred more churches have pledged to continue the campaign by meetings between this and the state convention in May.

Following is a list of city churches with their leaders:

Central, A. B. Philputt, pastor; R. W. Abberley, evangelist; Percy Parks, chorus leader; Mrs. J. E. Powell, soloist. Second (colored), H. L. Herod, pastor; W. E. Brown, evangelist; E. E. Winston, singer. Third; C. B. Newman, pastor; Chas. Reign Scoville, evangelist; P. M. Kendall, chorus leader; DeLoss Smith, soloist. Fourth, C. E. Underwood, pastor; E. L. Frazier, evangelist; Harry K. Shields, singer. Downey Avenue, F. W. Norton, pastor; Chas. A. Young, evangelist; A. I. Green, singer. Sixth, A. L. Orcutt, pastor; H. F. MacLane, evangelist; C. E. McVey, singer. Seventh, D. K. Lucas, pastor; J. P. Lucas, evangelist; Mrs. Mary Lucas Ade, singer. Hillside, O. E. Tomes, pastor; H. O. Pritchard, evangelist. Morris Street, C. A. Johnson, pastor; Thos. L. Cooksey, evangelist; Mrs. Nona Earhart, singer. Bismarck Avenue, G. F. Powers, pastor; Clay Trusty, evangelist; Carl Barnett, singer. North Park, Austin Hunter, pastor; M. W. Harkins, evangelist. Englewood, no pastor; J. O. Rose, evangelist; Harry Frank, singer. Olive Branch, F. P. Smith, pastor; T. J. Legg, evangelist; Mrs. Lola Calvert, singer.

The general management of the campaign in the city is under the direction of an executive committee of thirteen, of which the writer is chairman, and O. E. Tomes, secretary, having headquarters at room 34, Union Trust Building. The details of the work are cared for by the following sub-committees:

Public Meetings, A. B. Philputt, chairman; Publicity, A. L. Orcutt, chairman; Evangelists, C. B. Newman, chairman; Music, O. E. Tomes, chairman; Literature and methods, Austin Hunter.

chairman; Canvas, C. B. Coleman, chairman; Finance, Walter Lowe, chairman.

The general expenses of the work will be provided for by the Christian Church Union of the city. Mass meetings are to be held in Tomlinson Hall on three Sunday afternoons beginning November 4. Z. T. Sweeney will speak at the first meeting and John E. Pounds at the second. Arrangements have been perfected for receiving reports from all the meetings every night at headquarters for publication. We are hopeful for a great forward movement in the work.

F. W. NORTON.

West Virginia.

Most of the churches engaged in this state campaign began their meetings on October 21. West Liberty, on account of its pastor, J. W. Underwood being a student at Bethany began earlier and closed October 14; A. R. Davis being the evangelist. Wheeling First Church began early to enable Harlow and son to come to St. Louis. Montgomery, with F. L. Davis as evangelist, also began early and closed with seven additions. Wayne begins November 8; Fairmont, with Z. E. Bates, pastor, and W. F. Shearer, evangelist, begins November 11; Core, with G. H. Ellis as evangelist, starts November 18, and F. A. Bright cannot be with Pastor W. E. Pierce at Cameron until December 9. We regret that we have not space in this issue to give a full list of the churches and workers engaged but the early results of the campaign indicate an average attendance at 19 churches of 161 and 123 additions. We have made arrangements to be kept in touch with this campaign and will report it for the benefit of the churches engaged and the inspiration of all our readers.

Ministerial Exchange.

The Christian Church at Stuttgart, Ark., wants a preacher, a man of ability; prefer a married man about forty years of age. Salary $1,000 a year.

Robert E. Rosenstein has some time vacant during fall and winter. Any one in the Chicka-saw Nation wishing to correspond with him will address him at Norman, Okla.

Miss Mayme Eisenbarger, gospel singer, of Bethany, Mo., is open for engagements.

B. S. Harrison, Neosho, Mo., who has been out of regular work the past year because of sickness in his family, can be secured by some church willing to pay $600 or $700. He is 46 years old, highly commended, and counted both worthy and capable.

H. K. Shields, Rochester, Ind., helper and singer, has February open for engagements.

"After October 15 I will need some one to take charge of the music for my meetings. I want one who has had experience and who can and will take all the work of building up the chorus. One who can sing solos effectively, and can make others sing." Address O. D. Maple, evangelist, Cairo, Ill.

"We have installed electric lights in our church, and our fine acetylene plant, capable of lighting a house of 500, will be sold cheap. It cost $225 and is in good shape. Sale price $30."—R. A. Staley, Dinuba, Cal.

Charles Ford expects to do some evangelistic work this fall and winter. Any one desiring his services can address him at Brecksville, Ohio.

The church at Artesia, N. M., wants a pastor. Can pay the right man $900 to $1,000 per year. Prefer a middle aged man who has no family, and who wants western life and ways. Address D. W. Robertson, Sec. of the Board.

C. F. Rose expects to take up evangelistic work after January 1. Those interested can write him at Canton, Mo.

Esther W. Olive, Greenville, Ill., desires a situation as pastor's assistant.

C. R. L. Vawter, pastor of the First Church of Christ, Shelby, Ohio, can be had for a meeting or two this fall or winter. Brother Vawter has had good success in evangelistic work in several states, some of these meetings being exceedingly difficult pioneer tent work. Write for terms and plans to C. R. L. Vawter, Shelby, Ohio.

"Churches desiring meetings please write me at my permanent address, Bethany, Neb. I raise my own money. Can bring a singer."—Jas. S. Beem, general evangelist.

"I know a strong, fearless, gospel preacher of twelve years' experience in the ministry, whose services can be secured soon by some strong church in eastern Illinois or western Indiana. Any desiring the services of such a minister, write me at once."—G. Halleck Rowe, Sidell, Ill.

Charles W. Mabin and wife, evangelists have

an open date for a meeting in January, and will receive correspondence at Angola, Ind.

"As I shall have some vacant Sundays this fall and winter, I desire to fill pulpits for those who wish to be away in meetings. My limit would be about 100 miles from Kansas City. Address J. W. Monser, 1316 Broadway, Kansas City, Mo. References: T. P. Haley and W. F. Richardson.

"I have an open date for December and January meetings. Can furnish good song leader, $30 per week, and expenses for self, or the offerings and expenses. Address me at Wickliffe, Ky."—Wesley Campbell.

"I wish to commend the work of Miss Bertha Short, of Seymour, Ind. She is an excellent singer of sacred solos, a fine organist and a consecrated personal worker. Any evangelist or church in need of a singing evangelist should communicate with her."—A. W. Crabb.

The Christian Church at Lexington, Mo.

The Christian Church at Lexington, Mo., is one of the oldest congregations in the state. The church was organized on April 17, 1836, at the residence of Levi Van Camp, who then lived in the country, two miles south of the city. There were twenty charter members.

R. B. Briney, Pastor.

The first pastor to serve the young congregation was Duke Young, who preached for the church one Sunday in each month for two years. He was succeeded in the pastorate by Frank Palmer, of Independence, who for eight years continued preaching every third Lord's day. The first house in which the congregation worshiped was erected in 1840, on Main street, under the supervision of Samuel Hudson, an uncle of the oldest living member of the church, Aunt Hannah Waddell, as she is affectionately called by all the members, being in her 89th year. This old building, which in its day and generation was regarded as a marvel of church architecture, and of large dimensions for those primitive times, is still used as a church by a colored congregation of

Franklin, Alexander Proctor, Allen Wright, and a host of others whose voices are now hushed in death. It will be of interest to the whole brotherhood to recall the fact that John T. Johnson died here in November, 1856, while in the midst of a very successful meeting.

The church, being ministered to by able and consecrated men, continued to grow until the year 1847, when a personal quarrel arose in the congregation which resulted in a division, T. N. Gaines, the pastor, going with the seceders. Another church building was erected near the corner of Eleventh and South streets. This building is still used as a house of worship, being occupied by the German Methodists. Soon after this, however, better judgment and the Spirit of Christ having prevailed, the brethren saw the folly of trying to support two churches, and very nearly all of the seceding members returned to the mother church. In the year 1870, the church having outgrown the old building on Main street, a new edifice was erected on South street, in the very best residence portion of the city. This is a substantial brick building of two stories. Six years ago it was remodeled at a cost of $3,000. The beautiful auditorium has a seating capacity of 400 and the church has a membership of about 400. Since the year 1858 the congregation has enjoyed in its settled ministry the services of such eminent men as T. P. Haley, Henry H. Haley, Frank Allen, George Plattenburg, Jesse H. Huger, Chapman S. Lucas, G. W. Terrell, G. M. Goode, E. J. Fenstermacher, and others, whose splendid works follow them. Many successful meetings have been held, the most notable ones being conducted by Martin and Easton, when there were 252 added, and the one held by Northcutt and St. John, when 80 were added. On the first Lord's day in November, the Martin

family, of Chicago, will begin a meeting for this church. Great preparations are being made, and great results are confi-

dently expected. The present pastor, R. B. Briney, has been serving the church for the past four years, and was recently recalled by the congregation to continue that service indefinitely.

He is a son of J. B. Briney and a brother of W. N. Briney, now of Louisville, Ky. He is a graduate of the Bible college and Kentucky University, and served churches in Kirksville, Ky., Amarillo, Texas, and Monroe City, Mo., while he also at one time was state evangelist of Mississippi. He is a young man of promise and we feel sure he will garner and care for the sheaves that may be gathered by the successful evangelistic force he and his fine board of officers have called to their aid.

❀ ❀

If for any wish
  Thou darest not to pray,
Then pray to God
  To cast that wish away.

Evangelist Richard Martin and Miss Edna and Elbert Martin.

Baptists, they having remodeled it. Time was when its audience room rang with eloquent sermons, convincing logic, and powerful exhortations of such men as Alexander Campbell, "Raccoon" John Smith, Jacob Creath, John T. Johnson, T. M. Allen, Moses E. Lard, Benjamin

The Board of Officers.

THE BUFFALO CONVENTION

Flashes of Wit and Wisdom from the Convention.

BY JAMES SMALL.

Fire and facts, fun and fancy, wit and wisdom, story and song, prayer and praise, love, and laughter, song and solo, heart and head, graces and genius, goodness and greatness, gold and goodness, all have a place and a rightful one at our national conventions. Truth comes to us in humor as well as in homily; in fun as well as in fact.

Richard Abberley, of Walnut Hills, Cincinnati, a bright, brainy young Englishman who has never got the credit in the brotherhood that he deserves, said in a short speech at the English tea "that while he loved England, and perhaps if he had the choice of his birthplace he would want to be born there again, yet he preferred being an Englishman 'Yanked' over."

Another speaker this same evening congratulating the English as a sincere and sturdy people, remarked that they did not have the bright, witty element that the Irish did. He told this story to illustrate the point:

"Fred Douglas and an Irishman had been on the train for two hundred miles together. The hour came when they had to separate. The Irishman remarked on parting. 'Well, Mr. Douglas, I am glad that I got acquainted with you. We have talked politics and religion and we have not agreed on "aither." But you are a "gintleman", that's what you are. You are a Christian man and I can say that for you.' Then as Fred Douglas extended the hand to bid the Hibernian good-bye, he remarked, 'Well, Mike, I am sorry to say that I can't say the same about you.' Quick as a flash came the reply: 'Indade and ye could if ye had lied like the "devil" as I did.'"

W. T. Moore told a story to illustrate how plentiful the Englishmen were at this same tea. And if there is anybody in the country who can stop and tell a good story, it is this Moses of the brotherhood. A certain brother was extremely sensitive about his deafness. He never would allow people for a moment to think that he was deaf, and yet he was extremely so. He happened to be hunting one day and a stranger passed by as he was gazing up at a tree, gun in hand and half to his shoulder and in readiness for execution. The stranger called to him: "In what direction is Booneville?" "I believe it is up the tree," said our friend. "I said in what direction is Booneville?" "I believe it is behind the tree," answered our friend. For the third and last time which the deafest might have heard, the stranger remarked, "I want to know in what direction is Booneville?" "I believe," said our friend, once more, "it is in the hole." Walking away in disgust the stranger finally retorted, "You are a blank fool." "The woods are full of them," was the response.

The same speaker told a story on the woman's proverbial "tongue." It happened that a husband and wife got to quarreling before retiring and so far as the husband was concerned he would have settled the matter before going to rest. Not so the wife. She kept her side up until the husband dropped off to sleep. Some time in the night he awakened and the wife was still talking, but this time, to give the wife her proper due, she was talking in her sleep, but the husband not knowing this for a moment, inquired, "Nancy, are ye talking again, or—yet?"

One speaker told a good story on selfishness. Two little boys were swinging when one of them remarked: "If—one—of—us—would—get—out—there—would—be—more—room—for—me."

Richard W. Abberley told these on the train: An American and Englishman were talking in London and as the argument grew rather hot, the Englishman remarked: "If you don't look out, we will come over and lick you Americans!" "What?" replied the American—"again?"

A young lady in Toronto was talking against our flag and happened to remark in the presence of Senator Hoar that "it reminded her of one of these pieces of striped candy." "Yes," said the senator, "the kind that makes everybody sick that tries to lick it."

F. D. Power told a good story on himself that caused quite a ripple in the Convention. When he was a young man he went to preach at a place where the good believed in sending the preacher around instead of putting him up at one place. At this place it was difficult to place him at all. Finally an old lady rose and said: "Well, brethren, I can eat him, but I can't wash him." The ice being broken, another sister arose, and said: "Well, I can sleep him, but I am nothing on 'biled shirts.' Another one of the sisters was soon on her feet, remarking, "that as the other sisters were going to eat him and sleep him she could wash him."

One speaker gave as a definition for a hog: "A body built around an appetite." This speaker was illustrating the point that the brutes do not get as much good out of what they enjoy as we; because they feel their joys only along the rough lines of the material. Man has that and also the fine lines of the reason and the spiritual sensibilities. There are other exercises besides animal exercises. Faith and hope and love, said the speaker, are the loftiest exercises of the loftiest part of human nature. The righteous can make the best of both worlds. The good the Christian gets, the couches we rest on, the horses we drive, the homes we own, the pictures that we admire, the music we hear, the bread we eat, give us greater enjoyment when we are Christians and rest on the invisible things.

I am glad we all had a smile and a laugh at the Convention, for it is generally conceded that there is as much religion in these things as in tears and long faces. And then for most while it is bright and sunny on top, it is usually dark enough deeper down.

Britain at the Convention.

One of the sweetest meetings of the convention, to those privileged to participate in it, was the "tea" and reunion on Tuesday evening at the Touraine Hotel, of preachers and workers at various times connected with the work of the F. C. M. S. in England. Such gatherings have been held before in connection with the National conventions, but probably none so widely representative as this. Of the earlier workers in that field there were absent only M. D. Todd, who was taken to a higher fellowship twenty-one years ago, and H. S. Earl. After a doubtfully English "tea," the party adjourned to one of the drawing rooms to listen to speeches and reports and reminiscences. W. T. Moore, the venerable patriarch of the convention and J. H. Garrison told of the beginnings of the work in England and made our hearts burn as they reminded us of the sacredness and the abiding character of the friendships and attachments formed in such companionship in arms. J. J. Haley and J. M. Van Horn followed with reminiscences. Other speakers included B. H. Hayden, Geo. T. Walden (now of Australia), Jas. Small and Earle M. Todd. There were present also Mrs. J. H. Garrison, Mrs. Van Horn, Mrs. M. D. Todd and Miss Flora, Paul Moore, J. I. Tisdall, R. W. Abberley, Mathew Small, A. W. Taylor, and several from Australia and Canada whose names do not occur. Auld Lang Syne, sung with joined hands and prayer by W. T. Moore, closed the meeting, and all hurried away again to the urgent discussions at the Convention Hall.

E. M. TODD.

National Bible School Association.

The following board of directors was elected at Buffalo, for one year (expiring 1907): G. P. Coler, Ann Arbor, Mich.; Robt. H. Hopkins, Louisville, Ky.; W. H. McClain, St. Louis, Mo.; T. J. Legg, Indianapolis, Ind.; Chas. M. Fillmore, Cincinnati, Ohio.

For two years (expiring 1908): J. H. Bryan, Des Moines, Ia.; Herbert Moninger, Cincinnati, Ohio; I. W. Gill, Wichita, Kan.; Pres. T. E. Cramblet, Bethany, W. Va.; J. H. Hardin, Liberty, Mo.

For three years (expiring 1909): Prof. Clinton Lockhart, Waco, Tex; W. A. Moore, Tacoma, Wash.; P. H. Welshimer, Canton, O.; E. A. Cole, Washington, Pa.; W. A. Baldwin, Lincoln, Neb.

Eureka College Reception.

Mr. Chas. J. Phillips, superintendent of the D. L. & W. R. R., and his generous wife, both old Eureka students, tendered a delightful reception to the students and alumni of Eureka college attending the Buffalo convention. Forty-five responded to the invitation while a considerable number were prevented by previous engagements. Following refreshments, H. O. Breeden, of Des Moines, acted as toastmaster in his most happy way. Responding to his call, Prof. R. A. Gilcrest, of Missouri; G. A. Miller, of Kentucky; W. F. Richardson, of Kansas City; S. H. Zendt, of Iowa, A. W. Taylor, Finis Idleman and J. G. Waggoner, of Illinois. J. P. Lichtenberger, of New York City, gave most delightful reminiscences of college experiences and their influence upon one's life. A. E. Cory, of Po Chow, China, gave a happy talk of his college inspirations and his experiences in the Orient. The company returned to the convention in due time for the evening session, grateful to their host and hostess for their generous offices and to the good Father whose tender providences and loving care grants such rich fellowship and delightful occasions to his children.

J. G. WAGGONER.

Bethany Dinner.

The Bethany College dinner at the Y. M. C. A. cafe was the most largely attended and the most enthusiastic gathering of Bethany students, and friends ever held at one of our national conventions. Provision was made for 140 plates and before the hour arrived every ticket was sold and fifty more were at the banquet hall hoping to get in at the last moment. Many of these went elsewhere for their refreshments and returned to enjoy the toasts. A significant feature of the event was the prevailing spirit of hopefulness manifested by all present concerning the future of Bethany.

Among the speakers were Frank H. Main, A. McLean, Wallace Tharp, Allen Wilson, T. W. Phillips, S. M. Cooper, E. Lee Perry, W. B. Taylor, Will Loose, F. D. Power, T. E. Cramblet.

The most significant feature of the occasion was the enthusiastic passage of the following resolution: "Be it resolved by the Alumni, former students and friends of Bethany College in banquet at Buffalo assembled that we heartily endorse the Centennial aim to raise $100,000 additionl endowment and to increase the student body to 600 by 1909 and we hereby pledge ourselves to aid in making this effort successful.

The American Christian Education Society.

The meeting of the American Christian Education Society was held in Buffalo in convention with the other affiliated interests on October 17. An address was delivered by Pres. J. Hopwood, of Virginia Christian College. Prof. T. C. Howe, of Butler, read a statement in behalf of the directors of the Christian Education Society, and Pres. C. C. Rowlison of Hiram, read a short address emphasizing the need of a much larger interest in the brotherhood in the problem of education. According to the instructions of the directors of the society, those present were requested to become members of the society and to subscribe or give in cash the sum of $2 as their annual membership fee. About $100 in cash and pledges was the result of this appeal.

The society at present has for directors the executive heads of our educational institutions. The directors present at Buffalo held a conference in the Y. M. C. A. building and elected officers for the ensuing year; Pres. C. C. Rowlison, of Hiram, being made president, Prof. T. C. Howe, of Butler, vice-president, and Pres. R. E. Hieronymus, of Eureka, secretary-treasurer. Various committees were appointed and an aggressive program to be carried out by the executive committee was suggested.

The executive committee plans to have a day of conference in the near future to devise definite plans for the work of the society, and is determined to carry forward the interests of education among the Disciples in as vigorous a way as possible.

Much more money is needed and those who are interested in Christian education ought at once to indicate their willingness to become members of the society and to pay the small fee of $2 for such membership. It is hoped that many will immediately send to the secretary this membership fee.

NEWS FROM MANY FIELDS

Colorado's Convention.

It was the twenty-fourth annual meeting, and was held with the Central Church of Pueblo, October 2-4. The hospitality of the churches of Pueblo was abundant and hearty. D. W. Moore, pastor of the Central, had everything in readiness for the convention.

The Christian Woman's Board of Missions occupied the first evening and half day. Their reports were encouraging; they have had the best year in their history. We have not data at hand concerning it, but know that their record during the past year broke all previous ones. Their officers of the past year were re-elected, viz: President, Mrs. L. S. Brown, Denver; vice-president, Mrs. Olive Sanford, Littleton; secretary, Mrs. J. W. Maddux, Golden; treasurer, Mrs. Mary L. Parks, Denver; Superintendent of Junior Work, Mrs. Lizzie L. Sheely, Merino. Dr. Olivia A. Baldwin spoke at the evening session, on India.

The Colorado Christian Missionary Society and affiliated interests, viz, the Christian Endeavor and the Sunday-school, occupied a day and one-half and two evenings. Crayton S. Brooks presided with grace and dignity. The report of the State Board, read by Leonard G. Thompson, the corresponding secretary, recalled the fact that our conventions held with the Central Church at Pueblo have been epoch-making conventions. The first one was held here, in 1883, before the Central had a building; that of 1890 when they had only a chapel, and at that convention the first information was given which led to the coming of the Christian Woman's Board of Missions to Colorado; that of 1898 began the movement for larger self-support in our work, which is still growing, and this year has reached the highest point yet attained. The hope was expressed that this convention would take some worthy advance, and this was done later in determining to place an evangelist in the field to raise $3,500 this year for state work, to begin a campaign to enlist at least three thousand of our members as tithers, and to strive to bring several of our present mission churches to self-support during the year. Attention was called to our approaching silver anniversary, which comes in 1908, and plans will soon be inaugurated to suitably celebrate that event.

The Board aided in the support of 16 men in 14 fields a part of all of the year. R. M. Bailey labored most of the year at Rifle, although some time was given to Meeker and Grand Valley; a good house of worship was built and the membership more than doubled. W. E. Jones and J. K. Hester each labored a part of the year at Paonia. Plans are now being laid to build a new house of worship. The church at Delta was organized in March. Walter Carter served as supply pastor, and E. J. Harlow took permanent charge September 1. There are 62 members, and a good lot has been purchased. John Treloar has continued at Monte Vista. His health is very feeble, and he was tenderly remembered in the sessions of the convention. His work and influence at Monte Vista have been remarkable in view of his illness. His wife is now supplying the pulpit, while her husband is still confined to his bed most of the time. Ward Russell and J. W. Babcock each spent a part of the year at Florence, the latter now being in charge. The house has just been enlarged, and excellent congregations attend the services. The present building will serve temporarily. Wesley I. Houston began work at Lamar, December 1, and will close November 1, next. The church is making important improvements on their building, especially seating it with pews. H. M. Hale began at Colorado City with the year, but will have to remove November 1 on account of Mrs. Hale's health. It was hoped Brother Hale could have

completed their house of worship. The work has grown in nearly every department. Golden has exchanged its old property for a first-class central location, and has excavated for a new building. More funds had to be secured. At the convention G. W. Muckley told us that the Board of Church Extension had just granted a loan of $1,500 to this church. Work is now going forward on the foundation walls. J. W. Maddux is the capable leader and minister. Golden has the State School of Mines, one of the finest technical schools in this country. E. J. Harlow closed at Windsor with August, after two years' work. The church grew during his ministry. The house was seated with excellent pews. G. C. Johnson and Walter Carter each served a part of the year. The mortgage debt was paid in April. This church is but five years old. J. K. Hester and E. F. Harris have served at Sterling and Atwood, and meetings were held by Brother Hester and W. B. Clemmer, the latter assisted by Arthur Wake as singer. Under Brother Hester's ministry a house of worship was built at Sterling. We had had no organization for ten years, and the old property had been sold. John T. Stivers held meetings at La Junta, Rocky Ford, Rifle and Delta. At La Junta 96 were added, at Rocky Ford, 28; at Rifle, 88, and at Delta, 37. Ellis B. Harris, of Lind, Wash., held a meeting at Hillsboro, organizing with 26 members. E. F. Harris held a meeting at S. W. Ranch, with 7 additions. L. H. Humphreys, pastor at Greeley organized a church at Ault, north of Greeley, with 23 members, and located Virgil Walker as minister there at Hillsboro. Percy T. Carnes, of Laplata, Mo., held a meeting at Bayfield, Laplata county, in southwestern Colorado, and organized, but did not report the number of members. J. K. Hester and M. P. Givens held a meeting at Cripple Creek.

The report of the treasurer, A. E. Pierce, of Denver, covered thirteen and one-half months, and showed the following: Balance on hand August 11, 1905, $169.16; received from Christian Woman's Board of Missions, $1,512.50; received from Colorado, $2,167.22; total, $3,848.88. The year was closed with all obligations paid, and money in the treasury. The amount raised from October 21, 1905, to September 30, 1906, was $1,831.34, the largest amount in any year in the history of our Colorado work.

The Colorado Christian Herald, the eight-page monthly paper, published under the auspices of the state board, is now in its fourth year, and is filling a very important place in the development of the work.

Those well known in our work, who had passed on to their eternal reward during the year, were tenderly remembered. They are: Mrs. Katie Davis Mohorter, of Pueblo; Thomas A. Gunnell and Mrs. J. F. Lucas, of Colorado Springs; John W. Divers, of Salida; J. M. Miller, of Canon City; Jr. J. L. Edwards, of Florence, and Mrs. Emma Pickrell Craig, of Denver.

The report of the committee on summer assembly, stated that the meeting for the past summer was held, at Gato, 37 miles from Denver, where the permanent home of the institution is to be; that the total enrollment was 1441 while a little smaller than the previous year, yet better sustained throughout the sessions, and that more ministers were present this year than last. The development company which own the grounds has platted them, placing the most eligible lots on the market; a number of cottages have been built during the year; in platting the grounds the company has dedicated five acres to the use of the assembly, and it is hoped that before the meeting of next summer a beginning may be made on the auditorium, and accommodations provided for larger attendance. The committee confirmed the wisdom and expediency of maintaining the assembly, and is convinced that it may be made a potent factor in the development of our Colorado work.

The addresses were well prepared, and well delivered. D. B. Titus, of Longmont, spoke on "God's Portion," advocating the tithe system, and B. B. Tyler followed with an enthusiastic endorsement and discussion of the address. G. W. Muckley had preceded these addresses with one of his characteristically able addresses on Church Extension. This was Brother Muckley's second visit to a Colorado convention. He was most welcome, and will be at any time. M. M. Nelson, of Rocky Ford, spoke on "Sunday-school Work," and J. B. Hunley, of Canon City, on "The Christian Endeavor Pledge." David C. Peters, of Trinidad, addressed the convention on "Centennial Aims and Methods for Colorado." One thing he advocated brought forth hearty endorsement in the form of a motion which was unanimously passed, viz, that Colorado memorialize the National Benevolent Association to take immediate steps toward establishing in this state a sanitarium for tubercular patients. No state in the Union can more fully appreciate the need for such an institution than Colorado. The closing addresses were delivered by E. F. Harris, of Longmont and J. E. Pickett, of Denver. The former spoke on "The Gospel of the Helping

Hand," and the latter on evangelism, his theme being, "And They Went Everywhere."

The music was excellent throughout, Mrs. J. B. Hunley, of Canon City, was the chief soloist. Special numbers also were rendered by the quartet choir of Central Church, and by Mrs. W. T. Green, of the same church. Strong temperance and Christian citizenship resolutions were adopted.

The following are officers and state board for the year: President convention, David C. Peters, Trinidad; vice-president, B. C. Hilliard, Denver; recording secretary, J. E. Pickett, Denver, corresponding secretary, Leonard G. Thompson, Denver; treasurer, A. E. Pierce, Denver; other members of the board, Wm. Bayard Craig, Denver (chairman of the board), B. B. Tyler and Dallas J. Osborne, of Denver; Crayton S. Brooks, of Colorado Springs, and D. W. Moore, of Pueblo. Mrs. Laura B. Thompson was chosen superintendent of Sunday-school work, and Clifford H. White, superintendent of Christian Endeavor; both of Denver. The next convention goes to Colorado Springs. LEONARD G. THOMPSON,

Denver, Colo. Cor. Sec.

❁ ❁ ❁

We offer One Hundred Dollars Reward for any case of Catarrh that cannot be cured by Hall's Catarrh Cure.

F. J. CHENEY & CO., Toledo, O.

We, the undersigned, have known F. J. Cheney for the last 15 years, and believe him perfectly honorable in all business transactions and financially able to carry out any obligations made by his firm.

WALDING, KINNAN & MARVIN,
Wholesale Druggists, Toledo, O.

Hall's Catarrh Cure is taken internally, acting directly upon the blood and mucous surfaces of the system. Testimonials sent free, Price 75 cents per bottle. Sold by all Druggists.

Take Hall's Family Pills for constipation.

The New England Convention.

The forty-first annual convention of our churches in New England was held October 4-7 with the church at Manton a suburb of Providence, R. I. The convention opened with an able sermon by M. L. Streator, of Bridgeport, Conn., on "God's Elect. Who are they and am I one of them?"

The sessions of Friday began with a devotional service led by A. T. Remington, of Manton. The local pastor, Loren F. Sanford, welcomed the delegates, to which a happy response was given by G. A. Reinl, of Springfield, Mass. The president, A. L. D. Buxton, of Worcester, Mass., then spoke of the work of the year with suggestions touching the work in the year to come. An address by Harry Minnick, of Worcester, on "The Restoration Movement. What do we aim to restore?" followed by one by T. A. Manley, of West Pawlet, Vt., on "Union Through Restoration," gave us a clear presentation of the position we hold on the question of Christian union.

After a devotional service Friday afternoon, A. T. June, of Everett, Mass., spoke on "New England Missionary Needs." After this came the C. W. B. M. session, Encouraging reports of this work were given. Mrs. Newton Knox, of Worcester, was elected president. Mrs. I. W. Harrison, secretary of the Centennial committee, gave an address which was much appreciated.

Devotional service Friday evening was led by W. C. Crerie, of Haverhill, Mass. A. L. Ward, of Boston, gave an address on "Evangelization in New England," in which that feature of church work here was ably discussed. Following this Harry Minnick gave an interesting and helpful address on "The work of the Minister in New England."

Saturday morning after a devotional service led by R. H. Bolton, of Boston, came the Bible school session, in which Mrs. F. S. Fisher, of Worcester, spoke on "The Home Department," Miss Maud Phillips, of Worcester, on "The Primary," W. C. Crerie on "How to interest Young Ladies and Men in the Sunday-school." An open discussion on Sunday-school work was led by R. A. Spellman, of Manton. The superintendent's report, prepared by W. M. Nelson, of Boston, was read by F. H. Bailey, of Danbury, Conn. This session was closed by an able address by G. A. Reinl, on "The Teacher in the Scholar's Conversion." An able address on "The Authenticity of the Bible," prepared by Robert Pegram, now of Milton, N. S., was read by A. L. Ward, and it was voted to have it published.

After a devotional service Saturday afternoon, led by G. Wilton Lewis, the report of the Corresponding Secretary, R. H. Bolton was given. He reported the membership of our churches as 2917, a net gain of 112. Number of churches 20 not counting four anti-churches. Raised for foreign missions, $612.30; for home and New England missions, $740.42; for Church Extension, $111.81; for the C. W. B. M., $369.51; for all purposes, $23,318.52. Value of property, $143,140; indebtedness, $17,860. The debt of the Brockton church paid off, the debt of the Everett church reduced $1,000, and building funds started at Haverhill and Bridgeport.

This was followed by the business session of the New England Christian Missionary Society. R. H. Bolton was elected president; Harry Minnick, corresponding secretary and G. A. Reinl, treasurer. It was voted that the society send a delegate to each of the state councils of Massachusetts, Connecticut and Rhode Island of the Federation of Churches, to represent our plea for Christian union by a return to New Testament Christianity. The session closed with an address by G. B. Townsend of Troy, N. Y., representing the A. C. M. S.

The Saturday evening session began with a devotional service led by A. S. Heaney, of Manton, S. T. Willis, of New York, then spoke of the work of the Church Extension Board, and J. H. Mohorter, of St. Louis, of the work of the National Benevolent Association.

A meeting at which verbal reports from the churches were given was held early Sunday morning, presided over by S. M. Hunt, of Springfield. The sermon at the regular morning service was by J. H. Mohorter. J. W. Robbins, of Brockton, preached in the afternoon, after which came the communion service led by S. M. Hunt and A. S. Heaney. In the evening the Christian Endeavor service was led by the superintendent, H. A. Ling. The evening sermon was by Austin P.

Finley, the new pastor of the Highland Street church of Worcester.

The entire convention was harmonious and helpful. The attendance was not as large as usual because of the national convention being at Buffalo. The addresses were of a high order, and the spirit of the convention was inspiring and earnest. We were especially pleased to have with us Brother Mohorter who was identified with our work so long.   R. H. BOLTON.

Ohio.

After Buffalo what? In general, greater things everywhere! But in Ohio, the greatest thing immediately is the offering for Ohio missions November 4. There has never been as thorough a campaign put up in Ohio in behalf of Ohio missions as Secretary Bartlett has made this year. Sunday November 4 is the harvest time. Let every church be in line. "The biggest offering ever," should be the motto of each church.——A. A. Honeywell will assume the responsibilities of the work at Marietta, recently vacated by W. A. Brundige. Brother Honeywell leaves McConnellsville for Marietta.——E. E. Violett was to begin a meeting at Lorain with Pastor Hostetter October 21.——We are all rejoicing over the recovery of H. N. Allen from a recent operation.——Secretary Bartlett will preach regularly for the church at Painesville after November 4. His family will not move there till later, however. The daily press reports the call of Brother Mansfield at Millersburg. It does not state from whence he comes.——Grant Speer finds it impossible to get away permanently from the church at Hicksville, and will return after having

preached at Ashland for six months.——The Ohio letter is written this time from Pawnee, Neb., a thousand miles from the desk on which the letter is usually written. A ride from Ohio to Nebraska this time of year is a great treat. There is evidence of an abundant harvest of grain and fruit all along the way. A day was spent in Chicago with old Columbus friends, Prof. F. V. Irish and wife. A course was taken through Chicago university under Gates and Irish, and a diploma was promised by mail later. Several Ohio boys were met who are studying in the university. A game of croquet with Professor Irish and E. S. Ames clearly showed that they have the Rockefeller spirit—competitors were met and crushed without compunction of conscience. This is a great country out here in Nebraska. A black rich soil three feet deep covers every foot of Pawnee county. It is rolling enough to add beauty. Pawnee City has 2,000 people, and is a saloonless town with seven churches and a U. P. Academy. G. M. Weimer is bishop of "our folks" here and a jolly, scholarly, hard-working bishop he is. He ministers to a congregation of 175 of the best people in the community, men of business and affairs and ladies of culture. There is no lack of a topic for conversation here. Nearly everybody came from Ohio and all want to know all about the old Buckeye state. The meeting is taxing the capacity of the house, and the name of Christ is being confessed. But Pawnee for a western town is conservative. Yet for business thrift and moral and spiritual worth it is hard to find a better than Pawnee, Neb.—C. A. Freer, Painesville, Ohio.

Report of Committee on Union.
(Continued from Page 1402.)

(Continued from Page 1402.)

the Christian world must begin with
those separate denominations which are
nearest to oneness.

"In seeking and praying for union we
will not always find ourselves cheered
and welcomed; but for the world's sake
we must hold patiently and persistently
to the desire that all may be simply one
in Christ; and for our own sakes we must
keep the passion for unity. It will save
us from Pharisaism and bigotry, and the
deep hunger for oneness in itself will keep
us wondrous close to Christ.

"Respectfully submitted,
"E. B. Wakefield, Chairman.
"R. Moffett, Secretary."

Board of Ministerial Relief of the Church of Christ.

Aid in the support of worthy, needy, disabled ministers of the Christian Church and
their widows.
THIRD LORD'S DAY IN DECEMBER
is the day set apart in all the churches for
the offering to this work. If you make individual offerings, send direct to the Board.
Wills and Deeds should be made to
"BOARD OF MINISTERIAL RELIEF
OF THE CHURCH OF CHRIST, a corporation under the laws of the State of Indiana." Money received on the Annuity
Plan.
Address all communications and make
all checks, drafts, etc., payable to
BOARD OF MINISTERIAL RELIEF,
120 E. Market St., Indianapolis, Indiana.

Georgia Notes.

The "Southern Evangelist" of Atlanta has been
merged into THE CHRISTIAN-EVANGELIST and all
Southern Evangelist subscribers will now receive
THE CHRISTIAN-EVANGELIST, which is one of the
greatest weeklies in our brotherhood. It will be
a weekly treat for us to follow the pens of editor
J. H. Garrison, G. L. Snively, F. D. Power, B.
B. Tyler and others who make THE CHRISTIAN-
EVANGELIST one of the greatest religious weeklies
of this country. We trust that all "Southern-
Evangelist" readers will be delighted with the
change. I will continue to collect subscriptions
due the "Southern-Evangelist" and would be glad
if all who are behind with subscriptions would pay
up without further delay. My address is 187
Edgewood ave., Atlanta, Ga.
The Central and Northeast Georgia District
Conventions, the first at Toomsboro, October 17-19,
and the latter at Union Church, Oconee county,
October 23-25, were highly enjoyed by all who
attended. The entertainment was perfect and
the sermons and addresses of Brothers J. H.
Hughes, of Macon, B. P. Smith, of Atlanta, Cor.
Sec. Georgia Christian Missionary Society; Dr.
T. L. Harris, of Wrightsville; W. B. Shaw, of
Baldwin, secretary Southeastern Orphanage; S.
S. Landrum, of Winder, were enthusiastically re-
ceived. The preachers present who attended the
central district convention were: T. G. Linkous,
chairman; J. H. Hughes, Dr. T. L. Harris, G. R.
Cleveland, J. M. Boone, E. L. Shelnutt. The
preachers at the northeast district convention were:
E. L. Shelnutt, chairman; T. M. Foster, J. H.
Hughes, R. W. Simpson, Dr. W. B. Doster, S.
S. Landrum, W. B. McDonald, W. A. Chastain,
D. R. Piper, D. A. Brindle, J. H. Wood, P. H.
Mears, B. P. Smith. The C. W. B. M. of the
districts held splendid sessions during the conventions. The W. S. G. M. held an interesting
session during the northeast convention.
The State Convention will be held in Valdosta
November 19-22. A full delegation and a great
convention are expected and desired. If the editors of THE CHRISTIAN-EVANGELIST will attend,
they will receive a royal welcome. A full program will appear in this paper.
The Central Georgia Railway will give excursion
rates to St. Louis, Mo., November 15, 16, on account "Deep Waterway Convention," to be held
in that city. One fare plus $2, round trip.
A. Robert Miller has resigned as pastor of the
church in Savannah and may leave Georgia. We
can ill afford to give him up. He is a strong man
physically, mentally and religiously and Georgia
needs him and many more just such men.
Georgia has ten men, "boys," attending the Bible College at Lexington, Ky., preparing for the
ministry. Some of these "boys" are depending on
the "Georgia Christian Education Society" for financial assistance and should not be disappointed.
W. A. Chastain, of Athens is treasurer of this
society.
Don't neglect to take an offering for state missions between now and state convention. Every
church in the state should attend to this most
important matter. Write B. P. Smith, 58 Dunn
St., Atlanta, about it.
The South Carolina State Convention will be
held at Ellenton, just twenty odd miles from Augusta, Ga., and will begin the day the Georgia convention closes. Our national secretaries are expected to take in both conventions as well as all
the chicken and beefsteak they can get. Sugar
cane and "goobers" and "tater pie" will be added
to the bill of fare.   E. L. SHELNUTT.

Oregon.

September witnessed the closing of a good
meeting at Medford under Brother Kellems, and
the opening of a promising meeting at Ashland,
under S. M. Martin, and at St. John's (Portland), under City Evangelist J. F. Conder. The
latter is a joint mission of the City Joint Board
and the O. C. M. C.—I spent a large part of
the month with the churches of Southern Oregon.
Most of them are in fine working order and doing
good work. The mission church at Grant's Pass
is still advancing under the leadership of Brother
Bower. Roseburg is doing fine work under its
new pastor, B. E. Youtz. Brother Youtz is new
in Oregon, but not to the work. Brother Corbin,

who has been doing good service at Medford,
goes to Dallas. Dallas is a growing field and
Brother Corbin is a tried worker. We look for
great things from Dallas.——Oregon is to have
three district conventions this fall—Albany, October 4, 5; McMinnville, October 31, November
1; Roseburg, November 7, 8. Watch for reports.
Oregon means business for Christ and the Church.
—Let us all begin to rally our forces for the
offering for state missions November 4, and for
the winter campaign for souls. How many
churches are planning to hold missionary meetings
this winter?
         F. E. BILLINGTON, Cor. Sec.

Cottage Grove, Ore.

Evangelistic

We invite ministers and others to send reports of meetings, additions and other news of the churches. It is especially requested that additions be reported as "by confession and baptism," or "by letter."

Arkansas.

Prescott, Oct. 22.—Preached my annual sermon yesterday to a large audience. One addition.—Percy G. Cross.

California.

Pomona—Have closed a three weeks' meeting here with home forces. Twenty-eight additions—15 confessions, ten by letter and three from other religious bodies.—Madison A. Hart.

District of Columbia.

Washington, Oct. 22.—Present at ministers' meeting; Walter F. Scott, J. E. Stuart, F. D. Power, L. D. Riddell, of Memphis, Tenn.; B. E. Utz, of Spokane, Wash., and the writer. Additions: Vermont Ave. (F. D. Power), 7 by letter, 2 by confession and baptism; 34th St.(Claude C. Jones), 1 baptism.—Claude C. Jones, Sec.

Illinois.

Cairo, Oct. 18.—Ten added here to date.—O. D. Maple.

Lincoln, Oct. 23.—Eleven accessions to the church at Lincoln, where W. J. Lockhart and W. E. M. Hackleman are assisting W. H. Cannon in a meeting.

Rutland, Oct. 25.—C. L. Organ closed his meeting here October 24 with 50 additions—43 baptisms. This was the greatest meeting ever held in Rutland.—R. B. Doan, minister.

Fairfield, Oct. 22.—One addition yesterday by letter. Our second year here starts encouragingly. We begin a meeting on Nov. 7 with W. W. Yocom, of Martinsville, Ind., as evangelist.—Allen T. Shaw, minister.

Indiana.

Indianapolis, Oct. 22.—One added at Swayzee.—Willis M. Cunningham.

Nineveh, Oct. 22.—Commenced here October 22. Three accessions to date. Fine prospects.—Lee Tinsley.

Russellville, Oct. 24.—There have been 20 additions—16 baptisms, in a meeting here conducted by the Martin family.

Angola, Oct. 22.—We closed a splendid meeting with the church at Monrovia, last night, with 32 additions, 30 by baptism. This is the largest meeting in the history of the church. Our next meeting is at North Vernon.—C. W. Mahin and wife, evangelists.

Iowa.

Floris, Oct. 22.—Nineteen additions in our meeting at Ash Grove, 11 baptisms. Thirty have been added to the Pleasant Hill church that have not been reported, 15 by baptism.—E. A. Hastings.

Kansas.

Caldwell, Oct. 22.—One confession at last night's service.—L. H. Barnum.

Plainville, Oct. 22.—Work here improving. Five additions not reported; 1 by letter yesterday. Begin meeting Oct. 28. Neal Overman will assist.—N. Ferd Fagle.

LeRoy, Oct. +1.—Our meeting here with home forces is 14 days old, with 19 additions—16 by confession and baptism, and 3 by letter and statement.—F. H. Schmitt, pastor.

Manhattan, Oct. 22.—One added yesterday. We begin a union meeting here next Sunday with six churches, the pastors of the various churches preaching by turns.—W. T. McLain.

Stockton, Oct. 27.—N. A. Stull of Highland, Kan., closed a four weeks' meeting here which resulted in 15 additions—12 by confession and baptism, two by statement and one from another religious body.—W. W. Blanchard, minister.

Winfield, Oct. 26.—Have closed a 25 days' meeting here. J. B. Boen did the preaching and Leonard Daugherty led the singing. There were 38 additions—nine confessions, 21 by statement and letter, and eight from other bodies.—Albert Nichols.

Kentucky.

Valley View, Oct. 22.—We are in the midst of a good meeting here. Fifteen added last night; 37 the first week.—O. J. Young, evangelist; C. M. Hughes, singer.

Ashland, Oct. 22.—Our two weeks' meeting conducted by home forces, closed last night, resulting in a deepened spiritual life and increased zeal on the part of the church, and 18 additions

Send for our Holiday Catalogue.
CHRISTIAN PUBLISHING CO.,
       St. Louis, Mo.

---

to the membership—13 by primary obedience.—William D. Ryan.

Richmond, Oct. 26.—Our meeting here is two weeks old. Twenty-four additions to date. Expect to close in a few days.—H. A. Northcutt, evangelist.—John S. Zerin and wife, singers.

Massachusetts.

Everett, Oct. 23.—Two additions last Lord's day. Work is progressing well in all departments.—A. T. June, minister.

Michigan.

Sault Sainte Marie, Oct. 24.—Two added by baptism at Calumet and two at Marquette since last report.—R. Bruce Brown.

Missouri.

Brunswick, Oct. 26.—One confession yesterday.—E. H. Williamson.

Brunswick, Oct. 22.—One added yesterday by letter.—E. H. Williamson.

Foley, Oct. 24.—Closed at Davis, Mo., with 10 confessions.—S. J. Copher.

Middle Grove, Oct. 23.—Closed a meeting here with 19 added.—J. H. Crutcher.

Kirksville, Oct. 22.—Eight accessions yesterday; 13 since meeting closed.—D. A. Wickizer, pastor.

La Monte, Oct. 23.—The meeting with Pastor I. H. Fuller is a success.—Ben F. Hill and L. D. Sprague.

Appleton, Oct. 25.—Just closed a fine meeting here. I go next to Eldorado Springs.—J. J. Orison.

Two Mile Branch, Oct. 22.—Three confessions yesterday. Brother Miller preached, but leaves for another field to-day.—N. M. Field, singer.

Kansas City, Oct. 22.—Six added by letter at West Line; 44 added there in the last 5 weeks.—Clyde Lee Fife.

Cameron, Oct. 24.—I recently closed a meeting at Triplett, where I preach, with 58 additions, 49 by confessions, and 3 from another body.—W. D. McCulley.

Fayetteville, Oct. 22.—Have closed a meeting here with 11 additions—seven by baptism. Organized a Christian Endeavor Society with 30 members.—Clyde Sharp.

Canton, Oct. 26.—Closed a 17 days' meeting at Hazell Dell with seven additions—four by baptism, two by statement and one from another religious body. Church in good condition.—J. Tilden Sapp.

Montana.

Missoula, Oct. 18.—We had our autumn rally and roll-call Oct. 14. Splendid audience and 17 names added to the church roll. Commence a meeting Nov. 4, with H. S. Saxton as singer.—W. H. Bagby.

New Mexico.

Artesia, Oct. 27.—Our meeting with home forces

resulted in 8 additions; 4 added since meeting closed.—James A. Challenner.

Ohio.

Delta, Oct. 22.—Sixteen additions the past month, 13 by baptism and 3 by statement. All departments doing excellent work.—William B. Hendershot, minister.

Athens, Oct. 22.—Sixteen additions. We are expecting a great meeting with James Small in December.—T. L. Lowe.

Oklahoma.

Watonga, Oct. 24.—Ten accessions since last report. Church encouraged.—F. Douglas Wharton, pastor.

Oregon.

Corvallis, Oct. 19.—Fifteen added at regular services the last three Lord's days—four by confession and baptism. Begin revival services next Lord's day.—T. S. Handsaker.

Iowa.

Siam, Oct. 26.—Our meeting at Delphos closed with 38 added—30 by confession and baptism. Our meeting here is two weeks old with 33 additions—25 confessions. Brother Butler, of Mound City, Mo., is leading the singing. W. L. Dunlavey, is the pastor.—J. A. McKenzie, evangelist.

SUBSCRIBERS' WANTS.

Midweek Prayer-Meeting
November 7, 1906.

A CHURCH WITH A GREAT OP-PORTUNITY.—Rev. 3:7-13.

The Divine Call.

"Awake, my soul, stretch every nerve,
And press with vigor on;
A heavenly race demands your zeal,
And an immortal crown.

"'Tis God's all-animating voice
That calls thee from on high;
'Tis his own hand presents the prize
To thine aspiring eye."

That church that is concerned only with its internal affairs to the exclusion of interest in the progress of the kingdom throughout the earth looks not upon the ocean but over a land locked bay. It needs to sail through the "Golden Gate" of nobler streams and catch the inspiration of the universal sea.

It is worthy of note that in all these addresses to the seven churches the Holy Spirit in majestic language ascribes delectable qualities and omnipotent powers to Deity. With a reverence often lacking in us God contemplates his own beauty, holiness and glory. It is well for us to read these overtures to the "angels" for the sake of the veneration and adoration they will inspire within us.

To those worthily accepting these great opportunities studding like stars the Christian's horizon is everything the heart should hold dear—"Him that overcometh will I make a pillar in the temple of my God, and he shall go no more out: and I will write upon him the name of my God, and the name of the city of my God, which is New Jerusalem which cometh down out of heaven from my God: and I will write upon him my new name."

Philadelphia stood about twenty miles from Sardis and was the second city in importance in the province of Lydia. It is first mentioned in Revelation and the praises bestowed upon the church show that it was worthy of a city of "Brotherly Love." Though the old name has been laid aside by the Turks, the city still has 3,000 houses and a Christian population. There are five churches in the place, and it is the seat of a Greek bishop. —*Vision of the Ages.*

Opportunity is a nautical term. Literally it means "before the port." Philadelphia was before the harbor with anchor weighed and sails spread equipped for noble enterprises on every shore laved by the great oceans. Again she was approaching the haven apparently deeply laden with treasures for the king and all the city she had honorably acquired in Christian commerce with a world she had left richer and happier than she had found it. With what happy expectancy would she drift in with the twilight tide!

Such splendid opportunities are the heritage of every church that "hast kept the word of my patience."

No church has or has had a greater opportunity than our own. There is great praiseworthiness in a church's keeping its own garments of righteousness immaculate; in living in that atmosphere where the Spirit may say of it, Thou hast kept my word, and hast not denied my name; in caring for its own poor and sustaining its sorrowing through

hours of grief; in impressing the world with its faith in God, its loyalty to his will, and its confidence of an inheritance beyond Jordan. Let churches examine themselves and if self reformation is needed, let it be immediately begun. Then is it entering the channel that opens out into the sea of large opportunity.

Sunday-School
November 11, 1906.

JESUS IN GETHSEMANE.—Matt. 26:36-50.

Golden Text.—Not my will, but thine, be done.—Luke 22:42.

Memory verses, 38, 39.

The Garden of Gethsemane, to which Jesus and his eleven faithful disciples repaired after the supper in the upper room and after the betrayer had gone out from them, was an enclosure a short distance outside of the city on the slope of the Mount of Olives. Probably it was a place to which they had before frequently retired for rest and quiet, so that Judas, knowing his Master's love of the spot sought there for him after failing to find him in the house where the supper had been eaten.

Three of the eleven were chosen for a closer intimacy in this hour when all that was human in him needed the support of warm human hearts. These three were doubtless those best fitted to enter into fellowship with his sufferings through sympathy, though even they could not have been expected to understand them.

It is in this hour of his greatest suffering that we see Jesus most clearly exhibiting his divinity. His willing subjection to the Father's will, his agony over the approaching tragedy, whose true import he alone understood, his call for the strengthening sympathy of his friends, his tender thoughtfulness for his weary disciples—all these exhibit the divine qualities which fitted him to be the Savior of the world, more clearly than they could have been shown by any display of power in summoning legions of angels to his deliverance or by any exhibition of contempt or stoical disregard of the death and disgrace which were so soon to be inflicted upon him. Divinity is not spectacular. It is the greatest possible error to think of the agony in the garden as an exhibition of human weakness, a momentary and excusable lapse from his truly divine character. On the contrary, it helps us to see, in some measure, in what his divinity consisted.

What was the cause of that great agony which groaned out its expression in "If it be possible, let this cup pass." Surely we cannot make it depend solely upon the dread of physical death. That would be to credit him, whom all the world acknowledges as its chief of heroes, with less fortitude than has been exhibited by hundreds of martyrs from whom rack and flame have been unable to wring a word of pain or fear. That element of the sufferings must have been the least of all, or at least the best controlled.

But there were two great sources of suffering in the garden. The first was the sense of the ingratitude of his own nation, the knowledge that men loved darkness rather than light and so were about to put to death their best friend. This was akin to those pangs which a man may feel when those of his own house and blood turn against him without cause.

More deeply significant even than this was the suffering which came from the fact that he was dying for sin. Death is the triumph of sin, as well as its punishment. In some real sense—we shall not stop to discuss theories of the atonement—

Jesus Christ died for the sins of men. For an innocent being to take upon himself the penalty of the sins of others could not be without the keenest spiritual torture. It was probably this more than all else that wrung from the Savior in Gethsemane that cry of anguish and submission.

❊ ❊

Conversion and Pardon, or "Born of Water and the Spirit."

If water baptism be correctly represented as a birth in regeneration (John 3:5), does it not logically follow that life, spiritual life, precedes the birth, baptism? Thus it is in physical generation or birth.

S. J. Vance.

Again, if water baptism is correctly represented as a burial (Rom. 6:4), because of death to sin in conversion, does it not logically follow that death, death to sin, should precede burial, baptism? Hence baptism, the culminating act in the new birth or conversion, brings us to the pardoning power of God.

Conversion and pardon, therefore, are not synonomous terms but express separate and distinct acts, the first, human, in the heart and life of man; the second, divine, in the mind of God. Neither are the expressions "spiritual," and "dead to sin, equivalent to pardon, but rather describe a condition of heart wrought under the influence of the Spirit of God through faith in the Lord Jesus Christ (Jno. 6:63, Acts 15:9), which prepares man for baptism and leads on to the pardoning power of God. Hence conversion, which is wrought out in the human heart and life under the influences of teaching, faith, repentance, confession and baptism brings us to the pardoning power of God and the blessings and enjoyments of the new, the Christian life, into which we have been "born of water and the Spirit."

S. J. VANCE, Evangelist.

Carthage, Mo. ❊ ❊

Milk That is Wholesome.

Since the scientific handling and preservation of milk, originated by Gail Borden in the early '50s the use of Eagle Brand Condensed Milk has become general; but for those purposes where an unsweetened milk is preferred, Borden's Peerless Brand Evaporated-Cream fills every requirement.

November 11, 1906.

CHRIST'S LIFE.—XI. HIS SORROWS: HOW HE BORE THEM.
John 11:30-38; Isa. 53:3-5.

DAILY READINGS.

M. A Man of Sorrows.   Isa. 53:12-5.
T. A Place of Refuge.   Psa. 9:1-9.
W. A Blessed Promise.   Isa. 43:1-7.
T. The Broken-Hearted.   Isa. 6:11-11.
F. Promised Blessings.   Matt. 5:3-6, 10-12.
S. The God of Comfort.   2 Cor. 1:3-7.
S. Another Comforter.   John 16:6,7, 20-28.

"'Tis sorrow builds the shining ladder up
  Whose golden rounds are our calamities,
Whereon our firm feet planting, nearer God
The spirit climbs and hath its eyes unsealed."
—Lowell.

As persecution and sorrow grew darker and denser, the stars of heaven shone brighter, and through these windows he looked into whence he came, and whither he would soon return. For us also in sorrow the immortal lights are gleaming when we look upward.

Lincoln's sighs did more for the Republic than the Emancipation; McKinley's anguish contributed more for the brotherhood of the nations than his speeches or legislation bearing his name. In sorrow more than in triumphs is our own immortality wrought.

Christ bore his sorrows with resignation. Apparently he did not always understand why he suffered, but "Nevertheless not mine but thy will be done!" When wholly committed to God we beat not bleeding wings against the bars. When he would give us wider range his hand will open the doors.

Jesus suffered vicariously. "He hath borne our griefs and carried our sorrows." "He was wounded for our transgressions, he was bruised for our iniquities; the chastisement of our peace was upon him; and with his stripes we are healed." The consciousness of this character of his sufferings was in part his deliverance. The strength of all for whom he suffered helped sustain him; the necessary antipodal glory of such suffering multiplied by all the lives to whom blessing would come animated him. If suffering alone is more than you can bear, take on another's sorrow, too, and your burden is divided.

John 11:35 ("Jesus wept") is the shortest verse in the Bible, yet it spans the universe. It threads its way from the throne of God through stars and clouds till it reaches the sad heart, whether throbbing in palace or mine, and becomes to it a bright and living avenue to the great Comforter where one's tears are stanched and the heart that is broken is made whole again. No other Scripture makes the Son of God and the Son of Mary more realistically one. The former may be to us incomprehensible, the latter as too much one with us to deliver us, but as they blend in this verse we see the heavenly One omnipotent in power, divine in love and redeeming us for time and eternity.

"For it became him for whom are all things, and through whom are all things in bringing many sons unto glory to make the author of their salvation perfect through suffering." Jesus might have come to earth in the role of Caesar, Socrates, Croesus, or Lazarus. In either case he would have been in sympathetic touch with but a fraction of the race. But when he came as a sufferer he had immediate comradeship with all men. He suffered not for self-purification, but to draw us to himself in loving trust. Neither should we pass by on the other side of crosses if by suspending to them we can turn the thoughts of fellow-sufferers heavenward and to even one say, "This day shalt thou be with me in paradise."

❧ ❧

| ## The Home Department |

The Deserted Homestead.

Up on the hill, 'mid the blossoming trees,
  Stands the homestead, bare and tall;
The sunlight gleams on the broken panes,
  And shines through the silent hall;
The garden where the children played
  Is but a tangled maze,
And the cherry blossoms falling fast
  Bring thoughts of other days.

The woodbine climbs to the little porch,
  And taps on the dingy door;
It enters the room through the shattered pane
  And trails o'er the dusty floor;
It lovingly twines o'er the broken chair
  Where a mother used to rock,
And droops its leaves o'er the hanging door,
  And clings to the iron lock.

The roses that bloom in the summer house
  Nod their drooping heads and say:
"How long it is since the mother sang,
  And we watched the children play!
How long since the lovers wandered here
  And sat in the gloaming sweet!
How long since the garden echoed gay
  With the sound of little feet!"

But there's silence through the garden
  And through the orchard sweet;
No sound of happy singing.
  And no rush of little feet.
And the roses clustering gently
  O'er the window and the door
Listen vainly for the children,
  That are coming never more.

Up on the hill, 'mid the blossoming trees,
  Stands the homestead, bare and tall;
The sunlight gleams on the broken panes,
  And shines through the silent hall;
The garden where the children played
  Is but a tangled maze,
And the cherry blossoms falling fast
  Brings thoughts of other days.
         —*Springfield Republican.*

The Bronze Vase.

BY J. BRECKENRIDGE ELLIS.

PART IV.

CHAPTER III.

Raymund was prepared to find Ernest and Franz Geisthauser extremely dull, but they were far duller than he had anticipated. He had the consciousness of feeling that he earned, every penny of his salary in trying to start them along their educational career, but he felt that he got a good deal more out of it than the boys did. By endless repetition, the elder could be taught sundry rules of arithmetic and grammar, but he possessed a memory with a marvelous faculty of letting go. "Seems like I can't keep nothing on hands when I get it," he said good naturedly. "I knew that rule yestiddy, but as far as that rule is concerned now, Mr. Revore, my brains is just like a last year's birdnest, they ain't no aigs in it."

In October Jack Bellfield came to Kansas City to attend the University Medical. As it was as important for him as for Raymund, to live economically, he shared the little back room on Mrs. Bannerton's third floor, sharing the expense. "Until I get through," he said, "father will have to foot all the bills, and he's always drained to the last drop by the rest of us." They made a systematic study of the cheap restaurants of the city. Sometimes they found one which "reminded them of home cooking," but it would not be long before the food began to have a curious sameness. Then they ate in their own room, binging tongue, dried beef, bologna, weenerwurst, smoked halibut, sardines, by way of meat. Of course they did not revel in all these luxuries on the same day. For breakfast they enjoyed two heaping teaspoonfuls of cocoa cooked over the gas jet in a pint of something palely white which was sold to them under the general name, "cream." While living on the farm, Raymund had supposed "cream" a specific name, always meaning the same thing; but now he found it meant almost anything rather than the farm product. With the cocoa went a banana apiece, crackers that bent between your fingers and would not snap, and whatever scraps might have been left over from the day before; generally stringy, tenuous strips of dried beef. The round dark stain on the carpet by the washstand was where the cocoa had boiled over, the time Jack tried to read the daily paper while the gas jet was doing good work. Jack studied his medical notes and his anatomy, but he did not study them very hard. "I don't intend to put in all my time at this thing," he said. "I'm going to be a doctor, but not a doctor every minute of the day." As his memory was good, and as he had a knack of getting what had to be gotten, and of skimming what was not absolutely essential, and as he was always high-spirited, genial and kind, he was a general favorite. He was described as one who "could do anything if he would only try." It had been much harder for Raymund to acquire his education, but that was not without its compensation. Jack, in a general way, knew something on a multitude of subjects, but it is doubtful if he could have taught any one of them.

Jack went much in society. He seemed endowed with the genius of making friends among all classes. At night while Raymund sat dropping from intense application to the Geisthauser boys, while Jack should have been studying his lessons, the latter would detail his experiences of the day. This was a source of great enjoyment to Raymund, and to Jack as well. There would be a few words about the classes, and a good many about the football team, and a long account of some social function of the night before. These conversations usually took place on their "front porch." The "front porch" was the iron fire-escape at their back window. Its floor was formed of narrow square bars of iron, set about an inch and a half apart, running parallel to each other. There was thus formed an airy balcony almost on a level with the sill. To be sure there was but one iron rod about four feet from the floor, to serve as a railing, and a perpendicular iron ladder leading down to the second story that suggested possibilities of escape, but gave no pretense of security. Btu when one had again and again cautiously crawled out of the window upon the bars between which a fine glimpse of the basement yard was afforded, one at last ceased to cling convulsively to the window-ledge, or even to imagine that the frail-looking structure might presently fall from its dizzy height. To the bottom of the two front legs of an old stool, and to the bottom of its two hind legs, lathes were tacked, and when this stool was set upon the "front porch," the lathes prevented it from plunging down between the iron bars, to the rounds. Either Jack or Raymund would seat himself upon this stool while the other, having spread newspapers upon the grilled floor, would put a cushion upon the papers and take his ease with his legs dangling between earth and sky. They were thus sitting one warm autumn evening, when Jack informed Raymund that he had met Nelsie Loraine. "And, oh, my!" said Jack, "she is so pretty! I told her about your being here,' and she wants me to bring you around some time. They're in a fine house on Troost avenue, not far from the Geisthauser's." A few days later Jack reported having called upon Nelsie Loraine, and a week or so after that, he began abruptly one night with, "Say, Ray! what kind of a girl do you consider Nelsie Loraine?"

"She was very kind to me," said Raymund. It was November, now, and they were both muffled up in their overcoats, but loyal to their "front porch."

"In what way?" asked Jack, quickly. "Do you think she could ever care for a fellow who wasn't rich? That's what I mean. For instance—me."

"She never seemed at all proud of her wealth," said Raymund, slowly, "but I doubt if her father and mother—"

"Oh, never mind them," said Jack, impatiently. "It's just a question of Nelsie Loraine."

"Then you'd better ask her," Raymund laughed.

"Perhaps I shall," returned Jack seriously. "I was in love with her when I was a boy, and it's all coming back again, I'm afraid." It was not long after that when Jack took Raymund to the Omer's; Raymund suspected the visit was mainly to give Jack an excuse to see Nelsie Loraine. He found her more beautiful than when she missed her French and Latin lessons to Mrs. De Fer. She received him kindly, even graciously. She told him she did not think him much changed. She said, "And so you are a tutor! All that learning of yours is doing good after all! But wasn't it tiresome! It must be awfully monotonous, teaching young boys. How you would have enjoyed my course in Europe! It always seemed keeping me from having a good time, and now I laughed over it—I know."

"It was Mrs. De Fer who got me my position," Raymund told her. "She and I laughed over our old times—my birthday party, for instance."

"What was that?" asked Nelsie Loraine, kindly. "Oh, yes, I remember—that funny evening in the Hands' house. We were such ridiculous children! I really believe we thought all that was fun, you know!"

"I believe we did," said Raymund, with a sudden sense of disappointment in the beautiful young lady.

"Now, do you know," said Nelsie Loraine, languidly raising her jeweled hand to her deliciously tinted cheek, "sometimes I think people like those Hands—what were their names—Jim something?"

"Tom and Fred," Raymund reminded her.

"Yes," said Nelsie Loraine, with a tolerant smile, "Tom and Fred—do you know, I think that kind of people really get along, you know, and enjoy their sort of life, in a way? They went to so much trouble that night, and were so

embarrassed. Yes, I remember all about it now. I hadn't thought of it for years."

"And I went to your party the very next night," said Raymund. It was strange, looking now at the superbly dressed lady, to remember that of her own generous will, she had suggested the playing of "King William Was."

"Did you?" said Nelsie Loraine. "Do you know, all that time is so vague—so remote—I have been among such different scenes. I like Paris better than Berlin. Were you ever in Berlin, Mr. Jack?"

"No," said Jack, "but I've been in Paris, and I thought it great. I didn't hardly think it worth the money, but it was as good of its kind as anything on the Pike."

"Oh, yes, the World's Fair," said Nelsie Loraine. "Wasn't it tiresome! People tell me it was nothing like so good as the one at Chicago!"

Mrs. Omer presently came into the parlor. She was as stately and formal as ever, but kinder to Raymund than she had been in his lonesome boyhood. "It is so gratifying," she remarked, "to find you doing well, Raymund. So many orphans come to nothing. It is a terrible thing to be thrown out upon the world. I am glad you are able to teach and earn a good living. We are proud of you, Raymund. And your sister, too; Mr. Jack tells us she has a school at—at—ah—"

"Frog Bend," said Jack promptly. "Mighty fine place, Mrs. Omer."

"Ah, no doubt," said Mrs. Omer. "I, myself, have never been there. It is a source of great satisfaction to me to reflect that I was the means of getting Rhoda into the orphan home. Humble as was my assistance, it was no doubt of value. And we are glad we could give you asylum on our farm in your helplessness. You have realized our expectations, Raymund, and paid us for all our trouble. As for me, I may frankly say that you have done far, far better than I, myself, could have expected."

"But I always knew he would make his way," cried Nelsie Loraine, a slight flush beautifying her cheeks. And as her eye brightened, and fashionable languidity vanished, she seemed a good deal like the old friend of his lonesome boyhood. "You were always so industrious, Raymund, so dreadfully thorough! But you have your reward. And I am proud of you, and proud to know that we used to be such good friends." And she held out her hand with unwonted impulsiveness.

"For an orphan in destitute circumstances," said Mrs. Omer magnificently, "I, myself, consider the outcome a perfect marvel."

When they left the house Jack said, "What do you think of her, Raymund?"

"Jack," said Raymund, almost with a groan, "if she had been rescued from her mother when a child, she might have made a splendid woman!"

"Perhaps," said Jack slyly, "it is not yet too late to rescue her. At least here is your knight errant ready for a tilt with old I, MYSELF."

"Jack, I'm going to Crawley, Christmas," said Raymund abruptly. "My mind is made up." And his mind was also made up to keep his own opinion of Nelsie Loraine, because he wanted to keep Jack as his friend. Christmas week the Geisthausers rested from their labors, and Raymund went to Crawley. The tears smarted his eyes as he once more walked the familiar streets. Before he visited his mother's old home or looked up any friends, he went directly to the bank, and called for the tin box. On the lid was tacked this card: "To be given to Raymund or Rhoda Revore, when called for." There was a good deal of curiosity in the glances cast at him by the bank officials, but there was no renewing of acquaintanceship, as he had barely known the cashier and teller by sight. Having proved his identity, the box was placed in his hands. As he had no key, he broke it open. It contained nothing but a letter. He retired to a corner of the room to read it, having recognized the address of the envelope as his mother's handwriting.

(To Be Continued.)

❀ ❀

Advance Society Letters.

BY J. BRECKENRIDGE ELLIS.

In explaining about the Advance Society, two weeks ago, I forgot to say that we have no dues; that if we feel like contributing for our orphan and missionary we do so, but that it is not required. All that is asked is that you make the resolution to do the required reading and to memorize one good quotation each week; you don't even promise to do so; you make no pledge that you are presently going to break. Everybody is a free man or a free woman as the case may be, except of course Felix, who is my cat. I promised some time ago to present the readers of this page with a picture of your friend Felix. The delay is neither my fault nor his, though I must confess he tried his best to get away while the photographer was leisurely engaging him with his camera. The photographer is one of those persons—usually unknown to fame—who is in the chronic state of not being in a hurry. He has the "plate," however, and in due time I hope it may dish you up my cat for the feasting of your eyes. I'm afraid his old-gold tinge won't show in the cut, but I am sure his unwillingness to "sit" will be apparent. Edna Bear, Iberia, Mo.: "I am glad to tell you that I received my Av. S. gold pin this evening. I am well pleased with it. In this work of the Av. S. God bless you, your mother and father"—which, you understand, means everybody, who is helping Charlie and Drusie. Here is our old friend, Grace Everest, Oklahoma City: "I am cold and lonesome, too—lonesome because mamma is visiting in Los Angeles. She has been there three weeks." (I sympathize with your lonesome feeling; but why not make up the fire?) "Mamma will return on the 13th, and WON'T we be glad to see her?" (Yes, we WILL!) "You said we must always read 5 pp. history each week. Did you mean paragraphs? I have always read five, pages." (Pages it is.) "I am the one that can't find a history to interest me except Bill Nye's, and I've read that twice." (As soon as we learn to read history, not as if it were a story, but because we really want to know how people acted, thought and lived in the past, all histories become endurable and many interesting. The more you read Bill Nye's "history" the more you may fancy Bill, but the less you may care for history.) "What is Drusie's address? I want to write to her." (Drusie R. Malott, South Chihli Mission, Tai Mingfu, North China.) "The young women and girls of the church have organized a missionary society; we think a splendid plan to keep in touch with the missionaries by personal correspondence." (Yes, it is.) "Our president, a young woman, prepared herself to be a missionary in Mexico, but her health prevents." (That reminds me that we have a friend

What Sulphur Does

For the Human Body in Health and Disease.

COSTS NOTHING TO TRY.

The mention of sulphur will recall to many of us the early days when our mothers and grandmothers gave us our daily dose of sulphur and molasses every spring and fall.

It was the universal spring and fall "blood purifier," tonic and cure-all, and, mind you, this old-fashioned remedy was not without merit.

The idea was good, but the remedy was crude and unpalatable, and a large quantity had to be taken to get any effect.

Nowadays we get all the beneficial effects of sulphur in a palatable, concentrated form, so that a single grain is far more effective than a tablespoonful of the crude sulphur.

In recent years research and experiment have proven that the best sulphur for medicinal use is that obtained from Calcium (Calcium Sulphide) and sold in drug stores under the name of Stuart's Calcium Wafers. They are small chocolate coated pellets and contain the active medicinal principle of sulphur in a highly concentrated, effective form.

Few people are aware of the value of this form of sulphur in restoring and maintaining bodily vigor and health; sulphur acts directly on the liver and excretory organs and purifies and enriches the blood by the prompt elimination of waste material.

Our grandmothers knew this when they dosed us with sulphur and molasses every spring and fall, but the crudity and impurity of ordinary flowers of sulphur were often worse than the disease, and cannot compare with the modern concentrated preparations of sulphur, of which Stuart's Calcium Wafers is undoubtedly the best and most widely used.

They are the natural antidote for liver and kidney troubles and cure constipation and purify the blood in a way that often surprises patient and physician alike.

Dr. R. M. Wilkins, while experimenting with sulphur remedies, soon found that the sulphur from Calcium was superior to any other form. He says: "For liver, kidney and blood troubles, especially when resulting from constipation or malaria, I have been surprised at the results obtained from Stuart's Calcium Wafers. In patients suffering from boils and pimples and even deep-seated carbuncles, I have repeatedly seen them dry up and disappear in four or five days, leaving the skin clear and smooth. Although Stuart's Calcium Wafers is a proprietary article and sold by druggists and for that reason tabooed by many physicians, yet I know of nothing so safe and reliable for constipation, liver and kidney troubles and especially in all forms of skin diseases as this remedy.

At any rate people who are tired of pills, cathartics and so-called blood "purifiers" will find in Stuart's Calcium Wafers, a far safer, more palatable and effective preparation.

Send your name and address today for a free package and see for yourself.

F. A. Stuart Co., 57 Stuart Bldg., Marshall, Mich.

of the Av. S. 'way out in El Oro, Mexico. If any of you meet him speak him a kind word, for he gets rather lonesome at times, like Grace Everest; cold, too, like enough; I don't know. His name is George L. Gordon, and he has helped our orphan more than once.) Ferol Lester, Norwood, Mo.: "Ernest Hall and I send our dimes to orphan Charlie's ice cream social, hoping we are not too late to get cream. I think 'Bronze 'Vase' is fine, but Rhoda and Raymund do have such a hard time!" Mrs. Mollie B. Adams, Weldon, Ia.: "I have been an interested reader of your department ever since its conception, both letters and stories." (I hope none will be discouraged at "inception." Just look as if you knew what it meant and go on, for this letter is very cheering.) "I have long wished to express my appreciation of the grand work with the children. Training them to read to some advantage, and to be interested in missionary work is grand and noble. I am an invalid, and did not get to come to Charlie's social quite on time, but here is a quarter inclosed. When Charlie has his education and is earning his own money I hope he will remember others like himself and always be willing to give a portion of his earnings to help them along. May The Christian-Evangelist long be spared to carry on the good works it is forwarding in his name." Mrs. S. M. Gibbins, Garfield, Wash.: "As you have had some benches brought in from the old church to seat the tardy arrivals at Charlie's ice cream social, I have induced eight others to take a dish each, assuring them it will do Charlie just as much good as if they sat in the front row. My prayer is that Charlie may eventually be fitted to care for himself and to help others. I also send 50 cents for Drusie." (I like that note Mrs. Adams and Mrs. Gibbins strike about Charlie some day helping people; for anybody who thinks only of his own advantage is worse than nobody.) Mrs. Carrie Folk Johnston, Perrin, Mo. (who not long ago collected $3 for the social): "The above named send $1 for Charlie. Mrs. Creamer says her dime is for either Charlie or Drusie, as you think best." (I will take her dime under due consideration and advise you of the result later.) "Oliver has built a hay-frame today and dug dirt." (Oliver is Mrs. Johnston's youngest boy, who contributes a dime of the dollar, bless his heart!) "He is now the team to a little red cart with a lye-box for a bed. A little while ago I asked him to bring me some kindling. He said he would as soon as he had turned out. Mother has been telling me about her recent trip up the Columbia River, and about seeing the flag on the battlefield where General Richard Canby fell. Brother Frank was the first on board to spy it." (You who are familiar with our history may remember that General Canby was assassinated by the Modoc Indians while under a flag of truce. He had been sent by President Grant to negotiate a treaty with them. My aunt married General Canby's brother.) Hazel Power, Jefferson, Ore.: "My brother Bryant and I each send $1, half for Charlie, half for Drusie." (Charlie's social has taken in to date $159.80. I don't want to brag. I am not going to. But, honestly now, just honestly, did you ever hear of as successful a social as this one in all your life? Ashley S. Johnson has rebuilt the School of the Evangelists, at which ministerial students may work their way through college without any means but strength and purpose; but there is a debt on the new building, and it will not be opened till the debt is paid. So the Av. S. has just sent another dollar. President Johnson writes: "We have received you contribution, and we are indeed grateful for your assistance." Matilda B. Nickerson, Ethel, Mo.: "I send $1 for Drusie. I am a widow, and my income is small, but I feel it a duty and a blessed privilege to give of my mite to help send the Gospel to a sinful world.

May the Lord bless Drusie in her work; and I do hope and pray she may never lack funds to carry forward her mission." S. A. Seat, Mematite, Mo.: "I suggest a box supper for the benefit of our missionary, Miss Malott, as she is thousands of miles from home and in a strange land, showing her faith by her works. So I suggest Thanksgiving Eve as the time, and send 50 cents for two boxes, and now ask you" (viz., J, B, E.) "to help me enjoy the contents at that time. But this goes to the missionary, box supper or not." (I shall use S. A. Seat's suggestion as the foundation-stone of a new enterprise which I have on foot; but I have thought best not to have the event so soon as Thanksgiving Day. It is too close to Charlie's social; I don't want people who have already surfeited upon ice cream falling to at a lusty dinner of turkey and cranberries. Those who have sent me a dime for the social will have to get out and earn something before they can come again. But I have a plan, a brand new one. Let's have a Christmas Tree for our missionary!

A Christmas Tree for Drusie, right here in Bentonville. I'll furnish the tree if you will hang the presents upon it.

Now, Christmas is a good time off. We have nearly eight weeks to get ready for it. You say, How is this thing done? I'll tell you.

Just think of a present you would like to bring Drusie if you were coming to her tree sure enough, and if you knew she would be called in to take down the gift with her own hands. Suppose you wanted to give her a tin whistle—not that I suppose she would want a whistle —or a doll, so she could give it to one of the little children in her mission; or a book, or a game, or a box of candy, or something to wear. Well, whatever it is, you will know what it would cost if you really sent her that thing. Then you will send me how much the whistle, or doll, or book, or game, or candy, or garment comes to, telling me what you are sending. For instance, you will write: "I inclose for Drusie's Christmas tree three boxes of matches; they cost 5 cents." And you will inclose a nickel in your letter instead of the matches, for they might go off on the way and set the post-office department on fire.

But do you say, "I have no nickel"? But look here: It is nearly eight weeks off. Why not lay by your pennies till you have accumulated that nickel? Then along about December 25 here you send your nickel; or your dime, as the case may be. Twenty-five cents buys a beautiful cake of toilet soap. With 50 cents you can get lots of pretty things; and with a dollar you can make a dreadful gap in a 10-cent store. With two dollars— But there's no use talking about that!

Now, don't you think it will make interesting reading to know what the other people are sending to hang on the Christmas tree? And don't you think Drusie will bless the day as one of the sweetest of all her Christmases? And don't you know how good you will feel to be helping that much in converting the heathen in China, and in spreading the news about Jesus to thousands who have never heard his name? Why, as Brother Pinkerton says, "SURE!" (Brother Pinkerton is my preacher at my home town, Plattsburg, Mo. You ought to know him.) As I was going to say, it will be more fun than having a Christmas tree of our own. I'd lots rather hang that imaginary 10-cent whistle on the tree for Drusie than get that imaginary whistle myself. Wouldn't you?

Now, Drusie doesn't know a thing

about this plan. I don't even know if she would approve it—but she's rather too far off to help herself. Drusie has the idea—and it's a very good idea—that God is going to support her in her field, and that somehow she means will come, and she doesn't have to worry about it—just have faith. And I believe that, too. And I believe this Christmas tree is going to help do the business. I promised you two weeks ago that this would be a Drusie page this week. I thought I would print a lot of her letters, so I said our columns would "be packed and crammed with good things," and here I am handing out about all the things you are getting. I didn't know at that time that I should think of this tree plan. Anyway, I think I am turning out fairly interesting material, don't you? (I hope the St. Louis typographers won't run out of capital I's before I get done this piece!) Now, on the very topmost branch of our tree we will hang S. A. Seat's 50-cent present, for maybe I wouldn't have thought of the tree if he hadn't suggested the box supper. What do you say—will you change those two boxes of supper to boxes of candy, and let me hang 'em up on the tree?

And so maybe somebody who wants to give Drusie a good present will make something and sell it to get the means. Why not? And in making plans to give your kinfolks and friends gifts, maybe you will remember Drusie's tree and save out a little for that purpose. Why not?

Bentonville, Ark.

Graduate Courses at Home,

leading to degrees. If you can not come to the college, the college can go to you. Let us send you particulars. Write Pres. Chas. J. Burton, Christian College, Oskaloosa, Iowa.

Christian Publishing Company

2712 Pine St., St. Louis, Mo.

J. H. GARRISON, - - - - President
W. W. DOWLING, - - - - Vice-President
GEO. L. SNIVELY, - - - Sec. and Gen. Supt
R. P. CROW, - - - Tress. and Bus. Manager

—Through our book department you can get the best bread the mind of man feeds upon.

—A teachers' quarterly for each Bible school grade is among the charms of our next year's Sunday-school supplies.

—The increased cost of labor and publishers' materials forbids our selling THE CHRISTIAN-EVANGELIST for less than $1.50. Please do not ask it. Greatly inferior denominational papers sell readily at $2.

—If you send to the publishers of "Review of Reviews," you will pay $3 for it. We have arranged to sell that great "Review" and THE CHRISTIAN-EVANGELIST for $3. This we do, too, without discounting the latter.

—Our preachers have a golden opportunity to secure either "Helps to Faith," by J. H. Garrison, or "Victory of Faith," by E. L. Powell. Send us a new subscription and the $1.50 and by return mail we send you your choice of books.

—No other song book in use by our people approaches "Gloria in Excelsis" in learning, dignity, and universal value and charm. We also have a great variety of less expensive books for Sunday-school, Endeavor, and protracted meeting use.

—We are constantly pouring new wine into the Dowling Bible school publications, and not into old skins either. The books and papers are being constantly adapted to the ever-changing conditions of our schools and always anticipate the advancements being made through the consecrated efforts of

thousands of faithful teachers and superintendents.

—A good brother writes that he and a neighboring preacher agreed not to give a day's time to introducing one of our representatives to their people. We love these brethren well enough to tell them they stood hurtfully between the best interests of themselves and people and a great opportunity. W. J. Russell helped him place 53 papers at Frankfort, Ind.; E. L. Day, 64, at Brazil, Ind.; L. C. Howe, 106, at New castle, Ind.; T. J. Clark, 107, at Bloomington, Ind. Ask these able ministers if they ever rendered greater aid to their churches in the same length of time. Ministers, write us and we will try to get you some special assistance in placing a Christian paper in every Christian home.

—To help secure that "100,000 by 1909" we have secured some special temporary assistance. Minister James Mailley, of Greensburg, Ind., thus writes:

"Your representative was with me yesterday. I confess I dreaded the day, but to say I was agreeably disappointed is putting it mildly. I enjoyed every minute. He is a genius in his line. His presentation of THE CHRISTIAN-EVANGELIST was courteous without being 'oily.' I felt at ease everywhere for I could see he was making a good impression not for himself only, but for the cause of Christ. His coming and our day's campaign for THE CHRISTIAN-EVANGELIST was a positive blessing to this people. It is a matter of great personal satisfaction to me that he succeeded in getting a list of twenty-one subscribers for the paper; this will be a tremendous reinforcement to the ministry of the pulpit."

Pastors, receive as a brother and helper beloved any man bearing our credentials. He will do you only good and no evil.

—Our growth in circulation is not simply among the publishers' notes, but in the galleys. The old compositor in charge has been familiar with the lists for 24 years. His face shines with delight as the hundreds of new names are given him for the frequent revisions. He bends to his larger tasks delighted with his metallic proofs that the paper he has so faithfully

---

DR.PRICE'S
CREAM
Baking Powder

Has a dietetic value greatly beyond the conception of any one who has not used it. It will make your food of a delicious taste, a moist and keeping quality and a digestibility not to be obtained from any other baking powder or leavening agent.

But more important than all else, Dr. Price's Baking Powder carries only healthful qualities to the food.

Avoid the alum powders
Study the label

served is coming into its rightful inheritance of universal popularity and support. Here are the new clubs he added last week:

Chattanooga, Tenn., Ira Boswell, pastor...........5
Camp Point, Ill., H. J. Reynolds, pastor.........5
Keller, Tex., A. Christian, pastor...............3
Doniphan, Mo., W. A. Haynes, evangelist........6
Lexington, Ky...................................11
Greensburg, Ind., James Mailley, pastor........20
Winchester, Ky., Cecil J. Armstrong, pastor....20
Paris, Ky., Carey E. Morgan, pastor............22
At Buffalo Convention..........................24
Nicholasville, Ky., by special agent...........30
Wheeling, W. Va., W. H. Fields, pastor.........42
Bloomington, Ind., T. J. Clark, pastor........107

What Friends Are Saying.

I must tell you the Easy Chair has been of great profit, comfort and pleasure to me, and the sweet spirit of THE CHRISTIAN-EVANGELIST, its message of brotherly love, if carefully read, will make all life holier and sweeter, and bear rich fruit for our Master.—Mrs. Jessie W. Pierce, Belton, Texas.

THE CHRISTIAN-EVANGELIST has been part of my weekly fare for 14 years. The Easy Chair alone is worth the price of the paper, and especially is this true since I have learned to know the man in the "chair" on the Pacific Coast trip last summer. I should like to put THE CHRISTIAN-EVANGELIST in every home in our Church.—C. B. Townsend, Troy, N. Y.

I have been a regular subscriber and reader the greater part of the past 36 years. I began with "The Evangelist," published in Oskaloosa, Iowa.

We can't keep house now without the weekly visits of CHRISTIAN-EVANGELIST. It is at once conservative and conciliatory.—J. C. McReynolds, Asheville, N. C.

I write you a word of encouragement on the course THE CHRISTIAN-EVANGELIST has taken on the question of federation and other things. I hear it often remarked by the brethren that "THE CHRISTIAN-EVANGELIST gets better and better every issue." If you are a "mystic," as some have said, my prayer is that God may give us more of them.—J. A. Deatheridge (minister), Harrison, Ark.

We congratulate you on the fine issue of THE CHRISTIAN-EVANGELIST for the Buffalo convention. It is all that could be expected and in keeping with the dignity and carefulness of THE CHRISTIAN-EVANGELIST in every detail. I have already ordered a number of the papers for distribution. We shall fulfill all your expectations and promises for the National Convention.—R. H. Miller, chairman of the executive committee.

You can count on me to help you put THE CHRISTIAN-EVANGELIST in every home at this place if it is at all possible. There is some prejudice here against THE CHRISTIAN-EVANGELIST by those who do not know Bro. J. H. Garrison. They have never seen nor heard him nor read the valuable paper which he so ably edits. I believe THE CHRISTIAN-EVANGELIST, that I have read for many years, is the best paper extant, most ably edited and under the guidance of one whom I have learned to love.—Ferd F. Schultz (minister), Beallsville, Ohio.

THE
CHRISTIAN-EVANGELIST

A WEEKLY RELIGIOUS NEWSPAPER.

Volume XLIII. No. 45.

ST. LOUIS, NOVEMBER 8, 1906.

SOME ST. LOUIS CHURCHES ENGAGED IN THE SIMULTANEOUS CAMPAIGN.

1. (Center) Union Avenue, as it will be when completed. 2. (Left upper corner). Compton Heights. 3. (Right upper corner) Fourth. 4. (Lower left corner) First. 5. (Lower right corner) Hamilton Avenue.

THE CAMPAIGN IS NOW ON
FOR THAT
Centennial Fund of $250,000 for Land and Buildings on Mission Fields in Personal Gifts by 1909.

S. J. COREY,
Sec. F. C. M. S.

Interest is being aroused. Some are acting. Others are carefully considering. The friends of the Foreign Christian Missionary Society can be counted upon to do what is right. **Now** is the time to act!

IMPORTANCE OF SECURING LAND

Now on the foreign mission fields can hardly be overestimated. Land is rapidly advancing in value in all these countries, as it is wherever the Gospel is preached. Land the Foreign Society bought in Asia ten years ago is now worth many times what was paid for it. If we do not secure land and lots we need now, we will be compelled to pay much more in the near future.

The need in China and Japan and India and the Philippines and Africa—in a word, all our mission fields, is most pressing.

Our motto should be: "Not slothful in business, fervent in spirit, serving the Lord." The children of light should be as wise as the children of this world.

NEXT WEEK WE HAVE A WORD TO SAY ABOUT THE IMPORTANCE OF MISSION HOMES.

We ask the hearty, liberal and prompt co-operation of the readers of The Christian-Evangelist. Send cash if you are prepared to do so; if not sign the following pledge or copy on a postal card and return:

If you will move in this matter now, you will help to insure the Centennial Fund and help to move others. What is now needed is a movement!

Address,

F. M. RAINS, Sec.,
Box 884, Cincinnati, O.

WATCH THIS SPACE NEXT WEEK!

THE PLEDGE.

I agree to donate to the **Foreign Christian Missionary Society**, Cincinnati, Ohio, $................ per year for three years beginning june 1st, 1907, to aid in the creation of a special **Two Hundred and Fifty Thousand Dollar ($250,000)** Centennial Fund to be used for lands and buildings by the Society.

Name ....

P. O..

Date..................1906.　　Street. or R. F. D...................
　　　　　　　　　　　　　　State........................

The Christian-Evangelist.

J. H. GARRISON, Editor

PAUL MOORE, Assistant Editor

F. D. POWER,
B. B. TYLER, } Staff Correspondents.
W. DURBAN,

Subscription Price, $1.50 a Year.

For foreign countries add $1.04 for postage.

Remittances should be made by money order, raft, or registered letter; not by local cheque, unless 15 cents is added to cover cost of collection.
In Ordering Change of Post-Office give both old and new address.
Matter for Publication should be addressed to THE CHRISTIAN-EVANGELIST. Subscriptions and remittances should be addressed to the Christian Publishing Company, 2712 Pine Street, St. Louis, Mo.
Unused Manuscripts will be returned only if accompanied by stamps.
News Items, evangelistic and otherwise, are solicited, and should be sent on a postal card, if possible.
Published by the Christian Publishing Company, 2712 Pine Street, St. Louis, Mo.

Entered at St. Louis P. O. as Second Class Matter

CONTENTS.

Centennial Propaganda.......................1419
Current Events 1420
Editorial—
Where Jesus Placed the Emphasis—XI.....1421
The Formal and the Spiritual.............1421
Notes and Comments......................1422
Editor's Easy Chair.......................1423
Contributed Articles—
God's Purpose and Plan in Home Missions. E. P. Daugherty.................1424
What the Brethren Are Saying and Doing.
B. B. Tyler 1425
As Seen From the Dome. F. D. Power...1426
Church Federation. Rev. E. D. Sanford,
D. D. 1427
The Christian Church in St. Louis.......1428
Impressions of the Buffalo Convention....1430

Our Budget ....1433　　Christian Endeavor ....
News From Many Fields................1437　　Sunday-school ....
Evangelistic ....1440　　People's Forum ....
Midweek Prayer-meeting...............1441　　Home Department ....

Getting Ready for Business

Many schools are making arrangements for their winter's work along lines that help for all future work by organizing Normal Classes, and for which

The Normal Instructor

is just the help desired. It is in **seven** parts, as follows:
I. **The Book**, a general view and analysis of the books of the Bible, with numerous helpful diagrams and review questions.
II. **The Christ**, has general view of Names, Offices, Symbols, Types, with analytical view of the Prophecies concerning him, and a series of lessons covering his ministry.
III. **The Church** is considered in all its phases: The Church in Prophecy; The Church in Type; The Church's Name, Head, Foundation, Beginning, Membership, Ministry, Mission, Unity, and Future Glory.
IV. **The Land** treats of Bible Geography under "The Old Testament Land" and "The New Testament Lands." Has numerous maps and diagrams.
V. **The Institutions** are given close and careful study, in clear and simple style, classified as Patriarchal, Jewish and Christian, definitions of each.
VI. **The History** gives full and succinct views of the "Chosen People" of Bible Times, as also, the Nations coming into contact with them.
VII. **The People** includes all those brought into prominence in Bible History and the Nations about them and dealing with them.

QUALIFIED FOR SERVICE.

in any department of the Church if you will thoroughly master this course which can be had separately at 15 cents the copy, or $1.50 per dozen prepaid.

CHRISTIAN PUBLISHING COMPANY,

2712 Pine Street.　　　　　　　　　　St. Louis, Mo.

THE
CHRISTIAN-EVANGELIST

"IN FAITH, UNITY; IN OPINION AND METHODS, LIBERTY; IN ALL THINGS, CHARITY."

Vol. XLIII.　　　　　November 8, 1906　　　　　No. 45

1809
1909

CENTENNIAL PROPAGANDA
CHURCHES OF CHRIST
: : : GEO. L. SNIVELY : : :

Looking Toward Pittsburg.

—Brother J. E. Davis' article is entitled to consideration amid our Centennial plannings. Building in wood and stone is essential to the best and largest building in spirit, character and Zion. If some of our church financiers will help reduce his suggestions to the practice of the churches they will have accomplished great good.

—State Mission Day gives us one of the best possible viewpoints from which to see the Centennial that ought to be. Let us make it a high day and with eyes that have seen our duty fully done toward state missions behold the banners of all our commonwealth's victory crowned, as they are being borne down the applauding aisles of our great assembly.

November for State Missions.
W. R. WARREN.

One of the blessings for which all true Disciples will be giving thanks this month is the church home. At the same time we should remember those who are just as true and just as earnest but are living in towns within our own state where it is not possible to celebrate the Lord's Supper every week, where an earnest soul seeking the way of salvation can not find a simple and Scriptural answer, where a penitent believer repeating the Ethiopian eunuch's request can not be satisfied, where no voice is lifted in condemnation of divisions and traditionalism among the people of God, and no advocate ever appears for the one union. What consistency is there in our praise of the Christianity of Christ if we are unwilling to make sacrifices to see it established and advanced in every important community of our own commonwealth?

It is a good arrangement that puts the offerings for state missions in all the churches at the beginning of November, and children's day for Home Missions near the end of the same month. This enables us to consecrate all of November to state missions, for half of the latter offering goes directly back to the state from which it comes, and the rest of it is used in American missions. Before November closes every member of every church and every child in every Bible school should have borne a creditable part in helping to give America to Christ only.

The approach of our Centennial must deepen our gratitude for the great blessings we have received under God through the pioneers of this movement. But we fail of the finest, fruit, and the greatest blessings of their toils if we do not continue and complete what they began in the evangelization of America. Not only so, but it is imperatively incumbent upon us to train up our children to love the same holy cause and to give of their means and strength to its advancement.

Practice celebrating the Centennial in your church and Bible school this November.
Pittsburg.

Church Building and the Centennial.
J. E. DAVIS.

From my experience in church building there has been forced upon me a new idea I believe is worth developing.

In the last four years I have gone through two church building enterprises, and have become acquainted with the price and material of almost every necessity in church building. The average profit on a church building of $25,000 is from $4,000 to $5,000. On buildings costing $1,000 the profit ranges from $250 to $350. Out of the vast number of churches erected annually the same old story of shortage of funds affects ninety-eight per cent. Such shortages often destroy the larger vision of the work, and two-thirds of the churches underbuild in facilities for real church work. These two-thirds usually struggle along and get the auditorium, but the Bible school and its facilities for recruiting the ranks of the church and filling the auditorium are entirely eliminated. Thus the building is done and the work crippled, and in all probability the defect will never be remedied, whereas if the profits of said building could have been saved and put into the additional features needed, the work in that locality would have quadrupled in power.

The others over-build, that is, build beyond their means in their struggle to provide the proper facilities for church work, and either lose their property or a great debt hangs over them, a burden through decades, quenching every rising tide of missionary zeal and enthusiasm, while every society and Bible class in the church is put on a money-earning basis and is counted a success or failure according to the amount of money it can earn.

About two per cent of our churches build and either pay before the dedicator comes, or the cash to satisfy all obligations is handed over on dedication day.

Nearly all profits on these buildings could be saved and put into the building, thus affording not only the necessary facilities for church work, but avoiding the large and wearing debt that so often kills every buoyant ambition born in the zeal of a congregation.

My solution to this problem is to establish a Church Building Material Bureau in connection with our Board of Church Extension, and have it get in touch with manufacturing and producing firms, members of our church who love it, and secure concessions of cost on all materials used in building. The material is not to be bought locally by the church, but direct through the Church Extension bureau, from factories and foundaries.

This bureau could get in touch with architectural construction companies, foundries, lumber mills, nail factories, stone quarries, cement and lime factories, brick and terra cotta companies, and serve as a great wholesale firm to our brotherhood, furnishing at actual cost all material used in building.

The great and unnecessary profits of numerous middlemen the struggling church of God must pay. They should go to enhance the value of church buildings or diminish the cost.

Objections to such a project answered.

1. Will not local companies always furnish materials at cost? No. They seldom furnish them at actual retail cost. Then what some retail merchants consider cost (when selling at cost because it is a church) is the actual cost of goods to them and a per cent to support their business. Besides, what is the use of having the retail cost and profit, and the wholesale cost and profit, and back of that the factory cost of production, when the factory cost and actual cost of laying down the material is all that is necessary?

2. Would not the buying of lumber and other materials out of town antagonize and incur the displeasure of the local dealer? When any sensible or fair-minded man sees that the building material is being bought at the factory cheaper than he can buy it of the wholesale lumber companies he will not only not be offended but will urge the church to take advantage of the bargain. The good will or ill will of a man who loves the church only for what he can get out of it, does not affect very much. Besides, the man who joins or leans toward a church because he has sold that church a bill of hardware, lime or lumber, is actuated by purely commercial sentiments, and is not moved by faith or conviction. Such a man is not saved, is not a Christian, and is rather a hindrance than a help to any church.

Finally, the saving of the vast sums given out of charity's pockets for the original purpose for which the money was given (for building, instead of profits to money-making institutions), will greatly accelerate building enterprises among us and will provide a splendid saving to offer to various missionary enterprises, and will become a worthy twin sister in church building to the church loan, as well as to be a splendid accomplishment by the dawn of our Centennial.
Beatrice, Neb.

Centennial Helpers.

The subscriptions I send you herewith entitle me to the picture of Brother J. H. Garrison which I have been eager to obtain ever since your first announcement. I hope some time to meet him in the flesh. I hope he will live many years and edify his readers with his masterly editorials and the Easy Chair which has carried many a soul out of the shadows of discouragement into the glorious sunlight of peace and consolation. I hope I shall soon be able to persuade more of my brethren to come with us and enjoy these gracious feasts.—A. N. Noell, Asherville, Kansas.

Current Events

Because the Japanese children in San Francisco have been discriminated

Japan's Protest

against in the public schools of that city, the Japanese government, acting through its minister in Washington, has filed a formal protest with the state department. The incident seems a very trivial one but it is being magnified, in some quarters, into a possible, not to say probable, cause of war. The Japanese, to be sure, seem to be taking it rather seriously. They claim that it is in violation of the provisions of the treaty which gives them rights equal to those of any foreign people in this country. What is of even greater consequence, they resent being classed with the Chinese as an inferior race and having their children relegated to the separate schools which are maintained for orientals. Their war with China a dozen years ago convinced the Japanese that they were far superior to the Chinese, and their success in the war with Russia is, to their minds, evidence that they are in the vanguard of modern civilization. They are not in the mood to accept without protest the classification into which the San Francisco board of education has placed them. We have no apprehension of war, or even of serious diplomatic controversy on the subject. But the president is wise in taking the protest seriously. Secretary Metcalf, of the department of commerce and labor, has been dispatched to investigate the facts and find some way of removing the ground for Japan's grievance if any exists.

❀

Meanwhile, with Japan protesting against this slight discrimination against

Japanese Exclusion

her children in the public schools of one city, there is a growing movement in favor of passing a Japanese exclusion act. Such an act is favored by a certain labor element, but at the present time, at least, it would have but a small chance in congress and probably still less at the White House. Whatever may be the practical advantages of excluding the Chinese (and we strongly suspect that these are overestimated), there is a certain inherent absurdity in the theory of it. The principle of exclusion does not commend itself forcibly enough to the average citizen to make him anxious to extend it any further. The congestion of population is one of Japan's great problems. The war with Russia was undertaken chiefly to get in Korea a safety valve for the boiling pot of her population. Even with that, the value of America to Japan as a place for overflow is not small. Even worse than losing that, would be the sting and stigma of exclusion. Perhaps we would get war if we should undertake to keep out the Japanese. It has been hinted by some, who think they see possibilities of war in the present controversy, that Japan's splendid modern navy would be more than a match for ours and that the Philippines could be very quickly and easily wrested from our hands. Perhaps that would be as easy a way as any for us to escape from our obligation to the Philippines—to provoke a small war with Japan and let her take the islands away from us.

The eyes of the country are on New York. Before this paper reaches its

New York.

readers one of the most important political contests of recent years will have been decided. It is not in any ordinary sense a party contest. Each of the gubernatorial candidates has cut a wide swath in the ranks of his opponents. The conservative element is with Hughes. The discontented are with Hearst. Whether he is elected or not, Mr. Hearst's campaign has given him a standing and dignity which he did not have before. Before, he was admired by his followers and despised by his opponents. Now he has won the respect of his enemies for some, if not all, of his qualities. He is a good campaigner and he has—unexpectedly to his critics—shown entire good faith in his repudiation of Tammany in spite of Tammany's support of him. His personality has risen above the party. The party is only an incident in the campaign. Hearst himself is the platform, the ticket and the organization. The question to which two very different answers are returned is, "Is Hearst sincere?" The question to which there is now only one answer is, "Is Hearst a large factor to be considered in state and national politics?" The party of discontent is always formidable when it is in earnest; it is very formidable when it has an able leader. Discontent is not a bad thing, and it is not necessarily a disparagement upon any political group to call it a party of adullamites. What we need to do, as one editor remarks, is to "educate discontent." And that is about the truth. To vote down the discontented proves nothing and settles nothing. To help the discontented to direct their protests intelligently toward the removal of the real evils is to secure real progress. Whatever may be the degree of Mr. Hearst's sincerity or insincerity, a great part of his following is moved by the impulse of more or less intelligent discontent.

❀

Silver bullion is now selling at a trifle over 70 cents an ounce. Four years ago it was selling at 47 cents. This is one reason why Mr. Bryan, still believing in free coinage at the ratio of sixteen to one, does not think that the silver question is a live issue. Silver is taking care of itself without any legislative assistance.

❀

A new beauty doctor in New York announces that deep and correct breathing is the secret of both beauty and health. She ought to be a popular reformer, for she pronounces in favor of tight corsets and high heeled shoes.

❀

Mr. George B. Cortelyou has been transferred from the postoffice department to the impor-

Cortelyou.

tant post of secretary of the treasury. Mr. Cortelyou has been promoted with amazing rapidity from the position of stenographer and private secretary to the president under McKinley, to his present high station, but he has always made good in every place which he has held up to date. This last appointment will be the most severe test which his powers have yet had. The position at the head of the treasury department re-

Editorial

Where Jesus Placed the Emphasis.—XI.

His Unique Personality.

In coming now to this fundamental truth after dealing with many of the practical teachings of Christ, it may be thought that we have reversed the natural order, and that we should have dealt with this fundamental question first, and afterwards with the practical duties which Jesus taught. But this was not the method of Jesus. We are following his own order of procedure. It was not until the closing part of his ministry that he began to lay emphasis upon his own personality and to direct the thoughts of his disciples to himself in his unique relation to God and to humanity. It required no little teaching and training, under the personal influence and example of Jesus himself, to bring his disciples up to the point where they could understand his divine character and mission.

The student of the Gospels will recall his conversation with his disciples at Caesarea Philippi, the fullest account of which is given in Matthew's Gospel (16:13-21). In answer to the question, "Who do men say that the Son of Man is?" the disciples gave the different ideas which men entertained on this subject, which identified him either with John the Baptist, Elijah, Jeremiah, or one of the prophets. But making the question more direct Jesus asked, "But who say ye that I am?" Peter, no doubt speaking for the others as well as himself, said, "Thou art the Christ, the Son of the living God." Complimentary as the other ideas of Christ were, which identified him with the greatest characters in Jewish history, this answer of Peter transcends all of them by the distance of infinity. Peter had been so taught of God that he was able to see in Jesus not only the Christ foretold by the prophets—the anointed Prophet, Priest and King—but, also, the Son of God. It was a sublime reach of faith, nurtured under divine tuition, that enabled Peter to grasp this truth—the mightiest truth ever conceived by the mind of mortal man. Compared with it all philosophical systems and axioms pale into insignificance. On it hangs the destiny of a sinning and dying world. This truth accepted, then God's fatherhood and his redemptive purpose toward humanity are assured facts. The weary, groaning ages had been waiting for this revelation of God's love, and his gracious interposition to effect the recovery of the race from its thraldom of sin and sorrow. Now if this confession of Peter be true, the hour has struck, and the world has entered upon a new era. God has entered into humanity in the person of his Son and that for the purpose of restoring man to the divine image and thus bringing him into the inheritance of life everlasting.

Jesus puts the signet of his approval upon the truth confessed, pronounces a blessing upon Peter, and declares his purpose to build his church upon that divine, fundamental truth. It is here that the uniqueness of the method of Jesus comes out into prominence. No other religious teacher had ever proposed to build a church or found a religion upon his own personality. But the uniqueness of the method grows out of the uniqueness of the personality, for no other religious teacher in the world's annals had ever conceived himself to be the Son of the living God and convinced his immediate followers of the truth of his claim. If he be, indeed, God's only begotten Son and if this coming down of God into humanity was essential to the salvation of man, then it follows that the divine and unique sonship of Jesus is the basic truth of his religion, and the enduring foundation of the church which he established. This truth, standing out as it does in Himalayan proportions in the New Testament was obscured during the apostasy by human philosophy and speculation, creedal statements and traditions, and not until during the nineteenth century was it restored to its original supremacy as the central truth in Christianity. In many cases this restoration is even yet more theoretical than practical, as scarcely any of the creeds recognize the central and controlling place of this truth on which Jesus said he would build his church. But the cry "Back to Christ" has not been raised in vain, and steadily the great prophet of Galilee is rising toward the zenith of his power and influence in the church, and in proportion as he rises, his church is coming to greater unity and power.

The high claim which Jesus made for himself on the occasion referred to above, was always and everywhere insisted upon. To the caviling Jews who, in spite of the most convincing proofs, continued to deny his claim, he said, "Except ye believe that I am he ye shall die in your sins." (John 8:24). In his prayer, recorded in the seventeenth chapter of John, he prays, "And now, Father, glorify thou me with thine own self with the glory which I had with thee before the world was." Indeed, it was on the confession of this truth before the Jewish Sanhedrin and Pontius Pilate, that he was condemned to death. His resurrection from the dead was the vindication of all his claims, and made it possible to establish the Church on the rock-truth which had been confessed by Peter. The apostles, when they had received their enduement of power, not only testified to both Jews and Gentiles that Jesus was the Son of God, but they insisted that faith in him was the essential, saving faith.

Whatever, therefore, may be the readjustments of the future, of one thing we may rest assured: there can be no lowering of the high claims Jesus made for himself, for this would be to remove the very foundation upon which the Church is built. The religious reformation which we are urging has for its supreme note the exaltation of Christ to his true place as the center of the Christian system and the source of all authority in the realm of religion. On that basic truth we may plead successfully for Christian union in him, and for submission to his teaching in all that relates to the life and growth and work of the Church. From this impregnable Rock no criticism, or science, or philosophy, falsely so called, can dislodge us. It is the Rock of Ages, and whosoever builds thereon builds for eternity.

❋ ❋

The Formal and the Spiritual.

As man is a compound being made up of body and spirit, so Christianity which is adapted to man has also its body and its spirit—the formal and the spiritual. Just as the spirit is more important than the body which it inhabits, so the spiritual element in Christianity is vastly more important than the forms through which it manifests itself. But form is not without its important place and use to people dwelling in the body. To keep the right equipoise between these two elements of Christianity has been one of the real conflicts within the church through all its history. As a rule, we think it may be said that the tendency has generally been to exalt the external form above the internal or spiritual state. This has been especially true in ritualistic churches where the priest has usurped the function of the preacher and where transformation of character is less insisted upon than conformity to ecclesiastical rites and ceremonies. In such churches with all the devotion to forms, strange to say, the original New Testament forms which have real spiritual significance have been exchanged for others that lack such significance.

But while it is true, as we have stated, that the tendency has been to exalt the form at the expense of the spirit, just as it is natural for men to give vastly more thought proportionately to their bodies than to their spirits, yet there have come periods of reaction within the church when certain parts of it, revolting against the subordination of the spiritual to the formal, have reacted to an opposite extreme, and have entirely overlooked the significance and value of those few forms which in New Testament times were estimated of no little value.

Baptism and the Lord's Supper are the only two ordinances instituted by Christ and taught and practiced by his chosen apostles. The former of these as originally practiced was an impressive symbol of Christ's burial and resurrection, and, therefore, an enacted declaration of faith in his divinity. The Lord's Supper sets forth the relation of his death to the forgiveness of our sins and the life everlasting. It will be seen that the great gospel facts are thus embodied and symbolically set forth in these divine institutions. Indeed, baptism in New Testament times was the formal act of surrender to Christ and initiation into his church. As such it was associated with the remission of sins and the gift of the Holy Spirit. Of course this relation could only exist between an outward act and a spiritual blessing, where the former is an *act of faith* and of *allegiance* to Jesus Christ. In other words, baptism is faith seeking the divine blessing through obedience to a divine command. To separate baptism from faith is to rob it of all significance and value whatsoever.

The leading bodies of Protestants, except the state churches, in their revolt against the formalism of the Roman and Anglican churches, have generally tended to underestimate the value of these ordinances, and often to misplace them. It has been the purpose of this Reformation to avoid the extreme of sacramentarianism, which made the ordinances essential channels of saving grace, on the one hand, and the opposite extreme of regarding them as mere church ceremonies, subject to such changes in their manner of observance as might seem good to the church in any age. In other words, its aim has been and is, to restore these ordinances to the place which they hold in the New Testament. This is not to exalt the form above the spirit, but it is simply to maintain that the spirit of Christianity, if not misguided, will manifest itself in the same forms, so far as baptism and the Lord's Supper are concerned, as it did originally, seeing that these forms are designed to set forth the fundamental facts of the Gospel. The abnormal condition of things brought about by a departure from New Testament usage, for which the church of to-day is not responsible, may well cause us to be charitable toward all whose spirit is loyal to Jesus Christ; but it does not justify the approval of such departures by those seeking to restore the New Testament church in its constitutional features.

It is understood, of course, that the "form of godliness without the power," or spirit, is worthless. Infinitely more valuable in the sight of God is the spirit of obedience with a defective form than would be a perfect form of obedience without the spirit. Nevertheless, the *true ideal* is the spirit of obedience, submitting itself to God through divinely-ordained forms, or ordinances. For this ideal we must constantly strive, seeking, meanwhile, to be charitable to all who do not see as we do, and to be quick to recognize Christian faith and character wherever we see them. Such, it seems to us, should be the spirit and attitude of a religious movement seeking to be loyal to New Testament ideals, and to manifest, at the same time, the spirit of the Master.

Notes and Comments.

The claim which the "Argus" sets up is that the Disciples, so far as they are represented by the two papers indicated, are abandoning the ground hitherto occupied by them, and are lining up with Baptist teaching on the subject. This is the matter in regard to which we asked THE CHRISTIAN-EVANGELIST to declare itself, and state plainly and publicly whether it is correctly represented by the "Argus." We neither expressed nor felt any regret that THE CHRISTIAN-EVANGELIST is "sending forth the truth in connection with baptism." It would give us great pleasure to believe that it is engaged in such a task; but if it is giving currency to Baptist teaching on the subject, as the "Argus" claims, we are firmly convinced that it is sending forth error on the subject.—*The Christian Weekly*.

We have not seen the statements of the "Argus" referred to above. So far as THE CHRISTIAN-EVANGELIST is concerned, it has not "changed front" nor has it "abandoned the ground formerly occupied." It is headed exactly the same way, but hopes it is a little further along; it occupies the same ground, but hopes it is producing a little better crop from the soil. We are not alarmed if the "Baptist Argus" thinks we have "changed front," since that *appearance* of things may be entirely due to the clearer vision with which it now sees things.

❊

Here is the question, Bro. CHRISTIAN-EVANGELIST: Do you dissent from the views of the fathers and agree with those of the Baptists, and are you "coming straight," as the "Argus" claims, by forsaking the position of the fathers and heading toward the Baptist position? The "Argus" so declares. Will you please, *please*, PLEASE answer?—*The Christian Weekly*.

We are inclined to do almost anything to accommodate our venerable and esteemed Brother Briney. We are not conscious of any material "dissent" from the generally accepted view of the fathers touching baptism, though we dare say the emphasis is somewhat different in our columns from what it was in the "Christian Baptist" and "Millennial Harbinger," since we face a very different situation in our day. As to agreeing with the Baptists, we are glad to believe that both the Baptists and ourselves are learning how to take a more irenic view of baptism than was possible in the days of conflict, and that we are approximating each other's position. Has Brother Briney detected any teaching in THE CHRISTIAN-EVANGELIST on the subject of baptism which he thinks "dissents" from the teaching of *Jesus and his apostles?* If so, let him point it out in his own gentle, brotherly way, and we will try to profit by it. The New Testament is the only standard we recognize.

❊

Nothing of recent date has surprised us more than to see in some of our contemporaries, three of the greatest speeches delivered at our national convention at Buffalo, criticised as "attacks upon our plea." We have already printed President Cooper's address, and this week we print that of Brother Daugherty, of Wabash, Ind. The other was that of J. P. Lichtenberger, of New York City. We are free to confess

Editor's Easy Chair.

There is something pathetic in the fact that many people live their little life here on earth and pass away without having discovered anything beautiful and wonderful in the world in which they have lived. There is the daily panorama of the rising and setting sun, of floating clouds, of arching sky, of birds, of flowers, of laughing children, and the pageantry of the seasons in their stately procession, but in all this they see nothing that the eye or delight the soul. It is like a blind man standing in the midst of a magnificent art gallery, in which are displayed the great masterpieces of the world's best artists, and who sees them not, or a deaf man listening to the sublime oratorios and sweetest symphonies produced by the world's greatest musicians, but feeling no exaltation of soul, because his ear has not been attuned to these great melodies. There are eyes that can not see and ears that can not hear, and minds that can not appreciate, simply because they have not been educated and trained. Herein is the supreme office of education. It is not always received in schools, but in some way and through some experience, the inner eye and the inner ear must be opened if the soul is to receive the greatest messages that God wishes to convey to it. "Blessed are your eyes for they see, and your ears for they hear," said the great Prophet of Nazareth to his disciples who, under his tuition were beginning to catch a new meaning of life and its possibilities.

❀

But sometimes there is a sudden awakening of a soul that has hitherto been dead to its surroundings, to an appreciation of what had before been unnoticed. A recent author who has been making some "Adventures in Contentment", describes his own personal experience in undergoing such a change. Perhaps some of our readers have had such an experience. This is how he describes it:

"I can not well describe it save by the analogy of an opening door somewhere within the house of my consciousness, I had been in the dark; I seemed to emerge. I had been bound down; I seemed to leap up, and with a marvelous sense of freedom and joy, I stopped there in my field and looked up. It was as if I had never looked up before. I discovered another world. It had been there before, but I had never seen nor felt it. I saw a field, familiar, yet strangely new and unfamiliar, lying up to the setting sun, all red with autumn. Above it the incalculable height of sky, blue but not quite clear, owing to the Indian summer haze: I can not convey the sweetness and softness of that landscape, the airiness of it, the mystery of it, as it came to me at that moment. As I stood there I was conscious of the tang of burning leaves and brush heaps, the lazy smoke of which floated down the valley, and I heard, as though the sounds were then made for the first time, the vague murmurs of the country side, a cowbell somewhere in the distance, the

creak of a wagon, the blurred evening hum of birds, insects, frogs. And I said aloud to myself, 'I will be as broad as the earth. I will not be limited.'"

Who can tell what causes contributed to bring about a change like that? Here was a new revelation, not in the sense of a new world, but in the sense of a new vision of its beauty and meaning—a new power of appreciation, which brought with it a new joy in living.

❀

Is there not something analogous to this in relation to the spiritual world in the change which we call *conversion?* What is conversion but the waking up, more or less suddenly, to the sublime realities of the spiritual world? We have gone along in our careless, unseeing fashion, unmindful of any realities in the universe except the material things with which our time and attention have been engrossed. Heavenly voices have been speaking to us, but we heard them not. All life's tender relationships and all its high obligations have been calling us to a recognition of God, but their lesson has gone unheeded. The mystery of birth and of death, the experiences of sin and of sorrow, have sought to woo us to a higher and better life, but, alas, our hearts have resisted these appeals, and we have gone along the broad frequented way, heedless of all the higher and better things which life holds for us. One day we became conscious of new influences working in our heart, and of a change in our feeling and our point of view. At last, under the stress of some illuminating experience, which has brought home to us the vanity of all earthly glory, or under the moving appeal of the Gospel message, which has laid bare our spiritual poverty, and the unsearchable riches of Christ, the soul turned to God, as the flower lifts its face to the sunlight, and, behold! we live in a new world. Life has a new meaning and the world has a new beauty. All the relationships of life take on a new charm and sacredness because they have been lifted up into the light of God's countenance. "Old things have passed away, and behold all things have become new." This is conversion.

❀

Sometimes the process described above is very gradual, like the dawn of the morning, creeping over the eastern hilltops and brightening into the full tide of day. Sometimes the change comes with greater suddenness, as when some soul, beclouded and benumbed by sin, comes to a sudden realization of its guilt, and then of the pardoning love of God. But the genuineness of conversion does not depend upon these psychological differences. Whether it be sudden or whether it be a more gradual process, the change which we call conversion, by which the soul is turned to God and away from sin, is essential to true living, which, after all, is the life everlasting.

No scene in nature, however beautiful, can compare with the moral beauty of that change which we call conversion. It is the sunrise of the soul. The darkness and the mists roll away before the shining face of the Sun of Righteousness, as he rises with healing in his beams. As the wheeling of the earth into right relation with the sun brings on spring, with its flowers and birds, so the turning of the soul to the light of God causes it to bring forth the graces of Christian living which make the whole life fragrant and beautiful. This is what Christ can do for the soul when it commits itself to him. Is there anything more pathetic than the fact that there are so many millions of our human race whose hearts are sad and barren, whose lives are marred and maimed by sin, and who only need Christ to heal, strengthen, comfort; and make them whole, and they know it not? What holier task has earth for any one than to introduce the waiting and willing Christ to needy souls, to seek and to save whom he came into the world? This is evangelism. God make us worthy of so holy a work!

❀

What a vast gain it would be to religion and to humanity, if we could get rid of the notion that religion is something artificial and arbitrary, something unnatural and ghostly, something involved in intricate theological and ecclesiastical problems, and to conceive of it as simply the soul turning to God, its Author, the earthly child turning to its heavenly Father, for love and guidance! It is sin that is unnatural and abnormal, an interloper and intruder in God's world. Love and obedience to God are the normal and rightful conditions of the soul in which alone it can realize its destiny. In these days of evangelistic activity, when so many churches and evangelists are seeking to win men to God, let us strive to make it as plain and simple as it really is in the New Testament. Surely men can be made to see that sin has in it the seeds of sorrow and ruin, and that the soul that would be healthy and happy and whole, must get rid of sin and must come to him who can forgive sin, and who can impart to the soul the new life, which is infinitely superior to the old life of sin which ends in death. O, men of God, plead with sinners to turn away from what is destructive of both soul and body, and accept the life which is eternal! Plead with the prodigal sons and daughters to come home to the Father's house, where a warm welcome awaits them! Make it plain to them that they are not asked to solve theological or critical problems, but only to come to Christ, if they are weary and heavy laden, and he will give them rest unto their souls. It is a glorious evangel which God has committed to us, and may his gracious Spirit help us to present it in all its divine loveliness and winsomeness to a sinning and dying world!

God's Purpose and Plan in H

By E. F. Daugherty

From the beginning, and with whatever home-land he has specially dealt God's purpose has been none other than the purpose of loving, righteous sovereignty. His plan was, in the days of Israel as his chosen, and is, in these days of Americans as his favored, entrusted to human hands and hearts for its consummation.

The thread of that purpose may be traced backward through the noble army of Carey's imitators, past the Great Commission, and yet back through the Abrahamic covenant, to find its source in the word of hope which relieved the gloom of Eden's transgression; for the genesis of missions is in the birth of the Messianic hope. The merest commonplace in religious discussion affirms that the chosen people were guarded, shielded and preserved through all their tribal and national storms, that they might bequeath to civilization its spiritual heritage.

God's purpose had in view for them the preservation of the land of their fathers as the theater for the reclamation of humanity's lost heritage. Its frustration through human perversity is the one tragedy of fadeless interest in the world's past. Amidst the darkness of its apparent defeat, the star of Bethlehem swung out, presaging the rise of the sun of Righteousness—and universality, instead of nationality, became the compass of the plan divine.

No less of the chosen people than of their noblest representative, from whose birth history makes all its dates—"To this end were they born and for this purpose came they into the world, that they might bear witness unto the truth." With equal force will those words apply to whatever movement of reform a rational philosophy of history makes essential to the world's progress. So, supremely, triumphantly, and ceaselessly must it be asserted of the movement which this convention represents, "To this end were we born, and for this cause came we into the world, that we might bear witness unto the truth."

Up from the lowlands of obscurity, on toward the highlands of religious accomplishment we have come and are pressing. The dawn of the century finds us well in the morning of success toward the realization of our destiny as a conquering, unifying force in the world's religious life. Down the ages, the supreme problem with which God's people have dealt was and is—first, the willingness to accept God's sovereignty. Second, the enlistment of their disposition and power in the carrying out of his will. And with that problem we are face to face.

From one who stood in the forefront of faith's thinkers the last century through—from Gladstone— are these words: "I incline to think that the future of America is of more importance to Christendom than that of any other country." There breathes not a man in all this land with

soul so dead as to disagree. The struggles of the continent aside, men of keen vision, long vision, and sane, have declared the transference of world issues from the eastern to the western hemisphere, and asserted their focus in the destiny of the American nation. Out of an appeal to God for justice and liberty was the nation born; by loyalty to the spirit of its forefathers has its destiny unfolded, and it is not presumption but wisdom which declared "as goes America so goes the world." Grapple the facts, then, we must in relation to the purpose and plan of God and center them in the religious conditions of our national life.

These are the facts relating to the purpose and plan of God. A new earth wherein dwelleth righteousness. A new people whose distinction is righteousness, whose bond is peace, whose work is redemption, whose strength is unity, and whose heritage is glory. The simplicity that is in the old old story, the plan wherewith this purpose is to have its inevitable consummation.

These are the facts relating to the land we call home, and for whose conquest the society works and prays and plans and hopes. Within the land's borders—human nature of every conceivable type and condition. For the land's uplift, from every conceivable school of thought—Utopian plans afloat, and room for any and every new heresy that may arise, with the liberty to spread its bane or blessing. Contrasts here socially, morally, religiously, politically, financially, with all the variety ranging betwixt them which obtains between heaven and hell. Commercialism, the land's great fact—unconsecrated, entrenched, self-sufficient, subtle, omnipresent, and the nation *in toto* weighing to-day this dictum of God because the voice of the people has spoken it: "Graft must go!" Socialism—past the proportions of the cloud no larger than a man's hand on the horizon of affairs—with

*A speech delivered at the National Convention, Buffalo, by E. F. Daugherty, Wabash, Ind.

prevailing of short visions, self-launched by reactionaries within our own ranks.

So the scales of judgment are swung and the hour has struck for us to do God's will or fail in the path of our destiny by the weight of our own supine indifference and unbelief—for those are the clogs that have balked God's plan wherever it has made a tack. Though we have come into the strength of the giant, its method must be the gentleness of the Lamb, for our use of the jaw-bone belongs to the past and the love spirit in sacrifice alone can bring us victory. The call of the time is for love's service as manifested in the mind of the Christ, and in the balance of the world's need our movement is being held for answer to that need. We can say it nay by crystallizing into a self-righteous championship of legalistic forms; we can say it amen by exemplifying the spirit of fellowship with men and movements of worth, however little akin to us in methods they may be in the turmoil of the present.

Second—The facts mean this—that we will not be found wanting; for to the supreme test of these days have we aspired and conquered. Our hosts are of the common people, and the age-long distinction they have had is sanity! Concerning him whose cause we champion in its simplicity the saying has always been signal in its significance that "the common people heard him gladly." Of these in our age, no less than of them in his age, the same fact will hold, and the call we voice will be answered in grandly increasing acclaims of support, until the genius of the cause we plead, freed from its misinterpretations, shall leaven the body of the nation's believers and bring about their unity in the bonds of peace. Our vision must ever outrun our attainment, for where no vision is the people perish, and only the lack of vision can work our hurt. Seers we have never lacked and never will, for the purpose of God is inevitable, and from out the wavering ranks of the fickle, there will be, as there always has been, found the dependable. It is not, therefore, for us to quake

at the reality of clashing opinions within our ranks, for our heritage and shibboleth is liberty! It is not for us to wail and cynicize at the palpable fact of mistakes which may be charged against us, for our righteous pride is charity. It is not for us to be poisoned by that perverse spirit of our age, which from this party and the other affirms its own monopoly on truth, for the cause unto which we were born and which by God's grace we will see supreme is unity.

But it is for us, midst storm and calm, through progress or reverse, in weakness or in strength, to manifest a dauntless, persistent, unwavering, tireless faith, that God's hand and eye is on us, and we can not, we must not, we will not fail. No other spirit than this ever won a fight and the fight of faith is the fight supreme. If now and then a corporal deserts, take hold on the consolation that no army, however good and great its cause, has ever been without some deserters, whether salvation's forces with their Judas, or the forces of liberty with their Arnold. But the strength of a movement is in its loyal, and we can trust the common people with a trust, second only to the trust we place in God.

Third—The facts mean for us an inevitable centennial triumph. We have fought and won the battle for establishment, and now are wrestling with the problems of organization and education for a resistless advance. Pittsburg is the place and three years hence the time when the chronicle of a century's work of faith and labor of love will be written in figures that will glow and facts that will inspire. It will be, from the standpoint of evangelism, a record unrivalled since the conquering spirit of Pentecost went forth to prevail among the sin-smitten. From the regiments of home and foreign missions the spirit of Paul will have its increasingly honorable exemplification. From the brigade of the church extension wisdom will have her justification. Definite effectiveness will have possessed as a mantle of blessing the plans of ministerial relief. Education will have raised her eyes and taken a forward step in the path of endowment for mighty accomplishment. From every interest of the

brotherhood the news will be proclaimed that organization is prevailing over chaos, and the marshalling of our forces for the greatest accomplishments yet will there and then be made the fact of supreme rejoicing.

Therefore, the fourth and final meaning of the facts for us is this—that we must have and will a realized consecration of the brotherhood to the purposes and spirit of the kingdom. We have been preaching unity, while lacking it ourselves in effort. Co-operation we have applauded among others, while failing to demonstrate its power ourselves. We must rise to exemplify the vision, that from the great church to the obscure one, from the man of one talent to him of ten, concert of action in practicing the gospel of sacrifice as we have had it in preaching the gospel of conversion, is the royal path to follow in the fulfillment of our manifest destiny.

A realized consecration of the brotherhood will mean an intelligent and aggressive leadership in our pulpits and a loyal following from our membership in the pews on the pathway of concerted action. It will mean an enlistment of the dilatory in the support of short plans and long, the deepening of the spirit of sacrifice for the cause in all the faithful and doubled power in the prosecution of conquest aims.

Its burden is on the officers of our national organizations, that their plans be deep-laid and far-reaching. On our conquering evangelists in their mighty harvests that their converts be persuaded to the mastery of second principles of the faith when they have observed the first. Upon our pastors, to conserve and use the strength of their charges to its limit. Upon our membership, to claim the realization that no individual of this mighty army can be in good standing with it and fail to carry his portion of its honorable burdens.

Thus may God's purpose be realized—his plan exemplified and his nation's exhaustless riches in lives and means be consecrated to the work of the King.

"So, let it be in God's own might!
We gird us for the coming fight,
And, strong in Him whose cause is ours
In conflict with unholy powers,
We grasp the weapons he has given—
The Light, and Truth and Love of Heaven."

What the Brethren Are Saying and Doing

By B. B. Tyler

My body is in Denver. My spirit has been in Buffalo. My thoughts are of the tremendous progress of the Disciples of Christ. The victories that have been gained cannot be fully described by any pen. I know of no progress equal to that of the Disciples of Christ. I know of no victories greater than theirs.

I first visited Buffalo in 1868. I went out to Williamsville to worship. There was no body of evangelical believers, at that time in Buffalo, that desired to be known only as "Christians," "Believers," "Brethren," "Saints," "Disciples," "Fellow-Citizens," "Children of God." There are now a number of flourishing congregations of such persons in Buffalo, and in its immediate vicinity. They stand well, too!

If I understand this movement in the Church of Christ, it represents an earnest desire for unity and union among those who believe in the Christ, and this union in order to the speedy and successful evangelization of the world. "The Lord's Prayer" to "the fathers," was the seventeenth chapter of John. The golden text in this chapter were verses 20 and 21. "Neither for these only do I pray, but for

them also that believe on me through their word; that they all may be one; even as thou, Father, art in me, and I in thee, that they also may be in us; that the world may believe that thou didst send me." Repeat please, slowly and thoughtfully, the last ten words of this quotation.

"Thirty-one years ago we did not have in the wide field destitute of the gospel a single herald of the cross," is the language of the report of the Foreign Christian Missionary Society read in Buffalo. This society was organized in 1875 or '76. The first year only 29 churches sent in contributions. The aggregate offerings of congregations and individuals, the first year, amounted to $1,706.35. During the last year the receipts were $268,726.62. This is wonderful. My nerves tingle as I read this report. I am almost wild with excitement. Victory all along the line. Wholesome, healthy, sane, progress on the part of all societies, and boards, represented in the Buffalo convention. It is coming to be understood that the evangelization of the world is the one great work of the

church; this is a divine, not a merely human enterprise. To engage in it is for our good as well as for the benefit of those who are not Christians. There comes to the individual and to the church engaging in this work an enlargement. World-wide work for the bodies, the minds, the souls, of men is incongruous with sectarianism. This is genuine catholicity. Sectarianism and catholicity are antipodes. Missionaries and missionary enterprise is the foe of pessimism.

And the young men who are at the front! As I ran over the names of those who were announced to preach in Buffalo, convention Sunday, not more than two or three were in the work of the ministry when I began to try to tell the story of the Father's love toward his erring children. I am proud of our young men. A finer body can not be found on earth. Here is quality as well as quantity. The men are numerous and they are upon the whole, first-class fellows. There were no such young men in the ministry forty years ago. I am happy to see them increase while we who have been in the service a long time decrease. This is the order of nature. The God of all grace is in this movement of young men to the front. How it would have pleased me to have been in Buffalo to have looked into their faces, to have heard their voices, and to have pressed their hands. But I was there in spirit.

As Seen From the Dome By F. D. Power

I am once more on sacred soil. The Christian Missionary Society of Virginia is in session in the city of Richmond. I have the honor to be one of the founders of this society, and this is its thirty-first annual meeting. It succeeded the old state meeting, which was, a mass meeting, and resolved and re-resolved and died the same. Some of us felt the need of a more practical working organization and we got together, and here it is after thirty-one years of faithful and efficient service. The old state meeting was a great powwow. We always kept over Sunday, and in those days I preached in every Baptist church in this city at some one of these annual gatherings. My first exaltation to the dignity of introductory speaker was in 1871. I had been appointed alternate to Robert Cave. No one dreamed that the lot to preach that sermon would fall to me, but Cave escaped, and the young preacher was the victim. Peter Ainslie, of blessed memory, was the manager and called me and the congregation to the altar. Later they held a preachers' meeting, and he arose and said, as our young brother had preached the introductory he was the first subject of criticism, and he proceeded to review my maiden effort. When he sat down Dr. Chester Bullard arose and said: "Mr. Chairman, Brother Ainslie in his speech has made all the mistakes our young brother has been guilty of, and more," and he proceeded to review the critic. Of course my heart went out to the good doctor with a very warm feeling. There were sermons and songs, and prayers, and fellowship, and resolutions, and then we adjourned. The organization of the V. C. M. S. brought a new era. It has been more practical, businesslike, aggressive, truer every way to the Gospel ideal.

Richmond in itself makes any convention enjoyable. There is a flavor about this Virginia atmosphere that inspires the visitor. At the restoration of Charles II. Virginia's arms were quartered with those of the realm and the motto added *En dat Virginia Quartam*—"Behold Virginia gives the fourth," and Virginia was the oldest dominion of England in the new world, and so called "The Old Dominion." Here is a painting of Queen Elizabeth made in 1632 with the inscription in Latin, "The High and Mighty Princess Elizabeth, by the grace of God, Queen of England, France, Ireland and Virginia." Jamestown was the first capital and after Bacon burned it in 1676, then for a hundred years Williamsburg was the colonial capital, and then to get out of the way of the British they came up the river to this spot, and since 1779 it has been the seat of government. Here is the Capitol copied by Thomas Jefferson after the Maison Quarree of Nismes, an ancient Roman Temple, a wonderfully

impressive Ionic structure which cost only $120,000 in those good days, where so many great assemblies have met, among them the constitutional convention of 1829-30, when Alexander Campbell was the associate of such men as Madison, Monroe, Marshall and John Randolph, of Roanoke. Here came the confederate congress from Montgomery in 1862, and sat till April, 1865. Here is Hondon's statue of Washington, "the most perfect representation of the peerless man in existence." "A facsimile of Washington's person." said Lafayette. "Standing in the southeast corner of the rotunda and looking at this statue on a level with it," said Rembrandt Peale, who had often seen Washington, "you may well think you are beholding Washington himself. That is the man, sir; exactly." The figure seems over erect. Hondon came from Paris to Mt. Vernon in October, 1786, and Washington treated him with great consideration, but he staid, and made no sign of getting to work, and the great man began to weary of his guest. One day a pair of horses were sent to Washington for his inspection, and he and Hondon were looking at them. Expressing themselves much pleased with the horses, Washington asked their price and was told a thousand dollars! The father of his country at once assumed an attitude of indignation and Hondon cried triumphantly: "Ah! I 'ave him. I 'ave him!" and from that pose the statue was made.

This convention has been a good one. The report of the year's work is every way encouraging. The plans for the future mean worthy enlargement. First came a preacher's program, opened with a fine address by the president, J. T. T. Hundley, on the "Gospel Needed by Men." Others on the program were E. R. Kemm, H. W. Sublett, J. D. Hamaker, G. W. Remagen, W. R. Jinnett and Dr. R. H. Pitt, editor of the "Religious Herald." It was a profitable session, but there should be a more carefully prepared program, with timely notice to each speaker, and written addresses.

The woman's period was well filled. They have excellent C. W. B. M. workers here. I need only name Miss Kent, Miss Cary and Miss Orvis, Mrs. Jobson, Miss Shackelford and Miss Chiles, and Mrs. Haley, who were on the program. Miss Ella Maddock, the returned missionary, and Mrs. Ida Harrison made addresses that were received with great interest. The organization has in the state seventy-one auxiliaries and 1,309 members, who contributed the past year $2,581.69.

The State Society made a splendid record for 1906. H. C. Combs, the secretary, reports work done at Petersburg, Portsmouth, Harrisonburg, Blacksburg, Roanoke, Norfolk, Newland, Radford and Manchester. Six churches were

organized and eighty-one aided; 89 were added to the churches, and twenty two men were in the employ of the board. The sum raised for state missions was $7,350. There are many promising fields under cultivation and others are opened each year. Such men as Kemm, Woodward, Johnston, Burleigh, Morton, Culbertson, Coffey, Richards, Poage, Elmore, Henkel, Remagen Wade, Watson, and others are accomplishing much in building up the cause in the state, while the old workers like Hamaker, Hall, Spencer, Hopwood Hundley, Haley, Atkins and the rest are felt in all the counsels and labors of the brotherhood. The address of J. J. Haley on "New Testament Evangelism," was one of the great things of the convention. Reports of the "Field Workers' and a symposium on "Development," were two fine features of the meeting Our secretaries, McLean and Muckley Ranshaw and Mohorter, did splendid service for the general causes of the brotherhood. There were 140 delegates and a large attendance of brethren from the city churches. One hundred and ninety-three of the 225 churches contributed to the state work. W. F. Fox presided and was re-elected president of the society. The Centennial aims are

❦ ❦

"JUST A LITTLE"
Grape-Nuts Worked Wonders For An Unfortunate Woman.

"At last I was obliged to sit all day at a sewing machine in a factory," said an English lady who was once well and happy, but whose circumstances changed so that she was compelled to earn her living.

"I soon suffered dreadfully with indigestion, some days thought I would die from acute pain in front of the waist line. I took about everything for indigestion without any permanent relief; tried starvation but suffered just as much whether I ate anything or not.

"Curiosity caused me to try a package of Grape-Nuts food for a change. Then I got a second package and began to use it regularly. What was my surprise—bowels became regular, no more headaches, piles troubled me less frequently and best of all the stomach trouble was gone entirely. I wanted Grape-Nuts for luncheon as well as breakfast—seemed as if my system craved what was good for it.

"Everyone in the family has taken to eating Grape-Nuts. They said I ate it with so much relish they thought it must be very good—and so it is.

"My little girl has gained five pounds since she started eating Grape-Nuts—in about three months. I think everyone, sick or well, should eat Grape-Nuts at least twice every day." Name given by Postum Co., Battle Creek, Mich.

"There's a reason." Read the famous book "The Road to Wellville in pkgs.

30,000 Disciples, $10,000 annually for state work, $20,000 in their trust fund, which has now $8,000, Sunday-schools doubled, all homeless congregations housed, church debts paid, and pastorless churches supplied, and 250 Virginians at Pittsburg in 1909—all of which will be duly realized. The next convention goes to Norfolk, if satisfactory arrangements can be made. B. A. Abbott made the closing address.

Our Richmond churches seem to be in excellent condition. It is just seventy-four years since sixty-eight persons withdrew from the Baptist household and began to keep house for themselves. It was in 1832, and strangely enough the same month that the water was turned on in the city waterworks. Others were organized and soon that holy thing we call the cause was planted from the mountains to the sea. It had great prin-

ciples and great souls maintained them. It faced great difficulties and antagonisms, but it stood the test. It gave its spirit, its offerings, its sons and its daughters to work in Virginia and throughout the land. It has no reason to be ashamed of its contribution to the brotherhood, or to the larger religious life of humanity. It has had an illustrious past. It will have a more glorious future.

Church Federation   By Rev. E. B. Sanford, D. D.

A year has passed away since the great Inter-Church conference held its session in New York City. From that mount of spiritual vision where 500 delegates, representing the churches of our country holding to historical and evangelical Christianity came together, a mighty impulse has gone forth unifying spiritual forces in their work of advancing the Kingdom of God. Until the first meeting of the first "Federal Council of the Churches of Christ in America" in 1908, large responsibility was placed in the hands of the executive committee in which each of the thirty Christian bodies, by whose action the plan of federation was adopted, is represented. For that committee we make brief report.

The published volume containing the proceedings and addresses made at the conference is worthy of this assembly of which a great leader in the ranks of the laity has said, "I regard the result achieved by the Inter-Church conference on federation to be the greatest and most significant accomplished by any religious gathering ever held in North America." This book of nearly 700 pages contains the garnered thought of leaders in all the churches. The edition now on hand is limited but while it lasts a copy will be sent to every one that helps the work of the executive committee by the payment of an annual membership subscription of three dollars. Get this book and aid with your name and subscription sent to the office of the committee, 81 Bible House, New York, Alfred R. Kimball, treasurer.

What has been done since the conference? Correspondence world wide in scope has been cared for. Some of the leading Christian bodies in their national meetings have approved the plan of federation. Among these we note the unanimous and favorable action of the General Conference of the Methodist Episcopal Church, South, the General Assembly of the Presbyterian church in U. S. A. and the Reformed church in America. Several of the constituent bodies will take action in 1907. The federal council that will act in behalf of a united Protestant Christianity is assured.

The executive committee have not only given careful attention to this matter of organization, but under the resolutions passed by the conference they are securing fruitful practical results. The greetings to missionaries in foreign lands have brought cheering response. The federation in Japan composed of the represent-

atives of twenty-four denominational mission boards in its last annual meeting, referring to the Inter-Church conference, put on record these words, "We are of one mind that the missionary movements in Japan and in other countries will be directly influenced thereby and that there has been furnished by this meeting an impressive demonstration of the essential vital unity of Christianity to the non-Christian world."

Those who were present at the conference will recall the resolutions that were adopted regarding the conditions under which the helpless millions of the Congo River Basin in Africa are the victims of the worst form of slavery. Believing that our Government has a responsibility in this matter, the committee are making special efforts to secure action on the part of congress that will help at least in securing the creation of an impartial tribunal that can investigate and secure a change of the intolerable conditions that exist in that country where so many faithful missionaries are hampered in their work and compelled to witness suffering they are unable to relieve.

As suggested by the conference in its memorial to congress, faith has been kept with the civilized Indian tribes under the agreement by which they surrendered their tribal organization and the statehood bill under which Oklahoma comes into the Union contains a prohibition clause. The formal utterance of the conference regarding the social order and other matters in which all the churches are interested has given opportunity for counsel and action that promises to secure results that are only possible as the churches move toward.

It is impossible to estimate the influence both direct and indirect that has already followed the action of the conference. It is no exaggeration to say that this influence has been world wide in its scope and character.

In another message we shall tell the story of activities in connection with state and local federative movements that were covered by the following resolutions unanimously adopted by the conference:

1. That in pushing the frontiers of the kingdom of heaven on earth we earnestly urge all missionary bodies for work both at home and abroad that they establish methods of comity and co-operation, where they are not already begun, and in all cases carry out such methods to the fullest degree practicable.

2. That we urge upon the local churches that the same principles of comity and co-operation should be put in practice through the co-operative parish plan or similar ways of working together.

The executive committee that has in its care these most important matters would recall in all its labors the words of its chairman, Dr. Wm. H. Roberts, uttered at the close of the conference: "We recognize that the chief work of the organization we have approved is to bring salvation from sin to the lost races of man through Jesus Christ, our Divine Savior and Lord. This is our great work as churches of Christ. For this glorious end let us stand shoulder to shoulder, following him who 's the object of our supreme faith and love, at once man and God, the only begotten Son of God, the King immortal, eternal, invisible. Let his divine word of command be heard by every ear, be obeyed in every life; 'Go ye into all the world and preach the Gospel to every creature.'"

❦ ❦

HARD TO SEE

Even When the Facts About Coffee Are Plain.

It is curious how people will refuse to believe what one can clearly see.

Tell the average man or woman that the slow but cumulative poisonous effect of caffeine—the alkaloid in tea and coffee—tends to weaken the heart, upset the nervous system and cause indigestion, and they may laugh at you if they don't know the facts.

Prove it by science or by practical demonstration in the recovery of coffee drinkers from the above conditions, and a large per cent of the human family will shrug their shoulders, take some drugs' and—keep on drinking coffee or tea.

"Coffee never agreed with me nor with several members of our household," writes a lady. "It enervated, depresses and creates a feeling of languor and heaviness. It was only by leaving off coffee and using Postum that we discovered the cause and cure of these ills.

"The only reason, I am sure, why Postum is not used altogether to the exclusion of ordinary coffee is, many persons do not know and do not seem willing to learn the facts and how to prepare this nutritious beverage. There's only one way—according to directions—boil it fully 15 minutes. Then it is delicious." Name given by Postum Co., Battle Creek, Mich. Read the little book, "The Road to Wellville," in pkgs. "There's a reason."

The Christian Church i

Back in the '30s of the last century there were but seven people in St. Louis who could claim the honor of belonging to the Christian church. In the year 1837 these seven Disciples organized into a congregation and met every Lord's day. At first they met in their homes, then worshiped for two years with the Baptists, and after a time in a public schoolhouse, then in a public hall and finally in their first house of worship on

W. E. HARLOW AND HIS SON, CLYDE,
Evangelist and Singer, at Compton Heights.

the corner of Fifth and Franklin streets. The present church edifice on Locust street near Garrison avenue, is the first house of worship that was built by the First Christian Church of St. Louis. This church is the mother of several other congregations both in the city and surrounding states. Its present membership is about 900, its property is worth about $40,000 and its auditorium will seat about 1,000 people. It has been served by twenty-seven ministers during its history. John L. Brandt has been its pastor for more than five years, during which time more than 900 have been added to the membership and about the same number dismissed to serve the Lord elsewhere. Brother Brandt gathers

the largest congregations, perhaps, of any downtown minister and probably 80 per cent of his Sunday evening congregations are young people.

In 1862 the Second Church was organized. For some years past it has been under the care of W. D. Pittman. R. E. Alexander has lately entered upon the pastorate, owing to which fact the church will not participate in the simultaneous campaign.

The Fourth Church, on the corner of Penrose and Blair, was organized in 1881, with twenty-two members. It has a present membership of about 450. E. T. McFarland, the minister, will hold his own meeting, and will be assisted by an augmented choir and an orchestra.

The Hammett Place Church was organized in 1893 with thirty members. For a time the brethren met in a small hall over a saloon, but later a good piece of ground was secured and the chapel erected of an excellent church building which, it is hoped, will be built at no distant date. The present membership is about 300. During the pastorate of S. B. Moore, who has served the church for about three and a half years, the debt on the present building has been provided for. Brother Moore has just tendered his resignation but will remain with the church during the evangelistic meeting which will be conducted by C. C. Garrigues, of Albion, Ill., while W. T. W. Byrum, singer, of St. Louis, will contribute his help.

Compton Heights Church, on the corner of St. Vincent and California, was organized in 1894. It was in the spring of 1892 that the Central Christian Church decided to start a mission on the south side and begin a Sunday-school at Anchor Hall. For a time it flourished, being much aided by the faithfulness of

C. M. CHILTON,
Evangelist, Union Avenue.

C. H. ALTHEIDE,
Singer, Union Avenue.

JOHN L. BRANDT,
Pastor of the First Church.

HERBERT YEUELL,
Evangelist at First Church.

E. T. M'FARLAND,
Holding his own Meeting at the Fourth
Church.

W. F. TURNER,
Evangelist at Hamilton Avenue.

L. W. M'CREARY,
Pastor, Hamilton Avenue.

V. E. RIDENOUR,
Singer at Hamilton Avenue.

C. C. GARRIGUES,
Evangelist at Hammett Place.

S. B. MOORE,
Pastor, Hammett Place.

W. T. W. BYRUM,
Singer, Hammett Place.

Impressions of the Buffalo Conv

We asked a few of the veterans attending the convention at Buffalo to send us their impression tion with any suggestions for improvement in future conventions. We publish some of the replies this w follow:

By W. T. Moore.

In reply to your inquiry concerning my impressions of the Buffalo convention, I am free to say that the convention was great, and in some respects greater than any other convention I have ever attended. The fellowship was delightful, the speeches were nearly all good, and some of them rose to a very high level. A gratifying feature was the fact that most of these addresses were made by young men, some of them men who have never before delivered addresses at our conventions. It must be a source of gratification to the older men to find so many truly able young men coming on to take their places. Speaking for myself I can say that this was the most hopeful thing I saw in the Buffalo convention.

I have very few suggestions to make with respect to the future, and even these are more easily made on paper than they are likely to be made practical in our future conventions. Still, I believe that the changes I have to suggest would be helpful in every way, and they are certainly not impracticable, if seriously acted upon.

(1). I would make our conventions for business purposes wholly delegate meetings. While ample freedom should be given to the public generally to attend all the meetings, though, the delegates should occupy a specially appointed place in the hall and this place should be reserved for them.

(2). This would give opportunity for careful consideration and discussion of reports that may be made by the respective committees. The way these reports are at present disposed of is practically a farce, for everything is rushed through the convention without any consideration at all. I am not now even intimating that anything is passed by the convention which ought not to be passed.

It often happens that a report which everybody will agree to is the very one that ought to be emphasized by a friendly discussion. As these reports are now managed very few understand exactly what is contained in them, and nobody seems to care anything about them after they are once made. So far as I can see there is nothing really done in the convention that was not planned beforehand and adopted by the executive committee. I most sincerely believe that a little more "hastening leisurely" with the business features of our conventions would greatly improve their usefulness.

(3). There ought to be fewer set speeches. Each evening service should be set apart for hearing an address by one of the ablest men in our whole brotherhood. Those of us who pay our money to attend these conventions have a right to expect the best that can be given us in return for our sacrifice. These addresses should not be assigned to men simply for prudential reasons. In any case our editors might be allowed to have a rest for a time.

(4). Opportunity should be given to "hear from the counties." Let the people have a chance. Several symposiums might be arranged that would secure this end.

(5). A program committee should be appointed each year by the convention. We have committees on nearly every-

thing else, but the program is left to the executive committee. I say this as much for the benefit of the executive committee as for any other reason. The executive committee is blamed for the program by those who are disappointed in it because they are not on it. But for other reasons this change ought to be made.

(6). The return ticket should not be signed by the one in authority at the convention for a delegate to leave until the convention closes. After Tuesday evening the convention begins to break up and Wednesday is a day of unrest and depletion of attendance. It would be well, furthermore, to devise some plan by which sight seers should not break into the middle of the convention by going on excursions.

(7). Let there be more time given for spiritual culture. There is something in these great convocations, where the spirit has free course, that greatly augments spiritual life. Not the least value of the conventions is to be found in this fact.

Columbia, Mo.

By R. Moffett.

Forty-two years ago I had the pleasure and profit of attendance at the annual convention of the American Christian Missionary Society, held at the Eighth and Walnut Street Church in Cincinnati, and I have been present at most of the annual conventions since that time. It was the fourth year of a cruel civil war, during which nearly every fireside had felt the touch of sorrow and death. All the tender ministries of the Christian heart were in fever camps, and improvised hospitals, on brave battlefields, and in suffering prisons, and then beside the new-made grave in our own home cemetery. The mind of our brethren was not on missions. The corresponding secretary, B. W. Johnson, presented the annual report, which indicated a hard struggle for the year. About a half-dozen men had been employed at home, and about as many in Jamaica. Brother Beardslee, the chief missionary in the Jamaica field, had been called home that year. The cash income was about $7,000, and reports from three or four states swelled the total to about $30,000. Of course this is not a fair year for the campaign, but this embraced all our missionary work that year—state, home and foreign. The reports at Buffalo aggregated fully thirty times as much money, with corresponding missionary service and success. They tell us figures sometimes lie, but these figures tell a great truth, viz., that the "Disciples" have grown to be a great religious denomination—in numbers, in wealth, in character, and these together spell power.

Going back in memory to that meeting in 1864, I can call up the names of great men who were present, but who now are with Christ: A. Campbell, H. T. Anderson, L. L. Pinkerton, J. M. Henry, Love H. Jameson, George Campbell, D. S. Burnett, Aylette Rains, Robert Milligan, O. A. Burgess, Joseph King, A. I. Hobbs, J. M. Allen, A. S. Hayden, D. P. Henderson, Isaac Errett, E. Goodwin, Wm. Baxter, R. M. Bishop, H. W. Everest, W. A. Belding, Thomas Munnell, R. R. Sloan and B. W. Johnson. I do not think there were greater men at the Buffalo convention. In fact, the good men and women of each half a century simply "serve their generation,"

and serving their own they serve all the su The attendants at the are not serving their g the good men of They simply have larg does, not become one grams and plans for t his successors. If, how events and programs, the Church Extension incorporation. I wou culty in a better way, ple for union, but ever tice disintegration. O tions" are nothing bt ings. Nobody is aske gate or minister. It in liberative body. The done in the head churches, which pro think they have a rig and discussions. The know how to provid and did it well. The retaries of our missi how to set a literary f ing is the proof of th testify there were no to spoil the broth." T times.

May I suggest that convention is to be a and reunion combined, the Pittsburg meeting "camp fire", some aft admitting by ticket, convention does not any active part in s They have an oi side-half by themselv banquet.

I would have grea a hand-shake with ma and others whom I kn the convention, but no forded. Perhaps a vet remedy the matter, might be to keep the ju vention away from su wish was very often to see and hear some names have become ho

It was a great conv God and take courage. *Cleveland, O.*

By J. B.

The convention was ing points:

(1) In the harmony that prevailed there it indeed "good and pl to dwell together in have been a source of all present.

(2) In the charact livered. I do not thin standard reached in th

(3) In the reports during the year. T certainly encouraging

(4) In the determin fest on all hands to and better things for future.

I offer the followin improvements that ma

(1) By reducing th dresses. Convention p interests pertaining to prices discussed so oft they have come to gi tention to such address

been worn threadbare and their discussion in prepared speeches can no longer elicit much interest.

(2) By allowing more time for the discussion of board and committee reports. I believe that there is a very manifest and serious weakness in our convention at this point. Everything is railroaded through in a sort of perfunctory way and those who make up the bulk of the convention have no opportunity to do anything except to vote yes or no.

(3) By having as many as two warm, stirring, spiritual sermons that might be called "convention sermons." This would give opportunity for heart to heart talks that would lift us to the top of the Mount of Transfiguration, and cause us to see the glory of the Lord. Such sermons should

be delivered by men of ripe age and experience in the work of the Master.

(4) By omitting from all addresses half-concealed flings at brethren who may hold notions at variance with those entertained by the speakers.

Louisville, Ky.

By L. L. Carpenter.

The Buffalo Convention, in my judgment, was—with the exception of the jubilee convention at Cincinnati—the best one that I have ever attended. The business was well arranged, the addresses were exceedingly good. One or two speakers forgot to quit when they got through, which hurt what otherwise would have been exceedingly good speeches.

In future conventions I suggest that, how-

ever much we may be pleased with the singing, we do not take the time of the convention by encoring the singers. It is an injustice to the next speaker, as he has had just so much time allotted him, and he will have to cut his address just that much shorter. And here let me say that we could save a great deal of time, and feel a whole lot more religious, if we would say amen, when a good thing is said, and take much less time clapping our hands. We are over-doing the clapping of hands business. It has come practically to mean nothing at all in our conventions.

I suggest a little less time for addresses and more time for the discussion of the important business that should receive the careful consideration of the convention.

Wabash, Ind.

The Christian Church in St. Louis (Continued from Page 1428)

too small and was enlarged at a cost of nearly $1,000. During 1896 the foundation for a new building was put in and the effort well under way to raise the money for the building when the great cyclone came and this was one of the many churches almost destroyed. Many of the members being left homeless and some almost penniless, discouragement arose as to whether there should be a building erected on the same site, but on the Lord's day after the cyclone eighty-six members met in the midst of the ruins and with the help of the city mission board, our churches, THE CHRISTIAN-EVANGELIST and different interested brethren in and outside of St. Louis, the building was repaired and replaced at a cost of a little over $1,000. W. W. Sniff entered upon the pastorate and was followed by Sherman B. Moore and J. N. Crutcher. There was a steady growth. Part of the debt on the building was paid off by the raising of $2,000 cash and $3,500 was borrowed from the Church Extension fund. F. N. Calvin entered upon the pastorate in the fall of 1903, the present beautiful auditorium, which cost $12,454, being built just before his coming. During his pastorate the church has almost doubled its membership and every department has shown substantial growth. The building is too small to accommodate the great hive of workers. Compton Heights has been very fortunate in its ministers and is blessed with a harmonious, liberal, energetic membership. It has great opportunities in its neighborhood and there are evidences that the congregation is aware of these and determined to make itself a power for good on the south side of the city.

One of the most successful of all our evangelists, W. E. Harlow, with his son as singer, is leading the meeting.

Perhaps the wealthiest congregation is that now known as the Union Avenue Christian Church, which was formed by the combination of the Central and Mt. Cabanne churches. Central church, which met on Finney avenue, was organized in 1872 with thirteen members and had church property worth about $30,000. The Mt. Cabanne church, which had a good building on Kingshighway valued at about $28,000, was organized in 1892 with 37 members. The time came when it was felt that our cause in St. Louis needed a strong representative body, able to undertake greater tasks than any of our churches had ever attempted before, and local conditions seemed to point to a union of the Central with Mt. Cabanne as the combination that should supply this lack. James M. Philputt was called to the pastorate of the united congregation and entered upon his duties May

20, 1904. In September, a year later, Irving S. Chenoweth was called to be assistant pastor. A commodious chapel costing about $85,000 with seating capacity for 800 Sunday-school scholars was completed and entered in November, 1904. From the first there has been perfect unity and harmony and the congregation has made a record in missionary giving for the past two years. It is now a living link with three of the missionary boards and has a named loan fund with the Board of Church Extension. Plans are maturing for the completion of the main auditorium which will be one of the handsomest and most complete buildings in the brotherhood. C. M. Chilton, of this evangelistic campaign, and Chas. Altheide, of Bloomfield, Ia., has charge of the music.

Our newest church building in use is the Hamilton Avenue Christian Church, which is the outcome of a mission organized in 1894 by O. A. Bartholomew. Some account of its history was published in these columns under date of May 10, 1906. The handsome building was made possible by the liberality of Robert H. Stockton. The good result of enlargement and enterprise is seen in the growth of interest and in the large congregations that now attend the ministrations of L. W. McCreary, the present pastor. W. F. Turner, whose success at Joplin, Mo., is so favorably known, is the evangelist for this meeting and V. E. Ridenour, of Topeka, Kan., has charge of the music.

The Carondelet church, which was organized in 1897, and has been a mission church, will not be able to take part in this special effort. G. E. Ireland, who has been serving it as pastor, has resigned to become city missionary.

In the suburbs, Maplewood is the only church holding a meeting at present. Here F. A. Mayhall is pastor and E. M. Richmond is the evangelist. The church was organized in 1896 and has good property, all the indebtedness upon which was recently paid off.

Tuxedo, organized in 1895, is served by J. A. Bennett, who gives his week days to business, and Old Orchard, which is now worshiping in the building that was erected by the Christian churches on the World's Fair grounds, is proceeding quietly under the ministrations of R. L. Wilson. These two churches are unable at the present time to join in the campaign. The same is true of the newly established church at Landsdown, East St. Louis, where C. O. Reynard is trying to build up the cause. Our church at East St. Louis, however, under the leadership of Henry E. Jones, will participate, with E. A. Gilli-

land as the evangelist, and in about a week's time, or as soon as they can get their new building completed the little band at Granite City will fall into line with J. M. Hoffmann as the evangelist. G. A. Hoffmann has been giving his time to the work here for many weeks past. There are four towns contiguous to each other which will soon form one city. The present population is about 75,000. The church at Granite City has passed through sore trials, but during Brother Hoffmann's year of service the membership has grown from 88 to 112. The new church which is of concrete will, when completed, cost about $8,000.

The Campaign in St. Louis.

The simultaneous campaign in St. Louis has begun auspiciously. The First Church, where Brother Yeuell led off a week in advance of the others, has reported 40 additions up till last Sunday night, ten of them by letter and the others by confession and baptism. Most of the other churches began their evangelistic services last Lord's day, and at the ministers' meeting on Monday morning the reports were as follows: Compton Heights, four by confession, six by letter; Hamilton Avenue, eight by confession, two by letter; Fourth, one by confession, one by letter; Maplewood, four by confession, four by letter or statement; Union Avenue, five by confession, three by letter; East St. Louis, two by confession, two by letter; Hammett Place, two by letter. The Second Church, which is not holding special services, reported three by confession and two by letter. Several of the churches were without their special evangelists, these arriving in the city on Monday morning.

At the meeting of the ministers and evangelists engaged, which was held at the Christian Publishing Company's offices on Monday morning, plans for concerted action were discussed and it was agreed that a mass meeting should be called to be held at the First Church on Locust street near Garrison avenue, on Thursday morning of this week at 10:30, when there will be an interesting program rendered by the evangelists and singers in the campaign, and at which reports from several committees appointed to investigate the question of advertising and the holding of a great down-town union meeting will be considered. It is hoped that the members of the churches in the city will assemble in large numbers on Thursday morning of this week at the First Church. The meeting will last but one hour.

The Indiana State-Wide Campaign.

Brethren: The elections will be over November 6, and the state-wide simultaneous campaign will settle down to business. Don't fail to report daily by postal card, progress of meetings, so that the whole state may have benefit of the press reports.—T. J. Legg, state evangelist, 1402 Pleasant street, Indianapolis, Ind.

New Church to be dedicated soon at Granite City.

G. E. IRELAND,
City Missionary.

IRVING S. CHENOWETH,
Assistant Pastor, Union Ave.

J. M. HOFFMANN,   F. A. MAYHALL,
Evangelist, Granite City.   Pastor, Maplewood.

Hammett Place Church.
Only the Chapel has Been Completed.

Maplewood Christian Church.

Foreign Missionary Rallies.

The Foreign Christian Missionary Society' is planning the most comprehensive campaign of missionary rallies for this fall and winter, yet undertaken. Three months will be spent in this work, and the brotherhood will be covered as far as possible from New York to Texas and from Michigan to Alabama. A. McLean, Secretary Stephen J. Corey, Dr. Elliott I. Osgood, of China, and David Rioch, of India, will conduct the campaign. Several leading pastors will assist. The following is a list of the rallies to be held before the month ends:

November 19—Ashland, Ky., W. D. Ryan, pastor.

November 20—Paris, Ky., Carey E. Morgan, pastor.

November 21, Danville, Ky., H. C. Garrison, pastor.

November 22—Knoxville, Tenn., Robt. Stewart, pastor.

November 23—Kimberlin Heights, Tenn.

November 25—Chattanooga, Tenn.—P. M. Rally, pastor.

November 26—Atlanta, Ga., H. K. Pendleton, pastor.

November 26—Birmingham, Ala.—A. R. Moore, pastor.

November 27—Nashville, Tenn., R. L. Cave, pastor.

November 28—Memphis, Tenn., W. H. Shefer, pastor.

November 30—Hopkinsville, Ky., H. D. Smith, pastor.

Ministerial Exchange.

Churches needing a minister to begin work the first of next year should address James F. King, R. R. 2, box 75, Albion, Ill. Recommendations will be furnished.

Miss Helen C. Shoecraft, singing evangelist, Emporia, Kan., may be secured for a meeting in December.

E. W. Brickert, Sullivan, Ind., would be glad to hold one evangelistic meeting this fall and a couple next spring or early winter. He has held meetings in many states and has been richly blessed.

J. J. Cole, Galt House, Cincinnati, O., is open for engagements to hold meetings or, for regular employment.

M. F. Redlien, 300 Hall Bldg., Kansas City, Mo., is ready to hold meetings during fall and winter.

O. J. Young, evangelist and C. M. Hughes, singer, Valley View, Ky., are ready to make engagements for meetings.

Churches, or evangelists needing a singer to help in revival meetings can obtain the services of J. Ross Miller for December and January. His address is box 86, Gas City, Ind.

Miss Mayme Eisenbarger, Bethany, Mo., will be open for engagements as gospel singer after November 1.

Any church desiring a pastor of experience can be put in communication with one by addressing Evangelist Samuel Gregg, Jefferson, Ia.

Harold E. Monser wants a good pastor with a wife who is a good worker among women. Preacher must be a fair speaker and have patience. Salary, $600 to $850. Address, Findley, Ill.

The church at Rushville, Ia., has some good pews for sale. They are finished in walnut and there is a sufficient number of them to seat over 300 people. Address Walter E. Harmon, pastor.

Paul McReynolds, formerly of Illinois, but latterly of California and North Carolina, is now located at Marissa, Ill., as editor of a reform paper entitled "Uncle Sam," and is open for lectures and Sunday preaching.

S. J. Vance can now make engagements for meetings with or without a singer. Address Carthage, Mo.

D. G. Wagoner reports that the church at Chester, Neb., is a fine opening for some young married man. They pay a good salary and it is a healthy climate. Address R. L. Wilson, elder.

The Christian Church at Lake Charles is desirous of securing the services of a preacher. The church is able to pay about $75 per month, with the free use of a parsonage. For particulars address Henry B. Kane, chairman of board, Lake Charles, La.

"We are in need of a competent music teacher here. We desire to communicate with some Christian woman of experience, one who is willing to become a companion to my daughter, and live with us during the winter. I have just lost my wife and desire that my daughter study music at home. We can work up a large class for the right kind of an instructor. We would also expect the one who accepts the position to lead our church music."—R. S. Robertson, pastor Christian Church, Osborne, Kan.

Our Budget

—St. Louis simultaneous evangelistic campaign now on.

—Other campaigns in progress throughout the country. Success to them all!

—We are receiving many commendatory letters about our report of the Buffalo convention. We are glad to know that our efforts to adequately report the most important events in the brotherhood are appreciated.

—Geo. B. Van Arsdall will remain with the church at Cedar Rapids, Ia., notwithstanding the temptation to go to Des Moines to succeed Brother Breeden. They seem to have formed a sort of love-match at Cedar Rapids, that is not easy to break up.

—We regret to learn of the death of Carl Rash, son of Howard C. Rash, Salina, Kan., at Las Vegas, N. M., on October 29. Our sympathies are extended to the bereaved family.

—It was a large and enthusiastic gathering of ministers that assembled at the assembly room of the Christian Publishing Company on Monday morning last, reported results of the first day of simultaneous meetings, and discussed ways and means of advancing the success of same. At the close, after prayer and the benediction, and while they were greeting one another they were called to order by the chairman to listen to a number of telegrams received by THE CHRISTIAN-EVANGELIST, reporting success of meetings in Kansas City, Indianapolis, Lexington and other places, which were read by the Assistant Editor. The ministers then sang, "Praise God from Whom All Blessings Flow," with great zest, and separated with thankful hearts. ✧ ✧ ✧

—A. L. West, late of Carlinsville, has begun work at Mt. Vernon, Ill.

—A speaker recently said the right sort of personal consecration is spelled "purse-and-all" consecration.

—F. M. McCarthy, of Monroe, La., has been called to the church at Leesville, and is now actively at work there.

—Many improvements have just been made in the church building at Dinuba, Cal., where R. A. Staley ministers.

—The future for the Second Christian church at Houston, Texas, where F. B. Scrimshen is minister, seems very bright.

—The church at Girard, Ill., has called P. F. York, of Bloomington, to the pastorate and he has entered upon his duties.

—A new building at Marcus, Ia., where William Baier ministers, is to be dedicated this month. It is an $8,000 building.

—W. E. Bates has just closed his ministry at Hope, Kan., and enters at once upon the pastorate at Thomas, Okla.

—W. P. Murray has closed a three years' pastorate at Southington, O., and is now at work in his new field at Lucas, Ohio.

—The church at Roseville, Ill., has secured the services of J. M. Clemens, of Waverly, who will begin his new pastorate January 1.

—Thomas L. Cooksey made a brief call at THE CHRISTIAN-EVANGELIST office on his way to take part in the evangelistic campaign at Indianapolis.

—J. P. Furnish, ministers successfully to the brethren at Newark, Mo. A meeting just closed there by C. F. Rose, of Canton, will probably lead to a new church building.

—Clifford A. Cole has returned to his native state in going to the strong church at Abilene, Kan., where he has just entered upon the pastorate.

—It is hoped to have a fine building at Hawesville, Ky., by the early spring. Brother Self, the assistant minister of the church at Owensboro, preaches there once a month.

—W. T. Adams has recently closed a three years' pastorate at Waitsburg, Wash., and anticipates good results from his labors at Corona, Cal., upon whose pastorate he has just entered.

—"The Man with the Shovel, or Who Cares for the Stoker?" is the striking title of a sermon which we note on the church leaflet of the First Christian church, Pomona, Cal., of which M. A. Hart is pastor.

—Lee Tinsley has removed to Franklin, Ind., where he is dividing his time between the Union, four and one-half miles from there, and his recent church at Nineveh. He is taking this country work in order to benefit his health.

Miss Martha Stout.

The Missouri Superintendent of Juniors who won the C. W. B. M. National Banner at Buffalo.

—Work on the new building at Mayfield, Ky., has begun. The only charter member left, old Brother Thomas, was the first to use the spade. Roger L. Clark, the minister, is earnest in the work and leading it steadily to success.

—H. H. Shick, of Winfield, Kan., is to hold a meeting in Kaw City, Okla. Brother Shick has faith in the mission of good religious literature and will bring to his aid 300 copies weekly of THE CHRISTIAN-EVANGELIST.

—O. Wilkinson, after three months' vacation, has returned to Ukiah, Cal., and has found all the work in good condition. The brethren, he writes, are very active. They certainly have been treating Brother Wilkinson as he deserves.

—The church at Holliday, Mo., which is under the charge of Rolla G. Sears, is one of the best missionary churches in the state; contributing to all the societies. They also made themselves a life member in the permanent fund of Missouri.

—His own brother and his wife were among the converts in the meeting just held by F. W. Burnham at Chapin, Ill. Brother Burnham, of course, is now pastor of the Central church at Decatur, but Chapin is his native home and boyhood church.

—We are glad to announce to the friends of THE CHRISTIAN-EVANGELIST that Andrew J. Jones, of Enid, Okla., is representing the Christian Publishing Company in that great southwestern state and we commend him to the brotherhood there.

—Dr. J. B. Herbert, a song and anthem writer of international renown, spent several days with W. E. M. Hackleman at Lincoln, Ill., and assisted in the evangelistic services now being held at the First Christian Church by William J. Lockhart.

—J. Will Waters sends us a note of very cordial commendation of Charles E. McVay, singer and helper. Forty have been added to the church at Niantic, Ill., since Brother Walters began there last March. He can probably conduct one meeting during this or next month.

—C. B. Allison writes enthusiastically of the brethren worshiping at the Frederick Avenue Church, St. Joseph, Mo., where he has concluded a good meeting. He believes that this conservative community must ultimately feel the force of the faithful, fearless band in their midst.

—Harry E. Tucker's meeting at Excelsior Springs, Mo., was cut short on account of a message received by him announcing that his wife had typhoid fever. On account of his work at Platte City, Mo., he has been unable to accept no less than seven invitations to hold revivals this fall.

—We have received the following communication unsigned. "Please send my CHRISTIAN-EVANGELIST to Canton, Mo., as I am here now to attend Christian University." Will the Canton student who wrote this under date of October 17 please send his name and he will receive his CHRISTIAN-EVANGELIST.

—The Calhoun Street Church of Christ, Charleston, S. C., has pledged $1,700 on the $1,900 due to the Church Extension Board for the church lot. Enough cash was raised to take up the first note and the pastor, Marcellus R. Ely, writes us that it is expected the whole amount will be raised by June 1, 1907.

—R. R. Hamlin, of Fort Worth, probably holds the record for successful meetings held in Texas the past year. Brother Hamlin, assisted by Leonard Daugherty, of Louisville, Ky., began a meeting on Lord's day for the church at Nevada, Mo. These two evangelists can be had for winter meetings in the north or middle states.

—A note from Claude E. Hill explains that he was unable to write an account of the Christian Endeavor session at the Buffalo convention because the flesh was weak. He contracted a severe cold but is now at home again and hopes to be able soon to take up the active work incidental to the superintendency of our national Christian Endeavor work.

—J. H. O. Smith has been holding a good meeting at Billings, Mont. He has expressed himself as much pleased by the pluck, energy and courage manifested by the church there in its careful, thoroughgoing preparation. This is the church which the Editor of THE CHRISTIAN-EVANGELIST dedicated on his return last summer from the San Francisco convention.

Two Popular Songs.

Two of the most popular songs sung at Buffalo convention, by the Netz Sisters were "Were You There When They Crucified My Lord?" and "That Beautiful Land," both of which were arranged by W. E. M. Hackleman. The former is published in Concert Quartettes and the latter in Sacred Quartettes, by the Hackleman Music Co., Indianapolis.

—A new church has recently been built by the brethren at Lucerne, Mo. The $1,100 which it cost was all raised by subscription with the exception of $200 which Brother Abbott secured on dedication day. J. P. Noland writes us that Brother McKinley and Brother Blunt have just closed a good meeting there, when there were 39 additions to the membership. This leaves the church with very bright prospects for the coming year.

—Percy G. Cross has been holding a meeting where there has been no preaching for over a year. The population of Prescott, Ark., where he has just been, is over 3,200 and shows what a wide scope there is for establishing our cause, for there are hundreds of cities just as large where there is no Christian church. Brother Cross writes that he expects to secure a preacher for Prescott. The total number of baptisms he had during the past year was 122, not 112 as recently reported.

—H. E. Van Horn, who has taken charge of the East Side Church, Des Moines, Ia., finds it a promising field and reports accessions every Lord's day. "We hope that we will not lose a single number of THE CHRISTIAN-EVANGELIST." We hope he will not. The supply of our convention report issue was quickly ex-

hausted. So great is the demand that we can not supply a single copy of last week's issue. Brethren, preserve your CHRISTIAN-EVANGELISTS, or you will have to borrow from your neighbor.

—S. M. Martin has just held an excellent meeting at Ashland, Ore., when many persons listened to our plea for the first time. Members of the "CHRISTIAN-EVANGELIST Special" party who journeyed together from San Francisco to Portland will remember the beautiful situation and the fine fruit grown at Ashland. To W. L. Mellinger, pastor of the church there, should be given no little credit for the success of the meeting.

—Ona Jewyl Green, Ark., likens prayer to a telephonic communication with heaven. The wire should be "double-stranded, made of faith and love, and upheld by everlasting poles of good works. Make the message clear and plain and each and every one will be received." "Sometimes the wires are right but the poles are lacking." See that your connection with heaven is made secure and strong.

—A site for a new building needed for the growing suburb of Lindenwald, Hamilton, O., has been secured and at the second anniversary celebration of W. H. Hedges, the present minister, pledges were taken which clears off the present indebtedness. During the past year there were 109 additions, the membership a year ago being only forty-one. The Sunday-school shows an increase from 58 to 158, and about $2,000 was raised for all purposes during the year, $110 for missions.

—The local paper at Paxton, Ill., prints an account of a meeting recently held at Mt. Olivet church near Paxton by S. Elwood Fisher, who is pastor at Fisher, Ill. It speaks very highly of both the evangelist and Lewis G. Fisher, who is pastor of the church. The latter had been planning and working for the meeting since the beginning of the year and had all things in readiness for the evangelist. There were thirteen additions to the membership, which was strengthened for better work and knit closer together.

—On account of the serious illness of his wife, Leander Lane has closed a two years' pastorate at Santa Ana, Cal. During this time there were 188 additions to the church, 70 of them being by primary obedience. All departments have prospered and a new building has been planned for. Brother Lane and his family have sought a higher altitude and have been staying twelve miles north of Los Angeles at La Canada. His church very generously sent him a free-will offering of about $150. He is now in a position to accept another pastorate or to hold meetings.

—For several years past T. R. Hodkinson has been holding country pastorates in order that he might have time to prepare a book for the press. Brother Hodkinson is now ready to give all his time to some field having a wider outlook. While he is considerably past the period sometimes called the dead line, he is as vigorous in the Lord's work as he ever was and has the great advantage of much added knowledge and experience. He is, by no means, the kind of man whom we could afford to put "on the shelf." We trust some good church will at once get into correspondence with him at Palmyra, Ill.

—W. M. Stuckey, of Lebo, Kan., has just been holding a short meeting at Williamsburg, in the same state, and reports that not a family at that place was reading any of our church papers, which he says is a "deplorable state for any church to be in." He got the promise of

—The First Christian Church at Seattle, Wash., had just met to celebrate its financial independence and to burn the mortgage, but upon the advice of the Board of Church Extension the brethren did not burn the mortgage, but, as a substitute ceremony raised $1,000 as first payment on a new pipe organ which they hope to have installed in the spring. A. L. Chapman is the pastor and since the first of September, a year ago, 190 members have been received into fellowship, $1,000 spent on local debts and improvements, the pastor's salary increased $500, all current expenses met and over $2,700 paid on the building. The church is united, working and happy.

—F. F. Walters has accepted a call to the Central church, Springfield, Mo., opening his work there November 18, thus entering upon a larger and more active field. Brother Walters has nothing but good words and well wishes for the people at Neosho, which will now need a good pastor. This is a beautiful little town with 250 members in our church, over 100 of whom were added during Brother Walters' year of service. The greatest need is a new building, the present one being out of date. If that could be provided and a devoted pastor secured the church at Neosho would come into line with the progressive churches of this great state. O. F. Brockman is chairman of the board.

—We regret to report the death of Isaac H. Shaver, one of the best known pioneers of Cedar Rapids, Ia. He was a man who deserved in the highest sense the term well-beloved. Self-made, he took delight in doing good whenever he had opportunity, working in the Christian church which he loved so much. He always had a tender sympathy for the poor and many of them were the recipients of his benefactions. He was an earnest lover of his fellow men and zealously sought to promote their welfare by reducing intemperance, by promoting Christian education and by assisting in the distribution of the Scriptures. He loved the unity of the Church of Christ and yearned for and did all he could to hasten the coming of the better age. Brother Shaver was born in Sussex county, N. J., in 1825.

✸ ✸

AFTER MANY DAYS.
Cured with Five Bottles of Drake's Palmetto Wine, Costing $3.75.

Mrs. B. W. Smith, Maloy, Iowa, says: "Three doses of Drake's Palmetto Wine gave me the first relief from two years of constant Stomach distress. Five 75-cent bottles have cured me. The best doctors and largely advertised medicines utterly failed to give me any relief. I can now eat any wholesome food and have gained 20 pounds weight in three months. Our druggist sold nine bottles of Drake's Palmetto Wine one day to my friends who know what it has done for me. I am recommending it to all who suffer." The Drake Co., 314 Drake, Bldg., Wheeling, W. Va., will send a test bottle of Drake's Palmetto Wine free and prepaid to any one who suffers with Stomach Trouble or Constipation. One small dose a day gives prompt relief and cures to stay cured. For sale by all druggists.

—C. W. Mahin has had a good meeting at Angola, Ind., where there is a faithful and intelligent band of our brethren. Brother Mahin's record during the past years is a good one. Out of ten meetings held only three were at places where there were pastors or even regular preaching. Some of the churches had only a dozen members; and none of them had more than 150. The record of work accomplished shows three churches organized, pastors settled in seven churches, money pledged for all or a portion of the time, 200 additions—nearly all of them by baptism, and every church left in a healthy, united condition. Brother Mahin and his wife are now in a meeting at North Vernon.

—We are glad to know that J. J. Morgan, of Kansas City, Mo., has sufficiently recovered from a very serious illness, which kept him from his pastorate for some months, to enter upon a meeting with J. H. O. Smith as evangelist.

J. J. Morgan.

Howard Saxton as singer. The meeting began on Lord's day in the South Prospect Christian Church, Kansas City, Mo. With such a combination as the leadership of Brother Morgan, the strong preaching of Brother Smith, and Howard Saxton's musical ability, we look for another great meeting to follow the one that has just been completed and the other that is still in process in this go-ahead city on the big Missouri.

—M. M. Davis has just celebrated his sixteenth anniversary with the church at Dallas, Texas. During the past year there were 225 additions, over $8,100 raised, about half of which was spent for mission schools and benevolences. Brother Davis' work has been a very useful one, as will be seen from the following statistics: During the sixteen years he preached 2,212 sermons, had 3,143 additions to the church, and the money raised, amounted to $193,128.55. During these years five other congregations have been organized in Dallas and the organization of the sixth is under way. In 1890 when Brother Davis entered upon his present field of work there was but one congregation. It was during his pastorate that the present church edifice, costing $65,500, was erected. On his recent anniversary, to which we were invited, a sermon was preached giving a history of the pastorate and an outline of the work for the seventeenth year.

—H. C. Kendrick began his ministry at Georgetown, Ky., on the first Sunday in November. Brother Kendrick has written a pastoral letter to the members of the church which he goes to serve. We wish we had space to quote all of it. "I am coming to be your helper," he says. "I shall endeavor to inspire you with new courage for the daily battle, and seek to make you stronger for the wear of character that modern business necessitates. I hope to make this life of earth for you sublime by bringing to bear upon it the motives and sanctions of eternity. I shall study to so conduct

the services in the Lord's house that each of you may return from them with a feeling that in spite of the down dragging influences that are depressing you, there is something worth living for after all. Above all, I shall endeavor to get Christ before your eyes as the great helper and healer of men, the good Samaritan of humanity, who comes at the hour of our extremity with his tender sympathy and his ready assistance." This is a noble aim and we have no doubt that Brother Kendrick will do much to bring it into realization in the lives of the flock at Georgetown. The brethren at Hagerstown have treated him in a most noble way.

Board of Ministerial Relief of the Church of Christ.

Aid in the support of worthy, needy, disabled ministers of the Christian Church and their widows.

THIRD LORD'S DAY IN DECEMBER is the day set apart in all the churches for the offering to this work. If you make individual offerings, send direct to the Board. Wills and Deeds should be made to "BOARD OF MINISTERIAL RELIEF OF THE CHURCH OF CHRIST, a corporation under the laws of the State of Indiana." Money received on the Annuity Plan.

Address all communications and make all checks, drafts, etc., payable to BOARD OF MINISTERIAL RELIEF, 120 E. Market St., Indianapolis, Ind.

DR. J. W. BLOSSER,

Who sends by mail a free trial package of his Catarrh Cure to applicants.

It will cost you only a postal card (or two cent stamp) to get a liberal free trial package of this wonderful remedy. He will pay for everything, delivery charges and all. No offer could be more liberal than this, but he has such confidence in the remedy that he is willing to submit it to an actual test.

If you have catarrh of the nose, throat or lungs, if you are constantly spitting, blowing the nose, have stopped-up feeling, headache, head noises, deafness, asthma, bronchitis or weak lungs, write at once for a trial treatment, then you will soon know its effect for yourself. The full treatment is not expensive. A regular package containing enough to last one whole month is sent by mail for $1.00.

A postal card with your name and address, sent to Dr. J. W. Blosser, 475 Walton St., Atlanta, Ga., will bring you the free treatment and an interesting booklet about catarrh.

—R. O. Rogers, at Fredericktown, Mo., is with the brethren at Marshall, Ark., for a two weeks' meeting. W. T. Mills writes us that there is a great interest manifest, and as Brother Mills never fails to draw large audiences, there is nothing to hinder a religious awakening in Marshall. A great revival is expected.

—F. M. Rains made a big jump in going from Buffalo out to Los Angeles, where he has dedicated the handsome new Sunday-school room of the First Christian Church of that city. Brother Rains says it is the best in the brotherhood, and has nearly forty rooms. Last Lord's day he was to dedicate the new church at Kansas City, where S. W. Nay is pastor. While in California Brother Rains enjoyed a great missionary meeting with the church at Pomona, where M. A. Hart, late of Fulton, Mo., is doing a fine work.

—Herbert H. Saunders writes that a sentence in one of our evangelistic reports may be misleading. In his meeting at Union Star, Mo., he stayed to close the meeting on Monday and to baptize eighteen of the twenty confessions from Sunday night's service and three more who accepted Christ at the service on Monday morning.

—We have received many compliments on the thoroughness and the speed with which we have reported the convention for the benefit of THE CHRISTIAN-EVANGELIST readers. Although the other papers which may lay claim to covering the national field have this year given larger space than for several years to the convention, THE CHRISTIAN-EVANGELIST leads these by many columns in the space given to what is the most important meeting held by the Christian churches every year. Column for column, we have published as much as all the other papers put together, and we have not yet completed our report.

—We desire to call special attention to the advertisement of our Foreign Christian Missionary Society which appears opposite our Centennial page. This speaks of a special fund known as the Centennial Fund, which it is proposed to raise for the purpose of erecting buildings and thoroughly equipping them for the work in the foreign field. Read the advertisement, and regard it not as such but as a statement of an attempt to meet a condition that ought not to exist in a great brotherhood that has such a good opinion of itself and that is so easily able to supply a quarter of a million dollars for this special purpose, if it will but give serious thought to such an enterprise.

AS WE GO TO PRESS.

Special to THE CHRISTIAN-EVANGELIST.
Cincinnati, O., November 5—Brother Wharton, of India, dead; cablegram just received.—S. J. Corey.

Special to THE CHRISTIAN-EVANGELIST.
Lexington, Ky., November 4—Eighty-one added in twelve days in the Central Church meeting; thirty-eight came today. Brooks brothers are the evangelists.—I. J. Spencer, minister.

Special to THE CHRISTIAN-EVANGELIST.
Indianapolis, Ind., November 5—Twenty-seven yesterday, sixty in eight days—forty-four adults. Great audiences to hear Abberley and Mrs. Powell at Central church.—Allan B. Philputt.

Special to THE CHRISTIAN-EVANGELIST.
Kansas City, Mo., November 5—Meeting two weeks in continuance; 136 accessions; thirty to-day; immense audiences. Small and St. John have captured us completely. A truly great meeting is on.—George Hamilton Combs.

Special to THE CHRISTIAN-EVANGELIST.
Hamburg, Ia., November 4—Glorious meeting here; forty additions in fourteen days. Isaac Elder is the pastor of a great church. J. E. Lintt, singer. Through a misunderstanding we have November 22 open. What church wants us?—W. L. Harris, evangelist.

Special to THE CHRISTIAN-EVANGELIST.
Indianapolis, Ind., November 25.— At Sullivan, Ill., 755 conversions. Fifty-

seven here yesterday with Third church, Brother Newnan, pastor. Armory 100x 120 feet, yet overflow service filled church. Also 120 additions in eight days. Smith and Kendall, singers; 4,416 added so far this year.—Charles R. Scoville.

Special to THE CHRISTIAN-EVANGELIST.
Indianapolis, Ind., November 5—One hundred and fifty-eight additions on Lord's day in simultaneous campaign in Indianapolis—three hundred and thirty-four to date. Crowded houses throughout the city last night and many turned away. Z. T. Sweeney spoke to 4,000 in the afternoon on "The Peculiarity of the Disciples of Christ." Hundreds were turned away even before the hour for beginning. Splendid outlook all along the line.—F. W. Norton.

West Virginia Campaign.

Reports of the simultaneous revival issued on Friday last indicate the average attendance of 101 at sixteen different churches. The total additions at that time numbered 188. Below will be found a telegram giving later figures. The church having the largest number of additions is Wheeling First where 77 have been added. Huntington follows with twenty-two added. Wheeling Island has received thirteen to its number. Pine Grove twelve, Parkersburg four, New Cumberland four, Follansgee four, Williamson two, Mount Hope three, and Sistersville one. Hallowe'en and the political excitement have interfered this week with the meetings. All the churches, however, report a growing interest and much good done even where there have not been additions to the church. Brother Hanes, of the West Virginia Division who is acting as our special correspondent, believes that this movement has done a great deal of good towards the organized work of the state.

Special to THE CHRISTIAN-EVANGELIST.
Parkersburg, W. Va., November 5.— Latest reports from fourteen churches indicate an average attendance of 200, and forty-two more additions, making the total 230 added in this campaign.— B. E. Hanes.

Home Study College Courses,

leading to degrees. History, Evidences, Science, Languages, the Bible and sacred Literature. Over a thousand students enrolled. Full particulars free. Write Pres. Chas. J. Burton, Christian College, Oskaloosa, Iowa.

NEWS FROM MANY FIELDS

Good Work at Kirksville, Mo.

An excellent meeting was recently concluded at Kirksville, where Bruce Brown, of Mansfield, Ohio, assisted D. A. Wickizer. In three weeks there were 110 additions. Bruce Brown is known as an earnest gospel preacher without sensational

D. A. Wickizer.

methods, and he left the church strengthened in every way. Brother Wickizer has been with this congregation just fourteen months, and has found many faithful and earnest workers in its fold. The membership is now over 800, over 170 additions having been won in regular services since

Christian Church at Kirksville, Mo.

the present pastor took charge. With this meeting the record stands 280 additions in fourteen months. During this time over $3,200 was raised, $560 being given to missions. The church has just been arranging to have the building heated with hot water from the city heating plant.

New York and New Jersey.

The Disciples' Union of New York City held a mass meeting in the 56th Street church recently, the purpose being to bring the churches of Greater New York into line with our Centennial celebration. Brother Tharp, of Allegheny, came as our speaker and brought a most helpful message calculated to fire our hearts and enthuse us with greater zeal in the Master's service. Despite the terrific rain which continued most of the day, we had, I am told, the largest audience, save one, ever assembled by the Disciples' Union in this city. We think that this rally has done much to bring this extreme eastern district into touch, sympathy and co-operation with this, the greatest concerted effort ever made by our brotherhood.

Brother Rounds, of Crafton, Pa., has just been called to Flatbush, Brooklyn, and took up his new work October 21.

M. E. Harlan, of Sterling Place, Brooklyn, has been forced to resign on account of ill health, and thus another good church needs a pastor.

We are just located in our new field, and are well pleased with the people, place and general outlook. Miner Lee Bates is a good man to follow; the church is in splendid condition. Will any of our brethren knowing of Disciples coming into the territory of Greater New York, kindly send the address to me? I should also be grateful for information regarding any coming into New Jersey. Aside from our church here and a few brethren in Plainfield, there is not another organization of our people in the entire state. This ought not to be. Such information as I have requested, if sent to the pastors in our great centers, would tend to stop a large leakage from our brotherhood. L. N. D. Wells.
150 N. 15th St., E. Orange.

Another Field Man.

It is with much pleasure that I announce that W. S. St. Clair, of Columbia, Mo., has been engaged by the Missouri Christian Bible School Association as field man for North Missouri. He will enter actively upon the work in a short time. It is believed that Brother St. Clair possess qualifications of a very high order for the work to which he has been appointed. Let our ministers and superintendents co-operate with him, in order that he may accomplish worthy things for the Lord's cause. Address him at Columbia.
J. H. Hardin, State Supt.
311 Century Bldg., Kansas City, Mo.

Notes from Georgia's State Secretary.

Welcome to THE CHRISTIAN-EVANGELIST into Georgia. We shall miss our little home paper, but we shall soon become attached to the sweet-spirited, vigorous evangelist which will now visit us every week.

Our state convention is at hand. It meets in Valdosta, Nov. 19-22. Let every church send one or more delegates and let every preacher of the state be present. Reduced rates over the railroads have been secured. Buy your ticket at full price going and get a certificate from the agent. Get this certificate signed in Valdosta by the secretary, and you will get your return ticket at one-third rate. Two things remember: 1st. Get your certificate where you start. 2nd. Get it signed in convention at Valdosta.

Our program for the convention is good from start to finish. Monday night and Tuesday morning Brothers A. McLean and Dr. Osgood will have charge, and conduct a missionary rally. No one should miss this. Every delegate should go on Monday and stay till Thursday night. Let us all pray for the convention and go to it to see our prayers answered.

If any church has not yet taken the offering for Georgia missions, take it next Sunday and send to me or Dr. C. C. Stockard, 275 Capitol Ave., Atlanta, Ga. Our reports must go to the printer by Nov. 15, and all offerings should be in by that time.

Meet me at Valdosta November 19.
Bernard F. Smith, Sec. G. C. M. S.
P. S.—Don't fail to send me a report from your church.

A Meeting at Waynesville, Ill.

J. A. Barnett, who has closed a successful pastorate of nearly three years with the church at Pekin, Ill., has just begun, before entering upon his new pastorate at Freeport in December, a

J. A. Barnett.

special meeting with the church at Waynesville, Ill., where J. F. Smith is minister. The church considers itself fortunate in securing the services of one who is personally known to a large number of people in the community, and whose ability and successes assure the brethren of a treat of good things in a spiritual way. Brother Barnett is not only a forceful speaker and a fearless teacher of the truth, but he has the saving quality of not abusing people because they differ from him. During his ministry at Pekin there were 150 additions to the church, 70 of these being added in a revival which he himself conducted in February, 1905.

Although comparatively new in the field, Miss Manie B. Bowles, who is to help in this meeting, has had remarkable success as a singing evangelist. She is a musician of rare ability, having taken a lengthy course in a well known conservatory; but she decided to use her talents in singing the gospel. Her voice is a soprano of remarkable sweetness and power. Her last engagement was in a meeting with Evangelist Shearer at Heyworth, while she has twice assisted Brother Barnett in meetings that resulted in many additions. The church will be assisted in this evangelistic effort with copies of THE CHRISTIAN-EVANGELIST.

Columbia (Mo.) Bible College.

All the last year ministerial and missionary students have returned except Dr. Jennie Fleming, who has gone to Harda, India, with Dr. and Mrs. Drummond.——The new students are getting into regular places to preach.——On a recent Lord's Day four ministerial students reported fifteen additions.——Dr. Moore will soon begin a series of special lectures to the students.——Any church needing a preacher, within one hundred miles of Columbia, can be put in correspondence with a suitable one by writing me. It is a significant fact that all churches who are using student preachers are succeeding.——We are in correspondence with men of experience and ability, who will come to school if suitable churches can be found.   C. E. Burgess.

Louisiana.

Please allow me to congratulate and thank you for the splendid issue of October 11. It is just brim full of valuable information. I feel it is worth many times the subscription price of The Christian-Evangelist.——Our work in the Pelican state is moving on slowly but surely, and permanently. We have lost one valuable worker, G. W. Wise, of Leesville, who has gone to Illinois. George did a good work and our prayers go with him.——Brother Taylor is getting into his work nicely with the Soniat avenue Church in New Orleans. We hear many good things said of his work. We look for great things from Soniat Church, with a live church and a live minister generally make things move.——H. M. Polsgrove closed his first year at Jennings with very gratifying results, and starts on his second year full of hope. Brother Polsgrove is a strong man and full of the spirit. So look for a great work at Jennings.——O. L. Hawkins, of Crowley, has done a wonderful work considering the time he has been with the church. Otis is a live man and has message fresh from the Book.——L. A. Betcher and his estimable wife are the Sunday school powers in Louisiana. They not only go out and hunt up the children and bring them into Sunday-school, but they carry them on into the church and then lead them on in usefulness. In fact, they get them started and never allow them to stop.——F. M. McCarthey is bishop of Monroe and Ruston. He is doing a work as only an Irishman can, dividing time between two of the most important towns of North Louisiana.——

Roy Linten Porter and the Lake Charles Church are up on the firing line. Brother Porter preaches, visits the sick and edits the "Louisiana Christian" and, always finds time to meet his friends and never complains.——Claude L. Jones, of Shreveport, is a fixture. Shreveport would never be the same should Brother Jones leave. He is leading in every good work, both in and out of the church.——John A. Stevens and wife are preaching in the wilderness, writing letters, baptizing men and women, and building churches.——The work at Hammond is moving on smoothly. We are all working and praying and paying to get our church out of debt on Thanksgiving day, so it will be a real thanksgiving to us all. Then the money can go on to other fields to build houses for struggling bands of brethren who have no house.——Hammond is on a building boom. Men who have retired from active life in the North are building homes in Hammond.

Hammond, La.   Frank Lanehart.

Montana.

Our work in Montana has been organized for over twenty-six years. It dates from a meeting held by three of the leading brethren of the state, in the law office of Mossena Bullard in Helena. The progress of the work since that time has been hindered considerably by such cause as the terrible panic of 1893, but considering the many difficulties, Montana is able to make an excellent showing. The state is a mission field of the C. W. B. M., which organization is now supporting F. H. Groom as state evangelist. It is through the loyalty of the C. W. B. M. that the cause has been planted in such important cities as Butte, Helena, Anaconda, Missoula, Great Falls and Billings. The church at Corvallis, in the Bitter Root Valley, is the oldest in the state. Bozeman, Butte and Missoula churches are memorials, built by the various departments of the C. W. B. M., the latter being erected by the Junior builders. Bozeman church is the largest in the state.——The brethren of Montana are quite liberal. The entire membership is only about 1,500 and since last March there has been raised for state work over $1,100. And yet this amount is entirely inadequate for only about six of the twenty-three churches are able to support a minister without aid.——There are a number of strategic points yet to be occupied, Dillon, the seat of the state normal, Livingstone, Big Timber, Glasgow and other county seat towns.——The last state convention was held in Helena September 4-7 and was in many respects the best held since the work was organized. The following officers of the Montana Christian Association were elected for the ensuing year: Pres. S. W. Brown, Helena; vice-president, W. W. Beeman, Billings; corresponding secretary and evangelist, F. H. Groom, Helena; treasurer, E. Scharnikard, Deer Lodge. The next convention will be held in Billings in August, 1907.——Being the third state in the union in size, Montana is one of the most promising mission fields in America. Much of the desert land is being reclaimed, two Indian reservations are being opened with others soon to follow, and that with increased mining activities is bringing hundreds of immigrants to the state.——The C. M. & St. P. Railway, a great trunk line from the east, is building through from east to west on the way to the coast, and new towns are springing up. It is imperative that our great plea be heard constantly in this rapidly developing state, for a neglected opportunity now may require the work of years later on. The climate is as healthful as can be found anywhere and the mountain scenery surpasses description. Yellowstone park is a fair sample of what may be seen in many portions of the state. A strenuous effort to more firmly establish the primitive gospel in this great state now will certainly bring forth an abundant harvest in years to come.

     F. H. Groom.

From the Southwest.

Our work seems to be advancing. Will close a meeting to-night. Eleven additions under adverse circumstances.——We have a good church building and our Ladies' Aid Society will soon have money enough in the treasury to repaint and otherwise improve.——We have a large number of churches in this ("Panhandle") part of Texas and need several additional preachers. Our district and state boards are co-operating and we all look forward to better days. Our college at Here-

ford is under the efficient leadership of Pres. A. C. Elliott and has a twenty per cent larger attendance than last year. Jewell Howard is pushing ahead at Amarillo. J. N. Wooten, district secretary, is pastor at Hereford; Prof. Jno. V. Thomas is teaching and preaching at Pampa; J. P. Homes is preaching for the churches at Giles, Memphis, Estalline and Childress. J. C. Mullin is doing good work at Dalhart and Stratford. The field at Claude and Canyon City is in care of Brother Stockard, who is a master workman. Brother Nance is at Plainview. Just across in New Mexico we hear of good work being done. L. B. Grogan is at Tucumcari, C. C. Hill at Roswell. Texico and Carlsbad have ministers also.

     C. C. Bearden.

Bible School Work in Southwest Missouri.

At an institute with the Carthage school a fine interest was manifested and it was voted to form a Teacher-Training Class. It is almost certain that Superintendent Williams and his competent corps of teachers will show us something worthy our attention. With the institute began a month's rally in preparation for a meeting to begin about the first of November by W. H. Pinkerton. Pastor Sims is greatly loved by the Carthage church and the people in general.——Our next point was the Newton county meeting in session the same week at Seneca. At one meeting the children from the public school with their teachers came in a body, filling the church with one of the most delightful audiences it has fallen to our lot to address for many a day. The county meeting was a success.——The Monett church has long been struggling under a debt which it sometimes seemed impossible for them to pay; but something over a year ago they called Robert Simons to be their minister. He went to work with the purpose to clear the debt. He secured the assistance of J. W. Baker who has shown such splendid powers of leadership, and they, with the spirit of self-denial stirred up in the hearts of the members of the congregation, succeeded in securing subscriptions to provide for the payment of the debt. These subscriptions are now falling due and as they are paid in the debt is being paid off. The congregation is already taking on new life as the result of this relief from the incubus of so many years. That church and our entire brotherhood in the state owe Brother Simons a debt of gratitude.——W. E. Marion is superintendent of the Monett school, and is preparing for a campaign for larger things. Mrs. Buxton spoke once during the Monett institute and also at a special gathering at South street, Springfield, under the auspices of the Officers and Teachers' union of that city.—J. H. Hardin, state superintendent, Kansas City, Mo.

❖

Washington.

There are some churchless preachers and some preacherless churches in this state, and it is to be regretted. Every worthy minister ought to be kept busy. And churches practice poor economy and show little Christian spirit when they try to "get along" for months without a preacher. I recently returned from a two months' visit in Iowa, Kansas, Missouri and Nebraska. A summer spent with friends of other days is a delight that is greatly appreciated. My family are all much benefited by the recreation and rest. Large audiences have greeted us since our return and we have welcomed six good additions to the church. These things and the royal public reception given us review the thought that the best part of a journey is the home coming.——Spokane churches are prospering under the ministry of Brethren Stevens and Allen. Tacoma First Church is busy erecting a new building and the "Central" church is reported as moving to a location nearer the body of the membership.—— A beautiful bungalow, costing about $1,000, has been built by the little church at Wapato this summer. L. D. Green, who has preached for them since their organization by myself last January, planned the building and has led in its erection. J. T. Eshelman, of Tacoma, preached morning and afternoon to the delight and edification of all. A number of other ministers were present and took part in the exercises.—J. J. Handsaker and wife, returned missionaries from Jamaica, have taken charge of the church at Hoquiam and A. C. Vail has given up the evangelistic field and is now located at Ballard.—— P. R. Burnett, who has served some of our churches in eastern Washington, and who is an

able and worthy preacher, will soon be available for work. He ought not to be permitted to leave the state. We need such men here. The development of this state by means of new railroads now building and the rapid extension of the irrigation system under government direction and control, gives wonderful impetus to business, and it behooves the membership and ministry of the Church of Christ to prove true in this time of golden opportunity. The churches seem to be falling in line for 1909. These years should be the greatest in evangelistic and missionary effort of any in this glorious century.

MORTON L. ROSE.

North Yakima.

❖

Alabama Convention.

An excellent program has been arranged by the brethren of Alabama for their twenty-first annual meeting which will be held November 15-19, with the Christian church, Mobile, Ala. Claude E. Hill is the minister and the church will be found on the corner of Government and Dearborn streets. Lodging and breakfast will be furnished free. Other meals will be served by ladies of the church. E. C. Anderson, president of the Alabama Christian Missionary Co-operation, will call the meeting to order at 7 o'clock on Thursday evening, November 15. The C. W. B. M. session will be held that evening. Friday will be Alabama Day, when the reports of the executive committee, and evangelists, and churches will be presented. There is to be a general discussion on "The State Field." W. K. Warren is to speak on "The Revelation of the State Work to Our Centennial Movement," while there will follow a general discussion on "What Alabama can do in Celebration of Our First Centennial." On this day George W. Muckley will speak on State Missions and Church Extension. There is to follow a general discussion on "How Can Better Results Be Secured With Present Men and Means, and How Can the Efficiency of These Be Increased?" A number of other interesting items are on the program for this day. On Saturday there will be reports of standing committees, nominations, etc. Among the speakers will be J. A. Lord on "Christian Liberty," George B. Renshaw on "America for Christ," Mary Wisdom Grant of St. Louis, on "How I Teach a Bible Class," W. T. Moore on "The Education of Our Girls and Boys," and J. H. Garrison on "The Holy Spirit As Teacher and Monitor." On Sunday there will be preaching in many of the churches of the city. Among the speakers at special sessions will be W. T. Moore, J. H. Mohorter, A. McLean, and J. H. Garrison. The latter will speak on "The Present Status of Christian Unity." On Monday there is to be a preachers' open parliament, as well as a ladies' conference and business reports. Bro. J. W. Henry has been very busy in working up this convention which will not be interfered with by reason of the great storm through which Mobile recently passed. Claude E. Hill and the church there have sent out a very warm invitation to all the Disciples in Alabama to be present.

❖

A Country Church Meeting.

A good meeting has just been held at Two-Mile Branch Christian church, Montgomery county, Mo. There were ten additions—nine by confession and baptism and one by letter. Brother Lawrence, of Muncie, Ind., labored faithfully for two weeks and the pastor of the church, David Miller of Belleflower, filled his regular appointment on the following Sunday and Monday night, after which O. Waldron Jennings, of St. Louis, a representative of the Christian Publishing Co., took up the work for ten days, when there were six additions and an organization of a Y. P. S. C. E., with an enrollment of about 25 members, and a generally increased interest was the final result. The meeting was greatly assisted by the singing of N. M. Field and wife, of St. Louis.—O. Waldron Jennings.

Evangelistic

We invite ministers and others to send reports of meetings, additions and other news of the churches. It is especially requested that additions be reported as "by confession and baptism," or "by letter."

California.

Orange.—Nineteen additions here Oct. 28, at regular services.—14 by conversion and five by statement. The work here is harmonious and prosperous.—A. N. Glover, minister.

San Francisco, Oct. 30.—Work at "West Side" progressing. Additions at almost every service. Three confessions October 28. Audiences increasing. Interest in Sunday-school growing.—Robert Lord Cave.

Colorado.

Salida, Oct. 30.—Thirty-three additions last Lord's day, 23 baptisms. We recently held a union meeting with Evangelist Sunday.—W. B. Crewdson.

Illinois.

Eureka, Oct. 29.—Two added by letter, to the church at Ospur.—Lewis P. Fisher.

Lincoln.—Forty-one additions at First Christian Church with William J. Lockhart, evangelist.— W. E. M. Hackleman.

Clinton; Nov. 2.—Closed a four weeks' meeting with Ivanhoe Park Church, Kansas City, with 25 added. Begin at East St. Louis November 4.— E. A. Gilliland.

Niantic, Oct. 27.—Forty-one added here in twenty days. 'All by confession and baptism ex-cept six.—J. Will Walters, pastor, Charles McVay, song evangelist.

Nebo, Nov. 3.—I am in a good meeting here. Four confessions last night, six to date. Church much revived and encouraged. No preacher.—J. D. Williams, evangelist.

Blue Mound, Oct. 30.—Twenty-five have been added in our meeting. Interest is good. This is destined to become one of the strongest churches.—J. L. Thompson, evangelist.

Versailles, Nov. 1.—Closed a meeting at Coop-erstown, with 26 additions, nearly all of them by confession. Brotherly Bently, of Kansas, held a meeting at Ripley during October, which resulted in 33 additions—33 by confession.—Sheeler Camp-bell.

Decatur, Oct. 19.—Closed a three and one-half weeks' meeting at Chapin, Ill., with 37 additions almost all by confession and baptism. J. W. Por-ter filled the pulpit at Decatur during by ab-sence and four were added by letter.—F. W. Burnham.

Iowa.

Boone, Oct. 29.—Two by baptism and two from other religious bodies.—C. F. Ward, minister.

Indiana.

Indianapolis, Oct. 29.—Began revival at North Park church yesterday with M. W. Harkins as evangelist. Eleven added at first service.—Austin Hunter.

Indianapolis, October 29.—Our meeting at the Sixth Christian church began yesterday with much enthusiasm. Three additions. Brother Mac-Lane is the evangelist and A. Orcutt is pas-tor.—Charles McVay, song evangelist.

Salem, Oct. 28.—J. V. Coombs and J. Walter Wilson closed a 23 days' meeting here last night, with 69 additions—48 by confession and baptism, 19 by letter and statement, 4 from other re-ligious bodies.—W. Y. Allen, minister.

Indian Territory.

Chickasha, Oct. 29.—My first Sunday, after locat-ing, resulted in four additions.—J. E. Dinger, minister.

Japan.

Tokio, Oct. 11.—Five recent baptisms in the Yotsuya Mission. The work is prospering.—W. D. Cunningham.

Kansas.

Caldwell, Oct. 31.—Two confessions.—Lee H. Branum.

Geuda Springs, Oct. 29.—Two additions—one by confession and one from another religious body. —B. F. Stallings.

Kentucky.

Wickliffe, Oct. 23.—The meeting here, conduct-ed by J. J. Taylor and wife, resulted in 14 addi-tions.—George W. Reeves.

Massachusetts.

Everett, Oct. 31.—One addition last Lord's day. Thirty-six so far this year. Will begin an evan-gelistic meeting the last week in November.—A. T. June.

Michigan.

Owasso, Oct. 30.—There were 22 additions in a three weeks' meeting here, with home forces.

All departments prospering.—C. M. Keene.

Missouri.

Kansas City, Oct. 31.—One added by letter at Louisburg.—Clyde Lee Fife.

Hunnewell; Oct. 29.—Closed a three weeks' meeting last night, resulting in 15 additions. Bro. Millsap led the singing.—R. B. Havener.

Fredericktown, Oct. 29.—One baptism October 28, and one added at Mt. Oak church. A. W. Grisby preached in the morning.—S. P. Gross, minister.

Louisiana, Oct. 29.—Held a 12 days' meeting with the church at Center, Mo., with ten addi-tions—six confessions and five by letter.—E. J. Lampton.

Pittsburg, Oct. 29.—Seven additions at Cross Timbers, Sunday, at regular services—three con-fessions and baptisms, four by letter.—Pleasant Clark, minister.

St. Louis, Nov. 3.—Eighteen additions at Lib-erty, in Audrian county, in a meeting just closed, which greatly strengthened the church in every way.—W. 1- Kern.

Centralia, Oct. 31.—Closed a very successful meeting last night, with 12 additions. I begin November 4 with the Parkland church, Louis-ville, Ky.—H. G. Bennett.

Mountain Grove, Oct. 31.—Held a two weeks meeting at Rynumville, with 14 additions—7 by confession and 7 by letter and statement. Be-gin at Marshfield November 23.—E. W. Yocum.

Seneca, Oct. 31.—O. G. Blackwell and wife, of New Vienna, assisted by the pastor, E. J. Church, closed a meeting here Oct. 28. There were 4 additions and the church was greatly ben-efited.—A. R. Moore.

Ethel, Nov. 3.—LeBaron and Conrad closed their meeting at Ethel, October 29, with 64 added, and began at Grand River the following night. The attendance and interest is rapidly increasing.

Joplin, Nov. 5.—Our Crocker meeting closed at the end of two weeks with 33 additions—19 confessions, 3 from other religious bodies, and 11 otherwise. F. M. O'Neal led the singing.—Joseph Gaylor, evangelist.

Poplar Bluff.—Our three weeks' meeting re-sulted in 16 additions—four by acknowledgement, 10 by baptism, and two from other bodies. A. W. Kokendoffer, Mexico, Mo., was the singer.—E. J. Fenstermacher.

Grant City, Nov. 1.—A three weeks' meeting with home forces just closed with 35 additions. Splendid audiences every night. Church in fine spirits. V. E. Ridenour led the singing.—W. A. Shullenberger, pastor.

Newtown, Oct. 30.—Thirty-nine additions, 25 by confession, to the new West Liberty Chris-tian church in Putnam county, Mo., resulted from an 18 days' meeting conducted by the pastor, E. J. McKinley, and the writer.—Reuben W. Blunt.

Weaubleau, Nov. 2.—Closed a ten days' meeting at Hermitage with 5 additions—4 by primary obe-dience and one from another religious body. F. M. Hooten did the preaching. One confes-sion at Wheatland not reported.—S. E. Hen-drickson.

La Monta, oct. 31.—Our meeting of three and a half weeks closed to-night. B. F. Hill did the preaching and L. D. Sprague led the singing. There were 26 confessions, two by letter and one

by statement. The meeting was a splendid success. —I. M. Fuller.

Nebraska.

Chester, Oct. 31.—One confession last Lord's day.—D. G. Wagner.

Clay Center, Oct. 29.—Our meeting closed last night with 35 added to the church. Evangelists Melvin, Putnam and Miss Emma: Egbert conduct-ed the meeting. The church is now among the strongest in the state, and is in the best condi-tion in its history. A great field is before us.— A. G. Smith, pastor.

Oklahoma.

Ames, Oct. 26.—Revival here 18 days old with 28 additions to date, 25 of which are confessions. Will close October 28.—J. A. Tabor and wife.

Oregon.

Ashland, Oct. 22.—Our meeting with S. M. Martin closed last night with a total of 88 ac-cessions. This was the greatest meeting ever held by a single congregation in Ashland.—Mrs. Clara G. Esson, assistant pastor.

West Virginia.

Huntington, Oct. 26.—We are having a rousing meeting here. Fifteen additions first five days. Fine audiences.—R. H. Fife.

SUBSCRIBERS' WANTS.

A LUKEWARM CHURCH.—Rev.
3:14-22.

"Who at my door is standing,
　Patiently drawing near?
Entrance within demanding,
　Whose is the voice I hear?"

"Sweetly his tones are falling,
　'Open the door for me,
If thou wilt heed my calling,
　I will abide with thee.'"

The familiar nausea produced by lukewarm food that is rejected with loathing
expresses Christ's abhorrence for those
lacking zeal in his service.

A minister once remarked to a celebrated atheist, "I do not see how you
can have one moment's peace in the desperate state of atheism." The latter replied, "You are a greater surprise to me.
If I believed what you profess, no zeal,
no work, no sacrifice would seem sufficient to excuse me from responsibility
for the eternal weal or woe of my fellowmen."

How happy this hungry-hearted race
would be did it realize Jesus stands before every man as at a door seeking admission, and if sanctification has prepared for him a room will enter in and
abide with each of us, and make us to be
never lonely or afraid again. And how
smiles would make rainbows glitter in
our tears did we fully grasp the meaning of "Whom the Lord loveth he
chasteneth."

We are not to understand that in the
fifteenth verse Jesus expresses a desire
that any of the Laodiceans should be
cold or indifferent towards him; he is
rather looking forward to the judgment
day regretting that when they appeared before him they could not even
plead that they knew not the way of
righteousness. He saw them belonging
to a worse class, "which, after they had
known it, turned from the holy commandment delivered unto them." On that
great day how will all lukewarmness be
deplored! Then neutrality will appear in
its true light of open hostility to the
King of Kings and Lord of Lords.

Laodicea, situated twenty miles from
Ephesus and near Colosse. It was a
wealthy city, its trade consisting chiefly
in the preparing of woolen materials
whose raven blackness and durable dyes
made it famous. It was advantageously
situated, too, on the high road leading
from Ephesus into the interior. In common with other cities of Asia Minor, it
was subject to earthquakes. It was the
proud boast of Laodiceans that unlike
Ephesus and Sardis they required no
extraneous assistance to regain their
former prosperity after these destructive
shocks. As it is so often the case its material prosperity seems to have contributed rather to sinful pride than to
gratitude and grace.

The importance of this church continued many years. In Col. 4:16 we
learn the epistle was equally written to
the Laodiceans. The celebrated council
of Laodicea was held there in A. D.
361, and a century later its bishop held

a prominent position among the eccle-
siastics of his time, but soon after its
influence began to wane and it fell under the oppression of the Turks. In
Col. 2:4,8 and 1:8 we learn false doctrines
were lurking in the church and being
cherished by the membership. The warnings of John and Paul were unheeded.
Under these circumstances its ruin was
natural and inevitable. The heresy-
hunting spirit is deplorable but complacency in the midst of heresy is disaster.

Christian Endeavor
By GEO. L. SNIVELY.

November 18, 1906.

HOW THE BIBLE CONDEMNS IN-
TEMPERANCE.—Hab. 2:5-15.

DAILY READINGS.

M. Warning and Exhortation. Prov. 4:11-27.
T. The Sorrows of the Cup. Prov. 23:29-35.
W. Erring Through Drink. Isa. 28:1-13.
T. Disgrace of Intoxication. Hab. 2:15-20.
F. Servants of Corruption. 2 Peter 2:12-22.
S. Deliverance Promised. Rom. 8:16-21.
S. The Lord's Freemen. 1 Cor. 8:1-13.

Intemperance in tennis, novel reading,
traveling, entertaining, home keeping,
conversation, or artistic pursuits may
not be as disgraceful as wine bibbing,
but does become a sad reproach to the
Christian character of many otherwise
exemplary church members.

If wine inspires to social diversion, it
is to an indecent dance like Salome's; if
to art, it is to pictures or statuary mothers wish their sons to pass by on the
other side; if to idealism, it is of the sort
whose perfect expression is in the under
world; if to either eternity, it is where
the fire is not quenched and the worm
dieth not.

Much has been said of Christ's turning
water into wine. His Father did the
same before Jesus' pilgrimage through
Palestine. He does it to-day and hangs
the wine in purple buckets on thousands
of hillsides and mountain terraces. And
if men would drink only the kind of wine
Jesus made at Cana and that God makes
to-day, temperance reformers could take
up a new propaganda.

When the churches devote the time
and vitality now spent on maintaining
denominational prerogatives and party
organization to the overthrow of the
great iniquities and the redemption of
men from the despotism of Satan men
will cease buying rum, others will cease
making it; and the curse will exist only
in history and there as a horrid illustration of the depravity of sin.

He that transgresseth by wine is one
"who enlargeth his desire as hell, and is
as death and cannot be satisfied." He
that thirsteth after righteousness shall
never be satiated and yet he shall be
satisfied, while he that thirsteth for wine
or other distillations tinctured with the
spirit of Satan finds himself the victim
of desires growing ever more intense,
never more satisfied by indulgence than
flames are by fuel, that can not be
quenched by tears or blood, and that
constitute the horrors of living death.

Apologists for drunkenness have succeeded in arousing a maudlin sentiment
of sympathy for some drunkards on the
ground that they inherited an irresistible disposition to intemperance. Yet
the sisters of these degenerates with the
same blood flowing through their veins
are shining lights in the church. The

power of heredity for evil has been vast-
ly exaggerated. It can always be resisted by those who will struggle unto
blood. Upon the father was visited the
iniquity of his own sins and the sons will
be held strictly accountable for their
own.

A panther is loose in the haunts of men,
　Strong, crafty, and cruel, and none may know
What wooded valley shall hold his den,
　Or by what paths he will come and go.
In the shade tree boughs he may lie concealed,
　In wayside brambles, in flowery dell;
The father has taken his gun afield,
　And the mother watches the children well.
Birth, beauty and talent before him fall;
　He conquers the mighty again and again;
Will you guard by law King Alcohol?
　Will you set a price on the souls of men?
You would save the child from the panther's jaws,
　Will you leave him now to a fate far worse?
The strength of God for a righteous cause,
　Arise! and conquer the liquor curse!

JESUS BEFORE CAIPHAS.—Matt.
26:57-68.

Memory verses, 67, 68.

Golden Text.—He was despised and rejected of men.—Isa. 53:3.

The trial of Jesus, as recorded by the four evangelists, may be considered under the following simple analysis:

I. The Jewish Trial.
1. Before Annas (at night).
2. Before Caiaphas (at night).
    Buffeting and mockery.
    Peter's denial.
3. Before the council (early morning).
II. The Roman Trial.
1. Before Pilate (morning).
2. Before Herod.
    Mockery.
3. Before Pilate again.
    Scourging.
    Delivery to mob.

No one can read the Gospel narrative, or glance at such an outline as the above without feeling at once that the trial was no trial at all, in any legal sense. It was an effort of cruel and vindictive men to murder an innocent enemy without rendering themselves liable for an act of violence.

The trial began with an illegal and unauthorized arrest in the garden. It continued with a session before Annas, who held no office which gave them jurisdiction in such a case, an illegal midnight session before the high priest and the council, a meeting of the council in the morning to give some color of legality to the transactions of the night. Before Pilate there were no witnesses except a murderous mob, no charges except such as were palpably false, no condemnation except the sentence: "I am innocent of the blood of this righteous man. See ye to it." From the beginning to end there was a series of physical outrages and mockeries which wholly ignored the rights of the prisoner.

The examination of Jesus before Caiaphas, the high priest, was not a trial. It was an eager effort to secure evidence which would prove the prisoner guilty under the Jewish law. No one here is thinking of loyalty to Caesar or the apparently dangerous claim to kingship. Blasphemy is the charge. This, if honestly made, was not necessarily an unreasonable charge. The words and deeds of Jesus were either blasphemous or true. If he did not actually have that close relationship to God which he claimed, then he was guilty of blasphemy in claiming it.

The accusation based on Jesus' statement that he would destroy the temple and build it in three days, was a piece with the other wilful misunderstandings of his utterances. It was not altogether strange that they did not understand such a saying. Their fault was in making no real effort to understand it.

When the high priest asked Jesus if he were the Christ, the Son of God, he admitted it, and spoke of his future coming in glory. This was the climax of his blasphemy, in the eyes of his enemies, because it was the climax of the truth about himself. The world must ultimately range itself under one or two banners, either the banner of the one who said that he was "the Christ the Son of God," or that of his accuser who declared that such a statement was blasphemy.

People's Forum

"A New Idea."

To the Editor of THE CHRISTIAN-EVANGELIST:

A preacher whose name is quite familiar to the readers of THE CHRISTIAN-EVANGELIST under the above caption, says: "A preacher in THE CHRISTIAN-EVANGELIST of recent date has given to the world a new idea; that a man may have a Christian character and not be a Christian."

Now, if I were that preacher, I would like to reply to this preacher that he has given to the world an old idea. That Christian character "is that very thing that makes him a Christian." It is at least as old as the forming of that body of religious people wearing the name "CHRISTIAN CHURCH," and making "Christian character" the one condition of membership. They are consistent. They say Christian character is "that very thing that makes them Christians," and they open their doors to all recognized by them as being Christians.

Brother Editor, is your contributor as consistent? Will he take an unbaptized person with a Christian character into the local church for which he preaches? If he should do such a thing he would soon learn that he had introduced a "new idea" that would deprive him of a pulpit among our people.

The Apostle Peter at the home of Cornelius thought evidently it took something beside Christian character to make one a Christian.

May I ask that good man and preacher a question or two, that he may answer in your columns?

Is a man a Christian who is not "in Christ?" In order to get in Christ, is it yet necessary to be "baptized into Christ?" To the Galatian Christians, Paul said, "as many of you as have been baptized into Christ have put on Christ." Since Paul's day have we a "new idea," or revelation that the man who has a Christian character has already "put on Christ" and that it is "that very thing by which he has put on Christ?"

Is a man a Christian who is not in the Kingdom of God?

Can a man enter into the kingdom of God except he be born of water and the Spirit?

The preacher says: "I frequently meet an old soldier minus an arm or a leg. Does this defect outlaw him as a man or as a citizen or a patriot?"

No, sir. It emphasizes his manliness and patriotism. But the loss of that arm or leg did not make him a soldier. Do you think it did? That is your line of argument on what makes a man a Christian.

[Brother Jones' argument was that as these maimed soldiers were men in spite of their physical defects so a true believer may be a Christian in spite of some defect in the forms of his obedience.—EDITOR.]

The United States had a plan by which men were made soldiers. A citizen enlisted and was sworn in. Then the citizen became a soldier.

"The Pope of Rome with his claims to infallibility in his interpretations of Scripture, is not without his rivals even among Protestants." Agreed.

But who is this rival of the Pope? The man who brings out a "new idea" that the Scriptures do not teach.

Tricked by Dyspepsia

The Doctor Couldn't Tell Where The Trouble Lay.

"For the past seven years I have been a victim of dyspepsia and chronic constipation and have consulted the most noted specialists to be found on diseases of this character. None, however, seemed to locate the difficulty or give relief. In addition to this medical treatment, I have resorted to the use of many remedies and have given them faithful trial, but all to no purpose.

Upon the recommendation of a close friend, I purchased a 50c package of Stuart's Dyspepsia Tablets and in less than five days' notice that I was receiving more benefit than from any remedy I had used before. I continued to use the tablets after each meal for one month and by that time my stomach was in a healthy condition, capable of digesting anything which my increasing appetite demanded.

I have not experienced any return of my former trouble though three months have elapsed since taking your remedy."

We wish that you could see with your own eyes the countless other bona-fide signed letters from grateful men and women all over the land who had suffered years of agony with dyspepsia, tried every known remedy and consulted eminent specialists without result, until they gave Stuart's Dyspepsia Tablets a trial. Like the doctor above, they couldn't locate the seat of the trouble.

Dyspepsia is a disease which has long baffled physicians. So difficult of location is the disease that cure seems next to miraculous. There is only one way to treat dyspepsia—to supply the elements which nature has ordained to perform this function and to cause them to enter the digestive organs, supplying the fluids which they lack. Stuart's Dyspepsia Tablets alone fill these requirements, as is shown by the fact that 40,000 physicians in the United States and Canada unite in recommending them to their patients for stomach disorders.

We do not claim or expect Stuart's Dyspepsia Tablets to cure anything but disordered conditions of the stomach and other digestive organs, but this they never fail to do. They work upon the inner lining of the stomach and intestines, stimulate the gastric glands and aid in the secretion of juices necessary to digestion.

Stuart's Dyspepsia Tablets are for sale by all druggists at 50 cents a box. One box will frequently effect a perfect cure. If in doubt and wish more adequate proof send us your name and address and we will gladly mail you a sample package free. F. A. Stuart Co., 61 Stuart Bldg., Marshall, Mich.

As I read my Bible it takes Christian character plus putting on Christ to make a Christian. My Bible says: (and I do not have to interpret it, just read it), we put on Christ in baptism. These I recognize as Christians, and prove it by receiving them into the local church.

Whom do you receive? E. L. FRAZIER.

Morristown, Ind.

❀ ❀

Send for our Holiday Catalogue.
CHRISTIAN PUBLISHING CO.,
St. Louis, Mo.

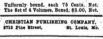

The Home Department

Lord, give the mothers of the world
More love to do their part;
That love which reaches not alone
The children made by birth their own,
But every childish heart.
Wake in their souls true motherhood,
Which aims at universal good.

Lord, give the teachers of the world
More love, and let them see
How baser metals in their store
May be transformed to precious ore
By love's strange alchemy.
And let them daily seek to find
The childish *heart* beneath the mind.
—*Ella Wheeler Wilcox.*

The Bronze Vase.

BY J. BRECKENRIDGE ELLIS.

PART IV.

CHAPTER IV.

On the back of the envelope was written, "For Raymund, or Rhoda." Raymund tore it open with trembling hands, and having turned that his face might be hidden from the bank officials, he read his mother's letter.

"My darling: You see I call you so, though I do not know whether this is Rhoda or Raymund. Whichever it is, God bless, you! As I write this, I think it may never be read. It is only to be read now, if something which you cannot explain has come between my darlings. If such a difference has arisen, something maybe that you cannot understand, then read on to the end. I need not tell you how much I love you as I write. And I think as you read, I will be looking down with love from my last dear home. I told you there is a secret in our little family. It is this: Raymund had reached the bottom of the first page. He turned it over and continued, "Only one of you is my very own child. The other one is adopted. When your father and I moved to St. Louis, we were very poor, but if your father's health had not failed, all would have gone well. We boarded on Washington avenue in a simple and cheap place. While there, a young couple came to lodge, a Mr. and Mrs. White. They had run away from home to marry, because Mr. White's father was opposed to the match. Mr. White's father was a very rich man; he lives in New York. They had come all the way, and young Mr. White, who was a lawyer, soon spent his little fortune. Your father and I loved them and did what we could to get Mr. White practice, but that was little, indeed. We were all attending the same church. My dear, have you come into the church? If you have not, take this as the warning and admonition of your dead mother who hopes to meet you with your father in heaven—that if you do not confess the name of Jesus before the people, God will not acknowledge you before the angels."

Amazed as Raymund was by the intelligence conveyed in the letter, he could not but murmur below his breath grateful thanks that both he and Rhoda were Christians. He continued the letter: "One thing helped to bind us and the Whites very closely together, our child and their child were born on the very same day. They wrote to the hardhearted parents in New York—the father, their only near relative. The elder Mr. White sent back the letter unopened. A year later they wrote to him again and this time the letter was not returned. We did not know if it was ever read. The letter informed Mr. White that his grandchild was a year old, but Mrs. White who wrote the letter, did not think to tell him whether it was a boy or a girl. We were very intimate. The Whites—we called each other by our first names—were the same kind of people we were. When you were three years old, one of the little darlings took the diphtheria. We hung over it day and night. Your father took it, so did Mr. and Mrs. White. All three died within fifteen days. It was left with my own child and with the other. They looked so much alike—the same color of eyes and hair—and they were both so sweet and dear and helpless—and born on the same day. I determined to raise you both as if you were my own children. I made no difference between you. I feel sure you could never have suspected the truth. There was one difficulty. Those at the boarding-house knew the truth. It is possible that one or more of them may some day meet you and tell you how it was. That is why I am writing this letter. There is another consideration: Old Mr. White is very rich. Our Mr. White was his only near relative. Of course his grandchild would inherit his money unless there is another marriage or a will. It may be necessary at some day to declare which one of you is his grandchild. There is still another possibility, though this I do not anticipate; should a cloud ever fall upon either of you, the one might wish to prove himself or herself of no kin to the other. This letter proves it. You are in no way related to each other, save by love.

"And now, my darling, should you still want to know which one of you is my very own child, go to that St. Louis boarding-house, whose number is at the bottom of this page, and ask permission to enter the second chamber of the cellar—where the coal was kept in our day. In the northeast corner of that cellar, directly beneath the second beam from the north end, there is buried a bronze vase. When you, my very own child, were two years old, Mr. and Mrs. White presented it to you as a birthgift. Around the upper surface of the pedestal is carved your name. I do not tell you here, whether that name is *Raymund* or *Rhoda*. If you *must* know, go and see for yourself. Whichever it is, is the name of very own child, and the one whose name is *not* upon that vase, is the heir or heiress of Mr. White of New York." The letter concluded with words of tender affection too sacred for any one save the one for whom the letter was intended.

Raymund left the bank, and although the day was cold and the fields white with snow, he set forth upon a long country walk. He desired to reflect upon what he had read, and he felt it necessary to be entirely alone. He read his mother's letter again and again. He grew to know parts of it by heart. The two important facts it contained were stamped vividly upon his mind: Rhoda was not really his sister; and on the bronze vase was the name of Mrs. Revore's only child! Was it his name? Was it Rhoda's name? He brought back his mother's voice—her tone and words—the look on her face—he remembered her tenderness and self-sacrifice. Surely she was his mother. Oh, it must be that he, not Rhoda, was the only child! He now thought he understood why Rhoda had changed toward him. She had learned they were not related. But how had she learned this? The bank president had assured him that the tin box had remained untouched since its deposit. How could Rhoda know? If she did now know, her change was inexplicable. But she had in some way discovered the truth of the change; was natural. She had shrunk from his embraces and kisses because he was not her brother. All alone in the wintry scene he wept because Rhoda was not really his sister. "But my mother!" he exclaimed aloud, "I am sure of her! I *know* she was my mother. I will never give up that belief, never!"

Although he had intended, when coming to Crawley, to visit the various men who were his mother's creditors, he found in his highly-wrought condition that he did not want to meet any one. He returned to Kansas City the same day, and sent drafts to Mr. Walker, Mr. Jennings and the others. Every cent of the debts were now paid, he wrote Rhoda, but he did not tell of his trip to Crawley. He must be while her face to face while relating that new After Christmas week, the Geisthauses were resumed. Raymund worked hard upon the improvement of the minds that at night as he and Jack about the coaloil stove in the little barroom, clad in their overcoats, and pretending it yas "warm enough" in order to save the coaloil, there was little time to brood over his discovery. Beside Raymund was not the sort of a man who broods over truths no matter how unwelcome. Already he accepted the fact of his mother's letter as final. Rhoda was not his sister! The bronze vase held the secret upon its pedestal. Jack was doing fairly well with his studies and even better with Nelsie Loraine. He open and joyous disposition, his frank acceptance of life's hardships, and his ability to skim along the heights of life and jump its hollows, were attractive to the daughter of the millionaire. They were so different that she found him interesting. He was not, of course, a young man whom Mrs. Omer could have considered for a moment as a possible son-in-law. But Jack felt that if, in few years, he could rise in his profession, and if Nelsie Loraine cared for him and would wait, everything might come out all right. "Anyhow," said Jack, as he humped himself over the coaloil stove and gnawed hungrily at a sapless heel ring, "I'm going to enjoy the days I have now, and if is isn't as pleasant later on it'll be time enough to kick, then." I'm sorry Jack used this slang, but you couldn't have been with him very long without hearing a little of that sort of thing; and he had to be in this story—was needed.

When summer came, the Geisthauses claimed a much needed rest, and Raymund and Jack went home together. They had scarcely taken their seats in the car when a well-dressed man in a tall silk hat touched Raymund on the shoulder. "Mr. Revore," he said, "pardon me, I am Horace Bridgewaite. Will you be seated with me a moment? I have a little business to discuss with you." Raymund followed him, wondering. "You do not know me," said the soothing voice, "but you are an old acquaintance of mine. In fact, I boarded with your mother and your—babe! But I go too fast. Perhaps it may be news to you to know that Rhoda is not—"

"I do not know you," Raymund interrupted with displeasure, "or why you should be interested in my affairs."

"You do not know me?" cried Mr. Bridgewaite. "You do not know Horace Bridgewaite? My dear young sir! it is my business to be interested in other people's affairs. That is how I make my living. No detail is too slight for me. Since a young man, I have made it my habit to learn everything I could about whomever I met. Sir, there is money in knowing things, there is much money!"

"There is no money in knowing anything about me," returned Raymund, half-rising, "and I do not care to discuss Rhoda with a promoter. And I do not think you can promote *me!*"

"Do not be sure, do not be too sure," said the soothing voice, as the man of the tall hat, laid a well-kept hand upon his coatsleeve. "You know Rhoda is not your sister?"

"I do," said Raymund coldly. The other was so astonished by this admission that Raymund felt rather sorry for him and sank back into the seat. The promoter said when he had recovered, "And-do-do you know which of you inherits Mr. White's money?"

"I am sure *I* do not," said Raymund, "for I feel certain that I am Raymund Revore."

"Ah, then you do not know!" cried the promoter triumphantly. "But I can prove that you are not her own son, and Rhoda is her own child; you are the heir to Mr. White's millions! What do you think of that? I can prove it. My young sir, there is money in knowing things! Mr. White has left his fortune to a hospital and a school in case his grandchild is not found—the will is in all the papers—but it is not known if his grandchild is a boy or girl, and it is not even suspected that you are in Missouri. My dear sir, you are that heir, and I can prove it! And if you will place a thousand dollars in my hands, I will turn you over a fortune of two millions!"

"Since it is in your power to hand me over this fortune," remarked Raymund, "why not keep out a thousand, or ten thousand, and hand over the balance."

"I do not do business that way," said the promoter. "My system demands that the customer shall pay down."

"Well, as I'm not a customer, you must excuse me," said Raymund. "I suppose your proof rests upon the bronze vase, does it not?"

For a second time the promoter was staggered. Seeking to hide his chagrin, he said, "Of course the bronze vase is a valuable clew. But reflect that I was boarding at that house on Washington Avenue at the time. I was at the breakfast table when Mr. White gave Rhoda the vase. It has your name on it. The following inscription was intended: "From Raymund to Rhoda." But through a mistake the rest of the engraving was not done. Your father, Mr. White, always meant to finish it; but he died when you were only three, and when Mrs. Revore adopted you, of course she didn't want the inscription changed. I was quite a friend of the Revores, and Mrs. Revore and I, after the sad epidemic, decided it would be a good thing to bury that vase as a clew in future years, should a proof ever be needed. It has never been disturbed. If you will go with me there, taking witnesses, that bronze vase will prove you a millionaire. Only a thousand down, young sir, only a thousand down to encourage me in the enterprise. Ah, my dear young sir, you will find out that I am well aware of that which I do speak, when I say that there is money in knowing things!"

(To be continued.)

Madeline's Message.

It would not have seemed so terrible, Madeline's friends told each other, if only Madeline had not from a child so exulted in the mere joy of motion. But to think of Madeline—Madeline—robbed in one cruel moment of all that eager, abounding life, and condemned for whatever years were left to her to an invalid's couch and constant suffering!

If, they said to each other, she had died and never known! But she had to know, and very soon. When, brokenhearted, her mother answered her questions, the girl asked to be left alone a while "to think it out." And the mother, knowing that it must be, closed the door and left her alone —in her wilderness.

The struggle lasted three days, while the mother waited and suffered with her. In those days Madeline went over and over it all—her happy past, the merry walk from school that windy afternoon, the sudden blow from a falling branch—and then the strange, dark world of imprisonment and pain. She would see no one in those days, not even the old minister who had loved her all her life.

"Tell him I've got to fight it out alone" she said. "He'll understand."

He did understand—they all did. And at last one morning Madeline drew her mother's face down to her's.

"It's all right, dear," she said. "Tell the girls I want them to come—everybody. Tell them they needn't think they can leave me out—I won't be left."

Everybody came eagerly, for Madeline's sake first; and very soon they were coming for their own. Madeline's room to all the "old crowd," and to others, who one by one found their way in, became the place where one turned instinctively with joy or hope or sorrow. And true to her word, Madeline did not let herself be "left out." She learned every kind of light and pretty work that weak hands could do; she kept up with all the new books, the

latest interests, even the fashions. More than one pretty party gown was planned in Madeline's room.

"You may go to parties," she would laugh, "but parties come to me all the time."

In those twelve years Madeline waited in her prison, she seldom, as the girls said, "talked religion," but soon after she knew what life would be to her she had a motto illuminated and hung at the foot of her bed. It was the old command to a people entering a strange land—"Be strong and of good courage, for the Lord thy God is with thee."

Madeline's eyes so often rested upon this as she talked that her friends began to notice it. And then they remembered that from the day Madeline's door had been opened to them no one had ever heard her complain.

But it was not until Madeline had gone that they understood what she had done for them. Rose Kenton began it by telling of a fine time when she was discouraged over her failure as a nurse.

"Madeline didn't pity me," she said. "She only said, 'Dear, there's always something left. One can always be brave, and—one doesn't have to be brave alone.' And when I thought of her and of her motto, I tell you, girls, I had to brace up."

Other experiences followed. One knew how George Alvord had gone to Madeline when Edith Marlow broke her engagement with him; another knew of one who had gone in the deep failure of sin, and many there were who had sought her in the loneliness death had made. To all her message had been the same. "One can always be brave—and one doesn't have to be brave alone."

So, having fought her fight and strengthened uncounted hearts, Madeline had passed into the light.—*Youth's Companion.*

He Swelled Up.

A little girl went for the first time to church with her mother. All went well during the service (Episcopal), but the child grew uneasy during the sermon, which was a long one.

The mother tried every way to keep the little girl quiet, but in vain.

Finally the child observed that the preacher had a pompous way of inflating his chest and lungs at a new paragraph or head. Just as the mother was assuring the child that the preacher would soon stop, he did, for another start, and the tired child burst out on her mother's assurance—"No, he won't; he's swelling up again."—*From the Rev. Silas B. Duffield, Somerfield, Mass.*

Should laugh instead of worry;
If we should grow—just you and I—
Kinder and sweeter-hearted.
Perhaps in some near by and by
A good time might get started;
Then what a happy world 'twould be
For you and me—for you and me!
Speak gently! 'tis a little thing
Dropped in the heart's deep well:
The good, the joy, that it may bring,
Eternity shall tell.

The Passion Flower.

This interesting flower, which has been specially cultivated in Gethsemane, beyond the Vale of Kedron, has been for many years looked upon by the Christian church as most symbolic of the passion of our Lord. Ten leaves, large, white, faintly tinted with violet, form the calyx. These are supposed to represent the ten commandments—the "outer court." In the center of the calyx we find a golden radiating circle. This represents the Sun of Righteousness that in the night of the dear Saviour's birth arose upon the world—the "holy place." Within the flower we find the implements of torture, hammer, nails, etc., used in the crucifixion. These represent the painful and atoning sufferings of our blessed Lord—the "holy of holies." This wonderful flower is sometimes called the "Rose of the South."—*Selected.*

A Failure of Contract.

Bishop Wilmer, of Alabama, was once asked by a colored man what he would charge to marry him just like white folks.

"Why," said the Bishop, "if you will get the wedding ring and meet me at the church, I'll marry you for—for five dollars just exactly like I do white folks."

"All right, sir," the darkey replied, "I'll get the ring and be at the church to-morrow morning at 6 o'clock."

The next morning, in the dim light, the Bishop, fully robed, stood in the chancel and read in his impressive voice the marriage service of the Episcopal church, joining together two loving hearts and dusky hands in the holy estate of matrimony, and blessed them as they knelt at the chancel-rail. When they arose, the groom paused for an instant as if in keen expectation of something further, then turned and hurried the bride away.

"Hold, John, wait a moment," cried the Bishop, "where is that five dollars?"

"'Scuse me, Bishop," replied the groom, "you ain't carried out the full contract."

"Not carried out the contract? What do you mean, sir? I said I'd marry you for five dollars just like white folks, and I have done it word for word," cried the justly indignant Bishop.

"Dere's one t'ing you've left out, sir," persisted the groom.

"And what is that, pray?"

"I notice, sir, dat you ain't salute de bride!"

For a minute the Bishop was stunned; then a great light of supreme amusement shone over his face, and he cried. "All right, John; that's all right about the five dollars, you just keep it—and I wish you much joy!"—*Claude Roberts.*

Canine Intelligence.

That a policeman on night duty in a great city would be more respected by criminals if accompanied by a powerful and sagacious dog, is a reasonable supposition; yet it remained for little Belgium to carry out this innovation in Antwerp, Ghent, Mons, Bruges and Ostend—an innovation which has now spread to other parts of Europe.

As time went on and the number of dogs was increased, it became apparent that night crimes, even in the worst quarters of Ghent, almost disappeared. Cunning ruffians had often contrived to outwit the soldiery patrol, but these big, swift, silent-footed and sagacious sheep-dogs inspired terror in the most desperate evil-doers.

The night service of the city is now made by about 120 guards, assisted by 50 or 60 perfectly trained dog police. The city is

Copyright, 1906, Perry Mason Co., Boston, Mass.

The Youth's Companion

250 Capital Stories; 2000 One-Minute Stories; The Children's Page; The Editorial Page; The Notes on Science; The Weekly Article on Hygiene and Emergency Treatment, Etc.

As much reading in the year as would fill twenty 400-page novels or books of history or biography ordinarily costing $1.50 each.

Send for Sample Copies and Illustrated Announcement for 1907, Free.

Every New Subscriber

Who cuts out and sends this slip (or mentions this publication) with $1.75 for The Companion for the 52 weeks of 1907 will receive

FREE ALL THE ISSUES OF THE COMPANION FOR THE REMAINING WEEKS OF 1906.

FREE THE THANKSGIVING, CHRISTMAS AND NEW YEAR'S DOUBLE NUMBERS.   BL 179

FREE THE COMPANION'S TWELVE-COLOR FOUR-LEAF HANGING CALENDAR FOR 1907.

$16,290 *in cash and many other special awards to subscribers who get new subscriptions. Send for information.*

THE YOUTH'S COMPANION ⫸ BOSTON, MASSACHUSETTS.

divided into 120 sections, so arranged
that man and dog can always count on
their neighbors' support if occasion should
arise. Careful check is kept upon the men,
that they visit every yard of their beat;
but even if the men are inclined to shirk
their work, the dogs will keep them to it.
If the night guards are used by day, they
get extra pay, and a corresponding number of hours is taken from their next night
watch.

Relating the achievements of his dogs,
M. Van Wesemael told of an arrest by one
of them named Beer. One night Beer came
upon five drunken fellows wrecking a saloon on the outskirts of the city. The men
were making a great uproar, and a resolute resistance to the law was feared.
Beer's muzzle was removed, and the fine
animal sprang forward without a sound.
When the patrol reaches the spot, four
of the men had fled, and Beer was clutch-
ing the fifth by the leg. The moment the
officer appeared, Beer gave up his prisoner,
and was off like the wind on the trail of
the fugitives. The patrol followed with
his prisoner, guided by a series of short,
sharp barks. Presently he came upon the
other four, who had turned at bay and
were trying to keep dauntless Beer from
tearing them to pieces. Thoroughly fright-

ened—sobered even—the men offered to
give themselves up if Beer were controlled
and muzzled. This was promptly done,
though not without a little protest from
Beer, and the procession started for the
central police bureau, with the victorious
Beer, now at liberty to give vent to his
joy, barking and racing round his prisoners, exactly as if they had been a flock of
sheep.

Tom is another dog no less alert. One
winter night in a quiet street near the
docks he met a man with a sack. Tom was
alone at the moment, but as both sack and
man seemed queer to him, he gave the
alarm, repudiating all attempts at anxious
conciliation. In a minute or two Tom's
colleague came along and asked about the
sack. The explanation being somewhat
lame, the man was invited to the police
bureau. There he confessed that he had
stolen a piece of beef and several dozen
eggs from a small store on the outskirts
of the city.

Tippo is another terror to burglars. He
is a record racer of great weight and
strength, long and lean of fang, a fast
swimmer, a high jumper and so daring that
not even point-blank revolver-shots will
turn him from his duty. He has been
wounded more than once and has narrowly
escaped death.—*The October Century.*

❀ ❀

It takes more than a heroic resolution
to resolve one into a hero.

Christian Publishing Company

2712 Pine St., St. Louis, Mo.

J. H. GARRISON,	President
W. W. DOWLING,	Vice-President
3RD. L. SNIVELY,	Sec. and Gen. Supt
R. P. CROW,	Treas. and Bus. Manager

—All books we sell of our own publication are of the very best grade. Among the premiers of this class is "Christian Union" by Editor Garrison, postpaid, $1.00.

—"John Doe, Sept. '06," on the yellow label of your paper means that John should send us $1.50 immediately, thus paying for his CHRISTIAN-EVANGELIST until September 1, 1907.

—Hoping it will bring us 5,000 new subscriptions within the next thirty days, we offer an excellent stereoscope and fifty high-class views for two new subscriptions to THE CHRISTIAN-EVANGELIST accompanied by $3.00. This premium will make an excellent Christmas gift.

—Are our preachers provident and enterprising? Some are—they sent us one new subscription and the $1.50 and secured "Helps to Faith" by Editor J. H. Garrison. Then they sent us another new subscription and secured as a premium "Victory of Faith" by E. L. Powell. Four thousand other preachers ought to avail themselves of this opportunity before January 1, 1907.

—Our Thanksgiving number will be a magnificent magazine of fifty-two pages. We will print all the people want. Single copies, 5c.; 6 for 25c.; and 50 to one address for $1.00. Orders will be filed and filled in order as received. Write us at once, enclosing remittance for this imperial number of America's best religious journal.

—A gratifying feature of the remarkable increase in the circulation of THE CHRISTIAN-EVANGELIST is that it is not being accomplished at the expense of any of our contemporaries. All our church papers are reporting gratifying numerical growth. Our special aim is a Christian paper in every Christian home and we much prefer being a pioneer than a supplanter.

—Few children are thoroughly indoctrinated into the principles of this Restoration in the home and none are in the world. If done at all it will be in the Bible school. It can not be done even there if the colorless interdenominational lesson helps are used. We commend those prepared by William Worth Dowling, one of the

most loyal and scholarly living Disciples.

—For twenty years an invaluable annual contribution this house has made to Bible school literature is W. W. Dowling's Christian Lesson Commentary. The 1907 volume is superb as respects its mechanical construction, skilful massing of helps, and scholarly interpretation of scripture. We recommend it as a Christmas gift by pupils to teacher, children to parents, schools to superintendents, churches to pastors, $1.00.

—While a larger percentage than usual of last week's new subscriptions came singly and in pairs at the regular $1.50 rate, we are pleased to report the following new clubs:

Stanford, Ky., L. M. Omer	4
Keokuk, Iowa, M. J. Nicoson, pastor	5
Enid, Okla., Andrew J. Jones, pastor	7
Portland, Ore., E. S. Muckley, pastor	10
Lancaster, Ky., F. M. Sinder, pastor	13
Wheeling, W. Va., W. H. Fields, pastor	13
Mt. Sterling, Ky., H. D. Clark, pastor	16
Danville, Ky., H. C. Garrison, pastor	28
Richmond, Ky., Hugh McLellan, pastor	42

—"Christian Union," by J. H. Garrison, is far more than a republication of his editorial serial. Every article has been elaborated, and one entire new chapter has been added, and there has been a rearrangement of matter. The book treats one of the livest subjects now before Christendom, and is certain to be widely read. Its statement of the present federation movement, its meaning and necessity; is a timely contribution to a better understanding of this great forward stride towards Christian unity.

—"Gloria in Excelsis" is a beautiful and complete hymnal. The hymns and tunes and chants have been judiciously selected. The responsive Scripture readings and the forms of words for special occasions add much to the value of the book. These will prove helpful to many. The editor-in-chief has spared no pains and no expense to produce a work that will meet all the needs of worship in the church and in the home. The printer and binder have done good work. This hymnal deserves and will doubtless secure a very wide sale.—A. McLean, Cincinnati, Ohio.

—Here is a list of excellent and acceptable Christmas gifts that may be secured as premiums by those securing subscriptions to THE CHRISTIAN-EVANGELIST: For one new subscription, large print New Testament; for two, large print New Testament bound in Morocco; or the American Kitchen set—bread knife, steel, large and small paring knives, cake turner and egg

THE
CHRISTIAN-
EVANGELIST

A WEEKLY RELIGIOUS NEWSPAPER.

Volume XLIII. . No. 46.

ST. LOUIS, NOVEMBER 15, 1906.

"When the frost is on the punkin, and the fodder's in the shock."

S. J. COREY.
Sec. F. C. M. S.

THE CAMPAIGN IS NOW ON
FOR THAT
Centennial Fund of $250,000 for Land and Buildings on Mission Fields in Personal Gifts by 1909.

Interest is being aroused. Some are acting. Others are carefully considering. The friends of the Foreign Christian Missionary Society can be counted upon to do what is right. Now is the time to act!

IMPORTANCE OF SECURING LAND

Now on the foreign mission fields can hardly be overestimated. Land is rapidly advancing in value in all these countries, as it is wherever the Gospel is preached. Land the Foreign Society bought in Asia ten years ago is now worth many times what was paid for it. If we do not secure land and lots we need now, we will be compelled to pay much more in the near future.

The need in China and Japan and India and the Philippines and Africa—in a word, all our mission fields, is most pressing.

Our motto should be: "Not slothful in business, fervent in spirit, serving the Lord." The children of light should be as wise as the children of this world.

NEXT WEEK WE HAVE A WORD TO SAY ABOUT THE IMPORTANCE OF MISSION HOMES.

We ask the hearty, liberal and prompt co-operation of the readers of The Christian-Evangelist. Send cash if you are prepared to do so; if not sign the following pledge or copy on a postal card and return:

If you will move in this matter now, you will help to insure the Centennial Fund and help to move others. What is now needed is a movement!

Address,

F. M. RAINS, Sec.,
Box 884, Cincinnati, O.

WATCH THIS SPACE NEXT WEEK!

THE PLEDGE.

I agree to donate to the Foreign Christian Missionary Society, Cincinnati, Ohio,
$............. per year for three years beginning June 1st, 1907, to aid in the creation of a special Two Hundred and Fifty Thousand Dollar ($250,000) Centennial Fund to be used for lands and buildings by the Society.

Name ....

P. O. ....

Street or R. F. D. ....

Date................1906. State...

The Christian-Evangelist.

J. H. GARRISON, Editor

PAUL MOORE, Assistant Editor

F. D. POWER, }
B. B. TYLER, } Staff Correspondents.
W. DURBAN, }

Subscription Price, $1.50 a Year.

For foreign countries add $1.04 for postage.

Remittances should be made by money order, draft, or registered letter; not by local cheque, unless 15 cents is added to cover cost of collection.

In Ordering Change of Post Office give both old and new address.

Matter for Publication should be addressed to THE CHRISTIAN-EVANGELIST. Subscriptions and remittances should be addressed to the Christian Publishing Company, 2712 Pine Street, St. Louis, Mo.

News Items, evangelistic and otherwise, are solicited, and should be sent on a postal card, if possible.

Published by the Christian Publishing Company, 2712 Pine Street, St. Louis, Mo.

Entered at St. Louis P. O. as Second Class Matte

CONTENTS.

Centennial Propaganda 1451
Current Events 1452
Editorial—
Where Jesus Placed the Emphasis........1453
A Pertinent Question........1453
Jesus and the Great Commission........1454
Notes and Comments........1454
Editor's Easy Chair........1455
Contributed Articles—
Where Jesus Placed the Emphasis. W. H. Bagby........1456
Visions of the English Bishop. William Durban........1457
As Seen from the Dome. F. D. Power........1458
Impressions of the Buffalo Convention....1459
The Outlook as Seen from Buffalo. W. J. Wright........1460
The Holy Spirit. F. M. Green........1460
Our Budget 1461
Carried Away in the Reading of a Hymn....1465

News from Many Fields.................1466
Evangelistic 1470
Sunday-school 1471
Midweek Prayer-meeting 1471
Christian Endeavor 1472
Obituaries 1473
Baptismal Dogma and the Great Commission.1474
Home Department 1475

THE
CHRISTIAN-EVANGELIST

--"IN FAITH, UNITY; IN OPINION AND METHODS. LIBERTY; IN ALL THINGS, CHARITY."

| Vol. XLIII. | November 15, 1906 | No. 46 |

1809 CENTENNIAL PROPAGANDA CHURCHES OF CHRIST 1909
: : : GEO. L. SNIVELY : : :

LOOKING TOWARD PITTSBURG.

One of the most picturesque Centennial missions· yet proposed is that of Brother David Millar's. We believe it is eminently practical and will·be crowned with gratifying success. The apostolic uniqueness, simplicity, and trustfulness of it makes the blood thrill with desire to have part in the apostolic triumph awaiting it. Who will be the Marks, Tituses and Timothies accompanying this twentieth century Paul on his first great missionary tour! The country is large and there' are other beckoning itineraries, who will claim them?

Our Centennial ·Secretary's clarion call to our sisterhood·will·strike chords in thousands of true hearts whose response will be, "We will, We are." As indispensable as women are to the successful development of religious, enterprises among all Christian bodies, the achievements of our own sisters is unparalleled outside our Disciple annals. Nor has the C. W. B. M. reached the zenith of its power for good. A saintly sister Burgess may·be called home, a Nancy E. Atkinson may relinquish leadership, but there will never fail an inspiring Mrs. M. E. Harlan to lead faster ·and 'farther and wider.

Woman and Missions.
BY W. R. WARREN.

The necessary part borne by women in the activities of missions may be clearly understood by a simple outline of the several fields in which the Christian Woman's Board of Missions is at work. Side by side with the Foreign Christian Missionary Society, mission stations, orphanages, schools and hospitals have been maintained in India. The growth and accomplishments of these have been most gratifying. On the island of Jamaica, in Mexico, South America and Porto Rico, the missionaries of this society have been laboring devotedly and successfully among our unfortunate neighbors. With industrial and other schools of the most approved types, ·its teachers have been serving among the negroes of the South and the neglected but capable white people of the mountains of·Eastern Kentucky. She has sought out also the states and ·cities of our country in which the apostolic plea was least known and has supported missionaries and evangelists there while they have been planting and developing ·churches of Christ. She has entered our great State Universities and established chairs for the teaching of the Bible on a par with other branches of learning. While maintaining these outward activities by her gifts systematically consecrated and accumulated, she has been devoting her time and attention with equal orderly care to increasing her own individual knowledge of missions and the Bible, training up the children of her community in the full appreciation of both the obligations and the privileges of the Savior's commission and exerting a constant influence in the church for aggressive righteousness throughout all the world.

Nothing further is needed to justify setting apart the first Lord's day of December as C. W. B. M. Day and devoting it to making the whole·church familiar with the way in which our modern Marys have done what they could. Such a public presentation of this service to which the love of Christ has constrained fifty ·thousand will lead as many more to choose the better part, and will help in many ways to prepare us all for the Centennial.

Centennial Secretary, Pittsburg, Pa.

Centennial Overland Campaign.

I am planning an ·evangelistic tour to begin about· May 1, 1907, to continue until the Centennial convention at Pittsburg in 1909.

That some such work as I am now planning is needed I am forced to believe by the fact that during the last few months I have been asked to hold meetings to strengthen weak churches and organize new ones, and had to decline owing to financial inability of the brethren. By this plan I expect to help at just such places.

The plan is to secure the co-operation or six consecrated young men (ministerial students) who can play some kind of instrument and sing, and who are possessed of hustling qualifications, grit, go and gumption. Our outfit will consist of an up-to-date wagonette built to accommodate comfortably seven persons, with the necessary rain and sun protection, drawn by a pair of strong horses, also a pair of lighter ones to be used as trace and saddle horses.

Our route will be through southeast Missouri, northwest Arkansas, into Indian Territory and· Oklahoma, as far as we can reach in five months, the time to be occupied in the outgoing trip. After which the young men will return by rail to their schools (if they are students), while I return over the course traveled for the purpose of confirming and strengthening the churches visited. Our work will be to hold meetings for weak churches and to organize new churches and Sunday-schools, staying a week or ten days at the most at each place. We will also stop at every ·village and· town we pass through and hold a service, and distribute tracts, etc. When we stay over to hold a meeting, we will drive to nearby. points in the daytime and on Lord's days the young men in pairs will hold meetings in school houses in the morning within a radius of five miles from town, while I preach there, and they will return for the meeting in town at night.

Our method will be in entering a town to drive around it, say seven times, for the purpose of getting the crowd from the very start. The band will play and signs will be conspicuously displayed upon the sides of the wagonette.

Our expenses and remuneration will be met by free will offerings and some help (I believe) from the missionary boards of the states we pass through, by advertising some of our schools and by the sale of bibles and other books. In fact each of the young men will be in charge of something·that will·prove remunerative.

Some one may ask why does it require a company of seven. Well, if I thought we could come out financially it would be a company of a dozen, so that when we entered a town we would not be handicapped by the attractions of the devil or the opposition of sectarians. We would have the right of way, and as our time will be limited this we must have. A center rush from start to finish. Do you know of any young men with the necessary qualifications? Do you know of any churches along the route given who need our services?

Have you any suggestion to offer, then please address, Yours in Christ,

Belleflower, Mo. DAVID MILLAR.

The Highest Journalism.
BY G. L. BUSH.

I write to congratulate you as General Superintendent upon the unprecedented increase in the circulation of THE CHRISTIAN-EVANGELIST. That it was growing and deserved to grow, I, knew like many others, but 30½ per cent in one year surprised me most delightfully. It is a fact of great significance to our movement and gives me as much joy as the increased receipts of our missionary societies. It indicates a growing appreciation of the best type of religious journalism by our ministers and members. This is one of the hopeful signs of the times and tends to optimism as to our future usefulness among the religious forces of the world.

Placing such a paper in every Christian home is an enterprise that should have the hearty co-operation of every minister in our ranks. It will give him an assistant pastor calling fifty-two times a year upon his members and keeping them well informed as to the progress of the gospel and the best thought of the times. It is high time for us to awake to the power of the press and help to supply the people with the right kind of literature. The wise shepherd seeks to *feed* as well as herd the flock, and· many know how easy it is to herd those who read our papers

Gainesville, Tex.

OUR CENTENNIAL HELPERS.

Last week's issue of THE CHRISTIAN EVANGELIST was great. If you have them on hand, please send me 100 copies. I want to distribute them here in the city and among my members.—L. A. Chapman, (minister) Mt. Pleasant, Ia.

Enclosed you will find order for my renewal of THE CHRISTIAN-EVANGELIST. I feel I can do without most anything else rather than do without THE CHRISTIAN-EVANGELIST.—Mrs. Sarah E. Stoops, Fullerton, Neb.

Current Events

Again the country has been saved. The patriots of both parties throughout

The Country Saved.

forty-two of our forty-five states have rallied to the defense of principle, party or persons, as the case happened to be, and the election is over. At the present writing, the returns show a Republican majority of something over fifty in the next house of representatives. This, of course, is for the sixtieth congress, which will meet a year from next December. We have many times commented on what seems to us the unfortunate arrangement of electing congressmen thirteen months before the time appointed for congress to assemble. In general interest the contest in New York overshadowed all other state campaigns. The election of Hughes (Rep.) by a plurality of about 75,000 over Hearst (Dem. and Ind.); while nearly all the remainder of the Democratic state ticket was elected, would be discouraging to any one less buoyant than Mr. Hearst. The contest hinged upon the popular opinion of Hearst's sincerity rather than upon any question regarding the principles which he professed. A candidate professing the same principles and admittedly sincere in the profession, would have been elected. But Hearst is still an unknown quantity and an undependable personality in the opinion of some thousands of people whose support he needed. For ourselves, we do not profess to know whether Hearst is sincere or not. But we are reasonably certain that in Mr. Hughes, New York will have an honest and capable governor who, in spite of inexperience in administrative work, will be efficient in his office. Most of the other states went about as they were expected to go. Missouri returned to the Democratic column. Nebraska, unmoved by the recent triumphal homecoming of the peerless leader, went Republican. Minnesota continued Democratic in the deserved re-election of Governor Johnson. The Republicans carried Colorado, which means the election of Buchtel as governor. He is a Methodist preacher (and a good one) and president of Denver University.

New Mexico and Arizona will wait a while longer for statehood. At last week's election

Statehood.

New Mexico voted to accept, but Arizona voted to reject, the proposition made by the last congress. In New Mexico the vote was about three to one in favor of joint statehood; in Arizona about three to one against it. Since New Mexico's vote is the larger, the proposition would have won but for the provision that each territory must accept

before the act could become effective. New Mexico has elected delegates to a constitutional convention. It is probable that these delegates will meet, frame a constitution and ask for separate statehood. Whether they will get it or not is another question. Probably not. But the expectation of getting separate statehood if New Mexico showed a disposition to accept what congress offered while New Mexico rejected it, was one factor in getting a large vote for joint statehood.

The Pennsylvania railroad has announced a 10 per cent increase in the pay of all of its

Prosperity.

employes who are receiving less than $200 a month. Here is a fine slice of the general prosperity handed out to some of the persons who are most deserving of it. Some other large employers ought to speak up to the same effect. And by the way, does it ever occur to church boards or school boards that preachers and teachers might appropriately be given a share of the prosperity of which we are all so proud. They get their share in the increased cost of living but they seldom have any other personal way of knowing that the times are prosperous.

That nine out of every ten Cubans entertain an unalterable prejudice against

Manual Labor.

manual labor as a means of obtaining a livelihood, is the answer which a recent visitor to the island gives to the question, "What's the matter with Cuba?" Cuba may have other and more original ailments. This one is certainly not confined to that island. But if it is so generally prevalent there it will inevitably be fatal to the infant civilization of that republic. Personally, we confess to a preference for intellectual toil. We would rather help to edit a newspaper than dig ditches. But most occupations (even newspaper work) require a combination, in varying proportions, of muscular and mental labor. The ideal work is one which calls into play both the gray matter and the long red fibers. The more successful workers generally find their work growing gradually more mental and less physical, for one good head can direct several pairs of hands and a head that can do that is better paid than one which can manage only one pair. But the man who starts in with the determination not to work with his hands is not choosing the right road to success. Nearly any soldier would rather be a colonel than a private, but it will be a poor army whose soldiers all insist on wearing the shoulder-straps. That's one thing that makes so many of the South American armies foolish and ineffective. The same principle applied in the industrial army produces no better results. A man of energy and ambition will say: I will

Editorial

Where Jesus Placed the Emphasis.—XII.

The Place of the Cross in Human Redemption.

We are still following Christ's own method of revelation. When he had brought his disciples to the clear recognition of his Messiahship and of his divine Sonship, "from that time began Jesus to show unto his disciples, that he must go unto Jerusalem and suffer many things of the elders and chief priests and scribes, and be killed, and the third day be raised up." (Matt. 16:21.) There were two reasons at least why this revelation of his humiliation and death was not made known to his disciples earlier. Not until their faith had grasped his divine character and mission were they able to stand such a revelation. It would have been too severe a shock for them. As the sequel shows they were imperfectly prepared even then, but the time had come when he could begin to take them into his confidence and let them know something of what awaited him. And then, in the second place, it is only in the light of Jesus' true nature, as "God manifest in the flesh," that his death can be seen in its vast significance, as essential to human salvation.

How foreign this thought of redemption through the sufferings of Christ was to the mind of the disciples, even at that period, is shown by Peter's rebuke to his Lord, saying: "Be it far from thee, Lord: this shall never be unto thee." This seemed to Peter, and no doubt to the others, as utterly inconsistent with the promise and hope that Christ should establish a kingdom and reign as king over that kingdom. But this was because Peter was looking at the problem from a purely human point of view. He expected his Master to come into the power of kingship, in the same way as other kings had come, and much in the same way, by which Satan had tempted Jesus to become a world-ruler. This was why Jesus rebuked Peter, calling him Satan, and bidding him get behind him. "Thou art a stumbling block unto me: for thou mindest not the things of God but the things of men." Christ had chosen the path of self-denial, humiliation, suffering, and death, as the way to universal dominion. This was contrary to all human ideas and methods. But nineteen centuries of Christian history have sufficed to show that the true way to dominion over the hearts and lives of men was indeed by the way of the cross.

While of course there is a uniqueness about the fact of Christ's death, in its relation to human salvation, the law of sacrifice which underlies it Jesus expands into a universal law; saying to his disciples, "If any man would come after me, let him deny himself, and take up his cross, and

follow me. For whosoever would save his life shall lose it: and whosoever shall lose his life for my sake shall find it." As there was no other way by which Christ could effect human redemption but the way of the cross, so he tells us, there is no other way to discipleship to him, except the way of the cross—the taking up of our cross and following him. As the principle of loyalty to his Father, and of love for men led him to offer his life for the sins of the world, so the principle of loyalty to God and of love for him and for our fellow men, will lead us to endure whatever sacrifice of time, money, reputation, and even of life itself, may be involved in doing the will of God and promoting the interests of our fellowmen. Whoever hesitates at any sacrifice however great, which is involved in discipleship to Jesus Christ, is unworthy to be his disciple. If this principle were emphasized more than it is, it would probably act as a sieve in keeping out of the church many who enter it, but the church would be stronger for the sifting, and would recruit its ranks none the less rapidly from those who are willing to follow Christ at all hazards.

The fundamental nature of Christ's death is graphically set forth in the scene in the Garden. "My Father, if it be possible, let this cup pass away from me: nevertheless, not as I will, but as thou wilt." Again, "If this can not pass away, except I drink it, thy will be done." The fact that the cup did not pass away, but that he drank it, even to its bitterest dregs, is evidence sufficient that not otherwise could the purpose of God in the salvation of men be realized. His language at the institution of the Lord's Supper is to the same effect. Concerning the loaf he said, "Take, eat; this is my body"; and of the cup he said, "Drink ye all of it; for this is my blood of the covenant which is poured out for many unto remission of sins" (Matt. 26:26-28). After his resurrection from the dead, on his walk to Emmaus with the two disciples, he said to them, "Thus it is written, that the Christ should suffer and rise again from the dead on the third day; and that repentance and remission of sins should be preached in his name unto all nations, beginning from Jerusalem" (Luke 24: 46, 47).

These passages suffice to show the fundamental importance of Christ's death in the plan of God for human redemption. They fully justify the statement of the greatest preacher of the first century: "But far be it from me to glory, save in the cross of our Lord Jesus Christ, through which the world hath been crucified unto me, and I unto the world" (Gal. 6:14). The cross of Christ is at once the highest expression of God's love for a sinning world, and the deepest revelation of the awful nature and consequences of sin, from the bondage and wages of which it was the purpose of Christ's death, to redeem men. No pulpit that minimizes the cross can be a pulpit of power, for the gospel is "the power of God unto salvation," and Christ's death for our sins is the very heart of the Gospel. Well may the church, in her on-

ward march through the centuries, continue to sing:

"In the cross of Christ I glory
Towering o'er the wrecks of time;
All the light of sacred story
Gathers round its head sublime."

A Pertinent Question.

An editorial from "The Examiner" (Baptist), New York City, entitled, "Why Not United?" which will be found elsewhere, raises a most pertinent and pressing question. The question why Baptists and Disciples are not united is a pressing one to all who feel that Christ's prayer for the unity of his followers expresses the will of God concerning us, and that it is our duty to do the will of God on earth as it is done in heaven.

If we were asked to answer the question raised by "The Examiner," "Why Not United?" we should say, first and chiefly, because they do not know each other well enough. Each body seems unaware, in the main, of the progress which the other has made and of the present state of religious feeling and conviction prevalent in each of the bodies. There ought to be, therefore, first of all, some plan for bringing the two bodies together in local, state and national gatherings for the purposes of interchange of thought and the promotion of mutual acquaintanceship. Why should we not plan to hold a common national congress in which there might be a discussion of the fundamental things of our common Christianity and an emphasis of things upon which we agree? One session might be devoted to disagreements which would tend to clear away the mists and reduce mountains to mole hills.

Another reason why the two bodies are not united is the existence of an extreme element in each, which magnifies the differences and minifies the agreements. This is a fact that must be reckoned with. It need not, however, be made a bar to mutual fellowship and co-operation among those who feel that we can not escape the displeasure of our Lord and Master, if we fail to carry out his desire that we should be one. Both the Baptists and Disciples have solved the problem of dealing with their anti-missionary society brethren by agreeing that all who believe in co-operation and missionary work should co-operate, and that those who are opposed to such a co-operation or prefer a different method of doing mission work, should pursue their own way, and we will have no quarrel with them. This same principle could be adopted in planning for such co-operation as is now practicable between the churches in both bodies prepared to enter into such co-operation. The others might be left free to come in later or permanently withhold their co-operation if they so preferred. There need be no quarrel nor separation, any more than there is in respect to our missionary methods. If this brief journey on shipboard with a company of our members on their way to the Buffalo convention, could create this impression on the mind of the editor of "The Examiner," think what a series of interdenominational gatherings would have in bringing about this feeling of unity.

The "Word of Approval," by Professor Hobart, called out by the editorial, which we also print, suggests that the Baptists as the older and larger of the two bodies, should take the initiative in bringing about this union. We feel perfectly safe in saying for the Disciples of Christ in general that "Barkis is willin." There was inaugurated at our last congress in Indianapolis, in which two eminent Baptists participated, a movement looking to a better understanding of each other, and we believe that Dr. Mullins, president of the Baptist Theological Seminary, at Louisville, took the initiative in this measure. If we will only be honest and open-hearted in trying to understand each other, the Lord, we are sure, will lead us into a closer unity and a sweeter fellowship.

Jesus and the Great Commission.

In another place we publish an article by Bro. J. S. Hughes, who believes he has a message on the above subject which the people should hear. We believe in freedom of speech and discussion and have agreed to permit Brother Hughes to state his position on this subject and his reasons therefor. The attempt of Brother Hughes to divorce baptism from the authority of Christ seems to us unavailing and unconvincing. Against it are the following facts: (1) Jesus himself was baptized, thereby setting us an example. (2) His disciples under his instruction practiced baptism. (3) He taught Nicodemus that "Except a man be born of water and of the Spirit, he can not enter into the kingdom of God," and (4) his apostles whom he trained and endowed with power from on high taught and practiced baptism, always connecting it with the name of Christ.

But we have not mentioned the fact that in the great commission as recorded by Matthew, Jesus commissioned his disciples to go and make disciples of all nations, "baptizing them into the name of the Father, and of the Son, and of the Holy Spirit." Brother Hughes gives certain reasons why he thinks Jesus did not give this commission to his disciples, but against all these reasons, stands the undisputed fact that Matthew's Gospel in all the oldest and best manuscripts, contains the passage quoted above, ascribing it to Christ. If we may annul the statement of Jesus contained in the received text of the New Testament, there is no end to this destructive process, except the fancy of each interpreter. As long as the scholarship of the world approves this passage as genuine no amount of subjective reasoning

nor arguments based on silences will suffice to separate that baptismal formula from the authority of Christ. That Brother Hughes has no proper appreciation of this fact is evidenced by his reference to the silence of the Scriptures concerning infant baptism, as a parallel case. But suppose there was an undisputed passage authorizing the baptism of infants: then to base an argument on the silence of the record concerning the actual cases of infant baptism, would be a very different proposition.

Hasting's Dictionary of the Bible, one of the ablest productions of modern scholarship, charged by no one with being too conservative, contains in its article on Baptism, page 241, the following statement which is given as the most satisfactory explanation of the formula mentioned in Acts of Apostles:

"When St. Luke says that people were 'baptized in (or into) the name of the Lord Jesus' he is not indicating the formula whch was used in baptizing, but is merely stating that such persons were baptized as acknowledged Jesus to be the Lord and the Christ; in short, he is simply telling us that the baptism was Christian. When Peter healed the cripple at the Beautiful Gate of the temple, the form of the words used is quoted: 'In the name of Jesus of Nazareth, walk.' No such form of words is quoted in any of the passages in which persons are said to be baptized in or into the name of Jesus Christ. There is no evidence against the supposition that in these and in all other cases the formula used was that which Christ rejoined. This is perhaps what Cyprian means when he says on Acts 2:38, Jesus Christi mentionem facit Petrus, non quasi Pater omitteretur, sed ut Patri Filius quoque adjungeretur (Eph. Lxx iii. 17). In I Cor. 10:2, where the Israelites are said to have been 'baptized into Moses, the meaning is that they were baptized into obedience to him and acknowledgment of his authority, not that his name was called over them in some formula."

With this view we concur, and with this brief statement we submit the article of Brother Hughes to our readers for their own judgment without further criticism.

Notes and Comments.

He is not a contributor to the peace and unity of the brotherhood, who magnifies the differences of opinion among brethren into articles of faith, and who speaks of the brethren, even those co-operating in missionary work, as divided into hostile camps and firing into each other! If we are going to adopt that sort of policy, and cultivate that sort of spirit, we may as well make up our minds to split into a number of little sects and parties, as many of the other Protestant bodies have done. It has generally been supposed that we have adopted a broader basis of fellowship than that, and had come into a larger inheritance of liberty not inconsistent with unity. And this we are persuaded is the conviction and guiding principle of the sanest and safest leaders among us.

We may have remarked before, but it will bear remarking again, that one of

Editor's Easy Chair.

Indian summer weather continues right along across the October line into November, regardless of our artificial divisions of time. There is as much haze and mystery about the origin of this phrase, "Indian Summer," as there is in the kind of weather which it designates. The most probable theory, however, is that the name was applied to the hazy, smoky, mild weather, which often comes in October and November and sometimes as late as December, because, in the early settlement of the country, the Indians committed their depredations in the white settlements at this season of the year, because their movements would be more or less concealed by the hazy condition of the atmosphere. But whatever may be the true theory about the *name*, the kind of weather which it designates is most charming. It brings to one who is fond of nature "The Call of the Wild." It is indeed a sort of imprisonment to be confined by one's duties indoors when

"There's a whisper on the hilltop and a murmur
  in the wood,
There's a dream of golden glory everywhere;
On the beech a russet cover, on the elm a scarlet
  hood,
But the walnut lifts her branches brown and
  bare.
When the squirrel's at his feasting in the old
  oak's top—.
And lo! the Indian summer, when the acorns
  drop!"

One picture comes clearly before our vision from boyhood days: It is the nutting season and November's "wailing winds" are bringing down the frost-loosened nuts from the great trees. And as they fall upon the ground the hulls burst and they lie in thick profusion. Sometimes when the wind did not suffice to bring them down fast enough, stones and clubs were improvised to assist nature in the work of harvesting the nuts. There were sacks full of hickory nuts, hazel nuts and walnuts, gathered from nature's own orchards, and laid away to dry for use in the long winter evenings around the blazing fire. Those were bright, halcyon days to us all, and the memory of them survives the wreck of many other scenes and incidents less congenial to the heart of boyhood and girlhood.

This is the era of simultaneous revival services. The phrase, as now used, means that the churches of the same religious body in a given district or state are engaged in evangelistic services at the same time. There is a great gain in this, both in the way of attracting public attention and in the mutual inspiration and encouragement which each church gets from the success of the others. The word "simultaneous" hardly expresses all that is involved in such meetings. The idea of *union* and of *co-operation* must enter into the plan as well as simultaneousness. The heart of these simultaneous revival movements is the union meeting in which the churches of a given city or district should meet together, at some central place, with as many people as they can bring together with them, for concentration of effort and for the mingling of hearts and voices in prayer and praise, for strengthening the bonds of unity, and for generating enthusiasm which can be transmitted to all parts of the movement. This feature of union added to that of *simultaneousness* will enable the weaker churches to share in the benefit, equally with the others, of all the advertising and all the general interest and enthusiasm. The simultaneous revival has probably come to stay, especially in the cities, for it is difficult for a single church in the city to make an impression upon the life of the city. But when a number of churches in different parts of the city join hands and hearts and make common cause in a great evangelistic campaign, the public attention is attracted, and many hear the Gospel and are drawn under the power of Christ, who would not otherwise be reached.

❦

But the idea of simultaneous evangelistic services needs to be enlarged. It should, occasionally, at least, embrace all the churches of the city that believe in the preaching of the Gospel for the conversion of sinners and the edification of saints. We can never make the impress upon our great cities which Christianity ought to make, until all the churches which acknowledge Jesus Christ as Lord, unite their efforts in preaching his Gospel and in bringing the knowledge of his truth and grace to the unevangelized masses. In the past it has been difficult, on account of excessive denominational zeal, to conduct such union meetings; but we have now reached a degree of Christian breadth and fellowship which makes it possible for Christian bodies, differing as yet in many things which would prevent their organic union, to unite in a common effort to bring men to repentance and to a saving faith in Jesus Christ as Savior and Lord. We are destined to witness more union evangelism in the future than has ever been possible in the past. Out of this united effort will come not only a larger influence for Christianity upon the thought and life of our cities, but a greater unity of feeling and fellowship among the several churches, which will greatly hasten the fulfillment of Christ's prayer for the oneness of his followers. These great union evangelistic meetings can alone solve the problem of city evangelization, and our cities must be evangelized if we are to perpetuate our free institutions and the life of the republic.

One of the changes needed to complete the preparation of all the churches for union evangelistic services, is the realization, to a much greater degree, of how much more important it is that men should be brought to a knowledge of God and to a living faith in him as he is revealed in Christ, than that they should have correct theories about forms of church government, theology, and methods of salvation. To put these things in the same class is to make all co-operation impossible. But he who so classifies them has yet to learn the deepest meaning of salvation as taught by Christ and his apostles. We are far from decrying the value of a correct knowledge of all questions that relate to Christian doctrine and to the progress of the church. But all this is a matter of growth after the soul has been brought into right relations with God by leaving off its sins, and, in a penitent faith coming to Christ for life and for pardon. This is the work of supreme value, and it is a work in which all churches can engage that are able to discriminate between things which are vital to salvation, and those which are useful and helpful in promoting the soul's growth and usefulness. After all, is not this the very distinction which our own religious movement has sought to emphasize from the beginning—the difference between faith and opinion, insisting that faith, in the New Testament sense, is confidence in and allegiance to Jesus Christ, and not the intellectual acceptance of a formulation of doctrines, either about Christ or about the church or the ordinances. Get Christ in the heart, we have said, and he will make everything else right. This is the basis on which we can hold union evangelistic services.

❦

It is a group of strong, forceful men of faith that is preaching the Gospel in our evangelistic campaign in St. Louis. They do not deal in negations. They have a positive message for the people. They believe and, therefore, speak. They have a clear grasp on fundamental truth, on the great spiritual realties, and these they present with a clearness of conviction that proceeds from faith quickened and intensified by personal experience. What a power it is to the preacher to commend to others that which he has experienced and found to be true in his own life! To lay a broad foundation for faith, to exalt Christ to his true place as the only Savior, and then to make the way unto him clear and plain—that is the program of true evangelism. Never since the apostolic age have men been truer to this New Testament method than are our own best evangelists today who are winning such victories for Christ. What this world needs is faith, not doubt.

"Talk faith. The world is better off without
  Your uttered ignorance and morbid doubt.
If you have faith in God, or man, or self,
  Say so. If not, push back upon the shelf
Of silence your thoughts till faith shall come;
  No one will grieve because your lips are dumb."

Where Jesus Placed the Emphasis* By W. H. Bagby

To become the Savior of the world Jesus had to become the Teacher of the world. Salvation in its broadest and best sense is education in its highest and most comprehensive sense. If Jesus had not taught, all else he did would have been in vain. Not because he wrought mighty works, but because he spake mighty words, has he been received by men as the Savior of the world. In making this assertion I in no wise minimize the importance of his works. On the contrary, I magnify it. If I wished to indicate by comparison, the loftiness of the Himalayas, I should choose the Alps or the Andes or the Rockies, the next loftiest mountains in the world.

To become the acknowledged Teacher of mankind Jesus had to meet the unrelenting demand the world makes upon him who aspires to be its teacher: that there shall be no mistake made in the placing of the emphasis. If he is the acknowledged Teacher of the world to-day it is because he met this demand by stressing only those things which the consensus of human intelligence and experience approves as worthy of emphasis. If he is the accepted Savior of men it is because he is the acknowledged teacher of saving truths and vital principles.

If what has just been affirmed be true, it follows as a vitally important conclusion, that the Church of Christ, to become, under her great head, the savior of the world, must become the acknowledged and accepted teacher of the world. In order to this, she must make no mistake in the point of emphasis. She must place the emphasis where Jesus placed it, and not be found stressing traditions and technicalities, and slurring vital principles and eternal verities. She must not be found like the Pharisees of old, magnifying matters of minor importance to the neglect of the weightier matters of the law. He sows in vain who sows but glittering grains of lifeless wind. In vain the Church of Jesus Christ expends all her precious strength and store scattering the seeds of dead dogmas, lifeless traditions, and powerless provincialisms. Only the seeds of living truth sown in good and honest hearts, can save this sinful world. There is no greater need than that the Church of Christ should be awakened to a realization of this great fact; for it would drive her to the task of seeking and stressing the vital things that Jesus stressed. Christ is the potential Savior of all men; but he is the actual Savior of only those who accept him as best they can with the light they have. Under Christ the Church is the potential savior of all; but to be the actual

savior of any, she must become the accepted source of saving, teaching and help. To become such she must teach truths and exemplify principles conceded by the best thought of the world, to be vital and essential. In a word, he must stress the things that Jesus stressed. In the limited space of this paper, only a few of the things that Jesus emphasized can be dwelt upon, and these but briefly. Those only have been selected the discussion of which is deemed most profitable at the present time.

I. Jesus placed the emphasis on the Function of the Church and not on its Form.

Like everything else in the world, the Church came into being for its highest function. Not to attain to a predetermined perfection of form, but to the perfect performance of a divinely prescribed function was to be its high aim and effort. As in the natural world, so in the spiritual realm, form is determined by function, and not function by form. As to its form, everything is a matter of what it does. There is no better illustration of the truth than is afforded by the Church herself. It is a matter of history that the Church came into being in the simplest possible form. There were but two classes in it—apostles and private members. This first simple form was adequate for the discharge of its first simple functions. As time passed on other demands arose and its form became inadequate to the full discharge of its functions. To meet this enlarged demand there was an enlargement of the form of the Church. In obedience to the law that says that function shall determine form, and in response to the voice of need, which is always and everywhere, the voice of God, the office of Deacon came into being. As came this office (organ) so came all the others that were later added. The need did not arise to meet the pre-existing office, but the office arose to meet the pre-existing need. The form of the Church at the close of the apostolic period was simply what its efforts to meet the needs of that period had made it. Was this to be its fixed and final form? Only to the extent to which that form had been determined by the demand of permanent need. It is a matter of history that there were offices in the apostolic Church that came into being in response to temporary demands. These ceased after the cessation of the demands that had called them into being. Among these were the offices of apostles and prophets. They departed in obedience to the law that says that no organ shall survive its function. If there should cease to be a demand for any office now in the Church, the same law that demanded the elimination of apostles and prophets from the Church of the first century would demand the elimination of that office from the Church of the twentieth century. If a demand unknown to the Church of the first century should arise in the twentieth century that same law would demand the

creation of an office unknown to the Church of the first century. The divine form of the Church is what the present demands upon it make it. Its fixed features are those only which exist in response to fixed demands. We have made a fetish of the form of the apostolic Church. We have attached an importance to it that does not belong to it. Assuming that it was constructed according to a divine pattern, we have made it the true test of the Scriptural Church. The possession of the form of the apostolic Church no more proves that an organization is the true Church of Christ than the possession of the form of a man proves that a marble statue is a living man. Only by the possession of his Spirit and the performance of its divinely-appointed functions can an organization establish its claim to be the Church of Christ. By her fruits and not by her form the Bride of Christ is known.

The Church could have no greater handicap than rigidity of form and inflexibility of method. Her task is world-wide and age-long. She is the hand of God for the accomplishment of this task. That hand must be characterized by the utmost freedom and flexibility. The conservatism that would sacrifice the work to save the form of the hand is as unreasonable as it is unscriptural. Christ was glad that demons were being cast out even by those who did not company with him. He is not in sympathy with the sentiment that would let the old ship of Zion remain forever becalmed rather than to convert her from a sailing vessel into a steamer. God's hand, is not with the Church that is standing guard over its form, but it is with the Church that is on a forced march in pursuit of its function. To eyes not blinded by prejudice, it is perfectly manifest that his hand is with bodies that, in their form, are wholly unlike the apostolic Church. The vital question to-day is not whether the Church has the form of the apostolic Church, but whether she has that form which best adapts her to meet the meeting of the demands of the present age. That form which does this is the most scriptural and the divinest. For the Church to eliminate the useless and to add the useful is to exercise the liberty wherewith Christ has made her free. In the eyes of Christianity nothing is sacred simply because it is conventional, but only because it met the demands of that period. If any feature of it is still divine (I speak reverently) it is because it is useful, and not because it was a feature of the Church of that period. Nothing can have any rightful place in the Christian Church on the mere ground of its conventionality. If it is useful the fact that it is conventional weighs nothing against it; but if it is not useful the fact that it is conventional weighs nothing in its favor.

❧ ❧

They who give according to their ability likely to have the ability to give again very soon.

*A paper read at the Texas Christian Lecture-ship. To be concluded next week.

Visions of the English Bishops By William Durban

The prophets are predicting, the pessimists are moaning, the optimists are indulging in dithyrambics and dances, the soothsayers are vaticinating, and the dictators of divinity are scattering broadcast the seeds of new controversies. It can not be said that the British people are religiously asleep. For never have I known livelier times than we are passing through. I have always felt deepest interest in the various and multitudinous conferences of all the great religious societies, for at these the representative men find opportunities of making authoritative statements of the opinions they are able to formulate after matured experience and protracted study. I shall not, of course, be able in the course of one short article to give any account of the vast volume of autumnal talk to which we are being treated by Anglicans, Baptists, Congregationalists, Presbyterians and Methodists in their fine assemblies. But I will make reference to certain extraordinary deliverances which I regard as most instructive and noteworthy signs of the times. In the buzzing and confusion of the oratorical chorus it is well to hearken specially to some few of the most suggestive dicta.

The Bishop of London on Christian Unity.

Dr. Winnington Ingram, the esteemed and intensely popular Bishop of London, has been delivering one of his characteristic utterances at a great gathering of young men at the London Polytechnic. After descanting on the immorality of great cities, the bishop observed that one of the greatest difficulties to be contended with to-day is the divided state of Christendom. He said that in the work of the Church one expected to encounter agnostics, sceptics, vice, crime, and drink, but the most miserable thing was the division among Christians. He would ask Christians of all denominations to be good members of the society to which they belonged, for the only way to heal the divisions in Christianity was for all to be enthusiastic working members of their several communities, but having tolerance, love and respect for those who differed from them, rather than feelings of bitterness.

The Bishop of Carlisle's Vision of Unity.

It is evident that some of the ablest and most influential of the English prelates are feeling troubled over this problem of Christian unity. I observe one singular phenomenon. A few years ago most of the great Anglican dignitaries were indulging in a roseate dream of what they styled the "Corporate Reunion of Christendom." The ring-leaders were Dr. King, Bishop of Lincoln, and the late accomplished Dr. Creighton, for a few years Bishop of London. This vision related to the reunion of the Roman, Greek and Anglican communions. It was fondly imagined by the great body of high churchmen, Lord Halifax being the most influential layman amongst them, that negotiations and overtures would bring about a great federation of Roman Catholics, Greek Catholics and Anglo Catholics. But we hear little of such aspirations now. The Pope of Rome has condescended only to make it clear that there can quickly enough be consummated a reunion of Christendom if all who are not Roman Catholics become such, and the great Russo-Greek church in all its actions insists on its right to swallow up all competitors. Now, the Bishop of Carlisle, Dr. Diggle, has at the great meetings of the church congress, just held at Barrow-in-Furness, launched a most uncomfortable sort of philippic against his own Anglican communion. Presiding as bishop of the northernmost English diocese at the congress, held within his own territory, Dr. Diggle talked in his address in a style that would have been unthinkable on the part of any prelate a few years ago. He struck out right and left in his unsparing criticisms of the Anglican church. He contended that the church must be both ancient and modern, primitive and progressive. One of the surest notes of a living religion is that as it grows older it also grows younger. The present peril to the church was that of going too near the middle ages, but not near enough to Christ. It was in danger, too, of falling behind the times, and so of being forsaken by the people. One of their shortcomings, accounting for the vast falling away of the people, was that the world was too much in the church and the church too little in the world. The world's knowledge was penetrating to the masses and becoming increasingly scientific in temper. Would the church welcome that temper as a friend, or treat it as a foe? Would she shut herself up behind tottering traditions? They stood at the parting of the ways, and the only choice was reform or ruin—fresh development or certain decay.

"In my young days," said the bishop, "I often dreamed dreams, and now I am growing old I sometimes see visions. Among my sweetest visions is that of a truly catholic and apostolic church. I seem to see all the churches marching into one flock. In the van of the procession I see our own beloved church of England, with a vast train of young and old, rich and poor, learned and ignorant, singly or pardoned, carried in her arms, holding on to her robes. Then I see the noncomformist and other reformed churches following close behind; then the Greek and other eastern churches, emancipated from their trammels and glowing with freedom; then the Roman church, purified as by fire, and, last of all, the hosts which no man can number. Then I wake and find it all a vision; yet not a vision of the black closing night, but of the red opening dawn. That God will grant to this congress the power to help forward, if only by a single step, the realization of this vision is my heart's most earnest prayer."

The Church that Most Impedes Unity.

It is not surprising that the magnificent oration of Bishop Diggle was greeted with the most enthusiastic applause. His eloquence carried away his immense audience. What is to be deeply regretted is that this same learned and aspiring dignitary seems utterly unconscious that he and an army of good men like him are the most formidable obstacles to the very thing that he so ardently longs for. It is certain that the Bishop of Carlisle will never, unless he becomes radically revolutionized, help to materialize his own vision. For only a few days before he delivered this harangue he was expressing himself vehemently in favor of sustaining the state establishment of the Anglican church, and he on the same occasion declared himself against the idea of mutual interchanges of pulpits by Anglican and free church preachers!! Truly such an attitude of mind as this makes his position on reunion an incomprehensible paradox. Here we have him in the same week declaring for the most emphatic symbols of separation and sectarian exclusiveness and also for a universal spiritual brotherhood. Well, I profoundly respect the learning and the earnestness of Bishop Diggle, but I absolutely despair of comprehending his meaning. I might as well endeavor—

(Continued on Page 1472.)

❀ ❀

IT'S THE FOOD

The True Way to Correct Nervous Troubles.

Nervous troubles are more often caused by improper food and indigestion than most people imagine. Even doctors sometimes overlook this fact. A man says:

"Until two years ago waffles and butter with meat and gravy were the main features of my breakfast. Finally dyspepsia came on and I found myself in a bad condition, worse in the morning than any other time. I would have a full, sick feeling in my stomach, with pains in my heart, sides and head.

"At times I would have no appetite for days, then I would feel ravenous, never satisfied when I did eat and so nervous I felt like shrieking at the top of my voice. I lost flesh badly and hardly knew which way to turn until one day I bought a box of Grape-Nuts food to see if I could eat that. I tried it without telling the doctor, and liked it fine; made me feel as if I had something to eat that was satisfying and still I didn't have that heaviness that I had felt after eating any other food.

"I hadn't drank any coffee then in five weeks. I kept on with the Grape-Nuts and in a month and a half I had gained 15 pounds, could eat almost anything. I wanted, didn't feel badly after eating and my nervousness was all gone. It's a pleasure to be well again."

Name given by Postum Co., Battle Creek, Mich. Read the book, "The Road to Wellville," in pkgs. There's a reason.

As Seen From the Dome

November 18 is to be observed throughout England by the "Day of Rest Movement." Simultaneous sermons, popular messages of representative leaders of Christianity through the press, Catholic and Protestant, united prayer and united effort in public meetings and house to house visitation, in which the established church and evangelical uniformity join hands; all are to promote better observance of the Lord's day.

A German reviewer spoke some time ago of "the religious Renaissance in London." One certainly sees great religious activity in the world's metropolis. The Welsh revival and the Torrey-Alexander meetings, and the ceaseless work of the churches show their effects to every visitor. Such an array of meetings as one sees announced by every individual church is amazing to an American. London has 2,700 places of worship. The church of England has 1,014; the Baptists, 283; Congregationalists, 219; Wesleyans, 159; Roman Catholics, 100; Presbyterians, 68; Christadelphians, 7; Disciples, 6. A religious census in 1902-3 shows in the population of 4,580,065, a Sunday attendance of 1,003,361; that is, a decrease since a similar census in 1886 of 163,951. The decline was almost entirely in the church of England. This showed a falling off of 139,519, while that of nonconformity was only 5,467. Of the attendance of 1,003,361, 323,735 were children, 412,999 women and 266,627 men.

A great change has come over London in twenty years—a revolt against formalism. The new century has its own spirit. Booth was laughed at once, his people mobbed and jailed, his religion characterized as corybantic. Salvation Army barracks now number 94 and Booth is classed with Loyola and Luther as the religious genius of his time. Earnestness and sacrifice have triumphed. But a decline in regular church attendance in sixteen years from 1,167,312 to 1,003,361 would mean that London is in a state of backsliding. Buckle said statistics will tear the heart out of every human system. The figures tell.

That this decline is a revolt against formalism is evident from the tremendous loss in the attendance upon the established church. The militant secularism, of which Bradlaugh was the chief protagonist, is dead. Scientists like Huxley and Tyndall descended into the arena of theological conflict as companions of agnosticism and tilted with Gladstone, Wace and Argyll. Now the scientists who deal with religion are not nearly so confirmed in their negations, many like Alfred Russell Wallace, Sir William Crookes and Oliver Lodge openly avowing their faith in the Bible and immortality. Evolution is no longer exempt from attack. Formalism is losing trust in its formulas and agnosti-

cism shows a more open mind. In the nonconformist churches, like Dr. Clifford's and Dr. Campbell's, and many others which I attended, I observed large congregations, and a devotion and enthusiasm one does not see in our American churches. Christian Endeavor has twenty-one unions, with 754 societies, and a membership of 33,570, and only five societies belonging to the church of England. It was Easter when the ritualistic organizations are at their best, and yet the audiences I noticed in Oxford and London in these churches did not seem large. Many vacant seats though the music was exceptionally fine and the millinery and ceremony as effective as might be desired. In Westminster Abbey Easter Sunday, April 15, I listened to Canon Henson. This historic place is a center of interest to strangers, and one always sees Americans here and tourists from everywhere, and the service is impressive by reason of the surroundings, more so than in St. Paul's or the city temple or the Westbourne Park Chapel, but even here there was no crowding. The people evidently do not care for formalism. They need New Testament Christianity.

The explanation of present religious conditions in the great metropolis was clear to me when I picked up the order of worship for the day in Westminster. On the first page of this bulletin with greatest prominence was printed the "Fides Catholica." It seems an archaism, but here it is, as placed in the hands of this twentieth century congregation. Perhaps you never read it:

The Catholick Faith is this: That we worship one God in Trinity, and Trinity in Unity;

Neither confounding the Persons: nor dividing the Substance.

For there is one Person of the Father, another of the Son: and another of the Holy Ghost.

But the Godhead of the Father, of the Son, and of the Holy Ghost, is all one; the Glory equal, the Majesty co-eternal.

Such as the Father is, such is the Son: and such is the Holy Ghost.

The Father uncreate, the Son uncreate; and the Holy Ghost uncreate.

The Father incomprehensible, the Son incomprehensible: and the Holy Ghost incomprehensible.

The Father eternal, the Son eternal: and the Holy Ghost eternal.

And yet they are not three eternals: but one eternal.

As also there are not three incomprehensibles, nor three uncreated: but one uncreated, and one incomprehensible.

So likewise the Father is Almighty, the Son Almighty: and the Holy Ghost Almighty.

And yet there are not three Almighties: but one Almighty.

So the Father is God, the Son is God: and the Holy Ghost is God.

And yet there are not three Gods: but one God.

So likewise the Father is Lord, the Son Lord: and the Holy Ghost Lord.

And yet not three Lords: but one Lord.

For like as we are compelled by the Christian Verity: to acknowledge every Person by himself to be God and Lord:

So are we forbidden by the Catholick Religion: to say there be three Gods, or three Lords.

The Father is made of none: neither created, nor begotten.

Impressions of the Buffalo Convention

We asked a few of the veterans attending the conventions at Buffalo to send us their impressions of the convention with any suggestions for improvement in future conventions. We published some of the replies last week. Others follow:

By S. C. Toof.

I first attended the general convention in 1870, and have attended or thoroughly read the reports of all the conventions since. My opinion is, that all our general conventions have been marvels of success in the manner of their order of proceedings. I see no cause for change in the preparation of the programs. A little more variety might be introduced by fewer set addresses, leaving time for some short impromptu talks by well-known men who might be in attendance, to be called upon by the presiding officer. I find no language to tell of the wonderful meetings held by the C. W. B. M. at the Buffalo Convention. The little talks by the returned missionaries were a source of information and inspiration to all.

Memphis, Tenn.

By Addison Clark.

The national convention of 1893, 1895, 1899, 1902, 1903, 1906, are the only ones which this far-away Texas teacher has had the privilege of attending. They have all seemed the best to me; that is, each seemed better than its predecessor. At the Buffalo Convention, the decorum seemed to me to be much better than at former conventions. Business seemed to be dispatched with greater ease and promptness. The addresses, though delivered, in the main, by the younger men, impressed me as being of a very high order, both as to matter and manner. The peace, unity and harmony that prevailed kept my mind filled with the 133d Psalm. So eager was the desire for harmony that the word "federation" was not spoken from the platform. If so, I did not hear it. For this condition of things, however, I did not rejoice, and do not rejoice. I mean that condition that held back from free expression of the readiness and eagerness of that great body of Disciples to take this long step toward that unity for which Christ prayed. I doubt the wisdom of holding the next convention, or any of our conventions, at the place of international expositions.

Thorp Spring, Texas.

By E. C. Browning.

My impression of the Buffalo Convention was generally good, and very good.

I think our conventions have improved in the devotional and reverential spirit. Perhaps there is still room for improvement in this regard. I heard a brother of reputation say, he would prefer "less clapping of hands and more Amens." If this would be more reverential he is probably right.

One very encouraging thing was that there were more young men on the program. The addresses were generally, if not universally, of a very high order. I am inclined to think that it is unwise to present the same names for special addresses, year after year. Of course the officers of the general boards must make their reports, but if suitable men can be found for special addresses, it seems to me expedient that different sections of our country should be represented.

I have little disposition to criticise a program, for it is one of the most difficult things to make a satisfactory program. All speakers should be held strictly to their time on the program.

It seems to me a wise provision to specify a portion of time for visiting places of special interest. There are certain phases of our convention work that relate to business, that I have thought could be improved, but I leave suggestions to others.

The spirit of harmony, good will and liberality that pervaded the convention is very encouraging.

No convention has been better cared for than the Buffalo meeting.

Little Rock, Ark.

By John H. Gordinier.

I was greatly pleased with the Convention. The arrangements for the care of the delegates were complete. The business management of the sessions was perfect. The leaders were the right ones in their places. The sermons and addresses by the speakers were very instructive and inspiring. Picked men and women gave us their best thoughts. The spiritual tone of the convention was pitched on a high key. The closing service was grand. The rapid firing guns electrified the audience. The interest was intense, the enthusiasm great. We thanked God and took courage for greater things in the future. We see more clearly in vision the world-wide empire of the Christ, and pray more fervently for its expansion among the nations.

Scio, N. Y.

By Charles Louis Loos.

What first of all profoundly impressed every one was the great assembly that had come from all parts of the United States and from the British dominions. The vast convention hall was filled to its utmost capacity. It presented a most inspiring sight. I said to myself, "Hitherto after so many years of conflict and waiting, the Lord has brought us."

We have gone far to overcome among our brotherhood the obstinate resistance to the cause of world-wide missions. What we have accomplished is a strong encouragement to go on to greater victories.

The spirit of the convention was all that could have been desired. A happier concourse of men and women could not be imagined. And all present had an intelligent conception and appreciation of the motives that had brought us together. Here was a fair representation of the best intelligence of our people in the holiest and most potent cause that can move human hearts.

We have learned much through the years that have passed since the national convention of 1849. And yet there is no religious people more free than we are in our judgments and in the expression of them. Wisdom presided over the convention. Nothing was brought before it but the great and holy themes that were supreme in the hearts of all. May it ever be so. May we ever guard with diligent care, with sleepless vigilance, the sacred trust of unity, of perfect fellowship of faith, of life and action that has been our strength.

One thought constantly passed through my mind as I observed the proceedings of the convention: of the

C. W. B. M. I said to myself: Here is a striking living exposition of the divine reason given in Genesis for the creation of woman: "It is not good that the man should be alone; I will make him an helpmeet for him."

It is certainly a most feeble and unworthy interpretation of these words to assume that they refer only to the office of woman in her conjugal and domestic relations. No! So great a word as evidently is this goes much farther; it certainly embraces in its widest scope all the social and all the moral and religious life of "the man," the "Adam," in even its greatest enterprises. In all these woman's assistance is needed to bring them to perfect completeness. And nowhere is this more manifest than in the work of the people of God on the earth. See what woman is accomplishing since she has been brought into special activity in her own particular sphere in the great enterprises of the church.

We must understand, once for all, that the vast enterprise of evangelizing "all the world" outside of christendom, including even many nations nominally Christian, must necessarily excite a supreme interest in the Christian church. Nothing can awaken in the hearts of God's people such strenuous motives for action, for liberal consecration of our substance and of ourselves, as the appeal to go forth and bring the whole pagan world to Christ; to save it. This must of necessity ever stand in the front of our missionary enterprises. The argument in behalf of our home missions cannot well be exaggerated. The A. C. M. S. demands and deserves a powerful support from a million and a quarter of Christian believers.

I know of no good ground for looking into the future otherwise than with hope and strong confidence in all our state and general missionary enterprises.

Lexington, Ky.

By W. S. Dickinson.

My mind and heart are so full of good impressions and thoughts of the convention that I am at a loss to specify its strongest points. It was a most inspiring, uplifting meeting; its personnel was excellent and harmonious beyond expectation, with not a note of discord. I was impressed by the careful preparation of the addresses of the various speakers, which, I think, have not been excelled in any of our former conventions; all breathed the spirit of Christ and Christian union; all strongly set forth the importance and necessity of missions—foreign and home—and a deeper spirit of consecration among all Christians.

There was no magnifying "our views;" there was no occasion for it. The arrangements of plans and details were most admirable and could hardly have been excelled. I regret to write of a lack of order during some of the sessions. I suggest that in the future a rule be adopted to have all doors of the hall locked a minute or two previous to the delivering of any address and until its close, none be permitted to pass in or out. An arrangement of this kind, I think, would add to the pleasure of both speaker and listeners.

I regard the Buffalo Convention as one of the most encouraging and helpful of any held by our churches—it so impressed me.

Cincinnati, O.

The Outlook As Seen From Buffalo

By W. J. WRIGHT,

Corresponding Secretary of American Christian Missionary Society.

"The morning cometh!" All signs indicate it. As a people we, are going forward rapidly. The missionary enterprises can not lag behind—least of all, home missions, the basis of all our organized work.

That every prospect brightens for the American Christian Missionary Society is evident in a few infallible signs much in evidence in Buffalo. Note a few of them: The attendance at the sessions of the home society. Instead of falling off, as at some other conventions, the great hall continued to be well filled at each session. Most of the people came early and got as near as possible to the speakers. Moreover, they stayed till the benediction was pronounced.

That makes the next point evident: They were interested. They knew something of the history of this society which is the mother of more than 3,000 churches in the United States. They wanted to hear her plans discussed and her claims set forth. They were ready, yea eager, for every good word. The flash of wit, the straight hard drive from the shoulder, the revelation of a great opportunity, the accusation that the home society was neglected and did not get the "square deal," the appeal for liberal things, the declaration that her work would be brought to the front—all these were instantly and heartily applauded in every session of the American society.

Her sessions were marked by great addresses. "The greatest day of sacred eloquence within my experience," was the verdict of the bishop of Washington; and men who were forward in the councils of the Disciples of Christ twenty years before, Brother Power was known declared the greatest day of speeches in the history of the society. The optimism of the speakers was contagious. Hundreds voluntarily expressed their firm hope that the new era had been entered upon by the home society, and that her progress would henceforth be many fold greater than in the past. The speakers presented great plans and made powerful pleas for their accomplishment; and the people responding in hearty and prolonged applause showed that they agreed with what was being said.

The convention confirmed the friendship of many and made a host of new friends for the American Christian Missionary Society. These friends, old and new, will take up her burdens as being their own, and will seek to increase greatly the number of individual churches, Sunday-schools and other organizations contributing to her support. Her receipts will swell. The volume of her work will increase, and its quality improve. The whole brotherhood will rejoice in her power and prosperity, and all our other work will go forward the more rapidly because the base of supplies, home missions, has been cared for as becomes wise men engaged in this spiritual warfare.

Without being unmindful of some mists, clouds and partial darkness, here in Buffalo I can not do otherwise than borrow for the American Christian Missionary Society an expression from one of the greatest missionaries, and declare that "The outlook is as bright as the promises of God." Will you help to keep them so?

[And let all the people say Amen!— EDITOR.]

the book that I like. First, I agree with him in most of the positions he takes and that makes me feel pleasantly when the other man agrees with me. Second, the author is not a dogmatist and does not seek to force any one to accept his dictum anyhow. Third, all the Scripture passages which bear on the subject are given with a commentary modest and conservative following. All in all I am pleased with the book and am glad I have no fear that "the foundations of the great deep" will be broken up if some of the positions taken by the Christian man who has written it should not be agreed to. The book has its value because it gives indirectly a history of the various stages in the progress of the discussion of the great question. Because of these characteristics the book can be read with profit by all. He who is really "filled with the Spirit" can not lead men astray and his prayer will ever be:

"O Church of Christ, to prayer; to prayer!
　Lean on thy sacred shrine,
　And there while lowly bowing down
　Receive the strength divine.
Then rise and let the Spirit's life
　Be healing for thy woes;
And let the Spirit's flaming sword
　Be lightning on thy foes."
Akron, Ohio.

❀　❀

"GOOD STUFF"

A Confirmed Coffee Drinker Takes to Postum.

A housewife was recently surprised when cook served Postum instead of coffee. She says:

"For the last five or six years I have been troubled with nervousness, indigestion and heart trouble. I couldn't get any benefit from the doctor's medicine, so finally he ordered me to stop drinking coffee, which I did.

"I drank hot water while taking the doctor's medicine, with some improvement, then went back to coffee with the same old trouble as before.

"A new servant girl told me about Postum—said her folks used it and liked it in place of coffee. We got a package but I told her I did not believe my husband would like it, as he was a great coffee drinker.

"To my surprise he called for a third cup, said it was "good stuff" and wanted to know what it was. We have used Postum ever since and both feel better than we have in years.

"My husband used to have bad spells with his stomach and would be sick three or four days, during which time he could not eat or drink anything. But since he gave up coffee and took to Postum, he has had no more trouble, and we now fully believe it was all caused by coffee.

"I have not had any return of my former troubles since drinking Postum, and feel better and can do more work than in the last ten years. We tell everyone about it—some say they tried it and did not like it. I tell them it makes all the difference as to how it's made. It should be made according to directions—then it is delicious."

Name given by Postum Co., Battle Creek, Mich. Read the book, "The Road to Wellville," in pkgs. "There's a reason."

The Holy Spirit. By F. M. Green

To the student of the New Testament there can be no question as to the important place the Holy Spirit holds in the conversion and sanctification of man. From first to last it is given large place; and "his personality, mission and modes of activity" are not confined in a "prison of words," but are declared in words so plain that the discussion of the subject since the apostolic age has added little, if anything, to the clear, clean-cut declarations of the Lord and his apostles. Books have been written almost without number; pamphlets have been written by the thousands; and a great multitude of orators have thundered their dogmas concerning the great subject. To-day the religious periodicals of nearly every "branch" of the Church of Christ are filled with almost numberless articles, pro and con, on some phase of the great question. I have no doubt that many of these speak or write with a sincere desire to explain what they think lacks clearness or needs explanation; but since the early days of my ministry, when I considered it my duty to enlighten the people on "The New Birth" and the "Doctrine of the Holy Spirit," I have dreaded the appearance of any new discussion of the subject. Most that appears is the "threshing of old straw" and the added dogmatism of men who are bound to have their way right, "whether or no." In looking through the pages of one religious newspaper which comes to me every week, I noticed a half dozen articles by as many different writers, each of them having a different view of the question and each one quite certain that he was right and the others wrong. But I suppose the discussion must needs go on, for "what has been must be," though "there is nothing new under the sun;" and I pray that no harm may come and the divine declarations concerning the great questions be obscured by clouds. I have read with interest Dr. J. H. Garrison's treatise on the subject. There are several things in

Our Budget

—The Evangelistic Campaign goes bravely on.

—"It is a glorious thing to rally souls to the cross of Christ."—Knowles Shaw.

—"God forbid that I should glory save in the cross of our Lord Jesus Christ."—Paul.

—"They that win many to righteousness shall shine as the stars, forever and ever."—Daniel.

—"There is more joy in heaven over one sinner that repenteth than over ninety and nine just persons who need no repentence."—Jesus.

—"Ho, every one that thirsteth, come ye to the waters, and he that hath no money, come ye, buy wine and milk without money and without price!"—Isaiah.

—Notice that thirst precedes coming to the waters. The sinner must feel his need of salvation before he will or can come to Christ. This indicates the divine order of procedure. O for the power to convict men of sin! This is the work of the Holy Spirit through the Gospel and the preacher who is most filled with the Spirit will succeed best in this vital work.

✦ ✦ ✦

—D. Y. Reavis is in a meeting at Linn Knoll, Mo.

—A Christian Endeavor Society will be organized at Lone Jack, Mo.

—J. L. Thompson has been asked to remain another year at Christian Temple, Decatur, Ill.

—Lewis R. Hotaling has re-engaged with the church at Catlin, Ill., for a period of two years.

—Joseph Gaylor reports as the result of a meeting held at Cracker, Mo., the trebling of the preacher's salary.

—Sherman B. Moore reports 440 additions to the First Church at Oklahoma City during twenty-six months.

—W. T. Hilton has just begun, at his church in Atchison, Kan., a winter series of sermons on the book of Acts.

—W. A. Dameron is holding a meeting with home forces at Shelbyville, Mo. Brother Dameron is energetic in the Lord's work.

—A. E. Cory and wife sail back to their mission work in China on the steamship Korea, leaving San Francisco on November 20.

—W. A. Fite has accepted a call to the church at Fulton, Mo., to begin December 1. The church at Windsor will, therefore, need a pastor.

—Lee H. Barnum has resigned at Caldwell, Kan., after three years of service, to take effect January 1, when he will be ready for other work.

—Milo Atkinson, of Marion, Ind., has accepted a call to succeed George A. Miller, at Covington, Ky., and will begin his work there January 1.

—The work at Litchfield, Ill., under M. S. Johnson is making great headway, but the dedication of the church has been postponed until December 2 or 9.

—Alson E. Wrentmore is to begin a meeting at Covington, Pa., November 17. Brother Wrentmore has recently changed his permanent address from Cleveland, O., to Litchfield, Ill., where he may be solicited for evangelistic work for any part of the country.

"CHRISTIAN UNION."

"AN IRREFUTABLE ARGUMENT; AN IRRESISTIBLE APPEAL."

DEAR BRO. GARRISON.

I have just finished reading your volume on Christian Union, and have laid it down with the feeling that it was surely suggested to your mind and heart by that Holy Spirit whose influence is so manifest on every page. The treatment of the subject is most happy, for no man can understand the problem of Christian Union who has not studied the history of the Church in its departure from and return towards the simplicity and unity of the Apostolic age. Every one of the five chapters is strong and clear, but the volume rises to a climax in the last chapter, The Period of Reunion. Here is found such vigor of thought, such lucidity of expression, such accuracy of discrimination, such sympathetic recognition of all that is good in other Christians than ourselves, as make an irrefutable argument and an irresistible appeal, for the real unity for which our fathers plead, and for which we, their children pray. The problem "How can we stand fast in the liberty wherewith Christ hath made us free, while standing fast also in the unity wherewith Christ hath made us one?" is answered by a sane and irenic setting forth of our appeal to the Christian world such as must have a profound effect upon all who read it. The volume ought to be placed in the hands of all our preachers, and might well be circulated widely among the ministers of all religious bodies. We are greatly your debtors for this delightful and inspiring book on the theme most dear to the heart of every true Disciple of our Lord. May its circulation be worthy of its merits! W. F. RICHARDSON.

Kansas City, Mo., Nov. 5, 1906.

—E. W. Thornton, who was elected at the Buffalo convention third vice-president of the American Christian Missionary

E. W. THORNTON.
Third Vice-President of A. C. M. S.

Society, has just begun his second year's work with the church at Long Beach, Cal. During the year there have been

321 additions that will retain membership. This does not include quite a number who came forward during the Scoville meeting, but who placed their membership elsewhere, not being residents of Long Beach. This church gave over $2,500 for missions and benevolence during the year.

—C. C. Hill is to remain the fourth year at Roswell, N. M., by the unanimous request of his congregation. During his labors there nearly 300 have been added to the membership of the church.

—D. Millar is in a good meeting at Mendon, Mo., with four additions on the day he reported. He would like to hold a few meetings for good town churches this winter.

—J. E. Dinger, minister at Chickasha, I. T., writes he expects to launch a local church paper and would like to receive specimen copies of those published by other churches.

—The remodeled church at Mt. Sterling, Ill., has just been rededicated, free from debt. We have no space in this issue to give particulars. J. E. Lorton is the present minister.

—The foreign society has received an annuity gift of $800 from a friend in Ohio. The society's new and attractive booklet about the annuity plan will be sent free upon application.

—F. M. Rains will dedicate a new building at Watertown, N. Y., December 9. The church extends a cordial invitation to all Christians in the vicinity. S. B. Culp is the minister.

—Lee H. Barnum reports the confession of an old lady who is one year short of 90 years. She came to witness the baptism of her son and during the invitation accepted Christ.

—R. A. Highsmith has started his work well at Prescott, Ark., where formerly there was but half-time preaching. W. D. Humphrey, the home missionary of the Hope Church, is now on the field.

—The prospects of the work at Nevada, Mo., where a meeting is now going on, were never brighter, writes Brother Burks. The membership is more nearly a unit in heart and purpose than for years.

—E. D. Long, who has recently taken charge at Atlanta, Ind., reports a good start there. A Sunday-school rally is to be held the first Sunday in December, and the church rally the first Sunday in January.

—J. H. Hammond, whose field of activity for many years has been in Michigan, paid THE CHRISTIAN-EVANGELIST a pleasant visit last week on his way to the Indian Territory, where he will spend the winter.

—Evangelist J. E. McKenzie, of Woodbine, Ia., has recently closed a meeting at Siam, resulting in 38 additions. Seventy-six have been added to the church since September 1. He is now in a meeting at Lacona, Ia., with Ben Alter.

—At the annual jubilee service at La Harpe, Ill., where L. H. Huff ministers, J. M. Elam, of Carthage and President R. E. Hieronymous, of Eureka, gave the principal addresses. The church is in good condition and doing excellent work.

—John Williams, who has resigned at Collingwood, Ont., is now visiting at Lacota, Mich. A good minister is wanted at once for the Collingwood church. The salary offered is $800 and Mrs. James Beecroft should be addressed.

—The Ohio Committee on Pulpit Supply will meet regularly, aid pastorless churches and preachers wanting locations may address J. P. Allison, 6416 Quinley avenue, Cleveland, O; J. E. Pounds, Hiram, or M. L. Buckley, Collingwood.

—Robert W. Lilley has entered upon his third year at Corydon, Ia., where every department of the work is prospering. Brother Lilley teaches a large Bible class on Friday evening.. He has held two meetings for his church, with good results.

—Cecil J. Armstrong will close his ministry at the First Christian Church, Winchester, Ky., November 30. Brother Armstrong has been in this pastorate for five years and has accomplished a fine work. His future is not yet definitely decided upon.

—William J. Russell, of Frankfort, Ind., sends out a note of warning against A. C. Babcock, who has been preaching at Battle Ground, Ind. He is about 35 years of age, with dark hair, of medium size, and a good talker. He is reported to be unfit for the ministry.

—James S. Beem, evangelist, and George W. Light, singer, will assist Hugh Gresham in a meeting at Cornell, Neb., which will begin November 20. They will make use of 300 copies of THE CHRISTIAN-EVANGELIST to help them in reaching the homes of the people.

—The motto for Oregon missions is 2,000 conversions and $6,000 for the work. F. E. Billington, the corresponding secretary, writes us that the state has been divided into five districts, and the effort is being made to put an evangelist into each one, besides aiding weak churches.

—Tally Defrees has concluded his first year's work at Greenville, Ill., with 170 additions, 31 of them being at regular services. Money raised for all purposes was $1,200, and $350 more for special revival services. Plans are being perfected for another meeting to be held by E. E. Violett.

—Thomas J. Nance, pastor of the church at Plainview, Texas, reports that the building there has been sold and a new one will be erected some time before spring. The present population is about 1,000, but as a railroad will enter the town, the number of residents is constantly increasing.

—It is a little late to hear from the church extension offering, but California is a long way off, and one lone report has just reached us; but as it is a good one we make it public now: The apportionment of the church at Orange was $50, and the offering was $106. A. N. Glover is the minister.

—A veteran minister writes: "I have read your book on 'Christian Union' with great pleasure. It ought to have a wide circulation, especially among our own people, and more especially among our preachers." This veteran is not alone in thinking that we need to make a fresh study of the subject of Christian union.

—The interior of the new house at Alexandria, La., is being completed, although the building has been used for three years. L. A. Betcher, the pastor, would like to know if a river scene suitable for a baptistry, can be purchased. There is a space 6 or 7 by 10 feet which can be used for such a purpose.

—G. B. Townsend, of Troy, N. Y., has accepted a call to Hagerstown, Md. Brother Townsend is one of our bright young preachers whom we learned to appreciate on "THE CHRISTIAN-EVANGELIST Special" going to San Francisco. We are sure that he will take up the work of Brother Kendrick in proper spirit and with great ability.

—A good meeting is under way at

Hamburg, Ia., where W. L. Harris and W. F. Lintt are helping Isaac Elder. At the close a number of meetings will be held in the country. The church at Hamburg has been going steadily forward. Their motto is to have in view to more than double their membership by April 1.

—H. A. Northcutt and Frank C. Huston are in a fine meeting at Brazil, Ind., with E. L. Day. This is part of the Indiana simultaneous campaign. Brother Huston is to assist P. H. Welshimer, who, by the way, has one of the largest Sunday-schools, if not the largest, in the brotherhood, in a great campaign at Canton, O., next February.

—John R. Golden won at the election last week at Gibson City, Ill., where he preaches, with a splendid majority, when he was elected by a good plurality to a seat in the state legislature on the Prohibition ticket. Brother Golden early in life worked on a farm and subsequently learned the carpenter's trade before he entered upon the ministry.

—Mr. Thomas Savage, a business man and one of our devoted workers in Sidney, Australia, visited St. Louis last week. Brother Savage started in company with George T. Walden, and was present at the Buffalo convention. He is on his way to San Francisco, whence he will sail for home before Brother Walden, who has several evangelistic meetings to conduct.

—J. H. Coil has just entered upon his fifth year's work with the church at Higginsville, Mo. During his ministry a new building has been erected at the cost of $1,500. All the offerings have been increased and there have been 80 additions to the church during the past three years. George H. Combs, of Kansas City, will hold a meeting in January, and a good singer is required.

—"'Gloria in Excelsis' is all right!" So writes O. C. Bolman, district secretary of Illinois fifth missionary district. Brother Bolman's church has just had the largest Sunday-school rally ever held in Mason City, and he is in a promising meeting with confessions every night. The church is using 200 copies of THE CHRISTIAN-EVANGELIST in their campaign.

—Leonard Daugherty, of Louisville, Ky., passed through St. Louis on his way to take part with R. R. Hamlin in a meeting with W. W. Burks, at Nevada, Mo. Brother Daugherty made a pleasant visit to the office of THE CHRISTIAN-EVANGELIST, and sang a solo at the First Christian Church, where Herbert Yeuell is leading one of the simultaneous meetings.

—There is good news from Sedalia, Mo. W. F. Hamann, pastor of the Broadway Christian Church, reports that over $2,100 on the debt has been raised during the past few months and the mortgage burned. Thus the church is free to spend its energy and money on other work and they are now planning for a special meeting in the near future.

—A. Martin planned for evangelistic work, January 1, after three years of pastoral work at Davenport, Ia., during which period 170 persons were received into membership, all the missionary activities doubled, and a beautiful parsonage erected, though the latter is not paid for. The church is at peace. Brother Martin has a good record for field work in twenty states, four Canadian provinces, and he also had several years experience in England. He is in his prime and believes he can yet do his best work. His church feels so, for they will not let him go.

—W. J. Russell, of Frankfort, Ind., has been absent from his church three weeks in a meeting at Rochester, Ky.

—H. C. Patterson, of Lexington, Ky., has decided to re-enter the evangelistic field. He has been engaged in business during the past two years, but has preached on an average three sermons a week, having filled pulpits for Carey Morgan, Mark Collis, P. H. Welshimer, and other well known brethren. He has had many calls during the past few months and has decided to enter upon this field of work.

—S. W. Elam has just closed his work at West Point and Fandon, Ill. During eleven months at the former place, fifteen were added to the church and the work is left in good condition. C. F. Pierce succeeded Brother Elam in leading this excellent little band of brethren. At Fandon forty-five were added, thirty-nine of them being by confession and baptism. This is a fine field and the congregation has not yet secured a pastor.

—J. W. Reynolds, who has been pastor at Saunemin, Ill., for the past sixteen months, has accepted a call to the First Church at Clinton, Ill., and is already on his new field, which is one of the strongest churches of the state. E. A. Gilliland recently resigned this pastorate, after nine years of service, in order to enter the evangelistic field. A reception was given the new pastor and his wife, when a large number of the membership greeted them.

—A. F. Reiter has closed a year's pastorate with the Calhoun Street Church, Baltimore, Md. He reports 91 additions, being an increase in membership from 71 to 153. For all purposes more than $1,700 was raised. Brother Reiter was handicapped by a siege of typhoid fever in the spring, and is just now recovering from an operation performed early in September. He is now available for meetings or other work, and may be addressed at Bluffton, Ohio.

—John S. Zeran and wife, who have been working with H. A. Northcutt as his singing evangelists, have given up this work to enter upon a settled pastorate at Gurney, Ill., where the brethren are building a parsonage for them and intend to rally round their new minister. There is scope for a good work at Gurney, and while Brother Zeran has not had much preaching experience, we feel confident that he will meet the expectations of those who have put their trust in him.

—H. A. Pearce has taken charge of the work at Larned, Kan., where we have a new $10,000 building. There are about 200 members in this church and there has just been inaugurated a "Twenty-five Club," one of the aims being twenty-five new subscribers to Christian papers before January 1. Brother Pearce writes us: "As I had edited secular papers for years before entering the ministry I can appreciate the power of so able and sweet spirited a publication as THE CHRISTIAN-EVANGELIST."

—There has been a corn shucking down in Kentucky. The church at Richmond has one of the most enterprising women's missionary societies in the state. Brother Elmer Deatheridge, one of the deacons, gave the society a load of corn, and nine of the members promptly repaired to the field and shucked six barrels which was sold, as missionary corn at $3.10 per barrel. It will appear from a report from Edwin Doerum that higher education does not interfere with manual labor, for on this occasion it was two school teachers, Misses Lela Harris and Miss Dorsey Stphton, who carried off the honors.

—J. P. Lichtenberger has been delivering three sermons on "The Disciples

of Christ." He recently spoke at the Madison Avenue Baptist Church for Dr. Kerr Boyce Tupper, a noted preacher of the Baptists, on "The Contribution of the Disciples to Religious Progress." This was the theme of Brother Litchenberger in his own pulpit in the morning. The other subjects were: "The Disciples: The Philosophy of Their History," and "The Disciples: Their Message to the Church of the Twentieth Century."

—For a period of more than six years the advisability of a new church on the west side of the river at Warren, O., has been under consideration. It remained for the Central Church, under the pastorate of J. E. Lynn, who built a church building at each of his former pastorates, to make a definite move in the matter, and the corner stone of a West Side Christian Church has just been laid. This new congregation will not be formed until the building is completed. Brother Lynn's church has entered upon a ten-weeks campaign of preparation for the decision meetings to be held in January, when he will be assisted by A. W. Taylor and Ida Mae Hanna.

—The sixtieth anniversary of the organization of the Hyde Park Christian Church, Kansas City, is to be celebrated on November 25. Incidentally an effort will be made to wipe out a $5,000 debt on that day. On the Friday night before a banquet for men will be given at the church, and on Lord's day afternoon a pioneers' meeting will be held. It will doubtless be a very enjoyable as well as a great occasion in the life of this congregation, to which Louis S. Cupp now ministers so faithfully. The Sunday-school of this church is now in competition with the South Side school, of course, is a satisfaction to them, but should not, by any means, be a discouragement to the South Side school.

—There are signs of progress at Kankakee, Ill. We like to receive such a report as this: "The church is not large or wealthy but we have a number of godly men and women who know what it means to sacrifice for the sake of Christ." Bro. M. G. O'Brien is the pastor, and he has just entered upon his second year's work. During his ministry forty-seven persons have united with the church, nearly all of them by confession and baptism. There has been a steady growth in the various departments of the church work. We are sure that with the spirit that is manifested under the leadership of the present pastor the coming year will show great progress.

—Austin Perry Finley has just entered upon his ministry at the Highland Street Church of Christ, Worcester, Mass. About a half column report of his sermon appeared in the daily paper of the city. None of the brethren at Worcester had ever seen Brother Finley until his arrival in New England, before entering upon the pastorate, but he was accepted because of his consecrated life and special training. In explaining the interpretation of the call to become a minister of the church Brother Finley said that his understanding of the mission of a minister "is primarily to preach the Gospel of Jesus Christ by which the thoughts of the church and community are elevated, their visions broadened and their lives made nobler as they flow into channels of Christianity and usefulness."

—Robert Stewart, who has been pastor of the Park Avenue church, Knoxville, Tenn, for eight years and three months,

will close his work there at the end of the year. The membership was 80 when he took charge of the work and 264 have been added to the fellowship, 37 in protracted meeings. Quite a number were lost by removal, death, etc., so that the present membership is 186. The current expenses have been kept up and the minister's salary doubled, the church repaired at considerable cost and a debt of $2,250 almost wiped out. The missionary offerings have increased from $150 to $400 per year. The separation will be with the kindest of feelings on all sides.

—Bro. J. W. Hopwood, of Springfield, Mo., who came to St. Louis a few weeks ago to visit his son here and undergo an operation for a long-standing disease, departed this life Thursday morning of last week. Brother Hopwood was a brother of Josephus Hopwood, president of Virginia Christian College, and both of them were students at Abingdon College with the Editor of this paper. Brother Hopwood has been a teacher and preacher of the Gospel since his graduation, having spent his life in Missouri, Kansas and Oklahoma. He removed from the last named place to Springfield about two years ago. From boyhood to the time of his decease he was characterized by his utter sincerity, humility and devotion to duty. All who knew him were impressed by his Christian character. He leaves, besides his widow, three children—two daughters and a married son, whom he was visiting at the time of his death. To his family he bequeaths the priceless legacy of a blameless life. They have our deep sympathy in their great loss. The body was removed to Springfield, Mo., the present home of the family, where the funeral services will be conducted and the body interred.

—The largest number of pulpits ever supplied at one of our national conventions, with one exception, were those placed at the disposal of preachers of Christian churches at Buffalo. There were about 135 services among twelve religious denominations. Bro. B. S. Ferrall deserves great credit for this. For the benefit, however, of future convention goers we wish to emphasize the necessity of having accurate lists of preachers participating. Several of our most widely known speakers were not advertised at all at some of our recent conventions. Of course we understand that preachers appointed sometimes fail to be at the convention. But when there are substitutes a supplementary list should be published. "The saloons are not five cents better off because of this great gathering," says Benjamin S. Ferrall, writing of the convention in his church paper.

—The new building of the School of Evangelists, Kimberlin Heights, Tenn., was dedicated with appropriate exercises Sunday, November 3, President Ashley Johnson presiding. It was erected at a cost of $30,000, and is said to be an imposing structure 86 feet front by 150 feet deep. The address was delivered by W. J. Wright, corresponding secretary of the American Christian Missionary Society. This building with the dormitories, including in the basement the machinery for heating and lighting the building, also a bakery, laundry, etc., are supplemented by a farm of 175 acres, which is cultivated by the students. The energy and enterprise manifested by President Johnson and his wife, in the founding of this school and in rebuilding after the fire, are worthy of all commendation. The design of this institution is well expressed by the inscription on the plate at the door, which reads as follows: "School of the Evangelists. Founded 1895—Rebuilt 1905. Open day and night to the poor young man who desires above every other desire to preach the Gospel of Christ. Ashley S. Johnson, Emma E. Johnson. Kimberlin Heights, Tenn., June 22, 1905."

✿ ✿

To Missouri Preachers.

My Brethren: We come to each one of you, asking that you will present the C. W. B. M. work to your people on "Our Day," December 2, or as near to that date as possible, whether you minister to one or several congregations.

The Christian Woman's Board of Missions is

E. M. RICHMOND,
Evangelist at Maplewood.

a power in the world, in the churches and more than all, in the individual life. All our sisters need its uplifting influences, and their families need the reflex good. If your church is unfortunate enough not to have an auxiliary to the work, all the more should the day be observed in your church. Shall they not learn of it from their pastor and leader? All needed literature will be gladly furnished promptly.

Mrs. L. G. Bantz, Cor. Sec.

✿ ✿

G. L. Wharton, Our First Missionary to the Heathen.

The death of G. L. Wharton at Jubbulpore, India, which was announced by telegram in our last issue, will be felt sorely by a very wide circle of brethren outside those intimately associated with the foreign society's work. His death was wholly unexpected and we have no further information other than it was due to cancer of the stomach. We are not informed whether he had undergone an operation. It may be remembered that Brother Wharton returned some time

G. L. WHARTON.

ago to bring his family, after having spent seventeen years in India as a missionary. His wife and children are now at Hiram, O., where the children are attending school. It was mainly because of his wife's health and his children that Brother Wharton gave up his work in India, but his heart was always on the mission field and he felt compelled to return there. This fact alone is a revelation of the character of the man. He was one of the most consecrated and sincere men we have ever met. He was the first missionary sent out by the foreign society to a heathen field and was, therefore, the pioneer of our work in India. He first went there in 1882. Brother Wharton was born in Monroe county, Ind., in 1847. He lived on a farm till he was 21 years of age. He attended the high school in Terre Haute and later took college work at Carbondale, Ill., after which he taught for two years, finally graduating at Bethany College in 1876. He married a daughter of Dr. R. Richardson. For six years he was minister at Buffalo, and for three years he had charge of the Hiram College church. Brother Wharton's first missionary work was especially along evangelistic lines, but on his return to India this last time he gave more time to the educational features of the work with a view to develop evangelists and preachers among the natives.

Carried Away in the Reading of a Hymn

Death of D. O. Smart.

Word has just reached us of the sudden death, on Friday evening last, while attending the revival service in his church at Kansas City, Mo., of our widely-known and well-beloved brother, D. O. Smart. He had just risen, the telegram in the paper states, to request that a certain hymn be read as a prayer, and died suddenly with apoplexy. This announcement will bring sorrow to thousands of hearts. As chairman of the Board of Church Extension, as president of the board of trustees of the Missouri Bible College, Columbia, as an elder in the Independence Boulevard Christian Church, of Kansas City, as a friend and supporter of all our missionary, educational and benevolent enterprises, as a fine business man and upright citizen who served his state faithfully one term in the legislature, as a Christian man who exemplified in his daily life the religion of Jesus Christ, he held a high place in the affections and confidence of a large number of the best people of the state and of our brotherhood. Although he was in his sixty-eighth year and his health had been impaired for several years, we had not thought of giving him up so soon. But the Father knoweth best. We do not doubt that our loss is his eternal gain. To the bereaved wife and children, and to the bereaved church our sincere sympathies are extended. To us it seems a personal loss, for he was our friend of many years and we have been associated together in the interests of our cause in Missouri so long that we had come to love him greatly and to trust him implicitly. Thank God for the hope of reunion with such noble spirits in the life that is immortal!

The Circumstances of the Death.

BY JAMES SMALL.

The meeting at the Independence Avenue Church, which has been in progress now nearly three weeks, came to its highest spiritual power Friday evening when ten persons came forward to unite with the church—six by letter and four to make the confession—when an incident, sad, sacred and sweet, took place which will never be forgotten by the 1,500 persons present. Brother Combs, Miss Pearl Denham, the assistant minister, and myself usually are in the corridors of the church half an hour before the service begins, and Friday night was no exception. The people were in an unusually happy and spiritual mood, filled with the spirit of expectancy that we were going to have a great meeting; so much so that Brother Combs remarked, "Brother Small, I feel we are going to have a number of additions to-night." The services began at 7:45 p. m. with rousing songs led by LeRoy St. John and sung heartily by the congregation. Song after song led the audi-

D. O. Smart.

ence into a spirit of praise and prayer and blessed fellowship. The writer then stepped to the front and led in prayer fixing the thought on the rich provision of God in Christ for all men. Another song, and Brother Combs read the story of the jailer's conversion with wonderful effect. While the minister was reading Brother St. John whispered to the writer, "Let the audience stand and sing one verse of 'In the Sweet Bye and Bye.'" I announced the verse, but remarked that it made me think of the comrades that are now over there, and how blessed the rest for the weary workers after a while. I went on to speak of heaven and remarked that if we like the country, why heaven would be a paradise and every desire in that direction would be gratified. If we loved the city, why heaven was the city with lights and commotion and companionship. Heaven, in a word, was all that was good and delightful; but far beyond golden streets in a city, far beyond harps and crowns and white robes, is the companionship of loved ones who developed the Christlike life here through "faith, hope and love." We will take all these with us. Then I talked about enduring as good soldiers here and serving God faithfully while we live, and quoted James Whitcomb Riley's poem on, "There, Little Girl, Don't Cry." Then we sang the song, "Just As I Am." Seven persons responded, and another exhortation on "Life's Greatest Question," with several illustrations for the young people present with candles and chemicals, brought three others to the front.

While we were singing the invitation Brother Smart waved his hand for me to come over to where he was standing in the midst of his class. He said, "Brother Small, I have found a beautiful song in this book which ought to be a prayer for all the teachers and officers in the school to repeat together so that we may do all we can in this service to save some mother's boy—some mother's daughter; will you give us a few moments at the close of this song?" I answered in the affirmative. Going to the front again, I remarked that I did not think the superintendent and officers of the school had had an opportunity in this service to do all they wished to do, and on this Brother Smart rose to his feet and made, in substance, the little talk he had made to me. His voice was tender but strong, and all could see he was full of subdued emotion and earnestness. "Let me read the song, and then I will ask all the teachers to read it as a prayer with me." He began: "My Scholars All for Jesus—" He only read this far when he sat down heavily on the seat. He grew pale and seemed to be at a loss for breath. I called on Dr. Forrester to attend him, but before he could reach him, the brave man had fallen in the strong arms of I. W. Gill, of Wichita, Kan., who was in the audience and sitting near Brother Smart. Brother Gill said afterwards that he could hear him say, as he fell, "It's over." It was but a few seconds when Dr. Forrester, Dr. Coffin, Dr. Thompson and Dr. Berry, who were in the audience, were around our stricken brother, aiding in every way possible, but all to no avail, as he died when they were carrying him across the street to his beautiful home.

It is useless to say that when we learned of the worst, the audience was terribly shaken, fully a thousand people bursting into tears.

So ended the life of a good man full of faith and the Holy Spirit. Some one else who has known him for many years will no doubt write you of his virtues that we might all do well to imitate. Brother Smart was a kind, honest, hospitable, liberal-hearted Christian gentleman. The hope we have in his death is without a cloud. He was not without some faults, to be sure; none of us are. But he was a Christian through principle and many are even saying now, "I have lost my best friend, the church and the world will feel lonelier without Brother Smart."

Our hearts are sore, sore. D. O. Smart is dead. This is loss to a host of friends, loss to a loving family, loss to a stricken church of which he was an honored and beloved elder, loss to the Church Extension Society of which he was the trusted president—loss, loss to the brotherhood. To me he was almost a father. To all men he was a brother. Yet his death was gloriously triumphant.   In sorrow,
November 10, 1906,   GEO. H. COMBS.

Why Not United?

It was our privilege, on a recent trip from Detroit to Buffalo through Lake Erie, to fall in with a company of some two hundred delegates en route to the great gathering of Disciples of Christ at Buffalo. This body of saints far outnumbered the other passengers on the great vessel that bore us, and in the evening literally took possession of the ship. Assembling at eight o'clock in the main saloon, they held an impromptu conference meeting, at which there were offhand addresses, singing, prayers, and testimonies, making up an evening of real spiritual delight and profit.

These brethren spoke, as Bunyan says, "the language of Canaan." Their hearts seemed charged and their lips overflowed with love for the Lord and Master of us all. It would have been impossible, but for the badges they wore, and an occasional allusion to the denomination they represented, to distinguish them from a similar body of Baptist men and women going on pilgrimage to their own anniversaries. Nor could the writer discover, in conversation after the meeting with a number of their leading men, in what essential respects they differed from their fellow-immersionists of the Baptist household. There were delegates from Canada, from the West and Southwest, from the extreme South, and from Australia, and all were, so far as we could discover, of one mind, and likeminded with us, to the great fundamentals of the faith. So impressed were we with this likemindedness, and with their fervid loyalty to Christ and to the Word of God, that we requested one of their number to favor the readers of "The Examiner" with a concise and precise statement of the fundamental doctrines held by them—a statement to the reading of which we look forward, as we are sure our readers will also, with great interest. If it shall appear that there are to-day no greater differences between these Christian brethren and us than were manifested in the addresses and conversations aboard the good ship Western States, we see no serious obstacle in the way of an essential union between the two bodies, at least in missionary work, at home and abroad. There may be—there certainly have been in the past—wider doctrinal differences between us than came to the surface at the gathering referred to; but it may be that they are not greater than is allowable under the law of Christian liberty, or than do actually exist both in the Baptist and the Disciples fold. It is well, it seems to us, that we should look carefully and with open mind into this matter, lest we thwart the desire of our common Lord that his loyal and obedient followers should be one not only in sympathy and in service, but in fellowship.—*The Examiner.*

A Word of Approval.

BY PROF. ALVAH S. HOBART, D. D.

Editors "Examiner:" Allow me to speak a word of approval of the editorial of October 25 headed "Why Not United?" The closing sentence is full of serious suggestion. "It is well that we look carefully and with open mind into this matter lest we thwart the desire of our common Lord that his loyal and obedient followers should be one in sympathy, service and fellowship."

All the signs of the times indicate that a spirit of fellowship and an increase of sympathy is at work in the hearts of the Christian world. In all denominations, in all parts of Christendom, among all classes of Christians, there is an uneasiness about these many distinctions and

sects. It is not too strong a statement to say that every good man deplores the divisions. But what is to be done about it? Continually to admit the wrong and yet make no move to stop it is not the highest kind of conduct. Why should Baptists, for example, be slow to propose and earnestly seek union both with Disciples and Free Baptists? They were once in the same connection: why not again? Why should there be hesitation and fears? "Ye can discern the face of the skies," said Jesus, "but ye can not discern the signs of the times." Does not this apply to some of this day as well? I confess that it grows upon me that we, the larger denomination, the older denomination, not only can secure the union, but we ought to seek it earnestly until it is accomplished.—*The Examiner.*

As We Go to Press.

Special to THE CHRISTIAN-EVANGELIST.

Huntington, W. Va., November 12.— Fifty-nine additions to date; hard field but interest good; pastor sick. I begin next week with Edmonds at Fort Smith, Ark. Singer H. H. Saunders goes to Carthage, Ill.—R. H. Fife, evangelist.

Special to THE CHRISTIAN-EVANGELIST.

Indianapolis, Ind., November 12.— Fifty-five additions in two weeks; twenty-one yesterday.—Cooksey and McHatten.

Special to THE CHRISTIAN-EVANGELIST.

Kansas City, Mo., November 12.— At South Prospect great meeting; fifty-two additions; thirty-two yesterday. Smith and Saxton, evangelists.—J. J. Morgan, minister.

Special to THE CHRISTIAN-EVANGELIST.

Kansas City, Mo., November 12.— Small and St. John meeting continues with great power; sixty-five came forward to-day; over 200 in nineteen days. We are pushing the battle to the gates.—George Hamilton Combs.

Special to THE CHRISTIAN-EVANGELIST.

Indianapolis, Ind., November 11.— Scoville, Smith and Kendall are with the Third Christian Church with C. B. Newnan. The Armory, where the meetings are held, is always filled and overflow meetings are held in the church across the street. Sixty added to-day, 226 to date.—P. M. Kendall.

Special to THE CHRISTIAN-EVANGELIST.

Indianapolis, Ind., November 12.—One hundred and eighty additions yesterday in Indianapolis meetings; 691 to date. Fine interest in all the churches. John E. Pounds spoke to the great Tomlinson Hall union meeting yesterday on "The Confession of Faith."—F. W. Norton.

Special to THE CHRISTIAN-EVANGELIST.

Indianapolis, Ind., November 12.— Great audiences; twenty-eight additions at Central yesterday in the Abberley-Powell meeting. One hundred and thirteen to date, including eighty adults, sixty heads of families.—A. B. Philputt.

Special to THE CHRISTIAN-EVANGELIST.

Hamburg, Iowa, November 11.— Nearly 5,000 chapters read this week in Bible school. Sixty-five conversions; twelve to-day. I am leading large chorus.—W. L. Harris, evangelist; J. E. Lintt, singing evangelist.

Special to THE CHRISTIAN-EVANGELIST.

Loraine, Ohio, November 12.—City of 30,000 with seven languages spoken; Catholics predominant; 130 saloons. Despite five denominational churches in a union meeting we had nineteen yesterday, and fifty-five to date; continue.

Hostetter, minister; Violett and Clarkson, evangelists.—W. G. Bliss.

Special to THE CHRISTIAN-EVANGELIST.

Lexington, Ky., November 11.—One hundred and thirty-one added in Central Church meeting; twenty-two came to-day. Interest deepens. Brooks brothers, evangelists.—I. J. Spencer, minister.

Special to THE CHRISTIAN-EVANGELIST.

Lincoln, Ill.—Sixty-five additions up to Sunday night, November 11.—W. E. M. Hackleman.

West Virginia.

The report of our special correspondent sent on Friday afternoon indicates that eleven churches in the West Virginia campaign had an average attendance of 201, with 36 new additions, bringing the total up to 284 at that time. We expect Brother Hanes to send us a telegram giving the latest figures up to the time of our going to press. Several of the churches have closed their meetings, some of them feeling that it was a mistake to do this, but special conditions demanded it. The interest is reported as growing in many quarters, and from nearly every source comes word that the churches have been strengthened and much good done even where there have not been large accessions.

St. Louis.

The simultaneous campaign in St. Louis has been in progress for a week, though the meeting at the First Church has run for two weeks. Weather conditions have been favorable and in most of the churches there has been a good attendance, with an increasing interest. The difficulty of advertising the meeting in a great city has been experienced and the chief reliance has been on personal work. There was reported at Saturday's meeting at the office of THE CHRISTIAN-EVANGELIST on Monday morning the following additions: First Church, 119; Union Avenue, 38; Compton Heights, 42; Fourth Church, 19; Hamilton Avenue, 16; Hammett Place, 6; Maplewood, 9; East St. Louis, 5; making a total of 254 up to and including Sunday night's service. On last Lord's day the First Church had the largest number of additions, 30 by confession and 9 otherwise; Union Avenue had 12 confessions and 11 otherwise; Compton Heights 13 by confession and 2 otherwise. At the Fourth there was one confession and 2 otherwise, while at Hammett Place 4 confessions are reported.

A great union meeting of all our churches was held at the First Christian Church on Lord's day afternoon, addressed by C. M. Chilton and Herbert Yeuell. Every member of the Christian Church in St. Louis is expected to be present next Lord's day, at 3 p. m., at the Odeon, when another great mass meeting will be addressed by W. E. Harlow. All the choirs of the different churches are invited to be present, and it is hoped that their numbers will be augmented by other good singers. The singing evangelists in the city will take part. At Indianapolis and other cities hundreds of people are being turned away from the Sunday afternoon meetings, and it is hoped that the St. Louis Disciples will come out in force and will give a demonstration to the city next Lord's day by their numbers and their enthusiasm. Brother Harlow, who will make the chief address, held with Brother Turner at Joplin, Mo., what is perhaps the greatest evangelistic meeting ever held in the state of Missouri. Last week was a week of disciplining. Most of the evangelists laid their emphasis on teaching and sowing the seed. It is expected that this week will produce some of the fruits of their faithful work.

GEORGIA STATE CONVENTION.

(Continued from Page 1464.)

the state and we are glad to hear that such men as A. McLean, Dr. Osgood, George W. Muckley, George B. Ranshaw and James H. Mohorter are to be here as the representatives of the various boards with which they are connected. Let every one who intends coming notify me in time for us to arrange for a place of entertainment before the convention begins. We wish that each church in the state might be represented, and, of course, our hospitality is by no means limited to the brethren who live in Georgia.

RICHARD W. WALLACE.

First Christian Church, Valdosta, Ga.

NEWS FROM MANY FIELDS

Illinois Notes.

The church at Pontiac has taken on new life since entering its beautiful new house. Everybody seems happy and ready for any task. Is it not the rule that those who work and sacrifice are happy? Wonder if the idea that religion makes people long-faced did not come from people of much profession but no work? If so, it is no wonder that a little church, mostly of poor people, after a half century of struggle in a little old church, is happy and joyful after spending nearly $16,000 for a new Christian home. W. G. McColey is the able, industrious and much-loved minister. The church now numbers 250, Sunday-school, 160; Christian Endeavor, 40; and all departments growing. The C. W. B. M. auxiliary was just beginning an institute guided by Misses Lura V. Thompson, state organizer, and Mary Monehan. These special institutes are of great value to the church as well as to the auxiliaries, when the members are wise enough to attend.

Flanagan is another royal church and it is especially happy because, although having but 150 members and all departments of home work to support it, gave to outside work the past year nearly $900. R. E. Thomas is the large-hearted and loyal minister.

The Rutland church, under the ministry of R. B. Doan, is properous and happy. He is in hearty sympathy with all our great enterprises and keeps his congregation well taught and informed, consequently the church is liberal and useful. No great cause appeals to it in vain. A splendid meeting was in progress, in which C. L. Organ, a former Eureka student, but now state evangelist of Iowa, was assisting the pastor.

I was happy, by invitation of several month's to enjoy the generous hospitality by S. G. Macartney and wife during the Buffalo Convention. He was one whom I had the pleasure of baptizing, among more than a hundred who obeyed the gospel while I was in Buffalo. It is clearly in the province of Illinois Notes to mention the contribution which Illinois made to the convention. I regret that the reports of the treasurers of all departments were not distributed so we could see how Illinois compares with other states in its offerings. Ohio, Indiana, Illinois, Kentucky, and Missouri figure usually about the same.

The church has great colleges, considering the small investment in them and the small attention given them, their work is almost miraculous in the production of great men. Had it not been for the guiding and blessing hand of the unseen Partner we would to-day be desperately embarrassed for want of men, ministers. W. J. Wright, secretary of home board, said "We ought to graduate 4,000 preachers from our colleges by 1909." We will need that many preachers by that time or sooner. Shall we give attention to their production? Our own college in Illinois has great reasons for joy and gratitude in the many strong men she has given to the world. Fifteen of the sermons delivered in the pulpits of Buffalo, October 14, were by men formerly connected with Eureka College. They were gathered from six states of the Union, Cuba, China and Africa, and the representatives of Eureka College on the general program acquitted themselves most honorably. Mrs. W. W. Wharton's address before the C. W. B. M. is characterized by a great journal as "Chaste in diction, poetic in conception and tender in pathos." Other good speeches were made by W. F. Richardson; W. W. Sniff; J. P. Lichtenberger; C. S. Medbury, and Pres. J. Hopwood. The delightful reception to former Eureka students and alumni, by Mr. C. J. Phillips and wife, has already been reported in THE CHRISTIAN-EVANGELIST.

There seem to be some good stayers among the Eureka men. W. F. Richardson has been with the

first church, Kansas City, for twelve years. G. A. Miller the same length of time at Covington, Ky., and H. O. Breeden, twenty-one years in Des Moines, Iowa. When we face the great results of the college efforts, made in our great state, it ought to furnish inspiration for larger patronage, greater gifts, and a holy zeal to multiply the power and usefulness of Eureka College. Shall we do it?   J. G. WAGGONER.

A Way to Law and Order.

A victory for law and order was recorded at the ballot box in St. Francois county, Mo., last week. St. Francois is one of the most wide open, lawless counties in the state. When the writer came to Farmington seventeen months ago, there were five murderers in the county jail waiting for trial. The eight saloons were, and are still open 365 days in the year, with all their attendant evils. Our first appeal was to the county officers, without effect. Then the county court was visited to ascertain, on what ground the saloon license was granted. We then attended the circuit court, and discovered the farce in dealing with cases brought before that body, under the liquor law. We then interviewed the judge of the court, to inquire from him the cause of this strange proceeding, and learned that he was acting under instruction from the governor to the prosecuting attorney. Not being satisfied with this, a letter was written to Governor Folk asking him if he had given such instructions. With his denial in hand, and many other facts, the case was presented to the people of the county, who decided in favor of law and order by defeating the prosecuting attorney by over 300 votes, and a general shake up in the political situation.

The writer conducted a single handed fight, with the exception of the good people who said, "Good, go on."   EDWARD OWERS.
Farmington, Mo.

North Carolina.

From October 8 to 18 I preached in a meeting with the church in Rural Hall, a village twelve miles from Winston-Salem and a point of vantage. It is also the station for Moore's Springs, a summer resort. Sister Moore and her family are Disciples and hundreds of people go there every summer to drink the healing waters. Our meeting was one of joy. There were two confessions and one Baptist brother took his stand under the broader name Disciple.——Lord's day, October 28, was a happy day with the church in Winston-Salem, the debt owed the Church Extension Board having been paid. We burned the mortgage. H. C. Bowen, who was minister when the house was built, was present and preached. The reports showed 50 members added from September 1, 1905, to September 1, 1906. Money expended for evangelistic meeting, $924.19; local preaching, $625; missions and benevolences, about $70; church debt, $928.35; the total was $2,863.37. The amount on the missionary side is too small to satisfy us. We have already increased our offering for state missions over three-fold and hope to make a better showing in other departments. We are considering the plan of making the first Lord's day in each month a day for a missionary or benevolent offering.
J. A. HOPKINS.

A Trip to Southeast Missouri.

This included a day at Libertyville at the St. Francois County Convention, and thirteen days at Poplar Bluff in a meeting. The convention was marred by the rains, but gave me a better acquaintance with the difficulties of the field and the faithfulness of some of these men of God. Owers and Judge Nations, of Farmington, Rogers of Fredericktown, Fenstermacher, of Poplar Bluff, G. T. Smith, of Dexter College, and several other ministers were in attendance. Here are some strong men, in one of the greatest missionary

sections of the middle west. Eastern capital by the tens of thousands is pouring into this part of the state. Here our devout souls, but the ungodly are doubtless in the majority. Many of the devout have had the culture of the non-progressive, but from a personal touch with these ministers and people I commend them to the brotherhood of the stronger sections of our state. They need sympathy, encouragement, prayer. They need greater concern on the part of our state boards.

At Poplar Bluff, we found a loyal few in town of 8,000 or more, with sixteen saloons and total protestant membership of perhaps less than one thousand. In the thirteen days there were three confessions, and two added by letter. Brother Fenstermacher continued one week longer, reaching a total of sixteen. Ten of these were by confession. This splendid result is to the praise of the pastor and the people.
Mexico, Mo.   A. W. KOKENDOFFER.

Jasper County (Mo.) Convention.

The Jasper county meeting was held this year with the church in Carterville. It was the best yet, sixty-four delegates being present. The sessions of the convention were held in the M. E. church, owing to the improvements being made on the Christian church. It will, when completed, be the most commodious and elegant church in that city.

The report of the work done by J. W. Baker, county evangelist, was enthusiastically received as it deserved to be. It showed, number of days, 303; sermons and addresses, 298; additions, 156; money raised, $5,140.08; one church organized, a house built and dedicated without debt; three dying churches revived, and four pastors located. This is a splendid showing, and one of which Jasper county is proud. Brother Baker enters the general evangelistic work, beginning at Granby November 8. The specific work of the county for the coming year will be to assist Purcell to have regular preaching and to organize a church at Oronogo and build a house of worship, and looking to the accomplishment of this, the convention adjourned to meet with the church in Oronogo the last Wednesday in October, 1907. The following officers were elected for the coming year: President, W. F. Turner, Joplin; vice-president, N. L. Simms, Carthage; secretary, W. E. Reavis, Webb City; treasurer, Geo. L. Peters, South Joplin.

Joplin, Mo. GEO. L. PETERS.

Georgia Notes.

THE CHRISTIAN-EVANGELIST has arrived in Georgia and the readers are delighted with it. I am sure that all "Southern Evangelist" friends now take advantage of the rich opportunities offered them through this famous weekly visitor. Send subscriptions to me or send direct to St. Louis.——R. G. Cross, of Rome, died almost suddenly November 5. Brother Cross was 75 years of age, and had been prominent in business affairs of Rome. He was one of the faithful of the Church of Christ at Rome and was a man above reproach. He will be greatly missed. He leaves a wife and one child. ——Georgia wants several good preachers to fill vacancies. If this should meet the eye of such men who desire to be numbered among the Georgia ministry, write to B. P. Smith, 58 Dunn street, Atlanta.——I have just read Brother J. H. Garrison's new book on "Christian Union," and I must say that it is the clearest and most suggestive book on the subject I have ever read. Every preacher in the brotherhood should read it.——J. H. Wood, now of Second church, Augusta, will move to Windsor December 1, and take charge of the churches at Winder, Statham and Mt. Vernon. On the same day P. H. Mears, of Winder, will take charge of the Second church, Augusta. Brother Mears is single now, but he will not be single then. Farewell, Brother Mears.——Of "Household Baptisms," a Baptist minister writes: "It is immense. Cannot be answered. By far the clearest and most conclusive treatise on the colossal and degrading error I've ever read." This 16-page tract for sale by the writer at $1.00 per hundred.——The state convention will take possession of Valdosta November 19. Everything is ready for the feast of good things.——S. S. Landrum continues to go over northeast Georgia eloquently preaching the Word.——The writer will preach at Central near Atlanta, Sunday the 11th.

E. L. SHELNUTT.

187 Edgewood avenue, Atlanta, Ga.

Idaho.

Before leaving the church at Caldwell I had begun a work at Emmett, Star and Wilson, Idaho, and Arcadia, Oregon. We have now at Star 63 members, and one who confessed yet to be baptized. Star is one of the oldest churches in this region and has been held together by a few faithful followers, among whom we find Brother and Sister O. W. L. Hall, Bro. J. S. Lankford and his good wife, Brother and Sister Palmer. Gilman, Neff, Bullock, Gray, Hart, Fry, Simon and other families have held together for a real live church at Star.——Last week two young ladies baptized in the Boise river at Star; this week one in Snake river at Wilson. At Emmett we have 15 members and one to be baptized. At Wilson we have 15 confessions ready for baptism in the Snake. There we have a little mission band of 20 believers united for work. At Arcadia we have 19 believers organized into a working band, and there, too, we have four or five confessions getting ready to put on Christ. At Caldwell there are two confessions arranging for further obedience in the way of putting on Christ in baptism. At Star and Emmett we are hoping for stationed ministers by spring or summer, and there are no better regions or health-ier in Idaho than Emmett and Star.

Caldwell, Idaho. B. W. RICE.

Meeting at Odessa, Mo.

We had large audiences all week-prior to the coming of Brother Fenstermacher, and the interest was unusually satisfactory. He joined us the first of the week. The chorus, led by Mr. Charles Gross, has been furnishing a song service that is inspiring. We held a union meeting for young men in our church at which the Rev. E. J. Hunt, presiding elder of the Sedalia district of the Methodist Episcopal church, who has been in a meeting with the Odessa M. E. church, delivered an inspiring address. This was followed by a sermon by the Rev. A. H. Kelso, pastor of the Presbyterian church, U. S. A. The service was unusually good in spirit and the attendance was large. Our prospects are splendid for the best evangelistic campaign in the history of the Odessa Christian church.   F. W. ALLEN, pastor.

❀ ❀

Kentucky Mission Work and Workers.

The Beattyville work is reported by the minister, J. Stuart Mill, as progressing satisfactorily. He expects the congregation to give more for support of local work than ever before.——Four additions at Latonia. H. C. Runyon and P. H. Duncan began in a meeting first Sunday in November. The house and lot adjoining the church lot has been deeded by Mrs. Whipps on the annuity plan to the congregation. She gave the lot on which the house of worship stands. The property just given is worth $1,600. This means more room on which to enlarge, or build houses of worship and a parsonage.——The veteran evangelist of Eastern Kentucky, D. G. Combs, had the best month of the year—58 baptisms and 117 added altogether; a house assured in Bath county, at Kendall Springs and $397.25 raised for this purpose. At time of report he was in a meeting in Rockcastle county.——W. J. Cocke reports 28 days in the field at Erlanger and Kirksville. Thirty added. He is to help at South Louisville. Arrangements are not made for filling his time with meetings after January first.——J. W. Masters says that the house at Harlan is progressing well. He has baptized 24 in a community where we have never been heard until now. A number of heads of families added and an organization and the building of a house of worship is assured. This will be our first house in the county outside of Pineyville and Middlesborough.——Walter E. Mill has begun the work at Bromley with prospect of growth.——Earl B. Barr has undertaken the Worthville work since the volunteer meeting of J. F. Mahoney. Prospects are favorable.——H. L. Atkinson began work with the Hazel Green and West Liberty congregations as special missionary of the church at Winchester. H. J. Derthick thinks he will do a fine work.——At Edmonson T. S. Buck has resigned to work under the auspices of the Anti-Saloon League. A good man is needed for Burksville and contiguous field; paying about $600.——Jellico, Tenn., is beginning to lift its head from the awful calamity caused by the explosion of a carload of dynamite. Our church building will have to be rebuilt; but the Sunday-school room can be repaired at a cost of about $50 so that it can be used until spring. The brethren are heroic and entitled to the help of the brotherhood.——H. W. Elliott was prevented from being away two Sundays during October on account of the sickness and death of his father-in-law. Much work was done in the way of sending out letters and literature relative to the November offering. About 25 per cent of the preachers or congregations replied and as about fifty per cent of those on the apportionment list give this is a very fair response at the present date. Many that have not replied can be as safely relied on to co-operate as those that have agreed in written statement to do so. The amount collected for October was $187.35—a gain of $148.90 over last October.——We urge all our churches and preachers to give all possible diligence to the matter of prime importance for November, namely, taking the offering for Kentucky missions. Remit as early as possible. The treasury is empty. H. W. ELLIOTT, Sec. and Treas. *Sulphur Ky.*

❀ ❀

Send for our Holiday Catalogue.
CHRISTIAN PUBLISHING CO.,
St. Louis, Mo.

Ministerial Exchange.

Edward O. Beyer, 1019 Cedar street, Pueblo, Colo., who has been assisting John W. Marshall the past year, can be secured for a meeting in December. John W. Marshall commends him as a splendid gospel singer and director.

J. M. Rhodes has the month of December open. Any church wishing him for a meeting address Newkirk, Okla.

"Any church in reach of Eldon, Mo., wanting my services for 1907 will write me at Eldon, Mo., R. F. D. 1, Box 54."—W. H. Scott.

Owing to a cancelled engagement, E. A. Gilliland, Clinton, Ill., is open for work in December.

The church at Harper, Kan., desires to correspond with a capable minister. Salary about $700. Write M. B. Ingle, Harper, Kan.

J. P. Hanes, general evangelist, Purdy, Mo., is ready to answer calls for evangelistic meetings this fall and winter. He prefers to hold a few meetings in eastern Texas. Terms, free will offerings and expenses.

F. M. O'Neal, 842 West Florida street, Springfield, Mo., can make engagements as leader of song in meetings during December and January, on reasonable terms.

Any church desiring the services of a young married minister of experience may be put in correspondence with one by addressing Box 593, Goodland, Kansas.

F. H. Groom, corresponding secretary, Box 695, Helena, Mont., can help two or three worthy young men secure work with congregations in Montana. Only those who can give good references need apply.

H. M. Barnett can make dates for meetings in February and March. He may be addressed at Smithville, Mo., or 1832 Norton avenue, Kansas City, Mo.

N. Rolla Davis, 211 North Twenty-first street, St. Joseph, Mo., is ready for employment, for 1907, with churches in reach of St. Joseph.

After November 15, Mr. and Mrs. R. R. Stevens, R. F. D. 4, Greenwich, Ohio, will be open for one or two engagements to serve as singing evangelists, or an evangelist and singer.

Frank C. Huston has an open date for December. Address him at Brazil, or Indianapolis, Ind. There is a most excellent young brother who has been preaching successfully for about two years, who desires to enter Butler College. January 1, 1907, it he can secure a church or church est within reach of the college. Any church interested can be put in touch with him by addressing Milo Atkinson, Marion, Ind.

❀ ❀

Changes.

Adams, W. T.—Waltsburg to Corona, Cal.
Bagby, E. B.—Washington, D. C., to 4518 Franklin avenue, Cleveland, Ohio.
Bennett, H. G.—Monroe, Wis., to Green City, Mo.
Bennett, R. J.—Shawnee, Ohio, to Bethany, W. Va.
Babb, J. D.—Buffalo, Mo., to Burlington, Colo.
Barnett, H. M.—1520 Harrison street to 1828 Norton avenue, Kansas City, Mo.
Cord, William C.—Hazel Green to Mt. Sterling, Ky.
Corbin, A. C.—Ashland to Dallas, Ore.
Couch, J. E.—Minier, Ill., to Pauls Valley, I. T.
Dameron, W. D.—Canton to Shelbyville, Mo.
Easterwood, Thomas J.—Temple, Tex., to box 855, South Haven, Kan.
Endres, W. D.—Moulton, Iowa, to 3826 Ingleside avenue, Chicago, Ill.
Freed, Theo J.—Rockville to Wolcott, Ind.
Fry, W. A.—Creal Springs to Spillertown, Ill.
Garm, H. M.—Lakewood, Ohio, to 575 East Sixty-second street, Chicago, Ill.
Green, T. W.—Arrowsmith, to Lincoln, Ill.
Honeywell, A. A.—McConnellsville, to 506 Woostter, street, Marietta, Ohio.
Hootman, N. E.—616 County Road, Martin's Ferry, Ohio, to Bethany, W. Va.
Howell, W. R.—Rocky Mount, N. C., to New Haven, Conn., care of Yale Divinity School.
Johnston, W. G.—Sinking Creek, to New Castle, Va.
Lockhart, Charles A.—Carthage, Mo., to North Waco, Texas.
Long, E. D.—Angola to Atlanta, Ind.
Love, E. R.—Arkansas City, Kan., to 660 Sixth street, San Bernardino, Cal.
Lowe, W. S.—701 Jackson street, Topeka, to Paola, Kan.
McCollough, J. H.—Irvington to Santa Clara, Cal.
McDaniel, Asa—Jonesville, to "The Lamar," Dayton, Ohio.
Moore, C. R.—Riverside, Arlington Station, Cal., to Eugene, Ore.
McKim, C. L.—Dallas City, Ill., to Oelwein, Iowa.
McKay, C. M.—Woodard, Mich., to St. Thomas, Ont.
McLead, James—Glenealrm, Ont., to Bethany, W. Va.
Moormaw, Orho C.—Clay Center, to Bonner Springs, Kan.
Orahood, Oren—Covington, Ind., to Martinsburg, W. Va.
Patterson, D. H.—Orange, to Milroy, Ind.
Porter, W. N.—Kinsley, Kan., to Lamar, Mo.
Post, W. L.—Kellogg, to Martelle, Ia.
Pace, LeGrand—Onawanda, Iowa, to Colby, Kan.
Roberts, G. E.—Maxwell, to Lake City, Iowa.
Roberts, Isom—Blackwell, to Weatherford, Okla.
Russell, Ward—Mabank, to Athens, Texas.
Sines, S. E.—Laomi, to Mechanicsburg, Ill.

South Carolina State Convention.

The twenty-seventh annual convention of the Churches of Christ in South Carolina is to be held at Ellenton November 22-25. Ellenton is twenty miles from Augusta, Ga., on the C. & W. C. railway. An attractive provisional program has been made out. It is earnestly desired that every church be represented. Let all delegates go prepared to make pledges for ensuing year. Any church not able to send a delegation, should be represented by letter, and if practicable by a contribution for the "state work;" also by pledges for ensuing year. Churches in arrears should send in their dues at once to Dr. C. W. Erwin, Allendale, S. C. We are expecting A. McLean, Geo. B. Ranshaw, G. W. Muckley and others from a distance. The public is cordially invited, and especially the ministers of Georgia, and brethren and sisters connected with any of the departments of church work. Brethren, let us unite and have the grandest convention in our history. Visitors coming by rail will be met at depot. Prospective delegates will please write to Capt. G. H. Bush, Ellenton, S. C., giving names and addresses who will provide for entertainment upon arrival. Watch CHRISTIAN-EVANGELIST for special rates. By order of J. C. Richardson, president; C. W. Erwin, corresponding secretary.
Allendale, S. C.

———

Send for our Holiday Catalogue.
CHRISTIAN PUBLISHING CO.,
St. Louis, Mo.

Evangelistic

We invite ministers and others to send reports of meetings, additions and other news of the churches. It is especially requested that additions be reported as "by confession and baptism," or "by letter."

Arkansas.

Paragould, Nov. 4.—Two added by statement.—Edward Owers.

Arkadelphia, Nov. 5.—I recently held a short meeting for the church at Amity, with six additions—three by confession and baptism, and three by statement.—E. S. Allhands.

Colorado.

Salida, Nov. 5.—Fifteen additions yesterday, 75 in last three weeks. House too small.—W. B. Crewdson.

Washington, Nov. 5.—Present at ministers' meeting: J. E. Stuart, F. D. Power, B. E. Utz, L. D. Riddell, and the writer. Additions: Vermont Avenue (F. D. Power), one by letter; Thirty-fourth Street (Claude C. Jones), one by letter; Fifteenth Street (J. E. Stuart and L. D. Riddell), three by letter and one confession. Meeting at Fifteenth Street, continues with live interest and fine sermons.—Claude C. Jones, Sec.

Illinois.

Mason City, Nov. 7.—Five baptisms and one other addition at Mount Pleasant.—O. C. Bolman.

Springfield, Nov. 9.—Our great meeting is drawing to a close. Seventy accessions.—F. M. Rogers.

La Harpe, Nov. 3.—Nine additions since last report. Four last Sunday by letter.—L. G. Huff, minister.

Decatur, Nov. 5.—There were seven additions at the evening service Lord's day, making a total of 104 this year.—J. L. Thompson.

Chicago, Nov. 9.—Ten added by confession and one by letter during a short meeting at Bushnton, Ill.—Will F. Shaw.

Coleta, Nov. 5.—I assisted Lewis Goos in a splendid meeting at Pine Creek near Polo. Thirteen added.—C. W. Marlow.

Eureka, Nov. 7.—Three added at Mt. Olivet Church near Clarence, last Lord's day—two by statement, one by letter.—Lewis P. Fisher.

Nebo, Nov. 7.—J. D. Williams, of El Dora, closed a two weeks' meeting here last night with ten additions to the church.—I. W. Pearson.

DuQuoin, Nov. 6.—T. S. Tinsley, of Louisville, Ky., closed a good short meeting with the church at Du Quoin with 13 additions.—R. H. Robertson, minister.

Waynesville, Nov. 10.—Meeting here five days old with good interest and large attendance. Five confessions last night, six additions to date.—J. A. Barnett, evangelist; Miss Manie B. Bowles, singer.

Litchfield, Nov. 7.—Closed a ten nights' meeting at Antioch, Okla., Oct. 15, with 18 accessions—14 baptisms, two from other religious bodies, one by statement and one reclaimed. Among these were eight of the leading men of the community, and three teachers. I begin a meeting with W. I. Burrell at Covington, Pa., November 17.—Alson E. Wrentmore.

Indiana.

Peru, Oct. 22.—Three more added last Lord's day. Fourteen in two weeks at regular services.—C. H. DeVoe.

Garrett, Ind., Nov. 6.—Five additions Lord's day—three by letter and two by confession.—O. L. Hull, minister.

New Albany, Oct. 22.—Three added yesterday at regular services. Church is united and doing a good work.—F. T. Porter, minister.

Brazil, Nov. 3.—Began a meeting with Northrun and Huston Thursday night. This is our second meeting this year.—E. L. Day.

Princeton, Nov. 10.—I assisted B. F. Hill in a good meeting at Lamonte, Mo., last month. Thirty added.—I. D. Sprague, gospel singer.

Indianapolis. Nov. 5.—The MacLane-McVay meeting at the Sixth Church is drawing large audiences. Thirty-four added in seven days.

Hamburg, Nov. 7.—We are in a great meeting here with evangelists Harris and Lintt leading our forces. Great crowds. Great interest. Forty-nine additions the first fifteen days.—Isaac Elder.

Ligonier, Oct. 22.—H. F. MacLane, of Hiram, has just closed a fine meeting for us. There were several additions and much good done otherwise. Mrs. B. F. Lindsley of Mansfield, O., led the singing.—I. N. Aldrich, pastor.

Indian Territory.

Tulsa, Nov. 6.—Four additions since last report. Our work prospers in all departments.—Cook.

Chickasha, Nov. 5.—Three more additions yesterday.—J. E. Dinger.

Iowa.

Keokuk, Nov. 5.—Our meeting with home forces started yesterday. Fine audiences and splendid interest. Baptized two at prayer-meeting last Wednesday night.—M. J. Nicoson.

Kansas.

Arkansas City, Nov. 7.—Seventy-two in first two weeks.—J. B. Boen.

Wellington, Nov. 5.—Seventeen additions not previously reported, at regular services.—L. T. Paulders.

Peru, Nov. 7.—Have begun a meeting here with Brother and Sister O'Neal, of Springfield, Mo., as singing evangelists. Interest good. Two additions since we began.—Elder J. P. Haner.

Kentucky.

Covington, Nov. 5.—Ten additions to the First Church yesterday. Seventeen the last three Sundays at regular services.—George Miller.

Clintonville, Nov. 7.—We had P. M. Finder, Lancaster, Ky., with us 16 days. Our church is revived and the whole community blessed. There were 24 baptisms and four more took membership.—Walter S. Willis.

Richmond, Nov. 10.—Our protracted meeting held by H. A. Northcutt closed last week and was an unqualified success. There were added to the church 54 by confession. We regard Mr. Northcutt as a man sent of God for such work. It was without reproach. Brother and Sister Zeran were admirable in the ministry of song.—Hugh McLellan.

Missouri.

Maitland, Nov. 5.—One by baptism yesterday.—B. F. Baker, pastor.

Kansas City, Nov. 5.—Seven added in last two Sundays.—J. J. Morgan.

Malden, Oct. 30.—Had fine services Sunday with three additions. My work at Fredericktown is growing.—R. O. Rogers.

Lathrop, Nov. 5.—Six added by letter and one by baptism Monday evening. Work is in good condition.—B. F. Creason.

Golden City, Nov. 10.—Received four by letter last Lord's day. One immersion at Kenoma. Outlook favorable.—J. D. Pontius.

Nevada, Mo., Nov. 4.—We have received fifteen new members in the last three Lord's days, six of these by baptism.—W. W. Burks, minister.

St. Joseph, Nov. 5.—Have just closed a meeting at Woodson Chapel in north St. Joseph with home forces. Twenty-eight were added to the church.—E. B. Bourland, minister.

Fayette, Nov. 6.—W. F. Shearer, of Angola, Ind., closed a successful meeting here Nov. 2. There were ten confessions and fourteen added by letter or statement.—R. B. Heiser, minister.

Kansas City, Nov. 11.—J. S. Clemons has just closed a nine days' meeting at Lone Jack, Mo., with nine added—eight by confession, one by letter, and the church is greatly improved.—G. C. Tomlinson.

Sheldon, Nov. 4.—Closed a three weeks' meeting at Altona last Sunday night with 18 additions —13 by baptism, four by statement, one from another religious body. R. A. Black did the preaching.—H. E. Carpenter.

Mexico, Nov. 9.—Four added to the church last Sunday, making 15 since the close of the Small-St. John meeting. Am now in a short meeting at the Hannibal church with Levi Marshall.—A. W. Kokendoffer.

Kansas City, Nov. 5.—E. A. Gilliland closed a revival at the Ivanhoe Park Christian church Thursday evening. His work can not be too highly commended. He left the church in good shape. Two by confession and two by statement at regular services yesterday.—Lewis P. Kopp, minister.

Michigan.

Fremont.—Two additions November 4, one baptism November 5. All departments progressing. Lord's day evening services largely attended by men.—Thomas W. Bellingham.

New Mexico.

Roswell, Nov. 5.—Seven additions here yesterday, five by confession, one by letter and one from another religious body. Fourteen added since the first Lord's day in October.—C. C. Hill.

Ohio.

Peebles, Nov. 3.—J. J. Taylor as evangelist and his wife as musical director, of Lexington, Ky., have just closed a two weeks' meeting with us with nine additions—all by confession and bap-

Sunday-School

November 25, 1906.

WORLD'S TEMPERANCE LESSON.
—Isa. 5:11-23.

Memory Verse, 11.

Golden Text.—I keep under my body, and bring it into subjection. I Cor. 9:27.

The prophets of Israel were all preachers of temperance. It was only rarely that they—or any other Biblical writers or speakers—had anything to say about the evils of strong drink, for that particular sort of intemperance had not assumed the proportions that it has to-day.

One may imagine, with but slight effort, how Amos or Isaiah would have poured out the vials of their holy wrath upon the saloon as an institution corrupting public life, controlling elections, serving as the rallying point for all the vicious, dangerous and destructive elements in social and political life.

The little wine shop of Isaiah's day sold wine and people who drank too much of it were rebuked. But the wine shop has grown into the saloon, which sells a dozen things worse than wine and has, besides, reared itself into a political institution and a great vested interest which must be protected.

In the early chapters of Isaiah, the prophet is reproaching Israel for her faithlessness and corruption. Although the chosen of the Lord, she has become an unfruitful vineyard (5:1-7). Therefore destruction shall come, and the vineyard shall be rooted up.

Some classes of people who had so lowered the moral and religious level of Israel are mentioned. There are the grasping and covetous who would increase their possessions even to crowding the poor from the very face of the earth. Woe to them! (5:8) There are those whose energies are all spent in revelry. Early and late they are at the wine. They have time and strength to spend in any debauch by day or by night, but they can spare no attention for the worship of God, the observation of his law, or even for attention to his handiwork in nature. Woe unto such! (5:11-12)

There are other classes of sinners also against whom the woe is pronounced: those given to falsehood (v. 18); those in whom falsehood has so far perfected itself that their moral judgments are wholly perverted and reversed, as Satan is made by Milton to say, "Evil, be thou my good" (v. 20); the self-righteous and self-satisfied (v. 21); again the drunken and riotous (v. 22); and finally those who pervert justice for a bribe. (v. 23).

"My people are gone into captivity for lack of knowledge." The nation's mistake. It is not on that account the less sinful, but it is the more pitiable. And that fact gives us a method for fighting it, not by scolding but by teaching. There is no captivity worse than that of intemperance, and those who are going into it are doing so from lack of knowledge. Let the church teach.

50 Years' Supremacy.

The supremacy of Borden's products is due to 50 years' scientific education of dairymen and employees with a fixed purpose to supply only the BEST Eagle Brand Condensed Milk and Peerless Brand Evaporated Cream fill every milk requirement.

Midweek Prayer-Meeting

November 21, 1906.

GOD'S PROVIDENT CARE. I Peter 5:7; Matt. 6:25-34.

"Yes, for me, for me he careth
With a brother's tender care;
Yes, with me, with me he snareth
Every burden, every fear.

"Yes, o'er me, o'er me he watcheth,
Ceaseless watcheth, night and day;
Yes, e'en me, e'en me he snatcheth
From the perils of the way.

"Yes, for me he standeth pleading
At the mercy seat above;
Ever for me interceding,
Constant in untiring love."

With all God's care for us he can not appear in our stead in the day of judgment. There amid its awful sublimities each man must appear for himself. But while God can not appear for us he will appear with us if through righteousness we have secured the advocacy of his Son.

Seeking first and exclusively the kingdom of God and his righteousness we become strangely exempt from the cares of life. Whether heretofore we have suffered from them on account of our fears (and out of mind, free from fear) or because God miraculously shields us from them, we know not, but we are free and full of peace and joy.

The same infinite love that prepared water for the fish, air for the wing, bread for hunger, beauty for the aesthetic taste within, has also prepared a glorious eternity in response to the soul's deathless longings for holiness and immortality. Yes, from the grave he will call his every child and in heaven invest him with the white robe and scepter and harp and the glad new song.

God's care does not fail when storm clouds lower and friends and good fortune flee. While he brings none of the sorrows of life upon us yet he does at times so utilize these apparent calamities as to bring us into nearer relationships to him and consequently into greater usefulness and happiness than we could otherwise have attained unto. If thoroughly committed unto God let us welcome the rain as well as the shine.

It does not in the least detract from our idea of the augustness of God that in his provident care the lower orders of life have share. The furs of polar fauna, the enlarged perspiratory glands of animals near the equator, the unfailing instinct that forewarns them of storm or drouth and that leads them to abstinence, to springs, or medical plants shows that the superabundance of loving care for all to which he has given breath is kindly conducted to those lower orders as physically sensitive as we. No one is like unto God who is unkind to any of the animal life beneath us.

Three great Bible texts are (1) For every man shall bear his own burden (2) Bear ye one another's burden and so fulfill the law. (3) Cast thy burden upon the Lord and he will sustain thee. These teach that there are some burdens each must bear for himself, others we may and ought to help each other bear, and others that will utterly crush us unless we commit them unto the Lord. Our Father solicitously pleads with us to let him help us. Let us enter into that

THE VALUE OF CHARCOAL.

Few People Know How Useful it is in Preserving Health and Beauty.

Costs Nothing to Try.

Nearly everybody knows that charcoal is the safest and most efficient disinfectant and purifier in nature, but few realize its value when taken into the human system for the same cleansing purpose.

Charcoal is a remedy that the more you take of it the better; it is not a drug at all, but simply absorbs the gases and impurities always present in the stomach and intestines and carries them out of the system.

Charcoal sweetens the breath after smoking, drinking or after eating onions and other odorous vegetables.

Charcoal effectually clears and improves the complexion, it whitens the teeth and further acts as a natural and eminently safe cathartic.

It absorbs the injurious gases which collect in the stomach and bowels; it disinfects the mouth and throat from the poison of catarrh.

All druggists sell charcoal in one form or another, but probably the best charcoal and the most for the money is in Stuart's Charcoal Lozenges; they are composed of the finest powdered Willow charcoal and other harmless antiseptics in tablet form or rather in the form of large, pleasant tasting lozenges, the charcoal being mixed with honey.

The daily use of these lozenges will soon tell in a much improved condition of the general health; better complexion, sweeter breath and purer blood, and the beauty of it is, that no possible harm can result from their continued use, but, on the contrary, great benefit.

A Buffalo physician, in speaking of Stuart's Charcoal Lozenges, says: "I advise Stuart's Charcoal Lozenges to all patients suffering from gas in stomach and bowels, and to clear the complexion and purify the breath, mouth and throat; I also believe the liver is greatly benefited by the daily use of them; they cost but twenty-five cents a box at drug stores, and although in some sense a patent preparation, yet I believe I get more and better charcoal in Stuart's Charcoal Lozenges than in any of the ordinary charcoal tablets."

Send your name and address today for a free trial package and see for yourself. F. A. Stuart Co., 56 Stuart Bldg., Marshall, Mich.

joyous estate possible only when self-reliant to the limit of our strength, fraternally disposed toward a needy world, and having our Father for our great burden bearer.

❀ ❀

THE COMING OF THE STORK
Reminds Mothers That One of the First and Most Important Requisites Is Cuticura Soap.

Physicians, nurses, pharmacists, and chemists throughout the world endorse Cuticura Soap, because of its delicate, medicinal, emollient, sanative, and antiseptic properties derived from Cuticura Ointment the great Skin Cure, united with the purest of cleansing ingredients and most refreshing of flower odors. For preserving, purifying, and beautifying the skin, for allaying itching, irritation and inflammation, for sanative, antiseptic cleansing, as well as for all the purposes of the toilet, bath and nursery, Cuticura Soap is invaluable. Guaranteed absolutely pure and may be used from the hour of birth.

November 25, 1906.

MISSIONS ON THE FRONTIER.—
Hab. 2:1-4.

DAILY READINGS.

M. A Family Missionary.　　　　John 1:35-42.
T. A Home Missionary.　　　　Mark 5:18-20.
W. A Neighborhood Missionary.　John 1:43-51.
T. A City Missionary.　　　　Acts 8:5-12.
F. A District Missionary.　　　Acts 8:26-40.
S. A Successful Missionary.　　John 4:31-42.
S. An Evening with Home Missions. Acts 1:6-8.

If not for America and Americans for what land and race will missionary martyrdom crown the cross with glory?

The San Francisco convention recommended that Idaho be made the special field for the missionary enterprise of our Endeavorers. Secretaries Wright and Ranshaw have referred the gathering of these special funds to Sarah Bird Dorman, Y. M. C. A. building, Cincinnati. Five thousand dollars are requested for this year. Let every society have at least a little part in this great ministry.

We need not seek arguments in justification of home missions. All we need is to open our eyes to the saloons and breweries, race tracks and gambling dens, the worship of mammon and the votaries of fashion, the unequal distribution of wealth and the heartlessness of the acquisitive, the desecration of the Lord's day, the neglect of Jehovah and the lost consciousness of eternity everywhere manifest and we see the necessity of more thoroughly evangelizing America.

We Disciples are said to have four frontiers in America. More than 1,000,-000 of our one and one-quarter million members live between Buffalo and Topeka, Kan., east and west, and between Chicago and Memphis, north and south. In the great regions lying on all sides of these bounds Disciples were long as rare as was the Word of the Lord in the days of Eli. Even as the love of God surged against the cross in Christ's time to enter into the larger life of Israel should we press against all these lines in order to bear the precious truths committed unto us to all our countrymen.

Our frontiers are not only geographical but moral as well. Custom, the sentiments of an age, our own disposition toward God, set bounds to Christian activity, to our consecration and visions of the higher life. When we scale some of these boundary walls, break through these limitations, struggle into larger liberty, we find other frontiers toward and through which the nobler will make their way in ceaseless endeavor to attain unto the liberty there is in Christ and to make all free. The last boundary line we cross will be the threshhold of the throne room of the eternal.

What Livingstone was to darkest Africa, Marcus Whitman was to wildest and most inaccessible America. In 1838 he established the first mission in the great northwest when there were but about fifty Americans in all that great empire now comprising Oregon, Washington, Idaho, Montana and Wyoming. In 1847 he was massacred by those red savages to whom he went to tell the story of the true happy hunting ground. Whitman College, at Walla Walla, was built over his grave and

helps commemorate one of the noblest lives in American history.

The home missionary is essentially a patriot. Whitman was notably so. When England was plotting to loop her border line beneath the imperial Oregon domain he rode horseback through the trackless wilds from the Pacific to the national capital to acquaint President Tyler, Daniel Webster and other statesmen of Britain's designs and of the natural resources of that great land many were disposed to surrender to England as the price of ignoble peace. While he added to the geographical and political puissance of our country other missionaries are adding to the wealth of American character, exalting its manhood, and making of it the noblest land that ere the sun shone on.

Visions of the English Bishops.

(Concluded from Page 1457.)

deavor to understand the most mystic passages of Browning in "Sordello," or the most sonorous pages of Carlyle's "Sartor Resartus," or some of the meanderings into philosophy of the Rev. R. J. Campbell in his fine but sublimated city temple sermons. All attempts to fathom such lucu-

brations are vain, for me at any rate; but to reconcile the extreme opposites of this Diggleism beats all other difficulties of the kind. It is encouraging, however, to note that the aspiration after Christian unity is everywhere in the air, although the majority of those who are thus longing for the consummation seem unable to see the only way to achieve it. The fact seems to be that they carefully shun the path of self-sacrifice which alone would lead them to it. They have no thought of surrendering their attachment to exclusive and privileged traditional ecclesiasticism. They would enjoy freedom while hugging the shackles of custom. How futile all the talk therefore is! Yet it may lead some who listen to it to the right reflections and put them in the path of candid inquiry. As to the Anglican bishops, there is only one real radical amongst them all—only one real progressive. He is that splendid liberal, Dr. Percival, Bishop of Hereford.

MARRIAGES.

Notices of marriages inserted under this heading at the rate of fifty cents for three lines or less (seven words to a line). Additional words at five cents per word. Cash must in each case accompany order.

CULP—GROVES.—S. B. Culp, minister of the Christian church at Watertown, N. Y., was married to Miss Lena J. Groves of that city, Wednesday, October 9, Joseph A. Serena, of Syracuse, performing the ceremony.

OLDHAM—DAVISON.—On October 24, 1906, at the M. E. church of Ebensburg, Pa., in the presence of about 300 invited guests, W. H. Oldham, minister of the East End Christian Church of East Liverpool, Ohio, and Miss Lyda J. Davison, of Ebensburg, Pa., were united in marriage by the Rev. Chicote and A. J. Welty. After the ceremony dinner was served at the home of the bride's parents and the contracting party was presented with a magnificent array of cut glass and silverware.   A. J. WELTY.

OBITUARIES.

[Notices of Deaths, not more than four lines, inserted free. Obituary memoirs, one cent per word. Send the money with the copy.]

JARRETT.

Thomas E. Jarrett died at his home in Salida, Colo., November 2, 1906, age 31 years, 10 months and 8 days. The funeral services by the writer at the Christian church.
W. B. CREWDSON.

PIPER.

Our dearly beloved brother, C. H. Piper, was called to the higher life Wednesday October 31, after a short illness with pneumonia. The neighborhood loses a genial friend, the church at Garden City a wise counsellor, and the family a devoted husband and father. The sincerest sympathy of all is with the stricken wife and family.
Garden City, Minn.

VAUGHN.

Alie E. Vaughn (nee Camplin) was born May 1, 1855, in Monroe county, Mo. She confessed Christ, and was baptized by Elder Rice when nearly 14 years old, and at her death, October 19, 1906, rounded out a true, beautiful Christian life and character. She married C. F. Vaughn January 22, 1880, and left, grieving over their loss, but rejoicing in heaven's gain, a husband, three sons, one sister, two brothers and her aged father. The funeral was held October 13, by the writer.
H. CAMPBELL CLARK, minister.
Ingersoll, Okla.

ROBERTSON.

Mrs. Sarah E. Mingle Robertson was born November 18, 1906, and, obedient to the gospel at the age of 21, has been faithful to the Master since. She was married to R. S. Robertson October 24, 1877, and of this union were born nine children, two having died in infancy. Brother Robertson had just moved from Malden, Mo., to Osborne, Kan., to take charge of the church where everything seemed so promising, when his wife was taken ill. She leaves a faithful husband, seven grown children, five grandchildren, a loving father and seven brothers to mourn her loss. She was always faithful to her family, and consecrated to her Master. Her spirit departed September 26, 1906, and the funeral was conducted by F. T. Roy, of Downs, in the Christian church.

HAYNES.

Miss Maria Frances Haynes, sister of our Veteran preacher, N. S. Haynes, died on October 12, 1906, at the home of her aunt, Mrs. Lucinda Rogers, Maysville, Ky., whither she had gone from Eureka, Ill., a few weeks before. Miss Haynes was born and raised at Eureka, where she was active in both church and college circles for many years. At fourteen years of age she became a member of the Christian church and in recognition of her active and helpful service in the church, a beautiful testimonial from the members of the Young Ladies' Auxiliary to the Christian Woman's Board of Missions of Eureka, Ill., was requested to be read at the funeral, which was held at the residence of her sister, Mrs. A. A. Major, on October 15, 1906, the remains having been brought to Eureka.
B. J. RADFORD.

FINCH.

One of our Sunday-school scholar, Mamie Finch, 12 years of age, went home to be with her Heavenly Father, Oct. 30. Through a long and painful illness she manifested a patient, loving spirit, and was most thoughtful of those who cared for her. She leaves a mother, brother, aged grandmother and stepfather of the immediate family; also a friend of the family, Mr. M. H. Selby, who deeply mourn her loss. Mr. Selby has loved her as his own. He has lived for her. His every thought has been for her welfare and his loss seems now irreparable. But she is now with One that will do everything that is for her best welfare and we may be with her in that home where there is no more pain. She cannot return to us to brighten our way with her presence, but we can go to her. DAVID N. WETZEL.
Mattoon, Ill.

HEROD.

William Erastus Herod was born in Boone county, Ky., September 30, 1821, and died at the home of his daughter, Mrs. W. D. Mowry in Kansas City, Kan., October 19, 1906, aged 85

years and 19 days. When ten years of age his parents located near Columbus, Ind. He was twice married. Brother Herod had been a liberal and devoted Christian for 68 years. He was a man of warm friendships and generous hospitality. His house was always the preacher's home. One brother, Robert Herod, of Chanute, Kan., three sons, Prof. E. A. Herod, of Alva, Okla.; A. L. Herod, of Thayer, Kan., and Dorcy Herod of Chanute, Kan.; and one daughter, Mrs. W. D. Mowry, of Kansas City, Kan. Several grandchildren and a host of brethren and friends were present at the funeral at the Christian church in Thayer, Kan., his late home.   C. W. YARD.
Buster Springs, Kan.

REGAL.

Mrs. Annie McGowan Regal was born October 29, 1841, and died October 20, 1906, aged 64 years, 11 months and 21 days. United in marriage to Miller McGowan in May 1861; of this union were born seven children, two sons and five daughters. One son and three daughters survive. Her husband, Miller McGowan, died December 18, 1876. She became the wife of Mark B. Regal on March 26, 1878. She has been a sufferer since 1881, and for the past four years she has been helpless. She was a niece of the well beloved Elder Jonas Hartzell. A faithful Christian for many years, and one of the most patient in her serious suffering the writer has ever known; she died strong in her faith that all is well. Services were conducted by the writer, assisted by Rev. E. G. Laughlin, on October 22, at North Benton, Ohio.   CHARLES E. TAYLOR.
Deerfield, Ohio.

PITNEY.

Drusilla Pitney was born in Coshocton county, Ohio, March 6, 1830. With her parents she went to Missouri where she grew to womanhood. In 1852 she returned to Ohio and on June 28, 1853, was married to John McElroy, who passed away February 9, 1869. They were the parents of eight children, but two of whom survive her. Mrs. Emma White, of Trenton, Mo., whose husband is pastor of the church there, and Mrs. Ada Fox, of Millersburg, who with her husband nursed and cared for her during her last illness. Early in life she became a Christian and for more than half a century she has been a member of the Christian church in Millersburg, O. She departed this life September 4, 1906, at the age of 76 years, 5 months and 28 days. Funeral services, conducted by the writer, were held at the home of her daughter, Mrs. J. C. Fox at Millersburg on Thursday, September 6.
P. H. WELSHIMER.
Canton, O.

CROWE.

Our much beloved brother, Eld. J. T. Crowe, departed this life on October 22, at the home of his daughter, Mrs. B. F. Sapp, of Joplin, Mo., of paralysis. John T. Crowe, was born at Bellaire, Ohio, on June 20, 1838; served through the rebellion with the Ohio Volunteer Infantry; was married October 22 (same date of his death) 1865, to Miss Maria Louise Davis, of which union were born five children, all being dead except the twins, James and Edna. His wife died April 23, 1883, and soon after he moved to Gravette, Ark., where he was largely instrumental in building and promoting the Church of Christ, and in it his labors never were irksome. He served five consecutive years in the superintendency of the Sunday-school, and the brethren regretted to have him withdraw from that office which he did on account of poor health; but he was ever ready to occupy a vacancy. We are grieved at his death, but knowing his life here realize that his departure means his eternal gain; for there certainly is a guttering crown in store for our good old Brother Crowe. He was married to Mrs. Anna C. Dunning in 1895. His wife dying in 1904, Brother Crowe has since lived with his daughter.   HERB. LEWIS.
Gravette, Ark.

McCLUNG.

Mary Ellen Scott McClung was born February 11, 1816, in Jefferson county, Ind. She was the second of seven children born to James and Mary Scott. Of these only one, J. M., now past eighty years of age, and living at Portland, Oregon, survives her. Mrs. McClung spent her early childhood on the farm in Jefferson county. While still a young girl her parents moved to Crawfordsville, Montgomery county. Here she lived until her marriage, May 16, 1837, to James C. McClung, when they settled on a farm three miles from Crawfordsville. Living there until 1847, they moved to Iowa, buying a claim near Dahlonega, Wapello county, upon which they lived until the death of Mr. McClung, July 23, 1892. Since his death Mrs. McClung has made her home with her children. The marriage of Mrs. and Mr. McClung proved to be a very happy one. Seven children were born to them, of whom five are living: Jno. S., of Dahlonega, Ia.; Susan Frances, living three miles south of Hedrick, Ia.; Martha M., of Hedrick, Ia.; Millard H., and Ryland, both of Portland, Oregon; Rebecca Ellen Kitterman, deceased December 28, 1860, and James Scott, deceased July 2, 1889. There were two step-children; by husband's former marriage: Mary Jane, deceased December, 1854, and Samuel McClung, deceased October 2, 1903. There are twenty-one grand-

children and twenty-four great grandchildren surviving her. Mrs. McClung confessed her Savior while yet in her teens, uniting with the Church of Christ. She was a devoted Christian, ever happy in the work of her Master. For many months before her death she had been unable to attend church, which was a source of much regret to her. However, in word and thought and deed she constantly held up to the world her Risen Savior as the world's model and at every opportunity expressed her confident expectation of meeting her Savior in heaven. About three weeks before her death, while visiting at the home of her grand-daughter, Mrs. Smith, of Linby, Ia., she experienced a severe fall which confined her to bed and was the probable cause of her death. Sinking very rapidly she died on Sunday, October 21, at 9 a. m. The funeral services were conducted from the house at 10 a. m. by Rudolph Heicke, pastor of the Church of Christ at Hedrick, assisted by Elder Jasper Smith, of Abbington, Ia. The remains were laid to rest by the side of her husband in Dahlonega cemetery.

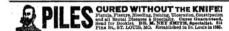

BAPTISMAL DOGMA AND THE GREAT COMMISSION

By J. S. HUGHES.

The words, "Baptizing them into the name of the Father, and of the Son, and of the Holy Spirit" (Matt. 28:19) are words that Christ never used. Look and see. We have a number of baptisms occurring in the New Testament, in the Acts and elsewhere related, and in not a single instance are the words, "Into the name of the Father and Son and Holy Spirit" used. That is the plain truth and ought of itself to settle it. But I am asked when I know it was not used. They did not use it because where any form of words was used it was another and not this form, as, "in the name of the Lord," and to have used the former they would have had to use both, and so have doubled, which we can not receive. To affirm they used such form is to speak where the Bible does not speak. And not only so, but it is bad form for those who have rejected infant baptism on the ground that no case is recorded of infants being present at household baptisms and who have said to the practicer of infant baptism, "It is your place to show, since you practice it, that there were infants in the families that were baptized," to now put themselves on this same ground of defense and with even less show for not only is the formula of Matthew absent in every recorded instance, but other forms take its place, and so exclude it. That Christ never spoke these words will further appear, if they are needed, by noting well the following facts:

1. Matthew's gospel is alone in using these words, no other book has them. Neither Luke nor John mention baptism in the commission.

2. "Baptizing the nations," is an idea entirely foreign to Christ's teaching which was so strictly personal. He never hinted at anything of the kind being done to nations as such.

3. How could Christ at that time speak of the Holy Spirit in such official way, the Holy Spirit not yet having come into his office!

The disciples had not yet even asked anything in his name and he had kept them in the Father's name.

This commission in Matthew, like that in Mark, has the appearance of having been tacked on at the end, and Matthew's commission as having been given in Galilee, while Luke and John refer to it as having been given at Jerusalem. But those long accustomed to regarding baptism not only as authorized by Christ, but as the one thing in which his authority was most centralized and expressed in the Great Commission, we go even further. There never existed, in fact, the thing we call "The Great Commission." There is nothing called a commission either great or small, and what we mean by it was not known to Christ's apostles, in fact.

We admit at once that Paul did not come under the same commission with the others and as he was more abundant in labors than they all the greater part of the work done had not baptism in its commission. There is no doubt that Christ said something very important to the apostles after his resurrection, to be noticed later; but we who have made "the Great Commission" our formal authoritative text for all great occasions and the beginning place for all great undertakings are a little surprised to learn that it was not at all so with the Christian church of the apostolic times. In not a solitary instance was this so-called "Great Commission" ever quoted or cited as the authority, or motive or incentive for any great movement of the church. On the other hand every one of its great beginnings and undertakings was started from a special, personal commission. I have just instanced Paul, who had never seen or heard Christ in the flesh, and who claimed no such authority in a common call with the other apostles. When he stood in the presence of King Agrippa to account for his ministry, he said, "I was not disobedient unto the heavenly vision." Beginning with the day of Pentecost we have the first occasion where the "Great Commission" should have been set forth. It was after the disciples had been speaking to one another in tongues "as the Spirit gave them utterance," and after this had been rumored outside among the people, and after they had gathered to the place to witness the spectacle, and after they had begun to mock and to accuse them who spake as the Spirit gave them utterance, of being drunk, that Peter rose to his feet to explain. Here was an occasion to cite "The Great Commission," for there were present people of all nations, but instead, Peter quotes Joel and gives the keyword to the heavenly campaign, "And it shall come to pass in the last days, saith God, I will pour out of my Spirit upon all flesh, and your sons and your daughters shall prophesy, and your young men shall see visions, and your old men shall dream dreams, and on my servants and on my handmaids I will pour out in those days of my Spirit, and they shall prophesy."

The "Great Commission" was not cited at all. As Peter is singled out as the one person above all others who was to be given this centralized authority, let us follow him to the next great occasion and beginning place. It was at the household of Cornelius. On his return to Jerusalem from this new step, the apostles and brethren said to him, "thou went'st in to men uncircumcised and didst eat with them." Peter rehearsed his experience and told of a vision that had been given to Cornelius to send for him, and instead of citing the "Great Commission" as any disciple preacher would have done, and which would have settled it with any church, Peter cited instead his own commission, his own personal commission to the exclusion of all other authority and all other apostles, and said, "What was I that I could withstand God?"

Neither Peter nor the "apostles and brethren" knew any other authority for settling it. If they had it would have been forthcoming on such demand. In fact the demand never could have been made. But again comes a test occasion, more decisive and far-reaching yet. It was the general council of the churches in Jerusalem. When the delegates from all the churches were met to consider the Gentile question with the apostles and elders, here Peter arose and again instead of quoting that "Great Commission" to all the world, and to every creature, and which placed the human family on equal grounds before God, and which would have at once settled it with every one who had ever heard of it, Peter entirely failed, and cited again his own personal and especial commission, saying, "Men and brethren, you know how that a good while ago God made choice among us that the Gentiles by my mouth should hear the word of the Gospel and believe." It is the same kind of answer he gave before when questioned for his authority. A commission to preach to the Gentiles could not have been given to all the apostles, or Peter could not have singled himself out as God's especial agent for this purpose. James being present arose and confirmed Peter's words, "Simon hath declared how God did at the first visit of the Gentiles." The notion that the so-called "Great Commission" was to be as the written will of a dead man to be carried out by administrators as in a court of law, or as the commission of a plenipotentiary in a foreign court to be carried out under a legal code of agreement, is a mistaken one, is grotesque, is a shallow and misleading fake, is a sophisticated propaganda of pitfalls to the unthinking and unsaved. Let us see, it is a question not of textual criticism, nor of interpretation of texts, but at bottom a question of method. Let us take Jesus Christ as our highest authority on method. He said, "You shall know a tree by its fruits," not by the tag which comes on it from the nursery, nor by the name the vendor may give it to sell in the market. Is the tree what it seemed to be and what it was declared would be? or what we have found it to be in fact, by seeing, handling and tasting its fruit? Christ said the latter; so say I. Now we find here what, by some means or other, got itself tagged as the "Great Commission," and there was imported into it all authority in heaven and on earth (really in the Roman church) and it placed all men for all time on equal grounds before God in a universal message of amnesty, and it enjoined baptism "into the name of the Father, and of the Son and of the Holy Spirit," for the remission of sins, and it alone was clothed with these names. We first discover that baptism was not so administered in the New Testament examples, and then still more evident that neither the apostles nor the brethren knew of the existence of any such authoritative declaration; but from Jerusalem where it began onward to the end the great movements followed the keynote given by Peter quoting from Joel. These last days were to be characterized by visions and prophesies among all classes. Hence Cornelius and Ananias and others received such visions. In fact every great movement of the Christian church was begun in personal visions and special mandates. The case of Philip follows Peter. By special revelation he went towards Gaza and by another joined himself to the chariot of the queen's treasurer, and through him sent the old Ethiopia. Peter by special and personal vision is ordered to go to Cornelius who has also seen a vision.

Paul on his way to Damascus is halted by a vision and sent henceforth to the Gentiles, and to Ananias who had also been given a vision.

Again, a second time while he is hunting a missionary field and is forbidden by the Spirit to enter this port and that and the other, Paul is given the vision of the man of Macedonia and being "not disobedient unto the heavenly vision" "goes to Philip, and there preaches Christ first in the western world, under the new special and personal commission.

Thus it stands in fact that the gospel was sent into Asia, into Africa and into Europe by personal special mandates given to individuals in visions,

and last of all the highest, holiest and greatest of them was given to John in the Isle of Patmos, saying to him "Thou must prophesy again concerning many peoples and nations and tongues and kings."

(CONCLUDED NEXT WEEK.)

SUBSCRIBERS' WANTS.

Advertisements will be inserted under this head at the rate of two cents a word, each insertion, all words, large or small, to be counted and two initials being counted as a word. Advertisements must be accompanied by remittance, to save bookkeeping.

YOUNG CHRISTIAN PHYSICIAN desires location in good Missouri towns. Address C., care Christian-Evangelist.

SEND $1.00 to J. A. Cunningham, Tupelo, Miss., for his twelve sermons pronounced "Masterpieces," and his "Blue and Gray."

SEND for catalog of Christian University, Canton, Mo. Departments—Preparatory, Classical, Scientific, Biblical, Commercial and Music. For ladies and gentlemen. Address Pres. Carl Johann, Canton, Mo.

CHURCHES or EVANGELISTS needing a singer with Stereopticon illustrating songs for revival meetings, can obtain the services of N. M. Field during the months of December and January. Best of references given. Address, No. 4439 St. Louis avenue, St. Louis, Mo.

THE NEW TEXAS-CALIFORNIA.—The Gulf Coast and Rio Grande Valley of Texas is the most attractive region known to us for both the Home-Seeker and the Investor. It is the home of the Citrus fruits, English walnuts, Figs and Grapes. The truck-farmer puts his products on the market from four to six weeks earlier than from any other portion of the country. He is 1500 miles nearer to the great markets than California. Our organization is especially trying to interest members of the Christian Church, so that the settler will have the advantage of his accustomed religious influence. For descriptive Literature, address Hallam Colonization Co., Denton, Texas. Sales office, Harlingen, Texas.

The Home Department

Cleaning House.

Dolly's clothes are on the line,
Dolly's dishes fairly shine;
Dolly's home is swept all through,
Chairs and table look like new—
Dolly's little mother, May,
Has been cleaning house to-day.
Picture books, a goodly row,
Such a pretty order show;
Games and blocks, ball put in place;
Pencils in the drawing case.
"I'm so tired," says little May;
"I've been cleaning house to-day."
—Children's Companion.

The Bronze Vase.

BY J. BRECKENRIDGE ELLIS.

PART IV.

CHAPTER V.

For awhile, Raymund did not reply to the elegantly dressed man of the high silk hat. He was thinking busily. According to this promoter, Mr. Horace Bridgewaite, the name on the bronze vase was "Raymund," and this same Raymund was the heir to the White millions. But according to his mother's letter, the child whose name was on the bronze vase, was not a White, but a Revore. Therefore if "Raymund" was on the vase, Rhoda must be the heiress. Raymund turned suddenly to Mr. Bridgewaite. "Where is that bronze vase buried?" he asked.

"At your mother's former boarding-house, my dear young sir. I can take you to the very spot."

"You will take me to that spot?"

"I will, good sir, when you have paid me down one thousand dollars."

"How can it be that you have never dug up that vase for private keeping, since you are so interested in other people's affairs?"

"Would I dig up property that does not belong to me?" cried the promoter indignantly. Then he added gently, "Besides, had it ever been disturbed, the proof would be gone. You might say I had had a vase made and engraved for my purpose. No, young sir, I will take you, with witnesses, to the spot which will show that it has remained undisturbed for years. Now, my friend, look at this." He thrust into Raymund's hands the morning paper. It contained an account of old Mr. White's recent death in New York and of his will which bequeathed all his property in case his grandchild was not found, to a hospital and a private school. The account stated that since the old widower's death, a letter dated eighteen years ago had been found among a bundle of private papers. The envelope was gone and the writer had neglected to give the name of the place from which it had been sent. The letter was given in the paper, as follows:

"Dear Father: Our little one is now one year old. If you can not forgive us, will you not have pity upon your innocent grandchild? Your son has been ill and we are partly depending upon the charity and kindness of a family of fellow-boarders. You returned my former letter unread. I pray you to treat this one more kindly.

Your daughter in need,
NELLIE RENNOLDS WHITE."

The newspaper went on to tell about the elopement of Mr. White's son with Miss Nellie Rennolds some twenty years ago. Nothing was known of them, except that they had gone west and that the son had died in Missouri.

"Now," said the promoter, as Raymund handed back the paper, I have only to prove your identity, and that hospital and private school can whistle for their money?" The train had stopped at a station and general attention was attracted by the entrance of an officer and deputies, who had two prisoners in charge. The prisoners were chained together, but a hand of each had been left free. They were smoking cigarettes, for on the small accommodation train, there was no private smoking car, and the entire forward coach was dedicated to tobacco fumes. Raymund instantly recognized one of the prisoners as Boggs. After four years, he had finally been sentenced to the state prison; but Mrs. Van Estry had been acquitted. As Bogg's mean, shifty eyes caught sight of Raymund, a sickly smile passed over his face. He moistened his lips with the tip of his tongue and inhaled his cigarette deeply. The next moment he saw Horace Bridgewaite. His countenance became livid and furious. He pointed his finger at the promoter and said in a husky voice, "There is the feller that was at the bottom of all my crookedness. I was low down, and he was high up. He moved with high-toners and I was a kid of the streets."

"Hush!" said one of the deputies.

"Let the man talk," retorted the sheriff. In fact, Horace Bridgewaite had pretended to promote a scheme of the sheriff's, and remembering what he had paid down in advance, the officer enjoyed Mr. Bridgewaite's discomfiture.

Boggs thus encouraged, raised his voice. "That white-livered promoter took me off the streets and made terms with me. I was to do business among the slums. He was to hoodwink the upper-tendums. We went halvers on what I made, and I got a bare pittance of what he made. I stood all the blame. I got all the kicks and curses. He sat at his ease. Did he come to me during my trial? Did he get me a good lawyer? He never did anything."

"This is insufferable!" cried the promoter, rising. "I shall retire to the other coach. Remember, Mr. Revore, if you want to clinch with my offer. I am at my office in the Junction building."

"Stand your ground!" cried the sheriff. "Why not demand protection from the railroad company?" The promoter left the coach followed by laughter and hisses.

"I'd serve two extra year in the pen, if it would put that villain in there with me," snarled Boggs.

"Never mind," said the sheriff, soothingly, "I think he will presently put himself in there."

Raymund felt that those on the car looked at him either sneeringly as a friend of the promoter, or pityingly as one of the promoter's victims. That, however, was not the reason of his suddenly changing his destination. When he left the train long before it reached Frog Bend, it was that he might make quick connection for St. Louis. He had resolved to go at once to the boarding-house on Washington avenue and examine the bronze vase. The Union Station looked pretty much the same as when he and Rhoda had left it to obey Mr. Willby's telegram. The Four Courts were so grimy and forbidding, the sounds from the elevated railroad threatened, as formerly, to descend upon his head. On reaching the boarding-house in question, he found that it was now a residence. When he explained that the bronze vase was buried in the coal cellar, without, of course, saying a word about the engraving upon it, or its connection with the mystery of Mr. White's heir, he was given sympathetic assistance. With a rapidly-beating heart the young man, obeying the directions of the letter of his dead mother, went to the northeast corner of the second cellar-chamber. Just as in his mother's time, coal stood in a pyramid as it had been cast through the narrow oblong pavement-window. Raymund locked overhead for the second beam from the north. Directly under it, the coal was half way on its pyramidal career. It was necessary to scoop away a great quantity, before the bare ground was revealed. The earth was very hard, but a spade was not long in discovering one spot where its blade preferred to go in. Raymund encouraged the blade, and although the weight of the coal had pressed the once loosened earth scraped suddenly against a hard object. Raymund dug around it, then resting upon his knees, groped in the semi-gloom. It was the bronze vase. Having deposited it in the bag which he had brought for that purpose, he gratefully acknowledged the kindness of the family, and departed to his hotel. Having locked himself in the bathroom, his first care was to wash the vase clean. The vase was two feet high, ornamented with two embossed cupids who were peering over the edge with smiles of delight at the flowers that should have been within. When the vase was clean and dry, Raymund carried it to a shop where he had the long slender stem cut half in two, with orders that the bowl should be wrapped up in one parcel and the pedestal in another. When these were given him, he left the shop and stood upon the pavement uncertain whether to go back at once, or to visit his uncle William.

As yet, he did not know what name was upon the pedestal of the bronze vase. It seemed an unfair advantage to examine it away from Rhoda. Why not carry it to her and unwrap it in her presence? In that way, both of them would learn at the same time which one of them was a Revore, and which one was a millionaire.

Raymund's heart was beating violently. His head seemed dizzy. He had not yet become used to the truth that Rhoda was not really his sister; that she was of no kin to him; that she was just like any other girl—say like Nelsie Loraine, with just that little claim upon him. And she had known that all this time, and had not hinted the fact. She had grown to regard him as a young man beyond the tie of blood—young man in the same class with Jack Bellfield. That was why she had drawn away from him whenever he sought to give her a brotherly embrace; for she knew he was not her brother. That was why she had refused to kiss him. As he recalled how she had torn herself away from his detaining hand, he felt a sudden resentment. Why had she not told him all? But he knew why well enough. She had not wanted to crush his spirit with the secret. Poor Rhoda! She knew they were not brother and sister, but she did not know which of them was the child of Mrs. Revore. The bronze vase would tell the story. If the name Raymund was upon it, that would mean that Raymund was Mrs. Revore's only child and that Rhoda was an heiress. If Rhoda was upon the vase then Raymund was not Mrs. Revore's son.

Impatient as he was to learn the truth, Raymund decided that it would be most magnanimous not to look at the vase until Rhoda was by his side. Until time for the train to leave for Frog Bend, a day must be spent in the city. It seemed something like a duty to go to see his uncle William. It was a painful pilgrimage to the narrow dark streets of the second-hand clothes. It was with no rapid or loving tread that he entered the long, dingy thoroughfare. He felt no ill will toward Mr. Hodges, but he could not but censure the old man for having cast him and Rhoda, helpless orphans but for the goodness of friends, out upon the mercy of a world that has little taste for orphans.

He paused, at last, before the familiar pawnshop, and summoned up the resolution to once more face Miss Pinns. The three golden balls seemed each a yellow eye of jealousy, gleaming unfriendly recognition. At last he grasped the iron handle his younger hand had so often felt, and pushed open the door. A Jew stood behind the counter, polishing the face of a silvermounted clock with a red silk cloth. There was the stove near which the young man had studied on winter nights while its iron sides grew dull and cold, and the night air crept in from under the door.

"I would like to see Mr. Hodges," said Raymund diffidently.

"I can't show him to you," said the Jew. "Is there something else you would like to see?"

"Perhaps you can tell me where Mr. Hodges is," suggested Raymund.

"Dead," said the man, rubbing violently and no longer looking up.

Raymund felt a shock of cold surprise. "Dead!" he repeated.

"Yes," said the new proprietor, "he married and then he died. What's the odds? That's pretty much all they is to life, as I look at it. He married late, and he died later. That was the end of him."

"Could you tell me where I could find Miss Pinns—I mean the woman he married?"

"You must have known 'em pretty good," said the other glancing up with more interest. "Yes, Miss Pinns, as you call her, is living on Vandeventer street, in handsome flats. She's set up an automobile and she's living at the top notch of luxury, spending as fast as she can all the old man left her. That black tooth —you remember it, hey?"

"Quite well," said Raymund.

"Well, she's carrying that black tooth to all the free festivities, and she's hovering on the outskirts of tony society

waiting for a chance to dash in." The Jew chuckled. "And I bet you she gets in by hook or crook," he added in admiration. "Let me tell you, Miss Pinns that was, is a genius. She ain't over particular, but she's a genius. Look how she come here as a plain, poor servant, and Mr. Hodges working his fingers to the bone laying up wealth. She married him out of hand. And now he's in his grave and she's in her automobile. That's what I call genius. Say, if you want to go to see her, I think I have the number here in my drawer."

He started to pull open the little drawer in which Rhoda used to keep her gloves, ribbons and the blank paper devoted to poetical purposes.

"No," said Raymund with decision, "I don't care to see her. Thank you. Good morning."

❀ ❀

The Funny Story Cure.

A case that came under my direction a few years ago was that of a professional man of middle age—conscientious, a hard worker and worrier ... much the hardest thing to get at was his mental condition. I knew that he couldn't be cured until that was changed. Finally I directed him to tell a funny story at each meal, with an extra two at dinner. That was because it was entirely impossible for him to control his own state of mind by will-power. A man can say to himself, "I will be optimistic" several hundred times a day and yet remain sad. He needs a handle—some objective way of getting at it. This man rebelled violently at the new orders, but finally consented to make the attempt. It was such a terrible undertaking for him that for the first few days he could not open his mouth. He forgot his stories completely. Then I made him write them down on a piece of paper and keep them in his lap for reference. When a pause in the conversation arrived he would become restless, look anxiously about, glance at his lap, clear his throat and begin. The prescription was a bitter one for him, but he had promised to make the attempt, and before a week was out the humor of the situation struck him, and he began to enjoy the fun. After that his recovery was sure. He became cheerful, light-hearted, approachable. The whole current of his life was changed.

❀ ❀

The Breakfast Table.

Even in families called intelligent the breakfast table is usually interrupted by a mad rush for the cars or for school. But if we want wholesome, beautiful children, we will follow the breakfast with a short period of leisure, and then go serenely about the day's work. One of the first needs in the child's day is for general bodily exercise, and this can better be given in the home than in the school; for in the home the exercise can be purposeful, some household service which will be of real use. Here, again, the service can be made a joy or a task, according to the spirit we put into it. It must be remembered that the childish will to do is rather fitful and uncertain, given to taking up occupations with enthusiasm and then dropping them before completion. The remedy is to fill out and complete the will, and this, it seems to me, can best be done by working merrily and joyfully with the child.

A small boy will help you make his bed and "tidy up" his room with the greatest pleasure if you give him your good company at the same time—the only sort of company you ought ever to give any one—while he would find it a

very dull and distasteful task if he had to do it alone. Tell him a story, sing a duet with him, try to outwhistle him—in short, see to it that you are merry workers in this merry, charming world. But do not rob him of the service, with its measure of health and good spirit, and do not teach him to look down on women while he is still in knickerbockers by forcing him to think that these homely, necessary tasks are unsuitable for him, but none too good for his mother, or sisters, or the women servants. In no case, however, may this service be paid for in other coin than loving appreciation, for that is to turn the child into a miserable little trader, and quite rob the service of value.

A day is well begun which has in it these wholesome elements of home life, this serenity and good comradeship and service. The home life is the primary thing and the school life quite secondary.—*Henderson in "Education and the Larger Life."*

A little kingdom I possess,
  Where thoughts and feelings dwell,
And very hard I find the task
  Of governing it well;
For passion tempts and troubles me.
  A wayward will misleads,
And selfishness its shadow casts
  On all my words and deeds.

I do not ask for any crown
  But that which all may win,
Nor seek to conquer any world
  Except the one within.
Be Thou my guide until I find,
  Led by a tender hand,
Thy happy kingdom in myself
  And dare to take command.
       —*Louisa May Alcott.*

❦ ❦
Advance Society Letters.

BY J. BRECKENRIDGE ELLIS.

The photographer has not yet finished up that new picture of Felix. He thinks he will do so to-day; I am still hoping we may have it in time to hang upon Drusie's Christmas Tree. Do our new readers know who Drusie is, and what we mean by her Tree? I will explain. A few years ago, the *Courier-Journal* had a department called "The Young Folks," and Drusie, just a girl, used to write letters for the page, as, for instance, Gerald Dever and the Per Lees used to write for this. I read her letters, and became interested in her. Two years ago she was fired with the sudden but overwhelming desire to be a missionary, and to be it right away. The church board at that time had no means to supply another vacancy, and Drusie decided to start for China, trusting to the Lord to see that she got there, since she was going for him.

Now listen at this: She left her Sunday-school class which she was teaching in a Christian church in Louisville, and asking them to pray for her work, bade her mother a hasty farewell, took the train for Chicago, told the passengers what she wanted to do, received enough on the car to pay for her ticket, reached Chicago with 75 cents, was taken care of by some kind woman till she received enough money to take her to the seacoast. Here she joined a band of men and women, all older than herself, people who had been Methodists and Presbyterians and Baptists and twelve other kinds, but who in going to China had resolved to all be of one and the same kind, to give up all differences, to take simply the requisites of the Bible and be for Christ instead of some particular party. People heard about this band who were waiting in faith at Los Angeles until means should come. Contributions began to roll in, and finally they lifted the ship off shore and carried her to China. That is what money will do; and that is what faith will do. I was particularly interested when I found out that one of that band was the little girl Drusie who used to write for the papers. I told the Advance Society about it; and you thought you could send her $5 a month. Of course $5 a month is not munificent, but we are hoping it goes farther in China than it does in Arkansas. And it is a good deal, when you stop to think about it, or whether you stop or not, I say, it is a good deal to expect of the dimes and nickels and stamps that come to me from little children. It is a good thing the old folks help us along. But at the same time, every one who ever contributed a penny should feel that he has done a certain part in this great work of sending the Gospel to the heathen; a great work indeed, if pennies are scarce; and a mighty stingy thing if they are scattered all about the house. Still, I had rather you'd be stingy than nothing. My point is this—and I hope it will stick nobody; when you are not able to give much for God, give a little in confidence and boldness; he will increase it. Do you know of anything bigger than those two mites of the poor widow? They are so big that

millionaires have been able to hide behind them, ever since they heard of them. Christmas I am going to have a Tree for Drusie, right here in Arkansas. Don't you want to hang something on it for Drusie? not literal gingerbread and popcorn, but the price of any present you would like to send. For instance, if you would like to present her with a souvenir-spoon or a needle-case, send the price of that object, and all you send will go to help Christianize the heathen. How much better that will be than giving the heathen the identical souvenir-spoon and needle-case. And how happy you will make Drusie, thus enabling her to spread the Word. Thing how many people you will make happy by such a gift; Drusie, the readers of this page, ME (what a consideration!) the heathen to be converted, you who send it, and God, for Whom all this labor is expended. Did you ever give a Christmas present and get so much out of it? I am not going to urge this matter, so please don't skip this page till Christmas is over. But send in your gift along about the middle of December and let's have a big time.

I told you that S. A. Seat, of Hematite, Mo., suggested a box-supper for Drusie on Thanksgiving, and I altered his suggestion to the Christmas Tree. Now there are some people who, if you don't take their suggestion, won't play. Ever notice that? You must do like they think and speak, or they are out of it. You can just go along and do the best you can. They told you how to do it, and you thought you knew better than they, and now you can simply manage it without their help. You ventured to have an opinion of your own; very well, then, *have* it, and do all the work yourself, and see how you like it! Did you ever know anybody like that in the church? Almost everybody is like that out of the church, but if you know any one in the church like that, why not take this and read it to 'em, for of course it isn't you. Nobody can accuse S. A. Seat of being that way, at all events, for just read his letter: "Yes, brother, have a Christmas tree. There's a heap more fun going to, and helping with, a Christmas Tree than an old box supper where they eat and eat and talk spoony. Sure, a Christmas Tree is most the thing. We can have a splendid time, and such a variety of presents and pretty candies, oranges, nuts—a thousand things! Get a large tree and trim it way up to the top. Somebody send us Christmas candles so we can see the presents; yes, and some ribbon to tie the presents on, with." The Fourth of July is rather late, as a matter of news, but I would like for you to compare the ordinary firecrackers display with Drusie's method of celebrating, as found in this extract from her letter: "We had a happy time in North China, on the Fourth; we celebrated our liberty in Christ Jesus. We had a picnic supper on the grass at the east end of our mission Farm. One of our number had prepared napkins, drawing with colored chalks the emblems of our national flags. The 'adopted children' of Uncle Sam had two flags side by side—in our band are two from Norway, one from Sweden, one from England and one from Ireland. Before eating, our General Director prayed for America, the President, Legislature and People, that they might glorify our God and Savior. Then we sung our national hymn, Columbia and Star Spangled Banner. One sees his country in a new light when he hears what foreigners have to say about it. May our United States never dishonor her glorious name by bringing dishonor upon our fathers' God, and our great Captain." Our orphan Dartie has recently written to my mother; I don't think he'll object if I give an extract: "I have been sick with malarial fever for a

week, but am up now. I received a letter from Drusie, Monday." (Bessie is his sister who has been adopted by a farmer and his wife; the Av. S. paid Charlie's way there last summer on a visit; Charlie had not seen her for three years; the Av. S. never took more satisfaction in any one of its acts, than the gift of this reunion for more than a week.) "I am studying hard. I hope to make the man that all the Av. S. members are wishing for. I received the underclothes. I thank Mr. Breck—was it he?—for sending them." No, it was the Av. S. These three heavy suits of underwear were procured at a great bargain for $1.50, so I bought them and forwarded same to Charlie, paying the bill out of Charlie's general expense fund—not the education fund, of course.) "I pass away my time reading. Since I came back from the summer vacation, I have read from 10 to 15 books which I get from the Public Free Library. You can have all the turkey you want, just so I get the same amount of chicken. That ice cream was a beautiful success. Just think, $146.55! I guess the people will stop buying, though, for the weather is cooler. I am going down to the depot this morning to take a little boy from here" (the orphan home). "I enjoyed my vacation ever so much while at your house and with Bessie, and with Mrs. Skinner and her friends and relations, and I am very thankful. . . The bell has rung for breakfast so I will close." Here is a note from Charlie's matron, Mrs. B. R. Brown, St. Louis: "Enclosed find $1 to add to Charlie's education fund, from Mrs. Arnold, Shamrock, Mo. Charlie is sick, but hope he will soon be well. He was so pleased with the underwear. I am so glad for him to have the woolen underwear for this winter, as he feels the cold forcibly." Here are tardy guests: Mrs. Flora Schenck, Basin, Wyo.: "My sister, Anna Seward, and I send a dime each for ice cream and as it is in one piece, we add a nickel to get it there. We should be glad to have Charlie visit us in the Big Horn Basin. We live on Shell creek, where there are lots of trout. We have no Church of Christ. Brother Banta is leading us in trying to build up the cause. I have not heard one of our preachers since coming to the Basin, six years ago, but all that time THE CHRISTIAN-EVANGELIST has been a great comfort to me. There are lots of good sermons in it besides the Easy Chair, which seem like letters from home. Av. S. letters have been a great help. We will eat our part of the ice cream at home this evening." Mrs. R. J. Naylor, Wal-

SCHOOLS AND COLLEGES.

dron, Mo.: "I send $1 for orphan Charlie and one for Drusie, also my prayers and best wishes." There is nothing like giving to teach the joy of giving; you can't get it out of books; you first give, then you *know*. Now comes our friend E. E. Herriman, Mooresville, Mo., who has already sent Charlie and Drusie $20 that I remember, and possibly by looking at my accounts I would find more to his credit. But does he feel, "Now I've done my part, let the others work?" Or does he say, "So-and so gave only a quarter; if he gives only a quarter, I'll make mine 10 cents?" Does he say that? No, somebody else says that, but not E. E. Herriman, for here he comes promptly to date with $5 more for Charlie, and $10 for Drusie. Of course, this goes on the education fund, but is not counted in the ice cream social, because that was not expressly stipulated.

In the meantime it must not be supposed that the regular Av. S. work is suffering—the daily reading and quotation-learning. Dorothy Brown, Medaryville, Ind.: "I have finished my seventh quarter and had done four weeks on the 8th, when I forgot a rule and had to begin all over again. I have some more S. S. cards for Drusie, if if she wants them." (I have written to ask her if she needs more, and will report on this page, later). Mrs. F. A. Potts, Chattanooga (who sends a beautiful post card illustrating Bluffs of Tennessee river): "Forgot my Bible verse last Sunday, but heard the Bible read. It is a miss?" (Hearing the Bible read would not meet the requirements if you had taken advantage of that to purposely save yourself the trouble of reading for yourself; but because you forgot to read, hearing it read makes it all right, and I am glad you were at a place Sunday where you could hear it.) Harry A. Stevens, Akita, Japan: "My reports are all right, if you think as I do about them. One day I was reading the history of a dog—Beautiful Joe—and that day I forgot to read in the Life of Lincoln. Now I do not call that a miss, do you? If you don't then please put me on the honor roll. It is pretty hard to keep the rules in summer time." (While the history of a dog is, strictly speaking, hardly a suitable substitute for Lincoln, yet, since you really forgot, I decide that it is all right to count it one time, in Japan; however, I do not think even in Japan that this ought to occur too often). Mrs. W. A. Mason, Nevada, Mo.: This is the third time—and this attempt a charm—on my eleventh quarter. After keeping the rules ten weeks, sickness prevented my reading the Scriptures, so recommenced right away and kept the rules nine weeks and owing to sickness missed my Scripture reading again; so I did not become discouraged, but recommenced again, and here I am with my report. You speak of having a Christmas tree for our missionary Drusie. I think that a wise suggestion. if all respond as readily as they did to Charlie's ice cream social, the tree will be paid for. May the Lord bless our orphan and missionary and every one interested in their welfare. I enclose my mite for each." Fannie A. Kellogg, Fairview, Mo.: "Here is Aunt Fannie Kellogg and her Sunday-school class for a share in Charlie's ice cream social. We think it the finest social we ever helped and send good wishes for Charlie's success and happiness; and we will not forget Drusie's Christmas tree. God bless the Av. S. and their work. Enclosed, draft for $1.50." (In two weeks we will print our new honor list, of which we are proud. We also have a batch of Drusie's letters to present. You will also be informed how the photographer is getting along. I think we may say definitely that the ice cream supper is over. When last reported, the receipts amounted to $159.80. That sum has now been increased to $162.55. Felix is still shedding hair.)

Bentonville, Ark.

SUNDAY SICKNESS.

BY C. M. AKERS.

The most insiduous of all ailments to which mortal flesh is heir, is the common disease known as "Morbus Sabbaticus," or Sunday Sickness. It is peculiar to church members and is periodic in its attacks. It is found in all stages from a slight indisposition to a dull, dead stupor of lethargy. Medical men so little understand the real nature of this disease that they are never sent for or consulted.

Symptoms.—Generally the patient arises on Sunday morning feeling as well as usual. After a hearty meal of beefsteak and biscuit he takes a stroll about the premises, or the depot, news stand, hotel or postoffice, as the case may be. He returns home about 9 or 10 a. m. so fatigued that he must seek the sofa or easy rocking chair. He feels the disease coming gradually upon him. He calls for the morning paper which is brought in post haste. He proceeds to devour it. He steadily grows worse until he sees his wife and children disappear on their way to church. This is the first relief he gets. The first attack begins to wear off, he gets easy and usually drops into a deep, sweet sleep; only to be aroused an hour or two later by the rattle of the dinner dishes and the appetizing odor of the kitchen. He arises to find his fever gone, his pulse normal and his appetite good. But this only indicates the treachery of the disease. Such contrasts in so short a space of time is experienced in no other disease known to the medical profession. He goes to the dinner table with a crocodillian appetite. After being served sumptuously to several courses of meats, vegetables, pastries, etc., he arises from the table feeling edified and strengthened for a long drive in the afternoon. He returns from his drive much fatigued but able to eat a hearty meal of cold hash and salad. After the repast he again feels that old disease tightening its grip upon him. Try hard as he may to ward off the soporific feeling of this dread disease, it finally gets complete possession of him and at exactly 7 p. m. he is in the same condition he was at 11 a. m. Feeling that sleep is nature's great restorative, he takes his bed and is not able to be about again until 6 a. m. Monday, when he arises ready for business. He is now free from another attack of "Morbus Sabbaticus" until the following Sunday, when the disease returns with augmented force and the last state of that man is worse than the first.

Prescription.—"If any man will come after me, let him deny himself, and take up his cross and follow me."—The Great Physician.—*St. Louis Christian Advocate.*

❋ ❋

His Savior.

John Newton tells of a night that he lay in his hammock on the Adriatic Sea after a fearful spell of wild debauchery. In a lurid dream, he saw himself throwing away his soul into the sea like a precious jewel at the daring of Satan, and as it sank beneath the waves, a fiendish shout went up from the pit and a flash of angry fire seemed to light up the mountain tops along the shore. His spirit sank within him and he felt that he had lost his soul, buried forever a treasure more precious than all the world.

Then, in his dream, his Savior seemed to stand before him and asked him if he wished to have that jewel recovered once more. He threw himself at his feet and earnestly pleaded for him to save it if he could. Then the Redeemer leaped into the

Christian Publishing Company

2712 Pine St., St. Louis, Mo.

J. R. GARRISON, - - - - President
W. W. DOWLING, - - - Vice-President
GEO. L. SNIVELY, - - Sec. and Gen. Supt
R. P. CROW, - - Treas. and Bus. Manager

—A stereoscope will make an acceptable Christmas gift. For two new subscriptions and the $3.00 we will send you a good one and 50 scenic cards.

—It would be nearly as reasonable to expect to make Disciples of your children by sending them to denominational churches, as to expect it while using interdenominational Bible school literature.

—No other book published by brother J. H. Garrison called out such immediate and numerous and heartfelt congratulations as his "Christian Union." The tribute by Brother Robert Moffett is only one of a multitude like unto it.

—"John Doe, Sept. 06" on the yellow label of THE CHRISTIAN-EVANGELIST means that John's time for his favorite paper expired Sept. 1, 06, and that he will enjoy his paper a great deal more by sending us $1.50 and having the label changed to "John Doe, Sept. 07."

—We deeply regret that our new "Southern Evangelist" readers were delayed in getting last week's CHRISTIAN-EVANGELISTS. They have now been fully adopted into THE CHRISTIAN-EVANGELIST

family, their names enrolled, and they will be served at the first table.

—According to the usual computations more than 150,000 people will read each issue of this paper hereafter. No wonder our editors are so often known to be in Bible study and silent prayer. The responsibility of addressing such an audience is almost staggering.

—The Garrison Library.—A reconstructive theology: "Helps to Faith," "The Holy Spirit," "Christian Union." Most helpful of devotionals: "Alone with God," "Half Hour Studies at the Cross," "The Heavenward Way." These great books by a great Christian man for $5.00.

—Great interest is expressed in our forthcoming Pioneer Number. The time of this is not determined, but the keenest anticipation will no more be disappointed in this than in our imperial Campbell Number. Here Scott, Stone, Smith, Henderson, the Haydens and others will be made to live and preach again.

—"Gloria in Excelsis" is our best hymnal. It is arranged to meet the needs of the entire church under all varying conditions. The order of arrangement is logical and comprehensive in its scope. It should have a great sale and have an influence thereby to unify our worship in the best hymns of the church. The hymns on Holy Spirit and Christian Union are the best ever pro-

duced.—Prof. W. B. Taylor, Bethany College.

—We never will be a "disappearing brotherhood," but to continue as a rapidly growing brotherhood we are dependent on Bible schools for recruits. Interdenominational Bible school literature does not contribute to our zeal for this Restoration that has no creed but the Bible. To experiment with this class of Bible helps is like playing with fire; it is dangerous. Among the most scholarly and loyal disciples is W. W. Dowling, editor of our Sunday school literature, and the best of schoolmasters to bring children into churches of Christ.

—Our club lists of new subscribers indicate that many more CHRISTIAN-EVANGELISTS are being read in the old Kentucky home; along the banks of the Wabash; amidst the green hills of West Virginia; where the Pilgrim fathers lived and wrought; and where rolls the mighty Missouri. In addition to a multitude of new subscriptions coming in by ones and twos, the following new lists were filed last week:

Everett, Mass., A. T. June, pastor............ 3
Danville, Ky., H. C. Garrison, pastor........ 4
Enid, Okla., A. Jay Jones, pastor............ 5
Murry, Okla., I. A. Clemens, evangelist...... 5
Hobart, Okla., W. A. Merrill, pastor......... 5
McKeesport, Pa., Howard Cramblet, pastor.... 7
Sullivan, Ind., E. R. Brickert, pastor....... 8
Norwalk, O., I. L. Deming, pastor............ 9
Elyria, O., J. P. Sala, pastor..............11
La Porte, Ind., M. H. Garrard, pastor.......12
Loraine, O., C. Manley Rice, pastor.........14
Rensselaer, Ind., G. H. Clarke, pastor......16
Geneva, O., Frank M. Field, pastor..........20
Wheeling, W. Va., N. H. Fields, pastor......20
Harrodsburg, Ky., M. G. Buckner, pastor.....25
Frankfort, Ky., C. R. Hudson, pastor.......111

"Christian Union," by J. H. Garrison.

I have been familiar with the many publications of the Disciples for more than a third of a century. I have seen tracts on Christian Union, but the volume just from the press of the Christian Publishing Company on Christian Union, by J. H. Garrison, is the first bound volume I have ever seen, from a Disciple, on this subject. And the reader will find it in the author's best style, and full of interest to all those who have made this subject a study. It will amply repay a careful reading, and specially so since there is an unusual up-to-dateness in the subject, and in the masterly manner of its treatment. Our preachers ought to get the book, and study its forceful lessons.

Cleveland, O.   R. MOFFETT.

THE CHRISTIAN-EVANGELIST

A WEEKLY RELIGIOUS NEWSPAPER

| Volume XLIII. | No. 47. |

ST. LOUIS, NOVEMBER 22, 1906.

THE GAUGE OF LIFE.

THEY err who measure life by years,
  With false or thoughtless tongue;
Some hearts grow old before their time;
  Others are always young.
'Tis not the number of the lines,
  On life's fast filling page;
'Tis not the pulse's added throbs
  Which constitute their age.
Some souls are serfs among the free,
  While others nobly thrive;
They stand just where their fathers stood;
  Dead even while they live!
Others, all spirit, heart and sense;
  Theirs the mysterious power
To live in thrills of joy or woe,
  A twelvemonth in an hour!
Seize, then, the minutes as they pass;
  The woof of life is thought!
Warm up the colors; let them glow
  With fire and fancy fraught.
Live to some purpose; make thy life
  A gift of use to thee:
A joy, a good, a golden hope,
  A heavenly argosy!

The Christian-Evangelist.

J. H. GARRISON, Editor

PAUL MOORE, Assistant Editor

F. D. POWER,
B. B. TYLER, } Staff Correspondents.
W. DURBAN,

Subscription Price, $1.50 a Year.

For foreign countries add $1.04 for postage.

Remittances should be made by money order, draft, or registered letter; not by local cheque, unless 10 cents is added to cover cost of collection.
In Ordering Change of Post Office give both old and new address.
Matter for Publication should be addressed to THE CHRISTIAN-EVANGELIST. Subscriptions and remittances should be addressed to the Christian Publishing Company, 2712 Pine Street, St. Louis, Mo.
Unused Manuscripts will be returned only if accompanied by stamps.
News Items, evangelistic and otherwise, are solicited, and should be sent on a postal card, if possible.
Published by the Christian Publishing Company, 2712 Pine Street, St. Louis, Mo.

Entered at St. Louis P. O. as Second Class Matter

CONTENTS.

Centennial Propaganda......................1483
Current Events 1484
Editorial—
   Where Jesus Placed the Emphasis—XIII...1485
   Lengthening Cords and Strengthening Stakes.1485
   Notes and Comments.......................1486
   Editor's Easy Chair.......................1487
Contributed Articles—
   Our Beloved Missionary, G. L. Wharton....1488
   Where Jesus Placed the Emphasis. W. H.
   Bagby 1490
   As Seen from the Dome. F. D. Power....1491
   The Lordship of Jesus. T. E. Winter....1492
   D. O. Smart, Our President. G. W.
   Muckley 1493

Our Budget 1493
News From Many Fields......................1498
Evangelistic 1503
Midweek Prayer-meeting 1504
Sunday-school 1505
Christian Endeavor 1505
People's Forum 1506
The Home Department 1507

THE
CHRISTIAN-EVANGELIST

"IN FAITH, UNITY; IN OPINION AND METHODS, LIBERTY; IN ALL THINGS, CHARITY."

| Vol. XLIII. | November 22, 1906 | No. 47 |

1809 — CENTENNIAL PROPAGANDA — 1909
CHURCHES OF CHRIST
: : : GEO. L. SNIVELY : : :

Looking Toward Pittsburg.

—Did we excell all other religious bodies in personal devoutness as we do in our ability to unfold the scheme of redemption very soon indeed could our statisticians announce our having passed the 2,000,000 mark. Brother Ryan's earnest appeal for the reinstitution of the family altar is timely and will receive hearty amens from all who realize that homes fragrant with the incense of adoration are the real resources of Centennial victory and all greatness.

—Never was it more necessary to preach all the Word and for all to preach the Word than now. Never has there been a time when faithful preaching was more generously rewarded by a harvest of souls than now. Let us preachers more highly magnify our office and wherever and whenever opportunity can be found, with all the unction possible to one who believes he is throwing the life line to men engulfed in ruin, preach. To this Brother Warren's following article will help us:

Preaching and the Centennial.
BY CENTENNIAL SECRETARY.

Only one thing is needed in order to attain the principal Centennial goals, and that is, more preaching of the gospel. But there are several ways in which this may be secured. First—by putting more of the Gospel and less of other things into the sermons that are preached. Second—by having all preachers engaged in preaching rather than in the pursuit of some secular calling. Third—by having those who are preaching give full time to the work. Fourth—by increasing the number of preachers.

Just now there seems to be occasion to strongly emphasize the third item. Few preachers are putting their entire strength unto preaching. Most of them are cumbered with much serving that ought to be done by the deacons and women of the churches. So exacting are these pastoral cares that strength is scarcely left for the preparation and delivery of two sermons on Lord's day. Would Paul have counted himself "instant in season, out of season," if preaching only twice a week? The world can never be saved by a one-day-in-seven Gospel. Instead of relapsing into material service the preacher should evermore be lifting other members to spiritual ministry.

If it seems desirable to hold a protracted meeting in the local church the preacher feels that it is absolutely necessary to call in an evangelist from the outside to assist him. Two men are not too many to conduct a revival in an important field. But if the church at A requires the full time of two men for a month, in justice to the general cause it should at least surrender the time of its one preacher for some other month in the year. Otherwise, when the balance is struck at the end of the year it will be found that this particular church has required more than one preacher for its work and that some other field has been left desolate for a part of the year on its account.

There ought to rest on the conscience of every preacher the duty of holding one meeting a year away from his own church. He owes it to himself. It will broaden his vision, quicken his pulse and intensify his zeal. It will give him a larger share of soul-saving joy. He owes it to the needy fields that are unable to secure one of our regular evangelists. "My people are destroyed for lack of knowledge." The loss of souls rests upon the messengers who will not respond to the call. What if Peter had not obeyed the summons of Cornelius? He owes it to his own church. This will save it from the selfishness through which it is liable to degenerate into a mere club. By sparing the preacher it will develop self-reliance and become a stronger church. There should be members able to lead the prayer-meeting. They are robbed of their privilege by the preacher. The problem of the country church is partially due to the regular tendency of the stronger churches to absolutely monopolize the time and strength of all the better preachers. No man of God has a right to sell himself to one church. Christ has sealed his bonds for wider, nobler, manlier service.

W. R. WARREN.

Family Prayers and the Centennial.
BY WILLIAM D. RYAN.

It may be true that the family altar is not so common as it once was. It is fact indisputable that it is not so common as it should be. Prayer can not be regulated by mathematics, nor can worshipping families be easily tabulated by the statistician, but visit the homes of the people of any congregation and you will long remember for their rarity those in which the family regularly, each day, listened to the Word, and together, on bended knee, communed with the Father.

For this dearth of family devotions reasons are adduced in sufficient profusion. In many homes time is at a premium. The old simplicity is gone. Every adult member of the family has engagements that fill the day more than full. Yet a man usually finds time to eat his breakfast. People usually find time to do the things they regard as necessary or even as really desirable. There are homes in which the husband is not a Christian. Yet, the wife proves herself thoroughly competent to direct the affairs of the family except in religion, which she professes to regard as most important of all.

There are men, a vast host of them, to-day, who look back upon the hour of worship in the old childhood home as the most sacred and precious that memory recalls, and their lives are mightily influenced by those prayers of long ago. Is it not the right of our boys and girls to-day to have a heritage like that? Shall they, thirty years from now, look back upon homes Christian only nominally, from which rose no incense of prayer, in which was found no time to worship God?

Alexander Campbell's boyhood was spent in an atmosphere of devotion. Richardson furnishes this glimpse of the home at Rich Hill: "While carefully superintending the literary education of his son, Thomas Campbell was by no means negligent of his religious training. It was made an essential part of his ministerial duty, as it was no less the dictate of his parental affection, to bring up his children 'in the nurture and instruction of the Lord,' in order that his family might be a pattern to others. To this end it was prescribed by the synod that the minister should worship God in his family by singing, reading and prayer, morning and evening. Of these obligations Thomas Campbell was carefully observant, and in all his regulations and efforts for the improvement and welfare of his family he was earnestly and ably seconded by the estimable woman he had married. It was their rule that every member of the family should memorize, each day, some portion of the Bible to be recited at evening worship. Long passages were often thus recited, but if only a single verse was correctly repeated by the smaller children, it was received with encouraging approbation. * * * * When Mr. Campbell was called away, as he often was, to assist other ministers at a distance, his pious wife constantly labored to keep up the regular order of religious worship and instruction in the family. It was in such influences, in the domestic circle, that Alexander Campbell passed his early years, and it can not be doubted that they had a most important bearing on his future life. To this fact he himself bore testimony in his declining years."

It is perhaps conservative to say that in 250,000 American homes there are Disciples of Christ. If the spirit of devotion and daily worship of the home in which this great movement had its inception were, even in some degree, reproduced in all these households of to-day, can any one conceive of blessedness half so great as that which would result? Back of vast missionary undertakings and church-building enterprises, and evangelistic ideals is the supreme need of deeply spiritual and truly consecrated Christians. And these will come from homes pervaded by the incense of daily prayer as naturally as fragrance comes from flower.

It is too much to expect that in all our homes the family altar will be established before our Centennial. Let our task be very much more humble. Let us try to double the present number of families with daily worship, in that time. This can be done. Through the influence of pulpit and press and personal endeavor it is quite possible. No Centennial enterprise could be of greater significance and value.

Ashland, Ky.

get it. This is the first case on record, so far as we remember, where the offending husband seriously tried to get alimony as a part of a divorce settlement. Count Boni's great ambition has been to become president of France. The loss of public esteem which he has suffered in connection with this divorce episode will set him back several kilometers on his journey to the Palace of the Elysee.

❋

Not less important than the recent political campaign is the campaign now being waged for the control of the great life insurance companies. The election will occur early in December. Most of the policy-holders will vote by mail. In each of the great companies there are two tickets, one representing the present directorate and the other the international policy-holders' committee. The "administration ticket" claims support on the ground that it represents experience and expert knowledge of the life insurance business and that the persons who were responsible for the bad management formerly prevailing in the companies have already been removed from them. The policy-holders' committee ticket is the result of the crusade started by Thomas W. Lawson. The thousands of proxies which Mr. Lawson obtained from policy-holders in the New York Life and the Mutual Life were invalidated by an act of the New York legislature postponing the elections and declaring void all proxies already given. At that time we advised against giving proxies to Mr. Lawson. It did not, and does not, seem wise to put into the hands of one man the control of interests so important and wide-spread. After the annulling of his proxies, Mr. Lawson organized a policy-holders' committee composed of eminent and trustworthy men. This committee has nominated a ticket of directors for each of the companies and has conducted a campaign of education to convince the policy-holders of the necessity of a complete change in the personnel of the directorates. They claim that men who were directors in the old days of mismanagement and who could not or dared not or, for any reason, did not oppose those methods, then, are poor material for directors now; and that the election of the administration tickets means the preparation of Wall street control. On this issue we are not at present disposed to take sides further than to say that the reasons which moved us to advise against giving proxies to Mr. Lawson obviously have no application to the question of voting for a group of directors nominated by a committee which was nominated by Lawson. The policy-holders' committee derives its standing not from the fact that Lawson nominated it but from the known integrity and ability of its members. Whatever one may think of Mr. Lawson—whether he is a hero or a fakir, a champion or a charlatan—and whether his motives be philanthropy, revenge, patriotism or greed, the fact is that he has gotten together a most estimable body of committeemen and they, in turn, have nominated an excellent body of directors. The policy-holder will choose his ticket according as he believes that the danger of experience with the new directorate would be greater or less than the danger of graft with the old.

The Insurance Campaign.

Cuba is restless again. The majority, believing that President Palma was re-elected by fraud, could not wait for the next election to right the wrong, but started a revolution. The result was that Palma resigned and the United States has to set up a provisional and temporary government to tide over until quiet should be restored sufficiently for another election to be held. One might have supposed that that would have satisfied even the impatient. But not so, Palma is gone, but many of his appointees remain in office. The insurgents are unhappy because these can not be legally removed before the election next June. They want Governor Magoon to take their side and put out Palma's appointees. Governor Magoon to do so and, since he is a man of much force and stability and of some experience with Latin-Americans, the matter will probably end right where it began. Richard Harding Davis, who professes that he was once an ardent admirer of the Cubans, has visited Cuba again since the recent American occupation and says that his admiration is turned to disgust by the ingratitude of the Cubans and their lack of self-control and capacity for self-government. But it is possible that even a brilliant writer of short stories, while seeing the dramatic, picturesque and humorous elements of the situation, may fail to make sufficient allowance for the frailties of a people in their political infancy. "Single men in barracks don't grow into plaster saints," and we still claim the liberty of believing that Cuba's case is not quite hopeless although we are driven to admit that the average Cuban patriot is no fit candidate for canonization.

Restless Cuba.

❋

Several cabinet changes have recently been made or will soon be made. One of the most important is the retirement of Secretary Hitchcock from the department of the interior. The secretary of the interior has a large position and Mr. Hitchcock in filling it has shown himself to be a large man. In no other department is eternal vigilance more necessary to prevent the robbing of the government. The public domain has always presented itself to the unscrupulous as an enticing object for speculation. There is land to be stolen by more or less subtle devices, which sometimes need and command the services of congressmen for their successful application, and there is timber to be stolen. Against all manner of crooks, whether in congress or out, who attempted to prey upon the public domain, Secretary Hitchcock has waged constant and successful war. His retirement will be hailed with joy by all such, on the chance that his successor, Garfield, will be less energetic and efficient. In that expectation, it is just possible that they may be disappointed.

Secretary Hitchcock.

❋

In Kentucky they are fighting the trusts with dynamite. Three trust-owned snuff warehouses were recently blown up by "night riders." It is reported that bloodhounds were put on the trail of the culprits. We should think that a bloodhound would labor under some disadvantages in attempting to follow a cold scent through the wreckage of a snuff warehouse.

Where Jesus Placed the Emphasis.—XIII.

The Coming and Work of the Holy Spirit.

It is in harmony with the order of development of the doctrine of Jesus, that we come now to the teaching concerning the Holy Spirit. It was not until the closing part of his ministry, and when he had practically retired from the world, and was teaching his disciples the great principles of his kingdom, that he disclosed to them the meaning and mission of the Holy Spirit. The occasion of his teaching was most natural. The hearts of his disciples were very sad at the thought of his going away from the world, and they felt themselves wholly unequal to the task of carrying forward his work in the world without his presence and aid. His promise, hitherto made, that he would be with them always even unto the end of the world, was not, of course, clearly grasped. It is easy to imagine, under these conditions, with what consternation they must have received his announcement of his approaching death and departure from the world. It was to meet a situation like that, that he gave to his disciples his great doctrine concerning the Holy Spirit, for the record of which we are chiefly indebted to the Fourth Gospel.

After assuring his disciples that the Father was in him and he in the Father, and that he was going now unto his Father, and they were to ask of the Father what they needed in his name, he adds to them this precious promise: "If ye love me, ye will keep my commandments. And I will pray the Father, and he shall give you another Comforter, that he may be with you forever, even the Spirit of truth; whom the world can not receive; for it beholdeth him not, neither knoweth him: ye know him; for he abideth with you, and shall be in you. I will not leave you desolate: I come unto you." (John 14:15-18)..

Was ever promise better adapted to comfort the hearts to which it was made? "Another Comforter?" That was exactly what they needed. What a comfort Jesus had been to them in solving all their problems and in leading them into an ever deepening and widening knowledge of the truth! Now that he was to leave them what they needed above everything else was "another Comforter," and one, too, who would be with them "forever," and who was none other than the "Spirit of truth," who would still be their Monitor and Teacher. The promise, "I will not leave you desolate: I come unto you," makes it clear that Jesus' promise to be with his disciples alway even unto the end of the world, was to find its fulfillment in the coming of the Holy Spirit whose mission would be to reveal Christ more fully to the disciples, especially as a divine force working within them.

Concerning the mission of this Com-forter Jesus further said, "But the Comforter, even the Holy Spirit, whom the Father will send in my name, he shall teach you all things, and bring to your remembrance all that I said unto you." (John 14:26). Again, "But when the Comforter is come, whom I will send unto you from the Father, even the Spirit of truth, which proceedeth from the Father, he shall bear witness of me." (John 15:26). Once more: "Nevertheless I tell you the truth: It is expedient for you that I go away; for if I go not away, the Comforter will not come unto you; but if I go, I will send him unto you. And he, when he is come, will convict the world in respect of sin, and of righteousness, and of judgment. * * * I have yet many things to say unto you but ye can not bear them now. Howbeit when he, the Spirit of truth, is come, he shall guide you into all the truth: for he shall not speak from himself; but what things soever he shall hear, these shall he speak: and he shall declare unto you the things that are to come. He shall glorify me, for he shall take of mine and shall declare it unto you (John 16:7, 8,12-14.)

It would be impossible to exaggerate the value of this teaching. The church has not yet risen to a full appreciation of its vast significance and value. It is clear from this that the coming of the Holy Spirit was as essential to the completion of the work of human redemption as was the coming of Christ to the inauguration of that work. God had a great work to do for men from without, which he did in the personal ministry of Christ and in his sacrificial death and resurrection from the dead. But he has a great work to do in men in bringing these great fundamental truths and facts to bear in the transforming of human lives to the likeness of God, and that is the work of the Holy Spirit.

In harmony with this promise of Jesus the Holy Spirit came on the Pentecost following Christ's resurrection, and began his mighty work which has continued even to the present day. To this fact we are indebted for the church and for all that it has accomplished in the world. Often the Holy Spirit has been grieved, his methods antagonized, his plans perverted, by human perverseness and ignorance. But he has never deserted the church. He has always found a dwelling-place in the humble, contrite hearts of those who were willing to know the truth and to obey the truth. He is the Spirit of unity, and how our divisions must have grieved him! And yet he has never wholly forsaken us, and is to-day seeking to breathe the spirit of unity and love into the hearts of Christ's disciples.

The question has often been raised as to the limitation of this promise of Christ concerning the Holy Spirit to his apostles. No doubt the apostles had some tasks to perform which do not need to be duplicated and for these tasks they received such measure of the Holy Spirit as would enable them to perform them. There is no reason to doubt that for all the tasks which the church as a whole, or which each individual member, may be called upon to perform, sufficient measure of the Holy Spirit will be given to-day just as in the apostolic age. Moreover we are fully justified by the teaching of Christ, supplemented by that of his apostles, in seeking the largest possible measure of the Holy Spirit by a loyal, trusting, obedient faith, by purity of heart and life, by prayer and communion with God, and by striving to do the will of God faithfully in all things. Just in proportion as we are "filled with the Spirit" will we come to the deepest knowledge of Christ, to the deepest experiences of Christian life, and exhibit the noblest type of Christian character. This is why our heavenly Father will, as Jesus taught, "give the Holy Spirit to them that ask him."

Nothing, we believe, is more needed among us to-day than greater emphasis upon the work of the Holy Spirit, as Comforter, as Teacher, giving to us a deeper knowledge of Christ, and as a life-giving agency, enabling us to bring forth the fruit of the Spirit in our lives, and to be channels of his convicting power in bringing others to the salvation which is in Christ.

❈ ❈

Lengthening Cords and Strengthening Stakes.

The general revival of interest in evangelistic work among all evangelical religious bodies is a matter for devout thanksgiving. This increased interest in the work of recruiting the army of the Lord is probably due as much to the success of the Disciples of Christ and their zeal in that work as to any other cause. We have always been an evangelistic people, and we, too, of late are experiencing a deepening interest in the work of evangelization which is manifesting itself in many hopeful ways.

There are those who scoff at the idea of a "new evangelism." It is a matter of small moment what name we call it, but there are some changes for the better for which we can not be too thankful. Not to speak now of the new evangelism, born with our reformatory movement, in contrast with the now outgrown forms of evangelism which prevailed at the time our movement began, we prefer to notice here some recent changes in our own evangelism which promise better and more enduring results. First of all, there is that wider view of evangelism which emphasizes the duty of each Christian to win others to the love and service of Christ. The new emphasis that is being laid upon our individual responsibility in this matter, and the training and development of a class of personal workers in all our churches, is a most helpful feature of present-day evangelistic work. No longer does an intelligent pastor or successful evangelist rely upon his own efforts to hold a successful meeting. He expects the active co-operation of all the members of the church, not merely in the way of attendance or contribution, but in direct personal work with their friends and others, with a view of bringing them to Christ. "Let him that heareth say come," is the phase of evangelism that is just now having great prominence.

In the next place, the work of evangelization is being better organized and systematized than ever before. In addition to an increasing corps of successful evangelists, many pastors are studying the methods of evangelism, and the singing evangelist, a development of modern times, is proving a most useful adjunct in this field of labor.

Again, it is no reflection on the past to say that a broader and sweeter spirit is entering into our evangelism. The evangelist that is in demand to-day preaches a full-orbed gospel, and seeks to do it in the spirit of brotherly love. He no longer feels it his duty to denounce those who hold different religious views, but is content to teach the whole gospel "speaking the truth in love" and beseeching men to be reconciled to God.

Finally, there is a change of emphasis, necessitated by the change of conditions and by a deeper and broader knowledge of the truth as it is in Christ. The hobbyist to-day, whether the hobby be baptism in water or "Holy Ghost baptism," is not in favor. Men want a fuller and richer gospel, that lays due emphasis upon the fundamental things of our common Christianity.

All this is well, but our evangelistic zeal and ardor must be supplemented by better methods of caring for and developing the converts, if we are to reap permanent benefits from our evangelism. The realization of this truth by many of our best evangelists, and by our pastors and church officials, is another most helpful feature of the new evangelism. Here has been our greatest weakness. We have been more successful in recruiting soldiers for Jesus Christ than in training and developing them for actual service. Now plans are being formulated for organizing, looking after and training, those who are brought into the church, that they may become active workers in saving others. This is the work that just now needs special emphasis. In vain do we add large numbers to our churches unless we retain them, and develop them, so that they shall be helps rather than hindrances. We do well in lengthening our cords, but we must also, in the same degree, strengthen our stakes, if we are to hold the ground gained and so make permanent progress.

The Anti-Saloon League of America has been holding its national convention and conference in St. Louis. To-day, Thursday, in the forenoon, there will be an address on "The Pastor's Relation to the League," and the evening session will be turned over to the Young People's Societies of St. Louis, to be addressed by John G. Woolley. The work of the league is a very important

one and is now thoroughly organized in forty-four states and territories, and it is rapidly becoming a strong factor in state and national politics. It works through all parties and all sects, its one main purport being to destroy the evil influence of the liquor interests.

✿ ✿

Notes and Comments.

The trustees of the Andover Theological Seminary are discussing the advisability of relocating that institution, which, having a million dollars of endowment, had only eleven students at the opening of the present year, with an entering class of only three. President Edward J. James, of the University of Illinois, has sent an open letter to the trustees of the seminary, urging them to relocate the institution contiguous to Urbana-Champaign, Ill., where its students may have the benefit of the courses offered by the State University, and where, in the great Mississippi valley, it would have a much wider field of usefulness than in its present isolated location. In this open letter President James says: "I can not help feeling that the church, using that term in a large sense, is losing one of the greatest opportunities in the present day in not planting itself in the form of an educational institution firmly and positively in the closest proximity to these great aggregations of students, with the idea of winning over to its service at least its fair proportion of this young and promising material." Concluding his letter the president says to the trustees: "You may set an example here and now, in this field of education, which other boards may follow and thus lead to that readjustment of our educational system to the conditions of modern life which is demanded alike by the interests of church and state." It is not likely, however, that local interests, and New England pride in the institution, will permit its removal to the Mississippi valley. Removal somewhere, however, would seem to be a necessity unless this great foundation shall be allowed to remain practically useless.

In another place we print an article by William Shaw, Treasurer of the United Society of Christian Endeavor, written at our request, concerning the Quarter-Century Christian Endeavor Memorial, to which we invite the attention of our readers. The movement to memorialize the twenty-fifth anniversary of Christian Endeavor by the establishment of an International Headquarters Build-

Day by Day.

Charge not thyself with the weight of a year,
Child of the Master faithful and dear.
Choose not the cross for the coming week,
For that is more than he bids thee seek.

Bend not thine arms for to-morrow's load—
Thou may'st leave that to thy gracious God.
Daily only be saith to thee,
"Take up thy cross, and follow me."

Editor's Easy Chair.

There is something very suggestive in the first snow of the season. It is nearly always unexpected. It breaks in on Indian summer with a suddenness which often finds us unprepared for it. We go to bed at night with the stars shimmering through fleecy clouds, and wake in the morning to find the earth carpeted in white, and all the trees bejeweled with the snowy crystals, presenting a scene of fairy-land. We are startled into the realization that winter is upon us. Other fair and bright days will come, but the earth has swung into that place in its orbit which makes possible snow, sleet and cold, any day. It is like the first gray hair which we discover on our heads, which is a premonition and prophecy of the time when they will all be gray, and old age shall have crowned us with its glory. There is something pathetic in the care with which that first gray hair is extracted, as if that would stop the flight of the years or stay the progress of age! Others come to take its place and soon they become so numerous that we cease all efforts to remove them, and seek to be reconciled to our lot. But let the first snow admonish us to complete our preparations for the winter, and the first gray hair remind us of the brief number of our days and lead on to a heart of wisdom.

❧

What is the "heart of wisdom" which the Psalmist hoped he might be led to secure through the realization of the brevity of life? Is it not a heart that views time in its relation to eternity? A heart that regards human conduct in its relation to God and the life beyond? A heart that recognizes that life on earth is fraught with eternal consequences, and that in the field of destiny we reap as we sow? Surely nothing can be more unwise or reckless than to think and plan and act to-day, without any reference to to-morrow, or to live our present life regardless of its effect upon the great hereafter. This is to ignore the universal law of cause and effect, which is the essence of folly. Whoso has a "heart of wisdom" will ponder well his steps, will look deep and with honest search into the motives which prompt his action, and bring his daily life to the supreme test of God's approval. If this, indeed, be the result of a "heart of wisdom," how many there are, alas, who have hearts of folly, living their lives here heedless of any divine standard of approval or of any eternal consequences! Oh, that all our Easy Chair readers may seek for a heart of wisdom, that their lives here on earth may be lived in the light which shines down upon them from the eternal world!

❧

These Easy Chair musings are written amid the deepening interest and pressure of our simultaneous evangelistic services, and naturally our thoughts center about the great problem of turning men to God. It is one of the strange things in a world full of mysteries, that any thoughtful human being can be content to live without God. As a matter of fact, no one does so live, for God is the sustaining power of every life, and in him we live, and move, and have our being. But the strange thing is that men will live without any recognition of the Being who sustains them and gives them all they have, and who has infinite blessings to bestow upon those who will open their hearts to him that he may bestow them. It is the glamour of this world, with its appeal to our lower natures, that holds men in its thralldom and blinds them to the realities of the spiritual world. To break the power of this strange spell and bring men to the recognition of God, of duty, and of destiny, is the task of the church through all its manifold agencies. But who is equal to this task? We cannot too often remind ourselves of the truth that Paul may plant, Apollos water, but that it is God that giveth the increase. The recognition of this fact should bring us all to our knees, and clothe us with the deepest humility. There can be no really successful evangelistic campaign that does not abound in prayer—real, vital prayer, that brings the workers into union with God, so that his divine power, acting through them, shall reach the unsaved and bring them to repentance and to life.

❧

We speak of failures and successes in these special religious services held with a view of winning men to Christ. It is well, however, for us to have a clear understanding of what is a successful meeting, and what is a failure in evangelistic effort. That meeting, we should say, is a failure in which unworthy motives prompt either the church or its evangelists, or in which wrong motives

Yesterday.

BY H. T. BAIRD.

O, God, I pray, that for this day
    I will not stray from Thee away;
And on the morrow have cause for sorrow,
    For any deed of yesterday.

O, Spirit sweet, guide Thou my feet,
    Keep Thou my heart from sin apart;
That on the morrow I'll have no sorrow
    For any deed of yesterday.

O, Christ, my king, speed the inbring
    Of Thy glad day of righteous sway;
When each bright morrow is free from sorrow
    For any deed of yesterday.

Father, Spirit, Son—wondrous Three in One—
    All earth acclaim Thy glorious name;
For pledge of morrow bereft of sorrow
    For any deed of yesterday.

To God, my stay—through Christ—the way,
    In faith I'll pray each blessed day;
"Till comes that morrow "surcease of sorrow,"
    For deeds of all the yesterday.

are urged upon men, as reasons for their uniting with the church. That meeting is a failure which does not make it clear to all who attend upon its services that baptism and church membership are unavailing and worse than useless unless preceded by a conviction of sin, by a genuine repentance, and by the sincere purpose to live the Christian life. No matter how many additions may be reported in a meeting of this kind, it is none the less a failure. That is a successful meeting which brings the message of God's love in Christ for a sinning world to the hearts of men; that makes known the will of God, as revealed in Christ, to sinful men; that makes plain the way of salvation through Christ to those who earnestly desire to be Christians. That is a successful meeting which, in addition to the foregoing, draws together, by the earnestness, energy, enterprise, and spiritual magnetism of the church and its evangelist, a large number of people to hear the divine message, from day to day. God will give the increase to such faithful presentation of the gospel. The immediate results may be large or apparently small, but God's word will not return unto him void. Where the "visible results" are small, we must believe that a necessary work of preparation has been accomplished, and that results must inevitably follow. There is no failure where Christ's gospel is preached in Christ's spirit.

❧

These lines are written on the eve of starting south where we hope to attend two of our southern state conventions; namely, that of Alabama at Mobile, and of Georgia at Valdosta. It is with regret that we leave for a week this evangelistic campaign in our own city, which is proving to be so fruitful a source of blessing to all our churches. And yet we of the stronger states owe something to our brethren in the south where our cause is weaker, and it is in the hope of contributing something, if it be but little, to the encouragement of our loyal and heroic brethren in the south, that we have agreed to make this visit. Our cause is one, north, south, east, west, and we are one people in spite of any little differences of opinion that may exist which do not at all impair our common faith nor sever the bonds of love. The exaltation of opinionism into bars to fellowship and co-operation has been the one evil that has beset our cause from the beginning, and it is the one evil against which we must be upon our guard continually. More and more let us emphasize the great cardinal principles of our movement which have made us one, and which have given us our success in the past, and discountenance every tendency to produce alienation and disaffection by magnifying differences of method or of opinion which do not affect Christian faith or character. So shall we transmit to those coming after us the priceless heritage we have received from those who have gone before us.

Our Beloved Missionary, G. L. Wharton*

"For he was a good man, and full of the Holy Spirit and of faith: and much people was added unto the Lord." Acts 11:23.

Another name must now be added to the long list of missionary heroes. Another hero has fallen at his post of duty joyfully bearing testimony for Jesus Christ. The Church of Christ at home has been exalted, and the cause of Christ in India has been advanced by the death, no less than by the life, of our beloved missionary, Bro. G. L. Wharton. He was one of the pioneer missionaries of our brotherhood. For four years he has been the "living-link" missionary of this congregation. The loftiness of his faith, the purity of his character, the closeness of his walk with Christ have blessed our churches as a whole and this congregation in particular. He has fought the good fight of faith; he has laid hold on eternal life.

I cannot help associating his name with that of that grand apostolic missionary, Barnabas, "the son of consolation." Many noble names adorn the pages of the Book of Acts, but none nobler than that of Barnabas. Could anything grander be said of a man than that "he was a good man, and full of the Holy Spirit and of faith: and much people was added unto the Lord"? Yet all this may be said of our beloved Brother Wharton whose earthly life has so recently closed.

Brother Wharton was a man of faith. Only a man of faith could labor for the redemption of India. Only a man of faith could leave wife and children to give his life to the uplift of that sad and oppressed people. He knew that his life and work, humanly speaking, could only be a small contribution to the ultimate redemption of India. He knew that weary years must pass, that his body must mingle with the dust, before India would be won to Christ. As he stood in the presence of the appalling need of India, his soul was wrung and his heart pierced by the indifference of the church at home. Yet he never complained, upbraided, or grew discouraged. Why? Because he was a man of faith. Faith always begets optimism. He saw with certain vision the rising tide of missionary enthusiasm in the home church, and he patiently waited; he looked beneath the repulsive exterior of the Hindu and saw the divine possibilities of his heart; his eyes pierced the thick clouds of heathenism that hung above the land, and he beheld God surely working out the redemption of that sad country; he looked into the future, and he beheld the temples crumbling and falling, he saw the land to which he had given his life dotted with churches and schools and inhabited by a happy, Christian people. With such a faith as that he waited patiently and labored hopefully. His was a strong faith that gripped firmly the throne of grace, that would not let go

*Sermon preached by Cecil J. Armstrong, pastor First Christian Church, Winchester, Ky., on Sunday morning, November 11, 1906. News of the death of Brother Wharton had been received a few days previous.

until he was blessed, and that led him to carry that blessing as a trust to the benighted sons of dark India.

There can be only one result to such a life, viz: "and much people was added unto the Lord." In this country and in India many under his personal ministry have turned to Christ for salvation, but the full harvest has not yet been gathered. The Word that he so faithfully preached shall not return unto God void, the life that he so patiently lived shall bear its fruitage throughout time, the sacrifices of his life shall touch the heart of the church at home, and she shall answer with her noblest sons and daughters, with ever increasing liberality, that the work to dear to his heart, the work for which he gave his life, may be carried on, that the people whom he loved may be "added unto the Lord!" He had the Christ-passion for souls. It was his greatest joy to see men and women turning unto Christ. God granted him many souls, but in the years to come; through the influence of his gentle spirit and pure life, through the instrumentality of the young men he has trained for the native ministry, through the generation and growth of the seed he has sown, God will grant him many more souls. His is truly a crown of rejoicing, for God has honored him, and the world is better for his life and labors.

Now the man who is "full of the Holy Spirit and of faith" will be willing to make any sacrifice for the sake of Christ and his Gospel. Sacrifice will become the law of his being. He looks upon the world with the vision of Christ, feels for the world with the heart of Christ, and enters into the work of human redemption with the zeal of Christ. Everything is held subservient to Christ. For the sake of the kingdom of God (if Christ cares) he will leave father and mother, wife and children, houses and lands. The one passion of his heart will be to be good in the name of Jesus.

Such a man was G. L. Wharton. At first we stood appalled when we learned that it was his purpose to go to India without his wife and family. But when we came to know the man intimately we discovered that he was one of those rare souls to whom sacrifice is a holy passion. To our protestations that such a sacrifice was not demanded of a man of his age and physical weakness, he had but one reply: "English army officers go to India, and for years are separated from their families for the sake of their King. Can I do less for my King?" To our earnest entreaties that he spend the rest of his life

in this country stirring up missionary interest among our home churches, he had, but one reply: "I long to join my comrades at the front." To our efforts to convince him that he should settle at Hiram, and there with wife and children enjoy well-earned years of peaceful labor, he had but one reply: "India needs me more than Ohio does!" He made this sacrifice at great cost to himself. Never did a man love wife and children more than Brother Wharton loved his. Step into his room quietly and nearly always you would find him upon his knees in prayer. What it cost him you and I will never know. It did seem that he had already given to India a mighty service. He had already spent over twenty years there as a missionary. He and his noble wife had passed through two of those awful famines. At the close of the second famine they were both so weak from overwork that they had to be carried on stretchers onto the ship. In the early "nineties" he had spent two years there without his wife and children. Yet he was not satisfied. He must do more for Christ yet. And so at fifty-six years of age he made the supreme earthly sacrifice: he left wife, children and native land for India.

Ah, friends, he was not the only one who made the sacrifice in this matter. Last February a year ago I spent two days and a night in that home at Hiram, Ohio. Would that I could tell you of the beautiful faith, the sweet resignation, the sublime courage of his noble wife. That woman's heart is the cruse of precious ointment over the feet of Jesus: the fragrance of her devotion must fill the "whole house" above. She had gladly yielded up the treasure of her own heart; she could make no greater sacrifice. She loved him as only a true woman can love a true man. Can you wonder if sometimes, when we talked of him, her eyes would fill with tears and she would leave the room? In a minute she would return with complete self-control to tell you how glad she and the children were to give him to such a noble work. O husband and father, what would it cost you to leave wife and children, and go alone to India as a missionary? O wife and mother, what would it cost you to have your husband, the father of your children, leave you for years that he might be a missionary? All that love can suffer when separated from the one loved Brother and Sister Wharton suffered in their separation. Yet they suffered gladly for Christ's sake.

In 1891 or 1892 they were in this country on furlough. They were living at Lexington, Ky. When the time of furlough was out the question of returning to India was considered. Mrs. Wharton could not then go. If he went he must go alone. While this battle was being fought out in his soul, one night as they talked it over, as he looked into the eyes of her whom he loved better than life and into the eyes of Grace and Lawrence whom he loved with the love of true fatherhood, and as he thought of the joy that would soon come to him with the child yet unborn, his eyes filled with tears, he turned to his wife and said: "I can not go." Little Grace's voice was heard as she said: "Papa, can not you do it for Jesus' sake?" Clasping Grace in his arms he said: "Yes, my child, for Jesus' sake I can and will go." Ah, there's the secret. "For Jesus' sake." Not for gain or pleasure, but for "Jesus' sake." Does it seem to you that they have made sacrifices you could not, or would not, make? The explanation is not that they love their loved ones less than you love yours, but that they are willing to do more "for Jesus' sake" than you are willing to do. With them nothing, even life itself, was too good to yield up for Jesus' sake. They had made the complete surrender, "had left all" to follow him. God help you and me to thus completely surrender ourselves to him.

But, now, what of the work to which he gave his strength, and for which he gave his life? I would not for a moment underestimate the value of the labors of Bro. Wharton for the redemption of India, but the whole history of the church proves that God takes care of his own cause. The work in India will go on. In life Brother Wharton did all he could for the elevation of that people; in death he has sealed his testimony with the sacrifices of his life. The conversion of India must be hastened by the life, labors, and the death of our beloved missionary. God will raise up others to take his place. Brother Wharton's example will inspire unnumbered hearts with the holy purpose that throbbed in his own noble soul. No, no, fear not for the future of missionary work in India. India shall be redeemed; her sadness turned to gladness, her darkness turned to light. The day will surely come when the temples shall crumble, the idols fall, the heathen worship cease and when all from the least unto the greatest, shall know the Lord. Only God knows how much to this grand consummation our beloved missionary, who has "burned out for Christ," contributed. So fear not for the missionary cause in India. God will not allow the efforts of his martyr-servants to come to naught. Upon the soil sanctified by their labors and enriched by their blood, the cause of Christ shall go forth conquering and to conquer. India has had many of God's noblemen upon her soil. The roll is too long to call. But she has never had a nobler man, a more faithful Christian, nor a more zealous missionary than him whose death we mourn to-day.

But what shall the attitude of THIS CHURCH—the church of which he was the "Living-Link Missionary"—towards the work so dear to his heart? This is a time of test. It will prove whether our missionary zeal has been devotion to a man or to God. We have committed no sin in loving Brother Wharton as we do (who could help loving such a Godlike man?), but we shall commit sin if we cease our missionary work because he has departed this life. Let us ever hold him in grateful remembrance. Never let that portrait of him be removed from the wall of this church. If spirits departed can hover around earthly scenes this is one spot where the spirit of our brother will frequently be. When the foreign society assigns us another missionary (it matters not whether his field be in India or elsewhere), it does not mean that we are to forget our beloved Brother Wharton. What would he have us do if he could speak to us to-day? There is but one answer to that question, viz: become more missionary than ever. I know not whether his body will finally rest in far-off India or in the soil of his native state. But wherever it does rest I hope that this congregation will erect above it a monument worthy of such a man. Brethren, place above his head a plain and simple shaft to express your debt of gratitude to him. But there is another monument that will be dearer to his heart than will be a marble or granite shaft above his grave. His quiet, humble soul yearns not for a costly headstone, but his soul was in travail for the salvation of the world. He labored for India, but he prayed for the whole world. The best monument that we can erect is that of increased liberality and increased prayerfulness and increased sacrifice for the conversion of the world. So far as we are concerned, Brother Wharton has lived in vain if in the days to come we do not do greater things for Christ than we have ever done in the past. Forget him not; think of him often; pray for his dear ones constantly; but the best evidence of your love for him and your devotion to his Christ will be increased missionary activity and liberality in the days to come.

It is said that during the battle of Waterloo one of Napoleon's Old Guard was brought to the hospital sorely wounded in the breast. It was before the days of the anaesthetic. As the doctor probed for the bullet the old soldier stoically endured untold suffering. At last he hissed between his teeth: "Probe deeper, Doctor, probe deeper, and upon my heart you will find the image of the Emperor." As our beloved missionary, far from native land and loved ones, lay in that hospital at Calcutta, if we could probe to the very center of his great soul we would thereon have found the image of Christ; nay, therein we would have found Christ. If we could probe to the heart of that noble wife, who to-day is most of all bereaved, we should thereon and therein find the image of Christ. I know not if Brother Wharton left a farewell message for this church. I have received no direct communication from his noble wife. But if a message from either or both were to come to us to-day it would be: "Do more than ever for the conversion of the world." Christ was in his heart; Christ is in her heart. If Christ be in our hearts we shall do his will, and in fulfilling the will of our Christ we shall do the will of our beloved missionary and his no less loved wife.

For him to live was Christ; therefore for him to die was gain. The mystery we can not solve, nor should we try. Let us thank God that we have for four years been in such intimate contact with such a noble life. "He was a good man, full of the Holy Spirit, and of faith." Let us follow him, even as he followed Christ. He left all for Jesus' sake. Let us devote our all to Christ. Let us not mourn for him as for one who went empty-handed into the presence of his Maker. Mourn not for him whose life was so pure, whose labor was so faithful, whose death was so triumphal. Let us rather rejoice that a saintly life has received its reward in heaven. Let us rather pray that a double portion of his noble spirit may rest upon each one of us. And, O friends, forget not to pray constantly for his wife and children. In the years to come—weary years to her—forget not to pray for them. I am going to ask you to sing that familiar, yet beautiful hymn, "Asleep in Jesus." Please notice how appropriate to this occasion is the last stanza:

"Asleep in Jesus! far from thee
Thy kindred and their graves may be,
But thine is still a blessed sleep,
From which none ever wakes to weep."

✿ ✿

BEAUTIFUL COMPLEXION
Lady of Fifty Looks Like Sixteen.

A Nashville lady found a way to beautify her complexion without the use of drugs or face creams.

"Before I began the use of Grape-Nuts," she writes, "I was convinced I could not live long. I was sick all the time; heart trouble, kidneys seriously affected, eyesight bad, sense of smell was gone and hearing very poor.

"My family thought I had dropsy and could not get well, and I ate Grape-Nuts because I slept better afterwards—did not dream I could be entirely cured, had quit all treatment and given up hope.

"After spending a large sum of money, and being under the best physicians for three years without relief, I commenced eating Grape-Nuts food three times a day and now I am sound as a dollar, am in perfect health, fifty years old and my complexion is better than some girls at sixteen.

"I never have headache, nerves are strong, sight so much improved I need no glasses, heart and kidneys in perfect condition.

"Your Grape-Nuts alone cured me and I cannot find words to express my thanks to the Postum Co. I have told hundreds of people what cured me. It was simple food that I could digest."

"There's a reason." Name given by Postum Co., Battle Creek, Mich.

It sometimes amazes persons what damage has been done by improper eating, not knowing any better way. A change to Grape-Nuts soon tells the story. Read the famous book, "The Road to Wellville," in pkgs.

Where Jesus Placed the Emphasis* By W. H. Bagby

(Concluded from Last Week.)

II. Jesus Placed the Emphasis on the Mission of the Church and Not on Its Method of Accomplishing It.

A number of years ago when that most intrepid explorer and missionary, David Livingstone, had been for many months lost to the world in the depths of Darkest Africa, the elder Bennett, then editor of the "New York Herald," cabled Henry M. Stanley at Cairo, Egypt, this brief message: "Find Livingstone!" The man who was capable of making that marvelous march of 999 days through the trackless jungles of the Dark Continent, on that memorable and most important mission could be trusted to devise the ways and means of its successful accomplishment. The splendid results that attended his effort more than justified the confidence of Mr. Bennett in the man he had chosen for the mission. Because he had been left absolutely free to choose his own methods in carrying out his great undertaking, Stanley emerged from the African wilderness a larger man, and bearing the map of a larger world.

In the beginning, God faced potentially perfect but wholly undeveloped man toward a potentially perfect but wholly undeveloped world and said: "Subdue it!". In the performance of this stupendous task man was left free to devise his own methods. It was manifestly the design of the Creator that through the effort to subdue the world man should attain to actual perfection. Out of the world's subjugation was to come man's sublimation. It is God's unwritten fiat that man's development shall be in direct ratio to his achievement. The Anglo-Saxon is what he is because of what he has done in the direction of subduing the earth. The Digger Indian is what he is because of his failure to do anything in this direction. To deprive man of his task, and to relieve him from the necessity to devise his own methods of operation, is to rob him of his only hope of development. This task of subduing the world was assigned to man, not as an end, but as a means to an end—the great end of human development. Out of the struggle to solve the world's problems and to subdue its forces has come the perfection of the race.

Nearly two thousand years ago, Jesus Christ faced the little group of men that formed the nucleus of the Christian church, toward a world spiritually unsubdued, and said: "Go, make disciples of all the nations!" As Stanley was left free to suit his methods to his ever varying circumstances, and as man was left free to devise the ways and means by which to accomplish his stupendous task, so the disciples of our Lord were left unhampered in the mat-

*A paper read at the Texas Christian Lecture-ship.

ter of the choice of methods for the carrying out of the great commission. And why should they not have been? If Stanley could be trusted to devise right methods for carrying out the commission of Mr. Bennett; if man could be trusted to devise wise and successful methods for carrying on to completion the task assigned him of God, could not the Spirit-filled, consecrated, Christ-enlightened church be entrusted with the freedom to choose her own methods in the prosecution of the great work she was commissioned to do? Are men free agents as citizens of the world and mere automatons as citizens of the kingdom of God? "Where the Spirit of Christ is there is liberty."

If Stanley, because of the privilege to use this liberty, came out of Africa a larger man and bearing the map of a larger world, and if man, in the enjoyment of this freedom, has subdued the world and sublimated himself, why may not a larger, spiritual growth come to the Christian church out of the freedom to exercise this same blessed privilege? Out of the struggle that commenced with the landing of the Pilgrims at Plymouth Rock have come the ingenuity, resourcefulness, vigor and virility of this American nation. If the Christian church is strong, vigorous and virile to-day, it is because, in the exercise of her blood-bought liberty, she has grappled with the problems that have confronted her, not asking "How would God have us do it?" but "How can it best be done?" knowing that the best way is always God's way. If world problems were designed to induce mental struggle that would result in intellectual development, are not spiritual problems designed to induce a struggle that will result in spiritual enlargement? Is the law of spiritual development diametrically opposed to the law of intellectual development? Upon him who affirms that it is rests the burden of proof.

III. Jesus Placed the Emphasis on the Spirit and Not on the Letter.

And this he did because of what they are and what they do. The letter is the form, the spirit the substance; the letter is the external, the spirit the internal; the letter is the shell, the spirit the kernel; the letter is the casket, the spirit the precious jewel in the casket. "The letter killeth, but the Spirit giveth life."

The letter of the worship is the time, the place, the order, the accessories. The spirit of worship is the sincerity and spirituality of it. "True worshipers shall worship the Father in spirit and truth." Zeal for the letter of worship is apt to blind the eyes to the spirit of it. Oft has the pearl of true piety been trampled under foot in an unseemly scramble over the casket of form.

The letter of the Lord's supper is the order, the attitude, the administration,

the emblems, the physical acts of eating and drinking. The spirit of it is the discernment of its deep spiritual meaning and the appropriation by faith of the grace symbolized. As the corner is a thing apart from the corner-stone, so the spirit of the supper is a thing apart from the letter of it. That symbolized is a thing apart from the symbols. Not he who partakes only of the symbols communes with God, but he who partakes of the thing symbolized. When the passover supper was instituted the people were commanded to partake of it standing. With no word of protest, Jesus partook of it, reclining. This indicates how much he cared for the letter. The spirit of the feast had been preserved. This was all for which he cared. In the light of this attitude of Jesus, how puerile the discussion over the propriety of using an individual communion service!

The letter of baptism is all connected with it that is merely external. The spirit of baptism is that intellectual and spiritual turning that brings the subject into vital union with Christ. Unaccompanied by this sincere, purposeful turning to God, baptism is an empty, valueless form, whether the subject be one or one hundred years old. The following paraphrase of a familiar passage of Scripture will serve to illustrate the difference between the letter and the spirit of baptism. (Rom. 2:25-29). "Baptism indeed profiteth if thou be a doer of the word; but if thou be a transgressor of the word thy baptism hath become invalid. If therefore the unbaptized keep the ordinances of the Gospel shall not their unbaptism be reckoned for baptism? And shall not the unbaptized who is so from lack of information or opportunity, if he fulfill the Gospel, judge thee, who with the letter and baptism, art a transgressor of the Gospel?. For he is not a Christian who is one outwardly; neither is that baptism which is outward and physical; but he is a Christian who is one inwardly; and baptism is that of the heart, in the spirit, not in the letter." That this paraphrase does no violence to the passage is clearly shown by this other passage from the same author: (Col. 2:11-12). "Ye were also circumcised with a circumcision not made with hands, in the putting off the body of the flesh, in the circumcision of Christ; having been buried with him in baptism, wherein ye were also raised with him through faith in the working of God, who raised him from the dead."

There is no greater menace to vital Christianity than literalism. It is a veritable Gorgon's head that turns into stone all that comes under the spell of its sinister power. A westerner but recently returned from a visit to the petrified forest in Arizona, was describing to a company of eager listeners, the strange things he had seen at that interesting spot. According to his story, the trees, the grass, the flowers, the stream, were all petrified. Even an eagle that had attempted to fly over the fatal spot had been arrested in its flight and hung suspended in mid-air, an agitated image of its former self. When reminded of the law of gravity he quickly replied, "O, the law of gravity was petrified too!" Thus the atmosphere of literalism turns into stone every vital thing that falls under its baneful influence. Its baleful breath blights and turns into adamant the beau-

(Continued on Page 1492.)

As Seen From the Dome   By F. D. Power

We are now a country without a president. Mr. Roosevelt is on the high seas. Traditions and precedents mean little to our present chief magistrate. He is doing what no president has dared to do before him. From the illustrious father of his country down to William McKinley no occupant of the presidential chair has ever set foot outside the United States. Washington going toward Massachusetts would not enter Rhode Island, because it had not subscribed to the constitution, and was therefore not a part of the country. President McKinley would not cross the bridge at El Paso for the same reason, and declined an invitation to be the guest of the city of Vancouver, or to return by the Canadian Pacific, as it would take him beyond our borders. But here is a man who flings such precedents to the winds. He is a law unto himself.

The constitution does not provide for the present situation. We have no arrangement for an acting president. No one can assume the duties and responsibilities of the executive head at this hour. "In case of the removal of the president from office, or of his death, resignation, or inability to discharge the powers and duties of the said office, the same shall devolve upon the vice-president," declares the constitution, but its framers meant physical "inability," and absence from the country is not contemplated in any case. To all intents and purposes we are a country without a president, but the machinery of the government moves smoothly enough without him and the prayers of the people go before the throne for a happy journey and a safe return. Mr. Roosevelt gets such thorough enjoyment out of these unusual undertakings, and turns them to such practical and useful ends, that nobody begrudges him either his outing or his adventure. We may say to the good ship Louisiana, in the historic words, "Quid times? Caesarem vehis," and we may rest assured we shall know more about the big ditch than we could possibly have learned from any other source. Mr. Roosevelt will see for himself, and he will speak with authority; and for some reason, when he speaks the country listens. If there is one thing the president possesses that compares with his boldness it is a keen foresight. He is a man of vision. Two imperative needs were emphasized by our scrap with Spain: the possession of the Hawaiian Islands as a naval base, and the canal to make communication between the Atlantic and Pacific seaboards safe and easy. Think of the Oregon's long, expensive, and dangerous voyage from San Francisco by way of Magellan Straits in 1898. The president will see things for the people when he gets to Panama.

The interchange of courtesies between the Baptists and Disciples of Maryland recently deserves more than a passing notice. Dr. Charles H. Dodd of the Eutaw Place Church, Baltimore, made a most fraternal address to our convention, which was heartily received. He was willing to take the position held by us with reference to the name and the Lord's Supper, and felt the two bodies should no longer stand apart. B. A. Abbott, our representative to the Maryland Association was warmly welcomed October 26. The brethren were as much delighted to receive our delegate as we were to greet Dr. Dodd, and Mr. Abbott found a strong sentiment among them for closer relations between us. Mr. Eugene Levering, the most prominent Baptist layman in the city, responded and favored the union of the two bodies, and rejoiced that in Baltimore arrangements had been made to extend the privileges of the communion to each other. Dr. Curtis Lee Laws, in whose church the association met, stated that for all differences existing between Mr. Abbott's church and his own, they might be merged into one. The stumbling-block, however, was which one. Certain it is, such fraternal intercourse between us must be promotive of the union spirit and should be encouraged. A congress of Baptists and Disciples would greatly help on the courtship. From appearances there is much less chance of union with the Free Baptist brethren than the regular Baptist churches of Christ. We would do well to spend our time on the easier problem. We have a freak Baptist brother here who rebaptizes Disciples, but there are freaks in both bodies. Education, information, and a better understanding every way may be reached by such incidents as this in which leading men like Dodd and Abbott have figured. Let us believe in and practice what we have been preaching. It is time. If we act not, others will get ahead of us. Our occupation will be gone. The procession is moving. Are we in the bandwagon?

One of the most distressing events in our recent history is the break-down in our beloved M. E. Harlan. He had done much to promote this cause of which I am writing. His addresses on this subject had a wide circulation, and accomplished much toward a better understanding between the Baptists and our people. He did a fine work in Brooklyn and was esteemed by all as a faithful preacher of the Gospel, and an upright, pure, and forceful man. In June last he had to give up his work; and the physicians tell him he can not resume it for a year. The trial is a sore one. His ministry was full of promise, and to be disabled, even temporarily, is a loss to our cause in the east and a great grief to Brother Harlan and his devoted wife. It is no wonder that the bearing of the heavy burdens and the incessant labors of a city pastorate should sometimes be too much for even the strongest. This has been true of this faithful man; and the heartfelt prayers of his brethren are with him in this hour of affliction. We appreciate his work and worth, and shall look anxiously for his restoration to the ranks where he loved to serve.

The strenuous age shows itself in our ministry. Few know the prodigious labors that are demanded of the man in the pulpit. If he works conscientiously he has cares and responsibilities and mental and physical strain such as no other servant of the public ever dreams of. Here goes Minot Savage, pastor of the Church of the Messiah, N. Y., a strong man of but sixty-five, a wreck in mind and body, and so with many others. It used to be thought preachers were long-lived, but the age is hard on the minister if he be a worker. It is not easy to suggest a remedy. One word of advice may be offered—give others something to do. The most successful pastor is he who can get the most work out of other people. He has burdens enough that are exclusively his without attempting to be the whole thing. Use the brethren. Use the sisters. Use the young people. Use the children. Some of them are longing to be called upon. Others are perishing from disuse. It is an absolute injury often to do yourself what you might as well have another do. Hunt for the buried talents. Dig them up, and send them about like Cromwell's statues of the apostles, doing good.

By the way, that was Houdon's statue of Washington, and not "Hondon's," as I was made to say last week.—"u" and not "n."

COFFEE IMPORTERS
Publish a Book About Coffee.

There has been much discussion as to Coffee and Postum lately, so much in fact that some of the coffee importers and roasters have taken to type to promote the sale of their wares and check if possible the rapid growth of the use of Postum Food Coffee.

In the coffee importers' book a chapter is headed "Coffee as a Medicine" and advocates its use as such.

Here is an admission of the truth, most important to all interested.

Every physician knows, and every thoughtful person should know, that habitual use of any "medicine" of the drug-stimulant type of coffee or whiskey quickly causes irritation of the tissues and organs stimulated and finally sets up disease in the great majority of cases if persisted in. It may show in any one of the many organs of the body and in the great majority of cases can be directly traced to coffee, in a most unmistakable way by leaving off the active irritant—coffee—and using Postum Food Coffee for a matter of 10 days. If the result is relief from nervous trouble, dyspepsia, bowel complaint, heart failure, weak eyes, or any other malady set up by a poisoned nervous system, you have your answer with the accuracy of a demonstration in mathematics.

"There's a reason" for Postum.

The Lordship of Jesus By T. E. Winter

Many people who acknowledge Jesus to be the Son of God do not accept him as their personal Savior; they may even admit that he "came to seek and to save that which was lost," he actually saves men, but still not accept him as *their* Savior by whole-hearted faith, and entire self-commitment. Others, again, accept him as the Son of God and as their own personal Savior by placing perfect confidence in him, and complying with his requirements, that they may be freed from their past sins, and become sons of God, but still they fail to acknowledge him as Lord. Now "the good confession," when made, is an acceptance of three great truths, viz: (1) The Sonship; (2) The Saviorship; (3) The Lordship of Jesus, the Christ. The last, logically an outgrowth of the two former truths, is equally as important; for while they have to do primarily with faith and doctrine, the latter has to do with the daily life.

Lordship implies both ownership and possession; in the parable of the wicked husbandman, "the lord of the vineyard" was its owner (Matt. 21:33-46.) Paul's teaching in Eph. 6:5-9 shows that the "servant" was owned and held in the possession of the "lord" or "master." As a consequence of this ownership and possession, the lord has authority to command and to compel obedience to his commands. God has delegated "all authority in heaven and on earth" to Jesus and Peter said to the Pentecostians, "God hath made this same Jesus, whom ye crucified, both Lord and Christ;" and again he says of Jesus, "He is Lord of all." (Acts 2:36; 10:36.) Since Jesus shed his blood to redeem us, (1 Peter 1:18, 19; 1 Cor. 6:20), and since we have committed ourselves to his service, he both owns and possesses us, and could well say therefore, "Glorify God in your bodies and in your spirits which are his." In harmony with this conception Paul calls himself "the bond-servant of Jesus Christ."

It is comparatively easy for one to acknowledge Jesus as "Lord of all," as "King of kings, and Lord of lords;" that is not sufficient; that does not necessarily affect one's own life. No, more than this is necessary. One must, like Thomas, cry out from the deepest conviction of one's own heart, "My Lord, and my God!" When, on the Damascus road, Saul of Tarsus was convinced that Jesus was the Christ, the Son of the living God, recognizing his Lordship he cried out, "Lord, what wilt thou have me to do?" The Lordship of Jesus always has to do with the practical side of the Christian life, with the doing of things—"Lord, what wilt thou have me to do?" From the time Saul asked this question, he was Christ's bond-servant; Jesus truly was the Lord of Paul's life. As Jesus "came to seek and to save that which was lost," Paul, as his bond-servant, said of himself, "I am made all things to all men that I might "by all means save some." (1 Cor. 9:22.) So touched by the infinite love of Christ as expressed

in the crucifixion, so filled with gratitude to him for this great sacrifice and salvation, was the apostle Paul, that his life was completely under the direction of his Redeemer and Lord; that question he asked on the Damascus road became his life-prayer. Think of what Paul gave up! Social, political and ecclesiastical position; his father's religion, his own faith. Summing it all up he says: "Whatsoever things were gain to me, those I counted loss for Christ." That is what the Lordship of Christ means.

Paul not only accepted Jesus as Lord, but he "preached Christ Jesus as Lord;" that is for you and me; it is our duty as fully to accept the Lordship of Jesus as did Saul of Tarsus. Oh, that every Christian would whole-heartedly inquire, "Lord what wilt thou come to do?" To him would come the answer, "Go ye into all the world and preach the gospel to every creature." "The servant is not greater than his lord." Jesus came to seek and to save and that is the chief mission of the church and of each Christian. As Paul says, become "all things to all men that you might by all means save some."

Jesus can not be Lord of a man's life unless he is Lord of his substance. We need to learn that the Lordship of Jesus must affect our use of material wealth committed to us. We ought carefully to consider this question—"How much owest thou unto thy Lord?" As Christians we are not

giving as we ought for the spreading of the Gospel. The members of the five principal religious bodies of the United States are giving on an average only one cent per member each week. Think of it! One cent a week!! The population of the United States now is three and one-half times greater than it was in 1850 while our wealth is fourteen times greater. Why should not the finances of the churches increase with a marvelous rapidity? In 1900 the Protestant church communicants were worth $22,066,317,000. During the period 1890-1900, these churches added to their permanent wealth each year on the average $684,754,410. Had they given even one-tenth of this amount, saved out of their net income they would have given 1250 per cent more to foreign missions than they did give. Why, if each member of our own brotherhood would give on the average only fifty cents we would have for foreign missions over $600,000. No one will dare say that amount could not be wisely and effectively used. Only ten packages of chewing gum, or one pound of tea, or a necktie, or ten car fares, denied ourself and the amount would be assured. Oh, my brother, recognize Jesus as Lord of your substance! Let him teach you that "It is more blessed to give than to receive," and be a giver for all our aggressive work. "Why call ye me Lord, Lord, and do not the things which I say unto you?" (Jesus.)

Greenwich, O.

WHERE JESUS PLACED THE EMPHASIS.

(Continued from Page 1490.)

tiful tree of life. It arrests in its flight the white dove of peace, and hardens its very heart into stone. Under its dread spell the laws of liberty, love and life become cold, inflexible, dead, "The letter killeth, but the spirit giveth life."

IV. Jesus Placed the Emphasis on Inward Transformation and Not on Outward Conformation.

All else that any one may be able to say is in vain if he can not say with Paul: "It is no longer I that live, but Christ that liveth in me." "Christ in you, the hope of glory." This is the *sine qua non* "Did you receive the Spirit after you were baptized?" is a much more important question than "Have you been baptized?" "And you (too) shall receive the gift of the Holy Spirit" was the highest note struck in the sermon on Pentecost. "That times of refreshing may come from the presence of the Lord" was the climax reached in the sermon in the temple court. "If any man have not the Spirit of Christ he is none of his."

It matters not what name is inscribed on the corner-stone of the house of worship if the Spirit of Christ dwells not in the hearts of those who worship within. It matters not what the order and the accessories of our worship may be, if it proceed not from hearts in which the Christ has been formed. It matters not when, nor where, nor how hard, nor by what plan we work, it will count nothing to our credit with God if it be not prompted by the unselfish love of Christ-filled hearts. It matters not when, nor

where, nor by whom, nor how, nor what for, nor how often we have been baptized if we have not the Spirit and the love and the life of Christ dwelling within us. These are the vital things. These are the things worthy of emphasis.

Our future as a factor among the religious forces of the world depends upon where we place the emphasis from this time on. If we would not be a "disappearing brotherhood" we must enlarge our field of emphasis. No religious movement can survive that does not learn in time to put first things first. A lady owned an imported canary. It was a beautiful singer, and she prized it very highly. But it began to droop and she feared it would die. With great care and regularity she provided it with the food upon which it had always been fed, but it got no better. One bright, sunny day she took it out into the garden, and removing it from the cage, placed it on the branch of a rose bush. Soon she observed it pecking eagerly at a small spider that hung suspended by its web. This was the food it needed—living food.

Brother ministers! Fellow-workers in the most glorious calling that ever enlisted the hearts and engaged the hands of men and women! The future of this splendid movement is in our hands! It lies with us to determine whether it shall go marching on to glorious victory, or whether it shall droop and die. The time has come when this bird of paradise must have a change of diet or commence to droop and die. We must feed it on the living truths and vital principles as abundantly provided as the other kind, and by the same beneficent hand.

D. O. Smart, Our President.   By G. W. Muckley

On Friday evening, November 9, at the evangelistic service held at the Independence Boulevard Church, Kansas City, Mo., David O. Smart, for eighteen years president of our Board of Church Extension, was stricken with heart disease and dropped to his seat, dead. The circumstances have been told in THE CHRISTIAN-EVANGELIST.

D. O. Smart was born in Independence, Mo., February 15, 1843, and would have been 64 years old next February. His parents were of Virginia stock, and, before moving to Missouri, lived in Kentucky. Brother Smart's father assisted in organizing the first Christian church in Jackson county, Mo., and he was early surrounded with Christian influences. He attended Bethany College for a few years. He was in college when the civil war broke out in 1861. As did many other young men he left college and hurrying home enlisted in Shelby's fighting brigade and remained in the confederate army until mustered out of service at the close of the war.

In October, 1866, he married Alice Walrond and moved to Kansas City. Two sons and a daughter, Mrs. Donaldson, were born to them, all workers in the Christian church. His wife has nobly and generously seconded him in all his work for the church. And, his services are now fully measured since we miss him at every turn. Mr. Smart led a very busy life. He told the writer that he had no time for vacations. He occupied very many responsible positions both in and out of the church and his judgment in business and church circles was always in demand. As a counselor in the affairs of the church his presence and appropriate words have always been conspicuous. Did you go to the morning or evening service Brother Smart was always there. If you attended prayer-meeting in heat or cold you rarely found him absent. At Sunday-school he always had a class of boys or girls. In the monthly meetings of the officers of the church Brother Smart's seat was rarely vacant. During the eighteen years that he was president of the Board of Church Extension he was at every meeting with but a half dozen exceptions. He was elected president of the Board of Church Extension for the nineteenth year at its meeting on Tuesday of the week he died. In everything he undertook he served as he did in the confederate army, "until he was mustered out." Death laid his cold hand upon him as he was about to make an exhortation to his fellow Sunday-school teachers to bring all their scholars to Jesus.

Here is the hymn he wanted to read with the teachers, after the reading of which by the teachers, on the following Sunday at the close of the Sunday-school, all of Brother Smart's class gave themselves to Christ. The hymn is certainly "beautiful" and is an "earnest prayer," to use Brother Smart's last words.

ALL MY CLASS FOR JESUS.

My scholars all for Jesus!
This be my earnest pray'r,
For they are souls immortal,
Entrusted to my care;
For each the Master careth,
I long, I long for each;
Grant, Lord, the heav'nly wisdom,
These wayward hearts to reach.

Chorus—

All, all my class for Jesus;
O which one could I spare?
All, all my class in heaven,
Let none be missing there!

My girls, light-hearted, tho'tless,
On trifling things intent,
These cost a priceless ransom,
On these my care be spent;
That each, a willing handmaid,
Be brought to own her Lord;
"Whate'er He saith" to "do it,"
Obedient to His word.

My boys I want for Jesus,
My wayward, wand'ring boys,
So full of life and beauty,
So charmed by earthly joys;
For them the Savior suffered,
For them His life was giv'n;
Lord, by that ransom, help me
Bring all my boys to heav'n.

Lord, be in ev'ry lesson,
Bless ev'ry lab'ring word;
My trembling lips may utter,
To bring them to the Lord;
So fleeting are the moments
Of opportunity!
O Jesus, Master, help me
Bring all my class to Thee.

This was the man's chief characteristic—he was in dead earnest in everything he did. His words and his work were therefore an inspiration to every one with whom he came in contact. He did not seek to be a counselor, but he was never happier than when his counsel was sought because he loved to serve people. When I came to Kansas City in 1890 to take the secretaryship of Church Extension he was the first man from whom advice and help was solicited. The first meeting we had together he looked upon me as a young man and said: "Do you think you can do it?" I said, "Yes, with help and counsel from men like you." His face fairly glowed as he said, "You shall have it." That counsel never failed through these eighteen years. In the councils of the Board of Church Extension his words always carried great weight. No minister among us, young or old, nor any man on the board, could possibly be more solicitous to realize all the aims of our Church Extension work than he. He was anxious to live and be present at our Centennial in Pittsburg and was in sympathy with all of its aims. He gave liberally but always in the name of the church. His other public office was the presidency of the trustees of our Bible college at Columbia, Mo. His most liberal public gifts were to that institution. He served for years on the state board of Missouri, also.

To our congregations in Kansas City he performed an indispensable service. He was first a deacon in the First Church and afterwards an elder. He was an elder of the Sixth and Prospect Church, now Independence Boulevard Church, from its beginning in 1888. He had a most liberal share in the erection of the Sixth and Prospect Church building and it could not have been built but for his large gifts. Here were laid the foundations deep and strong for the present work on Independence boulevard, now perhaps the greatest local church work in our brotherhood. While our pastor, Brother Combs, was absent on Sunday, October 14, at the national convention at Buffalo, Brother Smart took charge of the service at Independence Boulevard Church, and after an enthusiastic, sensible speech, raised $1,260 for the rebuilding of our stricken churches in San Francisco.

Writers of history tell us that in every decisive battle there have been a few moments of decision—a few moments, when by desperate fighting or skill of strategy the result of the battle is determined. It is so in the life work of men. Few of us realize how often the right word spoken at the proper time turns a man toward a great life work for Christ. Nearly every great and useful man has had words fitly spoken to him just at the moment in life when they counted for the most. It was so in the case of David O. Smart. As the work of the Christian church began to develop in Kansas City, men of the right calibre were needed. Brother Smart was put on boards and building committees and finally the church in the state needed his services on the state board. Just at that time Mr. Smart had taken on new business burdens and as he came into his office one morning he said with great emphasis to his associate and long time friend and adviser, E. P. Graves, "The church is thrusting too many burdens upon me. I can't neglect my growing business and assume these accumulating duties. I am going to resign from all these boards. They take too much of my time." Brother Graves saw that this was not the opportune moment to speak, but about two days later when Brother Smart came into the office in a splendid mood he saw the time had come to speak and he said: "David, I was very sorry to hear you speak as you did the other day about resigning your duties to the church. I don't want you to do it and these are my reasons:

"1. You have the ability to serve the cause.

"2. You have plenty of means to take the time.

"3. There are obligations resting upon you that should compel you.

"4. This will bring you in contact with the best and brightest men of the state among our people.

"5. They need you and you need them as much as they need you. By coming in contact with these men you will become a broader man and your vision of the Christian life will be widened."

Mr. Smart sat in a thoughtful mood for a moment, and, suddenly wheeling round to his desk he went to work and from that moment to the day of his death Brother Graves said he never heard a word of complaint from Brother Smart's lips about work that he was called to do for the church. The right word had been spoken at the critical time in Mr. Smart's life by an elder of the church who saw the moment and did not fail to do his duty and a conspicuously useful man was saved to the cause of Christ. Two years later, in 1888, when the Board of Church Extension was organized and located in Kansas City, he cheerfully accepted the presidency and gave it the wisest and best days of his life.

In all the places where Brother Smart worked his words and influence will linger for good. On Saturday morning after Brother Smart's death, an 11-year-old boy wakened his father at an early hour and said, "Wasn't that a fine death of Brother Smart's? I would like to die that way while I was telling people to do good." The influence of his work in the church and Sunday-school told on Sunday morning after his death, when, after the reading of that song, No. 124, by the teachers, twenty-nine young people made the confession and in the church services thirteen more, making in all forty-two for the day. Blessed are the dead who die in the Lord for their works certainly follow them.

Our Budget

—The Editor of THE CHRISTIAN-EVANGELIST is in the southland attending the Alabama and Georgia state conventions.

—The Christian churches of St. Louis will hold another great rally at the Odeon on Sunday next, at 3 p. m.

—The next issue of THE CHRISTIAN-EVANGELIST will be a special one. It will consist of 52 pages, or nearly double the usual size. In view of this fact and the Thanksgiving holiday period, we will be compelled to go to press on Saturday of this week and will, therefore, not be able to handle late news or telegrams as usual on Monday morning.

—Among the features of this special number, in addition to other Campbell matter, will be a reproduction of what we believe to be the latest photograph made of Alexander Campbell. The price for this number will be 5 cents per copy, six for 25 cents and $2.00 per hundred. The difficulty in producing so large a paper makes it imperative that we shall know before the edition is run off the press whether extra copies will be required by any of our readers. They should send in notice to the General Superintendent at once, if they wish extra copies.

❖ ❖ ❖

—F. M. McHale and Marie Brewer are in a meeting at Claflin, Kan.

—J. D. Williams reports that the church at Nebo, Ill., needs a minister.

—"Received a copy of 'Victory of Faith.' It is well worth reading."—F. M. McHale.

—H. A. Northcutt is to hold a meeting at Roswell, N. M., with C. C. Hill next spring.

—Walter S. Willis has received an increase of salary from the church at Clintonville, Ky.

—E. G. Merrill has been extended a unanimous call to preach for the church at Troy, Mo., next year.

—Thomas L. Cooksey has some open time for meetings and may be addressed at 143 Butler avenue, Indianapolis.

—Thomas Wallace has been making a preaching and lecture tour through New York, Pennsylvania and Ohio.

—J. D. McClure, of Albany, Mo., is starting west with his wife to find some relief from her asthma and heart trouble.

—C. A. Lowe expects "to follow up" what he calls a very good meeting just held by T. H. Capp for him at St. Joseph, Mo.

—S. M. Crutcher's engagements for 1907 will be as this year—two Sundays at Braymer, one at Cowgill, and one at Ludlow, Mo.

—W. T. Moore has gone to Mobile to address the Alabama convention. A bear hunt is also on the program of this 75-year-old youth.

—E. F. Leake closed, on October 28, a ministry of six years at Newton and began with the church at Onawa, Iowa, on November 4.

—L. L. Carpenter will dedicate the new building at Kellerton, Ia., on Nov. 25. Congregations in the vicinity are cordially invited to attend.

—J. F. Callahan is now on the Pacific Coast. A post card from him, written at Acampo, says the colony east of that place seems to be flourishing.

—F. D. Hobson, pastor at Kearney, Neb., commends the work of Melvin Putman and Miss Emma Egbert who have just assisted him in a meeting.

—C. H. DeVoe writes that the church at Peru, Ind., has just introduced the use of the individual communion set and is very much pleased with it.

—Since the dedication of the church at Lincoln, Ill., two years ago, there have been about 300 additions to the membership. W. H. Cannon is pastor.

—Reports at the annual meeting of the church at Peoria, Ill., where Harry Foster Burns is the minister, showed the work prospering in all departments.

—W. E. Harlow will close his meeting at Compton Heights Church, St. Louis, on Thursday evening with a lecture on "The New Thought: How to Live One Hundred Years."

—William M. Thomas, pastor of the Frederick Avenue Church, St. Joseph, Mo., commends highly Cassius V. Allison, of Mound City, who has just held a meeting for him.

—William Grant Smith reports that a large Young People's Society has just been organized at Rossville, Ill., where every department of the church seems to be successful.

—Thomas L. Cooksey will be at Henderson, Tenn., in a meeting during December. Owing to some churches changing their plans Brother Cooksey will have vacant dates from January to April when he goes to Texas.

—The number received at Niantic, Ill., since March last was 72 instead of 40 as stated in THE CHRISTIAN-EVANGELIST. Thirty-one of these were added at regular services. J. Will Walters, the pastor, thinks this is the best little church in central Illinois.

—The Chariton Christian Missionary Society will hold the next convention at Sumner, December 29, 30. E. H. Williamson, the secretary, writes us that these fifth Sunday meetings are found to be very helpful to the country churches of this Missouri district.

—The church at California, Pa., is making progress, there being additions, while the Bible school has more than doubled both in numbers and in collections. There is renewed interest in the Christian Endeavor and a Junior Society has just been started with 35 members. Thomas Martin is the pastor.

—Thomas J. Giddens reports the work at Miami, I. T., as in a prosperous condition. During his year of ministry 48 have been added, 25 during his regular appointments, lacking just two of doubling the membership. He commends John A. Brown, of Moline, who has just held for him a meeting, with 23 additions.

—W. J. Dodge writes us that the work of completing the church building at Jackson, Ky., goes forward and the basement will soon be ready for use. The Sunday-school has a good attendance and the prayer-meetings are full of profit. Brother Dodge has just entered upon his third year, by the unanimous request of the members.

—Charles E. Smith, state evangelist of South Carolina, has just organized a new church at Brunson with twenty-nine charter members. Brother Smith is now having splendid audiences in a tent meeting at Wagener, where, he says, is the greatest combination of Mormons, infidels, Millennialists and other "ites and isms" he has ever seen.

—Walter M. White, who is in the field in the interests of Kentucky University, is making good success also as an evangelistic preacher. His latest meeting was at Norwood, Ohio. Brother Armistead writes us that it accomplished all the most sanguine had hoped for. The church there has outgrown its facilities and will enlarge at once. The entire debt is now paid for.

—Geo. L. Snively, of the Christian Publishing Company, is to be with the Hyde

Park Christian Church, Kansas City, Mo., on the occasion of their sixty-eighth anniversary which is to be celebrated by a men's banquet on November 23, and all day meetings on the following Sunday, November 25. Brother Snively is glad to render service of this kind when he can.

—H. James Crockett, who has been with the church at Butler, Mo., for three years will close his ministry there in December. During his pastorate there have been over 150 accessions. The church is united and organized for aggressive work. Brother Crockett has not decided as to his future. He would like to hold a meeting or two before entering upon another pastorate.

—We regret to learn that the condition of Herbert Corwine is such that he has felt compelled to tender his resignation of the pastorate at Bartlesville, I. T., to which place he recently removed. He was only on his new field for about a week and he decided that it would be better to return to his old home at California, Mo. He will return to Bartlesville with his family if he improves to any noticeable extent.

—J. D. Hull has been asked to remain at Kendallville, Ind. The church building there has been much improved during the past year and 125 additions to the membership are reported during the eighteen months pastorate. A mission church has been supplied by Brother Hull during the year and he has acted as corresponding secretary of the First Missionary District of Indiana.

—In writing about "Gloria in Excelsis," R. S. Robertson, pastor at Osborne, Kan., says "the entire membership is greatly pleased with this hymn book. It is the only one that does justice to our great work. Brethren, throw away your cheap song books and secure 'Gloria in Excelsis.'" The church at Osborne has ordered new pews. Miss Lizzie Sprowl, of Indiana, is to take charge of the music.

—A very enjoyable union service arranged by all the churches of White City, Kan., has just been addressed by George E. Lyons, the new state secretary. On this occasion the church debt of $500 was pledged and enough more pledges taken to make a good beginning for a parsonage fund. C. E. F. Smith and wife, of Emporia, have been employed to labor with the church the coming year.

—C. H. Mattox, the efficient pastor at Albany, Mo., is being assisted by C. G. Stout, of Des Moines, Ia., in a meeting. Brother Stout has made quite a success in evangelistic work and we look forward to good results at Albany where the brethren will make use of THE CHRISTIAN-EVANGELIST in their campaign. During the past year Brother Mattox reports about 130 additions.

—H. L. Atkinson, pastor-evangelist at Hazel Green, Ky., writes that this mountain school church is in the midst of some needed repairs, and would like to learn of some richer church which could donate to them their discarded pews, if these be fairly usable. Hazel Green is unable, in view of the other repairs they have to pay for, to secure new pews.

—We regret to record the death of Mrs. Fannie L. Pannell, widow of the late F. Pannell, who was for many years associated with the musical department of Christian College, Columbia, Mo. She was a good woman and beloved by a wide circle of friends. Her pastor, C. H. Winders, conducted the funeral services in Columbia where the body was brought for interment.

—The Editor takes a little personal pleasure in the report elsewhere of the celebration of the twenty-first anniversary of the Society of Christian Endeavor in Boston, Mass., which he had the honor of organizing and which, so far as he knows, is the oldest Christian Endeavor Society among

us. It was a pleasant occasion—this celebration, and we regret that we could be present only by a message of greeting and congratulation.

—The Humboldt Street Church, at Brooklyn, N. Y., has just purchased a beautiful brick house of two stories and basement, which adjoins the church property, for a parsonage. J. Keevil and his family are now located there and appreciate a home all to themselves in this crowded section of the city. J. L. Keevil, of Johnson City, Tenn., has just closed a short meeting and three were added to the church. All departments are reported to be making progress.

—J. N. McConnell, who has just been holding a meeting at Pleasant Hill, Ore., speaks highly of the moral condition of that place, which, he says, is the result of the splendid church work that has been done there in days gone by, as well as under the present minister, M. F. Horn. Brother McConnell is now in a meeting at Aumsville, Ore., where Brother Messick is pastor. The latter, however, will go to Starbuck, Wash., to take charge of the church there.

—In another column will be found a report of some of the work of W. F. Richardson at the First Christian Church, Kansas City, Mo. Brother Richardson's church is in the down town district and it speaks well for him that he and his congregation can show such a fine report for the last year under all the difficulties incidental to a church placed as is this one. He has labored faithfully; he has labored intelligently, and he has won a host of friends because he deserves them.

—We hear excellent reports about Brother McKissock's interregnum ministry at Nashville, Tenn., where he has been supplying the Vine street pulpit. He has just commenced a protracted effort and Brother Linn Cave, of the Woodland Street Church, will assist. Bro. W. G. Mershon writes us that Dr. Torrey has just closed a meeting in Nashville which has stirred the city as no other ever has. Some 1,200 conversions are reported, the converts joining the different churches all of which will be helped as a result of this meeting.

—We regret to learn from Bro. Walter Scott Priest, of the Broad Street Church of Christ, Columbus, Ohio, that their building enterprise has sustained a severe loss in the destruction by fire of their splendid pipe organ. The organ was stored in a large dry goods house, on the fifth floor where the fire broke out, resulting in the complete destruction of the organ. It was a splendid instrument and was insured for only half its value. The new building is ready for the roof and the church hopes to be in it by March 1, when Charles Reign Scoville is to begin a meeting with them.

—S. R. Drake, of Columbus Junction, Iowa, would like to have some pastoral or evangelistic work. He would prefer work in the ministry, but if this does not open up wishes to do the next best thing so that he can support himself and family. He has had some experience in general merchandise and would be glad to enter a dry goods or hardware store. His chief desire is to get located in a town where he can have church privileges, for he has a family of four boys and one girl at home, the oldest boy being nineteen, and him he would like to get in some work where he would become a useful man.

—Zealous friends of THE CHRISTIAN-EVANGELIST should consider that THE CHRISTIAN-EVANGELIST can not be published in its present form and at the present price unless our great presses and numerous employes are kept busy during the intervals between publications of this paper. During these periods we print books and Bible school literature, and THE CHRISTIAN-EVANGELIST admirers are

How to Get Rid of Catarrh.

A Simple, Safe, Reliable Way, and it Cost Nothing to Try, Send for it and See.

Those who suffer from it well know the miseries of catarrh. There is no need of it. Why not get it cured? It can be done. The remedy that does this is the invention of Dr. J. W. Blosser, an eminent Southern doctor and minister, who has for over thirty-two years been identified with the cure of catarrh in all its worst forms.

He will send you, entirely free, enough to satisfy you that it is a real, genuine, "home" cure for catarrh, scratchy throat, stopped up feeling in the nose and throat, catarrhal headaches, constant spitting, catarrhal deafness, asthma, etc.

His discovery is unlike anything you ever had before. It is not a spray, douche, atomizer, salve, cream or any such thing, but a genuine, tried-and-true cure, that clears out the head, nose, throat and lungs, so that you can again breathe the free air and sleep without that choking, spitting feeling that all catarrh sufferers have. It saves the wear-and-tear of internal medicines which ruin the stomach. It will heal up the diseased membranes and thus prevents colds, so that you will not be constantly blowing your nose and spitting.

If you have never tried Dr. Blosser's discovery, and want to make a trial of it without cost, send your address to Dr. J. W. Blosser, 475 Walton St., Atlanta, Ga., and a good, free trial treatment and also a beautiful illustrated booklet, "How I Cure Catarrh," will be sent you at once, free, showing you how you can cure yourself privately at home.

Write him immediately.

helping in its development as they assist us in selling our other publications. One of the best expressions of friendship for THE CHRISTIAN-EVANGELIST is an order for books and B'ble school supplies.

—We very much regret to learn that an unexpected break-down of his health necessitates for H. C. Garrison, pastor of the church at Danville, Ky., a change of climate for awhile. His great-hearted church has given him an indefinite leave of absence and he has started for the mountains of North Carolina. Brother Garrison, who is not in any way related to the Editor of this paper, is one of our brightest young men, and has done an excellent work in his present field. It is sad to see such promising leaders as he, Burrus Jenkins, and others who could be mentioned, laid aside, at least temporarily, from active duties, largely, perhaps, through the great strain and incessant demands that are made upon them.

—The southwestern Minnesota convention, which recently closed, was an excellent one. The speeches and conferences were helpful. Among the resolutions adopted was one calling for closer co-operation among the churches of the district to advance the cause in so fruitful a field. The excellent work of District Evangelist Childs was endorsed, and a protest against the liquor traffic was made, while the people of the district were invited to make a candid investigation of the plea of the Disciples of Christ. Thanks were extended to J. H. Reaves and wife, who left their own work in South Dakota to take part in the convention. The next convention will be held at Mankato, Minn.

—J. W. Lowber, of Austin, Texas, has been invited to deliver an address before the American Anthropological Association.

—We have been unable until this moment to make mention of a very pleasant reunion of the Blunt family, which recently took place at their homestead near Brookfield, Linn County, Missouri. The family circle is a large one, embracing the parents, 12 children and 13 grandchildren. As two of the sons, John and Reuben, are ministers, a feature of the reunion was preaching in the Smyrna church nearby, while, of course, a basket dinner was part of the program. Visiting brethren were present from Linneus, Brookfield, Purdin, Antioch, Grantsville, Shelby and Browning and from Sullivan and Nodaway counties, as well as Kansas City. A meeting was carried on over the Lord's day and ten converts were added to the church. We are indebted to O. J. Bulfin for these facts.

—J. B. Scheitlin writes us that T. J. Shuey has completely surprised the congregation at Abingdon, Ill., by tendering his resignation, to take effect November 26. Brother Shuey and his family go to Seattle, Wash. He has been with the Abingdon church for about two years and eight months. Nothing definite can as yet be stated as to a successor. Any communications should be addressed to P. J. Murphy or C. N. Wright. Brother Scheitlin writes as follows: "Brother Shuey never preached a weak or poor sermon during his labors here and the entire community realizes that it must be an unusually able pulpit man to fill the place as acceptably as he has. Three Sisters Shuey, wife and daughters of the pastors, will be as much missed because of the extraordinary faithfulness manifested by them in the various departments of church work and especially in its music."

—F. O. Fannon, who recently paid the office of THE CHRISTIAN-EVANGELIST a pleasant visit while returning from an appointment, writes us that he has felt too busy preaching and helping on their feet weak churches to make regular reports to the paper. He is now in the hardest work of his life, yet he says it is the happiest. 'November 11, he writes, was a great day for the little church at Salem, Ill., when the cornerstone of a most complete church building to cost about $25,000 was laid. A new interest has been started. The church debt at Kinmundy has been provided for. The building erected four years ago has become too small and there is talk of enlargement. There are additions at nearly every service. Brother Fannon is now with a little band of 20 or 30 members at St. Elmo for a short meeting to help deepen the spiritual life, gathering in some new helpers, getting a pastor located and getting the world to feel the touch and uplift of another strong church.

❖ ❖

The Standard Adding Machine.

We wish to call attention of our readers to the advertisement in this issue of the Standard Adding Machine. The Standard Adding Machine has been on the market for a number of years and is to-day the leading commercial machine, having been adopted by a great many of the larges commercial institutions in the country, railroads, and the favorite machine of thousands of bankers.

The Standard is a very compact, durable machine, portable, and is never affected by change of position or change of temperature. Because of its simplicity, it is sold at a very low price in comparison to the make of others, and is far more satisfactory. The Standard is used in our offices, and has been for some time, and we are very willing to add our testimonial both as to the worth of the machine and the standing of the Company.

J. O. Shelburne.

Among the pastors who are resigning their regular work to enter the evangelistic field is J. O. Shelburne, of Toledo, O., who expects to resume his evangelistic work January 1. His past success in that field has been a constant motive to draw him back again into it, although his work as a pastor has been a valuable experience, enabling him to understand their problems which is an important feature of successful evangelism. Brother Shelburne has introduced in Toledo shop meetings which have been productive of great good. He has equipped himself for these noonday shop meetings with an organ, song books, posters, cards, etc., and an evangelistic sing-

J. O. Shelburne.

er who will have charge of this special feature of the work. This is really carrying the Gospel to the people and is a new departure of which we are glad to learn.

Improved financial methods, and a complete organization of forces to take care of new converts, are some of the features to which Brother Shelburne will give special attention in his work. It is a significant fact that the ministers of all the Protestant churches in the city have urged Brother Shelburne to undertake this work of evangelism. Brother Shelburne comes from a long line of preachers, his grandfather, Silas Shelburne, being one of the first preachers of the Reformation in Virginia. He had three sons who were preachers of the same primitive Gospel, and out of their families have come twelve preachers. The Shelburne family have given to the Reformation not less than twenty preachers.

We wish Brother Shelburne the greatest success in his evangelistic work and shall be glad to co-operate with him in carrying the Gospel into new fields.

❖ ❖

A Word of Greeting and Good-bye.

In common with many others, no doubt, we have received the following word of "greeting and goodbye" from two of our devoted missionaries, man and wife, who were just setting sail for China. We publish this greeting because we believe it expresses so well the spirit of all our missionaries, and because we hope it will help

W. F. Richardson's Twelve Years.

Having closed the twelfth year of my pastorate with the First Christian Church of Kansas City, Mo., it may be of some slight interest to some of your readers to know of the work done. During this period there have been 1,268 additions to the congregation, and 863 have been dismissed by letter and death, leaving a net increase of 445. More than half of the dismissals were to our sister churches in this city, as members moved from the downtown district into the residence neighborhoods. We have now a nominal membership of about a thousand, with an actual resident membership of 800.

The fiscal year of the church ended October 31 and the report showed that, despite our heavy losses during the year by the removal of many of our most liberal givers to other churches, we had raised more money than in any previous year of the church's history, except during the building of our house of worship, and the year when it was remodeled. Through the church and its auxiliaries $12,618.89 were contributed, of which $3,347.77 were for missions and benevolence. Many individual gifts were made for like purposes, not passing through our treasury. We start into the new year with every financial obligation of the church discharged, and a balance to our credit. To those who understand the situation here, this is counted worthy of commendation, and I want this faithful people to have their fidelity and sacrifices made known to their brethren. I began my thirteenth year as their pastor on October 1, and with the assistance of Barclay Meador, my faithful assistant, hope for even larger results in the future. We are to have R. H. Crossfield, of Owensboro, Ky., with us in January for a series of evangelistic meetings, and expect a great blessing from God.

Kansas City, Mo.   W. F. RICHARDSON.

A Meeting at Cornell, Neb.

James S. Beem, who is now in a meeting at Cornell, Neb., united with the Christian Church at the age of seventeen during a meeting conducted by M. C. Wilson. He had been a member of the M. E. church and, like many others, did not know that the Disciples of Christ make the plea for Christian union, their position having been misrepresented to him. He began preaching about seven years ago, three years of his ministry having been spent in active evangelistic work with the result that about 1,000 people have been added to the church under his labors. Much of his work has been held in difficult fields. He has a reputation of preaching the gospel in its purity and simplicity and yet without giving offense. Of his pastoral work we also hear a good report.

Brother Beem is to be assisted by George W. Light as leader of music. Brother Light has been training for this work and has received favorable commendations wherever he has labored. He was converted in one of Brother Beem's meetings, has

Jas. S. Beem, Evangelist.

assisted him in some of these, and is blessed, we hear, both with enthusiasm and ability for his special vocation.

Mr. Hugh Gresham, who is working as a missionary of the American Sunday School Union, with headquarters at Trenton, Neb., was instrumental in getting Evangelist Beem to go west. He will assist in the work in many ways.

Good News from the Foreign Field.

The Foreign Society has late and glorious news from our stations as follows: P. A. Davey, Tokio, Japan, reports two baptisms in Ota, and three in Hongo; H. P. Shaw, Shanghai, China, reports

two baptisms; C. E. Benjehr reports three baptisms in Damoh, India; Royal J. Dye reports twenty-two baptisms in Bolengi, Africa; Dr. A. L. Shelton reports seven baptisms at Ta Chien Lu on the borders of Tibet; W. H. Hanna reports twenty-five additions to the church in and around Laoag, province of Luzon, P. I.; H. P. Williams reports another church organized near Tisong, P. I., which church now has ninety-seven members; two new churches were dedicated in the Philippine Islands on September 9, one at Laoag and one at Loreta. The latest word from the Upper Congo, Africa, is as follows: "Chapel crowded yesterday. Twenty-two conversions. Very impressive immersional service afterward in the Congo river. Largest gathering around the Lord's table ever held here. Sunday-school crowded. All rejoice. Dr. Royal J. Dye."

R. O. Rogers.

R. O. Rogers of Fredericktown, Mo., has just held a successful revival meeting at Marshall, Ark. It lasted twelve days and was concluded because of another engagement of the evangelist.

T. J. Arnold, a lawyer of the town, who joined the Christian Church during this meeting writes enthusiastically of it. He says when he first began to attend it, being a member of the Missionary Baptist Church, he went more as a critic and as a spectator, but when the services had concluded he was compelled to say that they had wrought untold good to the town and people and a number of additions had been made to the churches.

St. Louis Simultaneous Campaign.

The interest in the simultaneous campaign held by most of the St. Louis churches has increased rather than shown any diminution. On Lord's day last, the services at all the churches were more largely attended than at any period during the meetings. It is unfortunate that, for local reasons, the meeting at the First Church, where 150 additions were reported under Herbert Yeuell, had to close the middle of last week, and that led by Bro. C. C. Garrigues at the Hammett Place Church had to close on Sunday when the meeting was really but getting under good way, because Brother Garrigues was compelled to return to his own church at Albion, Ill. At Compton Heights W. E. Harlow will conclude a good meeting on Thursday night with his lecture on "The New Thought." The other meetings will continue throughout the week. At Union Avenue Brother Chilton's preaching has had a most inspiring effect. Brother Turner has done good work at Hamilton Avenue, and we should not overlook the fact that Brother McFarland with home forces has had good results at the Fourth Church. We have not received details from some, but it is felt that even had there not been a single addition to the churches this effort has been well worth while.

A mass meeting of the St. Louis Disciples of Christ was held at the Odeon Theatre on Sunday afternoon. W. E. Harlow gave the address and there was special music by the combined choirs and the singing evangelists engaged in the campaign. Without any definite organization the body of the large hall was filled and it is expected that on next Lord's day afternoon, when a similar meeting will be held at the Odeon, the house will be packed to the doors. We can not, at this

As We Go to Press.

As We Go to Press.

Special to THE CHRISTIAN-EVANGELIST.

Kansas City, Mo., November 19.—We began at Forest Avenue yesterday; thirty-seven added first day; great crowds; everybody rejoicing.—H. E. Wilhite and E. C. Tuckerman, evangelists.

Special to THE CHRISTIAN-EVANGELIST.

Union Station, St. Louis, Mo., November 19.—Great day yesterday; big basket dinner; dedicated new church at Orestes, Ind., raising money for entire debt and to pay for new piano. Splendid meeting at Delphia, fifteen baptisms. On our way to Carlisle, Ark.—Clark Family, evangelists.

Special to THE CHRISTIAN-EVANGELIST.

Loraine, O., November 19.—Compelled to go to next meeting. One hundred and four added here in four weeks; nineteen last day. Sebring, O., next.—Violett and Clarkson.

Special to THE CHRISTIAN-EVANGELIST.

Indianapolis, Ind., November 19.—One hundred and thirty-seven additions in Indianapolis yesterday. One thousand to date. J. H. MacNeill spoke to the great union meeting yesterday afternoon.—F. W. Norton.

Special to THE CHRISTIAN-EVANGELIST.

Hamburg, Ia., November 18.—Great crowds and glorious interest. Isaac Elder leads this church as minister. J. E. Lintt is singing some stirring solos. I am preaching the Word. Eighty-eight conversions, fifteen to-night.—W. L. Harris, evangelist.

Special to THE CHRISTIAN-EVANGELIST.

St. Louis, November 19.—Great interest; 439 additions. See details in another column.

Special to THE CHRISTIAN-EVANGELIST.

Kansas City, Mo., Nov. 19.—Two hundred and forty at Independence Boulevard. With Bro. Haley now; church most hopeful of great meeting.—Small and St. John.

writing, say definitely who will be the speaker. The committee is making an effort to get a well known representative of our brotherhood from

Hugh C. Gresham.

outside the city. The following is the report of additions presented at the ministerial meeting on Monday morning:

	Confessions.	Other-wise.	Total to date.
Union Avenue	6	5	58
First	12	8	171
Compton Heights	12	6	72
Hamilton Avenue	2	7	34
Hammett Place	..	..	11
Granite City	3	3	3
Fourth	10	3	42
Second (not in campaign)	..	..	9
Maplewood	..	..	19
East St. Louis	..	..	20
Grand Total			439

NEWS FROM MANY FIELDS

Northwestern Ohio.

While we have a number of pastorless churches we hope we may soon have this problem solved. The work of constructing buildings is keeping with the cause seems to have taken hold on the hearts of our brethren. Bowling Green has a new $25,000 church under roof. Clyde Darsie, the pastor, has accomplished great things at this place.——Then comes the work under way as the church at Paulding, where our brother Myers holds forth; this also is to be a modern building.——At Fayette Brother Elwinger has just dedicated a new wing to the building, and made their building up to date. ——At Wauseon, where C. R. Oakley ministers, they have the plans for a new building and in the early spring a very fine church will be erected, and the South Church of Toledo has paid for an excellent lot where they are going to have a building ready for the Pittsburg Centennial.——Norwood Avenue, secured Brother Finch from Kansas as their preacher. We give him a hearty welcome. We understand that the East Side Church will soon have a pastor and this will fill up the broken ranks in this city.——Grant Speer has decided to remain at Hicksville, as the brethren will not let him go.——Brother Hendershot has had splendid success at Delta. ——I have resigned the work at Central to enter the field as an evangelist. I want to extend to my brethren my sincere thanks for the privileges they have given. I have no doubt made mistakes, but you have in a loyal way supported me.—— I have already received a number of calls. I have with me in my work Robert Knight, who, I think, will prove one of the strongest singing evangelists in the field. I will still remain in Toledo, O., and make it my headquarters. My first meeting will be January 1 at Salem, O.

J. O. Skelburne.

❈ ❈

Chicago Notes.

The month of October was the busiest month of my ministry in Chicago. The national conventions in Buffalo, a trip to Ohio to marry my niece and to spend a day with the dearest woman in the state, my old mother, now in her 76th year; the annual rally of the Chicago Christian Missionary Society, held in Willard Hall on Sunday, October 28, at 3 p. m., with H. L. Willett as chief speaker, and a crowded house full of members of our Chicago churches and missions, with the usual duties that come to me as minister of the West End Church and superintendent of missions, all conspired to give me enough to do to keep me out of mischief. In the Englewood church has just been held the annual business meeting and election of officers of the Chicago Christian Missionary Society. All the old officers were re-elected except a few who refused to permit their names to be voted on. E. M. Bowman was re-elected president and Edward B. Witwer, chairman of the board. At the annual rally the Larrabee fund, sacred to the memory of Brother Albert Larrabee, now deceased, who served the society for many years as superintendent of missions, was, augmented by offerings of nearly $300, of which $100 is to erect a suitable monument above his grave.——West Pullman is whittling down the debt and building up steadily in both church and Bible school. Guy Hoover is pastor.—— Chicago Heights was probably never in so prosperous and promising a condition as under the ministry of Brother Lockhart, and fostered by C. G. Kindred and the great Englewood church. ——Maywood and Humboldt Park are still looking forward to the location of a good preacher to live on the field and give full time to the work. Douglass Park is now enjoying the entire

time of their capable minister, F. C. Aldinger. ——Ernest M. Haile, late of Texas, is, ministering for South Chicago, while pursuing some studies in the university.——W. R. Moffett continues another year at Ashland Avenue, where he is doing a good work.——The West End is trying to be patient with a slow, but, we trust, a permanent growth. Last Lord's day was our best, both in Bible school and church attendance. We dedicate on Sunday, November 25, at 3 p. m., our house of worship recently acquired from the Presbyterians. On that day we expect to raise about $500 to pay off some outstanding obligations, and provide a fund for needed repairs and improvements. Friends are asked to send a contribution for the West End mission, or for the general work in this great city.—— The Monroe Street Church, which has been without regular pastoral care since the resignation of A. T. Campbell, now with the Metropolitan Church, has recalled their former minister, Charles C. Morrison, late of Springfield, Ill.

Sumner T. Martin, Supt. of Missions.

Chicago, Ill.

❈ ❈

Los Angeles Letter.

Southern California churches and preachers are again on the move. J. W. Utter goes from a successful ministry of ten years at Covina to become assistant pastor at the Broadway church, Los Angeles.——W. G. Cauley leaves Redlands after five years' successful work in that beautiful city and succeeds J. W. Utter at Covina. R. H. Bateman has closed his earthly ministry and entered upon his eternal reward. His pulpit at Whittier will be occupied by W. H. Martin, who has just closed a five years' fruitful pastorate at Santa Barbara.——Among the new men who are numbered among us are M. A. Hart, Pomona; E. E. Lowe, San Bernardino; W. T. Adams, Corona; Bailey, Downey; Oscar Sweeney, Rialto; E. C. Riley, assistant pastor at Pasadena, and Dr. A. S. Dabney, Vernon. It is expected that vacancies at Redlands, Santa Barbara, and Santa Ana will be supplied by the time these lines appear in print. Altogether our work in these parts is very prosperous.——The growth of population in southern California is immense. Los Angeles grows as by magic. The postal receipts for September, 1906, was 26 percent greater than for September, 1905. Public school buildings can not be erected fast enough to accommodate this rapidly increasing population.——Lord's day, October 28, was of special interest to the First Christian Church of this city, because on that day we formally dedicated our newly enlarged Sunday-school department. F. M. Rains, of Cincinnati, Ohio, was present and was master of ceremonies. This part of our church property as rebuilt is 76x68 feet in size. In the basement are found a banquet hall, 56 feet square, a boy's brigade room 20x56, with 100 lockers, the kitchen, the furnace room and several robing rooms. On the first floor are found the main Sunday-school room, which is 56 feet square, and built on the Akron plan with 20 class rooms opening into it from the first and second floors. Beside these down stairs there are six other rooms available for classes; the pastor's room, secretary's room, and the Sunday-school auditorium will comfortably seat 800 persons. Upstairs are to be found the ladies' parlors and dining rooms which are very spacious, a buffet kitchen for smaller social events, three class rooms beside those opening into the Sunday-school auditorium and the janitor's apartments of three rooms which are fitted up with every modern convenience. This part of our church property has 35 separate rooms in it and F. M. Rains says it is the most perfect building for Sunday-school work and social purposes that he knows in the brotherhood. The building is carpeted throughout except in the basement. The improvements cost $15,000. Our entire property and improvements are worth at least $80,000. It is our plan this year to lay greater stress than ever upon Sunday-school and

social work. We are convinced that the Sunday-school affords the most promising field for Christian work. It is both missionary and evangelistic and yields greater results for the investment of time and money of any line of church work. Located as we are in what is rapidly becoming the downtown church district of the city we must emphasize the social life of the church. Many are the young men coming to the city who need the friendly grasp of the hand. We shall strive to supply this need. This is an important and neglected line of church work in many of the cities of the country.

Los Angeles, Cal.   A. C. Smither.

❈ ❈ ❈

The Twenty-first Anniversary of Our Oldest C. E. Society.

The twenty-first anniversary of the Christian Endeavor Society of the Boston Church was fitly observed November 7. This is of more than local importance, because this is the oldest society among the Disciples of Christ. On November 3, 1885, under the efficient leadership of J. H. Garrison, who was then pastor of the Boston Church, this society was organized. The charter members were (order of names as they appear on secretary's book): J. H. Garrison, G. Wilton Lewis, Ida M. Marquis (now Mrs. Emery), Maurice Willis, E. M. Potter, George Marquis, Henry Bernard, A. O. Garrison, Mrs. J. H. Garrison, Mrs. E. M. Potter, George B. Howe, William M. Varney, W. E. Garrison. The first president was Maurice Willis; first secretary, Ida M. Marquis; first treasurer, Mrs. J. H. Garrison.

Mrs. Ida Marquis Emery, the first secretary, was present at our anniversary exercises, and read an excellent history of the society. From this I have gleaned some facts. In the beginning the society grew like many others, very rapidly. At the end of the first six months it had reached 42 active members; in 1890, there were 100 active members. For many years the society took first place in the work of the Boston Union. It was also influential in the organization of many other societies. Many students from our churches in the central portion of the country came to this city and coming in touch with this society, on returning to their home churches, began the Christian Endeavor work in them. This society, while not so large as in some former years, is still strong and doing good work.

Three of the charter members, George Marquis, G. Wilton Lewis, and Mrs. Ida Emery, were present and had places on our program. Greetings were read from Bro. J. H. Garrison, Maurice Willis and Mr. and Mrs. E. M. Potter.

The first Christian Endeavor Society in the Boston church sends greetings to all other societies in the brotherhood, praying that "They may all be one as thou Father art in me and I in Thee" and "May the Lord watch between me and thee while we are absent one from the other."

A. L. WARD.

※ ※

Nebraska.

T. B. McDonald has accepted the work at Waco.——Bert Wilson has resigned at Humboldt to take effect January 1. He will re-enter Cotner and will be ready for supply preaching then. He has done a splendid work at Humboldt.—— B. H. Whiston has resigned at Minden and accepted a call to Aurora. The change takes place December 1. The church at Minden has practically rebuilt its house during Brother Whiston's ministry.——Blue Hill has called P. T. Martin, of Nichols, Ia.——E. H. Longman has visited Bradshaw several times, and will very likely be called there regularly as supply.——W. L. Lodwig has been called to supply regularly at Ox Bow and Oak churches.——C. Kleihauer is visiting Dorchester. These young men are all Cotner ministerial students.——F. L. Pettit visited in Kansas recently and held a memorial service for an aged member of the Auburn church. There have been five confessions at Auburn since the last report. W. Mark Sexson is there in a meeting.——E. D. Eubank, of Broken Bow, preaches regularly for the Liberty church near Ansley. State Evangelist Adams will hold a meeting there in December.——Two confessions at Overton where C. F. Martin preaches. Will hold a meeting the present month.——The church at Grand Island, where J. R. McIntire ministers, gave a reception to the faculty and students of the business college, which was a decided success. During the seven months of Brother McIntire's ministry 35 additions. Some lingering debts were cleared up.——The Putman-Egbert meeting at Clay Center, where A. G. Smith preached, closed with thirty-five added, most of them from new homes, and a goodly number of men.——State Evangelist Whiston (Harvard special evangelist) closed the Norfolk meeting with seventeen added. The church will begin to build as soon as possible. John L. Stine preaches for the church half time, living at Wakefield.——State Evangelist E. von Forell (Clay Center special evangelist), held his first meeting at Vesta. There were six additions.——Brother and Sister Whiston are now at Guide Rock. He holds an independent meeting at Humboldt when through there.——State Evangelist O. A. Adams (Oberlie's special evangelist), has just closed a meeting at Mason City, resulting in an organization of thirty-three members.——Samuel Gregg began a meeting at Cerad, where H. F. Stevens is minister, October 21. He takes work at Fremont December 1. We give Brother Gregg a welcome to the state again.—— Kearney began a meeting with Putman and Egbert October 28. F. D. Hobson is the preacher there.——R. A. Schell is in a meeting with home forces at Hastings.——Two confessions at York, where Thomas Maxwell ministers, October 21.—— The church at Nelson liquidated all indebtedness in an offering taken October 7, and will make repairs on the building. There were two con-

fessions and one added otherwise on same date. The Ladies' Aid Society provided the funds to send their pastor, F. E. Day, to the national convention at Buffalo.——A county convention in Nuckolls county has been organized with F. E. Day as president.——A letter from S. D. Dutcher says that the First Church at Omaha is closing up contracts for its new building on Twenty-sixth and Harney streets. This will be a fine structure when completed, a credit to the city and state.——Nineteen people were added to the church at Blair, where F. Grant Hamm ministers, in the first half of October. Part of these the result of a union meeting. Brother Hamm has been called indefinitely and evidently he has been indefinitely called to a closer relationship with some good woman, as he reports that "Wife and

I received a good old-fashioned pounding Tuesday evening."——Knox P. Taylor held a Bible school institute at Belvidere. L. B. Cox is the preacher.——The church at Edison recently dedicated a new church costing about $3,000. J. Stuart Miller is the minister. This is a magnificent achievement for a small congregation. Brother Miller will hold a meeting at Bloomington.—— Gordon Lintt has entered the field as a singing evangelist, beginning at Mount Pleasant, Ia. Brother Lintt is a brother of W. F. Lintt.—— The Christian Endeavorers of the state sent State Superintendent Doward to the Buffalo convention.   W. A. BALDWIN.

※ ※

Send for our Holiday Catalogue.

CHRISTIAN PUBLISHING CO.,

St. Louis, Mo.

Oregon.

With October evangelistic work in Oregon begins in earnest and many of the churches have perfected their plans for the year's campaign for souls. As a rule, the churches will do their best to help the O. C. M. C. to realize the motto "2,000 souls for Christ and $6,000 for Oregon missions," by Turner, 1907.——During October I had the privilege of visiting most of the churches of eastern Oregon and attended the conventions of the central and northwest districts. That of the central has already been reported. The convention of the northwest district was the equal in every way of the Albany gathering. "The Field," "The Forces" and "The Obstacles," were some of the main questions considered in the convention.—As a result of this gathering G. C. Ritchey becomes evangelist for the district, opening his term of service with a meeting at Tillamook, where Brother Zimmerman is serving as missionary pastor.——The success of this convention was, in no small degree, due to the untiring energy of C. F. Swander and the hospitality of the McMinnville church. E. S. Muckley is the efficient leader of the work in this district and was chosen to succeed himself as its president.—— This district and the northeast have the distinction of having the only living link churches in the state. Portland, first, is a "living link" in the F. C. M. S. and Athena in the A. C. M. S. It would be a fine thing for some of the other Oregon churches to "go and do likewise."—— Now, brethren, may we not have a great gathering for Oregon missions during the first weeks of November, and have all "Debt Fund" pledges paid in before the first of the new year?—— Every Bible school in Oregon should send in a worthy offering the day following "Children's day for American Missions," November 25.
F. E. BILLINGTON, Cor. Sec. O. C. M. C.
Cottage Grove.

Oklahoma Christian University.

The Board of Trustees of this new institution, after careful discussion, decided to undertake the establishment of a general school or university. Enid, Oklahoma, was selected as the place for the location of the school. Determining factors were its natural and its superior railroad advantages, the flourishing condition of the city, and that the population is comparatively dense and the people prosperous and able to furnish a large local patronage.——The fact that we have a flourishing local church, and the further fact that our churches throughout the surrounding country are very numerous had great weight. We think that it will be possible for ministerial students to run out on Saturday to as many as two hundred churches and get back for work on Monday. The advantages Enid offers for student preaching are better than those offered by any other location in the new state, and Enid's bid for the school was the best proposition: One hundred 4-year scholarships at $200 each, $20,000. Two hundred one-year preparatory scholarships at $40 each, $8,000; one hundred music scholarships at $50 each, $5,000; water privilege for five years, worth at least $1,000; electric lights at Very much reduced rates, making it unnecessary for us to install our own plant; streets to be paved with asphalt and the promise to soon extend the pavement to the college campus; cars to run past the college campus, giving us a fifteen minute service; the city sewer or an independent sewer brought to our building at an estimated cost of $5,000. We also have the privilege of selling off twenty acres of our campus whenever we think it wise to do so, provided we invest the money in buildings and equipment. We estimate that this will be worth to us at least $0,000. The full value of Enid's bid, therefore, appears to be upwards of $150,000, allowing for the probable increase in the value of our land within the next two years. Option was also taken f r us on 160 acres of fine land within one-fourth mile of the college campus, at $12,000. This option has now been taken up and the farm secured, which will enable us to start an industrial department.

Our board required the city of Enid to put up a satisfactory guarantee for the payment of the cash bonus. We are proceeding at once with our plans for buildings, and we hope to be able to break ground not later than December 1. If we carry out the plans that we have in mind, we will have one of the finest educational plants in the new state. The next problem that we have on our hands after the erection of buildings, is to secure an adequate endowment for this great school. The aim will be to have the buildings ready for occupancy by September, 1907. The music department of the school will be opened at once in rented rooms, inasmuch as there is a strong local demand.

I will make my home in Enid from this time forward, and all correspondence may be addressed to me at that place.
E. V. ZOLLARS,
President Oklahoma Christian University.

North Carolina.

The North Carolina State Convention was held in the town of Dunn. The church there is comparatively young, but entertained the convention in a splendid manner. Dunn is on the outer rim of Disciple population in North Carolina. The strength of the brotherhood is in the Eastern counties. It was of the nature of an experiment to hold the convention with one of the frontier churches, but the attendance was good and the Convention itself several degrees better than any I have attended. The report of the Corresponding Secretary showed a considerable advance. Nearly four thousand dollars were raised from all sources. Three new churches were organized, and a fourth in embryo. An evangelist was sustained during the summer months and assistance was given, to a number of struggling churches.——The C. W. B. M. held its sessions the first day of the convention. Mrs. J. B. Jones has been the president for four years and has infused considerable vigor into the Women's work. This year the state officers are located at Kinston. The officers are, President, Mrs. Preston Bell Hall; Vice-President, Mrs. J. W. Granger; Recording Secretary, Mrs. J. F. Taylor; Treasurer, Mrs. W. B. Brown. Miss Bettie Tesh, of Winston-Salem, was chosen as Corresponding Secretary and organizer. The advisory members of the State Board are Mrs. N. J. Rouse, Mrs. M. E. Moseley, Mrs. Sarah E. Askew, Mrs. Julia Barrett and Mrs. R. F. Hill.——Dr. Longdon, of India, made a most interesting address as a fitting close of the C. W. B. M. day. Everybody was delighted with her. It was a rare treat for the people of this state to hear a consecrated missionary. It seems to bring the foreign fields nearer to our doors and but increase the interest in missions.——My fourth year with the church in Kinston has just closed. We have a unanimous call to remain. Our work has been successful and pleasant. The church has been strengthened in additions and in spiritual power. The ideal of worship has been advanced, and a continuous effort has been made by the pastor to get the church to realize its mission as a force for saving souls. This church is awake to all the interests of missions and benevolence. The Sunday School has vitality, system and order. The Christian Endeavor has enlisted a large number of young people and is doing a fine work. The prayer meetings are always interesting, but not largely attended. The prayer meeting is the pastor's cross. If, as some say, the prayer meeting is the gauge of the church's spirituality, then, alas! for the condition of most churches.——Our country churches in Eastern North Carolina have made their annual changes. This is a habit they have which has become a second nature. These churches seem to be content with one sermon a month and a week's prayer meeting in the summer time. Some of these have Sunday Schools, none have the Lord's Supper except on the preaching day. These churches are not grouped, each getting a pastor to its own taste, and the taste seems to get bitter or sour or both before a year ends. No preacher for the country churches is doing

much pastoral work. In many instances he is engaged in farming or some business or other. The churches are not progressive, and as the bulk of Disciples are in country churches and small towns, the State Work has never been aggressive. The belt of eastern churches does not extend much above the tide-water, and like the tide they ebb and flow, rising to some enthusiasm under a strong stimulus, but subsiding when the stimulus is removed.——I am very much pleased with THE CHRISTIAN-EVANGELIST. There are 20 copies coming to members of my congregation, and all like it very much. When I came here only one copy was received. I am glad to induce anyone to subscribe for THE CHRISTIAN-EVANGELIST, for I believe to be on the right course and desire to extend its influence. PRESTON BELL HALL.
Kinston, N. C.

Portland City Missions.

On September 16 I began work as Evangelist and superintendent of City Missions for the joint board of the Churches in Portland, Oregon, and the O. C. M. C. and A. C. M. S. Our first effort was a tent meeting at the rapidly growing center of St. Johns. The meeting lasted six weeks, with 35 additions, and I have the names and addresses of 26 more who are members of Christian churches, and who expect to come into the organization. There are others who have grown so cold and indifferent that they do not consider themselves members, and still others who have placed their membership with the denominational churches. During the six weeks, it rained almost continually, and the tent blew down several times.——The City Mission problem will be largely solved when our people realize, that, in order to enter a section of the city, it will be necessary to erect a splendid tabernacle building, for temporary use, such as the central church is now using, and the one that was erected where Brother Brooks is now holding a meeting at the very important field of Woodlawn.——There are now five congregations in the city of Portland, with a population of about 180,000. These churches will take an offering for city missions on the last Sunday in November, and it is hoped that at that time we will have a large offering, and plan for larger things in the city mission work.——The city mission committee held a meeting to-day, and decided that I should remain with, and take care of the young church at St. Johns, until a suitable man is secured for the work. It is the purpose of this board to plant a church, and to take care of it in every locality where a meeting is held this year. J. PERRY CONDER.

Victor Dorris at Springfield.

We have just closed at the West Side Christian Church, one of the most successful meetings ever held in Springfield, Ill., and, perhaps, the most successful ever held in the West Side Church. Of this we judge not by the number of accessions, of which there were eighty-one, but by the general impression made on the community and the church. However, when we take into consideration the fact that the church is located not among the unchurched masses, but among a people, with few exceptions, already churched, the results, in point of additions, were very satisfactory. These meetings were conducted by Victor W. Dorris, of Pendleton, Oregon, assisted by Chas. H. Altheide, of Bloomfield, Iowa, as director of music. Perhaps as high a compliment as I can pay Mr. Altheide would be to say that this was the third time within a year that he has been called to Springfield for such service, and the second time to the West Side Church.
Victor Dorris is quite well known, but as very little has appeared in print respecting his

Stockholders' Meeting.

Notice is hereby given that the annual meeting of the stockholders of the Christian Publishing Company will be held at the company's office, 2712 Pine street, St. Louis, Mo., Tuesday, January 1, 1907, at 10 o'clock, for the election of directors and for the transaction of such other business as may legally come before said meeting.
J. H. GARRISON, Pres.
GEO. L. SNIVELY, Sec.
St. Louis, Nov. 15, 1906.

---

work here or elsewhere, I feel inclined to say a word. His work was all that could be desired. He believes that the plea made by the fathers is the plea for the twentieth century. He never hesitated to preach the whole truth of God with respect to the sin of divisions and necessity for Christian union. I am quite sure that our pulpits would have a stronger hold upon the people to-day, and there would be less falling away after a great meeting, if sermons abounded more in instructions on the elementary principles of redemption. In this line of work Victor Dorris is a "professional"—that is, he knows the Book and preaches its doctrines with rare ability. Not a single sensational theme was announced throughout the entire series, yet the audiences were unparalleled in the history of the congregation. The West Side Church will be five years old January 1. In that time almost 700 have entered into the fellowship of the congregation. Our membership now is about 600. At present I am alone in our work in the city, but expect to be joined shortly by C. C. Sinclair, who comes to the Stuart Street Church December 2, and by Hugh McLellan, of Richmond, Ky., who comes to the First Church January 1; 1907. F. M. ROGERS.

Paxton's Meeting.

The Paxton (Ill.) church has been a problem for years. I came here as pastor in January, 1905. A reorganization was necessary. We reorganized the following September. Since then the church has prospered. The church is now respected and we have a place in the city. On October 14 Bros. H. A. Davis and Frank Charlton came to assist us in a three weeks' meeting. Both are Christian gentlemen and capable. This is not a great field. More than half of the population is Swedish. The church is only a year from the old organization. All of these things prevented a large ingathering. The church was strengthened and spiritualized and we are now better understood in the city. Thirty-eight had been added at regular services during the year. Twenty-three were added during the meeting.

Every department of the church was strengthened. The meeting closed with the largest audience and greatest service in the history of the church. Considering the field and the history of the church this was a great meeting.
M. L. PONTIUS.

"A True Revival."

We have just had a true revival of religion— the Christian religion—as the lamented L. B. Wilkes would say. Bro. H. D. Smith, of Hopkinsville, Kentucky, did the preaching. It is the universal opinion that his services were among the best ever heard in this town, where many able and distinguished men have preached. The pastors and many members of other churches joined in the services. The preaching, in thought, in spirit, and in expression, was all that could be desired. In fact the sermons were an education on many of the most vital themes of our holy religion. Just before the meeting began Mrs. Princess Long came and gave one of her inimitable recitals which did good like a revival meeting. It was our only regret that she could not remain and lead our singing after she had made such a deep and lasting impression. Seven choice spirits were received into the fellowship of the church during the meeting.
N. M. RAGLAND.
Fayetteville, Ark.

Why the Quarter-Century Christian Endeavor Memorial?

By William Shaw, Treasurer of the United Society of Christian Endeavor.

Because the object is a worthy one, and the United Society is entitled to it. I speak in no spirit of boasting, but with keen appreciation of the great things God hath wrought, and the small part men have had in the wonderful growth of Christian Endeavor.

Dr. Philip Schaff said on the platform of the great New York Christian Endeavor convention in 1892, "The historian of the nineteenth century will rank the Christian Endeavor movement as one of the greatest, if not the greatest movement in the history of the church."

Twenty-five years ago one society, to-day 67,800; then fifty members, to-day 3,500,000; then in one city, now in every country in the world; then in one denomination, now in sixty; then literature in one language, now in eighty; then in one church, now in scores of thousands of churches, missions, schools, hospitals, prisons, in the army and the navy, anywhere, everywhere that people need to know of the love of Christ.

Twenty-five years ago treated with distrust and suspicion, criticised and misunderstood; to-day praised by men high in affairs of church and state, at home and abroad, with a following as loyal as ever espoused a sacred cause.

These twenty-five years have witnessed the rallying of young men and women in unparalleled numbers in personal devotion to Christ and his church; in missionary work, both in going and giving (ten thousand societies in five years having given $2,187,000); in their interest in Christian citizenship, temperance and all moral reforms; in Christian fellowship, which is so marked a feature in the religious life of to-day, and in the promotion of international brotherhood among the young people of all nations.

During the years of theological unrest and readjustment through which our churches passed, and which witnessed great spiritual dearth and death, Christian Endeavor stood for faith in Christ and service for Christ, having confidence that if we would do his will, we should know of the doctrine.

It is giving to our churches, as fast as they make a place of service for them, young people trained to do things by doing them, trained in the church, for the church, and only outside the church when driven by opposition or lack of sympathy and wise leadership.

As to the future, we count not ourselves to have already attained, but we press toward the mark.

For seventeen years the United Society has carried the burden of extending the movement in all parts of this country and largely around the world, without soliciting or receiving a dollar from any society or individual. With the ever-broadening work expenses have increased, and new doors of opportunity have been opened.

Shall the future be more full of blessing to the young people of the world than the past has been? Your answer will be measured by your contribution to the Quarter-Century Christian Endeavor Memorial Fund, which is to be invested in an international headquarters building as a memorial of our first twenty-five years. This is to be no useless monument to a man, but an added equipment for service to the movement, so that Christian Endeavor may do a still larger work for Christ, and the church of the future.

Every society should give its members a chance to contribute. Every friend of the young people should have a generous share in this fund. Millions are given for the training of young people in secular studies. Here is your chance to invest in the training of young people in all lands for all times in religious life and practical service.

Let men of means join with the young people in generous gifts, that the resources of the society may be equal to the demands made upon it, and that gratitude for the past may be expressed not simply in words but in deeds and dollars as well.

※ ※

Georgia Notes.

Chas. E. Smith, state evangelist of South Carolina, writing from Wagner, says: "We recently organized a new congregation at Brunson with 29 charter members of the very best people of that thriving town. A tent meeting here at a brand new point with the finest interest and attention we ever had. It is too early to tell what can be done. There is not a 'Christian only' in the whole place, but the brethren come from Merritt's Bridge, ten to fifteen miles away." The report indicates that a denominational preacher there has misrepresented us.—Sectarianism in many places of our southland is still as far from the spirit of Christ as it is from the truth. Many sectarians have yet to learn that sectarianism does not make Christians and is not a part of Christianity. They thank God for divisions among God's people, but when preachers of another church go into their territory to establish a church they smell heresy and go about warning the people against "the new doctrine" and telling them to "stick to your bush" and let this "new thing" alone. But the truth told in love and practiced in daily life will prevail.—

T. F. Jones, of Newman, sent me the money to renew his subscription and said: "I am well pleased with our new paper." Brother Jones knows a good thing when he sees it. The weekly visits of this great paper will prove a blessing to any home. "Southern Evangelist" readers will soon become attached to THE CHRISTIAN-EVANGELIST and then the paper will come to our homes as a dear friend. In addition to the strong editorials and the news from many fields, the Sunday-school, prayer-meeting and Christian Endeavor come in for their share and assist us in these departments. Then if you try the Sunday-school literature gotten out by this paper, you will be perfectly delighted. So I consider that we are well fixed with our new paper and, like Brother Jones, I am well pleased with it. Convention news next week.   E. L. SKELLNUT.
187 Edgewood Avenue, Atlanta, Ga.

※ ※

Oregon S. W. District Convention.

The first annual convention of the Southwest District of the O. C. M. C. has held a most enthusiastic series of services at Roseburg. Plans for the year were formulated and heartily endorsed. It is hoped a "Dollar League" may be formed in all the churches, the proceeds of which shall support an evangelist in the district, which comprises Douglas, Coos, Curry, Josephine and Jackson counties. Reports show a good missionary interest and excellent work done by the churches. Officers for the current year chosen, were: B. E. Youtz, Roseburg, superintendent; Clark Bower, Grant's Pass, vice-superintendent; Frank

E. Alley, Roseburg, secretary and treasurer; F. E. Billington, our model corresponding-secretary; sister G. S. O. Humbert, C. W. B. M. president; and sister Clara G. Esson, Bible school superintendent. Each added greatly to the interest of the sessions by stirring addresses.   B. E. Youtz.
Roseburg, Ore.   Sec. of Convention.

Evangelistic

We invite ministers and others to send reports of meetings, additions and other news of the churches. It is especially requested that additions be reported as "by confession and baptism," or "by letter."

Arkansas.

Prescott, Nov. 10.—Closed the best meeting the church ever had here, last Wednesday night, with ten additions.—Percy G. Cross.

Siloam Springs, Nov. 1.—Just closed a two and half weeks' meeting here with 30 baptisms. Charles D. Purlee is the minister. Edward O. Beyer had charge of the music. We go next to Broadway church, Pueblo, Col.—John W. Marshall.

California.

Ventura, Nov. 13.—Three additions last Lord's day. Work growing nicely.—Dan Trundle.

San Francisco, Nov. 12.—One by baptism and by statement and letter the past week. Our opportunity here at West Side is appollingly great. Growth in all things increasing.—Robert Lord Cave.

Colorado.

Salida, Nov. 12.—Six added yesterday—5 baptisms; 83 in last three and one-half weeks.—W. B. Crewdson.

Illinois.

Greenville, Oct. 29.—Two additions at regular services yesterday.—Tally Defrees.

Maroa, Nov. 15.—Two baptized last night. Two added by letter recently.—W. H. Applegate.

Berlin, Nov. 12.—Meeting of three weeks closed last night. Nineteen additions. J. T. H. Stewart, Georgetown, Ill., helped nine days.—J. W. Bolton.

Rossville, Nov. 16.—One addition last Sunday. We are preparing for a meeting in February. Mrs. J. E. Powell will assist as singing evangelist.—William Grant Smith.

Alton, Nov. 16.—One addition by letter last Sunday night, one by statement two weeks ago. The attendance is growing with each service.—G. Washington Wise.

Nebo, Nov. 6.—Closed a two-weeks meeting here with 10 additions—9 baptisms and 1 restored. This is a good, loyal people but they need a minister.—J. D. Williams.

Waynesville, Nov. 12.—Fourteen added here in first week of meeting with J. A. Barnett, of Freeport, as evangelist, and has Mattie Bowles, of Ernden, as leader of song.—J. F. Smith, pastor.

Lincoln, Nov. 16.—William J. Lockhart and W. E. M. Hackleman have just closed a four-weeks meeting here which brought 76 people into the church—53 were by confession. Following so close upon the great meeting of Wilson and Lintt, our people regard this as another great victory.—W. H. Cannon.

Barry.—Closed a three-weeks meeting at Barry November 11. J. D. Dabney of Pittsburg, Pa., did the preaching. There were 23 additions—21 baptisms. This makes 58 additions since the beginning of the year—45 baptisms.—C. B. Dabney, pastor.

Allendale, Nov. 12.—A most excellent meeting of two weeks closed here last night, with 23 added, and the church greatly revived. J. W. Kilhorn, minister at Mt. Carmel, Ill., did the preaching. We have now the strongest church in town, and we have resolved to go forward to greater victories.—W. L. Morris, minister.

Charleston, Nov. 14.—Evangelists Davis and Chariton are in a good meeting with the First Christian Church here. Six additions to date. Prospects bright.—George H. Brown, pastor.

Irving, Nov. 12.—Closed a nineteen-days meeting with J. A. Mason, pastor, at Pleasant Hill, a country church in Edvar county, with 57 added—37 by confession and baptism and 20 by letter and restoration.—L. Hadaway.

Indiana.

Atlanta, Oct. 29.—Four added.—E. D. Long.

Driftwood, Nov. 12.—A nineteen-days meeting at this place last Sunday night, resulting in 19 additions, all by baptism except one.—Addison Willard Crabb.

Indianapolis, Nov. 15.—There have been 101 added in our meeting at the Sixth Church. Brother McLean is the evangelist. A. L. Orcutt is the minister.—Charles E. McVay, song evangelist.

Wabash, Nov. 13.—I recently closed a short meeting at Liston, Ind. There were 7 accessions—6 by confession and baptism and 1 from another religious body. Brother Alford is the pastor.—L. L. Carpenter.

Salem, Nov. 15.—The church at Salem has recently enjoyed a great meeting conducted by Evangelist J. V. Coombs and J. Walter Wilson. There were sixty-nine accessions to the church.—W. Y. Allen.

Flora, Nov. 11.—Closed a three-weeks meet-

ing with home forces, which resulted in 11 additions—5 by confession and baptism, 4 by letter, and 2 from other religious bodies. Church is left in fine condition.—A. B. Houze.

Indian Territory.

Tulsa, Nov. 12.—Two additions by letter and 2 by baptism yesterday.—Randolph Cook.

Sapulpa, Nov. 16.—Two additions since last report. All departments of the work in splendid condition.—A. M. Harral.

Miami.—John A. Brown, of Moline, Kan., conducted a sixteen days' meeting, which resulted in 23 additions.—Thomas J. Giddens, Oswego, Kan.

Iowa.

Richland, Nov. 6.—We are just beginning a meeting here. Frank Robey, of Drake University, is assisting in the singing and personal work. We go to Kentucky for our next meeting.—Lawrence Wright.

Des Moines, Nov. 12.—We are in a meeting now seven days old, the local minister conducting. Frank A. Wilkinson leads the singing. Ten additions to date, with many interested.—F. D. Macy.

Mount Pleasant, Nov. 17.—Large and enthusiastic audiences every evening. G. P. Lintt, evangelistic singer, of Lincoln, Neb., is assisting. Additions at nearly every service. Will continue one or two weeks longer.—L. A. Chapman.

Prairie City, Nov. 15.—W. E. Pitcher, of Blackton, Ia., assisted us in a three-weeks meeting, which closed last night, resulting in 19 additions—13 by baptism and 6 by statement. There had been 7 additions—2 by baptism—before the meeting, not reported.—C. H. Strawn.

North English, Nov. 15.—We closed a very successful three-weeks meeting at our country church, White Pigeon, on November 11, with 12 additions—11 by confession and baptism. The pastor did the preaching and was assisted by Mrs. J. H. Davis, of Oskaloosa, Ia., as leader of song.—J. C. Hanna, pastor.

Kansas.

Holsington, Nov. 12.—Three made the good confession November 11. Two of them were baptized.—F. M. McHale.

Wonsevu.—Closed my meeting with a crowded house. Four confessions, three baptized.—J. M. Cockrill.

Peru, Nov. 14.—Meeting here starts well, with large audiences, and the best of attention. Fourteen additions the first week. F. M. O'Neal and wife, of Springfield, Mo., are leading the singing.—J. F. Haner, evangelist.

Arkansas City, Nov. 12.—Great meeting in progress. Twelve added yesterday, 94 in seventeen days. Crowds every night. J. B. Boen is the evangelist.—M. Lee Sorey, minister.

Halstead, Nov. 12.—Began meeting here yesterday. Preparations perfect. H. W. Nicholson is the minister. Great audiences to start with.—M. B. Ingle, evangelist.

Kentucky.

Jackson, Nov. 12.—Four additions at regular services this last week—one baptism.—W. J. Dodge.

Missouri.

Kansas City, Nov. 15.—Prospects good for fine meeting. Fifty-five to date.—J. J. Morgan.

Brunswick, Nov. 11.—One baptized last night. Begin gospel meetings to-night at DeWitt.—E. H. Williamson, pastor.

Weston, Nov. 16.—Just closed a splendid meeting at Salem, Platte County, with 31 accessions—27 baptisms.—J. C. Howell.

Richland, Nov. 14.—I held a three weeks' meeting with the Mountain View Church resulting in three confessions and one added by statement.—George Thomas Smith.

Kansas City.—Four added—9 by confession and 1 by letter at Hyde Park Church.—S. S. Cupp.

Brazmer, Nov. 13.—Have baptized 5 since last report.—S. W. Crutcher.

Troy, Nov. 12.—Two additions at Elsberry Sunday—1 by confession and baptism and 1 by letter; 18 in the past ten months at the regular services.—E. G. Merrill.

St. Joseph, Nov. 12.—The Mitchell Park congregation has just closed a very successful revival. T. H. Capp, of Plattsburg, Mo., did the preaching. There were 38 additions, with 29 baptisms.—C. A. Lowe, pastor.

St. Joseph, Nov. 15.—One by letter last evening at the regular service, at Frederick Avenue Church. Church is in good order. Just closed a three weeks' meeting. Cassius V. Allison, of Mound City, Mo., did the efficient preaching.—William M. Thomas, pastor.

Warrensburg, Nov. 12.—Closed a meeting at Knobnoster last night with 20 additions—13 by confession, 3 by statement and 4 from other religious bodies. My brother, Phil L. Stark, is

pastor of the church, and conducted the music.—King Stark.

Canton, Nov. 14.—We closed a fifteen-days meeting at New Galilee, Lincoln county, last night, which resulted in 30 additions—24 confessions and baptisms, 3 from other religious bodies and 3 reclaimed. Oscar Marxs conducted the singing. Two added at Neeper since last report.—E. W. Carr, minister.

Nebraska.

Pawnee City, Nov. 15.—C. A. Freer, of Plainville, Ohio, lately closed a four weeks' meeting here. There were seven baptisms, all audiences through the whole meeting.—G. M. Weimer, pastor.

Stratton, Nov. 12.—Stratton meeting continued apart distance in country. Twenty-nine added in thirteen days—21 confessions. Cornell next.—James S. Beem and George Light.

Kearney,—Fifteen additions to date in a meeting a little more than a week old—6 by statement, 9 by confession. Melvin Putman is doing the preaching and is assisted by Miss Emma Egbert as singer. Meetings to continue indefinitely.—F. D. Hobson, pastor.

New Mexico.

Roswell, Nov. 12.—Three confessions yesterday at regular services—17 since Oct. 1.—C. C. Hill.

New York.

Niagara Falls, Nov. 13.—Four confessions in the last two Lord's days at regular services. One added by letter from another religious body.—J. A. Wharton.

Ohio.

Athens, Nov. 12.—Two baptisms last week. We begin a meeting with James Small in December. Outlook fine.—T. L. Lowe.

Norwood, Nov. 12.—Walter M. White, of Lexington, Ky., closed his meeting with us Sunday night, with 34 added—16 by confession.—Joseph Armistead, minister.

Oregon.

Aumsville, Nov. 8.—Just closed a meeting at Pleasant Hill with 44 additions. M. F. Horn is the efficient minister at that charge.—J. N. McConnell, evangelist.

Tillamook, Nov. 12.—Meeting eight days old, with 6 additions—two by confessions, 3 by statement and 1 from another religious body. Large chorus, great crowds and intense interest. Continue indefinitely.—Kitchey and Shaffer.

Pennsylvania.

California, Nov. 12.—We are expecting to begin a revival November 25. Will secure the assistance of a chorus leader.—Thomas Martin.

Philippine Islands.

Laoag, Oct. 8.—During August a new church was established in Claveria, with 17 members. During September 24 were baptized in Laoag, and 25 reported from other points in Ilocos Norte.—W. H. Hanna.

Tennessee.

Nashville.—Twelve additions at Vine Street Church to-day—6 by confession and 6 by letter, making about 40 additions in the past six weeks, during the temporary pastorate of Brother McKissock. He begins a protracted effort to-day. Three baptisms last evening.—W. G. Menninger.

West Virginia.

New Cumberland, Nov. 12.—W. S. Hoye, of Beaver Creek, Md., closed a two-weeks meeting here November 6, which resulted in 8 additions—4 by baptism and 4 otherwise. Much good was done.—Charles C. Cowgill, minister.

Texas.

Abilene, Nov. 16.—Five added at Abilene since last report.—Granville Snell.

❦ ❦

Send for our Holiday Catalogue.

CHRISTIAN PUBLISHING CO.,
St. Louis, Mo.

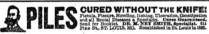

THANKSGIVING AND SERVICE.—

Ps. 116:12-19.

"What shall I render to my God
For all his kindness shown?
My feet shall visit thine abode,
My songs address thy throne.

"Among the saints that fill thy house,
My offerings shall be paid;
There shall my zeal perform the vows
My soul in anguish made.

"How happy all thy servants are,
How great thy grace to me!
My life, which thou hast made thy care,
Lord, I devote to thee."

One of the highest and most acceptable forms of service we can render to God is the dedication of ourselves to him—sanctified from sin and by education, culture and training nobly equipped for helping him usher in an age-long era of the ought to be. This ideal is fondly submitted to the prayerful consideration of all, and especially of our youth who may have decades of life to give him.

There is no thanksgiving apart from service. All that made worship of David's protestations of love for God and his frequent recitals of the Lord's goodness to him was their harmony with his love for God expressed by his earnestly striving to better the condition of Israel, to make of the people loyal and happy sons and daughters of the great King and to exemplify in his own life the dignity and grace of "a friend of God."

Brethren, it is not a question to-night of what returns China and Japan ought to make unto Jehovah for the emancipation from the furies of superstition he is marvelously effecting in them; of what our neighbor ought to give and do for the grace bestowed on them, nor of what we intend sometime to be for our own life-long blessings, but of what *we* shall do and give and be right now and henceforth. The summer is passing, soon harvest will be ended, the night is at hand and for us all is done or will be left forever undone.

The drops of praise we would have wafted up to God to-morrow are not sufficient returns for the great rivers of mercy everywhere flowing around us. Because of the great abundance of his kindnesses to us we ought to do infinitely more than we have to inaugurate his kingdom and make all our Father's children happy. Hezekiah's condemnation was that he returned not unto the Lord according to the kindness done unto him. Were we to stand in our houses and throw stones at the old king, doubtless we would hear the glass shiver.

Have we all done what we could to give all a generous share in the present era of material prosperity obtaining in our country? Land owners, money lenders, artisans, tradesmen, miners, railroad employes and all these crafts and clans are reveling in abundance. Little, if anything, has been done, however, to increase the compensation of clerks, land tenants, ministers, teachers, stenographers, house servants and unskilled laborers. Here is a new challenge to chivalry. It is ours to create a sentiment and to precipitate action that will result in a fairer distribution of the milk and honey with which our land is overflowing.

Millions of people will to-morrow rejoice in the amenities of home-coming and family reunions with their retold vows of love and helpfulness along the pilgrimage of life.

Many will not pause to thank the Founder of homes and the Preserver of their sanctities. Such homes as America knows are the direct gift of God through the church. But thanks to him for our homes and all the sweet privileges with which they are freighted will rise no higher than our roof tree unless we earnestly labor for the extension of a home-founding Christianity throughout the earth, and unless we try to make of every earthly home a beautiful type of the heavenly home beyond.

❀ ❀

Greek and Latin by Mail.

You can take the Normal, Classical or Bible course, leading to degrees, on the Home Study Plan. Catalogue free. Write Pres. Chas. J. Burton, Christian College, Oskaloosa, Iowa.

Christian Endeavor

By GEO. L. SNIVELY

December 2, 1906.

COURAGE OR COWARDICE—WHICH?—Luke 12:4, 5; Gal. 1:9-12; Jer. 1:6-10, 17.

(*Consecration Meeting.*)

DAILY READINGS.

M. Some Brave Spies.	Num. 14:6-10.
T. A Brave Leader.	Josh. 10:22-27.
W. A Brave Minister.	Deut. 6:7-10.
T. A Brave Queen.	Esther 5:1-14.
F. A Brave King.	Isa. 37:1-14.
S. A True Patriot.	Ezra 10:1-8.
S. A Brave Apostle.	Acts 28:11-15.

"What shall I do to gain eternal life?
  Discharge aright
The simple dues with which each day is rife?
  Yea with thy might.
Ere perfect scheme of action thou devise,
  Will life be fled,
While he who ever acts as conscience cries
  Shall live, though dead.—*Schuller.*

Fear is not necessarily ignoble. To fear God is one of the surest prophecies of glory and immortality. This fear really overcomes cowardice of men and evil spirits, of death and the grave, of resurrection and the judgment.

Courage is a higher quality than fearlessness. One soldier noticing another's blanched face, contemptuously said, "you must be afraid." "Yes," was the reply. "If you were as afraid as I, you would run away." Courage is that expression of nobility that holds one to his post and his principles in spite of his fears.

The writer once caught a bucket swinging from a windlass and was lowered hundreds of feet into a Cripple Creek mine for fear the miners would regard him as a very "tender foot" indeed. He manifested no bravery—simply indicated his lesser fear. It often requires more courage to descend than to rise, to sit than to stand, withhold than to give, to be silent than to speak, to retreat than to battle, to live than to die.

Joshua and Caleb were not blinded to the giants or other physical difficulties in the way of the conquest of Canaan, but they knew the Lord was mightier than they all. This sentiment made them invincible. If the Lord delight in us then will he bring us into this land which floweth with milk and honey. Only rebel not ye against the Lord, neither fear ye the people of the land; their defense is departed from them and the Lord is with us; fear them not. They may have shuddered at thought of the struggle and carnage, but that moral courage born of unfaltering trust enabled them to see Israel prosperous, happy and the religious light of the world after the ordeal was over and the victory won.

The pioneer who surrenders his just claim because lacking in physical powers or courage to hold it against the intrusions of others is not nearly so cowardly as the man who will equivocate or dissemble and thus relinquish a high moral or spiritual estate because the latter has more appealing to him to be brave, he ignobly surrenders infinitely more, he is the greater traitor to right and God.

Just to the extent of one's cowardice goes his practical atheism. Elisha's miracle of opening the eyes of his servant to the vision of a mountain full of horses and chariots was performed for his helpers once for all by our Savior on the cross. Now, all who will may see "God with us." Who can fear while marching beside the chariot of the Lord? The visions coming to us in earnest prayer will do far more to overcome our fears than gymnasiums, armories or diplomacy.

Sunday-School

December 2, 1906.

JESUS BEFORE PILATE.—Luke 23:13-25.

Memory verses, 20, 21.

Golden Text—Then said Pilate . . I find no fault in this man. Luke 23:4.

John tells us (18:28) that the mob which conveyed Jesus from the court of the high priest to the palace of Pilate "entered not into the palace, that they might not be defiled." Never was there a clearer contrast between real and ceremonial defilement. To enter the house of a Gentile would be a breach of the law of purity. To shed innocent blood was a matter of small concern.

Observe that the accusation before Pilate is quite different from the charge which was made against Jesus in the presence of the Jewish authorities. Then it was blasphemy; now it was treason. Before the Roman authorities it was necessary to have an accusation which would appeal to a Roman. Pilate would care little what Jesus had said about the temple. But the chief anxiety of a Roman governor was to keep the peace and prevent insurrection. So the accusers brought two charges: First, this man is a disturber of the peace; second, he claims to be a king and so wins away the loyalty of the people from Caesar.

Judea had always been a restless and turbulent province. The first charge was well calculated to arouse the fears of Pilate. It would have been a good charge if they could only have proved it. But even Pilate saw at once that it was a mere pretext. The second charge was equally transparent, Pilate saw that, whatever Jesus might say about being a king, he meant nothing prejudicial to Caesar's sovereignty. The accusation fell flat on both counts. The verdict was "Nothing worthy of death has been done by him."

Pilate's effort to escape responsibility was pathetic. He sent Jesus to Herod, but Herod, though appreciating the compliment, also shunned the responsibility and sent him back. He offered the release of Jesus or Barrabas. He suggested that he would scourge Jesus to satisfy the passions of the mob and then release him to satisfy his own sense of justice. But no argument or device could avail against the wild cry, "crucify him."

The weak magistrate gave way to the mob. He did not even profess to have a sentence upon Jesus, but in giving him up to be crucified he passed judgment upon himself. So does every one who answers the question, "What shall I do with Jesus?" It is still a question of life and death—not now the life or death of Jesus, but of the one who answers the question.

People's Forum

Who Are the Fathers?

I don't understand this paper racket over "Our Fathers." Who are they, that we should walk in their shoes? Shoes don't grow; feet do, I loved the good old pioneers of the Reformation, but their shoes don't fit. Let us go back to the apostles for "Our Fathers" and shape our feet to fit their shoes. Let us change your paraphrase of Kipling.

  Plea of our faith, our hope, our love,
    For whose dear sake the *Apostles* strove;
  O blessed Christ, we pledge to thee
  Head, heart and hand through years to be.
                  X. Y. Z.

[Our fathers in this Reformation had for their plea the restoration of apostolic teaching. We are safe in following them as they followed Christ, but no farther. The revised paraphrase is all right, but it means only what the paraphrase means. —Editor.]

Some Points and Questions.

To the Editor of The Christian-Evangelist:

Can a man have a Christian character and not be a Christian? All will agree that he may have a Christian character and not be a Catholic, or not be an Episcopalian, or Presbyterian or Methodist, or Baptist, or Disciple with a big D. But I affirm that every man who has a Christian character is a Christian. To be a Christian is to be *Christed*. A living faith in a saving Christ is the essential factor in a *Christian* character. A man may have a *religious* character and not be a Christian. This was the case with Cornelius. But Cornelius had no *Christian* character. He knew nothing of Christ as the Savior of man. When Peter set Christ before Cornelius as his Savior and Cornelius accepted him as such then Cornelius was Christed—made a Christian. Faith in the Son of God as the Savior of the soul transforms a man's ideas, transfigures his character, makes him a new creature—a Christian. If a man has not this faith—this character—we do not baptize him. Baptism does not give character to a man. It is the expression of a character already formed. This use of the expression "Christian character" does not convey the idea in its highest form. It requires time and experience, service and sacrifice, self-denial and suffering to produce Christian character in its nobler types. The thousands of men and women who have never been baptized and yet who have for long years been giving themselves faithfully in service to the Lord Jesus Christ, whose lives are influenced, guided and dominated by him, and whose characters are permeated by the Christ idea—are they not Christian?

* * *

Is a man a Christian who is not "in Christ?"

The phrase "in Christ" does not mean in his person. My body does not enter the body of Christ literally, nor my spirit enter his spirit. To be "in Christ" is to be under his influence as a leader, under his reign as Lord, under his dominion as Savior. No man is a Christian who is not thus "in Christ." Every man is a Christian who is thus in Christ.

In order to get in Christ is it necessary to be "baptized into Christ?"

In order to get into Christ formally or ceremonially it is necessary to be "baptized into Christ." In order to get into Christ really and spiritually it is not necessary to be baptized, since you cannot be Scripturally baptized until you have first entered into him spiritually and really.

And when a man enters into Christ spiritually he "puts on Christ" spiritually. When he enters into Christ ceremonially he "puts on Christ" ceremonially.

The Israelites were all baptized into Moses in the cloud and in the sea.". But they had already entered into Moses by faith, and had placed themselves under his leadership and followed him from Egypt to the Red Sea.

Is a man a Christian who is not in the kingdom of God? A man becomes a Christian and enters the spiritual kingdom of God simultaneously. The penitent believer is "begotten of God," if begotten of God he is God's child and hence in God's spiritual family or kingdom.

Can a man enter into the kingdom of God except he be born of water and the Spirit?

He can not enter the Kingdom of God on earth, the Church of Christ without being baptized or born of water. But he cannot be thus born of water until he has first been begotten of the Holy Spirit and been made a child of God.

Will I take an unbaptized person with a Christian character into the local church for which I preach?

I will not. Why? I am committed to the work of restoring apostolic Christianity to the world in doctrine, ordinances and life. The primitive church was composed of immersed believers. I could not bear my testimony to the truth nor be faithful to our restoration movement by endorsing a different course. I will recognize every man who has a Christian character as a Christian, will co-operate with him to the extent of my ability, and thus seek to win

him by love that I may teach him the way of the Lord more perfectly.

    Liberty, Mo.   A. B. Jones.

P. S.—The expression "baptized into Christ" occurs, I think, but once in the New Testament, while the phrase "believe into (*eis*) Christ," occurs about twenty-five times. And yet some men can never see how it is possible to get into Christ except through baptism.   A. B. J.

The Home Department

Prayer.

More things are wrought by prayer
Than this world dreams of. Wherefore let thy
  Voice
Rise like a fountain for me night and day,
For what are men better than sheep and goats,
That nourish a blind life within the brain,
If, knowing God, they lift not hands of prayer,
Both for themselves, and those who call them
  friend?
For so, the whole round world is every way
Bound by gold chains about the feet of God.
—*Tennyson.*

The Bronze Vase.

BY J. BRECKENRIDGE ELLIS.

PART IV.

CHAPTER VI.

Having left the pawnshop once owned by Miss Pinns while nominally under the ownership of Uncle William Hodges, Raymund wandered down one street and up another without much perception of his surroundings. A thought, strange, new but as yet not very pronounced, was beginning to take possession of him. He felt the need of being entirely alone; therefore he shrank from the idea of returning to Frog Bend. In his present disturbed state of mind he shuddered at the prospect of facing the inquisitive Mr. Willby. He shrank still more from meeting Rhoda. When he had last seen her he had believed her to be his sister; now he knew the truth and knew that she knew. He shrank most of all from learning what name was engraven upon the bronze vase. Either he was Mrs. Revore's son or he was a millionaire. He hesitated to know which. Could money compensate him for the loss of a mother? And if it proved that Rhoda was the heiress, would not the knowledge that Mrs. Revore was of no relationship, embitter her prosperity? Still, he had no right to maintain the secret. But for a while it might lie hidden—it had been hidden so many years. And what Raymund desired was time—time to think it over, to get used to the perplexing situation.

He found himself once more trudging along Washington avenue before the lodging house where his father had died. He came to the vacant lot where Wizzen had encamped with Mrs. Weed. He sat down upon the mouth of the crater, as it were, and gazed down upon the hollowed scene whose life had grown extinct. In yonder cavity had stood the old moving-wagon and the aged horses had been tethered in that distant frowsy growth of discouraged city weeds. It was curious how the young man's heart warmed as he thought of the dusty white-covered wagon and the listless attitude of the jaw-drooping horses. And Wizzen with his prodigal use of "which" and his manner of peering up from under his gazed cap—and old Mrs. Weed with her unerring gift of seizing the idea by the wrong word, and, as it were, seeking to force into its spiritual mouth a philological bit that never fitted—how Raymund would have rejoiced to see these simple friends again—to see any one, indeed in that desolate city with a kindly face. But no; Wizzen was gone, Mrs. Weed was gone. Rhoda was not only far removed in space, but had even ceased to be a sister. The coal soot like lazy snow in mourning, floated down upon him from the upper air. Beyond the concave vacant lot was the rear of various tenement houses, and from every porch and balcony swung lines of washing with a bold red obtrusiveness of nethermost garments. Raymund rose with a sigh and turned his back upon the scene. The hoarse-throated call of steamboats reminded him of the houseboat bearing his friends down to New Orleans. What had become of them?

At last Raymund had made his plans. He would not go to Frog Bend. He did not wish to meet Rhoda till he had thought and thought. Kansas City naturally occurred to him. In that little back room on the third floor of Mrs. Bannerton's lodgings on thirteenth street, he could be absolutely alone. Jack had gone to Frog Bend for his vacation. Mrs. De Fer, now the wife of the Columbia professor, had sailed for France. There would be no one to disturb his solitude. Raymund accordingly took the train for Kansas City.

Mrs. Bannerton was naturally surprised to see her "roomer" as she had understood his intention was to stay away all summer; but she was always more glad than surprised to see her old friend. Raymund took possession of his room with a certain snug feeling of satisfaction. It was no longer necessary to hump himself over a coal oil stove, pretending to be "warm enough." The weather was his stove now, and warmed him above the degrees of ease.

It was about six o'clock on the fourth day of his return to Kansas City and his resumption of the little rear room, that he heard a footstep on the stair that caused him to sit up in sudden surprise—he had been lying upon the side of the bed in abstracted thought. Suddenly the door was flung open and Jack Bellfield entered breezily.

"Why, hey there, Ray," cried Jack with a grin, "haven't got over the evil habit of lying on your bed in the daytime, I see. Tut, tut!" Jack flung himself upon the bed and added, "We got your letter telling us you'd been to St. Louis and would have to stay a week here in town. What's up?"

"I have been busy," said Raymund.

"Your look like you've been working hard," said Jack with a critical glance. "When did you eat last?"

"I—I don't know," said Raymund. "I haven't thought much about it. Don't you know, the little necessary acts and parts of life—eating and sleeping, you know—the links that hold the main parts together—oh, all that is a weariness!"

"You get weary without 'em," Jack commented. "Say, fellow, you are pale and thin and look like you've had a sickness. It's six o'clock and I'm hungry. Now you don't seem very communicative, but I'll tell you about me. Nelsie Loraine is visiting here for a few days, and I'm to take her to the opera house to-morrow night. And I'm to call around there to-night; and day after to-morrow, I'm to go with her to Westport to a sort of automobile meet. And the next day—by that time I calculate all my money will be spent—I'm to creep home to Frog Bend. Will you be ready to come home, by that time?"

"Yes," said Raymund listlessly, "I suppose so."

"Then we'll just batch here in the meantime as of old, hey? I'll go out and rustle us some provender."

Jack went out and Raymund flung himself upon the bed. Again his thoughts went back to this new light in which he stood to Rhoda. He was thinking of Rhoda when Jack returned. It was natural for him to ask about her.

"Awfully worried," said Jack, as he deposited various packages on the bed and washstand. "She can't imagine why you should streak off to St. Louis without a word. No more can I, but I'm not curious. Nelsie Loraine gives me all I can think about. I'm in love, that's what I am. Look out, fellow, that's pickles; don't tip it up that way. Do you want the bed floating in vinegar? Say! Don't roll on those bananas. They are soft. She's certainly the prettiest girl I ever saw in all my life. Now, I throw that out as a challenge. Pick up the glove. Did you ever know a prettier girl?"

"I never did," said Raymund promptly.

"And why?" cried Jack as he poured a bottle of cream into a tin pan and stirred in two heaping teaspoons of cocoa, "because they're not on the earth. That package you are trying to work up your trouser, leg, is the sugar. Heave it over this way."

Jack stirred the sugar into the mixture of cream and cocoa, then lit the gas. He had made a wire frame which fitted upon the bu_ler, just large enough for the tin pan, by the nicest of balancing, to rest upon it. When the cocoa was thus placed, Jack stood upon a chair in order to seize the pan the moment it began to boil. He looked down upon Raymund as the latter still moved restlessly upon the coverlet. "Ray," he said, "is it anything I can help?"

"No," said Raymund, dejectedly.

"All right, I'll not refer to it again," said Jack Bellfield. "Get out the crackers while I'm watching this cocoa, will you? Mixture you forgotten the old tricks? Pull out the wash-stand drawer and push it slightly in, upside down, for our table. Draw the bed around for our banqueting-bench. Unroll that smelly stuff; it's halibut."

"What! halibut?" cried Raymund with memory of other days and other halibut, "thank you, none for me."

"I guess you will," said Jack. "It's bought now—I didn't know how rank it was till I'd paid for it. We can't afford

to throw it away. We'll have to eat it to save it."

"Everything has its limit," said Raymund, "and the limit of economy is spoilt fish."

"It's not really spoilt," said Jack, "And we buy no more meat till this is eaten."

"And I eat no more, till more is bought!" Raymund declared.

Jack grinned at him and remarked, "I see all you've needed was for me to come to get you out of the dumps." Then he turned off the gas, bore the boiling cocoa to the upturned washstand drawer, and seated himself upon the banqueting bench. Cocoa was their first course, taken with bananas and crackers. Next followed halibut, in its dry or raw state, partaken of by Jack with bated breath and considerable rapidity.

"Now," he said, pushing the remainder of the odorous fish under the bed, "I've saved quite a hunk; I hope to dispatch the rest at supper, if you will lend a hand. If not, it goes into our breakfast, too, for the sooner it's done with the better for us and it, too. It's decomposing fast, but I think I can beat it to the goal. Now for our dessert."

The dessert consisted of a mixture of cream, raisens, pecan-kernels, a chopped-up orange, and two bananas, all stirred together in the water-pitcher. This was evenly portioned out in a couple of large pickle-jars and partaken of with much relish by Jack and with dawning interest in life on the part of Raymund. When the dishes, that is to say the jars, tins, and various lids of cans, and two tin spoons had been cleaned, it was growing dark. They repaired to their balcony, that is to say, the fire-escape. Seated upon newspapers, they swung their legs at the dizzy height, with nothing between them and the basement-ground, four stories below, but a few airy fairy bars of iron. Jack did his utmost to hearten up his friend and Raymund for a time put his new cares from him. On the other side of the basement-yard fence, a pug dog issued from the adjoining house —that house behind which Boggs had once alarmed Raymund. The pug caught sight of the two figures perched upon the fire-escape where no man, by his experience should be. He instantly burst forth into vociferous barking, rolling his eyes at them and pawing the ground in impotent wrath.

"Let's throw him the halibut," said Raymund slyly. "Let's make him madder."

"Ray," said Jack, "that's an inspiration!" And until time for Jack to go to see Nelsie Loraine they sat like children, throwing bits of fish at the dog, who would eat none of it. As Jack departed, after considerable primping, he said, "What do you say to coming along, Ray? Nelsie Loraine won't care, and your glumness will be a very effective foil to my high spirits." Raymund declined the part, and Jack went down stairs humming gayly—"Tell me pretty maiden, are there any more at home like you?"

But in reality, Raymund's thoughts were by no means glum. Because during the next four days he often seemed to Jack as solemn as a judge, was often abstracted, lost to the world, would hear his friend read a squib from the *Kansas City Star* with an unmoved countenance, therefore Jack imagined him melancholy. But it was not the sadness of his new reflections, it was their strangeness that affected Raymund. In the late afternoon his favorite walk was along the Passeo. He would sit for half an hour on the edge of the fountain staring at the circling water. He would lean over the high parapet, gazing down upon those passing below till a touch upon his shoulder was needed to bring him to the consciousness of city sounds.

The time came at last for Jack to return to Frog Bend.

"Yes, I am ready," said Raymund. "I will go with you." There was a new note in his voice. The clouds seemed suddenly to have vanished from his face.

"See here, fellow," said Jack, "you told me when I came to town that you were busy. But all the time I've been here, you haven't done a thing."

"That's where you're wrong," Raymund smiled with his old-time ease. "I've done a great work. I've come to a decision that will influence all my life—and Rhoda's." He smiled strangely.

"Well, I've done a good work, too," said Jack. "I'll tell you," he added joyously. "It's a secret, but you're my one friend, you know."

"I can guess," said Raymund. "And so yet get Nelsie Loraine? Strange how things come about?"

"Why don't you shake hands with me?" demanded Jack, suddenly. "Your thoughts never drifted that way, did they?"

"Perhaps when I was a boy," Raymund confessed. "But that ended long ago, one cold Christmas morning. No, indeed. I didn't shake hands, because I was thinking of—"

"Go ahead. Don't spare my feelings."

"Of the mother-in-law you are about to get. Not *that I, myself*, have any illwill toward that estimable Leader, but—"

Jack made a dive at him and Raymund nimbly fled to the fire-escape.

(To be Continued.)

❀ ❀

Checks Great and Small.

A short time ago the treasurer of the United States signed two checks, one for 2 cents and the other for $137,594,653.15. Their same routine was necessary for each. The 2-cent check gave just as much trouble in the clerical routine of the office as the check for millions. God gives thought to the poorest child as well as to the most famous man.

❀ ❀

Saying Grace Before a King.

When the late Commodore Foote was in Spain, he had upon one occasion the king on board his vessel as a guest. Like a Christian man, as he was, he did not hesitate in the royal presence to ask a blessing as the guests took their places at the table. "Why, that is just as the missionaries do," remarked the

The Pangs of Misprized Love.

BY MARY BARRETT HOWARD.

Mary Elizabeth, her feet bare, her frock torn and soiled, was tilting on the branch of an apple tree, the guest of Katrinka Knauber, the naughtiest little girl in town. Her costume and the hour—three o'clock in the afternoon—proclaimed her an exile from polite society, for although in that quiet village children of "the best families" were permitted during the morning hours to revel, unshod and unkempt in mud pies and tree-climbing, it was an unwritten law that at the approach of the sun's meridian they should submit themselves to the ministrations of the grownups, and appear for the remainder of the day in the garments of civilization.

But on this particular day, Mary Elizabeth, for the first time in her seven years of life was suffering the pangs of slighted love. Early that morning Nellie Ingraham, her most "intimate friend," had run across the street to impart the momentous fact that Chauncey Olcott, a hitherto loyal bondsman of Mary Elizabeth, had invited her, Nellie, to accompany him that afternoon to the village pharmacy, there to partake from a white marble soda fount of the delights of "strawberry and vanilla mixed."

Therefore had Mary forfeited her favorite dinner of broiled chicken, green peas and strawberry shortcake, and fled to the forbidden society of Katrinka Knauber; and in the desperate attempt to forget her wrongs she had, with the able assistance of that cheerful young outcast, been indulging in a perfect orgie of mischief.

Katrinka, frowned upon by mothers on account of an inexhaustible capacity for inventing original and unforgivable pranks, had her good points. She was a warm partisan, and her forcibly expressed sympathy and indignation were sweet to Mary Elizabeth's sore heart.

She was generous too, and when after some hours of lawless wanderings the two little Ishmaelites returned to the shabby, tumble-down habitation that Katrinka called home, she insisted on sharing her own small portion of the family's repast of bread and molasses.

Mary Elizabeth was fond of this delicacy, chiefly because it formed no part of her accustomed menu, and in the enjoyment thereof she had almost forgotten her troubles, when glancing down from her lofty perch she espied her perfidious friend mincing up the street arrayed in her best pink muslin frock and a triumphant smile. By her side, O, woeful sight! marched Chauncey Olcott, holding a diminutive pink parasol above Nellie, with an air of devotion that caused Mary Elizabeth to sink back among the apple blossoms in a state of collapse. Throwing her arms about the great tree she hid her face against the rough bark and sobbed so piteously that the alarmed Katrinka was at her wit's end to comfort her.

A sudden grunting from the pigsty below suggested to Katrinka a new idea.

"If you cry no more, Mary Elizabeth," she besought, "I vill gif you von of dose leetle pigs vor your own."

Like a flash Mary Elizabeth was out of the tree and down on her knees in the

rivulets of water that meandered through the muddy pen, her tears dried as if by magic. For Mary Elizabeth adored all dumb creatures, and the difficult task of deciding between ten little piglets, each more beautiful than the other, entirely banished her grievance from her mind.

"I tank you better vash him bevore you dake him home," recommended Katrinka, sagely.

Mary Elizabeth was embracing her newly acquired treasure with reckless fervor, but she acknowledged the soundness of Katrinka's advice, and notwithstanding piggy's protesting squeals he was held under the pump and thoroughly cleansed with the help of a scrubbing brush and soap surreptitiously obtained from the Knauber kitchen.

With her eyes shining like twin stars, Mary Elizabeth departed with the now snowy piglet under her arm. She did not trouble herself to imagine what Mrs. Knauber's feelings might be when she discovered that her too-generous daughter had given away one of the useful animals that formed the widow's chief means of support.

For some reason Mary Elizabeth deemed it wise to reconnoiter when she arrived at her own gate instead of rushing into the house in her usual impetuous fashion. Finding the coast clear, she stole quietly up the stairway to her own pretty room, and turning back the coverlets of her dainty white bed, she laid piggy to rest therein. Fearing that he might be chilly after his unaccustomed ablutions she went to her mother's wardrobe and confiscating a shawl of pale blue Canton crape, she proceeded to wrap it about her porcine prize until only a pink nose emerged from its folds.

When Master Piggy was worn out with his struggles, or whether he really appreciated the luxury of a soft clean bed will never be known, but certain it is that instead of attempting to escape he laid his head on the pillow as one who would say, "Leave, ah, leave me to repose."

Mary Elizabeth was unable to tear herself away from this entrancing pet. Dragging a chair to the bedside she began to sing, softly:

Hush, my babe, lie still and slumber,
Holy angels guard thy bed,
Heavenly blessings without number,
Gently falling on thy head.

Pretty red-haired Noah had been delegated to seek for the wanderer and had just completed a leisurely toilet, for it being the custom of Mary Elizabeth to "go traipsing off to goodness knows where," every time the world went awry with her, the family had felt no great anxiety when she did not appear at dinner.

Now as Noah stood before her glass she heard the voice of Mary Elizabeth chanting good Dr. Watts' cradle hymn. Hastening toward the sound she stood transfixed on the threshold of Mary Elizabeth's room. A shriek of housemaid stridency brought every member of the household to the spot where Mary Elizabeth was vigorously defying Noah's attempts to remove the uncanny occupant of the bed, and a chorus of shocked exclamations arose.

"O Mary Elizabeth—your lovely

Piles Quickly Cured at Home

Instant Relief, Permanent Cure—Trial Package Mailed Free to All in Plain Wrapper.

Piles is a fearful disease, but easy to cure if you go at it right.

An operation with the knife is dangerous, cruel, humiliating and unnecessary.

There is just one other sure way to be cured—painless, safe and in the privacy of your own home—it is Pyramid Pile Cure.

We mail a trial package free to all who write.

It will give you instant relief, show you the harmless, painless nature of this great remedy and start you well on the way to a perfect cure.

Then you can get a full-sized box from any druggist f r 50 cents, and often one box cures.

If the druggist tries to sell you something just as good, it is because he makes more money on the substitute.

Insist on having what you call for.

The cure begins at once and contigues rapidly until it is complete and permanent.

You can go right ahead with your work and be easy and comfortable all the time.

It is well worth trying.

Just send your name and address to Pyramid Drug Co., 65 Pyramid Building, Marshall, Mich., and receive free by return mail the trial package in a plain wrapper.

Thousands have been cured in this easy, painless and inexpensive way, in the privacy of the home.

No knife and its torture.

No doctor and his bills.

All druggists, 50 cents. Write to-day for a free package.

white bed! My best shawl!" wailed her mother.

"Of all the quare, outragious childer iver I seen, Mary Elizabeth bates Baniger," muttered Katy the cook, crossly.

"Where did you obtain the creature, child?" demanded her grandfather, adjusting his glasses with a judicial air.

"Katrinka Knauber gave him to me," the culprit faltered.

"Was it hers to give?"

"I—I don't know," Mary Elizabeth confessed.

"Don't you know that it belonged to her mother and you took it without her permission, that you practically committed a theft?" pursued Mr. Courtenay Owen with unprecedented severity.

"Yes, Mary Elizabeth, there isn't a cent's worth to choose between you and

'Tom, Tom the piper's son,'" agreed her father, frivolously.

Then Mary Elizabeth turned at bay, and in one impressive burst of oratory she chanted of her false friend, faithless vassal and heartless family.

"There doesn't a single person love me in all this world," she ended, tearfully, "and I can't even have a pig to comfort me."

She threw herself on the bed, clasping her one solace frantically to her heart. The expression of the faces about her changed with ludicrous swiftness.

"Come now, alannah," coaxed old Katy, "don't yez be failin' so bad. Sure an' I'll bake ye an illigant big little cakeen if yez'll take the little pig back to his mother who loikely be scratchin' fer him this same minyut."

"Faix, an' there's no nade to be tillin' the poor child such romances," broke in Norah, wrathfully, "sure an' it's me that'll be havin' the trouble of kapin' that crathur up here, but it's not me that ud be brakin' her heart deprivin' her of it."

"Norah may go over and purchase the little animal," conceded Mr. Owen hastily, slipping a silver dollar into the housemaid's hand, "and if your parents are unwilling that it should remain here"—

"She may keep it—of course she may," coaxed Mrs. Carr, vainly endeavoring to kiss the cheek hidden in a tangle of sunny curls, "only, darling, don't you think piggy would be happier in a nice little pen in the barn-yard?"

"Undoubtedly he would," interposed Mr. Carr, briskly. "Come, Mary Elizabeth, we'll go tell Peter where to build a pen, and then we'll have up the horses and drive to Fairview for some soda."

Mary Elizabeth's sobs ceased. Perhaps piggy would be happier out there in the warm sunlight. Moreover the soda water at Fairview was of a superior sort, much better than anything her native town could produce. She sat up and brushed aside her tangled curls.

"Will you go too, Grandfather?" she demanded.

It was the hour for the arrival of Mr. Owen's Tribune, and he loathed the sickish sweetness of the beverage which his prophetic soul warned him the small tyrant would require him to drink copiously, but he replied, with hesitation, "Most assuredly, dear child, if you wish me to do so."

Later, Mary Elizabeth sat enthroned in the old-fashioned "two-seater" enjoying the honor of driving, when two familar figures appeared in the distance. She stiffened perceptibly at the sight, and as they met she bowed in the manner of a justly offended princess.

Pink-frocked Nellie Ingraham was swinging her brief skirts with an air of smug satisfaction, but her escort was looking unmistakably bored, for Nellie's society seemed unutterably vapid to a boy who had delighted in the infinite variety of Mary Elizabeth. That he had slighted and grieved her to whom his inmost soul gave allegiance was merely an ebullition of "the eternal masculine" with its fondness for roving, its dislike of even silken fetters.

"Papa," questioned Mary Elizabeth after a solemn pause, "don't you think it is very much pleasanter for a little girl to be tooken by her own folks to get soda than to go with just a boy?"

"I do indeed," responded her father, giving Mary Elizabeth a great hug.

But the next instant she was leaning out of her carriage.

"Mamma," she said with a wistful look in her brown eyes, "Chauncey Ol-

cott just loves pink an'-my best frock is blue. Don't you s'pose that if you should buy me a pink one—pinker'n Nellie's, that Chauncey—p'raps"—

Mr. Carr laughed as his strong arm drew the child back into safety, but the eyes that met above the golden head held tears as well as smiles at the thought of what the coming years must bring to a nature so intense, so eager for love.—*The Congregationalist.*

❀❀

In Behalf of the Child.

The first law as regards the training of the child was thus phrased by Dr. Cuyler: "An ounce of honest praise is often worth more than many pounds of punishment."

The second law is no less worthy of acceptation: "Think twice and pray three times before punishing a child."—*Central Christian Advocate.*

Send for our Holiday Catalogue.
CHRISTIAN PUBLISHING CO.,
St. Louis, Mo.

A small brain that works is of more use than a massive intellect that balks.

Rest assured that most of your stray ideas have come over a neighbor's fence.

A naked truth offends the most sacred prejudices of society.

The domestic service problem is the pig in the clover problem—first to get the domestics into the circle, then to keep them there.

The family is a despotism governed by the meanest member. It is not the strongest, but the worst-tempered, who rules.—*Louise Herrick Wall in the Century.*

How Bob B—— Lived His Religion.

There are certain people who take every opportunity to make loud long professions of their religion, and, like the Pharisee of old, thank the Lord that they are better than others, but when you watch closely how they live, you will find that their lives don't tally with their professions.

Now I want to show you how Bob B—— lived his religion. The best thing about this little incident is that it is substantially true, though I may not be able to give it to you just as it was given to me.

Some years ago I had a brother working in the general offices of the G. P. R. R., at Birmingham, Ala., while Colonel S—— was general superintendent and Mr. G—— was assistant superintendent. My brother and Bob B—— worked in Mr. G——'s department.

Bob began work at a salary of $35 per month. He boarded at the same place where my brother did, and when he drew his first month's salary, that night at the boarding-house he counted out his money for this month."

"Now," said he, "that is my church money, and laid aside $3.50."

"You don't mean to give that much out of your own month's salary, do you?" said someone.

"No," replied Bob; "I am not giving that, I am only paying to the Lord. After that comes the giving."

After awhile Bob got a raise to $50 per month.

Some of the boys said, "Well, Bob, I suppose you will not give $5 out of your month's wages?"

"I'll pay my debts," said Bob.

Again he was raised to $60 per month, and it was the same thing.

But Bob was to be tested in another way. One Saturday afternoon Mr. G—— said: "Well, boys, I don't have you to work on Sunday, as a rule, but we are behind now, and you will all have to come down to-morrow and work to get things ready for the end of the month." But one of the boys had enough of the two G's—Grace and Grit —to object.

Bob spoke, quietly: "Mr. G——, I can't work on Sunday."

"Now, Bob," said Mr. G——, "this is the first time I have had you boys to do so, and we must work to-morrow to catch up."

"I'm sorry, sir," said Bob firmly, "but it is against my religion, and I can't do so."

"Well, Bob," said Mr. G——, sharply, if you can't do the work, I want you to do, at the time I want you to, I'll have to get a man that will."

Sunday morning every one but Bob went down to work; he went to Sunday-school and preaching. Monday morning he was "fired."

That night, when Bob brought in his part of a month's wages, some of the boys said: "Well, Bob, I guess you won't give any of that money to the church, but keep it to live on until you get another job." But Bob still paid his dues.

Bob started out at once to hunt him another job.

But days passed, and still he was out of a job, until the boys thought things pretty blue for him. But there was a brighter day ahead for him.

One day Col. S—— came into Mr. G——'s department. He knew Bob, and

missed him right away. "Where is Bob B——?" said he.

"I had to let him go," replied Mr. G——.

"What was the matter?"

"I had to work some on Sunday, we were so badly behind; Bob refused to work, so I had to let him out."

The colonel made no further remark then, but afterwards he saw my brother, and asked him about Bob—where he was, and what he was doing. He told the colonel that Bob boarded at the same place he did, and that he was still out of a job. Colonel S—— told him to tell Bob to come to his office next morning. Bob wept over next morning.

"Well," said the colonel, "you are the chap that preferred losing a job to working on Sunday?"

"Yes, sir."

"You are the very boy that I have been looking for—one that will stand by his principles. You can got to work at once in my office. What salary have you been getting?"

"Sixty dollars per month was my last salary."

"I'll start you at $75," said the colonel.

And little Bobbie went on climbing up, until he climbed up to New York, and the last I heard of him, he was getting $150 per month, and he may be still climbing, for I have lost sight of him for some years.

Boys, go and do likewise.—*Christian Observer.*

—Perhaps you *can* "get along" without the Dowling Bible school helps—but why should you? Our low prices put them within the reach of all.

—Correspondents will get better service by sending communications intended for our different departments on separate sheets of paper. Omnibus envelopes are unobjectionable, but the omnibus letter is a cause of delay.

—With 111 new CHRISTIAN-EVANGELISTS read by its members each week the historic church of C. R. Hudson and George Darsie at Frankfort, Ky., ought to and will attain even greater distinction in realms of Christian usefulness.

—Any preacher may get "Helps to Faith" by J. H. Garrison, one of the best books we have yet published, free of cost by sending us a new subscription accompanied by the $1.50. On the same terms he can get E. L. Powell's "Victory of Faith."

—Heretofore we have gone to press on Tuesday noons, but demands from all over the country for more CHRISTIAN-EVANGELISTS have forced us to close our forms early Monday p. m. Space will be reserved for telegrams and other brief and very important news till Monday noon. All other copy must be in the printers' hands by Saturday to insure its publication in the following week's paper.

—Every church contemplating a meeting should write at once for terms for 300, 500 or 1,000 CHRISTIAN-EVANGELISTS per week together with the pink circular containing pictures of ministers, evangelists and church together with appropriate local announcements. They not only insure large congregations, but fill the house with prepared listeners. Thousands of these are in use and are most important factors in many of our most successful revivals.

—Note churches that are dedicating new houses of worship, burning mortgages, holding great meetings, becoming living links, creating strong sentiment in favor of Christian union, preaching and exemplifying an optimistic, constructive, progressive Gospel, and you may depend upon it their ministers are reading THE CHRISTIAN-EVANGELIST and are in full sympathy and co-operation with its spirit and ideals. If these churches are greatly redounding in the virtues the probabilities are that the officiary and a large percentage of the membership are in the same literary boat with the minister.

—Our subscription clerk is working over time caring for the hosts of new subscriptions coming in these autumn days, and trying to get to the new members of our great constituency the earliest possible number of the paper. While the many coming by ones and twos help guarantee us an even distribution among the churches we are pleased to report the following new clubs at $1.50 each:

Mendon, Mo., David Millar, minister........ 3
Atlanta, Ga. 7
Munhall, Pa. 8
Lexington, Ky., Mark Collis, pastor.......... 13
Homestead, Pa., E. L. Allen, minister......... 25
N. Tonawanda, N. Y., E. A. Todd, pastor.... 25
Kansas City, Mo., W. F. Richardson, pastor...154

—"I consider 'Gloria in Excelsis' by far the most usable hymnal ever published by our brethren. It contains that which has been an insistent demand upon the part of the Church in a hymnal, viz., a large number of the hymns that will never die because born of the deepest thirstings of the human soul, with a liberal number of the more recent hymns which answer the heart cravings of the younger recruits to the army of God. The features of the hymnal which include the responsive readings for public services are a timely and helpful feature. The volume is, in binding and workmanship, most satisfactory. I trust it will have a large sale.—J. W. Hilton, Bethany, Neb.

A Constructive Paper.

Knowledge is always power. The man who *knows* always has work. The man who knows *wants* to work. Knowledge is the secret of the desire as well as the ability to work. People who know the most about the kingdom of Christ have the greatest desire to work. People not only need a knowledge of the kingdom of Christ scripturally, but they need to know the ongoing of it in all the world. This knowledge must come through good reliable religious literature. An increase of 30 per cent in circulation of a religious paper such as THE CHRISTIAN-EVANGELIST in one year is, therefore, a good omen. It means knowledge, which in turn means power. But to those who are students of the progress of the people who are contented to be called simply Disciples of Christ, this growth is not to be wondered at. THE CHRISTIAN-EVANGELIST is *worthy* of a larger circulation. It is a clean, aggressive, up-to-date religious *news* paper that is not too narrow to think and talk all the time about things within our own brotherhood, but keeps us in touch with what our neighbors are doing. It is an all-round paper, sound in faith, tolerant in spirit and constructive in teaching. Then it is conducted on good business methods. Its writers are the best. It is a valuable paper because of the many things it evidently does not print. Its growth is a demonstration of what the brethren *want*.

It is what the leading brethren want. If THE CHRISTIAN-EVANGELIST will aggressively "saw wood," keeping on the positive side of things, it will have a growth in the days to come that has not been dreamed of in the days that now are. All this present and promising growth means much to our brotherhood. It means that the best among us have no notion of settling down to be the meanest and narrowest of all sects, but rather to learn as we go, and keep our eyes, hearts and minds open to all the good things that look to the furtherance of our divinely-appointed mission—the union of all followers of the humble Nazarine. THE CHRISTIAN-EVANGELIST ought to be in every home in the brotherhood. One hundred thousand by 1909 will be a fine stride toward that end. For this I am willing to work.   C. A. FREER.
Painesville, O.

THE CENTENNIAL FUND

The following are some of the pledges we have received toward the $250,000 Centennial Fund. These start. Let us move a little faster. Let us hear from you.

C. M. Austin.................$ 15.00	Mr. and Mrs. B. F. Carr...$ 50.00	Cora B. and Margaret C.	Sumner T. Martin...
J. H. Alexander............ 15.00	G. P. Cofer............... 15.00	Harris............... 30.00	Chas. W. Kent.....
Geo. H. Anderson.......... 30.00	N. S. Carpenter.......... 15.00	Mrs. Mary F. Holbrook... 50.00	R. R. Keeler.....
Mrs. Martha Alcock....... 3.00	Mrs. E. Calhoun.......... 6.00	W. J. Henry............ 30.00	Dora L. Leichhardt..
Mrs. A. J. Applebee....... 6.00	W. A. Dameron........... 30.00	P. P. HasseNvander..... 15.00	R. P. Lambear.....
A. J. Applebee........... 15.00	Alicia Derthick.......... 15.00	A. Householder......... 3.00	Clas. Louis Loos....
E. L. Anderson........... 30.00	J. E. Davis.............. 6.00	Jos. W. Helms.......... 30.00	W. J. Loos.....
Mrs. E. J. Alden......... 75.00	Dr. A. G. Donst......... 9.00	In O. Herrold.......... 15.00	R. H. Lampkin.....
F. J. M. Appleman........ 15.00	E. F. Daugherty.......... 15.00	W. X. Hall............ 15.00	J. A. Lytle.....
Geo. Arbogast............ 3.00	F. H. DeVol............. 15.00	Anna Jamieson......... 15.00	Geo. E. Lane.....
Geo. Alexander........... 15.00	E. L. Day............... 15.00	Mrs. E. D. Jones....... 3.00	T. C. Morgan.....
A. R. Adams............. 15.00	Zulah Davis.............. 15.00	J. B. Jones............ 30.00	Melta O. Moninger...
C. P. Austin............. 30.00	B. C. Divers............. 15.00	Mrs. J. H. Johnston..... 15.00	Alex. McMillan.....
Miss Lillie Adams........ 3.00	N. W. Estill............ 15.00	Walter M. Jordan....... 7.50	Lulu L. Miner.....
J. F. Bryant............ 15.00	W. F. Eastman........... 15.00	G. C. Johnson.......... 7.50	Mrs. J. B. Merritt...
Briney's Monthly......... 30.00	Mrs. C. Evans........... 150.00	Mrs. Ida Jarvis........ 15.00	E. L. Miley.....
H. E. Brady............. 3.00	Simpson Ely............. 15.00	A. L. Jasper........... 5.00	S. P. Moody.....
A. M. Bird.............. 15.00	B. F. Farrar............ 15.00	Niles Jones........... 15.00	Mrs. P. Merrwether..
Will H. Barnes........... 15.00	Miss Kara Dora Ford..... 3.00	W. E. Jameson......... 15.00	Thos. Martin.....
B. M. Blount............ 15.00	S. G. Fisher............ 15.00	Frank V. Irish......... 15.00	J. F. Moody.....
A. Boyd................ 15.00	F. B. Fisher............ 15.00	Miss Jeanette King...... 15.00	John J. March.....
A. L. D. Buxton......... 75.00	J. H. Forsyth........... 15.00	E. B. Kemp............ 15.00	David Millar.....
Ira M. Boswell.......... 75.00	W. M. Forrest.......... 15.00	Glenn C. Kenyon....... 3.00	Carrie Lee Maus.....
Jas. Bartleson.......... 15.00	Mrs. F. W. Finley...... 15.00	Z. A. Kay............ 15.00	W. J. Morrison.....
Mrs. M. S. Bartlett...... 15.00	Miss M. Gascoyne....... 15.00		H. E. McMillen.....
W. C. Bogga............ 30.00	Jos. Geralin............ 30.00		
S. W. Baldinger......... 15.00	C. A. C. Gordon........ 3.00		
Matt Bradley............ 15.00	J. W. Giles............. 3.00		
H. E. Bunker........... 30.00	Medary Gorsuch......... 9.00		
K. W. Boring........... 15.00	J. E. Gordon........... 30.00		
Mrs. F. M. Bunting...... 75.00	A. C. Gray............. 24.00		
W. H. Coling........... 15.00	Nannie Gordon.......... 9.00		
John Campbell.......... 15.00	H. C. Groves........... 30.00		
E. K. Chapman......... 3.00	Nelson Gardner......... 15.00		
H. G. Connelly......... 15.00	Robt. D. Gardner....... 9.00		
Edwin F. Cornelius...... 7.50	Eliza J. Griswold...... 15.00		
Mrs. Collins............ 30.00	E. A. Henry........... 15.00		
S. J. Corey............ 75.00	H. S. Hale............ 15.00		
Mrs. Joshp Cox......... 15.00	Mrs. A. E. Hillman..... 15.00		
R. A. Chenoweth....... 15.00	O. L. Hall............ 15.00		
A. B. Crouch........... 15.00	Robt. E. Henry........ 3.00		
Mrs. C. J. Cowen...... 15.00	Mrs. W. L. Haskin..... 15.00		
A. J. Carrick......... 50.00	J. Hopwood........... 15.00		

┆ ....CUT HERE ....

¶ THE PLEDGE.
I agree to donate to the FOREIGN CHRISTIAN
ARY SOCIETY, Cincinnati, O.,$.........per yea
years beginning June 1, 19oo, to aid in the creatio
cial TWO HUNDRED AND FIFTY THOUSAN
($250,000) CENTENNIAL FUND) to be used for
buildings by the Society.

Name ....

P. O. ....

Street or R. F. D,.......................

Date........1906. ....State..

........CUT HERE ....

Please fill out the pledge to-day for what you are willing to give and address

F. M. RAINS, Sec.,

Box 884, Cin

WATCH THIS SPACE NEXT WEEK! WE HOPE FOR EVEN BETTER NEWS!

The Christian-Evangelist.

J. H. GARRISON, Editor

PAUL MOORE, Assistant Editor

F. D. POWER,
B. B. TYLER, Staff Correspondents.
W. DURBAN,

Subscription Price, $1.50 a Year.

For foreign countries add $1.04 for postage.

Remittances should be made by money order,
draft, or registered letter; not by local cheque, unless 10 cents is added to cover cost of collection.
In Ordering Change of Post Office give both old
and new address.
Matter for Publication should be addressed to THE
CHRISTIAN-EVANGELIST. Subscriptions and remittances should be addressed to the Christian Publishing Company, 2712 Pine Street, St. Louis, Mo.
Unused Manuscripts will be returned only if accompanied by stamps.
News Items, evangelistic and otherwise, are
solicited, and should be sent on a postal card, if
possible.
Published by the Christian Publishing Company,
2712 Pine Street, St. Louis, Mo.

Entered at St. Louis P. O. as Second-Class Matter

CONTENTS.

Centennial Propaganda 1517
Current Events 1518
Editorial—
  Where Jesus Placed the Em-
    phasis—XIV. 1519
  Let Us Give Thanks............1519
  Notes and Comments 1520
  Editor's Easy Chair...........1521
Contributed Articles—
  Thanksgiving. James Egbert....1522
  Thou Crownest the Year with
    Thy Goodness (poem). E. L.
    Allen 1522

The Future of Our Country and
  Our Contribution to it. W. H.
  Sheffer 1523
Minister Eighty Years—101 Years
  Old 1524
Why Should We be Thankful.....1525
England's Greatest Preacher. Wil-
  liam Durban 1526
As Seen from the Dome. F. D.
  Power 1527
The Art of Reading. James
  Mudge, D. D. 1529
Current Literature 1530
The Work of the Women.
  Ida W. Harrison..............1534
The Old and the New in Mexico.
  Jasper T. Moses..............1535

The Day of Salvation a
  B. M. Day. W. M. F
The Theology of Alexan
  bell W. E. Garrison
Where Thomas Campbel
  His Last Sermon i
  James Small ....
The Home Department..
Our Budget ....
News from Many Fields..
Evangelistic ....
Sunday-school ....
Christian Endeavor ......
Midweek Prayer-meeting
People's Forum ....

THE
CHRISTIAN-EVANGELIST

"IN FAITH, UNITY, IN OPINION AND METHODS, LIBERTY, IN ALL THINGS, CHARITY."

| Vol. XLIII. | November 29, 1906 | No. 48 |

1809 CENTENNIAL PROPAGANDA CHURCHES OF CHRIST 1909

: : : GEO. L. SNIVELY : : :

Looking Toward Pittsburg.

The honor of being Centennial President is worthy a king's quest.

Only thirty-four months till this greatest of our church festivals begins.

There are many reading this in hamlet and distant vale who shall not see death until they have witnessed our Centennial and told of the celebration to wondering crowds.

Men now unknown to fame among us have time to merge into prominence through the performance of good works and move like kings among the convention hosts. Spur, study, pray, sacrifice, win!

Among the dramatic incidents of Pittsburg it would not be surprising if some like A. M. Atkinson at Cincinnati saying, "Quit you like men," or Simeon at Jerusalem with his song—

Now lettest thou thy servant depart, O Lord,
For mine eyes have seen thy salvation,
And the glory of the people Israel

should never descend from the exalted spirit of the convention, but in an ecstasy breaking through the mantling flesh should in the presence of their brethren rise at once to the angel choir celebrating the triumphs of the church and the goodness of the Lord.

How fickle we are! Many like Isaac Errett, Alexander Procter, G. W. Longan and others now on earth and in heaven, whose hearts were often grieved by indictments of heresy framed in our own ecclesiastical courts and by the misconstruing of their motives, teachings and tendencies by their brethren will in that great convocation be enumerated among the prophets, heroes, and martyrs of this Restoration; and the mention of their names and the telling of their deeds will call forth thunderous applause.

Let not the thought that we may be mustered out of service or "fall asleep" abate in the least our zeal for achievements worthy the celebration by a great church. "God may bury his workmen, but his work will go on." Those who look down through the stars upon that triumphal scene and behold their own weaving in the fabric, seeing with clearer eyes and purified hearts and with fuller understanding of its significance to the culmination of God's plans, will doubtless rejoice ever more over the work of their hands than the visible participants in the convention.

After all the best way to "look towards Pittsburg," is to look to your own local congregation—to doubling its membership, to deepening its spiritual life, to enlisting the whole membership in all the benevolences of the brotherhood, to the putting of a Christian journal in every home, to erecting the family altar which has fallen, to the building up of the Sunday-school and the improvement of its methods, to looking after and building up the Christian Endeavor Society, the C. W. B. M. Auxiliary, the prayer-meeting and so promoting the welfare of the local congregations.

The Bible School and the Centennial.

Never before in our history has the consequence of the Bible school to the future of this Restoration been so fully and justly emphasized. We look there as never before for our numerical increase and for that intense loyalty, even unto proselyting zeal, for our Plea marking us as a "peculiar people" earnestly striving to make all like as we are and without bonds. We are not alone in placing an increased value on Bible school work. As never before the great religious denominations about us are beginning with the children to train their corps in the great armies of the Lord. It is surprising to many to learn the immense bibliography on this subject and to see what a large proportion of the space in our leading preachers' libraries is given over to literature on Bible school methods and inspiration. THE CHRISTIAN-EVANGELIST is fully awake to the trend of the times and has its columns open to helpful contributions on this great theme, and assures its correspondents that none other is more eagerly scanned. Not only so but "Our Young Folks"—the chief of its related publications—is now conducting a special department under the editorship of an experienced Bible school teacher on the best methods of teaching and training and recruiting those classes from which the flower and chivalry of this Restoration will go forth to work and win. "Our Young Folks" should be in the hands of every pastor, superintendent, teacher and the older among the student body. Resolutions should be adopted by the officiary of churches and schools to place this paper in the hands of all church and school workers not now privileged to read it. These evidences of appreciation of what has been done to bring this splendid paper for youths up to its present degree of excellence and what it is now doing to make it surpass all its past will call from us every possible effort to make it the best Bible school paper in all the land. It is now advocating an "each one win one" campaign to the end that within a year the membership of our Bible schools be doubled. We urge preachers, superintendents, pastors and evangelists to enthuse our schools with the Centennial propaganda, making the hearts of these young cadets to so glow with the fires of patriotism for the Father's kingdom that all impurities may be consumed and only love for the beautiful, good and true remain, that they not only become good soldiers of the cross themselves, but melt away the barriers keeping their parents and friends from the ranks, and that the church of to-day be assured that the world's youth of to-morrow will indivisibly be on the Lord's side.

Preacher, your richest ore is in the Bible school, and there, too, may multitudes hitherto seeking great opportunities for advancing the kingdom and patience of Jesus Christ and finding them not, attain their quest. Among the mighty captains honored at Pittsburg, from sanctums, pulpits, college faculties, or mission fields—none will be received with greater acclaim than our faithful and successful Bible school teachers.

A Pan-American Centennial.

Apropos the first Lord's day in December's consideration by our churches of our great missionary activities under the supervision of the National Christian Woman's Board of Missions, Centennial Secretary Warren sends an interesting article calling attention to three American open gateways to large usefulness. The first of these introduces us to millions of negroes and thousands of mountain people in the United States whose mental and moral culture have been almost entirely neglected save as they are being cared for by the women of this organization. At Edwards, Miss., we have an industrial school largely patterned after Booker Washington's Tuskegee institute. The Edwards' plannings are as wise and the ideals as high as at the more famous Alabaman seat, and money given there will yield as large returns as any other possible investment. At Louisville is a school for the preparation of young colored men for the Gospel ministry; at Hazelgreen and other points in the mountains, schools with vast possibilities for good are being ably conducted.

Another of these gateways opens into the West Indies. Porto Rico will soon be an integral part of these United States, giving those people added claim to our fraternal care; already we have a flourishing mission in Jamaica and the white banners of Immanuel float over another Disciple mission station in Cuba.

The third gate leads into continental America below the Rio Grande. Already in Mexico we have one prosperous mission; another has recently been established in the capital city of Buenos Ayres. The needs of these Latin lands as well as their geographical proximity to America rightfully place them under our religious as well as political tutelage. By consecrated, energetic missionary endeavor compensating for past delays, we might yet have statistics and representatives from these islands of the sea and hinter Americas most creditable to our first century's development and adding largely to the usefulness and glory of our first Centennial. We plead for a Pan-American Centennial; that all Disciples send to the corresponding secretary, Sister Harlan, financial evidences of their profound interest in the great work of our Christian Woman's Board of Missions, making the offering on the first Lord's day in December both of recruits to the membership and dollars to the treasury the largest in the history of that queenly organization.

Current Events

"The United States versus the Standard Oil Company," is a title for which we
have been waiting

The People Versus Oil.
for a long while. Now we have it in
the title of the suit instituted last week
by the authority of the president and
Attorney-General Moody. The suit is
on the ground of alleged conspiracy in
restraint of trade. The petition filed by
the government's attorneys in the federal court in St. Louis, recites the history of the oil trust's alleged proceedings, which it divides into three
periods: *First*, from
1870 to 1882, there
existed a conspiracy
among more than a
score of oil companies which had no
organic relation to
each other. The
present . Standard
Oil magnates were
the leaders in this
conspiracy and its
purpose was to prevent competition
and create monopoly. The trust idea
was in its infancy
then. It consisted
simply of an agreement among independent concerns resulting in the suppression of competition. *Second*, from
1882 to 1899 there
was conspiracy and
combination. A majority of the stock
of these forty or fifty co-operating oil
companies was
placed in the hands of nine trustees who
managed it all for the common good.
In this stage there was a definite and
formal unification of control while the
ownership of the several companies remained separate. This was declared an
illegal combination in 1892 and its dissolution was ordered by court, but the
parties appointed to wind up the affairs
of the combination carried them on by
the same method for seven years and
then escaped the law (temporarily) by
another form of still closer consolidation. *Third*, from 1899 to the present
time, the stock of the minor and subsidiary companies has been held by the
Standard Oil Company of New Jersey.
This corporation directly neither produces, owns, refines nor sells oil. It
owns stock in the companies that do
these things. It is a "holding corporation." The evasion of the laws against
combination have been always in the

direction of a closer consolidation, which
augmented the evils which the law
sought to remedy. Incidentally the petition charges that the company has
received rebates from the railroads. The
petition asks for an injunction and the
dissolution of the combination.

The new attorney-general, Mr. Bonaparte, who will succeed Mr. Moody before the Standard

A Bonaparte in the Field.
Oil Company files
its reply, has fighting blood in his veins. His grandfather,
Jerome Bonaparte, was a brother of one
Napoleon Bonaparte who, it will be remembered, gained some little reputation
in his day as a fighter. But he never
fought in half so good a cause as that

in which his grand-nephew will contend
with the oil trust. The old Bonaparte
fought for the restoration of absolutism.
The new Bonaparte is called on to conduct a fight against commercial and industrial absolutism. Strength to his
arm!

The committee appointed by the
American Bankers' Association met in
Washington and

A Currency Scheme.
has agreed upon a
plan of currency
reform which will be recommended to
the treasury department and to congress.
The grand desideratum of every currency
scheme is elasticity without inflation or
instability; to have some sort of money
which will automatically come into existence when money is scarce and dear,
will be safe and sound so long as it is
in circulation, will stay as long as there
is a real need for it to avert panic or
relieve stringency, and will modestly re-

THE THANKSGIVING PROCLAMATION.

YET another year of widespread well-being has passed. Never before in our history or in the history of any other nation has a people enjoyed more abounding material prosperity than is ours, a prosperity so general that it should arouse in us no spirit of reckless pride and least of all a spirit of heedless disregard of our responsibilities, but rather a sober sense of our many blessings and a resolute purpose, under Providence, not to forfeit them by any action of our own.

Material well-being, indispensable though it is, can never be anything but the foundation of true national greatness and happiness. If we build nothing upon the foundation, then our national life will be as meaningless and empty as a house where only the foundation has been laid. Upon our material well-being must be built a superstructure of individual and national life lived in accordance with the laws of the highest morality, or else our prosperity itself will in the long run turn out a curse instead of a blessing. We should be both reverently thankful for what we have received, and earnestly bent upon turning it into a means of grace and not of destruction.

Accordingly, I hereby set apart Thursday, the 29th day of November next, as a day of thanksgiving and supplication, on which the people shall meet in their homes or their churches, devoutly acknowledge all that has been given them, and pray that they may in addition receive the power to use these gifts aright.   THEODORE ROOSEVELT.

tire when normal conditions have be
restored. The plan now proposed is th
in addition to their bank-notes secur
by bonds, national banks shall be pe
mitted to issue unsecured emergen
notes to the amount of 40 per cent
their bond-secured circulation, and th
they shall pay a tax of 2½ per cent up
this emergency issue. Further, th
shall be allowed to issue a second cla
of unsecured notes equal to 12½ p
cent of their capital stock, and up
this issue a tax of 5 per cent is to be pa
These notes are to be guaranteed by t
government. The tax paid on them w
create a fund for the payment of a
losses arising through failure of ban
to redeem their notes. The theory
that the tax impos
will prevent t
issue of such not
except in times
stringency when i
terest rates go
high that the ban
will find a marg
of profit after pa
ing the tax; that t
issue of the not
will tend to relie
the stringenc
(which is the chi
purpose of it al
and thus to bri
the rate of intere
down to norma
and that decline
the interest rate w
then wipe out t
margin of profit f
the bank and indu
it to retire the issu
If it will work th
way it will be
ideal system of a
tomatic elastic cu
rency—unless one
disposed to object
a credit currency
principle. But it a
pears to our eyes
comparatively untrained as they are, v
must admit, to the intricacies of hig
finance—that the tax is scarcely hig
enough to secure prompt retireme
when the emergency is past. Would
not be almost or quite as cheap for
bank to pay 2½ per cent interest on i
issue of unsecured notes, as it is to bu
government bonds paying only 2 p
cent interest (thus using up good mone
which could have been loaned at 5 p
cent) and deposit these as security fo
a bank-note issue, as is done under t
present law? In one case the bank pays
tax on its notes; in the other, it los
part of the natural interest on the mone
which it invests in bonds to use as s
curity. Since ordinary secured ban
notes circulate with profit to the ban
in ordinary times, it appears that th
first class of emergency notes might d
the same. If this were true it woul
mean not elasticity, but permanent in
flation. If this argument is correct, th
defect in the newly proposed plan coul
easily be remedied by making the ta
higher.

Editorial

Where Jesus Placed the Emphasis.—XIV.

On the Life Hereafter.

[Concluding the Series.]

It might be expected that one who came into this world that men might have life and that more abundantly, and whose great mission was and is to bring men in right relations to God and to one another, whose kingdom is the kingdom of the spirit, would lay great stress upon the life beyond. Indeed the whole mission and ministry of Jesus Christ in this world assume the capacity of man for an eternal existence and justify themselves on the ground that man is to live forever.

The belief in a life beyond the grave is, of course, not peculiar to the teaching of Jesus. Such a belief, more or less vague, seems to have entered into the life and to have been a part of the religion of all nations. But these ideas, even among the Jews, were vague and unsatisfactory. It was Jesus Christ who "abolished death and brought life and immortality to light through the Gospel." (II Tim. 1:10.) His whole teaching was based on the assumption of life beyond the grave. His attitude toward that doctrine was not one of doubt or conjecture, but of absolute certainty and knowledge. He spoke of the world to come, as familiarly as we would speak of countries which we have visited and with whose inhabitants and customs we are acquainted. To quote here all the passages in which the future life is taught directly, or implied, would be to quote a large part of the teaching of Jesus. Let a few passages suffice.

To the Jews he said: "He that eateth my flesh and drinketh my blood hath eternal life; and I will raise him up at the last day." (John 6:54.) Again, meeting the objection of the Sadducees who did not believe in the life after death, he said: "But that the dead are raised even Moses showed, in the place concerning the Bush, when he called the Lord the God of Abraham, and the God of Isaac, and the God of Jacob. Now he is not the God of the dead but of the living: for all live unto him." (Luke 20:37, 38.) In the same connection he tells the Sadducees that "they that are accounted worthy to attain to that world in the resurrection from the dead, neither marry nor are given in marriage; for neither can they die any more: for they are equal unto the angels; and are sons of God, being sons of the resurrection." (Luke 20:35, 36.)

His repeated promise of giving "eternal life" to those who believed on him, and his instruction to his disciples not to fear him that can only kill the body, carries with it the inevitable conclusion

that in the thought of Jesus the grave is not the end of human life. To the penitent thief on the cross he promised "This day shalt thou be with me in Paradise." To the weeping sisters at Bethany, whose brother had died, when Martha had said, "I know that he shall rise again in the resurrection at the last day," Jesus replied: "I am the resurrection and the life; he that believeth on me, though he die, yet shall he live; and whosoever liveth and believeth on me shall never die." (John 11:25, 26.) It may be doubted whether the church has come to a full recognition of the meaning of this wonderful passage.

The one passage in the teaching of Jesus which, perhaps more than any other, has comforted the hearts of his disciples in the presence of death, is the following: "Let not your heart be troubled: believe in God, believe also in me. In my Father's house are many mansions; if it were not so I would have told you; for I go to prepare a place for you. And if I go and prepare a place for you, I come again, and will receive you unto myself; that where I am, there ye may be also" (John 14:1-3.) Than this nothing can be more explicit and satisfactory. Every element is here that is needed to comfort the heart troubled with the thought of death. There is the Father's house with its many abiding-places. We are not, then, to go out as strangers in a strange land, but rather we are going home to our Father's house where all our brothers and sisters will be gathered. Notice this assurance: "If it were not so I would have told you." Here our divine Lord pledges his own candor and veracity to the reality of the life beyond. He would not deceive us. He would not hold out great hopes of a glorious life hereafter, only to disappoint us. If it were not so he would have told us. On this solid rock we may place our feet and look, without a fear or a tremor, into that spiritual world whither we are going.

But as if all this were not enough to comfort and sustain the heart in the midst of the trials and tribulations, and the ravages of death, in this present world, he added demonstration to promise. He died for us, was buried, and rose again on the third day, appearing to his disciples, even to as many as five hundred at one time, demonstrating the reality of his resurrection. And then, one day leading his disciples out as far as Bethany, on the slope of Olivet, and giving them his parting blessing, he was parted from them, and under the bright shining of the Syrian sun, he ascended to his Father and our Father, to his God and to our God. Long did his disciples stand gazing up after him with wistful eyes, until the angel announced that this same Jesus who had ascended would in like manner descend again.

What more could Jesus say or do, to give assurance to his disciples of the reality and blessedness of the life that

lies beyond the grave. Before leaving the world he commissioned his disciples to go and preach the gospel to the whole creation, and this is now the great work which should engage the thought and resources and energies of the church. How vitally important it is that the world should come into possession of these great treasures of truth, and especially into possession of that eternal life which, beginning here on earth, stretches across the death-line with unbroken continuity into the very eternity of God!

If these brief studies in the teachings of our Lord shall serve to strengthen faith in, and reverence for him, and shall lead our readers to a more diligent study of his character and doctrine, and to a greater consecration to his service, our purpose in preparing them will have been realized. To his blessed name be glory, and honor, and majesty, and dominion, both now and forever. Amen.

❀ ❀

Let Us Give Thanks

For the loving kindness of our Common Father who has preserved our lives through the year past, and who has abundantly supplied all our needs. "For in him we live and move and have our being."

For the fruitful fields, the abundant harvests, and the bending orchards, with which the year has been crowned, rewarding the toils of the husbandmen and supplying food in abundance for man and beast. For he watereth the hills from his chariots and softeneth the furrows with showers from heaven.

For freedom from war, pestilence and famine, three of the great scourges of mankind, and the general prevalence of peace, health and prosperity, within all our borders.

For the spirit of brotherhood and charity which has manifested itself toward such cities or sections of the country as have suffered from earthquake, fire or flood. This growth of the altruistic spirit is of more value to the world than universal material prosperity.

For the rising tide of moral sentiment in the nation against all classes of evil-doers, and for the manifest purpose of the chief executive of the United States, to bring the great corporations of the country to the bar of justice, and compel them to respect and obey the laws regulating such organizations. There is nothing for which Christian people should be more grateful than for this higher ethical standard that the people are demanding both in public life and in commercial and industrial pursuits. In this we have the highest proof, perhaps, of the growing power of the kingdom of God over the common life of the people.

For the growing unity of the world, as manifested in friendly conferences between nations, in the Hague tribunal for preventing war, in numerous peace congresses, in growing commerce between nations, and in the universal condemnation of the aggressive policy of any nation against the territorial rights or political independence of another. Rapid transit and swift methods of communication are steadily unifying the world and bringing the family of nations into closer and more friendly relations.

For the growing unity of the church, as shown in the decay of the spirit of sectarianism in all enlightened communities, in closer co-operation between different religious bodies in advancing the common interests of the kingdom of God, in the waning power of human creeds and the increasing emphasis on the vital and fundamental truths on which the church is one. Christ's prayer for the unity of his followers moves steadily and irresistibly towards its fulfillment, and all "our little systems" that stand in the way of this grand consummation will soon "have their day and cease to be." For this fact the readers of this journal will be specially grateful, and for the humble part our own religious movement has had and is yet to have in bringing in the era of a united Christendom.

For our homes and the tender and sacred relationships of the family, where life has its sweetest and holiest charms, and whence issue those saving influences which make for good citizenship in the state, and in the kingdom of God.

For our public schools, our academies, colleges and universities, and all other institutions which stand for the general diffusion of knowledge and for the moral and intellectual development of the people.

For our churches, our hospitals and asylums, our homes for the orphan, the widow and the friendless and for all the sweet and tender ministries of benevolence alleviating human sorrow, rescuing neglected childhood, and soothing the pains of the unfortunate and afflicted.

For the advancement of science, which is giving us a better knowledge of the world in which we live, and of the universe, showing us how God has worked hitherto and is working in all the processes of life and growth, and which is revealing to us laws of health and of treating disease hitherto unknown, making new discoveries and inventions which contribute to human welfare and happiness and helping the race on toward a truer and more enlightened civilization. So from being an enemy of religion all right-thinking men now regard it as a helper and co-worker with religion in elevating the race.

For these and all other blessings which come down from above, let us give sincere and heart-felt thanks to Almighty God, while we confess our sins and shortcomings, and seek his forgiveness, and invoke his guidance and blessing in all the years to come.

Notes and Comments.

Is there to be another eruption so soon? Is the brotherhood to be thrown into a turmoil of controversy through newspaper attacks on brethren whose views are adjudged to be unsound? There are not wanting indications that we are threatened with such calamity. Surely if there were not an abnormal appetite for such literature among us it would cease to be forthcoming. If there is anything we need less than harsh and unbrotherly criticisms of those whose views are more liberal or more conservative than our own, we do not know what it is. If wrong positions be taken by any brother let them be pointed out in love. These general fusillades against the "new theology" and "destructive criticism," create false impressions and false alarms. We believe in discussion, but denunciation and insinuation are something very different.

Sometimes we have been asked why THE CHRISTIAN-EVANGELIST is not zealous in exposing error like some other religious journals. We have never felt it to be our duty to hunt up all the unwise, rash and skeptical things which rash and unwise men have said, and publish them for the sake of replying to them. Our journalistic policy has been different. Our ideal is that of the Apostle Paul, who said, "Whatsoever things are true, whatsoever things are honorable, whatsoever things are just, whatsoever things are pure, whatsoever things are lovely, whatsoever things are of good report; if there be any virtue, and if there be any praise, think on these things." Error has a wide enough circulation without our assisting it. Much more do we deprecate the tendency to magnify the faults of our brethren and to interpret what may seem to us to be an erroneous view, as a surrender of the faith and disloyalty to Christ. We want our readers to understand, what we believe to be true, that the great body of our brotherhood, both ministers and private members, are loyal to Christ and though differing in their views of certain aspects of truth, are one in their faith and loyalty to a common Lord. Sowing seeds of distrust among the brethren is one of the poorest ways to advance the kingdom of God.

We are in receipt of letters from several brethren who, referring to the outlook indicated above, are cast down in spirit and ask, what is to be done? We are bound to take the same optimistic view of this situation as we do of other things. There is an inherent power in truth and right, and an inherent weakness in error and wrong-doing, which is a sure ground for an optimistic view. Sooner or later error defeats itself and "truth crushed to earth will rise again." It is in the power of its friends to help it rise, but it is not in the power of its

Editor's Easy Chair.

We were hardly prepared for the difference in temperature between St. Louis and Mobile. When we left St. Louis we were having crisp late autumn weather with an occasional flurry of snow. We found Mobile sweltering in summer heat—an unusual temperature for even that southern city. The roses were blooming fresh in the yards and the people were wearing their summer costumes. Mobile's location, on the bay near the Panama Canal. The city does not yet appear, to a visitor, to be conscious of its great destiny, but inside of a decade great changes will be witnessed in real estate values, buildings, and other evidences of growth. We know of no better place for good investments. It still bears some of the marks of the great Caribbean storm which visited it September 27. But, after all, the city's loss was light as compared with the district down nearer the Gulf. A ride of thirty miles down the Bay to Coden, where we saw hundreds of acres of beautiful timber prostrated by the gale, impressed this fact on us. Captain Alba, at whose hotel we put up at Coden, but whose home is in Mobile, told us many remarkable incidents of the storm, resulting from the pushing back of the waters of the Gulf over all this part of the country. Other citizens also related thrilling personal experiences. This flood will be a distinct landmark in the history of this part of the state from which events are likely to be dated.

The people thereabouts are at work repairing their losses as far as possible, but the great need of this section of the country, as perhaps in many another section of the south, is intelligent, reliable labor, and additional capital. A gentleman who owns and conducts a large creamery down on the bay, said in our hearing that he was about to move his creamery elsewhere, simply for the lack of help which he could not get there. Everything else was ideal for the business. Our hostess in the residence part of the city, spent a half hour in telephoning various down-town firms for a messenger boy to carry our suit case to the station, but failed to find any one who could do so, and our host from his down-town business place sent one of his men to perform this service. This demand for help caused by temporary illness, impressed us with the need of a better organization of labor, as there are thousands of unemployed negroes in the city. The problem of transforming these freed men into reliable laborers is one of the great problems of the south. The problem would be more readily solved if the climate were less hospitable and the soil less productive. The old Confederate soldiers were having a reunion in Mobile on the day we left the city, and it was gratifying to us to know that these old grizzled veterans of many a hard-fought field were receiving hearty recognition, and a generous welcome from the people of that city. Their courage in battle, and their devotion to duty, both in war and peace, entitle them to this generous recognition. This is their only pension from the people whose cause they fought to maintain and it should not be withheld from them.

The state convention, which met in the First Christian Church, had well nigh completed its sessions before our arrival on the scene, late Saturday night. It was our privilege to speak twice on Lord's day, and to give the closing address on Monday morning. Another hand will report the entire convention. We believe it was regarded as one of the best which has been held in the state, and, judging from what we saw of it, the spirit was most admirable. The Alabama brethren who are engaged in co-operative missionary work, have their faces turned toward the future and are planning for larger and better things. There was a fine lot of earnest preachers present and a number of consecrated business men who are giving their time and thought to the advancement of the cause in the state. We have seldom addressed more responsive audiences anywhere than those we met in Mobile. It was a special delight to see the handsome new church building of the Christian Church on one of the great thoroughfares of the city—Government street—and to note the standing which the young church is already gaining in that conservative old city. Bro. Claude E. Hill, their minister, has done a monumental work in Mobile, and he is seconded in his efforts by a very efficient board of officers. Our home in the city was with Brother Wintersmith, one of the elders of the church, who, with his delightful family, discharged all the rites of Christian hospitality in a most charming manner. Only Christianity makes such a home possible.

An afternoon's fishing with Bros. W. T. Moore and C. E. Hill, in one of the bayous into the gulf, was a pleasant episode of our southern trip, and served as a brain rest after the fatiguing labors of the convention. We left the other two brethren mentioned down on the happy fishing and hunting grounds intent on further sport while we hastened back to Mobile with a view of taking in a part of the Valdosta, Ga., convention. On the eve of starting, however, a sudden illness necessitated the abandonment of our journey to Valdosta, and robbed us of the anticipated privilege of meeting with the Georgia brethren, which we very much regretted. If the Georgia brethren will pardon us, we will make amends for this at some future meeting. We had a painful journey home most of the way, but the kindness shown us by passengers on the train partially compensated for this, in showing, as we have often stated, how much of the milk of human kindness, after all, there is in the average human heart. Happily the illness proved temporary and by the time we reached St. Louis we were quite comfortable—thanks to Dr. Osgood of Mobile who provided us with remedies on leaving, and to a recuperative constitution for which we must thank the powers above. This Dr. W. W. Osgood is a brother of our missionary to China, Dr.

E. I. Osgood, who was a visitor at the convention. Among other visitors from outside the state, whom we recall, were President A. McLean, Assistant Secretary G. B. Ranshaw, Secretaries G. W. Muckley and J. H. Mohorter, W. T. Moore, of Columbia, and H. C. Bowen, of Cincinnati. Perhaps this convention may have been a little overloaded with outside visitors, but we heard no suggestion to that effect from those hospitable people. These intervisitations between residents of different sections of the country tend to break down provincialism and strengthen the bond of unity. Thank God we have no North and South churches.

THE CHRISTIAN-EVANGELIST comes to its readers this week in a special Thanksgiving number in honor of our national Thanksgiving day. Grateful for all the blessings which our heavenly Father has vouchsafed to us during the year past, we trust our readers are also in a grateful mood for the manifold favors they have received from the same source and will enter with us heartily into this Thanksgiving period. It is one of the customs which we should not allow to become stale with age. It springs from one of the noblest sentiments of the human heart—gratitude for blessings received. That man is low in the scale of moral development who feels no impulse of gratitude for undeserved favors which he has received. Even dumb animals show a sense of gratitude for kindnesses bestowed upon them. Let us then who wear the image of God see to it that we are not unmindful of all his benefits. Along with gratitude for blessings received, let there be acknowledgment of our sins and shortcomings and a deeper consecration to true and worthy living. So shall our annually-recurring Thanksgiving season prove a fountain of blessing to our individual, family and national life.

As we are closing early this week, because of an extra large edition, we are unable to report the full results of our simultaneous meetings, some of which have closed, but some of which are to run beyond the time of our going to press. We need not wait for the full results, however, to be able to say that the success has surpassed anything heretofore attempted in the way of evangelistic services in the city of St. Louis. The meetings have proved to be of incalculable benefit to all the churches co-operating. They have been strengthened greatly in the numbers added and, also, in the revival of the spiritual energy of former members. The experiment has convinced us of the wisdom of simultaneous meetings. Our mistake was in not undertaking it on a still larger scale, although we did seek to enlist a number of churches within reach of St. Louis which for one reason and another did not join with us. Other things being equal, the larger the number of co-operating churches the greater will be the spiritual momentum and the greater the results. Among the reasons for our gratitude on this Thanksgiving day is the success which has crowned our simultaneous evangelistic services in the city of St. Louis.

THANKSGIVING By JAMES EGBERT

Thankfulness is the state of which thanksgiving is the expression. It is usually associated with the emotional nature and expresses itself in poetry, song and prayer. Thanksgiving speaks of the harmony that exists between the Father lavishing his gifts and his children receiving them.

All true achievement in life is but an expression of thankfulness—the artist spreading on canvas his heart of fulness, the poet outpouring his love in song, the sculptor chiselling out of the rough stone the divine image, the artisan at his bench, the teacher before his class, the housewife in the home.

Thanksgiving is not a spasm coming one day in all the year. It is rather a habit of the soul. And every day is a thanksgiving day.

Our reasons for thanksgiving are based in the character of God. True recognition of the Father's love and care under all life's circumstances creates a trust which makes the heart constantly thankful. As said the Quaker poet:

"I know not where his islands lift,
Their fronded palms in air,
I only know I can not drift,
Beyond his love and care."

The Hebrews are a point in illustration. The Hebrew heart could always thank God and take courage. The most adverse circumstances only made evident their gratitude to Jehovah. Walk among the hymns in their Psalm Book and watch the stream of thanksgiving as it issues in "The Blessed Man" and winds its way among hills and through valleys in one unbroken stream of giving thanks until it finally reaches that climax, "Praise ye the Lord . . . Let everything that hath breath praise the Lord," and emerges into the great ocean of gratitude.

The Twenty-third Psalm is but an outburst of praise to the Shepherd who leads them in pleasant pastures and beside still waters. Even in the valley and shadow of death they are not unthankful, for his presence is there. Among enemies they find the spread table. In the Forty-sixth Psalm we find Israel in the midst of national calamity. The strong figure bespeaks its awfulness. Great mountains which have stood unmoved for ages are being hurled into the heart of the turbulent sea—but, says the Hebrew:

"God is our refuge and strength,
A very present help in trouble.
Therefore will we not fear."

One would think that the dark cloud of exile had quelled her thankful spirit. And, indeed, she did hang her harp on the willows and refuse to sing in a strange land. But the emotion was there and it must come forth. Under the power of this crushing of affliction Israel did sing. She re-sang her songs, reviewed her history, compiled and gave to the world that monumental literature which we find in the Old Testament.

Israel's deepest shame was famine, pestilence, and exile. Not that she was not hardy to endure but it cast reflection on Jehovah before other nations. She wanted all to recognize him as the Provider of every good. Hence she would ever say in affliction, "It is our own sin." Israel's greatest delight was in the well-filled granary, the overflowing larder, and hills feeding with flocks and herds. For in prosperity

Jehovah would be exalted among the nations.

The Hebrews were the hill-people, having flocks and herds. Living out under the open sky, they came in contact with God's rugged world. This largely accounts for their pure, simple emotion. Moses got the right vision of things from Pisgah's heights.

"THOU CROWNEST THE YEAR WITH THY GOODNESS."

By E. L. Allen.

For the year thou hast crowned with Thy goodness;

For Thy glory afar o'er the lea;
And the harvest which yielded its fullness;
The abundance we've "sucked of the sea;"

For the sunshine which gladdened the mountains;

For the dew and the soft falling rain—
Which, supplying the rivers and fountains,
Didst refresh each valley and plain—
We thank Thee, O Lord!

For the farmer who plowed the deep furrow

In hope, not in vain, a rich yield;
For the cattle which browsed o'er the meadow,
And the song-birds of forest and field;
For our ships which have sailed o'er the ocean,
Each bearing our commerce afar;
For our land preserved from commotion,
Rebellion and red-handed war,
We thank Thee, O Lord!

For our lives oft shielded from danger
In the ceaseless grind of the mill;
For the kindness of friend and of stranger
In the day of distress and of ill;
For our home life, so sweet and so tender;
The blessing of wife and of child—
All the gifts which we fail to remember
Of mercies so gentle and mild—
We thank Thee, O Lord!

Aye the year Thou hast crowned with Thy goodness;
For each season's sweet blessings rare;
For the Winter's brisk wholesome freshness,
And the Spring's budding blossoms so fair!
For the Summer's gay garland of flowers,
Gentle Autumn's rich burden of corn;
For old Time with his swift passing hours
Which fillest our life's sunny morn,
We thank Thee, O Lord!

For the Saviour's redemption from sorrow;
Thy comfort and peace from above—
Affording a glad golden morrow—
Aye ten thousand tokens of love—
For the hope when our journey is ended,
And Death with his dart lays us low,
That our lot with the glorified's blended,
We'll die the joys of eternity know,
We thank Thee, O Lord!

Homested, Pa.

He foresaw the danger of this simple people. Hence his warnings in Deut. 8. He feared that among the nations they would learn to trust in trained warriors, among the traders they would catch the spirit of commercialism, among the city mansions they would learn to trust in the material show of things—that they would vaunt themselves and forget God.

This is the danger of every age. The sadness of Greece is that in her beautiful scheme of culture she forgot God. In these days of gigantic intellect, and marvelous inventions, when art and literature and all good and beautiful things are being poured into our laps in abundance, let us not forget that God provides the life and the health, and inspires the thought. In these days of advanced thought, when we do not see God as a wonderworking magician, let us not fail to see him—see him in the great network of laws. Not only see that "all is law," but "all is God," and "all is love."

"God of our fathers, known of old—
Lord of our far-flung battle-line—
Beneath whose awful hand we hold
Dominion over palm and pine—
Lord God of Hosts, be with us yet,
Lest we forget, lest we forget."

Our daily living is so systematized and our system of distribution so perfect that all runs like clockwork. The farmer sows and cultivates his fields and reaps them with the ease of the best mechanism; hurries the grain off to mill, where it is ground on polished rolls and bolted on swing sifters; brought to our door by the delivery man at precisely the time wanted. Let us not forget that—

"Back of the loaf is the snowy flour,
And back of the flour is the mill;
And back of the mill is the sheaf—
And the shower
And the sun,
And the Father's will."

Jesus added another charm to giving thanks to God. He graced the reasons for thankfulness by taking things out of the material category and viewing them as spiritual values. His wilderness conflict was an inner struggle of conflicting ideals. He settled the matter once for all. Man was not to live by bread alone, but by the word of God; he would use his power for others; the realities of life are of first consideration. The issues of this struggle became his program for life, as well as the ideal program for every other son of God. He then set his face toward Jerusalem. The shadow of the cross ever hung over him. We think of him, and truly, as the Man of Sorrows—yet he was always thanking God. One day the disciples came in rejoicing because of their mastery over demons, Jesus told them not to rejoice over such things, but rejoice that their names are written in heaven. He then had joy in the Spirit and said, "Father I thank thee."

As they wended their way toward the Holy City, a man, struck by Christ's words of authority, said, "Master, bid my brother that he divide the inheritance with me." Jesus at once knew he had his mind set upon material things and said, "man's life consisteth not in the abundance of things possessed."

Likewise, the apostle Paul had such a firm grasp of the unseen realities that, utterly regardless of the appearance of material conflict, he could set his face toward the Roman prison not only to be bound but to die, with the song ever in his heart, "Rejoice in the Lord always, and again I say rejoice."

So the soul doth pierce the blackest night,
And smiles through the dash of tears;
For it knows, at the heart of thing is right,
And Time shows a Love that hears,

The Future of Our Country and Our Contribution To It[a]

By W. H. Sheffer

Born upon the shores of an untrod continent, wrapped in the swaddling clothes of adversity, and rocked in the cradle of oppression, yet soothed by the lullaby of a sustaining faith, our nation has grown until it takes its place among the sturdy peoples of the world. Its history is an open book and it is needless that I shall in any measure recite it to you. We are now a great people and living in a great age.

The permanent greatness of any nation depends upon its citizenship. Its people are its power. The American citizen is as unique as he is great. He is the compound product of many nations. In his veins flows the blood of many peoples. And the treasured wisdom of all the ages abides in his heart. The commingling of the blood of the different peoples of the world has strained out the narrowness peculiar to each, and given birth to a people larger and greater than any. And so we have of the many "one new man"—an American citizen. The word "American" has won its place in the ranks and thought of mankind. Those of other lands respect it and those of our country revere it with a sacred pride. Said Daniel Webster, pointing to the pillar on Bunker Hill, "That motionless shaft will be the most powerful of speakers. Its speech will be of civil and religious liberty. It will speak of patriotism and courage. It will speak of moral improvement and elevation of mankind. Decrepit age leaning against its base, and ingenuous youth gathering round it, will speak to each other of the glorious events with which it is connected, and exclaim, 'thank God, I also am an American.'"

Nor am I to speak of our present progress and power. Great as we are, and alluring as is the theme, it must be left to another. Our faces to-day are to the future. We must hear the marching orders of our king. And as he said to the wondering group on Olivet, "Go ye into all the world," so he has given to America an universal mission. We talk about our country's greatness, her size, her wealth, her physical prosperity and power, and recount with pride her material resources; but if these be all of which we have to boast we are poor indeed. These are but the outward evidences of an inward possession far more valuable. America is the incarnation of a divine purpose, the prophet of an ideal era wherein dwelleth peace, the herald of the Gospel of liberty as universal as mankind and commensurate in meaning and moment with that liberty of which our Master spoke when he said: "If the Son therefore shall make you free, ye shall be free indeed." It is ours to teach all men what freedom is, both civil and religious, and ours under God, to emancipate and redeem the human race. A vast horizon opens before us. Years ago with a kind of unconscious prophecy we declared: "We hold these truths to be self-evident—that all men are created equal; that these are endowed by their Creator with certain inalienable rights; that among these are life, liberty and the pursuit of happiness." Were the words "all men" meant only for that fragment of our race that dwells within the borders of our own land? Or must we

*An address delivered at Buffalo before the American Christian Missionary Society.

give them that universal reach that God meant them to have, even though our fathers, wise as they were, did not then discern it?

But before America could accomplish this mission, she must first establish herself as a great nation. This task she has fully and well performed. Another and higher task awaits her. What she has done for herself, she must do for others; and what she is and shall be must be recognized as a sacred trust for the entire race.

W. H. Sheffer.

No other nation is so fitted for this task as our own. Fleet of foot, she has outstripped all others in the race of progress; made wise by the experiences of older nations, she is to escape the pitfalls wherein many a promising people found ruin; bold as a gladiator, she is not to be intimidated by jealous rivals and opposers. The foundation principles of our government are world-wide and imperishable. America and Americanism must conquer the world; not indeed by force of arms or carnal conquest; but by the power of a success wrought out by modern and righteous methods of government; by the demonstration of a higher civilization, and by beneficent results that flow from our national life like streams of gladness which refresh and sweeten the lives of all the people, from the least to the greatest, and bless the poor and rich alike. No longer an experiment or an untried theory, America is to become the exemplar of the world, and by her example to lead all nations to a better life.

What I have said thus far has been, as I see it, the logical deductions from the fundamental principles of our government and a rational interpretation of our history. And in speaking thus I have not allowed myself to be blinded to the defects that exist or to the mistakes we have made in the applications of these principles. Being human we have erred, and at times our errors have been considerable. But we are encouraged just now by the wide-spread movement to correct many of our mistakes and to call our people to return to the first principles of our government as announced by the fathers and which have been the inherent power of our greatness. In this struggle to rectify our failures and to make the needed and proper advancement our nation de-

mands and must have every contribution of wisdom and service available. Her people must come forward with whatever they have for her betterment and place it willingly at her disposal, that her mission be not impeded, but that like an apostle clothed in light she may go forth among the nations both to her own and their eternal good.

In this day of our nation's need as well as of her hope; in this day when opportunity is pleading like an angel, what have we as a religious people to contribute to our nation's good? What have we to give to make more glorious her future, wherewith to bless the race, and wherewith to glorify our God? My brethren, I verily believe that to us God has given that which our nation most surely needs and that which above all else will contribute to her abiding greatness and which will through her bring the largest measure of good to all peoples. In my judgment what is most needed is the spiritual quality. We have become rampant in the matter of material prosperity and progress. Commerce, agriculture, finance, and an accompanying extravagance have set us wild, distorted our judgment, corrupted our ideals and led us away from the pillar of cloud that would not only have guided us through the seas of early struggle, but into the very promised land. Our national life seems to me to be abundant in body, in outward form, in material stature, but lacking in animating and directing spirit. What this huge body needs is a soul, a spiritual force, able to guide it in the proper way and to transform its material greatness into an intelligent spiritual power, and that will show us the difference between the real object of life and the incidents and means that lead thereto. The religious element was the bed-rock of our greatness. It was that on which we builded to our present heights. We should not treat it as,

"Ambition's ladder:
Whereto the climber upward turns his face;
But when he once attains the upmost round,
Then unto the ladder turns his back,
Looks into the clouds, scorning the base degrees
By which he did ascend."

It was faith in the living God and reverence for his holy name that made us a great and prosperous people; and it must be these that shall continue our greatness. Indeed, without these elements of spirituality we must inevitably pass into that withering blight and eternal doom that have passed upon all preceding nations that have forgotten God.

With this whole situation what have we as a people to do? Much every way: chiefly because unto us were committed the oracles of God. The Gospel of Christ has ever been and will be unto the end of time the power of God unto salvation. It is the savor of life to the individual and to the nation alike. These times need this gracious Gospel. But the conditions demand the real Gospel, the Gospel as revealed through the Christ and preached by his chosen apostles. This is no time for the vagaries and speculations of theology; these times are out of joint with the cold dead creeds that stand in our pathway like gaunt specters, whose clammy hand has chilled the warm blood of faith and thus confused the religious thought of mankind. The creed for this hour is the living Christ. Men who are unwilling or unable to believe many of the theological statements about the Christ, will gladly accept him as a personal Savior and admit him into their hearts as the Lord of their lives. The Christ is the religious center of gravity. When he is firmly fixed in the heart as the object of faith and love, all the other parts of the religious life are in perfect balance. He is the magnetic force which alone can unify all the religions, systems and peoples of the world. He, if lifted up, will draw men unto him, and secure that unity for which he both labored and prayed. This centering of the life in Christ assures stability and unity of faith and at the same time is a guarantee of that religious liberty which every growing life both craves and demands, and which is his by right of divine purpose and promise. Where the Christ binds us, we are every one willing to be bound; where he leaves us free, no man or method, no creed or council has the right to bind us. It is a Gospel that exalts the Son of God; that makes him the supreme source of authority in religion; that calls upon men everywhere to confess him and to wear his name; that makes his life and teaching the standard and example for the lives of all people.

This Gospel calls no man common or unclean, but makes of one blood all nations of men, and constitutes of the whole race an universal brotherhood with God our universal Father. It knows no distinction between what is commonly called sacred and secular, but demands that every man shall bear the principles and spirit of the Christ into all his affairs of life. This at once exalts business and government, giving them a spiritual significance and value, and at the same time regards them as but means to a far more intelligent, beneficent, and divine purpose, that the whole world may be filled with all the fullness of God.

This Gospel is strikingly adapted to the genius and conditions of our country. They both were born in the travail of a great opposition; grew to their present stature in spite of the combined forces of prejudice, ignorance and vice; and have gained their present eminence and power by virtue of a constant and

terrific warfare. And, as if by divine appointment, this same Gospel seems especially adapted to the intellectual, social, commercial and religious conditions of our present national life. This is an investigative age; and this Gospel has endured the light and scrutiny of nineteen centuries and constantly increased in popularity and power; it is a progressive age, ever taking on new forms, and this Gospel, while maintaining its truth and essence, adapts itself to the changing conditions of life; this age is indifferent to the theories and method of the past, asking only for the true and the good, and the Gospel of Christ is a genuine iconoclast, striking down the false and partial and giving the true and the universal; it comes bringing not peace, but a sword. Some cry for peace, but there is no peace, and can be none until it is reached in the clear wisdom, perfect righteousness and impartial love of the Son of God. He is the solvent of all doubts and of all problems, and is the one straight way through all the labyrinthian complexities of human life. He is the universal hope. Our social, commercial, political and religious life can all find their perfect adjustment and reconciliation in him. When we learn from him that men are of more value than things; that life is not to be measured by its accidents, that giving is better than getting, that service is valued above selfish ease, that love is the supreme law of God and man, then shall the middle wall of partition be broken down and we shall have that peace for which we have so long sought and which passeth all understanding.

To us who are called Christians has this Gospel been committed. It is ours in trust. By every demand of reason, of righteousness and of love we must not withhold it. If we more clearly than others see its light, the more imperative is our call. The American Christian Missionary Society is the medium through which we may co-operate in evangelizing our country. This society is to us a supreme opportunity. They do not relieve us of any responsibility; rather is it their mission to arouse us

and make us feel more profoundly this important duty. As a brotherhood and as individual Christians we must have fellowship with these chosen brethren. They have not chosen us, but we have chosen them, and in choosing them we have morally pledged our very best endeavor. Too long already have we withheld our worthy fellowship and full support; too long have we been almost criminal in our neglect. The blush of shame has burned its guilty spot deep enough into our cheeks. Let us awake ere it burn our souls.

Some day and all who now are here shall pass, I hope, to that immortal life which God in love hath promised to the faithful. Then, though far beyond this world, we still shall live again in the lives of those who still abide upon the earth: for every man may, if he will, enjoy two blessed immortalities.

"O may I join the choir invisible
Of those immortal dead who live again
In minds made better by their presence."

I stood at Memphis on the banks of the Father of Waters and watched the setting sun. As he sank low toward the west he cast from his glowing face a pathway of light across the surface of the stream. I saw him build with drifting clouds a palace of gold, all pillared and gabled with purple and crimson glory. He cast his mantle upon the lap of mother earth whereon he laid his head to rest. As the scene all shifted farther into the west there remained a lingering, streaming glory as if a band of angels had thrown aside their robes as they flew. And as I watched, one by one the stars came from their hiding places in the sky. The sun had set, but far beyond the horizon that bound my vision was shining in a new world; and yet in the world from which he had departed he was still living in ten thousand shining stars. So may we if faithful unto God and his call of service abide with him beyond the sky, and yet live on and forever in the lives of those whom we have blessed, like the lingering glory of a departing sunset reflected from a world of stars.

Minister 80 Years--101 Years Old

Perhaps John Schaeffer, the devout man of God and the eminent minister of His word, would estimate his life as modestly as did Jacob, "The wrestler with God," but he can say what Jacob could not say: "I have attained unto the days of the years of the life of my fathers in the days of their pilgrimage, and far beyond them." Only two of those who were contemporary with him in any part of his early ministry are now living—Prof. Charles L. Loos, of Lexington, Kentucky and Rev. Lathrop Cooley, of Cleveland, Ohio, both of them past their eightieth year. But they were far from the beginning of their ministry when John Schaeffer began his ministry of the Word.

Alexander Campbell, Walter Scott, William Hayden, Jonas Hartzel, Almon B. Green, John Henry, J. H. Jones, Adamson Bentley, William Collins, Marcus Bosworth, eminent preachers all, and a hundred other men of renown in their "day and generation" and contemporaries of his, have long since passed over to the "other side." He himself says, as he stands alone the representative of the Disciple preachers of his generation:

"No longer forward or behind, I look in hope or fear;
But grateful take the good I find,
The best of now and here."

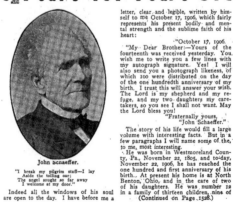

John Schaeffer.

"I break my pilgrim staff—I lay
Aside the toiling oar;
The angel sought so far away
I welcome at my door."

Indeed all the windows of his soul are open to the day. I have before me a

letter, clear and legible, written by himself to me October 17, 1906, which fairly represents his present bodily and mental strength and the sublime faith of his heart:

"October 17, 1906.

"My Dear Brother:—Yours of the fourteenth was received yesterday. You wish me to write you a few lines with my autograph signature. Yes! I will also send you a photograph likeness, of which 100 were distributed on the day of the one hundredth anniversary of my birth. I trust this will answer your wish. The Lord is my shepherd and my refuge, and my two daughters my caretakers, so you see I shall not want. May the Lord bless you!

"Fraternally yours,
"John Schaeffer."

The story of his life would fill a large volume with interesting facts. But in a few paragraphs we will name some of the, to me, most interesting.

He was born in Westmoreland County, Pa., November 22, 1805, and to-day, November 22, 1906, he has reached the one hundred and first anniversary of his birth. At present his home is at North Benton, Ohio, and in the care of two of his daughters. He was number 12 in a family of thirteen children, nine of (Continued on Page 1528.)

Why Should We Be Thankful?

What Is There for Which I as President of the Foreign Society Should be Thankful?

For the growing interest in missions on the part of the churches; for the manifest desire for fuller information shown by the number of missionary books bought and by the number of mission study classes formed; for the cultivated and consecrated young men in and entering the ministry, eager to assist the missionary cause according to the ability God has given them; for the prospect of a new generation in sympathy with missions almost from their birth; for the great and effectual doors opened on all sides; for the opportunities of service and sacrifice such as no previous age enjoyed; for the cheering reports that come from all the fields; for the new workers who have gone out; for those who having finished their course, having entered into the life that is life indeed. Our God has done and is doing great things for us and through us. He is honoring us by permitting us to have fellowship with himself and with Jesus Christ in the greatest and holiest of all enterprises. In his service he enriches and ennobles us; he greatens our souls. As we do our duty he puts it into our power to do still more, and thus he prepares us to receive larger blessings. We are not fighting a losing battle. The sure word of promise is that all the earth shall be filled with the glory of the Lord.   ARCHIBALD M'LEAN.

Things for Which a Corresponding Secretary Has to be Thankful.

For preserving me in safety while I traveled more than 20,000 miles during the missionary year. For giving me health and strength for the hardest year's work of my life. For giving me a great host of warm friends and supporters in my work, and permitting me to lay many of my burdens upon them. For giving me access to the hearts and purses of our brethren in two thousand churches, so that it was possible to raise a larger sum for home missions than in any former year.

For giving us the very best convention, with the best addresses, the best spirit, the best fellowship, the heartiest good will, the most ardent hope accorded the Home Society in many years. For driving dark clouds away from our work and making our prospects the brightest within our history. Hosts of our brethren indulge the conviction that in Home Missions we have entered upon a new era. Their belief will take an active form and thus bring it to pass. There will be a new and better era. For its advent we thank him and take courage.

Finally: For making life worth living in that he gives hard work to do, and ever matches the task by the increased power of the worker. "O let us exalt his name together."   W. J. WRIGHT, Cor. Sec.

Benevolence Inspires Thankfulness.

As we come to this Thanksgiving festival, I am especially grateful that it is my privilege to represent the Benevolent Association of our great brotherhood in its effort to restore apostolic benevolence in its purity and beauty. No ministry of the church is more beautiful and Christlike and none fraught with more interest to the final triumph of the truth of God's love to the world, than this in which the church by bearing one another's burdens fulfills the law of Christ. Of all the multitudes that bring their offering of Thanksgiving to God, none have greater reason for gratitude than those who are interested in the Gospel of the Helping Hand.

We may well be thankful for the help we have been permitted to bestow upon the helpless throughout the year. We have literally fed the hungry, clothed the naked, furnished homes to homeless, and healed the sick. More than 300 parentless children have found parental care and affection, and sixty faithful old brethren have been saved the humility of pauperism and the cruel pangs of cold and hunger by the love, loyalty and service of a great church. Instead

△△△△△△△△△△△△△△△△△△△△△△△△△

AN ANCIENT HYMN OF PRAISE.

Te Deum Laudamus.

We praise thee, O God;
We acknowledge thee to be the Lord.
All the earth doth worship thee, the Father everlasting.
To thee all angels cry aloud;
The heavens, and all the powers therein;
To thee cherubim and seraphim continually do cry—
Holy, holy, holy, Lord God of Sabaoth;
Heaven and earth are full of the majesty of thy glory.
The glorious company of the apostles praise thee.
The goodly fellowship of the prophets praise thee.
The noble army of martyrs praise thee.
The holy Church throughout all the world doth acknowledge thee;
The Father of an infinite majesty;
Thine adorable, true and only Son;
Also the Holy Ghost, the Comforter.
Thou art the King of Glory, O Christ;
Thou art the everlasting Son of the Father.
When thou tookest upon thee to deliver man,
Thou didst humble thyself to be born of a virgin.
When thou hadst overcome the sharpness of death
Thou didst open the kingdom of heaven to all believers.
Thou sittest at the right hand of God, in the glory of the Father.
We believe that thou shalt come to be our Judge.
We therefore pray thee, help thy servants,
Whom thou hast redeemed with thy precious blood.
Make them to be numbered with thy saints, in glory everlasting.
O Lord, save thy people, and bless thine heritage.
Govern them, and lift them up forever.
Day by day we magnify thee;
And we worship thy name ever, world without end.
Vouchsafe, O Lord, to keep us this day without sin.
O Lord, have mercy upon us, have mercy upon us.
O Lord, let thy mercy be upon us, as our trust is in thee.
O Lord, in thee have I trusted; let me never be confounded.

○▽▽▽▽▽▽▽▽▽▽▽▽▽▽▽▽▽▽

of becoming hardened under neglect and suffering they have grown sweet and grateful, invoking heaven's blessing upon their benefactors. Who would not be thankful for such a ministry?

We are thankful for the best year in the history of the association. The donations have been larger, and have been of a better quality. They have come from a larger number of persons. More have remembered this tender ministry in their wills. Our annuity plan was more popular by far. The offerings from individuals, churches and Sunday-schools were the largest we have ever received. The total amount received for the year was $91,794.76; about $12,000 in advance of last year. As we remember the words of the Master, "Inasmuch as ye have done it unto one of the least of these my brethren, ye have done it unto me," we have reason to rejoice and give thanks.

Then we have reason to be thankful for the growing interest in the mission of the association. There has never been such an interest in Christian benevolence since the days of the apostles. From everywhere over this broad land, from pulpits and pew come expressions of the warmest sympathy and heartiest approval, with pledge and promise that the Gospel of the Helping Hand shall occupy its divinely appointed place in the church. Manifestly the time

is at hand when the spirit of Christ dwelling in his church shall once more move among men in sympathy and helpfulness, when the dying mother will be eased in the pains of parting by committing her babies to the bosom of the church, and when no old saint shall suffer; but when the church having loved her own will love them to the end.   J. H. MOHORTER.

Why I, as a Christian Woman, am Thankful.

As a worker in the Christian Woman's Board of Missions I am thankful for the past year crowned with God's unfailing goodness, and for the present widening opportunities for service before our organization. I rejoice that work and hope and happy skies are ours, not only at this glad Thanksgiving time when autumn's gold is gathered and her harvest reaped, but in all seasons and in all service for him.

In the Thanksgiving joy for garnered harvests is the prayer that all may share the reaper's joy, that the Church of Christ may have the yearning heart of her great Captain and the divine illumination coming from a sanctified knowledge of his will. That she may be led by him to undertake with and for him the consummation of his plan—the Gospel taught in all lands and the union of all Christians. In this great work of the church we pledge ourselves to bear a part.
                    MRS. HELEN E. MOSES.

What Have I, as Secretary of the Board of Church Extension, to be Thankful For?

That God has seen fit to give me good health and to use me in some measure to help spread his kingdom has made me thankful every morning. I am thankful for the co-operation of my brethren in the ministry who have helped to build up a fund of nearly $600,000, and for the confidence of the churches. I treasure the confidence of my brethren in Christ more than all riches. I am profoundly grateful for the gains of last year—the first of our Centennial campaign. There was a gain of more than 25 per cent in receipts and a gain of 275 in the number of contributing churches.

I am thankful for my citizenship in a land so blest as ours, and for my membership in a brotherhood, with a plea so democratic that it is rapidly meeting the liberty-loving Americans who believe that in union there is strength.

I am, therefore, glad for the hosts of new churches that are born into this great family of God who are demanding for their housing a million dollar Church Extension fund which shall repeat itself in church-building work until the church militant shall become the church triumphant.

I rejoice in the fact that through this fund 1,027 congregations now have good church homes and that they have been so loyal in the use of this money that more than $580,000 has been returned to repeat its work and that only a few hundred dollars have been lost.

I am thankful, also, that we have over 1,200 homeless bands thus far loyal to Christ and our plea, who, though it would be easy to surrender and merge into sectarian congregations, yet will not hang their harps on the willows but who wait and work in faith and hope until that glad day when a tardy brotherhood will help them to strength and permanency with a church home.
                    G. W. MUCKLEY.

A Day with the Rev. J, H. Jowett, M. A.

England's Greatest Preacher

By William Durban

It has been often remarked, as Lord Chesterfield said in relation to Lady Hester Stanhope, that to know some men and women is a liberal education in itself. I have certainly greatly extended my own education as years have rolled on, by my immense privileges in making the acquaintance of very many wonderfully able and highly distinguished people, belonging to different walks in life. London affords its residents incomparable advantages in this respect. For this stupendous center of civilization attracts to itself, permanently or temporarily, the vast majority of the personalities who in this and other lands have deserved and achieved celebrity. It was my good fortune not long ago to spend a whole memorable day with Mr. J, H. Jowett. This popular Birmingham minister is, not only by his own people, but also by large numbers of others, considered the very greatest preacher now living in the world. Such an expression of appreciation when very wide-spread is surely a proof of a valid title to fame. But I have never met with a more unpretending or more easily accessible man, or one more utterly unconscious of his own towering merit.

Listening to the Pulpit Music.

A sermon by Jowett is a homiletic melody of indefinable fascination. I have been perhaps all my life peculiarly susceptible to the attractions of oratory. And I am sure that this sensitiveness to the charms of real eloquence has been a deepest source of pleasure. The versatile persuasiveness of Beecher, the torrential outpourings of that "volcano in a white necktie" (when he chose to wear one), T. DeWitt Talmage, the fine philosophic sermons of Dr. Hillis, the impressive declamation of Dr. Amory Bradford, the mingling of power and delicate humour in the addresses of Z. T. Sweeney, have taught me to understand the splendor of the finest American preaching. From my boyhood onward till now such men in the English ministry as Canon Liddon, the silver-tongued orator of St. Paul's for all too brief a career, the voice-voiced Henry Melvill of years before, styled the British Chrysostom, the matchless people's preacher, C. H. Spurgeon, the glittering Paxton Hood, the erudite and elegant Dr. Alexander McLaren, the stately Dr. Dale, of Birmingham, the potent and convincing Hugh Stowell Brown, the saintly Newman Hall, the soaring Morley Punshon, the master of wonderful whispers and sublime thunders, Dr. Joseph Parker—these have all in turn enchanted my admiration and enshrined themselves in my mental Valhalla of English pulpit princes. Alas, most of these have passed away! And in England today, though the number of excellent preachers never was so great, the number of really eminent and widely popu-

lar ministers of religion never in modern days has been so small. Dr. Campbell Morgan, of Westminster Chapel, has captured the West End of London; R. J. Campbell holds great crowds at the City Temple; Archibald Brown is the greatest pulpit force in South London, as he used to be in East London; the bishop of Stepney and Canon Scott Holland draw multitudes to St. Paul's; Canon Henson, in his parliamentary parish church of St. Margaret's, Westminster, is exceedingly attractive to the fashionable class, as is Archdeacon Wilberforce when he declaims in Westminster Abbey. But these stand out from the mediocre mass of preachers. They are bright stars in the homiletic firmament, but what a small galaxy it is!

Mr. Jowett's Style.

Why do many thoughtful people place Mr. Jowett higher as a pulpit orator than any of his companions in the clerical constellation? I think I can account for the priority. He is possessed of a rare and perhaps unequalled combination of the very qualities which captivate hearers of the best class. Most of the great preachers excel in one or two of these characteristics, but Mr. Jowett shines in them all. He is, of fine physique, but is not ponderous. He is given to natural gesture, but makes no attempt at histrionic display. He has a melodious and flexible voice, but never painfully exerts it. He is by turns impassioned, quiet, serene, excitable, pathetic, humorous, eloquent, simple, pungent, sarcastic, conciliatory and poetic. His argumentation is always somewhat declamatory, so that it never tries, but awakens the hearer to fresh interest. And his declamation is always argumentative, so that it never wearies the listener like a series of hollow thunderings. His thoughts are always expressed in the simplest possible diction, so that their crystalline clearness makes them at once apprehended. In illustration he excels perhaps all of his competitors. He plunges at one moment into classical allusions and presently takes his hearers on a flying excursion into some realm of nature. So that a sermon from this "Bishop of the Midlands" is a truly incomparable feast.

The Preacher's Views.

After hearing Mr. Jowett preach on one Sunday morning I spent the afternoon with him in conversation. The sermon was preached in Westminster, for on that day Dr. Campbell Morgan and Mr. Jowett were exchanging pulpits, the former having gone to Birmingham and the latter having come to London for that purpose. Long shall I recollect the grand utterance to which 3,000 delighted people listened. The subject was based on Matt. 16:13, "Whom do men say that I am?" The preacher dilated on the John the Baptist element, the Elijah ele-

ment, the Jeremiah element in the nature of Jesus. What did the man in the street of Christ's own day think of him? Evidently Jesus was not the kind of personality that we commonly imagine. He was not by any means simply or exclusively the "gentle Jesus, meek and mild," of our popular modern conception, but was rather known to his own generation as Knox, Oliver Cromwell, and other grand, majestic, stern and terrible reformers and denunciators of iniquity were known in their days. And just because of this element of majestic righteousness in Jesus which thundered out woes on hypocrites and oppressors, he also was ineffably tender in his love and compassion. For the water that trickles forth over granite rocks is always the purest and softest. Mr. Jowett declared that the chief want of

(Continued on Page 1528.)

❋ ❋

A DOCTOR'S TRIALS

He Sometimes Gets Sick Like Other People.

Even doing good to people is hard work if you have too much of it to do.

No one knows this better than the hardworking, conscientious family doctor. He has troubles of his own—often gets caught in the rain or snow, or loses so much sleep he sometimes gets out of sorts. An overworked Ohio doctor tell his experience:

"About three years ago as the result of doing two men's work, attending a large practice and looking after the details of another business, my health broke down completely, and I was little better than a physical wreck.

"I suffered from indigestion and constipation, loss of weight and appetite, bloating and pain after meals, loss of memory and lack of nerve force for continued mental application.

"I became irritable, easily angered and despondent without cause. The heart's action became irregular and weak, with frequent attacks of palpitation during the first hour or two after retiring.

"Some Grape-Nuts and cut bananas came for lunch one day and pleased me particularly with the result. I got more satisfaction from it than from anything I had eaten for months, and on further investigation and use, adopted Grape-Nuts for my morning and evening meals, served usually with cream and a sprinkle of salt or sugar.

"My improvement was rapid and permanent in weight as well as in physical and mental endurance. In a word, I am filled with the joy of living again, and continue the daily use of Grape-Nuts for breakfast and often for the evening meal.

"The little pamphlet, 'The Road to Wellville,' found in pkgs., is invariably saved and handed to some needy patient along with the indicated remedy." Name given by Postum Co., Battle Creek, Mich. "There's a reason."

As Seen From the Dome   By F. D. Power

One cause of thanksgiving that comes to every true heart to-day is found in the flowers. Consider the lilies; think upon them, take in their lessons. Millions of these lilies bloom in Galilee. The fine showy scarlet flowers abound everywhere. Jesus loves nature and teaches from nature, and looking upon the fields he exclaims, "Consider the lilies!" Consider the lily; it was a clod; it comes forth from the darkness; God fashions it. So he gives you life and beauty. Consider the lily; how the earth feeds it; and air fans it, and sun warms it, and heaven sends its dews upon it. Consider the lily; how it grows, from what it springs, to what it attains, how gratefully it lives and blooms and gives out its fragrance to bless the world. And from every grass blade, and every flower comes the lesson of praise and thanksgiving. *Deo gratiae,* "Thanks be to God," is the voice of all nature. Our word "thankful," from its Anglo-Saxon derivation, is allied to "thinkful," that is, to be thoughtful or mindful of benefits received, and thus every flower of the field seems to think, and to be of one mind with the poppy-anemones which in spring paint with bright scarlet the plains of Palestine. On a blue Monday recently I sauntered into the chrysanthemum show. It is worth a good deal to associate with these stately blooms and get their inspiration. I always go; and I preach better the next Sunday for an hour in such company. Here are the small-flowered pompons and the grotesque big-flowered Japanese sorts, the children of the Chusan daisy. Pompons are the small, flat and button-like outdoor plants, while the large, globular, Japanese blossoms are grown indoors. A single plant of the Japanese hairy type—the Mrs. Hardy—sold for $1,500 and started the American craze. Here are white flowers and golden flowers with long hairs, incurved and recurved; fantastic forms, freaks, oddities and curiosities; tubular and quilled varieties; flowers white and pink, amaranth and crimson, red and yellow, buff and bronze, and all seemingly brought to a stage of practical perfection, and growing to a height of five or six feet. What fanciful names! Golden Hair and Queen of Plumes, May Flower and Black Hawk, Good Gracious, Bronze Bride and Queen of Anemones, Golden Weddings and Silver Weddings. As my friend who shows me around is a canny Scot I am reminded by these last of the story of two old Scotch women in London during the queen's jubilee. One says to the other, "Can ye tell me, wumman, what is it they call a jubilee?" "Wele, it's this," said her neighbor, "When folk has been married twenty-five years, that's a silver wuddin', and when they have been fifty years that's a golden wuddin'. But if the mon's dead,

then, it's a jubilee."

Most of the beauties, however, are named after famous women. Here is Mrs Roosevelt and Mrs. Donald McLean, Mrs. Mary Mann, a deep pink of ample proportions, and Miss Alice Byron, a pure white, and Mrs. Senator Knox, a bright yellow; the pure white blossom, easily told by its rotundity and the glistening brilliancy of its petals, is the Beatrice, and the bloom, with many tints that change almost as the opaline hues of the seashell, is the Oklana; Mrs. Paul Sahnt is a floral curiosity with blossoms six inches in diameter, pure white, turning to a delicate pink, and Mrs. G. M. Wilson is a creamy white with lemon center and odd-shaped petals; Amoria is exquisitely pink and round while Ethel Fitzroy has red and yellow blooms; Magenta resembles a peony, and the Dazzler, a deep crimson, blushes like a June rose. Then here are our old friends, William Jennings Bryan and the Ducrosiets, and such freaks as the Rufus and the Brutus. Many a one might be named Fido, or, for the lack of a hair cut, "The Old Man of the Sea." They are enormous, some of them, measuring twenty-three inches in circumference.

Chrysanthemums are good to eat, they say. "The Golden Flower" is the flower of the east, as the rose is the flower of the west. The Chinese minister says they make an excellent salad, these "Mums." Mr. Chentung Liang-Cheng is authority for the statement that properly prepared the big bushy blooms are esteemed a delicacy in the land of Sinim. Mr. Sinzo Aoki, Japanese ambassador, says our chrysanthemums are larger and finer than those of Nippon, "the land of the chrysanthemums." But he is a diplomat, this little brown-skinned, black-eyed man from the land of the rising sun.

But there is more for my "Blue Monday" than these chrysanthemums in the show. Here are crotons that look like green plants streaked and spotted with white or yellow paint, palms and roses and carnations. Here my friend is creating a new lettuce, and in another place he is producing a new brand of oats, and in another, coaxing a new tomato to come into being that shall be smooth on top, and be worth 25 cents more on each plant. Here he has made a new rose which he says is worth —the single plant—a round thousand. Here is an old lady plant, a spray of which every old woman in his native country takes to church in her Bible to tickle her nose during the sermon and induce wakefulness. Here is a great hothouse given over entirely to my favorite carnations. Theophrastus, 300 B. C., gave the name Dianthus, Greek *Dios,* divine, and *anthos,* a flower, to this blossom because of its delightful fragrance.

Carnation, we call it, from the Latin, because of its flesh color. It is the old English "Gilly flower," and for two thousand years it has been cultivated, and they use the forceps on it as they do on the "Mums" and get nature to work it up in all forms and colors and scents. Here is the Dionaea, or "Venus Flytrap." It is an insectiverous plant and possesses an inexplicable fancy for flies. It is a wonder of the vegetable kingdom, and grows only in the sandy savannas of North Carolina. It has a large special literature, and everybody is interested to see and test it. So it is a much overworked plant. It delights in sunshine and sighs for "Tarheels." Its peculiarity is a little trap, formed by two leaves, with a border of sawlike filaments. Your *musca domestica,* overcome by curiosity ventures in the

❀ ❀

NO COFFEE
The Doctor Said.

Coffee slavery is not much different from alcohol or any other drug. But many people don't realize that coffee contains a poisonous, habit-forming drug—caffeine.

They get into the habit of using coffee, and no wonder, when some writers for respectable magazines and papers speak of coffee as "harmless."

Of course it doesn't paralyze one in a short time like alcohol, or put one to sleep like morphine, but it slowly acts on the heart, kidneys and nerves, and soon forms a drug-habit, just the same, and one that is the cause of many overlooked ailments.

"I wish to state for the benefit of other coffee slaves," writes a Vt. young lady, "What Postum Food Coffee has done for me.

"Up to a year ago I thought I could not eat my breakfast if I did not have at least 2 cups of coffee, and sometimes during the day, if very tired, I would have another cup.

"I was annoyed with indigestion, heart trouble, bad feeling in my head, and sleeplessness. Our family doctor, whom I consulted, asked me if I drank coffee. I said I did and could not get along without it.

"He told me it was the direct cause of my ailments, and advised me to drink Postum. I had no faith in it, but finally tried it. The first cup was not boiled long enough and was distasteful, and I vowed I would not drink any more.

"But after a neighbor told me to cook it longer I found Postum was much superior in flavor to my coffee. I am no longer nervous, my stomach troubles have ceased, my heart action is fine, and from 105 lbs. weight when I began Postum, I now weigh 138 lbs. I give all the credit to Postum as I did not change my other diet in any way." Name given by Postum Co., Battle Creek, Mich. Read the little book, "The Road to Wellville," in pkgs. "There's a reason."

open doorway, tickles the plant as he moves around, and it closes the trap with a jerk, and proceeds leisurely to devour its delicious morsel. Another curiosity is the "Ouvirandria Fenestralis," or lace plant of Madagascar, the leaves of which grow only under water and are like the most delicate lace of intricate pattern.

But there is no end to these attractions. The cerulean hue of my day is gone. Life is full of little joys. Nature teaches everywhere the goodness and love of God. It needs only an open mind and a grateful heart to receive the gifts. Sidney Smith said: "Never give way to melancholy, resist it steadily; for the habit will encroach. I once gave a lady two and twenty receipts against melancholy. One was a bright fire; another, to remember all the pleasant things said to her; another to keep a box of sugar plums on the chimney piece and a kettle simmering on the hob. I thought this mere trifling at the moment, but have, in after-life, discovered how true it is that these little pleasures often banish melancholy better than higher and more exalted objects; and that no means ought to be thought too trifling which can oppose it, either in ourselves or in others." But I never in all my life knew a "Blue Monday." Come, let us give thanks.

❀ ❀

England's Greatest Preacher.

(Continued from Page 1526.)

our times was a recovery of the accent of righteousness and of indignation against wrong inflicted on humanity.

An Afternoon Causerie.

I sat with Mr. Jowett on the Sunday afternoon, listening to his replies to certain queries that I addressed to him. These elicited some very original expressions of his individual ideas. He believes that the pulpit, so far from being superseded by the press, or becoming effete in an age of profusely poured forth literature, is a far greater power than ever before. For there is something in the souls of men which yearns for the efficient utterance by the living voice of the deepest and most vital truths. I asked Mr. Jowett what he considered should be the attitude of the ministry towards the various movements connected with criticism and modern thought. He replied thus: "I believe that the preacher's great Master places his disciples under no obligation to blind their judgment. Our preaching must be illumined, if it is to be effective. In the matter of the public ministry there are two things which we can only divorce at our peril—light and heat. It is very easy to display heated ignorance, and it is by no means difficult to exhibit non-fertilizing knowledge. I think that the Christian minister should guard against both these perils. In the realm of learning he must see to it that his zeal is according to knowledge. 'Speak, ing for myself," continued Mr. Jowett, "my indebtedness to modern scholarship is unspeakable. I believe that our Lord is lighting lamps all down the highway of the centuries, and the recent illuminations are by no means the least in the long succession. It may be that the critics are sometimes a little in advance of the discovered path, and I think they are on the open

moorland when they may be fancying that they have found the track across. And I quite agree that all revolutionary positions should be tested with scrupulous care before being accepted; but I am not prepared to shout an alarm simply because some pioneers have been a little premature in hailing unfounded discoveries. I am too much their debtor to be their thankless critic. There are some portions of the Old Testament which in these recent days have been vitalized as Carlyle vitalized the life of Oliver Cromwell."

A Fine Exegesis.

Mr. Jowett's evening sermon was as great a masterpiece of popular pulpit oratory as the discourse of the morning. It was on Luke 21:19. "In your patience ye shall win your souls." The authorized version reads, "In your patience possess your souls." But in the revised version it is "win." Mr. Jowett quoted from a letter by the late Bishop Westcott, one of the revisors, that of all the changes in the New Testament none had given him so much joy. For it is one thing to possess a Victoria Cross, quite another to win it. It is one thing to inherit a title, quite another to earn or win it. He added that the English people had only lately shown that they possessed South Africa, but had by no means won it. A country never is won by mere annihilation of our foes. The only way to win is by conversion, not destruction. The sword is not to be annihilated, but turned into a plowshare.

❀ ❀

Minister 80 Years—101 Years Old.

(Continued from Page 1524.)

whom grew to manhood and womanhood. His grandfather, John Schaeffer, arrived in the United States from Germany in 1763. The home in Germany was at Wittenberg where the university in which Luther and Melanchthon held professorships, was established in 1502, and where the colossal statue of Luther was erected in the market place in 1821. The father, also John Schaeffer, was born in Maryland, near Hagerstown. The family resting places after their arrival in America were, first near Hagerstown, Md.; then in Pennsylvania, on both the east and west sides of the Allegheny Mountains; then in Harrison county, O., where the family lived for thirty years; then in 1847 in Iowa where, in 1853, the father of the subject of this sketch died in the ninetieth year of his age. John Schaeffer, the third, was about 12 years old when his father's family came into Ohio. They were of the real pioneers of the eastern part of the state. The family was poor, and he had few advantages to obtain an education, and he never had the advantage of a collegiate education. But he was, nevertheless, a man of fine attainments in the line of scholarship, for he was fortunate in having, after he was 20 years of age, for an instructor, Rev. John Wagenhaltz, from Germany, a gentleman in the true sense of that word. This instruction was mainly theological—the theology of the Lutheran church—though the literary feature of an education was not overlooked. Writing of that period of his life in 1872, Mr. Schaeffer said: "I studied the theology of the Lutheran church one year, after which by the influence of Mr. Wagenhaltz, I obtained, when examined, a license to preach, sprinkle infants, catechise and solemnize marriage contracts, but was denied the right of administering the Lord's supper and a voice in the synodical and ministerial sessions. This was to assist me in the prosecution of my studies for another

The Art of Reading   By James Mudge, D. D.

Many people make shipwreck on the infinite sea of printer's ink. A pilot for that ocean, a professor of books and r ading, seems to be much needed. Goethe is reported to have remarked: "I have been fifty years trying to learn how to read and I have not learned yet." It may well be doubted then, if many common men can be accounted to have fully mastered this difficult art. Certainly not every one who is familiar with print knows how to read.

The immense multiplication of cheap reading matter, while commonly esteemed one of the glories of our time and land, has very serious drawbacks; and even the art of printing has not been a gift wholly unmixed with evil. It may easily become a clog on the progress of the human mind if not used with judgment and self-control. It has been said of some that they gave so much time to the minds of other men that they never found leisure to look into their own minds, and that they piled so many books upon their heads that their brains could not move. Who doubts that it was a blessing in the case of Lincoln, and some others, that they had so few books in their earlier years? Some are simply smothered by the weight of their accumulations. They do not possess their knowledge, they are possessed by it; they do not master their books, they are mastered by them. Great piles of fuel put out a little fire, though they only make a great fire burn brightly. When the mind is really on fire any and all material will feed the flame, But reading will do very little good to a mind which is sluggish, not thoroughly awake and alive and aware. Books give the mind stuff to work with—ideas, facts and sentiments—of which it is almost as bad to have too much as too little.

Advices? Rules? Yes, they can be given. No two persons would put them quite in the same way, nor would precisely the same formation be equally adapted to all. But, some things in the way of counsel may, perhaps, be ventured which those at least who are immature can find profit in pondering.

Read with a relish. It is not well, as a general thing, to lay out extended courses or attempt ambitious works of many ponderous volumes, unless there be a very decided taste for exploring some especial field of research. What is taken in when the mind is aglow, when it has by some means acquired an eager appetite, when curiosity is awake, is worth many times as much as that which is placed upon a dulled palate or received from a mere sense of duty. Hence a historical novel is frequently better for a young person than a dry history. It will often stimulate inquiry so that the sober history itself becomes afterwards attractive, whereas if the latter had been presented first, the only result would

have been a loathing for the whole thing.

Read with a purpose. He who works up a subject with the design of presenting it in a systematic form, in an essay or a lecture, or a newspaper article, a pamphlet, a book or a debate before some association, will take hold of it with a zeal otherwise unattainable, and will feel little fatigue after great labor. He has before him a definite end and is exceedingly stimulated by that thought. Random reading profits little, and is in most cases a mere waste of time.

Read with results. These will come only as pains are taken to digest the mental food. The mere act of reading will not be followed by lasting good any more than the mere act of eating. The voracious reader who races at express speed through whatever comes along, each volume wiping out the impression produced by its predecessor, is not a model for imitation. What is taken into the mind must be meditated upon and talked about until it becomes completely assimilated with previous stores and made one's own. The process of transformation must go on until the thoughts and facts received are no longer foreign substances, but have become incorporated with the intellectual system.

Read only what is worth reading; if, with the utmost care that precious thing can be ascertained. It needs a strong character and a resolute system to keep the head cool in the storm of literature around us. We are deluged with books, and, as to magazines and newspapers, they are without number. There are emptied upon the counters month by month whole libraries of print which are extremely unworthy to take the time of a busy man who has some respect for his brains. The wonder is, not that so few books outlive the year that gives them birth, but that they are born at all. One must be ignorant of much that is commonly talked about in order to have something in mind that is really worth talking about. The field is almost boundless and it is not surprising that we are extremely bewildered by the multiplicity of objects clamoring for a share of their attention. To find the few books that are really worth while is as difficult as to find the best companions.

Read with a pencil and make marginal notes, so that the main points may be rapidly reviewed and the mind concentrated on that which is most important. Some system of shorthand is a great help in this. "Reading with the fingers" has been called the most thorough test of active scholarship. It is no small art to know how to turn the pages of a thick volume quickly over and light easily on the exact spot where the thing wanted is to be found, picking out the valuable from the immense amount of useless ver-

biage that encumbers most books. Certain sections or chapters often embrace all that is really important, and it would be very foolish to feel it a duty to plod through the whole. Ordinary books contain a good deal of padding, a good deal that is very commonplace and that can just as well be omitted by one who has read widely. Much of literature is the mere pouring out of one bottle into another, the repetition in a slightly different form of what has been said over and over before. This makes the art of skipping and skimming exceedingly useful. One who has read much becomes able quite readily to get out of a new volume its real meat, its genuine contribution to the thought of the world, if it has any, to pluck out the heart of its mystery with speed, to suck its juice quickly and throw it aside like a squeezed orange. Very few books deserve prolonged study. He makes a great saving who has learned how to leap from point to point instead of painfully traversing the vast valleys of the commonplace which make up most of the pages.

The best reader is he, both thoughtful and purposeful, who reads to stimulate his mind that it may go to work on its own account to gather stores of information that he may have material to work upon, to purify his taste, improve his style, broaden his sympathies, enlarge his usefulness, and increase his power. He is glad to read quite often what he does not fully agree with that he may be roused to intellectual combat which will impart vigor to his reasoning faculties. He delights also to read very frequently those great poetical productions which expand his emotions, impart wings to his imagination and teach him both how to observe nature and how to comprehend the human heart. Such an one reads with close attention, reads a great deal aloud, reads with some system, reads with prayer and care, with patience and perseverance, for one's self and for other people, with diligence and determination, with enjoyment and exhilaration, and, while not altogether neglecting the current literature of the day (for once in a while there is a volume that has the breath of life in it), reads the solid, supreme books, the masterpieces of literature that have proved their right to be and commend themselves to us by the cumulative force of long-established prestige.

Blessings on books! They enlarge space and prolong time; they transfer us to former days and distant climes. Few men are happier than he who has both a taste for and a vocation among books. The winnowed and garnered wisdom of the past is his daily food. For him orators declaim, poets sing, and philosophers discourse. He has been made free of that rightly-named "republic of letters," that genuine republic where, without introduction or ceremony, the greatest and noblest of all ages may be met on terms of perfect equality. Fenelon said: "If the riches of both Indies, if the crowns of all the kingdoms of Europe were laid at my feet in exchange for my love of reading, I would spurn them all." Many others have said substantially the same. Next to a great university, as a means of culture, stands a great library; and even in the university the library is the central point. He who has learned how to make the best use of a large library has made excellent progress in his education.

Jamaica Plains, Mass.

Current Literature

Any book reviewed in these columns (except "net" books) will be sent postpaid by The Christian Publishing Company, St. Louis, on receipt of the published price. For "net" books, add ten per cent for postage.

SIDE-LIGHTS ON ASTRONOMY. By Simon Newcomb, LL. D. Harper Bros. 350 pages. $2 net.

Prof. Newcomb's name on any book dealing with the general subject of astronomy is guarantee of that book's worth and best of all, he is not only a specialist with a great fund of knowledge but, like Richard Proctor, he has the gift, rare in the man of science, of popularizing abstruse subjects and bringing them in language and treatment within the range of the common man. This book stimulates the imagination while it impresses one with the grandeur of astronomical conceptions. And though it calls for the exercise of the thinking powers, it is fascinating in its attractive qualities. Interest rather than unity of thought has determined the selection of these essays contributed originally to a number of the periodicals. A prominent theme in the collection is that of the structure, extent and duration of the universe. Prof. Newcomb discusses questions of this character in the light of the most recent knowledge. And it is worth while quoting this paragraph as showing how open-minded is the true scientist and how far short he feels he is from the final knowledge: "It is a curious fact that, although they (astronomers) were never learning so fast as at the present day, yet there seems to be more to learn now than there ever was before. Great and numerous as are the unsolved problems of our science, knowledge is now advancing into regions which, a few years ago, seemed inaccessible. Where it will stop, none can say." Although mainly astronomical, a number of discussions relating to general scientific subjects have been included in the book, the closing chapter being a lucid and sane presentation of the flying machine.

FAIREST GIRLHOOD. By Margaret E. Sangster. Fleming H. Revell Co. 263 pages. $1.50 net.

Mrs. Sangster's charming style is her sweet, winsome personality woven into words. She knows girlhood—its longings and hopes, its fears and frailties, its possibilities and its defeats, and its victories. She has been a girl and she has had opportunities to study the girls of to-day as few women have, and this, with her motherly instinct, has made her their best counsellor. This book, dedicated to Miss Grace Dodge, another friend of girlhood, has been written with love in every line for all sorts and conditions of girls, and it is beautifully presented with all the fine arts of the printer and drawings by Griselda Marshall McClure.

HIGHWAYS AND BYWAYS OF THE MISSISSIPPI VALLEY. By Clifton Johnson. The Macmillan Co. Pages 287. Price, $2 net.

Another volume of the "American Highways and Byways" series, which is as notable for its illustrations as it is for its charming character sketches and snap-shot descriptions. The author is a keen observer and an appreciative student of country manners and customs. He can see the greatness and pick out the oddities and he can make you see them. This is a book for the arm chair. Some of its meanderings are amid the "city behind the levee," the "land of rice and sugar," the cotton patches of Tennessee, down in Arkansas and the Ozarks, Mark Twain's country, the farms of Iowa, the prairies of Minnesota and Wisconsin and the headwaters of the great river. The half-tone illustrations are from really exceptionally artistic photographs. We can not name a more delightful gift book of this season.

RING IN THE NEW. By Richard Whiting. Century Company. Pages 347. Price $1.50.

Mr. Whiting became famous almost in a day by his story "No. 5. John Street," but he was known before that book appeared to some newspaper men as a sympathetic student of social conditions in the great city of London. It may be surmised, therefore, that his latest book now before us is concerned with the living and thinking of "the other half." "Ring in the New," is the story of a young girl orphaned, unworldly, unskilled, thrown into the maelstrom of a great metropolis. What life may mean to such a girl, what it does mean to thousands of gently bred, gentle natured, incompetent working girls in London is told in this book with the solution of the problem which the heroine found. Mr. Whiting's style would be the better were there a little more of poetry in it, but perhaps it is difficult to deal with such subjects in a poetical style. There are many bright sayings in it, many of which we would like to quote. For instance, "Most of her set are insane with the jumps—gadding about. The motor car has fixed it as the disease of the day. They never can stand still. They're all over the place on the lookout for the untried. That little study where she sits in the morning, is n soff of Clapham Junction (London railroad station) that leads to every place in the universe, a mere from and to. * * * They are all nice. I sometimes fancy they'll wriggle through with their manners at the Judgment Day." We give, but one more quotation: "Both were unfortunate in their papa, as he, too, was unfortunate in his progenitors. He had never had a chance until the kindly earth took him, in a last endeavor to make him useful in his grave. It is asserted, and plausibly, that even these by-products have a certain value as manure."

CONISTON. By Winston Churchill. The Macmillan Company. Price $1.50.

This is Mr. Churchill's best book. It is not his most interesting book to the young American girl. "The Crisis" or "The Crossing" have a more romantic love story as this is viewed by our set of sweet sixteen. But even as a love story "Coniston" is far ahead in the real delineation of human feelings than anything Mr. Churchill has written. But the love element is a feature of "Coniston," yet it is a very subsidiary one—except in its effects. It is character—character of great American womanhood, the character of rugged, untamed manhood, the despicable character of much that is allied with political ambition—that is the very soul of Mr. Churchill's presentation. There is less of the dramatic force in this book than in some of the author's productions, but it sounds a truer note and its principal figure is one that we can never forget, which can not be said of Richard Carvel and other of Mr. Churchill's characters. The book is interesting merely as a story, but as a study of political bossism it is opportune.

A CRITICAL AND EXEGETICAL COMMENTARY ON THE BOOK OF PSALMS. By Charles Augustus Briggs, D. D., D. Litt., and Emilie Grace Briggs, B. D. Vol. I. New York. Charles Scribner's Sons. Price, $3.00 net.

The great mass of humanity that finds itself mirrored in the sweet songs of Israel will not trouble itself about the questions discussed in this latest critical commentary

"WHEN friends grow cold and the converse of intimates languishes into vapid civility and commonplace, books only continue the unaltered countenance of happier days, and cheer us with that true friendship which never deceived hope nor deserted sorrow."
—Washington Irving.

✧ ✧ ✧

THE INSPIRATION OF OUR FAITH. By John Watson, D. D. (Ian Maclaren.) New York. A. G. Armstrong & Son. Pages 358.

Here we have a volume of sermons from the author of "Beside the Bonnie Brier Bush." It takes its title from the first sermon, which is as unlike the usual sermon as is the rest of the volume. There are not firstlies, secondlies, and thirdlies in this book. One great thought is in the preacher's mind, and with all the wealth of literary power with which he is gifted he makes it stand out before the mind of the hearer or reader. That the book is not commonplace may be taken for granted. That it is not always according to the accepted orthodoxy of conservative thinking is also true. Take, for instance, his sermon on Conversion. It is, he says, "impossible to standardize conversion because you can not reduce human nature to a uniformity. As long as every man has his own history and ancestry and idiosyncrasies there will be many kinds of conversion. There is only one God to return to, and one Father's house, but there are innumerable far countries, and John Bunyan is not the only man who has been converted. Perhaps, the most conventional conversion is moral, when man is turned from sin to holiness. Some people are kept from God, not by worldliness or unbelief, but by the power of fleshly sins. From their childhood they have been held in the bondage of the senses and they have been the slaves of their passions. They may not have sinned in act, but they have sinned in their imagination. It does not follow that their nature is coarser; it may be richer. Their blood may not be fouler; it may be redder. A spring of water, if it be banked, will water a glen; if it run at large it will make a morass. Their conversion will not be the destruction, but the redemption of their passion." Another form of conversion, he says, is spiritual, and it is the experience not of the publican and sinner, but of the scribe and Pharisee. He has not gone astray, as the sinners did. He has lived with God all his days, yet it is an inexplicable change when a Pharisee discovers that God is not hard and uncharitable, but that he is gracious and magnanimous. A third form of conversion, according to Dr. Watson, is intellectual, while there is another which is practical. One may be neither a sinner nor a Pharisee, and yet come short because he is doing nothing with his life. Dr. Watson is very positive when it comes to speaking of positive religion. He says that Christianity "is for every man, first, a venture, and then an experience," and that it is as positive as science. "Why," he says, "should a man not obey the conditions which Christ gave, and fulfill all conditions of obedience which he laid down? Let him suppose for the time that this Savior, who, according to testimony, has saved so many, is alive, and let him believe, in him for the time, at least, as so many have believed even unto death. It is a most supreme experiment, but there are reasons for making it, and also strong hope of its success."

✧ ✧ ✧

THE MENACE OF PRIVILEGE. By Henry George. The Macmillan Company, New York. Pages 420. Price $1.50 net.

Here is a book marked by vigor, sincerity, and clearness. It is a study of the dangers to the Republic from the existence of the favored class, and by it the author has made a place for himself independent of all the fame of his distinguished father. It is a book of the times and for the times. Lofty in tone, there is no appeal to passion and prejudice, though the writer has very pronounced views on the questions of which he treats. The book is replete with information gleaned from many sources in an exhaustive inquiry into existing social, industrial and moral conditions. Through these the author has sought to trace relations, secret or overt, between special privilege and commercial forces that make for personal aggrandizement in the republic. We have heard much of the muck-rake. Our country has been stirred by the revelations of magazine and newspaper writers. Here is a dispassionate presentation of "how privileges granted or sanctioned by government underlie the social and political, mental or moral manifestations that appear so ominous in the republic." Mr. George sets forth princes of privilege; how they live; their amusements, disposition; marital relations. He passes on to the victims of privilege, picturing to us the physical, mental and moral deterioration. Coming to resistance to privilege he writes of the organization of laborers and the dangers of unionism. There is a division on the weapons of privilege, and another on privilege as the corrupter of politics. Its influence over public opinion is discussed. Here the press, the university, and the pulpit are arraigned for their bondage to privilege. The last chapters of the book discuss the centralization of government, foreign aggression, civilizations gone before, and finally Mr. George states his remedy. He says we must first abolish private ownership of natural opportunities; second, abolish tariff, and third, taxation of production and on its fruits, thereby abolishing special government grants, such as public service charters; fourth, abolish grants under general laws and immunities in the courts, such as the New Jersey corporations, the great insurance corporations, etc. We cannot say that we accept all Mr. George's interpretations of the facts which he presents, but we can recognize the value of his book, and the sincere effort which its writer has made to deal with a question that is of paramount interest in this Republic.

✧

THE PHILOSOPHY OF CHRISTIAN EXPERIENCE. By Henry W. Clark, author of "Meaning and Methods of the Spiritual Life." "The Christ from Without and Within," etc., etc. With an appreciation by Marcus Dods, D. D. Fleming H. Revell Company, New York. $1.25 net.

This book has received very strong commendation from men who have a right to be heard with respect to theological questions. It is one of a class which just now seems to have a prominent place in religious literature. The Inductive method is undoubtedly the true method of investigation with respect to both nature and the Bible, but it is a method which must be handled carefully, or it will lead to destructive conclusions.

The subject of this volume is of vital importance. At least the latter part of the subject is, for undoubtedly "Christian experience" is vital in any Christian life that is worth consideration at all. It may be that we may never understand the philosophy of this experience, and doubtless very few will attain to this knowledge, but even the few will have comfort in the understanding which they may reach.

The literary style of the book is not to be commended. This is often rudely constructed, and is frequently so involved as to lead to obscurity. But the book is well worth reading very carefully, as it is, in its thought, frequently very suggestive. The author's treatment of the Fatherhood of God is an attempted irenicon between the two extreme views on that subject. He rather leans to the idea that sonship is potential rather than a real thing in the case of those who are not Christians. The following extract will give some idea of the author's style as well as the position for which he contends:

"Following this line of thinking, we reach a reconciliation of ideas which appear superficially irreconcilable, and find it a clear truth that the God who is or may be Father is the God who may also become the judge. As has been already said, the Fatherhood of God is truly fulfilled only for those who will on their side assume the attitude of self-affiliation, and who thus allow all that they are to be moment by moment born from what God himself is. God's love—God's eternal readiness for self-communication—passes into actual Fatherhood for those who let it have its way. But it is the correlative of this—it is, from this standpoint, a perfectly natural thing—that to the resisters the love which, had there been yielding in place of resistance, might have fulfilled itself as Fatherhood, should become a disturbing, even in a most real sense a hostile, influence instead. And man needs to remember, whenever the spiritual problem of his nature presents itself or is suggested to his thought, that just because God in his love has provided the solution for it, a refusal of the love-provided solution must turn God into a foe. God's enmity is but God's arrested love."

The reader will notice the clumsy style in this quotation and he will also not fail to see the want of clearness to which attention has already been called. The one thing for which the book should be most highly commended is its ringing advocacy of a close fellowship with God. The author urges that we must become "God-intoxicated," and that this will follow when we allow God to come into the quietude of our minds and hearts and there show himself as he is. The plea that we should get away from the rattle of wheels, the commercial friction, the rush and noise of the multitude into the quiet hour where we can hear the "still small voice" and come into possession of real power, for true living, is a plea which is becoming more and more a necessity of the present days. The reading of this book will help many souls to a higher and truer life.

✧

THE EPISTLES OF ST. PETER. By J. H. Jowett. New York. A. C. Armstrong & Son. Pages 345. Price, $1.25 net.

This is another volume of the practical commentary on the New Testament edited by Dr. Robertson Nicoll. Mr. Jowett is one of the foremost preachers of the British pulpit to-day, and is the successor of the famous theologian, Dr. Dale. There is as much difference, however, between Jowett and Dale as there is between R. J. Campbell and Dr. Parker, whom he has succeeded. Mr. Jowett is not so much a theologian as he is an expositor and a preacher. He is alive to the modern teaching, yet retains a healthy conservatism of judgment. He is fully devoted to Jesus Christ, and seeks to bring every thought into captivity to him. His book on the Epistles of St. Peter is an eminently worthy one.

✧

STUDIES IN THE BOOK OF PSALMS. By Lincoln Hulley, Ph. D., president of John B. Stetson University, DeLand, Florida. Fleming H. Revell Co., New York, Chicago and Toronto. $1 net.

The substance of these lectures was first given at a number of chautauquas and summer schools, and in response to many requests has been published in this form with much added comment by the author. These studies begin with a description of Hebrew poetry in general and then take up the Psalter as a "Book of Life." This is followed by a list of titles of the several psalms, and then a chapter is given to the "Traditional Setting of Some of the Psalms," pointing out the circumstances under which they were written. The book of Psalms is then divided into "Fifteen Psalm Groups," such as "The Messianic Psalms," "The Imprecatory Psalms," "Pilgrim Psalms," etc. Several of the individual psalms are taken up, analyzed, and treated most helpfully. On the whole, it is the most sympathetic, appreciative and illuminating study of this devotional book of the Old Testament which we have seen, and we can heartily commend the work to those who would like to make a special study of this remarkable collection of Hebrew poetry, which maintains, and ever will maintain, its hold upon the human heart.

✦

KEYWORDS IN THE TEACHING OF JESUS. By A. T. Robertson, D. D., Professor of New Testament Interpretation in the Southern Baptist Theological Seminary. Philadelphia. American Baptist Publication Society. 1906. Price, 75 cents.

The seven chapters forming this little volume were delivered first as lectures to the Jackson Springs Summer Assembly under the auspices of the Baptist State Convention of North Carolina in 1904. The following themes are discussed: God, the Father; The Son; Sin; The Kingdom; The Holy Spirit; The Future Life. The treatment of these important questions, while not strikingly brilliant, is safe and enlightened. It may be described further as conservative and yet in the light of modern scholarship. The publishers have done well to give these lectures to the public in their present form, and their circulation and careful reading cannot but accomplish good.

✦

PUTTING THE MOST INTO LIFE. By Booker T. Washington, author of "Up From Slavery." New York. Thomas Y. Crowell & Co. Price 75 cents.

Mr. Washington, who is Principal of the Tuskegee Institute, is in the habit of delivering Sunday evening talks to the students of the institute, on practical, moral and religious questions, and a number of these have been prepared for publication in this little volume. They are in Mr. Washington's characteristic style, clear, pointed, and practical, and, while they are especially adapted to his own race, are not without application to all students and young people. Here is a sentiment, for instance, that is applicable to all people:

"All industrial operations and material progress should be used not as ends but as means of making life more comfortable, more useful and more beautiful. The intelligent farmer as he plants and works and harvests the cotton must remember that the production of cotton is not the end of his effort. Every bale of cotton can be turned into books, into opportunities for travel and study. The man who grows corn must remember that that growing of corn is not the end of life, but that the corn can be turned into refinements and beauties of a civilized life and a Christian home."

The book is put up in artistic form and embraces six of these Sunday Evening Talks.

✦

TWO MINUTE TALKS. Short Discussions of Long Themes. By Amos R. Wells. American Tract Society, New York.

Whatever Amos R. Wells writes is well worth reading. We know of few men who possess his rare power of condensation, of seizing the salient points of a subject and stating them clearly in terse, vigorous English. This little volume of less than 200 pages has nearly half as many chapters, or different subjects, all of which are wisely stated and aptly illustrated. It is a splendid treasury of thoughts for Sunday-school and Christian Endeavor workers, and for ministers of the Gospel as well.

✦

THE EVOLUTION OF A CHRISTIAN. By David James Burrell, D. D., L. L. D., Minister of Marble Collegiate Church, New York. The American Tract Society, 150 Nassau street, New York.

This volume by Dr. Burrell was prepared in response to a request of the editor of the Christian Herald, New York, to prepare for publication "A plain statement of the steps to the Christian life." These are strong chapters, of course, for Dr. Burrell is a strong writer. We notice, however, in the opening chapter on "How to Begin" that same vagueness which has proved such a bar to successful evangelism among many of the great Protestant bodies. Faith, according to this author, is to believe certain things about Jesus, and it alone saves; but that it is faith in Jesus Christ himself as the Son of God, and involves the actual acceptance of Christ, and surrender to him in a definite confessional act, is not made clear. Many of the other chapters, however, are excellent, as those on "How to Hear," "How to Grow," "Character," "Imitation of Christ," etc.

✦

TARBELL'S TEACHERS' GUIDE TO THE INTERNATIONAL SUNDAY SCHOOL LESSONS FOR 1907. By Martha Tarbell, Ph. D. Indianapolis. Bobbs-Merrill Company, publishers.

A glance through this volume indicates that it is an up-to-date treatment of the Sunday-school lessons, the order being: The Bible Text; Words and Phrases Explained; Suggestive Thoughts from Helpful Writers; Light from Oriental Life. This is followed with: "Suggestions for Teaching the Lesson; Three Lesson Thoughts with Illustrations; Sentence Sermons; The Bible Its Own Interpreter." The work opens with an "Analysis of the First Nine Books of the Bible" and contains illustrations, maps, diagrams, reproductions of ancient mural decorations by Dore, Tissot, and other modern artists.

✦

THE SELF-CURE OF CONSUMPTION. By C. H. S. Davis, M. D., Ph. D. New York. E. B. Treat and Co. Pages 175. Price 75 cents.

We can cordially commend this little book, dealing with the White Plague. Consumption carries off perhaps more people than all other diseases in the United States combined. That we should seriously study its prevention and cure is a duty imposed upon every citizen, whether he be infected or not. It is said that the annual expense of consumption to the people of the United States is placed at $330,000,000, and there are over 150,000 deaths each year. The writer of this book, and many others, believe that there is not, a shadow of a doubt but that consumption can be practically stamped out. He discusses its causes, symptoms, and treatment with drugs. He realized that good results in a great majority of instances rest upon the institution of the correct treatment in the incipiency of the disease. The open-air treatment, and the use of proper diet are the points upon which he lays the greatest emphasis in the cure. The book is just a statement of the case, with some common-sense advice as to how to deal with it.

✦

STUDENTS AND THE MODERN MISSIONARY CRUSADE. New York. Student Volunteer Movement for Foreign Missions, 3 W. Twenty-ninth street. Pages 773. Price $1.50.

This large-size book contains a verbatim report of the addresses delivered at the Fifth International Convention of the Student Volunteer Movement for Foreign Missions at Nashville, Tenn., February 28, to March 4, 1906. The informal discussions and questions of the various sessions are also reprinted substantially as they were uttered. Condensation has been somewhat more conspicuous in the case of the sectional meetings. The introductory statement of the chairmen of the various meetings, and the prayers offered are omitted, while the denominational rallies are entirely unreported. As it is, the book is large enough, and it is packed with matter of great value to the student missions. We consider the convention held at Nashville as the most important meeting held this year in our country. We regretted exceedingly at the time of the convention that we were able to give so inadequate a report of its proceedings owing to the great pressure on our columns at that time. It was worth going all the way to Nashville to hear such a speech as that by Mr. Robert E. Speer, on "The Non-Christian Religions Inadequate to Meet the Needs of Men." And it would do every religious editor good to have been brought in touch with the viewpoint of such a secular editor as Mr. J. C. MacDonald, of the Toronto Globe. We cannot attempt to give a detailed survey of the contents of this book, but cordially commend it to every student of missions whether at home or abroad.

own contribution to the growing literature of the Nativity. This Caristmas Carol by Brother Allen is one of the ablest of these offerings of adoration to the new-born King. It is, indeed, a great poem, conceived in the spirit of reverence and devotion and tremulous with the joy and with the holy awe inspired by the same great event which inspired the angels' song. It is beautifully printed and illustrated, and deserves wide reading both on account of its literary excellence and for the life and joy which pulse through all its pages. Address the publishers as above, or Christian Publishing Company. We shall be glad to furnish it to readers at the publishers' price.

❖

THE CHURCH OF CHRIST," by a layman. Christian Publishing Co., Price, $1.

This lay writer is distinguished by three things. He has soul-saneness and simplicity of expression. The book is good literature then; for all literature has been described "as the best thoughts of the best writers in a manner to arouse emotion." "Nothing noble is ever born except in a passion." You are convinced before you read two pages of this book that the author has a deep conviction and his soul burns to tell the message. The first chapter is worth ten times the price of the book. It is on the "Newness of Christianity." He emphasizes the completeness and the originality of Christ's Gospel in a fashion that is at once unique and exhaustive. It is adapted, he says, as the only religion of the universal human heart.

The writer's next point is that it is new in its teaching concerning the fatherhood of God and the brotherhood of men. He has no faith in the "Carpenter" theory of the universe. He makes God eternally active in the world. He is the very life of the universe and infinite love is at the heart of it. So he makes Jesus teach. He quotes Max Muller in proof. He says, "that no such word as 'mankind' is found in human language before Christ—that there is nothing in human language to express the kinship of the race. Before Christ it was Egyptian, Mede, Persian, Grecian, Roman, Scythian, barbarian, bond and free, but no word to express the kinship of man."

It seems that no civilization ever existed before the Christian that learned the relation of one man to another, and the relation of both to God. Jesus he claims was the first to put men in right relation to world and to God and their fellowmen. The argument on this point is very strong. There is a great sermon here for the live preacher on: "What is Christianity?" He continues in this fashion: "The Christian religion alone teaches humility, as the road to greatness. He that is greatest among you shall be your servant." He emphasizes the originality of all this."

He points out that the religion of Jesus is positive. Repression is not its highest note, but service. The Christian method is not mutilation, but consecration. "Jesus, while restraining wrong, taught active goodness." Man must bear fruit. Jesus preached louder than any one on earth "good works." Once more: The Christian religion goes below the surface. It nips the rising thought in the bud. Its author makes the "intent" sinful. It alone can cleanse and transform the heart.

Furthermore, it is missionary. This alone is the dignity of all life inspired by the Master. "Christianity alone, of all religions, seems to possess the power of keeping abreast with the advancing civilization of the world. . . . It alone, of all the religions of mankind, has been capable of accompanying man in his progress from evil to good, from good to better." He holds that neither the Jewish nor the heathen religions are missionary. Christianity, in a word, "is alone swaying the world's destiny for nineteen hundred years, blessing and cheering the living, comforting the dying, and giving hope of eternal life beyond the grave." This has been a new world since Christ has been here. "All history is mystery without his story." In the same unique, fresh and original way he treats "The Kingdom of Heaven," "Preliminary Manifestations," "Christ as a Teacher," "Christ as the Word of God," "The Passion of Christ," "The Three Revelations," "The Church," "The Day of Pentecost," "The New Testament Scriptures," "The Great Salvation," "The Apostles' Preaching," "The Seven Chosen," "Miracles," (This is a great chapter,) "Conversions," "Saul and his Conversion," "Work of the Apostle Paul," "Call of the Gentiles," "What Shall I Do to be Saved?" "Operations of the Spirit," "Missionary Work of the Church," "The First Council," "The Decree of the Council," "Paul at Philippi," "The Thessalonians," "Opposition to Paul," "Paul at Athens," "Paul at Corinth," "The Prisoner of the Lord." In a second book and in the same volume he has short chapters on: "The Assurance of Pardon," "The Proof of Pardon," "The Church of Christ," "Church Ordinances," "The Church Complete," "The Apostasy," "Christian Unity," "What is Implied by Unity?" "Nature of Division," "Denominationalism," "The Uniqueness of Jesus."

JAMES SMALL.

The Work of the Women By Ida W. Harrison

On the first Sunday in December, the Christian Woman's Board of Missions not only asks for a presentation of its work and an offering for its support from auxiliaries, but from all the churches of our brotherhood. It has been said that because our board has its own constituency of women and children, who pay a stated sum into its treasury annually, that they should not ask for a collection from the churches at large like our other missionary, educational and benevolent organizations. The annual dues of to cents a month from our women and 5 cents a month from our children last year amounted to a little less than $75,000—our expenditures for our various enterprises in that time reached the sum of more than $200,000; so it can be seen that the yearly membership dues do not half cover the yearly expense. Though the women who belong to our societies are generally the active women in the churches, who make offerings to the other organizations on their annual days —so they are also the constituency of the Foreign Society, the American Society of Church Extension, and of all our agencies for doing good.

As long as our enterprises were few and our expenses comparatively small, the offerings of our members were sufficient to support them; but now that they have grown until we labor in five foreign countries with 195 workers in our employ there, and in 39 states and territories in our own land, with a total of 363 workers at home and abroad, the day of support by membership dues has passed.

While much of the growth in our work has come because our Father has prospered us, a large increase has also come because our brethren have felt such confidence in the business principles and economical management of our board that they have turned over some impor-

Orphanage Girls at Dinner, Deoghur, India.

tant departments of this work to us. The first of our missions, the Jamaica work, was begun by the American Society, and given to the Christian Woman's Board of Missions. In 1900, the work of negro evangelization and education was transferred from that society to ours— and in 1905, the evangelistic work in Porto Rico was also given to our board. The educational work in Eastern Kentucky was passed over to us by our good brethren—and the same has been done in less conspicuous instances. Should these splendid enterprises fail of assistance from our churches, merely because they have passed from one board to another?

There is no problem that looms larger on our national horizon than the race problem—what shall we do for these more than nine millions of negroes in our midst? Their presence here, while it is one of our great burdens, is also one of our great opportunities; it is our chance to minister to the heathen at

our very doors. Our mission in the Appalachian Mountain region asks for help from us. It has been shown that the intermittent evangelism practiced by the churches has not resulted in changing ideals of conduct there. The best solution of the mountain problem is Christian education—the mission school with enough money back of it to give good teachers, good equipment, and the necessary help to the worthy poor, is the hope for the permanent uplift of this great and needy section of our country. Those islands at our doors, Porto Rico and Jamaica, have rights to assistance at our hands. The only work being done by our church for them, for educational work in our great mountain section, for the training and teaching of the negro, is being done by the Christian Woman's Board of Missions. Certainly, the church at large desires fellowship in these noble undertakings, and they can do so by contributing to the offering on C. W. B. M. day.

In addition to this work, bequeathed to us by our brethren, our board has entered certain other fields of its own initiation, where no other agencies of our church labor—in Mexico, in South America, in Oriental work on the Pacific coast, in our Bible chairs at State Universities, and in other lines of work that I cannot pause to mention.

We trust that many besides the women in our membership will share in the support of the great work that has been committed to us on the first Sunday in December—and that churches which have no auxiliary to our board will count it an accepted time and a choice privilege to have fellowship with us in this gracious ministry.

Mrs. Helen E. Moses.
New President of the C. W. B. M.

Mrs. Nancy E. Atkinson,
Retiring President of the C. W. B. M.

Mrs. M. E. Harlan,
New Secretary of the C. W. B. M.

The Old and the New in Mexico   By Jasper T. Moses

Two photographs that I took recently seem to me to be fairly typical of the old and of the new Mexico. The first was taken on "All Souls' Day" at the common cemetery. It is a view looking from the spot where lies all that is earthly of our martyr missionary, A. G. Alderman. All around are the bare black crosses, grim and hopeless, rising out of the sterile ground as if to mock the resurrection hope. The scene is typical of the barren lives, the coldness and neglect that mark the old regime in Mexico. You can almost see the undertaker as, with indecent haste, he whips up his bony horse and the rude wagon jolts over the stony streets, carrying the rough pine box with its once human freight. We hear the rasping tones of the priest as he haggles with the bereaved ones for a higher fee than they are able to pay, and finally ungraciously takes what he can get or hurries off with a contemptuous shrug of his shoulders. If the service is read at all, it is rushed through in a mumbling undertone that seems less gracious than its omission. To cap the climax, if the family is very poor, the body is dumped from its coffin and the undertaker hurries off with the box, to use it over again and perhaps again.

vancement except his own ambition and ability. Thus we see that Mexico is free from that great and appalling problem of

Cemetery, Monterey, Mexico. The Grave of A. G. Alderman is in the Center of the Foreground.

the American nation, the race question. Some of the greatest of Mexico's statesmen have risen from the Indian class.

Making Bread (tortillas), Mexico.

The other picture that I have is one taken from my bedroom window looking out on our school playground. How happy and animated is the scene! Here are the boys and girls who are to make this a new Mexico. Do you suppose that after they have spent six years amid happy Christian surroundings, where both their minds and souls have been trained and uplifted they will ever be content to abide such scenes as the one we first presented?

The Mexican people have in them many of the elements of a great nation. Considering the limitations of environment and heredity, it is doubtful if any people have made greater progress in the last quarter of a century. Regarded in some ways, Mexico's great lower class, which we Americans are apt to look down upon, is an economic blessing to the country. No work is too hard nor too menial for the peon. He is more easily made content than even the negro, and is in many ways as good a workman. He has, moreover, the inestimable advantage of being able to rise above his condition. There is no barrier to his social or political ad-

Mexico is in a fair way to the solution of her political and industrial problems. She is making a fair beginning in edu-

cation; but to throw off the shackles of Romanism and to emerge into the glorious freedom of the Gospel is a thing not to be accomplished in a day. This is Mexico's real problem of problems. Were this in a fair way of solution, all else would be simple.

We believe that the best way to overcome and to counteract a bad environment is to supply a better one. This is what we are trying to do in our educational work in Mexico. We have found that no other ally of the Church is to be compared in efficiency with the school. Not only does it give us access to the pupils and an influence for good over them, but it opens unto us their homes, and it gives us standing and respect in the community. But this is only the beginning. The young man or woman who graduates from a Christian school will make a far more efficient and thorough-going disciple of Christ than could his ignorant father or mother. We are not only recruiting for the Church in the present, but we are building for her future as well.

Our one school in Monterey is doing all that could be expected of it under present conditions, but we must enlarge or lose our opportunity. We must have a new dormitory for boarding students, or the work will suffer. Our other stations are calling for schools, and the need in them is as great as it was in Monterey. We dare not let them go long without answering this pressing need. To-day is the day for action in Mexico. To-morrow our opportunity may have passed. Monterey, Mexico.

Playground of Mission School, Monterey, Mexico.

The Day of Salvation and C. W. B. M. Day
By W. M. Forrest.

Because the day of salvation has come nigh unto the hearts and homes of our women they desire to observe C. W. B. M. day. They would not be worthy of that salvation if they did not have such a desire. Nor would the men in our pulpits and pews be worthy of such women, as the grace of our God has made possible, if they were not anxious to help those women in the celebration of that day.

C. W. B. M. day affords an opportunity to express our gratitude to God for his great salvation. It is the call of the womanhood of our churches to the whole church. In every other work and offering of the year they have had a large share; now at the year's end they call upon men as well as women to help them celebrate their day. The occasion and the object are too important to be crowded into some time and place where all the church cannot be present to hear and to help.

Not only is it a day wherein we are to rejoice and be glad because of the salvation that has come unto us. It is a day that is to make possible the extension of that same salvation unto others. Therein is found its deepest significance and paramount importance. We meet not to thank God that we and our wives and daughters are not as other men and women. Rather do we meet to thank him for the opportunity to help extend the blessings of the day of salvation to others. How many, alas, even in our own land, have not yet seen the dawning of that day. And how great is the multitude in distant lands whose weary eyes have never caught the first glint of light heralding the coming of the day of our Lord.

There is India, for instance. It is claimed that even yet nine-tenths of its 300,000,000 people have never heard of Christ in a way that could make them responsible for rejecting him. About half of that 300,000,000 people are women and girls, too. Never yet have they been touched by the power which of old made pagan people cry, "What women these Christians have!" To this hour they are shackled and bound by the slavery and vice wherewith heathenism has been wont to curse its womanhood. In the pains and perils of motherhood the great physician has not been with them. When the sons of their land have been cruel to them the son of Mary has not come to comfort them. Through the long years of their bitter widowhood, and in the dread hour of death, he who wept with Mary, and said to his sorrowing disciples, "Let not your heart be troubled," and proclaimed for the dying and the dead, "I am the resurrection and the life"—he has not been known unto them.

Then bring an offering, all ye people of the Lord, and come into his courts to praise him. Yes, bring such an offering that the sheen of its gold shall shine afar in the rising of the Sun of Righteousness in benighted lands. And praise him in such wise that we shall speed the day when from the rising of the sun even to the going down of the same his name shall be glorious among all nations. Thus will the coming of the day of salvation for all peoples be hastened by the observance of C. W. B. M. day.

The Theology of Alexander Campbell
By W. E. Garrison

Mr. Campbell had a theology. His was an orderly and systematic type of mind which formed clear-cut conceptions and grouped them according to their relations. If such a mind gives its attention to plants, the result is botany; or if to animal life, zoology; or if to the great truths about God and man and their relations, the outcome is theology. This is equally true whether the material for the science is derived from experience or from books, from speculation or from Scripture.

Most, if not all, Protestant theologians have attempted to formulate a Biblical theology. Philosophy and (as we say) human speculation have had great influence in fixing the doctrines, but the results have always been validated, to the speculator's entire satisfaction, by an appeal to Scripture. With Mr. Campbell the appeal to Scripture was so constant, his criticism of his own previously held doctrines was so searching, and his rejection of his own former beliefs when they were seen to be out of harmony with Biblical teaching, was so unflinching, that it is impossible to doubt the sincerity of his effort to construct a purely Biblical system.

Every thinker whose brain is large enough to hold two ideas at a time finds it necessary to secure harmony between his theology and his general view of the world as he has obtained it through phy. If a man's personal experiences phy. If a man's personal experiences and deepest thinking have convinced him that this is the worst of all possible worlds, and that man is the victim of the higher powers, no amount of zeal for faithful exegesis can prevent him from having a gloomy and pessimistic theology. The text, "God is love," simply cannot become a part of such a man's system, though he may profess belief in it.

Mr. Campbell was in touch with the philosophy which was dominant in England in his time—the philosophy of John Locke. It was not the latest word of philosophy up to that date, but it was the latest philosophy that orthodox persons could comfortably accept. Hume was chiefly valuable as a horrible example. Kant was still considered dangerous and the later Germans, Hegel and his contemporaries, were still doing their work and were scarcely yet known in England or America. So Locke's influence was still dominant.

The philosophy of Locke dealt not chiefly with the problem of the nature of ultimate reality (metaphysics) or the principles of human duty (ethics), but chiefly with the problem of knowledge. Assuming that real things exist external to man, and that man and the world are about what they seem to be, how does man arrive at a true knowledge of reality? That was Locke's problem. His answer was that man gets all his materials for knowledge through sensation and organizes these materials into knowledge through reflection. Nothing is innate. Nothing is mystical or mysterious. Only what comes into the mind through the strait gates of seeing, hearing and touching is the honest stuff of knowledge. All else is delusion and fantasy.

This was the theory of knowledge.

which Mr. Campbell accepted. He was chiefly interested in applying it to the question of religious knowledge. How does man get his knowledge of the world? Through sensation. How does he get his knowledge of God and of the will of God and of the way of salvation and of the fact of forgiveness? Through sensation. It is not a question of emotion, or conscience, or inner light, or any sort of private mystical communication from the spirit of God to the spirit of man, but simply a question of information conveyed through the ordinary channels of the senses.

But how could man, by his senses, apprehend God? In the days of revelation, God appeared visibly and spoke audibly to men. So the inspiration of the Biblical writers was a special and miraculous extension of their sense-perceptions, or a special act of God by which things ordinarily unknowable (because beyond reach of the senses), were brought into the field of knowledge by being brought temporarily within the scope of the senses.

But this process of special revelation is a thing of the past and we are again living in a world where God is utterly unknowable. What saves us then from complete agnosticism? One thing only —the fact that these men of old, who had divine things brought within the range of their senses, left a written record of what was revealed to them. And, though we cannot, by sight or hearing, know directly the nature or the will of God, we can, by the exercise of our senses, learn what is written in this record. The record of revelation forms an object for sense perception and through it alone, therefore (without violating the Lockian psychology and theory of knowledge) man can arrive at any idea of God.

From this general view of the process by which man gets knowledge and especially knowledge of God, the working out of certain other positions followed naturally and inevitably.

1. A strict construction view of religious authority, that is, the authority of Scripture.

2. An emphasis (theoretically at least) on the knowing process, almost to the exclusion of the emotional process in religion.

3. A view of faith as the acceptance of the testimony of witnesses concerning matters of which we can never have first-hand knowledge.

4. The elimination of all mystical influences and mysterious emotional communications from God to man, whether in conversion or in giving assurance of forgiveness, or in the nature and guidance of the Christian after conversion.

The great value and strength of this type of theology was its clear, comprehensible and practical nature. It offered men something to believe on evidence, and something to do upon command. Faith in Christ as Saviour was made to appear as easy and natural and normal as belief in George Washington as the first president. In both cases it was merely a question of apprehending the testimony through the senses and digesting it through reflection.

For the time in which it was done, this was an inestimable service. It saved from the torments of uncertainty thousands of persons who were, by temperament, so unimaginative, or so unemotional, or so purely intellectual as to be incapable of being convinced of religious truth by any other than historical evidence. It reduced conversion to a rational process. It convinced men that faith and salvation were within their reach whenever they chose to lay hold upon them by the exercise of the

ordinary human powers, which God had given to all men. Although the philosophy from which it sprang has long since ceased to be current and the Lockian theory of knowledge no longer commands the allegiance of the thinking

world, these results—the clearing of the air from unwholesome mysticism and vague emotionalism and making the apprehension of religion a normal human process—have remained as an imperishable contribution to the present and the future.

"THE DAY NO ONE FORGETS"

Is called to mind every other day in the year by the book presented.

Books by J. H. Garrison:

Christian Union, 207 pages, cloth . . $1.00
The Holy Spirit, 211 pages, cloth . . . 1.00
Alone With God, 244 pages, cloth . .   .75
Heavenward Way, 100 pages, cloth . .   .75
Half Hour Studies at the Cross 75
The three above for 2.00
The Old Faith Re-stated, 500 pages,
 . . cloth 2.00
The Reformation of the 19th Cen-
 . tury 2.00
Helps to Faith, 245 pages, cloth 1.00
A Modern Plea for Ancient Truths.   .35

Books by W. W. Dowling:

The Bible Hand-book, fine, cloth,
 312 pages $1.00
The Lesson Commentary for 1907,
 just the thing for a Teacher or
 other Bible School Worker 1.00
The Christian Psalter, full of fine
 responsive readings and a very
 acceptable gift to the congrega-
 tion 50
The Lesson Helper for 1907, a gift
 to an Intermediate Teacher 35
The Lesson Mentor, for Junior
 Teachers 25
The Lesson Primer, for Primary
 Teachers 20

The Guide Book Manual on Sunday
 School Organization, for your
 Superintendent . . . .$ .25
The Helping Hand for Y. P. S. C. E .25
The Normal Instructor, in 7 parts,
 all needed by Bible Readers,
 Teachers, etc., each part 15

Books by B. W. Johnson:

The People's New Testament, with
 Notes, in 2 vols. making one re-
 member you for life $4.00
Young Folks in Bible Lands 1.00
A Vision of the Ages, on Revelation 1.00
Commentary on John 1.00

Books by W. T. Moore:

Man Preparing for Other Worlds, a
 book for thought $2.00
Fundamental Error of Christendom. 1.00
The Living Pulpit of the Christian
 Church 2.00
The Plea of the Disciples, postpaid .35

Books by E. L. Powell:

Savonarola, Sunday Evening Lec-
 tures, cloth $1.00
Victory of Faith 1.00

Any Name in Gold FREE on any $1.00 Book Ordered Before December 15, 1906

CHRISTIAN PUBLISHING COMPANY

2712 Pine Street   -   -   St. Louis, Mo.

Where Thomas Campbell Preached His Last Sermon in Ireland

By James Small

Six miles from Markethill, a little town of a few thousand people, in County Armagh, is the Lowland of Aghorey, and here in the open country stands this old Presbyterian church erected over a hundred years ago. The present minister, Mr. Kirkpatrick, who stands in the doorway of his "Manse," has been the faithful and honored minister for over fifty years. The Editors of THE CHRISTIAN-EVANGELIST have had special pictures taken of the old church, session house, and manse there and asked me to write of these which I visited six years ago. This church is only sixty miles from my old home over there. In my conversation with Mr. Kirkpatrick I found out that Mr. Campbell was well and favorably remembered in the community by the old settlers. Some of them remember well his last sermon, which was founded on the words, "Oh, Jerusalem, Jerusalem thou that killest the prophets. * * * How often would I have gathered thy children together as a hen doth her brood under her wings, but ye would not."

They remembered until even then the strong plea to awaken men to the higher interests of time and eternity. There were funerals, he said, over which an-

Two or three points were emphasized. Though Canaan was not a great journey from Egypt, yet the Israelites were kept forty years in the wilderness before they were allowed to enter it. It was necessary for them to undergo a process of education for their future destiny. In

this way they got acquainted with God and learned his holy laws. They were schooled to trust him and obey him. So Jesus prayed that the disciples should not be taken out of the world but kept from the evil. Here like the Israelites we are to be schooled for the honors and dignities of the future life that await us beyond the journey.

In the evening he preached on "The Prodigal Son," emphasizing the delu-

Thomas Campbell's Home at Aghorey.

The Church in Ireland where Thomas Campbell Preached.

gels only wept and deaths witnessed only by God. Jerusalem was dead in faith, in religion and men were in that house in the same condition. Mr. Kirkpatrick took me through the graveyard and showed me the graves of many who were once members of Campbell's congregation. The only knowledge this good old man had of Mr. Campbell was that he had gone to America and there organized a Baptist "sect" (?).

He listened attentively to the work accomplished by the Campbells as I tried to unfold it to him and remarked that he could agree to nine-tenths of it all himself. He said that the old "fatalistic" Calvinism was never preached any more now; and that the old view was not necessary even for preachers to hold before they were ordained to the Presbyterian ministry.

When asked what his themes were the previous Sunday, he replied that in the morning he preached on: "Israel as a Type," taking their wanderings as a basis.

sions of the youth and showing that the self-realization to which he came, of need and want, and of his sin against "his father" was the first step in his return.

The church is active yet in every good work and 400 people attend in the morning and 200 at night.

The old session house which appears in the picture is the one in which Mr. Campbell often met with his elders and officers and the "Manse" is the same residence which Mr. Campbell occupied. The country around is ideal. A few miles from this church John Hall, the noted preacher of New York for many years, was born and reared. Every year he made a journey to the old home and preached in this old church.

Nothing is changed but the pulpit. They have a new pulpit and new furnishings, but "as it was in the beginning, is now and ever shall be," is characteristic of many things besides the old sacred edifices in the old country.

The Old Session House.

The BRONZE VASE

By J. Breckenridge Ellis

PART IV.

Chapter VII.

When Raymund and Jack Bellfield returned to Frog Bend in each other's company, they were warmly received by the Bellfields and Willbys. Raymund's sudden trip to St. Louis and subsequent stay in Kansas City had been a surprise to all, but the young man offered no other word of explanation than that he had been very busy. From the instant Mr. Willby's house came into sight, Raymund had been on the outlook for Rhoda. He presently descried her rather shrinking behind the minister as had been her wont during the past few years, at his various returns. As the young man drew near, her face was colored with distress. She anticipated an effort on his part to seize her in his arms in the old time way and bestow hearty kisses upon her lips and cheeks. Formerly her holding back had deeply offended him, but he had not then learned, as she had, that she was not his sister. Now in an odd way, this very shy timidity upon her part pleased him. He offered her his hand so coolly and so casually, that Rhoda in her turn was surprised and hurt. So far from embarrassing her with a show of affection, he seemed hardly glad to see her.

"Raymund," she said reproachfully, "I would not have thought you'd have gone to St. Louis without me."

"Oh, yes," said Raymund with apparent indifference.

"At least," said Rhoda, "I should have thought that after being away from us a year, you would have come here first."

"Why?" Raymund asked.

Rhoda colored deeply. "If for no other reason," she said, "because your friends would want to see you."

"Oh, I didn't suppose my friends were in any hurry," observed Raymund serenely.

"And besides," Rhoda added gently, "you and I had so often planned our trip to St. Louis. We were to go together, some day, and look at the old places where we used to be so happy."

"Why, Rhoda!" cried Raymund. "Come, come! are you going to say that you were happy at that old second-hand store and pawnshop, with Miss Pinns sticking you with every sharp word her tongue could find?"

"Yes, I was happy!" cried Rhoda bravely, "because—" But she didn't finish.

Raymund turned away from her apparently in calm indifference, but in reality to hide the pleased light that he felt must be glowing in his eyes. The others had now gathered near, and Mr. Willby in particular bombarded the young man with eager questions. So Raymund told them about uncle William's death and about the social aspirations of her who had been Miss Pinns. They talked on and on as close friends may, each adding his part to the babel of speech, and few listening to what anybody else said.

This was especially true of Brother Bellfield's sister, who held a slip from a newspaper in her hand which she wanted to read to the entire assembly as she considered it timely and interesting. But she never got to read it aloud, though several times she ostentatiously read it to herself to whet curiosity.

When finally most of them had told what was on their own minds, and began to wake up to the consciousness that they had not learned anything from other minds, there came a lull. Raymund had purposely taken a remote seat from Rhoda, but now she crossed over to him and sat down by his side.

"Now," exclaimed Mr. Willby with his customary vivacity, "since Raymund has told us all he has to tell or, at least, all he is disposed to tell, we might as well go on with what we were doing before he came to throw us all out. Which was, to decide between three of Rhoda's poems. The fact is, Raymund, your sister has been requested by a magazine to contribute a poem; no money for it, lad, but immense honor. We are trying to decide. You and Jack cock your ears and help us."

"This," murmured Rhoda, "is embarrassing."

"Nonsense!" cried Mr. Willby, and he read from Rhoda's neat handwriting:

"Just simple living,
Loving and giving,
Home tasks doing
Duty pursuing,
Christ not denying,
Peacefully dying,
Heaven with spirits blest—
You may have all the rest."

"That's my favorite," said Brother Bellfield.

"It's too short," said Mr. Willby decidedly. "Now, I'll read the one I like best:

"Be sure you're right, then go ahead,
Tho' you strew your pathway with the dead.
If men your principles oppose,
Just knock 'em down; perfection goes!
The foolish may to this object.
What do you care? That, you expect.
Be sure you're right—Oh, cheering song!
Ha! everybody else is wrong!
So keep on going, never stop,
Tread others down to reach the top.
Weigh not advice of friend or foe,
You know you're right—away you go!
Turn not aside for weak man's plight—
Run over him—you know you're right.
Don't stop for wounded or for dead;
You know you're right—just go ahead."

"I do not particularly care for that," observed Mrs. Willby. "I don't like irony."

"Irony indeed!" cried Mr. Willby. "The piece is dead in earnest. And it expresses my sentiments exactly. If I'm right, I go ahead; and do I listen to anybody's advice? Not much! I'm too conscientious to be changing my mind! Now we'll have another." He read:

"There is only one road to To-morrow,
And the name of that road is To-day.
What needless heart-longings we borrow
To bridge o'er the ditch of Delay.

Farther on up the road to To-morrow,
There are numerous lanes of parting
There's a time no doubt for sorrow,
But now is the time for starting.

If a wish could bear us to To-morrow,
Who midst life's restless yearnings would stay?
We would pass in a breath from all sorrow—
But the road to To-morrow's To-day."

"That's all of 'em, isn't it?" queried the invalid sister, hopefully. "That's three."

"There's another, I find, mo'm," said Mr. Willby, with some decision, "and I purpose reading the same, mo'm." He did so:

"You spoke a simple word of cheer
When grief my heart did wildly wring,
And then I knew the Father near,
Because his messenger was here—
Yet you call that a little thing!

That day you turned to smile at me
What hope your sunny light did bring!
Blind in my selfish agony,
I thought a friend no more to see—
You call that smile a little thing!

Once, when maligned, in vengeful mood,
I sought to deal out sting for sting;
I melted when I understood
That you, one day, had called me 'good'—
And that, you term a little thing!

Call nothing 'little' that exists
In widest earth or heaven above
That love contains in slightest grasp,
Because the least of God is great,
And there is God, where there is love."

"Is that all?" asked the invalid sister.

"Yes, mo'm, it is," said Mr. Willby, "but we cannot hear your selection now, because we must decide upon these productions."

In the meantime, Rhoda, with the natural shyness of the poet who hears her poems under discussion, addressed Raymund.

"Raymund, you haven't asked me a word about how I liked my first year of teaching."

"Haven't I?" said Raymund carelessly, "well, how did you like it?"

"And—and you haven't asked me anything about my affairs." Suddenly there was a gleam in Rhoda's eyes. "Raymund! you don't seem interested in me!"

Raymund apologized politely, "Well, there are so many things on my mind."

Rhoda looked at him dumbly, then said with a catch in her voice, "We have what we consider a great piece of news for you. But perhaps you will not consider it of any importance, you seem so changed."

"Well, perhaps you have," said Raymund. "You know there are many things we once considered of importance, that are really of very little consequence."

THANKSGIVING.

By Clinton Scollard.

Thanksgiving for God's boundless blue
Above us brooding; for the hue
And perfumed pageant of the year;
For waters singing lyric clear,
And birds in choral retinue.

For all the varied life we view
About us bourgeoning; for the clue
To happiness beyond the Here—
Thanksgiving!

For chance the kindly deed to do
While dawn and dusk their paths pursue;
For hope and its attendant cheer;
For all that's noble and sincere;
For friends—but chiefly, love, for you—
Thanksgiving!

Rhoda's blue eyes stared at him reproachfully.

"Say, old man," spoke up Jack, who had been trying hard to make out his friend's queer behavior, "are you getting to be something of a prig? I never in my life knew you to act such an insufferable cub, you know!"

Raymund grinned. "By the way, Rhoda," he said, "I'm going back to our old home, Crawley, for a day or two. You've never been there since we left it as helpless orphans, have you?"

"You know I have not, or I should have told you," said Rhoda, quietly.

Mr. Willby, who had been gazing at his young friend with amazed curiosity, now spoke up. "That reminds me of news for you, Raymund, and as nobody seems disposed to open the subject—but are you well, Raymund?"

"Quite well, thank you, Mr. Willby."

"You don't seem well. But this is the news. Mr. Omer was here yesterday—left his daughter in Kansas City expressly to see you—didn't know you were in town; he is out on his Crawley farm, to be there a week. If you are going to Crawley you'd better look him up. He wants to see you bad. You don't think you've taken any malaria, do you, son?"

"Quite sure I haven't," said Raymund easily. "It's a wonder Mr. Omer didn't hunt me up in Kansas City last winter. He was on Troost avenue all the time. By the way, Rhoda, how would you like to go with me to Crawley and look over the old haunts—see our dear old home that used to be—drop in on Miss Glory Aggency and Mr. Merlin Aggency? It may be important for me to find Mr. Omer on his farm. Anyway, I'd decided to go, before I heard of his looking for me."

"Do you truly want me to go with you?" Rhoda asked with shy timidity.

"Why, yes, I do," said Raymund serenely. "Of course I do."

Rhoda felt an overpowering desire to see Crawley once more, the scene of her bright childhood and of her mother's love. Still, she hesitated, for Raymund was so odd.

"I am afraid I might be in the way," she hesitated. "You will be going out to Mr. Omer's farm, and you wouldn't know what to do with me."

Raymund faced her and she saw the steady purpose of his eyes. "I will know exactly what to do with you," he cried with sudden energy, "and you couldn't ever be in my way, Rhoda; and I want you to go; very much indeed."

"Now, you're talking!" cried Mr. Willby. "Now, you've said something! That's the way to plunk it down!"

"I will go," said Rhoda with a happy coo in her voice.

"I'll go along, too!" cried Jack.

"No," said Raymund, waving his hand, "you're not wanted."

He grinned at Jack and Jack grinned back at him.

"By the way, Ray," inquired Jack innocently, "when did you get a monopoly on this branch railroad?"

"That's all right," Raymund retorted laughing, "I mean to have a monopoly on Rhoda!"

❀ ❀

"Many are willing that God should lead them if they may show him the way.

The sunshine to the man of the world means something pleasant, useful or splendid; to the Christian it means all this and a heavenly Parent too; all this, and an infinitely loving and lovable heart besides.—*Samuel Penniman Leeds.*

❀ ❀

We need more of the temper of the lame man who used to thank God daily for what the world would have called his misfortune: "For, had I not been lame," he would say, "I would likely have run away from God."—*J. E. McFadyen.*

❀ ❀

Would you know who is the greatest saint in the world? It is not he who prays most or fasts most; it is not he who gives most alms or is most eminent for temperance, chastity or justice; but it is he who is always thankful to God, who wills everything that God willeth, who receives anything as an instance of God's goodness, and has a heart always ready to praise God for it.—*William Law.*

❀ ❀

A cheerful face, a contented mind, a grateful heart, belong to those who give their confidence and love and loyal service to the Lord Jesus Christ. His true disciples take no anxious thought for the morrow, and are profoundly grateful for today and yesterday. This is true even when yesterday was full of trouble, and today is a hard problem, and the morrow promises a storm. Yes; they give thanks always, for all things.—*George Hodges.*

❀ ❀

A six-year-old lass who has been dwelling in a Chicago flat, was housed up most of the winter with diphtheria. The ugly card in the front window represented to her imprisoning authority.

As soon as she was well, her parents had to carry into effect a delayed plan to move to another location. So the afternoon of the day that she was first able to return to school, she came home to find another great sign—"for rent"—staring her in the face from that front window.

The child ran breathlessly to her mother

DECORATIONS AND GAMES FOR THANKSGIVING.

BY RUTH VIRGINIA SACKETT.

For the clever hostess Thanksgiving offers all sorts of possibilities in the way of decorations. The table done in yellow, intermingled with green, and relieved by a touch of red is a charming suggestion.

An effective centerpiece is to have on a mat of greens a pumpkin carved to imitate a coach, with vines trailing over the sides and laden with golden-hued chrysanthemums. In front, a doll in colonial costume holding yellow ribbon reins and driving as many feathered roosters as there are tots present. These are found at most any toy store, and will make for the youngsters delightfully pleasing remembrances of the day.

Attach to the chandelier above a cluster of yellow and of red chrysanthemums combined with festoons of smilax, the ends reaching to the four corners and there held in the uplifted arms of jointed dolls attired in true Puritan style, close cap and all. It can easily be managed by using crepe paper for the gowns, and the result will be so pleasing that it will fully repay the small amount of labor involved. To carry out the color scheme still further, each place can be marked with tiny gilded baskets filled with yellow and white bonbons.

If there is an artist in the family, a charming idea is to have the guest cards illustrated in color with quaint figures of belles and beaux of a hundred years ago, and on the underside an amusing and appropriate quotation. If these lines are read aloud at the beginning of the repast it will doubtless cause much merriment and thus remove all formality.

Just the thing for an after-dinner aid to digestion, as it so mirth stirring, at least for the spectators, is to blindfold two persons, turn them around three times, and then request the couple to shake hands with one another.

A game in which young and old can join is played in this way: The company are seated in a circle, and the hostess begins by asking the one at her right, "What had we for dinner to-day?" and he or she must name something on the table, afterward ask her right-hand neighbor the same question, who mentions the dish already introduced and names another as well. In this manner the questions go around the ring, the menu increasing all the time, and all have to be on the alert, as the edibles have to be cited in the order given. The player who fails to do so has the pleasure of watching the others instead of taking part.

A pastime more adapted to the children of a larger growth is called Pro and Con. Divide the participants into two sets, as in the old-fashioned spelling match, call one division the pros and the other the cons. Start the game by the leader of the cons commencing a story of some kind, every sentence beginning with con, and he must continue as long as possible; but at the least hesitation the pros must be ready to go promptly on with the narrative, prefixing pro instead of con. If a word is wrongly chosen or mispronounced the one making the mistake must leave the game, but when he merely hesitates the story goes the other side and he remains in line ready to take his turn when it comes again. When only two remain the contest becomes intensely exciting. The one who is last to fail is considered the "victor," and he wins for himself, also for his side.—*N. Y. Observer.*

❋ ❋

THE FIRST THANKSGIVING.

FLORENCE I. SAUNDERS.

In these days of abundance and luxury, it is difficult to realize the severe want and many hardships of our forefathers in the earliest days of this great country though we may often have heard of them.

From the early records we learn that on November 9 of the year 1620 the "Pilgrim Fathers" in the ship "Mayflower," landed in a small bay near Cape Cod, and called the place Plymouth. There was formed the "Plymouth Colony."

After ten months of privations and sickness they gathered in their first harvest of twenty acres of corn and six of barley; enough to keep them supplied with food for the coming year.

The record says, "Our corn did prove well, and, God be praised! We had a good increase of Indian corn; and our barley was indifferently good; but our pease not worth the gathering; for we feared they were too late sown.

"They came up well, and blossomed, but the sun parched them in the blossom.

"Our harvest being gathered in, our Governor, William Bradford, sent four men out a-fowling; so we might after a more special manner rejoice together after we had gathered the fruit of our labors."

These men returned with water-fowl, wild turkey and venison, and the governor called the people together for a public expression of their gratitude in a day of feasting and thanksgiving and a week of rejoicing; during which they entertained ninety of the friendly Indians and their greatest chief, Massasoit; and these men, to show their appreciation of this feast, went out and killed five deer which they brought to the governor and his friends.

Thus we have the simple facts of the observance of the first special public Thanksgiving day, which has become for us one of national importance; and in the words of our ancestor, we may say, "By the goodness of God, we are so far from want that we wish all partakers of our plenty."

An Elusive Thanksgiving Dinner.

BY ELIZABETH A. MOORE.

"Laws sakes, if there ain't my Thanks-givin' dinner agoin' over the fence!"

Susan Hillary craned her neck out of the window and groaned.

"Now jest why didn't I clip the crit-ter's wings," she demanded of herself, ruefully. "There that turkey's gone right over into Mirandy Stebbins' gar-den, an' me tied up here by the foot with the rheumatiz. It jest beats all how con-trary things do go by spells."

The fence over which Miss Hillary's turkey had vanished was a tall structure of the variety known as "spite fence."

After Miss Hillary and Mrs. Stebbins had lived alongside each other for years in the closest of neighborly intimacy and companionship, Mrs. Stebbins, in an unluky moment, decided to embark in the chicken business.

The things that Mrs. Stebbins learned in the next few months would fill vol-umes, and the indignities that Miss Hil-lary and Miss Hillary's flower beds suf-fered through Mrs. Stebbins' new means of a livelihood would fill many more.

Miss Hillary expostulated—mildly at first, then with more vigor, for the sale of her flowers did considerable to eke out her own slender resources. Mrs. Stebbins, herself half frantic with the new modes of activity which her chick-ens were continually developing, replied tartly, and in an incredibly short time those miserable birds had brought about a rupture between the two elderly wom-en who really loved each other as sis-ters.

After this Miss Hillary expostulated no more, but when the next onslaught on her flower beds occurred, she be-took herself to the village carpenter, and, though it was a sore drain on her slen-der purse, she had erected between the two houses a high solid fence.

After that there was a cessation of hostilities, but the rupture remained. The two old ladies spoke stiffly when they met, but the old intimacy was a thing of the past.

It was the year following that one morning early in November a supercil-ious young traveler arrived at Miss Hil-lary's home. As to the donor there was no clue.

Susan regarded her gift with varying emotions. It was, unquestionably, a most acceptable one—but a live turkey, and three weeks before Thanksgiving day!

The next week that turkey led Miss Hillary a life better imagined than de-scribed. Josiah, the small boy that did the chores, had captured it several times when it had escaped the coop, only after the most exciting chase. A bed of asters had been ruined entirely, and Susan herself on one occasion, when ap-pearing in a crimson waist, had been put to flight most ignominiously.

"Dear, dear me." Miss Hillary had sighed to Josiah, "how am I a-goin' to keep that bird two weeks longer, I don't know."

This the bird himself had just now decided very much to his own satisfac-tion by again eluding the coop and van.

CRESCO FLOUR For DYSPEPSIA
(Formerly GLUTEN FLOUR)
SPECIAL DIABETIC FLOUR
K. C. WHOLE WHEAT FLOUR
Unlike all other goods. Ask grocers.
For book and sample, write
FARWELL & RHINES, WATERTOWN, N. Y., U. S. A.

ishing with a triumphant squawk over the "spite fence."

"If only Josiah would come," wailed Miss Hillary. "I simply can't go after that bird, crippled up as I am, an', be-sides, I wouldn't go to Mirandy Steb-bins' house, anyhow. She'd think I was tryin' to make up with her.

"The turkey's loose again," she screamed at Josiah as he entered the gate. "It's gone over the fence this time, an' goodness knows what it's been doin' all this time. Run, Josiah, an' oh, Josiah, jest say to Mrs. Stebbins—well, jest say as how Miss Hillary is s'orry to have to—er—intrude. You understand. Now run."

After a bad quarter of an hour for all concerned Josiah reappeared—without the turkey.

"Mrs. Stebbins says, ma'am, as how she's got the turkey fastened up good an' safe all right, an' as how you can have it when you pays for the truck it scattered out before she caught it. An' there's not much it ain't scratched out, I guess," volunteered Josiah.

"The sassy, impident piece!" exclaimed Susan, wrathfully. "After all I've took from her chickens, too. I'll jest see myself a-doin' it. I'll never, never pay for it, so there! But to think Mirandy would treat me so, she that used to be jest like a sister to me. Oh, dear, dear me!"

As Thanksgiving day drew near the thorn in Susan's flesh rankled more and more fiercely. It was becoming only too apparent that Mirandy Stebbins meant to steal that turkey. Susan blushed for her. But mortification over Mrs. Stebbins' downfall soon gave place to rage. Again and again she tried to form some plan to recapture the tur-key, but Mirandy seemed to have it safe this time, and besides, if the truth must be told, Susan was mortally afraid of that rampant, supercilious fowl.

But might there not be other ways to make good its loss. Susan paused sud-denly in her limping from the dresser to the stove and clapped her hands tri-umphantly.

"Of course, it's stealin'," she said, "but if Mirandy Stebbins can steal, why, so can I. It ain't no worse for me nor for her. But, laws sakes, I never thought I'd come to that, an' me a-professin' church member these thirty years. How-somever, I've either got to steal or go without any Thanksgivin' dinner, that's sure, so—I guess—well, I guess I'll jest have to steal."

That night, armed with a large market basket, Susan stole quietly out of her kitchen door into the crisp autumn night. Dead leaves rustled under her feet as she limped down the paths through her flower garden, and the purple Michael-

mas daisies along the fence shook their heads reproachfully as she passed.

Her heart beat wildly, but she pressed her lips tightly together and went stubbornly on. She climbed awkwardly over the old worm fence at the end of her garden and then into her neighbor's truck patch.

"Punkins—that's what I'm after," she said, softly. "An' here they be. Oh, what beauties! I reckon I didn't come none too soon, either. Mirandy'd been a-gatherin' these herself in a day or two an' I'd a-missed it all. Now, I'll have punkin' pies, anyhow, an' what's more, Mirandy won't unless she buys her pun-kins. They're big an' they're heavy, but not one do I leave. I guess to-morrow mornin' Mirandy Stebbins'll learn some-thin' that'll teach her a lesson. Mean old thing."

From the shadow of a friendly hedge Mirandy Stebbins watched her old neigh-bor as she plundered her pumpkin vines. Susan had overlooked the fact that it was bright moonlight.

"Poor old soul," she sighed, pityingly. "But it's a workin' all right, jest as I thought. Now, if I didn't know Susan Hillary's conscience better'n she does herself, I'd say good-bye to them pun-kins. But, good land, I know how it'll turn out without waitin' to see. Dear old Susan."

The next day Susan fairly reveled in Thanksgiving preparations. A delicious air of expectancy pervaded the kitchen, and, as she went on with her work, Susan tried hard to sing the old Thanks-giving hymn:

"Come, ye thankful people, come."

But somehow the words seemed to stick in her throat, and the twinges of rheumatism, greatly aggravated by her last night's exploit in the damp and cold, made her wince as she hobbled around the kitchen. Moreover, she started nerv-ously at every turn and in every sound she seemed to hear a whispered: "Thou shalt not steal."

As she opened the oven to look at the

great golden pies within, the delicious odor seemed to float out the tormenting words: "Thief—thief."

Susan shut the oven door with a snap and sprang up.

"I'm not the only one that's a thief, so there!" she said, defiantly. "It's no worse to steal punkins than turkeys." Then she sank into a chair with a groan wrung from her by the sudden twinge to her rheumatic joints.

"Goodness knows, I ain't none too much to be thankful for, nohow," she said, dismally, "what with the drought an' losin' my turkey an' the rheumatiz besides. Now, if I should get laid up entirely jest what's a-goin' to become of me, I wonder?"

Susan pondered over the situation a long while in silence. Her conscience refused absolutely to be quieted and the rheumatic pains grew more and more insistent. Sick and alone, old and poor, at enmity with her best friend and—and —a thief! This was the result of her meditation. She rose painfully and took out the great golden-brown pies from the oven and set them in a row on the table with her other Thanksgiving preparations. Then she hobbled miserably to a couch, and while all around her seemed to breathe out the very spirit of Thanksgiving, she, poor soul, buried her face in the cushions and wept.

Josiah, coming in later, found a strange Miss Hillary that he had never known before. From the lounge she gave him his orders.

"Do up your chores, Josiah, an' then take them punkin pies, every last one of 'em, an' them other things a-settin' there, an' carry 'em all over to Mirandy Stebbins' house. An' tell Mirandy Stebbins, Josiah, tell her—yes, tell her I stole 'em all an' here they be."

Josiah gasped.

"Stole 'em, Miss Hillary? Why, be you a thief?"

"Yes, I be; an' I might as well own up to it. But so's Mirandy Stebbins. Still, that's neither here nor there. But for me, I'll have a clear conscience if I do go hungry. An' mind, Josiah, that you don't tell her how bad my rheumatiz has got, now remember. I don't want none of her commiseration', that's sure."

When Josiah approached with his load Mrs. Stebbins was working, evidently with great enjoyment over a fat, overgrown turkey.

"Miss Hillary sends her compliments," he began, politely, for to his mind Susan's blunt message was not entirely in keeping with the season; "an sends you these 'ere punkin pies an' things for Thanksgivin', an' hopes as how you're right well. She's real bad sick herself, Miss Hillary is—got worse all of a sudden, jest sence yesterday somehow. But I forgot, she told me I wasn't to say nothin' about it, so I won't. Only I'm afraid she's a little out of her head, 'cause she said as how she'd been a thief an' stole all these things. If I was you, Mrs. Stebbins, I'd go over an' set awhile with her for fear——"

"You would, eh?" Mrs. Stebbins interrupted. "Well, you're a good little boy, an' here's a big apple for you. Now run along with you."

When Susan awoke late on Thanksgiving morning, after a miserable night, a heavenly odor even as of roast turkey pervaded the house, and a voice, presumably an angel's, was singing softly:

"The Lord's my shepherd, I'll not want."

"I guess I must a-died," murmured Susan, contentedly, "an' this is Heaven, I s'pose."

But something in the voice sounded strangely familiar, and Susan suddenly sat up in bed. With a groan she realized her mistake.

"I'm not in Heaven, after all, it seems," she said, resignedly. "I thought it was 'most too good to be true. But I do jest wonder what it all means, anyhow."

A large, cheery-faced woman appeared in the doorway, and a hearty voice, assuredly of the earth, exclaimed:

"Well, Susan Hillary, so you're awake at last, are you? I thought maybe you was a-goin' to sleep all day."

Too astonished to speak, Susan simply gaped at her visitor.

"Humph! You don't seem none too glad to see me, I must say," the intruder went on. "Anyhow, I heard as how you was took sick, so I come over to set awhile an' do for you."

"So it's you, Mirandy Stebbins, is it?" Susan managed to say at last. "I sent you back your old punkins, didn't I? Now, what more do you want, an' where's my turkey? That's what I'd like to know."

"Your turkey's in the oven a-cookin' for dear life, an' glad enough I am it is there at last, what with all I've suffered from that bird sense it flew over the fence yonder. Maybe you know somethin' about that yourself, though."

"Yes; I learned a lot about fowls lately," confessed Susan, grimly. "But I would like to know jest where it came from in the first place, I'll admit."

"Oh, Susan," Miranda's bravado wavered a little, 'don't you think maybe the good Lord prompted somebody to send you that turkey so you'd understand—?'

"Mirandy Stebbins," here Susan sat up in bed, despite the painful twinges in her swollen joints, "did you send that turkey here or didn't you? That's what I want to know."

"I did, Susan," admitted Miranda, meekly.

"For why?" demanded Susan, majestically, but with softened face.

"Well, I thought maybe as how you hadn't none too much an' might be glad of it. For, Susan, I've never really stopped carin' for you, much as I've tried. It was kind o' mean, but I'll admit too, I did think maybe if you knew somethin' of what jest one of the pesky things could do you might feel little different to me with all I've had to put up with. They've drove me nigh beside myself, there's no denyin'. An', Susan," here Miranda's big heart overflowed at last and her handkerchief went up to her eyes, "I did want you back again so much, for I've missed you so."

"Mirandy Stebbins, I've not spent a happy day sence that fence went up," confessed Susan. "And after that turkey come—well, Mirandy, sometimes I thought of what you must a had to contend with, an', honestly, I did feel awful guilty to think as how I'd helped. I was too hasty, an', Mirandy, I'm real sorry about it, 'deed, an' 'deed I am."

"Bless your heart, don't let's talk about it no more," said Miranda. "I always knew if we once got together we couldn't help but make up. Now that gobbler's done jest to a turn," she added briskly, as they both dried their eyes, "so let me help you get up."

"'God moves in a mysterious way,'" sang Miranda, blithely, as she bustled around among the Thanksgiving preparations. "Chickens is the most mysterious of all, though, I must say. Now, come, Susan, never mind your rheumatiz to-day. It's Thanksgivin', you know, an' this is a proper Thanksgivin' turkey. I picked him out a-purpose,

Tricked by Dyspepsia

The Doctor Couldn't Tell Where The Trouble Lay.

"For the past seven years I have been a victim of dyspepsia and chronic constipation and have consulted the most noted specialists to be found on diseases of this character. None, however, seemed to locate the difficulty or give relief. In addition to this medical treatment, I have resorted to the use of many remedies and have given them faithful trial, but all to no purpose.

Upon the recommendation of a close friend, I purchased a 50c package of Stuart's Dyspepsia Tablets and in less than five days' notice that I was receiving more benefit than from any remedy I had used before. I continued to use the tablets after each meal for one month and by that time my stomach was in a healthy condition, capable of digesting anything which my increasing appetite demanded.

I have not experienced any return of my former trouble though three months have elapsed since taking your remedy."

We wish that you could see with your own eyes the countless other bona-fide signed letters from grateful men and women all over the land who had suffered years of agony with dyspepsia, tried every known remedy and consulted eminent specialists without result, until they gave Stuart's Dyspepsia Tablets a trial. Like the doctor above, they couldn't locate the seat of the trouble.

Dyspepsia is a disease which has long baffled physicians. So difficult of location is the disease that cure seems next to miraculous. There is only one way to treat dyspepsia—to supply the elements which nature has ordained to perform this function and to cause them to enter the digestive organs, supplying the fluids which they lack. Stuart's Dyspepsia Tablets alone fill these requirements, as is shown by the fact that 40,000 physicians in the United States and Canada unite in recommending them to their patients for stomach disorders.

We do not claim or expect Stuart's Dyspepsia Tablets to cure anything but disordered conditions of the stomach and other digestive organs, but this they never fail to do. They work upon the inner lining of the stomach and intestines, stimulate the gastric glands and aid in the secretion of juices necessary to digestion.

Stuart's Dyspepsia Tablets are for sale by all druggists at 50 cents a box. One box will frequently effect a perfect cure. If in doubt and wish more adequate proof send us your name and address and we will gladly mail you a sample package free. F. A. Stuart Co., 61 Stuart Bldg., Marshall. Mich.

'cause I knowed he'd make so much trouble he'd have to make peace in the end, an' that's jest what he did, bless his contrary old heart. Have a leg, Susan. It jest does my heart good to carve this bird."—The Criterion.

Pure at the Source.

Milk is the chief article of food in the sick room and hospital. Every physician and nurse should know the source of supply before ordering in any form. It is not enough to know that it comes as "country milk." Borden's Eagle Brand Condensed milk, the original and leading brand since 1857.—Integrity and experience behind every can.

A Thanksgiving Reminder

By Mrs. Harriet A. Cheever

Mr. Howard Williams was walking from his house toward the "Exchange." His mind was pleasantly employed. The mind of a man is quite likely to be pleasantly employed with whom things have glided along with signal success for eleven months of the year. All at once something shot into his mind causing him to look more deeply thoughtful.

During a sermon of more than usual pungency the previous Sunday, Dr. Willis had said: "We none of us are thankful enough, or show thankfulness in the way we should for God's abounding mercies."

"Why, of course I am thankful," Mr. Williams had said to himself as he listened with ease and satisfaction to the remainder of the earnest discourse. What made the simple sentence recur to him now, he did not stop to inquire. He only walked along reviewing as with a bird's eye glance the prosperity of the waning year, and soliloquized mentally.

"Yes, I am getting pretty well fixed and no mistake! My wife and children are well fed, well dressed and happy. Wife Jennie enjoys the fine outlook as well as I do. Jennie is getting popular in choice circles, I notice. She should, too, for she is bright, intelligent and ladylike. Her paper on 'Moderation' in Society,' read at the club the other day, did her great credit. I happen to know. Willie and Susie are well trained. The home is paid for, handsomely furnished and full of comfort. Jennie shall have a seal-skin cloak for her Christmas present. And I am about to join the Croesus Club, a long coveted indulgence, never quite attainable until now.

"Really it is delightful, being able to train with the rich, and feeling yourself one of them! Phew! the 'International' has declared its dividend, and what glory—30 per cent! Now the splendid Thanksgiving dinner we will have, to be sure. We will invite that stunning couple, Colonel Rockingham and wife, now boarding temporarily, also Captain and Mrs. Ludington, who are expecting to be alone in their sumptuous apartments at the 'Buccleugh.' Here it is Monday, the invitations should have been sent sooner, but never mind, we can apologize on the grounds of everything being impromptu and informal.

Mr. Williams had reached a park which he must cross on the way, and it may be his lips moved as he ruminated on:

"I wonder if we could borrow a chef from the club house? Very likely; they say these fellows will sometimes give instructions to the under cooks, and go out for a 'special' if only the bait is large enough. Dear me, how enjoyable it will be: dinner coat, a few favors, flowers, the choicest Havanas. Yes, it is jolly even to think of and plan for."

Just then some one jostled him. A man so breathless with the news he was imparting as to collide with Mr. Williams without actually knowing it.

"Yes, sir, it is true! I heard the president himself talking about it!" The reply was like a hot challenge.

"Impossible! Why, man alive, it has just declared dividend of 30 per cent. You must be insane."

"I'm no more insane than you are!" was the passionate response. "The report is true."

"But what of its immense capital and assured surplus?"

"Don't know nor care anything about those bogus representations," was the dogged reply. "The 'International' has gone up, and Philbrook and Wetherell have come down like the stick of a rocket."

The excited speakers passed on, and Mr. Williams suddenly trembling as if palsied, sank onto an iron bench near the end of the park. It glanced through his mind, as his hand rested on the back of the bench, that its coldness was in touch with the iron that had entered into his soul. He knew the man well who had communicated the petrifying tidings. A "hanger on" who usually caught early in the day whatever was going "on the street."

He asked himself as in a dream, how the thing could have come about. 'The International!' The very soundest house of its kind in the country! It had been his pet dream to own a good clump of stock in it ever since he had become a man. No mushroom enterprise, no suddenly elevated company was the old and reliable 'International.' It was the summmum bonum of many a long-headed, sound business man's ambition to own stock in the fine old concern. A thing by no means easy to acquire. Only the strong, impelling influence of Mr. Wetherell of the banking house of Philbrook and Wetherell had eventually enabled Mr. Williams to avail himself of the handsome shares in the reputedly invincible concern.

How could it be? Mr. Williams ruminated now in the half stunned, half stupid way that people will, when a hard, benumbing shock mercifully dulls the sensibilities for the nonce, "No great Thanksgiving dinner," he murmured audibly, "no call for dinner coat, no favors, no flowers, no chef." Chef! He turned sick at the thought, it all at once seemed so presuming and so shallow.

"I've got the house anyway," he went on, "I'm sure of that. But Jennie can't swell at the club any longer. Great mercy. I hadn't joined the Croesus! Yet Jennie and the children are well. Thank God for that."

Then he thought he might as well go on, and find out how the disaster came about, and what prophecies were afloat as to what proportion of the investments might possibly be doled out in time.

Arrived at the splendidly equipped offices of the 'International,' he was languidly surprised to see things going on much as usual. "Just the least exasperating coolness," he thought bitterly. Mr. Wetherell was just sauntering out.

"What's this about the 'International?'" Mr. Williams asked grimly.

"Great news, isn't it?" answered Mr. Wetherell, voice jubilant, manner debonnaire.

"What news?" asked poor Mr. Williams.

"Why, haven't you heard?" asked the banker, wondering at Horace Williams' rigid appearance.

"Thirty per cent, man! Aren't you pleased?"

"Yes, but about the smash-up? Selkirk was telling just now about the 'International' having gone up."

Mr. Wetherell looked unpleasantly enlightened. "Oh, that flippant loon!" he cried. "I suppose he has confounded the petty failure of the International Coffee House, we were talking of this morning, with this concern. We must stop his mouth instanter before he creates a panic. Our 'International' is sound as a nut.

Advance Society Letters.

BY J. BRECKENRIDGE ELLIS.

This is our Thanksgiving edition of the Advance Society page for 1906. We are thankful for all those who have taken up our regular reading course, and for the splendid quarterly reports that have come in, some of them carefully typewritten, some illustrated, some tied in our society colors of blue and old gold, some occupying as many as 12 pages, with each day's Bible-reading, each week's quotation, etc., fully detailed. We are thankful for the wide extent of the Av. S., from New York to Lower California, and from South America to China and Japan. We are thankful for the great work of the Av. S., in taking up the disowned child, "Little Joe," paying his board and advertising him until he was adopted into a kind and refined home. We are thankful that orphan Charlie is given into our charge, that we may strive and write and talk and toil until we raise enough to educate him. We are thankful for Drusie taking the Gospel to benighted North China, and that we can help, by contributing to her support, in spreading that best of all Good News that ever came to earth. I, in particular, am thankful for the kind letters I so often receive—letters much too complimentary (I do not say, however, that they are undeserved), to be printed; and for the support from many readers who are not regular Av. S. members. But why do I try to tell all the things that make me thankful? I am thankful just to be sitting here alive, still on the earth. And I am thankful, I must not forget to say, that Felix's picture is finished. That picture would certainly have graced the great Thanksgiving number of THE CHRISTIAN-EVANGELIST, thus adding a charm and grace that no mere minister's likeness could impart, had not a delay come in the cut. There is trouble about the cut. This doesn't mean that Felix has been hurt. A 'cut' as we literary people use the word, has nothing to do with people pretending not to see you on the street car; because they are riding in a private automobile. It is thus: first we take a picture of Felix.—No, I should say first we chase and catch and hold Felix. Then we take him with a camera. When the photographer finds nothing else to do, and no more street carnivals to attend, he finishes the picture and you pay for it. You take that picture to your editor and ask him to send it to the engraver's to have a cut made. He says he will have it for you in four days. You then smile at this, you thank him and peacefully wait for the weeks to roll round. We are now in this stage of getting Felix presented to his numerous friends. It is a slow stage, but we are thankful to have any stage at all. However, it is not raining and it pleases me to say a kind word for Arkansas weather whenever it deserves it. It often deserves a compliment. It can't rain to-day, anyhow, for it is both sleeting and snowing and no weather, I care not in what state, can be expected to attend to more than these at the same time. As for Drusie's Christmas Tree, I think it promising. Let us hear from our dear old Av. S. comrade, Harry Buckley of Lawrenceburg, Ky.: "And

so it's to be a Christmas Tree? Well, that is a good idea, but I had set my heart on a Birthday Party for Drusie. A few weeks ago a dear friend was speaking to me of the splendid success of Charlie's Social, and said, 'Wouldn't it be nice if we could have a birthday party for our missionary? But I suspect Bro. Ellis has already thought of it, for after he gets through thinking there is very little left.'" (I like that friend of yours.) "But the Christmas Tree idea is all right, and here is a dollar for a present. As I am ignorant of the things a girl would like most to get for a Christmas present, I'll ask Grace Everest to kindly select something from the dollar counter and hang it on the tree for me. May God add His blessing to the Christmas Tree idea. The Bronze Vase is a delightful story, delightfully told, I think..." (It had been suggested some time ago that we have a birthday party for Drusie, I forget by whom, and it appeared a fine plan. But after long consideration, the Christmas Tree appealed to me more. Christmas has always been regarded by me as the very apex or crisis of the year; the time above all other times to eat too much with a good conscience, and to begin on candy immediately after breakfast, and to have relations even including the relations-in-law, to assem-

ble at your house, and blow horns and get every room on the place out of order. I don't see how I could possibly have been happier on my Christmases, unless there had been something like this Tree for our missionary; and yet, I never knew about Santa Claus. There was never a reindeer track on my father's roof, or a midnight visit down the stovepipe. It's all very well to hang your stocking at the open fireplace or even on the hinges of the coal stove. But it was always with my family quite out of the question that Santa should crawl out of a little door in the middle of a coal stove. All of which goes to show that no real happiness in this

world needs a myth or delusion to rest upon, and that if Santa Claus is a dear part in your past life, you would have had just as dear a time if he had been your father or mother; because Youth is the dear time, though not necessarily reindeer. But what has all this to do with Drusie? Why, just this: Christmas is such a delightful season that I want to be in some way the means of making it more delightful for you. And I know that if you help celebrate the coming Christmas by sending an imaginary gift for our missionary, that you will always look back upon this Christmas as a little different and in a sense a little better, than any you have known. Maybe it may seem a little selfish in me to want to have a hand in your holiday. That's all right, you send a present! So you see, this thing isn't entirely a Drusie affair, any more than Charlie's Social was a Charlie affair. No, not near all. It's the joy of giving to a great, noble purpose, the joy of taking something from yourself which could give you pleasure, and give it away where it will do good; something you will miss; something you will feel the want of. That makes a Christmas that is a Christmas! Mrs. J. O. Johnston, Stewartsville, Mo., in writing to my mother, says: "That ice cream social did fine for Charlie! I hope Drusie may have a grand Christmas tree. I hope it may be like the matches, 'go off in good shape. I did not expect any of my letter about that Social to be printed, but Oliver" (Oliver is her little boy) "was so proud when I showed it to him! he could find his name!" (Well, here it is again, Oliver—now how many times is that, Oliver?) Mrs. E. A. James, Long Beach, Cal.: "The Av. S. is certainly doing a grand work for the orphan boy and our missionary. The ice cream social was just the thing, though I was not there. But here I come to the Christmas Tree with a box of stationary for the dear girl who will want to write letters to the home folks." ($1.) "I am much interested in our orphan boy, and when he needs more funds I may have a few pennies. In order to go forward, I begin reading the dear CHRISTIAN-EVANGELIST at the back, so you see I soon get to the Av. S. pages. I always enjoy reading them so much. Then I soon turn to the Easy Chair. It's all good from first leaf to last. I hope the Christmas Tree will be bending down with good things," Lees Summit: "I enclose $1.25 for Charlie and Drusie; please do not publish my name, but accept the small amount for Christ's sake." Jennie Updike. Bellnap, Ia.: "I send 25 cents for Drusie and 10 for our orphan Charlie: I hope Drusie will be greatly blessed in her work of love and sacrifice in that far-away land; it is grand to have such faith as hers." Pasadena, Cal.: "I enclose $1, half for Drusie, half for Charlie. Plenty hot here for ice cream. The Christmas Tree is a fine idea. I trust every one will be generous. I want to thank you for your remarks about chain letters. It has been such a comfort to drop them in the waste basket without feeling a twinge of conscience. Since reading your opinion, I have felt so comfortable. May the Lord continue to bless the Av. S. work." Ann M. Thalker, Louisville, Ky.: "I am an old lady, 83 years of age, and yet I like ice cream, and you will please send me a dish of

Charlie's. God bless Charlie, and all who are kind to him; and may he grow up a good and useful man." Mrs. E. S. Stevens, Akita, Japan: "I am buying a foreign money order; when the notice is received, please send me one Av. S. gold pin. It is to be Henry's Christmas present. He has been very faithful in keeping the Av. S. rules. Please have the pin registered." (So I did; was it received? In printing the foregoing letter from Pasadena, I omitted the writer's name, Mrs. J. H. Byram, who sends a post card with picture of the Pasadena Christian Church as it will look when finished. It is a beautiful structure, of great towers, windows and entrances. In one corner something is growing, which in M'ssouri would suggest a large burdock; but no doubt being in California, it is a palm or banana-tree. No building can be too magnificent for the service of God, unless you sink over your head in debt on account of it; and no building, let us remember, however sublime, is so beautiful as the simple, childlike hearts that come to its portals in love.) Drusie R. Malott, Tai Ming-fu, North China: "My last days have been very busy ones, there was so much to do in preparing to move mission stations and to the city. Besides office work and this extra work, I have been putting up fruit for the station workers who could not do it for themselves,—wouldn't you like some apricots or peaches or apple marmalade" (um! mmh!) "or plum, apple or grape jelly? or watermelon preserves?" (Not m. w. preserves, but I thank you, I know you mean well.) "I am acknowledging the receipt of the books from Mrs. E. M. Rothwell, Moberly, Mo. The papers and cards are just what I desired. You need not send more than 15 papers of the same kind and date, as we have only 15 in our 'American' S. S. We are most grateful for both papers and cards. You may be sure we are glad to have all the cards we can get, for they can be used also in work among the Chinese. Does any one have the S. S. Evangelist to spare? Or the Christian Companion? Inland postage is charged for papers and packages, not because the homeland postage is not enough, but to pay overland expense from Shanghai. When the homeland postage is not sufficient, we have an extra fine of 12 cents Mexican for each half ounce. Your parcels have always had sufficient homeland postage. Our missionaries are about ready to return to their stations for another year's work. Pray the Lord to make this a glorious year of soul-winning. Pray for the gate-keepers, and cooks and language-teachers, that they may all be earnest witnesses for Jesus. And my dear mother misses me; please remember her in your petitions in my behalf. And I am asking the Lord to call my brother and sister into His service. I believe some day they are going to be with me in His work. I acknowledge with grateful thanks the $5-checks received from the Av. S. each month. The best wish I can send you, and them any any one is, that you may have as large a cup of the Lord's grace as I have. Praise His dear name!"

We have a splendid now Honor List this week; not that the names are so many, but nearly every report is very full and handsomely prepared. I wish you could see them. Bertha Beesley, Moselle, Mo. (31st quarter); Dorothy Brown, Medaryville, Ind (7th); Harry A. Stevens, Akita, Japan, (11th); Mrs. W. A. Mason, Nevada, Mo. (11th); Grace Everest, Oklahoma City (8th); Mabel E. Nicholas, 916 W. Oak St., Fort Collins, Colo.; Walter S. Whitacre, Mt. Vernon, Ill. (9th); Fanny Whitney, San Francisco, (2nd); Lucy Manfel, Orx, Mich. (2nd & 3rd); Mabel Tolliver, Portland, Ore. (5th); Will, Mary, James and Lucy Burton, North Roads, Ia.
Bentonville, Ark.

Our Budget

—"Bless the Lord, O my soul, and all that is within me, bless his holy name."

—"Bless the Lord, O my soul, and forget not all his benefits."

—Let all the readers of THE CHRISTIAN-EVANGELIST join in thanksgiving to God for his manifold kindnesses and mercies.

—THE CHRISTIAN-EVANGELIST is grateful among other things for the large increase in the number of its readers, showing that it is growing in favor with the people.

—Our cause of gratitude is that the things for which THE CHRISTIAN-EVANGELIST stands are growing more and more in favor with the brotherhood.

—Look out for "Our Pioneers" number of THE CHRISTIAN-EVANGELIST, the first week in January.

✥ ✥ ✥

Special to THE CHRISTIAN-EVANGELIST.

Barry, Ill., Nov. 24.—Illinois meeting at Eldora twelve days old; thirty-two conversions, fourteen last night, eight to-night.—W. E. Spicer, evangelist; J. D. Williams, minister.

—George P. Taubman has resigned at Portsmouth, Ohio.

—J. M. Plummer has accepted a call to begin work January 1, at Elk City, Kan.

—The dedication of the church at Litchfield, Ill., has been changed to December 16.

—News of the death of C. C. Boyd, of Covington, Ky., has been received. Further particulars next week.

—George A. Webb and wife, singing evangelists, are assisting S. M. Martin in a good meeting at Red Bluff, Cal.

—William M. Mayfield is being assisted in a good meeting at Dighton by J. B. Mayfield, evangelist, and G. A. Butler, singer.

—F. F. Walters, after his first Sunday in the Central church, Springfield, Mo., thinks the outlook is bright for a successful work.

—E. A. Gilliland has received a call to East St. Louis to succeed W. Henry Jones, whose views on Christian Science led to his resignation.

—L. L. Carpenter will dedicate the new church at Ottawa, Kan., December 2. The following night he will lecture on his tour through the Orient.

—O. P. Spiegel, who has just been elected state evangelist of Alabama, is to hold a meeting in North Tonawanda, N. Y., early in the new year.

—G. Washington Wise, who recently took up the work at Alton, Ill., thinks the outlook is very hopeful. The Sunday-school has more than doubled since October 1.

—We regret that T. J. Arnold did not, as indicated in our last "Budget," join the Christian church at Marshall, Ark., but commended Brother Rogers' meeting, though he remained a Baptist.

—A. M. Harral, of Sapulpa, I. T., is contemplating spending the winter on the gulf coast. He hopes to leave a capable minister at Sapulpa on his departure January 1.

—A. L. Ward is one of the secretaries of the interdenominational committee which has in charge the union meeting being held in Tremont Temple, Boston, by Gipsy Smith, the English evangelist.

It is reported that Boston is being shaken as never before.

—J. C. Howell reports that there are over one hundred young people in the Christian Endeavor Society at Salem, Mo., which is a church organized sixty-nine years ago.

—The church at Abilene, Texas, under Granville Snell is planning for both an education and a foreign missionary rally before long. The cause at Abilene seems to be full of promise.

—The brethren at Detroit express themselves as delighted with Lloyd Darsie, formerly of Chicago, who has been conducting for them evangelistic services both at the Central Church and the Woodward Avenue Church.

—R. E. Callihan is being assisted in a meeting with his church at Gallatin, Mo., by George L. Peters, who has lately entered the ranks of our Missouri preachers and has located at Joplin. Both Brother Peters and Brother Cal-

George L. Peters.

lithan are good workers and they will be assisted by 300 copies of THE CHRISTIAN-EVANGELIST weekly. Two other meetings are going on in the town.

—J. L. Thompson writes that it is gratifying to the workers in Decatur, Ill., to have N. S. Haynes and J. H. Smart become citizens of that place, for their presence will be a great inspiration to the brethren there.

—A good report has been made by the churches of Mayetta and Jeandale, Kan., where Nelson Gardner is the minister. They exceeded their apportionment for state missions, the former place more than doubling the amount expected.

—L. A. Chapman writes that notwithstanding the difficulty of the overshadowing influence of a Methodist state university our own church and people at Mt. Pleasant, Ia., are making due impression on the community.

—A Bible institute is announced by the Central Christian Church, Jacksonville, Ill., November 20-December 2. The school of this church is in competition with those of Paris and Akron. Each school has now made five points.

—George L. Snively's unusual success in securing funds for religious purposes is keeping his services in continual demand. Next Lord's day he will help Ivan Agee liquidate an old indebtedness hanging over the church at Atlanta, Ill.

—We received an invitation to the reception given by the First Christian

Church of Pittsburg, in honor of Pastor W. G. Winn and wife, which occurred Friday evening. We need not say we would have been delighted to be present.

—Harlow and Harlow began a meeting at Newman, Ill., November 25. The church there has averaged one addition a Sunday since January 15, at the regular services, and since that date the average attendance of the Bible school has been doubled.

—C. E. Chambers and the Davis Street Church at Ottumwa, Ia., are doing a good work together. There have been fifty additions and a debt of $750 paid off since Brother Chambers began his ministry there that April. Every missionary apportionment has been reached.

—To the very great grief of his large congregation at Paris, Ill., Finis Idleman has accepted a call to succeed H. O. Breeden at the Central Church, Des Moines, Ia. Brother Idleman has done a great work at Paris and is much beloved by the people there.

—B. G. Hostetter is pastor of the church at Loraine, O., and not C. Manly Rice, as appeared in some of our prints. Brother Hostetter's ministry is being greatly blessed. He has just concluded a revival with the assistance of Evangelist E. E. Violett, with 104 additions to the membership.

—R. B. Briney, minister at Lexington, Mo., was called to Louisville, Ky., last week, by the death of his mother, Sister J. B. Briney. We deeply regret to learn of this great loss to Brother Briney, and he and his family have our sincere sympathy in their bereavement of a faithful and loving wife and mother.

—T. Alfred Fleming, of the Miles Avenue Christian Church, Cleveland, O., is assisting Earl Wilfley in a good meeting at Crawfordsville, Ind. Brother Wilfley is a fine worker and we are not surprised that with a true and loyal following so many fathers and mothers are together taking their stand with the church.

—Mrs. Lee J. Harris writes of the encouragement which the little band at Moscow Mills, Mo., has derived from a visit of R. B. Havener, one of the Missouri state Bible school evangelists. He won the hearts there and $52 were contributed to the Bible school work and new life has been put into the congregation.

—Roy Linton Porter, who closed his work at Lake Charles, La., September 30, is at Chaneyville for a temporary stay, hoping to build up his health again, which he hopes to be able to do in two or three months so as to take some permanent work. The Lake Charles church gave him and his family a farewell social and remembered them with some things.

—J. D. Hull has been unanimously asked to remain the third year in the pastoral care of the church at Kendallville, Ind. The local newspaper not only speaks well of his effective work, both in and out of the pulpit, but gives a column and a half report of his sermon on Sunday evening under the title "What is This New Doctrine?" The theme was, "Christianity from the Bible Viewpoint."

—C. M. Mahin, who has just closed a second meeting at North Vernon, Ind., says the church there is in need of a minister for half time and the prospect is they can employ him soon for full time. It is one of the best fields in Indiana, and is ripe for an earnest, consecrated man. G. B. Baird, who has gone to China as a missionary, was the last minister. Correspondents may write to Capt. J. D. Hudson, enclosing recommendations.

—C. M. Schoonover, of Gainesville, Texas, who has been doing successful work in Texas as pastor and evangelist for the past six years, has come north and will evangelize in the states adjacent to Chicago while his wife takes some special work in music in the city. They are at present in a successful meeting at Boston Chapel, near Girard, Illinois.

—We do not know whether it was our fault or the sender of the news paragraph, but we reported last week a reception given to J. W. Reynolds and wife at Clinton, Ill. It should have been Saunemin, Ill. Brethren should be very careful when combining two or more news items to make perfectly clear the place and time and to write names very distinctly. This would save our office force a great deal of time and the probability of making an error.

—W. J. Kimbrough writes us from Richmond, Va., that B. H. Melton has begun his fifth year with the old Marshall church, under very favorable circumstances. During his four years' pastorate the church has doubled its power in every way. The building has been greatly enlarged and improved and the congregations are among the largest in this city of 100,000 people. The church is in the midst of a revival, he says, all the time, and the Lord adds members at nearly every service.

—We do not know who had charge of making known the program of the Texas Christian Lectureship. We regret that no communication was sent to THE CHRISTIAN-EVANGELIST office. The Lectureship was held last week at Palestine, Texas, the chief speaker being Dr. H. L. Calhoun, of the Bible College, at Lexington. Brother Calhoun passed through St. Louis on his way to Texas and we had the pleasure of his presence at the mass meeting of the Disciples of Christ at the Odeon.

—One of the most perfect church buildings ever erected in the south is fast being completed at Atlanta, Ga. When completed the property of the First Christian Church will be valued at not less than $100,000. It is the idea of pastor and congregation to make it the social headquarters and religious home of the young people of their congregation and of the city. For this purpose the institutional idea has been considered in the planning of the church building. King Pendleton is the pastor.

—W. H. Bagby, whose excellent address delivered before the Texas Christian Lectureship, appeared in our two last issues writes that the work at Missoula, Mont., is moving along nicely. He writes: "Old Nick has a strong grip on this region, and the church feels his squeeze, but the tide of civilization, morality and religion follows in the wake of the star of empire. No frontier can be too remote for it to reach nor too rough for it to revolutionize. We are waiting

and working for its coming to this fair and great but far northwest."

—Frank L. Van Voorhis is now on his new field at Shawnee, Okla., where he reports every one standing by the work with him. He has preached twice for a sister church at Tecumseh only four miles distant, and reports it will engage a minister soon. He has started a little monthly paper to cover the local field in the way of news announcements. We note that the motto suggested for the church is "Work." Brother Van Voorhis received the best kind of commendations from the church at Okmulgee, which he recently left to take up his present charge.

—"The Lucha," a Cuban American paper, published in Havana, announces that Rev. Lowell C. McPherson who has returned to that city after several months' vacation in the states, has announced his purpose to remove to Wellsville, N. Y., where he will reside in the future. The "Lucha" adds: "This news will be received with genuine regret by every person in Cuba who has met him. Americans and Cubans alike regard him not only as an able and devoted Christian worker, but as an upright gentleman and a warm and steadfast friend. Mr. and Mrs. McPherson came to Cuba with the first army of intervention and the extent of the good he has done can not be bounded by the imagination, for he labored with Americans and Cubans alike, working in the church, charities and educational fields. The best wishes of all will go with them in their new home."

—The congregation at Bedford Ind., has just had an enthusiastic meeting, it having been announced that $5,000 has been raised towards an aim recently decided upon to remove the present mortgage on the property, which is just double that amount. The church has been burdened with a very large debt, but the hearty co-operation of Pastor E. Richard Edwards and his people has enabled the congregation to pay off between $7,000 and $8,000, independent of the current expenses. One member of the church having agreed to assume the liabilities of interest and repairs, amounting to nearly $1,100, on condition that the other members of the church raise the mortgage, has led to the goal being half way reached.

—Aims for 1907: At least, 1. Four hundred in the Bible school. 2. Four hundred readers of Christian papers. 3. Four hundred givers to take pride in the finances of the church. 4. Seventy-five at the prayer-meeting. 5. One hundred accessions. In short, a membership who love the church and the Lord and one another. "The best is none too good." The above aims were found on a card the size of a calling card. On the reverse side there is printing to certify that the bearer is a member of "the four hundred" of the Central Church of Christ, Dayton, O., of which I. J. Cahill is minister. Each member agrees to help in some way to accomplish the aim set forth above. We will be glad to hear from a great many of our preachers what definite aims they and their congregations have for 1907. If replies to this invitation prove worth while, we shall be very glad to publish them in our first issue of the new year, and we cordially invite contributions that may be helpful and that will show definite work planned by different churches.

—It is a remarkable record that the East Dallas church has. It stands in the very forefront not only in Texas but throughout the country in the amount of money it raises and the work it does, considering all the facts of the case.

The third anniversary of the church has just been observed. During the past year there was raised more than $7,900, of which more than $2,800 went to missionary causes, partly itemized as follows: Home Missions, $438; Foreign Missions, $350; Church Extension, $150; Benevolent and Education, $1,500; State Missions, $350. The Ladies' Aid Society raised $1,791 for the new building. With a membership of seven less than 300, with no wealth, and worshiping in a low, flat roofed frame building, this is a remarkable financial statement. The secret of the fact that this congregation not only contributes to all good causes but is soon to erect a $30,000 building, is in its deep consecration and the fact that some of the members are tithers. During H. R. Ford's pastorate of twenty months there have been added 240 to the membership and sixty-five at regular services during the past year, though the net gain during the twelve months was only twenty-five. Brother Ford will begin his third year's pastorate January 1.

His Favorite Steed.

I received the copy of "Christian Union." I generally find it very difficult to get time for a reading of a book sent for review, and run over them enough to get a pretty good idea of them. But this was on a theme which lies very close to my heart. I have a pretty good stable full of well groomed hobbies, all of which I ride occasionally. My favorite steed from these stalls is Christian Union. You can, then, understand me when I tell you that I sat down soon after the book came, and read three-fourths of it before putting it down. I took it home with me and finished it before I slept! I can not tell how I enjoyed it, nor can I make you know how my soul was enriched by reading it. The Christian world would feel indebted to its author if only the book were read as I wish it were. The book evinces no little research in the data it contains, but the best is the Christ spirit that runs through the whole book.   G. A. FARIS.

Dallas, Tex., Nov. 6, 1906.

❋ ❋

A Wonderful Offer.

$25 to $50 per week. Lady or gentleman wanted in every locality for new line of staple goods. No canvassing. Apply quick. Mercantile Import Co., Dept. 43, 8-10-12 west 125th street, New York city, N. Y.

Gloria in Excelsis.—The New Christian Church Hymnal.

We have many song books, but this, as I view them, is the best. It is arranged to meet the needs of the entire church under all her varying conditions. The arrangement of this hymnal is the finest and most complete of any I have ever examined. It is progressive, orderly and easily accessible. The hymns have been selected not for the music only, but for the dictional value of each hymn. The wording of many has been changed to make them more perfectly in accord with the teaching of the Word of God.

The arrangements of the hymns which teach of the Christ illustrates this excellence of the book. The author begins with "The Incarnation and Advent;" then "The Life and Ministry of Jesus;" next "His Suffering and Death," "His Burial and Resurrection" and "His Ascension and Coronation." Then in order comes the hymns on "Christ's Reign and Mediation," and this part of the book closes with hymns of praise to Christ.

The next division of the book, "Hymns on the Holy Spirit," is perhaps the most distinguishing feature of the book. Here the author and committee take the largest liberty with the original poems to bring them in accord with the teaching of the word of God. The fact that they have chosen only fifteen hymns from the large number in this subject indicates the carefulness of selection. There could be a few more verbal changes to profit. But the fact that the subject is presented in a prominent way, is commendable. If we are under the guidance of the Holy Spirit and labor in His dispensation, if He abides in us and is our helper in time of need, if it is His mission through the Word and through the church to bear witness of Christ, then we as a people have not made enough of his ministry either in sermon or song. This collection and revision of hymns is not perfect, but it is a beginning in the right direction. It is a breaking away from that unscriptural custom of neglecting the Holy Spirit in our praise service and that spirit which would advise a young preacher not to preach on the work of the Holy Spirit for at least ten years. We had better make some mistakes than to neglect Him entirely.

The gospel of atonement is set forth in the same orderly manner. First are songs indicating "Our Need of Salvation," then "Salvation Provided" and "Salvation Offered." These constitute the songs of invitation while those of "Salvation Accepted" are arranged under the sub-headings of faith, repentence, confession and obedience. The same fine and scriptural analysis is followed under the general headings of "The Church," "The Christian Life," "Time and Eternity."

This hymnal furnishes songs and hymns suited for dedications, missionary meetings, ordination of officers and preachers, farewell services to ministers and missionaries; conventions, Thanksgiving and national celebrations; temperance, philanthropic and reform meetings, and special prayer-meetings. Indeed, I know of no place where songs are wont to be sung which this hymnal does not anticipate in select readings and songs.

The complete edition is some larger than we have been accustomed to, but not so unwieldy as the standard hymnals of other churches. The abridged edition presents the main features of the hymnal and is a beautiful book of convenient form and size. Since this is our greatest song book, it should have the greatest sale and have an influence to unify the worship of our people in the best hymns of the church.

Bethany, W. Va. PROF. W. B. TAYLOR.

—To our collection of Campbell photographs we add this week some more. On another page will be found some connected with the early days of Alex-

Alexander Campbell in 1857.

ander Campbell. Here we print a picture of Mr. Campbell, made from a daguerreotype taken in Mt. Vernon, O.,

The Last Portrait of Alexander Campbell.

in 1857 or 1858, and now in the possession of F. M. Rains. The other picture is from what we believe to be the last photograph ever taken of Mr. Campbell. This was taken in 1866, and as he died on March 4 of that year, there is every reason to regard this as his last portrait. It is in the possession of Mrs. A. J. Thompson, New Albany, Ind.

❀　❀

Stockholders' Meeting.

Notice is hereby given that the annual meeting of the stockholders of the Christian Publishing Company will be held at the company's office, 2712 Pine street, St. Louis, Mo., Tuesday, January 1, 1907, at 10 o'clock, for the election of directors and for the transaction of such other business as may legally come before said meeting.
　　　　　　　J. H. GARRISON, Pres.
　　　　　　　GEO. L. SNIVELY, Sec.
St. Louis, Nov. 15, 1906.

Foreign Society Rallies.

December 3—Henderson, Ky., Wm. Ward, pastor.
December 4—Centralia, Ill., J. F. Roseborough, pastor.
December 6—Vincennes, Ind., Wm. Oeschger, pastor.
December 7—Mattoon, Ill., D. N. Wetzel, pastor.
December 10—Crawfordsville, Ind., Earl Wilfley, pastor.
December 11—Terre Haute, Ind. (supper).
December 12—Bloomington, Ind., T. J. Clark, pastor.
December 13—New Albany, Ind., B. F. Cato, pastor.
December 14—Franklin, Ind., R. K. Ross, pastor.
December 16—Shelbyville, Ind.
December 17—Connersville, Ind., J. C. Burkhardt, pastor.
December 18—Wilmington, O.
December 19—Athens, O., T. L. Lowe, pastor.

❀　❀

Kentucky District Conventions.

We have just held the first series of district conventions that our people have ever held in southern Kentucky. We have reached fully five hundred people who had never attended a convention of any sort presenting our work. We have effected an organization in every district and selected time and place for the next convention. I give a list of the organizations.

(18) President, R. H. Crossfield, Owensboro; Vice-president, J. W. Berkshire; secretary and statistician, n. B. Self. Next convention, Calhoun, October 22-25, 1907.

(19) President, S. B. Taylor, Beaver Dam; Vice-president, Robt. Frazier; secretary and statistician, C. P. Austin. Next convention, Central City, November 9-10, 1907.

(20) President, W. T. Wells, Bowling Green; Vice-president, J. U. Potter; secretary and statistician, H. Wade Hampton. Next convention, Russellville, November 7-8, 1907.

(21) President, J. W. Ligon, Corydon; Vice-president, S. F. Fowler; secretary and statistician, S. L. Jackson. Next convention, Madisonville, October, 1907.

(22) President, John C. Gates, Princeton; Vice-president, John S. Crenshaw; secretary and statistician, W. H. Jones. Next convention, Cadiz, October, 1907.

(23) President, R. O. Hester, Mayfield; Vice-president, W. K. Hall; secretary, Henry Hazotte; statistician, Miss Jessie Hay. Next convention, Paducah, November, 1907. R. M. HOPKINS.
Louisville, Ky.

❀　❀

Big Returns From Small Investments.

That is just what people are looking for now. That is exactly what you can get from an investment in the work of Kentucky missions. If a man's soul is worth more than all the world —what is the value of many souls? During the first sixty days of our new year's work 528 have been added to our numbers through the labors of our workers in the Kentucky state mission field. One of the great missionary organizations set as its goal last year 1,000 souls added. They spent about $200,000 to accomplish this and it is considered well spent. You will note that more than half that number were added in two months in old Kentucky and at a very small cost. We believe a Kentuckian is worth as much as anybody on the globe. The writer believes that, and he is so unfortunate as not to be a Kentuckian—except by adoption. This work is a case of big returns from small investments.

WANTED—One hundred churches to take the state missionary offering in Kentucky at once. Will yours be among the number? The November offering has begun well—let us go unto perfection.　　　H. W. ELLIOTT, Sec.
Sulphur, Ky.

❀　❀

Kentucky Centennial Convention.

While all eyes are turned toward Pittsburg for 1909, let us not forget that our state conventions will be held in that year. There are thousands of earnest Disciples who for various reasons will not be able to attend the Pittsburg convention, and to those who go, a foretaste of the good things in the state convention will not come amiss. Many states are undertaking some special Centennial enterprise and they shall want to come to their state meetings to complete their undertakings and prepare for the Pittsburg convention.

In no state will it be more appropriate to hold a state Centennial convention in that year than in Kentucky. Here Barton W. Stone's work was done, and here much of Alexander Campbell's labor was expended.

After some careful consideration, the Bible school executive committee would like to sound the cry, "A Great Kentucky Gathering in 1909." Shall we have it, brethren? Let us hear what is thought about this. We ought soon to select the place for this Centennial convention, and possibly there is but one fitting place. We ought to prepare a program that would be appropriate for such a significant gathering. We cannot do too much in honor of our centenary.
Louisville, Ky.　　　R. M. HOPKINS.

A Most Remarkable List.

Bro. T. J. Clark has a record to be proud of. He has had just two pastorates in a ministry of thirty-five years. For twenty-two years he was with the church at Vincennes, Ind., and is now serving his thirteenth year as pastor at Bloomington.

One of our friends writes to us in the following strain:

"Brother Clark has just delivered to the publishers of THE CHRISTIAN-EVANGELIST a trainload of new readers—107 regular, bona-fide, one year, $1.50 subscribers; the kind that pay full fare and

T. J. Clark.

expect in return the best things—a ride in the 'Garrison coaches,' where the best articles are served regularly and in up-to-date style, with the sort of seasoning that strengthens faith in God, brings peace to the brotherhood, and inspires men to labor for precious souls.

May this substantial and commendable example of Brother Clark's cause many other pastor-conductors to say 'all-aboard, to their people and assist them into the great 'Union Train of Progress,' THE CHRISTIAN-EVANGELIST, whose engineer, firemen and brakemen are safe and sane. Every passenger is personally conducted through the brotherhood fifty-two times a year for $1.50. Purchase tickets before entering train. Day coaches only. Stops made at every Christian home. For additional information address Christian Publishing Company, General Passenger Agents, 2712 Pine street, St. Louis, Mo.

❀　❀

—From a Buffalo daily we make the following excerpt:

"Authority of Religion in the Plea of Our Fathers" was the subject of a very scholarly address delivered by the Rev. B. H. Hayden, of Buffalo. "The first question in religion is, What is right? If we succeed in finding this we shall have found the seat of authority. Conscience can not be an ultimate tribunal, for to make it a seat of authority would be to make each a law unto himself. The same is true of both the inner moral sense and the inner light theory. The written Word of God, as his will revealed objectively, is above the ultimate in religious authority. Without this we have no revelation of God that the savage 5,000 years ago did not possess. The sufficiency of the Scriptures as the ultimate in religious authority has from its inception been the plea of the restoration movement to which the Disciples of Christ are committed."

NEWS FROM MANY FIELDS

Another District Convention in Oregon.

The Southwest District is the third to hold a convention in Oregon. It was held at Roseburg, November 6-8, While not so large in numbers, it fully equals our other district conventions in the quality and character of its work. Its committee on nominations and future work has in view: that the district considers itself as a force auxiliary to the state organization; that the representatives to the Turner convention be authorized to select, at said convention, the district president for the ensuing year; that time and place of our next district convention, be left in the hands of the executive board; that the Southwest District put an evangelist into the field, a dollar-league being formed in each church, to provide the needed funds; and that the selection of the evangelist, and the time of service be left in the hands of the Executive Board, provided, however, that no debt be incurred; that the executive board establish the work in Marshfield and Oakland, and strengthen the weaker churches, it being the policy of the district to establish the cause in one field before taking it up in another; that each of the stronger churches undertake the establishment of a mission, in a nearby needy field, with a view of establishing the work—looking forward to further evangelism; that as a convention, we endorse the action of the state convention on benevolence in planning for the location, at Eugene, of a "Home" for old people and that we pledge our co-operation in its support. This report was unanimously adopted by the convention. All western Oregon is now in line.

F. E. BILLINGTON, Cor. Sec. O. C. M. C.

Ohio.

L. G. Walker has been holding his own meeting at Centerburg, with F. H. Cappa as singing evangelist. Brother Walker has preached for Centerburg for several years.—Bowman, Hosfetter, of Dundee, is holding a meeting at Tappan in Harrison county. This is the "Home church" of President Cramblet, of Bethany.—Ohio preachers still get married. This time it is W. H. Oldham, of East Liverpool. The happy bride was Miss Lyda Davidson, of Edensburg, O. Verily, he that getteth a wife getteth a good thing and obtaineth favor of the Lord.—John A. Armstrong, of McMechen, W. Va., has taken the church at North Eaton lately vacated by Robert Chapman. Alanson Wilcox, of Cleveland, supplied the North Eaton pulpit in the meantime. —Oliver McCully has been compelled to give up the work at Lancaster on account of ill health. He is seeking restoration in Colorado.—O. L. Cook will assist Dr. S. M. Cook in a meeting at Weston this month. One of the most pleasant recollections of this scribe's ministerial life is a meeting, the second he ever held, with Dr. Cook at Mungen. It is a benediction to any man to work with Dr. S. M. Cook for a month.——An offering for Ohio Missions will be in order any time this month if it has not already been taken. In fact, it is always in order any month of the year.—J. W. Kerns, of Massillon, has been holding a meeting at Homestead, Pa. The Massillon pulpit has been supplied by Prof. Wakefield, et al., during Brother Kern's absence.—John Mullen has returned to his first love, and again located with the church at McConnelsville. His sojourn in Texas restored his health.—The Ohio letter is written this time from Lovington, Ill. Our meeting here is two days old and two strong men have confessed Christ. This place felt the influence of the great meeting at Sullivan—only eight miles away. Lovington is a fine little town of 1,000 people. It is not over churched. The disciples who were first called Christians at Antioch have a splendid

meeting house here, and a fine lot of people. J. R. Parker is the faithful and much loved preacher. But his health causes him much anxiety and he may soon go to the southwest. This is the boyhood home of Finis Idleman, the efficient preacher at Paris, Ill. We have a promise of a visit from him during the meeting. Moultrie county, Illinois, of which Sullivan is the capital, and in which Lovington is situated, has no saloon within its borders. The new court house was dedicated at Sullivan yesterday and Charles Reign Scoville made the dedicatory speech.—We feel a great personal loss in the death of G. L. Wharton. Earth is poorer and heaven richer in the death of such men. May the Lord comfort his family.

Painesville, Ohio.   C. A. FREER.

North Carolina.

The North Carolina Christian Missionary Convention met with the church at Dunn. There was a large attendance, and the delegates were delightfully entertained. My lost was a good Baptist brother who did all he could to make me feel at home, and said that personally he wished we all were one.—The amount needed to pay interest on the bonds of Atlantic Christian College was pledged by churches. It was decided later in the convention that the corresponding secretary of the state should spend four months in the year in canvassing for the college.—A. B. Cunningham was made president of the state board and W. G. Walker, corresponding and field secretary. Brother Walker has been state evangelist the past year, and had a good report. Next year the convention goes to Bel Haven, and 500 delegates are expected. The feeling of the convention was for a greater move forward. Prof. J. C. Coggins spoke in the interests of the school at Black Mountain.—The state convention of the W. C. T. U. closed in Winston-Salem on Tuesday night. The principal attraction was the addresses of Mrs. Nannie Curtis, of Texas. She is a power on the temperance question. She will remain in the state until Christmas making temperance addresses.   J. A. HOPKINS.

Winston-Salem, N. C.

Kansas City Notes.

Many friends will learn with regret that Bro. J. A. Dearborn, who has been failing for many months, is now nearing the close of this life. He has awaited the summons with patience and with unwavering hope and trust.—Meetings already held here this fall with the results therefor are as follows: Jackson Avenue, W. J. Lockhart, evangelist, 308 added; Sheffield, E. V. Bond, pastor and evangelist, added; Ivanhoe Park, E. A. Gilliland, evangelist, 26 added; Budd Park, Mrs. Sarah McCoy Crank, evangelist, 40 added; Independence Boulevard Church, James Small, evangelist, closed with 240 added; South Prospect Church, J. H. O. Smith, evangelist, 52 added to date.—The Budd Park church, B. L. Wray, pastor, has just closed a four weeks' meeting. Forty were added. Sister Sarah McCoy Crank, of Paragould, Ark., the evangelist, made a very favorable impression upon the community. She has done a great deal of evangelistic work, having baptized more than a thousand persons with her own hands, but this is the first meeting she has ever held in a church that had a pastor. Her work has heretofore been in new fields. The Budd Park church has been greatly strengthened. —Meetings yet to be held here this season are as follows: Linwood Boulevard, James Small, evangelist, commencing Sunday, November 18; Forest Avenue, H. E. Wilhite, evangelist, commencing November 18; First, R. H. Crossfield, evangelist, commencing January 13; Hyde Park, John L. Brandt, evangelist, commencing in January.—The tenth annual convention of the Missouri branch of the International Order of the Kings' Daughters and Sons, was held at the First Church, November 6 to 9.—The preachers of the Churches of Christ of Kansas City continue to meet Monday mornings at 10 o'clock. Visiting

brethren are always welcome. Among those present this morning, were J. H. O. Smith, of Valparaiso, Ind., Geo. T. Walden, of Sydney, Australia and W. J. Lhamon, dean of the Bible College at Columbia. Each of them addressed the meeting.—The monthly meeting of the preachers held on the day of the state board meeting was last time addressed by James Small. 'A New Sermon on an Old Text" was his subject. His remarks assumed the form of a model sermon, in form, unity and matter. He was greatly enjoyed by all the brethren present, some of whom can but rarely hear a sermon delivered by another since their own pulpits require their presence continually.—Not least among the items of interest under "Kansas City Notes" is the mention of the work being done to increase the circulation of THE CHRISTIAN-EVANGELIST. Bro. J. M. Harris, accompanied by one after another of the pastors, is calling upon the members of each church in turn, beginning with the First. This campaign means much for the cause in Kansas City. It is succeeding even beyond expectations. One hundred and twenty-five names were secured in the First Church in addition to about 75 already on the list and the canvass goes on in the other churches.   BARCLAY MEADOR.

Kentucky University Notes.

Our college circles have been greatly saddened by the resignation of President Jenkins. After five splendid years of service, we have been forced to give him up. Probably no man ever connected with Kentucky University has enjoyed the esteem and admiration of so many local admirers. The popularity of President Jenkins is by no means confined to the local community, but wherever he went he made friends by the score for the institution over which he so honorably presided. Aside from his splendid scholarly attainments, President Jenkins is endowed with an unusual degree of personal magnetism and power. Thousands of earnest prayers are being offered for his complete restoration to health. He has for some time been at San Antonio, Texas, where he will remain during the winter.——Prof. Thomas B. McCartney, who has been connected with the university for several years as principal of the preparatory school of the university and assistant professor of Greek, has been elected to the position of dean, and until the president is chosen will perform the inside duties of that office. He has the confidence of the university faculty and of the entire student body. He is a man of splendid scholarship, a diligent student, and is thoroughly in love with his profession.—— We expect soon to begin work on the foundation of the science building, in order to have it ready for the fall term of 1907, by which time it is purposed to have raised a fund of $50,000 with which to endow and equip the scientific department of the university. With such a building, endowment and equipment, our scientific department will be second to none in all the south.

WALTER M. WHITE,
Secretary of Kentucky University.

Hiram College Notes.

The return of Prof. Charles T. Paul to Hiram, after a year in Nanking, China, has given fresh impetus to the mission study class. He is lecturing on the various countries through which he and Mrs. Paul and Justus passed on their journeying on the various countries from a missionary standpoint. The majority of the student body are regular attendants and it has become necessary to use the auditorium to accommodate the audience. The deep missionary interest at Hiram is significant of great things for the church.—— The warm sympathy of the whole Hiram community is with the bereaved wife and children of Brother C. L. Wharton, who was for several years the beloved pastor of the Hiram church. On his final return to India Mrs. Wharton and the children remained at Hiram. All three children are now in attendance at the college. At the special chapel service held on Tuesday, November 6, Professor Dean spoke in loving memory of his life and work. At the same chapel service, Professor Colton paid a tribute of respect and affection, in the name of the college, to another warm friend of Hiram, Capt. C. E. Henry, for many years a member of the board of trustees, and for some time president of the board. Capt. Henry gave much time and effort to the service of the college, and was one of its most loyal and enthusiastic supporters. Judge F. A. Henry, of Cleveland, his son, has been for a number of years a member of the board of trustees of the college.——Mrs. Norton, mother of F. W. Norton, '87, for many years pastor of the church at Irvington, Ind., passed away on November 15. The funeral was held November 17, Prof. G. A. Peckham officiating.—Students from four foreign countries are this year in attendance at Hiram. The majority are ministerial students. Churches desiring pulpit supply will do well to address the president or secretary.——The series of vesper services, so successfully inaugurated last year, are to be continued this year. E. B.

Bagby and R. H. Miller were the first speakers and a number of prominent preachers will, during this term, give of their best thought to the Hiram community.   J. O. NEWCOMB.

Entering the Battle at Wakefield, Neb.

We begin a meeting Sunday with Evangelists Putman and Miss Egbert. The decks have been cleared and we are ready for battle. The evangelist has been ordered to leave the "Blue Mantle" at home and to bring all the sunshine possible. The expense of battle has here provided and the armor has been brightened. We have thoroughly canvassed the field and every thing loose has been marked. Each soldier in our army will be given his man and we will fight it out in a hand to hand fight. The clouds will all be pushed back toward Norfolk, the snow banks will all be melted, the lips of tattlers will be sewed up, and we will endeavor to strengthen all the weak points —(Monday nights). In the first engagement the soldiers will cast the net on the right side of the ship while the captain fires over their heads at the enemy in the rear. If, when the smoke clears away and the net has been drawn in and we have caught and killed nothing, we will say it is a hard field and it was impossible to do anything.   JOHN L. STINE.

The City by the Sea.

Leaving New Orleans the last of May we passed through Shreveport, the city of Bro. Claude L. Jones. I use the expression advisedly, for there is probably no more prominent, certainly not a more influential, man in Shreveport than our Claude L. Jones. He has been pegging away there for more than half a dozen years and to-day he is the pastor of the largest Church of Christ in Louisiana. Shreveport is one of the prettiest hustling, bustling towns in the south.

At Joplin, visiting with relatives and friends we spent about a week. At Bro. W. F. Turner's request I spoke to the First Church on Home Missions in the South. I have the honor of being the "living-link" representative of this church on the home field. By the way, why should not the home society "echo" the foreign in this matter of "living-links." The more "living-links" churches at home the more there will be abroad. If the chains or links are not so big or long they are nevertheless important. Let such echoes sound and reverberate through our whole country.

Along the way to Charleston, riding along the beautiful French Broad river, and wondering how the mountaineers could possibly cultivate the vertical fields of corn which stood like green walls here and there, we got acquainted with a stranger, who was not a stranger, J. T. Boone, of Jacksonville, Fla. He had been visiting his mother in Tennessee and convalescing from an attack of typhoid fever. Brother Boone was once pastor of the First Church in Joplin. Everyone knows of the great work he is doing in Jacksonville.

C. E. Smith, my predecessor here, was one time located at Webb City, a suburb of Joplin. Counting Mrs. Ely Joplin has thus given this southeast region at least four workers. Brother Smith is now our state evangelist.

Yes, we are still in the Sunny South. 'Tis the sea that makes this city—Charleston—the beautiful

Charleston—the city rising out of the sea!—Old stone and brick and iron fences inclosing old colonial mansions give to it the name of Charleston the quaint. New Orleans was to a great extent a foreign city. Charleston is thoroughly American. Charleston is the typical southern city with the aroma of the times "befo' de wah" and the revolutionary period still in its atmosphere. Charleston is the city of Owen Wister's "Lady Baltimore" and the Lady Baltimore cake which his novel has made famous. Perhaps no other city in America has endured such terrible sufferings and no people have fought more bravely for what they believed to be the right. Charleston may be a little slow, but she is "getting a move on." The last six months have seen rapid strides forward. The U. S. Government is building a great navy yard here. New railroads are being projected. New steamship lines are being established. Just now the city is agog over the arrival of the North German Lloyd's immigrant ship with 476 European immigrants on board. This is the first time in 50 years that an immigrant ship has landed its passengers at the port of Charleston. It is expected that these immigrants and those that follow will help solve the labor problem in South Carolina and develop the marvelous resources of the state. South Carolina and the southeast now becomes the strategic center for the work of the American Christian Missionary Society. If the tide of immigration is turned toward the south where it is most needed then the churches of Christ should be prepared for the great opportunity which opens before them.——The Calhoun Street Church of Christ of Charleston (not Baltimore as one of our papers printed it) has a membership of about 100. They are mostly wage-earners getting from $5 to $18 per week. Not more than one or two have an income of $100 per month. But we have some splendid people and some who "seek first His

kingdom." On October 14, we began the work of paying off a debt of $1,900 due the Church Extension Board. $1,700 of the amount was raised in a few moments to be paid by June 2, 1907. Over $350 has already been received by the treasurer and one note taken up and the people's free-will offering to Church Extension in September was $50. On account of our debt-raising I was unable to get to Buffalo. But on November 5, by means of THE CHRISTIAN-EVANGELIST and "Christian Standard," I was able to give our people some stirring "echoes" of the convention. Some of the audience thought surely I had been to the convention. But I told them I had been to our papers. By the way, THE CHRISTIAN-EVANGELIST seems to have "scooped" the "Christian Standard" this time on convention news and addresses. We are glad that the convention goes to Norfolk next year. The brotherhood is hereby invited to go via Charleston.

MARCELLUS R. ELY.

3 Bennett Sts., Charleston, S. C.

Oregon Churches and Oregon Missions.

Already one church that made no offering last year, has sent in its gift. One brother, the offering from whose church is not yet in, writes: "Sunday we got two new life members and seven annual members, and a cash offering of $5.25." This church already has six life members. Life members pay $5 per year for five years and annual members pay $2 a year. If the other ministers and churches do likewise, and in proportion to their ability, there will be no question about the successful issue of our work in Oregon. May our vision of the field be continually enlarged, and may our gifts grow with our vision of the work to be done.   F. E. BILLINGTON.

Cottage Grove.   Cor. Sec. O. C. M. C.

The Christian Church in Carthage, Mo.

Set upon the Ozarks in a rich land, surrounded by the most lavish gifts of God, Carthage, a city of 13,000 people, is beautiful in appearance and cultured in its life. With lead and zinc producing districts and towns on every side, Carthage is the resident town, the city of homes.

Many years ago the Missouri State Board of Missions established a church in Carthage. The site of the first church house was on the ground now occupied by the Grand Opera House. Outgrowing its first home the congregation sought more ample accommodations a quarter of a cen-

Newell L. Sims.

tury ago, and in that building they still worship and here a meeting is now being held by W. H. Pinkerton, of Paducah, Ky., as evangelist, and F. H. Cappa and wife, of Louisville, Ky., in charge of the music.

The present membership of the church is about 400 and it includes many of the best families in the city. One of the church's deacons, and the former superintendent of the Bible school, was elected to congress from this district at the last election. The Hon. Thomas Hockney is the kind of a man needed in public life.

The church has launched out into larger things during the past year. It has lead the churches of Jasper county, excepting the First Christian Church of Joplin, in sending its own missionary, Dr. W. C. Widdowson, to Africa, and it is now working for a new $25,000 edifice which is to be built on the present site.

The congregation has been served by several able men as pastors, among them, W. A. Oldham, now of Kansas, and J. T. McGarvey, now of Warrensburg, Mo. The present pastor is Newell L. Sims who is in his second year's work. The meeting began November 18 and is to run at least one month. Extensive preparations have been made on the part of the church for a great revival. The aim of the congregation is to double its membership by 1909, at which time the Christian churches celebrate their Centennial Anniversary. The watchword of the Carthage church is, "The Christian Church the greatest church in Carthage. At least one hundred souls for Christ in this meeting, and a new house by 1909." We trust that all these aims will be more than realized and we wish the brethren in Carthage great success in their work.

A Great Day at Christian University.

To celebrate the clearing of the $15,000, already reported in the Christian-Evangelist, and to rededicate the Christian University, November 16 was set apart at Canton, Mo., as a gala day. All business in our little city was suspended from 2 to 6 p. m. At 2 o'clock all the church bells rang the glad joy that our college was free from debt. In the afternoon speeches were made by O. C. Clay and A. D. Lewis, both of Canton, and by Cor. Sec. T. A. Abbott, of Kansas City. All of these gentlemen are alumni of the institution. President Carl Johann also gave a concise synopsis of recent struggles. Professors Buxton and Sears participated. Preliminary to the evening session the crowd was treated to a display of fireworks managed by B. S. M. Edwards of the student body. The evening session was the climax of interest and enthusiasm. The first speaker was Prof. S. C. Barber, of Denver, Ill., a former member of the faculty and a firm friend of the institution. He was followed by former president J. H. Hardin. Then came Congressman J. T. Lloyd, a Christian University alumnus, a great favorite with us and one of our best friends. A pleasing feature of his remarks was the presentation at the close to President Johann of a handsome solid gold watch, the gift of the friends of the college as a token of their love and esteem.

The committee in charge had secured the finest easily obtainable; but there was remaining over, the sum of $45 which was also presented in gold coin. Pres. Johann for a time was speechless. Amidst the singing of the doxology, the room darkened, the veteran educator struck the match, and as the flame from the burnt mortgage smouldered out, the dedicatory prayer was offered by

President Carl Johann.

the writer. With social converse and delicate refreshments served by the ladies of the College Aid Society, a historic day for Christian university drew to a close.

Thus, up out of ashes, overcoming obstacle, we now have an excellent new modern in every respect, the best in t erhood, absolutely free from debt. T can not be said in praise of Presiden and his part in this. At a meetin ministerial association of the universit tions of Centennial ideals were adoptec same were unanimously ratified at the session of the celebration. The resolu to a gymnasium, two new dormitories, additional endowment, and 500 student whom shall be ministerial students.

Canton, Mo.　　　Geo. W. B

Pioneering in Wisconsin

For two years a voice has been com from the wilderness of Burnett county treme northwest county of the state "Come up, and preach the Word to came from Brother and Sister H. L. P of Moro Postoffice, who have been th homestead for six years, and have bee their neighbors in Bible study and wo is a very sparsely settled district, in w ning Disciples, most of whom Brother baptized.

I went up to them, the last 20 mil journey being made with team and s took with me W. L. Anderson, of Cam has had training and experience in e singing, and who is a devoted Christia held a 12 days' meeting, which result baptisms and five others added, unj neighborhood, forming a more comple ization, and making a start toward a worship. Most of the people of their v in the church, and they are a respons hearted people. The spirit of the Chr to prevail throughout.　　　H. F. E

Ladysmith, Wis.

The St. Louis Campaign.

The special simultaneous campaign eight of the St. Louis churches have gaged, will have closed by the time t reaches our readers. Weather condit bad the first part of last week and churches continued, and Compton Heig on Wednesday night, W. E. Harlow gi ture. As we write (Saturday) we t that the Fourth and Hamilton Avenue may continue until Thanksgiving. F and C. M. Chilton are the speakers at day afternoon rally in the Odeon the shall in our next issue give fuller report The total additions reported on Satur ing were:

	By Confession.	
Union Avenue	37	
First Church	115	
Compton Heights	65	
Fourth	42	
Hamilton Ave.	17	
Hammett Place	8	
Maplewood	5	
East St. Louis	7	
Granite City (just began)		
Second (not in campaign)	6	
Total		

Good Workers at Lebanon

The church at Lebanon, Mo., has four weeks meeting. Harold Bell W pastor, did the preaching. The serie moha was from the words of Jesus. was, "Heaven and Earth Shall Pa but My Words Shall Not Pass. At the suggestion of Brother Wright, a hand, a number of mottoes were pa the words of Jesus, and hung on the the church, and a large banner printe bearing the words, "What does Jesus it?" was hung across Commercial stre business portion of the town. This at attention of the people. Smaller no taining the same words adorned the w most of the business houses and ma dwellings of the city. Brother, Wrig the subject in a masterful way, entire most of his hearers, and he attracted until the capacity of the house was ta utmost. Brother Conrad Kundson, pas Lebanon Baptist church, led the music a solo every night, adding much to ivness of the services. There were 29 of which 25 were by confession. The tory services of each session were cor the members of the church and all er the work heartily. The church has bee erted and built up during this meetin look forward to a year of successful w Master.　　　　　　　　T. B.

Missouri Notes.

Knobnoster closed a meeting with about 20 additions. The meeting at Dresden has been working against the world, the flesh and the devil, and dark nights, and bad weather. One added by confession. John Jones, the county evangelist, is conducting the meeting.—W. H. Waggoner, with his maps and charts, and lantern, is at HughesVille, and will be at Knobnoster next week and here the week following. He is worth hearing.   I. H. FULLER.

La Monte, Mo.

Northwest Ohio Ministerial Association.

The Northwest Ohio Ministerial Association will meet with the Norwood Avenue church, Toledo, on Monday, December 3, at 10 a. m. Morning symposium on "Our Plea for Christian Union." 1. "To the Church of God," by A. C. Osborn. 2. "To the Presbyterians," by W. H. Artold. 3. Discussion, led by H. H. Elwinger. Afternoon, "The Missionary Training of the Churches," by C. H. Bass. Discussion, led by W. B. Hendershot.

Bays, O.   E. K. VAN WINKLE, Sec.

Ministerial Exchange.

D. Millar, Menden, Mo., would like to hold a few meetings for good town churches.

M. L. Anthony, new of Rogers, Ark., could be secured as evangelist or pastor in south Missouri.

A preacher is wanted for a very promising field. He must be single. Address J. I. Ellis, Baggs, Wyoming.

Have some open dates after January 1. Would like to arrange all dates for winter and spring, soon.—Lawrence Wright, Richland, Ia.

J. P. Haner, evangelist, Peru, Kan., is ready to answer calls anywhere in the United States. He would like to make a date for January.

The churches at Morrowville and Lowe Center, a country church, wish to employ a preacher together. An experienced man preferred. For particulars address D. W. Norris, Morrowville, Kan.

"Una Dell Berry, 527 Wood street, La Fayette, Ind., who for 18 months was assistant pastor of LaFayette church, has entered the field as singing evangelist, and I can most heartily commend her and her work. No church, pastor, or evangelist will regret securing her services."—A. W. Conner.

Changes.

Allen, John A.—Piedmont, Mo., to Gravette, Ark.
Baker, P.—Milford to Arrowsmith, Ill.
Bates, W. E.—Hope, Kan., to Thomas, Okla.
Callahan, J. P.—Euclid to 2223 Murray Hill, Cleveland, O.
Dennis, George F.—Morrison to Ceres, Okla.
Dinger, Mrs. J. E.—Means, O., to Chickasha, I. T.
Drake, D. H.—Lenore, Idaho to Delavon, Ill.
Elam, S. W.—Canten, Mo., to box 245, Dallas City, Ill.
Hartzog, William B.—Cleveland, O., to 5 Reed avenue, Bowling Green, O.
Hill, Sherman—Paola, Kan., to Centerville, Ia.
Jenner, R. H.—Washburn to New Bedford, Bureau County, Ill.
Leckhart, William J.—Des Moines, Iowa, to Webb City, Mo.
Lowe, J. M.—Galesburg, Ill., to 309 Western avenue, Topeka, Kan.
Lyon, George E.—Lyons to 701 Jackson street, Topeka, Kan.
Martin, W. H.—Santa Barbara to Whittler, Cal.
Manley, E. E.—7241 Race street, Pittsburg, to 1707 1-2 North Main street, Scranton, Pa.
McCully, Oliver—Warren to Middlefield, O.
Morrison, C. C.—Springfield to 1619 Jackson boulevard, Chicago, Ill.
Parker, J. E.—1188 W. Main to 535 Monmouth boulevard, Galesburg, Ill.
Pomeroy, C. E.—Arcadia to Chetopa, Kan.
Rounds, Walter S.—Crafton, Pa., to 2206 Beverly Road, Brooklyn, N. Y.
Schwan, Henry W.—400 Bailey avenue, Chattanooga, Tenn., to R. F. D. 3, Monroeville, O.
Sellards, D. F.—Leon to Gravity, Ia.
Smith, Thomas—Richland to Dexter, Mo.
Stebbins, Jas. E.—Richland, to Osage City, Kan.
Stevens, John A.—Helena, Ark., to Winnsboro, La.
Stevens, H. E.—Laurel to 103 S. E. street, Marion, Ind.
Thompson, W. H.—Flushing to West Austintown, R. D. 1, Ohio.
Utz, D. E.—Spokane Bridge, Wash., to 612 B. street, N. E. Washington, D. C.
Winters, W. H.—Eagle Lake, to Orange, Tex.
Zellar, A. Immanuel, Farmer City, to Cuba, Ill.

Evangelistic

We invite ministers and others to send reports of meetings, additions and other news of the churches. It is especially requested that additions be reported as "by confession and baptism," or "by letter."

District of Columbia.

Washington, Nov. 19.—Present at ministers' meeting; Pres. W. "F" Smith, B. E. Utz, F. D. Power, T. E. Stuart, and the writer. Additions: Vermont Avenue (F. D. Power), one by letter; Fifteenth Street (J. E. Stuart and L. D. Riddell), six by baptism and seven by letter or statement. Our ministers and churches are working in perfect harmony.—Claude C. Jones, Sec.

Iowa.

Elliott, Nov. 19.—Just closed a great meeting with 18 added.—Samuel B. Ross.

Keokuk, Nov. 19.—We are having a great meeting with home forces. Great crowds yesterday. Two made the good confession.—M. J. Nicoson.

Hamburg, Nov. 20.—W. L. Harris, evangelist, and J. E. Lhant, singer, are in a great meeting here. Eighty-nine conversions and the whole country stirred. Isaac Elder is the minister.

Illinois.

Waynesville, Nov. 17.—Meeting here now 2 weeks old, with 20 additions. J. A. Barnett, of Freeport, Ill., is the evangelist and Miss Mamie Bowles, of Emden, is soloist and leader of song. Large crowds and deep interest.—J. F. Smith, pastor.

Berlin, Nov. 19.—One addition yesterday by baptism.—J. W. Bolton.

Decatur, Nov. 19.—Three confessions Lord's day evening and two were baptized who had previously confessed.—J. L. Thompson.

Clinton, Nov. 19.—Three accessions. Work moving off well.—J. W. Reynolds, minister.

Eldora, Nov. 19.—A gracious revival in this church. Ten confessions the first week. Church aroused and community interested.—W. E. Spicer, evangelist; J. D. Williams, minister.

Indiana.

Indianapolis, Nov. 18.—There were 10 additions yesterday at the Olive Branch Christian church of this city. Seven other additions in the meeting not reported.—J. M. Canfield.

Franklin, Nov. 19.—Began a meeting at Union church yesterday, with 11 accessions.—Lee Tinsley, pastor.

Brazil, Nov. 27.—Closed our three weeks' campaign and full rally last night with interest at full tide. Northcutt and Huston were our efficient helpers. Twenty-two additions—11 baptisms. This is the second meeting for us this year and there have been over 200 additions.—F. L. Day.

Indianapolis, Nov. 19.—A three weeks' revival at North Park church closed last night with 73 additions. M. W. Harkins was evangelist. J. Ross Miller was the singing evangelist.—Austin Hunter, minister.

Stockwell, Nov. 19.—We have had a great meeting here, conducted by Evangelist R. C. Bulgin. There were 24 additions, and the church was reorganized and put in good condition.—W. C. McCollough.

Indianapolis, Nov. 16.—Meetings are progressing fine here. Sixty-nine to date at Morris street, where I am preaching.—Thomas L. Cooksey.

Indianapolis, Nov. 21.—Our meeting at the Sixth Church just closed with 127 additions. Brother McLain, of Ohio, was the evangelist. A. Orcutt, the pastor, made great preparations for the meeting and did much personal work. I sing next at Des Moines, Ia.—Charles E. McVay, song evangelist.

North Vernon, Nov. 15.—Closed our second meeting within eight months with the church at North Vernon with 37 additions—25 by baptism, seven by letter and statement.—C. W. Mahin and wife, evangelists.

Kansas.

Howard, Nov. 20.—Seven baptisms at our prayer-meeting Wednesday evening of last week.—J. M. Plummer.

Manhattan, Nov. 20.—Ten added since last report. W. T. McLain, minister.

Wichita, Nov. 19.—Third Lawrence Christian Church closed a five weeks' meeting last night. The preaching was done by the minister, Oliver W. Roth. Bert I. Beatly conducted the singing. The attendance was large and the interest good throughout the meeting. There were 49 additions, 34 confessions.

Peru, Nov. 19.—Meeting two weeks' old, with 20 added to date. Meeting continues.—J. P. Haner, evangelist.

Osage City, Nov. 19.—Meeting here is one week old. Eight confessions to date. There has been no service of any kind here for some time, and it is considered a hard field. We continue.—J. E. Stebbins and wife, evangelists.

Kentucky.

Riceville, Nov. 19.—Recently closed a meeting at South Louisville Christian church. There were 32 additions. This is a young church with a large field and magnificent promise. E. B. Richey is the deserving pastor.—W. J. Cocke, field agent K. C. M. C.

Massachusetts.

Boston.—The Boston church is in good condition. Three additions recently. Sunday-school larger than ever before. Planning for a campaign in the spring with Herbert Yeuell.

Everett, Nov. 19.—One confession, one baptism, and one otherwise last Lord's day.—A. T. June.

Michigan.

Detroit, Nov. 19.—S. L. Darsie has just closed a three weeks' meeting with the Central Church. There were 25 additions. He is now in a meeting with our church on Woodward avenue.—C. J. Tanner.

Minnesota.

Rochester, Nov. 15.—We recently closed an 18 days' meeting with 7 additions—5 by baptism, 2 by statement. Brother Baumer, of Pleasant Grove, did the preaching, and C. B. Osgood, of Winona, conducted a helpful Bible study and song service.—Rochester Irwin.

Missouri.

Napier, Nov. 19.—Have just closed a four weeks' meeting with the Walnut Grove Church with 13 additions—11 baptisms, three restored and one from another religious body. Circumstances considered, it was a good meeting.—James Anderson.

Bolivar, Nov. 19.—One by letter and one confession since last report.—J. H. Jones.

Frankford, Nov. 17.—Twenty-five to date. Continue.—C. S. Brooks.

Rockport, Nov. 18.—The Christian Church here has just closed a two weeks' meeting, resulting in three additions—one baptism and two by relation. The regular pastor, N. Rolla Davis, did the preaching. The church is much strengthened and prospects brighter than for two years past.—F. A. Sizemore.

Ridgeway, Nov. 17.—I closed a two weeks' meeting with a country church near Ridgeway, with additions—15 by confession and baptism, making 28 to this church and Ridgeway in the last month. Will commence a meeting for the church at Cainsville, Mo., November 19.—W. H. Hobbs.

Mendon, Nov. 15.—Held a two weeks' meeting with 28 additions—23 by confession and 5 by statement and letter. A church club was organized.—Davis Millar.

Festus, Nov. 20.—One confession. D. G. Cole.

Moberly, Nov. 19.—Six additions to Central Church here yesterday—3 by confession and 3 by letter.—W. B. Taylor.

Nevada, Nov. 19.—our meeting conducted by R. R. Hamlin and Leonard Daugherty, just through the first week. Fourteen added and everything indicates a great meeting.—W. W. Burks.

Mound City, Nov. 19.—One by confession and one by letter yesterday, making eight additions at regular services since last report.—Cassium V. Allison.

Columbia, Nov. 22.—B. E. Shively preached at the Mission Church here Sunday with a result of two additions. C. F. McCall and C. E. Burgess each report four additions, Sunday, at Friendship and Salem. Prof. Sharpe reports two additions last Lord's day.—C. E. Burgess.

Kansas City, Nov. 19.—Have just closed a two weeks' meeting for F. V. Loos at Smithville, Mo., with 30 additions, 20 baptisms and 10 by letter.—H. M. Barnett.

Gallatin, Nov. 19.—Had splendid audiences in

our meetings yesterday. Three have been added to date.—George L. Peters, evangelist; R. E. Callihan, minister.

Kansas City, Nov. 19.—Mrs. Sarah McCoy Crank, of Liberal, Mo., recently closed a four weeks' meeting with us at Budd Park with 40 additions—three by letter, 22 by baptism, and 15 otherwise. Also two added by baptism and three by statement before meeting began.—R. A. Wray, pastor.

Queen City, Nov. 20.—We held our meeting this year with home forces, I. N. Jett, the pastor, doing the preaching. We continued four weeks, with 55 additions and the work otherwise strengthened.

Nebraska.

Tecumseh, Nov. 19.—Following the McConnell-Jones union meetings, the church at Tecumseh held a week's meeting, in which 20 were added, 16 by baptism and four reclaimed. The pastor, A. J. Hollingsworth, was assisted by Dan C. Troxel, a baritone soloist.—D. C. Troxel.

Auburn, Nov. 21.—Evangelist W. Mark Sexson has been with us in a 19 days' meeting resulting in 20 additions—12 by primary obedience and eight by letter or statement.—F. L. Pettit, minister.

Stratton, Nov. 18.—Forty-two here in seventeen days.—James S. Beem.

Codger, Nov. 15.—Samuel Gregg, of Jefferson, Iowa, closed a four weeks' meeting for the church here last night, with 12 added—three by statement, nine by baptism.—H. F. Stevens, minister.

Ohio.

Mt. Vernon, Nov. 19.—We have had 24 additions here recently. We are planning now for a great meeting.—L. O. Newcomer.

Brilliant.—The Christian Church here is holding the most successful meeting in its history. The meeting is now three weeks old and 48 have confessed Christ. Miss Marguerite Virginia Hall, of Wheeling, W. Va., is the soloist and chorister. Brother Denslow was doing the preaching, but was called home and Brother Underwood took his place. Allan O. Hansen is the pastor.

North Royalton, Nov. 21.—Two by statement last Lord's day. One from another religious body.—Charles Ford, minister.

Sebring, Nov. 19.—Meeting starts off well with six in two days.—E. E. Violett.

Oklahoma.

Ames, Nov. 19.—We have had 24 additions here recently. J. A. Tabor and wife have just closed a five weeks' meeting here with 78 additions—62 by confession, 16 by statement, and eight from other religious bodies.—J. A. Sater, elder.

Ponca City, Nov. 21.—Seven have been added by letter since our last report.—R. H. Love, pastor.

Shawnee, Nov. 19.—Work going splendidly here. Fine audiences and few accessions yesterday, making fifteen since October 1.—Frank L. Van Voorhis.

Tennessee.

Nashville, Nov. 20.—Eleven yesterday. Ten confessions. Fifty-eight since October 7. Meeting nine days old with 30 added. E. Lin Cave assists much in the meetings.—James T. McKissick.

Washington.

Centralia, Nov. 16.—I closed a fine meeting November 11 with the church at Olympia, with 25 added. W. S. Crockett is the pastor.—A. D. Skaggs.

West Virginia.

Wheeling, Nov. 20.—On Thursday last W. H. Pinkerton, of Kentucky closed a most successful meeting of four weeks with the Island Church of Wheeling, having added 60 to our fold.—O. G. B.

Sunday School

December 9, 1906.

JESUS ON THE CROSS.—Luke 23:33-46.

Memory verses, 42, 43.

Golden Text.—Father, forgive them: for they know not what they do.—Luke 23:34.

The amazing thing about the record of the crucifixion is the simplicity of it. There is no indignation, no passion, no excitement on the part of the writer. There is no attempt to convey any impression of pathos or horror or sympathy or conviction, except such facts simply stated. This same self-restraint characterizes all of the gospels throughout, but nowhere is it more conspicuous or more effective than here where the temptation to give the narrative a strong emotional quality must have been greatest.

The journey from Pilate's judgment hall to the hill of Golgotha was by a route which has come to be known as the Via Dolorosa. The records give us no information about this mournful journey except the carrying of the cross, the compulsory service of Simon the Cyrenian, the following of the triumphant mob and the lamenting women, and the warning addressed to the "daughters of Jerusalem." Catholic tradition has elaborated this simple outline with many beautiful but unauthentic legends such as the story of the veil of St. Veronica and the meeting of Jesus with his mother and has systematized it by the nine stations of the cross.

The place of the crucifixion, Golgotha or the place of the skull, received its name either because of its accustomed use as a place of execution, or from the real or fancied resemblance of the low hill to the shape of a human skull, or (according to the pious imaginings of some of the fathers) because of a tradition that the skull of Adam, having been preserved by Noah, was buried at that place.

The most momentous fact in history is stated with all possible simplicity: "There they crucified him and the malefactors, one on the right hand and the other on the left."

The recorded sayings of Jesus on the cross are seven. In their probable order, they are:

1. "Father, forgive them." (Luke.)
2. "This day shalt thou be with me in Paradise." (Luke.)
3. "Woman, behold thy son!" (John.)
4. "My God, why hast thou forsaken me?" (Matt. and Mark.)
5. "I thirst." (John.)
6. "Father, into thy hands I commend my spirit." (Luke.)
7. "It is finished." (John.)

It will be observed that no evangelist reports more than three of the seven, and only one of the seven is given by as many as two of the gospels. Such passages where the gospels neither corroborate nor contradict each other in details furnish a strong evidence that they were written in good faith as historical documents. If the fourth gospel, for example, were a second century forgery, written after all the other gospels were in general circulation, its author would scarcely have dared to omit the four sayings given by the others and give three new ones of his own.

"Father, forgive them." The keynote of the life of Jesus was forgiveness. It would have nullified all his teaching if, in his own hour of supreme agony, he had not risen above thoughts of revenge to the plane of forgiveness.

"Save thyself," said the mocking Jews. That was just what Jesus could not do without being false to his mission. He did not come to save himself, but to sacrifice himself to save others. The cry "he saved others, himself he can not save," had more truth in it than its cruel authors knew.

We are not called upon to philosophize about the process or degree of salvation in the case of the penitent thief. The case was clearly exceptional. One thing it may fairly be taken to exhibit, and that is the boundless love of God which is ready to accept a penitent sinner whenever the sinner will truly turn to him.

Christian Endeavor

By GEO. L. SNIVELY

December 9, 1906.

WORDS FROM THE CROSS.—John 19:25-30; Luke 23:34-46; Mark 15:34.

DAILY READINGS.

M. A Prayer.		Luke 23:34.
T. A Promise.		Luke 23:43.
W. A Charge.		John 19:26, 27.
T. An Exclamation.		Mark 15:34.
F. A Request.		John 19:28.
S. A Declaration.		John 19:30.
S. A Commitment.		Luke 23:46.

As sunshine follows after the rain, so because of unfaltering loyalty, "Father, into thy hands I commit my spirit" follows after "My God, my God, why hast thou forsaken me?" So may it be with us. If not before, at least in our closing days, may all the storms have rolled away and an aurora of perfect trust and unalloyed joy suspend over every child of God.

Paul's thesis that suffering with Jesus necessarily precedes our glorification with him has an illustration in the relations of the dying thief and the crucified. Of that convict it may be said, "No cross no crown." While Christ's mercy to one who had so lately reviled him is conspicuous in the incident we should be no less impressed by its suggestiveness that through the shadows of the cross we must all pass to attain unto the gates of paradise.

Jesus not only seemed to suffer but actually endured all the pangs of dissolution in one of its cruelest forms. "I thirst" reveals to us that the pitiless irons had transformed his blood into molten fire for whose extinguishment every nerve was pleading. But he thirsted not in vain. Remembering how he thirsted for our sakes has helped his followers of every age to curb thirst for gold, place, power and all things that would lure us out of the straight and narrow way.

Christ's strange doctrine was, "Love your enemies, do good to them, that hate you, bless them that curse you, pray for them that despitefully use you." When the supreme test came his doctrine was also his practice. At the moment when those disciples who still had faith in him believed that with full proof of the criminality of his foes manifest to all the world and ages he would destroy them from the earth, with divine benignity he prayed "Father, forgive them; they know not what they do."

If there is one earth-born in heaven to whom Jesus accords more honor than another it must be the gentle Mary. She who was in such affectionate memory on the cross can not be forgotten from the throne. If there are yet others to be chiefly blessed among women in heaven, it must be those mothers who have reared sons to take Mary's. When Jesus said, "Behold thy mother," he was for all the ages proclaiming filial affection to be one of the most beautiful gems in the diadem of true manhood.

If there has been anything lacking to convince us that Christ was tempted in all

THE WORK OF CHRISTIAN WOMEN.—Phil. 4:3.

"Inspired with wisdom from above,
And with discretion blessed;
Displaying meekness, temperance, love,
Of every grace possessed:

"These are the ones we seek of thee,
O God of righteousness!
Such may thy servants ever be,
With such thy people bless."

One can not enumerate the heroes and martyrs of the sacred cause of temperance without reciting the names of Francis E. Willard and her colleagues. "In fact, call the women away and where is the great and holy empire in the world to-day that would not at once fall into ruin?"

A Christian star of the first magnitude now coming into ascendency is Sister M. E. Harlan, of Brooklyn, recently elected corresponding secretary of our C. W. B. M. We call upon all Disciples everywhere to co-operate with this gifted woman as she organizes and leads our forces for the conquest of all this world for Christ and his church.

Phoebe, deaconess of the congregation at Cenchrea, had no husband, but did have a great mission that kept her from living unto herself alone and fully redeemed her life from the commonplace. What a tribute Paul pays her: "For she herself also hath been a succorer of many, and of mine own self." When questions as to the scripturalness of women office bearers is raised, be it remembered Phoebe was a deaconess in an apostolic church. She is a representative of the unmarried but useful servants of our Lord as Priscilla is of those who also had family cares.

Mary never thought her act of adoration in anointing her Lord for his burial would be a memorial of her wherever his Gospel should be preached. Neither did Dorcas know the garments she made for the poor and all the good she did would be plead as reasons for a miracle raising her from the dead. They simply did their duty as they had light to see it and committed all the consequences to him who takes note of all things. So let us proceed, regardless of self, doing what we can in holiness for the saving of men through the upbuilding of the church and God will not only raise us from the dead, but memorialize us and signally honor us among the angels.

Even under the old dispensation were characters that to this day are part of the glory of the world's womanhood. Conspicuous among these was Hannah, wife of Elkanah a dweller of the hill country of Ephraim. To her was born little Samuel. Taking him to the great priest Eli in the holy temple she said: "For this child I prayed; and Jehovah hath given me my petition which I asked of him; therefore I also have granted him to Jehovah; as long as he liveth he is granted to Jehovah." This child thus dedicated unto the Lord became the first of the great prophets of Israel, one of the most helpful and sublime characters of history. O, the needs of the world are calling upon the ranks of motherhood for Hannahs to come to the altars of the Lord and consecrate sons to the ministry of prophets, priests and saviors of the race.

Among the most picturesque early Christians is Priscilla, wife of Aquila. Paul finds them in Corinth whither they had fled when Claudius banished the Jews from Rome. Paul abode with them a year and a half working at their common trade of weaving tent cloth. When Paul returns east, they accompany him as far as Ephesus. When the golden-mouthed Apollos comes to Ephesus knowing only the baptism of John, they took him and taught him the way of the Lord more perfectly. In Romans 16, we learn they have returned to Rome and their house is the assembly of Christians, and they are said to have endangered their lives for the apostle. In the first references to this couple Aquila is named first, but afterward Priscilla has the pre-eminence, indicating that she is the more energetic and devoted of the two. How different her life and glory from those of millions of her sisters of that and succeeding ages whose time and energies have been devoted to the rounds of fashionable idleness!

People's Forum

Why Silent?

To the Editor of THE CHRISTIAN-EVANGELIST:

I few days ago I was called to the country to see a sick member of my church, a fine young man and county superintendent of schools, who was thought by his physicians to be at the point of death. The young man had recently been received into our membership and came from the Brethren Church or Dunkards. When I arrived at the home I found three elders of the church who had been called together with myself for the purpose of anointing the young man. The elder, an excellent man and citizen, approached me saying, "Brother, we have been sent for to anoint this young man in the name of the Lord." Then turning to James 5:14, 15, he said: "Do you believe that Scripture?" Telling him that I did, he replied: "I can't understand why you people do not practice it." After assuring him that I believed the Scripture read, we proceeded to anoint the young man, who is to-day well. Was I not right and Scriptural in this, and why do our people believe it and not practice it? If "where the Bible speaks we speak," why are we silent on this passage that promises such a great blessing?

Huntington, Ind.　CEPHAS SHELBURNE.

A Bit of History.

To the Editor of THE CHRISTIAN-EVANGELIST:

Since the organization in western Pennsylvania of the movement known as the "Disciples of Christ," the organization has never been without a coterie of brethren who have acted as a committee of safety. They are distinguished for the anxious solicitude which they manifest for the purity and safety of the church and a strange lacking of confidence in the mental ability and Christian integrity of brethren who do not sympathize with them in their doubts and fears. Indeed they have indulged these feelings until they have become possessed with the idea entertained by an old Quaker who thought "everybody was queer but Jane and me, and sometimes thought Jane was a little queer." With this feeling in their minds and in their anxious solicitude for the purity and safety of the church, these brethren are ever on the lookout for signs of heresy, and ready to prevent its introduction into the church, by ambitious and designing men. Another virtue possessed by these brethren is their profound veneration for the teaching of the Fathers, *correctly interpreted,* but particularly for the "declaration," which reads: "Where the Scriptures speak we acquiesce, and where they are silent we interpret." There is, however, just one thing in which these brethren are a little "queer." It partakes largely of the nature of an hallucination. They are possessed with the idea that in the opposition they have made to every movement towards perfection that has been proposed in the church, *they represented the brotherhood,* as against a few ambitious and unscrupulous men, when, on the contrary, *it is a fact in the history of the Disciples that every such measure of prominent importance, notwithstanding this opposition, has been accepted by the brotherhood and is now in approved and successful working among all of the churches.* Notably among these measures may be mentioned the introduction of Sunday-schools; co-operation with the Society of "Evangelican Alliance;" admission of women into active work in the church; introduction of instrumental music into the worship; the organization of, first, the Home and later

Christian Publishing Company
2712 Pine St., St. Louis, Mo.

J. H. GARRISON, - - - - President
W. W. DOWLING, - - - - Vice-President
GEO. L. SNIVELY, - - - Sec. and Gen. Supt
R P. CROW, - - - Treas. and Bus. Manager

—Extra copies of this superb number for sale while the supply lasts—5 cents a copy, six for 25 cents, $2.00 per hundred.

—As well a farmer succeed without plows as preachers without books. We sell any book published on either side of the Atlantic, and at lowest prices.

—The Garrison Library—A reconstructive theology: "Helps to Faith," "The Holy Spirit," "Christian Union." Most helpful of devotionals: "Alone with God," "Half Hour Studies at the Cross," "The Heavenward Way." These great books by a great Christian man for $5.00.

—The pink subscription blank you will find in next week's paper is not a reminder of your delinquency (the yellow label tells the time to which you are paid) but an invitation for you to take part in the "each one win one" festivities of our friends. If this can be accomplished twice, we shall have passed the 100,000 mark.

—For one new subscriber before Jan. 1, 1907, we offer as a premium a large long primer, cloth bound New Testament. For two we offer the American kitchen set of six pieces, or a stereoscope and 50 scenic cards; or a seven piece Gold Coin initial fruit set, very beautiful. For five, half dozen quadruple plate silver teaspoons. These premiums will make excellent Christmas presents.

—In addition to our already large number of readers from Brothers Richardson's and Cupp's Kansas City congregations came a list of 152 new subscriptions at $1.50 each last week. We are advised "there are more to follow." To all appearances there will soon be a CHRISTIAN-EVANGELIST in nearly every Disciple's home in that city. Among other things this will guarantee our enterprising churches in that remarkable city will suffer no retrogression in faith and all good works.

—Notwithstanding the increased cost of labor, paper and other publishers' requisites, it is our intention to continue THE CHRISTIAN-EVANGELIST at the popular price of $1.50 per annum. Will not our friends aid us in this by doubling our present circulation. Greatly inferior denominational papers are being sold at $2.00. Patronizing our Bible school literature and book departments will greatly assist us in keeping the paper at a price easily within the reach of all.

—We much prefer having new Bible schools come to us from denominational publishing houses rather than from others of our own brotherhood in building up our rapidly growing business in this line. Any Disciple publications are better for making mature Disciples of Bible school children than are colorless inter-denominational teachings. And yet when our schools select from our own literature, why not get the best—which is a common name for the W. W. Dowling series?

—Many approving comments on the numerous evangelistic reports and editorials freight each day's mail. Terse, concise, scriptural articles on the various phases of Christian evangelism are highly prized by our editors and readers. We wish to be of the greatest possible assistance to all our evangelists, both by fostering zeal for conversions in the hearts of all Disciples and in helping them to growth in grace and the knowledge of the Lord Jesus when the meeting is over. Evangelists, make use of THE CHRISTIAN-EVANGELIST.

—300, 500, or 1000 CHRISTIAN-EVANGELISTS judiciously distributed each week in the vicinity where a revival meeting is in progress will insure not only a full house, but a large congregation of prepared listeners. Without extra cost we send with the first shipment a lot of pink circulars containing the pictures of pastor and evangelist and suitable local announcements. Concerning their use Frank W. Allen, of Odessa, Mo., writes: "Let me say how delighted I am with the plan of using THE CHRISTIAN-EVANGELIST during a meeting. It stimulates interest and adds a dignity to the local work."

—We have been fortunate enough to secure Miss Eva Lemert, formerly Geo. H.

THE ANALYSIS OF CHRISTIAN UNION

Our latest book from the pen of J. H. Garrison, will cause one to long to see into the heart of such a work. Hence the Analysis is given in full.

INDEX.

INTRODUCTION 13

I. THE APOSTOLIC AGE.
1. The Birth of the Church 25
2. An Undivided Church 32
3. Unity of the Early Church Tested . 37
4. Unity of the Early Church Imperiled 48
5. Divisions at Corinth 52
6. "I Am of Christ" 56
7. Was the Unity of the Early Church Organic? 61
8. Summing Up Results Our Study Thus Far 71

II. THE POST-APOSTOLIC AGE.
1. Change in Polity and Doctrine 79
2. Rise of the "Catholic" Church 85
3. Speculative Questions of That Age . 89

III. THE GRAECO-ROMAN PERIOD.
1. First Division in the Church 96
2. Condition of the Church in that Period 98

IV. THE PROTESTANT ERA.
1. From Ecclesiastical Despotism to Religious Liberty 103
2. Luther's Great Work 104

3. Other Reformations 109
(1) Presbyterian, (2) Independents, (3) Anglican, (4) Wesleyan, (5) Baptists.
4. Status of These Protestant Movements 115
5. Post-Reformation Advocates of Union 119

V. PERIOD OF REUNION.
1. A Seed-Truth Taking Root 129
2. Problem of Harmonizing Union and Liberty 135
3. Features of Catholicity in the Campbell Movement 140
4. Have the Disciples of Christ Been Loyal to Their Ideals? 146
5. Change of Attitude Toward the Movement 152
6. Forces Making for Union 158
7. Latest Step Toward Christian Union 170
8. Basis of Federation 170
9. Federation the Next Logical Step . 175
10. To What Conclusion? 180
11. The Inevitable Trend 184
12 External Motives to Union 186
13. How Shall Christian Union Come About? 192
14. When Christ's Prayer for Unity is Fulfilled 199

This work of 207 pages, in handsome silk cloth binding, postpaid, $1.00.

CHRISTIAN PUBLISHING COMPANY. St. Louis, Mo.

Combs' assistant in the Independence Boulevard Church, Kansas City, to assist in our Bible school department. Among her activities will be the direction of a school of methods in practical conduct of schools—a realm of usefulness in which she has been signally successful. "Our Young Folks" will have the benefit of her personal contributions on these important themes. This paper will continue its present low price of 75 cents per annum. Thousands of teachers and officers should have the help of Sister Lemert's writings.

—Each week for many months we have published a list of clubs of new subscriptions received at the unvarying price of $1.50 each. When the clubs fall below the average the symmetry of our growth is usually preserved by an unusual number of new subscriptions coming by singles and twos. We can not be said to be "booming" for there is nothing spasmodic or over-reaching about our growth. We have already passed many widely known journals and are pressing the leaders of circulation and believe that soon THE CHRISTIAN-EVANGELIST will be the most widely read church paper in America. Here are last week's clubs:

Kansas City, Louis S. Cupp, pastor 9
Englewood, Kan. 4
Washington, Pa. 10
Lexington, Ky., L. J. Spencer, pastor 17
Niagara Falls, N. Y., J. A. Wharton, pastor .. 21
Moundsville, W. Va., Percy Wilson, pastor ... 22
Marshall, Ark., R. O. Rogers, evangelist 23
Lexington, Ky. 33
Buffalo, N. Y., B. S. Ferrall, pastor 40

—In gratifying numbers the readers of the "Southern Evangelist" are sending remittances to continue their membership in THE CHRISTIAN-EVANGELIST family. The ideals of the "Southern Evangelist" can in no wise be likened to a "Lost Cause." In THE CHRISTIAN-EVANGELIST they will be presented to a vaster constituency, and through these columns Brothers Shelnutt and Adams will continue to fire the Southern heart with appeals for the chivalric defence of the faith once delivered, and the triumphs of primitive Christianity through all that fair region of our common inheritance. We hope to soon hear from each of these new members adopted into our family through our affiliation with the "Southern Evangelist."

THE
CHRISTIAN-EVANGELIST

A WEEKLY RELIGIOUS NEWSPAPER.

| Volume XLIII. | No. 49. |

ST. LOUIS, DECEMBER 6, 1906.

"Announced by all the trumpets of the sky
Arrives the snow; and, driving o'er the fields,
Seems nowhere to alight; the whited air
Hides hills and woods, the river and the heaven
And veils the farm house at the garden's end,
The sled and traveler stopped, the courier's feet
Delayed, all friends shut out, the housemates sit
Around the radiant fireplace, enclosed
In a tumultuous privacy of storm."
—Emerson.

THE CENTENNIAL FUND

continues to grow. Last week a friend in California agreed to give $5,000 to provide a hospital at Tung Chow, China. This is good, very good. We need land and three homes for missionaries in Tung Chow. The Foreign Society has three families there, but no land nor buildings. It is a city of about 100,000 inhabitants, and we have just opened the station.

Remember the Centennial Fund of $250,000 to be raised by 1909 is to come from personal gifts only and the whole amount is to be for land and buildings. We earnestly request your help.

Please fill out the pledge herewith and return or send cash.

Address

F. M. RAINS. Sec'y,

Box 884,

Cincinnati,

Ohio.

....................CUT HERE....................

A $250,000 Centennial Fund

I agree to donate to the FOREIGN CHRISTIAN MISSION-ARY SOCIETY, Cincinnati, O.,$..........per year for three years beginning June 1, 1907, to aid in the creation of a special TWO HUNDRED AND FIFTY THOUSAND DOLLAR ($250,000) CENTENNIAL FUND to be used for lands and buildings by the Society.

Name ....

P. O. ....

Street or R. F. D...........................

Date.............1906. State.............

....................CUT HERE....................

WATCH THIS SPACE NEXT WEEK!

The Christian-Evangelist.

J. H. GARRISON, Editor

PAUL MOORE, Assistant Editor

F. D. POWER,
B. B. TYLER,
W. DURBAN, } Staff Correspondents.

Subscription Price, $1.50 a Year.

For foreign countries add $1.04 for postage.

Remittances should be made by money order, draft, or registered letter; not by local cheque, unless 15 cents is added to cover cost of collection.

In Ordering Change of Post Office give both old and new address.

Matter for Publication should be addressed to The Christian-Evangelist. Subscriptions and remittances should be addressed to the Christian Publishing Company, 2712 Pine Street, St. Louis, Mo. Unused Manuscripts will be returned only if accompanied by stamps.

News Items, evangelistic and otherwise, are solicited, and should be sent on a postal card, if possible.

Published by the Christian Publishing Company, 13 Pine Street, St. Louis, Mo.

Entered at St. Louis P. O. as Second Class Matter

CONTENTS.

Our Centennial 1567
Current Events 1568
Editorial—
Is There a Missing Link? 1569
After the Meeting..................1569
The Religious Newspaper Problem..1570
Notes and Comments................1570
Editor's Easy Chair...............1571
Contributed Articles—
The Disciples and Evangelism. J. P. Lichtenberger 1572
As Seen From the Dome. F. D. Power 1573
A Divine Ordinance................1574

Our Budget 1576
Evangelistic 1579
News from Many Fields.............1580
The Georgia Christian Missionary Society 1581
The Alabama Convention............1583
Christian Endeavor 1586
Sunday-school 1586
Midweek Prayer Meeting...........1587
People's Forum 1588
Obituaries 1589
The Home Department...............1590

FAMOUS MEN OF THE OLD TESTAMENT

Table of Contents.

ABRAHAM, The Friend of God and Father of the Faithful.
JACOB, The Father of the Twelve Tribes.
JOSEPH, The Savior of His People.
MOSES, The Leader, Lawgiver and Literatus.
JOSHUA, The Father of His Country.
GIDEON, The Mighty Man of Valor.
JEPHTHAH, The Misinterpreted Judge.
ELI, The Pious Priest but Indulgent Parent.
SAUL, The First King of Israel.
DAVID, The Great Theocratic King.
SOLOMON, The Grand Monarch of Israel.
ELIJAH, The Prophet of Fire.
JONAH, The Recreant but Repentant Prophet.
DANIEL, The Daring Statesman and Prophet.
BALAAM, The Corrupt Prophet and Diviner.
ABSALOM, The Reckless and Rebellious Son.
NEHEMIAH, The Jewish Patriot and Reformer.

334 pages, silk cloth, postpaid, $1.50.

Christian Publishing Company, St. Louis, Mo.

Song Books

...FOR...

The Church, Sunday-School

...AND...

Endeavor Societies.

GLORIA IN EXCELSIS, The New Church Hymnal.

GOSPEL CALL, Published in Combined Edition, and Part One and Part Two.

CHRISTIAN HYMNAL Revised

GOSPEL MELODIES.

POPULAR HYMNS No. 2.

LIVING PRAISE.

SILVER AND GOLD.

PRAISES TO THE PRINCE.

CHRISTIAN SUNDAY-SCHOOL HYMNAL, Shape Note Edition Only.

Write us the kind of Song Book you are needing and we will take pleasure in giving you full particulars concerning our Music Books.

Christian Publishing Co., St. Louis, Mo.

THE
CHRISTIAN=EVANGELIST

"IN FAITH, UNITY; IN OPINION AND METHODS, LIBERTY; IN ALL THINGS, CHARITY."

| Vol. XLIII. | December 6, 1906 | No. 49 |

1809 CENTENNIAL PROPAGANDA CHURCHES OF CHRIST 1909
: : : GEO. L. SNIVELY : : :

Looking Toward Pittsburg.

—None of our Centennial Secretary's numerous recent clarion calls to duty and privilege is more timely or important than this one mustering our children into aggressive brigades for the evangelization of the home land. We commend this article especially to parents and Bible school superintendents.

—"A Brotherhood," by F. A. Wight (our roommate at the College of the Bible), is an able presentation of a splendid opportunity for Christian men to make great our Centennial. Brethren, write J. H. Allen, of St. Louis, president of our National Business Men's Association, for instructions in the matter of forming local auxiliaries. Write him, also, an appreciation of the great ministry in which he is enlisted.

The Home and the Home Land.
W. R. WARREN.

The fall and winter are particularly the home seasons. And possibly this character of the autumn is more appreciated because it comes earlier and brings with it the enjoyment of the first long evenings with ripened fruits and nuts, and the family circle drawn close for study, reading and conversation. It is a good time to emphasize the supreme claim which the homeland makes upon the home. Family affection, patriotism and religion are all of one piece; and the home is the place where all must be fostered. Whatever other agencies go for their up-building must be strengthened by the home or they fail of their purpose. If the homes throughout the states had been hostile to their governments the calls for volunteers would have gone unheeded, both north and south. The irrepressible conflict was the subject of conversation in the home and of preaching in the church and the recruits came thick and fast, because both the home and the church were fanning the flame of patriotic zeal. Now the evangelization of the states is more important than either states' rights or political union, and it would be well if this subject were uppermost at every fireside throughout the month of November. Talk of the plans and the campaigns of your state mission board and the American Christian Missionary Society. Mention by name the men who are at the front in this holiest of causes. Remember their needs, their opportunities and their trials in the home prayers. If this is done the funds for the support of these self-sacrificing men will spontaneously pour into the treasury of the Lord.

Fireworks and flags and bunting are very well for the expression of patriotism, but it will not be difficult to show even the children a more excellent way. It is righteousness and not military or naval strength which really exalts the nation. Indeed we have had ample evidence within the last few years that military power is impotent unless it is supported by religious patriotism.

Now this is not spontaneous; somewhere and somehow it must be carefully, diligently and persistently cultivated. Where else, if not in the Christian home? Where if not in the church of Christ?

How better than by the co-operation of the home and the church in the great Thanksgiving festival, children's day for home missions? Let every Bible school present the exercise prepared for this occasion, and let every home co-operate in making it a day fruitful of patriotism of a higher and better sort. The Centennial which we are beginning to celebrate would be worse than a failure if we should neglect this great fundamental labor.
W. R. WARREN.
Centennial Secretary.

A Brotherhood.
F. A. WIGHT.

One of the most important movements among us to bring to a full realization our highest hopes in 1909, received such little attention, through the absence of its officers at the Buffalo convention, that I am constrained to say something that I believe needed to be said on that occasion. I speak of the "Business Men's Association." We must not forget the words of our Savior, "Come, and I will make you fishers of men." The results of the first two Gospel sermons was the conversion of 5000 men. The Apostle John says, "I write unto you, young men, because ye are strong." He did not say, "I write unto young women." The Apostolic church was composed largely of men. Hear the Apostle in his exhortation to the church at Corinth, "Quit you like men; be strong." If we are to restore the New Testament church we must awake and become fishers of men, and enlist them in the mighty work of saving men, and build up in each church such a brotherhood, bound together by such bonds as are only possible to men. A brotherhood with its Andrews and Philips to go out with yearning hearts after the lost; with its holy fellowship like that of David and Jonathan, whose hearts become knit together because of like struggles against temptation and sin; and also a sustaining force like Aaron and Hur to support the work and be by the side of the preacher in the charge against the enemy as they unitedly capture the ramparts of sin. Are we not, by the very nature of the work we call "the pastorate," spending too much time in broadcloth, visiting the women and coddling the babies, while that which would give virility and sinew to our great plea is passed by with but little attention? Let us, together, open to Paul's address to the elders of Ephesus, where he tells them of his labors for them as an example and then see this strong man in the embrace of strong men, as they weep upon each other's necks and show their strong affection in kisses, showing such a feeling that would make such a brotherhood a mighty power for God. I am not sure that we have the best name for this association. It smacks too much of money, as if we wanted business men because they have means. What we want are the men themselves. Their stalwart support in every way. We want men to help save other men and hold them with bands of steel, for God. We want a brotherhood in each church that men find in the lodges and saloons. What means the multiplicity of lodges and the springing up of fraternities, like mushrooms in a night. Are not men combining in business and trades? Men do not like to stand alone, they want comradeship, and this yearning of men for a fellowship was abundantly met in the Apostolic church, where they were of one heart and mind and even had all things in common. Oh, that we, too, could so win men to Jesus Christ, that His love would possess them, as it did Paul, and this spirit of friendliness might not only be utilized, but cemented and augmented by the Holy Spirit, produce such a brotherhood that would put into the shade all other fraternities among men. Take your church record, my brother minister, and if it contains 300 names, there will probably be too men and boys. Write all these upon a paper by themselves and then take one name and pray, fully consider the possibilities of even one man as a man. Then think of him as a redeemed man purchased at a tremendous cost. Then think, that in that body there is also dwelling the mighty Paraclete making it his temple to strengthen with might the inner man and to reproduce in him the Christ life. Then think, I have not only one such man with such mighty possibilities, but too such men. Oh, what a power for God! And then as these men come before you in their true magnitude, pray for them, until your heart goes to each one, like that of Jonathan to David and Christ, your elder brother does to you. Keep on praying until you call these men together and tell them your vision and let them see your heart's desire for them and Christ's will concerning them, and organize them, in the simplest way possible, and send them out to do valiant work for Christ. Such a brotherhood would lift the finances out of the kitchen and fill the treasury with free-will offerings and build our much needed schools and colleges and hospitals in the foreign field and send missionaries into the needy east and the great west and south, and bring us up to Pittsburg with a mighty chorus of manly voices, an army that will shake the continent with their mighty tread, as they follow their elder brother—the mighty captain—as he leads them out to do valiant work for Christ. and century for the union of all Christians, and consequently the conquest of the world. There is no desire in this article to underestimate the noble part that women have borne and are bearing today in our great work. On them has fallen the heaviest part of the work. We love and ap-

(Continued on Page 1588.)

Current Events

The short session of the fifty-ninth congress opened on Monday, December 3. The short session is always overcrowded with business. Three months is a brief period in which to do a year's legislative business for a country as large as this. There is seldom opportunity for the passage of important new bills at a short session. The most that can be expected is the completion of the unfinished business and the passage of the necessary appropriation bills. The most important measures left over from the former session are the ship subsidy bill, the bill for the restriction of immigration, the bills requiring the publication of campaign subscriptions over $500 and prohibiting contributions by corporations, the Philippine tariff, the eight-hour bill, the bill to limit the working hours of railway employes in the interest of public safety, the anti-injunction bill. Besides, the senate will have to consider the San Domingo treaty, the Isle of Pines treaty by which that island is ceded to Cuba, and the case of Smoot. Mr. Smoot has now occupied his seat in the senate nearly four years, and the senate has not yet been able to determine whether or not he is properly entitled to it. No piece of legislation is more urgently demanded by every consideration of reason and justice than the Philippine tariff bill. The first Philippine assembly is to meet next summer, and it is highly desirable that, before that event, our government shall, by a reduction of the tariff, give substantial evidence of good faith toward the Filipinos and exhibit to them some tangible and appreciable benefits of a close connection with America. They have already received many benefits from that connection—far more than we have—in the way of restored order, improved local government and better education, but these are no excuse for further delay in doing justice to their industries by a re-adjustment of the tariff.

No Tariff for Them. The National Association of Thrasher Manufacturers does not care for any more protection. It has asked for a reduction of the tariff on the steel, iron and lumber which they use as raw material, and are willing to have their finished product compete with the imported article without the aid of a protective tariff. Considering the acknowledged supremacy of this country in the manufacture of farm implements, we should think this would be a very safe proposition. The names of McCormick and Deering are as familiar in Austria and Russia as is the name of Roosevelt. But it is pleasant to see an infant industry which voluntarily offers to surrender its nursing-bottle when it ceases to be an infant.

A Field for Hypnotism. A new field for the profitable practice of hypnotism has just been discovered. It has already been charged by some ruthless critics, who have no respect for either commerce or religion, that successful salesmen and popular evangelists win customers and converts by the exercise of hypnotic powers. Now it is invading the courts of justice and undermining the credibility of testimony. A man who was suing his wife for divorce and also trying to recover some property which he had given her, was telling his story on the witness stand. Suddenly he became confused, passed his hand across his brow with a gesture of bewilderment and came to a dead stop, from which neither the attorneys nor the judge could start him. Afterward he asserted that he had happened to meet the glance of his wife, who was in the court room, and that she had hypnotized him with a look and so rendered it impossible for him to proceed with his testimony. The woman in this case was a spiritualistic medium, which, of course, added to the potency of her glance. If hypnotism can cut off undesirable evidence, why can it not go a little farther and put into the lips of a controlled witness the statements which the hypnotist, seated inconspicuously among the spectators, may desire. Really, this is the submarine torpedo principle applied to the administration of justic

Bryce for Ambassador. There comes a pleasing but unconfirmed rumor that Mr. James Bryce, M. P., is to be appointed British ambassador at Washington. From the American point of view, no appointment could be more popular. Mr. Bryce is not only a real statesman, who represents what is best in English political life, but he is a distinguished scholar and litterateur. What is more, he knows American institutions and history as few Americans know them. His great work on "The American Commonwealth" has long been a standard text-book on American political institutions, and as such is perhaps more generally used than any other book in American colleges and universities. Mr. Bryce's lack of a title—for he is not even Sir James Bryce—will be no bar to his popularity and usefulness here.

Speculation. Mr. James J. Hill has been warning the farmers against the insidious dangers of speculation. Mr. Hill is, perhaps, not always right, but this time he is. He might widen the application of his advice and still be within safe limits. The farmers are not the only ones who need it. A financial writer says the country is in the vortex of a perfect cyclone of mining speculation. Certain millionaires have recently cleaned up thirty millions of easy money in "cobalt." Nevada is having a boom. Mining stock is being put on the market with no evidence of value except a nicely engraved stock-certificate, and is being eagerly bought up by persons whose greed for sudden and unearned gains is greater than their judgment as to ways of acquiring the same. Mining is a legitimate and often a profitable business. But it is a business —or a profession—and as such it requires expert knowledge and conservative management, as much as does any branch of commerce or manufacture. But buying mining stocks on the strength of glittering advertisements backed up by no stronger assurance of value than the bare word of the promoter that the price is about to soar, is pure folly, and generally very expensive folly. When any one tries to sell you stock in a mine in Nevada or Montana, bethink yourself what you would do if you were asked to buy a farm in Kansas or Ohio—a farm which you had never seen and about which you had never had any evidence more disin-

Editorial

Is There a Missing Link?

This does not refer to the missing link that science has been hunting for between man and the lower orders, but a missing link in the organization of our forces for effective work. With all right thinking people organization has ceased to be a bugaboo, and is everywhere recognized as an essential condition of all growing life and work. The only thing to guard against is that organization shall not hamper life or growth, but shall foster them. When any religious movement is sufficiently organized for the full and free expression of its life, and for the vigorous and orderly prosecution of its legitimate work in the world, it is adequately organized. Has our own religious movement attained to this degree of effectiveness in the way of national organization?

We have three general missionary organizations which hold their conventions annually, namely: the American Christian Missionary Society, the Christian Woman's Board of Missions, and the Foreign Christian Missionary Society. These are all designed to be simply methods of co-operation in missionary work, one in the home land, one in foreign lands, and the other peculiarly the work of women. Their constitutions limit their work to missions—the object for which they were formed. But there are several general interests vital to the welfare of the brotherhood that cannot strictly be classed as missionary, although, of course, they have either direct or indirect bearing upon the general work of extending the kingdom of God. We have no convention for the consideration of this class of general interests, and no convention of the brotherhood to which these several societies may report as constituent parts. Is there, or is there not needed a representative body from the churches of the brotherhood which would be a connecting link between the churches and the societies, and which could properly consider all those questions of general interest which do not belong especially to either of the missionary societies?

Some time ago we pointed out the necessity of such a convention unless there should be a widening of the scope of the convention of the American Christian Missionary Society beyond that which its constitution, strictly interpreted, calls for. Just now, when the revision of the constitution of this society is under consideration, it is timely to raise the question as to whether the new constitution should provide for the consideration of all questions deemed important to the welfare of the brotherhood, or whether it shall limit itself strictly to the work of home missions, and leave to another convention the consideration of other than missionary problems. We believe a majority of our brethren have been of the opinion that the convention of the American Christian Missionary Society may properly, with a liberal construction of its constitution, even as it is, consider all the questions that should come before a representative body of the brotherhood. There is a minority, however, who would cut out all these general questions, not strictly missionary, but they have made no suggestion, so far as we have seen, as to how such questions could be considered. The fact that there are some who are inclined to hold missionary societies responsible for any action taken at our national conventions, which does not meet with their approval, is leading many to believe that it will be better to make a clearer distinction between the missionary conventions proper, and a representative convention of the brotherhood whose object it would be to deal with questions other than missionary, which concern our future well being.

It is interesting to note that our Baptist brethren who have a similar organization to our own are just now confronting this same question. A correspondent of the "Standard" of Chicago, under the title of "A Convention for the Northern Baptists," urges the necessity of such an organization as we have indicated and quotes Dr. Rowland as favoring "A convention of Northern Baptists, to which each society should report when it met in annual session; thus giving one general constituency to which all should present reports and claims." Commenting on this, the question referred to, Dr. Spenser B. Meeser, says:

This is the ideal condition: a convention of northern Baptists, meeting in annual session, to hear reports of our missionary and publication work, to consider the policies and methods, to make recommendations (no legislative function being possible), and to consider other matters of profound and vital interest, educational, social, ethical, evangelistic, denominational policies, union with other bodies, federation with others, and many like things.

This describes a situation identical with our own. Such a convention could assemble at the same place where our three societies are holding their anniversaries, and would relieve the American Christian Missionary Society, from the consideration of many questions, and of many general interests which have hitherto taken up its time. It would, also, relieve the society of any criticism for any action taken by the convention on any subject outside the sphere of its own operations. The resolution on federation passed at the Omaha Convention, for instance, has been charged to the American Christian Missionary Society. But that society, as such, had nothing whatever to do with the action. It was the action of a mass meeting of the brethren.

The question arises, Who would be authorized to call such a convention? Any number of representative brethren could unite in such a call, but if the board of the American Christian Missionary Society should issue a request of this kind, we believe it would meet with a general response from the brethren. One thing at least we have the right to insist on, and that is that if such a convention be not provided for, then the revised constitution of the American Christian Missionary Society should include, within the scope of its annual convention, the duty of dealing with all questions relating to the welfare of the brotherhood, which require the action of a representative and deliberative assembly.

❋ ❋

After the Meeting.

In a great many churches throughout the brotherhood, as well as in our St. Louis churches, just now, special evangelistic services have closed and pastors and churches find themselves confronted with the problem, How can we best care for, develop, and train the young converts that have been brought into the church? No question can be more vital to the welfare of the churches than this and none is entitled to more prayerful consideration. A large majority of these young converts are young people with a limited knowledge of God and of spiritual things. They have been won to Christ by the love that has been awakened in their heart for him, and by the promises held out in God's word to those who believe in and obey him. But if their religious training should cease at this point their spiritual life would be dwarfed, their ardor would be chilled by contact with the world, their faith weakened, and their usefulness in the church ruined or largely curtailed. Several things are needed in order to their normal spiritual growth and future usefulness.

1. *They need encouragement.* The older members of the church should make it a point to get acquainted personally with these converts, invite them to their homes, and visit them in their homes. The bond of acquaintanceship and friendship should be formed inside the church. Special meetings at the church for this purpose are also helpful.

2. *They need feeding.* "Feed my lambs" was the charge which the risen Christ laid upon Peter. They need "the sincere milk of the word." For this purpose they should be gathered into the Sunday-school, into the Christian Endeavor Society, and into the prayer-meeting, and, as far as possible, special instruction adapted to their needs should be imparted to them by Christian men and women of experience and piety. If the Christian Endeavor Society, the Sunday-school, the prayer-meeting, the C. W. B. M. Auxiliary, and the Ladies' Aid Society, are not all increased in their membership, because of the ingathering, we may not anticipate permanent results.

3. *They need religious activity.* As far as practicable these converts should all be given something to do in some department of the church. There is nothing that develops strength like activity. There is nothing that develops interest in the church and in religion so much as some religious task to perform, some service for Christ. Just here there is great difference in the capacity of the religious leaders in the church. Some pastors and church officers have a special capacity for finding something to do for all the members, and oth-

ers, apparently, try to do all the work themselves, and have no genius for laying out the work for others. Some ministers are good preachers but lack in executive ability. This lack, however, should be supplemented by the co-operation of the official board.

4. *They need a healthy atmosphere.* If the spiritual atmosphere of the church is cold and formal, if there be lack of zeal and fidelity in church attendance on the part of the older members, if there be feuds or quarrels among church members, the young converts will be chilled, discouraged and blighted in their religious lives, by this condition of things. The lack of unity, and the spirit of fault-finding, are reasonsible for the loss of many young converts from the church.

We will be glad to welcome suggestions from pastors or others who have something to contribute out of their actual experience as to successful methods of retaining and developing into useful members the new converts which are brought into our churches every year by thousands. When we shall have become as successful in caring for and training young converts into spiritual manhood and womanhood as we are in winning them to Christ, our growth will be far more rapid and our spiritual power in the world greatly multiplied. To this problem we must address ourselves with a zeal and patience born of love for Christ and for all Christ's little ones.

The Religious Newspaper Problem.

We like to take our readers into our confidence on every question that relates to the welfare of THE CHRISTIAN-EVANGELIST. We wish to call their attention to a fact which has, perhaps, escaped their attention, namely: that during the last five or six years the wages of printers and the cost of material for making newspapers, have increased more than 40 per cent, according to an estimate based on high authority. In view of this fact many of the religious newspapers of the country are increasing their subscription price for the coming year. These facts affect THE CHRISTIAN-EVANGELIST just as they affect other religious papers. We had no margin of profit before. What ought we to do, therefore, in the face of this increase in the cost-price of producing the paper?

Wise or unwise, we have decided upon the heroic policy of continuing to offer THE CHRISTIAN-EVANGELIST to subscribers at the old rate of $1.50 per year. We are doing this, too, in the face of the fact that we are now cutting out thousands of dollars worth of advertising which we once published, believing them to be unsuitable for a high grade religious journal. Thus we are deliberately cutting down our income on the one hand, while the cost price of production is increasing. These are facts which our readers ought to know and, knowing them, ought to govern themselves accordingly.

These statements are made in view of

the fact that within the last week we received a few requests from local agents asking that they be permitted to receive subscriptions for the paper at a lower rate than the fixed price above mentioned, and giving as a reason that at one time in the past they received the paper at a reduced rate. We feel sure that these requests would not be made, nor would subscribers object to paying our regular price, if they were acquainted with the facts which we have stated above. It ought to be perfectly obvious to every intelligent reader of THE CHRISTIAN-EVANGELIST that such a paper as we are publishing can not be produced for the price at which we are selling it. Were the paper to stand alone on its own receipts, the price would have to be immediately advanced or its quality lowered, or the paper discontinued. Our readers are profiting by the fact that we are doing a large publishing business and that THE CHRISTIAN-EVANGELIST is carried at the expense of other departments. If the price of our paper were raised to $2.00, it would be cheaper still than it was five or six years ago at $1.50.

We leave it to our readers to decide what their duty is to the paper under these circumstances. We shall be disappointed if they do not decide that, in view of the fact that THE CHRISTIAN-EVANGELIST is offered at the same price, in spite of a great increase in cost of production and the cutting out of a large part of its income from advertising, they ought (1) to pay the full price of the paper promptly and cheerfully, and (2) lend their influence and efforts in securing additional subscribers so as to reduce the cost of furnishing the paper to each individual subscriber, and (3) patronize our general publishing business. Anything less than this would hardly be meeting us half-way in our efforts to supply a first-class religious journal at the lowest possible cost to its readers.

It gives us pleasure to add that the rapid increase in the circulation of THE CHRISTIAN-EVANGELIST—unprecedented in its past history—has greatly strengthened us in our purpose to continue the paper at its present low rate.

Notes and Comments.

When the Disciples refuse to receive to the fellowship of their churches a true Christian brother, because he does not agree with them as to the authorship of the Pentateuch, or the doctrine of baptism, or the inspiration of the Scriptures, what are they doing but making the organization of sects a necessity, and writing themselves down as the worst of sects. But the original mission of the Disciples was to find such a basis of fellowship as would make the creation of sects unnecessary.—*H. G. in The Scroll.*

There is a sense in which the above could be accepted as true. No opinion as to the authorship of the Pentateuch, the design or philosophy of baptism or as to the method of inspiration can rightly be made a condition of admission into our churches, because Jesus Christ has not made them conditions. But if we are to accept the New Testament as final authority, obedience to Christ in baptism by a penitent believer was a condition of ad-

mission into the churches of the apostolic age. The principle on which the Disciples acted was that if they would restore the New Testament terms of church membership they would have "such a basis of fellowship as would make the creation of sects unnecessary," so far as believers in Jesus Christ are concerned. They may have been wrong in this view, but it remains to be shown that they were wrong.

The "Scroll" of Chicago, quotes with its hearty endorsement the following statement from the "Christian Standard:"

"We occasionally come across the statement in correspondence, and in articles or speeches, that baptism is essential to salvation. This is neither the Scriptural doctrine nor statement, and with many people he prejudices the real Scriptural teaching on baptism who makes use of it. If baptism is essential to salvation, then no one can be saved who is not baptized. This denies salvation to infants, partially taught believers, and all who have mistaken sprinkling and pouring for Christian baptism. Now, the gospel does not require us to assume any such unnecessary burden as this extreme and virtually negative affirmation. The Scriptures clearly teach that, for the penitent believer, baptism is unto or for the remission of past sins. Affirming this, we buttress our position by the unmistakable teaching of New Testament Scripture. In giving the gospel doctrine, about which many are ignorant, it is most unwise to take an extreme position, especially if that position is not warranted by the law and the testimony. Let us not hesitate to preach and teach that he that believeth and is baptized shall be saved, that baptism for the penitent believer is for the remission of sins, and stop right there."

"How good and how pleasant it is for brethren to dwell together in unity!" If anything more were needed to show the near approach of the millennium, it is found in the statement of the "Scroll" that "B. B. Tyler and J. W. McGarvey are among the new subscribers!" "Blest be the tie that binds" is now in order. Prof. Willett may start the tune, and Prof. McGarvey sing bass!

An instructive volume might be written by some experienced journalist on the abuses of editorial power and position. The different forms which this abuse can take are too numerous to be enumerated and elaborated, except in a volume devoted to such work. One of the most common and reprehensible of these abuses is for an editor to wave his "big stick" or *little* stick, as the case may be, over the head of some man in an official or public position who dares to express an opinion contrary to that of the editor, with an implied threat of turning its columns against the official offender unless he straightway ceases to utter convictions which have not received the stamp of approval in the editorial sanctum. This sort of terrorism is supposed to be sufficient to suppress the convictions of brethren who, in a private capacity, would not be afraid to defend their positions, but who, as public servants, may feel a timidity in subjecting to criticism the public interests which they represent. Is there any way of protecting the personal rights and liberties of brethren whom we thrust into official positions to represent our general interest? Have they any rights which we editors are bound to respect?

Editor's Easy Chair.

Now the year passes into its twelfth and last division and hastens to its close. Spring, Summer and Autumn each in its turn has held sway but they must now give place to the reign of Winter. Fittingly enough Autumn ends her queenly reign, in this land at least, with the Thanksgiving festival. The nation has given thanks to the all bountiful Giver, has been reminded from thousands of pulpits and platforms of its manifold blessings and sins, its perils and prospects, and, sobered by these thoughts, it faces the perplexing problems and stern duties of the future. No doubt the prevailing note in all the Thanksgiving addresses and sermons was optimistic, for we are, above all things, a hopeful people. Americans believe in their destiny as they believe in God, but do not always consider the conditions upon which that great destiny is to be realized. In the hearts of the people, however, there is faith that the God who planted this nation in the New World, and whose hand has been manifest in all its past history, will lead it out of its commercialism, its bondage to low ideals, and on and upward to the fulfillment of his great purposes concerning it. One of the greatest reasons for thanksgiving, with thoughtful people, has been this very process of political and industrial purification, which is now going on before our eyes. There is one article of our political creed which is tenaciously held by the great body of Americans, and that is that no nation whose citizens do not cultivate and practice the virtues of honesty and integrity, of purity in private and public life, of courage and devotion to right, and are not patrons of religion and education, can attain to permanent greatness and power. No man that can not subscribe to that creed can ever be elected to any high office in these United States.

❧

On Thanksgiving morning the Easy Chair had the privilege of meeting with about seventy-five other young people in a sunrise prayer-meeting, at the Union Avenue Christian Church in this city. The morning was dark and lowering, and the clouds were dripping moisture, but in this young people's meeting there was nothing dark or dreary or dismal. Their bright faces, their hearty singing, their earnest prayers, their cheering, thoughtful talks, dispelled all exterior gloom and filled all the place with a heavenly radiance. As we listened to the prayers and talks of these young men and women, and observed how early in life they seemed to have caught the secret of joyous Christian living, in keeping close to Christ as a Friend and Brother, we could but feel that in the religiously-trained youth of the country lies the hope of the church and of the nation. The Christian Endeavor Society of the church mentioned above had invited the societies of two other churches to meet with them as their guests in this prayer

and praise service, and in the breakfast which followed. These young people all seemed to strike the same great notes of gratitude to God, and of love and service for Christ, heedless of denominational differences. They will never grow up to believe that all truth and loyalty to Christ are the special heritage of their own particular fellowship. The breakfast was like a great family meal, in which the brothers and sisters sat down together in happy, joyous converse and good fellowship. Thank God for Christian young people who have found in Christ the solution of all their life-problems, and who are making him their Guide and Counsellor in all the way of life! Of such the church of the future is to be made.

❧

Of all the crude, unwise, ill-digested, irreverent and barbarous theories, which unbalanced, would-be reformers are thrusting upon this generation, about the worst is the recent proposition for "trial marriages." And this from a woman! In the eyes of this social agitator, the teaching of Jesus, the past experience of the world, the moral sentiments of civilized peoples, and the very instincts of the human heart, amount to nothing. What does this woman know about the sacredness and tenderness of family relationships, and of the happiness that springs from these relations? Let us hope that the blasphemous proposition may at least serve the purpose of warning the people against the constant assaults that are being made upon the home, and upon Christian marriage which is the basis of the home. Much more teaching of a sane and safe character is needed in our homes, in our schools, and in our churches, on the meaning and sacredness of the marriage relation, and on the essential conditions of a true marriage and a happy home. The thoughtlessness with which many young people are entering into the marriage relation, and often out of Christian homes, is an alarming fact that should arrest the attention of all who believe that the home is the foundation of our civilization. The divorce evil, which attracts more attention and comment, is, after all, but the outcropping, in the main, of unwise marriages. The evil of divorce may be helped by legislation, but it cannot be cured except by beginning further back and impressing the minds of the young with the sacred obligations of marriage and with the necessity of a high standard of morality as an essential condition of marriage.

❧

Recently we had a letter from a most worthy minister who has been the object of a bitter and most unjust attack by an anonymous writer in one of our religious journals, asking whether it were better for him to suffer wrong in silence or to vindicate his reputation against unjust statements. That is a question which, unfortunately, many a worthy man has to face. The case is sufficiently common to justify a few observations on the subject. In the

first place, one who is feeling the sting of unjust criticism, is almost sure to overestimate its effect on the public mind. He is likely to imagine that every one will believe the statements of his accuser, when, as a matter of fact, such attacks usually answer themselves, and, unconsciously to their authors, reveal their real motive. Intelligent readers know how to discount such charges, and, to attribute them to other causes than the desire to promote truth and the welfare of the church. Again, if experience teaches any one lesson it is that any unjust assault on the character of another always reacts against the one making it. We are not saying that it is never proper to reply to misrepresentations of one's position and acts, but we do say that in a great majority of cases such replies are unnecessary. We often give too little credit to the discernment of readers, who are quite able to make a true estimate of such misrepresentations. A good man whose motives are true and who is seeking to do good and not evil in the world, need give himself but little concern about defending his reputation against the attacks of evil-minded persons. God and good people will take care of his reputation.

❧

Tennyson observed the fact long ago that "The thoughts of men are widened with the process of the suns," and he and many another poet and all true historians have noted the fact that this widening thought, this larger view of truth, this advancement in real knowledge, has come about through conflict of opinions. One mind sees one aspect of truth from its point of view, while another mind sees a different aspect of the same truth from another point of view, and these come into collision with each other—each perhaps mistaking its aspect of truth for the whole truth—and out of this conflict truth gets to be seen on all sides instead of on one side only, and so gets onward. So universal is this fact that it has come to be understood among thoughtful people that differing minds and differing theories, so far from being obstacles to the advancement of truth, are the very means which have been most used in the progress of knowledge. This is as true in the realm of theology as in the realms of science and philosophy. One would think that a recognition of this fact, and of the inevitableness of differing views, as long as there are differing minds, would teach us all the lesson of charity and tolerance, and enable us to see in our differing views an opportunity for enlarging our own knowledge, and not an occasion of strife or alienation. Other things being equal, that religious body that permits the largest freedom of thought and of utterance, consistent with loyalty to Christ, without interfering with the bonds of love and fellowship, will make the most rapid progress in the solution of current problems and in the application of Christianity to present-day conditions and needs.

The Disciples and Evangelism* B

Introduction.

The evangel of God's love is the most stupendous fact of human experience. Revealed by the incarnation, explained by the teachings, illustrated by the sinless life, and made efficacious by the sacrificial death of the Son of God, its propagation and spread throughout the world becomes at once the "raison d'etre" and the program of the church. Evangelism is fundamental. Institutions, movements, men, are of value in the direct ratio of their ability to extend the Kingdom. The Disciples of Christ fulfill their mission precisely in the extent to which they contribute to the world's evangelization.

The Nature of the Field.

The specific theme of this address is the contribution of the Disciples of Christ to the evangelization of America. But why talk of the evangelization of Christian America? The fact that 40,000,000 of our fellow citizens never cross the threshold of a church, Catholic or Protestant, gives sanity to the seeming paradox.

Facing this fact Dr. Hillis says: "The church is encamped on the edge of a dark continent of worldliness, and selfishness, and pleasure, and sin." But a moment of reflection reveals that it is not a dark continent of heathenism, nor of perverted religion. America is neither pagan nor unchristian. The realm of our conquest is an enlightened civilization based upon the very fundamental principles of Christianity. The ideals of Christ are exalted, only the people do not obey him as Lord. The dominant factors in our civilization are the undisciplined forces which Christianity has liberated. The twofold problem before us is the conversion of the individual and the christianization of society, and the solution is not easy. Theoretically the former task includes the latter. Practically, however, we have seen corporations, greedy, godless and vicious, composed of men famous for their piety; political parties controlled by eminent Christian statesmen go mad over the spoils of office. Society must be Gospelized.

In the new civilization of the present century with its material basis, its rapid social evolution, its intellectual progress, and its religious readjustment, our evangel is meeting its severest tests. Is it able for these things? We are of those who stand ardent, expectant, on the threshold of the greater opportunities for the larger conquests of the Gospel, believing devoutly in its power to master and control the forces of our modern life and ultimately to establish the kingdom of God on earth.

Paul characterized his age as "The Day

*An address delivered before the American Christian Missionary Society at Buffalo, N. Y.

of Salvation." However others may have viewed it, history has vindicated the great apostle. The dominant characteristic of his age is that it gave Christianity to the world. I venture the prophecy that when the story of the ages has been written, that which will characterize the present age will not be its modern inventions, its growth of scientific learning or its material prosperity, but missions and evangelism.

The Equipment of Our Forces.

Our restoration movement was born in the travail of a great religious awakening. It was led by men of keen intel-

J. P. Lichtenberger.

lectual perception and deep religious conviction. Men who faced the problems of the future resolutely, and who were not afraid to break with age-long traditions. Preachers who interpreted a first century message to nineteenth century men. Unfettered by creed, unhampered by tradition, the old Gospel was adaptable and acceptable to the new age and its marvelous growth bears testimony to its timeliness. For as "a man's gift maketh room for him," so any institution or movement among men finds acceptation ultimately in proportion to its worth.

Unlike other movements which were likewise the product of their times the plea of the Disciples of Christ refuses to be stereotyped and embalmed in the age that produced it. One glory of our cause is its mobility; its ready adaptability to the ever and rapidly changing conditions of our modern life. The protestant principle here finds its highest interpretation. Timorous souls who fear for the perpetuity of our cause on account of retrograde tendencies to crystalization need but to study anew, the genius of our history and aims. We are free men in Christ Jesus and we prize our liberty as one of our most priceless possessions. With a great price some of us obtained this freedom while others are free born, and we shall remain free.

As Seen From the Dome　By F. D. Power

Man digs up certain black stones from the bosom of the earth and says to them, "Transport me and this luggage at the rate of thirty-five miles an hour," and they do it. So Carlyle speaks of human control over nature. I have been among the black stones. I had a trip last week to the anthracite region, the richest black diamond region in the world, and had a descent into the bowels of the earth, where they coin $550,000,000 in a single year. It may seem incredible, yet it is absolutely true that while the gold and silver production of this country in 1904 was: Gold, $84,551,300, and silver, $53,603,000, a total of $138,154,300—great wealth to be extracted from the earth in one year's time—the value of the production of coal in a single state, for the same year, was $550,000,000.

Pennsylvania is the second state in the Union in point of wealth. During the four years ending in 1904; it gained over three billions. The total figures for the state, according to the census in 1904, were $11,473,620,306. And the Keystone State furnishes one-half of all the coal mined in this country. Practically all the anthracite is produced there. Think of 75,000,000 tons dug out in a single year! And the same year this great commonwealth mined over 99,000,000 tons of the bituminous coal. This is coal to burn! People are getting uneasy for fear the supply will be exhausted, but there is no occasion of uneasiness. Officials of the Geological Survey assure us there is no need for this generation to worry. They say there is enough in the United States to last four or five thousand years, yet some are really worrying about their fuel necessities for next year. Up to 1865 the total production had been 284,890,055 tons. The following decade it grew to 419,425,104, making the total to that time 700,000,000, and up to 1905 the grand total is figured at 5,970,773,571. According to the census of 1890 the production that year was only 6,445,681 tons, when the population was 23,000,000. From 1850 to 1900 the population increased 230 per cent, while the increase in coal production was 4,084 per cent.

It is worth a day's travel to visit the anthracite region in the Wyoming Valley. This is historic ground, for every school boy remembers that Indian massacre, and has been thrilled by the little wood cut of houses on fire, and women and children running for their lives, and painted and feathered-decked red men brandishing tomahawks, which used to appear in the school books. The story of Forty Fort, of the Tories and Senecas, and Zebulon Butler; of "Queen Esther" and little Frances Slocum, the poster web which saved the man in the log; of patriots spoiled by whiskey, and of English praise for the savages and English money appropriated for "scalping knives"—is not this written in the chronicles of 1778 and sung in the ears by the Susquehanna? And Catawissa, Wapwallopen, Nescopeck and Shickshinny,

Mocanaqua and Chillisquaque still speak of the time when poor Lo held sway. Now three or four hundred thousand busy white folks throng this valley—that is, they are white occasionally. Over 161,000 of them work in the mines and collieries, and periodically show that they are "pale faces." In 1904 there were 110,362 workmen employed here in the bowels of the earth, and over 50,000 outside employes, and among them were 596 fatal accidents, showing the dangerous character of the business. One can go miles and miles through shafts and chambers and slopes and workings, the veins running perhaps five miles across and fifty miles up and down the valley, the deepest shaft going down for 2,800 feet. And not only men, but more than 1,700 horses and mules are employed in the mines. Down in the Erebus-like abyss, where I was lowered by the cage, I visited a stable where fifty sleek, saucy looking mules were cared for, some of which had worked for twenty years on the subterranean railways. They seem to enjoy it, but cut up interesting capers when allowed a little freedom once in a while on the surface. They have the same tricks down below that characterize them above ground, and among the fatal accidents in 1904 fifty-eight are charged to the mules, and every now and then the cause of death is given "kicked by a mule." No women are employed, and no boy under 14, though 3,173 door boys and helpers of legal age are at work in the mines.

There is no other occupation as dangerous as mining, and none that requires more skill and care. Every mine must have its ambulance and stretchers as required by law. Accidents occur with alarming frequency. Falls of coal, slate and roof, and from the mine cars, are chief causes. On an average six lives are lost by "falls" to one by gas. The larger number come from negligence. Men become indifferent to danger. The state seeks to guard the miners by strictest regulations, and conditions are greatly improved, there being

MY CREED.

Charles Blanchard.

I sing the Angels' Song and dare
To pray the Saviour's prayer.
I fain would ever bear
Bravely my cross and care.
I hold the Christ's own creed—
My neighbor and his need—
That Love's best name is Deed!
And so I sing and go my way,
In humble pathways, day by day.
I know not why life's mysteries mock
Our wisdom. I would rather walk
With God, believing yet
That God is Love, and Love cannot
forget.

but one fatal accident to every 110,436 tons of coal mined in 1904. One sees all the world represented in these black cavernous recesses: English, Welsh, Polish, German, Hungarian, Italian, Slavonian, Lithuanian, Greek, Austrian, Russian, Swedish, Tyrolian, Bohemian, Assyrian; more Poles than any other people besides Americans. From 1892 to 1894 the death list foots up to 5,879. It would be interesting to know the loss of life through whiskey among these miners for the same period, a cause of slaughter which is legally protected by the great Keystone State. Looking over the list of men who have been mine victims in 1904 I am struck with such names as: Chanletski, Macajecke, Yascavage, Zatkeiwa, Malanofski, Bublovitski, and Gingloefski, Polihanis, Wocovitch, and Melechefski, Caposkus, Mismienskis, and Juncosky, Bjoglionio, and Laxzonio, and Syarcitues, Ovicavis, and Zenaweskie—names, the very mention of which to the red men at the time of the killing of the early settlers would have made them take to the tall timber. Yet with all the accidents and loss of life these people who delve in the bottom of things love their business, and won't consent to serve in the sunlight when once they have a taste of these black caverns, where grotesque trees and delicate ferns, huge mosses and tall reeds, engulfed in some ancient cataclysm, stored up the carbon for man, which they may bring out to warm and make cheery millions of homes and drive countless engines and machineries by day and night on sea and land. What a blessing is the sun, and what a treasure these stores of imprisoned sunlight!

We explored these dark passages and saw the various operations going on, and blew out our miner's lamps to feel the pitchy darkness, and got out with only a few bruises for my friend and guide—a young man, but not so sure-footed as his older companion. The manager who went through with us is John Dooley, a beloved worker in the Plymouth church, and the young man was L. O. Knipp, the successful pastor. He has a church now of 635 members, and last year held a meeting and added 105. Two years ago I dedicated their beautiful church. They are doing splendid service in one of the finest fields for missions in America. Think of being in a community where one can preach the Gospel in twenty-five tongues. We have two congregations in Scranton, with Richard Bagby and E. E. Manley as pastors, with 450 members. One at Wilkesbarre, where E. Cowperthwaite preaches, with a membership of 180; and one at Westmore, which C. A. Frick serves, with 150. These with the Plymouth church constitute our force in this anthracite region, and they are all doing well. It would be hard to find a harder worker than the Plymouth pastor. "A nipping and an eager air" he has about him, and there is always something doing in his parish. The end of the anthracite, they say, may be seen, but the work of the Lord goes on forever.

A Divine Ordi

"Where the Scriptures speak we speak, and where the Scriptures are silent we are silent," is a significant and an important statement, which was more used and perhaps better understood by the fathers of the "Restoration Movement" than by many now who wear only the name Christian. Not so with the phrase, "Ministerial relief," which is more used and better understood by the Disciples to-day than by the fathers, though many have yet to know its importance.

Ministerial relief is significant, not only of the needs of some of our good brethren in the ministry, but also of the obligation and responsibility of the church to supply that need. In that divine ordination, "those who preach the Gospel shal live of the Gospel," it is as certainly ordained that the church shall give as that the ministry shall receive. It is Christ's ministry, it is Christ's church. All belongs to him, and he is all in all. He can not use the ministry without the church, and he cannot use the church without the ministry. This divinely constructed bit of spiritual machinery is one of the most important agencies in all the universe. Upon it God depends for the final consummation of his holy purpose manifest in the gift of his Son. That we depend upon God is true; that God depends upon us is equally true. We can not live without his blessings; he can not save the world without our service. "We are laborers together with God," but only as we do his will.

The Whole Church.

It is often the case that some special mission work is undertaken and carried on by a single congregation; and where there is the ability this is a very good thing to do. But for the larger work in meeting the obligations the Lord has laid upon his people to preach the Gospel in all the world, we organize to systematically gather the funds and wisely work the fields. Hence, our missionary societies. A single congregation with the financial ability might elect to support some aged or disabled minister who has been forced into retirement, and this wheel within a wheel would work in perfect harmony with the divine will. Indeed, it would be a most Christlike thing to do. But only an occasional congregation would be able to do this, in addition to other financial obligations. Therefore, in order to meet the obligations of these larger demands we organize a department of the general work and call it ministerial relief. It is God's will and his order that this work be done, and our wisdom to do it through the agency of organization, the supreme thing before us being, not the organization, though it be essential, but the

A Message from the Board of Ministerial Relief.

observance of this divine ordinance, the support of the Lord's ministry.

There are among us good brethren who seem to think that "pioneer work" in this "Restoration Movement" is all done. That the pioneer preachers have all gone to their reward, and there is little or no need for this kind of work longer. In fact, that the term "pioneer" belongs to a bygone age. To recognize just two or three things will easily clear up this unfortunate misunderstanding. And to begin with, just as long as there is a mission field anywhere in all the world there will be pioneer work to be done. Just as long as preachers continue to live they will continue to grow old. And just as long as preachers so love the Lord and desire the salvation of their fellow men that they will do pioneer work without salary consideration, they will continue to come to the sunset of life like their Master with no place to call their own where they can lay their heads, or support provided save that only which God ordained. And this support is theirs, not as a charity or benevolence, but as their just dues for having laid their lives and their all upon the altar of the Kingdom in the long years of useful service they so freely gave the Master's cause. These noble men have hearts that have been pained and sensibilities that have been chagrined, not because they are poor and needy, but because the church which is now reaping from their sowing has failed in her sacred duty in making just returns to her Lord.

What We are Doing.

For a few years we have been pretending to support some of our worthy, worn-out, old preachers. We say pretending, for that is about all it has been. One hundred dollars a year for a man and his wife with no other income, cannot be called support. We may call it help, assistance, something, but not support. A brotherhood of more than a million, standing for the restoration of the practice of Apostolic Christianity, with the wealth of the Disciples, and the few men and women needing this support, doling out the pitiful sum of sixty to one hundred dollars a year for one, or it may be two persons, and call it support, brethren, is a travesty on Christianity, and makes "Our Plea" a mere pretense. We may not expect to influence the world by our preaching if it be not supported by our practice. It is not our pleasure, but our duty to say these things, for we do ourselves as a people and the plea we make an injustice by the insignificant support we give the work of Ministerial Relief. It is little less than a reproach that ten thousand churches of Christ averaged less than sixty cents each for this work last year.

It may be our duty to point out the sin

stand that it is the work of the church, and not simply the work of the Board of Ministerial Relief. That the Board is only the agency through or by which the church is supporting her aged and disabled ministers. To so regard this matter will prove a satisfactory solution of all the problems connected with the church.

Still another item of no small import is that the church recognize that her responsibility in this matter is not only to the aged and disabled ministers, but especially to the Father himself, for by his own ordination the duty of this ministry is laid upon his people. It is through the temporal blessings the Father gives his church that he expects to furnish the support he ordained for those who preach the gospel. God and his people are one when the people are with him in his plans and work.

$25,000 are needed in this work this year if we shall do our duty toward God and to the old preachers. And if we shall have a conscience void of offense before God, our next annual report will show even a much larger amount than this. Some of our annuitants ought to receive at least $300 a year; instead they are receiving $100. Others receiving $60 or $80 ought to receive $200. And, brethren, this half-hearted way of doing the Lord's will is not due to our inability, but to our indifference, and we must waken up. We cannot afford as a people, nor as individuals, to take such a record before the judgment throne. The old preachers can afford to go half clad and even half fed, but the church cannot afford to allow them to suffer such injustice. No! brethren, no! At least five thousand preachers ought to interest as many congregations to make their offerings to do this work December 16, and instead of hunger and cold, there would be joy and gladness. Where is the preacher among us who can expect the Father's blessing upon his work if he neglect this sacred duty? Help us, O God!

From the Other Side.

The following extracts were taken from some recent letters received and are given here to show the good spirit that prevails among those who compose our "Ministerial relief family." Aside from duty and religious obligation, it ought to be a pleasure to any true disciple of Jesus Christ to assist such people. If our spirit toward them in their need was like theirs toward us in our indifference, we ourselves would be happier, and they would be abundantly supplied with life's necessities; yea, they might even have a few of its comforts, for we would spare of our abundance.

"Dear Bro. Orcutt:

Your draft of October 1st received. I have no language that will fully convey to you and the Board of Ministerial Relief the gratitude of my heart for such relief in my need of help. I feel proud of my brethren for whom I labored for fifty years so assiduously and lovingly that they remember me now in my weakness. In the midst of my falling tears I say, God bless the dear brethren into whose hearts he has

put it to remember the old and needy. If I had the means I would enrich this fund, for I was hungry and you gave me meat.
Your humble brother, .

Dear Brethren in Christ:

My old heart was made to rejoice to-day on receiving the ten dollar check. You know you have my sincere thanks. It will enable me to have a few comforts which I could not have without it. I almost gave my life in caring for my dear husband so many long years ere he was called to rest, but God has been so good to me, and I rejoice in the hope of eternal life when

---

DECEMBER 16

Is the third Lord's day in December and means when the day arrives that every active preacher and every live church in the brotherhood should give attention and consideration to the interests of

MINISTERIAL RELIEF

Which means the support of our aged and disabled ministers and their wives, or widows, whose active, faithful consecrated lives have been given to the service of the Lord, who ordained it

THE CHURCH'S DUTY

To provide the means and care for these servants. No church is exempt from this divine obligation, and none should want to be. The coming of the day ought to fill all our hearts with gratitude, as our thoughts are turned

TO THE "OLD GUARD"

Into whose labors we have entered. And when we come to realize how much of their lives have come into our own lives, how their sacrifices made possible our service, and how we could not be what we are without them, we come to realize our obligation to them and to determine that they shall

NOT BE NEGLECTED

In the future as they have been in the past. By our offerings for their support we will make them to know our appreciation of their service. Whatever else we may undertake and whatever other interests may draw our attention, we will not forget

DECEMBER 16.

---

these pains and aches are over. Again thanking you, I am,
Your sister in the faith,

Dear Sirs:

I am truly grateful for the remittance you send me, and certainly appreciate the same. The amount just lacked $3.00 of paying my house rent and I am still unable to do anything in the way of work. Therefore your favors are thankfully received.
Gratefully yours,

Dear Bro. Orcutt:

Your very kind and welcome letter of October 2, containing draft for $25.00 received, for which I sincerely thank you. I can't tell you what a burden of care your timely remittance lifts just at this

time of the year when winter supplies are pressing upon us and to be able by the liberal help of the Board to meet these necessities is surely gratifying to me. But best of all comes to us your words of Christian sympathy and good cheer. God bless you and the Board for them, and may the Father's loving care ever guide you all in your work of love for his sake is the prayer of
Your grateful sister in Christ,

Dear Bro. Orcutt:

With grateful hearts we most thankfully acknowledge the receipt of your highly appreciated letter of the 2nd inst, with New York draft for $25.00. As you so kindly say, this sum can not meet all our necessities, but it does help us so much. We often regret we could not do without it and let some other faithful servant of our Lord have it. Wife joins me in sincere thanks and humble prayer to the kind heavenly Father to abundantly bless each member of your Board and every contributor thereto.
Your grateful sister in Christ,

❃ ❃

SCOFFERS

Often Make the Staunchest Converts.

The man who scoffs at an idea or doctrine which he does not fully understand has at least the courage to show where he stands. .

The gospel of Health has many converts who formerly laughed at the idea that coffee and tea, for example, ever hurt anyone. Upon looking into the matter seriously, often at the suggestion of a friend, such persons have found that Postum Food Coffee and a friend's advice have been their salvation.

"My sister was employed in an eastern city where she had to do calculating," writes an Okla. girl. "She suffered with headache until she was almost unfitted for duty.

"Her landlady persuaded her to quit coffee and use Postum and in a few days she was entirely free from headache. She told her employer about it, and on trying it, he had the same experience.

"My father and I have both suffered much from nervous headache since I can remember, but we scoffed at the idea advanced by my sister, that coffee was the cause of our trouble.

"However, we quit coffee and began using Postum. Father has had but one headache now in four years, due to a severe cold, and I have lost my headaches and sour stomach which I am now convinced came from coffee.

"A cup of good hot Postum is satisfying to me when I do not care to eat a meal. Circumstances caused me to locate in a new country and I feared I would not be able to get my favorite drink, Postum, but I was relieved to find that a full supply is kept here with a heavy demand for it." Name given by Postum Co., Battle Creek, Mich. Read "The Road to Wellville," in pkgs. "There's a reason."

Our Budget

—Thanksgiving Day is past but giving thanks is a perpetual duty.

—Gratitude for blessings received is a noble trait of character.

—December 16—Ministerial Relief Day—will be an opportunity for expressing our gratitude to the old preachers who have given their lives to the Cause we love and who now, in their old age, are dependent on their brethren for their support.

—We devote some space to this holy cause in this number of this paper and we earnestly wish that all our other churches might have fellowship in this ministry of love toward our aged and helpless veterans and their dependent families.

—One month now only remains of the year 1906. What we are to do in this year of our Lord must be done soon, if it is to have a place in the record.

—Let us fill this month with earnest labor and prayer.

✦ ✦ ✦

—C. D. Haskell has entered upon his second year with the church at Williamsville, Ill.

—B. L. Wray reports 101 additions at Budd Park, Kansas City, during the last fourteen months.

—F. W. Burnham has resigned at Decatur and accepted a call to the First Church, Springfield, Ill.

—Evangelist C. A. McDonald, of Akron, Ohio, is assisting S. P. Moody in a meeting at his church in Clinton, Ohio.

—L. L. Carpenter will dedicate at Marcus, Ia., December 9. The congregations in the vicinity are invited to attend.

—The West End Church of Christ, Chicago, has been dedicated. There is now a membership of about forty, all told.

—Jacob Waters has resigned at Ocean View, Del., and is now open for evangelistic work or a permanent engagement.

—H. K. Shields, of Rochester, Ind., will be the singer and helper in a meeting that is to be held at W. F. Richardson's church early in the new year.

—James M. Bell, formerly minister of the First Christian Church at Bellvernon, Pa., has accepted a call to McKinney, Tex., beginning there December 2.

—W. S. Mesnard, who has received an invitation to remain a third year at Mason, Ill., could take work for half time for some Illinois church after January 1.

—James N. Crutcher reports increasing audiences and additions at almost every service, as he enters upon his third year's pastorate of the church at Chillicothe, Mo.

—James T. Nichols, editor and publisher of the "Christian Union," Des Moines, Ia., has just recovered from a severe spell of typhoid fever, and has resumed his editorial work.

—A. W. Kokendoffer received a call to the South Prospect Church, Kansas City, to succeed J. J. Morgan, but he will not leave the work which he has so well in hand at Mexico, Mo.

—An increase of from $8 to $30 is the good report from the offering in the interests of Home Missions of the Bible School at Farmington, Mo., where Edward Owers is pastor.

—C. L. Organ, who is now one of the State evangelists of Iowa, preached on 288 days last year, had 390 additions to the churches, at an expense to the State Board of $1.12 each.

—R. B. Helser will begin a third year's service with the church at Fayette, Mo.,

on January 1, with his second increase of salary. There was a forward movement all along the line.

—J. Will Walters is to assist C. C. Taylor in a meeting at Norborne, Mo., and will lecture in Tina while in the state. N. S. Haynes will supply his pulpit at Niantic during his absence.

—The congregation at Brownington, Mo., is repairing its house of worship, and its minister, S. E. Hendrickson, reports that the outlook is brighter there than it has been for some time.

—Nearly every family represented in the church at Woodbine, Ia., is now visited weekly by one of our church papers. This church recently sent $25 to Iowa missions. B. F. Hall is its minister.

—The brethren at Malvern, Mills County, Ia., are encouraged in their work under Brother Utterback. They are rebuilding the church at a cost of $4,000, and expect to dedicate the first of the year.

●✦✦✦✦✦✦✦✦✦✦✦✦✦✦✦✦✦✦✦✦✦✦✦✦●

There is none of our Christian benevolences that makes a stronger appeal to the heart side of our religion than that which ministers to the necessities of our disabled and dependent ministers and their wives. In the days of their strength and vigorous manhood these men gave themselves unstintedly to the work of preaching the Gospel, regardless of any material compensation. So great was their zeal in ministering to the spiritual needs of the people of their day that they entirely overlooked the duty of the churches to minister to their temporal necessities. Old age or untimely weakness caused by disease has now cut off their ability to provide for themselves, and it remains with the churches which exist as the fruit of their labors and the labors of men likeminded to see that these aged and infirm veterans of the cross are not forgotten and neglected in the evening of their lives. To prevent this the Ministerial Relief Fund was organized by the initiative and unceasing labors of our lamented A. M. Atkinson. The third Lord's day in December is the day set apart for an offering from the churches for this fund. We trust that no church among us will be found wanting in its duty to this blessed ministry of love.

●✦✦✦✦✦✦✦✦✦✦✦✦✦✦✦✦✦✦✦✦✦✦✦✦●

—Stephen J. Corey writes us that some great missionary rallies are being held in the Southland. The Kimberlin Heights students have taken it upon themselves to support a native preacher in India.

—A note from Peter Ainslie says that the Baltimore brethren decided to lay the corner stone of the Christian Temple on December 2. We hope to give an illustration of this rather novel church home.

—C. E. Elmore, who has just been conducting a good meeting at Roanoke, Va., will assume the work at Crewe. Brother Elmore is a strong evangelist. His sermons are said to be models of simplicity and force.

—T. M. Myers, who has gone out to hold a meeting at Medical Lake, Wash., writes that the prospects are good. Although "our people" are few and far between, they seem to mean business in everything they do, he says.

—There is probably no truer philanthropy in which a church or other fraternity could engage than in assisting some unfortunate to the benefits promised by the New Hope Treatment referred to in another column.

—George C. Ritchey has been compelled to cancel meetings at Meridian, Idaho, and Falls City, Ore., in order to enter upon the work of state evangelist of the northwest district of Oregon, beginning in Jan-

—The longest pastorate in the history of the church at Fisher, Ill., has been that of S. Elwood Fisher, who has just completed four years of ministry there. During his incumbency there have been 161 additions with $6,800 raised for all purposes. The church will have an evangelistic meeting in January.

—Mrs. A. A. Buxton, State Primary Superintendent of Sunday-schools in Missouri, writes that the officers are anxious to secure a list of all the primary superintendents and teachers of the Christian churches in the State, and would like to receive names at once. Address 3001 East Sixth street, Kansas City, Mo.

—J. G. McNutt, who has just held a meeting at Cadwell, a little town ten miles from Sullivan, Ill., reports the church, which is in a wealthy country and has among its members people of influence, in need of a preacher. By combining with another church near by a salary of $1,000 might be assured, but none but a worker need apply.

—"Work for Men" is a keynote of John R. Ewers. Precisely twenty-five men between the ages of 18 and 35 have been received into the First Christian Church, Youngstown, Ohio, during the fourteen months of his pastorate. Eighty-three people in all have entered the fellowship in that time and a men's club numbering seventy has been organized.

—There is a better spirit in the south. For the first time in the history of the organizations fraternal messages were extended between the Georgia Baptist convention and our own. From the reports in our news columns it will be seen that our brethren in Georgia and Alabama are taking new courage and are lining up for aggressive work that shall have in it the spirit of Christ rather than the mere spirit of conquest and personal opinion, that has

frequently manifested itself in the past, not only in the south but in the north as well.

—J. J. Morgan, of the South Prospect Church, Kansas City, where a good meeting has just been held by J. H. O. Smith and H. H. Saxton, offered his resignation to the church at the beginning of the meeting. Brother Morgan's health has for some time been such that he has decided to seek a warmer climate and will take up the work at the First Church, Fort Worth, Tex.

—Many evangelists and preachers failed to remember the warning we printed in our Budget week before last and sent us telegrams on Monday which we could not print in view of the fact that our issue for that week had to go to press on Saturday because of its extra size and the Thanksgiving holiday. Until further notice we will again, as usual, be able to handle telegrams received on Monday morning.

—One dollar to missions for every $4.50 to current expenses is the account of the only church of the Disciples of Christ in McHenry County, Illinois. This is located at Nunda and the membership is small, and hence have to give liberally to sustain the local work. A building fund is being raised, but the brethren do not neglect, on that account, the preaching of the gospel to the wide world. H. B. Robison reports two baptized there November 25.

—"The Sphere and Work of Christian Women" was the title of the sermon preached by J. L. Hill at the Central Christian Church, Cincinnati, in observance of C. W. B. M. day, December 2. For breadth of view, clearness of vision, and vigor of thought, the sermon will linger long with those who were so fortunate as to hear it. This historic church is fortunate in having as its pastor a man so well equipped to carry forward the arduous work of a down town church, and under his wise leadership the church is advancing in every department of work.

—Nearly all our churches in Kansas City were represented at the celebration of the sixty-ninth anniversary of the founding of the Hyde Park Church, of which Louis Cupp is the greatly beloved pastor. George L. Snively, assisted on this happy occasion, and part of the worship consisted in the raising of $3,700 for the payment of debts contracted during the building of the beautiful new stone edifice. Brother Snively had the pleasure of meeting nearly all of the pastors of the Christian churches in the city, where our growth has been almost phenomenal and of which it may be said more truly, perhaps, than of any other city, that we have not many churches there, but rather one church meeting in many places.

—Cecil J. Armstrong, who has been for five years pastor of the First Christian Church, Winchester, Ky., has accepted a unanimous call to the River Street Church, Troy, N. Y. He will enter upon his new field of work December 9. Brother Armstrong has a fine record at Winchester, there having been 191 additions during his pastorate, $11,375 contributed to missions, and over $25,000 for all purposes. The officers have presented to the Winchester church a very commendatory statement concerning him and his work. We published in our issue of November 22 Brother Armstrong's sermon upon G. L. Wharton, who was the living link missionary of the Winchester church, while a few weeks prior to this we published his speech before the convention at Buffalo on "The Missionary Bump."

—Frank W. Allen, of Odessa, Mo., within the past few days had calls from the churches at Windsor, and at Twenty-second and Prospect, Kansas City. He will not go to Windsor, and is still in doubt about Kansas City. He says: "I love this little country town and its

people. It is about as near Kentucky as any place I know of in Missouri, and that is the highest praise." The meeting at Odessa closed with five confessions. From the first the house was crowded and the interest was unusual on the part of the other churches in town. Save on Sunday nights the Presbyterian pastor did not miss a service, even to dismissing his prayer meeting twice to be present. The audiences were from every denomination and the meeting looked very much like a union one. Brother Allen commends Brother Fenstermacher as a strong and faithful preacher of the Word.

❀ ❀

"Christian Union."

I recently read with care and interest Bro. J. H. Garrison's most recent book which bears the name "Christian Union," a book of 207 pages from the press of The Christian Publishing Company.

The major part of the book is given to facts with which very many of us are quite familiar. This, however, is used as the impregnable rock-foundation for the super-structure which deals with the present day phases of Church Union. Our theory of union is daily being cast into the crucible of practice. If we are to be taken seriously by our religious neighbors when we speak in behalf of union, we must discover a way in which to co-operate freely with them while we remain absolutely loyal to what is true. Loyalty and Liberty—both to be held firmly at the same time—Brother Garrison is both clear and strong in presenting this delicate aspect of the subject. What he says here is of great practical value since it is "the truth for the times."

The fidelity of our brethren for three-quarters of a century to the New Testament basis of unity, has borne fruit. Many things do not continue as in the time of our fathers. We are face to face with the new aspects of union. This book is a sane, honest treatment of the subject with these new aspects in view. I like the book, both for its spirit and for the views set forth, and heartily commend it to the younger men of our ministry as well as the great host who are not preachers.

WM. J. WRIGHT.

❀ ❀

As We Go to Press.

Special to THE CHRISTIAN-EVANGELIST.

Lexington, Ky., Dec. 2.—Thirteen hundred people packed Central church to-night. We have had 231 additions, including to-night. Brother Spencer is enthusiastic in his splendid leadership of this great congregation. Over 1,500 members now. We close Sunday night.—Arthur K. Brooks and W. T. Brooks.

Special to THE CHRISTIAN-EVANGELIST.

Meadville, Pa.—Clarence Mitchell began the most promising meeting in our history with twelve additions and plans to pay $2,300 indebtedness. He took ill with pneumonia and meeting had to close. Brother Mitchell more than met the demands of this critical college city.—W. D. Trumbull, minister.

Special to THE CHRISTIAN-EVANGELIST.

Sebring, Ohio, Dec. 3.—Meeting two weeks old; eighty additions. We continue. Homer Sala is pastor.—Violett and Clarkson.

Special to THE CHRISTIAN-EVANGELIST.

Toledo, Ohio, Dec. 3.—Buchanan and Gardner meeting one week old. Great crowds; thirty-four added, seventeen by confession; seventeen by letter; continue.—Charles R. Oakley, minister at Wauseon, Ohio.

Special to THE CHRISTIAN-EVANGELIST.

Kansas City, Mo., Dec. 3.—Meeting continues with great interest; 104 added in thirteen days, sixty-eight to-day. We are reaping from the sowing of T. P. Haley, that grand man of God and his co-workers. Kansas City is the most inviting field for

Stockholders' Meeting.

Notice is hereby given that the annual meeting of the stockholders of the Christian Publishing Company will be held at the company's office, 2712 Pine street, St. Louis, Mo., Tuesday, January 1, 1907, at 11 o'clock, for the election of directors and for the transaction of such other business as may legally come before said meeting.

J. H. GARRISON, Pres.
GEO. L. SNIVELY, Sec.

St. Louis, Nov. 15, 1906.

the Disciples we have seen in the United States.—Small and St. John.

Special to THE CHRISTIAN-EVANGELIST.

Nelson, Neb., Dec. 3.—The Christian Church is now having a meeting. The church building is too small. Opera house engaged and crowded twice Sunday. Confessions nightly.—F. Ellsworth Day.

Special to THE CHRISTIAN-EVANGELIST.

Indianapolis, Ind., Dec. 3.—To date, 532. Continuing. Have tried for two years to get Thomas Penn Ullom to join us in evangelism and have at last succeeded. He has resigned his pastorate and will be with us from this on. The Lord hath done great things for us, whereof we are glad.—Charles Reign Scoville.

❀ ❀ ❀

OUR SIMULTANEOUS CAMPAIGNS

St. Louis Campaign.

The special simultaneous effort in St. Louis was brought to a close Sunday before last, only four of the churches having held meetings during all of the week prior to that day. The total additions to eight churches actually engaged in the protracted meetings were 512, while this number would be swelled were we to include the additions at all the churches during the month of November. At no church did the meetings last over three weeks, other than the extra Sunday. Several of the churches, such as Maplewood and Hamlett Place, continued only two weeks, they being without the presence, during part of the meeting, of their regular pastors. At East St. Louis the resignation of the pastor was accepted during the meeting. Thus these places were somewhat handicapped by local conditions. Granite City did not begin until the other meetings were practically concluded and its remoteness makes it lose much of the effect of the benefit of the simultaneous effort. The reports of the different churches follow:

	By Confession.	Otherwise.	Total.
Granite City	5	18	23
Fourth	53	15	68
East St. Louis	7	11	18
Hammett Place	5		11
Hamilton Avenue	18	20	38
Union Avenue	41	40	81
Compton Heights	55	23	78
First	118	58	176
Maplewood			19
Totals	305	188	512

As to the value of the simultaneous campaign all the pastors are agreed.

L. W. McCreary, of Hamilton Avenue, where W. F. Turner and V. E. Ridenour helped him as evangelists, says: "These meetings have broadened our sympathies and deepened our love for the other churches of our own faith here in the city. We united our prayers for the one cause, in the various churches. We rejoiced in each other's successes. A victory for one was a victory for all, and thus the unity for which our Master prayed has been more perfectly established among all the churches of Christ in St. Louis."

James M. Philputt, of the Union Avenue Church, where C. M. Chilton and C. H. Altheide were the evangelists, says: "The church was thoroughly aroused and to hundreds of our members the Christian life will henceforth be a richer, broader and diviner thing because of the meetings. Brother Chilton's preaching was a revelation to us. A great soul back of the sermon is one of the secrets of his power. An exhaustive canvass of the neighborhood was made, yielding much good material. Brother Chilton and I made sixty calls on business men in their offices down town. Our congregation is now in fine shape to face the next great enterprise—the building of the auditorium."

John L. Brandt believes thoroughly in the simultaneous effort, so much so that he brought forward a motion requesting the state board to lay plans for a state-wide simultaneous campaign in Missouri. He says that the First Church has been strengthened not only in numbers but also financially and spiritually by Herbert Yeuell's efforts, which were ably seconded by a large body of personal workers in the church. Brother Brandt conducted the meeting after Brother Yeuell left, adding 25 more to the 151 won during the evangelist's presence.

F. N. Calvin, of Compton Heights, where W. E. Harlow is the evangelist, feels that this effort in St. Louis was not really a fair test of the simultaneous meetings, which might develop much more momentum.

W. W. Dowling, senior elder of the Hammett Place Church, where C. C. Garrigues preached for two weeks, says that the meeting "quickened the spiritual pulse of the membership, inspired them with new courage and determination, and the church was so well pleased with the evangelist that he was called to the pastorate and will take up the work at an early date."

E. T. McFarland was the only pastor who held his own meeting and he regards the campaign as a great victory for our cause in North St. Louis. He lays the stress of the success in his own church on preparation and prayer. This was continued two months before the meetings began and Brother McFarland preached a series of four sermons on soul winning. He made a special feature of the music and used printers' ink to advertise.

The churches in St. Louis are not as vitally associated as are our churches in some other cities, but it is felt that the campaign has done a great deal towards cementing the bonds of fellowship. The Sunday afternoon meetings, while not as thronged as they ought to have been, were well attended and did much towards instructing some of the membership in our history and aims and making us feel the greatness of our brotherhood and of our plea.

The Indianapolis Campaign.

Four weeks of the simultaneous evangelistic campaign in Indianapolis have passed into history. While the campaign is by no means ended, five churches continuing special services at the date this report is made, it is far enough advanced to warrant an expression as to the value of the movement. We were inspired to a large degree by the Pittsburg campaign to undertake the work in this city. We rejoice greatly in our successes, but if our victory can stimulate and increase the spirit of evangelism throughout our great brotherhood, our joy will be multiplied.

The total additions reported up to Monday morning, November 26, were:

	By Confession.	Otherwise.	Total.
Central	65	118	183
Second	14	6	20
Third	263	166	429
Fourth	28	29	57
Downey Avenue	8	13	21
Sixth	51	79	130
Seventh	14	8	22
Bismarck Avenue	53	50	103
Hillside	32	17	49
Morris Street	66	84	100
Englewood	2	9	11
Olive Branch	14	11	25
North Park	42	39	81
West Park	19	43	62
Totals	671	622	1,293

It is only fair to say that Olive Branch was one week late in starting, Downey Avenue two weeks late, and that Englewood was unexpectedly left without a pastor a few weeks before the time of beginning. The following churches are continuing with increasing interest: Third, Downey Avenue, Bismarck Avenue, Olive Branch and West Park.

Considering the number of churches engaged, we believe that this is the most successful simultaneous campaign ever carried on among the Disciples.

It is of interest to know how the campaign is regarded by the pastors of our churches. The following statements show:

"The simultaneous campaign has been a blessing to our churches. It has put us all on our metal and the result has been not only a tide of additions to our church, but an awakened church."—Allan B. Philput.

"The simultaneous campaign has proven itself a success. It is a mighty engine in the hands of God and a consecrated and united church for the saving of souls. Praise the Lord."—C. B. Newnan.

"It has laid the foundation for future united work in Indianapolis. It has given every member of each congregation a feeling of participation in every meeting. It has brought more religion out of the trunks than any former movement."—C. E. Underwood.

"We have certainly had a great meeting. A great and good impression was made upon our city. We are a stronger people now."—A. L. Orcutt.

"I think our campaign has been a great success. A complete Gospel has been preached and heard by thousands that would never have been reached in one great union meeting."—D. R. Lucas.

"There are at least two advantages over the old plan of evangelistic meetings. It is a business like way of doing the Lord's work and calls the attention of the public to the church and its message. By the co-operation of the large church, and through the general religious awakening of the community the smaller congregations have opportunities for strengthening their forces which they otherwise could not have."—G. F. Powers.

"The campaign has demonstrated the value of united effort. It placed our cause before the Indianapolis public as never before."—C. A. Johnson.

"The campaign was helpful in every way. It aroused an evangelistic enthusiasm, compelled public attention, and contributed to the unification of our work in such a way as could not have been done otherwise."—Austin Hunter.

"The evangelistic campaign has been a great success. We came before the people of a great city as a united church. More attention has been given in our city papers. But all advertising should be under one committee. Practice in

working together will solve many difficulties."—F. P. Smith.

J. M. Canfield was both pastor and evangelist at Olive Branch. He is a veteran. He has been in our city work for thirty-six years, having organized five of our fourteen churches. He says: "It is glorious, an unqualified success. I rejoice to have lived to see this day. The kindly feeling among the preachers is worth everything.

It would be almost miraculous if such a campaign were so conducted as to suit all, yet the spirit of criticism has been entirely absent. All have rejoiced in the victory of each church. The splendid spirit of unity among the ministers of the city has been deepened and strengthened. With fourteen churches and seven thousand or more members we are a great people and a force to be counted in this city.

Were we to begin the campaign over, I do not now see how we could make much improvement in our plans. Every committee did its work on time and well.

To me two features are especially gratifying. First, the marked success in the younger and smaller churches. I rejoice in the great meeting of the Third Church held in the Armory, under the leadership of Charles Reign Scoville, and commanding the attention of the whole city, but I rejoice also that it in no way interfered with the work in the other churches save to stimulate. One of the most remarkable of the meetings is that at Bismarck Avenue, conducted by three Butler College students as pastor, evangelist and singer, with 103 additions, and still continued with increased interest. Second, I rejoice in there having been not the slightest friction among the workers of the city, but on the contrary a growing feeling of love and confidence and unity.

F. W. Norton.

❦ ❦

Louisville Simultaneous Revivals.

The month of November marked a decided forward step for the cause in Louisville. Five churches were engaged in simultaneous revivals and 200 were added to the congregations interested. Another good result was that the Clifton church, for which T. S. Tinsley preaches, decided to become a living link in the home society, and Crescent Hill, a neighboring suburb, was chosen as the field of service. A Bible school has been organized and James T. McKissick is at present engaged in a very interesting revival fostered by the Clifton church, and the hope is to organize a congregation. The following is a tabulated report of the five revivals:

1. Broadway Church—W. N. Briney, minister; J. V. Coombs, evangelist. Seventy added. Church greatly pleased.

2. South Louisville Church—E. B. Richey, minister; W. J. Cocke, evangelist. Forty added. Our youngest church in a new house takes aggressive position among our sisterhood of churches. Church nearly out of debt.

3. Parkland Church—G. W. Nutter, minister.

H. B. Bennett, evangelist. Forty-four added.

4. Third Church—D. F. Stafford, minister; H. D. C. MacLachlan, evangelist. Twenty-six added. Evangelist did a great work in reconciling church to the event of sale and removal to a better location.

5. Clifton Church—T. S. Tinsley, minister; J. J. Castlebury, evangelist. Thirty added; $1,500 church debt paid and congregation becomes a living link in the Home Society. Church very happy.

The Louisville churches and preachers like the simultaneous idea and next time we hope to accomplish more, since this was our first experience. We needed the prestige and co-operation of our great First Church. While Brother Powell was friendly to the movement his engagements were such as to prevent his participation. If there is any truth in the widely known adage: "As goes America so goes the world," there must be more certainty in its paraphrase, "As goes the great First Church of any city so goes the city." But we expect not to look in vain to our First Church for leadership.   T. S. Tinsley.

❦ ❦

Convention Committee.

The brethren at Norfolk, Va., held a meeting last week with a view to shaping the work of arrangement for our next international convention which is to be held there in October, 1907. The report of the nominating committee was accepted. J. T. T. Hundley, of Norfolk, was elected general chairman, and the following brethren chairmen of committees: Publicity, R. E. Steed; finance, J. F. East; pulpit supply, D. S. Henkel, of Newport News; reception, Dr. R. H. Walker; registration, J. H. Schlegri; program, Thomas N. Miranda; credentials, C. N. Williams, of Hampton; halls, W. H. Phillips, of Port Norfolk; music, M. W. Mason; transportation, W. C. Humphreys; ushers, J. F. McGinnis; communion, W. R. Jennet, of Newport News; entertainment, J. G. Holladay; local excursions, A. B. Spicer.

The question of a Disciples' building at the Jamestown Exposition, similar to that of the St. Louis Exposition, was discussed. This matter was referred to a committee of five, appointed by the chairman, Messrs. M. W. Mason, Robert Burroughs, George A. Vaiden, R. E. Steed and J. F. East to act in conjunction with the general executive committee, with power to act and, if expedient, to form a stock corporation for the erection of said building, the idea being, if possible, to erect a structure that can be used for religious purposes after the close of the Exposition, and which will cost about $5,000.

The meeting adjourned to convene in Hampton the fourth Sunday in January.

NEWS FROM MANY FIELDS

Checking the Drifting at Burrton.

One of the best meetings held for several years has just been concluded at Burrton, Kan., by David Lyon. It seems that many of the young people were becoming skeptics, but Brother Lyon's sermons on evidences have strengthened the faith of all who heard and checked the drifting of many. The outlook for more additions to follow is good, for many think the meeting closed too soon. Burrton has been regarded as a hard place to hold a revival, but this meeting has shown that the Gospel ably presented has not

W. H. Pinkerton at Carthage, Mo.

The meeting which began at Carthage, Mo., November 18, is progressing nicely. W. H. Pinkerton and F. A. Cappa and wife, who are the evangelists, were delayed in their arrival by the storm. Pastor Newell L. Sims continued the meeting from Sunday and had ten additions up till the time of the arrival of the evangelists. Prospects are good for a fine meeting. A chorus of 100 voices is being organized and the city is being thoroughly canvassed and the meeting advertised everywhere.

The Meeting at Downs, Kan.

This meeting, led by H. E. Wilhite, closed with thirty-two additions. Considering the many things to contend with it is regarded as a very successful meeting. Brother Wilhite and his wife gained the love of all our workers and outsiders as well. Mrs. Wilhite conducted a Bible drill which was both helpful and instructive. During the last ten days Edgar Tuckerman, a graduate of Lincoln, Neb., led the song service and is now employed by Brother Wilhite. He left here to conduct a meeting at Forest Avenue, Kansas City. A reception was given to the evangelist and the new members in the home of Mr. T. M. Renfro.

F. T. Roy.

David Lyon.

W. H. Pinkerton.

F. A. Cappa.

lost its power. The Burrton Christian church is, in many respects, the best church in the town. At the reception given to the new members they were made to feel that they were in fellowship, and that they were to preach Christ by letting their light shine. Otto Shirley, the pastor, entered upon his second year's pastorate December 1 and feels the stronger for this meeting.

The Broadway Christian Church, Sedalia, Mo.

A jubilee service was held at this church on November 2, in celebration of the raising of $2,100 to pay for the debt on the building. The

mortgage has now been burned and, of course, the brethren are happy to be in a building free from all incumbrance. Erected during the pastorate of F. L. Cook, the cost of the building was about $8,000. Brother Cook is honored by the church as a man and for his faithful labors, and it was a cause of regret that he could not be with his former flock on this occasion. The city churches were invited and R. C. Miller, of the East Sedalia Baptist Church, and J. M. Rudy, of the First Christian Church, made helpful addresses. T. B. Young, chairman of the official board, gave a brief history of the church and Mrs. M. F.

Kaler, president of the Aid Society, spoke of the material part the women had taken in assisting the church. During the past eight years they have averaged $60 a month and during the last year they have raised over $1,000. Surely such an Aid Society is worthy of the name.

A meeting has just been begun at this church. A. N. Lindsey, of Clinton, Mo., who is well known in the state and has been very successful in revival work, is to assist Brother Hamann. This effort is being entered upon in the spirit of prayer. Twenty cottage prayer-meetings were planned for last Wednesday evening before the opening of the meeting.

W. F. Hamann, pastor.

Broadway Church, Sedalia, Mo.

A. N. Lindsey, of Clinton, Mo.

The Georgia Christian Missionary Convention.

The happiest, most harmonious and most enthusiastic state convention ever held by the churches of Christ in Georgia came to a close the night of November 22. Every address and speech and talk made during the convention was full of hope and harmony and progress. New zeal and new determination seemed to be in every heart and a new era is upon us in Georgia. Every preacher and every church in the state is ready for greater activity in the service of the Master. Valdosta, the beautiful city of 9,000 people, in which the convention was held, gave the convention delightful entertainment. The church and city were so much pleased with the convention that they asked to be allowed to entertain it again in 1907. The Georgia preachers present were: Howard T. Cree, president, Augusta; J. H. Wood, Augusta; H. King Pendleton, B. P. Smith, A. E. Seddon, E. L. Shelnutt, Atlanta; W. A. Chastain, Athens; P. H. Mears and S. S. Landrum, Winder; O. A. Moore, Texas; D. R. Piper, Watkinsville; T. G. Linkous, Sandersville; G. R. Cleveland, Wrightsville; J. A. Jenson, Tennille; A. B. Herring, R. I. Hinely, C. R. Miller, Lake Park; R. W. Simpson, Macon; R. W. Wallace, Valdosta; N. B. Buckley and A. D. Wade, Fitzgerald; W. B. Shaw, Baldwin. Visiting preachers were: A. McLean, Cincinnati; Dr. E. I. Osgood, missionary to China; George B. Ranshaw, Cincinnati; George W. Muckley, Kansas City; J. H. Mohorter, St. Louis; H. C. Bowen, Cincinnati; Sam J. White, Florida; Miss Mattie Pounds, Indianapolis. The convention regretted the absence of beloved J. S. Lamar, of Augusta; J. H. Hughes, of Macon, and J. H. Garrison, of St. Louis. These expected to be present but illness kept them away. They were tenderly remembered by the convention.

A brief outline of the proceedings is all I can give you here. The opening session of the convention was a missionary rally conducted by A. McLean and Dr. E. I. Osgood. It is useless to say that the large audience was simply electrified by these men upon the great theme so dear to their hearts. They made many deeper conversions to foreign missions. How can any one hear such men and such a theme and close his eyes, his heart and his pocketbook to the world's needs? Brother McLean and Dr. Osgood were given one hour Tuesday morning and again they charmed the convention with their missionary addresses. Georgia believes that A. McLean is one of the greatest men in the world and his presence was a benediction. We want Brother McLean and Dr. Osgood to attend our state convention in 1907.

Tuesday morning, November 20, from 10:30 to 12:30 the Woman's Society for Georgia Missions held an interesting session, presided over by the president, Mrs. B. O. Miller, of Augusta. This society, which confines its work to Georgia, showed prosperity and bright prospects for the future.

The sessions of the afternoon and evening were given to the Christian Woman's Board of Missions, with State President Mrs. B. P. Smith, of Atlanta, in the chair. This society reported the best year's work in its history. Miss Mattie Pounds, of Indianapolis, Ind., delivered two addresses and added much toward making these sessions very interesting, helpful and successful.

Wednesday morning the Georgia Christian Missionary Society held its first session, the popular president, Howard T. Cree, of Augusta, in the chair. The state board and corresponding secretary and treasurer made the best reports in the history of our work in Georgia and the convention was perfectly delighted over the reports and the fact that the society is out of debt and over $100 in the treasury. Georgia has adopted a new plan for state evangelization and it is working like a charm. The convention and visiting preachers were enthusiastic over the plan and no longer consider it an experiment.

From 11 to 12:30 George B. Ranshaw, of Cincinnati, field secretary of the American Christian Missionary Society, and George W. Muckley, secretary of the Church Extension, addressed the convention on the work of "Home Missions" and "Church Extension." Both addresses were considered masterpieces. These men are in their right places and no state loves them more than Georgia.

The afternoon session was devoted to Christian Endeavor and Sunday-school work. Mrs. Charles Goodman, of the First Church, Atlanta, presided over the Endeavor session and W. H. Ropey, of Macon, over the Sunday-school session. Both of these periods were very enthusiastic and helpful.

The evening address was delivered by the president, Howard T. Cree, of Augusta, and was one of the leading addresses of the convention. At the close of his address he called for pledges for state work and in a few minutes $1,500 were raised. The First Church, Atlanta, started the enthusiasm by pledging $300. Valdosta stepped in just behind and other churches and individuals followed with the above result. Such enthusiasm was never seen in a Georgia convention and everybody seemed happy. It was a fitting climax for the day.

Thursday, the last day, was another great day. "Our Country Churches, Their Importance, Their Needs, Their Officers, Their Preachers," were ably discussed by D. R. Piper, of Watkinsville; John H. Wood, Augusta; A. B. Wade, Fitzgerald, and O. A. Moore, Texas. These were followed by J. H. Mohorter, of St. Louis, who delivered the most touching address of the convention on "Benevolence." This was Brother Mohorter's first visit to Georgia and I must say he took possession. We could not resist. I wish these visiting brethren could know how much they helped us in our convention and how much we appreciated them and their help. But we will try to show them in December, in March, in May and in September.

Just at the close of the morning session a telegram of Christian courtesy was received from the Georgia state Baptist convention in session at Cartersville. This courtesy was gracefully accepted and acknowledged. This was the first time that fraternal greetings have been exchanged in Georgia between these two bodies in convention and such greetings indicate warmer feelings and closer relations between these bodies so closely allied.

About the same time a telegram was received from Dr. G. A. Nunnally, of La Grange, Ga., requesting the co-operation of the convention in the prohibition movement in Georgia. Such a resolution was adopted by the convention.

The afternoon session was devoted to the work in our cities in Georgia and to the work of the Georgia Education Society. Addresses and talks were made by Cree, Pendleton, Wood, who presided over the session of the education society, Chastain, Shelnutt, Linkous and Seddon.

At the evening session talks were made by W. B. Shaw, of Baldwin; J. H. Mohorter, of St. Louis, and J. H. Wood, of Augusta. Offerings were taken for the Orphanage at Baldwin and for the Georgia Christian Education Society. Then followed a great address by G. B. Ranshaw, on "Christian Union."

Quite a number of minute talks were then made by delegates and visitors, including Methodists and Baptists, and the happy convention closed. Much praise is due Brother R. W. Wallace, pastor of the splendid church in Valdosta, for the success of the convention. The delegates were delighted with Valdosta, the entertainment, the people and the climate and went away with happy recollections of the same.

The next convention goes to the First Church, Atlanta.

For the benefit of Georgia readers I want to say in conclusion that one surprising feature of the convention was the report of the committee on nominations, which was as follows: "In view of the fact that the present plan of work was inaugurated by the existing state board and that the members of this board are perfectly familiar with the conditions and needs of the field, we recommend the re-election of the officers and members without change." E. L. SHELNUTT.

Changes.

Bennett, J. C.—Kahoka, Mo., to Bisbee, Ariz.
Corey, N. E.—Augusta, to Colchester, Ill.
Deadman, Roy E.—Minburn, to Box 33, U. P. Station, Des Moines, Ia.
Crowden, A. M.—Carbondale, Ill., to Osceola, Ia.
Hubbell, H. H.—Lewiston, to Grangeville, Idaho.
Lindsey, Arthur, N.—New Franklin, to Clinton, Mo.
McGhee, N. B.—Gage, to Lordsburg, N. M.
Moore, W. A.—32 N. E., to S. Sixth and K., Tacoma, Wash.
O'Conner, T. J.—Eldora, to Sigourney, Ia.
Porter, Roy Linton—510 Kirby St., Lake Charles, to Cheneyville, La.
Reiter, A. F.—21 South Stricker St., Baltimore, Md., to Bluffton, O.
Smith, G. Lyle.—Waco, to Bor Rockwall Ave., Terrell, Texas.
Stivers, John T.—Dodge City, Kan., to La Junta, Colo.
Shelburne, W. J.—East Nashville, Tenn., to Tullahoma, Tenn.
Sharpe, Edward O.—Winchester, Ill., to 502 Oakland, San Antonio, Texas.
Tinsley, Lee—NineVeh, to R. F. D. 4, Franklin, Ind.
Warner, Gregory—McLemoresville, to Hollow Rock, Tenn.
Wagner, Clarence E.—Shelbyville, Mo., to Yates Center, Kan.

AT THE GEORGIA CONVENTION.

Southern California and Arizona Items.

For some time our missionary society has had under contemplation the matter of undertaking the work among the colored people in Los Angeles. E. F. Henderson, a well-known colored preacher, formerly of Missouri, has been employed as an evangelist to labor among his people. Headquarters have been found on what is known as the Furlong Tract in Los Angeles, on the Long Beach line. This is a community of about 100 families, with practically no convenient church privileges. Here a lot has been bought and a chapel will be erected. The evangelizing board desired to commend this work to the favorable consideration of the brethren in all the churches. Brother Henderson will, from time to time, be visiting the churches in the interest of this project. We hope he will be cordially received everywhere. His business is to solicit funds which will be turned over to a committee to be expended in this work. The standing committee to have charge of this is composed of Charles Goodwin, W. J. A. Smith, and Grant K. Lewis.——Leander Lane, of La Canada, recently held a short meeting at Hemet with good results.——J. W. Utter, who, for years has been the efficient minister of the church at Covina, has been called by the Broadway Church, Los Angeles, to assist Brother B. F. Coulter in the ministry of that great and growing congregation. He has already entered upon his duties.——W. G. Conley has resigned at Redlands and has already entered upon his work as pastor at Covina.——An open door is set before us in the seaside town of Redondo. Acting under instructions from our board, Eugene Burr, of Santa Monica, has begun a meeting which it is confidently expected, will result in the organization of a church.——Something like six months ago Mrs. Woolery, the state C. W. B. M. organizer, visited the Needles and organized an auxiliary. This was at the solicitation of a few faithful women who lived in this isolated city where we have no church. Now comes a call from this same devoted band for an evangelist that a meeting be held and a church organized. The secretary is under instructions to visit this place at an early date and see that their wishes are carried out. This reminds us of similar results attending an apostolic visit to a place by the river side where women were wont to gather for prayer. God be praised for faithful women.——Madison A. Hart's work at Pomona prospers greatly. He read a splendid paper before the ministerial association last Monday on

"The Training a Child Should Receive in the Sunday-school."——Jesse P. McKnight, the highly esteemed minister of Magnolia Avenue Church, Los Angeles, has been very ill for a few weeks. He is now recuperating and hopes are entertained that he may soon be able to be heard from his pulpit again. His work has been supplied by C. C. Bentley and Frank G. Tyrrell.—— At the magnificent property of the First Church, some account of which has appeared in THE CHRISTIAN-EVANGELIST, last Lord's day a special Sunday-school service brought the attendance at the Sunday-school hour to above 430. We congratulate Pastor Smither upon the success of this largest and latest venture of this great church.—— J. F. Sloan, who recently returned to the coast from Kansas, now serves the church at Sawtelle, the seat of Southern California's Old Soldiers' Home. He resides at Willowbrook.——Things are moving harmoniously and enthusiastically with the church at Pasadena. Here F. M. Dowling, assisted by Edgar C. Riley, is leading the church in a $50,000 building proposition. This is a great enterprise but the leaders and hosts in the "crown of the valley" are equal to the task.—— A good natured rivalry is about to begin between the Long Beach church and that of Magnolia Avenue, Los Angeles. It is in the nature of a contest in Sunday-school work. The average attendance of each is about 300.——The mother instinct of babies shows itself in their love for dolls. This is how it came that our baby church in Los Angeles presided over by the energetic E. H. Kellar, is founding a mission Sunday-school. The city's growth has proceeded in a southward course far beyond the neighborhood of the South Main Street Church. A lot has been selected in a new community where we already have about eighteen families. As soon as a chapel can be built the school will be organized.——At the August convention a simultaneous campaign in Southern California was postponed from the spring until the fall of 1907. The exact date to be fixed by the executive committee. At a recent meeting of this committee it was decided to fix the date for the last Sunday in October. Grant K. Lewis was made chairman of a committee on evangelism and instructed to take up the correspondence with both churches and evangelists that preparations may be forwarded.——A. F. Cory, missionary from China, was to address a rally of all our churches of Greater Los Angeles at Magnolia Avenue Church on November 18.—— W. T. Adams, of Washington, is winning his way into the hearts of the people at Corona and Arlington. Great interest is manifested already in the beginning of his vigorous work.——Oscar Sweeney and wife were among the new faces greeted at our preachers' meeting this month. They were given a royal reception by the Rialto

church the day after their arrival. This little band of Disciples are aglow with enthusiasm over their work. Brother and Sister Sweeney will also care for the church at Colton. H. Elliott Ward did splendid missionary service by holding the fort at these points the latter part of the summer.——The evangelizing board at its recent meeting decided to push vigorously the matter of Arizona missions. The secretary is under instructions to visit our Arizona churches and secure their advice and co-operation in the matter of evangelizing new fields. Among the growing communities which present great opportunities are Tucson, Prescott, Globe, San Carlos and a score of other towns of smaller magnitude. So the work presses upon us from every side. Let the prayers of a great brotherhood be for the spirit of understanding and wisdom and consecration to rest upon our workers everywhere.

Long Beach, Cal.   GRANT K. LEWIS.

THE DEVOTIONAL SPIRIT
Is quickened by, Alone With God, The Heavenward Way, Half Hour Studies at the Cross. Read them and meditate, then pass to a friend. Each, 75 cents, or the trio, postpaid, $2.00.

CHRISTIAN PUBLISHING CO.,
St. Louis, Mo.

☞ The Alabama Convention.

The greatest convention in the history of the brotherhood in the state is a thing of the past, closing yesterday at noon.

There were more than a hundred visitors from all portions of the state, representing about forty organized congregations that are in sympathy with our missionary work. The program, formerly published, was closely followed, and there were but few absentees. J. A. Lord, W. R. Warren and Mrs. Grant did not come. Mrs. Moses' place was filled by Miss Mattie Pounds, and the presence of Dr. E. I. Osgood, missionary to China; James C. Coggans, of Black Mountain, N. C., and H. C. Bowen, of "The Christian Weekly," Cincinnati, were agreeable surprises to all of us.

Great sermons and addresses were delivered by W. T. Moore, of Columbia, Mo.; J. H. Garrison, of St. Louis; A. McLean, of Cincinnati; George W. Muckley, of Kansas City; Miss Mattie Pounds, of Indianapolis; George B. Ranshaw, of Cincinnati; Dr. E. I. Osgood, of China; J. C. Coggins, of North Carolina; H. C. Bowen, of Cincinnati; Allen R. Moore, of Birmingham; J. C. Caldwell, of Selma; G. F. Cuthrel, of Oxford; J. R. McWane, of Birmingham; J. H. Hill, of Landersville; Belt White, of Anniston; J. H. Moborter, of St. Louis; H. Galt Braxton, of Birmingham; Thomas Lenox, of Athens, L. O. Herrold, of Jasper; J. B. Woodin, of Greenville; H. C. Sedinger, of Athens; B. F. Stiff, of Blocton; D. P. Taylor, of Bessemer; Dr. E. C. Anderson, of Anniston, and Claude E. Hill, of Mobile.

The new state bord is composed of Allen R. Moore, president; J. C. Caldwell, vice-president; E. C. Anderson, corresponding secretary and treasurer; D. P. Taylor, recording secretary; E. E. Linthicum, J. M. Cranford, H. G. Braxton, A. A. Oden and J. W. Henry.

Eighteen hundred dollars, including the $400 appropriated by the home board at Cincinnati, were raised for state missions for the ensuing year. This will be increased during the year to practically $2,500 by new subscriptions.

S. P. Spiegel, of Birmingham, was unanimously chosen state evangelist for the coming year, and many of the struggling congregations in destitute fields were aided by small appropriations. The prospects are very flattering indeed for a great year's work.

The initiatory steps were taken to establish a Bible school at Selma under the leadership of Jesse C. Caldwell, for the purpose of preparing young men for the ministry in Alabama at the least possible cost.

Our nonco-operating brethren are coming into this work, as fast as they understand it. And we were glad to welcome one or two able ministers, who attended a convention for the first time, and were thoroughly converted to state missions and all other missionary work, by what they heard and saw.

Jasper, Ala., where, under the efficient leadership of L. O. Herrold, they are completing an elegant new church, was chosen as the place for the twenty-second convention.

The committee on obituaries reported the deaths of twenty of our membership throughout the state. The other committees made appropriate reports and at noon Monday, after a splendid address on "The Holy Spirit," by Dr. J. H. Garrison, "God Be With You" was sung and the convention adjourned.　　J. W. HENRY.

Mobile, Ala.

❧ ❧

Kokendoffer at Hannibal.

A two weeks' meeting has just concluded at Hannibal, conducted by A. W. Kokendoffer, of Mexico. There were thirty-one accessions; twenty-two of these by confession. Levi Marshall, during whose pastorate at Hannibal there have been 937 accessions, writes that Brother Kokendoffer "has an evangelistic temperament and should be in the field all the time. He spoke with great

THE DEMAND CONTINUES

For The Victory of Faith, by E. L. Powell. Twenty-one Masterly Addresses, postpaid, $1.00.

CHRISTIAN PUBLISHING CO.,
St. Louis, Mo.

---

spiritual power from a well-stored mind and consecrated heart." The "Hannibal Journal" gave considerable space to the meeting, and at no service during the June convention was the house more densely packed than on the concluding Sunday night. Of the thirty-one additions twenty-seven were men and boys. Brother Marshall is, of course, a princely fellow and greatly beloved by all the Hannibal people.

❧ ❧

Cincinnati Letter.

Scoville, Smith and Kendall were in Cincinnati November 19, for a rally in the interest of an evangelistic campaign to be held next year. The brotherhood in the vicinity was well represented. Music Hall, the largest auditorium in the city, is the place selected. Cincinnati, as well as the whole brotherhood, will look forward to this meeting.——Good meetings have been held recently at Richmond Street, Norwood, Dayton, Ky., Lockland, Lawrenceburg, Ind., and at Central, with Pinkerton and Saxton leading. These meetings all resulted in about 125 additions. Latonia, Ky., came in about the time these closed and at last report had had twenty-five additions. P. H. Duncan is doing the preaching. S. Boyd White is being assisted in a good meeting now at Mt. Healthy by J. W. Hagin, of Covington.—— We are sorry to lose George A. Miller, who has been for nearly thirteen years at Fifth Street, Covington. He goes, to Washington to take up a great work and we wish him a happy and fruitful ministry there. Bro. Milo Atkinson, of Marion, Ind., who has been chosen to succeed him, is no stranger in our city and his return to us on January, 1907, will be the renewing of sweet fellowship.——The congregation at Camp Washington hopes to be in its new house in the near future.——The Central Church is enjoying splendid growth in numbers, and in the audiences at the Sunday services.　　W. G. Loucks,

Station R.

A Church "Absorbing" the Community.

For four years J. N. McConnell held a meeting at Pleasant Hill, Ore., with the result that forty-four were added to the church, twenty-eight of these being by confession. Many thought that nearly everybody in this community belonged to the church, for Pleasant Hill is one of the best moral and religious communities I have found. The people stand up for the neighborhood and the church with the result that Pleasant Hill is known far and wide, as a sociable and religious neighborhood. There is one church only—the Christian church, and when any one moves into the community the church immediately begins to absorb that one, and in a short time if he is at all "absorbable" the process of making a Christian only is completed. It is a pleasure and joy to work with such a body of believers. We were sorry to see Brother McConnell go, but he had another meeting to hold at Aumsville.

MARION F. HORN.

Indian Territory.

The summer is ended, the harvest is passed, the election is over. Crops have been abundant, all lines of commercialism pushing, and the weather ideal. Five circuses have been doing the territory, and minor attractions innumerable. We have held more revivals thus far during the autumn than were ever held by our people, I presume, during any autumn, and with less satisfactory results. The evil effects of political campaigns are already felt in the new state. R. E. Rosenstine succeeded in constituting a congregation at Ember, also one at Tuttle, and is now in a meeting at Sulphur.——George A. Wolf gathered in about 30 into the fold at Hartshorne. He is now at Haileyville. He baptized 23 Sunday afternoon, had three more confessions Sunday night, with others to follow. He goes to Dow next, thence to Poteau.——Brothers Wolf and Rosenstine are regular evangelists at this time in the employ of the Indian Territory Missionary Cooperation.——About ten other meetings have been held under the auspices of our cooperation with more or less success—more generally less. D. N. Manley, of New York, goes to Okmulgee, G. N. Guest to Ada, J. W. Hilderbrandt to Wealaka, J. S. Crouch to Pauls Valley and Lindsay.—J. T. Hawkins, Cor. Sec.

An Interesting Company.

We had the pleasure of a most interesting company at the Durham habitat in California a few days ago. One of our guests was Sister Eliza Swift Saxe, born in Bowling Green, Mo., in 1827, who came to California in 1862 by overland caravan. Her mother was one Margaret Campbell, a daughter of William Campbell, a younger brother of Alexander Campbell. This makes a relationship to that great family that is worthy of mention and a pride to any family ancestral history. Although our sister is in her eightieth year her mind is active and she is a great reader and thinker. She has reared a family of thirteen and of these four sons and one daughter are still living. Her brother, Hon. John Swift, was minister to Japan under President Harrison, and died in Tokio.

Another of our guests was Sister Sue E. Jones Grant, of Woodland, Cal. Sister Sue E. Grant's name is a household word in California, because of her great activity in the Christian women's work in our state. The Grant family came to California in 1873. Professor Grant was associated with President B. H. Smith in college work in Canton, Mo., for many years and for a number of years was in Hesperian College, California. But one of the most interesting features of Sister Grant's historic life is that she is the founder of Eureka College, Ill. It was in 1847, as a young teacher, that she opened a young ladies' select school with seventeen pupils in the little village of Walnut Grove. Returning to Jacksonville the next year to complete her course of study Brothers Lindsey and Fisher returned from Bethany and opened a mixed school called "Walnut Grove Academy," and after a time they named the place Eureka. Since the war our alma mater, Abing-

---

don College, was combined with Eureka, which has adopted our alumni. Sister Grant afterward was associated with Professor Williams in founding Columbia (Mo.) Female College, now Christian College, and one of the best schools in the United States. It was a pleasure to scatter flowers in the pathway of these worthy historic women.

Other important guests were Brother and Sister J. H. McCullough, who came to California in 1877. He was one of the founders of the

MRS. SUE E. GRANT,
Associated in the Founding of Eureka and Christian Colleges.

"Christian Standard." Brother McCullough is now the oldest of our preachers who is actively engaged in the ministry in California. He is now "holding the fort" for the united churches in San Jose, till their minister arrives from Indiana.

While Brother McCullough is the oldest preacher he has not been preaching in California as long as the writer of these lines, for the Durhams came out in 1871.

J. DURHAM.

DEDICATIONS.

Shiloh, Anderson County, Ky.

A new church building was recently dedicated here, all the necessary money to clear off the debt being raised with a fair balance on hand for new pews. I was assisted by the regular minister, D. W. Case, of Lexington, Ky. This dedication is part of the work of our Lawrenceburg church toward our Centennial aims. We have helped another church in the county with a meeting and two others by Sunday afternoon preaching, and our own work is much strengthened thereby.

WALTER C. GIBBS.

Jacksonville, Ill.

The dedicatory exercises of the Second Christian Church were carried out in the auditorium and not on the lawn as had been proposed. The auditorium was not large enough to accommodate all who wanted to attend and every foot of standing room was occupied. The Third Christian Church, of Bloomington, sent its choir to assist the local one. Evangelist R. A. Whittington

---

read the Scriptures. The opening prayer was made by John W. Kirk. E. M. Harlis made some pastoral remarks and J. R. O. Smith preached the sermon. After a talk by Russell F. Thrapp the collection was taken, which amounted to $278, though since then it has been increased to over $300.

E. M. HARLIS.

Salem, Ill.

The corner stone of the new Christian church at Salem, the birthplace of Hon. William Jennings Bryan, was laid on November 11. The exercises were under the direction of Elder F. O. Fannon, who has charge of the work at Salem. The edifice is to be a handsome structure, constructed of pressed brick with stone trimmings, and will cost when completed from $20,000 to $25,000. Senator Charles E. Hull, chairman of the building committee, stated that all financial obligations had been met to date. Elder John A. Williams, the first pastor of the Salem congregation, and who is in his 87th year, was the guest of honor. He delivered a reminiscent address relating incidents about the pioneer work of the Christian church in this, Marion county, which has sixteen active congregations at the present time. The Christian church is forging rapidly to the front in this section. There are 25,000 Disciples of Christ in Southern Illinois. New churches are being built while a number are contemplating erecting new buildings in the near future. A new church was recently erected at Carmi. Kimmundy will either build a new house or an addition in the near future. Mt. Carmel is about to decide in favor of erecting a new church house, while Centralia is contemplating the erection of a $20,000 edifice. J. F. Rosborough, pastor of the Centralia church, is president of the seventh district of southern Illinois, which includes twenty-two counties. R. H. Robertson, of DuQuoin, is president of the eighth district, which includes the remaining fourteen counties of southern Illinois, which are located in the extreme southern portion of the state. A good and effective work is being accomplished throughout both districts.

HARRIS DANTZ,
City Editor Centralia Daily Democrat.

Evangelistic

We invite ministers and others to send reports of meetings, additions and other news of the churches. It is especially requested that additions be reported as "by confession and baptism," or "by letter."

California.

Orange.—Two additions by conversion Nov. 11. Work here is prospering.—A. N. Glover, minister.

Red Bluff, Nov. 19.—The meeting at this place is doing well. S. M. Martin is stirring the community. Meeting two weeks old with 26 added to date, 19 yesterday.—George A. Webb, singer.

Dinuba, Nov. 26.—Our meeting with A. E. Mackey closed November 18 with 18 added—seven by baptism and 11 by statement. One confession and one by letter at yesterday's services.—R. A. Staley.

Colorado.

Colorado Springs, Nov. 26.—Three confessions here Sunday and one by letter. One confession at our last prayer-meeting. Last Tuesday night I closed a revival with Janus M. Bailey at Frankfort, Mo., with 26 additions, a goodly number considering the field. Brother Bailey is not only a good preacher but a fine singing evangelist.—Crayton S. Brooks.

Illinois.

Williamsville, Nov. 21.—Four baptisms at regular services Sunday evening.—C. D. Haskell, minister.

Greenville, Nov. 26.—Two confessions and baptisms at regular services yesterday. Outlook never so bright.—Tally Defrees.

Camp Point, Nov. 29.—An interesting meeting here. Gilbert Jones, of Marshall, Ill., is the evangelist.—A. R. Davis, singer.

Mason, Nov. 24.—Closed a ten days' meeting with the church of Springertown last night with nine confessions.—W. S. Mesnard.

El Dara, Nov. 27.—Meeting two weeks old. Forty-five confessions, two restored and one by statement. We continue.—W. E. Spicer, evangelist; J. D. Williams, minister.

Fairfield, Nov. 22.—We have had 15 additions to date in meeting here. Despite many obstacles the interest continues and crowds increase.—Allen T. Shaw, pastor; M. W. Yocum, evangelist.

Sullivan, Nov. 25.—Just closed a ten days' meeting at Cadwell, a little town ten miles from here. There were 27 additions in all and the church built up and strengthened.—J. G. McNutt.

Mason City, Nov. 30.—Seventeen added to date in our meeting here. Seventy added in past sixteen months. Seven at Mt. Pleasant in October. Membership of this church trebled in past sixteen months.—O. C. Bolman.

Edinburg, Nov. 24.—We have just returned from Chandlerville, where we assisted Brother Coleman, the preacher, in a two weeks' rally, which resulted in 22 accessions, 20 of whom were conversions.—D. W. Conner and E. E. Nelms.

Indiana.

Connersville, Nov. 26.—Meeting with home forces thirteen days old, with 26 added—22 by baptism. Continue.—James C. Burkhardt.

Indianapolis, Nov. 22.—Closed meeting of 21 days with 124 added at the Sixth Church. Begin meeting at Sharon, Pa., Nov. 25.—H. F. MacLane, evangelist.

Indianapolis, Nov. 27.—There were 25 additions in the meeting at the Olive Branch Christian Church of this city. Some of these were reported before.—J. M. Canfield.

Indianapolis, Nov. 26.—Our meeting with the Morris Street Church closed last night with 100 added—66 confessions. Thomas L. Cooksey did the preaching.—C. A. Johnson, pastor.

Middletown, Nov. 23.—L. E. Murray, minister of the church here, and myself, as leader of song and soloist, began a meeting Sunday last. There have been five additions thus far.—F. E. Trucksess.

Rensselaer, Nov. 26.—Wilson and Lintt have been here for a week and a great meeting is on. Forty additions yesterday and 13 previously, and one confession before the meeting began.—G. H. Clarke.

Indianapolis, Nov. 24.—Closed last night with over 50 added at the Fourth Christian Church. E. L. Frazier, as evangelist, did powerful and telling work and things were well organized by C. T. Underwood, the pastor.—H. K. Shields.

Plainfield, Nov. 27.—Our meeting closed last night. There were 29 additions, 18 by baptism, and it was, in many respects, a remarkable meeting, one of the best in the history of this church. A. L. Crim, of Irvington, Ind., did the preaching.—I. N. Grisso.

Shelbyville, Nov. 26.—Three confessions here yesterday. There have been 28 additions, including these three, not previously reported—11 by letter and statement and 17 by confession. Just closed a successful meeting with O. E. Tomes, the pastor, at Hillside church in Indianapolis.—H. O. Pritchard.

Indianapolis, Nov. 29.—There were 128 additions in the meeting at the Bismarck Avenue Christian Church. Eleven added the last night. The meeting was conducted by students of Butler College who were, at the same time, carrying full college work. Carl Barnett was the leader of song and Clay Trusty acted as evangelist. F. G. Powers is the pastor.—Clay Trusty.

Iowa.

Woodbine, Nov. 26.—Four additions by baptism recently.—B. F. Hall.

Altoona, Nov. 26.—One by baptism yesterday, making 11 in four months.—J. Windbigler, minister.

Des Moines, Nov. 26.—Just closed a meeting of 24 days at Elliott with 28 added. I am at Whiting for a short meeting.—C. L. Organ, state evangelist.

Elliott, Nov. 23.—Twenty-four days' meeting with 28 additions—17 baptisms, others by letter and statement. C. L. Organ, the evangelist, left a fine feeling among us.—Samuel B. Ross, minister.

Hamburg.—Have just closed a good meeting at Hamburg. Ninety-seven came into the church. The pastor, Isaac Elder, and his wife, deserve special mention. J. E. Lintt led the singing.—W. L. Harris, evangelist.

Moulton, Nov. 25.—Our meeting is one week old with 24 confessions and a deep spiritual interest. Nelson Trimble, minister; Arthur Stout, evangelist, and Hallie Fowler, director of music, are doing a good work.—G. T. Moore.

Des Moines, Dec. 1.—We closed a successful meeting at the Park Avenue Church on November 28, which ran over four Lord's days. The local minister did the preaching. There were 33 additions—12 by letter, 18 by baptism, and three from other sources. Frank A. Wilkinson, of Albia, Ia., proved an excellent leader of song and splendid soloist.—F. D. Macy, minister.

Kansas.

Eureka, Dec. 1.—Six additions here since last report.—G. F. Bradford, pastor.

Cherryvale, Nov. 26.—One baptism here last night. Three added by letter Nov. 4.—B. D. Gillispie.

Niotaze, Nov. 27.—Began meeting here last night. Good audience and splendid interest.—J. P. Haner, evangelist.

Farlington, Nov. 27.—Am in a good meeting here. In a meeting a few months ago there were nine additions which were not reported.—L. H. Koeprel.

Plainville, Nov. 23.—Fifty-two to date. Jubilee to-night. Large prospects ahead. Neal Overman with C. C. Gordner is the strong evangelistic team.—N. Ferd Engle.

Arkansas City, Nov. 20.—The meeting closed last Sunday with 138 additions. This has been a great meeting, in some respects the greatest the church has ever had.—M. Lee Sorey.

Dighton, Nov. 30.—J. B. Mayfield and George A. Butler have closed a meeting here. Three baptisms, three by letter or statement and the church greatly benefited.—William M. Mayfield, minister.

McPherson, Nov. 20.—Closed 18 days' meeting with the church at Potwin, Kan., where Oscar Hunsaker ministers. There were nine accessions. The church was put on a better financial footing and better organized for work.—W. A. Morrison.

Kentucky.

Lawrenceburg, Nov. 19.—Our work here is prospering. Four added by letter and four baptized since last report.—Walter C. Gibbs.

Massachusetts.

Everett, Dec. 1.—Three confessions this week. J. N. Robbins is evangelist.—A. T. June, pastor.

Michigan.

Bloomingdale, Nov. 26.—J. S. Raum, of Gale, Mich., has just closed a very successful meeting for us, resulting in 21 additions—17 by confession and baptism and four otherwise.—H. L. Maltman, minister.

Minnesota.

Fairmont, Nov. 26.—Closed a short meeting at Horicon Church, eight miles east. Thirteen were added by statement and immersion. Miss McBeth's singing was highly appreciated, as well as the helpfulness of brethren and friends.—J. P. Childs, district evangelist.

Missouri.

Webb City, Nov. 28.—Forty added in nine days.—W. E. M. Hackleman.

Clinton, Nov. 15.—Meeting closed, Twenty-four additions.—Arthur N. Lindsey.

Braymer, Nov. 24.—Two baptisms and one reclaimed since last report.—S. W. Crutcher.

Kansas City, Nov. 30.—Recently closed a meeting at Mt. Gilead. Direct result, 14 baptisms and one reclaimed.—J. T. Webb.

Randolph, Nov. 23.—I have received 20 into the congregations in my regular work this fall. Fourteen were baptized.—T. W. Cottingham.

Chillicothe, Nov. 22.—Three baptisms in last ten days. Eight additions last Sunday. The work is in a healthy and encouraging growth.—James N. Crutcher.

Missouri City, Nov. 24.—We closed our meeting at Missouri City with 34 additions—23 by primary obedience. Brother Ely, of Kansas City, Kan., did the preaching.—E. T. Davis.

Norborne, Nov. 23.—Just closed short meeting with church at Tina. Ten additions—seven by confession and baptism, two by statement and one from another religious body.—C. C. Taylor.

St. Joseph, Nov. 30.—We are assisting M. M. Goode in a meeting at the Wyatt Park Church in this city. Meeting has been in progress ten days. Sixteen confessions to date.—H. A. Northcutt, evangelist, Frank C. Huston, singer.

New Hampton, Nov. 22.—Our meeting is two weeks old with 14 added—two by letter, nine by confession, and three from another religious body. J. T. Alsip is the pastor here and is greatly beloved by this people.—J. S. Clements.

Kansas City, Nov. 25.—J. H. O. Smith and Professor Saxton conducted a three weeks' meeting at the South Prospect Church, which closed last Friday. There were several more accessions to-day, bringing the immediate results up to 80 additions.—F. R. Stutzman.

New Jersey.

East Orange.—Two accessions to the church here.—L. N. D. Wells.

Missouri City, Dec. 1.—I recently held a three weeks' meeting here, resulting in 34 additions, of which none were by letter, and the church [illegible]—E. L. Ely.

Ohio.

Lucas.—Am in a meeting at this place. Great interest. Four additions last night. Many turned away for lack of room. Asa Hull is leading the singing.—W. P. Murray.

Bellefontaine, Nov. 26.—Two added yesterday—one by letter and one by confession, making eight since we closed meeting. Great prospects for future work.—Roy L. Brown.

Youngstown, Nov. 26.—Recently closed a short but good meeting with Wilson and Lintt as evangelists. Accessions to the church 80, baptisms, 49.—Walter S. Goode, minister Central Church.

Oklahoma.

Sand Creek.—I preached one week at Hepler, Kan., with two additions. Discontinued on account of bad weather and sickness in the community. Begin here to-night.—Clyde Sharp.

Oregon.

Corvallis, Nov. 28.—Our three weeks' meeting closed November 11 with 16 additions, nine baptisms. There have been 51 added, 23 by confession and baptism, since we began here April 1.—T. S. Handsaker.

Tillamook, Nov. 22.—Have had extremely stormy weather for two weeks of meeting, but have had good crowds most of the time. Will continue until December 5. A. W. Shapper is doing fine work as chorus leader.—George C. Ritchey, evangelist for northwest district.

Texas.

Waco, Nov. 30.—Twenty-eight additions since October 1.—Charles A. Lockhart.

Llano, Nov. 19.—There were four additions to the church yesterday by letter.—J. J. Cramer.

Virginia.

Roanoke, Nov. 23.—We have just closed a meeting with the Church Avenue church, conducted by C. E. Elmore. The services continued two weeks, resulting in 27 accessions. The church was refreshed and strengthened.—R. E. Elmore.

Washington.

Waterville, Nov. 21.—The meeting at Ritzville was a pronounced success; not because of the large ingathering, but because of a spiritual development. The meeting at Pomeroy closed at the end of one week with four accessions to the church. Meeting here is three nights old. Attendance far exceeding our expectations. One addition the first night. Go next to Entiat.—O. M. Thomason, evangelist.

Waterville, Nov. 26.—Meeting here is one week old. Largest attendance in ten years. Seven additions. Waterville stirred as never before.—O. M. Thomason, evangelist.

West Virginia.

New Martinsville, Nov. 25.—Just closed a meeting here with 24 additions, 19 by baptism. Three confessions at closing service.—J. W. Stewart.

Christian Endeavor

By GEO. L. SNIVELY

December 16, 1906.

What Truth Has Chiefly Appealed to You from the Year's Bible School Lessons? — Matt. 13:52; Is. 52:13-15; 53:1-12.

DAILY READINGS.

M. Objects of the Scriptures. 2 Tim. 3:14-17.
T. Christ Proclaimed.   John 20:26-31.
W. Sin Rebuked.   Heb. 4:1-13.
T. Saints Built Up.   1 Cor. 14:21-28.
F. Lives Cleansed.   Isa. 6:1-9.
S. Unchangeable Word.   Rev. 22:18-21.
S. Continuance in Well-doing. Rom. 2:7.

The story of the crucifixion is not more a revelation of human and satanic malignity than it is of divine love.

The five thousand were fed not because the lad gave a great deal to the Lord, but because one in Israel had given his all to the Master. Our own unloading of ourselves of material things may enable us to feed even greater hosts on the Bread of Life.

Aside from their scriptural associations there is little attractiveness in the fishers' or shepherds' employ. They are invested with sacred romance to-day because engaged in by holy prophets and apostles and their relation to our Savior. In like manner we may ennoble the humblest tasks and positions if we nobly fulfill them. We may thus remove the stigma from occupations within which men may enter and achieve careers of splendid usefulness.

Peter was not a perfect man when he said, "Thou art the Christ, the Son of the living God," but he was facing in the right direction, and when close to the Master had the courage of his convictions. Under Christ's patronage he was on earth invested with the halo of martyrdom and is glorious in the heavens. Nor should men delay their public confession till they shall have attained perfection. Perfection is found only in Heaven, and on earth is not even approached outside the church.

1906, with its Bible school lessons, is like a golden cord strung with 52 beautiful gems on whose every facet is printed instruction in righteousness and life more precious than weighty gold or rarest stone. Let us hold these up to each other's admiration and scrutinize them closely for their innermost meaning. While we search for their spiritual significance, let us not yield to that tendency to "spiritualize away" their application to the practical affairs of this workaday world. They are intended for modern sinners as well as ancient Pilates, and the saints of to-day as well as the gentle Marys of old.

Were the rich young ruler living to-day, he would be one of the most exemplary young men in any city on earth; but until he had surrendered all and was following Jesus in the way the Master would still lovingly say, "One thing thou lackest." Perhaps none will ever on earth reach that stage where Jesus would not helpfully call attention to some lack in character. We will suppose he would each time name the most conspicuous defect. It is well we ask, "And what would mine be at the first?" In these closing days let us each overcome some present lack in the development of symmetrical Christian character.

In the few lessons from which specially helpful truths are to be recalled this evening, we must not forget the mountain of

transfiguration. Peter, James and John were taken with the Savior. Andrew naturally belonged with this division of the Apostles, and yet here and on other special occasions he was excluded from special privilege because, apparently, he fell just a little short of the requirements of being a witness to the resurrection of the ruler's daughter and of Christ's transfiguration glory. Doubtless, too, if we would grow just a little in grace, practice a denial of the flesh and an exaltation of spirit entirely within the range of our possibilities, we would enjoy many incomparably sweet and heavenly experiences, from which we are now excluded through lack of preparation.

Sunday-School

December 16, 1906.

Jesus Risen from the Dead.—Matt. 28:1-15.

Memory verses, 5, 6.

Golden Text.—He is risen, as he said. —Matt. 28:6.

It has often been remarked that the four accounts of the Resurrection, as found in the four gospels, not only differ in their report of the details of that event, but differ perhaps irreconcilably in some of the details. It is hard to say with any certainty that two statements are irreconcilable for the ingenuity of exegetes in harmonizing the apparently inharmonious is infinite.

To us it appears the most reasonable thing in the world that there should be variations in the report of the details of so marvelous an event. Did the angel roll away the stone before the women came (as Mark seems to say) or after their arrival and in their presence (as Matthew's account would lead one to imagine)? Were there "two men in dazzling apparel" standing in the tomb (Luke), or one sitting inside the tomb (Mark), or one sitting on the stone at the entrance (Matt.)? Who knows? Who cares, except as a matter of curious interest? The evangelists do not claim to have been witnesses of these first incidents of the resurrection. They got their information from the women. It is obvious that persons in a state of profound emotional excitement, as the women must have been, would not have been the best qualified to give a coldly accurate narrative of the details of such an event, though they were admirably qualified to report the scene in its general character and significance.

In regard to the Resurrection, therefore, as in regard to the Crucifixion, the variations of the different accounts are a confirmation of their substantial truth. The early defenders of Christianity considered the resurrection of Jesus as the most vital and essential of the gospel facts. Forgers would have taken good care to secure perfect agreement between their accounts of this event.

The Resurrection was the greatest but the most probable of the miracles of Jesus. Even thoughtful skeptics do not deny the possibility of the miraculous. If then, one admits the existence of a God by whose power miracles can be done, the acceptance of any particular alleged miracle as historically true will depend upon the evidence and the evidence must be judged, partly at least, in the light of the motive.

Mr. Huxley said that no conceivable evidence would make him believe that "a centaur had been seen trotting down Regent street." True enough, for such a marvel would have no meaning and value. It is the spiritual worth of the miracles of Jesus which gives them prob-

ability. This is pre-eminently true of the Resurrection. Granted that there is a God who can perform the miraculous, is any miracle more probable than the resurrection of such a person as Jesus. Considering the value which that event has had in the lives of men, and which it will continue to have—a value which was known in advance to the infinite wisdom—could any miracle be backed by a stronger motive? Does not such a miracle then have such an inherent probability that it commands belief more readily than would such a miracle as, for example, Huxley's "Centaur on Regent Street"?

The evidence for the resurrection is strengthened by the fact that the witnesses to it devotedly gave their lives and cheerfully met their deaths in defense of their testimony. Somehow, the disciples, who had believed at the time of the crucifixion that their master's mission was ended forever, gained a deep conviction that their Lord was alive again and would live on high forever. They proved the sincerity of their belief by dying for it. The fact that all early Christianity was based upon a belief in the resurrection is the strongest evidence of it as a fact of history.

One can not but protest against the tendency in modern nurseries and kindergartens to freight the memories of children with meaningless musical jingles instead of the sweet, trustful, solemn, and majestic "Rock of Ages," "Nearer My God to Thee," "Lead, Kindly Light," and similar sacred triumphs of our hymnology. A heart and memory thoroughly saturated with the tunes, words and sentiments of such songs are a priceless possession.

The emotions find expression in poetry as naturally as wants or reason do in prose, and when given voice they take the voice of song. Through the emotions we get the truest revelations of character. Thus in the songs we sing and the way we sing the world learns us as we are. But the peculiar ministry of song is not only to reveal, but also to form character. It is well then we be more concerned about the songs we sing than about the food we eat, the company we keep, the very air we breathe.

Such influence has song over life and character that a celebrated statesman once remarked: "Let me select the ballads of a people and I care not who writes their laws." This statement should at least suggest to teachers the propriety of expurgating from school songs all sentiments pitched to a low idealism, and to parents to eliminate from hearthstone music every chord inconsistent with ideals of noblest worth, and to preachers to banish from the sanctuary every song with bars discordant with "the form of sound words."

The psalmist laments that as the people were going into captivity and had hanged up their harps on the willows, their captors required one of the songs of Zion, but "How shall we sing the Lord's song in a strange land?" It would have been infinitely better for them had they sung. Nothing will do more to relieve the tense emotions, to make normal the suppressed heart, to clear the range of vision all the way up to God, and change defeat into victory than the new faith, courage, and hope that alwaye accompany the singing of the songs of Zion.

No other part of the worship will more richly repay careful preparation than will the song service. Often the impression is given that time is allowed for a song not so much for adoration as to occupy the hour. Again the selection is so little in harmony with the prevailing sentiments of the meeting or the spirit that ought to prevail there that music is permitted to render but a tithe of its natural helpfulness. Lack of discrimination is exhibited in persistently choosing the cheap and tawdry "sunshine" and "dewdrop" verses that creep into our books to the exclusion of the deeper and more dignified and majestic hymns that voice the greatest deeps of the heart and loftiest aspirations of the soul. Let us not neglect the great battle and martyr songs, those that celebrate new-born peace and hope, a faith emergent and triumphant, nor those that in the pro-

found language of God enshrine a spirit that makes the singer like unto him.

The scientist will reason from the wing and fin and the air and water that match them, from the hunger and the food that satisfies it up to the God whose designing intelligence and love they prove. Job's confidence is based on a yet more immediate and vivid consciousness. He sings,

"None saith, where is God my maker,
Who giveth songs in the night."

He who has supplied us with power to sing those songs in the night time of sickness and sorrow, of impending disaster and gloom, that assuage grief, restore faith and courage, and inspire us with hope for the morrow, has revealed a personal and paternal love more discerning and precious even than that manifested in providing the atmosphere for wings, rivers for fins, or bread for hunger.

People's Forum

Concerning "Trial Marriages."

To the Editor of The Christian-Evangelist.

In regard to a recent publication containing the suggestion of "trial marriages," with the privilege of breaking them off at will and marrying some one else, etc.—in other words, to stay married as long as one pleased, and then whenever one changed one's mind, to "marry" some one else; permit me to say, that this is precisely the system that was practised until recently, in one (or more) of the islands of the Pacific. A lady of delicate sensibilities, in trying to convey this condition of affairs to her readers, thus described it in her book. She had been some time on the island, learning the language, she said, before she became aware of the peculiar social conditions there; and the way she learned of them was this. She noticed the young son of the chief called several women "Mother." Inquiring of him why he called more than one by that name, he replied, that this one was his mother this year; that one was his mother last year; and still others had been his mother in previous years; and therefore, to avoid mistakes, he called all women "Mother."

This condition has however, I believe, through the missionaries and the intro-duction of Christianity, all been changed, until they now have permanent wives.

But we see that this supposedly novel advance in civilization has been practiced for ages by the pagans of the Pacific, and, if I am not mistaken, has been finally abandoned by them.

Mormonism is the taking of several permanent wives; and this most of Christendom reprehends and deplores. But trial marriages would be the taking of several temporary wives, and therefore be worse than mormonism. And as no length of time is prescribed for trial marriages, and as they are only to last until the parties or one of them changes their mind, they might change from day to day. This is about as the brute creation lives. But who before ever held the brute up as a model? Certainly the proposer of "trial marriages" is unique in the choice of ideals and progress!

There are just three questions I would like to ask the proposer:

1st. How can "trial marriages" be reconciled with Christ's command (Matt. 19:6) "What therefore God hath joined together, let not man put asunder," (save for the single cause which He Himself mentioned in Matt. 5:32)?

2nd. And how can they be reconciled with God's command (Ex. 20:14), "Thou shalt not commit adultery," in the light of what Christ said in Matt. 5:32, "But I say unto you, that everyone that putteth away his wife, saving for the cause of fornication, maketh her an adultress, and whosoever shall marry her when she is put away, committeth adultery?"

3rd. And finally, if one continually teaches or makes one's habit of life directly contrary to Christ's express commands, how can such a one be a Christian or expect heaven?

New York.　　J. B. M.

[The proposal of "Trial Marriages," by Elsie Clews Parsons is so manifestly barbarian and contrary to Christ's teaching and the experience of the world's civilization that it merits universal condemnation. Editor.]

A Brotherhood.

(Continued from Page 1567.)

preciate them none the less, but we love or should love the men the more, on whose shoulders rest the battle and heat of the day. Do not be particular about the form of organization. Twelve hundred dele-gates of the Presbyterian church met recently in Indianapolis to organize a brotherhood. But when they got on the mountain top of spiritual enthusiasm the delegates were told to go home with the life generated and let it work itself out. They would not deaden that splendid feeling with "whereases" and by-laws. "Go home," was the cry, "and let the life take its own form." They did what their fathers ought to have done two and a half centuries before—kept their profane hands off. One who was there went over to the Illinois delegation after the convention was over and heard a gray-haired man addressing a group as follows: "Men, I am going home to do better work for the Christ than ever before. All who will join with me in this determination, will you raise your hand," and every hand went up. "Then," he said, "draw your sword," and every hand went down to the imaginary sheath

and drew the sword and extended it high. Shall not we, who stand only, l the Christ draw our swords and do vali work for him who is mightily and able save to the utmost all who come un him?

Erie, Pa.

MAN'S FAREWELL ᵀᴼ LOW WAGES

GOOD-BY FOREVER TO HARD WORK—LITTLE PAY—HARD TIMES—JOB HUNTING! YOU CAN OWN AND BOSS THIS MONEY-MAKING BUSINESS! GET MONEY AS THIS MAN DID! CHANGE FROM WAGE EARNER TO WAGE PAYER--FROM SERVING OTHERS TO COMMANDING OTHERS

At it Would be Told at Home.

Pleasant Business.

Prosperity.

You may well rejoice, my wife, over our good fortune in getting-for almost nothing a business which made money the very first day and has grown better all along-until now after a few weeks the daily profits run from $8.00 to $12.00. You have just counted today's receipts and seem surprised that they amount to $15.00 plus some cents, but I have good reason to expect even larger returns as time goes on. Of that $15.00 you must take out about $3.00 for most of merchandise and the $12.00 remaining is profit. So business gets better as it gets older. I need have no worry about the future, because there remains many dollars' worth of unfinished work upon which I can calculate as in the past about 75c profit on the dollar and more orders coming in all the time. My trouble has not been the want of orders, but facilities to fill orders as fast as my many customers would like, and to make matters better have engaged a boy to help in the shop, including an extra solicitor.

If I has kept me hustling this far to take care of family customers whose orders range from $2.00 to $10.00, but increased facilities will enable me to get business in even larger quantities from hotels, restaurants and public institutions, manufacturers and retail stores, there being scarcely any person in business or out who does not at all times have urgent need for my services. I never thought it possible to

START A PROSPEROUS BUSINESS

like this with only a few dollars, for almost every business worth having requires several thousand dollars to begin with, and I was not in that class, in fact, we can both recall with sad regret the days of no work—no wages—debts piling up—nearly everyone and everything combined to keep me down. Then my siege of sickness—no work—laid up—laid off—almost laid away—nothing coming in—expenses going on—doctor bills and what not. Trouble, trouble, trouble, but that's the common hardship of every man who sells his time to others—hard work—long hours—little pay—enriching those who boss, but never himself. Verily, my good wife, we know from experience

that it's mighty inconvenient to be poor, and now after years of hard labor here and there and almost everywhere—from factory band to office clerk—teaching school or selling goods—town and city trades—now and then the farm—we find ourselves in prosperous circumstances, owning a pleasant business which promises to pay from

$1800 to $2500 ANNUALLY.

Goodness knows, we might still be slaving for a bare existence if this opportunity hadn't come as a God-send, but we know too well the need of money to get foolish or spoiled by sudden prosperity. I am happy to think that our days of self-denial and privations are over, that you and the children can have many things in the future which you craved but alas! didn't have the money to buy. You can dress better, visit more, work less, buy new things for the home and give the children a better education. What a blessing it is to have money coming in all the time, and how different the people treat a successful man.

It's really wonderful how people took to my business from the very start, just seemed that everyone had something for me to do—eager to have it done—a cordial welcome everywhere and people came from miles around—

GOODS WERE GOING OUT— MONEY COMING IN—

almost a dollar cleared every time a dollar taken in. You remember my starting here at home—set of one room which was soon filled with a great assortment of merchandise—some gold, some silver—big and little heaps—how things glistened when the sun came through—then the change to larger quarters owing to increased business with profits growing. It did

my heart good to receive such generous encouragement from people everywhere, for I can't forget my ups and downs —hard knocks—never a boost until this thing happened.

The people certainly looked kindly upon home industry, and because my business was conducted there in their very midst a feeling of confidence was immediately established. My work has always been well done and I do not fear to meet the same customer twice even ten years from now. I have never been the kind to deceive anyone and would not care to bring that disgrace upon my children even though success was the reward.

Yes, people do wonder at my sudden rise in the world, but there is nothing remarkable in my performance, simply a case of supplying something which the people did not have but wanted awful bad—never had before—it's a regular business in some large cities, but just as well suited to town and country places as my own success proved. My success has not been due to influence, business training, special schooling or technical knowledge, but to human endeavor, faithful work and earnest purpose. Had I failed to make good in this opportunity when everything was favorable to

success it would have been an ever lasting cause for self criticism. It would be an act of ingratitude on my part if I did not give

PRAISE TO THE MANUFACTURERS

who not only suggested the opportunity but furnished at slight cost everything needed to start the business, including special teaching, valuable instructions and trade secrets and did this so well that my ignorance of the business itself was no drawback at all. Quite a few people from other sections have already written them on my recommendation, for they

WILL START OTHERS

in all parts of the world, either men or women, in this business at home or traveling, all or spare time, but do not encourage business relations with drones or idlers. I am only one of thousands whom they have started in their twenty years of business experience, and I can't imagine a business which offers equal money-making opportunities to people of limited means —something easy to do, easy to get, easy to maintain, offering almost the only chance for people in moderate circumstances to better their position in life.

Though you, my wife, regard my success as remarkable in comparison with the old days it seems to be quite the regular order of things with their customers, as for example, one man claims $301.27 in two weeks, another $88.16 the first three days and hundreds of similar reports have come to my notice, which makes me feel that there is nothing of personal quality in my own success. You won't forget how skeptical I was at first, but these fears were unfounded, as we both know now, for I have found the business even better than their claim as a money-making chance which anyone without leaving home and without previous experience can manage successfully.

I shall continue advising people out of employment or working hard for a little money to send their name on a card to

GRAY & CO., 810 MIAMI BUILDING, CINCINNATI, OHIO,

and receive FREE as I did their proposition, valuable information, testimonials and samples.

They don't offer any impossible inducements, such as $50.00 a day without work, but simply claim that those willing to hustle have every reason to expect from

$30.00 TO $40.00 WEEKLY

to begin with and more than that as their business grows. I feel sure and believe that you, my wife, also believe that no one will ever regret the day they started with Gray & Co., for they are the largest concern of their kind in the world and are backed by $100,000.00 capital. It's well that you should know these things as I do so as to answer inquiries intelligently when visiting friends out.

The Home Department

"Look Unto Me."

Mine eyes were filled with bitten tears,
　My face I turned toward the sun;
My tears were changed to pearly drops,
　Of finest rainbow colors spun.

My heart bowed down with heavy grief,
　I raised my eyes to God's own Son;
The joy-bells rang within my soul,
　I murmured low, "Thy will be done."

With trouble sore within my heart,
　I in the deep'ning shadow walked,
I turned me t'ward the shining li*ht,
　And gaunt behind the shadow stalked.

When deep despair was in my soul,
　And I in darkness trod,
It vanished from before my face,
　When once I turned toward my God.
Britton, S. D.　　　　ALMA WILLISON.

The Bronze Vase.

BY J. BRECKENRIDGE ELLIS.

PART IV.

CHAPTER VI.

One the train to Crawley, Raymund and
Rhoda sat side by side. Raymund carried
his valise, and Rhoda a little bag. They
were to stay all night at the Crawley hotel
(it was, of course, called "the Laclede
Hotel,") and possibly two nights. It was
just a little pleasure trip back to the scenes
of their childhood. Rhoda looked at Raymund with dancing light in her blue eyes.
"We will see all our old friends!" she said,
"and as they'll know we have no need of
them, they'll all be glad to see us. It is
splendid! Don't you feel excited?"

"Oh, I don't know," said Raymund indifferently. "I've beeen here once already,
since you and I saw the town together."

"You have been here?" Rhoda echoed,
her blue eyes startled. "And you never
told me a word about it!"

"Why should I? You didn't seem to care
what I did," remarked Raymund. "I don't
mean to blame you, Rhoda, but really, you
know, you quite lost interest in me after
you started, to that Fulton school."

"I have never lost interest in you, never!" she protested, in her old-time impetuous fashion.

"It flowed very deep then," remarked
Raymund. "Oh, yes, I came back here.
I called for the tin box. In it was a letter
from mother to whichever of us should call
for it. I read it. I learned it by heart.
Then I destroyed it."

Rhoda turned pale in amazement and, as
it seemed in fear. "You called for that tin
box!" she faltered accusingly.

"Yes," said Raymund easily. "You know,
if a difference ever came between us, either
one was at liberty to open the tin box. The
difference came and so I went to Crawley.
It was quite natural and proper. Isn't that
a delightful prairie view? Look at that one
lonesome cottonwood tree in the middle of
the cornfield."

"What difference do you mean, Raymund?"

"The difference in you, of course, Rhoda.
How can you ask? The letter explained
it very satisfactorily. You are not my sister, Rhoda. In some way you learned that
fact. When you found I was not related
to you, of course you ceased to treat me
in a sisterly way."

Rhoda caught her breath. "The letter
told you that?"

"Yes. Mother explained just how it all
came about. It was a great shock at first,
but I've had nearly six months to adjust
myself to the truth. As for you, you've
known it for about three years. Now that
we meet again, we meet with our eyes

fully opened. We have grown used to the
thought that we are of no kin."

"Still, Raymund," said Rhoda gently, "we
can never forget how long we lived together as brother and sister, and how mother always treated each of us as her very
own child."

"Oh, yes, of course," said Raymund lightly, "we can not be exactly the same to each
other as other young ladies and gentlemen, I imagine, but all that is just sentiment, you know."

She looked at him with grieved eyes
and heightened color. "Of course," he
went on, "everybody will have to know the
truth in a short time. I'm sorry there will
have to be talk and poor dear Mr. Willby
will almost burst with questions! Let's
not spoil our little visit by referring to it
again."

"And shall we be brother and sister till
we go back to Frog Bend?" she asked
brightly.

"No," said Raymund, "we can never be
that, again. But we don't have to talk
about it." It was dinner-time, that is to
say, one o'clock, when they stopped at the
Laclede hotel. Side by side, but very
grave, and almost in silence they partook
of the white, tasteless "string-beans," the
hard plump peas with their insidious suggestion of soap, the unconquerable steak,
chicken that was game to the last, and the
high-roofed biscuits with their storage of
yellowish, clammy dough. Their first visit
was to Miss Glory Aggency. The old maid
was far more at her ease than when they
had approached her upon the lowly plain
of childhood. She took pride in their success, and was much interested in all they
had to tell. Mr. Merlin Agency remembered Raymund and claimed him as a congenial spirit. He showed him the latest
parlor ledger and dining-room ledger and
yard ledger. "I am still a very busy man,"
said Mr. Merlin Agency with great zest.
"I am compiling a record of my thermometer. I look at it every hour exactly at the
strike. Come, I will show you just how
hot it was on this day last year. See—
all in neat columns. Many a man, my
boy, lives through his day hardly knowing
if it is hot or cold, and certainly not knowing how the mercury is moving from hour
to hour. Alas, I cannot tell you what tricks
it plays at night! If I were rich, I would
hire some one to take observations through
the night."

"Brother," said his sister gently, "do not
excite yourself." As they stood on the
porch saying goodby, and just as Mr. Merlin with great heartiness was begging Raymund to come again and hear his discovery concerning the number 7," the
clock struck. "Ha!" cried Mr. Merlin
Agency and darted through the house;
for his thermometer, unluckily, hung at the
rear. The farewells were necessarily protracted. He returned panting to say, "We
cannot make it but 7½ this time, Sister
Glory."

Miss Glory complained that her brother
over-exerted himself in darting to his thermometer. She said he had thermometers that
hang thermometers at all likely places, that
the old accountant need but run to the
nearest station. "A capital suggestion!"
cried Mr. Merlin Agency. "I will han,
the premises with them! My boy, you
never come without giving me valuable assistance. Would that you lived in Crawley!"

"I think I shall live here some day,"
said Raymund; "at least on a farm near
town. I do not like city-life nearly so
well."

When they left, Rhoda turned to Raymund in surprise. "You surely do not
think of being a farmer, Raymund?"

"Yes, I do," said Raymund. "I believe
that in farming, my education can be utilized as thoroughly as in any other vocation.
And I love open air and independence.
I love the smell of the meadows in the
early dew, and the lowing of the cows at
evening, and the work—I like that; and
the appetite that comes after. If I can
rent a farm, I shall presently own one—
you'll see! And now, Rhoda, I'll leave
you to go out to the Omer farm. You can
visit your old school-mates, or just look
around, or stay at the hotel. I'll be back
in the morning, but I fancy if I find Mr.
Omer at the farm, he'll want me to stay
there all night."

Raymund was right in this supposition.
The lease of the eastern farmer would not
expire for another year, but the easterner
was only too willing to go; he had not
made the farm pay. "It is my purpose,"
said little Mr. Omer, always brief of speech,
and always conscious of the authority that
his million dollars carried, "to place this
farm in your hands, Raymund, if you will
undertake the work. I mean to move on
my Texas ranch with the family. I must
have some one here that I can trust. I have
watched you closely. I studied you when,
as a boy, you improved the yard of the
Hands' House and did every day a good
amount of work that was not required.
I've kept track of you in St. Louis, I know
about your tailoring at the university.
Geisthauser has explained how you labored
with his two pudding-heads. I propose to
leave everything in your hands, with the
advice of and aid of my faithful old hands,
Tom and Fred. Will you take this farm
for a thousand dollars a year, or will you
take it for half of what you can make?"

"I will take it for one year for a half of
what I can make," said Raymund, "but you

Send for our Holiday Catalogue
CHRISTIAN PUBLISHING CO.,
St. Louis, Mo.

COBALT

That Wonderful Silver Camp which is startling the world by its enormous riches.

Cobalt is the richest and most unique mining camp the world has ever seen. Millions of dollars of rich silver ores are being shipped monthly to the smelters. Stocks in operating companies which sold a few months ago for par have increased in value from five to twenty times. More millions have been made in the past year in the Cobalt Camp than in the first ten years of the celebrated Comstock Mines.

Powerful mining interests, notably the Guggenheims and American Smelting and Refining Company, are heavy investors in the Camp. Of course, as in all successful mining camps, the camp followers, fakirs and unprincipled promoters are an ever present menace to honest, sincere investment. Cobalt has its share.

The original discovery dates back from November, 1903, but it took a year for those conversant with the discovery to realize its importance, and it was only in May last that the camp began to get busy. Cobalt is to-day the scene of at least thirteen shipping mines. Nine of these have started up within the past three months, some of them within a month. And other mines will begin operations at no long intervals from now on.

The Railway Commission have built a handsome station at Cobalt and a substantial freight shed is now under construction.

Cobalt is situated 103 miles north of North Bay. It is on the Temiskaming & Northern Ontario Railway, and is easily accessible. The journey from Toronto to Cobalt is made in 16 hours, which includes a stop of two hours at North Bay. The Railway Station at Cobalt is practically the center of the camp. Cobalt is 330 miles from Toronto. It is an hour and a half's ride north of Temagami, which is being boomed as a summer resort. There is already a healthy paying traffic on the T. & N. O. Ry., and the commissioners are making it an up-to-date road. Before long the time between Toronto and Cobalt should be reduced to 10 or at most 12 hours

Three years ago the land about Cobalt would not have sold for ten cents an acre. To-day some of it would bring $100 a square inch. There is one tract of forty acres that you could not buy for $10,000,000 in cash. Through the district are other forty-acre tracts which their owners estimate at from hundreds of thousands to millions of dollars. Nevertheless, the land lies in the

Heart of the wildest woods on the continent. It is rocky and swampy, and it would take a quarter section to feed a goat.

Its value lies in the enormous silver deposits which have been recently discovered. The rock is streaked with great veins of almost pure silver ore. Three or four Million dollars' worth of this ore has already been shipped, and carloads of it are now on their way to New York, which are worth from $25,000 to $30,000 a car. A car-load of the best picked specimens from a certain mine is said to have sold for $90,000 and another car-load for $50,000 and another for $40,000.

A prominent engineer says:

"Nuggets of silver which are 80 and 90 per cent. pure have been taken out of the mines, and some of the nuggets weigh three and four hundred pounds each. I saw chunks of silver and rock the size of a paving brick which I could not lift. Indeed, much of the ore makes me think of the almost pure copper nuggets which one finds in the Lake Superior mines. These veins of silver are not regular in width nor do they run even through-out. Here and there branch veins jut out from the main one like the veins of a leaf, and the ore has everywhere soaked into the adjoining rocks."

THE COST OF MINING.

It can be taken from the mines for 8 per cent of the value of the product, an outlay of $2,000 bringing forth $25,000 or $30,000 worth of ore. So far it does not pay to ship anything that will yield less than $200 per ton and the most of the shipments are much richer.

The Premier Cobalt Company own in absolute fee 40 acres of most valuable territory of this most remarkable region, showing native silver on the surface; and a shaft down 120 feet in silver ore, increasing in value as depth is obtained. Steam hoists, buildings, all erected and in operation. Harry A. Lee, M. E., of Denver, Col., formerly Commissioner of Mines of the State of Colorado, is the consulting engineer. The Company is officered by men of unquestioned integrity who will conscientiously administer its affairs, and the engineers in charge of the operative department have been responsible for the success of some of the largest mines on this continent.

The Company has a capital of $1,000,000; shares par value $1.00. A limited amount of this stock will be sold at par, and may go to many times its present price within a few weeks, as the property bids fair to be one of Cobalt's largest producers.

Send subscription and make all checks payable to William Wiggins, President, 52 Broadway, New York, who will have charge of the allotment.

The books will close when the allotment is completed, as enough cash will be in hand to meet requirements.

WILLIAM WIGGINS, President,

52 Broadway, New York.

OFFICERS AND DIRECTORS:

WILLIAM WIGGINS, NEW YORK,
PRESIDENT.
COL. C. D. ROBBINS, PITTSBURG,
VICE PRESIDENT.
D. LOUIS SCHWARTZ, MADISON, N. J.,
SEC'Y and TREAS.

S. F. HECKERT, PITTSBURG.
WILLIAM FRANCY, PITTSBURG.
W. A. McCUTCHEON, PITTSBURG.
FREDERICK PFEFFER, NEW YORK.
EDWIN S. ROBINSON, NEW YORK.
WM. J. MATTHEWS, NEW YORK.
O. B. MILLER, NEW YORK.

ought to know, Mr. Omer, that it will always be my intention to buy a farm of my own."

"How much have you now?" Mr. Omer inquired with a smile.

"Two hundred dollars."

Mr. Omer smiled again. "I'll tell you what I'll do, Raymund," he said. "I never had any sentiment in my business before, but you're a man after my own heart. You shall have the privilege of buying this farm at sixty dollars an acre, no matter how much property is worth hereabouts, and you may buy it just as you are able." They had reached a final agreement when Tom and Fred were seen going to the Hands' House from their evening's work. They were attended by a lad of about nine years of age. "That little fellow is quite a help," said Mr. Omer, nodding his gray head toward the lad. "It's Tom's boy."

Raymund hurried toward the Hands' House, and was a little disconcerted to find that the weeds had overrun the yard and the washpan and soap had again taken up their posts on the front porch.

"If it ain't Raymond!" shouted Tom, redder of face than ever.

"Well, if it ain't!" cried Fred, working his ears and speaking in his thinnest squeak. "Howdy, Raymund, howdy!" It was evident, however, that they were not so much at their ease as formerly in his presence. But Raymund was so hearty in his welcome, and so demonstrative in his greeting of Baby (who now went by the name of "Babe") that the ice was presently thawed. The temperature did not, perhaps, rise to boiling point, but they were on very good terms when the young man went back to the brick house with pensive memories of Nelsie Loraine and Mrs. De Fer.

In the meantime, Rhoda had made a discovery in Crawley. In rambling over the familiar streets, after gazing at her mother's former home, and the house once occupied by Brother Bellfield, she visited the old cabin where she had gone with Jack and Raymund to ask Wizzen to help them run away. She was surprised to find that a neat latticework had been built about the once gaping space from under the house. The yard, too, was fenced off from the road, and showed considerable care. A garden thrived beyond the yard. The broken windows had been replaced by good ones, and before the door hung a little piazza. As Rhoda wondered, the door opened, and old Mrs. Weed looked out with a face of high excitement. She had caught sight of her friend from the window. "Come right out!" cried Mrs. Weed, "come right out, Rhoda!"

"She means it," said Wizzen, peeping over Mrs. Weed's shoulder, and, as in former times, acting as her annotater.

"Come right out!" repeated Mrs. Weed.

"Oh, Rhoda, this is such a joyful surprise! You must take supper with us. We're here to stay, here to stay! We're not going to move any more as long as we live! Henry, tell Rhoda the whole story."

"Yes," said Wizzen as Mrs. Weed sat down, still quivering with delight, "it's quite a story, and as the old lady is so deaf she can't hear me, I'll tell the whole of it. By the way, Rhoda, did you ever mention to Raymund or to anyone that the old lady's daughter was in the state prison?"

"No indeed, Wizzen, not a word."

"I knowed you wouldn't!" cried Wizzen, his face beaming. "I was shore of you, Rhoda. Let me tell you. We was in St. Louis back from our New Orleans trip which we found that you and Raymund had went, we couldn't git no satisfaction outen that Miss Pinns which she was but a head and sharp point to stick with, as I told the old lady here. And one night as I was prowling around I come to the police station, not that I had to go there, but viewing the sights, and a woman comes into the chief of police and she tells him how she was sent up for five years, but

being good was let off with two-third time, and comes back to the city to hunt work and live good and honest. But she had been two weeks hunting a job and them what knowed of her record wouldn't hire her, and them what didn't, wanted to know, which it wasn't no help when she told them. And she was half-starved, and her clothes no account, and her shoes wearing out, and she asks to be sent back to the pen for the balance of her five year. 'They'll feed me there,' says she, 'and keep me warm.' And she says several nights she slept in goods boxes, and on the benches at the Union Station till they drove her away, and such like. And she was desperate like. Well, the chief of police, he said she couldn't be took back into the penitentiary unless she did some crime agin, and he advised her not to give up, but to keep right, and he sent her out. She stood there on the street, a-cryin' desperate, and saying below her breath that it wasn't no use to try do right and she'd best go throw herself in the river. So I goes up and says, 'Lizzie,' I says. And she knowed me. They wasn't no particle of foolishness or sentimental bamboozle about it. She hadn't never loved me, I reckon though she said she had. But I says to her 'now without no poetry, Lizzie,' which I can make that, too, Rhoda, if at leisure, but I says, 'Without no poetry, and being your lawful husband though hitherto not a source of delight to either of us, but being so, why not come back to me?' And she sorter screamed out and says, 'Will you take me?' and I says, 'As to be a question of being took back into the state prison, maybe to come back as my wife might have some degrees of prefer, ence,' I says, 'and there is your old mother wearing out her heart to see you, which I have never let you know that you was ever sent to jail,' I says."

Wizzen paused and ducked his head and looked up at Rhoda as if peering from under a cap that was not there. "You see it was all dry, plain business-like proposition. She was so starved and ragged that she made a good deal more out of it than I did. And she cried and wailed like a wild creature, but she come, and here we are, and no more moving for your Uncle Wizzen! For which it is a good thing to move as a cure-all, no remedy is now needed, and Lizzie is satisfied to be tied down at last, which she was like a wild rabbit, for you chase it and try to tame it at first and away it goes. But she has been so drove by hard luck and hard life, that she's ready to crouch in her furrow even if the dogs was there to take her!"

"Oh, Wizzen!" cried Rhoda with a delight, "how proud you must be!"

"Well no, I can't say that proud is the word. Proud I am not, Rhoda, but middling contented."

Mrs. Weed, now perceiving that the news had been imparted, smiled rapturously at Rhoda and insisted that she should stay to supper and meet her long lost daughter. But Rhoda preferred to preserve her acquaintance of the prodigal through the medium of Wizzen. She departed, assuring them that Raymund would call in the morning.

(TO BE NEXT WEEK.)

※ ※

The Tyranny of Habit.

BY REV. WILLIAM J. DAWSON, D. D.

[Dr. Dawson has become well known in the United States through his evangelistic labors of the past few years, and American Christians are rejoicing that he has taken up a permanent abode among us. Our readers know of his successful career as preacher, lecturer, and author before he was turned in a remarkable way to his present labors. He has written many important books —Volumes of poems, sermons, literary essays, fiction, life of Christ. His journalistic powers are great, and he is a frequent contributor to the press. In all these ways, and especially by his effective preaching, he is a winner of souls to the Lord Jesus.—ED.]

The thing which we do once we find easy to do a second time. Such is the genesis of habit. The thing once done is a thing easy of repetition, and soon acquires a necessity of repetition. This is what is meant by the tyranny of habit.

Let us take a very simple and familiar illustration. Suppose I wake some night after two or three hours of sleep. I make no effort to compose myself. I say, "I am awake now; it is useless to attempt sleep again;" and so I turn up the light and begin to read. The chances are that the next night I shall awake at the same hour. Within a week I shall find the habit of waking at this hour firmly established. Within a month the habit will have become a tyranny; and, however weary I may be, or in need of rest, I shall be forced to spend a part of each night awake and reading. This is an experience so common that many of my readers will at once verify it.

The Slavery of Sin.

Suppose, again, that the habit in question has its root in appetite. I allow some indulgence that I know to be harmful or sinful. Precisely the same process will follow. At each repetition of the act the compulsion will become stronger. In the end I become its slave. Never was there truer word than the word of Christ, "He who sinneth is the servant or the slave of sin." The plea and the attraction of evil usually is that it comes to us disguised as freedom. We break a law, thinking that in doing so we assert our freedom. On the contrary, we impose upon ourselves a bondage. It is not long before we discover that we are the slaves of our iniquity. The thing we would not, that we do, and we cry in misery, "Who will deliver me from the body of this death?"

The great thing to be observed, then, is extreme care in the formation of habits. An act is not necessarily a habit, though it is the beginning of one. Take, again, the instance of waking at a certain hour in the night. If I resolutely compose myself to sleep, in all probability I can regain my sleep. It will be difficult and annoying, but I can do it, I may toss miserably upon my bed, but by dint of effort I can wear out my enemy. But, if I do not make the effort at once, it will be much harder on the second occasion.

Good Habits are as Easily Formed as Bad Ones.

It is also clear that good habits are as easily formed as bad ones. Habit itself knows no morality; it has no preferences. A man may as readily form the habit of sleeping at a certain hour as waking.

Thus, to give a personal instance, I formed years ago the habit of sleeping by the clock at any time during the day. I can take my watch in my hand, say to myself, "I can afford fifteen minutes' sleep," and I am asleep almost as soon as I have said it. In the same way, I can wake at the very moment I wish, and am rarely behindhand by a minute. If I wish to wake in the morning at a given time, I can do so; I have only to give orders to my brain over night. To make assurance doubly sure, I often give instructions to some one to wake me when I have a journey to take or an engagement to keep, but in nine cases out of ten I need no calling.

The brain never sleeps; it stands sentinel through the long hours of unconsciousness. If I trust it, it will not betray my confidence. We are essentially self-governing creatures, and we can control our habits just as we control our limbs, our speed, our actions.

Many people who practise the art of letters set out with a stupid idea they can write only when "the afflatus" comes. They wait for a mood, for an inspiration; and the consequence is that they often wait in vain, and waste great quantities of time.

But the greatest literary workers know better. Huxley defined genius as a mind always under control, always kept at heel, and ready to meet any demand that might be made upon it. Harriet Martineau said that she soon discovered that it was folly to wait for an inspiration. She accustomed herself to begin writing at a certain hour each morning, whether she had anything to say or not, and she soon found that her brain responded to her demand upon it like an obedient machine. Anthony Trollope wrote early each morning before he went to business, and with such regularity that he never failed to produce exactly the amount of manuscript which he desired. Walter Scott wrote his novels in the early morning, long before any one but himself was awake.

Almost all great writers have been methodical workers. They have accustomed their minds to obey the call of habit, and habit has thus become to them second nature. The tyranny of habit has been in this way turned to good account, and has become a source of strength.

The Habit of Diligence.

When John Wesley called his followers Methodists, he meant no more than this—that they were a people who lived upon a method. They lived by rule, and the rule applied to their time, to their thought, and to the general disposition of their life. Wesley himself was the example of what he taught. He found that by the parsimonious use of time he could get through an enormous quantity of work without fatigue. Some of his maxims are wise enough to be far better known than they are. For example, "Never be unemployed, and never be trifingly employed."

It is a matter of perpetual wonder to the biographers of Wesley that one man was able to accomplish so much. He not only governed with wisdom and personal vigilance a vast and growing community, but he preached regularly from three to four times a day, travelled yearly many thousands of miles, read all the current literature that was worth reading, engaged in public controversies, wrote with his own hand an immense number of letters every year, and finally published about a hundred books, including many departments of literature not immediately connected with his religious work, such as grammars, histories, treatises on physics, and even abridgements of works of fiction. How was all this done? By making diligence a habit. If habit was for him a tyranny, it was a beneficent tyranny.

We need not quarrel, then, with the term, "the tyranny of habit," since it stands for much that is best in life as well as for much that is painful. The thing is, to make right habits our tyrants, for in good

and evil alike we are the children of habit. Virtue is a habit as well as vice, industry as well as indolence, truth as well as falsehood, high and noble thought as well as sordid and vulgar imagination.

It is not really more difficult to do right than to do wrong. There are many persons I have known who would find it much harder to do wrong than to do right, simply because they have established in their lives, by long practice and discipline, the habit of pure thought, high sentiment, and honorable conduct. Cynicism smiles at the man who cannot tell a lie; yet there are multitudes of men and women who have that noble incapacity. The profligate, who takes all men to be as himself, sneers at the man who has no taste for sensuality; yet there are multitudes of men who are genuinely incapable of feeling anything but pleasure. The business knave assumes that all business is knavery; yet all around him are men who would rather be beggared than prosper by falsehood and injustice.

When Joseph said in the hour of his great temptation, "How can I do this great wickedness?" he simply expressed that invincible repugnance to evil which comes from the habit of righteousness. When Luther said, "Here I take my stand; I can do no other," he expressed the incapacity for cowardice which was the result of the habit of courage and clear thinking. If our habits make us, we make our habits; and it is possible for us to acquire habits that in the day of temptation are our defence, our anchorage, our invincible city of refuge.

Breaking Bad Habits.

But what if we have acquired evil habits? What if little by little we have allowed ourselves to be entangled in habits which debase and corrupt us? The answer is that habit is the creature of will. The will that makes the habit can unmake it.

An excellent illustration on this point is the story of the great scientist who was lowered into the crevasse of a glacier to observe its formation, and found that when he signalled to be drawn up, his assistants could not draw him up, because they had forgotten *the weight of the rope*. We are all apt to forget the weight of the rope.

I think that it is well for us, even in habits of sense which may have no distinct wrong in them, every now and again to test the weight of the rope; or, in other words, to ascertain whether we are free. I know smokers who at intervals put their pipes away for a month, just to assure themselves that they *can* do so. There are many other things in which the same renunciation would be wise—renunciation or abstention for a time, just to ascertain that our freedom is not impaired. I imagine that this is the principle which underlies the habit of periodic fasting, once recognized as a plain duty of religion, but now almost totally ignored in Protestant communities; it is the assertion of the freedom of the spirit against the encroachment of the flesh.

No one finds these acts easy, but no wise man will deny that they have great spiritual uses. And the fact that men can do these things is the encouragement to us to attempt them. Let no one then, be hopelessly dismayed because some evil habit has fastened on him. Let him believe that it can be broken, and all things are possible to him that believeth. Fight the good fight, and fight it to a finish. Re-enforce the will by prayer, and set about the task of your deliverance with faith in God, and reliance on His grace. And remember always, when the fight is hardest, the great lines of Emerson:

"So near is glory to our dust,
  So close is God to man,
When Duty whispers low, 'Thou must,'
  The youth replies, 'I can.'"
    —*Christian Endeavor World.*

Wock 'O Bages.

k o' Bages, keft for 'me"—
hrough the house the words are ringing,
red by a lisping tongue;
sten! 'Tis our darling singing—
ck o' Bages, keft for me,
me hide myse'f in thee."

i, In his study writing,
a he hears the sweet refrain,
aes in his work to listen,
'aits to catch the words again·
ock o' Bages, keft for me,
me hide myse'f in thee."

ock o' Bages, keft for me"—
nd the Voice is soft and low,
, we bend to catch the meaning,
or the breath comes hard and slow;
ock o' Bages, keft for me,
A me hide myse'f in thee."

i darkened room ·he lies,
et the same sweet song is singing,
, into our breaking hearts
eace and resignation bringing:
ock o' Bages, keft for me,
me hide myse'f in thee."

ock o' Bages, keft for me"—
Mamma, sing it; you know how;
rlie's—dying—mamma, darling—
/on't you—sing it—for—him—now?"
ock—o'—Bages—keft—for—me.
—me—hide—my—se'f—in—thee."

ick af Ages, cleft for me"—
t'is a mother sings it now;
th has marked her precious baby,
.nd the damp is on his brow—
ock o' Bages, cleft for me,
me hide myse'f in thee."

t me hide myself in thee;
hou who, hast the wing-press, trod;
is is all we have, O God!
her, must we drink the cup?
st we give our darling up?"

'ock o' Bages"—and our baby
lang the rest to Christ alone,
the angels tenderly
bore him to the great white throne.
ock o' Bages, keft for me,
d be hid himself in thee.
—Hans Gobel, in Good Housekeeping.

A Grumbling Snowflake.

1e little snowflakes were sleeping· in
home in cloud-land.
Father sent a cold wind·to awaken
As soon as they were awake,·the
told them they must go on a long
y—away down to the earth to help
up the little seeds and plants that
sleeping there.
me, my dears, you must hurry, for
lants have· not a single blanket or
to keep them warm. Jack Frost is
d down there, and he will freeze
sure if you don't hurry. Then what
he little girls and boys say when the
: comes, and there are no plants·and
s for them, and no wheat to make
iour for their bread? My, my! You
hurry!"
.kind but noisy old wind blustered
doing his best to get ·them, all
med and dressed for their journey.
k Frost came to help him. He gave
each a lovely white dress, made from
beautiful patterns.
the snowflakes were glad to go, for
did so want to help the little roots
ieeds. Did I say all? Well, there
one little grumbler-flake who seemed
int to stay in the cloud, for he kept
bling away all the time the rest were
g ready. This is what he said;
ie idea! Just think of me, going
down to that big earth! I was down
before, and I know it's like—the big.
place you ever saw. I'm so small
I never see me there, and as for help-
o keep the plants from freezing, I'd
to help keep the poor little things
i until spring comes, but you see I'm
mall. I could not cover the tiniest
· of ground. One little flake on the
big brown earth! He, ha! who ever
l of such a thing! But if you're all
;, I suppose I'd better go, too, although
w I can't do any good."
e other little snowflakes just laughed

at the grumbling snowflake and said, "Just
wait and see, just wait and see!"
Such a jolly time as they had going
down through the air, dancing and playing
—down—down, till it seemed as if they
would never get to the end of their journey.
They talked and laughed about how glad
the little seeds and plants would be when
they covered them up·so snug and warm,
and one little flake said, "Oh, I'm so happy,
to think that I'm really going to be of use
in the big world!"
All the way down the little grumbler kept
grumbling, and the other little flakes
jostled and ·danced against him in ·their
play to try to brighten ·him up. But he
only said, "Oh, if I were only bigger—
only bigger!"
. And this is the chorus the other little
snowflakes sang to answer him with:

"The Father knows best,
The Father knows best;
He sent us,
He sent us;
He'll do all the rest."

At last they came in sight of the brown
earth, and the little grumbler said:
"Just look! just look! What did I tell
you?"
Nearer and nearer they came—oh, such
a big place to cover! Could the grumbler
be right?. But no, still they sang:

"The Father knows best,
The Father knows best:
He sent us,
He sent us;
He'll do all the rest."

Faster and faster they went; nearer and
nearer, down, down—at last one little flake
touched, another little flake touched, and,
just as he touched, the grumbler said:
"Now, wasn't I right?"
He turned his head, expecting to see ·so
many fields ·left bare and brown and cold,
but—everywhere he looked was beautiful
white snow, the whitest; thickest, warmest
blanket you ever saw—not a speck of
brown earth to be. seen.
You see, it happened like this: when this
little grumbler was turning his head, one
little. snowflake touched and covered just
one tiny ·little speck of ground. Another
touched and covered another tiny little
speck. Each one did his own little part,
and when ·they had done that there was
nothing else left to do, for all was done,
and the earth had .on her winter blanket
of snow.
Then the grumbler said: "I was wrong—
foolish and wrong. I will never grumble
again."

"For nothing's too small,
For nothing's too small;
Do your part,
Do your part;
'Littles' make 'all.'"
.   .   .   —S. S. Times.

Christian Publishing Company

2712 Pine St., St. Louis, Mo.

J. H. GARRISON, - - - - President
v. W. DOWLING, - - - Vice-President
JNO. L. SNIVELY, - - Sec. and Gen. Supt
R P. CROW, - - Tress. and Bus. Manager

—What fuel is to engines books are to preachers. Better order our catalog.

—We supply the best unfermented communion wine at 75 cts. per quart. Purchaser pays express.

—For a Christmas present we suggest one of our flexible, silk sewed, leather lined, American Standard Revised Bibles, printed on linen paper—$5, and will last a lifetime.

—There is just one price to all our readers, save preachers. When you pay $1.50 for your CHRISTIAN-EVANGELIST you have the satisfaction of knowing you are getting it at the lowest price.

—Ample expositions of the mid-week prayer-meeting, Endeavor, and Bible school lessons are found in each issue of "Our Young Folks," together with a department devoted to special instruction in the upbuilding and development of our schools.

—"The Little Ones," as its name indicates, is a paper for the nursery. It is printed in colors, and contains short stories, merry jingles and lesson talks that will from the beginning inculcate in the children taste and love for the best literature. Only 50 cents.

—The Garrison Library, series one—A reconstructive theology: "Helps to Faith," "The Holy Spirit," "Christian Union." Series two—Most helpful of devotionals: "Atone with God," "Half Hour Studies at the Cross," "The Heavenward Way." These great books by a great Christian man for $5.00.

—For one new subscription before January 1, 1907, we give as a premium a large, long primer New Testament, or a large picture of Editor Garrison. For two, we will send either a stereoscope with 50 scenic cards, or a flexible cover Teachers' Bible. What excellent Christmas gifts these premiums will make!

—"The Round Table" is a paper for bright boys and girls. It is filled with entertaining stories, travel sketches, and familiar talks on important themes that will greatly enrich the lives of our star-eyed youth. It costs but 50 cents per annum. We suggest to parents that in ordering literature for the children it is well to require an editorial supervision that is concerned about the moral culture of the young reader.

—Friends write that if we would lower the price of THE CHRISTIAN-EVANGELIST they could displace a paper whose casuistic and litigious spirit they do not wish disseminated in their community. Labor, paper and other publishers' requisites have so advanced in cost of late as to make it impossible to publish THE CHRISTIAN-EVANGELIST in its present form for less than $1.50. We ask our friends to help us on this basis to make it a fixture in 100,000 homes before 1909.

—We believe that soon our own Bible school literature will be reinstated in practically all our churches. There is a value in the form of sound words our people are beginning to appreciate as never before. Our doctrines are enshrined in words and sentences with which even children should be familiarized. The Christian Publishing Company's Bible school supplies are edited by one of the most loyal and scholarly living Disciples. Why not procure the best since it is just as convenient and no more expensive?

—300, 500, or 1,000 CHRISTIAN-EVANGELISTS judiciously distributed each week in the vicinity where a revival meeting is in progress will insure not only a full house, but a large congregation of prepared listeners. Without extra cost we send with the first shipment a lot of pink circulars containing the pictures of pastor and evangelist and suitable local announcements. Concerning their use Frank W. Allen, of Odessa, Mo., writes: "Let me say how delighted I am with the plan of using THE CHRISTIAN-EVANGELIST during a meeting. It stimulates interest and adds a dignity to the local work."

—"Our Young Folks" may suggest a juvenile paper to those not familiar with it, but for the juvenile world we publish "The Little Ones," "The Young Evangelist," and "The Round Table." "Our Young Folks" is not regulated by the almanac—it is for the youthful-hearted even if old age has frosted their locks. In addition to its already valuable features a new department on practical Bible school methods and training is now conducted by a talented teacher of many years' experience. Every pastor, superintendent and teacher should immediately become possessed of this invaluable help. Annual subscription, 75 cents.

—Perhaps more new subscriptions at the regular $1.50 rate are coming now by singles and twos than ever before, but in addition to these we are pleased to report the following new clubs from representative churches.

Dayton, O., Asa McDaniel, pastor 5
Odessa, Mo., F. W. Allen, pastor 6
Mobile, Ala., Claude E. Hill, pastor 7
Washington, Pa., E. A. Cole, pastor 10
Stockwell, Ind., R. R. Bulgin, evangelist, ... 12
Lima, O., J. N. Scholes, pastor 16
Hamilton, O., Wesley Hatcher, pastor 20
Philadelphia, Pa., D. T. Stanley, minister 20
Kansas City, Geo. H. Combs, pastor 29
Lexington, Ky., I. J. Spencer, pastor 75

—A subscriber in sending $4.50 in payment of two years' arrearages and the renewal of his subscription adds 30 cents interest. This is rather unique. Many delinquents are inclined to think it exceedingly meritorious to pay arrearages in full. Among the encouragements of the life journalistic are such evidences of an appreciative constituency.

❈ ❈

There is only one real failure in life possible, and that is not to be true to the best one knows.
—*F. W. Faber.*

THE CHRISTIAN-EVANGELIST

A WEEKLY RELIGIOUS NEWSPAPER.

Volume XLIII.   No. 50.

ST. LOUIS, DECEMBER 13, 1906.

THE CHRISTIAN TEMPLE, BALTIMORE,
Whose corner stone has just been laid, and where a rather unique Christian work
will be carried on. See page 1606.

A $250,000 CENTENNIAL FUND

In Personal Offering for Land and Buildings by

Our Centennial in Pittsburg, 1909

The friends of the Foreign Society express themselves enthusiastically in favor of this important move

---

A STRIKING CONTRAST

Contrast this grass hut with the home of F. E. Hagin at Tokyo, Japan, a picture of which is below.

To compel the missionaries to live in century-old, vermin-infected, unventilated buildings is to handicap them in their work and endanger their health and their very lives.

GRASS HOUSE AT DAMOH, INDIA.

Where J. G. McGavran and family lived for a time. They are missionaries of the Foreign Society. They uttered no word of complaint. It is evident they could not do their best work living here. It is not sufficient protection from the extreme heat and heavy rains, and besides there is not sufficient room. We ought not ask our missionaries to live in a place like this. Their health and lives are endangered.

Contrast this home with the grass hut at Damoh, India, the picture of which is above.

This home is a signboard to Heaven for the natives and a means of grace to the missionary.

HOME OF F. E. HAGIN, TOKYO, JAPAN.

This is a modern, up-to-date home, recently built by the Foreign Society at a cost of about $2,000. It is commodious and convenient. It will last many years. Here the missionary and his family can live in comfort and do their best work. Their health and lives will be protected. Besides a good example to the native population, it helps to give them a higher estimate of Christianity.

GOOD NEWS.

A good man and wife have just turned over $8,450 to the Foreign Society on the Annuity Plan. This goes into the Centennial Building Fund. We hope others will take this step. We are receiving cash and pledges every day for a great Centennial Fund. Will you not join the friends in this mighty movement? Please let us hear from you at once.

Address

F. M. RAINS, Sec'y,

Box 884,

Cincinnati,

Ohio.

Date.................1906.

What Some of the Friends Think.

The call for building equipment seems a most modest one on the part of our Foreign Society. With the increase and development of the work there must be increasing demands for such a building plant to insure permanency.   F. D. POWER.
Pastor Vermont Avenue Church.
Washington, D. C.

I hope the Foreign Society will be successful in providing additional building equipment in foreign fields. Necessary buildings are a great help anywhere, but especially on the foreign field.
R. E. HIERONYMUS,
President of Eureka College.
Eureka, Ill.

I am in perfect accord with the proposition of the Foreign Society to secure $250,000 for buildings and equipment in foreign fields. It is timely, and if accomplished will be a great stride in advance in our foreign work.   C. J. TANNAR.
Pastor of Central Church.
Detroit, Mich.

I can say without hesitation that I think no part of the work of the Foreign Board is more important than that of erecting proper buildings for the missionaries in foreign fields. It seems to me scarcely possible to build up a church of influence in any heathen land, or even in any civilized land, without a suitable house in which to hold their meetings, and suitable apartments in which to reside. I hope that you will very soon realize your purpose and expectations in this matter.
J. W. McGARVEY.
President of the College of the Bible.
Lexington, Ky.

To provide homes for our missionaries is the sanest business policy introduced into the realm of the Lord's work. Properly housed, all their forces and resources are conserved, wastes are avoided, and the missionaries are ever at their best. When to comfortable homes there is added complete working equipment in chapels, schools, hospitals and orphanages, we are only multiplying the power of our representatives at the front. Churches at home should share the sadness of our missionaries in often facing great opportunities with their hands tied by lack of proper equipment.
CHAS. S. MEDBURY.
Pastor University Place Church.
Des Moines, Ia.

.... Cut here ....

THE PLEDGE.

I agree to donate to the Foreign Christian Missionary Society, Cincinnati, Ohio, $............... per year for three years beginning June 1st, 1907, to aid in the creation of a special Two Hundred and Fifty Thousand Dollar ($250,000) Centennial Fund to be used for lands and buildings by the Society.

Name ....

P. O. ....

Street or R. F. D. ....

State ....

THE
CHRISTIAN-EVANGELIST

"IN FAITH, UNITY; IN OPINION AND METHODS, LIBERTY, IN ALL THINGS, CHARITY."

Vol. XLIII. December 13, 1906 No. 50

1809 CENTENNIAL PROPAGANDA CHURCHES OF CHRIST 1909
: : : GEO. L. SNIVELY : : :

LOOKING TOWARD PITTSBURG.

No other enterprise in which we are engaged as a people will do more to popularize the church, enthrone Christ in all hearts, and create a Christian enthusiasm that will not fall short of splendid success, than "The Gospel of the Helping Hand" that is being so ably advocated by Secretary Mohorter. God grant him and his faithful co-laborers even more than they have dared to ask in their Centennial program printed below.

Last week the Foreign Society received a pledge for $5,000 from a generous friend in California with which to erect a hospital in Tung Chow, China. This is the kind of Centennial preparation that is needed. Tung Chow is a city just recently entered by our missionaries. We have no land or buildings there. The three families stationed in that important point need homes; suitable homes will conserve their health and their very lives. Read the foreign missionaries' appeal on the opposite page and have fellowship with this generous Disciple that the new hospital may be completed as soon as possible. There should be many of these dedicated to the glory of the Great Physician by 1909.

For forty-three years THE CHRISTIAN-EVANGELIST has continuously, enthusiastically and most effectively advocated and supported every great Disciple enterprise, save the Christian Publishing Company. "Why don't you say a word for yourself, John?" Friends have complained that while we have helped carry on to victory every other crowning enterprise of our brotherhood, we have neglected this on which depend vast interests and in the estimation of many our hopes of ever realizing the religious and church ideals of the "fathers" of this Restoration. THE CHRISTIAN-EVANGELIST has never aspired to be the chief conservator or repository of the faith once delivered, but we are assured that tens of thousands of Disciples fear for the future of our plea should the influence of THE CHRISTIAN-EVANGELIST ever wane. We confess that most that has been done for advancing the interests of this House has had initiation and completion with its friends. Henceforth in the same spirit we advocate Christian missions, Church Extension, Christian education and benevolence we will aid our friends in the enterprise of placing THE CHRISTIAN-EVANGELIST in 100,000 homes and its related literature in churches and Bible schools. "What Our Friends are Saying" is evidence of the spirit of the people and that the popular heart is with us. Come, go, let us all work together and by 1909 so intrench THE CHRISTIAN-EVANGELIST and its collateral interests in the hearts and patronage of 100,000 homes, and 11,000 churches that earnest souls need not be anxious lest the future be without its inspiration and guidance.

If you believe the aid of this House to be essential to a great Centennial victory, will you not show your faith by your works and keep our subscription clerks busily engaged in enlisting new readers and have thousands of additional children studying the Bible school lessons prepared by eminent, loyal and scholarly Disciples. In confidence that it will mean much to the brotherhood we await responses to this appeal.

Benevolent Association and the Centennial.

BY J. H. MOHORTER.

The steadily rising tide of interest in the work of restoring apostolic benevolence is one of the most comforting, encouraging omens of our Centennial. Twenty years ago almost no one in this great religious movement was giving serious thought to this most Christ-like ministry. How remarkable the change wrought by these years. Our National Benevolent Association has come into existence. Through its agency we have opened two hospitals, two homes for aged, dependent brethren, and six orphanages. Twenty years ago, the people who claim to stand for the simple faith of the apostolic church and the beautiful spirit of the Christ were giving $85 for purely benevolent work. Last year they freely gave $91,797.03 to feed the hungry and clothe the naked in the name of him who said, "Inasmuch as ye have done it unto one of the least of these, my brethren, ye did it unto me." In these years seventy-eight helpless old brethren and 4,065 homeless, parentless children have found salvation from hunger, cold and, possibly, crime, under the protecting love of this great brotherhood. Through this ministry 2,207 little neglected waifs have found Christian homes of their own. At the present time sixty dependent old brethren are growing mellow and sweet for the home above, and 225 parentless children are blossoming into beautiful manhood and womanhood under the fostering love of a loyal church.

The most hopeful sign, however, is in the growing appreciation of the value of this ministry in this intensely practical age. It is clearly recognized that the most effective antidote for the prevalence of the lodge spirit and the spread of certain religious crazes is found in this ministry of helpful deeds. Everywhere men are saying, "The best way to restore the church to her primitive place and power is to restore the spirit of apostolic benevolence." From all parts of the country calls are coming for the opening of homes and hospitals. If this enthusiasm can be wisely guided for the next few years we can cover the land with this ministry of love, and so save every homeless child and worthy saint from the almshouse and thrill this whole brotherhood with the spirit that made victorious the church of the apostles. To guide this growing enthusiasm the association has set before the brotherhood the following splendid Centennial aims::

1. To raise a special fund of $40,000 to clear all our institutions of debt.

2. To secure a building adequate for the work of our Central orphanage in St. Louis.

3. To provide a good home for incurables, centrally located.

4. To open at least two more homes for the aged, one on the Pacific slope, and one in the south.

5. To establish an open air sanitarium in Colorado or New Mexico, for those afflicted with tubercular troubles.

6. To open at least five orphanages, one in the southwest, one in the northwest, and three in the section of the country where our people are most numerous.

7. To erect a great memorial hospital in Pittsburg.

8. To raise at least $100,000 with which to begin the endowment of our various institutions.

What more worthy aim can we have than to be able to say at Pittsburg, in 1909, no homeless child, no helpless Disciple need be left to suffer. All are protected in Christ's name.

What Our Friends are Saying.

I am sure our membership will be greatly benefited through their reading THE CHRISTIAN-EVANGELIST.—Una Dell Berry, Lafayette, Ind.

Enclosed find $1.50 for my CHRISTIAN-EVANGELIST. I have only been taking it one year, but like it so well that I can not possibly get along without it.—James Gresham, Glasgow, Mo.

I send one new subscription and my renewal to THE CHRISTIAN-EVANGELIST. I would deny myself many things in preference to giving up my CHRISTIAN-EVANGELIST.—N. D. Evans, Clinton, Mo.

I think THE CHRISTIAN-EVANGELIST is the greatest Christian worker I have ever known. I am in full accord with its teachings and wish it the greatest success. Enclosed find express order for $1.50.—W. H. Smith, Cottage Grove, Ore.

I congratulate THE CHRISTIAN-EVANGELIST force on the make-up and matter of the Alexander Campbell number. As an introductory service, I read extracts from it to my congregation Sunday evening.—W. F. Reynolds, (minister) Cleburne, Texas.

I enclose $1.50 for my CHRISTIAN-EVANGELIST. I like its fraternal spirit so much. It is so helpful to me, as there is no organization of our people where I live, and I must worship with other religious bodies.—Mrs. Olive Thompson, Williams, Iowa.

It is hard to state in finite terms the value of THE CHRISTIAN-EVANGELIST to a preacher or to any Christian worker. As for me, I never want to be without it and, more than that, I do not want others to be without it.—G. W. Woodbury, minister, Hiram, O.

I want to commend your plan on behalf of the State Mission's offering and thank you for the interest THE CHRISTIAN-EVANGELIST is taking in this fundamental work for the support of world-missions.—J. O. Rose, Cor. Sec., Indianapolis.

D. F. Hendrickson, of Glendora, Cal., has recently suffered the loss of his saintly and now sainted mother. He thus writes: No matter how old or how young, there is no good time to lose a mother and no time but what you need her. I shall take THE CHRISTIAN-EVANGELIST if for no other reason than because she loved it so.

We did not get to the Buffalo convention, but we want you to know how much we appreciate the excellent report of the great meeting in last week's CHRISTIAN-EVANGELIST. You have a large circle of readers here and all have words of praise for the effective way you have brought this convention to our very doors.—W. W. Burks, (minister) Nevada, Mo.

The Christian-Evangelist.

J. H. GARRISON, Editor
PAUL MOORE, Assistant Editor

F. D. POWER,
B. B. TYLER, } Staff Correspondents.
W. DURBAN,

Subscription Price, $1.50 a Year.

For foreign countries add $1.04 for postage.

Published by the Christian Publishing Company,
2712 Pine Street, St. Louis, Mo.

Entered at St. Louis P.·O, as Second Class Matter

CONTENTS.

Centennial Propaganda :.....................1599
Current Events 1600
Editorial—
 Sanctification a Condition of Unity......1601
 Progress in Christian Union Sentiment....1601
 The State Must Protect Its Business......1601
 Notes and· Comments 1602
 Editor's Easy Chair 1603
Contributed Articles—
 "Is There a Missing Link?"..............1604
 Problems of Evangelization. J. P. Lich-
  tenberger 1605
 As Seen from the Dome. F. D. Power...1606
 The Elderburg Association 1607
 The Psychology of Baptism. W. J.
  Lhamon 1609
Books that Have Interested Me..........1609
Our Budget 1610
News from Many Fields...................1615
Evangelistic 1619
Christian Endeavor 1620
Midweek Prayer-meeting 1620
Sunday-school 1621
People's Forum 1622
The Home Department 1624

Current Events

Congress is in session again. It has become a custom for Congress to wait (and

Congress. waste) a day before having the President's message. The President scandalized the old-timers by sending in a batch of appointments to be acted upon before the message was read, thus preventing the usual adjournment and saving a day. The message deals with the topics which it was expected to deal with. Much of it has to do with economic and industrial questions. Some of the lines of legislation which are recommended to Congress are: The prohibition of campaign contributions by corporations; to give the government the right of appeal on technical points in criminal cases; to limit the use of injunctions and prevent their abuse especially in labor cases; to limit the hours of labor of railway employes; to establish more thorough and effective control by the Federal Government over all capital, and over all corporations engaged in interstate commerce; to secure an amendment to the Constitution giving the Federal Government jurisdiction over the question of marriage and divorce; to revise and reform the currency laws (the need stated but no specific suggestions offered); to give the Philippines a lower tariff or free trade with the United States; to provide for the naturalization of Japanese. The President's message includes an excellent sermon on moral obligations in international politics, with special reference to the present flurry of anti-Japanese feeling.

❦

The soap trust in England has gone down to a sudden death and a dishonored grave.

How They Do It in England. There is a high degree of effectiveness about the indignant protest of the thoroughly aroused Englishman. When the soap trust was organized as "a working arrangement between the leading soapmakers of the United Kingdom," its promoters thought they had taken into consideration every element in the situation and that their success was sure. They had, in fact, considered everything, except public opinion. The public was against it. The papers smote it, and the soap-buyers sought out obscure and inferior brands rather than patronize the trust. The fever of indignation did not die till its work was done. The boycott did not stop till the trust was defunct. The leaders of this busted trust, in announcing the discontinuance of the "working arrangement of the leading soapmakers," said that it "has been received with such disfavor by the trade and public as to make it unworkable." When a working arrangement becomes unworkable, there is nothing for it but to confess failure. This true story of a trust that failed shows that the people can come pretty near to getting anything they want if they want it enough to undergo some inconvenience in getting it and if they keep on wanting it until they do get it. This is a very practical application of President Hadley's publicity-and-ostracism cure for trusts. But the successful application of this remedy requires a continuity as well as a fervor of indignation which it is hard for the average American to maintain.

❦

One of the perennial railway projects, which thrill the imagination, is the plan of

Pan-American Railway. constructing a continuous line of railroad from New York to Buenos Ayres. Of course a large part of this road is already in existence and in operation. The total distance between the two cities named by the best route is 10,400 miles. The building of 3,700 miles of road would make the connecting link between the North American and the South American railroads. But that is a good deal of railroad. It would cost, we are told, $185,000,000. Would it pay? Probably not. The competition with the water route would prevent it from getting much through freight. The through passenger business would not pay interest on the investment—it never does. And over a great part of the route there would be practically no local business, either freight or passenger. There is no insurmountable engineering difficulty in the way of such a pan-American railroad. In fact, one is scarcely justified in admitting that there are any insurmountable engineering difficulties nowadays. But the economic difficulties would be very great. Perhaps, until some great and unlooked-for change of conditions comes, we will have to be content to call such enterprises economically impossible, except in cases like the trans-Siberian railroad, where a political and military motive is added to the financial.

❦

Secretary Wilson's report issued upon the eve of Thanksgiving day, was a timely doc-

The Backbone of Progress. ument. The statement that the prosperity of the farmer is the basis and foundation of the prosperity of everybody else, is old and hackneyed, but that does not keep it from being true. It is a fact that among those who earn their living honestly here can not ordinarily be much prosperity unless the farmer is getting his show. And this year he is getting it. The value of the farm products of this country for the present year, on the basis of the prices which the farmer will receive for his goods, is estimated by the Secretary of Agriculture at $6,794,000,000. It is a comfort to reflect that in spite of the vast aggregations of capital in the hands of the oil king and others of his kind, the American farmer collectively could buy out the biggest of them a dozen times over out of a single year's income. And it is pleasing to remember also that by far the greater part of this vast agricultural wealth belongs not to great landlords, but to small farmers, to whom the profits of the year will mean not the means for indulgence in senseless and demoralizing luxury, but the opportunity for better and more wholesome living.

❦

A few weeks ago a ship-load of immigrants from Europe arrived at Charleston,

Immigration to the South. S. C. The event was celebrated with much rejoicing, because it was the first ship to land a large number of immigrants at a southern port. If in some way we could get our incoming millions from Europe to go south instead of stopping in New York and a few other cities of the north and east, the immigration problem would solve itself for a few years. The south needs the workers and the immigrants need the opportunities which are offered by the south's need: There is truth in every word said by the opponents of free immigration about the danger of this great mass of undigested and unassimilated foreign population. And there is truth in all that is said on the other side about the vastness of this country and its almost infinite capacity to furnish homes and work for all comers. The trouble is that the comers and the work do not get together. An immigrant who is a peril in New York might be a blessing in Colorado or Alabama. It seems superficially probable also, that an influx of foreign labor into the south would contribute something to the solution of the race problem by freeing the south from its complete dependence upon negro labor.

Editorial

Sanctification a Condition of Unity.

It is a significant fact that in the great intercessory prayer of our Lord, just before he prays for the unity of his disciples, to the end that the world may be converted, he makes this petition for them: "Sanctify them in the truth: thy word is truth. * . * . * * And for their sakes I sanctify myself that they themselves also may be sanctified in truth." Here, then, is a condition precedent to unity, namely: the sanctification of believers in Christ to the will and service of Christ.

The word *sanctify* here means the setting apart to holy uses. Christ devoted himself wholly to the will and work of God, in accomplishing human redemption. To this sublime task he consecrated the infinite resources of his mind and heart, and for this end he sacrificed his life. Indeed sanctification of himself to this work began when he, "existing in the form of God, counted not the being on an equality with God a thing to be grasped, but emptied himself, taking the form of a servant, being made in the likeness of men; and being found in fashion as a man, he humbled himself, becoming obedient even unto death, yea, the death of the cross." The human mind is lost in bewildering awe and admiration in seeking to fathom the fathomless depths of this language. Such was the complete consecration or sanctification of Christ to human salvation.

Now his prayer is that his disciples may be sanctified to this same work. Indeed his sanctification was in order that they might be sanctified. It is clear, too, from the connection in which this petition occurs, and from the very nature of the case, that in the thought of Jesus this complete surrender to the will of God, implied in sanctification, was a condition of that unity for which he prayed. Our word *consecration* expresses very well what Jesus means by our sanctification in the truth. It means putting ourselves at his service, and the abandonment of whatever hinders us from doing his will.

What is involved in our sanctification to the work of saving the world? Nothing less than our complete submission to the will of God, and the putting of all that we have and are at the service of God to be used by him for the world's redemption. It involves, certainly, the putting away of whatever hinders the progress of the kingdom of God in the world. If our worldliness, our indifference, our carnality, our divisions, our party names, party creeds, and party spirit, are obstacles to the triumph of God's reign over man, then our consecration to the work that brought Christ into the world, involves the surrender of all of these things for his sake, and for humanity's sake.

Is this asking too much of us? Shall it be said of those who claim to be followers of him who disrobed himself of glory and took the form of a servant, and died the death of the cross for our redemption, that they are unwilling to abandon their denominational pride and ambition, their divisions and all that perpetuates these divisions, in order to promote the triumph of the church and the redemption of the race? It is written, "God so loved the world that he gave his only begotten Son that whosoever believeth on him might not perish but have everlasting life." O, when will it be written that the church, the bride of Christ, so loved the world that she gave up her denominational pride, her party names, her sectarian aims and worldly ambitions, in order that Christ's followers might be united and the world converted.

This is the relation, then, between our sanctification or complete consecration to the work of God, and the fulfillment of Christ's prayer for the unity of his disciples. Just so long as the church loves the things which divide it, weaken it, and destroy its influence, more than it loves Christ and the unity for which he prayed, its consecration is incomplete and its complete unity can not be realized. Is it not evident that we have had a good deal of unsanctified zeal in behalf of unity? The cause is too holy to be helped by unsanctified efforts. Is there not reason for honest self-examination on the part of all who own Christ as Lord?

Perhaps, the emphasis needed just now is on *consecration* rather than on efforts to formulate bases of union. Let us get closer to the great, throbbing, bleeding heart of Christ, enter into fellowship with his sufferings, and share in the joy of doing his will, and our divisions will melt away like frost before the rising sun, and we shall flow together as kindred drops, and heart will touch heart, and hand grasp hand in a united effort for the salvation of the lost. To this complete consecration we are called by the prayer of Christ, by the needs of the world, by the great providential movements of our time, and by the sweet pleadings of the Holy Spirit now working in a multitude of human hearts to bring about a united church and a redeemed world.

❀ ❀

Progress in Christian Union Sentiment.

Rev. William States Jacobs of the First Presbyterian Church in Houston, Texas, preaching on the question of our differences and divisions, points out the fact that there are as great differences among the members of his own congregation as exist between members of different denominations. He further emphasizes the fact that persons are not required to affirm their belief in predestination and other doctrines of the church, in order to be a Christian or even a member of that church. "All believe and hold to the great essential —the divinity of Jesus Christ." The sermon closes with the following statement:

"The differences are being forgotten. We are coming to see that the things that divide us are not nearly so great as the things that unite us. And so a new era has come. A few months ago I sat in a great convention of young men in Nashville, and saw there the splendid sight of hundreds of the choicest of our Christian college youth uniting in one great cause and that the evangelization of the world. I saw a young man, one of the leaders in the movement, stand before his fellow young men and tell of the tremendous possibilities of the work in the world to-day, of the opportunities which the field offers, and there I saw them fired with the determination which they so aptly expressed in their motto, 'The world for Christ in this generation.' And there sat Presbyterians, and Methodists, and Baptists, and Episcopalians, and people of other shades of Christian belief, all uniting in one common effort.

"The era of strife and dissension has thus given way to the missionary era. The church is fired with the determination to carry the gospel to the uttermost part of the earth, and as one solid army it is united in heart and purpose. The time is past for dogmatic contentions. The work, the vast work that the world offers, is before us and we must be about our Father's business."

This is the key note that is everywhere being sounded and in this kind of atmosphere the church will ultimately grow out of its differences "into the unity of the faith and of the knowledge of his will, spiritual growth—that is to be growth in the knowledge of Christ and of his will, spiritual growth—that is to be the death of sectarianism and the efficient cause of a united church.

❀ ❀

The State Must Protect Its Business.

Attorney-General Hadley of Missouri has recently given an opinion in the case of the Harvest King Distilling Company of Kansas City, which had lodged complaint with the state board of railroad and warehouse commissioners against the American Express Company, because the latter would not accept from it C. O. D. packages of liquor for transportation, that ought to be instructive and suggestive. The Attorney-General holds that the companies can not refuse to receive these shipments, on the following ground:

"The complainant is engaged in a business, the legality of which is recognized by the fact that the state receives from it a license fee, for which it is permitted to engage in the sale of liquor in Jackson county, Mo. Consequently to deprive it of the right to have the liquor that it sells in Jackson county carried by an express company C. O. D. to some local option county would constitute a prejudice and disadvantage to such company which would deprive it of a privilege enjoyed by companies engaged in other kinds of business."

Here is food for reflection. Notice, please, that because the state receives a "license fee" for the sale of liquor in Jackson county the men holding this liquor license are entitled to ship the liquor which they sell into local option counties where the people have decided against the sale of intoxicating drinks. The state may then override the wish and will of the people of any county opposed to the liquor-traffic, in order to uphold a business from which it receives revenue!

Was there ever a stronger indictment against the license system than this decision of our Attorney-General? The decision, too, let us say, seems quite logical and consistent. If the state legalizes a business and receives from it a license fee it would seem that it puts itself under obligations to protect that business. But suppose the *effects* of that business are such that the good citizens in many parts of the state have seen proper to prohibit it within their respective counties, ought the state then to legalize a business so evil in its influence as to work such disaster and ruin, that the good people of the state seek to protect themselves against it? Certainly not. It has no right to the protection enjoyed by "other kinds of business." It curses, others bless and benefit the people. This is the root of the whole matter. It is an iniquitous business, injurious to the welfare of the individual, of the family, and of society, and the state has no moral right to put the seal of legitimacy upon such a traffic. If it does so, it places itself under legal obligations to protect it, even when it overrides the will of counties and communities opposed to it.

How long will it take the law-makers and the courts of this country to see this truth, and to act in accordance with it? Unless our civilization goes backward, it can not be very long.

But our civilization is not going backward, for Jesus Christ is in it, and is leading it forward to a glorious consummation.

Notes and Comments.

The Christian Church in Austin, a suburb of Chicago, has adopted a resolution "prohibiting any money-getting function under the auspices of the church and declaring a higher plane of spirituality could be attained thereby." The pastor, George A. Campbell, in explaining this action, is reported as saying:

"It will give the ladies more time for charitable work. It will increase Volunteer gifts, and put the responsibility of the church upon the members, and stop the running of an opposition to bakeries and restaurants. The ladies were forever talking about bazaars, suppers and entertainments instead of religious subjects. 'Money functions,' said the pastor, 'were branded at our meeting this morning as stomach religion and mercenary religion.'"

The president of a bank in Indiana clipped the foregoing and addressed it to THE CHRISTIAN-EVANGELIST asking, "Does the inclosed correspond with your views?" We answer most emphatically, it does. We believe it to be a poor financial policy to resort to these methods of money-getting, and, worst of all, we believe it to be detrimental to the spiritual interests of the church to rely on these schemes for getting the necessary funds to carry on its operations. The grace of giving, which brings a spiritual blessing to the giver, is one that needs to be cultivated, and direct giving is the best method of cultivating this grace.

But having said this much concerning the advisability of churches engaging in money-making functions, it is only just and proper to say that sometimes under exceptional conditions the ladies of the church, or in a community where we have no church, and

where the male members are few and unable or unwilling to give, are compelled to face the question of doing something to secure funds for the church or to see the cause go down. They sometimes give suppers or make garments or other useful articles with their own hands and hold bazaars with the view of helping the church. We can not find it in our heart to censure these Christian women who give expression to their loyalty to the church and their religious interest by doing such things. The thing which we wish to discountenance, and which we hope to see discontinued, is the resort to fairs and festivals for money-making purposes on the part of churches whose members are able to give directly all the money necessary for carrying forward the operations of the church. It is direct instead of indirect giving that we would advocate as the best means of spiritual growth and the surest path to financial success in church management.

The personal experience which Brother Shelnutt relates in his "Georgia Notes," concerning his change of views on the subject of federation is that hundreds, yea thousands of others who, having a wrong impression of what it is and what it aims at, were opposed to it as inimical to our plea for Christian union, but who, on coming to a true understanding of its spirit and purpose, see in it a powerful agency for hastening the realization of Christ's prayer for the unity of his disciples. This open-mindedness to truth is the glory of the Disciples of Christ, and if they should ever lose that, their history as a reformatory movement is ended and "Ichabod" may be written across what remains.

The very zeal for the principles which distinguish us as a religious body often leads our members to oppose certain movements and measures, the nature and spirit of which they do not understand. As soon, however, as they come to see that the principle, measure or movement, is in perfect harmony with what we are seeking to accomplish, their open-mindedness and love for the truth cause them to fall in heartily with what they had at one time suspected and opposed. This, at least, is the rule. It is perfectly proper that we should be thus zealous in behalf of principles which we hold in trust, but we must see to it that our zeal for the cause we plead is not without knowledge, and especially that it is not without love, which is even greater than knowledge. The Jews were looking for the Messiah, but rejected him when he came, because he did not come in the way they supposed he would come. It would indeed be a lamentable mistake if a religious body, championing the cause of Christian union, should reject it, because it comes in a guise somewhat different from that which we expected it to wear.

In a kindly notice of the Editor's book on "Christian Union" the *Baptist Argus* of Louisville, says:

Dr. J. H. Garrison, Editor of THE CHRISTIAN-EVANGELIST, St. Louis, is making a statesmanlike and Christian effort to restate the positions of the Christian church with a view to Christian union. This book is his formal effort in that direction. If the Christian denomination would appoint a commission in accord with Dr. Garrison to approach the Baptist denomination with a view to a combined restatement we think something of notable moment would happen. This book is a historical exposition of the question involved. When the author comes to the history of his own people his book grows particularly interesting.

If the Baptist denomination had only such newspaper organs as the *Baptist Argus*, The *Examiner*, and some others, and our own religious papers were all like-minded, "something of notable moment would happen" very soon. But it is going to happen anyway, sooner or later, for God reigns.

We, like this manifestation of *esprit de corps* from our esteemed neighbor, the *Central Baptist*:

"The religious weekly can not afford to be shabby. Least of all can Baptist papers afford to lag behind. Baptists do not have to be content with inferior boards or colleges or books or papers. It is a criticism they ought to resent, and one which they will resent, to tell them that any sort of old print is good enough for them. We have no right to discredit our cause and our people in our own eyes and in the eyes of the world by worshiping in tumbled down meeting houses or by handing out papers that are below the common standard in the world of periodicals."

It is interesting to note the fact that our Baptist and Presbyterian brethren in St. Louis have caught the spirit of simultaneous evangelistic meetings and are now making plans for such meetings some time in the near future. It is an encouraging fact that the spirit of evangelism is rising in all the churches, and along with this fact, there is another not less encouraging, namely: the tendency in all the churches to conform more closely to the simple New Testament method of evangelization. A distinguished Baptist evangelist recently held a series of meetings in this city in which there were several conversions, and his method of receiving the confession of those who came forward was substantially that which prevails in our own evangelistic services.

We had a call recently from an able and widely known minister and lecturer, in one of the so-called "liberal" churches who, in the course of a religious conversation, told us his heart was hungering to preach the Christ of the New Testament, and that he was tired of the thin air of human philosophy and speculation which he had been breathing, and his face was "steadfastly turned toward Jerusalem." It is marvelous —this modern hungering and thirsting after the Christ of Galilee. What an infinite advantage have they whose sole mission it is to preach Christ to a weary, heart-hungering world! "And I," said Jesus, "if I be lifted up from the earth will draw all men unto me." Let us lift him up in our pulpits, in our daily lives, in art, in music, in government, and in all that makes up our Christian civilization.

Editor's Easy Chair.

Each season of the year has its own perplexities and cares. The questions now which cause most anxiety and concern in domestic circles is not how to conciliate Japan in relation to the San Francisco school question, nor the discharge of the colored troops without honor, and not even the question of trusts. These all hold a subordinate place now to the main question, which is, What does he or she want for a Christmas present? It is complimentary to human nature that very few are concerned about what they are going to receive, and are anxious only about what they are going to give. They want to give something and they would like to give something appropriate, and that would be appreciated by the receiver. What that particular thing is in each particular case is just now causing a good many people to lie awake of nights. The Easy Chair would be glad to help its readers in their Christmas troubles as in all others, but can only do so in the way of general suggestions. One of these is to avoid costly gifts, as a rule, which to most of us would prove burdensome. Let us not make Christmas a festival to be dreaded on account of the exorbitant demands it makes upon our purses. The value of a Christmas gift, as we all know, does not consist in its cost price, but in the spirit of friendship which it expresses. Then, again, we can not give gifts to all the people whom we admire and esteem. That would bankrupt most of us. Once more, may we suggest that if we remember the poor and the destitute, our gifts are more certain to be appreciated and it is far easier in such cases to decide what to give. A broken, soiled and castaway doll will give more joy to some poor child, than a diamond or a necklace would give to the rich.

❀

We are conscious, however, of having evaded the main question in the foregoing. What shall we give? Can we help each other to solve this problem? Some people have an intuitive gift in this direction, but others have not. The Easy Chair belongs to the latter class, and usually falls back on its lady friends for advice. This is a suggestion which many of our male readers might use with profit. It is a custom in some households to converse very freely in the weeks preceding Christmas about their needs, in which suggestions are thrown out not without a purpose to guide other members of the family in their selection of gifts. These suggestions are always welcomed and mental notes made of them. We have heard of a clever device between husbands and wives for insuring mutual satisfaction in their gifts. Each one purchases for the other some article which he wishes for himself or herself, with the understanding that they would exchange gifts. We do not recommend this method, as it is too utilitarian in its spirit for real gift-making. The more our Christmas-giving is limited to little love-tokens and made the expression of sincere, kindly feeling, the more they will accord with the true spirit of Christmas, and the more joy they will give, both to those who give and to those who receive. And the more unselfish our gifts are—that is, giving where we can not hope to receive in return—the more Christ-like it will be, and the more happiness we shall get out of it. Let the spirit of him whose birth is commemorated by the Christmas festival rule all our giving and all our conduct, if we would get most out of the Christmas season.

❀

"I had not thought of it before," writes one of our readers, "but since reading your editorial on 'The Religious Newspaper Problem,' I am sure it is true that by patronizing your publishing house in its Sunday-school supplies and book business we are making it possible for you to furnish us such a paper as THE CHRISTIAN-EVANGELIST at the low price at which you are offering it." We have no doubt there are many of our friends who fail to connect in their minds the two things which our brother mentions above, as having just seen. In a letter just received from a minister whose name is familiar throughout our brotherhood, he says: "I would despair of the future of our movement if it were not for the commanding influence of THE CHRISTIAN-EVANGELIST, and I think thousands of others feel as I do." While we feel that this is complimentary to the paper we do not quote it for that reason. Such a sentiment, often expressed in letters and in conversation, fills us with a profound sense of our unworthiness and of our responsibility. We do not believe the future of the great cause we plead is dependent on any one religious journal, for God is over all and he raises up agents and agencies for carrying forward his truth. We do believe, however, most profoundly, that those ideals and principles for which THE CHRISTIAN-EVANGELIST stands are essential to the future usefulness and success of our movement. Now this is the point: If this be true, as thousands of our brethren believe it is true, there are some duties and obligations involved in it that the brotherhood ought to recognize. Just in proportion as we receive their co-operation and patronage in all the lines of our publication business, can we propagate those truths and principles, and realize those ideals, which they and we alike believe to be essential to the well-being of the cause we plead.

❀

Jehovah said to his ancient people,

"Oh that my people would hearken unto me,
That Israel would walk in my way!
I would soon subdue their enemies,
And turn my hand against their adversaries."—Psalm 81:13, 14.

God had chosen Israel for a certain work, and if they had been true to their divine calling how much mightier their influence would have been in the world! But God has chosen other peoples in later times to execute his will and carry forward his work. In proportion as these have been loyal to him who has called them, their work has prospered; and in so far as they have departed from his counsel, weakness and confusion have resulted. We who plead for a united church on the New Testament basis of fellowship, believe we have been called of God to this work. He is saying to us, no less than he said to ancient Israel, that if we will walk in his ways and do the work which he has called us to do, he will subdue our adversaries and lead us on to triumph. The only possible failure that can come to us must come through unfaithfulness to God, and the consequent cutting off of his blessing. To his dull and unresponsive people of old Jehovah said, "Open thy mouth wide and I will fill it." God prefers to be generous in his gifts to us. We are not limited in our asking. He wishes us to open our mouths wide that he may fill them. We must expect large things from God. We must plan large things, and work for large things. According to our faith so will it be unto us.

❀

All day the sun has hid his face behind the clouds and the shadowed earth reflects the somberness of the sky. How often it happens that these gray days have their counterpart in our own spirits. It is well at such times to remember that "somewhere the sun is shining," and that it is likely to shine again out of our own sky. If it be better, as the wise man hath said, to visit the house of mourning than the house of mirth, no doubt these somber days minister to our deeper needs better than continuous sunshine. Among other things, they teach us that the roots of our joy and gladness are not to find their exclusive or chief nourishment in our external environment, no matter how pleasant it may be, but in the consciousness of seeking daily to do the work which God has given us to do, and in filling the place in life which he intends us to fill. One who feels himself thus fitted into those eternal relationships and fulfilling his alloted task, may cherish a feeling of joy even in the cloudy days, and sing his songs in the night. It is in the nature of faith to paint every cloud that hangs above us a golden hue, or beautify them at least with a silver lining.

❀

There is probably no more inspiring chapter in the annals of missionary movements than the rise and progress of the Christian Woman's Board of Missions. Its "Day," which has just passed, has been more generally recognized among the churches probably than ever before, and this is as it should be, for no missionary organization among us better deserves our confidence and assistance. The enthusiasm combined with practical wisdom which marks their history is giving a new impetus to all departments of our work. It is emancipating, developing and glorifying our Christian womanhood and making it a most powerful factor, as Christ intended it should be, in the redemption of the world. A child is said to have made this criticism on "Christian" in Bunyan's immortal work: "I like 'Christiana' better than 'Christian,' because he went to the celestial city alone, while she took the children with her." The beauty about the work of our Christian women is that they are taking the children with them through the juniors, and in the home circle, in their march to the city of God.

"Is There a Missing Link?"

[The attention of a number of leading brethren having been called to the editorial in last week's CHRISTIAN-EVAN-GELIST under the above title, with a request for an expression of opinion on the subject, the following replies have been received in time for this issue. Others will follow in later issues, and we will welcome a brief expression of opinion on this question from any of our readers who may feel an interest in it.—EDITOR.]

By W. F. Richardson.

Inasmuch as our general convention has already considered in its annual sessions such diverse interests as those of missions, education, benevolence and Christian union, it seems to me needless to form another organization for that purpose. Rather let us so amend our constitution as to recognize the competency of the general convention of the A. C. M. S. to consider these and other matters, carefully guarding against the consideration of questions of the faith of the church, or the fundamentals in practice. By all means it ought to be possible for us to speak in behalf of our brotherhood on such questions as that of the closer co-operation of the people of God in common moral and social movements for the betterment of our race.
Kansas City, Mo.

By Allan B. Philputt.

I believe there should be a delegate body representing the churches, whose function it would be to pass on questions such as you mention in your editorial. The present acephalous condition of our general conventions has obtained long enough. There are times when the decent and dignified thing to do is to pass on a question and we should not any longer have to make the humiliating confession that we have no tribunal or body competent to do it. We are the only people in the world organized for any purpose whatever, that I know of, without such a representative assembly or head. The details can be worked out so as to safeguard all dangers, and we can still retain our mass conventions where all the people may come; but for certain purposes we need a representative and responsible delegate body. As I see it now, this end can be gained without creating an additional organization, by so amending the constitution of the A. C. M. S. as to provide for what is desired.
Indianapolis, Ind.

By Herbert L. Willett.

I have long felt that the limitations under which our national conventions are organized do not permit of any representative expression of sentiment on subjects which may be of as vital interest to our work as are those of missionary and philanthropic character. I am satisfied that one of two things must transpire: Either we must widen the scope of the missionary conventions, especially that of the American Christian Missionary Society, so that it may consider matters of general Christian teaching as part of its program, or else there must be organized upon a separate foundation a convention which will be thoroughly representative of all the interests of the brotherhood. I see no reason why the former of these two courses is not the better one. There are probably few questions likely to arise at any particular time demanding serious consideration, beyond those which concern missionary work. If, therefore, the constitution of the American Christian Missionary Society can be so amended or interpreted as to include matters of this character, there is no need for further organizations. If, however, it can not, then there must be some plan devised, as we found necessary in the case of the Congress. As the brotherhood grows in diversity of interests and activities we are in great need of some opportunity for expression of opinion on questions which are neither specifically matters of missionary, educational and philanthropic nature, such as the conventions now handle, nor those of doctrinal and social interest such as the Congress discusses. It would seem unfortunate to multiply machinery merely to meet this demand, provided it can be met by a more elastic arrangement of our convention interests. If this is impossible, then the new organization must be projected.
Chicago.

By Robert Moffett.

I have read with much interest your editorial entitled, "Is There a Missing Link?" I am in favor of giving the American Christian Missionary Society the old and well established liberty to consider questions which have to do with the advancement and prosperity of the cause of Christ. I take it for granted that in changing the constitution, the Norfolk convention will not discard state delegations. A by-law can fix the matter beyond dispute that all such

[We call attention to the foregoing comments on the editorial, "Is There a Missing Link." It will be noticed that while there is a slight divergence of opinion concerning the best method of reaching the end desired there is perfect unanimity of sentiment on the essential principle involved, namely: that we must have a representative body competent to deal in a purely advisory and non-legislative way with all questions which have an important bearing upon our present and future well-being, and which may properly come before a deliberative body. That is the point which THE CHRISTIAN-EVANGELIST has emphasized. Whether this end be reached by such a revision of the constitution of the American Christian Missionary Society as will place beyond question its competency, in general convention assembled, to deal with all such matters of general interest, or by the calling of a separate convention, is not a question of vital importance. But that we must have such a representative body to act upon great questions affecting the whole brotherhood, and having to do with the progress of the kingdom of God, admits of no reasonable doubt. It would be a most anomalous and undignified position for any great religious movement to occupy, to plead its inability to discuss, and take any advisory action upon questions of great public concern, because it has no representative body authorized to give an expression of sentiment! And if we were to add to this the statement that we were afraid to trust ourselves to consider such questions of general interest in convention lest we be tempted to legislate and bind the churches by our ecclesiastical edicts, the confession would be as humiliating as it would be ridiculous and unfounded.—EDITOR.]

subjects as temperance education, Christian union, civic righteousness and temperance shall be considered as germane and can be turned over to these state delegations, if necessary, in a separate meeting, but their resolutions not to be binding on the local churches. If the Norfolk convention should go back on the numerous precedents already established, I would favor an organization to be called "The American Disciples' Union," to give voice to any measures which have alliance with whatever makes for righteousness. As a religious body we can not afford to withhold hand or voice for the world's uplift.
Cleveland, Ohio.

By F. D. Power.

That at some time and place other questions beside missions, pure and simple, need consideration by a representative gathering of our people, there can be no doubt. These matters are constantly coming up, and it seems hardly fair to expect our much overworked editors to settle them all infallibly. The Congress answers a purpose, but is not sufficiently representative, as from the very nature of things we can not assemble in large and representative numbers twice yearly. Our great missionary gatherings bring together the largest numbers possible, and the men that lead in these meetings could speak for the churches on other great interests that concern our people. Why may there not be a day, or two days, added to the time of the conventions, which shall be devoted to other matters than missions? Then the consideration of these matters, and any action thereon, could not be chargeable to the missionary societies, and would in no way interfere with their usefulness. We desire harmony among the brethren on all measures, and a conference of this kind would aid greatly to the unity of the brotherhood and clear up many misunderstandings.

By E. L. Powell.

Referring to the editorial in this week's CHRISTIAN-EVANGELIST, it seems to me that a representative convention apart from those of the missionary societies would be more desirable than revising the constitution of the A. C. M. S. in order to make it practicable in dealing with questions other than those which are strictly missionary. Of course, such a representative convention would have no binding authority on any of our churches. It would be purely advisory and to this extent helpful. It would give to those who should be sent as delegates to the convention an opportunity to express themselves on very many questions with which our people should deal. I should like a convention in which the very largest liberty of utterance could be granted, and one not too formal in its exercises. We have not the time at our national conventions, as at present arranged, to do anything more than carry out a definitely prepared program. I should think that such a convention as you suggest would be largely attended, and would make its influence felt throughout the entire brotherhood. I like the idea of another convention separate and distinct from those which assemble on the occasions of our national meetings.
Louisville, Ky.

Problems of Evangelization

Being the Second Part of the Address before the Buffalo Convention on "Disciples and Evangelism."

By J. P. Lichtenberger

That we are facing new problems in present day evangelism is apparent. The times are different. We are now in the 20th century. "We go forth conscious that the Faith confronts the civilization not of a hundred, of fifty, of ten years ago." This is the sublime and awful present.

The Evangelization of the City.

In the new evangelization the city is the centre. It is the product of present social and economic conditions. It is constantly assuming larger proportions and influence. In 1790, 3.4 per cent of our people lived in cities of 8,000 and over; in 1890, 29.2 per cent; to-day over 35 per cent, while in the North Atlantic division more than 60 per cent. The rate of growth (Weber, "Growth of Cities"), increases from the rural districts, which tend to decrease, to the metropolis. Small towns are about stationary. Large cities are making rapid growth while the cities of the first rank are marvelously increasing. Recent attempts to show that an opposite tendency has set in are unscientific and abortive. They are but eddies in the stream of population flowing into the cities, or else they prove to be merely movements toward the suburbs of the greatest cities. There is no reason to think the present trend will change under present economic conditions.

The modern city is the test and opportunity for the church. Its conditions are new and untried. Many have considered them inimical to the progress of Christianity, and not a few have been willing that we should turn hopelessly to the stationary or diminishing populations of the village and country as our field because they offer larger present gains. To do this is to abandon the real issue. It is to concede the impotency of our evangel and that it stands helpless on the threshold of the new civilization.

WHAT CHRIST SAID.

I said, "Let me walk in the fields,"
He said, "No, walk in the town."
I said, "There are no flowers there,"
He said, "No flowers, but a crown."

I said, "But the skies are black;
There is nothing but noise and din."
And He wept as He sent me back;
"There is more," He said: "there is sin."

I said, "But the air is thick,
And fogs are veiling the sun."
He answered, "Yet souls are sick,
And souls in the dark undone."

I said, "I shall miss the light,
And friends will miss me, they say."
He answered, "Choose to-night
If I am to miss you, or they."

I pleaded for time to be given.
He said, "Is it hard to decide?
It will not seem hard in heaven
To have followed the steps of your Guide."
—George MacDonald.

To concede that the cities are ultimately unfavorable and that modern civ-ilization is detrimental to the cause of Christ is to surrender faith in the power of the Gospel. If this be true, then the Church must inevitably decline with the growth of cities and the march of progress. It is to put the church on the defensive and consign it to the task of counteracting an increasingly hostile environment. It is to impose the church against progress.

Such are not the facts. Such is not the fate of the Gospel against which the gates of Hades shall not prevail. The church is not to be repudiated by the best product of the civilization it has been the most instrumental in creating. Brethren, it is time we cease beating ourselves against invisible and imaginary barriers like a frightened bird in its cage, but with more intelligence and faith apply ourselves to the solution of the problem. The seeming obstacles in the cities are neither essential nor permanent and constitute the challenge of the church to improve them. Shelley said "Hell is a city much like London," and we have made a program of his pessimism. Canon Freemantle uttered the word of wisdom for the age in reference to the city when he said "It is a vain thing to go back upon human progress. The industrial revolution which has made our great cities, and which through them supplies the needs of mankind, is part of God's providence; and what we have to do, the real task of our generation, is to face the problems which the city life presents, applying to them the light which the Bible gives us, and determining, so far as in us lies, and by the power of God and of Christ, that London and New York shall not be as Babylon, but as the New Jerusalem."

Where has our evangelism won its greatest victories? According to the statistics of our Year-Book, in ten cities of the first rank, (Buffalo, Chicago, Cleveland, Des Moines, Kansas City, Pittsburg, St. Louis, Washington, Los Angeles, and New York); we have grown in ten years from 41 to 107 churches, and from 11,424 to 32,353 communicants —a growth of 183 per cent, while in the country at large the growth in the same decade did not exceed 60 per cent.

We have the message for the modern city. Let us attack the problem with faith in God, and the Gospel with a heroism worthy of our sires.

Adjustment to Present Conditions.

Precisely in the same manner in which the severest tests of Christianity arise out of the forces which it itself has released, so we as a people are being tested as to our ability to adjust ourselves in the midst of influences to which we have contributed more than any other religious body. If we have been the pioneers in the plea for Christian union we are not to-day its sole advocates. Others have joined us with the enthusiasm of the champions of a new cause. The battle has not been won, nay, in some quarters it has not even been heard that there has been any progress. This is for reasons akin to those prevailing in China, where, we are told, there are millions of Chinese who do not so much as know that there ever was a Japanese-Chinese war, and millions more who think they whipped the Japs. But among the leaders and in the enlightened portions of the kingdom conquests for Christian union have been won and large progress achieved.

In a Christian country, therefore, where the people are neither ignorant nor opposed to our policy our advocacy of it must be different from the plea of 1840.

Our theories are being judged by our practices. Our friends, "the enemy," are estimating the genuineness of our convictions upon the union question by our attitude toward the honest efforts of others to accomplish the same task. They desire to perceive whether our interests are chiefly the kingdom, or the building of a strong religious party; whether Christian union is a passion with us or a denominational slogan. Strange enough to excite the wonder of many outside our ranks and significant enough to create some interest among us, is the fact that practical efforts for the actual accomplishment of Christian union in the last decade, have not arisen with us, but with others whose professions have been less pretentious, while an attitude of unfriendliness has sometimes been perceptible among us. Our tree is being judged by its fruit.

Are we equal to this new test? I think we are, but our hope lies not in the way of a polemic defense of the logic of our position, but in a new wave of evangelistic fervor, not inspired by a party shibboleth, but by the love of Christ for lost men, which shall sweep us forward with all who share that love, to the conquest of the world for him. Let us, then, in sympathy with every worthy effort to unite God's people for the sake of the world's redemption, join hands, touch shoulders, keep step with the ongoing of the great army of God, and prove the sincerity of our profession and the righteousness of our plea.

For this we need educated evangelists as we need an educated ministry. Too long a zeal of God, and ability to exhort, have been considered the chief requisites of the evangelist. Our colleges are rendering a service for which we are not adequately compensating them, either in appreciation or means, for the character of men they have trained and are training for our evangelists. We are coming more and more to consecrate our best trained men for this holy service to-day. We have happily fallen upon a time, when the once opprobrious title of "Dr." may be worn with perfect propriety by the peer of our evangelists, and it has not seemingly detracted from his power. The plea for an educated ministry has now become a universally recognized need with us. I plead earnestly, brethren, the same necessity for the evangelist who shall represent us in this all important work.

The Wider Scope of the Term.

Another problem confronting our evangelism is our frightful waste and loss. Our statisticians tell us we have a gross increase of 100,000 per year, while we have a net increase of 31,000. Many churches reporting large increase in evangelistic meetings show no larger membership as the result. Much of this loss is unavoidable. Nor do I think the difficulty lies in the over-emphasis of *numbers.* Men who decry numbers are usually men who have few additions. To win the multitudes is our mission. The cry of "Not numbers, but souls," is a thoughtless and foolish alarm. Our evangel is for the world. The man who fears numbers lacks the spirit of Pentecost. Furthermore, I am a pastor,

and have not forgotten that the care of the numbers rests heavily on the pastors. I do not seek to escape responsibility. Still, the vital matter has not been touched.

The connotation of our term "Evangelism" is too narrow. Often the evangelist turns over to the pastor a host of "additions" (a much abused word), neither converted nor added to the Lord, and for whom the Lord himself would likely refuse to be responsible. We have no word in our religious vocabulary to define the result of a great meeting. We need a new terminology. Many are not converted, in any ordinary acceptation of that term. They are not added to anything. They simply came forward and immediately slid backward. Moved to their repentence, by "a godly sorrow," but rather by the emotional appeal of the evangelist and the mental suggestion of the mind of the crowd, they are not prepared for the experience of the "morning after."

What can be done to evade the religious reaction and spiritual dearth which frequently follows in the wake of the "great" meeting? I answer: Substitute an *intelligent Christianization* for an over *emotional*

evangelism. See to it that faith in the Divine Person becomes the dynamic in conversion. Let love for him be the compelling force rather than hypnotic suggestion. Inspiration is better than perspiration. The sufferings of Jesus produce a more lasting effect on the heart than the contortions of the evangelist. Transformation of life by Christ's spirit is the object to be attained rather than formal obedience to positive commands. Confession and baptism are essential as initiatory acts, but the ultimate test is not obedience, but "Holiness, without which no man can see God." The final proof of our loyalty in the sight of Jesus is a life invested for humanity, "inasmuch as ye did or did it not to one of the least of these, my brethren." To serve Christ is to serve men. To follow in his steps is to go about doing good. To call him Lord we must do the thing which he says. His mission in the world was not to be baptized, but to do the will of God on earth as it is done in heaven. Formally to make the good confession makes an "addition." Sincerely to obey him as Lord and to live by his spirit constitutes a Christian.

(To be Continued.)

As Seen From the Dome   By F. D. Power

Once more Congress is with us. For three months it is to be on our hands. Congress is our peculiar joy, our annual wonder. From the first Monday in December new faces appear on our streets, new people throng our hotels, new animation stirs our official atmosphere, new turnouts dash along our avenues, new impulses and fads and functions awaken society. The whirl is on and we all enjoy it. The District of Columbia appreciates the nation's aggregation and watches with ever renewed interest the interplay of social and political ambitions, the clash of rival parties, and the sharp contests for the best places in the limelight. In these thirty-one years I have watched the play. It has varied little. These mortals are men of like passions with those who preceded them. Solons they are as were their fathers, patriots of the same quality, politicians for the most part, but God reigns still and the government shall live.

It is not presumable that things will be dull. The man who runs things at the other end of the avenue is likely to prevent inertia. He has things to say that will stir as goads the indolent. What if he insists upon the "Nu Spelin'." Some of our representatives have not yet fully mastered the old, and a revision of the dictionary is sure to arouse such standpatters. Tariff revision, the currency, a larger navy, the insular possessions, the big ditch, Smoot, the discharge "without honor" of the negro companies, the Algeciras treaty and the Santo Domingo treaty, the River and Harbor bill, the war cloud over the Japanese and San Francisco, the immigration and ship subsidy questions, the labor bills, the Cuban revolution—everything but the abolition of the traffic in intoxicating drinks, will receive attention and even this will come up in the House, for our Brother Webber of Ohio, is determined to push his bill for prohibition

in the District of Columbia. Webber for President would suit us.

There have been some changes. There are many lame ducks, some of whom have been long in the service. My friend, Mr. Wadsworth, of New York, one of the few left of the 47th Congress when I served as chaplain, "Farmer Jim," is allowed to retire. Another man of prominence, but one we could well spare, Babcock of Wisconsin, becomes a private citizen. There are a number from Wisconsin. Grosvenor of Ohio, a grim old warrior of many hard-fought fields, is turned down by his people. Fred Landis is another. New men will come in their places. Three months more and these will pass out of the public eye. The King is dead, long live the King. It is astonishing, after all, how easy it is to drop out of sight, when we have felt the poor world could not get along without us. With all its gratification at the coming of the annual show within its gates, Washington knows but few of these gentlemen, and does not seriously miss the great majority when they retire from service. The makeup of the procession changes, but it is the procession that interests us, and the procession keeps moving. Some of the oldest members went to their last home since the first session of the Fifty-ninth. Among them Hitt and Ketcham of my old flock, the Forty-seventh. They were strong men. Only two or three are left of the Congress I served. Speaker Cannon is one, Keifer is another. As I personally know every member of that House I have watched their careers with interest. They have gone—they have all passed by, and that is only a quarter of a century in the past. The history made since I have known Congress would fill many volumes, and the future promises even greater things.

The President is vigorous enough in

his message. There is too much about war for an old-fashioned Quaker, and too little about rum for a latter day Prohibitionist. Social-politics and world-politics are treated well. California is disgruntled; but Nippon is delighted. He begins with corporations and ends with rifle clubs. He pleases the believers in a strong central government, and disgusts the states-rights people. He has been in touch with the Spanish thought recently enough to say "Mánana! Manana!" and thinks about many things that "it may best to wait," and "in the near future" tackle them. He is sound on the divorce question, and his dissertations on righteousness, peace, and international unselfishness will meet general approval. He has stirred up the animals to a remarkable degree. The outcome will be watched with eagerness.

Meantime the Kingdom of God advances. Our own Zion is busy. Sunday, December 2, I had the privilege of assisting Peter Ainslie, of Baltimore, in laying the corner stone of his Temple. After a good program in the chapel five hundred Sunday-school children paraded and swung the 1700 pound stone in place and buried it in roses and carnations. The Cardinal himself could not have gotten up a prettier spectacle. The new addition to the Temple will cost $3,000 and will be a most attractive edifice. Two years ago I was with this congregation at the corner stone laying of their chapel. Then in the stone they put a list of 237 members and 101 Sunday-school scholars, while in this case the figures are 445 and 626 respectively. Catholics and Protestants, Jews and Gentiles have shared in the good work. The new building will accommodate 1400 when complete. There are crowds attending the Temple services and constant additions. It is a veritable hive of industry and thoroughly united

(Continued on Page 1608.)

The Elderburg Association

[This association is, as Brother Doctor has said, "in its existence and in its component parts a remarkable phenomenon, a portent, perhaps." We began this series of reports of the meeting on the green of the court house, of the twelve preachers of Elderburg in our issue of March 8, 1906. They ran on until early summer when they were discontinued for the time being, owing to the difficulty of finding space for a regular series of articles. The difficulty of finding this space is as great as ever, but we are making an effort to conclude the series because we believe they are well worth while. They discuss problems and situations that effect more or less every church and every preacher and these are presented in a humorous and quaint style. Brother Doctor suggested that the association ought to spend some time each day in the discussion of the topic "Why we are where we are, or what is the matter with us?" An arrangement for carrying his idea into effect was instantly made. Brother Notary and J. P. was appointed to preside at all discussions. Brother Lawyer was appointed official critic and reviewer, while Brother Schoolmaster was made secretary.—EDITOR.]

CHAPTER VIII.

Experiences of Brother Paper-Hanger.

Brother Paper-Hanger was a medium-sized man whose hair, now of a beautiful silver-gray color, had once been a very deep auburn. He had keen, shrewd blue eyes, and whenever he smiled little wrinkles, like marks of parenthesis, appeared at the corners of his eyes and on either side of his mouth. He was a Scotch-Irishman, and he spoke with a slight burr. When he took off his hat before beginning his story, a tuft of white hair stood up aggressively above his forehead.

"I don't mind telling you, gentlemen, that I am in my present state of extinguishment because I have found it easier to guide a paste brush over the church walls than to guide my own tongue in the pulpit. I'm not without pretensions to scholarship, as some of you know. I have had debates with Mormons, Spiritualists, Universalists, and divers other heretical persons, and I've no reason to be ashamed of the outcome of those battles. I admit that I have met, in my public discussions, men who were my equals in logic and my superiors in eloquence; but for roasting a respected adversary over a slow fire of irony, or for filling his skin full of the barbed arrows of wit, sarcasm, innuendo, I am the peer of any man of my generation.

"Though I have never preached to empty benches, in any place where I have labored, it is a singular fact that I could never hold a pulpit long. 'My hair is gray, but not with years;' and this premature grayness is due to the hot water in which I have lived almost constantly, from the first day I entered the ministry until the day I left it. I perceive, brethren, that what the apostle foretold has come to pass: The so-called Christians of our day have itching ears, and they will no longer endure sound doctrine. Yet sound doctrine is the only thing I would ever consent to preach. I, too, Brother Lawyer, am one of those unfortunates, one of those embryonic martyr-heroes to whom the Lord has added keenness of vision to discern evil, and from whom he has subtracted that nice, wise, discreet power to sugar-coat the truth so that men shall swallow it 'unbeknownst' to themselves, so characteristic of the popular preachers of the day. Set me front to front with mine adversary, and I smite—suddenly, swiftly, unsparingly, without preliminary flourish of trumpets or exchange of cartel.

"I need not, I suppose, catalog for your information the manifest, crying evils of our time: drunkenness, gambling, prostitution, corruption in public and private life; nor need I call your attention to the cowardice of Christians in the face of them. In every congregation where I have worked there have been people, few or many, who needed admonition on these subjects. Toward such people my attitude has been that of Solomon: 'How long wilt thou sleep, O sluggard? When wilt thou arise, out of thy sleep?' I have prodded such sluggards with all spiritual implements at hand; prodded them till the blood came, sometimes, but it was for their good. Thank goodness, it was never possible for any weak-kneed professor to go to sleep under my preaching when once I had got him located. For he could never foresee, no matter what my subject might be, what sudden, red-hot thunderbolt, barbed with wit or sarcasm might be aimed at his guilty heart. Many a time have I seen the unhappy one turn pale and writhe; and let him seek to conceal the wound as he might, I would know that his heart's blood was flowing. You do not know, brethren, if you have never given attention to the matter, how abundant are the opportunities for that sort of execution open to any man with a fair wit and a reasonably good command of our language—if only he will cultivate firmness of heart and a sure aim. For example:

"At Wayback there were old Brother and Sister Willyum, who used tobacco; at Wollyville there was Brother Bourbon, who had once signed a petition for a saloon; at Speedy there was Sister Uppity, who gave balls and progressive card parties; at Degeneracy there were several young people who danced and certain old people who kept private demijohns. Ah, me! the white-hot Gospel thunderbolts I have fired at each one of them, without ever failing to score the bull's-eye! I launched truth, every time; truth from the great arsenal of truth. Observe now: Every one of those people, instead of becoming convicted of sin, instead of amending his life, quit coming to church; each of them had influence enough to stir up a party against me; and the influence that each had he used to injure me! Am I not justified when I say the time is come when the people who call themselves Christians will no longer endure sound doctrine?

"The defeat which finally disheartened me was when I entered into a fight against the saloons, brothels, and gambling hells in Flodden. Have you, any of you, ever tried to move a dish of moral skim-milk to action, in an enterprise like that? If so, you know something of the weaknesses, imbecilities, skulkings, and cowardices that may suddenly develop in men and women who should be veterans of the Cross. The man who has the job of leading that undisciplined rabble of incompetents against the wary, unscrupulous, well-organized, well-appointed hosts of evil, is not to be envied. Certainly, in this fight, as in most other fights of that kind, there were many true, brave, resourceful people; but the work of overcoming the cowardice of the cowards and the folly of the fools so occupied the time and attention of the capable few that they had but little time left to devote to the common enemy.

"I cannot say I have been wary of entering into quarrels, as old Mr. Polonius advises, yet being in, I have tried to so bear myself that the enemy might beware of me. In this particular battle I bore myself like a valiant man and true; fought with pen, tongue, and (once) with bare knuckles; fought it from the pulpit, on the stump,

❀ ❀

A FRIEND'S ADVICE.

Something Worth Listening To.

A young Nebr. man was advised by a friend to eat Grape-Nuts because he was all run down from a spell of fever. He tells the story:

"Last spring I had an attack of fever that left me in a very weak condition. I had to quit work; had no appetite, was nervous and discouraged.

"A friend advised me to eat Grape-Nuts, but I paid no attention to him and kept getting worse as time went by.

"I took many kinds of medicine but none of them seemed to help me. My system was completely run down, my blood got out of order from want of proper food, and several very large boils broke out on my neck. I was so weak I could hardly walk.

"One day mother ordered some Grape-Nuts and induced me to eat some. I felt better and that night rested fine. As I continued to use the food every day, I grew stronger steadily and now have regained my former good health. I would not be without Grape-Nuts as I believe it is the most health-giving food in the world." Name given by Postum Co., Battle Creek, Mich. Read the book, "The Road to Wellville," in pkgs. "There's a reason."

in the press. Well, we were whipped. We were defeated because the tie of party was stronger with some Christian voters than any plea we could make for civic righteousness. Among these voters was an elder of our congregation. This man did actually try to control nominations in his party so that decent men might be put up as candidates. Bless your life, the wise ones in that party just played with this good man; snowed him under ten deep. Yet he went on and voted for and with the gang that had routed him. When it was all over I fired a parting shot through the columns of a local paper. (Five cents a line, one insertion.) I fired it in the form of a song. I believe I can repeat it from memory:

SINGULAR SONG OF A SUBDUED SAINT.

(Apologies to Savitar.)

(Air.—"Mountains of Hepsidam.")

With the east wind at large in his whiskers,
(Ho, the storm-wind Euroclydon!)
The church-member old stood alone in the cold
And sang as the gale howled on—
Sang thus as the gale howled on:—
"This here ain't no song of no sixpence,
Nor a song of a tank full of rye;
But the theme of these walls as I'm running
these scales,
Is the boys and the party and I.

(Chorus after each verse:)

I'm innocuous, tame, inefficient,
When it comes to affairs of state;
I am flaccid, obese, and torpid;
And I'm classed as an invertebrate.)

"There are statesmen abroad in this nation,
Wise to most things on land or on sea;
Yet I venture to bet you ain't never met
Any statesman aware of me.

"You're supposed to be nice where a gal is,—
Yes; you have to walk-chalk with your wife,
But you're free to make free with yours truly,
you see,
'Cause I never engage in strife.

"I'm saddle-broke, bridle-wise, gentle,
And I shore seldom balks or kicks:
But I'm aye in a fix when invited to mix
Religion with pol-i-tics.

"Yes, yes; as a large tax-payer
I am back of the whole shebeen;
But the dough-faced gossoon who runs the
saloon
Attends to the party machine.

"No; they don't mind me—I'm a Christian;
My work is to fast and to pray
And to dig up the stuff for the tough and the
rough,
To 'blow' on election day."

"You may not think much of this, as poetry, brethren, but I assure you that it was much discussed in Flodden—created there the literary sensation of the year. It also was a contributing cause to my resignation as pastor of that congregation. The elder of whom I have spoken was pleased to consider himself satirized in that poem; some of his friends in the church and some of my enemies outside of the church encouraged him in the notion. Taken along with my other fearless utterances in the course of that campaign, those verses got me into a little of the hottest hot water I have ever been in. A saloon-keeper there chose to identify himself as the 'dough-faced gossoon' of the poem. He assaulted me one day, so that I had to defend myself with the arm of flesh. A result of that encounter was the appearance of my name in a daily paper, under large, black headlines.

A more or less witty reporter characterized the affray as 'The second battle of Flodden field, only, in this case, he said, the battle was not between the English and the Scots, but between the Irish and the Dutch.

Of 'course you easily guess what happened. A pressure was brought to bear on the church board by my enemies in the congregation, and the board could not, or would not, resist the pressure. They respected me, they said, believed me to be sincere, etc. Other churches, hearing of my troubles at Flodden, fought shy of me. Fortunately for me, there was, about that time, an opening for an artistic paper-hanger in Elderburg. I leave my patrons to say how well I have filled that opening.

(To be Continued.)

As Seen From the Dome.

(Continued from Page 1606.)

under the pastor's leadership. Numerous societies and lines of work keep every member busy. There is a Bible Seminary with sixty students. There is an orphanage work with twenty children who are wards of the Temple. There is the Tribune home for working girls. There is a living link missionary in Miss Edna P. Dale at Wuhu, China. Peter has no time to play golf, though a Scotchman by descent, and yet he is like an enthusiastic golf player of whom the story is related that one day with an older man, as they wended their way homeward from the links, the older enthusiast said: "We have had a fine day, laddie, a grand day. Shall we play to-morrow?" "Weel, I had arranged to be married, but I can put it off," said the younger. Peter has no time even to get married. His centennial aim is 1000 in the membership of the Temple, 1000 in the school, 100 in the Seminary, two living links on the foreign field. Peter has served in Baltimore for fifteen years, and three churches tell the story. Perhaps his only recreation is to act as chaplain of the St. Andrew's Society of the city, an organization of men from "the land o' cakes," or their descendants, for which he has been chosen three times in succession. He is a good representative of the fisherman and enjoys Acts II.

Our other churches in Baltimore are prospering. B. A. Abbott, C. M. Kreidler and E. C. Baker helped in the corner stone ceremonies. The last is a recent addition through Brother Abbott's preaching from another communion, and is in charge of the Calhoun Street work. Washington is not idle. W. G. Oram, late of Brooklyn, has accepted a call to our H Street Church and is already on the field. B. E. Utz is conducting excellent service at the Ninth Street Church. J. E. Stuart had a fine meeting with L. D. Riddell as evangelist and the Fifteenth Street Church is growing steadily. Vermont Avenue has taken on its winter aspect. The Sunday-school under the able leadership of E. A. Gongwer, is in a lively contest with that of

the First Church, Philadelphia, and the Quaker city, where they do not eat snails because they cannot catch them, is stirring.

Some Things.

Did you forget last Lord's day that your Savior had said "Do this in remembrance of me"? It is as if this request is repeated to you every week.

Did you forgive that brother who had sinned against you before you asked your heavenly Father to forgive you? If not you would better go again.

Are you on the committee "To secure the pastor's resignation"? If so, do you know how to do your work? Never give up until you bring in a favorable report. Verily, you will have your reward. Part of your reward will come now, for you will gain your end and drive the pastor out of town. But part of your reward you will have to wait for, but it is sure. The Lord never forgets.

An elder has been heard in a prayer-meeting apologizing for, and defending the licensing of saloons. His political party is committed to license. This is why. What ought to be done to him? What will the Lord do with him?   E. L. FRAZIER.

"PROUD AND GLAD"

Because Mother Looked So Well After Quitting Coffee.

An Ohio woman was almost distracted with coffee dyspepsia and heart trouble.

Like thousands of others, the drug in coffee—caffeine—was slowly but steadily undermining her nervous system and interfering with natural digestion of food.

"For 30 years," she writes, "I have used coffee. Have always been sickly—had heart trouble and dyspepsia with ulcers in stomach and mouth so bad sometimes, I was almost distracted and could hardly eat a thing for a week.

"I could not sleep for nervousness, and when I would lie down at night I'd belch up coffee and my heart would trouble me. At last, when I would want to drink coffee, it would gag me. It was like poison to me. I was thin—only weighed 125 lbs., when I quit coffee and began to use Postum.

"From the first day that belching and burning in my stomach stopped. The Postum went down so easy and pleasant. I could sleep as soundly as anyone and, after the first month, whenever I met any friends they would ask me what was making me so fleshy and look so well.

"Sometimes, before I could answer quick enough, one of the children or my husband would say, 'Why, that is what Postum is doing for her'—they were all so proud and glad.

"When I recommend it to anyone I always tell them to follow directions in making Postum, as it is not good to taste if weak, but fine when it is boiled long enough to get the flavor and rich brown color." Name given by Postum Co., Battle Creek, Mich. Read the little book, "The Road to Wellville," in pkgs. "There's a reason."

The Psychology of Baptism　By W. J. Lhamon

In the October number of "Religious Education" John Dashell Stoops, Ph.D a professor in Iowa College, Grinnell, Iowa, presents an article under the caption "The Psychological Basis of Religious Nurture."

Among other suggestions of value one finds the following: There is a view of religion and salvation according to which they are the gifts of the church through her sacraments. This is the institutional method of salvation. The church has baptized the man—therefore he is saved. Or, the church has bestowed extreme unction—therefore the dying one is saved.

This method, Professor Stoops says, "fails to take account of the fact, which is absolutely vital, that religion springs out of the fundamental instincts of the mind itself. The church is not a means of bringing religion from some outside source to the individual; it is rather the expression of a common religious experience. The rite of baptism, accordingly, must be regarded as a symbol of an inner transition of experience, a fully conscious giving up of self to the divine life. There is implied a development of will sufficient to enable the individual to understand the nature of the transition through which he is passing. Infant baptism belongs to the institutional or sacramental theory. The baptism of Jesus, symbolizing the personal consecration of his adolescent self to the Kingdom of God is the ideal type of true baptism."

This is putting in a psychological way what we have been saying all along in our Christological way. It is comforting indeed to see twentieth century psychology rising up to confirm first century theology. Is infant baptism coming under the ban of science as it has been under that of Scripture? Then, its day is practically past. And adult baptism also, as a mere sacramental conveyance, of salvation, must pass out of our thought and teaching. Baptism, real baptism, must be an act of the soul rather than of the church; it must be psychological. It must spring from the enlightened, believing, responsive heart. It must not be an imposition of the church, but an inspiration of the child of God to respond to the will of God.

Bible College of Missouri.

Books That Have Interested Me

I have been especially interested in Brierly's books this year. My regret is that I did not find him earlier. Why? Well, who can put an answer to such a question as that! I like Brierly because I like him, that's all. If I were to add, because he is provocative of thought, incisive in style, fresh and vigorous and unconventional and free, my neighbor might read the book and truthfully say: "It seems not so to me." So after all it's a question of taste, a fundamental matter of palate. I like Brierly. He has helped me. No doubt many have already tasted him and know. Books are like soup. My friend likes bean soup. I abhor it. Every man to his liking.

GEORGE H. COMBS.

※

I have read the following books this year, but I haven't time now to tell you why they have interested me: "Immanence of God" (Bowne), "Rational Living" (King), "Life of Gladstone," two volumes, (John Morley), "Jesus Christ and Christian Character" (Peabody), "Old Testament Criticism" (Orr), "Old Testament Religion" (Kent), "Strength and Weakness of Christian Science," "Primitive Traits in Revivals" (Davenport), "Finality of the Christian Religion" (Foster).

JAMES M. PHILPUTT.

※

The two books that have helped me most are Stalker's "Trial and Death of Jesus," and "The Life of David Livingstone." The first has added to my appreciation of both the humanity and the divinity of our Saviour, and the last has made me understand God's wonderful persistence and devotion expressed in a man.

STEPHEN J. COREY.

※

"The Bible, Nature and Origin," by Dods; "Immanence of God," by Bowne; "Democracy and Social Ethics," by Jane Addams; "Rational Living," by King; "The Reconstruction of Religious Belief," by Mallock; "Jesus Christ and the Christian Character," by Peabody, and "The School and Society," by Dewey, are some of the most interesting books which I have read during the past year.

These are books which "find me." Their authors are masters of the subjects upon which they have written and bring to us the results of their ripened thought. If one desires to have his own opinions

confirmed these volumes may prove disappointing; but if, on the other hand, he is looking for a sane and luminous discussion of the most vital questions of the day by writers who are jealous only for the truth, he will feel more than repaid.

FREDERICK F. GRIM.

EXPOSITIONS OF HOLY SCRIPTURE. By the Rev. Alexander McLaren, D. D., Litt. D. A. C. Armstrong & Son, New York. Price per volume, $1.25 net. Sold only in sets.

Under the title of "Expositions of Holy Scripture" the publishers have arranged for the collection in permanent form of Dr. McLaren's Expositions which, when completed, will form a commentary on the Bible in thirty volumes, to be published in an annual series of six volumes. For fifty

Dr. Alexander McLaren.

years Dr. McLaren has been preaching the unsearchable riches of Christ. For forty years of that period he occupied one pulpit. For at least twenty-five years of that period he has been recognized as the greatest British expositor. Not as brilliant, not as unique as Dr. Parker, whose "People's Bible" was one of the greatest religious productions of the latter part of the nineteenth century, Dr. McLaren has a strength that was lacking in the great English preacher. The Scotchman has always the sane point of view, and a wonderful gift of illustration. He has been primarily a student of the Book, and one who has waited on the Master. His sermons are the production of the study and a thoughtful mind. There is little of the market-place about them. He has gone to the great mine of Holy Scripture and digged deep into it, uncovering treasures that can not be found

by the surface skimmer. And yet there is humanity and a heart power about Dr. McLaren which weaves itself into his studies so that they grapple with those problems which are at the very center and the circumference of a man's life. The six volumes of the first series are: "The Book of Genesis," "The Prophecies of Isaiah," "The Prophecies of Isaiah" (chapters XLIX-LXVI), and the "Prophecies of Jeremiah," and the three volumes of "The Gospel of Matthew." Each volume numbers from 338 to 420 pages, and is published in the very best style. They should be in every preacher's library. The man who has not read McLaren has missed some of the choicest expositions of the Word of God. It is a delight for us to know that one with whom the present reviewer has had intimate relations is completing a noble life work by giving his most mature thought to the preparation of this series, being assisted by Dr. Robertson Nicoll, editor of "The Expositor's Bible." Necessarily such a series must be sold in sets.

P. M.

※

THE HOPE OF IMMORTALITY. By Charles Fletcher Dole. The Ingersoll Lecture, 1906. New York, Thomas Y. Crowell & Co., publishers.

The author does not base his argument for immortality on the fact of Christ's resurrection, though he does not question that fact. "The only sure ground for the hope of immortality must be in the fact that we are in some true sense immortal by nature. For unless we thus possess immortality, no miracle could demonstrate this fact." This gives the author's point of view. The fact that "man's life not only belongs to the realm of the senses and what all call material things, but it belongs essentially, in respect to all that concerns us as human to the invisible realm of thought or spirit;" the presence and prevalence of the idea of immortality; a glance over the brink, if we deny immortality; the reasonableness that the most valuable things should be preserved; what is involved in personality; a purposeful universe; a moral world—these are some of the facts on which the author bases his argument in his strongly-written book.

J. H. G.

Our Budget

—Let us make the few weeks that remain of 1906 "tell on ages, tell for God."

—THE CHRISTIAN-EVANGELIST is nearing the half-way mark towards its 100,000 goal. Let's all pull together for the next few weeks, in reaching that mark. That will insure the 100,000 by 1909.

—C. W. B. M. day we hope was generally observed. If any of the churches have omitted doing so, let them do it yet. The women are doing a great work.

—Next Lord's day we must remember the plea on behalf of disabled ministers and their dependants.

—We shall be glad to consider any photographs or interesting material that would prove of value for our "Pioneer Number." These should be sent to us at once.

—We have great difficulty in publishing all the good things that come to us. Many brethren make the mistake of writing at too great length. The short article is the one that stands the best chance of being published, as well as the short news item.

—Read the 'Elderburg Association." You will get some amusement, as well as some instruction on a sad state of affairs.

—The address we are now publishing by J. P. Lichtenberger is one of the three which some good brethren who do not seem able to see two sides of a question have called "an attack on our plea." We have already published two of these addresses. We can trust the good sense of the vast majority of the brotherhood not to hunt for "heresy" in men who are loyal to Jesus Christ, even though they may sometimes differ from us about certain methods or interpretations.

—Our serial story, "The Bronze Vase," is concluded in this issue. We shall publish some short stories between now and the new year, when another serial story will be started from the pen of J. Breckenridge Ellis. We shall give further particulars of this in our next issue. It will run only six months and will be in independent divisions. We hope to improve our Home Circle department in our new volume.

—There are some interesting contributions in the "Forum" that should be read by the women as well as the men.

—The Centennial fund of $250,000 in personal gifts proposed by the Foreign Society is making a good start. Nearly $20,000 in cash and pledges have been secured since the national convention. Read the announcement of the Foreign Society on our inside cover page this week. It is an interesting and convincing statement. Now is the time to secure real estate in all the far eastern world, for it is advancing in value and we will be compelled to pay much more in the not distant future.

✠ ✠ ✠

—M. B. Madden, Sendai, Japan, reports six baptisms at that place. The work is in a most prosperous condition.

—The foundation of the beautiful new church at Omaha, of which S. D. Dutcher is pastor, is finished and the walls are rising.

—J. L. Thompson has taken the work at the Forest Avenue Church, Kansas City, where H. E. Wilhite is now engaged in a fine meeting.

—The Violett-Clarkson meeting at Loraine, O., closed with 104 added. A report next week.

—THE CHRISTIAN-EVANGELIST force enjoyed a call from Jas. T. Nichols of the "Christian Union."

—Frank Thompson, of the First Chris-

tian Church, Carmi, Ill., has accepted a call to the Temple Place Church of Decatur, to be effective January 1.

—George E. Jones has resigned his work at Turtle Creek, Pa., and is now on the editorial staff of the "Christian Worker," published in Pittsburg.

—R. A. Staley, of Dinuba, Cal., is delivering Sunday evening lectures on "The Church and Reformatory Movements," which are being largely attended.

—Charles H. Caton is doing some itinerary preaching in Arkansas. Brother Caton is one of our brightest pulpit men and ought to find a settled pastorate.

—R. L. McHatton, of Santa Rosa, Cal., reports 56 additions in his recent evangelistic work at various points, over 30 of these being by confession and baptism.

—Interest is increasing under the ministrations of C. L. McKim, who recently took the work at Oelwein, Ia. Large space was given in the daily paper to his Thanksgiving address.

—The brethren at Lawrenceburg, Ky., appreciate Walter C. Gibbs, having just extended to him a unanimous call for an indefinite period, and presented him with a fine new suit as a Christmas gift.

—Rochester Irwin reports the apportionment for state missions as passed at the church in Rochester, Minn. The children's program for home missions was an effective one and an offering was taken.

—E. A. Gilliland, who conducted the recent evangelistic meeting at the East St. Louis church, has accepted a call to the pastorate there, to begin work just as soon as he can complete evangelistic engagements already made.

—R. R. Eldred will return to Bolengi, Africa, this month. Miss Alice Ferrin and Miss Ella Ewing, of Illinois, will go out to the field with him. Glorious news comes from the Bolengi missions. Twenty-two baptisms recently reported.

—Mary R. Hawkins, of Cuckoo, Va., writes that Brother Forrest, of the University of Virginia, preached for the church at Gibboa on C. W. B. M. Day. It was a fine address from John 10:10, which was followed by a good offering.

—The "Artesia Advocate," N. M., gives a report of a sermon by Bro. James A. Challener, of Byran, on "Love the Great Power," in which love is finely analyzed and its various characteristics noted. It was a sermon worth preaching and worth hearing.

—The work at East Liverpool, Ohio, moves steadily forward. E. P. Wise writes that the question as to who shall be their living link missionary in the foreign field is now up for decision. Preparations are going forward for a series of meetings in January when the Netz Sisters will help Brother Wise.

—Hugh C. Gresham has resigned as missionary of the American Sunday-school Union and is assisting Bro. Beem in his evangelistic work. He reports the meeting at Cornell a good one. He will, with the new year, go west to take up other work and preach for our scattered brethren as he may have opportunity.

—L. L. Carpenter will dedicate a newly repaired and greatly beautified house at Newville, Ind., December 16. This is one of the first churches for which Brother Carpenter preached when he began his ministry nearly fifty years ago. It is hoped that the churches in DeKalb County will send large delegations to this opening service.

—The seventy-fifth anniversary of the church at Eureka, Ill., of which Alva W. Taylor is pastor, will be celebrated next April. Brooks Brothers are to hold a meeting for this church at an early date. Miss

Ella Ewing, one of the girls from the church, leaves this month to be a living link missionary of the church, at Bolengi, Africa.

—M. J. Thompson, of Dayton, Ore., writes us that the brethren there made preparation for a meeting, but their evangelist failed them. W. P. Mayrs is now located there, though not as pastor. Brother Patterson, of Portland, came to the rescue, but being compelled to return, the meeting was closed until January 15, when another meeting will be held. Brother Muckley, of Portland, visited the brethren and preached for them one week night.

—On resigning the work at the Carondelet church, St. Louis, recently, in order to take up the work of city evangelist, G. E. Ireland was presented with a handsome gold watch and a testimony of warm and loving appreciation of Brother and Sister Ireland and their work. To Mrs. Ireland a handsome fur was presented with words of high regard. These are faithful servants of the Master, and among the most earnest Christian workers we know.

—The church at Ocean View, Delaware, one and one quarter miles from Bethany Beach, needs the pastoral care of a young man who would be willing to accept $400 per year. The church was dedicated about five years ago and has a membership of forty. There will be no debt, as the members will pay off the Church Extension loan before the new preacher gets there. Mrs. D. C. France writes us that she believes it is a good place for a tactful young man to advance the cause and to advance himself.

—The wedding bells are ringing merrily in Kansas City, Mo. The following announcements have been received: Miss Martha E. Stout to Rev. Nelson Hastings Trimble, at South Prospect Church of Christ, 8 p. m., December 18. Miss Bessie S. Fife (daughter of Bro. and Sister R. H. Fife), to Rev. Arthur K. Brooks, at Hyde Park Christian Church, Christmas evening. Our heartiest congratulations to these young people, and especially to the two young preachers, who have so wisely chosen.

—We are under obligations to many of our ministers and other readers for extracts from sermons of note or newspaper articles, and from different sources, which they clip and inclose to us in an envelope, for such use as we may wish to make of them. In this way many things are brought to our knowledge which would otherwise escape our attention. We appreciate this method with the desire to accomplish good, the way will be found.

—Writing from a sparsely populated part of Nebraska, among scattered and struggling Disciples, Bro. B. A. Wilkinson says: "I seize every opportunity, and create as many more as possible, to federate. I plan for union meetings of various kinds and persuade the pastors as far as I can, that the people want something of the kind." He tells about driving the saloons out of Gordon by this co-operation among the churches. Wherever there is the spirit of co-operation with the desire to accomplish good, the way will be found.

—F. P. Arthur will close his work at Grand Rapids, Mich., January 1, to enter the state work in the hope that Michigan is now ready for a forward move into new cities. He has had a pleasant service in Lyon Street Church of nearly eight years, and finds it hard to leave that field. A new church was built in 1901 on Fifth Avenue, and William Bellamy is now the pastor with Sister Workman as helper. This new cause promises to outgrow the First Church. The tone of the work, Brother Arthur reports, is better than ever.

—Now and then a copy of the editor's book on "The Holy Spirit" falls into the hands of a Philistine, and it is to him a red rag that stirs up all his theological pugilism. One such writes: "Mr. ——. Sir: From under your hand I have just seen some of the rotted theological lies about the holy Spirit, and the continuity of that indefinite something you call the church." He has not learned so much as that there be any Holy Spirit who has anything to do with men to-day, and as to the fruit of the Spirit, he appears not to have even tasted thereof. No wonder it all seems like a lot of "theological lies" to him.

—Prof. Errett Gates, of the University of Chicago, is going to work in a new direction. He will be open to engagements for evangelistic meetings during the months of April, May, and June, 1907. His plan is to spend two weeks in a place holding two meetings a day. There will be a lecture study each afternoon of the first week on the "Teachings of Jesus," and of the second week on the "Teachings of the Disciples." He proposes to use very freely the question box, and will preach an evangelistic sermon every evening with the purpose of bringing men to a decision for the Christ. Professor Gates can be addressed at the University of Chicago.

TO KEEP POSTED

Read The Literature of the Disciples, by J. W. Monser, for it tells you of the books written by the Disciples and an epitome of their contents. Postpaid, 35c.
CHRISTIAN PUBLISHING CO.,
St. Louis, Mo.

—It is always a delight to receive such a communication as: "I find the congregation willing to work and am much encouraged with the outlook." This is what L. E. Chase says of the brethren at LeRoy, Ill., with whom he has been a little less than two months. He reports seven added and the organization perfected. The attendance at all services is greatly increasing. The attendance at the Bible school, he reports, is 100 per cent greater than a year ago, and much development work is planned in this department. The offering for State missions this year was the largest ever taken by the congregation for any missionary work, it being $53 as compared with $5 last year.

—One of the best attendances at Sunday-school was that at the First Christian Church, Akron, Ohio, on what is called Patriotic Day, Sunday when there were present by actual count 1,401 people, and the offering for American missions amounted to $200.17. Pastor Darsie's class had an attendance of 405 and the collection was $75. We are not at all surprised that Superintendent Kelly H. Hays, under whose direction the day was planned, was unusually happy. This school is contesting with the one at Jacksonville, Ill. The following Sunday was a big day for Jacksonville, with 976 present and an offering of $150.23.

—J. W. Beach, writing from Batavia, Ark., says that three Seventh Day Advent preachers were holding meetings in that community and that they were making quite a number of converts, mainly from the Methodists and Baptists, and he adds that there is no one there able to meet their arguments. The New Testament is a sufficient refutation of their arguments. The resurrection of Christ on the first day of the week, the descent of the Holy Spirit, and the introduction of the new dispensation are all facts inconsistent with the Sabbatarian theory. A proper distinction between the Jewish Sabbath and the Christian Lord's day is generally sufficient to undermine the position of these Sabbatarians.

—Samuel B. Moore, who recently resigned the pastorate of the Hammett Place Church, St. Louis, is now ready to locate in another field where his good preaching ability and experience in the Christian ministry can count. During Brother Moore's three and a half years' pastorate in St. Louis, the membership has doubled and he left with the happy thought that all the indebtedness of the church had been provided for. W. W. Dowling, the senior elder of the church, is glad to commend Brother Moore and feels that he is just the man that a great many churches need. C. C.

Garrigues, who was called to the Hammett Place Church, had great difficulty in getting his congregation at Albion, Ill., to release him, but they finally agreed to let him come to St. Louis as soon as they can get a suitable successor.

—John D. Zimmerman, minister at Horton, Kan., writes that the congregation there has raised more than $1,000 on the church debt.

—J. W. Davis has an unusual record. For the last twenty years he has preached for the Concord church in Macon, Mo., most of the time. He has just closed his ministry there and leaves the church in better condition for work than he has ever known it. He also leaves Illinois Bend church, in Adair county, where he began work twenty years ago. This, also, is in good condition. He writes that the work with these churches has been a very pleasant one and he is stronger and better able for the Christian ministry than ever, and is now ready for other new fields. He may be addressed at Kirksville, Mo.

—The dedication of the new church at Litchfield, Ill., will definitely take place on December 16, the decorators having at last completed their work. J. Fred Jones will preach on Saturday night as well as at both services on Sunday. Friends are invited to meet and rejoice with M. S. Johnson, the pastor, and this faithful congregation. All departments of the work are flourishing, and more room had come to be a necessity. The old house is comparatively new, having been erected only five years ago, but it was wholly inadequate to the work of the growing congregation. At the Endeavor meeting the other night when missions was the subject, the audience was almost equal to one of Brother McLean's rallies. Every department is full of life. The last report of the Sunday-school attendance was 322.

CUTICURA OINTMENT.

—Up till December 6 Charles Reign Scoville was able to count 4,888 reached by him in his meetings this year. This is a most happy and inspiring record which we trust will be an inspiration to every evangelist and preacher of the good news of salvation. Let us be careful, however, not to make a race merely to report so many hundreds of converts. We have met some evangelists and preachers who seem to give the impression that they are striving after a "record." Let us remember that results are with God, and that it is for us to be faithful in seeking to change men from the sinful and worldly life, rather than to establish a record surpassing that of some preacher or evangelist who has been on the field before. The evangelist has a great responsibility to men. He has, also, a great responsibility to God. The day is not passed when our converts need to be "pricked in their hearts."

—It was not the Editor's privilege to hear all the evangelists who assisted in our simultaneous campaign in St. Louis, but we did hear with only a few breaks, the series of sermons by Bro. C. M. Chilton, pastor of the First Christian Church in St. Joseph, Mo., who assisted Dr. J. M. Philputt at the Union Avenue Church. We are glad to say that we have never heard an abler series of evangelistic sermons from anyone. The Gospel he preaches is clothed with a sublimity, a power, a meaning, a beauty, that makes it not only winsome, but convincing and effective. The motives he urges, why men should become Christians, are the very highest, and appeal to reason, to conscience and to the will. He won the confidence and esteem of all who heard him. His masterly sermon at the union meeting at Odeon Hall on the last Sunday will not soon be forgotten. The sample sermons we heard from Herbert Yeuell at the First Church and W. F. Turner at the Hamilton Avenue Church sufficed to show that these were the right men at the right place.

—"I was turned down because part of the congregation insisted upon a younger man. It is a sad (and to me a new thing) to find our churches refusing to consider any man after he gets to be 50 years old. I am in better health than in past years, and fully competent for effective service, but I do not feel like being humiliated in this way, and I fear that I shall be compelled to turn to other work. That was a fine sermon for an old man,' I have been twice told of late and, hearing that, realized there would be no call nor has there been." This is a specimen of the communications we sometimes receive to our very deep sorrow. A man who has for thirty years or more been qualifying himself for the best work of his life may be "turned down" by some church for no other reason than that he has passed a certain mark in the number of his years. Other reasons do not seem to enter into the question of the selection of the preacher when he is on the wrong side of even forty years of age. The folly of such action on the part of the church is so manifest to those who have opportunities of wide experience that one has difficulty in exercising his patience sometimes. Of course, it is possible for a minister to cease growing intellectually and spiritually and to become entirely out of touch with the work demanded, but there seem to be few who through laziness come to such a pass. Many are put on the shelf by the unwise action of churches. There is such a thing as a church cultivating and helping its preacher, and this is just as much a duty as for the preacher to be the leader and the most active worker in the church.

Send for our Holiday Catalogue

CHRISTIAN PUBLISHING CO.,

St. Louis, Mo.

He "Felt No Interest"—But Afterwards.

The Christian Publishing Company was kind enough to send me a copy of "Christian Union," by J. H. Garrison. When I first received the book I felt no interest in it, did not think I would read it. The theme was an old one, and I was familiar with the arguments in its favor; had been all over the ground again and again, and did not think I cared to go over it another time. But after looking at the book lying on my desk for several days, I concluded to read the introductory chapter—just to sample its style. After this there was no inclination to let go until the last chapter was read. The whole subject of Christian union in its historical, ecclesiastical, economic, ethical and spiritual phases is here presented with a freshness and cogency that is inspiring. And this is all done with a style so direct, limpid, fluent and concise as to make this little book a literary gem. You have the subject of Christian union here, up to date, and in a nutshell. My ideas on this subject have been clarified, verified, fructified and intensified. . . .

Liberty, Mo. A. B. Jones.

Built by its own Members.

F. M. Rains recently dedicated the Central Christian Church, West Side, Kansas City, Mo. Twice had this congregation lost its home by foreclosure sales, but the men and women would not be discouraged. We reprint here from the columns of the Kansas City "Star" its account of this plucky church and present also the picture of S. W. Nay, the go-ahead present minister:

"By the grace of God we will build it our-

S. W. Nay.

selves. We haven't $10,000 to pay out so we'll save $10,000."

Men and women with that sort of spirit could not long be without a church. No useless repining for them. They didn't believe in committees to worry people for subscriptions. They saw the practical side of the question, 'and that was: "We are without a church; we have no money, no credit; we believe in our own congregation. We'll keep on trying. Success must come."

That was the kind of men and women that made up the large part of the membership of the Central Christian Church, West Side, two years ago. They had lost two church buildings—sold to other denominations to satisfy mortgages. They were in debt. There was strife and dissension in the membership until the Rev. S. W. Nay be-

G. L. Wharton's Death and Burial

At noon, Lord's Day, November 4, in Caleutta, Brother Wharton died from cancer of the duodenum, or lower stomach. His life needs no praise from me; but I can not refrain from saying, that when we, as a people, cease to cherish his memory, as the hero of our Foreign Missions, and especially of our India Mission, it will be a day which the Master will regard as a day of retrogression. He was our first missionary to the heathen. He was our prince of pleaders for the cause of missions among the heathen. He emphasized his plea by being a missionary. He knew the meaning of being a missionary. For over two years he had been separated from his family, that he might do the work of a missionary. He remained at his post until his strength failed him. In order to go to his work, he had to rest twice on the roadside, so weak in body had he become. At the time of his death, he was a teacher in the Bible College at Jubbulpore. He was the first to start this school, when he lived and worked at Harda. He promoted its interests by raising $25,000 for its buildings and equipment. While on the threshold of realizing his fond wish for this school, he was taken away from earth and its work. The building is now in process of erection; but before it is completed he has entered into a house not made with hands.

But my purpose how is to tell of his last illness. Many hearts will ache when they know the peculiarly sad circumstances under which his life ended. He was away from home and friends. Among those who ministered to him at the time of his death, I was the only one not a stranger to him. Mrs. Wharton and his children are in Hiram, Ohio. For four months, without understanding fully the nature of his disease, he had been trying to recover his health. To this end he had gone from Jubbulpore to the mountains, and then to a Sanitarium in Calcutta. Until within a few weeks of his death he did not think that he had any serious ailment. On October 12 I received from him the following letter:

"The Sanitarium," 50 Park Street, Calcutta, Oct. 11, '06.

Dear Brother Adams:—I feel that I should tell you, as Secretary of the Mission, more particularly of my condition and movements. I have been doing my best, since July 9 when I went to Simla, to regain the strength I lost during May and June on the plains. After being in Simla nearly a month, as I was not gaining satisfactorily, I called on a physician for advice and treatment. He examined me rather carefully, and said there was nothing much the matter with me, and that all I needed was a little tonic and good weather. I got dyspepsia from the commencement of his medicine. Not being satisfied, I called on the best physician in Simla. He asked me carefully of my symptoms and pronounced it nothing but atomic dyspepsia, which would soon pass away. He gave me some medicine, but I got no better, and suffered intensely with indigestion, notwithstanding all my careful dieting at his order. I finally went to him on September 24 and told him that his medicine was worse than a failure. He then examined me carefully and to his surprise found what he called a growth in the stomach. He called another doctor to consult. They agreed in their diagnosis, and had but one suggestion—"exploratory operation." Dr. McNab is a perfect gentleman and admitted that, if

it were himself, he would not allow any one in India to operate upon him. I remained in Simla until October 5, and then went to Ludhiana and consulted two doctors there and was advised to come here.

This is, as you know, a kind of "Battle Creek Sanitarium." Dr. Ingersoll and his wife, who are in charge, are graduates of the Ann Arbor School of Medicine. They have been examining me to-day. The substance of the matter is, that all agree to the presence of a tumor in the stomach, as the cause of my trouble.

This will give you some correct idea of my condition. I have written the above to Mrs. Wharton, but to no one else. I believe I will, by God's help, overcome the whole trouble, without either the knife or going home. At any rate, I believe that I am doing right to make a fair effort to get well here, before going home to the surgeon. I will keep you posted. If I do not get better here in three weeks, I will go to Jubbulpore and see what the cool dry climate and dieting will do for me there. I am cheerful and mean to make the most of my disappointments. God knows all.

Lovingly,
G. L. Wharton.

In a few days after this letter was written, he sent for me and J. G. McGavran, and came to the decision to submit to an operation, with the hope that the trouble was being caused by something which the surgeons could remove. The day for the operation was fixed; but when it came his fever was so high and his condition so bad that they decided to wait until he should be better prepared for the ordeal. But it never came. He rapidly grew worse and with the light of the morning of November 4, I saw that death was at work. The end came about noon. I had a post mortem examination and the growth, which was so evident to the touch, proved to be cancer of the lower stomach. In his brave effort to recover, he had not the shadow of a chance. No surgeon's knife could have brought him any relief. It now looks as if we were providentially kept from having the operation. On the morning of November 5 I buried him in Lower Circular Road Cemetery, Calcutta. I feared I should have to do this task alone, as none of our missionaries were within reach; but,

just as we entered the cemetery gate, Brother and Sister Monroe arrived from Deoghar. The new friends of the Sanitarium were also with us, and this for the most part, strange hands committed his body to the earth. Our hearts are broken over the loss of our comrade and for the sorrowing wife and children, who are just now receiving the sad message which I cabled to Cincinnati. It was a hard duty to say, "Brother Wharton is dead;" but we are consoled with the fact that in life he lived in fellowship with God, and that, in death, God the Father was his comfort. "Yea, though I walk through the valley of the shadow of death, I will fear no evil, for thou art with me."   Morton D. Adams.

❧

For the Nursery—For the Table.

Whether as an ideal food for infants or for general household use, Borden's Eagle Brand Condensed Milk has no equal; of no other food product can this be truthfully said.

"The Helpful" Paper.

A well known minister writes: ."THE CHRIS-TIAN-EVANGELIST is the most helpful journal, that comes to my table, and is always the first one read." We like that word *helpful*. It expresses exactly what we are trying to make THE CHRISTIAN-EVANGELIST—helpful to every one of its readers in their efforts to live the Christian life and do their Christian work in the world. We have no higher ambition than to make THE CHRISTIAN-EVANGELIST helpful to its readers in realizing their highest aims and aspirations.

❦ ❦

Report Children's Day.

Offerings from children's day for home missions are coming in slowly this year. A larger number of contributing Sunday-schools is reported this year than so far. The amount of the offerings is a little below that for the same period last year. With the splendid gain made last year the home board is more than justified in its appeal for $15,000 this year. From the enthusiasm already shown by our preachers in the Centennial campaign, we are sure that they will heartily join in the movement to enlist every Sunday-school for an offering for home missions this year.

❦ ❦

The New University.

Referring to the article which we published from President E. V. Zollar's concerning the Oklahoma Christian University, which has been located at Enid, our readers may judge of the interest attached to the location of such an institution when the city of Enid was willing to pay a cash basis of $85,000 and to donate a campus worth at least $20,000. Other cities made generous bids, but this excelled them all, it was thought, and so secured the school. That the institution, under such an administration as President Zollars will give it, will be a powerful factor in the future development of New Testament Christianity, not only in Oklahoma but throughout the great southwest, can not be doubted. The brotherhood at large will watch with interest the growth of this rising educational star in the southwestern horizon, and will rejoice to see it become a star of the first magnitude, shedding a bright and steady light for the intellectual, moral and religious enlightenment of the people.

❦ ❦

Winona's Church Destroyed.

The little church at Winona, Miss., has suffered a great loss. Only a handful, not a dozen members, and perhaps not over three men in the number, they had a good house in that beautiful little city of 5,000 people, and it was well located. In the hurricane that swept over parts of the south, the building was completely destroyed. Having no money and no preacher, they were preparing to sell the pile of lumber to the highest bidder and give up, though they had been planning for a meeting to be held by our state board. But Bro. H. K. Coleson persuaded them to wait and see if their brethren would come to their rescue. If we were able in Mississippi we would be glad to look after our own unfortunate family, but as you know, we are a very feeble folk. Now, if the brethren will come to the aid of this little band and help them to stand upon their feet they will be in better condition than they were before the storm. For, first, they will feel stimulated by the help of others to do more heroic things for themselves; and their religious neighbors and outside friends will have much more respect for them when they see they are counted worthy by their brethren. They had a good house. Now they have only a heap of broken planks. They

are positively not able to put these together and make a house again.

W. W. PHARES, Cor. Sec,
McComb, Miss.

As We Go to Press.

Special to THE CHRISTIAN-EVANGELIST.
Nelson, Neb., Dec. 10.—Forty confessions, twenty baptisms in past ten days. We continue.—Richard Martin.

Special to THE CHRISTIAN-EVANGELIST.
Barnesville, O., Dec. 10.—Great crowd; in nine days 29 confessions. Haley my singer. Ministers, Wayt—Clarence Mitchell.

Special to THE CHRISTIAN-EVANGELIST.
Ft. Smith, Ark., Dec. 9.—Sixty-three added in eighteen days. Great interest. We continue another week.—Roger H. Fife, evangelist.

Special to THE CHRISTIAN-EVANGELIST.
Louisville, Ky., Dec. 10.—Rejoice with us over new church born in Louisville. Over fifty charter members.—McKissick and Tinsley.

Special to THE CHRISTIAN-EVANGELIST.
Webb City, Mo., Dec. 10.—Seventy-seven added in three weeks. W. E. M. Hackleman is singing. W. E. Reavis is the earnest pastor. We continue.—Wm. J. Lockhart, evangelist.

Special to THE CHRISTIAN-EVANGELIST.
Kansas City, Mo., Dec. 9.—Twenty to-day; one hundred and twenty in three weeks at Forest Avenue Church. Wilhite and Tuckerman doing great work.—J. L. Thompson.

Special to THE CHRISTIAN-EVANGELIST.
Wauseon, O., Dec. 10.—Buchanan and Gardner meeting here has added sixty-nine

in two weeks—forty-eight by confession. We continue.—Chas. R. Oakley.

Special to THE CHRISTIAN-EVANGELIST.
Washington, Pa., Dec. 10.—First Church closed three weeks' meeting with home forces; fourteen baptisms; five by letter, one reclaimed. Begin my sixth year here.—E. A. Cole, minister.

Special to THE CHRISTIAN-EVANGELIST.
Lexington, Ky., Dec. 9.—Closed to-night. Last week 81; to-day 58, there coming 28 at last invitation; total 312. An unusual number of adults. Comparatively few by affiliation. Many things contributed to the victory. Brother Spencer is a past master in his work. James Small's meeting, the help of a host of preachers and college professors, a great chorus, an efficient force of Sunday-school teachers all helped. New converts pledged nearly a thousand dollars annually to current expenses. We will be at Eureka, Ill., for two weeks.—Brooks Brothers.

❦ ❦

Changes.

Sparks, J. R.—Hawkins to Raven, Va.
Speer, Grant W.—Ashland to Hicksville, Ohio.
Smith, W. H.—Cos Cob, to 99 Edgewood avenue, New Haven, Conn.
Sorey, M. Lee—Cerida Springs, to 525 North Second, Arkansas City, Kan.
Stout, Arthur—Kansas City, to 1329 Twenty-sixth street, Des Moines, Ia.

NEWS FROM MANY FIELDS

Illinois.

Passing through Chicago I took time to call on Brother Parker Stockdale, who is new among us, and preaches to the great satisfaction of the Jackson Boulevard Church. His loyalty to the Scriptures and his faithful Gospel preaching are very highly appreciated by his people. He was at the Buffalo convention, the first he has attended with us. He was greatly delighted with the large purposes and growing work of the church, as well as by the profound addresses which he heard.——A. T. Campbell has recently taken the work of the Metropolitan church and seems to fit well the conditions. He is thoroughly interested in Christian education and hopes soon to have some of his young people in Eureka college.——S. G. Buckner is in the midst of church building at Harvey. The house is under roof and will cost about $12,000, including the lot. This was a heroic undertaking for such a small weak company, but success is practically assured and much will be due to the noble young preacher.—— At Waukegan E. N. Tucker is also in the building stage. The first story is up, covered, finished and is in use. The company numbers but 90, but they have a Sunday-school of 200 enrolled and are pressing forward. We also have another church, meeting in the old house, in Waukegan, numbering about 80 souls, with a good Sunday-school, and regular preaching, but previous engagements hurried me away without meeting with the church. From some cause the work has been unusually difficult for us in northern Illinois, but we are making steady gains and the people are strong for the truth when they once understand it.——Milwaukee, Wis., the center of the west's beer interest, as Peoria is of the whisky interest, has a splendid Church of Christ. Claire L. Waite, late of Chicago, is the able and much loved minister. The church has been fortunate in selecting pastors, among whom have been the late G. L. Brokaw, M. B. Ryan, P. N. Calvin, Brother Kreidler and others, through whose able coöperation to the work the church has its strength of 400 members, 200 in Sunday-school, 35 in Christian Endeavor and C. W. B. M., 25, and a good modern house costing perhaps $20,000. The church is gaining in influence and has good standing in the city. It was the church that discovered B. H. Sealock, sent him to Eureka College, and he is now our minister at Lexington, Ill. How many boys in the churches are yet undiscovered who might be a great power in the world's life if encouraged to commit themselves to the service of the Master! While we "pray the Lord of the harvest to send more laborers into the field," we ought to be looking after it a little ourselves. It seems to me that every purposeful boy or girl, whatever his possible profession, should be looked after by the church and its pastor, with a view to utilizing his strength also for righteousness and the church by at least encouraging a Christian education.—— The church at Lewistown has always struggled, yet kept the lights burning, sometimes feebly, but now it is having an era of prosperity and blessing. Walter Kline, one of our strong, wise and industrious young men, who is also president of the Third District Missionary Society, has been with the church about nine months. He has added 25 to the church membership, which is now 200, with 200 in the Sunday-school and 16 in the C. W. B. M. The church is investing about $1,800 in church improvements. While this is being done, the sheriff very generously tendered the church for its meetings, the use of the circuit court room of the beautiful court house of Fulton county. The church highly appreciates this liberal favor. Indeed here is seen the fellowship of law and Gospel. The jury box becomes the choir loft for the praise of God; from the judge's stand is proclaimed pardon and life and in the idle spectators' chairs sit the listeners, in-terested in the greater and larger trial of life, through which we all are passing.——At Ipava the church is enjoying a season of refreshing and prosperity under the strong and mature ministry of J. T. Craig. He came over into Illinois two years ago from Missouri, but is as loyal to the interests of our state, both educational and evangelistic, as if native born. This is one of the strong older churches, having about 300 members with 200 enrolled in the Sunday-school. This is the home of our venerable brother, Dr. J. H. Breeden, to whose ministry and help the churches in this region are much indebted. He is the father of H. O. Breeden, for twenty-one years leader of our forces in Des Moines, Iowa. M. T. Cooper, after a useful ministry, in the regions round about is, quietly living near Ipava. May the Lord bless our veterans in Israel as well as those now on the firing line in the midst of the fight.——At Astoria J. W. Keefer is closing a three years' ministry. This is one of our good older congregations, that has contributed many households to the larger new west. Death has claimed many of the veterans and those remaining are standing loyally by the work.—— At Baders L. R. Thomas was in a good meeting. The church has had only irregular preaching for a year and with some other unfortunate occurrences has become much weakened, but the valor and loyalty and perseverance of those that remain are truly heroic and commendable. If the meeting fills the present prophecy, the church will be soon on its feet again, and will hold forth the Word of life regularly, to the people. There is a choice company of young people here, faithfully filling their part in the Master's service.—— Removals and deaths have so weakened the Frederick church that the Sunday-school is all that is doing regular business. John Fagan, formerly of Eureka College, a business man, and his estimable wife, lead in the Sunday-school, which is in a prosperous condition.——The Table Grove Church of about 70 members and 100 enrolled in Sunday-school, 30 in the Christian Endeavor, 25 Juniors, has recently completed a $2,800 improvement, giving them a beautiful modern house, as good as new. It has an unusually strong board of officers and a faithful membership, rich, not in means, but in faith and good works. E. J. Stanley has just closed a very successful pastorate and F. S. Nichols, a senior in Eureka College, succeeds him. He will make his home with the church after his graduation. It is difficult to hold students in college, when the field is so ripe for the harvest. We have in Illinois about 425 more churches than preachers. The college must train more men.

Eureka, Ill.　　　　　　　J. G. WAGGONER.

Oregon.

Since November a twenty-two churches have sent in offerings for Oregon missions. The list is as follows: Albany First, $13.40; Ashland, $19.70; Athena, $24.25; Corvallis, $5.50; Cottage Grove, $29.20; Dallas, $17.25; Dayton, $5; Drain, $5; Falls City, $5.20; Forest Grove, $22; Harrisburg, $5; heppner, $8.75; Hillsboro, $5.20; Hood River Valley, $24.55; La Grande, $79.50; McMinnville, $12; Monmouth, $20.15; Nashville, $3.35; Pleasant Hill, $7.30; Richland, $5; Scio, $3.20, and Aumsville, $18.45.——Although not on the list in 1905, Aumsville, Dayton, Harrisburg, Heppner, Richland and Scio are among the first contributors for this year. Of the above named churches, on the offering list for both years, only Ashland, Falls City, Forest Grove and Hood River Valley have gone ahead of last year's offering. This does not include payments on five year pledges, some of which are included in the above figures. Although six churches are here added to the offering list, not on last year, the general offering is still short of that for last year from the churches here named. We are hoping, however, that the payments on pledges and the gifts from other churches will materially change the prospect for a large advance over last year's gift.——Several churches might follow the good example of Albany, McMinnville, Portland First, Roseburg and Silverton, who loaned their ministers to the state board for a meeting, turning the proceeds over to the treasury of the O. C. M. C. The district work is proceeding nicely, and we hope to report more evangelists at work in the near future. The year 1909 will soon be here.　　F. E. BILLINGTON, Cor. Sec.

Cottage Grove.

❀ ❀

Virginia.

The renewed and enlarged house of the Manchester congregation was used for service the last Sunday in November, and rededicated to the Lord's work. This is a great victory for this congregation. C. O. Woodward is the pastor. They have the largest Virginia Sunday-school, 400. ——W. G. Johnston has held a good meeting at Blacksburg, the seat of Virginia Polytechnic Institute, in which there are 800 students. The congregations were very large, and there were quite a number added. This congregation is doing splendid work in this college town. E. R. Kemm is the minister.——Virginia has set us as one of her centennial mottoes 30,000 Disciples in Virginia by 1909. The present membership is 25,000.——Virginia Christian College is making a great effort to secure $50,000 for two needed buildings. The college deserves the support of all good men.——A new building has just been completed at Sheva. The congregation has heretofore worshipped in a hall. A. F. Ramsey is pastor.——D. M. Austin has accepted a call for a second year in the Perseverance field.——The new building at Blackstone is a beauty, and a great credit to this young congregation.——H. D. Coffey expected to organize the third church in Bristol, Va. and Tennessee, by December 1.—— The Roanoke church is planning to purchase the property for a third congregation in the magic city.——Wm. Burleigh and the Portsmouth church are planning an aggressive work. Virginians should look out for Portsmouth.——B. H. Melton, of Marshall street, Richmond, is in a meeting with J. T. T. Hundley and the Norfolk church.　　　　　　　　H. C. COMBS,

Financial Secretary of V. C. M. S.

❀ ❀

Georgia Notes.

Two 'Sotthern Evangelist" subscribers, who are now readers of THE CHRISTIAN-EVANGELIST, have written me that they object to the latter's position on " federation." For their benent, as well as for the benefit of others, I want to say that they are passing through my own experience on the subject. Like them, I was uninformed as to what federation is, and, consequently, was prejudiced against it, but since knowledge has taken the place of ignorance concerning it. I am a full convert to its purposes. My ignorance of it produced the prejudice against it and caused me to draw hasty and unjust conclusions respecting it. I thought I was right in condemning it until I read Brother Garrison's explanation of it in his matchless book on "Christian Union." I am now thoroughly convinced that while "federation" is not the real thing desired, it is a step toward it and that is all that is claimed for it. Read and see, and if we do not take a front seat on this subject, we will soon have to take a back seat in religious progress. To take this front seat requires no sacrifice of truth, but it does require love for God and man and a desire for the world's redemotion. This love and this desire, which naturally follows, will enlarge our vision, right the wrongs in religion, exalt God's word, unite heart

the great needs of that portion of our state. The pocket change, potatoes, apples and woolen socks received sound like the days of "Raccoon" John Smith in Kentucky, I am sure that Brother Presley needs and deserves another pair of socks as well as an increase in the other things mentioned. But here is the report: "I have been requested to report my work to THE CHRISTIAN-EVANGELIST. This report is from August 1. My first meeting was at Ludville. Two made the good confession' and the church was left in good working order. I went to Bethel next with C. C. Goodson and D. Anderson. Had good meeting with five additions. I then held a meeting at Pleasant Hill, my home congregation, assisted by Brother Goodson. Brother Anderson was with us two days. At the close of a week's meeting I baptized six. My next preaching was at Antioch, Cherokee county, I only preached a few days. The church seemed greatly revived but no additions. From Antioch I went to Adairsville and held a five days' meeting and had four additions. I had to close the meeting to meet the executive committee of the North Georgia district held at Pleasant Hill, Pickens county.' The committee then employed me to visit all the churches I could during the next month. The first church I visited was Pisgah, Gilmer county. I found the church with no regular supply. I preached one sermon. They will

The Christian Church, Valdosta, where the Georgia convention was held.

and soul in Jesus Christ and answer his prayer for the unity of his people. If there are Christians to unite, as we claim, and if love begets love then we must love if we expect the offspring of love. In order to love we must become acquainted. Acquaintance is not love but it is necessary in order to reach love. So "federation" is not Christian union, but it leads to acquaintance, acquaintance leads to love and love leads to unity. Federation, acquaintance, love, unity. This is the whole thing in a nutshell as I see it. Let us investigate before we condemn.

The following report from Bro. C. P. Presley, of Sherman, Ga., will give our readers an idea of what it means to be an evangelist in the mountain counties of Georgia, as well as an idea of

be represented in the next annual meeting of the district to be held at Ludville. From here I went to Stanley's Creek, Fannin county, and preached six sermons. They are highly in favor of the co-operative work. Wilscot was my next point. Preached four sermons and added three to the membership. This church has no regular preacher. I then preached one sermon at Big Creek school house and went to Dial, in the same county, and preached two sermons. This part of the district is badly in need of help. For twenty-five miles square we haven't a brother who will lead in prayer. On this round I was gone thirteen days, preached fourteen sermons, baptized three and received $3.25, one bushel of potatoes, one peck of apples and one pair of woolen socks,

first month's report shows eleven added and much other good done. He will do good there and Broadway church, Lexington, will not be ashamed of the work of their evangelist.——D. G. Combs has gone to Florida and will preach the Gospel at Leesburg, while he is resting. Listen—"I will come back at once if you don't want me to lose the time. I have been in the work forty years and never took a vacation. Let me know how long you are willing for me to stay, sure." His report for November shows 19 days, 31 sermons, 38 additions, a divided congregation united and an unfinished house of worship to be completed. May the Lord bless this tireless and loyal servant of the Cross.——H. W. Elliott was at work all the month at home and abroad. We have not received very large returns from the November offering; $452.57 received, an increase of $110.83 over last November, and this is a gain of $295.15 since the Louisville convention as compared with the same period in 1905.——We urge prompt remittance on the part of all who have taken the offering and plead with the congregations that have not done so to lose no time in taking the offering. Do not allow another month to pass without paying your respects to this great work. Directly other interests will be demanding your attention and dollars and Kentucky missions will be kicked and cuffed out of the way like a Thanksgiving football. Lend a hand now.

H. W. Elliott, Sec.

Sulphur, Ky.

New York City.

During November our Disciples' union held a joint meeting with the evening session of the semi-annual convention of the C. W. B. M. The attendance and enthusiasm was the greatest in many months. Miss Helen F. Clark, director of the New York Foreigners' Mission, told of her work among the Chinese, Italians and Jews on the lower east side. It was a revelation to us all. Some of us did not know that the purchase price of girls in the metropolis of free America ranges from a few hundreds for the very young to $1,500 to $2,000 for the most attractive girls of 16 or 18 years.——At Fifty-sixth street we recently baptized five Chinese men, four of whom take membership with us. This gives us seven faithful members, fruits of our Chinese Bible school. Three of them desire further education in both the English and Chinese Bible in order that they may be of greater service among their own peo-

ple. The possibilities of our work among the Chinese seems to be limited only by the scarcity of available teachers.——The Second Church at One Hundred and Sixty-ninth street, expects to dedicate their new building December 16. They will then have one of the best appointed churches of our people in Greater New York. This splendid work is a tribute to the seventeen years' ministry of S. T. Willis. He has staying qualities. ——Walter S. Rounds, the new pastor at Third Church, Brooklyn, is already engaged in a protracted meeting.——The serious illness and consequent resignation of M. E. Harlan at Sterling Place, Brooklyn, cast a cloud over all our preachers and workers which does not lift. He was an efficient pastor and a strong preacher, but he was greater still as a man. Every one respected him, honored him, loved him. He left his impress upon us all. His improvement is very slow, but we hope for more speedy recovery with prolonged rest.

New York City.　　MINER LEE BATES.

Ohio.

It ought not to be forgotten that Ohio is looking forward to a simultaneous evangelistic campaign next November to February, 1907-1908. Much has been said about it, but now is the time to lay the plans by securing your evangelists and singers and also preparing the church. Let this year be a year of purging in the church. Let every congregation clean house. Get the dead wood out. Heal up all the old sores, purify the church life. Let it be a year of fasting and prayer. Let the church get right with God.—— Geo. P. Taubman has resigned at Portsmouth. He has been there several years and made a large showing. It will be hard to find just the right man to follow him.——E. B. Barnes, of Noblesville, Ind., has been holding a good meeting with the church at Monterey.——W. H. Boden, of Washington Court House, is doing quite a little evangelistic work by holding a meeting at New Holland, with 23 additions. He is now in a meeting at his old parish, Marshfield.——W. A. Brundige held a good meeting at Buford, in Highland county, with 24 at last account. He goes in December to Cambridge.——Brother John Shaeffer, of North Benton, held one pulpit for 60 years, and has lived in one house for 70 years. He is very spry for a man of his age, taking a walk daily about the home. He reads without glasses and takes an active interest in all current events.——I have recently given J. H. Garrison's book on "The Holy Spirit," a second

careful reading. This was done in view of some recent utterances against it. If I were writing that book there are two or three things that I might put differently, but they are not serious things. The author does not close the volume with "ne plus ultra." We have altogether too many editorials, articles and books in our religious literature that do close thus. This one thing is clearly apparent—most of the critics of this book need to read it carefully. It will do you good to read this book even if you do not keep step all the way. J. H. Garrison is still a student on the subject of the Holy Spirit. So am I. Some among us evidently are not. They know it all to a mathematical accuracy.　　C. A. FREER.

Painesville, Ohio.

Our Birthday Party.

The Bay Union of Auxiliaries to the Christian Woman's Board of Missions celebrated its second birthday anniversary by holding the eighth quarterly convention at the West Side Christian Church, San Francisco. There were 75 delegates who responded to roll call and a new auxiliary reported from South Berkley.

When Mrs. R. P. Shepherd finished her "Tidings Talk" one felt strongly impelled to go right home and put into practice her excellent suggestions. One entire column would be required to do justice to the paper by Mrs. J. H. Wood on "Immediate and Ultimate Aims for the Bay Union." All were pleased to listen to the greeting from our first president, Mrs. Agnew, of Chicago. Officers were elected as follows: For president, Mrs. Hiram Van Kirk; for vice-president, Mrs.

R. L. Cave and C. A. Murdock; for treasurer, Mrs. J. H. K. Bell; for corresponding secretary, Mrs. M. A. Nash; for recording secretary, Mrs. Alonso J. Wagner. Mrs. Van Kirk announced that a brief history of the Alameda Church had just come from the press and was being sold for the enlargement of its Building Fund. We wish friends to send for this book and learn from its pages what a consecrated band of 'ten women can do. It will encourage strong and weak churches alike. First the C. W. B. M. Auxiliary, then a church organized and now a splendid work requiring a $17,000 structure to house the activities of a growing congregation.

The two addresses of the afternoon were of equal merit, both emphasizing the need of co-operation among the Christian women for the betterment of the great heathen sisterhood. Dr. Mary B. Ritter's "Recent Observations in Japan" opened up a vista of usefulness for workers in a field ripe unto the harvest. "The Great Sisterhood," treated in Dwight E. Potter's forceful style, was very helpful. It was a day of good fellowship, beautifully crowned by the Vesper Service. The secretary's reports show a membership of 165 women in the auxiliaries about the Bay. Let each woman plan her duties so as to save the second Tuesday in February for the enjoyment of the Ninth Convention.

Mrs. Alonzo J. Wagner, Sect.

Alameda, Cal.

The Huntington (W. Va.) Meeting.

Our revival closed at Huntington with 66 additions to the church. There were 40 baptisms, and over fifty of the entire number were net gains. We had a good hearing all of the time. We were seriously interrupted by sickness among the members, the pastor being confined to his bed a part of the time. We had a very large hearing from other religious bodies, and some co-operated in the meeting. We received the most courteous attention from the daily papers of the city, and they even urged us to give larger reports of our meetings daily. The church at Huntington, after passing through the perils of the past, is on the road to victory. The congregation seems to be in perfect harmony, and is planning for greater things. The beautiful building which was saved some months ago by the timely aid of the Church Extension Board, has been newly frescoed, and presents a very attractive appearance. The present prosperity of the church is largely due to the wise leadership of the pastor, Orilas G. White and his good wife who are very much loved by the entire congregation. R. H. Fife, Evangelist.

Winning in a City.

Some years ago, in the city of Indianapolis, a great religious convention was in session. The ministers held a meeting with discussion of the theme, "How to Reach the Masses." At that time Messrs. Moody and Sankey were in this city. They went down on one of the main street corners and entering a store, Mr. Moody borrowed a dry goods box. Taking it out on the street corner, he said to Mr. Sankey, "Now, mount and sing a song." Mr. Sankey sang one or two earnest Gospel songs, and when a great throng of passers-by had paused to listen, Mr. Moody mounted the box and made a brief, earnest and impassioned address. In closing his address he said: "The ministers are discussing the question: How to Reach the Masses. Let's go down and help them. I will speak and Mr. Sankey will sing." And in a few moments later a great crowd which filled the church to overflowing pressed in with Moody and Sankey to the meeting.

Can a great meeting be held in a city church? For years we have been discussing this question: The pros and cons have been very ably given. For six weeks now an Indianapolis church has been giving a demonstration of the possibilities of such a meeting. In a city of over 200,000 population, the Third Christian Church, under the leadership of Charles Reign Scoville, has been holding a great meeting. We have shown that, while it might take a little longer time than in smaller places, the same faith and prayer and consecration that win the towns, will win the

---

cities. Thus far 579 people have stepped out, either to confess Christ, or to re-consecrate themselves in the service, and the meeting still goes on with an appointment to close. The church board of thirty-five good men, and true, has stood loyally and as one man, by the evangelist in these meetings. We are glad to report progress, thus far, and will make full report at the close.—Chas. B. Newnan.

Chicago Letter.

The Jackson Boulevard Church, Parker Stockdale, minister, had a Harvest Home Festival November 25. The doors had to be locked to prevent over-crowding. This church is growing in all departments.—C. C. Morrison is installed again at Monroe Street, and additions are being reported already.—The First Church, H. L. Willett, minister, and R. L. Handley, associate, is planning to build in the near future. They have been meeting in a hall. About $25,000 has just been pledged. As much more is expected soon. Evanston, Irving Park and Garfield Boulevard Church are putting forth special effort in Bible school work, and most cheering growth is being realized.——The Englewood Church has outgrown its Sunday-school room, and is planning to erect a new and modern Sunday-school building.—The Sheffield Avenue, Ashland, and West Pullman Churches are making good progress in wiping out their debts.——Douglas Park is raising a fund for a new building.——E. M. Haile, lately chosen minister of South Chicago Church, has been in the hospital for several weeks. He is now about recovered and occupied his pulpit last Sunday.—Harvey expects to dedicate its new church, a splendid structure, near the first of the year.—The new Executive Board of the C. C. M. organized by electing Carl Bushnell chairman, Mrs. F. M. Jackson secretary. See. W. J. Wright, of the A. C. M. S. will meet with the Board Saturday.—The West End Church's rally day in S. S. and Dedication was a great day. Bible School went far beyond the best previous attendance. The offering at night of nearly $25 was for Home Missions. What do you think of that for a little Mission school of about 50 scholars?—In spite of rain the house was full for the dedicatory exercises in the afternoon. A little over $300 was pledged. Englewood, Ashland, Irving Park, Evanston, Sheffield Avenue, First and Jackson Boulevard Churches were represented in the offering. Individuals from Monroe Street, Austin, Hyde Park and perhaps others gave. The little church was greatly cheered by this kindly fellowship giving.

Sumner T. Martin,

Chicago.   City Evangelist.

The Abberley-Powell Meeting.

The Central Church of Indianapolis has had a season of refreshing in a month's meeting (in the simultaneous campaign) held by R. W. Abberley, of Cincinnati, as evangelist, and Mrs. J. E. Powell, of Bloomington, Ill., as singer. The majority of the 183 additions were adults and heads of families. Our membership was stirred to activity as never before and we now have, a larger and better conception of what we ought constantly to be, doing in looking after the people within the sphere of our influence.

I had never heard Brother Abberley preach until he came to us. He proved himself a strong, self-possessed and satisfying man. He has the English instinct for a finished sermon, homiletically speaking. His analysis is clear and complete. His points are all buttressed by Scripture, illustrated by anecdote and incident and often beautifully reflected in some hymn or poetry quoted, of which he seems to have an exhaustless store. His voice is pleasant and well modulated. He rarely rises into impassioned discourse but when he does it makes a much greater impression than if "tearing a passion to tatters" were a common thing with him. His sermons average better than any one's I have listened to. There is nothing of the professional evangelist, so-called, about him, but we will be sure to have a "protracted meeting" if you get Abberley. Our people were delighted with him and, many preachers

---

came to listen to him, a number of them young men studying for the ministry. In many respects he is a good model for young men. Another point in which Brother Abberley sets a good example is, that he does not attempt difficult intellectual "stunts."

Of Mrs. Powell I am glad to say that her presence as well as her singing was a great help to the meeting. Always dignified and sympathetic, she endeared herself to many and was popular with all because of her sincere devotion to the work. Her sweet songs will linger long in memory.

Allan B. Philputt.

The Hastings Meeting.

A three weeks' meeting with the home forces of the Hastings (Neb.) church close, with 34 added to the Lord, the majority by primary obedience, and all but four or five were adults and a number of heads of families. The plain, direct preaching of the Old Story by Pastor R. A. Schell, who has recently come upon the field, has won again and has opened up an unlimited field for future work. The music was in charge of Professor Ralph E. Boileau, of this congregation. Within the present year this congregation has enlarged the present building at an expense of over $1,000 and purchased a choice lot for $4,000 upon which it is planned to erect a new church building within the next few years. J. H. Galloway.

Wheeling (W. Va.) Island Church.

This church has just been passing through a season of refreshing. A sad calamity came just about the time plans laid for a revival with W. H. Pinkerton as evangelist were to be executed, viz.: the death of C. Manley Rice, the pastor, and G. S. Naylor, the senior elder. Sept. 9, I was called to do some supply work. Grasping the true situation I agreed to take the pastorate of the church for a time. In a few weeks we had over $600 in the bank for our meeting. Brother Pinkerton came. It took two full weeks to wake the church up to catch the vision of this modern Josiah, but they finally saw it and our old men had dreams in broad daylight and our young men saw visions at noon time. Brother Pinkerton, while in the pulpit, bends his tall body forward, stretches out his long arms, opens his great hands, mouth and heart until he embraces his audience, lifts them to a wondrous vision of the Christ, whom seeing, men desire to accept and imitate. Two great mass meetings were held at one of the opera houses with far-reaching results. Mrs. C. A. Hill had charge of the music. Although this was Mrs. Hill's first attempt at singing since her long illness Brother Pinkerton expresses his fullest satisfaction with her work. The meeting resulted in 60 additions and $1,050 were raised the last night to apply on the church debt. Brother Pinkerton was asked to return in May when a large tabernacle will be built and a great meeting expected.

Clarence A. Hill, Pastor.

Evangelistic

We invite ministers and others to send reports of meetings, additions and other news of the churches. It is especially requested that additions be reported as "by confession and baptism," or "by letter."

Arkansas.

Hope, Dec. 1.—Three additions since last report, two by statement and one by confession and baptism.—Percy G. Cross.

California.

Red Bluff, Dec. 1.—S. M. Martin stirring the town. Fifty-eight additions. Continue two weeks.—George A. Webb.

Ventura, Dec. 2.—New added. Bro. Ogburn is with us in a tent meeting, but the weather is against us.—Dan Trundle.

Illinois.

Benton, Dec. 3.—One added by letter yesterday.—Mrs. Lew D. Hill.

Berlin, Nov. 30.—One added last Sunday by letter.—J. W. Bolton.

Taylorville, Dec. 4.—Six have united with us since last report, four by letter and two by obedience.—Z. Moore.

Quincy, Dec. 3.—On Nov. 28 we closed our four and and one-half weeks' meeting with 29 additions—19 by baptism, seven by letter and three by statement. H. A. Denton, of Maryville, Mo., and J. Will Landrum, of Emporia, Kan., were our evangelistic team. The spiritual uplift of the meeting will be lasting.—Walter M. Jordan, minister.

Nebo, Dec. 7.—Two confessions at Mozier last Sunday.—J. W. Pearson, minister.

Fairfield, Dec. 7.—Short meeting here closed with 23 additions, nearly all of them by primary obedience. Exchanged pulpits with M. W. Yocum, of Martinsville, Ind., who conducted meeting here.—Allen T. Shaw, pastor.

Normal, Dec. 3.—We closed a six weeks' meeting last Thursday evening. Forty-six added, 28 by baptism, 14 by letter or statement, two from other churches and two reclaimed. Nearly all adults. This is the second successful meeting during the year. S. E. Fisher, of Champaign, Ill., did the preaching.—R. H. Newton, pastor.

Camp Point, Dec. 5.—I am in a meeting here with H. J. Reynolds, the minister, and A. R. Davis as singer. A number of additions so far, but greatly hindered by rainy weather.—Gilbert Jones, evangelist.

Waynesville, Dec. 8.—A total of 52 added to date.—J. A. Barnett.

Indiana.

Connersville, Dec. 7.—Meeting of 23 days with home forces. Fifty-two added. L. V. Hegwood led the music.—J. C. Burkhardt.

Indianapolis, Nov. 30.—Two baptisms at Jerome, and four confessions elsewhere not reported.—Willis M. Cunningham.

Iowa.

Moulton, Dec. 7.—Our meeting closed with 54 additions in 17 days. Thirty-eight confessions.—G. T. Moore.

Oelwein, Dec. 4.—Two baptisms.—C. L. McKim.

Vinton, Dec. 5.—Five additions here—four by letter, one by baptism. Begin a revival next Lord's day with Evangelist C. G. Stout.—A. B. Elliott, minister.

Clarksville, Dec. 4.—Great interest in the meeting here. We wish to locate a pastor at the close. Write us.—Joel Brown.

Boone, Dec. 12.—Two baptisms and one by statement not reported. Will hold union meeting in January.—C. F. Ward, minister.

Moulton, Dec. 7.—Our meeting is two weeks old with 51 added—25 confessions. Arthur Stout is doing good preaching.—G. T. Moore.

Lacona, Nov. 19.—Four baptisms and two by letter since coming here.—J. A. McKenzie.

Indian Territory.

Sapulpa, Dec. 4.—One addition by statement at our Wetumka mission last Sunday.—A. M. Harral.

Kansas.

Dresden, Dec. 2.—Meeting two weeks old. Four added by statement. Frances Zimmer, of Randall, is conducting the song service.—A. R. Poe, pastor.

Asherville, Dec. 3.—Our three weeks' meeting conducted by Evangelist J. W. Garner, of Perkins, Okla., closed last night with 12 additions—five by baptism, four reclaimed, three from other religious bodies. Notwithstanding the inclement weather the audience and the interest was good throughout.—A. N. Noell.

South Haven, Dec. 1.—Two confessions and two otherwise. Am preaching here and at Hunnewell.—Thomas J. Easterwood.

Osborne, Dec. 3.—Four additions yesterday, two confessions, one reclaimed and one from another religious body. All departments of work improving.—R. S. Robertson, minister.

Barnes, Dec. 6.—Revival meeting 23 days old with 27 added. No preacher here for six months and not one baptism before for three years. Continue the meeting with fine prospects.—Orwin L. Adams, evangelist; Charles Henning, song leader.

Kentucky.

Lawrenceburg, Dec. 4.—Two added by letter since last report. Outlook is very encouraging.—Walter C. Gibbs.

Mississippi.

Meridian.—On Nov. 29 we closed one of the most successful revivals this church has ever had. Fifty-one were added. R. H. Crossfield, of Owensboro, Ky., was the evangelist, and J. E. Hawes, of Ada, O., chorus leader.—W. M. Baker, minister.

Missouri.

Braymer, Dec. 4.—Baptized two since last report.—S. W. Crutcher.

Sedalia, Dec. 6.—Have had four additions during our meeting.—W. F. Hamann.

St. Joseph, Dec. 6.—Twenty-five additions to date in our meeting at the Wyatt Park Church.—H. A. Northcutt, evangelist; Frank C. Huston, singer.

Creighton, Dec. 3.—Seventy-four added in a big meeting here.—J. P. Andrews.

Clarence, Nov. 26.—Nine added at Lemonville, 12 at Brashear and ten at Illinois Bend since last report.—J. B. Lockhart.

Liberty, Nov. 28.—Elder Barnett, of Kansas City, has just closed a fine meeting of two weeks with the church at Smithville, Mo. There were 32 additions.—Fred V. Loos.

Michigan.

Ann Arbor, Dec. 6.—For the months of October and November we have had 21 additions—two by baptism and 19 by letter and statement, several of whom have come from other Christian bodies.—A. C. Gray.

Detroit, Dec. 3.—Meeting with Lloyd Darsie closed with 30 additions to the church. Membership increased by 50 per cent.—S. G. Fisher.

Minnesota.

Rochester, Dec. 3.—Baptized five persons yesterday. Four of them had been sprinkled, but were desirous to have "the answer of a good conscience," so concluded to be "buried with their Lord in baptism."—Rochester Irwin.

Nebraska.

Trenton, Dec. 3.—The meeting at Cornell is progressing. Large crowds and good interest. Up to date three reclaimed, three confessions, one by letter.—Hugh C. Gresham.

Cozad.—Our meeting resulted in 12 accessions. H. F. Stevens is the pastor.—Samuel Gregg.

Ohio.

East Liverpool, Dec. 4.—Three confessions recently, not reported.—E. P. Wise.

Bellaire, Nov. 27.—The meeting at New Martinsville closed after a little over four weeks' of effort with 24 added—19 confessions and five by statement. The preaching of the pastor, J. W. Stewart, was highly commended. During the last week the preaching was done by F. A. Bright, of Waynesburg, Pa. The writer had charge of the music.—George E. Hopkins.

New Richmond, Dec. 7.—J. M. Helm, of Parkersburg, W. Va., has just closed a very successful meeting here with 24 additions.—M. D.

Oklahoma.

Watonga, Nov. 30.—Our meeting at Ames closed with 78 additions.—J. A. Tabor and wife.

Pennsylvania.

Rogersville, Dec. 7.—Six accessions recently—three by baptism and three otherwise. Began at Holbrook with seven accessions to date, five confessions and two by restoration.—G. F. Assiter.

California, Dec. 7.—Are in a good meeting with home forces. Five accessions to date and interest is growing. Elmer W. Martin is leading the singing.—Dr. Thomas Martin.

Washington.

Waterville, Dec. 3.—Meeting two weeks old. Eighteen accessions. Close Wednesday night then go to Entiat.—O. M. Thomason, evangelist.

Christian Endeavor

By GEO. L. SNIVELY

December 23, 1906.

The Christmas Spirit.—Luke 2:8-20.

DAILY READINGS.

M. The Birth of Christ. Luke 1:26-35.
T. The Song of the Angels. Luke 2:1-14.
W. The Visit of the Shepherds. Luke 2:15-20.
T. The Visit of the Wise Men. Matt. 2:1-12.
F. The Holy Child Jesus. Luke 2:25-38.
S. The Star of Prophecy. Num. 24:11-18.
S. The Wonderful Name. Isaiah 9:1-7.

"O never failing splendor!
O never, silent song!
Still keep the green earth tender,
Still keep the gray earth strong."

In all the wide world it will be true that the happiest among the celebrants of Christmastide will be those who have given most rather than those who have received most.

The purse may be so thin that our Christmas gift may lie lightly on the scales and yet they may be so surcharged with love that in God's sight and in the opinion of the recipient they may be heavier than loveless stars.

There is no Christmas for him whose heart is not at peace with all mankind. He may be warred against, but he must not be warring if he would have fellowship with those angels singing, "Glory to God in the highest, and on earth peace and good-will among men, in whom he is well pleased."

Benevolence is inextricably a part of the Christmas spirit. No sooner had God given to those shepherds of Bethlehem the world's first Christmas gift till they began sharing it with all—"And when they saw it they made known concerning the same which was spoken to them about this child." Our best expression of thanks for the blessings of Christmas and all others will be our sharing them with those having not.

Fear is one element of the true Christmas spirit—"And the glory of the Lord shone round about them and they were sore afraid." As our own figure casts a shadow on the glory of the Lord shining around us at Christmas time, may we have a saving fear of our own unworthiness and in penitential tears and Jesus' blood wash away our own guilt, and be pure in His sight as the angels who first sang the Nativity.

There is no other gift many of us grown older in the affairs of life would prize more highly through these Christmas days than to see again these angels such as the shepherds saw hovering over the storied hills of Bethlehem and such as in fond fancy we ourselves saw in childhood's innocent days. O ruby lipped, pink cheeked, radiant winged, angel bands, come again with your sweet songs and heavenly chorus and enchant our eyes to the skies and in all ways lure us home!

❋ ❋

THE DEMAND CONTINUES

For The Victory of Faith, by E. L. Powell. Twenty-one Masterly Addresses, postpaid, $1.00.

CHRISTIAN PUBLISHING CO.,
St. Louis, Mo.

Midweek Prayer-Meeting

December 19, 1906.

The Danger of Apostasy.—Heb. 6:4-6.

"A charge to keep I have,
A God to glorify,
A never-dying soul to save,
And fit it for the sky.

"To serve the present age,
My calling to fulfill;
O, may it all my powers engage
To do my Master's will!

"Arm me with jealous care,
As in thy sight to live;
And O, thy servant. Lord, prepare
A strict account to give!

"Help me to watch and pray,
And on thyself rely,
Assured, if I my trust betray,
I shall forever die."

There are many apostates whose statements of belief are faultless; they can formulate scholarly statements of doctrine, but they are apostates—"their hearts are far from me"; they know but do not do; they believe but do not live.

Paul asks no more of others than he himself did to maintain loyalty to the Crucified. He testifies, "I buffet my body and keep it under subjection lest having preached the Gospel to others, I myself should become a castaway." This emphasizes that eternal vigilance is the price of liberty in Jesus, even for those who have looked through rifted skies and held converse face to face with Christ.

To realize our constant peril of apostasy, look around. In every community are aged men and women who in earlier years were devout, enthusiastic, sacrificing, disciples on whose altars the fires have burned low and whose ardor has grown dim amidst the falling shadows and mists of age. The heavenly inheritance that once was theirs by right of faith and sacrifice is falling out of their grasp, and they seem unconscious of profound loss. "Be thou faithful unto death and thou shalt receive the crown of life."

Among the awful words of the Scriptures are these: "It is impossible to renew them again unto repentance: seeing they crucify to themselves the Son of God afresh and put him to open shame." It is not ours to philosophize about this dictum, but to accept it as a statement of truth from on high. Let us know that it is fearfully true that having once been enlightened and made partakers of the heavenly gifts, we can leave them and have no more ties binding us to the throne and the life eternal.

Paul is referring in the lesson to apostates, who had once enjoyed sweet spiritual privileges—"They were once enlightened" and "tasted the heavenly gift" and "were made partakers of the Holy Spirit," and "tasted the good word of God and the powers of the age to come," but notwithstanding all "fell away." Surely if such blessings did not anchor those first century disciples fast to the faith and the throne we of the twentieth century ought to give the more earnest heed to the things we have heard and felt and tasted lest haply we drift away from them.

There is one apostasy of heart and another of mind, and they are different. David's frequent apostasies were of the former sort. Sin's dangerous blasts frequently diverted his course from God, but his heart was true, and when the sudden tempest ended, like the needle that points again to the polar star when the intruding

What Sulphur Does

For the Human Body in Health and Disease.

COSTS NOTHING TO TRY.

The mention of sulphur will recall to many of us the early days when our mothers and grandmothers gave us our daily dose of sulphur and molasses every spring and fall.

It was the universal spring and fall "blood purifier," tonic and cure-all, and, mind you, this old-fashioned remedy was not without merit.

The idea was good, but the remedy was crude and unpalatable, and a large quantity had to be taken to get any effect.

Nowadays we get all the beneficial effects of sulphur in a palatable, concentrated form, so that a single grain is far more effective than a tablespoonful of the crude sulphur.

In recent years research and experiment have proven that the best sulphur for medicinal use is that obtained from Calcium (Calcium Sulphide) and sold in drug stores under the name of Stuart's Calcium Wafers. They are small chocolate coated pellets and contain the active medicinal principle of sulphur in a highly concentrated, effective form.

Few people are aware of the value of this form of sulphur in restoring and maintaining bodily vigor and health; sulphur acts directly on the liver and excretory organs and purifies and enriches the blood by the prompt elimination of waste material.

Our grandmothers knew this when they dosed us with sulphur and molasses every spring and fall, but the crudity and impurity of ordinary flowers of sulphur were often worse than the disease, and cannot compare with the modern concentrated preparations of sulphur, of which Stuart's Calcium Wafers is undoubtedly the best and most widely used.

They are the natural antidote for liver and kidney troubles and cure constipation and purify the blood in a way that often surprises patient and physician alike.

Dr. R. M. Wilkins, while experimenting with sulphur remedies, soon found that the sulphur from Calcium was superior to any other form. He says: "For liver, kidney and blood troubles, especially when resulting from constipation or malaria, I have been surprised at the results obtained from Stuart's Calcium Wafers. In patients suffering from boils and pimples and even deep-seated carbuncles, I have repeatedly seen them dry up and disappear in four or five days, leaving the skin clear and smooth. Although Stuart's Calcium Wafers is a proprietary article and sold by druggists and for that reason tabooed by many physicians, yet I know of nothing so safe and reliable for constipation, liver and kidney troubles and especially in all forms of skin disease as this remedy."

At any rate people who are tired of pills, cathartics and so-called blood "purifiers" will find in Stuart's Calcium Wafers, a far safer, more palatable and effective preparation.

Send your name and address today for a free trial package and see for yourself.

F. A. Stuart Co., 57 Stuart Bldg., Marshall, Mich.

finger is removed, he stands forth loyal and devout. "For Demas hath forsaken me, having loved this present world, and is departed unto Thessalonica," portrays the other. With Demas it is a settled conviction that the Christian life is not worth while. There is hope for the Davids, but only "farewells" for the Demases. And yet the Davids must strive unto blood against sin.

Sunday-School
December 23, 1906.

Jesus Ascends Into Heaven.—Luke 24:36-53.

Memory verses: 46-48.

Golden Text.—While he blessed them, he was parted from them, and carried up into heaven. Luke 24:51.

During the forty days which intervened between the resurrection and the ascension, Jesus appeared seven times, according to the records of the evangelists. In the following list of the appearances, with the gospels in which they are narrated, note how incomplete is any one gospel by itself:

1. To the women at the tomb. (Matt., John.)
2. On way to Emmaus. (Mark.)
3. To the ten at Jerusalem. (Luke, John.)
4. To the eleven, including Thomas. (Mark, John.)
5. To seven by Sea of Galilee. (John.)
6. To eleven on a mountain in Galilee. (Matt.)
7. The ascension. (Mark, Luke.)

Mark's account of the ascension is given in the closing verses which were probably not a part of the original gospel. Luke's account of that remarkable event therefore stands alone.

The nature of this miracle we need not discuss. The ideas of "up" and "down" with reference to extra-terrestrial space do not mean as much to us as they meant when the Ptolemaic astronomy was in vogue. We feel less justified in feeling that heaven is always directly "up" from us, in view of the fact that up from the other side of the globe would be precisely the opposite direction in space.

But these quibbles touch only the physical envelope and not the spiritual kernel of the matter. In regard to the resurrection we said that the great fact was that, in some way, and quite against their expectations, the disciples received the undying conviction that, in spite of his crucifixion, their Master was not a dead but a living Lord. This was not primarily a fact for science or history. It was primarily a fact for faith. So now, in some way, the men who were nearest to Jesus, reached the conviction that the one whom they had gradually learned to know as the Son of God, was again with his Father.

Both of these facts are not only supported historically by all the evidence that is available, but also supported spiritually by the experience of the apostles and of millions of disciples in all subsequent ages. The testimony of the Christian consciousness is that we have a living Lord who, as our mediator and intercessor, stands in the presence of God.

Send for our Holiday Catalogue.
CHRISTIAN PUBLISHING CO.,
St. Louis, Mo.

Ministerial Exchange.

A. A. Doak, Kent, O., has resigned his charge at that place in order to give all his time to evangelistic work. He has held many successful meetings. Address him at Kent, O.

W. D. Trumble and wife, of Meadville, Pa., are available as evangelists. A local paper speaks very highly of the singing of Sister Trumble. Evangelists who know Brother Trumble speak well of him, both as a Christian gentleman and pastor.

Two or three good men are wanted for the work in Montana. None but those who can furnish satisfactory references as to character and work, need apply. Write F. H. Groom, box 695, Helena, Mont.

J. P. Myers, a successful pastor of Paulding, O., is available for an occasional meeting; at present he is immediately available. His success in this line of work argues that he should be kept busy all the time.

Our churches in Steuben county, Indiana, are desirous of securing an evangelist to give all his time to that field. The salary will be from $800 to $1,200 per year, according to ability. He must be a man of character and must have had sufficient success in this line of work to commend him to the brethren. Address Vernon Stauffer, Angola, Ind.

W. G. Johnson, Roanoke, Va., who has had unusual success, both as a settled minister and as an evangelist, desires to locate. Here is an ideal man for some good church.

R. R. Watson, Fort Worth, Texas, is giving all his time to evangelistic work, having recently resigned his church in that city. He is one of the ablest in our recent accessions to the evangelistic ranks and is capable of holding good meetings in our southland. We cheerfully commend him to the consideration of the brethren.

The western half of the great state of Washington is in need of an absolutely first-class evangelist. The brethren desire a man whose spiritual qualities will be as marked as his purely evangelistic traits. This is one of the greatest fields in America and is worthy of one of the best men. Write to Mrs. J. A. C. Merriman, 1116 Bishop Court, Spokane, Wash.

Miss Una Dell Berry, Lafayette, Ind., has resigned as pastoral helper and intends spending all her time in the work of singing evangelist. She is one of the best soloists in our brotherhood; her singing being very much like that of Mrs. Princess Long's. Write her at 527 Wood street.

Henry P. Keltch, Wadsworth, Ohio, is available for a meeting at almost any time during the winter. Churches in Ohio, especially are invited to write to him.

S. K. Tomlinson, of Fairland, Ind., is desirous of changing location. He has been in charge of several of our most important churches in that state.

A. R. Miller has resigned at Savannah, Ga., having ministered there for several years. A good church ought to secure his services at once.

Charles E. Schultz and wife, evangelists, Newcastle, Ind., are holding successful meetings. They have some open dates which ought to be filled immediately.

M. D. Sharpless, Stronghurst, Ill., is desirous of settling as pastor. Many good and able brethren speak highly of his character and ability.

C. A. McDonald, Akron, O., is ready to do evangelistic work either occasionally or all the time, according as there are opportunities. He is a capable man and can also as well as preach.

A. K. Dubber, Fort Worth, Texas, is ready to give all his time to evangelistic work or to settle as a pastor. He prefers a northern or western charge. He is one of the ablest men in our Texas ministry.

Mart Gary Smith, Douglas, Ariz., is ready to enter evangelistic work. President Zollars speaks highly of him and says he is a young man of more than ordinary ability.

C. M. Farnham, Newbury, Ind., is giving all his time to holding meetings and has a few dates for winter and spring and would be pleased to hear of places desirous of meetings.

Brother Flourney Payne recently resigned at Berkeley Church, Denver, and is available for work in almost any part of the country. He has succeeded both in Denver and Baltimore, Md.

J. Frank Green, Mt. Pleasant, Mich., has finished his term of service with the church in that place and is ready for work elsewhere. He is a good man with a successful record.

L. E. Murray, Middletown, Ind., is available for evangelistic work. He prefers going to the southwest.

J. A. Pine, Dayton, Wash., is writing for a good evangelist to succeed Bro. L. F. Stevens, who has just left that field. None but an able man could do the work which Brother Stevens has been doing.

Walter Mansell, 1232 Neal avenue, Columbus, O., can go away for three or four weeks' meeting during January or February. Brother Mansell's well known ability ought to result in him securing many calls.

Bertha A. Short, 413 East Fifth street, Seymour, Ind., can be secured as singing evangelist for meetings in December and January.

Owing to disarranged dates, L. H. Koeprel, Farlington, Kan., is open for a meeting in December.

The church at Great Bend, Kan., would like to employ a minister. Address J. W. Sodenstrom.

J. Windbigler, Altoona, Iowa, wants a singer for a meeting in January.

H. M. Barnett, 1832 Norton avenue, Kansas City, Mo., can hold a meeting for some church before the holidays.

People's Forum

Old Scotty on Theology.

To the Editor of THE CHRISTIAN-EVANGELIST.

I ain't much fur theology an' don't know much about it nohow, but it 'peers to me that we ain't on the rite track when good religious papers have so much stuff that don't do nobody any good. You know that the Disciples (excuse the big D) is a-gettin' to be a mighty powerful people, an' quite respectful in the eyes of uther folks. We had a grate convention way off at Buffalo, near where the Falls is, an' say! what do you think? After it was over or perhaps befor, if some of them fellers didn't go an' pile rite on to Bro. Cooper, an' ther was nuthin' to make people do it, except some folks ain't never satisfied unless they are a-steppin' round a-lookin' for a chip on some body's shoulder, an' if they can't find one, they pick up anything an' hit at it. Now, I read not long ago in that splendid paper, the "Standard"—always read in our house first—how in about seven pages of good space, an elder in a De Fence, tried with tears an' sighs, as it were, to save a church. The preacher was one of them there smart Alecks what works so hard but knows too much, a higher kritter so to speak. Now, elders ot to always keep kopies of letters fur themselves so they can tell what they write. Do you remember the big meetin' they had? There set the town preachers in a row across our pulpit—the horrid sects—an' perhaps a-laffin' in thers sleeves. Jes' like 'em. That "presiding elder"—well, is that the New Testament name? Well, he was a queer chap to be a preacher an' preach "Ther ain't no hell any more." Perhaps he came from Ann Arbor fur they sing that ther when they beat in foot-ball. Now, I ain't a-goin' to say wher the troubel was, fur I don't know, only I am sorrie they had such a time. But I think we ot to pass a law that elders ot to be in fur jes' so long, an' if the church wanted them agen, why, put 'em in agen. An election is always better than a quarrel.

I got another thing to say. That man from Harper, Kan., has got that higher kriticism all straightened out. Why, it is a "psychic phenomenon," pure and simple. All of them fellers—critics—every one, no exception (take a long breth now—Garrison, Peckham, Willett, Ames, S. Jones, Gates, C. M. Sharp, B. A. Jenkins, Rowlison, Hieronymus, etc.) are "egotists of the most intense and absurd type." Now, you see what learnin' an' education does. No, it is that "psychic phenomenon" that makes you an' all uther higher critics act up so. Do you know the meanin' of these big words? The Kansas man tells us "it is a species of hysteria or hallucination, perpetuating itself by suggestion upon the subjective faculties of men." This makes men "dreamers," who don't say nuthin' back, or do nuthin' but jes' let on like you don't see artikles by men who are tryin' to enlighten people. How unsimpathetic an' unkind higher kritics are! They are in the subjective case while some folks is in the objective case. Now, I know sum of these dreamers an' sum I don't. I know that Bro. Garrison is too busy writin' good things to waste time in enterin' the arena to defend himself. He found out long ago that there ain't no Christianity in that. Bro. Willett is too busy teachin', preachin', bringin' folks into the kingdom of God—immersin' every one of 'em too—an' gettin' redy fur a trip to Palestine, to bother hisself with things that don't need to be done. The sort of religion this ole world wants ain't the disputin' kind, but a lovin' kind. Not the kind that is a-pullin' all the time, but the kind that is a-liftin'. We say we love each uther, but it ain't the kind of love that the Carpenter of Nazareth had fur men.

Now, this is all I have to say, Mister Editor, this time, only I am glad to know what higher kriticism is. It is a releef after tryin' to find out what the kritter looked like. Thanks. It is a "psychic phenomenon."

❀

An Appeal to Women From an Eclipsed Man.

To the Editor of THE CHRISTIAN-EVANGELIST:

It is not often that I feel inspired, really inspired; but whenever I am in that condition, I must write, or talk to some one who will listen, and I have picked you out from among some fifteen million men in the United States to mention the matter that is upon my mind.

I have been in New York City for about five or six weeks, and, as my custom is, I have regularly attended church services, especially on the Lord's day. For a few weeks I attended our churches on 56th street and on 119th street, but lately I have been visiting around, seeing how other folks conduct their services, and hearing some of the great divines.

Now it so happens that the people out here are not aware of the fact that I am a great preacher (!) and ought to be given some prominent seat, either on the pulpit or, "up front," where I would be both comfortable and conspicuous, so I have had to enter the sanctuary and take what ordinary folks who go to church get fifty-two times a year (if they go that often), and in doing this, I have learned a great deal that I never knew before.

I will not trespass upon your valuable time to mention a great many things that have impressed me; but will confine this inspired epistle to the consideration of one subject, namely, the average woman's hat in church.

At first I attended our 56th street church, and I believe the first Lord's day I had an open view; but the second time I attended that church, a very sweet and beautiful young lady sat in front of me with a hat on her head about two feet in diameter, and try as hard as I could, I just could not see either around, over or through that hat, so I gave it up and heard Brother Bates deliver a splendid sermon as one would hear some great preacher through the means of a phonograph.

Then I began visiting about a little and I observed that the higher up I went in church society, the higher and wider and more top-heavy was the headgear of the daughters of men, or more properly speaking, the daughters of millionaires. At what is called Mr. Rockefeller's church I just gave up in despair at once; as I was seated way back behind a wilderness of hats—hats! HATS!! HATS!!! Never saw so many hats before in my life, and I almost had the blind staggers before the service was half through. In this church they have just called a new minister, a Mr. Aked from England, and I heard the voice, but saw no man." I saw him after the service was over, so am reasonably sure that he preached in person, but could not make oath to it.

When last Lord's day arrived says I to myself, says I, "I'll just go over to hear a preacher who is much spoken of, who preaches for a congregation of poor folks, and maybe the wash-women there will have shawls over their heads and I will get a chance to see and to hear." But I was a little late and the usher gave me a nice seat in the extreme back of the church, but fortunately no one was in the seat just in front of me, and I fairly revelled in sight seeing, as one who had been healed of blindness. Alas, alas, I enjoyed that blessed vision only about five minutes when a late comer was shown the seat just in front of me, and she was a poorly clad girl with a very ordinary hat on; but the hat had a green bunch of drooping feathers that waved right in front of me—between me and the preacher, and I know she moved her head and tossed that green plume a hundred times a minute, until I could neither see nor hear anything. My eyes pained me so that I closed them for long periods, but as soon as I opened them again, that same green plume was waving defiance in my face, so I finally gave up in despair and left.

It is unnecessary that I go on and multiply cases, which I could do. I have said enough to make my case, and now I plead for reforms in the style of hats worn by women in church, and ask you to take your pen in hand and "suggest" the inconvenience to others, and maybe our great, great grand-daughters will do differently.

As every one knows, the state laws compel women to remove their hats in theaters and other places of amusement, where people would not stand for such interference after they had paid to see and to hear. So why would it not be becoming to the gentler sex to be a little considerate in this matter? If the Apostle Paul's admonition is still understood to apply to such cases, then let our women devise some "dear little bonnet" that will fit so close and not in the least interfere with the view of those behind them.

I will not attempt to describe the modern hat in all of its shapes and glory; but if you or any one else will look over the next audience (if it is a bright day, especially), you will see—oh, I won't begin to catalog the multitude of things of all sizes, shapes, colors and texture that one will see on the beautiful heads of our lovely women.

I guess I've said enough to give you a start on this subject, and I hope you will have the courage (or audacity) to open your big guns on this great and inconsiderate evil.

W. DAVIESS PITTMAN.

New York City, Dec. 3, 1906.

OBITUARIES.

[Notices of Deaths, not more than four lines, inserted free. Obituary memoirs, one cent per word. Send the money with the copy.]

McCURDY.

Melissa A. McCurdy (maiden name Deck), died at her late home near Edmond, Okla., Nov. 17. She was a daughter of Isaac and Leah Deck. and was born near Alton, Ill., Aug. 6, 1850. She was married to Joseph McCurdy Dec. 31, 1872. The burial was at Bunker Hill, Ill. Sister McCurdy was a faithful member of the Dorchester church until its disruption in 1897.   J. K. MASTERS.
Dorchester, Ill.

TANKSLEY.

William Albros, second born of Bro. and Sister R. H. Tanksley, of the church at Mound Valley, Kan., went home to God on his eighth birthday, November 16, 1906. He was a bright boy, leading his class in school, but was promoted to be happy in a heavenly company. Brother Tanksley was with us when our only boy, Errett, went home New Year's day, this year. May the Lord comfort the sorrowing ones.   E. E. LOWE.

CROSS.

Robert Gollop Cross, who died November 5, 1906, was born in Axminster, England, April 6, 1833. At the age of 20 he came to America, first to Canada and later to the United States, making his home in Nashville, Tenn. He fought through the civil war with bravery, for which he was awarded many places of honor and trust. Brother Cross was for a number of years a consistant member of the Cumberland Presbyterian church, but on September 4, 1904, he was baptized into Christ and united with the Christian church. This godly man found much happiness in his Christian life. In a recent talk with him about the story of his gallant life he said: "I can not understand why our young men and women put off the acceptance of Christ so long. The call is urgent and we need good strong men and women to press forward this great and glorious work." He is survived by a devoted wife and two daughters, who for many years have been members of the Christian church. Many friends join these dear ones in tenderest sympathy in their hour of grief.   B. F. ARCHER.
Rome, Ga.

FRAZIER.

William Frazier was born in Shelby county, Kentucky, September 23, 1828. At the age of nine years he came with his father to Lincoln county, Missouri, settling near New Hope, The most of his life service was spent in Lincoln county, except sixteen years in Colfax, California and two years in Iowa. His father died when William was fifteen years old and for many years the care of the family fell upon him. He confessed his faith in his divine Lord and Savior under the preaching of Elder Joseph Errett at New Hope. Brother Frazier was united in marriage to Fannie Blanton in the early 50's, which union continued about six years. His second marriage was with Sarah Robinson, and several years later he was again called to part with a loved companion. His last marriage was to Orpha Virginia Cash, nee Brown, on November 16, 1873, and his death occurred on the thirty-third anniversary of this marriage, November 16, 1906.

In his death we have lost one of nature's noblemen, a generous friend, a genial companion, a man of sound judgment, prompt in action, faithful in matters of truth, an earnest and devoted Christian worker and an ardent lover of the plea for the union of all of God's children. Let us ever treasure the memory of his blameless Christian life, his wise counsels, his faithful waning, and his zeal for the cause of Christ. We deeply sympathize with his widow. The funeral was held in the church of which Brother Frazier was a much beloved elder for many years, on November 17. Rev. B. D. Kennedy, pastor of the Troy Presbyterian church, offered a memorial tribute followed by the pastor of the church, F. G. Merrill. The body was then laid to rest in the Troy cemetery.   E. G. MERRILL.

THE DEVOTIONAL SPIRIT

Is quickened by, Alone With God, The Heavenward Way, Half Hour Studies at the Cross. Read them and meditate, then pass to a friend. Each, 75 cents, or the trio, postpaid, $2.00.

CHRISTIAN PUBLISHING CO.,
       St. Louis, Mo.

Stockholders' Meeting.

Notice is hereby given that the annual meeting of the stockholders of the Christian Publishing Company will be held at the company's office, 2712 Pine street, St. Louis, Mo., Tuesday, January 1, 1907, at 10 o'clock, for the election of directors and for the transaction of such other business as may legally come before said meeting.
     J. H. GARRISON, Pres.
     GEO. L. SNIVELY, Sec.
St. Louis, Nov. 15, 1906.

The Home Department

On the Line.

Do not surrender, e'en though stricken down;
    The battle's never lost
Till you admit defeat. The fates may frown
    And sorely tried and crossed
Your wounded soul and weary may still cry
    Against all further strife;
But—it remains always to bravely die—
    Else, little worth were life.

"A man must live;"
    That is the coward's cry,
Excuse that recreants for their actions give;
    Let us be brave and say, "A man must die,"
And so die worthily, with front to foe
    And striving still; aye, to the latest breath.
Is it not better, mortal, thus to go,
    Paying to God his debt, a true man's death?

Death comes to all; must come; why, then, post-
    pone,
    By craven suppliance to the things we hate,
The inevitable end. Is death itself alone
    The dreadful fact of life? Should we await
The hurts, the chains, dishonor and disgrace
    That do attend or yielding? In God's plan,
Whose is the higher and the nobler place,
    Who lives a slave; or dies free—and a man?
                    —T. K. H. in Globe-Democrat.

❧ ❧

A new serial story, by J. Breckenridge Ellis,
will begin in THE CHRISTIAN-EVANGELIST January
3, 1907. Other stories will also be published during the year. Next week there will be short
stories.

The Bronze Vase.

BY J. BRECKENRIDGE ELLIS.

The Last Chapter.

The next morning Raymund returned
to the Laclede hotel in time to take
breakfast with Rhoda. She was full of
bright information about their old
friends; she had been to sit with Miss
Glory Agency again, and the old lady
was much more at her ease with her
than she had been when the orphan was
a little girl. She told about Wizzen, and
said, "You must be sure to go to see
him."

"Of course I shall," said Raymund
with a smile, "but in the meantime—
how would you like to go for a walk
with me—not to see anybody, you understand, except each other?"

Rhoda thought she should like that
very much, so they set forth and having lingered past their old home, with
softened reminders of their mother, they
came to the stream at the edge of town
over which the railroad started on its
way to Kansas City. There was a wagon
bridge farther down, and when they
were half-across, Raymund stopped. All
this time he had been carrying his valise, but now he placed it upon the dusty
floor. They leaned upon the railing and
watched the swirling water as they had
watched it in childhood. Raymund
suddenly turned his face to Rhoda and
asked her to tell him how she had
learned that she was not his sister.

"It was while I was at Fulton," Rhoda
answered gravely. "A gentleman called
at the dormitory who proved to be an
old acquaintance of my mother's. He
was Mr. Horace Bridgewaite."

"The promoter!" Raymund exclaimed;
"yes, I've met him."

"I supposed so," Rhoda nodded gravely. "Many years ago—at least they
seem many years ago,—a man had come
to me at Crawley—the creature named
Boggs—and had let fall words that
hinted of a bronze vase, which in some
way concerned us."

"You never told me that," Raymund
remarked.

"No, I thought it best not to disturb
your mind with useless imaginings.
Brother Bellfield advised the same

course. Well, this Mr. Horace Bridgewaite was boarding where our mother
boarded in St. Louis, when a bronze
vase was given you. It was from me,
but of course I was so little that our
parents did the giving. Anyway, the
name on it was Rhoda. Your father had
asked that the inscription, 'From Rhoda to
Raymund' be engraved on the vase, but
through a mistake only my name was put
on it. And that is how he showed me that
you was not the son of—of my mother.
I mean, I am Rhoda Revore, but you are
Raymund White. Even had he said otherwise, I must have always known that I am
Rhoda Revore. Something within seems
to tell me that I could have no mother but
the one we both called by that dear name."

"That's exactly the way I feel about
her," said Raymund. "And it may astonish you a good deal to learn that Mr.
Bridgewaite told me the word 'Raymund'
was on that vase, and not 'Rhoda'!"

Rhoda stared incredulously. "Why, Raymund! I was so sure my name was on
that vase, and so afraid he would go and
tell you, that I gave him the $150 Uncle
William gave me, to bind him to secrecy."

"The wretch," muttered Raymund.

"I knew how it would grieve you,"
Rhoda went on with exceeding gentleness,
"to learn that you are only mother's
adopted child. I would have given more
than that, if I'd had it—indeed, Mr.
Bridgewaite wanted more—to have kept the
truth from you."

"But, Rhoda," Raymund expostulated,
"Mr. Bridgewaite told me, and only a few
days ago, that my name is on that vase!
And mother's letter says that whosever's
name is on that vase, that one is her only
child."

Rhoda began to tremble and her face
turned deathly pale. She grasped the
bridge-railing for support, and stared dumbly at the other.

"Now, Rhoda," said Raymund slowly,
"listen attentively, for all depends upon
your decision; I think it is pretty evident
that we cannot believe that promoter, no
matter what he says. He has contradicted
himself, and even if he hadn't, we could
neither of us accept his word as final, because each feels—at least I feel, I am the
only child of our dear mother; and you tell
me you feel the same about yourself."

"Oh, yes!" Rhoda gasped.

"You wondered why I went to St. Louis,"
Raymund continued. "It was to dig up
that bronze vase."

"Did you do so?" she asked quickly.

"I did."

"Whose name is on it?"

"I do not know."

Still trembling with suspense, she looked
at him for an explanation.

"I carried a bag to the cellar," Raymund
said, speaking every word slowly, and all
the time keeping his eyes upon the other,
"and as soon as it was dug up, I put it in
the bag. I carried it to my hotel, and
washed it thoroughly in the bath tub, having first bound my eyes with a handkerchief
to prevent myself from seeing the inscription. In washing away the dirt, my hand
encountered the first letter of the name. It
was a rounded capital 'R.' After that, I
was extremely careful not to touch that
place. When the vase was clean and dry,
I put it in another bag and then removed
my bandage. I carried it to a work shop
and ordered it to be cut in two, the separate halves to be done up securely and then
given business. When I came back, the
work was finished. In this valise are the

bowl and the pedestal, in diffe
just as I received them from
man."

Raymund stooped and opene
He tore off the wrapper fro
and presented it to Rhoda. H
up the pedestal but did not
wrapper. "Rhoda," he said w
"this pedestal tells which of
adopted child. Shall I open th

"No," said Rhoda faintly.

"Each of us claim that belo
said Raymund, his voice trem
when this inscription has one
one of us can never claim that
ilege again."

"Do not open it," Rhoda w
"The one whose name is not
estal," said Raymund, "is the
a vast fortune. We have bu
this name, to know which of
Mr. White's millions. But tha
claim Mrs. Revore as a moth
why she told us on her death

knowledge of the secret might make us rich, and at the same time very unhappy. Do you agree with me, dear"—he had studiously avoided any show of affection since learning that she was not his sister, but now he spoke tenderly, quite unconscious that he did so—"Do you agree with me, dear, that there is something in this world of more value than millions?"

"I do," said Rhoda, her eyes glowing.

"Oh, Raymund, I am so proud of you, so proud, oh, so proud!" She burst into tears.

Raymund handed her the pedestal. "Dear Rhoda," he said softly, "the stream beneath our feet will hide the secret forever."

Rhoda dropped the pedestal, still in its brown paper wrapping, over the railing. It splashed in the water. Ripple after ripple was sent from the spot till they were lost among the high flags along the banks.

"Now," said Raymund, "this upper part of the bronze vase belongs equally to us both, for we are both to claim the mother of our childhood as the mother of our maturity. No one will ever know which one of us is related to her by right of birth; but we know that each has an equal right of love. We will cherish this part of the bronze vase as long as we live.

And so they did, for when, twelve years later, Jack Belifield and Mrs. Jack Bellfield—a lady once known to her friends simply as Nelsie Loraine—visited the farm that had once been Mr. Omer's, and was now Raymund's, they found the upper portion of the bronze vase fastened high up on the wall in the sitting-room. Resting across the mouth of the bowl was Rhoda's first book of poems, just from the press.

"What you got that bronze vase up there for?" asked the brilliant young physician (we speak of Jack) who always addressed Raymund and Rhoda with the delightful familiarity of an old friend—a familiarity, to say truth, to which Mrs. Omer had never grown accustomed.

"That," said Rhoda with a smile, "is where we keep our marriage certificate."

THE END.

My Friend Jack Louis.

BY S. S RETLAW.

We were college chums, Jack and I, and no finer young man attended the old North Western C. U. at Indianapolis. We were together in the geometry and rhetoric classes, members of the same (Pythonian) literary society, joined the church in the same great meeting, and always attended the young people's prayer meeting. I have no more vivid memory of that Monday night meeting than Jack's earnest prayer. I graduated a year ahead of Jack, on account of his enlistment in the army. He was older than I; and, so, old enough to enlist; whereas I was but 20 when the war closed. I thus gained a year on him, and there was the year's difference, when in 1866, the month of February, we enlisted in the good fight of faith.

We met a few times in meetings of the alumni, but otherwise I saw nothing of Louis after I entered the world as a teacher, and he as a scientific farmer. I had my turn as country teacher, village principal, county superintendent, college professor, normal instructor, expert institute worker, etc. And while in the course of this routine I one day chanced to meet Jack all rosy and plump, and showing that he had been well fed.

Of course, our greeting was cordial, and our talk ran on for an hour or more. Jack listened with admirable good manners to my recital, smiling over the pleasant features and dropping a tear over my sorrows; and then he told me of himself, of the best and sweetest wife in the world, and his three children; just beaming with pride as he recounted their graces. He had settled near his county seat, the popular young man of his country; and, while pursuing his course in agriculture, mingling with the young of his neighborhood, he incidentally fell in with Nettie Clare, who in his and her childhood had seemed the sweetest and prettiest of little girls. She had undergone that miracle of transmutation that takes place in the life of every lass, and now spoke maturely, and carried herself as a woman. Their glance was electric, and Jack was now a bondman. The Clares were a good family, and Nettie was the flower of the family. Jack made timid advances, and Nettie blushingly encouraged them. In short, they were soon betrothed, and Jack put new energy into all his plans. All he lacked of naming the day for the nuptials was the assurance that he could properly provide for her.

As the stars would have it, the county convention was at hand, and one of Jack's army chums proposed his name for treasurer. It was a popular chord; and he received the nomination, practically without effort on his part. As his party was "two to one" in the county his nomination had been regarded as equal to an election. But here is his pathetic story in his own words: "I virtually knew, I would be elected, for there was only one township in the county in which my opponents had a majority. But try as I would, I could not rest contented. What if my opponent should prove more popular? What if he should spring a scandal against me? What if some unknown force should assail me, and I should be defeated? There is my Nettie to grieve and weep, and myself reduced to shame! And oh! think of it; another year or two before I could call her my very own! These reflections began to tell on my health and I lost many hours of sleep.

"One Lord's day evening I was out on the street, when I ought to have been in the church at worship. I had a headache—a true headache, and convinced my heart that I was staying out of the meeting house to take the air. But the serious fact was I staid out to see voters and hear their words of flattery and encouragement, in

REV. J. W. BLOSSER, M. D.

A Noted Minister and Doctor of Atlanta, Ga., is Meeting with Wonderful Success.

Those who have long doubted whether there really is a permanent cure for catarrh will be glad to learn that a southern physician, Rev. J. W. Blosser, M. D., of Atlanta, Ga., has discovered a method whereby catarrh can be cured to the very last symptom without regard to climate or condition. So that there may be no misgivings about it, he will send a free sample to any man or woman without expecting payment. The regular price of the remedy is $1.00 for a box containing one month's treatment.

The Doctor's remedy is radically different from all others, and the results he has achieved seem to mark a new era in the scientific cure of catarrh, foul breath, hawking and spitting, stopped-up feeling in nose and throat, coughing spells, difficult breathing, catarrhal deafness, asthma, bronchitis and the many other symptoms of a bad case of catarrh.

If you wish to see for yourself what this remarkable remedy will do, send your name and address to Dr. J. W. Blosser, 475 Walton St., Atlanta, Ga., and you will receive the free package and an illustrated book.

other words, I was soliciting votes; not, perhaps, in very words but in smiles and handshakes, and silly platitudes of esteem.

"The sermon must have been well on the way, and I had just made up my mind to go into the house, when a tough from Quarry township stepped out of an alley and squared himself before me. 'Hello, Jack!' 'Why, how are you, Ned!'—with an extension of my hand to shake his filthy member. 'How are you? And how's Quarry?'

"'Oh! Quarry's all hunk; but they's a few of us a-feelin' pretty all-fired dry.' And here he squeezed my hand and winked in the most supercilious fashion. I felt no heart either in my shake of that hand or in his address to me.' In fact, I would have felt more comfortable had I been touching the cold skin of a toad.

"I was about to withdraw my hand and leave him, when he gave me a too familiar jerk and swore I was not in so great a hurry. Just then, too, a half dozen others came out of the alley, and seemed to me like so many vultures about to settle and begin to tear me.

"Ned was the leader; and when he appealed to the crowd with 'Is he, boys?' they answered in a breath: 'No! not by a long shot!'

"I then, in a hypocritical manner of sympathy and interest in their affairs put the question, 'Well, what can I do for you, boys?' They all looked at Ned, and he answered: 'Why, Jack, we want a drink, and we've lit on you as the chap to get it for us.' 'O boys,' I answered, 'that will never do. I have nothing to give you for drinks.'

"'We all know that; but we know you kin git 'em, and we cain't!' 'Why, boys,' I answered, 'I never drink a drop myself, and I'm under a solemn pledge not to help any one to get a drink.'

"'D—n your pledge!' said the leader. 'Ef ye don't take no interest in Quarry township you kin go to thunder! Come orn, boys! Jack ain't our kind!' And the whole tough gang started away. Here was my supreme moment. 'Shall I lose Quarry Township? Why not have that, too?'—and I felt all my manhood leaving me. 'Say, boys! Isn't there some other way to fix this matter? I don't want you to be offended!'

"'Et's jist as you please! Et's a drink fer the crowd, right now, 'er yer cake's dough in Quarry!' I do not know why I did not despise the whole tramp of them; but I answered: 'If nothing else will do, come on!'

"I led them past the church, and hurried a little lest some of the brethren see me, and halted not till we reached the drug store door. There Ned alone followed me in, and I advanced to the druggist, with 'here,' Doc, this gentleman wants a quart of rye whisky!'—throwing down a dollar. 'It is for medical purposes, of course?'

"And I drew my hat down over my eyes and answered 'yes!'

"I immediately hurried out and my very frame shook with excitement, as I darted off down the street; but not in time to avoid the cackle of exultation, meant for my coward ears.

"That night the six toughs made a pandemonium of our little city, and did not subside till they were all shut up in the station house. And I; I cried like a woman when I reached a lonely place; and begged the Lord to pardon my perjured soul. I walked the floor, and wrung my hands, and vowed repentance and it was not a moment that I slept until almost day-break. It was only after I clambered out of bed and on my knees promised my Maker on pain of death never to allow myself debauched again, that I slept at all. In the morning I wakened late; but I felt relieved. My vow had fixed it; and I did not believe I would ever violate it.

"But O, Retlaw, I was mortgaged to the Devil! And before noon, I had done the same thing over! In the course of the campaign I had prostituted my honor a hundred times. I never saw the slightest indication of interest on the part of the Quarry gang; and I had only the usual vote in that township; and in the other townships I had no more than the usual majority. I was elected, and re-elected; and in my two terms, I have made thirty thousand dollars; but I would gladly give it all if I could get back again the peace of mind I enjoyed when we used to sing and pray in the old chapel prayer meeting."

❊ ❊

Over a Thousand Enrolled

for fall and winter work in our Bible correspondence courses. Let us tell you about it. Catalogue free. Write Pres. Chas. J. Burton, Christian College, Oskaloosa, Iowa.

A Sunset.*

A picture, eh? Methinks not long ago
One eve at sunset on a mount that lol.
As rare a scene unfolded as man's eyes
Have ever witnessed in the sea or skies.
Calm 'twas—Far out upon the waters lay
Sailboats at rest. The breezes of the day
Gave place to nature's quiet and the deep
Calm and untroubled walked in its sleep.
Beauty! If ever from a mountain's brow
Mine eyes beheld it I behold it now,
As I recall the memories of that sky,
So filled with marvels for my wondering eye,
Such colors blended! Crimson, red and gold,
Canvas ne'er yet hath yielded power to hold.
Clouds sun-appareled! Yet did some appear
Dark and prophetic that a storm was near.
We watched it there together—you and I
Daylight's departing glory—Saw day die
Saw the great orb which lighted up the day
Dip into darkest cloud and sink away—
A picture wouldst? Well, if I should incline
To label one so matchless and so fair
I'd call it God's most perfect, most divine,
And bow my head and bathe my soul in prayer.
—C. R. W.

❀ ❀

Advance Society Letters.

BY J. BRECKENRIDGE ELLIS.

This week, the readers of THE CHRIS-
TIAN-EVANGELIST are presented with the
very last (or, in the language of modern
orators, the last, final and concluding)
chapter of the "Bronze Vase." Some will
doubtless be glad that it *is* the last, final
and concluding chapter of that story.
Where is the gentleman from Blooming
Grove, Tex., who chortled with glee when
"A Week With the Woodneys" finished its
protracted span? Let him now hold another thanksgiving service. (The reader
will observe how his scathing denunciation
still rankles.) But those who liked the
"Bronze Vase" may be pleased to know
that there is another story in the air. I will
tell you more about it next week. Here
comes a letter from one of our religious
houses: "Dear Friend—You want a book
by E. L. Powell, the famous orator of the
Christian Church of Louisville, Ky." (Yes,
sir; I didn't know it, but I suppose I do. I
wish he wanted one of my books, and
would get one of 'em. The Christian Publishing Company handles four: "King
Saul," "In the Days of Jehu," "Shem" and
"Adnah," the last two being novels of adventure.) The letter continues: "We have
one to give free." (Now, I like that and
am sorry I can't return the compliment.
Famous novelists, however, are worse
handicapped financially than famous orators; at least that's the explanation I have
thought out.) "It is beautifully bound, it
is highly commended. This offer is made
only to preachers." (Then why was this
alluring prospect held out to *me?* Why
whet my appetite thus, then place the dish
out of my reach? This is mockery, and
there is no need to finish the epistle.) I
have recently received illustrated post cards
representing Billings' Library, Burlington,
Vt., and the Public Libraries of Joplin, Moberly and Chicago. The one at Moberly is
by far the most attractive to my eyes, for
I prefer a choice collection of books to
additional stories and stone pillars; and
the card from Moberly informs me that
"Jehu," "Adnah" and "Shem" are in *that*
library. Here also is a card from foreign
parts, beginning, "La Colonia Americana
tiene el honor de invitar a Ud. y a su
apreciable familia al Baile." In other
words, I am invited by the American colony
to a ball in the Escuela Santa Marina; but
as I do not dance, nor any of my
"apreciable" family, I shall remain in Arkansas. Our orphan Charlie writes from
St. Louis: "I have been nlanning to write
to you for the last two weeks." (It must
certainly have taken deep scheming on your
part to plot your way to a final triumph.)
"I received your picture. Felix seems to be
taking it easy." (Charlie refers to a kodak
sketch, not to the picture which has been

*A sunset over Lake Michigan as seen from the
"Mount of Vision," "Garrison Park," Pentwater,
Mich.

so long promised the A. S. As for *that*
picture, we are still waiting for the "cut."
It has been a long, long time since Felix
sat, or, rather, squatted for the photographer, but we trust to get his likeness
upon this page in his life-time. I may be
accused of a too hopeful disposition, but
you know cats can throw away several lives
and still have enough to go on. Charlie,
excuse, me; I forgot you were talking.)
"It has not been very cold in St. Louis yet.
How about the Arkansas hills?" (They are
wet to-day.) "I think my ice cream social
was a great success, and I hope the Christmas tree for Drusie will do as much more.
I am studying hard on my books, especially
on grammar and spelling. I got 99½ in
writing and the same in deportment; that
is as high as our teacher gives, therefore it
is as near perfect as we can get." (That
reminds me of keeping the clock a few
minutes fast to make ourselves hurry. We
never have the time exactly right, but we
aren't late, unless we make too great an
allowance.) "I never got any lower than
95. We are having evangelistic services at
our church. There have been several additions already (November 7). I guess
you read in the papers where Rev. Sam P.
Jones died." (Charlie and I heard Mr.
Jones lecture, when our orphan was here
last summer. Mr. Jones, who was a personal friend, reviewed old times and was
as genial and kind [off the platform] as
we had ever known him. On the platform
he was—Sam Jones.) J. D. Dillard writes
from Agency, Mo.: "I inclose you 50c to
go on Charlie's Educational Fund, from
two little boys near Wellington, Mo—Earl
and James A. Emerson. Did you get my
money order ($5) from the Grandin Inter.
C. E. Society? I guess I missed the paper
telling about it." (I guess you did, too.
Why, I told all about that $5 and about my
family's friendship for you, and how we
missed your yearly visits to Plattsburg
when you came to take collections for the
Orphan Home. I have received interest
on annuity bond from Mrs. J. K. Hansbrough, who sends me best wishes; and
this is addressed to Plattsburg, Mo. That
reminds me of a minister who recently
made Bentonville, and who said: "I just
felt that I had to meet J. Breckenridge
Ellis. I'd heard of him for years, but I
didn't have any idea he was down in Arkansas." This is fame. Reader, seek for
it not. 'Tis but a bubble, my word for it.)

Mabel E. Nicholas, Fort Collins, Colo.:
"Inclosed please find my first quarterly
Av. S. report. I enjoy keeping the rules
and think it is helpful as we become better
acquainted with the Bible and can easier
find the references that our Sunday-school
teachers give us for test questions." (By
the way, that sounds as if there were something going on in that Sunday-school.) "I
have interested another little girl so she
has commenced keeping the Advance Society rules, and I hope she will prove faithful. Brother Findley is our pastor and we
think him the best in the land. Our town
has a population of 8,000. It is four miles
east of the mountains. It is a pleasant trip
to go there and take dinner and spend the
day." Eva Mildred Coors, Russellville,
Ark.: "Inclosed find $6.30 for Drusie's
Christmas tree. Some of our teachers have
been telling us of Drusie and the tree, and
the Sunday-school superintendent suggested
that we donate the collection of two Sundays as a present to Drusie. We hope other Sunday-schools will follow our example,
and that Drusie will have a thousand dollar
tree." (Please observe how we do things
down in Arkansas. As for the Sunday-
school here at Bentonville, it has pledged
itself to raise $100 on the $4,000 church
debt. Every penny of the big debt is provided for, but you can see the excuse we
have for not doing outside work. But if
your church hasn't a debt of $4,000 on it,
why not imitate the example of Russell-

ville?) Bertha Beesley, Moselle, Mo.:
"Here I am with my thirty-second report
and our mite for Drusie. Mamma sends
25c to buy ribbon with, so you can tie Mr.
Seat's boxes of candy on the tree. Papa
sends 10c for a handkerchief, and I send
25c for stationary. If Drusie's like me,
that is something she can find use for.
May God's richest blessings rest upon
Drusie, Charlie and all the Av. S. members." Mrs. Dora Griffith, Emida, Idaho:
"I have come to Charlie's ice cream social
and will take a back seat right beside Sister
Gibbins. Give me $2.50 worth if ice cream.
It's like the Savior's wine, the last is best,
and Charlie will appreciate it just as much.
I also send $2.50 for Drusie; put a parasol
on the Christmas tree for Drusie, as I
imagine it may be raining about Christmas
time. I appreciate very much the letters
Drusie sends me from China. Such faith
as hers will never be forsaken. The Lord
give her strength and courage." Drusie
Drusie R. Malott, North China: "THE
CHRISTIAN-EVANGELIST grows more interesting every day. Do you remember that I
wrote about our missionaries' children, and
how we hold a Sunday-school? We meet
together each Tuesday and each Friday
evening to read a story and have prayer
together. We have been reading 'Probable
Sons,' but let me tell you they are more
interested in THE CHRISTIAN-EVANGELIST
than the books, and each time they want
the 'Bronze Vase' and the Av. S. Letters
read before anything else. Their first
question on meeting days is, 'Did you get
another paper?' And now, about our work:
The boys from the boys' school went home
one by one for the summer. How I wish
you could have seen the bright, manly lads
and heard them sing. Last Easter they sang
for us 'Christ Arose.' It was the first time
I had ever heard that sung by Chinese. Do
you not realize how much that meant to
me? But, of course, you do! Think of how
you would feel to hear that song from fifty
boys who were heathen one year ago!
Pray for our missionaries out here; that
will strengthen and inspire them, for the
greatest work the Lord can do in our
midst. Pray the Lord to raise up more
faithful native helpers to witness in each
of our twelve stations. I forward receipt
for the Av. S. $5. May the Lord bless each
one who gave a part, and each one who is
praying for me. Little Lawrence Grimes
has a light case of smallpox; the family
are under quarantine. Smallpox is very
common here. The Chinese women tell
me that grown people never have it, because all who are susceptible to it have it
when young. Just refer to me that person
who wants to know if you are doing anything for missions; I can tell him how you
and the Av. S. are helping and cheering
this little missionary. Oh, what a joy and
privilege to be an ambassador of the King!
Hallelujah! I am rejoicing." (Those who
intend sending a present for Drusie's tree
had better be making preparations. I'd like
to know whether I'd better get a big tree,
or whether a little one will hold all the
gifts. Charlie's social has amounted to
$166.95.)

Bentonville, Ark.

these evangels in hundreds of homes silently yet continuously and effectively pleading for the higher life, Christian union and an immediate alliance with God your meeting house will be filled with earnest and prepared listeners from the start. We also send pink circulars with the papers containing pictures of pastors and evangelists and local announcements.

—"I am anxious to say what I feel about your new hymn book 'Gloria in Excelsis.' You have labored earnestly and the result is the best song book in the brotherhood. The responsive readings are well selected and classified; the order of services will do much to enrich the worship of the church; the splendid selection of hymns and appropriate music can not be excelled. You are to be congratulated on having produced such a book; and our brotherhood is to be congratulated on having such a superb addition to its song library.—Geo. W. Henry, Tipton, Ind.

—Week after week we are pleased to enumerate churches testifying to the world through the exhibition of clubs of CHRISTIAN-EVANGELIST readers that they have their faces toward the sunrise, that they are progressive, aggressive, and profoundly in earnest in their attempts to disseminate primitive Christianity throughout the earth, multiply apostolic churches and edify individual Disciples. Here are last week's clubs:

California; Pa., Thos. Martin, pastor............ 3
Homestead, Pa., E. L. Allen................... 3
Chicago, Ill............................. 4
Woodland, W. Va........................... 5
Shelbyville, Ind., H. O. Pritchard, pastor...... 6
Grand Rapids, Mich., F. P. Arthur.......... 7
Waynesville, Ill., E. E. Nichola, pastor......10
Kansas City, Geo. H. Combs, pastor.........13
Indianapolis, C. B. Newnan, pastor..........19

—This company has suffered a severe loss through the withdrawal of Bro. B. M. Stoddard from our corps of propagandists. His thorough preparation for his ministry, the conscientiousness with which he fulfilled every obligation, his popularity with our preachers wherever he went, and his Christian enthusiasm made him an invaluable assistant. We are not surprised at his call to become General Superintendent of the Great Western Printing and Publishing Co. Success to him. We trust others will school themselves in this work as for the dignified and useful profession it is.

THE
CHRISTIAN-
EVANGELIST

A WEEKLY RELIGIOUS NEWSPAPER.

Volume XLIII.　　　　No. 51.

ST. LOUIS, DECEMBER 20, 1906.

BETHLEHEM

From the painting by Dobson.

"Silent night! Hallowed night!
Land and deep silent sleep;
Softly glitters bright Bethlehem's star,
Beck'ning Israel's eye from afar,
Where the Savior is born."

The Christian-Evangelist.

J. H. GARRISON, Editor

PAUL MOORE, Assistant Editor

F. D. POWER,
B. B. TYLER,
W. DURBAN, } Staff Correspondents.

Subscription Price, $1.50 a Year.

For foreign countries add $1.04 for postage.

Remittances should be made by money order, draft, or registered letter; not by local cheque, unless 10 cents is added to cover cost of collection.
In Ordering Change of Post Office give both old and new address.
Matter for Publication should be addressed to THE CHRISTIAN-EVANGELIST. Subscriptions and remittances should be addressed to the Christian Publishing Company, 2712 Pine Street, St. Louis, Mo.
Unused Manuscripts will be returned only if accompanied by stamps.
News Items, evangelistic and otherwise, are solicited, and should be sent on a postal card, if possible.
Published by the Christian Publishing Company, 2712 Pine Street, St. Louis, Mo.

Entered at St. Louis P. O. as Second Class Matter

WHAT WE STAND FOR.

For the Christ of Galilee,
For the truth which makes men free,
For the bond of unity
  Which makes God's children one.

For the love which shines in deeds,
For the life which this world needs,
For the church whose triumph speeds
  The prayer: "Thy will be done."

For the right against the wrong,
For the weak against the strong,
For the poor who've waited long
  For the brighter age to be.

For the faith against tradition,
For the truth 'gainst superstition,
For the hope whose glad fruition
  Our waiting eyes shall see.

For the city God is rearing,
For the New Earth now appearing,
For the heaven above us clearing,
  And the song of victory.

            J. H. Garrison.

CONTENTS.

Centennial Propaganda 1631
Current Events 1632
Editorial—
  Christmas in the Air..............1633
  When Christ Was Born............1633
  Some Vexed Questions............1633
  Notes and Comments 1634
  Editor's Easy Chair...............1632
Contributed Articles—
  The Christmas Heart. Frank Waller Allen 1636
  "A Little Child Shall Lead Them."
    Thomas J. Clark.................1638
  "Come to Us, Christmas, Good Old Day"—A Symposium 1638
  Methods of Evangelization. J. P. Lichtenberger 1639
  The Elderberg Association 1640
  Good News from the Dark Continent. Mrs. Dr. R. J. Dye, Bolengi.1641
Our Budget 1642
News From Many Fields...........1646
Evangelistic 1651
Midweek Prayer-meeting 1652
Sunday-school 1653
Christian Endeavor 1654
People's Forum 1654
The Home Department....,........1655

THE CHRISTIAN-EVANGELIST

"IN FAITH, UNITY, IN OPINION AND METHODS, LIBERTY, IN ALL THINGS, CHARITY."

Vol. XLIII. December 20, 1906 No. 51

1809 CENTENNIAL PROPAGANDA 1909
CHURCHES OF CHRIST
: : : GEO. L. SNIVELY : : :

LOOKING TOWARD PITTSBURG.

—"Blest be the tie that binds" England and America into a closer fellowship than is known to diplomacy—our common Christianity. · Nor are there anywhere found more beautiful sentiments than those cherished for one another by the Disciples of Christ trying to exemplify the graces of primitive Christianity on either continent. We all deeply sympathize with our English brethren in the difficulties of establishing our "nonconformist" cause in that land of ancient precedents and prejudices against innovations in things religious, and we rejoice in their triumphs. We welcome them into our Centennial Propaganda and hope multitudes of them will help in our Pittsburg celebration.

The American people cheerfully pay millions per annum for the care of the old veterans in earlier years offered their lives as a defense to our government and the perpetuation of its hard-won liberties. If the amount of their pensions were left to popular vote, under stirring appeals to gratitude and patriotism, the people would doubtless enthusiastically ratify a resolution to treble the amounts being placed in the trembling hands of the old heroes and their wives. Our Centennial secretary eloquently portrays this week another band of soldiers, heroes everyone, who are walking in the shadows of the years with faith and zeal undimmed but with natural strength abated by the resistless processes of time. Our commerce with them is not of statutes but of grace. The law of the land prescribes what the U. S. treasurer must give those who once followed the stars and stripes. A higher law impels us to give even more generously to our brethren who have helped us into our rich spiritual heritage through their loyalty to the white banners of Prince Immanuel. A quarter million endowment for ministerial relief should be one of our Centennial victories to celebrate in 1909.

Christmas and Centennial hardly constitute an alliteration, but there should be a closer than a merely euphoneous connection between the two suggestive terms.

The Union Avenue Church of this city is earnestly engaged in building a church home. At a recent business meeting the old problem of securing funds was under consideration. One of the elders, J. H. Garrison—known at least by reputation to some of the brethren—remarked that a characteristic of all great achievements among us was a heroic initiative by some one man. When the most beautiful South Broadway Church was devised for Denver one man dedicated his fortune to it and afterward lived in the church and served as its janitor. George H. Combs' splendid edifice on Independence boulevard, Kansas City, was made possible by an R. A. Long's $75,000; and so he plead for some one whom God had endowed with the power to perform a great and distinguishing sacrifice for the cause of the Disciples of Christ in this city. His address to that local assembly ought to be sounded throughout the land this Christmastide. Will not some man this Christmas place $100,000 upon the altar for the endowment of a great missionary, benevolent or educational enterprise? Will not others make wholehearted dedication of lives and all their talents to the glory of Immanuel? Let heroes of initiative stand forth in this Christmas light and inspire us all to nobler ideals and loftier achievements as part of the record of our first century as a peculiar people.

The Old Preacher's Christmas.
BY SEC. W. R. WARREN.

In the Kingdom of God no man liveth to himself. And not one of us is able to make provision for his own Christmas and that of his immediate family without considering a wider circle of persons in whose happiness he must be interested. Each of our lives has been touched and profoundly influenced by more than one minister of the gospel. The treasures which some of these have brought into our lives cannot be estimated in dollars and cents, and yet they have been allowed to pass beyond the limits of our knowledge, and to-day we are unable to tell where or how most of them are living, or whether they have passed on to the reward of the just.

In the nature of things one of them somewhere is old and poor and helpless. During the years of his successful and popular labor his needs were provided for with reasonable regularity by the people to whom he ministered in spiritual things. Christmas every year he and his devoted wife were remembered with many little luxuries and tokens of affection and appreciation. During the last few years he has passed in rapid succession from one church to another, each a little smaller and a little poorer than the one before until none was found willing to provide even a scant living for the service that he rendered. To-day there is no congregation that looks to him as its spiritual minister. Each of those that he has served has another man in his place, who receives not only the regular support of the congregation, but all the special gifts and donations that its members bestow.

You would expect these two aged saints to complain bitterly of the ingratitude of Christ's disciples and churches. Instead, to your surprise you find them heroically cheerful. They look back to the cross to which our Savior was nailed by his own people, and they look forward to the glorious heaven into which he is waiting to receive them. They have learned, in whatsoever state they are therewith to be content. The burden of their prayer is that the kingdom for which they can no longer labor should be more gloriously advanced. Daily thanksgiving rises from their hearts as they hear the news of gospel victories! They are satisfied with their lot and its privations.

But can we be satisfied to leave them so? Are they not in the most intimate sense of "our own"? Failing to care for them would brand us worse than infidels. Can we plead with men to become Christians and ourselves remain so unchristian? Can we urge our religious neighbors to be Christians only when they so far surpass us in this fundamental Christian grace? Let us make consistency one of the Centennial virtues as we approach 1909?

England's Centennial Plans.
SECRETARY L. W. MORGAN.

The twenty-sixth annual conference of our churches in Britain recently closed at Tasso Tabernacle, Fulham, London. The President for the year, Mark Wayne Williams, West London Tabernacle, presided and on the opening evening gave an excellent address on "The Church of Christ." W. Durban was elected president for the coming year, for the tenth time, after an absence from the chair for five years. Great regret was expressed at his enforced absence from the conference through illness. E. H. Spring, of Gloucester, was also absent, through illness in his family.

The reports from our seventeen churches and missions were very satisfactory. More money has been raised than in any previous year in the history of our work in England. The Liverpool church freed itself of a mortgage of nearly $5,000 and other churches also did well in paying off mortgage debts or in raising money for their building funds. The churches are in earnest concerning these two things. In this connection the completion of the organization of a building loan society is significant. The society will do its work very much on the lines of the Church Extension Society in America, and has not been born too soon. F. Coop, of Southport, was elected president, with the support of a strong board of management.

Our new mission was started during the year and another just after the conference year closed. At least two others will be opened in a few weeks time. If all of these develop into churches it will mean more accomplished in this line than during several years past.

Plans are being considered for celebrating the Centennial in 1909 and a three years' campaign is to be entered upon. The proposals of the executive committee include the doubling of our self-supporting churches, the paying of half the mortgages on our churches, the opening of at least eight new missions, the raising of $2,000 per annum for home missions, the erection of at least three "Centenary" church buildings, and the raising of a special fund of $25,000 in commemoration of the departure of Thomas and Alexander Campbell for America, to be administered by the Building Loan Society. Concerning the last item more will be written later as it is desired to enlist the sympathy and help of our American brethren. It is proposed also to organize a great convention to meet in London to follow immediately upon the Pittsburg convention.

Current Events

The quarrel between the French government and the Catholic church reached

France and the Church.
its most acute stage on December 12, the date set for putting into effect the law passed a year ago separating church and state. The law renders it necessary for every church to secure a government license in order to conduct service. As a concession, it has been decided that churches may secure permits under the general law of 1881 for the licensing of public meetings. But the church does not admit that its services, its masses and high masses, can properly be brought under the law of public meetings. It is only another and more acute phase of the demand of two years ago requiring religious associations to be registered in accordance with law. Registration in one case or the securing of a license in the other involves no special hardship. It is the theory of the thing that is objected to. If the government can impose any sort of regulation upon the church it can, if it pleases, impose regulations which would be fatal to the church's freedom and effectiveness. The place to make the fight, the church argues, is at the point where the principle only is involved, without waiting for specific acts of oppression. The Pope's late encyclical makes 't evident that the church will not yield. The government shows no sign of receding from its position. The church hopes to provoke the state to violence and thus to cause an uprising of popular sympathy in favor of the church. Meanwhile the priests are waiting, half in hope, half in fear, to see whether they will be put out of their churches by violence.

❀

It is rumored again that there is prospect of a break between the president and the senate.

The President and the Senate.
The senate's delay in confirming the appointments of Moody, Bonaparte and Cortelyou to their new cabinet positions gives a color of probability to the rumor. The senate's charge is that the president has "ignored senatorial customs and precedents in the executive management of public affairs." So he has. He has demoralized the system of senatorial patronage, has robbed senators of their immemorial right to pay their private political debts with appointments to public office, and has set the senate to work on the very first day of the session. We all know (Kipling told us) what happened to the "fool who tried to hustle the east"—meaning the far east. The east is celerity itself compared with that highly deliberative body which we call the senate, and when a president tries to hustle the senate he is tolerably certain to make himself unpopular with the senate, however much

his actions may be approved by the public. It is customary for the senate to confirm cabinet appointments as soon as they are received. The delay this time is said to be partly as a means of conveying to the president a delicate hint that he has been too swift. Then there is some ostensible opposition to the appointees themselves. The objection to Mr. Cortelyou is that, as chairman of the Republican national committee, he received campaign funds from insurance companies. Mr. Garfield, the appointee as secretary of the interior, has the misfortune to be *persona non grata* to Senator Foraker. Mr. Moody is charged, by the Democrats, with having favored the reduction of representation in the southern states which have disfranchised the negroes—a measure which most of us think it would be unwise to push, but which nearly every one admits to be exactly in keeping with the provision of the constitution. Mr. Bonaparte—O, crowning joke—is opposed because of his alleged pro-trust sympathies. Fancy the senate holding up a Roosevelt appointment because the appointee is suspected of sympathy with the trusts. Well, the senate's delay is probably only a sort of naval demonstration in the enemy's waters. The appointments will doubtless go through in good time.

❀

The Nobel prize, of $40,000, for the promotion of peace, has been awarded

The Nobel Prize.
by the Norwegian parliament to President Roosevelt. Dr. Nobel, a wealthy Swedish scientist who died a few years ago, left the bulk of his fortune to establish five prizes to be given annually to the persons who have made the most valuable contributions to the sciences of physics, chemistry and medicine, to pure idealistic literature and to the cause of international peace and arbitration. The award to the president is made on the ground of his services in bringing the Russo-Japanese war to an end. The president, in acknowledging the award of the prize, announces that he has decided to use the money in establishing at Washington a permanent industrial peace commission to be an agency for the promotion of arbitration between capital and labor.

❀

The altercation which has arisen between the president and Mr. Bellamy

The Storer Case.
Storer, late minister to Vienna, is unfortunate. It suggests to the plain citizen, who has not time to make exhaustive research into the merits of a purely personal question, that first Mr. Storer and then the president have put some things in print which it would have been just as well to leave in manuscript—and then destroy the manuscript. Mr. Storer, who is a convert to Catholicism, and has all the zeal of a proselyte, was summarily dismissed from the diplomatic service because he persisted in making official efforts to have the Pope make Archbishop Ireland a cardinal and in representing to the Pope that these efforts were in obedience to the president's orders. The president denies that he ever gave such orders, admits that per-

Editorial

Christmas in the Air.

Five more days and then Christmas! The happy season is again with us. Its spirit for weeks has been in the air. Its benign influence has been softening men's hearts. The best thing Christmas does is to quicken the generous impulse of natures chilled by selfishness. The peace and good will it brings make the hardest and most tight-fisted Scrooges of society to be touched by the tenderness and beneficence that show their influence in the stores and markets, on the street cars and trains, in the nursery and kitchen—everywhere. The great lesson: "It is more blessed to give than to receive," taught by him who, ascending on high, "led captivity captive and gave gifts unto men," pervades the whole atmosphere.

The first characteristic of the Christmas spirit is that of giving. Tokens of affection and esteem are stored up sometimes months ahead, or purchased at the time without reference to cost. Remembrances trifling in value, it may be, are gathered together and sent out on the festal morning to show our friends we love them and think of them. Boyhood chums, old people, servants, children, neighbors, people with whom life has been a struggle, the sick, the troubled—all come to mind under the impulse of the Christmas spirit. It is a time of thankfulness, and gratitude to God prompts to good deeds to men.

"Now that the time is come wherein
Our Savior Christ was born,
The larders full of beef and pork,
The garners filled with corn;
As God hath plenty to thee sent,
Take comfort of thy labors,
And let it never thee repent
To feast thy needy neighbors."

The second characteristic of the Christmas spirit is that of child-likeness. We are all brought into closer touch with the children. The oldest bends lowest to the little child. The coldest is warmed by memories of far-away childhood. Every home blessed with children is a house of mysteries. Parents are consulting in whispers. Mysterious packages are being smuggled in, and hidden away on shelves and in closets. Stockings are being darned. Confiding letters are being written and addressed: "S. Claus, Esq., North Pole." Childish eyes stare and childish minds are filled with wonder and childish hearts beat with quickened expectations. It is the children's festival and the poor man's festival—everybody's festival.

"Take courage soul, in grief cast down,
Forget the bitter dealing;
A Child is born in David's town,
To touch all souls with healing.
Then let us go and seek the Child,
Children like him, meek, undefiled."

The third characteristic of the Christmas spirit is its tone of cheer and hope. It could not be the spirit of benevolence, or of childhood, or of Christ without this. It tells of glad tidings of great joy. It recalls the gospel—the only thing known distinctively as "gospel" that ever broke in upon the darkness of this world. It fills the whole earth wherever it has gone with the angel chorus. It promises the fulness of joy eternal. Were this spirit always in the air; were this loving kindness ever leavening human society everywhere, this earth would be heaven. As it is, it inspires men on every return of its benediction with hope for themselves and hope for the race.

"Build thee more stately mansions, O my soul,
As the swift seasons roll;
Leave thy low-vaulted past;
Let each new temple, nobler than the last,
Shut thee from heaven with a dome more vast
Till thou at length be free,
Leaving thine outgrown shell by life's unresting
sea."

❦ ❦
When Christ Was Born.

When the world was dark with the night of sin and no star of hope shone above the horizon of time, save the promise of the coming Deliverer, there was born in Bethlehem of Judea, a child whose birth was also the birth of a new era in the world's history. That was a cold, cruel, despairing world, upon which the star of Bethlehem rose. Human wisdom, philosophy, learning, art in its highest form, law, government —all these had sought to arrest the world's moral degeneracy, and stem the tide of human corruption, but in vain. Hebrew, Greek and Roman, had struggled with the problem of human deliverance without success. The world was sinking under the weight of its woe and its guilt.

There was no such thing in the world as a free government by a free people when Christ was born. There was no recognition of equality of rights and of the sacredness of human life, as we now view it, when Jesus came into the world. Childhood was neglected, womanhood unhonored, marriage a name, and the home, as we know it, unknown throughout the Roman world. Pagan religions without love, worshiping gods without pity and without righteousness, brought no relief to a sin-sick world. It was a world without churches, without Christian homes, without hospitals and asylums for the unfortunate, without the softening and purifying influence of that religion which dominates our civilization.

In an age like that Jesus was born. His coming was the birthday of a new age. The song of the angel-choir which echoed over the Judean hills, was the prelude to the great anthem of human redemption. The birth of Jesus was the coming of God into the life of man. It was the union of humanity and divinity. It was the entering into the stream of human history of a divine element destined to change its whole current and to make it ultimately the very river of God.

To compare the world of to-day with that into which Jesus was born, is to get some measure of his greatness and of his influence on humanity. His hand, pierced for human sin, has not only lifted ancient empires off their hinges, but it has opened the gate of life and progress to all mankind. It has planted the flower of hope in the heart of despair. His love has evoked from human hearts sweeter music and nobler songs than the world had ever known. His triumph over death has lifted the leaden weight of sorrow from the heart of humanity, and opened up a vista of endless life. His character has revolutionized the ideals of the world, and is leading humanity upward to nobler heights. His influence is girdling the globe. His name is honored and adored, and his praises are sung among nearly all the tribes and peoples of earth.

Jesus' birth opened a fountain of life in the world's desert of sin and death. Wherever that fountain sends its healing streams the beautiful and fragrant flowers of Christian virtue grow and flourish. Wherever these streams have not flown because the channels have been choked by the indolence and unbelief of the church, there sterility and death still abound. This fountain of life is also a fountain of hope whose joyous notes are the marching-song of the world's progress.

We best honor the day and season associated with his birth by imbibing his spirit of love toward all, and emulating his example of doing good to all, and especially to those most in need, as we have opportunity. May the spirit expressed in the refrain of that angelic song which announced his birth soon pervade the entire world: "Peace on earth, good will among men!"

❦ ❦
Some Vexed Questions.

Paul must have been tried with troublesome questions in his day, judging from his advice to Timothy to "shun foolish and ignorant questions." No doubt we have plenty of them in our day. Some of these hard questions, however, naturally grow out of the anomalous condition of a divided church, and in answering them one must be guided by the general principles of the gospel, as there are of course no specific New Testament answers to such questions. Here are a few that frequently come to our desk:

"If God knows all things, why should we pray?" This, of course, is based on a misconception of what prayer is. It is not a means of communicating information to God, though some prayers might lead one to think so.

2. "Why didn't God make man so he couldn't sin?" Because he did not want to make a machine, but a free, rational, moral and responsible being.

3. "What would become of a man who should suddenly die on his way to be baptized?"

This "poser" used to be put to Disciples of Christ by their denominational critics, who supposed our position involved the damnation of all who were not baptized, regardless of conditions or circumstances!

They forgot that other New Testament principle—"It is required of a man according to what he hath, and not according to what he hath not"—which we also believe.

4. "Is a man a Christian who has not been baptized (immersed), although he be a sincere believer who has obeyed Christ to the best of his knowledge?"

The principle mentioned in the foregoing would seem to answer this question. Alexander Campbell's definition of a Christian, as one who believes in Christ with his whole heart and obeys him to the full measure of his knowledge of his will, is one that is not likely to be disproved or greatly improved. He is a Christian who has been Christed—anointed by Christ's Spirit.

5. 'But is such a one as described above 'in Christ?' Paul says we are 'baptized into Christ,' but, if only immersion is baptism, how can those who have not been immersed be in Christ?"

Surely a Christian is 'in Christ,' and unless one is prepared to deny that only immersed believers can be Christians, he must admit that all sincere believers in Christ who obey him according to their understanding of his will, are 'in Christ,' by virtue of such faith and obedience. To deny this is formalism, pure and simple.

6. "Why not then receive into our churches those who have been conscientiously sprinkled or poured, for baptism, and who believe these are Scriptural 'modes' of baptism?"

Because we can not make the conscience of others a guide for ourselves, nor a substitute for what we believe to be the New Testament conditions of church membership. The local church, acting collectively, must be true to its 'understanding of Christ's will for the local church, just as each individual must be true to his 'understanding of Christ's will for the individual. As the individual believer must be true to his understanding of Christ's will in order to be saved, so must the local congregation, which has a collective life to maintain and develop, conform to its knowledge of Christ's will, in order to be saved from disintegration and sterility.

7. "Is the local congregation, then, the highest court of appeal in settling such questions?"

The will of Christ, as contained in the New Testament, is of course the ultimate authority in all matters relating to his religion. The local congregation is composed of those who have reached a common mind, or unity of faith and knowledge concerning the vital things of the Kingdom of God and the constitutional features of the church which Christ established. This makes it possible and profitable for them to associate themselves together for worship and for Christian service in extending Christ's reign. All congregations, however, similarly constituted, having a common faith and a common understanding of Christ's will as regards the terms of membership in his church, are bound together by the ties of a common faith and a common work, and constitute a larger brotherhood, whose consensus of judgment on any question of practice or policy becomes a regulative force and a safeguard against extreme tendencies. It cannot be doubted that it is Christ's will that his local churches should co-operate in mutual fellowship and service.

But such a mutuality in fellowship and service, implies, not necessarily unity of opinion on all questions or in all methods of service, but it does imply loyalty to a common faith, and conformity to the general consensus of judgment in the body as to the constitutional features of the church. It would be a grave mistake for any local church, sharing in the general life and activities of the brotherhood, and being nurtured and strengthened by this wider fellowship and broader activity, to forfeit these benefits by adopting any policy which cuts it off from such benefit. This has been the serious mistake of the churches known as anti-missionary society churches. It may become the mistake of churches at the other extreme, who, guided by some question of local expediency, or following an opinion as to conditions of membership not shared by the brotherhood at large, may alienate itself from the larger life and wider fellowship of the body as a whole. Of course if a local congregation should so change its conscientious convictions of truth, as to make this conformity to the consensus of judgment in the brotherhood as to what is essential to the integrity and unity of the church an impossibility without being disloyal to its understanding of Christ's will, that is another matter. The time has then arrived for a readjustment of relationships.

"No man liveth unto himself and no man dieth unto himself." So no local church lives or dies to itself. It is an integral part of a common body whose growth and influence are affected by the fate of each particular part.

Notes and Comments.

Rev. Samuel L. Boston, of Pittsburg, Pa., who is writing a series of articles on "Baptism; Its Significance and Mode," for the "Presbyterian Banner," says, among other things: "Immersion is out of harmony with the whole genius and simplicity of the gospel plan of salvation." A little further on he says: "Will Presbyterians immerse? Yes, there is no reason why they cannot." That is, there is no reason why they cannot adopt a practice which is "out of harmony with the whole genius and simplicity of the gospel plan of salvation!" Whether sincere and honest believers can ever agree upon what Christ meant when he commanded baptism, or not, they ought to be able to agree, at least, upon so plain and self-evident a proposition as this: That any form of baptism that is scriptural enough to be practiced, ought not to be denounced by those who practice it. If our Pedo-baptist brethren are going to continue to practice immersion—and they will be compelled to continue it—they ought to cease their opposition to it for consistency's sake and for truth's sake. We are sure that a large number of intelligent and fair-minded Pedo-baptists will concur in this view of the matter.

Rev. William Frost Bishop, pastor of Clifton Heights Presbyterian church, replying to a sermon by Archbishop Glennon whose sermon on "The Origin of Creed and Dogmas" was printed in the Republic sends to that paper the following apt and sufficient refutation of the Archbishop contention:

"One reads with amazement your report Archbishop Glennon's sermon at Richmond, Va., on a recent occasion. It makes him say that Christ founded the Roman Catholic Church, and that other churches were founded by mere men. Yet make his contention to be that in the same sense in which Catholics claim Christ as the founder of their church, in that same sense Alexander Campbell was the founder of the 'Christian Church, Wesley the founder of the Methodist Church, Luther the founder of the Lutheran Church, Calvin the founder of the Presbyterian Church, and so on.

"Alexander Campbell founded no church. He merely undertook to reform a church which already claimed Christ as its divine founder.

"Luther founded no church. He reformed a church which for centuries had claimed Christ as its only foundation.

"Wesley was merely a reformer, and a form and a re-former are celestial diameters apart. The vast movement of the sixteenth century was not a 'formation,' but a 'reformation.' John Calvin did not found a church in the same sense which Catholics claim that Christ founded the Roman Church."

The attempt of the Roman Catholic Archbishop to make it appear that Christ founded the Roman Catholic Church, and that the great reformers mentioned established other churches, is absurd in the light of history. Every one acquainted with the history of the church knows that these reform movements mentioned were efforts to recover the church from the apostasy of Roman Catholicism. Not one of these reformers attempted to establish a church of his own, but to restore to the church of Jesus Christ those principles and practices which had been lost in the great apostasy.

Kentucky is often made the butt of jokes referring to the fondness of its citizens for old bourbon, mint juleps, etc. It may surprising, therefore, to our readers know that of the 119 counties in the state 94 are now totally "dry," to use a current phrase to express the illegality of saloons. Twelve of these counties voted against the saloon within the last two months. A special dispatch of the 16th inst., from Louisville, Ky., commenting upon this situation says:

"This remarkable spread of temperance in Bourbon commonwealth, the home and stronghold of Kentucky whisky, has been more striking shown in the last ten days than ever before. In one county in Kentucky is entirely 'wet,' The are only four counties that are approximately urated. These are all along the Ohio river in the northern part of the state. There are ninety-five counties without any saloons, eighteen with loons in only one place, eight with saloons in places and six where liquor is sold in three more places."

Our hearty congratulations to the people of Kentucky for this remarkable growth of temperance sentiment. How has this good work been accomplished? Such reforms do not come about by accident. Is the Anti-Saloon League behind this local option agitation? What has been the relation of the churches to this movement?

Editor's Easy Chair.

Once in each year the little hill-town of Bethlehem outshines all the capitals of the world. London, Paris, St. Petersburg, Berlin, Vienna, Tokio, Pekin, Washington—all are eclipsed by the ancient town near which Ruth gleaned barley in the fields, where David spent his boyhood days tending his father's flocks, and where later, in the fullness of time, the Christ-child was born. Other cities may crumble into ruins and their very names and places be forgotten. Macaulay's New Zealander may stand upon a broken arch of London Bridge and sketch the ruins of St. Paul. But as long as the race endures men will make pilgrimages to Bethlehem of Judea and stand in awe at the spot where the Savior of mankind was born. At this season of the year the whole world, in imagination, not only makes its pilgrimage to that far-famed city of David, but it traverses nineteen centuries of time to get back to that auspicious and historic night when Jesus was born. What marvelous power there must be in a personality which can thus draw all the ages to itself, and render forever sacred the place of its advent into the world! No wonder the world sings with Phillips Brooks:

> "O little town of Bethlehem,
> How still we see thee lie;
> Above thy deep and dreamless sleep
> The silent stars go by:
> Yet in thy dark streets shineth
> The everlasting light;
> The hopes and fears of all the years
> Are met in thee to-night."

Brooding over these holy memories, and remembering the mission which brought Christ into the world, who of us can not breathe the prayer:

> "O holy child of Bethlehem,
> Descend to us, we pray;
> Cast out our sin, and enter in,
> Be born in us to-day.
> We hear the Christmas angels
> The great glad tidings tell;
> O come to us, abide with us,
> Our Lord, Immanuel!"

⁂

Of all the anniversaries of the year—the great days that stand out like mountain peaks across the plains of Time—there is none that stirs the imagination and quickens the memory, and warms the heart like Christmas. It is the magician whose mysterious wand wakens all the holier impulses of the heart, sends the memory back along the shining track of the years to childhood days, and fills all the earth and the heavens once more with the awe and mystery of life's early morning. It summons before us once more the faces and forms of the loved and the lost of long ago. We see once more in the light of the glowing fire the radiant faces of a family circle long since broken up, to be gathered no more on earth. We hear again the merry shouts and laughter of the light-hearted and hope-filled boys and girls whose heads are now silvered with age. We live over again in imagination, those bright,

halcyon days, and find ourselves half regretting that we can not live them over in reality. While this can not be, we may retain the faith of childhood, youthfulness and buoyancy of spirit, and keep in touch and sympathy with childhood and youth and with all that goes to make life beautiful and the future bright and hopeful. In so far as Christmas helps us to do this it is a blessing to age and a benediction to childhood. There is eternal youth in the heart of one who has learned the true meaning of Christmas and has entered into the secret of that marvelous Life which, manifesting itself in the flesh, on that first Christmas morning, has filled all subsequent ages with its influence and is destined yet to fill the whole world with its glory.

⁂

What is the greatest thing about Christmas? What is it that gives it its dominant spirit and makes it a glad, joyous season? When we stop to think of it, it is love, which has been truly called "the greatest thing in the world." Why should this spirit of love and good will among men find expression in a special manner at Christmastide? Because love became incarnate in the birth of Jesus. God is love, but the world would never have known that if love had not become flesh and dwelt among us. St. John was no doubt thinking of Jesus, and of the Father whom he had revealed, when he uttered that great truth, "God is love." Love as a law of life was a new principle which Christ brought into the world. The birth of Christ marks the beginning of a new era, because it marks the introduction of love as a substitute for all those evil passions which had hitherto so largely controlled the actions of men. How slowly, after all, does love win its way as a controlling factor in life against the opposing forces of hatred, envy, malice, selfishness, revenge, avarice, lust and worldly ambition! And yet not more surely does the sun advance along his conquering way, from the winter solstice to the height of summer, than does love advance as a dominating factor in the life of the world, influencing laws, customs, and governmental policies, and asserting its regnancy in all the relationships among men. Yes, it is love that creates the atmosphere of Christmas, which we all like to breathe. What a blessed world this will be to live in, when all the days of all the months, in all the years, shall be dominated by love, in all the spheres of human activity, and in all the manifold relationships of life!

⁂

If Christmas shall remind us that love must become incarnate to accomplish its beneficent purposes, it will serve a most useful end. We are too apt to allow our kindly feeling toward all, at the Christmas time, to fritter itself away in mere good wishes. Put it into deeds. Clothe it with flesh and blood, and send it about

on errands of mercy. What love needs to bless the world is continuous incarnation in human form. It wants human hands and feet with which to minister to those in need. It needs human speech to utter the word of sympathy and good cheer. It needs embodiment in all those who claim to be Christ's followers in order that he may continue going about doing good. This is the great lesson of Christmas. It was not enough that God should love the world from afar. That love must take a human body and tabernacle with men to accomplish its purposes. Our love for our fellowmen, and our love for God must also be embodied. This is the deepest meaning of Christmas. Christ's Church, which is called his body, was intended to be a re-incarnation of Christ. Through it Christ would still minister to the world's needs. This is the great demonstration for which the world is waiting. When Christ's love for humanity finds itself incarnate in the lives of his professed followers, then every day will become a Christmas in which Christ will be born anew in human hearts, and all the hills and valleys of earth will echo with angelic songs of "peace on earth, good will among men."

⁂

It remains for the Easy Chair to wish all its readers "a Merry Christmas," and even more than that, a happy Christmas. Nothing more delights us than the real joy and happiness of our readers. No motive for living is stronger than the desire to minister to their well-being and happiness. The Easy Chair craves a place, in memory at least, at your festal boards and around your radiant hearth-stones when the yule log burns brightly in the fireplace. It wishes to share in all your domestic joys and, as far as possible, mitigate or help you to bear your burdens and sorrows. But in this happy Christmas season we trust that joy will be the dominant note in all the homes which THE CHRISTIAN-EVANGELIST has the privilege of entering. If anything found in these pages shall serve to make Christmas a gladder and happier season for you, we shall be glad in your gladness. In the preceding paragraphs we have indicated how we may make the most of Christmas, and get the most joy out of it. It is by putting our love and good will for others into deeds of practical kindness. One way of doing this, is, if you have found THE CHRISTIAN-EVANGELIST a source of strength and comfort to you by its weekly visits through the year, to send it as a Christmas present to some one whom you love, that it may be a weekly messenger of light and love to your friend or loved one through all the coming year. In what other way can you, with so small an outlay, confer so great a blessing upon any one for whom you cherish a kindly personal feeling? In any event, the Easy Chair wishes its readers, one and all, a very happy Christmas!

The Christmas Heart.   By Frank Waller Allen.

"For unto us a child is born,
Unto us a son is given."

The worthiness of a religion is to be measured, not by the mere logic of its creed or the beauty of its theology, but by the result of the practice of its teachings upon human character. That doctrine which does not sink from the mind down into the heart, and thence out to serving and teaching through kindly lips and ministering fingers is of no value whatever to a world of ignorant and suffering men and women crying for life. And of necessity the indisputably best religion is that which, when lived, makes for the most good for the most of men.

History has never chronicled the life of a more active man than that of Jesus of Nazareth. There has never been a life more vital, more positive, busier with doing the work within his hands than was that of the Master during his public career. And he never preached, told men of a principle, or instructed them in a truth, but his message was potent with the command to do things. To work, to serve, to teach, to love, and thus to taste the joys of immortality.

Yet with all of this force in the personality of Christ, and the very practicalness, and every-day-service found in his teaching, there was much in him, too, which appealed directly to the poetic instinct of the heart. There was much tender sentiment within the man, and there was a deal of that sense of the eternal fitness of things, which makes men companionable. In a word: Jesus was not only the Man of Sorrows, and a man of action; but he was as equally the Man of Joys, and, perhaps most of all, a Man of Heart. Therefore, because too much business, too much mind and over much logic is not good for the soul, it behooves us betimes to sit down face to face with our hearts, for there is much strength to be gotten out of God's Dream-World. And of all seasons where logic is out of place it is at Christmastide. Then, at least, for once in the whole year's round, let doctrine, chapter and verse be banished for a good, impulsive, right warm Christmas Heart.

The greatest blessing God ever gave the world was the first Christmas Gift. "Unto us a son is given." And therefore are we impressed with the truth of it being far, far better to give than to receive. Still more wonderfully strange is it, that the only way we may have and keep within our lives this Gift of God is by giving the gift away. The only Christmas Heart you may call your own is the Christmas Heart you give to the men and the women of the world. . . . Of the good within him man cannot give either to his God or his fellows other than that which has already been given of the Father-friend. . . . As a man treats men so does he behave toward his God. . . . Therefore the greatest gift for you, for me, to give to God is to give to men the Christmas Heart—the Christ Heart. And the only way to have Christ in the heart is to give him to those who are in need. Likewise the Father has made it beautifully strange that the more of the Christ-principle we give away the more have we yet within the treasure of our own heart.

A pure heart inactive is not a Christmas Heart, but purity at work to leaven the life about it by the service of mere contrast is indeed giving the gift of the Christ. Likewise to give to our friendships sincerity; to make forgiveness an active principle inasmuch as we give those who have wronged us an opportunity to forget; to remember that the giving of strength is the gentlest of all service; to keep in mind that to give cheerful hands to the sorrowful is of as much importance as to give blessing-prayers; and more than all else to understand that not love, but love at work, given even as the Father gave in the long ago, is the greatest and best thing in the world; in a word: to love as Jesus loved, this is to have within the Christmas Heart.

These things form the characteristics which were of the heart of Christ. To know them is a splendid thing; to have them a part of your own heart is to have within you so much of divinity.

Odessa, Mo.

"A Little Child Shall Lead Them"   By Thomas J. Clark

(Isa. 11:6; 9:6,7.)

There are given to us by the Prophet Isaiah two pictures of the Messiah who was to come. In the first, we have a little child set in the midst of the animal world. This picture fitly represents the brutal animal forces of human nature that were dominant at the coming of Christ. The lion, the leopard, the bear, the asp, all represent the cruel, fierce, untamed forces or elements of human nature. The cow, the calf, the lamb, the kid, represent the patient, serviceable, domestic side of life. A child in the midst, leading, restraining, taming, unifying the spirit of all. A child, the most helpless of all creatures infusing a new spirit into life, changing the whole spirit and nature of human kind. The other picture presents a child born, as growing into a great and expanding spiritual force that permeates all life and institutions of mankind, changing for the better all things. "Wonderful, Counsellor, Mighty God, Everlasting Father, Prince of Peace." All these convey the idea of spiritual force in different forms. In both figures is the promise of redemption for humanity. It is well on the return of the Christmas occasion, while our minds are full of the joys and festivities, to consider the deeper meaning of the event that we thus celebrate.

I. Let us then consider the Child and the world into which he came. Here are two distinct ideas: First, the world into which he came. What kind of a world was it? The picture of the prophet fairly represents it. The lion, the wolf, the leopard, the cow, the lamb, the kid; it was a world in which brutal forces were regnant, the weak the prey of the strong.

Take the Roman world of that day as an illustration. Pagan Rome stands for an all-conquering power. In his letter to the Romans, Paul said: "I am not ashamed of the Gospel of Christ, for it is the power of God." It was one kind of power matched against another. Paul thought of power as the dominant idea of Rome. The tread of her armies and the force of her arms had shaken the world. The were masters, the many were slaves. Her generals came back from the wars of conquest, dragging the bodies of their vanquished foes through the streets of Rome, behind their chariots. To afford their people pleasure, gladiators were trained to kill each other and to fight wild beasts in the arena. Gluttony and starvation existed side by side. Ruler after ruler came to the throne through assassination. In the immediate locality to which the Christ-child came, a Herod ruled. The highest Jewish court abounded in men who did not scruple to set aside justice, and to resort to subornation to condemn one whom they desired to destroy. Power counted for everything. One has said of the spirit of that time: "Roman religion was faith in the magic of the Roman name, and the irresistibleness of the Roman arms, a worship of brute force, hard, unfeeling, coarse." Rome's dominion was universal, and it was a reign of brute force.

That was the character of the Roman world; what of the Jewish? From the New Testament story we know what a pitiful spectacle it presented. In the fact that the leaders demanded the death of Jesus, the brutal spirit is shown. One or two sentences will tell something of the feeling the nation had toward other peoples. The Jew, speaking in the Fourth book of Esdras, thus addresses God: "On our account thou hast created the world. Other nations, sprung from Adam, thou hast said, are nothing and are like spittle, and thou hast likened their multitude to the droppings of a cask. But we are thy people whom thou hast called thy firstborn, thine only begotten, thy well beloved. A single Israelite is of more worth in the sight of God than all the nations of the world; every Israelite is of more value before him than all the nations who have been or will be." It was indeed a hard, brutal, cruel world into which Christ came.

Second, "A little child shall lead them." The most helpless thing imaginable is a little child. The child of a humble Jewish peasant girl, the reputed son of a carpenter. The child of a people who were regarded with loathing and contempt by the Romans. When one came to Rome from the scenes of battle at Jerusalem and told of the slaughter of many thousands of Jews in two battles waged by Vespasian, a Roman is reported to have said: "Have you nothing more worth talking about than that?" Look upon the world dominated by such brutal ideas as that, then look upon this child of apparent weakness, and what promise can you see for the future of humanity? Look at the problem from that end and where is the ground of hope? Yet the prophet saw a gleam of light and hope for mankind. "A little child shall lead them." The savage beasts shall under his

or it was a sacrifice made to reconcile God to man, or to propitiate his favor. Christ said "God so loved the world that he gave his only begotten son." Paul said, "God commendeth his love toward us." John said "Hereby we perceive the love of God," and "Herein is love." According to this view the death of Christ was an expression of that same divine force that is predominant in the little child, love. It is through the power of love that God would reconcile, save, and uplift the world. That is what Napoleon said of Christ's kingdom

his lofty precepts to apply in the world is the most distinctive feature of the Christian faith. And how was this done? Simply by putting behind every glorious law one supreme motive, Christ set every law, every duty, against a background of love. He nailed them to the cross. How many soldiers hear the command who will follow it only when some loved leader goes with them. Even so the world hears Christ's commands because the loved Master has gone with the world. Therein lies the sharpest line of division between Christianity and any other faith, that was ever preached." So against this background of love Christ has put the duties of the home

lead, consort together in peace and quiet with the domestic animals, the strength of the one shall be given to the other. As each recurring Christmas comes the marvel grows. The contrast, the brutal world and the little Child, the one to be tamed by the other—that is the marvel of the ages. But the little Child is to lead, the world is to be tamed and made tender and glorious. That is the task.

II. By what force is this to be accomplished? By a Divine spiritual force. Both prophecies tell us that. By a force that finds its characteristic expression in the little Child. Malachi said, "I will send you Elijah the prophet before the great and terrible day of the Lord come, And he shall turn the heart of the fathers to the children and the heart of the children to the fathers, lest I come and smite the earth with a curse." That means that there shall be a blending of the child life and the mature life of mankind by the power of love. Love is a heart power. The qualities that are characteristic of the little child are heart qualities. Love is the highest expression of life. So in adult life, when normal, the qualities that respond to the presence of the little child are heart qualities. Love is the natural response. It is often said that it is not on the birth of Christ, but on his death that the divine scheme of salvation rests. On this basis theological systems and theories rest. The death of Christ was in payment of a debt,

in contrast with his own: "Alexander, Cæsar, Charlemagne, and myself founded empires. On what did we rest the creations of our genius? Upon force. Jesus Christ alone founded his empire upon love; and at this hour millions of men would die for him." The difference in the two empires is in the kind of force employed to upbuild and maintain them. That relying upon physical force will fall to pieces when the master is withdrawn, but that which rests upon love will abide. What are the truths that Christ brought into the world to save it? They are three.

First, the universal Fatherhood of God. Love is the highest expression of this relationship.

Second, the universal brotherhood of man, with good will and service as its highest expression.

Third, eternal life as the supreme gift, result, and reward. and this springing out of love in the heart of God and man.

Now, Christ brought these great ideas into the world where brute force was enthroned, and they have been working as a leaven to the changing of the spirit of humanity. One has said: "Christianity differentiates itself from other religions more by its motive than by its commands. The laws of duty and morality, which are beautifully expressed in the Old and New Testaments, can often be found beautifully expressed in other religions. The difference seems to be in that one word which Matthew Arnold said characterized the teachings of Marcus Aurelius, beautiful, righteous, but 'ineffectual.' The effectiveness with which Christ has brought

life, industrial life, governmental life, all life. The great message of the Christmas time is love. A poet has expressed this truth for us in these words:

At first I prayed for light; could I but see the
    way,
  How gladly would I walk to everlasting day!
  I asked the world's deep law before my eyes to
    ope',
And let me see my prayer fulfilled, and realize
    my hope.
    But God was kinder than my prayer,
    And darkness veiled me everywhere.

And next I prayed for strength, that I might
    tread the road,
  With firm unfaltering pace to heaven's abode;
That I might never know a faltering, failing
    heart,
But manfully go on and reach the highest part,
    But God was kinder than my prayer,
    And weakness checked me everywhere.

And then I asked for faith, could I but trust my
    God,
  I'd live, in heavenly peace, though foes were
    all abroad,
His light thus shining round, no faltering should
    I know,
And faith in heaven above would make a heaven
    below.
    But God was kinder than my prayer,
    And doubts beset me everywhere.

And now I pray for love, deep love to God and
    man,—
  A love that will not fail, however dark His
    plan;
That sees all life in Him, rejoicing in His power,
And faithful though the darkest clouds of gloom
    and doubt may lower.
    But God is kinder than my prayer,
    Love fills and blesses everywhere."

Let us pray evermore for love, "deep love to God and man," and we shall not only have love, but we shall also have light and strength and faith, and indeed all things else that we need, for this love is the greatest thing in the world, and being the greatest it includes the less.

Bloomington, Ind.

"Come to Us Christmas, Good Old Day"

Christ, the Revealer.

The Babe of Bethlehem! May he be enshrined in our hearts, showing us those things that are hid from the wise and prudent and revealed unto babes!

Carthage, O.   CHAS. M. FILLMORE.

"The Prince of Peace!"

"And on earth peace, good will toward men." These words, spoken by the angelic host on the night of the Nativity, were a prophecy of the great blessing of the kingdom that was soon to be inaugurated upon the earth and whose spread among the nations would surely hasten the day when men "shall beat their swords into plowshares and their spears into pruning-hooks; when nation shall not lift up sword against nation, neither shall they learn war any more." Just as the spirit of the Christ fills the souls of men and dominates their life, so will men be at peace among themselves, the schisms in the body of Christ healed; international differences arbitrated, resulting in disarmament, and the kingdoms of this world become the kingdom of our Lord and of his Christ. Hasten, thou, thy reign of peace in all the earth, O Christ.

Columbus, O.   WALTER SCOTT PRIEST.

The First Great Gift.

What am I doing with God's great gift, Jesus Christ, himself? This is a question which always comes to me, over and over, with increasing interest, at Christmas time. Am I showing my gratitude to God for his unspeakable gift, by giving him lovingly, unselfishly, and unstintingly the best service of my life? Am I bestowing my gifts of whatever sort, entirely careless of my own happiness? In our giving, we should be moved only by the needs of others. We should not give because someone else has given to us, or because we expect them to give in return for our gifts. "God maketh the sun to rise on the evil and on the good, and sendeth rain on the just and on the unjust." If we shall give thus unselfishly, we shall be the children of our Father.   S. D. DUTCHER.

Omaha, Neb.

The Joy of Sacrifice for Others.

Christmas is a benediction to all humanity. All alike rejoice and are made better in the celebration of the birth of our Lord and Saviour, Jesus Christ. The beautiful spirit of the Christ rules in us and we love to have a part in making just as many of God's children happy as possible. Sacred memories of other Christmases fill our minds, and we live over again the glad days of our childhood. We give expression to our joy in the bestowal of gifts and love tokens. We are remembered with gifts, and are glad, but the exquisite joys of the season come to those only who gladly give and sacrifice as did the Christ.

Drake University, Des Moines, Ia.
   HILL M. BELL.

A Christmas Meditation.

Christmas night. Night of the advent of our Lord. Blessed night of the beginning of peace. Night of the world's hopes. Night of the poor man's enrichment. Morning of the world's redemption. The angels sang a sweeter and a fuller story than anyone then knew, and far sweeter than many thousands now living have ever realized. God is among men. His mercy is embodied in that matchless life. His holiness shines forth from every page of the wonderful story of Jesus' birth and life. Let cold materialism; let over-fed sensualism and luxury; let pinching mammonism; let languishing indifference and shiftlessness—and every other blight upon the world—within or without the church—be purged away from me as I meditate upon the sacrifice and humiliation, and the glory that followed, which had their beginning on the night of our Lord's advent.

Maryville, Mo.   H. A. DENTON.

The Significance of Song.

Is it not significant that the first proclamation of the Savior's birth was made in song? Is this not a standing proof of its inspiration to life's noblest ideals? Doubt does not sing. Fear fits none of the harmonies of music. Hate finds no expression in anthems of praise. Only faith, hope, and love sing. The highest evidence of the divinity of our Lord is that his entrance into the world was heralded by a burst of song and that its echoes have been heard in all lands and in every age. May the power of this message fill our hearts.

Bethany, Neb.   W. P. AYLSWORTH.

Givers of Gifts.

Christmas is the season of good cheer. It means vastly more than mere feeding and feasting, and the lavish bestowal of gifts. It is beyond all else a time when the poor should be clothed and warmed, and the hungry be fed. The happiness that comes to all relieved sufferers is shared by those who help to relieve the suffering. The giver is himself the richer for his gift. It is more blessed to give than to receive. The greatest joy of the Christmastide is the quickening of the life into full sympathy with him who brought peace on earth, good will to men.

Eureka, Ill.   R. E. HIERONYMUS.

Our Christmas Gifts.

The list of friends has been selected with care. We have remembered the favors received in days gone by and tried to select presents worthy of them. Are we sure that no one has been omitted from our list? Not one? What have you selected for your best friend? The one to whom you owe everything? But you say, "I have been paying my part all year." Yes, you have also been feeding, clothing and educating your children all year, but you will give them, something extra for Christmas. Why not make Christmas a time when we will give something extra for the Lord's work?   J. A. LONGSTON.

Independence, Kas.

The Children's Festival.

Jesus coronated childhood and Christmas is, above all else, the children's festival. The holiday season, as it is in our cities, both large and small, is an exhibition of commercialism rampant; tradesmen vying with one another in keen competition and salespeople wearing themselves out in the mad rush of Christmas shoppers. Moreover, with many this is the season for dissipation and carousal. How unseemly all this! If there is any one day above all others in the year when the drunkard should go home sober and in his right mind it is at blest Christmastide. Nor is this the season for the exchange of costly gifts. It is the children's festival and if one has the money only to purchase a single gift, let it be a toy for a child. Tell the little tots what Christmas means. Repeat the "old, old story" of Jesus cradled in a manger and dying at last on Calvary for the sin of the world. Make the day one of sunshine and good cheer and redolent with the spirit of the Christ-teaching.   EDGAR D. JONES.

Bloomington, Ill.

Making Hearts Happy.

Our thought should be Christ blessed. Our whole being should be keenly awake to the wonderful life. Let us open our eyes and we will behold the King in his beauty just in measure as we see the needs of our fellows. Let our ears be unstopped and we will hear the Master's voice in our inmost soul just in measure as we hear the cry of human distress—the call of the hungry, the naked, the sick and the prisoner. Somehow the Prince of Peace had a way of knowing how hearts could be made happy. Have we caught the spirit?

Shelbina, Mo.   J. H. WOOD.

What Does Christmas Mean to Me?

Does it mean that I am to have a jolly good time in much merry-making, feasting with friends, in which there is a round of physical dissipation? If this is the meaning, all that I get out of it, then it is a detriment and not a blessing.

But it means to me this: I have a precious Savior who is able to cleanse me from all unrighteousness; able to keep that which I have committed unto him against that day; able to lead me in the way of life; able to give me the best of this world, and a home in heaven, when I have finished my course.

If it means this much to me (and I think it does, and more), then I can not afford to be disloyal to such a Savior. I must take up my cross daily and follow after him.   J. H. SMART.

Decatur, Ill.

"What Means this Lowly Birth?"

The Magi wondered as they worshipped the Christ on that first Christmas morning, and for all then there is increasing charm in the significance of this lowly birth. Born amid plainest surroundings, it was revealed that redemption is not through riches; without the show of learning, thus proving that salvation is not through wisdom; without the presence of the military power, thus evidencing that the Kingdom does not come by force of arms. In a word, such a birth makes Jesus a brother to the race.

He identifies himself with us in all the varied experiences of our lives. And we can feel that no social nor intellectual barrier keeps us from him, since he was reared in such a lowly estate.

And up from this manger birth he rose with the flight of the days to the divine task of human redemption.

Terre Haute, Ind.   L. E. SELLERS.

It Closes the Chasm.

Since the coming of God into human nature, the chasm that separated God from man has been closed. All human nature has now the offer of striking a higher level of being in Christ, through Christ and by means of Christ. Jesus Christ has therefore become not simply a dead stepping stone to a higher level, but he has become "a new and living way"—an avenue of approach to the mind and heart of the living God. Since the incarnation man becomes "partaker of the divine nature." In all other religions man is left to search after God, but in the Christian religion God is seen to be searching after man. A great writer has expressed the thought in the following words: "It is the teaching alike of the Scriptures and of philosophy that it is primarily God who seeks man, not primarily man who seeks God."

Sedalia, Mo.   J. M. RUDY.

Methods of Evangelization

Being the Third Part of the Address before the Buffalo Convention on "Disciples and Evangelism."

By J. P. Lichtenberger

Paul was the first great Methodist; becoming all things to all men, that he might gain some. Method is nothing, to gain men is everything. Yet, because all men are to be won by some method, method is everything.

1. Conforming Practice to Theory.

Dr. J. Wilbur Chapman began his address before the federation conference in New York last November with this significant sentence: "If the church should maintain the position which in the plan and purpose of God she was ever meant to hold, special evangelistic meetings would be unnecessary." The doctrine of the open door into the church, "which no man can shut," has been a tremendous power in the growth of our movement. But there has been a diminution in evangelistic effort in our regular services, and a growing tendency to depend upon the revival method. Some of us have been so long teachers, historians, lecturers, that we have lost the art of evangelistic preaching. Has not the hour come for a revival of evangelism in our regular services? The tree of life yields its fruit every month. Let the centennial crusade be characterized by a regular, persistent, perennial revivalism in all our churches. Our membership can not be doubled by the time of the centennial celebration by the protracted meeting method. Some of our best evangelistic preachers seldom hold meetings, and the growth of many of our churches at regular services exceeds those which rely upon the meeting method. I am not decrying the revival. I believe in the revival, but, with Dr. Chapman, as an expedient and not as the natural method. Our custom of receiving members at any of our services has often been the envy of some of the brethren in other churches. Shall we cease to use it to the full extent of its value?

2. The Undenominational Plea.

Another tremendous advantage in our evangelism is our undenominational plea. The large experience in union evangelistic work throughout America led Dr. Chapman in that same address to say: "One does not require very much experience to realize that it is vastly easier to make Christians of the unconverted than to manufacture Presbyterians, or Methodists, or Baptists." He is nearly a century late in this discovery. This has been our universal experience. Again, many among our religious neighbors have discovered that the shoemaker in "Hiram Goff's Religion," "that if they lose Christ in the church and simply hold to the denomination they have very little left; but if they lose the denominational mark, and hold to the Christ, which is the heart of the church, they have lost very little."

And yet, brethren, have we not frequently proclaimed an undenominational gospel in a sectarian spirit? Have we always impressed a community that our chief aim was to win men to Christ rather than build up a particular church? Has our plea always seemed unsectarian to those who heard it? Has not our theory sometimes outrun our practice?

Of all the religious peoples in America we should be the leaders in union evangelistic effort. We should be supplying the country with union evangelists. As a matter of fact we have often lagged behind the procession. We have witnessed the peculiar enigma of all the churches in a community engaged in union evangelistic effort but the church committed to that plea. We are only now beginning to come into our estate. Let the recent union meetings of Wright, Scoville, Rudy and others be the beginning of a great wave of union evangelistic effort instituted, fostered, generaled by men who are heart and soul committed to an undenominational plea, and not only will the religious world take us seriously, but God will pour out upon us a blessing such as we have not hitherto received. Let us become the initiators of such a movement. Let us hesitate only before conditions that compromise conviction or limit the evangel. The most significant event in evangelism among the Disciples in a decade, is the decision of H. O. Breeden to resign the pastorate of his great church in Des Moines to enter the field as a union evangelist.

A union meeting arrests the attention of a city. It creates a religious atmosphere. It commands the united force of the whole church. It forestalls prejudice and strengthens the conviction among the unchurched, that after all, we are more interested in saving them than in the perpetuation of our sectarian rivalries. A positive constructive work of a few weeks, heartily entered into by all Christian people in any community, will advance the kingdom. Destructive denunciation will hinder its progress. Simultaneous campaigns have demonstrated the power of a united host. But how tremendously more effective would such campaigns be were the whole church of God enlisted in the enterprise.

But some will say, How shall we do this and preserve our individuality and our distinctive plea? In the name of God, brethren, are we here to preserve an individuality and a plea, or to win the world to Christ? Have we come to the kingdom at such a time as this, with the religious world aglow with evangelistic fire, and our hands so tied by precedent and tradition that we can not participate our full share in the mighty ongoing triumphs of the army of God? Are we so wedded to our idols that we shall permit others with more modest pretensions to lead us in this glorious crusade?

3. The New Evangelism.

Within a year in our religious papers there have been articles on "The Old Evangelism," "The New," "The Newer," and "The Newest Evangelism." This serves to emphasize the diverse needs of different fields. Any kind of evangelism in our age will be selective. There is no semblance of a universal type of religious thought in America to-day. In their religious conceptions men range all the way from ultra-conservatism to ultra-radicalism. Estimated in terms of mass, conservative views largely predominate. If in terms of intellectual culture, progressive views are in the ascendency. Our gospel has a mighty message for the masses and must still be proclaimed in the spirit and power of Wesley, Whitefield, and Finney. But it has likewise a message for the cultured and the educated. I have heard recently two evangelists in our city. They addressed different audiences. One delivered a message in thunderous tones on the terrors of the judgment, of which Jonathan Edwards would have had no reason to be ashamed, and rough men trembled with fear. The other, with calm, yet passionate logic, drove home the arrows of conviction to the hearts of a cultured throng. Both were greatly blessed of God. Both had an important message and mission. Those who decry either are men of narrow vision.

New methods of presenting the old message are being greatly blessed to-day. Perhaps the time has come for some of us to make fundamental changes in our methods. In the great cities, street meetings, tent meetings, theatre meetings, are attracting wide attention.

As a method applicable to cities of almost every rank I wish particularly to advocate the use of theatres for religious services. On this subject Dr. Newell Dwight Hillis recently said: "The forty closed theatres on Sunday afternoon and Sunday night are challenges to the preachers of New York—either we can go into these theatres on Sunday nights and reach the people or we will find within ten years that Sunday night will be a theatre night from New York to San Francisco. In the 18th century, when the country people were unreached, God raised up Wesley in England to reach them by open air preaching. In the 19th century God raised up Gen. Booth to reach the submerged classes of the great cities. Now the hour has come, in a country where open air preaching is impossible for eight months in the year, for some new apostle of evangelism to rise up and organize a new denomination to utilize all the theatres of the country in the great cities and small factory towns for evangelistic preaching on Sunday afternoons and evenings. If we are going to keep the

Sunday in American life we must use the Sunday."

Is not this our challenge? What greater impetus could be given our centennial crusade than that from every theatre throughout the land our plea for the simple gospel should be sounded forth. What was done in Manchester may be done in a thousand cities. In our Scoville meetings in the Lenox Avenue Union Church last spring, while our building was ample for all our audiences, Harlem Opera House, the largest and best theatre building above Fifty-ninth street, on Sunday evening, April 22, was entirely inadequate. The doors were open but twenty minutes until they had to be closed against hundreds who sought admission. The offering was ample to cover the expense of the meeting (over $200) and allowed us to send $50 to the relief of the brethren in San Francisco. Let us make the experiment in a thousand theatres. Let us send out the message which God has committed to us from these great gathering places of the people.

(To be Continued.)

The Elderburg Association

CHAPTER IX.

Brother Paper-Hanger Reviewed.

"I can imagine conditions," said Brother Lawyer, "under which a bull in a china shop would be the right 'critter' in the right place, even from the standpoint of the owner of the shop. Assume that business is stagnant, expenses certain and collections uncertain, and that the owner has an accident policy on his stock; then let a bull invade the premises, and the owner may soon cash his policy; and he will have, moreover, a good excuse for making an assignment. It is conceivable also, that in any china shop there will be accumulations of things that ought to be smashed, if only to make room for more merchantable stuff. For that purpose, however, somebody with more judgment than a bull would be required; some one with a better knowledge of values, with a better eye, for artistic effects; some one whose knowledge of china would prevent costly mistakes.

"Also I can imagine communities where aggressive reformers, of the bull-in-the-china-shop type, may come as great, heaven-sent blessings. There are communities and churches where the people have grown torpid, fat-hearted, somnolent, lazy, their moral faculties tending to atrophy for lack of exercise. Such people need to be stirred up by something sudden and strenuous; something like a hawk in the barn yard, a bear in the hog pen, a nigger in the hen house, a lizard at the camp-meeting, or, as aforesaid, a bull in a china shop. The man who is content to serve them in that way will be sure to interest them, will probably make them angry, may throw them into fits, may or may not do them good,

but he can not hurt them. Nevertheless, evanescence and strenuousness—that kind of strenuousness—are closely related qualities. If we stop to think we perceive that this must be so. I suppose that when we come to understand all things as they are, we shall see the beneficent purpose of the cyclone—shall understand the particular great mission it has to perform. Yet we know, right now, without waiting for all the mysteries to be unveiled, that no matter what good a cyclone does, it can not expect to be permanently employed in any community. Whatever it does it must do quickly; it must pass rapidly on to the next job; and we seldom or never see that the people in whose midst it has done a great work are anxious to have it come back. So with the bull in the china shop; he may work acceptably for a season, but the season is necessarily brief.

"If a man desires to distinguish himself as a moral cyclone; if he is willing to be a bull in the social and moral china shop, who shall say him nay? Who shall say he has not been called and chosen to that work before the foundation of the world?

"Once, in my boyhood, I was going home, with what my father called a 'small jag of hay,' on a wagon. A cloud was rising in the west and I felt sure it would rain before I could get home; but a gad-fly stung the oxen, causing them to run away, so that I and the wagon and some of the hay got home before the shower. Up to that time I had never been able to see where there was any use for a gad-fly. I dare say that for ages and ages nobody could guess why the Lord had taken the trouble to make the hornet, until he sent him to labor for a season with the Hivites, the Canaanites, and Hittites. Always, however, the labors of the cyclone, the bull-in-the-china-shop, the gad-fly, and the hornet, while bitter and keen and thorough-going, must be done hurriedly; and if a preacher elects, or is irresistibly impelled, to do that sort of work, let a brief, busy, nerve-thrilling season of labor suffice him—in any given field. Thrice is that human hornet armed who knows that, whatever happens, he has the trade of paper-hanging to fall back on; a rebellious and stiff-necked generation of elders and deacons may 'fire' him from his pulpit, but they can not starve him.

"Our brother spoke of 'hurling thunderbolts' at various offenders, and perhaps the verbal weapons he used may very well be likened to thunder-bolts, in their devastating effects. To be witty; to have fine powers of sarcasm; to be master of irony; and to be able to use all these so as to cause the most possible pain to a given victim; if any man have these gifts in any appreciable measure, let his prayer be, 'Lord, lead me not into temptation.' A man might obtain from these things results not unlike the effects of thunderbolts, but they are so apt to scorch the fingers of the man who hurls them. I can not imagine anything more dangerous to a preacher of the Word than to possess such gifts and to know that he possesses them. They must be a constant temptation to him; and if the grace of God dwell not richly in his heart, at all times, he is sure to do mischief to himself and others. Most of us, I suppose, would like to wield the thunderbolts of Jove, but we should be almost certain to abuse the privilege, if we had it. We should like to see the dust (or the fur) fly, and hear the racket; and the Lord only knows what mischief we might do.

"Could great men thunder
As Jove himself does, Jove would ne'er be quiet,
For every pelting, petty officer
Would use his heaven for thunder: nothing but thunder."

"No; I reckon nobody but Jove himself has the requisite wisdom and judgment to go into the thunderbolt business. Let us take counsel of something higher than ourselves before we go to blazing away too recklessly at our fellows. If irony, wit, sarcasm, are to be classed among the thunderbolts, and if we will use them, let us practice exclusively on men of straw or on wooden dummies: the heart of a fellow-mortal, the heart of a fellow-Christian, especially, is no fit target for our marksmanship."

(To be Continued.)

A Christmas Prayer.

THOMAS CURTIS CLARK.

O'er far Judæa's sacred hills
A joyous cry was heard,
"A king is born in Bethlehem;"
All men took up the word.
Unto the lowly manger crib
Came peasant, seer, king;
And, bending low, by love inspired,
Brought each his offering.

* *

O Saviour, on this Christmas day,
Our gifts we bring to thee;
No gold, no frankincense and myrrh
We bear on bended knee:
Our minds we bring, to make them thine;
Our hearts, to know thy love;
Our hands—O teach them ever, Lord,
At thy command to move.

Two Babes of Bethlehem.

BY LOUIS S. CUPP.

Ruth, the Moabitess, gleaning in the fields of Boaz, a wedding such as had not been seen for many a day in Bethlehem, then another harvest; but Ruth goes no more out to glean. There is a baby in the house. It is a house of joy. The village women gather to bless Jehovah that a child is born in Bethlehem. The kinsmen come to rejoice that a son is given, saying, "He shall be a restorer of life." And this babe became the grand-father of King David, ancestor of the Messiah.

As we listen to the story, the bells of that far-off Christmas begin to echo through the years. Another babe is in Bethlehem, in a stable, lighted by a star. And everywhere there is joy. This world loves childhood more since Jesus came, and the bells of gladness can never cease their ringing.

Hyde Park Church, Kansas City, Mo.

Good News From Darkest Africa   By Mrs. R. J. Dye

Two weeks ago we had the pleasure of entertaining a party of the Baptist Missionary Society's missionaries over Lord's day. They arrived Saturday noon, a party of ten on their new steamer, "The Endeavor," en route to their up-river stations, Bopoto and Yakusu, which we visited a year ago on our vacation trip. This party was made up partly of old and partly of new missionaries so what comments they made on the Bolengi work were especially interesting to us, and I thought, perhaps, would be to you. Because of my illness they insisted that they should have all their meals on the steamer so we enjoyed their dropping in all times of day and having a quiet chat.

All attended the morning services at 10 a. m. save Mrs. Kirby, of Bopoto, who remained with me until time for the communion service when Bro. Hensey came for her to go. Mr. and Mrs. Kirby are just returning from a furlough home, where they left little Vera. On their way up-river they heard of the very impressive communion service at Bolengi and were anxious to see it. It must be impressive for its very simplicity for it is observed in the good old way. Every absent member is remembered by name. On their return from this meeting they found my room full of visitors, many very old women and most of our Christian babies, as we term the children of Christian parents, who can me after the service. They had been struck with the number of white-haired women especially, none of them ever having seen them in church before anywhere.

Mrs. Kirby said she had not come out with any definite work in view for this term, but she had seen her vision and it should be her purpose now to endeavor to win the aged mothers at Bopoto. Mr. and Mrs. Wilford, of Yakusu (Stanley Falls), were also interested in this, and as she is coming out for the first time it gave her an incentive also, for what has been done here can be done elsewhere. As they were gathered about me I pointed out a white-haired mother, her older sister, her middle-aged daughter and three grandchildren, all of the older three being Christians, three generations reached in that one family.

One other thing noted by them was the Christian men and their wives seated together in the middle row of seats, a custom not observed elsewhere, usually the men being seated all on one side and the women on the other. Mr. Howell has seen many years' service in Congo, having come out under the L. I. M. and later transferring to the B. M. S. He is a missionary steamer captain and sees all the stations on the main river at least twice yearly. He was surprised to see the large audience and deep attention and said that our people were much more anxious for the gospel than those on the lower river. He was greatly pleased with the outlook here and interested in the numbers of Bosira workmen seeking salvation, seeing as do we a possible opening to that great unopened country. The natives were pleased to see so many white teachers at the service and several expressed the wish that Bolengi alone could have as many as that.

At 3 p. m. all gathered in my room informally to have an English tea, more that we might all be together once. Just a cup of black tea, bread and butter, cake (made by Bolengi's famous white-boy cooks) and an enjoyable half hour of happy fellowship.

At 4 p. m. Sunday-school was called and all went back but were not prepared for what they found. There are a few Sunday-schools in Upper Congo, but ours is unique in that it is conducted on the European plan being divided into classes with native teachers, who have been given the lesson previously. Every one felt this to be the best service of all, there being such a crowd of children as well as older people. When walking about the "park," as they call our station, they had wondered at the wooden benches out under the trees by the chapel, and now they saw their purpose, for all the younger classes have their class rooms in the beautiful shady gallery over-arched by the palms and mammoth tropical trees. They were surprised to see Christian girls and women teaching classes so intent upon the lesson that nothing distracted their attention. Here again the class of grandmothers attracted the most notice, there being about thirty present. Mrs. Kirby told them of her purpose to help their sisters at Bopoto, which pleased them very much and I heard of it from several who said she should have a special meeting for them such as we used to have, then she would get them to come. The Wilfords were enthusiastic over it all and are writing an article for the London Sunday-school Times, the greatest Sunday-school paper of England, describing it, for which we gave them some pictures.

Mr. Dodds is one of the older missionaries, previously stationed at Monsembe, which was abandoned last year, the village depopulated by State depredations and the sleeping sickness. He is now working at Bopoto also and had been down to meet his new bride at Boma. He knows this station well and was as much surprised as the home folks to know that the native church supported so many evangelists and seemed to think it almost incredible, as their evangelists and teachers all receive home support.

In the evening while the native church had their regular service, all the missionaries met together in our library where Mr. Kirby had charge of the meeting. Though not present I could enjoy the music and enter into the spirit of the hour. As they came to say good night and good-bye, I believe every one felt that it had been a day of rich blessing and sweet fellowship.

Early the next morning they steamed away leaving only the usual group of sick folk from the down river stations brought to see the doctor. "The Endeavor" is the finest mission steamer yet launched on the Congo, costing $35,000 raised by the Christian Endeavorers of Great Britain.

You will be glad with us to know that during the month of June I gained faster than for several previous months. We feel greatly encouraged as we now seem able to ward off the hard heart spells which kept me so long in the valley of shadow. The turn for the better came unexpectedly and suddenly and we feel that it has been an answer to offering of prayer being raised for us in the home land. During the last few months we have received several letters from total strangers both in Canada and America, who though not knowing of our extremity, had felt peculiarly drawn to think of us and write to us. Surely God's mysteries are still most wonderful.

During the recent trip of the S. S. Livingstone down river it waited over here a few days and one day I was bundled up, carried in a hammock on board where a traveling bed was prepared on deck to receive me, and Captain McDonald, missionary of the C. B. M., took us up and down the river while I drank in the sweet fresh air and felt once more that I was really alive.

We are happy and encouraged to hear of reinforcements. We shall stay as long as possible, you may be sure. Since last spring our little daughters have been very well. Polly is enjoying her school and being a little mother to Dorcas. She is trying to save up $5 for Children's day offering so she is beginning her missionary life already.

TWENTY-TWO CONVERTS RECENTLY BAPTIZED AT BOLENGI.

Our Budget

—"A merry Christmas" to all our readers!

—May your stockings all be filled, on "the night before Christmas"!

—If not, however, we are sure they will all be filled on Christmas morning—before breakfast!

—But the main thing is to see that your hearts are filled with joy and gratitude for God's great Christmas gift to the world.

—Kindly greetings to all our fellow editors of the religious press. May they all have a prosperous year to come, even according as their prosperity maketh for the welfare of Zion.

—"Agnes of the Bad Lands." This is the title of the new serial story which will begin in The Christian-Evangelist of January 3, 1907. We think it will prove a very interesting story from the story standpoint, while the moral will not be lost because of the fiction element. We trust that a great many new subscribers may be obtained to start in with the new story.

—There were 70 names on the annuitant list of the Board of Ministerial Relief last year. These men and women have been through the fight and have come out as heroes and heroines, but they are lacking in this world's goods. If you had no part in the regular Sunday offering last Lord's day and want to help support the old preachers and their wives or widows, send a contribution to the Board of Ministerial Relief, 120 E. Market street, Indianapolis, Ind.

✦ ✦ ✦

—The brethren at Princeton, Ind., will repair their building.

—The dedication of our church at Granite City will be held December 27.

—W. W. Sniff has resigned at Rushville Ind., and accepted a call to Paris, Ill.

—A meeting at Ames, Okla., resulted in almost the doubling of the membership.

—L. E. Murray will begin a meeting with F. D. Muse at Daleville, Ind., December 30.

—W. S. Hood is to be employed as evangelist of the Dade county (Mo.) convention.

—Clyde Sharp is in a meeting at Sand Creek, Okla., and will be at Wakita in January.

—D. M. Harris was to enter upon the ministry of the church at Galena, Kan., last Lord's day.

—Thomas Wallace has accepted a call to Croton, Ohio, where there is an average attendance of about 200.

—A full house, notwithstanding four churches holding meetings near ours, is the report from Bellefontaine, O.

—W. G. Oram has accepted a call to the pastorate of the H Street Church, Washington, D. C., and is on his new field.

—The church at Dixon, Ill., with H. H. Peters as pastor, is making a special effort in the interest of the Sunday-school.

—T. L. Lowe has resigned at Athens, O., where he has ministered for six years, and has accepted a call to Union City, Ind.

—William Ross Lloyd, who has been supplying for the church at Salt Lake City for some months past, has removed to Lexington, Ky.

—We regret to learn from a post card from George Lobingier that he is seriously ill at Lincoln, Neb., and must undergo an operation.

—T. A. Abbott, state secretary of Missouri, passed through St. Louis on his way to St. Francis county, in the work of organization.

—Eleven young men from the Missouri Bible College and the University spent their Thanksgiving holidays in gospel work at Paris, Mo.

—We have that a deep spiritual impression was made by the meeting conducted by J. M. Helm, of Parkersburg, W. Va., at Richmond, O.

—George E. Hopkins writes enthusiastically of the meeting held by F. A. Bright, formerly evangelist of Western Pennsylvania, at Bellaire, Ohio.

—The church at Dresden, Kan., has never had any pastoral care, writes A. R. Poe, but he believes that in a year's time he will have it in a good condition.

—The Central Church, Wichita, Kan., is planning for a great forward movement January 27, when Joseph Powell, of Buffalo, N. Y., and Z. T. Sweeney will be with them.

—Charles A. Lockhart's work at the Central Christian Church, Waco, Texas, has started auspiciously and plans are being made for a great meeting one year hence.

—A man 95 years of age has just united with our church at Caldwell, Kan., where Lee H. Barnum's pastorate will close January 1. Brother Barnum has not accepted any other work as yet.

—J. M. Rhodes, of Newkirk, Okla., has been called to the pastorate of the church at New Franklin, Mo., where A. N. Lindsey did such a good work, and will enter upon the field January 1.

—O. L. Adams has just held a good meeting at Barnes, Kan., where there had not been a baptism for three years. There are five church buildings in the town but only three, if our information be correct, being used.

—The Christian-Evangelist force enjoyed the pleasure of a call from A. M. Harral while visiting friends in St. Louis. The women of his church this year observed C. W. B. M. day for the first time and had a fine service.

—Edward Clutter has just closed a year's work at Irvington and Florence, suburbs of Omaha. There were 71 additions to the churches. He is now in Cotner University and will be ready to make dates for meetings after June 15, 1907.

—The church at Marshall, Mo., is planning for a meeting to begin January 1, in which the pastor, B. T. Wharton, who is, by the way, a brother of the lamented Bro. G. L. Wharton, will be assisted by A. N. Lindsey, of Clinton, Mo.

—A number of contributions on "The Missing Link," bearing on the proposed revision of the constitution of the A. C. M. S., coming in a little late, are necessarily laid over till next week, as Christmas has the right of way.

—The average Sunday-school attendance at Jacksonville, Ill., where R. F. Thrapp is pastor, and C. B. DePew is superintendent, has been over 600 for this year, while, as reported in our last issue, the attendance was nearly 1,000 a week or two ago.

—H. L. Maltman, minister at Bloomingdale, Mich., writes us that among those who joined the church, at a recent meeting of J. S. Raum, was Mr. R. A. Stokes, of Toronto, Canada, who will devote his life to the work of singing evangelist.

—J. H. Hardin, who has just been holding a Bible Institute at Lamar, Mo., where he organized a Teachers' Training Class, and had three additions to the church, reports S. G. Clay working in such a way as to insure great results in the near future.

—T. J. Golightly, of Bethany, Mo., recently held a meeting at Oakland, a country church, in which there were 26 additions, 20 being by baptism. James E.

Hawes, of Ada, O., is now with him in a meeting at Bethany as leader of the chorus.

—O. D. Maple will hold a meeting at Parker, Ind., in January, and at Clarinda, Ia., in February. On March 1 he goes to Cairo, Ill., for a period of nine months during which time a $12,000 church will be built and a big meeting held.

—W. D. Trumbull and wife, who are going into the evangelistic work for a time, can count 74 added to the membership at Meadville, Pa., at the conclusion of their second year there, $3,000 raised for all purposes and an increase in the different organizations.

—P. C. MacFarlane, who had been compelled to go into a sanitarium, was brought home to have Thanksgiving dinner with his family. Though much improved, the weakness caused by a long siege of inflammatory rheumatism still forces him to remain at home.

—H. C. Littleton has announced his resignation at Fairfield, Ia., to be effective January 1. During his twenty-five months' pastorate there were 165 additions. Brother Littleton has excellent recommendations and will be ready for the evangelistic field or for a pastorate.

—J. P. Childs' work during the past year was the organization of a church at Fairmont, Minn., which has increased to a membership of 77, the Sunday-school 50, and the Endeavor Society 70. A lot has been purchased and about $900 in money and subscriptions pledged for a new church. Brother Childs has resigned to go into the

·evangelistic work and a man of spiritual power is wanted to succeed him.

—We regret that the pressure on our space is still so great that items have to be held over or much curtailed. Among these is the report of the Violett-Clarkson meeting at Lorain, Ohio. A brief report of Brother Violett's Ohio meetings will be found under "As we go to press."

—The church at Benton, Ill., is going forward under the ministration of Lew D. Hill and wife. There has been a large increase in the Endeavor work and a gradual increase in the Sunday-school. The church not only contributed to the national offerings, but paid the pastor's expenses to the convention.

—George Darsie, minister of the First Christian Church of Christ, Akron, Ohio, writes: "The work is going splendidly here. There were 690 in the Bible school yesterday and large audiences at church. Miss Mary Graybiel spoke in the morning and more than $100 was raised as the C. W. B. M. offering."

—J. L. Callahan, writing from California, which he calls "the land of golden opportunities," says he has found many friends of other days out there in the far west and among others Bro. H. Kirk, of Berkeley, who was formerly of Akron, O., with whom he is having a royal time in talking over "the days gone by."

—Mr. and Mrs. Barton Campbell Hagerman announce the marriage of their daughter, Mary Virginia, to Dr. Halford A. Watson, Saturday evening, December 29, Argyle Hall, Lexington, Ky. The bride and groom will be at home after January 15 at the Auditorium Hotel, Chicago, Ill. Our congratulations to all parties concerned.

—If "pounding" is an evidence of appreciation, then Isaac Elder is held in very high esteem by his church at Hamburg, Ia., for many tokens of love have been left at the pastor's house again and again, according to W. L. Harris, who has just held a meeting of this church. But we know that Brother Elder and his wife are thoroughly worthy.

—Ivan Agee, writing from Atlanta, Ill., expresses great appreciation for himself and the church of the sermons and the services of George L. Snively, upon whose call $1,000 was raised in a few minutes to wine out a debt of $800 that had been standing for several years. We are glad to learn that the future of Atlanta is so full of promise.

—N. G. Buckley, minister at Fitzgerald, Ga., writes that the brethren there expect to have their chapel finished in 90 days, when it will be one of the largest and best Christian church buildings in the state. This church was organized only two years ago with 37 members and went to work in a rented hall. Brother Buckley will enter upon his third year, January 1.

—The work under the leadership of W. B. Slater at N. Fairfield, O., moves steadily forward. The brethren are expecting to hold a good meeting after the holidays. This church has a membership of 135 and the observance of C. W. B. M. day has revealed the fact that the two auxiliaries with a membership of 46 paid last year $244 and much more, in the way of largeness of heart and missionary zeal.

—There will be a meeting of the National Christian Bible School Association in the Central Church, Indianapolis, December 27, 28. Addresses will be made by J. H. Hardin, W. H. McClain, J. H. Bryan, Marion Stevenson, Herbert Moninger, and Robert M. Hopkins—all leaders in Sunday-school work. The full attendance of the national executive committee is expected, writes Robert M. Hopkins, the secretary, and all Bible school workers are invited.

—Herbert Yeuell has been preaching and lecturing to crowded houses at Hutchinson,

Kan., since leaving St. Louis. His aim has been the deepening of the spiritual life of the membership. Elmer Ward Cole, the popular pastor, has been on a lecture tour through the state while Brother Yeuell has occupied his pulpit. Arthur Wake is to be associated with Brother Yeuell as singer in the future, their first meeting together being at Elwood, Ind., where Robert Sellers is pastor.

—Brethren sometimes complain because we publish only two or three lines of a report that would take a column of space. It often happens that it is impossible for us to find room for the more lengthy report and we give the essential facts immediate publication reserving other details worthy of publication until a better opportunity presents. It is quite impossible for us to publish all the news that we receive, and we ask correspondents to make their reports just as brief as is consistent with the importance of the news.

—J. E. Lynn is delivering a series of Sunday evening sermons from his pulpit at the Central Church, Warren, Ohio, on "Great facts of faith in the light of modern thought," while in the morning he is giving a series of expository sermons entitled "On the way to Pentecost." All this is in preparation for the decision meetings to be held in January when A. W. Taylor, of Eureka, Ill., is to do the preaching. Brother Lynn has just led a conference at the ministerial association on plans for a co-operative effort among the churches of Warren.

—There are a great many churches that need a revival and that could be brought into usefulness did they receive any adequate care. Nelson Trimble writes of a visit to Exline, Ia., where there had not been an addition for over two years and where, since the organization of the church over fifty years ago, there had been but one missionary sermon and never congregational offering. As a result of Brother Trimble's visit there were five additions to the church, a missionary sermon, and the church as a body made an offering of $4.46 which, under the conditions, is a good start.

—Robert Simons has closed his pastorate with the church at Monett, Mo., where he had been less than two years. He found them discouraged with a mortgage of $500, but that has just been burned and it was the privilege of Joseph Gaylor to be with the brethren on this occasion to present the cause of state missions, and an offering of $300 was made. Brother Simons will go into the field as a living-link evangelist of this church, his district being southwest Missouri. He is a consecrated man and ready to hold meetings for weak churches and enter new fields. He will doubtless be a great help in bringing forward our cause in this needy district.

—I. J. Cahill's tenth anniversary of his pastorate at the Central Church, Dayton, Ohio, was recently celebrated. When Bro. Cahill became pastor of this church there was a debt of $9,000, all of which has been removed. In addition to this about $50,000 has been raised for different purposes and the additions to the church have numbered 1035. One hundred from this congregation went to the new church on the west side, and the present membership is about 800. One of the pleasant features of the anniversary was the presentation by Prof. C. L. Loos of a beautiful bouquet of American Beauty roses to the pastor as a recognition of Brother Cahill's ability and faithfulness.

—David C. Peters and his family expect to spend Christmas with the home folks at Versailles, Mo. Four years ago Brother Peters had a long siege of typhoid fever which left him with a crippled heart. This has caused him considerable trouble and at times it seemed as if he would have to surrender his work at Trinidad, Colo., and

seek a lower altitude, but so far he has continued in the mountains where the work is prosperous and he is just as happy as he can be. He has recently been helping in a meeting at Rocky Ford, pastor Nelson and he assisting each other in a special evangelistic effort in both churches. Brother Peters has hopes of making an Oriental tour in February, 1908.

—Word has come to us that Bro. John L. Dearborn, so long and favorably known as one of the leading ministers in the western part of Missouri, has passed away. Years ago when the organization known as the A. P. A. was making itself felt, he was prominent in its counsels and at one time was assaulted by thugs in Kansas City who nearly killed him. No man was more tender, none more true. His ministry was a blessing and he was loved by everyone that knew him. For several years he had been making his home with his son in Kansas City, and it was there that death found him. W. F. Richardson conducted the funeral services.

—A telegram announces the conclusion of the great meeting of the Third Church in Indianapolis with 760 additions. This is the largest city meeting our brotherhood has ever held, we believe. We shall hope to publish fuller particulars of it than we have space for in this edition. Brother Scoville's evangelistic plan now consists of six workers. Thomas Penn Ullom, as announced in our columns last week, "a spiritual dynamo," as Brother Scoville calls him, has been secured to superintend the personal work. DeLoss Smith, Mr. and Mrs. P. M. Kendall, Evangelist Scoville and wife, complete the staff, independent of the pastor and workers in a church where they may be engaged.

—J. W. Monser has chosen as a special work the filling of pulpits for those who wish to be absent on Lord's day. He can go out for 50 to 75 miles from Kansas City in any direction. Brother Monser has succeeded in giving satisfaction to the preachers in that city and those within reach of his help may be glad to know that they can secure it on reasonable notice. He may be addressed at 514 Quincy avenue. Brother Monser is one of the tried and true preachers of our restoration movement and is author of the very valuable little book just brought out by the Christian Publishing Company, entitled, "The Literature of the Disciples," which, by the way, should be in the library of all our preachers, not only as a matter of information but to inspire them to try to discover whether they have any gift in writing.

—Miss Gertrude Ward, formerly of the Central Christian Church this city, who went to Paonia, Colo., three or four years ago, writes of a great work that has been accomplished recently in that town under the leadership of J. K. Hester, who began his work there in June last. The church is erecting a new building and by wise financial management is likely to complete it with little or no indebtedness. The Christian Endeavor Society, she writes, has pledged $100 on the building fund. She asks the prayers of other Christian Endeavorers on their work out there "where the young cowboy and the ranchman may find pleasure in the Christian Endeavor meeting, instead of a saloon, pool room, and billiard hall." We congratulate this little band of Disciples and their preacher on their faithful and successful work for the Master.

—F. W. Burnham, who has accepted a call to Springfield, Ill., writes us from his present pastorate at Decatur, as follows: "The Central Church here counts itself fortunate in securing O. W. Lawrence, of

Rock Island, Ill., as pastor to begin February 1. The pulpit will be vacant not more than one month, and a successor is secured some weeks before the present pastor retires. An unanimous call was extended Brother Lawrence upon the occasion of his visit to an informal reception last Monday evening, and, after carefully canvassing the matter, the call has been accepted. Our people rejoice, and I rejoice with them. The work of the year will not be seriously interrupted by our departure, and we feel that, for the future, continued prosperity is assured. This is a great church, rich in faith and zeal and is a strong factor in the life of this city. I have never seen a better spirit manifest at a critical time like this. We go to Springfield, January 1."

—We know from personal experience that where there are a number of ministers in the same vicinity and bearing the same name confusion frequently arises. This is especially true when several of the same family are in the ministry. In our issue of November 29 it was announced that O. P. Spiegel, who had been recently elected state evangelist of Alabama, is to hold a meeting early next year in North Tonawanda. Brother Spiegel is to hold a meeting, but it is his younger brother, S. P. Spiegel, who was elected state evangelist of Alabama. The information came to us through a press dispatch and the initials were not correct. S. P. Spiegel did four years of fine work as state evangelist of Alabama, but four years ago resigned, since which time he has built a beautiful church in West Point, Ga. At the recent Alabama convention, however, he was re-elected state evangelist. O. P. Spiegel was state evangelist of Alabama from 1894 to 1898 and has recently been general southern evangelist of the home board, but he is now an independent general evangelist. Another brother, J. E. Spiegel, is pastor of the First Christian Church, Corsicana, Texas, while the youngest brother, R. O. Spiegel, who was educated at Lexington, Ky., preached for a while, but his health was not good, and he now superintends an excellent Sunday-school in Alabama. The oldest brother is an active elder and "exhorter" in the home church of the Spiegels.

—The Weekly Guide, Dunn, N. C., of November 29, which has come to hand, contains a beautiful tribute to the venerable Dr. William B. Harrell, of that place, who recently departed this life. Dr. Harrell was a minister of the gospel in the Baptist church and a man of eminent piety and of most lovable character, according to the tribute paid him in his home paper. He had been a reader of THE CHRISTIAN-EVANGELIST for many years and sometimes contributed to its columns. Dr. J. H. Foy, of this city, who was his friend and ardent

admirer, and to whom we are indebted for this paper containing the tribute, says in a letter to the editor:

"Such lives and such deaths are exhortations to steadfastness. While earth may not be poorer since the departed 'live again in lives made better by their presence,' yet those who linger behind feel that heaven is richer and more inviting for them. Brother Harrell had learned to hold you in high esteem through THE CHRISTIAN-EVANGELIST and through a book of yours. He was a good man and full of the Holy Spirit. While dying he summoned his forces, called his children around him, blessed them singly and collectively in patriarchal style, then calmly announced that he saw beyond the veil, beheld Jesus whom he loved, and the dear wife who had preceded him into the enduring life three days before. Then sank to rest,

'Calmly as to a night's repose
Like flowers at set of sun.'"

Our sympathies are extended to the bereaved family.

How an Ohio Church was Established.

A new auditorium at Springfield, O., was dedicated December 9.

About eighteen years ago the church at Springfield was organized and after a brief life a meeting was held by J. V. Updike, which resulted in a large ingathering. The church at first met in a rented building, but finally purchased a lot and erected a house of worship. It was a large undertaking for the young church and conditions were not hopeful in many ways. The church appealed to the brotherhood throughout Ohio for funds to help pay for the building, but even with the help received from outside the problem could not be solved and the burden of debt was so heavy that through the influence of Alanson Wilcox, then secretary of the Ohio Christian Missionary Society, the property was deeded over to that society.

There were various pastors in charge of the work for some years but the situation grew worse and worse until seven years ago, when the writer became secretary of the O. C. M. S., the field was about hopeless. It was one of the few missions that were being supported by the state board and received also some support from the Tenth Missionary District. The church was left pastorless very soon after the beginning of my secretaryship, and I determined to make Springfield one of the points where we should centralize our efforts in the building of a church. W. A. Harp, then of Portsmouth, where he had done a splendid work for a number of years, signified his willingness to leave Portsmouth provided a suitable field opened. I wrote to him asking him to meet me at Springfield to look that field over with a view to locating with that mission church. I wrote to Springfield calling the church together and on the evening that Brother Harp and I were there about a dozen people gathered in the dingy church building, about as hopeless a band as I have ever seen. We asked them how much they could pay toward the support of a pastor, and they said, "Nothing," that they had all they could do to keep up the expense of the church. Brother Harp saw the opportunity and consented to take the work provided the state board would stand back of him.

The first Sunday of November he entered the field. The situation was so hopeless that property owners hesitated about renting him a house because they felt he would stay but a short time. Eighteen were present at his first church service. The Sunday-school consisted of the same number and was divided into three classes. On every hand were debts annd unpaid bills. When Brother Harp suggested that the church should pay the old bills, people laughed and said they had given up all hopes of ever having them paid, but Brother Harp began paying them and paid them all. Allen Wilson was then state evangelist of Ohio and held a meeting resulting in nearly a hundred accessions and the work began to take on new life. The Sunday-school grew and little by little repairs and enlargements were made to the church building to give room to the Sunday-school. Finally the old church debt to the Church Extension Board which had been standing for years with some interest was taken up and paid, the writer being present the day the money was raised and having charge of the service. The Endeavor Society became the best in Clark County and held the banner for years in succession. Brother Harp and his good wife were giving their lives completely to the work of the Springfield church and all of its victories came through their earnest labors. After the debt was out of the way the problem of a new church building was taken up in earnest. The writer was again called to Springfield to assist in this enterprise and a little over $2,000 was raised to be paid within a year to be a sort of nest egg for the new building. The building cost more than was anticipated. It was thought at first that $5,000 was all the church could raise, but the total cost was about $8,400 for repairs to the old building and for the new auditorium. The day of the

corner-stone laying came and the writer again went to Springfield, laid the corner-stone and raised for furnishing the building that day a little over $2,000. The ladies of the church for more effective service were divided into four sections or divisions, and each of these divisions went to work and raised as much or more money than is frequently raised by all of the ladies of the church for a building enterprise. Two hundred dollars a year for each division is a splendid record. Finally the church was completed; a new auditorium, beautiful to look upon, substantially built, was placed in front of the old building, a great sliding partition opening up between them, with a completely equipped basement under the whole structure.

Dedication day was rainy but the house was filled with people. There was yet $4,300 to be raised, a hard problem, but the people, under the splendid leadership of Brother Harp, went at it with a will and a little more than the necessary amount was pledged and will be paid for inside of two years.

Never had I attended a dedication service that was so enthusiastic, that had so much joy and fellowship in it. The afternoon service was remarkable. About a dozen of the preachers of the city were present and with one united voice declared that the Springfield Church of Christ is the most active and aggressive church in the whole city and set the pace in every good word and work. We that had seen it seven years ago, hopeless, discouraged and almost dead, could scarcely believe our ears. This splendid victory is the result of the consecrated efforts of W. A. Harp and his good wife and to them is due the largest measure of praise. My own relationship with the church during these seven years has been very close. I have held for them one meeting. I have been with them on every occasion when money was to be raised for debt or building. I have been asked for counsel and advice at all times, and the O. C. M. S. during the seven years paid $2,700 for pastor's support; but all of this effort has paid and paid abundantly and the result is indeed a great victory for Christ and his church in Springfield.　　　　S. H. BARTLETT.

Cleveland, O.

Something in the Interest of Bethany Assembly.

In 1849 the Indiana Missionary Society was organized. In 1863 the Ministerial Association was organized and L. L. Carpenter is the only surviving charter member. In 1868 the Indiana Sunday-school Association was organized at Wabash, and eight years later the C. W. B. M. came into existence. These different organizations held great conventions, sometimes exceeding 1,000 delegates. These proved to be a great burden on the churches entertaining and in 1881 and 1882 Island Park Assembly Grounds were used as a meeting place. At the last gathering Bethany Assembly was organized. This association bought the present grounds in the winter of 1882-1883, and during the spring of 1883 the hotel tabernacle, lake and some cottages were constructed, and in the summer of that year the first assembly was held, at which time the different state organizations held their conventions.

To-day Bethany Assembly and all that it stands for is close to the hearts of those who are most interested in the cause in Indiana. This is

shown by the increase in attendance and by the many words of appreciation which we hear on every hand. The grounds have been improved from year to year, there being some splendid improvements made last year. As it now stands the assembly is out of debt, and property valued at $50,000 is the result of twenty-three years' work. Many improvements will be made this next year. The entire park has been replatted, and the plat will be recorded as prescribed by law. Many new lots are now for sale, the best on the ground. Many have been sold recently. The year 1908 will be the silver anniversary of Bethany Assembly and we suggest that we keep abreast of the spirit of the times and celebrate it. Now is the time to begin our plans for this purpose. Committees should and will be appointed in a few days. Let the aim be increase of capitalization with large amount of stock sold; new cottages in large numbers; and last and most important, a substantial endowment to insure the Bible conference and summer schools now contemplated for next year to become permanent features of the assembly. These things are plausible and a steady pull by all means that they will be accomplished.　　　　W. E. M. HACKLEMAN,
Secretary of Bethany Assembly.
Indianapolis, Ind.

Ministerial Exchange.

Congregations near Kansas City wanting preaching can address T. W. Cottingham, Randolph, Mo.

"Miss Maybelle Barrett, a member here, wants work as evangelistic singer. She has a strong, beautiful voice, is able to lead a choir or do solo work. Fine personal worker. Churches would do well to give her a trial."—W. D. Trumbull, pastor, Meadville, Pa.

Mr. and Mrs. W. D. Trumbull, evangelist and singer, Meadville, Pa., are now ready for work anywhere. They still have March and February open.

J. S. Clements, Lees Summit, Mo., will be free Jan. 1 to take work, either as pastor or to engage in meetings.

E. T. Davis, 2634 Myrtle street, Kansas City, Mo., can preach one-half time for some church not too far from Kansas City next year, beginning Jan. 1.

Miss Mabel Ridenour, daughter of V. E. Ridenour, is now engaged in a meeting assisting Duncan and MacFarlane at Thayer, Kan. For terms address her at Topeka, Kan.

A preacher is wanted to take charge of four churches in Georgia. Two of these are in small towns and the other two in the country. They want a single man, want him to begin work Jan. 1, if possible, and will pay about $400. Write Dr. T. L. Harris, Wrightsville, Ga., or C. D. Shelnutt, Sandersville, Ga.

The services of J. Ross Miller, singer and helper, of Milroy, Ind., can be obtained for meetings in January.

Evangelist J. H. Beard, 216 East Mark street, Marion, O., is ready for meetings in any part of the country. He has an open date for January.

F. B. Elmore is ready to close his work at Sweet Springs, Mo., and invites correspondence with any congregation seeking a pastor or an evangelist for next year.

Any church desiring the services of a first-class lady preacher can secure the same by addressing Minister, care of William Belton, Waukomis, Okla.

F. M. O'Neal, 840 West Florida street, Springfield, Mo., can be engaged now as song leader for meetings in February, March and April.

Miss Mayme Eisenbarger, Gospel singer, of Bethany, Mo., has an open date for January, 1907.

W. W. Harris, New Holland, O., can hold a meeting after the holidays. Will furnish his own tracts and preach chart sermons if desired.

Owing to a change of dates Charles E. McVay, song evangelist, Benkelman, Neb., can sing in a meeting in February.

Niatzae and Peru, Kan., need a minister.

"Will some wide-awake young man who will preach for two churches for a fair salary, and knows how to preach without being unkind to other religious bodies, please correspond with J. M. Lowe, evangelist, Savonburgh, Kan."

Edward Clutter, president of Ministerial Association, Bethany, Neb., can put churches in too miles of Lincoln in touch with experienced preachers for Sunday supply work.

Petersburg and Bullitsville, Ky., two adjacent towns, 25 miles from Cincinnati, wish to locate with them a good preacher at a good salary. Address John Berkshire, Petersburg; Thomas Willis, Bullitsville.

"Correspondence solicited with any young man who wishes to study for the ministry, in a classical course, and to work his way. Also, with any young woman looking toward missionary or pastoral work, and willing to work her way through college." Address President Dexter Christian College, Dexter, Mo.

The church at Lyons, Kan., wants a good, live preacher for a good, live church. It has about 400 members, 310 enrolled in Sunday-school, a new house of worship and everything in first-class shape. Good salary to the right man.

The church at Tuxedo Park, a suburb of St. Louis, wants a pastor for full time, January 1. Can pay $600 with parsonage. Young married man preferred. Good field, united church, convenient to public libraries, city preachers' meeting, etc. Address Charles H. Brown, 400 South Fourth street, St. Louis, Mo.

"State, district or county boards or churches wanting tabernacle meetings will write me at 943 Clinton avenue, Carthage, Mo. I have an open date for a February meeting. I will have associated with me a first-class singing evangelist and will be ready for work, north or south, as soon as the weather will permit."—S. J. Vance, evangelist.

"Churches, pastors, or evangelists needing a singer and all round helper may find in Ernest E. Bilby, of Frankton, Ind., what they desire. He is the possessor of a deep bass voice and is consecrated in his work."—H. K. Shields.

The churches at Havensville and Soldier, Kan., will want some one to take charge of the work the first of the year. T. J. Richardson, Havensville, Kan., would like to correspond with a good man who is willing to take the work at a salary of $650 for the coming year.

❊ ❊ ❊

We will send you the Campbell Library, by prepaid express, $8.00.

CHRISTIAN PUBLISHING CO.,
St. Louis, Mo.

As We Go to Press.

Special to THE CHRISTIAN-EVANGELIST.

Indianapolis, Ind., Dec. 16.—Eighty-one added to Third Church to-day—65 at last invitation; 760 to date. Closing reception Tuesday night. This is the greatest large city meeting and the second largest meeting of the brotherhood. Scoville addressed big Y. M. C. A. meeting of 2149 men at English opera house. Scores stood for Christ not counted above. He has had $112 during 1906.— C. B. Newnan, pastor.

Special to THE CHRISTIAN-EVANGELIST.

Litchfield, Ill., Dec. 17.—Dedicated church seating 1,000 people here yesterday. More than enough money raised. M. S. Johnson is the minister.—J. Fred Jones, Cor. Sec., of Illinois.

Special to THE CHRISTIAN-EVANGELIST.

Lahoma, Okla., Dec. 16.—Sixty-three additions to date, nine last night. The previous membership was forty-five; town population 350.—Tabor and McKinney.

Special to THE CHRISTIAN-EVANGELIST.

Eureka, Ill., Dec. 16.—In six days sixty-five additions—over fifty confessions and many grown young men. A. W. Taylor is in his fifth year as pastor of this splendid church.—Brooks Brothers.

Special to THE CHRISTIAN-EVANGELIST.

Wauseon, O., Dec. 17.—One hundred and nineteen in three weeks. C. R.

Oakley is the beloved pastor. Buchanan and Gardner, evangelists.

Special to THE CHRISTIAN-EVANGELIST.

Nevada, Mo., Dec. 16.—One hundred and thirty-one additions here; great crowds; we continue a few days. W. W. Burks is pastor.—R. R. Hamlin and L. Daugherty, evangelists.

Special to THE CHRISTIAN-EVANGELIST.

Lorain, O., Dec. 16.—Closed Ohio meetings with 340 additions; Minerva, 114; Lorain, 104; Sebring, 122. Greenville, Ill., next—E. E. Violett.

Special to THE CHRISTIAN-EVANGELIST.

Kansas City, Mo., Dec. 16.—Thirty-five to-night, 172 in four weeks; greatest meeting in the history of Forest Ave. church. Wilhite and Tuckerman are the evangelists.—J. L. Thompson, pastor.

Special to THE CHRISTIAN-EVANGELIST.

Ft. Smith, Ark., Dec. 17.—Closed with 80 additions. Rained out last two days.—E. T. Edmonds, pastor; Roger H. Fife, evangelist.

Special to THE CHRISTIAN-EVANGELIST.

Harrisville, N. Y., Dec. 17.—Great meeting; thirteen confessions yesterday. Evangelist W. D. Trumbull and wife efficient workers.—A. Hay Owens, minister.

Special to THE CHRISTIAN-EVANGELIST.

Barnesville, O., Dec. 17.—Fifty additions in fifteen nights. Clarence Mitchell, evangelist, Arthur Haley, singer. Great interest—Hugh Wayt, minister.

NEWS FROM MANY FIELDS

Nebraska.

Wilber has been repairing its church building. They are looking forward to a meeting with State Evangelist Whiston.——At Ashland there have been 22 added by baptism and five by letter and statement during the current year.——J. K. Simpson gives half time each to Eddyville and Riverdale. The church building at Riverdale is being repaired.——Samuel Gregg is now located at Fremont.——District No. 8 held a meeting of its ministerial association at Oxford. This district, with few preachers and far apart, is the only one that supports such an association. W. E. Rambo is president and J. G. Slick secretary.——J. W. Sapp, minister at Shubert, is in a meeting.——The Broken Bow church, L. N. Early, minister, is preparing to build a $4,000 church on a lot recently purchased.——A new singing evangelist has taken up her residence with C. F. Martin, of Overton. No outside engagements accented for the present.——Six additions to the Grand Island Church where J. R. McIntire ministers. That church has paid off its outstanding obligations and repaired the furnaces.—— There were three baptisms at Davis City recently. Lee Furgeson is the preacher.——Falls City is repairing its house to the extent of $400. T. A. Lindenmeyer is the minister.——Edison Church is waiting for the seats for its new church. T. S. Miller is the minister. Brother Miller held a meeting at Bloomington, where G. C. Johnson preaches, with 41 additions.——I. C. Swan, missionary of the state society at North Platte, held a short meeting there with home forces, resulting in six baptisms and one added by statement. The B. & M. railroad has surveyed its new line directly through the new church. Whether the company means to stop its trains there for much needed religious refreshment or not, does not appear. It probably means a new location for our people there.—— S. A. Kopp held a short meeting at Gross recently. There were 12 baptisms. Nine united at Cross and two at Pleasantview church not far from Gross.——W. R. Burbridge, of Danbury, will assist Mrs. Clara Hazelrigg in a meeting at Lenora, Kan. Brother Burbridge is ready to preach for some church in Nebraska.——The meeting at Firth, N. T. Harmon, evangelist, and Jean Cobbey, regular supply, with Brother Troxel as singer, has developed a deep interest. Sixteen additions and the meeting is still in progress at this writing. The church itself has been revived. ——A meeting at Fairview Church, where J. W. Walker ministers, resulted in a considerable increase. Brother Walker also preaches at Miller where the church is growing into usefulness again.——A. L. Ogden is assisting C. F. Martin in a meeting at Overton. F. W. Emerson is engaged in the national reform work. The corresponding secretary spent December 2 at Mason City, where Evangelist Adams recently organized a new congregation. Two very good audiences gathered in a very poor hall. The church is seeking lots on which to build. Brother Adams is highly thought of in that little town.——State Evangelist Whiston closed his meeting at Guiderock with 18 added. The church was just in much better working order. George Aydelotte is supplying there. Brother Whiston is in an independent meeting at Humboldt, where Bert Wilson is the minister. The meeting is still going on and a number of additions have resulted. Brother Wilson will hold his next meeting for the board at Murray, where L. P. Bush is regularly supplying.——The Humboldt Church is seeking to persuade Evangelist Forell to remain with them.—— Evangelist Forell closed the Alliance meeting after five weeks of hard labor; 29 added, and a lot purchased at $1,000 and the money raised to pay for it. The members have sent in a very glowing letter regarding Brother Forell's work. He is now at Scottsbluff, where D. A. Youtzy

and R. A. Given had already begun a meeting.—— Evangelist Adams is now at Liberty Church in Custer county. Miss Josephine Poynter is leading the singing. The house is crowded, and there were 19 added the first eight days. Brother Adams goes next to Louisville.——H. C. Foxton has located at Rising City. He has moved there and will give full time to the work at the present. H. Maxwell Hall has taken supply work at Palmer for half time. Was at Vesta December 9. W. M. Reese preached at Hebron on December 2. W. L. Harris is temporarily at home from his evangelistic work and could supply for some church.——T. C. McIntire is in a meeting with his home church at Ansley. J. E. Lintt is leading the music. W. A. BALDWIN.

Southern California and Arizona.

Arizona must be evangelized! It is a great, rich, undiscovered land to the Disciples. The secretary is out prospecting and found a rich vein of free gold the very first strike. It is at The Needles on the boundary between California and Arizona. It is 310 miles from Los Angeles and a twelve-hour run on the Santa Fe overland. To the tourist it is but a little oasis in a great desert, being one of the celebrated Fred Harvey dining stations. I was surprised to find it a thriving city of 2,500 inhabitants. It is an important division point on the Santa Fe system. A $65,000 social and amusement hall for employes is just being finished. A new $50,000 station is in project. Six hundred Americans are employed here by the railroad, not to mention the Mexicans, Indians and Japanese. Many mines are located in this vicinity and enough ore is shipped here to keep a smelter busy. I found as many Disciples in the town as representatives of any other Protestant body. Considering their loyalty, ability and influence, they would make the strongest moral and religious factor in all this great section, if organized into a church and equipped with pastor and building. Men and their families, holding positions of trust and responsibility, such as the chief dispatcher, section master, conductors and clerks, belong to "that despised and first called Christians at Antioch." Nearly a year ago Mrs. Mattie Woolery, the C. W. B. M. organizer, came here and organized the faithful women into an auxiliary. They have more than twenty members and recently had an open meeting, which even the Catholic priest did himself the honor of attending and giving expression to his good wishes for their moral and spiritual worth to the community. It is not a question of organizing a new church in "an overchurched town;" it is a question of maintaining a church already there. The church entered The Needles when these Disciples, by the providence of God were led there. Their duty, and ours, in the matter is plain. And so I told them when the honor and opportunity of preaching the first sermons ever proclaimed in the region round about from the point of view of one who is "simply and only a Christian," fell to me. They were promised a protracted meeting in January and if faith, courage and loyalty can do it, regular Lord's-day services will be maintained thereafter.

The secretary continues his prospecting tour in Arizona. For one who had scarcely seen frost for seven years, and with the scent of roses and orange blossoms still clinging to his garments, to be dropped suddenly from a Santa Fe overland in the middle of the night on a lonely mountainside, miles and miles from anywhere, and into snow eighteen inches deep, with the thermometer eight degrees below zero, is a hard experience. But here in a cozy "box-car Pullman" lives one of our preachers. While he regales his spent energies on the pine-flavored ozone of Arizona, he serves the Santa Fe as its faithful sentinel on this lonely mountain side. One is surprised what a neat and comfortable home a box car makes, when presided over by a Christian woman. J. Welborn Rose and wife know more about conditions and the Disciples in Arizona than any

one else in the great territory, and the work is under many obligations to him for information and helpful suggestions.——A possible half dozen "scattered Disciples" can be found at Flagstaff, but conditions are not such as to warrant any organized effort just now. Flagstaff is a little city of 1,500 people, made important by its railroad, normal school and sawmill. Like all these cities, it is as wicked as hell, and in it the way that leadeth to destruction is broad, and wide the gate. In such a community the Disciples who in some way align themselves with the Christian forces already established, certainly do right.—— A day was profitably spent in the beautiful little city of Prescott. This is a distributing center for a great mining district. It is the home of 5,000 American citizens. This "city a mile high" is coming to enjoy a good reputation on account of its good climate. Having no other source of information, the pastor of the largest Protestant church was called upon. He supposed there were as many as twenty "Christians" who had become identified with his church. He gave me to understand that the town was already "overchurched" and somewhat nervously inquired as to the object of my visit. By his courtesy I "got scent" of "fresh tracks" of my "game," and in the course of the afternoon I had "bagged" several choice specimens of the germ "Christian only." The county superintendent of schools and wife are of the good old Kentucky brand of Disciples; the leading physician and his wife, and her

father and mother; the assistant cashier of the bank and his wife; the bookkeeper of a great retail and wholesale firm; the head of an assay office and mining engineer, family of merchant and others might be named. While these people wish for a church of their own faith and order, they hesitate to Venture, and are even becoming inoculated with the notion that the town is already "overchurched." Now such a condition is possible, but the impression a stranger gets is decidedly otherwise. The town is under-churched and over-salooned. The fact is that the very conditions existing at Prescott are the grounds that warrant the Disciples entering the field. When four weak, ineffective Protestant organizations can scarcely maintain themselves in a community of 5,000 Americans, it shows something radically faulty with the position, method, or spirit of the church. What is coming to be recognized as the fundamental weakness of Protestantism is to be observed as under microscope in a western town. When will God's church learn that to maintain rival denominations, or seek to group the Lord's disciples about any other principle or name than faith in and loyalty to him is an act of treason to the kingdom? Scarcely a conversion is reported from the churches of Prescott this year. This of itself would justify the Disciples in entering the town. The churches already there need the leavening power of our presence to inspire them with the spirit of burning loyalty to Christ and zealous evangelism for souls. With a good evangelist for a lever, with the following we already have there as a fulcrum, the Disciples can move mightily the un-churched multitudes in Prescott.

Arizona must be evangelized.

GRANT K. LEWIS,

Tempe, Aris.   Secretary.

Texas.

The late lectureship, held at Palestine, November 19-23, was one of the most delightful ever held in Texas. For harmony and good fellowship, it was complete. The papers given were all of very high order. Dr. Hall Calhoun, of Kentucky University, was the chief lecturer. He is scholarly, a very fine speaker. I mean by that he is distinct in his enunciation, clearly understood by all and, without trimmings and trappings, tells in a modest way of the subjects to which he has given deep thought and careful research. While announcing himself as conservative, we found him broad-minded, sweet-spirited, and giving evidence that he understood that there is more beyond. Dr. Clinton Lockhart's address on "Evangelism" was perhaps the most eloquent. Ellsworth Faris gave us a very thoughtful address on the "Immanence of God." This address brought out some discussion, but all in the best spirit. J. B. Holmes, of Beaumont, gave us a strong and timely address on the subject of the "Divorce Evil." This address should indeed have a wide reading. A. E. Dubber, of Fort Worth, gave us a tender address on the "Risen Life." But time will forbid my mentioning each of the addresses. Not one fell below a high average. The next lectureship goes to Abilene, the geographical center of Texas. It was a pleasure to the writer to meet with and preach to these brethren on the Sunday preceding the lectureship, since Palestine was the last church I served as pastor. L. D. Anderson, the present minister, is doing an excellent work there, and is popular with the entire city. The brethren have recently completed the best church building in Palestine, and the outlook they have is very bright, indeed.

W. A. Boggess, one of our state evangelists, is in a fine meeting at Huntsville, with Mrs. M. R. Cox as singing evangelist. Some 25 persons have been added and the "end is not yet." Spicer and Douthitt are aiding T. F. Weaver at Port Arthur in a missionary meeting. Some 30 addi-

tions have been reported and it is believed that within a few months this new church, in an important and growing city, will dwell in its own house and become self-sustaining.

Our summer and fall campaign, as will be noted by our semi-annual report, has been the most successful ever made in Texas. More churches have responded to the November offering than ever before in this state, the receipts up to December 7 being fully 25 per cent above that of any prior November offering. Texas is receiving some excellent men from other states; one of the latest is W. J. Battenfield, of Illinois, who locates with the church at Beeville. A. J. Chowning, of Oklahoma, will probably locate at Blooming Grove. J. J. Morgan, of Kansas City, is with the First Church at Fort Worth. Charles Lockhart is leading the Central at Waco, W. R. Montgomery is at Belton, W. H. Winters at Orange, Brother Horne at Midland. S. W. Jackson is the Panhandle district evangelist and William Monday is at work as the Northwest Texas evangelist. There are still others whose names do not occur to me just now, but we are receiving a number of first-class men. We need still others, but they must be men who can work for $50 to $75 per month, and who will be willing to serve two or more churches. Let any one applying for work write me with the first letter about the amount of salary he can work for, whether or not he is willing to take more than one church, and send commendation from your home church and state secretary. To observe these rules will save unnecessary correspondence.

J. C. MASON.

Report of J. C. Mason, corresponding secretary to the Texas Christian Mission Board, six months' work, June 1 to November 30, 1906: Men employed, 35; days, 3,662; sermons, 2,207; baptisms, 853; by letter and statement, 534; from the denominations, 71; net gain, 924; total additions, 1,458; cash raised by and for Texas missionary support, $9,966.03; cash for all, purposes, $17,476.65; pledges, $9,143.65; places visited, 313; churches organized, 18; houses built, 4; "Texas missions," 103.

Report of the personal work of J. C. Mason, June 1 to November 30, six months: Total days, 184; sermons and addresses, 79; baptisms, 7; by letter, 22; net gain, 71; total additions, 29; cash raised in the field, $1,038.55; total cash raised, $3,768.12; pledges, $2,457; places visited, 23; "Texas missions," 63; Sunday-schools organized, 2; church, 1.

Denver, Colo.

The Central, the mother church of Denver and Colorado, is now a downtown church and only a block from the Brown Palace Hotel. The new $250,000 Y. M. C. A. building is in process of construction just across the street. Our auditorium is one of the most attractive in the city and our music and order of services in harmony with Christian devotion and culture. The church is renewing its youth. In the past two years the Bible school has grown from 150 to 400. A class of young people of both sexes enrolls 150. There are no other classes to match these in Colorado.

——We start a simultaneous evangelistic campaign January 6. All our churches are doing well. No man in the city is more popular and beloved than B. B. Tyler. J. E. Pickett has done heroic work in North Denver. The Berkeley church plans continued progress when their new pastor comes. Brother Haston is bringing the East Side church into line.——The love that Mrs. Craig had everywhere elicited has manifested itself in every gracious way. Love inspires to right words and deeds. Her memory is inspiring us all to greater Christian devotion and service. I am grateful to the host of friends who have written in loving sympathy. Christian faith is sustained and comforted beyond the power of words to tell. The motive and inclination inciting to Christian preaching and work are stronger than ever, but loneliness oppresses. I began this work in Denver twenty-five years ago and the result, while not what it might be, is cause for thanksgiving. Our aim is to have Denver share in the great victories in city work. We have recently reorganized a Denver union of our churches on Kansas City lines.   WM. BAYARD CRAIG.

A New Church at Helena, Ark.

My wife and I are just now returning to Louisiana from Helena, Ark., where we closed a short meeting, resulting in the organization of a new church, and the buying of a lot for $1,050 cash. Helena is a town of 10,000 people, 3,000 being whites. Helena is at the upper edge of the greatest hard wood country now known to me. When the hard wood is removed this region will be as fertile as any section of the Mississippi swamp. Traveling over the "Vinegar Central" railroad just built through this vast undeveloped region we went eighty-two miles without passing a town with more than one store in it. Helena lies at the upper end of this vast region of undeveloped wealth. It is to be a great river city. Edgar Graham, of Louisville, Ky., moved to Helena about two years ago and began to hold communion services with whoever would come out in a justice of the peace's office. He finally wrote to W. J. Wright and Brother Wright sent us from Louisiana up to Helena and told us to do what we could in the short time we had to work and the A. C. M. S. would stand for half the expense. We could only get an upstairs hall at first, and after that an old store down stairs for our services. We organized, secured the best available lot, and prepared for a meeting next May which will be called the "house building meeting."　　　JOHN A. STEVENS,
　　　　　　　　　　　　　　　Cor. Sec.

❀ ❀

Virginia.

Minor J. Ross, a Virginian by birth, a graduate of Milligan College, and also of the college of the Bible, Lexington, Ky., who has preached acceptably in Kentucky for some years, begins work in the Harrisonburg, Va., field the second Sunday of 1907.——H. D. Coffey, in the employment of V. C. M. S., has held a meeting in East Bristol, organizing a new congregation with 120 members, only 19 of whom had been members of the first church, Bristol; 25 others made the confession, some of whom will unite with this congregation.——The enlarged house at Manchester has been opened, the dedication to be in January.——The new church at Blackstone is at last ready; the present need is a preacher for this good field.——The Roanoke congregation has just purchased a church property in the northwest unchurched section of the city, where there is promise of rapid growth for this third church.——The new building at Petersburg, seating 500 people was formally opened for service December 2.
　　　　　　　　　　　　　　　H. C. COMBS,
　　　　　　　　　　　Fin. Sec. V. C. M. S.

❀ ❀

A New Building in the Philippines.

Yesterday, September 9, we dedicated the chapel built in Laoag, Philippines, by the Foreign Christian Missionary Society. A storm rendered it impossible for the missionary in Vigan, Hermon P. Williams, to be present and deliver the Spanish sermon. Three successful meetings were held. In the morning more than five hundred persons were present, among whom were provincial and municipal officials, members of the bar and priests of the Aglipayano church. Good attention was given to the discourse preached in Ilocano by W. H. Hanna on "The Uses of a Chapel." Many remained for the Lord's supper and witnessed for the first time that which has been altered into a sacrifice for the sins of the living and dead by the Romish church.

In spite of the rain which came at the hour of the afternoon service the seats were well filled by American teachers, pupils of the high school and intermediate school and residents of Laoag. Dr. C. L. Pickett preached a fine sermon on "Christ, the Centre." Brother Will Jessup, of the auditing department of the Philippines, assisted at the service.

At night the Stygian darkness did not keep the people away. Three native preachers delivered short addresses and your reporter let down the Gospel net. Three men made confession—a Spaniard, a native opium-smoker and an old man. Two of these were baptized the same hour of the night. So a glorious close was given to the inauguration day. Mrs. Hanna presided at the organ and Mrs. Pickett assisted in special music. Dr. Pickett's Bible school class of high school boys sang "Wonderful Story of Love."

The chapel is neatly and substantially built of Oregon pine, rests on posts of molave, has a tower, dressing-rooms and baptistry, galvanized iron roof and is painted in two shades of green. The sides are wainscoted and the ceiling and walls are lined with woven bamboo or *swali*. The principal timbers have been painted with a preparation called carbolineum, so they will not become a prey to white ants, which are almost the supreme pest of our province. The building is much admired by all who enter or pass by, and is accepted by the Ilocanos as an evidence that American Christians love them and have a deep interest in their eternal welfare. We are hopeful that with the opening of this chapel will come enlargement of the missionary interests in all our province. The native congregation purchased (with some outside help) a fine twenty-eight-inch bell to call people to worship. The members have very small possessions and are strangers to free-will giving for religious purposes, but this example of American liberality will surely inspire them to assist the congregations in nearby towns in the erection of houses of worship.
Laoag, Philippines.　　　　W. H. HANNA.

❀ ❀

Oriental Missions.

(Pacific Coast.)

San Francisco.—Dr. L. H. Dott, a Chinese medical graduate of seven years' standing, has been engaged to take charge of the medical work here. At first he will practice in Oakland, just across the bay, where most—some 12,000—of the Chinese now reside. He will thus establish our reputation and make friends. Later he will work in the hospital in San Francisco. Great difficulty is being experienced in securing the lot for the hospital, largely on account of high prices. We need $5,000 more than we have. Would that some good brother or sister might supply this amount to the C. W. B. M. There is a great future for the medical work among the Chinese and Japanese. It is a crying need. It will be blessed.

Berkeley.—The Japanese night school is flourishing. The volunteer corps of teachers is doing a truly missionary work and deserve all praise. The Japanese have made formal application to our board to take over all forms of work among them. This is an unusual opportunity, and ought to be embraced.

Portland and Los Angeles.—Plans are being laid in both these cities for an enlarged work among Chinese and Japanese. It may take the form of medical ministrations, and associated evangelistic and educational efforts.

Lectures.—A course of lectures on Missions is being given to the students of the seminaries in Berkeley.

Addresses.—At least six "C. W. B. M. Day" addresses will be given this year. Richmond and Sacramento have already been visited. The churches at Berkeley and Oakland will be addressed next Lord's day, and Santa Rosa and Napa, later.　　　　W. P. BENTLEY.
Berkeley, Cal.

SCHOOLS AND COLLEGES.

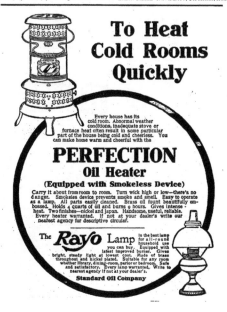

Our Only Church in Utah.

Salt Lake is a beautiful city, and destined in this respect to be the Washington of the West. Mormonism has reached its zenith, and is now about 3 o'clock toward sunset. Non-Mormons control the city, and will soon dominate the county, and could now, if they would agree. The writer has been supplying the pulpit of the Central Christian Church for six months, and found one of the very best churches of over 200 members in the brotherhood. In church attendance, liberality, loyalty to the minister, zeal and good Christian sense, they are as good as anybody I know of. There have been additions nearly every Sunday. They keep up their finances well, the church has all the modern conveniences. That valuable and good man, B. F. Clay, and his wife deserve great praise for this organization and building. The church has had men of ability from the first—the zealous W. H. Bagby, eloquent T. H. Pinkerton and the consecrated W. M. Taylor, the latter for only five months. I must be leaving soon. I only promised to stay three months, but their kind entreaties have kept me. They are looking for the right preacher, but have not found him yet. Inquiries should address J. C. Campbell, Monarch Hardware Co., Salt Lake City. It is no harder for us to work and get fine results here than anywhere else. A strong, able, energetic preacher is the need, a good man, full of the Holy Spirit and wisdom will find here one of the greatest and most inviting fields in the United States.

W. ROSS LLOYD.

[Since writing the above Brother Lloyd has gone to Lexington, Ky. We presume the pulpit is still open, as we have had no further advice.—EDITOR.]

India Notes.

Brother Wharton and his wife came to India in the year 1882, in company with Albert Norton, and Misses Graybiel, Kinsey, Boyd and Kingsbury. Of this group Brother Wharton is the first to pass from this life. Mr. Norton is now in another mission, but at the time of writing none of the others named are in India. Miss Kingsbury is expected on the 16th of this month, Misses Boyd and Graybiel are on furlough at home, Mrs. Wharton is with her children at home, and Miss Kinsey, now Mrs. Mitchell, is also in America. The party of missionaries first went to Harda in 1883. From that time until his return to America in 1899, with the exception of a short time spent in Bilaspur, Brother Wharton's missionary home was Harda. While never strong since his return to the field in 1904, he entered into all the work and its plans and expressed great regret when it was impossible to do what he wanted to do. The one work which was upon Brother Wharton's heart more than any other was the Bible college for the preparation of preachers. He began a work of this kind before he went to America in 1899. Before returning in 1904 he canvassed the country for funds for this work. Thousands will remember his speeches in behalf of this work. Since his return he has been connected with it at Jubbulpore.

Another of our missionaries, Dr. Anna Gordon, of Mungeli, is seriously ill. She was attacked with what was pronounced appendicitis in its acute form. Though there was no doctor within thirty miles she passed through the crisis, but an operation was decided upon. She has since gone to Bombay for that purpose, but the results are not yet known.

Several others have been ill. Brother Davis, of Bilaspur, has been having a hard time with fever. So have Misses Pope and Drake. Miss Mills has had a severe attack of measles. Having had the disease once before she was considered immune, but the measles of India is no respecter of immunes and frequently attacks for a second or even a third time.

There have lately been four baptisms in Harda and three in Ruth. Most of these—five I think—were converts from heathenism. We have just had a joint convention of Christian Endeavor, Sunday-school and Epworth League workers in Jubbulpore. Our mission is the most prominent in the central provinces in the first two lines of work. It was all held in the vernacular. About 100 native brothers and sisters were present at the mission. They were profitable to all present. Seventeen boys walked over from Damoh, representing that society, preaching the gospel in the

villages along the route of 266 miles, and camping at night along the roadside.

Our Bible college has now twenty-one students in it. The new building is being erected, and it is hoped to dedicate it in March. What friend of missions wishes to be present at the dedication? Send your name and we shall be most happy to entertain you. GEO. V. BROWN.

Jubbulpore, India.

South Dakota.

Though there is but little from the Dakotas in the papers, there is a number of quiet, consecrated workers whose work shall come to light in the future. We get some help from the American Christian Missionary Society and some from the National C. W. B. M. We hope to have a state evangelist at work soon. He will devote some time in North Dakota since the A. C. M. S. has made a small appropriation to be used in that state under the direction of our South Dakota board.——Ellendale, N. D., is the only field in that state where a pastor is located and a small amount of assistance will be rendered there. Fargo, Mandan, Gladstone and other points need help and encouragement. Calls are coming in daily from all over South Dakota for meetings and assistance in pastoral support. It is doubtful if the Disciples throughout the country have yet realized the open door in the Dakotas—the vast extent and developing wealth of the country. It would be almost impossible to plant a sectarian type of Disciples in this soil for they have not so much as heard whether there be such a thing as anti-ism, to say nothing of a much worse thing—a standard of orthodoxy set up in an editorial sanctum. Men of faith and vision should come this way, not to defend the faith or word, but to preach the Gospel of life.

THE CHRISTIAN-EVANGELIST, like old wine, grows richer with age and may God use her Editors many years to come. Other national papers come, too, and we love them all, like we do our boys who sometimes scrap in the church yard. A redeeming feature is, that our people generally read only those pointed briefs which concern the progress of the kingdom and care but little as to the length of beard requisite to the eldership.

The church at Sioux Falls burned their mortgage on November 17 and the writer regrets that he could not be there to speak as expected.—— The church at Carthage where J. H. Reeves labors, will dedicate their new house of worship within a few weeks. The church at Presho is also building. Since locating at Aberdeen, April 1, there have been some improvements. A new parsonage with modern equipments has been

built and every dollar subscribed paid. Some improvements have been made on the church property in way of furnace, etc. Within the past few weeks five have been added by letter and others coming. The work is difficult, but our people are liberal and those who work at all are faithful. Aberdeen now has nine departures by rail and the building enterprise has not yet closed for winter. To-day at our ministerial association Rev. C. Knoll, who was a student under Professor Harnack at Berlin, gave a paper on the noted scholar. F. B. SAPP,

Aberdeen, S. D. Cor. Sec.

OBITUARIES.

[Notices of Deaths, not more than four lines, inserted free. Obituary memoirs, one cent per word. Send the money with the copy.]

WILLIAM FRAZIER

was born in Shelby county, Ky., September 23, 1848. At the age of 9 years he came with his father to Lincoln county, Mo., who settled near New Hope. The most of Elder Frazier's life service has been spent in Lincoln county, except sixteen years in Colusa, Cal., and two years in Iowa. His father died when William was 15 years old and for many years the care of the family fell upon him. He confessed his faith in his divine Lord and Savior under the preaching of Elder Joseph Errett at New Hope and presented himself to Brother Errett for baptism, saying: "See, here is water what doth hinder me to be baptized?" and was "buried with his Lord by baptism," and received into the fellowship of the church at New Hope. Early in his Christian life he was set apart to the office of elder in the Church of Christ and he served the church in that capacity most conscientiously and faithfully. Brother Frazier was united in marriage to Orpha Virginia Cash, nee Brown, on November 16, 1873, and his death occurred on the thirty-third anniversary of this marriage, falling sweetly asleep in Jesus at 3:30 p. m. on November 16, 1906.

The funeral was held in the church of which Brother Frazier was a much beloved elder for many years, on Saturday, November 17, at 2 p. m. The house was full of sympathizing friends. Rev. B. D. Kennedy, pastor of the Troy Presbyterian Church, offered a memorial tribute followed by the pastor of the church, after which a short sermon was preached by the pastor, Elder E. G. Merrill, from Isa. 40:6. The body was then laid to rest in the Troy cemetery.

"Precious in the sight of the Lord is the death of his saints."—E. G. Merrill, pastor of the Christian Church, Troy, Mo.

Evangelistic

We invite ministers, and others to send reports of meetings, additions and other news of the churches. It is especially requested that additions be reported as "by confession and baptism," or "by letter."

California.

Chico, December 9.—Twenty-eight additions since we began work here the middle of last September. Eighteen of these are by statement, seven by letter, three baptisms, one reclaimed and two from another religious body.—G. L. Lobdell, minister.

Lodi, Dec. 7.—R. E. McKnight, of Bakersfield, recently closed a meeting with us resulting in 18 additions—15 by letter and three by confession. Three additions since, two by confession and one by letter.—John Young.

Red Bluff, Dec. 5.—The meeting conducted by S. M. Martin continues with increasing interest. Seventy-four additions to date, nearly all confessions.—George A. Webb.

Colorado.

Boulder, Dec. 15.—Our splendid meeting here about to close. Sixty-four added to date. S. M. Bernard is the pastor.—Evangelist J. Bennett.

Florence, Dec. 11.—Just closed a meeting here with 27 additions, 17 baptisms. Work is in the best shape it has been for years. Meeting held with home forces.—J. W. Babcock.

Georgia.

Fitzgerald, Dec. 14.—Seven additions last Lord's day, to the Central Church. Largest audiences we have ever had. All departments of the work in fine shape.—N. G. Buckley, minister.

Illinois.

Sullivan, Dec. 15.—Have just returned from a ten days' meeting with the church in Patricksburg. The community was stirred and 25 added to the church.—E. W. Brickert.

Sullivan, Dec. 2.—Two additions.—J. G. McNutt.

Camp Point, Dec. 10.—The Jones-Davis meeting closed on account of the bad weather. We had six additions.—H. J. Reynolds.

Mattoon, Dec. 3.—We are in a good meeting with Combs and Wilson as evangelists.

Girard, Dec. 14.—Closed a short meeting at Boston Chapel last Sunday. There were four confessions. Mrs. Schoonover directed the music.—C. M. Schoonover, evangelist.

Freeport, Dec. 15.—Meeting at Waynesville closed last night with a total of 64 additions. The church is entering an era of prosperity under the efficient ministry of J. F. Smith.—J. A. Barnett.

Clinton, Dec. 15.—One accession last Sunday morning. This makes four additions since the first of November.—J. W. Reynolds.

Indiana.

Frankton, Dec. 10.—Thirty-two added in fourteen days. Thirty-one of those baptisms. Great interest manifested. I. N. Grisso, pastor-evangelist.—H. K. Shields.

Middletown, Dec. 14.—Closed here last night. Forty-one additions. Eight by letter and statement, 31 by baptism, and one from another religious body. F. E. Truckness was in charge of the music.—L. E. Murray.

Jerome, Dec. 10.—One addition from another religious body last night—Willis M. Cunningham.

Brazil, Dec. 15.—Three recently added.—E. L. Day.

Terre Haute.—Closed a quiet revival with sixty additions. I. E. Sellers did masterly work in the pulpit and in management of forces. One added by letter was a preacher from another religious organization.—Herbert A. Carpenter, assistant.

Indian Territory.

Tulsa, Dec. 13.—Have just closed a ten nights' meeting assisted by George H. Farley, part of the time, with eight additions, making 133 during the past fifteen months of my pastorate.—Randolph Cook.

Chickasha, Dec. 10.—Twelve additions not previously reported. Three congregations. Additions every Sunday since I have been here.—J. E. Dinger, minister.

Iowa.

Des Moines, Dec. 9.—In eight days we have had 18 confessions. We are holding services in the Highland Park College Chapel. W. J. Wright is the evangelist.—Charles E. McVay, song evangelist.

Osceola, Dec. 11.—Two added December 9. Am

preaching to fine congregations.—A. M. Growden.

Keota, Dec. 12.—Brother Davis is holding a glorious revival at our church in Kinross with 40 additions.—Mrs. M. E. Nays.

Kansas.

Niataze.—Closed a short meeting at Niataze Sunday night. All things considered, we had a very successful meeting. We had eight additions and closed with a growing interest.—J. P. Haner, evangelist.

Wichita, Dec. 10.—Our meeting at the Central closed with 40 additions. During the four months E. W. Allen has been with us there have been 70 additions.

Osborne, Dec. 10.—Three additions to the church here yesterday. One by confession, one by statement and one from another religious body. Many people attending our services that never entered the church before. Congregation and minister rejoicing.—R. S. Robertson, minister.

Savonburg.—Meeting here growing in interest. Several accessions to date. Meeting at Leona closed November 15. The purpose of the meeting, to unite a sadly divided church, was happily accomplished and converts won.—J. M. Lowe.

Kentucky.

Sebree, Dec. 13.—Began here December 9. Attendance is good and interest fine. Brother Pittman is the preacher here.—Lawrence Wright.

Massachusetts.

Everett, Dec. 8.—One confession and two baptisms this week. J. W. Robbins, evangelist.—A. T. June.

Missouri.

St. Joseph, Dec. 14.—Forty-five additions to date.—Northcutt, Huston and Goode.

Bloomfield, Dec. 13.—Have just closed a meeting at this place. R. H. Lamkin, of Dexter, did the preaching. The church was helped, and one made the good confession.—J. H. Tiller, pastor.

Shelbina, Dec. 11.—Have closed a four weeks' meeting with 47 additions, 26 by baptism, R. E. L. Prunty, of Brookfield, did the preaching for about three weeks. I am in my ninth year preaching for this church.—J. H. Wood, pastor.

Fredericktown, Dec. 11.—Four added Sunday.—R. O. Rogers.

Chillicothe, Dec. 11.—Two confessions last Sunday. Six added the week before.—James N. Crutcher.

Warrensburg, Dec. 11.—Closed a two weeks' meeting last night at Rich Hill, Mo., with 12 additions, all, except one, by confession.—King Stark.

Salem, Dec. 13.—We closed our four weeks' meeting here on the 9th with 26 added—18 by baptism, five by statement, and three by letter. Good crowds and fine interest throughout.—W. T. Walker.

Marshall, Dec. 8.—Five added to church within last two weeks, four by letter and one by baptism.—B. T. Wharton.

Lebanon, Dec. 8.—Meeting closed at Conway with 31 added.—Joseph Gaylor.

Nebraska.

Firth, Dec. 10.—Just closed a very successful meeting here with 18 additions. Besides these the church has been greatly built up and strengthened. N. T. Harmon, evangelist, and D. C. Troxel, singer; Jean A. Cobbey, pastor.

Ohio.

Sullivan, Dec. 11.—Nineteen additions—18 by confession and baptism. C. E. Babcock is the minister.—Charles W. Mahin.

Lucas, Dec. 12.—Meeting at Lucas continues with great interest. Twenty added to date.—Asa Hull, singer; W. P. Murray, pastor.

Bellefontaine, Dec. 10.—Baptized two last night. Work was never in more prosperous condition and outlook is very promising.—Roy L. Brown.

Philippine Islands.

Vigan, Oct. 22.—Since last report 34 have been baptized in Bullagao district.—Hermon P. Williams.

Vigan, Oct. 26.—Fourteen baptisms reported from Cabugao, three from Pilar, one from Bugay and nine from Bongued.—Hermon P. Williams

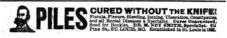

Midweek Prayer-Meeting
December 26, 1906.

The Christmas Group.—Luke 2:1-16.

The Babe of Bethlehem.

"Behold the Child of Promise!
Behold the new-born King!
To-day his glorious advent
Let every creature sing.
Around his manger-cradle
Adoring bend the knee;
For, though his birth is humble,
There's none so great as he.

"He comes to lift the burden
From every soul oppressed;
To heal the broken-hearted,
And give the weary rest;
He comes the world to ransom,
And set its captives free;
He comes, the Lord anointed—
There's none so great as he."

Have we rendered unto the Lord according to all his benefits during the year whose sands are nearly run? In giving unto the poor we are committing unto the Lord that which he will return to us, before another Christmas, in large measures, pressed down and running over.

We never will know the full significance of the Savior's coming until with eyes not of flesh, we behold the appointments of our heavenly home in the Father's house of many mansions. The angels never can know all because subject to limitations from which the sons of God are exempt, but they knew enough to sing joy to all of earth who would be redeemed by the blood of the cross.

The angels sang peace the first Christmas, let us pray and make for peace this Christmastide. It is true Christ has made impossible another "Thirty Years' War," or Napoleonic era, but still kings are more interested in drilling soldiers than husbandmen, and general disarmament can not be secured. Let us help the sentiments of peace among the nations, between religious cults, communities, families, around all hearthstones, and particularly between ourselves and God.

The coming of the wise men to Joseph's humble home was not so much a miracle as an accentuation of the universal quest for God and the instinct guiding men to him. That intuition has impelled millions to pagan fane and temple, the Greeks to an image of "The Unknown God," Socrates to nobler conceptions of God, and "the wise men of the east" to the Savior's cradle. It is impelling the world Godward to-day. This comment must not disparage miracles, but if "the wise men's" coming was "miraculous," the day of miracles is not ended.

Doubts concerning the Nativity do not relate to whether God could introduce the Prince of Glory to the world through Judean peasantry, but to whether he would. If the effect will justify it, God, who controls all causes, will withhold none. If for one hour we look over the brink down into the world of ruin into which the incorrigible have fled from the serene light of heaven and listen to the wailing over wasted opportunities, we will all agree that the coming of the Son of Man would have been justified if only one soul had been saved. Students of human nature will tell us that his manner of coming and living was the one best adapted to his accomplishing the work the Father gave him to do.

When Jehovah sought a mother for his holy Child he did not pass Mary by on the other side because she was a poor peasant girl, nor was that estate the reason for her selection. To her was given the highest honor ever conferred on mortal because she was heavenly minded and the noblest

response the world contained to God's overtures for man's return to the original design of the race. And to-day he goes neither to palaces nor cottages in quest of a medium through which to work wonders of grace, but where character is resplendent with the virtues. Station, wealth, heredity and other considerations that the world may highly prize are merely incidental, and not at all determining in the bestowal of divine honors.

Sunday-School
December 30, 1906.

Fourth Quarterly Review.

Memory verse, Psa. 90:12.

Golden Text.—His name shall be called Wonderful, Counselor, the Mighty God, the Everlasting Father, the Prince of Peace.—Isa. 9:6.

The lessons of this quarter cover a period of only a few days, but the most important few days in the history of the world. Beginning on Tuesday of Passion Week, three days before the crucifixion, we trace the course of Jesus in his last days with his disciples, his warnings and blessings and exhortations to them, the last touches in their three years course of training; the last conflicts between the pettiness of scribes and Pharisees and the breadth and depth of the Master's wisdom; the base and cowardly plot of the chief priests and their illegal procedure in carrying it out; the weakness and cowardice of the Roman governor in abdicating in favor of a mob and delivering to death a prisoner whom he had acquitted; the dark hour of the crucifixion; the glad day of the resurrection; and finally the triumphant ending of the Savior's earthly career in the ascension.

The effect of these closing events of the life of Jesus upon the disciples indicates at least one reason why the Christ must die. In no other way than by his death could their minds have been so completely cleared of every thought of a material kingdom. In no other way than by his resurrection could they have gained the assurance that they had a living Lord, still potent in the world though not visible in it, who was the head of a spiritual and eternal kingdom to which they were all heirs. The price, great as it was, was not too much for such a conviction, not only in the minds of the disciples but perpetuated in the world as a transforming power in the lives of men.

❊ ❊

ALL THAT THE FONDEST

Of Fond Mothers Desires for the Alleviation of her Skin-Tortured Baby is to be Found in Warm Baths with Cuticura Soap.

Assisted by Cuticura Ointment, the great Skin Cure. These pure, sweet and gentle curatives afford instant relief, permit rest and sleep, for mother and child, and point to a speedy cure in the most distressing of torturing and disfiguring humors, eczemas, rashes, itchings, and chafings of infants and children, when the usual remedies and even the best physicians fail. Cures made in infancy and childhood are in most cases speedy, permanent, and economical.

Christian Endeavor

By GEO. L. SNIDELY

December 30, 1906.

Carey and Missions In India.—Isa. 54:2,3.

DAILY READINGS.

M. Workers for Missions.	Matt. 28:16-20.
T. Money for Missions.	2 Cor. 9:6-11.
W. Prayer for Missions.	Luke 11:1-4.
T. Missionary Obstacles.	Acts 18:5-11.
F. Missionary Triumphs.	Phil. 1:12-18.
S. Missionary Promises.	Ps. 27:1-9.
S. Topic.	Isa. 54:2,3.

If one is interested in the religious redemption of but a small part of earth, it is evidence of his heavenly inheritance being co-extensive with but a small portion of the eternal ages. God's plans for men and worlds have rather to do with spheres than segments. We must be lovers and Saviors of the whole round world, of which India is a part.

"Now, o'er the waters,
Burns the crimson after glow,
From a hundred temples
Fades the day so slow;
Where the palm tree rises,
Telling of a foreign strand,
Turn our hearts in sorrow
For this stranger land.
India, sad India,
Let the dead years speak no more.
India, sad India,
Open now thy door."

There is a Christian's peace that passeth all understanding that the world can neither give nor take away, but there is also a divine discontent in the breast of true Christians that gives no rest until the utmost is done to make known to those living in benighted regions God, the Father, Holy Spirit, the Comforter, and Jesus, the "friend that sticketh closer than a brother."

While William Carey was apprenticed to a cobbler a fellow workman effected his conversion. The name of his obscure mentor is not now known to man, but it certainly is to the angels, and to him will accrue in heaven no small part of the glory and honor won by his great protege who translated the Bible into twenty-four languages and dialects and gave the Scriptures to 300,000,000 men and women.

Though very poor, William Carey was a great student and mastered Latin, Greek, Hebrew, French and German. In India he finally became professor of Indian languages at Fort William College at Calcutta. His salary was $7,500 per annum. It is said that himself and family lived on $200 a year and gave the rest to missions. One-tenth for missions is more than most of us can bear, but this over-soul rejoiced in the self denial that enabled him to give nine-tenths to far-away evangelization.

In the eighteenth century were born Washington, Franklin, Napoleon and others whose names were pre-eminent in war and statecraft, art and science, but none of them so mightily affected this world and the one to come as has William Carey, the son of a Paulerspury (England) weaver, born August 17, 1761. Through his consecration to the redemption of India, not only has that sad land been lifted up into the sunshine of hope and joy, but inspiration has been given to heroes and martyrs to endue other continents and islands of the sea with the glorious privileges of Christian civilization. His is a name that ought not to die and which the ages will never permit to die, and chanting hosts around the great white throne will blend it in

their ascriptions of praises to Father, Son and Holy Spirit.

One of the goals toward which Carey pressed his way in India was the overthrow of the pagan institution of the "Suttee," which required the incineration of widows on the funeral pyre of their husbands. In 1829 the English government declared all priests and others engaged in this institution should be held guilty of murder. It is said Carey was gowned for his Sunday sermon when the carrier brought him the decree for translation. Recognizing the significance of the manuscript, he removed his ministerial garb and entered immediately upon the work of translation in the hope that his haste might save some from the cruel "Suttee." This was characteristic. Neither considerations of personal ease or established forms or precedents would deter him from doing what he could for the greatest good to the greatest number.

People's Forum

Brother Garrison on Inspiration.

To the Editor of THE CHRISTIAN-EVANGELIST:

Having read with interest and some degree of profit your book entitled "The Holy Spirit," especial attention was given to the chapter on the "Inspiration of the Holy Scriptures;" and I find some questions forcing themselves into my thinking which I am very anxious to set before you.

Before formulating these questions permit me to say that I am disappointed at the attitude you have taken toward the inspiration of the Holy Scriptures. Your treatment is remarkable for a lack of Scripture quotations, and therefore unsupported by the Word of God. You have not set before your readers the Bible facts in the case.

You say the sacred writers distinctly claim inspiration for their writings and you have used the familiar formula, "The word of the Lord came to," to prove that fact. There are others, such as "The Word of the Lord came to Jeremiah," "The Word that the Lord spake against Babylon," and again, "I heard a voice of one that spake unto me, saying, Son of man stand upon thy feet and I will speak unto thee." (Ezek. 1:28 and 2:1.) In the face of these quotations from Jeremiah and Ezekiel, you say, "the prophets were under and simply conscious of a divine impulse moving them to write or speak." You ignore the idea of verbal inspiration of the Scriptures as taught in the formulae quoted, and heartily endorse and promulgate the "dynamic theory" as you are pleased to call it, because you do not know "a single great thinker in the church of to-day who holds the verbal or mechanical theory."

Brother Garrison, in this you may be correct—the verbal theory may be without such advocates, but there are others who do some thinking and can not be satisfied with your disposition of the question. We crave satisfaction on this question of inspiration, and we are anxious to know if the prophets and apostles were any more inspired than Shakespeare, Bacon, Macaulay and others? We may claim these meh had a divine impulse for their messages to the age in which they lived. How can we think without words or intelligible signs? Has the Lord spoken to men by the 'use of intelligible speech? Did he speak to Moses and Israel from Mount Sinai? Did he speak to John the Baptist and

How to Get Rid of Catarrh.

A Simple, Safe, Reliable Way, and it Cost Nothing to Try, Send for i. and See.

Those who suffer from it well know the miseries of catarrh. There is no need of it. Why not get it cured? It can be done. The remedy that does this is the invention of Dr. J. W. Blosser, an eminent Southern doctor and minister, who has for over thirty-two years been identified with the cure of catarrh in all its worst forms.

He will send you, entirely free, enough to satisfy you that it is a real, genuine, "home cure" for catarrh, scratchy throat, stopped up feeling in the nose and throat, that clears out the head, nose, throat and catarrhal headaches, constant spitting, catarrhal deafness, asthma, etc.

His discovery is unlike anything you ever had before. It is not a spray, douche, atomizer, salve, cream or any such thing, but a genuine, tried-and-true cure, so that you can again breathe the free air and sleep without that choking, spitting feeling that all catarrh sufferers have. It saves the wear-and-tear of internal medicines which ruin the stomach. It will heal up the diseased membranes and thus prevent colds, so that you will not be constantly blowing your nose and spitting.

If you have never tried Dr. Blosser's discovery, and want to make a trial of it without cost, send your address to Dr. J. W. Blosser, 475 Walton St., Atlanta, Ga., and a good, free trial treatment and also a beautiful illustrated booklet, "How I Cure Catarrh," will be sent you at once, free, showing you how you can cure yourself privately at home.

Write him immediately.

the disciples at Jordan and on the Mount of Transfiguration and declare, "This is my beloved Son in whom I am well pleased"? Is it not possible for God to speak through men without destroying their individuality? Has he not done so? He surely could do so and violate no law of reason, and these men would not necessarily be considered "mere agents" in the sight of their fellow-men, as they voiced the messages of the Almighty rather than unintelligible impulses. How are we to understand the address of Jesus to the disciples? He tells them, "They shall deliver you up; take no thought how or what ye shall speak, for it shall be given you in that same hour what ye shall say, for it is not ye that speak, but the spirit of your Father which speaks in you." (Matt. 20:19-20.)

Again, how are we to understand the apostles speaking on the day of Pentecost, in languages they had never learned of nations assembled at Jerusalem? Representatives of every nation under heaven at that time were there. More nations were represented than there were apostles, and still they heard them speak, every man in his own tongue in which he was born. The apostles spake the wonderful works of God. Who enabled them so to speak? If the men had nothing more than a divine impulse or sudden feeling, here is a marvelous thing! The Holy Spirit took of the things of Jesus and revealed them unto the apostles and the apostles to the people—a people whose speech they had never learned. The same is true of Cornelius and those who were with him when Peter came to instruct them in the way of life. The twelve Ephesians also, whom Paul baptized and upon whom he laid his hands that they might receive the Holy Ghost, "spake with tongues and prophesied." The Holy Spirit came upon them in a miraculous way and they spake with tongues and glorified God. The miracle was in the speech of the apostles and not in the hearing of the multitude. Paul, in Corinthians, speaks of "the gift of tongues" and "thanked God he spake with tongues more than they all." Is not this more than a divine impulse unexpressed? Again you say (page 39), "The theory, for instance, that has no room for the fact of minor errors in matters of detail and genealogical dates, is too narrow for facts that are well known to every intelligent Bible student." Here, it seems to me, is a positive reflection on the intelligence of all who accept the verbal inspiration of the Scriptures. Is it to be inferred that narrowness and weakness are in the position of those who believe the messages of our Lord came to those who uttered them in well worded and well-rounded sentences? If verbal errors there are and some incorrect genealogical dates, may they not have crept into the text in the work of transcribing the Scriptures? However, these errors, or apparent errors, by no means interfere with the sense and truth of the message and may yet be reasonably accounted for.

Your attempt, by seemingly a very weak argument, to support the so-called "dynamic theory" of inspiration is set forth as follows: "The man who does not see more of the Holy Spirit in the 13th chapter of 1st Corinthians than in a chapter of the imprecatory Psalms is perhaps the unfortunate victim of a theory which prevents him from so doing." Is it reasonable to suppose that inspiration depends upon the degrees of truth revealed? Did it not require as much inspiration for Moses to say, "A prophet shall the Lord your God raise up unto you of your brethren, like unto me, Him shall ye hear in all things," as it did for Isaiah to say, "Unto us a child is born, unto us a son is given, and the government shall be upon his shoulder and his name shall be called, Wonderful, Counsellor, The Mighty God, the Everlasting Father, the Prince of Peace," and also describe his sufferings and death?

You grant that the men who wrote "were to some degree inspired, or under partial control of the Divine Guide, which would assure substantial accuracy of the inspired record and thereby furnish an infallible guide to one seeking the way of salvation." You could not have said much less than this, with any reasonable expectation that your treatment of the subject would find any sympathy and acceptance by your readers. The apostles in many ways were fallible men, and as you teach, "under a partial divine impulse," how can any reasonable man expect infallibility from such a source? How are we to determine that they correctly worded that partial divine impulse or sudden feeling? How do we know that the partial divine impulse was revealed at all? Luke writes to Theophilus that he might know the certainty of those things wherein he had been instructed. The apostles no doubt voiced the mind of God and Christ in the very language of the Holy Spirit.

Dear Brother, there are some things in your treatment of the inspiration of the Holy Scriptures that are hard to be understood which the unlearned may wrest to their own confusion as they do other Scriptures.   R. W. STEVENSON.

[The best reply we could make to the foregoing criticism would be to have our readers turn to the chapter of our work on "The Holy Spirit," entitled "Inspiration of the Holy Scriptures," and give it a careful reading. We could wish that Brother Stevenson might do the same. We append a few remarks:

1. Brother Stevenson complains that we did not quote all the passages claiming inspiration for the Bible. Certainly not. We quoted enough, however, to show that the Scriptures do claim inspiration for themselves. That was the point aimed at.

2. Our critic says "Is it reasonable to suppose that an inspiration depends upon the degree of truth revealed?" It is quite reasonable to suppose that more inspiration was needed for writing the 13th chapter of 1 Corinthians than one of the imprecatory psalms, or some purely historical record. This was our contention, aimed against the dead-level idea of revelation.

3. Our correspondent inadvertently puts into quotation marks statements which we did not make, which is a great injustice to any writer. Thus the words quoted as if from the chapter criticised—"Were to some degree inspired, or under partial control of the divine Guide," e.c.—are not our words, but our critic's. There are other inaccurate quotations.

4. In discarding the mechanical theory of inspiration which holds that the Bible writers were only amanuenses of the Holy Spirit, we distinctly stated: "Nor can any theory of inspiration which has in it no room for occasional direct communications from God of certain facts and words, be considered broad enough for all the facts. For such communications there seem to have been." ("The Holy Spirit," page 40). This statement is completely ignored by the article in which we are asked whether or not certain words were not communicated on certain occasions, as if our view took no note of that fact.

5. Again our critic says: "We are anxious to know if the prophets and apostles were any more inspired than Shakespeare, Bacon, Macaulay, and others?" And this in the face of our statement in the very chapter criticised, as follows: "Nor is that theory broad enough to meet all the facts which limits the degree of inspiration of the Bible writers to that possessed by other men of great talent and genius. There are characteristics about the Scriptures not to be accounted for without the presence of a superhuman agency." ("The Holy Spirit," page 40).

6. Again Brother Stevenson cites passages where the "gift of tongues" is mentioned, as instances where men spoke in languages intelligible to others, which they had never learned. A careful study of the New Testament, especially of 1 Corinthians, the 14th chapter, would show our brother that this is not the meaning of the "gift of tongues," which is speaking in ecstatic language. The case of Pentecost seems different.

7. Finally our brother says, "There are some things in your treatment of the inspiration of the Holy Scriptures that are hard to be understood which the unlearned may wrest to their own confusion as they do other Scriptures." This is not a serious charge, seeing it is one which Peter made against the writings of Paul; but notice that Paul's writings were wrested, that is, distorted from their true meaning, intent, and application, by the unlearned to their own confusion.

The chapter criticised was an effort to emphasize the fact of inspiration, and to vindicate it from certain false theories, which have caused many to reject the fact, and we have had many testimonials of help in this direction from this chapter.—EDITOR.]

A CHRISTMAS GIFT

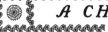

By FRANK H. SWEET

So long the road was up the hill,
Beyond the town, beyond the mill,
That few in summer took that way;
But when the winter snows came down
Upon the hills beyond the town,
None passed the door of Peter Shay.

A low, gray house, whose scanty cheer
Grew scantier with each passing year;
So hard and homely was his lot,
So little had his heart to hold,
His life before its time grew old;
He seemed by all his kind forgot.

Close by the busy village street,
The pastor sat with question meet
Of work to bring the Master gain.
His head was bowed, but not with years;
His eyes but clearer were for tears;
His heart was richer for its pain.

"Show me, dear Lord, a lamb to feed,"
So prayed he, "'tis the shepherd's need;
Or tempted feet that go astray!"
He rose, and led by circumstance,
Went where by providential chance
He heard the name of Peter Shay.

He slept and woke; the Christmas light
Lay in his chamber still and bright;
"Give me," he cried, "a gift, O Christ!
A soul for thy dear love to win
Out of its sorrow and its sin,
A gift of love and joy unpriced!"

The midday found him on the hill,
Where snow untracked lay drear and
chill,
And knocking at the lonely door;
Welcomed with wonder as a guest,
He entered where no feet had pressed
With Christmas message e'er before.

And now what words of Christly cheer
Greeted the unaccustomed ear:
With human sympathy addressed,
The old, sweet story, newly told,
Was sweeter for the dark and cold
That gloomed around the hillside nest.

The stranger passed, but on the air
Lingered the fragrance of his prayer
"As if an angel shook his wings."
So beautiful on hills of God
Are feet that bear through earthly road
Glad tidings of the heavenly things.

The days wore on till spring was brown
Upon the hills beyond the town,
And green in warmer valleys lay;
When in the house of God was seen,
In true right mind and heart I ween,
The form and face of Peter Shay.

Eyes questioned wondering eyes to tell
What hap of change or chance befell
That drew him to the holy place:
But he who led with reverent air
The worshippers in praise and prayer,
Gave thanks for gift of Christly grace.
Waynesboro, Va.

Where Christ was Born.

BY JEAN K. BAIRD.

The First Place.

The night was oppressively hot, even for a Judean night. The breeze had shifted from the direction of the sea, and now came from the rocky desert places of the southeast. But for the most part, the air was still, so still that not a leaf upon the olive trees at the foot of the hills moved. The moon looked like a great cartwheel of silver suspended upon high.

Nathan could not rest within doors. The air was heavy in the sleeping-room. There were so many little bodies to fill up the space in the house. He looked upon his sleeping brothers, Reuben, Levi, Benjamin—a whole half dozen, all bearing the good orthodox names of the Israelites. No drop of the blood of mixed races was in their veins. Nathan was proud that this was so. There was nothing so fine in all this wide world as being a Hebrew—to be the chosen ones of the Lord.

His mind dwelt much on such matters. He was a dreamer. He would sit for hours to listen to the history and legends of his people. The boys of his age jeered at his taking no part in their play or work. His brothers laughed, declaring that Nathan was as old as Eleazar, who lived out from the town, and who was so old that he could not see or hear, nor could he eat meat, having no teeth to tear it. He sat all day and mumbled. Surely Nathan was as old as he.

At this, the mother had patted his dark curly hair, telling them to hold their tongues; Nathan, perhaps, might be chosen for greater things. She had thoughts of the Temple service in her mind. She was ambitious for Nathan.

Now, he slipped away from his sleeping brothers. Going out into the moonlight, he picked his way to the sloping hillside, throwing himself down, his clasped hands

under his head, his face upturned to the sky. The blue dome was covered with stars, steady, clear, looking down upon him. Far in the distance were the olive-covered hills about Brook Kedron. Their shadows were black lines in the moonlight. Judean nights are quiet, but this night was more than that. A great calm pervaded all space. Nature was not asleep, but hushed into an awesome silence. Some mighty presence had its finger-tips upon the lips of all living things.

Nathan felt the spell. He was uplifted in spirit. He raised his eyes from the distant landscape to fix them again upon the heavens. A feeling of exultation awoke within him. To his people had the promise been given that they should be as the stars; and the promise had been fulfilled. He knew how many millions had come back from Egypt. His heart was sore because of their separation, and their wrong-doings. He grieved that they had been blind; that they had not seen what had weakened them.

His people suffered now. Some had crossed the seas into other lands. All was not well with them. But the time was coming when this would pass. He knew the prophecy. The Lord had promised to send a king to them. All other prophecies and promises had been fulfilled within their time, and why not this? He wondered the King would come in his time! His heart throbbed at the thought of that great One who would rule the Israelites! How he would serve him! The meanest, most servile place in the King's service would be his honor. Yet when this came to fulfillment he, Nathan, might be an old, old man, blind, deaf, and mumbling like Eleazar, who lived out on the road from Bethany.

"But even then, even then," he whispered to himself, "I shall serve him in my heart! I shall sing his praises, and all that I have shall be his. I will build a little hut for myself; but my flocks and the olive groves shall be the King's."

His lips paused. He held his breath. What strange thing was this! A mighty presence filled all space. He could not cry out! His heart was bounding within his breast. His whole being was singing though he made no sound.

His eyes, filled with a strange new light, were fixed upon the far distant eastern sky. From the millions of tiny, steady lamps hung there, one moved, moved on and on, as though a path had been marked out for it. His gaze followed. It paused not, but moved in a line across the heavens. The way was cleared before it. All other lights grew pale. There were millions there, but this one alone filled the heavens.

And now the moon itself faded into insignificance before its presence.

How long it continued its course, Nathan knew not. It might have been hours. It may have been, but a few minutes. Time was no consideration. Then it stopped, and hung like a suspended jewel.

Nathan watched it long. It remained stationary. Then he breathed deeply. The intensity of his emotions relaxed. "It's over in the direction of Bethlehem," he said.

He arose, standing erect, his eyes still upon the suspended star. He was young. His dark locks lay in soft curls upon his forehead. He was strong of limb, and straight as an arrow. His head was flung back, and his eyes, filled with a strange light born of the inspiration of the hour, were fixed on the star. As he stood so, there swept through his mind the memory of the old prophecies, centuries before fulfilled.

"I know not what it is," he said. "But the star calls me. I must go. It may be that the God of our fathers, the God who guided my father Abraham has read my heart, and knows how great has been its desire to see him who is to come as King of the Jews. It may be that over there in Jerusalem or Bethlehem the new King holds his court. I know not what awaits me there. But the star draws me and I must go."

He descended the hill, passed without a backward glance the house wherein Reuben and Levi and the other brothers lay sleeping. Down between the vine-covered hills of Judea, he hurried on, and on, each step bringing him nearer to the stable at Bethlehem over which the star, like a suspended jewel, yet hung.

The Second Place.

Breon arose with a dull pain in his head. He crawled from his bed and into a bath robe. With a discontented, fretful expression his eyes wandered over his bed-room and the apartment adjoining. Disorder was the prevailing mark. His evening clothes, which he had worn the previous night were scattered about on chairs and tables. His watch, face downward, lay on the floor. Mechanically, he stooped to pick it up. Walking to the window, where the light was better, he held the time-piece in his hand, examining it critically. The crystal was broken. It had stopped going the instant of its fall.

"Whew," he exclaimed. "It was pretty early—or late when I got in. Two o'clock. I didn't intend staying out so late when I started. I wonder what time it is now. Late enough, I reckon. No office for me to-day, and the boss to-morrow ready to give me fits. Oh, well, all goes in a life-time. 'A short life and a merry cne,' is my motto."

His expression, as he set about dressing, belied his words. Dissatisfaction and dis-content had written themselves upon his face. His head ached. He worried about the money he had spent the evening before. Although he would have repudiated the suggestion had any one else presented it to his mind, he was troubled about what would be said at the office when he re-turned.

"It's no use going anywhere for lunch," he said, drawing on his overcoat, and with hat and gloves starting forth. "I couldn't eat anything now. I'll walk out some place where I can get air that isn't smoke thick."

He made his way down the traffic-filled street. He elbowed his way through the mass of pedestrians, hurrying along. He picked his way among street-cars and ve-hicles. He came face to face and passed by hundreds of people, yet he neither saw nor heard. The confusion made his head worse. The pain in his eyes was almost maddening.

He turned suddenly at a corner. He would leave the busy thoroughfare and go down some quiet street. He wheeled about, coming full against some hurrying pedes-trian. Bundles fell in all directions. He stammered an apology, as he stooped to gather up the parcels. "Don't apologize. It was as much my fault as yours," cried a cheery, girlish voice. "I wasn't paying any attention to where I was going, and I had really more than I should have attempted carrying. But at Christmas time, one can not wait to have everything sent home from the shops."

She, too, had stooped to pick up her belongings. In a moment more, with arms laden, she had gone on her way.

At Christmas time! she had said. He had forgotten. To-morrow was Christmas, to be sure. But a stranger in a big selfish city tries to forget about such holidays. At Christmas time! At Christmas time! the words kent ringing in his ears. He strode forward, He was annoyed with him-self that the words of a stranger would ring in his ears like this. He walked still faster. The street was quiet. Brick houses with their white marble steps rose high on both sides of him. In the windows, wreaths of holly tied with crimson bows were hanging.

From one of these houses came an old gentleman with silver hair. He stopped before Breon, extending his hand. "I'm glad I met you, my boy," he said. "You have been in my mind all morning. I would have gone to your rooms before this but I supposed you were in the office. I tried to read and write a little, but your face came up before all. I started out hoping

to see you." He still retained the boy's hand in his own firm clasp. Breon could not look at him. He turned his eyes away, fixing his glance upon the street with its unbroken walls of brick and marble.

"Have you been ill, my boy?"

"No; not ill. My head has ached to-day." The old man relaxed his clasp. Placing both hands upon his shoulders, he turned the boy about so that he might look into his face. Breon's glance fell, but the old gentleman compelled him to look up into his face.

"I'm sorry, my boy. Your face and man-ner tells me all I feared. Your eyes have lost their clear light. You are ashamed to look your friends—look me—in the eyes. I have watched and guarded you all the while you have been in the city. I leave you for a month or more, and you go down. Isn't there enough manhood in you to stand alone? Must you always be propped up?

"I have been patient long enough. I thought there was enough good material in you to make a man"—the boy broke from under the restraining hands. He moved backward. This was harder to bear than a blow in the face. He moved away, but the words of the old man fol-lowed him. "But, I shall not give you up, Breon, I'll never do that. A boy with God-fearing parents such as yours will come back to the right way. The blood of your ancestors is bound to tell, and thank God, they were men and women worthy of the name. I'll hunt you up—" But Breon was beyond hearing.

The blood of his ancestors would tell! What did Dr. Clec mean by that! The boy was angry, defiant. He should like to have a quarrel with the old man, but he could not. The words of anger were checked on his lips. He was angry, de-fiant, ashamed. The blood surged against his temples like the beating of hammers, his anger hurried his footsteps. He passed from the residence streeets into narrow, straggling thoroughfares where the houses sagged at the beams, and had a general air of being about to tumble on the heads of passers-by. No Christmas wreaths were in the windows here. No Christmas ring was in the voices of those he met. Angry and unhappy though he was, this difference impressed him. The at-mosphere of this section was not pleasant. He hurried from it as quickly as his feet could carry him. A feeling of relief came, when, passing the last house, he entered on the country road. He threw back his head and drank deep of the air which was free from factory smoke. He walked slower now. The quiet rested him. As he came to the knolls, with their leafless trees stand-ing like sentinels, he quitted the road, mak-ing his way through the lifeless wood.

He gave no thought to how long or how far he was walking. A fallen tree half-buried in dead leaves gave him a resting-place. The walk in the bracing air had freed his head from pain. He thought of Dr. Clec's words. He wondered if this old friend would write back home to tell how their boy had been living.

What did Dr. Clec mean in saying that the blood of his ancestors would tell? He would come back to the right way. His ancestors! He brought to mind all that he could remember of them; fearless men who marked out a way and followed it; men whose word was as good as a bond; women of whom no one could speak light-ly; women to whom all in distress came. These, his ancestors—plain folk, calm, se-rene and happy. So far as the world was concerned, he, a mere boy, had more than they, yet they had been happy.

From point to point, detail after detail, he brought back their lives. The whole long afternoon, he sat searching in his mind for that which had made them con-tented and happy. The blood of his an-

Advance Society Letters.

BY J. BRECKENRIDGE ELLIS.

Hurrah! I have every reason to believe that the picture of Felix will appear upon this page next week—our Christmas edition of the Advance Society. The "cut" is finished and I have seen it. It is good. Here comes a letter addressed to "J. Breckenridge Ellis, pastor Christian Church." Don't know 'im, so will have to pass this over to somebody else. Please don't ever anticipate a reply from "Rev." J. B. E. I am just an ordinary mortal with a cat. A lady told me not long ago that in Lawrence county, Mo., they held a convention, and she asked some of the preachers if they had heard of me. One said, "Ye-e-es, isn't he that man that writes about a cat?" This is fame. W. R. Warren writes for advice concerning the Centennial Campaign—how to make the churches strong and enthusiastic, the contributions for missions large, and in a word, how to best build up the cause. My advice is to live it. We've been preaching it a long time, and preaching it well, and let no preacher preach it less; but we who are not preachers—suppose we start into living it awhile, just to show the world what Christianity means when we don't bear grudges and don't give grudges, but forbear and forgive and love. Of course that would do away with the ridiculous anomaly of having any sort of a division in a church, or the absurdity of any sort of a quarrel among children of God. I don't know anything that would build up the cause quicker, or surprise the world more. Now, you take Felix, and some people he likes on sight, while others seem to turn his hair the wrong way whenever he sees them. Cats, too, he dislikes, and especially dogs. You take Felix as he is as I see him now, lying by the fire with his nose wedged between the joints of his two hind-legs and his tail sandwiched between all three, and his forepaws doubled up under his breast. There is not a soul in the house but the family—he knows that, you may be sure. There's a delightful rich odor upon the air that insinuates the fact that we are going to have meat to-day. Presently the dinner will be served. Felix purrs with satisfaction. His whiskers sweep over his tailtip with a graceful air of friendship for all the world. He reminds me of a church-member when nobody is bothering him. There's nothing that will keep an organization "harmonious" like each member having things just as he wants it. Now, if a dog should enter—a dog, for instance, who isn't believe in cats —you would see Felix's tail bristle; and if the scent of meat proves a delusion, and it turns out that we have but our customary spread of baker's bread, potatoes and other vegetable products, Felix will stalk away in wrath and go to hold a meeting by himself over some unfortunate mouse. But is Felix a type for Christians to imitate? He is only a cat; let us be something more. What do you think of this, Mr. Warren? Think you can get this idea worked up?

Drusie R. Malott, South Chihli Mission, China: "While looking through a box of papers to-day, I came across this letter which I thought I had mailed long ago. I am sorry for the delay." (Then comes the letter referred to): "It is six o'clock in the morning. I have just come in from the Mission Farm ready for a long day's work, preparing copy for our circular letter, and finished the addressing of letters and booklet. The little booklet tells the story of our mission up to the present time. May God add his blessing to it in calling other missionaries out here to the harvest, for oh! they are so badly needed. You would have enjoyed my drive through the

country and city this morning. The sun was just peeping above the horizon, the birds were singing a sweet carol, and, everything seemed as fresh and happy as could be." (This was received in July.) "One of our Chinese men pulled the rickisha—something like a two-wheeled buggy or cart, but smaller and much lighter. In the country the farmers were beginning their work. In the city the men were lined up on each side of the street, eating their breakfast—they buy a bowl of food and sit down on the ground or stand out on the sidewalk to eat. In the suburbs the women and children as well as men, were gathered about the front entrance, eating their bowl of food. I loved the farm more than ever as I came into the city with its many odors. On the streets the dogs are so numerous that we almost had to run over them. Many Chinese do not kill dogs, believing that the spirits of their ancestors pass into the body of dogs, and that every dog one sees may contain the soul of one's grandfather, or some other relative." (I was wondering what was in that "bowl of food" you mentioned; I wish you had told us; but I know from what you say here, that it was without one ingredient that had occurred to me. I believe, however, the most orthodox Chinaman would scout the idea of his ancestor's soul entering the form of a mouse!) "It would have interested you to see our harvest reaped and threshed. The grain is cut by hand, with a sickle. When the last sheaf has been cut and gathered together, the word is given and dozens of gleaners rush in with rakes made from limbs of trees, and rake and sweep until not a sheaf is left. One can always tell when the gleaners begin because they rush in with such zeal that a big cloud of dust immediately envelops the field. When they quiet down a little, you can see them through the dust, dragging their rakes." (Now, I want to ask the people of Arkansas—what do you think of people "rushing" to do any sort of work?) "I often see 100 gleaners swoop down upon a little field not larger than a medium-sized garden in the homeland." (Just think of "swooping" down upon toil!) "They sit around the border of the field, waiting for the work to begin." (Now, I can understand that. It was that sort of thing, I fancy, that delayed the appearance of Felix's picture.) "The threshing-place is usually a piece of hard ground where the grain is spread and tramped" (as we do our apples for tinned-butter, I suppose, only we keep our boots on) "and tossed into the air until it is free from chaff. Last Tuesday was our day of fasting and prayer. We met from 6 to 10 a. m., and again from 11 to 6 p. m. It lasted 11 hours, but did not seem long. We did not want to stop even at the last, though the clock rang the supper-gong five times. He just had to wait till we came. Oh, it was such a blessed day! All study and work was put aside except the daily Christian prayer-meetings, morning and afternoon; at such times, we have a whole day of waiting before the Lord in prayer, song, testimony. After supper we had a baptismal service. One of the lesser officials was baptized. He had witnessed the murder of one of the missionaries during the Boxer uprising at Paoting Fu, and the impression made then never left him. And now at last he came and asked for baptism. Pray for him. He says he is different from the other officials, and would like to be in the Lord's service. Oh, if you could only have been present at our meeting! He gave such a blessed testimony, so simple and childlike, so earnest and clear. About 25 Chinese Christians were present, and seven of us; and every one of us spoke for the Lord,' of his wonderful goodness— spoke in Chinese, of course. Why I could not have kept from it! Two women were present who had that day walked nineteen miles to hear about Jesus. They asked to be baptized. After hearing them express knowledge and confidence in Christ, they were baptized, too. Would you walk more than eighteen blocks to hear a message from God?" (Yes, many of us.) "When I heard about the awful earthquake and fire at San Francisco, it seemed to me but another sign of the times, telling us that the coming of our Lord is ever near. I want to 'go up' to meet him from this place where he has so marvellously brought me. What joy it will be to take some precious souls with me! Benton county, Arkansas, is not the only place that has fruit; we had some of the best apricots I ever tasted. They are one cent a dozen. We had peas and beets from our own garden. Let me assure all friends as well as members of the Av. S. that I ALWAYS rejoice over their letters."

Mrs. J. P. Cameron, Hockman, Va.: "I have been reading some of the Av. S. letters and am much interested in the orphan Charlie, and missionary Drusie. I am sending $1 from the Ladies' Aid Society, Graham Church, for Charlie; and I send $1 for Drusie's Christmas tree; any present will suit me that you think she will like. I only wish it were more, but hope she may get many dollars on the tree. May the Lord bless Drusie that she may win many souls to Christ." Mrs. A. P. Camren, Peoria, Ill.: "I send $1, half for Charlie, half for Drusie's Christmas tree. I hope they may be permitted to do much good in their lives. I do greatly enjoy reading about the grand work of the Av. S.; and the stories are fine. May you all be spared many days for the great work that is yet to be done." The Christian Pub. Co. forwards me 50 cents which Mrs. Mary E. Bradfield, New Metamoras, O., sends as Drusie's Christmas present. Mrs. D. M. Scott, Mr. and Mrs. H. L. Carter, Hamilton, Mont., send 75 cents for Charlie and Drusie "wishing very much we could send more." Geo. W. Dawson, Kansas City, Mo.: "I failed to get any of Charlie's ice cream, but I want something on that Christmas tree! I inclose $2; divide it or give it to either as you see fit." (I will divide it.) "God bless the Av. S. for the noble work it is engaged in." Mrs. S. M. Gibbins, Garfield, Wash.: "Here we are again with five dimes for five more saucers of ice cream. That orphan social has done me so much good that I keep asking others to partake, knowing the effects are as la 'ng as the benefit is mutual. Makes us realize the meaning of 'And in helping others, we ourselves of God are blessed.' One of these dimes is given by a dear little orphan boy who has been adopted; the others are from dear friends of mine. How it gladdens my heart to see the sum swell!"

Bentonville, Ark.

Greek and Latin by Mail.

You can take the Normal, Classical or Bible course, leading to degrees, on the Home Study Plan. Catalogue free. Write Pres. Chas. J. Burton, Christian College, Oskaloosa, Iowa.

Who Is Santa Claus?

It was just before Christmas, and the four little Wolseys were at work making presents. Baby John's work was peculiar; he was hammering tacks into a bar of kitchen soap, and he had to be constantly furnished with tacks to keep him from pounding the soap itself. Dorothy was stringing beads, with an apprehensive eye upon John, who, in spite of the mother's utmost efforts and the attractiveness of the soap, would make a dive for the beadbox every now and then. Norman was gilding a very unsymmetrical clay vase which he had made for his grandmother, and Carleton was putting the last links to a long "daisy chain" of colored paper, wherewith to decorate a certain Christmas tree. He was ensconced behind a barricade of chairs, together with Norman and the gold paint, as the only means of escaping the too appreciative fingers of that diminutive tyrant, John.

Every one heaved a sigh of relief when Inga, the nurse, appeared to take the baby. He was borne off, howling indignantly; but, once outside the door, he stopped with ludicrous promptitude. Soon after he might have been heard shouting with laughter as he knocked down the blocks, which, with Inga's aid, he had laboriously piled up.

"Mamma," said Norman, breaking the blissful silence which followed John's departure, "the little boy next door said there was no such thing as Santa Claus. There is, isn't there?"

"Yes, dear," said mamma.

"A real, live man with 'cheeks' like a cherry,' with 'eyes how they twinkled, and dimples, how merry?'" persisted Norman.

"I never saw him," said mamma. "I should suppose that would be a pretty good picture of what he means."

"Oh, does he mean something?" asked Norman, in a disappointed tone.

"Yes, he does. Everybody does. You do."

"What do I mean?" he asked, looking puzzled.

"That's a riddle for you to find out. You've got all your life to work it out. You'll be lucky if you get it then."

"You're such a funny mamma," sighed Carlton. "Am I a riddle, too?"

"Yes, indeed, you are!" laughed his mother. "You're a riddle that's too much for me, every once in a while."

"Am I a riddle?" asked Dorothy. She didn't know what a riddle is, but she wanted to be in the game.

"Yes, you are, and I am, and everyone is. Santa Claus is."

"Is he just the kind of a riddle we are?" asked Norman.

"No, not exactly. But the difference is another riddle for you to guess."

"I know!" cried Norman. "I can see myself, but I can't see Santa Claus."

"Can you see yourself?" asked the mother.

"Of course."

"What can you see?"

"I can see my legs, and my arms, and my hands, and my stomach."

"Is that yourself?" interrupted his mother.

"They are parts of myself."

"Yes; but can you see all of yourself? Can you see your eyes, for instance?"

Norman ran to the looking-glass.

"There!" said he, pointing to the blue eyes that looked back at him, alive with intelligence.

"Are those your eyes?" asked the mother. "Your very eyes? If I should break the looking-glass, or cover it up, should I make you blind?"

The three children laughed like a chime of bells. Childlike, they loved an argument.

"Then you can't see yourself, can you?

Stomach Sufferers Squander Millions.

In Search of Relief.

The world is full of disordered stomachs and 90 per cent of the money spent upon physicians and drugs goes in an attempt to cure the stomach.

People are made to believe that in order to gain health they must doctor their stomachs and use cathartics. So the doctor gets his fee for the stomach treatment and the druggist for the physic, until the savings of a life time are exhausted and yet no cure.

Let's be reasonable.

The sick stomach is in every case the result of over-eating, hurried mastication and improper choice of foods. The mucous lining all the way down the food tract loses its sensitiveness, and when food is forced down the muscles fail to respond. They do not churn the food as they should. The glands no longer give out gastric juice to dissolve the food and render it capable on assimilation. The man has become a dyspeptic.

There is one sure way and only one to bring positive relief. Put into that stomach of yours the very elements that it lacks to get that food into liquid form. It takes pepsin, diastase, golden seal and other ferments to accomplish this. The healthy stomach contains these elements. The dyspeptic stomach lacks part or all of them. Stuart's Dyspepsia Tablet is made up of just what the dyspeptic stomach lacks—nature's digestives.

Stuart's Dyspepsia Tablets are not a medicine, not a drug, not a cathartic. They do not cure anybody of anything but Dyspepsia and Indigestion and such ailments as arise from poorly digested food.

While they digest the food the stomach recuperates. The mucous membrane is coming out of its stupor, the gastric juice is coming to the surface, the muscles are regaining their power. Every organ of the body takes on new life, the skin gains color, and the eyes are no longer tinged with yellow. You live.

Why doctor and why drug yourself? Stuart's Dyspepsia Tablets will take care of your food while Nature cures you.

Try a box at your druggists, 50 cents. Or, if you prefer a free trial package before buying, send your name and address to-day, F. A. Stuart Co., 68 Stuart Bldg., Marshall, Mich.

Neither can you see Santa Claus. But you can see parts of yourself, and you can see parts of him."

"Can we? Where? Where?" they all cried.

"Whenever you look into a kind person's eyes; whenever you see any one giving another pleasure. When Dorothy gives John a bite of her apple, then as you look at her, you catch a tiny glimpse of Santa Claus. When you get a surprise ready for mamma to welcome her home from down town, then any one looking at you sees a little bit of Santa Claus."

"Then he is just kind people, as Arthur said?" cried Norman, bitterly disappointed.

"No, indeed. All the kind people in the world put together wouldn't make Santa Claus. I said you could see parts of him, but not himself. The kind people are parts of him, sometimes. He whispers kind thoughts to them, one after the other. He flies from one to the other, like a bee from flower to flower, only instead of taking away sweetness, he gives it. His presents on Christmas day are only a few of his presents. He gives better ones every day, but he gives them so quietly that no one seems to know it. On Christmas day every one suddenly recognizes him, and his invisible gifts become visible."

"What's visible?" asked Dorothy.

"You can't see his gifts of every day, but his Christmas gifts-you can see," explained her mother.

"But I want- to see, him, myself," said Dorothy. "I am going to hold my eyes open and watch when I hang up my stockings."

"You would never see him if you should," answered her mother. "Santa Claus is a fairy, dear, and you can never see fairies, nor quite understand them. When you think you are just going to catch them they vanish away. Santa Claus hides in many ways. He hides in the people you know. If you should stay awake you would probably see what would look like mamma and papa filling your stockings, yet all the time it would be Santa Claus."

A Legend for Christmas.

BY JAMES SMALL.

Hope was a young man, Memory was a young damsel. Hope wanted to marry Memory, but Memory refused, saying that Hope was a deceiver. Hope remonstrated. Memory was unmoved. Well, said Hope, let us take a journey around the world together. To this Memory agreed.

When they returned they met a man that was much younger when they started off, and into whose heart Hope had poured bright anticipations. Memory at once recognized him and began to question him. She found that every hope had been realized and everything Hope had spoken to him had come to pass.

Memory at once said: "Hope, sname wronged you, let us wed." They wed. Since that day Hope and Memory have been linked in eternal embrace.

Memory can look back to the day that Jesus slept upon a mother's knee and remember how he grew in wisdom and stature and in favor with God and man and how the Son of Man pitied and toiled and suffered to win man's love, and Hope looks to the future with "inspiring thoughts of raptures yet to be" and with Campbell in "The Pleasures of Hope," say:

Eternal Hope, when yonder spheres sublime,
Pealed their first note to sound the march of time,
Thy joyous youth began but not to fade,
When all the sister planets have decayed,
When wrapt in fire the realms of ether glow,
And heaven's last thunder shakes the world,
Thou, undismayed shall o'er the ruins smile,
And light thy torch at nature's funeral pile.

Wishing the boys and girls, and all a happy Christmas and a prosperous New Year with Jesus as our leader and partner.
Columbus, Ind.

Christ came as a child, to be guarded and cared for through all those early years. And that manger cradle has given sacredness to every cradle since. Motherhood has a different meaning since Mary held her first-born in her arms.

A man whose house adjoined the railway kept a goat tethered in his garden. A friend asked him one day what was the use of the goat. "Use of the goat!" he replied. "Man, that goat keeps me in coals. Never a train passes but the fireman throws a bit of coal at it."—Glasgow Evening Times.

Christ's kingdom is growing. In the days when he walked in Galilee, Rome was mistress of the world. The victories of Napoleon mean nothing now. Time has undone his work. It is only Christ whose glory grows with the centuries, whose power increases, whose kingdom spreads. And "of the increase of his government and peace there shall be no end."

The Riding Song of the Magi.

With a quick little chime like a ripple of rhyme,
A shake from our camel's small bells;
With a song on our lips as the soft night slips
We come as the Star compels.

From slumber and feast, from far out of the East,
We ride, for we can not but choose
To seek through the earth the place of the birth,
Of this mystical King of the Jews.

We have gifts in our hands for this child of far ands,
Three gifts for the child that's thrice great;
Bright gold have we brought for the King we have sought,
Red gold for the King's high state.

And myrrh do we bring for his burying,
For his delicate body's behoof,
When as man in the ground with the fair linen bound,
They house him with earth for a roof.

And frankincense we bear as the Godhead's share,
A tribute for God-head divine;
Its savor that stays while the years go their ways
Is of life everlasting the sign.

So ride we along with offering and song
To kneel at the door where he dwells,
Through deserts and marts with a prayer in our hearts,
We come as the Star compels.
—*Home Magazine.*

DISCOVERY OF CHRISTMAS TREES.

How the Worthless Balsam-fir Became the Christmas Tree.

It is natural for us to take it for granted that there have always been Christmas trees, yet fifty years ago there were few in America, save in the homes of foreigners. About thirty years ago a number of duck-hunters cruising along the coast of Maine noticed the millions of young balsam firs which grew along the shores, and the brilliant idea occurred to one member of the party that these symmetrical evergreens would make excellent Christmas trees. At this time the "abandoned farm" era had begun and it looked as if the whole state would grow up to firs. The balsam fir used to be a synonym for worthlessness. Nowadays "Canada balsam" is made from this tree, and thousands of vacation tourists gather its young twigs for "balsam pillows." But the wood has always been useless to the lumberman. Therefore, when the New York yachtsman offered to buy a few shiploads of young firs, the honest Maine farmers failed to see the joke. But when the city man opened his purse they fell to with a will.

The first venture proved a success, and others hurried into the business. Ten years

later the whole coast of Maine was stripped of firs and the business moved inland. From this beginning the trade has grown until now a million and a half of Christmas trees are sold every year in New York and New England, of which about a million come from Maine alone.

Home Readings.

M. The Character of the Messiah.—Isa. 9.1-7.
T. The Branch.—Isa. 11:1-10.
W. The Deliverer.—Isa. 42:1-8.
T. The Comforter.—Isa. 61:1-6.
F. The King.—Ps. 72:1-17.
S. The Redeemer.—Isa. 59:16-21.
S. The Savior.—John 3:5-16.

Dark Outlook.

"Mamma," asks the little boy, "how can Santa Claus get into our flat, when we haven't any chimney—nothing but a steam radiator?"

"He will probably slip in by the basement door, darling."

"It's all off, then," said the lad, with a surprising vigor in the use of slang. "That janitor will put him out of business before he can unpack his sack."
WILBUR NESBIT.

The fool worries because he can't have what he would like, and the wise man takes comfort in enjoying the things he has.

Christian Publishing Company

2712 Pine St., St. Louis, Mo.

J. H. GARRISON,	- - -	President
J. W. DOWLING,	- - -	Vice-President
GEO. L. SNIVELY,	- -	Sec. and Gen. Supt
R. P. CROW,	- -	Treas. and Bus. Manager

—Don't forget your friend's library at Christmas time. We have books that will help them into new careers of happiness and usefulness.

—In these closing days of the year make out your book list for 1907 and send it to us. We will submit to you prices enabling you to get the very most and best for your money.

—For two new subscriptions, accompanied by the $3 we will give the sender choice of either an excellent stereopticon and 50 scenic cards, or an initial-letter fruit set consisting of seven beautiful plates.

—If you will send the 1907 CHRISTIAN-EVANGELIST to a friend for a Christmas present, you will be reduplicating a most delectable gift 52 times and bring your name and face to his memory as often.

—There ought to be great improvement in the Bible schools of the land during 1907, for the W. W. Dowling literature is being received for the first time into so many of them. We have a right to expect it.

—"If you will authorize me to do so I can get you a big club of trial subscribers here for 25 cents for two months."—L. S. D.

Brother: Don't fool with "trial" subscribers now. We are too busy enrolling yearly subscriptions for $1.50.

—There is an actual ministerial "dead line"—not determined by age, but by stagnation. Readers of THE CHRISTIAN-EVANGELIST and the new books advertised in its columns do not become conscious of it nor do their hearers think of them as being in near proximity to it.

—We wish to again commend to the consideration of the "Committee on Supplies" our new Teachers' Quarterlies. These help the teachers to quickly grasp the main points of the lesson and suggest the best methods of presenting them to the bright minds and receptive hearts before the teacher.

The Alexander Campbell number is most excellent. Couldn't you get all those pictures on one nice card for framing and sell us all a copy? I would be a premium many would work for too. I am sure. That issue of THE CHRISTIAN-EVANGELIST will certainly be very helpful to all our young ministers, and there ought to be several thousand extra copies for our pastors to give to fellow pastors of the other churches.—Geo. C. Ritchey, (evangelist) Monmouth, Oregon.

If our friends desire it, we will.

—Preacher, don't miss this opportunity of adding one or both these great books to your library free of cost to you. For one new subscription accompanied by the $1.50, we send you postpaid either "Helps to Faith," by J. H. Garrison, or "Victory of Faith," by E. L. Powell. Any preacher in the land can easily thus secure one or both these dynamic books. "Do it now."

—The "Herald and Presbyter" thus speaks of one of our most popular books: The Holy Spirit. By J. H. Garrison, Editor of THE CHRISTIAN-EVANGELIST. Cloth, 12mo. $1. Christian Publishing Company, St. Louis. It is very gratifying to find this treatise, which the Editor says, in his preface, "is written from the general point of view of the Disciples of Christ," so close to the faith generally held by evangelical Trinitarian believers. So vital is the Scriptural truth as to the Holy Spirit in his person, office and work, that it is a joy to see that truth so clearly expressed as it is in this volume.

—"Our Young Folks" and THE CHRISTIAN-EVANGELIST $2.00; a fountain pen and THE CHRISTIAN-EVANGELIST, $2.00; "The American Boy" (a splendid paper for boys) and THE CHRISTIAN-EVANGELIST, $2.00; "The Ladies' Home Companion" and THE

CHRISTIAN-EVANGELIST, $2.25; a self-filling fountain pen, warranted by makers 10 years and THE CHRISTIAN-EVANGELIST (to a new subscriber), $2.50; "The Review of Reviews" (price $3) and THE CHRISTIAN-EVANGELIST, $3.00. Both the paper and the premiums make choice Christmas gifts. They may be ordered now and we will hold and later send labeled "For Christmas."

—Christmas diversions have interfered with the composition of new clubs for the past few days, but in addition to the larger number coming by ones and twos we are pleased to report the following new lists:

Cowderly, Ky., H. C. Ford	3
Hopkinsville, Ky., H. C. Ford	3
Rogers, O., G. W. Woodbury	3
Lisbon, O., G. W. Woodbury	3
Moulton, Ia.	3
Tillamook, Oreg., Geo. C. Ritchey, pastor	4
Neho, Ky., H. C. Ford	4
Indianapolis, Ind., F. P. Smith, pastor	5
Crafton, Ky., H. C. Ford	7
Lovington, Ill.	7
Madisonville, Ky., H. C. Ford	9
Wellsburg, W. Va., E. H. Hart, pastor	13
Kansas City, Mo., Geo. H. Combs, pastor	15
Charleroi, Pa., H. H. Connelly	24
Indianapolis, Ind., A. B. Philputt, pastor	38
Indianapolis, Ind., C. B. Newnan, pastor	46

The Christian Lesson Commentary for 1907.

For the twenty-second consecutive year, this Christian Commentary has come before the Sunday-school public offering its aid in the study of the International Series of Lessons. It has gained and holds a high place in the schools of the brotherhood as a safe, sound, practical Bible school commentary, embodying the best thoughts of the best thinkers, as well as those of the author on the lessons studied. The volume for 1907, now lying before us, is not inferior to any of its predecessors. Like wine, it seems to grow better with age. Brother Dowling is, of course, a past master in the art of Sunday-school work and in the preparation of literature for the schools. The lessons for 1907 are all in the Old Testament. As the year 1906 was devoted to the study of the Words and Works of Jesus the coming year will be devoted to the Stories of the Patriarchs and Judges, beginning with Creation and ending with Samuel. Besides the lesson material proper, with its ample illustrations which are numerous and its maps, there are the quarterly class records, and the pronouncing dictionary of Bible names. The owner of this volume will be well-equipped for his Sunday-school work for 1907. Price, $1. Address Christian Publishing Company.

THE
CHRISTIAN-
EVANGELIST

A WEEKLY RELIGIOUS NEWSPAPER.

Volume XLIII.	No. 52.
ST. LOUIS, DECEMBER 27, 1906.	

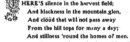

HERE'S silence in the harvest field;
And blackness in the mountain glen,
And cloud that will not pass away
From the hill tops for many a day;
And stillness 'round the homes of men.

—*Mary Howitt.*

A $250,000 CENTENNIAL FU

In Personal Offering for Land and Buildings by

Our Centennial in Pittsburg, 1909

The friends of the Foreign Society express themselves enthusiastically in favor of this important move

A STRIKING CONTRAST

Contrast this grass hut with the home of F. E. Hagin at Tokyo, Japan, a picture of which is below.

To compel the missionaries to live in century-old, vermin-infected, unventilated buildings is to handicap them in their work and endanger their health and their very lives.

GRASS HOUSE AT DAMOH, INDIA.

Where J. G. McGavran and family lived for a time. They are missionaries of the Foreign Society. They uttered no word of complaint. It is evident they could not do their best work living here. It is not sufficient protection from the extreme heat and heavy rains, and besides there is not sufficient room. We ought not ask our missionaries to live in a place like this. Their health and lives are endangered.

Contrast this home with the grass hut at Damoh, India, the picture of which is above.

This home is a signboard to Heaven for the natives and a means of grace to the missionary.

HOME OF F. E. HAGIN, TOKYO, JAPAN.

This is a modern, up-to-date home, recently built by the Foreign Society at a cost of about $2,000. It is commodious and convenient. It will last many years. Here the missionary and his family can live in comfort and do their best work. Their health and lives will be protected. Besides a good example to the native population, it helps to give them a higher estimate of Christianity.

GOOD NEWS.

A good man and wife have just turned over to $8,450 to the Foreign Society on the Annuity Plan. This goes into the Centennial Building Fund. We hope others will take this step. We are receiving cash and pledges every day for a great Centennial Fund. Will you not join the friends in this mighty move. ment? Please let us hear from you at once.

What Some of the Friends Think.

THE call for building equipment se most modest one on the part of our eign Society. With the increase an velopment of the work there must b creasing demands for such a building to insure permanency.   F. D. POW
Pastor Vermont Avenue Chu WASHINGTON, D. C.

I hope the Foreign Society will be cessful in providing additional bui equipment in foreign fields. Nece buildings are a great help anywhere, especially on the foreign field.
R. E. HIERONYMUS,
President of Eureka Colle EUREKA, ILL.

I am in perfect accord with the pr sition of the Foreign Society to s $250,000 for buildings and equipment in eign fields. It is timely, and if ac plished will be a great stride in adv in our foreign work.   C. J. TANNA
Pastor of Central Chur DETROIT, MICH.

I can say without hesitation that I t no part of the work of the Foreign Bo is more important than that of erec proper buildings for the missionaries foreign fields. It seems to me scarcely sible to build up a church of influenc any heathen land, or even in any civil land, without a suitable house in which hold their meetings, and suitable apartm in which to reside. I hope that you very soon realize your purpose and pectations in this matter.
J. W. McGARVEY,
President of the College of the Bibl LEXINGTON, KY.

To provide homes for our missiona is the sanest business policy introduced the realm of the Lord's work. Prop housed, all their forces and resources conserved, wastes are avoided, and the r sionaries are ever at their best. Wher comfortable homes there is added comp working equipment in chapels, schools, pitals and orphanages, we are only mu plying the power of our representative the front. Churches at home should sh the sadness of our missionaries in o facing great opportunities with their ha tied by lack of proper equipment.
CHAS. S. MEDBURY.
Pastor University Place Churc DES MOINES, IA.

Address

F. M. RAINS, Sec'y,

Box 884,

Cincinnati,

Ohio.

.... Cut here ....

THE PLEDGE.

I agree to donate to the Foreign Christian Missionary Society, Cincinnati, C $................. per year for three years beginning June 1st, 1907, to aid in creation of a special Two Hundred and Fifty Thousand Dollar ($250,000) Centen Fund to be used for lands and buildings by the Society.

Name ....
P. O. ....
Street or R. F. D. ....
Date .... 1906.   State ....

THE
CHRISTIAN-EVANGELIST

"IN FAITH, UNITY; IN OPINION AND METHODS, LIBERTY; IN ALL THINGS, CHARITY."

Vol. XLIII. December 27, 1906 No. 52

1809 CENTENNIAL PROPAGANDA CHURCHES OF CHRIST 1909

: : : GEO. L. SNIVELY : : :

CENTENNIAL GLEAMINGS.

The information Brother Rains gives us concerning the great philanthropy proposed by the curators of Hiram college is most inspirational. That Home and its supplemental scholarships are evidences that we are rapidly passing the tentative stages of our missionary activities beyond the seas. We are not sending preachers and their wives abroad on holiday jaunts, nor merely to stay till their little ones have come to school age. This is notification to candidates for missionary careers that permanence is part of the fruitage expected of their ministry. It is confidently expected that the reflex influence of this strengthening of stakes will enable our enterprising Foreign Missionary Society to greatly lengthen its cords before 1909.

In expressing such sentiments as glow in Brother Lowe's "Passing of the Partisan," one must "walk delicately" lest he convey the impression that he is not contending earnestly for the faith once delivered, and as it was comprehended by "the fathers" of one hundred years ago; or rather as some of us think they comprehended it. Constituted as we are, it is difficult for us to keep from becoming partisan; but free from it we must be to overcome the partisanship that has divided the body of Christ and weakened the church in the presence of the Canaanite who is still in the land. They only who have largely eradicated the "I am for Cephas" spirit from their hearts, will trail the cord of extension, dyed in the Saviour's blood, as a boundary line around the land of the denominationalist, annexing it as a province to the growing empire of primitive Christianity. Let us prepare ourselves to do this to a notable degree before our Centennial celebration begins. Presbyterians are consolidating; Congregationalists, United Brethren and Methodist Protestant are uniting; are there not some segments of the great circle of the church universal we can altogether persuade to walk in the more excellent way, and become Christians only before the century's close? Let us work and pray to the end that at Pittsburg reports may be made of actual, practical beginnings of Christian unions being accomplished by denominations also as well as by units.

The Passing of the Partisan.

BY J. M. LOWE.

Denomination is less and less and the Kingdom of God is more and more. Gradually we are freeing ourselves from the tangle of tiresome discussion and seeing and grasping the things that abide. Beneath the turbulent tide there is the all-supporting sea. Many different lights glimmer and gleam on earth, but the sun is above them all. Humanity is larger than family, state and nation, and no thought, social or religious, can come to its best without relating itself to the whole. To cherish for ourself a set of ideas while ignoring the whole, is a species of selfishness which, though it may wear the "livery of heaven," we are at a loss to know how possession was secured, unless the Bard of England has informed us. But not even the livery of heaven can long conceal the hopeless impotence of a doctrine which vainly supposes itself a master instead of a servant, and which fails to see that it cannot be of value unless it expresses itself in ever more increasing sympathy and comprehensiveness. The end is not doctrine but character, not creed, but deed, not party, but humanity. No more surely will a pond of water, cut off from supply, dry up and disappear, than will the party that exists for itself decay, for truth has a most resistless way of disposing of things it does not need, for truth is the invisible and eternal life of the universe.

With these thoughts in mind, it is easy to see that our great brotherhood, pursuing one course will find a locked gate, going another direction we will behold an open pathway into ever enlarging fields of service. Yonder is the field of battle. The hosts are gathering. The ranks are closing. Let us on to the conflict, lest we "disappear."

A Commendable Enterprise.

BY F. M. RAINS.

Hiram College, Hiram, O., proposes to raise a special fund of $25,000 with which to provide a home for the children of the missionaries of the Foreign Christian Missionary Society and to grant them free tuition while they pursue their studies. The proposed home is to be deeded to the Foreign Society, free of charge, and the society is to furnish and equip and support and manage it for the exclusive use of the children of missionaries while their parents continue their work on the foreign field. After the home has been secured, the rest of the fund is to be used as an endowment to provide the free tuition. This is a generous proposition on the part of Hiram College and one which the society, on behalf of the missionaries, fully appreciates. Hiram is a great center of missionary interest and enthusasm.

The education of the children of missionaries has now come to be a serious problem. In the early days of our foreign work before the families of the missionaries had grown up, we did not have to face this perplexing situation. At the present time there are some ten or a dozen children of missionaries in this country attending school and away from their parents. Others are coming soon and still others ought to come. Satisfactory homes and home surroundings with proper school and church advantages are hard to combine. We believe the new arrangement fully meets all the difficulties.

It is hoped that the friends of Hiram College will give the agents of the institution a cordial reception and generous aid in the very laudable undertaking of providing the $25,000 at the earliest possible date. School facilities are very limited on the various mission fields. This important step has been under consideration for a long time. The children must be educated in America. The missionaries can not abandon their work while the children are in school.

The New Hope.

George Hamilton Combs, in an address that ought never to be forgotten, delivered at Hannibal last summer, called it "The Newest Evangelism." It is another name for the limitless opportunities of extending the Kingdom through the medium of our Bible schools.

"The newest evangelism is all permeating and inclusive. Unify your Bible school and you unify the church as a whole. Get the man or the woman and you have gotten one; get the child and you have gotten both man and woman.

"We are approaching our Centennial. We would double our membership to two and a half million members by 1909. Along the present lines of effort we shall not even come within sight of such accomplishments. We are but toying with a battle cry. We have no confidence in our undertaking. And yet it is practicable. We can, if we will, double our membership by that centennial hour. If every church in our great brotherhood shall concentrate its efforts on our Bible schools, putting time into them, putting work into them, striving earnestly and heroically to double their membership and convert them into fire-hot evangelistic forces and agencies—if every church would but do this there would arise to us such Pentecostal awakenings as this old world has never seen before, and when that memorable year should have rolled around we should turn a mighty host two and a half million strong toward the gates of Pittsburg and with jubilation and with song praising God for his wonderful works among the children of men."

In keeping with this sentiment we are pleased to announce that beginning with our next issue Bro. J. H. Hardin will inaugurate in this paper a new department, "The Practical Bible School," in which will appear brief and pointed hints on matters that concern the organization and management of Bible schools and all matters pertaining to "The New Hope." This, we believe, will be one of our most valuable contributions to the Centennial propaganda.

The Christian-Evangelist.

J. H. GARRISON, Editor
PAUL MOORE, Assistant Editor

F. D. POWER,
B. B. TYLER, } Staff Correspondents.
W. DURBAN,

Subscription Price, $1.50 a Year.

For foreign countries add $1.04 for postage.

Published by the Christian Publishing Company,
2712 Pine Street, St. Louis, Mo.

Entered at St. Louis P. O. as Second Class Matter

CONTENTS.

Centennial Propaganda 1663
Current Events 1664
Editorial—
  The Circuit of the Year.................1665
  A Backward Glance 1665
  Notes and Comments 1665
  Editor's Easy Chair 1667
Contributed Articles—
  What Lack We Yet? H. H. Hubbell....1668
  Is There a Missing Link? 1668
  Inspiration for Evangelization. J. P.
    Lichtenberger 1669
  The Parthenogenic Controversy. William
    Durban 1670
  The Elderburg Association 1671
  What the Brethren are Saying and Doing.
    B. B. Tyler 1672
  As Seen from the Dome. F. D. Power..1673
  A Specimen of "Modern Courtesy"....1674
Our Budget 1675
News from Many Fields 1678
Evangelistic 1682
Sunday-school 1683
Midweek Prayer-meeting 1683
Christian Endeavor 1684
Obituaries 1686
The Home Department 1687

Current Events

If any one is surprised at the attitude of Congress, particularly of the Senate,

Roosevelt and Congress. towards President Roosevelt, it must be because he is not a close student of current political history. The dismissal of the colored troops for their disgraceful conduct in the Brownsville, Texas, affair, and the president's attitude toward the Japanese question in San Francisco are only occasions which certain political leaders have been anxiously looking for to make war on the president and lower his prestige and popularity in the country. His aggressive opposition to trusts, his recommendation of the inheritance tax, his views on railroad regulation and other measures of similar character, are not popular with many of the political leaders of his own party, nor with the political bosses in any party. They dare not make an issue with him on these questions, however, and so are glad to find their opportunity in the matters above referred to. The ultimate decision of the Brownsville episode will turn on the facts in the case, which are now being newly investigated. The San Francisco school question has probably been unduly magnified. No doubt some way will be found by which Japan's treaty rights will be enforced, as the president desires, without interfering seriously with the local question of where the few dozen Japanese children in San Francisco shall go to school. But when these questions are settled other occasions will be found for antagonizing the president, whose policy does not commend itself to the grave and reverend senators, with whom politics is more than statesmanship.

It is difficult for the people of this country to get a clear idea of just what

France and the Roman Catholics. is involved in the present issue between the government in France and the Roman Catholic Church. On the one hand it is urged by the government and its friends that the effort is simply to effect a separation between Church and State, and to prohibit any interference with the government of France by an outside religious potentate. Americans are apt to think of this as analogous to what we have in this country. Archbishop Ireland, however, says that the separation of Church and State "has a totally different signification" in France to what it has in this country. "The separation of the Church from the State in America means liberty and justice; there it means oppression." He also quotes from Pius X, who said: "We are ready to submit to separation, but it must be a fair separation, such as obtained in the United States, in Brazil, in Great Britain, in Holland, and not a subjection.". The archbishop thinks it is a party of infidels and atheists that is making war against religion, and not simply against the Roman Catholic Church. It is difficult to understand, however, how France, after the experience of the revolution of 1789, would undertake again to put down religion as an abiding force in human life. No doubt there are complications in this question that Americans do not yet fully comprehend. It is certain, however, that any legislation aimed against Christianity, or even any unjust legislation against the rights of the Roman Catholic Church will ultimately fail, and Archbishop Ireland is probably right in predicting a happy issue to the present struggle with a clearer understanding between the Church and State.

That the federal government is destined to play a larger, and the state

More Centralization. governments a smaller, part in the control of affairs in this country, is the opinion voiced by Secretary Root in his speech last week at the dinner of the Pennsylvania Society in New York City. The tendency, he says, is toward the obliteration of state lines. It is true that many influences are working in this direction. The increase of facilities for transportation, the movements of population from one state to another, the volume of interstate commerce and business and social relations generally—all tend to create a homogeneity of population and of governmental problems which has no parallel in the conditions of the thirteen states when the present scheme of federal and state government was formulated. Bad corporation laws, bad divorce laws, or bad administration of any laws in one state are an injury to all the other states. The question ultimately is not one of constitutionality, but of efficiency. If state governments permanently fail to govern with due regard to the welfare of the citizens of the nation, then some way will be found by which the federal government can take on those functions which the states show themselves unable to discharge. Meanwhile it will be the very important business of the party of the opposition to sound the note of alarm against dangerous encroachments of the federal power. It would not be strange if, when the Democratic party finds itself after its recent wanderings in the wilderness, the issue between the two great parties should be drawn upon the question of states rights more clearly than it has since the days of the Civil War.

The complaint of the people in the Northwest, especially in the Dakotas, of a coal

Car Shortage. famine and the dissatisfaction of shippers in the south with railroad facilities caused the president to institute an official inquiry as to the reasons of this alleged shortage of cars. Judge Prouty has been in St. Louis for several days taking the testimony of prominent railroad men and of shippers with a view of getting at the bottom facts. According to the evidence submitted the responsibility for this shortage in cars must be distributed between the railroads, the shippers and some of the middle men, who come between the railroads and the shippers. No doubt the roads have an inadequate supply of cars, but there is also lack of a wise use of the supply on hand. Cars are allowed to stand loaded with coal for several days in the yards, because the demurrage fees are less than the cost of storage. In talking with a railroad expert on this subject he claims that it is the speculator who comes in between the railroad and the consumers who causes this delay of cars in the yards, and that if the shipments could be made direct to the men for whom they are intended, this delay would be avoided. Another remedy he suggests would be to raise the price of demurrage to $3 a day per car instead of $1 per day. Already the good effects of the inquiry are being seen, and when the evidence is all in, there will probably be needed some legislation to avoid the evil from which the country has been suffering.

We are not afraid of Japan but that is no reason why we should pick a fight

America and the Japs. with her. Doubtless Japan is slightly megacephalous just at present as the result of her war with Russia, and unduly sensitive upon small points of national dignity like the segregation of her children in separate schools in San Francisco. But if so, it is no reason why we should choose precisely this time to take any measure which, while only slightly beneficial to us, would be highly offensive to them. One of the six special messages which the president sent to Congress last week (rather a big week's work even for our vigorous executive) conveyed the report of Secretary Metcalf who is investigating the situation on the coast. Mr. Metcalf reports that there have been numerous violent and riotous attacks on the persons and property of Japanese government, has not as yet shown its ability to give adequate protection. If they fail to do so, the federal government will be compelled to interfere. The objection which the people of San Francisco make to allowing Japanese adults to attend the public schools with American children is well founded. It would be objectionable to permit adults of any race to do so. Suit has already been brought to determine the right of the local authorities to exclude Japanese children on the score of their race alone, but the government hopes that the school boards will see their way to admit Japanese children, to whom there can be no serious objection, while excluding adults from the schools.

Editorial

The Circuit of the Year.

The calendar reminds us we are at the close of another year. The revolving earth, in its circuit around the sun, has brought us through the changing seasons, and is now completing its annual course, as it has been doing since time began. For

"Just as of old the seasons come and go.
The spring with its flowers, and the winter with its snow."

Time, the great tomb-builder, moves on his resistless way, neither quickening his speed to gratify the desire of youth, nor retarding it to suit the plans of age. Men come and go like bubbles on a stream, but the world goes on forever. Empires rise and fall. Generation follows generation with rapid pace, and the world moves on to its far-off destiny. How infinite must be the plan of God which embraces all these diverse and short-lived movements and agencies, and holds them all in subjection to the divine purpose! When one pauses, as he must at this season of the year, to think of the brevity of his own little life, of the immensity of God's universe, of the infinite scope of the all-embracing purpose of God, he can but feel humbled and awed into silence, as he realizes how infinitesimally small must be the place which any one life can fill in bringing about the realization of God's plan and purpose.

The year past has been an eventful one in the history of the world. A simple narration of the events of historic value would occupy more space than we can give. In our own nation events of far-reaching importance have taken place. The political and industrial life of the nation seems to be undergoing a process of regeneration. We are still in the midst of the process, however, and how long it will continue, and just what the outcome will be, no human mind can foresee. Of one thing we may be assured, and that is that God's hand is in all these movements, and that out of them we shall come, ultimately, a purer, juster, and more enlightened nation. Nor less certain may we feel that the great world-movement among the nations of the earth to secure a larger measure of rights and of equality among men will issue in greater freedom for the masses, who will be given a larger share of power and responsibility in government. In all the struggles of the past, the rights of the common people have ultimately triumphed over the tyranny of despots and the intrigues of courts. This is only saying, after all, that the kingdom of God is growing in the world, and asserting its power more and more over the affairs of human life. God is as surely with his people in their affliction and oppression, to-day, as he was with his ancient people in the brick kilns of Egypt. He is behind all movements for the betterment of human conditions, for the alleviation of suffering, for the promotion of righteousness, peace and unity among men, and for whatever makes for the progress of mankind. It is for us to be co-workers with God in carrying out his beneficent designs for the redemption of the world. The time is short in which any of us can do our little part to bless the world. In a little while we shall have accomplished our brief course on earth and have passed on to fulfill God's purpose in other spheres of activity that lie beyond. The swiftly-passing years remind us that what we do must be done quickly. They ought to remind us, also, that only that which is done for God will live as an abiding force for good in the world.

A Backward Glance.

One can scarcely close the arduous labors of a year without a look backward over what has been accomplished within the year. No man's work, perhaps, ever looks so large in retrospect as it does in prospect. We rarely, if ever, accomplish within the limits of a year all that we had hoped to do. We notice from the number, as well as from the date which THE CHRISTIAN-EVANGELIST bears this week, that this number completes its forty-third volume. There is not a large number of religious papers in the country that date back beyond the birth of this journal. Most of those that came into existence "to meet a long-felt want," as was supposed, have died young. Only now and then one survives the vicissitudes of time, and the diseases incident to newspaper infancy and childhood and attains its majority. Although the religious newspaper is not subject to the limitations of a human life, few have surpassed the period of three score and ten which the psalmist allotted to man.

In this backward glance over the year that has passed we can but feel thankful that we have been able, during each of the fifty-two weeks, to perform our allotted tasks. In the vast amount of matter we have written for the paper during the year, under all sorts of conditions, and often under depressing or disturbing influences, there has no doubt been much that has failed to come up to a high standard of literary excellence, and here and there, perchance, there has been a sentence or a phrase which, on maturer reflection, might have been left unwritten. It would be strange, at least, if this were not the case. As we look back over the work of the year in retrospect, however, it is a matter of no small comfort to us that we are conscious of having been actuated, in all that we have written and published, by the sincere desire to promote truth, build up our readers in the faith and service of God, and advance the reign of Christ among men.

It has been a year marked by earnest discussion in our journals, in which all have not seen alike but in which substantial progress has been made in solving some of the great problems which confront us. Time, which tests all things, will put its seal of approval or disapproval on what has been said on the one side and on the other. The winds of God which winnow out the chaff, leave all the wheat; and the fire which tests every man's work, of what sort it is, will burn up only the wood, hay and stubble, leaving unharmed, and only purified by trial, the gold, silver and precious stones. On all these questions we have tried to write in view of these tests of God. But whatever may be the fate of the work we have accomplished, we look confidently for his approval of the motive which prompted it.

We can not look back, in retrospect, without feeling our debt of gratitude, not only for the divine help and guidance, but for the earnest co-operation of many hearts and many hands of those who have wrought with us for the same common ends. A religious journal worthy of the name is vastly more than the personal organ of any one man or group of men; it is the medium of expression for a great body of believers, who use its columns for mutual interchange of thought, and for reporting what the Lord has wrought through them. We are profoundly grateful, too, for that vast body of friends whose names and contributions do not appear on our pages, but whose sympathy and endorsement have been expressed in their patronage and in assisting us in extending our circulation. In no year of its existence has THE CHRISTIAN-EVANGELIST had so many marks of public approval, nor so many new readers, as in the year now closing.

In the heat of the discussions of the year this paper's position has been grossly misrepresented, and some bitter partisans have accused its editor of abandoning the faith and betraying the sacred cause which has been committed to our hands. These things have not moved us from our straightforward course of advocating those movements and principles which we believe Christ approves and which are necessary to the triumph of the kingdom of God. Nor have we cherished any feeling of bitterness towards those who have thus misrepresented us. They may be as conscientious as we have tried to be. We are sure we could not have pursued a different course and maintained a good conscience toward God. We do not impugn the motive of others. God has made some things very clear to us. We can but be true to the light He has shown us. But we shall go out of the Old Year into the New Year, God willing, "with malice toward none and with charity for all."

And so, looking back over the year, we can but thank God for the past, and commit ourselves to Him for the future. His grace and wisdom, which have been our reliance in the past, are our hope in the years to come.

Notes and Comments.

The "Religious Herald" of Richmond, Va., prints an able address delivered by Dr. E. Y. Mullins, president of the Southern Baptist Theological Seminary, at Louisville, Ky., at the General Baptist Association in Richmond, Va., entitled "A New Defense of the Baptist Position." The address is an elaboration of the six axioms, which he stated at the Disciples' Congress at Indianapolis, namely:

1. The theological axiom: *The holy and loving God has a right to be sovereign.*
2. The religious axiom: *All souls have an equal right to direct access to God.*
3. The moral axiom: *To be responsible man must be free.*
4. The ecclesiastical axiom: *All believers have a right to equal privileges in the Church.*
5. The social axiom: *Love your neighbor as yourself.*
6. The religio-civic axiom: *A free Church in a free State.*

These propositions Dr. Mullins rightly affirms are "self-evident. They are the axioms of religion. The instructed religious consciousness cannot and will not repudiate them, however inconsistent men may be in applying them." They exclude infant baptism, all systems of hierarchy, and the union of church and state, as Dr. Mullins contends.

As to the relation of Baptists and other religious bodies to these axioms of religion, Dr. Mullins says:

Now, two of these axioms Baptists have not been alone in holding—viz.: the theological and the social. But four of them they alone have consistently held throughout their history. Three of them they alone consistently hold to-day— viz.: the religious, the moral, and the ecclesiastical. The soul's right to deal with God directly, the soul's freedom in obeying the ordinances, and the equal ity of believers in Church life, Baptists alone consistently hold. One wing of the Church of the Disciples agree with us in holding them, but the other wing puts baptism between the soul and God, by making baptism a condition of remission of sins.

This statement by so able and fair-minded a man as Dr. Mullins concerning the attitude of "one wing" of the Disciples of Christ to one of these axioms, will be certain to interest all our readers, among whom we take it are both "wings." Dr. Mullins' remark raises this question: Does he mean that the position that baptism is *in any sense* for remission of sins, conflicts with the axiom of "the soul's freedom in obeying that ordinance"? He does not, for he himself believes that baptism is for the *ceremonial* remission of sins.' In what *sense*, then, must one view baptism in relation to remission of sins, to conflict with "the soul's freedom in obeying the ordinances"? The view that baptism is absolutely essential in all cases to remission of sins, whether one understands the command and his duty to obey it or not. The "wing" among the Disciples of Christ that holds that arbitrary view of baptism is so small as to be a negligible quantity. It is only one of the *pin-feathers* of undeveloped the ological birdlings.

But Dr. Mullins' statement raises another question: Is the position that baptism is

"unto remission of sins" in the sense that it is a help which God has given to the believer to enable him, by actual self-commitment to Him in that overt act, to gain the assurance of divine forgiveness, in conflict with the axiom referred to above? Hardly, we should say. And yet such a view "puts baptism between the soul and God," not as a fence to keep him away, however, but as a gate to admit him into closer fellowship with God. In other words, if baptism be regarded as a condescension on the part of sovereign love to human need in helping men, by means of a definite, concrete act of self-surrender, to commit themselves to Christ as Saviour and Lord, and thus to come into a relation of peace with God, it is in perfect harmony with the soul's freedom, and with every other axiom of religion, as well as with the clearest New Testament teaching. Does Dr. Mullins hold that such a view is contrary to his axiom? We would be glad to know.

In his department of Biblical Criticism in the "Christian Standard," Bro. J. W. McGarvey, after quoting and commenting on a paragraph from "The Scroll," says:

I think it now in order to ask J. H. Garrison, who is an honorary member of the Institute by which this *Scroll* is published, whether he is really in sympathy with it. I have a right to ask this; for it is declared in the constitution of the Institute, as I have already quoted, that before one is elected to honorary membership he must be investigated by the nominating committee to make sure that he is in sympathy with the organization. If he is not, he owes it to himself, and to the cause of Christ, to say so publicly and positively. This is also the duty of every member whose sympathies are misrepresented; and I am glad to know that some members have withdrawn their membership on the ground that it grossly misrepresents them.

If this were from some one for whom we feel less respect than we do for Brother McGarvey, we should not feel called upon to notice it. Neither Brother McGarvey nor any intelligent, fair-minded reader of the above paragraph, needs to be told that sympathy with these young men and with the general purpose of their organization to keep up their scholarly habits and to pursue certain lines of investigation, does not commit one to an endorsement of all their views. Otherwise we would all be found in a most embarrassing position. Few of us could remain connected with any missionary organization, or with any church, if such connection involved an endorsement of all the views of all the other members. On this principle think how many readers of the "Christian Standard" would be compelled to stop the paper! We know personally many of the young men of the Campbell Institute, and admire their characters and ability. They understand quite well that we do not share all their views, for we have met with them once or twice and have contested their positions. Nor do they all agree among themselves. They do not have to. Recently we criticised an utterance of "The Scroll," and shall feel perfectly free to do so in the future. When they notify the Editor that this attitude of freedom to crit-

Editor's Easy Chair.

This is the night for the annual meeting of our circle of Easy Chair readers. Stir the fire; put on another backlog, and widen the circle, for many new faces have joined us since we last gathered in annual council. How swiftly the months have fled! This is the last night of the Old Year! "It is a time for memory, and for tears." The dying year rises before us and calls us to account for the manner in which we have spent it. In thinking over the matter certain questions have come to us as if they had fallen from the lips of the great Judge before whom we shall stand in the last day, and before whom, in a very real sense, we stand every day. Have we a clearer and truer vision of God than we had a year ago? Have we a stronger grip on Christ, and do we enjoy his companionship more than we did at the beginning of this year? Do we grasp more firmly the reality of the life eternal, as having its beginning in us already? In the power of this quickened faith do we find it easier to conquer self, resist temptation, and hold in subjection the body with its appetites and passions? Do we relish more keenly the word of God and the privilege of prayer? These are testing questions and each one may answer them to his own conscience. It is not always easy for us to see that we have made any actual progress in the spiritual life, and these questions may help us to decide whether we have been simply marking time, or whether we are really following Christ. These questions as to our attainments, imply others relating to our achievements that are perhaps more easily answered. Have we done good, for evil, prayed for our enemies, conquered our tempers, controlled our tongues, practiced charity towards our neighbors, and entered the doors of opportunity which God's providence has opened to us? These questions have to do with practicing Christianity rather than with merely professing it. They will serve as the basis for a profitable meditation for each of our readers on the closing night of the Old Year.

❀

There now! It is good to bring our lives frequently to the bar of conscience, but it is not intended that we should always live in the white light that beats upon the judgment throne. There are other voices speaking to us to-night and they, too, must be heard. Memory and Hope each has its message for us. Each of them sings to us its own sweet songs. Memory sings:

"How dear to my heart are the scenes of my childhood
When fond recollection presents them to view!
The orchard, the meadow, the deep-tangled wildwood
And all the loved scenes which my infancy knew."

And then there rises before our vision that dear old home, about which cluster a thousand hallowed memories. It was perhaps a very humble home, but father, mother, brothers and sisters, were there, and love, which sweetens and ennobles all life, and hallows the humblest abodes, was there. That humble cottage home

rises out of the dim mists of the past, this last night of the Old year, and fills our hearts with its holy memories. We think of those who were but are not. Some of those who started with us on life's journey have grown weary and laid down to rest. Why are we here yet? The long, toilsome journey over which we have come, stretches away behind us to the distant past. Would we go back and live it all over again? Here Hope raises her triumphant note and sings of "a land that is fairer than day," that lies "further on." And "the Father waits over the way to prepare us a dwelling-place there." No, we would not go back, for all the heart holds fondest is to be regained and enjoyed forever in the Father's house that is before us. Thank God for Memory and Hope! The one holds all the best treasures of the Past, and the other opens to us the infinite possibilities of the Future.

❀

What are we going to do with this New Year that is soon to dawn? Shall we not try to use it as a gift from God? Shall we not seek to have the sins of the past blotted out, and make a new beginning? Some people are afraid of them. But how can any conscientious man, realizing his sins and mistakes in the past, avoid making new resolutions for the future? Can he deliberately compromise with sin and purposely lower his ideals to his life, instead of trying to lift up his life to his ideals? The mistake is in limiting our resolutions to New Year. Each day is a new leaf in our life-volume and each morning we should resolve with God's help to make that day better than the preceding one. But there is something impressive in the passing of an old year and the birth of a new one that strikes the imagination and causes us to realize the awful brevity of life and its deep solemnity. This fact makes it a peculiarly appropriate time for a man to look himself squarely in the face and ask himself a few plain questions about his soul's health and the tendencies of his life. Men take stock in business to see how they stand. Why should they not do so in religion? We know one prince merchant who has a skilled physician employed to call at his office at stated times and make a thorough examination of his physical condition, lest some insidious disease should make such an inroad into his system before it was detected as to shorten his life. Is it not a wiser precaution to look after the health of the spiritual man, lest sin in its insidious way undermine the soul, corrupt the heart and lead us into spiritual bankruptcy? Let us take stock.

❀

We say "Time flies." What is time? The dictionaries can not tell you. They give you words without ideas. To say that "it is a system of those relations which one event sustains to another, as past, present or future," is not to add one iota of information to what is known by a child. We may think of it as a stream flowing by, or we may think of time as stationary, and the world and all therein as moving on. Time, one authority says, "is a measured portion of dura-

tion;" but as duration is time, that is only to say that "time is a measured portion of time!" It may be said that time is that part of eternity that is measured off into years, months and days. But years, months and days are determined by planetary revolutions. How do we know that these measurements will ever cease? What we do know is that the period of our sojourn here in the body is brief, and that our future existence is to bear a very close and vital relation to the life we are now living. Death is not the end of one being or personality, and the birth of a new one, but an event in the life of a deathless spirit whose continuity is unbroken by it. As we who pass from the Old Year into the New will not thereby lose our identity, nor be released from debts and obligations we have contracted, so the human spirit in its passage from its earthly tabernacle to its "house not made with hands, eternal in the heavens," does not lose its identity or change its character. Whatsoever a man sows, in the soil of his earth-life, he will reap in the field of destiny. That makes it a very solemn thing to live. And yet it makes life seem worth living. If no generous deed, no noble thought, no high aspiration, no worthy effort, no act of self-sacrifice for the true and the right, no truth gained, no victory over self, can possibly be lost, but is to bring its harvest of good through the eternal years, then, indeed, "to be living is sublime."

❀

The hour is late and the hands on the clock point to the closing moments of the year, 1906. Soon the Old Year will be gone forever. Well, we have had a good time together, have we not, during the year that is now taking its flight? When the year was young we took you all with us on a journey to New Mexico, and together we traversed its valleys and scaled its mountains, visited some of its pueblos, noted some of its scenic attractions and climatic advantages and prophesied of its future. Later in the season you went with us to the pine woods of Michigan, where the great lake meets the forest-crowned hills, and the two pool their charms in forming an ideal summer resort. There we spent several weeks together in the delightful haunts of Garrison Park at Pentwater, keeping close to the heart of Nature, and seeking to understand something of its deeper meaning. You have gone with us to our Congress, and to our National Conventions and shared with us the glorious fellowship of these great occasions. Many a quiet chat we have had together, sometimes on the deeper things of the spiritual life, and sometimes in lighter vein. Sometimes, perhaps, the quiet waters of this department have been slightly disturbed by the waves of controversy beating on the outside, but ordinarily we have reserved the Easy Chair musings as a quiet haven where storm-tossed vessels may enter and find rest from wind and wave. You, kind readers, have been a great help to us during the year, and if the Easy Chair has brought some good cheer and strength to you in bearing your burdens, and in performing your tasks, we give thanks to Him whose help we constantly seek, that we may others bless. If you choose to journey with us another year, as we trust you all may, we shall strive to do thee good, and only good. Good-bye, Old Year! Welcome, the New!

What Lack We Yet?   By H. H. Hubbell

This is a time of great rejoicing. From the Buffalo host has come the sound of battle and the pean of victory. How it stirs the hearts of the brethren who are contending for the simple faith and obedience in the neglected fields to receive such messages of advancement and to catch a heavenly vision of brotherly fellowship in God's great work! May we not be pardoned, when surrounded with so much that hinders our cause in the west, if down in our hearts we rejoice in numbers and figures, which tell of unprecedented growth? Surely we may hear the benediction of "Well done, good and faithful servant" for what has been accomplished. This is not taking the satisfaction that our labor is ended now that victory has come to our banners, but only putting into our hearts that faith and courage which come with the realization that our labor is not in vain in the Lord.

It seems to me most appropriate that at this time our great brotherhood should come unto the Captain of our Salvation, realizing the struggle and victories of the past and in the spirit of humility and with holy desire, asking, wherein lack we yet? Like the questioner of old, we have been walking in God's commandments from our youth up. But we do not come with this question with the feeling of perfection attained. Nay, realizing our shortcomings and that we should be wholly prepared for the work whereunto God has called us, we can say with the Apostle Paul: "For to this end we labor and strive, because we have our hope set on the living God." As one of the young men of our ministry, I have ever rejoiced in the foundation work of our fathers. They were the peers among God's people and, it is no slight upon their ability or devotion to the truth to say that the present hour finds us—their children in the Gospel—lacking in some things. He who is blind to his faults has no opportunity of correcting them. For more than ten years I have been trying to preach Jesus Christ to our churches in Iowa, Kansas and Idaho, and I believe I am well acquainted with their doctrine, conversation and manner of life.

In loyalty to God's word, in obedience to many of the commandments, we have led the Christian world, but, brethren, the prayer of my heart is that we should be not one whit lacking in the spiritual things of God. Not that we should rightly divide the Word or preach faith, repentance, confession and baptism the less, but that we lay a greater emphasis upon the spiritual life. In our own daily living we can well afford to take the advice of the writer of Hebrews: "Wherefore leaving the doctrine of the first principles of Christ, let us go on unto perfection." Brethren, think you that prayer, that great boon of living with God as companion, friend and helper, has its full place in the daily living? Have we but speaking acquaintance with our blessed God and Saviour Jesus Christ? When I see so many of our brethren merely tasting of God's goodness or refusing altogether to enter into the joys of spiritual fellowship, I can not help but pray that the time has come for a strong plea for a deepening of the life in Christ Jesus. What would it mean for our churches to have such a blessing? It would mean an enlargement of our hearts, one for the other. We be brethren. It would mean joy and happiness to all who love the holy cause of missions, for one can not dwell with Jesus and not catch the burden of his heart—the salvation of the world. It would mean that the church of the Lord Jesus Christ would receive such a blessing as not to be able to contain it. We would be caused to cry out with Paul in the joy of our hearts: "O the depth of the riches and the wisdom and the knowledge of God! For of him, and through him, and unto him, are all things. To him be the glory forever, Amen."

Grangeville, Idaho.

"Is There a Missing Link?"

By W. J. Wright, Cor. Sec. of the American Christian Missionary Society.

The speed of a fleet is that of its slowest vessel. Something similar, not identical, may be affirmed of the church and her organizations. The Good Shepherd keeps pace with those that can not move rapidly. He carries the feeble lambs and gives special care to the old and lame. Herein is a lesson. Even if tastes and ability enable us to travel rapidly in perfect safety, sympathy and love constrain us to be patient and to stay in the company of those who "make haste slowly." However, if some insist on a more rapid gait, my verdict is, "They are not lost, but gone before." I have sufficient faith, charity or credulity to think of those who out-travel me, as walking in old paths, good ways, and finding rest for their souls.

I fully believe that any thoroughly representative body of our brotherhood is sane and safe; and that, call it mass meeting, convention or what you may, it will do what is right, provided time and opportunity be given for full discussion. I am not afraid of temperance resolutions because passed by a missionary society. If the mass meeting or convention should act or resolve contrary to my principles, I am not bound. I am free and will act just as if the assembly had not spoken.

But some of my brethren are afraid to trust men in a missionary convention, even though they might trust the same men in a mass meeting. For their sake, let us move slowly, and let missionary conventions be missionary only.

1. Because "This one thing I do," is a good motto even for a missionary society.

2. Because for me to enjoy my full liberty in this matter, offends my brother. For his sake I must put away what he regards as an idol.

3. Because in present conditions, for the convention to be anything more than missionary, hurts the society and retards the work of the Lord. A man offended by something said or done in a session of the American Christian Missionary Society, acts as if the offensive thing were done "by the determinate counsel and foreknowledge" of the acting board. He withdraws his support and induces others to do the same. This is like the stupid and cowardly boycott which "starves out" the preacher. The offended gains his point but the issue is not settled.

To attack one society for such a thing is to attack all, for the conventions of all the societies are made up of the same men; and a mass meeting would have the same identical constituency. The same men can not be paragons of wisdom when you call them the Foreign Society, and dolts and ninnies when you call them the Home Society. Their qualities and characters are constant. For that reason, if I may trust them at one time under one name, I can trust them at whatever time or under whatever name.

But some of the brethren do not see this. I am unwilling to offend them. If our Father can wait so long for the consummation of his plans, surely we can possess our souls in patience while gray matter grows in our heads and grace in our hearts.

Supply the missing link in a mass meeting apart from the sessions of all our societies. Let it wrangle or hold love-feasts, according to its moods. To it let the man go who would have passed a resolution of sympathy with the starving people in a fire, flood or famine-swept region, to it send the friend of temperance, education and beneficence; from it send forth the message of fraternal greeting to the M. E. conference or general assembly of Presbyterians who are in session at the same time in distant cities; for, strictly interpreted, none of these things is missionary.

And if some wise man laughs at me for my formality; if he reminds me that whatever we call ourselves for three hours, we are the identical persons who made up the various conventions; if with remorseless logic he points out that we who theoretically are the freest of all religious peoples, are in danger of binding ourselves with the cast-off chains of our religious neighbors, I am not silenced. I can answer neither his laugh nor his logic. He holds the stronger position there. But I shall say to him, "I can more easily bear your laughter, and can more easily forget your logic and warnings, than I can endure seeing the work of the American Christian Missionary Society suffer. Therefore, for the present, and until more of the brethren are convinced that liberty and loyalty will walk hand in hand, and that love will never work ill to his neighbor, let our missionary conventions be missionary and nothing more."

By William Bayard Craig.

Undoubtedly we need a convention of a representative character to deal with matters of general interest outside the scope of the present missionary societies. Such a convention might not need to meet oftener than once in three years. It would be better in my judgment to organize such a convention on a more strictly representative basis than anything we now have and as such a convention might at some time wish to consider questions involving the relationship of the present societies to each other and the whole church, it would seem best that it should not be an enlarged Home Missionary Society.

The present conventions are necessarily conducted and dominated by the needs of the special work and presented as seen from that peculiar viewpoint. We need a convention organized in the interest of a viewpoint central to our whole work in all its varied aspects, that would naturally consider the happiest co-ordination of all special interests. It is high time we were considering the best means of accomplishing this desirable result.

Denver, Colo.

❖

By S. R. Drake.

I am in favor of "a conference or congress of Christians" to convene two days before the general conventions, or in connection with the "Congress of Disciples" in which any Christian in America, or on the globe can meet and have a voice in the discussion of any and all great questions pertaining to the kingdom of heaven, that may come before such a "conference of Christians." I would prefer the word "congress" to "conference." I favor a separate organization by all means, where every Christian can become a member and have a voice in the discussion of these great questions affecting the interests of the Church of Christ.

Inspiration for Evangelization

Being the Final Part of the Address before the Buffalo Convention on "Disciples and Evangelism."

By J. P. Lichtenberger

A great tidal wave of evangelism is sweeping over the country. The Welsh revival and the Torrey and Alexander meetings in England, Australia and America have attracted world-wide attention, and quickened the evangelistic pulse. Continent-wide campaigns have been organized by several religious bodies. The readiness of the people to hear the Gospel is attested by evangelists everywhere. Dr. Hillis tells this incident to illustrate this condition. He said: "Standing in a cart a while ago, at the noon hour, I told a group of several hundred men to go on smoking while I was speaking. Do you say that these men are not interested in the great themes of God and the soul? I answer that before my 25 minute address was complete the pipes had all gone out. When I was through I saw from 200 to 400 men reach for matches, scratch them on their thighs, and fight their pipes, while they stood and discussed, and talked for a few minutes before hastening back to their work."

In Brooklyn there are fifteen noon meetings with groups of from 50 to 300 men who give up thirty minutes of their noon hour to a study of the life of Christ. Recently 20,000 men in one week heard the gospel in shop meetings in the city of Cleveland. Two weeks ago 1,000 Methodist ministers and laymen met as a great committee in New York to consider plans for their winter's evangelistic campaign.

Among our own forces the situation is encouraging. All our leading evangelists are engaged for a year ahead. Our papers often report a thousand additions in the telegrams of a single issue, and the evangelistic season has scarcely opened.

Our centennial campaign arises to supply the need of the hour, to organize, to systematize, and to direct our forces. A state-wide program as in Ohio should be arranged in every state and these all marshalled in one great simultaneous, continent-wide campaign for our centennial year. Thus will it be the year of our jubilee and a million souls shall be won for the glory of our risen Lord.

Other great enterprises have been organized well worthy of our attention and effort as appropriate centennial memorials. These let us do, but not to the neglect of the one great and supreme work of the church. That which most honors the Christ and blesses the world, is not stately edifices, gorgeous rituals, or monuments made with hands, but lives won and consecrated to the cause of God and humanity.

It is the evangelistic note in all our preaching that is to save us from formalism and from crystalization. The Gospel is not a system of morals nor a theology, but a Divine Passion. The church stands hesitant on the threshold of the 20th century, (1) not because she lacks knowledge. The knowledge of the Lord covers America as the waters cover the sea. Men know the truth. Pulpit and press have not been recreant to their trust as the teachers of the people. (2) Not because she lacks opportunity. The multitudes hear the message gladly. Doors of opportunity stand wide open on every hand. The home-land is white for the harvest; the Macedonian cry has become the cry of continents; and the isles of the sea wait for his law. (3)

Nor does she lack equipment. Never was the church so well organized for effective service. We have ample means and men. But the church of God is in camp. Our moral machinery is complete but it does not work. Our engine is perfect but it lacks steam. Our dynamo is installed but it fails of the current. The one thing needful is motive, passion, power! The sermon is to be "not so much an essay with a subject, as a theme with an object." The Christian is not merely to live a correct moral life but to be a vital, active force for righteousness. The church is to be, not so much a cold storage plant of correct doctrine as a power house of spiritual dynamics.

It is evangelistic fervor for the salvation of men that is to thrill the preacher and send him out to do His will on earth as it is done in heaven. Culture, education, equipment, are of value only when lit up by a holy passion to complete for men what He began to do and teach.

It is evangelistic fire that is to take the church, organized, drilled, equipped as an army with banners and hurl it with the abandon of a conquering host against the indifferent, pleasure seeking, selfish civilization of our time, not with the spirit of repression, not with the desire or hope of turning backward the march of progress, but of guiding it along the highway that leads to God.

THE ANGELS' SONG.

Into the silence of our world dropt the Angels' Song,
And the mystery and the marvel are with us long!

*   *   *   *   *   *

No change of time can spoil Him of His claim—
The Son of God—but with the human name.
Love leaps to love across the loveless years,
Sobbed through with sorrows, trembled through with tears!
There is a sweetness in that song that stills
The whirlwind of our woes and soothes our ills;
Though we are slow of heart to understand
All that the Lord hath spoken; yet in every land
The Angels' Song has bent the pitying skies
A little nearer to the shepherds' eyes!

And evermore may those who listen hear
The chorus of the heavenly host who brought good cheer
To earth so long ago. And those who sought have found
The place where He was born still holy ground!
The manger and the cross, the empty grave
Are symbols of the power of Christ to save!
The world can never be the same to them
Whose hands have touched the seamless hem
Of holy garments; whose eyes have seen the vision fair
Are born of God, and such may not despair!

—*Charles Blanchard.*

The Parthenogenic Controversy By William Dur[ban]

An extraordinary sensation has been created here in England throughout the whole religious world. It has been aroused through a discussion at the annual assembly of the Congregational Union, held at Wolverhampton, the great Midland town which is a centre of the iron industry and was the scene of the ministry of the lamented and beloved Dr. Berry, who was designated by Henry Ward Beecher as his successor. The Congregationalists in Britain have of late years not given so much attention to doctrinal theology (at any rate in polemic fashion) as to evangelization and to practical church and mission enterprise amongst the masses at home. They have rivalled the Methodists in planting institutional centres and great halls for the accommodation of the working people, and have been achieving magnificent success. Yet theologically they have not been by any means inert, for I think that, as in the days of Brock, Landels, Hugh Stowell Brown, C. M. Birrell, Nathaniel Haycroft, the elder Mursell, Rosevear, Aldis, Charles Clark, Charles Stovell, Howard Hinton (with Charles Williams, Alexander McLaren, Archibald Brown, E. G. Gange, and one or two other splendid pulpit orators then in their prime, but now in the sunset years), the Baptists possessed an eclipsing galaxy of eminent preachers; so now, Congregationalism is adorned with a larger number of popular ministers than any other English body. R. J. Campbell, Horton, Horne, Jowett, Barrett and Campbell Morgan certainly take the first place in popularity. No other denomination is able to match these Congregationalist preachers, although the Baptists have in the magnificent personality of Dr. Clifford, who has recently been receiving world-wide honors on attaining his 70th birthday anniversary, perhaps the most striking figure in the whole of the English Christian ministry of the day. But, though the Congregationalist ministry was never, perhaps, as brilliant as it is at this juncture, it is to the credit of the denomination that it has been for several years showing paramount solicitude about all-round practical religious efforts for the stolid and unevangelized myriads of the common people.

A Darkening Discussion.

Deep regrets prevail in the ranks of Free Churchmen in view of the strange unwisdom—as I believe most thoughtful minds consider it—of introducing into a great public conference so difficult and delicate a topic as the theological problem of the Virgin Birth. For the utmost logical confusion soon marked the debate that ensued. The occasion was opened by a fine paper on orthdox and conservative lines, by the able minister of Norwich, Dr. Barrett. Now, this East Anglian preacher is no obscurantist. He has never been reckoned

amongst the ministerial fossils, but is always adding some worthy contribution to any topic that he treats with tongue or pen. But he was doubtless not a little astonished and distressed, to judge by his remarks at the close of the discussion, at the tempestuous clashing of opinions that his paper provoked. There has never, I venture to assert, occurred so momentous a controversy at a religious gathering in England, since the distressing and calamitous Downgrade discussion at the Baptist Union Assembly, raised by the vehement protests of the late C. H. Spurgeon, who seceded from the Baptist Union with the great majority of his collegians immediately after. The controversy on the Virgin Birth is not likely to cause actual disruption in the Congregational denomination, any more than in the Anglican Church, but in both bodies it is simply raging furiously as a matter of theological opinion. It is singular that the Congregationalist authorities who arranged the program of the Wolverhampton proceedings should have incorporated so difficult a problem. No better man than Dr. Barrett could have been found to deal with it. Yet he immediately had on his back, fiercely tearing at his position, some of the most noted collegiate professors and preachers present. The uttermost confusion reigned. And consternation has been spread through the churches at discovering that Congregationalist ministers, as well as instructors of ministerial students, are all at sea over this physiological and psychological problem of the New Testament. Some of the speakers took up the position, in direct opposition to Dr. Barrett, that the incarnation may be a matter of devout faith without the acceptance of the dogma of the Virgin Birth; though they were densely nebulous in attempting to explain this way of dodging the miraculous. Other clever gentlemen tried to make out that it is the resurrection, not the incarnation at all, which is doctrinally essential, seeing that Paul and the other writers of the Epistles, as well as the writers of the Acts of the Apostles, lay stress on the resurrection of Christ, not at all on his birth.

A Hideous Quagmire.

I must confess that personally I am lost in amazement at the precipitation of these undoubtedly able controversialists. It is singular indeed that they do not seem to perceive that they are in the hands of the most dangerous of all the modern infidels, the atheistic biologists of the school of Ernst Haeckel, who in his chair as one of the scientific professors at the University of Jena, as well as in his great and imposing books, "The Riddle of the Universe," and "Monism," has not only sought to establish the eternity of matter as an infallible dogma, eliminating all notion of any pos-

sible Creator, but has taken special to pour scurrilous derision on the doctrine of the incarnation, especially reference to the Virgin Birth. that during long years of observ[ation] have seen and heard nothing th[at] seemed so painful and so humilia[ting] the reverent Christian mind as thi[s] tacle, and this widely circulated re[port of] proceedings at Wolverhampton, a number of doctors of divinity tumbled over each other in order to the hungry wolves of the not and ravening Jena menagerie. only yesterday talking with an old loved C. H. Spurgeon. Said he, perhaps as well, after all our mo[urning] that dear Spurgeon was taken awa[y] though he sorrowed so deeply ov[er] recklessness of the chief promot[ers of] the Downgrade, this new departure the straight paths of the Puritanism exalted England and made her must have simply broken his hea[rt] will prove by "verifying my refere[nce] as Lord Salisbury exhorted us all that this astounding Congregatio[nalist] escapade leads in a direction whic[h] scalpers of a venerable dogma s[eem] unable to realize. In his "Riddle [of the] Universe" Haeckel goes out of his to rake up an ancient fable abou[t] Virgin Mary, concocted by blasphe[mous] Jewish enemies of the Christian This outrageous myth, ascribing di[vine] our to Mary in terms I dare not here, alleges that she became the m[other] of Jesus after being deceived by a R[oman] centurion named Panders. And H[aeckel] actually quotes this dastardly slanc[er as] authentic history. Even in his own try this called forth unspeakable nation although our German cousi[ns] fairly accustomed to heresy. O[n] book shelves stands beside the vol of Haeckel the book entitled " Haeckel," written by Dr. Frie[drich] Loofs, professor of church histo[ry at] Halle University, who is style[d by] Prof. Sanday, of Oxford, "that scientific of German theologians." withering chapters Loofs ex cient documents and his shameful lessness in referring to fables as his[tory.] The comparison of these two book[s of] the Jena and the Halle professors have been neglected by the gentl who rushed into the fray at W[olver]hampton ready to trample both o[n] Barrett and on the Evangelists Ma and Luke. Otherwise they might discovered that Haeckel was so di[scredited] fited that in a later edition he pa[rtly] modified his notorious and blasphe[mous] Chapter 17 of the "Riddle." Now, is a new "Riddle," not of the uni but of the "Free Churches and of E[van]gelical Protestantism." Where ar going? What are we likely to hear and who is to be the next trusted leader to betray his sacred trust? I have refrained from mentioning the names of the professors and the well-known preachers who at Wolverhampton astounded the assembly. For I do not wish this letter to be in any sense personal. But I honor and admire Dr. Barrett the more. He will stand to his guns. Lastly, is it not strange that there should be so widespread an ignorance of elementary biology amongst cultured theologians? Huxley, when asked whether he could believe in the Virgin Birth and

the resurrection, replied that whatever difficulty might attach to the idea of the resurrection, there was none about the Virgin Birth, because there are among the lowest orders of creatures millions of virgin births. Parthenogenesis is the commonest of all facts low down in creation. As to the easy notion of accepting the resurrection while rejecting the miraculous element in the incarnation, this device is laughed to scorn by all infidels. The Anglican Church is distracted by this very dispute on the Virgin Birth. Last year the Rev. C. E. Beeby avowed his

disbelief in the doctrine and was constrained by the bishop of Birmingham, Dr. Gore, to give up his living. Canon Henson took fire at this and vehemently denounced Bishop Gore's action, but this was sustained by an overwhelming consensus of opinion. Mr. Percy Gardner, a prominent broad churchman, steps forward and declares in defending Mr. Beeby that both the Virgin Birth and the resurrection lie right across the path of modern historic criticism. Yes, it is certain that both miracles must find credence or neither.

The Elderburg Association

CHAPTER X.

Brother Editor Tells a Frenzied Story of Fragmentary Finance.

Brother Editor, who was next on the program, was a middle-aged man whose appearance affected the beholder strangely. He somehow suggested a man at a health resort, recovering, almost recovered, from a long and wasting illness. One saw that his form was bent, but not so much as it had been; that his cheeks were hollow, but not so hollow as formerly; that his expression was careworn, yet less careworn than of yore. He was a living hieroglyph, decipherable by all men: the ideograph for convalescence.

"You behold in me," he said, "no victim of frenzied finance, but a victim of petrified finance, paralyzed finance, idiotic, unstable, hand-to-mouth, inhuman, unblushing, scandalously inefficient and inadequate finance; finance without rhyme or reason or truth; finance the methods of which, applied to the affairs of any business concern in this land, would spell bankruptcy, sooner or later—with the odds two to one in favor of sooner.

"I keep, or rather my wife keeps a little canvas-bound book. In that book, for many years, I entered the items of my accounts with the churches where I labored. Therein may be found, in the beautiful, small, ladylike handwriting which has since become so dear to the printers in my office, entries of all items of money, meal, mutton, merchandise and milk received by me from church boards and individual Christians in payment of my salary. This book is not cherished by me as a blessed memento of my past. On the contrary, I hate the sight of it. But my wife keeps it and uses it judiciously as a whip to keep me pulling steadily in the editorial traces. For there are times when my soul is not at ease in Zion; times when I have an uncomfortable feeling that I ought to be at work preparing a sermon for Sunday. When my wife detects any symptoms of this uneasiness she gets out that old book and says: 'Dear, let us go over this together, and go back in imagination to the delightful, dead past, and recall old times and places, and play that we are preaching again.' That cures me.

"In that book are entered credits for cream, cabbages, and carrots; for potatoes,

pickles and pork; for sauer-kraut, sausage and sorghum; for butter, bran and bacon; for mackerel, melons and middling-meat: all turned in on my salary, the average amount opposite each item being thirty-four and seven-eighths cents.

"I never see that book without an involuntary sinking of the heart such as I used to feel after my settlements with the board at the end of each month. I had my dreams sometimes—who has not? I used to have visions of a small surplus after settlement, enough to get my wife a pair of shoes, after paying the rent; but usually it happened that some one had turned in an account for lard, lettuce or 'lasses to the amount of eighty cents, while another had demanded credit for turnips, tomatoes, or 'taters—items which had eluded the drag net of my book-keeping. In these particulars, however, the associations are with things painful rather than with things disastrous; they are connected with the days when I was young and tender-hearted, too apt to sympathize with the hard-times plaint of the churches. As to these particulars, also, the experiences, while painful, were perhaps not unwholesome. Once I heard a preacher say, 'If the Lord will keep me humble, my congregation will keep me poor.' I amend that by saying, 'If the congregation will keep me impoverished, the Lord need not bother about keeping me humble: the humiliation will take care of itself.' The book is not only associated with things painful, but it has its chapters of disaster.

"I was called to the work at Spickspan. A pretty little village, with a pretty little church, a pretty little organ and a pretty little choir. They had a pretty little standard set for their preacher, as to manners, social qualities, pulpit ability, and dress for himself and family: for which they paid the pretty little salary of $800 a year. It was an 'up-to-date' little church, but it was seldom quite on-date with the cash for its pastor's salary. Quite abreast of the times in choir music, but away behind time with the preacher's stipend. Yet in any commercial agency this congregation would be rated solvent, able to make good its contracts. Moreover, it boasted, with good reason, that it had never allowed a pastor to leave there with his salary unpaid. Bear in mind the fact that this congregation was solvent. Bear in mind, also, the facts that my work was acceptable to the people and

that the church really prospered under my care, except in one particular.

"My arrangement with the board was for monthly settlements. After the first few months, payments fell behind, and from that on to the end of the year there was seldom a time when the amount those people owed me was not considerable. The money came in driblets.

"Under a system like that it was necessary for me to go in debt for the necessaries of life. Naturally, the people with whom these debts were contracted asked for their money when I did not, after a reasonable time, pay without asking. I need not point out to intelligent men like you all the elements of danger there is in the deadly store account for necessaries; how the debt exceeds the expectations and intentions of the debtors; how, especially, the driblet income is fatally inadequate to the meeting of financial obligations of any considerable amounts. I am making no excuse for my own mistakes, understand, or for any carelessness or lack of business capacity I may have shown in the management of my own affairs. If there were faults of my own I paid for them at last, in currency, and in heartache and humiliation. There may be here or there a Napoleon of finance who can husband the penny and hoard the nickel until the driblet becomes a full-sized drib, big enough to discharge the largest store account; and also there may be here and there a housewife who can borrow a bucket of water from the rain-barrel, replacing it at last with water caught in a pint cup held under the drippings of the eaves: the one task is as easy as the other; but I am equal to neither. I do not mind admitting that I am not a Napoleon of finance.

"When the duns came—and they began at last to come thick and fast—what was I to do if I had not the money to pay? For my reputation's sake I must give some reason for failure to pay; and for my soul's sake I could give no reason but the true one. Invariably, almost, I would tell the bill-collector the church owed me more than enough to pay: and in every instance I would make an honest effort to collect the money. It was inevitable that the owners of accounts would investigate, at last; they would go to leading members of the congregation and ask if the church owed me money; and they would casually remark that they had a small account, which, etc., etc. This would perhaps annoy the members. The disastrous thing, however, was the fact that the private affairs of the preacher, and the financial affairs of the congregation became at last matters of common gossip on the street.

"When shall I forget that bitterest day of my life when the elders called on me in a body and remonstrated with me about my debts? A man to whom I owed a bill to the amount of thirty dollars had complained to them. This, taken in connection with previous complaints from others, had caused them to investigate, and they had gone about town and had ascertained from various sources the gross sum of my obligations. In the aggregate, that sum was rather large, yet not beyond my resources, if my people would only be prompt in meeting their obligations to me. At that moment they owed me enough to discharge one-half of my indebtedness; the other half was not beyond my means to pay, with economy on my part and promptness on the part of the church; and my creditors were reasonable men, personally friendly to me.

"I shall never forget the pain of that hour. I had tried to lead a harmless, cleanly life, there as elsewhere, and I could not but feel the humiliation keenly. It was then that I showed those elders my book—the dear little, canvas-covered book which my wife guards under lock and key to keep me from burning it. I showed them how, in one year, they had paid me more than 50 per cent of my salary in sums of *less than ten dollars: in average payments of less than seven dollars.* I asked them to tell me, if they could, what would happen to any business firm in that town if it should adopt, in the management of its financial affairs, the business methods in use in that church. I reminded them that I had a family to support; that I had children to house, clothe, feed and educate; and that I was expected to house and clothe them at least in a manner that would not make the people ashamed of their pastor.

"You imagine, I presume, that this board, after this interview, speedily amended its financial methods. Well, you are wrong. They did no such thing. It is true that, by a special effort, they managed to pay me what they then owed, but after that they went on in the same old hand-to-mouth way. At the end of the year they asked for my resignation. They mercifully

deadened the effect of this blow by telling me that while I had been a good pastor, I had proved a poor financier etc., etc. It cost me one hundred dollars to move to the next field.

"In the next field I made an iron-clad, triple-plated, steel-riveted rule to the effect that rather than go in debt for the necessaries of life, we would live on bread and water. These sunken cheeks and hollow eyes, brethren, witness my stern adherence to that rule. There have been days in my home when the phrase 'bread and water' was no mere poetical figure of speech. In that last church I demanded a certain stipulated sum of cash each week, for housekeeping expenses; settlement in full at the end of each month. Sometimes, especially when the Sunday collections were good, I got the stipulated amount on Monday. Sometimes I got half; sometimes less than half. Yet the Lord gave me strength of purpose to adhere to my iron-clad, etc., rule. I have spent a whole week, neglecting all other business, trying to secure from the treasury, each day, enough to keep me in provisions until the next day. A rainy Sunday was a calamity to our household, invariably. I have gone to the officers of that church feeling like a beggar, when I was merely asking them to procure for me enough of my hard-earned salary to keep my family from actual hunger.

"It may be that you are saying to yourselves that I am a bad financier; that a man with any management need not live in this hand-to-mouth way. Say what you will, I am not posing as a Morgan or Rockefeller. Nevertheless I have done very well since I quit the pulpit. In that last church my salary was $20 per week. I left it to do the work of reporter for a small daily newspaper at a salary of $15 per week. The newspaper, fortunately, was solvent, so that I got that $15 every Saturday. Big difference in salary, you think. Yes; the dif-

✃ *What the Brethren are Saying and*

The Editor of THE CHRISTIAN-EVANGELIST has said a good many excellent things, on a live question, in his book just from the press of the Christian Publishing Company on "Christian Union." It is a meaty book. I read and relished every word in its more than two hundred pages on a train yesterday afternoon between Denver and Colorado Springs. This is the most practical testimony I can give of my appreciation of the things that Brother Garrison says on the problem of union in this latest product of his brain and pen. Christian union is in the air. It is in the air because it is in the minds and hearts of a multitude of Christly men and women as never before. This is the time, therefore, to speak on the subject sanely and sweetly. And this is what Brother Garrison has done in this volume. It is a thought-provoking and quotable book.

Many influences have been at work during the last third of a century to bring those who believe in the Christ into closer fellowship. The following is a partial list: The uniform Sunday-school lesson system, the Woman's Christian Temperance Union, the Young Men's Christian Association, the Young Women's Christian Association, the work of evangelization in non-Christian lands, the American Bible Society, the American Tract Society, the American Sunday-school Union, the action of the House of Bishops of the Protestant Episcopal church some years ago, with the discussion to which it gave rise, the Christian Endeavor movement, and the persistent discussion of the union question by the Disciples of Christ. In season, out of season, in private and in public, with tongue and with pen, formally and informally, wisely and unwisely, the Disciples have

insisted that schism is a sin, and that Christians must unite on Christ, in Christ, under Christ, in order to receive the blessing of the Head of the Body leading on to the successful evangelization of the world. There is no way of estimating accurately and fully the influence of the Disciples in bringing about the present state of mind on the part of the public in respect to this, as Mr. Bryan would say, "paramount issue." There is no great danger that the average Disciple will under-estimate this influence. J. H. Garrison certainly does not; yet, he gives credit to others for what they have done. He, of course, believes in "federation" as an influence coming to the front, the effect of which will mightily promote the unity and union for which our dear Lord fervently prayed. I have been federated for so long a time, and so happily, that I find it difficult to understand why any person who claims to be a Christian should oppose federation. There is reason at the present time to thank God and take courage. The Church of the First Born is putting itself in order, that it may move forward in the conquest of the world. This little book, circulated and read, will promote this good cause.

Francis E. Clark, D. D., the originator of the Christian Endeavor movement, has recently given to the world the book entitled, "Christian Endeavor in All Lands." This is a fascinating book. It contains nearly 200 half-tone engravings, portraits, and etchings. This is a well-told story of a great movement, "for Christ and the church," which has spread over all the earth from a small beginning in America, about twenty-five years ago. The Christian Endeavor societies literally encircle the earth. Dr. Clark tells the story of this wonderful movement in fine style. There are more than 600 pages in this book. If

Boston and C. E. As Seen From the Dome
By F. D. Power

A trip to Boston is always somewhat of an event in any man's life. Last week I was at "the Hub," and found the universe spinning around it with usual fuss and rattle, while it serenely holds its own and suffers the universe to enjoy this honor. Bunker Hill Monument, and the great Public Library with its 1,000,000 volumes, and the Old State House with its statues and paintings and memorials and volumes of history are still here. Boston Common, an ancient "trayning field and for the feeding of cattell," where they put to death witches in 1648, '56 and '60, and Quakers, Indians and prisoners of war, from the branch of the great elm; where they fought duels, and where Whitefield held his great meetings; where common scolds were punished by ducking in the Old Frog Pond which never was known to have a frog in it; where John Hancock had Rachel Wall executed on the charge that "Rachel Wall on the 18th day of March, 1789, at Boston, on the public highway, attacked Margaret Bender and with bodily force seized and put on the bonnet of said Bender at the value of 7 shillings. This did she carry away against the public peace of the commonwealth." Boston Common with all its story is still here. Faneuil Hall, the Cradle of Liberty, looks as it did in 1762 with some reconstruction. Healy's picture of "Webster's Reply to Hayne," with its 130 portraits, still looks down upon the visitor and scores of other faces. The Massachusetts State Grange was in session and I looked in upon "the embattled farmers," being something of a granger myself. They had the air of their ancestors, to whom Captain Parker, that April day in 1775, at Lexington, said: "Stand your ground. Don't fire unless fired upon. But if they mean to have a war, let it begin here." The gilded grasshopper on the cupola of the building, under which the farmers were deliberating, is the original one of 1742, reconstructed and rejuvenated. This was fashioned from sheet copper by the "cunning artificer," Deacon Shendroune immortalized by Hawthorne in "Drowne's Wooden Image." The Ancient and Honorable Artillery Company has its armory above the hall and one sees there many relics of colonial, provincial, and revolutionary times. Eighteen of their flags show the colonial colors, the oldest having been carried in 1663. Quincy market is here, and as I strolled through it, the Christmas holiday dress was on, and wreaths, flower bells, holly and mistletoe and thousands of Christmas trees from Maine and Vermont, and all over New England were on exhibition.

The old churches after all, however, are the most interesting things here except the people, and the beans and brown-bread, and other deities. Christ Church is the most ancient. On a tablet one reads: "The signal lanterns of Paul Revere displayed in the steeple of this church, April 18, 1775, warned the country of the march of the British troops to Lexington and Concord." Here is a

THE OLD STATE HOUSE, BOSTON.

communion set presented by George II in 1732 and an organ imported from London in 1759 and beside the organ is a gallery built for the use of slaves. The chimes were the first used in America. A number of British officers killed at Bunker Hill are interred here. Kings Chapel is another old shrine. In 1689 the authorities compelled the town to tolerate, and provide a place for, those who desired to worship according to the ritual of the Church of England, and here in a small frame church the royal governors and British officers were provided with pews, and services were conducted with great pomp. This went hard with the old puritan. It had the hour glass on the pulpit to mark the length of the sermons, and still has the high-back pews and lofty pulpit with winding stairs. It is now a Unitarian church.

Old South Meeting House is the most interesting of these antiques. It is built on the site of Winthrop's home on a corner of the famous Milk street. The first meeting house was built in 1670 where Benjamin Franklin was christened January 17, 1706. He was born just across the street at No. 17. In 1730 the present structure was erected. The congregation moved to the New Old South. Twenty-five women organized the Old South Preservation Committee, and purchased it when about to be torn down, and it is now a museum. The tea party was organized and started from the door of the Old South. Judge Sewall, who burned the witches publicly, expressed his contrition for the deed here in 1697. Warren made his address from its pulpit after the Boston massacre, coming in through the window behind the desk. In the museum are countless relics of Indian and colonial and revolutionary times, and whole volumes of the old time sermons, dry, enough, many of them, the first preached in Boston, and the writing as clear and legible as if written ten years ago. The longest word in Elliot's Indian Bible, which I noted here, will delight the intelligent compositor. It is in Mark 1:40, and for the English "kneeling down to him," and is this: Wutappesittukqussunnookwehtunkquoh. How Mr. Evarts would have rolled that trippingly on his tongue! By the way, I have one on Boston. I observed on their printed cards in the Old South the statement that "the Father of his Country" addressed the people there and had to come through the window to the platform, so great was the pressure of the people to see and hear him. Passing out I said to the lady in charge: "Have you any evidence that General Washington ever spoke in this building?" "Why, no sir, he never spoke here." "Well," said I, "here is your printed declaration to that effect." "Let me see it," said the lady. "Gracious, that's awful! I will correct it at once." Here is a call for the D. A. R. and, at the Hub itself.

But my business was not to set Boston right on its own history, but to attend a meeting of the executive committee of the trustees of Christian Endeavor. It was a delightful privilege to meet with the leaders at Tremont Temple at the Christian Endeavor headquarters. My visit convinced me of their need of a new building. So far $35,000 have been contributed for this purpose. Secretary Vogt having resigned, our special work was to select his successor. Mr. William Shaw was unanimously chosen. Mr. Shaw has for twenty years been the treasurer of the United Society. In this office he has been greatly successful. He is thoroughly imbued with the Christian Endeavor spirit. He is universally popular in Christian Endeavor circles. He combines with sound judgment and excellent administrative ability a devout character and a full knowledge of the history and principles and genius of the Endeavor movement. To us there

seemed no other name to suggest itself and we feel our action will meet with universal approval.

Mr. Vogt has done good service. In his three and a half years we have gained a net increase of 5,000 societies. The figures are now 67,811 societies. He retires of his own choice to take a position with the Home Society of the Presbyterian Church.

Dr. Clark leaves January 19 for an extended tour in South America. Begin-

ning in Jamaica he will visit the new Costa Rica Union, and after holding a number of meetings in the canal zone, will visit for several months the workers in the different South American republics, closing in Brazil in May. Everything is hopeful at headquarters. A new assistant secretary will be chosen. Mr. Hiram Lathrop, of Boston, becomes treasurer and two new departments of work will soon be opened. Merry Christmas to all Christian Endeavorers and all readers of THE CHRISTIAN-EVANGELIST.

A Specimen of "Modern Courtesy"

It will be remembered that a short time ago I had a friendly discussion with "The Christian Standard" with respect to the historical position of the fathers of our religious movement with special reference to the question of federation. During that discussion "The Christian Standard" charged Brother Garrison with contending that Pedobaptist churches are "Scriptural" churches. This I emphatically denied, and went so far as to say that if the "Christian Standard" would quote from Brother Garrison's writings anything he had ever said even like that, I would at once publicly repudiate his position and help the "Christian Standard" to break down his influence. At the same time the "Christian Standard" intimated that my position was the same as that of Brother Garrison. When the "Christian Standard" replied to me, it suggested that I was not competent to speak for Brother Garrison, and still clearly intimated that I was mistaken with regard to his position, though not a single line or word was quoted to justify any such intimation. The discussion was just about to close, but I thought it was only fair to all parties that my representation of Brother Garrison should be fully sustained before the readers of the "Christian Standard." With this view I wrote to Brother Garrison, asking him whether I had fairly represented his position or not. To this inquiry I received the following:

"Replying to your question, whether you have correctly represented my position in your reply to the 'Christian Standard,' I would say, most certainly you have. I have myself declined to deny a charge so manifestly absurd as that which you have denied for me. Do I need to deny for the benefit of Disciples of Christ that I hold and teach that Pedobaptist churches are 'Scriptural,' while holding to infant baptism, affusion and creed-prescription? What then would be the meaning and mission of our reformatory movement? Is it not a self-evident truth to every unbiased mind that all churches—our own included—are 'Scriptural' only as they conform to the teaching and life of Christ, and that they are un-scriptural to the extent that they depart from his example and teaching? So I believe, and I have therefore not felt called upon to deny, for our readers, statements which I felt sure the brethren would properly estimate. I must do the brethren the justice to say that not one of them, so far as I now recall, has ever written to me to know whether the statements which you deny for me were actually true. From this I infer that they were not taken seriously."

When I received Brother Garrison's letter I wrote to the "Christian Standard," incorporating so much of his letter as is contained in the preceding paragraph, and

suggested to the "Christian Standard" that I thought that this final statement ought to be made in order to level up everything in our discussion.

After waiting several weeks for my article to appear, I wrote to the "Christian Standard" and enclosed a stamp asking that my article should be returned. To my request no attention was paid whatever. After waiting some considerable time I again addressed a letter to the "Christian Standard" asking for the return of my manuscript. I still received no answer. I then wrote a private letter to Brother Errett, asking him to give his personal attention to the matter, and see that my manuscript was returned, but for some reason he has not replied, and so I am shut up to the necessity of making this explanation through the columns of THE CHRISTIAN-EVANGELIST.

Now one reason why I was anxious for the "Christian Standard" to publish my letter was that during my discussion with the "Christian Standard" I received many intimations that the main reason of the "Christian Standard's" position was to be found in its hostility to Brother Garrison. I was anxious for it to vindicate itself from this charge by publishing Brother Garrison's repudiation of the position which the "Christian Standard" had ascribed to him. As the "Christian Standard" refuses to publish my article, I fear that many brethren will now feel justified in the suspicion which they entertained. I regret this exceedingly, for my whole purpose in writing the articles I did was to bring about an irenicon between brethren who ought to be as one in the advocacy of our great cause. I must now leave the matter for others to judge as to whether the "Christian Standard's" "courtesy" is what the Apostle Paul would call Christian or not.   W. T. MOORE.

P. S.—After sending the foregoing to the CHRISTIAN-EVANGELIST I received the following letter from Russell Errett:

Cincinnati, O., October 6, 1906.
Mr. W. T. Moore, Columbia, Mo.:

Dear Brother Moore—Your note received, and I find you have blamed Brother Lord for what is due to my own delinquency. On taking the matter up with him again, he thinks it best to publish your article, and will do so the coming week, without reply, but with a small editorial explanation.

Trusting that you will prefer this to the return of the manuscript, as you request, I am,

Faithfully yours,   RUSSELL ERRETT.

It will be seen that this letter was writ-

ten October 6, before our National Convention at Buffalo. At Buffalo I reminded Brother Lord that my article had not yet appeared as had been promised. He said that Brother Errett had gone off some place, and that this was why my article had not appeared, as he had promised, but that it would appear very shortly. I waited until last week, when I wrote Brother Errett another letter, telling him that he had failed to comply with his promise, and that I now felt compelled to publish some explanation of the matter if I did not hear from him by telegram at once. Several days have already passed since I wrote this letter, and I have not received either telegram or anything else with respect to the matter. I now feel that I can wait no longer, and I must leave the general public to decide upon the treatment I have received.

The correspondence has developed at least one feature which was already assured to myself, but which was perhaps not suspected by the general public. That feature is that J. A. Lord is not the responsible editor of the "Christian Standard," and that he did not write the articles in reply to mine that appeared in the "Christian Standard." I understood this matter from the beginning, and now Brother Errett's letter practically acknowledges that he has been responsible for the "Christian Standard's" part of the controversy with me. I state this fact because I want the public to understand the whole truth in this case. Brother Errett conducted the controversy in the main with skill and courtesy, and I want him to have the credit for his work, and now that he has refused to admit to his columns my article vindicating Brother Garrison, I want the blame to rest where it belongs.   W. T. M.

Columbia, Mo., November, 1906.

[We give place to the foregoing regretfully, because it refers to a discussion that is now in the past. We do so, however, at the request of Brother Moore, whose whole aim, as he says, has been to bring about a better understanding between brethren, and who feels that its publication is due to the brotherhood, who are entitled to a knowledge of the facts therein stated. We must take this occasion to say, however, that for the editor of the "Christian Standard" we have none but the kindest feeling, personally, and we do not judge his motive in making statements that seemed to fairminded brethren to do us serious injustice. For us the incident is closed, and we assure the editor of the "Christian Standard" that nothing will give us more satisfaction than that we should be able to co-operate, as the two papers once did, in the furtherance of our common cause and in promoting the peace and unity of the brotherhood.—EDITOR.]

Our Budget

—Farewell, Old Year, a long farewell!

—How often Pilate's words recur to us, at this season, "What is written, is written!"

—The year's deeds have gone to record, and no power in the universe can change that record.

—Let that solemn and impressive fact be kept in memory as we begin the record of the New Year.

—Suggestion to readers: The more thoroughly you read your paper the more profit you will get out of it and the deeper will be your attachment to it.

—Suggestion to writers: Let us all be briefer the coming year. Boil down, down, down! There's a great demand in this office for column and half column articles.

—Our assistant editor will be gray long before the time if he be compelled to use his blue pencil, as he is doing now, much longer. Help him by leaving out half your words.

—We have a great many rare good things on hand and in mind for the coming year, and the shorter the articles you write, the more of these special features will appear. More writers and shorter articles is our motto for 1907.

—The article which appears on the opposite page from W. T. Moore, is one that we have held in type since before the Buffalo Convention, the article to which he refers having been sent to Cincinnati about five months ago. After Brother Moore had given up the matter of getting that article in the "Standard," we personally wrote to Brother Lord asking whether he was going to publish the article, as in that case we did not care to do it, as it relates to a discussion conducted in the "Christian Standard." He replied that they would publish it soon; but as three issues of the paper have since appeared, without the article, Brother Moore feels we ought not to wait longer, and, desiring to close this matter up with the year, without carrying it over into the new, we give place to it this week, and, so far as we are concerned, this must end the matter.

—We have in type a lengthy report of Scoville's recent meeting received too late for this week's "make-up."

✢ ✢ ✢

—R. W. Mills has been called for full time at Highmore, S. D.

—Harold E. Monser has been organizing a new church at Findley, Ill.

—G. B. Townsend has entered upon his ministry at Hagerstown, Md.

—W. I. Burrell expects to close a five years" ministry at Co_ington, Pa., January 1.

—F. V. Kearns has begun work at Whitten and Garwin, Ia., leaving Mt. Auburn.

—Joseph Gaylor will preach for the church just dedicated at Conway, Mo., for a time.

—Baker and Daugherty will begin a meeting January 1 for G. F. Bradford at Eureka, Kan.

—B. F. Hill is the new minister at California, Mo. H. J. Corwine returns to Bartlesville, I. T.

—J. W. Campbell has taken the work at Milton, Ill. Pearl, Pleasant Hill and Nebo are not supplied.

—J. B. Lockhart will leave Unionville to take charge of the church at Clarence, Mo., January 1.

—J. B. Mayfield, of Clarksville, Mo., has been spending December with the church at Scott City, Kan.

—Miss Alice Miller, who spent a year in Kentucky and Missouri, returned to the Yotsuya Mission November 6.

—W. L. Waggoner, formerly of Port Jefferson, O., has been in charge of the work at Houston, Mo., since October 1.

—The First Church, St. Louis, Mo., recently joined the living-link churches of the Foreign Society. John L. Brandt, the pastor, led in the enterprise.

—The Medicine Lodge church has called Lee H. Barnum from Caldwell, Kan., to become their pastor, and he will take up the work January 1.

—E. L. Kirtley, who has taken up the work at Ada, I. T., writes that the prospects are fine. He speaks well of his old field at Polo and Sumner, Okla.

—J. R. Perkins, after a year's ministry at Huntsville, Mo., succeeded J. H. Wright at Paris, and has been in charge of the work there since December 1.

—L. L. Carpenter has just dedicated at Ohio Grove, Ill., and will dedicate at Eminence, Ind., December 30. Surrounding churches are invited to participate.

—J. D. Hull, who begins his third year with the congregation at Kendallville, Ind., January 1, has been elected president of the ministerial association of the city.

—While at High Hill, Mo. recently, R. B. Havener, began the work of building a church, pledges reaching $850. To secure a building to cost $1,200 is the purpose of the congregation.

—The Foreign Society has received $2,500 from Charles C. Chapman, of California, for a new hospital in Nan Tung Chow, China. He will furnish an additional $2,500 as the building progresses.

—The Foreign Society has received a gift of $8,450 on the annuity plan from a brother and sister in Missouri. The Society is hoping that others will take this liberal step in the near future.

—W. N. Porter has been spending a few weeks in Christian County, Mo., preaching at Ozark, Sparta and Billings. He will be glad to hold meetings or locate, and may be addressed at Lamar.

—R. L. Mobley has resigned at Springfield to begin work January 1 at Alamo, Tenn. The church at the former place is in a prosperous condition, and will want a minister to take charge at once.

—Our sympathies are extended to the "Religious Herald," of Richmond, Va., which has recently lost its venerable editor, Dr. Dickinson, who for more than forty years has been associated with that paper.

—The Foreign Society has just appointed Miss Edna E. Kurs, of Hiram College, a member of the Franklin Circle Church, Cleveland, O., a missionary to Nankin, China. She will go out next September.

—Sheeler Campbell, who has had 89 additions, 47 of them being within the past six months, at Versailles, Ind., and other points, writes that the new building at the former place will soon be dedicated.

—H. Clay Shields, who recently helped I. N. Grisso in a meeting, writes that the latter has decided to give his time to evangelistic work. Brother Shields writes very enthusiastically of his abilities. We understand that efforts are being made to induce Brother Grisso to enter a wider field and many will rejoice at his decision to do this. He

may be addressed at Plainfield, Ind., for dates and terms.

—A telegram from T. P. Haley about the Small-St. John meeting reached us too late for the "As We Go to Press" columns. There were 164 additions in three weeks. We shall expect a fuller report from Brother Haley.

—J. W. Reynolds writes that the C. W. B. M. organization at Clinton, Ill., was organized less than a year ago with five charter members; these have grown to thirty and the prospects are that this membership will soon be doubled.

—J. Frank Green has accepted the pastorate of the Columbia Avenue Christian Church of Rochester, N. Y., and will enter upon the field in January. M. S. Becker, of Ohio, has been chosen as his successor at Mt. Pleasant, Mich.

—Now that H. H. Cushing has taken charge of the Bleecker Street Church of Christ, Gloversville, N. Y., which has suffered because there has been no regular minister through the summer and autumn season, a pleasant and profitable ministry is anticipated.

❀ ❀

Infant and Adult.

For the upbuilding of the infant and sustaining the adult, milk is essential and to be wholesome must be pure. Eagle Brand Condensed Milk and Peerless Brand Evaporated-Cream have no equals for purity, flavor and richness.

—"We rejoice with S. T. Willis and all of the Disciples in New York City over the dedication of a handsome church edifice on 169th street. An account of this has been received, but we must defer its publication until next week.

—Clay T. Runyon, has recently accepted the pastorate at Richmond, Cal., for one year during the absence of the pastor, who is taking a post-graduate course at Harvard. Brother Runyon is enjoying post-graduate work in Berkeley Bible Seminary and the University of California.

—A. Sterling, who has been pastor of the church at Richards, Mo., during the past three years, has resigned to accept work near his home in Warrensburg. O. L. Fouts writes us that he leaves with the best wishes of his congregation, and that it can truly be said that he lives as he preaches.

—It is with regret that we note that A. L. Bush has relinquished the Benevolent Association work in Texas, but we can appreciate the feeling that makes him decide that he cannot remain away from home all the time. Brother Bush goes to Wichita Falls as pastor.

—We have received a notice from F. M. McCarthy, minister at Leesville, Ind., to the effect that the official board of our church there has been compelled to withdraw fellowship from W. H. Hill, and state that he is no longer a minister or member of the congregation.

—Joseph Lowe, of Kansas City, Mo., goes to California to hold some meetings during the winter, so as to avoid the cold weather in Missouri and Kansas. His first meeting will be held in Poplars, California, where he has now gone. We commend Brother Lowe to brethren on the coast.

—L. A. Chapman, who has recently visited his mother and other relatives in Ohio, writes that Uriah Wells has been superintendent of the Sunday-school for over forty years. Plans are being made for a big revival at Mt. Pleasant, Ia., during the coming year.

—The brethren at Lafayette, Ind., recently burned a mortgage for $800, while bank notes were placed in the hands of the treasurer to meet another mortgage for $2,100. For over nine years the church has only been able to pay the interest on these mortgages. Within the last 28 months the membership has increased from 200 to 500. A. W. Connor is the pastor, and with the load just lifted the members have great hope for the future.

—John Kendrick Ballou has been asked by the church at Sioux City, Ia., to remain indefinitely. During his two years of service with them a neat house of worship has been erected. The church is fast becoming one of the leading churches in this city of forty congregations. A tabernacle campaign is planned for next autumn, the best site in town having been selected by Brother Muckley. The present building will be enlarged, it is hoped, in time for this special forward move.

—F. R. Liddell writes us that since

THE DEVOTIONAL SPIRIT

Is quickened by Alone With God, The Heavenward Way, Half Hour Studies at the Cross. Read them and meditate, then pass to a friend. Each, 75 cents, or the trio, postpaid, $2.00.

CHRISTIAN PUBLISHING CO.,
St. Louis, Mo.

M. H. Garrard took charge of the work at LaPorte, Ind., the beginning of September, there has been a new interest, the attendance increasing and the membership being thoroughly united. Brother Liddell has been with this church for eleven years and says he cannot recall a time that the outlook was more promising. Preparations are being made for a special meeting to begin January 13, the pastor to do the preaching and Arthur L. Haley, singing evangelist, to assist.

—Harold Bell Wright, of Lebanon, Mo., has received a call to Redlands, Cal., and will enter upon that work not later than February 1. Brother Wright makes the change for health reasons, it being thought that the climate of Southern California will suit him better than that of the Ozark hills. He stopped off and visited THE CHRISTIAN-EVANGELIST office during a recent visit to Chicago, where he has made arrangements for the publication of his new novel which will appear next autumn. "That Printer of Udell's," has had a very large sale and is now being published in a cheap edition. The assistant editor had the pleasure of having Brother Wright read to him the manuscript of his new book, while on a camping expedition together in the Missouri hill country. The story is an interesting one and its author has grown in his craftsmanship. We have every confidence that Redlands will be delighted with the minister, whom we shall be very sorry to lose from Missouri. We have Brother Wright's promise that he will write for THE CHRISTIAN-EVANGELIST during the coming year.

A Campaign at Bloomfield, Ia.

A great effort in the interest of Christian union and New Testament Christianity will be made in Iowa at the beginning of the year, and the Christian church at Bloomfield will be among those to begin on Sunday, January 6. The pastor, F. D. Ferrall, will be assisted by Evangelist

H. A. Northcutt.

H. A. Northcutt, of Knox City, Mo., who is doing some of the best evangelistic work in our country. He has held meetings in many states of the Union and is well-known in Bloomfield, as he was for several years the efficient pastor of this church. Nor does he need an introduction as evangelist, for twice he has held interesting meetings there and led hundreds to Christ. He is the type of evangelist who unifies and who leaves no unpleasant things behind him. With forces well organized and the meeting well advertised the brethren have great faith that they will get and be a blessing. H. A. Northcutt comes fresh from other victories to this church with a building holding more than one thousand people, with a splendid chorus choir, and a coun-

our Zion be restored. Because the appeal of God comes last shall it lose its effect? God forbid.

Our Reconstruction Commission at San Francisco is composed of wise and godly men appointed by the Northern California State Convention. It remains now for our churches to do their duty on the first or second Sunday of January and send such offerings as will enable us to put our work on a respectable footing at San Francisco. Other religious bodies are providing new buildings on a liberal scale. Now is our opportunity to demonstrate for Christ's sake and for Christ's Plea that we love the cause for which we stand so well, that we will, once for all, do things worthy of a great people with a great plea. Send all offerings to The American Christian Missionary Society, Y. M. C. A. Bldg., Cincinnati, O.

H. A. Northcutt's Labors Ended.

Mexico, Mo., Dec. 20, 1906.

DEAR BROTHER GARRISON: Say through THE CHRISTIAN-EVANGELIST to the great host that knew and loved Bro. H. A. Northcutt, that his earth labors are done. He reached Mexico Tuesday afternoon, having closed his meeting with M. M. Goode at St. Joseph Monday night. I met him by chance at the train. I thought he was looking well. He came to rest a few days with his only daughter, Mrs. E. R. Locke, took ill Tuesday night and died at 1:30 p. m., Wednesday afternoon, December 19. The physician says death came from heart failure, as a result of an overwrought and thoroughly exhausted nervous system. He was a princely man. His life was a benediction. His labors as an evangelist eminently successful. His heart was richly endowed with love, and his mind stored with the Scriptures. He was an example of his oft-repeated exhortation to others, "be thou faithful unto death." He has the crown.

Assisted by Brothers Headington and A. A. Wallace, the Presbyterian minister, we conducted a very sweet, though sad service here to-day, and then they took the body to Knox City for interment. He was by the side of his wife, deceased over thirty years ago. A. W. KOKENDOFFER.

[The foregoing announcement will bring sorrow to the heart, and tears to the eyes of thousands of the devoted friends of this loving and loveable evangelist. He was a sort of forerunner among us of that type of evangelists of which there are now many, who know how to preach Christ both loyally and lovingly. Of him it may be said, as it was written of Barnabas: "He was a good man, full of the Holy Spirit and of faith, and much people was added to the Lord." He was a true "son of consolation," and his name will long remain as a sweet fragrance in the memory of thousands whose lives have been blessed by his ministry. We share the sorrow of all who mourn his departure, and our sincere sympathy is extended to his loving daughter.—Editor.]

Evangelize Iowa.

All Iowa is awake! There are great possibilities for the plea of the Disciples in Iowa. We are entering upon a state-wide campaign. Possibly more than 250 evangelistic meetings will be conducted this season. The offerings to state work are large. I have a tract of practical suggestions on, "How to Have a Revival," also cards and advertisements used in our meetings to great advantage. If you would like some of these for "pointers," I will send them for five cents in stamps. They may be suggestive.

Des Moines, Ia. I. L. ORGAN.
State Evangelist.

Following Dewey's Victory.

"The Way of Reconciliation," is the title of a bi-monthly paper published in Vigan, Ilocos, Sur., Philippine Islands, by Hermon P. Williams, our missionary to those islands. We have been interested in several things in it. Here is a report of conversions:

"Baptisms are reported as follows: Laoag, 17; Aparri, 14; Cainyoon, 11; Tallungan, 7; Paruddan, 8; Pilar 2; Bangued, 3; Vigan, 1; San Ildefonso, 1; Cabugao, 19."

Mrs. Beulah Williams reports the conversions: "A class for Bible women was undertaken last month at Vigan. Justa Oliva and Teodora Izbarra came down from Sinait to study the Bible under my instruction. The congregation of which they are members is one of the most faithful in Ilocos Sur. Ruperto Inis, one of the evangelists there,

loaned them his ox and cart for the trip. Their neighbors, not of the congregation, asked them what wages they would receive. 'A clearer knowledge of God's word, nothing more,' Teodora answered; but they would not believe her.'"

"These women, after their Bible course was completed, went back home, Mrs. Williams says, to begin teaching there. Teodora was intending to start a children's class at Sinait, and Justa a class for women, each to meet three times a week. This item then, too, will be read with interest: 'The following letter was received not long ago from a distant town in Ilocos Sur.—I have been, Sir, for a short time a subscriber to the paper "Dalan Ti Cappia," and during these past few months for the first time I have examined the "New Testament of our Lord Jesus Christ," which was loaned by Sr. Esteban Paredes, correspondent of this paper. Through earnest reading the light has come quickly to me, to my darkened mind. Here now I am, repentant of my many sins. I believe in Christ. And that my evil deeds may be cleansed or wiped out, once for all, and that I may be saved send me, Sir, a John Bateo (Dipper), that I may be buried with Christ my Lord.

'Yours, desirous of entering into the new life, "ANTONIO ACOSTA.'"

These are some of the indirect results of Dewey's victory in Manila Bay. "God moves in a mysterious way his wonders to perform."

As We Go to Press.

Special to THE CHRISTIAN-EVANGELIST.

Watertown, N. Y., Dec. 23.—Successful dedication by F. M. Rains. Outlook bright. Two additions.—S. B. Culp.

Special to THE CHRISTIAN-EVANGELIST.

Des Moines, Ia., Dec. 23.—Closed at Webb City Wednesday with 105. Conditions unfavorable, but a good meeting. New converts contribute over $400. Pastor Reavis complimented with $200 raise in salary. Begin at Central Church, Denver, January 6. Brother Hackleman accompanies me.—Wm. J. Lockhart.

Special to THE CHRISTIAN-EVANGELIST.

Eureka, Ill., Dec. 23.—Thirteen days, 107 additions. Eureka has 1,800 inhabitants; church seats 600; a very fruitful meeting, length and conditions considered. Eureka has no saloons, theatre, dancing, card parties, or billiards yet. Prosperous, happy college has furnished us such men as Breeden, Haynes, Richardson, Aylsworth, Gilliland, Sniff, Burnham, Ideman, Fisher, Shaw, Thrapp, Stewart, Garrison, Rowlison, Lichtenberger, Miller, and Cobb. A new evangelistic team of two tried and true men is announced. Crim and Shields, of Indianapolis, glory! A. W. Taylor is building a great body here, nine hundred members now. Campaign next.—W. F. Brooks.

Special to THE CHRISTIAN-EVANGELIST.

Banesville, O., Dec. 24.—Seventy additions in meeting with Clarence Mitchell and Arthur Haley, singer. One hundred during the year; $2,000 worth church improvements; more additions this year than the combined results eight previous years.—Hugh Wayt, minister.

NEWS FROM MANY FIELDS

One Hundred Words from Moulton, Ia.

We began our meeting November 18 and closed December 5 with 54 additions—37 confessions, 15 by letter and statement, and two reclaimed. Our meeting closed earlier than we had expected because of the illness of Evangelist Arthur Stout. One other church here just closed a three weeks' meeting with nine additions. They are equipped as well as we, in some particulars, better, having a good minister and splendid people. I can see no other reason for our larger success than our plea, the world-winning plea of unity on Christ. Let's be worthy of God's greater blessings.

NELSON TRIMBLE, minister.

From Idaho.

Two confessions, at Star. One baptism in Boise river. The church there is to be dedicated during the last days of December and will be free of debt.—On the parsonage there will be one hundred dollars debt.—At Emmett we are moving the church building a few blocks to the permanent location. A protracted series of sermons will doubtless begin about January 10, and continue indefinitely, or until a resident minister is called. —At Arcadia arrangements are being made for Brother Clore, of the Caldwell laity to preach each Lord's day. The Oregon state board is being asked to stand a part of the car-fare for these services. Only a few workers can be mustered at Arcadia.

B. W. RICE,
Caldwell, Idaho.

Violett-Clarkson Meeting.

Lorain is a city of 30,000 where twenty-seven languages are spoken. There are 130 saloons. Catholics predominate, with eight churches. Of the Protestant bodies the Methodists are strongest, having four churches with resident pastors. Commercialism has so taken hold of the people in this rapidly-growing city that ministers all wished that something might be done to arouse interest in the work of the churches.

Our church ranked third among the Protestant bodies in strength. In cleanness of life and freedom from the modern popular sins it stands first. The membership was 150. The building is practically new, is well located, but has a debt of $4,000. The seating capacity is 500. An effort has been made to cut out all paid socials and circus methods of raising money. The past year has seen none of it and all bills have been paid though the budget increased. The church had six months of preparation. A revival association was formed, the purpose of which was to raise funds and to create interest in every way possible. More than half the money was raised before the meeting. A hopeful list was gathered, but not as large as expected. Conferences were held between the evangelist and pastor. The pastor made allusion to the meeting in some way at every service for months. Prayer-meetings pointed toward it. Sermons in reference to it were preached. We were compelled to pay at advertising rates for our newspaper notices, but we used the papers anyway. Window cards were placed in the homes of the people a month before the meeting. Cards were placed in the business houses and street cars. E. E. Violett is undoubtedly one of the cleanest, most energetic, tactful evangelists among us. He has more of the Bible committed than any man I ever met. Its words fall from his lips with a burning eloquence that brings conviction. He believes the Bible and preaches its truths. His spirit is always kindly, even under bitter attacks. Song leader Clarkson is a young man of good voice and a personality which wins wherever he goes. He was prevented from doing his usual work here on account of an attack of fever.

One hundred and four came forward during the meeting. Business men expressed surprise that such a thing could be accomplished in Lorain. One of the editors declared that if we had seventeen additions in two weeks he would give us a half page advertisement. There were nineteen

the last day of the meeting. The church is strengthened in every way. We will begin at once to prepare for our next meeting. Hundreds heard of our plea who never before knew the object of our existence. We now stand second among Protestant bodies in strength. Among business men we have come to the point where we can do business on the cash basis and that without begging for favors "just because it is the church."

VICTOR G. HOSTETTER,
Lorain, O.
Minister.

Growth in Portland.

All of our Portland churches have this year enjoyed unprecedented prosperity. There has been practically no report of the work of the Rodney Avenue Christian Church, of this city, since I was called to serve it last January. It has been a mission point of the Oregon Missionary Society and C. W. B. M. for several years. Since last January 48 have been added to the membership. The $500 indebtedness has been paid, the mortgage burning celebrated. Much of the credit of improvements upon the interior of the church is due to our Ladies' Aid. There has been a decided increase in contributions for local work and for missions. The spiritual growth of the congregation is most gratifying. I have been called to serve the church another year at substantially increased salary, which the church will pay without the aid of these missionary boards. The steady growth indicates that a more commodious building will soon be required. We are planning for a meeting this winter. The field seems ripe. With a united, self-supporting congregation of nearly 200 members, free from all indebtedness, we feel assured of a splendid future.

Portland, Ore. F. ELMO ROBINSON, minister.

The Fourth Church in the Simultaneous Campaign in Indianapolis.

E. L. Frazier preached the simple Gospel with unusual power. It was said by our people that the church had never had such clear exposition of the Gospel way. Harry K. Shields led the chorus of sixty voices admirably, and stirred the people with his hymn solos. We commend him to the brotherhood as a leader and soloist of the first rank. The church had thoroughly organized personal work, and well planned advertising. Every detail of the public service was worked out in advance. A pleasing feature of our work was the maintenance of a rest room for the babies, where the Cradle Roll ladies cared for the children while the mothers heard the sermon. We feel that some of the mothers came to Christ because this arrangement enabled them to listen to the Word. In a field thoroughly gleaned, and cramped, where failure was predicted, there were 57 additions, with four since the meeting closed, up till writing this report. There were six not reported before the meeting began, making a total of 67 not reported. Of these 32 are by confession and baptism, and 35 by letter and statement. We are now ready for an increase campaign in our Sunday-school.

CHAS. E. UNDERWOOD, Pastor.

Oregon.

Since last report Albany First, Ashland, Cottage Grove and Dallas have supplemented their gifts to Oregon missions and eight other churches have sent in their offerings; viz.—Halfway, $4.30; Santa Clara, $3; Thurston, $4; Elmira, $12.50; Hood River City, $7; Stayton, $7.50; Grant's Pass, $8.55 and Roseburg, $26.51. We are very glad to enroll Thurston and Elmira this year with their gifts. Of the other churches reported here Santa Clara alone reaches last year's offering. Her gift shows a gain of 20 per cent. The gift from Roseburg for 1905 was augmented by the proceeds of a missionary meeting.

In this report I wish to mention the report of the Committee on Future Work at the Northwest District Convention held at McMinnville in No-

vember, which recommended that be employed; that he raise what h the field meetings; that we have mittee composed of the pastors who shall solicit the churches for the evangelist; that first work be de at the earliest possible moment; the ings with such churches as Day and others, where the church enough to support a pastor and meeting; that we co-operate in the "Home of the Aged" at Eug ern Oregon join with Southern California in a series of simulta during the winter of 1907 and 19

Delegates enrolled, 60; ministe churches represented, 16, and 3 reported and only 3 not heard fr Dow at Central Point for a short are starting well. T. E.

Cottage Grove, Ore.

C. W. B. M. in Misso

The Missouri State Board hel meeting at Kansas City on Dece home of Mrs. W. F. Richardson was present. We were glad to Sister Lampton, whose absence fro meetings, through illness, was so r A delicious luncheon was served by of the hostess, Misses Olive and Jo The state of our cause was reviewe er upbuilding planned. One chief Centennial. Our auxiliaries are n this as we hope they will. The cor Centennial secretaries as well as t ier, were instructed to push this fast as possible. One cause of regr our beloved young Junior superi Martha Stout. She has served the fully and so wisely, that we are her up. But Cupid was to be com as our state work, and the love a of the whole state follow her in tions. We were fortunate in securi cessor, until the state convention, A. Walker, of St. Louis, who takes Y. P. department immediately. A ence in regard to this department dressed to Miss Walker at her hor Belle Place, St. Louis. Miss Walk crated young woman, anxious to high standard of the work in Mis ask the help and co-operation of al petent one may be, and carry it f cess. Miss Walker must have y your prayers.

A most delightful day was spent in attendance on the Federation of Kansas City and vicinity. Mrs. G. sided. The program was full. On ture was a greeting from the pre Federation of Presbyterian Missio in Kansas City, who spoke of the g had learned from the methods of A splendid luncheon was served by the Independence Boulevard Chur more than two hundred sat at the many others were yet to serve.

MRS. L.

What Can Be Done in the South.

Meridian, Miss., has just had the experience of a really great meeting. The brief results in additions were promptly reported in THE CHRISTIAN-EVANGELIST and from W. M. Baker, the minister of our church at Meridian, we received further particulars which we are glad to present for the joy of the brotherhood and the encouragement of other churches with hard fields to conquer for the Master. Mississippi is said to be the most conservative state in the south, and Meridian has been one of the most difficult fields for our plea. As Brother Baker says, when the board of the A. C. M. S. becomes discouraged it can be agreed that the work is very hard, and when some of the ablest preachers get no apparent results, there is some reason for concluding that conservatism is king. To have a meeting with 51 additions, meaning an increase of 33 1-3 per cent in eighteen days, is a great victory. The meeting was begun under difficulties, Pastor Baker and Singer Hawes starting it contemporaneously with a Methodist meeting and a street fair, Evangelist R. H. Crossfield coming two days later. Brother Hawes rendered good service and Brother Crossfield showed his strength in personal work as well as in the pulpit, while he made a fine impression on the citizens. The meeting has given our brethren a stronger hold in the city, while the congregation has received fresh inspiration and has been built up spiritually. The papers were generous, giving all desired space free. With 23 additions in regular services the increase in membership since January 1 has been 74, or nearly 50 per cent. A new house of worship by 1909 is now the desire.

Illinois Notes.

At Rushville, the beautiful county seat of Schuyler county, the brethren are putting $2,500 in repairs on their substantial brick building, which will make of it a convenient modern house. It seems like nearly half our churches in Illinois are building, repairing or paying for improvements. A better class of buildings are replacing the old, much to the credit of the churches. W. E. Harman, the much loved minister, is not only caring for the improvements and the spiritual interests of the church, but he and his wife who also preaches, take care of the Bethany and Pleasant View churches, a few miles distant in the country. In many parts of our state such effort has become a necessity where we have 425 more churches then preachers. This also is the residence of Bro. Alpheus Brown, a venerable pioneer on the verge of the grave, through whose ministry, several thousand people have entered the kingdom of God. With proper care and work and sacrifice there seems to be a great and useful future before this church.——At Vermont a large and intelligent audience assembled at the regular service, where G. W. Ross for some 12 years has been the devoted minister. He is pre-eminently a gospel preacher and gives the people the message of truth which feeds their souls.——Ins for many years was the home of the late J. B. Royal, whose memory is precious in all this region. Here was raised Miss Nell Dougherty, who laggidly made her way through Eureka College, went to China as a missionary and there became the wife of Dr. Butchart. Here W. E. Spicer, our minister at Pittsfield, found his excellent wife. Here also were born and raised the Gillilands; one, J. H., has been preaching in Bloomington about eighteen years; the other, E. A., recently closed a nine years' pastorate at Clinton, and is now at East St. Louis. Brother Rose's daughter is the wife of a preacher and his son, still in college, is beginning to preach.——Marshall, in Clark Co., is getting some benefit and prominence on account of a recent discovery of oil and gas in the vicinity, and the church is sharing somewhat in the increased population. The house has been recently repaired, reseated and much beautified. Gilbert Jones, in his six months ministry, has endeared himself to the people and is doing a fine work for the church. He is also a well-known evangelist of power, and expects in connection with his regular work, to hold several meetings for weak churches in the county. The church has a good C. W. B. M., and all other auxiliaries for church usefulness. This is the boyhood home of J. W. Kilborn and where his parents still live.

He has recently returned from a successful pastorate in Keokuk, Iowa, and is now doing fine service for the church at Mt. Carmel, Ill. Casey and Martinsville are in the new oil regions. Business is booming, but the great enterprises of the Church of Christ have not yet received dividends. Although the head of the church is the chief depositor, he will probably be the last to realize on the stock. Is it irreverent thus to speak of our Savior's love in bestowing wealth upon his people? What shall it profit that he make his people rich, if they honor him not with their substance? In this case, however, our brethren are not large owners.——Casey has gone to Indiana. His place, however, will soon be filled and prosperity will follow faithful service. At Martinsville removals and death have almost depopulated this once excellent church. But the few splendid families which remain will surely see that Gospel light is not removed from the community.——The church at West Union is under the splendid guidance of J. J. Van Houton, who visits them once a month from Paris, his home. There are some splendid people here, with a commodious house and a good Sunday-school.——Hutsonville has been having a series of meetings, with W. W. Jacobs in the lead. There seemed to be but little interest so far, but the church is getting good instruction. The faithful preaching of the Gospel will not be lost. R. Layton, of West York, is about completing a year's faithful service for the church.——Palestine is taking on new life in the additions ot the Illinois Central railroad shops coming to it. G. S. McGaughey is entering upon his second year of efficient service. He is a splendid man, and takes hold of the enterprises of the state like a native born. The church is old and strong, much stronger than it knows. It numbers 150 members, with all useful auxiliaries, and recognizes all public days by its ministry and offerings. Walter S. Goode, of Youngstown, O., began his ministry here. M. H. Garrard, of Laporte, Ind., entered the ministry from this church as also did L. E. Murray, of Middletown, Ind. If all the churches had been as fruitful in putting ministers in the churches as the Palestine church we would not be so scarce of preachers.——Robinson, after many years of struggle and varied history, is beginning to glow with the purpose of a new church building. How a purpose and enterprise for the Master brings life and power. John W. Moody is the splendid young minister who came over from Kentucky to help us and takes up Illinois work in a truly loyal way. The little city is growing rapidly and if the 130 Christians will crowd the work as the wave comes in, we may expect a strong, enterprising church here in a short time.——In the country, some twelve miles from Robinson, in the midst of the oil region, is the old Hardinsville church. For half a century or more it has held forth the word of life, in such a manner that a large proportion of the people are on the Lord's side. They are in a new church building with a fine Sunday-school and prospects for enlarged usefulness. P. C. Cauble, of Vincennes, Ind., preaches for them part of the time.——At Oblong, Brother Cauble gives half his time, greatly to the satisfaction and profit of the church. This is the old home of Hale Johnson, the great temperance leader and worker, whom the church still mourns and greatly misses. J. W. Hanly has moved from Newton, and other removals and

deaths have seriously weakened the church. This is also the home of B. W. Tate, now in a meeting at Smithsborough. He is a successful evangelist.——At Wheeler, J. C. Williams was just beginning a meeting with good prospects. The church is a little discouraged on account of recent removals and deaths, but there are plenty good people left to carry on the Lord's work in good order with proper efforts and sacrifice, and a good opportunity for growth, especially among the young people. T. H. Wilson, of Centralia, is the regular minister and is spoken of as a good preacher.——The brethren at Mason have recently repaired their house of worship and are enjoying prosperity. John S. Read, one of the members, after a clean, sober campaign, has just been elected to the state legislature. It is not always true that a man must treat and buy votes to be elected. The election of Mr. Read is a compliment to his entire district and an honor worthy of emulation. It ought to be prima facie evidence of a man's unfitness to be a law maker who so debases our ballot as to buy votes with liquor or money. The vote so bought is an un-American and base as the guilty candidate. The ballot box should give the unbiased expression of the best judgment of every voter, and he who corrupts it degrades our nation and imperils the Republic.

Eureka, Ill. J. G. WAGGONER.

A Sane Investment

Also RARE; SAFE because sane; EXCEEDINGLY PROFITABLE; six per cent interest up to dividend paying period; secured by real estate. If dissatisfied at any time within one year money will be refunded with six per cent interest. A very unusual opportunity. For particulars address THOMAS KANE & CO., 64 Wabash Ave., Chicago.

FAMOUS MEN
OF THE OLD TESTAMENT

Table of Contents.

ABRAHAM, The Friend of God and Father of the Faithful
JACOB, The Father of the Twelve Tribes.
JOSEPH, The Savior of His People.
MOSES, The Leader, Lawgiver and Literatus.
JOSHUA, The Father of His Country.
GIDEON, The Mighty Man of Valor.
JEPHTHAH, The Misinterpreted Judge.
ELI, The Pious Priest but Indulgent Parent.
SAUL, The First King of Israel.
DAVID, The Great Theocratic King.
SOLOMON, The Grand Monarch of Israel.
ELIJAH, The Prophet of Fire.
JONAH, The Recreant but Repentant Prophet.
DANIEL, The Daring Statesman and Prophet.
BALAAM, The Corrupt Prophet and Diviner.
ABSALOM, The Reckless and Rebellious Son.
NEHEMIAH, The Jewish Patriot and Reformer.

334 pages, silk cloth, postpaid, $1.50.

Christian Publishing Company, St. Louis, Mo.

For Over 60 Years

Mrs. Winslow's Soothing Syrup
has been used for over FIFTY YEARS by MILLIONS of Mothers for their CHILDREN while TEETHING, with perfect success. IT SOOTHES the CHILD, SOFTENS the GUMS, ALLAYS all pain, CURES WIND COLIC, and is the best remedy for DIARRHŒA. Sold by Druggists in every part of the world. Be sure and ask for Mrs. Winslow's Soothing Syrup and take no other kind. 25 Cents a Bottle.

An Old and Well-tried Remedy

When You Take Cold

One way is to pay no attention to it; at least, not until it develops into pneumonia, or bronchitis, or pleurisy. Another way is to ask your doctor about Ayer's Cherry Pectoral. If he says, "Just the thing," then take it. Do as he says, anyway.

We have no secrets! We publish the formulas of all our preparations.

J. C. Ayer Co., Lowell, Mass.

Evangelizing in Mexico.

I am making my first evangelistic trip unaccompanied by a native preacher. Our churches and outstations in the frontier are in most promising condition, but greatly in need of more workers. I have preached in Fuente, Nava, Sabinas and Nacional this week, with two baptisms in Fuente and one confession in Nacional. The people are hungry for the Gospel, and our new converts are splendid examples of fidelity. Brothers Jiminez and Camacho, our preachers in this field, are an inspiration in their sacrifice and hard work. One gets $30 (gold) per month, the other $15, paying house rent out of this; yet they are cheerful and contented and enthusiastic in preaching the Word.

Sabinas, Coap, Mexico.   S. G. INMAN.

No Harsh Words—126 Converts.

One of the most successful revival meetings held in the Christian Church at Charleston, Ill. in recent years closed with 126 additions—32 coming the last Lord's day and four on the night of the reception. The meeting was of four weeks' duration and was conducted by H. A. Davis, who spoke the truth in love and notwithstanding the fact that the other Protestant churches in town united in a meeting after we began and continued until we closed, he never uttered a harsh word against them, nor did anything that would in any way lower the dignity of his message. As one of the local papers expressed it, "his message breathed not only love for the sinner, but good will to all Christian people engaged in the building up of the Master's kingdom. His doctrinal sermons were plain and unequivocal, yet in the entire series of meetings not a single word was uttered by the evangelist to which an exception could be taken by even the most sensitive." A notable circumstance connected with the additions is that at least seventy-five per cent are adult men and women. Many normal students are included in the list. Brother Charlton rendered us splendid service; he bids fair to become one of our greatest singing evangelists. The meeting was a blessing to the church in every way.

GEORGE H. BROWN, pastor.

Ohio.

Ohio has captured two of Indiana's preachers. They are M. G. Long, who comes from Warsaw, Ind., and H. C. V. Wilson, from Lyons, Ind. to Mt. Victory and Big Springs. We extend a most cordial greeting to these two brethren and hope they will soon become full-fledged Buckeyes and be greatly blessed in their work.——Charlie Pearce has been called to the church at Ashland recently vacated by Grant Speer and will leave Galion for Ashland Jan. 1. Ashland will find Brother Pearce and his good wife pure gold and genuine Christians.——Indiana, we are sorry to say, has captured one of our good Ohio preachers. Thos. L. Lowe goes from Athens, where he has been for six years, to Union City, Ind., with the new year. But so long as we can trade one for two, we ought not complain too much. But we didn't want Lowe to go at all. We submit, though, and wish all the blessings of heaven upon him. He will "make good" even on Hoosier soil.——E. D. Salkeld, of Homestead, Pa., has found favor in the sight of the saints at Lakewood, Cleveland, and will soon take up his abode in that bishoprick. A hearty welcome to him. He will find a great field in Lakewood.——E. B. Bagby will begin a meeting at Franklin Circle, Cleveland, December 30. A singer will assist if one can be found.——Isaac J. Cahill, of Dayton, will preach in a meeting at Uhrichsville where parson Darsie is leading on and on to better and better things, beginning Jan. 13.——T. J. White, the very faithful and aggressive builder at North Baltimore, has recently held a good meeting with home forces.——Violett and Clarkson stirred up Sebring. A pastoral help has been installed in the person of the new wife of bishop Sala.——W. A. Harp and wife, of Springfield, deserve the thanks of the state.——The Ohio man recently closed a very successful meeting at Lovington, Ill. Ninety-one people responded to the invitation. Of these fifty-three were men. Thirty-one

young men. It was an ideal meeting. It stirred the whole community deeply. There was no excitement. People were not auctioned into the church. Only high motives were appealed to. It was a deep, devotional uplifting meeting from start to finish. The people worked like beavers. They prepared in a faultless way for the meeting. It was a joy to work with them. Some man will find a great opportunity there.——J. H. Garrison's new book on "Christian Union" and President King's "Rational Living" are furnishing good reading just now. Every preacher ought to read

these books. This is especially true of each one of them. They are intensely interesting and greatly helpful. By the way, did you note Prof. McGarvey's criticism of Brother Garrison's book? It reminds us of the mixed figure of a certain sophomoric orator, "I smell a mouse; I see it floating in the air, I'll nip it in the bud."——We wish for all THE EVANGELIST family, which by the way is getting to be almost like the descendants of Abraham, a very Merry Christmas and a Happy New Year.   C. A. FREER.

Painesville, O.

A GREAT MEETING AT NEVADA, MO.

The Pastor's Side of It.

Hamlin and Daugherty have just closed one of the best meetings ever held in our city. One hundred and fifty persons came out—nearly one

W. W. Burks, Nevada, Mo.

Leonard Daugherty, Louisville, Ky.

Texas, where for sixteen years he has labored for some of the strongest churches both as an evangelist and pastor.

We made no mistake in calling him. He is an

R. R. Hamlin.

hundred of these by confession. This was the first meeting Brother Hamlin ever held in Missouri and before coming to us he was practically unknown here. He has done a great work in

ideal evangelist because he is both a strong preacher and a great personal worker. Brother Daugherty is well known to our brethren of Missouri and the central states as one of the most efficient singing evangelists in the field. Our church is now one of the largest in western Missouri, having had a net increase of over 200 members in 1906. We plan for larger things at once. The organization of our young men and women into the Daraca-Philathea classes has contributed very much to our great success. Our "prayer-list people" and personal workers committee are entitled to praise for their faith and persistence.

W. W. BURKS.

From the Evangelist.

Months ago when the call came to me to conduct the Nevada meeting my expectations were high. Two Texas preachers—M. M. Davis and J. J. Lockhart—were former pastors there and I had heard many good things of the church and people. My experience of six weeks' justifies all that had been told me and more. We were delightfully entertained and tasted of Missouri's best hospitality. The audiences were large and the interest and attention, together with an ever-deepening current of spiritual feeling, were enough to inspire any man to do his best. Men and women worked publicly and privately for the salvation of the lost. The G. W. B. M. banded themselves together before the meeting for prayer and work taking vows before God and keeping them. There was much praying and splendid singing. Brother Daugherty lead the great chorus, until every heart was singing, and often men, women and children were heard singing the revival songs in homes and on the street. W. W. Burks is a prince of pastors and in his aid to the evangelist. He is intellectual, hopeful, tactful, cheerful, spiritual—a rare combination of qualifications, and such as can be mightily used of God in his work. The Methodist said "Burks has got religion and belongs to us." His hearty "Amens" were like the cheers of friends to the soldier in battles. I never worked with a pastor who gave me better support or who watched more vigilantly to relieve the evangelist of the scores of things that demand time and attention which ought to be given elsewhere. I have nothing but good words to say of the church and its official board. I have confined my labors to Texas in the past, as there is quite a good-sized, territory for one there, but if Nevada is a sample of Missouri churches, I hope to hold many more meetings in the state. Among the 150 who came forward during the meeting, were many adults, prominent men and women in business and social circles.

R. R. HAMLIN.

A Village Church Has 57 Additions.

The El Dara church, of which J. D. Williams is minister, closed a three weeks' meeting in which I was called to assist. It gives me pleasure to report the fine work of this church and minister. The building had been repaired and beautified at more than $300 expense. The congregation rallied to the lifting of all its debt, a liberal offering to state missions, and a liberal return for my ser-

vices as evangelist. Notwithstanding bad weather there was a well sustained interest. Fifty converts were baptized. Seven were received otherwise. Brother Williams has organized an Endeavor society with 50 members, and a Bible study class that will meet on a week day night during the winter. Brother Williams came to us from the Baptists a few years ago. He is doing a splendid work at El Dara and New Hartford. The new converts have pledged themselves to a definite financial support of the church.

Pittsfield, Ill. W. E. SPICER.

[We have received a report of this meeting also from Brother Williams, who says that Brother Spicer won the hearts of his people by a manly, pleasing presentation of the Gospel. This meeting indicates what a village church may accomplish by a united effort.—EDITOR.]

CHURCHES RECENTLY DEDICATED.

Litchfield, Ill.

The church here rejoices in a great victory realized on dedication day. Our motto was: 400 at Sunday-school and a collection of $100; a full house at dedication and $3,000 in good pledges

M. S. Johnson, Pastor.

to cover balance on our new building. We realized 417 present at Sunday-school and a cash collection of $115.50, while the pledges to the new building reached $3,363.25 and volunteer pledges and cash contributions are still coming in. This will give us a little margin with which to pay interest until pledges are all collected. The church property is now worth over $15,000. With more

triple arch, the rear arch supported by gothic columns and capitals, and the background consisting of a large picture of the river Jordan, the work of one of the best scenic artists in the state. Visitors admire the building and wonder that we could secure so much at so small any outlay. J. Fred Jones did excellent service for us on dedication day. He has the two essentials of a good solicitor and dedicator, viz., humor and tact. We now have the largest and most modern building in town. M. S. JOHNSON, pastor.

Marcus, Iowa.

The new house of worship was dedicated December 9 by L. L. Carpenter. The property represents a cost of $10,000. The sum of $4,000 was asked for the day of dedication which amount was more than secured. The building is a substantial frame structure arranged with every modern church convenience. The basement consists of reception hall, dining room and kitchen. On the main floor is the auditorium and lecture room (which can be made into one), pastor's and robing rooms. The audience room is seated with circular oak pews, the rest of the rooms with chairs. We have the best and most convenient house of its size in Cherokee county.

WILLIAM BAIER, pastor.

Little Rock.

At the request of the Third Street Christian Church, Little Rock, Ark., I aided them in opening up and dedicating their new house of worship. This is the second church in the city and it already numbers over 100 members. A year ago they purchased 100 feet of ground on the corner of Cross and Third streets for $3,900. On this lot they erected a beautiful, commodious building. They needed still $1,000 to pay for it. After the sermon I made an appeal and $1,147 were quickly raised. All seemed to be happy. The afternoon communion service and night meeting were both well attended. I was glad to meet J. N. Jessup, who ministers to the Tenth Street Church, which has just completed at a cost of $20,000, the chapel end of a $50,000 church property. Our cause in Little Rock is doing far better than formerly and since Brother Jessup has taken hold of the work great and permanent progress has been made. E. C. Browning, secretary of state missions, was also on hand. He appears as young as he was twenty years ago, while in Missouri.

George D. Weaver, who has for a year ministered to the Third Christian Church, has resigned and returns to Canada. The church will be temporarily supplied by Brother Browning. It was very kind in the Third Street Church to dismiss

New Church at Litchfield, Ill.

money at our disposal we might have made the exterior of our church more pleasing and imposing, but it is difficult to see how the interior could be made more beautiful or more convenient. It will accommodate 1,000 people. The auditorium is connected with rooms on either side by large sliding doors. The rostrum is made beautiful by a large

their morning service and Brother Jessup, with quite a number of his flock, attend the dedication. They were not only an inspiration, but aided substantially when the call for funds was made. I was never more favorably impressed with the fact that Little Rock, and, in fact, the whole state of Arkansas is a great and needy mission field. G. A. HOFFMANN.

Conway, Mo.

Taking the place of Brother Abbott, whose little daughter had diphtheria, I preached the dedication sermon of the church at Conway, Laclede county. Joseph Gaylor, evangelist in the southwest district, led this undertaking to the splendid consummation of dedication day. When Gaylor takes hold in a town, a new church, a good congregation, and all things that spell success are sure to follow. The week preceding the dedication, I attended three county conventions in Missouri, and conducted institutes, etc. Our people are more aggressive in that part of the state than ever before. J. H. HARDIN.

Deweese, Neb.

The church here was dedicated December 16, Joel Brown, of Des Moines, Ia., being master of ceremonies. Twenty-seven hundred dollars

Joel Brown.

were pledged in a remarkably short time and the church dedicated without debt. This church owes its origin to Mrs. E. E. Jenkins, who in 1898 circulated a subscription paper for a new church before there was an organization.

Evangelistic

We invite ministers and others to send reports of meetings, additions and other news of the churches. It is especially requested that additions be reported as "by confession and baptism," or "by letter."

Foreign Missions.

R. P. Anderson reports two baptisms at Christiana, Norway, and Anders Johnsen reports eleven baptisms at Frederickshald, Norway, and C. S. Weaver reports two baptisms at Osaka, Japan. The Foreign Society is greatly encouraged over the recent large number of conversions in the different fields.

Arkansas.

Hope, Dec. 18.—Two baptisms. One addition by statement.—Percy G. Cross.

California.

Berkeley.—Two baptisms at Richmond.—Clay T. Runyon.

Rialto.—Two have been added by letter.—Oscar Sweeney.

Colorado.

Rocky Ford.—Our meetings of three weeks closed December 10 with 36 additions—15 by baptism. David C. Peters, of Trinidad, did the preaching and Mrs. W. T. Green, of Pueblo, led the singing.—M. M. Nelson, pastor.

District of Columbia.

Washington, D. C., Dec. 17.—Present at ministers' meeting: President Walter F. Smith, F. D. Power, B. E. Utz, J. E. Stuart, W. G. Oram, Lewis and the writer. Reports: Vermont avenue (F. D. Power) 4 by letter and 1 confession; Ninth street (B. E. Utz), 1 by statement; H street (W. G. Oram), 1 by letter; 34th street (Claud C. Jones), 1 confession. Vermont Avenue Sunday-school is in contest with the school of First church, Philadelphia. F. D. Power is delivering illustrated sermons on his travels.—Claude C. Jones, Sec.

Illinois.

Redmon, Dec. 20.—I have just closed a revival here with 12 by confession and baptism and 22 by letter. Brother Mason led the song service.

We organized on the 17th with 34 charter members. Officers and committees were appointed and a building will be erected in the early spring. This is a new field with great prospects. The Gospel is new to most of the town and was a revelation to those who had never heard the Bible without modification.—L. Hadaway.

Minonk, Dec. 17.—Charles D. Hougham, of Streator, Ill., has just closed a four weeks' meeting here. There were 13 additions, all adults except three, 7 confessions, 5 reclaimed and 1 from the M. E's. A reception was held last evening for the new members.—J. H. Bullock, minister.

Maroa, Dec. 17.—Eleven additions within the last month; 8 baptisms, 2 letters and one statement.—W. H. Applegate.

Williamsville, Dec. 23.—One addition by confession and baptism Sunday.—C. D. Haskell, minister.

Pittsfield, Dec. 18.—Three additions at regular services—all by baptism. Two of them from denominations.—W. E. Spicer.

Lovington.—I spent Lord's day, December 16, with this good church. J. R. Parker has been the faithful pastor. But failing health has caused him to seek a milder climate for the winter. This church has just closed a most successful meeting under the direction of Evangelist Charles A. Freer, of Ohio. There were almost 100 additions. The church is an old one, and quite substantial in membership and means. They have a good modern house, costing about $10,000. This is the home of Brother Finis Idleman, where he was brought up. His parents still live here. Also Bro. J. P. McKnight, of Los Angeles, Cal., was brought up at Lovington, and his father still resides here. They need a good man to locate with them, and the right men can do a great work with this church. In a quiet way they are seeking the man they need.—J. H. Smart, Decator, Ill.

Danville, Dec. 16.—I have been very busy for a number of weeks in a social meeting with home forces, with the Second church, in this city. There have been 70 additions to date, forty-six by baptism, the others by letter, reclaimed, and from the denominations. Among the additions were an M. E. minister and his wife, about the average in ability, who are proving of great help to us.—Andrew Scott.

Freeport, Dec. 16.—Five added, four by letter, including pastor and wife, who began their work with the church, and one by confession. The new church looks hopefully toward the future. The Sunday-school has increased 5 per cent in the three months of its life.—J. A. Barnett.

Indiana.

Rensselaer, Dec. 21.—Our meeting closed with 114 additions, 68 baptisms. Wilson and Lintt preach the gospel in sermon and song with great power. The Bible truths that were set forth will yield a harvest after many days. The church is revived and is looking hopefully into the New Year.—G. H. Clarke.

Milroy, Dec. 20.—In a meeting of 18 days there were 6 accessions—2 baptisms, 4 otherwise. J. Ross Miller, of Gas City, gave universal satisfaction as leader of song and general helper.—D. H. Patterson.

Terre Haute.—Twenty-four added at Kingman in a four weeks meeting, representing a gain of 19 to the cause. Nine were by confession and 10 from other folds. Two added at Scott's Prairie, not reported.—Oscar E. Kelley.

Iowa.

Des Moines, Dec. 2.—Assisted in the services at the Central Church this morning; 2 additions. W. J. Wright preached a fine sermon. To-night we began our revival in the Highland Park district. Four churches co-operating. Many people were turned away at this our first service.—Charles E. McVay, song evangelist.

Mt. Pleasant, Dec. 18.—There have been nine added here recently—1 by baptism and 2 otherwise.—L. A. Chapman.

Delta, Dec. 17.—Our meeting closed with 56 additions. The attendance and interest were remarkable and would have justified a continuation of the services, but because of bronchial trouble and hoarseness on my part we were obliged to close.—W. B. Wilson, minister.

Des Moines, Dec. 19.—Twenty-five added in 6 days at Granger; 23 of these confessions. Mrs. Boggess preached Sunday at Washington chapel and had 4 confessions; this made 29 for us during the week.—E. F. Boggess.

Des Moines, Dec. 17.—Our meeting at Highland Park College chapel closed with 40 confessions. The meeting lasted 15 days. W. J. Wright, of Cincinnati, O., was the evangelist. This meeting was a part of the Chapman campaign.—Charles E. McVay, song evangelist.

Kansas.

Salina, Dec. 17.—Baptisms at both services.—T. C. McArthur.

Cherryvale, Dec. 17.—One baptism and one by statement.—B. D. Gillispie.

Hoisington, Dec. 17.—Eight yesterday—1 by letter, 7 confessions.—F. M. McHale.

Asherville, Dec. 17.—Three added from other religious brotherhoods.—J. P. Clark, minister.

Barnes, Dec. 18.—Closed a five weeks' meeting with 21 added by baptism, 8 by statement and 1 reclaimed; a Catholic girl made confession, who has not yet been baptized because of parental objection. Eight of those baptized were from other organizations. Arrangements were made for regular preaching services. Charles Henning of Bethany, Neb., was the song leader and helper.—Orwin L. Adams, Bethany.

Centralia, Dec. 20.—A three weeks' meeting conducted by the pastor, J. F. Rosborough, closed with 25 additions to the church, 20 confessions and 5 by letter. F. O. Fannon preached at Kinmundy last Sunday with four additions.

Wichita, Dec. 20.—Our meeting at the Central closed with 40 additions. During the four months E. W. Allen has been with us there have been 70 additions.

Smith Center, Dec. 13.—November 30 I closed a meeting of 11 days in a school house near Reamsville. There were only 2 members living in the community when I went there, and to-day there are 15 members of Christ's body there. Eight were baptized on Thanksgiving day and 5 came from the denominations who had previously been baptized. There has been one added to the Smith Center church by baptism and to the Dewey church 1 by baptism, 1 reclaimed and 1 by letter. Sister Hazelrigg comes to help us in a meeting through January.—F. E. Blanchard.

Kentucky.

Sadieville.—I have just closed my fifth meeting with this church. The meeting continued two weeks. Twenty-five baptized.—E. L. Frazier, Morristown, Ind.

Louisville, Dec. 2.—Closed meeting at Vine street, Nashville, with 51 added—80 during two months' stay there. Good beginning here at Crescent Hill. One confession Sunday night and five additions last night; audiences are large. This work is done under the auspices of the Clifton church, led by that tireless, consecrated and capable minister, T. S. Tinsley.—J. T. McKissick.

Massachusetts.

Boston, Dec. 18.—Nine additions recently—5 confessions. Sunday-school larger than ever. Work is moving with enthusiasm.—A. L. Ward.

Everett, Dec. 17.—Had 3 confessions, a baptisms and two additions this week. We continue another week. J. W. Robbins, evangelist.—A. T. June.

Michigan.

Adrian, Dec. 17.—We have held a short evangelistic meeting with local forces. The meeting stopped sooner than it otherwise would on account of the union revival meeting by C. H. Yatman. We had five baptisms, two other bap.

Sunday-School

January 6, 1907.

God the Creator.—Gen. 1:1-25.

Memory verses, 1-3.

Golden Text.—In the beginning God created the heavens and the earth.—Gen. 1:1.

Every race which has a religion has also a more or less complete tradition to explain the origin of all things. The round of the seasons, the sequence of seed, plant, fruit and seed again, the succession of generation from generation, suggest even to the faintly philosophical mind of the savage the inquiry as to the beginning of things. The idea that things have always been as they are now, or that they just happened, is not a natural product of human reason. It comes only when men are diligently trying to dispense with the idea of a creator.

The Hebrew story of the creation is, in some respects, like those of other races; in other respects, it is different. It is like them in representing that the different elements of the physical universe came into existence in some sort of orderly sequence and by the exercise of a power above man. It is unlike the others in its freedom from gross and absurd polytheistic and pantheistic elements and in the pure and lofty view which it presents of the nature of God and his relation to man.

There has been much unnecessary discussion of the alleged "conflict," and more of the alleged "harmony," between Genesis and modern science. It is no part of the purpose of divine revelation to convey scientific information about astronomy, geology or biology. When Paul tells what inspired scriptures are profitable for he does not mention these subjects.

In giving to the writer of this splendid record the idea of creation by the will of a personal and righteous God and of man as made in the image and likeness of God, the divine spirit necessarily kept the record free from those absurd and preposterous elements which mark the pagan cosmologies and render it impossible for a modern man to take them seriously. But it is nowhere indicated that the inspiration of this document was of a nature to enable its author to anticipate scientific discoveries which were yet thousands of years in the future.

What it did give him was an insight into spiritual truths which are wholly beyond the reach of science and which are vastly more important than any scientific discoveries. The truth stated in the words "God created," is vastly more vital than any details as to how or in what order the universe came into existence.

When the author spoke of the "first day," the "second day," and so on, he evidently meant days in the common meaning of the word. No one ever suspected that he meant anything else until the science of geology revealed the fact that vast periods of time were involved in the making of the world. It

Free from harmful drugs. Cure coughs and hoarseness. Prevent sore throat.

---

is not dealing frankly with Scripture to compel it, by an unnatural interpretation, to say what it clearly never meant to say, in the interest of a theory which requires that somehow Genesis and geology be brought into harmony.

One has but to read together the Hebrew and the Babylonian accounts of the creation to see that, while some of their details may have been derived from a common Semitic tradition, the spirit of God was moving uniquely in and through the Hebrew record to make it the vehicle of a revelation of himself.

Midweek Prayer-Meeting

By Charles Blanchard.

January 2, 1907.

Enlistment for Service.—Matt. 20:1-16; 21:28-32.

This householder was interested in his vineyard. And we ought to be. The vineyard of the Lord—ah! How big a thing it is! We need a vision of bigness along with the blessedness of service. We need to get out early in the morning for the Master. He is looking for us—has been looking for some of us a long while and wondering why we don't come! He wants laborers. He is willing to pay for them. He wants us to pray for more laborers. But while we are praying he expects us to get busy!

"The kingdom of heaven is like unto a man that was an householder, who went out early in the morning to hire laborers into his vineyard." This householder was a man of affairs. The kingdom of heaven is not all singing and praying. It's an affair of business. It was a busy man that the Master had in mind. He was an early riser. He didn't lay abed on Sunday morning. He was up with the robins in the summer time, and rousting about when the first street-car motorman's merry whistle cut the winter winds around the corner.

"So, when the even was come the lord of the vineyard said unto his steward, Call the laborers." O, friends, the night is coming. The burden is heavy, the way seems long? Patience. It will only be a little while. "They received every man a penny." It is of the Lord. I am glad for myself and for you that it is that way. We dream of equality on earth, but are far from realizing it. It will please me to just let the "Good" man of the house" even things up for us. I reckon there will be some kicking. But remember, the kickers are last—and don't!

Some have never had an invitation to go into his vineyard. "No man hath hired us," those said whom the Lord found waiting at the eleventh hour. Does the Lord expect men—us—to go out and hunt up fellows to help do his work. It looks that way. Some things are not getting done because we haven't done it, haven't invited others to help us. What about these eleventh hour folks? They are the ones that didn't have a chance. It does not mean the one who trifled away his day of grace and usefulness and then came around whining because no man cared for his soul. But there are a lot of neglected folks and some of us are to blame! We didn't invite them to come with us and share in the sweat and sweet of the Master's service.

A penny a day is mighty small wages, you think? Well, it's a divine rule that

---

in the sweat of our brows we shall eat our bread. But the bread of the laborer is sweet. Sweat if you want your bread to be sweet. It's a part of the recompense of toil, like the sleep of the just. "Whatsoever is right I will give you." And we can afford to trust him, who holdeth the wealth in his hands for his children. We can trust him who makes the apple bloom blow in the May of the world, who makes the grass to grow, and the flowers to spring up in the desert. He is more than just. He is generous, as the parable shows, to every one but the grumbler and the fault-finder. Let's quit—not working—but grumbling. There is no grace in grouchiness, no faith in finding fault.

"And he saw others standing idle in the market-place." O, the idlers in the market-place of souls! Souls being sold? Yes! But more simply lost by indifference, while we squander the Lord's time and money, or labor all our years for that which is not bread and can not satisfy. The command is, "Go into the vineyard." It is the command of love. It is the constraint of the Christ. It is the invitation of the Master of the household. Of course he expects us to work, honestly, faithfully and till nightfall. But all the sweet of the vineyard we may have for the taking. Help yourselves! "All things are yours," Paul says. Why won't we take and eat? Some of us actually starve to death right in the vineyard, because we are too lazy to eat or to gather the grapes of his grace for ourselves and others.

❧ ❧

January 6, 1907.

BEGINNING WITH GOD AND CONTINUING WITH HIM. (Consecration Meeting.)—Gen. 1:1.

Jno. 1:11-14, 15:4-7.

DAILY READINGS.

M. The new birth. . . . . John 3:1-8.
T. Babes in Christ. . . . . 1 Pet. 2:1-5.
W. Pressing forward. . . . . Phil. 3:8-14.
T. Kept by Him. . . . . Jude 20-25.
F. Having His Peace. . . . . John 14:27-31.
S. Ever with Him. . . . . 1 Thess. 4:13-18.
S. Topic.

Build thee more stately mansions
O my soul, as the swift seasons roll!
Leave thy low-vaulted past,
Let each new temple—
Nobler than the last—
Shut thee from heaven
With a dome more vast,
Till thou at length art free—
Leaving thine out-grown shell
By life's unresting sea.

Starting right is very commendable, but holding fast is most praiseworthy.

The years have come and gone and there is so much common to all that there is little to distinguish one from the other. But a closer walk with Jesus, more reliance upon the Father, greater love for man, complete consecration to the All-good will make 1907 be to the years of the past like an apple of gold in a picture of silver.

Guard against the slightest divergence from righteousness in the early days of the year. Tracks go out of the great union station almost parallel. Their separation at first is scarcely observable as they bear southward but soon one is seen reaching to the east and the other diametrically opposite. Determine now that you will never get further than a hand grasp away from the Saviour.

Every new year comes to us with possibilities for the creation of new spiritual worlds in which we may live and love and labor. If we permit, God will create these worlds for us and with us and pronounce them "very good," and if we will dress the garden and keep it, and disregard the tempter—tempt he ever so wisely—this paradise on earth and the city that lieth four square will so nearly resemble and our preparation here for the one there be so complete, the transition will cost us no apprehension nor scarce a pang—there will only be a joyous looking forward to glory to come.

What are you bringing over with you from 1906? Leave behind every weight and the sin that doth so easily beset you; bury with the decrepit old year all enmities and hatreds, envies and malice, avariciousness and narrowness, and renounce the card playing, dancing and every form of frivolity that offends the conscience of those living closest to Christ. But bring with you your trust in God and faith in man; your hopefulness, sanguineness and cheer; your Bible and prayers, and your zeal for the Gospel, liberality to the church and exemplification of the life of the Master.

God made the world beautiful and helpful in all its appointments. Satan's baneful influence sharpened thorns and scattered thistles; it distilled poison under the serpent's tongue and murder into the hearts of men. Satan can mar the non-resisting earth, but since Christ came he can not degrade a resisting

man. God will make for you a new world and call it 1907. If you will resist Satan he will flee from you and your new world. Therein you may live a useful, happy, unsullied life, and when it is

filed away with other years and at submitted to the final inspection of Judge of all it will be such as to mi ily prevail toward securing for you coveted "well done" and "enter in."

OBITUARIES.

[Notices of Deaths, not more than four lines, inserted free. Obituary memoirs, one cent per word. Send the money with the copy.]

ALLEN.

Francis Withers Allen was born April 1, 1832, in Howard county, Mo. When a small boy the family moved to Monroe county. He attended the State University and Bethany College, graduating in 1854. In 1859 he was married to Susan J. Reid, who died in 1857. After teaching school he commenced practicing medicine in 1864. In December, 1864, he was married to Amanda Malvina Pearl. His first patient was Uncle John Clarkson, 42 years ago, who was also his last patient before his death. Bro. Doc. Allen, as he was commonly called, served as an elder in the Concord Church in Macon county for more than a quarter of a century. The funeral was preached at the Christian Church in Callao, Mo., and the body was laid to rest in the beautiful cemetery at that place.   E. J. WRIGHT.
Macon, Mo.

BARBEE.

Mrs. J. A. Barbee passed to her reward Sunday, December 9, age 71 years, 3 months and 21 days. She had been a member of the Christian church for 56 years. She leaves a husband and seven children, one sister, and two brothers to mourn her death. She was one of God's good women and was the mother of a noble family. Funeral services by our pastor on December 11.   Z. MOORE.
Taylorville, Ill.

CHAIN.

Mrs. Mary S. Chain, widow of the lamented Hugh Chain, Jr., fell asleep in Christ December 15, 1906, in her 53d year. She was in apparent good health, and had prepared her Sunday-school lesson and attended to her other duties on the Saturday when she was stricken. Brother and Sister Chain founded the Third Church in West Philadelphia in 1878, and worked together in its interests until the husband entered into rest. September 20, 1892. Since then, Sister Chain has constantly striven to advance the cause that was so sacred and near to her heart. We will miss her presence in our meetings and her counsel in our deliberations. She leaves a daughter, three sons and two grandchildren to mourn her departure.   G. P. RUTLEDGE.
Philadelphia, Pa.

DEARBORN.

Our venerable and beloved brother John A. Dearborn, died in Kansas City, Mo., on Thursday, November 22, 1906, aged 81 years, 3 months and 17 days. He had preached the gospel for nearly sixty years, and his name was a household word among the Disciples of Christ. He was born in Cynthiana, Ky., but his parents moved to Paris, in that state, while he was an infant, and his early years were spent there. He was educated at Bethany college, graduating in the first class that went out from that institution, in 1847. He was married in 1852 to the eldest daughter of Dr. B. S. Lawson, of Cincinnati, and survived his wife fourteen years and three days. Brother Dearborn served many of our prominent churches, either in pastoral or evangelistic work, and had few superiors in the pulpit. With a mind rarely endowed by nature and improved by culture, he was an elegant and forceful speaker, and as an expositor of the word of God had few equals among his brethren. Pure in heart and life, chaste in speech, courteous in manners and spotlessly clean and neat in person, the church was indeed blessed that enjoyed his ministry. Among his pastorates were churches in Baton Rouge, La.; Cincinnati, O.; Harrodsburg and Princeton, Ky.; Marshall and Liberty, Mo.; Richmond and Newport News, Va. The last named was his last pastorate, from which he resigned some five years ago because of falling health. Since that time Brother Dearborn has made his home with his son, Clarence, in this city, and has preached as supply in many churches in this city and vicinity. For about a year he was unable to leave his room, and suffered much, but always with patience and resignation. The end came peacefully, with two of his children, his son Clarence and his daughter, Mrs. J. L. Hill, of Richmond, Va., by his side. His other son, whose home is in Chicago was unable to come. The funeral services were held in the First Christian church, of which he had been a member since his return to the city, and were conducted by the writer, assisted by T. P. Haley. His body was laid to rest in beautiful Elmwood cemetery, beside his wife and son, Lawson. He rests from his labors, and his works do follow him. His presence with us during these latter years was a benediction, and his memory is blessed.
   W. F. RICHARDSON.

FORD

Edwin Allen Ford, son of Elder G. W. and S. E. Ford, was born in Mt. Vernon, Ind., September 24, 1896, and died in West Salem, Ill. December 4, 1906. Allen was a bright boy, a general favorite among his companions and a loving, obedient son. He suffered greatly during his last illness and he bore his affliction with much fortitude. Father, mother, five brothers, one sister and many friends mourn his death. Brother and sister Ford have lost five children. Four of these have died in a little over three years. Their oldest daughter, wife of J. T. Davis, died August 23, 1903; their daughter, Minnie, December 20, 1903, and the third daughter, wife of O. E.

France, July 19, 1906. Brother and Sister Ford have the esteem and the sympathy of many friends. May our Father comfort and sustain them.
   C. C. GARRIGUES.

HUTCHISON.

Sarah Hutchison was born in Cape Girardeau county, Mo., on November 15, 1875, and died in St. Louis on December 8, 1906—31 years of age. Her parents were members of the hardshell Baptist church—"Old Bethel"—the first protestant church west of the Mississippi which celebrated its centennial a few weeks ago. In 1844 she joined the Christian church at Memphis, Tenn., and was a member continuously to the time of her demise. Two children survive—Dr. R. M. Hutchison, of Palms, Cal., and Mrs. W. J. Miller, of St. Louis; also, a grand-daughter, Miss Anna Hutchison, of St. Louis. Burial December 12, at the old family burying place near Jackson.

STARR.

Sister Harriet Starr was called to the higher life November 30, 1906, aged 62 years, 1 month and 27 days. She was a constant member of the Christian church at Harmony, O. The funeral service was held at the home Sunday, December 2; and was attended by a large number of friends.   A. M. HURD.
Byesville, Ohio.

WITHERS.

Charles Washington Withers, son of Thomas and Jane Withers, was born near Marshfield, O., September 11, 1850, and died at his home at Marshfield December 3, 1906. Three brothers and five sisters, and five of his seven children survive him. October 29, 1871, he was married to Susan Swain. In 1879, he became a Disciple of the Christ. Though there was a period of a few years when he was negligent of his duty, he many years ago renewed his vows and became one of the most active and faithful members of the Marshfield church, where he was a deacon and a worker in all departments of the church.
   HARRY F. RECTOR.

❧ The Home Department ❧

The End of the Year.

Thou crownest the year with thy goodness.

Remember all that time has brought—
  The starry hope on high,
The strength attained, the courage gained,
  The love that can not die.
Forget love bitter, brooding thought,
  The word too harshly said;
The living blame; love hates to name
  The frailties of the dead!
  —*Oliver Wendell Holmes.*

O friend, it has been a strange year for you; sin in it, folly in it, neglect of duty and of God in it; but if the heart is crying, "I will not let thee go except thou bless me," if the interests of life are moral ones for you, if the one worth of being alive at all is daily self-conquest to the glory of God—then bid defiance to your sin and failure, in the name of Christ forget the things that are behind, there is a year worth living ahead of you. —*G. H. Morrison.*

No man can pass into eternity for he is already in it. The dull brute globe moves through its ether and knows it not; even so our souls are bathed in eternity and we are never conscious of it.— *F. W. Farrar.*

What thou has done, thou hast done; for the
  heavenly horses are swift.
Think not their flight to o'ertake—they stand at
  the throne even now.
Ere thou canst compass the thought, the immortals
  in just hands shall lift,
Poise and weigh sweetly thy deed, and its weight
  shall be laid on thy brow;—
  For what thou has done, thou hast done.

What thou hast not done remains; and the heaven-
  ly horses are kind.
Till thou has pondered thy choice, they will
  patiently wait at thy door.
Do a divine deed, and, behold! they are farther
  away than the wind.
Returning, they bring thee a crown, to shine on
  thy brow evermore;
  For what thou hast done, thou hast done.
  —*Mary Wright Plummer.*

"What does it signify whether I go to the bottom or not, so long as I didn't skulk?—or rather," and here the old man took off his hat and looked up, "so long as the Great Captain has his way, and things is done to his mind?"—*George Macdonald.*

Grace is of a growing nature: in the way to Zion they go from strength to strength.—*Thomas Boston.*

Most gracious God, who hast been infinitely merciful to us, not only in the year past, but through all the years of our life, be pleased to accept our most unfeigned thanks for Thine innumerable blessings to us; graciously pardoning the manifold sins and infirmities of our life past, and bountifully bestowing upon us all those graces and virtues, which may render us acceptable to Thee. And, every year which Thou shalt be pleased to add to our lives, add also, we humbly implore Thee, more strength to our faith, more ardor to our love, and a greater perfection to our obedience; and grant that, in a humble sincerity and constant perseverance, we may serve Thee most faithfully the remainder of our lives, for Jesus Christ's sake. Amen.

A Camp Visitor.

BY ORPHA BENNETT HOBLIT.

He rode into camp just as the preparations for dinner were well under way. The kettle was bubbling on the little camp stove; the rice was swelling in the pot; already inviting whiffs of coffee floated out to the waiting ones under the trees, and the odor of frying ham was in the air. Madame, her white locks bound snugly beneath a grey veil, was putting the finishing touches on some lemon pies, while the young ladies were setting the table, and the invalid, into whose pale cheeks the dry, invigorating mountain air had already brought a faint tinge of pink, looked expectantly from her wheeled chair, delighted with the idea of once more dining with the family.

Then arrived the cowboy—our first real cowboy—riding a beautiful dappled-grey horse, which picked its way carefully down the incline among the stones and boulders, across the little *arroyo* and under the clump of oak and juniper trees that sheltered our tents. A chorus of delighted welcome from the young ladies, New Mexican damsels every one, greeted him, as he swung out

A NEW SERIAL STORY

The Home Department will be delighted with the new serial story which will begin next week. We are not going to tell you what it is all about. But you will like it, for it will be by J. Breckenridge Ellis, who wrote "A Week With the Woodneys" and "The Bronze Vase."

"AGNES OF THE BAD LANDS"
WILL BE ITS TITLE.

Do not fail to begin with the first chapter next week. It will be a story of child life and of grown-up life, and of church life. This is only one of the stories that will be published next year.

of the saddle and, dropping the reins on the ground before the horse—strode? —no, limped painfully toward us.

He was tall, spare and sinewy. A week's growth of thin, sandy beard covered the lower part of his face, which was burned and tanned to a leathery texture and to the color of the reddish sands of his own *mesa.* Ordinary in feature, the face was yet lighted by a pair of keen, friendly blue eyes, and, when he removed a much soiled and battered grey felt hat, bound about the crown with a carved leather band, we saw a shock of curly, sandy hair flattened down about a high, narrow forehead.

"Why, Will," said one of the afore-mentioned damsels as she brought him a chair, "What makes you so lame?"

"Horse fell on me," said Will briefly. "Haven't been out for a week before to-day."

Here the dinner claimed my attention

and I left him chatting with the girls, old friends of his, until it was on the table. Then, seated opposite, I found time to observe him more closely, to notice that the light-colored cotton shirt he wore was clean and fresh, as was also the bandanna loosely tied about his throat, and found my own enjoyment of the repast heightened by his evident appreciation of it, as he satisfied the hunger that his fifteen mile ride from the ranch had left with him.

In his conversation, however, I found the greatest entertainment. It became almost a monologue—just a question here and there to start a new subject, as he finished one picture after another of life on the plains and hills. His speech was correct in the main, for, although he had been born on the ranch and bred to the life of herdsman and cowboy, the F——s were a "good family" and Will had been to public school and had even spent a few terms in the territorial agricultural college, so that now, except for a few words such as "varmints," "stompede," "krel," and "that-a-way," his speech and pronunciation were fairly good.

"Yes, ma'am," he said, in answer to my question. "This is papa's land, this canyon where you're camping." (It was odd to hear the great fellow speak of "papa" as a little child might have done.) "We have three perpetual watering places on the range and this is one of them. We can always get water in the big *arroyo* here by digging down a few feet and most always it is running along on top like it is now."

"Then your cattle never dies of thirst."

"Not often, no ma'am, except in very dry seasons when the feed is pretty short they sometimes get too weak to go to water. You see our range runs the whole distance along the west side of the mountains and in through these canyons, and, when all the springs are dry except these three, we are pretty sure to find some cattle 'down' on their way here. We can't do much for them then, no ma'am, only kill them right away to put them out of their misery. We have a gasoline engine for the pump at the ranch now and that helps out some. Can't anybody run it but us though, seems like. If we leave it half a day with a Mexican he's sure to get to monkeying with it and it stops on him."

"No, ma'am, I don't ever carry a gun, or a lunch or a canteen. I travel just as light as I can with just my rope and branding iron and so do all the other fellows. It is just the eastern city chaps who come out here and think they're cowboys, who pile on the decorations. They always carry such things, but most of us don't want to be bothered when we are at work."

"We have to carry the branding iron for the mavericks and the yearlings. That's most of our work, except at the round-ups, riding the range and branding. We come across an unbranded yearling, rope it and tie its legs, then build a fire and brand it. Papa's brand is J. E. F. Mine is W. F. W. on the shoulder, F. on the hip. No, we don't always brand a maverick. If we know the mother and that she belongs to another range we don't brand it; (if we're honest.) There's never any dispute over mavericks, though, for the law gives the animal in question to the state, so it isn't worth while.

"Four of us are going to work this

canyon next week. We'll camp in that old cabin down the *arroyo* and you'll see us pretty often for a while."

"Yes, ma'am, Bird is a pretty good horse," in answer to some question about his nag. "He's getting pretty old now, though. He's ten years old. I broke him and no one else ever rides him. The men know better than to try. If he's the only horse at the krel they'll walk first. Why, I can't even put a lady on him. I tried once, lifted her 'most into the saddle, and he jumped out from under her and she went onto the ground."

"Feed your horse, Will," urged one of the young ladies. "It's hungry, poor thing. There's some hay left from what the horses had that brought us out. But don't get up, tell Felipe."

"I don't like to air my Spanish before the professor," said Will, but when the professor had assured him that the boy would probably understand his Mexican better than he would his own Castillian, he called out to our shy little dish-washer, in the soft Mexican dialect: "Oyes, Felipe, llevale el caballo por el agua y dale de comer." As the boy started to perform his bidding, he said apologetically: "I know it isn't correct, but it does to talk to the men. I can talk to them and understand, but it is different with the women. Maybe it's their voices, or perhaps they use different words or talk about different things—anyway, I can't understand a Mexican woman or make her understand me."

"No, ma'am, we have only cattle and horses now. Cattle won't feed after sheep or goats. I've herded both though. Papa began with them and when I was about ten years old I herded a flock of five hundred goats in this very canyon. I had sheep before that, but I hate sheep—can't bear the sight of one even now. They're so stupid and it's so monotonous working with them that I've known fellows to go crazy at it. Now goats are different. I had mine all named, every one, and they knew me. If the mountain lions got one, or I found one hung up dead by its wool in the bushes I could always tell papa which one it was by name. I knew every day just how they were going to act. I don't know how I could tell, but some mornings, when they started out to feed, I would just stay 'round here in camp. I knew by the way they acted, as I watched them climb up over that ridge there that the old leader would bring them back at night. Then again, other times, I knew I had to go along with the dog. They were different, some way. Yes, I was all alone here with them. I herded them and looked after them myself and sheared them all myself. I'd rather shear sheep. It's about the only thing I do like about sheep, their fleece comes off so pretty, all in one piece, but a goat's doesn't. They were fine stock, most of them Angora, but some just common goats. They gave us most of our living in those days besides the wool we sold, for they were all we needed for meat and milk, and meal for bread was cheap."

"I like cattle best though. They are some like the goats, but there is more doing with cattle. I can't explain it, but I can tell right off how a cow is going to act and how I've got to work her. Sometimes all she needs is a little rope and coaxing; then again you get one that has to be driven, and sometimes we find one that can't be coaxed or driven. She'd die first. That kind?—well, we just have to leave them till next time. It is no use trying to do anything with them. They're not many though. Yes, I can tell right off how

to treat them, but I don't know how I do it."

"I don't really know when I learned to rope things. Seems as if I always knew. You see, when I was a little fellow, I had no one to play with at home and I used to go out into the krels after supper and play with the goats and calves. I guess I must have learned then. The hardest thing I ever tried to rope was a centipede. Yes, ma'am, I've done it with a horsehair for a lasso, but it isn't easy. This morning at the ranch my sister's little boy—he's four years old—found a tarantula and was trying to rope it with a string when I went out into the yard. I guess he'll be a cowboy all right."

"Will," said the invalid, "we saw a fox last night creeping along past the camp. I thought at first it was a mountain lion. Are there many wild animals in these mountains?"

"Not many now, foxes and deer, a few, and once in a great while, a mountain lion, but you needn't be afraid. A lion wouldn't come near your camp, especially these bright, moonlight nights. I never saw one in the day time and we always hunt them in the dark of the moon. They don't trouble us now any to amount to anything. Once in a great while a colt will disappear, (they take horses every time in preference to cattle.) They used to be plenty, though, and we had to watch out for them. We have fifty-four pelts at the ranch. The last one papa killed with a six-shooter. We'd tracked it for hours with the dogs, and finally they backed it up against a rock and closed in on it, but it cuffed them off and sent them flying. There wasn't one in the whole thirteen that wasn't badly torn and scratched. Then it came after papa and backed him almost to the edge of the cliff. I was down below and yelled to him to drop over, but he said he was going to have a shot first, and he did, and that was the last of that lion. There's supposed to be a big bounty for their scalps, but we never could get anything. I guess this territory is dead broke."

"Please tell me, Mr. F——" I said, as we rose from the table, "what those leather overalls you wear over the others are called, and why you wear them."

"Most of the boys call them 'chaps,' but I guess that's short for some other word," he replied. "We have to wear them to protect us from the cactus and thorn bushes, for we can't pick our way when we're riding after a bunch of stampeded cattle. That's what these leather cuffs are for too. The leggins are pretty expensive. These of mine cost fifteen dollars, but they have the *conchas*. Some of them are just plain and cheaper."

The *conchas* were flat disks of metal, perforated in two places and fastened in a line down the outside of the leg with thongs of leather tied through the perforations.

"See what a handsome fob I have for my watch," he said, drawing a good gold watch from his pocket and displaying a notched leather fob. "An old Mexican we have down at the ranch cut the ear off my boot last week and made that for me—for luck, he said, but my horse stepped into a hole that very morning and nearly broke my leg."

"That would not have been a new experience for you, though, Will," remarked one of the girls.

"No, not exactly. One leg, both collar bones, two ribs, both arms, one of them twice, and, last summer, my neck twisted until I wished it had been broken and done with it. It isn't that I'm reckless, or ride wild horses for the fun

ing, the little creature left a part of its tail in the horny hand of its captor. "But it doesn't hurt him," he assured us. "They always do that-a-way and he'll grow another in just a little while."

He described to us the other canyons of the mountains. Rucker, so wild and broken that even the poinés, trained to rough riding in the hills, found it difficult to get up into it laden with "just enough bedding to keep a man from freezing to death at night;" Fillmore, famous for its mine, its beautiful little waterfall and the great clumps of wild columbine that grew beside it; and Van Patten's, noted for the early romance in the life of its owner, when, an adventurous young soldier, he wooed, won and stole away from her father and her tribe the daughter of an Indian chief and hid her away in the canyon till he could make his peace with her people. "I like Soledad best of all, though," he said, and, looking about the well-wooded hollow, divided by the boulder-bordered *arroyo* and rimmed about by heights, whose jagged, sunlit peaks pierced the wonderful sky of New Mexico and shut us completely away from the world, we agreed with him.

A true lover of nature he showed himself to us, and a brave and manly character, strong, yet tender and affectionate, and when finally he rode away he carried with him our genuine respect and admiration.

"If they are all like that," I began, as he disappeared behind the rocks.

"But they are not, unfortunately," said the invalid. "Many are, perhaps most of them. You will see another side sometime, perhaps."

I saw it sooner than she had expected. The very next day three brutes in human form came riding down the canyon. For an hour we had heard their shouts and cries above us, and when they appeared we understood the cause. The one riding in front was dragging at a rope, the other end of which was fastened about the neck of a cow, half strangling her as she pulled back and resisted, emitting continuously a piteous, groaning noise, while the two burly fellows behind belabored her with their ropes and quirts, Her face was covered with blood, for they had knocked off one of her horns, and her body was bruised and scarred with their blows. Dragged slowly past our camp, at the top of the incline she lay down and then began a torture that was sickening to witness; kicks from their heavy spurred boots, blows from rocks and whips, until finally, in desperation, she struggled to her feet and they dragged her over the hill. Not far. Evidently she lay down again, for in a few minutes one of the men appeared at the tents and, explaining that they were compelled to kill her, asked us to lend him an axe and a knife. This we gladly did, thankful that the poor beast's torture was to end. A few hours later they rode back, the meat from her carcass dangling from each side of their saddles.

"However," said our gentle invalid, as we sat discussing the affair, "Give even the devil his due. Those men had self-control enough not to swear in our hearing. Not one oath during the whole miserable business. Do you remember?"

We remembered, but down in the canyon the next day the bleating of a calf robbed of its mother reminded us too forcibly of their cruelty to make that memory weigh very heavily in the scales of our opinion.

Advance Society Letters.

By J. BRECKENRIDGE ELLIS.

Here he is at last—Felix of Missouri. Please notice his disturbed expression. This is not habitual with him, but he is like many people who dislike reading; put a book before him, and he is miserable. If the book could only have been a mouse, he would have perked up more; but it was impossible to secure a mouse for this occasion; it was all we could do to secure the photographer. I do not know, but possibly Felix has caught sight, in that paper, of the word, "Federation," and is saying in his own way, "Please stop my subscription." That is a silk tie just above Felix's crook of the neck, and above the tie is my own countenance, concerning which it would

FELIX AND THE WRITER OF OUR NEW STORY AND THE "ADVANCE SOCIETY."

be unbecoming in me to speak at length, The tie is not one of those bought things, ready-made, but is just a long string that I did up with my own hand. You can find the hand in the picture if you look carefully. The hand seems to have the mumps, but in reality it is straining every vein (pray observe the veins) in an effort to hold Felix at bay. Felix is exerting every muscle to escape being kept at bay, for he dislikes water, especially in large quantities. He is not so timid, however, about milk. Yet even about milk he is particular. When the girl brings the warm, fresh milk in the evening (we do not keep a cow because we cannot afford it—if this touches any one's heart, please don't send me a cow, for none of us can milk), it is useless to offer Felix any of the pale-blue liquid left over from the noon lunch; he *will*

have the unskimmed article, and he cries and waves his tail until he gets it. I am sorry you can't see his tail in the picture, but you can imagine it at the other end of him.

My mother and I were talking about this page not long ago, and she thinks it ought to be broken up more—that we have been printing it too solid. That's why I have made a new paragraph here, not because I am done with Felix. Of course if breaking up the page will lead more people to read it, it ought to be broken up. Perhaps it will look like conversation. Anyway, at Christmas time, all things should be different, and even the children ought to go in and out

at the front door, and eat peanuts in the house. I am glad this is Christmas-time, and I wish a lot of people who read this, might get just one tiny bit more of pleasure out of the holidays on account of the Advance Society. I don't say I wish *every* one who reads this might enjoy it, because I don't think it much fun wishing for the impossible, and it is simply impossible to please everybody, whether it's about a church-choir, or the way you cook corn bread (so many insist on putting salt in it.) As to a church-choir needing salt—better make another break here.

I told you long ago that when Brother Pinkerton went to the general conference at San Francisco, he found that Felix was better known there than himself. And when I came here to Arkansas, the fame of Felix had preceded him. And yet that cat cares nothing for fame. The great evangelist, S. M. Martin, who had 376 converts at a meeting at Plattsburg, Mo., has just written my father, saying, among other things (his home is Red Bluff, Calif., a name, by the way, that suggests the Ozarks): "I always read what 'Breck' has in THE CHRISTIAN-EVANGELIST. I can just see him in it all. He amuses me very much at times. And Felix!" Here language fails him; and those who know Brother Martin know that he is indeed overwhelmed when he has no more words.

The great evangelist Herbert Yeuell, who has recently established our first church in New Hampshire—what do you think? He is here in Bentonville holding a meeting for us. We trust he will have a mighty effect for good, and it does seem that he has already affected the weather, for it is beautiful with snow. He and Felix picked up a warm friendship from the first, and he is now carrying some old-gold hairs around on his trousers, unless he worked mighty hard since I last saw him.

You want to hear about our missionary's Christmas tree, I know you do. But just remember, please, that although you are reading this at Christmas time, I am writing it a good while before Christmas. That's the way we editors have to do—pretend that we've feasted upon brown turkey when in reality that turkey 's still gobbling in the coop; and as for me, I haven't a turkey even to gobble. I will have to do the gobbling myself. In that picture—

I say, in that picture, you have a view of part of our front porch. You look right through the hall and see the square window opposite the front door. That is a doorbell just over my shoulder, but it doesn't ring loud enough to be heard, so it is not so annoying as it might be. However, sometimes the company comes around to the back door. I think we ought to have a poem at Christmas time, if you don't mind, so I have written one. I can't say that it is exactly cheerful, but nobody wants to laugh all the time. It's considered quite the thing to dedicate one's poems to somebody, so we'll say that this one is dedicated to E. M. R., of Moberly, Mo., not that it is personal to her, or that it expresses any history in my own life; you may just consider it as a mood, or fancy—or you can skip it if you please; for you'll find me waiting for you at the end of it. We will call it

CHRISTMAS MEMORIES.

One goal there was toward which I toiled,
  One point where every purpose met,
As in old times the exile strove
  To gain his rightful coronet.
I failed—ah, weary length of days!
  Seemed life's dear radiance to have set.
I cast myself in the low grass—
  (Did not ask, then, to forget)

Behold! there bloomed the Violet—
The one I loved I knew—too well!
  Would soon be putting out to sea.
The tide was ebbing—ebbing fast,
  It slipped my bark away from me.
Lost in the mist his farewell smile,
  His hand in mine no more to be;
But through my tears God sent the light
  The rainbow arch of heav'n to see.
    (Sure promise of eternity.)

The years have crumbled all away
  Till prostrate in the dust is lain
That arch of Triumph that was reared,
  Reared, for the one I loved, in vain.
The world is young, but I grow old,
  And friends are sweet, but friendships wane.
It almost seems, in my small world,
  That only Christ and I remain.
    (He bore alone His pain.)

What could I do, since youth is fled—
  Which he who wears bears brightest gem—
Since friends are gone—who courage gave
  Life's blackest shadows to condemn—
Since dream of power is fled—with which
  Life's current once I thought to stem—
If Christ had not, on Christmas morn,
  Been born long since, in Bethlehem!
    (For then, for then my Hope was born,
    Was cradled there in Bethlehem.)

I have a letter from Mrs. Helen E. Moses, the honored President of the C. W. B. M. She writes from Indianapolis, among other tidings: "I feel almost like one of your Advance Society members, although I will soon be — years old." (Now, let no one think the number I have omitted larger than it is!) "I like your work thoroughly (namely, the Av. S.) and sympathize with you in it. I like cats, too, and am waiting with the rest of the folks, for he promised picture." (Just feast your eyes aloft.) Here comes, also, an illustrated post card from Mrs. Moses, showing the mission house at Oberlin, Jamaica, and saying: "I am glad we may look for Felix's picture soon. Have just read the last chapter of the 'Bronze Vase.' You are simply dreadful. Have you no thought of a woman's curiosity? WHICH? Well, you are hopeless! Christmas greetings to all."

Let's make another paragraph. This is from Lena Beamer, Smithfield, Mo.: "I am writing you again, you see. I have just finished the 'Bronze Vase.' It is a fine story." (You are right, there.) "Congratulations. I am very anxious to see Felix. Witch, Winks and Mother Goose send greetings. I don't think it fair for you not to keep the rules of the Av. S." (Now who said I didn't?—or is this an insidious way of trying to find out if I do?). "Have you had snow in Arkansas, yet?". (Yes, we have it yet, but as it fell only last night, we must not be impatient.) ("We had a large snow before Thanksgiving. If you didn't —well—I always did like Missouri best for everything, and I always did say Missouri leads. Hurrah for the 'best-ever' state! Where are Carl and Clarence Pet Lee? I smell apples and that means goodby." (Are there any apples outside of Arkansas? But I suppose they are some we shipped to Missouri. I do not deny that for a varied assortment of snows, hails, sleets, north winds and muddy roads without bottom, and east winds and incredulity, Missouri leads the earth. We may beat 'er on rains, but we simply have to throw up our hands before her other specialties).

Mrs. J. R. Goodwin, Abilene, Kan.: "I have been unable to get an appropriate book for Drusie, so will ask you to get and send it, as I know you have nothing else to do." (Aye, aye!). "I send one dollar for some book, 25 cents for mailing, and 50 cents for a box of stationary to be put on Drusie's Christmas tree." (I hope, considering all the stationary Drusie is getting, that she'll write a little oftener for our page! By the way, I have mailed to her five handsome books, all interesting and appropriate, I think; they ought to help out her Christmas in lonesome China. After all, though, it is not so lonesome for her; she has always heavenly company.)

"Grace Everest, Oklahoma City: "Well, Harry Buckley, I've been to the dollar counter, but I couldn't find a suitable present for Drusie there; however, I can get her a good pair of gloves for $1.25, so with your money and mine together, we will keep our missionary's hands warm through the winter. I have to give an oration before the English class this week—it makes me shiver just to think of it; we are allowed to choose our own subject." (Why not speak in French or German, then, they won't know whether it's good or bad.) "I selected a quotation that I used a month ago: 'For the chance to help some other, keep an open eye.'"

I trust each will keep an eye open for Drusie's Christmas tree. Next week our new continued story begins, and the week after that we will tell about what hung on our missionary tree, so that will

AS WE PASS THROUGH THE WORLD.

BY LIDA C. TULLOCH.

Amy Stewart and Edith Lacy, two young teachers in a city school, were on their way to the dining-room the morning after their arrival at a new boarding place. As they passed through the lower hall, Amy noticed a little child who seemed to shrink within the shelter of some coats hanging in a recess.

"Good-morning," she said pleasantly. The child did not reply, so she said again: "Good-morning, dear."

Only a scowl of the child's brows rewarded her.

"Don't notice such an unmannerly child, Amy," urged Edith. "Breakfast is waiting."

"Poor little chap!" said Amy, pityingly as she followed Edith. "Perhaps he's sick."

"More likely cross," returned Edith.

The next morning the same sharp face looked out from among the coats, and again Amy said, "Good morning, dear." There was no answer.

"Do you not say 'good morning' to anyone?" she asked.

The child shook his head.

"Why not?"

"Don't want to!" was the reply, in a curious, guttural tone.

"Oh, but you must want to. It will make you feel better all day, and people will like you, and you will like them. Now, think it over to-day, dear, and to-morrow see if you cannot find that little tongue of yours and make it say 'good mornin.'"

With a kind smile and a soft pat on his tumbled hair, Amy passed on to the dining-room, with Edith grumbling beside her.

"I should think we have enough in school to worry us without seeking children outside," said Edith.

"This little fellow appeals to me for some reason," replied Amy. "I am sure he is not happy. He looks like some elf who has wandered out of his sphere, and is not yet adjusted to his surroundings. I am determined to make friends with him."

"Why not give him candy? That is what usually brings children around."

"I do not like to buy a child's friendship."

"Well," laughed Edith, "it's your own affair, but I'm afraid you'll have only your labor for your pains."

"I wonder if your elfin friend will be waiting for you," was Edith's remark the following morning, as the two girls went down to breakfast.

"I hope so," said Amy. "We are earlier than usual and I can give him more time. Oh, see, there he is! Good-morning, my dear. How do you do?"

After a moment's waiting there came from among the coats something that sounded like "mornin."

"Why, we've found that nice tongue!" she said brightly. "Now, see this card I've brought you. Here's a picture of a boy just about as big as you, and he's out in the sunshine running and playing."

The child shyly put out a thin hand for the card.

"Take it in to the front window where you can see it," Amy urged. "Don't stay in that dark corner. Come, we will go in together."

Much to the astonishment of Edith, who was looking on, the child suffered himself to be drawn from among the coats and led to the parlor. Thus seen outside of his shelter he proved to be a thin fellow, whose small, sallow face wore an unhappy expression.

"What an unattractive child!" said Edith, unsympathetically, when Amy, af-

ter settling the boy in the parlor, rejoined her.

"Yes, poor little fellow!" was the response. "I am more than ever sorry for him. His mother told me last night that since he was ill with scarlet fever he has not been able to speak distinctly. He doesn't want to play with other children, and hides in corners by himself."

"Why doesn't she take him out of doors more?"

"How can she, when her time and energy are given to earning a living for her family? What the child needs is to be cheered up; to be made happy. And by the way, his name is Felix, which means happiness, you know! What a misnomer!"

"Isn't it! Well, I must say you seem to be gaining a quick victory!"

"I do not consider victory won yet. I have made a beginning though."

It was not long before Felix, instead of hiding behind the coats, posted himself at the front window to watch for his friend's return from school. Shyly, at first, and still with something of a frown on his brow, but gradually growing bolder, until he even ran to the door to greet her, his face bright, and a pretty smile on his lips.

True to her theory, Amy forebore to buy these concessions. A caress, a little story, were varied only occasionally with candy or a toy, and one never-to-be-forgotten day she took him for a trolley ride into the country.

His devotion to her grew with each day, as did his mother's gratitude.

One evening when the two girls were seated in their room, a timid little knock was heard at the door. When Amy opened it there was Felix.

"Why, Felix!" she said. "I thought you were in bed long ago!"

"Mit Amy," the child said, slipping his little hand in hers, with pretty faith, "will you come wif me to get water? I 'fraid."

"Yes, I'll go with you this time," Amy said, as they went downstairs together. "But my Felix mustn't be afraid of the dark; he must learn to be brave."

When she returned to the room Edith said, "you give up entirely too much of your few hours of leisure to that child. He will get to be a nuisance. Why do you do it?"

"Do you remember, Edith," said Amy gently, "those lines you read the other day and liked; 'I shall pass through this world but once! Let me do what good I can'? I have taken them for my watchword."

A change came over Edith's face and she did not speak for a moment. Then she said: "I remember. I thought the sentiment beautiful, and had much to say about it. But you, Amy, instead of talking, put it into practice. I am sure this world will be better for your having passed through it.'"

DO YOU KNOW A BARGAIN?

An Exposition of the Bible

A series of expositions covering all the chapters and books of the Old and New Testament by the most eminent divines and Biblical scholars.

The Scriptures are analyzed, illuminated and interpreted in a graphic and thoroughly interesting manner. The highest order of scholarship is manifested throughout the entire work, and it is written in a style that is essentially popular and positively fascinating.

The knowledge imparted through this work can not be overestimated. It is an invaluable aid to Ministers, Expositors, Teachers and Students of the Bible.

THE EXPOSITION OF EACH BOOK OF THE BIBLE IS WRITTEN BY AN EMINENT SCHOLAR:

Genesis, St. John, First Corinthians, Marcus Dods, D. D. Exodus, St. Mark, G. A. Chadwick, D. D. Leviticus, S. H. Kellogg, D. D. Numbers, Judges, Ruth, Job, R. A. Watson, D. D. Deuteronomy, Andrew Harper, D. D. Joshua, First and Second Samuel, W. G. Blaikie, D. D. LL. D. First and Second Kings, Daniel, Dean F. W. Farrar, D. D. First and Second Chronicles, W. H. Bennett, M. A. Ezra, Nehemiah, Esther, Song of Solomon, Lamentations, W. F. Adeney, M. A. Psalms, Colossians, Philemon, Alexander MacLaren, D. D. Proverbs, R. F. Horton, D. D. Ecclesiastes, Samuel Cox, D. D. Isaiah, Twelve Minor Prophets, George Adam Smith, D. D. LL. D. Jeremiah, C. J. Ball, M. A. Ezekiel, John Skinner, M. A. St. Matthews, J. Monro Gibson, D. D. St. Luke, Henry Burton, M. A. Acts of the Apostles, G. T. Stokes, D. D. Romans, H. C. G. Moule, D. D. Second Corinthians, Thessalonians, James Denney, D. D. Galatians, Ephesians, G. G. Findlay, D. D. Philippians, Rober Rainy, D. D. First and Second Timothy, Titus, James, Jude. A. Plummer, D .D. Hebrews, T. C. Edwards, D. D. First and Second Peter, J. R. Lumby, D. D. First, Second and Third John, W. Alexander, D. D. Revelation, W. Milligan, D.D.

The whole work contains 5,261 double column pages, averaging 877 to each volume. It is printed on fine, clear paper, from new electrotype plates (brevier type,) costing $17,000; is strongly and handsomely bound in dark green genuine buckram cloth, with flexible back, so that each volume will readily lie open.

STRONGLY AND HANDSOMELY BOUND IN GENUINE BUCKRAM CLOTH.

Each volume measures 10¾ x 7½ x 1⅞ inches

PRICE COMPLETE IN 6 VOLS., $10.00.

CHRISTIAN PUBLISHING COMPANY, ST. LOUIS, MO,

Christian Publishing Company

2712 Pine St., St. Louis, Mo.

J. H. GARRISON, - - - - President
.¬. W. DOWLING, - - - Vice-President
GEO. L. SNIVELY, - - Sec. and Gen. Supt
R P. CROW, - - Treas. and Bus. Manager

—While Christmas sales have been enormous, we can yet supply all our patrons with the world's best books promptly and at lowest prices.

—When in doubt, turn to the safe side. That is another way of saying—order your Bible school supplies of this House. Otherwise there is little room for choice, but ours cost no more than inferior grades.

—One Kentucky preacher sent us twenty-seven new subscribers and secured three sets of our porcelain china, semi-vitreous dinner sets of forty-two pieces each. We have more of these beautiful table services that we offer as premiums for nine new subscribers to THE CHRISTIAN-EVANGELIST.

—The enterprising F. J. Yokley, of Canton, will wait for the opening of the doors at Pittsburg with his lamps trimmed and burning. He already has numerous credits on his transportation account to Pittsburg, 1909, by reason of helpful co-operation with this House. Let others emulate his foresightedness.

—Multitudes of our preachers are securing "Helps to Faith," by J. H. Garrison, by sending us one new subscriber accompanied by $1.50. Most of them add "Victories of Faith," by E. L. Powell, by sending another new subscriber. Any preacher can in a similar manner secure one or both of these literary and spiritual gems.

—The 1907 volume of THE CHRISTIAN-EVANGELIST will doubtless be the most splendid trophy of religious journalism the world will have seen this side of January 1, 1908. Renew your subscription at once and secure entrance for the entire volume into as many new homes as possible. This is a form of missionary activity most commendable.

—We gained as many new Bible schools during November as during the entire previous year. This signifies that the people are learning they can purchase the Dowling supplies at as low prices as are being asked for other literature greatly inferior in scholarship, adaptability to modern conditions, and even in mechanical make-up. Samples sent on application.

—Notwithstanding the great haste in filling orders for Bible school literature the eye must momentarily linger on the beautiful testimonials paid to our Bible school literature by superintendents, secretaries and treasures whose schools have used them for from one year to a quarter of a century. Such expressions of gratitude and fellowship constitute a large part of the reward coming to the modern publisher.

—It is gratifying to know that many schools heretofore using denominational Sunday-school publications of different names and types have learned that they are not nearly so helpful as those of their "own faith and order," and are returning for supplies to this House, whose Bible school literature is designed to transform the children of the Disciples of this generation into the stalwart Disciples of Christ of next generation.

—Miss Eva Lemert, formerly of Kansas City, perhaps the most successful Bible school worker in our ranks, has a department in "Our Young Folks" for studies in methods and reports of successes in the actual management of Bible schools, that makes this paper one of our most valuable publications. It is only 75 cents per an-

num. Sister Lemert makes single issues of her department worth more than that to busy teachers and perplexed superintendents.

—During the last week we received perhaps the largest number of new subscribers by singles and twos ever coming to this House in the same space of time. Notwithstanding this and the usual Christmas festivities, we are pleased to note the following new clubs at $1.50 each. Men and women, deeply in earnest seem determined to continue their efforts to place THE CHRISTIAN-EVANGELIST into 100,000 homes until this Centennial aim has been fully achieved.

Kansas City, Mo., Jas. Small, evangelist...... 3
Ridgeway, Mo., W. H. Hobbs, pastor........ 5
Marble Falls, Tex., M. H. Reed, agent....... 30
Liberal, Kan. 17
Indianapolis, C. B. Newman, pastor..........62

—Discriminatingly compare our news service with that given by any other Christian newspaper and the palm will be awarded us. We may not have chronicled that Bros. K. L. Sects and Hit M. Hard of Postem and Knockem exchanged arenas last Saturday night, but movements of men in whom the brotherhood is interested are reported as well as all that pertains to the real progress of the kingdom of God's dear Son. We believe THE CHRISTIAN-EVANGELIST is the best real news vender among us.

—The St. Louis "Republic" thus comments on one of our books that is coming into large appreciation by the reading public—a book that ought to be studied by every man who sees but dimly through the vail intervening between earth and heaven:

RELIGIOUS AND SOCIOLOGIC.

"Helps to Faith" is the work of J. H. Garrison. He terms it a contribution to theological reconstruction. It is an effort to carry the argument in favor of Christianity further back than it is usually carried, so as to meet every man on his own ground where he is, and to lead him thence, step by step, to the acceptance of Jesus Christ as affording the only revelation of God and the only religion which can fully satisfy the needs of men. Beginning with the foundation fact of human nature itself, with its religious instincts and religious needs, it aims to lead the sincere and honest searcher for truth from fact to fact until the mind is prepared to receive the Christ of the Bible as the fulfillment of the prophecies of man's inner being—its intuitions, its capacities, its needs—as well as the fulfillment of the prophecies written by holy men of old. It is the author's belief that it is a timely book, adapted to the religious needs of many, who, to-day, are disturbed in their inherited beliefs, and are seeking for some more substantial basis for their faith. It is his sincere hope, too, that the book will in some humble measure meet the wants of this class of people and serve to lead many a doubting soul into the light and joy and strength of a larger and stronger faith. It is published by the Christian Publishing Company of St. Louis.

—All that is needed is simply "precipitation" to secure from the preachers of this brotherhood a public and almost unanimous declaration that the intelligent loyalty of THE CHRISTIAN-EVANGELIST to the true principles of this Restoration and the spirit in which its propaganda is conducted is most conducive to this cause we all love and for which we plead. Reports come to us from every realm of the brotherhood

that as never before preachers are looking to THE CHRISTIAN-EVANGELIST as our chief newspaper hope for the future. If in this respect those preachers would give their sentiments expression in the form of lists of subscribers they would quickly make of this paper a medium of sufficient power to make this current Reformation conform to the ideals of its founders and, what is more desirable, to the will of God, as water conforms to the outlines of the pitcher. Why postpone? The hour has struck. Let all who believe in the principles advocated by THE CHRISTIAN-EVANGELIST act unanimously, enthusiastically and right now, and the future will soon be assured.

A Morning Star.

I am rejoiced to note the evidences of THE CHRISTIAN-EVANGELIST's prosperity. An increasing subscription list for THE CHRISTIAN-EVANGELIST is a "morning star" of promise. I think that we can go on a while longer, feeling that "life is worth living." It means much to this great brotherhood of whose mind and spirit the paper is the loftiest exponent. With a religious journal the dollars and cents prosperity is secondary (albeit without it no paper can accomplish its mission). The prosperity is only a symptom. It indicates that the advocacy of the paper is growing in favor. In this case it is another demonstration of the truth that "the letter killeth, but the spirit giveth life." THE CHRISTIAN-EVANGELIST has been leading us out into the spirit that giveth life.
Little Rock, Ark. J. N. JESSUP.

WHAT OUR FRIENDS ARE SAYING

I am sending you herewith $3.00 for a new subscriber whose name you will find on enclosed pink slip. Wish also to renew my own subscription. I wish I could secure for your paper one hundred new subscribers and have them all enjoy the paper as much as I do. I hope to send a few more names soon and thank you in advance for the large returns I know I will receive for money invested.—Lydia Hadler, Bloomington, Ills.

I enclose $1.50 for my renewal. I have been reading THE CHRISTIAN-EVANGELIST for more than fifteen years and words can not express my appreciation of the good I feel it has done me. I have always been thankful that I happened to start with it instead of a paper with a harsh, critical spirit so that the paper I read has more influence over my life perhaps than any other one thing. I shall always speak words of praise of it and insist on people reading it.—Mrs. R. A. Mingle, Chattanooga, Tenn.

I wish at this time to thank the editors of THE CHRISTIAN-EVANGELIST for the surpassingly fine reports which have appeared of the convention. We could ask nothing better. The reports are written in the spirit which characterized the convention throughout and nothing can be presented to the brotherhood concerning the Buffalo Convention which will please us more than that the spirit of harmony, fellowship and prayerful desire for the full coming of the Kingdom which pervaded every session, shall pervade the churches also as a result of the meeting. The convention was not only missionary, it was a mission in this city, the influence of which will abide to the advancement of the church.—R. H. Miller, Buffalo.

| 1907 | THE CHRISTIAN | 1907 |

LESSON COMMENTARY

On the International Bible Lessons.
BY W. W. DOWLING.

Twenty-second Volume Now Ready. Better than ever! Full of good things for Pastors, Teachers and Advanced Pupils. Every Lesson Thoroughly Analyzed.

$1.00 per copy, postpaid. $9.00 per Dozen, not prepaid.

CHRISTIAN PUBLISHING COMPANY.
St. Louis, Mo.

9 780483 474420